To the Student:

This text was created to provide you with a high-quality educational resource. As a publisher specializing in college texts for business and economics, our goal is to provide you with learning materials that will serve you well in your college studies and throughout your career.

The educational process involves learning, retention, and the application of concepts and principles. You can accelerate your learning efforts utilizing the supplements accompanying this text:

- Study Guide for use with Federal Taxation, 1992 Edition;
- Two 1990 Individual Tax Return Practice Problems;
- Federal Tax Return Preperation with TurboTax (includes ten individual tax return problems); and
- 1990 Tax Return Practice Problems for Corporations, S Corporations, and Partnerships.

These learning aids are designed to improve your performance in the course by highlighting key points in the text and providing you with assistance in mastering basic concepts.

Check your local bookstore, or ask the manager to place an order for you today.

We at Irwin sincerely hope this text package will assist you in reaching your goals, both now and in the future.

Full Name (as appears on credit card): _

Signature: _

Permanent Address (cannot ship to P.O. Box): _ _ _ _ _ _ _ _ _ _ _ _ _ _ _

_ _

Circle One: VISA   MC   AMEX

Complete Card Number: _

Expiration Date: _

Please send me the following:

☐ Individual Taxation, 1993 Edition/ISBN 0-256-10849-8/Bk # 01-2654-06

☐ Federal Taxation, 1993 Edition/ISBN 0-256-10832-3/Bk # 01-2650-06

☐ Corporate, Partnership, Estate
   and Gift Taxation, 1993 Edition/ISBN 0-256-10842-0/Bk # 01-2656-06

For information, call 1-800-634-3961 - Melissa Mizner
$60.00 includes shipping and handling per book

IRWIN

Full Name (as appears on credit card): _

Signature: _

Permanent Address (cannot ship to P.O. Box): _ _ _ _ _ _ _ _ _ _ _ _ _ _ _

_ _

Circle One: VISA   MC   AMEX

Complete Card Number: _

Expiration Date: _

Please send me the following:

☐ Individual Taxation, 1993 Edition/ISBN 0-256-10849-8/Bk # 01-2654-06

☐ Federal Taxation, 1993 Edition/ISBN 0-256-10832-3/Bk # 01-2650-06

☐ Corporate, Partnership, Estate
   and Gift Taxation, 1993 Edition/ISBN 0-256-10842-0/Bk # 01-2656-06

For information, call 1-800-634-3961 - Melissa Mizner
$60.00 includes shipping and handling per book

IRWIN

Melissa Mizner
Customer Service
Richard D. Irwin, Inc.
1820 Ridge Road
Homewood, IL 60430

IRWIN

Melissa Mizner
Customer Service
Richard D. Irwin, Inc.
1820 Ridge Road
Homewood, IL 60430

FEDERAL TAXATION

1992 Edition

FEDERAL TAXATION

1992 Edition

GENERAL EDITORS

James W. Pratt, D.B.A., C.P.A.
Jane O. Burns, Ph.D., C.P.A.
William N. Kulsrud, Ph.D., C.P.A.

CONTRIBUTING AUTHORS:

Jane O. Burns, Ph.D., C.P.A.
Texas Tech University

Marguerite R. Hutton, Ph.D., C.P.A.
Western Washington University

Sally M. Jones, Ph.D., C.P.A.
University of Texas at Austin

William N. Kulsrud, Ph.D., C.P.A.
Indiana University

Michael A. O'Dell, Ph.D., C.P.A.
Arizona State University

Nathan Oestreich, Ph.D., C.P.A.
San Diego State University

James W. Pratt, D.B.A., C.P.A.
University of Houston

Edward J. Schnee, Ph.D., C.P.A.
University of Alabama

Jerrold J. Stern, Ph.D.
Indiana University

Steven C. Thompson, Ph.D., C.P.A.
University of Houston

John C. Tripp, Ph.D., C.P.A.
University of Denver

Michael J. Tucker, J.D., Ph.D., C.P.A.
George Mason University

James L. Wittenbach, D.B.A., C.P.A
University of Notre Dame

TAXATION SERIES

Homewood, IL 60430
Boston, MA 02116

IBM® PC and PS/2® are registered trademarks of International Business Machines Corporation.

Lotus® and 1-2-3® are registered trademarks of Lotus Development Corporation.

Sponsoring editor: Ron M. Regis
Project editor: Margaret S. Haywood
Production manager: Irene H. Sotiroff
Compositor: Publication Services, Inc.
Typeface: 11/13 Times Roman
Printer: R.R. Donnelley & Sons Company

ISBN 0-256-10044-6
ISSN 0742-7816

Printed in the United States of America

1 2 3 4 5 6 7 8 9 0 DO-W 8 7 6 5 4 3 2 1

PREFACE

This ninth edition of **Federal Taxation** is designed for use by undergraduate or graduate accounting, business, or law students in their study of Federal taxation. The numerous examples and computational illustrations used to explain the more complex rules concerning the Federal income taxation of individuals, corporations, partnerships, estates, and trusts should also make this text suitable for use in a self-study program.

The primary emphasis of the text is the Federal income taxation of individuals (17 chapters). In addition, abbreviated coverage of the other basic areas of taxation is also provided. Three chapters are devoted to the income taxation of regular corporations and shareholders—from formation to liquidation; and one chapter each is provided for partnerships and S corporations. Federal estate and gift taxation is discussed in one chapter; and two additional chapters contain the related topics of the income taxation of estates, trusts, and beneficiaries and the major aspects of family tax planning. Our goal in covering all these topics in a single volume is to give instructors maximum flexibility in the design of their own courses. It is neither our intention nor our belief that all this material should be covered in a traditional three-hour, one-semester course.

The *1992 Edition* has been revised to reflect the changes introduced by the Revenue Reconciliation Act of 1990 as well as other significant judicial and administrative developments during the past year. In the event that other significant changes in the tax law occur during the year, we will continue our policy of providing users with timely update supplements.

In addition to revisions reflecting changes in the tax law, previous users will notice several other modifications. On the outside, the 1992 Edition has a different look than its predecessors—a new cover design and expanded size. On the inside, the 1992 Edition has a fresh format. At the beginning of each chapter, the reader will now find a list of learning objectives, identifying the goals of the chapter and providing a brief glimpse of the topics covered. Immediately following these objectives is a summary outline of the chapter, complete with major chapter headings and their page numbers. These outlines not only make specific subjects easier to find, but, like the learning objectives, offer an overview of what the chapter contains.

Former users will also note changes in the contents of several chapters and the arrangement of certain topics within the text. These changes were made to improve the presentation of these subjects and make the materials in the chapters more manageable. For example, the complex rules governing the deduction of certain investment expenses and losses (interest, passive losses, and vacation homes) are now consolidated into a separate chapter (Chapter 12), and the coverage of the passive loss rules is expanded. This change enables those wishing to avoid these rather technical areas to do so by simply pruning this chapter from the course. Another significant change in the text can be found in the chapters dealing with property transactions. Formerly covered by three chapters (old Chapters 13, 14, and 15), this material is now presented in four chapters. The opening chapter introducing basis determination and gain and loss recognition (new Chapter 14) has been expanded with the addition of a complete discussion of the installment sales rules (formerly found in old Chapter 16). The second chapter in the property transaction sequence continues to be devoted to nontaxable exchanges. It remains intact but has been christened with a new number (Chapter 15). The principal change in this area was a division of the chapter on gain characterization (old Chapter 15) into two chapters: Chapter 16 on capital gains and losses, and Chapter 17 on Section 1231 gains and losses and the depreciation recapture rules. The final alteration concerns the chapter previously devoted to accounting periods and methods. This chapter has been eliminated and the topics shifted to other appropriate chapters in the text, generally in an abbreviated form.

For those students planning careers as tax professionals—and for those instructors who believe, as do the contributing authors, that the only way to be a successful tax practitioner is to be capable of conducting tax research—Chapter 2 of this text provides an introduction to tax research sources, and most later chapters contain one or more tax research problems.

In addition to the standard discussion questions and computational problems contained at the end of every chapter of this text, several chapters contain comprehensive tax return problems and cumulative problems that require an understanding of material presented in earlier chapters and completion of some tax forms. Also, Appendix E contains two comprehensive tax return problems for individual taxpayers. These problems require completion of some of the most common tax forms and are ideal for course projects. Each of these problems requires approximately 6 to 10 hours for completion. These tax return problems are intended to supplement other end-of-chapter problems by requiring students to relate tax rules to actual tax return compliance procedures.

Several chapters have problems labeled "Computerized Tax Analysis." These problems, which require the use of an IBM-PC or IBM-compatible microcomputer and a Lotus 1-2-3® electronic spreadsheet software program, are designed to help students learn to solve tax computation and tax planning problems in a step-by-step manner. For those who adopt this text, a master disk containing the Lotus-based templates required for solving these problems will be made available, along with the publisher's permission to make an appropriate number of copies for student use. Instructions for using these materials are contained in Appendix D of the text. The self-instruction orientation of these new problems is intended to prevent the need for using in-class time for directions.

A comprehensive package of instructional aids is available with this text.

■ *Solutions Manual:* containing solutions to the discussion questions and computational problems at the end of each chapter. These solutions are referenced to specific pages and examples from the text, and where appropriate, to supporting statutory or administrative authorities.

- *Instructor's Guide:* containing solutions to the tax research problems, tax return problems (including the two comprehensive tax return problems contained in Appendix E), and a test bank containing over 1000 objective questions (true-false and multiple choice), with answers referenced to specific pages and examples in the text.

- *Chapter Lecture Outlines:* containing a summary of the key points of each chapter and *Transparency Masters* for selected illustrations, with a large typeface for easier viewing.

- *CompuTest III:* a microcomputer testing system for use with an IBM-PC or IBM-compatible, along with data disks containing all the questions from the test bank included in the Instructor's Guide. This software package can be used to create quizzes or exams in a minimum amount of time.

- *CompuGrade:* a microcomputer software program designed to maintain test scores for several different classes on a floppy disk. This program disk comes in the package with CompuTest III.

- *A Student Study Guide,* written by Professor Nathan Oestreich (San Diego State University). It provides students with chapter highlights and self-review exams and answers.

- *Two 1990 Individual Tax Return Practice Problems,* written by Professor Marguerite R. Hutton (Western Washington University). It contains original data source forms (e.g., Forms W-2, 1099-DIV, 1099-INT, real estate closing statements) for the manual preparation of 1990 Form 1040 for two married couples. It also contains blank copies of the tax return forms required to be completed by students.

- *Tax Return Practice Problems for Corporations, S Corporations, and Partnerships,* written by Professor Marguerite R. Hutton. It contains one practice problem for each of these tax entities and blank copies of the 1990 tax return forms required to be completed by students.

- *Federal Tax Return Preparation with TurboTax,* prepared by Professor Edmund D. Fenton, Jr. (Gonzaga University). It contains ten Federal tax return problems for individuals, ranging in difficulty from simple to complex, which can be prepared and printed using one of the best tax return preparation programs available.

We are greatly indebted to those who have made many useful suggestions regarding the prior editions of this text. We specifically thank Professors Shirley M. Arbesfeld (Rutgers University), Kathleen R. Bindon (University of Alabama), Thomas L. Davies, (University of South Dakota), Edmund D. Fenton, Jr. (Gonzaga University), and Barry Greenwald (Missouri Western State College) for their excellent suggestions; their comments greatly aided our editorial efforts. In this regard, we continue to invite all readers—students and instructors—to call errors and omissions to our attention. As with any work of this magnitude, it is extremely difficult to identify all errors and shortcomings without help, particularly in the dynamic area of Federal taxation. Because this text is revised annually, errors can be *quickly* corrected and constructive criticism will be incorporated on a *continuing* basis.

Finally, we are most appreciative of the professional and technical services received from the staff at Publication Services. This *1992 Edition* would not have been possible without their help.

April, 1991   *James W. Pratt*
                                                 Jane O. Burns
                                         William N. Kulsrud

CONTENTS IN BRIEF

PART V

PROPERTY TRANSACTIONS

PART VI

EMPLOYEE COMPENSATION

PART VII

CORPORATE TAXATION

PART VIII

FLOW-THROUGH ENTITIES

PART IX

FAMILY TAX PLANNING

Appendices and Index

CONTENTS

3   TAXABLE ENTITIES, TAX FORMULA, INTRODUCTION TO PROPERTY TRANSACTIONS

4   PERSONAL AND DEPENDENCY EXEMPTIONS; FILING STATUS; DETERMINATION OF TAX FOR AN INDIVIDUAL; FILING REQUIREMENTS

PART II
GROSS INCOME

5   GROSS INCOME

6 GROSS INCOME: INCLUSIONS AND EXCLUSIONS

PART III
DEDUCTIONS AND LOSSES

7 OVERVIEW OF DEDUCTIONS AND LOSSES

8 EMPLOYEE BUSINESS EXPENSES

9 CAPITAL RECOVERY: DEPRECIATION, AMORTIZATION, AND DEPLETION

10   CERTAIN BUSINESS DEDUCTIONS AND LOSSES

11   ITEMIZED DEDUCTIONS

12 DEDUCTIONS FOR CERTAIN INVESTMENT EXPENSES AND LOSSES

PART IV

ALTERNATIVE MINIMUM TAX AND TAX CREDITS

13 THE ALTERNATIVE MINIMUM TAX AND TAX CREDITS

PART V

PROPERTY TRANSACTIONS

14 PROPERTY TRANSACTIONS: BASIS DETERMINATION AND RECOGNITION OF GAIN OR LOSS

15   NONTAXABLE EXCHANGES

16 PROPERTY TRANSACTIONS: CAPITAL GAINS AND LOSSES

17 PROPERTY TRANSACTIONS: DISPOSITIONS OF TRADE OR BUSINESS PROPERTY

PART VI

EMPLOYEE COMPENSATION

18 EMPLOYEE COMPENSATION AND RETIREMENT PLANS

PART VII

CORPORATE TAXATION

19 CORPORATIONS: FORMATION AND OPERATION

20 CORPORATE DISTRIBUTIONS, REDEMPTIONS, AND LIQUIDATIONS

21 TAXATION OF CORPORATE ACCUMULATIONS

PART VIII

FLOW-THROUGH ENTITIES

22   TAXATION OF PARTNERSHIPS AND PARTNERS

23 S CORPORATIONS

25

INCOME TAXATION OF ESTATES AND TRUSTS

26

FAMILY TAX PLANNING

Appendices and Index

FEDERAL TAXATION

1992 Edition

PART I

INTRODUCTION TO THE FEDERAL TAX SYSTEM

CONTENTS

LEARNING OBJECTIVES

Upon completion of this chapter you will be able to:

- Trace the historical development of our Federal income tax system

- Explain the key terms used to describe most taxes

- Identify the different types of Federal taxes found in the United States, including

  - Income taxes

  - Wealth transfer taxes

  - Employment taxes

  - Excise taxes

- Understand the relationship between estate and gift taxes

- Explain the differences in the employment taxes levied on employees versus those levied on self-employed individuals

- Indentify some of the more common social and economic goals of our Federal tax system

CHAPTER OUTLINE

Chapter 1

AN OVERVIEW OF FEDERAL TAXATION

INTRODUCTION

The system of Federal taxation that has been developed in the United States is among the most sophisticated and complex national tax programs in the world today. This system of taxation has an impact on almost every business and investment decision as well as many personal decisions. Decisions a business enterprise must make, such as the form it will take (i.e., sole proprietorship, partnership, or corporation), the length and nature of its operations, and the manner in which it will be terminated cannot be made without consideration of the tax consequences. An individual's decisions regarding employment contracts and alternative forms of compensation, as well as place and duration of employment, will be affected by the Federal tax structure. Even such personal choices as housing, family size, marital relationships, and termination of these relationships by divorce or death involve some of the most complex rules of the Federal tax law. This complexity places a *premium* on knowledge of the various types of Federal taxes imposed on those who by chance or choice must operate within the system's boundaries.

The purpose of this book is to introduce the reader to the major elements of Federal taxation. A corollary objective of the authors is to aid the reader in the development of his or her *tax awareness* (i.e., ability to recognize tax problems, pitfalls, and planning opportunities). Such an awareness is not only an important attribute of accountants and lawyers—it is *essential* for everyone who chooses a career in business.

THE NATURE OF A TAX

The Supreme Court of the United States has defined a *tax* as "an exaction for the support of the Government."[1] Thus, what a tax does is to provide a means through which the government derives a majority of the revenues necessary

---

[1] *U.S. v. Butler,* 36-1 USTC ¶9039, 16 AFTR 1289, 297 U.S. 1, 70 (USSC, 1936). An explanation of case citations such as this is presented in Chapter 2.

to keep it in operation. A tax is not merely a source of revenue, however. As discussed in a later section of this chapter, taxes have become a powerful instrument which policymakers use to attain social as well as economic goals.

A tax normally has one or more of the following characteristics:

1. There is no *direct relationship* between the exaction of revenue and any benefit to be received by the taxpayer. Thus, a taxpayer cannot trace his or her tax payment to an Army jeep, an unemployment payment, a weather satellite, or any of the myriad expenditures that the Federal government authorizes.

2. Taxes are levied on the basis of *predetermined criteria*. In other words, taxes can be objectively determined, calculated, and even planned around.

3. Taxes are levied on a *recurring* or *predictable* basis. Most taxes are levied on an annual basis, although some, like the estate tax, are levied only once.

4. Taxes *may be distinguished* from regulations or penalties. A regulation or penalty is a measure specifically designed to control or stop a particular activity. For instance, at one time Congress imposed a charge on the products of child labor. This charge was specifically aimed at stopping the use of children in manufacturing and thus was a regulation rather than a tax, even though it was called a "tax." Also, taxes can be distinguished from licenses and fees, which are payments made for some special privilege granted or services rendered (e.g., marriage license or automobile registration fee).

The major types of taxes imposed by taxing authorities within the United States (e.g., income, employment, and wealth transfer taxes) are discussed later in this chapter. As will be noted, one or more of the above characteristics can be found in each of these various taxes.

DEVELOPMENT OF U.S. TAXATION

The entire history of the United States, from its beginnings as a colony of England to the present day, is entwined with the development of Federal taxation. From its infancy until well into the current century, the United States Federal tax system closely paralleled the tax laws of its mother country, England.[2]

---

[2] The states in turn have developed their own systems of taxation which often parallel— but sometimes diverge from—the Federal tax system.

EXCISE AND CUSTOMS DUTIES

Shortly after the colonies won independence and became the United States of America, tariffs became the Federal government's principal revenue-raising source.[3] At the time of its adoption in 1789, the U.S. Constitution gave Congress the power to levy and collect taxes. Promptly exercising this authority, Congress passed as its first act the Tariff Act of 1789, which imposed a system of duties (called excise taxes) on imports.

FEDERAL INCOME TAX

As time passed and the Federal government enlarged the scope of its activities, it became more and more apparent to political leaders that additional sources of revenue would have to be devised to supplement the tariff system. A tax on income was a likely alternative, but Congress was limited by constitutional constraints imposed on its power to levy and collect taxes. Under the original Constitution, any *direct* tax imposed by Congress was required to be *apportioned* among the states on the basis of relative populations. Under such a system it would be possible, and indeed likely, that each state would have a different Federal tax rate for its citizens because the sizes of the states' populations differed. If such a system had been tried, it would have been politically and practically unworkable.

> **Example 1.** Assume that Congress imposed a $50,000 tax on income. Assume further that the United States was composed of only three states with populations as follows: Vermont—2,000; Texas—3,000; and New York—5,000. Under the original Constitution, if the income tax were a direct tax, it would be allocated among the states according to population, and each state's tax burden would be as follows: Vermont, $10,000 (20% of total population × $50,000 tax); Texas, $15,000 (30% of $50,000); and New York, $25,000 (50% of $50,000).

> **Example 2.** Assume the sum of the residents' income in each state above was as follows: Vermont—$100,000; Texas—$300,000; and New York—$1,000,000. In such a case, the average rate of tax on income in each state would be as follows: Vermont, 10% ($10,000 tax ÷ $100,000 income); Texas, 5% ($15,000 ÷ $300,000); and New York, 2.5% ($25,000 ÷ $1,000,000). Since incomes are not distributed among the states in the same proportion as residents, the Federal government would be required to assess taxes on citizens of different states at *different rates*—a resident of Vermont might pay taxes at a rate of 10% while a resident of New York paid only 2.5%.

---

[3] A tariff is a duty imposed on an importer. Since it is a cost of the product being imported, it usually is passed on to the consumer as part of the product's price. Thus, the higher the tariff imposed on a product, the higher must be its price if importation is to be profitable.

Despite the apportionment requirement, Congress enacted the first Federal income tax in 1861 to finance the vastly increased expenditures brought on by the Civil War. The tax was applied uniformly to all residents—the apportionment requirement being ignored, apparently on the belief that the income tax was not a direct tax. In *Springer v. U.S.*,[4] however, a taxpayer challenged the Civil War income tax, asserting that the tax was unconstitutional because it was direct, and that any direct tax required apportionment.

The distinction between *direct* taxes and indirect taxes has never been completely clarified. According to some, a direct tax is one that cannot be avoided or at least shifted to another with ease. Two taxes generally considered direct taxes are head taxes and property taxes; neither of these can be escaped without difficulty. Customs duties and other excise taxes are normally considered indirect taxes, since they can be avoided by not purchasing the particular good. Beyond these examples, however, the issue is unresolved. In *Springer,* the Supreme Court specifically addressed the question of whether an income tax was a direct tax. Upholding the constitutionality of the income tax, the Court indicated that only head taxes and real estate taxes were direct taxes and that all others were indirect. Although this case dealt squarely with the issue, the decision did not end the controversy.

The income tax was allowed to expire shortly after the Civil War, in 1872, but was reenacted in almost identical form in 1894. Upon reinstatement, it again was attacked as a direct tax requiring apportionment. In *Pollock v. Farmers' Loan and Trust Co.*,[5] the Supreme Court focused specifically on the income tax as it applied to income from real estate. The Court believed this case to be different from *Springer* and held that a tax on income from real estate was the equivalent of a tax on the real estate itself. Accordingly, the Court held that the tax was unconstitutional because it was a direct tax imposed without apportionment. After this decision, the constitutionality of an income tax was again suspect.

Undaunted by the *Pollock* decision, proponents of a Federal income tax continued their efforts and in 1909 were successful in bringing about a corporate income tax. This tax was upheld by the Supreme Court in *Flint v. Stone Tracy Co.*[6] when the Court held that it was an excise tax measured by corporate income, rather than a direct tax.

Concurrent with its passage of the 1909 corporate income tax, Congress proposed an amendment to the Constitution that would allow it to levy a tax on *all* incomes *without* apportionment among the states based on population. This effort culminated in the passage of the Sixteenth Amendment on February 25, 1913, which provided that,

> The Congress shall have the power to lay and collect taxes on incomes from whatever source derived, without apportionment among the several States, and without regard to any census or enumeration.

---

[4] 102 U.S. 586 (USSC, 1880).

[5] 3 AFTR 2602, 157 U.S. 429 (USSC, 1895).

[6] 3 AFTR 2834, 220 U.S. 107 (USSC, 1911).

Without hesitation, Congress enacted the Revenue Act of 1913 on October 3, 1913 and made it retroactive to March 1, 1913.

Because of special exemptions and the progressive tax rates of the 1913 income tax law, it too was challenged as a denial of due process of law as guaranteed by the Fifth Amendment to the Constitution. In 1916 the Supreme Court upheld the validity of the new income tax law in *Brushaber v. Union Pacific Railroad Co.*[7] Although many changes have taken place, the United States has not been without a Federal income tax since 1913.

As historical conditions changed and the Federal government's need for additional revenues increased, Congress exercised its income taxing authority by the passage of many separate pieces of legislation that resulted in greater complexity in the Federal income tax law. Each new revenue act was a reenactment of a previous revenue act with added amendments. This process created great confusion for those working with the law, since it could be necessary to research over 100 separate sources to determine exactly what law was currently in effect. In addition, the reenactment of a statute sometimes suggested that any intervening interpretation of that statute (law) by the courts or the Treasury was approved by Congress, although no such Congressional approval was expressly stated. Congress resolved the confusion in 1939 with its systematic arrangement of all tax laws into the Internal Revenue Code of 1939, a permanent codification that required no reenactment.

The 1939 Code was revised in 1954 and again in 1986. Thus, today's governing Federal tax law is the *Internal Revenue Code of 1986*. The 1986 Code has already been amended by the Revenue Act of 1987, the Technical and Miscellaneous Revenue Act of 1988, the Revenue Reconciliation Act of 1989, and the Revenue Reconciliation Act of 1990, and will continue to be amended to incorporate changes in the tax law as those changes are enacted.

FEDERAL WEALTH TRANSFER TAXES

In 1916, the very same year the Supreme Court upheld the constitutionality of the Federal income tax, Congress enacted the first Federal law to impose a tax on the transfer of property triggered by the death of an individual. The value of the transfer was measured by the fair market value of the various assets included in the decedent's estate, and consequently the tax imposed on the transfer is referred to as the estate tax. The Federal estate tax imposed a progressive tax on the value on the decedent's taxable estate.

Because an individual could avoid the imposition of the Federal estate tax simply by giving away his or her property before death, Congress enacted the first Federal gift tax in 1924[8] to prevent full scale avoidance of the estate tax.

---

[7]   240 U.S. 1 (USSC, 1916).   [8]   Although repealed in 1926, the Federal gift tax was reinstated in 1932.

Like the Federal income tax, these Federal wealth transfer taxes have undergone significant changes since first enacted, adding to their complexity. Also, like the Federal income tax, there is little likelihood that Congress will abandon them in the foreseeable future.

FEDERAL TAXES AS A SOURCE OF REVENUE

As sources of revenue, only the Federal income tax can claim a dominant role in providing the funds with which the U.S. government operates. The chart in Exhibit 1-1 illustrates the role of the Federal income tax in providing funding for the 1991 fiscal year proposed budget submitted by President Bush to the Congress in January, 1991. Note the limited role of excise taxes. Federal transfer taxes are even less significant and are included in the "other" category as a revenue source.

KEY TAX TERMS

Before examining the various types of Federal taxes in more detail, the reader must first become familiar with basic tax terminology. Some of the more common terms are briefly presented below.

Tax Base.   A tax base is that amount upon which a tax is levied. For instance, in the case of Federal income taxation the tax base is *taxable income*. Taxable income is the taxpayer's total income *less* deductions, exclusions, and exemptions

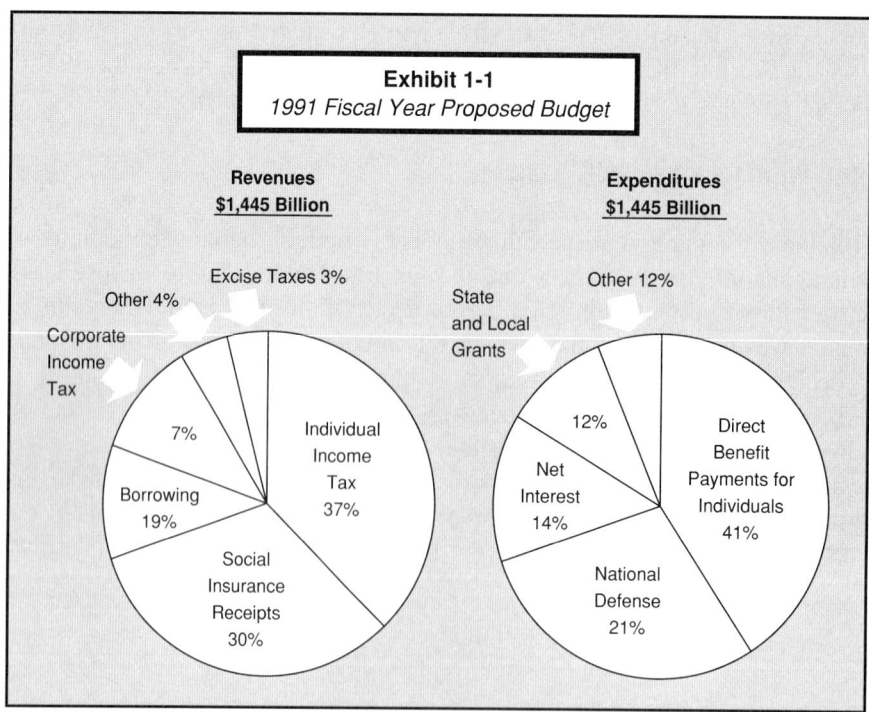

that might be available to a particular taxpayer. In the case of the Federal wealth transfer taxes, the tax base is the fair market value of the property transferred by gift or at death *reduced* by certain exclusions, exemptions, or deductions allowed by Congress.

Income. Any *permanent* increment to wealth generally is defined as income. Temporary increments such as loans are not considered to be income. Sometimes income is subject to Federal taxation and other times it is not. The taxability of these increments to wealth generally depends upon whether Congress has *exempted* a particular form of income from taxation. Increments to wealth take many forms. Such increments may take the form of cash, property other than cash, or even services that are rendered to the taxpayer. As a general rule, Congress—and the various Federal courts assigned to interpret its laws—consider *any* increment to wealth to be taxable income *unless* it is *excluded* by definition (e.g., loans that must be repaid), by specific statutory authority in the Internal Revenue Code of 1986, or by the Constitution. Each of these possibilities is examined in detail in Chapters 5 and 6, which deal with gross income.

Deduction. A deduction is a reduction in the gross (total) amount which must be included in the taxable base. For instance, when an individual taxpayer incurs expenses such as medical expenses, interest on a loan or home mortgage, or property taxes, he or she generally will be allowed to deduct these expenses to arrive at taxable income for Federal tax purposes. Similarly, corporations are allowed to deduct most of their costs of doing business to determine corporate taxable income. It is *extremely important* to note, however, that deductions are a matter of legislative grace—unless Congress has specifically authorized a particular deduction, the expense will not be deductible.

> **Example 3.** Individual T purchased his family residence in 1987 for $70,000. T sells his residence in 1991 for $60,000. T may not take a deduction for the $10,000 loss (a permanent reduction in wealth) in determining his taxable income *because* Congress has not authorized a deduction for this particular type of loss.

Most deductions available to individual taxpayers and to other taxable entities (i.e., corporations, estates, and trusts) are discussed in detail in Chapters 7, 8, 9, 10, 11, and 12 of this text.

Exclusions. Certain increments to wealth that are *not included* in a particular Federal tax base are referred to as exclusions. Since the Constitution grants Congress the authority to tax income *from whatever source derived,* exclusions obviously are the creations of Congress. For various social, political, or economic reasons, Congress has chosen to exclude many sources of income and wealth transfers from their usual Federal tax base. The more common Congressional objectives of exclusions are discussed in a later section of this chapter.

> **Example 4.** N receives a $10,000 graduation gift from her aunt. N does not have to include this amount in determining taxable income because Congress has specifically excluded gifts from income. If N had

received the $10,000 in exchange for rendering services to her aunt, or if N had received the $10,000 for appearing on a television game show, then in both cases she would have to include (report) the amount in income subject to taxation.

Example 5.   Refer to *Example 4* above. If N's aunt transfers $10,000 to N in the current year as a graduation gift, and this is the only gift made by the aunt to N in the current year, this transfer will not be subjected to the Federal gift tax. Congress has provided an annual exclusion from gift taxation of $10,000 per donee per year.

Tax Rates.   A tax rate is some percentage applied to the tax base to determine a taxpayer's liability. Tax rates usually are either proportional or progressive. A *proportional* tax rate is one that remains at a constant percentage regardless of the size of the tax base. A *progressive* tax rate structure is one in which an increasing percentage rate is applied to increasing increments of the tax base. A *regressive* tax rate structure is one in which a decreasing percentage rate is applied to increasing increments of the tax base.

Example 6.   A has a tax base of $5,000 and pays a tax of $500, or 10%. B's similar tax base is $10,000 and the tax on this amount is $1,000, or 10%. If the same constant rate of 10% is applied to any amount of tax base, the tax is proportional.

Example 7.   R has a tax base of $10,000 and pays a tax of $500 on the first $5,000, and a tax of $1,000 on the next $5,000. The total tax of $1,500 was calculated by applying a 10% rate to the first $5,000 increment of the tax base and then applying a 20% rate to the excess tax base over $5,000. Since a higher percentage rate is applied as the tax base increases, this is a progressive rate structure.

Most excise taxes (e.g., sales taxes) employ a proportional tax rate. However, both the Federal income and transfer tax rates, as well as most state income tax rates, are progressive. The 1991 Federal income tax rate schedules for individual taxpayers appear on the inside front cover of this text for ready reference. The tax rates for corporations, estates, and trusts are presented on the inside back cover of the text. The Federal gift and estate tax rates are reproduced in Appendix A at the back of the text. A glance at either of these sources will indicate the progressive nature of the Federal tax system.

Marginal, Average, and Effective Tax Rates.   The *marginal* tax rate of any rate structure is that percentage at which the *next* dollar added to the tax base will be taxed. For example, under the 1991 Federal income tax rate structure for individuals, the highest marginal tax rate is 31 percent (i.e., no one will be taxed on income at a rate greater than 31 percent).

Example 8. H, an unmarried taxpayer, has taxable income of $18,000 for 1991. Referring to tax rate Schedule X on the inside front cover of this text, an unmarried taxpayer with taxable income of $18,000 has a tax of $2,700. H's marginal tax rate is therefore 15%. If H is a married taxpayer filing a separate tax return but reporting the same $18,000 of taxable income, his marginal tax rate would be 28%.

A taxpayer's knowledge of his or her marginal tax rate is essential in any tax-planning effort to minimize taxes. Without it, the tax impact of an additional dollar of the tax base or an additional dollar deduction could not be determined.

Example 9. Refer to *Example 8.* If unmarried taxpayer H is considering depositing $2,000 in an Individual Retirement Account, an amount currently allowed as a deduction for Federal income tax purposes, he could determine his immediate tax savings to be $300 (the 15% marginal tax rate × the $2,000 income not taxed). Similarly, if H had a 31% marginal tax rate and wanted to know the after-tax amount of a proposed $6,000 increase in salary, he would simply multiply 69% (100% − 31%) times the $6,000.

Many individuals, including those who are highly educated, do not understand the marginal tax rate concept. All too often one hears the expression, "I can't afford to earn more because it will throw me into a higher tax bracket and I will keep less than I do now after taxes." This theoretically cannot occur unless the marginal tax rate exceeds 100 percent.

Marginal tax rates are also confused with *average* tax rates (tax divided by tax base) and *effective* tax rates (tax divided by total economic income). In decrying the harshness of the income tax, people often point to their marginal rate and declare that they are paying that percent (e.g., 28%) of their income to the government. Such is clearly not the case.

Example 10. K, an unmarried taxpayer, has taxable income of $25,000 and pays a tax of $4,355. Although her marginal tax rate is 28%, K's average tax rate is 17.4% ($4,355 ÷ $25,000), a far cry from 28%.

Example 11. Assume the same facts as in *Example 10* except that K's total economic income is $35,000, the $10,000 difference between total income and taxable income being attributable to exclusions and deductions (e.g., interest on tax-exempt bonds and the personal exemption). In such case, K would pay taxes at an effective rate of 12.4% [$4,355 ÷ ($25,000 + $10,000)].

Tax Credits. A tax credit is a dollar-for-dollar offset against a tax liability. A credit is quite different from a deduction, since it directly reduces the tax liability itself, whereas a deduction simply reduces the base amount subject to the tax.

Example 12.   T is a single taxpayer with a 31% marginal tax rate. An additional $100 tax deduction would result in a tax reduction to T of $31 (31% × $100). If the $100 qualified as a tax credit, however, T would have a $100 tax reduction—the equivalent of a $323 tax deduction at a marginal tax rate of 31%.

Tax credits are discussed in detail in Chapter 13 of this text.

MAJOR TYPES OF TAXES

Taxing authorities within the United States have a wide array of taxes with which they raise revenues or attempt to effect social, political, or economic change. The average individual will feel the impact of quite a number of taxes during his or her lifetime. Any attempt to accumulate wealth requires diligent tax planning, and to ignore the growing size of the Federal, state, and local taxes will serve no useful purpose toward this end. Although the principal thrust of this text is aimed at the Federal income and wealth transfer taxes, some of the other types of taxes merit a brief introduction.

INCOME TAXES

An income tax is an extraction of some of the taxpayer's economic gain, usually on a periodic basis. In addition to the Federal government, many states and some local governments impose a tax on income. As noted earlier in Exhibit 1-1, the individual income tax is expected to provide 37 percent of the Federal government's revenues in 1991. Of all the sources providing revenues to the Federal government, the individual income tax is the largest. In contrast, the corporate income tax is expected to provide only 7 percent of the Federal government's projected revenues for 1991.[9]

The Federal government imposes an income tax on individuals, corporations, estates, and trusts. Usually, a final tax reckoning (reporting and paying taxes due) is made at the end of each year. In order to ensure tax collections, however, Congress has created a pay-as-you-go requirement. Basically, this process requires employers to withhold and remit to the Federal government income taxes

---

[9]   Such heavy reliance on the income tax as a source of government revenues is peculiar to the United States. Most Western European nations have turned to a Value Added Tax (VAT). A VAT is a system of taxing the increment in value of goods as they move through the production and manufacturing process to the market place. The VAT operates very much like a national sales tax and has occasionally been proposed, though unsuccessfully, for the United States.

on wages paid to employees. Individuals with income from sources other than wages, and most other tax entities are required to make estimated tax prepayments during the year.[10]

Application of the Federal income tax to individuals is discussed in Chapters 3 and 4. Computation of a corporation's Federal income tax is explained in Chapter 19. The Federal income taxation of partnerships, estates, and trusts is examined in Chapters 22 and 25. For now, the procedures for determining the Federal income tax liability of corporate and individual taxpayers are reduced to computational formulas presented in Exhibits 1-2 and 1-3 as follows. The components of these formulas are introduced and discussed in greater detail in Chapter 3.

Most states of the United States impose an income tax of some sort.[11] Generally, state income taxes are designed to operate much like the Federal income tax. Almost all the states have a tax-withholding procedure and most use the income determination for Federal income tax purposes as the tax base. Some states allow a deduction for Federal income taxes, while others exclude income that is subject to Federal income taxation. Interest income from Federal government obligations is not subject to state income taxation, and interest income from state and local government obligations generally is not subject to either Federal or state income taxation. Most states have developed their own set of rates, exemptions, and credits; however, the filing date for the state income tax return generally coincides with the due date of the taxpayer's Federal income tax return.[12]

One particular problem that has developed in the area of state taxation is the so-called "unitary tax." Several states[13] tax businesses on the basis of their global activities, not just their local operations. This asserted right to tax income that has not been earned within the state's boundaries has been subjected to many challenges in the courts; but, as of this date, the unitary tax has not been

---

[10] This procedure was developed by Congress during World War II to accelerate annual tax payments needed to finance the war effort. The process served so well to increase compliance with and facilitate administration of the Federal income tax law that Congress chose not to abandon it at the close of the war.

[11] States *not* currently imposing an income tax on individuals are Alaska, Florida, Nevada, South Dakota, Texas, Washington, and Wyoming. Tennessee and New Hampshire impose an income tax on an individual's dividend and interest income. Every state imposes either a corporate income tax or a tax on the privilege of conducting

business within the state's boundaries. See subsequent discussion of franchise taxes.

[12] For individuals and partnerships, the due date of the Federal income tax return is the fifteenth day of the fourth month following the close of the tax year. For corporate taxpayers, the due date of the Federal return is the fifteenth day of the *third* month following the close of the tax year.

[13] Among those states that tax businesses on the basis of worldwide income are Alaska, California, Colorado, Florida, Idaho, Illinois, Indiana, Massachusetts, Montana, New Hampshire, New York (oil companies only), North Dakota, Oregon, and Utah.

Exhibit 1-2
Tax Formula for Corporate Taxpayers

Income (from whatever source)	$xxx,xxx
Less: Exclusions from gross income	− xx,xxx
Gross income	$xxx,xxx
Less: Deductions	− xx,xxx
Taxable income	$xxx,xxx
Applicable tax rates	xx%
Gross tax	$ xx,xxx
Less: Tax credits and prepayments	− x,xxx
Tax due (or refund)	$ xx,xxx

Exhibit 1-3
Tax Formula for Individual Taxpayers

Income (from whatever source)		$xxx,xxx
Less: Exclusions from gross income		− xx,xxx
Gross income		$xxx,xxx
Less: Deductions *for* adjusted gross income		− xx,xxx
Adjusted gross income		$xxx,xxx
Less: 1. The larger of		
a. Standard deduction	$x,xxx	
or	*or*	− x,xxx
b. Total itemized deductions	$x,xxx	
2. Personal and dependency exemption deduction		− x,xxx
Taxable income		$xxx,xxx
Applicable tax rates (from Tables or Schedules X, Y, or Z)		xx%
Gross tax		$ xx,xxx
Less: Tax credits and prepayments		− x,xxx
Tax due (or refund)		$ xx,xxx

struck down as unconstitutional.[14] Foreign corporations object to this worldwide combined reporting for many reasons, the most obvious being that it may result in the imposition of state taxation even when no taxable income has been generated by intrastate operations.

WEALTH TRANSFER TAXES

Unlike Federal and state income taxes, wealth transfer taxes are not significant revenue producers. For example, collection of the Federal transfer taxes for 1989 represented less than 2 percent of Federal income.[15] Historically, the primary function of wealth transfer taxes has been to *hinder* the accumulation of wealth by family units. Thus, the goal of wealth redistribution generally underlies the design of estate and gift tax systems.

The Federal Estate Tax. Since 1976, the Federal estate tax and Federal gift tax have been combined into one tax known as the unified transfer tax. The unified transfer tax eliminates the distinction previously required between taxable lifetime transfers and transfers at death. Like the Federal income tax rate structure, the unified transfer tax rates are progressive. Unlike the income tax, however, the Federal transfer tax is *computed cumulatively* on taxable gifts made during a donor's lifetime and taxable transfers made at the donor's death. This is done by adding taxable gifts for the current year to all taxable gifts made in prior years (since 1976), calculating the gross tax on the sum of the gifts, and *subtracting* gift taxes assessed on the prior years' gifts. Under this system, a decedent's taxable estate is treated as the decedent's *final* gift.

Although discussed in detail in Chapter 24, the procedure for computing the Federal estate tax liability is reduced to summary form in Exhibit 1-4 as follows.

A decedent's gross estate includes the value of *all* property owned at date of death, wherever located. This includes the proceeds of an insurance policy on the life of the decedent if the decedent's estate is the beneficiary, or if the decedent had any ownership rights[16] in the policy at time of death. Property included in the gross estate generally is valued as of the date of death.[17]

The taxable estate is the gross estate reduced by deductions allowed for funeral and administrative expenses, debts of the decedent, certain taxes and losses, and charitable gifts made from the decedent's estate. It is important to note that there

---

[14] The U.S. Supreme Court upheld California's system of taxing global profits of U.S.-based multinational businesses in *Container Corporation of America v. Franchise Tax Board,* 103 S.Ct. 2933 (USSC, 1983).

[15] Commissioner of Internal Revenue, *1989 Annual Report,* IRS Publication 55.

[16] Ownership rights in a life insurance policy include the power to change the policy's beneficiary, the right to cancel or assign the policy, and the right to borrow against the policy.

[17] An executor of a taxable estate may elect an alternative valuation date of six months after death. See Chapter 24 for greater details.

Exhibit 1-4
Computation of Federal Estate Tax Liability

Gross estate................................		$x,xxx,xxx
Less the sum of:		
Expenses, indebtedness, and taxes...............................	$ xx,xxx	
Losses...................................	x,xxx	
Charitable bequests.......................	xx,xxx	
Marital deduction..........................	xxx,xxx	− xxx,xxx
Taxable estate...............................		$ xxx,xxx
Plus: Taxable gifts made after December 31, 1976................		+ xx,xxx
Total taxable transfers.........................		$ xxx,xxx
Tentative tax on total transfers................		$ xxx,xxx
Less the sum of:		
Gift taxes paid on post-1976 taxable gifts......................................	$ x,xxx	
Unified transfer tax credit...................	xx,xxx	
Other tax credits............................	x,xxx	− xx,xxx
Estate tax liability.............................		$ xx,xxx

is no limit imposed on the charitable deduction.[18] If an individual is willing to leave his or her entire estate for public, charitable, or religious use, there will be no taxable estate. Finally, an *unlimited* marital deduction is allowed for the value of property passing to a surviving spouse. Thus, if a married taxpayer, no matter how wealthy, is willing to leave all of his or her property to the surviving spouse, no Federal transfer tax will be imposed on the estate. Only upon the subsequent death of the surviving spouse will the couple's wealth be subject to taxation.

Under current Federal estate tax laws, taxable gifts made after 1976 are added to the taxable estate to arrive at total taxable transfers. A tentative transfer tax is then computed on the base amount. All gift taxes paid on post-1976 gifts, as well as certain tax credits, are subtracted from this tentative tax in arriving at the Federal estate tax due, if any. Most estate tax credits have a single underlying purpose—to reduce or eliminate the effect of multiple taxation of a single estate. Estate taxes paid to the various states or foreign countries on property owned by the decedent and located within their boundaries are examples of estate tax credits. However, the major credit available to reduce the Federal estate tax is the *unified credit.*

---

[18] Planning for maximizing the benefit of the unlimited marital deduction is discussed in Chapter 26.

The unified credit is a lifetime credit available for all taxable transfers, including taxable gifts made after 1976. It must be used when available; a taxpayer may not decide to postpone use of the credit if he or she makes a taxable transfer in the current year. Currently, the unified credit is $192,800. This amount of credit completely offsets the tax on $600,000 of taxable transfers (see Appendix A for the Unified Transfer Tax Rate Schedule currently in effect). Thus, an individual may make substantial transfers of wealth *before* any tax liability is incurred.

> **Example 13.** T had never made any taxable gifts prior to her death in 1991. The tentative tax on T's taxable estate is $250,000, and tax credits *other than* the unified tax credit total $5,000. The Federal estate tax due on T's estate will be $52,200 ($250,000 tentative tax − $192,800 unified tax credit − $5,000 other credits).

The Federal Gift Tax. As stated earlier, the purpose of the Federal gift tax was to prevent the avoidance of the Federal estate tax by lifetime transfers of property. Until 1977, the Federal gift tax rates were 75 percent of the Federal estate tax rates. This rate differential encouraged taxable lifetime transfers, which in effect accelerated transfer tax payments to the Federal government. The Tax Reform Act of 1976 eliminated this rate difference, and as discussed above, there now is only *one* Federal transfer tax rate structure.

The procedure for computing the Federal gift tax liability is presented as a formula in Exhibit 1-5. To arrive at taxable gifts for the year, the taxpayer's total gifts may be reduced by the annual exclusion and by the deductions allowed for property transferred to a spouse or charity. In computing taxable gifts for the current year, note that a donor is allowed an annual exclusion of $10,000 per donee. The annual exclusion is allowed *each year* even if the donor had made gifts in the prior year to the same donee.

> **Example 14.** T, a widower, wanted his son, daughter-in-law, and their five children to share his wealth. On December 25, 1991, he gave $10,000 to each family member. He repeats these gifts in 1992. Although T has transferred $140,000 [$10,000 × 7 (number of donees) × 2], he has not made taxable gifts in either 1991 or 1992.

The marital and charitable deductions for Federal gift tax purposes are the same as for the Federal estate tax—*unlimited*. Thus, if a taxpayer gives his or her spouse a $2,000,000 anniversary present or transfers $100,000 to his or her church, a taxable gift has not been made.

If taxable gifts have been made for the current year, the cumulative computational procedure of the unified transfer tax must be applied.

Exhibit 1-5
Computation of Federal Gift Tax Liability

Fair market value of all gifts made in the current year..............................		$xxx,xxx
Less the sum of:		
Annual exclusions ($10,000 per donee)................................	$xx,xxx	
Marital deduction............................	xx,xxx	
Charitable deduction	x,xxx	− xx,xxx
Taxable gifts for current year......................		$xxx,xxx
Plus: Taxable gifts made in prior years...........................		+ xx,xxx
Taxable transfers to date.........................		$xxx,xxx
Tentative tax on total transfers to date		$ xx,xxx
Less the sum of:		
Gift taxes computed at current rates on prior years' taxable gifts..........	$ x,xxx	
Unified transfer tax credit....................	x,xxx	− x,xxx
Gift tax due on current gifts......................		$ xx,xxx

---

Example 15. In 1987 R made her first taxable gift of $350,000. Tax (before credits) on this amount was $104,800. In 1991 R makes a second taxable gift of $350,000. The tax (before credits) on the second gift is $125,000, computed as follows:

Taxable gift in 1991	$350,000
Plus: Taxable gift in 1987	+ 350,000
Cumulative taxable gifts................	$700,000
Tax on $700,000	$229,800*
Less: Tax on 1987 gift..............	− 104,800*
Tax on 1991 gift........................	$125,000

* See the unified transfer tax rate schedules contained in Appendix A. Also, note that the current year's tax rate is used to compute the tax reduction for the 1987 gift.

Note that the cumulative system of wealth transfer taxation *and* the progressive rate schedule cause a higher tax on the 1991 gift, even though the gift was the same amount as the 1987 gift.

Computation of the current year's gift tax liability is a two-step process. First, a tentative tax is calculated by applying the unified tax rates in effect for the current year to the cumulative lifetime taxable transfers made by the individual. Next, the tentative tax liability is reduced by (1) the taxes attributable to prior years' taxable gifts, and (2) the unified transfer tax credit. Note that in computing the reduction for prior years' taxable transfers, the unified tax rates in effect in the current year are used—even though the tax reduction so computed may exceed the actual gift taxes paid on the prior transfers. This procedure was developed in 1977 when the gift tax rates were increased to the same level as the estate tax rates. Since the tentative tax liability is calculated by applying the current tax rates to *all* lifetime taxable transfers, any gifts made before 1977 are included at rates substantially higher than those in effect for the year the gifts were made. Without the procedure, the current year's gift tax liability would include some additional tax on prior years' gifts—in effect, a double taxation of pre-1977 gifts.

The only credit available to offset the Federal gift tax liability is the unified transfer tax credit. As illustrated previously (in Examples 13 and 14), a taxpayer's unified transfer tax credit for any given year is the scheduled unified credit available for that particular year.

Example 16. Assume the same facts in *Example 15*. The tax on R's 1987 gift is $104,800, and she must use $104,800 of her available unified credit so that the actual gift tax due is reduced to zero. The tax on R's 1991 gift is $37,000, computed as follows:

Taxable gift for 1991		$350,000
Plus: 1987 taxable gift		+ 350,000
Taxable transfers to date		$700,000
Tentative tax on total transfers to date (see Exhibit 1-5)		$299,800
Less: Gift taxes on 1987 gift		− 104,800
Tentative tax on 1991 gift		$125,000
Less: Remaining unified transfer tax credit:		
Total credit available	$192,800	
Less: Unified transfer tax credit used in 1987	− 104,800	− 88,000
Gift tax due on 1991 gift		$ 37,000

Another unique feature of the Federal gift tax involves the *gift-splitting* election available to a married donor. If a donor makes the election on his or her current gift tax return, one half of all gifts made during the year will be considered to have been made by the donor's spouse. The election is valid *only if* both spouses *consent* to gift-splitting.

Example 17. In 1991 husband H makes two gifts of $100,000 each to his son and daughter. His wife W makes a gift of $5,000 to the daughter only. H and W elect gift-splitting on their 1991 gift tax returns. As a result, H will report a gift to the son of $50,000 and a gift to the daughter of $52,500 [1/2 of ($100,000 + $5,000)], and will claim two $10,000 gift tax exclusions. W will report exactly the same gifts and claim two $10,000 exclusions.

Without gift-splitting, H would still be entitled to $20,000 of exclusions, but W could only claim an exclusion of $5,000 for her gift to the daughter. Thus by electing to split gifts, a married donor can, in effect, make use of any annual exclusions not needed by his or her spouse. More importantly, if taxable gifts are made under a gift-splitting arrangement, *two* lifetime unified credits (i.e., one for each spouse) will be available to reduce the resulting gift tax liability.

State and Local Transfer Taxes. Many states and some local jurisdictions impose an inheritance tax on the *right to receive* property at death. Unlike an estate tax, which is imposed on the estate according to value of property transferred by the decedent at death, an inheritance tax is imposed on the recipient of property from an estate.[19] The amount of an inheritance tax payable usually is directly affected by the degree of kinship between the recipient and the decedent. The inheritance tax typically provides an exemption from the tax, which increases as the relationship between the recipient (e.g., surviving spouse, children, grandchildren, parents, etc.) and the decedent becomes closer. In addition, as the relationship becomes closer, the transfer tax rates decrease. Thus, the more closely related one is, the smaller the inheritance tax will be. Generally, little if any inheritance tax exemption is available for transfers to unrelated recipients, and the highest rate is imposed.

State estate taxes take one of two forms. One type, similar to the Federal estate tax, permits deductions from the gross estate such as the marital deduction, funeral and administrative expenses, and debts of the decedent. The rates imposed on the resulting taxable estate are considerably lower than those of the Federal unified transfer tax rates. The more common form of a state estate tax, however, is based on whatever amount qualifies for the *maximum* state death tax credit allowed for Federal estate tax purposes. Section 2011 of the Internal Revenue Code contains a schedule of the maximum amount of a credit that may be taken against the Federal estate tax for any estate, inheritance, legacy, or succession taxes actually paid to a state. This schedule is presented below in Exhibit 1-6. States imposing an inheritance tax usually will have an estate tax so that they will collect the maximum amount of transfer taxes allowed as a credit under Code § 2011.

> **Example 18.** At his death, T resided in a state that imposes an estate tax based on the maximum amount allowed as a credit for Federal estate tax purposes. If T's Federal adjusted taxable estate is $1,540,000, the state's estate tax will be $70,800.

States that impose *both* an estate and inheritance tax, and which impose their estate tax based on the maximum amount allowed as a credit for Federal estate tax purposes, will reduce the state estate tax by any inheritance tax imposed on the heirs.

---

[19] It is not uncommon for the decedent's will to provide that his or her estate pay any inheritance tax imposed on the recipient of property from the estate.

Exhibit 1-6
Federal Estate Tax Credit for State Death Taxes

**Table for Computation of
Maximum Credit for State Death Taxes**

(A) Adjusted* Taxable Estate Equal to or More Than—	(B) Adjusted Taxable Estate Less Than—	(C) Credit on Amount in Column (A)	(D) Rates of Credit on Excess Over Amount in Column (A)
$ 40,000	$ 90,000	$ 0	0.8%
90,000	140,000	400	1.6
140,000	240,000	1,200	2.4
240,000	440,000	3,600	3.2
440,000	640,000	10,000	4.0
640,000	840,000	18,000	4.8
840,000	1,040,000	27,600	5.6
1,040,000	1,540,000	38,800	6.4
1,540,000	2,040,000	70,800	7.2
2,040,000	2,540,000	106,800	8.0
2,540,000	3,040,000	146,800	8.8
3,040,000	3,540,000	190,800	9.6
3,540,000	4,040,000	238,800	10.4
4,040,000	5,040,000	290,800	11.2
5,040,000	6,040,000	402,800	12.0
6,040,000	7,040,000	522,800	12.8
7,040,000	8,040,000	650,800	13.6
8,040,000	9,040,000	786,800	14.4
9,040,000	10,040,000	930,800	15.2
10,040,000	. . . . .	1,082,800	16.0

*The adjusted taxable estate is the Federal taxable estate reduced by $60,000.

Example 19.   At her death, F resided in a state that imposed both an estate and inheritance tax. The state's estate tax is based on the maximum allowed credit for Federal estate tax purposes. If the state imposed an inheritance tax of $7,000 on the heirs of F's $440,000 adjusted taxable estate, the state estate tax would be $3,000 ($10,000 minimum state death tax credit − $7,000 inheritance tax).

Nine states impose a state gift tax.[20] Like the Federal gift tax, state gift tax laws usually provide for lifetime exemptions and annual exclusions and very often incorporate by reference the Federal gift tax law. For instance, the New York State statute permitting a state gift tax deduction for charitable contributions reads as follows:

> New York adopts the Federal provisions permitting deductions for charitable, public, and similar gifts less exclusions. The Federal figure is reduced by the gifts, less exclusions, which are not qualified charitable New York gifts (e.g., gifts of out-of-state real property).[21]

State gift tax rates usually follow the pattern of state inheritance taxes. That is, the closer the relationship between donee and donor, the lower the gift tax rate and the larger the gift tax exemption.

EMPLOYMENT TAXES

The Federal government and most states impose some form of employment tax on either self-employed individuals, employees,[22] or employers. The most common form of state employment tax is levied on wages, with the proceeds used to finance the state's unemployment benefits program. State unemployment taxes are imposed on employers who have employees working within the state's boundaries, but only if the employees would be eligible for unemployment benefits from the state. Most states' unemployment taxes are based on the same taxable wage base as that used for the Federal unemployment tax (see discussion below), and employers are allowed to take state unemployment taxes paid as a credit against the Federal unemployment tax liability.

The Federal government imposes two types of taxes on employment—a social security tax and an unemployment tax. The Federal Insurance Contribution Act (FICA) imposes a tax on self-employed individuals, employees, and employers. The FICA tax (commonly known as the Social Security tax) is paid by both an employee and his or her employer if the employee is eligible for Social Security benefits. Although subject to a different tax rate, self-employed individ-

---

[20] Delaware, Louisiana, New York, North Carolina, Oregon, Rhode Island, South Carolina, Tennessee, and Wisconsin.

[21] § 1009, Tax Law (CCH New York Tax Reports, No. 88-937). See Chapter 2 for an explanation of citation symbols.

[22] The term "employee" is used to identify persons whose work effort, tools, place of work, and work time periods are subject to the supervision and control of another (the employer). A person who provides his or her own tools and who has the *right* to exercise control over when, where, and for whom services are rendered (i.e., an independent contractor) generally is classified as self-employed rather than as an employee. See Chapter 8 for a discussion of the importance this classification has in the deductions allowed to individuals for Federal income tax purposes.

uals are required to pay FICA taxes on net earnings from self-employment. The Federal Unemployment Tax Act (FUTA) imposes a tax *only* on the employer. Self-employed individuals are not eligible for unemployment benefits and thus are not subject to the FUTA tax. The tax base and rate structure of both these Federal employment taxes are presented below.

FICA Taxes. Proceeds from the FICA tax are used by the Federal government to finance its payment of Social Security benefits [i.e., old age, survivors' and disability insurance (OASDI) payments and Medicare health insurance (MHI) payments]. The tax base and tax rates have increased annually since 1978. In recent years, Congress has set the tax base each year—a few months before the beginning of the year—rather than determine an extended base to be applicable for several subsequent years.

Beginning in 1991, the FICA tax imposed on wages and self-employment income has two components: (1) a 1.45 percent tax for Medicare health insurance (MHI), and (2) a 6.2 percent tax for old age, survivors' and disability insurance (OASDI). In the past, these two taxes have always applied to the same base, and it was therefore common to combine the two and simply speak of an FICA tax of 7.65 percent (6.2% + 1.45%). However, the Revenue Reconciliation Act of 1990 extended the base that is taken into account for calculating the Medicare health insurance portion of the FICA tax to $125,000. The base for the portion of the FICA tax based on old age, survivors' and disability insurance was increased to $53,400 for 1991.

Employees and Employers. FICA taxes are imposed at the combined rate of 7.65 percent (6.2% OASDI + 1.45% MHI) on each dollar of an employee's wages up to $53,400 *plus* an additional 1.45 percent on each dollar of wages from $53,400 to $125,000. Thus, the maximum amount of an employee's FICA taxes for 1991 is $5,123.30 [(7.65% × $53,400 = $4,085.10) + ($125,000 − $53,400 = $71,600 × 1.45% = $1,038.20)].[23] The employer is required to pay a *matching amount* of FICA taxes for each employee (i.e., the same tax rates on each employee's wage base up to the same limits).

> **Example 20.** During 1991, employee E earns wages of $24,000. As a result, E will pay $1,836 (7.65% × $24,000) FICA taxes, and her employer must pay the same amount as an employment tax.[24]

---

[23] Another way to calculate the maximum FICA tax to be paid by an employee for 1991 is to add the maximum amounts of the two components of the tax. The maximum OASDI portion of the FICA tax is $3,310.80 (6.2% × $53,400), and the maximum MHI portion is $1,812.50 (1.45% × $125,000). Thus, the maximum FICA tax for an employee is $5,123.30 ($3,310.80 + $1,812.50).

[24] Employers are allowed a tax deduction for all payroll taxes. See Chapter 7 for a discussion of business deductions.

An employer is required to withhold both Federal income taxes and FICA taxes from each employee's wages paid during the year. The employer is then required to pay these withheld amounts plus the employer's matching FICA taxes for each employee to the IRS on a regular basis, usually weekly or monthly.[25] Employers also are required to file Form 941, Employer's Quarterly Federal Tax Return, by the end of the first month following each quarter of the calendar year (e.g., by April 30, 1991 for the quarter ended March 31, 1991), and pay any remaining amount of employment taxes due for the previous quarter.[26]

In some instances, an employee who has had more than one employer during the year may have paid *excess* FICA taxes for the year and will be entitled to a Federal income tax credit or refund for the excess.

> **Example 21.** During 1991, E earned $30,000 from his regular job and $30,000 from a part-time job. Both of E's employers withheld $2,295 ($30,000 × 7.65%) from his wages, and with a matching amount, made payments to the IRS. Since E has paid a total of $4,590 FICA taxes and the maximum amount due for 1991 is $4,180.80 [$3,310.80 OASDI portion (6.2% × $53,400) + $870 MHI portion ($30,000 + $30,000 = $60,000 × 1.45%)], E will be entitled to a tax credit or refund of the $409.20 excess ($4,590 − $4,180.80).

Self-Employed Taxpayers. Like employees, self-employed individuals are required to pay FICA taxes (commonly known as self-employment tax). For 1991, the OASDI portion of the self-employment tax rate is 12.4 percent and the MHI portion is 2.9 percent. These rates are *twice* the FICA tax rates imposed on an employee's wages, and the $10,246.60 maximum self-employment tax is the *sum* of the maximum $5,123.30 FICA tax imposed on *both* an employee and his or her employer. Apparently in order to provide some relief from this "doubling-up effect," self-employed taxpayers are allowed an income tax deduction for one-half the amount of self-employment taxes actually paid.[27] In addition, a self-employed taxpayer is allowed to *reduce* net earnings from self-employment by an amount equal to one-half the combined 15.3 percent tax rate times net earnings from self-employment (i.e., 7.65% × net earnings from self-employment) in arriving at each of the self-employment tax bases.[28] As illustrated in Example 22, this last so-called deduction may not be of benefit to some self-employed taxpayers.

---

[25] The frequency of these payments depends on the total amount of Federal income taxes withheld and the FICA taxes due on the employer's periodic payroll. The amount of Federal income and FICA taxes to be withheld from each employee's wages, and the reporting and payment requirements are specified in Circular E, *Employer's Tax Guide,* a free publication of the Internal Revenue Service.

[26] Because of significant penalties for underpayment of these Federal employment taxes, most employers exercise great care to make payments on a timely basis. See Circular E for a discussion of these penalties and due dates.

[27] § 164(f). See Chapter 2 for an explanation of citations to the Internal Revenue Code of 1986.

[28] § 1402(a)(12).

Each component of the self-employment tax required to be paid is computed as follows:

First: Multiply one-half the self-employment tax rate times net earnings from self-employment.

Second: Subtract the amount determined in step 1 from net earnings from self-employment.[29]

Third: Compare the result in step 2 with each seperate maximum base amount ($53,400 for OASDI and $125,000 for MHI) for self-employment tax purposes and select the smaller amount.

Fourth: Multiply the amount from step 3 by the tax rate for each separate component.

Fifth: Add the amounts of the separate components from step 4. This is the amount of self-employment tax required to be paid.

Example 22. Individuals C and D have net earnings from self-employment for 1991 of $50,000 and $150,000, respectively. Self-employment taxes for C and D are determined as follows:

C

	OASDI	MHI
Net earnings from self-employment	$ 50,000	$ 50,000
Subtract: 7.65% of net earnings from self-employment	(3,825)	(3,825)
	$ 46,175	$ 46,175
Smaller of maximum tax base or amount determined above	$ 46,175	$ 46,175
Times: Each component's tax rate	× 12.4%	× 2.9%
Tax on each component	$5,725.70	$1,339.08

OASDI tax	$5,725.70
Plus: MHI tax	1,339.08
Equals: C's self-employment tax	$7,064.78

	D	
	OASDI	MHI
Net earnings from self-employment..............	$ 150,000	$ 150,000
Subtract: 7.65% of net earnings from self-employment................	(11,475)	(11,475)
	$ 138,525	$ 138,525
Smaller of maximum tax base or amount determined above	$ 53,400	$ 125,000
Times: Each component's tax rate	× 12.4%	× 2.9%
Tax on each component.........................	$6,621.60	$3,625.00
OASDI tax......................................		$ 6,621.60
Plus: MHI tax.................................		3,625.00
Equals: D's self-employment tax		$10,246.60

C will be allowed to deduct $3,532.39 (one-half of $7,064.78 self-employment tax paid) for income tax purposes, and D will be allowed to deduct $5,123.30 (one-half of $10,246.60). Although both will receive a benefit from the income tax deduction, note that only C has received any benefit from the so-called second deduction in arriving at his self-employment tax bases. Because D's reduced net earnings for self-employment for each component is still greater than the maximum tax base, she is required to pay the maximum amount of each component of the self-employment tax for 1991.

Self-employed individuals are required to pay quarterly estimated Federal tax payments, including self-employment taxes, if the estimated amount is $500 or more. A self-employed taxpayer also is required to file Schedule SE, Computation of Social Security Self-Employment Tax, with his or her annual Federal income tax return (Form 1040).

In some instances, a self-employed individual may also earn wages subject to FICA withholding while working as a full or part-time employee. In such a case, the maximum earnings base subject to each component of the self-employment tax is reduced by the wages earned as an employee.

Example 23. During 1991, T received wages of $30,000 and had self-employment income of $40,000. In computing T's self-employment tax, the maximum taxable base for *both* the OASDI tax and the MHI tax is reduced by the wages paid because T's employer has already withheld the appropriate FICA amount on these wages.

	OASDI	MHI
Maximum tax base	$ 53,400	$ 125,000
Less: Wages subject to FICA tax	(30,000)	(30,000)
Reduced maximum tax base	$ 23,400	$ 95,000
Net earnings from self-employment	$ 40,000	$ 40,000
Subtract: 7.65% of net earnings from self-employment	(3,060)	(3,060)
	$ 36,940	$ 36,940
Smaller of reduced maximum tax base or amount determined above	$ 23,400	$ 36,940
Times: Each component's tax rate	× 12.4%	× 2.9%
Tax on each component	$2,901.60	$1,071.26

OASDI tax	$2,901.60
Plus: MHI tax	1,071.26
Equals: T's self-employment tax	$3,972.86

T will also have an income tax deduction of $1,986.43 (one-half of the $3,972.86 self-employment taxes paid).

FUTA Taxes. A Federal unemployment tax is imposed on employers who pay wages of $1,500 or more during any calendar quarter in the calendar year, or who employ at least one individual on each of some 20 days during the calendar year or previous year.[30] Certain exceptions are made for persons employing agricultural or domestic workers.

FUTA tax revenues are used by the Federal government to augment unemployment benefit programs of the various states. The current FUTA tax rate is 6.2 percent of the first $7,000 of wages paid during the year to each covered employee. This translates into a *maximum* FUTA tax of $434 (6.2% × $7,000) *per employee* per year. Since most states also impose an unemployment tax on employers, a credit is allowed against an employer's FUTA tax liability for any similar tax paid to a state. Currently, the maximum FUTA tax credit allowed for this purpose is 5.4 percent of the covered wages (i.e., maximum of $378 per employee). Thus, the maximum FUTA tax paid is normally $56 ($434 − $378, or 0.8% × $7,000) per employee.

All employers subject to FUTA taxes must file Form 940, Employer's Annual Federal Unemployment Tax Return, on or before January 31 of the following year. If the employer's tax liability exceeds certain limits, estimated tax payments must be made during the year.[31] Most states require an employer to file unemployment tax returns and make tax payments quarterly.

---

[30] § 3306(a)(1).

[31] See instructions in Circular E, *Supra*, Footnote 27.

EXCISE TAXES

The purpose of an excise tax is to tax certain privileges as well as the manufacture, sale, or consumption of specified commodities. Federal excise taxes are imposed on the sale of specified articles, various transactions, occupations, and the use of certain items. This type of tax is not imposed on the profits of a business or profession, however. The major types of excise taxes are as follows:

1. Occupational taxes;

2. Facilities and services taxes;

3. Manufacturers' taxes;

4. Retail sales of products and commodities taxes; and

5. Luxury taxes.

Occupational Taxes. Some businesses must pay a fee before engaging in their business. These types of businesses include, but are not limited to, liquor dealers, dealers in medicines, and dealers in firearms.

Facilities and Services Taxes. The person who pays for services and facilities must pay the tax on these items. The institution or person who furnishes the facilities or services must collect the tax, file returns, and turn over the taxes to the taxing authorities. A few of the common services subject to the facilities and services excise tax include air travel, hotel or motel lodging, and telephone service.

Manufacturers' Taxes. As a rule, certain manufactured goods are taxed at the manufacturing level to make collection easier. Most of these items are of a semi-luxurious or specialized nature, such as sporting goods or firearms. This excise tax applies to the sale or use by the manufacturer, producer, or importer, of specified articles. The taxes may be determined by quantity of production (e.g., pounds or gallons) or by a percentage of the sales price. When sales price is used as an index, the tax is based on the sales price of the manufacturer, producer, or importer.

Retail Sales of Products and Commodities Taxes. This excise tax applies to the retail sale or use of diesel fuel, special motor fuels, and fuel used in noncommercial aviation. The tax is collected from the person buying the product by the seller, and the seller must file and pay the tax unless the buyer purchased it tax-free.

Luxury Taxes. This excise tax is merely an extension of the excise taxes imposed on certain retail sales of products. In an obvious attempt to obtain more revenue from those with greater ability to pay, Congress added this new excise tax as part of the Revenue Reconciliation Act of 1990. The 10 percent luxury tax applies to the portion of the sales price that *exceeds* a set price for selected luxury items. The items subject to the tax and their respective set prices are listed below.

Item	Price in Excess of
Passenger cars, vans, and light trucks	$ 30,000
Boats	100,000
Aircraft	250,000
Jewelry	10,000
Furs	10,000

As an example, the luxury tax on a car with a cost of $35,000 would be $500 ($35,000 − $30,000 = $5,000 × 10%). The tax is collected and remitted to the IRS by the retailer.

State Excise Taxes.   Many states and local governments also have excise taxes. They vary in range of coverage and impact, but most parallel the Federal excise taxes. For instance, most states have an excise tax on gasoline, liquor, and cigarettes, as does the Federal government.

ADDITIONAL TYPES OF TAXES

Many other types of taxes are used to augment state, local, and Federal income, employment, excise, and wealth transfer taxes. All three levels of government have never been reluctant to exercise their imagination in creating and developing new ways of supplementing governmental revenues. A few of the other more common types of taxes are briefly explained below.

Franchise Tax.   A franchise tax is a tax on the privilege of doing business in a state or local jurisdiction. The measure of the tax generally is the net income of the business or the value of the capital used within the taxing authorities' jurisdictions.

Sales Tax.   A sales tax is imposed on the gross receipts from the retail sale of tangible personal property (e.g., clothing, automobiles, and equipment) and certain services. Each state or local government determines the tax rate and the services and articles to be taxed. The seller will collect the tax at the time of the sale, and then periodically remit the taxes to the appropriate taxing authority. It is not uncommon for a state or local government to allow the seller to retain a nominal percentage of the collected taxes to compensate for the additional costs incurred by the seller in complying with the tax requirements.

Use Tax.   A use tax is a tax imposed on the use within a state or local jurisdiction of tangible property on which a sales tax was not paid. The tax rate normally equals that of the taxing authority's sales tax.

Doing-Business Penalty. This penalty tax is imposed on a business that has not obtained authorization from the state or local government to operate within its border. Usually, a business must pay a fee for a state charter or some other kind of license as permission to enter business within the state.

Real Property Tax. A real property tax is a tax on the value of realty (land, buildings, homes, etc.) owned by nonexempt individuals or organizations within a jurisdiction. Rates vary with location. This type of tax normally supports local services, such as the public school system or the fire department, and is levied on a recurring annual basis.

Tangible Personal Property Tax. This tax is levied on the value of tangible personalty located within a jurisdiction. Tangible personalty is property not classified as realty and includes such items as office furniture, machinery and equipment, inventories, and supplies. The tax normally must be paid annually, with each local jurisdiction determining its own tax rate and the items to tax.

Intangible Personal Property Tax. This tax is imposed on the value of intangible personalty (i.e., stocks, bonds, and accounts and notes receivable) located within a jurisdiction. The tax generally is paid annually, with each local jurisdiction setting its own tax rate and items to be taxed.

GOALS OF TAXATION

In subsequent chapters, the specific provisions that must be followed to compute the tax will be discussed in detail. Some may view this discussion as a hopeless attempt to explain what seems like an endless barrage of boring rules—rules that, despite their apparent lack of "rhyme or reason," must be considered if the final tax liability is to be determined. The frustration that students of taxation often feel when studying the rules of Federal tax law is not completely unfounded. Indeed, a famous tax scholar, Boris Bittker, once commented on the increasing intricacy of the tax law, saying, "Can one hope to find a way through a statutory thicket so bristling with detail?"[32] As this statement suggests, many provisions of the law are, in fact, obscure and often appear to be without purpose. However, each provision of the tax law originated with some goal, even if no more than to grant a benefit to some Congressman's constituency. A knowledge of the goals underlying a particular provision is an important first step toward a comprehension of the provision. An understanding of the purpose of the law is an invaluable tool in attacking the "statutory thicket." In studying taxation, it becomes apparent that many provisions have been enacted with similar objectives. The following discussion reviews some of the goals of taxation that often serve as the reasons behind the rule.

---

[32] Boris I. Bittker and Lawrence M. Stone, *Federal Income Taxation*, 5th Ed. (Boston: Little, Brown & Co., 1980) liii.

ECONOMIC OBJECTIVES

At first glance, it seems clear that the primary goal of taxation is to provide the resources necessary to fund governmental expenditures. At the Federal level, however, this is not entirely true. As many economists have pointed out, any taxing authority that has the power to control the money supply—as does our Federal government—can satisfy its revenue needs by merely creating money. Nevertheless, complete reliance on the Treasury's printing press to provide the needed resources is not a viable alternative. If the government's expenditures were financed predominantly with funds that it created rather than those obtained through taxation, excess demand would result, which in turn would cause prices to rise, or inflation. Thus, taxation in serving a revenue function also operates along with other instruments of policy to attain a stable price level.

Although Congress can create its own resources, revenue objectives often can explain a particular feature of the law. Consider the personal and dependency exemption deductions, the purpose of which is to free from tax the income needed to maintain a minimum standard of living. Although the cost of living has risen substantially over the years, Congress has been reluctant to increase the amount of these exemptions. The exemption deduction was set at $600 from 1948 to 1969 and was only recently increased over $1,000. In effect, the deduction changed very little over the past 38 years, despite significant increases in the price level during this time. The reluctance to alter the exemption amount derives primarily from the potential impact on revenues.[33] A slight increase in the exemption without a corresponding increase in revenues from other sources would result in a tremendous revenue loss because of the number of exemptions taxpayers claim—approximately 227 million in 1980. For similar reasons, Congress has refrained, until recently, from adjusting the tax rate schedules to compensate for inflation, since to do so would significantly reduce its inflow of resources. In 1985, however, both the personal and dependency exemption amount *and* the individual tax rate schedules were adjusted (indexed) for the increase in the Consumer Price Index that occurred during the previous year.

Revenue considerations also can explain why tax accounting methods sometimes differ from those used for financial accounting. Prior to 1954, an accrual basis taxpayer could neither defer taxation of prepaid income nor deduct estimates of certain expenses, such as the expected costs of servicing warranty contracts. In 1954, the treatment of such items was changed to conform with financial accounting principles that permit deferral of income and accrual of expenses in most situations. The expected revenue loss attributed to this change was $50 million. Within a year after the change, however, the Treasury requested Congress

---

[33] In order to keep pace with price level changes since 1949, the personal and dependency exemptions would have to be approximately $6,000 each in 1987. The Tax Reform Act of 1986 increased the exemption amount to $1,950 for 1988 and indexed for inflation thereafter. For 1991 the exemption amount is $2,150—still a far cry from $6,000.

to repeal the new provisions retroactively because estimates of the revenue loss were in excess of several billion dollars. In short, Congress responded and, as a result, the treatment of prepaid income and certain accruals for tax and financial accounting purposes differs—a difference attributable to revenue considerations.

The role of Federal taxation in carrying out economic policy extends beyond the realm of revenue raising and price stability. Taxation is a major tool used by the government to attain satisfactory economic growth with full employment. The title of the 1981 tax bill is illustrative: *The Economic Recovery Tax Act of 1981* (ERTA). As the title suggests, a major purpose of this legislation was directed toward revitalizing the health of the economy. ERTA significantly lowered tax rates to spur the economy out of a recession. Its objective was to place more *after-tax* income in the hands of taxpayers for their disposal. By so doing, it was hoped that taxpayers would consume more and thus increase aggregate demand, resulting in economic growth.

Congress also has used the tax structure to directly attack the problem of unemployment. In 1977 employers were encouraged to increase employment by the introduction of a general jobs tax credit, which effectively reduced the cost of labor. In 1978 Congress eliminated the general jobs credit and substituted a targeted jobs credit. This credit could be obtained only if employers hired certain targeted groups of individuals who were considered disadvantaged or handicapped. This credit was expanded in 1983 to stimulate the hiring of economically disadvantaged youth during the summer. As the credit for jobs suggests, Congress believes that major economic problems can be solved using the tax system.

A subject closely related to economic growth and full employment is investment. To stimulate investment spending, Congress has enacted numerous provisions. For example, accelerated depreciation methods—the accelerated cost recovery system (ACRS)—may be used to compute the deduction for depreciation, thus enabling rapid recovery of the taxpayer's investment.

Congress encourages certain industries by granting them favorable tax treatment. For example, the credit for research and experimental expenditures cited above clearly benefits those engaged in technology businesses. Other tax provisions are particularly advantageous for other groups such as builders, farmers, and producers of natural resources. Special privileges also are available for exporters. As will become clear in later chapters, the income tax law is replete with rules designed to encourage, stimulate, and assist various enterprises as Congress has deemed necessary over the years.

SOCIAL OBJECTIVES

The tax system is used to achieve not only economic goals but social objectives as well. Some examples are listed below:

1. The deduction for charitable contributions helps to finance the cost of important activities that otherwise would be funded by the government.

2. The deduction for interest on home mortgages subsidizes the cost of a home and thus encourages home ownership.

3. The targeted jobs credit noted above exists to fight unemployment problems of certain disadvantaged groups of citizens.

4. Larger standard deductions are granted to taxpayers who are 65 or over, or are blind, to relieve their tax burden.

5. Deductions for contributions to retirement savings accounts encourage individuals to provide for their future needs.

These examples are representative of the many provisions where social considerations provide the underlying rationale.

The above discussion is but a brief glimpse of how social and economic considerations have shaped our tax law. Interestingly, most of the provisions mentioned have been enacted in the past 20 years. During this time, Congress has relied increasingly on the tax system as a means to strike at the nation's ills. Whether the tax law can be used successfully in this manner is unclear. Many believe that attacking such problems should be done directly through government expenditure programs—not through so-called *tax expenditures*. A tax expenditure is the estimated amount of revenue lost for failing to tax a particular item (e.g., scholarships), for granting a certain deduction (e.g., charitable contributions), or for allowing a credit (e.g., targeted jobs credits). The concept of tax expenditures was developed by noted tax authority Stanley S. Surrey. While Assistant Secretary of the Treasury for Tax Policy during 1961–1969, Surrey and his supporters urged that certain activities should not be encouraged by subsidizing them through reduced tax liabilities. They argued that paying for government-financed activities in such a roundabout fashion makes their costs difficult if not impossible to determine. In addition, they asserted that such expenditures are concealed from the public eye as well as from the standard budgetary review process. Others, however, argued that the tax system could be used effectively for this purpose. Whether either view is correct, Congress currently shows no apparent signs of discontinuing use of the tax system to influence taxpayers' behavior.

OTHER OBJECTIVES

Although social and economic goals provide the rationale for much of our tax law, many provisions can be explained in terms of certain well-established principles of taxation. These principles are simply the characteristics that "good" taxes exhibit. Most tax experts agree that a tax is good if it satisfies the following conditions:[34]

1. The tax is *equitable* or fair;

2. The tax is *economically efficient* (i.e., it advances a goal where appropriate and otherwise is as neutral as possible);

---

[34] These qualities were first identified by Adam Smith. See *The Wealth of Nations,* Book V, Chapter II, Part II (New York: Dutton, 1910).

3. The tax is *certain* and not arbitrary;

4. The tax can be administered by the government and complied with by the taxpayer at a *low cost* (i.e., it is *economical* to operate); and

5. The tax is *convenient* (i.e., administration and compliance can be carried out with the utmost simplicity).

These five qualities represent important principles of taxation that must be conformed with in pursuing social and economic goals. As discussed below, these criteria have greatly influenced our tax law.

Equity. A tax system is considered equitable if it treats all persons who are in the same economic situation in the same fashion. This aspect of equity is referred to as *horizontal equity*. In contrast, *vertical equity* implies that taxpayers who are not in the same situation will be treated differently—the difference in treatment being fair and just. There are two major obstacles in implementing the equity concept as explained. First, there must be some method to determine when taxpayers are in the same economic situation. Second, there must be agreement on reasonable distinctions between those who are in different situations. The manner in which these obstacles are addressed explains two significant features of our tax system.

As indicated above, the first major difficulty in implementing the equity concept is identification of some technique to determine when taxpayers are similarly situated. For tax purposes, it is well settled that similarity is measured in terms of a taxpayer's *ability to pay*. Hence, taxpayers with equal abilities to pay should pay equal taxes. To the dismay of some tax policymakers, however, there is no simple, unambiguous index of an individual's ability. A taxpayer's ability to pay is the composite of numerous factors including his or her wealth, income, family situation, health, and attitude. Clearly, no one measure captures all of these factors. This being so, tax specialists generally have agreed that the best objective measure of ability to pay is income. This agreement, that income is a reasonable surrogate for ability to pay and thus serves the equity principle, explains in part why the primary tax used by the Federal government is an *income* tax.

The second obstacle in implementing the equity concept concerns the treatment of taxpayers who are differently situated. In terms of income, the problem may best be explained by reference to two taxpayers, A and B. If A's income (e.g., $100,000) exceeds B's (e.g., $20,000), it is assumed that A has more ability to pay and thus should pay more tax. The dilemma posed is not whether A and B should pay differing amounts of tax, but rather, what additional amount may be fairly charged to A. If a proportional tax of five percent is levied against A and B, A pays $5,000 (5% of $100,000) and B pays $1,000 (5% of $20,000). While application of this tax rate structure results in A paying $4,000 more than B absolutely, A pays the same amount in relative terms; that is, they both pay the *same* 5 percent. Those charged with the responsibility of developing Federal tax policy have concluded that paying more tax in absolute terms does not adequately serve the equity goal. For this reason, a progressive tax rate structure is used, requiring relatively more tax to be paid by those having more income. With respect to A and B above, this structure would require that A pay a greater percentage of his income than B.

The equity principle explains (at least partially) not only the basic structure of our predominant tax device—an income tax and its progressive tax rate structure—but also explains many other provisions in our law. In fact, some of the factors mentioned earlier that affect a taxpayer's ability to pay are recognized explicitly by separate provisions in the Code. For example, a taxpayer may deduct medical expenses and casualty losses—items over which the taxpayer has little or no power—if such items exceed a certain level. Similarly, a taxpayer's family situation is considered by allowing exemption deductions for dependents whose support is the taxpayer's responsibility.

There are many other specific situations where the equity principle controls the tax consequences. For example, fairness dictates that taxes should not be paid when the taxpayer does not have the *wherewithal to pay* (i.e., the money to pay the tax). This is true even though the transaction results in income to the taxpayer.

> **Example 24.** Upon the theft of valuable machinery, LJM Corporation received a $20,000 insurance reimbursement. Assuming the machinery had a cost (adjusted for depreciation) of $5,000, LJM has realized a $15,000 gain ($20,000 − $5,000). Although the corporation has realized a gain, it also has lost the productive capacity of the machinery. If LJM reinvests the entire $20,000 proceeds in similar assets within two years of the theft, the gain is not taxed. This rule derives from Congressional belief that equity would not be served if taxes were levied when the taxpayer did not have the wherewithal to pay. In addition, the taxpayer's total economic situation has not been so materially altered as to require recognition of the gain.

Administrative Concerns. The final three qualities of a good tax—certainty, economy, and simplicity—might be aptly characterized as administrative in nature. Numerous provisions exist to meet administrative goals. Some of these are so obvious as to be easily overlooked. For example, the certainty requirement underlies the provision that a tax return generally is due each April 15, while economy of collection is the purpose, at least in part, for withholding. Similarly, provisions requiring the taxpayer to compute the tax using tables provided by the IRS are motivated by concerns for simplicity.

Perhaps the most important aspect of the administrative principles is that they often conflict with other principles of taxation. Consequently, one principle must often be adhered to at the expense of another. For example, our tax system could no doubt be more equitable if each individual's ability to pay was personally assessed, much like welfare agents assess the needs of their clients. However, this improvement could be obtained only at a substantial administrative cost. The administrative principle is first in importance in this case, as well as in many others.

A PRELUDE TO TAX PLANNING

Although taxes affect numerous aspects of our lives, their impact is not uncontrollable. Given an understanding of the rules, taxes can be managed with considerable success. Successful management, however, is predicated on good tax planning.

Tax planning is simply the process of arranging one's actions in light of their potential tax consequences. It should be emphasized that the tax consequences sometimes turn on how a particular transaction is structured—that is, *form* often controls taxation.

> **Example 25.** Z is obligated to make monthly payments of interest and principal on a note secured by his car. During the year, he was short of cash so his mother, B, made the payments for him. Since B made the payments directly, she may not deduct the interest expense because interest is deductible only if it relates to a debt for which the taxpayer is personally liable. Moreover, her son cannot deduct the expense since he did not make payment. Note that the deduction could have been obtained had the payment been structured properly. If Z had received a gift of cash from his mother and then made payment, he could have claimed the interest deduction. Alternatively, if B had been jointly liable on the note, she could have deducted the interest payments she made.

In the example above, note that regardless of how the transaction is structured, the result is the same *except for* the tax ramifications. By merely planning and changing the form of the transaction, tax benefits are obtained. Before jumping to the conclusion that form always governs taxation, a caveat is warranted. Courts often are obliged to disregard form and let substance prevail. Notwithstanding the form versus substance difficulty, the point to be gained is that the pattern of a transaction often determines the tax outcome.

The obvious goal of most tax planning is the minimization of the amount that a person or other entity must transfer to the government. The legal minimization of taxes is usually referred to as *tax avoidance*. Although the phrase "tax avoidance" may have a criminal connotation, there is no injustice in legally reducing one's taxes. The most profound statement regarding the propriety of tax avoidance is found in a dissenting opinion authored by Justice Learned Hand in the case of *Commissioner v. Newman*. Justice Hand wrote:[35]

> Over and over again courts have said that there is nothing sinister in so arranging one's affairs so as to keep taxes as low as possible. Everybody does so, rich or poor, and all do right, for nobody owes any public duty to pay more than the law demands: taxes are enforced exactions, not voluntary contributions. To demand more in the name of morals is pure cant.

---

[35] 159 F.2d 848 (CA-2, 1947).

This statement is routinely cited as authority for taking those steps necessary to reduce one's taxes. It should be emphasized that tax planning and tax avoidance involve only those actions that are legal. *Tax evasion* is the label given to illegal activities that are designed to reduce the tax liability.

The planning effort for Federal income taxation (the principal area covered in this text) requires an understanding of the answer to *four* basic questions regarding the flow of cash and cash equivalents into and out of various tax entities. These questions regard the amount, character and timing of income, deductions and credits, and recognition (reporting) of these items. The answers depend upon the tax entity that receives or transfers the cash or cash equivalents, its tax accounting period and methods, and whether the entity is considered a taxpayer separate from its owners or simply a conduit through which items of income, gain, loss, deduction, or credit flow to its owners. The tax entities recognized for Federal tax purposes, and the tax planning questions, are presented in Exhibit 1-7 as follows.

Tax planning efforts often involve deferring the recognition of income or shifting the incidence of its tax to a lower tax bracket entity (e.g., from parents to children), or accelerating, deferring, or shifting deductions and credits to tax periods or among tax entities with higher or lower tax rates. Keeping this overall scheme of tax minimization in mind, many of the subsequent chapters of this text conclude with a discussion of tax planning considerations.

Exhibit 1-7
Tax Planning Perspective

Tax Entities

INFLOWS   *OUTFLOWS*

Cash and cash   *Cash and cash*
equivalents (property   *equivalents (property*
and services)   *and services)*

Questions on   **Questions on**
Inflows: **Outflows:**

                            Individuals
1. Is it included in   (See Chapters 3–18)   1. Is it deductible or does
   income?   it result in a credit?
   (See Chapters 5   Corporations   (See Chapters 7, 8, 9,
   and 6)   (See Chapters 19–21)   10, 11, 12, and 13)

2. If so, when?   2. If so, when?
   (See Chapter 5)   Partnerships   (See Chapter 7)
                            (See Chapter 22)
3. Character of   3. Character of
   income?   deduction or
   (See Chapter 16)   Estates and Trusts   credit?
                            (See Chapters 24–26)   (See Chapters 13
                                                                and 16)

4. Reported by   4. Reported by
   whom?   whom?

PROBLEM MATERIALS

DISCUSSION QUESTIONS

1-1 *Tax Bases.* Describe the tax bases for the Federal income tax and for each of the Federal wealth transfer taxes.

1-2 *Tax Rates.* Distinguish between a proportional tax rate and a progressive tax structure. What is the significance of the marginal tax rate under either a proportional or a progressive rate structure?

1-3 *Progressive, Proportional, and Regressive Taxes.* The media often refer to sales taxes as regressive. Similar comments are made when discussing Social Security taxes (FICA). Are the media correct? Include in your comments an explanation of the different types of tax rate structures.

1-4 *Deduction vs. Credit.* Distinguish between a deduction and a credit. If a credit is allowed for 20 percent of an expenditure in lieu of a deduction for the total expenditure, under what circumstances should you prefer the credit? The deduction?

1-5 *Individual vs. Corporate Taxable Income.* Based on the tax formulas contained in Exhibits 1-2 and 1-3, what are the significant differences in computing a corporation's taxable income as opposed to computing an individual's taxable income?

1-6 *Withholding Taxes at Source.* What do you believe is the principal reason that Congress continues the pay-as-you-go requirements of employers' withholding Federal income taxes from the wages paid their employees?

1-7 *Marital Deduction.* Describe the marital deduction allowed for Federal estate and gift taxes. How might an individual use this deduction to avoid all Federal wealth transfer taxes?

1-8 *Unified Credit.* How is the unified transfer tax credit applied in determining taxable wealth transfers?

1-9 *Annual Gift Tax Exclusion.* What is the amount of the annual Federal gift tax exclusion? If a widow were interested in making gifts to her daughter and seven grandchildren, how much could she transfer to them in any given year before incurring a taxable gift?

1-10 *Gift-Splitting Election.* What is the gift-splitting election allowed for Federal gift tax purposes? How might the marital deduction be used to explain why Congress allows this election?

1-11 *Estate vs. Inheritance Taxes.* Distinguish between an estate and an inheritance transfer tax. How are these two taxes often integrated by a state in its wealth transfer tax system?

1-12 *Federal Employment Taxes.* Distinguish between FICA and FUTA taxes. Between an employee and his or her employer, who bears the greater burden of these taxes?

1-13   *Unemployment Taxes.*   For 1991, what is the maximum FUTA tax an employer can expect to pay if he or she has three employees during the year and the minimum salary paid is $10,000? If the employer also is subject to state unemployment taxes, what is the maximum amount of credit he or she will be allowed against the FUTA tax liability?

1-14   *Sales vs. Use Tax.*   Distinguish between a sales and a use tax. Assume you live in state A but near the border of state B and that state A imposes a much higher sales tax than does state B. If you were planning to purchase a new automobile, what might you be tempted to do? How might state A discourage your plan?

1-15   *Tax Expenditures.*   It is often suggested that many of our social problems can be cured through use of tax incentives.

a.   Discuss the concept of tax expenditures.
b.   Expand on the text's discussion of the pros and cons of tax expenditures vis-à-vis direct governmental expenditures.

1-16   *Goals of Taxation.*   In a recent discussion concerning what a fair tax is, the following comments were made: (1) the fairest tax is one that someone else has to pay; (2) people should be taxed in accordance with the benefits they obtain (i.e., taxes are the price paid for the benefit); (3) a head tax would be the fairest; and (4) why tax at all, just use the printing press. Discuss the first three of these comments in terms of equity and explain whether the fourth represents a viable alternative.

PROBLEMS

1-17   *Marginal Tax Rates.*   T, a single taxpayer, has taxable income of $40,000 for 1991. If T anticipates a marginal tax rate of 15 percent for 1992, what income tax savings could she expect by accelerating $1,000 of deductible expenditures planned for 1992 into the 1991 tax year?

1-18   *Tax Rate Schedules and Rate Concepts.*   An examination of the tax rate schedules for single taxpayers (see the inside cover of the text) indicates that the tax is a "given dollar amount" plus a percentage of taxable income exceeding a particular level.

a.   Explain how the "given dollar amounts" are determined?
b.   Assuming the taxpayer has a taxable income of $50,000 and is single, what is his tax liability for 1991?
c.   Same facts as (b). What is the taxpayer's marginal tax rate?
d.   Same facts as (b). What is the taxpayer's average tax rate?
e.   Assuming the taxpayer has tax-exempt interest income from municipal bonds of $30,000, what is the taxpayer's effective tax rate?

1-19   *Tax Equity.*   Taxpayer R has a taxable income of $20,000. Similarly, S has a taxable income of $20,000. Each taxpayer pays a tax of $1,000 on his income.

    a.   Discuss whether the tax imposed is equitable. Include in your discussion comments concerning horizontal and vertical equity.

    b.   Assume S has a taxable income of $40,000 and pays a tax of $2,000 on his income. Discuss whether the tax imposed is equitable in light of this new information.

1-20   *Taxable Gifts.*   M made the following cash gifts during 1991:

To her son	$50,000
To her daughter	50,000
To her niece	10,000

    a.   If M is unmarried, what is the amount of taxable gifts she has made in 1991?

    b.   If M is married and her husband agrees to split gifts with her, what is the total amount of taxable gifts made by M and her husband for 1991?

1-21   *Taxable Estate.*   R dies in 1991. R made taxable gifts during his lifetime in 1979, 1980, 1982, 1985, and 1988 but paid no Federal transfer taxes due to the unified transfer tax credit. What effect will these taxable gifts have on determining the following:

    a.   R's Federal taxable estate?

    b.   The rates imposed on the Federal taxable estate?

1-22   *Estate Tax Computation.*   T died in a car accident on January 4, 1991. He owned the following property on his date of death:

Cash	$ 75,000
Stocks and bonds	400,000
Residence	230,000
Interest in partnership	450,000
Miscellaneous personal property	25,000

Upon T's death, he owed $80,000 on the mortgage on his residence. T also owned a life insurance policy. The policy was term life insurance which paid $100,000 to his mother upon his death. Its value immediately before his death was $0. T had all of the incidents of ownership with regard to the policy.

During his life, T had made only one gift. He gave a diamond ring worth $30,000 (it was an old family heirloom) to his daughter in 1986. No gift taxes were paid on the gift due to the annual exclusion (gift-splitting was elected) and the unified transfer tax credit. The ring was worth $50,000 on his date of death.

T's will contained the following provisions:

    a.   To my wife I leave all of the stocks and bonds.

    b.   To my alma mater, State University, I leave $50,000 to establish a chair for a tax professor in the Department of Accounting in the School of Business.

    c.   The residue of my estate is to go to my daughter.

Compute T's estate tax. Assume that his state imposes a state death tax equal to the maximum credit allowable for state death taxes. No other credits are available.

1-23 *State Estate Taxes.* At the time of her death, T resided in a state that imposes an estate tax based on the maximum amount allowed as a credit for Federal estate tax purposes.

a. If T's Federal taxable estate is $500,000, how much estate taxes will be imposed by the state?

b. If the state also imposes $3,000 of inheritance taxes on the heirs of T's estate, what will its estate tax levy be?

1-24 *Excess FICA Taxes.* During 1991, E earned $38,000 of wages from employer X and $20,000 of wages from employer Y. Both employers withheld and paid the appropriate amount of FICA taxes on E's wages.

a. What is the amount of excess taxes paid by E for 1991?

b. Would it make any difference in the amount of E's refund or credit of the excess of FICA taxes if he was a full-time employee of each employer for different periods of the year, as opposed to a full-time employee of X and a part-time employee of Y for the entire year?

1-25 *Self-Employment Tax.* During 1991, H had earnings from self-employment of $30,000 and wages of $38,000 from employer X. Employer X withheld and paid the appropriate amount of FICA taxes on H's wages. Compute H's self-employment tax liability for 1991. What is the amount of H's income tax deduction for the self-employment taxes paid?

1-26 *Tax Awareness.* Assume that you are currently employed by Corporation X in state A. Without your solicitation, Corporation Y offers you a 20 percent higher salary if you will relocate to state B and become its employee. What tax factors should you consider in making a decision as to the offer?

COMPUTERIZED TAX ANALYSIS

1-27 *Wage and Self-Employment Income—1991.* Use computer file T102 for this problem.

a. Review computer file T102. Work to understand each computation in the analysis section. Note that the self-employment tax deduction for adjusted gross income is always 50 percent of the total self-employment tax.

b. Compute the total self-employment tax for the following cases:

Case	Wages	Net Income from Self-Employment	Total Self-Employment Tax
1	$ 0	$40,000	_____
2	40,000	40,000	_____
3	53,400	40,000	_____
4	60,000	40,000	_____
5	70,000	40,000	_____
6	70,000	70,000	_____
7	70,000	80,000	_____

c. Compare the computer analyses for Cases 1 and 2. Why is the self-employment tax lower for Case 2?

d. Compare the computer analyses for Cases 2 and 3. Why is the self-employment tax lower for Case 3?

e. Compare the computer analyses for Cases 3, 4, and 5. Why does the self-employment tax stay constant even though wages steadily rise?

f. Compare the computer analyses for Cases 5 and 6. Why does the self-employment tax rise for Case 6?

g. Compare the computer analyses for Cases 6 and 7. Why does the self-employment tax stay constant even though net income from self-employment rises?

LEARNING OBJECTIVES

Upon completion of this chapter you will be able to:

- Describe the process in which Federal tax law is enacted and subsequently modified or evaluated by the judiciary

- Interpret citations to various statutory, administrative, and judicial sources of the tax law

- Identify the source of various administrative and judicial tax authorities

- Locate most statutory, administrative, and judicial authorities

- Evaluate the relative strength of various tax authorities

- Understand the importance of communicating the results of tax research

CHAPTER OUTLINE

Chapter 2

SOURCES AND APPLICATIONS OF FEDERAL TAX LAW

Mastery of taxation requires an understanding of how and where the rules of taxation originate. What might be called the "body of tax law" consists not only of the legislative provisions enacted by Congress, but also court decisions and administrative (Treasury Department) releases that explain and interpret the statutory provisions. In the aggregate, the statutes, court decisions, and administrative releases constitute the *legal authority* that provides the consequences given a particular set of facts. The tax treatment of any particular transaction normally must be based on some supporting authority. The tax rules contained in each of the later chapters all have their origin in some authoritative pronouncement.

This chapter introduces the sources of tax law and explains how these and other information relating to taxes may be accessed and used in solving a particular tax question. This process of obtaining information and synthesizing it to answer a specific tax problem is referred to as *tax research*. The importance of tax research cannot be overemphasized. The vast body of tax law and its everchanging nature place a premium on knowing how to use research materials.

AUTHORITATIVE SOURCES OF TAX LAW

Sources of tax law can be classified into two broad categories: (1) the law, and (2) official interpretations of the law. The law consists primarily of the Constitution, the Acts of Congress, and tax treaties. In general, these sources are referred to as the *statutory* law. Most statutory law is written in general terms for a typical situation. Since general rules, no matter how carefully drafted, cannot be written to cover variations on the normal scheme, interpretation is usually required. The task of interpreting the statute is one of the principal duties of the Internal Revenue Service (IRS) as representative of the Secretary of the Treasury. The IRS annually produces thousands of releases that explain and clarify the law. To no one's surprise, however, taxpayers and the government do not always agree on how a particular law should be interpreted. In situations where the taxpayer or the government decides to litigate the question, the courts, as final arbiters, are given the opportunity to interpret the law. These judicial interpretations, administrative interpretations, and the statutory law are considered in detail below.

STATUTORY LAW

The Constitution of the United States provides the Federal government with the power to tax. Disputes concerning the constitutionality of an income tax levied on taxpayers without apportionment among the states were resolved in 1913 with passage of the Sixteenth Amendment. Between 1913 and 1939, Congress enacted revenue acts that amounted to a complete rewrite of all tax law to date, including the desired changes. In 1939, due primarily to the increasing complexity of the earlier process, Congress codified all Federal tax laws into Title 26 of the *United States Code,* which was then called the *Internal Revenue Code of 1939.* Significant changes in the Federal tax laws were made during World War II and the post-war period of the late 1940s. Each change resulted in amendments to the 1939 Code. By 1954, the codification process had to be repeated in order to organize all additions to the law and to eliminate obsolete provisions. The product of this effort was the *Internal Revenue Code of 1954.* After 1954, Congress took great care to ensure that each new amendment to the 1954 Code was incorporated within its organizational structure with appropriate cross-references to any prior provisions affected by a new law. Among the changes incorporated into the 1954 Code in this manner were the Economic Tax Recovery Act (ERTA) of 1981, the Tax Equity and Fiscal Responsibility Act (TEFRA) of 1982, and the Deficit Reduction Act (DRA) of 1984. In 1986, Congress again made substantial revision in the tax law. Consistent with this massive redesign of the 1954 Code, Congress changed the title to the *Internal Revenue Code of 1986.* Like the 1954 Code, the 1986 Code is subject to revisions introduced by a new law. Recent changes incorporated into the 1986 Code were the Revenue Act of 1987, the Technical and Miscellaneous Revenue Act (TAMRA) of 1988, the Revenue Reconciliation Act of 1989, and the Revenue Reconciliation Act of 1990.

The legislative provisions contained in the Code are by far the most important component of tax law. Although procedure necessary to enact a law is generally well known, it is necessary to review this process with a special emphasis on taxation. From a tax perspective, the *intention* of Congress in producing the legislation is extremely important since the primary purpose of tax research is to interpret the legislative intent of Congress.

THE MAKING OF A TAX LAW

Article I, Section 7, Clause 1 of the Constitution provides that the House of Representatives of the U.S. Congress has the basic responsibility for initiating revenue bills.[1] The Ways and Means Committee of the House of Representatives must consider any tax bill before it is presented for vote by the full House of Representatives. On bills of major public interest, the Ways and Means Committee holds public hearings where interested organizations may send representatives

---

[1] Tax bills do not originate in the Senate, except when they are attached to other bills.

to express their views about the bill. The first witness at such hearings is usually the Secretary of the Treasury, representing the President of the United States. In many cases, proposals for new tax legislation or changes in existing legislation come from the President as a part of his political or economic programs.

After the public hearings have been held, the Ways and Means Committee usually goes into closed session, where the Committee prepares the tax bill for consideration by the entire House. The members of the Committee receive invaluable assistance from their highly skilled staff, which includes economists, accountants, and lawyers. The product of this session is a proposed bill that is submitted to the entire House for debate and vote.

After a bill has been approved by the entire House, it is sent to the Senate and assigned to the Senate Finance Committee. The Senate Finance Committee may also hold hearings on the bill before its consideration by the full Senate. The Senate's bill generally differs from the House's bill. In these situations, both versions are sent to the Joint Conference Committee on Taxation, which is composed of members selected from the House Ways and Means Committee and from the Senate Finance Committee. The objective of this Joint Committee is to produce a compromise bill acceptable to both sides. On occasion, when compromise cannot be achieved by the Joint Committee or the compromise bill is unacceptable to the House or the Senate, the bill "dies." If, however, compromise is reached and the Senate and House approve the compromise bill, it is then referred to the President for his approval or veto. If the President vetoes the bill, the legislation is "killed" unless two-thirds of both the House and the Senate vote to override the veto. If the veto is overridden, the legislation becomes law.

It should be noted that at each stage of the process, information is produced that may be useful in assessing the intent of Congress. One of the better sources of Congressional intent is a report issued by the House Ways and Means Committee. This report contains the bill as well as a general explanation. This explanation usually provides the historical background of the proposed legislation along with the reasons for enactment. The Senate Finance Committee also issues a report similar to that of the House. Because the Senate often makes changes in the House version of the bill, the Senate's report is also an important source. Additionally, the Joint Conference Committee on Taxation issues its own report, which is sometimes helpful. Two other sources of intent are the records of the debates on the bill and publications of the initial hearings.

The following diagram illustrates the normal flow of a bill through the legislative process and the documents that are generated in this process.

Committee reports and debates appear in several publications. Committee reports are officially published in pamphlet form by the U.S. Government Printing Office as the bill proceeds through Congress. The enacted bill is published in the *Internal Revenue Bulletin* and the *Internal Revenue Cumulative Bulletin*. The debates are published in the *Congressional Record*. In addition to these official government publications, several commercial publishers make this information available to subscribers.

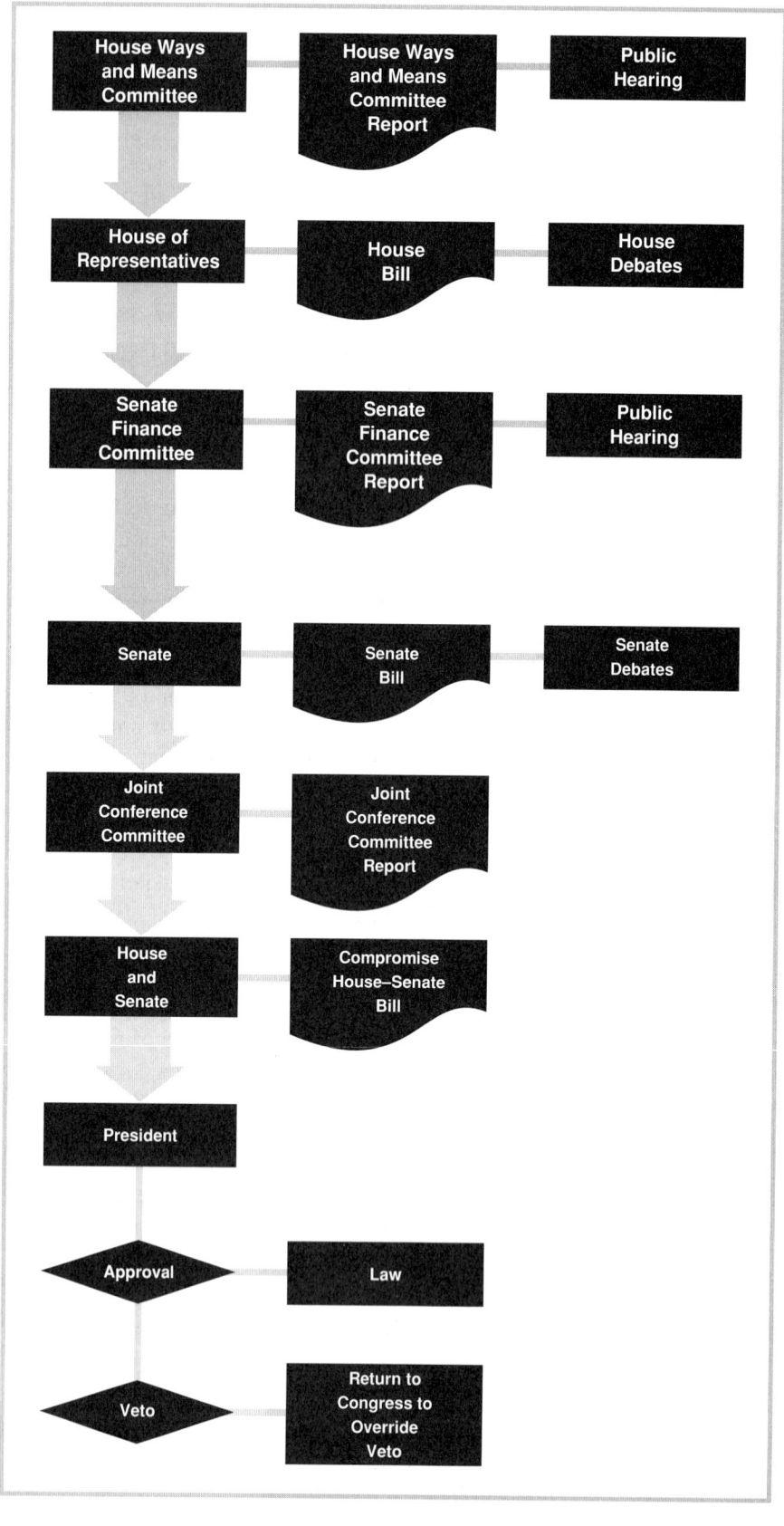

ORGANIZATION OF THE CODE

Once a tax bill becomes tax law, it is incorporated into the existing structure of the *Internal Revenue Code*.[2] The ability to use the Internal Revenue Code is essential for all individuals who have any involvement with the tax laws. It is normally the starting point for research. The following format is the basic organization of the Code.

Title 26 of the United States Code (referred to as the Internal Revenue Code)

  Subtitle A—Income Taxes

    Chapter 1—Normal Taxes and Surtaxes

      Subchapter A—Determination of Tax Liability

        Part I—Tax on Individuals

          Sections 1 through 5

When working with the tax law, it is often necessary to make reference to or *cite* a particular source with respect to the Code. The *section* of the Code is the source normally cited. A complete citation for a section of the Code would be too cumbersome. For instance, a formal citation for Section 1 of the Code would be "Subtitle A, Chapter 1, Subchapter A, Part I, Section 1." In most cases, citation of the section alone is sufficient. Sections are numbered consecutively throughout the Code so that each section number is used only once. Currently the numbers run from Section 1 through Section 9602. Not all section numbers are used, so that additional ones may be added by Congress in the future without the need for renumbering.[3]

Citation of a particular Code section in tax literature ordinarily does not require the prefix "Internal Revenue Code" because it is generally understood that, unless otherwise stated, references to section numbers concern the Internal Revenue Code of 1986 as amended. However, since most Code sections are divided into subparts, reference to a specific subpart requires more than just its section number. Section 170(a)(2)(B) serves as an example.

---

[2] All future use of the term Code or Internal Revenue Code refers to the *Internal Revenue Code of 1986*.

[3] It is interesting to note that when it adopted the 1954 Code, Congress deliberately left section numbers unassigned to provide room for future additions. Recently, however, Congress has been forced to distinguish new sections by alphabetical letters following a particular section number. See, for example, Sections 280, 280A, 280B, and 280C of the 1986 Code.

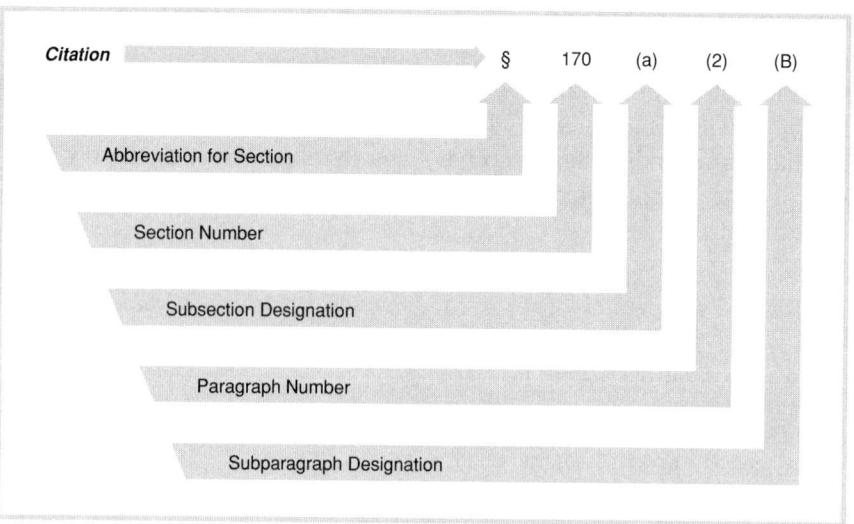

All footnote references used throughout this text are made in the form given above. In most cases, the "§" or "§§" symbols are used in place of the terms "section" or "sections," respectively.

Single-volume or double-volume editions of the Internal Revenue Code are published after every major change in the law. Commerce Clearing House, Inc. (CCH), Prentice Hall (PH), and the Research Institute of America (RIA) all publish these editions. Additionally, the Code is included in each of the major tax services that are discussed in a later section of this chapter.

TAX TREATIES

The laws contained in tax treaties represent the third and final component of the statutory law. Tax treaties (also referred to as tax conventions) are agreements between the United States and other countries that provide rules governing the taxation of residents of one country by another. For example, the tax treaty between the United States and France indicates how the French government taxes U.S. citizens residing in France and vice versa. Tax treaties, as law, have the same authority as those laws contained in the Code. In fact, treaty provisions normally take precedence over those contained in the Code. For example, § 7852(d) specifically provides that none of the Code's provisions apply in any case when such provisions are contrary to any treaty obligation. For this reason, persons involved with an international tax question must be aware of tax treaties and recognize that the Code may be superseded by a tax treaty.

ADMINISTRATIVE INTERPRETATIONS

After Congress has enacted a tax law, the Executive branch of the Federal government has the responsibility for enforcing it. In the process of enforcing the law, the Treasury interprets, clarifies, defines, and analyzes the Code in order to apply Congressional intention of the law to the specific facts of a taxpayer's situation. This process results in numerous administrative releases including the following:

1. Regulations
2. Revenue rulings and letter rulings
3. Revenue procedures
4. Technical advice memoranda

REGULATIONS

Congress has authorized the Secretary of the Treasury to prescribe and issue all rules and regulations needed for enforcement of the Code.[4] The Secretary, however, usually delegates the power to write the regulations to the Commissioner of the Internal Revenue Service. Normally, regulations are first published in proposed form—*proposed regulations*—in the Federal Register. Upon publication, interested parties have 30 days for comment. At the end of 30 days, the Treasury responds in light of the comments in any of three ways: it may (1) withdraw the proposed regulation; (2) amend it; or (3) leave it unchanged. In the latter two cases, the Treasury normally issues the regulation in its final form as a *Treasury decision* (often referred to as TDs) and it is published in the Federal Register. Thereafter, the new regulation is included in Title 26 of the *Code of Federal Regulations*.

The primary purpose of the regulations is to explain and interpret particular Code sections. Although regulations have not been issued for all Code sections, they have been issued for the great majority. In those cases where regulations exist, they are an important authoritative source on which one can usually rely. Regulations can be classified into three groups: (1) legislative; (2) interpretive; and (3) procedural.

Legislative Regulations. Occasionally, Congress will give specific authorization to the Secretary of the Treasury to issue regulations on a particular Code section. For example, under § 1502, the Secretary is charged with prescribing the regulations for the filing of a consolidated return by an affiliated group of corporations. There are virtually no Code sections governing consolidated returns, and

---

[4] § 7805(a).

the regulations in effect serve in lieu of the Code. In this case and others where it occurs, the regulation has the force and effect of a law, with the result that a court reviewing the regulation usually will not substitute its judgment for that of the Treasury Department unless the Treasury has clearly abused its discretion.[5]

Interpretative Regulations. Interpretative regulations explain the meaning of a Code section and commit the Treasury and the Internal Revenue Service to a particular position relative to the Code section in question. This type of regulation is binding on the IRS but not on the courts, although it is "a body of experience and informed judgment to which courts and litigants may properly resort for guidance."[6] Interpretive regulations have considerable authority and normally are invalidated only if they are inconsistent with the Code or are unreasonable.

Procedural Regulations. Procedural regulations cover such areas as the information a taxpayer must supply to the IRS and the internal management and conduct of the IRS in certain matters. Those regulations affecting vital interests of the taxpayers are generally binding on the IRS, and those regulations stating the taxpayer's obligation to file particular forms or other types of information are given the effect of law.

Citation for Regulations. Regulations are arranged in the same sequence as the Code sections they interpret. Thus, a regulation begins with a number that designates the type of tax or administrative, definitional, or procedural matter and is followed by the applicable Code section number. For example, Treasury Regulation Section 1.614-3(f)(5) serves as an illustration of how regulations are cited throughout this text.

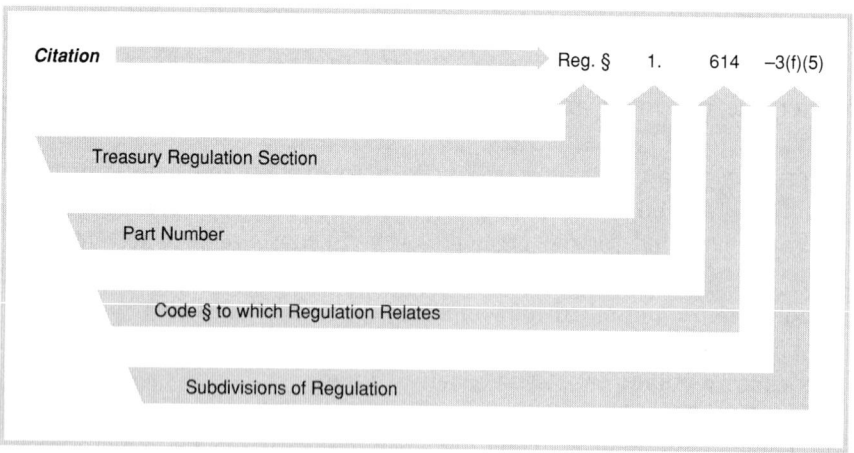

---

[5] *Anderson, Clayton & Co. v. U.S.*, 77-2 USTC ¶9727, 40 AFTR2d 77-6102, 562 F.2d 972 (CA-5, 1977), *Cert. den.* at 436 U.S. 944 (USSC, 1978).

[6] *Skidmore v. Swift and Co.*, 323 U.S. 134 (USSC, 1944).

The part number of a Treasury regulation is used to identify the general area covered by the regulation as follows.

Part Number	Law Subject
1	Income Tax
20	Estate Tax
25	Gift Tax
31	Employment Tax
48–49	Excise Tax

The various subdivisions of a regulation are not necessarily related to a specific subdivision of the Code.

Sometimes the Treasury issues temporary regulations when it is necessary to meet a compelling need. For example, temporary regulations are often issued shortly after enactment of a major change in the tax law. These temporary regulations have the same binding effect as final regulations until they are withdrawn or replaced. Such regulations are cited as Temp. Reg. §.

Temporary regulations should not be confused with proposed regulations. The latter have no force or effect.[7] Nevertheless, proposed regulations provide insight into how the IRS currently interprets a particular Code section. For this reason, they should not be ignored.

REVENUE RULINGS

Revenue rulings also are official interpretations of the Federal tax laws and are issued by the National Office of the IRS. Revenue rulings do not have quite the authority of regulations, however. Regulations are a direct extension of the law-making powers of Congress, whereas revenue rulings are an application of the administrative powers of the Internal Revenue Service. In contrast to rulings, regulations are usually issued only after public hearings and must be approved by the Secretary of the Treasury.

Unlike regulations, revenue rulings are limited to a given set of facts. Taxpayers may rely on revenue rulings in determining the tax consequences of their transactions; however, taxpayers must determine for themselves if the facts of their cases are substantially the same as those set forth in the revenue ruling.

Revenue rulings are published in the weekly issues of the *Internal Revenue Bulletin*. The information contained in the *Internal Revenue Bulletins* (including, among other things, revenue rulings) is accumulated and usually published semiannually in the *Cumulative Bulletin*. The *Cumulative Bulletin* reorganizes the material according to Code section. Citations for the *Internal Revenue Bulletin* and the *Cumulative Bulletin* are illustrated on the following page.

---

[7] Federal law (i.e., the Administrative Procedure Act) requires any federal agency, including the Internal Revenue Service, that wishes to adopt a substantive rule to publish the rule in proposed form in order to give interested persons an opportunity to comment. Proposed regulations are issued in compliance with this directive.

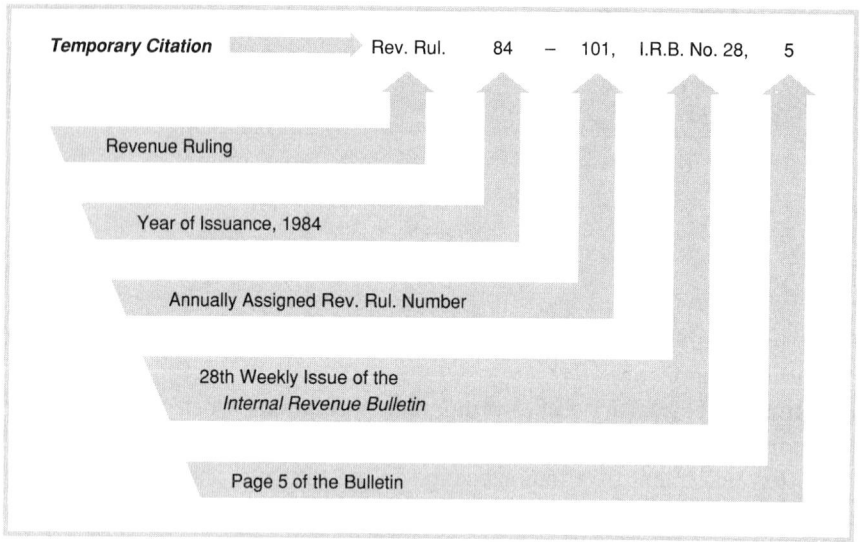

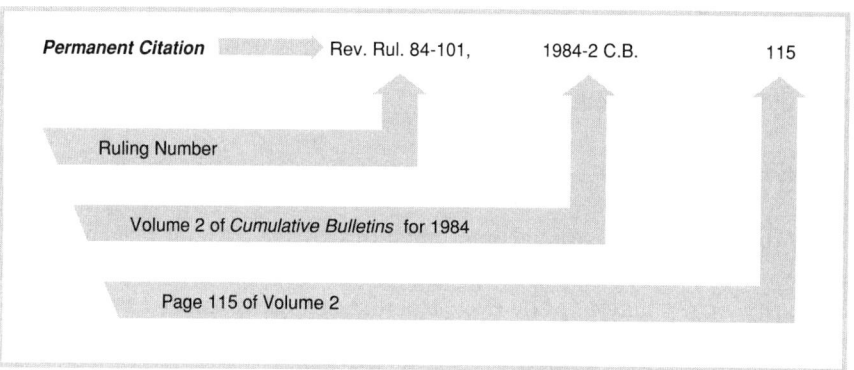

REVENUE PROCEDURES

Revenue procedures are statements reflecting the internal management practices of the IRS that affect the rights and duties of taxpayers. Occasionally they are also used to announce procedures to guide individuals in dealing with the IRS or to make public something the IRS believes should be brought to the attention of taxpayers. Revenue procedures are published in the weekly *Internal Revenue Bulletins* and bound in the *Cumulative Bulletin* along with revenue rulings issued in the same year. The citation system for revenue procedures is the same as for revenue rulings except that the prefix "Rev. Proc." is substituted for "Rev. Rul."

LETTER RULINGS

Taxpayers who are in doubt about the tax consequences of a contemplated transaction may ask the National Office of the IRS for a ruling on the tax question involved. Generally, the IRS has discretion about whether to rule or not and has issued guidelines describing circumstances under which it will issue a ruling on a

Judicial Interpretations 2-11

question posed by a taxpayer.[8] Unlike revenue rulings, letter rulings (or private rulings) apply *only* to the particular taxpayers asking for the ruling and are not applicable to all taxpayers. For those requesting a ruling, the response might provide insurance against surprises because, as a practical matter, a favorable ruling should preclude any controversies with the IRS on a subsequent audit. During the process of obtaining a ruling, the IRS may recommend changes in a proposed transaction to assist the taxpayers in achieving the result they wish. Since 1976, the IRS has made individual rulings publicly available after deleting information that tends to identify the taxpayer. Such rulings appear in digests by the leading tax commentators and by publishers such as CCH and PH.

TECHNICAL ADVICE MEMORANDA

Either a taxpayer or an IRS district's Appeals Division may request advice from the National Office of the IRS about the Code, Regulations, and statutes and their impact on a specific set of facts. Generally, such requests take place during an audit or during the appeals process of the audit, and give both the taxpayer and the revenue agent an opportunity to resolve a dispute over a technical question. If the National Office renders advice favorable to the taxpayer, normally it must be applied. However, if the advice is against the taxpayer, the taxpayer does not lose his or her right to further pursue the issue in question with the IRS.

Citations for letter rulings and technical advice follow a multi-digit file number system. IRS Letter Ruling 9042002 serves as an example.

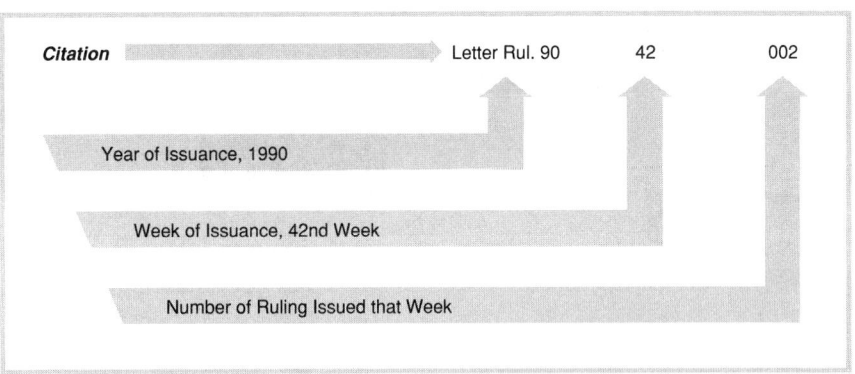

JUDICIAL INTERPRETATIONS

The Congress passes the tax law and the Executive branch of the Federal government enforces and interprets it, but under the American system of checks and balances, it is the Judiciary branch that ultimately determines whether the

---

[8] See Rev. Proc. 82-22, 1982-1 C.B. 469 for a description of the areas in which the IRS has refused to issue advanced rulings. Note, also, that the IRS is required to charge tax- payers a fee for letter rulings, opinion letters, determination letters, and similar requests. The fees range from $50 to $1,000. See § 6591.

Executive branch's interpretation is correct. This provides yet another source of tax law—court decisions. It is therefore absolutely essential for the student of tax as well as the tax practitioner to have a grasp of the judicial system of the United States and how tax cases move through this system.

Before litigating a case in court, the taxpayer must have exhausted the administrative remedies available to him or her within the Internal Revenue Service. If the taxpayer has not exhausted his or her administrative remedies, a court will deny a hearing because the claim filed in the court is premature.

All litigation begins in what are referred to as *courts of original jurisdiction*, or *trial courts*, which "try" the case. There are three trial courts: (1) the Tax Court; (2) the U.S. District Court; and (3) the U.S. Claims Court. Note that the taxpayer may select any one (and only one) of these three courts to hear the case. If the taxpayer or government disagrees with the decision by the trial court, it has the right to appeal to either the U.S. Court of Appeals or the U.S. Court of Appeals for the Federal Circuit, whichever is appropriate in the particular case. If a litigating party is dissatisfied with the decision by the appellate court, it may ask for review by the Supreme Court, but this is rarely granted. The judicial system is illustrated and discussed below.

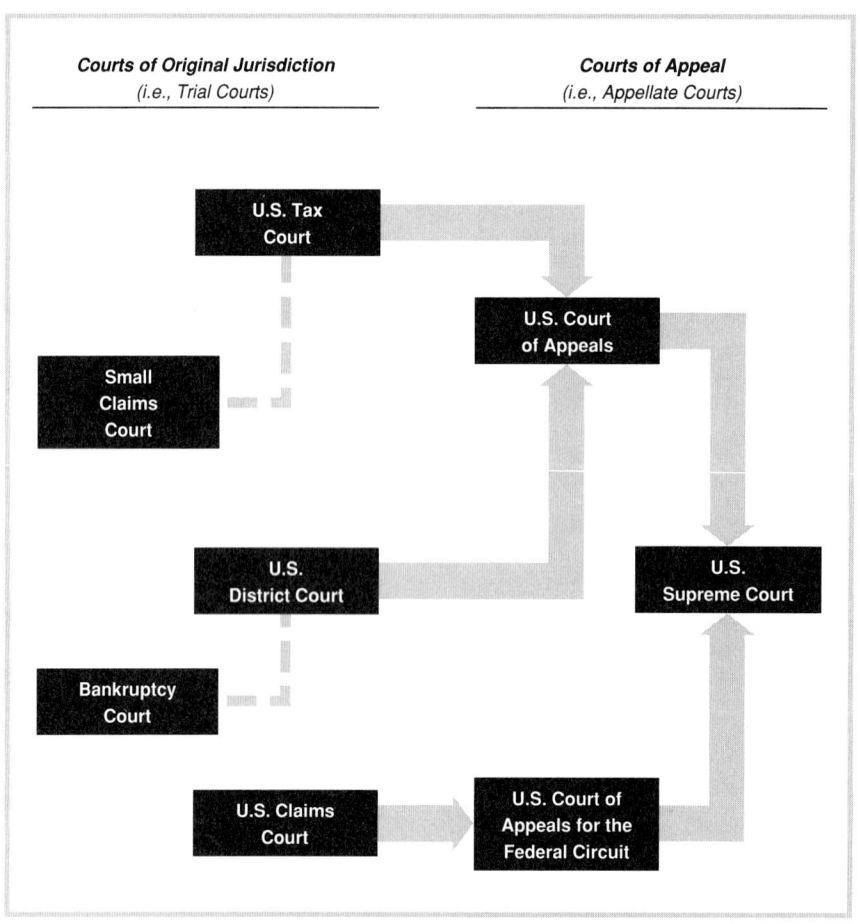

TRIAL COURTS

U.S. Tax Court.   The Tax Court, as its name suggests, specializes in tax matters and hears no other types of cases. The judges on the court are especially skilled in taxation. Usually, prior to being selected as a judge by the President, the individual was a practitioner or IRS official who was noted for his or her expertise. This Court is composed of 19 judges who "ride circuit" throughout the United States (i.e., they travel and hear cases in various parts of the country). Occasionally, the full Tax Court hears a case, but most cases are heard by a single judge who submits his or her opinion to the chief judge, who then decides whether the full court should review the decision.

Besides its expertise in tax matters, two other characteristics of the Tax Court should be noted. Perhaps the most important feature of the Tax Court is that the taxpayer does not pay the alleged tax deficiency before bringing his or her action before the court. The second facet of the Tax Court that bears mentioning is that a trial by jury is not available.

U.S. District Courts.   For purposes of the Federal judicial system, the United States is divided into 11 geographic areas called circuits which are subdivided into districts. For example, the second circuit, which is composed of Vermont, Connecticut, and New York, contains the District Court for the Southern District of New York, which covers parts of New York City. Other districts may include very large areas, such as the District Court for the State of Arizona, which covers the entire state. A taxpayer may take a case into the District Court for the district in which he or she resides, but only after the disputed tax deficiency has been paid. The taxpayer then sues the IRS for a refund of the disputed amount. The District Court is a court of general jurisdiction and hears many types of cases in addition to tax cases. This is the only court in which the taxpayer may obtain a jury trial. The jury decides matters of fact but not matters of law. However, even in issues of fact, the judge may, and occasionally does, disregard the jury's decision.

U.S. Claims Court.   The United States Claims Court was established on October 1, 1982. Prior to that time it was called the "U.S. Court of Claims." The U.S. Claims Court hears cases involving certain claims against the Federal government, including tax refunds. This Court is made up of 16 judges and usually meets in Washington, D.C. A taxpayer must pay the disputed tax deficiency before bringing an action in this court, and may not obtain a jury trial. Appeals from the U.S. Claims Court are taken to the U.S. Court of Appeals for the Federal Circuit, an appellate court created at the same time as the U.S. Claims Court.

The following chart illustrates the position of the taxpayer in bringing an action in these courts.

	U.S. Tax Court	U.S. District Court	U.S. Claims Court
Jurisdiction	Nationwide	Specific district in which court is sitting	Nationwide
Subject Matter	Tax cases only	Many different types of cases, both criminal and civil	Claims against the Federal government, including tax refunds
Payment of Contested Amount	Taxpayer does not pay deficiency, but files suit against IRS Commissioner to stop collection of tax	Taxpayer pays alleged deficiency and then files suit against the U.S. government for refund	Taxpayer pays alleged deficiency and then files suit against the U.S. government for refund
Availability of jury trial	No	Yes	No
Appeal taken to	U.S. Court of Appeals	U.S. Court of Appeals	U.S. Court of Appeals for the Federal Circuit
Number of Courts	1	95	1
Number of Judges Per Court	19	1	16

Small Claims Cases. When the amount of a tax assessment is relatively small, the taxpayer may elect to submit the case to the division of the Tax Court hearing small claims cases. If the amount of tax at issue is $10,000 per year or less, the taxpayer can obtain a decision with a minimum of formality, delay, and expense; but the taxpayer loses the right to appeal the decision. The Small Claims Court is administered by the chief judge of the Tax Court, who is authorized to assign small claims cases to special trial judges. These cases receive priority on the trial calendars, and relatively informal rules are followed whenever possible. The special trial judges' opinions are not published on these cases, and the decisions are not reviewed by any other court or treated as precedents in any other case.

Bankruptcy Court. Under limited circumstances, it is possible for the bankruptcy court to have jurisdiction over tax matters. The filing of a bankruptcy petition prevents creditors, including the IRS, from taking action against a taxpayer, including the filing of a proceeding before the Tax Court if a notice of deficiency is sent after the filing of a petition in bankruptcy. In such cases, a tax claim may be determined by the bankruptcy court.

APPELLATE COURTS

U.S. Courts of Appeals. The appropriate appellate court depends on which trial court hears the case. Taxpayer or government appeals from the District Courts and the Tax Court are taken to the U.S. Court of Appeals that has jurisdiction over the court in which the taxpayer lives. Appeals from the U.S. Claims Court are taken to the U.S. Court of Appeals for the Federal Circuit, which has the same powers and jurisdictions as any of the other Courts of Appeals except that it only hears specialized appeals. Courts of Appeals are national courts of appellate jurisdiction. With the exceptions of the Court of Appeals for the Federal Circuit and the Court of Appeals for the District of Columbia, these appellate courts are assigned various geographic areas of jurisdiction as follows:

Court of Appeals for the Federal Circuit (CA-FC)	*District of Columbia Circuit (CA-DC)*	*First Circuit (CA-1)*	
U.S. Claims Court	District of Columbia	Maine Massachusetts New Hampshire Puerto Rico Rhode Island	

Second Circuit (CA-2)	*Third Circuit (CA-3)*	*Fourth Circuit (CA-4)*	*Fifth Circuit (CA-5)*
Connecticut New York Vermont	Delaware New Jersey Pennsylvania Virgin Islands	Maryland N. Carolina S. Carolina Virginia W. Virginia	Canal Zone Louisiana Mississippi Texas

Sixth Circuit (CA-6)	*Seventh Circuit (CA-7)*	*Eighth Circuit (CA-8)*	*Ninth Circuit (CA-9)*
Kentucky Michigan Ohio Tennessee	Illinois Indiana Wisconsin	Arkansas Iowa Minnesota Missouri Nebraska N. Dakota S. Dakota	Alaska Arizona California Guam Hawaii Idaho Montana Nevada Oregon Washington

Tenth Circuit (CA-10)	*Eleventh Circuit (CA-11)*
Colorado New Mexico Kansas Oklahoma Utah Wyoming	Alabama Florida Georgia

Taxpayers may appeal to the Courts of Appeal as a matter of right, and the Courts must hear their cases. Very often, however, the expense of such an appeal deters many from proceeding with an appeal. Appellate courts review the record of the trial court to determine whether the lower court completed its responsibility of fact finding and applied the proper law in arriving at its decision.

District Courts must follow the decision of the Appeals Court for the circuit in which they are located. For instance, the District Court in the Eastern District of Missouri must follow the decision of the Eighth Circuit Court of Appeals because Missouri is in the Eighth Circuit. If the Eighth Circuit has not rendered a decision on the particular issue involved, then the District Court may make its own decision or follow the decision in another Circuit.

The Tax Court is a national court with jurisdiction throughout the entire country. Prior to 1970, the Tax Court considered itself independent and indicated that it would not be bound by the decisions of the Circuit Court to which its decision would be appealed. In *Golsen,*[9] however, the Tax Court reversed its position. Under the *Golsen rule,* the Tax Court now follows the decisions of the Circuit Court to which a particular case would be appealed. Even if the Tax Court disagrees with a Circuit Court's view, it will decide based upon the Circuit Court's view. On the other hand, if a similar case arises in the jurisdiction of another Circuit Court that has not yet ruled on the same issue, the Tax Court will follow its own view, despite its earlier decision following a contrary Circuit Court decision.

U.S. Courts of Appeals generally sit in panels of three judges, although the entire court may sit in particularly important cases. They may reach a decision that affirms the lower court or that reverses the lower court. Additionally, the Appellate Court could send the case back to the lower court (remand the case) for another trial or for rehearing on another point not previously covered. It is possible for the Appellate Court to affirm the decision of the lower court on one particular issue and reverse it on another.

Generally, only one judge writes a decision for the Appeals Court, although in some cases no decision is written and an order is simply made. Such an order might hold that the lower court is sustained, or that the lower court's decision is reversed as being inconsistent with one of the Appellate Court's decisions. Sometimes other judges (besides the one assigned to write the opinion) will write additional opinions agreeing with (concurring opinion) or disagreeing with (dissenting opinion) the majority opinion. These opinions often contain valuable insights into the law controlling the case, and often set the ground for a change in the court's opinion at a later date.

U.S. Supreme Court. The Supreme Court of the United States is the highest court of the land. No one has a *right* to be heard by this Court. It only accepts cases it wishes to hear, and generally those involve issues that the Court feels are of national importance. The Supreme Court generally hears very few tax cases. Consequently, taxpayers desiring a review of their trial court decision find it solely at the Court of Appeals. Technically, cases are submitted to the Supreme

---

[9] *Jack E. Golsen,* 54 T.C. 742 (1970).

Court through a request process known as the "Writ of Certiorari." If the Supreme Court decides to hear the case, it grants the Writ of Certiorari; if it decides not to hear the case, it denies the Writ of Certiorari. It is important to note that there is another path to review by the U.S. Supreme Court—*by appeal*—as opposed to by Writ of Certiorari. This "review by appeal" may be available when a U.S. Court of Appeals has held that a state statute is in conflict with the laws or treaties of the United States. The "review by appeal" may also be available when the highest court in a state has decided a case on grounds that a Federal statute or treaty is invalid, or when the state court has held a state statute valid despite the claim of the losing party that the statute is in conflict with the U.S. Constitution or a Federal law. Review by the U.S. Supreme Court is still discretionary, but a Writ of Certiorari is not involved.

The Supreme Court, like the Courts of Appeals, does not conduct another trial. Its responsibility is to review the record and determine whether or not the trial court correctly applied the law in deciding the case. The Supreme Court also reviews the decision of the Court of Appeals to determine if the court used the correct reasoning.

In general, the Supreme Court only hears cases when one or more of the following conditions apply:

1. When the Court of Appeals has not used accepted or usual methods of judicial procedure or has sanctioned an unusual method by the trial court

2. When a Court of Appeals has settled an important question of Federal law and the Supreme Court feels such an important question should have one more review by the most prestigious court of the nation

3. When a decision of a Court of Appeals is in apparent conflict with a decision of the Supreme Court

4. When two or more Courts of Appeals are in conflict on an issue

5. When the Supreme Court has already decided an issue but feels that the issue should be looked at again, possibly to reverse its previous decision

CASE CITATION

Tax Court Decisions. Prior to 1943, the Tax Court was called the Board of Tax Appeals. The decisions of the Board of Tax Appeals were published as the *United States Board of Tax Appeals Reports* (BTA). Board of Tax Appeals cases are cited as follows:

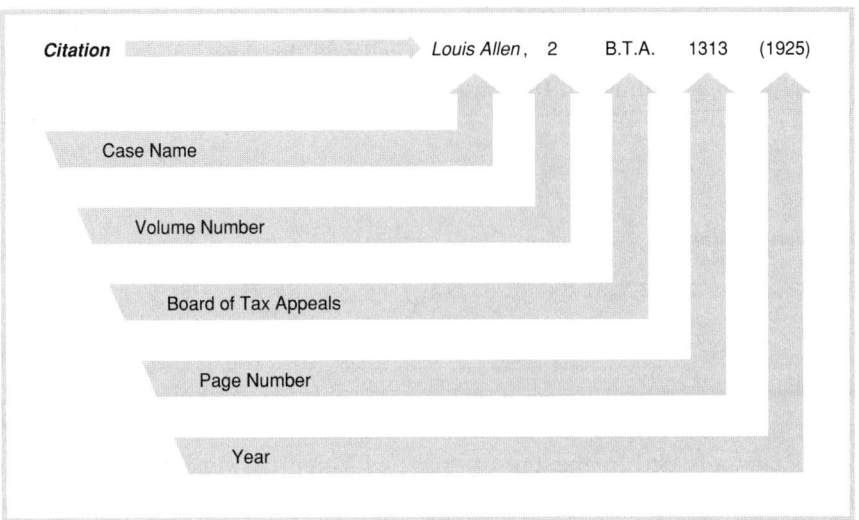

The Tax Court renders two different types of decisions with two different citation systems: regular decisions and memorandum decisions.

Tax Court *regular* decisions deal with new issues that the court has not yet resolved. In contrast, decisions that deal only with the application of already established principles of law are called *memorandum* decisions. The United States government publishes regular decisions in *United States Tax Court Reports* (T.C.). Tax Court regular decisions are cited as follows:

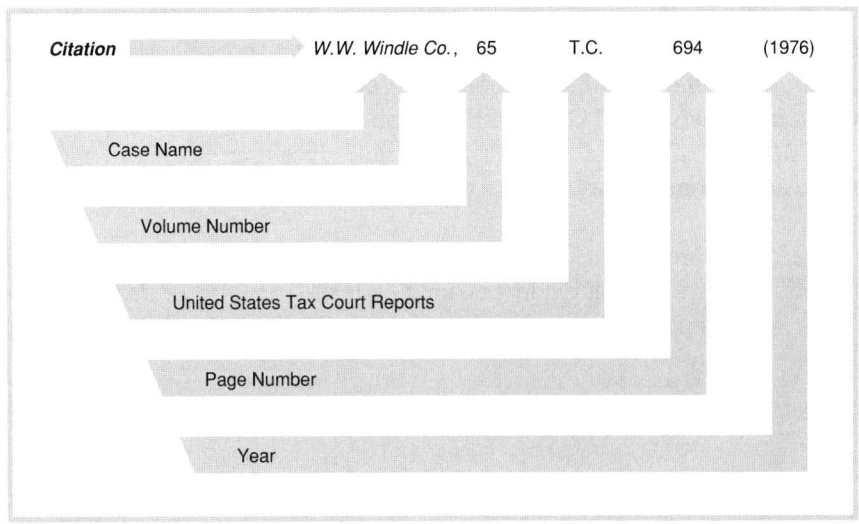

Like revenue rulings and the *Cumulative Bulletins*, there is a time lag between the date a Tax Court regular decision is issued and the date it is bound in a *U.S. Tax Court Report* volume. In this case, the citation appears as follows:

Temporary Citation:

W.W. Windle Co., 65 T.C. _____, No. 79 (1976).

Here the page is left out, but the citation tells the reader that this is the 79th regular decision issued by the Tax Court since Volume 64 ended. When the new volume (65th) of the Tax Court Report is issued, then the permanent citation may be substituted for the old one. Both CCH and PH have tax services that allow the researcher to find these temporary citations.

The IRS has adopted the practice of announcing its acquiescence or nonacquiescence to the regular decisions of the Tax Court that are adverse to the position taken by the government.[10] That is, the Service announces whether it agrees with the Tax Court or not. The IRS does not follow this practice for the decisions of the other courts, or even for memorandum decisions of the Tax court, although it occasionally announces that it will or will not follow a decision of another Federal court with a similar set of facts. The IRS may withdraw its acquiescence or nonacquiescence at any time and may do so even retroactively. Acquiescences and nonacquiescences are published in the weekly *Internal Revenue Bulletins* and the *Cumulative Bulletins*.

Although the U.S. government publishes the Tax Court's regular decisions, it does not publish memorandum decisions. However, both CCH and PH publish them. CCH publishes the memorandum decisions under the title *Tax Court Memorandum Decisions* (TCM), while PH publishes these decisions as *Prentice Hall TC Memorandum Decisions* (T.C. Memo). In citing Tax Court memorandum decisions, some authors prefer to use both the PH and the CCH citations for their cases.

In an effort to provide the reader the greatest latitude of research sources, this dual citation policy has been adopted for this text. The case of *Jerome Prizant* serves as an example of the dual citation of Tax Court memorandum decisions.

---

[10]   The IRS' acquiescence is symbolized by "A" or "Acq." and its nonacquiescence by "NA" or "Nonacq."

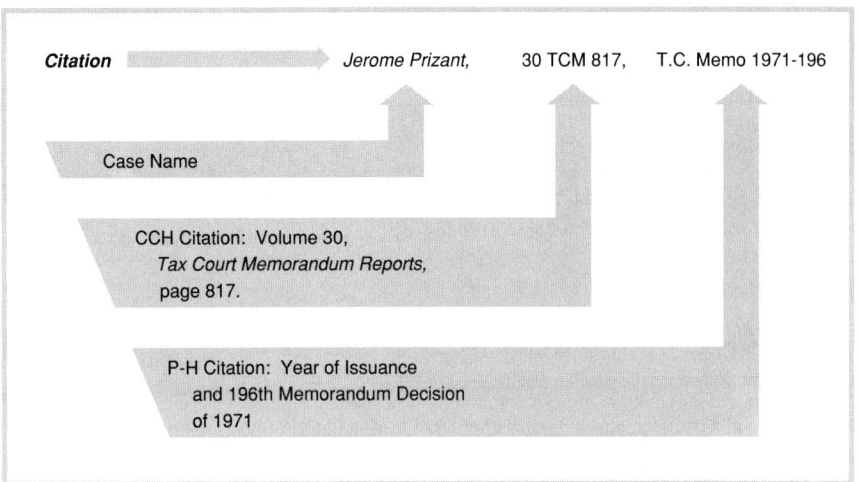

Citations for U.S. District Court, Court of Appeals, and Claims Court. Commerce Clearing House, Prentice Hall, and West Publishing Company all publish decisions of the District Courts, Courts of Appeals, and the Claims Court. When available, all three citations of a case are provided in this text.[11] CCH publishes the decisions of these courts in its *U.S. Tax Cases* (USTC—not to be confused with the U.S. Tax Court Reports) volumes, and PH offers these decisions in its *American Federal Tax Reports* (AFTR) series. West Publishing Company reports these decisions in either its *Federal Supplement Series* (F. Supp.—District Court decisions), or its *Federal Second Series* (F.2d—Claims Court and Courts of Appeals decisions).

The citation of the U.S. District Court decision of *Cam F. Dowell, Jr. v. U.S.* is illustrated for each of the three publishing companies as follows:

---

[11] When all three publishers do not print the case, only the citations to the cases published are provided.

CCH Citation:

    Cam F. Dowell, Jr. v. U.S., 74-1 USTC ¶9243, (D.Ct. Tx., 1974).

Interpretation: This case is reported in the first volume of the *U.S. Tax Cases,* published by CCH for calendar year 1974 (74-1), located at paragraph (¶) 9243, and is a decision rendered in 1974 by a U.S. District Court located in Texas (Tx).

PH Citation:

    Cam F. Dowell, Jr. v. U.S., 33 AFTR2d 74-739, (D.Ct Tx., 1974).

Interpretation: Reported in the 33rd volume of the second series of the *American Federal Tax Reports* (AFTR2d), published by PH for 1974, and located at page 739.

West Citation:

    Cam F. Dowell, Jr. v. U.S., 370 F.Supp. 69 (D.Ct. Tx., 1974).

Interpretation: Located in the 370th volume of the *Federal Supplement Series* (F.Supp), published by West Publishing Company, and located at page 69.

The multiple citation of the U.S. District Court case illustrated above appears as follows:

    Cam F. Dowell, Jr. v. U.S., 74-1 USTC ¶9243, 33 AFTR2d 74-739, 370 F.Supp. 69 (D.Ct. Tx., 1974).

Decisions of the Claims Court (Ct. Cls.), the Courts of Appeals (e.g., CA-1, CA-2, etc.), and the Supreme Court (USSC) are published by CCH and PH in the same reporting source as District Court decisions (i.e., USTCs and AFTRs). Claims Court and Court of Appeals decisions are reported by West Publishing Company in its *Federal Second Series* (F.2d). Supreme Court decisions are published by West Publishing Company in its *Supreme Court Reports* (S.Ct.), and the U.S. Government Printing Office publishes Supreme Court decisions in its *Supreme Court Reports* (U.S.).

An example of the multiple citation of a Court of Appeals decision follows:

Citation:

    Millar v. Comm., 78-2 USTC ¶9514, 42 AFTR2d 78-5246, 577 F.2d 212 (CA-3, 1978).

A multiple citation of a Supreme Court decision would appear as follows:

Citation:

Fausner v. Comm., 73-2 USTC ¶9515, 32 AFTR2d 73-5202, 413 U.S. 838 (USSC, 1973).

Note that in each of the citations above, the designation "Commissioner of the Internal Revenue Service" is simply abbreviated to "Comm." In some instances, the IRS or U.S. is substituted for Comm., and older cases used the Commissioner's name. For example, in *Gregory v. Helvering,* 293 U.S. 465 (USSC, 1935), Mr. Helvering was the Commissioner of the Internal Revenue Service at the time the case was brought to the Court. Also note that the citation contains a reference to the Appellate Court rendering the decision (i.e., CA-3, or USSC) and the year of issuance.

Exhibits 2-1 and 2-2 summarize the sources of case citations from various reporter services.

Exhibit 2-1
Reporters of Tax Court Decisions

Reporter	Abbr.	Type	Publisher
Tax Court Reports	TC	Regular	Government Printing Office
Tax Court Memorandum Decisions	TCM	Memorandum	Commerce Clearing House
Tax Court Memorandum Decisions	PH TC Memo	Memorandum	Prentice Hall, Inc.

Exhibit 2-2
Reporters of Decisions Other Than Tax Court

Reporter	Abbr.	Courts Reported	Publisher
Supreme Court Reports	U.S.	Supreme Court	Government Printing Office
Supreme Court Reporter	S. Ct.	Supreme Court	West Publishing
Federal Supplement	F. Supp.	District Courts	West Publishing
Federal Reporter	F. F. 2d	Cts. of Appeal and Claims Ct.	West Publishing
American Federal	AFTR	District Courts	Prentice Hall, Inc.
Tax Reports	AFTR 2d	Claims Court, Cts. of Appeal, and Supreme Ct.	Prentice Hall, Inc.
United States Tax	USTC	Same as AFTR and AFTR2d	Commerce Clearing House

SECONDARY SOURCES

The importance of understanding the sources discussed thus far stems from their role in the taxation process. As mentioned earlier, the statutory law and its official interpretations constitute the legal authorities that set forth the tax consequences for a particular set of facts. These legal authorities, sometimes referred to as *primary authorities,* must be distinguished from so-called *secondary sources* or *secondary authorities.* The secondary sources of tax information consist mainly of books, periodicals, articles, newsletters, and editorial judgments in tax services. When working with the tax law, it must be recognized that secondary sources are unofficial interpretations—mere opinions—that have no legal authority.

Although secondary sources should not be used as the supporting authority for a particular tax treatment (except as a supplement to primary authority or in cases where primary authority is absent), they are an indispensable aid when seeking an understanding of the tax law. Several of these secondary materials are discussed briefly below.

TAX SERVICES

"Tax service" is the name given to a set of books that contains a vast quantity of tax-related information. In general, a tax service is a compilation of the following: the Code, regulations, court decisions, IRS releases, and explanations of these primary authorities by the editors. As the listing of contents suggests, a tax service is invaluable since it contains, all in one place, a wealth of tax information, including both primary and secondary sources. Moreover, these materials are updated constantly to reflect current developments—an extremely important feature given the dynamic nature of tax law. The major tax services are

Publisher	Name of Publication
Commerce Clearing House	Standard Federal Tax Reporter—Income Taxes
Prentice Hall	Federal Taxes—Series D, including Citator
The Bureau of National Affairs, Inc.	Tax Management Portfolios—U.S. Income
Research Institute of America	Federal Tax Coordinator—2nd Series
Mertens	Law of Federal Income Taxation

The widespread use of computers also has found its way into tax research. For example, *LEXIS* is a computerized data base that a user can access through his or her personal computer. The *LEXIS* data base contains almost all information available in an extensive tax library. Suppliers of tax services are currently making their own computer-based system available to their customers, or are in the process of perfecting such a system. Undoubtedly computers will be basic to tax research in the future, particularly within the large law and accounting firms that have enough work to make the use of such a system economical.

Commerce Clearing House, Prentice Hall, and other publishers issue weekly summaries of important cases and other tax developments that many practitioners and scholars find helpful in keeping current with developments in the tax field. The Bureau of National Affairs publishes the *Daily Tax Bulletin,* a comprehensive daily journal of late-breaking tax news that often reprints entire cases or regulations of particular importance. *Tax Notes,* published by Tax Analysts, is a weekly publication addressing legislative and judicial developments in the tax field. *Tax Notes* is particularly helpful in following the progress of tax legislation through the legislative process.

TAX PERIODICALS

In addition to these services, there are a number of quality publications (usually published monthly) that contain articles on a variety of important tax topics. These publications are very helpful when new tax acts are passed, because they often contain clear, concise summaries of the new law in a readable format. In addition, they serve to convey new planning opportunities and relay the latest IRS and judicial developments in many important sub-specialities of the tax profession. Some of the leading periodicals include the following:

Estate Planning	*Taxation for Lawyers*
Journal of Corporate Taxation	*Taxes—The Tax Magazine*
Journal of Real Estate Taxation	*The International Tax Journal*
Journal of Taxation	*The Review of Taxation of Individuals*
Journal of the American Taxation Association	*The Tax Adviser*
Tax Law Journal	*The Tax Executive*
Tax Law Review	*The Tax Lawyer*
Taxation for Accountants	*Trusts and Estates*

In addition to these publications, many law journals contain excellent articles on tax subjects.

Several indexes exist that may be used to locate a journal article. Through the use of a subject index, author index, and in some instances a Code section index, articles dealing with a particular topic may be found. Three of these indexes are

Title	Publisher
Index to Federal Tax Articles	Warren, Gorham and Lamont
Federal Tax Articles	Commerce Clearing House
The Accountant's Index	American Institute of Certified Public Accountants

In addition, the PH tax service contains a section entitled "Index to Tax Articles."

TAX RESEARCH

Having introduced the sources of tax law, the remainder of this chapter is devoted to working with the law—or more specifically, the art of tax research. Tax research may be defined as the process used to ascertain the optimal answer to a question with tax implications. Although there is no perfect technique for researching a question, the following approach normally is used:

1. Obtain all of the facts

2. Diagnose the problem from the facts

3. Locate the authorities

4. Evaluate the authorities

5. Derive the solution and possible alternative solutions

6. Communicate the answer

Each of these steps is discussed below.

OBTAINING THE FACTS

Before discussing the importance of obtaining all the facts, the distinction between closed-fact research and open or controlled-fact research should be noted. If the research relates to a problem with transactions that are complete, it is referred to as closed-fact research and normally falls within the realm of tax practice known as tax compliance. On the other hand, if the research relates to contemplated transactions, it is called controlled or open-fact research and is an integral part of tax planning.

In researching a closed-fact problem, the first step is gathering all of the facts. Unfortunately, it is difficult to obtain all relevant facts upon first inquiry. This is true because it is essentially impossible to understand the law so thoroughly that all of the proper questions can be asked before the research task begins. After the general area of the problem is identified and research has begun, it usually becomes apparent that more facts must be obtained before an answer can be derived. Consequently, additional inquiries must be made until all facts necessary for a solution are acquired.

DIAGNOSING THE ISSUE

Once the initial set of facts is gathered, the tax issue or question must be identified. Most tax problems involve very basic questions such as these:

1. Does the taxpayer have gross income that must be recognized?

2. Is the taxpayer entitled to a deduction?

3. Is the taxpayer entitled to a credit?

4. In what period is the gross income, deduction, or credit reported?

5. What amount of gross income, deduction, or credit must be reported?

As research progresses, however, such fundamental questions can be answered only after more specific issues have been resolved.

> **Example 1.** R's employer owns a home in which R lives. The basic question that must be asked is whether the home constitutes income to R. After consulting the various tax sources, it can be determined that § 61 requires virtually all benefits to be included in income unless another provision specifically grants an exclusion. In this case, § 119 allows a taxpayer to exclude the value of employer-provided housing if the housing is on the employer's premises, the lodging is furnished for the convenience of the employer, and the employee is required by the employer to accept the housing. Due to the additional research, three more specific questions must be asked:
>
> 1. Is the home on the employer's premises?
>
> 2. Is the home provided for the employer's convenience?
>
> 3. Is R required to live in the home?

As the above example suggests, diagnosing the problem requires a continuing refinement of the questions until the critical issue is identified. The refinement that occurs results from the awareness that is gained through reading and rereading the primary and secondary authorities.

> **Example 2.** Assume the same facts in *Example 1*. After determining that one of the issues concerns whether R's home is on the business premises, a second inquiry is made of R concerning the location of his residence. (Note that as the research progresses, additional facts must be gathered.) According to R, the house is located in a suburb, 25 miles from his employer's downtown office. However, the house is owned by the employer, and hence R suggests that he lives on the employer's premises. He also explains that he often brings work home and frequently entertains clients in his home. Having uncovered this information, the primary authorities are

reexamined. Upon review, it is determined that in *Charles N. Anderson*,[12] the court indicated that an employee would be considered on the business premises if the employee performed a significant portion of his duties at the place of lodging. Again the question must be refined to ask: Do R's work and entertainment activities in the home constitute a significant portion of his duties?

LOCATING THE AUTHORITIES

Identification of the critical issue presented by any tax question begins by first locating, then reading and studying the appropriate authority. Locating the authority is ordinarily done using a tax service. With the issue stated in general terms, the subject is found in the index volume and the location is determined. At this point, the appropriate Code sections, regulations, and editorial commentary may be perused to determine their applicability to the question.

> **Example 3.**   In the case of R above, the problem stated in general terms concerns income. Using an index, the key word, *income,* could be located and a reference to information concerning the income aspects of lodging would be given.

Once information relating to the issue is identified, the authoritative materials must be read. That is, the appropriate Code sections, regulations, rulings, and cases must be examined and studied to determine how they relate to the question. As suggested above, this process normally results in refinement of the question, which in turn may require acquisition of additional facts.

EVALUATING THE AUTHORITY

After the various authorities have been identified and it has been *verified* that they are applicable, their value must be appraised. This evaluation process, as will become clear below, primarily involves appraisal of court decisions and revenue rulings.

The Code.   The Internal Revenue Code is the final authority on most tax issues since it is the Federal tax law as passed by Congress. Only the courts can offset this authority by declaring part of the law unconstitutional, and this happens rarely. Most of the time, however, the Code itself is only of partial help. It is written in a style that is not always easy to understand, and it contains no examples of its application. Accordingly, to the extent the Code can be understood as clearly applicable, no stronger authority exists, except possibly a treaty. But in most cases, the Code cannot be used without further support.

---

[12] 67-1 USTC ¶9136, 19 AFTR2d 318, 371
     F.2d 59 (CA-6, 1966).

Treasury Regulations. As previously discussed, the regulations are used to expand and explain the Code. Because Congress has given its authority to make laws to the Executive branch's administrative agency—the Treasury—the regulations that are produced are a very strong source of authority, although not as strong as the Code itself. Normally, the major concern with regulations is whether they are consistent with the Code. If the regulations are inconsistent, the Court will not hesitate to invalidate them.

Judicial Authority. The value of a court decision depends on numerous factors. On appraising a decision, the most crucial determination concerns whether the outcome is consistent with other decisions on the same issue. In other words, consideration must be given to how other decisions have evaluated the one in question. An invaluable tool in determining the validity of a case is a *citator*. A tax citator is a volume containing an alphabetical listing of virtually all tax cases. After the name of each case, there is a record of other decisions that have cited (in the text of their facts and opinions) the first case.

> **Example 4.**   Assume the same facts as in *Example 2*. Examination of the *Anderson* case in a citator reveals that it has been cited by courts in other decisions numerous times. For example, two cases in which the *Anderson* decision was discussed are *U.S. Jr. Chamber of Commerce*[13] and *Jan J. Wexler.*[14]

It is important to note that tax citators often use abbreviations for subsequent case history. For example, the abbreviations *aff'g* and *aff'd* mean "affirming" and "affirmed" and indicate that an appeals court has upheld the decision in question. Similarly, *rev'g* and *rev'd* mean "reversing" and "reversed" and indicate that a trial court's decision was overturned. Finally, *rem'g* and *rem'd* mean "remanding" and "remanded" and indicate that the case has been sent back to a lower court for reconsideration.

The validity of a particular decision may be assessed by examining how the subsequent cases viewed the cited decision. For example, subsequent cases may have agreed or disagreed with the decision in question, or distinguished the facts of the cited case from those examined in a later case.

Another important factor that must be considered in evaluating a court decision is the level of the court that issued it. Decisions issued by trial courts have less value than those issued by appellate courts. And, of course, decisions of the Supreme Court are the ultimate authority.

A court decision's value rises appreciably if the IRS agrees with its result. As discussed earlier, the IRS usually indicates whether it acquiesces or does not acquiesce to regular Tax Court decisions. The position of the Service may also be published in a revenue ruling.

[13]   64-2 USTC ¶9637, 14 AFTR2d 5223, 334 F.2d 660 (Ct. Cls., 1964).

[14]   75-1 USTC ¶9235, 35 AFTR2d 75-550, 507 F.2d 842 (CA-6, 1975).

Rulings. The significance of revenue rulings lies in the fact that they reflect current IRS policy. Since agents of the IRS are usually reluctant to vary from that policy, revenue rulings carry considerable weight.

Revenue rulings are often evaluated in court decisions. Thus, a tax service should be used to determine whether relevant rulings have been considered in any decisions. By examining the Court's view of the ruling, possible flaws may be discovered.

Private letter rulings issued to the taxpayer must be followed for that taxpayer by the IRS as long as the transaction is carried out in the manner initially approved. Variation from the facts on which the ruling was based permits the Service to revise its position. With its enactment of the Revenue Reconciliation Act of 1989, Congress has established that all taxpayers can rely on letter rulings even though they are issued to specific taxpayers.

DERIVING THE SOLUTION

Once all the relevant authorities have been evaluated, a conclusion must be drawn. Before deriving the final answer or answers, however, an important caveat is warranted: the researcher must ensure that the research reflects all current developments. The new matters section of a tax service can aid in this regard. The new matters section updates the textual discussion with any late-breaking developments. For instance, the section will contain any new cases, regulations, or pronouncements of the Internal Revenue Service that may bear on the discussion of the topic covered in the main text.

After the current validity of the research is verified, the questions that have been formulated must be answered. In some cases the answers are clear; all too often, however, they are not. In such cases, it seems that from a practical viewpoint the issue should always be resolved in the taxpayer's favor, since the probability that a particular return will be subject to audit is very low. This decision also depends on several other factors, such as a taxpayer's personal attitudes, the amount of the tax at issue, and whether the tax return contains other items that might be at risk. Prior to enactment of the Tax Equity and Fiscal Responsibility Act (TEFRA), this was often the result. Under the rules enacted by TEFRA, however, the taxpayer may be subject to a penalty. This penalty is levied if there is a substantial understatement of tax attributable to a particular treatment for which the taxpayer does not have substantial authority.[15] (No penalty is imposed if the treatment is disclosed on the return.) Although the criterion of substantial authority has yet to be defined, the standard probably

[15]   § 6661.

lies somewhere between "reasonable support" and "more likely than not." In any event, it is clear that taxpayers must be concerned with their conclusion and its supporting authority more than ever before.[16]

COMMUNICATING THE FINDINGS

The final product of the research effort is a memorandum recording the research and a letter to the interested parties. Although many formats are suitable for the memorandum, one technique typically used is structured as follows:

1. Description of the facts
2. Statement of the issues or questions researched
3. Report of the conclusions (brief answers to the research questions)
4. Discussion of the rationale and authorities that support the conclusions
5. Summary of the authorities consulted in the research

A good tax memorandum is essential. If the research findings are not communicated intelligently and effectively, the entire research effort is wasted.

---

[16] It should be noted that the Internal Revenue Code contains penalties for improper conduct by tax return preparers as well. These penalties run the gamut from offenses such as failing to furnish a completed copy of a return to the taxpayer to penalties for negligence and fraud.

PROBLEM MATERIALS

DISCUSSION QUESTIONS

2-1   *Making a New Tax Law.*   Describe the Congressional process of making a tax bill into final law.

2-2   *Legislative vs. Interpretative Regulations.*   Explain the difference between a legislative Treasury Regulation and an interpretative Regulation.

2-3   *Proposed vs. Final Regulations.*   Distinguish between proposed and final Regulations. How would either type of Regulation involving Code § 704 be cited?

2-4   *Revenue Rulings and Revenue Procedures.*   Distinguish between a Revenue Ruling and a Revenue Procedure. Where can either be found in printed form?

2-5   *Private vs. Published Rulings.*   Distinguish between a private letter ruling and a Revenue Ruling. Under what circumstances would a taxpayer prefer to rely on either of these sources?

2-6   *Technical Advice Memoranda.*   What are Technical Advice Memoranda? Under what circumstances are they issued?

2-7   *Trial Courts.*   Describe the trial courts that hear tax cases. What are the advantages or disadvantages of litigating a tax issue in each of these courts?

2-8   *The Appeals Process.*   A taxpayer living in Indiana has exhausted her appeals within the IRS. If she chooses to litigate her case, trace the appeals process assuming she begins her effort in each of the following trial courts:

    a.   The U.S. Claims Court
    b.   The U.S. District Court
    c.   The U.S. Tax Court
    d.   The Small Claims Division of the U.S. Tax Court

2-9   *Tax Court Decisions.*   Distinguish between a Regular Tax court decision and a Memorandum decision.

2-10   *Authority of Tax Law Sources.*   Assuming that you have discovered favorable support for your position taken in a controversy with an IRS agent in each of the sources listed below, indicate how you would use these authoritative sources in your discussion with the agent.

    a.   A decision of the U.S. District Court having jurisdiction over your case if litigated
    b.   Treasury Regulation
    c.   The Internal Revenue Code
    d.   A decision of the Supreme Court
    e.   A decision of the Small Claims Court
    f.   A decision of the U.S. Tax Court
    g.   A private letter ruling issued to another taxpayer
    h.   A Revenue Ruling
    i.   A tax article in a leading periodical

2-11 *Tax Services*. What materials are generally found in leading tax services? Which does your library have?

PROBLEMS

2-12 *Interpreting Citations*.   Interpret each of the following citations:

a.   Reg. § 1.721-1(a).
b.   Rev. Rul. 60-314, 1960-2 C.B. 48.
c.   Rev. Proc. 81-54, 1981-2 C.B. 44.
d.   Rev. Rul. 90-104, I.R.B. 1990-52, 5.
e.   § 351.

2-13 *Citation Abbreviations*.   Explain each of the abbreviations below.

a.   B.T.A.
b.   Acq.
c.   D. Ct.
d.   CA-9
e.   F. Supp.
f.   NA.
g.   Ct. Cls.
h.   USTC
i.   AFTR
j.   *Cert. Den.*
k.   *aff'g* and *aff'd*
l.   *rev'g* and *rev'd*
m.   *rem'g* and *rem'd*

2-14 *Interpreting Citations*.   Identify the publisher and interpret each of the following citations:

a.   41 TCM 289.
b.   93 S. Ct. 2820 (USSC, 1973).
c.   71-1 USTC ¶9241 (CA-2, 1971).
d.   236 F. Supp. 761 (D. Ct. Va., 1974).
e.   T.C. Memo 1977-20.
f.   48 T.C. 430 (1967).
g.   6 AFTR2d 5095 (CA-2, 1960).
h.   589 F.2d 446 (CA-9, 1979).
i.   277 U.S. 508 (USSC, 1928).

2-15 *Citation Form*.   Record the following information in its proper citation form.

a.   Part 7, subdivision (a)(2) of the income tax Regulation under Code § 165
b.   The 34th Revenue Ruling issued March 2, 1987, and printed on pages 101 and 102 of the appropriate document
c.   The 113th letter ruling issued the last week of 1986

2-16 *Citation Form.* Record the following information in its proper citation form.

    a.   A 1982 U.S. Tax Court case in which Roger A. Schubel sued the IRS Commissioner for a refund, published in volume 77 on pages 701 through 715 as a regular decision

    b.   A 1974 U.S. Tax Court case in which H. N. Schilling, Jr. sued the IRS Commissioner for a refund, published by (1) Commerce Clearing House in volume 33 on pages 1097 through 1110 and (2) Prentice Hall as its 246th decision that year

    c.   A 1966 Court of Appeals case in which Boris Nodiak sued the IRS Commissioner in the second Circuit for a refund, published by (1) Commerce Clearing House in volume 1 of that year at paragraph 9262, (2) Prentice Hall in volume 17 on pages 396 through 402, and (3) West Publishing Company in volume 356 on pages 911 through 919.

RESEARCH PROBLEMS

2-17 *Using a Citator.* Use either the Commerce Clearing House or Prentice Hall Citator in your library and locate *Richard L. Kroll, Exec. v. U.S.*

    a.   Which Court of Appeals Circuit heard this case?

    b.   Was this case heard by the Supreme Court?

    c.   James B. and Doris F. Wallach are included in the listing below the citation for Kroll. In what court was the Wallach case heard?

2-18 *Using a Citator.* Using any available citator, locate the case of *Corn Products v. Comm.*, 350 U.S. 46. What effect did the decision in *Arkansas Best v. Comm.* (58 AFTR2d 86-5748, 800 F.2d 219) have on the precedential value of the *Corn Products* case?

2-19 *Locating Court Cases.* Locate the case of *Robert Autrey, Jr. v. United States*, 89-2 USTC ¶9659, and answer the following questions.

    a.   What court decided the case on appeal?

    b.   What court originally tried the case?

    c.   Was the trial court's decision upheld or reversed?

2-20 *Locating Court Cases.* Locate the case of *Estate of James C. Freeman*, 67 T.C. 202, and answer the following questions.

    a.   What court tried the case?

    b.   Identify the various types of precedential authority the judge used in framing his opinion.

2-21 *Locating Court Cases.* Locate the cited court cases and answer the questions below.

    a.   *Stanley A. and Lorriee M. Golantly,* 72 T. C. 411 (1979). Did the taxpayers win their case?

    b.   *Hamilton D. Hill,* 41 TCM 700, T.C. Memo ¶71,127 (1971). Who was the presiding judge?

    c.   *Patterson (Jefferson) v. Comm.*, 72-1 USTC ¶9528, 29 AFTR2d 1181 (Ct. Cls., 1972). What was the issue being questioned in this case?

2-22 *Completing Citations.* To the extent the materials are available to you, complete the following citations:

  a. Rev. Rul. 85-153, _____ C.B._____.
  b. *Lawrence W. McCoy,* _____ T.C. _____ (1962).
  c. *Reginald Turner,* _____, TCM _____, T.C. Memo 1954-38.
  d. *RCA Corp. v. U.S.,* _____ USTC _____ (CA-2, 1981).
  e. *RCA Corp. v. U.S.,* _____ AFTR2d _____ (CA-2, 1981).
  f. *RCA Corp. v. U.S.,* _____ F.2d _____ (CA-2, 1981).
  g. *Comm. v. Wilcox,* _____ S. Ct. _____ (USSC, 1946).
  h. _____, 79-1 USTC ¶9139 (USSC, 1979).
  i. _____, 34 T.C. 842 (1960).
  j. *A. V. Johnson,* 23 TCM 2003, T.C. Memo _____.
  k. *Samuel B. Levin v. Comm.,* 43 AFTR2d 79-1057(_____).

2-23 *Examination of Tax Sources.* For each of the tax sources listed below, identify at least one of the tax issues involved. In addition, if the source has a temporary citation, provide its permanent citation (if available).

  a. *Battelstein Investment Co. v. U.S.,* 71-1 USTC ¶9227, 27 AFTR2d 71-713, 442 F.2d 87 (CA-5, 1971).
  b. *Joel Kerns,* 47 TCM, _____ T.C. Memo 1984-22.
  c. *Patterson v. U.S.,* 84-1 USTC ¶9315 (CA-6, 1984).
  d. *William Sennett,* 80 T.C. 825 (1983).
  e. *Thompson Engineering Co., Inc.,* 80 T.C. 672 (1983).
  f. *Towne Square, Inc.,* 45 TCM 478, T.C. Memo 1983-10.
  g. Rev. Rul. 85-13, I.R.B. No. 7, 28.
  h. Rev. Proc. 85-49, I.R.B. No. 40, 26.
  i. *William F. Sutton, et al. v. Comm.,* 84 T.C. _____ No. 17.
  j. Rev. Rul. 86-103, I.R.B. No. 36, 13.
  k. *Hughes Properties, Inc.,* 86-1 USTC ¶9440, 58 AFTR2d 86-5015, _____ U.S. _____ (USSC, 1986).
  l. Rev. Rul. 87-105, I.R.B. No. 43, 13.

2-24 *Office in the Home.* T comes to you for advice regarding the deductibility of expenses for maintaining an office in his home. T is currently employed as an Executive Vice President for Zandy Corporation. He has found it impossible to complete his job responsibilities during the normal forty-hour weekly period. Although the office building in which he works is open nights and weekends, the heating and air conditioning systems are shut down at night (from 6 p.m.) and during the entire weekend. As a result, T has begun taking work home with him on a regular basis. The work is generally done in the den of T's home. Although T's employer does not require him to work at home, T is convinced that he would be fired if his work assignments were not completed on a timely basis. Given these facts, what would you advise T about taking a home-office deduction?

Partial list of research aids:

§ 280A
Reg. § 1.280A
M.G. Hill, 43 TCM 832, T.C. Memo 1982-143

2-25 *Journal Articles.* Refer to Problem 2-24 above. Consult an index to periodicals (e.g., AICPA's *Accountants Index*; Warren, Gorham, and Lamont's *Index to Federal Tax Articles*; or CCH's *Federal Tax Articles*) and locate a journal article on the topic of tax deductions for an office in the home. Copy the article. Record the citation for the article (i.e., author's name, article title, journal name, publication date, and first and last pages of the article) at the top of your paper. Prepare a two-page summary of the article, including all relevant issues, research sources, and conclusions. Staple your two-page summary to the article. The grade for this exercise will be based on the relevance of your article to the topic, the accuracy and quality of your summary, and the quality of your written communication skills.

2-26 *Deductible Medical Expenses.* B suffers from a severe form of degenerative arthritis. Her doctor strongly recommended that she swim for at least one hour per day in order to stretch and exercise her leg and arm muscles. There are no swimming pools nearby, so B spent $15,000 to have a swimming pool installed in her back yard. This expenditure increased the fair market value of her house by $5,000. B consults you about whether she can deduct the cost of the swimming pool on her individual tax return. What do you recommend?

> **Hint:** You should approach this problem by using the tax service volumes of either Prentice Hall, Commerce Clearing House, or Research Institute of America. Prentice Hall and Commerce Clearing House are organized according to Code Sections, so you should start with Code § 213. You will find the Code Sections on the back binding of the volumes. Research Institute of America has a very extensive index, so look under the term "medical expenses."

2-27 *Deductible Educational Expenses.* T is a CPA with a large accounting firm in Houston, Texas. He has been assigned to the international taxation group of his firm's tax department. As a result of this assignment, T enrolls in an international tax law course at the University of Houston Law School. The authorities of the University require T to enroll as a regular law student; and, theoretically, if he continues to attend courses, T will graduate with a law degree. Will T be able to deduct his tuition for the international tax law course as a business expense?

> **Hint:** Go to either the Prentice Hall or Commerce Clearing House tax service and use it to find the analysis of Code § 162. When you have found the discussion of § 162, find that part of the subsection dealing with educational deductions. Read the appropriate Regulations and then note the authorities listed after the Regulations. Read over the summaries provided and then choose those you think have the most relevance to the question asked above. Read these cases and other listed authorities, and formulate a written response to the question asked in light of these cases and other authorities. Finally, for the authorities you choose, go to the Prentice Hall or Commerce Clearing House Citator and use it to ensure that your authorities are current.

LEARNING OBJECTIVES

Upon completion of this chapter you will be able to:

- Identify the entities that are subject to the Federal income tax

- Explain the basic tax treatment of individuals, corporations, partnerships, S corporations, and fiduciary taxpayers (trusts and estates)

- Understand the basic tax formulas to be followed in computing the tax liability for individuals and corporations

- Define many of the basic terms used in the tax formula such as gross income, adjusted gross income, taxable income, exclusion, deduction, and credit

- Calculate the gain or loss on the disposition of property and explain the tax consequences, including the special treatment of capital gains and losses

CHAPTER OUTLINE

Chapter 3

TAXABLE ENTITIES, TAX FORMULA, INTRODUCTION TO PROPERTY TRANSACTIONS

INTRODUCTION

The amount of income tax ultimately paid by any taxpayer is determined by applying the many rules comprising our income tax system. This chapter examines some of the fundamental features of this system. Those features specifically considered concern the following:

1. *Taxable Entities*—those entities that are subject to taxation and those that are merely *conduits*

2. *Tax Formulas*—the mathematical relationships used to compute the tax for the various taxable entities

3. *Property Transactions*—the tax treatment of sales, exchanges, and other dispositions of property

THE TAXABLE ENTITY

The income tax must be imposed on the income of some type of entity. Unfortunately, those concerned with tax policy over the years have been unable to agree on what is the theoretically correct unit of taxation. There are a variety of legal, economic, social, and natural entities that could be chosen as the appropriate subject of taxation. Some of the entities that could be selected include the following: individuals (natural persons), family units, households (those living together), sole proprietorships, partnerships, corporations, trusts, estates, governments, religious groups, nonprofit organizations, and other voluntary or cooperative associations. Despite the disagreement over which of these or other entities are the proper choices, Congress has provided that only certain entities are responsible for actually paying the tax. According to the Code, individuals, most corporations, and fiduciaries (estates and trusts) are taxable entities. Other entities, such as sole proprietorships, partnerships, and so-called "S" corporations, are not required to pay tax on any taxable income they might have. Instead, the taxable income of these entities is allocated to their owners, who bear the responsibility for paying any tax which may be due.

> **Example 1.** R and S are equal partners in a partnership that had taxable income of $50,000 in the current year. The partnership would not pay tax on the $50,000. Rather, the income would be allocated equally between R and S. Thus, both R and S would report $25,000 of partnership income on their individual returns and pay the required tax.

In the following sections, the general tax treatment of the taxable entities—individuals, corporations, and fiduciaries—is explained along with the treatment of partnerships and "S" corporations. The specific tax treatment of entities other than individuals is discussed separately in later chapters of this text. However, it should be emphasized that many of the tax rules applying to one entity also apply to other entities. These similarities will be pointed out as the various rules are discussed.

TAXABLE ENTITIES

INDIVIDUAL TAXPAYERS

Citizens and Residents of the United States. Section 1 of the Internal Revenue Code indicates that a tax is imposed on the taxable income of all individuals. The term *individuals* includes not only U.S. citizens, but also any other persons who are considered residents (resident aliens). The definition ascribed to residents may cause some foreign visitors to become unexpectedly subject to U.S. tax. According to the regulations, any alien present in the United States who is not a mere transient or sojourner is a resident.[1] Thus, a foreign individual who is merely visiting in the United States is not normally subject to U.S. tax. However, even visitors do not escape U.S. taxation if they are indefinite as to the length of their stay, since such persons qualify as residents.[2] As discussed below, the tax would be levied on both their U.S. income and any foreign income.

Foreign Taxpayers. Individuals who are not U.S. citizens and who do not qualify as residents may be subject to U.S. tax. These persons referred to as nonresident aliens are taxed on certain types of income that are received from U.S. sources.[3] These amounts are taxed at a flat rate of 30 percent.

Age. It should be noted that the age of the individual is not a factor in determining whether he or she is a taxpaying entity. Whether the individual is eight years old or eighty years old, he or she is still subject to tax on any taxable

---

[1] Reg. § 1.871-2(b).

[2] See § 7701(b) for a definition of the "substantial presence test" that is used to determine if an individual is a resident alien and subject to U.S. tax.

[3] § 871.

income he or she might receive. Contrary to the belief of some people, a child's income is taxed to the child and not the parent. As explained later, age may have an impact on *both* the method of computing the tax and the amount of tax owed; it does not, however, affect the individual's status as a taxpayer.

Sole Proprietorship.   Another aspect of individual taxation requiring consideration is the taxation of sole proprietorships. For financial accounting purposes, the business activities of the proprietor are treated as distinct from other activities. The sole proprietorship is considered a separate accounting entity for which separate records and reports are maintained. For tax purposes, however, the sole proprietorship is not a separate entity subject to tax. The sole proprietorship does not file its own tax return. Rather, the taxable income of the proprietorship is reported on the individual's personal income tax return along with any other tax items. In essence, the sole proprietorship serves as a conduit; that is, any income it has flows through to the individual.

> **Example 2.**   K is employed as an accounting professor at State University, where she earns a salary of $42,000. K also operates a consulting practice as a sole proprietorship, which earned $10,000 during the year. The sole proprietorship does not file a separate return and pay tax. Instead, K reports the sole proprietorship's income along with her salary on her individual return and pays the tax required. Specifically, the operations of the sole proprietorship are reported on a special form, Schedule C, which accompanies Form 1040 where the salary is reported.

Worldwide Income.   The Federal income tax on individuals applies not only to domestic (U.S.) source income, but also to income from foreign sources. It is therefore possible to have foreign source income taxed by more than one country. Several provisions exist to prevent or minimize double taxation, however. For example, U.S. citizens and residents living abroad may take either a direct reduction in U.S. tax (foreign tax credit)[4] or deduct such taxes.[5] In lieu of taking a credit or deduction for foreign taxes, any U.S. citizen who works abroad may exclude from his or her U.S. income certain amounts of income earned abroad.[6] This exclusion is limited to $70,000 for any 12-month period. To qualify, the taxpayer (referred to as an *expatriate*) must either be a bona fide resident of a foreign country (or countries) or be physically present in a foreign country for 330 days in any 12 consecutive months.

---

[4]   § 901.   [6]   § 911(a).

[5]   § 164(a).

Example 3. Z, a U.S. citizen, is an aircraft mechanic who was temporarily assigned to a lucrative job in Seoul, South Korea. Z lived in Seoul all of 1991 except for two weeks when he came back to the United States to visit relatives. From his Korean job, he earned $90,000 in 1991. Because Z was present in the foreign country for 330 days during 12 consecutive months, he meets the physical presence test and may exclude $70,000 of his $90,000 salary.

In addition to the relief measures mentioned above, tax treaties often exist that deal with the problem of double taxation by the United States and foreign countries.

CORPORATE TAXPAYERS

Section 11 of the Code imposes a tax on all corporations. The tax applies to both domestic and foreign-owned corporations and their foreign and domestic source income.[7] Although § 11 requires all corporations to pay tax, other provisions in the law specifically exempt certain types of corporations from taxation. For example, a corporation organized not for profit, but for religious, charitable, scientific, literary, educational, or certain other purposes generally is not taxable.[8] However, if a nonprofit organization conducts a business unrelated to the purpose for which its exemption was granted, any taxable income resulting from that business would be subject to tax.[9] In addition to the special provisions governing taxation of nonprofit corporations, the rules applying to S corporations vary from those applying to C or "regular" corporations as explained below.

The overall income tax treatment of corporations is quite similar to that of individuals. In fact, all of the basic rules governing income, exclusions, deductions, and credits apply to individuals as well as C corporations and, for that matter, fiduciaries. For example, the general rule concerning what is deductible, found in Code § 162, allows *all* taxpayers a deduction for trade or business expenses. Similarly, § 103 provides that *all* taxpayers are allowed to exclude interest income from state and local bonds. Although many of the general rules are the same for both individuals and corporations, there are several key differences.

The most obvious difference can be seen by comparing the corporate and individual formulas for determining taxable income as found in Exhibits 3-1 and 3-2. The concepts of adjusted gross income and itemized deductions common to the individual tax formula are conspicuously absent from the corporate formula. Other major differences in determining taxable income involve the treatment of particular items, such as dividend income and charitable contributions. These and other differences are discussed in detail in Chapter 19. It should be emphasized once again, however, that most of the basic rules apply whether the taxpayer is a corporation or an individual.

---

[7] § 822(a). See Chapter 19 for more details.   [9] § 501(b).

[8] § 501(a).

One difference in the taxation of individuals and corporations that is not apparent from the basic formula, but which should be noted, concerns the tax rates that each uses in computing the tax liability (see the inside back cover of the text). A comparison of the individual and corporate tax rates reveals a much different progression: 15 to 31 percent for individuals and 15 to 39 percent for corporations. The difference between individual and corporate tax rates has spawned a great deal of planning over the years as taxpayers have tried to arrange their affairs in such a way as to minimize the applicable tax rate.

Perhaps the most critical aspect of corporate taxation that is generally not shared with any other taxable entity concerns the potential for double taxation. When a corporation receives income and subsequently distributes that income as a dividend to its shareholders, the effect is to tax the income twice: once at the corporate level and again at the shareholder level. Double taxation can occur because the corporation is not allowed to deduct any dividend payments to its shareholders. As one might suspect, many have questioned the equity of this treatment, arguing that it penalizes those who elect to do business in the corporate form. Note, however, that this treatment is consistent with the fact that the corporation is considered a separate taxable entity. Moreover, it is often argued that the corporation and its owners in reality do not bear the burden of the corporate tax. According to the argument, corporations are able to shift the tax burden either to consumers by charging higher prices or to employees by paying lower wages. In addition, those who reject the double tax theory often note that closely held corporations, whose owners are also employees of the business, are able to avoid double taxation to the extent they can characterize any corporate distributions as deductible salary payments rather than nondeductible dividends. Whether in fact double taxation occurs, it appears that this feature, which has been part of the U.S. tax system since its inception, is unlikely to change in the immediate future.

Special rules apply to the formation of a corporation, corporate dividend distributions, and distributions made to shareholders in exchange for their stock. Penalty taxes also may be assessed against corporations that fail to pay dividends to their shareholders. These topics and others related to the income taxation of corporations and their owners are discussed in Chapters 19, 20, and 21.

FIDUCIARY TAXPAYERS

A *fiduciary* is a person who is entrusted with property for the benefit of another, the *beneficiary*. The individual or entity that acts as a fiduciary is responsible for managing and administering the entrusted property, at all times faithfully performing the required duties with the utmost care and prudence.

Two types of fiduciary relationships are the trust and the estate. The trust is a legal entity created when the title of property is transferred by a person (the *grantor*) to the fiduciary (the *trustee*). The trustee is required to implement the instructions of the grantor as specified in the trust agreement. Typically, the property is held in trust for a minor or some other person until he or she reaches a certain age or until some specified event occurs.

An estate is also recognized as a legal entity, established by law when a person dies. Upon the person's death, his or her property generally passes to the estate, where it is administered by the fiduciary until it is distributed to the beneficiaries. Both trusts and estates are treated as taxpaying entities.

The Code specifically provides for a tax on the taxable income of estates and trusts.[10] Determining the tax for such entities is very similar to determining the tax for individuals, with one major exception.[11] When distributions are made to beneficiaries, the distributed income is generally taxed to the beneficiary rather than to the estate or trust.[12] In essence, the trust or estate is permitted to reduce its taxable income by the amount of the distribution—acting as a *conduit*, since the distributed income flows through to the beneficiaries.

> **Example 4.**   T is the trustee of a trust established for the benefit of A and B. The trust generated $4,000 of income subject to tax for 1991 and no distributions were made to either A or B during the year. The trustee files an annual fiduciary tax return for 1991 and pays the tax based on the $4,000 taxable amount.

> **Example 5.**   Assume that for 1992 the trust in *Example 4* had $4,500 of income subject to tax and that distributions of $1,200 each were made to A and B. The trustee files an annual trust return for 1992 and pays a tax based on $2,100 ($4,500 taxable income − $2,400 distribution). A and B each include $1,200 in their income tax returns for 1992.

Distributions made by a trust or estate from its corpus (also called the trust property or principal), including undistributed profits from prior years, generally are not taxable to the beneficiary.[13] This is because these distributions are part of a gift or inheritance or have been taxed previously. Similarly, the trust or estate is not entitled to deductions for these non-taxable distributions.[14] These and other provisions related to the Federal income taxation of estates, trusts, and beneficiaries are discussed in Chapter 25.

PARTNERSHIPS

The partnership is a conduit for Federal income tax purposes. This means that the partnership itself is not subject to Federal income tax and that all items of partnership income, expense, gain, loss, or credit pass through to the partners and are given their tax effect at the partner level.[15] The partnership is required to file an information return reporting the results of the partnership's transactions

---

[10]   §§ 1(e) and 641(a).

[11]   § 641(b).

[12]   §§ 651 and 661.

[13]   § 662.

[14]   § 661.

[15]   § 701.

and how those results are divided among the partners. Using this information, the partners each report their respective shares of the various items on their own tax returns.[16] Because a partner pays taxes on his or her share of the partnership income, distributions made by the partnership to the partner generally are not taxable to the partner.[17]

> **Example 6.** For its calendar year 1991, EG Partnership had taxable income of $18,000. During the year, each of its two equal partners received cash distributions of $4,000. The partnership is not subject to tax, and each partner must include $9,000 in his annual income tax return, despite the fact that each partner actually received less than this amount in cash. The partnership must file an annual income tax return reporting the results of its operations and the effect of these operations on each partner.

In some respects, the partnership is treated as a separate entity for tax purposes. For example, many tax elections are made by the partnership,[18] and a partnership interest generally is treated as a single asset when sold.[19] In transactions between the partners and the partnership, the partners generally are treated like nonpartners.[20] However, an individual partner who performs services in his or her role as a partner is not an employee for tax purposes. As a result, the partner does not qualify for the favorable tax treatment of employee fringe benefits (see Chapter 6), and his or her share of any trade or business income is generally subject to self-employment taxes. These and other controlling provisions related to the Federal income tax treatment of partnerships are discussed in Chapter 22.

ELECTING SMALL BUSINESS CORPORATIONS: "S" CORPORATIONS

The Internal Revenue Code allows certain closely held corporations to elect to be treated as conduits (like partnerships) for Federal income tax purposes. The election is made pursuant to the rules contained in Subchapter S of the Code.[21] For this reason, such corporations are referred to as *S corporations*. Not all corporations are eligible to select S status. Only corporations that have 35 or fewer shareholders and meet certain other tests may qualify.

---

[16] § 702(a).

[17] § 731(a).

[18] § 703(b).

[19] § 741 states that the sale or exchange of an interest in a partnership shall generally be treated as the sale of a capital asset.

[20] § 707(a).

[21] §§ 1361 through 1379.

If a corporation elects S corporation status, it is taxed in virtually the same fashion as a partnership. Like a partnership, the S corporation's items of income, expense, gain, or loss pass through to the shareholders to be given their tax effect at the shareholder level. The S corporation files an information return similar to that of a partnership, reporting the results of the corporation's transactions and how those results are allocated among the shareholders. The individual shareholders report their respective shares of the various items on their own tax returns. Chapter 23 contains a detailed discussion of the taxation of S corporations and their shareholders.

The preceding discussion has focused on the common accounting entities and their role in our tax system. As explained, there are only three taxable entities—individuals, corporations, and fiduciaries.

TAX FORMULA

Computing an income tax liability is normally uncomplicated, requiring only a few simple mathematical calculations.[22] These steps, referred to as the tax formula, are shown in Exhibits 3-1 and 3-2. The tax formula is presented here in two forms: the simpler general formula that establishes the basic concepts as applicable to corporate taxpayers (Exhibit 3-1) and the more complex formula for individual taxpayers (Exhibit 3-2). The formulas in Exhibits 3-1 and 3-2 will be useful references while studying the various aspects of Federal income tax law in the subsequent chapters. To make such reference easier, both formulas are reproduced on the inside back cover of the text.

The tax formula for each type of entity is incorporated into the Federal income tax forms. Exhibit 3-1 may be compared with Form 1120 (the annual income tax return for corporations) and Exhibit 3-2 with Form 1040 (the return for individuals). These forms are included in Appendix B at the back of the text.

Examination of the two formulas reveals the importance of tax terms such as *gross income*, *deductions*, and *exemptions*. Each of these terms and countless others used in the tax law have very specific meanings. Indeed, as later chapters will show, taxpayers often have been involved in litigation solely to determine the definition of a particular term. For this reason, close attention must be given to the terminology used in taxation.

---

[22] §§ 1 and 63.

Exhibit 3-1
Tax Formula for Corporate Taxpayers

Total income (from whatever source)	$xxx,xxx
Less: Exclusions from gross income	− xx,xxx
Gross Income	$xxx,xxx
Less: Deductions	− xx,xxx
Taxable income	$ xx,xxx
Applicable tax rates	xx%
Gross tax	$ xx,xxx
Less: Tax credits and prepayments	− x,xxx
Tax due (or refund)	$ xx,xxx

Exhibit 3-2
Tax Formula for Individual Taxpayers

Total income (from whatever source)		$xxx,xxx
Less: Exclusions from gross income		− xx,xxx
Gross Income		$xxx,xxx
Less: Deductions *for* adjusted gross income		− xx,xxx
Adjusted gross income		$xxx,xxx
Less: 1. The larger of		
a. Standard deduction	$x,xxx	
or	*or*	− x,xxx
b. Itemized deductions	$x,xxx	
2. Personal and dependency exemption deduction		− x,xxx
Taxable income		$xxx,xxx
Applicable tax rates (from Tables or Schedules X, Y, or Z)		xx%
Gross tax		$ xx,xxx
Less: Tax credits and prepayments		− x,xxx
Tax due (or refund)		$ xx,xxx

ANALYZING THE TAX FORMULA

Income.   Tax computation begins with a determination of the taxpayer's total income, both taxable and nontaxable. As the formula in Exhibit 3-2 suggests, income is defined very broadly to include income from any source.[23]   The list of typical income items in Exhibit 3-3 illustrates its comprehensive nature. A specific definition of income is developed in Chapter 5.

Exclusions.   Although the starting point in calculating the tax is determining total income, not all of the income identified is taxable. Over the years, Congress has specifically exempted certain types of income from taxation, often in an attempt to accomplish some specific goal.[24]   In tax terminology, income exempt from taxation and thus not included in a taxpayer's gross income is referred to as an "exclusion." Exhibit 3-4 shows a sample of the numerous items that can be excluded when determining gross income. Exclusions are discussed in detail in Chapter 6.

Gross Income.   The amount of income remaining after the excludable items have been removed is termed *gross income*. When completing a tax return, gross income is usually the only income disclosed, because excluded income normally is not reported. (See line 8b of Form 1040, however, which requires disclosure of tax-exempt interest income.)

> **Example 7.**   E is divorced and has custody of her only child. E's income for the current year is from the following sources:
>
> | | |
> |---|---:|
> | Salary | $34,000 |
> | Alimony from former spouse | 12,000 |
> | Child support for child | 6,000 |
> | Interest from First Savings & Loan | 1,200 |
> | Interest on U.S. Government Treasury Bonds | 1,600 |
> | Interest on State of Texas Bonds | 2,000 |
> | Total | $56,800 |
>
> Even though E's total income is $56,800, her gross income for tax purposes is only $48,800 because the child support and the interest income from the State of Texas are excluded. All the other items are included in gross income. Note that the interest from the Federal government is taxable, even though that from state and local governments is generally excluded from gross income.

---

[23]   § 61(a).

[24]   See Chapter 6 for a discussion of the social and economic reasons for excluding certain items of income from taxation.

Exhibit 3-3
Partial List of Items Included in Gross Income

Alimony and separate maintenance payments
Annuities
Awards
Bonuses
Commissions
Debts forgiven to debtor by a creditor
Dividends from corporations
Employee expense reimbursements
Fees and other compensation for personal services
Gains from illegal transactions
Gains from transactions in property
Gross profit from sales
Hobby income
Income from an interest in an estate or trust
Income from rental operations
Income in respect of a decedent
Interest
Pensions and other retirement benefits
Prizes and gambling or lottery winnings
Pro rata share of income of a partnership
Pro rata share of income of an S corporation
Punitive damages
Rewards
Royalties
Salaries and wages
Tips and gratuities
Trade or business income
Unemployment compensation

Exhibit 3-4
Partial List of Exclusions from Gross Income

Amounts received from employer-financed health and accident insurance to the extent of expenses
Amounts received from health, accident and disability insurance financed by the taxpayer
Amounts received under qualified educational assistance plans
Certain death benefits from employers
Certain specified employee fringe benefits
Child support payments received
Contributions by employer to employer-financed accident and health insurance coverage
Dependent care assistance provided by employer
Gifts and inheritances
Group prepaid legal service plan benefits
Improvements by lessee to lessor's property
Interest on most state and local government debt
Meals and lodging furnished for the convenience of one's employer
Personal damage awards
Premiums paid by employer on group-term life insurance (for coverage up to $50,000)
Proceeds of life insurance paid on death
Proceeds of borrowing
Qualified transportation plan benefits
Scholarship and fellowship grants (but only for tuition, fees, books, and supplies)
Social security benefits (within limits)
Veteran's benefits
Welfare payments

Deductions. *Deductions* are those items that are subtracted from gross income to arrive at taxable income. The deductions normally allowed may be classified into two major groups:

1. *Business and Production-of-Income Expenses*—deductions for expenses related to carrying on a trade or business or some other income-producing activity, such as an investment[25]

2. *Personal Expenses*—deductions for certain expenses of an individual taxpayer which are primarily personal in nature such as charitable contributions and medical expenses[26]

A comparison of the general tax formulas used by corporations and by individuals reveals some differences in the treatment of deductions. For a corporate taxpayer, all deductions are subtracted directly from gross income to arrive at taxable income. In contrast, the individual formula divides deductions into two groups:[27] one group of deductions is allowed to reduce gross income, resulting in what is referred to as adjusted gross income (A.G.I.), while a second group is subtracted from A.G.I. As explained more fully below, the first group of deductions is generally composed of certain business expenses and other special items. The deductions in this group are referred to as deductions *for* adjusted gross income. The second group of expenses consists of two categories of allowable deductions: (1) deductions *from* adjusted gross income, and (2) deductions for personal and dependency exemptions. Deductions from adjusted gross income, normally referred to as *itemized deductions*, may be deducted only if they exceed a stipulated amount known as the *standard deduction* (e.g., $3,400 for single taxpayers in 1991). The deduction for any personal and dependency exemptions claimed (e.g., $2,150 per exemption in 1991) is deductible regardless of its amount.

Dividing deductions into two groups is done primarily for administrative convenience. Congress substantially reduced the number of individuals who claim itemized deductions because they need to be reported only if they exceed the taxpayer's standard deduction. This reduction in the number of tax returns with itemized deductions significantly reduced the IRS audit procedures involving individual taxpayers. Since corporate taxpayers have only business deductions, no special grouping was needed and thus the term *adjusted gross income* does not exist in the corporate formula.

Adjusted Gross Income. The amount of an individual taxpayer's adjusted gross income (A.G.I.) serves two primary purposes. First, it is simply a point of reference used for classifying deductions: deductions are classified as either for or from A.G.I. Second, the calculation of the amount of several itemized deductions is made with reference to A.G.I. For example, medical expenses are deductible only if they exceed 7.5 percent of A.G.I., while personal casualty losses may be deducted only if they exceed 10 percent of A.G.I. In addition,

---

[25] §§ 162 and 212.   [27] § 62.

[26] §§ 170 and 213.

recent changes in the tax law make A.G.I. even more important for some taxpayers. As explained below, beginning in 1991, most itemized deductions and the deduction for exemptions are reduced if adjusted gross income exceeds certain levels.

Example 8. This year proved to be very difficult for T; his divorce became final, and shortly thereafter he became very sick. For the year, he earned $45,000 and paid $5,000 in alimony to his ex-wife and $10,000 for medical expenses that were not reimbursed by insurance. T's A.G.I. is $40,000 ($45,000 − $5,000) because alimony is a deduction for A.G.I. As computed below, T's medical expense deduction is limited to $7,000 because he is allowed to deduct only the amount that exceeds 7.5% of his A.G.I.

Medical expenses (unreimbursed)		$10,000
Adjusted gross income	$40,000	
Times:	× 7.5%	
Threshold	$3,000	(3,000)
Deductible medical expenses		$ 7,000

Deductions for Adjusted Gross Income. Code § 62 specifically lists the deductions allowable in arriving at A.G.I. This listing is a potpourri of items, as illustrated in Exhibit 3-5. They have been given various names besides deductions for A.G.I. For example, on Form 1040 they are referred to as "adjustments

---

Exhibit 3-5
List of Deductions for Adjusted Gross Income

Alimony and separate maintenance payments paid
Certain deductions of life tenants and income beneficiaries of property
Certain portion of lump-sum distributions from pension plans subject to the special averaging convention
Certain required repayments of supplemental unemployment compensation benefits
Contributions to pension, profit sharing, and other qualified retirement plans on behalf of a self-employed individual
Contributions to the retirement plan of an electing Subchapter S corporation on behalf of an employee/shareholder
Deductions attributable to property held for the production of rents and royalties
Individual retirement account contributions (within limits)
Losses from the sale or exchange of property
Penalties for premature withdrawal of deposits from time savings accounts
Reforestation expenses
Reimbursed trade or business expenses of employees
Trade or business deductions of self-employed individuals (including unreimbursed expenses of qualified performing artists)

to income." In contrast, practitioners often refer to this category of deductions as being "above the line"—the line being A.G.I. Classification of a deduction as one for A.G.I. is significant for numerous reasons, as explained fully in Chapter 7. The most important of these reasons, however, is that unlike itemized deductions, deductions for A.G.I. need not exceed a minimum level before they may be subtracted when computing taxable income.

Itemized Deductions and the Standard Deduction. Itemized deductions are all deductions other than the deductions for A.G.I. and the deduction for personal and dependency exemptions.[28] While deductions for A.G.I. are deductible without limitation, itemized deductions are deducted only if their total exceeds the taxpayer's *standard deduction*. For example, if T has total itemized deductions of $3,000 and his standard deduction amount is $3,400, he normally would claim the standard deduction in lieu of itemizing deductions. In contrast, if T's itemized deductions were $5,000, he would no doubt elect to itemize in order to maximize his deductions.

The standard deduction was introduced along with the concept of adjusted gross income and deductions *for* and *from* A.G.I. as part of the overall plan to eliminate the need for every taxpayer to list or itemize certain deductions on his or her return. As suggested above, by allowing the taxpayer to claim some standard amount of deductions in lieu of itemizing each one, the administrative problem of verifying the millions of deductions that otherwise would have been claimed has been eliminated. The standard deduction also simplifies return preparation in that most individuals no longer have to determine the amount of deductions to which they are entitled. For this reason, the amount of the standard deduction is theoretically set at a level that equals or exceeds the average person's expenditures for those items qualifying as deductions from A.G.I. Consequently, the great majority of taxpayers claim the standard deduction in lieu of itemizing deductions.

The amount of each taxpayer's standard deduction differs depending on his or her filing status.[29] The amounts for each filing status are adjusted annually for inflation. For 1990 and 1991, the amounts are as follows:

Filing Status	Standard Deduction Amount	
	1990	1991
Single	$3,250	$3,400
Unmarried head of household	4,750	5,000
Married persons filing a joint return (and surviving spouse)	5,450	5,700
Married persons filing a separate return	2,725	2,850

[28] § 63.

[29] § 63(c) contains the standard deduction amounts for 1988. The amounts for subsequent years are adjusted for inflation and announced by the IRS annually. Filing status is discussed in Chapter 4.

Exhibit 3-6 contains a partial list of itemized deductions. The most common itemized deductions are those granted for a few personal expenses: medical expenses, state and local property taxes, casualty and theft losses, moving expenses, and interest expense related to a home mortgage and investments. Itemized deductions are also allowed for a group of other expenses referred to as *miscellaneous itemized deductions*. Miscellaneous itemized deductions include the deductions for unreimbursed employee business expenses (e.g., dues to professional organizations, subscriptions to professional journals, travel), tax return preparation fees and related costs, and certain investment expenses (e.g., safety deposit box fees, investment advice). The classification of an expense as a miscellaneous itemized deduction is extremely important because a limitation is imposed on their deduction. Only the portion of miscellaneous itemized deductions exceeding 2 percent of adjusted gross income is deductible. Congress imposed this limitation in hopes of simplifying the law. The floor is intended to relieve taxpayers from the burden of recordkeeping (unless they expect to incur substantial expenditures) and relieve the IRS of the burden of auditing these expenditures.

Exhibit 3-6
Partial List of Itemized Deductions

Not Subject to 3 Percent Cutback Rule

Medical expenses (amount in excess of 7.5 percent of A.G.I.):
    Prescription drugs and insulin
    Medical insurance premiums
    Fees of doctors, dentists, nurses, hospitals, etc.
    Medical transportation
    Hearing aids, dentures, eyeglasses, etc.
Investment interest (to extent of investment income)
Casualty and theft losses (amount in excess of 10 percent of A.G.I.)
Wagering losses (to the extent of wagering income)

Subject to Cutback Rule

Certain state, local, and foreign taxes:
    State, local, and foreign income taxes
    State, local, and foreign real property taxes
    State and local personal property taxes
Mortgage interest on personal residences (limited)
Charitable contributions (not to exceed 50 percent of A.G.I.)
Moving expenses
Miscellaneous itemized deductions (amount in excess of 2 percent of A.G.I.):
    Costs of preparation of tax returns
    Fees and expenses related to tax planning and advice
    Investment counseling and investment expenses
    Certain unreimbursed employee business expenses (including
       travel and transportation, professional dues, subscriptions,
       continuing education, union dues, and special work clothing)

Example 9. R, single, is employed as an architect for the firm of J&B Associates, where he earned $25,000. His itemized deductions for the year were interest on his home mortgage, $3,000; charitable contributions, $900; tax return preparation fee, $200; and professional dues, $400. R's total itemized deductions are computed as follows:

Miscellaneous itemized deductions:		
Tax return preparation fee	$200	
Professional dues	400	
Total miscellaneous itemized deductions...........	$600	
A.G.I. limitation (2% × $25,000).................	(500)	
Total deductible miscellaneous itemized deductions ..		$ 100
Other itemized deductions:		
Interest on home mortgage.......................		3,000
Charitable contributions...........................		900
Total itemized deductions...........................		$4,000

Because R's itemized deductions of $4,000 exceed the standard deduction for single persons, $3,400 (1991), he will deduct the entire $4,000. Note that only $100 of R's miscellaneous itemized deductions are deductible, whereas all his other itemized deductions are deductible.

In search of more revenue, Congress imposed a new limitation on the amount of itemized deductions that high-income taxpayers may deduct. Beginning in 1991, taxpayers must reduce total itemized deductions otherwise allowable (*other than* medical expenses, casualty and theft losses, and investment interest) by 3 percent of their A.G.I. in excess of $100,000 ($50,000 for married individuals filing separately). However, this reduction cannot exceed 80 percent of the deductions. This ensures that taxpayers subject to the cutback can deduct at least 20 percent of their so-called "3 percent" deductions. As a result, a taxpayer's itemized deductions are never completely phased out.

Example 10. In 1991, Mr. and Mrs. J had an adjusted gross income of $300,000. Ms. K, single, had adjusted gross income of $500,000. Both the couple and Ms. K had the following itemized deductions: charitable contributions ($4,000), home mortgage interest ($4,000), and medical expenses ($3,100 after the 7.5% limitation). The amount of itemized deductions that these taxpayers may deduct is computed below.

	J	K
Itemized deductions subject to 3% cutback:		
Charitable contributions....................	$ 4,000	$ 4,000
Home mortgage interest...................	+ 4,000	+ 4,000
Total 3% deductions.......................	$8,000	$8,000
Tentative cutback:		
Adjusted gross income.....................	$300,000	$500,000
Threshold.................................	− 100,000	− 100,000
Excess...................................	$200,000	$400,000
Times: 3%................................	× 3%	× 3%
Tentative cutback.........................	$ 6,000	$ 12,000
80% limit:		
Itemized deductions subject to limit.........	$8,000	$8,000
Times: 80%...............................	× 80%	× 80%
Maximum reduction........................	$6,400	$6,400
Cutback: Lesser of tentative cutback or maximum reduction..............	− 6,000	− 6,400
Deductible "3%" itemized deductions.........	$2,000	$1,600
Medical expense deduction..................	+ 3,100	+ 3,100
Total itemized deductions....................	$5,100	$4,700

Note that in the case of Ms. K, the 80% limitation on the cutback enables her to deduct at least 20% of her deductions, or $1,600. Also observe that Ms. K would itemize her deductions because her total itemized deductions of $4,700 exceed her standard deduction of $3,400. In contrast, Mr. and Mrs. J would use the standard deduction because total itemized deductions of $5,100 do not exceed their standard deduction of $5,700.

The 3 percent cutback of certain itemized deductions affects virtually all the itemized deductions cherished by most taxpayers, including home mortgage interest, charitable contributions, state and local income taxes, property taxes, moving expenses, and unreimbursed employee business expenses. It should be observed that the effect of reducing these itemized deductions is simply a disguised tax rate increase for those earning above $100,000. Assume a taxpayer has 3 percent deductions and an A.G.I. of $100,000. In such case, $100 of additional taxable income causes a decrease in 3 percent deductions of $3. As a result, the taxpayer effectively has additional taxable income of $103. The tax in such case would be $31.93 (31% × $103). Thus, the 3 percent cutback generally increases the taxpayer's marginal tax rate by 0.93 percent.

Additional Standard Deduction for Elderly or Blind Taxpayers. Congress has traditionally extended some type of tax relief to the elderly and blind, presumably to take into account their special situations. Currently, an unmarried taxpayer who is either blind or age 65 at the close of the taxable year is allowed to increase his or her standard deduction by an additional $850 ($800 for 1990). If an unmarried taxpayer is *both* blind and 65 or older, he or she is allowed to increase the standard deduction by $1,700. A married couple is allowed $650 for each status for a maximum increase on a joint return of $2,600.

> **Example 11.** In 1991, S celebrated her sixty-fifth birthday. Instead of using the $3,400 standard deduction amount allowed for single taxpayers for 1991, S will be allowed a standard deduction of $4,250 ($3,400 basic standard deduction + $850 additional standard deduction) for 1991.
> If S were married filing a joint return for 1991, the standard deduction amount allowed would be $6,350 ($5,700 + $650). If both S and her husband were 65 or older, the standard deduction would be $7,000 [$5,700 standard deduction + (2 × $650 additional standard deduction)].

Both age and blindness are determined at the close of the taxable year. Guidelines are provided for determining whether an individual is legally blind, and specific filing requirements must be met.[30] An individual is considered to have attained age 65 on the day *preceding* his or her sixty-fifth birthday.[31] Thus, if a taxpayer's sixty-fifth birthday is January 1, 1992, he or she is considered to be 65 on December 31, 1991.

Not all individuals are entitled to the full benefit of the standard deduction. No standard deduction is allowed for the following individuals:

1. A married person filing a separate return if his or her spouse itemizes deductions;[32]

2. A nonresident alien;[33] and

3. An individual filing a return for a period of less than 12 months because of a change of accounting period.[34]

In addition, the standard deduction is limited for an individual who is claimed as a dependent on another taxpayer's return. This limitation is discussed in Chapter 4.

[30] §§ 151(d) and 151(d)(3). A taxpayer is legally blind if he or she cannot see better than 20/200 in the better eye with corrective lenses, or the taxpayer's field of vision is not more than 20 degrees. A statement must be attached to the tax return for the year. The statement must be prepared by a physician or optometrist when a taxpayer is less than totally blind. Reg. § 1.151-1(d)(2).

[31] Reg. § 1.151-1(c)(2).

[32] If one spouse elects to itemize deductions on a separate return, the other spouse *must* also itemize deductions. § 63(c)(6)(A).

[33] § 63(c)(6)(B).

[34] § 63(c)(6)(C).

Exemptions. Congress has always recognized the need to insulate from tax a certain amount of income required by the taxpayer to support himself and others. For this reason, every individual taxpayer is entitled to a basic deduction for himself and his dependents. This deduction is called an exemption. For 1991, an individual taxpayer is entitled to a deduction of $2,150 for each *personal* and *dependency* exemption.[35] *Personal exemptions* are those allowed for the taxpayer. Generally, every taxpayer is entitled to claim a personal exemption for himself or herself. However, taxpayers *cannot* claim a personal exemption on their own return if they can be claimed as a dependent on another taxpayer's return.[36] If husband and wife file a joint return, they are treated as two taxpayers and are therefore entitled to claim two personal exemptions. *Dependency exemptions* may be claimed for qualifying individuals who are supported by the taxpayer.[37] In addition to the 3 percent cutback in itemized deductions, high-income taxpayers are required to reduce the amount of their total deduction for personal and dependency exemptions. All the special rules governing the deduction for exemptions are discussed in detail in Chapter 4.

Taxable Income and Tax Rates. After all deductions have been identified, they are subtracted from gross income to arrive at taxable income. Taxable income is the tax base to which the tax rates are applied to determine the taxpayer's gross tax liability (i.e., the tax liability before any credits or prepayments).

The tax rate schedule to be used in computing the tax varies, depending on the nature of the taxable entity. For example, one set of tax rates applies to all regular corporations (see inside back cover of text). In contrast, individuals use one of four tax rate schedules (see inside front cover) depending on their filing status, of which there are four. These are

1. Unmarried individuals (i.e., single) who are not surviving spouses or heads of households

2. Heads of household

3. Married individuals filing jointly and surviving spouses

4. Married individuals filing separately

These tax rate structures are all graduated with the rates of 15, 28, and 31 percent. Although the rates in each schedule are identical, the degree of progressivity differs. For example, in 1991 the 31 percent marginal rate applies to single taxpayers when income exceeds $49,300, but this rate does not apply to married individuals filing jointly until income exceeds $82,150. The various filing statuses and rate schedules are discussed in Chapter 4.

---

[35] § 151(d)(1). For 1989, the exemption was $2,000. For years *after* 1989, the amount is indexed for inflation ($2,050 for 1990).

[36] § 151(d)(2).

[37] § 152.

Credits. Unlike a deduction, which reduces income in arriving at taxable income, a credit is a direct reduction in tax liability. Normally, when the credit exceeds a person's total tax, the excess is not refunded—hence, these credits are referred to as *nonrefundable* credits. In some instances, however, the taxpayer is entitled to receive a payment for any excess credit. This type of credit is known as a *refundable* credit.

Credits have frequently been preferred by Congress and theoreticians because they affect all taxpayers equally. However, credits often have complicated rules and limitations. A partial list of tax credits is included in Exhibit 3-7, and most of these are discussed in detail in Chapter 13.

Prepayments. Attempting to accelerate the collection of revenues for the war effort in 1943, Congress installed a "pay-as-you-go" system for certain taxes. Under this system, income taxes are paid in installments as the income is earned.

Prepayment, or advance payment, of the tax liability can be made in several ways. For individual taxpayers, the two most common forms of prepayment are Federal income taxes withheld from an employee's salaries and wages and quarterly estimated tax payments made by the taxpayer. Certain corporate taxpayers must make quarterly estimated tax payments as well. Quarterly estimated tax payments are required for taxpayers who have not prepaid a specified level of their anticipated Federal income tax in any other way, and there are penalties for failure to make adequate estimated prepayments.

These prepayments serve two valuable purposes. As suggested above, prepayments allow the government to have earlier use of the tax proceeds. Secondly, prepayments reduce the uncertainty of collecting taxes since the government, by collecting at the source, gets the money before the taxpayer has a chance to put it to a different use. In effect, the government collects the tax while the taxpayer has the wherewithal (ability) to pay the tax.

Other Taxes. There are several types of other taxes that must be reported and paid with the regular Federal income tax. A partial list of these taxes is included in Exhibit 3-8. The alternative minimum tax is discussed in Chapter 13. Most of the other taxes are discussed later in the text.

Exhibit 3-7
Partial List of Tax Credits

Foreign tax credit
Earned income credit
Child and dependent care credit
Credit for the elderly
Credit for producing fuel from a nonconventional source
Credit for increasing research activities
Employee stock ownership credit
Credit for employment of certain new employees
Low income housing credit
Credit for rehabilitating certain buildings

Exhibit 3-8
Partial List of Other Taxes

Alternative minimum tax on corporations
Alternative minimum tax on individuals and fiduciaries
Self-employment tax
Social security tax on tip income not reported to employer
Tax on premature withdrawal from an Individual Retirement Account
Tax from recapture of investment credit
Uncollected employee F.I.C.A. and R.R.T.A. tax on tips

INTRODUCTION TO PROPERTY TRANSACTIONS

The tax provisions governing property transactions play a very important part in our tax system. Obviously, their major purpose is to provide for the tax treatment of transactions involving a sale, exchange, or other disposition of property. However, the basic rules covering property transactions can also impact the tax liability in other indirect ways. For example, the amount of the deduction granted for a charitable contribution of property may depend on what the tax result would have been had the property been sold rather than donated. As this example suggests, a basic knowledge of the tax treatment of property transactions is helpful in understanding other facets of taxation. For this reason, an overview of property transactions is presented here. Chapters 14, 15, 16, and 17 examine this subject in detail.

The tax consequences of any property transaction may be determined by answering the following three questions:

1. What is the amount of gain or loss *realized*?

2. How much of this gain or loss is *recognized*?

3. What is the *character* of the gain or loss recognized?

Each of these questions is considered in the following sections.

GAIN OR LOSS REALIZED

A realized gain or loss results when a taxpayer sells, exchanges, or otherwise disposes of property. In the simple case where property is purchased for cash and later sold for cash, the gain or loss realized is the difference between the purchase price and the sale price, adjusted for transaction costs. The determination of the realized gain or loss is more complicated when property other than cash is received, when liabilities are involved, or when the property was not acquired by purchase.

The formal method used for computing the gain or loss realized is shown in Exhibits 3-9, 3-10, and 3-11. As these exhibits illustrate, the gain or loss realized in a sale or other disposition is the difference between the *amount realized* and the *adjusted basis* in the property given up. The amount realized is a measure of the economic value received for the property given up. It generally includes the amount of any money plus the fair market value of any other property received, reduced by any selling costs.[38] In determining the amount realized, consideration must also be given to any liabilities from which the taxpayer is relieved or which the taxpayer incurs. From an economic standpoint, when a taxpayer is relieved of debt, it is the same as if cash were received and used to pay off the debt. In contrast, when a taxpayer assumes a debt (or receives property that is subject to a debt), it is the same as if the taxpayer gave up cash. Consequently, when a sale or exchange involves the transfer of liabilities, the amount realized is increased for the net amount of any liabilities discharged or decreased for the net amount of any liabilities incurred.

The adjusted basis of property is similar to the concept of "book value" used for accounting purposes. It is the taxpayer's basis at the time of acquisition—usually cost—increased or decreased by certain required modifications.[39] The taxpayer's basis at the time of acquisition, or original basis, depends on how the property was acquired. For purchased property, the taxpayer's original basis is the property's cost. When property is acquired by gift, inheritance, or some form of tax-deferred exchange, special rules are applied in determining the original basis. Once the original basis is ascertained, it must be increased for any capital improvements and reduced by depreciation and other capital recoveries. The adjusted basis represents the amount of investment that can be recovered free of tax.

Example 12.   This year, L sold 100 shares of M Corporation stock for $41 per share for a total of $4,100. He received a settlement check of $4,000, net of the broker's sales commission of $100. L had purchased the shares several years ago for $12 per share for a total of $1,200. In addition, he paid a sales commission of $30. L's realized gain is $2,770, computed as follows:

Amount realized ($4,100 − $100)..........	$4,000
Less: Adjusted basis ($1,200 + $30)......	− 1,230
Gain realized.............................	$2,770

---

[38]   § 1001(b).   [39]   §§ 1011 through 1016.

Exhibit 3-9
Computation of Amount Realized

Amount of money received (net of money paid)
Add: Fair market value of any other property received
        Liabilities discharged in the transaction (net of
        liabilities assumed)
Less: Selling costs
Equals: **Amount realized**

Exhibit 3-10
Determination of Adjusted Basis

Basis at time of acquisition:
  For purchased property, use cost
  Special rules apply for the following methods of acquisition:
    Gift
    Bequest or inheritance
    Nontaxable transactions
Add: Capital improvements, additions
Less: Depreciation and other capital recoveries
Equals: **Adjusted basis in property**

Exhibit 3-11
Computation of Gain or Loss Realized

Amount realized from sale or other disposition
Less: Adjusted basis in property (other than money) given up
Equals: **Gain or loss realized**

Example 13. During the year, T sold his office building. As part of the sales agreement, T received $20,000 cash, and the buyer assumed the mortgage on the building of $180,000. T also paid a real estate brokerage commission of $7,000. T originally acquired the building for $300,000 in 1980, but since that time had deducted depreciation of $230,000 and had made permanent improvements of $10,000. T's gain realized is computed as follows:

Amount realized:		
Cash received......................	$ 20,000	
Liability assumed by buyer...........	+180,000	
Selling expenses....................	− 7,000	
		$193,000
Less: Adjusted basis		
Original cost.......................	$300,000	
Depreciation claimed................	−230,000	
Capital improvements...............	+ 10,000	
		− 80,000
Gain Realized.........................		$113,000

GAIN OR LOSS RECOGNIZED

The gain or loss *realized* is a measure of the economic gain or loss that results from the ownership and sale or disposition of property. However, due to special provisions in the tax law, the gain or loss reported for tax purposes may be different from the realized gain or loss. The amount of gain or loss that affects the tax liability is called the *recognized* gain or loss.

Normally, all realized gains are recognized and included as part of the taxpayer's total income. In some instances, however, the gain recognition may be deferred or postponed until a subsequent transaction occurs.

Example 14. M exchanged some land in Oregon costing $10,000 for land in Florida valued at $50,000. Although M has realized gain of $40,000 ($50,000 − $10,000), assuming certain requirements are satisfied, this gain will not be recognized, but rather postponed. This rule was adopted because the taxpayer's economic position after the transaction is essentially unchanged. Moreover, the taxpayer has not received any cash or wherewithal with which she could pay any tax that might result.

Chapter 15 contains a discussion of the more common types of property transactions in which the recognition of an individual taxpayer's realized gains are postponed.

Any loss realized must be specifically allowed as a deduction before it is recognized. Individuals generally are allowed to deduct *three* types of losses. These are

1. Losses incurred in a trade or business (e.g., an uncollectible receivable)

2. Losses incurred in an activity engaged in for profit (e.g., sale of investment property such as stock at a loss)

3. Casualty and theft losses

Losses in the first two categories generally are deductions for adjusted gross income. Casualty and theft losses from property used in an individual's trade, business, or income-producing activity also are allowed as deductions for adjusted gross income. However, casualty and theft losses from personal use property are classified as itemized deductions and are deductible only to the extent they exceed $100 per casualty or theft and other specific limitations. Other than casualty and theft losses, all other losses from dispositions of personal use assets are *not* deductible. The rules governing the deductibility of losses in the first three categories are covered in Chapter 10. The special rules governing the deduction of "capital" losses are introduced below and covered in greater detail in Chapter 16.

CHARACTER OF THE GAIN OR LOSS

From 1913 through 1921, all includible income was taxed in the same manner. Since 1921, however, Congress has provided special tax treatment for "capital" gains or losses. As a result, in determining the tax consequences of a property transaction, consideration must be given to the character or nature of the gain or loss—that is, whether the gain or loss should be classified as a *capital* gain or loss or an *ordinary* gain or loss. Any *recognized* gain or loss must be characterized as either an ordinary or a capital gain or loss.

Capital Gains and Losses.   Although capital gains and losses arise in numerous ways, they normally result from the sale or exchange of a *capital asset*. Any gain or loss due to the sale or exchange of a capital asset is considered a capital gain or loss.

Capital assets are defined in § 1221 of the Code as being anything *other* than the following:

1. Inventory, or other property held primarily for sale to customers in the ordinary course of a trade or business

2. Depreciable property or real property used in a trade or business of the taxpayer

3. Trade accounts or notes receivable

4. Certain copyrights, literary, musical, or artistic compositions, and letters or memorandums held by the person whose personal efforts created them, and certain specified other holders of these types of property

5. U.S. Government publications acquired other than by purchase at the price at which they are sold to the general public

The term *capital assets*, therefore, includes most passive investments (e.g., stocks and bonds) and most personal use assets of a taxpayer. However, property used in a trade or business is not a capital asset and is subject to special tax treatment, as discussed later in this chapter.

Holding Period. The exact treatment of the results of sales and exchanges of capital assets depends on how long the assets were held by the taxpayer. A long-term gain or loss is one resulting from the sale or disposition of an asset held for *more than one year*.[40] A short-term gain or loss occurs when an asset is held for *one year or less*.[41] The length of time that a property is held is called the *holding period*.[42] The distinction between long-term and short-term capital gains and losses is required as part of the netting process described below.

Combining Capital Gains and Losses: Netting Process. Generalization about the treatment of capital gains and losses is difficult because the actual treatment can be determined only after the various capital gains and losses for a taxable year are combined, or netted, to determine the net gain or loss during the year.

The first step in the netting process is to classify the gains and losses as either short-term capital gains or losses (STCG or STCL) or long-term capital gains or losses (LTCG or LTCL). Short-term capital gains and losses are combined to arrive at a *net* short-term capital gain or loss (NSTCG or NSTCL). Similarly, long-term capital gains and losses are combined to arrive at a *net* long-term capital gain or loss (NLTCG or NLTCL). The final step in the netting process concerns the netting of NSTCG or NSTCL with NLTCL or NLTCG. There are six possible combinations of a taxpayer's capital gains and losses. These combinations and the results are summarized in Exhibit 3-12.

---

[40] § 1222(3) and (4).   [42] § 1223.

[41] § 1222(1) and (3).

Exhibit 3-12
*Taxation of Individual Taxpayer's
Capital Gains and Losses*

<u>Netting Process</u>	<u>General Tax Treatment</u>
Case 1. NSTCG[1] and NLTCG[2] cannot be combined	NSTCG is treated as ordinary income; NLTCG is taxed at a maximum of 28%
Case 2. NSTCG > NLTCL = Overall NSTCG[1]	Treated as ordinary income
Case 3. NLTCG > NSTCL = Overall NLTCG[2]	Taxed at a maximum of 28%
Case 4. NSTCL > NLTCG = Overall NSTCL	Deduct up to $3,000 from ordinary income; unused NSTCL carried forward until exhausted and treated as if incurred in year to which carried; the loss retains its character as NSTCL
Case 5. NLTCL > NSTCG = Overall NLTCL	Deduct up to $3,000 from ordinary income; unused NLTCL carried forward until exhausted and treated as if incurred in year to which carried; the loss retains its character as NLTCL
Case 6. NSTCL and NLTCL cannot be combined	Deduct NSTCL from ordinary income first, up to $3,000; if full $3,000 has not been offset by NSTCL, offset ($3,000 − NSTCL) by NLTCL; unused NSTCL and NLTCL carried forward until exhausted and treat as if incurred in year to which it is carried; NSTCL and NLTCL retain their character when carried forward

[1] The term *capital gain net income* is used by the Code to describe a NSTCG with no further netting allowed as well as the excess of a NSTCG over a NSTCL.
[2] The term *net capital gain* is used by the Code to describe a NLTCG with no further netting allowed as well as the excess of a NLTCG over a NSTCL.

Tax Treatment of Capital Gains. Beginning in 1991, favorable treatment is extended to an *individual* taxpayer's long-term capital gains. The Code provides a special tax calculation that ensures that a taxpayer's long-term capital gains are taxed at a maximum marginal tax rate of 28 percent instead of the 31 percent rate that could otherwise apply. This calculation is covered in detail in Chapter 16. Note that this special tax treatment is reserved solely for the taxpayer's long-term capital gains, or more precisely, the taxpayer's *net capital gain* [i.e., the excess of NLTCG over NSTCL (if any)]. In contrast, no special treatment is extended to a taxpayer's short-term capital gains [i.e., *capital gain net income*, the excess of NSTCG over NLTCL (if any)]. Net short-term capital gains receive the same treatment as ordinary income.

Example 15. Assuming taxpayers A and B realized the following capital gains and losses, netting would be performed as follows:

	Taxpayer A		Taxpayer B	
	Short-term	Long-term	Short-term	Long-term
STCG	$8,000		$14,000	
STCL	(3,000)		(9,000)	
LTCG		$1,000		$1,000
LTCG		5,000		
LTCL				(3,000)
NSTCG	$5,000		$5,000	
NSTCL				
NLTCG		$6,000		
NLTCL				($2,000)

Taxpayer A has both a NSTCG and a NLTCG, and no further netting of these transactions occurs. This is *Case 1* in Exhibit 3-12. A will combine her NSTCG with other income and receive no special treatment. A's NLTCG will be taxed at a maximum rate of 28%. In contrast, taxpayer B has a NSTCG of $5,000 and a NLTCL of $2,000, which are combined to yield an overall NSTCG of $3,000 (technically referred to as capital gain net income). This overall NSTCG receives no special treatment.

Tax Treatment of Capital Losses. When the result of an individual's capital asset transactions is a net capital loss (i.e., *Cases 4, 5,* and *6* in Exhibit 3-12), the loss is deductible up to an *annual limit* of $3,000.[43] The deductible capital loss is a deduction *for* adjusted gross income. Any losses in excess of the annual limit are carried forward for an indefinite period.

Example 16. In 1991, T has a net short-term capital loss of $2,000, a net long-term capital loss of $5,000, other includible income of $40,000, and no other deductions for adjusted gross income. In arriving at his $37,000 A.G.I., T is allowed to deduct only $3,000 of the $7,000 net capital loss. The remaining $4,000 net capital loss must be carried forward to future years.

When an individual has both a net short-term and net long-term capital loss, the net short-term capital loss must be used first toward the $3,000 capital loss deduction limit.

Example 17. Assume the same facts in *Example 16*. In arriving at his $3,000 capital loss deduction, R must use all $2,000 of the net short-term capital loss and only $1,000 of the net long-term capital loss. The remaining $4,000 net long-term capital loss may be carried forward to future years.

---

[43]　§ 1211(b).

Details of capital gain and loss treatment and the capital loss carryover rules are discussed in Chapter 16.

Corporate Taxpayers. Although corporations net their capital gains and losses in the same manner as individuals, there are important differences in the tax treatment of the overall results. Corporate taxpayers receive no special treatment for long-term capital gains. Long-term capital gains of corporations are taxed in the same manner as other income. Corporations are also not allowed to deduct capital losses against ordinary income. A corporate taxpayer's capital losses can be used *only to offset* its capital gains.[44]   Any excess losses are first *carried back* to the three preceding years and offset against any capital gains. Absent any capital gains in the three prior years, or if the loss carried back exceeds any capital gains, the excess may be *carried forward* for five years.[45] The rules related to the treatment of a corporate taxpayer's capital gains and losses are illustrated and further discussed in Chapter 19.

TRADE OR BUSINESS PROPERTY

Depreciable property and real property used in a trade or business are not capital assets, but are subject to several special provisions. Any depreciation of properties sold or exchanged may be subject to the depreciation recapture provisions if the property transaction results in a gain. Any other gains and any losses are netted under a separate netting process, and the net result generally is subject to favorable treatment.

Depreciation Recapture. All or part of depreciation related to real property and all depreciation related to other property used in a trade or business are subject to the depreciation recapture provisions. In effect, any gain on the sale of depreciable properties is ordinary income to the extent of all or a part of the depreciation deductions claimed on the property. This amount is referred to as the "depreciation recapture potential."[46] Any additional gain is subject to a special netting process under § 1231.

Section 1231 Gains and Losses. Section 1231 provides for an elaborate netting process of the results of certain casualties and thefts with the gains and losses from sales or exchanges of § *1231 assets*. Section 1231 assets generally include depreciable property and land used in a trade or business and held for more than one year. The results of such sales or exchanges are included in the netting process *only* after the application of the above recapture provisions.

If after the netting process is complete, a gain results, the *overall gain* generally is treated as a long-term capital gain. That gain is combined with other capital gains and losses for the year. In the case of an *overall loss*, the net loss is treated as an ordinary loss rather than a capital loss.

The special rules related to depreciation recapture and § 1231 gains and losses are examined in detail in Chapter 17.

---

[44]   § 1211(a).   [46]   §§ 1245 and 1250.

[45]   § 1212(a).

TAX PLANNING CONSIDERATIONS

CHOICE OF BUSINESS FORM

One of the major decisions confronting a business from a tax perspective concerns selecting the form in which it conducts its operations. A taxpayer could choose to operate a business as a sole proprietorship, a partnership, an S corporation, or a regular C corporation. Each of these entities has its own tax characteristics that make it more or less suitable for a particular situation. The following discussion highlights a number of the basic factors that should be considered.

Perhaps the most important consideration in choosing a business form is the outlook for the business. A business that expects losses will typically opt for a business form different from the one that expects profits. A key advantage of a conduit entity (i.e., partnership or S corporation) applies in years in which a business suffers losses. Like income, losses flow through to the owners of the entity and generally can be used to offset other income at the individual level. In contrast, losses suffered by a regular C corporation are bottled up inside the corporate entity and can benefit only the corporation. Losses of a regular corporation generally are carried back 3 years and carried forward 15 years to offset income that the corporation has in prior or subsequent years.

A profitable business may also benefit from its choice of the proper form. For example, a taxpayer with an extremely high income may wish to use an S corporation or a partnership to conduct business in order to avoid the high corporate tax rates. At the top end, income of a corporation is taxed at a rate of up to 34 percent while income of an individual is taxed at a maximum of 31 percent. However, a corporation may save its owner taxes relative to the flow-through entities if its income is not extremely high. For example, a glance at the tax rate schedules for corporations and individual taxpayers reveals that the first $50,000 of income of a corporate taxpayer is taxed at a 15 percent rate while single taxpayers receive the benefits of a 15 percent rate on a maximum of $20,350 (in 1991). As one might expect, careful planning enables the taxpayer to obtain the best of both worlds.

A major disadvantage of partnerships and S corporations concerns the treatment of certain fringe benefits. As explained in Chapter 6, the Code contains a host of fringe benefits that generally are deductible by the employer and nontaxable to the employee. For example, a corporation is entitled to deduct the costs of group-term life insurance provided to an employee, and the benefit (i.e., the payment of the premiums) is not treated as taxable compensation to the employee but is tax-free. Note that if the employee purchases the insurance directly, it is purchased with compensation that has been previously taxed. As a result, the employee acquires the benefit with after-tax dollars. The favorable tax treatment of fringe benefits is generally available only to employees of a business. Unfortunately, partners and shareholders in S corporations who work in the business are not considered employees for this purpose and consequently cannot obtain many of the tax-favored fringe benefits. In contrast, shareholders in regular C corporations who work in the business are treated as employees and are therefore able to take advantage of the various benefits.

ITEMIZED DEDUCTIONS VS. STANDARD DEDUCTION

A typical complaint of many taxpayers is that they have insufficient deductions to itemize and therefore cannot benefit from any deductions they have in a particular year. Nevertheless, with a little planning, not all of those deductions will be wasted. Taxpayers in this situation should attempt to bunch all their itemized deductions into one year. By so doing, they may itemize one year and claim the standard deduction the next. By alternating each year, total deductions over the two-year period are increased. This could be accomplished simply by postponing or accelerating the payment of expenses. Cash basis taxpayers have this flexibility because they are entitled to deduct expenses when paid.

> **Example 18.** Last year, X, a widow age 71, made the final payment on her home mortgage. As a result, she no longer has the interest deductions that in the past enabled her to itemize. In fact, the only deductible expenses she anticipates are property taxes on the house and charitable contributions to her church. However, these expenses together do not exceed the standard deduction as her estimates below show.
>
> | | 1991 | 1992 |
> |--------------------------|---------|---------|
> | Property taxes .... | $1,200 | $1,200 |
> | Charitable contributions ...... | 2,000 | 2,000 |
> | Total .... | $3,200 | $3,200 |
>
> If the pattern above continues, X will not benefit from any of the itemized deductions since they do not exceed the standard deduction for single taxpayers, $3,400. In short, she would obtain a total of $6,800 ($3,400 × 2) of deductions over the two-year period. Note, however, what would happen if X simply shifted the payment of the charitable contributions from one year to the other by paying it either earlier or later. In such case, total itemized deductions in one year would be $5,200 and she could itemize, while in the other year she could claim the standard deduction. As a result, she would obtain total deductions over the two-year period of $8,600 ($5,200 + $3,400), or $1,600 more than if she merely claimed the standard deduction.

PROBLEM MATERIALS

DISCUSSION QUESTIONS

3-1 *Taxable Entities.* List the classes of taxable entities under the Federal income tax. Identify at least one type of entity that is not subject to the tax.

3-2 *Double Taxation.* It has been stated that corporate earnings are subject to double taxation by the Federal government. Elaborate.

3-3 *Fiduciary.* In some regards, the fiduciary is a conduit for Federal income tax purposes. Explain.

3-4 *Partnership Return.* The partnership tax return is often referred to as an information return only. Explain.

3-5 *Tax Formula.* Reproduce the tax formula for individual taxpayers in good form and briefly describe each of the components of the formula. Discuss the differences between the tax formula for individuals and that for corporations.

3-6 *Gross Income.* How is gross income defined in the Internal Revenue Code?

3-7 *Deductions.* Distinguish between deductions *for* and deductions *from* adjusted gross income.

3-8 *Standard Deduction.* What is the standard deduction? Explain its relationship to itemized deductions. Which taxpayers are entitled to additional standard deductions?

3-9 *Itemized Deductions.* List seven major categories of itemized deductions. How and when are these reduced? Is the standard deduction reduced? If so, under what circumstances?

3-10 *Exemptions.* Differentiate between personal exemptions and dependency exemptions. Which taxpayers are denied a personal exemption?

3-11 *Credits.* There are numerous credits that are allowed to reduce a taxpayer's Federal income tax liability. List at least four such credits.

3-12 *Credits.* Credits of equal amount affect persons in different tax brackets equally, whereas deductions of equal amount are more beneficial to taxpayers in higher tax brackets. Explain.

3-13 *Prepayments.* What is meant by the concept of "wherewithal to pay" for tax purposes? How do prepayments of an individual's income taxes in the form of withholding and quarterly estimates represent the application of this concept?

3-14 *Amount Realized.* What is meant by "the amount realized in a sale or other disposition?" How is the amount realized calculated?

3-15 *Adjusted Basis.* Describe the concept of adjusted basis. How is the basis in purchased property determined?

3-16 *Gain or Loss Realized.* Reproduce the formula for determining the gain or loss realized in a sale or other disposition of property.

3-17 *Gain or Loss Recognized.* Differentiate between the terms "gain or loss realized" and "gain or loss recognized."

3-18 *Losses.* Which losses are deductible by individual taxpayers?

3-19 *Capital Assets.* Define the term "capital asset."

3-20 *Holding Period.* The determination of the holding period is important in determining the treatment of capital gains and losses. What is the difference between a long-term holding period and a short-term holding period?

3-21 *Capital Gains.* Describe the capital gain and loss netting process and identify the two results with *overall* capital gains. How are these gains treated?

3-22 *Capital Losses of Individuals.* There are "limitations" on the capital loss deduction for individuals. Identify these limitations.

3-23 *Capital Losses of Corporations.* What is the limitation on the deduction for excess capital losses of a corporate taxpayer?

3-24 *Carryover of Excess Capital Losses.* Excess capital losses of individuals may be offset against gains for other years. Specify the carryover and/or carryback period for such excess losses. How do the carryover/back provisions differ for corporate taxpayers?

3-25 *Section 1231 Assets.* Generally, what assets are included in the classification "Section 1231 assets?"

3-26 *Section 1231 Netting Process.* Give an overall description of the netting process for § 1231 gains and losses and describe the treatment of the net result.

PROBLEMS

3-27 *To Whom Is Income Taxed?* In each of the following separate cases, determine how much income is to be taxed to each of the taxpayers involved:

a. Alpha Partnership is owned 60 percent by William and 40 percent by Patricia, who agree to share profits according to their ownership ratios. For the current year, Alpha earned $12,000 in ordinary income and made no cash distributions.

b. Beta Trust is managed by Susan for the benefit of Gregory. The trust is required to distribute all income currently. For the current year, Beta Trust had net ordinary income of $5,500 and made cash distributions to Gregory of $7,000.

c. Gamma Corporation earned net ordinary income of $24,000 during the current calendar year. The corporation is a regular U.S. corporation. Heather and Kristie each own 50 percent of the stock and received dividend distributions of $1,350 each during the year.

3-28 *Selecting a Form of Doing Business.* Which form of business—sole proprietorship, partnership, S corporation, or regular corporation—is each of the following taxpayers likely to choose? An answer may include more than one business form.

a.   Edmund and Gloria are starting a new business that they expect to operate at a net loss for about five years. Both Edmund and Gloria expect to have substantial incomes during those years from other sources.

b.   Robin would like to incorporate her growing retail business for non-tax reasons. Because she needs all of the net profits to meet personal obligations, however, Robin would like to avoid the corporate "double tax" on dividends.

c.   After investigating, Edith learned that her grandchildren currently have no source of income. Edith would like to reduce the amount of income taxes she currently pays. She plans to give her income-producing investments to her minor grandchildren someday.

3-29 *Tax Treatment of Various Entities.* Office Supplies Unlimited is a small office supply outlet. The results of its operations for the most recent year are summarized as follows:

Gross profit on sales.............................	$95,000
Cash operating expenses........................	43,000
Depreciation expense...........................	16,500
Compensation to owner(s).......................	20,000
Distribution of profit to owner(s).................	5,000

In each of the following situations, determine how much income is to be taxed to each of the taxpayers involved.

a.   The business is a sole proprietorship owned by T.

b.   The business is a partnership owned by R and S with an agreement to share all items equally. S is guaranteed a salary of $20,000 (see above).

c.   The business is a corporation owned equally by U and K. K is employed by the business and receives a salary of $20,000 (see above).

3-30 *Determining Adjusted Gross Income and Taxable Income.* Fred and Susan are married and file a joint income tax return. Neither is blind or age 65. They have two children whom they support, and the following income and deductions for 1991:

Gross income	$40,000
Deductions for A.G.I.	1,200
Total itemized deductions......................	5,600
Credits and prepayments......................	1,350

Determine Fred and Susan's adjusted gross income and taxable income for their calendar year 1991.

3-31 *Tax Formula.* The following information is from the 1991 joint income tax return of Gregory and Stacy Jones, both of good sight and under 65 years of age.

Gross income	$64,000
Adjusted gross income	55,350
Taxable income.................................	31,050
Number of personal exemptions................	2
Number of dependency exemptions.............	2

Determine the amount of the Jones' deductions for A.G.I. and the amount of their itemized deductions.

3-32 *Tax Formula.* Complete the following table of independent cases for a single person in 1991:

	A	B	C
Gross income	$50,000	$65,000	$_____
Deductions for A.G.I.............	_____	8,000	7,000
Adjusted gross income (A.G.I.)..	42,000	_____	68,000
Itemized deductions.............	7,500	3,000	_____
Standard deductions.............	_____	_____	_____
Exemptions......................	2	1	1
Taxable income..................	_____	_____	59,000

3-33 *Worldwide Income Subject to Tax.* T, a U.S. citizen, has income that was earned outside the United States. The income was $20,000, and a tax of $2,000 was paid to the foreign government. Determine the general treatment of this income and the tax paid under the following circumstances:

a. The tax paid was on income earned on foreign investments, and the U.S. tax attributable to this income is $2,800.

b. Same as (a), except the U.S. tax attributable to this income is $1,800.

c. Same as (a), except the income is from services rendered while absent from the United States for 13 successive months.

3-34 *Itemized Deductions and the Cutback Rule.* W is single and has the following itemized deductions for the year:

Medical expenses.............................	$4,000
State and local taxes..........................	3,000
Interest paid on home mortgage................	8,000
Investment interest paid	1,000
Charitable contributions........................	5,000

Determine W's itemized deductions, assuming the following levels of adjusted gross income for 1991:

a. $50,000

b. $150,000

c. $600,000

3-35 *Asset Classification.* For each of the assets in the list below, designate the appropriate category using the symbols given:

> C – Capital asset
> T – Trade or business asset (§ 1231)
> O – Other (neither capital or § 1231 asset)

a. Personal residence
b. Stock in Xerox Corporation
c. Motor home used for vacations
d. Groceries held for sale to customers
e. Land held for investment
f. Land and building held for use in auto repair business
g. Trade accounts receivable of physician's office
h. Silver coins held primarily for speculation

3-36 *Gain or Loss Realized.* During the current year, W disposed of a vacant lot which he had held for investment. W received cash of $12,000 for his equity in the lot. The lot was subject to a $32,000 mortgage that was assumed by the buyer. Assuming W's basis in the lot was $23,000, how much is his gain or loss realized?

3-37 *Adjusted Basis.* M owns a rental residence that she is considering selling, but she is interested in knowing her exact tax basis in the property. She originally paid $39,000 for the property. M has spent $8,000 on a new garage, $2,500 for a new outdoor patio deck, and $4,500 on repairs and maintenance including painting. M has been allowed depreciation on the unit in the amount of $7,500. Based on this information, calculate M's basis in the rental residence.

3-38 *Gain or Loss Realized, Adjusted Basis.* S sold a rental house for $72,000. She received cash of $6,000 and a vacant lot worth $30,000. The buyer assumed the $36,000 mortgage loan outstanding against S's property. S had purchased the house for $52,000 four years earlier and had deducted depreciation of $12,000. How much are S's amount realized, her adjusted basis in the house sold, and her gain or loss realized in this transaction?

3-39 *Capital Gain and Loss Netting Process.* Individual D executed the following transactions during 1991:

Transaction	Sales Price	Adjusted Basis	Holding Period
Sale of 100 shares of XYZ	$2,000	$1,000	Long-term
Sale of land held for investment	9,000	3,000	Long-term
Sale of silver held for speculation	5,000	7,000	Short-term
Sale of personal jewelry	4,000	6,000	Long-term

Based on these transactions, calculate D's net capital gain or net capital loss for 1991.

3-40 *Excess Capital Loss.* T, an individual taxpayer, had a short-term capital gain of $4,000 and a long-term capital loss of $9,000 during 1991. How much is T's allowable capital loss deduction for 1991? What is the treatment of the short-term gain?

3-41   *Excess Capital Loss.*   Individual R completed the following transactions during 1991:

Transaction	Sales Price	Adjusted Basis	Holding Period
Sale of 150 shares of LMK...............	$1,800	$2,400	Long-term
Sale of land held for investment.........	8,000	6,800	Long-term
Sale of gold held for speculation.........	4,000	7,000	Short-term

Based on these transactions, calculate R's capital loss deduction, if any, for 1991.

3-42   *Individual's Tax Computation.*   Richard Hartman, age 29, single with no dependents, received a salary of $23,000 in 1991. During the year, he received $700 interest income from a savings account and a $1,500 gift from his grandmother. At the advice of his father, Richard sold stock he had held as an investment for five years, for a $3,000 gain. He also sustained a loss of $1,000 from the sale of land held as an investment and owned for four months. Richard had itemized deductions of $1,300. For 1991, compute Richard's:

a.   Gross income.

b.   Adjusted gross income.

c.   Taxable income.

d.   Income tax before credits and prepayments (use the appropriate 1991 tax rate schedule located on the inside front cover of this text).

e.   Income tax savings that would result if Richard made a deductible $2,000 contribution to a qualified Individual Retirement Account.

3-43   *Tax Treatment of Income From Entities.*   The G family—Mr. G, Mrs. G, and G Jr.—owns interests in the following successful entities:

1.   X Corporation is a calendar year regular corporation owned 60 percent by Mr. G and 15 percent by G Jr. During the year, it paid salaries to Mr. G of $80,000 to be its president and to G Jr. of $24,000 to be a plant supervisor. The company earned a net taxable income of $75,000, and paid dividends to Mr. G and G Jr. in the amounts of $42,000 and $10,500, respectively.

2.   Mrs. G owned a 60 percent capital interest in a retail outlet, P Partnership. The partnership earned a net taxable income of $60,000 and made distributions during the year of $72,000. The profit and the distributions were allocated according to relative capital interests.

3.   Mr. G and G Jr. each own 25 percent interest in H Corporation, an electing S Corporation. The corporation is a start-up venture and generated a net tax loss of $28,000 for the calendar year. No dividend distributions were made by H. Both Mr. G and G Jr. have bases in their H Corporation stock of $30,000.

4.   G Jr. is the sole beneficiary of G Trust created by Mrs. G's father. The trust earned a net taxable income of $16,000 and made distributions of $4,500 to G Jr.

Determine the amount of income or loss from each entity that is to be reported by the following:

a.   Mr. and Mrs. G on their joint calendar year tax return.
b.   G Jr. on his calendar year individual return.
c.   X Corporation.
d.   P Partnership.
e.   H Corporation.
f.   G Trust.

3-44   *Comprehensive Taxable Income Computation.*   Indy Smith, single, is an anthropology professor at State University. His tax records that he brought to you for preparation of his return revealed the following items.

Income

Salary from State University	$58,000
Part-time consulting	5,000
Dividend income	500
Reimbursement of travel to Denver by State University	200

Expenses

Interest on personal residence	$ 7,000
Travel expenses related to consulting	1,000
Tax return preparation fee	500
Safety deposit box to hold bonds	50
Travel and lodging to present academic paper in Denver related to his teaching position	450

In addition, Indy claims a dependency exemption for his father. Compute Indy's taxable income for the current year.

3-45   *Comprehensive Taxable Income Computation.*   Eli and Lilly have been happily married for 30 years. Eli, 67, is a research chemist at Pharmaceuticals Inc. Lilly, 64, recently retired but stays busy managing the couple's investments, including a duplex. The majority of the couple's income is derived from Eli's employment, from which he received a salary of $100,000 this year. Other income includes dividends from stocks of $5,000 and interest on State of Illinois bonds of $1,000. In addition, rents collected from the duplex were $10,000 while rental expenses (e.g., maintenance, utilities, depreciation) were $6,000. Eli contributed $2,000 to his individual retirement account. The couple also paid the following expenses: unreimbursed medical expenses, $7,000; interest on the home mortgage, $10,000; property taxes on the home, $3,000; charitable contributions, $4,000; and rental of safety deposit box, $100. Determine the couple's taxable income for 1991.

RESEARCH PROBLEM

3-46 *Using the Internal Revenue Code.*   Locate an *Internal Revenue Code of 1986*. Read §§ 61 through 65, 67, 151 and 152. Read the titles of §§ 71 through 135, 161, and 162.

    a.   Describe how Congress defined "gross income."

    b.   Why is the "exemption deduction" properly called a deduction from adjusted gross income?

    c.   A taxpayer is self-employed and incurs an ordinary and necessary expense in his business endeavor. What is the authority for deducting the expense? Why is it considered a deduction *for* adjusted gross income?

    d.   A taxpayer pays alimony to her former husband. Within limits, it is deductible *for* adjusted gross income. Why?

COMPUTERIZED TAX ANALYSIS

3-47 *Capital Gain and Loss Netting Process.*   Use computer file T301 for this problem. Assume the taxpayer is single and has adjusted gross income (A.G.I.) of $50,000 *before* taking account of capital transactions. For the independent situations below, compute the net increase (decrease) in A.G.I., the long-term capital loss carryforward (if any), and the short-term capital loss carryforward (if any).

a.	Long-term capital gains (LTCGs)	$33,000
	Long-term capital losses (LTCLs)	2,000
	Short-term capital gains (STCGs)	3,200
	Short-term capital losses (STCLs)	0
b.	Long-term capital gains (LTCGs)	$22,000
	Long-term capital losses (LTCLs)	2,000
	Short-term capital gains (STCGs)	5,000
	Short-term capital losses (STCLs)	15,000
c.	Long-term capital gains (LTCGs)	$30,000
	Long-term capital losses (LTCLs)	45,000
	Short-term capital gains (STCGs)	3,000
	Short-term capital losses (STCLs)	5,000
d.	Long-term capital gains (LTCGs)	$5,000
	Long-term capital losses (LTCLs)	1,000
	Short-term capital gains (STCGs)	10,000
	Short-term capital losses (STCLs)	50,000
e.	Long-term capital gains (LTCGs)	$5,000
	Long-term capital losses (LTCLs)	12,000
	Short-term capital gains (STCGs)	10,000
	Short-term capital losses (STCLs)	50,000

LEARNING OBJECTIVES

Upon completion of this chapter you will be able to:

- Identify the various requirements that a taxpayer must meet in order to claim a personal or dependency exemption

- Explain the phase-out of the deduction for personal and dependency exemptions

- Apply the rules to determine the taxpayer's filing status

- Compute the tax liability of an individual taxpayer using the tax rate schedules and the tax tables

- Explain the special approach used in computing the tax liability of certain children

- Describe the filing requirements for individual taxpayers and the role of the statute of limitations as it applies to the filing of tax returns

- Explain when taxes must be paid and the penalties that apply for failure to pay on a timely basis

CHAPTER OUTLINE

Chapter **4**

PERSONAL AND DEPENDENCY EXEMPTIONS; FILING STATUS; DETERMINATION OF TAX FOR AN INDIVIDUAL; FILING REQUIREMENTS

As seen in Chapter 3, numerous factors must be considered in the determination of an individual's net tax liability. Beginning in this chapter and continuing through Chapter 18, a detailed examination of these factors is conducted. This chapter is devoted to four particular concerns of individual taxpayers:

1. Personal and dependency exemptions;

2. Filing status;

3. Calculation of the tax liability using the tax rate schedules and tax tables; and

4. Filing requirements.

PERSONAL AND DEPENDENCY EXEMPTIONS

Since the inception of the income tax, policymakers have recognized the need to protect from tax some minimum amount of income that could be used for the support of the taxpayer and those who depend on him. The device used to accomplish this objective is the deduction allowed for exemptions. There are two types of exemptions for which deductions are allowed: personal exemptions and dependency exemptions.[1] Taxpayers may deduct the *exemption amount* for each of their exemptions. The exemption amount for 1991 is $2,150.[2] Each of the types of exemptions is discussed below.

PERSONAL EXEMPTIONS

There are *two* types of personal exemptions:

1. Exemption for the taxpayer
2. Exemption for the taxpayer's spouse

Each individual taxpayer normally is entitled to one personal exemption. When a *joint return* is filed by a married couple, *two* personal exemptions may be claimed. This occurs not because one spouse is the dependent of the other, but because the husband and wife are each entitled to their own personal exemption. If a married individual files a *separate return*, however, a personal exemption may be claimed for his or her spouse only if the spouse has no gross income and is not claimed as a dependent of another taxpayer.[3]

Disallowance of Personal Exemption. A taxpayer is denied a personal exemption if he or she qualifies as a dependent of another taxpayer (see discussion below).[4] This rule prevents two taxpayers (e.g., a child and his or her parent) from benefitting from two exemptions for the same person.

> **Example 1.** J is 21 years of age and a full-time college student. J receives a partial scholarship and works part-time, but the majority of his support is received from his parents. Assuming J is eligible to be claimed as a dependent on his parents' return, he is not entitled to a personal exemption deduction on his own return. This rule applies *regardless* of whether J's parents actually claim an exemption for him.

---

[1] §§ 151(a), 151(b), and 151(c). For 1988, the deduction allowed for each personal and dependency exemption was $1,950.

[2] For years after 1989, the $2,000 exemption amount is to be increased to reflect price level changes based on changes in the consumer price index. The exact amount is to be announced by the IRS in the fall of the preceding year. For instance, the exemption amount for 1992 will be announced by December 15, 1991. §§ 1(f) and 151(d)(3).

[3] § 151(b).

[4] § 151(d)(2).

DEPENDENCY EXEMPTIONS

As indicated above, an individual taxpayer also is entitled to an exemption for each person who is considered a *dependent*—generally one who depends on the taxpayer for his or her support. Technically, an individual qualifies as a dependent only if *all* five of the following requirements are satisfied.

1. *Support Test.* The taxpayer must provide more than 50 percent of the dependent's total support.

2. *Gross Income Test.* The dependent's gross income must be less than the exemption amount. An exception is provided for a child of the taxpayer who is under age 19 or a child of the taxpayer who is a full-time student *and* is under age 24.

3. *Relationship or Member of the Household Test.* The dependent must be a relative of the taxpayer or a member of the taxpayer's household.

4. *Joint Return Test.* The dependent must not have filed a joint return with his or her spouse.

5. *Citizenship or Residency Test.* The dependent must be a U.S. citizen, resident, or national, or a resident of Canada or Mexico.

In reporting dependency exemptions, the taxpayer must provide the Social Security number of every dependent who has reached the age of one as of the close of the taxable year. Failure to do so results in the imposition of a small penalty.[5]

Support Test. To satisfy the support requirement, the taxpayer must provide over half of the amount spent for the dependent's total support.[6] Total support includes not only amounts expended by others on behalf of the dependent but also any amounts spent by the dependent. Note that only the amount *actually spent* for support is relevant. Income and other funds available to the dependent for spending are ignored unless they are spent.

> **Example 2.** During the year, C paid $10,000 to maintain her father, F, in a nursing home that provides all of his needs. No other amounts were spent for his support. C made these payments, even though her father could afford them since he has cash in the bank and tax-exempt bonds valued at $200,000. Although F has funds available for providing his own support, they are not considered in applying the support test because the funds were not spent. Consequently, the support test is satisfied.

---

[5] Although some parents may be skeptical, the year that this requirement became effective the number of exemptions dropped 7 million below what had been expected, resulting in about $2.8 billion in additional tax revenue. Interestingly, over 48 percent of the drop was attributable to single taxpayers. See IRS Pub. 1500 (August 1990).

[6] § 152(a).

Support is generally measured by the cost of the item to the individual providing it. However, when support is provided in a noncash form, such as the use of property or lodging, the amount of support is the fair market value or fair rental value.

What constitutes an item of support is not always clear. If, for example, a child receives a stereo or car, are these items considered support, or do only necessities qualify? The Regulations provide some guidance as to the nature of support, indicating that it includes food, shelter, clothing, medical and dental care, education, recreation, and transportation.[7] Support is not limited to these items, however. Examination of the numerous cases and rulings reveals a hodge-podge of qualifying expenditures. Exhibit 4-1 presents a sampling of those items that constitute support. For example, the costs for boats, life insurance, and lawn mowers are not considered support. Additionally, the value of any services performed for the dependent by the taxpayer is ignored.[8]

The determination of support also is complicated by several items accorded special treatment. For example, scholarships and fellowships received by the taxpayer's child or step-child are not considered support items. Accordingly, such amounts are not treated as being provided by either the taxpayer or the dependent.[9]

Exhibit 4-1
Partial List of Support Items

Automobile	Lodging
Care for a dependent's pet	Medical care
Charitable contributions by or on behalf of dependent	Medical insurance premiums
	Singing lessons
Child care	Telephone
Clothing	Television
Dental care	Toys
Education	Transportation
Entertainment	Utilities
Food	Vacations
Gifts	

---

[7] Reg. § 1.152-1(a)(2)(i).

[8] *Markarian v. Comm.*, 65-2 USTC ¶9699, 16 AFTR2d 5785, 352 F.2d 870 (CA-7, 1965).

[9] Reg. § 1.152-1(c). Note that G.I. Bill benefits are not treated as scholarships and therefore are included as support items provided by the recipient.

Example 3. J was the recipient of an athletic scholarship that covered 100% of her tuition, books, supplies, room, and board. In addition, J was paid a small cash allowance. J's parents also provided her with $2,000 cash to be used for clothing, entertainment, and miscellaneous expenses.

The scholarship package, which was related to J's continued scholastic activity, was valued at $5,500 per year. Nevertheless, assuming the other four tests are met, J's parents are entitled to a dependency exemption, since the scholarship is not included in her support.[10]

Although Social Security benefits generally are not taxable income to the recipient, they are considered as provided by the person covered by Social Security. Thus, Social Security benefits are included in determining support to the extent they are spent for support items.[11] State welfare payments are considered provided by the state, and therefore are not treated as provided by the parent or any other taxpayer. This is true even though the parent is entrusted to oversee the prudent expenditure of the funds.[12]

Example 4. F received support during the current year from various sources, including amounts contributed by his son, S. The amounts spent toward F's support were provided as follows:

F's Social Security benefits	$5,500
Taxable interest income	400
Amount provided by S	2,100
Total	$8,000

S is not entitled to a dependency exemption for F because he did not provide more than 50% of F's total support ($2,100 is not greater than 50% of $8,000).

Example 5. This year M received Social Security benefits of $6,000, $3,500 of which was immediately deposited in a savings account. The amounts spent toward M's support were provided as follows:

M's Social Security benefits spent	$2,500
Taxable interest income	600
Amount provided by M's brother, B	4,000
Total	$7,100

---

[10] For scholarships awarded after August 16, 1986, any part of a scholarship providing benefits other than tuition, fees, and supplies, is includible in the recipient's gross income to the extent of those benefits. See Chapter 6 for a discussion of taxable scholarships.

[11] Reg. § 1.152-1(a)(2)(ii).

[12] See Rev. Rul. 71-468, 1971-2 C.B. 115 and *Helen Lutter*, 61 T.C. 685, *aff'd*. at 75-1 USTC ¶9439, 35 AFTR2d 75-1414, 514 F.2d 1095 (CA-7, 1975), *cert. den.*

Assuming the other tests are met, B is entitled to a dependency exemption for M since he provided more than one-half of her support expenditures ($4,000 is > 50% of $7,100).

In many instances, an individual who is not self-supporting is supported by more than one taxpayer. Generally, no dependency exemption is allowed for such persons; however, two exceptions exist. Exemptions may be allowed under multiple support agreements or to divorced or separated parents with respect to their children.

Multiple Support Agreements.   A dependency exemption may be assigned to a taxpayer under a multiple support agreement if *all* of the following tests are met:[13]

1.   No one person contributed over half the support of the individual.

2.   Over half the support was provided by a group, all of whose members must be qualifying relatives of the individual.

3.   The citizenship, joint return, and gross income requirements are met by the individual.

4.   The dependency exemption is assigned by agreement to a group member *who contributed more* than 10 percent of the total support.

The assignment is effective only if each of the members contributing more than 10 percent signs a declaration to the effect that he or she will not claim the exemption. This declaration is made on Form 2120 (see Appendix B), which is then filed with the return of the taxpayer claiming the exemption.

Example 6.   M is single and received her support of $12,000 for 1991 from the following sources:

	Amount	Percentage
Social Security benefits....................	$ 4,000	33.33%
Taxable interest income....................	800	6.67
From D, M's daughter......................	4,700	39.17
From S, M's son...........................	1,500	12.50
From G, M's grandchild....................	1,000	8.33
	$12,000	100.00%

Together, D, S, and G contribute more than 50% of M's support for 1991 ($7,200 > 50% of $12,000). If a multiple support agreement is executed, either D or S may be allowed the exemption deduction. G is not eligible since he did not contribute more than 10% of the total support. Also, note that S may claim M as a dependent even though D provided more of M's support.

---

[13]   § 152(c).

Children of Divorced or Separated Parents. Special rules apply to children of parents who are divorced or legally separated under a decree of divorce or separate maintenance, or separated under a written separation agreement, or live apart at all times during the last six months of the calendar year. If over half of a child's support is provided by one parent or collectively by both parents (including amounts contributed by the new spouse of a parent), and the child is in custody of one or both parents for more than half of the year, the dependency exemption generally is allowed to the parent with custody for the greater portion of the year.[14] Thus, the custodial parent ordinarily receives the exemption regardless of the amount paid by either parent. Under certain conditions, however, the *noncustodial parent* may claim the exemption.

The noncustodial parent is entitled to the dependency exemption if the custodial parent signs a written declaration that he or she will not claim the exemption for the child, *and* the declaration is attached to the tax return of the noncustodial parent.[15]

> **Example 7.** R and S were divorced in early 1991. S has custody of their only child. R paid child support of $3,600 in 1991. Since S is the custodial parent, she is entitled to the dependency exemption. However, if S signs a statement granting the dependency exemption to R and he attaches the statement to his 1991 tax return, R is entitled to the dependency exemption for the child.

Gross Income Test. The second test that must be satisfied before an individual may be claimed as a dependent concerns his or her gross income. A dependency exemption generally is not allowed for a person whose gross income equals or exceeds the exemption amount ($2,150 for 1991).[16] In applying this test, the technical definition of "gross income" must be heeded.[17] It does not include items that are excluded from income. Accordingly, a person whose only sources of income are excluded from gross income (e.g., Social Security and municipal bond interest) may qualify as a dependent.

It also should be noted that gross income is not always synonymous with includible gross receipts. Regulation § 1.61-3 indicates that gross income for a merchandising business generally means the total sales less the cost of goods sold *plus* any income from investments or other sources. The importance of this distinction between gross receipts and gross income is demonstrated in the following example.

---

[14] §§ 152(e)(1) and 152(e)(5).

[15] § 152(e)(2). A special rule applies to agreements executed before 1985. See § 152(e)(4).

[16] § 151(c)(1)(A).

[17] See Chapters 5 and 6 for detailed discussion of "gross income."

Example 8.   T provides 60% of the support for his single brothers, R and S, for the 1991 calendar year. R's sole source of income is from the sale of fireworks. During the year, he sold fireworks costing $4,000 for $5,500. S's sole source of income is derived from rental property. During the year, he collected rents of $3,200 while incurring expenses of $1,700 for repairs, maintenance, and interest. Although R and S each earned $1,500 (R: $5,500 − $4,000 = $1,500; S: $3,200 − $1,700 = $1,500), R's *gross income* was $1,500, whereas S's was $3,200. As a result, T can only claim an exemption for R, since R's gross income was less than the $2,150 exemption amount for 1991.

Absent a special rule, the gross income limitation might cause a taxpayer to discourage his or her children from working, since even a modest income would cause the loss of the dependency exemption for the parent. Accordingly, Congress provided that the gross income limitation *does not apply* to a child of the taxpayer who has not attained age 19 during the year or a child of the taxpayer who is a full-time student *and* has not reached age 24.[18] *Child* means a natural or adopted child of the taxpayer. Foster children and children placed in the taxpayer's home by an authorized agency pending adoption by the taxpayer are also included.[19] *Student* means that the child was enrolled full-time during at least five calendar months of the year in a qualifying educational institution. A student satisfies the full-time condition if he or she is enrolled for the number of hours or courses that the school requires for a student to be considered in full-time attendance. School attendance only at night does not qualify. However, attendance at night as a part of a full-time program is acceptable.[20]

Relationship or Member of the Household Test.   The third of the five hurdles that must be cleared before an individual can be claimed as a dependent concerns the individual's relationship to the taxpayer. Regardless of the amount of support that the taxpayer provides for another person, no exemption is allowed unless the prospective dependent is properly related to the taxpayer.[21] Apparently the authors of the dependency rules believed that the tax law should not grant an exemption unless there is some obligation on the part of the taxpayer to support an individual. Such an obligation normally exists between relatives or

---

[18]   § 151(c)(1)(B).

[19]   Reg. § 1.151-3(a).

[20]   Reg. § 1.151-3(b).

[21]   § 152(a). Note: Recall that there is no dependency exemption for spouses. The exemption for spouses is the *personal* exemption.

others who are members of the taxpayer's household. Therefore, to qualify as a dependent, an individual must satisfy one of nine qualifying relationship tests. All of these are familial (i.e., related by blood, marriage, or adoption) except one. These are:

1. A son or daughter (including an adopted child, a foster child who lives with the taxpayer the entire taxable year, or a child placed with the tax-payer by an authorized agency pending legal adoption by the taxpayer), or a descendent of either

2. A stepson or stepdaughter

3. A brother, sister, stepbrother or stepsister

4. The father or mother, or an ancestor of either

5. A stepfather or stepmother

6. A niece or nephew[22]

7. An aunt or uncle[23]

8. A son-in-law, daughter-in-law, father-in-law, mother-in-law, brother-in-law, or sister-in-law

9. Any person who lives in the taxpayer's home and is a member of the tax-payer's household for the entire taxable year. Even though such a person is not legally related to the taxpayer (i.e., a familial relative), he or she is treated the same as one who satisfies one of the legal relationships as long as he or she lives with the taxpayer the entire taxable year; for this purpose, temporary absences due to illness, school, vacation, business, or military service are ignored; in addition, a person cannot be claimed as a dependent if the relationship with the taxpayer violated local law (e.g., cohabitation).[24]

A relationship created by marriage does not cease upon divorce or the death of the spouse. Thus, for tax purposes, a divorce would not terminate an individual's relationship with his or her mother-in-law.[25] Additionally, if a dependent dies before the close of the tax year, the taxpayer may still claim a dependency exemption.

[22] A niece or nephew must be a daughter or son of a brother or sister of the taxpayer. § 152(a)(6).

[23] An aunt or uncle must be a sister or brother of the father or mother of the taxpayer. § 152(a)(7). For example, the person married to your mother's sister would be her brother-in-law, but he would not qualify as your uncle for purposes of this definition. Technically, such a person would be your "uncle-in-law," a relationship not defined in Code § 152.

[24] § 152(b)(5).

[25] Reg. § 1.152-2(d).

Example 9. This year F provided all the support for several individuals, none of whom had more than $2,150 of income. These persons and their status as relatives are shown below:

1. S, F's son, living in Los Angeles and attending UCLA. S is a relative; a son is a familial relative and such persons need not live in the home.

2. B, F's 29-year-old brother who moved in with F on November 1 after leaving the military. B is a relative; a brother is a familial relative and such persons need not live in the home.

3. C, F's 27-year-old cousin who moved in with F on October 1 after being unemployed for 10 months. C is not a relative; a cousin is not considered a familial relative and therefore qualifies only if he lives with the taxpayer the entire taxable year.

4. BL, the brother of F's former wife. BL is a relative; BL is F's brother-in-law, a familial relative; such a relationship continues to exist whether F is divorced or his wife dies.

5. Z, a friend who has been living with F since December 1 of the prior year. Z is a relative; a person who lives with the taxpayer the entire taxable year qualifies as a relative even though such person is not related by blood or marriage.

Joint Return Test. A married dependent for whom an exemption is claimed may not file a joint income tax return with his or her spouse.[26] Therefore, it may be beneficial to parents of newlyweds and certain other couples for their child to file a married, separate return.

If a joint return is filed *solely* for a refund (i.e., the tax is zero and all withholding is refunded), the joint return test is met. In this case, the IRS will treat the return as a claim for refund rather than a filed return.[27]

Example 10. B and C were married on December 21, 1991. B, a budding 25-year-old attorney, earned $34,000 for the year. C, age 23, is a full-time graduate student. Because C was fully supported by her parents, she was eligible to be claimed as a dependent on her parents' return. However, C's parents may not claim C as a dependent if B and C elect to file a joint return. The family must determine whether or not they are better off if: (1) B and C file a joint return and C claims her exemption on their joint return; or (2) B and C each file married filing separately and they relinquish C's exemption to her parents. A partial analysis would suggest the first alternative is far superior. If a joint return is filed, all of B's income would be taxed at 15% (see inside front cover of text for rates). Alternatively, the filing of separate returns would cause a substantial portion of B's taxable income to be taxed at 28%. In this case, it would appear that the additional tax caused by filing separate returns would more than offset any savings to be derived from shifting the exemption to C's parents.

Example 11. D and E were married on December 28, 1991. During 1991, D, age 22, attended State University full time. In addition, she worked part-time, earning $5,000 for the year. E, age 21, was also a full-time student, fully supported by his parents. In this case, E's parents are entitled to claim an exemption for E even if D and E elect to file a joint return. The joint return requirement would not be violated because the couple owes no tax (the couple's standard deduction eliminates their taxable income). Consequently, under the IRS view, they would be filing merely to obtain a refund of any withholding and not filing an actual return.

Citizenship or Residency Test. A dependent must be a citizen or national (e.g., an American Samoan) of the United States or a resident of the United States, Canada, or Mexico. An adopted child of a citizen qualifies, even though not a resident, if he or she was a member of the taxpayer's household for the entire taxable year.[28]

Return Filed by a Dependent. The fact that a person files his or her own tax return does not bar another taxpayer (who otherwise meets all the necessary tests) from claiming him or her as a dependent. This is true as long as the dependent does not file a joint return for any reason other than to claim a refund of the entire amount of taxes withheld. Otherwise, the joint return test would not be met and the dependency exemption would be denied.

Phase-out of Personal and Dependency Exemptions. Since 1986, Congress has reduced the benefits that high-income taxpayers receive from their personal and dependency exemptions. Under § 151(d), taxpayers must reduce their deduction for personal and dependency exemptions by 2 percent for each $2,500 or fraction thereof ($1,250 for married persons filing separate returns) by which a taxpayer's A.G.I. exceeds the applicable threshold. These thresholds depend on the taxpayer's filing status, as shown below.

Filing Status	Threshold A.G.I.
Single individuals (not surviving spouse or head of household)	$100,000
Married filing jointly or surviving spouse	150,000
Head of household	125,000
Married filing separately	75,000

The threshold amounts will be adjusted for inflation for years beginning after 1991.

[28] § 152(b)(3).

The reduction in the exemption deduction may be computed as follows:

$$\frac{\text{A.G.I.} - \text{threshold}}{\$2,500 \text{ (or }\$1,250)} = \frac{\text{Factor}}{\text{(round-up)}} \times \frac{2}{\text{percentage points}} = \frac{\text{Percentage}}{\text{reduction}}$$

Example 12. H and W are married with four children. They are entitled to claim six exemptions. In 1991, their A.G.I. is $191,000. The reduction in the couple's exemption deduction is computed as follows:

A.G.I.	$191,000
Threshold	−150,000
Excess	$ 41,000

$$\frac{\$41,000}{\$2,500} = 16.4, \text{ rounded to } 17 \times 2 = 34\%$$

H and W are required to reduce their exemption deduction by 34%. Assuming the total exemption deduction is $12,900 ($2,150 × 6), the deduction is reduced by $4,386 (34% × $12,900) to $8,514 ($12,900 − $4,386). In effect, the couple receives only 66% of their normal exemption deduction.

Note that the exemption deduction is completely eliminated if A.G.I. exceeds the threshold by more than $122,500. For example, if a married couple's A.G.I. exceeds $272,500, their total deduction for exemptions would be eliminated [($272,501 − $150,000 = $122,501) ÷ $2,500 = 49.004, rounded up to 50 × 2 = 100% reduction].

FILING STATUS

EVOLUTION OF FILING STATUS

The tax rates that are applied to determine the taxpayer's tax liability depend on the taxpayer's filing status. From 1913 to 1948, there was only one set of tax rates that applied to individual taxpayers. During this period, each taxpayer filed a separate return, even if he or she were married. For example, if both a husband and wife had income, each would file a separate return, reporting their respective incomes. This system, however, proved inequitable due to the differing state laws governing the ownership of income (or property).

In the United States, the rights that married individuals hold in property are determined using either the common law or community property system. There are nine community property states: Arizona, California, Idaho, Louisiana, Nevada, New Mexico, Texas, Washington, and Wisconsin. In a community property state, income generated through the personal efforts of either spouse is generally owned *equally* by the community (i.e., the husband and wife). In common law states, income belongs to the spouse that earns the income. The differing treatments of income by community property and common law states produced the need for a special rate schedule for married taxpayers.

Married Status.   The category of married couples filing jointly and its unique rate schedule were added to the law because of an inequity that existed between married couples in community property states and non–community property jurisdictions (separate or common law property states). As noted above, earnings derived from personal services performed by married persons in community property states generally are owned jointly by the two spouses. Accordingly, both husband and wife in a community property state would file returns showing one-half of their earned income, even though only one may have been employed. Note that the total income of the couple would be split equally between the husband and wife regardless of who earned the income. If a couple in a non–community property state relied on one spouse's earnings, the employed spouse filed a return showing the entire amount of those earnings.

Since the tax rates are progressive, a married couple in a non–community property state would bear a larger tax burden than one in a community property state if only one spouse was employed outside the home or one spouse earned substantially more than the other. To eliminate this inequity, Congress elected to grant the benefits of income splitting to all married couples. This was accomplished by authorizing a new tax schedule for married persons filing jointly. A joint return results in the same amount of tax as would be paid on two "married, filing separate" returns showing half the total income of a married couple.

> **Example 13.**   L and M are married and reside in California with their two children. L is an executive with a major corporation and M works in the home. Under state law, L's salary of $70,000 is owned equally by L and M. Each may file a separate return and report $35,000 of the salary.

> **Example 14.**   S and T are married and reside in Virginia with their two children. S is an executive with a major corporation and T works in the home. If S were to file a separate return, she would report the entire $70,000 salary on that return. Since the tax rate schedules for individuals are progressive, S would pay a higher tax than the total paid by L and M in *Example 13*. Consequently, the total tax burden on S and T is greater than that on L and M. By filing a joint return, S and T are placed in a position equivalent to that of L and M.

Head-of-Household Status.   Introduction of the joint return in 1948 was not viewed by the public as only a solution to a problem caused by differing state laws. In addition, it was seen as a tax break for those who had family obligations. As a result, single parents and other unmarried taxpayers with dependents tried to persuade Congress that they should be entitled to some tax relief due to their family responsibilities. Their arguments were based on the fact that they suffered a greater tax burden than single-earner married couples. In 1957, a tax reduction was allowed in the form of a new tax rate schedule for taxpayers who qualify as a *head of household*. The rates were designed to be lower than the original rates, which applied to all taxpayers, but *higher* than the rates for married persons filing jointly.

Single Status.   The most recent change in the overall tax rate structure was the addition of a separate tax rate schedule for single persons. This change was made because a single person was paying a higher rate of tax on the same income than married persons filing jointly and heads of households. The reduced rates for single taxpayers still are higher than those for a head of household, but lower than those in the original rate structure. As a result of this final change, the original tax rate structure that once applied to all taxpayers now applies only to married persons filing separately.

Summary.   The Federal income tax on individuals is based on four tax rate schedules. Taxpayers must file under one of the following classifications, listed in order from lowest to highest in tax rates:

1.   Married filing jointly (including surviving spouses)

2.   Head of household

3.   Single

4.   Married filing separately

The 1991 tax rate schedules for these classifications are reproduced on the inside front cover of this text.[29]

MARRIED INDIVIDUALS

Marital status is determined on the last day of an individual's taxable year. A person is married for tax purposes if he or she is married under state law, regardless of whether he or she is separated or in the process of seeking a divorce. However, if two formerly married individuals are legally separated under a final decree of divorce or a court decree of separate maintenance, they are considered unmarried.[30]

In the case of a taxpayer whose spouse dies during the taxable year, filing status is determined at the time of death rather than the last day of the tax year.[31] Thus, a joint return may be filed by the taxpayer and a deceased spouse for the year of the spouse's death even though the taxpayer is not married at the close of the year. This is true unless the taxpayer remarries before the end of the year.[32] If the surviving spouse remarries, he or she may file a joint return with the new spouse, but the decedent is denied the benefits of a joint final income tax return. In this case, the decedent's status is married filing separately.

---

[29]   The 1991 tax tables had not been issued by the IRS at the date of publication of this text. However, the 1990 tax tables are reproduced in Appendix A.

[30]   § 7703(a)(2).

[31]   § 7703(a)(1).

[32]   § 6013(a)(2).

Joint Return. A husband and wife generally may file a return using the rates for married persons filing jointly.[33] If a joint return is filed, husband and wife are jointly and severally (individually) liable for any tax, including any later assessments of tax, related to *that* joint return. As a result, one spouse may be held liable for paying the entire tax, even though the other spouse earned all the income. For this reason, a spouse should be cautious in signing a joint return. However, under the *innocent spouse rule*, a spouse will not be held liable for tax and penalties attributable to misstatements by the other spouse if the assessment is large relative to his or her financial situation, he or she did not know of the misstatements in the return, and he or she did not have reason to know of it.[34]

Surviving Spouse. Certain widows and widowers may use the tax rates for married persons filing jointly. In order to use these lower rates, the person must qualify as a *surviving spouse*. There are two requirements. First, the spouse must have died within the two taxable years preceding the current taxable year. Second, the taxpayer must provide over half the cost of maintaining a home in which he or she and a *dependent* son, stepson, daughter, or stepdaughter live.[35] Remarriage terminates surviving spouse status. Of course, a joint return can be filed with the new spouse.

> **Example 15.** H and W were married in 1982 and had two children, S and D. H died in 1991. After H's death, W continued to provide a home and all the support of S and D. As a result, W is entitled to claim S and D as dependents. For 1991, H may file a joint return with W. W may file as a surviving spouse in 1992 and 1993, using the same rates as married persons filing jointly. In subsequent years, W may file as a head of household.

Separate Returns. Normally, it will be advantageous for married persons to file a joint return because it is simpler to file one return than it is to file two, and the tax will be as low or lower than the tax based on the rules for married persons filing separately. In some situations, a taxpayer may prefer to file a separate return. For example, a person may wish to avoid liability for the tax on the income of his or her spouse. Similarly, a husband and wife who are separated and are contemplating divorce may wish to file separate returns.

Separate returns may be to the taxpayers' advantage in certain circumstances. Although rare, use of the separate rate schedules may result in a lower total tax than by using the rates applicable to a joint return. Filing of separate returns may also prove beneficial when the filing of a joint return would prevent another taxpayer (e.g., a parent) from claiming a dependency exemption deduction for either the husband or the wife (see *Example 10* above).

[33] § 6013(a). However, a special rule applies if the spouse is a nonresident alien. See § 6013(g).

[34] § 6013(e). Generally, the understatement of tax must exceed $500 and certain other tests must be met.

[35] § 2(a).

HEAD OF HOUSEHOLD

Head-of-household rates may be used if the taxpayer satisfies two conditions. First, the taxpayer must be unmarried or considered unmarried (i.e., an abandoned spouse) on the last day of the tax year. The second condition generally requires that the taxpayer provide over one-half of the cost of maintaining the home in which a *qualifying relative* lives for more than half the taxable year.[36] Qualifying relatives include the taxpayer's child, grandchild, stepchild, or adopted child, whether or not the child is married. Exhibit 4-2 contains a list of other relatives who may qualify the taxpayer for head of household status.

An individual is normally a qualifying relative *only* if he or she is the taxpayer's dependent *and* lives in the taxpayer's household. Three exceptions exist to this general rule.

1. A parent need not live in the taxpayer's home; however, the taxpayer still must pay more than half of the cost of keeping up a home for his or her mother or father. For example, the taxpayer qualifies if he or she paid more than half the cost of the parent's living in a rest home or home for the elderly.

    Example 16. D, an unmarried individual, lives in San Francisco and pays more than half of the cost of maintaining a home in Reno for her dependent parents. Although her parents do not live with her in San Francisco, D qualifies for the head of household rates.

2. An *unmarried* child, grandchild, stepchild, or adopted child of the taxpayer need not be a dependent. This exception permits a divorced parent to qualify as head of household even though the former spouse claims the exemption for the child.

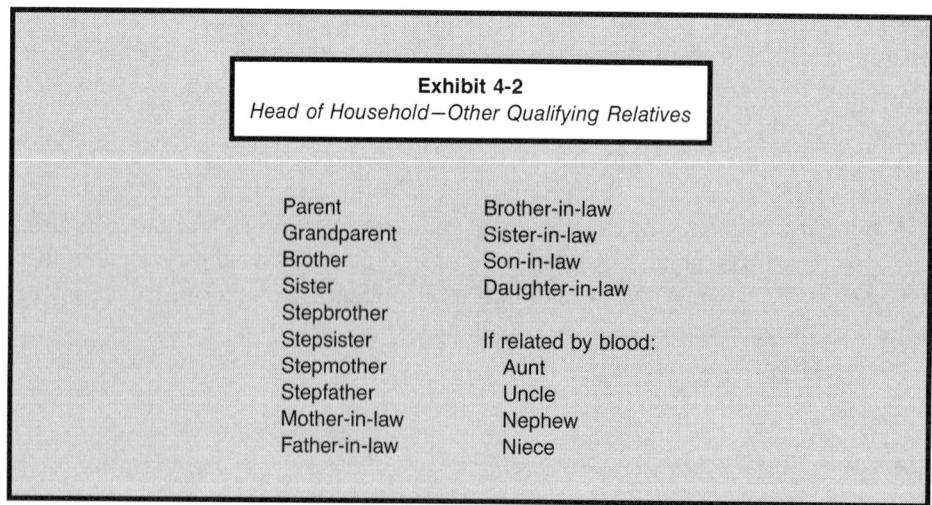

Exhibit 4-2
Head of Household—Other Qualifying Relatives

Parent	Brother-in-law
Grandparent	Sister-in-law
Brother	Son-in-law
Sister	Daughter-in-law
Stepbrother	
Stepsister	If related by blood:
Stepmother	Aunt
Stepfather	Uncle
Mother-in-law	Nephew
Father-in-law	Niece

---

[36] § 2(b)(1).

Example 17.   M is divorced and maintains a household for herself and her 10-year-old daughter. Although M is the custodial parent, she allows her former husband to claim the exemption for the child. M still qualifies for the head of household rates.

3.   A *married* child, grandchild, stepchild, or adopted child of the taxpayer who *could* be claimed as a dependent except that the taxpayer has signed a written declaration allowing the noncustodial parent to claim the dependent.

It should be noted that a person for whom a dependency exemption is claimed solely because he or she lived in the taxpayer's home for the entire taxable year (e.g., not a relative) or under a multiple-support agreement (e.g., the taxpayer did not provide over half the cost of maintaining the home) is not considered a qualifying relative and *cannot* qualify the taxpayer as a head of household. In addition, a nonresident alien cannot be a head of household.[37]

Costs of Maintaining a Home.   In determining whether a taxpayer qualifies for head-of-household status, it is necessary to determine whether he or she pays over half of the cost of maintaining a home for the taxable year. This determination must also be made for surviving spouse filing status. The costs of maintaining the home include the costs for the mutual benefit of the occupants and include such expenses as property taxes, mortgage interest, rent, utilities, insurance, repairs, upkeep, and food consumed on the premises. The cost of maintaining a home does not include clothing, educational expenses, medical expenses, or transportation.[38]

Abandoned Spouse Provision.   Without a special provision, an individual whose spouse has simply abandoned him or her might be forced to file using the high rates for married individuals filing separately. Aware of this problem, Congress has provided that a married individual who files a separate return may file as head of household if he or she qualifies as an *abandoned spouse*. To qualify, the individual must provide over half the cost of maintaining a home that houses him or her and a son, stepson, daughter, or stepdaughter for whom a dependency exemption deduction is *either* claimed or could be claimed by the taxpayer except for the fact that the exemption was assigned to the noncustodial parent. The child or stepchild must live in the home with the taxpayer for more than half the taxable year and the taxpayer's spouse must not live in the home at any time during the last six months of the year.[39] If each of these requirements is met, an abandoned spouse qualifies as a head of household.

---

[37]   §§ 2(b)(3), 152(a)(9), and 152(c).

[38]   Reg. § 1.2-2(d).

[39]   § 2(c) and § 7703(b). An adopted child of the taxpayer is considered a son or daughter for this test.

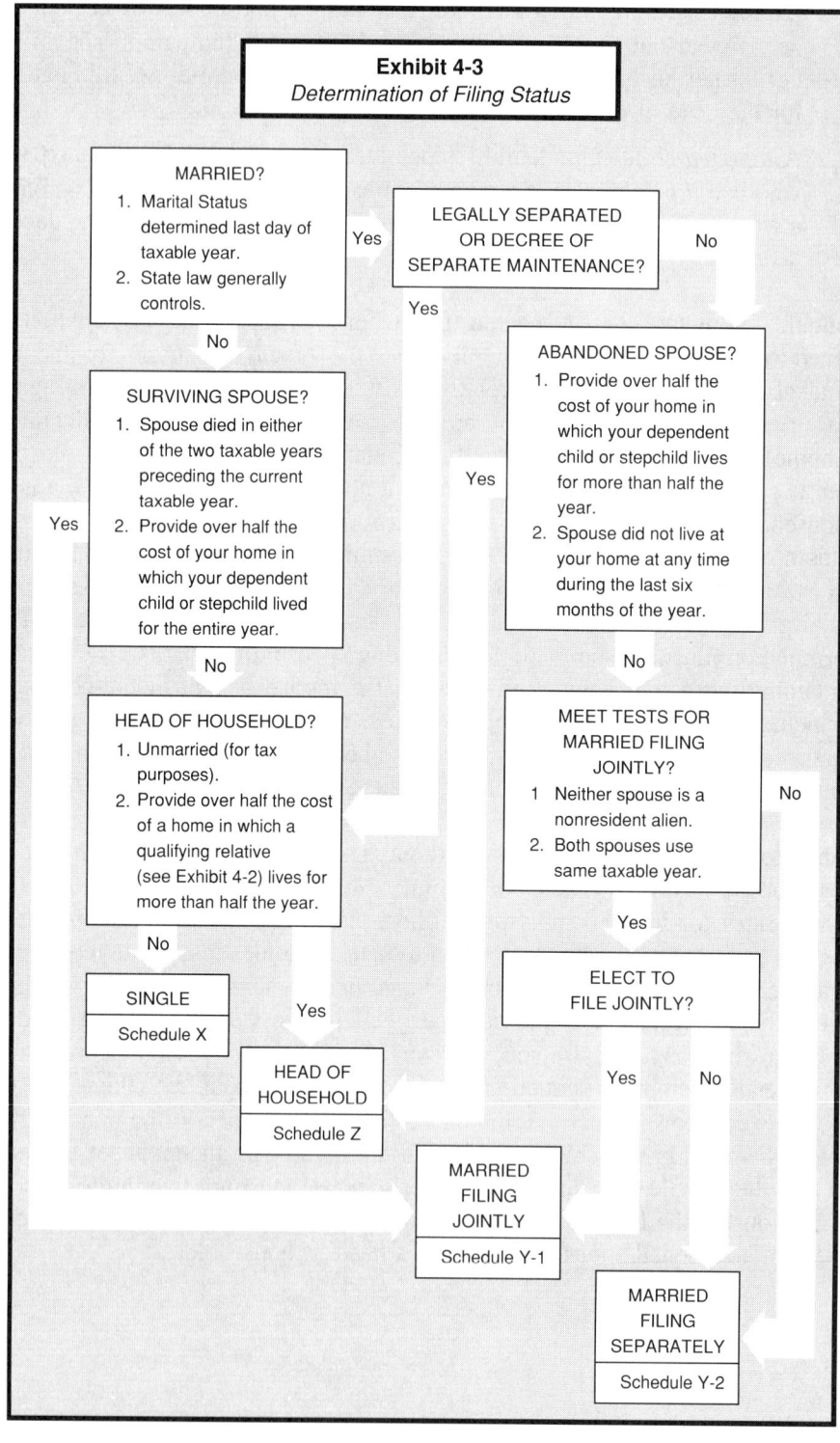

Exhibit 4-3
Determination of Filing Status

MARRIED?
1. Marital Status determined last day of taxable year.
2. State law generally controls.

LEGALLY SEPARATED OR DECREE OF SEPARATE MAINTENANCE?

Yes → Yes / No

No

SURVIVING SPOUSE?
1. Spouse died in either of the two taxable years preceding the current taxable year.
2. Provide over half the cost of your home in which your dependent child or stepchild lived for the entire year.

ABANDONED SPOUSE?
1. Provide over half the cost of your home in which your dependent child or stepchild lives for more than half the year.
2. Spouse did not live at your home at any time during the last six months of the year.

Yes

No

HEAD OF HOUSEHOLD?
1. Unmarried (for tax purposes).
2. Provide over half the cost of a home in which a qualifying relative (see Exhibit 4-2) lives for more than half the year.

MEET TESTS FOR MARRIED FILING JOINTLY?
1. Neither spouse is a nonresident alien.
2. Both spouses use same taxable year.

No

Yes

No

SINGLE
Schedule X

Yes

HEAD OF HOUSEHOLD
Schedule Z

ELECT TO FILE JOINTLY?

Yes   No

MARRIED FILING JOINTLY
Schedule Y-1

MARRIED FILING SEPARATELY
Schedule Y-2

Example 18. M and N are married with six children. In October, M stormed out of the house, saying he would never return. N was hopeful that M would return and consequently had not taken action to obtain a divorce by the end of the year. Although M and N are eligible to file a joint return, M indicated that he would not. Consequently, N's filing status is married filing separately. She does not qualify as an abandoned spouse since her husband lived in the home during the last six months of the year. In the following year, however, N could qualify and file as head of household.

Single. Single filing status is defined by exception. A single taxpayer is anyone who is unmarried and does not qualify as a head of household or surviving spouse. Even though these rates are somewhat lower, they may not be used by married persons filing separately.[40]

COMPUTATION OF TAX FOR INDIVIDUAL TAXPAYERS

Once taxable income has been determined, the tax computation for most individuals is fairly straightforward. The gross tax is computed using the tax tables or the tax rate schedules. This amount is then reduced by any tax credits available to the taxpayer and any tax prepayments in arriving at the tax due or the refund. Children under age 14 with unearned income and all persons claimed as dependents are subject to special rules in the computation of their income tax.

TAX TABLES

The vast majority of individuals must determine their tax using *tax tables*, provided by the IRS along with the instructions for preparing individual income tax returns. The tables are derived directly from the rate schedules to simplify compliance and reduce taxpayer errors. The tax for any particular range of taxable income is determined by using the midpoint of the range and the appropriate rate schedule. For example, the tax in the 1990 tables for a single taxpayer with taxable income of $19,010 is $2,854, which is the tax computed on $19,025 (see Exhibit 4-4 for an excerpt and Appendix A for the complete 1990 Tax Tables).

The tables cover taxpayers in each filing status with taxable incomes less than $50,000. A taxpayer who qualifies generally is required to use the tax tables.[41]

---

[40]   Single filing status is referred to in Code § 1(c) as "Unmarried individuals (Other Than Surviving Spouses and Heads of Households)."

[41]   § 3.

Exhibit 4-4
Excerpts From Tax Tables for 1990

If line 36 (taxable income) is—		And you are—				If line 36 (taxable income) is—		And you are—			
At least	But less than	Single	Married filing jointly *	Married filing sepa-rately	Head of a house-hold	At least	But less than	Single	Married filing jointly *	Married filing sepa-rately	Head of a house-hold
		Your tax is—						Your tax is—			
19,000						**31,000**					
19,000	19,050	2,854	2,854	3,218	2,854	31,000	31,050	6,159	4,654	6,578	5,301
19,050	19,100	2,861	2,861	3,232	2,861	31,050	31,100	6,173	4,661	6,592	5,315
19,100	19,150	2,869	2,869	3,246	2,869	31,100	31,150	6,187	4,669	6,606	5,329
19,150	19,200	2,876	2,876	3,260	2,876	31,150	31,200	6,201	4,676	6,620	5,343
19,200	19,250	2,884	2,884	3,274	2,884	31,200	31,250	6,215	4,684	6,634	5,357
19,250	19,300	2,891	2,891	3,288	2,891	31,250	31,300	6,229	4,691	6,648	5,371
19,300	19,350	2,899	2,899	3,302	2,899	31,300	31,350	6,243	4,699	6,662	5,385
19,350	19,400	2,906	2,906	3,316	2,906	31,350	31,400	6,257	4,706	6,676	5,399
19,400	19,450	2,914	2,914	3,330	2,914	31,400	31,450	6,271	4,714	6,690	5,413
19,450	19,500	2,925	2,921	3,344	2,921	31,450	31,500	6,285	4,721	6,704	5,427
19,500	19,550	2,939	2,929	3,358	2,929	31,500	31,550	6,299	4,729	6,718	5,441
19,550	19,600	2,953	2,936	3,372	2,936	31,550	31,600	6,313	4,736	6,732	5,455
19,600	19,650	2,967	2,944	3,386	2,944	31,600	31,650	6,327	4,744	6,746	5,469
19,650	19,700	2,981	2,951	3,400	2,951	31,650	31,700	6,341	4,751	6,760	5,483
19,700	19,750	2,995	2,959	3,414	2,959	31,700	31,750	6,355	4,759	6,774	5,497
19,750	19,800	3,009	2,966	3,428	2,966	31,750	31,800	6,369	4,766	6,788	5,511
19,800	19,850	3,023	2,974	3,442	2,974	31,800	31,850	6,383	4,774	6,802	5,525
19,850	19,900	3,037	2,981	3,456	2,981	31,850	31,900	6,397	4,781	6,816	5,539
19,900	19,950	3,051	2,989	3,470	2,989	31,900	31,950	6,411	4,789	6,830	5,553
19,950	20,000	3,065	2,996	3,484	2,996	31,950	32,000	6,425	4,796	6,844	5,567

Example 19.   William W. Bristol was single for 1990 and had no dependents. Bill's only income was wages of $24,160 and taxable interest of $150. Since his itemized deductions totaled only $1,650, Bill claims the $3,250 standard deduction allowed for 1990. Federal income tax of $3,020 was withheld from Bill's salary. Bill's taxable income and tax for 1990 are calculated as follows:

Salary..		$24,160
Taxable interest..................................		+ 150
Equals: Adjusted gross income..................		$24,310
Less: Standard deduction for 1990..............	$3,250	
Personal exemption for 1990..............	2,050	− 5,300
Equals: Taxable income.........................		$19,010
Tax on $19,010 for 1990 (See Exhibit 4-4)........		$ 2,854
Less: Income tax withheld.......................		− 3,020
Equals: Tax due or (refund).....................		($166)

A completed Form 1040EZ for William W. Bristol, based on the information in this example, is shown in the Appendix at the end of the chapter.

Example 20. Clyde F. and Delia C. Cooper were married during all of 1990 and had income from the following sources:

Salary, Clyde		$31,145
Federal income tax withheld	$2,970	
Part-time salary, Delia		16,450
Federal income tax withheld	1,280	
Interest from City Savings		950
Interest from U.S. Government		150

Clyde and Delia are the sole support for their two children, ages 2 and 7. During 1990, they paid job-related child care expenses of $3,500 and made deductible contributions of $4,000 to their Individual Retirement Accounts ($2,000 each). Their itemized deductions for the year do not exceed their standard deduction of $5,450. The Cooper's taxable income and tax for 1990 are calculated as follows:

Salary ($31,145 + $16,450)		$ 47,595
Plus: Taxable interest ($950 + $150)		+ 1,100
Less: Contributions to IRAs		− 4,000
Equals: Adjusted gross income		$ 44,695
Less: Standard deduction for 1990	$5,450	
Personal exemptions for 1990	8,200	− 13,650
Equals: Taxable income		$ 31,045
Tax on $31,045 for 1990 (See Exhibit 4-4)		$ 4,654
Less: Child care credit (.20 × $3,500)		− 700
Equals: Net tax		$ 3,954
Less: Income tax withheld ($2,970 + $1,280)		− 4,250
Equals: Tax due or (refund)		($296)

A completed Form 1040A based on this information is included in the Appendix at the end of the chapter.

TAX RATE SCHEDULES

A taxpayer who is unable to use the tax tables uses the tax rate schedules in computing his or her tax. These schedules contain the rates as stated in § 1 of the Internal Revenue Code. The 1990 tax rate schedules are included, along with the 1990 tax tables, in Appendix A. The 1991 tax rate schedules are summarized in Exhibit 4-5. For future reference, the tax rate schedules for 1991 are also reproduced on the inside front cover of this text.

A typical example illustrating the use of the tax rate schedules is given below.

> **Example 21.**   R, single, has taxable income of $60,000 for 1991. R's gross tax liability is $14,475.50, computed as follows:

Tax on $49,300................................	$11,158.50
Plus: Tax on income above $49,300	
[($60,000 − $49,300) × 31%]..............	3,317.00
Tax liability......................................	$14,475.50

SPECIAL TAX COMPUTATION RULES

Unfortunately, the computation of the tax is not always as straightforward as shown in *Example 21* above. For certain individuals, special rules must be followed.

Persons Claimed as Dependents.   As one might deduce from the brief introduction to tax rates, one of the most fundamental principles of tax planning concerns minimizing the marginal tax rate that applies to the taxpayer's income. The significance of this principle is easily understood when it is recognized that Federal marginal tax rates have at times exceeded 90 percent. Even with the reduction of marginal rates to their current levels, minimizing the tax rate can provide benefits—although the potential for savings clearly diminishes when the top rate is 31 percent.

Historically, one of the most popular techniques to minimize the tax rate has been to shift income to a lower bracket taxpayer such as a child. As discussed in Chapter 5, this could be accomplished most easily by giving the child income-producing property. For example, a parent might establish a savings account for a child. In this way, the income would be taxed to the child at his or her low rate rather than the parents' high rate. In addition, this strategy—absent any special rules—takes advantage of the personal exemption and standard deduction available to a child.

Exhibit 4-5
Individual Tax Rate Schedules for 1991

SINGLE

If taxable income is		Tax liability	Of the
Over	But not over		Amount over
$ 0	$ 20,350	15%	$ 0
20,350	49,300	$ 3,052.50 + 28%	20,350
49,300	—	11,158.50 + 31%	49,300

MARRIED FILING JOINTLY AND QUALIFYING WIDOWS AND WIDOWERS

If taxable income is		Tax liability	Of the
Over	But not over		Amount over
$ 0	$ 34,000	15%	$ 0
34,000	82,150	$ 5,100.00 + 28%	34,000
82,150	—	18,582.00 + 31%	82,150

HEADS OF HOUSEHOLDS

If taxable income is		Tax liability	Of the
Over	But not over		Amount over
$ 0	$ 27,300	15%	$ 0
27,300	70,450	$ 4,095.00 + 28%	27,300
70,450	—	16,177.00 + 31%	70,450

MARRIED FILING SEPARATELY

If taxable income is		Tax liability	Of the
Over	But not over		Amount over
$ 0	$ 17,000	15%	$ 0
17,000	41,075	$2,550.00 + 28%	17,000
41,075	—	9,291.00 + 31%	41,075

Congress has long recognized the tax-saving potential inherent in such plans. For this reason, it is not surprising that it has taken steps to limit the opportunities. These are:

1. **Personal exemption.** A taxpayer who can be claimed as a dependent on another taxpayer's return is not entitled to a personal exemption. This rule effectively prohibits all children from claiming a personal exemption. Observe that *without this rule*, a child could currently receive up to $2,150 income tax free.

2. **Standard deduction.** The standard deduction available to a taxpayer who can be claimed as a dependent on another taxpayer's return is limited to the greater of $550 ($500 for 1990) or his or her earned income. Without this rule, a child could receive unearned income such as interest of up to $3,400 (i.e., the normal standard deduction in 1991) tax free.

3. **Kiddie tax.** The *unearned income* of a child under age 14 is generally taxed as if the parent received it to the extent it exceeds $1,100 ($1,000 for 1990).[42] Absent this provision, affectionately known as the *kiddie tax*, a parent could shift up to $20,350 in income to the child in 1991, who would pay taxes at a 15 percent rate rather than at the parents' rate.

The effect of these provisions is to severely limit the success of any schemes designed to shift income.

Example 22. V, age 15, lives at home and may be claimed as a dependent on her parents' return. Several years ago, V's grandfather died, leaving her with a tidy sum to help send her to college. For 1991, V received interest income of $2,900. Her taxable income is computed as follows:

Adjusted gross income		$2,900
Less: Standard deduction	$550	
Personal exemption	+ 0	− 550
Taxable income		$2,350

Note that, in computing V's taxable income, her standard deduction is limited to $550 (the larger of earned income, $0, or $550). The limitation is imposed because she is eligible to be claimed as a dependent on another taxpayer's return. For the same reason, she is not allowed to claim her own personal exemption deduction. Although the benefits of the normal standard deduction and personal exemption are denied, she avoids the kiddie tax because she is over 13 years of age. Consequently, her tax is $353 (15% × $2,350). By escaping the kiddie tax, some tax savings are probably achieved since the income is taxed at her 15% rate rather than a higher rate (e.g., 31%) had her parents actually received the income.

---

[42] § 1(i).

Example 23. Assume the same facts in *Example 22*, except that V also earns $2,000 from a part-time job. V's taxable income is determined as follows:

Adjusted gross income:		
Earned income...............	$2,000	
Interest income..............	+ 2,900	$4,900
Less: Standard deduction........	$2,000	
Personal exemption........	+ 0	− 2,000
Taxable income..................		$2,900

As in *Example 22*, because V is a dependent, she is not allowed to claim her personal exemption deduction, nor may she claim the full standard deduction of $3,400. Note, however, that her standard deduction has increased because of her earned income. Her standard deduction is now $2,000 (the *larger* of earned income, $2,000, or $550). In effect, V is able to shelter income from tax to the extent it is earned.

Kiddie Tax. The kiddie tax provisions apply only to children who have not attained the age of 14 before the close of the taxable year and who have at least one living parent (or foster parent). If the child becomes 14 before the close of the year, he or she is treated as being 14 for the entire taxable year and the rules do not apply. Moreover, the kiddie tax rules are triggered only when the designated child has *net unearned income*. For this purpose, unearned income generally includes dividends, interest, rents, and royalties. Net unearned income is unearned income in excess of $1,100 ($1,000 for 1990).[43] In short, when a child under 14 has unearned income exceeding $1,100, the special tax computation must be made. The effect of this calculation is that the first $550 of unearned income is offset by the standard deduction and the second $550 of unearned income is taxed at the child's rates (currently 15%). Any unearned income exceeding $1,100 is taxed at the parents' top rates.

---

[43] § 1(i)(4). If greater than $1,100, the sum of $550 and the allowable itemized deductions specifically allocable to production of the unearned income is used.

Example 24. J is 12 years old. Each year he receives interest income from a savings account and earned income from his paper route. The table below shows several sample calculations of J's taxable income assuming various amounts of earned and unearned income. In addition, the amount taxed at his rates and his parents' rates is computed.

	A	B	C	D
Unearned income	$1,400	$ 400	$1,400	$2,600
Earned income	350	700	700	5,000
Total	$1,750	$1,100	$2,100	$7,600
Standard deduction: Greater of $550 or earned income not to exceed $3,400 standard deduction	−550	−700	−700	−3,400
Personal exemption	−	−	−	−
Taxable income (a)	$1,200	$ 400	$1,400	$4,200
Taxed at parents' rates Unearned income > $1,100 (b)	$ 300	$ 0	$ 300	$1,500
Taxed at child's rates [(a) − (b)]	$ 900	$ 400	$1,100	$2,700

In case B, there is no net unearned income because J's unearned income was less than $1,100. J has net unearned income in cases A, C, and D. In each case, the amount taxed at the parents' rate is the amount by which the child's unearned income exceeded $1,100. Any other income is taxed at the regular rates for the child.

When the child has net unearned income, the tax must be computed as if such income had been the parents' income. The child is required to pay the tax computed using his or her parents' rates except in rare cases where the tax computed in the normal manner is greater (in which case, the higher tax must be paid).

Although the thrust of the kiddie tax is to tax income that would be taxed at a 15 percent rate at a 28 or 31 percent rate, determination of the child's actual tax is somewhat complicated. The tax is computed on Form 8615 (see Appendix A) using the following approach:

Tax on child excluding net unearned income	$x,xxx
+ Tax on net unearned income at parent's rates:	
Tax on parent including net unearned income of child	$x,xxx
− Tax on parent computed in the normal manner	(x,xxx)
Parental tax	+x,xxx
= Child's total tax	$x,xxx

The first tax simply computes the child's tax by eliminating net unearned income. The second tax—called the *parental tax*—represents the tax that would be imposed on the net unearned income had the parents received it. In those situations where the parents are divorced, the tax is computed using the taxable income of the custodial parent (or joint income if he or she has remarried). Where the parents file separate returns, the tax is computed using the greater of the two taxable incomes.

In computing the tax on the parent *including* the child's net unearned income, such income is not considered when computing any of the parents' deductions or credits (e.g., the deduction for miscellaneous itemized deductions, which is limited to the amount that exceeds 2 percent of adjusted gross income).

Where there is more than one child under 14 with net unearned income, the parental tax must be computed using the net unearned income of all children. As shown below, the tax so computed is then allocated pro rata based on each child's relative contribution to total net unearned income.

$$\frac{\text{Child's net unearned income}}{\text{All children's net unearned income}} \times \frac{\text{Parental}}{\text{tax}} = \frac{\text{Child's share}}{\text{of parental tax}}$$

Example 25. During 1991, T, age 11, received $4,500 in dividends from stock given to him in 1987 by his now deceased grandfather. Similarly, his sister, V, age 6, had $1,700 of dividend income. Since T and V are under 14 and have net unearned income of $3,400 ($4,500 − $1,100) and $600 ($1,700 − $1,100), respectively, their tax must be computed in the special manner. The children's parents had income of $60,000. In addition, due to special medical problems of the father, they incurred $9,500 of medical expenses. The couple also has other itemized deductions of $10,000. T's tax is computed as follows:

1. Tax on parents computed in the normal manner:

Adjusted gross income	$ 60,000
Deductions:	
Medical expenses [$9,500 − (7.5% × $60,000)]	− 5,000
Other itemized deductions	− 10,000
Exemptions (4 × $2,150)	− 8,600
Taxable income computed in the normal manner	$ 36,400
Tax [$5,100 + 28% ($36,400 − $34,000)]	$ 5,772

2. Tax on parents including net unearned income of all children:

Parents' taxable income computed in the normal manner	$ 36,400
Net unearned income of children:	
($3,400 + $600)	+ 4,000
Taxable income including net unearned income	$ 40,400
Tax [$5,100 + 28% ($40,400 − $34,000)]	$ 6,892

3. Parental tax:

Tax on parents including net unearned income	$ 6,892
− Tax on parents computed in the normal manner	− 5,772
= Parental Tax	$ 1,120

4. T's share of parental tax ($1,120 × ($3,400 ÷ $4,000)] = $ 952.00

5. Tax on T excluding net unearned income:

Dividend income		$ 4,500
− Net unearned income		− 3,400
− Standard deduction (as limited for dependents)		− 550
− Exemption deduction (none for dependents)		− 0
Taxable income		$ 550
Tax (15% × $550)		$ 82.50

6. Total tax on T:

Tax on T excluding net unearned income		$ 82.50
+ Parental tax		+ 952.00
= T's total tax		$1,034.50

Note that in this case the total parental tax of $1,120 is simply the product of the net unearned income of $4,000 and the parents' marginal tax rate of 28%. Also note that the parents' deduction for medical expenses is computed without including the net unearned income of the children (i.e., the percentage limitation is based on $60,000 rather than $64,000).

Election to Report Child's Income on Parents' Return. In order to simplify the return filing process, parents may elect to include on their own return the unearned income of a child if certain conditions are satisfied.[44] Note that this is contrary to the normal procedure where the child files his or her own return and pays the tax computed with respect to the parents' rates. This election eliminates the hassle of filing separate returns for each child. However, the election can only be made where the child is under age 14, his or her income is between $550 and $5,000, and consists solely of interest or dividends. The election is not available if estimated taxes have been paid or taxes have been withheld on dividend or interest income (i.e., the child is subject to back-up withholding).

DETERMINATION OF NET TAX DUE OR REFUND

Once the tax is determined using the tax tables, tax rate schedules, or the special tax computation procedures described above, it is reduced by the amount of any credits or prepayments. These items were mentioned in Chapter 3 and are discussed in detail later in this text. The primary prepayments are the Federal income tax withheld from the taxpayer's salary or wages by an employer, quarterly estimated tax payments, and the estimated tax paid when an extension of time to file a return is requested. Estimated tax payments and extensions of time to file are discussed later in this chapter.

Numerous credits are allowed in computing the Federal income tax. The credit most frequently encountered on an uncomplicated income tax return is the child care credit. This and other credits are discussed in detail in Chapter 13.

---

[44] § 1(i)(7).

FILING REQUIREMENTS

Individual taxpayers with extremely low levels of income are not required to file a Federal income tax return. In general, a taxpayer is not required to file an income tax return for the year if his or her gross income is less than the *total* of his or her standard deduction (including the additional amount for the elderly but not the blind) *plus* personal exemptions (but not dependency exemptions).[45] These taxpayers generally are not liable for any Federal income tax. The filing requirement is based on gross income, so taxpayers who have larger gross incomes *must* file even if they owe no Federal income tax. A partial list of filing requirements for 1991 and how they are computed are illustrated in Exhibit 4-6:

Exhibit 4-6
Gross Income Filing Requirements for 1991

	Personal Exemption +	Standard Deduction +	Elderly Standard Deduction =	1991 Gross Income
Single person < 65 years old	$2,150	$3,400	–	$ 5,550
Single person ≥ 65 years old	2,150	3,400	$ 850	6,400
Head of household < 65	2,150	5,000	–	7,150
Head of household ≥ 65	2,150	5,000	850	8,000
Married filing jointly, both < 65	4,300	5,700	–	10,000
Married filing jointly, both ≥ 65	4,300	5,700	1,300	11,300
Married filing separately	2,150			2,150
Surviving spouse < 65	2,150	5,700	–	7,850
Surviving spouse ≥ 65	2,150	5,700	650	8,500
Dependents				Special Rules

---

[45]   § 6012(a)(1).

In addition to the general requirement for filing (gross income is at least as much as the taxpayer's standard deduction + personal exemptions), certain individuals *must* file returns. These include

1. Any taxpayer who has self-employment income of $400 or more

2. An individual who is claimed as a dependent on another taxpayer's return *and* who has unearned income at least equal to his or her minimum standard deduction (i.e., generally $550, but increased by the additional amount for elderly or blind taxpayers)[46]

3. Any person who receives any advance payments of earned income credit

Form 1040. The individual taxpayer is required to file Form 1040, along with related forms and schedules. A complicated return involves many forms and schedules in addition to the Form 1040, whereas a simpler return may require only a few or no attached schedules.

Two simplified forms are provided for taxpayers with uncomplicated tax calculations. The Form 1040EZ is available for taxpayers who are single and have no dependents. To qualify, the taxpayer's income must consist only of salaries and wages plus interest income of $400 or less. The only allowable deductions on this form are the personal exemption amount and the standard deduction.

The Form 1040A is available for a large number of taxpayers who do not itemize their deductions and have no income other than salaries and wages, dividends, interest, and unemployment compensation. This form provides for deductions for individual retirement account (IRA) contributions, personal and dependency exemptions, and the earned income credit.

---

[46] § 6012(a)(1)(C)(i). As stated earlier, certain children under the age of 14 are not required to file a tax return *if* their parents *elect* to include the child's income on their return and pay the appropriate additional tax.

Example 26.   Jeremy S. Allen, a registered nurse, and Shelly R. Allen, an air traffic controller, are married and file a joint income tax return for 1990. They are the sole support of their three children: William, Susan, and Gregory. The following information is from their records for 1990:

Salaries and wages, Jeremy......................		$30,975
Federal income tax withheld....................	$4,900	
Salaries and wages, Shelly.......................		43,000
Federal income tax withheld....................	5,600	
Interest income—Mercantile National Bank.........		1,800
Interest income—U.S. Government Bonds..........		600
Interest income—Ben Franklin Savings.............		400
Dividends—GRE, Inc.		
(A Kansas corporation).........................		200
Itemized deductions are as follows:		
Hospitalization insurance.......................		700
Unreimbursed fees of doctors, hospitals, etc......		2,100
Unreimbursed prescription drugs.................		200
Real estate taxes on residence....................		1,200
State income taxes paid..........................		3,500
Interest paid on original home mortgage...........		8,500
Investment interest..............................		400
Charitable contribution—First Church..............		1,300
Charitable contribution—		
Home State University..........................		200

The Allens' adjusted gross income is $76,975 ($30,975 + $43,000 + $2,800 interest income + $200 dividend income) since there were no deductions for A.G.I. The deductible amount of their itemized deductions is $15,100, summarized as follows:

Medical expenses exceeding $5,773		
(i.e., 7.5% × $76,975 A.G.I.)........................	$	0
Deductible taxes ($1,200 + $3,500)....................		4,700
Qualifying home mortgage interest....................		8,500
Investment interest....................................		400
Charitable contributions...............................		1,500
Total itemized deductions..............................		$15,100

The Allens' taxable income, gross tax, and tax due or refund for 1990 are determined as follows:

Adjusted gross income		$76,975
Less: Itemized deductions	$15,100	
Personal and dependency		
exemptions ($2,050 × 5)	+10,250	−25,350
Equals: Taxable income		$51,625
Gross Tax (from 1990 Tax Schedule):		
Tax on $32,450 (rounded)	$4,867	
Tax on excess [($51,625 −		
$32,450) × 28%	+5,369	$10,236
Less: Prepayments ($4,900 + $5,600)		−10,500
Equals: Tax due or (refund)		($ 264)

The Allens' completed 1990 tax return is shown in the Appendix at the end of the chapter. It consists of a Form 1040 plus Schedules A and B.

The more common tax forms and schedules used by individual taxpayers are listed in Exhibit 4-7. Copies of these forms are contained in Appendix B at the end of the text.

DUE DATES FOR FILING RETURNS

The day on which a Federal return must be filed with the IRS depends upon what type of return is involved. Generally the tax returns must be filed on or before the due dates, which are as follows:[47]

Type of Return	Due Date
Annual Individual Income Tax Returns	Fifteenth day of the fourth month following the close of the tax year (April 15 for calendar year individuals)
Annual C Corporation and S Corporation Income Tax Returns	Fifteenth day of third month following the close of the tax year (March 15 for calendar year corporations)
Annual Partnership, Estate, and Trust Income Tax Returns	Fifteenth day of the fourth month following the close of the tax year (April 15 for calendar year entities)
Estate Tax Returns	Nine months after the date of the decedent's death
Gift Tax Returns	April 15 (All gift tax returns are for a Calendar year)

Any return that is mailed via the U.S. Postal Service is deemed to be delivered when mailed, so any return postmarked on or before the above due dates is timely filed. If any of these due dates fall on Saturday, Sunday, or a legal holiday, the return must be filed on the succeeding day that is not a Saturday, Sunday, or legal holiday.

---

[47] § 6072(a).

Exhibit 4-7
*List of Common Forms and Schedules
Used by Individual Taxpayers*

Form 1040   **U.S. Individual Income Tax Return**

Accompanying Schedules:

Schedule A	Itemized deductions
Schedule B	Interest and dividend income
Schedule C	Profit (or loss) from business or profession
Schedule D	Capital gains and losses
Schedule E	Supplemental income schedule (rents, royalties, etc.)
Schedule F	Farm income and expenses
Schedule R	Credit for the elderly
Schedule SE	Computation of social security self-employment tax

Accompanying Forms:

Form 2106	Employee business expenses
Form 2119	Sale or exchange of principal residence
Form 2210	Underpayment of estimated tax by individuals
Form 2441	Credit for child and dependent care expenses
Form 3800	General business credit
Form 3903	Moving expense adjustment
Form 4562	Depreciation
Form 4684	Casualties and thefts
Form 4797	Supplemental schedule of gains and losses
Form 6251	Alternative minimum tax computation
Form 6252	Computation of installment sale income
Form 8582	Passive activity losses
Form 8615	Computation of tax for children under age 14 who have investment income of more than $1,000
Form 8814	Parents' election to report child's interest and dividends

Other Common Forms:

Form 1040A	U.S. Individual Income Tax Return
Form 1040EZ	Income tax return for single filers with no dependents
Form 4868	Application for automatic extension of time to file
Form 2688	Application for extension of time to file

Extension of Time to File. The Internal Revenue Code provides extensions of time for filing returns. The extension must be requested on or before the due date of the return. Currently, there is an *automatic* four-month extension for filing the individual income tax return (Form 1040). Thus the extended due date for calendar year individuals is August 15. If the taxpayer desires to use the four-month extension, he or she simply fills out Form 4868 and mails it to the IRS by the original due date along with a check covering the estimated balance due. It should be noted that an extension of time to file is not an extension of time to pay. There is *no extension* of time to pay estimated tax due.[48]

If the taxpayer needs additional time to prepare the return after the automatic four-month extension, he or she must file Form 2688 or write a letter explaining the circumstances. This extension is discretionary with the IRS and probably will not be granted unless unusual circumstances indicate that the taxpayer is laboring under "undue hardship" in compiling the necessary records.

> **Example 27.** As a result of a severe flood in early April, T lost all records necessary for the filing of his Federal income tax return for the prior year. T should file Form 4868 and pay any income tax he estimates to be due. If T requires more than four months to gather duplicate copies of his records (e.g., bank statements, cancelled checks, and prior years' Federal income tax returns), he should file Form 2688 or write a letter to the District Director of the IRS requesting another extension of time. Under these circumstances, there is no doubt that T will be granted his request.

Interest and Penalties. Whenever a taxpayer fails to pay the amount of tax owed by the due date of the return, interest is charged at a rate 3 percent higher than the Federal short term rate. For the first quarter of 1991, the annual interest rate charge on such a deficiency is 11 percent (8% + 3%), compounded daily on the unpaid balance.[49] An interest charge normally results when the taxpayer files for an extension and pays the estimated tax due that ultimately turns out to be less than that due when the return is actually filed. In addition, if the balance due is more than 10 percent of the tax shown on the taxpayer's return or the amount due is not paid by August 15, the IRS charges a late-payment penalty. This *failure-to-pay* penalty is one-half of 1 percent (0.5%) per month (or any fraction of a month), up to a maximum of 25 percent of the amount due.[50] However, no penalty for failure to pay is assessed when there is reasonable cause or an extension of time to file is properly obtained and the tax due is less than 10 percent of the total tax shown on the return.

[48] Reg. § 1.6081-4(a).

[49] § 6601(a). The 11 percent rate is scheduled to remain in effect until April 1991, at which time it will be increased, reduced, or allowed to remain unchanged, based on a predetermined formula.

[50] § 6651(a)(2).

Example 28. W was simply too busy to file his Federal tax return for the most recent calendar year. Thus on April 15 he requested an automatic extension of time to file until August 15. W had prepaid taxes of $5,800 in the form of withholding, and he estimated that his total tax would be $6,200. Therefore, he paid $400 when he filed the request for an extension. When he finally did file on June 15, W's return showed a total tax of $6,850 and a tax due of $650. W is not required to pay the penalty for failure to pay since his tax due is less than 10 percent of the total tax [$650 < 10%× $6,850]. However, assuming the current rate of interest on underpayments is 11%, W must pay interest of $12 ($650 at 11% annually, compounded daily for 61 days).

In the event a tax return is not filed by the due date (including extensions), the IRS will impose a *failure-to-file* penalty of 5 percent per month—up to a maximum of 25 percent—on the amount of tax due on the return.[51] Like the failure-to-pay penalty, any fraction of a month is counted as a full month. A minimum penalty of $100 (limited to the total tax on the return) applies if the return is not filed within 60 days of the due date.

When both of the preceding penalties apply, the penalty for failure to file is reduced by the amount of the penalty for failure to pay. Since both penalties are technically an addition to the tax, interest must be paid on the penalty as well as the unpaid tax.

Example 29. K forgot to file her Federal tax return for the most recent calendar year. K had prepaid taxes of $4,600 in the form of withholding. When she finally filed the return on June 15, K's return showed a total tax of $5,200 and a tax due of $600. Assuming the current rate of interest on underpayments is 11 percent, K must pay the following:

Tax due		$600
Penalty for failure to pay ($600 × .005 × 2)		+ 6
Penalty for failure to file ($600 × .05 × 2)	$ 60	
Net of penalty for failure to pay	− 6	+54
Interest [($600 + $54 + $6) at 11 percent annually, compounded daily for 61 days, rounded]		+12
Total due		$672

Many other penalties exist to ensure proper compliance with the tax laws. For example, the Code provides for an *accuracy-related* penalty of 20 percent of the amount of understatement due to negligence or intentional disregard of the rules (e.g., failing to report income), or substantial valuation infractions.[52] In addition, severe penalties, both civil and criminal, exist for fraud.[53] Still another important penalty to be considered is that for failure to pay estimated taxes during the year. This penalty is discussed below.

---

[51] § 6651(a)(1). If the failure to file is fraudulent, the penalty is 15 percent per month up to a maximum of 75 percent. § 6551(f).

[52] § 6653(a)(1).

[53] § 6653(b).

Amended Return.   After the original return has been filed, an individual tax-payer generally has until the later of three years from the date of filing the original return, or two years from the time the tax was paid, to amend his or her return.[54] This is done by filing Form 1040X (see Appendix B).

ESTIMATED TAX PAYMENTS

Under the "pay-as-you-go" system for collection of taxes, taxpayers are required to prepay Federal income taxes in the form of withholding from certain types of income and estimated tax payments. Withholding is normally adequate for taxpayers receiving only salaries and wages. However, those taxpayers with other income *must* estimate the tax which will be due (including the self-employment tax, the alternative minimum tax, and certain other taxes) and make periodic payments of the estimated tax. Corporations are also required to make estimated tax payments.

A penalty is imposed for taxpayers who fail to make adequate estimates. This penalty is separate from the penalty for failure to pay the tax and the interest which is charged.[55] The failure-to-pay penalty applies to underpayments of tax due as of the due date (e.g., April 15) of the return. The estimated tax penalty is charged from the date the estimated tax installment was due (e.g., June 15th) until the tax was paid (or, if the tax is paid late, the due date of the return). The penalty is assessed at the same rate as the interest which is charged on tax deficiencies; however, it is not assessed where the net tax due after withholding is less than $500.

The estimates are due on April 15, June 15, September 15, and January 15 for a calendar year taxpayer. To avoid penalty, the total prepayments must generally equal or exceed the lesser of the following:

1. Ninety percent of the tax shown on the return

2. One hundred percent of the tax shown on the return for the individual for the preceding year

However, whether the payments are adequate or not is determined at the end of each quarter. For this purpose, withholding is treated as if it occurred proportionately throughout the year. At the end of each quarter, the payments to date are compared to the appropriate portion of the amount required to be paid.

---

[54]   § 6511(a).   [55]   § 6654(a).

Example 30. For 1990 and 1991, G's gross tax was $12,000 and $16,000, respectively. G's withholding for 1991 was $6,500 and his estimated tax payments were $1,500 on April 15 and June 15 and $500 on September 15 and January 15. G's underpayment is determined as follows:

	Payment due date			
	4/15	6/15	9/15	1/15
Percentage due........................	25%	50%	75%	100%
Ninety percent of current year's tax ($16,000 × .90 × percentage due).............	$3,600	$7,200	$10,800	$14,400
One hundred percent of prior year's tax ($12,000 × percentage due).........	$3,000	$6,000	$9,000	$12,000
Payments to date:				
Withholding..........................	$1,625	$3,250	$4,875	$6,500
Estimated tax payments..............	+1,500	+3,000	+3,500	+4,000
Total................................	$3,125	$6,250	$8,375	$10,500

G's payments are adequate for the first quarter and the second quarter, since the payments up to each date exceed the lesser of the two required amounts (the prior year's tax in both cases). As of the third payment date, G is underpaid by $625 ($9,000 − $8,375); and as of the last payment date, he is underpaid by $1,500 ($12,000 − $10,500). The penalty is computed based on these amounts from the due date until the day they are paid (or April 15, if earlier).

Assuming the current rate of penalty is 11 percent and G does not pay his tax early, G's penalty would be $64, which is the penalty on $625 from September 15 through January 15 [$625 × (.11 × 122 days/ 365 days) = $23] *plus* that on $1,500 from January 15 through April 15 [$1,500 × (.11 × 90 days / 365 days) = $41].

The penalty for failure to make adequate estimated tax payments is calculated on Form 2210 (see Appendix B for a sample form). Unless a taxpayer can reduce the penalty by applying the annualized income installment or otherwise, he or she may simply let the IRS calculate this penalty and assess a deficiency for it. In addition, the IRS may waive the underpayment penalty in the event of a casualty or unusual circumstances where it might be inequitable to impose the additional tax. The IRS may also waive the penalty for retired taxpayers who are age 62 or disabled where the underpayment was due to reasonable cause rather than willful neglect.

Annualized Income Installment. If the income for a year is earned disproportionately during the year, the taxpayer may be able to avoid penalty for one or more of the first three payments under the *annualized income installment* method.[56] Under this method, no penalty is imposed when the payment to date exceeds the tax which would be due on the income for the months preceding the payment date on an annualized basis.

---

[56] § 6654(d).

Example 31. F, a calendar year individual, is engaged in a seasonal business which earns most of its income during the fourth quarter. F is able to demonstrate that the income was earned as follows:

	Payment due date			
	4/15	*6/15*	*9/15*	*1/15*
Months preceding payment......	3	5	8	12
Net income earned for the months preceding the payment......................	$10,000	$18,000	$25,000	$50,000
Annualized amount [Net income × (12 ÷ No. of months to date)]........	$40,000	$43,500	$37,500	$50,000

To apply this exception, the tax on the annualized income is determined. There is an underpayment only if the estimated tax payments are less than the appropriate portion of the tax on the annualized income.

The required payment for April 15 is the fraction 3 months ÷ 12 months times the tax on $40,000. If the tax on $40,000 is $8,000, F has no underpayment for the first payment so long as she paid $2,000 ($8,000 × 3/12) or more. If she had paid less, the underpayment would be the amount by which $2,000 exceeded the payments. A similar process would be followed for each quarter.

To apply the annualized income installment calculations, a taxpayer completes a worksheet that accompanies the Form 2210. If this method is used to the benefit of the taxpayer for one payment, it must be used for all four payments.

STATUTE OF LIMITATIONS

Even in the administration of the Federal tax laws, all things must finally come to an end. As the U.S. Supreme Court has stated,

> Congress has regarded it as ill advised to have an income tax system under which there would never come a day of final settlement and which required both a taxpayer and the Government to stand ready forever and a day to produce vouchers, prove events, and recall details of all that goes into an income tax contest.[57]

Accordingly, there are certain time periods within which the IRS must take action *against* a taxpayer. If the Service does not take action within the prescribed time period, it is *barred* from pursuing the matter further. Technically the period in which an action must be commenced is called the Statute of Limitations. If the Statute of Limitations runs (expires) without any action on the part of the IRS, then the government is prohibited from assessing additional taxes for the expired periods.

[57] *Rothensies v. Electric Storage Battery Co.,* 47-1 USTC ¶9106, 35 AFTR 297, 329 U.S. 296, 301 (USSC, 1946).

Under the general rule, the IRS has three years from the date a return is filed to assess an additional tax liability against the taxpayer. If the tax return is filed before its due date, the three-year period for assessment begins *on* the due date.

> **Example 32.** R, a calendar year taxpayer, files a 1991 income tax return (due April 15) on March 7, 1992. The IRS will be prevented from assessing R additional taxes for 1991 any time after April 15, 1995.

> **Example 33.** Refer to *Example 32*. If R files a 1991 income tax return on October 15, 1992, the IRS may assess additional taxes for 1991 at any time through October 15, 1995.

There are several important exceptions to the three-year time period for assessing additional taxes. First, if the taxpayer has filed a false or a fraudulent return with the intention to *evade* the tax, then the tax may be assessed (or a proceeding may be initiated in court without assessment) at *any time* in the future. Similarly, if the taxpayer fails to file a return, the Statute of Limitations will not begin to run. Interestingly, a willful failure to file, a negligent failure to file, or an innocent failure to file are all treated the same. Thus, under any of these circumstances there is no limit to the time in which the IRS may make an assessment or begin a court proceeding against the taxpayer.

In the case of a *substantial omission of income* from a tax return, the Statute of Limitations is extended to six years. A substantial omission is defined as an omission of income in excess of 25 percent of the gross income *reported* on the return.[58] If the omission of gross income was committed with the intent of evading the tax, however, the assessment period would be unlimited.

> **Example 34.** T, a calendar year taxpayer, unintentionally failed to include $8,000 of dividends in his 1991 tax return filed on April 15, 1992. If the $8,000 omitted is more than 25 percent of the gross income reported on T's 1991 return, the IRS may assess an additional income tax liability against him at any time until after April 15, 1998.

The periods within which assessments must be made are summarized in Exhibit 4-8, which follows.

INDEXATION AND THE FEDERAL INCOME TAX

Inflation has significant effects on a progressive tax rate structure stated in terms of a *constant* dollar. Taxpayers whose *real* incomes remain constant will have increasing levels of income, stated in terms of *nominal* dollars. Accordingly, their incomes will *creep up* into higher tax brackets. This *bracket creep*, as it has been labeled, results in a larger portion of the taxpayer's earnings being paid to the Federal government. In effect, unlegislated tax increases occur.

[58] § 6501(e).

Exhibit 4-8
Periods within Which Assessments Must Be Made

Circumstances of Return	Period of Assessment
Normal return has been filed	Three years from date of filing or due date, whichever is later
Return filed with substantial omission of gross income	Six years from date of filing or due date, whichever is later
No return is filed	No time limit
False or fraudulent return	No time limit

The tax reductions in 1981 and 1986 were intended to stimulate the economy. They also tend to offset the bracket creep that has been allowed to occur over the last several decades. These specific tax rate adjustments have been followed by a permanent remedy for bracket creep.

Congress added indexation to the Internal Revenue Code for 1985 and subsequent years. Adjustments were made to the standard deduction, the personal and dependency exemption amounts, and the tax rate schedules (by indexing the brackets). Following the tax rate reductions in 1986, Congress specified the amounts of the standard deduction, exemption amounts, and tax brackets for 1987 and 1988 (and the exemption amount for 1989). Thereafter, each of these amounts is annually adjusted for price level changes as measured by the Consumer Price Index.[59]

---

[59]   See §§ 1(f), 1(g)(4), 639(c)(4), and 151(d)(3).

APPENDIX

TAX RETURN ILLUSTRATIONS

The following pages provide realistic examples of uncomplicated tax returns for individual taxpayers. The information from *Examples 19*, *20*, and *26* of this chapter is used.

Form 1040EZ
Return for William W. Bristol
(Example 19)

Department of the Treasury · Internal Revenue Service

Form 1040EZ

Income Tax Return for Single Filers With No Dependents **1990**

OMB No. 1545-0675

Name & address

Use IRS label (see page 9). If you don't have one, please print.

Print your name (first, initial, last)
WILLIAM W. BRISTOL
Home address (number and street). (If you have a P.O. box, see page 9.)   Apt. no.
651 SOUTH HAMPTON
City, town or post office, state, and ZIP code. (If you have a foreign address, see page 9.)
LITTLE CITY, KS   62228

Please see instructions on the back. Also, see the Form 1040EZ booklet.

Presidential Election Campaign (see page 9)
Do you want $1 to go to this fund?

Note: Checking "Yes" will not change your tax or reduce your refund. ▶

Please print your numbers like this:
1 2 3 4 5 6 7 8 9 0

Your social security number
1 8 7 | 5 2 | 9 0 3 4

Yes No
[✓]

	Dollars	Cents

Report your income

Attach Copy B of Form(s) W-2 here. Attach tax payment on top of Form(s) W-2.

Note: You must check Yes or No.

1 Total wages, salaries, and tips. This should be shown in Box 10 of your W-2 form(s). (Attach your W-2 form(s).)   **1**
24,160.00

2 Taxable interest income of $400 or less. If the total is more than $400, you cannot use Form 1040EZ.   **2**
150.00

3 Add line 1 and line 2. This is your **adjusted gross income.**   **3**
24,310.00

4 Can your parents (or someone else) claim you on their return?
  ☐ **Yes.** Do worksheet on back; enter amount from line E here.
  ☑ **No.** Enter 5,300.00. This is the total of your standard deduction and personal exemption.   **4**
5,300.00

5 Subtract line 4 from line 3. If line 4 is larger than line 3, enter 0. This is your **taxable income.**   **5**
19,010.00

Figure your tax

6 Enter your Federal income tax withheld from Box 9 of your W-2 form(s).   **6**
3,020.00

7 **Tax.** Use the amount on **line 5** to find your tax in the tax table on pages 14–16 of the booklet. Enter the tax from the table on this line.   **7**
2,854.00

Refund or amount you owe

8 If line 6 is larger than line 7, subtract line 7 from line 6. This is your **refund.**   **8**
166.00

9 If line 7 is larger than line 6, subtract line 6 from line 7. This is the **amount you owe.** Attach your payment for full amount payable to "Internal Revenue Service." Write your name, address, social security number, daytime phone number, and "1990 Form 1040EZ" on it.   **9**

Sign your return

Keep a copy of this form for your records.

I have read this return. Under penalties of perjury, I declare that to the best of my knowledge and belief, the return is true, correct, and complete.

Your signature   Date
X *William W. Bristol*   3/7/91

For IRS Use Only—Please do not write in boxes below.

For Privacy Act and Paperwork Reduction Act Notice, see page 4 in the booklet.   Form 1040EZ (1990)

Form 1040A
Return for Clyde F. and Delia C. Cooper
(Example 20)

Form **1040A**	Department of the Treasury—Internal Revenue Service **U.S. Individual Income Tax Return** **1990**		OMB No. 1545-0085

Step 1
Label
(See page 14.)

Use IRS label. Otherwise, please print or type.

L A B E L H E R E	Your first name and initial CLYDE F.　Last name COOPER	Your social security no. 234 : 56 : 7890
	If a joint return, spouse's first name and initial DELIA C.　Last name COOPER	Spouse's social security no. 345 : 67 : 8901
	Home address (number and street). (If you have a P.O. box, see page 14.) 1234 FINE STREET　Apt. no.	**For Privacy Act and Paperwork Reduction Act Notice, see page 3.**
	City, town or post office, state, and ZIP code. (If you have a foreign address, see page 14.) DESIRABLE, OK 66666	

Presidential Election Campaign Fund (see page 15)
Do you want $1 to go to this fund? . . . . ☑ Yes ☐ No
If joint return, does your spouse want $1 to go to this fund? ☑ Yes ☐ No

Note: *Checking "Yes" will not change your tax or reduce your refund.*

Step 2
Check your filing status
(Check only one.)

1 ☐ Single. (See page 16 to find out if you can file as head of household.)
2 ☑ Married filing joint return (even if only one had income)
3 ☐ Married filing separate return. Enter spouse's social security number above and spouse's full name here ▶ _____
4 ☐ Head of household (with qualifying person). (See page 16.) If the qualifying person is your child but not your dependent, enter this child's name here ▶ _____
5 ☐ Qualifying widow(er) with dependent child (year spouse died ▶ 19___). (See page 17.)

Step 3
Figure your exemptions
(See page 17.)

6a ☑ **Yourself** If your parent (or someone else) can claim you as a dependent on his or her tax return, do not check box 6a. But be sure to check the box on line 18b on page 2.
6b ☑ **Spouse**

c Dependents: 1. Name (first, initial, and last name)	2. Check if under age 2	3. If age 2 or older, dependent's social security number	4. Dependent's relationship to you	5. No. of months lived in your home in 1990
GARY R. COOPER		777:99:6541	SON	12
DEBORAH D. COOPER		456:99:8765	DAUGHTER	12

No. of boxes checked on 6a and 6b **2**

No. of your children on 6c who:
● lived with you **2**
● didn't live with you due to divorce or separation (see page 21) _____

No. of other dependents listed on 6c _____

If more than 7 dependents, see page 20.

d If your child didn't live with you but is claimed as your dependent under a pre-1985 agreement, check here . . . . ▶ ☐
e Total number of exemptions claimed.

Add numbers entered on lines above **4**

Step 4
Figure your total income

Attach Copy B of your Forms W-2 and W-2P here.

Attach check or money order on top of any Forms W-2 or W-2P.

7 Wages, salaries, tips, etc. This should be shown in Box 10 of your W-2 form(s). (Attach Form(s) W-2.)	7	47,595 00
8a **Taxable** interest income (see page 23). (If over $400, also complete and attach Schedule 1, Part I.)	8a	1,100 00
b **Tax-exempt** interest. (DO NOT include on line 8a.) 8b		
9 Dividends. (If over $400, also complete and attach Schedule 1, Part II.)	9	
10a Total IRA distributions. 10a	10b Taxable amount (see page 24). 10b	
11a Total pensions and annuities. 11a	11b Taxable amount (see page 25). 11b	
12 Unemployment compensation (insurance) from Form(s) 1099-G.	12	
13a Social security benefits. 13a	13b Taxable amount (see page 28). 13b	
14 Add lines 7 through 13b (far right column). This is your **total income.** ▶	14	48,695 00

Step 5
Figure your adjusted gross income

15a Your IRA deduction from applicable worksheet. 15a	2,000 00	
b Spouse's IRA deduction from applicable worksheet. 15b	2,000 00	
Note: *Rules for IRAs begin on page 30.*		
c Add lines 15a and 15b. These are your **total adjustments.**	15c	4,000 00
16 Subtract line 15c from line 14. This is your **adjusted gross income.** (If less than $20,264, see "Earned income credit" on page 38.) ▶	16	44,695 00

Return for Clyde F. and Delia C. Cooper
Continued

1990   **Form 1040A**   Page 2

Step 6 | **17** Enter the amount from line 16. | 17 | 44,695 | 00

18a Check if: ☐ **You** were 65 or older   ☐ Blind   } **Enter number of boxes checked** ▶ 18a ☐
        ☐ **Spouse** was 65 or older   ☐ Blind

b If your parent (or someone else) can claim you as a dependent, check here . . . . ▶18b ☐

c If you are married filing separately and your spouse files Form 1040 and itemizes deductions, see page 34 and check here . . . ▶18c ☐

Figure your standard deduction,

19 Enter your standard deduction. **See page 35 for the chart (or worksheet) that applies to you. Be sure to enter your standard deduction here.** | 19 | 5,450 | 00

exemption amount, and

20 Subtract line 19 from line 17. (If line 19 is more than line 17, enter -0-.) | 20 | 39,245 | 00

taxable income

21 Multiply $2,050 by the total number of exemptions claimed on line 6e. | 21 | 8,200 | 00

22 Subtract line 21 from line 20. (If line 21 is more than line 20, enter -0-.) This is your **taxable income.** ▶ 22 | 31,045 | 00

Step 7

Figure your tax, credits, and payments

23 Find the tax on the amount on line 22. Check if from: ☐ Tax Table (pages 49–54) or ☐ Form 8615 (see page 36) | 23 | 4,654 | 00

24a Credit for child and dependent care expenses. Complete and attach Schedule 2. | 24a | 700 | 00

b Credit for the elderly or the disabled. Complete and attach Schedule 3. | 24b

c Add lines 24a and 24b. These are your **total credits.** | 24c | 700 | 00

If you want IRS to figure your tax, see the instructions for line 22 on page 36.

25 Subtract line 24c from line 23. (If line 24c is more than line 23, enter -0-.) | 25 | 3,954 | 00

26 Advance earned income credit payments from Form W-2. | 26

27 Add lines 25 and 26. This is your **total tax.** ▶ 27 | 3,954 | 00

28a Total Federal income tax withheld. (If any is from Form(s) 1099, check here ▶ ☐ .) | 28a | 4,250 | 00

b 1990 estimated tax payments and amount applied from 1989 return. | 28b

c Earned income credit. See page 38 to find out if you can take this credit. | 28c

d Add lines 28a, 28b, and 28c. These are your **total payments.** ▶ 28d | 4,250 | 00

Step 8

Figure your refund or amount you owe

29 If line 28d is more than line 27, subtract line 27 from line 28d. This is the amount you **overpaid.** | 29 | 296 | 00

30 Amount of line 29 you want **refunded to you.** | 30 | 296 | 00

31 Amount of line 29 you want **applied to your 1991 estimated tax.** | 31

Attach check or money order on top of Form(s) W-2, etc. on page 1.

32 If line 27 is more than line 28d, subtract line 28d from line 27. This is the **amount you owe.** Attach check or money order for full amount payable to "Internal Revenue Service." Write your name, address, social security number, daytime phone number, and "1990 Form 1040A" on it. | 32

33 Estimated tax penalty (see page 42). | 33

Step 9

Sign your return

Keep a copy of this return for your records.

Under penalties of perjury, I declare that I have examined this return and accompanying schedules and statements, and to the best of my knowledge and belief, they are true, correct, and complete. Declaration of preparer (other than the taxpayer) is based on all information of which the preparer has any knowledge.

Your signature   *Clyde F. Cooper* | Date 4/2/91 | Your occupation PROFESSIONAL MODEL

Spouse's signature (if joint return, BOTH must sign)   *Delia C. Cooper* | Date 4/2/91 | Spouse's occupation COMPUTER PROGRAMMER

Paid preparer's use only

Preparer's signature ▶ | Date | Check if self-employed ☐ | Preparer's social security no.

Firm's name (or yours if self-employed) and address ▶ | E.I. No. | ZIP code

Return for Clyde F. and Delia C. Cooper
Continued

Schedule 2 (Form 1040A) (0)	Department of the Treasury—Internal Revenue Service **Child and Dependent Care Expenses for Form 1040A Filers** 1990	OMB No. 1545-0085

Name(s) shown on Form 1040A: CLYDE F. AND DELIA C. COOPER
Your social security number: 234 : 56 : 7890

- If you are claiming the child and dependent care credit, complete Parts I and II below. But if you received employer-provided dependent care benefits, first complete Part III on the back.
- If you are not claiming the credit but you received employer-provided dependent care benefits, only complete Part I, below, and Part III on the back.

Part I

Persons or organizations who provided the care

You MUST complete this part. (See page 46.)

1	a. Name	b. Address (number, street, city, state, and ZIP code)	c. Identifying number (SSN or EIN)	d. Amount paid (see instructions)
	HAPPY TRAILS PRESCHOOL	2391 BRONCO ST. DESIRABLE, OK 66789	74-3966431	3,500 00

(If you need more space, attach schedule.)

2 Add the amounts in column d of line 1 and enter the total. **2** | 3,500 00

Note: *If you paid cash wages of $50 or more in a calendar quarter to an individual for services performed in your home, you must file an employment tax return. Get Form 942 for details.*

Part II

Credit for child and dependent care expenses

3 Enter the number of qualifying persons who were cared for in 1990. You must have shared the same home with the qualifying person(s). (See page 47 for the definition of a qualifying person.) **3** | 2

4 Enter the amount of **qualified** expenses you incurred and actually paid in 1990. See page 47 to find out which expenses qualify. **Caution:** *If you completed Part III on page 2, DO NOT include on this line any excluded benefits shown on line 23.* **4** | 3,500 00

5 Enter $2,400 ($4,800 if you paid for the care of two or more qualifying persons). **5** 4,800 00

6 If you completed Part III on page 2, enter the **excluded benefits,** if any, from line 23. **6**

7 Subtract line 6 from line 5. (If line 6 is equal to or more than line 5, STOP HERE; you cannot claim the credit.) **7** | 4,800 00

8 Compare the amounts on lines 4 and 7. Enter the **smaller** of the two amounts here. **8** | 3,500 00

9 You **must** enter your **earned income.** (See page 48 for the definition of earned income.) **9** | 31,145 00

10 If you are married filing a joint return, you **must** enter your spouse's earned income. (If spouse was a full-time student or disabled, see the instructions for the amount to enter.) **10** | 16,450 00

11 If you are married filing a joint return, compare the amounts on lines 9 and 10. Enter the **smaller** of the two amounts here. **11** | 16,450 00

12 • If you are married filing a joint return, compare the amounts on lines 8 and 11. Enter the **smaller** of the two amounts here.

   • All others, compare the amounts on lines 8 and 9. Enter the **smaller** of the two amounts here. **12** | 3,500 00

13 Enter the decimal amount from the table below that applies to the **amount on Form 1040A, line 17.**

If line 17 is:		Decimal amount is:	If line 17 is:		Decimal amount is:
Over—	But not over—		Over—	But not over—	
$0	10,000	.30	$20,000	22,000	.24
10,000	12,000	.29	22,000	24,000	.23
12,000	14,000	.28	24,000	26,000	.22
14,000	16,000	.27	26,000	28,000	.21
16,000	18,000	.26	28,000		.20
18,000	20,000	.25			

13 | × .20

14 Multiply the amount on line 12 by the decimal amount on line 13. Enter the result here and on Form 1040A, line 24a. **14** = | 700 00

For Paperwork Reduction Act Notice, see the Form 1040A instructions. Schedule 2 (Form 1040A) 1990

Return for Clyde F. and Delia C. Cooper
Continued

Schedule 1 (Form 1040A) (0)	Department of the Treasury—Internal Revenue Service **Interest and Dividend Income for Form 1040A Filers**	**1990**	OMB No. 1545-0085

Name(s) shown on Form 1040A	Your social security number
CLYDE F. AND DELIA C. COOPER	234 : 56 : 7890

Part I

Interest Income

(See pages 23 and 44.)

Complete this part and attach Schedule 1 to Form 1040A if:
- You have over $400 in taxable interest, or
- You are claiming the exclusion of interest from series EE U.S. savings bonds issued after 1989.

If you are claiming the exclusion or you received, as a nominee, interest that actually belongs to another person, see page 45.

Note: *If you received a Form 1099–INT, Form 1099–OID, or substitute statement, from a brokerage firm, enter the firm's name and the total interest shown on that form.*

1 List name of payer		Amount	
CITY SAVINGS	1	950	00
U.S. GOVERNMENT		150	00
2 Add the amounts on line 1.	2	1,100	00
3 Enter the excludable savings bond interest, if any, from Form 8815, line 14. Attach Form 8815 to Form 1040A.	3		
4 Subtract line 3 from line 2. Enter the result here and on Form 1040A, line 8a.	4	1,100	00

Part II

Dividend Income

(See pages 24 and 45.)

Complete this part and attach Schedule 1 to Form 1040A if you received over $400 in dividends.

If you received, as a nominee, dividends that actually belong to another person, see page 45.

Note: *If you received a Form 1099–DIV, or substitute statement, from a brokerage firm, enter the firm's name and the total dividends shown on that form.*

5 List name of payer		Amount	
	5		
6 Add amounts on line 5. Enter the total here and on Form 1040A, line 9.	6		

For Paperwork Reduction Act Notice, see the Form 1040A instructions.   Schedule 1 (Form 1040A) 1990

Form 1040, with Schedules A and B
Return for Jeremy S. and Shelly R. Allen
(Example 26)

Form **1040** — Department of the Treasury—Internal Revenue Service
U.S. Individual Income Tax Return 19**90**

For the year Jan.–Dec. 31, 1990, or other tax year beginning ____ , 1990, ending ____ , 19 ____   OMB No. 1545-0074

Label
(See Instructions on page 8.)

Your first name and initial: **JEREMY S.**   Last name: **ALLEN**
Your social security number: **123 45 9875**

If a joint return, spouse's first name and initial: **SHELLY R.**   Last name: **ALLEN**
Spouse's social security number: **456 85 2147**

Use IRS label. Otherwise, please print or type.

Home address (number and street). (If you have a P.O. box, see page 9.): **8473 SMITHSON PLACE**   Apt. no.

City, town or post office, state, and ZIP code. (If you have a foreign address, see page 9.): **BORING, OR 97832**

For Privacy Act and Paperwork Reduction Act Notice, see Instructions.

Presidential Election Campaign
(See page 9.)

Do you want $1 to go to this fund? . . . . [✓] Yes / [ ] No
If joint return, does your spouse want $1 to go to this fund? . . . [✓] Yes / [ ] No

Note: Checking "Yes" will not change your tax or reduce your refund.

Filing Status

Check only one box.

1 [ ] Single. (See page 10 to find out if you can file as head of household.)
2 [✓] Married filing joint return (even if only one had income)
3 [ ] Married filing separate return. Enter spouse's social security no. above and full name here. ▶
4 [ ] Head of household (with qualifying person). (See page 10.) If the qualifying person is your child but not your dependent, enter this child's name here. ▶
5 [ ] Qualifying widow(er) with dependent child (year spouse died ▶ 19 ____). (See page 10.)

Exemptions
(See Instructions on page 10.)

6a [✓] Yourself If your parent (or someone else) can claim you as a dependent on his or her tax return, do not check box 6a. But be sure to check the box on line 33b on page 2 .
b [✓] Spouse . . . .

No. of boxes checked on 6a and 6b: **2**

No. of your children on 6c who:
• lived with you: **3**
• didn't live with you due to divorce or separation (see page 11)

c Dependents:

(1) Name (first, initial, and last name)	(2) Check if under age 2	(3) If age 2 or older, dependent's social security number	(4) Dependent's relationship to you	(5) No. of months lived in your home in 1990
WILLIAM A.		789 65 4321	SON	12
SUSAN B.		456 65 9874	DAUGHTER	12
GREGORY C.		321 65 9873	SON	12

If more than 6 dependents, see Instructions on page 11.

No. of other dependents on 6c ____

d If your child didn't live with you but is claimed as your dependent under a pre-1985 agreement, check here ▶ [ ]
e Total number of exemptions claimed . . . .

Add numbers entered on lines above ▶ **5**

Income

Attach Copy B of your Forms W-2, W-2G, and W-2P here.

If you do not have a W-2, see page 8.

Attach check or money order on top of any Forms W-2, W-2G, or W-2P.

7 Wages, salaries, tips, etc. (attach Form(s) W-2) . . . . | 7 | **73,975** 00
8a Taxable interest income (also attach Schedule B if over $400) . . . . . | 8a | **2,800** 00
b Tax-exempt interest income (see page 13). DON'T include on line 8a | 8b |
9 Dividend income (also attach Schedule B if over $400) . . . . | 9 | **200** 00
10 Taxable refunds of state and local income taxes, if any, from worksheet on page 14 . . . . | 10 |
11 Alimony received . . . . | 11 |
12 Business income or (loss) (attach Schedule C) . . . . | 12 |
13 Capital gain or (loss) (attach Schedule D) . . . . | 13 |
14 Capital gain distributions not reported on line 13 (see page 14). . . . . | 14 |
15 Other gains or (losses) (attach Form 4797) . . . . | 15 |
16a Total IRA distributions . | 16a | | 16b Taxable amount (see page 14) | 16b |
17a Total pensions and annuities | 17a | | 17b Taxable amount (see page 14) | 17b |
18 Rents, royalties, partnerships, estates, trusts, etc. (attach Schedule E) . . . . . | 18 |
19 Farm income or (loss) (attach Schedule F) . . . . | 19 |
20 Unemployment compensation (insurance) (see page 16) . . . . . . | 20 |
21a Social security benefits . | 21a | | 21b Taxable amount (see page 16) | 21b |
22 Other income (list type and amount—see page 16) . . . . | 22 |
23 Add the amounts shown in the far right column for lines 7 through 22. This is your **total income** ▶ | 23 | **76,975** 00

Adjustments to Income

(See Instructions on page 17.)

24a Your IRA deduction, from applicable worksheet on page 17 or 18 . | 24a |
b Spouse's IRA deduction, from applicable worksheet on page 17 or 18 | 24b |
25 One-half of self-employment tax (see page 18) . . . . . | 25 |
26 Self-employed health insurance deduction, from worksheet on page 18 | 26 |
27 Keogh retirement plan and self-employed SEP deduction . . | 27 |
28 Penalty on early withdrawal of savings . . . . . | 28 |
29 Alimony paid. Recipient's SSN ▶ | 29 |
30 Add lines 24a through 29. These are your **total adjustments** . . . . ▶ | 30 |

Adjusted Gross Income

31 Subtract line 30 from line 23. This is your **adjusted gross income**. If this amount is less than $20,264 and a child lived with you, see page 23 to find out if you can claim the "Earned Income Credit" on line 57 . . . . ▶ | 31 | **76,975** 00

Return for Jeremy S. and Shelly R. Allen
Continued

Form 1040 (1990)   Page **2**

Tax Compu-tation	32	Amount from line 31 (adjusted gross income)	32	76,975 00
	33a	Check if: ☐ **You** were 65 or older ☐ Blind; ☐ **Spouse** was 65 or older ☐ Blind. Add the number of boxes checked above and enter the total here . . . . ► 33a		
If you want IRS to figure your tax, see Instructions on page 19.	b	If your parent (or someone else) can claim you as a dependent, check here . . . ► 33b ☐		
	c	If you are married filing a separate return and your spouse itemizes deductions, or you are a dual-status alien, see page 19 and check here . . . . ► 33c ☐		
	34	Enter the larger of: { • Your **standard deduction** (from the chart (or worksheet) on page 20 that applies to you), **OR** • Your **itemized deductions** (from Schedule A, line 27). If you itemize, attach Schedule A and check here. . . ► ☐ } . . .	34	15,100 00
	35	Subtract line 34 from line 32	35	61,875 00
	36	Multiply $2,050 by the total number of exemptions claimed on line 6e	36	10,250 00
	37	**Taxable income.** Subtract line 36 from line 35. (If line 36 is more than line 35, enter -0-.)	37	51,625 00
	38	Enter tax. Check if from: a ☐ Tax Table, b ☐ Tax Rate Schedules, or c ☐ Form 8615 (see page 21) (If any is from Form(s) 8814, enter that amount here ► d _____) . . .	38	10,236 00
	39	Additional taxes (see page 21). Check if from: a ☐ Form 4970 b ☐ Form 4972 . .	39	
	40	Add lines 38 and 39 . . . . ►	40	10,236 00
Credits (See Instructions on page 21.)	41	Credit for child and dependent care expenses (attach Form 2441)	41	
	42	Credit for the elderly or the disabled (attach Schedule R) . . .	42	
	43	Foreign tax credit (attach Form 1116)	43	
	44	General business credit. Check if from: a ☐ Form 3800 or b ☐ Form (specify) _____ .	44	
	45	Credit for prior year minimum tax (attach Form 8801)	45	
	46	Add lines 41 through 45	46	
	47	Subtract line 46 from line 40. (If line 46 is more than line 40, enter -0-.) . . . . . . ►	47	10,236 00
Other Taxes	48	Self-employment tax (attach Schedule SE)	48	
	49	Alternative minimum tax (attach Form 6251)	49	
	50	Recapture taxes (see page 22). Check if from: a ☐ Form 4255 b ☐ Form 8611 . .	50	
	51	Social security tax on tip income not reported to employer (attach Form 4137)	51	
	52	Tax on an IRA or a qualified retirement plan (attach Form 5329)	52	
	53	Advance earned income credit payments from Form W-2	53	
	54	Add lines 47 through 53. This is your **total tax** . . . . ►	54	10,236 00
Payments Attach Forms W-2, W-2G, and W-2P to front.	55	Federal income tax withheld (If any is from Form(s) 1099, check ► ☐).	55	10,500 00
	56	1990 estimated tax payments and amount applied from 1989 return	56	
	57	**Earned income credit** (see page 23)	57	
	58	Amount paid with Form 4868 (extension request)	58	
	59	Excess social security tax and RRTA tax withheld (see page 24) .	59	
	60	Credit for Federal tax on fuels (attach Form 4136)	60	
	61	Regulated investment company credit (attach Form 2439) . .	61	
	62	Add lines 55 through 61. These are your **total payments** . . . . ►	62	10,500 00
Refund or Amount You Owe	63	If line 62 is more than line 54, enter amount **OVERPAID** . . . . ►	63	264 00
	64	Amount of line 63 to be **REFUNDED TO YOU** . . . . ►	64	264 00
	65	Amount of line 63 to be **APPLIED TO YOUR 1991 ESTIMATED TAX** ►	65		
	66	If line 54 is more than line 62, enter **AMOUNT YOU OWE.** Attach check or money order for full amount payable to "Internal Revenue Service." Write your name, address, social security number, daytime phone number, and "1990 Form 1040" on it . . . . ►	66	
	67	Estimated tax penalty (see page 25)	67	

Sign Here	Under penalties of perjury, I declare that I have examined this return and accompanying schedules and statements, and to the best of my knowledge and belief, they are true, correct, and complete. Declaration of preparer (other than taxpayer) is based on all information of which preparer has any knowledge.		
Keep a copy of this return for your records.	Your signature *Jeremy S. Allen*	Date 4/15/91	Your occupation *REGISTERED NURSE*
	Spouse's signature (if joint return, BOTH must sign) *Shelly R. Allen*	Date 4/15/91	Spouse's occupation *AIR TRAFFIC CONTROLLER*
Paid Preparer's Use Only	Preparer's signature	Date	Check if self-employed ☐	Preparer's social security no.
	Firm's name (or yours if self-employed) and address		E.I. No. ZIP code

Return for Jeremy S. and Shelly R. Allen
Continued

SCHEDULES A&B	Schedule A—Itemized Deductions	OMB No. 1545-0074
(Form 1040)	(Schedule B is on back)	**1990**
Department of the Treasury Internal Revenue Service	► **Attach to Form 1040.** ► **See Instructions for Schedules A and B (Form 1040).**	Attachment Sequence No. **07**

Name(s) shown on Form 1040: JEREMY S. AND SHELLY R. ALLEN

Your social security number: 123 45 9875

Medical and Dental Expenses	**Caution:** *Do not include expenses reimbursed or paid by others.*			
	1 Medical and dental expenses. (See page 27 of the Instructions.)	1	3,000 00	
	2 Enter amount from Form 1040, line 32 ⌐2⌐			
	3 Multiply the amount on line 2 by 7.5% (.075). Enter the result .	3	5,773 00	
	4 Subtract line 3 from line 1. Enter the result. If less than zero, enter -0-	4		-0-
Taxes You Paid	5 State and local income taxes	5	3,500 00	
(See Instructions on page 27.)	6 Real estate taxes	6	1,200 00	
	7 Other taxes. (List—include personal property taxes.) ►	7		
	8 Add the amounts on lines 5 through 7. Enter the total	8		4,700 00
Interest You Paid	9a Deductible home mortgage interest paid to financial institutions and reported to you on Form 1098. Report deductible points on line 10 .	9a	8,500 00	
(See Instructions on page 27.)	b Other deductible home mortgage interest. (If paid to an individual, show that person's name and address.) ►			
	....			
	....	9b		
	10 Deductible points. (See Instructions for special rules.) . . .	10		
	11 Deductible investment interest (attach Form 4952 if required). (See page 28.)	11	400 00	
	12a Personal interest you paid. (See page 28.) ⌐12a⌐			
	b Multiply the amount on line 12a by 10% (.10). Enter the result .	12b		
	13 Add the amounts on lines 9a through 11, and 12b. Enter the total	13		8,900 00
Gifts to Charity	**Caution:** *If you made a charitable contribution and received a benefit in return, see page 29 of the Instructions.*			
(See Instructions on page 29.)	14 Contributions by cash or check	14	1,500 00	
	15 Other than cash or check. (You **MUST** attach Form 8283 if over $500.)	15		
	16 Carryover from prior year	16		
	17 Add the amounts on lines 14 through 16. Enter the total	17		1,500 00
Casualty and Theft Losses	18 Casualty or theft loss(es) (attach Form 4684). (See page 29 of the Instructions.) . ►	18		
Moving Expenses	19 Moving expenses (attach Form 3903 or 3903F). (See page 30 of the Instructions.). ►	19		
Job Expenses and Most Other Miscellaneous Deductions	20 Unreimbursed employee expenses—job travel, union dues, job education, etc. (You **MUST** attach Form 2106 if required. See Instructions.) ►	20		
(See Instructions on page 30 for expenses to deduct here.)	21 Other expenses (investment, tax preparation, safe deposit box, etc.). List type and amount ►			
	....	21		
	22 Add the amounts on lines 20 and 21. Enter the total	22		
	23 Enter amount from Form 1040, line 32. ⌐23⌐			
	24 Multiply the amount on line 23 by 2% (.02). Enter the result .	24		
	25 Subtract line 24 from line 22. Enter the result. If less than zero, enter -0-. . . ►	25		
Other Miscellaneous Deductions	26 Other (from list on page 30 of Instructions). List type and amount ►			
	....			
	....			
	.... ►	26		
Total Itemized Deductions	27 Add the amounts on lines 4, 8, 13, 17, 18, 19, 25, and 26. Enter the total here. Then enter on Form 1040, line 34, the **LARGER** of this total or your standard deduction from page 20 of the Instructions . . . . ►	27		15,100 00

For Paperwork Reduction Act Notice, see Form 1040 Instructions.   Schedule A (Form 1040) 1990

**Return for Jeremy S. and Shelly R. Allen
Continued**

Schedules A&B (Form 1040) 1990   OMB No. 1545-0074   Page **2**

Name(s) shown on Form 1040. (Do not enter name and social security number if shown on other side.)

JEREMY S. AND SHELLY R.

Your social security number: 123 45 9875

Schedule B—Interest and Dividend Income

Attachment Sequence No. **08**

Part I Interest Income

(See Instructions on pages 13 and 30.)

If you received more than $400 in taxable interest income, or you are claiming the exclusion of interest from series EE U.S. savings bonds issued after 1989 (see page 31), you must complete Part I. List ALL interest received in Part I. If you received more than $400 in taxable interest income, you must also complete Part III. If you received, as a nominee, interest that actually belongs to another person, or you received or paid accrued interest on securities transferred between interest payment dates, see page 31.

Interest Income	Amount
1 Interest income. (List name of payer—if any interest income is from seller-financed mortgages, see Instructions and list that interest first.) ►	
MERCANTILE NATIONAL BANK	1,800 00
U.S. GOVERNMENT BONDS	600 00
BEN FRANKLIN SAVINGS	400 00

Note: If you received a Form 1099-INT, Form 1099-OID, or substitute statement, from a brokerage firm, list the firm's name as the payer and enter the total interest shown on that form.

2 Add the amounts on line 1. Enter the total	2	2,800 00
3 Enter the excludable savings bond interest, if any, from Form 8815, line 14. Attach Form 8815 to Form 1040	3	
4 Subtract line 3 from line 2. Enter the result here and on Form 1040, line 8a ►	4	2,800 00

Part II Dividend Income

(See Instructions on pages 13 and 31.)

If you received more than $400 in gross dividends and/or other distributions on stock, you must complete Parts II and III. If you received, as a nominee, dividends that actually belong to another person, see page 31.

Dividend Income	Amount
5 Dividend income. (List name of payer—include on this line capital gain distributions, nontaxable distributions, etc.) ►	
GRE, INC.	200 00

Note: If you received a Form 1099-DIV, or substitute statement, from a brokerage firm, list the firm's name as the payer and enter the total dividends shown on that form.

6 Add the amounts on line 5. Enter the total	6	200 00
7 Capital gain distributions. Enter here and on Schedule D*	7	
8 Nontaxable distributions. (See the Inst. for Form 1040, line 9.)	8	
9 Add the amounts on lines 7 and 8. Enter the total	9	
10 Subtract line 9 from line 6. Enter the result here and on Form 1040, line 9 ►	10	200 00

*If you received capital gain distributions but do not need Schedule D to report any other gains or losses, see the Instructions for Form 1040, lines 13 and 14.

Part III Foreign Accounts and Foreign Trusts

(See Instructions on page 31.)

If you received more than $400 of interest or dividends, OR if you had a foreign account or were a grantor of, or a transferor to, a foreign trust, you must answer both questions in Part III.

	Yes	No
11a At any time during 1990, did you have an interest in or a signature or other authority over a financial account in a foreign country (such as a bank account, securities account, or other financial account)? (See page 31 of the Instructions for exceptions and filing requirements for Form TD F 90-22.1.)		✓
b If "Yes," enter the name of the foreign country ►		
12 Were you the grantor of, or transferor to, a foreign trust that existed during 1990, whether or not you have any beneficial interest in it? If "Yes," you may have to file Form 3520, 3520-A, or 926		✓

For Paperwork Reduction Act Notice, see Form 1040 Instructions.   Schedule B (Form 1040) 1990

PROBLEM MATERIALS

DISCUSSION QUESTIONS

4-1 *Personal and Dependency Exemptions.* Distinguish between personal and dependency exemptions.

4-2 *Tests for Dependency Exemptions.* List and briefly describe the five tests that must be met before a taxpayer is entitled to a dependency exemption for another individual. Must all five tests be met?

4-3 *Support.* Briefly describe the concept of support. As part of your definition, include examples of support items.

4-4 *Support—Special Items.* With respect to the support test, discuss the treatment of each of the following items: athletic scholarships, social security survivors benefits paid to an orphan, and aid to dependent children paid by the state government.

4-5 *Gross Income Test.* Describe the gross income test that is applied to the dependency exemption. Must all dependents for whom a dependency exemption is claimed meet this test?

4-6 *Community Property Law.* How does the treatment of earned income differ between a community property state and a noncommunity property (i.e., separate property) state for Federal income tax purposes? Why?

4-7 *Filing Status, Tax Schedules.* List the four sets of rate schedules that apply to individual taxpayers. Refer to them by filing status and schedule designation (e.g., Schedule Z). Which taxpayers must use the rate schedules rather than the tax rate tables?

4-8 *Determination of Marital Status.* Married taxpayers are subject to a separate set(s) of tax rates. When is marital status determined? What authority (state or federal) controls marital status?

4-9 *Exceptions—Marital Status.* In certain instances, a person who is married may use the rates for unmarried persons. In another instance, a single person may use the rates for married persons filing jointly. Elaborate.

4-10 *Head of Household—Requirements.* What are the specific requirements for head-of-household status? List at least ten relatives who may qualify the taxpayer for head-of-household filing status.

4-11 *Head of Household—Divorced Parents.* May a divorced parent with custody of a child qualify as a head of household even though his or her former spouse is entitled to the dependency exemption for the child? Explain.

4-12 *Head of Household—Taxpayer's Home.* Must the person who qualifies a taxpayer as a head of household (i.e., the taxpayer's child or other dependent) live in the taxpayer's home? Are there any exceptions to this rule?

4-13 *Standard Deduction.*   List the standard deduction for each filing status. What is the effect of the standard deduction in the determination of one's tax liability? Which taxpayers are allowed an additional standard deduction?

4-14 *Tax Tables.*   Are taxpayers required to use the tax tables? Which taxpayers are ineligible to use the tables?

4-15 *Limited Standard Deduction.*   W is 16 years old, single, and claimed as a dependent by his parents. His gross income is $4,000.

    a.   If W's taxable income is $3,450, what is the character of his income, earned or unearned?

    b.   If W's taxable income is $2,500, what is the character of his income, earned or unearned?

    c.   If W's taxable income is $600, what is the character of his income, earned or unearned?

4-16 *Kiddie Tax.*   G is 13 years old and claimed as a dependent by her parents. G's top marginal tax rate is 15 percent and her parents' is 28 percent. Calculate G's taxable income and the rate at which it will be taxed in the following instances:

    a.   Interest of $950

    b.   Interest of $1,600

    c.   Interest of $600 and wages of $2,400

    d.   Interest of $3,400 and wages of $500

4-17 *Filing Requirements.*   Which individuals are exempted from filing a Form 1040 (or equivalent Form 1040A or Form 1040EZ)?

4-18 *Due Date.*   What is the due date for the individual income tax return? Are extensions of time to file the return allowed?

4-19 *Interest and Penalties.*   Briefly describe the interest and penalty rules for failure to file a return and failure to pay the tax.

4-20 *Estimated Tax Payments.*   Which taxpayers are required to make quarterly estimated tax payments? In the case of taxpayers who make inadequate payments, how is the underpayment determined? Is a penalty assessed? How is it calculated?

4-21 *Statute of Limitations.*   What is the importance of the Federal Statute of Limitations to the taxpayer? To the IRS?

4-22 *Six-Year Statute of Limitations.*   Under what circumstances will the regular three-year statutory period for assessments be extended to six years?

4-23 *Indexation and the Individual Income Tax.*   Congress has provided for indexation of certain deductions beginning in 1989. What items are subject to indexation? What index is to be used as an estimate of price-level changes? What items are to be indexed after 1989?

PROBLEMS

4-24 *Exemptions.* In each of the following situations determine the proper number of personal and dependency exemptions available to the taxpayer. Unless otherwise implied, assume that all tests are satisfied.

a. R's mother, age 85, lives in his home. R figures that including the value of the lodging, he provides support of about $6,000. The remainder of her support is paid for with her Social Security benefits of $4,000.

b. This year D sent his father, F, monthly checks of $200 or $2,400 for the year. F used these checks along with $2,200 of rental income ($4,000 of rents less $1,800 of expenses) to pay all of his support.

c. H and W are married with one daughter, D, age 7. D models children's clothing and earned $3,000 of wages this year. D also has a trust fund of $50,000 established by her grandparents. All of D's wages were saved and none were used to pay for her support. Similarly none of the funds of the trust were used to pay for D's support.

d. Professor and Mrs. Smith participated in the foreign exchange student program at their son's high school. In December of 1990, a student, Hans, arrived from Germany, spent the spring of 1991 with the Smiths, then returned to Germany.

e. B and C are happily married with one son, S. S, age 20, is a full-time student at the University of Cincinnati. S worked as a painter during the summer to help put himself through school. He earned wages of $3,000, $2,500 of which was used to pay for his room and board at school and $500 for miscellaneous living expenses (e.g., gas for his car, dates, laundry, etc.). He lived with his parents during the summer. The value of their support including meals and lodging was $4,000. He also received a National Merit Scholarship which paid for his tuition of $5,000.

4-25 *Personal and Dependency Exemptions.* In each of the following situations determine the proper number of personal and dependency exemption deductions available to the taxpayer.

a. A is single and 44 years of age. He provides full support for his mother, who is 67 and lives in a small retirement community in A's hometown.

b. D and K are married and file a joint return for the year. D is 67 years of age and K is 62. They have no dependents.

c. E and O are married and file a joint return for the year. They provide all the support for their two younger children for the entire year. E and O also provided all the support for their oldest child (age 19) for the eight months she was a full-time student. After graduating from high school, she accepted a job that paid $3,000 in salaries. Nevertheless, her parents contributed over one-half of her support for the entire year.

4-26 *Exemption Phase-out.* H and W are married with two children, ages 3 and 5. Compute the couple's deduction for exemptions assuming they have adjusted gross income as follows:

a. $100,000
b. $176,000
c. $300,000

4-27 *Married Dependents.* In November of this year, Jim Jenkins married his college sweetheart, Kate Brown. Jim was 24 and Kate was 22. Jim had graduated two years ago. Kate still had one more year of school. The majority of Kate's support this year was provided by her parents. Jim earned $15,000 during the year while Kate received $900 of interest from her savings account. Assume Kate's parents are in the 28 percent tax bracket and would give the couple any tax savings to be derived from claiming Kate as a dependent.

 a. May Kate's parents claim an exemption for Kate assuming the couple files a joint return?

 b. Would the couple be better off filing separate returns (and thus receiving any taxes saved by Kate's parents) or filing a joint return? Show all computations you must make to determine your answer.

4-28 *Itemized Deductions and Exemptions.* G and H are married and file a joint return for 1991. They have A.G.I. of $197,400 for the year and the following itemized deductions and personal and dependency exemptions:

State and local taxes	$ 5,300
Residence interest	14,500
Investment interest	500
Charitable contributions	6,200
Personal and dependency exemptions	4

 a. Calculate G and H's taxable income for 1991.

 b. Calculate G and H's taxable income for 1991 assuming their A.G.I. was $207,400, a $10,000 increase over (a).

 c. By what amount did taxable income increase due to this $10,000 increase in adjusted gross income? Why wasn't it $10,000?

4-29 *Multiple Support Agreements.* G's support is provided as follows:

Social Security benefits	$3,600
Taxable interest income	800
Support from:	
A, G's oldest son—Cash	1,600
B, G's daughter—Fair value of lodging and cash	2,300
C, G's youngest son—Cash	700

 a. Who is entitled to a dependency exemption for G in absence of any agreement as to who gets the deduction?

 b. Who may claim a dependency exemption for G under a multiple support agreement?

 c. How would your answer to (b) differ if A contributed $650 instead of $1,600?

4-30 *Children of Divorced Parents.* For each of the following, determine whether M or F is entitled to the dependency exemption in 1991 for their only child, S. M and F were divorced in 1988 and M has custody, except when F has visitation privileges. Together, M and F provide 100 percent of S's support.

    a.   M was granted the dependency exemption under the divorce decree. F pays child support for the year totaling $1,500. Total support expenditures for S are $3,600.

    b.   No mention of the dependency exemption was made in the divorce decree. F pays child support for S of $2,400, and the total support for S is $4,500.

    c.   F was granted the dependency exemption in the divorce decree and he paid child support of $1,800 for the year. The total support for S for the year was $3,500.

4-31 *Filing Status and Standard Deduction.* Determine the most beneficial filing status and the standard deduction for each of the following taxpayers for 1991:

    a.   M is a 54-year-old unmarried widow whose spouse died in 1986. During all of 1991, M's son, for whom she claims a dependency exemption, lives with her.

    b.   S is a 67-year-old bachelor who lives in New York City. S pays over half the cost of maintaining a home in Tampa, Florida for his 89-year-old mother. He is entitled to a dependency exemption under a multiple support agreement executed by his brother, his sister, and himself.

    c.   R is a widower whose wife died in 1990. R maintained a household for his three dependent children during 1991 and provided 100 percent of the cost of the household.

    d.   J is divorced and has custody of his 9-year-old child. J provides over half the cost of the home in which he lives with his child, but his ex-wife is entitled to the dependency exemption for the child for 1991.

4-32 *Head of Household.* Indicate whether the taxpayer would be entitled to file using the head of household rate schedule.

    a.   Y is divorced from her husband. She maintains a home in which she and her 10-year-old son live. Her ex-husband pays child support to her that she uses to provide all of the support for the child. In addition, Y has relinquished her right to claim her daughter as a dependent to her former spouse.

    b.   C is divorced from his wife. He provides 75 percent of the support for his mother who lives in a nursing home. His mother receives $5,000 of interest income annually.

    c.   J's grandson, L, had a falling-out with his parents and moved in with him this year. J did not mind because he had grown lonely since his wife died three years ago. L is 17 years old and earned $5,000 this year as a part-time grocery clerk.

d.   B's wife died four years ago and he has not remarried. Last year his daughter, D, graduated from Arizona State University and moved to Hawaii. Unfortunately, D was unable to earn enough money to make ends meet and had to rely on checks from dad. B paid for D's own apartment and provided the majority of her support.

e.   M's wife died last year. This year he maintains a home for his 25-year-old daughter, E, who is attending graduate school. E earned $8,000 as a teaching assistant. Nevertheless, M provided the majority of E's support.

f.   Same as (e) except E is the taxpayer's sister.

g.   F's husband died this year. She continues to provide a home for her two children, ages 6 and 8.

4-33   *Dependent's Personal Exemption and Standard Deduction.*   K is 16 years old and is claimed as a dependent on her parents' income tax return. She earned wages of $2,800 and collected interest of $1,200 for the year. What is the amount of K's taxable income for the year?

4-34   *Dependent's Personal Exemption and Standard Deduction.*   B is 20 years old and is claimed as a dependent on his sister's tax return. B earned $1,600 from a part-time job during the year. What is B's taxable income?

4-35   *Computation of Tax.*   R and S are married and have two dependents. Compute their 1991 tax liability, assuming their taxable income is

a. $75,000
b. $175,000

4-36   *High-Income Taxpayer.*   H and W are married and file a joint return for 1991. They have no dependents and both are under age 40. H earned a salary of $120,000. W is self-employed and earned a net profit from business of $89,000. H and W have personal itemized deductions totaling $14,800 (all subject to the 3% cutback problem).

a.   What are the amounts of their adjusted gross income and taxable income on their joint income tax return?

b.   Calculate the 1991 tax liability, including W's self-employment tax. Assume that the 1991 self-employment tax is 15.3 percent on income up to $53,400 (2.9% MHI up to $125,000).

4-37   *Tax Tables.*   S earned a salary during 1990 of $24,600. She is single and had no dependents for the year. Her only other income was taxable interest income of $560. Determine S's taxable income and her Federal income tax. (**Note:** This tax table computation is for 1990 because the 1991 tax tables will not be available until late 1991.)

4-38 *Tax Rate Schedules.* W and T were married and filed a joint return for 1991. Their adjusted gross income for the year was $72,000. Their total itemized deductions were $9,700 and they were entitled to three personal and dependency exemptions. Neither W nor T is 65 years old and both have good sight. Determine W and T's taxable income and their Federal income tax liability before prepayments and credits for 1991.

4-39 *Application of the "Kiddie" Tax.* For each of the following situations, determine the child's taxable income and the amounts that would be taxed at the child's and parents' rates.

  a. When J's rich uncle died, he left her 1,000 shares of stock. This year the stock paid J $1,200 in dividends, her only income. J is seven years old and her parents claim an exemption for her.

  b. L, age 13, works in his father's record shop on weekends. During the year, he earned $900 from this job. In addition, L had $700 of interest income attributable to a gift from his grandfather. L's father claims an exemption for him.

  c. Same as (b) except L's earned income was $1,900 and interest income was $1,700.

4-40 *Computation of the "Kiddie" Tax.* G's great aunt gave her a certificate of deposit which matures in ten years when she is 21. The certificate pays interest of $2,000 annually. G's parents file a joint return. Their taxable income is $75,000. Compute G's tax.

4-41 *Failure-to-File Penalty.* T, overwhelmed by other pressing concerns, simply forgot to file his tax return for 1991 until July 20, 1991. When filed, T's 1991 return showed a tax due before withholding and estimated taxes of $10,000.

  a. Will T be penalized for failure to file his return if the total income taxes withheld by his employer were $11,000?

  b. Assuming T's employer withheld $8,000, what is the amount of the failure-to-file penalty, if any?

4-42 *Failure-to-Pay Penalty.* On April 13, 1992, R, a calendar year taxpayer, sat down to prepare his 1991 tax return. Realizing that he simply did not have time to accumulate all of his records, R decided to file for an extension. R's tax liability for the previous year, 1990, was $8,000. During 1991, R's employer withheld $2,500 and R paid estimated taxes of $500. R estimates that his final tax liability for 1991 will be $12,000.

  a. Assuming R obtains an extension to file his 1991 return, when will his return normally be due?

  b. Based on the facts above, what amount must R pay by April 15 to avoid a failure-to-pay penalty?

  c. R completed and filed his return on July 20, 1992. Unfortunately, his initial estimate of his tax was low and his final tax (before withholding and estimated tax payments) was $15,000. What is the amount of the failure-to-pay penalty, if any?

4-43   *Estimated Taxes.*   K works as a salesman for the National Hospital Supply Corporation, selling surgical and other hospital supplies. He receives a salary plus a percentage commission on sales over a certain threshold. In 1991, K's tax liability before prepayments was $20,000. His 1990 tax liability was $12,000. What is the lowest required tax installment (including withholding) that K can make and avoid the penalty for underpaying his taxes during the year? (Ignore the annualized income installment.)

4-44   *Underpayment Penalty.*   Refer to the facts in Problem 4-43 above. Assume that K paid estimated taxes of $1,000 on each due date. In addition, K's employer withheld a total of $3,000 during the year. K filed and paid the balance of his liability on April 15, 1992. Assume the applicable interest rate charged on underpayments for each period in 1991 is 10 percent. Compute K's penalty, if any, for failure to pay estimated taxes. Compute the penalty for the first installment only.

4-45   *Estimated Taxes: Fluctuating Earnings.*   Refer to the facts in Problem 4-44 above. Assume that K works solely for commissions and that he had no income through March 31, 1991 because he decided to take a winter vacation. Income for the remainder of the year was sufficient to generate a tax liability before prepayments of $20,000. What implications do these facts have on the calculation of the underpayment penalty for 1991?

4-46   *Statute of Limitations.*   T, a calendar year taxpayer, filed her 1990 Federal income tax return on January 29, 1991 and received a tax refund check for overpaid 1990 taxes on May 17, 1991.

   a.   Assuming that T did not file a false return or have a substantial omission of income, what is the last date on which the IRS may assess an additional income tax liability against her for the 1990 tax year?

   b.   If T unintentionally had a substantial omission of income from her 1990 return, what is the last day on which the IRS may assess her an additional 1990 income tax liability?

   c.   If T had never bothered to file her 1990 tax return, what is the last day on which the IRS may assess her an additional 1990 income tax liability?

TAX RETURN PROBLEMS

4-47   *Form 1040EZ.*   Samuel B. White was single for 1991 and had no dependents. Sam's only income was wages of $16,500 and taxable interest of $65. Federal income tax of $2,430 was withheld from Sam's salary.

   Calculate Sam's Federal income tax and his tax due or refund for 1991. A Form 1040EZ may be completed based on this information. Supply fictitious occupation, Social Security number, and address. (**Note:** If the 1991 tax forms are not available, use 1990 forms.)

4-48   *Form 1040A.*   Charles D. and Alice A. Davis were married during all of 1991 and had income from the following sources:

Salary, Charles....................................		$22,000
Federal income tax withheld....................	$2,660	
Part-time salary, Alice............................		11,400
Federal income tax withheld....................	1,280	
Interest from Home Savings......................		320
Interest from U.S. Government Bonds............		430

Charles and Alice provide the sole support of their two children. During 1991, they paid job-related child care expenses of $2,200. Their itemized deductions for the year are insufficient for them to itemize, but a deductible $2,000 was deposited in each of their individual retirement accounts.

Calculate the Federal income tax and the tax due (or refund) for Mr. and Mrs. Davis, assuming they file a joint return. If the 1991 tax tables are not available, use the tax rate schedules on the inside front cover of the text. A Form 1040A may also be completed. Supply fictitious information for the address, occupations, social security numbers, and children's names. (**Note:** If the 1991 tax forms are not available, use 1990 forms.)

4-49   *Form 1040.*   William A. Gregg, a high school educator, and Mary W. Gregg, a microbiologist, are married and file a joint income tax return for 1991. Neither William nor Mary is over 50 years old, and both have excellent sight. They provide the sole support of their three children: Barry, Kimberly, and Rachel. The following information is from their records for 1991:

Salaries and wages, William.......................		$32,000
Federal income tax withheld.....................	$3,420	
Salaries and wages, Mary.........................		44,000
Federal income tax withheld.....................	4,730	
Interest income—Home Savings and Loan.........		410
Interest income—City Bank.......................		220
Tax-exempt interest income.......................		1,400
Dividends—Alto, Inc. (a Florida company)..........		180
Itemized deductions as follows:		
Hospitalization insurance........................		320
Unreimbursed fees of doctors, hospitals, etc.....		740
Unreimbursed prescription drugs................		310
Real estate taxes on residence..................		1,350
State income taxes paid.........................		1,440
State sales taxes paid...........................		720
Interest paid on original home mortgage.........		8,430
Charitable contribution—Faith Church............		1,720
Charitable contribution—State University.........		200
Quarterly estimated taxes paid....................		3,500

Calculate the 1991 Federal income tax and the tax due (or refund) for the Greggs assuming they file a joint return. Form 1040, along with Schedules A and B, may be completed. Supply fictitious information for the address and social security numbers. (**Note:** If the 1991 tax forms are not available, use 1990 forms.)

RESEARCH PROBLEMS

4-50 *Support by Noncustodial Parent.*   G incurred several expenses while exercising visitation rights with his children from a dissolved marriage. Determine which, if any, of the following expenses are treated as provided by G toward the support of his children: travel by G to visit the children, transportation and entertainment for children, lodging in G's residence, and gifts of toys and clothing.

Research aids:

Brandes v. Comm., 29 TCM 1436, T.C. Memo 1970-313.
Gilliam v. Comm., 28 TCM 956, T.C. Memo 1969-188.
Hout v. Comm., 25 TCM 1468, T.C. Memo 1966-281.
Hastings v. Comm., 16 TCM 928, T.C. Memo 1957-202.

4-51 *Nonresident Alien Spouse.*   C is a citizen of the United States who resides indefinitely in Europe. C is married to N, a citizen of Greece. C has $32,000 of gross income subject to United States tax and would like to file jointly with N. Can C accomplish this goal? If so, what steps are necessary? How is the income of N treated?

Research aids:

Code § 6013(g) and Reg. § 1.6013-6.

COMPUTERIZED TAX ANALYSIS

4-52 *Phase-out of Personal and Dependency Exemptions—1991.*   Use computer file T402 for this problem.

  a.   Review computer file T402. Work to understand each computation in the analysis section.

  b.   Compute the missing items for the following cases:

Case	A.G.I.	Filing Status	Exemptions	A.G.I. Threshold	Percentage Reduction of Exemptions
1	$161,000	MFJ	2	_____	_____
2	161,000	H of H	2	_____	_____
3	161,000	Single	2	_____	_____
4	161,000	MFS	2	_____	_____
5	140,000	MFJ	2	_____	_____
6	140,000	H of H	2	_____	_____

  c.   Compare the computer analyses for Cases 1–4. Why does the percentage reduction of exemptions continually rise?

  d.   Compare the computer analyses for Cases 5 and 6. Why is there no percentage reduction of exemptions for Case 5 while exemptions are partially phased out for Case 6?

  e.   If A.G.I. exceeds the threshold by more than $122,500 ($61,250 for MFS), the percentage reduction of exemptions becomes 100 percent, causing personal and dependency exemptions to be eliminated. At what levels of A.G.I. does the percentage reduction *first* reach 100 percent for MFJ, H of H, single, and MFS taxpayers?

4-53 *Kiddie Tax—1991.* Use computer file T403 for this problem. In all cases, assume the children are younger than 14 years old and are claimed as dependents on their parents' tax return.

  a.   Enter the following information in the input section of the program:

INPUT:
Parents' taxable income computed in the
  normal manner... $50,000

	Child #1	Child #2
Children's earned income........................	$4,000	$0
Children's unearned income.....................	$0	$0

Review computer file T403. Work to understand each computation in the analysis section. What are Child #1's taxable income, total tax, and average tax rate? Why is the child's taxable income $600, rather than $4,000 (the amount of earned income)? Why does the kiddie tax not apply?

b.   Enter the following information in the input section of the program:

INPUT:
Parents' taxable income computed in the
normal manner.. $50,000

	Child #1	Child #2
Children's earned income........................	$0	$0
Children's unearned income	$2,000	$0

What are Child #1's taxable income, total tax, and average tax *rates*? Work to understand each computation in the analysis section. Explain the key tax rules and computations behind each of the three average tax rates.

c.   Enter the following information in the input section of the program:

INPUT:
Parents' taxable income computed in the
normal manner.. $50,000

	Child #1	Child #2
Children's earned income........................	$3,000	$0
Children's unearned income	$2,000	$0

What are Child #1's taxable income, total tax, and average tax *rates*? Work to understand each computation in the analysis section. Explain the key tax rules and computations behind each of the three average tax rates.

d.   Enter the following information in the input section of the program:

INPUT:
Parents' taxable income computed in the
normal manner.. $50,000

	Child #1	Child #2
Children's earned income........................	$5,000	$0
Children's unearned income	$2,000	$0

What are Child #1's taxable income, total tax, and average tax *rates*? Work to understand each computation in the analysis section. Explain the key tax rules and computations behind each of the three average tax rates.

e.   Enter the following information in the input section of the program:

INPUT:
Parents' taxable income computed in the
normal manner.. $50,000

	Child #1	Child #2
Children's earned income........................	$5,000	$6,000
Children's unearned income	$2,000	$3,000

What are each child's taxable income, total tax, and average tax *rates*? Work to understand each computation in the analysis section. Explain the key tax rules and computations behind each average tax rate for each child.

f.   Enter the following information in the input section of the program:

INPUT:
Parents' taxable income computed in the
   normal manner.. $81,000

	Child #1	Child #2
Children's earned income.........................	$5,000	$6,000
Children's unearned income......................	$2,000	$3,000

Note the *only* new input is the parents' taxable income of $81,000. What are the *differences* in the computer analyses for parts (e) and (f) of this problem and the reasons for those differences?

PART II

GROSS INCOME

CONTENTS

Upon completion of this chapter you will be able to:

■ Define income for tax purposes and explain how it differs from the definitions given to it in accounting or economics

■ Explain the concept of the taxable year and identify who is eligible to use fiscal years

■ Apply the cash and accrual methods of accounting to determine the tax year in which items are reported

■ Determine the effect of a change in accounting method

■ Describe some of the special rules governing the treatment of prepaid income, interest income, interest-free loans, and income from long-term contracts

■ Identify which taxpayer is responsible for reporting income and paying the taxes on such income

██████ CHAPTER OUTLINE ██████

Chapter 5

GROSS INCOME

INTRODUCTION

Determination of the final income tax liability begins with the identification of a taxpayer's gross income. Before identification can occur, however, one obviously must understand what constitutes *income* for tax purposes. The primary purpose of this chapter is to examine the income concept and thus provide some general guidelines regarding what is and what is not subject to taxation. The uninitiated should be forewarned that determining whether a particular item is income sometimes proves difficult. This difficulty has been the subject of much commentary, but perhaps was summarized best by the Supreme Court in a case regarding the income status of embezzled funds. In this decision, the Court stated:

> In fact, no single conclusive criterion has yet been found to determine in all situations what is sufficient gain to support the imposition of an income tax. No more can be said in general than that all relevant facts and circumstances must be considered.[1]

Notwithstanding the Court's observations, two important generalizations developed in this chapter are

1. "Income" is broadly construed for tax purposes to include virtually any type of gain, benefit, or profit that has been realized.

2. Although the scope of the income concept is broad, certain types of income are exempted from taxation by statute, administrative ruling, or judicial decree.

Once it has been determined that a particular item should be treated as income, consideration must be given to *when* the income must be reported and *who* must report it. The second part of this chapter focuses on the timing of income recognition and the identification of the reporting entity.

---

[1] *Comm. v. Wilcox*, 46-1 USTC ¶9188, 34 AFTR 811, 327 U.S. 404 (USSC, 1946).

GROSS INCOME DEFINED

The definition of income found in the Internal Revenue Code reflects the language of the constitutional amendment empowering Congress to impose taxes on income.[2] Section 61(a) of the Code defines *gross income* as follows:

Except as otherwise provided in this subtitle, gross income means all income from whatever source derived, including (but not limited to) the following items:

1. Compensation for services, including fees, commissions, fringe benefits, and similar items;
2. Gross income derived from business;
3. Gains derived from dealings in property;
4. Interest;
5. Rents;
6. Royalties;
7. Dividends;
8. Alimony and separate maintenance payments;
9. Annuities;
10. Income from life insurance and endowment contracts;
11. Pensions;
12. Income from discharge of indebtedness;
13. Distributive share of partnership gross income;
14. Income in respect of a decedent; and
15. Income from an interest in an estate or trust.

Despite the statute's detailed enumeration of income items, the list is not comprehensive. The items specified are only a sample of the more common types of income. Taxable income includes many other economic benefits not identified above.

As a practical matter, Code § 61 furnishes little guidance for determining whether a particular benefit should be treated as income. The statute provides no criteria or factors that could be used for assessment. For example, the general definition does not provide any clue as to whether a gift or an inheritance constitutes taxable income. Similarly, the statute is not helpful in determining whether income arises upon the discovery of buried treasure. These and similar issues, as will be seen, are often answered by reference to other, more specific, sections of the Code. On the other hand, many questions cannot be resolved by reference to the statute or the regulations. In situations where clear statutory guidance is absent, the difficult task of ascertaining how far the definitional boundary of income extends falls to the courts. To this end, the courts have utilized the meanings given income in both economics and accounting to mold a workable definition of income for tax purposes.

[2] See Chapter 1.

ECONOMIC CONCEPT OF INCOME

Economists define income as the amount that an individual could have spent for consumption during a period while remaining as well off at the end of the period as at the beginning of the period. This concept of income may be expressed mathematically as the sum of an individual's consumption during the period plus the change in the individual's net worth between the beginning and end of the period.[3]

Example 1. K's records revealed the following assets and liabilities as of December 31, 1991 and 1992:

	12-31-91	12-31-92
Assets (fair market value)	$100,000	$140,000
Liabilities	(20,000)	(30,000)
Net worth	$ 80,000	$110,000

During the year, K spent $25,000 on rent, food, clothing, entertainment, and other items. From an economic perspective, K's income for 1992 is $55,000 determined as follows:

Consumption	$25,000
Change in net worth ($110,000 − $80,000)	30,000
Economic income	$55,000

From a tax perspective, the critical aspect of the economist's definition of income is the notion that consumption and the change in net worth must be computed using market values on an accrual basis rather than on a realization basis. For example, economists include in income any increase in the value of an individual's shares of stock during the period, even though the shares are not sold and the individual does not *realize* the increase in value. In addition, economists would include in income the rental value of one's car or home, as well as the value of food grown for personal use, since such items constitute consumption. Gifts and inheritances would also be considered income by an economist since these items would affect an individual's net worth. Although the economist's approach to income is theoretically sound, it has significant drawbacks from a practical view.

For practical application, the meaning given to income must be objective to minimize controversies. The economist's reliance on market values to measure net worth and consumption violates this premise. Few assets have readily

[3] The economic definition of income given here is often referred to as the Haig-Simons definition as derived from the following works: Robert M. Haig, "The Concepts of Income—Economic and Legal Aspects," *The Federal Income Tax* (New York: Columbia University Press, 1921); Henry C. Simons, *Personal Income Taxation* (Chicago: University of Chicago Press, 1921).

determinable and accurate values. Valuation of most assets would be a subjective determination. For example, an individual may be able to value shares of stock by referring to an active publicized market, but how is the value of a favorite chair to be computed? The difficulty in making such valuations would no doubt lead to countless disputes and administrative hassles. These practical problems of implementing the economic concept of income have caused the courts to adopt a different interpretation.

It should be pointed out, however, that the economist's approach to measuring income—the so-called "net worth method"—is sometimes used when the IRS decides that the taxpayer's records do not adequately reflect income.[4] Application usually occurs where the taxpayer has not maintained records, or has falsified or destroyed any records that were kept. In these situations, the IRS reconstructs income by determining the change in net worth during the year and adding estimated living expenses.

ACCOUNTING CONCEPT OF INCOME

The principle of realization distinguishes the accountant's concept of income from that of the economist. Under this principle, accountants recognize income when it is *realized*. Income is generally considered realized when (1) the earnings process is complete, and (2) an exchange or transaction has taken place.[5] These two criteria provide the objective determination of value traditionally believed necessary for the work that accountants perform. As a result, accounting income usually does not recognize changes in market values of assets during a period (as would economic income) unless such changes have been realized.

INCOME FOR TAX PURPOSES: THE JUDICIAL CONCEPT

The landmark decision of the Supreme Court in *Eisner v. Macomber* in 1918 provided the first glimpse of how the concept of income would be interpreted for tax purposes.[6] In this case, the court embraced the realization principle of accounting, indicating that income must be *realized* before it can be taxed. As later decisions suggested, the primary virtue of the realization principle is not that it somehow yields a better or more theoretically precise income figure. Rather, it provides an objective basis for measuring income, eliminating the problems that would arise if income were determined using subjective valuations. In short, the realization principle is a well-entrenched part of the tax law because it makes the law so much easier to administer.

[4] *Holland v. U.S.,* 54-2 USTC ¶9714, 46 AFTR 943, 348 U.S. 121 (USSC, 1954). Net worth, however, is to be determined using the tax basis in assets and not their fluctuating market values [*S. Bedeian,* 54 T.C. 295 (1970)].

[5] "Basic Concepts and Accounting Principles Underlying Financial Statements of Busi-ness Enterprises," *Accounting Principles Board Statements No. 4* (New York: American Institute of Certified Public Accountants, 1970), ¶134.

[6] 1 USTC ¶32, 3 AFTR 3020, 252 U.S. 189 (USSC, 1920).

A second issue addressed by the *Eisner* decision concerned the scope of the income concept. How far did it reach? Did income include gifts, scholarships, court-awarded damages, a personal secretary, and other types of benefits? In essence, the Court again followed the accounting approach, stating that income was restricted to gains realized from property or personal services.

Hence, finding a $10 bill, receiving a prize or award, or profiting from a canceled debt would not have been taxable under *Eisner,* since the benefits were obtained without any effort by the taxpayer. Later decisions, however, expanded the concept of income by rejecting the notion that only gains derived from capital or labor are recognized. The courts have taken what is often referred to as an "all-inclusive" approach; that is, *all* gains are presumed to be taxable except those specifically exempted. The Supreme Court's opinion in *Glenshaw Glass Co.* provides the definition of income that is perhaps most commonly accepted today.[7] This case involved the treatment of punitive damages awarded to Glenshaw Glass for fraud and antitrust violations of another company. In holding that such awards were income, the Court stated:[8]

> Here we have instances of undeniable accessions to wealth, clearly realized, and over which the taxpayer has complete dominion. The mere fact that the payments were extracted from wrongdoers as punishment for unlawful conduct cannot detract from their character as taxable income to the recipients.

Thus, income for tax purposes is construed to include any type of gain, benefit, profit, or other increase in wealth that has been realized and is not exempted by statute.

It should be noted that, notwithstanding this expansive approach to income, the tax base is far from comprehensive because of the numerous exclusions and exemptions that have crept into the law over the years.[9] The provisions concerning statutory exclusions are discussed in detail in the following chapter. In addition to these exclusions, other refinements have been made relating to the concept of income for tax purposes.

REFINEMENTS OF THE
GROSS INCOME DEFINITION

In the early years of the Federal income tax, the courts were often confronted with the problem of determining whether or not a particular item should be considered taxable. In rendering their verdicts, the judiciary established numerous precedents that served to shape and refine the notion of income. Due to their significance, some of the principles established by these early court decisions have since been given statutory effect; that is, the rule evolving from the decision was

---

[7]   55-1 USTC ¶9308, 47 AFTR 162, 348 U.S. 426 (USSC, 1955).

[8]   *Ibid.*

[9]   For an excellent discussion of the concept of income and the notion of a comprehensive tax base see Boris Bittker, "A Comprehensive Tax Base as a Goal of Income Tax Reform," 80 *Harvard Law Review* 925 (1967).

subsequently enacted as part of the law, or codified. Other court rulings have been incorporated into the Regulations either directly or by way of reference. Several of these rulings, however, have not found their way into the Code or Regulations. Nevertheless, they provide authoritative guidance for the determination of taxable income. This section examines three major principles that are relevant to the income concept. These concern

1. *Form of Benefit.* Must income be realized in a particular form, such as cash, before it becomes taxable?

2. *Return of Capital.* Does gross income mean gross receipts or net gain after allowance for a tax-free recovery of the taxpayer's capital investment?

3. *Indirect Economic Benefits.* Are benefits provided by an employer (such as a company car) taxable where they are not intended as compensation?

FORM-OF-BENEFIT PRINCIPLE

Many taxpayers erroneously believe that income need be reported only when cash is received. The Regulations clearly state, however, that gross income includes income realized in any form.[10] Thus, income is not limited to receipts of cash but also extends to receipts of property, services, and *any other economic benefits*. For example, taxpayers may realize income when their debts are canceled or they purchase property at a price less than its fair market value—a so-called *bargain purchase*. In situations where income is received in a form other than cash, a cash-equivalent approach is adopted.[11] Under this method, the measure of income is its fair market value at the time of receipt.

> **Example 2.** A dentist performed a root-canal for a plumber in exchange for some repair work. Both the dentist and the plumber recognize income equal to the fair market value of the services received. Barter transactions of this nature are subject to taxation.

> **Example 3.** Taxpayer A owed B $10,000, evidenced by a note payable due in six months. If B allows A to cancel the note for a payment of $9,000, A must normally recognize gross income of $1,000.

---

[10] Reg. § 1.61-1(a).   [11] Reg. § 1.446-1(a)(3).

RETURN OF CAPITAL DOCTRINE

The return of capital doctrine is best illustrated by a simple loan transaction. When a taxpayer lends money and it is later repaid, no income is recognized since the repayment represents merely a *return of capital* to the taxpayer. Although there is no statutory provision to this effect, it is a well-recognized rule. However, any interest on the loan that is paid to the taxpayer would be income.

The application of the return of capital doctrine is not limited to loans, however. One of the first refinements made to the income concept concerned the use of the return of capital principle to determine the income from a sale of property. In 1916 the Supreme Court held that the total proceeds received on a sale were not to be treated as income.[12] Rather, the portion of the proceeds representing the taxpayer's capital (i.e., adjusted basis) could be recovered tax free. Thus, it is the return of capital doctrine that allows the taxpayer to determine the income upon a sale or disposition of property by reducing the amount realized (cash + the fair market value of other receipts such as property) by the adjusted basis of the property. Using this approach—now contained in § 1001(a)—the taxpayer's income on dispositions of property is limited to the *gain* realized.

> **Example 4.** R sold XYZ stock for $10,000. He purchased the stock for $6,000. R's realized gain is $4,000 ($10,000 amount realized − $6,000 adjusted basis) rather than the gross amount of the sales price, $10,000, since the return of capital doctrine permits him to recover his $6,000 investment tax free.

The return of capital doctrine also stands for the important proposition that gross income is not the same as gross receipts. This is reflected in Regulations, which provide that in the manufacturing, merchandising, or mining business, *gross income* means total sales less costs of goods sold.[13]

Damages. Another situation where the return of capital doctrine may have application concerns amounts awarded for injury inflicted upon the taxpayer. Section 104, discussed in the following chapter, specifically excludes from income the amount of any damages awarded for personal injury on the grounds that the amount received represents a return of the personal capital destroyed. For this same reason, early rulings and decisions held that compensatory damages awarded for such personal wrongs as breach of contract to marry, slander and libel, and alienation of affection are nontaxable.[14] In many cases, amounts are also awarded to penalize the party responsible for the wrongdoing. These

---

[12] *Doyle v. Mitchell Bros.*, 1 USTC ¶17, 3 AFTR 2979, 247 U.S. 179 (USSC, 1918). See also, *Southern Pacific Company v. Lowe*, 1 USTC ¶19, 247, 3 AFTR 2989, 247 U.S. 330 (USSC, 1918).

[13] Reg. § 1.61-3(a).

[14] For example, see *C.A. Hawkins*, 6 B.T.A. 1023 (1927); *L. McDonald*, 9 B.T.A. 1340 (1930); and Rev. Rul. 74-77, 1974-1 C.B. 33.

so-called punitive damages are fully taxable.[15]   Similarly, where the damages awarded represent reimbursement for lost profits, the amounts are considered taxable since they are merely substitutions for income.[16]

Example 5.   After ten consecutive losing seasons as head football coach at Trample University, Coach F was fired. Shortly thereafter, F developed an ulcer, which forced him to have surgery. It was subsequently determined that the operation had been improperly performed. F sued the university for lost wages and the court awarded him $25,000. The $25,000 is fully taxable since it represents a substitution of income. F also sued the surgeon for $200,000 for malpractice and won. The $200,000 is not taxable since it represents a return of capital.

Example 6.   G, an aging Hollywood starlet, sued a national gossip publication for malicious and defamatory remarks concerning how she made her way to the top. The suit demanded $800,000 for compensatory damages and $200,000 for punitive damages. The court only awarded her $500,000. In absence of any court allocation, the amount representing punitive damages, $100,000, is taxable, whereas the amount representing compensatory damages, $400,000, is nontaxable. These amounts were determined as follows:

$$\frac{\$200,000}{\$200,000 + \$800,000} \times \$500,000 = \$100,000 \text{ taxable}$$

$$\frac{\$800,000}{\$200,000 + \$800,000} \times \$500,000 = \$400,000 \text{ nontaxable}$$

Damages awarded to businesses are generally subject to the same tests applied to individuals. Awards or settlements for antitrust violations or patent infringements are examples of substitutions for income and thus are taxable. This is true for both actual and punitive damages. Compensation for damages to property are taxable to the extent that amounts received exceed the adjusted basis of the assets. Where the award is for damages to the goodwill of the business, the entire amount is usually taxable since the taxpayer normally does not have any recoverable basis in the goodwill.[17]

Example 7.   Business Computer Corporation sued PC Clones Inc. for infringing on certain patented aspects of computers they manufactured. The court awarded BCC $200,000. This amount is fully taxable since it represents lost profits.

[15]   Rev. Rul. 85-98, 1985-2 C.B. 51 and Rev. Rul. 58-418, 1958-2 C.B. 18.

[16]   *Phoenix Coal Co. v. Comm.,* 56-1 USTC ¶9366, 49 AFTR 445, 231 F.2d 420 (CA-2, 1956).

[17]   *Raytheon Production Corp. v. Comm.,* 44-2 USTC ¶9424, 32 AFTR 1155, 144 F.2d 100 (CA-1, 1944).

Example 8. M left her car running and ran inside the bank to make a deposit. When she came back, she stopped in shock as she watched her car plunge through the front of a furniture store. The furniture store ultimately received $50,000 in damages for property for which it had a basis of $35,000. The store realized a gain of $15,000. This gain must be recognized unless certain special rules concerning involuntary conversions discussed in Chapter 13 are followed.

Other Considerations. The scope of the return of capital doctrine extends beyond situations involving damages and simple sales transactions. Numerous Code sections are grounded on this principle, and often contain detailed rules for ascertaining how a receipt should be apportioned between capital and income. For example, amounts received under a life insurance policy are not taxable on the theory that the proceeds—at least in part—represent a return of the taxpayer's premium payments.[18] Similarly, where the taxpayer purchases an annuity (i.e., an investment which makes a series of payments to the investor in the future), the return of capital doctrine provides that each payment is in part a tax-free return of capital.[19] In addition, somewhat intricate provisions exist to determine whether a corporate distribution represents a distribution of earnings (i.e., a dividend) or a tax-free return of the taxpayer's investment.[20] The special rules governing life insurance, annuities, and dividends are covered in detail in Chapter 6.

INDIRECT ECONOMIC BENEFITS

Another refinement to the otherwise all-inclusive definition of gross income concerns certain benefits provided by employers for employees. Early rulings and decisions exempted those benefits conferred to employees that did not represent compensation and were provided for the convenience of the employer. For example, in 1919, the IRS ruled that lodging furnished seamen aboard ship was not taxable.[21] Similarly, in 1925, the Court of Claims held that the value of quarters provided an Army officer was not includible in income.[22] Explanations offered for exempting the lodging from income emphasized that the employee was granted the benefit solely because the employer's business could not function properly unless an employee was furnished that benefit on the employer's premises. In addition, it was observed that the benefits were not designed as a form of compensation for the employee, but rather were an outgrowth of business necessity. These early holdings established the view that certain benefits

---

[18] § 101.

[19] § 72.

[20] §§ 301 and 316. See Chapter 20 for coverage of these provisions.

[21] O.D. 265, 1 C.B. 71 (1919).

[22] *Jones v. U.S.*, 1 USTC ¶129, 5 AFTR 5297, 60 Ct.Cls. 552 (1925). Section 119, discussed in Chapter 6, currently provides specific rules that must be satisfied before meals and lodging may be excluded.

an employee receives indirectly from his or her employer are nontaxable. Recent decisions indicate that before the benefit may be excluded, the employee must demonstrate that the benefit served a business purpose of the employer other than to compensate the employee.[23]

> **Example 9.** In the following situations an employee is permitted to exclude the benefit received under the rationale discussed above.
>
> 1. An employer provides the employee with a place to work and supplies tools and machinery with which to do the work. Similarly, an employee is not taxed when his or her secretary types a letter.
>
> 2. An employer provides tuition-free, American-style schools for its overseas employees.
>
> 3. An employer provides an executive with protection in response to threats made by terrorists.
>
> 4. An employer requires its employees to attend a convention held in a resort in Florida and pays the travel costs to the employees.
>
> 5. An employee uses a company car to travel from the office to business appointments.

It is often difficult to determine whether a particular benefit represents compensation or, alternatively, serves the business needs of the employer. For example, free parking places and similar fringe benefits provided by an employer could arguably fall into either category, depending upon the circumstances. After many years of controversy concerning the taxation of fringe benefits, Congress addressed the problem in 1984. To emphasize that fringe benefits are taxable, Congress modified the listing of typical income items found in § 61 to specifically include "fringe benefits and similar items." However, several exceptions exempting certain benefits still exist. These exceptions are discussed in Chapter 6 concerning exclusions.

REPORTING INCOME:
TAX ACCOUNTING METHODS

Once the taxpayer has realized an item of taxable income, he or she must determine *when* the income should be reported. This determination, however, requires an understanding of the nature of accounting periods and accounting methods that may be used for tax purposes. This section examines some of the fundamental rules of tax accounting and how they govern the timing of income recognition.

---

[23] *George D. Patterson v. Thomas*, 61-1 USTC ¶9310, 7 AFTR2d 862, 289 F.2d 108 (CA-2, 1960).

ACCOUNTING PERIODS

Taxable income is usually computed on the basis of an annual accounting period commonly known as the taxable year.[24] There are two types of taxable years: a calendar year and a fiscal year. A calendar year is a 12-month period ending on December 31, whereas a fiscal year generally is any period of 12 months ending on the last day of any month other than December.[25] Any taxpayer may use a calendar year. Fiscal years, however, may be used only by taxpayers who maintain adequate books and records. A taxpayer filing his or her *first* return may adopt either a calendar year or a fiscal year without IRS consent. After adoption, however, any change does require IRS consent.[26]

Income from Partnerships, S Corporations, Fiduciaries. Reporting income derived from an interest in a partnership, an S corporation, or an estate or trust presents a special problem. As explained in Chapter 3, income realized by a partnership or an S corporation is not taxable to either of these because they are not treated as separate taxable entities. Rather, the partnership or S corporation merely serves as a conduit through which the income flows. Consequently, partners or S shareholders report their distributive shares of the entity's income in their taxable year within which (or with which) the partnership or S corporation tax year ends. Partners or S shareholders must report their share of the income regardless of the amounts distributed to them.

> **Example 10.** DEF Company, a fiscal year taxpayer, is a partnership owned equally by D, E, and F. For the taxable year ending September 30, 1991, the company had net income of $90,000. During the 12-month period ending on September 30, 1991, D withdrew $20,000 from his capital account. For his year ending December 31, 1991, D must report his share of partnership income, $30,000 ($1/3$ of $90,000), even though he only received a distribution of $20,000. Note that any income earned by the partnership from October 1991 through December 1991 is not reported until D files his 1992 tax return, which is normally due on April 15, 1993.

Income realized by a trust or an estate is generally taxed to the beneficiaries to the extent it is actually distributed or required to be distributed. Income that is not taxed to the beneficiaries is taxed to the estate or trust.

Limitation on Fiscal Years. One effect of allowing fiscal years for reporting is to enable certain taxpayers to *defer* the taxation of income. For instance, in *Example 10* above, the election by the partnership to use a fiscal year creates an

---

[24] § 441(a) and (b).

[25] Reg. § 1.441-1(d) and (e). The taxpayer may elect to end the tax year on a particular day of the week rather than a date, resulting in a tax year that varies in length between 52 and 53 weeks. See Reg. § 1.441-2.

[26] A request for a change is made on Form 1128. The initial selection of, or a change in, tax year may result in a short tax year, in which case the tax may have to be computed on an annualized basis. See §§ 442 and 443.

opportunity for D. Note that D's share of the partnership's income for October 1991 through December 1991 is not reported until D files his 1992 tax return, which is normally filed on April 15, 1993. A small corporation that primarily provides personal services could obtain a similar deferral.

> **Example 11.** G&H Inc., a law firm, is a regular C corporation owned by two attorneys, G and H. The corporation reports using a fiscal year ending on January 31. During 1991, the corporation paid G and H small salaries. Just before the close of its taxable year ending January 31, 1992, the corporation paid a bonus to G and H equal to its taxable income. By deducting the bonus, the corporation reports no income for its taxable year ending January 31, 1992, and G and H defer reporting the bonus until they file their 1992 tax return on April 15, 1993.

In 1986, Congress felt that the use of fiscal years to create deferral of income as shown above was improper. As a result, provisions were enacted that restrict the use of fiscal years by partnerships, S corporations, and so-called personal service corporations (i.e., corporations where the principal activity is the performance of services, substantially all of which are performed by employees who are also the owners of the business). Although certain exceptions enable these entities to use a fiscal year on a limited basis, as a general rule, these taxpayers normally must use the calendar year.[27]

Annual Accounting and Progressive Rates. The use of an annual accounting period in combination with other features of the taxation process causes numerous difficulties. For example, consider the effect of the tax system's use of both an annual accounting period and a progressive tax rate structure. Each year the taxpayer computes his or her taxable income for that period and applies a progressive rate structure to the income of that year. If income varies from one year to the next, taxes paid on the *total* income of those two years are likely to exceed the total taxes that would have resulted had the taxpayer earned the income equally each year.

> **Example 12.** Taxpayer R is a salesman whose income is derived solely from commissions. Taxpayer S earns a salary. Both taxpayers are single. In 19X1 and 19X2 R's taxable income was $83,200 and $16,800, respectively, while S had taxable income of $50,000 each year. The tax effect on R and S (rounded to the nearest dollar and using 1991 tax rates) is as follows:

	R		S	
	Taxable Income	Tax	Taxable Income	Tax
19X1	$ 83,200	$21,668	$ 50,000	$11,375
19X2	16,800	2,520	50,000	11,375
Total	$100,000	$24,188	$100,000	$22,750

---

[27] §§ 441(i), 444, 706(b), and 1378.

Note that although R and S have the same total income of $100,000 for the two year period, R's total tax bill of $24,188 exceeds S's bill of $22,750 by $1,438.

As the above example demonstrates, the use of an annual accounting period may create inequities. In this particular case, R could reduce his tax bite if he could defer some of his income from one year to the next so as to split his income between years as equally as possible. In other cases, Congress has responded by enacting special provisions. For example, where a taxpayer has a loss during the year, the net operating loss rules allow the taxpayer to utilize the loss by permitting it to be carried back or forward to profitable years.[28] Without these carryback and carryover provisions, the taxpayer would receive no benefit from any losses realized.

ACCOUNTING METHODS

Once the tax year is identified, the taxpayer must determine in which period a transaction is to be reported. The year in which a particular item becomes part of the tax calculation is not a trivial matter. The time of recognition can make a substantial difference in the taxpayer's total tax liability not only because of the time value of money but also because other changes may occur from year to year. For instance, tax rates may go up or down from one year to the next. Such change does not necessarily take an act of Congress. A taxpayer may simply marry, divorce, incorporate, or change from a taxable to tax-exempt entity. In such case, deferral of income to the low-rate year and acceleration of deductions to the high-rate year could produce significant savings. Similarly, Congress may completely revise the treatment of an item. For example, in 1986 Congress eliminated the deduction for sales tax, increased the limitation on deductible medical expenses, and also axed the favorable treatment for long-term capital gains. These and other similar changes make the time of reporting critical.

The rules that determine when a particular item is reported are generally referred to as accounting methods. The Code identifies four permissible methods of accounting:[29]

1. The cash receipts and disbursements method

2. The accrual method

3. Any other method permitted by the Code (e.g., a method for a specific situation such as the completed contract method or the use of LIFO to value inventories)[30]

4. Any combination of the three methods above permitted by the Regulations

---

[28] § 172. See Chapter 8 for a discussion of the net operating loss rules.

[29] § 446(c).

[30] Reg. § 1.446-1(c)(1)(iii).

The term "accounting method" is not limited to the overall method of accounting used by the taxpayer (e.g., the cash or accrual method). It generally includes the treatment of *any particular item* if such treatment affects *when* the item will be reported. For example, the use of LIFO to value inventories would be considered an accounting method since the use of this method determines when the cost of a product will become part of costs of goods sold.

It should be emphasized that the taxpayer is not required to adopt one overall method of accounting. For example, a taxpayer with inventories must use the accrual method to account for inventories and related sales. However, the same taxpayer could use the cash method to report interest income or other items. This approach (referred to as the *hybrid method*) is completely acceptable as long as the taxpayer applies the same methods consistently.

Taxpayers are generally allowed to select the methods of accounting they wish to use. In all cases, however, the IRS has the right to determine if the method used *clearly reflects income*, and, if not, to make the necessary adjustments.[31] For example, assume that each year a taxpayer changes the way it computes the amount of overhead that it capitalizes as part of inventory (e.g., on the basis of direct labor hours one year, machine hours the next). In such case, the IRS might require the taxpayer to use one method consistently so that income would not be distorted from year to year but would be clearly reflected.

Tax Methods vs. Financial Accounting Methods. At first glance, many people—particularly accountants—would no doubt conclude that a method of accounting that conforms with generally accepted accounting principles (GAAP) would be regarded as clearly reflecting income.[32] Although this is ordinarily true, it is not always the case.[33] Conflicts sometimes exist because the objectives of the income tax system differ from that of financial accounting. The primary goal of financial accounting is to provide useful information to management, shareholders, creditors, and other interested parties. In contrast, the goal of the income tax system is to ensure that revenues are fairly collected. Due to these different goals, the tax law may disregard fundamental accounting principles. Perhaps the most obvious example can be found in the tax law's allowance of the cash method of accounting. Despite its failure to properly match revenues and expenses, the cash method is normally tolerated because from an administrative view it is simple and objective. Such administrative concerns often dictate a different approach for tax purposes. For example, an accrual basis taxpayer is often required to report prepaid income when received rather than when earned. Although this practice violates the matching principle, it ensures that the tax is imposed when the taxpayer has the cash to pay it.

[31] § 446(b).

[32] Reg. § 1.446-1(a)(2).

[33] For an excellent example, see *Thor Power Tool Co.*, 79-1 USTC ¶9139, 43 AFTR2d 79-362, 439 U.S. 522 (USSC, 1979).

The operation of differing objectives can also be seen in the use of estimates. One of the major responsibilities of financial accountants is to ensure that financial statement users are not misled. This demand normally encourages accountants to be conservative, which in turn may cause them to understate rather than overstate income. Although the government does not want taxpayers to overstate income, it certainly does not want to endorse principles that would tend toward understatement. Thus, the tax law generally does not allow taxpayers to estimate future expenses such as bad debts or warranty costs and deduct them currently, as is the case with financial accounting. Instead, the deduction is allowed only when there is objective evidence that a cost has been incurred. In general, the government frowns on estimates of expenses, presumably because taxpayers would tend to overstate them.

Reporting of prepaid income and the treatment of estimated expenses are just two examples of where financial accounting principles deviate from tax accounting. The key point to recognize is that a particular item may be treated one way for financial accounting purposes and another way for tax purposes. As a practical matter, this may mean that two sets of books are maintained, or what is perhaps more likely, one set based on financial accounting principles to which adjustments must be made to arrive at taxable income.

CASH METHOD OF ACCOUNTING

General Rule. Virtually all individuals—as well as many corporations, partnerships, trusts, and estates—use the cash method of accounting. Its prevalence is no doubt attributable to the fact that it is easy to use. Under the cash method, taxpayers simply report items of income and deduction in the year in which they are received or paid.[34] In effect, the cash method allows taxpayers merely to refer to their checkbooks to determine taxable income.

In using the cash method, items of income need not be in the form of cash but need only be capable of valuation in terms of money. Under this rule, sometimes termed the *cash equivalent doctrine,* the taxpayer reports income when the equivalent of cash is received.[35] Thus, where property or services are received, the fair market value of these items serves as the measure of income.

Due to the cash equivalent doctrine, reporting of income arising from notes and accounts receivable differs. Notes received by a cash basis taxpayer are usually considered property and hence constitute income equal to the value of the note.[36] Where a promise to pay is *not* evidenced by a note (e.g., credit sales resulting in accounts receivable), no income is recognized by a cash basis taxpayer until payment is received.[37] This treatment results because unsupported promises to pay normally are not considered as having a fair market value.

---

[34]   Reg. § 1.446-1(c)(1)(i).

[35]   Reg. § 1.446-1(a)(3).

[36]   *A.W. Wolfson,* 1 B.T.A. 538 (1925).

[37]   *Bedell v. Comm.,* 1 USTC ¶359, 7 AFTR 8469, 30 F.2d 622 (CA-2, 1929).

Constructive Receipt Doctrine. As may have been observed, taxpayers using the cash method of accounting appear to have substantial control over income recognition in that they may control the timing of the actual receipt of cash. If the requirement calling for *actual* receipt were strictly adhered to, the cash basis taxpayer could easily frustrate the purpose of progressive taxation. For example, taxpayers could select the year with the lowest tax rate and simply cash their salary or dividend checks or redeem their interest coupons in that year. To curtail this practice, the doctrine of constructive receipt was developed. Under this principle, a taxpayer is *deemed* to have received income even though such income has not actually been received. It should be noted that there is no corresponding doctrine for deductions (i.e., there is no constructive payment doctrine).

The constructive receipt doctrine is currently expressed in Regulation § 1.451-2(a) as follows:

> Income, although not actually reduced to the taxpayer's possession, is constructively received by him in the taxable year in which it is credited to his account, set apart for him or otherwise made available so that he could have drawn upon it during the taxable year if notice of intention to withdraw had been given. However, income is not constructively received if the taxpayer's control of its receipt is subject to substantial limitations or restrictions.

As the Regulation suggests, the taxpayer is treated as having received income where three conditions are satisfied:

1. The taxpayer has control over the amount without substantial limitations and restrictions

2. The amount has been set aside or credited to the taxpayer's account

3. The funds are available for payment by the payer (i.e., the payer's ability to make payment must be considered)

Some of the common situations to which the rule is applied are illustrated in the following examples.

Example 13. B refereed a football game on Saturday night, December 31, 1991 and did not receive the check for his services until after the banks had closed. He cashed the check on January 3, 1992. B must report the income in 1991. In the case of a check, a taxpayer is deemed to have received payment in the year the check is received rather than when it is cashed.[38]

Example 14. T mailed a check on December 29, 1991 to S, which S received in January, 1992. S is not in constructive receipt of the check since it was not available to him for his immediate use and enjoyment. However, if S requested that T mail him the check so that he receive it in 1992, or if S could have received the check by merely appearing in person and claiming it, S would be deemed to have received the payment in 1991.

---

[38]   *C. F. Kahler,* 18 T.C. 31 (1952).

Example 15.   When G made a deposit on January 15, 1992, the bank updated her passbook to show that $200 of interest was credited to her account for the last quarter of 1991. G withdrew the interest on January 31. G must report the interest in 1991. Interest credited to the taxpayer's account is taxable when credited, regardless of whether it is in the taxpayer's possession, assuming that it may be withdrawn.[39]

Example 16.   B Corporation mailed dividend checks dated December 20 on December 28, 1991. R, a shareholder in B, received her check on January 4, 1992. R reports the dividend income in 1992 as long as the payer customarily pays dividends by mail so that the shareholder receives it after the end of the year.[40]

Example 17.   R's secretary received several checks for services that R had performed. Payments received by a taxpayer's agent are considered constructively received by the taxpayer.[41]

Example 18.   A taxpayer who agrees not to cash a check until authorized by the payer is not considered to have constructively received it where the payer does not have sufficient funds in the bank to cover the check.[42]

The tax treatment of many deferred compensation arrangements between employers and employees is tied to the constructive receipt doctrine. The Service has ruled that where the taxpayer has entered into a deferral agreement *before* the services are performed, such income is not considered received.[43] This is true even though the taxpayer has control over whether the payments are to be made currently or are to be deferred. The Service's conclusion rests on the principle that once the employee has made the agreement, he or she does not have the right to receive currently the deferred amounts. This presumes, however, that the taxpayer has not received cash equivalents such as notes and that the payments are not secured in any fashion. Similarly, the taxpayer cannot be protected through some type of escrow or trust account to which funds are transferred since such amounts may be treated as having been set aside for withdrawal by the taxpayer.

---

[39] Reg. § 1.451-2(b).

[40] *Ibid.; S.L. Avery,* 4 USTC ¶1277, 13 AFTR 1168, 292 U.S. 210 (USSC, 1934). See also *H.B. McEuen v. Comm.,* 52-1 USTC ¶9281, 41 AFTR 1169, 196 F.2d 127 (CA-5, 1952).

[41] *T. Watson,* 2 TCM 863 (1943).

[42] *A.V. Johnston,* 23 TCM 2003, T.C. Memo 1964-323.

[43] Rev. Rul. 60-31, 1960-1 C.B. 174. For further discussion, see Chapter 18.

Example 19. F Corporation employs R as a major league baseball player. They enter into a contractual arrangement whereby F promises to pay R $500,000 this year and $100,000 annually for five years after he retires. R will not be treated as having constructively received the deferred payments when the employment contract is signed because he has no legally enforceable right to demand payment currently. In addition, R has not received a negotiable note but merely an unsecured promise to pay.

Limitations on the Use of the Cash Method. As a method of accounting, the cash method's principal advantage lies in its simplicity. On other counts, however, the cash method scores poorly, ranking a distant second to the accrual method. From an accounting perspective, the cash method is entirely inappropriate since income and expense are recognized without regard to the taxable year in which the economic events responsible for the income or expense actually occur. Similarly, when some parties to a transaction use different methods of accounting, there may be a mismatching of income and deductions. For example, an accrual basis corporation could accrue expenses payable to a cash basis individual. In such case, the corporation could obtain deductions without ever having to make a disbursement and, moreover, without the individual taxpayer recognizing any offsetting income.

While the above are clearly shortcomings, the major flaw found in the cash method is that it is easily abused. Taxpayers have often secured benefits by merely timing their transactions appropriately: recognizing income in one year, deductions in the next, or what is more likely, deductions in years in which the taxpayer is in a high tax bracket and income in years in which the taxpayer is in a low tax bracket.

To attack these problems, Congress has limited the use of the cash method of accounting. The following entities are normally prohibited from using the cash method:[44]

1. Regular C corporations

2. Partnerships that have regular C corporations as partners (other than certain personal service corporations described below)

3. *Tax shelters,* generally defined as any enterprise (other than a regular C corporation) in which interests have been offered for sale in any offering required to be registered under Federal or State security agencies

---

[44] § 448(a).

Despite these general restrictions, Congress believed that the simplicity of the cash method justified its continued use in certain instances. For example, Congress felt that it would be costly for small businesses to switch to the accrual method. Similarly, it recognized that the accrual method would create undue complexity for farming businesses if such a method were required to account for growing crops and livestock. In addition, Congress believed that personal service corporations, which have traditionally used the cash method, should be allowed to continue their use. Accordingly, the following entities are allowed to use the cash method.[45]

1. Any corporation or partnership whose annual *gross receipts* for *all* preceding years do not exceed $5 million. This test is satisfied for any prior year only if the average annual gross receipts for the three-year period ending with such year does not exceed $5 million. Once this average *exceeds* $5 million, the corporation cannot use the cash method for the following year.

2. Certain farming businesses.

3. Qualified personal service corporations. A regular C corporation is qualified if substantially all of the activities consist of performing services in the fields of health, law, engineering, architecture, accounting, actuarial science, performing arts, or consulting, *and* at least 95 percent of its stock is held by the employees who are providing the services. The latter test is considered satisfied if the stock is owned by a retired employee or by the estate or heirs of a deceased employee.

Example 20. G's Grocery, a regular C corporation, started business in 19X1. Since that time it has had annual gross receipts as follows:

Year	Gross Receipts	Average Annual Gross Receipts*
19X1	$ 4,000,000	$4,000,000
19X2	2,000,000	3,000,000
19X3	6,000,000	4,000,000
19X4	10,000,000	6,000,000

* Current + Prior two years / 3 (or if less, years in existence)

It initially adopted the cash method in 19X1. It was able to use the cash method through 19X4 because the average annual gross receipts for all prior years did not exceed $5 million. Note that although its gross receipts were $6,000,000 in 19X3, its *average annual* gross receipts for that year

[45] § 448(b).

were only \$4,000,000 [(\$4,000,000 + \$2,000,000 + \$6,000,000) ÷ 3]. Consequently, the cash method could be used for 19X4. It will be denied use of the cash method for 19X5 since the average annual gross receipts for 19X4 exceed \$5 million [(\$2,000,000 + \$6,000,000 + \$10,000,000) ÷ 3 = \$6,000,000].

It should be noted that the above exceptions do not apply to tax shelters. Any enterprise considered a tax shelter must use the accrual method.

ACCRUAL METHOD OF ACCOUNTING

Taxpayers using the accrual method of accounting report income in the year in which it is considered earned under the so-called *all events test*. Under this test, income is earned when all the events have occurred that fix the right to receive such income and the amount of income can be determined with reasonable accuracy.[46] As the all events test indicates, income generally accrues only if the taxpayer has an unconditional right to receive the income. This right normally arises when the title to the property passes to the buyer.[47] With sales of inventory, however, taxpayers may accrue income when the goods are shipped, when the product is delivered or accepted, or when title passes, as long as the method is consistently used.[48]

The accrual method *must* be used in accounting for sales, purchases, and inventories if inventories are an income-producing factor. However, the taxpayer who must use the accrual method in this instance may still account for other items of income and expense using the cash method. The accrual method, as noted earlier, must be used by regular C corporations and partnerships with C corporations as partners unless one of several exceptions is satisfied.

There are several special rules relating to the accrual method of accounting that cause variations in the normal scheme. For example, dividends would normally accrue under the all events test on the date of record. An exception exists, however, so that dividends are reported when received.[49] In addition to this exception, others exist that are discussed later in this chapter.

CHANGES IN ACCOUNTING METHODS

Taxpayers are initially given great freedom in the methods of accounting they may use. However, once a particular method has been adopted (e.g., when it is first used to account for an item), it may not be changed unless consent is granted by the IRS.[50] Taxpayers seeking a change must apply for permission

---

46 Reg. § 1.451-1(a).

47 *Lucas v. North Texas Lumber Co.*, 2 USTC ¶484, 8 AFTR 10276, 281 U.S. 11 (USSC, 1929).

48 Reg. § 1.446-1(c)(1)(ii).

49 Reg. § 1.451-2(b), *Tar Products Corp. v. Comm.*, 42-2 USTC ¶9662, 29 AFTR 1190, 130 F.2d 866 (CA-3, 1942).

50 § 446(f) authorizes the IRS to impose penalties if consent is not secured.

by filing Form 3115, Application for Change in Accounting Method, within 180 days of the beginning of the tax year when the change is to become effective. The IRS does not rubber-stamp these requests. Permission is granted only if the taxpayer is willing to make any adjustments required by the IRS. Under Code § 481, the IRS is authorized to require adjustments if a change in method would result in the omission of income or the duplication of deductions.

> **Example 21.** T, Inc. operates a computer consulting company. It has always used the cash method to account for its income from services. In 1991, it decided that it should switch to the accrual method. At the end of 1990, T's outstanding receivables were $10,000. If T were allowed to switch to the accrual method and no adjustment were required, the $10,000 would escape taxation. The $10,000 would not be taxed in 1990 since T was on the cash basis in that year and no collections were made. Similarly, the $10,000 would not be taxed in 1991 because T is on the accrual method in that year and the income did not accrue in 1991 but rather 1990. Thus, without an adjustment, the $10,000 of income would be omitted from both the 1990 and 1991 returns, never to be taxed.

Example 21 illustrates why the law requires taxpayers who wish to change to agree to an adjustment. Prior to 1954, however, taxpayers were normally not required to make an adjustment for duplications or omissions. For this reason, if the *IRS* requires the taxpayer to change accounting methods, any portion of the adjustment attributable to years prior to 1954 is disregarded. In contrast, if the taxpayer voluntarily changes an accounting method, any portion attributable to years before 1954 must be taken into account.[51]

Accounting for the Adjustment. Taxpayers are normally required to report the entire adjustment in the year of the change and pay any additional tax due (or receive a refund).[52] In certain situations, this may create a severe hardship for the taxpayer (e.g., the required inclusion of several years' income in a single year). However, § 481(c) allows the IRS to alter this approach. The IRS has used this authority to develop a system that encourages taxpayers to switch from a clearly erroneous method they may be using to a correct method.[53] For this purpose, a clearly erroneous method—a so-called *Category A method*—is a method not permitted by the Code, Regulations, or Supreme Court decision. For example, if the taxpayer failed to use the accrual method to account for inventories or did not use the uniform capitalization rules to account for indirect costs, the methods that were used would be considered clearly erroneous. The system devised by the IRS to govern changes also contains rules for changes from one permissible method of accounting—a *Category B method*—to another permissible method.

---

[51] § 481(a).

[52] *Ibid.*

[53] Rev. Proc. 84-74, 1984-2 C.B. 736.

Under the procedures prescribed by the IRS, the treatment of the adjustment depends on who initiates the adjustment (a voluntary change by the taxpayer or an involuntary change required by the IRS) and the type of adjustment (Category A, clearly erroneous, or Category B, permissible). Taxpayers who voluntarily change from a Category A method are treated far more favorably than those who are forced to change by the IRS as part of an audit proceeding. If the IRS requires the taxpayer to change from a Category A method, the entire adjustment is taken into account in the year of the change. In contrast, if the taxpayer voluntarily changes from a Category A method to a correct method of accounting, a positive adjustment is normally spread over three years (the year of the change and the following two years) and a negative adjustment is brought into income entirely in the year of change. When the change involves a Category B method, the taxpayer is usually allowed to spread the adjustment over six years, the year of the change and the following five years. Special rules may apply, however.

> **Example 22.**   J has operated a small hardware store as a sole proprietorship since 1970. This year the IRS audited J's 1988 tax return and determined that J had failed to use the accrual method of accounting for inventories. Instead, J had expensed all of his inventory as it was acquired. Consequently, the IRS required J to change his method of accounting. Based on a physical count and valuation of his inventory, the IRS determined that J had understated his income in prior years by $300,000. Because the change was initiated by the IRS and involved a Category A (i.e., clearly erroneous) method, J must pay all of the tax attributable to the $300,000 adjustment this year.[54] Had J voluntarily changed to the proper method, he would have been entitled to a forward spread of three years, reporting $100,000 in each of 1988, 1989, and 1990. By so doing, he would have deferred the tax to 1988, 1989, and 1990.

> **Example 23.**   During 1990, R asked and obtained permission to change from the cash method to the accrual method. This change resulted in a positive income adjustment of $60,000. Because this is a Category B method and was initiated by the taxpayer, R could spread the $60,000 of income over six years, $10,000 in 1990 and $10,000 in each of the following five years.

Changes in accounting method are not to be confused with correction of errors. Errors such as mathematical mistakes or the improper calculation of a deduction or credit can be corrected by the taxpayer without permission of the IRS by simply filing an amended return. Alternatively, the IRS may discover the mistake and require the taxpayer to make a correction. However, if the statute of limitations has run on a return containing an error, no correction can be made. In these cases, the taxpayer's income is forever over- or understated, as the case may be.

---

[54]   In computing the tax that must be paid, § 482(b) provides special rules.

ACCOUNTING FOR INCOME:
SPECIAL CONSIDERATIONS

CLAIM OF RIGHT DOCTRINE

Occasionally income may be received before the taxpayer's rights to such income have been clearly established. The tax difficulty posed in these instances concerns whether the taxpayer should report the income currently or wait until the proper claims to the income have been identified. For these situations, the courts have established a rule of law termed the *claim of right doctrine*. Under this rule, if a taxpayer actually or constructively *receives* income under a claim of right (i.e., he claims the income is rightfully his) and such income is not restricted in use, it must be included in gross income.[55] In other words, earnings received must be included in income if the taxpayer has an *unrestricted claim*, notwithstanding the possibility that the income may be subsequently relinquished if the taxpayer's claim is later denied.

> **Example 24.** Television station WXYZ received $100,000 from KLM Company to air the firm's commercials during a local talk show in the month of December. During this month, the ratings dropped sharply when the star of the show quit. Shortly thereafter, KLM contacted the station, indicating that it wanted to discontinue its sponsorship and requesting return of $75,000 of the payment. In view of their interpretation of the agreement, the station continued to air the firm's commercials and retained the $100,000. KLM brought suit to recover the $75,000. Under the claim of right doctrine, WXYZ must include the entire $100,000 in income even though it may have to repay the amount or a portion thereof to KLM. The amount is included because WXYZ received the money and could use the amount without restriction.

The claim of right doctrine applies to both cash and accrual basis taxpayers. As previously discussed, income is usually reported by an accrual basis taxpayer only when all the events have occurred that fix the taxpayer's right to receive such income. Hence, in the case of contested income, the taxpayer's rights to such amounts have not been fixed, and under the all events test he or she would not report it. The claim of right doctrine, however, carves out an exception to this rule for contested income the taxpayer has *received*. An accrual basis taxpayer who *receives* contested income under a claim of right without restrictions on its use must report the amount in income even though his or her rights to the income have not been fixed.[56] Alternatively, if the accrual basis taxpayer has *not received* the contested income, it will not be included because his or her rights thereto have not been fixed.[57] Thus, an *accrual basis* taxpayer's reporting of contested income depends on whether or not the taxpayer has received it.

---

[55] *North American Oil Consolidated v. Burnet,* 3 USTC ¶943, 11 AFTR 16, 286 U.S. 417 (USSC, 1932).

[56] *Ibid.*

[57] Reg. § 1.446-1(c)(1)(ii).

Example 25. RST, Inc., an accrual basis taxpayer, shipped parts to MNO Corporation and sent a bill for $25,000. MNO used the parts and reported that they did not perform according to specifications. If MNO had paid the $25,000 and subsequently sued to recover the purchase price, RST would be required to include the $25,000 in income since the amount was received and the claim of right doctrine applies (i.e., RST has an unrestricted claim to the income). On the other hand, if MNO had not paid the $25,000, RST would not be required to accrue the income because the amount was *not* received and the all events test has not been satisfied (RST's rights to the income have not been fixed).

The claim of right doctrine has been used in many differing instances to cause the inclusion of income in the year received. Some examples where the rule has been applied to make the income taxable are

1. Contingent legal fees that must be returned upon a reversal by an appellate court[58]

2. Illegal income and gains (e.g., embezzled amounts)[59]

3. Bonuses and commissions that were improperly computed and had to be subsequently repaid[60]

The claim of right doctrine does not apply where the taxpayer receives the income but recognizes an obligation to repay.[61] For example, a landlord would not be required to report the receipt of a tenant's security deposit as income because the deposit must be repaid upon the tenant's departure if the apartment unit is undamaged.

In those situations where the taxpayer repays an amount that previously had been included in income, a deduction is allowed. Section 1341 provides a special rule for computing the deduction, which ensures that the tax benefit of the deduction is the equivalent to the tax paid on the income in the prior year.

---

[58] *Michael Phillips v. Comm.*, USTC ¶10,067, 50 AFTR 718, 238 F.2d 473 (CA-7, 1956).

[59] *James v. U.S.*, 61-1 USTC ¶9449, 7 AFTR2d 1361, 366 U.S. 213 (USSC, 1961).

[60] *U.S. v. Lewis*, 51-1 USTC ¶9211, 40 AFTR 258, 340 U.S. 590 (USSC, 1951).

[61] *Comm. v. Turney*, 36-1 USTC ¶9168, 17 AFTR 679, 82 F.2d 661 (CA-5, 1936).

PREPAID INCOME

Over the years, a web of exceptions and special rules have developed regarding the reporting of prepaid income by an *accrual basis* taxpayer. Absent these rules, the accrual basis taxpayer (in accordance with the all events test) would defer recognition of prepaid income until it becomes earned, as is the case in financial accounting. For tax purposes, however, accrual basis taxpayers often report prepaid income in the year received. This treatment normally results from application of the claim of right doctrine, which requires income recognition when the taxpayer receives earnings under an unrestricted claim. For example, prepaid rental income must be reported when received since the taxpayer accepts the money under a claim of right without restrictions on its use. Unfortunately, no general rule is completely reliable to determine when prepaid income must be reported. Rather, the reporting procedure depends on the type of income received. As discussed below, special rules exist for prepaid income from rents, interest, services, warranties, goods, dues, subscriptions, and similar items. Note, however, these rules apply to *accrual basis* taxpayers only. A *cash basis* taxpayer reports all of these prepaid items of income in the year received.

Prepaid Interest, Rents, and Royalties. Several types of advance payments are included in income when received without question. For example, prepaid interest is income when received.[62] Prepaid rent and lump-sum payments, such as bonuses or advanced royalties received upon execution of a lease or other agreement, are also income when received.[63] As subsequently explained, however, the term *rent* does not include payments for the use or occupancy of rooms or space where significant services are also rendered to the occupant (e.g., hotels, motels, and convalescent homes are not considered as having received rents).[64] These prepayments are reported using the rules applying to prepaid service income. Prepaid rents must be distinguished not only from services but also from lease or security deposits. Amounts received from a lessee that are refundable provided the lessee complies with the terms of the lease are not income since the lessor recognizes an obligation to repay.[65] The deposits become income only when the lessor becomes entitled to their unrestricted use upon the lessee's violation of the agreement.

---

[62] *Franklin Life Insurance v. U.S.*, 68-2 USTC ¶9459, 22 AFTR2d 5180, 399 F.2d 757 (CA-7, 1968).

[63] *South Dade Farms, Inc. v. Comm.*, 43-2 USTC ¶9634, 31 AFTR 842, 138 F.2d 818 (CA-5, 1943); *W.M. Scott,* 27 B.T.A. 951.

[64] Rev. Proc. 71-21, 1971-2 C.B. 549.

[65] *Clinton Hotel Realty Corp. v. Comm.*, 42-2 USTC ¶9559, 29 AFTR 758, 128 F.2d 968 (CA-5, 1942).

Prepaid Service Income.   For many years, the IRS argued that the claim of right doctrine required taxpayers to report prepayments for service income in the year received. After much litigation, however, the Service relented and created special rules. Revenue Procedure 71-21 explains that the procedures used for reporting advance payments for services vary, depending on when the services will be performed.[66] The income is reported as it is *earned* where under an agreement all of the services are required to be performed by the end of the next tax year (i.e., the tax year following the year of receipt). If services *may* be performed after the next tax year, all income is reported when received.

> **Example 26.**   AAA Inc. is an accrual basis, calendar year taxpayer that sells riding lawn mowers. The company sells one-, two-, and three-year service contracts. In a late September sale in 1991, the company sold the following contracts, the income from which would be reported as follows:

		Income Recognition	
Contract Terms	Proceeds	1991	1992
One-year	$ 2,400	$ 600	$1,800
Two-year	8,000	8,000	0
Three-year	10,000	10,000	0

> For the one-year contracts the taxpayer reports $600 ($3/12$ of $2,400) of income, representing that amount earned for the last three months of the year. Deferral is permitted since all of the services are required to be performed by the end of the succeeding year, 1992. Deferral is not permitted in the case of two- and three-year contracts because the services may be performed after the close of the next year.

As previously noted, the treatment accorded service income also applies to rents where significant services are also rendered for the occupant. This treatment permits hotels, motels, and the like to enjoy the deferral provision as outlined above for services. For example, a calendar year, accrual basis ski lodge need not report prepayments received in November for rooms to be used in February but may defer income recognition until the rooms are actually used.

Advanced Payments for Goods.   Normally, an accrual basis taxpayer reports advanced payments for sales of merchandise when they are earned (e.g., when the goods are shipped). This treatment enables the taxpayer to defer recognition of the prepayments. However, this approach is allowed only if the taxpayer follows the same method of reporting for financial accounting purposes.

---

[66]   *Supra,* Footnote 64.

Example 27. C Corporation, a calendar year taxpayer, manufactures kitchen appliances. In late December, 1991, it received $50,000 for kitchen appliances that it will produce and ship in May, 1992. The corporation may postpone recognition of the income until 1992, assuming that such income is also reported on the financial accounting income statement in 1992.

The Regulations require reporting of advanced payments for goods earlier (e.g., before they are shipped) if[67]

1. The goods are on hand or are available from normal channels; and

2. *Substantial advanced payments* have been received (i.e., payments that exceed the seller's costs of the goods).

If both of these conditions exist, the advanced payments must be reported at the earlier of (1) the year reported for financial accounting purposes, or (2) the second tax year following the year of receipt. This special rule adopts the view that at the time when these two conditions exist—the payment exceeds cost *and* the goods could have been delivered out of inventory—the sale is essentially complete with respect to those goods, and income recognition is therefore appropriate.

Example 28. In 1991, D Corporation received $100,000 for guaranteed delivery of special airplane parts in 1995. The parts, which were in inventory at the close of 1991, cost $70,000 to produce. Because the payment exceeds D's cost and the parts are currently in inventory, D must report the income in 1993, the earlier of (1) the year accrued for financial purposes, 1995, or (2) the second tax year following the year of receipt, 1993.

Example 29. Refer to the facts in *Example 27*. The special reporting rule illustrated in *Example 28* does not apply since the kitchen appliances are not on hand at the close of the year.

Notwithstanding the government's method for reporting prepaid income from sale of goods, the courts have drawn certain distinctions. For example, refundable advance payments, such as deposits relating to a future contract, were not income when received.[68] Similarly, advance payments that constituted loans were not income when received.[69] As suggested above, however, deferral problems should rarely arise in light of current policy.

---

[67] Reg. § 1.451-5(c)(1).

[68] *Sophia M. Garretson,* 10 B.T.A. 1381 (1928).

[69] *Summit Coal Co.,* 18 B.T.A. 983 (1930).

Long-Term Contracts.   Section 460 contains special rules for the reporting of income from long-term contracts. A long-term contract is defined as any contract for the manufacture, building, installation, or construction of property that is not completed within the same taxable year in which it was entered into. However, a *manufacturing* contract is still not considered long-term unless it also involves either (1) the manufacture of a unique item not normally carried in finished goods inventory (e.g., a special piece of machinery), or (2) items that normally required more than 12 months to complete. If a manufacturing contract does not qualify as a long-term contract, deferral may still be available under the rules regarding advance payments for goods discussed above. Note that contracts for services normally do not qualify for treatment as long-term contracts.

The tax law has long allowed taxpayers who enter into a long-term contract to use the percentage of completion method or the completed contract method (subject to certain limitations) to account for advance payments.[70] The percentage of completion method requires the taxpayer to recognize a portion of the gross profit on the contract based on the estimated percentage of the contract completed. In contrast, the completed contract method allows the taxpayer to defer income recognition until the contract is complete and acceptance has occurred. When available, taxpayers usually opted to use the completed contract method in order to postpone recognition of income. In some extreme cases, taxpayers have been able to postpone income for many years on the claim that the contract was not complete.

Over the years, Congress became concerned about the opportunities for deferral as well as the potential for abuse. Consequently, it took various steps, slowly but surely limiting the use of the completed contract method. These actions culminated with the virtual repeal of the method in 1989. As a result, long-term contracts currently entered into normally must be accounted for using the percentage of completion method.[71] However, there are several situations where the completed contract method can still be used. These include[72]

1. *Home construction contracts.* Contracts in which 80 percent of the costs are related to buildings containing four or fewer dwelling units. Special rules apply to contracts if the buildings contain more than four units (i.e., so-called residential construction contracts).[73]

2. *Contracts of small businesses.* Construction contracts that are completed within two years of commencement and are performed by a contractor whose average annual gross receipts for the three preceding tax years do not exceed $10 million.

---

[70]   Reg. § 1.451-3.

[71]   § 460(a).

[72]   § 460(e).

[73]   A 70% percentage of completion method may be used for certain residential construction contracts.

When using the percentage of completion method, the portion of the total contract price reported during the year and matched against current costs is computed as follows.

$$\text{Total contract price} \times \frac{\text{Direct and allocable indirect costs incurred this period}}{\text{Total estimated costs of contract}}$$

Note that if less than 10 percent of the contract's costs have been incurred, the taxpayer may elect to defer reporting until the year in which the 10 percent threshold is reached.[74]

> **Example 30.** In October 1991, W Corporation entered into a contract to build a hotel to be completed by May 1993. The contract price was $1 million. The company's estimated total costs of construction were $800,000. W's average annual gross receipts exceed $10 million, and it is therefore required to use the percentage of completion method. Total costs incurred during 1991 were $600,000. The income reported in 1991 is $150,000 [($600,000 ÷ $800,000 = 75% × $1,000,000 = $750,000) − $600,000]. In 1992, the contract was completed at a total cost of $840,000. The income reported in 1992 is $10,000 ($1,000,000 − $750,000 − $240,000).

Any contract for which the percentage of completion method is used is subject to the special *look-back* provisions.[75] Under these rules, once the contract is complete, annual income is recomputed based on final costs rather than estimated costs. Interest is then paid to the taxpayer if there was an overstatement of income. Conversely, the taxpayer must pay interest if income was understated.

> **Example 31.** Same facts as in *Example 30* above. Based on total actual costs of $840,000, W's 1991 income should have been $114,000 [($600,000 ÷ $840,000 = 71.4% × $1,000,000 = $714,000) − $600,000]. Thus, W overstated income in 1991 by $36,000 ($150,000 − $114,000). Consequently, the IRS is required to pay the taxpayer interest on the overpayment of the related tax.

Prepaid Dues and Subscriptions. Amidst much controversy concerning the reporting of prepaid income, Congress provided specific rules for the reporting of prepaid dues and subscriptions. Section 455 permits the taxpayer to elect to recognize prepaid subscription income (amounts received from a newspaper, magazine, or periodical) ratably over the subscription period. Section 456 provides that taxpayers may elect to report prepaid dues ratably over the membership period.

[74] § 460(b)(5).   [75] § 460(b)(2).

INTEREST INCOME

The period in which a taxpayer recognizes interest income usually follows the basic tax accounting rules for cash and accrual basis taxpayers. In some cases, however, these taxpayers must observe special provisions that may cause reporting to vary from the normal pattern.

General Rules. As a general rule, cash basis taxpayers recognize interest income when received, while accrual basis taxpayers recognize the income when it is earned. As previously noted, both accrual and cash basis taxpayers that receive interest before it is earned (prepaid interest) must report the income when it is received.

> **Example 32.** T operates a small business that manufactures pottery dishes. When one of her customers was unable to pay her bill, T accepted a $10,000 note, dated October 1, 1991, payable with 6% interest on October 1, 1992. Assuming T is a cash basis taxpayer, she will report $600 of interest income ($10,000 × 6%) in 1992. If T uses the accrual method, she would include $150 ($10,000 × $3/12$ × 6%) in her gross income for 1991 and $450 ($10,000 × $9/12$ × 6%) in 1992. Had the customer paid all of the interest, $600, in 1991 as a showing of good faith, T would report the entire $600 in 1991 regardless of whether she is a cash or accrual basis taxpayer.

In many instances, a taxpayer will purchase an interest-bearing instrument between payment dates. When this occurs, it is assumed that the purchase price includes the interest accrued to the date of the purchase. Thus, when the buyer later receives the interest payment, the portion accrued to the date of purchase is considered a nontaxable return of capital that reduces the taxpayer's basis in the instrument. On the other hand, the seller must include as interest income the amount accrued to the date of the purchase, regardless of the seller's method of accounting.

> **Example 33.** S owned a $1,000, 12% AT&T bond that paid interest semi-annually on November 1 and May 1. He purchased the bond at par several years ago. On September 1, 1991, S sold the bond for $1,540 including $40 of the accrued interest ($1,000 × 12% × $4/12$). S must report $40 of interest income accrued to the date of sale. In addition, S will report a capital gain of $500 ($1,540 − $40 interest − $1,000 basis). The result is the same if S is a cash or accrual basis taxpayer.

> **Example 34.** Assume B purchased for $1,540 the bond that S sold in the example above. On November 1, B receives an interest payment of $60 ($1,000 × 12% × $6/12$). B treats the interest accrued to the date of purchase, $40, as a nontaxable return of basis. Thus, B's basis is reduced to $1,500 ($1,540 − $40). The remaining $20 of interest is included in B's gross income.

Discount. When accounting for interest income, any discount relating to the debt instrument—the excess of the face value of the obligation over the purchase price—must be considered. Discount typically results when the rate at which the instrument pays interest is less than the market rate. In such case, the discount essentially functions as a substitute for interest. Consistent with this view, the tax law attempts to ensure that the discount is treated as interest income and is normally reported currently. Special provisions have been introduced over the years to clarify the reporting of the discount income as well as to prohibit taxpayers from converting the discount income into capital gain.

> **Example 35.** During 1989, T purchased a $10,000, 8% corporate bond for $8,000, or a $2,000 discount. In 1991 the bond matured and the taxpayer redeemed the bond for its par value of $10,000. The redemption is treated as an exchange, and the taxpayer recognizes a long-term capital gain of $2,000 ($10,000 redemption price − $8,000 basis). In this case, the taxpayer has converted the discount of $2,000, which from an economic view is ordinary interest income, to capital gain. Moreover, the taxpayer has deferred the reporting of such income from the time it accrues to the time the bond is sold. Although this opportunity still exists for certain older bonds, some of the provisions discussed below (and in greater detail in Chapter 16) eliminate this possibility for bonds issued in the future.

The tax treatment of discount depends in part on when it arises. The discount often occurs at the time the instrument is issued. For example, certain instruments such as U.S. savings bonds, Treasury bills, and so-called zero coupon bonds do not bear interest and are usually *issued* at discounts. Other debt obligations that do bear interest (such as corporate bonds) also may be issued at a discount, usually if the coupon rate is set lower than the current rate. Discount could also result after the instrument is issued. For example, where interest-bearing instruments are issued at par, discount may arise upon a subsequent purchase. The specific treatment of discount is examined below.

Non–Interest-Bearing Obligations Issued at a Discount. The Code provides special rules for non–interest-bearing obligations that are issued at a discount and redeemable for a fixed amount that increases over time. The instruments to which these rules would normally apply are Series E and EE U.S. savings bonds. Series E bonds were issued between 1941 and 1980, having maturities up to 40 years. Beginning in 1980, these bonds were replaced by Series EE bonds. These bonds are issued at a discount and are generally redeemable at any time up until the final maturity date at a price that increases with the passage of time. No interest payments are made while the bond is held. The holder's interest income is represented by the difference between the redemption price and purchase price. For reporting purposes, taxpayers may elect to include in income the annual increase in the redemption price of the bond.[76] In essence, this election allows a cash basis taxpayer to use the accrual method with respect to these bonds. If income is not reported on an annual basis, the taxpayer reports the entire difference between the redemption and issue prices as income when the bond is redeemed.

> **Example 36.** S purchased Series EE bonds with a face value of $10,000 at a cost of $8,000. The redemption price of the bonds increases during the year by $100. If S elects to report the income annually, she will include $100 in her gross income. Alternatively, S could wait until she redeems the bond to report the income. For example, if S later redeemed the bonds for $9,500, she would report $1,500 income (the difference between the redemption price of $9,500 and her cost of $8,000).

The taxpayer may make the election to report the interest annually at any time. When the election is made, all interest previously deferred on all Series E and EE bonds must be reported. This procedure effectively allows the taxpayer to choose the year in which the interest income is to be reported. However, once the election is made, it applies to *all* Series E and EE bonds subsequently acquired. Should the taxpayer desire to change to reporting the income at redemption, consent from the IRS is required.

Series E and EE bonds may be exchanged within one year of their maturity date for Series HH bonds that *pay* interest semiannually. By exchanging the Series E or EE bonds for Series HH bonds, the taxpayer is able to postpone the recognition of any unreported income attributed to the Series E or EE bonds to the year in which the Series HH bonds are redeemable.[77]

> **Example 37.** In June 1959, B purchased Series E bonds at a cost of $6,000. He did not report the income annually. When the bonds mature in 1991, B will receive $40,000 and will have to report a gain of $34,000 ($40,000 − $6,000). B could effectively shift the $34,000 of income to a year of his choice by exchanging the Series E bonds for Series HH and redeeming the Series HH bonds at a later date. By so doing, B may be able to create a significant tax savings by recognizing the income in a year in which a lower tax rate would apply (e.g., his retirement years).

[76]   § 454(a).

[77]   § 454(c); Reg. § 1.454-1(a); § 1037.

Educational Savings Bonds. In 1988, Congress took steps to help taxpayers finance the rising costs of higher education by offering a special tax break for those who save to meet such expenses. Code § 135 generally provides that accrued interest on Series EE savings bonds issued after 1989 is exempt from tax when the accrued interest and principal amount of such bonds are used to pay for *qualified educational expenses* of the taxpayer or the taxpayer's spouse or dependents (but only if these relationships are satisfied in the year of the redemption). For this purpose, qualified education expenses include those for tuition or fees to attend college or certain schools offering vocational education. Costs which otherwise qualify must be reduced by any scholarships or fellowships that may be received, as well as any employer provided assistance.

The interest exclusion is allowed only to the extent that the taxpayer uses the proceeds of the bond redemption to pay qualified educational expenses during the year that he or she redeems a bond. If the redemption proceeds received during the year exceed the amount of education expenses paid during the same year, the amount of the interest exclusion must be reduced proportionately. The amount of the exclusion may be computed as follows:

$$\frac{\text{Qualified educational expenses paid during the year}}{\text{Total redemption proceeds of qualified bonds during the year}} \times \text{Accrued interest} = \text{Exclusion}$$

Example 38. Mr. and Mrs. T purchased Series EE savings bonds in 1991 for $4,000. On June 2, 2005, they cashed in the bonds and received $10,000, $6,000 representing accrued interest and $4,000 representing their original investment. Three months later on September 2, they paid the college expenses for their daughter, D. The expenses included tuition of $9,000 and dorm fees of $5,000. In November, D received a scholarship of $1,000 for being an outstanding accounting major. Only $8,000 ($9,000 tuition − $1,000 scholarship) of D's expenses are considered qualified educational expenses. Since this amount represents only 80% ($8,000/$10,000) of the total redemption proceeds, Mr. and Mrs. T may exclude only 80% of the $6,000 accrued interest, or $4,800.

Note that to qualify for the exclusion, the savings bonds need not be transferred directly to the educational institution. The exclusion applies to interest on any post-1989 Series EE savings bond which is realized during the taxable year as long as the taxpayer pays sufficient qualified educational expenses during the same taxable year.

The special exclusion is designed to benefit only those who have moderate incomes. To achieve this objective, the exclusion is gradually reduced once the taxpayer's A.G.I. (as determined in the taxable year when the bonds are redeemed) reaches a certain level. The income level at which the phase out begins depends on the taxpayer's filing status as shown below.

Filing Status	Phase out range Modified A.G.I.*
Single (including heads of household)............	$40,000-$55,000
Married filing jointly..............................	60,000- 90,000

*To be adjusted annually for inflation

The reduction of the exclusion otherwise allowed is computed as follows:

$$\frac{\text{Excess A.G.I.}}{\substack{\$15,000 \\ (\$30,000 \text{ for joint returns})}} \times \text{Otherwise Excludable Interest} = \text{Reduction}$$

Married taxpayers filing separately are not eligible for the exclusion. Taxpayers who are married must file a joint return to secure the exclusion.

Example 39. Mr. and Mrs. B have an A.G.I., after proper modifications, of $70,000. As a result, the amount of any interest that would otherwise be nontaxable must be reduced by one-third

$$\frac{(\$70,000 \text{ A.G.I.} - \$60,000 \text{ threshold} = \$10,000)}{(\$90,000 - \$60,000 = \$30,000 \text{ phase out range})}$$

Assume the couple redeemed qualified bonds this year with accrued interest of $10,000. Only 90% of the proceeds of the bonds (i.e., interest and principal) were spent on qualifying education expense. They could exclude $6,000 of the interest, computed as follows:

Excludable interest (90% × $10,000)........................	$9,000
Exclusion phase-out	
(1/3 × $9,000)...	(3,000)
Amount of interest excluded.................................	$6,000

Note that the exclusion would not be available to the couple if their A.G.I. in the year they redeemed the bonds was at least $90,000.

Without any special provision, taxpayers with high incomes might try to circumvent the income limitation to obtain the exclusion. For example, a father earning an income of $100,000 might give $10,000 to his 10-year-old daughter who would then be instructed to buy the bonds. When the daughter started college, she would redeem the bonds to pay for her tuition. Absent any restrictions, the daughter could secure 100 percent of the available exclusion since she would have little or no income. To prevent such schemes, the exclusion is available only for bonds that are issued to individuals who are at least 24 years old. In addition, the exclusion is available only to the original purchaser of the bond or his or her spouse. This rule prohibits gifts of qualified bonds.

Example 40. Mr. and Mrs. C have an A.G.I. of $100,000. Assume they currently hold qualified Series EE bonds with $10,000 of accrued interest. To avoid the income limitation, the bonds are given to Mr. C's father, GF, who has little income. This year, GF cashes the bonds in and pays for his grandson's tuition. The payment is sufficient to qualify the grandson as GF's dependent. Even though the redemption proceeds are used to pay for education expenses of the taxpayer's dependent, no exclusion is available for the interest since GF was not the original purchaser of the bond. Had GF originally purchased the bonds for his grandson, the exclusion would be allowed (assuming his grandson is his dependent).

Government Obligations. Special rules also govern the treatment of the discount arising upon the purchase of short-term government obligations such as Treasury bills. Typically, a taxpayer purchases a short-term Treasury bill at a discount and redeems it for par value shortly thereafter. In this instance, Code § 454(b) applies to cash basis taxpayers to ensure that the gain on the redemption—in effect, the discount—is treated as ordinary interest income. Specifically, any gain realized by cash basis taxpayers from the sale or redemption of non–interest-bearing obligations issued by governmental units that have a fixed maturity date that is one year or less from the date of issue is always ordinary income. This ordinary income is reported *in the year* of sale or redemption. In contrast, accrual basis taxpayers are required to amortize the discount (i.e., include it in income) on a *daily* basis under Code § 1281(a).

Example 41. On December 1, 1991, B, a cash basis calendar year taxpayer, purchased a $10,000 non–interest-bearing Treasury bill. She purchased the bill at 97 ($9,700) and redeemed the bill on March 1, 1992 at par. B recognizes a $300 gain ($10,000 − $9,700) on the redemption, and the entire gain is treated as ordinary income in 1992. The same result would occur if B had *sold* the Treasury bill for $10,000 on January 15, 1992. Note that if B were an accrual basis taxpayer, the $300 discount would have been included in income on a daily basis. Consequently, a portion of the income would be reported in 1991 and the remainder in 1992.

Original Issue Discount. When interest-bearing obligations such as corporate bonds are *issued* at a discount, a complex set of provisions operates to prevent taxpayers from not only deferring the discount income but also converting it to capital gain as depicted in *Example 35*. These rules apply only to discount which arises when the bonds are originally issued. This discount is technically referred to as *original issue discount* (OID) and is determined as follows:

Redemption price	$x,xxx
− Issue price	− xxx
= Original issue discount	$x,xxx

The thrust of the provisions is to require the holder of the bond to amortize the discount into income during the period the bond is held. A complete discussion of the treatment of OID is provided in Chapter 16.

IDENTIFICATION OF THE TAXPAYER

A final consideration in the taxation of income concerns identification of the taxpayer to whom the income is taxed. Generally, this determination is easily made. As discussed below, however, receipt or nonreceipt of income does not necessarily govern who must report it.

INCOME FROM PERSONAL SERVICES

In the famous case of *Lucas v. Earl,* the Supreme Court was required to determine whether a husband was taxable on earnings from personal services despite a legally enforceable agreement made with his wife that the earnings would be shared equally.[78] At the time of this decision, such agreements effectively split income between a husband and wife; this resulted in a reduced tax liability since each individual was treated as a separate taxable entity and a progressive income tax rate structure existed. The Court eliminated the usefulness of this technique, however, by holding that the income is taxable to the taxpayer who earns it. Thus, anticipatory assignments of income that one has a *right* to receive are an ineffective device to escape taxation. In explaining what has become the assignment of income doctrine, the Court gave birth to the well-known *fruit of the tree* metaphor. According to Justice Holmes, the fruit (income) must be attributed to the tree from which it grew (Mr. Earl's services).

---

[78]   2 USTC ¶496, 8 AFTR 10287, 281 U.S. 111
(USSC, 1930).

Section 73 directly addresses the treatment of a child's earnings. This provision indicates that amounts received for the services of a child are included in the *child's* gross income. Thus, a parent or a guardian who collects income earned by a child would not report the income; rather the income would be reported by the child since he or she earned it. As discussed in Chapter 4, however, the *unearned* income of a child under age 14 may be reported on his or her parents' tax return and taxed at the parents' rates.

INCOME FROM PROPERTY

The assignment of income doctrine also applies where income from property is received. Under this rule, income from property is included in the gross income of the taxpayer who owns the property. This principle was derived from another famous case, *Helvering v. Horst*.[79] In this case, Mr. Horst clipped the interest coupons from bonds he owned and gave them to his son, who later collected them. The Supreme Court held Mr. Horst taxable since he owned and controlled the source of income (i.e., the bonds). Accordingly, income from property can be effectively assigned only if the taxpayer relinquishes ownership of the property.

When ownership of income-producing property is transferred, special rules must be followed in determining who reports income accrued to the date of the transfer. This problem arises, for example, when a gift or a sale of interest-bearing bonds occurs between payment dates. As noted earlier, upon a sale of property on which interest has accrued, the selling price is assumed to consist of accrued interest that must be reported in the year of sale. Where property is transferred by gift, the IRS has ruled that interest income accrues daily.[80] Thus, a cash basis donor of property reports any interest accrued to the date of the gift as income, as would the accrual basis taxpayer. The cash basis donor, however, does not report this income until the donee collects it.

Example 42. On December 25, 1991, T, a cash basis taxpayer, gave his daughter, P, a bond with a face value of $1,000 and an interest rate of 10%. Interest is paid semiannually on November 1 and May 1. Interest accrued to December 25, 1991, $15 ($^{54}/_{365} \times 10\% \times \$1,000$), will be reported by T on his *1992* tax return, assuming P collects the interest on May 1, 1992. P will report the remaining interest income.

[79] 40-2 USTC ¶9787, 24 AFTR 1058, 311 U.S. 112 (USSC, 1940).   [80] Rev. Rul. 72-312, 1972-1 C.B. 22.

A different set of rules applies for determining who reports dividends when stock is transferred since dividends do not accrue daily. The taxpayer who reports the dividend income depends on when the transfer is made. For this purpose, two dates are important: (1) the declaration date, that is, the date on which the board of directors of the corporation declares that dividends will be paid; and (2) the date of record, the date used for determining exactly who owns the stock and who is entitled to receive the dividend. The Tax Court has ruled that in the case of a *gift,* the donor is taxed on any dividends if the transfer is made after the declaration date and before the date of record.[81]

> **Example 43.** X Corporation declared a dividend on May 10 payable to shareholders of record on June 1. R transferred all of his stock in X to his son, S, on May 15. Although S collects the dividend income, it will be taxable to R since the stock was transferred after the declaration date.

The reporting of dividend income in the case of a *sale* presents no difficulty since income automatically follows ownership. Specifically, the person who owns the stock on the date of record is the person who ultimately receives the dividends and consequently is taxed on them.

UNEARNED INCOME OF CHILDREN UNDER 14

Perhaps the most fundamental principle in tax planning concerns minimizing the marginal tax rate that applies to the taxpayer's income. The significance of this principle is easily understood when one realizes that Federal marginal tax rates have at times exceeded 90 percent. Even with the recent reduction of marginal rates, minimizing the tax rate can provide benefits—although the potential for savings clearly diminishes when the top rate is 31 percent.

Minimizing the tax rate is normally accomplished by shifting income to a lower bracket taxpayer. As discussed above, the assignment of income doctrine makes it virtually impossible for taxpayers to shift income arising from services. Opportunities do exist, however, for shifting income through transfers of property. The most popular technique in this regard has traditionally involved transferring income-producing property to a child. In this manner, not only is the tax rate applying to the income reduced, but the income also stays within the family unit, normally to be used as the parent directs.

---

[81]   *M.G. Anton,* 34 T.C. 842 (1960).

As part of the tax overhaul in 1986, Congress took steps to reduce tax avoidance opportunities available through income shifting to a child. This was accomplished by enacting a special provision affectionately referred to as the "kiddie" tax.[82] The thrust of this rule—as explained in Chapter 4—is to tax the *unearned* income of a child under the age of 14 as if it were the parents' income and thus at the parents' rates. By limiting the tax to unearned rather than earned income, Congress was taking direct aim at parents and others who shifted income by making gifts of property. Accordingly, shifting techniques based on gifts of property such as stocks, bonds, and rental property that produce unearned income (e.g., dividends, interest, and rents) are now severely limited.

INTEREST-FREE AND BELOW-MARKET LOANS

To be successful in shifting income to another, the assignment of income doctrine generally requires that the taxpayer transfer the income-producing property itself, not merely the income from the property. Consequently, shifting income normally requires a completed gift of the property. Taxpayers, however, are understandably reluctant to forever relinquish ownership and control of the property. For this reason, taxpayers have attempted to design techniques that enable them to retain ownership of the property yet shift income.

Prior to 1984, one popular method for shifting income from one family member to another, or from a corporation to its shareholders (or employees), utilized interest-free loans. Under the typical arrangement, a father who was in the 50 percent tax bracket would make a loan to his son who was in a tax bracket far lower than his father's (or who perhaps paid no taxes at all). Upon receipt of the loan, the son (or his representative if he was a minor) would invest the funds. As a result, any income earned on the investment would be taxed to the son at a lower rate than would have been paid had the father received the income directly. This arrangement could secure substantial tax savings, particularly where there was a great disparity between the tax rates of the two family members.

The success of the tax saving technique described above was attributable to the terms of the loan agreement. These terms required the son to repay the loan on demand *without interest*. Had the father charged interest, he would still have income attributable to the amount loaned, and no income shifting would have occurred. By not charging interest, however, the interest income that the father would have earned was successfully shifted to the son and tax savings resulted. In addition, the interest that was not charged, a valuable benefit for the son, was not considered a taxable gift. Moreover, this arrangement was extremely appealing because it did not require the father to part with the property forever. Since he had only loaned the funds to his son, he could demand repayment of the funds at any time.

---

[82] § 1(i).

The IRS did not view interest-free loans as a valid means to shift income, but rather a tax avoidance device designed to circumvent the assignment of income rules. After much unsuccessful litigation, the Service finally struck a severe blow in 1984, when the Supreme Court decided in *Dickman* that the interest-free use of the loan amount (i.e., the foregone interest) did constitute a taxable gift by the lender.[83] Despite this victory, the decision did not preclude income shifting. Instead, it merely imposed a cost on using the tax-saving technique equal to the gift tax—which could be zero if the gift of the forgone interest was less than the amount of the annual exclusion of $10,000. As a result, the use of interest-free loans to shift income still appeared viable. However, Congress eliminated this opportunity in 1984 by enacting Code § 7872, which imputes interest income to the lender where the actual interest is considered inadequate.

Treatment of Below-Market Loans.   In general, § 7872 applies to loans when the interest charged is below the current market rate of interest. When such a loan is made, the treatment is determined *assuming* the following: the borrower pays the interest to the lender at the market rate which the lender is then deemed to transfer back to the borrower. This hypothetical scenario results in the following tax consequences:

1. The borrower may be allowed a deduction for the interest hypothetically paid to the lender, while the lender reports the fictitious payment as *interest income*.

2. The lender treats the hypothetical payment to the borrower as either compensation, dividend, or gift depending on the nature of the loan. Similarly, the borrower treats the payment as either compensation, dividend, or gift as the case may be. In determining the character of the lender's hypothetical payment, the Code classifies loans into three types according to the relationship between the lender and the borrower.

   Gift loans—those where the forgone interest is in the nature of a gift

   Compensation-related loans—those made by an employer to an employee or an independent contractor

   Corporation-shareholder loans—those made by a corporation to a shareholder.[84]

---

[83]   84-1 USTC ¶13,560, 53 AFTR2d 84-1608, 104 S.Ct. 1932 (USSC, 1984).

[84]   In this regard, Proposed Reg. § 1.7872-4(d)(2) indicates that a payment to a shareholder-employee is presumed to be a dividend if the corporation is (1) closely held and such person owns more than 5 percent of its stock, or (2) publicly held and such person owns $1/2$ of one percent of the stock.

The thrust of these rules is to treat the borrower as having paid the proper amount of interest, which is funded by the lender through compensation, dividends, or gift.

Example 44.   Lender L loaned $100,000 to borrower B payable on demand without interest. Assume the statutory rate of interest required to be charged is 10 percent compounded semiannually. Thus, the interest hypothetically paid by B and which must be imputed to L is $10,250. The following table shows the effect on L and B, assuming the loan is

1.   A gift loan

2.   A compensation-related loan

3.   A corporation-shareholder loan

Lender L				Borrower B			
Interest Income	Gift Made	Comp. Expense	Dividend Paid	Interest Expense	Gift Received	Comp. Income	Dividend Received
(1) $10,250	$10,250			($10,250)	$10,250		
(2) 10,250		($10,250)		(10,250)		$10,250	
(3) 10,250			$10,250	(10,250)			$10,250

The first situation reveals the effects where the interest foregone by the lender is considered a gift (e.g., loans between family members). In this case, income shifting is prohibited since L does not avoid taxation on the income from the loan. Rather, he or she is deemed to receive an interest payment from B on the amount loaned. In addition, L is treated as having made a taxable gift to B of $250 ($10,250 gift − $10,000 annual exclusion). On the other hand, B is entitled to exclude the $10,250 gift from income. B's hypothetical interest payment may or may not be deductible, depending on whether it is treated as investment interest, business interest, or personal interest (see Chapter 11 for a discussion of interest).

The second situation assumes that the loan is made by an employer to an employee, and, thus, the hypothetical payment by the lender is considered compensation. In this case, the lender is treated as having received interest income that is offset by a deduction for compensation expense to B. Note, however, that if B is an employee, L would be responsible for employment taxes and withholding. The effect on the borrower, B, depends on whether the hypothetical interest payment is deductible. If so, there generally will be no effect since such deduction offsets B's compensation income.

The third situation demonstrates the undesirable consequences that a corporation encounters when its deemed payment is considered a dividend rather than compensation. This problem would normally arise where the loan is made to an individual who is both a shareholder and an employee of the corporation. In this situation, like the second situation above, L (a corporation) has income from the deemed payment. In contrast to the second situation, however, L receives no offsetting deduction since dividend payments are not deductible. The effect on B again depends on whether the hypothetical interest payment is deductible.

These provisions govern not only the treatment of gift, compensation-related, and corporate-shareholder loans, but also any other type of below-market loan designed to achieve tax avoidance or affect the tax liability of the lender or the borrower.

Example 45.   During the year, J joined a country club. The club requires each member to loan the club $10,000 without interest. Assuming interest rates are currently 8 percent, the club is effectively receiving annual dues of $800 from each member. More importantly from the member's standpoint, the dues are paid with tax-free dollars.

Had J received the $800 directly, she would be required to pay taxes. By making the loan to the club, she has effectively converted taxable income to tax-exempt income. Under Code § 7872, however, this arrangement would not be effective since J would be treated as having received the $800 income and would have no offsetting deduction for the payment to the club.

Exempted Loans.   To restrict the application of § 7872 to predominantly abusive situations, Congress carved out several exceptions to the rules described above. Under the first exception, § 7872 does not apply to *gift* loans as long as the loans outstanding during the year do not exceed $10,000 *and* the borrower does not use the loan proceeds to purchase or carry income-producing assets. Without this latter requirement, income of small amounts could still be shifted. The effect of this provision is to exempt small loans where income shifting is absent.

Congress also granted compensation-related and corporation-shareholder loans an exemption from the onerous rules of § 7872 if they do not exceed $10,000. The exemption does not apply to these loans, however, if tax avoidance is one of the principal purposes of the loan.

Interest Income Cap.   Another special rule imposes a limit on the amount of imputed interest income for loans between individuals. Generally, if the amount of outstanding loans does not exceed $100,000 and their principal purpose is not tax avoidance, the deemed payment by the borrower to the lender is limited to the borrower's investment income. This rule follows from the theory that the amount of income shifted by the lender is limited to that which the borrower actually earns. In addition, to enable loans where tax-avoidance is obviously not a motive, the lender is treated as having no imputed interest income if the borrower's investment income does not exceed $1,000. However, the lender is still deemed to have made a gift of the foregone interest.

> **Example 46.**   R has a son, T, who earns a salary and has $800 investment income. During the year, R loaned T $90,000 without interest to purchase a home. Interest imputed at the IRS rate is $12,000. R has no interest income since the loan is less than $100,000 and investment income is less than $1,000. However, R is charged with a taxable gift of $2,000 ($12,000 − $10,000 exclusion). Note that if T had $7,000 of investment income, R also would have been charged with interest income of $7,000.

INCOME FROM COMMUNITY PROPERTY

In the United States, the rights that married individuals hold in property are determined using either the common law or community property system. The community property system developed in continental Europe and was adopted in several states having a French or Spanish origin. The nine states currently recognizing the community property system are Arizona, California, Idaho, Louisiana, Nevada, New Mexico, Texas, Washington, and Wisconsin. The remaining 41 states use the common law system, which originated in England.

The community property system categorizes property into two types: separate property, which is considered belonging separately to one of the spouses, and community property, which is considered owned equally by each spouse. In general, separate property consists only of those assets owned before marriage or acquired by gift or inheritance while married. All property acquired during a marriage except by gift or inheritance is community property.

Income from separate property may be community property or separate property depending on the state of jurisdiction. In Texas, Louisiana, and Idaho, income from separate property is community property. Accordingly, for Federal tax purposes each spouse is responsible for one-half of the income. In the other six states, income from separate property is separate property and must be reported by the person owning the property. Income from personal services is generally treated as belonging to the community. The following example illustrates how these differing rules must be taken into account.

Example 47. A husband and wife elect to file separate returns. The husband received a $30,000 salary and $1,000 dividends on stock he had purchased prior to the couple's marriage. The husband also receives $500 of taxable interest from a certificate of deposit that he had purchased in his own name while married. The wife's income would vary depending on the state in which she lived:

	Texas	Arizona	Common Law States
Salary.................	$15,000	$15,000	$0
Dividends..............	500	0	0
Interest................	250	250	0
Wife's income..........	$15,750	$15,250	$0

Community Income Where Spouses Live Apart. The treatment of community income can create financial problems, particularly where spouses live apart during the year and are later divorced before the end of the taxable year. For example, consider R and S, who were married but lived apart during the first half of the year before their divorce became final. Under these circumstances, the property settlement should consider the accrued tax liability that arises due to any community income. Accounting for the liability may be difficult or impossible, however, if one of the spouses has abandoned the other. In such cases, the abandoned spouse becomes liable for the tax on income earned by a spouse who cannot be located to share the financial responsibility. To eliminate these difficulties, special provisions were enacted.

Section 66 provides that a spouse will be taxed only on the earnings attributed to his or her personal services if during the year the following requirements are satisfied:

1. The two married individuals live apart at all times.

2. The couple does not file a joint return with each other.

3. No portion of the earned income is transferred between the spouses.

This rule only applies to income from personal services and not income from property.

Example 48. M and N, residents of Texas, decided in November 1990 to obtain a divorce, which became final on March 31, 1991. N earns $2,000 each month and M is unemployed. N has a savings account that yielded $200 of taxable interest during the first three months of 1991. Assuming the two live apart during all of 1991 and none of the earned income is transferred between them, N will report all of the $6,000 ($2,000 × 3) attributable to her personal services and $100 of the interest. M will report his $100 share of the taxable interest.

TAX PLANNING

TIMING INCOME RECOGNITION

The proper timing of income recognition can reap great benefits for the taxpayer. As a general rule, postponement of income recognition is wise since the tax on such income is deferred. The major advantage of tax deferral is that the taxpayer has continued use of the funds that otherwise would have been used to pay taxes. Deferral of the tax is in essence an interest-free loan from the government.

When considering deferral, attention must be given to the marginal tax rates that may apply to the income. For example, taxpayers often postpone income until their retirement years, when they are usually in a lower tax bracket. Although deferral may be wise in this situation, it may be unwise where tax rates rise by operation of law or because of the taxpayer's increase in earnings. Ideally, the taxpayer should attempt to level out taxable income from one year to the next and equalize the tax rate that applies annually (to avoid the situation of R in *Example 12* and duplicate that of S).

The opportunities for most individuals to postpone income are limited, particularly in light of the constructive receipt doctrine. Several techniques do exist, however, as outlined below:

1. Taxpayers who own securities may postpone the sale of investments at a profit. Methods exist for locking in the gain in the current year without having to realize it (selling short against the box or "put" options).

2. Installment sales of property enable the taxpayer not only to avoid the bunching of income in a single year but also to defer the tax.

3. Income on Series E and EE bonds, Treasury bills, and certain certificates of deposit may be deferred until they are redeemed.

4. Investments in Individual Retirement Accounts (IRAs), Keogh plans, and qualified retirement plans are all made with before-tax dollars (since these contributions are deductible), and earnings on these investments are not taxed until they are withdrawn.

5. Deferred compensation arrangements may be suitable, as in the case of a professional athlete, celebrity, or executive (see Chapter 18).

INCOME-SPLITTING TECHNIQUES

As stressed earlier, the most fundamental rule in tax planning concerns minimizing the marginal tax rate that applies to the taxpayer's income. Minimizing the applicable rate is usually accomplished through use of some type of income splitting or shifting technique.

Example 49. Mr. and Mrs. J pay taxes at a rate of 31%. The couple helps support Mr. J's 67-year-old retired mother, M, by giving her $5,000 annually. Such gifts do not entitle the couple to claim M as a dependent. Consequently, in 1991, M may claim an exemption deduction of $2,150 and a standard deduction of $4,250 ($3,400 regular + $850 additional for unmarried and over 65 years of age), for total deductions of $6,400. In providing M's support through gifts, the couple is using after-tax dollars. That is, the couple would have to earn $7,246 to provide M with $5,000 in support [$7,246 − (31% of $7,246) = $5,000]. Instead, the couple could transfer income-producing property to M to provide the needed support. By so doing, the income would not be subject to tax (assuming M's only other income is tax-exempt such as social security benefits), and the cost of support would be far less expensive. Although this arrangement requires the couple to give up the property permanently (since any type of reversionary interest would cause the income to be taxed back to the couple), in many family situations, M would probably give the property back when she no longer needs it or when she dies. In addition, other techniques are available that can circumvent the problem of permanently departing with the property.

The above example demonstrates how income can be shifted successfully. Where income is to be shifted to children, however, the taxpayer must contend with the "kiddie" tax.

The "kiddie" tax clearly limits opportunities for shifting unearned income to children. However, it does not eliminate them. It should be emphasized that the "kiddie" tax does not apply to children 14 and over. Thus, tax savings similar to those illustrated in *Example 49* can be obtained with little difficulty where the children have reached 14. Moreover, the "kiddie" tax does not apply until unearned income exceeds $1,100 (in 1991). Consequently, for a child under 14, the first $550 of unearned income bears no tax because of the standard deduction, and the next $550 is taxed at the child's rates. Although the "kiddie" tax severely curtails the amount of tax that could otherwise be saved through shifting income to children, taxpayers attempting to shift modest amounts of income are not affected.

Example 50.   In 1991, Father, who is in the top tax bracket (31%) decided to start a college fund for his seven-year-old, Son. To this end, he opened a savings account for Son and deposited $1,000 in the account annually. Assuming the account pays 10% interest annually, interest income for the next several years would be determined as follows:

Son's Age	Balance	Interest	Son's Tax	Son's After-Tax Income
7	$ 1,000	$ 100	$ 0	$100
8	2,100	210	0	210
9	3,310	331	0	331
10	4,641	464	0	464
11	6,105	610	9	601
12	7,706	771	33	738
13	9,444	944	59	885
14	11,329	1,133	87	1,046

As the table shows, Son pays no taxes at all for the first four years due to the $550 standard deduction. Moreover, for the next several years Son pays taxes at his low 15% rate because his unearned income does not exceed $1,100 and consequently is not subject to the "kiddie" tax. Note that in this case the "kiddie" tax never applies since Son's unearned income begins to exceed $1,100 only after he turns 14. In contrast, if Father had embarked on a similar program for himself, all income would have been taxed at a rate of 31%.

For taxpayers wanting to shift more unearned income to their children, other techniques are available. One way of coping with the "kiddie" tax is by making investments with income that is deferred until the child becomes 14 or older. For example, the taxpayer could give a child Series EE savings bonds. The income from these bonds can be deferred by not electing to report the accumulated interest until after the child turns 14. Interest thereafter would be reported annually. Similarly, discount bonds—those *without* original issue discount—could be purchased. In this case, the interest is not reported until the bond is sold.

The "kiddie" tax applies to unearned income and not earned income. As a result, earned income can be successfully shifted by paying the child for performing some task. Of course, shifting does not occur unless the payment is deductible by the parent. Such payments, when made by a parent directly to a child under 18, have the added benefit of not being subject to social security taxes.

EXCLUDED ECONOMIC INCOME

In arranging one's affairs, it should be observed that certain "economic" income does not fall within the definition of income for tax purposes and thus can be obtained tax free.

Example 51.   Taxpayer R received a gift from her rich uncle of $100,000, which she is considering investing in either a condominium or corporate stocks. The condominium in which she is interested is the one in which she currently lives and rents for $8,000 annually. In lieu of purchasing the condominium, she could continue to rent and invest the $100,000 in preferred stocks paying dividends of 10% annually, or $10,000 of income per year. Assume that R pays taxes at a marginal rate of 50%. The return after taxes on the preferred stock will be 5%, or $5,000. The return from the investment in the condominium is represented by the rent that she does not pay of $8,000, which is nontaxable. In essence, the condominium pays a dividend-in-kind (i.e., shelter), which is tax-exempt. Consequently, R would obtain a higher yield on her investment by purchasing the condominium. Note that income for tax purposes does not include the value of the condominium which would be considered income in the economic sense because the use of the condominium's shelter represents consumption. This same type of analysis applies to all types of investments in consumer goods that provide long-term benefits, such as washers and refrigerators.

PROBLEM MATERIALS

DISCUSSION QUESTIONS

5-1 *Economic versus Tax Concept of Income.* It has been said that the income tax discriminates against the person who lives in a rented home as compared with the person who owns his or her own residence. Comment on the truth of this assertion and why such discrimination may or may not be justified.

5-2 *Net Worth Method.* Explain the circumstances in which the economist's approach to measuring income might be used for tax purposes and what specific steps might be taken to implement such an approach.

5-3 *What Is Income?* Listed below are several items that may or may not constitute income for purposes of economics and income taxes. Indicate whether each item would be considered income for each of these purposes, including comments on why differences, if any, might exist.

   a.   Beef raised and consumed by a cattle rancher.
   b.   Interest received on state or local bonds.
   c.   Air transportation provided by an airline to one of its flight attendants.
   d.   Appreciation of XRY stock from $1,000 to $6,000 during the year.
   e.   Proceeds collected from an insurance company for a casualty loss and reinvested in similar property.
   f.   A loan obtained from a friend.
   g. $105 received from sale of stock purchased one year ago for $100; inflation during the past year averaged 5 percent.
   h.   A gift received as a Christmas present.

5-4 *Cash Equivalent Doctrine.* A financial newsletter recently reported the many advantages that may be obtained from belonging to a barter club or organization. Would tax benefits be included among these advantages (e.g., no taxable income realized on the exchange of services)?

5-5 *Return of Capital Doctrine—General.* Explain the return of capital doctrine and discuss three situations in which the doctrine operates.

5-6 *Indirect Benefits.* S is vice president of a car manufacturer. His employer regularly provides him with a new automobile which he is to evaluate. Is the value of the car's use income?

5-7 *Indirect Benefits.* A, an assistant manager for a department store, often is required to work overtime to help mark down merchandise for special sales. On these occasions, her employer pays the cost of her evening meal. Does the meal constitute income? Explain.

5-8 *Annual Accounting Period-Planning.* Briefly explain the notion of "income bunching" and why it is a problem.

5-9   *Relationship between Tax and Financial Accounting Methods.*   Does conformity with generally accepted accounting principles satisfy the requirement of § 446(c) that income must be clearly reflected? Explain, including some illustrations where income for tax purposes will differ from that for financial accounting purposes.

5-10   *Cash Basis Taxpayer's Receipt of Notes.*   Does a cash basis taxpayer recognize income when a note is received or when collections are made?

5-11   *Constructive Receipt Doctrine.*   Discuss the planning opportunities related to the cash method of accounting and how these are affected by the constructive receipt doctrine.

5-12   *Accrual Method of Accounting.*   Address the following questions:

   a.   When does a taxpayer using the accrual method of accounting normally report income?

   b.   Under what circumstances is an accrual basis taxpayer treated like a cash basis taxpayer for purposes of reporting income?

5-13   *Category A vs. Category B Methods.*   T Corporation is considering altering the way in which it accounts for a particular item. Its accountant has stated that the ultimate disposition of the item and the effect of the change on income depend on whether the method is considered a Category A or Category B method of accounting as well as who initiates that change. Explain.

5-14   *Change in Accounting Method—Pre-1954 Balances.*   J has operated a furniture store in Littleville, Ohio, since 1947. This year, he hired an accountant who immediately discovered that J was not using the accrual method to account for his inventory costs. According to the accountant, a change to this method will result in additional income of $200,000, a portion of which is attributable to the years 1947 through 1953. What would you advise J to do?

5-15   *Changing Accounting Methods: Procedures.*   F files the tax returns for his three-year-old son, S. Up until this year, F had always reported the interest on S's Series E savings bonds annually. F now wishes to report the interest income when the bonds are redeemed (e.g., when the child reaches age 14). Can F change the way he reports the interest? If so, how?

5-16   *What Is an Accounting Method?*   This year, T hired a new accountant, A. As part of A's routine review procedures, A determined that T's previous accountant had improperly computed the gross profit percentage to be used in recognizing income on an installment sale. Based on the previous accountant's calculation, 40 percent of each year's receipts were to be included in income, whereas according to A's calculation the proper percentage was 50 percent. Explain what A should do upon finding the discrepancy.

5-17   *Claim of Right.*   Consider the questions below.

   a.   Is the application of the claim of right doctrine limited to situations that involve only contested income? Explain.

   b.   Explain the difference between the claim of right and constructive receipt doctrines.

5-18   *Claim of Right versus Clear Reflection of Income.*   Which doctrine has priority: claim of right or clear reflection of income? Explain.

5-19 *Prepaid Rent.* In light of the tax treatment, should landlords of apartment complexes characterize an initial $500 deposit from their tenants as a security deposit or as a payment of the last month's rent in advance? Explain.

5-20 *Prepaid Services.* Identify several types of services where the accrual-basis provider will not be permitted to defer any prepayments of income related to such services. Explain.

5-21 *Advanced Payment for Goods.* The Regulations provide complex rules governing an accrual basis taxpayer's privilege of deferring income arising from advance payments for goods. Why might these rules have little relevance for most accrual basis taxpayers? In what type of situation might the rules become operable?

5-22 *Long-Term Contracts.* Indicate which method of accounting for long-term contracts—completed contract or percentage of completion—the taxpayer may use in the following situations. Assume each contract is considered a long-term contract unless otherwise implied.

   a.   A contract to build an office building. The taxpayer's annual gross receipts for the last five years have exceeded $11 million.

   b.   A contract to build a home to be finished next year. The taxpayer's annual gross receipts for the last five years have exceeded $11 million.

   c.   A contract to build a high-rise apartment complex containing 120 units. The contractor's average gross receipts are $11 million.

   d.   A contract to manufacture 15,000 seats for a football stadium. The taxpayer has several contracts for this type of seat. Average gross receipts are $12 million.

   e.   A contract to manufacture a special part for the Space Shuttle. Average annual gross receipts were $12 million.

5-23 *"Kiddie" Tax.* R has been advised that due to recent changes in the tax law he can no longer save taxes by shifting income to his children.

   a.   Explain the origin of such advice.

   b.   Refer to *Example 50*. Determine how much more Father is able to accumulate for Son's education by using the savings account over the period shown in the example.

5-24 *Taxpayer Identification—Family Trusts.* In recent years, many taxpayers have fallen victim to vendors of the so-called "family trust" tax shelter. Under this arrangement the taxpayer signs a contractual agreement entitling the trust to all of the taxpayer's income which is subsequently distributed to the beneficiaries of the trust. Explain how this arrangement is supposed to save taxes and why it fails.

5-25 *Income Reporting by Partnerships and S Corporations.* Explain how partners and shareholders in S corporations may defer the reporting of income by having their respective entities select fiscal years for reporting rather than calendar years.

5-26 *Income from Community Property.* Under what circumstances will knowledge of the community property system be relevant? Is it necessary for persons residing in common law states to understand the community property system?

5-27 *Planning—Timing Income Recognition.* Although it is generally desirable to defer income recognition and the related taxes, when would acceleration of income be preferred?

5-28 *Planning—Income Splitting.* How might R, who operates a shoe store as a sole proprietorship, reduce the taxes that are imposed on his family using income-splitting techniques?

PROBLEMS

5-29 *What Is Income?* In each of the following situations indicate whether taxable income should be recognized.

a.   Q purchased an older home for $20,000. Shortly after its purchase, the area in which it was located was designated a historical neighborhood, causing its value to rise to $50,000.

b.   R, a long-time employee of XYZ Inc., purchased one of the company's cars worth $7,000 for $3,000.

c.   I borrowed $10,000 secured by property that had an adjusted basis of $3,000 and a fair market value of $15,000.

d.   S, a 60 percent shareholder in STV Corporation, uses a company car 70 percent of the time for business and 30 percent for personal purposes. The rental value of the car is $200 per month.

5-30 *What Is Income?* In each of the following situations indicate whether taxable income should be recognized.

a.   R discovered oil on his farm, causing the value of his land to increase by $100,000,000.

b.   While jogging, L found a portable stereo radio valued at $200.

c.   E agreed to rent his lake cottage to F for $1,000 during the summer. After living there for two weeks, E and F agreed that E would only charge $700 if F made certain improvements.

d.   D borrowed $100,000, $20,000 each from S, T, U, V, and W. He gave them each a one-year note bearing interest at a rate of 25 percent. At the end of the year, D borrowed $200,000 from X, promising to pay him back in one year plus 30 percent interest. D used part of the $200,000 from X to pay the interest due to S, T, U, V, and W. D also convinced them to extend the original notes for another year. D has no intention of ever repaying the principal of the notes.

5-31 *What Is Income?* In each of the following situations indicate whether taxable income should be recognized.

a.   L sued her former employer for sex discrimination evidenced in his compensation policy. She was awarded $100,000, $39,000 of which represented reimbursement for mental anguish.

b.   M, a sales clerk for a department store, purchased a microwave oven from the store's appliance department. The store has a policy allowing employees a 10 percent discount. This discount results in $45 savings to M.

c.   R received a bottle of perfume and a case of grapefruit from her boss at the annual Christmas party. The items were valued at $25.

5-32 *Constructive Receipt.* When would a cash basis taxpayer recognize income in the following situations? Assume the taxpayer reports on a calendar year.

    a. R, a traveling salesman, was out of town on payday, December 31. He picked up his check when he arrived back on January 3.

    b. C owns a bond with interest coupons due and payable on December 31. C clipped the coupons and redeemed them on January 7.

    c. R is an officer and controlling shareholder in XYZ Corporation. In December the corporation authorized bonuses for all officers. The bonus was paid in February of the following year.

5-33 *Constructive Receipt.* For each of the following situations, indicate whether the taxpayer has constructively received the income.

    a. R received a bonus as top salesman of the year. He received the check for $20,000 at 10 P.M. on December 31 at a New Year's Eve party. All the banks were closed.

    b. On January 3, D received the check for January's rent of her duplex. The envelope was postmarked December 31.

    c. On December 25, C Corporation rewarded its top executive, E, with 100 shares of stock for a job well done. E was unable to find a buyer until March 15 of the following year.

    d. Immediately after receiving her check on December 31, Z went to her employer's bank to cash it. The bank would not cash it since the employer's account was overdrawn.

5-34 *Constructive Receipt.* For each of the following situations, indicate whether the taxpayer has constructively received the income.

    a. X Corporation declared a dividend on December 15 and mailed dividend checks on December 28. R received her check for $200 on January 4.

    b. F owns a small apartment complex. His son, S, lives in one of the units and manages the complex. Several tenants left their January rent checks with S during the last week of December. S delivered the checks to his father in January.

    c. This year, the cash surrender value of L's life insurance policy increased by $500. In order to obtain the value, L must cancel the policy.

5-35 *Changes in Accounting Method.*   JB and his sons have operated a small "general store" in Backwoods, Idaho, since 1947. This year, JB hired a new accountant, who immediately told him he should be using the accrual method to account for his inventories and related sales. According to the accountant's best guess, as of January 1, 1954 the store's balances in accounts receivable and inventory were $40,000 and $50,000, respectively. On that same date, JB owed $10,000 in accounts payable related to his inventory. The receivables were primarily attributable to sales of seed to farmers as well as appliances. JB has always used the cash method of accounting, reporting all of his income when he receives it and deducting all costs when paid. According to the accountant, as of the close of the current year, JB had $70,000 in receivables outstanding (none of which had been reported in income), inventory of $130,000 (all expensed), and outstanding accounts payable for recent purchases of inventory of $20,000.

a. If JB is audited, what method of accounting will the IRS claim that he should be using? Is the method he is currently using a Category A or Category B method?

b. If the IRS audits JB and requires him to change his method of accounting, what is the adjustment amount and when will JB report it?

c. Same as (b) except JB voluntarily changes his method of accounting.

d. If JB changes to the accrual method of accounting to account for inventories and sales, may he continue to report other items of income (e.g., interest income) and expense (e.g., supplies) using the cash method?

5-36 *Advanced Payments for Goods.*   HIJ Furniture, an accrual basis company for both tax and financial accounting purposes, normally does not sell the items displayed in its showrooms, nor does it keep those items in stock. Instead, it obtains partial payment from the customer and orders the items directly from the manufacturer. During 1991, HIJ collected $60,000 with respect to furniture sales still on order at the close of the year. The partial payments collected by HIJ do not exceed their cost for the items ordered.

a. Must HIJ report any of the $60,000 as income in 1991?

b. Would your answer above differ if the partial payments collected by HIJ exceeded their cost and the items were in stock?

5-37 *Percentage of Completion.*   THZ Corporation is a large construction company. This year it contracted with the city of Old York to build a new performing arts center for a price of $5,000,000. Estimated total costs of the project were $4,000,000. Annual costs incurred were as follows:

1992	$2,000,000
1993	500,000
1994	1,000,000
Total	$3,500,000

a.   What method(s) of accounting may the corporation use to report income from the project?
b.   How much income would be reported each year under the percentage of completion method?
c.   Would any interest be due to (or from) the IRS as a result of this contract? If so, compute for the first year only, assuming the taxpayer is in the 34 percent tax bracket and the interest rate is 10 percent.
d.   Assume that the costs incurred in 1992 were $100,000. How much income is the taxpayer required to report in 1992?

5-38   *U.S. Savings Bonds.*   During 1991, S purchased U.S. Government Series EE Bonds for $700. The redemption value of the bonds at the end of the year was $756.

a.   What options are available to S with respect to reporting the income from the bonds?
b.   What advantage might be obtained by exchanging the Series EE Bonds for Series HH Bonds?

5-39   *Educational Savings Bonds Requirements.*   H and W have twin sons, S and T, and two daughters, D and E. The couple purchased Series EE savings bonds, hoping to take advantage of the interest exclusion for their children's education. This year, they cashed in some of the bonds, receiving $5,000. Of this amount, $2,000 represented interest. For each of the following independent situations, indicate how much, if any, of the exclusion is allowed this year.

a.   D enrolled at Michigan State University and paid tuition of $4,000 and fees for room and board of $3,000. To help defray some of these expenses, she used an academic scholarship of $1,000.
b.   While on her way to the first day of class, D fell and broke her leg. She withdrew from classes and received all of her money back.
c.   S is 25 and entered the Ph.D. program at the University of Texas this year. As a teaching assistant, he receives a salary of $7,000 during the year. His parents paid $1,000 of his tuition.
d.   H and W paid for all of T's tuition to attend Arizona State University. The couple's A.G.I. for this year was $100,000. When the couple purchased the particular bonds used to pay for T's tuition, their A.G.I. was $55,000.
e.   E, 22, redeemed bonds this year, receiving $5,000. E used all of the proceeds to pay for her tuition. She received the bonds as a gift from her parents last year. E's A.G.I. for this year is $3,000.

5-40   *Contested Income.*   In 1991, GLX Company, an accrual basis taxpayer, received $10,000 for supplying running shoes to T for sale in his sporting goods store. During 1991, T claimed the shoes had defective soles and requested GLX to refund the $10,000 payment.

a.   Must GLX report any of the $10,000 as income in 1991?
b.   Had GLX not received payment in 1991, would your answer in (a) change?
c.   Assume GLX and T resolved their dispute in 1992 and GLX refunded $2,000 to T. What would be the effect, if any, on GLX?

5-41 *Deposits and Prepaid Rents.* Q owns several duplexes. From each new tenant she requires a $150 security deposit and $300 for the last month's rent. The deposit is refundable assuming the tenant complies with all the terms of the lease. During the year, Q collected $1,000 in deposits and $2,400 of prepaid rents for the last month of occupancy. In addition, she refunded $400 to previous tenants but withheld $300 due to damages. How much must Q include in income assuming she is an accrual basis taxpayer?

5-42 *Prepaid Service Income: Accrual Method.*

a. LL Corporation, a calendar year and accrual basis taxpayer, is engaged in the lawn care business, providing fertilizer treatments four times a year. It sells one- and two-year service contracts. On September 1, 1991, it sold a contract for $100 and provided one treatment for the customer in 1991. What amount must be included in income in 1991 and 1992 if the contract is a one-year contract?

b. Same as (a) except that the contract is for two years.

c. A professional basketball team that reports on the calendar year and uses the accrual method collected $700,000 in pre-season ticket sales in August and September of 1991. Of its 41-game home season, 15 games were played prior to the end of the year. What amount must be included in income in 1991?

d. A posh resort hotel in Florida reports on the calendar year and uses the accrual method. During 1991, it collected $10,000 in advance payments for rooms to be rented during the winter of 1992. What amount of income must be included in 1991 and 1992?

5-43 *Income from Transferred Property.* E's grandmother owns several vending machines on campus. To help him through college, she allows E to collect and keep all the receipts from the machines. During the year, E spent approximately two hours a month to collect $5,000. Who must report the income and what is the amount to be included?

5-44 *Partnership Income.* QRS, a partnership, had taxable income of $120,000 for the fiscal year ended September 30, 1991. For the first quarter ending December 31, 1991, taxable income was $30,000. During 1991, Q, a partner with a 30 percent interest in profits and losses, withdrew $1,000 per month for a total of $12,000. What is Q's taxable income from QRS for 1991?

5-45 *Reporting Interest Income.* On November 1, 1990, G received a substantial inheritance and promptly made several investments. Indicate in each of the following cases the amount of interest income that he must report and the period in which the income is properly reported, assuming that G uses (1) the cash method of accounting, or (2) the accrual method of accounting. G reports using the calendar year.

a. G purchased a $10,000, 90-day U.S. Treasury bill at 99. The bill matured on January 30, 1991, when G redeemed it at par.

b. G purchased $100,000 of AFN Inc. 10 percent bonds for $95,000. The bonds were issued at par in 1982. The bonds pay interest semiannually on March 1 and September 1. On March 1, 1991, G received an interest payment of $5,000.

5-46 *Interest-Free Loans.* F is chief executive officer of CVC Corporation and has taxable income in excess of $200,000 annually. During the year, he loaned his 20-year-old son, S, $30,000, payable on demand without interest. S promptly invested the $30,000 and earned $1,200, which was his only income during the year.

    a.   Assuming the interest that should have been charged under applicable rate is $3,000, compute the effect of the loan on the taxable income of both F and S.

    b.   Would F be able to shift income to his son if he had made a loan of only $9,000?

5-47 *Code § 7872: Exceptions.* For each of the following independent cases, indicate the income and gift tax consequences for both the lender and the borrower.

    a.   J loaned his 19-year-old son, K, $8,000 interest-free which K used to purchase a car. K had $400 investment income from a savings account for the year.

    b.   Same as (a) except K decided to invest the money in a certificate of deposit yielding $800 of interest income producing a total net investment income of $1,200 for the year.

    c.   G loaned her 29-year-old daughter, D, $50,000 interest free to help her acquire a franchise for a fast-food restaurant. All of D's funds were invested in the business and consequently she had no investment income for the year.

    d.   P Corporation loaned its sole shareholder, Q, $150,000 interest free.

    e.   Same as (d) except Q owns no stock in P but is simply a key employee.

5-48 *Gifts of Income.* In each of the following cases, indicate who must report the income and the amount to be reported.

    a.   E's grandmother gave him a $10,000 certificate of deposit on April 30 this year. The certificate pays 10 percent interest semiannually on January 1 and July 1.

    b.   On June 6, 1991, M gave 100 shares of XYZ stock to D and also sold 100 shares in the market. On June 1, XYZ had declared a dividend of $2 per share payable on June 30 to shareholders of record as of June 15.

5-49 *Cash Method Eligibility.* Given the facts below, indicate whether the taxpayer may use the cash method for 1991 in the following situations.

    a.   Sweatshirt Corporation, a publicly traded corporation: annual gross receipts prior to 1988 were $1 million annually; gross receipts for 1989 were $3 million; and for 1990, $8 million.

    b.   Dewey, Cheatham and Howe, a national public accounting firm, operated as a partnership. Annual gross receipts for the last five years have exceeded $50 million.

    c.   McSwane, McMillan, and McClain, Inc., an architectural firm, operated as a regular C corporation. Annual gross receipts for the last two years have exceeded $7 million. McSwane, McMillan, and McClain own all of the stock and perform services for the firm.

    d.   Buttons and Bows, Inc., an S corporation.

    e.   A trust established for John Doe.

    f.   Plantation Office Park, a publicly traded limited partnership: annual gross receipts have never exceeded $2 million.

5-50 *Shifting Income to Children.*   Mr. and Mrs. D wish to shift income to their seven-year-old son, C, to be used for his college education. Explain whether the following would serve their goals or, alternatively, how they impact on any technique designed to shift income.

a.   Paying C an allowance for making his bed and picking up his clothes.

b.   Paying C for helping to wash cars at his dad's car wash.

c.   Buying C Series EE savings bonds.

d.   Arranging to have Mrs. D's employer pay C part of her salary.

e.   The social security rules.

f.   The rules governing personal exemptions.

CUMULATIVE PROBLEM

5-51 David K. Gibbs, age 37, and his wife Barbara, age 33, have two children, Chris and Ellen, ages 2 and 12. David is employed as an engineer for an oil company, and his wife recently completed a degree in accounting and will begin working for a public accounting firm next year. David has compiled the following information for your use in preparing his tax return for 1991.

1.   For the current year, David received a salary of $50,000. His employer withheld Federal income taxes of $9,000 and the appropriate amount of F.I.C.A. taxes.

2.   At the annual Christmas party, he received a card indicating that he would receive a bonus of $3,000 for his good work during the year. The bonus check was placed in his mailbox at work on December 30. Since David was out of town for the holidays, he did not pick up the bonus check until January 2.

3.   A bond issued by AM&T Inc. was sold on May 30, 1991 for $9,700, $700 of which represented interest accrued to the date of the sale. The Gibbs had purchased the bond (issued at par value of $10,000 on March 1, 1978) in 1988 for $10,000.

4.   Because of some financial difficulties the couple had encountered, Barbara was able to obtain an advance from her new employer of $1,500. Her first paycheck in January 1992 was to be reduced by this amount.

5.   The couple has a $500 U.S. savings bond, which they purchased for $300 and gave to their daughter several years ago. The proper election to report the income from the bond annually was made. The bond's redemption value increased $30 this year.

6.   David was an instant winner in the state lottery and won $50.

7.   The couple's only itemized deductions were interest on their home mortgage, $6,500; and property taxes on their home of $900.

Compute Mr. and Mrs. Gibbs' Federal income tax liability (or refund) for 1991. If a tax return is required by your instructor, prepare Form 1040, including Schedules A and B.

RESEARCH PROBLEMS

5-52 During the year, J, a college accounting professor, received complimentary copies of various textbooks from numerous publishers. J gives some of these books to students and the school library. J also keeps some of the books for his personal use and reference. A few times during the year J sold an unwanted text to a wholesale book dealer who periodically checked with him and other professors for texts. Must J report any income related to receipt of these books?

5-53 R recently became a member of a religious order. As a member, she was subject to the organization's complete control. The organization often required its members to terminate their employment in order to work in other jobs consistent with the organization's philosophy. For example, the organization supplied personnel to missions, hospitals, and schools. The organization also requires all members to take an oath of poverty and pay over all their earnings to it. Members' living expenses are paid for by the organization out of its own funds. Is R taxable on her earnings?

5-54 In each of the following cases, indicate who is responsible for reporting the income.

  a.   Dr. A instructed the hospital for which he worked to pay his salary to his daughter C.

  b.   H, age 16, agreed with his father to share equally any bonus he might receive for signing a professional baseball contract in exchange for his father's coaching, business management, and agent services. H signed a contract when he was 19.

  c.   R, a famous entertainer, agreed to perform at a concert gratuitously (without fee) for the benefit of a charitable organization.

  d.   In a contest for the best essay on why education is important, T, age 25, won the right to designate a person under 17 to receive $1,000.

Research aid:

   Rev. Rul. 76-323, 1976-2 C.B. 18.

5-55 M owed her good friend, F, $20,000. In addition, M planned on making a charitable contribution to her church of $10,000. Instead of using cash to pay her friend and to make the contribution, M is considering transferring stock to each in the appropriate amount. The stock is currently worth $100 per share. M had purchased the 300 shares of stock several years ago for $6,000 ($20 per share). Will M realize any income if she transfers the stock rather than paying cash?

5-56   Sam Sellit is a salesman for Panoramic Pools of St. Louis, a construction company that builds and sells prefabricated swimming pools. Over the past several years, Sam has progressed to become the top salesman for the St. Louis franchise. Sam has done so well that he is considering purchasing his own franchise and starting a company in San Antonio. This year he contacted the home office in Pittsburgh about the possibility of opening up his own shop. The vice president in charge of expansion, Greg Grow, suggested that the two of them meet at the company's annual meeting of franchisees in Orlando. Greg knew that Sam, although not a franchisee, would be attending because he was the top salesman in the St. Louis office, and the company invites the top salesman from each office as well as his or her spouse to attend the meeting.

While at the four-day meeting (Tuesday through Friday) in Orlando, Sam and his wife, Sue, met with Greg and discussed the potential venture. In addition, Greg allowed Sam and Sue to attend the parts of the meeting that were only for franchisees so that they could get a glimpse of how the company operated. Of course, while they were in Orlando, Sam and his wife visited all of the tourist attractions. On Tuesday, there were no meetings scheduled and everyone spent the day at Disney World and Epcot Center. On Thursday afternoon, no meetings were scheduled and the couple went with Greg and his wife to Sea World. Sam attended meetings for several hours on Friday while his wife played golf. The couple stayed over through Sunday and continued their sightseeing activities.

The company picked up the tab for the couple's trip, reimbursing Sam $3,500 which included the costs of air fare, meals, lodging, and entertainment. What are the tax consequences to Sam?

5-57   Large Corporation manufactures computers. Its total sales of computers last year were well over $100 million. With each computer it offers a three-year warranty, covering parts and labor. The company estimates the future costs of warranty work related to current year sales and defers the recognition of income until such time that it expects the warranty work will be done. Currently, the corporation reports 60 percent of the warranty income in the year of sale because the majority of warranty work occurs shortly after the computer has been sold. Thirty percent of the warranty income is reported in the second year of the warranty, and the remaining 10 percent is reported in the last year of the warranty. The company's estimates were based on sophisticated statistical techniques. Such techniques have produced estimates that appear extremely accurate based on the last 10 years of data. Upon audit this year, the IRS agent indicated that the company cannot defer the warranty income and assessed a large tax deficiency. Advise the taxpayer as to whether it should pay the additional tax or pursue the matter in court.

LEARNING OBJECTIVES

Upon completion of this chapter you will be able to:

- Identify which items an individual taxpayer must include in the computation of gross income

- Determine which items an individual taxpayer can exclude from the computation of gross income

- Understand generally what goals Congress had in mind in passing the applicable rules and exceptions for inclusions and exclusions

- Recognize tax planning opportunities related to the more common types of income inclusions and exclusions available to individual taxpayers

CHAPTER OUTLINE

Chapter 6

GROSS INCOME
Inclusions and Exclusions

INTRODUCTION

Gross income includes *all* income unless specifically exempted by the U.S. *Constitution*, by *statute*, or by the evolving but authoritative *definition* of income (outlined in Chapter 5). Both the Sixteenth Amendment and Code § 61(a) grant this broad approach to Federal income taxation. Consequently, it is the taxpayer's responsibility to (1) prove that a particular type of income is excluded, and (2) to provide the specific authority that permits the exclusion.

Income can be (1) taxable (includible) in total, (2) taxable in part and nontaxable (excludable) in part, or (3) nontaxable in total. In most instances, income that is nontaxable in total is completely omitted from the tax return. For example, it is not possible to determine who received certain nontaxable employee benefits by looking at the tax returns. In contrast, some income that is partially taxable and partially nontaxable is reported in full on the tax return and the nontaxable portion is subtracted in arriving at gross income. For instance, income included on certain brokerage statements is reported in full on the tax return, the nontaxable portion is subtracted, and the taxable portion remains a part of gross income.

This chapter contains a discussion of the more frequently encountered sources of income. To provide some order and logic to the discussion, these sources are classified in the following pages as (1) investments, (2) employee compensation and other benefits, (3) personal transfers between individuals, (4) transfers by unrelated parties, (5) business gross income, and (6) miscellaneous items.

INVESTMENTS

Gross income from investments includes the taxpayer's share of gross income from a partnership (see Chapter 22) and an S corporation (see Chapter 23). Although only the net income or loss is actually recorded on the tax return, the taxpayer is deemed to have reported each item individually, including the business's gross income.[1] This distinction, for example, can be important in determining whether an individual qualifies as a dependent. Gross income also includes the total amount of rents and royalties before any expenses are deducted.[2] In contrast, only the gain on investments in stocks, bonds, and annuities is treated as gross income. Depending on the source, all the interest may be nontaxable.

DIVIDENDS

Corporate distributions may be of several types. Those commonly received are

1. Cash or property dividends
2. Return of capital
3. Stock dividends

Cash and Property Dividends. A *dividend* is a distribution of cash or other assets to a shareholder with respect to the individual's stock. Dividends are taxable to the extent the distribution comes from the corporation's current or accumulated earnings and profits (E&P). [Basically, current E&P is a corporation's taxable income for the current year after certain specified adjustments are made. Accumulated E&P is a corporation's undistributed E&P from previous years. (In general, see Chapter 19.)] In the case of noncash assets, the value of the dividend received for individuals is the fair market value, but for corporations it is the lesser of fair market value or the distributing corporation's basis in the assets.[3] The taxable amount becomes the asset's basis. To avoid double taxation at the corporate level, corporate shareholders are allowed a special dividend-received deduction (discussed in Chapter 19).[4]

In contrast to a regular corporation, a mutual fund is usually treated as a conduit in that dividends distributed to its shareholders are deductible in computing the mutual fund's taxable income. As a result, a mutual fund is taxed only on its undistributed income. *Ordinary dividends* received by shareholders of a mutual fund are included in gross income in the years of receipt.[5] *Capital gain dividends* are treated as long-term capital gains irrespective of how long the shareholder has owned the stock in the mutual fund.[6] Furthermore, undistributed capital

---

[1] § 702(b) and (c). Business gross income is revenues or net sales less cost of goods sold.

[2] § 61(a)(5) and (6) and Reg. § 1.61-8.

[3] § 301(b)(1)(A) and (B).

[4] §§ 243 through 246. Generally, the deduction is a percentage of the dividends re-ceived from a domestic corporation determined as follows: (1) 70% when the stock ownership percentage (SOP) is less than 20%, (2) 80% when the SOP is 20% or more but less than 80%, and (3) 100% when the SOP is 80% or more.

[5] Reg. § 1.852-4(a).

[6] Reg. § 1.852-4(b).

gain dividends that have been allocated to shareholders by the mutual fund are taxable.[7] Corporate shareholders of a mutual fund are entitled to the dividend-received deduction with respect to ordinary dividends only. A mutual fund is required to provide each shareholder with Form 1099-DIV detailing the types of dividends paid or allocated during the year.

Return of Capital. Distributions of cash and other assets to shareholders by corporations in *excess* of their current and accumulated E&P do not qualify as dividends.[8] Instead, they are a return of capital, and are therefore nontaxable to the extent of the shareholder's basis in the stock. After the shareholder's basis in the stock is reduced to zero, additional distributions in excess of E&P are capital gains.[9]

> **Example 1.** C, Inc. distributes $100,000 to shareholders when its current E&P is $60,000 and it has no accumulated E&P. T, a 10% shareholder, has a basis in C, Inc. stock of $3,000. T receives $10,000, of which $6,000 (10% × $60,000) is from C's current E&P. Thus, T has a $6,000 taxable dividend; the $3,000 equal to his basis in the stock is a nontaxable return of investment, and the remaining $1,000 is capital gain.

There are a number of other types of distributions that do not qualify as dividends.[10] Some of these are listed below.

1. In some instances, earnings on deposits with banks, credit unions, investment companies, and savings and loan associations are referred to as dividends when they actually possess all the characteristics of interest. These dividends are reported as interest.[11]

2. Mutual insurance companies distribute amounts referred to as dividends to owners of unmatured life insurance policies. These dividends are treated as a nontaxable return of a portion of the insurance premium paid.[12]

3. Cooperatives distribute patronage dividends to cooperative members. These dividends are treated as a return of part of the original price paid for items purchased by members.[13]

4. As noted above, dividends from regulated investment companies (mutual funds) that represent gains on sales of investments from the fund are treated as long-term capital gains.[14]

---

[7] § 852(b)(3)(D).

[8] § 316(a).

[9] § 301(c)(3).

[10] § 116(c).

[11] Reg. § 1.116-1(d)(2)(ii).

[12] § 316(b)(1).

[13] Reg § 1.116-1(d)(1).

[14] Reg. § 1.116-1(d)(2)(iii).

Stock Dividends. In some instances, corporations wish to pay dividends but have insufficient cash or other assets to distribute. One approach is to issue stock dividends to shareholders without giving them an opportunity to receive cash, other assets, or other stock. If the stock dividend is common stock distributed to common shareholders, it is nontaxable.[15] Shareholders simply increase the number of common shares held. The basis in their original holdings is divided equally among all shares of common.[16] The holding period for the new common stock is the same as the holding period of the original common stock.

> **Example 2.** V owns 100 shares of Z common with a basis of $2,200 ($22 per share). He receives 10 shares of Z common as a stock dividend. If V did not have the right to receive cash or other assets in lieu of the stock, he has no taxable income and his $2,200 basis is allocated among the 110 shares of common for a $20 per share basis ($2,200 ÷ 110).

When nonconvertible preferred stock is distributed to common shareholders as a stock dividend, it too is nontaxable.[17] After the distribution, shareholders own both common and preferred stock. The basis in their original holdings of common stock is allocated between the common and the preferred stock based on their relative fair market values. The holding period for the preferred stock is the same as the holding period of the common stock.[18]

> **Example 3.** Q owns 100 shares of S common with a basis of $2,200. She receives 10 shares of S preferred as a stock dividend. The market value is $4,000 ($40 per share) for common and $1,000 ($100 per share) for preferred. If Q did not have the right to receive cash or other assets in lieu of the stock, she has no taxable income. Her basis for the preferred stock is $440 [$1,000 ÷ ($4,000 + $1,000 = $5,000 total value) = 20% × $2,200] and her basis for the common stock is $1,760 [either ($2,200 − $440) or ($4,000 ÷ $5,000) × $2,200].

Reinvested Dividends. Shareholders who have the right to choose between receiving their dividends in cash *or* in additional shares of stock do not qualify for the stock dividend exclusion. Regardless of whether these shareholders elect to receive cash or stock, they have taxable dividend income (to the extent of E&P, as discussed above).[19] This same treatment applies to all situations in which a dividend can change a common shareholder's proportionate ownership interest in the common stock.[20]

---

[15] § 305(a).

[16] § 307(a).

[17] § 305(a) and (b)(5). However, § 306 may require a taxpayer to recognize ordinary income for all or a portion of the gain when the preferred stock is sold.

[18] § 1223(5).

[19] § 305(b)(1).

[20] § 305(b)(2).

INTEREST

Generally, interest is taxable income regardless of (1) its source (a bank, business, friend, or relative), (2) the form of the interest-bearing instrument (savings account, bond, or note), or (3) how the funds were used. Two exceptions are (1) the exclusion for interest on certain state and local government obligations, and (2) the exclusion for interest on educational savings bonds.

Interest on State and Local Government Obligations. From the inception of the Federal income tax law, interest on obligations of a state, a territory, a U.S. possession, or any of their political subdivisions has been *nontaxable*.[21] This treatment stems from an uncertainty about whether taxing this interest would be unconstitutional and also from political pressure exerted by the affected governments.[22] The exclusion is exceedingly beneficial to these governments because it means they can pay a lower interest rate and still attract investors, especially those investors who are subject to taxes at the highest marginal rates.

> **Example 4.** K, Inc. invests $10,000 in corporate bonds that pay 13% annually and $10,000 in state bonds that pay 9% annually. If K, Inc.'s marginal tax rate is 34%, its after-tax earnings on the corporate bonds is less than its earnings on the state bonds.

	Corporate Bonds	State Bonds
Annual interest income............	$1,300	$900
Federal income tax (34%).........	442	0
After-tax income	$ 858	$900

If K's marginal tax rate is 15%, however, its after-tax earnings for the corporate bonds increases to $1,105 ($1,300 − $195).

A break-even point between taxable and nontaxable rates of return may be calculated with the following formula:

$$\text{Taxable interest rate} \times (1 - \text{Marginal tax rate}) = \text{Tax-free rate}$$

Applying the numbers in the example above when K, Inc.'s tax rate is 34 percent, the break-even point for the taxable bond is

$$13\% \times (1 - 0.34 = 0.66) = 8.58\%$$

---

[21] § 103(a)(1).

[22] In *National Life Insurance Co.*, 1 USTC ¶314, 6 AFTR 7801, 277 U.S. 508 (USSC, 1928), the Supreme Court indicated that Federal taxation of *interest* paid by state and local governments was unconstitutional.

However, in *Willcuts v. Bunn*, 2 USTC ¶640, 9 AFTR 584, 282 U.S. 216 (USSC, 1931), the Supreme Court reversed a Court of Appeals decision and held that Federal taxation of *gain* (not representing interest) from a sale of state and local securities was constitutional.

Thus, at the 34 percent marginal tax rate, a 13 percent taxable return is equal to an 8.58 percent tax-exempt return.

The formula can be converted to compute the break-even point for the tax-exempt bond as follows:

$$\text{Tax-free rate} \div (1 - \text{Marginal tax rate})$$

or

$$9\% \div (1 - 0.34 = 0.66) = 13.6\%$$

Thus, at the 34 percent marginal tax rate, a 9 percent tax-exempt return is equal to a 13.6 percent taxable return.

In recent years, Congress has reacted to the criticism that this exclusion subsidizes the wealthy (i.e., those subject to the highest tax rates) and has also reacted to the increasing number and complexity of financial offerings developed by state and local governments. Originally, these governments sold securities to fund public projects. In recent years, however, bonds have been issued to fund business construction and other industrial development projects. When this occurs, a governmental unit retains ownership of the facilities and leases them to a business. Because the interest rate on these bonds is lower than it would be on bonds issued by the corporation, the negotiated lease payments can be lower. Congress has curtailed the tax-exempt status of industrial development bonds. With certain specified exceptions, interest on industrial development bonds issued after April, 1968 is taxable income.[23]

There are numerous restrictions intended to curb the use of state and local bonds to finance business activities. For example, tax-exempt bonds can no longer be issued to finance airplanes, gambling facilities, liquor stores, health clubs, sky boxes, or other luxury boxes. Nor can the bonds be issued to finance the acquisition of farmland or existing facilities, with certain exceptions.

It should be noted that any exclusion on state and local obligations is for *interest* income received by the bondholder. Thus, *gain* on the sale of tax-exempt securities that does not represent interest is taxable income.[24] In addition, interest received for late payments of tax refunds, trade accounts receivable, or condemnation awards are taxable income.[25]

Educational Savings Bonds. As discussed in Chapter 5, § 135 provides a tax exemption for interest on U.S. Series EE savings bonds that are issued after December 31, 1989 and are used to finance higher education expenses

[23] § 103 (b).

[24] *Willcuts v. Bunn*, 2 USTC ¶640, 9 AFTR 584, 282 U.S. 216 (USSC, 1931). (See footnote 22.)

[25] *U.S. Trust Co. of N.Y. v. Anderson*, 3 USTC ¶1125, 12 AFTR 836, 65 F.2d 575 (CA-2, 1933) and *American Viscose Corp. v. Comm.*, 3 USTC ¶881, 10 AFTR 1478, 56 F.2d 1033 (CA-3, 1932).

incurred by the taxpayer, his or her spouse, or dependents. The exclusion is available only for taxpayers who (1) purchased the bonds after reaching age 24 and (2) are the sole owners of the bonds or own them jointly with their spouse. Consequently, the exclusion will not be allowed for bonds purchased by a parent or grandparent and put in a child's name. The bonds must be redeemed by the owner, rather than the educational institution, and the total accrued interest is exempt provided the aggregate redemption amount (i.e., principal plus interest) does not exceed the student's qualified educational expenses (i.e., tuition and required fees). Should the aggregate redemption amount exceed the student's qualified educational expenses for the year, the interest exclusion is determined by the following formula:

$$\frac{\text{Qualified education expenses}}{\text{Total redemption amount}} \times \text{Total accrued interest}$$

Furthermore, for 1991 the interest exclusion phases out for single taxpayers with modified A.G.I. exceeding $41,950 and for joint filers with modified A.G.I. exceeding $62,900.

ANNUITIES

An annuity is an investment contract that requires a fixed amount of money to be paid to the owner at specific intervals for either a certain period of time or for life. Annuities may be purchased either by an individual or for an employee by the employer. In addition, a beneficiary may elect to receive life insurance proceeds under an annuity arrangement. When the annuity is purchased by an individual, the interest earned on the investment is tax-deferred. This means the interest is taxable income but not during the current year when it is earned. Instead, the interest is included in gross income at some future date when the annuitant receives cash payments. Until then, the interest is automatically reinvested in full, without payment of Federal income taxes, to earn tax-deferred interest.

Example 5.   H invests $20,000 in a single-premium deferred annuity. The interest earned in the first year totals $2,000. Since this is tax-deferred, H has no taxable income, and the $2,000 is added to the $20,000 to continue to earn interest.

When earnings are reinvested, as they are for an annuity, the value of the asset grows at an increasing rate. A formula may be used to determine the *approximate* time period required to double the original investment in these circumstances:

$$72 \div \text{Compound interest rate}$$

If the compound interest rate used is an annual one, the solution provides the number of years required. Or, if the compound interest rate is a monthly one, the solution is in number of months.

Example 6. An annuity's annual compound interest rate is 12%. At this rate, the original investment will be doubled in approximately six years (72 ÷ 12).

Since the formula provides an *approximate* period, it should be used as a quick "rule of thumb" only. Greater accuracy is obtained by using annuity tables or by making the detailed computations.

Investors are discouraged from withdrawing funds before annuity benefits are scheduled to be received on contracts issued after August 13, 1982. Not only are early withdrawals treated as being distributions of the interest earned on the contract, a 10 percent penalty is assessed on the deferred income. The penalty is waived if the taxpayer satisfies certain requirements provided in the Code.[26]

Annuity payments are commonly scheduled to begin on retirement when the recipients' marginal tax rates are lower. Because of the lower rates, these individuals actually pay less total taxes in addition to receiving the benefits from tax deferral. Annuitants, similar to beneficiaries of life insurance contracts, may elect to receive the principal plus accumulated interest in installments for a stipulated number of years or for the annuitant's lifetime. The important point to remember is that the individual has taxable income equal to the amount of interest received. As discussed in Chapter 5, the portion that is a return of capital is nontaxable.[27] The formula for determining the portion that is a *nontaxable return of capital* for the current period is

$$\frac{\text{Investment in the contract}}{\text{Expected return from the contract}} \times \text{Amount received currently}$$

The taxable portion is the amount received currently less the portion that is a return of capital. When the annuity will be received over a stipulated number of years, the expected return from the contract is the amount to be received each year (or month) multiplied by the number of years (or months) payments are to be received.

Example 7. W invests $20,000 in a single-premium deferred annuity. At the end of 15 years, W elects to receive the $20,000 principal plus interest over the next ten years. She receives $7,000 in the current year and will receive $7,000 each of the following nine years. W's nontaxable return of capital each year is

$$\frac{\$20,000}{\$7,000 \times 10 \text{ years} = \$70,000} \times \$7,000 = \$2,000$$

W's taxable income each year is $5,000 ($7,000 − $2,000).

---

[26] See § 72(q)(2).   [27] § 72(b)(1).

Example 8.   Refer to *Example 7*. If W receives only three payments in the first year totaling $1,750 ($7,000 × $^3/_{12}$), the computation remains the same except the amount received currently is $1,750 (instead of $7,000). Consequently, her nontaxable return of capital in the first year is $500 [($20,000 ÷ $70,000) × $1,750] and her taxable income is $1,250 ($1,750 − $500).

Note that the solution to *Example 7* is the same if W had simply divided the $20,000 principal by the 10 years (and to *Example 8* if W adjusted the annual amount to months). This is not true, however, when an individual elects to receive the annuity payments over his or her lifetime. For these situations, the Regulations contain several tables based on contract payment terms and the annuitant's age.[28] Because of the Supreme Court decision in *Arizona Governing Committee v. Norris,*[29] tables V through VIII were added to the Regulations; these tables ignore a taxpayer's gender in calculating the expected return. In general, these tables became effective July 1, 1986, and must be used by those taxpayers making post–June 1986 contributions to the annuity contract. A portion of table V, which contains the new multiples, is reproduced in Exhibit 6-1.

Exhibit 6-1
Ordinary Life Annuities—One Life—Expected Return Multiples

Age	Multiple	Age	Multiple	Age	Multiple
21	60.9	58	25.9	95	3.7
22	59.9	59	25.0	96	3.4
23	59.0	60	24.2	97	3.2
24	58.0	61	23.3	98	3.0
25	57.0	62	22.5	99	2.8
26	56.0	63	21.6	100	2.7
27	55.1	64	20.8	101	2.5
28	54.1	65	20.0	102	2.3
29	53.1	66	19.2	103	2.1
30	52.2	67	18.4	104	1.9

[28]   Reg. § 1.72-9.

[29]   *Arizona Governing Committee v. Norris*, 82-52 Slip Op. (USSC, 1983). The case specifically dealt with whether monthly retirement benefits received under an employer's deferred compensation plan could be lower for a woman than for a man when the contributions to the plan were equal. In 1978, the Supreme Court held that an employer could not require women to make larger contributions than men in order to obtain the same monthly benefits. *Los Angeles Dept. of Water & Power v. Manhart*, 435 U.S. 702 (USSC, 1978).

When the payments will be received over the life of the annuitant, the expected return from the contract is the amount to be received each year times the multiple that corresponds to the annuitant's age in the Table.[30] It also is important to note that the portion of any annuity payment to be excluded from gross income cannot *exceed* the unrecovered investment in the contract immediately before the receipt of the payment.[31] In addition, if the annuitant dies before the entire investment is recovered, the amount of the *unrecovered investment* is allowed as a *deduction* for his or her final tax return.[32]

> **Example 9.** T, 65 years old, purchased a single-premium immediate life annuity on January 1, 1991 for $11,400. It will pay $100 a month for the rest of her life (i.e., annual payment of $1,200). From Exhibit 6-1, her multiple is 20.0. T's nontaxable return of capital each year is
>
> $$\frac{\$11,400}{\$1,200 \times 20 = \$24,000} \times \$1,200 = \$570$$
>
> T's taxable income is $630 ($1,200 − $570). The $570 is considered a return of capital until T recovers her $11,400 investment. Note that if she lives 21 years, the total amount she excludes is limited to $11,400 ($570 × 20 years = $11,400). Thus, T's taxable income for year 21 is the entire $1,200 received. In contrast, if she lives just 15 years, the total amount she excludes is $8,550 ($570 × 15 years), and the unrecovered amount of $2,850 ($11,400 − $8,550) is allowed as a deduction on T's final tax return.

Some employers with qualified pension or profit-sharing plans (see Chapter 18) purchase annuity contracts for their employees' retirement. The taxable income to the employee is dependent on the employee's total *after-tax* investment in the annuity. After-tax funds generally exclude contributions, for example, to certain Individual Retirement Accounts (when individuals are allowed a deduction for the contribution) and to qualified employer retirement plans (since these contributions are made from amounts that are excluded from gross income in the current year). Investments that are not from after-tax funds are ignored in determining the individual's capital investment in the annuity. In some situations, employees may not have invested any after-tax funds in the employer's plan. Consequently, their basis in the annuity contract is zero and all amounts are included in gross income when received by them. In all other instances, calculations for return of capital and taxable income are identical to the procedure outlined in the above paragraphs.

---

[30] § 72(c)(3). Two common types of life annuities are the *single-premium deferred life annuity* and the *single-premium immediate life annuity*. The former provides for annuity income after a specified future date (i.e., when the annuitant retires), whereas the latter provides the annuitant with income for life beginning at once.

[31] § 72(b)(2).

[32] § 72(b)(3).

Safe Harbor for Some Annuities. The Internal Revenue Service has provided taxpayers with a simplified safe harbor method for computing the nontaxable portion of annuity distributions from qualified plans.[33] In addition, the safe harbor method should enable distributees (i.e., recipients) to exclude a larger portion of each annuity payment. The simplified method may be elected if the annuity payments

1. Start after July 1, 1986;

2. Depend on the life of the distributee or the joint lives of the distributee and his or her beneficiary;

3. Are made from a qualified employee plan [under § 401(a)], an employee annuity [under § 403(a)], or an annuity contract [under § 403(b)]; and

4. Start when the distributee is under age 75 or, if older, there are less than five years of guaranteed payments remaining.

A taxpayer electing to use the safe harbor method will find the computations less onerous than those previously described for computing the exclusion ratio under § 72. Under this method, the total number of monthly annuity payments expected to be received is based on the distributee's age at the annuity starting date. Consequently, the life expectancy tables (such as Exhibit 6-1) can be ignored. Instead, Exhibit 6-2 is used, and is applicable whether the annuity is single life or joint and survivor type.[34]

The portion of each monthly annuity payment that is nontaxable is determined using the following formula:

$$\frac{\text{Investment in the contract}}{\text{Number of monthly payments}} = \text{Nontaxable return of capital}$$

Exhibit 6-2
Monthly Payments Table

Age of Distributee	Number of Payments
55 and under	300
56–60	260
61–65	240
66–70	170
71 and over	120

[33] Notice 88-118, 1988-2 C.B. 450.

[34] A single life annuity pays a fixed amount at regular intervals for the remainder of one person's life. A joint and survivor annuity pays a fixed amount at regular intervals to one individual for life, and on his or her death, the payments continue over the life of a designated person such as a spouse or child.

Example 10. H, an employee, retired on January 1, 1991 at the age of 65. He started receiving retirement benefits in the form of a joint and 50% survivor annuity to be paid for the joint lives of H and W (his spouse), who is 60. H contributed $48,000 (after-tax contributions) to the plan and will receive a retirement benefit of $2,000 a month. Upon H's death, W will receive a survivor retirement benefit of $1,000 each month. The nontaxable portion of each monthly annuity payment to H is calculated as follows:

$$\frac{\$48,000 \text{ investment}}{240 \text{ payments (see Exhibit 6-2)}} = \$200 \text{ nontaxable return of capital}$$

Should H die prior to receiving his entire investment of $48,000, W will likewise exclude $200 from her $1,000 monthly payment. As explained earlier, after 240 annuity payments have been made, any additional payments will be fully taxable. Should both H and W die prior to receiving 240 payments, a deduction is allowed in the amount of the unrecovered investment in the last income tax return.

The safe harbor method should help reduce the number of requests the IRS receives each year from retirees and beneficiaries asking the Service to make the necessary computations.

EMPLOYEE COMPENSATION AND OTHER BENEFITS

Employee compensation is included in gross income whether it is in the form of cash or other assets and whether it is salary, commissions, bonuses, tips, vacation pay, or severance pay.[35] In addition, employers incur a number of other expenses for the benefit of their employees. These may be classified as (A) generally includible in, or (B) generally excludable from, the employees' gross income when the expenses are incurred by the employer.

A. *Generally Includible in Gross Income*

Reimbursement for
    Business transportation and travel
    Business entertainment
    Moving expenses
    Educational expenses
Employer gifts
Employer awards

---

[35] § 61(a)(1) and Reg. § 1.61-2(a).

B.   **_Generally Excludable from Gross Income_**

Employee taxes
   Social Security (FICA) taxes
   State and Federal unemployment taxes
Premiums paid on
   Group-term life insurance (up to $50,000 coverage)
   Health insurance
   Accident insurance
   Disability insurance
Death benefits (first $5,000)
Meals and lodging (on the premises at the employer's convenience)
Supper money
Legal plans
Educational-assistance plans
Child or dependent care facilities
Benefits that would qualify as deductible expenses by the employee
Parking
Use of company facilities or services
Purchase discounts
De minimis benefits
Tuition reduction by educational institutions

Most employee fringe benefit plans must meet rigid rules to enable the employer to deduct contributions to the plans and for employees to exclude these amounts. Basically, the plans must (1) not discriminate in favor of highly compensated employees, (2) be in writing, (3) be for the exclusive benefit of the employees, (4) be legally enforceable, (5) provide employees with information concerning available plan benefits, and (6) be established with the intent that they will be maintained indefinitely. In addition, several eligibility and benefit tests provide detailed rules that must be met to ensure employer costs are nontaxable income for employees. Additional employment benefits involving stock option, profit-sharing, and pension plans are discussed in Chapter 18.

REIMBURSEMENT OF EMPLOYEE EXPENSES

Amounts received from employers as reimbursement of expenses are included in an employee's gross income regardless of whether the employee has an offsetting business deduction (see Chapter 8 for an exception when the employees have accounted to their employers). The most commonly reimbursed items are business-related expenses such as transportation, out-of-town travel, entertainment, and moving expenses for a new or transferred employee. In addition, some employers reimburse employees for all or part of their educational expenses. This is likewise included in income (unless it is made under an educational-assistance plan—discussed later in this chapter). Generally, when reimbursement of these items equals the employee's deductible expense, the net effect on adjusted gross income (A.G.I.) is zero. An excess of reimbursement over deductible expenses increases A.G.I. Under-reimbursement also has a zero effect on A.G.I. but may reduce taxable income if the amounts qualify as itemized deductions (see Chapters 8 and 11).

EMPLOYER GIFTS

The inclusion or exclusion of *employer gifts* depends on several factors: (1) whether a legal obligation exists, (2) whether the employer intends to make a gift, (3) whether the employer deducts the cost for tax purposes, and (4) whether the amount is nominal. The existence of a legal obligation generally means the transfer is taxable compensation, not a gift. In contrast, the absence of a legal obligation to make the transfer is favorable, but not conclusive, evidence that the transfer is a gift. The employer's intent also is important. For the transfer to be a gift, it must be made with detached or disinterested generosity and not be a reward for past services nor made in expectation of future services.[36] Intent also is evidenced by how the employer handles the gift on the business's tax return. Compensation is deductible whereas a gift is not. An exception is made when the value of the gift is nominal.[37] For example, a holiday gift of a turkey, ham, umbrella, or inexpensive pen may be deducted by the employer but is nontaxable by the employee.

This same reasoning applies to all business-related gifts whether made to employees, clients, or other business contacts.[38] Although the word *nominal* (or *de minimis*) is not defined for employee gifts, it is defined for gifts to nonemployees as being $25 or less. Thus, the $25 limitation is presumed to be applicable to all types of gifts. This does not mean that a larger amount cannot qualify as a gift if other factors are favorable. It does mean, however, that both parties benefit when the gift is nominal; the employer deducts the cost as a business expense and the employee excludes the income. This two-sided benefit does not exist for amounts above $25.

EMPLOYER AWARDS

Employer awards to employees, other than de minimis fringe benefits (discussed later in this chapter), are generally treated as compensation with two exceptions: if they are provided (1) for length-of-service or safety achievements, or (2) under a nondiscriminatory qualified award plan. To be nontaxable, the awards must be made with tangible personal property. No exclusion is available for cash payments or the equivalent. The award must be given as part of a meaningful presentation and under conditions and circumstances that do not create a significant likelihood of the payment of disguised compensation. Also, no exclusion for the length-of-service award is available if it or a similar award is made within the individual's first five years of employment with the employer. To be nontaxable, safety awards cannot have been made to more than 10 percent of a company's eligible employees. All employees are considered to be eligible except those in managerial, professional, and clerical positions.[39]

---

[36] *Comm. v. Duberstein,* 60-2 USTC ¶9515, 5 AFTR2d 1626, 363 U.S. 278 (USSC, 1960).

[37] Rev. Rul. 59-58, 1959-1 C.B. 17.

[38] §274(b).

[39] See §§74(c) and 274(j).

Qualifying awards are deductible by the employer and nontaxable by the employee if the amount does not exceed the statutory limits. Under these limitations, the cost of property cannot exceed $400 per employee annually for length of service and safety achievements or $1,600 annually for all qualified plan awards, including length of service and safety achievements. For example, an employee achievement award (other than a qualified plan award) that costs the employer $390 and has a fair market value of $440 would be fully excluded from the employee's gross income. Excess costs are taxable income to the extent of the *greater* of (1) the non-deductible cost to the employer due to the limitations, or (2) the property's market value in excess of the limitations. This taxable income must be reported on the employee's Form W-2.

> **Example 11.** R, Inc. pays $525 ($640 market value) for a brooch that it awards to L in recognition of her 15 years of service to the company. No other awards are given to L during the year. R's deduction is limited to $400, and L has taxable income of $240 (the greater of $525 − $400 = $125 and $640 − $400 = $240). The $240 will appear on L's Form W-2 as taxable income.

SOCIAL SECURITY BENEFITS

When taxpayers (employees, self-employed, and others) collect Social Security benefits, these receipts generally are excludable from gross income.[40] For high-income bracket recipients, however, a portion of the social security benefits received must be included as taxable income. Thus, in effect, these amounts are taxed to some individuals twice; first when included as gross wages and second when included as social security benefits received.

Basically, social security recipients must include in gross income the lesser of (1) one-half the benefits received, *or* (2) one-half the excess *combined income* (adjusted gross income + interest on tax-exempt bonds + one-half of benefits received) over a specified base amount. The specified base is $32,000 for married filing jointly, $0 for married filing separately, and $25,000 for other individuals.[41] Deductions are allowed for legal fees incurred in perfecting social security claims, and adjustments are allowed for catch-up and repayment situations. Congress has earmarked all income tax generated by this new law for the social security trust fund.

---

[40] Rev. Rul. 70-217, 1970-1 C.B. 12.   [41] § 86.

Example 12. Taxpayers H and W are married and file a joint return. Their income for the year is as follows:

Taxable interest	$15,000
Dividend income	5,000
Net rental income	7,000
Tax-exempt bond interest	18,000
Social security benefits	10,000

Assuming they have no deductions *for* adjusted gross income, H and W must include $5,000 of their social security benefits in taxable income, computed as follows:

Taxable interest		$15,000
Dividends		5,000
Net rental income		7,000
Adjusted gross income		$27,000
Taxable social security benefits:		
Adjusted gross income	$27,000	
Plus: Tax-exempt interest	18,000	
One-half of social security		
benefits	5,000	
	$50,000	
Less: Specified base	(32,000)	
Excess combined income	$18,000	
Social security benefits		$10,000
Includible social security benefits:		
Lesser of $9,000 (1/2 of $18,000		
excess combined income) or		
$5,000 (1/2 of $10,000 benefits)		$ 5,000

UNEMPLOYMENT BENEFITS

Employers only, not employees, are subject to Federal and State unemployment taxes. These *taxes* are deductible business expenses for the employer and are not gross income for the employee. However, unemployment benefits *received* under a government program are included in gross income.[42]

EMPLOYEE INSURANCE

It is common for employers to have group insurance coverage for employees. Premiums may be paid by the employer only, by the employee only, or by both the employer and employee under some shared cost arrangement. Generally, employer-paid premiums for health, accident, and disability insurance are deductible business expenses and are excluded from the employee's gross income. On the other hand, life insurance premiums paid by the employer generally are included by the employee and deductible by the employer. As may be expected, however, there are exceptions.

---

[42] § 85(a).

Life Insurance Premiums and Proceeds. Employer-paid life insurance premiums are nontaxable by an employee but *only* for the first *$50,000* of *group-term life insurance* protection.[43] Premiums paid by an employer for any other type of life insurance are fully included in each employee's gross income. In order to qualify as group insurance, the employer must provide coverage for all employees with a few permitted exceptions based on their age, marital status, or factors related to employment. Examples of employment-related factors are union membership, duties performed, compensation received, and length of service.[44] Acceptable discrimination, however, is limited by the Regulations. Thus, employers may establish eligibility requirements that exclude certain types of employees, such as those who work part-time, who are under age 21, or who have not been employed at least six months. But omitting older employees or those with longer service records generally is not permitted.

When group-term insurance protection exceeds $50,000, the employee's taxable income is an amount set forth in the Regulations rather than actual premiums paid. The taxable amount for each $1,000 of insurance in excess of $50,000 is based on the employee's age as of the last day of his or her tax year. For group-term life insurance provided after 1988, the Technical and Miscellaneous Revenue Act of 1988 required the IRS to prescribe higher monthly rates for taxpayers over age 64. Under prior law, taxpayers over age 64 received a favorable tax break, in that the premium cost was computed as if they fell in the 60 to 64 age bracket. Accordingly, the IRS has provided a new table (see Exhibit 6-3) for determining the cost of group-term life insurance provided employees after December 31, 1988.[45]

Example 13. BC, Inc. provides all full-time employees with group-term insurance. Records for three of the employees show the following information. All three were employed by BC for the full year.

Employee	Age	Insurance Coverage	Coverage in Excess of $50,000
D	56	$80,000	$30,000
E	38	62,000	12,000
F	35	40,000	0

D's taxable income is $270 ($9.00 × $30,000 ÷ $1,000). E's taxable income is $15.84 ($1.32 × $12,000 ÷ $1,000). F has no taxable income from group-term life insurance, since the coverage does not exceed $50,000.

[43] § 79(a). The $50,000 is eliminated for retired employees who are disabled.

[44] Reg. §§ 1.79-0(c) and 1.79-1(a)(4).

[45] Temp. Reg. § 1.79-3T. Beginning in 1988, the cost of group-term life insurance that an employee must include in his or her gross income must also be treated as wages for social security withholding purposes.

Exhibit 6-3

| | Includible Income per $1,000 | |
Employee's Age	Monthly	Annually
Under 30	$0.08	$ 0.96
30 to 34	0.09	1.08
35 to 39	0.11	1.32
40 to 44	0.17	2.04
45 to 49	0.29	3.48
50 to 54	0.48	5.76
55 to 59	0.75	9.00
60 to 64	1.17	14.04
65 to 69	2.10	25.20
70 and over	3.76	45.12

Regardless of whether life insurance is provided by the employer or not, proceeds received by a beneficiary on the death of the insured ordinarily are excludable from gross income.[46] There are some exceptions, however. For example, insurance proceeds are taxable if the proceeds are a *substitute for taxable income* or if the policy was transferred in exchange for *valuable consideration*.[47] Each of these exceptions is discussed below.

Substitute for Taxable Income. In some instances, life insurance is used to protect a creditor against a bad debt loss on the death of the insured. However, the fact that the debt is offset by life insurance proceeds on the death of the insured does not cause otherwise taxable income to be nontaxable. For example, amounts equal to unreported interest due on the debt are taxable interest income.[48] Similarly, proceeds offsetting debt that was previously written off as uncollectable, or proceeds representing gain not previously reported, are included in gross income.[49]

---

[46] § 101(a)(1).

[47] Insurance proceeds are also taxable if the policy is an investment contract with little or no *insurance risk* or the owner of the policy does not have an *insurable interest* in the insured. In addition to the insured, a spouse, dependents, business partners, and in some instances, creditors and employers are considered to possess the requisite insurable interest.

[48] *Landfield Finance Co. v. Comm.*, 69-2 USTC ¶9680, 24 AFTR 2d 69-5744, 418 F.2d 172 (CA-7, 1969), *aff'g.* 69-1 USTC ¶9175, 23 AFTR2d 69-601, 296 F. Supp. 1118 (DC, 1969).

[49] *St. Louis Refrigerating & Cold Storage Co. v. Comm.*, 47-2 USTC ¶9298, 35 AFTR 1477, 162 F.2d 394 (CA-8, 1947), *aff'g.* 46-2 USTC ¶9320, 34 AFTR 1574, 66 F. Supp. 62 (DC, 1946) and Rev. Rul. 70-254, 1970-1 C.B. 31.

Transfer for Valuable Consideration.   If a policy is transferred to another party in exchange for valuable consideration, any *gain* from the proceeds on the insured's death is taxable income.[50] Gain is defined as the insurance proceeds less the owner's basis. Basis is the total purchase price plus all premiums paid by the subsequent owner after the transfer.

> **Example 14.**   XY Corporation purchased a $15,000 life insurance policy from S, the insured, for $7,300. The corporation made five annual premium payments of $600 each on the policy. S died at the end of the fifth year and XY collected $15,000 insurance. Since XY's basis in the policy is $10,300 [($600 × 5 payments) + $7,300], its taxable income is $4,700 ($15,000 − $10,300).

There are four exceptions to *Example 14.* All gain is nontaxable if the purchaser is (1) a partner of the insured, (2) a partnership in which the insured is a partner, (3) a corporation in which the insured is a shareholder or officer, or (4) the insured.[51]

Health Insurance Benefits.   With few exceptions, all medical insurance benefits are excluded from income regardless of who pays the premiums.[52] Any reimbursement of medical costs simply reduces the amount of medical expenses that can be itemized (as deductions from A.G.I.—discussed in Chapter 11).[53] However, in some instances the expenses are paid in one year but reimbursement is not received until a later year. Taxpayers have a choice when this occurs. One, they may anticipate the reimbursement and not deduct any of the reimbursable expenses. This decision means the reimbursement is nontaxable when received. Alternatively, these taxpayers may choose to itemize all medical costs in the year paid even though reimbursement is expected. This decision means the reimbursement is included in gross income when received to the extent a *tax benefit* was obtained for the prior year's deduction.[54] Since only the amount of medical expenditures that exceed 7.5 percent of A.G.I. provides a tax benefit (i.e., reduces an individual's taxable income), it is possible that part of the reimbursement is nontaxable.

---

[50]   § 101(a)(2).

[51]   § 101(a)(2)(B).

[52]   § 106.

[53]   §§ 105(b) and 213.

[54]   § 111.

> **Example 15.** J pays $4,000 medical expenses in 1991 and receives reimbursement of $1,100 in 1991 and $2,900 in 1992 from the insurance company. J's 1991 A.G.I. is $20,000. If J chooses to deduct all unreimbursed medical expenses in 1991, her itemized deduction is $2,900 ($4,000 − $1,100 reimbursed in 1991) and her *tax benefit* is $1,400 [$2,900 − (7.5% × $20,000 A.G.I. = $1,500)]. Thus, only $1,400 of the $2,900 reimbursement received in 1992 is included in gross income. Alternatively, if J decides to forgo the deduction in 1991, she has no taxable income in 1992. In this example, the important factors in J's decision are (1) her marginal tax rates for both years, and (2) the present value to her of the tax deferral for one year.

In contrast to the above, reimbursement received in one year for a medical expense not paid until a future year is nontaxable.

> **Example 16.** L pays medical expenses of $1,100 in 1991 and $2,900 in 1992. However, he is reimbursed in 1991 by the insurance company for the entire $4,000. L may not deduct the medical expenses, but he also does not have taxable income for the reimbursement.

If medical coverage is financed by the employer, any reimbursement in excess of medical expenses incurred by an employee for himself or herself, a spouse, and dependents is included in gross income.[55] These excess amounts, however, are not included if the premiums were paid by the individual.

Corporations that finance their own medical benefit plans from company funds (instead of through insurance) are required to establish plans that do not discriminate in favor of certain officers, shareholders, or highly paid employees. If the plan is discriminatory, individuals in these three categories must report taxable income equal to any medical reimbursement they received that is not available to other employees.[56] Thus, the purpose is to encourage corporations to extend medical coverage to all of their employees.

Accident and Disability Insurance Benefits. As a general rule, all amounts received under an *employer-financed* accident or disability plan are taxable with few exceptions. When payments are for permanent loss or use of a function or member of the body or for permanent disfigurement, however, they are nontaxable.[57]

> **Example 17.** G lost two fingers while making repairs to her automobile. She received $2,500 from her employer-provided accident insurance policy. The $2,500 is nontaxable income and is not considered to be a reimbursement of any medical expense.

---

[55] § 105(b).

[56] § 105(h).

[57] §§ 105(a) and (c).

In contrast with employer-financed disability plans, all disability income is *nontaxable* if the taxpayer paid for the disability coverage.[58] Consequently, those employees with long-term disabilities may incur substantial tax costs if their disability income is received from employer-financed plans.

> **Example 18.** After graduation from high school, R was employed by WW Manufacturing Company. The company's employee benefits included disability insurance. R's disability insurance premiums averaged $250 annually. After 15 years with WW, R became seriously ill. The illness left him permanently disabled. After a three-month wait, required by the insurance company, R began receiving $800 monthly disability income. Whether the $800 is taxable income depends on who paid the $250 annual premium on the disability policy. If WW paid the premium, the $800 monthly disability income is taxable income. If R paid the premium, the $800 is nontaxable. If R paid a portion of the premium, for example 40%, then that portion, $320 (40% × $800), is nontaxable, and the remaining $480 is attributable to the employer's contribution and is, therefore, taxable income.

DEATH BENEFITS

When an employee dies, payments to the deceased's beneficiaries by an employer may qualify as either death benefits, compensation, or gifts. The first $5,000 of payments that qualify as death benefits is deductible by the employer but is excluded from income for the beneficiaries. (Amounts in excess of $5,000 are either compensation or gifts, based on the employer's intent, as discussed earlier in this chapter.) To qualify for this exclusion, the payment must be made *solely* because of an employee's death.[59] It does not matter, however, whether the payment is a legal obligation or a voluntary act of the employer. Any amounts earned by the employee, or amounts that represent other nonforfeitable rights vested in the employee prior to death, would have been paid regardless of death, and consequently, do not qualify for the exclusion. Examples of amounts earned by the employee before death are accrued salaries, bonuses, commissions, and vacation pay. All of these are taxable compensation. An exception occurs, however, when lump-sum distributions are made from qualified pension, profit-sharing, or stock bonus plans. These distributions qualify for the exclusion even if the benefits are nonforfeitable.

In most instances, death benefits in excess of $5,000 are deducted by the employer, and are therefore taxable to the beneficiary. The $5,000 limit is per employee and is unaffected by the number of employers or beneficiaries. The exclusion also covers beneficiaries of self-employed individuals but only if lump-sum distributions are made.[60] When more than one beneficiary is involved, the $5,000 exclusion is allocated among all of them, regardless of their relationships to the deceased, based on each one's percentage of the total death benefit paid.

---

[58] § 104(a)(3) and Reg. § 1.104-1(d).

[59] § 101(b) and Reg. § 101-2(a).

[60] § 101(b)(3).

Example 19. A corporation distributes $8,000 in death benefits to a deceased employee's beneficiaries as follows: $4,000 to the spouse; $2,000 to a son, and $2,000 to a daughter. The exclusion for the spouse is $2,500 ($4,000 ÷ $8,000 = 50% × $5,000) and for each child is $1,250 ($2,000 ÷ $8,000 = 25% × $5,000). Thus, taxable income for the spouse is $1,500 ($4,000 − $2,500) and for each child is $750 ($2,000 − $1,250). The entire $8,000 is a deductible business expense for the corporation.

In some instances, employer distributions in excess of $5,000 qualify as business gifts. This means the employer can deduct only $5,000 as a death benefit and the remainder is subject to the $25 business gift limitation discussed previously in this chapter.[61] Since both the $5,000 death benefit and the gifts are nontaxable, beneficiaries have no gross income.

EMPLOYER-PROVIDED MEALS AND LODGING

The value of meals and lodging provided by an employer to an employee and the employee's spouse and dependents is excluded from income if

1. Provided for the *employer's convenience*;

2. Provided *on* the employer's *business premises*; and

3. In the case of lodging, the employee *is required* to occupy the quarters in order to perform employment duties.[62]

Generally, meals and housing furnished to employees without charge are considered to be for the employer's convenience if a substantial noncompensatory business purpose exists.[63] For example, there may be substantial business reasons to provide meals and lodging to the manager of a motel who is on 24-hour call.[64] But, if the employee has the option to receive other compensation instead, the value of the meals and lodging is included in income.[65]

If all requirements for exclusion are met, the value of meals and lodging is nontaxable for all *employees*, even those who are major shareholders.[66] This provision, however, does not apply to owners who do not qualify as employees.

---

[61] § 274(b).

[62] § 119 and Reg. § 1.119-1(b).

[63] Reg. §§ 1.119-1(a)(2) and (b).

[64] *J.B. Lindeman*, 60 T.C. 609 (1973), *acq.*

[65] Reg. § 1.119-1(c)(2).

[66] See *Comm. v. Wilhelm, et al.*, 66-2 USTC ¶9637, 18 AFTR2d 5563, 257 F. Supp. 16 (DC, 1966); but see *Atlanta Biltmore Hotel Corp. et al. v. Comm.*, 65-2 USTC ¶9573, 16 AFTR2d 5285, 349 F.2d 677 (CA-5, 1965).

Since it has been held that owners of proprietorships and partnerships cannot be employees of their businesses, the exclusion is not available to them. Consequently, the costs of meals and lodging furnished a proprietor or partner generally are nondeductible business expenses.[67]

Some employees who are required to accept employer-provided meals or housing must pay for them. If the fee is a fixed assessment, employees have nontaxable income equal to the charges.[68] Otherwise, these payments are personal expenses. Special rules apply to qualified campus lodging, primarily covering lodging on or near an educational institution provided for its employees.

> **Example 20.** Employees of the Q Recreational Spa are required to accept housing on the grounds as a condition of employment. Employee N's monthly salary is $1,000. In addition, she pays monthly rent of $200 for housing on the grounds; the housing has a rental value of $450. N's monthly taxable compensation is $800 ($1,000 − $200). If N were *not* required to live on the grounds to perform her duties, her monthly taxable compensation would be $1,250 ($450 − $200 = $250 + $1,000).

Nontaxable meals and lodging must be furnished on the employer's premises. The term *business premises* has been interpreted to be either the primary place of business (e.g., the hotel, restaurant, or construction site) or elsewhere as long as it is near the place of business and where a significant portion of the business is conducted.[69] However, employer-owned housing located two blocks from the primary place of business, a motel, was disallowed because it was not considered to be on the employer's premises.[70] This contrasts with employer-owned housing located across the street from the primary place of business, a hotel, that was held to be on the premises.[71] Apparently, taxpayer success in this second case was based on the amount of business conducted in the home rather than its location.

Definitions of what constitutes meals and lodging are broadly interpreted. For example, lodging includes operating costs such as utilities, as well as the rental value of housing.[72] In addition to restaurant meals, purchases of unprepared food and nonfood items such as napkins and paper towels from grocery stores have been allowed by the courts.[73] However, a 1977 Supreme Court decision

---

[67] Rev. Rul. 53-80, 1953-1 C.B. 62 and *Wilson v. Comm.*, 67-1 USTC ¶9378, 19 AFTR2d 1225, 376 F.2d 280 (Ct. Cls., 1967); but see *George A. Papineau*, 16 T.C. 130 (1951), *nonacq.*

[68] Reg. §§ 1.119-1(a)(2), (a)(3), and (b) and Rev. Rul. 59-307, 1959-2 C.B. 48.

[69] Rev. Rul. 71-411, 1971-2 C.B. 103.

[70] *Comm. v. Anderson*, 67-1 USTC ¶9136, 19 AFTR2d 318, 371 F.2d 59 (CA-6, 1966), *cert. denied.*

[71] *J.B. Lindeman*, 60 T.C. 609 (1973), *acq.*

[72] See *Comm. v. Dole, et al.*, 65-2 USTC ¶9688, 16 AFTR2d 5756, 351 F.2d 308 (CA-1, 1965), *aff'g.* 43 T.C. 697 (1965), *acq.*, and Rev. Rul. 68-579, 1968-2 C.B. 61.

[73] See *Jacob v. Comm.*, 74-1 USTC ¶9316, 33 AFTR2d 74-972, 493 F.2d 1294 (CA-3, 1974).

seems to end disagreement over whether employer cash reimbursement of meals and groceries qualifies for the exclusion. In *Kowalski*, the Supreme Court ruled that the exclusion applies only to meals (and presumably lodging) furnished *in kind*, and not to cash reimbursements.[74] The full effect this decision will have on the issue of employer-provided meals and lodging is yet to be known. For example, it has long been held that cash allowances or "supper monies" infrequently paid to employees working overtime are nontaxable.[75] A footnote in *Kowalski* specifically states this issue was not considered in the decision. In addition, exclusions for cash allowances paid to military personnel also could be in question as a result of *Kowalski*.

ADDITIONAL EMPLOYEE BENEFITS

The types of fringe benefits a firm provides its employees can be a very important factor in attracting and retaining key people. Fortunately, the Internal Revenue Code contains a number of provisions granting employers and employees favorable tax treatment. For example, to encourage employers to underwrite the cost of child care, the Code allows an employer a deduction and an employee an exclusion for child and dependent care assistance provided through an employer plan.[76] The employee's exclusion, however, is limited to $5,000 annually (and $2,500 for married filing separate returns). Many of the requirements relating to this exclusion parallel those found in the child and dependent care tax credit provisions (discussed in Chapter 13).[77]

The Revenue Reconciliation Act of 1990 extends the § 127 exclusion for employer-provided educational assistance benefits of $5,250 per year per employee to December 31, 1991. Furthermore, for taxable years beginning after December 31, 1990, the term "educational assistance" is extended to graduate level courses. Prior law (i.e., tax years beginning after 1987 and before 1991) did not apply to courses leading to advanced academic or professional degrees. To the extent that the educational assistance is not excludable because it exceeds the maximum dollar limitation, it may be excludable as a working condition fringe benefit (discussed below) under Code § 132(d), assuming the education is job related. In addition, the new law extends the Code § 120 exclusion for employer-provided group legal service plans through taxable years beginning before January 1, 1992.

---

[74] *Kowalski v. Comm.*, 77-2 USTC ¶9748, 40 AFTR2d 6128, 434 U.S. 77 (USSC, 1977).

[75] O.D. 514, 2 C.B. 90 (1920).

[76] § 129.

[77] § 44A.

In 1984, Congress enacted legislation that, in general, codified many of the fringe benefits allowed in the past but not specified in the Code or Regulations.[78] Beginning with 1985, only the following additional employee benefits are excluded from income by employees:

1. Working condition fringe benefits

2. No-additional-cost services

3. Qualified employee discounts

4. De minimis fringe benefits

5. Qualified tuition reduction by educational institutions

Working Condition Fringe Benefits. This exclusion provides that fringe benefits are nontaxable to the extent that employees could deduct the costs if they reimbursed their employer or otherwise paid the costs.[79] For example, many businesses furnish some of their employees with company-owned automobiles. Expenses related to the business usage of the cars are deductible by employers and are excluded from income by the employees. In contrast, personal use of the cars, which includes commuting between the employees' home and work, is taxable compensation (unless it is nontaxable under the de minimis rule discussed later in this section).[80] This income is reported as other compensation, and thus not subject to withholding taxes.[81] If, however, employees reimburse their employers for all personal use of the automobiles, there is no auto-related taxable compensation. Other items qualifying for this exclusion are professional dues and subscriptions. These benefits need not be provided to all employees (i.e., they may be reserved for officers, owners, and highly paid employees).

Several other types of benefits that result in deductible costs for employers and nontaxable income for employees have been available for many years. For example, some employees enjoy free or low-cost parking. Although this expense is not deductible when paid by an employee, the exclusion was extended to cover this fringe benefit when paid by the employer. Thus, the value of parking provided on or near the business premises is nontaxable as a working condition fringe benefit.[82] In addition, the Code contains an exclusion for the use of athletic facilities provided on the employer's premises primarily for employees, their spouses, and their dependent children.[83]

---

[78] § 132.

[79] § 132(d).

[80] § 61 and Reg. § 1.61-2(d)(1).

[81] Reg. § 1.6041-2 and Ltr. Rul. 8122017. Although not subject to withholding taxes, this income is subject to social security taxes.

[82] § 132(h)(4).

[83] § 132(h)(5).

No-Additional-Cost Services.   Some employers allow employees to use company facilities or services without charge or for a minimal maintenance fee. Unlike the situation with most other benefits, in this case employees have nontaxable income only if the company incurs no additional cost as a result of the employees' usage and the benefit does not discriminate in favor of officers, owners, or highly paid employees.[84]   These benefits range from use of company meeting rooms to free tickets in the entertainment industry for seats that would otherwise be empty. The exclusion is limited to services sold in the normal course of business in which the employee works. For example, the value of a hotel room is nontaxable if used by an employee (and/or a spouse or dependent children) who works in the employer's hotel business. It is taxable, however, if the employee works for another line of business of an employer with diversified interests such as hotels and auto rentals.[85]   Those employees identified with more than one line of business may exclude the benefits received from all of them. The exclusion is extended to benefits provided under a written reciprocal agreement by another employer that is in the same line of business.[86]   Thus, the hotel employee has nontaxable income for free use of a hotel room provided by another company that has a qualified reciprocal agreement with the employer.

The line of business limitation is relaxed for companies that, on January 1, 1984, were providing substantially all employees with these benefits regardless of the employees' line of business. Such companies may elect to continue the practice, but they must pay a nondeductible 30 percent excise tax. The tax is levied each year on the amount that the total value of the exclusion for these services plus employee discounts (discussed below) that exceed 1 percent of total compensation. The election can be revoked by the company at any time.

Qualified Employee Discounts.   It is common practice for companies to allow employees to purchase inventory items at a discount. For example, a department store may allow its employees to purchase merchandise at the selling price less a stipulated discount. Such discounts seldom result in taxable income unless they discriminate in favor of highly compensated employees.[87]   The exclusion, however, is not available for discounts on investment property nor on real estate.

The rules governing nondiscrimination, the requirement that items must be offered for sale in the normal course of business and line of business, and the rules governing coverage of spouses and dependent children discussed above for nontaxable services also pertain to nontaxable discounts. In contrast with services, however, discounts under reciprocal agreements are taxable income. The merchandise discount exclusion is limited to the employer's normal profit (i.e., the discount may not exceed the employer's gross profit). In the case of employer services, the discount may not exceed 20 percent of the price charged to customers. Any discount beyond that amount is taxable income to the employee.

---

[84] § 132(b).

[85] TAMRA of 1988 clarified that airline employees who are involved in cargo transportation (e.g., baggage and handling) are treated as being in the same line of business as those in the passenger transportation. Therefore, an employee working in the cargo area can receive nontaxable air travel. § 132(h).

[86] § 132(g)(2).

[87] § 132(c).

Example 21. V, an employee of an auto mechanic business, has her automobile repaired by the company. Accounting records show the following information for the parts and service necessary to repair V's car:

	Normal Selling Price	Firm's Cost	V's Cost
Parts	$200	$120	$112
Service	90	81	70

V's taxable income for the parts is $8 ($120 − $112) and for the service is $2 [($90 − $70 = $20) − ($90 × 20% = $18)].

De Minimis Fringe Benefits. Exclusion of employee benefits also extends to items of minimal value such as the occasional use of a company's photocopy machines, other equipment, or typing services; annual employee picnics, cocktail parties, or occasional lunches; and inexpensive holiday gifts such as a turkey at Thanksgiving. No dollar amount is specified in determining what qualifies as *de minimis*. The general guideline is that the value of these benefits is so small that accounting for them is unreasonable or administratively impractical.[88] The exclusion also covers discounts on food served in an eating facility provided by an employer *if* (1) the facility is located on or near the employer's business premises, (2) its revenue equals or exceeds its direct operating costs, and (3) the nondiscriminatory rules discussed above are met.

Qualified Tuition Reduction by Educational Institutions. Employees of educational institutions have nontaxable income for reduction in tuition costs provided by their employer or other educational institution *below* the graduate level. This exclusion is available to the employee, a spouse, and dependent children and is extended to these individuals even if the employee is retired, disabled, or deceased.

Under § 117(d), *graduate* students who are engaged in teaching or research activities (e.g., graduate assistants) for an educational institution are allowed to exclude tuition costs provided by the institution for graduate level work as well as undergraduate work. In effect, this new rule extends favorable nontaxable treatment to tuition reduction arrangements for graduate students who teach or serve as a research assistant.[89]

MILITARY PERSONNEL

Military personnel are employees subject to most of the same provisions as nonmilitary employees. However, the character and tax treatment of some military benefits differ from those of nonmilitary employee benefits. All compensation is taxable unless specifically excluded. Examples of taxable compensation are

---

[88] § 132(e).

[89] § 117(d) is subject to the compensation limitation in § 117(c).

active duty and reservist pay, reenlistment bonuses, lump-sum severance and readjustment pay, and retirement pay. Examples of nontaxable benefits are allowances for subsistence, uniforms, and quarters; extra allowances for housing and living costs while on permanent duty outside the United States, and family separation allowances caused by overseas duty; moving and storage expenses; combat pay for commissioned officers; and all pay while a prisoner of war or missing in action.[90] Benefits provided to military veterans by the Veterans Administration also are nontaxable. Examples of these are allowances for education, training, and subsistence; disability income; pensions paid to veterans or family members; and grants for specially equipped vehicles and homes for disabled veterans. In addition, bonuses paid from general welfare funds by state governments to veterans are nontaxable.

PERSONAL TRANSFERS BETWEEN INDIVIDUALS

Assets are transferred from one individual to another as a result of *personal relationships* under many different circumstances. Commonly, cash and other assets are received as gifts, inheritances, child support, and alimony. With the exception of alimony, these asset transfers are nontaxable for Federal income tax purposes. That is, the transferor has no deduction and the transferee has no taxable income.

GIFTS AND INHERITANCES

Section 102 excludes the value of property received as a gift, bequest, devise, or inheritance from gross income.[91] However, this exclusion does not extend to income earned on the property.[92] For example, the value of bonds inherited or received as a gift is nontaxable, but any interest income earned on the bonds by the new owner is taxable unless specifically exempted by the Code (e.g., interest on tax-exempt bonds issued by a municipality).

Ordinarily, the source of assets inherited or received as a gift is not relevant. For example, it does not matter if cash received is paid from the donor's *principal* or *income*.[93] There are two exceptions, however. One, this exclusion does not apply to a gift or assignment of income. Thus, a qualifying gift of interest earned on corporate bonds placed in a nonreversionary trust (i.e., the assets will not revert to the grantor) is taxable to the party *receiving* the interest. Two, a gift or bequest of a specific sum of money that is paid from a trust or estate in more than three installments is included in income to the extent it is paid from income.

---

[90] The TRA of 1986 consolidated existing military benefits and provided the Treasury with the authority to expand the list.

[91] § 102(a).

[92] Reg. § 1.102-1.

[93] § 663(a)(1).

Example 22. P inherits $30,000 from his grandmother's estate. The estate consists primarily of stocks in a family-owned business. To avoid forcing the sale of these stocks, P agrees to receive the $30,000 in installments as cash is accumulated in the estate. Eventually, P receives $10,000 from estate principal and $20,000 from estate earnings. If the $30,000 is received in three or fewer installments, the entire amount is excluded from P's income. However, if the $30,000 is received in four or more installments, it is included in P's income to the extent of the $20,000 paid from earnings.

As discussed previously in this chapter, the nontaxability of gifts is determined by the intent of the donor. A nontaxable gift or inheritance must be a voluntary transfer of property and not an exchange for adequate consideration such as services or other property. Thus, a donor is expected to be motivated solely by affection, admiration, sympathy, or similar emotion.

ALIMONY AND SEPARATE MAINTENANCE

Alimony and separate maintenance agreements provide for the transfer of funds between two people. The substance of these transfers is reflected in the Code. That is, amounts that qualify as alimony or separate maintenance are deductible by the payor (hereinafter referred to as the husband) in arriving at A.G.I. and are taxable income to the payee (hereinafter referred to as the wife).[94] As long as all requirements are met, this tax treatment occurs even in states that do not specifically recognize alimony payments.[95] On the other hand, amounts that qualify as property settlements are not deductible by the husband or taxable to the wife. A property settlement is a transfer of property to a spouse in exchange for the release of her marital claims (i.e., claims to property accumulated during marriage). No deduction is allowed for property transfers because, unlike alimony payments, they are not made by the ex-husband in discharge of his "general obligation to support" his ex-wife.

Provisions governing payments and property transfers incident to divorce were changed substantially in 1984. The rules discussed in this section reflect these changes and often are not applicable to agreements made prior to their effective date.[96]

---

[94] § 215(a) and 71(a)(1). Identifying the husband as the payor spouse is for illustration purposes only. In reality, the wife may be the payor spouse, in which case the same rules apply.

[95] *Douglas G. Benedict*, 82 T.C. 573 (1984).

[96] These changes apply to a pre-1985 divorce decree *only* if both parties expressly agree. Ltr. Rul. 8634040.

Payments qualify as alimony or separate maintenance only if[97]

1. They are made in *cash*;

2. They are made as a result of a divorce or separation under a *written decree* of separate maintenance or support;

3. They are *required* under a decree or a written instrument incident to a divorce or separation;

4. The spouses or court do *not* elect that they be designated as not qualifying as alimony;

5. The husband and wife do not live together nor do they file a joint return together; and

6. Payments cease with the death of the *recipient*.

Payments meeting these requirements, however, are not treated as alimony if the divorce or separation agreement clearly states they are not alimony for Federal income tax purposes.

As indicated above, the payments from the ex-husband to the ex-wife must be in cash, not property. The following types of payments qualify as alimony or separate maintenance payments:

1. Payments made in cash, checks, and money orders payable on demand.[98]

2. Payments of cash by the ex-husband to the ex-wife's creditors in accordance with the terms of the divorce or separation instrument such as payments of the ex-wife's mortgage (i.e., on house ex-wife owns), taxes, rent, medical and dental bills, utilities, tuition, and other similar expenses.[99]

3. Premiums paid by the ex-husband for term or whole life insurance on the ex-husband's life made pursuant to the terms of the divorce or separation instrument, provided the ex-wife is the owner of the policy.[100]

4. Payments of cash to a third party on behalf of the ex-wife, if they are made at the written request of the ex-wife, such as a contribution to a charitable organization.[101]

5. Payments required to be made to ex-wife's parents or other relatives in discharge of ex-wife's obligation to provide support.[102]

---

[97] § 71(a) and (b) and Reg. § 1.71-1.

[98] Temp. Reg. § 1.71-1T(b), Question 5.

[99] Temp. Reg. § 1.71-1T(b), Question 6.

[100] *Ibid.* See also *Lemuel A. Carmichael*, 14 T.C. 1356(1950) and Rev. Rul. 70-218, 1970-1 C.B. 19.

[101] Temp. Reg. § 1.71-1T(b), Question 7.

[102] *Christiansen*, 60 T.C. 456(1973) *acq.*

However, the following *do not* qualify as alimony or separate maintenance payments:

1. Assets transferred as a part of the property settlement, such as a home, car, stocks and bonds, life insurance policies, annuity contracts, and so forth.

2. Any payments to maintain property owned by the ex-husband and used by the ex-wife, including mortgage payments, real estate taxes, insurance premiums, and improvements.[103] Such payments increase the ex-husband's equity in the property.

3. Fair rental value of residence owned by ex-husband but used exclusively by ex-wife.[104]

4. Repayment by the ex-husband of a loan previously made to him by his ex-wife as part of the general settlement.[105]

5. Transfers of services (i.e., professional or otherwise).[106]

6. Voluntary payments not required by the divorce or separation agreement.

7. Payments made prior to a divorce or separation.

Example 23. D and G are divorced. The divorce decree requires D to transfer personal assets valued at $30,000 to G, to pay G $2,400 per year until G remarries or dies, and to pay G $50,000 over a period of 12 years. During the year, D pays G the following amounts:

1. $1,000 separate maintenance, voluntarily made prior to their separation or divorce

2. $2,400 separate maintenance, made in accordance with the divorce agreement

3. $30,000 of personal assets, transferred in accordance with the divorce agreement

4. $6,000 of the $50,000 to be paid over 12 years

G's alimony is $8,400 ($2,400 + $6,000). The $1,000 separate maintenance is not alimony because it was paid voluntarily and before any divorce or separate maintenance agreement was made. The $30,000 transfer of personal assets is not alimony since it is a property settlement. Since G has taxable alimony of $8,400, D has a deduction for A.G.I. of $8,400.

---

[103] Temp. Reg. § 1.71-1T(b), Question 6.

[104] Temp. Reg. § 1.71-1T(b), Question 5.

[105] Reg. § 1.71-1T(b)(4).

[106] Temp. Reg. § 1.71-1T(b), Question 5.

Limitations on Front Loading. To discourage "excessive" amounts from being treated as alimony in the early years, Congress redesigned § 71 to preclude the early deduction of large payments that may, in reality, represent property settlements.[107] Moreover, the provision prevents the payor spouse from taking advantage of tax savings that are worth more when larger payments are deducted early as opposed to deferring the deductions to later years. These rules are effective for all instruments executed after 1986 and for pre-1987 instruments that are modified after 1986.

Alimony paid in the first and second years must be *recaptured* in the third year if, during this three years, alimony payments decreased by more than $15,000. Amounts recaptured are included in gross income by the payor and deductible by the payee in arriving at A.G.I. To compute the recapture, the years must be considered in reverse order. Thus, the recapture formula for the second post-separation year is (1) total payments made in the second year less (2) payments made in the third year less (3) $15,000. The recapture formula for the first year is similar with one exception. In the second step, an *average* is computed of the second-year payments (less excess payments for that year, determined in the preceding computation above) plus the third year payments.

> **Example 24.** Alimony payments by W to H for the first three years after divorce are $25,000, $20,000, and $15,000. Since payments did not decrease by more than $15,000, no recapture is required. Both W's deductions for A.G.I. and H's taxable income are $25,000 the first year, $20,000 the second year, and $15,000 the third year.

> **Example 25.** Alimony payments by M to F for the first three years after divorce are $50,000, $20,000, and $0. Since payments decrease by more than $15,000, recapture is required in the third year. The recapture from the second year is $5,000 ($20,000 paid in the second year − $0 paid in the third year − $15,000). The recapture from the first year is $27,500 [$50,000 paid in the first year − ($20,000 paid in the second year − $5,000 excess from the first calculation = $15,000 + $0 paid in the third year = $15,000 ÷ 2 = $7,500 average for the two years) − $15,000]. M's deduction for A.G.I. and F's taxable income are $50,000 the first year and $20,000 the second year. In the third year, the recaptures exceed payments; thus, M's taxable income and F's deduction for A.G.I. is $32,500 ($5,000 + $27,500).

Different rules apply to divorce instruments executed during 1985 and 1986. There are no front loading provisions for years prior to 1985.

---

[107]   § 71(f).

Recapture rules do not apply for post-1984 divorce instruments if payments

1. Cease because of the death of either spouse during the three-year period;

2. Cease because the payee remarries during the three-year period;

3. Are made under a support agreement, and thus do not qualify as alimony; or

4. Are a fixed portion of income to be paid for at least three years and based on revenues from a business, from property, or from employee or self-employment compensation.

In all situations, the tax effect of payments between divorced or separated individuals must be offsetting. That is, (1) payments that do not qualify as alimony are neither taxable income to the ex-wife nor deductible by the ex-husband, and (2) payments that qualify as alimony are taxable income to her and deductible by him. There is one type of exception to this approach but the outcome remains the same. An alimony obligation may be satisfied by transferring income-producing property to the ex-wife. When this occurs, the income is taxable to her, but instead of a deduction, he excludes the income.[108] Regardless of the method, her A.G.I. is increased by the same amount as his A.G.I. is reduced.

Transfers of property between spouses or former spouses incident to a divorce are nontaxable regardless of the type of property, if liabilities are involved, or if it is an equal exchange or unequal transfer. Consequently, neither party recognizes any gain or loss and the former owner's basis and holding period transfers with the property.[109]

> **Example 26.**   H and W are divorced. The divorce decree transfers investments owned by H to W. The investments have a market value of $24,000 and a basis for H of $16,000. Neither H nor W has taxable income, and W's basis in the investments is $16,000.

Prior to 1985, transfers between former spouses often resulted in gain being recognized by the former owner; the recipient's basis in the property was its market value.

---

[108] §§ 71(d) and 215.   [109] § 1041(b)(2).

Child Support.　If there are children, it is reasonable to assume that a portion of the husband's payments will be for their care and support. Amounts that qualify as child support are nondeductible personal expenses for the husband and nontaxable income to the wife.[110] Funds qualify as child support *only* if

1. A specific amount is fixed or is contingent on the child's status (e.g., reaching a certain age);

2. Paid solely for the support of minor children; and

3. Payable by decree, instrument, or agreement.

If all three requirements are not met, the payments are treated as alimony with no part considered to be child support.[111] All other factors are irrelevant to the issue. For example, the intent of the parties involved, the actual use of the funds, and state or local support laws have no bearing on whether payments qualify as child support. Also, even though state law may be to the contrary, a minor child is anyone under age 21.[112]

> **Example 27.**　A divorce decree states that B is to pay $300 per month as alimony and support of two minor children. The agreement also states that the payments will decrease by one-third (1) if the former spouse dies or remarries, and (2) as each child reaches 21 years of age. This type of agreement meets the contingency rule for child support. Consequently, $100 per month qualifies as alimony and $200 per month qualifies as child support.

If child support is not properly established in the original agreement, the parties involved may amend the agreement retroactively.[113] This retroactive amendment is allowed, however, only if taxpayers produce convincing evidence that the amendment corrects a mistake, inadvertence, or clerical error. If such evidence does not exist, it is unlikely that any retroactive adjustment will be accepted.[114] Once child support is established, no payments are considered to be alimony until all past and current child support payments are made.[115]

---

[110]　Reg. § 1.71-1(e).

[111]　See § 71(c)(2) and Temp. Reg. § 1.71-1T, Questions 16 and 17. Also, see *Arnold A. Abramo*, 78 T.C. 154 (1983) *acq.* and *Comm. v. Lester*, 61-1 USTC ¶9463, 7 AFTR2d 1445, 366 U.S. 299 (USSC, 1961).

[112]　*W.E. Borbonus*, 42 T.C. 983 (1964).

[113]　Rev. Rul. 71-416, 1971-2 C.B. 83 and *Margaret R. Sklar*, 21 T.C. 349 (1953), *acq.*

[114]　Rev. Rul. 58-52, 1958-1 C.B. 29 and *A.Z. Gordon*, 70 T.C. 525 (1978).

[115]　§ 71(b) and Reg. § 1.71-1(c).

Example 28. A divorce decree states that H is to pay $100 per month as alimony and $200 per month as support of two minor children. The first payment was due October 1. H paid $150 in October, $300 in November, and $350 in December. These payments are allocated between child support and alimony as follows:

	Payment	Child Support	Alimony
October	$150	$150	$ 0
November	300	250	50
December	350	200	150
Total	$800	$600	$200

The above allocation is made even if H or state law stipulates that payments are to cover alimony first.

TRANSFERS BY UNRELATED PARTIES

Taxpayers also receive cash and other assets from unrelated parties. That is, neither a family nor business relationship exists between the transferor and transferee. Such transfers include assets received as prizes, awards, scholarships, fellowships, and government transfer payments.

PRIZES AND AWARDS

Prizes and awards generally are taxable income. Thus, winners of sweepstakes, lotteries, employer service awards, contests, door prizes, and raffles held by charitable organizations have taxable income to the extent the fair market value of the winnings exceeds the cost of entering the contests.[116] Fair market value of property won is not necessarily the list price or even the cost to the purchaser. For example, the Tax Court held that the taxable amount for an automobile won was less than its purchase price but more than the amount allowed as a trade-in ten days later, after the car was driven several hundred miles.[117] When property won has no resale market or is nontransferable, the Tax Court has estimated the value that the particular winner could and would pay for similar goods.[118]

---

[116] Reg. § 1.74-1(a)(2).

[117] *Lawrence W. McCoy*, 38 T.C. 841 (1962), acq.

[118] *Reginald Turner*, 13 TCM 462, T.C. Memo. 1954-38.

An exception is provided in the Code for prizes and awards that are made in recognition of religious, charitable, scientific, educational, artistic, literary, or civic achievements, but only if

1. The recipient was selected without any direct action on his or her part to enter the contest or proceeding;

2. The recipient is not required to perform substantial future services as a condition of receiving the prize or award; and

3. The prize or award is given by the payor to a governmental unit or tax-exempt organization.[119]

When these rules are met, the award has no impact on the winner's tax liability; it is neither taxable income nor a deductible charitable contribution.

SCHOLARSHIPS AND FELLOWSHIPS

Although scholarships and fellowships are considered to be prizes and awards, they are specifically exempted from the above provisions.[120] Instead, § 117 excludes all qualifying scholarships and fellowships that are required to be used and, in fact, are used for (1) tuition and fees necessary for enrollment or attendance at an educational institution; and (2) fees, books, supplies, and equipment required for the course of study. Any amounts not used for these purposes are taxable income unless returned to the grantor. However, recall from the earlier discussion in this chapter for employee benefits that certain tuition reductions for employees of educational institutions (including graduate students engaged in teaching or research activities) are nontaxable.[121]

When recipients are degree candidates, the educational activities may take place away from the school. Nevertheless, they must be pursued for the purpose of meeting requirements at a degree-granting institution. Ordinarily, the educational institution must have a faculty, a curriculum, and an organized student body participating in the educational function.[122] Degree candidates also are not subject to dollar limitations.

Regardless of whether the recipient is a degree candidate or not, educational benefits from an employer generally are taxable income to the employee.[123] Even though a current employment relationship may not exist, scholarships

---

[119]   § 74(b).

[120]   Rev. Rul. 59-80, 1959-1 C.B. 39.

[121]   § 117(d).

[122]   Reg. § 1.117-3(b) and § 151(e)(4).

[123]   Rev. Rul. 76-71, 1976-1 C.B. 308 and Reg. § 1.117-4(c).

granted with the expectation of future services generally are taxable to the recipient. For example, a beauty contest winner of a scholarship was considered to have taxable income since she participated in the televised pageant and was expected to perform promotional services in the future.[124]

Finally, the exclusion does not apply to scholarships provided by individuals who are motivated by family or philanthropic reasons.[125] In any event, taxpayers with taxable scholarship or fellowship income may be allowed a deduction for educational expenses (see Chapters 8 and 11).

GOVERNMENT TRANSFER PAYMENTS

Many government transfer payments are excluded from income. For example, earlier discussion in this chapter revealed that all or a portion of Social Security benefits are excluded from income. Since medicare benefits are considered to be Social Security, they also are nontaxable. Supplementary medicare payments received as reimbursement of medical expenses deducted in a prior year are taxable, however, to the extent the taxpayer received a *tax benefit* in that year.[126]

Workmen's compensation received as a result of a work-related injury is excluded from income.[127] Similar to the typical accident insurance policy discussed earlier in this chapter, workmen's compensation provides the injured employee with a fixed amount for the permanent loss of use of a function or member of the body. For example, an individual who loses a hand, fingers, or hearing in a work-related accident receives a nontaxable amount, according to a schedule of payments. This exclusion is extended to compensation received by the survivors of a deceased worker. Other workmen's compensation benefits are taxable unless the requirements for accident or health plans, previously discussed, are met.

Both state and Federal government transfer payments that are classified as public assistance (e.g., food stamps) or paid from a general welfare fund (e.g., welfare payments) are nontaxable.[128] Among others, these include payments to foster and adoptive parents, to individuals who are blind, to victims of crimes, for disaster relief, to reduce energy costs for low-income groups, and for urban renewal relocation payments.[129]

---

[124] Rev. Rul. 68-20, 1968-1 C.B. 55.

[125] Reg. § 1.117-3.

[126] Rev. Rul. 70-341, 1970-2 C.B. 31.

[127] § 104(a)(1).

[128] Rev. Rul. 71-425, 1971-2 C.B. 76.

[129] Rev. Ruls. 78-80, 1978-1 C.B. 22; 74-153, 1974-1 C.B. 20; 77-323, 1977-2 C.B. 18, 74-74, 1974-1 C.B. 18; 76-144, 1976-1 C.B. 17; 78-180, 1978-1 C.B. 136; and 76-373, 1976-2 C.B. 16.

Benefits to participants in government programs designated to train or retrain specified groups are frequently nontaxable. Whether these benefits are nontaxable or not is dependent upon the primary purpose of the programs. Thus, if the objective of the program is to provide unemployed or under-employed individuals with job skills that enhance their employment opportunities, amounts received are nontaxable.[130] But, if the primary purpose is to provide compensation for services, participants are government employees with taxable wages.[131]

Most government transfer payments to farmers are included in income.[132] For example, gross income from farming includes government funds received for trees, shrubs, seed, and certain conservation expenditures, and for reducing farm production.[133] If materials are received instead of cash, their fair market value is taxable income. In addition, taxpayers receiving government funds under qualifying conservation cost-sharing plans may elect to exclude the reimbursement of capital improvements. However, the capitalized cost of the projects must be reduced by the excluded amount.[134]

BUSINESS GROSS INCOME

The amount to be included in gross income for proprietorships, partnerships, and corporations is total revenues plus net sales less cost of goods sold. This same concept is applicable even if the business conducted is illegal or if the activities do not qualify as a trade or business but constitute a hobby. Many of the other includible and excludable business gross income items are discussed earlier in this chapter. Additional income items peculiar to business that deserve discussion are classified as (A) generally includible in, or (B) generally excludable from, gross income.

A. *Generally Includible in Gross Income*

Agreement not to compete
Goodwill
Business interruption insurance proceeds
Damages awarded
Debt cancellation
Lease cancellation payments

B. *Generally Excludable from Gross Income*

Leasehold improvements (unless made in lieu of rent)
Contributions to capital

---

[130] Rev. Ruls. 63-136, 1963-2 C.B. 19; 68-38, 1968-1 C.B. 446; 71-425, 1971-2 C.B. 76; and 72-340, 1972-2 C.B. 31.

[131] Rev. Rul. 74-413, 1974-2 C.B. 333.

[132] Reg. § 1.61-4(a).

[133] *R.L. Harding*, 29 TCM 789, T.C. Memo. 1970-179 and Rev. Rul. 60-32, 1960-1 C.B. 23.

[134] See §126 and Temp. Reg. § 16A.126-1.

AGREEMENT NOT TO COMPETE AND GOODWILL

The sale of a business often contains an agreement that the seller will not compete with the buyer in the same or similar business within a particular area or distance. The amount assigned to the agreement is included in ordinary income. The purchaser may amortize (deduct) this amount over the life of the agreement on a straight-line basis.

When the net selling price of the business exceeds the fair market value of all identifiable net assets, the business generally is considered to possess *goodwill*. That is, its potential value exceeds its net assets because of the business name, location, reputation, or other intangible factor. Goodwill is taxable as a capital gain. However, the purchaser of the business may not deduct any part of the goodwill until the business is sold or discontinued. If the contract includes a single amount for both goodwill *and* a noncompetition agreement, the entire amount is treated as goodwill.

BUSINESS INTERRUPTION INSURANCE PROCEEDS

Some businesses carry insurance policies that provide for the loss of the use of property and of net profits sustained when the business property cannot be used because of an unexpected event such as fire or flood. The Regulations state that the insurance proceeds are included in gross income regardless of whether they are a reimbursement for the loss of the use of property or of net profits.[135] Similarly, insurance proceeds that are to reimburse the business for overhead expenses during the period of interruption are taxable.[136]

DAMAGES AWARDED

Cash may be awarded by the courts or by insurance companies for damages suffered by businesses because of patent infringement, cancellation of a franchise, injury to a business's reputation (see later discussion concerning professional reputation), breach of contract, antitrust action, or unfair competition. Punitive damages are included in gross income.[137] However, compensatory awards may be used *first* to offset any litigation expenses or other expenditures in obtaining the award.[138] *Second*, funds that represent a recovery of capital when damages are awarded because of a loss in value to a business's goodwill or other assets are used to offset or write down the capitalized asset costs.[139] Remaining damages

---

[135] Reg. § 1.1033(a)-2(c)(8).

[136] Rev. Rul. 55-264, 1955-1 C.B. 11.

[137] *Comm. v. Glenshaw Glass Co.*, 55-1 USTC ¶9308, 47 AFTR 162, 348 U.S. 426 (USSC, 1955).

[138] *State Fish Corp.*, 49 T.C. 13 (1967), *mod'g*. 48 T.C. 465 (1967).

[139] *Farmers' and Merchants Bank of Cattletsburg, Ky. v. Comm.*, 3 USTC ¶972, 11 AFTR 619, 59 F.2d 912 (CA-6, 1932) and *Thomson v. Comm.*, 69-1 USTC ¶9199, 23 AFTR2d 69-529, 406 F.2d 1006 (CA-9, 1969).

generally are considered to be a reimbursement for a loss of profits and are included in gross income.[140] An exception to the latter classification occurs when compensatory damages are awarded in an antitrust suit. While the punitive damages in these cases are taxable, the compensatory damages are taxable only to the extent that losses sustained by the business resulted in a tax benefit.[141]

LEASE CANCELLATION PAYMENTS

Early termination of lease agreements may result in a lease cancellation payment. Either a lessor or a lessee may receive these payments, depending on which party cancelled the lease. In *Hort*, the Supreme Court held that lease cancellation funds received by a lessor are a substitute for rent.[142] Consequently, these receipts are taxable income. Amounts received by a lessee on cancellation of a lease are considered proceeds from the sale of the lease.[143] Thus, the gain is included in gross income. Whether the gain is ordinary or capital depends on the use of the property (see discussion in Chapter 16).

DEBT CANCELLATION

A business's tax consequences when creditors cancel all or part of its debt are determined by whether the business is in bankruptcy proceedings or is insolvent.[144] When debt is cancelled under bankruptcy proceedings, there is no taxable income currently. The taxpayer has a choice in how the reduction is recorded. First, the decrease in debt may be offset by five tax attributes: (1) net operating losses; (2) general business tax credits; (3) capital losses; (4) basis of depreciable and nondepreciable assets; and (5) foreign tax credits.[145] All of these attributes are discussed in later chapters. Any debt reduction exceeding these five tax attributes is ignored. Alternatively, the decrease in debt may be offset by a reduction in the debtor's depreciable assets or real estate held as inventory.[146] These lower asset bases are used for future depreciation and gain or loss calculations (see discussion in Chapters 9 and 16). Thus, the asset reduction represents a tax deferral rather than an exclusion.

[140] *Durkee v. Comm.*, 1950-1 USTC ¶9283, 35 AFTR 1438, 162 F.2d 184 (CA-6, 1947), rem'g. 6 T.C. 773 (1946).

[141] § 186 and Reg. § 1.186-1.

[142] *Hort v. Comm.*, 41-1 USTC ¶9354, 25 AFTR 1207, 313 U.S. 28 (USSC, 1941).

[143] § 1241.

[144] § 108(a).

[145] § 108(b).

[146] § 108(b)(5).

Although not in bankruptcy proceedings, a business may be insolvent (i.e., liabilities exceed the value of its assets). If the business continues to be insolvent after debt cancellation, the decrease in debt is offset by the five tax attributes listed above.[147] If, however, the business is insolvent before but solvent after the cancellation, the cancellation to the extent of solvency is subject to the rules governing solvent businesses.[148] In contrast, when debt of a solvent business not in bankruptcy is cancelled, the taxpayer must report the reduction as taxable income.[149]

LEASEHOLD IMPROVEMENTS

A lessee often makes improvements to leased real estate. These may range from minor improvements up to the construction of a building on the leased land. If these improvements are made in lieu of rent payments, they are included in the lessor's gross income.[150] Otherwise, the lessor has no taxable income either at the time the improvements are made or at the time the lease is terminated, even if the improvements substantially increase the property's value.[151] The lessor's only taxable income from these improvements will occur indirectly on the sale of the property to the extent the improvements result in a higher net selling price.

CONTRIBUTIONS TO CAPITAL

Cash or other property received by a business in exchange for an ownership interest are nontaxable transactions for the business. These assets are treated as contributions to capital and not income.[152] Contributions to capital that are not in exchange for an ownership interest also are nontaxable.

MISCELLANEOUS ITEMS

As stated in the first paragraph of this chapter, gross income includes *all* income unless specifically exempted. Although this chapter is not intended to discuss every income item, some additional items are classified for discussion purposes as miscellaneous.

---

[147] §§ 108(b), (d)(3), and (e)(1).

[148] § 108(a)(3).

[149] § 61(a)(12).

[150] Reg. § 1.109-1.

[151] § 109.

[152] §§ 118 and 721.

FEES RECEIVED

Ordinarily, fees received for services performed are included in gross income. Thus, fees paid to corporate directors, jurors, and executors are reported as miscellaneous gross income. However, if executor fees are paid regardless of whether the taxpayer performs any services, they may qualify as nontaxable gifts.[153]

ASSET DISCOVERY

Cash or other assets found by a taxpayer are taxable income even if found accidentally, with no effort expended in discovering them.[154] For example, taxpayers were held to have taxable income equal to cash found in a used piano they had purchased.[155]

CAR POOL RECEIPTS

One type of earned income is nontaxable. Vehicle owners operating car pools for fellow commuters may exclude all the revenues received.[156] Car pool expenses are *personal* commuting expenses, and therefore are not deductible. If, however, the car pool activities are sufficient to qualify a taxpayer as being in a trade or business, all revenues are taxable. How much activity constitutes a trade or business is a question of fact not easily answered but, in this type of situation, the definition of trade certainly requires considerably more activity than a single automobile or small van making one round trip daily.

INCOME TAX REFUNDS

All income tax refunds are nontaxable except to the extent the taxpayer received a tax benefit in a prior year.[157] A corporation receives a tax benefit for all business expenses, including state and local income taxes but not Federal income taxes, unless the corporation incurs a net operating loss for the year of deduction. State and local income taxes paid by individuals, however, provide a tax benefit only if the taxpayer itemized these deductions in the year paid. There is no tax benefit for the expense if the standard deduction was used instead of itemized deductions.

[153] Rev. Rul. 57-398, 1957-2 C.B. 93.

[154] Rev. Rul. 53-61, 1953-1 C.B. 17.

[155] *Cesarini v. Comm.*, 70-2 USTC ¶9509, 26 AFTR2d 70-5107, 428 F.2d 812 (CA-6, 1970).

[156] Rev. Rul. 55-555, 1955-2 C.B. 20.

[157] § 111(a).

TEMPORARY LIVING COSTS

If an individual receives insurance to cover temporary living costs incurred because the principal residence was destroyed or damaged by fire, flood, or other casualty, the funds are nontaxable to the extent they are offset by *extra* living costs.[158] These funds also may be excluded if the government prevented the individual from using an undamaged residence because of the existence or threat of a casualty. Extra living costs are limited to those additional costs actually incurred for temporarily housing, feeding, and transporting the taxpayer and members of the household. Typical qualifying costs are hotel or apartment rent and utilities, extra costs for restaurant meals, and additional transportation necessitated by having to live outside the immediate area of the residence.

DAMAGES AWARDED TO INDIVIDUALS

Cash may be awarded by the courts or by insurance companies as damages to individuals because of job discrimination or personal injuries suffered due to alienation of affection, breach of promise to marry, and slander or libel. Job discrimination damages are considered to be for backpay that was lost because of discrimination. Consequently, they are included in gross income.[159] In contrast, the awards received for personal injuries due to alienation of affection, breach of promise to marry, and slander or libel represent nontaxable income.[160] When damage amounts for these personal injuries are specified as reimbursement for medical expenses, they reduce any itemized medical deduction. If any of these medical expenses were deducted in a prior year, they are included in gross income to the extent the taxpayer received a *tax benefit* for them.[161]

In a recent decision, the Sixth Circuit Court in *Threlkeld*[162] lined up with the Ninth Circuit Court in *Roemer*[163] in holding that damages received for injury to an individual's professional reputation were excludable from income as personal injury damages under § 104(a)(2). In both cases, the courts concluded that the harm to the individual's reputation was a personal injury even though it affected the professional relationships of the victim. The Tax Court changed its original position and now agrees with the Ninth Circuit. However, the Internal Revenue Service has announced that it will not follow the Ninth Circuit's decision in *Roemer*.[164] In the opinion of the IRS, a taxpayer cannot sustain a personal

---

[158] § 123.

[159] Rev. Rul. 72-341, 1972-2 C.B. 32.

[160] Rev. Rul. 74-77, 1974-1 C.B. 33.

[161] Rev. Rul. 75-230, 1975-1 C.B. 93.

[162] *James E. Threlkeld v. Comm.*, 88-1 USTC ¶9370, 61 AFTR2d 1285, 848 F.2d 81(CA-6, 1988), *aff'g.* 87 T.C. 1294 (1986).

[163] *Roemer, Jr. v. Comm.*, 83-2 USTC ¶9600, 52 AFTR2d 5954, 716 F.2d 693 (CA-9, 1983), *rev'g.* 79 T.C. 398 (1982).

[164] Rev. Rul. 85-143, 1985-2 C.B. 55.

injury within the meaning of § 104(a)(2) when the primary harm suffered is a loss of business income. Therefore, the IRS will continue to tax amounts received for damages to professional reputation.

The Revenue Reconciliation Act of 1989 amends § 104(a) with respect to punitive damages received on account of personal injuries. Such amounts, if received after July 10, 1989, are excluded from gross income only if a physical injury or sickness is involved. Consequently, determining the nature of the damage (i.e., compensatory or punitive) has important tax implications.

TAX PLANNING

In *Gregory v. Helvering*, Judge Learned Hand stated: "Any one may so arrange his affairs that his taxes shall be as low as possible; he is not bound to choose that pattern which will best pay the Treasury; there is not even a patriotic duty to increase one's taxes."[165] Individuals and businesses have many opportunities to arrange their affairs in ways that decrease their annual Federal income tax liability. Tax advisers must be both knowledgeable and imaginative in order to provide their clients with good tax-planning information. But then, it is the taxpayers' responsibility to use this information wisely to meet their own needs and desires.

INVESTMENTS

Tax-planning strategy must be viewed in terms of each taxpayer's own financial position. When considering investments, both the after-tax return and the risk involved must be evaluated. Before-tax income frequently is lower for tax-exempt and tax-deferred investments than it is for taxable investments with the same degree of risk. Consequently, tax-exempt investments should be most attractive to those in the higher tax bracket. They may not be beneficial to those in the lower bracket. Tax-deferred investments should be most attractive to those expecting a lower tax bracket when the deferral period ends. In addition, investors must consider whether any gains will be taxed as ordinary income or capital gains (see Chapter 15), and whether capital gains will be needed to offset capital losses.

Taxpayers have a variety of investment opportunities available to them. In order to arrive at informed investment decisions, comparative evaluations are necessary. However, such evaluations must be viewed with caution. The very nature of this type of analysis means that tentative assumptions must be made about the future. For example, when comparing a possible stock purchase with an annuity purchase, assumptions must be made about (1) future cash flows for the two investments, (2) future marginal tax rates, and (3) the discount rate to be used in determining the present value of the expected cash flows. A decision should never be based on a simple nonmathematical tax comparison of the total of annual dividend exclusions plus capital gains for the stock, as opposed to the total deferred ordinary income for the annuity. A tax adviser should always remember that while taxation is a very important factor, it is just one of several that must be considered.

On the death of an insured person, life insurance companies ordinarily allow beneficiaries to receive the proceeds in one lump sum, or in installments for a stipulated period or over the beneficiary's life. Tax concerns aside, some beneficiaries may elect to leave the proceeds with the insurance company simply because they like the security of receiving a periodic payment from an established

---

[165] 35-1 USTC ¶9043, 14 AFTR 1191, 55 U.S. 266 (USSC, 1935).

financial institution. Each installment contains a ratable portion of the proceeds plus interest. This interest is taxable income. Thus, life insurance proceeds received in installments are treated the same as annuities.

> **Example 29.**   M is the sole beneficiary of her husband's $60,000 life insurance policy. She elects to receive the proceeds in monthly installments for 10 years. Her monthly installment is $500 plus interest on the unpaid principal. In the current year, she receives $6,000 plus $3,700 interest. Her taxable interest income is $3,700.

One feature of life insurance that has enticed many investors over the years is its tax-free cash build-up. Taxpayers have taken advantage of this by borrowing against the policy—in effect receiving use of the income without having to pay tax on it. To discourage the purchase of life insurance as a tax-sheltered investment vehicle, special rules have been established. As a result, taxpayers must closely scrutinize the type of insurance they purchase with respect to its tax treatment. Under the revised rules, a taxpayer who receives amounts before age $59\frac{1}{2}$, including loans, from certain single premium and other investment-oriented life insurance contracts (modified endowment contracts) is treated as receiving income first and then a recovery of basis. In addition, the recipient is subject to an additional 10 percent income tax on the amounts received that are includible in gross income. This provision affects only "modified endowment contracts" entered into on or after June 21, 1988.

An investor who desires nontaxable income may choose to purchase assets such as

1. Qualifying state and local government bonds to obtain the full interest income exclusion

2. Stocks in companies with net income for accounting purposes, but no earnings and profits for tax purposes, to obtain the full exclusion for distributions that are treated as a return of capital

Investors who wish to defer income may choose to purchase

1. Annuities (or to elect that life insurance proceeds be received as annuities) to obtain the deferral of all interest income until received

2. Assets that are expected to appreciate, such as stocks, real estate, and collectables, to obtain the deferral of all appreciation until it is realized

If the taxpayer does not dispose of the assets, the deferral becomes permanent. That is, no one recognizes the income and the assets are inherited at their market values, including the deferred income.

EMPLOYEE BENEFITS

Company fringe benefits can provide employees with tax consequences that range from excellent to actually being a disadvantage. From a tax viewpoint, the best fringe benefits are those that are deductible by the employer and convert otherwise taxable income to nontaxable income for the recipient. For example, payments made to beneficiaries on behalf of a deceased employee are nontaxable up to $5,000 if they qualify as death benefits but are taxable compensation otherwise. In addition, most employee benefits that are provided in lieu of additional salary convert taxable compensation to nontaxable benefits.

> **Example 30.** W is a new employee of Z Corporation. Her compensation package is $20,000. However, she may choose to receive (a) $20,000 salary and no benefits, or (b) $19,000 salary and Z will pay premiums of $600 for medical insurance and $400 for group-term life insurance. If W chooses the first option, she has $20,000 taxable income, but if she selects the second option, she has $19,000 taxable income.

Another very valuable type of fringe benefit is one that is nontaxable income if provided by the employer but is a nondeductible expenditure if paid by the employee. Most fringe benefits are of this type. These include premiums paid for group-term life insurance up to $50,000, qualifying meals and lodging on the premises, supper money, company parking, use of company facilities, and employee discounts. All of these benefits are deductible costs by the employer but nontaxable income to the employee when the necessary requirements discussed in this chapter are met. If, however, the employees pay these costs instead of the employer, there is no tax deduction for them.

A third type of fringe benefit includes expenditures that are deductible expenses, when paid by individuals, but are subject to restrictions. For example, health insurance premiums are deductible for employees who itemize their deductions but *only* to the extent that all qualifying medical expenditures exceed 7.5 percent of A.G.I. (see Chapter 11). Thus, employer-paid health insurance represents different tax savings to different employees.

> **Example 31.** L's compensation includes a salary of $30,000 plus employer-paid health insurance premiums of $600. L's taxable income is $30,000 since the $600 is nontaxable. If the company policy is changed so that L pays the $600 health insurance premiums and the company increases his salary to $30,600, the tax effect on L depends on his individual tax situation.
>
> 1. If L does not itemize medical expenses, he has taxable income of $30,600 salary and no deduction for the $600.
>
> 2. If L itemizes deductions and his medical expenditures before the health insurance premiums exceed 7.5% of A.G.I., he still has taxable income of $30,600 salary but now has a deduction of $600.

Assume L has a 28% marginal tax rate. In situation 1 above, his tax benefit from employer-paid health insurance premiums is $168 ($600 × 28%). In the second situation, L appears to receive no tax benefit when his company pays the health insurance premiums. However, his A.G.I. is $600 higher when L pays the premium. Since medical expenses equal to 7.5% of A.G.I. are not deductible, this increases the nondeductible portion by $45 ($600 × 7.5%). Thus, at the 28% tax rate, his tax increases by $12.60 ($45 × 28%).

Some employer-provided benefits can be a disadvantage to employees. Recall, for example, that disability income is taxable if the premiums were paid by the employer but nontaxable if they were paid by the individual. The best tax-planning advice when employers pay disability insurance premiums is for employees to convince employers to provide another benefit and let employees pay their own disability premiums.

Considerable leeway in tax planning is available to those employees who are allowed to select their own fringe benefits. Simply looking at the cost of each benefit to the company, however, is inadequate. Each employee should carefully evaluate personal needs and the tax effect of each desirable benefit before selection is made.

EMPLOYEE VERSUS SELF-EMPLOYED

The numerous favorable tax results received with fringe benefits are available only if an employer/employee relationship exists. When all necessary requirements are met, it does not matter if the employees are major shareholders of the employer. This situation creates an incentive to operate some businesses as corporations rather than as proprietorships or partnerships.

One of these fringe benefits, employer-furnished meals and lodging, has been of increasing interest to closely held businesses in recent years. Farming represents a particularly good example of a business that requires someone to be available on the property 24 hours a day. When the working owner lives on the farm, a business deduction plus an employee exclusion for the cost of meals and lodging provided to the farmer can be significant.

Example 32. A farm owned by M has the following information for the current year:

Gross income	$130,000
Cost of food consumed by M	2,000
Cost of lodging used by M	4,200
Salary to M	20,000
Other farm expenses	85,000

If the farm is a proprietorship, net farming income is $25,000 ($130,000 − $20,000 − $85,000) and M has an A.G.I. of $45,000 ($25,000 + $20,000).[166] Similar results occur if the farm is a partnership, except M will report only his share of the $25,000. In contrast, if the farm is a corporation, net income is $18,800 ($130,000 − $2,000 − $4,200 − $20,000 − $85,000) and M has an A.G.I. of $20,000. Thus, M, the proprietor, has $45,000 A.G.I. compared with a combined income of $38,800 ($18,800 + $20,000) for the M Corporation and M, the employee.

Although the above example seems to result in a tax advantage for the corporate farm, such a conclusion is over-simplified. Other tax factors are important. For example, corporate net income is taxed to the corporation currently and again as dividend income to shareholders when distributed to them (see Chapters 19 and 20). Another important factor is that individuals and corporations are subject to different tax rates. Also, if farming losses occur, the results may be very unfavorable with a corporate entity. The important point to remember is that the tax advantage achieved with the corporation for meals and lodging (and other employee benefits) is just one of the necessary ingredients when evaluating whether a business should be incorporated.

DIVORCE

Insufficient attention usually is given to tax planning during separation and divorce. Of course, favorable tax results are easier to accomplish when the individuals are parting amicably, but good results still can occur amid animosity. The more disparate the husband's and wife's tax brackets, the greater the benefits to be achieved. This is because payments classified as alimony or separate maintenance are deductible by the payor and are taxable income to the recipient. In contrast, all other asset transfers are neither deductible expenses nor taxable income.

> **Example 33.** H and W are divorced. H's marginal tax rate is 28% while W's is 15%. Every $10 of alimony costs H $7.20 after taxes [$10 paid − $2.80 tax savings ($10 × 28%)] and is worth $8.50 to W after taxes [$10 received − $1.50 tax due ($10 × 15%)]. Thus, H pays $7.20 for W to receive $8.50. If W requires $425 after taxes each month, she must receive $500 if the payments qualify as alimony [$500 − ($500 × 15% = $75)] or $425 if they do not. On the surface, it seems that H would rather pay $425 a month than $500 but $500 in alimony results in an after-tax cost of $360 [$500 − ($500 × 28% = $140)] for a monthly savings of $65 ($425 − $360). Naturally, the closer the two marginal rates, the less there is in tax savings.

---

[166] Technically, a proprietor's salary is not a farming expense but is shown in the example for comparison purposes. Thus, net income is $45,000 ($130,000 − $85,000) and M's A.G.I. is $45,000.

PROBLEM MATERIALS

DISCUSSION QUESTIONS

6-1 *Basic Concepts.* Determine whether each of the following statements is true or false. If false, rewrite the statement so that it is true. Be prepared to explain each statement.

a. Receipts are included in gross income only if specifically listed in the Code.

b. Tax returns show (1) gross receipts from all sources, less (2) excludable income, which equals (3) taxable income.

c. Interest earned on tax-exempt municipal bonds is nontaxable income regardless of whether it is received by an individual or by a corporation.

6-2 *Investments—Stocks v. Bonds.* C has $10,000 to invest but is uncertain whether to purchase H, Inc. stocks or tax-exempt bonds issued by the State of Illinois. List the relevant types of information that C must obtain or estimate in order to make a mathematical calculation of her after-tax return on the two investments she is considering.

6-3 *Investments—Bonds.* D, Inc. bonds are selling for $1,000 each with an interest rate of 11 percent. Tax-exempt bonds issued by the State of Kentucky are selling for $1,000 each with an interest rate of 8 percent. Which bond provides a taxpayer with the higher after-tax return when the marginal tax rate is

a. 28 percent?

b. 15 percent?

6-4 *Investments—Dividend Income.* Corporate distributions may qualify as dividends, return of capital, or stock dividends. Explain the tax treatment of each of these three distributions. What determines whether a distribution is a dividend, a return of capital, or a stock dividend?

6-5 *Employee Benefits.* Z, Inc. owns and operates several businesses, including six hotels and two real estate agencies. R, an employee of Z, spends three nights free of charge in one of Z's hotels in Indiana. Is the value of the lodging nontaxable to R, assuming the information below? Explain.

a. R works for one of the real estate agencies.

b. R tends bar in one of the hotels in Maine.

c. R is a tax accountant in Z's corporate headquarters where the tax records of all of Z's businesses are maintained.

6-6 *Employee Benefits—Comparison.* Compare the tax treatment for each of the items listed below assuming they are paid by (1) the employer, or (2) the employee.

    a. Parking in the company lot during working hours

    b. Health insurance premiums

    c. Disability insurance premiums

    d. Meals eaten in the company cafeteria when the employee must remain on the premises for job reasons

6-7 *Employee Benefits—Meals and Lodging.* Employer-provided meals and lodging that qualify as nontaxable income can be an exceedingly valuable employee benefit.

    a. When do employer-provided meals and lodging qualify as nontaxable income?

    b. List at least 10 types of occupations in which employer-provided lodging and/or meals could qualify for the exclusion. Explain why these occupations are appropriate for the exclusion.

6-8 *Employee Benefits.* Over the years, the list of employee benefits that qualify as deductible expenses by the employer and nontaxable income for the employee has expanded. Assume Congress is interested in further expanding the list of benefits available for this special tax treatment. Prepare a list for Congress of at least three items not discussed in this chapter that would provide many employees with valuable benefits. Explain why these three would be logical additions.

6-9 *Gifts.* How can gifts to family members reduce the family's income tax liability?

6-10 *Alimony and Child Support.* A husband and wife who are obtaining a divorce disagree whether certain periodic payments should be classified as alimony or child support.

    a. What difference does it make how the payments are classified?

    b. What if the agreement states the payments are for both alimony and child support without making a specific distinction in dollar allocation between the two?

    c. List three types of compromise offers that could be made by the husband to reach an allocation that might satisfy both the husband and wife. Explain the tax consequences of each of the three possible solutions.

6-11 *Alimony.* A husband (H) and wife (W) are obtaining a divorce. He agrees to pay alimony of $25,000 in each of the two years after the divorce to enable her to attend graduate school. No alimony will be paid after the second year.

    a. What are his deductible and her taxable amount of alimony for each of the two years, and what are the tax effects in year three?

    b. How could the payment schedule be restructured to maximize his deductions?

    c. How could the payment schedule be restructured to minimize her taxable income?

6-12 *Prizes and Awards.* Contest winners must report the value of prizes won as taxable income.

a.   What arguments could the taxpayer use to convince the IRS and the courts that the values of the prizes are less than their retail selling prices?

b.   Are any prizes or awards ever nontaxable? Explain.

6-13 *Scholarships and Fellowships.* CPA firms are interested in encouraging practical research that explores accounting issues with an objective of developing better accounting methods for the profession. Assume the XY firm decides to establish a fund that will support individual research efforts. Recipients of these grants will be selected based on the quality of their past work and on a written proposal of a specific research project to be completed with funds from the XY firm. Do recipients of these grants have taxable or nontaxable income? Explain.

6-14 *Goodwill versus Agreement Not to Compete.* A preliminary agreement covering the sale/purchase of a dental practice includes an allocation of $40,000 to goodwill and the agreement that the seller will not practice dentistry within a five-mile radius for five years.

a.   What are the tax consequences of this $40,000 allocation?

b.   What advice should a tax adviser give the seller?

c.   What advice should a tax adviser give the buyer?

6-15 *Damages Awarded.* As the result of a newspaper article, V claims his character was damaged beyond repair, he lost his job, and he incurred medical expenses for psychiatric care. His lawsuit requested the court award him the following amounts: $500,000 for personal injury due to slander; $30,000 in lost wages; and $5,000 for psychiatric care.

a.   What are the tax consequences to V if he is awarded the $535,000?

b.   V decides to accept an out-of-court settlement of $150,000. The newspaper and its insurer are willing to allocate the $150,000 in any manner that V requests. How should V have the amount allocated?

PROBLEMS

6-16 *Basic Concepts.* Calculate the amount to be included in gross income for the following taxpayers.

a.   T is self-employed as a beautician. Her records show

Receipts:	
Services	$21,000
Product sales	3,000
Expenditures	
Cost of products sold	1,800
Cost of supplies used	2,600
Utilities	2,400
Shop and equipment rent	3,600
Other expenses	1,000

b.   R owns rental property. His records show

Gross rents	$6,000
Depreciation expense	4,200
Repair expense	2,100
Miscellaneous expense	300

c.   S is an employee with the following tax information:

Gross salary	$15,000
Social security (FICA) taxes withheld (rounded for simplicity)	1,000
Federal income tax withheld	2,200
Health insurance premiums withheld	500
Net salary received in cash	11,300
Employer's share of social security taxes	1,000

6-17 *Investments—Cash Dividends.* Three years ago, Z purchased 50 shares of L common stock for $6,000. Although Z is married, the stocks are recorded in his name alone. The current market value of these shares totals $7,200. He and Mrs. Z file a joint return and neither of them owns any other stock. Mr. Z wants to know what effect each of the following totally separate situations has upon (1) his taxable income and (2) his basis in each share of stock.

a.   L distributes a cash dividend and Z receives $330.

b.   L distributes cash as a return of capital and Z receives $330.

6-18 *Investments—Stock Dividends.* A, who is single, purchased 100 shares of N Corporation common stock four years ago for $12,000. The stock has a current fair market value of $14,400. A asks how each of the following separate situations affects her (1) taxable income and (2) her basis in each share of stock.

a.   N distributes common stock as a dividend and A receives 10 shares.

b.   N distributes nonconvertible preferred stock as a dividend and A receives 10 shares. The preferred stock has a current fair market value of $100 per share.

6-19 *Investments—Cash Dividends.* D, Inc. had accumulated earnings and profits at January 1 of the current year of $20,000. During the taxable year, it had current earnings and profits of $10,000. On December 31 of the current year, D, Inc. made a cash distribution of $40,000 to its sole shareholder, G. G paid $25,000 for his stock three years ago.

a.   How will G treat the $40,000 he received on December 31?

b.   Assume G sold all of his stock for $36,000 on January 1 of the following year. Compute his capital gain.

6-20 *Investments—Interest.*   Mr. K died at the beginning of the year. Mrs. K received interest during the year from the following sources:

Corporate bonds	$1,100
Bank savings account	200
Personal loan to a friend	500
City of Maryville bonds (issued to build a new high school)	600

In addition to the above, Mrs. K was the beneficiary of her husband's $50,000 life insurance policy. She elected to receive the $50,000 proceeds plus interest over the next 10 years. She receives $7,500 in the current year and will receive a like amount each of the following nine years. Calculate the taxable portion of the interest income received by Mrs. K during the year.

6-21 *Investments—Annuities.*   P is single, 65 years old, and retired. On August 1, 1987, he purchased a single-premium deferred life annuity for $40,000 using after-tax funds. This year, P received $5,000 in annuity benefits. He will receive a like amount each year for the rest of his life. (Note: In answering the following questions, use the information in Exhibit 6-1 of the textbook.)

a. Calculate P's taxable income from the annuity for the current year.
b. Calculate P's taxable income from the annuity for year 5.
c. Calculate P's taxable income from the annuity for year 22.
d. Assume P lives just 15 more years. Calculate the deduction that would be allowed on P's final tax return.
e. Assume the annuity was purchased by P and his employer jointly. P contributed $12,000 in after-tax funds, and the employer contributed $28,000. Calculate P's taxable income from the annuity for the current year.

6-22 *Annuities.*   A, age 66, retired after 30 years of service as an employee of the XYZ Corporation. He started receiving retirement benefits in the form of a single life annuity on January 1, 1991. A's total after-tax contributions to the plan amounted to $34,000, and his retirement benefit is $1,500 per month.

a. Determine A's nontaxable portion of each monthly payment, assuming he elects the simplified safe-harbor method.
b. Assume A lives another 20 years. Will there be a time period in which A will be required to fully include the monthly payments in gross income? If so, when?

6-23 *Investments—Life Insurance.*   L is 65 years old and retired. Her husband died early in the year. L was the beneficiary of his $20,000 life insurance policy. L elected to receive $5,200 annually for five years rather than receive a single payment of $20,000 immediately. Calculate L's taxable income from the first payment.

6-24 *Social Security Benefits.* X, who is single and retired, has the following income for the current year:

Taxable interest	$20,000
Dividend income	10,000
Tax-exempt bond interest	8,000
Social security benefits	7,200

   a. Compute the taxable portion of X's social security benefits.

   b. Assume the above information remains the same, except X's taxable interest amounted to $10,000. Compute the taxable portion of his social security benefits.

6-25 *Employee Benefits.* Determine the (1) deductible employer amount, and (2) taxable employee amount for each of the following employer-provided benefits.

   a. Reimbursement of expenses paid by an employee to entertain a client of the business, $200.

   b. Bonus paid an employee when a sales quota was met, $300.

   c. Watches given employees at Christmas, $38 each.

   d. Free parking provided on company property, $500 market value and $220 cost per employee.

   e. Supper money of $15 paid to an employee for each of 10 nights that she worked past 6 P.M., $150.

6-26 *Employee Benefits.* Determine the (1) deductible employer amount, and (2) taxable employee (or beneficiary) amount for each of the following employer-provided benefits.

   a. A death benefit of $6,000 paid to the wife and $4,000 to the son of a deceased employee.

   b. Premiums of $700 paid on $70,000 of group-term life insurance for a 52-year-old woman employee.

   c. Ten percent discount employees are allowed on the retail price of all merchandise purchased from the employer. During the year, sales to employees totaled $18,000 ($20,000 retail price − $2,000 discount) for merchandise that cost the employer $14,000. The employer reported the $18,000 as sales and the $14,000 as cost of goods sold.

6-27 *Employee Benefits—Medical Insurance.* F's $400 annual health insurance premium is paid by his employer. During the year, F received $870 reimbursement of medical expenses; $650 for this year's expenses and $220 for last year's expenses. Determine F's taxable income from the reimbursement in the current year if

   a. F never itemizes any medical expenses.

   b. F deducted medical expenses from his A.G.I. this year of $900 and last year of $450.

6-28   *Tax Benefit Rule.* During 1990, K had adjusted gross income of $30,000. A list of itemized deductions available to K in preparing her 1990 return is shown below:

State income taxes paid	$2,000
Property taxes on residence	600
Charitable contributions	400
Medical expenses	2,500
Interest paid on residence	1,200

K is single, and her son M, who is 8 years old, lives with her. She qualifies as a head of household. In 1991, K received $2,500 from an insurance company for reimbursement of her 1990 medical expenses. Is K required to include any of the $2,500 reimbursement in her gross income in 1991?

6-29   *Fringe Benefits versus Compensation.* P is a 46-year-old professor at Z University, a private school in the Midwest. P is married and has triplets who are freshmen at Z University. Among others, P is provided with the following fringe benefits during the current year:

Group-term life insurance coverage of $75,000. Premium cost to Z University is $300. Tuition reduction of $30,000 for the triplets.

a.   How much does the group-term life insurance cost Professor P? Assume his marginal tax bracket is 31 percent.

b.   Would P be equally well off if the university simply paid him an additional $300 in compensation to cover the term insurance?

c.   Is the tuition reduction for the triplets taxable?

d.   Assuming tuition remains constant, how much will Professor P save in tuition payments by remaining on the faculty at Z University until the triplets graduate?

e.   What would be the result for the current year if the university increased Professor P's salary by $30,000 a year to pay for the triplets' tuition?

6-30   *Unemployment Compensation and Disability Income.* Mr. and Mrs. B are married filing jointly. Mrs. B was permanently disabled the entire year and Mr. B was unemployed part of the year. Both are 55 years old. Their receipts for the year were

Disability income—Mrs. B	$ 6,200
Social security income—Mrs. B	1,000
Salary—Mr. B	16,500
Unemployment compensation—Mr. B	4,500

Calculate their taxable income for the year assuming the disability insurance premiums were paid

a.   Entirely by Mrs. B.

b.   Entirely by Mrs. B's employer.

6-31   *Damages Awarded and Disability Income.*   D works for the XYZ Tool and Die Shop. On March 1, 1991 a stamping press that D was operating malfunctioned, resulting in the loss of the index finger on his right hand. D, claiming the machine was not properly maintained, sued XYZ for the following damages:

Medical expenses during D's one-week stay in the hospital	$ 8,000
Loss of D's finger	50,000
Punitive damages	5,000
Total	$63,000

On April 1, 1992 the court awarded D $63,000.

a.   Assuming D did not deduct the $8,000 of medical expenses he incurred in 1991, what portion of the $63,000 settlement is included in D's gross income in 1992?

b.   D did not return to work for three months. During this time period, he received $3,000 in disability income payments. Assuming D paid the annual premium on the disability insurance, how much of the $3,000 is taxable income to D?

6-32   *Meals and Lodging.*   Mr. and Mrs. G own and operate a small motel near Big Mountain resort area. Their only employees are two maids and one cook. The rest of the work is done by Mr. and Mrs. G. In order to be on 24-hour call, they live in a home next to the motel. The home is owned by the business. Both Mr. and Mrs. G eat most of their meals in the motel restaurant. Answer the questions below assuming the business is (1) a corporation, or (2) a partnership.

a.   Are any of the costs for the meals and lodging deductible by either the business or Mr. and Mrs. G?

b.   Is the value of the meals and lodging included in Mr. and Mrs. G's gross income?

c.   Answer the questions in (a) and (b) again, but assume Mr. and Mrs. G paid the business for all their meals in the restaurant and for rent of the home.

6-33   *Military Compensation.*   After graduating from high school last year, K, who is single, joined the U.S. Air Force. Her military compensation for the current year is

	Cash	Market Value
Salary	$10,000	
Military housing		$2,500
Computer training on the job		1,800
Uniforms		800
Meals on the base		3,600
Reimbursement of moving expenses	500	

Calculate K's taxable income for the year.

6-34   *Inheritances.*   In each of the following independent situations, determine how much, if any, the taxpayer must include in gross income.

    a.   At the beginning of this year, a taxpayer inherited rental property valued at $87,000 from his grandmother. Rental income from the property after the transfer of title totaled $6,000, and rental expenses were $5,200.

    b.   A taxpayer inherited $50,000 from her employer. She was his housekeeper for ten years and was promised she would be provided for in his will if she continued employment with him until his death.

    c.   A taxpayer lent $15,000 to a friend. To protect the loan, the taxpayer had his friend make him beneficiary on her $20,000 life insurance policy. Six months later the friend died and the taxpayer received $20,000 from the insurance company.

6-35   *Gifts.*   In each of the following independent situations, determine how much, if any, the taxpayer must include in gross income.

    a.   A taxpayer often visits her uncle in a nursing home. In addition, she manages his investment portfolio for him. To show his gratitude, he has given her stock valued at $5,000. He has also implied that if she continues these activities, he will transfer other shares of stock to her.

    b.   A taxpayer saved a child's life during a fire. The child's parents gave him land valued at $5,000 to show their gratitude. They paid $2,200 for the land several years ago.

    c.   Taxpayer's employer gave him $1,200 in recognition of his 20 years of service to the company. The employer deducted the $1,200 as a business expense.

6-36   *Awards.*   In each of the following independent situations, determine how much, if any, the taxpayer must include in gross income.

    a.   The taxpayer, a professional basketball player, was voted as the outstanding player of the year. In addition to the honor, he received an automobile with a sticker price of $16,000. He drove the car for six months and sold it for $12,000. The taxpayer's employer also gave him a gold watch worth $1,200. He wears the watch. Both donors deducted their respective costs for the automobile and the watch as business expenses. The costs of the automobile and watch were $13,500 and $800, respectively.

    b.   The taxpayer was selected by the senior class as the most outstanding classroom teacher. The high school presented her with a $1,000 check in recognition of her significant accomplishments. She used the money to take a well-earned vacation to Cancun.

    c.   M, Inc. gave T a watch in recognition of her 20 years of service to the company. The watch cost the employer $400.

6-37 *Child Support and Alimony.* Determine the effect on A.G.I. for the husband (H) and wife (W) in each of the following *continuous* situations. H and W are divorced and do not live in a community property state. They have three children.

  a. H pays W $400 per month as alimony and support of the three children.

  b. W discovers her attorney did not word the agreement correctly. H and W sign a statement that the *original* agreement is retroactively amended to hold that H pays $100 per month as alimony to W and $300 per month as support of the three children. All other language remains unchanged. What is the effect of this change on future and past payments?

  c. Assume the original agreement contained the wording in (b) above. In the first year, H makes only 10 of the 12 payments for a total of $4,000. In the second year, H pays the $800 balance due for the prior year and makes all 12 payments of $400 each on time.

  d. On their divorce, W was awarded an automobile. H is required to pay the loan outstanding on the car, $94 per month for 20 months. During the year, H pays $94 for 12 months. This includes $130 interest and $998 loan principal.

  e. H owns the home in which W and the children live free of charge. H's mortgage payments are $360 per month for the next 20 years. During the year, his expenses on the home are $2,900 interest, $800 property taxes, $340 insurance, $280 loan principal, and $218 repairs. The rental value of the home is $425 per month.

  f. In addition to the monthly alimony and support payments above, H is to pay W $30,000 over a period of 11 years. H pays $2,500 of this amount the first year and $3,600 the second year.

  g. H inherits considerable property. As a result, he voluntarily increases the alimony to $150 and child support to $450 per month. He makes 12 payments of $600 each during the year.

6-38 *Alimony.* Determine the effect on A.G.I. for the husband (H) and wife (W) in each of the three years. W is to pay H alimony of $100,000 as follows:

Year	Amount
1	$56,000
2	26,000
3	18,000

6-39 *Divorce—Property Settlement.* Husband (H) and wife (W) are divorced this month. The divorce agreement states that all jointly owned property will be transferred as follows:

	Cost	Market Value	Transferred to
Home	$35,000	$65,000	W
Investments	3,000	5,000	W
Cash	7,000	7,000	H and W equally

W will occupy the home and H will rent an apartment. Determine the recognized gain or loss and the basis of the assets to H and W after the transfer. Explain.

6-40 *Divorce—Property Settlement.*   H and W, who live in Michigan (a common law state), decided to end their troubled 30-year marriage. Pursuant to the divorce decree, the following assets are transferred from H to W on March 1, 1991:

	Basis to H	Market Value
Stocks (purchased by H on April 10, 1986)	$300,000	$400,000
Land (purchased by H on June 2, 1982)	200,000	500,000

In addition to the above, H transferred a life insurance policy on his life with a face value of $200,000 to W, who assumed responsibility for the annual premium.

W sold the stocks for $500,000 on November 1, 1991 and the land for $550,000 on December 1, 1991. H died on December 20, 1991.

a.   Determine W's gain on the sale of the stocks and land in 1991.

b.   Are any of the life insurance proceeds taxable to W? Explain.

6-41 *Unrelated Party Transfers.*   In each of the following independent situations, determine how much, if any, the taxpayer must include in gross income.

a.   Taxpayer has been very active as a volunteer hospital worker for many years. In the current year, the city named her as the Outstanding Volunteer of the Year. She later discovered that she was nominated for the award by two nurses at the hospital. The honor included a silver tray valued at $400. In addition, the two nurses collected $700 from hospital personnel and gave her a prepaid one-week vacation for two people.

b.   Taxpayer, an undergraduate degree candidate, was selected as one of five outstanding sophomore students in accounting by the National Association of Accountants. Selection was based on an application submitted by eligible students. The winner received $15,000. Although there was no stipulation of how the money was to be used, the award was given with the expectation that the money would be used for tuition, books, and fees in the student's junior and senior years.

c.   Taxpayer won the bowling league award for the highest total score over a five-week period. Taxpayer received a trophy valued at $65 and $100 cash.

d.   Taxpayer purchased church raffle tickets in her eight-year-old son's name and gave the tickets to him. One of the tickets was drawn. The prize was a $600 color television.

e.   Taxpayer receives a $20,000 grant from the National Association of Chiefs of Police to conduct a research study on crowd control. The grant stipulates that the research period is for eight months and that $8,000 of it is for travel and temporary living costs.

f.   An accounting student accepted an internship with a CPA firm and is paid $3,000. The stated purpose of the internship is to provide students with a basic understanding of how accounting education is applied. It is believed this understanding will help students in remaining course work and later job selection. Although the faculty believes internships would benefit all students, only 40 percent of the accounting majors participate in the program.

6-42 *Businesses.* In each of the following independent situations, determine how much, if any, the taxpayer must include in gross income.

a. A taxpayer sold a beauty shop operated as a proprietorship for $60,000. The assets were valued as follows: tangible assets, $45,000; agreement not to compete, $10,000; and goodwill, $5,000. The seller's basis for the tangible assets is $45,000 but there is no basis for the other two assets.

b. The building in which a drug store is located is damaged by fire. The store had to be closed for two weeks while repairs were made. As a result, the insurance company paid the store $50,000 for lost profits during the period and $15,000 to cover overhead expenses.

c. E, Inc. leases land to V, Inc. The agreement states that the lease period is for five years and the annual lease payment is $1,000 per month. Under the terms of the lease, V immediately constructs a storage building on the land for $40,000. E receives $12,000 from V each year for three years. At the end of the third year, V cancels the lease and pays a cancellation penalty of $6,000. At this time, the building's market value is $30,000. Thus, in the third year, E received $18,000 cash and a building worth an additional $30,000. Determine E's taxable income from the lease for each of the three years.

d. A corporation accepted $100,000 from an insurance company as an out-of-court settlement of a law suit for patent infringement.

6-43 *Debt Cancellation.* DEF, Inc. is in the van conversion business. Due to stiff competition and a declining economy in the region served by DEF, the company has incurred significant operating losses during the past year. As of December 31, 1991, DEF's financial statements reflect the following pertinent information:

Total assets...	$ 750,000
Total liabilities..	1,000,000
Tax attributes	
Adjusted basis of depreciable assets.....................	300,000
NOL carryover...	100,000
Capital loss carryover...................................	25,000

In an attempt to rescue the company from going out of business, DEF's suppliers have agreed to forgive $180,000 of indebtedness.

a. Assuming DEF is not in bankruptcy proceedings, what are the tax consequences to the corporation resulting from the cancellation of the debt?

b. Would your answer to part (a) change if DEF makes an election under Code § 108(b)(5)?

c. Would your answer to part (a) change if the $180,000 of debt is cancelled under bankruptcy proceedings?

d. Assume that the facts in the problem remain the same, except that DEF has total assets of $1 million and total liabilities of $750,000. What impact does the cancellation of $180,000 in debt now have on DEF?

6-44   *Miscellaneous Items.*   In each of the following independent situations, determine how much, if any, the taxpayer must include in gross income.

   a.   A taxpayer's round trip mileage to and from work is 50 miles. Five fellow employees live near him and pay to ride with him. The taxpayer's records for the current year show $3,900 receipts and $3,120 automobile expenses.

   b.   While walking across campus, a taxpayer found a diamond ring. She notified the authorities on campus and paid $10 for an ad in the lost-and-found section of the newspaper. When six weeks went by with no response, she had the ring appraised. It was valued at $1,200. After six more weeks with no response, she sold the ring for $850.

   c.   A taxpayer was injured on the job and was out of work for most of the year. He received the following government benefits during the year: $800 in food stamps; $1,500 workmen's compensation for the injury; and $1,800 in welfare payments.

   d.   A taxpayer sued her neighbor for malicious slander. The court awarded her $30,000 for personal injury due to indignities suffered as a result of the slander; $3,500 in lost income; and $200 reimbursement for medical expenses incurred. The taxpayer does not itemize deductions.

6-45   *Cumulative Problem.*   H, age 40, and W, age 38, are married with two children: M, age 15, and N, age 16. H, who is president of a local bank, is paid a salary of $125,000. He also is the sole proprietor of a jewelry store that had a net profit for 1991 of $75,000. W, a registered nurse at a large hospital, is paid a salary of $50,000. In addition to the above income, H and W received the following during 1991:

   a. $6,000 cash dividend on ABC, Inc. stock, which they own jointly. They paid $25,000 for the stock three years ago and it has a current market value of $40,000. ABC, Inc. has $300,000 of current and accumulated E&P.

   b. $750 in interest on State of Michigan bonds that H owns.

   c. $7,000 in interest on corporate bonds that H and W purchased two years ago at face value for $100,000.

   d.   W received a check for $400 from her employer in recognition of her outstanding service to the hospital during the past 10 years.

   e.   The bank provides H with $90,000 of group term life insurance protection. The bank provides all full-time employees with group term insurance.

   f.   1,000 shares of XYZ common as a stock dividend. Prior to the distribution, H and W owned 9,000 shares of common with a basis of $15,000. H and W did not have the right to receive cash or other assets in lieu of the stock.

   g.   Because W must be available should an emergency arise, she is required to eat her lunches in the hospital cafeteria. The value of the free meals provided by her employer during 1991 was $1,100.

   h.   H's grandfather passed away in February 1991, leaving H a 400-acre farm in southern Illinois valued at $500,000. H rented the land to F, a neighboring farmer, for $13,000.

   i.   In order to drain off the excess surface water from 10 acres, F (see h above) installed drainage pipe at a cost of $1,500.

   j.   W sold 50 shares of DEF stock for $100 per share. She bought the stock four years ago for $1,800.

k. H received a dividend check for $280 from the XYZ Mutual Life Insurance Company. H purchased the policy in 1980, and W is the primary beneficiary.

l. H and W's only itemized deductions were interest on their home mortgage, $18,000; property taxes on their home, $4,000; and charitable contributions, $6,000.

m. The hospital withheld $9,500 of Federal income taxes on W's salary and the appropriate amount of FICA taxes. The bank withheld $14,000 in Federal income taxes from H's salary and the appropriate amount of FICA taxes. Furthermore, H's quarterly estimated tax payments for 1991 total $25,000.

Part I: Computation of Federal Income Tax. Calculate H and W's 1991 Federal income tax liability (or refund) assuming they file a joint return.

Part II: Tax Planning Ideas. H and W are very concerned about the amount of Federal income tax they now pay. Because they want to send M and N to private universities, they have come up with the following strategies, which they hope will reduce their family's total tax liability.

1. In 1992, M and N will begin working at the jewelry store two nights a week and on Saturdays throughout the school year and 20 hours a week during the summer months. Each child will be paid $4,500 for services during the year.

2. On January 1, 1992, H and W will sell their corporate bonds for $100,000 and invest the cash proceeds in Series EE savings bonds. H and W will use the bonds to pay for M and N's qualified educational expenses.

3. On January 1, 1992, H and W will gift their stock in ABC, Inc. to M and N equally.

4. Beginning in 1992, H will instruct the farmer who is leasing his Illinois farm to pay the $13,000 in rent directly to M and N (i.e., $6,500 each).

H and W have asked for your opinion concerning the above strategies. For each idea, explain why it will or will not reduce the family's total tax liability. Assuming H and W implement only the strategies that will reduce taxes, how much will the family save in taxes in 1992 compared to 1991?

RESEARCH PROBLEMS

6-46 *Divorce.* J and M are obtaining a divorce after ten years of marriage. They have two children. A draft of the divorce agreement and property settlement between them states that they will have joint custody of the children. They plan to live in the same general area and each child will live half of each year with each parent. Since J's A.G.I. is $40,000 and M's $15,000, he will pay her $100 per month for each child ($2,400 per year) and $500 per month for her support. The $500 ceases on his or her death, her remarriage, or when her A.G.I. equals his. In addition, J agrees to continue to pay premiums of $50 per month on his life insurance policy payable to her. All jointly owned property will be distributed as follows:

	Basis	Market Value	Transfer to
Home	$50,000	$80,000	M
Furnishings	20,000	15,000	M
Investments	10,000	30,000	J

Each will keep his or her individually owned personal items and an automobile. This is an amicable divorce and they both request your advice. Their objective is to maximize total tax benefits without making too many changes to the agreement. Use tax-planning techniques when possible in responding to the following questions.

a.   Who will be able to claim the children as dependents?

b.   What is each one's filing status for the current year if neither one remarries?

c.   Does the $500 per month qualify as alimony? Does the $50 per month qualify as alimony?

d.   J expects to make the $500 and $50 payments for three months while legally separated before the divorce. What are the tax effects during this period?

e.   What is the tax effect of the distribution of jointly owned property to J and to M?

f.   What tax planning advice could you give to J and M that would decrease their combined tax liability?

6-47 *Meals and Lodging.* H and W are married with three children. The children are 8, 10, and 15 years old. H and W are purchasing a 500-acre farm, which they will manage and operate themselves. In addition, they will employ one full-time farmer year round and several part-time people at peak times. H will be responsible primarily for management of the operations, the crops, and the dairy herd and other farm animals. W will be responsible primarily for the garden, the chickens, providing meals for the family and farm hands, and maintaining the family home. The children are assigned farm chores to help their parents after school and weekends.

The taxpayers prefer to operate the farm as a partnership but, after all factors are considered, are willing to incorporate the farm if it seems to provide greater benefits. Presently, they ask for detailed information about the residence on the farm and the groceries that will be purchased to feed them and their employees on the farm. Some of their specific questions are listed below.

a. What are the benefits and requirements covering meals and lodging provided by the business?

b. Is it possible to meet the requirements and obtain all or at least some of the benefits if the farm is operated as a proprietorship or partnership, or must it be operated as a corporation?

c. If full benefits are obtained, are any adjustments required for the children, for personal entertainment and meals shared with friends and relatives in the farm home, or any other personal use? If any adjustments are required, which ones, and are they made at cost or market value?

d. If full benefits are obtained, exactly what qualifies? For example, do all groceries qualify, including supplies that are not eaten, such as freezer bags to store frozen foods from the garden, soap, and bathroom supplies? Do all expenses for the home qualify, such as utilities, insurance, and repairs?

e. Should the business or should H and W own the home?

f. Is it acceptable for H and W to purchase the food and be reimbursed by the business?

Some suggested research materials:

Code § 119 and accompanying Regulations.
Kowalski v. Comm., 77-2 USTC ¶9748, 40 AFTR2d 6128, 434 U.S. 77 (USSC, 1977).
Armstrong v. Phinney, 68-1 USTC ¶9355, 21 AFTR2d 1260, 394 F.2d 661.
Rev. Rul. 53-80, 1953-1 C.B. 62.

6-48 *Discharge of Indebtedness.* T, who is single, purchased a new home in 1976 from the XYZ Construction Co. for $55,000. She received a 7.25 percent mortgage from the Federal Savings and Loan Association (FS&L). Currently, the home's fair market value is approximately double its original purchase price. Since interest rates have risen significantly in recent months, FS&L wants to rid itself of the low 7.25 percent mortgage. Lending to others at a much higher interest rate would clearly enhance FS&L's profits. Consequently, during the current year FS&L sent a letter to T offering to cancel the mortgage (which had a remaining principal balance of $35,000) in return for a payment of $29,000. T took advantage of the prepayment opportunity, thus receiving a discount equal to the difference between the remaining principal balance of $35,000 and the amount paid by T of $29,000, or $6,000.

a. Although T is pleased she no longer has a monthly mortgage payment, she is concerned about the possible tax consequences resulting from the discharge of indebtedness. T has come to you for your advice.

b. Assume that the fair market value of T's residence has declined to $25,000 due to the construction of a nearby land fill operation. Does this fact change your answer?

Some suggested research materials:

Code §§ 61(a)(12), 108(a)(1), and 108(e)(5).
Sutphin v. U.S., 88-1 USTC ¶9269, 1 AFTR2d 88-990, 14 F.2d 545 (Ct. Cls., 1988).
Hirsch v. Comm., 40-2 USTC ¶9791, 25 AFTR 1038, 115 F.2d 656 (CA-7, 1940).

6-49   *Compensatory Damages.*   T. J. Taxpayer, CLU, has owned an insurance agency in Santa Rosa, California since 1960. As an independent agent, he represented five companies selling auto, home, commercial, and life insurance. Because of his excellent reputation in the community, T. J. has built a very successful agency. In 1985, T. J. applied for an agency license from the American Life Insurance Co. in order to broaden his life insurance business. In reviewing his application, American requested a credit report from Federal Credit. Federal Credit provided copies to American Life as well as other insurance companies.

The credit report contained numerous false accusations. In addition to questioning Taxpayer's integrity, the report stated that T. J. seldom returned phone calls from clients and lacked understanding of basic insurance practices and concepts. As a result, American Life denied T. J. a license to sell its life insurance. Because the report adversely affected his ability to work with existing clients and to attract new business, T. J.'s profits declined considerably.

T. J. sued Federal Credit for libel, claiming that the credit report was issued with intent to damage his business or professional reputation. The jury found that Federal Credit had committed libel and awarded him $100,000 in compensatory damages. T. J. has heard conflicting comments from various sources about whether the $100,000 is taxable and comes to you for help. When researching this issue, you come across a number of cases and rulings.

a. Two Circuit Courts of Appeal have expressed their opinion concerning the taxability of damages received for injury to an individual's business or professional reputation. What was their conclusion? Give a summary of the analysis each court used in arriving at its decision.

b. What is the Tax Court's position concerning compensatory damages? Is the Tax Court's current position a reversal of its previously held position? If so, explain why the Tax Court changed its mind.

c. What is the Internal Revenue Service's position with respect to compensatory damages?

d. What advice would you give T. J. Taxpayer concerning the taxability of the $100,000?

COMPUTERIZED TAX ANALYSIS

6-50 *Investments—Bonds.* Use computer file T601 for this problem.

a.   For the independent situations listed below, compute the missing values.

	(1)	(2)	(3)	(4)	(5)
Amount of investment in bonds	$12,000	$12,000	$12,000	$12,000	$12,000
Annual interest rate on corporate bonds	10%	10%	10%	10%	10%
Annual interest rate on municipal bonds	8%	7.2%	6%	8%	8%
Marginal tax rate of investor	28%	28%	28%	33%	15%
Annual ATCF from corporate bonds	___	___	___	___	___
Annual ATCF from municipal bonds	___	___	___	___	___
Breakeven interest rate	___	___	___	___	___

b.   Given the results obtained in question (a)(1), should the investor buy the corporate bonds or the municipal bonds? Why?

c.   Given the results obtained in question (a)(2), should the investor buy the corporate bonds or the municipal bonds? Why?

d.   Given the results obtained in question (a)(3), should the investor buy the corporate bonds or the municipal bonds? Why?

e.   In questions (a)(1) through (a)(3), the annual rate of interest on the municipal bonds declines from 8 percent to 7.2 percent, and then to 6 percent. The breakeven interest rate, however, remains constant. Why?

f.   Notice the trend of the results for questions (a)(4) and (a)(5). What does this trend imply regarding the wisdom of investing in municipal bonds (versus corporate bonds of equivalent risk) by investors who are in low or moderate tax brackets?

PART III

DEADUCTIONS AND LOSSES

CONTENTS

LEARNING OBJECTIVES

Upon completion of this chapter you will be able to:

- Recognize the general requirements for deducting expenses and losses
- Define the terms *ordinary*, *necessary*, and *reasonable* as they apply to business deductions
- Recognize tax accounting principles with respect to deductions and losses
- Explain the proper treatment of employee business expenses
- Describe the importance of properly classifying expenses as deductions *for* or *from* adjusted gross income
- Classify expenses as deductions *for* or *from* adjusted gross income
- Recognize statutory, administrative, and judicial limitations on deductions and losses
- Explain tax planning considerations for optimizing deductions

CHAPTER OUTLINE

Chapter 7

OVERVIEW OF DEDUCTIONS AND LOSSES

As explained in Chapter 3, the income tax is imposed on taxable income, a quantity defined as the difference between gross income and allowable deductions.[1] The concept of gross income was explored in Chapters 5 and 6. This chapter and the following four chapters examine the subject of deductions.

There is little doubt that when it comes to taxation, the questions asked most frequently concern deductions. What is deductible? Can this expense be deducted? How much can I deduct? This is a familiar refrain around taxpaying time, and rightfully so, since any item which might be deductible reduces the tax that otherwise must be paid. Many of the questions concerning deductions are easily answered by merely referring to the basic criteria. On the other hand, many items representing potential deductions are subject to special rules. The purpose of this chapter is to introduce the general rules which are in fact used for determining the answer to that age-old question: Is it deductible?

DEDUCTION DEFINED

In the preceding chapters, the definition given for income was described as being "all inclusive" (i.e., gross income includes *all* items of income except those specifically excluded by law). Given this concept of income, it might be assumed that a similarly broad meaning is given to the term deduction. Deductions, however, are defined narrowly. Deductions are only those *particular* expenses, losses, and other items for which a deduction is authorized.[2] The significance of this apparently meaningless definition is found in the last word—"authorized." *Nothing is deductible unless it is allowed by the Code.* It is a well-established principle that before a deduction may be claimed the taxpayer must find some statutory provision permitting the deduction. The courts consistently have affirmed this principle, stating that a taxpayer has no constitutional right to a deduction. Rather, a taxpayer's right to a deduction depends solely on "legislative grace" (i.e., Congress has enacted a statute allowing the deduction).[3]

---

[1] § 63.

[2] § 161.

[3] *New Colonial Ice Co. v. Helvering*, 4 USTC ¶1292, 13 AFTR 1180, 292 U.S. 435 (USSC, 1934).

Although a taxpayer's deductions require statutory authorization, this does not mean that a particular deduction must be specifically mentioned in the Code. While several provisions are designed to grant the deduction for a specific item, such as § 163 for interest expense and § 164 for taxes, most deductions are allowed because they satisfy the conditions of some broadly defined category of deductions. For example, no specific deduction is allowed for the advertising expense of a restaurant owner, but the expense may be deductible if it meets the criteria required for deduction of *business expenses*.

The remainder of this chapter examines those provisions authorizing several broad categories of deductions: § 162 on trade or business expenses, § 212 on expenses of producing income, and § 165 on losses. In addition to these deduction-granting sections, several provisions that expressly deny or limit deductions for certain items are considered. The rules provided by these various provisions establish the basic framework for determining whether a deduction is allowed. Once the deductibility of an item is determined, an additional problem exists for individual taxpayers—the deduction must be classified as either a deduction *for* adjusted gross income or a deduction *from* adjusted gross income (itemized deduction). The classification process is also explained in this chapter.

DEDUCTIONS FOR EXPENSES: GENERAL REQUIREMENTS

Given that the taxpayer can deduct only those items that are authorized, what deductions does Congress in fact allow? The central theme found in the rules governing deductions is relatively straightforward: those expenses and losses incurred in business and profit-seeking activities are deductible while those incurred in purely personal activities are not. The allowance for business and profit-seeking expenses stems in part from the traditional notion that income is a *net* concept. From a conceptual perspective, income does not result until revenues exceed expenses. It generally follows from this principle that it would be unfair to tax the revenue from an activity but not allow deductions for the expenses that produced it.

In light of the Code's approach to deductions, many commentators have aptly stated that the costs of *earning* a living are deductible while the costs of living are not. Although this is a good rule of thumb, it is also an over-generalization. As will become clear, the Code allows deductions not only for the costs of producing income, but also for numerous personal expenses such as interest on home mortgages, property taxes, medical expenses, and charitable contributions. To complicate matters further, the line between personal and business expenses is often difficult to draw. For this reason, the various rules governing deductions must be examined closely.

GENERAL RULES: CODE §§ 162 AND 212

Two provisions in the Code provide the authority for the deduction of most expenses: § 162 concerning trade or business expenses and § 212 relating to expenses for the production of income. Numerous other provisions of the Code pertain to deductions. These other provisions, however, normally build on the basic rules contained in §§ 162 and 212. For this reason, the importance of these two provisions cannot be overstated.

Section 162(a) on trade or business expenses reads, in part, as follows:

> In General.—There shall be allowed as a deduction all the ordinary and necessary expenses paid or incurred during the taxable year in carrying on any trade or business, including—
> (1) a reasonable allowance for salaries or other compensation for personal services actually rendered;
> (2) traveling expenses (including amounts expended for meals and lodging other than amounts which are lavish or extravagant under the circumstances) while away from home in the pursuit of a trade or business;
> (3) rentals or other payments required to be made as a condition to the continued use or possession, for purposes of the trade or business, of property to which the taxpayer has not taken or is not taking title or in which he has no equity.

Although § 162(a) specifically enumerates three items that are deductible, the provision's primary importance lies in its general rule: ordinary and necessary expenses of carrying on a trade or business are deductible.

Section 212 contains a general rule very similar to that found in § 162. Section 212, in part, reads as follows:

> In the case of an individual, there shall be allowed as a deduction all the ordinary and necessary expenses paid or incurred during the taxable year—
> (1) for the production or collection of income;
> (2) for the management, conservation, or maintenance of property held for the production of income. . . .

Production of income expenses are normally those related to investments, such as investment advisory fees and safety deposit box rentals.

An examination of the language of §§ 162 and 212 indicates that a deduction is allowed under either section if it meets *four* critical requirements. The expense must have all of the following properties:

1. It must be related to carrying on a trade or business or an income-producing activity.

2. It must be ordinary and necessary.

3. It must be reasonable.

4. It must be paid or incurred during the taxable year.

It should be emphasized, however, that satisfaction of these criteria does not ensure deductibility. Other provisions in the Code often operate to prohibit or limit a deduction otherwise granted by §§ 162 and 212. For example, an expense may be ordinary, necessary, and related to carrying on a business, but if it is also related to producing tax-exempt income, § 265 prohibits a deduction. This system of allowing, yet disallowing, deductions is a basic feature in the statutory scheme for determining deductibility.

RELATED TO CARRYING ON A BUSINESS OR AN INCOME-PRODUCING ACTIVITY

The Activity.   Whether an expense is deductible depends in part on the type of activity in which it was incurred. A deduction is authorized by § 162 only if it is paid or incurred in an activity which constitutes a trade or business. Similarly, § 212 permits a deduction only if it is paid or incurred in an activity for the production or collection of income. The purpose of each of these requirements is to deny deductions for expenses incurred in an activity which is *primarily personal* in nature. For example, the costs incurred in pursuing what is merely a hobby, such as collecting antiques or racing automobiles, normally would be considered nondeductible personal expenditures. Of course, this assumes that such activities do not constitute a trade or business.

The Code does not provide any clues as to when an activity will be considered a trade or business or an income-producing activity rather than a personal activity. Over the years, however, one criterion has emerged from the many court cases involving the issue. In order to constitute a trade or business or an income-producing activity, the activity must be *entered into for profit*.[4] In other words, for the taxpayer's expenses to be deductible, they must be motivated by his or her hope for a profit. For this reason, taxpayers who collect antiques or race automobiles can deduct all of the related expenses if they are able to demonstrate that they did so with the hope of producing income. In such case, they would be considered to be in a trade or business. If the required profit motive is lacking, however, expenses of the activity generally are not deductible except to the extent the activity has income.

As may be apparent, the critical question in this area is what inspired the taxpayer's activities. The factors to be used in evaluating the taxpayer's motivation, along with the special provisions governing activities which are not engaged in for profit—the so-called hobby loss rules—are considered in detail later in this chapter.

A profit motive is the only requirement necessary to establish existence of an *income-producing* activity. However, the courts have imposed an additional requirement before an activity qualifies as a *trade or business*. Business status requires both a profit motive and a sufficient degree of taxpayer involvement in the activity in order to distinguish the activity from a passive investment. No clear guidelines have emerged indicating when a taxpayer's activities rise to the level of carrying on a business. The courts, however, generally have permitted business treatment where the taxpayer has devoted a major portion of time to the activities or the activities have been regular or continuous.[5]

> **Example 1.** C owns six rental units, including several condominiums and townhouses. He manages his rental properties entirely by himself. His managing activities include seeking new tenants, supplying furnishings, cleaning and preparing the units for occupancy, advertising, and bookkeeping. In this case, C's involvement with the rental activities is sufficiently continuous and systematic to constitute a business.[6] If the rental activities were of a more limited nature, they might not qualify as a trade or business. The determination ultimately depends on the facts of the particular situation.[7]

> **Example 2.** H owns various stocks and bonds. Her managerial activities related to these securities primarily consist of maintaining records and collecting dividends and interest. She rarely trades in the market. These

---

[4] *Doggett v. Burnett*, 3 USTC ¶1090, 12 AFTR 505, 65 F.2d 192 (CA-D.C., 1933).

[5] *Grier v. U.S.*, 55-1 USTC ¶9184, 46 AFTR 1536, 218 F.2d 603 (CA-2, 1955).

[6] *Edwin R. Curphey*, 73 T.C. 766 (1980).

[7] *Ibid.*

activities are those normally associated with a passive investor, and accordingly would not constitute a trade or business under § 162 (they would be considered an income-producing activity under § 212).[8] On the other hand, if H had a substantial volume of transactions, made personal investigations of the corporations in which she was interested in purchasing, and devoted virtually every day to such work, her activities could constitute a trade or business.[9] Again, however, the answer depends on the facts.

Distinguishing between §§ 162 and 212. Prior to enactment of § 212, many investment-related expenses were not deductible because the activities did not constitute a business. The enactment of § 212 in 1942 allowing for the deduction of expenses related to production or collection of income enabled the deduction of investment-oriented expenses. This expansion of the deduction concept to include so-called "nonbusiness" or investment-related expenses eliminates the need for an activity to constitute a business before a deduction is allowed. As a result, the issue of deductibility (*assuming* the other requirements are met) is effectively reduced to a single important question: Is the expense related to an activity engaged in for profit?

It may appear that the addition of § 212 completely removed the need for determining whether the activity resulting in the expense constitutes a business or is merely for the production of income. However, the distinction between business and production of income expenses remains important. For example, the classification of the expense as a deduction for or from adjusted gross income may turn on whether the expense is a trade or business expense or a production of income expense. Production of income expenses (other than those related to rents or royalties) are usually miscellaneous itemized deductions and can be deducted only to the extent they *exceed* 2 percent of adjusted gross income. In contrast, most business expenses are deductions for adjusted gross income and are deductible in full.

> **Example 3.** Refer to *Example 2*. In the first situation, where H is considered a passive investor, her investment-related expenses (e.g., subscriptions to stock advisory services and investment newsletters) would be miscellaneous itemized deductions and deductible only to the extent they exceed 2% of adjusted gross income. In the second situation, however, the same type of expenses would be deductions for adjusted gross income since H's trading activities qualify as a trade or business.

---

[8] *Higgins v. Comm.*, 41-1 USTC ¶9233, 25 AFTR 1160, 312 U.S. 212 (USSC, 1941).

[9] *Samuel B. Levin v. U.S.*, 79-1 USTC ¶9331, 43 AFTR2d 79-1057, 597 F.2d 760 (Ct. Cls., 1979). But see *Joseph Moller v. U.S.*, 83-2 USTC ¶9698, 52 AFTR2d 83-6333 (CA-FC, 1983) where, for purposes of the home office deduction, the court held that the taxpayer's management of his substantial investment portfolio could not be a trade or business regardless of how continuous, regular, and extensive the activities were.

Another reason for ascertaining whether the activity constitutes a business relates to the use of the phrase "trade or business" in other Code Sections. The phrase "trade or business" appears in at least 60 different Code Sections, and the interpretation given to this phrase often controls the tax treatment. For example, whether an activity is an active business or a passive investment affects the tax consequences related to losses (deductible or limited), bad debts (short-term capital loss vs. ordinary loss), property sales (capital gain or loss vs. ordinary gain or loss), expenses for offices in the home (deductible vs. nondeductible), and limited expensing of depreciable property (allowed vs. disallowed).[10]

The Relationship. Before an expense is deductible under §§ 162 or 212, it must have a certain relationship to the trade or business or income-producing activity. The Regulations require that business expenses must be directly connected with or must pertain to the taxpayer's trade or business.[11] Similarly, production of income expenses must bear a reasonable and proximate relationship to the income-producing activity.[12] Whether an expenditure is directly related to the taxpayer's trade or business or income-producing activity usually depends on the facts. For example, the required relationship for business expenses normally exists where the expense is primarily motivated by business concerns or arises as a result of business, rather than personal, needs.[13]

> **Example 4.** While driving from one business to another, T struck a pedestrian with his automobile. He paid and deducted legal fees and damages in connection with the accident that were disallowed by the IRS. The Court found that the expenses were not directly related to, nor did they proximately result from, the taxpayer's business. The accident was merely incidental to the transportation and was related only remotely to the business.[14]

Whether a particular item is deductible often hinges on whether the expense was incurred for business or personal purposes. Consider the case of a law enforcement officer who is required to keep in top shape to retain his employment. Is the cost of a health club membership incurred for business or personal purposes? Similarly, can a disc jockey who obtains dentures to improve his speech deduct the cost as a business expense? Unfortunately, many expenses—like these—straddle the business-personal fence and the final determination is difficult. In both the cases above, the Court denied the taxpayers' deductions on the theory that such expenses were inherently personal.

---

[10] See §§ 166, 1221, 280A, and 179.

[11] Reg. § 1.162-1(a).

[12] Reg. § 1.212-1(d).

[13] *U.S. v. Gilmore*, 63-1 USTC ¶9285, 11 AFTR2d 758, 372 U.S. 39 (USSC, 1963).

[14] *Julian D. Freedman v. Comm.*, 62-1 USTC ¶9400, 9 AFTR2d 1235, 301 F.2d 359 (CA-5, 1962); but see *Harold Dancer*, 73 T.C. 1103 (1980), where the Tax Court allowed the deduction when the taxpayer was traveling between two locations of the *same* business. Note how the subtle change in facts substantially alters the result!

Another common question concerns expenses paid or incurred prior to the time that income is earned. In the case of § 212 expenses, it is not essential that the activity produce income currently. For example, expenses may be deductible under § 212 even though there is little likelihood that the property will be sold at a profit or will ever produce income.[15] Deductions are allowed as long as the transaction was entered into for profit.

> **Example 5.** B purchased a vacant lot three years ago as an investment. During the current year she paid $200 to have it mowed. Although the property is not currently producing income, the expense is deductible since it is for the conservation or maintenance of property held for the production of income.

ORDINARY AND NECESSARY EXPENSES

The second test for deductibility is whether the expense is ordinary and necessary. An expense is *ordinary* if it is normally incurred in the type of business in which the taxpayer is involved.[16] This is not to say that the expense is habitual or recurring.[17] In fact, the expense may be incurred only once in the taxpayer's lifetime and be considered ordinary. The test is whether other taxpayers in similar businesses or income-producing activities would customarily incur the same expense.

> **Example 6.** P has been in the newspaper business for 35 years. Until this year, his paper had never been sued for libel. To protect the reputation of the newspaper, P incurred substantial legal costs related to the libel suit. Although the taxpayer has never incurred legal expenses of this nature before, the expenses are ordinary since it is common in the newspaper business to incur legal expenses to defend against such attacks.[18]

It is interesting to note that the "ordinary" criterion normally becomes an issue in circumstances which are, in fact, unusual. For example, in *Goedel*,[19] a stock dealer paid premiums for insurance on the life of the President of the United States, fearing that his death would disrupt the stock market and his business. The Court denied the deduction on the grounds that the payment was not ordinary but unusual or extraordinary.

---

[15] Reg. § 1.212-1(b).

[16] *Deputy v. DuPont*, 40-1 USTC ¶9161, 23 AFTR 808, 308 U.S. 488 (USSC, 1940).

[17] *Dunn and McCarthy, Inc. v. Comm.*, 43-2 USTC ¶9688, 31 AFTR 1043, 139 F.2d 242 (CA-2, 1943).

[18] *Welch v. Helvering*, 3 USTC ¶1164, 12 AFTR 1456, 290 U.S. 111 (USSC, 1933).

[19] 39 B.T.A. 1 (1939).

A deductible expense not only must be ordinary, but also necessary. An expense is *necessary* if it is appropriate, helpful, or capable of making a contribution to the taxpayer's profit-seeking activities.[20] The necessary criterion, however, is rarely applied to deny a deduction. The courts have refrained from such a practice since to do so would require overriding the judgment of the taxpayer.[21] The courts apparently feel that it would be unfair to judge *currently* whether a previous expenditure was necessary at the time it was incurred.

It should be emphasized that not all necessary expenses are ordinary expenses. Some expenses may be appropriate and helpful to the taxpayer's business but may not be normally incurred in that particular business. In such case, no deduction is allowed.

> **Example 7.** W was an officer in his father's corporation. The corporation, unable to pay its debts, was adjudged bankrupt. After the corporation was discharged from its debts, W decided to resume his father's business on a fresh basis. In order to reestablish relations with old customers and to solidify his credit standing, W paid as much of the old debts as he could. The Supreme Court held that the expenses were necessary in the sense they were appropriate and helpful in the development of W's business. However, the Court ruled that the payments were not ordinary since men do not usually pay the debts of another.[22]

REASONABLE EXPENSES

The third requirement for a deduction is that the expense be reasonable in amount. An examination of § 162(a) reveals that the term "reasonable" is used only in conjunction with compensation paid for services (e.g., a reasonable allowance for salaries). The courts have held, however, that reasonableness is implied in the phrase "ordinary and necessary."[23] In practice, the reasonableness standard is most often applied in situations involving salary payments made by a closely held corporation to a shareholder who also is an employee. In these situations, if the compensation paid exceeds that ordinarily paid for similar services—that which is reasonable—the excessive payment may represent a nondeductible dividend distribution.[24] Dividend treatment of the excess occurs if the amount of the excessive payment received by each employee closely relates to the number of shares of stock owned.[25] The distinction between reasonable compensation and dividend is critical since characterization of the payment as a dividend results in double taxation (i.e., it is taxable to the shareholder-employee and not deductible by the corporation).

---

[20] *Supra*, Footnote 18. See also *Comm. v. Heininger*, 44-1 USTC ¶9109, 31 AFTR 783, 320 U.S. 467 (USSC, 1943).

[21] *Supra*, Footnote 18.

[22] *Supra*, Footnote 18.

[23] *Comm. v. Lincoln Electric Co.*, 49-2 USTC ¶9388, 38 AFTR 411, 176 F.2d 815 (CA-6, 1949).

[24] Reg. § 1.162-7(b)(1).

[25] Reg. § 1.162-8.

Example 8. B and C own 70 and 30% of X Corporation, respectively. Employees in positions similar to that of B earn $60,000 annually while those in positions similar to C's earn $20,000. During the year, the corporation pays B a salary of $130,000 and C a salary of $50,000. The excessive payment of $100,000 [($130,000 + $50,000) − ($60,000 + $20,000)] is received by B and C in direct proportion to their percentage ownership of stock (i.e., B's salary increased by $70,000 or 70% of the excessive payment). Because the payments are in excess of that normally paid to employees in similar positions and the excessive payment received by each is closely related to his stockholdings, the excessive payment may be treated as a nondeductible dividend.

Some of the factors used by the IRS when considering the reasonableness of compensation are [26]

1. Duties performed (i.e., amount and character of responsibility)
2. Volume and complexity of business handled (i.e., time required)
3. Individual's ability and expertise
4. Number of available persons capable of performing the duties of the position
5. Corporation's dividend policies and history

PAID OR INCURRED DURING THE TAXABLE YEAR

Sections 162 and 212 both indicate that an expense is allowable as a deduction only if it is "paid or incurred during the taxable year." This phrase is used throughout the Code in sections concerning deductions. Use of both terms, "paid" and "incurred," is necessary because the year in which deductions are allowable depends on the method of accounting used by the taxpayer.[27] The term *paid* refers to taxpayers using the cash basis method of accounting while the term *incurred* refers to taxpayers using the accrual basis method of accounting. Accordingly, the year in which a deduction is allowed usually depends on whether the cash or accrual basis method of accounting is used.

Cash Basis Taxpayers. For those taxpayers eligible to use the cash method (as discussed in Chapter 5), expenses are deductible in the taxable year when the expenses are actually paid.[28] However, there are numerous exceptions to this rule that are designed to restrict the flexibility a cash basis taxpayer would otherwise have in reporting deductions. Without these restrictions, a cash basis taxpayer

---

[26] Internal Revenue Manual 4233, § 232.

[27] § 461(a).

[28] Reg. § 1.446-1(a)(1).

could choose the year of deductibility simply by appropriately timing the cash payment. Before examining these restrictions, it is important to understand when the taxpayer is considered to have paid the expense.

Time of Payment. For the most part, determining when a cash basis taxpayer has paid an expense is not difficult. A cash basis taxpayer "pays" the expense when cash, check, property, or service is transferred. Neither a promise to pay nor a note evidencing such promise is considered payment. Consequently, when a cash basis taxpayer buys on credit, no deduction is allowed until the debts are paid. However, if the taxpayer borrows cash and then pays the expense, the expense is deductible when paid. For this reason, a taxpayer who charges expenses to a credit card is deemed to have borrowed cash and made payment when the charge is made. Thus, the deduction is claimed when the charge is actually made and not when the bank makes payment or when the taxpayer pays the bill.[29] If the taxpayer uses a "pay-by-phone" account, the expense is deductible in the year the financial institution paid the amount as reported on a monthly statement sent to the taxpayer.[30] When the taxpayer pays by mail, payment is usually considered made when the mailing occurs (i.e., dropping it in the post-office box).[31]

Restrictions on Use of Cash Method. Under the general rule, a cash basis taxpayer deducts expenses when paid. Without restrictions, however, aggressive taxpayers could liberally interpret this provision to authorize not only deductions for routine items, but also deductions for capital expenditures and other expenses that benefit future periods (e.g., supplies, prepaid insurance, prepaid rent, and prepaid interest). To preclude such an approach, numerous limitations have been imposed.

One of the more fundamental restrictions applying to cash basis taxpayers concerns inventories. For example, if no limitation existed, a cash basis owner of a department store could easily reduce or eliminate taxable income by increasing purchases of inventory near year-end and deducting their cost. To prevent this possibility, the Regulations require taxpayers to use the accrual method for computing sales and costs of goods sold if inventories are an income producing factor.[32] In such cases, inventory costs must be capitalized, and accounts receivable and accounts payable (with respect to cost of goods sold) created. The taxpayer could continue to use the cash method for other transactions, however.

Provisions of both the Code and the Regulations limit the potential for deducting capital expenditures, prepaid expenses, and the like. As discussed later in this chapter, Code § 263 specifically denies the deduction for a capital expenditure; such costs as those for equipment, vehicles, and buildings are normally recovered through depreciation, as discussed in Chapter 9.

---

[29] Rev. Rul. 78-39, 1978-1 C.B. 73.

[30] Rev. Rul. 80-335, 1980-2 C.B. 170.

[31] See Rev. Rul. 73-99, 1973-1 C.B. 412 for clarification of this general rule.

[32] Reg. § 1.446-1(c)(2).

The Regulations—at least broadly—deal with other expenditures that are not capital expenditures per se, but which do benefit future periods. According to the Regulations, any expenditure resulting "in the creation of an asset having a useful life which extends *substantially beyond the close of the taxable year* may not be deductible when made, or may be deductible only in part."[33] In this regard, the courts agree that "substantially beyond" means a useful life of more than one year.[34] Perhaps the simplest example of this rule as so interpreted concerns payments for supplies. Assuming the supplies would be exhausted before the close of the following tax year, a deduction should be allowable when payment is made. In regard to other prepayments, however, the application of this principle has spawned a hodgepodge of special rules.

Prepaid Rent.   An Appeals Court decision suggests that prepayments of rents and prepayments for services may be deducted in the year paid when two conditions are present: (1) the period for which the payment is made does not exceed one year, and (2) the taxpayer is contractually obligated to prepay an amount for a period extending beyond the close of the year.[35]   Other advanced payments of rentals can be deducted only during the period to which they relate.

> **Example 9.**   R, a farmer, pays taxes based on the calendar year. In 1991 he leases farm land for the twenty-year period December 1, 1991 to November 30, 2011. The lease agreement provides that annual rent for the period December 1 to November 30 is payable on December 20 each year. The yearly rent is $24,000. On December 20, 1991 R pays the $24,000 rental for the next year. The prepayment is deductible because it is for a period not exceeding a year and R is obligated to pay for the entire year in advance on December 20. However, if the lease agreement required only monthly rentals of $2,000 each (instead of an annual payment of $24,000), only $2,000 would be deductible (representing the rent allocable to the month of December) because the remainder of the payment was voluntary.[36]

Prepaid Insurance.   Prepayments of insurance premiums normally are not deductible when paid. Instead, the IRS holds that this expense must be prorated over the period that the insurance covers.[37]   However, the "one year" exception noted above with respect to prepaid rent may also apply here.

> **Example 10.**   On December 15, 1991 T purchased an insurance policy covering theft of his inventory. The policy cost $3,000 and covered 1992–1994. T may not deduct any of the cost in 1991. In each of the following three years, he will deduct $1,000.

---

[33]   Reg. § 1.446-1(a)(1).

[34]   *Martin J. Zaninovich*, 69 T.C. 605, *rev'd* in 80-1 USTC ¶9342, 45 AFTR2d 80-1442, 616 F.2d 429 (CA-9, 1980).

[35]   *Supra*, Footnote 34.

[36]   *Bonaire Development Co.*, 83-2 USTC ¶9428, 679 F.2d 159 (CA-9, 1983), *aff'g.*, 76 T.C. 789 (1981).

[37]   Rev. Rul. 70-413, 1970-2 C.B. 103.

Other Prepayments. Perhaps the Service's current view of the proper treatment of most prepayments is best captured in a ruling concerning prepaid feed. In this ruling, the taxpayer purchased a substantial amount of feed prior to the year in which it would be used.[38] The purchase was made in advance because the price was low due to a depressed market. The IRS granted a deduction for the prepayment because there was a business purpose for the advanced payment, the payment was not merely a deposit, and it did not materially distort income. Based on this ruling and related cases, prepayments normally should be deductible if the asset will be consumed by the close of the following year, there is a business purpose for the expenditure, and there is no material distortion of income.

Prepaid Interest. For many years, cash basis taxpayers in need of a deduction would simply prepay the interest on a home mortgage or take out a loan and pay the interest in advance. The Code now expressly denies the deduction of prepaid interest. Prepaid interest must be capitalized and deducted ratably over the period of the loan.[39] The same is true for any costs associated with obtaining the loan. The sole exception is for "points" paid for a debt incurred by the taxpayer to purchase his or her principal residence. In this regard, the IRS has ruled that points incurred to refinance a home must be amortized over the term of the loan.[40] However, a recent Appeals Court case allowed a taxpayer to deduct the amount of points paid on refinancing a home. The proceeds were used to pay off a 3-year, temporary loan that was made to allow the borrower time to secure permanent financing for the home.[41] The court stated that, since the temporary loan was merely an integrated step in securing permanent financing for the taxpayer's residence, the points were deductible currently.

> **Example 11.** K desires to obtain financing for the purchase of a new house costing $100,000. The bank agrees to make her a loan of 80% of the purchase price, or $80,000 (80% of $100,000) for thirty years at a cost of two points (two percentage "points" of the loan obtained). Thus, she must pay $1,600 (2% of $80,000) to obtain the loan. Assuming it is established business practice in her area to charge points in consideration of the loan, the $1,600 in points (prepaid interest) is deductible. However, if the house is not the principal residence of the taxpayer, then the prepaid interest must be deducted ratably over the 30-year loan period.

---

[38] Rev. Rul. 79-229, 1979-2 C.B. 210. See also, *Kenneth Van Raden*, 71 T.C. 1083 (1979), *aff'd* in 81-2 USTC ¶9547, 48 AFTR2d 81-5607, 650 F.2d 1046 (CA-9, 1981).

[39] § 461(g).

[40] Rev. Rul. 87-22, 1987-1 C.B.146.

[41] *James R. Huntsman*, 90-2 USTC ¶50,340, 66 AFTR2d 90-5020, 905 F.2d 1182 (CA-8,1990).

Accrual Basis Taxpayers.   An accrual basis taxpayer deducts expenses when they are incurred. For this purpose, an expense is considered incurred when the *all events test* is satisfied and *economic performance* has occurred.[42] Two requirements must be met under the all events test: (1) all events establishing the existence of a liability must have occurred (i.e., the liability is fixed); and (2) the amount of the liability can be determined with reasonable accuracy. Therefore, before the liability may be accrued and deducted, it must be fixed and determinable.

> **Example 12.**   In *Hughes Properties, Inc.*, an accrual basis corporation owned a gambling casino in Reno, Nevada that operated progressive slot machines that paid a large jackpot about every four months.[43] The increasing amount of the jackpot was maintained and shown by a meter. Under state gaming regulations, the jackpot amount could not be turned back until the amount had been paid to a winner. In addition, the corporation had to maintain a cash reserve sufficient to pay all the guaranteed amounts. At the end of each taxable year, the corporation accrued and deducted the liability for the jackpot as accrued at year-end. The IRS challenged the accrual, alleging that the all events test had not been met, and that the amount should be deducted only when paid. It argued that payment of the jackpot was not fixed but contingent, since it was possible that the winning combination may never be pulled. Moreover, the Service pointed out the potential for tax avoidance: the corporation was accruing deductions for payments that may be paid far in the future, and thus—given the time value of money— overstated the amount of the deduction. The Supreme Court rejected these arguments, stating that the probability of payment was not a remote and speculative possibility. The Court noted that not only was the liability fixed under state law, but it also was not in the interest of the taxpayer to set unreasonably high odds, since customers would refuse to play and gamble elsewhere.

The all events test often operates to deny deductions for certain estimated expenditures properly accruable for financial accounting purposes. For example, the estimated cost of product guarantees, warranties, and contingent liabilities normally may not be deducted—presumably because the liability for such items has not been fixed or no reasonable estimate of the amount can be made.[44] However, the courts have authorized deductions for estimates where the obligation was certain and there was a reasonable basis (e.g., industry experience) for determining the amount of the liability.

---

[42]   § 461(h).

[43]   *Hughes Properties, Inc.*, 86-1 USTC ¶9440, 58 AFTR2d 86-5015, 106 S. Ct. 2092 (USSC, 1986).

[44]   *Bell Electric Co.*, 45 T.C. 158 (1965).

The condition requiring *economic performance* was introduced in 1984 due to Congressional fear that the all events test did not prohibit so-called premature accruals. Prior to 1984, the courts—with increasing frequency—had permitted taxpayers to accrue and deduct the cost of estimated expenditures required to perform certain activities *prior* to the period when the activities were actually performed. For example, in one case, a strip-mining operator deducted the estimated cost of backfilling land which he had mined for coal.[45] The court allowed the deduction for the estimated expenses in the current year even though the backfilling was not started and completed until the following year. According to the court, the liability satisfied the all events test since the taxpayer was required by law to backfill the land and a reasonable estimate of the cost of the work could be made. A similar decision involved a taxpayer that was a self-insurer of its liabilities arising from claims under state and Federal workmen's compensation laws.[46] Under these laws, the taxpayer was obligated to pay a claimant's medical bills, disability payments, and death benefits. In this situation, the taxpayer was allowed to accrue and deduct the estimated expenses for its obligations even though actual payments would extend over many years. In Congress' view, allowing the deduction in these and similar cases prior to the time when the taxpayer actually performed the services, provided the goods, or paid the expenses, overstated the true cost of the expense, because the time value of money was ignored. Perhaps more importantly, Congress recognized that allowing deductions for accruals in this manner had become the foundation for many tax shelter arrangements. Accordingly, the economic performance test was designed to defer the taxpayer's deduction until the activities giving rise to the liability are performed.

The time at which economic performance is deemed to occur—and hence the period in which the deduction may be claimed—depends on the nature of the item producing the liability. A taxpayer's liabilities commonly arise in three ways, as summarized below.

1. *Liability of taxpayer to provide property and services.* When the taxpayer's liability results from an obligation to provide goods or services to a third party (e.g., perform repairs), economic performance occurs when the taxpayer provides the goods or services to the third party.

2. *Liability for property or services provided to the taxpayer.* When the taxpayer's liability arises from an obligation to pay for services, goods, or the use of property provided to (or to be provided to) the taxpayer (e.g., consulting, supplies, and rent), economic performance occurs when the taxpayer receives the services or goods or uses the property. Note that in this case, economic performance occurs when the taxpayer *receives* the consideration bargained for, while in the situation above it occurs when the taxpayer *provides* the consideration.

---

[45] *Paul Harrold v. Comm.*, 52-1 USTC ¶9107, 41 AFTR 442, 192 F.2d 1002 (CA-4, 1951).

[46] *Crescent Wharf & Warehouse Co. v. Comm.*, 75-2 USTC ¶9571, 36 AFTR2d 75-5246, 518 F.2d 772 (CA-5, 1975).

3. *Liability for payment arising under workmen's compensation laws or any tort.* If the liability arises from an obligation to pay another person under any worker's compensation law or due to the taxpayer's tort, economic performance occurs as the payments are made.

Example 13. In 1991 C, an accrual basis corporation, contracted with P, a partnership, to drill 50 gas wells over a five-year period for $500,000. Absent the economic performance test, C could accrue and deduct the $500,000 fee in 1991 because the obligation is fixed and determinable. However, because economic performance has not occurred (i.e., the services have not been received by C), no deduction is permitted in 1991. Rather, C may deduct the expense when the wells are drilled.

Example 14. Same facts as above. Although P is obligated to perform services for C over the five year period, P cannot prematurely accrue the cost of providing these services because economic performance has not occurred. Deduction is permitted only as the wells are drilled.

To prohibit the disruption of normal business and accounting practices, certain recurring expenses are exempted from the economic performance rules. The expense may be accrued and deducted if all of the following conditions are met.[47]

1. The all events test is satisfied.

2. Economic performance does in fact occur within a reasonable period after the close of the taxable year not to exceed eight and one-half months.

3. The item is recurring in nature and the taxpayer consistently treats such items as incurred in the taxable year.

4. The item is either immaterial, or accrual in the earlier year results in a better match against income than accruing the item when economic performance occurs.

Example 15. Z, who uses the accrual basis and reports using the calendar year, operates a small construction business. He has engaged a CPA firm to prepare monthly financial statements for the business for $300 a month. The financial statements for December are normally prepared by the end of January of the following year. Under the exception for recurring expenses, Z may accrue the charge for December even though the services are not performed until the next accounting period. In this case, economic performance occurs shortly after year-end and the item is recurring and probably immaterial.

---

[47] § 461(h)(3).

EMPLOYEE BUSINESS EXPENSES

The definition of *trade or business* also includes the performance of services as an employee. In other words, an employee is considered to be in the business of being an employee. As a result, the ordinary and necessary expenses incurred by an employee in connection with his or her employment are deductible under § 162 as business expenses. Examples of deductible expenses typically incurred by employees include union dues, dues to trade and professional societies, subscriptions to professional journals, small tools and supplies, medical exams required by the employer, and work clothes and uniforms as well as their maintenance (where required as a condition of employment and not suitable for everyday use).[48] Expenses such as travel, entertainment, and education may also be deducted as employee business expenses under certain conditions explained in Chapter 8. As explained later in this chapter, employee business expenses—other than those which are reimbursed—are considered miscellaneous itemized deductions and thus deductible only to the extent they exceed 2 percent of A.G.I.

DEDUCTIONS FOR LOSSES

The general rules concerning deduction of losses are contained in § 165. This provision permits a deduction for any loss sustained which is not compensated for by insurance. The deductions for losses of an individual taxpayer, however, are limited to

1. Losses incurred in a trade or business

2. Losses incurred in a transaction entered into for profit

3. Losses of property not connected with a trade or business if such losses arise by fire, storm, shipwreck, theft, or some other type of casualty

Note that personal losses—other than those attributable to a casualty—are not deductible. For example, the sale of a personal residence at a loss is not deductible.

Before a loss can be deducted, it must be evidenced by a closed and completed transaction. Mere decline in values or unrealized losses cannot be deducted. Normally, for the loss to qualify as a deduction, the property must be sold, abandoned, scrapped, or become completely worthless. The amount of deductible loss for all taxpayers cannot exceed the taxpayer's basis in the property. Special rules related to various types of losses are discussed in Chapter 10.

---

[48] Rev. Rul. 70-474, 1970 C.B. 35.

CLASSIFICATION OF EXPENSES

Once the deductibility of an item is established, the tax formula for individuals requires that the deduction be classified as either a deduction *for* adjusted gross income or a deduction *from* adjusted gross income (itemized deduction).[49] In short, the deduction process requires that two questions be asked. First, is the expense deductible? Second, is the deduction for or from adjusted gross income (A.G.I.)? Additional aspects of the first question are considered later in this chapter. At this point, however, it is appropriate to consider the problem of classification.

The classification process arose with the introduction of the standard deduction in 1944. The standard deduction was introduced to simplify the return form for the majority of individuals by eliminating the necessity of itemizing primarily personal deductions such as medical expenses and charitable contributions. In addition, the administrative burden of checking such deductions was eliminated. Although these objectives were satisfied by providing a blanket deduction in lieu of itemizing actual expenses, a new problem arose. The standard deduction created the need to classify deductions as either deductions that would be deductible in any event (deductions for A.G.I.), or deductions that would be deductible only if they exceeded the prescribed amount of the standard deduction (deductions from A.G.I.).

IMPORTANCE OF CLASSIFICATION

The classification problem is significant for several reasons. First, itemized deductions may be deducted only to the extent they exceed the standard deduction. For this reason, a taxpayer whose itemized deductions do not exceed the standard deduction would lose a deduction if a deduction for A.G.I. is improperly classified as a deduction from A.G.I. This would occur since deductions for A.G.I. are deductible without limitation.

A second reason for properly classifying deductions concerns the treatment of miscellaneous itemized deductions. As part of the tax overhaul in 1986, Congress limited the deduction of miscellaneous itemized deductions—defined below—to that amount which exceeds 2 percent of A.G.I. This new limitation is extremely important. Under prior law, taxpayers who itemized deductions could misclassify a deduction for A.G.I. as an itemized deduction with little or no effect, since the expense would be deductible either one place or the other. Under the current scheme, however, misclassification of a deduction for A.G.I. as a miscellaneous itemized deduction would subject the expense to the 2 percent floor, making it partially nondeductible.

---

[49] § 62.

A third reason for properly classifying deductions concerns A.G.I. itself. Limitations on deductions such as medical expenses and charitable contributions are expressed in terms of the taxpayer's A.G.I. For example, miscellaneous itemized deductions are deductible only to the extent they exceed 2 percent of A.G.I., medical expenses are deductible only to the extent they exceed 7.5 percent of A.G.I., and charitable contributions are deductible only to the extent of various limitations (50, 30, or 20 percent) based on A.G.I.

As discussed in Chapter 3, Congress has created two new limitations that are based on A.G.I. and begin in 1991. First, the amount of itemized deductions (other than for medical expenses, casualty and theft losses, and investment interest) must be reduced by 3 percent of a taxpayer's A.G.I. in excess of $100,000. In addition, the deduction for personal exemptions is phased-out as the taxpayer's A.G.I. exceeds a threshold amount (e.g., $150,000 for joint returns and $100,000 for a single taxpayer). Thus, the misclassification of a deduction for A.G.I. as an itemized deduction would result in a higher A.G.I. and could result in a lower deduction for itemized deductions and personal exemptions.

Adjusted gross income for Federal income tax purposes also serves as the tax base or the starting point for computing taxable income for many state income taxes. Several states do not allow the taxpayer to itemize deductions. Consequently, misclassification could result in an incorrect state tax liability.

Still another reason for properly classifying expenses concerns self-employment tax. Under the Social Security and MediCare programs, self-employed individuals are required to make an annual contribution based on their net earnings from self-employment. Net earnings from self-employment include gross income from the taxpayer's trade or business less allowable trade or business deductions attributable to the income. Failure to properly classify a deduction as a deduction for A.G.I. attributable to self-employment income results in a higher self-employment tax.

DEDUCTIONS FOR A.G.I.

The deductions for A.G.I. are specifically identified in Code § 62. It should be emphasized, however, that § 62 merely classifies expenses; it does *not* authorize any deductions. Deductions *for* A.G.I. are

1. Trade or business deductions except those expenses incurred in the business of being an employee (e.g., expenses of a sole proprietorship or self-employment normally reported on Schedule C of Form 1040)

2. Two categories of employee business deductions:

   a. expenses that are reimbursed by an employee's employer (and included in the employee's income); and

   b. expenses incurred by a qualified performing artist (see below)

3. Losses from sale or exchange of property

4. Deductions attributable to rents or royalties

5. Deductions for contributions to Individual Retirement Accounts or Keogh retirement plans

6. Alimony deductions

7. Deductions for penalties imposed for premature withdrawal of funds from a savings arrangement

8. Deduction for 25 percent of premiums for family medical care insurance paid by qualified self-employed persons

9. Deduction for 50 percent of self-employment tax paid by self-employed persons

10. Certain other deductions

All of the above are deductible for A.G.I., while all other deductions are from A.G.I. (i.e., itemized deductions).

ITEMIZED DEDUCTIONS

As seen above, only relatively few expenses are deductible for A.G.I. The predominant expenses in this category are the deductions incurred by taxpayers who are self-employed (i.e., those carrying on as a sole proprietor) and any reimbursed employee business expenses. All other expenses are deductible from A.G.I. as itemized deductions.

Itemized deductions fall into two basic categories: those that are *miscellaneous itemized deductions* and those that are not. The distinction is significant because miscellaneous itemized deductions are deductible only to the extent they exceed 2 percent of A.G.I. Miscellaneous itemized deductions are all itemized deductions *other than* the following:

1. Interest

2. Taxes

3. Casualty and theft losses

4. Medical expenses

5. Charitable contributions

6. Moving expenses

7. Gambling losses to the extent of gambling gains

8. Deduction where annuity payments cease before investment is recovered

9. Amortizable bond premium

10. Certain other deductions

The miscellaneous itemized deductions category is comprised primarily of *un-reimbursed* employee business expenses, investment expenses, and deductions related to taxes such as tax preparation fees. Examples of these (assuming they are not reimbursed by the employer) include:

1. Employee travel away from home (including meals and lodging)

2. Employee transportation expenses

3. Outside salesperson's expenses [except that "statutory employees" (e.g., full-time life insurance salespersons and traveling salespersons) are allowed to report their income and expenses on a separate Schedule C and avoid the 2 percent of A.G.I. limitation]

4. Employee entertainment expenses

5. Employee home office expenses

6. Union dues

7. Professional dues and memberships

8. Subscriptions to business journals

9. Job-seeking expenses (in the same business)

10. Education expenses

11. Investment expenses, including expenses for an investment newsletter, investment advice including management fees charged by a mutual fund, and rentals of safety deposit boxes

12. Tax preparation fees or other tax-related advice including that received from accountants or attorneys, tax seminars, and books about taxes

SELF-EMPLOYED VERSUS EMPLOYEE

Under the current scheme of deductions for and from A.G.I., an important—and perhaps inequitable—distinction is made based on whether an individual is an employee or self-employed. As seen above, employees generally deduct all unreimbursed business expenses as itemized deductions. In contrast, self-employed taxpayers (i.e., sole proprietors or partners) deduct business expenses for A.G.I. At first glance, the difference appears trivial, particularly for those taxpayers who itemize their deductions. Recall, however, that as part of the tax reform package of 1986 an employee's business expenses are treated as miscellaneous itemized deductions and thus deductible only to the extent that these and all other miscellaneous itemized deductions collectively exceed 2 percent of the taxpayer's A.G.I. Due to this distinction, deductibility often depends on the employment status of the taxpayer.

Example 16.   T is an accountant. During the year she earns $30,000 and pays dues of $100 to be a member of the local CPA society. These were her only items of income and expense. If T practices as a self-employed sole proprietor (e.g., she has a small firm or partnership), the dues are fully deductible for A.G.I. However, if T is an employee, none of the expense is deductible since it does not exceed the 2% floor of $600 (2% × $30,000). If T's employer had reimbursed her for the expense and included the reimbursement in her income, the expense would have been completely deductible, totally offsetting the amount that T must include in income. If T is employed, but at the same time does some accounting work on her own, part-time, the treatment is unclear.

The logic for the distinction based on employment status is fragile at best. According to the committee reports, Congress believed that it was generally appropriate to disallow deductions for employee business expenses because employers reimburse employees for those expenses that are most necessary for employment. In addition, Congress felt that the treatment would simplify the system by relieving taxpayers of the burden of recordkeeping and at the same time relieving the burden of the IRS of auditing such deductions.

Reimbursed Expenses.   As emphasized above, an employee's business expenses are generally deductible as itemized deductions unless a reimbursement is received. Where the employee is fully reimbursed and the reimbursement is included in income, the deduction is fully deductible for A.G.I. If only a portion of the expense is reimbursed and included in income, that portion is deductible for A.G.I. and the remainder is a miscellaneous itemized deduction.

Example 17.   Professor K is employed by State University in the finance department. The department has a policy of reimbursing up to $50 for his costs of subscribing to finance journals. During the year, K spent $75 on subscriptions and received a $50 reimbursement. K's A.G.I. is $40,000 (including the $50 reimbursement). He may deduct $50 for A.G.I. The remaining $25 is a miscellaneous itemized deduction which may or may not be deductible depending on whether this amount *plus* all other miscellaneous itemized deductions exceeds the 2% floor of $799 ($39,950 × 2%).

The discussion to this point assumes that all employee reimbursements are included by the employer in the employee's income. This is usually not the case, however. As discussed in Chapter 8, the employee may omit both the reimbursement and the expense from the return if, as is generally true, the reimbursement equals such expense and an adequate accounting is made to the employer. In fact, the IRS does not require the employer to file an information return under such circumstances.[50] As a result, an employee expense reimbursement is generally not included in income, and the related expense is not deductible either as a deduction for A.G.I. or as an itemized deduction.

---

[50]   Reg § 1.6041-3(i).

Whether a reimbursement is or is not included in the income of the employee, the effect on A.G.I. is the same. That is, there is no effect on A.G.I. The transaction is a "wash" economically for the employee and is, therefore, a "wash" on the employee's tax return. This concept is demonstrated below.

Example 18. Dr. R is employed by General Hospital. The hospital reimburses employees for the cost of subscribing to medical journals. During the year, Dr. R spent $100 on subscriptions and, after an adequate accounting, received a $100 reimbursement. If the reimbursement is included in Dr. R's income, she is allowed an offsetting deduction for A.G.I. If the reimbursement is not included in her income, she does not take any deduction with respect to the subscription cost.

	Reimbursement included in income	Reimbursement not included in income
Gross income	$ 100	$ −0−
Deduction for A.G.I.	(100)	(−0−)
A.G.I.	$ −0−	$ −0−

Expenses of Performing Artists. As noted above, most employee business expenses were relegated to second-class status in 1986 as they became subject to the 2 percent limitation. However, one group of employees, the struggling performing artists, escaped this restriction. These actors, actresses, musicians, dancers, and the like are technically employees but exhibit many attributes of the self-employed. They often work for several employers for little income yet incur relatively large unreimbursed expenses as they seek their fortunes. For these reasons, "qualified performing artists" are permitted to deduct their business expenses *for* A.G.I. To qualify, the individual must perform services in the performing arts as an employee for at least two employers during the taxable year, earning at least $200 from each. In addition, the individual's A.G.I. before business deductions cannot exceed $16,000. Lastly, the artist's business deductions must exceed 10 percent of his or her gross service income, otherwise they too are considered miscellaneous itemized deductions.

Example 19. Z is an actress. This year she worked in two Broadway productions for two different employers earning $7,000 from each for a total of $14,000. Her expenses, including the fee to her agent, were $2,000. She may deduct all of her expenses for A.G.I.

Self-Employed or Employee? The above discussion illustrates the importance of determining whether an individual is self-employed or is treated as an employee. However, whether an individual is self-employed or is an employee is often difficult to determine. An employee is a person who performs services for another individual subject to that individual's direction and control.[51] In the employer-employee relationship, the right to control extends not only to the result to be accomplished but also to the methods of accomplishment. Accordingly, an employee is subject to the will and control of the employer as to both what will be done and how it will be done. In the case of the self-employed person, the individual is subject to the control of another only as to the end result, and not as to the means of accomplishment. Generally, physicians, lawyers, dentists, veterinarians, contractors, and subcontractors are not employees. An insurance agent or salesperson may be an employee or self-employed, depending on the facts. The courts have developed numerous tests for differentiating between employees and self-employed persons. Each of the following situations would suggest that an employer-employee relationship exists.[52]

1. Complying with written or oral instructions (an independent contractor need not be trained or attend training sessions)

2. Regular written or oral reports on the work's status

3. Continuous relationship—more than sporadic services over a lengthy period

4. Lack of control over the place of work

5. No risk of profit or loss; no income fluctuations

6. Regular payment—hourly, weekly, etc. (an independent contractor might work on a job basis)

7. Specified number of hours required to work (an independent contractor is master of his or her own time)

8. Unable to delegate work—hiring assistants not permitted

9. Not independent—does not work for numerous firms or make services available to general public

---

[51] Reg. § 31.3401(c)-1(a).

[52] See Stewart and Kramer, "An Empirical Answer to the Problem of Determining 'Employee' or 'Independent Contractor' Status," *Taxes* (November, 1980) p. 747–757.

LIMITATIONS ON DEDUCTIONS

Some provisions of the Code specifically prohibit or limit the deduction of certain expenses and losses despite their apparent relationship to the taxpayer's business or profit-seeking activities. These provisions operate to disallow or limit the deduction for various expenses unless such expenses are specifically authorized by the Code. As a practical matter, these provisions have been enacted to prohibit abuses identified in specific areas. Several of the more fundamental limitations are considered in this chapter.

HOBBY EXPENSES AND LOSSES

As previously discussed, a taxpayer must establish that he or she pursues an activity with the objective of making a profit before the expense is deductible as a business or production of income expense. When the profit motive is absent, the deduction is governed by § 183 on activities not engaged in for profit (i.e., hobbies). Section 183 generally provides that hobby expenses of an individual taxpayer or S corporation are deductible only to the extent of the gross income from the hobby. Thus, the tax treatment of hobby expenses substantially differs from profit-seeking expenses if the expenses of the activity exceed the income resulting in a net loss. If the loss is treated as arising from a profit-motivated activity, then the taxpayer ordinarily may use it to reduce income from other sources.[53] Conversely, if the activity is considered a hobby, no loss is deductible. Note, however, that hobby expenses may be deducted to offset any hobby income.

Profit Motive. The problem of determining the existence of a profit motive usually arises in situations where the activity has elements of both a personal and profit seeking nature (e.g., auto racing, antique hunting, coin collecting, horse breeding, weekend farming). In some instances, these activities may represent a profitable business venture. Where losses are consistently reported, however, the business motivation is suspect. In these cases all the facts and circumstances must be examined to determine the presence of the profit motive. The courts have held that the taxpayer simply is required to pursue the activity with a bona fide intent of making a profit.[54] The taxpayer, however, need not show a profit. Moreover, the taxpayer's expectation of profit need not be considered reasonable.[55] The Regulations set out nine factors to be used in ascertaining the existence of a profit motive.[56] Some of the questions posed by these factors are

1. Was the activity carried on in a businesslike manner? Were books and records kept? Did the taxpayer change his or her methods or adopt new techniques with the intent to earn a profit?

---

[53] The limitations imposed on losses from passive activities should not be applicable in this situation since the taxpayer materially participates in the activity. See discussion in Chapter 12 and § 469.

[54] Reg. § 1.183-2(a).

[55] Ibid.

[56] Reg. § 1.183-2(b).

2. Did the taxpayer attempt to acquire knowledge about the business or consult experts?

3. Did the taxpayer or family members devote much time or effort to the activity? Did they leave another occupation to have more time for the activity?

4. Have there been years of income as well as years of loss? Did the losses occur only in the start-up years?

5. Does the taxpayer have only incidental income from other sources? Is the taxpayer's wealth insufficient to maintain him or her if future profits are not derived?

6. Does the taxpayer derive little personal or recreational pleasure from the activity?

An affirmative answer to several of these questions suggests a profit motive exists.

Presumptive Rule. The burden of proof in the courts is normally borne by the taxpayer. Section 183, however, shifts the burden of proof to the IRS in hobby cases where the taxpayer shows profits in any three of five consecutive years (two of seven years for activities related to horses).[57] The rule creates a presumption that the taxpayer has a profit motive unless the IRS can show otherwise. An election is available to the taxpayer to postpone IRS challenges until five (or seven) years have elapsed from the date the activity commenced. Making the election allows the taxpayer sufficient time to have three profitable years and thus shift the burden of proof to the IRS. This election must be filed within three years of the due date of the return for the taxable year in which the taxpayer first engages in the activity, but not later than 60 days after the taxpayer has received notice that the IRS proposes to disallow the deduction of expenses related to the hobby. The election automatically extends the statute of limitations for each of these years, thus enabling a later challenge by the IRS. It should be emphasized that this presumptive rule only shifts the burden of proof. Profits in three of the five (or two of seven) years do not absolve the taxpayer from attack.

> **Example 20.** T enjoys raising, breeding, and showing dogs. In the past, she occasionally sold a dog or puppy. In 1991, T decided to pursue these activities seriously. During the year, she incurred a loss of $4,000. T also had a loss of $2,000 in 1992. If T made no election for any of these years (i.e., within three years of the start of the activity), the IRS may assert that T's activities constitute a hobby. In this case, the burden of proof is on T to show a profit motive, since she has not shown a profit in at least

---

[57]   § 183(d).

three years. If T made an election, then the IRS is barred from assessing a deficiency until five years have elapsed. Five years need to elapse to determine whether T will have profits in three of the five years and, if so, shift the burden of proof to the IRS in any litigation which may occur. If an election is made, however, the period for assessing deficiencies for all years is extended until two years after the due date of the return for the last taxable year in the five-year period.[58] In T's case, an election would enable the IRS to assess a deficiency for 1991 and subsequent years up until April 15, 1998, assuming T is a calendar year taxpayer. If an election were not made, the statute of limitations would normally bar assessments three years after the return is due (e.g., assessments for 1991 would be barred after April 15, 1995).

Deduction Limitation. If the activity is considered a hobby, the related expenses are deductible to the extent of the activity's gross income as reduced by *otherwise allowable deductions*.[59] Otherwise allowable deductions are those expenses relating to the hobby that are deductible under other sections of the Code regardless of the activity in which they are incurred. For example, property taxes are deductible under § 164 without regard to whether the activity in which they are incurred is a hobby or a business. Similarly, interest on debt secured by the taxpayer's principal or secondary residence is deductible regardless of the character of the activity. Consequently, any expense otherwise allowable is deducted *first* in determining the gross income limitation. Any other expenses are deductible to the extent of any remaining gross income (i.e., other operating expenses are taken next, with any depreciation deductions taken last). Otherwise allowable deductions are fully deductible as itemized deductions, while other deductible expenses are considered miscellaneous itemized deductions and are deductible only to the extent they exceed 2 percent of A.G.I. (including the hobby income).

> **Example 21.** R, an actor, enjoys raising, breeding, and racing horses as a hobby. His A.G.I. excluding the hobby activities is $68,000. He has a small farm on which he raises the horses. During the current year, R won one race and received income of $2,000. He paid $2,300 in expenses as follows: $800 property taxes related to the farm and $1,500 feed for horses. Additionally, R calculated depreciation with respect to the farm

---

[58] § 183(d)(4).

[59] § 183(b). On classification of the deductions, see Rev. Rul. 75-14, 1975-1 C.B. 90 and Senate Finance Committee Report on H.R. 3838, S. Rep. No. 99-313 (5/29/86), p. 80, 99th Cong., 2nd. Sess.

assets at $6,500. Assuming the activity is considered a hobby and R itemizes deductions, he would compute his deductions as follows:

Gross income	$2,000	
Otherwise allowable deductions:		
Taxes	800	$ 800
Gross income limitation	$1,200	
Feed expense:		
$1,500 limited to remaining gross income .		1,200
Total		$2,000

Note that because depreciation is taken last, there is no deduction for this item.

R would include $2,000 in gross income, increasing his A.G.I. to $70,000. Of the $2,000 in deductible expenses, the property taxes of $800 are deductible in full as an itemized deduction. The remaining $1,200 is considered a miscellaneous itemized deduction. In this case, none of the $1,200 is deductible since this amount does not exceed the 2% floor of $1,400 (2% of $70,000). No deduction is allowed for the remaining feed expense of $300 ($1,500 − $1,200) due to the gross income limitation.

Example 22. Assume the same facts as in *Example 21* except that R's expense for property taxes is $2,400 instead of $800. In this case, because the entire $2,400 is deductible as an otherwise allowable deduction and exceeds the gross income from the hobby, none of the feed expense is deductible. Thus, R would include $2,000 in gross income and the $2,400 of property taxes would be fully deductible from A.G.I.

PERSONAL LIVING EXPENSES

Just as the Code specifically authorizes deductions for the costs of pursuing income—business and income-producing expenses—it also denies deductions for personal expenses. Section 262 prohibits the deduction of any personal, living, or family expenses. Only those personal expenditures expressly allowed by some other provision in the Code are deductible. Some of the personal expenditures permitted by other provisions are medical expenses, contributions, qualified residence interest, and taxes. Normally, these expenses are classified as itemized deductions. These deductions and their underlying rationale are discussed in Chapter 11.

The disallowance of personal expenditures by § 262 complements the general criteria allowing a deduction. Recall that the general rules of §§ 162 and 212 permit deductions for ordinary and necessary expenses *only where a profit motive exists*. As previously seen in the discussion of hobbies, however, determining whether an expense arose from a personal or profit motive can be difficult. Some of the items specifically disallowed by § 262 are:

1. Expenses of maintaining a household (e.g., rent, utilities)

2. Losses on sales of property held for personal purposes

3. Amounts paid as damages for breach of promise to marry, attorney's fees, and other costs of suits to recover such damages

4. Premiums paid for life insurance by the insured

5. Costs of insuring a personal residence

Legal expenses related to divorce actions and the division of income-producing properties are often a source of conflict. Prior to clarification by the Supreme Court, several decisions held that divorce expenses incurred primarily to protect the taxpayer's income-producing property or his or her business were deductible.[60] The Supreme Court, however, has ruled that deductibility depends on whether the expense arises in connection with the taxpayer's profit-seeking activities. That is, the *origin* of the expense determines deductibility.[61] Under this rule, if the spouse's claim arises from the marital relationship—a personal matter—then no deduction is allowed. Division of income-producing property would only be incidental to or a consequence of the marital relationship.

> **Example 23.** R pays legal fees to defend an action by his wife to prevent distributions of income from a trust to him. Because the wife's action arose from the marital relationship, the legal expenses are nondeductible personal expenditures.[62]

Legal expenses related to a divorce action may be deductible where the expense is for advice concerning the tax consequences of the divorce.[63] The portion of the legal expense allocable to counsel on the tax consequences of a property settlement, the right to claim children as dependents, and the creation of a trust for payment of alimony are deductible.

[60] F.C. Bowers v. Comm., 57-1 USTC ¶9605, 51 AFTR 207, 243 F.2d 904 (CA-6, 1957).

[61] Supra, Footnote 13. Also, compare Comm. v. Tellier, 66-1 USTC ¶9319, 17 AFTR2d 633, 383 U.S. 687 (USSC, 1966) with Boris Nodiak v. Comm., 66-1 USTC ¶9262, 17 AFTR2d 396, 356 F.2d 911 (CA-2, 1966).

[62] H.N. Shilling, Jr., 33 TCM 1097, T.C. Memo 1974-246.

[63] Rev. Rul. 72-545, 1972-2 C.B. 179.

CAPITAL EXPENDITURES

A capital expenditure is ordinarily defined as an expenditure providing benefits which extend beyond the close of the taxable year. It is a well-established rule in case law that a business expense, though ordinary and necessary, is not deductible in the year paid or incurred if it can be considered a capital expenditure.[64] Normally, however, a capital expenditure may be deducted ratably over the period for which it provides benefits. For example, the Code authorizes deductions for depreciation or cost recovery, amortization, and depletion where the asset has a determinable useful life.[65] Capital expenditures creating assets that do not have a determinable life, however, generally cannot be deducted. Assets such as land and goodwill are considered as having an indeterminable life and thus cannot be depreciated or amortized. These types of capital expenditures are recovered (i.e., deducted) only when there is a disposition of the asset through sale (e.g., cost offset against sales price), exchange, abandonment, or other disposition.

> **Example 24.**   B has decided to purchase a newspaper business in a small town for $100,000. It can be determined that $80,000 of the purchase price is allocable to the assets of the business and $20,000 is attributable to land and goodwill. B will be able to recover $80,000 of the cost through deductions for depreciation, amortization, etc. The $20,000 attributable to land and goodwill is not deductible because such assets have an indeterminable life. If B subsequently disposes of the land or the business, she may be able to recover the remaining $20,000.

As a general rule, assets with a useful life of one year or less need not be capitalized. For example, the taxpayer can write off short lived assets with small costs such as supplies (e.g., stationery, pens, pencils, calculators), books (e.g., the Internal Revenue Code), and small tools (e.g., screwdrivers, rakes, and shovels).

Capital Expenditures vs. Repairs.   The general rule of case law disallowing deductions for capital expenditures has been codified for expenditures relating to property. Code § 263 provides that deductions are not allowed for any expenditures for new buildings or for permanent improvements or betterments made to increase the value of property.[66] Additionally, expenditures substantially prolonging the property's useful life, adapting the property to a new or different use, or materially adding to the value of the property are not deductible.[67] Conversely, the cost of incidental repairs that do not materially increase the value of

---

[64] *Supra*, Footnote 18.

[65] §§ 167, 168, 169, 178, 184, 188, and 611 are examples.

[66] § 263(a).

[67] Reg. § 1.263(a)-1(b).

the property nor appreciably prolong its life, but maintain it in a normal operating state, may be deducted in the current year.[68] For example, costs of painting, inside and outside, and papering are usually considered repairs.[69] However, if the painting is done in conjunction with a general reconditioning or overhaul of the property, it is treated as a capital expenditure.[70]

> **Example 25.** L operates his own limousine business. Expenses for a tune-up such as the costs of spark-plugs, points, and labor would be deductible as routine repairs and maintenance since such costs do not significantly prolong the car's life. In contrast, if L had the transmission replaced at a cost of $600 allowing him to drive it for another few years, the expense must be capitalized.

Acquisition Costs. As a general rule, costs related to the acquisition of property must be capitalized. For example, freight paid to acquire new equipment or commissions paid to acquire land must be capitalized. For tax years beginning after 1987, Code § 164 requires that state and local general sales taxes related to the purchase of property be capitalized. Under prior law, such taxes could be capitalized at the election of the taxpayer. The costs of demolition or removal of an old building prior to using the land in another fashion must be capitalized as part of the cost of the land.[71] Costs of defending or perfecting the title to property, such as legal fees, are normally capitalized.[72] Similarly, legal fees incurred for the recovery of property must be capitalized unless the recovered property is investment property or money that must be included in income if received.[73]

Advertising. Under a strict interpretation of the capitalization rules, the cost of advertising could be considered a capital expenditure because such costs may benefit future periods. Despite the theoretical merits of this argument, this approach generally has been rejected due to the difficulty in determining the amount that each future period benefits. For this reason, advertising costs are ordinarily deductible in the year paid or incurred.

Elections to Capitalize or Deduct. Various provisions of the Code permit a taxpayer to treat capital expenditures as deductible expenses, as deferred expenses, or as capital expenditures.[74] For example, at the election of the taxpayer, expenses for research and experimentation may be deducted currently, treated as deferred expenses and amortized over at least 60 months, or capitalized and included in the basis of the resulting property.[75]

---

[68] Reg. § 1.162-4.

[69] *Louis Allen*, 2 BTA 1313 (1925).

[70] *Joseph M. Jones*, 57-1 USTC ¶9517, 50 AFTR 2040, 242 F.2d 616 (CA-5, 1957).

[71] § 280B.

[72] Reg. § 1.263(a)-2.

[73] Reg. § 1.212-1(k).

[74] §§ 174, 175, and 180 are examples.

[75] § 174.

BUSINESS INVESTIGATION EXPENSES
AND START-UP COSTS

Another group of expenses which arguably may be considered capital expenditures are those incurred when seeking and establishing a new business, such as costs of investigation and start-up. Business investigation expenses are those costs of seeking and reviewing prospective businesses prior to reaching a decision to acquire or enter any business. Such expenses include the costs of analysis of potential markets, products, labor supply, and transportation facilities. Start-up or pre-opening expenses are costs which are incurred after a decision to acquire a particular business and prior to its actual operations. Examples of these expenses are advertising, employee training, lining up distributors, suppliers, or potential customers, and the costs of professional services such as attorney and accounting fees.

Historically, the deductibility of expenses of business investigation and start-up has turned on whether the taxpayer was "carrying on" a business at the time the expenditures were incurred. Notwithstanding recent changes, the basic rule still remains: when the taxpayer is in the same or similar business as the one which he or she is starting or investigating, the costs of investigation and start-up are wholly deductible in the year paid or incurred.[76] The deduction is allowed regardless of whether the taxpayer undertakes the business.[77] However, this rule often forces taxpayers to litigate to determine whether a business exists at the time the expenses are incurred. Prior to recent changes, if the taxpayer could not establish existence of a business, the expenditures normally were treated as capital expenditures with indeterminable lives.[78] As a result, the taxpayer could only recover the expenditure if and when he or she disposed of or abandoned the business.

In 1980 Congress realized that the basic rule was not only a source of controversy but also discouraged formation of new businesses. For this reason, new provisions permitting amortization of these expenses under certain conditions were enacted.[79] Before examining these provisions, it should be emphasized that the traditional rule still continues to be valid. Thus, if a taxpayer can establish that the investigation and start-up costs are related to a similar existing business of the taxpayer, a deduction is allowed.

> **Example 26.** S owns and operates an ice cream shop on the north side of the city. A new shopping mall is opening on the south side of the city and the developers have approached her about locating a second ice cream shop in their mall. During 1991, S pays a consulting firm $1,000 for a

[76] The Colorado Springs National Bank v. U.S., 74-2 USTC ¶9809, 34 AFTR2d 74-6166, 505 F.2d 1185 (CA-10, 1974).

[77] York v. Comm., 58-2 USTC ¶9952, 2 AFTR2d 6178, 261 F.2d 421 (CA-4, 1958).

[78] Morton Frank, 20 T.C. 511 (1953).

[79] § 195(a).

survey of the potential market on the south side. Because S is in the ice cream business when the expense is incurred, the entire $1,000 is deductible regardless of whether she undertakes the new business.

Amortization Provision. Section 195 sets out the treatment for the startup and investigation expenses of taxpayers who are *not* considered in a similar business when the expenses are incurred *and* who actually enter the new business. Eligible taxpayers may elect to treat qualified expenditures as deferred expenses and amortize them over a period not less than 60 months. Amortization starts in the month the taxpayer begins or acquires the business. Expenses for research and development, interest payments, and taxes are not considered start-up expenditures.[80] Consequently, these costs are not subject to § 195 and may be deducted under normal rules.

> **Example 27.** J, a calendar year, cash basis taxpayer, recently graduated and received $10,000 from his wealthy uncle as a graduation gift. J paid an accountant $1,200 in September to review the financial situation of a small restaurant he desired to purchase. In December, J purchased the restaurant and began actively participating in its management. J may deduct $20 ($1/60$ of $1,200) for the current year.

> **Example 28.** S, a famous bodybuilder, has decided to build his first health spa. While the facility is being constructed, a temporary office is set up in a trailer next to the site. The office is nicely decorated and contains a small replica of the facility. S hired a staff who will manage the facility but at this time are calling prospective customers. Elaborate brochures have been printed. All of these costs, including the salaries paid to the staff, the printing of the brochures, and the costs of operating the trailer such as depreciation and utilities, are start-up costs and must be amortized over a period not less than 60 months.

As suggested above, the taxpayer must enter the business to qualify for amortization. Whether the individual is considered as having entered the business normally depends on the facts in each case.

If the taxpayer (who is not in a similar, existing business) does not enter into the new business, the investigation and start-up expenses generally are not deductible. The Tax Court, however, has held that a taxpayer may deduct costs as a loss suffered from a transaction entered into for profit if the activities are sufficient to be considered a "transaction"[81] The IRS has interpreted this rule to mean that those expenditures related to a *general search* for a particular business or investment are not deductible.[82] Expenses are considered general when they are related to whether to enter the transaction and which transaction to enter. Once

---

[80] § 195(c)(1).

[81] *Harris W. Seed*, 52 T.C. 880 (1969).

[82] Rev. Rul. 77-254, 1977-2 C.B. 63.

the taxpayer has focused on the acquisition of a *specific* business or investment, expenses related to an unsuccessful acquisition attempt are deductible as a loss on a transaction entered into for profit.

> **Example 29.** L, a retired army officer, is interested in going into the radio business. He places advertisements in the major trade journals soliciting information about businesses which may be acquired. Upon reviewing the responses to his ads, L selects two radio stations for possible acquisition. He hires an accountant to audit the books of each station and advise him on the feasibility of purchase. He travels to the cities where each station is located and discusses the possible acquisition with the owners. Finally, L decides to purchase station FMAM. To this end, he hires an attorney to draft the purchase agreement. Due to a price dispute, however, the acquisition attempt collapses. The expenses for advertising, auditing, and travel are not deductible since they are related to the taxpayer's general search. The legal expenses are deductible as a loss, however, since they occurred in the taxpayer's attempt to acquire a specific business.

Job-Seeking Expenses. The tax treatment of job-seeking expenses of an employee is similar to that for expenses for business investigation. If the taxpayer is seeking a job in the same business in which he or she is presently employed, the related expenses are deductible as miscellaneous itemized deductions subject to the 2 percent floor.[83] The deduction is allowed even if a new job is not obtained. No deduction or amortization is permitted, however, if the job sought is considered a new trade or business or the taxpayer's first job.

> **Example 30.** B, currently employed as a biology teacher, incurs travel expenses and employment agency fees to obtain a new job as a computer operator. The expenses are not deductible because they are not incurred in seeking a job in the profession in which she was currently engaged. Moreover, the expenses are not deductible even though B obtained the new job. However, the expenses would be deductible if she had obtained a new job in her present occupation.

PUBLIC POLICY RESTRICTIONS

Although an expense may be entirely appropriate and helpful, and may contribute to the taxpayer's profit-seeking activities, it is not considered necessary if the allowance of a deduction would frustrate sharply defined public policy. The courts established this longstanding rule on the theory that to allow a deduction for expenses such as fines and penalties would encourage violations by diluting the penalty.[84] Historically, however, the IRS and the courts were free to restrict deductions of any type of expense where, in their view, it appeared that the

---

[83] Rev. Rul. 75-120, 1975-1 C.B. 55, as clarified by Rev. Rul. 77-16, 1977-1 C.B. 37.

[84] *Hoover Motor Express Co., Inc. v. U.S.*, 58-1 USTC ¶9367, 1 AFTR2d 1157, 356 U.S. 38 (USSC, 1958).

expenses were contrary to public policy—even if the policy had not been clearly enunciated by some governmental body. As a result, taxpayers were often forced to go to court to determine if their expense violated public policy.

Recognizing the difficulties in applying the public policy doctrine, Congress enacted provisions in 1969 specifically designed to limit its use.[85] The new rules identified and disallowed certain types of expenditures that would be considered contrary to public policy. Under these provisions no deduction is allowed for fines, penalties, and other illegal payments.

Fines and Penalties. A deduction is not allowed for any fine or similar penalty paid to a government for the violation of any law.[86]

> **Example 31.** S is a salesman for an office supply company. While calling on customers this year, he received parking tickets of $100. None of the cost is deductible because the violations were against the law.

> **Example 32.** Upon audit of T's tax return, it was determined that he failed to report $10,000 of tip income from his job as a maitre d', resulting in additional tax of $3,000. T was also required to pay the negligence penalty for intentional disregard of the rules. The penalty—20% of the tax due—is not deductible.

Fines include those amounts paid in settlement of the taxpayer's actual or potential liability.[87] In addition, no deduction is allowed for two-thirds of treble damage payments made due to a violation of antitrust laws.[88] Thus, one-third of this antitrust "fine" is deductible.

Illegal Kickbacks, Bribes, and Other Payments. The Code also disallows the deduction for four categories of illegal payments:[89]

1. Kickbacks or bribes to U.S. government officials and employees if illegal

2. Payments to governmental officials or employees of *foreign* countries if such payments would be considered illegal under the U.S. Foreign Corrupt Practices Act

> **Example 33.** R travels all over the world, looking for unique items for his gift shop. Occasionally when going through customs in foreign countries, he is forced to "bribe" the customs official to do the necessary paperwork and get him through customs as quickly as possible. These so-called grease payments to employees of foreign countries are deductible unless they violate the Foreign Corrupt Practices Act.

---

[85] S. Rep. No. 91-552, 91st Cong., 1st Sess. 273-75 (1969); Note, however, that the Tax Court continues to utilize the doctrine despite Congress' attempt to restrict its use— see *R. Mazzei*, 61 T.C. 497 (1974).

[86] § 162(f).

[87] § 162(g).

[88] Reg. § 1.162-21(b).

[89] § 162(c).

3. Kickbacks, bribes, or other illegal payments to any other person if illegal under generally enforced U.S. or state laws that provide a criminal penalty or loss of license or privilege to engage in business

4. Kickbacks, rebates, and bribes, although legal, made by any provider of items or services under Medicare and Medicaid programs

Those kickbacks and bribes not specified above would still be deductible if they were ordinary and necessary. The payment, however, may not be necessary and thus disallowed if it controverts public policy.

Kickbacks generally include payments for referral of clients, patients, and customers. However, under certain circumstances, trade discounts or rebates may be considered kickbacks.

> **Example 34.** M, a life insurance salesman, paid rebates or discounts to purchasers of policies. Since such practice is normally illegal under state law, the rebate is not deductible.[90]

Expenses of Illegal Business. The expenses related to an illegal business are deductible.[91] Similar to the principle governing taxation of income from whatever source (including income illegally obtained), the tax law is not concerned with the lawfulness of the activity in which the deductions arise. No deduction is allowed, however, if the expense itself constitutes an illegal payment as discussed above. In addition, Code § 280E prohibits the deduction of any expenses related to the trafficking in controlled substances (i.e., drugs).

LOBBYING AND POLITICAL CONTRIBUTIONS

Although expenses for lobbying and political contributions may be closely related to the taxpayer's business, Congress has traditionally limited their deduction. These restrictions are usually supported on the grounds that it is not in the public's best interest for government to subsidize efforts to influence legislative matters.

Lobbying. Prior to 1962, no deduction was permitted for any type of lobbying expense. In 1962, however, Congress altered its position slightly with the addition of § 162(e), which carved out a narrow exception for certain lobbying expenses. This provision allows a deduction for the expenses of appearing before or providing information to governmental units on legislative matters of *direct interest* to the taxpayer's business. Similarly, a deduction is permitted for expenses of providing information to a trade organization of which the taxpayer is a member where the legislative matter is of direct interest to the taxpayer and

---

[90] *James Alex*, 70 T.C. 322 (1978).

[91] See *Max Cohen v. Comm.*, 49-2 USTC ¶9358, 176 F.2d 394 (CA-10, 1949) and

Neil Sullivan v. Comm., 58-1 USTC ¶9368, AFTR2d 1158, 356 U.S. 27 (USSC, 1958).

the organization. The portion of dues paid to such an organization attributable to the organization's allowable lobbying activities are also deductible.

The taxpayer must have a direct interest in the legislation before lobbying expenses may be deducted. Although the definitional boundaries of the term "direct" are vague, a taxpayer is considered as having satisfied the test if it is reasonable to expect that the legislative matter affects or will affect the taxpayer's business. However, a taxpayer does not have a direct interest in the nomination, appointment, or operation of any legislative body.[92]

The deduction for lobbying *does not* extend to expenses incurred to influence the general public on legislative matters, elections, or referendums.[93] Expenses related to the following types of lobbying are not deductible:

1. Advertising in magazines and newspapers concerning legislation of direct interest to the taxpayer.[94] However, expenses for "goodwill" advertising presenting views on economic, financial, social, or similar subjects of a general nature, or encouraging behavior such as contributing to the Red Cross, are deductible.[95]

2. Preparing and distributing to a corporation's shareholders pamphlets focusing on certain legislation affecting the corporation and urging the shareholders to contact their representatives in Congress.[96]

> **Example 35.** T owns a restaurant in Harris County, Texas. Legislation has been introduced to impose a sales tax on food and drink sold in Harris County to be used for funding a dome stadium. T places an ad in the local newspaper stating reasons why the legislation should not be passed. He drives to the state capitol and testifies on the proposed legislation before several committees. He pays dues to the Association of Restaurant Owners organization which estimates that 60% of its activities are devoted to lobbying for legislation related to restaurant owners. T may deduct the cost of travel and 60% of his dues since the legislation is of direct interest to him. He may not deduct the ad since it is intended to influence the general public.

Political Contributions. No deduction is permitted for any contributions, gifts, or any other amounts paid to a political party, action committee, or group or candidate related to a candidate's campaign.[97] This rule also applies to indirect payments, such as the payments for advertising in a convention program and admission to a dinner, hall or similar affair where any of the proceeds benefit a political party or candidate.[98]

---

[92] Reg. § 1.162-20(b).

[93] § 162(e)(2).

[94] Rev. Rul. 78-112, 1978-1 C.B. 42.

[95] Reg. § 1.162-20(a)(2).

[96] Rev. Rul. 74-407, 1974-2 C.B. 45, as amplified by Rev. Rul. 78-111, 1978-1 C.B. 41.

[97] § 162(e).

[98] § 276.

EXPENSES AND INTEREST RELATING
TO TAX-EXEMPT INCOME

Section 265 sets forth several rules generally disallowing deductions for expenses relating to tax-exempt income. The best known rule prohibits the deduction for any *interest* expense or nonbusiness (§ 212) expense related to tax-exempt *interest* income.[99] Without this rule, taxpayers in high tax brackets could borrow at a higher rate of interest than could be earned and still have a profit on the transaction.

> **Example 36.** D, in the 28% tax bracket, borrows funds at 15% and invests them in tax-exempt bonds yielding 12%. If the interest expense were deductible, the after-tax cost of borrowing would be 10.8% [(100% − 28% = 72%) × 15%]. Since the interest income is nontaxable, the after-tax yield on the bond remains 12%, or 1.2 percentage points higher than the effective cost of borrowing. Section 265, however, denies the deduction for the interest expense thus eliminating the feasibility of this arrangement. It should be noted, however, that business (§ 162) expenses (other than interest) related to tax-exempt interest income may be deductible.

If the income that is exempt is *not* interest, none of the related expenses are deductible.[100]

> **Example 37.** A company operating a baseball team paid premiums on a disability insurance policy providing that the company would receive proceeds under the policy if a player were injured. Because the proceeds would not be taxable, the premiums are not deductible even though the expenditure would apparently qualify as a business expense.[101]

As a practical matter, it would appear difficult to determine whether borrowed funds (and the interest expense) are related to carrying taxable or tax-exempt securities. For example, an individual holding tax-exempt bonds may take out a mortgage to buy a residence instead of selling the bonds to finance the purchase price. In such case, it could be inferred that the borrowed funds were used to finance the bond purchase. Generally, the IRS will allow the deduction in this and similar cases unless the facts indicate that the primary purpose of the borrowing is to carry the tax-exempt obligations.[102] The facts must establish a *sufficiently direct relationship* between the borrowing and the investment producing tax-exempt income before a deduction is denied.

[99]   § 265(2).

[100]   § 265(1).

[101]   Rev. Rul. 66-262, 1966-2 C. B. 105.

[102]   Rev. Proc. 72-18, 1972-1 C.B. 740 as clarified by Rev. Proc. 74-8, 1974-1 C.B. 419, and amplified by Rev. Rul. 80-55, 1980-2 C.B. 849.

Example 38. K owns common stock with a basis of $70,000 and tax-exempt bonds of $30,000. She borrows $100,000 to finance an investment in an oil and gas limited partnership. The IRS will disallow a deduction for a portion of the interest on the $100,000 debt because it is presumed that the $100,000 is incurred to finance all of K's portfolio including the tax-exempt securities.[103]

Example 39. R has a margin account with her broker. This account is devoted solely to the purchase of taxable investments and tax-exempt bonds. During the year, she buys several taxable and tax-exempt securities on margin. A portion of the interest expense on this margin account is disallowed because the borrowings are considered partially related to financing of the investment in tax-exempt securities.[104]

Business Life Insurance. Absent a special rule, premiums paid on insurance policies covering officers and employees of the business might be deductible as ordinary and necessary business expenses. However, to ensure that the taxpayer is not allowed to deduct expenses related to tax-exempt income (i.e., life insurance proceeds) a special provision exists. Under § 264, the taxpayer is not allowed any deduction for life insurance premiums paid on policies covering the life of any officer, employee, or any other person that may have a financial interest in the taxpayer's trade or business, if the taxpayer is the *beneficiary* of the policy. Thus premiums paid by a business on a key-person life insurance policy where the company is beneficiary are not deductible. In contrast, payments made by a business on group-term life insurance policies where the employees are beneficiaries are deductible.

RELATED TAXPAYER TRANSACTIONS

Without restrictions, related taxpayers (such as husbands and wives, shareholders and their corporations) could enter into arrangements creating deductions for expenses and losses, and not affect their economic position. For example, a husband and wife could create a deduction simply by having one spouse sell property to the other at a loss. In this case, the loss is artificial because the property remains within the family and their financial situation is unaffected. Although the form of ownership has been altered, there is no substance to the transaction. To guard against the potential abuses inherent in transactions between related taxpayers, Congress designed specific safeguards contained in § 267.

---

[103] *Ibid.*

[104] *B.P. McDonough v. Comm.*, 78-2 USTC ¶9490, 42 AFTR2d 78-5172, 577 F.2d 234 (CA-4, 1978).

Related Taxpayers. The transactions that are subject to restriction are only those between persons who are considered "related" as defined in the Code. Related taxpayers are[105]

1. Certain family members: Brothers and sisters (including half-blood), spouse, ancestors (i.e., parents and grandparents), and lineal descendants (i.e., children and grandchildren)

2. Taxpayer and his or her corporation: An individual and a corporation if the individual owns either directly or *indirectly* more than 50 percent of the corporation's stock[106]

3. Personal service corporation and an employee-owner: A corporation whose principal activity is the performance of personal services which are performed by the employee-owners (i.e., an employee who owns either directly or indirectly *any* stock of the corporation)

4. Certain other relationships involving corporations, partnerships, trusts, and individuals

In determining whether a taxpayer and a corporation are related, the taxpayer's direct and indirect ownership must be taken into account for the 50 percent test. A taxpayer's indirect stock ownership is any stock that is considered as owned, or "constructively" owned by the taxpayer but not actually owned. Section 267 provides a set of constructive ownership rules, also referred to as *attribution rules*, indicating the circumstances when the taxpayer is considered as owning the stock of another. Under the constructive ownership rules, a taxpayer is considered owning indirectly[107]

1. Stock owned directly or indirectly by his or her family as defined above

2. His or her proportionate share of any stock owned by a corporation, partnership, estate, or trust in which he or she has ownership (or of which he or she is a beneficiary in the case of an estate or trust)

3. Stock owned indirectly or directly by his or her partner in a partnership

In using these rules, the following limitations apply: (1) Stock attributed from one family member to another *cannot* be reattributed to members of his or her family, and (2) stock attributed from a partner to the taxpayer *cannot* be reattributed to a member of his or her family or to another partner.[108]

---

[105] § 267(b).

[106] A partner and a partnership in which the partner owns more than a 50 percent interest are treated in the same manner. See § 707(b).

[107] § 267(c).

[108] § 267(c)(5).

Example 40.   H and W are husband and wife. HB is H's brother. H, W and HB own 30, 45, and 25% of X Corporation, respectively. H is considered as owning 100% of X Corporation, 30% directly and 70% indirectly (25% through HB and 45% through W, both by application of attribution rule 1 above). W is considered as owning 75% of X Corporation, 45% directly and 30% indirectly through H by application of attribution rule 1 (note that HB's stock cannot be attributed to H and reattributed to W). HB is considered as owning 55% of X Corporation, 25% directly and 30% indirectly through H by application of attribution rule 1 and the reattribution limitation.

Losses.   The taxpayer is not allowed to deduct the loss from a sale or exchange of property directly or indirectly to a related taxpayer (as defined above).[109] However, any loss disallowed on the sale may be used to offset any gain on a subsequent sale of the property by a related taxpayer.[110]

Example 41.   A father owns land that he purchased as an investment for $20,000. He sells the land to his daughter for $15,000 producing a $5,000 loss. The $5,000 loss may not be deducted because the transaction is between related taxpayers. If the daughter subsequently sells the property for $22,000, she will then realize a $7,000 gain ($22,000 sales price − $15,000 basis). However, the gain may be reduced by the $5,000 loss previously disallowed, resulting in a recognized gain of $2,000 ($7,000 realized gain − $5,000 previously disallowed loss). If the daughter had sold the property for only $19,000, the realized gain of $4,000 ($19,000 − $15,000) would have been eliminated by the previous loss of $5,000. The $5,000 loss previously disallowed is utilized only to the extent of the $4,000 gain. The remaining portion of the disallowed loss ($1,000) cannot be used. Had the father originally sold the property for $19,000 to an outsider as his daughter subsequently did, the father would have recognized a $1,000 loss ($19,000 sales price − $20,000 basis). Note that the effect of the disallowance rule does *not* increase the basis of the property to the related taxpayer by the amount of loss disallowed.

Example 42.   S owns 100% of V Corporation. She sells stock with a basis of $100 to her good friend T for $75, creating a $25 loss for S. T, in turn, sells the stock to V Corporation for $75, thus recouping the amount he paid S with no gain or loss. The $25 loss suffered by S, however, is not deductible because the sale was made *indirectly* through T to her wholly owned corporation.

---

[109]   § 267(a)(1).   [110]   § 267(d).

Unpaid Expenses and Interest. Prior to enactment of § 267, another tax avoidance device used by related taxpayers involved the use of different accounting methods by each taxpayer. In the typical scheme, a taxpayer's corporation would adopt the accrual basis method of accounting while the taxpayer reported on a cash basis. The taxpayer could lend money, lease property, provide services, etc., to the corporation and charge the corporation for whatever was provided. As an accrual basis taxpayer, the corporation would accrue the expense and create a deduction. The cash basis individual, however, would report no income until the corporation's payment of the expense was actually received. As a result, the corporation could accrue large deductions without ever having to make a disbursement and, moreover, without the taxpayer recognizing any offsetting income. The Code now prohibits this practice between "related taxpayers" as defined above. Code § 267 provides that an accrual basis taxpayer can deduct an accrued expense payable to a related cash basis taxpayer *only* in the period in which the payment is included in the recipient's income.[111] This rule effectively places all accrual basis taxpayers on the cash method of accounting for purposes of deducting such expenses.

> **Example 43.** B, an individual, owns 100% of X Corporation which manufactures electric razors. B uses the cash method of accounting while the corporation uses the accrual basis. Both are calendar year taxpayers. On December 27, 1991 the corporation accrues a $10,000 bonus for B. However, due to insufficient cash flow, X Corporation was not able to pay the bonus until January 10, 1992. The corporation may not deduct the accrued bonus in 1991. Rather, it must deduct the bonus in 1992, the year in which B includes the payment in his income.

> **Example 44.** Assume the same facts as above, except that B owns only a 20% interest in X. In addition, X is a large law firm in which B is employed. The results are the same as above because B and X are still related parties: a personal service corporation and an employee-owner.

PAYMENT OF ANOTHER TAXPAYER'S OBLIGATION

As a general rule, a taxpayer is not permitted to deduct the payment of a deductible expense of another taxpayer. A deduction is allowed only for those expenditures satisfying the taxpayer's obligation or arising from such an obligation.

> **Example 45.** As part of Q's rental contract for his personal apartment, he pays 1% of his landlord's property taxes. No deduction is allowed because the property taxes are the obligation of the landlord.

---

[111] § 267(a)(2).

Example 46. P is majority stockholder of R Corporation. During the year, the corporation had financial difficulty and was unable to make an interest payment on an outstanding debt. To protect the goodwill of the corporation, P paid the interest. The payment is not deductible and P will be treated as having made a contribution to the capital of the corporation for interest paid.

An exception to the general rule is provided with respect to payment of medical expenses of a dependent. To qualify as a dependent for this purpose, the person needs only to meet the relationship, support, and citizen tests.[112] If the taxpayer pays the medical expenses of a person who qualifies as a dependent under the modified tests, the expenses are treated as if they were the taxpayer's expenses and are deductible subject to limitations applicable to the taxpayer.

SUBSTANTIATION

The Code requires that taxpayers maintain records sufficient to establish the amount of gross income, deductions, credits, or other matters required to be shown on the tax return.[113] As a practical matter, recordkeeping requirements depend on the nature of the item. With respect to most deductions, taxpayers may rely on the "*Cohan* rule."[114] In *Cohan*, George M. Cohan, the famous playwright, spent substantial sums for travel and entertainment. The Board of Tax Appeals (predecessor to the Tax Court) denied any deduction for the expenses because the taxpayer had no records supporting the items. On appeal, however, the Second Circuit Court of Appeals reversed this decision indicating that "absolute certainty in such matters is usually impossible and is not necessary." [115] Thus, the Appeals Court remanded the case to make some allowance for the expenditures. From this decision, the "*Cohan* rule" developed, providing that a reasonable estimation of the deduction is sufficient where the actual amount is not substantiated. In 1962, however, Congress eliminated the use of the *Cohan* rule for travel and entertainment expenses and established rigorous substantiation requirements for these types of deductions. Substantiation for other expenses, however, is still governed by the *Cohan* rule. Despite the existence of the *Cohan* rule, records should be kept documenting deductible expenditures since estimates of the expenditures may be substantially less than actually paid or incurred.

---

[112] § 213(a)(1).

[113] Reg. § 1.6001-1(a).

[114] *Cohan v. Comm.*, 2 USTC ¶489, 8 AFTR 10552, 39 F.2d 540 (CA-2, 1930).

[115] *Ibid.*

TAX PLANNING CONSIDERATIONS

MAXIMIZING DEDUCTIONS

Perhaps the most important step in minimizing the tax liability is maximizing deductions. Maximizing deductions obviously requires the taxpayer to identify and claim all the deductions to which he or she is entitled. Many taxpayers, however, often overlook deductions which they are allowed because they fail to grasp and apply the fundamental rules discussed in this chapter. To secure a deduction, the taxpayer needs only to show that the expense paid or incurred during the year is ordinary, necessary, and related to a profit-seeking activity. Notwithstanding the special rules of limitation that apply to certain deductions, most deductions are allowed because the *taxpayer* is able to recognize and establish the link between the expenditure and the profit-seeking activity. The taxpayer is in the best position to recognize that an expenditure relates to his or her trade or business, not the tax practitioner. Practitioners typically lack sufficient insight into the taxpayer's activities to identify potential deductions. Thus, it is up to the taxpayer to recognize and establish the relationship between an expenditure and the profit-seeking activity. Failure to do so results in the taxpayer paying a tax liability higher than what he or she is required to pay.

The taxpayer should not only maximize the absolute dollar amount of deductions, but also the value of the deduction. A deduction's value is equal to the product of the amount of the deduction and the taxpayer's marginal tax rate. Because the taxpayer's marginal rate fluctuates over time, the value of a deduction varies depending on the period in which the deduction is claimed. When feasible, deductions should normally be accelerated or deferred to years when the taxpayer is in a higher tax bracket. In timing deductions, however, the time value of money also must be considered. For example, in periods of inflation, the deferral of a deduction to a high bracket year may not always be advantageous, since a deduction in the future is not worth as much as one currently.

An individual taxpayer's timing of itemized deductions is particularly important in light of the standard deduction and the floor on miscellaneous itemized deductions. Many taxpayers lose deductions because their deductions do not exceed the standard deduction in any one year. These deductions need not be lost, however, if the taxpayer alternates the years in which he or she itemizes or uses the standard deduction. For example, in those years where the taxpayer itemizes, all tax deductible expenditures from the prior year should be deferred while expenditures of the following year should be accelerated. By so doing, the taxpayer bunches itemized deductions in the current year to exceed the standard deduction. In the following year, the taxpayer would use the standard deduction. Itemized deductions are considered in detail in Chapter 11.

Maximizing deductions also requires shifting of deductions to the taxpayer who would derive the greatest benefit. For example, if two sisters are co-obligees on a note, good tax planning dictates that the sister in the higher tax bracket pay the deductible interest expense. In this case, either sister may pay and claim a deduction.

TIMING OF DEDUCTIONS

In the previous section, the importance of maximizing the absolute amount of deductions was emphasized. However, because of the time value of money it is equally important to consider the timing of deductions.

> **Example 47.** R, who pays Federal, state, and local taxes equal to 50% of his income, makes a cash expenditure of $10,000. If the $10,000 is deductible immediately, R will realize a tax benefit of $5,000 ($10,000 × 50%). Moreover, because the tax savings were realized immediately, the present value of the benefit is not diminished. On the other hand, if R is not able to deduct the $10,000 for another five years, the benefit of the deduction is substantially reduced. Specifically, assuming the annual interest rate is 10%, the present value of the $5,000 tax savings decreases to $3,105 ($5,000 × [1 ÷ (1 + 0.10)^5]), a decrease of almost 38%.

As the above example illustrates, accelerating a deduction from the future to the present can substantially increase its value. Awareness of the provisions permitting acceleration of deductions allows taxpayers to arrange their affairs so as to reap the greatest rewards. For example, a taxpayer may choose an investment which the tax law allows him or her to deduct immediately rather than an investment which must be capitalized and deducted through depreciation over the asset's life.

EXPENSES RELATING TO TAX-EXEMPT INCOME

Although expenses related to tax-exempt income are not deductible, expenses related to tax-deferred income are deductible.[116] For example, income earned on contributions to Individual Retirement Accounts are not taxable until the earnings are distributed (usually at retirement). If the taxpayer borrows amounts to contribute to his or her Individual Retirement Account, interest paid on the borrowed amounts may be deductible because the income to which it relates is only tax-deferred, not tax-exempt.

---

[116] *Hawaiian Trust Co., Ltd. v. U.S.*, 61-1 USTC ¶9481, 7 AFTR2d 1553, 291 F.2d 761 (CA-9, 1961). See also, Letter Rul. 8527082 (April 2, 1985).

"POINTS" ON MORTGAGES

"Points" paid to secure a mortgage on a principal residence normally are deductible in the year paid or incurred. In many cases, however, the points are not paid out of independent funds of the taxpayer but are withheld from the mortgage proceeds. For example, where a lender is charging two points on a $50,000 loan, or $1,000 (2% of $50,000), the $1,000 is withheld by the lender as payment while the remaining $49,000 ($50,000 − $1,000) is advanced to the borrower. The Tax Court has ruled that in these situations, the taxpayer has not prepaid the interest (as represented by the points) and thus must amortize the points over the term of the loan.[117] To avoid this result and obtain a current deduction, the taxpayer should pay the points out of separate funds rather than having them withheld by the lender.

HOBBIES

Several studies suggest that the factor on which the hobby/business issue often turns is the manner in which the taxpayer carries on the activity.[118] For business treatment, it is imperative that the taxpayer have complete and detailed financial and nonfinancial records. Moreover, such records should be used in decision-making and in constructing a profit plan. The activity should resemble a business in every respect. For example, the taxpayer should maintain a separate checking account for the activity, advertise where appropriate, obtain written advice from experts and follow it, and acquire some expertise about the operation.

Although the taxpayer is not required to actually show profits, profits in *three* of *five* consecutive years create a substantial advantage for the taxpayer. Where the profit requirement is satisfied, it is presumed that the activity is not a hobby and the IRS has the burden of proving otherwise. For this reason, the cash basis taxpayer might take steps which could convert a loss year into a profitable year. For example, in some situations it may be possible to accelerate receipts and defer payment of expenses. However, the taxpayer should be cautioned that arranging transactions so nominal profits occur has been viewed negatively by the courts.

---

[117]   *Roger A. Schubel*, 77 T.C. 701 (1982).

[118]   See, for example, Burns and Groomer, "Effects of Section 183 on the Business/Hobby Controversy," *Taxes* (March, 1980) pp. 195–206.

PROBLEM MATERIALS

DISCUSSION QUESTIONS

7-1 *General Requirements for Deductions.* Explain the general requirements that must be satisfied before a taxpayer may claim a deduction for an expense or a loss.

7-2 *Deduction Defined.* Consider the following:

    a. It is often said that income can be meaningfully defined while deductions can be defined only procedurally. Explain.

    b. The courts are fond of referring to deductions as matters of "legislative grace." Explain.

    c. Although deductions may only be defined procedurally, construct a definition for a deduction similar to the "all inclusive" definition for income.

    d. Will satisfaction of the requirements of your definition ensure deductibility? Explain.

7-3 *Business versus Personal Expenditures.* Consider the following:

    a. If the taxpayer derives personal pleasure from an otherwise deductible expense, will the expense be denied? Explain.

    b. Name some of the purely personal expenses which are deductible, and indicate whether they are deductions *for* or *from* A.G.I.

7-4 *Business versus Investment Expenses.* Two Code sections govern the deductibility of ordinary and necessary expenses related to profit-motivated activities. Explain why two provisions exist and the distinction between them.

7-5 *An Employee's Business.* Is an employee considered as being in trade or business? Explain the significance of your answer.

7-6 *Year Allowable.* The year in which a deduction is allowed depends on whether the taxpayer is a cash basis or accrual basis taxpayer. Discuss.

7-7 *Classification of Expenses.* F is a self-employed registered nurse and works occasionally for a nursing home. G is a registered nurse employed by a nursing home. Their income, exemptions, credits, etc. are identical. Explain why a deductible expense, although paid in the same amount by both, may cause F and G to have differing tax liabilities.

7-8 *Above and Below-the-Line Deductions.* At a tax seminar, F was reminded to ensure that he properly classified his deductions as either above or below-the-line. After the seminar, F came home and scrutinized his Form 1040 to determine what the instructor meant and why it was important. Despite his careful examination of the form, F could not figure out what the instructor was talking about or why it was important. Help F out by explaining the meaning of this classification scheme.

7-9 *Performing Artists.* V hopes to become a movie star someday. Currently, she accepts bit parts in various movies waiting for her break. What special tax treatment may be available for V?

7-10 *Classification of Deductions.* J and K are both single, and each earns $30,000 of income and has $2,000 of deductible expenses for the current year. J's deductions are for A.G.I. while K's deductions are itemized deductions.

    a.   Given these facts, and assuming that the situation of J and K is identical in every other respect, will their tax liabilities differ? Explain.

    b.   Same as (a) except their deductions are $5,000.

7-11 *Constructive Distributions.* D owns all of the stock of DX Inc. which manufactured record jackets. Over the years, the corporation was very successful. This year, D placed his 16- and 14-year-old sons on the payroll, paying them each $10,000 annually. The boys worked in the assembly line a couple of hours each week. Explain D's strategy and the risks it involves.

7-12 *Disguised Distributions.* E owns all of the stock of EZ Inc., which operated a nursery. During the past several years, the company had operated at a deficit and E finally sold all of his stock to C. C drew a very low salary before he could turn things around. Now the business is highly profitable and C is paying himself handsomely. As C's tax advisor, what counsel if any should be given to C?

7-13 *Income and Expenses of Illegal Business.* B is a bookie in a state where gambling is illegal. During the year, he earned $70,000 accepting bets. His expenses included those for rent, phone, and utilities. In addition, he paid off a state legislator who was a customer and who obviously knew of his activity.

    a.   Discuss the tax treatment of B's income and expenses.

    b.   Same as (a) except B was a drug dealer.

7-14 *Permanent and Timing Differences.* Financial accounting and tax accounting often differ in the manner in which certain expenses are treated. Identify several expenditures which, because of their treatment, produce permanent or timing differences.

7-15 *Capital Expenditures.* Can a cash basis taxpayer successfully reduce taxable income by purchasing supplies near year-end and deducting their cost?

7-16 *Independent Contractor versus Employee.* Briefly discuss the difference between an independent contractor (self-employed person) and an employee and why the distinction is important.

7-17 *Hobby Expenses.* Discuss the factors used in determining whether an activity is a hobby and the tax consequences resulting from its being deemed a hobby.

7-18 *Public Policy Doctrine.* A taxpayer operates a restaurant and failed to remit the sales tax for August to the city as of the required date. As a result, he must pay an additional assessment of 0.25 percent of the amount due. Comment on the deductibility of this payment.

7-19 *Constructive Ownership Rules.* Explain the concept of constructive ownership and the reason for its existence.

7-20 *Expenses Relating to Tax-Exempt Income.* Discuss what types of expenses relating to tax-exempt income *may* be deductible.

7-21 *Substantiation.* Explain the *Cohan* rule.

PROBLEMS

7-22 *General Requirements for Deduction.* For each of the following expenses identify and discuss the general requirement(s) (ordinary, necessary, related to business, etc.) upon which deductibility depends.

    a. A police officer who is required to carry a gun at all times lives in New York. The most convenient and direct route to work is through New Jersey. The laws of New Jersey, however, prohibit the carrying of a gun in the car. As a result, he must take an indirect route to the police station to avoid New Jersey. The indirect route causes him to drive ten miles more than he would otherwise. The cost of the additional mileage is $500. (Note: commuting expense from one's home to the first job site is a nondeductible personal expense).

    b. The current president of a nationwide union spends $10,000 for costs related to reelection.

    c. The taxpayer operates a lumber business. He is extremely religious and consequently is deeply concerned over the business community's social and moral responsibility to society. For this reason, he hires a minister to give him and his employees moral and spiritual advice. The minister had no business background although he does offer solutions to business problems.

    d. The taxpayer operates a laundry in New York City. He was recently visited by two "insurance agents" who wished to sell him a special bomb policy (i.e., if the taxpayer paid the insurance "premiums," his business would not be bombed). The taxpayer paid the premiums of $500 each month.

7-23 *Accrual Basis Deductions.* In each of the following situations assume the taxpayer uses the accrual method of accounting and indicate the amount of the deduction allowed.

    a. R sells and services gas furnaces. As part of his sales package, he agrees to turn on and cut off the buyer's furnace for five years. He normally charges $35 for such service, which costs him about $20 in labor and materials. Based on 1991 sales, R sets up a reserve for the costs of the services to be performed, which he estimates will be $4,500 over the next five years.

    b. At the end of 1991, XYZ, a regular corporation, agreed to rent office space from ABC Leasing Corp. Pursuant to the contract, XYZ paid $10,000 on December 1, 1991, for rent for all of 1992.

    c. RST Villas, a condominium project in a Vermont ski resort, reached an agreement with MPP Pop-Ins providing that MPP would provide maid services for 1992 for $20,000. RST transferred its note payable for $20,000 at the end of 1992 to MPP on December 1, 1991.

7-24 *Accrual vs. Cash Method of Accounting.* D operates a hardware store. For 1991, D's first year of operation, D reported the following items of revenue and expense:

Cash receipts	$140,000
Purchase of goods on credit	90,000
Payments on payables	82,000

By year-end, D had unsold goods on hand with a value of $25,000.

a. Using the cash method of accounting, compute D's taxable income for the year.

b. Using the accrual method of accounting, compute D's taxable income for the year.

c. Which method of accounting is required for tax purposes? Why?

7-25 *Prepaid Interest.* In each of the following cases, indicate the amount of the deduction for the current year. In each case, assume the taxpayer is a calendar year, cash basis taxpayer.

a. On December 31, P, wishing to reduce his current year's tax liability, prepaid $3,000 of interest on his home mortgage for the first three months of the following taxable year.

b. On December 1 of this year, T obtained a $100,000 loan to purchase her residence. The loan was secured by the residence. She paid five points to obtain the loan bearing a 13 percent interest rate.

c. Same as (b) except the loan was used to purchase a duplex which she will rent to others. The loan was secured by the duplex.

7-26 *Prepaid Rent.* This year F, a cash basis taxpayer, secured a ten-year lease on a warehouse to be used in his business. Under the lease agreement he pays $12,000 on September 1 of each year for the following twelve months' rental.

a. Assuming F pays $12,000 on September 1 for the next 12 months' rental, how much, if any, may he deduct? How would your answer change if F were an accrual basis taxpayer?

b. In order to secure the lease, F also was required to pay an additional $12,000 as a security deposit. How much, if any, may he deduct?

7-27 *Prepaid Expenses.* D, a cash basis taxpayer, operates a successful travel agency. One of her more significant costs is a special computer form on which airline tickets are printed as well as stationery on which itineraries are printed. Typically, D buys about a three-month supply of these forms for $2,000. Knowing that she will be in a lower tax bracket next year, D would like to accelerate her deductions to the current year.

a. Assuming that D pays $12,000 on December 15 for forms which she expects to exhaust before the close of next year, how much can she deduct?

b. Same as above except D purchases the larger volume of forms because D's supplier began offering special discounts for purchases in excess of $3,000.

7-28 *Expenses Producing Future Benefits.* B took over as chief executive officer of Pentar Inc. which specialized in the manufacture of cameras. As part of his strategy to increase the corporation's share of the market, he ran a special advertising blitz just prior to Christmas that cost over $1,000,000. The marketing staff estimated that these expenditures very well could increase the company's share of the market by 10 percent over the next three years. Speculate on the treatment of the promotion expenses.

7-29 *Capital Expenditure or Repair.* This year, Dandy Development Corporation purchased an apartment complex with 100 units. At the time of purchase, it had a 40 percent vacancy rate. As part of a major renovation, Dandy replaced all of the carpeting and painted all of the vacant units. Discuss the treatment of the expenditures.

7-30 *Identifying Capital Expenditures.* K, a sole proprietor, made the following payments during the year. Indicate whether each is a capital expenditure.

a. Sales tax on the purchase of a new automobile
b. Mechanical pencil for K
c. Mops and buckets for maintenance of building
d. Freight paid on delivery of new machinery
e. Painting of K's office
f. Paving of dirt parking lot with concrete
g. Commissions to leasing agent to find new office space
h. Rewiring of building to accommodate new equipment

7-31 *Hobby Expenses—Effect on A.G.I.* C is a successful attorney and stock car racing enthusiast. This year she decided to quit watching the races and start participating. She purchased a car and entered several local races. During the year, she had the following receipts and disbursements related to the racing activities:

Race winnings	$3,000
Property taxes	2,800
Fuel, supplies, maintenance	1,000

Her A.G.I. exclusive of any items related to the racing activities is $100,000.

a. Indicate the tax consequences assuming the activity is not considered to be a hobby.
b. Assuming the activity is treated as a hobby, what are the tax consequences?
c. Assuming the activity is deemed a hobby and property taxes are $4,000, what are the tax consequences?
d. What is the critical factor in determining whether an activity is a hobby or a business?
e. What circumstances suggest the activity is a business rather than a hobby?

7-32 *Hobby—Presumptive Rule.* In 1989, R, a major league baseball player, purchased a small farm in North Carolina. He grows several crops and maintains a small herd of cattle on the farm. During 1989, his farming activities resulted in a $2,000 loss which he claimed on his 1989 tax return, filed April 15, 1990. In 1991 his 1989 return was audited, and the IRS proposed an adjustment disallowing the loss from the farming activity, asserting that the activity was merely a hobby.

a. Assuming R litigates, who has the burden of proof as to the character of the activity?

b. Can R shift the burden of proof at this point in time?

c. Assume R filed the appropriate election for 1989, and reported losses of $3,000 in 1990 and profits of $14,000 in 1991, $5,000 in 1992, and $6,000 in 1993. What effect do the reported profits have?

d. When does the statute of limitations bar assessment of deficiencies with respect to the 1989 tax return?

7-33 *Investigation Expenses.* H currently operates several optical shops in Portland. During the year he traveled to Seattle and San Francisco to discuss with several doctors the possibility of locating optical shops adjacent to their practices. He incurred travel costs to Seattle of $175 and to San Francisco of $200. The physicians in Seattle agreed to an arrangement and H incurred $500 in legal fees drawing up the agreement. The physicians in San Francisco, however, would not agree and H did not pursue the matter further.

In the following year, H decided to enter the ice cream business. He sent letters of inquiry to two major franchisers of ice cream stores and subsequently traveled to the headquarters of each. He paid $400 for travel to Phoenix for discussions with X Corporation and $500 for travel to Los Angeles for discussions with Y Corporation. He also paid an accountant $1,200 to evaluate the financial aspects of each franchise ($600 for each evaluation). H decided to acquire a franchise from Y Corporation. He paid an attorney $800 to review the franchising agreement.

a. Discuss the tax treatment of H's expenses associated with the attempt to expand his optical shop business.

b. Discuss the tax treatment of the expenses incurred in connection with the ice cream business assuming H acquires the Y franchise and begins business.

c. Same as (b). Discuss the tax treatment of these expenses assuming H is forced to abandon the transaction after being informed that there is no franchise available in his city.

7-34 *Investigation Expenses.*   P incurred significant expenses to investigate the possibility of opening a Dowell's Hamburgers franchise in Tokyo, Japan. Her expenditures included hiring a local firm to perform a feasibility study, travel, and accounting and legal expenses. Her 1991 expenditures total $25,000. With respect to this amount:

   a.   Assuming this was P's first attempt at opening a business of her own, how much may she deduct in 1991 if she decides *not* to acquire the franchise?

   b.   Assuming this was P's first attempt at opening a business of her own, how much may she deduct in 1991 if she decides to acquire the franchise?

   c.   Assuming P was already in the fast food business (she owns a Dowell's franchise in Toledo, Ohio), how much may she deduct in 1991 to acquire the franchise?

7-35 *Capital Expenditures.*   Consider the following:

   a.   A corporate taxpayer reimbursed employees for amounts they had loaned to the corporation's former president who was losing money at the racetrack. Comment on the deductibility of these payments as well as those expenditures discussed in *Example 7* of this chapter (relating to payments of debts previously discharged by bankruptcy) in light of the rules concerning capital expenditures.

   b.   The tax treatment of expenditures attributable to goodwill often gives rise to controversy. Explain.

   c.   How are the costs of expenditures such as goodwill and land recovered?

   d.   Distinguish between a capital expenditure and a repair.

7-36 *Classification of Deductions.*   M works as the captain of a boat. His income for the year is $20,000. During the year, he purchased a special uniform for $100. Indicate the amount of the deduction and whether it is for or from A.G.I. for the following situations:

   a.   M's boat is a 50-foot yacht and he operates his business as a sole proprietorship (i.e., he is self-employed).

   b.   M is an employee for Yachts of Fun Inc.

   c.   M is an employee for Yachts which reimbursed him $70 of the cost (included in his income on Form W-2).

7-37 *Computing Employee's Deductions.* T, who is single, is currently a supervisor in the tax department of a public accounting firm in Milwaukee. T's total income for the year consisted of compensation of $32,000 and dividend income of $2,100. During the year, she incurred the following expenses:

AICPA dues...	$ 200
State Society of Accounts dues....................	100
Subscriptions to tax journals......................	300
Tax return preparation.............................	200
Pen and pencil set................................	50
Cleaning of suits..................................	189
Safety deposit box (holds investment documents)...	30
Annual fee on brokerage account..................	20
Qualified residence interest........................	4,000

T's employer reimbursed her $50 for the AICPA dues (included in her income).

a. Compute T's taxable income.

b. Assuming T expects her expenses to be about the same for the next several years, what advice can you offer?

7-38 *Computing Employee's Deductions.* Z, a single taxpayer, is employed as a nurse at a local hospital. Z's records reflect the following items of revenue and expense for 1991:

Gross wages.....................................	$20,000
Expenses:	
Employee travel expenses, not reimbursed.......	1,100
Cost of commuting to and from work,	
reimbursed (included in gross wages)..........	520
Charitable contributions...........................	700
Interest and taxes on personal residence...........	3,900
Nurse's uniform, reimbursed (included in	
gross wages).................................	250

a. What is Z's A.G.I.?

b. What is Z's total of itemized deductions?

7-39 *Interest.* Mr. E operates a replacement window business as a sole proprietorship. He uses the cash method of accounting. On November 1, 1991 he secured a loan in order to purchase a new warehouse to be used in his business. Information regarding the loan and purchase of the warehouse is shown below. All of the costs indicated were paid during the year.

Term.......................................	20 years
Long origination fee.........................	$ 2,000
Points......................................	6,000
One year's interest paid in advance.........	20,000
Legal fees for recording mortgage lien.......	500

What amount may E deduct in 1991?

7-40 *Insurance.* Hawk Harris owns and operates the Waterfield Mudhens, a franchise in an indoor soccer league. Both Hawk and the corporation are cash basis, calendar year taxpayers. During 1991, the corporation purchased the following policies:

Policy Description	Cost	Date Paid
Two-year fire and theft effective 12/1/91	$2,400	12/15/91
One-year life insurance policy on Jose Greatfoot, star forward; the corporation is beneficiary; effective beginning 11/1/91	1,000	11/1/91
One-year group-term life insurance policy covering entire team and staff; effective 1/1/91	9,000	1/15/91
One-year policy for payments of overhead costs should the team strike and attendance fall; effective beginning 11/1/91	3,600	9/1/91

In addition to the policies purchased above, the corporation is unable to get insurance on certain business risks. Therefore the corporation has set up a reserve—a separate account—to which it contributes $5,000 on February 1 of each year.

How much may the corporation deduct for 1991?

7-41 *Life Insurance.* The Great Cookie Corporation is owned equally by F and G. Under the articles of incorporation, the corporation is required to purchase the stock of each shareholder upon his or her death to ensure that it does not pass to some undesirable third party. To finance the purchase, the corporation purchased a life insurance policy on both F and G, naming the corporation as beneficiary. The annual premium is $5,000. Can the corporation deduct the premiums?

7-42 *Business Life Insurance.* L, 56, has operated her sole proprietorship successfully since its inception three years ago. This year she has decided to expand. To this end, she borrowed $100,000 from the bank, which would be used for financing expansion of the business. The bank required L to take out a life insurance policy on her own life which would serve as security for the business loan. Are the premiums deductible?

7-43   *Public Policy—Fines, Lobbying, etc.*   M is engaged in the construction business in Tucson. Indicate whether the following expenses are deductible.

a.   The Occupational Safety and Health Act (OSHA) requires contractors to fence around certain construction sites. M determined that the fences would cost $1,000 and the fine for not fencing would be only $650. As a result, he did not construct the fences and paid a fine of $650.

b.   M often uses Mexican quarry tile on the floors of homes that he builds. To obtain the tiles, he drives his truck across the border to a small entrepreneur's house and purchases the materials. On the return trip he often pays a Mexican customs official to "expedite" his going through customs. Without the payment, the inspection process would often be tedious and consume several hours. This year he paid the customs officials $200.

c.   M paid $100 for an advertisement supporting the administration's economic policies which he felt would reduce interest rates and thus make homes more affordable. In addition, he paid $700 for travel to Washington, D.C. to testify before a Congressional Committee on the effects of high interest rates on the housing industry. While there, he paid $100 to a political action committee to attend a dinner, the proceeds from which went to Senator Q.

7-44   *Limitations on Business Deductions.*   This is an extension of Problem 7-22(d). In that problem, you are asked to determine if the following case contains expenditures that are ordinary, necessary and reasonable under the provisions of Code § 162. Assume the positive criteria of § 162 are met (i.e., the expenditures are ordinary, necessary, and reasonable). Are there any additional provisions in § 162 that will cause the expenditures to be disallowed?

7-45   *Related Taxpayers—Sale.*   E sold stock to her son for $8,000. She purchased the stock several years ago for $11,000.

a.   What amount of loss will E report on the sale?

b.   What amount of gain or loss will the son report if he sells the stock for $12,000 to an unrelated party?

c.   If the son sells for $10,000?

d.   If the son sells for $4,000?

7-46   *Related Taxpayers—Different Accounting Methods.*   G, a cash basis, calendar year taxpayer, owns 100 percent of XYZ Corporation. XYZ is a calendar year, accrual basis taxpayer engaged in the advertising business. G leases a building to the Corporation for $1,000 per month. In December, XYZ accrues the $1,000 rental due. Indicate the tax treatment to XYZ and G assuming the payment is

a.   Made on December 30 of the current year; or

b.   Made on April 1 of the following year.

c.   Would your answers above change if G owned 30 percent of XYZ?

7-47 *Constructive Ownership Rules.* How much of RST Corporation's stock is B considered as owning?

Owner	Shares Directly Owned
B...	20
C, B's brother..............................	30
D, B's partner..............................	40
E, B's 60 percent-owned corporation........	100
Other unrelated parties.....................	10

7-48 *Expenses of Another Taxpayer.* B is the only child of P and will inherit the family fortune. P, who is in the 28 percent tax bracket, is willing to give B and his wife $500 a month. Comment on the advisability of P paying the following directly in lieu of making a gift.

a. Medical expenses of B who makes $20,000 during the year; P (the father) provides 55 percent of B's support.

b. Interest and principal payments on B's home mortgage on which B and his wife are the sole obligees.

c. Same as (b) except that P is also an obligee on the note.

7-49 *Losses.* This year was simply a financial disaster for Z. Indicate the effects of the following transactions on Z's taxable income. Ignore any limitations that may exist.

a. After the stock market crash, Z sold her stock and realized a loss of $1,000.

b. Z sold her husband's truck for $3,000 (basis $2,000) and her own car for $5,000 (basis $9,000). Both vehicles were used for personal purposes.

c. Z's $500 camera was stolen.

d. The land next to Z's house was rezoned to light industrial, driving down the value of her home by $10,000.

7-50 *Planning Deductions.* X, 67, is a widow, her husband having died several years ago. Each year, X receives about $30,000 of interest and dividends. Because the mortgage on her home is virtually paid off, her only potential itemized deductions are her contributions to her church and real estate taxes. Her anticipated deductions are:

Year	Contribution
1992	$2,000
1993	3,000
1994	1,000

What tax advice can you offer X?

7-51 *Timing Deductions.* T currently figures that Federal, state, and local taxes consume about 30 percent of his income at the margin. Next year, however, due to a tax law change his taxes should increase to about 40 percent and remain at that level for at least five or six years. Assuming T buys a computer for $4,000 and he has the option of deducting all of the cost this year or deducting it ratably through depreciation over the next five years, what advice can you offer?

7-52 *Classification and Deductibility.*   In each of the following independent situations, indicate for the current taxable year the amounts deductible *for* A.G.I., *from* A.G.I., or *not deductible* at all. Unless otherwise stated, assume all taxpayers use the cash basis method of accounting and report using the calendar year.

  a.   M spent $1,000 on a life insurance policy covering her own life.

  b.   G is an author of novels. His wife attempted to have him declared insane and have him committed. Fearing the effect that his wife's charges may have on him and his book sales, G paid $11,000 in legal fees resulting in a successful defense.

  c.   Taxpayer, a plumber employed by XYZ Corporation, paid union dues of $100.

  d.   Q Corporation paid T, its president and majority shareholder, a salary of $100,000. Employees in comparable positions earn salaries of $70,000.

  e.   L operates a furniture business as a sole proprietorship. She rents a warehouse (on a month-to-month basis) used for storing items sold in her store. In late December, L paid $2,000 for rental of the warehouse for the month of January.

  f.   M is a self-employed security officer. He paid $100 for uniforms and $25 for having them cleaned.

  g.   N is a security officer employed by the owner of a large apartment complex. He pays $150 for uniforms. In addition, he paid $15 for having them cleaned. His employer reimbursed him $60 of the cost of the uniforms (included in his income on Form W-2).

  h.   K owns a duplex as an investment. During the year, she paid $75 for advertisements seeking tenants. She was unable to rent the duplex and thus no income was earned this year.

  i.   P paid $200 for subscriptions to technical journals to be used in his employment activities. Although P was fully reimbursed by his employer, his employer did not report the reimbursement in P's income.

7-53 *Classification and Deductibility.*   In each of the following independent situations, indicate for the current taxable year the amounts deductible *for* A.G.I., *from* A.G.I., or *not deductible* at all. Unless otherwise stated, assume all taxpayers use the cash basis method of accounting and report using the calendar year.

  a.   O paid the interest and taxes of $1,000 on his ex-wife's home mortgage. The divorce agreement provided that he could claim deductions for the payments.

  b.   P paid an attorney $1,500 in legal fees related to her divorce. Of these fees, $600 is for advice concerning the tax consequences of transferring some of P's stock to her husband as part of the property settlement.

  c.   R paid $10,000 for a small warehouse on an acre of land. He used the building for several months before tearing it down and erecting a hamburger stand.

  d.   H and his wife moved into the city and no longer needed their personal automobiles. They sold their Chevrolet for a $1,000 loss and their Buick for a $400 gain.

e.   C is employed as a legal secretary. This year he paid an employment agency $300 for finding him a new, higher-paying job as a legal secretary.

f.   X operates his own truck service. He paid $80 in fines for driving trucks which were overweight according to state law.

g.   T, an employee, paid $175 to an accountant for preparing her personal income tax returns.

7-54 *Classification and Deductibility.*   In each of the following independent situations, indicate for the current taxable year the amounts deductible *for* A.G.I., *from* A.G.I., or *not deductible* at all. Unless otherwise stated, assume all taxpayers use the cash basis method of accounting and report using the calendar year.

a.   B sold stock to his mother for a $700 loss. B's mother subsequently sold the stock for $400 less than she had paid to B.

b.   Same as (a) but assume the mother sold the stock for $500 more than she had paid to B.

c.   D operates three pizza restaurants as a sole proprietorship in Indianapolis. In July he paid $1,000 in air fares to travel to Chicago and Detroit to determine the feasibility of opening additional restaurants. Because of economic conditions, D decided not to open any additional restaurants.

d.   T owns and operates several gun stores as a sole proprietorship. In light of gun control legislation, he traveled to the state capitol at a cost of $80 to testify before a committee. In addition, he traveled around the state speaking at various Rotary and Kiwanis Club functions on the pending legislation at a cost of $475. T also placed an advertisement in the local newspaper concerning the merit of the legislation at a cost of $50. He pays dues to the National Rifle Association of $100.

e.   D is employed as a ship captain for a leisure cruise company. He paid $1,000 for rent on a warehouse where he stores smuggled narcotics which he sells illegally.

f.   M, a plumber and an accrual basis taxpayer, warrants his work. This year he estimates that expenses attributable to the warranty work are about 3 percent of sales or $3,000.

g.   G, a computer operator, pays $75 for a subscription to an investment newsletter devoted to investment opportunities in state and municipal bonds.

7-55 *Employee Business Expenses: Planning.*   J is employed as a salesman by Bigtime Business Forms Inc. He is considering the purchase of a new automobile that he would use primarily for business. Are there any tax factors that J might consider before purchasing the new car?

CUMULATIVE PROBLEMS

7-56 Tony Johnson (I.D. No. 456-23-7657), age 45, is single. He lives at 5220 Grand Avenue, Brooklyn, NY 46289. Tony is employed by RTI Corporation which operates a chain of restaurants in and around New York City. He has supervisory responsibilities over the managers of four restaurants. An examination of his records for 1991 revealed the following information.

1. During the year, Tony earned $33,000. His employer withheld $3,200 in Federal income taxes and the proper amount of F.I.C.A. taxes. Tony obtained his current job through an employment agency to which he paid a $150 fee. He previously was employed as a manager of another restaurant. Due to the new job, it was necessary to improve his wardrobe. Accordingly, Tony purchased several new suits at a cost of $600.

2. On the days that Tony works, he normally eats his meals at the restaurants for purposes of quality control. There is no charge for the meals which are worth $2,000.

3. He provides 60 percent of the support for his father, age 70, who lived with Tony all year and who has no income other than social security benefits of $7,000 during the year. Tony provided over one-half of the cost of maintaining the home.

4. Dividend income from General Motors Corporation stock which he owned was $350. Interest income on savings was $200.

5. Tony and other employees of the corporation park in a nearby parking garage. The parking garage bills RTI Corporation for the parking. Tony figures that his free parking is worth $1,000 annually.

6. Tony subscribes to several trade publications for restaurants at a cost of $70.

7. During the year, he paid $200 to a bank for a personal financial plan. Based on this plan, Tony made several investments, including a $2,000 contribution to an individual retirement account, and also rented a safety deposit box for $30 where he stores certain investment-related documents.

8. Tony purchased a new home, paying three points on a loan of $70,000. He also paid $6,000 of interest on his home mortgage during the year. In addition, he paid $650 of real property taxes on the home. He has receipts for sales taxes of $534.

9. While hurrying to deliver an important package for his employer, Tony received a $78 ticket for violating the speed limit. Because his employer had asked that he deliver the package as quickly as possible, Tony was reimbursed $78 for the ticket which he paid.

Compute Tony's taxable income for the year. If forms are used for the computations, complete Form 1040 and Schedule A. (Use 1990 tax forms if the 1991 forms are not available.)

7-57   Wendy White (I.D. No. 526-30-9001), age 29, is single. She lives at 1402 Pacific Beach Ave., San Diego, CA 92230. Wendy is employed by KXXR television station as the evening news anchor. An examination of her records for 1991 revealed the following information.

1.   Wendy earned $110,000 in salary. Her employer withheld $22,000 in Federal income taxes and the proper amount of F.I.C.A. taxes.
2.   Wendy also received $10,000 in self-employment income from personal appearances during the year. Her unreimbursed expenses related to this income were: transportation and lodging, $523; meals, $120; and office supplies, $58.
3.   Wendy reports the following additional deductions: home mortgage interest, $6,250; charitable contributions, $1,300; state and local income taxes, $3,100; and employment-related expenses, $920.

Compute Wendy's taxable income for the year and her tax due (including any self-employment tax). If forms are used for the computations, complete Form 1040, Schedule A, Schedule C, and Schedule SE.

Reminder: F.I.C.A. and self-employment taxes are composed of two elements: Old Age, Survivor, and Disability insurance (OASDI) and Medicare health insurance (MHI). In 1991, OASDI is paid at a rate of 6.2 percent (12.4 percent for self-employed individuals) on the first $53,400 of earned income; MHI is paid at a rate of 1.45 percent (2.9 percent for self-employed individuals) on the first $125,000 of earned income.

RESEARCH PROBLEMS

7-58   T and two associates are equal owners in LST Corporation. The three formed the corporation several years ago with the idea of capitalizing on the fitness movement. After a modest beginning and meager returns, the corporation did extremely well this year. As a result, the corporation plans on paying the three individuals' salaries which T believes the IRS may deem unreasonable. T wonders whether he can avoid the tax consequences associated with an unreasonable compensation determination by paying back whatever amount is ultimately deemed a dividend.

a.   What would be the effect on T's taxable income should he repay the portion of a salary deemed a dividend?
b.   Would there be any adverse effects of adopting a payback arrangement?

Partial list of research aids:

Vincent E. Oswald, 49 T.C. 645.
Rev. Rul. 69-115, 1969-1 C.B. 50.

7-59   C, a professor of film studies at State University, often meets with her doctoral students at her home. In her home, C has a room which she uses solely to conduct business related to the classes she teaches at the university. In the room she and her students often review the movies the students have made to satisfy requirements in their doctoral program. Can C deduct expenses related to her home office?

7-60   R moved to St. Louis in 1990 and purchased a home. After living there for a year, his family had grown and required a much larger home. On August 1, 1991 they purchased their dream house which cost far more than their first home. Shortly before he closed on the new residence, he put his first house on the market to sell. After two months had passed, however, he had received no offers. Fearing that he would be unable to pay the debt on both homes, R decided to rent his old home while trying to sell it. Surprisingly, he was able to rent the house immediately. However, in order to secure the party's agreement to rent monthly, he was required to perform a few repairs costing $500. Seven months after he had rented the home, R sold it. During the rental period, R paid the utilities and various other expenses. R has come to you for your advice on how these events in 1991 would affect his tax return.

7-61   In November of 1991, B, employed as a life insurance salesman for PQR Insurance Company in Newark, New Jersey, purchased a personal computer for use in his work. B has come to you for help in deciding how to handle this purchase on his 1991 tax return. He, of course, wants to expense the full price of the computer under Code § 179.

B relates the following salient information to you with respect to this purchase:

1.   B files a joint return with his wife, L. They have a combined A.G.I. of $65,000 before considering this item. They have sufficient qualified expenditures to itemize deductions on Schedule A but they have no miscellaneous itemized deductions.

2.   B paid $3,000 for the lap-top computer that will be used 100% for business use.

3.   B bought the computer to analyze client data. He figures this will help him increase his sales because he can analyze the results of various insurance options at the client's home or office (all personalized, of course).

4.   PQR does not provide B with company-owned computing equipment. In fact, they refused to pay for B's computer because the expense of providing computers for all of PQR's agents would be too great.

How should B treat this purchase on his 1991 tax return?

7-62 On January 28, 1991, S comes to you for tax preparation advice. She has always prepared her own return, but it has become somewhat complicated and she needs professional advice.

During your initial interview, you discover that S is a teacher at a high school in Chicago, Illinois. She is also the coach of the golf team. In 1988, S decided she wanted to be a professional golfer. So, when she was 32 years old, she began a part-time apprenticeship program with the Professional Golfers' Association of America (PGA) where she was an unpaid assistant to the pro at a local country club. Then, in 1989, she became a member of the PGA and began her professional career.

S has not made much money as a professional golfer. In fact, her expenses exceeded her income in both 1989 and 1990 ($4,000 loss in 1989; $3,500 loss in 1990). Believing she was actively engaged in a trade or business (she kept separate records for her golf activities, practiced about 10 hours each week, and worked with a pro whenever she could), S deducted her golf-related expenses on Schedule C and reported her losses from this activity on her prior returns.

The IRS has challenged S's 1989 and 1990 loss deductions, calling them non-deductible "hobby" losses. Is the IRS correct in this matter? Would she win if the matter is taken to court? What planning steps can S take to ensure that any future losses are deductible trade or business losses?

LEARNING OBJECTIVES

Upon completion of this chapter you will be able to:

■ Discuss the rules governing the deduction of several common expenses incurred by employees and self-employed persons

■ Recognize when educational expenses are deductible

■ Explain the rules concerning the deduction of moving expenses

■ Describe when expenses of maintaining a home office are deductible

■ Distinguish between deductible transportation expenses and nondeductible commuting costs

■ Understand the differences between deductible travel expenses and deductible transportation costs

■ Determine when entertainment expenses can be deducted

■ Describe the 80% limitation on the deduction of meals and entertainment

■ Explain the special record-keeping requirements for travel and entertainment expenses

■ Discuss the two types of reimbursement arrangements: accountable and nonaccountable plans

CHAPTER OUTLINE

Chapter **8**

EMPLOYEE BUSINESS EXPENSES

Over the years, many rules have been developed to govern the deductibility of specific business expenses. These rules normally augment the general requirements of § 162 (identified in Chapter 7) by establishing additional criteria that must be satisfied before a deduction may be claimed. As a practical matter, the primary purpose of many of these rules is to prohibit taxpayers from deducting what are in reality personal expenditures. For example, consider a taxpayer who uses a room at home to work or a taxpayer who takes a customer to lunch. In both cases, the expenses incurred very well may be genuine business expenses and deductible under the general criteria. On the other hand, such expenses could simply be *disguised* personal expenditures. As these examples suggest, some of the expenses that are likely to be manipulated are those often incurred by employees in connection with their employment duties. Such common employee expenses as those for travel and entertainment, education, moving, and home offices have long been the source of controversy. Of course, such costs are incurred by a self-employed person as well as by employees and raise similar problems. This chapter examines the special provisions applicable to these items.

EDUCATION EXPENSES

Historically, the tax law has taken the view that most education expenses are not deductible. For example, an art appreciation course for the taxpayer's cultural enrichment is purely personal in nature. Consequently, its cost is not deductible. Similarly, no deduction is granted for expenses of a college education on the theory that they are costs of preparing the taxpayer to enter a new business—not the costs of carrying on a business. Therefore, such general education expenses are nondeductible capital expenditures for which no amortization is allowed. Other education expenses, however, such as those incurred by an accountant to attend a seminar on a new tax law, are considered essential costs of pursuing income and are deductible like other ordinary and necessary business expenses. To ensure that deductions are permitted only for education expenses that serve current business objectives and are not personal or capital in nature, special tests must be met.

The Regulations allow a deduction if the education expenses satisfy *either* of the following conditions *and* are not considered personal or capital in nature, as discussed below.[1]

1. The education maintains or improves skills required by the taxpayer in his or her employment or other trade or business.

2. The education meets the express requirements imposed by either the individual's employer or applicable law, and the taxpayer must meet such requirements to retain his or her job, position, or rate of compensation.

Education expenses that meet either of these conditions are still not deductible if they are considered personal or capital expenditures under either of the following two tests:[2]

1. The education is necessary to meet the minimum educational requirements of the taxpayer's trade or business.

2. The education qualifies the taxpayer for a new trade or business.

REQUIREMENTS FOR DEDUCTION

Maintain Skills. For the expense to qualify under the first criterion, the education must be related to the taxpayer's present trade or business and maintain or improve the skills used in such business. The taxpayer must be able to establish the necessary connection between the studies pursued and the taxpayer's current employment. To illustrate, a personnel manager seeking an M.B.A. degree was allowed to deduct all of her education expenses when she ingeniously related each course taken to her job (e.g., a computer course enabled her to be more effective in acquiring information from and communicating with computer personnel).[3] In contrast, the Tax Court denied the deductions of a research chemist's cost of an M.B.A. indicating that courses such as advanced business finance, corporate strategy, and business law were only remotely related to the skills needed for his job.[4]

Refresher and continuing education courses ordinarily meet the skills maintenance test.

---

[1] Reg. § 1.162-5(a).

[2] Reg. §§ 1.162-5(b)(2) and (3).

[3] *Frank S. Blair, III,* 41 TCM 289, T.C. Memo 1980-488.

[4] *Ronald T. Smith,* 41 TCM 1186, T.C. Memo 1981-149.

Example 1. T repairs appliances. To maintain his proficiency, he often attends training schools. The costs of attending such schools are deductible because the education is necessary to maintain and improve the skills required in his job.

Required by Employer or Law. Once the minimum education requirements are met to obtain a job, additional education may be required by the employer or by law to retain the taxpayer's salary or position. Costs for such education are deductible as long as they do not qualify the taxpayer for a new trade or business.

Example 2. This year, R took a new job as a high school instructor in science. State law requires that teachers obtain their masters degree within five years of becoming employed. Expenses for college courses for this purpose are deductible even though they lead to a degree since such education is mandatory under state law.

New Trade or Business. If education prepares the taxpayer to enter a new trade or business, no deduction is permitted. In this regard, a mere change of duties usually is not considered a new business.[5] For example, a science teacher may deduct the cost of courses enabling him or her to teach art since the switch is a mere change in duties. The taxpayer becomes qualified for a new occupation if the education enables the taxpayer to perform substantially different tasks, regardless of whether the taxpayer actually uses the skills acquired.

Example 3. R was hired as a trust officer in a bank several years ago. His employer now requires that all trust officers must have a law degree. R may not deduct the cost of obtaining a law degree because the degree qualifies him for a new trade or business.[6] No deduction is allowed even though it is required by his employer and R does not actually engage in the practice of law.

Minimum Education. Expenses of education undertaken to gain entry into a business or to meet the minimum standards required in a business are not deductible. These standards are determined in light of the typical conditions imposed by the particular job. This rule operates to prohibit the deduction of such expenses as those for a review course for the bar or C.P.A. exam and fees to take such professional exams.[7] Similarly, education expenses related to a pay increase or promotion may not be deductible under this rule if the increase or promotion was the primary objective of the education.

---

[5] Reg. § 1.162-5(b)(3).   [7] Rev. Rul. 69-292, 1969-1 C.B. 84.

[6] Reg. § 1.162-5(b)(3)(ii), Ex. 1.

TRAVEL AS A FORM OF EDUCATION

Prior to 1986, travel in and of itself was considered a deductible form of education when it was related to a taxpayer's trade or business. For example, an instructor of Spanish could travel around Spain during the summer to learn more about the Spanish culture and improve her conversational Spanish. In such case, the travel cost would have been deductible since it was related to the taxpayer's trade or business. In 1986, Congress became concerned that many taxpayers were using this rule to deduct what were essentially the costs of a personal vacation. Moreover, Congress believed that any business purpose served by traveling for general education purposes was insignificant. To eliminate possible abuse, no deduction is allowed simply because the travel itself is educational.[8] Deductions are allowed for travel only when the education activity otherwise qualifies and the travel expense is necessary to pursue such activity. For example, a deduction for travel would be allowed where a Professor of French literature travels to France to take courses that are offered only at the Sorbonne.

TYPES AND CLASSIFICATION OF EDUCATION DEDUCTIONS

Education expenses normally deductible include costs of tuition, books, supplies, typing, transportation, and travel (including meals, lodging, and similar expenses). Typical education expenses are for college or vocational courses, continuing professional education programs, professional development courses, and similar courses or seminars.

The costs of transportation between the taxpayer's place of work and school are deductible. If the taxpayer goes home before going to school, however, the expense of going from home to school is deductible, but only to the extent that it does not exceed the costs of going directly from work. The cost of transportation from home to school on a nonworking day represents nondeductible commuting.

Unreimbursed educational expenditures of an employee are treated as miscellaneous itemized deductions subject to the 2 percent floor. In contrast, if an employer reimburses an employee for such expenses or the expenses are incurred by a self-employed person, the expenses are deductible *for* A.G.I.

---

[8]   § 274(m)(2).

MOVING EXPENSES

For many years, moving expenses were viewed as nondeductible personal expenses. In 1964, however, Congress revised its position, believing that moving expenses necessitated by the taxpayer's employment should be regarded as a deductible cost of earning income. To this end, Code § 217 was enacted, expressly authorizing a deduction for moving expenses. Section 217 allows self-employed individuals and employees to deduct moving expenses incurred in connection with beginning employment or changing job locations. To ensure that the deduction is allowed only for moves required by the taxpayer's employment, the taxpayer must satisfy *both* a distance test and a time test before the deduction may be claimed.

DISTANCE REQUIREMENT

Congress apparently believes that moves of short distances are motivated primarily by personal rather than business desires. For this reason, a somewhat misleading 35-mile distance test must be met if moving expenses are to be deductible. The taxpayer does not satisfy the requirement simply by moving 35 miles to a new residence in connection with a new job location. To satisfy this requirement, the distance between the old residence and the new job site must be at least 35 miles greater than the distance between the old residence and the old job site. Note that both distances are measured from the taxpayer's *former residence*. Thus, if the taxpayer's old commute was four miles, the new commute (absent a move) would have to be at least 39 miles (39 − 4 = 35) before the test is satisfied.

> **Example 4.** During the year, R was promoted to district sales manager, requiring her to move from Tucson to Phoenix. To determine whether the 35-mile test is met, the distances shown below must be compared.

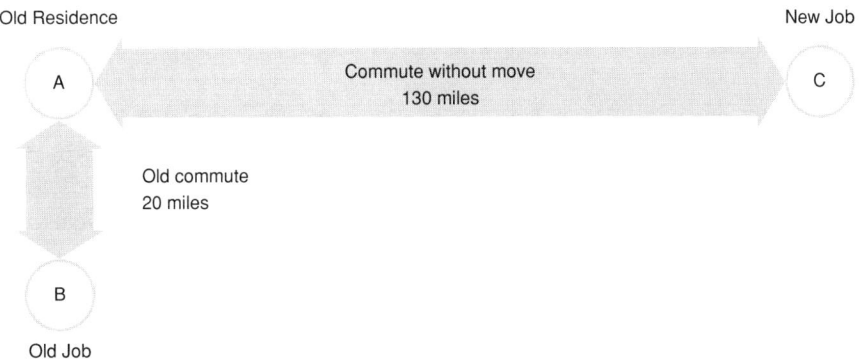

Since the distance between R's old residence and new job (AC = 130 miles) exceeds the distance between R's old residence and old job (AB = 20 miles) by more than 35 miles (130 − 20 = 110), the distance requirement is satisfied.

If the taxpayer has no old job site, the test is satisfied if the new job site is 35 miles from the old residence.[9] The test is designed to allow a deduction where the taxpayer's change in employment requires the taxpayer to move his or her residence.

TIME TEST

If taxpayers were not required to maintain employment for a minimum amount of time, they could move from place to place taking temporary jobs in each location to justify the deduction of what in effect are personal travel expenses. To prohibit this possibility, the second test generally requires the taxpayer to work for a *sustained period* of time upon arrival at the new job location. This condition is met if the taxpayer is a full-time employee in the area of the new job location for at least 39 weeks during the 12-month period immediately following arrival.[10] Alternatively, the taxpayer may satisfy the test by being an employee or self-employed on a full-time basis for at least 78 weeks during the 24-month period after arrival. Note, however, that—like the first test—39 of these 78 weeks must be during the first 12-month period. In either case, the taxpayer need not work for the same employer or for 39 weeks in a row. The time requirement is waived if the taxpayer dies, becomes disabled, is involuntarily dismissed, or is transferred by the new employer.[11]

> **Example 5.** N, an accountant, left his job in Boston to take a new job with a firm in Orlando. After working for the firm for eight months, he became dissatisfied and quit to open his own practice as a sole proprietor. Due to a lack of business, N closed the business after six months and moved to Denver. N may not deduct his expenses of moving to Orlando. Since he was employed for only 32 weeks (eight months) during the 12-month period after arrival in Orlando, he does not meet the test for employees. Similarly, he does not meet the alternative test since he was employed or self-employed only 56 weeks (14 months) of the 24-month period in Orlando after his arrival. Whether the costs of moving to Denver are deductible depends on whether either of the tests can be satisfied.

In many instances, taxpayers do not know by the end of the tax year whether they will be able to satisfy the time test. Accordingly, the law permits the taxpayer to claim the deduction on the assumption that the test will be satisfied. If the test is subsequently failed, the taxpayer must increase income in the year of failure by the amount of the previous deduction. In lieu of claiming the deduction prior to satisfaction of test, the taxpayer may wait until the test is satisfied and file an amended return for the year of the moving expense.

---

[9] § 217(c)(1).

[10] § 217(c)(2).

[11] § 217(d).

DEDUCTIBLE MOVING EXPENSES AND LIMITATIONS

For the purpose of determining the deduction, moving expenses are classified into two categories: direct and indirect. The distinction is important because direct moving expenses are deductible without limitation while indirect expenses are subject to several limitations, discussed below.

Direct Moving Expenses. Direct moving expenses include the following:[12]

1. Costs of moving household goods and personal belongings

2. Costs of traveling from the old location to the new location

Such costs include expenses for transporting or hauling the taxpayer's possessions, packing, insurance, costs of connecting and disconnecting utilities required by the moving of the taxpayer's appliances, and in-transit storage and insurance.[13] An expense is considered "in-transit" if it occurs within any consecutive 30-day period after the day the items are moved from the taxpayer's home. Losses sustained on dispositions of memberships in clubs, expenses of refitting rugs and drapes, mortgage prepayment penalties (although these are usually deductible as interest), and similar expenses are not deductible. Travel expenses include meals and lodging en route within one day after the former residence has been made unsuitable for occupancy (e.g., the furniture has been removed) and including the day of arrival. As discussed later in this chapter, in computing the deduction for meal costs, only 80 percent of the cost is allowed *regardless* of whether the expenses are reimbursed by the taxpayer's employer. Normally, when the employee is reimbursed for meal expenses, the 80 percent limitation applies to the employer and not the employee. In the case of moving expense meals, however, the limitation always applies to the employee even if he or she is reimbursed for such costs.

In computing transportation costs, the taxpayer may use actual expenses (i.e., the costs for oil, gasoline, tolls, and parking—but not for general repairs or maintenance) or an optional allowance of 9 cents per mile. Travel expenses are permitted only for the taxpayer and the taxpayer's household, including pets but excluding servants.

Indirect Moving Expenses. Indirect moving expenses are classified into three types:

1. *Pre-move house-hunting trips.* After obtaining employment, expenses of traveling to and from the old residence to the new job location to search for a new residence are deductible subject to certain dollar limitations discussed below.[14] House-hunting need not be successful nor is there any limit on the number of trips.

[12] §§ 217(b)(1)(A) and (B).

[13] Reg. § 1.217-2(b)(3).

[14] § 217(b)(1)(C); Reg. § 1.217-2(b)(5).

2. *Temporary living expenses.* Lodging and 80 percent of any meal costs incurred while occupying temporary quarters at the *new* job location for *any* consecutive 30-day period after the taxpayer has obtained a job may be deducted.[15] These expenses do not include the cost of entertainment, laundry, or other personal expenses. Dollar limitations on the deduction are explained below.

3. *Qualified residence, sale, purchase, or lease expenses.* Allowable expenses include[16] (a) costs related to selling the old home, such as the realtor's commission, attorney's fees, and points; (b) costs related to purchasing a new home, including legal and appraisal fees, title costs, and points not representing interest; (c) costs related to settling an unexpired lease on the taxpayer's old residence, including the cost of subleasing; and (d) costs related to acquiring a new lease, excluding security deposits.

The total amount of indirect expenses that may be deducted is limited to $3,000.[17] In addition, nested within the overall $3,000 limit is a separate limit on pre-move house-hunting expenses and temporary living expenses. These expenses when combined cannot exceed $1,500.[18]

The taxpayer may elect to treat the costs related to buying or selling a home either as moving expenses, or in the case of buying expenses, as additions to the new home's basis, or in the case of selling expenses, as reductions in the amount realized on the sale of the home.[19] Typically, taxpayers should treat selling expenses as moving expenses, because the gain on the sale of a personal residence normally is not recognized (see Chapter 15 for a discussion of deferring gain on the sale of a personal residence).

If an employee is reimbursed for moving expenses by his or her employer, the reimbursement must be reported by the employee as gross income from services.[20] The moving expense deduction must be taken according to the rules above—*without* netting the expenses against the reimbursement.

---

[15]   § 217(b)(1)(D); Reg. § 1.217-2(b)(6).   [18]   § 217(b)(4).

[16]   § 217(b)(1)(E); Reg. § 1.217-2(b)(7).   [19]   § 217(e).

[17]   § 217(b)(3).   [20]   § 82.

Example 6. H incurs the following deductible moving expenses:

Moving van	$5,000
Travel to new location	500*
Pre-move house-hunting	900*
Temporary living	800*
Real estate commission on sale of old residence	4,000

*After reduction for 20% of meal costs.

H's moving expense deduction is computed as follows:

Direct expenses:		
Moving van		$5,000
Travel		500
Indirect expenses:		
Pre-move house-hunting	$ 900	
Temporary living	800	
	$1,700	
Limited to		1,500
Real estate fee	$4,000	
Remaining indirect limit:		
$3,000 − $1,500	1,500	1,500
Remaining real estate fee not deductible	$2,500	
Total moving expense deduction		$8,500

H may deduct $8,500. In addition, she may treat the remaining $2,500 real estate fee (disallowed as a deductible moving expense) as a reduction in the amount realized on the sale of her old home. Note that her expenses for pre-move house-hunting and temporary living exceeding the limitation, $200 ($1,700 − $1,500), are not deductible and provide no tax benefit.

CLASSIFYING AND REPORTING THE MOVING EXPENSE DEDUCTION

Moving expenses of an employee or a self-employed person are deductible as itemized deductions. Moving expenses are *not* considered miscellaneous itemized deductions, and therefore are *not* subject to the 2 percent floor. All moving expenses are reported on Form 3903.

Reimbursements. Any reimbursements received for moving expenses must be included in gross income as compensation. Such reimbursements and other amounts paid on the employee's behalf normally are included in the employee's total income reported on Form W-2.

Potential Inequity.   Before leaving moving expenses, it should be emphasized that their current tax treatment may create hardships for certain taxpayers. For example, taxpayers that do not itemize their deductions still must include the reimbursement in their income *yet* receive no corresponding deduction. As a result, these taxpayers pay taxes on income that is somewhat illusory. Also note that employers often reimburse moving expenses that either exceed the deductible thresholds for indirect expenses (that have not been increased since 1977) or simply are not deductible. Taxable income would result in these cases as well, even though the taxpayer is not better off.

HOME OFFICE EXPENSES

It is currently estimated that over 24 million Americans—24 percent of the labor force—work at home either full or part time. However, simply working at home does not automatically enable a taxpayer to write off the costs of owning or renting. Very narrow standards must be met before a deduction is permitted.

Prior to 1976, expenses relating to use of a portion of the taxpayer's home for business purposes were deductible without limitation when they were merely appropriate and helpful in the taxpayer's business. In 1976, however, Congress felt that the appropriate and helpful test was insufficient to prevent the deduction of what were really personal expenses. For example, under the helpful test, a university professor who was provided an office by his employer could convert personal living expenses into deductions by using a den or some other room in his residence for grading papers. In such a situation, it was unlikely that any additional expense was incurred due to the business use. To prevent the deduction of disguised personal expenses, Congress enacted § 280A, severely limiting the deduction of expenses related to the home. Section 280A generally disallows deduction of any expenses related to the taxpayer's home except those otherwise allowable, such as qualified residence interest and taxes, and those for certain business and rental use (the exception for rental use is discussed in Chapter 12).

REQUIREMENTS FOR DEDUCTIBILITY

Under the business use exception, a deduction is allowed for a home office if a portion of the home is "exclusively" used on a "regular" basis for any of three types of business use:[21]

1.   As the principal place of business for *any* business of the taxpayer

2.   As a place of business used regularly by patients, clients or customers in meeting or dealing with the taxpayer in the normal course of his or her trade or business

3.   In connection with the taxpayer's trade or business when the office is located in a separate structure

---

[21]   § 280A(c).

If the taxpayer is an employee, the deduction is allowed only if the use is for the convenience of the employer. To meet this condition, the home office must be more than appropriate and helpful. The Tax Court has suggested that satisfaction of this test requires the taxpayer to show that he or she was unable to do the work performed at home at the employer's office.[22] For example, the Second Circuit has held in *Weissman* that this standard is met if the employer does not provide the employee with space to properly perform his or her employment duties.[23] In this case, a college professor who shared an office and did extensive research at home satisfied the test because in the Court's view the home office was necessitated by lack of suitable working space on campus.

The home office must be exclusively used for business. This condition does not require physical separation of the home office from the remainder of the home. Rather, the home office activities must be confined to a particular space within a room.[24] The exclusive use test prohibits personal activities in the home office; and the office must be used regularly in contrast to occasionally or incidentally.[25]

Principal Place of Any Business. A taxpayer satisfies the first business use test if the home office is the principal place of business for any business of the taxpayer. Most taxpayers, as employees, fail this test since their only business is that of being an employee and the principal location of that business is at the employer's office. This rule is not foolproof, however. In one decision, the court held that the principal place of business of a taxpayer employed as a concert musician was his home practice room rather than where he gave performances.[26] In contrast, employees who have a *second* business (e.g., selling cosmetics or vitamins) or self-employed persons who operate these activities out of their home normally satisfy the first business use test as long as they can show that the home is in fact the principal place of business.

Whether the home is the principal place of business has created much controversy over the years. However, the Tax Court recently revised its view in this regard. Under the court's new three-prong test, a home office is deemed to be the principal place of business if (1) it is essential to the taxpayer's business; (2) the taxpayer spends substantial time there; and (3) there is no other location available to perform the office function of the business.[27]

[22] *Robert Chauls,* 41 TCM 234, T.C. Memo 1980-471.

[23] *David J. Weissman v. Comm.,* 85-1 USTC ¶9106, 55 AFTR2d 85-539, 751 F.2d (CA-2, 1984).

[24] *George Weightman,* 42 TCM 104, T.C. Memo 1981-301.

[25] § 280A(c)(1).

[26] *Drucker v. Comm.,* 83-2 USTC ¶9550, AFTR2d 83-5804 (CA-2, 1983).

[27] *Nader E. Soliman,* 94 T.C.__, No. 3 (1990).

Example 7.   One of the first decisions to consider the principal-place-of-business issue was a 1980 case involving Joan Baie, who operated a hot dog stand several blocks from her home. In this case, all of the sandwiches sold at the stand were prepared by Baie in her kitchen. In addition, she used another room exclusively to do the paperwork of the business. No deduction was permitted by the Tax Court for expenses allocable to her kitchen because it was not *exclusively* used for business. Moreover, the Court did not allow any deduction for expenses allocable to the kitchen or the room in which the paperwork was done because it believed the principal place of business was the hot dog stand. Unfortunately, it appears that Baie's timing was bad. Under the Tax Court's recently enunciated view, she might have obtained a deduction for the expenses related to the room in which the paperwork was done if she could demonstrate that the room was essential to her business, she spent substantial time there, and there was no place in the hot dog stand to perform the necessary work.[28]

No deduction is permitted for home office expenses if the activities to which they relate do not constitute a business.[29]

Example 8.   T, an engineer, regularly uses a room in his home exclusively for evaluating his investments. No deduction is permitted since the activity does not constitute a business.

Meeting Place.   The second exception for business use is less restrictive than the first. Under this exception, the home office qualifies if clients regularly meet with the taxpayer there. Interestingly, in *John W. Green,* the taxpayer ingeniously argued that this exception should be satisfied where he regularly received phone calls in his home office. Although a majority of the Tax Court agreed with the taxpayer, the decision was reversed on appeal. The Appellate Court believed that the statute required that the taxpayer *physically* meet with clients in the home office.[30]

Separate Structure.   The third exception for business use is the least restrictive of the three. If a separate structure is the site of the home office, it need be used only in connection with the taxpayer's work (e.g., a converted detached garage). Additional exceptions are provided for certain storage use and use in providing day care services.

---

[28]   *Rudolph Baie,* 74 T.C. 105 (1980).

[29]   S. Rep. No. 94-938, 94th Cong., 2d Sess. 147-49 (1976).

[30]   78 T.C. 428 (1982).

AMOUNT DEDUCTIBLE

If the taxpayer qualifies for the home office deduction, an allocable portion of expenses related to the home may be deducted. The allocation of expenses generally must be based on square footage. Typical expenses include utilities, depreciation, insurance, interest, and taxes. It should be emphasized that the home office deduction is limited to the gross income from the home business as reduced by allowable deductions. This computation is very similar to that for determining deductible hobby expenses. The taxpayer may deduct expenses equal to the extent of gross income reduced by (1) expenses allowable without regard to the use of the dwelling unit (e.g., interest—assuming it is a primary or secondary residence—and taxes), and (2) business or rental expenses incurred in carrying on the activity other than those of the home office (e.g., supplies and secretarial expenses).[31] Any home office expenses that are not deductible due to this limitation may be carried over and used to offset income from the business which led to the deduction, even if the taxpayer does not use the unit in the business in subsequent years.

Where the taxpayer is self-employed (i.e., a sole proprietor), all of the taxpayer's expenses, including those attributable to the home office, are deductible for A.G.I. In contrast, if the taxpayer is an employee, the otherwise allowable expenses are deductible in full as itemized deductions. The other business expenses, including the home office expenses, are considered miscellaneous itemized deductions and are subject, along with other miscellaneous itemized deductions, to the 2 percent floor.

> **Example 9.** K maintains a qualifying home office. During this year, she earned only $2,000 from the home office activities. Her expenses included the following: interest and taxes allocable to the home office, $600; secretarial services, miscellaneous supplies and postage, $900; and expenses directly related to the home office including insurance, utilities, and depreciation, $1,700. K's potential deduction is $2,000 computed as follows:

Gross income.........................	$2,000	
Otherwise allowable deductions:		
Interest and taxes....................	(600)	$ 600
Other business expenses..............	(900)	900
Gross income limitation................	$ 500	
Home office expenses:		
$1,700 limited to remaining gross income		500
Total potential deduction................		$2,000

---

[31] See § 280A(c)(5).

Whether the $2,000 of deductible expenses are deductible for or from A.G.I. depends on whether K is self-employed or an employee. If K is self-employed, the entire $2,000 is deductible for A.G.I. If the taxpayer is an employee, the $600 of interest and taxes allocable to the home office are deductible as itemized deductions and would be subject to the 3% cutback provision. The remaining $1,400 is considered a miscellaneous itemized deduction subject (along with other miscellaneous itemized deductions) to the 2% floor. Of course, any miscellaneous itemized deductions exceeding the 2% floor are still subject to the 3% cutback provision. The home office expenses that are not deductible this year, $1,200 [($600 + $900 + $1,700 = $3,200) − $2,000], may be carried over to the following years to be offset against future home office income.

RENTAL OF RESIDENCE

The *business use* requirements explained above do not apply when the taxpayer simply rents a part of his or her home to a third party. In such case, the taxpayer reports the income from the rental and deducts the expenses without limitation.

In *Feldman,* the taxpayer used the rental exception to avoid the home office rules.[32] Mr. Feldman operated an accounting practice as a separate corporation. Pursuant to an agreement between him and the corporation, Feldman leased a room in his home to the corporation which then provided it for Feldman's use. By so doing, Feldman was able to deduct all expenses allocable to the "rental property." Because the deductions offset the rental payment, no tax was paid on the amount received. In effect, Feldman was able to receive part of his corporation's earnings tax free. Note that had Feldman simply used the home office related to his employment, no deduction would have been allowed since it would not have satisfied the principal place of business or convenience of the employer tests. To eliminate this avoidance possibility, Congress amended the home office provisions. Under the amendment, no home office deduction is allowable where an employee leases a portion of the home to the employer. For this purpose, an independent contractor is treated as an employee for the party for whom the work is performed.

RESIDENTIAL PHONE SERVICE

For many years, taxpayers who used their home phone for business or income-producing purposes deducted a portion of the basic charge for local service on the grounds that it was business-related. In 1988, however, Congress saw the issue differently. Apparently it believed that in this day and age the cost of basic phone service to a taxpayer's residence would have been incurred in any event— without regard to any business that the taxpayer might otherwise conduct. As a result, a taxpayer may no longer deduct any charge (including taxes) for local

---

[32]   84 T.C. 1 (1985).

phone service for the *first* phone line provided to any residence. The taxpayer may still deduct the costs of long-distance phone calls or optional phone services such as call waiting or call forwarding, when such costs are related to business. In addition, the costs of additional phone lines into the home that are used for business are deductible.

TRANSPORTATION EXPENSES

Before examining the deduction for transportation expenses, the distinction between transportation expenses and travel expenses should be explained. In tax jargon, transportation and travel are not synonymous. Travel expenses are broadly defined to include not only the costs of transportation but also related expenses such as meals, lodging, and other incidentals when the taxpayer is in a travel status. As discussed below, the taxpayer is in travel status when he or she is *away from home overnight* on business.[33] In contrast, transportation expenses are defined narrowly to include only the actual costs of transportation—expenses of getting from one place to another while in the course of business when the taxpayer is *not* away from home overnight.[34] Transportation expenses normally occur when the taxpayer goes and returns on the same day. The most common transportation expense is the cost of driving and maintaining a car, but the term also includes the cost of traveling by other forms of transportation such as bus, taxi, subway, or train.[35]

> **Example 10.** M is an architect in Cincinnati. At various times during the year, he drove to Cleveland to inspect one of his projects. He often ate lunch and dinner in Cleveland before returning home. M is allowed to deduct only the costs of transportation. None of the meals is deductible since he was not away from home overnight. Had he spent the night in Cleveland and returned the next day, the costs of meals and lodging as well as transportation would be deductible.

The deduction for transportation is allowed under the general provisions of §§ 162 and 212. Therefore, to qualify for deduction, the transportation expense must be ordinary, necessary, and related to the taxpayer's trade or business or income-producing activity. Personal transportation, of course, does not qualify for deduction. Like many other expenses, however, the boundary between business and personal transportation is often difficult to identify. Some of the common problem areas are discussed below.

---

[33] § 162(a)(2).

[34] Reg. § 1.62-1(g).

[35] *Ibid.*

DEDUCTIBLE TRANSPORTATION VERSUS NONDEDUCTIBLE COMMUTING

The cost of transportation or commuting between the taxpayer's home and his or her place of employment may appear to be a necessary business expense. It is settled, however, that commuting expenses generally are nondeductible personal expenses. This rule derives from the presumption that the commuting expense arises from the taxpayer's *personal preference* to live away from the place of business or employment. This presumption persists even though there often is no place to live within walking distance of employment, much less one that is suitable or within the taxpayer's means. The fact that the taxpayer is forced to live far away from the place of employment is irrelevant and does not alter the personal nature of the expenses.

> **Example 11.**   In *Sanders v. Comm.*, the taxpayers were civilian employees working on an air force base.[36] Despite the fact that they were not allowed to live on the base next to their employment and could only live elsewhere and commute, the transportation costs were not deductible. The Court found it impossible to distinguish between these expenses and those of a suburban commuter, both being personal in origin.

> **Example 12.**   In *Tauferner v. Comm.*, the taxpayer worked at a chemical plant that was located 20 miles from any community due to the dangers involved.[37] The taxpayer was denied deductions for his commuting even though he lived in the nearest habitable spot. Arguably, the nature of his job—not personal convenience—produced additional transportation costs. Nevertheless, the Court did not believe that such hardship changed the personal character of the expenses.

The taxpayer is permitted to deduct the costs of commuting in several situations, however. These exceptions to the general rule are discussed below.

Commuting with Tools and Similar Items.   The fact that the taxpayer hauls tools, instruments, or other equipment necessary in pursuing business normally does not cause commuting expenses to be deductible. The Supreme Court has ruled that only the *additional* expenses attributable to carrying the tools are deductible.[38] The IRS determines the taxpayer's "additional expenses" by applying the so-called "same mode" test.[39] Under this test, a deduction is allowed for the extra cost of commuting by one mode with the tools over the cost of

---

[36]   71-1 USTC ¶9260, 27 AFTR2d 71-832, 439 F.2d 296 (CA-9, 1971).

[37]   69-1 USTC ¶9241, 23 AFTR2d 69-1025, 407 F.2d 243 (CA-10, 1969).

[38]   *Fausner v. Comm.*, 73-2 USTC ¶95-15, 32 AFTR2d 73-5202, 413 U.S. 838 (USSC, 1973).

[39]   Rev. Rul. 75-380, 1975-2 C.B. 59.

commuting by the same mode without the tools. Thus, a carpenter who drives a truck would not be allowed a transportation deduction simply by loading it with tools since carrying the tools created no additional expense. The fact that tools may have caused the carpenter to drive a truck, which is more expensive than some other type of transportation, is irrelevant under the IRS view. The courts, however, appear to have rejected this test in certain cases.[40]

Example 13. T plays second trumpet in the Dallas orchestra. During the year, his employer indicated they no longer needed a second trumpet and thus T would have to switch to the tuba to retain his job. If, in order to transport the tuba, T had to change from driving to work in a small car costing $3 per day to driving to work in a van costing $5 per day, the IRS would not allow a deduction for the additional cost. Under the same mode test, the cost of driving the van with the tuba is the same as without the tuba. The courts, however, may allow a deduction for the $2 increase in cost. On the other hand, if T had rented a trailer to carry the tuba at a cost of $2 per day, the IRS would allow the deduction because the cost of driving the van with the tuba is now $2 more than without the tuba.

Commuting between Two Jobs. The transportation cost of going from one job to a second job is deductible.[41] The deduction is limited to the cost of going *directly* from one job to the other.

Example 14. R works for X Corporation on the morning shift and for Y Corporation on its afternoon shift. The distances he drives are diagrammed below.

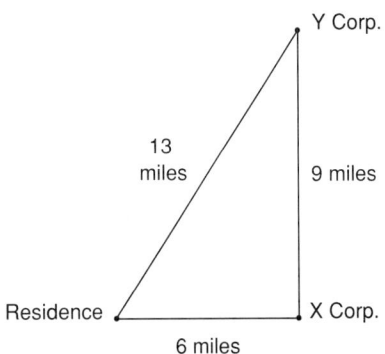

If R leaves X and goes home to eat lunch before going to Y, he actually drives 19 miles to get to Y, or 10 more miles than if he had driven directly (19 − 9). However, only the cost of driving directly, 9 miles, is deductible.

[40]   *J.F. Grayson,* 36 TCM 1201, T.C. Memo 1977-304. See also *H.A. Pool,* 36 TCM 93, T.C. Memo 1977-20.

[41]   *Supra,* Footnote 39.

Commuting to a Temporary Assignment.   Individuals are often assigned to work at a location other than where they regularly work. When a taxpayer commutes to a *temporary work location,* the commuting expenses are deductible transportation costs if either of the following tests are satisfied:

1.   The temporary assignment is *within* the general area of the taxpayer's employment *and* he or she otherwise has a *regular* place of business (e.g., an office);[42] or

2.   The temporary assignment is *outside* the general area of the taxpayer's employment (i.e., his or her tax home).[43]

Example 15.   C is an auditor for a public accounting firm that has its office in downtown Chicago. C works about 30% of the time in her employer's office, and the remaining 70% is spent at various clients' offices around the city. C may deduct the costs of commuting between her residence and a client's office because the client's office is a temporary work location and C otherwise has a regular place of business (i.e., her employer's office).

Example 16.   M is a carpenter. He works for a construction company that builds houses in subdivisions in various areas of Houston. Most of his assignments are located within about 25 miles of downtown Houston. During the year, M worked at two different locations, one on the north side of Houston and the other on the west side. Although M is assigned to temporary work locations, he is not allowed to deduct any of his commuting expenses because he does not otherwise have a regular place of business.

Example 17.   Assume the same facts as above except that M was temporarily assigned to a job in Galveston, 60 miles from Houston. He drove to Galveston daily and returned home in the evenings. Under these circumstances, M may deduct the cost of driving the entire 120-mile round trip from his home to Galveston. The following diagram illustrates this approach.

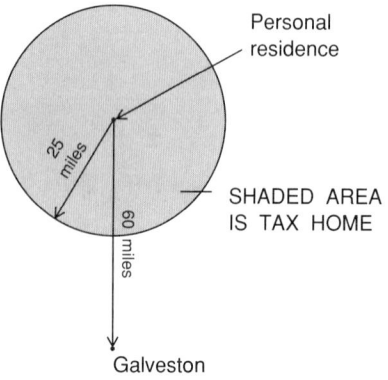

[42]   Rev. Rul. 90-23 I.R.B. No. 11, 4.   [43]   Rev. Rul. 190, 1953-2 C.B. 303.

The IRS draws an important distinction between temporary and regular work locations. A work location is temporary if the taxpayer performs services on an irregular or short-term basis (e.g., a matter of days or weeks).[44] In contrast, a work location is considered a *regular* place of business if—as one might expect—the taxpayer performs services there on a regular basis. According to the IRS, a taxpayer may have more than one regular place of business even though he or she does not perform services at that location every week or on a set schedule. When the taxpayer commutes to these different locations on a "regular" basis, the costs of commuting would not be deductible because such locations are not temporary.

Example 18. Dr. T, a podiatrist, has an office on both the north side and south side of Indianapolis. In addition, she performs services at a clinic and a hospital with which she is associated. T may not deduct the costs of transportation between her residence and these various locations because each is considered a regular place of business and not a temporary work location. As discussed below, however, the costs of going between two business locations (e.g., a clinic and a hospital) are deductible.

Transportation between Job Sites. While the transportation costs between a taxpayer's home and the first and last job sites generally are considered non-deductible commuting expenses, transportation costs between two job sites are deductible.[45] Accordingly, once the taxpayer arrives at the first job site any business travel thereafter usually is deductible.

Example 19. R is employed as a tax accountant and works primarily in his employer's office downtown. R drives 34 miles round-trip from his home to the office. After arriving at work one day, R drove 6 miles to a client's office and returned to his employer's office. In this case, R may deduct the cost of driving 12 miles.

Example 20. Assume R drives 17 miles to work in the morning. In the afternoon, he drives 15 miles to a client's office where he conducts some business. From the client's office he drives 9 miles home. In this situation, R may deduct the cost of driving 15 miles because transportation between two job sites is deductible. In addition, it appears that he may deduct the cost of driving 9 miles since transportation between the taxpayer's residence and a temporary work location (i.e., the client's office) is deductible.

[44] An assignment beyond the taxpayer's tax home is not considered to be temporary if it is expected to last for a year or more. Rev. Rul. 83-82, 1983-1 C.B. 45.

[45] Rev. Rul. 55-109, 1955-1 C.B. 261.

Although transportation expenses between the taxpayer's home and work normally are not deductible, the rule concerning travel between job sites creates a favorable exception for taxpayers who maintain a separate trade or business at home. For these taxpayers, the transportation from the first job site—the home—and the second job site would be deductible.

> **Example 21.** V is a landscape engineer and works out of his home. Transportation costs from his home to a client's place of business are deductible since the expenses are incurred in traveling from his principal place of business to a job site.[46]

COMPUTING CAR EXPENSES

Deductions relating to driving and maintaining a car may be computed using actual expenses or a standard mileage rate (automatic mileage method). Under either method, if the car is used for both business and personal purposes, only the car expenses attributable to business or income production are deductible.

Actual Expenses. Actual car expenses normally deducted include the costs for gas, oil, repairs, insurance, depreciation, interest on loans to purchase the car (other than that of an employee), taxes, licenses, garage rent, parking fees, and tolls. Calculating actual expenses usually requires determining the portion of the nondeductible expenses attributable to personal use. Under the actual expense method, the total actual expense is allocated based on mileage.

> **Example 22.** R, self-employed, drove 20,000 miles during the year: 16,000 on business and 4,000 for personal purposes. Total actual expenses were as follows:

General expenses:	
Gas	$ 800
Maintenance (oil, repairs)	200
Insurance	400
Interest expense	600
Depreciation	2,000
Total	$4,000
Other business expenses:	
Tolls incurred on business trips	$ 10
Parking fees when calling on clients	90
Total	$ 100

---

[46] See *Raymond Garner*, 42 TCM 1181, T.C. Memo 1981-542, and *Joe J. Adams,* 43 TCM 1203, T.C. Memo 1982-223.

Since R used the car 80% (16,000 ÷ 20,000) for business, he may deduct 80% of the general expenses, $3,200 (80% × $4,000). In addition, he may deduct the entire $100 cost for the parking and tolls since they were incurred solely for business purposes, for a total deduction of $3,300. Note that the nonbusiness portion of the interest expense would not be deductible, assuming it is not attributable to a loan secured by his first or second home. If R were an employee, none of the interest would be deductible because business interest of an *employee* is not deductible.

Standard Mileage Rate. The automatic mileage method generally allows a deduction of 27.5 cents per mile for *all* business miles driven during the year.[47] The business portion of expenses for interest (if self-employed), state and local property taxes, parking, and tolls also may be added to the amount computed using the mileage rate. Other expenses such as depreciation, insurance, and maintenance are built into the mileage rate and cannot be added.

Example 23. Same facts as in *Example 22*. R's deduction using the standard mileage rate would be $4,980, as computed below.

Business mileage (16,000 × $0.275)................	$4,400
Interest ($600 × 80%).............................	480
Parking and tolls....................................	100
Total..	$4,980

Note that in arriving at the deduction, gas, maintenance, insurance, and depreciation are not added to the amount computed using the standard rate since they are built into the rate. Conversely, interest (if self-employed), parking, and tolls are added since they are not included in the rate.

The standard mileage rate may be used *only* if it is adopted in the first year the car is placed in service. In addition, the following conditions must be satisfied:[48]

1. The car must be owned by the taxpayer, not leased.

2. The car must not be one of two or more cars being used simultaneously in a business, such as in a fleet operation. When a taxpayer alternates in using different cars on different occasions, the cars are treated as one and the mileage is combined.

3. The car must not be for hire, such as a taxi.

4. Additional first year depreciation or depreciation using an accelerated method must not have been claimed in a prior year.

---

[47] Rev. Proc. 90-59 I.R.B. No. 52. Special rules apply to rural letter carriers.

[48] *Ibid.*

If these conditions are satisfied, the taxpayer may switch methods from year to year. However, use of the standard mileage method precludes the taxpayer from using the Modified Accelerated Cost Recovery System (MACRS) for computing depreciation in a subsequent year, and depreciation must be computed under one of the alternative methods.[49] Note that selecting the actual method in the first year generally *prohibits* the taxpayer from ever using the standard mileage rate for that automobile.

Taxpayers who use the standard mileage rate are required to reduce the adjusted basis of their automobiles just as if they had claimed depreciation. For example, for 1990 and 1991, the basis is reduced by 11 cents per mile for each mile driven.[50]

CLASSIFICATION OF TRANSPORTATION AND TRAVEL EXPENSES

The *unreimbursed* transportation and travel expenses of an employee are treated as miscellaneous itemized deductions subject to the 2 percent floor. In contrast, if an employee is reimbursed for such expenses under a qualified arrangement or the expenses are incurred by a self-employed person, the expenses are deductible for A.G.I. An employee reports the expenses on Form 2106, a copy of which is reproduced in the last section of this chapter.

Travel and transportation expenses related to property held for the production of income are also considered miscellaneous itemized deductions unless the income is rents or royalties, in which case the deductions would be for A.G.I. In addition, the deduction for meals may be limited to 80 percent of their cost. This limitation is discussed in detail with entertainment expenses later in this chapter.

TRAVEL EXPENSES

Section 162 of the Code provides for the deduction of travel expenses while "away from home" in the pursuit of a trade or business.[51] A similar deduction is allowed for travel expenses connected with income-producing activities not constituting a business.[52] The definition of travel expenses is not as narrow as that of transportation expenses. Travel expenses include not only the costs of transportation but also the costs of meals (but limited to 80 percent of actual costs, as discussed later), lodging, cleaning, and laundry, telephone, and other similar expenses related to travel.[53] Whether these additional expenses such as meals and lodging are deductible depends on whether the taxpayer is considered "away from home."

[49] *Supra*, Footnote 47.

[50] *Supra*, Footnote 47. For previous years, see Rev. Proc. 89-66.

[51] *Supra*, Footnote 34.

[52] §§ 212(1) and (2).

[53] Reg. § 1.162-2(a).

AWAY-FROM-HOME TEST

The taxpayer must be *away from home* before travel expenses are deductible. The "away-from-home" test poses two questions: For what period does the taxpayer need to be away from home, and where is the taxpayer's home for tax purposes? With respect to the first question, the Supreme Court has ruled that the away-from-home test generally requires the taxpayer to be away from home *overnight*.[54] Later interpretations of this decision have indicated that the taxpayer will be considered to be "overnight" when it is reasonable for the taxpayer to stop for needed sleep or rest. A trip where the taxpayer leaves and returns the same day is not travel and, consequently, only the transportation cost would be deductible. Meals eaten during the trip, lodging, etc., would not be deductible.

The second and more critical aspect of the away-from-home test concerns the determination of the taxpayer's *tax home*. As in the transportation area, this question is continually debated. The IRS and the Tax Court have defined the term *tax home* to mean the business location of the taxpayer or the general vicinity of the taxpayer's employment, regardless of the location of the taxpayer's personal residence.[55] The Court of Appeals in several circuits, however, has held that "home" should be interpreted in the normal fashion (i.e., as the place where the taxpayer normally maintains his or her residence;[56] see *Example 25*). The interpretation problems usually arise when taxpayers live in one location but also conduct substantial business at another location where they often stay because it is impractical to return to the residence. As an illustration, consider a construction worker who lives in Detroit but obtains a job to work on the construction of a nuclear power plant near Chicago. The issue here is the location of the taxpayer's tax home. If the individual normally works in Chicago, the IRS would take the position that his tax home is in Chicago. In such case, the IRS would not allow the deduction of any travel costs (including meals and lodging in Chicago) because the taxpayer, in its view, is not considered away from his tax home. However, the IRS would permit the taxpayer to deduct his travel costs if the taxpayer could demonstrate that the taxpayer's work away from his principal place of employment, Detroit, is temporary.[57] As previously explained, an assignment is considered temporary if it is not indefinite (e.g., not more than a year).

> **Example 24.** D is employed as an engineer, living and working in Kansas City. Her employer assigned D to a job in El Paso where she lived and worked for five months before returning to Kansas City and resuming her regular employment. The IRS would permit D to deduct her travel expenses since the assignment is temporary. If D's assignment in El Paso was

[54] *U.S. v. Correll*, 68-1 USTC ¶9101, 20 AFTR2d 5845, 389 U.S. 299 (USSC, 1967).

[55] G.C.M. 23672, 1943 C.B. 66, superseded by Rev. Rul. 74-291, 1974-1 C.B. 42.

[56] For example, see *Rosenspan v. U.S.*, 71-1 USTC ¶9241, 27 AFTR2d 71-707, 438 F.2d 905 (CA-2, 1971).

[57] *Supra*, Footnote 44.

extended beyond the original period to exceed a year, D would have to establish that the assignment was temporary and not indefinite before her travel expenses would be deductible.

If the taxpayer has no principal place of employment, the tax home is normally his regular place of abode.[58] However, if the taxpayer has no permanent place of residence, the courts have consistently denied the taxpayer's deductions for meals and lodging since there is no "home" to be away from. This rule has been applied to itinerant construction workers and salespeople whom the courts view as being *at home* wherever their work may take them.[59]

The purpose of the away from home provision is to reduce the burden of the taxpayer who, because of business needs, must maintain two places of abode and consequently incurs additional and duplicate living expenses. The rule is based on the principle that a taxpayer normally lives and works in the same general vicinity. Thus, when taxpayers choose to live in an area other than where they work, the resulting expenses normally are considered personal. This rule often is difficult to apply in particular situations. For this reason, the deduction of travel expenses ultimately depends on the facts.

> **Example 25.**   C works at a testing laboratory in a remote mountain area of New Mexico, 70 miles from his home. His residence, however, is the closest place to the laboratory to live. C normally commutes to work but sometimes stays at the testing facilities' quarters overnight when he works overtime. In this situation, the IRS would not allow a deduction for travel expenses since C's tax home is at the testing laboratory, and when staying there he is not away from home. Some Appellate Courts, however, may permit the deduction for meals and lodging since he is away from his residence.[60]

COMBINED BUSINESS AND PLEASURE TRAVEL

As discussed above, travel costs are deductible only while away from home in pursuit of business or income-producing activities. When traveling away from home, however, taxpayers often combine business with pleasure. In these situations, the question arises as to how much of the travel expenses are deductible. The rules governing combined business and pleasure travel differ depending on whether the taxpayer is traveling inside or outside of the United States.

---

[58] Criteria exist for determining whether a taxpayer has a regular place of abode. See Rev. Rul. 73-529, 1973-2 C.B. 37.

[59] *George H. James v. U.S.,* 62-2 USTC ¶9735, 10 AFTR2d 5627, 308 F.2d 204 (CA-9, 1962).

[60] For example, see *Lee E. Coombs,* 79-2 USTC ¶9719, 45 AFTR2d 80-444, 608 F.2d 1269 (CA-9, 1979).

Domestic Travel. The taxpayer who travels within the United States (all 50 states and the District of Columbia) may deduct all of the costs of travel to and from the destination if the trip is primarily for business. [61] If the trip is primarily for business, making a personal side-trip or extending the stay for a vacation does *not* make the cost of traveling from home to the business destination partially or totally nondeductible; however, the costs of any personal side-trips are not allowed. Travel which is primarily for personal purposes is not deductible even though some business is conducted. Note that the taxpayer either deducts *all* of the *to-and-from* travel expenses or deducts *none* of them—there is no allocation. Of course, any travel expenses (e.g., meals and lodging) directly related to business upon arriving at the destination qualify.

> **Example 26.** F, a CPA, flew from Dallas to Denver for the annual convention of the Texas Society of Certified Public Accountants. The air fare was $500. Meals and lodging for the three days she attended were $150 and $230, respectively. Upon conclusion of the convention, F drove to the mountains and skiied for two days before returning home. The travel to the mountains, including meals and lodging, cost $350. F may deduct all of the air fare, $500, because costs of transportation are fully deductible without allocation when the trip is primarily for business. In addition, F may deduct 80% of the meal costs, $120 (80% × $150), and $230 for lodging because these travel expenses are directly related to business. The expenses of $350 for the ski trip are nondeductible personal expenses.

> **Example 27.** Assume the same facts as in *Example 26,* except that F skied for five days. In this case, the trip may be treated as primarily personal thus preventing any deduction of the $500 air fare from Dallas to Denver. Eighty percent of the expenses for meals and all of the lodging costs while at the convention on business are still deductible.

Obviously the most troublesome question concerning domestic travel is whether the nature of the trip is primarily business or pleasure. In this regard, the Regulations, Rulings, and reported decisions offer little guidance—saying only that the answer depends on the facts and circumstances in each case. Among the factors normally considered, the amount of time devoted to business as compared to personal activities is often decisive. Another factor emphasized is the type of location where the business occurs (e.g., a resort hotel or a more businesslike setting). The increasing number of professional organizations that schedule their conventions and seminars in resort areas has caused the IRS to closely scrutinize deductions for alleged business trips which are merely disguised vacations. Congress took action regarding expenses related to nonbusiness conventions (e.g., investment and tax seminars), completely disallowing their deduction after 1986.[62] For a business meeting, however, if it can be clearly shown that the expenses were incurred for business purposes, the deduction is not disallowed merely because the meeting occurs at a resort.

---

[61] Reg. § 1.162-2(b)(1).   [62] § 274(h)(7).

Example 28. This year, Dr. H, a surgeon, attended a week-long course on arthroscopic surgery in Palm Beach. His wife accompanied him and attended a seminar on personal financial planning. H may deduct his costs of transportation as well as the travel expenses incurred after arriving in Palm Beach because the expenses are related to business. None of his wife's expenses are deductible because they relate not to her trade or business but to investments and taxes.

Taxpayers often travel with family members when making business trips. The travel expenses of the family member are not deductible unless the taxpayer can adequately demonstrate that the family member's presence has a bona fide business purpose.[63] Performance of incidental services does not cause the family member's expense to qualify. The courts, however, have allowed a deduction for a spouse's expenses when the facts have shown that the spouse's presence enhanced the image of the taxpayer or the spouse acted as a business assistant.[64]

Foreign Travel. When the taxpayer travels outside the United States, the travel expenses must satisfy more stringent requirements for deduction. Generally, the costs of transportation to and from the foreign destination and other travel expenses must be allocated between business (or income-producing activities) and personal activities. If the travel is *primarily* business, the costs of transportation are fully deductible without allocation if one of the following conditions is satisfied:[65]

1. *Travel outside the United States does not exceed one week* (seven consecutive days). In counting the days out of the United States, the day of departure from the United States is excluded while the day of return to the United States is included. (For example, leaving on Sunday and returning on the following Sunday is exactly seven days.)

2. *More than 75 percent of the days on the trip were devoted to business.* A day is treated as a business day if during any part of the day the taxpayer's presence is required at a particular place for a business purpose. Moreover, the day is considered a business day even though the taxpayer spends more time during normal working hours on nonbusiness activity than on business activity. Weekends, holidays, or other "stand-by" days that fall between the taxpayer's business days are also considered business days. However, such days are not business days if they fall at the end of the taxpayer's business activities and the taxpayer merely elects to stay for personal purposes. The day of departure and the day of return are both treated as business days.

3. Taxpayer has no substantial control over arranging the business trip.

4. Personal vacation is not a major consideration in making the trip.

---

[63] Reg. § 1.162-2(c); Rev. Rul. 55-57, 1955-1 C.B. 315.

[64] See *Fraser Wilkins*, 72-2 USTC ¶9707, 30 AFTR2d 72-5639, 348 F. Supp. 1282 (D.Ct.

Neb. 1972); *Pierre C. Warwick*, 64-2 USTC ¶9864, 14 AFTR2d 5817, 236 F. Supp. 761 (D.Ct. VA., 1974).

[65] § 274(c); Reg. § 1.274-4.

If the travel is not primarily for business or fails to satisfy one of the above conditions, an *allocation* of the to-and-from travel expenses must be made. In such cases, the deductible travel expenses are determined by the following allocation formula:

$$\frac{\text{Business days on trip}}{\text{Total days on trip}} \times \begin{array}{c}\text{Total}\\\text{to-and-from}\\\text{Travel Expenses}\end{array} = \begin{array}{c}\text{Deductible}\\\text{to-and-from}\\\text{Travel Expenses}\end{array}$$

A deduction for the to-and-from travel expenses is not allowed if the trip is primarily personal. However, travel costs (e.g., meals and lodging) directly related to business upon arriving at the destination are deductible.

Example 29.   B, an executive, arranged a trip to Japan primarily for business. He left Chicago flying for Tokyo on July 1 and returned on July 20. During his trip, he spent 15 days on business (including the two travel days) and five days sight-seeing. His air fare was $1,000 and his lodging plus 80% of the meal costs totaled $100 per day. Unless B can show that a personal vacation was not a major consideration for the trip, he must allocate his expenses because none of the other conditions are satisfied. In such case, B may deduct $2,250 [(15 business days ÷ 20 total days = 75%) × $3,000 total expenses]. If B had returned July 8 or spent one less day sight-seeing, no allocation would be required since he would have been out of the United States less than a week or would have spent more than 75% of his time on business activities.

Luxury Water Travel.   When lawmakers lowered the boom on entertainment and meal expenses in 1986, they also took a swipe at unhurried businesspersons who travel by cruise ships, ocean liners and other luxury water transportation. As a general rule, deductions for transportation by water are limited to *twice* the highest per diem amount allowed to Federal employees while away from home but serving in the 48 contiguous states.[66]

Example 30.   To conduct a business meeting in London, T traveled by ocean liner, taking five days at a total cost of $3,000. Assuming the top per diem rate for Federal employees serving in the United States is $200 per day, T's deduction is limited to $2,000 ($200 × 2 × 5).

---

[66]   § 274(m)(1).

FOREIGN CONVENTIONS

Notwithstanding the restrictions imposed on deductions related to foreign travel, substantial abuse existed until 1976. Most of this abuse involved travel to foreign conventions, seminars, cruises, and the like, which if properly scheduled amounted to government-subsidized vacations. To eliminate this possibility, specific safeguards were enacted in 1976 and revised in 1978. Currently, no deduction is allowed for travel expenses to attend a convention, seminar, or similar meeting outside of North America *unless* the taxpayer establishes the following:[67] (1) the meeting is directly related to the active conduct of his or her trade or business, and (2) it is as reasonable to hold the meeting outside North America as within North America. North America includes the United States, its possessions, Canada, Mexico, the Trust Territory of the Pacific Islands, and qualifying Caribbean Countries and Bermuda.

> **Example 31.** B, a professor of international business, traveled to Spain to present a paper on tax incentives for exports at the International Accounting Convention. Since it is as reasonable to hold an international meeting in Spain as in North America, and presentation of the paper is directly related to B's business, she may deduct her travel expenses subject to the normal rules for travel outside the United States.

CRUISE SHIPS

No deduction is allowed for the cost of attending meetings conducted on a cruise ship unless the following requirements are met:[68] (1) the ship is a vessel registered in the United States and it sails *only* between ports in the United States or its possessions; (2) the meeting is directly related to the taxpayer's business; and (3) certain detailed information regarding the cruise is submitted with the return. For qualifying cruises, the maximum deduction is $2,000 per calendar year for each taxpayer. An employer, however, may deduct the cost of sending an individual to a foreign convention or on any type of cruise if the amount is included in the employee's income.

ENTERTAINMENT EXPENSES

Perhaps no single deduction has created as much controversy as that for entertainment expenses. The difficulty lies in the fact that there is no simple way to distinguish entertainment expenses incurred out of business necessity from those incurred for personal purposes. The problem is the dual personality of entertainment. Entertainment can be purely for fun and amusement. Or it can be used to

---

[67]　See § 274(h)(1), (3), and (6).　　　　[68]　§ 274(h)(2).

break the ice with a potential customer, to relax, or to create an engaging atmosphere for closing the sale or getting the contract. Over the years, Congress and various administrations have continually struggled to devise the proper test that would prohibit taxpayers from deducting what might be a personal expenditure.

The Kennedy administration was the first to have some success in limiting the entertainment deduction. In 1961, President Kennedy recommended abolishing the deduction for entertaining customers at parties, night clubs, and the like, as well as disallowing the deduction for country club dues. Although Kennedy's suggestions were not enacted, Congress did move to make it more difficult to deduct entertainment expenses with the enactment of Code § 274. This provision—discussed below—still stands as the major hurdle that must be overcome before entertainment expenses may be deducted. Under § 274, entertainment expenses must not only satisfy the normal criteria for business and income-producing expenses but also several additional requirements, including certain recordkeeping standards. Despite these additional conditions, the so-called *Kennedy rules* still were viewed by many to be an inadequate policeman.

President Carter's administration ventured into the battle over entertainment deductions in 1977, blasting the taxpayer's right to deduct the cost of what is now the infamous "three martini lunch." The Carter attacks were generally unsuccessful, however. It was not until President Reagan's term that the entertainment deduction was drastically curtailed. Present law now presumes that virtually every entertainment and meal expense contains a personal element that is not deductible. As discussed below, only 80 percent of the cost of allowable meals and entertainment is currently deductible.

DEDUCTION REQUIREMENTS

To be deductible, an entertainment expense must first survive the gauntlet of tests applied to all potential deductions by § 162. That is, the expense must be ordinary and necessary and incurred in carrying on a trade or business.

> **Example 32.** D is a sales representative of M Corporation, a manufacturer of cookware. Twice a month, she takes buyers from the leading retail department stores to lunch where they discuss the corporation's new products. Business meals are customary, appropriate, and helpful in commissioned sales and thus are deductible.

> **Example 33.** P, the public defense attorney of South City, occasionally takes all of his staff to lunch. The entertainment expenses are not deductible because public defenders—unlike those in private practice—normally do not take their associates to lunch.

As a practical matter, most entertainment expenses satisfy the ordinary and necessary tests with little difficulty. It is the additional requirements of § 274 that provide the greatest obstacles.

The restrictions contained in § 274 apply to any expense related to an activity customarily considered to provide entertainment, amusement, or recreation.[69] The provision applies to expenses for entertaining guests such as those for the following: food, liquor, sporting events, movie and theater productions, social, athletic and country clubs, yachts, hunting and fishing trips, and company-provided vacations. Business gifts also are governed by this provision.[70] It should be emphasized that expenses ostensibly for other purposes also are subject to the requirements of § 274 if they are of an entertaining nature.

> **Example 34.** A national magazine desiring publicity often sends the company president flying in a hot air balloon emblazoned with the corporation's logo. Although the expense is for advertising, § 274 applies since the activity constitutes entertainment.

As might be expected, when the IRS questions the taxpayer about his or her deductions for entertainment, the auditor does not ask whether the taxpayer had a good time. Unfortunately, the agent is concerned with whether the taxpayer has satisfied either of two principal tests. Under § 274, no deduction is allowed unless the taxpayer can adequately substantiate that the entertainment expense is *either* "directly related to" or "associated with" the taxpayer's business or falls within one of ten exceptions.[71]

Directly-Related-To Expenses. The Regulations set forth what the taxpayer must establish for an entertainment expenditure to be considered *directly related to* the taxpayer's business or income-producing activity. Expenses are treated as directly related under the so-called *general test* if the taxpayer shows all of the following:[72]

1. More than a general expectation of deriving some income or other specific benefit (other than goodwill) existed as a result of making the expenditure; no resulting benefit must be shown, however.

2. Business was actually discussed or engaged in during the entertainment.

3. The combined business and entertainment was principally characterized by business.

Business Benefit. Prior to the enactment of § 274, entertainment deductions were liberally granted where they were shown to promote the customer's goodwill. Section 274 rejects this prior standard. Under current law, the taxpayer must have more than just a general expectation of deriving some income or some specific business benefit. Although this standard is hardly the epitome of clarity, it is clear that the likelihood of a benefit must be greater than a remote possibility.

---

[69]   § 274(a)(1).

[70]   § 274(d).

[71]   *Supra*, Footnote 69.

[72]   Reg. § 1.274-2(c)(3).

Example 35. T, an insurance salesman, sees his old college chum, C, in a bar. T buys his buddy a few drinks then takes him to a ballgame, using an extra ticket T has. Before the night is over, T mentions that if C ever needs insurance he should give T a call. In this case, T's prospect of a business benefit is slight, too distant, and thus not directly related. It simply creates goodwill, which is insufficient to obtain a deduction. However, T may be able to benefit from hindsight. If C later calls him about insurance, T could rightfully claim the deduction.

Actively Engage in Business. Under the general test, the taxpayer must actually discuss or engage in business. This means that at some point during the entertainment—at half-time, during the intermission, between innings—the taxpayer must forsake the merriment of the moment and get down to business, negotiating, dealing, bargaining with respect to a bona fide business transaction. Since this is obviously difficult to police, the Regulations have given the IRS two helpful presumptions.[73] First, it is presumed that no business can take place if the taxpayer is not present. If the taxpayer is at home mowing the lawn while the client is enjoying the game using tickets given to him by the taxpayer, the implication is that no business can take place. (In such case, the taxpayer may be able to deduct the cost of the tickets as a business gift as discussed below.) Second, it is presumed that no business can take place where there are substantial distractions. The Regulations insist that such distractions are present at night clubs, sporting events, social gatherings, cocktail lounges, theaters, and wherever the taxpayer meets with a group including not only business associates but others. Despite these presumptions, a deduction is still allowed if the taxpayer can establish to the contrary that he or she actively engaged in the discussion of business. As a practical matter, most taxpayers take advantage of this latitude, claiming the deduction and hoping that they will never be called upon to justify it.

Principal Character Is Business. During the entertainment, business must predominate. This does not mean that the taxpayer must spend more time on business than enjoying the activity. It does mean that the business aspects must be more than incidental. As above, the Regulations rest on the rebuttable presumption that the primary character of certain activities—those on a hunting or fishing trip, a yacht or pleasure boat—is not business.

The Regulations also specify several other situations where the entertainment expense will be considered directly related. For example, entertainment is directly related if it is provided in a clear business setting—a setting where the guest recognizes the taxpayer's business motive (e.g., a hospitality room provided by a book publisher at a convention of accounting professors).[74] Expenditures for entertainment provided for those who render services for the taxpayer also are regarded as directly related. For example, a vacation trip awarded by a manufacturer to the retailer selling a number of its products qualifies.[75]

---

[73] Reg. § 1.274-2(c)(7).

[74] Reg. § 1.274-2(d)(4).

[75] Reg. § 1.274-2(d)(5).

Associated-With Expenses. It is often difficult to qualify the entertainment under the directly related test, generally due to the presumption regarding distractions or simply because the taxpayer could not squeeze in any business during the show or game. However, the entertainment may still qualify for deduction if it satisfies the *associated-with test*. Entertainment expenses are considered *associated with* the taxpayer's business if the entertainment is immediately before or after a substantial business discussion.[76] The key distinction between associated-with and directly-related-to expenses concerns when the business activity occurs. The associated-with test allows the business to occur immediately preceding or following the entertainment while the directly-related-to standard requires business during the entertainment. Note that to satisfy the "immediately preceding or following" requirement it is sufficient that the entertainment merely takes place on the same day as business. In some cases, the entertainment may be on the day before or after the business activity.

> **Example 36.** B operates a chain of sporting goods stores in Dallas. Before school begins each fall, he invites area coaches to one of his stores, where he presents his new lines of equipment. Immediately afterwards, he takes them to a Cowboy football game. B may deduct the costs of tickets to the game since there was substantial business activity immediately before the entertainment. Note that due to the distractions presented by the game no deduction would be permitted if B merely took the coaches to the game and discussed business there.

Business Meals. For many years, taxpayers were allowed to deduct the cost of meals with business associates regardless of whether they satisfied the directly-related-to or associated-with requirements. More importantly, the costs could be deducted even if business was not discussed. The effect of these rules was to allow a deduction for entertaining that created goodwill. In 1986, Congress believed that this favorable treatment was no longer justified and therefore tightened the rules.

Currently, expenses for meals, like other entertainment expenses, are not deductible unless they satisfy the directly-related-to or associated-with tests.[77] Under these criteria, the business meal is not deductible unless there is a substantial and bona fide business discussion either before, after, or during the meal.[78] In addition, the taxpayer or an employee of the taxpayer normally must be present at the meal.[79] For example, if the taxpayer merely reserves a table for dinner at a restaurant for a customer, but neither the taxpayer nor one of his or her employees attends the dinner, no deduction is allowed. For purposes of this rule, an independent contractor who performs significant services for the taxpayer such as an attorney or accountant is considered an employee.

---

[76] *Supra,* Footnote 69; Reg. § 1.274-2(d).

[77] An individual who is *away from home* on business and eats alone need not satisfy these tests.

[78] §§ 274(a) and (b).

[79] § 274(k)(1)(B).

A common question regarding the deduction for business meals concerns the costs of the taxpayer's own meals. From a purely theoretical view, the cost would presumably be a nondeductible personal expense since the taxpayer has to eat in any event. In *Richard A Sutter,* the Tax Court took just such a view in disallowing a taxpayer's deduction for his own meals at business lunches.[80] The Court said:

> We think the presumptive nondeductibility of personal expenses (the taxpayer's meals) may be overcome only by clear and detailed evidence as to each instance that the expenditure in question was *different from* or *in excess* of that which would have been made for the taxpayer's personal purposes (emphasis supplied).

Despite the Court's holding, the IRS has been quite gracious. The Service permits the taxpayer to deduct the *entire cost* of his or her own meal except in abusive situations where it is evident that a substantial amount of personal expenditures are being deducted.[81] Where abuse is apparent, the IRS would invoke the *Sutter* rule and allow a deduction only to the extent it exceeds the amount the taxpayer would normally spend.

Another common question concerns the costs of entertaining those who are not directly involved in the business activities to which the entertainment relates. The portion of any entertainment expense attributable to the customer's and the taxpayer's spouses is deductible where the purpose is business rather than personal or social.[82] For example, when the taxpayer entertains a business client and it is impractical to entertain the client without the spouse, the expenses of both the taxpayer's spouse and the client's spouse are deductible. Any expenses of other persons not closely connected with those who attended the business discussion are not deductible.

ENTERTAINMENT FACILITIES

For many years, the costs of owning and maintaining such status symbols as airplanes, luxury skyboxes, yachts, and hunting and fishing lodges could be subsidized by deducting them as entertainment expenses. Typically, taxpayers would deduct expenses like depreciation, utilities, maintenance, insurance, and salaries (e.g., that of the yacht's captain) that were allocable to business usage of the property. In 1978, however, Congress imposed severe restrictions. Currently, costs such as those listed above that are related to any entertainment facility are not deductible.[83] Additional special rules apply to expenses incurred in using a luxury skybox.[84]

---

[80] 21 T.C. 170 (1953).

[81] Rev. Rul. 63-144, 1963-2 C.B. 129.

[82] Reg. § 1.274-2(d)(4).

[83] § 274(a)(1)(B); Reg. § 1.274-2(e)(2).

[84] § 274(l)(2).

These rules governing entertainment facilities do not prohibit the deduction of out-of-pocket expenses incurred while at the entertainment facility. Expenses for such items as food or beverage would be deductible, assuming they meet the directly-related-to or associated-with tests.

Although Congress has outlawed the deduction of most expenses related to entertainment facilities, one important exception is preserved. Dues or fees paid for a membership in a country club, athletic club, or social club may be deducted on a limited basis if the club is primarily used for business purposes.[85]

A club is considered primarily used for business purposes if more than 50 percent of the number of days of actual use are for business. A day is treated as a business day if the facility is used for entertainment that satisfies the directly-related-to or associated-with tests or that meets the business meal exception.[86] In those instances when the club is used for business and personal purposes on the same day, the day normally is regarded as a business day. If the 50 percent test is satisfied, only the portion of the dues allocable to the days for directly-related and business meal use is deductible.

Example 37.   B pays dues of $1,000 to a country club. Her records reveal the following usage:

Type of Use	Number of Days	
Business:		
Directly-related...........	10	
Business meals...........	15	
Associated-with..........	35	60
Personal..............		40
Total days actually used........		100

Business usage (60 ÷ 100)............................		60%
Deduction:		
Dues...		$1,000
× Directly related and		
business meal use (25 ÷ 100).....................		× 25%
Dues deduction.......................................		$ 250

Since B's total business usage, 60%, exceeds the 50% threshold, she may deduct a portion of the dues. Note that the business-use percentage of 60% is *not* used for this purpose but only the amount attributable to directly-related and business meal use, 25%.

---

[85]   § 274(a)(2)(C).   [86]   Reg. § 1.274-2(e)(4)(i).

Any fees for initiation or membership that are refundable or capital in nature are not deductible.

The various exceptions of § 274 discussed below may enable an employer to deduct expenses connected with entertainment facilities. For example, an employer may deduct the costs of vacation condominiums, swimming pools, tennis courts, and similar facilities if such entertainment facilities are provided primarily for employees.[87]

EXCEPTIONS TO DIRECTLY-RELATED-TO AND ASSOCIATED-WITH TESTS

In certain innocent situations, entertainment and meal expenses need not meet either the directly-related-to or associated-with requirements. These include expenses for the following:[88]

1. Food and drink furnished on the business premises primarily for employees (e.g., costs of a holiday office party)

2. Recreational or social activities, including facilities primarily for employees (e.g., a summer golf outing, a company health club, an annual picnic)

3. Entertainment and meal expenses for an employee if the employee reports their value as taxable compensation (e.g., a company-provided vacation for the top salesperson)

4. Entertainment and meal expenses at business meetings of employees, stockholders, and directors (e.g., refreshments at a directors' meeting)

5. Costs of items made available to the general public (e.g., soft drinks at a grand opening, free ham to the first 50 customers)

6. Costs of entertainment and meals sold to customers (e.g., costs of food sold at an event)

EIGHTY PERCENT LIMITATION ON ENTERTAINMENT AND MEAL EXPENSES

Opponents of the deduction for entertainment and meal expenses have long argued that, despite their business relationship, such expenses are inherently personal and should not be deductible. These same critics typically declare that businesspersons should not be able to live high-on-the-hog at the expense of the government. In 1986 the critics had their way.

---

[87] § 274(e)(5).   [88] § 274(e)(1)-(9).

Currently, § 274(n) generally limits the amount that can be deducted for meals and entertainment to 80 percent of their actual cost. In effect, 20 percent of the cost is disallowed. For employees whose entertainment expenses are *not reimbursed,* the 80 percent limitation is applied before the 2 percent floor for itemized deductions.

Example 38. B, an employee, pays $3,000 for business entertainment for which he is not reimbursed. B's A.G.I. is $50,000 for the year and he has no other miscellaneous itemized deductions. B's deduction is $1,400 computed as follows:

Total unreimbursed entertainment expenses..........	$3,000
Less 20% reduction (20% × $3,000)..............	(600)
Miscellaneous itemized deductions...................	$2,400
Less 2% of A.G.I. (2% × $50,000)...............	(1,000)
Itemized deduction.................................	$1,400

Expenses subject to the 80 percent limitation include the costs of taxes, tips, and parking related to a meal or an entertainment activity. In contrast, the costs of transportation to and from the activity are not subject to limitation.

Example 39. B is the agent of L, who recently signed a lucrative contract with the New York Jets. After successfully negotiating L's contract, B and L took a cab to a local restaurant where they toasted their success. After dinner, they walked to a nearby nightclub. For the night, B spent $207 for the following:

	Limited Expenses	Other
Meal..................................	$120	
Tax...................................	12	
Tips..................................	30	
Cover charge	38	
Cab...................................		$7
Total..............................	$200	$7

The cost of the cab ride, $7, is not subject to limitation and thus can be deducted in full. Of the remaining $200, only $160 is deductible (80% of $200).

It should be emphasized that the percentage reduction rule applies to meals while away from home overnight on business as well as the traditional quiet business meal. In addition, meal expenses incurred during a work-related move, which are otherwise deductible as moving expenses, are also limited.

The 80 percent limitation does not apply in several situations, thus allowing the taxpayer to deduct the meal or entertainment in full. These exceptions are discussed below.

Reimbursed Expenses. When the taxpayer is reimbursed for the meal or entertainment, the limitation is imposed on the party making reimbursement, not the taxpayer.[89]

> **Example 40.** N, a salesman for Big Corporation, took a customer to lunch after he secured a large order. He paid $30, for which he was totally reimbursed. N includes the $30 in income and may deduct the entire $30. The corporation can deduct only $24 (80% of $30).

As noted earlier, in the case of meals qualifying as a deductible moving expense the limitation always applies to the employee, even if he or she is reimbursed for such costs.

If an employee has a reimbursement or expense allowance arrangement with the employer, but under the arrangement the full amount of business expenses is not reimbursed, special problems arise. These problems are considered along with recordkeeping requirements later in this chapter.

Excludable Fringe Benefit. The 80 percent limitation does not apply where the food or beverage provided is excludable as a de minimis employee fringe benefit (e.g., holiday turkeys, hams, fruitcakes, and the like given to employees or to subsidized cafeterias).[90]

Code § 274(e) Exceptions. The percentage reduction rule generally is not imposed on entertainment and meal costs which are exempted from the directly-related-to and associated-with tests noted above.[91] For example, there is no reduction required for the deductible costs of an annual employee Christmas party, summer golf outings, or company-provided vacations treated as compensation. Similarly, the costs of promotional items made available to the general public (e.g., 100 baseball tickets given by a radio to the first 100 callers) or the salaries of comedians paid by a nightclub are not subject to the 80 percent limitation.

Charitable Sporting Event. The costs of tickets to a sporting event are not subject to the reduction rule if the event is related to charitable fund-raising.[92]

---

[89] §§ 274(n)(2) and 274(e)(3).

[90] § 274(n)(2)(B).

[91] § 274(n)(2).

[92] § 274(n)(2)(C).

Specifically, the event must be organized for the primary purpose of benefiting a tax-exempt charitable organization, must contribute 100 percent of the proceeds to the charity, and must use volunteers for substantially all work performed in putting on the event. For example, the costs of attending a golf or tennis celebrity tournament sponsored by the local chapter of the United Way would normally satisfy these requirements and would be fully deductible. Tickets for high school, college, or other scholastic events (e.g., a football game or theater tickets) do not qualify for this exception on the grounds that volunteers do not do all the work (e.g., coaches, their assistants, and other paid individuals provide substantial work such as coaching and recruiting).

LIMITATIONS ON DEDUCTIONS FOR TICKETS

In the entertainment fracas of 1986, lawmakers also struck a blow at the deductible costs of tickets. This deduction is limited to the face value of the ticket.[93] This rule is aimed at amounts paid to a ticket scalper in excess of the regular price of the ticket. Such excess is not deductible. The rule also makes nondeductible any fee paid to a ticket agency for arranging tickets. Note, however, that this rule does not apply to tickets to qualified charitable fundraisers.

BUSINESS GIFTS

In hopes that their generosity will someday be rewarded, taxpayers often make gifts to customers, clients, and others with whom they have a business relationship. Such business-connected gifts are deductible under the general rules of § 162. Under prior law, taxpayers wanting to create goodwill could shower their business associates with gifts and deduct these instruments of goodwill. Moreover, the recipient of such bounty could arguably exclude the presents. Currently, § 274(b) curbs such practice by limiting the deduction for business gifts to $25 per donee per year.[94] For this purpose, the following items *are not* considered gifts:

1. An item costing $4 or less imprinted with the taxpayer's name (e.g., pens)

2. Signs, display racks, or other promotional materials to be used on the business premises of the recipient

Incidental costs such as engraving, mailing, and wrapping are not considered part of the cost of an item for purposes of the $25 limit.

---

[93]   § 274(l)(1).

[94]   § 274(b). It is unclear whether the 80 percent limitation applies to gifts. See § 274(n)(1) and Reg. § 1.274-2(b)(1)(iii).

Example 41. J, a saleswoman of hospital supplies, computes her deduction for business gifts during the year in the following manner.

Description of Gift	Amount	Deduction
H, head of purchasing at St. Jude hospital:		
Perfume	$10	
Solar calculator	30	
Total	$40	$25
Dr. Z:		
Box of golf balls	$18	
Gift wrap	2	
Total	$20	20
Total business gift deduction		$45

Assuming J is an employee, she may deduct the $45 as a miscellaneous itemized deduction.

Employee Achievement Awards. When a business expresses its gratitude for an employee's performance with a gift, special rules allow amounts greater than $25 to be transferred. The effect of these rules is to allow an employer to make and deduct gifts of up to $1,600 to an employee who is allowed to *exclude* the amount of the gift. The Code generally allows an employer to deduct up to $400 per employee for an *employee achievement award.*[95] An employee achievement award is defined as an item of tangible personal property (e.g., a television or watch, not cash or a gift certificate) transferred to the employee for length of service or for safety achievement. To help ensure that such awards are not merely disguised compensation, the award must be transferred as part of a meaningful presentation. When the employer has a qualified plan in effect—a nondiscriminatory written plan where the average annual award to all employees does not exceed $400—a deduction of up to $1,600 for a particular award is allowed.

TRAVEL AND ENTERTAINMENT RECORDKEEPING REQUIREMENTS

Travel and entertainment expenses (including business gifts) are not deductible unless the taxpayer properly substantiates the expenses.[96] The *Cohan* rule permitting a deduction for an unsupported but reasonable estimation of an expense does not apply in regard to travel and entertainment.[97]

---

[95] § 274(j).

[96] § 274(d).

[97] Reg. § 1.274-5(a)(3).

Section 274(d) specifically requires the taxpayer to substantiate each of the following five elements of an expenditure:

1. Amount
2. Time
3. Place
4. Business purpose
5. Business relationship (for entertainment only)

In most cases, each item must be supported by adequate records such as a diary, account book, or similar record, *and* documentary evidence including receipts or paid bills. Where adequate records have not been maintained, the taxpayer's personal statement will suffice—but only if there is other corroborating evidence, such as the testimony of the individual who was entertained.[98] Congress has indicated that oral evidence would have the least probative value of any evidence and has also authorized the IRS to ask certain additional questions concerning substantiation on the return (see Part II, lines 19–21 of Form 2106, discussed below). In addition, the legislative history makes it clear that the IRS and the courts will invoke the negligence and fraud penalties in those cases where the taxpayer claims tax benefits far in excess of what can be justified.

A receipt is necessary only for lodging expenses and any other expenses of $25 or more. Cancelled checks, without other evidence, may not be sufficient. In the well-known blizzard case of 1975, the importance of properly substantiating each element of the expense was made clear.[99] In this case, the taxpayer did not keep a diary or other record of his substantial travel and entertainment expenses, but he presented the District Court with over 1,700 bills, chits, and memos, as well as 20 witnesses. The District Court allowed the deduction holding that the virtual "blizzard" of bills, etc., met the required tests. The Appellate Court, however, disagreed, indicating that the District Court did not determine whether the elements of each expense were substantiated. Lacking sufficient information on the specific purpose of each expenditure, deductions were denied. A written statement of the purpose is unnecessary, however, where the business purpose or business relationship is obvious from other surrounding facts.

In lieu of substantiating expenses of meals while away from home on business, taxpayers may elect to compute the deduction using a standard daily allowance rate. The standard meal rate is usually $26 per day and is not reduced by the 80 percent limit on meals.[100]

---

[98] Reg. § 1.274-5(c)(3).

[99] *Cam F. Dowell, Jr. v. U.S.,* 75-2 USTC ¶9819, 36 AFTR2d 75-6314, 522 F.2d 708 (CA-5, 1975), *vac'g.* and *rem'g.* 74-

1 USTC ¶9243, 33 AFTR2d 74-739, 370 F. Supp. 69 (D.Ct. TX., 1974).

[100] "Travel, Entertainment and Gift Expenses," IRS Publication 463 (1989), p. 2.

REPORTING BUSINESS EXPENSES AND LOSSES

SOLE PROPRIETORS AND SELF-EMPLOYED PERSONS

Sole proprietors and self-employed persons are not treated as separate taxable entities. Rather, their income and expenses are compiled and reported simply as a part of their individual return. This information is reported on Schedule C of Form 1040. Page 1 of Schedule C appears on the following page. An examination of Schedule C reveals that it is relatively straightforward and self-explanatory. The net income or loss as reported on line 31 of Schedule C is transferred to Page 1 of Form 1040 and is added to the taxpayer's income. The net income or loss on Schedule C also is used in the computation of self-employment tax. Accordingly, the net amount on Schedule C must also be transferred to Schedule SE.

EMPLOYEES

Both the treatment and reporting of an employee's business expenses vary significantly depending on whether the expenses are reimbursed. As explained in Chapter 7, employee business expenses that are *not* reimbursed are treated as miscellaneous itemized deductions, and are therefore deductible only to the extent that total miscellaneous itemized deductions exceed 2 percent of A.G.I. In addition, such deductions would be subject to the 3 percent cutback. On the other hand, reimbursed expenses are usually fully deductible for A.G.I. This latter treatment normally applies to most employee expense accounts, including those arrangements where the employer reimburses an employee for a particular expense as well as those where the employer gives the employee a fixed allowance (e.g., a per diem amount such as $15 per day for meals and $25 per day for lodging). It should be emphasized, however, that even though an expense may appear to be reimbursed in the normal sense, it may not be treated as reimbursed for determining whether it is deductible for or from A.G.I.

Accountable and Nonaccountable Plans. Beginning in 1989, an employee's business expenses are treated as reimbursed only if his or her employer has a reimbursement or allowance arrangement that qualifies as an *accountable plan*. An arrangement generally qualifies as an accountable plan if the employee properly substantiates the expenses to the employer, and, in the case of advances or allowances, is required to return to the employer any amount in excess of that which is substantiated.[101] If the arrangement does not meet the accountable plan requirements, it is considered a *nonaccountable plan*. As might be expected, the tax treatment of payments under the two different plans differs drastically.

---

[101] Temp. Reg. 1.62-2T.

SCHEDULE C (Form 1040)	**Profit or Loss From Business**	OMB No. 1545-0074

SCHEDULE C (Form 1040)

Department of the Treasury
Internal Revenue Service

Profit or Loss From Business
(Sole Proprietorship)
Partnerships, Joint Ventures, Etc., Must File Form 1065.
▶ Attach to Form 1040 or Form 1041.   ▶ See Instructions for Schedule C (Form 1040).

OMB No. 1545-0074
19**90**

Attachment
Sequence No. **09**

Name of proprietor | Social security number (SSN)

A Principal business or profession, including product or service (see Instructions) | **B** Enter principal business code (from page 2) ▶

C Business name and address ▶ .... (include suite or room no.) | **D** Employer ID number (Not SSN)

E Accounting method: **(1)** ☐ Cash **(2)** ☐ Accrual **(3)** ☐ Other (specify) ▶ ....

F Method(s) used to value closing inventory: **(1)** ☐ Cost **(2)** ☐ Lower of cost or market **(3)** ☐ Other (attach explanation) **(4)** ☐ Does not apply (if checked, go to line H)

		Yes	No
G	Was there any change in determining quantities, costs, or valuations between opening and closing inventory? (If "Yes," attach explanation.)		
H	Are you deducting expenses for business use of your home? (If "Yes," see Instructions for limitations.)		
I	Did you "materially participate" in the operation of this business during 1990? (If "No," see Instructions for limitations on losses.) . . .		
J	If this is the first Schedule C filed for this business, check here . . . . ▶ ☐		

Part I Income

1	Gross receipts or sales. *Caution: If this income was reported to you on Form W-2 and the "Statutory employee" box on that form was checked, see the Instructions and check here* . . . . ▶ ☐	**1**	
2	Returns and allowances	**2**	
3	Subtract line 2 from line 1. Enter the result here	**3**	
4	Cost of goods sold (from line 38 on page 2)	**4**	
5	Subtract line 4 from line 3 and enter the **gross profit** here	**5**	
6	Other income, including Federal and state gasoline or fuel tax credit or refund (see Instructions)	**6**	
7	Add lines 5 and 6. This is your **gross income** . . . . ▶	**7**	

Part II Expenses

8	Advertising	**8**		**21** Repairs and maintenance . . .	**21**	
9	Bad debts from sales or services (see Instructions)	**9**		**22** Supplies (not included in Part III) .	**22**	
				23 Taxes and licenses	**23**	
10	Car and truck expenses (attach **Form 4562**) .	**10**		**24** Travel, meals, and entertainment:		
11	Commissions and fees	**11**		**a** Travel	**24a**	
12	Depletion	**12**		**b** Meals and entertainment .		
13	Depreciation and section 179 expense deduction (not included in Part III) (see Instructions). .	**13**		**c** Enter 20% of line 24b subject to limitations (see Instructions) .		
14	Employee benefit programs (other than on line 19)	**14**		**d** Subtract line 24c from line 24b	**24d**	
15	Insurance (other than health) . .	**15**		**25** Utilities	**25**	
16	Interest:			**26** Wages (less jobs credit)	**26**	
	a Mortgage (paid to banks, etc.).	**16a**		**27a** Other expenses (**list type and amount**):		
	b Other	**16b**		....		
17	Legal and professional services .	**17**		....		
18	Office expense.	**18**		....		
19	Pension and profit-sharing plans .	**19**		....		
20	Rent or lease (see Instructions):			....		
	a Vehicles, machinery, and equip. .	**20a**				
	b Other business property. . . .	**20b**		**27b** Total other expenses	**27b**	

28	Add amounts in columns for lines 8 through 27b. These are your **total expenses** . . . . ▶	**28**	
29	**Net profit or (loss).** Subtract line 28 from line 7. If a profit, enter here and on Form 1040, line 12. Also enter the net profit on Schedule SE, line 2 (statutory employees, see Instructions). If a loss, you MUST go on to line 30 (fiduciaries, see Instructions)	**29**	

30 If you have a loss, you MUST check the box that describes your investment in this activity (see Instructions). . .
} **30a** ☐ All investment is at risk.
} **30b** ☐ Some investment is not at risk.

If you checked 30a, enter the loss on Form 1040, line 12, and Schedule SE, line 2 (statutory employees, see Instructions). If you checked 30b, you MUST attach **Form 6198**.

For Paperwork Reduction Act Notice, see Form 1040 Instructions.   Schedule C (Form 1040) 1990

Reimbursements or advances made under an accountable plan are treated far more favorably than those under a nonaccountable plan. Amounts paid under an accountable plan are normally excluded from gross income, not reported on the employee's Form W-2, and are exempt from employment taxes (i.e., social security and unemployment). In contrast, reimbursements and advances made under a nonaccountable plan must be reported in the employee's gross income, included on Form W-2, and are subject to employment taxes. More importantly, the expenses for which the employee is reimbursed under a nonaccountable plan are *not* deductible for A.G.I. but must be claimed as miscellaneous itemized deductions subject to the 2 percent floor. Under either plan, the employee normally summarizes employee business expenses on Form 2106 (shown on pp. 8-46 and 8-47). When this form is properly completed, expenses not considered reimbursed flow to Schedule A and are deducted as miscellaneous itemized deductions. The reporting of employee business expenses is summarized in Exhibit 8-1 (shown on pp. 8-44 and 8-45).

Under an accountable plan, an employee who substantiates his or her expenses and returns any excess reimbursement reports neither the reimbursements nor the expenses because there is a complete wash. (See Exhibit 8-1, Item 1). *However,* if the employee fails to return any excess reimbursement, a different accounting is required. In this case, the excess reimbursement is treated *as if* paid under a nonaccountable plan. Therefore, the employer must report the excess in the employee's Form W-2 as well as pay the related employment taxes. On the other side, the employee can deduct only the substantiated expenses for A.G.I. and any remainder as a miscellaneous itemized deduction. (See Exhibit 8-1, Item 3.)

Example 42. R is a salesman for C Corporation and has an expense account arrangement. Under this arrangement, R fills out an expense report every two weeks, documenting all of his expenses, and submits it for reimbursement. This year R submitted travel expenses of $5,000, all of which were reimbursed. Assuming this is an accountable plan and R has properly substantiated expenses of $5,000, there is nothing included on his Form W-2 and none of the expenses are reported on his return. In effect, there is no effect on R because the reimbursement and expenses wash. (See Exhibit 8-1, Item 1.)

Example 43. Assume the plan in *Example 42* was not properly structured and did not require R either to substantiate his expenses or to return any excess reimbursement. In this case, the arrangement would be a nonaccountable plan. Consequently, the $5,000 reimbursement would be included as income in R's Form W-2 and he could deduct the $5,000 as a miscellaneous itemized deduction. In this case, the income and deduction do not necessarily wash (e.g., if R does not itemize), and R ends up with taxable income that economically he does not have. (See Exhibit 8-1, Item 4. The Form 2106 shown on pp. 8-46 and 8-47 reveals how this information would be reported.)

Exhibit 8-1
*Reporting Travel, Transportation, Meal, and
Entertainment Expenses and Reimbursements*

Type *of Reimbursement or Other Expense Allowance Arrangement*	**Employer** *Reports on Form W-2*
1. **Accountable** *Adequate accounting and excess returned*	*Not reported*
2. *Per diem or mileage allowance (up to government rate)* *Adequate accounting and excess returned*	*Not reported*
3. *Per diem or mileage allowance (exceeds government rate)* *Adequate accounting up to the government rate only and excess not returned*	*Excess reported as income.[3] Amount up to the government rate is reported only in Box 16—it is not reported in Box 10 or in Box 13*
4. **Nonaccountable** *Adequate accounting or return of excess either not required or required but not met*	*Entire amount is reported as wages in Box 10 but not in Box 13[3]*
5. *No reimbursement*	*Normal reporting of wages, etc.*

Notes:

[1]Any allowable expense is carried to line 20 of Schedule A and deducted as a miscellaneous itemized deduction.

[2]These amounts are subject to the applicable limits including the 80% limit on meals and entertainment expenses and the 2% of adjusted gross income limit on the total miscellaneous itemized deductions.

[3]Beginning in 1990, these amounts will be subject to income tax withholding and to all employment taxes such as FICA and FUTA.

Source: "Travel, Entertainment and Gift Expenses," IRS Publication 463 (1989) p. 12.

Employee *Shows on Form 2106*	**Employee** *Claims on Schedule A*
Not shown	*Not claimed*
All expenses and reimbursements only if excess expenses are claimed.[1] *Otherwise, form is not filed*	*Expenses the employee can prove and which exceed the reimbursements received*[2]
All expenses, and reimbursements equal to the government rate, only if expenses in excess of the government rate are claimed.[1] *Otherwise, form is not filed*	*Expenses the employee can prove and which exceed the government rate*[2]
All expenses[1]	*Expenses the employee can prove*[2]
All expenses[1]	*Expenses the employee can prove*[2]

Form **2106**	**Employee Business Expenses**	OMB No. 1545-0139
Department of the Treasury Internal Revenue Service	▶ See separate Instructions. ▶ Attach to Form 1040.	19**90** Attachment Sequence No. **54**

Your name R	Social security number	Occupation in which expenses were incurred

Part I   **Employee Business Expenses and Reimbursements**

STEP 1   Enter Your Expenses

		Column A Other Than Meals and Entertainment		Column B Meals and Entertainment
1	Vehicle expense from line 22 or line 29	1		
2	Parking fees, tolls, and local transportation, including train, bus, etc. . .	2		
3	Travel expense while away from home overnight, including lodging, airplane, car rental, etc. **Do not** include meals and entertainment . . .	3	*5,000*	
4	Business expenses not included on lines 1 through 3. **Do not** include meals and entertainment	4		
5	Meals and entertainment expenses. (See the separate Instructions.) . .	5		
6	Add lines 1 through 5 and enter the **total expenses** here	6	*5,000*	

Note: *If you were not reimbursed for any expenses in Step 1, skip line 7 and enter the amount from line 6 on line 8.*

STEP 2   Enter Amounts Your Employer Gave You For Expenses Listed In STEP 1

7	Enter amounts your employer gave you that were **not** reported to you in Box 10 of Form W-2. Include any amount reported under code "L" in Box 17 of your Form W-2. (See Instructions.)	7	*—0—*

STEP 3   Figure Expenses To Deduct on Schedule A (Form 1040)

8	Subtract line 7 from line 6	8	*5,000*	
	Note: *If both columns of line 8 are zero, stop here. If column A is less than zero, report the amount as income and enter -0- on line 10, column A. See the separate Instructions for how to report.*			
9	Enter 20% (.20) of line 8, Column B	9		
10	Subtract line 9 from line 8	10	*5,000*	
11	Add the amounts on line 10 of both columns and enter the total here. **Also enter the total on Schedule A (Form 1040), line 20.** (Qualified performing artists and individuals with disabilities, see the separate Instructions for special rules on where to enter the total.) . . . . ▶	11	*5,000*	

For Paperwork Reduction Act Notice, see the separate Instructions.   Form **2106** (1990)

Form 2106 (1990)

Part II Vehicle Expenses (See Instructions to find out which sections to complete.)

Section A.—General Information

			(a) Vehicle 1	(b) Vehicle 2
12	Enter the date vehicle was placed in service	12	/ /	/ /
13	Total mileage vehicle was used during 1990	13	miles	miles
14	Miles included on line 13 that vehicle was used for business . .	14	miles	miles
15	Percent of business use (divide line 14 by line 13)	15	%	%
16	Average daily round trip commuting distance	16	miles	miles
17	Miles included on line 13 that vehicle was used for commuting .	17	miles	miles
18	Other personal mileage (add lines 14 and 17 and subtract the total from line 13).	18	miles	miles

19 Do you (or your spouse) have another vehicle available for personal purposes? . . . . ☐ Yes ☐ No

20 If your employer provided you with a vehicle, is personal use during off duty hours permitted? . . ☐ Yes ☐ No ☐ Not applicable

21a Do you have evidence to support your deduction? ☐ Yes ☐ No. 21b If "Yes," is the evidence written? ☐ Yes ☐ No

Section B.—Standard Mileage Rate (Use this section only if you own the vehicle.)

22	Multiply line 14 by 26¢ (.26). Enter the result here and on line 1. (Rural mail carriers, see the separate Instructions.).	22

Section C.—Actual Expenses

			(a) Vehicle 1		(b) Vehicle 2	
23	Gasoline, oil, repairs, vehicle insurance, etc..	23				
24a	Vehicle rentals.	24a				
b	Inclusion amount	24b				
c	Subtract line 24b from line 24a	24c				
25	Value of employer-provided vehicle (applies only if 100% annual lease value was included on Form W-2. See Instructions.) .	25				
26	Add lines 23, 24c, and 25 . . .	26				
27	Multiply line 26 by the percentage on line 15	27				
28	Enter amount from line 38 below .	28				
29	Add lines 27 and 28. Enter total here and on line 1.	29				

Section D.—Depreciation of Vehicles (Use this section only if you own the vehicle.)

			(a) Vehicle 1		(b) Vehicle 2	
30	Enter cost or other basis. (See Instructions.)	30				
31	Enter amount of Section 179 deduction. (See Instructions.) .	31				
32	Multiply line 30 by line 15. (See Instructions if you elected the Section 179 deduction.) . . .	32				
33	Enter depreciation method and percentage. (See Instructions.) .	33				
34	Multiply line 32 by the percentage on line 33. (See Instructions.) . .	34				
35	Add lines 31 and 34	35				
36	Enter the limitation amount from the table in the line 36 instructions.	36				
37	Multiply line 36 by the percentage on line 15.	37				
38	Enter the **smaller** of line 35 or line 37. Also enter it on line 28 above.	38				

As the above examples illustrate, most employers should opt to establish reimbursement arrangements that meet the accountable plan requirements so that employees are not unduly penalized. Nevertheless, as noted above, even if the employer has an accountable plan, the employee must still substantiate any expenses and return any reimbursements in excess of the expenses substantiated to avoid unfavorable treatment.

Substantiation. A plan generally satisfies the substantiation requirement if the employee meets the normal rules for substantiation of expenses. For example, travel and entertainment expenses must be substantiated under the special rules of § 274(d) discussed earlier in this chapter. Note that an employee whose reimbursement is based on some type of fixed allowance (e.g., a per diem for meals and lodging or a mileage allowance) is *deemed* to have substantiated the amount of his or her expenses up to the amount set by the IRS for per diem, mileage, or other expense allowances.[102] Generally, the only expense substantiation for such plans is the number of business miles traveled and the number of days away from home spent on business. Due to this rule, employees who receive allowances within the IRS guidelines will have no reimbursements in excess of their substantiated expenses and, therefore, will not have any excess to return.

> **Example 44.** K works as an accountant for a public accounting firm in Tampa. This year she attended a continuing education course in Jacksonville. The firm gives its employees a meal allowance of $12 per diem, which is within the IRS guidelines. K attended the course for five days. When she returned from the trip, she submitted her expense report requesting reimbursement for meals of $60 (5 × $12). In reality, K, wanting to save as much as she could, spent only $40 on meals. Although K has actually received $20 more than she spent ($60 − $40), she does not have to return the excess because she is deemed to have substantiated expenses of $60.

If the employee has expenses that the employer did not reimburse, the employee should file Form 2106 to claim a deduction for the unreimbursed expenses. Proper completion of this form results in the unreimbursed expenses being claimed as miscellaneous itemized deductions on Schedule A. (See Exhibit 8-1, Item 2.)

> **Example 45.** Under an accountable plan, T is reimbursed 26 cents per mile for all business miles driven. For the year, he received $1,000. After consulting his records, T determined that his actual expenses exceed 26 cents per mile for a total of $1,200. None of the reimbursement is included on T's Form W-2 because this is an accountable plan and the allowance does

---

[102]   See Regs. §§ 1.62-2T(e)(2) and 1.274-5T(g).

not exceed the government rate. T should report the $1,200 of expenses on lines 1–6 of Form 2106. The $1,000 reimbursement is entered on line 7 and subtracted from the $1,200 expense amount to leave $200. The $200 (the amount for which T did not receive a reimbursement) flows through to Schedule A and is treated as a miscellaneous itemized deduction. (See line 11 of Form 2106 and Exhibit 8-1, Item 2.)

Example 46.   J's employer pays her a flat $100 per month to cover her car expenses. The employer does not have an accountable plan. Thus the employer must include the $100 as income in J's Form W-2, and J may deduct her car expenses as miscellaneous itemized deductions. (See Exhibit 8-1, Item 4.)

In certain instances, the employer may give the employee a per diem allowance that exceeds the Federal government allowable rate (e.g., 30 cents per mile instead of the allowable 26 cents per mile). In such cases, special reporting rules apply.[103]

Partial reimbursements.   Occasionally, the reimbursement received by an employee does not cover all of his or her deductible business expenses. This often occurs when the taxpayer is on a per diem allowance. Because of the 80 percent limitation imposed on meal and entertainment expenses, when there is only a partial reimbursement the employee must determine the particular expenses that were reimbursed. As noted above, the employee is able to deduct 100 percent of any reimbursed meal or entertainment expense. In contrast, either of these which is not reimbursed must be reduced by 20 percent and then may be deducted along with other miscellaneous itemized deductions subject to the 2 percent floor. The portion of the meals and entertainment expenses deemed reimbursed is determined in a manner similar to that under prior law, as follows:[104]

$$\frac{\text{Entertainment and meal expenses (before 80\% limit)}}{\text{Total reimbursable expenses}} \times \text{Reimbursement}$$

For this purpose, total reimbursable expenses represent those expenses which the reimbursement was intended to cover.

---

[103]   *Supra,* Footnote 100, p. 11.   [104]   Reg. § 1.62-1(f).

Example 47.   H, a salesman for XYZ corporation, paid the following expenses for which he was reimbursed $700:

Meals...	$ 600
Lodging...	400
Total expenses....................................	$1,000

After allocating the reimbursement, R may deduct $420 [$700 × ($600 ÷ $1,000)] of the meals and $280 [$700 × ($400 ÷ $1,000)] of the lodging for A.G.I. Of the remaining $180 ($600 − $420) of meal expenses, $36 is not deductible under the 20% disallowance rule for meal expenses, and $144 is a miscellaneous itemized deduction subject to the 2% floor. The remaining $120 ($400 − $280) of lodging expenses is also a miscellaneous itemized deduction.

TAX PLANNING CONSIDERATIONS

MOVING EXPENSES

Upon retirement, many individuals move to another location. Normally, the moving expenses would not be deductible. If the taxpayer can obtain a job at the new location, however, the costs of moving become deductible. In this regard, the taxpayer must be sure to satisfy the 39- or 78-week test.

TRAVEL AND ENTERTAINMENT EXPENSES

The rules governing deductions for combined business and pleasure travel permit some vacationing on business trips without jeopardizing the deduction. As long as the trip is primarily for business, the entire cost of traveling to the business/vacation destination is deductible. Although the expenses of personal side-trips are not allowed, these expenses may be incidental to the major costs of getting to the desired location. For example, a taxpayer living in New York can deduct a major portion of the cost of a vacation in Florida—the cost of getting there—by properly scheduling business in Miami. In those situations where vacation time exceeds time spent on business, the taxpayer must be prepared to establish that the trip would not have been taken *but for* the business need.

When traveling, the taxpayer may also be able to deduct the expenses of a spouse if a business purpose for the spouse's presence can be established. Even where a spouse's travel expenses are clearly not deductible, only the *incremental* expense attributable to the spouse's presence is not allowed. When an automobile is used for transportation, there is no incremental expense. In the case of lodging, the single room rate would be fully deductible and only the few extra dollars added for a double room rate would not be deductible.

The importance of adequate records for travel and entertainment expenses cannot be over-emphasized. However, the *actual cost* of travel expenses need not be proved when a per diem or a fixed mileage allowance arrangement exists between the employee and the employer. In these situations, the other elements of the expense—time, place, and business purpose—must still be substantiated by the employer and employee. Moreover, the taxpayer must substantiate the cost of travel where the employee is "related" to the employer (an employee is considered related when he or she either owns more than 10 percent of a corporate employer's stock or is the employer's spouse, brother, sister, ancestor, or lineal descendant). Notwithstanding the relaxation of the substantiation requirements for travel costs, it is advisable to maintain receipts and other records to substantiate the other elements of the expenditure.

The taxpayer should get in the habit of contemporaneously recording the required elements for each expenditure. Although a bothersome task, this must be done to secure deductions for travel and entertainment expenses. *Each* element of each expenditure must be established.

With respect to vehicle expenses, the taxpayer cannot simply deduct the expenses and hope that he or she will never be asked to produce evidence supporting the deduction. Form 2106 (Part II, line 21) specifically asks whether the taxpayer has proper written evidence. Thus, failure to maintain such documentation would mean that the taxpayer could not answer this question in the affirmative, increasing the probability of audit. Of course, indicating that such evidence exists when it in fact does not could subject the taxpayer to negligence or fraud penalties.

HOME OFFICE DEDUCTION

Generally, reporting any gain realized on the sale of a residence may be postponed if the taxpayer purchases another residence with a sales price equivalent to that of the residence sold (see Chapter 15 for details). Claiming the home office deduction in the year of sale, however, results in loss of the deferral privilege for any gain on the sale of the residence attributable to the home office. Thus, before claiming the deduction, the trade-off between a current deduction and subsequent gain recognition must be considered.

> # PROBLEM MATERIALS

DISCUSSION QUESTIONS

8-1 *Requirements for Education Expenses.* J has been told that, as a practical matter, most education expenses are considered nondeductible personal expenses. Under what conditions, if any, may J deduct expenses for education?

8-2 *Education: Degrees, Promotion, and Employer Assistance.* Y is currently employed as the manager of a fast-food restaurant, earning $29,000. In order to improve her upward mobility in the company, Y decides that she should go to college and earn her degree.

   a. Can Y deduct any of the cost of obtaining her bachelor's degree in business?

   b. Same as above, except Y already has her bachelor's degree and now decides to take courses which could lead to her receiving an M.B.A.

   c. What is the effect on Y if her employer pays for her education costs this year of $6,000? Answer for both a bachelor's degree and an M.B.A.

8-3 *Expenses of Education.* F, vice president of sales for a large corporation, is in the executive M.B.A program at the University of Michigan. F lives in Chicago and travels to Ann Arbor and Detroit to take certain courses.

   a. F's employer reimburses F for the tuition, which is $8,000 per year. Explain how F will treat the reimbursement and the expense. What if F was not reimbursed?

Indicate whether the following expenses incurred by F would be deductible:

   b. Meals and lodging when he stays overnight

   c. Transportation costs from Chicago and back

   d. Books

   e. Secretarial fees for typing term projects

   f. Copying expenses

   g. Value of vacation time used to take classes

   h. Tutor

8-4 *Qualifying Educational Expenses.* Indicate whether education expenses would be deductible in the following situations:

   a. H, a practicing tax accountant, is taking a correspondence course to become a certified financial planner.

   b. J is currently an elementary school teacher. State law requires beginning teachers to have a bachelor's degree and to complete a master's degree within five years after first being hired. This year he took two courses toward the master's degree.

   c. R is a full-time engineering student and has a part-time job as an engineer with a firm that will employ him as an engineer when he graduates.

   d. C is an airline pilot and is presently taking lessons to become a helicopter pilot.

   e. H retired from the finance department of the Army and now is getting his M.B.A. He plans to get a job with a financial institution.

8-5 *Moving Expenses.*   Address the following:

a.   What two tests must be satisfied before moving expenses may be deducted?

b.   Explain the differences between direct and indirect moving expenses, and why the distinction is important.

c.   Are moving expenses deductible *for* or *from* adjusted gross income?

8-6 *Moving Expenses: Real Estate Commissions.*   B's employer transferred him during the year. As a result, B sold his home in North Dakota and moved to New York, where he lives in an apartment. He does not plan to move into a new home. B's real estate commissions were $6,000. B has asked how he should treat the real estate commissions. Give him some advice regarding his options, and describe the factors that should be considered in making a choice.

8-7 *Home Office Expenses.*   The enactment of the restrictive rules related to home office deductions caused many commentators to conclude that the home office deduction had been essentially eliminated and that the tax advantages of vacation homes had been severely curtailed. Which particular requirement(s) of § 280A prompted such a conclusion?

8-8 *Computing Car Expenses.*   Briefly answer the following:

a.   With respect to a business car, can the taxpayer claim depreciation in addition to the expense determined using the standard mileage rate?

b.   Can a taxpayer switch to the automatic mileage method after using MACRS to compute depreciation? If so, when does the car become fully depreciated?

8-9 *Transportation vs. Travel.*   Explain the distinction between transportation expenses and travel expenses.

8-10 *U.S. Travel vs. Foreign Travel.*   Compare and contrast the rules governing travel in the United States to those rules governing travel outside of the United States.

8-11 *Limitations on Entertainment and Meals.*   T is employed by KL Publishing Corporation. He is a sales representative with responsibility for college textbook sales in Georgia, Florida, and Alabama. T lives in Atlanta. For each of the following situations, indicate whether T's or the corporation's deduction for entertainment or meals would be limited, and if so, how?

a.   T flew to Birmingham on a Tuesday night. After checking in at the hotel, he caught a cab to his favorite restaurant where he ate by himself. The cost of the meal was $20, including a $1 tax and a $3 tip. The cost of the cab ride was $10. The next day he called on a customer.

b.   Same as (a), except that T's employer reimbursed him under an accountable plan for all of his costs.

c.   Same as (a), but further assume that T's A.G.I. for the year was $30,000 and that he has other miscellaneous itemized deductions of $700.

d.   At the year-end Christmas party for employees, the corporation gave T a 10-pound, honey-baked ham, costing $40. The cost of the party (excluding the ham), which was held at a local restaurant, was $300.

e.   During the annual convention of college marketing professors in New Orleans, the corporation rented a room in the convention hotel for one night and provided hors d'oeuvres. The room cost $200 while the food and drink cost $1,000.

8-12 *Reimbursed Expenses.* Explain the reporting requirements relating to expenses that are reimbursed.

8-13 *Entertainment Expenses.* Distinguish between entertainment expenses that are considered "directly related to" the taxpayer's business and those that are "associated with" the taxpayer's business.

8-14 *Business Meals.* Can the taxpayer deduct the costs of his or her own meal when he or she pays for the lunch of a customer and no business is discussed?

8-15 *Entertainment Facilities.* Under what circumstances are expenses related to an entertainment facility deductible?

8-16 *Substantiation of Travel and Entertainment Expenses.* What information must the taxpayer be prepared to present upon the audit of his or her travel and entertainment expenditures? Does the taxpayer need to maintain records if he or she has a per diem arrangement with the employer?

8-17 *Foreign Convention.* Dr. B recently learned that a world famous plastic surgeon will be making a presentation concerning her area of expertise at a convention of physicians in Switzerland. If B attends, can she deduct the costs of airfare, meals, lodging, and registration? Explain.

8-18 *Cruise Ship Seminars.* The American Organization of Dental Specialists is offering a seven-day seminar on gum disease aboard a cruise ship. Dr. D, a dentist, would like to attend. If D attends, can he deduct his expenses?

8-19 *Reporting Reimbursements.* R is regional sales manager for a large steel manufacturing corporation. His job requires him to travel extensively to call on customers and salespeople. As a result, he incurs substantial expenses for airfare, hotel, meals, and entertainment, for which he is reimbursed. Under what conditions may R simply ignore reporting the reimbursements and the expenses for tax purposes?

8-20 *Reporting Employee Business Expenses.* T is a salesperson for Classy Cosmetics Inc. During the year, she incurred various business expenses for which she was reimbursed under an accountable plan. Indicate how T must report the reimbursements and expenses in the following situations, assuming an adequate accounting was made.

   a. T was on a per diem of $25 per day for lodging and $15 per day for meals. She received $2,000 under the per diem arrangement for expenses totaling $2,200.
   b. T was reimbursed $3,800 for expenses totaling $3,000.

8-21 *Per Diem Arrangement.* Al was recently hired by a public accounting firm as a staff accountant. When Al is out of town on business (e.g., staff training or an audit at a client's place of business), the firm gives him $12 a day for dinner. Al normally spends $5 and banks the rest. What are the tax consequences?

8-22 *Substantiation Requirements.* Indicate whether the following is required in order to properly substantiate a deduction:

   a. Purpose of an entertainment expenditure
   b. Date of entertainment expenditure
   c. Receipt for business meal with client, which cost $15
   d. Receipt for lodging at Motel Cheap, which cost $12

e.   Description of what the taxpayer wore on the day he lunched with client

f.   Diary detailing information normally required for substantiation of entertainment expenses

g.   Cancelled check for $12 for tickets to baseball game that was attended with customer

h.   Social security number of client entertained

PROBLEMS

8-23   *Education Expenses.*   Indicate the amount, if any, of deductible education expenses in each of the following cases. Comment briefly on your answer and state whether the deduction is deductible *for* or *from* adjusted gross income:

a.   C is employed as a plumber, but is training to become a computer programmer. During the year, he paid $500 for tuition and books related to a college course in programming.

b.   E is a licensed nurse. During the year, she spent $300 on courses to become a registered nurse.

c.   R paid a $75 fee to take the C.P.A. exam and $800 for a C.P.A. review course. R currently is employed by a public accounting firm.

d.   R is an IRS agent. This year, he began taking courses toward a law degree emphasizing tax. Tuition and books cost $1,000.

e.   H is a high school instructor teaching European history. On a one-year sabbatical leave from school, he traveled to Europe, taking slides which he planned on using in his classes. The trip cost $7,000, including $1,000 for meals.

8-24   *Moving Expenses.*   In May of the current year, M found a new job, forcing him to move from Tulsa to Seattle. On June 1, the moving company picked up all of M's possessions. M and his family stayed in a hotel on June 1, left the morning of June 2, and arrived in Seattle on June 4. They incurred the following expenses.

1.   Air fare and meals for him and his wife while traveling to Seattle to look for a new house, $260 and $50 respectively. They failed to find a home. Consequently, they moved into an apartment, from which they continued their search.

2.   Lodging in Tulsa on the day they moved out of their house, $70.

3.   Expenses on the way to Seattle included meals, $80; and lodging, $100.

4.   Mileage to Seattle, 2,000 miles.

5.   Car repair on trip to Seattle, $175.

6.   Moving van, $4,000.

7.   Storage charges for furniture that would not fit in the apartment: $3 per day for the period June 5–July 31.

8.   Temporary living expenses for period June 5–July 31: apartment, $10 per day; meals, $20 per day; and cleaning and laundry, $25.

9.   Realtor's commission on sale of old home, $1,000.

a.   Compute M's moving expense deduction (Form 3903 may be helpful).

b.   How would you treat the real estate commission had it been $8,000 rather than $1,000?

8-25 *Home Office.* In each of the following independent situations, indicate whether the taxpayer is entitled to deduct expenses related to the home office:

a. C, a dermatologist employed by a hospital, also owns several rental properties. He regularly uses a bedroom in his home solely as an office for bookkeeping and other activities related to management of the rental properties.

b. R, an attorney employed by a large law firm, frequently brings work home from the office. She uses a study in her home for doing this work as well as paying bills, sorting coupons and conducting other personal activities.

c. M is a research associate employed by the Cancer Research Institute. His duties include designing and carrying out experiments, reviewing data, and writing articles and grant proposals. His employer furnishes M a laboratory but due to insufficient space cannot provide an office for him. Thus, for about three hours each day, M uses a portion of his bedroom (where he and his wife sleep) to do the writing, reviewing, and other related activities.

d. T is a self-employed tax consultant. He has an office downtown and a home office. He occasionally meets with his clients in the home office since it is often more convenient for the clients to meet there.

e. S, an artist, converted a detached garage to a studio for painting. She sells her paintings at her own gallery located in town.

8-26 *Home Office.* R is considering purchasing a home priced somewhat over her budget. Her brother has suggested that converting a room to a home office would enable her to deduct a substantial part of the costs related to the home, thus making the purchase feasible. R is a sales manager for X Corporation, which transfers its middle management employees frequently. Comment on the following advice given to R by her brother:

a. Establishing a home office is an effective method for reducing the costs of home ownership by the amount of the tax benefits received.

b. There are no disincentives for claiming the home office deduction.

8-27 *Home Office Computations.* T is employed as a law professor at State University. Outside of her university work she teaches continuing education courses for attorneys and occasionally provides legal services. T does all her work for these outside pursuits in her home office. Income and expenses relating to these were

Income:	
Fees for services...............................	$2,000
Expenses:	
Depreciation on home office furniture and	
computer.......................................	400
Miscellaneous supplies, books, etc................	500
Expenses attributable to home office:	
Depreciation, insurance, and utilities..............	1,200
Taxes...	300
Interest...	700

Determine the tax consequences resulting from T's part-time activities.

8-28 *Deductible Moving Expenses.*   Indicate whether the following expenses qualify as deductible moving expenses:

a. Costs of meals and lodging while en route to new location.

b. Insurance on household and personal effects being transported—an option provided by the moving company.

c. Costs of driving the family car to new location.

d. Costs of storing items that would not fit in apartment at the new location; the apartment served as a temporary residence until a home was purchased.

e. Costs of new carpeting and wallpaper to prepare old home to be sold.

f. Real estate commission on sale of former residence.

g. Loss on sale of residence.

h. Payment of six months' rent to settle lease obligation at old location; the lease had six more months to run.

i. Cost of appraisal of new home required as part of loan application.

8-29 *Moving Expenses: Time Test.*   On September 1, 1991, L left her former employment in Indianapolis to seek her fortune in Cincinnati. Indicate whether L could deduct the cost of her moving expenses to Cincinnati under the following conditions.

a. L found a teaching job for the public school system for which she worked ten months, September through June. After school was out, L took a three-month vacation. She then decided to leave Cincinnati and move to Atlanta.

b. Same as (a) except L found a job as a substitute teacher and was considered self-employed.

c. L moved to take a new position as product manager with P&G Corporation. After working three months, she and her new employer had a falling out over what she considered unethical advertising. She quit her job and moved to New York.

8-30 *Moving Expenses: Distance Test.*   P is an accountant for L Corporation. This year, his employer moved from its downtown Manhattan location to a new office in New Jersey. As a result, P decided to move to be closer to the office.

a. Assuming P did not change jobs, is he allowed to deduct any moving expenses?

b. Regardless of your answer to (a), indicate whether P satisfies the distance test in light of the following information:
   —Old office building to new building: 60 miles
   —Old home to new home: 45 miles
   —New home to old office: 51 miles
   —Old home to old office: 30 miles
   —New home to new office: 15 miles
   —Old home to new office: 58 miles

8-31   *Standard Mileage Rate.*   R, self-employed, elects to compute her deduction for car expenses using the standard mileage rate. Indicate whether the following expenses may be deducted in addition to expenses computed using the standard rate:

     a.   Depreciation
     b.   Interest on car loan
     c.   Insurance
     d.   Parking while calling on customers
     e.   Parking tickets incurred while on business
     f.   Major overhaul
     g.   Personal property taxes on car
     h.   Tolls

8-32   *Transportation Expenses.*   Indicate the amount, if any, deductible by the taxpayer in each of the following cases. (Ignore the floor on miscellaneous itemized deductions.)

     a.   R works in downtown Denver, but chooses to live in the mountains 90 miles away. During the year, he spent $2,700 for transportation expenses to and from work.

     b.   Q, a high school basketball coach, liked to scout his opposition. On one Friday afternoon, he left school and drove 40 miles to attend the game of the team he played next. On the way, he stopped for a meal ($5). He watched the game and returned home.

     c.   R, a carpenter, commutes to work in a truck. He drives the truck in order to carry the tools of his trade. During the year, R's total transportation costs were $5,000. R estimates that his costs of transportation without the tools would have been $4,000, since he otherwise would have taken public transportation.

     d.   G, an attorney, works downtown. She is on retainer, however, with a client who has offices two miles from her home. G often stops at the client's office before going to work. The distance between these locations is as follows: home to office, 20 miles; home to client, 2 miles; and client to office, 22 miles. During the year, G drove directly to work 180 days and via the client's office 50 days.

8-33   *Transportation to Temporary Assignments.*   For each of the following cases, indicate the number of business miles driven by the taxpayer. (Ignore the floor on miscellaneous itemized deductions.)

     a.   K is employed as a salesperson for Midwest Surgical Supply Company. The company's offices are in downtown Chicago. K's sales territory is the northwest side of Chicago and the adjacent suburbs. During Monday through Thursday, K drives directly from her residence to call on various customers. She sees each customer about once a month. On Friday of each week, she goes directly from her home to her office downtown to turn in orders, attend the weekly sales meeting, and do any other miscellaneous work. A portion of K's trip diary appears below.

| | | Odometer Reading | | |
Date	Destination	Begin	End	Mileage
3-17	Springmill Clinic	470	482	12
	Dr. J	482	485	5
	Home	485	500	15
3-18	Office	500	530	30
	Home	530	560	30

b. F, an electrician, works for EZ Electrical. He lives and works in the Los Angeles area. For 200 days of this year, he was assigned to do the wiring on a 30-story office building in downtown Los Angeles. His mileage from his home to the building was 20 miles. For 50 days during the year, he was assigned to a job in San Diego. Most of F's assignments are 20 miles closer than San Diego. F commuted 70 miles from his home to San Diego.

8-34 *Travel Expenses.*   Indicate the amount, if any, deductible by the taxpayer in each of the following situations. (Ignore the floor on miscellaneous itemized deductions.)

a. P, a steelworker, obtained a job with XYZ Corporation to work on a nuclear reactor 200 miles from his residence. P drove to the site early on Monday mornings and returned home late Friday nights. While at the job site he stayed in a boarding house. P anticipates that the job will last for eight months. During the year, he traveled 4,000 miles in going to and from the job. Other expenses while away from home included the following: meals, $1,000; lodging, $900; and laundry, $75.

b. Same as (a), except P anticipates the job to last for three years.

c. W plays professional football for the Minnesota Vikings. He has an apartment in St. Paul but he and his wife's permanent personal residence is in Tucson. During the season, W usually stays in St. Paul. In the off-season he returns to Tucson. Expenses for the year include travel between St. Paul and Tucson, $2,000; apartment in St. Paul, $1,800; meals while in St. Paul, $900.

d. R takes a trip to New York primarily for business. R's husband accompanied her. She spent two weeks on business and one week sightseeing in the city. Her train fare was $400 and meals and lodging cost $30 and $50 per day, respectively. R's husband incurred similar expenses.

e. L flew from Cincinnati to Chicago for $300 round-trip. She spent one day on business and four days shopping and sight-seeing. Her meals and lodging cost $30 and $50 per day, respectively.

8-35 *Car Expense Computation.*   E, a salesperson for T Corporation, incurred the following expenses for transportation during the year:

Gas and oil	$ 900
Repairs	200
Insurance	300
Interest on car loan	400
Depreciation	2,000
License	100

In addition, he spent $70 on parking while calling on customers. E drove the car 20,000 miles during the year, 18,000 for business.

a.   Compute E's deduction, assuming the standard mileage rate is elected.

b.   Compute E's deduction, assuming he claims actual expenses.

8-36 *Travel Outside of the U.S.*   S, an executive for an automotive company, traveled to Paris this year for business meetings with a European subsidiary. Prior to the trip, she thought that the meetings presented an ideal opportunity for her to vacation in Paris as well as to conduct business. For this reason, she scheduled the trip. S's air fare to Paris was $1,000 and her daily meals and lodging were $30 and $50 respectively. Given the additional facts below, indicate the amount, if any, of the deduction that S may claim.

a.   S's trip was primarily business. She spent two days on business (including travel days) and four days sightseeing.

b.   Her itinerary revealed the following:

Thusday, May 1:	Depart New York, arrive Paris
Friday, May 2:	Business 9-11 a.m.; remainder of day sightseeing in Paris
Saturday and Sunday, May 3-4:	Tour French countryside
Monday and Tuesday, May 5-6:	Business 9-5
Wednesday-Sunday, May 7-11:	Tour Germany
Monday, May 12:	Business 9-5
Tuesday, May 13:	Depart Paris, arrive New York

c.   Same as (a) except the travel was to Paris for the International Car Exposition, a foreign convention.

d.   Same as (a) except the business meetings took place on a luxury liner cruising the Caribbean.

e.   Same as (a) except S had no control over arranging the trip.

f.   Same as (a) except the trip was primarily personal.

8-37 *Entertainment Expenses.*   R is president of X Corporation, a company that manufactures and distributes office supplies. During the year, he and the company incurred various expenses relating to entertainment. In each of the following situations, indicate the amount of the deduction for entertainment expenses. Briefly explain your answer and classify the deduction as either *for* or *from* adjusted gross income. (Assume all the substantiation requirements are satisfied.)

a.   R and his wife took a potential customer and his wife to a night club to hear a popular singer. Tickets for the event cost $10 each. R was unable to discuss any business during the evening.

b.   After agreeing in the afternoon to supply S's company with typing paper, R took S to a baseball game that evening. Tickets were $8 each. X Corporation reimbursed R $16 for the tickets under an accountable plan.

c.   R and S, a client, went to lunch at an expensive restaurant. R paid the bill for both his meal, $30, and S's meal, $40. No business was discussed during lunch.

d.   X Corporation purchased a vacation condominium for use primarily by its employees. Expenses relating to the condominium, including depreciation, maintenance, utilities, interest, and taxes, were $7,000.

e.   R joined an exclusive country club this year. The membership fee, which is not refundable, was $1,000. In addition, R paid annual dues of $3,600. During the year, R used the club 100 days, 70 days for entertainment directly related to business and 30 days for personal use.

f.   R gave one of the company's best customers a $100 bottle of wine.

g.   X Corporation gave one of its retailers 1,000 golf balls ($1 each) to distribute for promotional purposes. X Corporation's name was imprinted on the balls.

8-38 *Convention and Seminar Expenses.* Dr. F, a pediatrician, is employed at a hospital located in Chicago. He also operates his own practice. During the year, he attended the following seminars and conventions. In each case, he incurred expenses for registration, travel, meals, and lodging. Indicate whether such expenses would be deductible assuming he attended.

a.   "The Care and Feeding of New Borns," a seminar in Honolulu sponsored by the American Family Medical Association.

b.   While Dr. F was attending the meeting above, his wife attended a concurrent seminar entitled "Tax Planning for Physicians and their Spouses."

c.   "The Economics of a Private Practice: Make Your Investment Count," sponsored by the American Management Corporation in Chicago.

d.   "Investing and Inside Information," sponsored by National Association of Investment Specialists in Orlando.

CUMULATIVE PROBLEM

8-39   George (445-42-5432) and Christina Campbell (993-43-9878) are married with two children, Victoria, 7, and Brad, 2. Victoria and Brad's social security numbers are 446-75-4389 and 449-63-4172, respectively. They live at 10137 Briar Creek Lane, Tulsa, OK 74105. George is the district sales representative for Red Duck, a manufacturer of sportswear. His principal job is to solicit orders of the company's products from department stores in his territory, which includes Oklahoma and Arkansas. The company provides no office for him. Christina is a maker of fine quilts which she sells in selected shops in the surrounding area. The couple uses the cash method of accounting and reports on the calendar year. Their records for the year reveal the following information:

    1. George received a salary of $35,000 and a bonus of $5,000. His employer withheld Federal income taxes of $6,000 and the proper amount of F.I.C.A. taxes.

    2. Christina's income and expenses of her quilting business, Crazy Quilts, include

Quilt sales	$7,000
Costs of goods sold	600
Telephone (long distance calls)	100

Christina makes all of the quilts at home in a separate room that is used exclusively for her work. This room represents 10 percent of the total square footage of their home. Expenses related to operating the entire home include utilities, $2,000; and insurance, $500. Depreciation attributable to the home office is $800.

    Christina computes her deduction relating to use of her car using actual expenses, which included gas and oil, $900; insurance, $300; and repairs, $100. The car is fully depreciated. Her daily diary revealed that, for the year, she had driven the car a total of 20,000 miles, including the following trips:

Trip Description	Miles
Home to sales outlets and return	10,000
Between sales outlets	2,000
Miscellaneous personal trips	8,000

    3. George incurs substantial expenses for travel and entertainment, including meals and lodging. He is not reimbursed for these expenses. This is the second year that George has used the standard mileage rate for computing his automobile expenses. During the year he drove 50,000 miles, 40,000 of these were directly related to business. Expenses for parking and tolls directly related to business were $90. Total meal and lodging costs for days that he was out of town overnight were $600 and $1,200, respectively. Entertainment expenses were $400.

4. This is George's second marriage. He has one child, Ted (age 11), from his first marriage to Hazel, who has custody of the child. He provides more than 50 percent of the child's support. The 1979 divorce agreement between George and Hazel provides that George is entitled to the exemption for Ted. George paid Hazel $4,800 during the year, $1,600 as alimony and the remainder as child support. Ted's social security number is 122-23-3221.

5. The couple's other income and expenses included the following:

Dividends (IBM stock owned separately by George)..	$ 400
Interest on redeemed Treasury bills..................	700
Interest on City of Reno bonds......................	566
Interest paid on home mortgage.....................	8,000
Real property taxes on home........................	900
Safety deposit box fee..............................	50

6. Both taxpayers elect to give to the Presidential campaign fund.

Compute the couple's tax liability for the year. If forms are used, complete Form 1040 for the year, including Schedules A, B, C, SE, and Form 2106.

RESEARCH PROBLEMS

8-40   *Travel Away from Home.*   M is a traveling salesperson who lives with his family in Cincinnati. His sales territory consists of Indiana, Illinois, and Kentucky. Most of his business, however, is in the Louisville area. For this reason, he normally travels to Louisville weekly and spends three or four days there living in a hotel. He also spends considerable time traveling throughout his territory. M completes the paperwork and other tasks incidental to his work at his home in Cincinnati. M's wife has a good job in Cincinnati and consequently M has never considered moving to Louisville. May M deduct the costs of traveling between his residence in Cincinnati and Louisville (including the costs of meals and lodging while in Louisville)?

8-41   *Business Gifts.*   R is product manager for a large pharmaceutical company. At the annual Christmas party, he handed out $50 gifts (checks from his personal account) to each of the 10 employees that work in his division under his supervision. R's group had been highly successful during the year and he felt that each person contributed to the division's profitability. He also gave his secretary $100. What amount, if any, may R deduct?

COMPUTERIZED TAX ANALYSIS

8-42 *Moving Expense Deduction.* Assume that both the 35-mile distance test and 39/78-week time test have been met, thereby enabling the taxpayer to deduct qualified moving expenses. The taxpayer is assumed to have enough itemized deductions without the moving expense deduction to justify itemizing. In other words, the taxpayer's itemized deductions without the moving expense deduction already exceed the standard deduction. The taxpayer's marginal tax rate is 28 percent. Use computer file T901 for this problem.

a. For the independent situations listed below, compute the missing values.

	(1)	(2)	(3)	(4)	(5)	(6)
Transportation expenses in moving household goods and personal effects	$ 6,000	$6,000	$6,000	$6,000	$6,000	$6,000
Travel and lodging expenses in moving	500	400	300	300	300	300
Meal expenses in moving	0	100	200	200	200	200
Pre-move house-hunting expenses	1,000	1,000	1,000	1,000	1,000	1,000
Temporary living expenses	1,850	1,550	1,250	850	850	850
Meal expenses from pre-move househunting and temp. living	0	300	600	600	600	600
Expenses related to the old or new residence	2,400	2,400	2,400	2,400	5,000	0
Reimbursement received for moving expenses	11,750	9,500	2,000	2,000	2,000	2,000
Marginal tax rate of taxpayer	28%	28%	28%	28%	28%	28%
Sum of moving expenses						
Moving expense deduction						
Tax liability increase (decrease)						

b.   What is the sum of *all* moving expenses for question (a)(1)? How does the total compare with the size of the reimbursement?

c.   Given your answer for question (b), why is there an excess of reimbursement over the moving expenses deduction?

d.   For question (a)(1), what is the effect of having the reimbursement exceed the moving expense deduction on the taxpayer's tax liability?

e.   For question (a)(2), the reimbursement is $9,500. What is the effect on the moving expense deduction and the tax liability? Why is there an increase in the tax liability?

f.   Based on the results of questions (a)(1) and (a)(2), should the taxpayers ask their employers not to reimburse them for moving expenses in excess of their moving expenses deduction? Why, or why not?

g.   For question (a)(3), the reimbursement drops to $2,000. Explain how and why this affects the tax liability.

h.   For question (a)(4), temporary living expenses decrease to $850, yet there is no change in the moving expense deduction or tax liability. Explain the tax rules that keep this decrease from affecting the results.

i.   Expenses related to the old or new residence increase to $5,000 for question (a)(5), yet there is no change in the moving expense deduction or tax liability. Explain the tax rules that keep this increase from affecting the results.

j.   For question (a)(5), assume the $5,000 item is for a broker's commission from selling the old residence. How much of the $5,000 is left to be deducted in computing the gain (loss) on the sale of the old residence?

k.   For question (a)(5), the taxpayer has the option of deducting *all* of the $5,000 in computing the gain (loss) on the sale of the old residence (thereby leaving none left to increase the moving expense deduction). Would you recommend the taxpayer take advantage of this option? Why, or why not?

l.   The expenses related to the old or new residence decline to 0 for question (a)(6). Compare the ANALYSES questions (a)(6) and (a)(5). Discuss the tax rules that cause the differences in the ANALYSIS.

LEARNING OBJECTIVES

Upon completion of this chapter, you will be able to:

- Identify the various depreciation methods and accounting conventions available under the Modified Accelerated Cost Recovery System (MACRS)

- Make recommendations concerning the selection of an appropriate depreciation method and accounting convention

- Compute a taxpayer's depreciation deduction under each of the various depreciation methods and accounting conventions

- Explain the depreciation rules for listed property

- Identify property eligible for the election to currently expense rather than depreciate its cost

- Determine the current depletion deduction for various assets

- Explain the options available in selecting the appropriate tax treatment of research and experimentation expenditures

- Recognize tax planning opportunities related to depreciation, amortization, and depletion deductions

CHAPTER OUTLINE

Chapter 9

CAPITAL RECOVERY
Depreciation, Amortization, and Depletion

The concept of capital recovery originated with the basic premise that income does not result until revenues exceed the capital expended to produce such revenues. For example, consider the situation where a taxpayer purchases an asset at a cost of $1,000 and subsequently sells it. Generally, the sale produces no income unless the asset is sold for a price exceeding $1,000. This result derives from the principle that the taxpayer first must *recover* his or her $1,000 of capital invested (basis) before he or she can be considered as having income. Here, the recovery occurs as the taxpayer offsets the basis of the asset against the amount realized on the sale. This same principle operates where an asset, instead of being sold and providing a readily identifiable benefit, provides benefits indirectly (e.g., a machine used for many years as part of a process to manufacture a product). In this case, the cost of the asset or the capital invested is *recovered* by offsetting (deducting) the asset's cost against the revenues the asset helps to produce. Thus, in the absence of a sale or other disposition of an asset, capital recovery usually occurs when the taxpayer is permitted to deduct the expenditure. Certain capital expenditures such as research and experimental costs are recovered in the year of the expenditure since the tax law allows immediate deduction. For other types of capital expenditures, the taxpayer is allowed to deduct or recover the cost over the years for which the asset provides benefits.

This chapter examines the various cost allocation methods allowed by the Code. These are depreciation, amortization, and depletion. Although each of these methods relates to a process of allocating the cost of an asset over time, different terms for the same process are used because each method relates to a different type of property. Depreciation concerns *tangible property*, amortization concerns *intangible property*, and depletion concerns *natural resources*. Tangible property means any property having physical existence (i.e., property capable of being touched such as plant, property, and equipment). Conversely, intangible property has no physical existence but exists only in connection with something else, such as the goodwill of a business, stock, patents, and copyrights. There are two types of tangible property: real property and personal property. Real property (or *realty*) is land and anything attached to the land such as buildings, curbs, streets, fences, and other improvements. Personal property is property that is not realty and is usually movable. The concept of personal property or *personalty* should be distinguished from property that a person owns and uses for his or her benefit—usually referred to as *personal-use* property.

In addition to the cost recovery methods mentioned above, this chapter discusses the tax treatment of other capital expenditures such as those for research and experimentation, and certain expenses of farmers.

DEPRECIATION AND AMORTIZATION FOR TAX PURPOSES

GENERAL RULES FOR DEPRECIATION DEDUCTIONS

The Code allows as a depreciation deduction a reasonable allowance for the exhaustion, wear and tear, and obsolescence of property that is either used in a trade or business or held for the production of income.[1] This rule makes it clear that not all capital expenditures for property are automatically eligible for depreciation. Rather, like all other expenditures, only those that satisfy the initial hurdles can be deducted.

Exhaustion, Wear and Tear, and Obsolescence.   Only property that wears out or becomes obsolete can be depreciated. As normally construed, this requirement means that depreciation is allowed only for property that has a *determinable life*.[2] Property such as land which does not wear out and which has no determinable life cannot be depreciated. Similarly, goodwill and works of art cannot be amortized or depreciated since both have an indefinite life. In contrast, intangible assets with definite lives such as covenants not to compete, patents, copyrights, and licenses that cover a fixed term can be amortized.

Business or Income-Producing Property.   Like other expenses, no deduction is allowed for depreciation unless the property is used in a trade or business or an income-producing activity. Property used for personal purposes cannot be depreciated. In many instances, however, a single asset may be used for *both* personal purposes and for profit-seeking activities. In these cases, the taxpayer is permitted to deduct depreciation on the portion of the asset used for business or production of income.

> **Example 1.**   N is a salesman who uses his car for both business and personal purposes. He purchased the car this year for $9,000. During the year, N drove the car 50,000 miles, 40,000 miles for business and 10,000 miles for personal purposes. Under these circumstances, 80% (40,000 ÷ 50,000) of the cost of the car is subject to depreciation.

---

[1]   § 167(a).   [2]   Reg. §§ 1.167(a)-2 and 1.167(a)-3.

Property held for the production of income, even though not currently producing income, may still be depreciated. For example, a duplex held out for rental which is temporarily vacant may still be depreciated for the period during which it is not rented. Similarly, if the taxpayer's trade or business is suspended temporarily, rather than indefinitely, depreciation can be continued despite the suspension of activity.

Depreciable Basis.   The basis for depreciation is the adjusted basis of the property as used for computing gain or loss on a sale or other disposition.[3] This is usually the property's cost. Where property used for personal purposes *is converted* to use in business or the production of income, the basis for depreciation purposes is the lesser of the fair market value or the adjusted basis at the time of conversion.[4] This ensures that no deduction is claimed for declines in value while the property was held for personal purposes.

> **Example 2.**   R purchased a home computer for $1,000 while attending college. He used it solely for personal purposes. After graduation, R went into the consulting business and began using the computer for business purposes. At the time he converted the computer to business use, its value was $400. R may compute depreciation using a basis of $400 (the lesser of the adjusted basis, $1,000, or its value, $400, at the time of conversion).

The basis for depreciation must be reduced by depreciation allowed or allowable.[5] Thus, where a taxpayer fails or forgets to claim a depreciation deduction to which he or she was entitled in prior years, future depreciation charges may not be increased to correct for the error. However, this failure does not prohibit the taxpayer from claiming the proper amount of depreciation in the current year.

> **Example 3.**   In 19X1, D purchased a typewriter to use in her business for $1,000. The typewriter has an estimated useful life of 10 years and no salvage value. D did not claim depreciation to which she was entitled in 19X1 because she was temporarily in a low tax bracket. In 19X2, D elects to use the double declining-balance method of depreciation. D's depreciation deduction for 19X2 is $160 [20% of $800 ($1,000 cost − $200 allowable depreciation)]. Note that in 19X2 D must reduce the depreciable basis of $1,000 by the $200 of depreciation she did not claim in 19X1, since she was entitled to it. However, D can file an amended return for 19X1 to claim the depreciation not taken in that year. This is available as long as the three-year statute of limitations has not run out for 19X1.

---

[3] § 167(g).

[4] Reg. § 1.167(g)-1.

[5] Reg. § 1.167(a)-10.

HISTORICAL PERSPECTIVE

Prior to 1981, taxpayers could compute depreciation using either of two approaches: (1) the facts-and-circumstances method or (2) the Class Life System. Depreciation methods such as straight-line, declining balance, and sum-of-the-years'-digits were available for most assets under each system. The facts-and-circumstances method enabled taxpayers to choose useful life and salvage value estimates for depreciable assets based on their experience and judgment of all surrounding facts and circumstances. There were no predetermined or prescribed guidelines. Conflicts often arose between taxpayers and the IRS over useful life selections because taxpayers were motivated to employ short useful lives in order to maximize the present value of tax savings from depreciation deductions.

As an alternative to the facts-and-circumstances system, the Class Life System became part of the law in 1971. It was developed primarily to minimize IRS-taxpayer conflicts over useful life estimates. The system prescribed depreciable life ranges for numerous categories of assets. For example, office furniture and fixtures could be depreciated using lives from 8 years to 12 years under the Class Life System.[6] Taxpayers electing this system were not challenged by the IRS. However, IRS-taxpayer conflicts were not eliminated because many taxpayers continued to employ the facts-and-circumstances system, seeking depreciable lives that were shorter than those available with the Class Life System.

In 1981, the facts-and-circumstances system and Class Life System were all but eliminated for assets placed in service after 1980. In the Economic Recovery Tax Act of 1981 (ERTA), Congress substantially revised the method for computing depreciation by enacting Code § 168 and the Accelerated Cost Recovery System (ACRS). Altered several times since 1981, the current version of this system is known as the Modified Accelerated Cost Recovery System (MACRS). An alternative to MACRS, called the Alternative Depreciation System (ADS), is also available.

A major benefit of MACRS and ADS is the elimination of previous areas of dispute between taxpayers and the IRS. Under these systems, the taxpayer is required to choose from a small set of predetermined options regarding depreciable life and depreciation method. Salvage value is ignored in all cases. Thus, depreciation calculations are more uniform for all taxpayers.

It should be emphasized, however, that some assets may not be depreciated using either of these systems. For this reason, the facts-and-circumstances approach and the Class Life System have continuing validity in certain instances.

MODIFIED ACCELERATED COST RECOVERY SYSTEM

AN OVERVIEW OF MACRS

Once it is determined that property is eligible for depreciation, the amount of the depreciation deduction must be computed. Under current law, taxpayers are required to calculate depreciation for most property using the Modified Accelerated

---

[6] Rev. Proc. 77-10, 1977-1 C.B. 548.

Cost Recovery System (MACRS). As suggested earlier, MACRS is a radical departure from traditional approaches to depreciation. Under MACRS, useful lives for assets are termed *recovery periods* and are prescribed by statute. These recovery periods are for the most part arbitrary, determined without regard to how long the asset may actually last. Regardless of the effects of nature and outside forces, each asset is deemed to have a particular useful life of 3, 5, 7, 10, 15, 20, 27.5, or 31.5 years. In addition, salvage value is ignored under MACRS. With these rules, possibilities for abuse using unrealistic values for useful life and salvage value are essentially eliminated.

The basic machinery of MACRS that is used to compute depreciation can be summarized as follows:

1. The system establishes eight classes or categories of property (e.g., 3-year property).

2. For each class of property, a specific useful life and depreciation method are prescribed (e.g., for 3-year property the useful life is three years and either the 200 percent declining-balance or straight-line method must be used).

To actually compute depreciation, taxpayers must first determine whether the property is subject to MACRS, then—based on the property's classification—determine the applicable method, recovery period, and accounting convention. These elements of the depreciation calculation are discussed below.

PROPERTY SUBJECT TO MACRS

Taxpayers generally must use MACRS to compute depreciation for all *tangible* property, both real and personal, new or used.[7] MACRS is not used to amortize *intangible* assets such as patents or copyrights, which are amortized using the straight-line method. In addition, the revamped version of MACRS may not be used with respect to the following property:[8]

1. Property depreciated using a method that is not based on years (e.g., the units-of-production or income forecast methods)

2. Automobiles if the taxpayer has elected to use the standard mileage rate (such an election excludes the property from MACRS)

3. Property for which special amortization is provided and elected by the taxpayer in lieu of depreciation (e.g., amortization of pollution control facilities)

4. Certain motion picture films, video tapes, sound recordings, and public utility property

5. Generally, any property that the taxpayer—or a party related to the taxpayer—owned or used (e.g., leased) prior to 1986

---

[7] § 168(a).   [8] § 168(f).

As a practical matter, MACRS is mandatory for all tangible property. But, as will be seen, the taxpayer is allowed to elect out of MACRS and use the Alternative Depreciation System (ADS). In addition, in lieu of depreciation, the taxpayer may be allowed to expense up to $10,000 annually of the aggregate costs of certain assets placed in service during the year. It should be emphasized, however, that there are no elections available enabling the taxpayer to use the facts-and-circumstances method typically used for financial accounting purposes. Exhibit 9-1 identifies the depreciation methods and accounting conventions available under the MACRS and ADS systems.

CLASSES OF PROPERTY

As indicated in Exhibit 9-1, all property subject to MACRS is assigned to one of eight classes.[9] Classification is important because the recovery periods, methods, and accounting conventions to be used in calculating depreciation can vary among the different classes of property. Property is assigned to a particular class based on its *class life* as prescribed in Revenue Procedure 87-56.[10] This Revenue

Exhibit 9-1
Depreciation Methods and Accounting Conventions under MACRS and ADS

8 MACRS Property Classes	Modified Accelerated Cost Recovery System (MACRS): Use MACRS Property Class Life	Alternative Depreciation Sysem (ADS): Use ADS Life	Accounting Convention[1]
3-year, 5-year, 7-year, 10-year[2]	Choices: 200%DB or SL[3]	Choices: 150%DB or SL	Half-year or mid-quarter
15-year, 20-year	Choices: 150%DB or SL	Choices: 150%DB or SL	Half-year or mid-quarter
Residental rental real estate	27.5 years SL	40 years SL	Mid-month
Nonresidental real estate	31.5 years SL	40 years SL	Mid-month

Notes:
(1) Taxpayers do *not* have the option of choosing either the half-year or mid-quarter convention. As explained later in this chapter, either the half-year or mid-quarter convention is *required* depending on the timing of asset purchases during the year.
(2) Under certain conditions, $10,000 immediate expensing under Code § 179 is available for most 3-, 5-, 7-, and 10-year assets (i.e., depreciable tangible personal property).
(3) Abbreviations:
   DB = declining balance
   SL = straight-line

---

[9] § 168(e).

[10] 1987-2 C.B. 674, as modified by Rev. Proc. 88-22, I.R.B. No. 18, 38.

Procedure, an excerpt of which is provided in Exhibit 9-2, specifies not only the class lives of various assets but also the recovery periods to be used for both MACRS and ADS. Note that the "General Depreciation System" column of Exhibit 9-2 pertains to MACRS. Exhibit 9-3 provides examples of property in each of the eight MACRS property classes.

CALCULATING DEPRECIATION

Under MACRS, depreciation is a function of *three* factors: the recovery period, the method, and the accounting convention.

Recovery Periods. As seen in Exhibit 9-1, recovery periods run various lengths of time depending on the class of property.[11] Although the current recovery periods more closely resemble assets' actual useful lives than did recovery periods of prior years, the relationship is still more arbitrary than real.

In examining the different classes, several features should be observed. First, certain property is assigned to a class without regard to its class life. The most notable example of this is cars, which are assigned to the five-year class (see asset class 00.22 in Exhibit 9-2). Note also that the current structure provides different recovery periods for real property, depending on whether it is residential or nonresidential real estate. As a result, when a building is used for both residential and nonresidential purposes (e.g., a multilevel apartment building with commercial space on the bottom two floors) it must be classified as one or the other. For this purpose, realty qualifies as residential real estate if 80 percent of the gross rents are for the dwelling units.[12]

Depreciation Method. The depreciation method to be used—like the recovery period—varies depending on the class of the property. A closer look at Exhibit 9-1, however, reveals that the variation is actually between real and personal property. Real property is depreciated using the straight-line method, while personal property is depreciated using either straight-line or a declining-balance method. If a declining balance depreciation method is elected, a switch to straight-line is made in the first year in which a larger depreciation would result. Example 4 illustrates this procedure.

Accounting Conventions. The final factor to be considered in computing depreciation is the accounting convention. The Code establishes three conventions to handle the computation of depreciation when property is placed in service or sold (or otherwise disposed of) during the year.[13] These are the half-year, mid-month, and mid-quarter conventions.

Half-Year Convention. The half-year convention applies to all property *other than* nonresidential real property and residential rental property. From a practical perspective, the half-year convention applies to *all personal property*. Under the half-year convention, one-half year of depreciation is allowed regardless of when the asset is placed in service or sold during the year (e.g., $1/2 \times$ the annual depreciation as normally computed).[14] Since only one-half year's depreciation is allowed in the first year, the recovery period is effectively extended one year so that the remaining one-half may be claimed.

---

[11] § 168(c).

[12] § 168(e)(2).

[13] § 168(d).

[14] § 168(d)(4).

Exhibit 9-2
Excerpt from Revenue Procedure 87-56

Asset Class	Description of Assets Included	Class Life (in years)	Recovery Periods (in years) General Depre-ciation System	Recovery Periods (in years) Alternative Depre-ciation System
SPECIFIC DEPRECIABLE ASSETS USED IN ALL BUSINESS ACTIVITIES, EXCEPT AS NOTED:				
00.11	**Office Furniture, Fixtures, and Equipment:** Includes furniture and fixtures that are not a structural component of a building. Includes such assets as desks, files, safes, and communications equipment. Does not include communications equipment that is included in other classes...........................	10	7	10
00.13	**Data Handling Equipment, except Computers:** Includes only typewriters, calculators, adding and accounting machines, copiers, and duplicating equipment	6	5	6
00.21	**Airplanes (airframes and engines), except those used in commercial or contract carrying of passengers or freight, and all helicopters (airframes and engines)**...........................	6	5	6
00.22	**Automobiles, Taxis**...............................	3	5	5
00.23	**Buses**	9	5	9
00.241	**Light General Purpose Trucks:** Includes trucks for use over the road (actual unloaded weight less than 13,000 pounds)	4	5	5
00.242	**Heavy General Purpose Trucks:** Includes heavy general purpose trucks, concrete ready-mix truckers, and ore trucks, for use over the road (actual unloaded weight 13,000 pounds or more)..	6	5	6
DEPRECIABLE ASSETS USED IN THE FOLLOWING ACTIVITES:				
01.1	**Agriculture:** Includes machinery and equipment, grain bins, and fences but no other land improvements, that are used in the production of crops or plants, vines, and trees; livestock; the operation of farm dairies, nurseries, greenhouses, sod farms, mushroom cellars, cranberry bogs, apiaries, and fur farms; the performance of agriculture, animal husbandry, and horticultural services.........................	10	7	10
01.11	**Cotton Ginning Assets**..	12	7	12
01.21	**Cattle, Breeding or Dairy**..	7	5	7
01.22	**Horses, Breeding or Work**......................................	10	7	10
01.221	**Any horse that is not a race horse and is more than 12 years old at the time it is placed in service**...........................	10	7	10
01.223	**Any race horse that is more than 2 years old at the time it is placed in service**...	*	3	12
01.23	**Hogs, Breeding**...	3	3	3
01.24	**Sheep and Goats, Breeding**.....................................	5	5	5
01.3	**Farm buildings except structures included in Class 01.4**.....	25	20	25
01.4	**Single-purpose agricultural or horticultural structures [within the meaning of section 48(p) of the Code]**....................	15	7	15

Exhibit 9-3
Examples of MACRS Property

MACRS Property Class	Examples
3 years	Special tools, race horses, tractors, and property with a class life of 4 years or less
5 years	Automobiles, trucks, computers, and peripheral equipment (such as printers, external disk drives, and modems), typewriters, copiers, R&E equipment, and property with a class life of more than 4 years and less than 10 years
7 years	Office furniture, fixtures, office equipment, most machinery, property with a class life of 10 years or more but less than 16 years, and property with no assigned class life
10 years	Single-purpose agricultural and horticultural structures, assets used in petroleum refining and manufacturing of tobacco and certain food products, and property with a class life of 16 years or more but less than 20 years
15 years	Land improvements (such as sidewalks, roads, parking lots, irrigation systems, sewers, fences, and landscaping), service stations, billboards, telephone distribution plants, and property with a class life of 20 years or more but less than 25 years
20 years	Municipal sewers and property with a class life of 25 years or more
27.5 years	Residential rental real estate, including apartment complexes, duplexes, and vacation rental homes
31.5 years	Nonresidential real estate, including office buildings, warehouses, factories, and farm buildings

Example 4. On March 1, 1991, T purchased a car to be used solely for business for $10,000. It was his only acquisition during the year. The car had an estimated useful life of four years and an estimated salvage value of $2,000. Although these estimates might be used for financial accounting purposes, under MACRS, salvage value is ignored and T is required to use the recovery period, depreciation method, and accounting convention prescribed for 5-year property, the class to which cars are assigned. T elects to compute his depreciation using the 200% declining-balance method (switching to straight-line where appropriate), a 5-year recovery period, and the half-year convention. The 200% declining-balance rate would be 40% (200% × straight-line rate, $^1/_5$ or 20%). The declining-balance method would be used until 1995, when a switch to straight-line maximizes the depreciation deduction. Due to the half-year convention, the cost is actually recovered over six years rather than the 5-year recovery period. Depreciation would be computed as follows:

Year	Depreciation Method	Basis for Depreciation Computation	Rate	Depreciation
1991	200% D.B.	$10,000	20%*	$ 2,000
1992	200% D.B.	8,000	40%	3,200
1993	200% D.B.	4,800	40%	1,920
1994	200% D.B.	2,880	40%	1,152**
1995	S.L.	1,730	$^{1.0}/_{1.5}$	1,152***
1996	S.L.	1,730	$^{0.5}/_{1.5}$	576
				$10,000

*Half-year allowance (40% × $^1/_2$ = 20%).

**Note that straight-line depreciation is the same ($2,880 × $^1/_{2.5}$).

***Declining-balance depreciation would have been $692 ($1,730 × 40%); since straight-line depreciation over the remaining 1$^1/_2$ years is $1,152 and greater than $692, the switch to straight-line is made.

Example 5. Same facts as above except the property was sold on December 20, 1993. In computing depreciation for personal property in the year of sale or disposition, the half-year convention must also be used. Thus, depreciation for 1993 would be $960 ($4,800 × 40% × $^1/_2$).

To simplify the computation of depreciation, the IRS provides optional tables as shown in Exhibits 9-4 to 9-7.[15] The percentages (or rates) shown in the tables are the result of combining the three factors used in determining depreciation—method, rate, and convention—into a single, composite percentage to be used for each class of property.[16]

---

[15]   Rev. Proc. 87-57, 1987-2 C.B. 687.

[16]   Depreciation percentages in the tables are rounded to one-hundredth of a percent for recovery property with a recovery period of less than 20 years, and one-thousandth of a percent for all other property. See Rev. Proc. 87-57 *supra*.

Example 6. The depreciation rate for the year that 5-year property is placed in service and for the following year is determined as follows:

Year 1

Straight-line rate (1/5)........................	20%
× Declining-balance rate........................	× 200%
200 percent declining-balance rate............	40%
× Half-year allowance............................	× 1/2
Depreciation rate per table.....................	20%

Year 2

Basis of asset remaining (100% − 20%)......	80%
× 200 percent declining-balance rate.............	× 40%
Depreciation rate per table.....................	32%

Example 7. Same facts as in *Example 4*. Depreciation computed using the table in Exhibit 9-4 would be the same as above, computed as follows:

Year	Unadjusted Basis	×	Accelerated Recovery Percentage	Annual Depreciation
1991	$10,000		20.00%	$ 2,000
1992	10,000		32.00	3,200
1993	10,000		19.20	1,920
1994	10,000		11.52	1,152
1995	10,000		11.52	1,152
1996	10,000		5.76	576
			100.00%	$10,000

Exhibit 9-4
MACRS Accelerated Depreciation Percentages Using the Half-Year Convention for 3, 5, and 7-Year Property

Recovery Year	Property Class		
	3-Year	5-Year	7-Year
1	33.33%	20.00%	14.29%
2	44.45	32.00	24.49
3	14.81	19.20	17.49
4	7.41	11.52	12.49
5		11.52	8.93
6		5.76	8.92
7			8.93
8			4.46

Source: Rev. Proc. 87-57, Table 1.
Appendix C has additional depreciation tables.

Example 7 illustrates the basic steps necessary to compute annual depreciation. These steps are as follows:

1. Identify the *depreciable basis* of the asset (generally its cost): $10,000 in *Example 7*.

2. Determine the MACRS *property class*: 5-year property in *Example 7*.

3. Identify the *depreciation convention* (either half-year or mid-quarter for personal property; mid-month for real estate): half-year convention in *Example 7*.

4. Determine the *recovery period* and *method*. See Exhibit 9-1 for a summary of the available choices: 5-year 200 percent declining balance in *Example 7*.

5. Locate the *appropriate table* based on the depreciation convention, recovery period, and method: Exhibit 9-4 for *Example 7*. (Note the depreciation convention is already reflected in the table percentages for the year of acquisition, but *not* for the year of disposition.)

6. Choose the *table percentages* relating to the recovery period of the asset: 5-year property percentages for *Example 7* (i.e., 20 percent, 32 percent, etc.).

7. Multiply the table percentages by the depreciable (cost) basis of the asset to *compute annual depreciation* amounts: $10,000 multiplied by 20 percent provides $2,000 of depreciation for 1991 in *Example 7*.

When using the depreciation tables, a special adjustment must be made if there is a disposition of the property before its cost is fully recovered. As noted above, under the half-year convention the taxpayer is entitled only to a half-year of depreciation in the year of disposition. Therefore, where the half-year convention applies and the property is used for only a portion of the disposition year, only one-half of the amount of depreciation determined using the table is allowed.

Example 8.   Same facts as *Example 7* except the taxpayer sold the property on December 1, 1993. Since the taxpayer did not hold the property the entire taxable year and the half-year convention is in effect, only one-half of the amount of depreciation using the table is allowed. Therefore, depreciation for 1993 would have been $960 ($10,000 × 19.2% × $^1/_2$). Note that this is the same result as obtained in *Example 5* above.

Mid-Month Convention.   This convention applies only to real property (i.e., nonresidential real property and residential rental property).[17] Under the mid-month convention, one-half month of depreciation is allowed for the month the

---

[17]   § 168(d)(2).

asset is placed in service or sold and a full month of depreciation is allowed for each additional month of the year that the asset is in service.[18] For example, if a calendar year taxpayer places a building in service on April 3, the fraction of the annual depreciation allowed is $^{8.5}/_{12}$ (half-month's depreciation for April) and eight months depreciation for May through December.

Example 9. The first-year depreciation rate for residential rental realty that is placed in service in April is determined as follows:

Straight-line rate ($^1/_{27.5}$).....................	3.636%
× Mid-month convention......................	× $^{8.5}/_{12}$
Depreciation rate per table.................	2.576%

Due to the mid-month convention, the recovery period must be extended one month to claim the one-half month of depreciation that was not claimed in the first month. For example, the entire cost of residential rental property is recovered over 331 months ($27^1/_2$ years is 330 months + 1 additional month to claim the half-month of depreciation not claimed in the first month). As a result, depreciation deductions are actually claimed over either 28 or 29 years depending on the month in which the property was placed in service. This can be seen by examining the composite depreciation percentages for real property reflecting the mid-month convention given in Exhibits 9-5 and 9-6.

Example 10. S purchased a duplex as an investment for $110,000 on July 17, 1991. Of the $110,000 cost, $10,000 is allocated to the land. The estimated useful life of the duplex is 30 years—the same period as her mortgage—and the estimated salvage value is $15,000. Despite these estimates, under MACRS salvage value is ignored and S is required to use the recovery period, depreciation method, and convention prescribed for residential rental property, the class to which the duplex is assigned. Therefore, S uses a 27.5-year life, the straight-line method, and the mid-month convention. Using the table in Exhibit 9-5, depreciation for the first year would be $1,667 ($100,000 × 1.667%).

When using the depreciation tables, an adjustment must be made if there is a disposition of the real property before its cost is fully recovered. This adjustment is similar to that required where the half-year convention applies, but not identical. In the year of disposition, the taxpayer may deduct depreciation only for those months the property is used by the taxpayer. In addition, under the mid-month convention, the taxpayer is entitled to only a half-month of depreciation for the month of disposition.

Example 11. Same facts as *Example 10* except the taxpayer sold the property on May 22, 1993. Depreciation for 1993 would be $1,363 ($100,000 × 3.636% × $^{4.5}/_{12}$).

---

[18]   § 168(d)(4)(B).

Exhibit 9-5
MACRS Depreciation Rates
Residental Rental Property

Month Placed in Service	Recovery Year						
	1	2	3	...	27	28	29
1	3.485%	3.636%	3.636%		3.636%	1.970%	0.000%
2	3.182	3.636	3.636		3.636	2.273	0.000
3	2.879	3.636	3.636		3.636	2.576	0.000
4	2.576	3.636	3.636		3.636	2.879	0.000
5	2.273	3.636	3.636		3.636	3.182	0.000
6	1.970	3.636	3.636		3.636	3.485	0.000
7	1.667	3.636	3.636		3.637	3.636	0.152
8	1.364	3.636	3.636		3.637	3.636	0.455
9	1.061	3.636	3.636		3.637	3.636	0.758
10	0.758	3.636	3.636		3.637	3.636	1.061
11	0.455	3.636	3.636		3.637	3.636	1.364
12	0.152	3.636	3.636		3.637	3.636	1.667

Source: Rev. Proc. 87-57, Table 6.
Appendix C has additional depreciation tables.

Exhibit 9-6
MACRS Depreciation Percentages
Nonresidental Property

Month Placed in Service	Recovery Year						
	1	2	3	...	31	32	33
1	3.042%	3.175%	3.175%		3.174%	1.720%	0.000%
2	2.778	3.175	3.175		3.175	1.984	0.000
3	2.513	3.175	3.175		3.174	2.249	0.000
4	2.249	3.175	3.175		3.175	2.513	0.000
5	1.984	3.175	3.175		3.174	2.778	0.000
6	1.720	3.175	3.175		3.175	3.042	0.000
7	1.455	3.175	3.175		3.174	3.175	0.132
8	1.190	3.175	3.175		3.175	3.174	0.397
9	0.926	3.175	3.175		3.174	3.175	0.661
10	0.661	3.175	3.175		3.175	3.174	0.926
11	0.397	3.175	3.175		3.174	3.175	1.190
12	0.132	3.175	3.175		3.175	3.174	1.455

Source: Rev. Proc. 87-57, Table 7.
Appendix C has additional depreciation tables.

Mid-Quarter Convention. The mid-quarter convention applies only to *personal property*. However, it applies only if more than 40 percent of the aggregate bases of all personal property placed in service during the taxable year is placed in service during the last three months of the year.[19] Property placed in service and disposed of during the same taxable year is not taken into account. If the 40 percent test is satisfied, the mid-quarter convention applies to *all* personal property placed in service during the year (regardless of the quarter in which it was actually placed in service).

Example 12. During the year, K Company, a calendar year taxpayer, acquired and placed in service the following assets:

Assets	Acquisition Date	Cost
Office furniture	March 28	$20,000
Machinery......................	October 9	80,000
Warehouse....................	February 1	90,000

Of the total *personal* property placed in service during the year, more than 40% [$80,000 ÷ ($20,000 + $80,000)] occurred in the last quarter (i.e., October through December). As a result, K must use the mid-quarter convention for computing the depreciation of both the furniture and the machinery.

When applicable, the mid-quarter convention treats all personal property as being placed in service in the middle of the quarter of the taxable year in which it was actually placed in service.[20] Therefore, one-half of a quarter's depreciation — in effect one-eighth ($1/2 \times 1/4$) or 12.5 percent of the annual depreciation — is allowed for the quarter that the asset is placed in service or sold. In addition, a full quarter's depreciation is allowed for each additional quarter that the asset is in service. For example, personal property placed in service on March 3 would be treated as having been placed in service in the middle of the first quarter and the taxpayer would be able to claim $3 1/2$ quarters — $3.5/4$ or 87.5 percent — of the annual amount of depreciation. The percentages of the annual depreciation allowed under the mid-quarter convention for a year in which an asset is placed in service are

	Quarter Placed in Service			
	First January–March	*Second* April–June	*Third* July–September	*Fourth* October–December
Percentage of annual depreciation allowed............	87.5%	62.5%	37.5%	12.5%

---

[19] § 168(d)(3).   [20] § 168(d)(3).

The above chart illustrates that where an asset is placed in service in the first quarter and the mid-quarter convention applies, the taxpayer is allowed to deduct 87.5 percent of the annual depreciation. In contrast, for personal property placed in service during the fourth quarter only 12.5 percent of the annual depreciation may be deducted. Note that the recovery period must be extended by one year so that the balance of the depreciation not claimed in the first year may be deducted. Composite depreciation percentages to be used for 3-year and 5-year property where the mid-quarter convention applies are provided in Exhibit 9-7. Appendix C has depreciation tables for all categories of personal property under the mid-quarter convention.

Example 13. In 1991, T, a calendar year taxpayer, purchased four automobiles to use in his business at a cost of $10,000 each. These purchases were his only acquisitions of personal property during the year. Three of the cars were purchased in December while the other car was purchased in January. Since more than 40% of the property placed in service during the year was placed in service in the last quarter ($30,000 ÷ $40,000 = 75%), the mid-quarter convention applies in computing depreciation. Thus, the depreciation allowed on the auto purchased in January would be limited to 87.5% of a full year's depreciation, and the depreciation allowed on the three cars purchased in December would be limited to 12.5% of a full

Exhibit 9-7
MACRS Accelerated Depreciation Percentages Using the Mid-Quarter Convention for 3- and 5-Year Property

3-Year Property:

Recovery Year	Quarter Placed in Service 1	2	3	4
1	58.33%	41.67%	25.00%	8.33%
2	27.78	38.89	50.00	61.11
3	12.35	14.14	16.67	20.37
4	1.54	5.30	8.33	10.19

5-Year Property:

1	35.00	25.00	15.00	5.00
2	26.00	30.00	34.00	38.00
3	15.60	18.00	20.40	22.80
4	11.01	11.37	12.24	13.68
5	11.01	11.37	11.30	10.94
6	1.38	4.26	7.06	9.58

Source: Rev. Proc. 87-57.
Appendix C has additional depreciation tables.

year's depreciation. Since a full year's depreciation would be 40% of cost (straight-line rate of 20% per year × 200% declining-balance = 40%), the depreciation for the January purchase would be limited to 35% of cost (40% × 87.5%), or $3,500 (35% × $10,000). Similarly, the depreciation for the December purchases would be limited to 5% of cost (40% × 12.5%), or $1,500 (5% × $30,000). Total depreciation under the mid-quarter convention is limited to $5,000 ($3,500 + $1,500). These amounts are easily computed using the tables in Exhibit 9-7.

Note that had the mid-quarter convention *not* applied, the depreciation percentage would have been 20%—reflecting the half-year allowance for 5-year property (40% × $1/2$ = 20%), or $8,000 ($40,000 × 20%). Due to the timing of the acquisitions, T's depreciation for the year is reduced by $3,000 ($8,000 − $5,000).

When using the depreciation tables, a special adjustment must be made if there is a disposition of the property before its cost is fully recovered. This adjustment is similar to that for the half-year and mid-month conventions. As noted above, under the mid-quarter convention, the taxpayer is entitled to only one-half of a quarter's depreciation—in effect one-eighth ($1/2$ × $1/4$) or 12.5 percent of the annual depreciation—for the quarter that the asset is sold. In addition, a full quarter of depreciation is allowed for each quarter that the asset is in service. For example, if property was sold on August 2, the taxpayer could claim $2 1/2$ quarters— $2.5/4$ or 62.5 percent—of the annual amount of depreciation. The percentages of annual depreciation allowed under the mid-quarter convention for the year an asset is sold are

	Quarter Property Sold			
	First January–March	*Second* April–June	*Third* July–September	*Fourth* October–December
Percentage of annual depreciation allowed............	12.5%	37.5%	62.5%	87.5%

Example 14. Same facts as in *Example 13* above except the car acquired in January, 1991 was sold on August 9, 1993. Since T did not hold the property the entire taxable year and the mid-quarter convention is in effect, only 62.5% of the amount of depreciation using the table is allowed. Therefore, using the table in Exhibit 9-7, T's depreciation for this car would have been $975 ($10,000 × 15.6% × 62.5%).

STRAIGHT-LINE METHODS

The accelerated depreciation methods prescribed by MACRS are normally desirable since they allow taxpayers to recover their costs more rapidly than the straight-line method. However, there may be circumstances where the slower-paced straight-line method may be more rewarding. For example, if the taxpayer is currently in the 15 percent tax bracket, he or she may want to defer depreciation deductions to years when he or she is in the 28 or 31 percent tax bracket. By doing this, the taxpayer may be able to maximize the present value of the tax savings from depreciation deductions (depending upon the taxpayer's discount rate).

Taxpayers can elect to use the straight-line method in lieu of the accelerated method. Two different approaches are available: straight-line under MACRS, or straight-line under ADS.

MACRS Straight-Line. Although it may seem inconsistent, the *Accelerated Cost Recovery System* offers taxpayers a straight-line method of depreciation.[21] If the taxpayer so elects, the straight-line method is used in conjunction with all of the other rules that normally apply under MACRS; that is, the taxpayer simply uses the straight-line method (in lieu of the accelerated method) along with the applicable recovery period and accounting convention. The depreciation percentages to be used where the taxpayer elects the straight-line method are contained in Exhibit 9-8 (half-year convention property) for 3-, 5-, and 7-year property. Appendix C has straight-line depreciation tables for all categories of personal property under the half-year convention. The depreciation percentages for the straight-line method when the mid-quarter convention applies can be found in Revenue Procedure 87-57.[22]

> **Example 15.** On June 1, 1991, L purchased 5-year property (to which the half-year convention applies) for $50,000. Using the table in Exhibit 9-8, depreciation for the year would be $5,000 ($50,000 × 10%). Depreciation for 1992 would be $10,000 (20% × $50,000). If L sold the property on January 22, 1993, depreciation would be $5,000 ($50,000 × 20% × $1/2$).

Exhibit 9-8
*MACRS and ADS Straight-Line Depreciation Percentages
Using the Half-Year Convention
for 3, 5, and 7-Year Property*

Recovery Year	Property Class		
	3-Year	5-Year	7-Year
1	16.67%	10.00%	7.14%
2	33.33	20.00	14.29
3	33.33	20.00	14.29
4	16.67	20.00	14.28
5		20.00	14.29
6		10.00	14.28
7			14.29
8			7.14

Source: Rev. Proc. 87-57.
Appendix C has additional depreciation tables.

---

[21] § 168(b)(3)(C).

[22] 1987-2 C.B. 687.

The election to use the straight-line method is made annually by class (of course, the straight-line method must be used for realty). For example, if in 1991 the taxpayer makes the election for 7-year property, *all* 7-year property placed in service during the year must be depreciated using the straight-line method. The election does not obligate the taxpayer to use the straight-line method for any other class. Similarly, the taxpayer need not use the straight-line method for such class of assets placed in service in the following year.

Alternative Depreciation System. As part of the 1986 reform package, Congress established the Alternative Depreciation System (ADS) as an option for taxpayers.[23] This system is similar to MACRS in two ways: salvage value is ignored, and the same averaging conventions must be followed. The major differences between MACRS and ADS consist of longer recovery periods for most assets and, in some cases, slower rates of depreciation. The recovery period to be used for ADS is normally the property's class life. The class life—which is usually longer than the MACRS life—is used unless no class life has been prescribed for the property or a specific class life has been designated in Code § 168. For example, as shown in Exhibit 9-2, the ADS class life for typewriters (asset class 00.13) is six years while the MACRS life is five years. Thus, depreciation under ADS would be computed using a 6-year life while depreciation for MACRS would be computed using a 5-year life. The recovery periods to be used for ADS are summarized in Exhibit 9-9.

Taxpayers electing ADS for real property are restricted to straight-line depreciation. Thus, an office building (nonresidential real property) would be depreciated using straight-line and a 40-year recovery period under ADS. The ADS depreciation percentages for real property are found in Exhibit 9-10.

In contrast, either straight-line or 150 percent declining balance depreciation may be chosen for personal property. The ADS straight-line depreciation percentages for personal property, which in fact have class lives of 3, 5, and 7 years, are the same as those for MACRS straight-line and can be found in Exhibit 9-8.

For personal property, a taxpayer may have as many as four different depreciation options. For example, the ADS options for a typewriter consist of straight-line over six years or 150 percent declining balance over six years. The MACRS alternatives for a typewriter are straight-line over *five* years or *200* percent declining balance over five years. Which of these four choices would be best for depreciating the typewriter? In general, the taxpayer should select the depreciation method that maximizes the present value of tax savings from depreciation deductions. For taxpayers who expect their future marginal tax rate to either remain constant or decline, the fastest depreciation method over the shortest time period will maximize the present value of tax savings from depreciation.

---

[23] § 168(g).

Exhibit 9-9
Alternative Depreciation System
Recovery Periods

General Rule: Recovery period is the property's class life unless

1. There is no class life (see below), or
2. A special class life has been designated (see below).

Type of Property	Recovery Period
Personal property with no class life	12 years
Nonresidential real property with no class life	40 years
Residential rental property with no class life..................	40 years
Cars, light general purpose trucks, certain technological equipment, and semiconductor manufacturing equipment.................................	5 years
Computer-based telephone central office switching equipment...	9.5 years
Railroad track...	10 years
Single purpose agricultural or horticultural structures...........	15 years
Municipal waste water treatment plants, telephone distribution plants..	24 years
Low-income housing financed by tax-exempt bonds............	27.5 years
Municipal sewers	50 years

Exhibit 9-10
ADS Straight-Line Depreciation Percentages
Real Property
Using the Mid-Month Convention

Month Placed in Service	Recovery Year		
	1	2–40	41
1	2.396%	2.500%	0.104%
2	2.188	2.500	0.312
3	1.979	2.500	0.521
4	1.771	2.500	0.729
5	1.563	2.500	0.937
6	1.354	2.500	1.146
7	1.146	2.500	1.354
8	0.938	2.500	1.562
9	0.729	2.500	1.771
10	0.521	2.500	1.979
11	0.313	2.500	2.187
12	0.104	2.500	2.396

Source: Rev. Proc. 87-57, Table 13.

The mechanics of the election to use ADS—except for real property—are identical to those of MACRS discussed above. Except for real property, the taxpayer may elect to use ADS on a class-by-class, year-by-year basis.[24] For realty, the election is made on a property-by-property basis. In addition, the taxpayer *must* use ADS straight-line for depreciating certain property. Such property includes certain "listed property" (discussed later in this chapter), foreign use property (i.e., property used outside the U.S. more than half of a taxable year), property leased to a tax-exempt entity (and foreign persons unless more than 50 percent of the income is subject to U.S. tax), and property that is financed either directly or indirectly by the issuance of tax-exempt bonds (i.e., tax-exempt bond-financed property).[25] ADS is also used for computing depreciation for purposes of the alternative minimum tax (discussed in Chapter 13) and a corporation's earnings and profits (discussed in Chapter 20).

DISPOSITIONS OF ASSETS FROM GENERAL ASSET ACCOUNTS

Quite often, it is impractical for a taxpayer to account for so-called mass assets. The term *mass assets* is defined as a group of individual items of property not necessarily homogeneous but so numerous in quantity that separate identification is impractical. In addition, each asset's value is minor relative to the total value of the group. Examples of mass assets include returnable containers, railroad ties, portable tools, and minor items of office furniture. Despite their relatively minor value, each asset represents a capital expenditure recoverable through depreciation. To simplify accounting for these items, the Code allows the taxpayer to establish *general asset accounts*.[26] Under this accounting procedure, depreciation is computed in the normal manner. However, upon disposition of the asset the entire amount of the proceeds realized (undiminished by the basis of the asset disposed of) is recognized as income. For this reason, the unadjusted basis of the asset disposed of is left in the general asset account to be fully recovered through depreciation in future years.

> **Example 16.** P Corporation, a nation-wide painting company, purchased 1,000 portable paint sprayers at a cost of $300 each (total cost of $300,000). P uses a general asset account to account for the sprayers. The sprayers were shipped to branches of the company in over 50 cities including Miami. During the year, P closed its Miami branch and sold all of the sprayers to local companies for $9,000. P will report the entire $9,000 in income and continue to depreciate whatever sprayers were sold until they are fully depreciated.

---

[24] § 168(g)(7).

[25] § 168(g)(1).

[26] § 168(i)(4).

LIMITED EXPENSING
ELECTION: CODE § 179

When Congress introduced MACRS, it also enacted a provision allowing taxpayers (other than estates or trusts) to *elect* to treat the cost of qualifying property as a currently deductible expense rather than a capital expenditure subject to depreciation.[27] This measure was intended primarily to eliminate the need for maintaining depreciation records where the taxpayer's annual acquisitions were not substantial. The limitation on the amount that can be expensed annually by a taxpayer is normally $10,000. However, two limitations may restrict the amount that the taxpayer may otherwise expense.

1. *Acquisitions of Eligible Property Exceeding $200,000.* Where the aggregate cost of *qualifying* property placed in service during the year exceeds $200,000, the $10,000 amount must be reduced $1 for each $1 of cost in excess of $200,000. For example, taxpayers purchasing $204,000 of property could expense up to $6,000 of the cost while taxpayers purchasing in excess of $210,000 could not benefit from § 179 at all.

2. *Taxable Income Limitation.* The deduction under § 179 cannot exceed the amount of taxable income (prior to consideration of this deduction) derived from all of the taxpayer's trades or businesses. Any amount that cannot be deducted can be carried over indefinitely to following years to be used against future income. The maximum amount that can be expensed in subsequent years is not increased by the carryover amount, however.

The taxpayer may elect to expense all or a portion of an asset so long as the total amount expensed does not exceed the dollar limitation. If only a portion of an asset is expensed, the remaining portion is subject to depreciation.

---

[27]   § 179.

Example 17.   T purchased 5-year property for $17,000 and 7-year property for $13,000 during the current year. Both assets are eligible to be expensed subject to the limitations of § 179. Assume T expects her future marginal tax rate to remain constant. To maximize the present value of the tax savings from limited expensing and depreciation deductions, T should expense $10,000 of the 7-year property rather than the 5-year property since the cost of the 5-year property could be recovered more quickly, thus resulting in higher depreciation deductions in the current year. Assuming T elects to expense $10,000 of the 7-year property, her deduction for such property would be $10,429 computed as follows:

	Original cost.............................	$13,000	
−	Expensed portion........................	(10,000)	$10,000
	Remaining depreciable basis..............	$ 3,000	
×	Depreciation percentage..................	× 14.29%	
	Depreciation deduction...................	$ 429	429
	Total deduction.........................		$10,429

In addition, the taxpayer could claim a deduction for *depreciation* of the 5-year property.

Eligible Property.   Only property that satisfies certain requirements is eligible for expensing. To qualify, the property may be new or used and must be[28]

1. Recovery property;

2. Property that would have qualified for the investment credit (e.g., most property other than buildings and their components);

3. Property used in a trade or business, as distinguished from property held for the production of income; and

4. Property acquired by purchase from someone who is generally not a "related party" under § 267 (e.g., gifted or inherited property usually does not qualify nor would property acquired from a spouse or parent).

Recapture.   Without any special rule, taxpayers could use an asset in business for a short period (e.g., one day), expense it for tax purposes, then convert it to nonbusiness use. To prohibit this possible abuse, a special rule applies. If the property is converted to nonbusiness use *at any time*, the taxpayer must *recapture* the benefit derived from expensing.[29] Recapture requires the taxpayer to *include* in income the difference between the amount expensed and the MACRS deductions that would have been allowed for the actual period of business use.

---

[28] §§ 179(d)(1) and (2).   [29] § 179(d)(10).

Example 18. On January 1, 1991, F purchased a computer for $5,000. He used it for business for one year, then gave it to his teenage son as a graduation present and bought himself another computer. F may expense the entire $5,000 cost of the computer. However, in 1992 he must recapture and include in income the difference between the expensed amount and the deduction computed under MACRS, $4,000 [$5,000 expensed − MACRS deduction of $1,000 ($5,000 × 20%)]. Note that the net effect in this case is to allow F a deduction equal to what he otherwise could have claimed under MACRS, $1,000.

LIMITATIONS FOR AUTOMOBILES

Over the years, Congress has become more and more concerned about taxpayers who effectively use the benefits of the tax law to reduce the cost of what are essentially personal expenses. For example, a taxpayer may justify the purchase of a luxury rather than standard automobile on the grounds that the government is helping to defray the additional cost through tax deductions and credits allowed for the purchase. In 1984 Congress enacted Code § 280F to reduce the benefits of depreciation and limited expensing for certain automobiles and other properties that are often used partially for personal purposes. In addition, the recordkeeping requirements for travel and entertainment were tightened and extended to certain property used for personal purposes.

Section 280F carves out a special set of limitations for *passenger automobiles*. A passenger automobile is defined as any four-wheeled vehicle manufactured primarily for use on public streets, roads, and highways that weighs 6,000 pounds or less unloaded.[30] (Normally, a standard sedan weighs approximately 4,500 pounds while vans typically weigh about 5,000 pounds.) For purposes of § 280F, the term *passenger automobiles* does not include vehicles for hire, such as taxi cabs, rental trucks, and rental cars.[31] Ambulances and hearses directly used in a trade or business are also unaffected by the § 280F limitations. In addition, the IRS has prescribed Regulations exempting certain trucks and vans.

For passenger automobiles, § 280F generally imposes a ceiling on the amount of annual depreciation and first-year expensing deductions. The *maximum* depreciation and/or § 179 expense for autos placed in service during 1990 is limited as follows:

Taxable year	Limit
1	$2,660
2	4,200
3	2,550
Thereafter	1,475

---

[30] § 280F(d)(5).   [31] § 280F(d)(5)(B).

Pre-1989 limitations under § 280F restricted the annual depreciation amounts for autos costing $12,800 or more (assuming 200 percent declining balance depreciation was selected). However, a similar rule of thumb cannot be used with current § 280F limitations. For instance, depreciation on an auto costing less than $13,300 would not be limited in the first year but would be limited in the second year. The second-year limitation would affect a car costing more than $13,125, and the third-year limitation would affect a car costing over $13,281. Moreover, note that if the taxpayer selects (or is required to use) straight-line depreciation, depreciation on an auto costing more than $7,375 would be restricted by the $1,475 limitation for years following the third year of ownership (i.e., $7,375 × 20 percent = $1,475).

Where the car is used less than 100 percent of the time for business—including the portion of time the car is used for production of income purposes—the maximum amounts given above must be reduced proportionately.

> **Example 19.** T purchased a car for $20,000. She used it 60% of the time for business purposes and 20% of the time traveling to her rental properties. Depreciation and limited expensing may not exceed $2,128 (80% × $2,660) for the first year, $3,360 (80% × $4,200) for the second year, and so on.

If the property's basis has not been fully deducted by the close of the normal recovery period (i.e., apparently the extended recovery period of six years), a deduction for the *unrecovered basis* is allowed in subsequent years. Deductions for the property's unrecovered basis are limited to $1,475 annually until the entire basis is recovered.

> **Example 20.** On October 1, 1991, R purchased a new automobile for $20,000 which he uses solely for business. As a result of depreciation deduction limits, his recovery period is extended an additional five years to 2001.

	1991	1992	1993	1994	1995	1996	*Annually* 1997–00	2001
Unadjusted basis.........	$20,000	$20,000	$20,000	$20,000	$20,000	$20,000		
Depreciation percentage...	20%	32%	19.2%	11.52%	11.52%	5.76%		
MACRS depreciation..	$ 4,000	$ 6,400	$ 3,840	$ 2,304	$ 2,304	$ 1,152		
Limit............	$ 2,660	$ 4,200	$ 2,550	$1,475	$ 1,475	$ 1,475	$ 1,475	$ 1,475
Deduction	$ 2,660	$ 4,200	$ 2,550	$1,475	$ 1,475	$ 1,152	$ 1,475	$ 588

In examining the above schedule, notice that in the sixth year, 1996, the depreciation actually calculated, $1,152, is less than the $1,475 limitation. The taxpayer can only deduct $1,152 despite the fact that there is additional basis remaining to be recovered.

Leasing. Without any special rule, the taxpayer could lease a car and circumvent the limitations on depreciation since the restrictions would appear to apply only to the deduction for depreciation and not lease payments. For instance, in *Example 20* above, the taxpayer might lease the car for $400 per month and claim a deduction of $4,800 for the year—far in excess of the amount allowed for depreciation. To prohibit this possibility, lessees may deduct the amount of the lease payment (applicable to business or income producing use)—but must *include* certain amounts in income to bring their deductions for use of the car in line for owners. Note that the above limitations do not apply to cars leased 30 days or less, or lessors who are regularly engaged in the auto leasing business.[32]

LIMITATIONS FOR PERSONAL USE

Section 280F also restricts the amount of depreciation that may be claimed for so-called "listed property" that is not used predominantly—more than 50 percent—for business. If the property is not used more than 50 percent *for business* in the year it is placed in service, the following restrictions are imposed:[33]

1. Limited expensing under § 179 is not allowed.

2. MACRS may not be used in computing depreciation. Property not qualifying must be depreciated using ADS. As explained above, ADS depreciation is computed using the straight-line method and the asset's class life (except in the case of certain property such as automobiles and computers, where the life to be used is specifically prescribed as five years).

Note that these restrictions are imposed if the property is not used primarily for business in the *first* year. Subsequent usage in excess of 50 percent does not permit the taxpayer to amend the earlier return or later use accelerated depreciation or limited expensing. On the other hand, if qualified usage initially exceeds 50 percent but subsequently drops to 50 percent or below, benefits previously secured must be relinquished. The recapture of these benefits is discussed below. Exhibit 9-11 identifies the depreciation methods available for listed property.

[32] § 280F(c).   [33] § 280F(b).

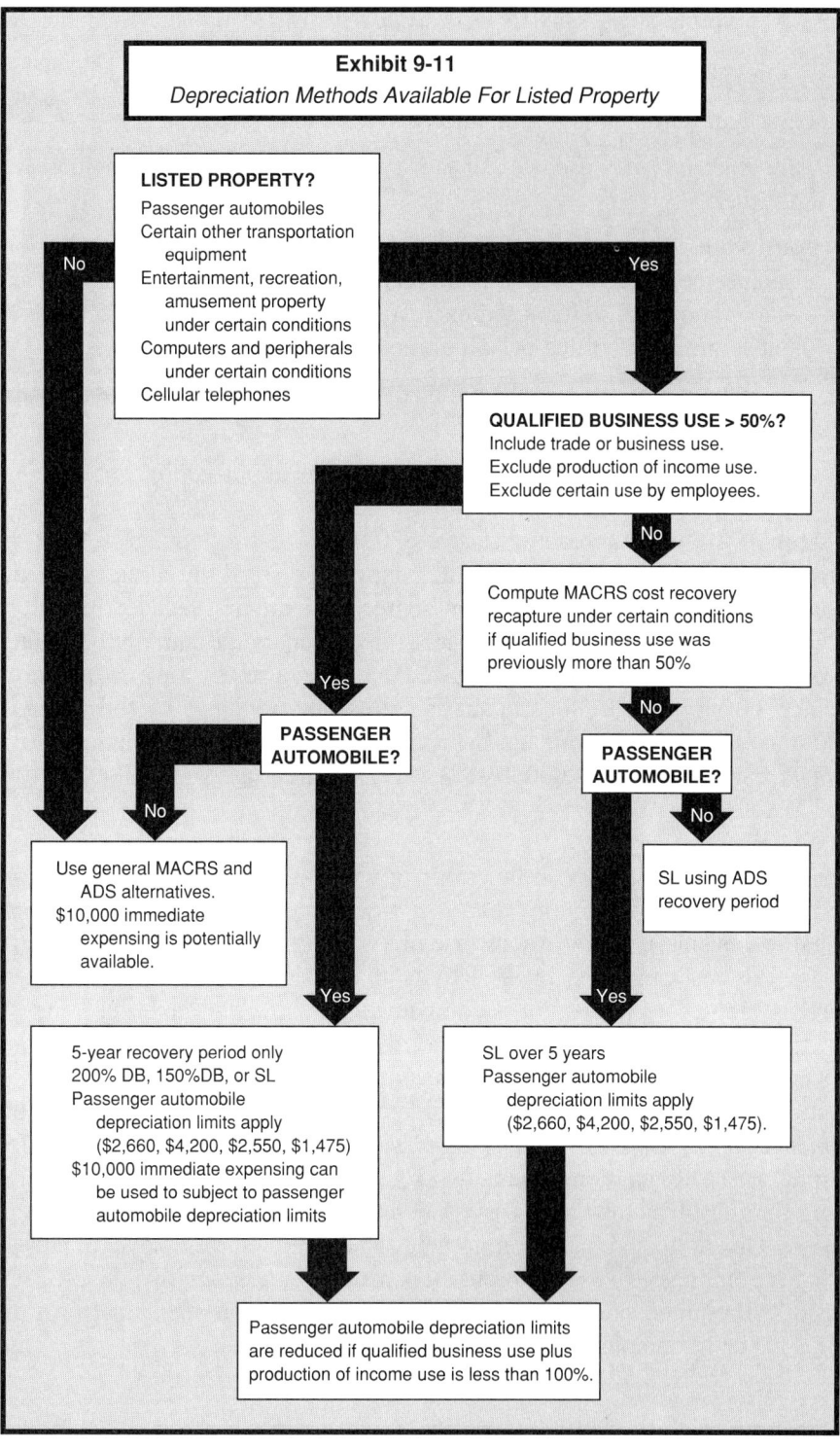

Exhibit 9-11

Depreciation Methods Available For Listed Property

LISTED PROPERTY?

Passenger automobiles
Certain other transportation
  equipment
Entertainment, recreation,
  amusement property
  under certain conditions
Computers and peripherals
  under certain conditions
Cellular telephones

No   Yes

QUALIFIED BUSINESS USE > 50%?
Include trade or business use.
Exclude production of income use.
Exclude certain use by employees.

No

Compute MACRS cost recovery
recapture under certain conditions
if qualified business use was
previously more than 50%

No

Yes

**PASSENGER
AUTOMOBILE?**

**PASSENGER
AUTOMOBILE?**

No   No

Use general MACRS and
ADS alternatives.
$10,000 immediate
  expensing is potentially
  available.

SL using ADS
recovery period

Yes   Yes

5-year recovery period only
200% DB, 150%DB, or SL
Passenger automobile
  depreciation limits apply
  ($2,660, $4,200, $2,550, $1,475)
$10,000 immediate expensing can
  be used to subject to passenger
  automobile depreciation limits

SL over 5 years
Passenger automobile
  depreciation limits apply
  ($2,660, $4,200, $2,550, $1,475).

Passenger automobile depreciation limits
are reduced if qualified business use plus
production of income use is less than 100%.

These restrictions apply only to *listed property*. Listed property includes the following:[34]

1. Passenger automobiles (as defined above)

2. Any other property used as a means for transportation (e.g., motorcycles and trucks)

3. Any property generally used for purposes of entertainment, recreation, or amusement (e.g., yacht, photography equipment, video recorders, and stereo equipment) *unless* used exclusively at a regular business establishment (e.g., at the office or at a home office)

4. Any computer or peripheral equipment *unless* used exclusively at a regular business establishment

5. Any cellular telephones and similar communications equipment

> **Example 21.** K purchased a car for $20,000. She uses her car 40% of the time for business and the remaining time for personal purposes. Since the property is a car, the limitations on depreciation are first reduced in light of the personal usage. In the first year, depreciation would initially be limited to $1,064 ($2,660 maximum allowed × 40% business use). In addition, since the car is listed property and is not used more than 50% for business, K must use ADS to compute depreciation. Therefore, depreciation in the first year is $800 ($20,000 cost × 40% business use = $8,000 × 10% ADS rate).

Qualified Business Use. In determining whether the property is used more than 50 percent for business, only *qualified business use* is considered.[35] Generally, qualified business use means any use in a trade or business of the taxpayer.[36] Thus, for this test *only*, use in an activity that does not constitute a trade or business is ignored (e.g., use of a computer to monitor the taxpayer's investments does not count toward the 50 percent threshold since the activity is not a business).[37] Additionally, an employee's use of his or her own property in connection with employment is not considered business use unless it is for the *convenience of the employer* and is *required as a condition of employment*.[38] According to the Regulations, these two requirements generally have the same meaning for § 280F as they have for § 119 relating to the exclusion for meals or lodging.[39] Given this interpretation, a mere statement by the employer expressly requiring the employee to use the property is insufficient. Ordinarily, the property is considered required only if it enables the employee to properly perform the duties of his or her employment.

---

[34] § 280F(d)(4).

[35] § 280F(b)(1) and (2).

[36] § 280F(d)(6).

[37] Temp. Reg. § 1.280F-6T(d)(2).

[38] § 280F(d)(3).

[39] Temp. Reg. § 1.280F-6T(a)(2).

Example 22.   T is employed by X, a newspaper company, to deliver papers in a rural area where the homes are widely scattered. The company does not provide T with a car and does not require T to own a car for employment. Since the car enables T to properly perform his duties and is for the convenience of X, T's use should qualify for purposes of the 50% test even though he is not explicitly required to own a car.

Example 23.   J is a budget analyst in the accounting department of a large construction firm. She owns a personal computer that is identical to the one she uses at work. Instead of staying late at the office, J occasionally brings home work for which she uses her computer. J's use of her computer for her work does not qualify.

Recent rulings indicate that the IRS takes a very narrow view regarding what satisfies the convenience-of-the-employer and condition-of-employment tests. In one instance, the Service held that a professor's use of her home computer for writing related to her research—which was required for continued employment—did not satisfy the tests.[40]   Although the Service agreed that the use of the computer was related to her work, it found no evidence that employees who did not use home computers were professionally disadvantaged. The Service also felt that her employer did not explicitly require use of the home computer before she was hired. Apparently, the Service will require taxpayers to demonstrate that the work could not properly be performed without the computer or at least that they will be professionally disadvantaged if they do not use the computer. In addition, under the IRS view, taxpayers will be obliged to show that use of the computer was mandatory and not optional.

The reach of this and other rulings goes farther than it first appears. As brought out by the Service, a literal interpretation of the statute indicates that if an employee does not satisfy the convenience-of-the-employer and condition-of-employment tests, *none* of the employee's use is treated as business use. This view does *not* mean that the employee is merely relegated to using ADS for depreciation. Rather, with no business use, the employee is prohibited from claiming any deductions relating to the listed property. Only time will tell whether this interpretation is consistent with Congressional intent.

In those cases where qualified business use exceeds 50 percent, any usage for the production of income or other business purposes is included in determining the percentage of the asset that may be depreciated using MACRS. Similarly, if business use is 50 percent or less, the usage for production of income or other nonqualified business purposes is still included in determining the percentage of the asset that may be depreciated using ADS. Note that depreciation is still allowed where the 50 percent test is not met, assuming there is business or investment usage.

---

[40]   Letter Ruling 8615024.

Example 24. V, a financial consultant, purchased a car for $20,000. She uses the car 25% of the time for business and 55% for production-of-income activities that do not qualify as a business. V must use ADS since business usage is only 25%. Although the time spent for the production of income cannot be counted towards the 50% test, it may be considered in the depreciation computation. Thus, V's depreciation would be $1,600 [$20,000 × (55% + 25%) × 10%]. It should be noted that where the listed property is an automobile, the limitations on depreciation also apply. Here the depreciation limitation is $2,128 [(55% + 25%) × $2,660; note that the production-of-income usage is considered in making the proper reduction]; thus it does not restrict the amount of the depreciation deduction. Had the usage percentages been reversed, the depreciation deduction would still have been limited to $2,128 ($20,000 × 80% business and investment usage = $16,000 × 20% depreciation percentage = $3,200 but limited to $2,128).

Employer-Provided Cars. The qualified business use rules directly address the problems of the company-owned car and other company-owned property used by employees. In the case of automobiles, employers typically provide company-owned cars to their employees principally for use in the employer's business. Normally, however, the employee also uses the car for personal purposes if only to commute to work. Under prior law, the employer claimed deductions and credits for the car without limitation (i.e., 100 percent of the car's basis was taken into account) while employees were required to treat the personal use as compensation. In most cases, the compensation income was avoided as long as the employee reimbursed the company for the value of the personal use, which the company in turn reported as income. Section 280F now prescribes specific rules governing depreciation where listed property is used by someone *other than* the owner—such as an employer-provided automobile. The following discussion examines these rules as they apply to employer-provided automobiles; however, such rules extend to other listed property as well.

Where an employee uses an automobile, an *employer* is able to secure 100 percent qualified business use—and thus depreciate the entire cost of the automobile—in one of four ways.[41]

1. The employee's actual business usage is disregarded and the *entire value* of using the vehicle is included in the employee's income.

2. The employee's actual business usage is combined with inclusion of the value of any personal use by the employee as income.

3. The employee's actual business usage is combined with a reimbursement arrangement where the employee reimburses the employer for any personal use (i.e., a fair rent is paid).

4. The use falls under one of four exceptions.

---

[41] Temp. Reg. § 1.280F-6T(d)(4)(iv).

Conditions 2 and 3 cannot be applied to qualify the use of a person owning greater than a 5 percent interest in the business (e.g., the company president, who is also a 30 percent shareholder). In this case, the employer can depreciate the car based only on the employee's actual business usage.

Before looking at several examples of these rules, it should be noted that each requires a valuation of the vehicle's use to the employee. The value can be determined using a facts-and-circumstances approach (e.g., considering such variables as geographic location, make and model, etc.) or one of several safe harbors provided by Temporary Regulations.[42] For example, the Regulations provide a table (i.e., a lease value table) based on the car's total value which provides values for personal use. Another alternative that can be used to value personal use under certain circumstances is the standard mileage allowance.

Example 25. During the year, X Corporation provided T, an employee, with a new car costing $10,000. T drove the company car 15,000 miles, 9,000 miles or 60% for business purposes, and 6,000 miles or 40% for personal purposes. X Corporation may use any of the first three alternatives to account for the car.

Alternative No. 1. Under this full inclusion method, the employee's actual use is disregarded and the employee must include 100% of the value of the car's use in income, $4,125 (15,000 × 27.5 cents—the standard mileage rate for 1991)[43] just as if it were salary (i.e., X Corporation includes it on T's Form W-2 and withholds income and FICA taxes). Therefore, all of T's use qualifies and X may depreciate 100% of the car using MACRS. T may then deduct any substantiated business use as a miscellaneous itemized deduction subject to the 2% floor. One advantage of this method for the employer is that it shifts all of the substantiation burden to the employee.

Alternative No. 2. Under this partial inclusion method, only T's personal use is treated as income, or $1,650 (6,000 × 27.5 cents). X could depreciate the car in the same manner as above. T may be better off under this method since the amount of compensation is reduced. This may have an effect on the amount of deductions or credits T may otherwise claim (e.g., the 2% floor on miscellaneous itemized deductions would be smaller due to the lower amount of income). In this case, X must be able to substantiate the employee's actual business use.

Alternative No. 3. Under the rental reimbursement method, T would pay X Corporation for his personal use, $1,650. X could depreciate the car in the same manner as above. T would be worse off in this situation. Each dollar of reimbursement costs T one dollar, while inclusion of the value of the personal use costs the employee only the tax on the value. Again, X must be able to substantiate the employee's actual business use.

[42] Temp. Reg. § 1.61-2T(d)(2)(iii).

[43] Rev. Proc. 90-59, I.R.B. No. 52,1. The rate was 26 cents per mile for 1990.

Five Percent Owner. If T owns 5% or more of the business (i.e., X Corporation), the only alternative is to compute depreciation using T's actual business mileage. In this case, X could depreciate 60% of the car using MACRS. Had T's business usage been 50% or less, X would be required to use ADS to compute depreciation.

Additional rules for determining qualified business usage exist for other situations. For example, leasing the property to a 5 percent owner of the business or a related person is not considered qualified business use. Similarly, special rules are provided for aircraft.

Recapture Provisions. If the 50 percent test is satisfied in the year property is placed in service but failed prior to the time when the cost of the asset would be completely recovered using the listed property recovery rules, the taxpayer is required to relinquish the benefits of MACRS. Technically, the taxpayer must recompute the depreciation in the prior years using ADS and include in income the excess of the depreciation actually claimed over the ADS amounts. Depreciation in future years is computed using the straight-line method.

> **Example 26.** In 1991 G purchased a car for $10,000 and used it entirely for business. Depreciation for 1991 was $2,000 ($10,000 × 20%). In 1992 G's business usage dropped to 40%. Since G's business usage is no longer greater than 50%, he must recapture the benefits of accelerated depreciation. Depreciation using the straight-line method in 1991 would have been $1,000 ($10,000 × 10%). Thus, G must include $1,000 ($2,000 original depreciation − $1,000 straight-line depreciation) in income in 1992. Depreciation for 1992 and all subsequent years must be computed using the straight-line method.

Recordkeeping Requirements. Not only has Congress severely restricted tax benefits for listed property, it also has imposed strict recordkeeping requirements for such property. The substantiation rules contained in Code § 274(d), which were formerly reserved solely for travel and entertainment expenses, now extend to expenses related to "listed property." For listed property, the taxpayer is required to substantiate the following: [44]

1. The amount of each expenditure related to the property, including the cost of acquisition, maintenance, and repairs

2. The date of the use of the property

3. The amount of each business or investment use as well as total use [the number of miles—in the case of a car or other means of transportation— or the amount of time that the property was used for other listed property (e.g., a computer)]

4. The purpose of the use of the property

---

[44] Temp. Reg. § 1.274-5T(b)(6).

In those cases where the overall use of the property for a taxable year can be definitely determined without entries, nonbusiness use need not be recorded. For example, in the case of a car, total miles can be determined by comparing the odometer readings at the beginning and the end of the taxable year. Consequently, the taxpayer needs to make entries only for business and investment use.

OTHER CONSIDERATIONS

Anti-Churning Rules. In some cases, a taxpayer's depreciation deductions under MACRS would be higher than those that the taxpayer may currently have. For this reason, Congress believed that some taxpayers would engage in transactions that might enable them to secure the advantages of MACRS.

> **Example 27.** In 1980 H acquired an apartment building as an investment that she chose to depreciate using the straight-line method over 35 years. H made this decision because the use of accelerated depreciation caused a portion of any gain from the subsequent sale of such property to be treated as ordinary income rather than favorable capital gain. With the elimination of favorable capital gain treatment in 1986, there no longer was any disincentive to use the accelerated method. Therefore, H created a plan to benefit from the change. She sold the property to her son who immediately leased it back to her. The rental payments to be paid by H were structured in light of the higher depreciation deductions (27.5-year life instead of 35 years) that her son would be able to take as the new owner of the property.

Sales, exchanges, and other dispositions of assets such as that illustrated above are referred to as "churning" transactions—exchanges of used property solely to obtain the benefits of MACRS.

The thrust of the anti-churning rules is to preclude the use of MACRS for property placed in service prior to the enactment of either version of MACRS, unless the property is transferred in a transaction where not only the owner changes but also the user.[45] In *Example 27* the anti-churning rules prohibit H's son from using MACRS since ownership did not truly change.

There are three sets of rules designed to police churning. For practical purposes these provisions should be given close review whenever the taxpayer is involved in a leasing or nontaxable transaction. For example, a taxpayer would typically be subject to the anti-churning rules in the following situations:

1. Sale followed by immediate leaseback

2. Like-kind exchange

3. Formation and liquidation of a corporation or partnership, including transfers of property to and distributions from these entities

---

[45] § 168(e)(4).

Component Depreciation and Improvements. Before 1981, taxpayers accelerated depreciation deductions on real property by separating the property into various components and depreciating them separately using different useful lives. For example, the structure or shell of a building might be assigned a life of 35 years while such items as carpeting, wiring and plumbing would be assigned lives of perhaps 5, 10, and 12 years. Component depreciation is not allowed under MACRS. Note also that any addition or improvement is to be depreciated using the same method as the property improved. For example, if in 2000 a new roof was added to an apartment building that was placed in service in 1990, the roof would be depreciated using a 27.5-year life and would be fully depreciated in 2028. No consideration is given to the fact that at the time of the improvement the remaining useful life of the original property is only 17.5 years.

Although MACRS rules preclude using component depreciation for structural components of buildings, taxpayers may still be able to accelerate real estate depreciation deductions by segregating certain costs associated with their buildings. See the section titled "Accelerating Depreciation with Cost-Segregation" in the "Tax Planning Considerations" section at the end of this chapter.

Property Leased to Tax-Exempt Entities. Prior to 1984, property leased to a tax-exempt entity such as a school, hospital, or government organization normally qualified for depreciation using ACRS (the predecessor of MACRS). Because depreciation provided no tax benefits for tax-exempt entities, these entities often structured arrangements to lease the properties they needed from taxable entities that could utilize the depreciation deductions. By so doing, the tax-exempt entity's effective cost of leasing the property was lower than the cost of purchasing the property outright. In 1984, however, Congress addressed the depreciation issue. As a general rule, depreciation of "tax-exempt use property"—most property leased to a "tax-exempt entity"—must be depreciated using ADS with special rules to determine the applicable recovery period.[46] However, the restrictions described above do not apply to a variety of situations. For example, the rules are inapplicable to "short-term leases."

AMORTIZATION

As previously discussed, MACRS does not apply to intangible property. Therefore, intangibles are subject to the rules existing prior to enactment of ACRS and MACRS. Generally, intangibles are amortized using the straight-line method over their estimated useful life. Special amortization and depreciation rules apply to certain expenditures, however.

GOODWILL AND COVENANTS NOT TO COMPETE

As mentioned in Chapter 6, buyers of a going concern often pay an amount in excess of the fair market value of the concern's tangible assets. This excess purchase price normally is attributable to intangible assets such as goodwill and/or

[46] § 168(g)(1)(C).

a covenant not to compete. Since goodwill is considered as having an unlimited life, any cost assigned to it may not be amortized. Recovery of a taxpayer's basis in goodwill occurs only when the business is subsequently sold or abandoned. In contrast, a covenant not to compete usually has an ascertainable life since the seller typically agrees to refrain from conducting a similar business or some other activity for a certain number of years. As a result, any cost attributable to the covenant may be amortized over the appropriate period using the straight-line method.

5-YEAR ELECTIVE AMORTIZATION

To accomplish certain economic and social objectives, Congress has enacted various optional 5-year (60-month) amortization procedures from time to time over the last 40 years. During certain periods, a 5-year amortization election (in lieu of regular depreciation) has been available for expenditures made in connection with child care facilities (§ 188), pollution control facilities (still an option under § 169), railroad rolling stock (§ 184), and rehabilitation of low-income housing [§ 167(k)]. A 60-month amortization election is currently available for qualifying expenditures associated with starting up a business (see Chapter 7).

LEASEHOLD IMPROVEMENTS

Taxpayers often lease property and improve the property while leasing it. In this situation, the lessee is entitled to recover the investment in the improvement.[47] After 1986, the cost of any leasehold improvement made by a lessee is depreciated in the normal manner without regard to the term of the lease. Any unrecovered cost at the end of the lease term would increase the taxpayer's basis for determining gain or loss. The recovery of the costs of acquiring a lease is determined under special rules in Code § 178.

DEPLETION

A taxpayer who invests in natural resources that are exhausted over time is entitled to recover his or her capital investment. Depletion is the method of recovering this cost and is similar to depreciation.[48] Depletion usually is claimed for investments in oil, gas, coal, copper, and other minerals. Land is not subject to depletion.

To qualify for depletion, the taxpayer must have an economic interest in the mineral deposits.[49] Typically, both the owner of the land who leases the property and the operator to whom the land is leased have the requisite interest since they both receive income from the severance or extraction of the minerals.

---

[47] § 168(i)(8); also see § 178(a) when the lease permits renewals.

[48] § 611.

[49] Reg. § 1.611-1(b).

COMPUTING THE DEPLETION DEDUCTION

Taxpayers generally are permitted to compute their depletion deduction using either the cost or percentage (statutory) depletion method. The taxpayer computes both cost and percentage depletion and is required to claim the higher amount.[50]

Cost Depletion.   Using cost depletion, the taxpayer recovers the actual investment (adjusted basis in the natural resource) as the mineral is produced. The following formula is used:[51]

$$\begin{array}{c} \text{Annual cost} \\ \text{depletion} \end{array} = \frac{\text{Unrecovered adjusted basis}}{\text{Estimated recoverable units}} \times \begin{array}{c} \text{Number of units } \textit{sold} \\ \text{during the year} \end{array}$$

This formula generally matches the cost of the investment against the revenues produced.

> **Example 28.**   On June 3, 19X1, D, a coal producer, paid $150,000 to acquire the mineral rights in a property which contains coal. He estimates that 90,000 tons of coal are recoverable from the property. During the year, 58,000 tons of coal were produced and 30,000 were sold. D's cost depletion would be $50,000 computed as follows:
>
> $$\frac{\$150,000 \text{ basis}}{90,000 \text{ units}} \times \begin{array}{c} 30,000 \\ \text{units sold} \end{array} = \begin{array}{c} \$50,000 \\ \text{depletion} \end{array}$$

Similar to depreciation, total *cost* depletion can never exceed the taxpayer's adjusted basis in the property.

Percentage Depletion.   For large oil and gas producers, cost depletion is the only depletion method allowed. However, both cost depletion and percentage depletion are available to small "independent" oil and gas producers as well as royalty owners.[52] In contrast, percentage depletion is allowed to *all* producers of certain types of minerals (e.g., gold, silver, gravel).

Under the percentage depletion method, the taxpayer's depletion deduction is computed without reference to the taxpayer's cost of the investment. Rather, percentage depletion is based on the amount of income derived from the property.[53] For this reason, the taxpayer may deduct percentage depletion in excess of the adjusted basis of the investment. Thus, the taxpayer is entitled to a deduction for percentage depletion as long as the property continues to generate income.

To compute percentage depletion, a percentage specified in the Code (see Exhibit 9-12) is applied to the *gross* income from the property. The resulting product is the amount of percentage depletion unless limited. For oil and gas properties, percentage depletion is generally limited to the taxpayer's *taxable* income before

---

[50]   § 613(a); Reg. § 1.611-1(a).

[51]   Reg. § 1.611-2(a).

[52]   § 613A(c).

[53]   § 613.

```
                    Exhibit 9-12
                Summary of Various
              Percentage Depletion Rates


                                                    Percentage
                  Natural Resource                     Rate

  1.  Gravel, sand, and other items..........................      5
  2.  Shale and clay used for sewer pipes; or
        brick and clay, shale, and slate used
        for lightweight aggregates............................    7.5
  3.  Asbestos, coal, sodium, chloride, etc....................    10
  4.  Gold, silver, oil and gas, oil shale, copper,
        and iron ore from deposits in the United States...........   15
  5.  Sulfur and uranium and a series of minerals
        from deposits in the United States.....................    22
  6.  Metals, other than those subject to 22%
        or 15% rate.........................................    14
```

depletion. Percentage depletion is limited to 50 percent of the taxpayer's taxable income from mineral properties. Gross income is the value of the natural resource when severed from the property before any processing. Taxable income from the property is the difference between income and operating expenses including overhead.

Example 29. Assume the same facts in *Example 28* and that the 30,000 tons sold were sold for $10 per ton (gross income of $300,000). Further, operating expenses attributable to the coal operation were $260,000. Percentage depletion is computed as follows:

Gross income..................................	$300,000
Statutory percentage for coal...................	× 10%
Percentage depletion before limitation...........	$ 30,000
Taxable income limitation:	
Gross income................................	$300,000
Less: Operating expenses.....................	− 260,000
Taxable income before depletion..............	$ 40,000
Limitation percentage........................	× 50%
Percentage depletion limit....................	$ 20,000
Percentage depletion allowable.................	$ 20,000

In this situation, D would use cost depletion of $50,000 as computed in *Example 28* because it exceeds allowable percentage depletion.

Example 30. Assume the same facts in *Example 29* except that barrels of oil are being produced, rather than tons of coal. Cost depletion computations are the same as in *Example 28*. Percentage depletion is computed as follows:

Gross income.............................	$300,000
Statutory percentage for oil...................	× 15%
Percentage depletion before limitation.........	$ 45,000
Gross income.............................	$300,000
Less: Operating expenses....................	− 260,000
Taxable income before depletion..............	$ 40,000
Percentage depletion limit....................	$ 40,000
Percentage depletion allowable...............	$ 40,000

D would use cost depletion of $50,000 (computed in *Example 28*) rather than percentage depletion of $40,000 because cost depletion is larger.

Whether percentage or cost depletion is used, the taxpayer must reduce the property's basis (but not below zero) by the amount of depletion claimed. Note that once the basis of the property is reduced to zero, only percentage depletion may be claimed, and *no* adjustment is made to create a negative basis.

RESEARCH AND EXPERIMENTAL EXPENDITURES

At first glance, it may appear that the proper tax treatment for research and development expenses requires their capitalization as part of a project's cost. This approach seems appropriate since these costs normally yield benefits only in future periods. Under this theory, the capitalized costs could be recovered over the period during which the project provides benefits or when the project is disposed of or abandoned. Upon closer examination, however, it becomes apparent that this approach is fraught with problems. Since it is difficult to establish any direct relationship between costs of research and development and the actual period benefited, it may be impossible to determine the appropriate period for recovery. For example, establishing a useful life for a scientific discovery that has numerous applications and which continually contributes to later research would be guesswork at best. A similar problem exists for unsuccessful efforts. Although a particular effort may not prove fruitful, it may at least indicate what does not work and thus lead to other, perhaps successful, research. In such case, it is not clear whether the costs should be written off or capitalized as part of the subsequent project.

Due to the administrative difficulties inherent in these determinations, the IRS historically granted research and experimental costs favorable treatment by generally allowing the taxpayer to deduct the expenses as incurred or to capitalize the expenses and amortize them over whatever period the taxpayer desires. Although this approach encountered difficulties in the courts, Congress eliminated the problems with enactment of special provisions in 1954.

RESEARCH AND EXPERIMENTAL EXPENDITURES DEFINED

The Code provides separate rules for research and experimental costs.[54] It should be emphasized that the provisions apply to research and *experimental* costs, not to research and development costs. The term *experimental* was used instead of *development* to limit the special treatment to laboratory costs.[55] Qualified costs generally include those incident to the development or improvement of a product, a formula, an invention, a plant process, an experimental or pilot model, or similar property. Research and experimental costs do *not* include expenditures for ordinary testing or inspection of materials or products for quality control, efficiency surveys, management studies, consumer surveys, advertising, or promotion. Costs of obtaining a patent, such as legal fees, qualify. However, the costs of acquiring an existing patent, model, or process are not considered research and experimental costs. Expenditures for depreciable property do not qualify but the depreciation allowable on the property is eligible for special treatment.

ALTERNATIVE TAX TREATMENTS

Three alternative methods may be used to account for research and experimental expenditures. The expenses may be deducted as they are paid or incurred, deferred and amortized, or capitalized. Immediate deduction usually is the preferred method since the present value of the tax benefit is greater using this method. Deferral may be preferable in two instances, however. If the taxpayer's income is low in the current year, the tax benefit of the deduction might be increased by deferring the deduction to high-income years when the taxpayer is in a higher marginal tax bracket. Deferral also may be better if an immediate deduction creates or adds to a net operating loss since such losses may be carried over and used only for a limited period of time. The general rule for selecting the best alternative is to choose the one that maximizes the present value of the tax savings from the research and experimental expenditures.

Expense Election. The taxpayer can elect to deduct all research and experimental expenditures currently.[56] Note, however, that expenditures for depreciable property cannot be expensed currently.[57] If the taxpayer adopts this method in the first tax year in which research and experimental expenses are incurred, the method must be used for all such expenditures in all subsequent years, unless permission is secured to change methods of part or all of the expenditures.[58] The IRS does not need to approve the method the taxpayer adopts initially. Consent is required, however, if the taxpayer wishes to change methods.

---

[54] § 174.

[55] Reg. § 1.174-2(a).

[56] § 174(a).

[57] § 174(c).

[58] § 174(a)(2).

Deferral Option. Research and experimental expenditures may be deferred and amortized at the election of the taxpayer.[59] The expenses must be amortized ratably over a period not less than 60 months beginning in the period in which benefits from the expenditures are first realized. It should be emphasized that costs of depreciable property are not deferred expenses; rather, the depreciation expense must be capitalized and amortized over 60 months. Also, if the taxpayer elects to defer the expenditures and a patent is subsequently obtained, the cost must be amortized over the life of the patent, 17 years. If the deferral method is initially elected, the taxpayer must use this method for all future expenses in subsequent tax years unless permission to change methods is obtained.[60]

Election to Capitalize. A taxpayer who does not elect either to amortize research and experimental expenditures over 60 months or to deduct them currently must capitalize them. Capitalizing the expenditure increases the basis of the property to which the expense relates. No deduction is permitted for the capital expenditure until the research project is considered worthless or abandoned. A disposition of the research project such as a sale or an exchange enables the taxpayer to offset the capitalized expenditures—the basis of the project—against any amount realized.

> **Example 31.** L Corporation, a drug manufacturer, is an accrual basis, calendar year taxpayer. During 1991, the corporation performed research to improve various cold and flu medications. On December 1, 1991, a new cold and flu product line was successfully introduced on the market. In connection with this project, L incurred the following costs:
>
> | | |
> |---|---:|
> | Lab equipment (5-year property) | $50,000 |
> | Salaries | 90,000 |
> | Laboratory materials | 5,000 |
>
> If L Corporation elects to expense the research and experimental costs, it may deduct $105,000 in 1991 as follows:
>
> | | |
> |---|---:|
> | MACRS depreciation on lab equipment (20% of $50,000) | $ 10,000 |
> | Salaries | 90,000 |
> | Laboratory materials | 5,000 |
> | Total deductions | $105,000 |

---

[59] § 174(b).   [60] § 174(b)(2).

Note that only the depreciation on the lab equipment may be deducted as a research and experimental cost, *not* the entire cost of the equipment. If L Corporation elects to defer the expense, its monthly amortization beginning December 1, 1991 would be

$$\frac{\$105,000}{60} = \$1,750$$

Alternatively, L could capitalize all the expenses as an asset (including the $10,000 of depreciation) and receive no deduction until a later disposition or abandonment.

OTHER RELATED PROVISIONS

Several other provisions exist relating to the treatment of research and experimental expenditures. In 1981 Congress created a tax credit for research and experimentation. Generally, the credit is 20 percent of the current year's expenditures after adjustments (see Chapter 13).[61] Taxpayers electing the credit are generally required to reduce their research and experimentation expenses by 50 percent of the credit for purposes of computing the amount to either be expensed, deferred, or capitalized.[62] Special rules also exist for contributions of research property by corporations (see Chapter 11).[63]

EXPENSES OF FARMERS AND RANCHERS

Special provisions exist for certain types of expenditures incurred by those engaged in farming and ranching. The rules examined below generally differ from the treatment of expenses that normally would be considered capital expenditures subject to depreciation.

EXPENSES RELATED TO LIVESTOCK

Costs of acquiring animals used for breeding, dairy, work, or sport are treated as capital expenditures and are depreciable under MACRS unless such animals are primarily held for sale and would be appropriately included in inventory. Where a farmer raises his or her own livestock, however, expenses incurred such as feed normally can be deducted as paid, assuming the taxpayer uses the cash basis method of accounting.[64] This rule is in sharp contrast to that applying to other self-production costs. Costs incurred by farmers and others in constructing their own equipment and buildings must be capitalized and depreciated.

---

[61] § 41.

[62] § 280C(c).

[63] § 170.

[64] Reg. § 1.162-12.

SOIL AND WATER CONSERVATION, FERTILIZER, LAND CLEARING

Farmers often incur expenses for soil and water conservation. Examples of these expenses are the costs of leveling or terracing the soil to control the flow of water, irrigation and drainage ditches, ponds, dams, eradication of brush, and planting windbreaks. Although normal tax rules would require these expenses to be capitalized, Code § 175 permits a deduction when such expenses are paid or incurred as long as such expenses are consistent with a conservation plan approved by the Soil Conservation Service of the Department of Agriculture. To encourage these practices and still restrict the availability of this benefit, the Code requires that the taxpayer be engaged in the business of farming. In addition, the annual deduction for these expenses is limited to 25 percent of the taxpayer's gross income from farming. This limitation prohibits a taxpayer from using the deductions to reduce nonfarm income. Expenditures exceeding this limitation may be carried over to subsequent years.

Like soil and water conservation expenditures, Code § 180 provides that the cost of fertilizer, lime, and other materials used to enrich farmland can be deducted in the year paid or incurred by those engaged in the business for farming. There is no limitation imposed on the amount of the deduction.

Taxpayers engaged in the farming business must capitalize expenses of clearing land in preparation for farming. These expenses include any cost of making the land suitable for farming such as those for removing and eradicating brush or tree stumps and the treating or moving of earth. Routine brush clearing and other ordinary maintenance related to the land may be expensed, however.

DEVELOPMENT EXPENSES

Expenses incurred in the development of farms and ranches prior to the time when production begins may be capitalized or expensed at the election of the taxpayer.[65] Examples of these expenses are costs of cultivation, spraying, pruning, irrigation, and management fees.

The expensing of development and other farm-related costs prior to the period in which the farm begins to produce income provides an attractive device for high-bracket taxpayers—who have no interest in farming—to shelter their income from other nonfarm sources. These and other tax advantages offered by farming in the sixties brought such an influx of "urban cowboys" to the farming industry that several farm groups protested and demanded protection. Congress first responded to these groups in 1969. Currently, this provision prohibits the immediate expensing of any amount attributable to the planting, cultivation, maintenance, or development of any citrus or almond grove. Any of these development costs that are incurred in the first four years of the grove's life must be capitalized.

---

[65] *Ibid.*

Congress adopted additional safeguards in 1976. Section 447 generally requires that corporations (and partnerships having a corporate partner) engaged in the business of farming must use the accrual method of accounting. Since this provision was intended to protect small farmers and family-owned farms, the following are not treated as corporations: (1) S corporations; (2) family-owned corporations (at least 50% of the stock is owned by family members); and (3) any corporation that did not have gross receipts exceeding $1 million in any prior year. In addition, farming syndicates may deduct the costs of feed, seed, fertilizer, and similar farm supplies only as they are actually used.[66] A farming syndicate generally is defined to include partnerships and S corporations where the sale of their interests are specifically regulated by state or local securities laws, or more than 35 percent of their losses during any period are allocated to limited partners or persons who do not actively participate in the management of the business.

In 1986 the prohibition against the deduction of prepaid farming expenses was extended to all farmers that prepay more than 50 percent of their expenses such as feed, seed, and fertilizer.[67] Farmers cannot deduct such expenses until the items are consumed or used. Several exceptions exist, however.

---

[66]   § 464.   [67]   § 464(f).

TAX PLANNING CONSIDERATIONS

DEPRECIATION AND AFTER-TAX CASH FLOW

Many taxpayers, when analyzing an investment, fail to consider the tax aspects. For example, a taxpayer who looks solely to the cash flow projections of investing in a rental property might overlook the effect of depreciation. The depreciation deduction does not require an outlay of cash, but does produce a tax benefit.

Example 32. In January 1991, L purchased a duplex for $80,000 which she rented to others. Of the $80,000 purchase price, $70,000 was allocable to the building and $10,000 was allocable to the land. L financed the purchase with a $5,000 downpayment and a mortgage calling for monthly payments of interest and principal of $400. During the year, L rented the property for $7,000. Expenses for the year were as follows:

Mortgage interest	$4,000
Taxes	1,200
Insurance	500
Maintenance and utilities	300
Depreciation (MACRS: $70,000 × 3.485%)	2,440
Total expenses	$8,440

The net taxable loss from the real property would be

Rental income	$ 7,000
Less: Rental expenses	(8,440)
Net taxable loss	$ 1,440

Note that the taxable loss contains depreciation expense of $2,440, a noncash expenditure. Assuming L is in the 28 percent tax bracket, the net cash flow from the project would be computed as follows:

Cash inflow:		
Rental income	$7,000	
Tax saving from loss		
($1,440 × 28%)	403	
Total cash inflow		$7,403
Cash outflow:		
Total expenses	$8,440	
Less: Depreciation	(2,440)	
	$6,000	

Debt service
  Mortgage payments ($400 × 12)............. $4,800
  Less: Interest (included in
        expenses above).................   (4,000) + 800

  Total cash outflow...........................   (6,800)

  After-tax cash flow............................. $ 603

Therefore, L has a positive cash flow of $603 on the project notwith-standing the taxable loss that she suffered of $1,440.

Under certain circumstances, limitations are imposed on the deduction of losses from rental property. These limitations are discussed in Chapter 12.

ACCELERATING DEPRECIATION WITH COST-SEGREGATION

Prior to 1981, some taxpayers used a technique called "component depreciation" to accelerate real estate depreciation deductions. These taxpayers separated the costs of their depreciable buildings into various components with useful lives shorter than the rest of the building. For example, structural components such as wiring, plumbing, and roofing were depreciated over periods of 10 or 15 years rather than the much longer periods typically associated with the useful life of the building shell.

Although MACRS rules do not allow component depreciation for structural components of buildings, taxpayers may still be able to accelerate depreciation on some costs that might otherwise be depreciated over 27.5 or 31.5 years with the rest of the building's cost. Examples of assets that taxpayers should segregate from the cost of the building and depreciate over five or seven years include movable partitions, computers, separate fire protection systems, manufacturing equipment, and built-in desks and cabinets. Separate humidity-control and air conditioning systems installed specifically for special equipment can also be depreciated over seven years. A rule of thumb for identifying these separate depreciable assets is to assess whether the items would be removed if the business were to relocate. If so, the removable assets can have their own depreciation schedules.

Land improvements represent another set of costs that should be separated since they can be depreciated over 15 years. These include parking lots, landscaping, sewers, and irrigation systems.

To segregate costs successfully, taxpayers or their advisors should work closely with building contractors to document the costs of fast-depreciating assets. Early involvement with the contractor or architect could even lead to building designs that maximize the number of separate depreciable assets while not reducing the productive use of the building.

PROBLEM MATERIALS

DISCUSSION QUESTIONS

9-1   *Requirements for Depreciation.*   Indicate the basic requirements that must be satisfied before property may be depreciated.

9-2   *Depreciation and Amortization: Eligible Property.*   Indicate whether a taxpayer could claim deductions for depreciation or amortization of the following property:

  a.   Land used in the taxpayer's farming business.
  b.   A duplex—the taxpayer lives in one-half while he rents the other half out.
  c.   The portion of the taxpayer's residence that she uses as a home office.
  d.   The taxpayer's former residence, which he listed for rental temporarily until he is able to sell it. The residence was listed in late November and was not rented as of the end of the taxable year.
  e.   A mobile home that the taxpayer initially purchased and used while he was in college and this year began renting to several students.
  f.   The costs attributable to goodwill and a covenant not to compete.
  g.   An automobile used for business. The taxpayer accounts for his deductible car expenses using the standard mileage rate.

9-3   *Definitions: Cost Allocation Methods and Types of Property.*   Explain the terms depreciation, amortization, and depletion. Include in your discussion an explanation of tangible and intangible property as well as personal and real property.

9-4   *Depreciation Systems.*   Briefly describe the depreciation systems (e.g., MACRS) for computing tax depreciation that one may encounter in practice.

9-5   *Ineligible Property.*   What types of property are not depreciated using MACRS? How can the taxpayer avoid MACRS?

9-6   *Depreciation Methods and MACRS Statutory Percentages.*

  a.   Briefly explain the three basic depreciation methods.
  b.   Indicate the first-year depreciation percentage applicable to office furniture and show how it is determined.
  c.   Same as (b) except the property is an apartment building.

9-7   *MACRS and Straight-Line Depreciation.*   Assuming a taxpayer desires to use the straight-line method of depreciation, what alternatives, if any, are available?

9-8   *Alternative Depreciation System.*   Typically, all depreciation is computed using MACRS. However, Code § 168 also establishes an alternative depreciation system (ADS). As a practical matter, when will use of ADS be most likely?

9-9 *Depreciating Recovery Property.*   During the year, X purchased land and a building for a total of $500,000 and furniture for the building for $100,000. He intends to lease the building. Indicate whether the following factors are taken into account in computing the depreciation of these assets.

  a. Each asset's useful life as estimated by the taxpayer in light of industry standards.
  b. Salvage value.
  c. The month in which the property was placed in service.
  d. The use of the building by the lessee.
  e. The taxpayer is a corporation.
  f. The property is used for investment rather than business use.
  g. The acquisition cost of the building including the land.
  h. The lessee.

9-10 *Half-Year Convention.*   Indicate whether the following statements are true or false regarding the half-year convention.

  a. Depreciation can be claimed for the *entire* year if the asset has been in service for more than six months.
  b. The half-year convention applies to *all* property placed in service during the year.
  c. The half-year convention applies *both* in the year of acquisition and the year of disposition of the asset.
  d. The convention must be considered when expensing an asset under Code § 179.

9-11 *Acquiring a Business.*   L has worked as a salesman in the outdoor advertising business for ten years. This year he decided to go into business for himself. To this end he purchased all of the assets of Billboards Unlimited Corporation for $2 million. The value of the tangible assets such as the office building, furniture, and equipment was $1.4 million. Explain how L will recover the cost of his investment.

9-12 *Luxury Cars.*   Indicate whether the following statements are true or false. If false, explain why and show supporting calculations.

  a. W purchased a car used solely for business for $12,000. The limitations imposed by Code § 280F on deductions related to automobiles do not alter what W could claim in the year of acquisition.
  b. P Corporation is a distributor of hospital supplies. During the year, it purchased a $20,000 car for its best salesperson. Section 280F does not alter the total amount of depreciation deducted while P owns the car. Section 280F alters only the timing of the depreciation deductions.

9-13 *Listed Property.*   Indicate whether the following statements are true or false. If false, explain why.

    a.   J is a part-time photographer. This year she purchased a camera that cost $1,000 for her video cassette recorder. Thirty percent of her usage was for business while the remainder was personal. J may use the accelerated depreciation recovery percentages of MACRS.

    b.   P, a proprietor of a lighting store, purchased computer equipment for $10,000 which he uses 50 percent of the time for business. Under Code § 280F, the maximum deduction for depreciation and limited expensing in the first year is $500, while without § 280F the deduction would be $5,000.

    c.   C purchased computer equipment that he uses 60 percent for managing his investments and 35 percent of the time in connection with a mail-order business he operates out of his home. C may claim straight-line depreciation deductions based on 95 percent of the cost of the asset.

    d.   G is employed as a research consultant for RND Corporation, a research institute. G uses the company's computer at the office but often takes home work, which she does on her home computer. G's use of her home computer for work done for her employer is considered qualified business use.

    e.   T is a college professor who uses a computer, for which he properly claims deductions, to write textbooks in his home office. It is unnecessary for T to maintain records on business usage of the computer.

    f.   WS Corporation, a large clothing manufacturer, provides a car for each of its salespeople. It charges each of its salespersons 27.5 cents for each mile of personal use. WS may disregard any personal use of the cars by its salespeople in computing depreciation.

    g.   WS Corporation also provides a car for its chief executive officer, C, who owns 10 percent of the company's stock. All of C's use is for business except for commuting to work, which represents 60 percent of the car's use. C reimburses the company for the personal use. WS may claim accelerated depreciation for the car based on 40 percent of the car's cost.

9-14 *Amortization.*   How are the costs of patents, copyrights, and goodwill recovered?

9-15 *Leasing Restrictions.*   Address the following:

    a.   Construct a numerical example illustrating why a tax-exempt entity would rather lease than buy.

    b.   R acquired a ten-year ground lease on three acres on which it constructed a small office building. Explain how R will recover its cost of the building.

9-16 *Depreciation—Allowed or Allowable.*   R inherited her mother's personal residence in 1958 and converted it to rental property. Her basis for depreciation was $30,000. The residence had an estimated useful life of 30 years. This year, R sold the residence for $40,000. During the time R held the property, she never claimed a deduction for depreciation on the residence. What amount of gain will R report upon the sale?

9-17 *Salvage Value.* How is salvage value used in computing the depreciation deduction using MACRS?

9-18 *Depreciable Basis and Limited Expensing.* Explain how the taxpayer's depreciable basis may be affected by the amount expensed under the limited expensing election of § 179.

9-19 *Anti-Churning Rules.* Explain the purpose of the anti-churning rules and when they normally will apply.

9-20 *Component vs. Composite Depreciation.* Answer the following:

   a. Distinguish component depreciation from composite depreciation.
   b. May the taxpayer use either method? Explain.

9-21 *Mid-Quarter Convention.* T company, a calendar year taxpayer, purchased $100,000 of equipment on December 3 of this year.

   a. Under what circumstances will the mid-quarter convention apply in computing depreciation of the equipment?
   b. Assume that T can purchase the equipment at any time during the year. How will T time the acquisitions if it wants to maximize the firm's depreciation deductions for the year?

9-22 *Depletion.* Address the following:

   a. Briefly describe how cost and percentage depletion are computed and determine which is used in a particular year.
   b. Assuming the taxpayer has completely recovered her depletable cost basis (e.g., her basis is zero), is she entitled to further depletion deductions?

9-23 *Farming Expenses.* N plans on stepping down from his position of president of a large energy company in five years. At that time, he and his wife would like to move to the country where they would retire and perhaps operate a small dairy farm. N has spotted some land through which a sparkling creek runs. His accountant has suggested that he purchase the land now and begin to operate it despite initial losses. Explain the rationale behind the accountant's advice.

PROBLEMS

9-24 *Depreciation of Converted Personal-Use Property.* F purchased a mobile home to live in while at college. The home cost $12,000. When he graduated, he left the home in the trailer park and rented it. At the time he converted the home to rental property, it had a fair market value of $10,000.

   a. What is F's basis for depreciation?
   b. F now lives 75 miles away from his alma mater. Can he deduct the cost of traveling back to check on his rental property (including those trips on which he also attended a football game)?

9-25 *MACRS Accelerated Depreciation.*   In 1991, T, a calendar year taxpayer, decided to move her insurance business into another office building. She purchased a used building for $70,000 on March 15. T also purchased new office furniture for the building. The furniture was acquired for $20,000 on May 1. The first-year expensing option is not elected, yet T wants to depreciate her assets as rapidly as possible. MACRS depreciation tables are located in Appendix C.

    a.   Compute T's depreciation deduction for 1991.
    b.   Compute T's depreciation deduction for 1992.
    c.   Assuming that T sold the office building and the furniture on July 20, 1993, compute T's depreciation for 1993.
    d.   Answer (a), (b), and (c) above assuming that the furniture was purchased on October 20.

9-26 *Mid-Quarter Convention.*   Q Corporation anticipates purchasing $300,000 of office furniture and fixtures (7-year property) next year. This will be Q's only personal property acquisition for the year. Q Corporation management is willing to purchase and place the property in service any time during the year to accelerate its depreciation deductions. In addition, management wants to depreciate the property as rapidly as possible. MACRS depreciation tables are located in Appendix C.

    a.   Compute depreciation for the first two years of ownership assuming *all* of the property is purchased and placed in service on February 2.
    b.   Compute depreciation for the first two years of ownership assuming *all* of the property is purchased and placed in service on December 6.
    c.   Compute depreciation for the first two years of ownership assuming $177,000 (59%) of the property is purchased and placed in service on February 2 and $123,000 (41%) is purchased and placed in service on December 6.
    d.   Based on the results of (a) through (c) above, what course of action do you recommend for Q Corporation?

9-27 *MACRS Straight-Line Depreciation.*   G Corporation operates a chain of fast-food restaurants. On February 7, 1991, the company purchased a new building for $100,000. In addition, on May 5, 1991, G purchased a used stove for $5,000 and refrigeration equipment for $30,000 (both 7-year property). G does not elect to use the limited expensing provision. The company does elect to compute depreciation using the straight-line method under MACRS. MACRS depreciation tables are located in Appendix C.

    a.   Why might G elect to use the straight-line method?
    b.   Assuming G elects to use the straight-line method and a 7-year recovery period for depreciating the stove applies, can it use MACRS accelerated recovery percentages for the refrigeration equipment? For the building?
    c.   Compute G's depreciation for the stove and building in 1991 assuming it elects the straight-line method for the 7-year property.
    d.   Compute the depreciation for the stove and building in 1992.
    e.   If G does not dispose of either the stove or building, what is the final (i.e., last year's) depreciation deduction for the stove and the building?
    f.   Assuming G disposes of both the stove and the building on October 18, 1992, what is the depreciation for each of these assets in 1992?

9-28 *ADS Depreciation.* P retired several years ago to live on a small farm. To supplement his income, he cuts wood and sells it in the nearby community. This year he purchased a new light duty truck to haul and deliver the wood. He used the truck 20 percent of the time for business. Assuming the truck cost $9,000, compute P's depreciation for the year.

9-29 *Section 179 Election.* Although K is currently a systems analyst for 3L Corporation, her secret desire is to write a best-selling novel. To this end, she purchased a computer for $3,000 this year. She used the computer only for writing her novel. Can she deduct the entire cost of her computer this year? Next year?

9-30 *Limitations on § 179 Expensing.* In each of the following situations, indicate whether T may elect to use the limited-expensing provisions of § 179. Assume the acquisition qualifies unless otherwise indicated.

a. T is a corporate taxpayer.
b. This year, T purchased a $300,000 building and $50,000 of equipment.
c. T suffered a net operating loss of $40,000 this year before consideration of the § 179 deduction.
d. T purchased the asset on the last day of the taxable year.

9-31 *Limited-Expensing Election: Eligible Property.* For each of the following assets, indicate whether the taxpayer may elect to expense a portion or all of the asset's cost.

a. A $10,000 car used 75 percent for business purposes and 25 percent for personal purposes.
b. A home computer used by the taxpayer to maintain records and perform financial analyses with respect to her investments.
c. An apartment building owned by a large property company.
d. A roll-top desk purchased by the taxpayer's father, who gave it to the taxpayer to use in her business.

9-32 *Limited-Expensing Election Calculations.* N, a single taxpayer, purchased duplicating equipment to use in his business. He purchased the equipment on June 3 of the current year for $12,000. N elects to expense the maximum amount allowable with respect to the equipment.

a. What portion of the cost of the equipment may N expense for this year?
b. Compute N's depreciation deduction for the current year.

9-33 *Section 280F Calculations.* In the current year, H purchased a new automobile for $15,000. The first-year expensing election is not made.

a. Assuming the car is used solely for business, prepare a depreciation schedule illustrating the amount of annual depreciation to which H is entitled assuming he holds the car until the entire cost is recovered.
b. Assume the same facts as (a) except the car is used 80 percent of the time for business and 20 percent of the time for personal purposes. Compute the current year's depreciation deduction.
c. Same as (b) except the car is used 70 percent of the time for business, 10 percent of the time for production of income activities, and 20 percent of the time for personal purposes.
d. Same as (a) except the car is used 40 percent of the time for business and 60 percent of the time for personal purposes.

9-34 *Section 280F Calculations.*   M purchased a new automobile for $30,000. The first-year expensing election is not made. The car is used solely for business. M is in the 28 percent tax bracket. The present value factors for a 10 percent discount rate are as follows: year 1, .91; 2, .83; 3, .75; 4, .68; 5, .62; 6, .56; 7, .51; 8, .47; 9, .42; 10, .39; 11, .35; 12, .32; 13, .29; 14, .26; 15, .24; 16, .22; 17, .20.

a.   Prepare a depreciation schedule.

b.   Compute the total tax savings M will receive throughout the recovery period from depreciation deductions.

c.   Using an after-tax discount rate of 10 percent, compute the present value of tax savings from depreciation deductions under § 280F.

d.   Using an after-tax discount rate of 10 percent, compute the present value of tax savings from depreciation deductions under MACRS *as if* § 280F were repealed.

e.   Compare the results of (b) and (c) above. What impact does discounting have in assessing the tax benefits of depreciation?

f.   Compare the results of (c) and (d) above. What is the discounted after-tax cost of the § 280F limitations for this taxpayer?

9-35 *Research and Experimental Expenditures.*   ABC Corporation is developing a new process to develop film. During the year, the company had the following expenditures related to research and development:

Salaries...	$60,000
Laboratory equipment (5-year property)..........	30,000
Materials and supplies..........................	10,000

Compute ABC's deduction for research and experimental expenditures under each of the alternative methods.

9-36 *Depletion.*   DEF Company produces iron ore. It purchased a property for $100,000 during the year. Engineers estimate that 50,000 tons of iron ore are recoverable from the property. Given the following information, compute DEF's depletion deduction and undepleted cost basis for each year.

Year	Units Sold (tons)	Gross Income	Taxable Income before Depletion
1	15,000	$300,000	$124,000
2	20,000	400,000	50,000
3	10,000	250,000	90,000

9-37 *Depletion.*   Assume the same facts in Problem 9-36 except that barrels of oil are being produced rather than tons of iron ore. Compute DEF's depletion deduction and undepleted cost basis for each year.

CUMULATIVE PROBLEMS

9-38   David and Lauren Hammack are married with one child, Jim, age 12. The couple lives at 2003 Rolling Drive, Indianapolis, Indiana 46222. David is a product manager for G&P corporation, a food company. Lauren operates a clothing store as a sole proprietorship (employer identification number 35-123444). The couple uses the cash method of accounting except where the accrual method is required. They report on the calendar year.

David earned a salary of $60,000 during the year. G&P also provides health insurance for David and his family. Of the total insurance premium, the company paid $750. Income taxes withheld from David's salary were $7,000. The couple paid $10,000 in estimated taxes during the year.

Lauren's father died on June 20. As a result, Lauren received $40,000 as beneficiary of a life insurance policy on her father. In addition, her father's will provided that she receive all of his shares of IBM stock. The stock was distributed to her in October when it was worth $30,000.

On August 1 of this year, the couple purchased a six-month Treasury Bill for $9,700. They redeemed it on February 1 of the following year for its face value, $10,000. In addition, the couple purchased a previously issued AT&T bond with the face value of $1,000 for $890 on June 1. The bond pays interest at 6 percent per year on January 1 and July 1. On July 1 they received an interest payment of $30, which was also reported on Form 1099-INT, sent to them shortly after year-end. The couple plans on reporting any accrued market discount in taxable income when they sell or redeem the bond, in some future year.

Several years ago, the couple invested in Nedco Corporation, acquiring 100 shares of stock for $10,000. They were two of the original 10 investors that helped start the corporation. Unfortunately, the corporation was never successful and the stock became worthless this year. Only $500,000 of stock was ever issued. All of Nedco's stock is considered small business stock under Code § 1244.

Each year, Lauren travels to Paris to attend the annual fashion shows for buyers. When scheduling her trip for this year, Lauren decided to combine business with pleasure. On Thursday, March 6, Lauren departed for Paris, arriving on Friday morning. Friday afternoon was devoted to business discussions with several suppliers. Since the shows began on Monday, she spent the weekend touring Paris. After attending the shows Monday through Wednesday, she returned to Indianapolis on Thursday, arriving late that night. The cost of her round-trip air fare to Paris was $500. Meals were $30 per day and lodging was $100 per day for Friday through the following Wednesday.

In addition to running her own shop, Lauren teaches an M.B.A. course in retailing at the local university. She received a $6,000 salary for her efforts this year. The university withheld $429 in F.I.C.A. taxes, but did not make additional tax withholdings related to the salary. The school is ten miles from her office. Normally, she goes home from her office to get dinner before she goes to the school to teach (16 miles from her home). According to her log, she made 80 trips from home to school. In addition, the log showed that she had driven 20,000 miles related to her clothing business. She uses the standard mileage rate to compute her automobile expenses.

Lauren's records, which she maintains for her business using the cash method of accounting, reveal the following additional information:

Sales	$120,000
Cost of goods sold	(50,000)
Gross profit	$ 70,000
Advertising	6,000
Insurance	1,400
Rent	9,000
Wages	15,000
Employment taxes	2,000

The insurance included (1) a $200 premium paid in September for coverage of her car from October through March of the following year; and (2) a $1,200 payment for fire insurance for June 1 through May 31 of the following year. Similarly, rent expense includes a $4,500 payment made on November 1 for rent from November through April. She has a five-year lease requiring semiannual rental payments of $4,500 on November 1 and May 1.

Lauren allows several of her customers to buy things on credit. This year, she sold $2,000 of merchandise to X and allowed him to charge it to his account. To Lauren's dismay, X declared bankruptcy during the year and the debt is now worthless.

During the year, David purchased a new automobile for $15,000 which he uses 60 percent of the time for business (i.e., "qualified business usage" is 60 percent). His actual operating expenses, excluding depreciation, were $3,000.

In addition to the information provided earlier in this problem, the couple paid the following amounts during the year:

State income taxes	$5,500
County income taxes	500
Real estate taxes	2,400
Mortgage interest on their home	3,600
Charitable contributions	2,000

David and Lauren's social security numbers are 445-54-5565 and 333-44-5789, respectively. Their son Jim's social security number is 464-57-4681.

Compute David and Lauren's tax liability for the year. Make all computations (including any special elections required) to minimize the Hammacks' tax liability based on *current* tax law. If a tax return is to be prepared for this problem, complete the following forms: 1040 (including Schedules A, C, and SE), and 2106.

9-39 Michelle Kay purchased a small building on February 1 of the current year for $650,000. In addition, she paid $15,000 for land. Ms. Kay obtained a $640,000 mortgage for the acquisition. She and five of her employees use the property solely to manufacture and sell a variety of gift items. The following information pertains to the business:

Sales	$950,000
Cost of goods sold	625,000
Wages for employees ($20,000 each)	100,000
Payroll taxes for five employees	?
Depreciation	?
Advertising	25,000
Mortgage interest	60,000
Legal services	20,000
Real estate taxes	4,000
Fire insurance	3,000
Meals and entertainment	2,500

During the year, Ms. Kay purchased the following assets for the business. She wants to depreciate all business assets as rapidly as the law allows.

	Cost	Month/Day of Acquisition
Personal computer	$14,000	March 31
Printer for computer	2,000	April 2
Office furniture and fixtures	20,000	April 29
Machinery (7-year property)	30,000	May 12

Michelle Kay was divorced from Benjamin Kay two years ago. The divorce decree stipulates that Benjamin Kay would receive the dependency exemption for their son, Eric (now 12 years old), even though Eric lives full-time with Ms. Kay in a home she maintains. During the year, Ms. Kay provided 25 percent of Eric's support and Mr. Kay provided 75 percent. Ms. Kay received $15,000 of alimony and $10,000 of child support from Mr. Kay during the year.

Unrelated to her business, Ms. Kay paid the following amounts during the year:

Estimated federal income taxes	$25,000
State income taxes	3,500
County income taxes	1,500
Real estate taxes	2,000
Mortgage interest on her home	5,600
Charitable contributions	2,900
Deductible contribution to individual retirement account (Note: This is a deduction *for* A.G.I. It is one of the "adjustments to income" on page 1 of Form 1040.)	2,000
Health insurance for Ms. Kay	1,000

Compute Ms. Kay's tax liability for the year based on *current* tax law. (Hint: Ms. Kay's adjusted gross income is less than $100,000.) If a tax return is to be prepared for this problem, complete the following forms: 1040 (including Schedules A, C, and SE) and 4562. For grading purposes, attach a sheet to Schedule C showing supporting calculations for payroll taxes.

RESEARCH PROBLEMS

9-40 *Depreciation.* S is a land developer. During the year, he finished construction of a complex containing a new shopping mall and office building. To enhance the environment of the complex, substantial landscaping was done including the planting of many trees, shrubs, and gardens. In addition, S acquired a massive sculpture that served as the focal point of the complex. S also purchased numerous pictures, which were hung in the shopping center and office building. Can S claim depreciation deductions for any of the items noted above?

9-41 *Amortization.* During the year, the metropolis of Burnsberg accepted bids from various cable television companies for the right to provide service within its city limits. The accepted bid was submitted by Cabletech Inc. in the amount of $500,000. For this amount, the city granted the company a license to operate for 10 years. The terms of the agreement further provided that the company's license would be renewed if the city was satisfied with the services provided. May Cabletech amortize the cost of the license?

COMPUTERIZED TAX ANALYSIS

9-42 *Depletion.* Use computer file T901 for this problem.

a. In the first section of the ANALYSIS, "taxable income (loss) before depletion" is computed *before* percentage or cost depletion is calculated. For one of the two depletion items the "taxable income (loss) before depletion" calculation is necessary, but for the other it is not. Explain why.

b. Percentage depletion is $52,800 and cost depletion is $22,500. Which one is used as the depletion allowed? Why?

c. The percentage depletion rate is 22 percent. To what natural resources does this rate pertain?

d. What amount of operating expenses would cause percentage depletion to be equal to cost depletion? Explain the tax rules that cause this result.

e.

INPUT: Beginning basis of natural resources	
(excluding cost of land)	$100,000
Estimate of recoverable units (e.g., total	
estimated barrels of oil to be recovered)	60,000
Number of units sold this year	25,000
Property type (Enter 1 for oil and gas.	
Enter 2 otherwise)	2
Sale price per unit	$ 30
Operating expenses	$500,000
Percentage depletion rate (e.g., enter 10%	
as .10)	15%

1. The rules for percentage depletion enable the taxpayer to deplete (write off) more than the cost of the natural resources. Explain the tax rules that allow this.

2. If only cost depletion were allowed (and percentage depletion were repealed), would it be possible for the taxpayer to deplete more than the cost of the natural resources? Why, or why not?

3. Assume the taxpayer is a corporation in the 34 percent tax bracket and *all* of the taxable income from this natural resource activity is taxed at 34 percent. How much tax would be payable as a result of this year's operations?

4. Assume the taxpayer is a corporation in the 34 percent tax bracket and *all* of the taxable income from this natural resource activity is taxed at 34 percent. Further assume that Congress repealed percentage depletion (thereby causing the taxpayer to use cost depletion). By how much would the taxpayer's tax liability increase?

5. The input for "property type" should now be 2. This indicates the property subject to depletion is *not* an oil or gas property. Produce an analysis for an oil or gas property by changing this input to 1. Note that only *one* of the outputs changes while all of the others remain constant. Explain why.

6. Do you think those in the business of natural resource exploration would be in favor of repealing the percentage depletion rules? Why, or why not?

LEARNING OBJECTIVES

Upon completion of this chapter you will be able to:

- Determine when a deduction is allowed for a bad debt
- Understand the different tax treatment for business and nonbusiness bad debts
- Explain what constitutes a deductible casualty or theft loss
- Compute the amount of the deduction for casualty and theft losses
- Explain the basic tax accounting requirements for inventories
- Identify the costs that must be capitalized as part of inventory and the role of the uniform capitalization rules in making this determination
- Explain how inventory costs are assigned to costs of goods sold using the FIFO and LIFO assumptions
- Compute ending inventory using double-extension dollar-value LIFO
- Apply the lower of cost or market rule in valuing ending inventory

CHAPTER OUTLINE

Chapter 10

CERTAIN BUSINESS DEDUCTIONS AND LOSSES

The rules governing the treatment of expenses and losses discussed in Chapter 7 set forth the general requirements that must be met if the taxpayer wishes to claim a deduction. As already seen, the basic test—whether the item was incurred in carrying on business or profit-seeking activities—is often just the initial hurdle in obtaining a deduction. Other provisions in the Code may impose additional conditions or limitations that must be considered. This chapter examines some of the special rules that relate to certain business losses and expenses of the taxpayer, including the provisions for bad debts, casualty losses, the net operating loss deduction, and inventories.

BAD DEBTS

Loans are made for a variety of reasons. Some are made in connection with the taxpayer's trade or business while others are made for purely personal purposes. People also make loans hoping to make a profit. Regardless of the motive, with the extension of credit comes the possibility—as every lender knows—that the loan will never be repaid. When the borrower, in fact, cannot repay the loan, the taxpayer has what is termed a *bad debt* and may be entitled to a deduction. For tax purposes, a bad debt is considered a special form of loss subject to the specific rules of Code § 166. This provision governs the treatment of all types of bad debts: those that arise from the sale of goods or services such as accounts receivable, as well as those resulting from a direct loan of money. Moreover, § 166 applies regardless of the form of the debt (e.g., a secured or unsecured note receivable or a mere oral promise to repay).[1]

---

[1]   Notes issued by a corporation (with interest coupons or in registered form) that are considered capital assets in the hands of the taxpayer are treated as worthless securities, as discussed in Chapter 12.

TREATMENT OF BUSINESS VERSUS NONBUSINESS BAD DEBTS

The tax treatment of a bad debt vastly differs depending on whether it is a *business* or *nonbusiness* bad debt. Business bad debts may be deducted without limitation. In contrast, nonbusiness bad debts are deductible only as short-term capital losses and are therefore subject to the limitation on deductions of capital losses (i.e., to the extent of capital gains plus $3,000).[2] Congress provided this distinctive treatment for nonbusiness bad debts in part to ensure that investments cast in the form of loans are handled in virtually the same manner as other investments that become worthless. As a general rule, an investment in a company's stock or bonds that becomes worthless also receives capital loss treatment.

Another difference between business and nonbusiness bad debts concerns the method allowed to claim a deduction. For some debts, it may be apparent that a portion of the loan will become uncollectible but determination of the exact amount must await final settlement. In the case of a nonbusiness bad debt, there is no deduction for partial worthlessness.[3] A deduction is postponed until the ultimate status of the debt is determined.

> **Example 1.** R loaned his neighbor $5,000 in 1990. During 1991, his neighbor declared bankruptcy, and it is estimated that R will recover no more than 20 cents on the dollar or a maximum of $1,000 from the debt. Although R can establish that he has a bad debt of at least $4,000 ($5,000 − $1,000), no deduction is permitted in 1991 since the debt is nonbusiness, and it is partially worthless. If in 1992 R settles for $500, without any capital gains or other capital losses, he may deduct $3,000 of this loss as a *short-term* capital loss and carry over the remaining $1,500 ($5,000 − $3,000 − $500) to the following year. On the other hand, if the debt had arisen from R's business, R could deduct $4,000 in 1991 based on his estimate of the uncollectible amount, and the $500 remainder of the loss, in 1992, all against ordinary income.

Because of their significantly different treatments, the determination of whether a particular debt is a business or nonbusiness bad debt has produced substantial controversy.

Business Bad Debts. Business bad debts are defined as those that arise in connection with the taxpayer's trade or business.[4] To qualify, the loan must be closely related to the taxpayer's business activity. Simply making a loan to a

---

[2] § 166(d)(1)(B). See Chapter 16 for a detailed discussion of capital gains and losses.

[3] Reg. § 1.166-5(a)(2).

[4] § 166(d)(2).

business associate does not make the loan business related; it must support the business activity. Common business bad debts include the following:

1. Uncollectible accounts receivable (for accrual basis taxpayers only)

2. Loans to suppliers to ensure a reliable source of materials

3. Loans to customers, clients, and others to preserve business relationships or nurture goodwill

4. Loans to protect business reputation

5. Loans or advances to employees

6. Loans by employees to protect their employment

7. Loans made by taxpayers in the business of making loans

It is important to note that corporate taxpayers are not subject to the nonbusiness bad debt rules.[5] All loans made by a corporation are deemed to be related to its trade or business. Thus, any bad debt of a corporation is considered to be a *business* bad debt.

Nonbusiness Bad Debts. A nonbusiness bad debt is defined as any debt other than one acquired in connection with the taxpayer's trade or business.[6] From a practical perspective, nonbusiness bad debts are simply those that do not qualify as business bad debts.

The most common nonbusiness bad debts are losses on personal loans, such as those made to friends or relatives. As suggested above, however, nonbusiness bad debt treatment also extends to loans that are made to make a profit and that essentially function as investments. For example, a loan to an acquaintance to start a new business is in effect an investment and thus a nonbusiness debt. Similarly, a loan to a business to protect an investment in such enterprise would be considered a nonbusiness debt. For example, an investor may loan funds to a struggling corporation in which he owns stock, hoping that the infusion of cash might sustain it and save the original investment.

Although the dividing line between business and nonbusiness bad debts usually is clear, controversy typically arises in several common situations. One troublesome area involves taxpayers who frequently make loans to make a profit but who do not make such loans their full-time occupation. In such cases, the Service takes the view that the taxpayers are not in the business of making loans and thus any bad debts are not business bad debts. These situations can become even more difficult when the taxpayer devotes substantial time and energy to establishing and developing the business.

---

[5] § 166(d)(1).   [6] § 166(d)(2).

Example 2. In *Whipple v. Comm.*, Whipple had made sizable cash advances to the Mission Orange Bottling Co., one of several enterprises that he owned.[7] He spent considerable effort related to these enterprises but received no type of compensation, either salary, interest, or rent. When these advances subsequently became worthless, Whipple deducted them as a business bad debt. The Supreme Court held that the loans made by the shareholder to his closely held corporation were nonbusiness bad debts even though Whipple had worked for the company. According to the Court:

> Devoting one's time and energies to the affairs of a corporation is not of itself, and without more, a trade or business of the person so engaged. Though such activities may produce income, profit or gain in the form of dividends—this return is distinctive to the process of investing—as distinguished from the trade or business of the taxpayer himself. When the only return is that of an investor, the taxpayer has not satisfied his burden of demonstrating that he is engaged in a trade or business.

Despite the Court's holding in *Whipple*, taxpayers have achieved limited success where they have convinced other courts that they were in the business of organizing, promoting, and financing businesses.

The other prominent area of controversy concerns a situation common to many new struggling corporations: loans made to corporations by employees who are also shareholders. Here, the issues are similar to that above. Is the taxpayer making the loan to protect an investment or to protect his or her job (i.e., the business of being an employee)? When employee-shareholders have been able to show that a loan was made to protect their jobs rather than their investment, they have been able to secure business bad debt treatment.

GENERAL REQUIREMENTS

To be deductible, the debt must not only be partially or totally worthless but must also represent a bona fide debt and have a basis.[8]

Bona Fide Debt. A debt is considered bona fide if it arises from a true debtor-creditor relationship. For this relationship to exist, there must be a promise to repay a fixed and determinable sum, and the obligation must be enforceable under local law.

The question of whether there is valid debtor-creditor relationship usually arises when it appears that the taxpayer made the loan with little expectation of being repaid. This is typically the case where there is a close relationship between the taxpayer and the borrower. For example, loans to relatives or friends are likely to be viewed as nondeductible gifts rather than genuine debts. Such treatment is most likely where the lender makes little attempt to enforce repayment of the loan—a common occurrence when the borrower is a child or parent.

---

[7]   63-1 USTC ¶9466, 11 AFTR2d 1454, 373 U.S. 193 (USSC, 1963).

[8]   Reg. §§ 1.166-1(c) and (e).

In a similar fashion, advances to a closely held corporation that are not repaid may be considered nondeductible contributions to capital. On the other hand, loans made by a corporation may be something other than what they purport to be. For example, a loan to a shareholder may be treated as a disguised dividend distribution while a loan to an employee could be considered compensation.

To determine whether a bona fide debtor-creditor relationship exists requires an assessment of all of the facts and circumstances related to the debt. Besides the relationship of the parties, factors typically considered are (1) whether the debt is evidenced by a note or some other written instrument (in contrast to a mere oral promise to repay that has not been reduced to writing); (2) whether the debt is secured by collateral; (3) whether the debt bears a reasonable interest rate; and (4) whether a fixed schedule for repayment has been established.

Basis. A taxpayer may deduct a loss from a bad debt only if he or she has a basis in the debt.[9] For this reason, cash basis taxpayers who normally do not report income until it is received are not entitled to deductions for payments they cannot collect. Their loss is represented by the unrecovered expenses incurred in providing the goods or services. Conversely, accrual basis taxpayers who engage in credit transactions usually report income as it is earned. Accordingly, they may deduct bad debts for those amounts previously included in income. Uncollectible loans (as distinguished from accounts receivable) made by either cash or accrual basis taxpayers may be deducted, assuming the taxpayer has a basis for the loan.

> **Example 3.** R is a tailor and uses the cash method of accounting. This year he made two suits for B for $300, which he never collected. In addition, he loaned $1,000 to a material supplier who left the country. Assuming both debts are worthless, R may deduct only the loan to the supplier for $1,000. No deduction is allowed for the uncollected $300 since R does not report the amount as income until he collects it and therefore has no basis in the debt. However, any expenses incurred in producing the suits (i.e., materials, etc.) are deductible.

Worthlessness. Whether a debt is worthless ultimately depends on the facts. The Regulations indicate that a taxpayer does not have to undertake legal action to enforce payment or obtain an uncollectible judgment with respect to the debt to prove its worthlessness.[10] It is sufficient that the surrounding circumstances suggest that legal action would not result in recovery. Among the circumstances indicating a debt's worthlessness are the debtor's bankruptcy or precarious financial position, consistent failure to pay when requested, or poor health or death. As noted above, a *business* bad debt need not be totally worthless before a deduction is allowed. When events occur which suggest that the debt will not be recoverable in full, a deduction for partial worthlessness is granted.

---

[9] Reg. §§ 1.166-1(d) and (e). [10] Reg. §§ 1.166-2(a) and (b).

DEDUCTION METHODS

For taxable years beginning after 1986, deductions for bad debts must be claimed using the specific charge-off method.[11] This method—often called the direct write-off method—allows a deduction only in the year when the debt actually becomes worthless. The reserve method, which allows deductions for estimated bad debts and is typically used for financial accounting purposes, was repealed for all businesses except certain financial institutions and service businesses by the Tax Reform Act of 1986.

The direct write-off method provides some flexibility in accounting for business bad debts. Where the facts indicate that a specific debt is partially worthless, the portion considered uncollectible may be deducted, but only if such portion is actually written off the taxpayer's books for financial accounting purposes.[12] Any remaining portion of the debt that later becomes worthless can be deducted in subsequent years. Using this approach, taxpayers need not wait until the debt becomes totally worthless before any deduction is claimed. Alternatively, taxpayers can wait until the debt becomes totally worthless and claim the entire deduction at that time. Note that when the debt is totally worthless (in contrast to partially worthless), there is no requirement that the debt actually be written off the taxpayer's books.

> **Example 4.** K Company is a major supplier of lumber to homebuilders. One of its customers, which owed the company $10,000, fell on hard times in 1991 and declared bankruptcy. Because this event suggests that the debt is partially worthless, a deduction is permitted. K estimated that it would recover $7,000 of the debt, and therefore claimed a $3,000 bad debt deduction in 1991. The $3,000 amount was also charged off the taxpayer's books as required. In 1993, K Company actually received $1,000 and deducted the remainder of the loss, $6,000 ($10,000 − $3,000 previously deducted − $1,000 actually received). Alternatively, K may opt to claim no deduction for 1991 and deduct the entire $9,000 loss in 1993. Note that when the debt became totally worthless in either case, the taxpayer is not required to write the debt off its books for financial accounting purposes.

Experience Method for Service Businesses. Although the 1986 Act ostensibly eliminated the reserve method of accounting for bad debts, it provided an equivalent—but not identical—technique for service businesses. If a business uses the *accrual method* to account for income from services, the business is not required to accrue any amount that, *based on experience*, it knows will not be collected.[13] Businesses can take advantage of this exception only if they do not charge interest or a late charge on the amount billed.

---

[11]   § 166(a).

[12]   Reg. § 1.166-3(a).

[13]   § 448(d)(5).

As a practical matter, the actual use of this technique may be limited, since most service businesses are allowed and typically do use the cash method rather than the accrual method of accounting. Service businesses usually are exempt from the rule requiring use of the accrual method,[14] falling under the exceptions for sole proprietorships, S corporations, qualifying partnerships, personal service corporations, or taxpayers with gross receipts that generally do not exceed $5 million.

CASUALTY AND THEFT LOSSES

GENERAL RULES

The Code generally provides that an individual's losses arising from casualty or theft are deductible regardless of the activity in which the losses are incurred. An individual's casualty and theft losses related to profit-seeking activities may be deducted under the general rules, which provide that losses incurred in a trade or business or a transaction entered into for profit are deductible.[15] In addition, § 165(c)(3) expressly allows a deduction for losses related to property used for *personal* purposes where the loss arises from fire, storm, shipwreck, theft, or other casualty.

A deduction is allowed only for casualty losses related to property owned by the taxpayer; no deduction is allowed for damages the taxpayer may be required to pay for inflicting harm upon the person or property of another.[16] Further, the casualty must damage the property itself. A casualty that indirectly reduces the resale value of the property normally does not create a deductible loss (e.g., a mud slide near the taxpayer's residence).[17] Any expenses of cleanup, or similar expenses such as repairs to return the damaged property to its condition prior to the casualty, are normally deductible as part of the casualty loss. Incidental expenses that arise from the casualty, such as the cost of temporary housing or a rental car, are considered personal expenses and are not deductible as part of the casualty loss.

CASUALTY AND THEFT DEFINED

Casualties. The Code permits a deduction for losses arising not only from fire, storm, or shipwreck, but also from other casualties. While the terms *fire*, *storm*, and *shipwreck* are easily construed and applied, such is not the case with the phrase "other casualty." Interpretation and application of this phrase is

---

[14] Subject to certain exceptions, § 448 requires corporations, partnerships with corporate partners, or tax shelters to use the accrual method of accounting.

[15] §§ 162 and 212.

[16] *Robert M. Miller*, 34 TCM 528, T.C. Memo 1975-110.

[17] *Pulvers v. Comm.*, 48 T.C. 245, *aff'd.* in 69-1 USTC ¶9272, 23 AFTR2d 69-678, 407 F.2d 838 (CA-9, 1969).

a continuing subject of conflict. The courts and the IRS generally have agreed that to qualify as a casualty the loss must result from some *sudden, unexpected, or unusual event, caused by some external force.*[18] Losses deductible under these criteria include those resulting from earthquakes, floods, hurricanes, cave-ins, sonic booms, and similar natural causes.[19] On the other hand, losses resulting from ordinary accidents or normal everyday occurrences (e.g., breakage due to dropping) are not considered unusual and consequently are not deductible.[20] Similarly, no deduction is allowed for losses due to a gradual process, since such losses are not sudden and unexpected.[21] For this reason, losses suffered because of rust, corrosion, erosion, disease, insect infestation, or similar types of *progressive deterioration*, generally are not deductible. Unfortunately, the casualty criteria are vague, and the taxpayer often is forced to litigate to determine if his or her loss is sufficiently sudden or unusual to qualify. For example, the IRS has ruled that termite damage does not occur with the requisite swiftness to be deductible.[22] The courts, however, have found the necessary suddenness to be present in several termite cases and have allowed a deduction for the resulting losses.[23]

Thefts. Losses of business or personal property due to theft are deductible. The term *theft* includes, but is not limited to, larceny, embezzlement, and robbery.[24] If money or property is taken as the result of kidnapping, blackmail, threats, or extortion, it also may be a theft. Seizure or confiscation of property by a foreign government does not constitute a casualty or theft loss but may be deductible if incurred in profit-seeking activities.[25] Losing or misplacing items is not considered a theft but may qualify as a casualty if it results from some sudden, unexpected, or unusual event.[26]

> **Example 5.** H slammed a car door on his wife's hand, dislodging the diamond from her ring never to be found. The Tax Court held that the loss was deductible as an "other" casualty.[27]

---

[18] *Matheson v. Comm.*, 2 USTC ¶830, 10 AFTR 945, 54 F.2d 537 (CA-2, 1931).

[19] *Your Federal Income Tax*, IRS Publication 17 (Rev. Nov. 90) p. 140.

[20] *Diggs v. Comm.*, 60-2 USTC ¶9584, 6 AFTR2d 5095, 281 F.2d 326 (CA-2, 1960).

[21] *Supra*, Footnote 18.

[22] Rev. Rul. 63-232, 1963-2 C.B. 97.

[23] *Rosenberg v. Comm.*, 52-2 USTC ¶9377, 42 AFTR 303, 198 F.2d 46 (CA-8, 1952).

[24] Reg. § 1.165-8(d).

[25] *W.J. Powers*, 36 T.C. 1191 (1961).

[26] Rev. Rul. 72-592, 1972-2 C.B. 101.

[27] *John P. White*, 48 T.C. 430 (1967).

LOSS COMPUTATION

The loss computation is the same whether the casualty or theft relates to property connected with profit-seeking activities or personal use.[28] As explained below, however, limitations on the amount of deductible loss may differ depending on the property's use.

The *amount* of the loss is the difference between the fair market value immediately before the casualty and the fair market value immediately after the casualty as reduced by any insurance reimbursement. Of course, when the property is completely destroyed or stolen, the loss is simply the fair market value of the property as reduced by any insurance reimbursement. Although appraisals are the preferred method of establishing fair market values, costs of repairs to restore the property to its condition immediately before the casualty may be sufficient under certain circumstances.[29]

For many years, a controversy existed concerning the deductibility of insured casualty losses for which taxpayers chose not to file a claim. The problem typically arises when taxpayers avoid filing a claim for fear that their insurance coverage may be canceled or its cost may increase. When this occurs, the Treasury is effectively acting as an insurance company, partially subsidizing the taxpayer's loss. In 1986 Congress eliminated the controversy for *nonbusiness* property by providing that no deduction is permitted for casualty losses of such property for which the taxpayer is insured, unless a timely insurance claim is filed.[30]

The amount of the deductible loss generally is limited to the lesser of the property's adjusted basis or fair market value (decline in value if a partial casualty).[31] The lesser of these two amounts is then reduced by any insurance reimbursements. There are two exceptions to this general rule, however. First, for property used in a trade or business *or* for the production of income that is *completely* destroyed or stolen, the deductible loss is the property's adjusted basis reduced by insurance reimbursements. Second, losses to property *used for personal* purposes are deductible only to the extent they exceed a $100 floor. The $100 floor does not apply to property used in a trade or business or for the production of income. The $100 floor applies to each event, not each item. Further, if spouses file a joint return, they are subject to a single $100 floor. If spouses file separately, each one is subject to a $100 floor for each casualty.[32]

In 1982 Congress added a further limitation on the deduction for casualty or theft losses of property used for personal purposes. In addition to the $100 floor on personal losses, only total losses (after reduction by the $100 floor) in excess of 10 percent of adjusted gross income are deductible.[33] This limitation does not apply to property used in a trade or business or an income-producing activity. The computation of the casualty and theft loss deduction is summarized in Exhibit 10-1.

---

[28] Reg. § 1.165-7(a).

[29] Reg. § 1.165-7(a)(2)(ii).

[30] § 165(h)(4)(E).

[31] Reg. § 1.165-7(b)(i).

[32] Reg. § 1.165-7(b)(4)(iii).

[33] § 165(h)(2).

Exhibit 10-1
*Computation of Casualty and
Theft Loss Deduction*

Smaller of

    (1) Decline in value; or
    (2) Adjusted basis*

Less:

    Insurance reimbursement
    $100 floor/casualty if personal
    10% of A.G.I. if personal

Equals: Deductible casualty loss

*Adjusted basis, rather than decline in value,
must be used if business or income property is
completely destroyed or stolen.*

Example 6. R had four casualties during the year:

| | | | Fair Market Value | |
| | | Adjusted | Before | After |
Casualty	Property	Basis	Casualty	Casualty
1. Accident	Business car	$ 3,000	$ 9,000	$ 5,000
2. Robbery	Ring	500	800	0
	Suit	95	75	0
3. Tornado	Residence	50,000	60,000	57,000
4. Fire	Business			
	computer	3,000	4,000	0

R received a $600 insurance reimbursement for his loss on the residence. The deductible loss for each casualty is as follows:

1. The loss for the business car is $3,000 [lesser of the decline in value $4,000 ($9,000 − $5,000) or the adjusted basis of $3,000]. The deduction is *for* adjusted gross income unless it is related to R's business as an employee, in which case the deduction would be an itemized deduction.

2. The loss for the ring and suit is $475. The loss for the ring is $500 [lesser of decline in value of $800 ($800 − $0) or the adjusted basis of $500]. The loss for the suit is $75 [lesser of decline in value of $75 ($75 − $0) or the adjusted basis of $95]. The total loss attributable to the robbery is $575 ($500 + $75). This loss must be reduced by the $100 floor to $475 ($575 − $100). Note that the $100 floor is applied to the event, not to each item of loss. The loss, subject to the 10% overall limitation, is deductible *from* adjusted gross income.

3. The loss for the residence is $2,300 [lesser of decline in value of $3,000 ($60,000 − $57,000) or the adjusted basis of $50,000, reduced by the insurance reimbursement of $600 and the $100 floor]. The loss, subject to the 10% overall limitation, is deductible *from* adjusted gross income. Assuming R's adjusted gross income is $20,000, $775 is deductible [$2,300 + $475 − $2,000 (10% × $20,000)].

4. The loss for the computer is $3,000. Since the computer is used for business and is completely destroyed, the loss is the adjusted basis of the property regardless of its fair market value. The loss is deductible *for* adjusted gross income.

CASUALTY GAINS AND LOSSES

Upon the occurrence of some casualties, the insurance reimbursement may exceed the taxpayer's adjusted basis for the property resulting in a gain. As discussed in Chapter 15, the Code provides some relief in this case, permitting the taxpayer to postpone recognition of the gain if the insurance proceeds are reinvested in similar property. Where the gain must be recognized, however, Code § 165(h) sets forth special treatment.

Under § 165(h), all gains and losses arising from a casualty unrelated to business or a transaction entered into for profit—*personal casualty gains and losses*—must first be netted. For this purpose, the personal casualty loss is computed after the $100 floor but before the 10 percent limitation. If personal casualty gains exceed personal casualty losses, each gain and each loss is treated as a gain or loss from the sale or exchange of a capital asset. The capital gain or loss would be long-term or short-term depending on the holding period of the asset. In contrast, if losses exceed gains, the net loss is deductible as an itemized deduction to the extent it exceeds 10 percent of the taxpayer's adjusted gross income.

Example 7. T had three separate casualties involving personal use assets during the year:

			Fair Market Value	
Casualty	Property	Adjusted Basis	Before Casualty	After Casualty
1. Accident	Personal car	$12,000	$ 8,500	$ 6,000
2. Robbery	Jewelry	1,000	4,000	0
3. Hurricane	Residence	60,000	80,000	78,000

T received insurance reimbursements as follows: (1) $900 for repair of the car; (2) $3,200 for the theft of her jewelry; and (3) $1,500 for the damages to her home. Assuming T does not elect (under § 1033) to purchase replacement jewelry, her personal casualty gain exceeds her personal casualty losses by $300, computed as follows:

1. The loss for the car is $1,500 [(lesser of $2,500 decline in value or the $12,000 adjusted basis = $2,500) − $900 insurance recovery − $100 floor].

2. The gain for the jewelry is $2,200 ($3,200 insurance recovery − $1,000 adjusted basis).

3. The loss from the residence is $400 [(lesser of $2,000 decline in value or the $60,000 adjusted basis = $2,000) − $1,500 insurance recovery − $100 floor].

T must report each separate gain and loss as a gain or loss from the sale or exchange of a capital asset. The classification of each gain and loss as short-term or long-term depends on the holding period of each asset.

Example 8. Assume the same facts in *Example 7* except the loss for the personal car was not insured. In this case the loss on the car is $2,400 and the personal casualty losses exceed the gain by $600 ($2,400 + $400 − $2,200). T must treat the $600 net loss as an itemized deduction subject to the limitation of 10% of A.G.I.

YEAR DEDUCTIBLE

A casualty loss usually is deductible in the taxable year in which the loss occurs.[34] A theft loss is deductible in the *year of discovery*. If a claim for reimbursement exists and there is a reasonable prospect of recovery, the loss must be reduced by the amount the taxpayer *expects* to receive.[35] If later receipts are less than the amount originally estimated and no further reimbursement is expected, an amended return is *not* filed. Instead, the remaining loss is deductible in the year in which no further reimbursement is expected. If the casualty loss deduction was reduced by the $100 floor in the prior year, the remaining loss need not be further reduced. However, the remaining loss is subject to the 10 percent limitation of the later year.

> **Example 9.** G's watch was stolen on December 4, 1991. Her loss was $700 before taking into account any insurance reimbursement. She expects the insurance company to reimburse her $400 for the loss. In 1991 G may deduct $200 ($700 loss − the expected reimbursement of $400 and reduced by the $100 floor) subject to the 10% limitation for 1991. If G actually receives only $300 in the following year, she may deduct an additional $100 (the difference between the expected reimbursement of $400 and the $300 received) subject to the 10% limitation for 1992. If the reimbursement was greater than that expected, the excess is included in gross income.

A special rule exists for the reporting of casualty losses sustained within an area designated by the President as a "disaster area." This rule permits the taxpayer to accelerate the tax relief provided for casualty losses by electing to deduct the disaster loss in the taxable year immediately preceding the year of the disaster loss.[36]

> **Example 10.** F, a calendar year taxpayer, suffered a loss in a "disaster area" from a flood on March 4, 1991. F may elect to deduct the loss on his 1990 return. If he has not filed the return by the casualty date, he may include the loss on the original 1990 return. If the 1990 return has been filed prior to the casualty, an amended return or refund claim is required. Alternatively, F could claim the loss on his 1991 return. In determining which year to claim the loss, F should consider the effect of the 10% limitation. For example, assume F had no other casualty losses in 1991 and his casualties in 1990 exceeded 10% of his 1990 adjusted gross income. F would derive greater tax benefits by deducting the loss in 1990 since the *entire* loss would be deductible, while the loss deduction in 1991 would be reduced by 10% of his 1991 adjusted gross income.

---

[34] Reg. § 1.165-7(a).

[35] Reg. § 1.165-1(d)(2)(i).

[36] § 165(i).

NET OPERATING LOSSES

In a year during which the taxpayer's deductions exceed gross income, the taxpayer is allowed to use the excess deductions to offset taxable income of prior or subsequent years.[37] Technically, the excess of deductions over income, as modified for several complex adjustments, is referred to as the taxpayer's *net operating loss* (NOL).[38] The Code generally permits the taxpayer to carry back the NOL 3 years and forward 15 years to redetermine taxable income.

Allowance of the net operating loss deduction reduces the inequity that otherwise exists due to the use of an annual reporting period and a progressive tax rate structure. For example, consider a situation involving two taxpayers, R and S, who over a two-year period have equivalent taxable incomes of $100,000 each. R earned $50,000 each year while S earned $300,000 in the first year and had a loss of $200,000 in the second year. Without the NOL provisions, S would *not* be able to offset his $200,000 loss against his $300,000 income and consequently would pay a substantially greater tax than R. Such a result clearly would be unfair since both taxpayers had identical taxable incomes over the two-year period. The NOL provision partially eliminates this inequity by allowing a loss in one year to offset income in other years.

CARRYBACK AND CARRYFORWARD YEARS

As mentioned above, an NOL resulting in the current year is generally carried back 3 years and forward 15 years.[39] The loss is first carried back to the third prior year (i.e., the earliest year first) and taxable income is recomputed for that year. If any loss remains after reducing that year's tax liability to zero, the remaining loss is carried to the second prior year and then the first prior year. If a loss still remains, the taxpayer carries it forward to the first year after the loss and so on up to the 15th year following the loss year. For example, a loss occurring in 1991 would be applied to taxable income of these years as follows: 1988, 1989, 1990, 1992, 1993, 1994, . . . , 2005, 2006. It should be emphasized that if a taxpayer does not carry back a loss to the earliest prior year, the amount eligible for carryback may not be deducted in a later year except to the extent that such loss would not be absorbed in the prior year.[40]

> **Example 11.**   B had a net operating loss in 1991 of $10,000. She incorrectly carried the loss forward to use in 1992 and 1993. Upon audit of the 1993 return, it is determined that she did not properly carry the loss back to 1988, 1989, and 1990 before carrying it forward. If B had carried back the loss of 1991 to 1988, it would have been entirely absorbed in offsetting the

---

[37]   § 172.

[38]   § 172(c).

[39]   § 172(b)(1).

[40]   *Bessie Eisenberg*, 22 TCM 333, T.C. Memo 1963-78.

income of that year. Consequently, B does not receive a deduction for the loss in 1992 or 1993. Moreover, because of her error she may be barred by the statute of limitations from using the loss in 1988, resulting in no tax benefit from the loss.

The taxpayer may *elect* to forgo the carryback period and carry forward the loss instead.[41] The election is made simply by attaching a statement to the tax return for the year to indicate the taxpayer's intention of forgoing the carryback period. This election must be made by the due date of the return (including extensions) in which the net operating loss is reported. The election *cannot* be subsequently claimed or revoked by filing an amended return. This election normally is appropriate only where the taxpayer expects future profits. If future profits are anticipated, the taxpayer must determine whether carrying the loss back or forward will yield the greater tax benefit. This decision is often difficult since the taxpayer may be unable to predict the future with any certainty.

When the taxpayer carries the loss back to a prior year, the loss deduction is claimed on an amended return for the earlier year (Form 1040X). For this purpose, the statute-of-limitations period for returns of the earlier years normally is extended to three years after the due date (including extensions) of the return in which the loss is reported.[42] Alternatively, the loss may be claimed using Form 1045 (Form 1139 for corporations) for a so-called "quick refund." This form must be filed *after* the return of the loss year is filed and *within* one year after the *close* of the loss year. If the taxpayer fails to file Form 1045, an amended return (Form 1040X) may still be filed.

> **Example 12.** B, a calendar year taxpayer, reported a loss for 1991. He filed his 1991 return April 15, 1992. Under normal conditions, B must file an amended return for 1988 (the year to which the loss is carried) by April 15, 1992 (three years after April 15, 1989, the due date for the 1988 return). The Code, however, extends the period for filing an amended return for 1988 until April 15, 1995, three years after the due date of the return for the loss year. Alternatively, B may claim the loss using Form 1045 by filing the form before December 31, 1992, one year after the close of the loss year.

Where the taxpayer carries the loss forward, the loss deduction is claimed on the subsequent year's normal return (Form 1040).

If the taxpayer has losses occurring in two or more years, the loss occurring in the earliest year is used first. When the loss from the earliest year is absorbed, the losses from later years may be claimed.

---

[41] § 172(b)(3)(c).   [42] § 6511(d)(2).

NET OPERATING LOSS COMPUTATION

The term *net operating loss* is defined as the excess of the deductions allowed over gross income, computed with certain modifications.[43] The purpose of the modifications is twofold. First, the net operating loss provisions are designed to permit a taxpayer a deduction for his or her true economic loss. Thus, certain artificial deductions that do not require cash outlays (such as the deductions for personal and dependent exemptions) are added back to negative taxable income. Second, the net operating loss provisions were enacted to provide relief only in those cases where there is a business loss. Therefore, restrictions are imposed on the amount of nonbusiness expenses that may be deducted.

The net operating loss deduction of an individual taxpayer is computed by making the following modifications in computing taxable income.[44]

1. Any net operating loss deduction carried forward or carried back from another year is not allowed.

2. The deduction for personal and dependent exemptions is not allowed.

3. Deductions for capital losses and nonbusiness expenses are limited as explained below.

To determine the extent of any deduction for capital losses and nonbusiness expenses, gross income must be classified into *four* categories: (1) capital gains from business; (2) other income from business; (3) capital gains not from business; and (4) other income not from business. With income so classified, the following rules are applied with respect to nonbusiness expenses and capital losses in the following order: [45]

1. Nonbusiness capital losses may be deducted to the extent of any nonbusiness capital gains; thus, any excess is added back to taxable income.

2. Nonbusiness expenses may be deducted to the extent of any nonbusiness income, including any excess of nonbusiness capital gains over nonbusiness capital losses (as determined in step 1); thus, any excess is added back to taxable income.

3. Business capital losses may be deducted to the extent of any business capital gains; any excess business capital losses may be deducted to the extent of any excess of nonbusiness capital gains over nonbusiness capital losses and nonbusiness expenses (as determined in step 2).

---

[43] *Supra*, Footnote 38.

[44] § 172(d)(1) through (4).

[45] § 172(d)(4).

For purposes of applying these rules, business income generally includes salaries, wages, and rents. Further, casualty losses are always treated as business deductions. In contrast, contributions to individual retirement accounts (IRAs) or self-employment retirement plans are considered nonbusiness deductions. Similarly, the deduction for alimony is treated as a nonbusiness deduction. Finally, the taxpayer's nonbusiness expenses are his or her itemized deductions (or standard deduction if the taxpayer does not itemize). Exhibit 10-2 summarizes the operation of these rules to compute the net operating loss deduction.

Exhibit 10-2
Computation of Net Operating Loss

Taxable loss shown on return

Add back:
  Exemptions

  Nonbusiness deductions
    Less:
      Nonbusiness ordinary income
      Nonbusiness net capital gain

  Nonbusiness capital losses
  Less:
      Nonbusiness capital gains

  Business capital losses
    Less:
      Nonbusiness net capital gains
        Less: (Nonbusiness deductions - nonbusiness income)

Equals: Net Operating Loss Deduction

Example 13.   In 1991 G quit his job and opened a car repair shop. G's filing status is married, filing jointly, and he reported the following income and deductions for the year:

Income

Business income...	$40,000
Salary from previous job	10,000
Business capital gains—long term.............................	7,000
Business capital losses—long term............................	(2,000)
Nonbusiness capital gains—long term.........................	5,000
Nonbusiness capital losses—long term........................	(3,000)
Interest income on nonbusiness investments..................	1,000

Expenses

Business expenses...	70,000
Casualty loss on personal car	5,100
Intertest on home mortgage	8,000

Taxable income is computed as follows:

Net business loss ($40,000 − $70,000).......................		($30,000)
Salary...		10,000
Interest earned		1,000
Net long-term capital gain...................................		7,000
Adjusted gross income (loss)		($12,000)
Less: Itemized deductions		
Mortgage interest paid	8,000	(13,000)
Less: Personal exemptions		(4,300)
Taxable income (loss)..		($29,300)

* *$5,100 − $100 floor. Note that the 10 percent limitation does not apply since A.G.I. is a negative number.*

Following the format of Exhibit 10-2, G's net operating loss for 1991 is computed as follows:

Taxable income (loss)...........................			($29,300)
Modifications			
Add back:			
Personal exemptions.........................			4,300
Nonbusiness expenses:			
Mortgage interest..........................		$8,000	
Nonbusiness income:			
Interest	$1,000		
Nonbusiness net capital			
gain ($5,000−$3,000)	+ 2,000	(3,000)	5,000
Net operating loss for 1990			($20,000)

Computation of the real dollar loss or economic loss results in a similar deduction:

Business loss		($30,000)
+	Salary	10,000
+	Business capital gains	5,000
−	Casualty loss	(5,000)
Net operating loss		($20,000)

Note that the nonbusiness income (capital gains of $2,000 and interest income of $1,000) is not considered in this computation of economic loss since it is offset by nonbusiness expenses.

RECOMPUTING TAXABLE INCOME FOR YEAR TO WHICH NET OPERATING LOSS IS CARRIED

Once the net operating loss deduction is computed, it is carried to the appropriate year and used in the recomputation of taxable income for that year. The net operating loss deduction is a deduction *for* A.G.I. As a result, the deduction may have an effect on the amount of the deduction for certain items such as medical expenses, which are based on the taxpayer's A.G.I. All expenses based on A.G.I. except charitable contributions must be *recomputed* in determining the revised taxable income.[46] The net operating loss deduction also may have an effect on any tax credits originally claimed. For example, if a 1994 net operating loss deduction completely eliminates the taxable income of 1991, any credit originally claimed in 1991 becomes available for use in another year.

After the effect on the tax of the earliest year is computed, the amount of any loss remaining to be carried forward must be determined. In other words, a computation is required to determine how much of the net operating loss is absorbed in the year to which it is carried and how much may be carried to subsequent years. Although this calculation is somewhat similar to that explained above, additional nuances exist making the computation somewhat complex. For this reason, further reference should be made to the Regulations and Form 1045.

INVENTORIES

As might be expected, taxpayers who buy or produce merchandise for subsequent sale are not allowed to deduct the costs of the merchandise *at the time* the goods are produced or purchased. Instead, such costs normally must be capitalized (i.e., inventoried) and deducted when the goods are sold. The following example illustrates what might occur if taxpayers were not required to captalize the costs of inventory.

---

[46] Reg. § 1.172-5(a)(3)(ii).

Example 14. C Corporation began business in 1991 and purchased 10,000 gizmos at $10 each for a total of $100,000. In 1991, the corporation sold 6,000 gizmos for $120,000. In 1992, the corporation made no further purchases and sold the remaining 4,000 gizmos for $80,000. Gross profit reported with and without inventories is computed below.

	No Inventories		Inventories	
	1991	1992	1991	1992
Sales...	$120,000	$80,000	$120,000	$80,000
Cost of goods sold:				
Beginning inventory.........................	—	—	—	$40,000
+Purchases.............................	$100,000	—	$100,000	—
−Ending inventory.........................	—	—	(40,000)	—
Costs of goods sold (4,000 @ $10)..........	$100,000	—	$60,000	$40,000
Gross profit.................................	$20,000	$80,000	$60,000	$40,000

Although the total income for the two-year period is the same under either method ($100,000), the time when it is reported differs significantly. The use of inventories produces higher income and higher taxes in the first year because only the costs of goods actually sold are deducted.

As the preceeding example shows, the lack of inventories causes a mismatching of revenues and expenses and with it the possibility of widely fluctuating incomes. Without inventories, the income reported in any one year would in most cases represent a distorted picture—not a clear reflection—of how well the firm was doing. Perhaps what is more crucial, at least from the Treasury's point of view, is that taxpayers would be able to postpone the payment of taxes if inventories were not required. Note in *Example 14* that absent inventories, the taxpayer is able to defer $40,000 ($60,000 − $20,000) of income and the corresponding tax from 1991 to 1992. Congress recognized these possibilities at an early date and in 1918 took corrective action that is still intact today. Currently, Code § 471 provides the following:

> Whenever in the opinion of the Secretary the use of inventories is necessary in order clearly to determine the income of any taxpayer, inventories shall be taken by such taxpayer on such basis as the Secretary may prescribe as conforming as nearly as may be to the best accounting practice in the trade or business and as most clearly reflecting income.

With the enactment of § 471, Congress delegated its rulemaking authority concerning inventories to the IRS. The IRS has responded with a number of regulations indicating when inventories are necessary as well as what methods are acceptable for tax purposes.

The Regulations require taxpayers to maintain inventories whenever the production, purchase, or sale of merchandise is an income-producing factor.[47] As a practical matter, this means virtually all manufacturers, wholesalers, and retailers must keep track of inventories while service businesses are usually exempt. Note that inventories are required regardless of the taxpayer's method of accounting. Cash basis taxpayers must account for inventories as do accrual basis taxpayers. However, the mandatory use of the accrual method for purchases and sales does not prohibit taxpayers from using the cash method to account for other items such as advertising costs or interest income.[48]

A close reading of § 471 reveals that Congress has given the IRS two criteria to be followed in determining what inventory accounting methods are acceptable for tax purposes: (1) the method should conform as nearly as possible to the best accounting practice used in the taxpayer's trade or business; and (2) the method should clearly reflect income. Because of these requirements, the tax rules for inventory are quite similar to those used for financial accounting. Nevertheless, it is important to recognize that the IRS is the ultimate authority on determining what method represents the "best accounting practice" as well as what method most clearly reflects income. Consequently, as will be seen, taxpayers are sometimes required to adopt methods that vary from generally accepted accounting principles and cause differences between book income and taxable income.

There are three steps that must be followed in accounting for inventories and computing costs of goods sold: (1) identifying what costs (e.g., direct and indirect) are to be inventoried or capitalized; (2) evaluating the costs assigned to the ending inventory and determining whether reduction is necessary to reflect lower replacement costs (i.e., lower of cost or market); and (3) allocating the costs between ending inventory and costs of goods sold (e.g., specific identification, FIFO, LIFO). Each of these steps is discussed below.

COSTS TO BE INVENTORIED

The first step in determining costs of goods sold and ending inventory is identifying the costs that should be capitalized as part of inventory. Without guidance, taxpayers no doubt would be inclined to expense as many costs as possible. However, over the years, the IRS with help from Congress has established strict guidelines concerning what can be deducted currently (i.e., period costs) and what must be capitalized (i.e., product costs). The most recent development in this continuing debate was the enactment of the *uniform capitalization rules* (unicap) in 1986. As discussed below, the unicap provisions narrow further what the taxpayer is able to treat as a period cost.

---

[47]   Reg. § 1.471-1 and Reg. § 1.446-1(a)(4)(i).   [48]   Reg. § 1.446-1(c)(1)(iv).

As a general rule, the costs that must be capitalized depend on whether the taxpayer manufactures the goods (e.g., a producer of razor blades) or purchases the items for later resale (e.g., a wholesaler or a retailer such as a department store). When merchandise is bought for resale, the taxpayer must capitalize as a cost of inventory the invoice price less trade discounts plus freight and other costs of acquisition. Cash discounts may be deducted from the inventory cost or reported as a separate income item. In addition, certain retailers and wholesalers are subject to the unicap rules that require capitalization of particular indirect costs as discussed below. For manufactured items, inventory cost includes costs of raw materials, direct labor, and certain indirect costs. The unicap rules apply to all manufacturers.

Many of the problems concerning inventory involve the treatment of indirect costs. Various methods have been devised to account for these costs. For example, under the *prime costing* method only the costs of direct materials and direct labor are capitalized; all indirect costs are expensed. Another method, often advocated by cost accountants, is the *variable* or *direct costing* approach. This method capitalizes only those costs varying with production and expenses all fixed costs. Despite the acceptance of these methods for managerial and internal reporting, the IRS has outlawed their use. In 1974, the IRS issued regulations requiring all manufacturers to use the *full absorption costing* method.[49] Retailers and wholesalers were not subject to the full absorption rules, and, therefore, were not required to capitalize any indirect costs.

Under the full absorption method, direct costs of material and labor must be capitalized. The treatment of indirect costs depends on which of three categories they fall: *Category 1* includes costs that must be capitalized; *Category 2* includes costs that can be expensed; and *Category 3* includes costs whose tax treatment must conform with their financial accounting treatment. A summary of these categories and what they include appears in Exhibit 10-3.

The search for additional tax revenues brought about a substantial revision of the treatment of indirect costs in 1986 with the enactment of § 263A containing the *uniform capitalization rules*. The unicap rules apply to all manufacturers. They also apply to any retailers and wholesalers if their average annual gross receipts for the past three years exceed $10 million. Although these rules replace the full-absorption costing method, in practice many manufacturers continue to use the full-absorption method with certain modifications to meet the unicap requirements.

---

[49]   Reg. § 1.471-11. Absorption costing is currently used for financial statement purposes.

Section 263A requires the capitalization of direct material, direct labor costs, and, most importantly, any indirect costs that, in the words of the Regulations, "directly benefit or are incurred by reason of the performance of a production or resale activity."[50] The effect of these rules was to require taxpayers to capitalize many costs that they previously deducted. The Regulatory scheme is shown in Exhibit 10-3. In general, the Regulations categorize costs as (1) those that benefit only production and resale activities (must capitalize); (2) those that benefit only policy and management functions (do not capitalize); and (3) those that benefit both production and resale activities and policy and management functions, referred to as mixed service costs (capitalized by using any reasonable basis to allocate costs between production and policy functions).

The practical effect of the enactment of the uniform capitalization rules was to require taxpayers to adjust their accounting systems to capture the additional costs required to be capitalized. This was no small task, particularly for retailers and wholesalers that previously had never had to capitalize any indirect costs. As can be seen in Exhibit 10-1, the current scheme requires large retailers and wholesalers to capitalize any costs related to offsite storage (e.g., operating a warehouse), purchasing, handling and an allocable portion of general and administrative costs. To provide all affected taxpayers with some relief, the IRS has provided several simplified techniques to account for these costs detailed in the Regulations.

ALLOCATING INVENTORIABLE COSTS

After total product costs for the year have been identified, these costs along with the cost of beginning inventory must be allocated between the goods sold during the year and ending inventory. If each item sold could be identified (e.g., a car or jewelry) or all items had the same cost, there would be little difficulty in determining the cost of items sold and those still on hand. As a practical matter, however, these conditions rarely exist. Consequently, the taxpayer must make some assumptions regarding which costs should be assigned to costs of goods sold. Like financial accounting, the tax law does not require the cost flow assumption to be consistent with the physical movement of goods. There are several acceptable approaches for allocating costs: specific identification, first-in first-out (FIFO), last-in first-out (LIFO), and weighted averaged.

---

[50] Reg. §1.263A-1T(b)(2)(ii).

Example 15.   K Corporation's inventory records revealed a beginning inventory of 300 units acquired at a cost of $3 per unit. This year the corporation purchased 400 units for $4 per unit, and it sold 500 units for $5,000. Gross profit using FIFO and LIFO are computed below.

	FIFO	LIFO
Sales (500 units @ $5).........................	$5,000	$5,000
Costs of goods sold:		
Beginning inventory (300 @ $3)..............	$900	$900
Purchase (400 @ $4).....................	1,600	1,600
Goods available..........................	$2,500	$2,500
Ending inventory:		
FIFO (200 @ $4).........................	(800)	
LIFO (200 @ $3).........................		(600)
Costs of goods sold.........................	$1,700	$1,900
Gross profit..................................	$3,300	$3,100

If K uses FIFO it is assumed that goods are used in the order that they are purchased (i.e., the first goods in are the first goods to be sold). Thus, the ending inventory consists of the most recent purchases, $800 (200 at $4 per unit). The effect of FIFO is to assign the oldest costs to costs of goods sold. In contrast, LIFO assumes that the last goods purchased are the first sold. As a result, under LIFO the most recent costs are assigned to costs of goods sold and the oldest costs to ending inventory. Thus, ending inventory under LIFO is $600 (200 at $3).

The preceding example illustrates the principal advantage of LIFO. In periods of rising prices, LIFO matches current costs against current revenue. From a financial accounting perspective, it can be reasoned that this produces a better measure of current income since both revenues and costs are stated on a comparable price basis, thereby reducing the inflationary element of earnings.[51] From a tax perspective, LIFO appears preferable because taxable income is typically lower and the corresponding tax is reduced. In effect, taxable income is not "overstated" by fictitious gains. Interestingly, LIFO became part of the tax law in 1939 for just this reason—to help businesses reduce the "paper profits" that conventional methods were yielding and that were being taxed at wartime rates of close to 80 percent.

---

[51] Arguably, income results only to the extent that the sales price exceeds what it will cost to buy a replacement item for the merchandise sold. LIFO approximates this approach.

It must be noted, however, that the advantage of LIFO is lost to the extent that sales in any one year exceed puchases (see *Example 15* above). In this case, the lower prices of goods purchased in previous periods are charged to costs of goods sold. This dipping into the past LIFO layers creates inventory profits, the specific problem that LIFO was designed to address. In a worst case scenario, a company that adopted LIFO in 1939 might unexpectedly liquidate all of its LIFO layers, matching 1939 costs with 1991 revenues. This would no doubt lead to an unforeseen tax liability with little "real" income to pay the tax. This is a significant risk when LIFO is used. At the same time, it may represent an opportunity. Companies may be able to create income, if desirable, by liquidating LIFO layers (e.g., to absorb an expiring net operating loss).

DOLLAR VALUE LIFO

As a practical matter, applying the LIFO procedure to specific goods can be quite cumbersome and costly. In contrast to the simple one item example above, most firms have hundreds or thousands of individual inventory items, and the number of units purchased and sold each period may amount to hundreds of thousands or more. Pricing each separate unit at the oldest costs and properly accounting for the liquidation of any LIFO layers might be a recordkeeping nightmare. Moreover, the major advantage of LIFO could be lost if old LIFO layers had to be liquidated because a specific item was discontinued or replaced. To address the problems of specific-goods LIFO, variations of LIFO have been developed. Perhaps the most widely used version of LIFO is the dollar-value method.

The dollar-value method reaches the desired result—eliminating the inflationary element of earnings attributable to inventory—in a unique way. Ending inventory is priced using the prices at the time LIFO was adopted (base-year). This value is then compared to beginning inventory to determine if there is a real increase or decrease in the pool of dollars invested in inventory. If there is no real change (i.e., ending inventory at base-year prices is the same as beginning inventory at base-year prices), the effect is to charge costs of goods sold with an amount reflecting current prices. On the other hand, if there is a real increase in inventory in terms of base-year dollars, the increase is valued at current prices and added to beginning inventory as a separate LIFO layer to determine ending inventory.

Example 16. T Corporation had an ending inventory on December 31, 1991 of 10,000 units at a cost of $20,000. During the year, T sold the original units and purchased another 10,000 units for $24,000. On December 31, 1992 ending inventory valued at current prices was $24,000. In such case, costs of goods sold would be $20,000, computed as follows.

Beginning inventory.....................................	$20,000
Purchases...	24,000
Ending inventory.......................................	(24,000)
Costs of goods sold....................................	$20,000

But what if, as the facts suggest, prices have increased by 20%? If so, the real amount invested in inventory has not changed ($24,000 ÷ 120% = $20,000). Consequently, valuing ending inventory at current year prices of $24,000 (as above) effectively assigns the oldest costs of $20,000 to costs of goods sold, resulting in an inflationary profit of $4,000. Dollar-value LIFO eliminates this artificial gain—the objective of LIFO—by restating ending inventory at base-year prices. In this case, ending inventory would be restated at $20,000 ($24,000 ÷ 120%). This restatement would yield a cost of goods sold of $24,000, and would properly match current year costs against current year revenues.

The important difference between dollar-value and specific-goods LIFO is that increases and decreases in inventory are measured in terms of dollars rather than physical units. This approach allows goods to be easily combined into pools and effectively treated as a single unit. Consequently, the likelihood of liquidating LIFO layers is reduced.

Although there are various methods of dollar-value LIFO, the most frequently used is the *double-extension method*.[52] The steps to be used in applying the double-extension method are summarized in Exhibit 10-4 and applied to the following example.

---

[52] Taxpayers may use the link-chain method or certain simplified procedures. See Code §§ 472(f) and 474 and the applicable regulations.

Exhibit 10-4
Double-Extension Dollar-Value LIFO
Computation of Ending Inventory

Step 1.   *Extension #1.* Value *ending inventory at current year prices* (actual cost of most recent purchases, average cost or other acceptable method).

Step 2.   *Extension #2.* Value *ending inventory at base-year prices*.

Step 3.   Compute current year quantity increase or decrease by comparing beginning and ending inventories at base-year prices.

   Ending inventory at base-year price (Step 2)
   −Beginning inventory at base-year price
   _____
   Current year quantity increase (decrease) at base-year price

Step 4.   Calculate current year price index.

$$\text{Index} = \frac{\text{Ending inventory at current year price (Step 1)}}{\text{Ending inventory at base-year price (Step 2)}}$$

Step 5.   Compute the quantity increase or decrease to be added to or subtracted from beginning inventory.

   a.   For a quantity increase: convert the increase measured at base-year prices (Step 3) to current year's prices using the current year price index (Step 4).

   Quantity increase at   Index   New
      Base-year price   ×   (Step 4)   =   LIFO
         (Step 3)   Layer

   b.   For a quantity decrease: a current year decrease consumes the layer(s) of inventory in LIFO fashion (i.e., the decrease must be subtracted from the most recently added layer). Previous layers are peeled off at the prices at which they were added.

Step 6.   Ending LIFO inventory is the beginning inventory increased by the new LIFO layer [Step 5(a)] or decreased by any liquidation of LIFO layers [Step 5(b)].

Example 17. In 1991, T Corporation elected to value inventories using double-extension dollar-value LIFO. Beginning inventory for 1991 consisted of the following:

Date	Pool Items	Ending Quantity	Current Cost Per Unit	Total at Current Cost
1-1-91	A	3,000	$3	$ 9,000
	B	4,000	6	24,000
Total base-year cost				$33,000

Inventory information for 1991–1993 and the computation of ending inventory using the steps in Exhibit 10-4 are shown below.

Steps 1 and 2: Double extend ending inventory.

			Ending inventory at current year prices			Ending inventory at base-year prices	
Date	Pool Items	Ending Quantity	Current Cost Per Unit	Total at Current Cost		Base-Year Cost Per Unit	Total at Base-year Cost
12-31-91	A	2,000	$4	$ 8,000		$3	$ 6,000
	B	5,000	7	35,000		6	30,000
				$43,000			$36,000
12-31-92	A	6,000	$5	$30,000		$3	$18,000
	B	7,000	9	63,000		6	42,000
				$93,000			$60,000
12-31-93	A	4,000	$6	$24,000		$3	$12,000
	B	5,000	10	50,000		6	30,000
				$74,000			$42,000

Step 3: Determine quantity increase (decrease) at base-year price.

	1991	1992	1993
Ending inventory base-year price	$36,000	$60,000	$42,000
Beginning inventory base-year price	(33,000)	(36,000)	(60,000)
Quantity increase at base-year price	$ 3,000	$24,000	($18,000)

Step 4: Calculate current year price index.

$$\text{Index} = \frac{\text{Ending inventory at current year price}}{\text{Ending inventory at base-year price}}$$

	1991	1992	1993
	$43,000	$93,000	Decrease: use index at
	$36,000	$60,000	which units were added
=	1.19	1.55	1.55

Step 5: Compute quantity increase or decrease to be
added or subtracted from beginning inventory.

	1991	1992	1993
Quantity increase at base-year price	$3,000	$24,000	($18,000)
× Index	× 1.19	× 1.55	× 1.55
= Increase or decrease to beginning inventory	$3,570	$37,200	($27,900)

Step 6:   Compute ending inventory.

	1991	1992	1993
Base-year	$33,000	$33,000	$33,000
1991 layer	3,570	3,570	3,570
1992 layer	—	37,200	9,300*
Total ending inventory	$37,570	$73,770	$45,870

* $37,200 − $27,900 = $9,300

THE LIFO ELECTION

Taxpayers may elect to use LIFO by filing Form 970 with the tax return for
the year in which the change is made. Unlike most other changes in accounting
method, prior approval by the IRS is not required. Conversely, the LIFO election
cannot be revoked unless consent is obtained. As explained below, the lower of
cost or market procedure may not be used with LIFO. Consequently, in the year
LIFO is elected, all previous write-downs to market must be restored to income.
For many years, the IRS required that all of the income due to the change had to
be reported in the year of the change. In 1981, Congress expressed its disfavor
with this view and enacted Code § 472(d). This provision allows the taxpayer to
spread the adjustment equally over three years, the year of the change and the
two following years. Nevertheless, if substantial write-downs have been made,
there may be a considerable cost to elect LIFO.

Another ramification of the LIFO election concerns the *conformity requirement*. Under § 472(c), taxpayers who use LIFO for tax purposes must also
use LIFO in preparing financial reports to shareholders and creditors. Failure to
comply with this rule terminates the LIFO election and requires the taxpayer to
change the method of accounting for inventory. As a result, taxpayers not con-
forming may be forced to give back any income tax savings previously obtained
with LIFO.

The conformity requirement appears to have stifled the use of LIFO, presumably because during periods of rising prices it produces lower income and
earnings per share than other inventory methods. This is true notwithstanding
the tax savings that are available with LIFO and the relaxation of the rule over
the years. The Regulations now permit the taxpayer to disclose income using
an inventory method other than LIFO if the disclosure is made in the form of a
footnote to the balance sheet or a parenthetical on the face of the balance sheet.[53]
No comparative disclosures are allowed on the face of the income statement.

---

[53]   Reg. § 1.472-2(e).

LOWER OF COST OR MARKET

In certain instances, the value of an inventory item may have dropped below the cost allocated to such items. When this occurs, financial accounting has traditionally abandoned the historical cost principle and allowed businesses to write-down their inventories to reflect the decline in value. The tax law has adopted a similar approach. Under the Regulations, taxpayers may value inventory at either (1) cost, or (2) the lower of cost or market.[54] However, the lower of cost or market approach may not be used if the LIFO method is used. Note that the lower of cost or market procedure deviates from the normal rule that losses are not deductible until they are realized.

In the phrase *the lower of cost or market,* "market" generally means replacement cost, or in the case of manufactured products, reproduction cost. When the rule is applied, the value of *each* similar item must be compared to its cost, and the lower is used in computing ending inventory.

Example 18. J's inventory records reveal the following.

Item	FIFO Cost	Market	Lower of Cost or Market
A	$3,100	$3,500	$3,100
B	5,100	3,000	3,000
C	6,000	7,500	6,000
	$14,200	$14,000	$12,100

If J elects to value inventories at cost, the inventory value is $14,200. Alternatively, if the lower of cost or market approach is elected, the inventory is valued at $12,100. This value is used because unsimilar items cannot be aggregated for tax purposes. For financial accounting purposes, J could combine the various items. Consequently, a difference may arise between book and taxable income.

The approach used above is that prescribed in the Regulations for normal goods. Note that these rules only allow a write-down to replacement cost. What if the firm believes that it will ultimately sell the item for less than what it would cost to replace it? Financial accountants refer to estimated sales price less costs of disposition as net realizable value. A write-down below this value is allowed only for what are often referred to as "subnormal" goods.[55]

---

[54] Reg. § 1.471-2(c).

[55] See Reg § 1.471-2(c) Note that reduction of net realizable value by an allowance for a normal profit margin is not allowed for tax purposes.

Subnormal goods are those items in inventory that cannot be sold at normal prices because of damage (e.g., a dent in a file cabinet), imperfections (e.g., a thousand sweatshirts with the logo improperly spelled), shop wear, changes of style, odd or broken lots, and so on. The Regulations allow the taxpayer to value these "subnormal" goods at a bona fide selling price less direct costs of disposition. However, this lower value is acceptable only if the goods are actually offered for sale at such price 30 days after the inventory date (e.g., cars with severe hail-damage are actually on the lot with a sales price slashed below replacement cost within 30 days of when inventory is taken).

Example 19.   In the landmark decision of *Thor Power Tool Co.*,[56] the taxpayer manufactured power tools consisting of 50 to 200 parts. Thor followed the common practice of producing additional parts at the same time it manufactured the original tool. This practice helped the company to avoid expensive retooling and special production runs as replacement parts were actually required. When accounting for these spare parts, the company initially capitalized their costs and—consistent with GAAP—subsequently wrote them down to reflect the decline in their expected sales price. The Supreme Court ultimately denied the write-down because Thor could not show that the parts (i.e., the excess inventory) were a subnormal good, and even if they had, the company had not actually offered the parts for sale at the lower price. The effect of this decision is to prohibit companies from writing down the value of slow moving inventory.

---

[56]   79-1 USTC ¶9139, 43 AFTR2d 79-362, 439 U.S. 522 (USSC, 1979).

TAX PLANNING CONSIDERATIONS

CASUALTY AND THEFT LOSSES

Much of the controversy surrounding casualty losses results from insufficient documentation of the loss. For this reason, taxpayers should give careful attention to accumulating the evidence necessary to establish the deduction. Such evidence would include, where appropriate, pictures, eyewitnesses, police reports, and newspaper accounts. The taxpayer also should gather evidence regarding the value of the property damaged or destroyed. In situations where an item is not repaired or replaced, an appraisal may be the only method of adequately valuing the loss.

In some cases, a taxpayer may suffer a casualty loss and in seeking insurance reimbursement incur appraisal costs. Even if the casualty loss is not deductible due to the 10 percent limitation, the appraisal costs are deductible as a cost of preparing the tax return and are therefore claimed as a miscellaneous itemized deduction.

Taxpayers often measure the amount of their casualty losses by the amount paid for repairs that are necessary to bring the property back to its condition before the casualty. This method of measuring may be inappropriate, however, if the repairs do not restore the property to its same condition before the casualty. In such case, an additional loss representing the decline in value should be claimed.

The rules for determining the deductible casualty loss have important implications for the amount of insurance that a taxpayer should maintain.

Example 20. T purchased a home in Boston for $70,000 15 years ago. This year, the home burned to the ground and the taxpayer received a $70,000 reimbursement from the insurance company. The cost of rebuilding the house was $200,000. Although T's economic loss was $130,000 ($200,000 − $70,000), none of the loss is deductible as a casualty loss. The casualty loss deduction is the *lesser of* the decline in value, $200,000, or the taxpayer's adjusted basis, $70,000, less the insurance reimbursement. Since the insurance reimbursement of $70,000 completely offset T's basis, there is no deductible loss.

BAD DEBTS

It is not uncommon for family members or friends to make loans to each other that are never repaid. This often occurs when a son or daughter is embarking on a business venture in which a parent is willing to invest. If the taxpayer wishes to claim a deduction if the debt is not paid, steps should be taken upon making the loan to ensure that the loan is not considered a gift. For example, the taxpayer should document the transaction in such a way that it is clear that both parties intend that repayment of the loan will occur. The best method of documenting the parties' wishes is to have a formal note drafted. Such a note would lend support to the argument that a debtor-creditor relationship existed between the parties. The note also should have a definite payment schedule, and each payment should be made on time. Collateral could be included as well. In addition, the note should call for a reasonable amount of interest. Failure to charge adequate interest could cause the imputed interest rules discussed in Chapter 5 to operate.

> **Example 21.** In 1991, F loaned his friend K $10,000 to start a chocolate chip cookie business. The business struggled along, requiring K to ask F for another $5,000, which he gladly loaned her. The business failed after six months. If F documented the loans and sought repayment, he may claim a bad debt deduction. If he failed to do so, any deduction may be disallowed.

NET OPERATING LOSSES

When a taxpayer suffers a net operating loss, a decision must be made whether to carry the loss back or elect to carry it forward only. Due to the time value of money, a carryback is usually more advantageous since an immediate tax refund can be obtained. However, this gain must be weighed against the future benefits to be obtained by a carryforward. If the taxpayer expects to be in a higher tax bracket in the future, the present value of the higher savings may be greater than the value of an immediate refund.

PROBLEM MATERIALS

DISCUSSION QUESTIONS

10-1 *Business vs. Nonbusiness Bad Debts.* R is employed as the chief executive officer of XYZ Corporation. Believing the company's future to be bright, he has acquired 75 percent of XYZ's stock. During the year, R loaned XYZ $10,000. Explain the tax consequences assuming XYZ is unable to repay all or a portion of the loan.

10-2 *Bad Debt Requirements.* Under what circumstances, if any, is a cash basis taxpayer allowed to claim a deduction for a bad debt? An accrual basis taxpayer?

10-3 *Identifying Bad Debts.* For each of the following situations, indicate whether the taxpayer would be able to claim a deduction for a bad debt.

   a.   Several years ago, F advanced $30,000 to his wholly owned corporation, which was experiencing financial difficulties. Last year he loaned it another $10,000. No notes were executed and no payments have been made. During the current year, the company declared bankruptcy.

   b.   T worked as a secretary for P Corporation for 25 years. When the company began struggling this year, she worked without pay. The company finally went out of business owing T six months of back pay.

   c.   E quit his old job as a salesman to become a sales manager for K Corporation this year. As part of his arrangement with K, he was to receive a $10,000 bonus if the company reached $1 million in sales for the year. Sales for the year were $900,000, and K Corporation did not pay E a bonus.

   d.   B and C each own 50 percent of ABC Incorporated. Over the years, ABC made loans to C. When C died he was penniless. He owed the company $20,000.

10-4 *Is There a Bad Debt?* In 1988 R's son, S, got in the restaurant business. R loaned S $10,000 to help him get the business going. No note was signed nor was any interest charged. The business was initially a huge success but as time passed, it began having financial problems. This year the son's business failed.

   a.   Can R claim a bad debt deduction? If so, is the debt a business or nonbusiness bad debt and how much is the deduction?

   b.   Same as (a) except R obtained a signed note from his son.

10-5 *Bad Debt of Related Party.* H loaned her son $10,000 to enter the car repair business. If the son subsequently abandons the business and does not repay the loan, what are the tax consequences to H?

10-6 *Casualty Losses.* Explain the rationale underlying the rules (lower of basis or value with certain exceptions) for computing the amount of the deduction for a casualty loss.

10-7 *Casualty Losses.* During the year, R had various losses. Explain whether each of the following would qualify as a casualty loss.

a.   Loss of stove due to electrical fire.

b.   Damage to water pipes from freezing temperatures in Southern California.

c.   Loss of tree from Dutch elm disease.

d.   Ruined carpeting from clogged sewer line.

e.   Hole in his suit from cigarette ashes he dropped.

f.   Damage to both his and his neighbor's car while R's son drove R's car.

g.   Luggage and contents seized by a foreign government during a European vacation.

10-8 *Theft Loss Calculation.* If taxpayers could plan their taxes to account for thefts of their own personal use property (e.g., theft of their stereo and television), would they want the burglar to take all the property at once or take some property the first time and return for more later?

10-9 *Net Operating Losses in General.* Comment on each of the following:

a.   The purposes of the net operating loss deduction.

b.   The rationale underlying the complex calculation of the net operating loss deduction.

c.   How a net operating loss occurring in 1991 is utilized (i.e., the carryover process).

10-10 *Inventoriable Costs: § 263A.* HHG operates a chain of retail appliance stores. The company has grown tremendously over the last several years. It expects that its gross receipts will exceed $10 million this year. What are the implications of this growth for the company's method of accounting for inventories?

10-11 *LIFO vs FIFO.* During the 1970s, there was a tremendous shift from the FIFO method of inventory to LIFO. Nevertheless, not every company shifted to the LIFO method. Discuss why some might shift to LIFO although others might not.

PROBLEMS

10-12 *Treatment of Bad Debts.* AAA Computer Company, an accrual basis corporation, installed a new computerized accounting system for a customer and billed him $1,500 in June, 1991. When aging its accounts receivable at year-end, the company found that the customer was experiencing financial difficulties.

a.   Assuming the company estimated that only $1,000 of the account would be collected, what is the amount of the bad debt deduction, if any, that it can claim in 1991?

b.   Would the answer to (a) change if the debt were a nonbusiness bad debt?

c.   In 1992 the company actually collected $200 and the remainder of the debt was worthless. What is the amount of the bad debt deduction, if any, that it can claim in 1992?

10-13 *Bad Debts and Accounting Methods.* Dr. D, a dentist, performed a root canal for a patient and charged him $300. The patient paid $100, then left town, never to be seen again. What is the amount of bad debt deduction, if any, that D may claim assuming that she is a cash basis taxpayer?

10-14 *Uncollectible Loan.* Several years ago, L loaned his old high-school friend B $5,000 to help him start a new business. Things did not go as well as B planned, and late in 1991 B declared bankruptcy. L expects to collect 40 cents on the dollar. In 1992, all of B's affairs were settled and L received $1,000. What are the tax consequences to L in 1991 and 1992?

10-15 *Personal Casualty.* When the waters of the Mississippi began to overflow their banks and flood the surrounding area, M was forced to leave her home and head for higher ground. On December 2, she returned to her home to find that it had been vandalized as well as damaged from the flood. After cleaning up, she determined that the following items had been stolen or damaged:

Item	Adjusted Basis	FMV Before	FMV After	Insurance Reimbursement
Fur coat	$6,000	$7,000	$0	$7,000
Computer	4,000	3,000	0	Uninsured
Couch	1,200	800	See below	500
Van	7,000	5,000		

The couch had been damaged and M had it reupholstered for $700. The insurance company reimbursed her for the amounts shown on December 27. Under M's insurance policy, the company did not reimburse her for loss on the car until 45 days had passed. M expected to recover $4,000 but subsequently received a check for $2,000 on January 25, 1992. While she was waiting for reimbursement for her van, she rented a car at a total cost of $700. Although M received value for the coat, she did not replace it. In addition to the losses shown above, her real estate broker advised that even though her house had not been damaged by the flood, the value had dropped by $20,000 since it was evident that it was located in an area prone to flooding.

a. Compute M's casualty loss deduction, assuming her A.G.I. in 1991 was $18,000 and in 1992, $20,000.
b. Assume the loss occurred on January 2, 1992, and the location was officially designated a disaster area by the President. Explain when the loss could be deducted.

10-16   *Casualty Loss: Business and Investment Property.*   H is a private detective. While sleuthing this year, his car was stolen. The car, which was used entirely for business, was worth $7,000 and had an adjusted basis of $12,000. H received no insurance reimbursement for his car. Also this year, his office was the victim of arson. The fire destroyed only a painting that had a basis of $1,500 and was worth $3,000. H received a reimbursement of $800 from his insurance company for the painting. H suffered yet another misfortune this year as his rental property was damaged by a flood, the first in the area in 70 years. Before the casualty, the property—which had greatly appreciated in value—was worth $90,000 and afterward only $40,000. The rental property had an adjusted basis of $30,000. He received $20,000 from the insurance company, the maximum amount for which homes in a flood plain could be insured. Compute H's casualty loss deduction assuming his A.G.I. is $30,000. Can a casualty loss create a net operating loss?

10-17   *Casualty Gains and Losses.*   This year, C's jewelry, which cost $10,000, was stolen from her home. Luckily, she was insured and the insurance company reimbursed her for its current value, $19,000. In addition, while she was on vacation all of her camera equipment was stolen. The camera equipment had cost her $3,500 and was worth $3,100. She received no reimbursement since she carried a large deductible on such items. C's A.G.I. for the year was $15,000.

a.   What is the effect of the casualty losses on C's taxable income?
b.   Same as above except the jewelry was worth $11,000.

10-18   *Casualty and Theft Loss Computation.*   In each of the following cases, compute the taxpayer's casualty loss deduction (before percentage limitations) and indicate whether it is deductible *for* or *from* adjusted gross income.

a.   While G was at the theater, his house (adjusted basis $60,000, fair market value $80,000) was completely destroyed by fire. The fire also completely destroyed both his skiing equipment (cost $300, fair market value $90) and a calculator (adjusted basis $110, fair market value $80) used for business. He was reimbursed for $30,000 with respect to the house.
b.   B owned a duplex which she rented. A tornado demolished the roof but did not damage the remainder of the duplex. The duplex's value before the tornado was $45,000 and after the tornado was $40,000. B's adjusted basis in the property was $30,000. The President declared the entire city a "disaster area."
c.   Assume the same facts in (b) except that instead of B's duplex being partially damaged it was her personal cabin cruiser, and she received a $2,000 reimbursement from the insurance company.
d.   L backed his car out of the garage and ran over his 10-speed bicycle (cost $400, fair market value $300). The bicycle is worthless.

10-19   *NOL Items.*   Indicate whether the following items can *create* a net operating loss for an individual taxpayer.

a.   Business capital loss
b.   Nonbusiness bad debt
c.   Casualty loss
d.   Interest expense on mortgage secured by primary residence
e.   Employee business expenses
f.   Contribution to Individual Retirement Account
g.   Alimony
h.   Personal exemption

10-20   *Items Considered in Computing an NOL.*   Indicate whether the following items are considered in computing the net operating loss deduction for an individual.

a.   Salary
b.   Capital gain on the sale of investment property
c.   Interest income
d.   Interest on a mortgage on a primary residence

10-21   *Net Operating Loss Computation.*   R, a single taxpayer, operates a bicycle shop. For the calendar year 1991, he reports the following items of income and expense:

Gross income from business	$150,000
Business operating expenses.	210,000
Interest income from investments	7,000
Casualty loss.	4,000
Interest expense on home mortgage	9,000
Long-term capital gains (nonbusiness)	3,000
Long-term capital loss (nonbusiness)	5,000
Long-term capital gains (business)	1,000

The casualty loss represented the uninsured theft of R's personal auto worth $4,100 ($9,000 adjusted basis).

a.   Compute R's net operating loss for 1991.
b.   Assuming R carries the loss back to 1988, when must the corrected return for 1988 be filed?

10-22 *Net Operating Loss Computation.* V, married with two dependents, owns a hardware store. For the current year, her records reveal the following:

Gross income from sales..................	$180,000
Business operating expenses..............	230,000
Royalties from investment.................	6,000
Nonbusiness expenses....................	9,000
Long-term capital gain (nonbusiness).......	5,000
Long-term capital gain (business)..........	3,000
Long-term capital loss (business)..........	3,500

What is V's net operating loss?

10-23 *Valuing Inventories.* Chapters Inc., a large publishing house, prints a variety of titles, some of which are best sellers and others of which are duds. Because it is very difficult for Chapters to estimate with any accuracy which books will be successful, and because the marginal cost of printing an additional book is small, it typically prints 5,000 more copies than it expects to sell. Books that are not sold within a year of release are stored. The company's experience has shown that 95 percent of the books stored are never sold. Consequently, the company writes off any excess copies once they are delivered to storage. This practice appears permissible for financial accounting purposes. Can the same procedure be used for tax purposes?

10-24 *Applying Lower of Cost or Market.* Fitness Galore specializes in selling physical fitness equipment. The company's inventory at the close of 1991 revealed the following:

Merchandise	Cost	Replacement Cost
Weight machines	$40,000	$43,000
Stationary Bicycles	10,000	8,000
Stair climbers	24,000	27,000

a. Compute the company's inventory assuming it uses the lower of FIFO cost or market.

b. Assume the company adopts LIFO next year. Explain the tax consequences.

10-25 *Double Extension Dollar-Value LIFO.* Unwound Sound has recently engaged an accountant to evaluate its inventory procedures and determine whether it should change from using FIFO to LIFO to account for inventories. The company's inventory records for 1990 and 1991 are shown below. Assume that the company had adopted double-extension dollar-value LIFO in 1990, and compute the ending inventory for:

a. 1990
b. 1991

Inventory Pool	1-1-90 Units	1-1-90 Cost per unit	12-31-90 Units	12-31-90 Cost per unit
Records	5,000	$2	3,000	$2
Tapes	4,000	3	6,000	4
Compact Discs	2,000	6	5,000	7

Inventory Pool	12-31-91 Units	12-31-91 Cost per unit
Records	2,000	$3
Tapes	3,000	5
Compact Discs	4,000	7

10-26 *LIFO Pooling.* As shown in Problem 10-25 above, the inventory of Unwound Sound consists of records, tapes, and compact discs. Over the last 15 years, the components of the company's inventory have changed dramatically. Whereas once the company only carried records, now it also carries tapes and CDs. Unwound Sound expects that in the very near future it will discontinue selling records. Assuming the company uses LIFO, explain the advantages of having one single pool containing all three items rather than three different pools.

RESEARCH PROBLEMS

10-27 R has had several minor automobile accidents in the last two years. During the current year, R demolished his car (value, $7,000; adjusted basis, $8,000) when he ran into a telephone pole. He used the car solely for business. R decided not to report the accident to the insurance company and claim his reimbursement because he believes his insurance rates will be raised if he does. Will R's deduction of his unreimbursed casualty loss be allowed?

10-28 T, a cash basis taxpayer, paid a swimming pool contractor, C, the sum of $10,000 in advance for improvements that C agreed to make to T's personal residence. C performed part of the contract and then ceased activity, leaving much of the work uncompleted.

T seeks your advice concerning whether she may claim a deduction for a bad debt.

LEARNING OBJECTIVES

Upon completion of this chapter you will be able to:

- Identify the personal expenses that qualify as itemized deductions

- Explain the rules regarding deductible medical expenses and compute the medical expense deduction

- Distinguish between deductible taxes and nondeductible fees or other charges

- Explain the rules regarding deductible state income taxes, including the proper treatment of such taxes by married persons filing joint or separate returns

- Distinguish between currently deductible and nondeductible interest expenses

- Explain the requirements for the deductibility of charitable contributions and compute the contribution deduction

- Identify the personal expenditures that qualify as either miscellaneous itemized deductions or other itemized deductions

- Explain the cutback rule applicable to certain itemized deductions of high-income taxpayers and compute their total deduction allowed

CHAPTER OUTLINE

Chapter **11**

ITEMIZED DEDUCTIONS

Although the vast majority of deductions are those for trade or business expenses, a taxpayer's deductions are not confined to these alone. As noted in Chapter 7, since 1942 Congress has also allowed taxpayers to deduct expenses relating to profit-seeking activities—thus creating a *second* category of so-called investment or nonbusiness expenses. In addition, despite the fact that Code § 262 expressly prohibits the deduction of personal expenditures, Congress has created various exceptions. As a result, a *third* category of deductible expenses exists, which contains such personal items as medical expenses, casualty losses, interest on home mortgages, taxes on real and personal property, charitable contributions, and tax return preparation costs. The last four chapters have focused primarily on business expenses. This chapter continues the discussion of the three types of deductions by examining the specific statutory and administrative authority relating to personal itemized deductions. As defined in Chapter 3, these personal expenses are deducted by a taxpayer only if (1) they exceed the available standard deduction, or (2) the taxpayer is not eligible for the standard deduction.

Before considering these deductions in detail, it should be emphasized that a particular type of expense (e.g., interest) does not necessarily receive the same treatment in all situations. More often than not, the expense is treated differently depending on whether it is business, investment, or personal in nature. For example, the deductibility of interest expense generally depends on whether it is related to a loan that was used to make a business, investment, or personal expenditure. In contrast, real property taxes are deductible regardless of whether the property is used for business, investment, or personal purposes. The character of the expense may also affect the deduction's classification. Generally, trade or business expenses (other than the unreimbursed expenses of an employee) and expenses related to producing rents or royalties are deductions *for* A.G.I., while other expenses are *itemized deductions* which may or may not be subject to the 2 percent floor.

MEDICAL EXPENSES

IN GENERAL

Deductible medical expenses include amounts paid for the diagnosis, cure, relief, treatment, or prevention of disease of the taxpayer, his or her spouse, and dependents.[1] The status of a person as the taxpayer's spouse or dependent must exist *either* at the time the medical services are rendered *or* at the time the expenses are paid.[2] A spousal relationship does not exist if the taxpayer is legally separated from his or her spouse under a decree of separate maintenance because the two parties are not considered married.[3] For purposes of dependency status, however, *both* the gross income test and the joint return test are waived.[4]

> **Example 1.** T pays all the medical expenses of his mother, M, during the current year. Although M had gross income in excess of the exemption amount ($2,150 in 1991) for the current year, all other dependency tests are met by T. Even though T cannot claim M as a dependent, he will be allowed to deduct all medical expenses paid on her behalf (assuming T itemizes his deductions and they exceed the percentage limitations imposed on medical deductions).

Medical expenses for children of divorced parents are deductible by the parent who pays for them, regardless of which parent is entitled to the dependency exemption. Additionally, if a taxpayer is entitled to a dependency exemption under a multiple support agreement, the taxpayer will be allowed to deduct any medical expenses which he or she actually pays on behalf of the claimed dependent.[5]

Medical expenses also include payments for treatment affecting any part or function of the body,[6] expenditures for certain medicines and drugs,[7] expenses paid for transportation primarily *for* and *essential* to the rendition of the medical care,[8] and payments made for medical care insurance for the taxpayer, his or her spouse and dependents.[9] Again, the term *dependent* includes any person who would otherwise qualify as the taxpayer's dependent even though the gross income or separate return tests are not met, and any person claimed as a dependent under a multiple support agreement.

---

[1] See §§ 213(a) and 213(d)(1).

[2] Reg. § 1.213-1(e)(3).

[3] § 143(a).

[4] See Reg. § 1.213-1(a)(3)(i) and Chapter 4 for a discussion of the dependency tests.

[5] See § 213(d)(5) and Reg. § 1.213-1(a)(3)(i). Medical expenses taken into account under § 21 in computing a credit for the care of certain dependents are not allowed to be treated as deductible medical expenses. See § 213(e) and Reg. § 1.213-1(f) and Chapter 13 for a discussion of the tax credit allowed under § 21.

[6] § 213(d)(1)(A) and Reg. § 1.213-1(e)(1)(i).

[7] § 213(d)(2) and Reg. § 1.213-1(e)(2).

[8] § 213(d)(1)(B) and Reg. § 1.213-1(e)(1)(iv).

[9] § 213(d)(1)(C) and Reg. § 1.213-1(e)(4).

Partial lists of deductible and nondeductible medical expenses are presented in Exhibits 11-1 and 11-2. The most recent addition to the list of nondeductible medical expenses involves cosmetic surgery or other similar procedure. Cosmetic surgery is defined as any procedure which is directed at improving the patient's appearance and does not meaningfully promote the proper function of the body or prevent or treat disease. Thus, the costs of face lifts, liposuction, hair transplants, and other similar elective procedures undertaken primarily to improve the taxpayer's physical appearance are not deductible. However, deductions are allowed for procedures necessary to ameliorate a congenital deformity, a personal injury arising from an accident or trauma, or a disfiguring disease.

WHEN DEDUCTIBLE

In computing the medical expense deduction for a given tax year, the taxpayer is allowed to take into account *only* those medical expenses *actually paid* during the taxable year, regardless of when the illness or injury which occasioned the expenses occurred, and regardless of the method of accounting used by the taxpayer in computing his or her taxable income (i.e., cash or accrual).[10] Consequently, if the medical expenses are incurred but not paid during the current

---

Exhibit 11-1
Partial List of Deductible Medical Expenses[11]

Fees paid for doctors, surgeons, dentists, osteopaths, opthalmologists, optometrists, chiropractors, chiropodists, podiatrists, psychiatrists, psychologists, and Christian Science practitioners

Fees paid for hospital services, therapy, nursing services, (including nurse's meals while on duty), ambulance hire, and laboratory, surgical, obstetrical, diagnostic, dental, and X-ray services

Meals and lodging provided by a hospital during medical treatment, and meals and lodging provided by a center during treatment for alcoholism or drug addiction

Medical and hospital insurance premiums

Medicines and drugs, but only if prescribed by doctor (includes vitamins, iron, and pills or other birth control items)

Special foods and drinks prescribed by doctor, but only if for the treatment of an illness

Special items, including braces for teeth or limbs, false teeth, artificial limbs, eyeglasses, contact lenses, hearing aids, crutches, wheelchairs, and guide dogs for the blind or deaf

Transportation expenses for needed medical care, including air, bus, boat, railroad, and cab fares

---

[10]   Reg. § 1.213-1(a)(1).

[11]   See *Your Federal Income Tax*, IRS Publication 17 (Rev. 1990), pp. 115–117.

Exhibit 11-2
Partial List of Nondeductible Expenditures[12]

Accident insurance premiums
Bottled water
Care of a normal and healthy baby by a nurse*
Cosmetic surgery (with limited exceptions)
Diaper service
Funeral and burial expenses
Health club dues
Household help*
Illegal operation or treatment
Maternity clothes
Programs for weight loss or to stop smoking
Social activities, such as dancing lessons, for the general improvement of health, even
    though recommended by doctor
Toothpaste, toiletries, cosmetics, etc.
Trip for general improvement of health
Vitamins for general health

Note: A portion of these expenditures may qualify as expenses for the child or dependent care tax credit allowed under § 21. See Chapter 13 for further discussion of this credit.

---

tax year, the deduction for such expenses will not be allowed *until* the year of payment. The IRS has ruled, however, that the use of a bank credit card to pay for medical expenses *will* qualify as payment in the year of the credit card charge regardless of when the taxpayer actually repays the bank.[13]

The *prepayment* of medical expenses does not qualify as a current deduction unless the taxpayer is required to make the payment as a condition of receiving the medical services.[14] Accordingly, the IRS has ruled that a taxpayer's nonrefundable advance payments required as a condition for admission to a retirement home or institution for future lifetime medical care are deductible as expenses in the year paid.[15]

> **Example 2.** As a prerequisite for prenatal care and the delivery of her child, M prepays $1,750 to her doctor on November 15, 1991. Even though much of the prenatal care and the delivery of the child does not occur until 1992, M will be allowed to treat the prepayment as a medical expenditure in 1991.

---

[12] *Supra,* Footnote 11, p. 116.

[13] Rev. Rul. 78-39, 1978-1 C.B. 73.

[14] See *Robert S. Basset,* 26 T.C. 619 (1956). Absent such a prohibition, a taxpayer could maximize the tax benefits of medical deductions simply by timing the year of payment.

[15] Rev. Rul. 75-303, 1975-2 C.B. 87.

DEDUCTION LIMITATIONS

The medical expense deduction was created by Congress with the stated social objective of providing individual taxpayers relief from a heavy tax burden during a period of medical emergency and thereby encouraging the maintenance of a high level of public health. However, the deduction was designed to provide relief for only those expenditures in excess of a normal or average amount. Currently, the medical expense deduction is allowed only to the extent medical expenditures exceed 7.5 percent of the taxpayer's adjusted gross income. This limitation ensures that only extraordinary medical costs will result in a deduction.

In addition to the percentage limitation imposed on the medical expense deduction, it is important to note that most of the everyday type of expenditures incurred by an individual for items incident to his or her general health and hygiene are excluded from the definition of qualifying medical expenses. For example, medicine and drug expenditures are deductible only if they are for insulin and *prescribed* drugs.[16] Over-the-counter medicines and drugs such as aspirin, cold remedies, skin lotions, and vitamins are not deductible. Other nondeductible expenditures are listed in Exhibit 11-2.

Example 3.   F had adjusted gross income of $30,000 for 1991 and paid the following medical expenses:

Doctors	$ 500
Dentist	600
Hospital	1,300
Medical insurance premiums	800
Medicines and drugs:	
Prescription drugs	300
Nonprescription medicines	150

Assuming F is not reimbursed for any of the medical expenditures during 1991, her medical expense deduction is computed as follows:

Medical insurance premiums	$ 800
Fees paid doctors and dentist	1,100
Hospital costs	1,300
Prescription drugs only	300
Total medical expenses taken into account	$3,500
Less: 7.5% of $30,000 (A.G.I.)	− 2,250
Allowable medical deduction for 1991	$1,250

---

[16]   § 213(b) and Reg. § 1.213-1(b)(2)(i).

SPECIAL ITEMS AND EQUIPMENT

The term *medical care* includes not only the diagnosis, treatment, and cure of disease, but the mitigation and prevention of disease as well. Thus, a taxpayer's expenditures for special items such as contact lenses, eyeglasses, hearing aids, artificial teeth or limbs, and ambulance hire would also qualify as medical expenditures.[17] Similarly, the cost of special equipment (e.g., wheelchairs and special controls or other equipment installed in an auto for use by a physically handicapped person) purchased *primarily* for the prevention or alleviation of a physical or mental defect or illness will be allowed as medical deductions. If the purchase of special equipment qualifies as a medical expenditure, the cost of its operation and maintenance is also a deductible medical expense.[18]

Capital expenditures generally are not deductible for Federal income tax purposes (i.e., depreciation is allowed only for property or equipment used in a taxpayer's trade or business or other income-producing activity). However, if a capital expenditure would otherwise qualify as a medical expense (i.e., it is incurred primarily for medical care), it will not be disqualified as a deduction. If the capital expenditure is for the permanent improvement or betterment of property such as the taxpayer's home, *only* the amount of the expenditure which *exceeds* the increase in value of the property improved will qualify as a medical expense.[19]

> **Example 4.**   After suffering a heart attack, T is advised by his physician to install an elevator in his residence rather than continue climbing the stairs. If the cost of installing the elevator is $6,000 and the increase in the value of his residence is determined to be only $1,000, the difference of $5,000 will be deductible by T as a medical expense in the year paid. Annual operating costs (i.e., utilities) and maintenance of the elevator also qualify as deductible medical expenses.

In two specific situations, any increase in value of the improved property is ignored (or deemed to be zero) for purposes of measuring the medical expense deduction. First, if permanent improvements are made to property *rented* by the taxpayer, the *entire* costs are deductible (subject to the 7.5% floor).[20] Likewise, the entire cost of certain home-related capital expenditures incurred by a physically handicapped individual qualifies as a medical expense. Qualifying costs

---

[17] Reg. § 1.213-1(e)(1)(ii). The IRS has ruled that the costs to acquire, train, and maintain a dog that assists a blind or deaf taxpayer are deductible medical expenses (see Rev. Rul. 55-216, 1955-1 C.B. 307 and Rev. Rul. 68-295, 1968-1 C.B. 92). In the Committee Reports for the Technical and Miscellaneous Revenue Act of 1988, Congress indicated its approval of this IRS position and stated that similar costs incurred with respect to a dog *or* other service animal used to assist individuals with *other physical disabilities* would also be eligible for the medical expense deduction.

[18] *Supra*, Footnote 11, p. 116.

[19] Reg. § 1.213-1(e)(1)(iii).

[20] Rev. Rul. 70-395, 1970-2 C.B. 65.

include expenditures for (1) constructing entrance or exit ramps to the residence; (2) widening doorways at entrances or exits to the residence; (3) widening or otherwise modifying hallways and interior doorways to accommodate wheelchairs; (4) railings, support bars, or other modifications to bathrooms to accommodate handicapped individuals; (5) lowering of or other modifications to kitchen cabinets and equipment to accommodate access by handicapped individuals; and (6) adjustment of electrical outlets and fixtures.

SPECIAL CARE FACILITIES

Expenses paid for emergency room treatment or hospital care of the taxpayer, his or her spouse, or dependents qualify for the medical deduction.[21] However, the deductibility of expenses for care in an institution other than a hospital depends upon the medical condition of the individual *and* the nature of the services he or she receives. If the *principal reason* an individual is in an institution (such as a nursing home or special school) is the availability of medical care, the *entire cost* of the medical care qualifies as a medical expenditure. This includes the cost of meals and lodging as well as any tuition expenses of special schools.[22]

> **Example 5.** T enrolled his dependent son, S, in a special school for children with hearing impairments. If the principal reason for S's attendance at the school is his medical condition *and* the institution has the resources to treat or supervise training of the hearing impaired, the entire cost of S's attendance at the school qualifies as a medical expense. This includes tuition, meals and lodging, and any other costs that are incidental to the special services furnished by the school.

If an individual's medical condition *is not* the principal reason for being in an institution, only that part of the cost of care in the institution which is attributable to medical care will qualify as a medical expense.[23]

> **Example 6.** T placed her dependent father, F, in a nursing home after F suffered a stroke and partial paralysis. Of the $6,000 total nursing home expenses, only $2,500 is attributable to the medical care and nursing attention furnished to F. If F is not in the nursing home for the principal reason of the medical and nursing care, only $2,500 will be deductible by T.

---

[21] This includes the cost of meals and lodging incurred as an in-patient of a hospital. See Reg. § 1.213-1(e)(1)(v).

[22] Reg. § 1.213-1(e)(1)(v)(a). See also *Donald R. Pfeifer*, 37 TCM 817, T.C. Memo 1978-189; *W.B. Counts*, 42 T.C. 755 (1963);

Rev. Rul. 78-340, 1978-2 C.B. 124; and Rev. Rul. 58-533, 1958-2 C.B. 108.

[23] Reg. § 1.213-1(e)(1)(v)(b). This *excludes* meals and lodging and any other expenses not directly attributable to the medical care or treatment.

MEDICAL TRAVEL AND TRANSPORTATION

Expenses paid for transportation to and from the office of a doctor or dentist or to a hospital or clinic usually are deductible as medical expenses. This includes amounts paid for bus, taxi, train, and plane fares, as well as the out-of-pocket expenses for use of the taxpayer's personal vehicle (i.e., gas and oil, parking fees, and tolls). If the taxpayer uses his or her personal automobile for medical transportation and does not want to calculate actual expenses, the IRS allows a deduction of 9 cents a mile *plus* parking fees and tolls paid while traveling for medical treatment.[24]

Travel costs include *only* transportation expenses and the cost of lodging. For these expenses to qualify as a medical deduction, a trip beyond the taxpayer's locale *must* be "primarily for and essential to medical care."[25] Meal costs are deductible only if provided by a hospital or similar institution as a necessary part of medical care. Thus, meals consumed while en route between the taxpayer's home and the location of the medical care are not deductible.

If an individual receives medical treatment as an outpatient at a clinic or doctor's office, the cost of lodging while in the new locality may be deductible— but not the cost of meals. The cost of lodging will qualify as a medical expense if (1) the lodging is not lavish or extravagant under the circumstances; and (2) there is no significant element of personal pleasure, recreation, or vacation in the travel away from home. If deductible, the amount of lodging costs includible as a medical expense may not exceed *$50* for *each night* for each individual.[26] It is important to note that travel costs of a companion (including parents or a nurse) are included as medical expenses if the individual requiring medical treatment could not travel alone, or if the companion rendered medical treatment en route.[27] Thus, the lodging costs of such a person while in the new locality should also be treated as a part of any medical expenses (subject to the $50 per night limitation).

> **Example 7.** At the advice of a doctor, T travels with his three-year-old daughter, D, from Lincoln, Nebraska to Houston, Texas. D has a rare blood disease and a hospital in Houston is the nearest facility specializing in treatment of her disorder. The transportation costs and lodging for both T and his daughter while en route to and from Houston are deductible. If they stay at a nearby hotel while D receives treatment as an outpatient, the costs of lodging (but not meals) incurred in Houston—up to $100 per night—are also deductible.

---

[24] Rev. Proc. 85-49, 1985 I.R.B. 40, 26.

[25] See § 213(d)(2), Reg. § 1.213-1(e)(1)(iv), and *Comm. v. Bilder,* 62-1 USTC ¶9440, 9 AFTR2d 1355, 369 U.S. 499 (USSC, 1962).

[26] § 213(d)(2).

[27] See Rev. Rul. 75-317, 1975-2 C.B. 57.

MEDICAL INSURANCE COSTS AND REIMBURSEMENTS

Amounts paid for medical care insurance for the taxpayer, his or her spouse, and dependents qualify as medical expenses. If premiums are paid under an insurance contract which offers coverage beyond medical care (e.g., coverage for loss of life, limb, or sight, or loss of income), only the portion of the premiums paid that is attributable to medical care is deductible. To be deductible, however, the medical care portion of the premiums paid must either be separately stated in the contract itself, or included in a separate bill or statement from the insurer.[28]

Taxpayers receiving reimbursements for medical expenses in the *same year* in which the expenses were paid must reduce any medical expense deduction to a net amount. However, if the reimbursement is for medical expenses in a prior year, the income tax treatment of the reimbursement depends upon whether the taxpayer claimed a medical expense deduction for the year in which the expenses were actually paid. If no medical expense deduction was taken in the year in which the expenses were paid (e.g., taxpayer used the standard deduction or total medical expenses did not exceed the required percentage of A.G.I.), any reimbursement for such expenses will not be included in gross income. If the taxpayer claimed a deduction for the medical expenses in the prior year, however, the reimbursement must be included in gross income to the extent of the *lesser* of: (1) the previous medical expense deduction, or (2) the excess of the taxpayer's itemized deductions over his or her standard deduction. The inclusion in gross income of all or a part of the reimbursement is in accordance with the tax benefit rule.

> **Example 8.** T has adjusted gross income of $20,000 for 1991. During the year, T pays the following medical expenses:
>
> | | |
> |---|---:|
> | Hospitalization insurance premiums........... | $1,100 |
> | Doctor and dental bills....................... | 800 |
> | Eyeglasses................................... | 75 |
> | Medical transportation .... | 25 |
>
> T's medical expense deduction is computed as follows:
>
> | | |
> |---|---:|
> | Total medical expenses................... | $2,000 |
> | Less: 7.5% of $20,000 (A.G.I.).......... | − 1,500 |
> | Medical expense deduction from 1991..... | $ 500 |
>
> T's itemized deductions (including the $500 medical expense deduction) for 1991 exceeded his standard deduction by $1,500. In 1992 T received $400 as a reimbursement from his insurance company. T must include the *entire* $400 in gross income for 1992. If T had received the $400 reimbursement in 1991, his medical expense deduction would have been limited to $100.

---

[28] Reg. § 1.213-1(e)(4). Participants in the Federal Medicare program are entitled to treat as medical care insurance premiums the amounts withheld for voluntary doctor-bill insurance.

Example 9. Assume the same facts as in *Example 8* except that the medical expense reimbursement was $700 instead of $400. If the reimbursement was received in 1992, T would be required to include *only* $500 in gross income—the amount of the medical expenses included in his itemized deductions. If the amount by which T's itemized deductions exceeded his standard deduction was *less* than $500 for 1991, he would include in gross income for 1992 only so much of the reimbursement represented by the prior year's itemized deductions in excess of the standard deduction amount. However, if T had used the standard deduction in 1991, none of the $700 reimbursement would be included in 1992 gross income because T received no tax benefit in 1991.

The situations illustrated in *Examples 8* and *9* occur quite often because taxpayers are *not required* to reduce a current year's medical expense deduction by *anticipated* insurance reimbursements. Notice that this can result in a taxpayer receiving reimbursements early in the next tax year and not being required to pay income taxes on the reimbursement until April 15 of the following year.

HEALTH INSURANCE COSTS OF SELF-EMPLOYED TAXPAYERS

As part of the Tax Reform Act of 1986, Congress introduced a special rule allowing self-employed individuals to deduct 25 percent of the amounts paid for health insurance on behalf of a self-employed individual, his or her spouse, and dependents.[29] The deduction is allowed in determining adjusted gross income (i.e., a deduction *for* A.G.I.) rather than being treated as an itemized medical expense deduction subject to the 7.5 percent floor. The deduction may not be claimed, however, *unless* the self-employed individual provides coverage for all employees in his or her business and certain nondiscrimination requirements are satisfied.[30] Also, no deduction is allowable to the extent it *exceeds* the taxpayer's net earnings from self-employment.[31] Thus, the deduction cannot create a loss. More important, the deduction does not reduce the income base for which the taxpayer is liable for self-employment taxes.

Example 10. K, a self-employed individual, paid $1,600 during 1991 for health insurance for himself, his wife, and their two children. K had no employees during the year. K is entitled to deduct $400 ($1,600 × 25%) in determining adjusted gross income, provided the deduction does not exceed his net earnings from self-employment, and his A.G.I. before the deduction is at least $400.

---

[29] § 162(m). This provision was scheduled to expire after September 30, 1990, but has been extended through 1991 by the Revenue Reconciliation Act of 1990 [§ 162(m)(4)].

[30] § 162(m)(2)(B).

[31] § 162(m)(2)(A).

Absent a special rule, self-employed individuals who are also employees might be tempted to opt out of an employer-provided medical insurance plan. By so doing, the 7.5 percent floor on medical expenses could be avoided and taxpayers could deduct 25 percent of what normally would be nondeductible premium payments. To prevent this course of action, the deduction is not allowed if a self-employed individual or spouse is eligible to participate in a health insurance plan of an employer.[32]

PERSONAL CASUALTY AND THEFT LOSSES

As discussed in Chapter 10, Congress has provided for a deduction of losses related to property used for *personal* purposes where the loss arises from fire, storm, shipwreck, or other casualty, or theft.[33] Like the medical expense deduction, the deduction for personal casualty and theft losses is designed to provide relief for only extraordinary losses. Thus, an individual taxpayer's deduction for personal casualty and theft losses is allowed only to the extent such losses exceed $100 per occurrence *and* the sum of all losses (after reduction by the $100 floor) for a given tax year exceeds 10 percent of the taxpayer's adjusted gross income. These deduction limitations were discussed and illustrated in Chapter 10.

YEAR DEDUCTIBLE

A personal casualty loss is generally deductible in the taxable year in which the loss occurs. Recall, however, that a theft loss is deductible only in the year of discovery. If a claim for insurance reimbursement (or any other potential recovery) exists and there is a reasonable prospect of recovery, the loss must be reduced by the amount *expected* to be received.[34] If later receipts are *less* than the amount originally estimated and no further reimbursement is expected, an amended return is not filed. Instead, the remaining loss is deductible in the year in which no further reimbursement is expected. Most important, if the casualty loss deduction claimed in the prior year was reduced by the $100 floor and exceeded the 10 percent A.G.I. limitation, the remaining loss is not further reduced. However, the remaining loss is subject to the 10 percent limitation of the later year.[35]

REPORTING CASUALTY LOSSES

Individual taxpayers are required to report and compute casualty losses on Form 4684,[36] which is to be filed with Form 1040. The casualty loss deduction, if any, is reported with other itemized deductions on Schedule A, Form 1040.

---

[32] § 162(m)(2)(C).

[33] § 165(c)(3).

[34] Reg. § 1.165-1(d)(2)(i).

[35] See *Example 9* of Chapter 8.

[36] See Appendix B for a sample of this form.

TAXES

Code § 164 is the statutory authority which permits taxpayers to deduct several types of taxes for Federal income tax purposes. If the taxes are related to an individual taxpayer's trade or business or income-producing activity, the deduction is generally allowed in arriving at adjusted gross income. However, both the IRS and the courts have taken the position that state, local, and foreign *income* taxes are deductible by an individual taxpayer *from* his or her adjusted gross income—even though it could be argued that such taxes are related to his or her trade or business. Likewise, if *property* taxes are related to personal use property (e.g., residence, car, etc.), such taxes are deductible only if the individual itemizes his or her deductions. If taxes are deductible by taxpayers other than individuals, the deductions simply reduce gross income to taxable income.[37]

The types of taxes specifically allowed as deductions under § 164 are

1. State, local, and foreign real property taxes;

2. State and local personal property taxes;

3. State, local, and foreign income, war profits, and excess profit taxes; and

4. The generation-skipping transfer tax.[38]

The generation-skipping transfer tax is imposed on income distributions from certain trusts. Discussion of this tax is beyond the scope of this text. However, each of the other three types of deductible taxes is discussed in detail below.

GENERAL REQUIREMENTS FOR DEDUCTIBILITY

A tax is deductible *only* if (1) it is imposed on the taxpayer's income or property; and (2) it is paid or incurred by the taxpayer in the taxable year for which a deduction is being claimed. Even if these two requirements are met, deductions for certain Federal, state, and local taxes are expressly denied. Exhibit 11-3 contains a list of nondeductible taxes. The most recent addition to the list of nondeductible taxes involves state and local sales taxes. Prior to 1987, if such taxes were paid or incurred in connection with a trade or business or for the production of income, taxpayers could either deduct the expenses or elect to capitalize the costs as part of the tax basis of the property purchased. Similarly, state and local sales taxes paid on purchases of personal use property (e.g., home furnishings, clothes, autos and trucks) were allowed as deductions if the taxpayer elected to itemize his or her deductions. Since 1986, however, no business *or* personal deduction is allowed for any tax paid or incurred in connection with

---

[37]   See the later section in this chapter entitled "Reporting Deductions for Taxes."

[38]   § 164(a).

an acquisition (i.e., a sales tax) or disposition (i.e., a transfer tax) of property. Instead, such tax *must* be treated as a part of the cost of the acquired property, or, in the case of a disposition, as a reduction in the amount realized on the disposition.[39]

In addition to the nondeductible taxes listed in Exhibit 11-3, deductions for *fees* (whether or not labeled as taxes) paid by taxpayers usually are denied *unless* the fees are incurred in the taxpayer's trade or business or for the production of income. Fees paid or incurred in connection with a trade or business, if ordinary and necessary, are deductible as business expenses under § 162. Similarly, fees related to the production of income generally are deductible expenses under § 212.[40]

The IRS distinguishes a "tax" from a "fee" by looking to the *purpose* of the charge.[41] If a particular charge is imposed upon the taxpayer for the purpose of *raising revenue* to be used for public or government purposes, the IRS will consider the charge to be a *tax*. However, if the charge is imposed because of either *particular acts or services* received by the taxpayer, such charge will be considered as a *fee*. Thus, fees for driver's licenses, vehicle registration and

---

Exhibit 11-3
Nondeductible Taxes[42]

Nondeductible Federal taxes:
  Federal income taxes (including those withheld from an individual's pay)
  Social security or railroad retirement taxes withheld from an individual by his or her employer (includes self-employment taxes)
  Social security and other employment taxes paid on the wages of the taxpayer's employee who performed domestic or other personal services
  Federal excise taxes or customs duties, *unless* they are connected with the taxpayer's business or income-producing activity
  Federal estate and gift taxes

Nondeductible state and local taxes:
  Motor vehicle taxes (*unless* they qualify as ad valorem taxes on personal property)
  Inheritance, legacy, succession, or estate taxes
  Gift taxes
  Per capita or poll taxes
  Cigarette, tobacco, liquor, beer, wine, etc., taxes
  Sales taxes

---

[39] *Supra*, Footnote 38.

[40] See Chapter 7 for a discussion of the requirements that must be met in order to deduct business and nonbusiness expenses of this nature.

[41] See § 275, Reg. § 1.164-2 and *Your Federal Income Tax*, IRS Publication 17 (Rev. 1990), pp. 120–21.

[42] See § 275, Reg. § 1.164-2 and *Your Federal Income Tax*, IRS Publication 17 (Rev. 1990), pp. 120–21.

inspection, license tags for pets, hunting and fishing licenses, tolls for bridges and roads, parking meter deposits, water bills, sewer and other service charges, and postage fees are not deductible *unless* related to the taxpayer's trade or business, or income-producing activity.[43]

Since most individual taxpayers use the cash receipts and disbursements method of accounting for tax purposes, the following discussion of income and property tax deductions concentrates on cash basis taxpayers and the requirement that taxes be *paid* in the year of deduction. Bear in mind throughout this discussion, however, that accrual method taxpayers are allowed a deduction for taxes in the tax year in which the obligation for payment becomes fixed and determinable (i.e., the all-events test is met).

INCOME TAXES

Most state, local, or foreign income taxes paid or accrued by a taxpayer are deductible in arriving at taxable income. For individual taxpayers, however, a deduction for state and local income taxes is allowed only if the taxpayer itemizes his or her deductions. Although the income taxes may be related solely to the individual's business income (e.g., income from a sole proprietorship or partnership), or income from rents and royalties, these taxes are considered personal in nature. Since income taxes paid to a foreign country or a U.S. possession may either be deducted as an itemized deduction or claimed as a credit against the U.S. income tax, an individual who does not itemize deductions should elect to claim foreign income taxes as credits.[44]

Cash basis taxpayers are allowed to deduct state and local income taxes *paid* during the taxable year, including those taxes imposed on interest income that is exempt from Federal income taxation. Amounts considered paid during the taxable year include

1. State and local income or foreign taxes withheld from an individual's salary by his or her employer;

2. Estimated payments made by the taxpayer under a pay-as-you-go requirement of a taxing authority; and

3. Payments made in the current year on an income tax liability of a prior year.

[43] *Your Federal Income Tax*, IRS Publication 17 (Rev. 1990), p. 120. No matter how strong an argument a taxpayer can make that his or her marriage was for business or income-producing purposes, fees for marriage licenses are considered nondeductible personal expenses.

[44] See § 27. For further information on this and other matters regarding the Federal income taxation of foreign source income, see *Corporate, Partnership, Estate and Gift Taxation*, 1992 Edition (Homewood: Richard D. Irwin, Inc.), Chapter 9.

Example 11. During 1991, Z, a cash basis taxpayer, had $1,500 of Illinois state income taxes withheld by her employer. In 1991 she paid the remaining $450 in state income taxes due on her 1990 Illinois tax return, and also paid $300 in estimated state income tax payments during 1991. If Z itemizes her deductions for Federal income tax purposes, she is entitled to a $2,250 ($1,500 + $300 + $450) state income tax deduction for 1991.

If a cash basis taxpayer receives a refund of state, local, or foreign income taxes in the current year, the refund must be included in the current year's gross income to the extent a deduction in an earlier tax year provided a tax benefit.[45]

Example 12. Assume the same facts as in *Example 11*. While preparing her 1991 Illinois state income tax return in early 1992, Z determined she had overpaid the state tax liability by $375. She received a refund of the entire overpayment on August 10, 1992. If Z claimed the total $2,250 state income taxes paid as a deduction on her 1991 Federal income tax return and her itemized deductions exceeded the standard deduction amount by at least $375, she must include the entire refund in gross income on her 1992 Federal income tax return.

Married taxpayers filing *separate* state or Federal income tax returns are subject to the following rules regarding the deduction for state income taxes:[46]

1. If separate state *and* Federal returns are filed, each spouse may deduct on his or her Federal income tax return the amount of state income tax imposed on and paid by such spouse during the tax year.

2. If separate state returns *but* a joint Federal return will be filed, the married couple may deduct on the joint Federal income tax return the sum of the state income tax imposed on both husband and wife, regardless of which spouse actually paid the tax.

3. If a joint state return *but* separate Federal returns are filed, each spouse is allowed to deduct on his or her Federal income tax return that *portion* of the total state tax imposed and paid during the year that the gross income of each spouse contributes to their total combined gross income.

---

[45] § 111.

[46] *Your Federal Income Tax*, IRS Publication 17 (Rev. 1990), p. 119.

PROPERTY TAXES

Personal property taxes paid to a state, local, or foreign government are deductible *only* if they are *ad valorem* taxes.[47]   Ad valorem taxes are taxes imposed on the *value* of property. Quite often, state and local taxing authorities impose a combination tax and fee on personal property. In such cases, only that portion of the charge based on value of the property will qualify as a deductible tax.[48]

> **Example 13.**   State A imposes an annual vehicle registration charge of 60 cents per hundredweight. X, a resident of the state, paid $24 in 1991 for the registration of his personal automobile. Since this charge is not based on the value of the auto, X has not paid a deductible tax.

> **Example 14.**   State B imposes an annual vehicle registration charge of 1% of value plus 50 cents per hundredweight. Y, a resident of the state, owns a personal use automobile having a value of $10,000 and weighing 4,000 pounds. Of the $120 [(1% × $10,000) + (50¢ × 40 hundredweight)] total registration charge paid by Y, only $100 would be deductible as a personal property tax.

Real property (real estate) taxes are generally deductible only if imposed on property owned by the taxpayer and paid or accrued by the taxpayer in the year the deduction is claimed. If real property taxes are imposed on jointly held real estate, each owner may claim his or her portion of the taxes. For example, if cash basis, married taxpayers file separate Federal income tax returns and real property taxes are imposed on jointly held real estate, each spouse may claim *half* of the taxes paid.

If real estate is sold during the year, the deduction for real estate taxes *must* be *apportioned* between the buyer and seller according to the number of days in the year each held the property, regardless of which party actually paid the property taxes.[49] The taxes are apportioned to the seller up to (but not including) the date of sale, and to the buyer beginning with the date of sale.

---

[47]   § 164(b)(1) and Reg. § 1.164-3(c).

[48]   § 164(b)(2)(E). States known to include some ad valorem tax as part of auto and boat registration fees are Arizona, California, Colorado, Indiana, Iowa, Maine, Massachusetts, Nevada, New Hampshire, Oklahoma, Washington, and Wyoming.

[49]   § 164(d) and Reg. § 1.164-6(b).

Example 15. The real property tax year in Colorado County is April 1 to March 31. X, the owner on April 1, 1991 of real property located in Colorado County, sells the real property to Y on June 30, 1991. Y owns the real property from June 30, 1991 through March 31, 1992. The real property tax is $730 for the county's tax year April 1, 1991 to March 31, 1992. For purposes of § 164(a), $180 (90 ÷ 365 × $730 = $180 taxes for April 1, 1991 through June 29, 1990) of the real property tax is treated as imposed on X, the seller. The remaining $550 (275 ÷ 365 × $730 = $550 taxes for June 30, 1991 through March 31, 1992) of such real property tax is treated as imposed on Y, the purchaser.[50]

When both buyer and seller of real property are cash basis taxpayers and only one of the parties *actually* pays the real property taxes for the period in which both parties owned the property, *each* party to the transaction is entitled to deduct the portion of the real property taxes based on the number of days he or she held the property. As a practical matter, real property taxes are usually allocated during the closing process, and the details are provided in the closing statement for real property sales. A taxpayer need only acquire the closing statement to ascertain the proper allocation and how the sales price has been affected by the allocation.

Unless the actual real property taxes are apportioned between buyer and seller as part of the sale/purchase agreement, adjustments for the taxes must be made to determine the amount realized by the seller, as well as the buyer's cost basis of the property.[51] The treatment of the adjustments depends upon which party actually paid the real estate taxes.

Example 16. Assume that buyer and seller are both cash basis, calendar year taxpayers, and real estate taxes for the entire year are to be paid at the end of the year. Real property is sold on October 1, 1991 for $30,000, and B, the buyer, pays the real estate taxes of $365 on December 31, 1991. The real estate taxes attributable to and deductible by B are $92 (92 ÷ 365 × $365). The remaining $273 ($365 − $92) of the taxes will be apportioned to and deductible by S, the seller. As a result of this apportionment, the seller must increase the amount realized from the sale to $30,273, and the buyer will have an adjusted cost basis for the property of $30,273.

Example 17. Assume the same facts as in *Example 16*, except that the real property taxes are payable in advance for the entire year and that S, the seller, paid $365 in January of 1991. The real estate taxes are apportioned in the same manner, and the buyer, B, will be entitled to deduct $92. However, B must adjust his cost basis of the property to $29,908 ($30,000 purchase price − $92 taxes paid by seller). The seller, S, is entitled to deduct $273 of the taxes and reduce his amount realized from the sale to $29,908.

---

[50] Reg. § 1.164-6(b)(3), Example 1.

[51] Reg. § 1.164-6(d); Reg. § 1.1001-1(b); and Reg. § 1.1012-1(b). A similar result should occur if buyer and seller are using different accounting methods.

Real property taxes assessed against local benefits of a kind tending to increase the value of the property assessed (e.g., special assessments for paved streets, street lights, sidewalks, drainage ditches, etc.) are not deductible.[52] Instead, the property owner simply adds the assessed amount paid to his or her cost basis of the property. However, if assessments for local benefits are made for the purpose of maintenance or repair, or for the purpose of meeting interest charges with respect to such benefits, they are deductible.[53] If an assessment is in part for the cost of an improvement and in part for maintenance, repairs or for interest charges, only *that* portion of the tax assessment relating to maintenance, repairs, or interest charges will be deductible. Unless the taxpayer can show the allocation of the amounts assessed for the different purposes, *none* of the amount paid is deductible.[54]

REPORTING DEDUCTIONS FOR TAXES

Deductible state and local taxes are reported on different forms depending on the taxpaying entity claiming the deduction. Corporations report their deductions for these taxes on Form 1120. Fiduciaries (trusts and estates) report deductible taxes on Form 1041. Partnerships and S corporations report deductible taxes on Forms 1065 and 1120S, respectively. Individuals report deductible taxes on Form 1040, but the particular schedule used depends upon whether the taxes are business expenses or personal itemized deductions.

An individual's deduction for taxes (other than income taxes) related to his or her trade or business is reported on Schedule C of Form 1040 (Schedule F for farmers and ranchers). Deductible taxes (other than income taxes) related to rents and royalties are reported on Schedule E. All other deductible taxes, including state and local income taxes on business income or income from rents or royalties, are reported by an individual taxpayer on Schedule A of Form 1040.

INTEREST EXPENSE

The deductibility of interest expense has been a controversial issue for many years. Much of the controversy centered around the wisdom of continuing to allow interest deductions on loans to finance personal consumption of goods and services and nonbusiness related investments. Many economists argued that continuation of such a Federal tax policy encouraged spending at the expense of current savings and contributed to taxpayers' willingness to make investments in marginally profitable or even unsound ventures. In 1986, Congress responded to the criticism by phasing out the deduction for interest on most consumer debt and further restricting deductions related to investments.

---

[52]   § 164(c)(1), Reg. § 1.164-2(g), and Reg. § 1.164-4(a).

[53]   § 164(c)(1) and Reg. § 1.164-4(b)(1).

[54]   Reg. § 1.164-4(b)(1).

Beginning in 1991, no deduction is allowed for *personal* (consumer) *interest*. For this purpose, the term "personal interest" is defined as any interest other than[55]

1. Trade or business interest;

2. Investment interest;

3. Interest from a passive activity; and

4. Qualified residence interest.

Thus, nondeductible consumer interest includes any interest on personal automobile loans, interest related to an employee's business expenses, and interest paid on delinquent tax payments and penalties. Also included as nondeductible personal interest are the finance charges from department store and bank credit card purchases, gasoline credit card purchases, and interest on student loans. It is important to note, however, that an exemption remains for the deduction of interest on a taxpayer's personal residence.

> **Example 18.** In 1988, T purchased a new home for $150,000 by paying $15,000 cash and taking out a mortgage on the home for the $135,000 balance. During the current year, T paid $9,850 interest on his home mortgage. Even though the interest is personal in nature, T will be allowed to deduct the entire $9,850 interest expense, assuming he itemizes his deductions and will not be subject to the 3% cutback rule discussed later in this chapter.

Unfortunately, there are certain restrictions imposed on some taxpayers' home-mortgage interest. These restrictions, as well as limitations imposed on other interest expense deductions and losses from certain investments, are discussed in Chapter 12.

CHARITABLE CONTRIBUTIONS

To encourage the private sector to share in the cost of providing many needed social services, Congress allows individuals, regular corporations, estates, and trusts deductions for charitable contributions (or gifts) of money or other property to certain qualified organizations. Partnerships and S corporations are not allowed to deduct charitable contributions. Instead, these conduit entities pass the contributions through to the partners and shareholders who must claim the deduction on their own Federal income tax returns.[56]

---

[55] § 163(h).

[56] See §§ 702(a)(4) and 1366(a)(1).

Code § 170 contains the rules regarding deductions for charitable contributions made by individuals and regular corporations. Code § 642(c) sets forth the rules regarding the amount and timing of charitable contribution deductions claimed by estates and trusts. The rules related to the measurement, timing, and qualification of contribution deductions claimed by individuals and corporations are discussed below. A discussion of the percentage limitations imposed on current deductions by individual taxpayers is also included. The specific rules regarding limitations imposed on a corporation's annual charitable contribution deduction are discussed in Chapter 19.

DEDUCTION REQUIREMENTS

Individual taxpayers are allowed a deduction for contributions of cash or other property *only if* the gift is made to a qualifying donee organization. Additionally, individuals are required to actually pay cash or transfer property before the close of the tax year in which the deduction is claimed. An exception to the payment requirement is made in the case of contribution deductions which, due to deduction limitations, have been carried over from prior years. The deduction limitations and carryover rules are discussed later in this chapter.

Qualifying Donees. To be deductible, contributions of cash or other property must be made to or for the use of one of the following:[57]

1. A state, a U.S. possession, a political subdivision of a state or possession, the United States, or the District of Columbia, if the contribution is made solely for public purposes;

2. A community chest, corporation, trust, fund, or foundation that is organized or created in, or under the laws of, the United States, any state, the District of Columbia, or any possession of the United States *and* is organized and operated exclusively for religious, charitable, scientific, literary, or educational purposes or for the prevention of cruelty to children or animals;

3. A war veterans' organization;

4. A nonprofit volunteer fire company or civil defense organization;

5. A domestic fraternal society operating under the lodge system, but only if the contribution is to be used for any of the purposes stated in item 2 above; and

6. A nonprofit cemetery company if the funds are to be used solely for the perpetual care of the cemetery as a whole, and not for a particular lot or mausoleum crypt.

---

[57] See § 170(c) and *Your Federal Income Tax,* IRS Publication 17 (Rev. 1990), p. 125.

If the taxpayer has not been informed by the recipient organization that it is a qualifying donee, he or she may check its status in the *Cumulative List of Organizations* (IRS Publication 78). This publication contains a frequently updated listing of organizations which have applied to and received tax-exempt status from the IRS. To be a qualifying donee, however, the organization is not required to be listed in this publication.

Disallowance Possibilities. Direct contributions to needy or worthy individuals are not deductible. In addition, contributions to qualifying organizations must not be restricted to use by a specific person; if so, deductions generally are disallowed.

> **Example 19.** F contributed cash of $10,000 to his son, S. S is a missionary for a church that is a qualified organization, and the gift proceeds were used exclusively by S to further the charitable work of the church. F is not entitled to a charitable contribution deduction since the gift was not made to a qualifying donee. Similarly, F would be denied a deduction if he made the gift to the church but restricted the use of the funds only for his missionary son.[58]

A taxpayer's contribution to a qualified organization that is motivated by the taxpayer's expectation and receipt of a significant economic benefit will not be deductible as a charitable contribution. The receipt of an unexpected and indirect economic benefit as a result of the gift should not disqualify the taxpayer's deduction, however.

> **Example 20.** T donated two parcels of land to a nearby city for use as building sites for new public schools. The location of the building sites was such that the city had to construct two access roads through the taxpayer's remaining undeveloped land in order to make use of the gifted property. Construction of the access roads significantly enhanced the value of T's remaining acreage, and as a result, his charitable contribution deduction may be denied.[59]

---

[58] *White v. U.S.*, 82-1 USTC ¶9232, 49 AFTR2d 82-364, 514 F. Supp. 1057 (D.Ct. Utah, 1981). For a similar result, see *Babilonia v. Comm.*, 82-2 USTC ¶9478, 50 AFTR2d 82-5442 (CA-9, 1982).

[59] See *Ottawa Silica Co. v. U.S.*, 83-1 USTC ¶9169, 51 AFTR2d 83-590, 699 F.2d 1124 (CA-Fed. Cir., 1983) where, under similar circumstances, the taxpayer's claimed contribution deduction was disallowed.

Apparently because Congress does not believe that the benefit received by a taxpayer is of great significance, 80 percent of the amount paid by a taxpayer to a college or university that either directly or indirectly entitles the taxpayer to purchase tickets to the institution's athletic events is allowed as a deduction.[60] However, any amount actually paid for the tickets will not be deductible.

LIMITATIONS ON DEDUCTIONS

Unlike the requirement that an individual's medical expenses and casualty losses *exceed* some minimum percentage of adjusted gross income (referred to as the *floor* amount) *before* any deductions are allowed, deductions for charitable contributions are subject to *ceiling* limitations (i.e., not to *exceed* a percentage of A.G.I.). Generally, an individual's current deduction for charitable contributions is limited to 50 percent of the taxpayer's adjusted gross income. A 30 percent ceiling limitation is imposed on an individual's contributions of *certain appreciated property*; and a 20 percent overall limitation is imposed on an individual's contributions to *certain qualifying organizations*.

Under the general rule, the amount of a taxpayer's charitable deduction (before any percentage limitation) is the *sum* of money *plus* the fair market value of any property other than money which is contributed to a qualifying donee. However, both the gift of property to certain organizations and the gift of certain types of property other than money may result in a deduction of an amount *less than* the property's fair market value. These exceptions to the general rule are explained below, followed by a discussion of the various percentage limitations imposed on an individual's deduction for charitable contributions.[61]

Contributions Other than Money or Property. No charitable contribution deduction is allowed for the value of time or services rendered to a charitable organization.[62] Likewise, no deduction is allowed for any "lost income" associated with the rent-free use of a taxpayer's property by a qualifying charity. However, *unreimbursed* (out-of-pocket) *expenses* incurred by the taxpayer in rendering services to a charitable institution or allowing rent-free use of property by such an organization *qualify* as charitable contributions.[63] For example, a taxpayer is allowed a deduction for the cost and upkeep of uniforms required to be worn while performing the charitable services, but only if the uniforms are not suitable for everyday use. Similarly, a taxpayer is generally allowed to deduct

---

[60] See § 170(m), introduced into the Code by the Technical and Miscellaneous Revenue Act of 1988. This provision was made retroactive to tax years beginning after 1983, and set aside a longstanding position of the IRS that denied any portion of such payments as deductions.

[61] Regular corporations are subject to an overall limitation of 10 percent of taxable income, determined without regard to certain deductions. See Chapter 19 for more details.

[62] Reg. § 1.170A-1(g).

[63] *Ibid.*

amounts paid for transportation to and from his or her home to the place where the charitable services are performed.[64] This includes the costs for gasoline, oil, parking, and tolls incurred by a taxpayer using his or her own vehicle in connection with the charitable services. In lieu of deducting the actual expenses for gasoline and oil, a taxpayer is allowed to use a standard mileage rate of 12 cents per mile in calculating the cost of using an automobile in charitable activities.[65] In either case, no deduction is allowed for insurance, depreciation, or the costs of general repairs and maintenance.

Example 21. T is the scoutmaster of a local troop of the Boy Scouts of America. During the current year, T incurred the following expenses in rendering his services to this charitable organization:

Cost and upkeep of uniforms..............	$ 80
Gasoline and oil expenses.................	200
Parking and tolls..........................	30
Estimated value of rent-free use of den in home........................	1,000
Estimated value of services (500 hours @ $50 per hour).............	25,000
Total...................................	$26,310

T is entitled to a $310 charitable contribution deduction for his out-of-pocket expenses ($80 + $200 + $30) incurred in rendering the charitable services as a scoutmaster. No deduction is allowed for the estimated value of his services or the rent-free use of his home.

Example 22. Assume the same facts as in *Example 21*, except that T drove his automobile 3,000 miles in connection with the charitable services. If he did not keep records of the actual expenses for gasoline and oil, T could use the standard mileage rate of 12 cents per mile. In this case, he will be allowed to deduct $470 [(3,000 miles $\times$ 12¢ per mile for charitable use of auto = $360) + $30 for parking and tolls + $80 related to uniforms].

Fair Market Value Determination. The IRS defines fair market value as "the price at which the property would change hands between a willing buyer and a willing seller, neither being under any compulsion to buy or sell and both having reasonable knowledge of relevant facts."[66] Determination of this amount usually means the taxpayer must make an educated guess or incur the cost of an independent appraisal. Since the IRS requires that the taxpayer attach a statement to his or her return when a deduction exceeding $500 is claimed for a charitable

---

[64] The Tax Reform Act of 1986 added § 170(k) to the Code to disallow a deduction for travel expenses related to charitable services where there is a significant element of personal pleasure, recreation, or vacation in such travel.

[65] § 170(j).

[66] Reg. § 1.170-1(c)(1).

gift of property (Form 8283, Noncash Charitable Contributions), many taxpayers seek independent appraisals to support their claimed deductions. Independent appraisals are *required*—and the donee must *attach* a summary of the appraisal to his or her return—if the claimed value of the contributed property exceeds $5,000.[67] Appraisal fees are not deductible as contributions. However, they are deductible by individuals as miscellaneous itemized deductions (subject to the 2% floor).[68]

Ordinary Income Property. The term *ordinary income property* is used to describe any property which, if sold, would require the owner to recognize gain *other than* long-term capital gain. As such, ordinary income property includes a donor/taxpayer's property held primarily for sale to customers in his or her trade or business (i.e., inventory items), a work of art created by the donor, a manuscript prepared by the donor, letters and memorandums prepared by or for the donor, and a capital asset held by the taxpayer for not more than one year (i.e., short-term capital gain property). The term also includes property which, if sold, would result in the recognition of ordinary income under any of the depreciation recapture provisions.[69]

The charitable deduction (without regard to any percentage limitations) for the gift of ordinary income property is equal to the property's fair market value *reduced* by the amount of ordinary income that would be recognized if the property had been sold at its fair market value (this amount is often called the *ordinary income potential*).[70]

> **Example 23.** F donated 100 shares of IBM stock to his church on December 15, 1991. F had purchased the stock for $9,000 on August 7, 1991, and it was worth $12,000 on the date of the gift. Since F would have recognized a short-term capital gain if the stock had been sold on December 15, 1991 (i.e., holding period not more than one year), the stock is ordinary income property. As a result, F's charitable contribution deduction is limited to $9,000 ($12,000 fair market value − $3,000 ordinary income potential).

In most cases, the charitable deduction for ordinary income property will be limited to the taxpayer's adjusted basis in the property since its fair market value is reduced by the *unrealized appreciation* in value (fair market value − adjusted basis) which would not result in long-term capital gain if the property were sold. There are, however, four important instances when this would not be the case.

---

[67] § 6050L. A donee charity that sells or otherwise disposes of such property within two years of the donation *must* report the disposition (and amount received, if any) to the IRS and the donor.

[68] Under § 212(3), individuals are allowed to deduct expenses associated with the determination of their tax liability. This includes appraisal fees paid in valuing property contributions.

[69] See § 170(e)(1), Reg. §§ 1.170A-4(b)(1) and (b)(4).

[70] § 170(e)(1). For an application of this rule, see *William Glen*, 79 T.C. 208 (1982).

First, the charitable deduction for *any property* which, if sold, would result in a *loss* (i.e., adjusted basis > fair market value) is limited to the property's fair market value. Second, any depreciable property held by the taxpayer for more than one year and used in his or her trade or business is § *1231 property*. The amount of gain from the sale of such property that exceeds any depreciation recapture is referred to as "§ 1231 gain." Potential § 1231 gains are treated as long-term capital gains for purposes of measuring a taxpayer's charitable contribution deduction.[71] As such, any unrealized appreciation in the value of property that is attributable to § 1231 gain will not be considered ordinary income potential for purposes of the above-described limitation.

The two remaining exceptions apply to the deduction allowed a corporation which contributes inventory items (ordinary income property) to certain qualifying charities. In one situation, the inventory must be donated to a public charity or private operating foundation *and* used by the charitable organization for the care of children, the ill, or the needy.[72] The other situation requires that the inventory item be manufactured by the corporate taxpayer, constitute scientific property, and be donated within two years of its construction to an educational institution for use in research.[73] In each of these situations, the corporate taxpayer is permitted to claim a contribution deduction in excess of the property's adjusted basis.

Capital Gain Property. Any property which, if sold by the donor/taxpayer, would result in the recognition of a long-term capital gain or § 1231 gain is *capital gain property*.[74] A taxpayer is generally allowed to claim the fair market value of such property as a contribution deduction. There are two important exceptions to this rule, however. *First*, if capital gain property is contributed to or for the use of a private nonoperating foundation [as defined in § 509(a)], the donor must *reduce* the contribution deduction by the *entire* amount of any long-term capital gain or § 1231 gain which would be recognized if the property were sold at its fair market value.[75] In effect, this exception treats the contribution of capital gain property to private nonoperating foundations exactly like contributions of ordinary income property, since the donor must reduce the contribution deduction to the basis of the property.

> **Example 24.** G donates stock worth $10,000 to a private nonoperating foundation on November 17, 1991. G had purchased the stock for $4,000 on August 23, 1988. G's charitable-contribution deduction must be reduced to $4,000 ($10,000 fair market value − entire $6,000 appreciation).

---

[71] Reg. § 1.170A-4(b)(4).

[72] § 170(e)(3).

[73] § 170(e)(4).

[74] § 170(e)(1).

[75] § 170(e)(1)(B)(ii).

It is important to note that this limitation *generally* does not apply to donations of capital gain property to public charities.

> **Example 25.** Assume the same facts as in *Example 24*, except that G donated the stock to her alma mater, State University (a public charity). G's charitable contribution would be $10,000 because the reduction requirement applies only to contributions to private foundations.

The *second* exception to the general rule that taxpayers are allowed to claim a deduction for the fair market value of contributed capital gain property involves contributions of tangible personalty.[76] If tangible personalty is contributed to a public charity (i.e., a university, museum, church, etc.) and the property is put to an *unrelated use* by the donee organization, the charitable contribution must be reduced by the entire amount of the property's unrealized appreciation in value (i.e., to the property's basis). For purposes of this limitation, the term *unrelated use* means that the property could not be used by the public charity in its activities for which tax-exempt status had been granted. For example, if antique furnishings are donated to a local museum that either stores, displays, or uses the items in its office in the course of carrying out its functions, the use of such property is a related use.[77] The fact that the charity later sells or exchanges the property does not alter the contribution deduction. Thus, if the taxpayer can reasonably anticipate that the tangible personalty donated to the charitable organization will be put to a related use, this limitation will not be applicable.[78]

> **Example 26.** J contributes a painting to the local university. He had purchased the painting in 1979 for $10,000, and it was appraised at $60,000 on the date of the gift. The painting was placed in the university's library for display and study by art students. J's charitable contribution will be measured at $60,000 (the painting's fair market value) since the property was not put to an unrelated use. This is true even if the university later sells the painting.

> **Example 27.** R donates her gun collection to the YWCA (a public charity). R had paid $8,000 for the collection 10 years ago, and the guns were appraised at $18,000 on the date of the gift. The YWCA immediately sold the collection for $18,000 to a local gun dealer. Although the property had appreciated by $10,000, R's charitable contribution must be reduced to $8,000 (the property's basis) since the property was not (and most likely could not be) put to a related use.

---

[76] As described in Chapter 9, tangible personalty is all tangible property *other than* realty (i.e., land, buildings, structural components).

[77] Reg. § 1.170A-4(b)(3).

[78] Reg. § 1.170A-4(b)(3)(ii).

Fifty Percent Limitation. An individual's deduction for contributions made to public charities may not exceed 50 percent of his or her adjusted gross income for the year.[79] This "ceiling" deduction limitation applies to contributions made to the following types of public charities:[80]

1. A church or a convention or association of churches;

2. An educational organization that normally maintains a regular faculty and curriculum;

3. An organization whose principal purposes or functions are the providing of medical or hospital care (hospitals) or medical education or medical research (medical schools);

4. An organization that receives support from the government and is organized and operated exclusively to receive, hold, invest, and administer property for the benefit of a college or university;

5. A state, a possession of the United States, or any political subdivision of any of the foregoing, or the United States or the District of Columbia;

6. An organization that normally receives a substantial part of its support from a government unit (described in item 5 above) or from the general public; and

7. Certain types of private foundations discussed below.

Private foundations are organizations that, by definition, do not receive contributions from the general public. Examples of well-known private foundations include the Ford, Carnegie, Cullen, and Mellon Foundations. For charitable deduction purposes, private foundations are classified as either operating or nonoperating foundations. Contributions to *all* private operating foundations are subject to the 50 percent ceiling limitation.[81] The 50 percent limit also applies to contributions to certain private, nonoperating foundations if the organizations

1. Distribute the contributions they receive to public charities and private operating foundations *within* $2^1/_2$ months following the year the contributions were received; or

2. Pool all contributions received into a common fund, and distribute *both* the income and the principal from the fund to public charities.

---

[79] § 170(b) and Reg. § 1.170A-8(b).

[80] § 170(b)(1).

[81] See § 4942(j) for the requirements for classification as a private operating foundation. For all practical purposes, an operating foundation is recognized as a public charity.

An individual's contributions of cash and ordinary income property to public charities, private operating foundations, and the above described nonoperating foundations which exceed the 50 percent limitation are carried forward and deducted in subsequent years. The carryover rules are discussed in a later section of this chapter. Contributions of capital gain property *and* contributions to private nonoperating foundations (other than those described above) are subject to *either* the 30 percent or 20 percent limitation. These limitations are discussed below.

Thirty Percent Limitation.   The annual deduction allowed for contributions of capital gain property that have not been reduced by the unrealized appreciation will generally be limited to 30 percent of the taxpayer's adjusted gross income.[82] This limitation was imposed by Congress in 1969 to reduce the amount of charitable contribution deductions allowed taxpayers for gifts of substantially appreciated capital or § 1231 assets. Contributions to private nonoperating foundations of cash and ordinary income property also are subject to the 30 percent limitation. In applying the limitation rules, contributions subject to the 30 percent limit are considered only after the amount of contributions allowed under the 50 percent limitation has been determined.[83] Contributions in excess of the 30 percent limit can be carried forward and deducted in subsequent years.

> **Example 28.**   K has adjusted gross income of $30,000 for the 1991 tax year. The only contribution made by K in 1991 consisted of stock worth $10,000, which she had purchased for $4,000 in 1986. The stock was given to her church. Although the contribution does not exceed 50% of her adjusted gross income, K's deduction is limited to $9,000 (30% × $30,000 A.G.I.) since the stock is capital gain property. The $1,000 excess contribution can be carried over to subsequent years.

> **Example 29.**   Assume the same facts as in *Example 28*, except that K's 1991 adjusted gross income is $40,000 and she also gave $14,000 cash to her church. In this case, her deduction for the gift of the stock is limited to $6,000 (50% × $40,000 A.G.I. = $20,000 − $14,000 cash contribution) since the 50% overall limitation is applied before the 30% limitation. The remaining $4,000 ($10,000 fair market value of stock − $6,000 deduction allowed) will be carried forward to subsequent years.

The 30 percent limitation can be avoided if the taxpayer *elects* to reduce his or her claimed deduction for the capital gain property by the property's unrealized appreciation.[84] This may result in a larger deduction in the current year since the reduced amount will be subject to a higher ceiling limitation (i.e., 50% of A.G.I. rather than 30%). It is important to note that this election, if made, applies to all contributions of capital gain property made during the year.

---

[82] § 170(b)(1)(C)(i). In addition, the amount of the deduction related to unrealized appreciation is generally treated as a tax preference item for purposes of the alternative minimum tax. See Chapter 13 for more details.

[83] *Ibid.*

[84] § 170(b)(1)(C)(iii).

Example 30.   T has adjusted gross income of $50,000 for the current year and contributes stock worth $23,000 to the American Heart Association (a public charity). T had purchased the stock for $19,000 two years earlier. Assuming this is T's only contribution for the current year, he can either claim his deduction subject to the 30% limitation and carry over any excess, or *elect* to reduce the claimed deduction by the capital gain property's unrealized appreciation and forego any carryover. T's deduction choices are

1. $15,000 current deduction (30% × $50,000 A.G.I.) and $8,000 ($23,000 − $15,000) contribution carryover; or

2. $19,000 current deduction ($23,000 − $4,000 unrealized appreciation) and no carryover.

Obviously, the decision to reduce a current deduction by the property's unrealized appreciation *or* to claim the deduction subject to the 30 percent limit and carry over any excess amount will depend on several factors. Among the factors to be considered are

1.   The difference between the capital gain property's fair market value and its adjusted basis to the taxpayer (i.e., unrealized appreciation);

2.   The taxpayer's current marginal income tax bracket compared to his or her anticipated future marginal tax rates; and

3.   The expected remaining life of the taxpayer and his or her anticipated future contributions.

Twenty Percent Limitation.   The 50 percent ceiling limitation imposed on an individual's annual charitable contribution deduction is an "overall" limitation. The 30 percent limitation applies to most contributions of capital gain property and to contributions of cash and ordinary income property contributed to nonqualifying private nonoperating funds. However, a more severe restriction is imposed on deductions for contributions of capital gain property to such private nonoperating foundations. In addition to the required *reduction* of the contribution by any unrealized appreciation in value, the deduction allowed for contributions to *private charities* (i.e., organizations not included in the seven categories listed earlier) is limited to the *lesser of*

1.   Twenty percent of adjusted gross income; or

2.   An amount equal to 50 percent of adjusted gross income, and reduced by contributions qualifying for the 50 percent and 30 percent limitations, including any amount in excess of the 30 percent limitation.[85]

---

[85]   § 170(b)(1)(B)(i).

Like excess contributions to public charities, any contributions to private non-operating foundations that exceed the 20 percent limitation are carried forward and deductible subject to the 20 percent limit, in subsequent years.[86]

> **Example 31.** D contributed $8,000 to his church (a public charity) and IBM stock worth $15,000 to a private nonoperating foundation in 1991. D had purchased the stock for $11,000 in 1986. His adjusted gross income for the year is $20,000. D's contribution deduction for 1991 is $10,000 [$8,000 contribution to church + $2,000 of the eligible $11,000 contribution to private foundation ($15,000 market value − $4,000 unrealized appreciation = $11,000)]. The deduction allowed for the contribution to the private foundation is limited to the *lesser* of
>
> 1. $4,000 (20% × $20,000 A.G.I.); or
>
> 2. $2,000 [(50% × $20,000 A.G.I. = $10,000) − $8,000 contribution qualifying for the 50% limitation].
>
> Note that D's total contribution deduction of $10,000 does not exceed 50% of his 1991 adjusted gross income. If D had contributed $10,000 or more to his church, *none* of the $11,000 contribution to the private foundation would have been allowed. In either case, the excess contributions can be carried over to subsequent years.

CONTRIBUTION CARRYOVERS

An individual's contributions that exceed either the 20 percent limitation, the 30 percent limitation, or the 50 percent overall limitation may be carried over for five years.[87] All excess contributions due to the 20 and 30 percent limitations will *again* be subject to these limitations in the carryover years.[88] Although contribution carryovers are treated as having been made in the year to which they are carried, contributions *actually* made in the carryover year must be claimed before any carryover amounts are deducted.[89]

> **Example 32.** In 1991 D contributes $10,000 cash to State University (a public charity). Her adjusted gross income for 1991 is $15,000. D's contribution deduction for 1991 is limited to $7,500 (50% × $15,000 A.G.I.) and she may carry over the remaining $2,500 to 1992. If she does not make contributions in 1992 that exceed the 50% limitation, D can claim the $2,500 carryover as a deduction. If the contributions actually made in 1992 exceed 50% of D's 1992 adjusted gross income, she must carry over the 1992 excess contributions *and* the $2,500 carryover from 1991.

---

[86] § 170(d)(1).

[87] § 170(d)(1)(A) and Reg. § 1.170A-10(a).

[88] Reg. § 1.170A-10(b)(2).

[89] Reg. § 1.170A-10(c)(1).

Example 33. Assume the same facts as in *Example 32*, except that D's contribution was a capital gain property worth $10,000 instead of cash. Her 1991 deduction would be limited to $4,500 (30% × $15,000 A.G.I.) and she would have a $5,500 contribution carryover. Since this carryover resulted from the 30% limitation, it will be subject to the 30% limit in any carryover year. Thus if D has adjusted gross income of $10,000 and does not make contributions in 1992, she can claim a deduction of $3,000 (30% × $10,000 A.G.I.) and carry over the remaining $2,500.

All charitable contribution carryovers are applied on a first-in, first-out basis in determining the amount of any carryovers deductible in the current year.[90] Since such carryovers will expire if not deducted within five succeeding tax years, taxpayers obviously should limit actual contributions until the carryovers are used.

MISCELLANEOUS ITEMIZED DEDUCTIONS

As discussed in Chapter 7, two major changes regarding miscellaneous itemized deductions were introduced into the tax laws in 1986. Perhaps the most significant change involves the inclusion in this category of all *unreimbursed* employee business expenses. Prior to 1987, an employee's unreimbursed travel and transportation expenses were allowed as deductions in arriving at adjusted gross income. Since 1986, only reimbursed employee business expenses are deductible *for* A.G.I.[91] Additionally, an employee's unreimbursed costs for business entertainment and meals (whether or not incurred in connection with travel) must first be reduced by a 20 percent disallowance since only 80 percent of these costs qualify for deduction.[92] It is also important to remember that interest on any indebtedness to finance an employee's business expenses is treated as *nondeductible* personal interest expense.

The second major change involves the introduction of a deduction *floor* on the total of all expenses in this category similar to the approach taken for medical and casualty loss deductions. After 1986, miscellaneous itemized deductions are deductible only to the extent they *exceed* 2 percent of A.G.I.[93] The obvious intent of this change in the law is to limit the number of taxpayers who will be able to deduct miscellaneous itemized deductions—and thereby reduce the administrative cost of policing such deductions. Exhibit 11-4 contains a partial list of items qualifying as miscellaneous itemized deductions.

---

[90]   Reg. § 1.170A-10(b)(2).

[91]   § 62(a)(2)(A).

[92]   § 274(n).

[93]   § 67(a).

Exhibit 11-4
*Partial List of Miscellaneous
Itemized Deductions*

Unreimbursed employee expenses for
    Travel away from home (lodging and 80% of meals)
    Transportation expenses
    Entertainment expenses (after 20% reduction)
    Home office expenses
    Outside salesperson's expenses
    Professional dues and memberships
    Subscriptions to business journals
    Uniform costs, cleaning, and maintenance expenses
    Union dues

Investment expenses for
    Investment advice
    Investment newsletter subscriptions
    Management fees charged by mutual funds
    Rentals of safety deposit boxes

Qualifying education expenses

Job seeking expenses (in the same business)

Tax determination expenses for
    Appraisal costs incurred to measure deductions for medical expenses (capital improvements), charitable contributions, and casualty losses
    Tax return preparation fees
    Tax advice, tax seminars, and books about taxes

Example 34. T has $40,000 of adjusted gross income in 1991. His unreimbursed employee business expenses and other miscellaneous itemized deductions include

Unreimbursed business travel expenses	$ 90
Subscription to the Wall Street Journal	110
Professional dues	250
Safety deposit box rental	50
Tax return preparation fee	250
Total	$750

Since T's total miscellaneous itemized deductions of $750 do not exceed $800 (2% × $40,000 A.G.I.), he will not be able to claim any deduction for these expenses.

OTHER ITEMIZED DEDUCTIONS

The final category of itemized deductions includes certain personal expenses and losses that cannot be classified in any of the other categories discussed thus far. Some of the items in this category—referred to as "Other Miscellaneous Itemized Deductions"—are discussed in other chapters.

1. Unrecovered investment in an annuity where the taxpayer's death prevents recovery of the entire investment. As discussed in Chapter 6, this deduction is allowed on the taxpayer's final tax return.

2. Impairment-related work expenses of persons with disabilities.

3. Moving expenses that meet the requirements for deduction that were discussed in Chapter 8.

4. Amortizable premium on bonds purchased before October 23, 1986. Amortization of bond premium is discussed in Chapter 16.

5. Gambling losses to the extent of gambling winnings.

It is important to note that each of these items may be subject to its own unique set of limitations (e.g., moving expenses). Unlike miscellaneous itemized deductions, however, these deductions *are not* subject to the 2 percent limit.

THREE PERCENT CUTBACK RULE

As discussed in Chapter 3, the total itemized deductions of certain high-income taxpayers are subject to another limitation beginning in 1991. Basically, taxpayers must reduce total itemized deductions otherwise allowable (*other than* medical expenses, casualty and theft losses, and investment interest) by 3 percent of their A.G.I. in excess of $100,000 ($50,000 for married individuals filing separately)[94] However, this reduction cannot exceed 80 percent of the deductions. Again, this ensures that taxpayers subject to the cutback rule can deduct at least 20 percent of their so-called "3 percent" deductions. Consequently, a taxpayer's itemized deductions are never completely phased out.

Exhibit 11-5 identifies the itemized deductions that are subject to the cutback rule. Again, it is important to note that a taxpayer's medical expenses, investment interest expense, and casualty and theft losses are not subject to this new limitation.

---

[94]   § 68.

Exhibit 11-5
Itemized Deductions Subject to Cutback Rule

Taxes paid, including
   State, local, and foreign income taxes
   State, local, and foreign real property taxes
   State and local personal property taxes
Mortgage interest on personal residences
Charitable contributions
Miscellaneous itemized deductions (in excess of 2% of A.G.I.)
Moving expenses
Other itemized deductions, including
   Gambling losses (to extent of gambling winnings)
   Hobby losses

Example 35. Z is single and has adjusted gross income of $250,000 for the current year. Z has the following itemized deductions: medical expenses ($1,200 after the 7.5% limitation), real estate taxes paid ($3,000), state income taxes ($7,400), home mortgage interest ($10,300), charitable contributions ($2,500), and miscellaneous itemized deductions ($800 after the 2% limitation). The amount of itemized deductions that Z may deduct for the current year is computed as follows:

Itemized deductions subject to cutback:		
Taxes paid ($3,000 + $7,400)	$10,400	
Home mortgage interest	10,300	
Charitable contributions	2,500	
Miscellaneous itemized deductions	800	
Deductions subject to 3% cutback rule		$24,000
Tentative cutback:		
Adjusted gross income	$250,000	
Threshold amount	(100,000)	
Excess A.G.I.	$150,000	
Times: 3%	× 3%	
Tentative cutback	$ 4,500	
Cutback limit:		
Itemized deductions subject to cutback	$ 24,000	
Times: 80%	× 80%	
Maximum cutback	$ 19,200	
Cutback: *Lesser* of tentative cutback		
or maximum cutback		(4,500)
Amount deductible after 3% cutback		$19,500
Plus: Itemized deductions not subject		
to cutback (medical expenses)		1,200
Total deduction for itemized deductions		$20,700

Example 36. Assume the same facts in *Example 35* above, except that Z's adjusted gross income for the current year is $800,000.

Total itemized deductions subject to cutback......................		$24,000
Tentative cutback:		
Adjusted gross income...	$800,000	
Threshold amount..	(100,000)	
Excess A.G.I..	$700,000	
Times: 3%..	$\times$ 3%	
Tentative cutback...	$ 21,000	
Cutback limit:		
Itemized deductions subject to cutback........................	$ 24,000	
Times: 80%...	$\times$ 80%	
Maximum cutback..	$ 19,200	
Cutback: *Lesser* of tentative cutback		
or maximum cutback		(19,200)
Amount deductible after 3% cutback............................		$ 4,800
Plus: Itemized deductions not subject		
to cutback (medical expenses)		1,200
Total deduction for itemized deductions........................		$ 6,000

Note that in this case Z's tentative cutback ($21,000) exceeds the maximum cutback ($19,200). Thus, Z is allowed to deduct at least 20% ($24,000 $\times$ 20% = $4,800) of the itemized deductions subject to the cutback rule.

It should be obvious from the above examples that relatively few taxpayers will suffer drastic cutbacks in their itemized deductions. However, those taxpayers with adjusted gross incomes above $100,000 will find that they face another complexity in computing their itemized deductions.

PROBLEM MATERIALS

DISCUSSION QUESTIONS

11-1 *Medical Expenses and Dependency Status.* Under what circumstances is a taxpayer entitled to deduct medical expenses attributable to other persons?

11-2 *Medical Expenses.* F and M are the divorced parents of three minor children. M, the custodial parent, has proposed to F that the current child-support payments be increased in order to pay the expected dental costs of having braces put on their oldest son's teeth. F's tax advisor has suggested that F agree to pay these costs directly to the dentist rather than increasing the support payments. From a tax perspective, why has F's advisor made this suggestion?

11-3 *Medical Expenses.* K and her two brothers currently provide more than half the support of their mother. For the past several years, they have taken turns claiming a dependency exemption deduction for their mother under a multiple support agreement. This year, K will be entitled to the exemption, and her mother needs money for cataract surgery and new eyeglasses. K's accountant has suggested that she can double-up on the tax benefits by directing her share of her mother's support toward these expenses. How is this possible?

11-4 *Medical Expenses.* For the past several years, L's total itemized deductions have barely exceeded his standard deduction amount, and this pattern is not expected to change in the near future. L is currently faced with elective surgery to repair a hernia, and the procedure is not covered under his health insurance policy. Strictly from a tax perspective, and assuming that this ailment is not life-threatening, what advice would you give to L concerning the timing of the surgery?

11-5 *Prepaid Medical Expenses.* What is the requirement imposed on taxpayers who wish to deduct prepaid medical expenses? What potential abuse is prevented by this requirement?

11-6 *Medical Deductions—Percentage Limitation.* The only medical expenditures made by taxpayer T during 1991 were for prescription drugs costing $800. If T has adjusted gross income of $10,000 for the year and itemizes his deductions, how much, if any, medical expense deduction will he be allowed?

11-7 *Medical Travel Expenses.* W resides in Gary, Indiana and suffers from chronic bronchitis. At the advice of her doctor, W spends three months each year in Flagstaff, Arizona. Under what circumstances would W be entitled to claim the costs incurred for these trips as deductible medical expenses? If deductible, which costs?

11-8   *Casualty Losses.* Taxpayer F has adjusted gross income of $20,000 during the current year and he asks you the following questions regarding the deductibility of damages to his home caused by a recent hurricane. (Hint: See Chapter 10 for discussion of limitations on casualty loss deductions.)

     a.   If F does not have home insurance, how much must his loss be before any deduction is available?

     b.   If F repairs the damage himself, what amount can he deduct for the value of his time?

     c.   If the area in which he resides is declared a disaster area, what options are available to F as to when to claim a deduction for the casualty loss?

11-9   *Taxes versus Fees.* What is the distinction between a deductible tax and a fee? If an individual taxpayer paid appraisal fees in connection with the determination of his personal casualty loss and charitable contribution deductions, would these payments be deductible?

11-10   *Deductible Income Taxes.* Which income taxes are deductible by an individual taxpayer? Does it make any difference whether the taxes are paid directly by the taxpayer as opposed to being withheld from his or her salary and paid by an employer to the appropriate taxing authority?

11-11   *Filing Status and State Income Taxes.* If married taxpayers file separate state or Federal income tax returns, how is the Federal tax deduction for state income taxes determined?

11-12   *Personal Property Taxes.* What is an ad valorem tax? What difference does it make to a taxpayer if he or she pays a tax on nonbusiness property and the tax is based on weight or model year as opposed to value?

11-13   *Real Estate Tax Apportionment.* How are real estate taxes apportioned between the buyer and seller in the year real property is sold? What effect does the apportionment have on the seller if the buyer pays the real estate taxes for the entire year?

11-14   *Special Tax Assessments.* Under what circumstances can a property owner claim a deduction for a special tax assessment?

11-15   *Personal Interest.* What is the current limitation imposed on the deductions of personal interest? What impact do you suppose this restriction might have on debt-financed consumer purchases?

11-16   *Charitable Contribution Requirements.* What are the two basic requirements imposed on an individual taxpayer's deduction for charitable contributions?

11-17   *Contributions of Ordinary Income Property.* What is ordinary income property? Does this contribution deduction limitation apply to all taxpayers? Explain.

11-18   *Contributions of Capital Gain Property.* Under what circumstances must a taxpayer reduce his or her contribution deduction by the unrealized appreciation in value of capital gain property donated to a qualifying charity? How might this limitation be avoided?

11-19 *Contribution Deduction Percentage Limitations.* What are the percentage limitations imposed on an individual taxpayer's annual charitable contribution deduction? In what order must these percentage limitations be applied to current contributions?

11-20 *Contribution Carryovers.* Which excess contributions may be carried forward by an individual taxpayer? For how many years? In determining the amount of his or her contribution deduction for the current year, how must the taxpayer treat the carryovers from prior years?

11-21 *Miscellaneous Itemized Deductions.* E's employer has offered her the option of a $50 monthly pay raise or a reimbursement plan to cover her current subscriptions to professional journals ($200) and her dues to professional organizations ($350). E files a joint return with her husband, and they expect their adjusted gross income to be $50,000 for the upcoming year. Assuming that their only miscellaneous itemized deductions are from E's subscriptions and professional dues, is this a good offer? Explain.

11-22 *Three Percent Cutback Rule.* Explain the difference between the tentative cutback and the maximum cutback amounts related to the total deduction allowed for itemized deductions. Which itemized deductions are not subject to the cutback rule?

PROBLEMS

11-23 *Medical Expense Deduction.* R, an unmarried taxpayer, has adjusted gross income of $20,000 for 1991. During the year, he paid the following amounts for medical care: $300 for prescription medicines and drugs, $600 for hospitalization insurance, and $1,100 to doctors and dentists. R filed an insurance reimbursement claim in December of 1991 and received a check for $1,200 on January 24, 1992.

   a.   Assuming R itemizes deductions, determine the deduction allowed for the medical expenses paid in 1991.
   b.   What effect does the insurance reimbursement have on R's deduction for 1991? How should the reimbursement be treated in 1992 if R's itemized deductions for 1991 (including the medical expense deduction) were $4,500 greater than his standard deduction?
   c.   How should the reimbursement be treated in 1992 if R's itemized deductions for 1991 were $700 greater than his standard deduction?

11-24 *State Income Taxes.* During 1991, K paid $500 in estimated state income taxes. An additional $400 in state income taxes was withheld from her salary by K's employer and remitted to the state. K also received a $200 refund check during 1991 for excess state income taxes paid in 1990. K uses the cash method of accounting and has adjusted gross income of $50,000 for the year.

   a.   If K itemizes her deductions, how much may she claim as a deduction for state income taxes on her 1991 Federal tax return?
   b.   If K's itemized deductions for 1990 were $1,900 greater than her standard deduction, how must the $200 refund be treated for Federal income tax purposes?

11-25 *Real Estate Tax Apportionment.* S sells her home located in Carrolton County, Kansas, on March 1, 1991. Carrolton County assesses real property taxes at the beginning of each calendar year for the entire year, and the property tax becomes a personal liability of the owner of real property on January 1. The tax is payable on April 1, 1991. Buyer B paid $80,000 for the home on March 1, 1991 and also paid the $1,200 real estate taxes on April 1. Both S and B are cash basis, calendar year taxpayers.

   a.   How much of the $1,200 in real estate taxes is deductible by S? What adjustment must S make to the amount she realized from the sale?

   b.   How much of the $1,200 in taxes is deductible by B? How will he treat any of the taxes paid which are attributable to S?

11-26 *Charitable Contributions.* Determine the amount of the charitable deduction (without regard to percentage limitations) allowed in each of the following situations:

   a.   Rent-free use of building for three months allowed for the United Way fund drive. The building normally rents for $900 per month, and the owner paid $1,100 for utilities during this period.

   b.   Gift of General Motors stock valued at $9,000 to State University. Taxpayer purchased the stock five months ago for $11,000.

   c.   Donation of stamp collection valued at $4,000 to local museum for display to the general public. Taxpayer had paid $1,000 for the stamps many years ago.

   d.   Gift of paintings by local artist to local hospital to be placed on the walls of a remodeled floor. The paintings were appraised at $20,000.

   e.   Donation of Civil War relics to American Heart Association to be sold at its current fund-raising auction. Taxpayer paid $1,000 for the relics ten years ago and an expert appraiser valued them at $7,000 on the day of the gift.

11-27 *Contribution Deductions—Percentage Limitations.* J contributed $10,000 to the University of Miami and a long-term capital asset worth $10,000 (basis of $5,000) to a private nonoperating foundation during 1991. Assuming his adjusted gross income for the year is $24,000, answer the following:

   a.   What is the amount of J's contribution deduction for 1991?

   b.   How must any excess contributions be treated?

   c.   If J had come to you for advice before making the gifts, what advice would you have offered?

11-28 *Contribution Deductions—Percentage Limitations.* During 1991, R donated land to her church (a public charity) to be used as a building site for a new chapel. R had purchased the land as an investment in 1980 at a cost of $10,000. The land was appraised at a fair market value of $30,000 on the date of the gift. Assuming R's adjusted gross income for 1991 is $60,000, answer the following:

   a.   If R made no additional charitable contributions during 1991, what is the amount of her contribution deduction for the year?

   b.   If R contributed cash of $20,000 to her church in addition to the land, what is the amount of her charitable contribution deduction for 1991?

   c.   Calculate the amount of R's excess contributions from (a) and (b) and explain how these amounts are to be treated.

11-29 *Contribution Deductions—Percentage Limitations.* T, a single taxpayer, had adjusted gross income of $20,000 for 1991. During the year, T contributed cash of $1,000 and Xerox Corporation stock worth $10,000 to his church (a public charity). T inherited the stock during 1991 when it was valued at $8,000.

a. Calculate T's total contribution deduction for 1991.

b. How must any excess contributions be treated?

c. If T does not anticipate being able to itemize his deductions in any future years, what might he do in 1991 to increase his current contribution deduction?

11-30 *Miscellaneous Itemized Deductions.* R, single, has the following miscellaneous itemized deductions for the current year.

Unreimbursed employee business expenses	$1,350
Professional dues and subscriptions	650
Job-seeking expenses	800
Tax return preparation fee	250
Safe-deposit box rental	50

Assume that R itemizes his deductions for the current year.

a. What is the amount of R's deduction for the above items if his adjusted gross income is $70,000 for the current year?

b. What is the amount of R's deduction for these items if his adjusted gross income is $100,000 for the current year?

11-31 *Three Percent Cutback Rule.* H and W are married and file a joint return for the current year. They have the following itemized deductions (before any percentage limitations) for the year.

Medical and dental expenses	$8,000
Real estate taxes on home	3,500
Deductible interest on home mortgage	9,000
State income taxes paid	5,500
Charitable contributions	4,000
Miscellaneous itemized deductions	2,500

Determine H and W's itemized deductions, assuming the following levels of adjusted gross income for the current year.

a. $100,000

b. $400,000

c. $800,000

d. What effect will an additional $10,000 of adjusted gross income have on your answer to (c) above?

11-32   *Calculating Itemized Deductions.*   Robert and Jean Snyder have an adjusted gross income of $30,000 for 1991. Their expenses for 1991 are

Prescription drugs	$ 300*
Medical insurance premiums	900
Doctor and dental bills paid	1,400*
Eyeglasses for Robert	155
Hospital and clinic bills paid	450*
Property taxes paid on home	900
State income taxes paid:	
Remaining 1990 tax liability	125
Withheld from wages during year	875
State and local sales taxes paid:	
Amount paid on new automobile	800
Amount paid on other major purchases	280
Personal property taxes paid	100
Interest on home mortgage**	4,750
Interest paid on personal auto loan	1,100
Interest paid on credit card purchases	400
Interest paid on E.F. Hutton	
margin account***	120
Cash contributions to church	2,000
Fair market value of Hightech Corp. stock	
contributed to church (purchased for	
$1,000 three years ago)	5,000
Labor union dues paid by Robert	200
Qualifying education costs paid by Jean	300
Safe deposit box rental	50
Fee paid accountant for preparation of 1990	
state and Federal tax returns	350

> *These amounts are net of insurance reimbursements received during 1991.
>
> **This mortgage was created at the time the home was purchased.
>
> ***This investment interest expense is related to the production of $1,500 of net investment income.

The Snyders drove their personal automobile 500 miles for medical and dental treatment and an additional 1,000 miles in connection with charitable services performed for their church. Assuming Robert and Jean are both under age 40 and plan to file a joint income tax return for the year, determine their total itemized deductions. If a tax form is used for the computations, complete Schedule A (Form 1040).

COMPUTERIZED TAX ANALYSIS

11-33   *Real Estate Tax Apportionment.* Use computer file T1101 for this problem.

a.   For the independent situations (1) through (5), compute the missing values.

	(1)	(2)	(3)	(4)	(5)
Real estate taxes paid by seller	$ 365	$ 0	$ 65	$ 365	$ 365
Real estate taxes paid by buyer	0	365	300	0	0
Sale price of real estate (unadjusted)	50,000	50,000	50,000	50,000	50,000
Year in which real property tax year begins	1991	1991	1991	1991	1991
Month in which real property tax year begins	Jan.	Jan.	Jan.	Jan.	Jan.
Day on which real property tax year begins	1	1	1	1	1
Year in which real property is sold	1991	1991	1991	1991	1991
Month in which real property is sold	April	April	April	May	Dec.
Day on which real property is sold	1	1	1	1	31
Real estate taxes deductible by seller					
Real estate taxes deductible by buyer					
Amount realized on sale (adjusted)					
Amount paid for real property (adjusted)					

b.   For question (a)(1), the amount realized on sale adjusted for real estate taxes is equal to the amount paid for the real estate property adjusted for real estate taxes. Explain the tax rules that cause this.

c.   For question (a)(2), the buyer, rather than the seller, pays the real estate taxes. The real estate taxes deductible by the buyer and seller remain unchanged, yet the amounts realized and paid adjusted for real estate taxes have increased. Explain why.

d.   Question (a)(3) provides another variation regarding the payment of real estate taxes. Explain the tax rules that account for the differences between the *analyses* for questions (a)(2) and (a)(3).

e.   For question (a)(4), the sale of the property occurs one month later than for the previous questions. Explain the tax rules that account for the differences between the *analyses* for questions (a)(1) and (a)(4).

f.   What do the results for question (a)(5) emphasize regarding the manner in which we count the days of ownership for the buyer and seller?

LEARNING OBJECTIVES

Upon completion of this chapter you will be able to:

- Discuss the basic rules governing the deduction of investment expenses

- Explain the limitations imposed on the deduction of losses incurred in an activity in which a taxpayer does not materially participate (i.e., passive losses)

- Identify the five different types of interest expense (personal, investment, business, qualified residence, and passive) and explain their treatment

- Discuss the restrictions imposed on deductions related to vacation homes

CHAPTER OUTLINE

Chapter **12**

DEDUCTIONS FOR CERTAIN INVESTMENT EXPENSES AND LOSSES

Since 1942 Congress has generally allowed taxpayers to deduct expenses and losses incurred in connection with investment activities. As explained in Chapter 7, Code § 212 currently authorizes the deduction of investment-oriented expenses. This provision specifically allows a deduction for expenses incurred for the production or collection of income or for the management, conservation, or maintenance of property held for the production of income. Deductible investment expenses typically include such items as fees paid to rent a safety deposit box to hold securities, cost of financial advice, and travel expenses incurred in managing property. Expenses incurred in operating rental property such as those for maintenance, depreciation, utilities, and insurance are also deductible under § 212. Similarly, deductions for interest expense incurred by taxpayers to finance their investments also are deductible under § 212, although certain restrictions apply, as discussed in this chapter. Investment expenses are normally classified as miscellaneous itemized deductions and are subject to the 2 percent limitation and the 3 percent cutback. However, expenses related to property held for the production of rents or royalties are deductible *for* A.G.I.

For many years, the general rule of § 212 adequately governed the deduction of most investment expenses. In recent times, however, Congress has enacted additional provisions to restrict investment-type deductions where it found the general rule to be insufficient. This chapter examines three areas where the Congressional axe has fallen: the deduction for losses from passive investment activities, the deduction for interest expense, and the deductions related to the rental of vacation homes.

PASSIVE ACTIVITY LIMITATIONS

For many years, taxpayers were generally free to use deductions from one activity to offset the income of another. Similarly, most credits could be used to offset tax attributable to income from any of the taxpayer's activities.

Example 1.   R earns $50,000 annually working as vice president of marketing at Plentiful Products, Inc. Over the years, he has accumulated a modest portfolio of stocks which generates dividends of about $10,000 a year. In addition, he is a 10% limited partner in a partnership which owns an apartment complex consisting of 200 units. During the year, the apartment complex had operating expenses which exceeded rental income, creating a $100,000 loss. Prior to 1987, R could use his share of the loss, $10,000, to offset his other income, both salary and dividends. Assuming R's marginal tax rate was 30%, the loss produced tax savings of $3,000.

The above example illustrates the essentials of what is now a well-publicized phenomenon: under prior law, an individual could reduce his or her tax liability—even eliminate it—by investing in "tax shelters" that produced losses which could be offset against other income. The attraction of such losses for taxpayers wishing to avoid taxes was so great that the tax shelter business grew into a thriving industry.

A typical tax shelter is organized as a limited partnership. From a tax perspective, use of this form allows the losses of the activity to flow through to the individual partners to be used to reduce the investor's other taxable income. Assuming the activity carried on by the partnership is economically sound, the losses which result are artificial. They are normally attributable to a mismatching of expenses and revenues which occur in the early years of a shelter. For example, in the initial years of a traditional real estate tax shelter, expenses for interest, taxes, and accelerated depreciation normally exceed the rental income, which is often low because of the time it takes for the project to become fully occupied. Moreover, interest and accelerated depreciation are greater initially simply because of the manner in which the computations are made. As a result, in the first several years, the project "throws off" losses—many of which do not require a cash outlay due to depreciation and accrued expenses. In later years, however, these events reverse, and taxable income is produced.

Over the years, the number of stories about how taxpayers, particularly high-income taxpayers, have used tax shelters to avoid paying taxes has been legion. The February, 1986 cover of *Money* magazine was illustrative. The cover pictured three highly successful individuals, and indicated that each had made over a million dollars but paid no taxes. In light of this and other similar reports, it is not surprising that taxpayer confidence in the fairness of the tax system had badly eroded. Many taxpayers had come to believe that tax was paid only by the naive and the unsophisticated. This belief, in turn, was leading to noncompliance and providing incentives for expansion of the tax shelter market, often diverting investment capital from productive activities to those principally or exclusively servicing tax avoidance goals.

In order to prevent what it considered the harmful and excessive use of tax shelters, Congress took action—albeit indirect—in 1986. Perhaps fearing that they would alienate certain constituencies, Congress opted not to eliminate or limit the provisions on which shelters are built (e.g., special benefits for low-income housing and rehabilitation of old and historic buildings). Instead, Congress enacted Code § 469 which places far-reaching restrictions on how deductions and losses of a passive activity can be used to offset the income of another activity. Although these restrictions were aimed principally at losses from a limited partnership interest, they also limit losses from rental activities, as well as losses from any trade or business in which the taxpayer does not materially participate.

GENERAL RULE

The thrust of § 469 is to divide a taxpayer's income into three types: (1) wages, salaries, and other active income; (2) portfolio income (e.g., interest, dividends, capital gains and losses); and (3) passive income—the sort deemed to be produced by most tax shelters and rental activities. Expenses related to passive activities can be deducted only to the extent of income from *all* such passive activities. Any excess expenses of these passive activities—the passive activity loss—may not be deducted against portfolio income or wages, salaries, or other active income. Losses which cannot be used are held in suspension and carried forward to be used to offset passive income of future years.[1] Suspended losses from a passive activity can be used in full to offset portfolio or active income *only* when the taxpayer disposes of his or her entire interest in the activity. Upon disposition, any current and suspended losses (including any loss realized on the disposition) are used to offset income in the following order:[2]

1. Any gain on the disposition of the interest

2. Any *net* income from all passive activities (after taking into account any suspended losses)

3. Any other income or gain (i.e., active and portfolio income)

Observe that this special ordering rule requires the taxpayer to use up the suspended losses against gain on the disposition and any passive income before offsetting such losses against active or portfolio income. Without this rule, a taxpayer would use all of the suspended loss against active income, thus freeing up the passive gain on the disposition to absorb other passive losses.

> **Example 2.** T owned and operated her own construction company as a sole proprietorship. For the year, the company had net income of $120,000. T has a substantial portfolio that produced dividends of $15,000 and a short-term capital loss from the sale of stock of $7,000. In addition, her investment in Pleasant Properties, a limited partnership, produced a passive loss. T's share of the loss was $30,000. Her investment in Restful Recordings, another limited partnership, generated passive activity income. T's share of

---

[1] Suspended losses are carried forward to the following year, where they are treated as if they were incurred in such year. Temp. Reg. § 1.469-1T(f)(4)(B).

[2] § 469(g). To date, Regulations have not been issued on dispositions, leaving many unanswered questions. See Erickson, "Passive Activity Disposition," *The Tax Adviser* (May 1989), p. 338.

the income was $5,000. Under the capital gain and loss provisions, T may deduct $3,000 of the capital loss and carry over the remaining $4,000. The $30,000 passive loss is deductible only to the extent of passive income, which is $5,000. In effect, income and loss from the passive activities are netted, and the net loss attributable to Pleasant Properties, $25,000, is carried over to the following year.

Example 3.   Same facts as above. T held on to her investment in Pleasant Properties until this year, when she sold her entire interest, producing a gain of $40,000. Total suspended losses attributable to her investment were $70,000. Net income from Restful Recordings was $20,000 for the year. T may deduct the entire $70,000 loss: $40,000 against the gain, $20,000 against the net income from Restful Recordings, and $10,000 against any other income. Note that had there been a suspended loss from Restful Recordings, none of it would be deductible. Due to the ordering rules, the suspended loss must be used against current passive income before any active income.

As a practical matter, many taxpayers will have investments in several passive activities, some that produce income and some that produce losses. If the taxpayer has losses from more than one activity, the suspended loss for *each* activity must be determined in the event that the taxpayer subsequently disposes of one of the activities. The suspended loss of each activity is determined by allocating the total loss disallowed for the year, including any suspended losses, pro rata among the loss activities using the following formula.[3]

$$\text{Total disallowed loss for year} \times \frac{\text{Loss for this activity}}{\text{Total losses from all activities with losses}} = \frac{\text{Suspended loss}}{\text{for this acitvity}}$$

Note that this fraction simply represents the percentage of the total loss attributable to a particular activity. In effect, each loss activity absorbs this fraction of any passive income from other activities.

Example 4.   T owns an interest in three passive activities: A, B, and C. For 1991, activity B reports income of $2,000 while activities A and C report losses of $6,000 and $4,000, respectively. T is allowed to deduct the passive losses from A and C to the extent of the passive income from B. Thus he may deduct $2,000 of the losses. The remaining loss of $8,000 cannot be used to offset T's income from other sources (e.g., wages, dividends, or interest income) but must be suspended and carried forward to the following year. The suspended loss of $8,000 must be allocated between the loss activities pro rata. Since 60% ($6,000/$10,000) of the net loss was attributable to A, the suspended loss for A is $4,800 (60% ×

---

[3]   Temp. Reg. § 1.469-1T(f)(2).

$8,000). Similarly, the suspended loss for C is $3,200 [($4,000/$10,000) × $8,000]. Alternatively, the loss activities could be viewed as absorbing the passive income. Using this approach, the suspended losses would be computed somewhat differently but with the same result.

	A	C	Total
Loss for the year......................	$(6,000)	$(4,000)	$(10,000)
Loss absorbed:			
$2,000 × ($6,000/$10,000).........	1,200	–	1,200
$2,000 × ($4,000/$10,000).........	–	800	800
Suspended loss.......................	$(4,800)	$(3,200)	$(8,000)

These losses are carried over and treated as if they were a deduction in the following year.

Example 5. Assume the same facts as in *Example 4*. The income and loss for 1992 of the three activities is shown below.

Activity	Current Net Income (Loss)	Carryforward from Prior Years	Total
A	$(5,200)	$(4,800)	$(10,000)
B	12,000	–	12,000
C	(1,800)	(3,200)	(5,000)
Total	$ 5,000	$(8,000)	$ (3,000)

The total passive loss disallowed in 1992 is $3,000. The $3,000 disallowed loss is allocated among the activities with total losses (taking into account both current operations and losses suspended from prior years) as follows:

Activity	Total Disallowed Loss	×	Percentage of Total Loss	=	Allocable Portion of Loss
A	$3,000	×	$10,000/($10,000 + $5,000)	=	$2,000
C	3,000	×	5,000/($10,000 + $5,000)	=	1,000

In making the allocation, the disallowed loss is allocated based on an activity's net loss including suspended losses (e.g., $10,000 for A) rather than the loss that actually occurred in the current year (e.g., $5,200 for A).

Example 6. J has three passive activities: R, S, and T. The suspended losses and current income and losses for each activity for 1991 are shown below. In addition, J sold activity S for a $10,000 gain in 1991. Because there has been a complete disposition of S, J is able to deduct all of the suspended losses as shown below.

	R	S	T
Suspended loss............................	$ (9,000)	$(12,000)	$(15,000)
Current income (loss).......................	(5,000)	(6,000)	(7,000)
Total.......................................	$(14,000)	$(18,000)	$(22,000)
Gain on disposition of S.....................		10,000	
Excess loss deducted against other income...		$ (8,000)	

J must first offset the suspended and current losses of $18,000 from Activity S against the $10,000 gain on the sale. The next step is to offset the $8,000 balance of losses against any net passive income for the year. In this case, the activities have no income, and thus none of the loss is absorbed by passive income. At this point, the remaining loss of $8,000 is no longer considered passive and can be used to offset any active or portfolio income that J may have.

Example 7. K has three passive activities: X, Y, and Z. The suspended losses and current income and losses for each activity for 1991 are shown below. In addition, in 1991 K sold activity Y for a $21,000 gain. K is able to deduct all of the suspended losses of Y as shown below.

	X	Y	Z
Suspended loss............................	$ (7,000)	$(10,000)	$(18,000)
Current income (loss).......................	(8,000)	(6,000)	8,000
Total.......................................	$(15,000)	$(16,000)	$(10,000)
Gain on disposition of Y.....................	—	21,000	—
	$(15,000)	$5,000	$(10,000)
Loss absorbed:			
$5,000 × ($15,000/$25,000)...............	3,000		
$5,000 × ($10,000/$25,000)...............			2,000
Suspended loss............................	$(12,000)		$(8,000)

K must first offset the current and suspended losses of $16,000 against the $21,000 gain on the sale. Note that the balance of the gain is considered passive income that can be combined with the net losses (the sum of current income or loss and suspended losses) from the other passive activities for the year.[4]

---

[4]   § 469(g)(1)(A) and Temp. Reg. § 1.469-2T(c)(2)(i)(A)(2).

Rules similar to those for passive losses apply to tax credits produced by passive activities (e.g., the low-income housing credit, rehabilitation credit, research credit, and jobs credit). Passive credits can be used *only* to offset any tax attributable to passive income. Any unused credit may be carried forward to the next taxable year to offset future taxes. In contrast to passive losses, however, credits being carried over may be *lost* when a passive activity is sold. This occurs if there is no tax attributable to passive income (including any gain on the sale of the activity) in the year of disposition.

> **Example 8.**   T invested in a limited partnership that rehabilitated a historic structure. In 1993, T sold his interest, realizing a gain of $5,000. At that time, T had suspended losses of $20,000 and credits of $10,000. T is able to use $5,000 of the losses to offset the gain and the other $15,000 to offset other active or portfolio income. None of the credit can be used, however, because there is no income from the passive activity. Had T sold the property for a gain of $50,000, he would have had $30,000 of passive income. Assuming T is in the 28% tax bracket, he could have used $8,400 ($30,000 × 28%) of the credit. The remaining credit of $1,600 is lost.

TAXPAYERS SUBJECT TO LIMITATIONS

The new provision applies to individuals, estates, trusts, personal service corporations, and certain closely held C corporations.[5] Partnerships and S corporations are not subject to the limitations per se. However, their activities flow through to the owners who are subject to limitation.

The passive loss rules generally do not apply to regular C corporations. Presumably, their immunity is based on the theory that individuals generally do not benefit from losses locked inside the corporate form. Congress, however, did not want taxpayers to be able to circumvent the passive loss rule merely by incorporating. Absent a special rule, a taxpayer could utilize corporate immunity to shelter income derived from personal services. Taxpayers would simply incorporate as a personal service corporation and acquire tax shelter investments at the corporate level. The losses produced by the tax shelters would offset not only the service income but also income from any investments made at the corporate level. Consequently, the passive loss rules apply to *personal service corporations*. For this purpose, a personal service corporation is one where the principal activity is the performance of personal services and such services are substantially performed by employee-owners. In addition, the employee-owners must, *in the aggregate,* own more than 10 percent of the stock of the corporation either directly or indirectly (e.g., through family members). Common examples of personal service corporations are professional corporations such as those of doctors, accountants, attorneys, engineers, actors, architects, and others where personal services are performed.

---

[5]   § 469(a)(2).

Without additional restrictions, any taxpayer—not just one who derives income from services—could incorporate his or her portfolio and offset the investment income with losses from tax shelters. To prohibit this possibility, the passive loss rules also apply in a limited fashion to all closely held C corporations (i.e., a regular C corporation where five or fewer individuals own more than 50 percent of the stock either directly or indirectly). Note that some personal service corporations which might escape the tests above may still be subject to the rules due to their status as closely held corporations. A closely held corporation may not use passive losses to offset its portfolio income. However, such corporations may offset losses from passive activities against the income of any active business carried on by the corporation.[6]

> **Example 9.** R and his two brothers own Real Rustproofing Corporation. This year the corporation suffered a loss from operations of $10,000. In addition, it received interest income from short-term investments of working capital of $20,000. The corporation also had a passive loss from a real estate venture of $30,000. In determining taxable income, the passive activity limitation rules apply since the corporation is closely held (i.e., five or fewer individuals own more than 50 percent). As a result, none of the loss can be deducted since the loss cannot offset portfolio income of the corporation and the corporation did not have any income from operations. Had the corporation had $50,000 of operating profit, the entire loss could be deducted since passive losses can be used by a closely held corporation to offset active income—but not portfolio income.

PASSIVE ACTIVITIES

Assuming the taxpayer is subject to the passive activity rules, the most important determination is whether the activity in which the taxpayer is engaged is passive. The characterization of an activity as passive generally depends on the level of the taxpayer's involvement in the activity, the nature of the activity, or the form of ownership. Section 469(c) provides that the following activities are passive:

1. Any activity (other than a working interest in certain oil and gas property) which involves the conduct of a trade or business in which the taxpayer *does not materially participate*; and

2. *Any* rental activity regardless of the level of the taxpayer's participation.

---

[6] § 469(e)(2).

Given these definitions, several questions must be addressed to determine whether a particular endeavor of the taxpayer is a passive activity.

1. What is an activity?
2. Is the activity a rental or nonrental activity?
3. What is material participation?

Unfortunately, none of these questions are easily answered. An exceedingly complex set of Regulations exists that, in large measure, creates intricate definitions designed to prohibit wily taxpayers from deducting their passive losses. The basic rules are considered below.

DEFINITION OF AN ACTIVITY

The definition of an activity serves as the foundation for the entire structure of the passive loss rules. Virtually all of the important determinations required in applying the passive loss rules are made at the activity level. Perhaps the most significant of these concerns the taxpayer's level of participation. As discussed later in this chapter, if the taxpayer participates for more than 500 hours per year in a nonrental activity, he or she is deemed to materially participate in the activity, and the activity is therefore not passive. As the following example illustrates, this test requires an unambiguous definition of an activity.

> **Example 10.** Mr. R. Rock owns and operates 10 restaurants in 10 different cities. In addition, in each of those 10 cities he owns and operates 10 movie theaters. R spends 80 hours working in each restaurant during the year for a total of 800 hours. R spends 70 hours working in each movie theater for a total of 700 hours. If *each* restaurant and each movie theater are treated as separate activities, it would appear that R would not be treated as a material participant in any one of the businesses because he devoted only a minimum amount of his time during the year, 80 or 70 hours, to each. On the other hand, if all the restaurants are aggregated and deemed a *single activity,* R's total participation in all the restaurants, 800 hours, would in fact be considered material. A similar conclusion could be reached for the movie theaters. In addition, if the restaurants are adjacent to the movie theaters (or in fact are concession stands in the theaters), it might be appropriate to treat the restaurant operation and the movie theater operation as a single activity.

The definition of an activity is not only important for the material participation test, but it is also significant should there be a disposition. As noted above, a complete disposition of an activity enables a taxpayer to deduct any suspended losses of the activity.

Example 11.   Same facts as in *Example 10* above. Also assume that there are suspended losses for each restaurant. If each restaurant is treated as a separate activity, a sale of one of the restaurants would enable R to deduct the suspended loss for that restaurant. In contrast, if the restaurant is not considered a separate activity, none of the loss would be triggered.

Examples 10 and 11 demonstrate not only the importance of the definition of an activity but also the problems inherent in defining what constitutes an activity.

The authors of § 469 obviously anticipated the difficulty in defining an activity and therefore provided no working definition in the Code. As a result, the formidable task of defining an activity fell in the laps of those who write the Regulations. Defining an activity would not be difficult if all taxpayers were engaged in a single line of business at one location. As a practical matter, this is not always the case. Some taxpayers, such as Mr. Rock in *Example 10,* are involved in several lines of business at multiple locations. Consequently, any definition of an activity had to consider such situations. In fixing the scope of an activity, the Treasury feared that a narrow definition would allow taxpayers to generate at will passive income that could be used to offset passive losses. For example, if Mr. Rock were able to treat each restaurant as a separate activity, he could easily manipulate his participation at each restaurant to obtain passive or active income as he deemed most beneficial. To combat this problem, the IRS designed a broad definition that generally requires a taxpayer to aggregate various endeavors into a single activity. By establishing a broad definition that treats several undertakings as a single activity, the material participation test is more easily met, resulting in active rather than passive income. Unfortunately, the actual definition is quite complicated, as evidenced by the Regulations, which contain 196 pages of intricate rules and examples devoted to the subject.

Perhaps the easiest way to explain the definition of an activity is by analogy. Like a chemical compound that consists of various elements, activities consist of various components. An activity is made up of one or more *undertakings*. In other words, one undertaking might constitute a single activity, or several undertakings might be aggregated to make a single activity. An undertaking is the smallest unit that can constitute an activity.[7] Undertakings themselves consist of operations.[8] There are two types of income-producing operations: rental operations and business operations (i.e., nonrental operations). Using this building-block approach, a single activity may consist of one or more undertakings that are in turn made up of one or more operations. This relationship of operations, undertakings, and activities is illustrated in Exhibit 12-1. The practical problem in identifying an activity is determining (1) whether two or more operations

---

[7]   Temp. Reg. § 1.469-4T(a)(2).

[8]   Only income-producing operations can be undertakings. Special rules address the treat- ment of so-called support operations that do not independently produce income but merely support other income-producing operations. See Temp. Reg. § 1.469-4T(c)(2).

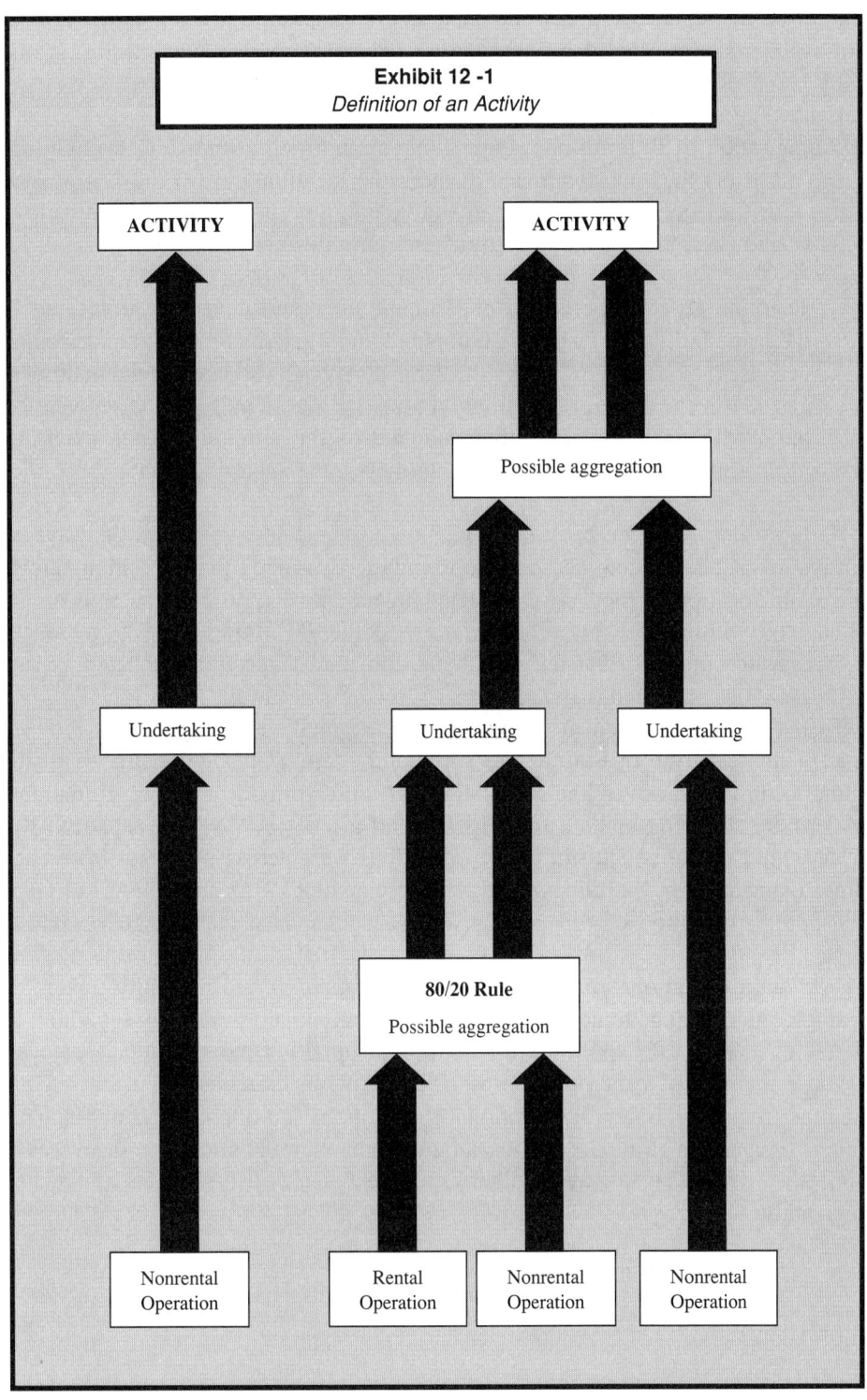

Exhibit 12 -1
Definition of an Activity

ACTIVITY

ACTIVITY

Possible aggregation

Undertaking

Undertaking

Undertaking

80/20 Rule

Possible aggregation

Nonrental
Operation

Rental
Operation

Nonrental
Operation

Nonrental
Operation

should be aggregated and considered a single undertaking; (2) whether two or more undertakings should be aggregated and considered a single activity; and (3) whether two or more activities should be aggregated and treated as a single activity. The aggregation rules are considered below.

Aggregation of Operations. Operations are normally treated as a single undertaking if (1) they are conducted at the same location and (2) they are owned directly by the same taxpayer (e.g., an individual, S corporation, or partnership).[9] This is true even though the operations are quite different in nature.

> **Example 12.** L operates a department store and a restaurant located in the same building. These are combined and treated as a single undertaking because they are (1) owned by the same person, (2) both nonrental activities, and (3) in the same location. In contrast, if the department store were on the north side of town and the restaurant on the south side, each would be a separate undertaking since they are not in the same location.

Determining whether operations are in the same location is not always as simple as in the example above. The Regulations provide that operations are in the same location if they are conducted in the same physical structure or are conducted within close proximity of one another.[10] Based on this guidance, it is easy to conclude that a department store and a restaurant located in two different cities or in two different parts of town are not in the same location. But what if they were located in the same shopping mall? The Regulations indicate that in this case the operations are sufficiently "close" to be considered in the same location. However, the Regulations go on to provide that two restaurants in separate shopping malls a few blocks apart are not in the same location. But what would be the conclusion if the operations were across the street from each other or in different buildings on the same city block? As these few examples illustrate, application of this rule in any particular case may be guesswork at best.

Although operations conducted in the *same location* are normally treated as a single undertaking, rental and nonrental operations are treated as separate undertakings. This rule applies even if they are in the same location. However, if more than 80 percent of the gross income of an undertaking is attributable to either rental or nonrental operations, the predominant operation controls. This rule is intended to eliminate accounting problems with the allocation of overhead and other items that taxpayers otherwise face when two operations are treated separately.

---

[9]   Temp. Reg. § 1.469-4T(c)(2)(ii).   [10]   Temp. Reg. § 1.469-4T(c)(2)(iii)(A) and (B).

Example 13. PB&K, an accounting firm, operates its practice out of an office building that it owns. The firm occupies two floors of the building and leases the other three floors to third parties. This year, 90% of the firm's income is from its accounting practice and 10% is from rental of the office space. Because the income of the nonrental operation predominates (i.e., it is more than 80% of the total), the rental and nonrental operations are aggregated into a *single nonrental* undertaking. Note that any net loss on the rental activity is effectively combined with the income of the accounting operation.

Example 14. Same facts as above except that 70% of the firm's gross income comes from its practice and 30% from rent. In this case, there would be no aggregation, and there would be two separate undertakings.

Rental and nonrental operations normally must be separated because they are subject to different rules. For example, rental activities are always passive, whereas nonrental activities are passive only if the taxpayer does not materially participate in such activities. In addition, owners of rental real estate are normally entitled to deduct up to $25,000 of rental losses annually without limitation, whereas there is no comparable rule for nonrental activities.

Aggregation of Undertakings. Once operations have been identified and properly converted to undertakings, the taxpayer must consider another round of possible aggregation. Undertakings are generally treated as separate activities; however, aggregation may be permitted or required. Aggregation is mandatory in applying the material participation tests. On the other hand, the taxpayer may elect to treat the undertakings as separate activities for all other purposes (e.g., for purposes of applying the disposition rules).

The thrust of the aggregation rules is to require the combination of undertakings into a single activity if, in the words of the legislative history, they constitute an "integrated and interrelated economic unit." The Regulations provide two methods to ascertain whether two or more undertakings must be aggregated and treated as a single activity. The first method uses an objective mechanical test, and the second method is a subjective test based on certain facts and circumstances.

Aggregation of Similar Undertakings. Under the first test, undertakings generally must be aggregated if they are similar.[11] Undertakings are similar if their *predominant operations* are in the *same line of business*. In applying the same-line-of-business test, the first step is to determine the predominant operations of the undertaking. Recall that an undertaking may consist of several different operations that have been aggregated because they are in the same location and owned by the same person. For example, one undertaking might consist of a department store and a grocery store. According to the Regulations, the

---

[11] Temp. Reg. § 1.469-4T(f). Certain tests concerning ownership and control must also be met before aggregation is required.

predominant operation is that which produces more than 50 percent of the business' gross income. If there is no predominant operation, the undertaking usually cannot be aggregated and is treated as a separate activity. If an undertaking has a predominant operation, its predominant operation is compared to that of other undertakings. To determine whether the predominant operations of two or more undertakings are in the same line of business, reference is made to Rev. Proc. 89-38, which identifies 79 lines of business. These lines of business are based on the Standard Industrial Classification (SIC) codes contained in the Office of Management and Budget's *Standard Industrial Classification Manual*. In short, if two businesses have the same SIC code, they are similar. The categories are quite broad. For example, the real estate category contains virtually every type of business related to real estate, including construction companies (those that build skyscrapers as well as those that construct single-family residences), title companies, real estate management companies, and businesses that operate cemeteries, to name a few. Some of the other categories are communications industry (e.g., television, motion pictures, radio), food stores (e.g., retail bakeries, donut shops, and candy stores, but not restaurants), agriculture, and automobile (repair, service, and parking, but not sales).

Example 15. Several years ago, B opened a restaurant, a movie theater, and a gift shop in a small shopping mall. After much success, she opened the same three stores in three other malls around the Dallas–Ft. Worth area. B has four undertakings because the operations at each mall are aggregated since they are at the same location and have the same owner. The percentage of each undertaking's gross income attributable to each of its operations is shown below:

	Operations and SIC Code			
Undertaking	Gift shop (#49)	Restaurant (#45)	Theater (#75)	Total
1	80%	15%	5%	100%
2	65%	20%	15%	100%
3	10%	70%	20%	100%
4	40%	50%	10%	100%

In this case, the predominant operation of undertakings 1 and 2 is the gift shop, whereas the predominant operation of undertaking 3 is the restaurant. Undertaking 4 has no predominant operation. Undertakings 1 and 2 have predominant operations with the same SIC code and are therefore deemed to be similar. Because 1 and 2 are similar and are commonly controlled, they are aggregated and treated as a single activity. Because undertaking 3 is not similar to 1 and 2, it is treated as a single activity. Because undertaking 4 has no predominant operation, it cannot be aggregated with any of the other undertakings; consequently, it is treated as a separate activity.

Undertakings are also considered similar if one undertaking (the supplier undertaking) provides more than 50 percent of its property or services to another undertaking (the recipient undertaking) and both are controlled by the same interests. For example, consider a taxpayer that owns a business that produces milk and other dairy products, all of which are sold to a chain of convenient stores owned by the same taxpayer. Even though the two undertakings would not be considered in the same line of business, they would be treated as similar and be aggregated because more than 50 percent of the supplier's product was sold to another business owned by the same taxpayer.

Aggregation under the Integration Rule. The authors of the Regulations were concerned that aggregation required under the mechanical line-of-business test might lead to the separation of undertakings that in reality operated as a single unit. For this reason, the Regulations contain a second aggregation rule that looks to the facts and circumstances surrounding the situation to determine whether undertakings as well as activities should be aggregated. Under this subjective test, undertakings and activities must be combined into one activity if they constitute a *single integrated business* and they are controlled by the same interest.[12] The Regulations identify various factors to be used in making this determination, including the following:

1. *Location:* Whether the operations are conducted at the same location

2. *Accounting records:* Whether the operations are treated as a unit in the primary accounting records reflecting the results of the operations and the extent to which other persons treat similar operations as a unit in the primary accounting records

3. *Ownership:* Whether such operations are owned by the same person

4. *Product or services:* The extent to which the operations involve products or services that are commonly provided together

5. *Same customers:* The extent to which the operations serve the same customers

6. *Personnel, facilities, or equipment:* The extent to which the same personnel, facilities, or equipment are used to conduct such operations

7. *Interdependence:* Whether the operations are conducted in coordination with or reliance upon each other; whether the economic success of one operation depends on the other; whether one operation is merely incidental to the other

8. *Trade name:* Whether the operations are conducted under the same trade name

The following example, based on the Regulations, illustrates the operation of this super-aggregation rule.[13]

---

[12] Temp. Reg. § 1.469-4T(g)(2).   [13] Temp. Reg. § 1.469-4T(g)(4)(Ex. 1).

Example 16.   Smith owns a number of department stores and auto-supply stores. Some of the department stores include auto-supply departments, in which case the department stores are the predominant operation. In other cases, department store and auto-supply operations are at different locations. Under the line-of-business test, the department stores are treated as a separate activity, as are the auto-supply stores. The department stores all operate under the trade name of Smith's, and the auto supply stores use the name Smith's Auto Supplies. Smith's sends out a monthly catalogue, which contains ads for Smith's Auto Supplies. Smith's Auto Supplies honors the Smith's credit card issued by the department stores. They jointly conduct sales and other promotional activities. Sales personnel generally work in one particular store, but other employees (e.g., cashiers, janitorial and maintenance workers, and clerical staff) may work for either operation. The management of store operations is organized on a geographical basis, and managers above the level of the individual store supervise operations in both types of store. A central office provides payroll, financial, and other support services to all stores. Most inventory is acquired through a central purchasing department, and inventory for all stores in an area is stored in a common warehouse. Based on these circumstances, the department store activity and auto supply activity constitute a single integrated business, and they are consequently aggregated and treated as one activity.

Other Aggregation Rules.   Before leaving the aggregation rules, it should be mentioned that special aggregation rules exist for several particular situations. For example, unique provisions apply to undertakings that are considered *professional service undertakings* (i.e., more than 50 percent of the undertaking's gross income is derived from services performed in the fields of health, law, engineering, architecture, accounting, actuarial science, performing arts, or consulting).[14] If an undertaking is characterized as a professional service undertaking, it can be aggregated with other professional service undertakings if they are controlled by the same interests or provide similar services. However, professional service undertakings or activities cannot be combined with other nonrental or rental undertakings or activities. Other aggregation rules apply to oil and gas operations and certain other situations.

---

[14]   Temp. Reg. § 1.469-4T(h).

RENTAL VERSUS NONRENTAL ACTIVITIES

Under the general rule described above, all rental activities are deemed to be passive, regardless of whether the taxpayer materially participates. Congress adopted this view based on the belief that there is seldom any significant participation in rental activities. Therefore, it created a presumption that all rental activities would be passive. For this purpose, a rental activity is defined as any activity whereby a taxpayer receives payments that are principally for the use of property owned by the taxpayer (e.g., apartments or equipment).

Observe that this blanket rule effectively classifies many rental activities as passive even though an owner might render significant services in connection with the rental. For example, renting video tapes would be considered passive under the general rule even though the owner might perform substantial services. This approach would be unfair to those who participate yet suffer losses. Moreover, the rule creates a huge planning opportunity for those seeking passive income given that many rental businesses are profitable. Recognizing these problems, the authors of the Regulations identified six situations where what is normally a rental is to be treated as a nonrental activity.[15]

1. *1–7 Days Rental*. The activity is not a rental if the average rental period is seven days or less. Under this exception, short-term rentals of such items as cars, hotel and motel rooms, or video cassettes are not considered rental activities.

2. *8–30 Days Rental*. The activity is not a rental if the average rental period is 30 days or less and *significant services* are performed by the owner of the property. In determining whether significant services are provided, consideration is given to the type of service performed and the value of the services relative to the amount charged for the use of the property. In this regard, the Regulations indicate that telephone service and cable television are to be ignored as are those services commonly provided in connection with long-term rentals of commercial and residential property (e.g., janitorial services, repairs, trash collection, cleaning of common areas, and security services). Unfortunately, the Regulations provide few other clues as to what constitutes significant services.

---

[15] Temp. Reg. § 1.469-1T(e)(3)(ii).

Example 17.   T owns and rents a resort condominium in Florida. He provides telephone, cable, trash removal, cleaning of the common areas, and daily maid and linen service. The cost of the maid and linen services is less than 10% of the amount charged to tenants occupying the apartments. In determining whether significant services are provided, the telephone, cable, trash, and cleaning services are disregarded. Moreover, according to the Regulations, the maid and linen services would not be considered significant in this case. Because there are no significant services under the Regulations' view, the activity would be considered a rental (*assuming* the average rental use exceeds seven days).

3. *Extraordinary Services.* The activity is not a rental if extraordinary personal services are provided by the owner of the property. Services are considered extraordinary if the use of the property is merely incidental to the services performed.

    Example 18.   Nathan Hale Military Academy, a private college preparatory school, provides housing for its students. The school's rental of such facilities would be considered incidental to the educational services provided and therefore be treated as a nonrental activity.

4. *Incidental Rentals.* The activity is not a rental activity if the rental of the property is merely incidental to the nonrental activity.

    Example 19.   S owns unimproved land that she is holding for future appreciation. To defray the costs of the land, she leases the land to a rancher for grazing his cattle. According to the Regulations, if the rent is less than 2% of the basis of the property (or value if less), the activity is not treated as a rental.

5. *Nonexclusive Use.* The activity is not a rental activity if the taxpayer customarily makes the property available during defined business hours for the nonexclusive use of various customers. For example, this exception would apply to a golf course that sells annual memberships but which is also open to the public on a daily basis.

6. *Property Made Available for Use in a Nonrental Activity.* The activity is not a rental activity if the taxpayer owns an interest in a partnership, S corporation, or joint venture to which the property is rented. For example, if T rents equipment to a partnership in which he is a partner, the rental is treated as a nonrental activity.

As noted above, any operation constituting a "rental" is a passive activity. Note, however, that those activities not classified as rentals (i.e., nonrental activities) may still be considered passive. Whether a *nonrental* activity is a passive activity depends on whether the taxpayer has materially participated in the activity.

MATERIAL PARTICIPATION

Material participation serves a crucial role in the application of the passive loss rules. It is the criterion that distinguishes between "passive" and "active" non-rental activities. The Code provides that an individual meets the material participation test only if he or she is involved in the operation of the activity on a regular, continuous, and substantial basis. Without further guidance, applying this nebulous criterion would essentially be left to the subjective interpretation of the taxpayer. However, the Regulations establish objective standards that look to the actual number of hours spent in the activity.

Under the regulatory scheme, a taxpayer materially participates in an activity if he or she meets one of seven tests.[16]

1. *More Than 500 Hours.* An individual materially participates if he or she spends more than 500 hours in the activity during the taxable year. Apparently the authors of the Regulations believed that this threshold (e.g., about 10 hours per week) appropriately distinguished those who truly were involved in the business from mere investors. Note that the work of a spouse is counted if it is work typically done by owners. For example, if B owned a football team (e.g., that suffered losses), he would materially participate if he devoted more than 500 hours to the activity. However, if he spent only 300 hours and hired his wife as a receptionist who spent 250 hours, the test is not met because her work is not normally done by owners.

2. *Substantially All of the Participation.* The individual and his or her spouse materially participate if they are the sole participants or their participation constitutes substantially all of the participation of all individuals (including nonowners and nonemployees) who participate in the activity. This test, as well as the next, takes into account the fact that not all businesses require 500 hours to operate during the year. For example, if S operates a snow removal service by himself and spends only 50 hours in the activity this year because of light snow, the test is met because he was the sole participant.

3. *More Than 100 Hours and Not Less Than Anyone Else.* An individual materially participates if he or she participates for more than 100 hours and no other individual spends more time on the activity. For example, assume that S, above, occasionally hires E to help him remove snow. If S spent 160 hours and E 140, S qualifies because he spent more than 100 hours and not less than anyone else. Had S spent only 60 and E 40, S would not qualify under either this or the previous test.

---

[16] Temp. Reg. § 1.469-1T(a).

4. *Significant Participation in Several Activities (SPAs).* An individual materially participates if his or her total participation in all significant participation activities (SPAs) exceeds 500 hours. A significant participation activity is defined as a trade or business in which the taxpayer participates more than 100 hours, but fails the other six tests for material participation. Thus a taxpayer must spend more than 100 hours in each activity and greater than 500 in all. The rule derives from the view that an individual who spends more than 500 hours in several different activities should be treated the same as those who spend an equivalent amount of time on a single activity.

Example 20. T spends 140 hours overseeing his car wash, 160 hours supervising his quick-lube operation, and 499 hours managing his gas station. Each activity qualifies as a SPA because T spends more than 100 hours in each. More importantly, T is treated as materially participating in each because the total hours in all SPAs exceeds 500. However, if T spent 2 more hours in his gas station, then he would not be a material participant in either the car wash or quick-lube business. This occurs because the gas station would no longer be a SPA since the activity by itself satisfies the more-than-500-hours test. As a result, T's total hours in all SPAs, 300 (160 + 140), would not exceed the 500-hour benchmark.

The Regulations provide what at first glance is a curious treatment of SPAs. As expected, losses from SPAs failing to meet the 500-hour test are passive and generally not deductible. However, income from SPAs failing to meet the 500-hour test is not passive. Note that the IRS obtains the best of both worlds when a taxpayer is unable to combine his or her SPAs to get over the 500-hour threshold: passive loss but not passive income. This "heads I win, tails you lose" approach was designed to prevent taxpayers from creating passive income that could be used to absorb passive losses by spending small amounts of time in unrelated activities that are profitable.[17]

5. *Prior Participation.* An individual materially participates if he or she has materially participated (by tests 1 through 4) in an activity for five of the past ten years. This test prevents the taxpayer from moving in and out of material participation status. For example, D and son are partners in an appliance business that D started 30 years ago. D has essentially retired, leaving the day-to-day operations with his son. Without a special rule, D could tailor his participation year by year to obtain passive or nonpassive income as fits his needs.

---

[17]   See Reg. § 1.469-2T(f)(2).

6. *Prior Participation in a Personal Service Activity*. An individual materially participates in a personal service activity if he or she has materially participated in the activity for at least three years. Like the previous test, this rule eliminates the flexibility those working for personal service businesses have in tailoring their participation to obtain passive or nonpassive income as they need. For example, if a general partner in a law firm retired and converted her interest to a limited partnership interest, she would still be treated as a material participant in that law firm.

7. *Facts and Circumstances*. Based on the facts and circumstances, the individual participates in the activity on a regular, continuous, and substantial basis.

Rental Real Estate Exception. An extremely important exception to the passive activity rules is carved out in § 469(i) for rental real estate activities of the small investor. In many cases, the real estate held by a taxpayer is a residence that is used part-time, was formerly used, or may be used in the future. Relief was provided for this type of rental real estate because it is often held to provide financial security to individuals with moderate incomes. In such a case, these individuals share little common ground with the tax shelter investors. The relief is provided solely to individuals and certain trusts and estates. Regular C corporations are ineligible.

Under the exception, a taxpayer who *actively* participates (in contrast to materially participates) may deduct up to $25,000 of losses attributable to rental real estate annually. The $25,000 allowance is reduced by 50 percent of the excess of the taxpayer's A.G.I. over $100,000. Consequently, high-income taxpayers (i.e., those with A.G.I. of $150,000 or more) cannot take advantage of this provision. A.G.I. for this purpose is computed without regard to contributions to individual retirement accounts, taxable social security, and any net passive losses that might be deductible. Any portion of the loss that is not deductible may be carried over and deducted subject to the same limitations in the following years.

> **Example 21.** L moved to a new home this year. Instead of selling his old home, L decided to rent it out to supplement his income. During the first year, rents were $3,000 while expenses including maintenance, depreciation, interest, utilities, and taxes were $10,000. L's A.G.I. is $40,000. L may deduct the $7,000 loss for A.G.I. Had L's A.G.I. been $140,000, he could have deducted only $5,000 [$25,000 maximum − 50% × ($140,000 − $100,000)] and carried over $2,000 to the following year.

It should be emphasized that the taxpayer can use this exception only if the property is considered rental real estate. It cannot be used for losses from rental of personal property. More importantly, the real estate is not considered a "rental" activity where the rental period is either 1 to 7 days or between 8 and 30 days and significant services are performed.[18] For example, consider the typical investor who owns a vacation condominium. If the average rental of the condominium is 1 to 7 days, the condominium is not considered rental property and the $25,000 exception does not apply. The result is the same if the average rental period is between 8 and 30 days and significant services are provided. Note that even though the $25,000 exception is not available in either case, all is not necessarily lost. In both situations, the condominium could be treated as a nonrental activity. In such case, the taxpayer will be able to deduct all losses if there is material participation.

> **Example 22.**   M lives in Orlando, where she practices law. M owns a condominium which she rents out on a daily basis to tourists. M runs ads in the local newspaper, makes arrangements for the rental, and cleans the unit as needed. In this case, it appears that the activity is not a rental business because of the short-term rental. As a result, the $25,000 exception for rentals does not apply. However, the property is not considered a rental activity, and because of M's material participation the passive activity rules should not apply.

As noted above, the Code draws a distinction between material and active participation. The primary difference concerns the taxpayer's degree of involvement in operations. For example, a taxpayer is actively involved if he or she participates in management decisions such as approving new tenants, deciding on rental terms, approving capital or repair expenditures, or if he or she arranges for others to provide services such as repairs. In all cases, the taxpayer is not treated as actively participating in the activity if less than a 10 percent interest is owned. On the other hand, the taxpayer is not presumed to actively participate if the interest is 10 percent or more. The above standard still must be satisfied.

RECHARACTERIZED PASSIVE INCOME

As is evident throughout the passive loss Regulations, the IRS was concerned that taxpayers might create passive income which could be used to absorb otherwise nondeductible passive losses. Nowhere is this more evident than in the recharacterization rules. In certain situations, income that is characterized under the general rules as passive is recharacterized under a special rule and treated as active. An example of the type of recharacterization that can occur was discussed earlier in connection with SPAs. As noted in that discussion, income from SPAs that fail to meet the 500-hour test would normally be treated as passive, but under the special recharacterization rule it is treated as active. There are several other situations when this might occur. Consequently, before it can be concluded that

---

[18]   For an excellent discussion of this topic and issue see Bomyea and Marucheck, "Rental of Residences," *The Tax Adviser* (September 1990), p. 543.

income is passive, the recharacterization rules must be considered. The recharacterization rules operate to convert the following types of income to nonpassive or active income (rather than passive).[19]

1. *Significant participation activities:* Income from significant participation activities that fail to meet the 500-hour test

2. *Rental of nondeductible property:* Income from rental activities where less than 30 percent of the basis of the property rented is not depreciable (e.g., rental of land)

3. *Developer sales of rental property:* Rental income, including gain on the sale of rental property, if (1) gain on the sale is included in income during the taxable year; (2) rental of the property commenced less than 24 months before the date of disposition; and (3) the taxpayer performed sufficient services that enhanced the value of the rental property

4. *Self-rented property:* Income from rental of property to an activity in which the taxpayer materially participates, other than related C corporations

5. *Licensing of intangible property:* Royalty income from a pass-through entity that the taxpayer acquired after the entity created the intangible property

6. *Equity-financed lending activity:* Income from the trade or business of lending money if certain conditions are satisfied

INTEREST EXPENSE

Interest expense is an amount paid or incurred for the use or forebearance of money.[20] Under the general rule of Code § 163(a), all interest paid or accrued on indebtedness within the taxable year is allowed as a deduction. As with most general rules in the tax law, however, there are limitations imposed on the deduction of certain interest expense as well as the complete disallowance of deductions for interest related to certain items. These restrictions are discussed below.

LIMITATIONS ON DEDUCTIONS OF INTEREST EXPENSE

Prior to 1987, interest expense for most taxpayers was totally deductible. As part of the tax reform package of 1986, however, Congress substantially limited the deduction for interest.

---

[19] Temp. Reg. § 1.469-2T(f).

[20] *Old Colony Railroad v. Comm.*, 3 USTC ¶880, 10 AFTR 786, 284 U.S. 552 (USSC, 1936).

Over the years, Congress became concerned that by allowing a deduction for all interest expense the tax system encouraged borrowing and, conversely, discouraged savings. This problem was exacerbated by the fact that the "economic" income arising from the ownership of housing and other consumer durables is not subject to tax. For example, when a taxpayer purchases a residence, the return on the investment—the absence of having to pay rent for the item—is not subject to tax. Had the taxpayer invested in assets other than housing or other durables, the return (e.g., interest or dividends) would have been fully taxable. In those situations where the investment is financed by borrowing, allowing a deduction is equivalent to allowing a deduction for expenses related to tax-exempt income—which is expressly prohibited under Code § 265. The net result of this system is to provide an incentive to consume rather than save.

In rethinking the approach to interest in 1986, Congress believed that it would not be advisable to impute income on investments in durables and tax it. However, Congress did feel that it was appropriate and practical to address situations where consumer expenditures are financed by borrowing. Accordingly, Congress enacted rules that prohibit the deduction for personal interest (other than certain home mortgage interest). As a result, interest expense on personal auto loans, credit card purchases, and the like are no longer deductible.

In eliminating the deduction for personal interest, Congress effectively established *five* categories of interest expense, each of which is subject to its own special set of rules. The different categories of interest expense are (1) personal interest, (2) qualified residence interest, (3) trade or business interest, (4) investment interest, and (5) passive activity interest. As explained in detail below, interest (other than qualified residence interest) is classified according to how the loan proceeds are *spent*. Consequently, taxpayers are required to determine the nature of an expenditure from loan proceeds before the amount of the interest deduction can be determined.

Personal Interest.   Beginning in 1991, taxpayers may no longer deduct any *personal interest*. Personal interest is defined as all interest arising from personal expenditures *except* the following:[21]

1. Interest incurred in connection with the conduct of a trade or business (other than the performance of services as an employee);

2. Investment interest;

3. Qualified residence interest;

4. Interest taken into account in computing the income or loss from passive activities; and

5. Interest related to payment of the estate tax liability where such tax is deferred.

---

[21]   § 163(h)(1).

The effect of these rules is to severely limit the deduction for interest on consumer debt. For example, if a taxpayer borrows $2,000 from the bank and uses it to take a Caribbean cruise, none of the interest on the loan is deductible. Similarly, interest and finance charges would not be deductible on the following:

1. Automobile loans;

2. Furniture and appliance loans;

3. Credit card debt;

4. Student loans;

5. Life insurance loans;

6. Loans from qualified pension plans [including § 401(k) plans]; and

7. Delinquent tax payments and penalties.

It should be emphasized that interest incurred by an *employee* in connection with his or her trade or business is treated as consumer interest and is not deductible. In contrast, interest incurred by a self-employed person in his or her trade or business is fully deductible.

> **Example 23.**   K sells cosmetics for Fantastic Faces, Incorporated. Her job involves calling on department stores all over the state of Ohio and soliciting their orders. She uses her car entirely for business. Interest on her car loan for the year was $2,000. Since K is an employee, none of the interest is deductible.

> **Example 24.**   R is a real estate agent working for Bungalow Brokers. All of his compensation is based on the number of homes he sells during the year. He uses his car entirely for business. Under the employment tax rules (Code § 3508), real estate agents and direct sellers are not considered employees where their remuneration is determined by sales. Since R would not be considered an employee, all of the interest on his car loan would be deductible.

> **Example 25.**   P is a reporter for the *News-Gazette*. She purchased a portable computer for $1,000, charging it on her bank credit card. She uses the computer entirely for business. Finance charges attributable to the purchase are $25. Even though the finance charges are incurred in connection with P's business, they are not deductible since she is an employee.

Qualified Residence Interest. The elimination of the deduction for personal interest in 1986 did not extend to interest on most home mortgages. As a general rule, interest on any debt secured by a taxpayer's first or second home is deductible. The interest is normally deductible whether the interest is on an original, second, or refinanced mortgage. Moreover, the interest is deductible regardless of how the taxpayer uses the money as long as the debt is *secured* by a mortgage on his or her primary or secondary residence. Unfortunately, tucked behind these seemingly simple rules are several complex restrictions.

Qualifying Indebtedness. Technically, only "qualified residence interest" is deductible. There are two types of qualified residence interest:[22]

1. Interest on *acquisition indebtedness:* interest on debt that is incurred in acquiring, constructing, or improving a qualified residence and that is secured by such residence

2. Interest on *home equity indebtedness:* interest on debt secured by a qualified residence to the extent that the debt does not exceed the property's fair market value reduced by its acquisition debt

Note that in both cases, the crucial element in determining whether the interest qualifies is whether the debt is secured by a residence. Unsecured debt and debt secured by other property does not qualify even though the debt proceeds may be used to acquire a personal residence.

> **Example 26.** J borrowed $50,000 from her pension plan and $10,000 from her father to buy a new home. None of the interest on the debt is deductible because neither of the debts is secured by the residence. This is true even though the borrowed amounts were used to buy a residence.

Also observe that in the case of both acquisition and home equity debt, the debt must be secured by a *qualified* residence. A qualified residence is the taxpayer's principal home and one other residence of the taxpayer.[23] This rule effectively allows taxpayers to deduct the interest on only two homes: their first home and a second of their choosing. A taxpayer with more than two homes must designate which is the second home when the return is filed. Different homes can be selected each year.

> **Example 27.** After winning the New York State lottery, T retired from her job and purchased a home in Tampa, Florida. She also purchased a motor home and a condominium in Vail, Colorado. All purchases were debt-financed and secured by the property. Within certain dollar limitations, T can treat the interest paid on her home in Tampa *and* the interest paid on *either* the motor home *or* the condominium as qualified residence interest.

---

[22] § 163(h)(3).   [23] § 163(h)(4).

Example 28.   Assume the same facts as above except that T converted the condominium into rental property at the advice of her tax accountant. In this case, the condominium will not qualify as T's secondary residence.[24]

In determining the deductibility of interest on a second home, special rules must be considered if the taxpayer *rents* it out. These rules are examined in conjunction with vacation homes discussed later in this chapter. If the second home is not rented out, no personal use is actually needed in order to meet the qualified residence test.

Congress also took steps to ensure that a taxpayer could not convert nondeductible interest into qualified residence interest simply by pitching a tent on the property and calling it a second home (e.g., vacant land or a car). In determining whether the debt is incurred with respect to a qualified residence, the term *residence* includes a vacation home, condominium, mobile home, boat, or recreational vehicle as long as the property contains basic living accommodations (i.e., sleeping space, toilet, and cooking facilities).

Limitations on Deductible Amount.   To prevent taxpayers from taking undue advantage of the deductibility of home mortgage interest, Congress imposed limits on the maximum amount of debt qualifying under either definition. The aggregate amount of debt that can be treated as acquisition indebtedness for any taxable year cannot exceed $1 million ($500,000 in the case of a married individual filing a separate return),[25] whereas the aggregate amount of debt that will be treated as home equity indebtedness for any taxable year cannot exceed $100,000 ($50,000 if married and filing separately).[26] Collectively, the total amount of debt in any one year on which the interest paid or accrued will be treated as qualified residence interest cannot exceed $1.1 million.

Example 29.   During the current year, T purchases a principal residence in Boston for $900,000 and a vacation home in Tampa for $500,000. Mortgages secured by both properties total $1.3 million. T may treat *only* the interest paid on $1 million of acquisition indebtedness as qualified residence interest. In addition, he may treat $100,000 of the loans as home equity indebtedness and, therefore, the related interest is deductible as qualified residence interest. Whether interest on the balance of the debt, $200,000, is deductible depends on how the funds are used.

---

[24] This does not mean that a taxpayer's interest expense on rental property is not deductible. As discussed later, however, losses from rental property (including interest expense) may be subject to deduction limitations.

[25] Any qualified residence indebtedness incurred before October 14, 1987—whether it is acquisition debt, home equity debt, or a combination of both—is to be treated as acquisition debt and is not subject to the $1 million limitation. If the property is later refinanced, however, the new indebtedness will be subject to this limitation. § 163(h)(3)(D).

[26] § 163(h).

Example 30. C purchased his present residence several years ago at a cost of $1.9 million. The present balance on his home mortgage is $800,000 and the property is valued at $2.5 million. This year, C borrowed $300,000 secured by a second mortgage on his home. Even though the total indebtedness does not exceed $1.1 million, C may deduct the interest on the $800,000 unpaid acquisition indebtedness and the interest on only $100,000 of the home equity mortgage. Any excess interest paid during the year will be treated as personal interest.

It is important to note that the interest paid on qualifying home equity indebtedness is allowed as a deduction *regardless* of how the taxpayer uses the loan proceeds. Thus, the obvious reason for the $100,000 limit on qualifying home equity debt is to impose a limit on the amount of an interest deduction the taxpayer may claim on loan proceeds used for personal purposes.

Example 31. K purchased her present residence 10 years ago at a cost of $70,000. The present balance on her home mortgage is $40,000 and the property is appraised at a value of $150,000. This year, K borrowed $80,000 secured by a second mortgage on her home. She used the loan proceeds to purchase new clothes and a new automobile, and to take a vacation to Hawaii. The interest on the $80,000 loan is deductible since it is qualified residence interest. The fact that K used the loan proceeds for personal purposes is irrelevant. Also note that K's original cost of $70,000 is not used to limit the amount of her $80,000 home equity loan.

Finally, any attempt to refinance acquisition indebtedness should be undertaken with caution. A qualifying residence's acquisition debt is *reduced* by principal payments and *cannot be increased* unless the loan proceeds are used for home improvements. Thus, the acquisition debt can be refinanced only to the extent that the principal amount of the refinancing does not exceed the principal amount of the acquisition debt immediately before the refinancing.[27] The interest paid on any excess refinanced debt will not be treated as acquisition indebtedness. However, any excess may be treated as home equity indebtedness. As noted above, the total qualifying indebtedness (acquisition and home equity) cannot exceed the value of the residence.

Example 32. In 1957, G purchased her California bungalow for $25,000. The house is now worth $350,000. G paid off the mortgage on the home several years ago. This year, G mortgaged her house for $120,000 and subsequently loaned the money to her grandson to enable him to buy his first home. None of the loan qualifies as acquisition debt because the balance of acquisition debt refinanced was zero. However, G may deduct interest on $100,000 of the loan, which qualifies as home equity debt.

---

[27]   §163(h)(3)(B).

Example 33.   R purchased his present residence in 1988 for $250,000 and borrowed $210,000 on a 14% mortgage secured by the property. In 1994, R refinanced the balance of his mortgage, $190,000, by securing a new mortgage of $230,000 at 10%. Unless R used the additional loan proceeds to substantially improve the residence, only $190,000 of the new mortgage constitutes acquisition indebtedness, and the corresponding interest is therefore deductible. In addition, the $40,000 balance of the debt may be treated as home-equity debt. In such case, the interest on the entire $230,000 mortgage would be deductible as qualified residence interest.

Trade or Business Interest.   While the taxpayer normally cannot deduct interest of a personal nature, interest related to a trade or business expenditure is totally deductible. Perhaps the most common example of business interest is that arising from loans used to acquire fixed assets such as buildings and equipment that are used in the business. Business interest also includes that attributable to loans used to acquire an interest in an S corporation or a partnership in which the taxpayer materially participates. Recall, however, that interest incurred in connection with performing services as an employee is not considered business interest, and thus is considered nondeductible personal interest.

As explained below, the fact that a business incurs interest expense does not necessarily mean that such interest is classified as business interest. If interest expense incurred by a business arises from an investment considered unrelated to the business, it will not be business interest (e.g., a closely held corporation purchases stock on margin).

Investment Interest.   The fourth category of interest expense subject to limitation is investment interest. This limitation is imposed on taxpayers, other than regular corporations, who have paid or incurred interest expense to purchase or carry investments.[28]   Common examples include interest on loans to purchase unimproved land and interest incurred on margin accounts used to purchase stocks and other securities. Congress imposed the investment interest limitation to eliminate what it perceived was an unfair advantage to certain wealthy investors. For example, consider the taxpayer who borrows to acquire or carry investments that produce little or no income currently but pay off handsomely when the investment is sold. This is commonly the hoped-for result with investments in such assets as growth stock or land. Without any restrictions, the taxpayer would be able to claim an immediate deduction for interest expense yet postpone any income recognition until the property was ultimately sold. Moreover, the income that the taxpayer would realize on the sale would normally be favorable capital gain. Congress apparently felt that this mismatching of income and expense was unwarranted and reacted by limiting the taxpayer's deduction for investment interest to the taxpayer's current investment income.

Before examining the investment interest limitation, the definition of investment interest should be clarified. *Investment interest* is generally any interest expense on debt used to finance property held for investment. It does not in-

---

[28]   § 163(d).

clude, however, qualified residence interest or any interest related to a passive activity. As discussed below, interest related to a passive activity is allocated to the passive activity and is taken into account in computing the activity's income or loss. As a result, such interest is effectively limited by the passive loss rules. Note, however, that any interest incurred by a passive activity that is related to its portfolio income would normally be considered investment interest subject to the investment interest limitation. Because rental activities are usually treated as a passive activity, interest expense allocable to a rental activity is normally subject to the passive loss rules.

The annual deduction for investment interest expense is limited to the taxpayer's *net investment income,* if any, for the tax year.[29] Any investment interest that exceeds the limitation and is disallowed may be carried forward until it is exhausted. Operationally, the disallowed interest is carried forward to the subsequent year, where it is combined with current year interest and is once again subject to the net investment income limitation. (Note that a sale of the financed property does not trigger the allowance of any disallowed interest.)

Net Investment Income. Net investment income is the excess of the taxpayer's investment income over investment expenses. For this purpose, *investment income* is defined as the gross income from property held for investment, including any net gain on the disposition of such property. Common examples of investment income include

1. Interest

2. Dividends

3. Royalties

4. Net short-term or long-term capital gains attributable to the disposition of investment property

5. Ordinary income from the recapture of depreciation or intangible drilling costs under §§ 1245, 1250, and 1254

6. Portfolio income under the passive loss rules

7. Income from a trade or business in which the taxpayer did not materially participate (but which is not a passive activity, e.g., a working interest in an oil or gas property)

Note that income from rental property and income from a passive activity (other than portfolio income) are not considered investment income. As noted above, any interest expense incurred in rental or passive activities is allocated to those activities and is used in computing the passive income or loss of such activity.[30] For example, mortgage interest on rental property would be deductible only to the extent of passive income.

---

[29]   § 163(d)(1).   [30]   § 163(d)(4)(E).

Investment expenses are generally all those deductions (except interest) that are directly connected with the production of the investment income. Any investment expenses that are considered miscellaneous itemized deductions are considered only to the extent they exceed the 2 percent floor. For this purpose, the 2 percent floor is first absorbed by all other miscellaneous expenses.

Example 34. G's records for 1991 revealed the following information:

Salary...	$ 40,000
Dividends and interest...........................	3,500
Long-term capital gain...........................	1,000
Short-term capital gain..........................	2,000
Short-term capital loss..........................	(900)
Share of partnership income:	
Partnership ordinary income....................	700
Portfolio income:	
Dividends..................................	50
Interest.....................................	80
Rental income from duplex........................	15,000
Rental expenses..................................	(14,000)
Adjusted gross income............................	$ 47,430
Qualified residence interest.......................	$8,000
Real estate taxes on home........................	4,000
Property tax on land held for investment..........	1,000
Miscellaneous itemized deductions:	
Safety deposit box rental......................	50
Financial planner..............................	1,500
Fee to maintain brokerage account.............	100
Unreimbursed employee business expenses...	725

G is a limited partner in the partnership and thus treats the partnership as a passive activity. G also paid $7,700 of interest expense on the land held for investment. G's net investment income is computed as follows:

Investment income:			
Dividends and interest.........................		$3,500	
Net capital gain................................		2,100	
Partnership income:			
Portfolio income:			
Dividends.................................		50	
Interest....................................		80	
Total investment income...........................			$5,730
Investment expenses:			
Property tax on land...........................		$1,000	
Safety deposit box rental......................		50	
Financial planner..............................		1,500	
Fee to maintain brokerage account............		100	
Miscellaneous itemized deductions disallowed			
2% floor (2% × $47,430)...................	$ 949		
Unreimbursed employee business expenses.	(725)		
Investment expenses classified as			
miscellaneous itemized deductions disallowed		(224)	
Total investment expenses........................			(2,426)
Net investment income............................			$3,304

For 1991, G may deduct $3,304 of investment interest expense. The balance of $4,396 ($7,700 − $3,304) is carried over to the next year, 1992, and is treated as if it were paid in 1992. There is no limit on the carryover period. Note that in computing investment expenses, only investment expenses exceeding the 2% floor are allowed. In computing the disallowed portion, investment expenses are deemed to come last. Also note that rental income is not considered investment income.

Passive Activity Interest. As noted earlier in this chapter, deductions attributable to so-called *passive activities* (e.g., those in which a taxpayer does not participate in a material fashion) are subject to special rules. Interest expense incurred by a passive activity itself (e.g., a limited partnership), or by investment in a passive activity, is treated as a deduction relating to the passive activity and is limited by the passive loss rules.[31]

> **Example 35.** Dr. P borrowed $50,000 and invested it by acquiring an interest in a limited partnership which produces movies. Interest on the loan for the year is $5,000. P can deduct the interest only to the extent of any passive income that he may have.

> **Example 36.** The partnership incurs interest expense related to loans made to acquire equipment used in its operations. The interest is treated as a normal deduction and is used in arriving at the partnership's net income or loss for the year. This year, the partnership suffered a net loss including deductions for interest expense. Dr. P is allowed to deduct his share of the loss only to the extent he has passive income from other activities.

CLASSIFICATION OF INTEREST EXPENSE

The different rules for different types of interest expense force taxpayers to classify and allocate their interest expense among appropriate categories. The classification procedure established by the Treasury is very straightforward in principle. Under the Temporary Regulations, interest is generally classified according to how the loan proceeds are spent—that is, the character of the expenditure determines the character of interest.[32] The type of collateral that may secure the loan is irrelevant in the classification process—except in the case of the qualified residence interest which is deductible regardless of how loan proceeds are spent.[33]

---

[31] § 163(d)(3)(B).

[32] Temp. Reg. § 1.163-8T.

[33] Temp. Reg. § 1.163-8T(c)(1). For purposes of the alternative minimum tax, however, qualified housing interest is deductible only if the debt is spent on the residence. See Chapter 13 for further discussion.

Example 37. This year, T pledged IBM stock held as an investment as collateral for a loan which he uses to purchase a personal car. Any interest expense on the loan is considered nondeductible personal interest since the debt proceeds were used for personal purposes. The fact that the debt is secured by investment property is irrelevant. If the loan were secured by T's primary residence, the interest could be deductible as qualified residence interest.

The classification scheme demands that the taxpayer trace how any loan proceeds were used. To simplify this task, specific rules exist for debt proceeds that are (1) deposited in the borrower's account, (2) disbursed directly by the lender to someone other than the borrower, or (3) received in cash.

Proceeds Deposited in the Borrower's Account. In most cases, taxpayers borrow money, deposit it in an account, and write checks for various expenditures. Since money is fungible (that is, one dollar cannot be distinguished from another) it would be impossible without special rules to determine how the loan proceeds were spent and therefore how the related interest should be allocated. The Temporary Regulations create such rules.[34]

The first presumption created by the Regulations concerns the treatment of interest on funds that have not been spent. To the extent borrowed funds are deposited and not spent, interest attributable to such a period is considered *investment interest* regardless of whether the account bears interest income.[35]

Example 38. On November 1, K borrowed $1,000 which she intends to use to fix up her boat. She deposited the $1,000 in a separate account. No expenditures were made during the remainder of the year. In this case, K is subject to the interest allocation rules since the interest expense is considered attributable to an investment and is therefore investment interest.

Example 39. Same as above except K makes several personal expenditures during the next three months. Interest must be allocated between investment interest and personal interest.

Example 40. R borrows $100,000 on January 1 and deposits it in a separate account where it remains until April 1 when he purchases an interest in a limited partnership for $20,000. On September 1, R purchases a new car for $30,000. Interest expense attributable to the $100,000 is allocated in the following manner:

| Period | Debt Proceeds | | |
	Investment Interest	Passive Interest	Personal Interest
1/1-3/31	$100,000		
4/1-8/31	80,000	$20,000	
9/1-12/31	50,000	20,000	$30,000

---

[34] Temp. Reg. § 1.163-8T(c)(4).   [35] *Ibid.*

Commingled Funds. In most situations, a taxpayer has one account in which all amounts are deposited. When this occurs, all expenditures from the account after the loan is deposited are deemed to come first from the borrowed funds.

> **Example 41.** On October 1, B borrowed $1,000 to purchase a snowplow attachment for the front of his truck. He plans to make some extra money this winter by plowing driveways and parking lots. B deposited the $1,000 in his only checking account. On October 20, he bought the attachment for $1,500. Prior to October 20, he wrote $700 in checks for groceries and other personal items. Of the $1,000 loan, $700 is deemed to have been spent for personal items while the remaining $300 is allocated to the snow plow. Consequently, B may deduct only the interest expense on $300.

If proceeds for more than one loan are deposited into an account, expenditures are treated as coming from the borrowed funds in the order in which they were deposited (i.e., first-in, first-out).

> **Example 42.** Dr. T has a personal checking account with a current balance of $3,000. On November 1, T obtained a $1,000 one-year loan (Debt A) from her bank, which it credited to her personal account. She planned to use the loan to purchase a small copier for her dental practice. After shopping, T determined she would need additional funds. Therefore, on November 30 she obtained another $1,000 loan (Debt B). On December 12, T wrote a check for $800 to pay for her husband's Christmas present, a diamond ring. On December 19, she wrote a check for $2,100 to purchase the copier. These transactions are summarized as follows:
>
> | Date | Transaction | |
> |------|-------------|------|
> | 11/1 | Borrowed (Debt A) | $1,000 |
> | 11/30 | Borrowed (Debt B) | 1,000 |
> | 12/12 | Purchased ring | (800) |
> | 12/19 | Purchased copier | (2,100) |
>
> For purposes of determining the deduction for the interest on the loan, $800 of Debt A is deemed to be used for personal purposes (i.e., the ring purchase) and $200 towards the copier. All of Debt B is used for the copier. Thus, interest attributable to $800 of Debt A is nondeductible personal interest (10% in 1990 is deductible) while that attributable to $200 is totally deductible. All of the interest on Debt B is deductible business interest. This may be summarized as follows:
>
> | Expenditure | 11/1 Debt A $1,000 Personal | 11/1 Debt A $1,000 Business | 11/30 Debt B $1,000 Personal | 11/30 Debt B $1,000 Business | Other |
> |-------------|------|------|------|------|------|
> | $ 800 ring | $800 | | | | |
> | 2,100 copier | | $200 | | $1,000 | $1,100 |

15-Day Rule. In lieu of allocating the debt proceeds in the above manner, an alternative method is available. A borrower can elect to treat any expenditure made within 15 days after the loan proceeds are deposited as having been made from the proceeds of that loan.

> **Example 43.** C borrowed and deposited $5,000 in his checking account on December 1. On December 2, he wrote a check for $6,000 for his estimated income taxes. On December 10, he wrote a check for $5,000 for furniture for his business. Under the normal allocation rule, the entire $5,000 proceeds from the debt would be considered spent for personal purposes. Under the 15-day rule, however, C may treat the $5,000 as used to purchase the furniture since the proceeds were spent within 15 days of deposit.

Loan Proceeds Received Indirectly. In many transactions, a borrower incurs debt without receiving any loan proceeds directly. For example, if the taxpayer borrowed $100,000 from a bank to purchase a building, the bank typically disburses the $100,000 directly to the seller rather than to the borrower. Similarly, the borrower may purchase the building and assume the seller's $100,000 mortgage. In this and similar situations, the borrower is treated as having received the proceeds and using them to make the expenditure for the property, services, or other purpose.[36]

Loan Proceeds Received in Cash. When the borrower receives the loan proceeds in cash, the taxpayer may treat any cash expenditure made within 15 days after receiving the cash as made from the loan. If the loan proceeds are not spent within 15 days, however, the loan is deemed to have been spent for personal purposes.

Debt Repayments, Refinancings, and Reallocations. Loans that are used for several purposes present a unique problem when a portion of the loan is repaid. In this case, repayments must be applied in the following order:[37]

1. Personal expenditures

2. Investment expenditures and passive activity expenditures (other than rental real estate in which the taxpayer actively participates)

3. Rental real estate expenditures

4. Former passive activity expenditures

5. Trade or business expenditures

---

[36] Temp. Reg. § 1.163-8T(c)(3).   [37] *Ibid.*

Example 44. R borrows $10,000, $6,000 of which is used to purchase a personal automobile and $4,000 of which is used to invest in land. On June 1 of this year she paid $7,000 on the loan. Of the $7,000 repayment, $6,000 reduces the portion of the loan allocated to personal expenditures and the remaining $1,000 reduces the portion allocated to investment.

If the taxpayer refinances an old debt, interest on the new debt is characterized in the same way as that on the old debt.

Example 45. In 1989, S borrowed $10,000 at an annual interest rate of 14%. He used $8,000 to purchase a new boat and $2,000 to purchase a computer to use in his business. This year, he borrowed $6,000 from another bank at 10% to pay off the balance of the old loan. At the time the original loan was paid off, $4,000 of the $6,000 balance was allocated to the boat purchase and $2,000 was allocated to the computer purchase. The new debt will be allocated in the same manner as the old debt.

If the taxpayer borrows to finance a business asset, the debt must be recharacterized whenever the asset is sold or the nature of the use of the asset changes.

Example 46. Several years ago, B, a traveling salesman, borrowed $12,000 to buy a car which he uses entirely for business. This year, B gave his car to his wife who uses it solely for personal use. The loan and interest thereon must be reclassified.

Computation and Allocation of Interest Expense. The special rules governing the taxpayer's deduction for interest expense do not affect its computation. Interest is computed in the normal manner. However, allocation of the interest expense among the different categories does present certain difficulties. As a general rule, interest expense accruing on a debt for any period is allocated in the same manner as the debt. Interest which accrues on interest—that is, compound interest—is allocated in the same manner as the original interest.[38]

Example 47. On January 1, R borrowed $100,000 at an interest rate of 10%, compounded semiannually. She deposited the loan in a separate account and on July 1 used the funds to purchase a yacht. On December 31, R paid the accrued interest of $10,250 computed as follows:

Period	Principal		Rate		Time		Interest
1/1-6/30	$100,000	×	10%	×	6/12	=	$ 5,000
7/1-12/31	105,000	×	10%	×	6/12	=	5,250
							$10,250

---

[38] Temp. Reg. § 1.163-8T(c)(2).

Under the allocation rules, R's loan is classified as an investment loan from January 1 through June 30 and, therefore, the interest accruing for that period of $5,000 is investment interest. In addition, the interest expense which accrues on this $5,000 from July 30 through December 31 of $250 ($5,000 × 10% × $^6/_{12}$) is considered investment interest for a total of $5,250. This $250 of "compound interest" accruing from July 31 through December 31 is allocated to the investment category even though the original loan has been assigned to a new category for the same period. The remaining $5,000 of interest expense accruing from July 1 through December 31 ($100,000 × 10% × $^6/_{12}$) is personal interest.

To simplify the allocation of interest expense, the taxpayer may use a straight-line method. Using this technique, an equal amount of interest is allocated to each day of the year. For this purpose, the taxpayer may treat a year as consisting of twelve 30-day months.

Example 48. Assume the same facts as in *Example 47* above, except that R elects to allocate the interest expense on a straight-line basis, treating the year as consisting of twelve 30-day months. As a result, interest expense of $5,125 ($^{180}/_{360}$ × $10,250) would be investment interest while the remaining $5,125 of interest expense would be personal interest.

WHEN DEDUCTIBLE

The taxpayer's method of accounting generally controls the timing of an interest expense deduction. Accrual method taxpayers generally may deduct interest over the period in which the interest accrues, regardless of when the expense is actually paid. However, cash basis taxpayers must *actually* pay the interest before a deduction is allowed. Many situations arise in which the "actual payment" requirement imposed on cash basis taxpayers delays the timing of a deduction. Other situations concern measurement of the amount of interest actually paid. The most common of these situations are briefly discussed below.

   Interest Paid in Advance. If interest is paid in advance for a time period that extends beyond the end of one tax year, *both* accrual method and cash basis taxpayers generally are required to spread the interest deduction over the tax years to which it applies.[39] An important exception is made for cash basis individual taxpayers who are required to pay interest "points" in connection with indebtedness incurred to *purchase* or *improve* the taxpayer's principal residence (i.e., taxpayer's home).[40] The term *points* is often used to describe charges imposed on the borrower under such descriptions as "loan origination fees," "premium charges," and "maximum loan charges." Such charges usually are

---

[39] § 461(a).   [40] § 461(g).

stated as a percentage (point) of the loan amount. If the payment of any of these charges is *strictly* for the use of money *and* actual payment of these charges is made out of *separate funds* belonging to the taxpayer, an interest deduction is allowed in the year of payment.[41]

> **Example 49.** R borrowed $15,000 from State Bank to make improvements on his home. The loan is payable over a 10-year period, and the bank charged R a loan origination fee of $300 (2 points). If R pays the $300 charge from separate funds, it is currently deductible as an interest expense (assuming R itemizes his deductions). However, if the $300 charge is added to the amount of the loan, R has not currently paid interest. Instead, R will be required to treat the charge as note discount interest (see discussion below).

Note-Discount Interest. Taxpayers often sign notes calling for repayment of an amount greater than the loan proceeds actually received. This occurs when the creditor subtracts (withholds) the interest from the face amount of the loan and the taxpayer receives the balance, or when the face amount of the note simply includes add-on interest. In either case, cash basis taxpayers are not allowed a deduction until the tax year in which the interest is actually paid. Accrual method taxpayers are allowed to deduct the interest over the tax years in which it accrues.

Graduated Payment Mortgages. A creature of the high interest rate mortgage market of recent years, graduated payment mortgages provide for increasing payments in the early years of the mortgage until the payments reach some level amount. Under these plans, the payments in the early years are less than the amount of interest owed on the loan. The unpaid interest is added to the principal amount of the mortgage and future interest is computed on this revised balance. As should be expected, cash basis taxpayers may deduct *only* the interest actually paid in the current year; the increases in the principal balance of the mortgage are treated much the same as note discount interest.

Installment Purchases. Individual taxpayers who purchase personal property or pay for educational services under a contract calling for installment payments in which carrying charges are separately stated but the interest charge cannot be determined are allowed to *impute* an interest expense. The imputed expense is allowed whether or not a payment is actually made during the tax year, and is

---

[41] See *Roger A. Schubel*, 77 T.C. 701 (1982), and *James W. Hager*, 45 TCM 123, T.C. Memo 1982-663. Note, however, that this interest deduction is subject to the rules regarding qualified residence interest.

computed at a rate of 6 percent of the *average unpaid balance* of the contract during the year.[42] The average unpaid balance is the sum of the unpaid balance outstanding on the first day of each month of the tax year, divided by 12 months.[43] Credit card and revolving charge account finance charges are generally much greater than 6 percent. Fortunately, these charges are usually stated separately at a *predetermined* interest rate (e.g., finance charge of $1\frac{1}{2}\%$ of unpaid monthly balance). Recall, however, that this type of interest expense is generally personal interest and thus subject to deduction limitations discussed earlier.

WHERE REPORTED

Like the deductions for taxes, the appropriate tax form or schedule on which deductible interest is reported depends upon the entity entitled to the deduction and the nature of the indebtedness to which the interest relates. A corporation's deductible interest is reported on its annual tax return Form 1120. Estates and trusts report interest deductions on Form 1041; partnerships and S corporations claim interest deductions on Forms 1065 and 1120S, respectively. Individuals claiming a deduction for interest expense must report the amount on the appropriate schedule of Form 1040. If the interest is related to business indebtedness—and the business is self-employment—the individual will claim his or her deduction on Schedule C (Schedule F for farmers and ranchers). Interest on debt incurred in connection with the production of rents or royalties is reported on Schedule E. Deductible interest on indebtedness incurred for personal use must be reported as an itemized deduction on Schedule A. However, any individual who has refinanced his or her home, or is otherwise subject to the limitations imposed on qualified residence interest, should see IRS Publication 936 for instructions in computing the home mortgage interest deduction.

An individual's current deduction for investment interest expense should be calculated on Form 4952 (see Appendix B), and any disallowed deduction reported as a carryover amount. The deductible amount from Form 4952 should be transferred to and claimed as a deduction on the individual's Schedule E, Form 1040 if the interest relates to the production of royalties; otherwise, the deductible amount is reported on Schedule A. Partnerships and S corporations are not allowed to deduct investment interest expense in determining income or loss. Instead, these conduit entities are required to set out and separately report each partner's or shareholder's share of *both* investment interest expense *and* net investment income for the current year. Each partner or shareholder must claim his or her deduction subject to the previously described limitations. Recall, however, that a partner that is a regular corporation will not be subject to the investment interest expense limitation.

---

[42] § 163(b)(1).   [43] *Ibid.*

RENTAL OF RESIDENCE (VACATION HOME RENTALS)

Section 280A imposes restrictions on the deduction of expenses related to rental of a residence if the taxpayer is considered as using the residence primarily for personal purposes rather than for making a profit. These restrictions are aimed at the perceived abuse existing in the area of vacation home rental. Prior to the enactment of § 280A, many felt that personal enjoyment was the predominant motive for purchasing a vacation home. Any rental of the vacation home served merely to minimize the personal expense of ownership and not to produce income.

BASIC RULES

In 1976, Congress prescribed an objective method for ascertaining the purpose of the rental activity as well as the amount of the deduction. According to this approach, the expenses incurred by the taxpayer in owning and operating the home (e.g., interest, taxes, maintenance, utilities, and depreciation) must first be allocated between personal use and rental use. The deductibility of the expenses then depends on whether the home is considered the taxpayer's *residence* or *rental property*. This latter determination is made based on the owner's personal use and the amount of rental activity.[44]

1. *Nominal Rentals:* If the residence is rented out fewer than 15 days, all rental income is excluded from gross income and no deduction is allowed for rental expenses. Otherwise allowable deductions, such as those for qualified residence interest, real estate taxes, and casualty losses may be deducted *from* A.G.I.

2. *Used as a "Residence":* If the taxpayer uses the vacation home for more than 14 days or 10 percent of the number of days the property is actually rented out, whichever is greater, the home is treated as his or her residence and deductions are restricted as explained below. A typical taxpayer caught by this rule is the owner of a vacation home who uses it for more than two weeks and rents it out to defray the cost.

   a. *Expenses allocable to the rental use:* These expenses are deductible to the extent of gross income less otherwise allowable deductions. Any deductions in excess of gross income can be carried over and deducted to the extent of any future income. These expenses are deductible *for* A.G.I. since they are related to rental use.

   b. *Expenses allocable to personal use:* Since these expenses are considered personal, they may be deducted only if they are specifically authorized by the Code. Allocable property taxes are deductible with-

---

[44] §§ 280A(c)(5) and 280A(d) through (g).

out limitation as an itemized deduction since such expenses are fully deductible regardless of the activity in which they are incurred. Interest expense may be deductible as an itemized deduction. Allocable interest is normally qualified residence interest since the home—*in this case*—is considered the taxpayer's residence (e.g., because it is used greater than 14 days). However, if the home is not the primary or secondary residence of the taxpayer (e.g., the taxpayer has several vacation homes), no deduction would be available. The other operating expenses are not deductible.

3. *Used as "Rental Property":* If the taxpayer does not use the property extensively (i.e, more than the greater of 14 days or 10 percent of the number of days rented out), then the property is effectively treated as rental property.

    a. *Expenses allocable to the rental use:* These expenses are deductible subject only to the restrictions on passive losses. If the property is rented for either (1) 1–7 days or (2) 8–30 days *and* significant services are provided, the property is *not* rental property under the passive loss rules. Thus, the treatment of any loss depends on whether the taxpayer materially participates in this "nonrental activity." If the taxpayer materially participates, any loss would not be passive and would therefore be fully deductible. (See *Example 22* earlier in this chapter). If the property is considered a rental (e.g., perhaps under the facts and circumstances test or if the rental is 8–30 days and *no* significant services are provided) and the taxpayer is considered as having met the active participation standard, the taxpayer may qualify for the rental exception under the passive loss rules. This would allow the taxpayer to deduct up to $25,000 in losses annually. Any deductions would be for A.G.I.

    b. *Expenses allocable to personal use:* As noted above, since these expenses are personal, they may be deducted only if they are specifically authorized by the Code. In this case, property taxes would continue to be fully deductible. On the other hand, none of the interest expense would be deductible as qualified residence interest since the vacation home is not considered a "residence" (because the taxpayer did *not* use it more than 14 days). However, the excess interest expense would be treated as investment interest and could be deducted to the extent of investment income. Other operating expenses would not be deductible.

This treatment is summarized in Exhibit 12-2.

For purposes of the owner use test, the number of days a unit is rented out does not include any day the unit is used for personal purposes. The unit is generally treated as used for personal purposes on any day where the owner or a member of his or her family uses it for any portion of the day for personal purposes

Exhibit 12-2
Vacation Homes
Summary of §280A Rules

Character of vacation home:	Residence	Rental property
Characterization: Personal use exceeding the greater of 1. 14 days, or 2. 10 percent of days rented out	Yes	No
Expenses allocable to rental use:	Limited to gross income by § 280A	Limited by passive loss rules Rental exception may apply
Expenses allocable to personal use: Taxes	Deductible	Deductible
Interest	Qualified residence interest	Investment interest
Other	Not deductible	Not deductible

or the unit is rented at less than a fair rental.[45] A day on which the taxpayer spends at least two-thirds of the time at the unit (or if less than two-thirds then at least eight hours) on repairs is not counted as a personal day. This is true even though individuals who accompany the taxpayer do not perform repairs or maintenance.[46]

ALLOCATION OF EXPENSES

In allocating the expenses between personal and rental use, two different methods are used. Prior to 1987, allocation of otherwise allowable deductions such as interest and taxes assumed that such expenses *accrued daily* regardless of use. Consequently, the fraction for allocating these items to the rental use was[47]

$$\text{Otherwise allowable deduction} \times \frac{\text{Number of rental days}}{365} = \text{Portion attributable to rental use}$$

---

[45] § 280A(d)(2).

[46] Prop. Reg. § 1.280A-1(e)(4) and § 280A(d)(2).

[47] *Dorance D. Bolton*, 77 T.C. 104 (1982), *aff'd.* at 82-2 USTC ¶9699, 51 AFTR2d 83-305 (CA-9, 1982).

In contrast, expenses such as utilities, maintenance, and depreciation were considered a *function of use*. As a result, the fraction used for allocating these items to the rental use was

$$\frac{\text{Operating}}{\text{expenses}} \times \frac{\text{Number of rental days}}{\text{Rental + Personal days}} = \frac{\text{Portion attributable}}{\text{to rental use}}$$

In allocating any interest and taxes, it is unclear whether the first fraction shown—which was approved by the courts prior to 1987—should still be used in light of the 1986 revisions.[48] The Senate Finance Committee Report indicates that the allocation of interest is to be made under rules similar to prior law. Yet, immediately thereafter the Report states that "interest" is to be allocated based on relative use (i.e., the second fraction above). The following example takes the approach under prior law.

> **Example 50.**   A owns a condominium in a ski resort. During the year, A uses the condominium as a secondary residence for 30 days and rents it out for 90 days. The condominium is not used the remainder of the year. A's gross rental income is $3,500. Total expenses for the entire year include maintenance and utilities of $1,000, interest of $6,200, taxes of $1,100, and $2,000 depreciation on the entire cost of the unit.
>
> A's use for 30 days is more than 14 days, the greater of 14 or 9 days (10% of the 90 days rented). For this reason, expenses attributable to the rental are deductible to the extent of gross income as reduced by otherwise allowable deductions (the interest and taxes). Deductions are computed and deducted *in the following order*:

Gross income..	$3,500
Deduct allocable portion of otherwise allowable deductions:	
Interest and taxes [$7,300 × (90 ÷ 365)]....................	− 1,800
Gross income limitation...	$1,700
Deduct allocable portion of deductions other than those otherwise allowable and depreciation:	
Utilities and maintenance	
[$1,000 × 90 ÷ (30 + 90)]...............................	− 750
Gross income limitation...	$ 950
Deduct allocable portion of depreciation:	
Depreciation [$2,000 × 90 ÷ (30 + 90)] = $1,500	
but limited to $950 balance of gross income..............	− 950
Net income..	$ 0

All of the above deductions are *for* A.G.I. The balance of interest and taxes not allocated to the rental use, $5,500 ($7,300 − $1,800), is deductible if the taxpayer itemizes deductions. Note that the interest in this case is

---

[48] § 280A(e).

qualified residence interest since the unit is treated as A's residence. The deduction for maintenance and utilities is not limited by gross income since all of the expenses attributable to the rental activity are deductible. The $250 ($1,000 − $750) remaining balance of maintenance and utilities would not be deductible in any case since it represents the expenses attributable to personal use. Of the remaining depreciation balance of $1,050 ($2,000 − $950), $550 ($1,500 − $950) attributable to the rental is not deductible due to the gross income limitation but may be carried over to subsequent years. The other $500 of depreciation is not deductible since it is the portion attributable to personal use. Also note that only the $950 of depreciation allowed is treated as a reduction in the basis of A's condominium.

Example 51. Assume the same facts as in *Example 50*, except that A used the condominium for 10 days rather than 30. Also assume that the rental is on a three-month basis to locals and no services are provided. In such case, the condominium would be treated as rental property rather than as a residence since A stayed less than 14 days. In addition, the $25,000 rental exception of the passive loss rules would apply since there is a long-term rental and no significant services are provided. A's deduction would be computed as follows:

Gross income	$3,500
Deduct allocable portion of otherwise allowable deductions	
($7,300 × 90 ÷ 365)	− 1,800
Deduct allocable portion of utilities and maintenance	
[$1,000 × 90 ÷ (90 + 10)]	− 900
Deduct allocable portion of depreciation	
[$2,000 × 90 ÷ (90 + 10)]	− 1,800
Loss	$(1,000)

In this case, a loss is created which may offset any other income of the taxpayer. In contrast to *Example 50* above, however, the balance of the interest expense, $5,500 ($7,300 − $1,800), would not be deductible as qualified residence interest since the property does not qualify as a residence. Nevertheless, the taxpayer may be able to deduct the amount as investment interest to the extent of any net investment income that he may have from other investments. Lacking investment income, the taxpayer would be better off by using the condominium more, in order that he could qualify it as a second residence and deduct the interest. The balance of the other expenses would not be deductible.

The vacation home rules, as discussed above, could operate to eliminate legitimate deductions for those taxpayers who convert their personal residence for rental during the year. In these cases, the owner usually uses the residence for more than 14 days and thus, deductions are limited. However, § 280A(d) provides relief for taxpayers in these situations. The provision accomplishes this goal by not counting as personal use days any days of personal use during the year immediately before (or after) the rental period begins (or ends). This rule, often referred to as the *qualified rental period exception*, applies only if the rental period is at least a year (or if less than a year, the house is sold at the end of the rental period).

Example 52.   B lived in her home from January through July. In August, she moved into a condominium and decided to convert her old home to rental property. B was able to find a tenant who leased the old home for a year. Under the normal rules of § 280A, B's deductions related to the old home would be limited to gross income since her personal use exceeded 14 days. The relief measure of § 280A(d) removes this limitation because the seven months of personal use preceding the one-year rental period are not counted as personal use days.

PROBLEM MATERIALS

DISCUSSION QUESTIONS

12-1 *Tax Shelters and the Solution.*   In 1982, T purchased for $10,000 an interest in Neptune III, a limited partnership created by Dandy Development Company to finance and build a 25-story office building in downtown Houston. T, who was in the 50 percent tax bracket, hoped that this investment would significantly cut her taxes.

a.   Explain the features of the investment that during that period made such investments attractive and might produce the benefits desired by T.

b.   Explain what steps Congress took in 1986 to eliminate the benefits of investments in such activities as Neptune III. Comment in some detail on the approach used by Congress to accomplish its objective.

c.   What steps might you have suggested had you been advising Congress on the restriction of tax shelters?

12-2 *Effect of Code § 469.*   D owns and operates several ski rental shops in Vail, Aspen, Beaver Creek, and Steamboat Springs. Over the years, the shops have had their ups and downs—profits some years, losses in others. Recently, D has spent less and less time at the shop, letting his employees do most of the work.

a.   What is the significance should the business be characterized as a passive activity?

b.   Should D worry about his business being treated as a passive activity? When is an activity considered passive?

c.   Does the fact that D's business is a rental operation have any bearing on the nature of the activity?

d.   What are the aggregation rules and why might they be important in D's case?

12-3 *Taxpayers Subject to § 469.*   Dr. R has been quite successful over the years. She left St. James hospital in 1973 and started her own sports medicine practice, The Sports Institute Inc., a regular C corporation. After building this operation into a thriving practice, she branched out. In 1982, she and a good friend opened their own restaurant, The Diner, a partnership. In 1985, her college roommate persuaded R to invest and buy stock in a new venture, Compatible PCs, a corporation that manufactured personal computers. Compatible PCs was owned by R and three other individuals and operated as a regular C corporation until this year, when it converted to S status. Dr. R's other investments include a single-family house that she rents out, a limited partnership interest in an oil and gas operation, and a limited partnership interest in a business that develops land into shopping centers. Explain how R is affected by the passive loss rules.

12-4 *Definition of an Activity and Planning.* D owns several businesses, including an indoor soccer facility, a gas station adjacent to the soccer facility (he bought it with the intention of someday expanding the soccer facility), and a fast-food restaurant across the street from the soccer facility. Within the soccer facility, he has rented space to a local soccer retail store. He also rents space in the facility to another company, which operates a small bar and restaurant. In any one year, each business may be profitable or may have losses. For simplicity, assume each business is operated as a sole proprietorship.

    a.   Assuming one of the businesses is profitable, would D prefer passive or active income?

    b.   Assuming one of the businesses has losses, would D prefer a passive or active loss?

    c.   Discuss the passive loss rules, how they might apply to D, and what planning might be considered. Identify as many questions as possible that might be asked in determining how the passive loss rules apply to D.

12-5 *Aggregation Rules.* Aggregation is mandatory for purposes of the material participation tests.

    a.   Explain the general rules concerning aggregation and their purpose.

    b.   Explain when this rule is beneficial and when it is detrimental for the taxpayer.

12-6 *Rental Activities and Material Participation.* T owns a 10-unit apartment complex. He not only manages the apartments but also performs all of the routine maintenance and repairs as well as keeping the books. Most of the leases that he signs with tenants are for one year. This year the complex produced a loss of $30,000. How will T treat the loss, assuming his adjusted gross income from other sources is $90,000?

12-7 *Recharacterization.* Briefly explain the purpose of the recharacterization rules and why they must not be overlooked when dealing with passive activities.

12-8 *Credits from a Passive Activity.* P is considering rehabilitating a home in a historic neighborhood. She hopes to qualify for both the rehabilitation credit as well as the low-income housing credit.

    a.   Assuming she qualifies, explain how she will compute the amount of credit that she may claim.

    b.   P's accountant has explained the limitations that apply to losses and has indicated to P that any losses on the rental that are denied currently will ultimately be allowed once P sells the property. Can the same be said of credits?

12-9 *Types of Interest Expense.* D is a spender, not a saver. In fact, he spends money he doesn't even have. This year he borrowed over $50,000 and paid interest of close to $7,000. D was shocked when his accountant told him that only certain types of interest were deductible.

    a.   Identify the different types of interest expense and explain the treatment of each.

    b.   How will D classify the interest expense that he paid?

12-10 *Deductible Interest.*   Your neighbor has come up with an excellent tax plan and he asks you for advice on structuring his scheme. He plans to give each of his five children a $10,000 promissory note, due in 20 years and bearing interest at 10 percent per year. The interest will be paid annually and he plans to claim a $5,000 interest expense deduction. Do you see any flaws in this plan? What advice would you give to your neighbor?

12-11 *Personal Interest.*   What is the current limitation imposed on the deductions of personal interest? What impact do you suppose this restriction might have on debt-financed consumer purchases?

12-12 *Classifying Interest Expenses.*   The local bank has just introduced a new loan program entitled "Home Equity Credit Line" under which individuals can either borrow funds or finance credit card purchases based on the equity they have in their homes. What is the tax incentive offered by this arrangement?

12-13 *Investment Interest Expense.*   What is the investment interest expense limitation? Which taxpayers are not subject to this limitation? What is the purpose of the limitation?

PROBLEMS

12-14 *Identifying Activities.*   For each of the following situations, indicate the number of activities in which the taxpayer participates.

   a. S owns and operates an ice cream store in Southwoods Mall. He is also a camera buff and owns a camera shop in the same mall.

   b. T owns a small "strip" shopping center that houses 10 businesses, including T's own video store. This year T received $40,000 in income from renting out space in the shopping center and grossed $60,000 from her video store.

   c. O owns five greeting card stores spread all around Denver.

   d. P owns 10 gas stations throughout the state of Georgia. Each station not only sells gas but also sells groceries. Seven of the stations derive 60 percent of their income from gas sales and 40 percent from food sales. Two of the stations derive 55 percent of their income from food sales and 45 percent from gas sales. One station also provides auto repair services and consequently derives one-third of its income from each operation.

   e. E owns a beer distributorship and ten liquor stores throughout Minneapolis. Sixty percent of the distributorship sales are to the liquor stores.

12-15   *Combining Activities.*   T owns a 70 percent interest in each of three partnerships: a radio station (WAKO), a minor league baseball team (the Harrisville Hippos), and a video and film company (Dynamite Productions) that produces short subjects for television, including advertisements. In any particular year, one business may be profitable while another may be unprofitable. Each business is at a different location. Each business also prepares its own financial statements and has its own management, although T participates extensively in the management of all three partnerships. Any financing needed for the three partnerships is usually obtained from Second National, a local bank. The radio station broadcasts all of the Hippo games, and the production company often prepares material for local television spots on the Hippos. Occasionally, some employees in one partnership assist the other partnership in periods of peak activity or emergency. Explain how the passive loss rules apply to T in this case.

12-16   *Material Participation.*   During the week, A is a mild-mannered reporter for the local paper. On the weekends, he is a partner with his brother-in-law, B, in a small van-conversion operation in Elkhart. The two typically work seven or eight hours on most Saturdays during the year. This year, the partnership suffered a loss of $10,000.

    a.   How will A treat the loss?

    b.   What planning might you suggest?

12-17   *Participation Defined.*   Three recent Purdue graduates—C, D, and E—formed their own lawn treatment company. Each of the three participates on a part-time basis because each is otherwise employed on a full-time basis. In this, their first year of operations, C spent 40 hours, D spent 70 hours, and E contributed 80 hours. E's wife also kept the books for the partnership. Explain whether C, D, and E satisfy the material participation test.

12-18   *Material Participation.*   F is an accountant with a large C.P.A. firm. She also has an interest in two partnerships: a night club and a family-owned drugstore. F maintains the accounting records for each partnership, spending 200 hours working for the night club and 400 hours for the drugstore.

    a.   How will F treat any losses that the partnerships might have?

    b.   How will F treat any income that the partnerships might have?

12-19   *Material Participation.*   In 1972, H started his own replacement window business, Sting Construction, an S corporation. Up until 1985, H had been the sole shareholder. In 1985, he sold 90 percent of his stock to J and K, who continued the business. From time to time, H still provides advice to J and K. This year, H spent 300 hours working for the company. J and K each devoted 1,500 hours to the business. Unfortunately, the corporation suffered a loss this year because of a downturn in the economy. How will H treat the loss?

12-20   *Rental or Nonrental Activities.*   Indicate whether the following are rental or nonrental activities.

    a.   P owns an airplane. She has an arrangement with a flying club at a small airport to lease the plane out on a short-term basis to its students. Most of the time the plane is rented for two to three hours.

    b.   Q owns a condominium in Aspen that he rents out during the year. The average stay is one week. Q has arranged to provide daily maid and linen service for the unit. In addition, his monthly condominium fee pays for maintenance of the common areas.

c.   S and his wife, T, own White Silver Sands, a posh resort on the coast of Florida. As part of its package, the resort provides everything a vacationer could want (daily maid service, free use of the golf, tennis, and pool facilities, an on-site masseuse, etc.). The average stay is two weeks.

d.   Z owns a duplex near the University of Texas that she normally rents out to students on a long-term basis. The average stay is nine months. Z provides typical landlord services such as repairs and maintenance.

e.   B owns Quiet Quarters, a retirement home for the elderly. The home's staff includes a physician and several nurses.

f.   C owns and operates Body Beautiful, a fitness club. The club has over 1,000 members, who have use of the club daily from 6 A.M. to 11 P.M.

g.   D owns a 200-acre parcel of land on the outskirts of Lubbock. The land is worth $700,000 (basis $200,000). During the year, D leased the land to a local car enthusiast who used it as a raceway. D collected rents of $5,000.

12-21   *Passive Activities.*   G is the head chef for TWF Airlines making a salary of $70,000 a year. In addition, his investment income is about $20,000 a year. Over the years, G has made numerous investments and has been a participant in many ventures. Indicate whether the passive activity rules would apply in each of the following situations.

a.   A $10,000 loss from G's interest in Flimsy Flims, a limited partnership. G is a limited partner.

b.   A $5,000 loss from G's interest as a shareholder in D's Bar and Grill, an S corporation. G and his wife operate the bar. Each spent 300 hours working there in the current year.

c.   G and his friend, F, are equal partners in a partnership that produces and markets a Texas-style barbecue sauce. G leaves the management of the day-to-day operations to F. However, G spent 130 hours working in the business during the current year. For the year, the partnership had income of $15,000. Assume that this is G's *only* investment.

d.   Same as (c) except G has an ownership interest in three other distinctly different activities (e.g., construction and consulting). He spends 130 hours in each of the four activities.

e.   G is a 10 percent partner in a restaurant consulting firm. The firm operates the business on the bottom floor of a three-story building which it owns. The firm leases the other two floors to a law firm and a real estate company. The consulting side of the business reported a $100,000 profit from consulting, $5,000 in interest income, and had a loss from the rental operation.

f.   G is the sole owner of Try, Inc., a regular C corporation which produces G's special salad dressing. The corporation had an operating profit of $4,000. In addition, Try, Inc. had interest income of $5,000 and a $7,000 loss from its investment in a real estate limited partnership in which it was a limited partner.

12-22 *Passive Activity Limitations.* M is a successful banker. Two years ago, M's 27-year-old son, J, asked his dad to become his partner in opening a sporting goods store. M agreed and contributed $50,000 for a 50 percent interest in the partnership. J operates the store on his own, receiving little advice from his father. Information regarding M's financial activities reveals the following for the past two years:

Year	Salary	Interest Income	Partnership Income (Loss)
1992	$100,000	$20,000	$(40,000)
1993	100,000	20,000	12,000

All parties are cash basis, calendar year taxpayers. Answer the following questions.

  a. How did M's investment in the partnership affect his A.G.I. in 1992?
  b. How did M's investment in the partnership affect his A.G.I. in 1993?
  c. Would your answer to (b) change if the partnership had a loss in 1993 and the income shown was from M's interest as a limited partner in a real estate venture?
  d. On January 1, 1994, M sold his interest in the partnership to his son for a $40,000 gain. What effect?

12-23 *Passive Activity Limitations: Rental Property.* L, single, is the chief of surgery at a local hospital. During the year, L earned a salary of $120,000. L owns a four-unit apartment that she rents out unfurnished. The current tenants have one-year leases, which expire at various times. This year, the property produced a loss of $30,000 due to accelerated depreciation. L is actively involved in the rental activity, making many of the decisions regarding leases, repairs, etc.

  a. How much of the loss may L deduct?
  b. Would the answer to (a) change if L materially participated?

12-24 *Suspended Losses.* When tax shelter activity was at its highest, G was one of its biggest proponents. Currently, she still owns an interest in several limited partnerships. She is now considering what she should do in light of the passive loss rules. To help her make this decision, she has put together her best guess as to the performance of her investments over the next two years. These are shown below.

Activity	1991	1992
X	$(7,000)	$(2,000)
Y	(3,000)	(9,000)
Z	6,000	1,000

  a. Determine the amount of suspended loss for each activity at the end of 1991 and 1992.
  b. Assume the same facts as in (a) above, except assume that in 1992 G sells the Y activity for a $4,000 gain. Explain the effect of the disposition on any suspended losses G might have, including the amount of suspended losses to be carried forward to 1993.

12-25 *Characterizing Income.*   Indicate whether the income in the following situations is passive or nonpassive.

   a.   Ten years ago, T purchased a strip of land for $300,000. Shortly thereafter, he built an office building on the land for $100,000. He currently leases the entire building to a large corporation on a ten-year lease for $90,000 annually. This year he sold the building for $700,000.

   b.   Q owns a real estate development business that she operates as an S corporation. In 1990, she purchased a vacant lot for $100,000. Q proceeded to put in roads, sewers, and other amenities at a cost of $50,000. Shortly thereafter, she contracted for the construction of a warehouse at a cost of $1 million. Upon completion of the building in September 1990, Q began leasing the space. It was completely leased by June 1991. In December 1992, she sold the property for $2 million.

   c.   T owns 100 percent of the stock of Z Corporation, an S corporation that operates a construction company. This year T purchased and leased a crane to the corporation. T received total rents of $10,000.

   d.   X operates a travel agency and an office supply store to which she devotes 300 and 100 hours, respectively. The travel agency produced a profit of $10,000 while the office supply business sustained a loss of $40,000.

12-26 *Interest Expense—Note Discount.*   Taxpayer T signed a note for $2,000 on August 30, 1991, agreeing to pay back the loan in 12 equal installments beginning September 30, 1991. The 12 percent interest charge ($2,000 $\times$ 12% = $240) was subtracted from the face amount of the note and T received $1,760, all of which was used to purchase furniture for his business. T uses the calendar year as his taxable year.

   a.   If T is a cash basis taxpayer and he makes the four payments scheduled for 1991, what is his deduction for interest on the note in 1991? In 1992?

   b.   Would your answers to (a) change if T were an accrual method taxpayer? Explain.

12-27 *Investment Interest Expense.*   R, a cash basis, single taxpayer, paid $17,000 of investment interest expense during 1991. R uses the calendar year for tax purposes and reports the following investment income: $1,500 interest income, and $3,500 long-term capital gain on the sale of investment property.

   a.   How much of the investment interest expense is deductible by R in 1991?

   b.   What must R do with any investment interest expense deduction which is disallowed for 1991?

   c.   Would it make any difference in your answers to (a) and (b) above if R were married and filing a separate tax return? Explain.

12-28 *Investment Interest Expense Limitation.* L is an engineer. This year, she borrowed $300,000 and purchased 40 acres south of Houston. For the year, L paid interest of $30,000 on the loan. Her tax records revealed the following additional information.

Income:	
Salary	$ 50,000
Dividends....................................	8,000
Long-term capital gain	3,000
Short-term capital loss	(1,000)
Share of partnership income:	
Ordinary loss	(3,000)
Portfolio income:	
Interest and dividends....................	1,000
Rental income	8,000
Expenses:	
Rental expenses.............................	7,000
Qualified residence interest	10,000
Property tax on land	5,000
Investment publications	400
Professional dues, licenses and subscriptions..	1,100

The items noted concerning the partnership result from L's limited partnership interest in Country Homes, a real estate development. The rental income is derived from a four-unit apartment complex that is currently filled with tenants with one-year leases. The related rental expenses include $2,000 of interest expense on the debt to acquire the apartments. Compute L's deduction for investment interest expense this year.

12-29 *Business Interest Expense.* R is an employee of a television repair shop. He uses his own truck solely for business, making customer service calls. During the year, he paid $900 interest on a loan on his truck. According to R, the interest is deductible since it is an ordinary and necessary expense incurred in carrying on his business. Comment.

12-30 *Interest Expense Limitations.* Indicate in each of the following cases the amount of interest expense that the taxpayer is allowed to deduct.

a. During the year, H used his bank credit card to purchase a new stereo for his teenage daughter. Finance charges for the year were $70.

b. Over the years, G has consistently borrowed against her insurance policies because of their low rates. This year, she paid interest of $1,100 on the loans.

c. D lives and works in Birmingham. He owns a house there as well as a summer home at Hilton Head and a condominium at Sun Valley. He paid interest expense of $6,000 on loans on each unit.

d. B owns a home in Denver which she purchased in 1977 for $70,000. The current balance on B's mortgage loan is $60,000 and the property is worth $150,000. During the year, B obtained a second mortgage on her home, receiving $20,000 which she used to pay off her two outstanding car loans. Interest on the first mortgage was $4,000 while interest on the second mortgage was $1,000.

e. M is a heavy trader of stocks and bonds, using his margin account frequently. This year, interest expense charged on his margin purchases was $1,200. M's investment income was $900.

12-31   *Rental versus Nonrental Activities.* Identify rental activities that would not be considered "rental activities" for purposes of the passive loss rules.

12-32   *Vacation Home Rental.*   S owns a condominium in Florida which he and his family use occasionally. During the year, he used the condominium for 20 days and rented it for 40 days. The remainder of the year, the condominium was vacant. S compiled the following information related to the condominium for the entire year:

Rental income	$1,000
Expenses:	
Interest on mortgage	3,650
Maintenance	900
Depreciation	6,000

a.   Compute the tax effect of the rental activity on S.

b.   Assuming S only used the condominium personally for ten days, compute the tax effect.

c.   Assuming S only rented the condominium for 14 days, compute the tax effect.

12-33   *Vacation Home—Personal Use Days.*   Indicate the number of personal use days in each of the following situations.

a.   Saturday morning, March 3, S drove to Vail to replace a hot water heater in his vacation home. He arrived in Vail at 9 A.M. and skied until late afternoon when he retired to his condominium at 6 P.M. After dinner, he worked on replacing the hot water heater until midnight when he went to sleep. The following morning he awoke and went skiing until 5 P.M. when he returned home.

b.   Same as (a) except S's wife and family accompanied him. S's family also skied but did not perform any repairs or maintenance related to the vacation home.

c.   T owns a duplex which he rents. On February 1 of this year, the one-year lease of the tenant living upstairs expired and she moved. Unable to rent the upstairs unit, T moved in on December 1 and remained through the end of the year.

PART **IV**

ALTERNATIVE MINIMUM TAX AND TAX CREDITS

CONTENTS

LEARNING OBJECTIVES

Upon completion of this chapter you will be able to:

- Explain the tax policy reasons underlying the Alternative Minimum Tax (AMT) system

- Understand the conceptual framework of the system and understand the terminology necessary to communicate AMT issues or concerns to a tax professional

- Determine the amount of AMT adjustments, preferences, and exemptions, and calculate the alternative minimum taxable income, the tentative minimum tax, and the AMT

- Complete Form 6251, Alternative Minimum Tax - Individuals

- Explain the tax policy reasons for enacting recent tax incentives in the form of tax credits rather than deductions

- Distinguish between nonrefundable tax credits subject to dollar limitations and refundable tax credits, which have no such limitations

- Understand the components of the general business credit and be able to calculate the amount of credit allowable with respect to each separate component

- Identify and calaculate the nonbusiness tax credits, including the child and dependent care credit, the credit for the elderly, the earned income credit, and the minimum tax credit

- Understand and apply the tax credit carryover, carryback, and recapture rules

CHAPTER OUTLINE

Chapter **13**

THE ALTERNATIVE MINIMUM TAX AND TAX CREDITS

INTRODUCTION

Congress has for many years utilized the income tax system to affect the behavior of the U.S. citizenry. Congressional concerns are usually translated into statutory language that provides special tax incentives[1] for taxpayers to make expenditures in furtherance of the prescribed goals. Tax incentives (also known as tax preferences) can take the form of a current deduction for some expenditures,[2] accelerated cost recovery or amortization for other expenditures,[3] and income tax credits that directly reduce the income tax liability for still other expenditures.[4] As the number of tax preferences grew, adroit tax advisors were able to devise legal methods of structuring business and investment deals that utilized the statutory incentives so well that it became common for very wealthy individuals with large gross incomes to pay little or no income tax. Recognizing that a problem existed with the perceived fairness of the income tax system in 1969, Congress took action to ensure that all wealthy individuals paid at least some Federal income tax. However, instead of removing from the Code the original tax preferences which created the tax savings opportunities, Congress chose to add another layer of taxation, referred to as the minimum tax. Since 1969, the minimum tax has steadily grown in scope and importance in the Federal income taxation scheme. Major changes were made in the minimum tax in 1976, 1978, 1981, 1982, and again in 1986. The Tax Reform Act of 1986 overhauled the minimum tax rules, making it still more difficult for both individuals and corporations to use certain tax preference expenditures to avoid paying tax.

---

[1] See "Goals of Taxation" discussion in Chapter 1.

[2] See for example, expenditures for research and experimental purposes (§ 174), circulation (§ 173), and intangible drilling and development costs [§ 263(c)].

[3] In general, ACRS deductions (§ 168) and amortization of pollution control facilities (§ 169).

[4] As examples, expenditures for child care (§ 21), qualified clinical testing expenses (§ 29), or qualified expenditures on low-income housing [§ 42(a)].

One of the purposes of this chapter is to provide an overview and a working knowledge of the current alternative minimum tax as it applies to individuals and corporations. This chapter also examines the incentives giving rise to the income tax credits. Tax credits are identified and their operational rules are illustrated.

ALTERNATIVE MINIMUM TAX

POLICY OBJECTIVES

The Tax Reform Act (TRA) of 1986 overhauled the minimum tax provisions for all taxpayers for taxable years after 1986. Noncorporate (i.e., individuals, estates, and trusts) and corporate taxpayers are subject to the new and tougher alternative minimum tax (AMT) imposed by Code § 55. The policy underlying the tightened rules is explained in the following excerpt taken from the Senate Finance Committee Report on the TRA of 1986.

Reasons for Change

> The committee believes that the minimum tax should serve one overriding objective: to ensure that no taxpayer with substantial economic income can avoid significant tax liability by using exclusions, deductions, and credits. Although these provisions may provide incentives for worthy goals, they become counterproductive when taxpayers are allowed to use them to avoid virtually all tax liability. The ability of high-income individuals and highly profitable corporations to pay little or no tax undermines respect for the entire tax system and, thus, for the incentive provisions themselves. In addition, even aside from public perceptions, the committee believes that it is inherently unfair for high-income individuals and highly profitable corporations to pay little or no tax due to their ability to utilize various tax preferences.[5]

Accordingly, the revised AMT was designed to ensure that the tax liability is at least a minimum percentage of a broad-based concept of income, less related expenses and certain personal or unavoidable expenditures. The intent of the legislation is to increase tax levies on certain wealthy taxpayers.

Under the new AMT rules, taxpayers must make a completely separate tax calculation to determine the *tentative minimum tax*; if the tentative minimum tax is greater than the regular tax liability, the taxpayer will have to pay the higher amount. The upshot of the new rules is that the separate tax calculations force taxpayers to keep a separate set of books just to compute the AMT.

---

[5] Senate Finance Committee Report. H.R. 3838, Page 518, U.S. Government Printing Office, May 29, 1986.

OVERVIEW OF AMT

Calculation of the tentative minimum tax requires several steps: (1) determination of alternative minimum taxable income (AMTI), (2) computation of the exemption amount, and (3) determination of the gross AMT—but the starting point is the regular taxable income of the taxpayer.[6] (A conceptual framework of the AMT calculation is presented in Exhibit 13-1.) In the first step, regular taxable income is *adjusted* for several items that may have been subject to accelerated deductions for regular tax but which must be capitalized and deducted over a longer period for AMT purposes. Adjustments in this category include cost recovery deductions, mining exploration and development costs, and deductions for pollution control facilities. Additional adjustments are required for income items that may have been deferred or excluded from the regular tax but are required to be included in current income for AMT purposes. For example, when incentive stock options (ISOs) are exercised, the "spread" between the option price and the fair market value of the stock—the so-called bargain element—may be included as current income for AMT purposes in the year of exercise, but is not included in regular taxable income until the year in which the stock acquired with the ISOs is sold. For individuals, the AMT system imposes severe limits on the allowable

---

Exhibit 13-1
*The Alternative Minimum Tax
Conceptual Framework*

Start with:	Regular taxable income..............................	$xxx,xxx
Plus/Minus:	AMT adjustments (see Exhibit 13-2).................	± xx,xxx
	Adjustment for passive activity losses................	+ x,xxx
	Adjustment for farm shelter losses...................	+ x,xxx
Equals:	AMT adjusted taxable income........................	$xxx,xxx
Plus:	Sum of tax preference items (see Exhibit 13-3).......	+ xx,xxx
Equals:	Alternative minimum taxable income (AMTI)..........	$xxx,xxx
Less:	Exemption amount (adjusted for phase-out)..........	− xx,xxx
Equals:	AMTI base..	$xxx,xxx
Times:	AMT rate...	× xx%
Equals:	Gross alternative minimum tax......................	$ xx,xxx
Less:	AMT foreign tax credit.............................	− x,xxx
Equals:	Tentative alternative minimum tax...................	$ xx,xxx
Less:	Regular tax liability................................	− x,xxx
Equals:	Alternative minimum tax............................	$ xx,xxx

---

[6] § 55(b)(2).

itemized deductions, and for corporations a special inclusion in AMT income is required for 75 percent of the adjusted current earnings of the corporation that exceed the corporation's alternative minimum taxable income otherwise subject to the AMT. The first step also includes making adjustments to losses allowed for regular tax purposes on passive activities and farm shelter activities. The AMT system requires that the passive activity loss (PAL) and farm activity loss (FAL) be calculated separately using allowable AMT accounting rules. The difference between the loss computed under the regular tax rules and that computed under the AMT rules is the amount of the adjustment that must be taken into account in the computation of the alternative minimum taxable income. The AMT adjustments are summarized in Exhibit 13-2.

The second step requires certain items of tax preference to be added to the AMT adjusted taxable income—resulting in alternative minimum taxable income (AMTI). Tax preference items include the tax incentives related to the deduction for percentage depletion and intangible drilling and development costs, certain charitable contributions of appreciated capital gain property, and certain tax-exempt interest income. Tax preference items are summarized in Exhibit 13-3.

> **Example 1.** K has taxable income of $92,500, on which she is required to pay a regular income tax of $24,551. In computing her regular taxable income, she utilized regular tax incentives that resulted in $55,000 of AMT adjustments and $35,000 of AMT tax preference items. K's alternative minimum taxable income is $182,500 ($92,500 + $55,000 + $35,000).

After the AMTI is computed, it is reduced by an exemption amount (which is phased out for AMTI in excess of certain ceiling amounts) and the result is multiplied by the AMT tax rate to arrive at the gross AMT. The tentative AMT is equal to the gross AMT reduced by the allowable AMT foreign tax credit, if any. If the tentative AMT is greater than the regular tax liability, the excess tax is imposed on the taxpayer and is referred to as the AMT. In general, the regular tax for this purpose means the regular income tax imposed by § 1 or § 11, reduced only by the foreign tax credit. While this nomenclature may be confusing, it is important to recognize that even though the regular income tax and the alternative minimum tax are imposed by different statutory provisions, the amount that the taxpayer will have to pay the IRS is equal to the tentative AMT.

Implicit in the AMT formula is the fact that regular income tax credits (other than the foreign tax credit) *cannot* be used to reduce the AMT liability. There is, however, one exception applicable to corporations. Up to 25 percent of a corporate taxpayer's AMT can be offset with prior years' investment tax credit carryovers.[7] Investment tax credit computations and carryovers are discussed in a later section of this chapter.

---

[7]   § 38(c)(3).

AMT RATES AND EXEMPTIONS

Tax Rates. The AMT rate for individuals, estates, and trusts is currently 24 percent.[8] For corporate taxpayers, the minimum tax rate is 20 percent.

AMT Exemptions. In order to shield taxpayers with small tax preference amounts from the minimum tax, the Code provides an *exemption* that shelters some AMTI from the minimum tax.[9] The exemption amount for a noncorporate taxpayer is based on the taxpayer's filing status. The exemption amounts are

1. $40,000 if married filing jointly or a surviving spouse;

2. $30,000 for single individuals; and

3. $20,000 if married filing separately or an estate or trust.

Exemption Phase-Out. To prevent taxpayers with large AMT tax preferences and adjustments from taking advantage of these exemptions, the Code contains an "exemption phase-out rule." Specifically, the exemption amounts are reduced (but not below zero) by 25 cents for each $1 that the AMTI *exceeds* (1) $150,000 for joint filers and surviving spouses; (2) $112,500 for single taxpayers; and (3) $75,000 for married taxpayers filing separate returns and for estates and trusts.

Example 2.   Assume the same facts as in *Example 1*. Because K's $182,500 AMTI exceeds the $112,500 threshold by $70,000, her exemption amount must be reduced by $17,500 ($70,000 × 0.25). Thus, the allowable exemption for the year is equal to $12,500 ($30,000 − $17,500).

K's AMT is $16,249, computed as follows:

Regular taxable income	$ 92,500
Plus: AMT adjustments	+ 55,000
AMT adjusted taxable income	$147,500
Plus: AMT preference items	+ 35,000
AMTI	$182,500
Less: Exemption amount	− 12,500
AMTI base	$170,000
Times: AMT rate	× 24%
Gross AMT	$ 40,800
Less: AMT foreign tax credit	− 0
Tentative AMT	$ 40,800
Less: Regular tax liability	− 24,551
AMT	$ 16,249

---

[8] § 55(b). For taxable years beginning before January 1, 1991, the minimum tax rate was 21 percent for individuals, estates, and trusts.

[9] § 55(d).

The phase-out rule will completely eliminate the $40,000 exemption at $310,000 [($310,000 − $150,000 = $160,000) × 0.25 = $40,000] of AMTI, the $30,000 exemption at $232,500 of AMTI, and the $20,000 exemption at $155,000 of AMTI.

The exemption amount for corporate taxpayers is $40,000. The exemption is phased out at the rate of 25 cents for each dollar of corporate AMTI in excess of $150,000. The exemption amount is completely phased out for corporations with AMTI of at least $310,000 or more.

ADJUSTMENTS IN COMPUTING AMTI

All taxpayers must determine their alternative minimum taxable income (AMTI) as an integral part of determining the alternative minimum tax liability. As previously mentioned, this determination involves two types of modifications to taxable income, known as *adjustments* and *tax preference items*. Adjustments usually result in a disparity in basis between the regular tax and the minimum tax and, therefore, require a separate accounting supported by a permanent record which is used to determine the minimum tax in a subsequent year. The separate records are required to compute future deductions for minimum tax purposes and to determine the gain or loss on the disposition or abandonment of an asset for minimum tax purposes. Thus, adjustments can generally be thought of as timing differences, where the accounting treatment of an item increases AMTI for minimum tax purposes in the early years, reverses, and actually reduces the amount included in the AMTI in later years.

The second type of modification, tax preference items, generally requires only a side calculation made independently on an annual basis to determine an amount of preference, which is added to the adjusted taxable income to determine AMTI. Generally, tax preference items are analogous to permanent differences between the regular tax and the minimum tax.

The adjustments for AMTI are listed in Exhibit 13-2 and examined in detail below. The adjustments applicable to all taxpayers are discussed first, followed by a discussion of those adjustments applicable only to individuals, then those applicable only to corporations, and finally, the special tax shelter loss adjustments. Tax preference items are discussed in the next section of this chapter.

Adjustments Applicable to All Taxpayers. There are *six* adjustments in determining the AMTI applicable to all taxpayers.[10] Each of these is discussed below.[11]

---

[10]   § 56.

[11]   The adjustment for installment sales of certain inventory property is of limited applicability and is not covered in this text. See § 56(a)(6) for details. Also, the Revenue Reconciliation Act of 1990 added an adjustment based on energy preferences available to taxpayers engaged in oil and gas exploration, development, or operations other than integrated oil companies. This adjustment is equal to the lesser of the alternative tax energy preference deduction or 40 percent of AMTI. It is industry specific and is therefore not covered in detail in this text . For more details on the alternative tax energy preference deduction see § 56(h).

Exhibit 13-2
AMT Adjustments Requiring Separate Calculations

Applicable to All Taxpayers

Cost recovery deductions
Mining exploration and development costs
Gains reported on the completed-contract method
Pollution control facility expenditures
Net operating losses
Gains or losses recognized on asset dispositions

Applicable Only to Individuals

Itemized deductions
Circulation and research expenditures
Standard deduction
Personal exemptions
Adjustment to income for tax refunds
Gains from incentive stock options (ISOs)

Applicable Only to Corporations

Corporate adjustment for current earnings

Special Tax Shelter Loss Adjustments

Farm shelter losses
Passive activity losses

1. *Cost Recovery.* Taxpayers who use MACRS for cost recovery purposes for property *placed in service after* 1986 must recompute their recovery deductions for minimum tax purposes under the Alternative Depreciation System (ADS). As discussed in Chapter 9, the Alternative Depreciation System requires straight-line depreciation, utilizing the appropriate convention, over the class life of the property for personal property, or 40 years for real property. There is, however, a major exception to this system for minimum tax purposes. For all personal property (other than films and video tape, sound recordings, public utility property, and assets depreciated using unit-of-production method), the Code allows a 150 percent declining-balance method over the ADR class life of the asset, switching to straight-line for the first taxable year that using the straight-line method will yield a higher

allowance.[12] The 150 percent declining-balance method will not apply to assets for which the taxpayer has elected the straight-line method for regular tax purposes. An adjustment for accelerated depreciation deductions is not required for assets placed in service before 1987, but the accelerated deductions may give rise to tax preference items, as discussed in the following section.

As a rule of thumb, if the asset is depreciated under old ACRS or pre-ACRS, the accelerated depreciation will give rise to a tax preference item. However, if the asset is depreciated under the MACRS system, an adjustment will be required.

Example 3.   T placed an asset costing $100,000 in service on February 5, 1991. Assume the asset is "3-year property" and has an ADR class life of 3 years. The effect on the minimum tax is computed below assuming that the 150 percent declining-balance method was used for AMT purposes.

	1991	1992	1993	1994
Regular tax deduction 200%	$33,330	$44,450	$14,810	$ 7,410
AMT deduction (150%)......	− 25,000	− 37,500	− 25,000	− 12,500
Effect of adjustment on AMTI	$ 8,330	$ 6,950	($10,190)	($ 5,090)
	increase	increase	decrease	decrease

As illustrated in *Example 3*, as property ages, the regular tax deduction will be less than the AMT deduction, and the excess AMT depreciation deduction with respect to a specific asset will reduce AMTI in 1993 or 1994. The amount of the adjustment is even greater if the ADS system is used for AMT purposes.

Using a different deduction for AMT causes a taxpayer to have a different adjusted basis for regular tax purposes and AMT purposes. Accordingly, the amount of gain or loss if the property is sold may be different. In essence, the taxpayer must maintain a *second set of books* for depreciable assets.

---

[12]   § 56(a)(1)(A)(ii).

Example 4.   Assume the same facts as in *Example 3*, except that the taxpayer uses the ADS system. Also assume that the property has an ADR class life of 3 years.

	1991	1992	1993	1994
Regular tax deduction (200%)...	$33,330	$44,450	$14,810	$ 7,410
AMT deduction (ADS)...........	− 16,670	− 33,330	− 33,330	− 16,670
Effect of adjustment on AMTI	$16,660	$11,120	($18,520)	($ 9,260)
	increase	increase	decrease	decrease

Recognizing the burdensome task of maintaining one set of depreciation books for each tax system, Congress provided taxpayers an *election* that allows the Alternative Depreciation System (ADS) to be used for regular tax purposes. If the administrative burden of maintaining two sets of books for depreciation is substantial, and the taxpayer agrees to stretching out the depreciation deduction for regular tax purposes, an election to use the ADS for all purposes can simplify the reporting procedures required by the AMT by eliminating this adjustment.[13]

Example 5.   Assume the same facts as in *Example 4*, except that T elects to use the ADS for all purposes. In this case, the need for an adjustment for AMT purposes is eliminated.

	1990	1991	1992	1993
Regular tax deduction (ADS)	$16,670	$33,330	$33,330	$16,670
AMT deduction (ADS).......	− 16,670	− 33,330	− 33,330	− 16,670
Effect of adjustment on AMTI	$ 0	$ 0	$ 0	$ 0

Taxpayers can obtain the same results in *Example 5* above by electing to depreciate an asset over its ADR class life at the 150 percent (declining balance) rate.[14]

Given this elaborate scheme to curtail accelerated depreciation deductions for AMT purposes, it is surprising that the election to expense property under § 179 does not give rise to an AMT depreciation adjustment, but current first year § 179 depreciation deductions allowed for regular tax purposes are also allowed for AMT purposes.[15]

---

[13]   § 168(g)(7).

[14]   See §§ 168(b)(2), 168(c)(2), and 56(a)(1)(A)(ii).

[15]   *Supra*, Footnote 5, page 552, note 5.

2. *Mining Exploration and Development Costs.* Mining exploration and development costs that are currently expensed[16] on a mineral property for regular tax purposes are required to be capitalized and amortized ratably over a ten-year period for minimum tax purposes. However, for minimum tax purposes the taxpayer is allowed to use the higher adjusted basis in the mineral property for reporting gain or loss on a disposition or an abandonment. The "extra set of books" is required to account for the disparity in basis between the two tax systems (i.e., regular tax versus AMT).

3. *Long-Term Contracts.* The taxable income from long-term contracts must be determined under the percentage-of-completion method of accounting for minimum tax purposes.[17]

4. *Pollution Control Facilities.* Taxpayers using the 60-month amortization rule[18] on certified pollution control facilities are required to compute depreciation under the Alternative Depreciation System for minimum tax purposes.[19] The basis of the property and the amount of gain or loss upon disposition is to be computed for minimum tax purposes by taking into account the depreciation deduction allowable for minimum tax purposes.[20]

5. *Alternative Tax Net Operating Loss (ATNOL) Deduction.* An ATNOL is allowed as a deduction for minimum tax purposes.[21] The procedure for computing the ATNOL parallels its cousin, the regular tax NOL, but the ATNOL must be determined taking into consideration all of the AMT adjustments and tax preference items. In addition, the amount of the ATNOL is *limited* to 90 percent of the AMTI determined without regard to this deduction.

6. *Gains or Losses on Asset Dispositions.* If the adjusted basis of an asset is different for the regular tax system and the AMT system and the asset is disposed of in a taxable transaction, an adjustment to regular taxable income will be required in the computation of the AMTI. The amount of the adjustment is equal to the difference in recognized gain or loss attributable to the disposition in each separate tax system.[22]

---

[16] §§ 616 and 617 allow a current deduction for these expenditures.

[17] § 56(a)(3).

[18] § 169.

[19] § 56(a)(5).

[20] § 56(a)(7).

[21] § 56(a)(4).

[22] § 56(a)(7).

Adjustments Applicable Only to Individuals. Each of the *six* adjustments applicable only to individual taxpayers are discussed below.

1. *Alternative Tax Itemized Deductions.*   With two exceptions and two modifications, the majority of the itemized deductions for regular tax purposes are allowed as alternative tax itemized deductions (ATIDs). The regular tax deductions not allowed as ATIDs are miscellaneous itemized deductions and itemized deductions relating to the payment of any tax. In addition, any limitations applicable to a specific regular itemized deduction also apply to the ATID, and two of these deductions (medical and interest) are subject to further modifications. However, the 3 percent cutback rule applicable to certain regular tax itemized deductions *does not* apply under the minimum tax system.[23] ATIDs include the following items:[24]

   a. Medical expenses, but *only in excess* of 10 percent of A.G.I.

   b. Interest expense consisting of

      (1) Qualified housing interest

      (2) Investment interest expense to the extent of net investment income

   c. Charitable contributions

   d. Theft, casualty, and wagering losses

   e. Moving expenses

   f. Estate tax deductions resulting from reporting income in respect of a decedent under § 691

   g. Impairment-related work expenses[25]

   h. Bond premium amortization deductions

   The above list is self-explanatory with the exception of the amount of interest that will be allowed as an ATID. Several new terms and concepts regarding the deduction for interest were developed and incorporated into the alternative minimum tax scheme. *Qualified housing interest* is interest paid or accrued on indebtedness incurred after June 30, 1982, in acquiring, constructing, or substantially rehabilitating property that is a principal

---

[23] § 56(b)(1)(F).

[24] See § 67(b) for a complete list of itemized deductions that are allowed as ATIDs. Also

note that a standard deduction is not allowed for AMT purposes.

[25] § 67(d).

residence (as defined in Code § 1034) or qualified dwelling.[26] For indebtedness incurred *before* July 1, 1982, a deduction can be taken for interest paid or accrued on a debt that, at that time, was secured by a qualified dwelling without regard for the purpose or use of the proceeds of the indebtedness. The essence of this rule is that interest on home second mortgages established after 1982 will not be deductible for AMT purposes as qualified housing interest *unless* the proceeds were used to improve the principal residence.

When interest rates fall, taxpayers often refinance their homes, and a question had arisen about the interest paid on a loan (new loan) the proceeds of which were used to pay off the original qualified housing indebtedness (old loan). The TRA of 1986 resolved the issue by allowing an interest expense deduction for AMT purposes on the new loan used to refinance the principal residence, but only to the extent that the new loan does not exceed the outstanding balance of the old loan.[27]

Investment interest expense is allowed as an ATID, but only to the extent of qualified *adjusted* net investment income.[28] The adjustment in computing the net investment income is required for AMT purposes as a result of including a portion of the tax-exempt interest income from specified private activity bonds (SPAB) as a tax preference item that increases the AMTI (see *Example 11* for details relating to the tax-exempt income preference item). If exempt interest income from SPABs is included as a preference item for AMT purposes, the interest expense incurred with respect to it will be allowed as a deduction for AMT purposes. These adjustments for tax-exempt income and its related interest expenses are also allowed in computing the "adjusted" net investment income for AMT purposes.

2. *Circulation and Research Expenditures.* Amounts paid or incurred that are allowable as a deduction for circulation [29] expenditures in computing the regular tax must be capitalized and amortized over a three-year period beginning with the taxable year in which the expenditures were made. The same rule applies to research and experimental expenditures, except the amortization period is ten years.[30] However, the Revenue Reconciliation Act of 1989 repealed the AMT adjustment for research expenses of indi-

---

[26] A qualified dwelling is a house, apartment, condominium, or mobile home (not used on a transient basis). Qualified dwelling for AMT is a narrow definition and differs from that of Code § 280A(f)(1), which broadly defines a dwelling unit as a house, apartment, condominium, mobile home, boat, or similar property.

[27] § 56(e)(1).

[28] See Chapter 12 for a discussion of the investment interest deduction limitation.

[29] § 173.

[30] § 56(b)(2)(A)(ii).

viduals who materially participate in the activity in which research expenses are incurred. The repealer is effective for taxable years beginning after December 31, 1990.[31] As with other adjustments that create a disparity between basis for regular tax and basis for AMT, separate records must be maintained to determine the allowable amortization deduction in subsequent years or the gain or loss on disposition or abandonment.

3. *Gains from Incentive Stock Options (ISOs).* For regular tax purposes, the bargain element of ISOs is *not* required to be included in income either at the time the option is granted or when the option is exercised;[32] however, an income adjustment may be required for the AMT. The income adjustment with respect to stock received from options exercised after December 31, 1987 is determined under the principles of Code § 83. Assuming the stock acquired is not subject to substantial risk of forfeiture, the adjustment to AMTI is equal to the amount by which the value of the share at the time of exercise exceeds the option price.[33] If the stock is disposed of in the option year, however, this income adjustment is not required because the income attributable to the bargain element will be reported under the regular tax system in the same year.

Example 6. D receives an option to purchase 1,000 shares of her employer's stock at $50 per share. Three years after the receipt of the option, D exercises her option when the stock is selling for $70 per share. When D exercises the option, she has an AMT adjustment of $20,000 ($70,000 − $50,000).

Since the AMT adjustment amount computed above increases the AMTI, an upward basis adjustment of an equal amount is allowed for AMT purposes. This disparity in the stock's basis for regular tax and the AMT requires the *extra set of books* to determine the amount of gain recognized upon a subsequent disposition of the stock for AMT purposes.

Example 7. Assume the same facts as in *Example 6* and that D holds the stock until it further increases in value to $85,000. If D sells the stock for $85,000, she has a $35,000 gain for regular tax purposes ($85,000 − $50,000), and an AMT gain of $15,000 ($85,000 − $70,000).

4. *Standard Deduction Not Allowed.* Individuals are not permitted to take into account the standard deduction in computing the alternative minimum taxable income.[34]

---

[31] § 56(b)(2)(D).

[32] See Chapter 18 for a discussion of ISOs and § 83.

[33] § 56(b)(3). Although no direct authority exists, arguably a § 83(b) election may be made for AMT purposes.

[34] § 56(b)(1)(E).

5. *Personal Exemptions.* Personal exemptions authorized under § 151 are not allowed as deductions in computing the AMTI.[35]

6. *Adjustment to Income for Tax Refunds.* Generally, taxpayers who itemize deductions must report a refund of a prior year's state or local income tax as gross income in the year of receipt.[36] However, since itemized deductions for all tax expenditures are not allowed for AMT purposes, the refund or recovery in *all cases* is excluded from AMTI.

Adjustment Applicable Only to Corporations. For years beginning after 1989, the only adjustment applicable solely to corporate taxpayers is the adjustment based on a corporation's *adjusted current earnings*—commonly referred to as the ACE adjustment.[37] Consistent with the philosophy of the alternative minimum tax system, the ACE adjustment is deemed necessary to ensure that corporations having large economic incomes will be forced to pay at least some tax under the alternative minimum tax system.

The ACE adjustment requires that a corporation's AMTI include 75 percent of the adjusted current earnings in excess of the corporate AMTI computed without regard to the ACE adjustment.[38] Adjusted current earnings are calculated using the corporation's AMTI as a starting point to which other certain specified adjustments are made.[39] A discussion of each specified adjustment required to compute the ACE adjustment is beyond the scope of this text, but the rationale for the collective specified adjustments is to determine the corporation's actual economic earnings so that the corporation's true ability to pay a tax can be determined.

---

[35] *Ibid.*

[36] See Chapter 6 for an exception based on the tax benefit rule.

[37] This adjustment *does not* apply to certain corporations, including S corporations, regulated investment companies, real estate investment trusts, or real estate mortgage investment conduits. § 56(g)(6).

[38] § 56(g)(1).

[39] § 56(g)(4).

Example 8. T corporation has AMTI of $200,000 without regard to the ACE adjustment. T's adjusted current earnings are determined to be $400,000. T's regular income tax liability is $41,750. T has AMTI of $350,000, a tentative AMT of $70,000, and AMT of $28,250, computed as follows:

AMTI before ACE...	$200,000
Plus: ACE adjustment [($400,000−$200,000) × 75%]..........	+150,000
AMTI...	$350,000
Less: Exemption amount	
(completely phased out).....................................	− 0
AMTI base...	$350,000
Times: AMT rate..	× 20%
Gross AMT...	$ 70,000
Less: AMT foreign tax credit..................................	− 0
Tentative AMT...	$ 70,000
Less: Regular tax liability....................................	− 41,750
AMT...	$ 28,250

This portion of the alternative minimum tax system has been crafted to make certain the AMT is imposed on corporate taxpayers having an economic ability to pay.

Special Tax Shelter Loss Adjustments. Certain losses that may be deductible for regular tax are *denied* for purposes of computing the AMTI. Specifically, tax shelter farm losses and passive activity losses allowed as deductions for regular tax purposes must be recomputed under the AMT system, taking into account all of the AMT tax accounting rules.[40] Clearly, a separate set of books will be required for each activity. The amount of the AMT adjustment required by the statute is the difference between the loss allowed for the regular tax system and the loss allowed under the AMT system.

1. *Tax Shelter Farm Losses.* Noncorporate taxpayers and personal service corporations are not allowed to deduct losses from a tax shelter farm activity in computing AMTI.[41] For the AMT system, the disallowed loss will be treated as a deduction allocable to such activity in the *first* succeeding taxable year, and will be allowed to offset income from that activity in any succeeding year. Under this rule, each farm is treated as a separate activity. In the year that the taxpayer disposes of his or her entire interest in any tax shelter farm activity, the amount of previously disallowed loss related to that activity is allowed as a deduction for the year under the AMT system.

---

[40] These rules are specified in §§ 56 and 57.   [41] § 58(a).

2. *Passive Activity Losses.* As discussed in Chapter 12, there are limitations on the use of losses from passive activities to offset other income of the taxpayer for regular tax purposes.[42] For AMT purposes, similar rules apply, except for AMT purposes a loss generated from a passive activity must be recomputed to reflect the AMT rules. This means that depreciation, intangible drilling and development costs, percentage depletion, and other adjustments and preferences must be reflected in computing the loss for AMT purposes. Because of the differences in the treatment of such items, the amount of suspended losses relating to an activity may differ for minimum tax and regular tax purposes and may require that two sets of books be kept in order to track the passive loss carryover on each activity.[43]

Example 9. C has $200,000 of salary income, $50,000 of gross income from passive activities, and $170,000 of deductions from passive activities for the current year. C's loss with respect to the passive activities is $120,000 for regular tax purposes. Because the recomputed expenses for AMT purposes are only $130,000, the passive activity loss is $80,000 for minimum tax purposes. For regular tax purposes, the taxpayer has taxable income of $200,000 and a suspended passive loss in the amount of $120,000 ($170,000 passive deductions − $50,000 passive income). For minimum tax purposes, the taxpayer has AMTI of $200,000 and a suspended passive loss of $80,000 ($130,000 − $50,000).

As illustrated in the example above, the recomputed passive loss using the AMT rules can be significantly different from the regular tax passive loss with respect to an activity. In fact, in some situations it is possible to have a regular tax passive loss amount *and* an AMT passive income amount on the same activity!

Example 10. Assume that taxpayer C in the example above had passive activity deductions of $80,000 for regular tax purposes and $40,000 for minimum tax purposes. C would have regular taxable income of $200,000 and a suspended passive loss of $30,000 ($80,000 − $50,000) for regular tax purposes. For AMT purposes, C has alternative minimum taxable income of $210,000 [$200,000 salary + ($50,000 − $40,000)] and no suspended passive loss for minimum tax purposes.

---

[42]   See Chapter 12 for a discussion of passive losses.

[43]   P.L. 99-514, Tax Reform Act of 1986, Conference Committee Report, Act § 701.

TAX PREFERENCE ITEMS

Since tax preference items are required to be identified and computed for both corporate and noncorporate taxpayers, all the preference items are listed in Exhibit 13-3; however, only the most common items are explained below.[44]

Items of tax preference include

1. Depletion in excess of basis with respect to natural resources.

   The amount of the preference item is the excess (if any) of the percentage depletion claimed for the taxable year over the adjusted basis of the property at the end of the taxable year (determined without regard to the depletion deduction for the taxable year). This computation must be made for each unit of property.

Exhibit 13-3
Alternative Minimum Tax
Tax Preference Items

Percentage depletion in excess of cost basis

Intangible drilling and development costs (in excess of 65 percent of net oil and gas income)

Reserves for losses on bad debts of financial institutions in excess of the deduction computed on the basis of actual experience*

Specified tax-exempt interest

Unrealized gain on certain charitable contributions of appreciated capital assets

Accelerated depreciation on certain property placed in service prior to January 1, 1987

* Applies only to corporate taxpayers

---

[44] § 57 sets forth all of the tax preference items and the specifics of each calculation.

2. Intangible drilling and development costs.[45]

In general, the amount of the tax preference is equal to the intangible drilling costs (IDC) incurred and deducted on productive oil, gas, and geothermal wells reduced by the sum of

a. The amount allowed as if the IDCs had been capitalized and amortized over a 10-year period, and

b. Sixty-five percent (65%) of the net income for the year from these properties.

If the intangible drilling and development costs are capitalized and amortized in accord with special rules contained in § 59(e), they are not treated as a preference item.[46]

3. Excess reserves for losses on bad debts of financial institutions.

4. Tax-exempt interest income.

This preference item pertains to interest income on specified private activity bonds (SPABs) issued after August 7, 1986.[47] The term *private activity bond* means any bond issued if 10 percent of the proceeds of the issue are used for private business use in any trade or business carried on by any person that is not a governmental unit. Where interest income on SPABs is includible in AMTI under the above rule, the regular tax rule of Code § 265 (denying deductions for expenses and interest relating to tax-exempt income) does not apply, and expenses and interest incurred to carry SPABs are deductible for minimum tax purposes.

Example 11.   Taxpayer P is required to include in AMTI $10,000 of otherwise tax-exempt interest income on SPABs as a preference item. She incurred $900 of interest expense on a temporary loan in order to purchase the bonds. Code § 265 disallows a deduction of this $900 for regular tax purposes, but it is deductible for minimum tax purposes.

---

[45] § 57(a)(2) contains several unique concepts specific to the oil and gas industry (in statutory language, the productive well "excess intangible drilling and development costs" over "net income from oil and gas properties" constitutes a tax preference item). For a detailed explanation of these concepts, see 1991 *Income Taxation of Natural Resources*, by Russell, Prentice Hall, at Para. 11.02.

[46] Code § 59(e) was enacted to provide relief to taxpayers that are subject to the AMT, but through proper planning want to maximize the regular tax deductions and at the same time minimize the impact of the AMT. This section provides an election to capitalize "qualified expenditures" and deduct them ratably over a 10-year period (3 years in the case of circulation expenditures). Qualified expenditures include IDCs, circulation, research and experimentation, and mining exploration and development costs.

[47] § 57(a)(5)(C)(iv).

5. Charitable contributions.

    The untaxed appreciation in charitable contributions of certain appreci-ated long-term capital gain property represents another preference item. A taxpayer who makes a charitable contribution of capital gain property must determine the amount of the tax preference for purposes of the AMT. The preference amount is the amount by which the charitable contribution claimed for regular tax purposes exceeds the property's adjusted basis.[48]

    Example 12. J donated stock worth $10,000 to Central University during the current year. J purchased the stock three years ago for $6,000. He claimed a regular tax charitable contribution of $10,000 (the property's FMV).[49] J has a tax preference item of $4,000 ($10,000 − $6,000 adjusted basis) as a result of the contribution claimed for the capital gain property.

    For taxable year 1991 only, contributions of appreciated tangible personal property will not generate a tax preference. Thus, charitable contributions of tangible personal property (other than inventory or ordinary income property, or short-term capital gain property), the use of which is related to the donee's tax-exempt purpose, will give rise to a deduction equal to the fair market value of the asset for both regular tax purposes and AMT purposes. The deduction for charitable contributions of inventory or other ordinary income property and short-term capital gain property continues to be limited to the adjusted basis of the property for both regular tax and AMT systems.

6. Excess accelerated depreciation on nonrecovery real property placed in service before 1981.

    The amount of this preference item is the depreciation deducted for the year less the amount that would have been allowed if the straight-line method had been used. This computation must be made for each property.

7. Excess accelerated cost recovery deductions on 19-year (also includes 18- and 15-year) real property placed in service before 1987.

    The amount of this preference item is the cost recovery deduction taken for the year less the amount that would have been allowed had the property been depreciated using a 19-year (18- or 15-year) life, the straight-line method, and no salvage value.

---

[48] The Conference Committee Report on the TRA of 1986 specifies that this preference does not apply to charitable contribution carryovers if the contribution was made prior to August 16, 1986. *Supra*, Footnote 43.

[49] This example assumes that J is not subject to any limitations on his charitable contribu-tions for regular tax purposes. See Chapter 11 for a discussion of charitable contribu-tions of capital gain property.

Example 13. On January 5, 1986, C purchased a rental house for $110,000. She allocated $10,000 to the land and elected the accelerated cost recovery method. C's tax preference resulting from this transaction for 1991 is $400, computed in the following manner:

1991 tax preference item:

Allowable cost recovery deduction using a 19-year life ($100,000 × 5.7% from table in Appendix C)............	$5,700
Less: Straight-line depreciation using a 19-year life ($100,000 × 5.3% from table in Appendix C)......	(5,300)
Tax preference item for 1991.......................................	$ 400

8. Excess accelerated cost recovery deductions on low-income housing. The preference item is computed as in (7) above except the straight-line recovery period is 15 years.

9. Excess accelerated depreciation on leased personal property (applicable to individual taxpayers only).

   a. For leased nonrecovery personal property, the preference item is computed as in (6) above.

   b. For leased recovery personal property, the preference item is the cost recovery deduction taken for the year less the depreciation that would have been allowed for the year if the straight-line method with a half-year convention, no salvage value, and the following recovery periods had been used:

3-year property...	5 years
5-year property...	8 years
10-year property..	15 years
15-year public utility property......................................	22 years

ALTERNATIVE MINIMUM TAX COMPUTATIONS

Before the alternative minimum tax calculations can be made, the taxpayer's current taxable income and Federal income tax liability must first be determined. As illustrated in Exhibit 13-1, a taxpayer's AMT liability is the excess of the tentative AMT over the regular tax liability. To further examine this interaction, a factual situation is presented below in *Example 14* where the taxpayer's regular tax liability is determined. The same facts are then used to compute the ATIDs in *Example 15*, the taxpayer's AMT liability in *Example 16*.

Example 14.   T is a married taxpayer filing a joint return for 1991. He had the following items of income, expenses, and regular tax liability for the year.

Income:		
Salary...	$ 88,000	
Interest..	2,000	
Dividends......................................	8,000	
Short-term capital gain........................	2,000	
Adjusted gross income...........................		$100,000*
Itemized deductions:		
Medical expenses [$9,500 total − (7.5%		
of $100,000 A.G.I.)].........................	$ 2,000	
Real property taxes on home....................	12,000	
Real property taxes on mountain		
range property...............................	8,000	
Personal property taxes........................	4,000	
Interest expense:		
Qualified residence interest..................	20,000	
Investment debt on mountain range		
property ($12,000 total,		
but limited to)............................	4,000**	
Charitable contributions.......................	10,000***	
Casualty loss [$13,000 total − (10%		
of A.G.I.)]..................................	3,000	
Miscellaneous itemized		
deductions [$11,000 total − (2%		
of A.G.I.)]..................................	9,000	
Total itemized deductions......................		(72,000)
Personal exemptions (2 × $2,150)..............		(4,300)
Taxable income....................................		$ 23,700
Regular tax.......................................		$ 3,555

  * Although not required to be included in his taxable income, T exercised an incentive stock option for $20,000 when the fair market value of the stock was $80,000.

  ** The mountain range property was acquired as a speculative investment and was 90% debt-financed. Recall that interest on investment indebtedness is allowed as a deduction under § 163(d) to the extent of net investment income. Net investment income = $2,000 interest + $8,000 dividends + $2,000 capital gain − $8,000 property taxes = $4,000. Thus the $12,000 interest expense is limited to $4,000.

  *** The charitable contribution deduction results from T's gift to his church of Ford Motor Company stock worth $10,000. T had purchased the stock two years earlier for $2,000.

Example 15.   Refer to *Example 14*. T's 1991 alternative tax itemized deductions (ATIDs) and the resulting AMT adjustments are determined as follows:

	Allowed ATIDs for AMT	Allowed Itemized Deductions for Regular Tax	AMT Adjustments
Medical expenses (in excess of 10% of A.G.I.).................	$ 0	$ 2,000	$ 2,000
Itemized deductions for taxes (not allowed) ...	0	24,000	24,000
Qualified housing interest......................	20,000	20,000	0
Other qualified interest (limited to net investment income, = $2,000 + $8,000 + $2,000 − $8,000) ...	4,000	4,000	0
Casualty losses...............................	3,000	3,000	0
Charitable contributions.......................	10,000	10,000	0
Miscellaneous itemized deductions (not allowed)................................	0	9,000	9,000
Totals for 1991...............................	$37,000	$72,000	$35,000

Note that the computations for ATIDs are similar to those in *Example 14* for itemized deductions except (1) the reduction in medical expenses is 10% rather than 7.5%, (2) deductions for state and local taxes are not allowed in the alternative tax calculations, and (3) the miscellaneous itemized deductions are not allowed in the calculation of the AMT liability. The differences between the ATIDs allowed for AMT purposes and the itemized deductions allowed for regular tax purposes result in AMT adjustments. These adjustments are added back to T's regular taxable income to arrive at AMT adjusted taxable income and are reported on Form 6251, Computation of Alternative Minimum Tax for Individuals.

Example 16. Refer to *Examples 14* and *15*. T's alternative minimum tax (AMT) liability for 1991 is computed as follows:

Regular taxable income		$ 23,700
Plus: Net adjustment for itemized deductions		+ 35,000[1]
Net adjustment for exercise of ISO		+ 60,000[2]
Adjustment for personal exemptions		+ 4,300
AMT adjusted taxable income		$123,000
Plus: Tax preference item [due to charitable contribution of capital gain property ($10,000 FMV − $2,000 adjusted basis)]		+ 8,000
Alternative minimum taxable income (AMTI)		$131,000
Less: Exemption amount (married filing jointly)		− 40,000
AMTI base		$ 91,000
Times: AMT rate		× 24%
Gross alternative minimum tax		$ 21,840
Less: AMT foreign tax credit		− 0
Tentative AMT		$ 21,840
Less: Regular tax liability		− 3,555
AMT liability for 1991		$ 18,285

[1]Regular tax itemized deductions	$ 72,000
ATIDs allowed for AMT	(37,000)
Disallowed itemized deductions increase the AMTI	$ 35,000
[2]Stock FMV when ISO exercised	$ 80,000
Option price	(20,000)
Excess is AMT adjustment that increases AMTI	$ 60,000

Since the tentative AMT of $21,840 *exceeds* his $3,555 regular tax liability (computed in *Example 14*), T must pay the difference of $18,285 for 1991 because of the alternative minimum tax.

The previous example illustrates an unfortunate consequence of the strict application of the AMT provisions. The tax benefits of longstanding regular-tax incentive provisions such as home ownership (e.g., deductibility of interest and real property taxes) and charitable contributions of capital gain property are either decreased or totally eliminated by the AMT. Although Congress continues to support the objectives of these incentives, their use by individuals to avoid all or most of their Federal income tax liability is not the intent of the law. Recent changes are an attempt to minimize such perceived abuses. As illustrated in *Example 16*, because of the limited definition of ATIDs and the decreasing Federal income tax rates, it is possible that some unsuspecting individuals (like T) will be subject to the AMT. Consequently, tax planning to avoid or minimize the AMT is becoming more important for a growing number of taxpayers. As an adjunct to planning for the impact of the AMT, it should be remembered that each taxpayer has the responsibility to maintain adequate records to support the accuracy of the amounts of tax preferences and adjustments used in the AMT computation.[50]

A completed Form 6251, based on the facts from *Examples 14*, *15*, and *16*, is contained in Exhibit 13-4. Note that the 1990 form is used because the 1991 form was not available at the publication date of this text.

With all of the potential complexity and extra reporting work required by the AMT provisions, it is noteworthy that Congress has made an attempt to make another area of the Federal tax laws more orderly—the part specifying credits against the tax liability. The remainder of this chapter is devoted to the tax incentives provided by the tax credit provisions.

INCOME TAX CREDITS

One reason tax credits are popular is that a credit is viewed as providing a more equitable benefit than a comparable deduction. This is because a credit is a direct reduction of the tax liability, while a deduction merely reduces the amount of taxable income. This difference is illustrated in *Example 17*.

---

[50]   Reg. § 1.57-5(a).

	Exhibit 13-4

Form 6251

Department of the Treasury
Internal Revenue Service

Alternative Minimum Tax—Individuals
► See separate Instructions.
► Attach to Form 1040 or Form 1040NR. Estates and trusts, use Form 8656.

OMB No. 1545-0227

1990

Attachment Sequence No. **32**

Name(s) shown on Form 1040: **MR. & MRS. T**

Your social security number: **457 89 6132**

1	Taxable income from Form 1040, line 37. (If Form 1040, line 37 is zero, see Instructions.)	1	23,700
2	Net operating loss deduction, if any, from Form 1040, line 22. (Enter as a positive amount.)	2	
3	Combine lines 1 and 2	3	23,700
4	**Adjustments:** (See Instructions before completing.)		
a	Standard deduction, if any, from Form 1040, line 34	4a	
b	Personal exemption amount from Form 1040, line 36	4b	4,300
c	Medical and dental expenses	4c	2,000
d	Miscellaneous itemized deductions from Schedule A (Form 1040), line 25	4d	9,000
e	Taxes from Schedule A (Form 1040), line 8	4e	24,000
f	Refund of taxes	4f ( )	
g	Personal interest from Schedule A (Form 1040), line 12b	4g	
h	Other interest adjustments	4h	
i	Reserved	4i	
j	Depreciation of tangible property placed in service after 1986	4j	
k	Circulation and research and experimental expenditures paid or incurred after 1986	4k	
l	Mining exploration and development costs paid or incurred after 1986	4l	
m	Long-term contracts entered into after 2/28/86	4m	
n	Pollution control facilities placed in service after 1986	4n	
o	Installment sales of certain property	4o	
p	Adjusted gain or loss §.83 INCOME FROM ISD	4p	60,000
q	Certain loss limitations	4q	
r	Tax shelter farm loss	4r	
s	Passive activity loss	4s	
t	Beneficiaries of estates and trusts	4t	
u	Combine lines 4a through 4t	4u	99,300
5	**Tax preference items:** (See Instructions before completing.)		
a	Appreciated property charitable deduction	5a	8,000
b	Tax-exempt interest from private activity bonds issued after 8/7/86	5b	
c	Depletion	5c	
d	Accelerated depreciation of real property placed in service before 1987	5d	
e	Accelerated depreciation of leased personal property placed in service before 1987	5e	
f	Amortization of certified pollution control facilities placed in service before 1987	5f	
g	Intangible drilling costs	5g	
h	Add lines 5a through 5g	5h	8,000
6	Combine lines 3, 4u, and 5h	6	131,000
7	Alternative tax net operating loss deduction. (Do not enter more than 90% of line 6.) See Instructions	7	
8	Alternative minimum taxable income. Subtract line 7 from line 6. If married filing a separate return, see Instructions	8	131,000
9	Enter: $40,000 ($20,000 if married filing separately; $30,000 if single or head of household)	9	40,000
10	Enter: $150,000 ($75,000 if married filing separately; $112,500 if single or head of household)	10	150,000
11	Subtract line 10 from line 8. If zero or less, enter -0- here and on line 12 and go to line 13	11	0
12	Multiply line 11 by 25% (.25)	12	0
13	Subtract line 12 from line 9. If zero or less, enter -0-. If completing this form for a child under age 14, see Instructions for amount to enter	13	40,000
14	Subtract line 13 from line 8. If zero or less, enter -0- here and on line 19 and skip lines 15 through 18	14	91,000
15	Multiply line 14 by 21% (.21) (24% in 1991)	15	21,840
16	Alternative minimum tax foreign tax credit. See Instructions	16	
17	Tentative minimum tax. Subtract line 16 from line 15	17	21,840
18	Enter your tax from Form 1040, line 38, minus any foreign tax credit on Form 1040, line 43. If an amount is entered on line 39 of Form 1040, see Instructions	18	3,555
19	**Alternative minimum tax.** Subtract line 18 from line 17. If zero or less, enter -0-. Enter this amount on Form 1040, line 49. If completing this form for a child under age 14, see Instructions for amount to enter	19	18,285

For Paperwork Reduction Act Notice, see separate Instructions.

Form **6251** (1990)

Example 17. Assume that in 1991 A is single with taxable income of $49,400 and that B is single with taxable income of $11,000. Also assume that tax policymakers are evaluating whether a tax credit or a tax deduction is more equitable. For comparison purposes, the policymakers restrict their options to allow all taxpayers either a special $100 tax *credit* or a $100 tax *deduction*.

	Taxpayer A		Taxpayer B	
	Credit Method	Deduction Method	Credit Method	Deduction Method
Taxable income....	$49,400	$49,400	$11,000	$11,000
Special deduction..	0	(100)	0	(100)
Taxable income.... (adjusted)........	$49,400	$49,300	$11,000	$10,900
Tax liability.........	$11,190	$11,159	$ 1,650	$ 1,635
Special credit......	(100)	0	(100)	0
Tax liability (adjusted)........	$11,090	$11,159	$ 1,550	$ 1,635
Tax savings........	$ 100	$ 31[a]	$ 100	$ 15[b]

[a]$11,190 − $11,159 = $31.
[b]$1,650 − $1,635 = $15.

Note that the marginal tax rate is 31% for A and 15% for B. This difference in rates does not affect the tax credit method. But under the deduction method, A saves 31% of the $100 while B saves just 15% of the $100.

The results from *Example 17* can be generalized for tax policy purposes as (1) taxpayers receive more benefit from tax credits than from tax deductions of the same amount; (2) all taxpayers receive the *same dollar benefit* from credits, regardless of marginal tax rates; and (3) taxpayers with higher marginal tax rates benefit more from tax deductions than do those with lower marginal rates. In addition, the argument has been made that credits are of more benefit to those with lower incomes. This is based on the reasoning that the $100 tax saved has more relative value for those with low incomes than it has for those with high incomes. However, this line of reasoning is questionable since taxable income is just one inexact measure of a person's economic situation.

OVERVIEW OF TAX CREDITS

In recent years, the number of tax credits has been significantly increased by Congress. Most of them have been enacted into law to achieve a specified social, economic, or political goal. These goals range from encouraging taxpayers to engage in scientific research (the research credit) and the conservation of energy (energy tax credits) to providing compensatory tax reductions for those individuals who may carry greater burdens than others (credits for the elderly and for individuals with low earned incomes).

As the table in Exhibit 13-5 illustrates, the credit provisions are divided into *five* major groups or subparts. Subpart A consists of nonrefundable individual tax credits and Subpart B contains nonrefundable specific business credits. All of these nonrefundable credits may be used to reduce the tax liability, but *only* to the extent of the "regular tax liability." Subpart C contains the *refundable* credits. The new credits for enhanced oil recovery and access for disabled individuals have been combined with five previously enacted credits into the "general business credit" in Subpart D. Finally, the minimum tax credit is contained in Subpart G.

Limitation on Nonrefundable Credits. The TRA of 1986 amended the definition of *regular tax liability* for purposes of applying the credits. Under revised Code § 26, a taxpayer's "regular tax liability" does not include (1) the minimum tax (§ 55); (2) the additional tax imposed on distributions from certain annuities [§ 72(m)]; (3) the additional tax imposed on income from certain retirement accounts [§ 408(f)]; (4) the accumulated earnings tax (§ 531); (5) the personal holding company tax (§ 541); (6) the tax on certain capital gains of S corporations

---

Exhibit 13-5
Table of Tax Credits

	Code Section	Specific Credit
Subpart A:	§ 21	Child and Dependent Care Credit
	§ 22	Credit for the Elderly
	§ 25	Credit for Interest on Certain Home Mortgages*
Subpart B:	§ 27	Possession and Foreign Tax Credit
	§ 28	Credit for Clinical Testing of Certain Drugs*
	§ 29	Credit for Nonconventional Fuel Production
Subpart C:	§ 31	Credit for Taxes Withheld on Wages
	§ 32	Earned Income Credit
	§ 33	Credit for Taxes Withheld at Source on Nonresident Aliens and Foreign Corporations
	§ 34	Credit for Certain Uses of Gasoline and Special Fuels
Subpart D:	§ 38	General Business Credit

Includes
1. Investment Tax Credit (§ 46)
2. Targeted Jobs Credit (§ 51)*
3. Alcohol Fuels Credit (§ 40)
4. Research Credit (§ 41)*
5. Low-Income Housing Credit (§ 42)*
6. Enhanced Oil Recovery Credit (§ 43)
7. Disabled Individual Access Credit (§ 44)

	Code Section	Specific Credit
Subpart G:	§ 53	Credit for Prior Year Minimum Tax Liability

* These credits are scheduled to expire on December 31, 1991.

(§ 1374); or (7) the tax on passive income of S corporations (§ 1375).[51] This definition is significant because the nonrefundable credits may only be used to reduce the § 26 tax liability. Thus, the nonrefundable credits cannot be used to offset penalty taxes imposed by the Code (e.g., personal holding company and accumulated earnings penalty taxes).

For taxpayers to whom two or more credits apply, the Code specifies an ascending order for the use of nonrefundable credits. Nonrefundable credits are to be used to reduce the § 26 tax liability in the following order: §§ 21, 22, 25, 27, 28, 29, 38, and 53. This order is important because some of the credits may be carried forward or back and utilized in different tax years, while others "fall through the cracks" (i.e., provide no tax benefit) if they exceed the § 26 tax liability in the year they originate.

Refundable Credits. Refundable credits are accounted for *after* the nonrefundable ones and may be applied against *any* income tax imposed by the Code—including the penalty taxes. As the name suggests, refundable credits may result in the taxpayer receiving a refund check for an amount in excess of any Federal taxes paid or withheld. In a sense, these credit provisions may result in a "negative income tax."

Due to the magnitude and relative importance of the business credits, they are examined first. A discussion of the tax credits available only to individual taxpayers follows.

GENERAL BUSINESS CREDIT

The investment tax credit, targeted jobs credit, alcohol fuels credit, research credit, low-income housing credit, enhanced oil recovery credit, and the disabled access credit have been combined to form the general business credit. Each of these seven components is separately computed under its particular set of rules, and then the total of these credits becomes the current year's business credit.

In order to prevent taxpayers from using business credits to avoid paying all income taxes, the general business credit is limited each year by the taxpayer's *net regular tax liability*. The net regular tax liability is the § 26 tax liability reduced by the credits allowed in §§ 21 through 29.[52] In addition, taxpayers with a net regular tax liability exceeding $25,000 are subject to a second limitation.

---

[51] Other taxes imposed in special circumstances are also excluded from the regular tax liability. See § 26(b)(2) for a complete list of taxes that are excluded.

[52] § 38(c)(2).

The business credit is limited to $25,000 *plus* 75 percent of the net regular tax liability in excess of $25,000.[53] Generally, credits that are unused because of these limits can be carried back three years and then forward 15 years, applied on a first-in, first-out basis.[54]

> **Example 18.** In 1991, F has a potential general business credit of $92,000 and a net regular tax liability of $100,000. The maximum allowable business credit for 1991 is $81,250 [$25,000 + (75% × $75,000 = $56,250)]. The unused credit of $10,750 ($92,000 − $81,250) is subject to the carryover rules.

The common rules for computing the separate components of the general business credit, beginning with the investment tax credit, are detailed in the following sections.

INVESTMENT TAX CREDIT

The investment tax credit (ITC) is made up of four distinct parts: (1) the regular investment credit, (2) the credit for rehabilitation expenditures, (3) the business energy credit, and (4) the reforestation credit. Each part of the ITC is computed separately under its own specific rules. The actual amount of each part of the ITC is the function of two factors: the taxpayer's basis in property qualifying for the credit, and the rate of the credit. The three most frequently encountered components of the ITC are discussed below.

Regular Investment Tax Credit. Prior to 1986, the regular investment credit was available for most tangible personal property placed in service for use in a trade or business. In order to partially offset the significant loss of Federal tax revenues resulting from the TRA of 1986 tax rate reductions, Congress terminated the regular ITC for assets placed in service after December 31, 1985.[55] However, a 10 percent credit is still available for certain transition property, qualified

---

[53] § 38(c)(1). Married taxpayers filing separate returns are limited to $12,500 plus 75 percent of the tax liability in excess of $12,500 [§ 38(c)(4)].

[54] § 39(a). Note that credits allowed for enhanced oil recovery or disabled access expenditures *cannot* be carried back to years beginning before 1991.

[55] The regular ITC rules have been changed many times, resulting in several unique sets of rules applicable to different time periods in which the assets were placed in service. Because the recovery period, and thus the ITC recapture period, for all assets placed in service prior to 1986 has expired, much of the complexity and detail involved in computing and recapturing the regular ITC have been omitted.

progress expenditures, and qualified timber property. Basically, this exception applies to property acquired or progress expenditures made under a binding, written contract in effect on December 31, 1985. Based on the acquired property's class life, it must be placed in service no later than a specific date in order to qualify for the regular investment credit. These dates are[56]

Property's Class Life	Placed in Service Before
Less than 5 years	July 1, 1986
At least 5 but less than 7	January 1, 1987
At least 7 but less than 20	January 1, 1989
20 years or more	January 1, 1991

Rehabilitation Investment Credit.   The Economic Recovery Tax Act of 1981 grafted onto the regular investment credit an additional tax credit designed to encourage the restoration of certain older buildings. The credit represents a unique tax incentive for the restoration of old buildings.

With an emphasis on urban renewal, the rehabilitation investment credit is limited to substantial *rehabilitation expenditures* (excluding the purchase price) of *commercial buildings* and *historic structures*.[57] *Substantial* is defined to mean qualifying expenditures that exceed the greater of (1) the property's basis, or (2) $5,000.[58] To prevent destruction of these buildings, the amended legislation requires that

1. Fifty percent (50%) or more of the existing external walls of the buildings are retained in place as external walls;

2. Seventy-five percent (75%) or more of the external walls of the building are retained in place as internal or external walls; and

3. Seventy-five percent (75%) or more of the existing internal structural framework of the building is retained in place.

If these requirements are met, the credit is available for qualified expenditures on *both* nonresidential real property and residential rental property or an addition or improvement to either type of property. However, if the rehabilitation credit is taken, the property *must* be depreciated under the straight-line method or the alternative depreciation system.[59]

---

[56] Transition rules also apply to constructed or reconstructed property and equipped buildings if the taxpayer had made a substantial investment in these assets prior to December 31, 1985.

[57] § 47(a).

[58] § 47(c)(1)(C).

[59] § 47(c)(2)(B).

The rate of rehabilitation credit is

Rate	Type of Structure
10%	Commercial building originally placed in service prior to 1936
20	All certified historic structures[60]

Example 19. On January 3, 1991, R purchases a commercial building that was constructed in 1920. In addition to the $300,000 of the purchase price allocated to the building, the entire core of the building is renovated at a cost of $600,000. R's rehabilitation credit is $60,000, computed as follows:

Start with: Qualified investment............	$600,000
Times: Rate of credit......................	× 10%
Equals: Current credit (before limitations)...	$ 60,000

In some instances, rehabilitation expenditures also qualify for the energy investment credit (discussed below). When this occurs, taxpayers *must choose* between the two credits because both credits cannot be claimed for the same expenditure.[61]

Energy Investment Credit. With rising concern about conservation of energy use, Congress added *energy investment credit* provisions to the Code. The objective of these credits is to encourage taxpayers to incur certain expenditures that decrease energy consumption or change the type of energy used. After 1986, the incentives are applicable to business property only.[62]

---

[60] § 47(c)(3). The designation as a certified historic structure is made by the Secretary of the Interior.

[61] § 48(a)(2)(C).

[62] One exception is the 10 percent investment credit for qualified reforestation expenditures, enacted by the RRA of 1990. See §§ 48(b) and 194 for details of this new credit.

To encourage businesses to utilize *alternative energy sources*, a business energy tax credit is available for certain new depreciable property acquired during the period from January 1, 1986 to December 31, 1991. The rate of the credit is dependent on the type of energy source and the year of the expenditure, as follows:[63]

Type of Property	Year of Expenditure	Rate
Solar property	1/1/86 to 12/31/86	15%
	1/1/87 to 12/31/87	12
	1/1/88 to 12/31/91	10
Geothermal property	1/1/86 to 12/31/86	15
	1/1/87 to 12/31/91	10
Ocean thermal property	1/1/86 to 9/30/90	15

Example 20. S is the owner of a deluxe print shop. In March 1991, S installed four solar panels to heat water to be used in a photographic development process. The panels, pumps, valves, storage tanks, control system, and installation cost a total of $80,000. S's energy tax credit is $8,000.

Qualified investment......................	$ 80,000
Rate of credit.............................	× 10%
Current ITC (before limitations)............	$ 8,000

Basis Reduction of Qualified Property. At one time, taxpayers were allowed to take a full 10 percent ITC and any applicable energy tax credit and still recover their entire cost basis of qualifying property under ACRS. In 1986 Congress decided that this treatment was too liberal with respect to rehabilitation property[64] and required the basis of the property to be reduced by the amount of ITC taken with respect to the property.[65] A similar rule requires that the basis of energy property be reduced by one-half of the amount of the ITC taken on such energy property.[66]

---

[63] § 48(a)(2)(B), as amended by the RRA of 1990.

[64] § 50(c)(1). These changes also helped fund a portion of the cost of the rate reduction enacted by Congress in the TRA of 1986.

[65] Note that for determining the amount and character of gain on the disposition of the property, the downward basis adjustment is treated as a deduction allowed for depreciation. Accordingly, the amount of the basis adjustment will be subject to the § 1245 depreciation recapture rules discussed in Chapter 17.

[66] § 50(c)(3).

Example 21. Refer to the facts in *Example 19*, where R's rehabilitation credit is $60,000. R purchased the property for $300,000 and incurred $600,000 of rehabilitation expenditures. R's basis in the rehabilitated property is $840,000 ($300,000 + $600,000 − $60,000).

Example 22. Refer to the facts in *Example 20*, where S's energy tax credit is $8,000. S purchased the solar property for $80,000. S's basis in the energy property is $76,000 ($80,000 − $4,000).

The regular ITC calculations discussed here provide the background for computing the recapture of ITC on early dispositions still required by the Code.[67] The amount of ITC recapture should be an economic consideration in planning the disposition of any asset upon which the ITC was claimed.

ITC Recapture. When taxpayers place qualified investment property into service, they claim the full amount of ITC regardless of how long they intend to use the property. However, if an asset ceases to be qualified property during the recovery period (due to a sale or other disposition, or a change in the purpose or use of the asset), taxpayers are required to recapture a portion of the "unearned" ITC.[68] The recapture percentages illustrated in Exhibit 13-6 must be used to calculate the amount of unearned credit that is recaptured as an additional tax in the year of early disposition. As a general rule, 20 percent of the credit is "earned" for each full year the property is held. For example, a qualified rehabilitation property placed in service on December 20, 1990, qualified for the rehabilitation credit in 1990 and was taken on the taxpayer's return for the year. However, none of the credit was *earned* until December 20, 1991. On that date, 20 percent of the credit allowed in 1990 was earned and thus no longer subject to recapture.

Exhibit 13-6
ITC Recapture Percentages[69]

If qualified property ceases to be qualified property—	The recapture percentage is:
Before one full year, after placed in service	100%
After one year, before two full years	80
After two years, before three full years	60
After three years, before four full years	40
After four years, before five full years	20

---

[67] § 47. Note that when ITC is recaptured, an increase in basis will result.

[68] § 50(a).

[69] § 50(a)(1)(B).

Example 23. Assume that the commercial building in *Example 19* was sold by R on February 1, 1991. The ITC recapture is computed as follows:

Property	ITC Claimed	×	Recapture Percentage	=	Amount Recaptured
Commercial bldg.	$60,000	×	80%	=	$48,000

This amount is reported on Form 4255 and is treated as an additional tax imposed on the taxpayer in the year in which an early disposition occurs. Because the building's basis was originally decreased by the entire credit claimed, its basis is increased by the amount of the recapture for purposes of computing the gain or loss to be recognized on the sale.

In addition to sales and exchanges, dispositions generally include gifts, dividend distributions from corporations, cessation of business usage, and involuntary conversions.[70] Even though the recaptured ITC is referred to as an "other tax" on Form 1040, the amount recaptured will not be treated as a tax for purposes of determining the amount of nonrefundable tax credits allowed under § 26.[71]

The recapture rules do not apply to transfers by reason of death or to assets transferred in certain corporate acquisitions.[72] The recapture rules also will not apply to transfers of property between spouses, even if the transfer is made incident to divorce.[73] Finally, property is not treated as ceasing to be qualified property when a mere change in form of conducting the trade or business occurs, so long as the property continues to be qualified property in the new business and the taxpayer retains a substantial interest in this trade or business.[74]

Reduction of ITC Carryovers. The portion of the general business credit carry forward attributable to a regular ITC from a tax year before June 30, 1987, *and* any ITC allowed after 1986 on transition property must be *reduced* by 35 percent for tax years after June 30, 1987.[75] This reduction was introduced by Congress to correspond with the reduction of both individual and corporate tax rates. The amount of the credit reduction is not allowed as a credit for any other taxable year. In addition, in determining the extent to which an investment credit is used in a taxable year, the regular investment tax credit is deemed to be used *before* the rehabilitation and energy investment credits.

---

[70] Reg. § 1.47-2.

[71] § 50(a)(5)(C).

[72] § 50(a)(4).

[73] § 50(a)(5)(B).

[74] § 50(a)(4) and Reg. § 1.47-3(f).

[75] With respect to transition property, the basis of the qualifying property is required to be reduced *only* by the amount of credit that is allowable after the cutback. See § 49(d) before the amendments made by the RRA of 1990.

TARGETED JOBS CREDIT

The original jobs tax credit was scheduled to expire on December 31, 1981, but it has been extended annually by various revenue acts. The current rules apply to qualified wages paid or incurred prior to December 31, 1991.[76]

In 1984, the jobs credit was incorporated into the general business credit. As such, the § 38 rules limiting the amount of credit to the net regular tax liability (the first $25,000 + 75% of the tax liability in excess of $25,000) are applicable as well as the three-year carryback and 15-year carryover rules.

The targeted jobs credit is an elective credit that an employer may take for wages paid to individuals from specified target groups who have historically had difficulty in obtaining employment. The maximum credit is an amount equal to 40 percent of the first $6,000 of qualified first-year wages paid to each qualified individual. The employer's wage expense must be *reduced* by the amount of the jobs tax credit.

Members of Targeted Groups. The purpose of the job credit legislation is to encourage employers to hire individuals who are members of certain targeted groups. These individuals are[77]

1. Vocation rehabilitation referrals

2. Economically disadvantaged youths (between the ages of 18 and 22, inclusive)

3. Economically disadvantaged Vietnam-era veterans

4. Social Security Supplemental Income Benefits recipients

5. General assistance recipients

6. Youths participating in cooperative education programs (between the ages of 16 and 19, inclusive)

7. Economically disadvantaged ex-convicts

8. Eligible work incentive employees

9. Qualified summer youth employees

In addition, the law requires that each individual obtain certification from a designated local agency specifying that the individual is a member of one of the targeted groups. If such certification is incorrect because it was based on false information provided by the individual, certification will be revoked and wages paid after the notice of revocation is received by the employer will not be treated as qualified wages.

---

[76] § 51(c)(4).

[77] § 51(d).

Special Rule for Qualified Summer Youth Employees.   Employers are allowed to claim the jobs credit for wages paid for the summer employment of economically disadvantaged youths. These individuals must be 16 or 17 years of age on the hiring date and not have worked previously for the employer. To qualify for the credit, the services must be attributable to any 90-day period between May 1 and September 15. The summer youth employment credit is 40 percent of the first $3,000 of eligible wages, for a maximum credit of $1,200 per youth.[78] If a summer youth employee continues to work after the 90-day period, his or her wages may qualify for the general targeted jobs credit previously discussed. However, certification of this employee as a member of a second target group must be determined as of the date of the second certification rather than on the basis of the employee's original certification as a qualified summer youth employee. In addition, the $6,000 wage limit for the targeted job credit must be reduced by the qualified summer wages.

> **Example 24.**   On July 29, 1991, the owners of a farm hired 10 youths as certified summer employees to help harvest crops. The owners paid the youths $150 a week for eight weeks (through September 22). The amount of targeted jobs credit in 1991 without regard to additional certifications is $4,200, computed in the following manner:
>
> | | |
> |---|---:|
> | Qualifying wages ($150 × 10 youths × 7 weeks) | $10,500 |
> | Percent of credit............................... | ×   40% |
> | Amount of credit................................ | $ 4,200 |
>
> The wage expense deduction attributable to the youths' salaries would be $7,800, computed as follows:
>
> | | |
> |---|---:|
> | Total wages paid ($150 × 10 youths × 8 weeks) | $12,000 |
> | Reduced by allowable credit.................... | − 4,200 |
> | Allowable wage expense........................ | $ 7,800 |

Note that the eighth week does not qualify for the credit since it occurs after the September 15th cutoff date.

---

[78]   § 51(d)(12)(B).

ALCOHOL FUEL CREDIT

The third component of the general business credit is the alcohol fuels credit. To foster the production of gasohol, an income tax credit for alcohol and alcohol-blended fuels applies to fuel sales and uses before January 1, 2000. The alcohol fuels credit is computed and reported on Form 6478. Generally, the credit is $0.60 per gallon of alcohol used in a qualified alcohol mixture or as a straight alcohol fuel.[79]

RESEARCH AND EXPERIMENTAL (R&E) CREDIT

The fourth component of the general business credit is the *research credit*—commonly called the R&E credit. This is a 20 percent credit that applies to *incremental* expenditures paid or incurred that are classified in either of two categories: (1) qualified research expenditures, or (2) basic research payments.[80] The rules applicable to the expenditures of each category are separately discussed below. The Revenue Reconciliation Act (RRA) of 1989 significantly changed the rules for determining the R&E credit for expenditures incurred after December 31, 1989.[81] These new rules are discussed in the text, with footnote disclosure regarding rules for expenditures prior to January 1, 1990. First, however, the impact of the R&E credit on the taxpayer's current deduction for research and experimental expenditures should be examined.

Impact of R&E Credit on Current Deductions. In addition to extending the R&E credit to expenditures incurred through December 31, 1991, the RRA of 1990 continues to require a *reduction* in the amount to be accounted for under the taxpayer's adopted method of accounting for R&E costs. A collateral provision allows the taxpayer to elect not to have the R&E credit section apply for any taxable year.

For taxable years beginning after December 31, 1989, § 280C(c) disallows a deduction for the taxable year equal to the amount of the R&E credit determined for the year.[82] For taxpayers using the deferred asset method of accounting for R&E costs, the amount capitalized as a deferred asset to be amortized over a 60-month period is likewise reduced by the amount of the R&E credit determined for the year. In the event the credit is not utilized by the taxpayer within the 15-year carryover period, a deduction equal to the amount of the expiring credit is allowed in the year *following* the expiration of the tax credit carryover period.[83]

---

[79] § 40. The RRA of 1990 added another credit applicable to small ethanol producers.

[80] § 41(a).

[81] The RRA of 1990 extended the termination date of the R&E credit from December 31, 1990 to December 31, 1991.

[82] For taxable years beginning before January 1, 1990, the R&E deduction was reduced by an amount equal to 50 percent of the R&E credit determined for the year.

[83] § 196. The deduction allowed is 50 percent of the expired R&E credits attributable to taxable years beginning before 1990.

Because of the forced reduction in the amount otherwise allowable as a current tax deduction by the taxpayer taking the R&E credit, the taxpayer is allowed to *elect* to claim a reduced credit and thereby avoid an unnecessary reduction of the R&E deduction.[84] This election was provided as a relief provision for taxpayers caught by the limitation on the full use of the credit imposed by the alternative minimum tax. The election must be made at the time for filing the tax return for the credit year, including extensions.

Qualified Research Expenditures. Qualified research expenditures are *in-house* research expenses incurred by a taxpayer in carrying on a trade or business. The Revenue Reconciliation Act of 1989 expanded this definition so that start-up companies not yet in a trade or business would be entitled to the credit. Under the new law, a taxpayer is treated as meeting the trade or business requirement with respect to in-house research expenses if, at the time the expenses are incurred, the principal purpose of the taxpayer in making such expenditures is to use the results of the research in the active conduct of a future trade or business of the taxpayer.[85] The credit applies only to the extent that the current year's qualified research expenditures exceed the *base amount* of qualified research expenditures.[86] Generally, the base amount is the product of the fixed-base percentage and the average annual gross receipts of the taxpayer for the four taxable years preceding the taxable year for which the credit is being determined.[87] See Exhibit 13-7 for a conceptual overview of the R&E credit calculation.

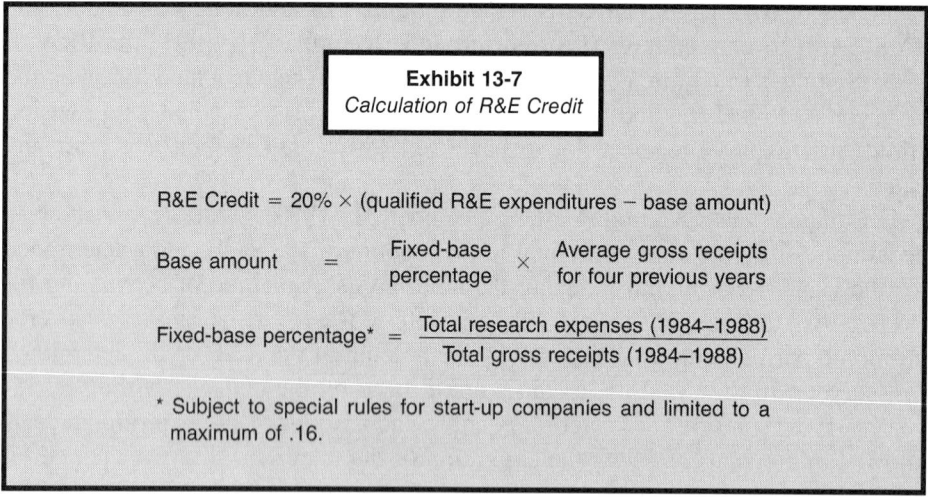

Exhibit 13-7
Calculation of R&E Credit

R&E Credit = 20% × (qualified R&E expenditures − base amount)

$$\text{Base amount} = \text{Fixed-base percentage} \times \text{Average gross receipts for four previous years}$$

$$\text{Fixed-base percentage*} = \frac{\text{Total research expenses (1984–1988)}}{\text{Total gross receipts (1984–1988)}}$$

* Subject to special rules for start-up companies and limited to a maximum of .16.

[84] § 280C(c)(3).

[85] § 41(b)(4).

[86] § 41(a)(1).

[87] § 41(c). The RRA of 1989 radically changed the method of computing the base amount for taxable years beginning after December 31, 1989. For rules applying to years prior to 1990, refer to old § 41(c).

Qualified research expenditures must satisfy the conditions of Code § 174, which allows a current deduction for research expenditures. Generally, the requirements are directed at research and development in the experimental or laboratory sense. This includes (1) the development of an experimental or pilot model, plant process, formula, invention, or similar property, and (2) the improvement of such types of property already in existence.[88] In addition, the expenditures must be technological in nature *and* must relate to establishing a new or improved function, or improving the performance, reliability, or quality of a product.[89] Finally, the credit is *denied* for certain expenditure items,[90] including

1. Research undertaken outside the United States

2. Research conducted in the social sciences or humanities

3. Ordinary testing or inspection of materials or products for quality control

4. Market and consumer research

5. Research relating to style, taste, cosmetic, or seasonal design

6. Advertising and promotion expenses

7. Management studies and efficiency surveys

8. Computer software for internal use of the taxpayer

9. Research to locate and evaluate mineral deposits, including oil and gas

10. Acquisition and improvement of land and of certain depreciable or depletable property used in research (including the annual depreciation deduction)

Amount of Credit. A 20 percent tax credit is allowed to the extent that a taxpayer's qualified research expenditures for the current year exceed its base amount for that year. The credit does not apply to amounts paid or incurred after December 31, 1990.[91]

---

[88] Reg. § 1.174-2(a).

[89] § 41(d)(1)(B).

[90] § 41(d)(4).

[91] § 41(h).

In order to determine the "base amount," the statute requires taxpayers to first compute a "fixed-base percentage," which is then multiplied by the average amount of the taxpayer's gross receipts for the four preceding years.[92] The "fixed-base percentage" is computed differently for existing firms with a history of doing research than for firms that do not have such a history. For taxpayers reporting both qualified research expenses and gross receipts during each of at least three years from 1984 to 1988, the "fixed-base percentage" is the ratio that its total qualified research expenses for the 1984 to 1988 period bears to its total gross receipts for this period, subject to a maximum ratio of .16. "Start-up companies" and those taxpayers not meeting the R&E expenditures and gross receipt requirements above are assigned a fixed-base percentage of .03.

Example 25. Assume R Corporation reported the following research expenditures and gross receipts:

	1986	1987	1988	1989	1990	1991
Research expenditures..	$ 90,000	$100,000	$110,000	$120,000	$130,000	$ 180,000
Gross receipts...	700,000	900,000	800,000	700,000	900,000	1,000,000

Since the base amount is dependent on the fixed-base percentage, the calculations necessarily begin by determining the fixed-base percentage, which is then used to determine the base amount. R Corporation's R&E credit is computed as follows:

(1)   Fixed-base percentage = $300,000/$2,400,000 = .125

(2)   Base amount = .125 × $3,300,000/4 = $103,125

(3)   Qualified R&E expenditures for 1991 = $180,000

(4)   R&E Credit = 20% × ($180,000 − $103,125)

= $15,375

Note that R Corporation must reduce its current deduction for research expenditures by $15,375, or if the deferred asset method of accounting is used, the $180,000 R&E costs must be reduced to $164,625 ($180,000 − $15,375) before being capitalized and amortized over a period not less than 60 months.

---

[92]   See generally, new § 41(c).

Basic Research Expenditures. The second category of expenditures qualifying for the research credit includes *basic research payments* made to universities and other qualified organizations. Basic research means any original investigation for the advancement of scientific knowledge not having a specific commercial objective. The term "basic research payment" means any amount paid in cash during the taxable year by a corporation to a qualified organization for basic research, but only if such payment is made pursuant to a written agreement and the basic research is to be performed by the qualified organization. Qualified organizations include educational institutions, certain scientific research organizations, and certain grant organizations.[93]

The R&E credit applies to the *excess* of corporate cash expenditures in a year over the qualified organization base period amount. The qualified organization base period amount is the *sum* of (1) the minimum basic research amount, plus (2) the maintenance-of-effort amount.[94] The *minimum basic research amount* is the greater of two fixed floor amounts: (1) the amount of average base period basic research payments, *or* (2) an amount equal to 1 percent of the average sum of all in-house research expenses, contract research expenses, and credit-eligible basic research expenditures for the base period. The *maintenance-of-effort amount* prevents the corporation from shifting its historical charitable contribution to any qualifying educational organization over to a creditable basic research payment. It is an amount equal to the *average* nondesignated university contributions paid by the corporation during the base period, increased by the cost of living adjustment for the calendar year over the amount of nondesignated university contributions paid by the taxpayer during that year. Any portion of the basic research payments that does not exceed the qualified organization base period amount will be treated as qualified research expenditures for computing the incremental qualified research expenditures discussed under "qualified research expenditures" above.[95]

Credit Limitations. In an effort to prevent the research credit from being exploited by tax shelter promoters, additional limitations are imposed. For individuals with ownership interests in unincorporated businesses (i.e., partners of a partnership), trust or estate beneficiaries, or S corporation shareholders, any allowable pass-through of the credit cannot exceed the *lesser of* (1) the individual's net regular tax liability limitation discussed earlier, or (2) the amount of tax attributable to the individual's taxable income resulting from the individual's interest in the entity that earned such credit.[96]

The final unique characteristic of the R&E credit is applicable to changes in business ownership. Special rules apply for computing the credit when a business changes hands, under which qualified research expenditures for periods prior to the change of ownership generally are treated as transferred with the trade or business that gave rise to those expenditures.[97]

---

[93] § 41(e)(6).

[94] § 41(e)(3).

[95] § 41(e)(1)(B).

[96] § 41(g).

[97] § 41(f)(3).

LOW-INCOME HOUSING CREDIT

The fifth component of the general business credit is the low-income housing credit. This credit is available for low-income housing that is constructed, rehabilitated, or acquired after 1986 and before 1992. The credit is claimed over a 10-year period, with an annual credit of approximately 9 percent of the qualifying basis of low-income units placed in service. If Federal subsidies were used to finance the project, the credit is limited to approximately 4 percent.[98] The exact amount of the credit is determined by the IRS on a monthly basis. The percentages for any month are calculated to yield, over a 10-year credit period, amounts of credit that have a present value equal to (1) 70 percent of the qualified basis of new buildings that are not Federally subsidized for the tax year, and (2) 30 percent of the qualified basis of existing buildings and new buildings that are Federally subsidized.[99]

> **Example 26.** In December 1990, H Corporation constructed and placed in service a qualified low-income housing project. The qualified basis of the project was $1 million. The 70% present value credit for buildings placed in service in December 1990 is 9.06%.[100] Thus, the annual credit that H would be entitled to before consideration of the general business credit limitations is $90,600.

Each year, the sum of allowed low-income housing credits is subject to a nationwide cap. The cap amount is allotted between all of the states so that each state will have a cap on the amount of low-income housing credits it can authorize. A credit allocation from the appropriate state credit authority must be received by the owner of the property eligible for the low-income housing credit. The credit is available on a per-unit basis; thus, a single building may have some units that qualify for the credit and some that do not. In order to qualify, a low-income housing project must meet a host of exacting criteria throughout a 15-year compliance period.[101]

---

[98] § 42(b)(1).

[99] § 42(b)(2)(B). A formula for making such computations is provided in Rev. Rul. 88-6, 1988-1 C.B. 3.

[100] Rev. Rul. 90-99, I.R.B. 1990-49.

[101] See §§ 42(g) and 42(l). The RRA of 1990 allows taxpayers who had an investment in low-income housing credit property before October 26, 1990 to elect to claim a low-income housing credit of 150 percent of the credit otherwise available for the first year ending after October 24, 1990. The election is irrevocable and applies to successors in interest. The low-income housing credit available in future years must be reduced ratably by the amount of increased credit taken in 1991. See RRA of 1990 Act § 11407(c) for more details.

The Revenue Reconciliation Act (RRA) of 1990 created an enhanced oil recovery credit and a credit for expenditures to provide access to disabled individuals that were incorporated into the general business credit.[102] Whereas the enhanced oil recovery credit is narrowly focused on existing oil and gas properties requiring secondary or tertiary methods of production, and therefore has limited applicability to general taxpayers,[103] the disabled access credit is available to all eligible small businesses.

DISABLED ACCESS CREDIT

Under new § 44, an eligible small business can elect to take a nonrefundable tax credit equal to 50 percent of the amount of the eligible access expenditures for any taxable year that exceed $250 but do not exceed $10,250. An eligible small business is defined as one having gross receipts for the preceding taxable year that did not exceed $1,000,000, or having no more than 30 full-time employees during the preceding taxable year. Eligible access expenditures are defined as amounts paid or incurred by an eligible small business to comply with applicable requirements of the Americans With Disabilities Act of 1990. Eligible access expenditures generally include amounts paid or incurred for the following:

1. Removing architectural, communication, physical, or transportation barriers that prevent a business from being accessible to, or usable by individuals with disabilities

2. Providing qualified interpreters or other effective methods of making aurally delivered materials available to individuals with hearing impairments

3. Providing qualified readers, taped texts, and other effective methods of making visually delivered materials available to individuals with visual impairments

4. Acquiring or modifying equipment or devices for individuals with disabilities

5. Providing other similar services, modifications, materials, or equipment

In cases where the eligible business is being conducted as a partnership or an S corporation, the dollar limitations are applied at both the entity and the owner level. Any portion of the unused general business credit attributable to the disabled access credit may not be carried back to any taxable year ending before 1990.

---

[102] New §§ 43 and 44.

[103] For details of this credit, see RRA of 1990 Act § 11511 and the accompanying Conference Committee Report beginning on page 139.

Example 27.   J, a sole proprietor, had gross receipts of $700,000 last year and incurred $5,250 of eligible access expenditures this year. J's disabled access credit for this year is $2,500 [($5,250 − $250) × 50%].

As is the case with other components of the general business credit, the depreciable basis of assets acquired using access expenditures must be reduced by the amount of credit claimed with respect to those expenditures. Alternatively, any current deduction attributable to the access expenditures must be reduced by the amount of credit claimed.[104]

GENERAL BUSINESS CREDIT CARRYOVER RULES

Prior to 1984, each component of the general business credit contained its own separate limitations regarding the amount of tax that could be offset by each credit. As a transitional rule, § 38 provides for pre-1984 unused credits to be combined into a single credit at the end of 1983. The resulting general business credit was allowed to be carried forward to 1984—the first year of the combined 15-year carryover period.

If the business credit carryover cannot be used within the stipulated time period, the credit expires. This is a double loss for taxpayers who used the full investment tax credit percentages or other credits and who decreased the basis of property for ACRS computations. Not only have they lost the credit but they also were unable to deduct the full cost of the assets. Because of this possibility, taxpayers are allowed to deduct the amount of the previous reductions from basis stipulated by the expired ITC or other credits. This deduction may be taken in the year *following* the expiration of the tax credit carryover period.[105]

Example 28.   Q originally claimed an ITC of $10,000 and reduced the basis in the assets by $5,000. After the expiration of the 15-year carryforward period, an unused ITC of $3,000 expires. In the first taxable year after the expiration of the credit carryover period, Q may deduct $1,500 ($1/2$ of $3,000). This amount equals the original decrease in basis for the expired investment credit.

OTHER BUSINESS CREDITS

Three other business credits are available to taxpayers. A foreign tax credit is authorized by § 27. A discussion of this credit and other aspects of international taxation is beyond the scope of this text. The credit for clinical testing of certain drugs (§ 28) and the credit for producing fuel from a nonconventional source (§ 29) are of limited applicability and are not covered in this text.

---

[104]   § 44(c)(7).   [105]   § 196.

MINIMUM TAX CREDIT

As previously discussed, a significant feature of the new alternative minimum tax (AMT) system is that many taxpayers will be required to pay the AMT long before they would have had to pay the regular income tax from certain investments. For example, taxpayers with substantial investments in depreciable personal property are *denied* the tax reduction benefits of MACRS for purposes of computing the AMT.[106] Likewise, a taxpayer who exercises an ISO must recognize income for AMT purposes to the extent the fair market value of the stock exceeds its option price, but for regular income tax purposes the taxpayer does not recognize income until the stock acquired with the ISO is sold. Without some form of relief, a taxpayer could be subject to the AMT in one year and the regular tax in a later year on the same item.

In order to alleviate the possibility of double taxation under the two tax systems, Congress introduced an alternative minimum tax credit. Basically, the alternative minimum tax credit paid in one year may be used as a credit against the taxpayer's *regular* tax liability in subsequent years. The credit may be carried forward indefinitely until used; however, the credit cannot be carried back *nor* can it be used to offset any future minimum tax liability.[107] In effect, the minimum tax credit converts the AMT from a permanent out-of-pocket tax to a prepayment of regular tax to the extent the AMT is attributable to deferral or timing preferences and adjustments rather than to exclusion items.[108]

For noncorporate taxpayers, the AMT credit for any year is the amount of the taxpayer's *adjusted net minimum tax* for all tax years after reduction for the minimum tax credit utilized for all such prior years. The adjusted net minimum tax, generally the amount of the minimum tax credit, is the difference between the AMT actually paid and the amount of AMT that would have been paid if only exclusion items were taken into account. The exclusion items are listed below:

1. Itemized deductions

2. Personal exemptions

3. Percentage depletion

4. Tax-exempt interest

5. Appreciated property charitable deductions that created a tax preference item

---

[106] Recall that depreciable personal property placed in service after 1986 can be depreciated using either the 150 percent declining balance or the ADS straight-line method over the asset's class life for AMT purposes.

[107] § 53(a).

[108] § 53(d)(1)(B)(iv) authorizes corporate taxpayers to use the entire minimum tax liability as the minimum tax credit. However, this rule applies only to minimum tax credits arising in taxable years beginning after December 31, 1989.

Example 29.   J is married and files a joint return for the current year on which she reports $80,000 of taxable income and claims the standard deduction. In computing her taxable income, J claimed a $56,000 depletion deduction, which creates a $56,000 AMT preference item, and she claimed a $100,000 deduction for research expenses from an activity in which she does not materially participate, which creates a $90,000 AMT adjustment for research and experimental expenditures. J's minimum tax credit to be carried forward is $26,760 as computed below.

The amount of AMT actually required to be paid is $34,220, determined as follows:

Regular taxable income...............................	$ 80,000
Plus: AMT adjustment for research expenses....... +	90,000
AMT adjustment for personal exemptions..... +	4,300
AMT adjustment for standard deduction ...... +	5,700
AMT preference item for depletion............ +	56,000
AMTI..	$236,000
Less: Exemption amount [after $21,500 phase-out ($236,000 − $150,000 = $86,000 × 0.25)] −	18,500
AMTI base...	$217,500
Times: AMT rate.................................. ×	24%
Tentative AMT.......................................	$ 52,200
Less: Regular tax liability.......................... −	17,980
AMT liability for current year..........................	$ 34,220

The amount of AMT that would have been required to be paid if only exclusion items were taken into account is $7,460, determined as follows:

Regular taxable income...............................	$ 80,000
Plus: AMT adjustment for personal exemptions..... +	4,300
AMT adjustment for standard deduction ...... +	5,700
Tax preference for depletion.................. +	56,000
AMTI..	$146,000
Less: Exemption amount (no phase-out)........... −	40,000
AMTI base...	$106,000
Times: AMT rate.................................. ×	24%
Tentative AMT.......................................	$ 25,440
Less: Regular tax liability.......................... −	17,980
AMT using only exclusions............................	$ 7,460
AMT actually paid....................................	$ 34,220
AMT using only exclusion items...................... −	7,460
Minimum tax credit..................................	$ 26,760

The $26,760 minimum tax credit may be carried forward and used to offset (reduce) the regular tax liability in subsequent years.

NONBUSINESS CREDITS

In addition to the numerous business credits discussed thus far, there are several nonbusiness credits available to individual taxpayers only. These credits include (1) the child and dependent care credit, (2) the credit for the elderly, (3) the credit for interest on certain home mortgages, and (4) the earned income credit and other refundable credits. Each of these credits is discussed below.

CHILD AND DEPENDENT CARE CREDIT

Congress has encouraged entry into the work force by providing a tax credit for individuals who must pay to have certain dependents cared for while they are at work. A taxpayer who maintains a household for a qualified dependent may claim the credit. A *qualified dependent* is a child under the age of 13 or any physically or mentally incapacitated dependent or spouse. Special rules apply to divorced parents—*only* the custodial parent qualifies for the credit.[109]

The *child and dependent care credit* is computed by multiplying the applicable percentage times the lesser of employment-related expenses or earned income. The *applicable percentage* begins at 30 percent and is reduced (but not below 20%) by one percentage point for each $2,000 (or fraction thereof) that the taxpayer's adjusted gross income exceeds $10,000. Thus, the rate for a taxpayer with A.G.I. of $12,500 is 28 percent. The rate for taxpayers with adjusted gross incomes in excess of $28,000 is 20 percent.

Employment-Related Expenses. Employment-related expenses are those expenses for the care of a qualified individual incurred by the taxpayer in order to be gainfully employed or to seek employment.[110] The expenses must be incurred for household services or for the care of a qualifying individual. The maximum amount of employment-related expenses that may be taken into account for purposes of computing the credit are $2,400 for one qualifying individual and $4,800 for two or more qualifying individuals.[111] The computation of the child and dependent care credit requires a three-step approach, as illustrated in the following example.

---

[109] § 21(e)(5).   [111] § 21(c).

[110] § 21(b)(2).

Example 30. F is a widower and maintains a household for his two small children. He incurs $5,000 as employment-related expenses and reports A.G.I. of $27,300 for the current year. F's child care credit is determined as follows:

Step 1: Determine the applicable percentage:

Adjusted gross income............................	$27,300
Less: Ceiling on 30% rate........................	(10,000)
Adjusted gross income over $10,000 limit............	$17,300

Divided by $2,000 and rounded up:
($17,300 ÷ $2,000) = 8.65%
Rounded up to 9%

Maximum rate.......................................	30%
Subtracted from 30%...............................	(9%)
Allowable percentage...............................	21%

Step 2: Determine the allowable employment-related expenses:

Lesser of $5,000 paid or $4,800 limit..............	$ 4,800

Step 3: Determine the dependent care credit:

Allowable employment-related expenses...........	$ 4,800
Times: Applicable percentage .... ×	21%
Dependent care credit............................	$1,008

Earned Income Limitation. Employment-related expenses are limited to the individual's earned income for the year. A married couple must file a joint return in order to claim the credit.[112] The employment-related expenses may not exceed the lesser of the taxpayer's earned income or the earnings of the taxpayer's spouse. In determining the lesser earned income for married couples, special rules apply if one spouse is either a full-time student[113] or an incapacitated person. The student or incapacitated spouse will be deemed to have earned income of $200 a month if there is one qualified dependent or $400 a month if there are two or more qualified dependents. This deemed income does not increase A.G.I. when determining the applicable percentage. These rules are illustrated in the following example.

---

[112] § 21(e)(2).

[113] § 21(d)(2). For this purpose, a full-time student is defined exactly the same as for the dependency test (i.e., for at least five months, partial months count as full months).

Example 31.   B and G are married, have one dependent child, age 9, incur employment-related expenses of $2,700, and have A.G.I. of $22,500 for the current taxable year. G is employed full-time and earns $27,000 a year. B returned to graduate school and was a full-time student for ten months during the year. He was not employed during the year.

Step 1: The applicable percentage is determined to be 23% [30% − ($22,500 − $10,000 = $12,500 ÷ $2,000 = 6.25%, rounded up to 7%)]

Step 2: The allowable employment-related expenses are $2,000. This is determined by the lesser of three amounts: (1) the $2,700 spent, (2) the $2,400 limit, and (3) B's deemed earned income of $2,000 ($200 for one dependent × 10 months).

Step 3: Determine the dependent care credit:

Allowable employment-related expenses....	$2,000
Applicable percentage (30% − 7%)......... ×	23%
Dependent care credit........................	$460

The credit may be claimed for child or dependent care expenses paid to any relative who is *not* the taxpayer's dependent. If the relative is the taxpayer's child, the child must be at least 19 years of age. In addition, if care is provided in the taxpayer's home, the person providing the care may do household chores as long as the predominant purpose is care of the qualified dependent(s). Also, the name, address, and taxpayer identification number of the care provider must be reported on any return claiming a credit for dependent care.

Amounts paid for care outside the home in dependent care centers[114] and in nursery schools for preschool children also qualify for the credit. In fact, most care outside the home is acceptable for the credit if it is for a qualifying dependent who is a member of the taxpayer's household and regularly spends at least eight hours a day in the taxpayer's home. However, school tuition, other than nursery school, does not qualify—nor will amounts paid to send a qualifying dependent to summer camp. In addition, transportation costs for the dependent between the taxpayer's home and the care location are not qualifying expenses.

For years beginning after 1981, employers have been allowed to establish qualified dependent care assistance plans.[115] These plans allow employers a current deduction for contributions to the plans and allow employees to *exclude* from gross income any payments received under the plan to the extent that the expenses would qualify as child and dependent care expenses incurred to enable an employee to work. Of course, any amount excluded by an employee as a dependent care assistance payment will not qualify for any other type of income tax deduction or credit.[116]

---

[114] § 21(b)(2)(C).   [116] § 21(c).

[115] See § 129 and the discussion in Chapter 6.

The child and dependent care credit is nonrefundable and is used to offset the tax liability determined under Code § 26. It is the *first* credit to be used in reducing an individual's tax liability and there is no carryover or carryback available for unused credits.

CREDIT FOR THE ELDERLY AND PERMANENTLY DISABLED

A nonrefundable tax credit is available to certain taxpayers who are either 65 years of age or older or are permanently and totally disabled.[117] The credit is 15 percent of an individual's earned and investment income that does not exceed the taxpayer's appropriate § 22 amount.[118] The maximum § 22 amount is

1. $5,000 for single individuals

2. $5,000 for a joint return where only one spouse is at least 65 years old

3. $7,500 for a joint return where both spouses are 65 years or older

4. $3,750 for a married individual filing separately[119]

The maximum amount from above is then reduced by excludable pension and annuity income received during the year, including social security and railroad retirement benefits, and by one-half of the taxpayer's A.G.I. that exceeds

1. $7,500 for unmarried individuals

2. $10,000 if married filing jointly

3. $5,000 if married filing separately[120]

> **Example 32.** P is single, 65 years old, and has A.G.I. of $8,300 from interest and dividends. During the taxable year, she also received social security of $1,500. Her credit for the elderly is computed as follows:

Maximum § 22 amount..........................		$5,000
Less: Social security received	$1,500	
50% of A.G.I. over $7,500 ($8,300 − $7,500 = $800 × 50%)..............................	+ 400	(1,900)
Section 22 amount available for credit...........		$3,100
Multiply by rate.................................		× 15%
Amount of credit.................................		$ 465

---

[117] Limited rules apply to taxpayers who are under 65 years old if they are certain governmental retirees subject to the Public Retirement System and elect to have this section apply [see § 22(c)].

[118] § 22(a).

[119] § 22(b)(2).

[120] § 22(d).

There are a number of additional special rules, and because these rules are quite complicated, individuals are allowed to file their return with a request that the IRS compute their tax liability and tax credit. However, few people are able to take advantage of the credit for the elderly since social security receipts commonly exceed the maximum § 22 amount.

The credit for the elderly or permanently disabled is limited to the § 26 tax liability reduced by the child and dependent care credit. Like the child and dependent care credit, this credit is nonrefundable and may not be carried back or forward.

CREDIT FOR INTEREST ON CERTAIN HOME MORTGAGES

Code § 25 was intended to curb state and local governments' usage of *tax-exempt mortgage and subsidy bonds*. The ability of state and local governments to issue the tax-exempt qualified mortgage bonds is scheduled to expire on December 31, 1991. Code § 25 allows the states to exchange qualified mortgage bond authority for authority to issue home mortgage credit certificates (MCC). Under this provision, home purchasers receiving MCCs are entitled to a credit equal to a specified percentage of the interest paid or accrued during the taxable year on the qualifying mortgage.[121] This percentage may not exceed 50 percent, but may not be less than 10 percent of the interest on qualifying indebtedness. The maximum amount of credit allowed is $2,000.[122] The amount of the home purchaser's interest deduction in any year is reduced by the amount of the MCC for that year. The credit will offset the § 26 tax liability after it has been reduced for credits with a lower Code section number. Excess credits may be carried forward for three years.[123]

REFUNDABLE CREDITS

Refundable credits are those credits that are recoverable even though an individual has no income tax liability in the current year. They are treated as payments of taxes. Included in this category are the credit for taxes withheld at the source (§ 31), the earned income credit (§ 32), the credit for tax withheld at source on nonresident aliens and foreign corporations (§ 33), and the gasoline and special fuels credit (§ 34).

---

[121] § 25(a)(1)(B).

[122] § 25(a)(2).

[123] § 25(e).

TAX WITHHELD AT THE SOURCE

The first and most important of the refundable credits is styled "Credit for Tax Withheld on Wages" and obviously includes the amount withheld by an employer as a tax on wages earned.[124] However, the credit has broader application with respect to certain taxes withheld by the payor at the source of payment, including

1. Tax on pensions and annuities withheld by the payor[125]

2. Overpaid FICA taxes (in cases where a taxpayer has two or more employers in the same year)

3. Amounts withheld as backup withholding in cases where the taxpayer fails to furnish a taxpayer identification number to the payor of interest or dividends[126]

4. Quarterly estimated tax payments

Refundable credits may be used to offset all taxes imposed by the Code, including penalty taxes. This result is accomplished by combining all the refundable credits and accounting for them after all the nonrefundable credits have been used to offset the § 26 tax liability.

EARNED INCOME CREDIT

A tax credit on *earned income* is available to certain low-income taxpayers. The RRA of 1990 significantly modified the earned income credit by increasing the percentages over a four-year period, authorizing a higher percentage if there is more than one qualifying child and/or if a child is less than one year old at the end of the taxable year and expanding the credit to include a supplemental credit for health insurance premiums paid.[127]

For years beginning in 1991, the maximum basic earned income credit is equal to the appropriate percentage (see Exhibit 13-8) times the first $7,140 of earned income for a maximum credit of $1,192 (.167 × $7,140) for a taxpayer with one qualifying child and $1,235 (.173 × $7,140) for a taxpayer with two or more qualifying children.[128] If either A.G.I. or earned income exceeds $11,250 in 1991, the credit is subject to reduction by a specified percentage of the excess amount.[129] As a result, the basic earned income credit is eliminated when the A.G.I. or the earned income for a taxpayer exceeds $21,244.

---

[124] §§ 31(a) and 3401.

[125] §§ 31(a) and 3405.

[126] §§ 31(c) and 3406.

[127] § 32(a).

[128] § 32(b)(1) and Rev. Proc. 90-64.

[129] § 32(b)(2) and Rev. Proc. 90-64.

```
┌─────────────────────────────────────────┐
│              Exhibit 13-8                 │
│  Earned Income Credit and Phase-out       │
│              Percentages                  │
└─────────────────────────────────────────┘
```

Tax Year Beginning In	Number of Qualifying Children	Credit Percentage	Phase-out Percentage
1991	1 child	16.7	11.93
	2 or more children	17.3	12.36
1992	1 child	17.6	12.57
	2 or more children	18.4	13.14
1993	1 child	18.5	13.21
	2 or more children	19.5	13.93
1994	1 child	23.0	16.43
	2 or more children	25.0	17.86

Example 33. D and M are married, file a joint return for 1991, and maintain a household for their dependent son, who is three years old. D has earned income of $15,000 and M has none. The couple own investments that produce $2,475 of includible income for the year and have an A.G.I. of $17,475 ($15,000 + $2,475). The earned income credit is computed as follows:

Maximum credit (16.7% × $7,140)	$1,192
Less: Reduction for A.G.I. over $11,250	
($17,475 − $11,250 = $6,225 × 11.93%)	(743)
Earned income credit.....................................	$449

Supplemental Young Child Credit. In the case of a taxpayer with a qualifying child who has not attained one year of age as of the close of the taxable year, the credit percentage is increased by 5 percentage points, and the phase-out percentage is increased by 3.57 percentage points. If the taxpayer elects to take a child into account for this purpose, the child will not be treated as a qualifying individual for purposes of the child and dependent care credit.[130]

---

[130] § 32(b)(1)(D).

The income base eligible for the credit, $7,140, and the phase-out levels, $11,250 and $21,244, are adjusted annually for inflation.[131] The IRS provides a work sheet and an earned income credit table to aid taxpayers in making the earned income credit calculation. The work sheet and table are included with the instructions for completing Form 1040 and Form 1040A (see Appendix B for a copy of the 1990 Table).[132]

As a refundable credit, qualified individuals may receive tax refunds equal to their earned income credit even in years when they have no tax liability.[133]

> **Example 34.**   Y has earned income and A.G.I. of $5,600, has three exemptions (including two qualified children), and files as head of household. As a result, she has no tax liability for the year. However, she is entitled to a tax refund equal to the earned income credit of $969 ($5,600 × 17.3%) plus any taxes (other than FICA taxes) withheld from her wages.

Earned income is wages, salaries, tips, and other employer compensation plus earnings from self-employment. It does not include pension and annuity income even though provided by an employer for past services. An individual's earned income is computed without regard to any community property laws.

Eligibility Requirements.   Any individual that has a qualifying child will be eligible for the earned income credit. A child will be considered a *qualifying child* if four requirements are satisfied: a relationship requirement, an age requirement, a residency requirement, and an identification requirement.[134] The relationship test is satisfied if the child is a son or daughter of the taxpayer or a descendent of either, or if the child is a stepson or stepdaughter, a foster child, or a legally adopted child of the taxpayer. Married children will not satisfy the relationship test unless the taxpayer is entitled to claim a dependency exemption for the married child. The age requirement is met if the child has not attained the age of 19 as of the close of the calendar year, is a full-time student who has not attained the age of 24 as of the close of the calendar year, or is permanently and totally disabled any time during the taxable year. The residency test is satisfied if the child has the same principal place of abode as the taxpayer for more than one-half of the taxable year and that abode is located in the United States. To satisfy the identification requirement, the taxpayer must indicate the name, age, and taxpayer identification number of the qualified child on the taxpayer's tax return.

---

[131] § 32(i).

[132] Note that the earned income credit table prepared annually by the IRS reflects the credit based on a mid-point of each $25 increment of an income range.

[133] The taxpayer is required to reduce his or her earned income credit by the amount of the alternative minimum tax imposed on that individual.

[134] § 32(c).

Health Insurance Credit.   The Revenue Reconciliation Act of 1990 added an additional credit for health insurance premiums paid by the taxpayer on a health insurance policy that covers a qualified child. The credit is determined in the same manner as the basic earned income credit except that the credit percentage is 6 percent and the phase-out percentage is 4.285 percent.[135]

In certain situations, employers can make advanced payments of the earned income credit to an eligible employee.[136] An eligible employee who elects to receive advanced payments of the credit from his or her employer *must*

1.   File a certificate of eligibility (i.e., Form W-5) with the employer, and

2.   File a tax return for the year the income is earned.

If the taxpayer receives advances that exceed the allowable credit, the excess is treated as an increase in the Federal income tax imposed on the taxpayer for that year.

OTHER REFUNDABLE CREDITS

Three other refundable credits are allowed. Code § 33 allows as a credit the amount of tax withheld at the source for nonresident aliens and foreign corporations. Code § 34 provides an income tax credit for the amount of excise tax paid on gasoline, where the gasoline is used on a farm, for other nonhighway purposes, by local transit systems, and by operators of intercity, local, or school buses. Finally, Code § 35 provides that an overpayment of taxes resulting from filing an amended return will be treated as a refundable credit.

---

[135]   § 32(b)(2).   [136]   §§ 32(g) and 3507.

PROBLEM MATERIALS

DISCUSSION QUESTIONS

13-1 *Alternative Minimum Tax.* It has been said that a taxpayer must maintain a second set of books to comply with the AMT system. Why is the extra set of books necessary?

13-2 *Alternative Minimum Tax.* The AMT requires taxpayers to keep an extra set of books for several adjustment items. What action can a taxpayer take to minimize the recordkeeping requirements with respect to depreciation deductions?

13-3 *Alternative Minimum Tax.* Assume a taxpayer has a regular tax liability of $25,000, a tentative AMT of $28,000, and an AMT of $3,000 for the current year. How much does the taxpayer actually owe the IRS?

13-4 *Alternative Minimum Tax.* A taxpayer has an AMT liability of $50,000 and a general business credit of $50,000. He is not concerned about paying the AMT because he thinks the general business credit can be used to offset the AMT. Is he correct? What if the taxpayer were a corporation?

13-5 *Alternative Minimum Tax.* Is it safe to assume that only wealthy individuals who have low taxable incomes are subject to the alternative minimum tax? Are any taxpayers whose marginal rates exceed 24 percent subject to the alternative minimum tax? Explain.

13-6 *Alternative Minimum Tax.* G will be subject to the alternative minimum tax in 1991 but not in 1992. G's property tax on her residence is due November 15, 1991. If she defers payment of the property tax until 1992, she must pay a 5 percent penalty. When should G pay the property tax? Explain.

13-7 *Alternative Minimum Tax.* Some interest expense can be taken as an itemized deduction for regular tax purposes but different rules control the interest expenses allowable as an AMT itemized deduction. Explain the differences in these rules and note which rules are more restrictive.

13-8 *Alternative Minimum Tax.* Is the § 179 (first-year expensing) deduction allowed as a deduction for the AMT system?

13-9 *Credits vs. Deductions.* Assume taxpayers have a choice of deducting $1,000 for A.G.I. or taking a $250 tax credit for the current year. Which taxpayers should choose the deduction? Why?

13-10 *Rehabilitation and Energy Investment Tax Credits.* A taxpayer purchases an old train station, which was placed in service in 1935, for $20,000. He plans to tear the building down and erect a new office building for $100,000. Will any of this qualify for the rehabilitation or energy investment tax credit? What tax advice could you give the taxpayer for his consideration in maximizing these credits?

13-11 *Rehabilitation and Energy Investment Tax Credit.* When a taxpayer claims a rehabilitation tax credit, what impact does the credit have on basis of the property for cost recovery purposes? What is the impact on the basis when a business energy credit is claimed? What if the disabled access credit is claimed?

13-12 *ITC Recapture.* Explain two possible consequences if a taxpayer claims an investment tax credit on property and then makes an early disposition of the property.

13-13 *Minimum Tax Credit.* If a taxpayer pays an AMT in the current year, what consequences does that payment have on the AMT liability that may be owed in subsequent years? What impact does the payment of the AMT in the current year have on the regular tax liability in subsequent years?

13-14 *Dependent Care Credit.* A husband and wife both work and employ a babysitter to watch the children during their work hours. How much of the babysitter's salary qualifies for the child and dependent care credit if

    a.   The babysitter performs cooking and cleaning services while she is watching the children.

    b.   The babysitter also performs services around the house including gardening, bartending, and chauffeuring.

13-15 *Earned Income Credit.* A husband and wife with A.G.I. and earned income of $7,000 maintained a household for their son but were unable to claim him as a dependent because he was 20 years old and earned $3,500. Can the son or his parents qualify for the earned income credit? Explain.

13-16 *Research Credit.* Two college students work in a garage during 1991 doing research for a new patent. They spend $15,000 on the research in 1991. In January 1992, they form an S corporation, each controlling 50 percent of the stock, and apply for the patent, which is granted in 1992. How much credit for research expenditures will the taxpayers be allowed and in what year?

13-17 *Targeted Jobs Credit.* The purpose of the targeted jobs credit is to encourage the employment of certain groups of people with high unemployment rates. The credit has not quite achieved the desired objectives. What changes should be made to the present credit to increase its effectiveness?

PROBLEMS

13-18 *Alternative Minimum Tax—Computation.* T is single and has taxable income of $47,050 and a regular tax liability of $10,529 for the current year. T uses the standard deduction for regular tax purposes and has $60,000 of positive adjustments for AMT purposes.

    a.   Determine T's tentative AMT and her AMT.

    b.   Determine the amount that T actually has to pay the IRS this year.

13-19 *Alternative Minimum Tax—Computation.*   V and W are married and file a joint return for the current year. They have no other dependents and they take the standard deduction. V and W's taxable income is $78,400 and their regular tax liability is $17,532. They have $60,000 of AMT preference items and $32,050 of AMT positive adjustments. Determine V and W's tentative AMT and their AMT liability.

13-20 *Alternative Minimum Tax—Charitable Contribution Preference.*   J contributes a painting to the local university. He had purchased the painting in 1980 for $10,000, and it was appraised at $60,000 on the date of gift. The painting was placed in the university's Art Building for display and study by art students. J's A.G.I. for the year of contribution is $300,000.

a.   Determine J's allowable charitable contribution deduction for the regular tax system.

b.   Determine J's allowable charitable contribution deduction for the AMT system.

c.   Determine J's AMT charitable contribution preference amount with respect to the contribution of the painting.

13-21 *Alternative Minimum Tax—Charitable Contribution Preference.*   J contributed stock to the local university. He had purchased the stock in 1980 for $10,000, and it was appraised at $60,000 on the date of gift. The stock was sold shortly after the contribution was made, and a painting was purchased by the university with the proceeds from the sale. The university placed the painting in its Art Building for display and study by art students. J's A.G.I. in the year of contribution is $300,000.

a.   Determine J's allowable charitable contribution deduction for the regular tax system.

b.   Determine J's allowable charitable contribution deduction for the AMT system.

c.   Determine J's AMT charitable contribution preference amount with respect to the contribution of the stock.

13-22 *Alternative Minimum Tax—Computation.*   B is single and reports the following items of income and deductions for the current year:

Salary...	$ 50,000
Net long-term capital gain on sale	
of investment property	200,000
Medical expenses...............................	17,500
Casualty loss....................................	4,500
State and local income taxes....................	10,000
Real estate taxes................................	15,000
Charitable contributions (all cash)	15,000
Interest on home mortgage......................	12,000
Interest on investment loans	
(unimproved real property)	10,000

The only additional transaction during the year was the exercise of an incentive stock option of her employer's stock at an option price of $12,000 when the stock was worth $100,000. Compute B's tax liability for the current year.

13-23   *Alternative Minimum Tax.*   Refer to the facts in Problem 13-22 and assume B holds the stock acquired by exercising her ISO for two years and sells it for $105,000. Determine the amount of gain that must be reported for regular tax purposes and the gain that must be reflected in the AMT calculations in the year the stock was sold.

13-24   *Alternative Minimum Tax—Cost Recovery Adjustment.*   In 1986, T placed in service two heavy-duty trucks (Truck A and Truck B), which cost $40,000 each. In 1991, T placed two light-duty trucks (Truck C and Truck D) in service, also at a cost of $40,000 each. T uses the applicable ACRS and MACRS methods of depreciation for all his assets.

   a.   Identify and calculate the minimum tax adjustments that must be made for AMT purposes in 1991.
   b.   Identify and calculate the amount of tax preferences, if any, that must be included in the AMT calculation for T.

13-25   *Alternative Minimum Tax—Cost Recovery.*   Refer to the facts in Problem 13-24, but assume Truck C and Truck D, which were placed in service this year at a cost of $40,000 each, were heavy-duty trucks. Identify and calculate the minimum tax adjustments that must be made for AMT purposes in 1991.

13-26   *Alternative Minimum Tax—Cost Recovery Adjustment.*   In January 1991 A purchases nonresidential property for $200,000, excluding the cost of the land. For regular tax purposes, the 1991 depreciation on the building is $6,085 ($200,000 $\times$ $^{11.5}/_{12}$ $\times$ $^{1}/_{31.5}$). For AMT purposes, depreciation is $4,792 ($200,000 $\times$ $^{11.5}/_{12}$ $\times$ $^{1}/_{40}$). Determine the AMT adjustment for cost recovery for 1991 and 1992.

13-27   *Alternative Minimum Tax—Computation.*   O is married to G and they file a joint return for 1991. O and G have A.G.I. of $70,000. One of the deductions from gross income was $50,000 of percentage depletion. Cost depletion on their oil and gas property was zero because the cost basis of the property was reduced to zero by prior years' depletion deductions. They do not itemize deductions. Determine O and G's tax liability for 1991.

13-28   *Alternative Minimum Tax.*   T is an unmarried real estate entrepreneur. In 1988 he purchased constructed properties and leased them to tenants on long-term leases. In 1991, T has rental losses on his real estate activities of $100,000 and income from his brokerage business of $100,000. T also has a $25,000 general business credit carryover from 1990. Determine T's tax liability for 1991, assuming he does not itemize his deductions.

13-29   *Minimum Tax Credit.*   Refer to the facts in Problem 13-22 and determine the minimum tax credit, if any, that is available to offset the regular tax liability in 1992.

13-30   *General Business Credit—Limited by Tax Liability.*   K's tax liability before credits is $35,000. She earned a general business credit of $40,000. Determine K's tax liability after credits and any general business credit carryback or carryforward that may exist.

13-31 *Energy Investment Credit.*   In the current year, J invested $60,000 in a solar system to heat water for a production process.

  a.   Determine the amount of business energy credit available to J.
  b.   Determine the basis of the energy property that J must use for cost recovery purposes.

13-32 *Rehabilitation Investment Credit.*   During the current year, T incurred $300,000 of qualified rehabilitation expenditures with respect to 75-year-old property.

  a.   Determine the amount of rehabilitation investment credit available to T.
  b.   Determine the basis of the rehabilitated property that T must use for cost recovery purposes.

13-33 *Rehabilitation Credit—Computation.*   During the current year, K incurred $200,000 of qualified rehabilitation expenditures with respect to property placed in service in 1930. The entire block where his property is located has been designated as a Certified Historical District.

  a.   Determine the amount of credit allowable to K if his structure is recognized as a historical structure.
  b.   Assuming that K paid $180,000 for his building in the current year and that he would like to maximize his cost recovery deductions, calculate his adjusted basis in the building at the end of the year. Assume that the property was placed in service in July of the current year.

13-34 *ITC Recapture.*   Assume D claimed a business energy credit of $30,000 for property placed in service on December 18, 1988 and that D sold this property on January 7, 1991. Determine the amount, if any, of ITC recapture that D should report as an additional tax in 1991.

13-35 *ITC Recapture.*   Assume L claimed rehabilitation investment credit of $80,000 on property placed in service on February 18, 1988 and that L exchanged this rehabilitated property for like-kind property (a § 1031 exchange) on March 17, 1991. Determine the amount of ITC recapture that L should report as an additional tax in 1991, if any.

13-36 *Research and Experimentation Credit.*   M, a sole proprietor, has been in business only two years but is very successful. He has average annual gross receipts of $150,000 for this period and incurred $40,000 in qualified R&E expenses this year.

  a.   Determine M's R&E credit for the current year.
  b.   Determine the current deduction for R&E expenditures that M is entitled to, assuming he elects to deduct R&E expenditures currently.

13-37 *Disabled Access Credit—Computation.*   P Corp. had gross receipts of $500,000 last year and incurred $9,000 of eligible access expenditures to build a wheelchair ramp this year.

  a.   Determine P's disabled access credit.
  b.   Determine the basis of the wheelchair ramp that will be eligible for cost recovery deductions.

13-38 *Dependent Care Credit.* V and J are married and file a joint return for the current year. Because they both work, they had to pay a babysitter $5,200 to watch their three children (ages 7, 8, and 9). V earned $17,000 and J earned $21,200 during the year. They do not have any other source of income nor do they claim any deductions for adjusted gross income. Determine the allowable dependent care credit for V and J.

13-39 *Dependent Care Credit.* M and B are married, have a son three years old, and file a joint return for the current year. They incurred $500 a month for day care center expenses. During the year, B earned $23,000 but M did not work outside the home. They do not have any other source of income nor do they claim any deductions for adjusted gross income. Determine the allowable dependent care credit for the year if

    a.   M enrolled as a full-time student in a local community college on September 6 of the current year.

    b.   M was in school from January through June, and from September through December of the current year.

13-40 *Dependent Care Credit.* C is a single parent raising a son who is eight years old. During the current year, C earned $19,500 and paid $3,000 to a sitter to watch her son after school. Determine C's dependent care credit for the current year.

13-41 *Earned Income Credit.* R is 43, divorced, and maintains a household for his 7-year-old dependent daughter. R was laid off in 1990 and his unemployment benefits have run out. During 1991, he worked at part-time jobs earning $5,500. He has no other sources of income.

    a.   Determine R's allowable earned income credit.

    b.   Determine R's tax payment due or his refund, assuming that nothing was withheld from his wages and that he did not make any quarterly estimated tax payments.

12-42 *Earned Income Credit.* S, who is 24 and a single parent, maintains a household for her 3-year-old dependent daughter and her 10-month-old son. S earned $11,500 during this calendar year. S has no other source of income and does not itemize her deductions.

    a.   Determine S's allowable earned income credit.

    b.   Determine S's tax payment due or her refund, assuming that $200 was withheld from her wages and that she did not make any quarterly estimated tax payments.

13-43 *Integrative Credit Problem.* J, who is 32 and a single parent, maintains a household for his six-year-old dependent son. J earned $13,500 and paid $3,000 in child care payments during the calendar year. J did not have any Federal income tax withheld from his check. Determine the amount of J's refund check from the IRS, if any, or the amount that J must pay the IRS, if required.

13-44 *Credit for the Elderly.* P and D are 66 years old, married, and file a joint return. The only sources of income they have are dividend income of $14,000 and Social Security of $2,500.

a. Determine the allowable credit for the elderly for the current year.

b. Determine the tax payable or refund due, assuming that no withholding was made on the dividends and that no quarterly estimated payments were made.

CUMULATIVE PROBLEM

13-45 R and S, married and the parents of two children ages 10 months and 6 years, file a joint return. R is a college professor of civil engineering and teaches at State University. R applied for a one-year visiting professorship with International Engineering Corporation (IEC) and was selected for the position. The visiting professor position was available from July 1 to June 30 of the following year and required R to move his family from Detroit to Los Angeles at a total cost of $6,500 during the last week in June. IEC reimbursed R only $5,000 for the move. R rented his Detroit home for the last six months of the year at a net loss of $6,000 for regular tax purposes. Due to the longer life of the residential real property for AMT purposes, and therefore a smaller cost recovery deduction, the net loss for AMT purposes was only $4,000.

S was employed by the government and was able to get a temporary transfer to Los Angeles. S earned $12,000 for the year. During the year, R and S paid $6,000 in child care expenses.

R and his family incurred expenses of $2,500 a month to rent a furnished apartment (assume $1,000 a month was attributable to R and $1,000 a month was attributable to S) for the last six months of the year. R and his family incurred expenses of $800 a month for food during the last six months of the year (assume 25% of the food is specifically attributable to R and that 25% is attributable to S). In addition, R incurred transportation expenses, parking fees, and laundry expenses of $2,500, and he spent $1,200 on lunches on work days during the last half of the year. S incurred transportation expenses of $500 and took her lunch to work with her. R earned $25,000 from State University for teaching half of the year and $60,000 from IEC for practicing half of the year. Together, R and S had $12,000 of Federal income tax withheld from their paychecks.

During the year, R and S also incurred the following expenses:

Unreimbursed medical expenses................	$7,000
Charitable contribution of stock	
to State University (adjusted basis $1,000).....	5,000
State and local income taxes....................	4,000
Real estate taxes on lake property..............	3,000
Real estate taxes on principal residence	
(one-half year)...............................	2,000
Interest on principal residence	
(one-half year)...............................	4,800

The couple also had these additional income items:

State tax refund from previous year..............	$1,500
Interest income from private activity bonds..	7,000

R and S have a minimum tax credit carryover from last year of $5,000. Determine R and S's tax liability for the year.

RESEARCH PROBLEMS

13-46   *Rehabilitation Credit.*   Taxpayer S, a real estate developer, rehabilitated an old commercial building and was entitled to an investment tax credit based on the rehabilitation expenses incurred. Prior to placing the new offices into service, S is approached by P, who is interested in purchasing the building. As an inducement to get P to buy the property, S offers to transfer the ITC to P. That is, S agrees not to claim the credit on his tax return with the expectation that P can claim the credit instead. Will P be allowed to take credit on her tax return in the year she places the office building into service?

13-47   *Dependent Care Credit.*   B is a single parent and his child is enrolled in a public school. The school administrators have scheduled a supervised trip to Dearborn, Michigan for one full week for the students to see Greenfield Village and the Henry Ford Museum. Total trip costs per student is $800. If B pays for his child to make the trip, will he be entitled to a child care credit for the expenditures? If so, how much of the costs will qualify?

PART V

PROPERTY TRANSACTIONS

CONTENTS

Upon completion of this chapter you will be able to:

■ Understand the concepts of realized and recognized gain or loss from the disposition of property

■ Explain the process of determining gain or loss required to be recognized on the disposition of property, including computation of the following:

   ■ Amount realized from a sale, exchange, or other disposition

   ■ Effect of liabilities assumed or transferred

   ■ Adjusted basis of property involved in the transaction

■ Identify the most common types of adjustments to basis of property

■ Define an installment sale and identify taxpayers eligible to use the installment method of reporting gain

■ Compute the amount of gain required to be recognized in the year of installment sale and the gain to be reported in any subsequent year

■ Explain the limitations imposed on certain installment sales, including

   ■ The imputed interest rules

   ■ Related-party installment sales

   ■ Gain recognition on the disposition of installment obligations

   ■ Required interest payments on deferred Federal income taxes

■ Identify various transactions in which loss recognition is prohibited

Chapter **14**

PROPERTY TRANSACTIONS
Basis Determination and Recognition of Gain or Loss

Section 61(a)(3) of the Code provides that gross income includes gains derived from dealings in property. Similarly, § 165 allows a deduction, subject to limitations, for losses incurred in certain property transactions. The term *dealings in property* includes sales, exchanges, and other types of acquisitions or dispositions of property. This chapter examines the determination of the amount of gains and losses from dealings in property. Specific rules regarding gain recognition are addressed, as are the gain-deferral possibilities associated with certain installment sales. Various limitations on the deductibility of losses also are addressed.

Other topics dealing with property transactions are examined in the next three chapters. Chapter 15 deals with certain nontaxable exchanges. Chapter 16 covers the special treatment accorded gains and losses from sales or exchanges of capital assets. The unique rules governing the disposition of property used in a trade or business are examined in Chapter 17.

DETERMINATION OF GAIN OR LOSS

INTRODUCTION

Determining the gain or loss realized in a property transaction is usually a simple computation. It is the mathematical difference between the amount realized in a sale or other disposition and the adjusted basis of the property surrendered (see Exhibit 14-1). The amount realized is a measure of the consideration received in the transaction. It represents the economic value *realized* by the taxpayer.

Sale or other disposition essentially refers to any transaction in which a taxpayer realizes benefit in exchange for property. It is not necessary that there be a sale transaction or that cash be received for gain or loss to be realized by the taxpayer surrendering property other than cash.

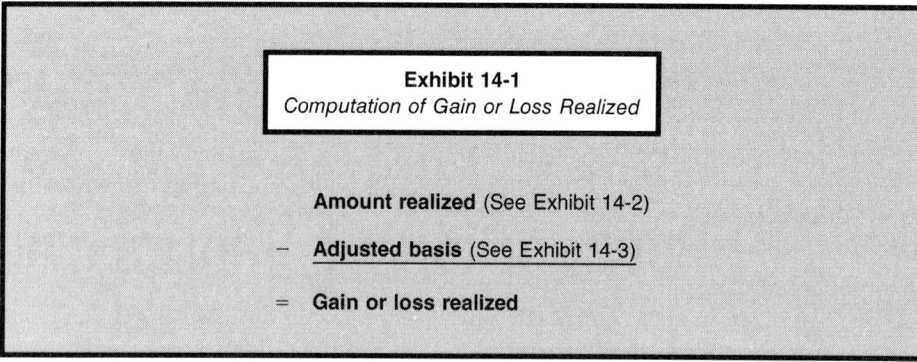

Exhibit 14-1
Computation of Gain or Loss Realized

Amount realized (See Exhibit 14-2)

− **Adjusted basis** (See Exhibit 14-3)

= **Gain or loss realized**

The adjusted basis of purchased property is generally cost, plus or minus certain adjustments. Computing gain or loss realized is similar to determining gain or loss for accounting purposes, and adjusted basis is similar in concept to book value. However, the adjusted basis of a property will not always be, and frequently is not, equal to its book value for accounting purposes.

In effect, the adjusted cost, or adjusted basis, of a given property is the amount that can be recovered tax-free upon its disposition. For example, if property is sold for exactly its cost, as adjusted, there is no gain or loss realized. This concept is referred to as the *recovery of capital* or *recovery of basis* principle. If a taxpayer receives more than the adjusted basis in exchange for property, gain is realized only to the extent of that excess. The adjusted basis is recovered tax-free. The following examples illustrate this concept:

> **Example 1.** K transferred 30 acres of land to ZX Company for $42,000 cash. K had purchased the 30 acres five years earlier for $35,000, which is his adjusted basis. As a result of this "sale or other disposition," K has a realized gain of $7,000 ($42,000 − $35,000). His $35,000 basis in the land is recovered tax-free.

> **Example 2.** In 1989, L purchased 300 shares of W Corporation stock for $3,600 cash, including brokerage fees. When the market outlook for W Corporation's product began to weaken in 1991, L sold her shares for $3,100. The broker deducted a commission of $48 and forwarded $3,052 cash to her. L has a realized loss on this transaction of $548 ($3,052 − $3,600) in 1991.

> **Example 3.** R transferred 200 shares of C Corporation stock worth $4,000 and $2,000 cash for an auto which he will use for personal purposes. The C Corporation stock had been purchased two years earlier for $4,600. R realizes a loss of $600 [($6,000 − $2,000) − $4,600] on the "sale or other disposition" of the stock.

GENERAL RULE OF RECOGNITION

Any gain or loss realized must be recognized unless some provision of the Internal Revenue Code provides otherwise. A *recognized gain* is reported on a tax return. For example, a gain on the sale of stock generally is recognized in full in the year of sale (i.e., the gain is reported on a tax return, included in gross income, and considered in determining the tax liability for the year). In determining taxable income, the recognized gain is either offset against losses for the year or included in the computation of taxable income.[1]

A *recognized loss* also is generally given its full tax effect in the year of realization. Depending on the type of loss, it may be either offset against gains or deducted against other forms of income in determining taxable income. Some losses, however, are not deductible[2] and others are limited.[3] For example, losses on the sale of property used for personal purposes are disallowed. Certain other losses are deferred to later tax years. Some examples of nontaxable exchanges are listed in Exhibit 14-2.

COMPUTING AMOUNT REALIZED

The amount realized from a sale or other disposition of property includes the amount of money received plus the fair market value of any other property received in a transaction. Other property includes both tangible and intangible property.

> **Example 4.** P received $20,000 and a motor home worth $80,000 in exchange for a sailing yacht that she had used for personal enjoyment. P's amount realized on the disposition of the yacht is $100,000 ($20,000 + $80,000).

The amount realized also includes any debt obligations of the buyer, and if the contract provides for inadequate interest or no interest, interest must be imputed and the sales price reduced accordingly.

> **Example 5.** Y sold his vintage Dodge automobile to C for $10,000 and a note payable from C to Y for $15,000 plus interest compounded monthly at 9%. Y's amount realized in this transaction is $25,000, the down payment plus the value of C's note.

---

[1] Capital gains must be offset by capital losses, and only net capital gains are included in taxable income. See the discussion of capital gains and losses in Chapter 16.

[2] Losses on certain sales to related parties are disallowed under § 267, and losses on the sale of personal use property are not allowed under § 165(c).

[3] The deduction for capital losses is limited under § 1211(b).

Exhibit 14-2
Partial List of Nontaxable Exchanges

Type of Transaction	Action Required	Tax Result
Sale of Principal Residence	Reinvest in a New Principal Residence	Gain Is Deferred* See Chapter 15 and § 1034
Casualty, Theft, Condemnation (Involuntary Conversion)	Reinvest in Similar Property	Gain May Be Deferred* See Chapter 15 and § 1033
Like-Kind Exchange	Exchange Directly for Like-Kind Property	Gain or Loss Is Deferred* See Chapter 15 and § 1031
Formation of a Corporation or Subsequent Stock Issues	Transfer Property in Exchange for Stock or Securities by Controlling Shareholders	Gain or Loss Is Deferred* See § 351
Reorganization of Corporation(s)	Examples Include Mergers, Consolidations, Divisions, Recapitalizations	Gain or Loss Is Deferred* See § 368
Formation of a Partnership	Transfer Property in Exchange for a Partnership Interest	Gain or Loss Is Deferred* See § 721

*When gain or loss is deferred, the deferral is only until the replacement property is sold or otherwise transferred (i.e., the deferred gain or loss is recognized along with any subsequent gain or loss when the replacement property is sold). In addition, a taxpayer who is at least 55 years of age and has owned and occupied his or her principal residence for three years may totally avoid tax on any gain on the sale of that residence up to $125,000.

Example 6.   Z sold a parcel of real estate for $100,000. Her basis in the land was $60,000. The sales contract called for $10,000 to be paid upon transfer of the property and the remaining $90,000 to be paid in full two years later.

   Since no interest was provided for in the contract, interest must be imputed on the buyer's $90,000 obligation (in this case, 9% interest, compounded semiannually, is used).[4] Accordingly, the sales price is reduced to $85,471 [$10,000 cash down payment + $75,471 (the discounted present value of the $90,000 payment in two years)]. Z will report an amount realized of $85,471 and a gain realized of $25,471 ($85,471 − $60,000 basis). When Z collects the $90,000, she must report interest income of $14,529 ($90,000 face value − $75,471 present value on date of sale).

The amount realized also includes the amount of any existing liabilities of the seller discharged in the transaction. Specifically, it includes any debts assumed by the buyer and any liabilities encumbering the property transferred which remain with the property in the buyer's hands.[5] Exhibit 14-3 illustrates the computation of *both* the amount realized and the gain or loss realized from the sale or other disposition of property.

Example 7.   B purchased a rental house for $40,000 in 1983. She paid $8,000 down and signed a mortgage note for the balance. During the years she owned the property, B deducted depreciation totalling $16,000 and made principal payments on the note of $4,000, leaving a mortgage balance of $28,000.

   During 1991, B sold the house for $62,000. The buyer paid $34,000 cash and assumed the $28,000 mortgage liability. B's amount realized is $62,000 ($34,000 cash + $28,000 relief of liability), and her adjusted basis is $24,000 ($40,000 cost reduced by $16,000 depreciation). Her gain realized is therefore $38,000 ($62,000 amount realized − $24,000 adjusted basis).

Any expenses of selling the property reduce the amount realized. Selling costs include many costs, paid by the seller, associated with offering a property for sale and transacting the sale. For example, selling costs include advertising expenses, appraisal fees, sales commissions, legal fees, transfer taxes, recording fees, and mortgage costs of the buyer paid by the seller.

---

[4]   The actual rate is determined with reference to current market rates and is announced periodically by the IRS. For transactions involving $2.8 million or less, the rate cannot exceed 9 percent compounded semiannually.

[5]   Reg. § 1.1001-2. Also, see the following discussion of the effect of liabilities in property transactions.

Exhibit 14-3
*Computation of Amount Realized
and Gain or Loss Realized*

Amount realized:

Amount of money received		$xxx,xxx
Add: Fair market value of other property received	+	x,xxx
Liabilities discharged:		
Liabilities assumed by the buyer	+	xx,xxx
Liabilities encumbering the property transferred	+	x,xxx
Less: Selling expenses	−	xx,xxx
Amount of money given up	−	x,xxx
Liabilities incurred:		
Liabilities assumed by the taxpayer	−	xx,xxx
Liabilities encumbering the property received	−	x,xxx
Equals: Amount realized		$xxx,xxx
Less: *Adjusted basis* in property other than money given up	−	xx,xxx
Equals: *Gain or loss realized*		$xxx,xxx

BASIS DETERMINATION RULES

The adjusted basis of property may be determined in several ways, depending on how the property is acquired and whether any gain or loss is being deferred in the transaction. Various methods of acquiring property and their specific basis determination rules are discussed below.

PROPERTY ACQUIRED BY PURCHASE

Cost Basis.   In a simple purchase transaction, basis is the cost of the property acquired. Cost is the amount of money paid and the fair market value of any other property transferred in exchange for a given property.[6] The cost basis includes any payments made by the buyer with borrowed funds and any obligations (i.e., promissory notes) of the buyer given to the seller or any obligations of the seller assumed by the buyer in the exchange.[7]

---

[6] Reg. § 1.1012-1(a).

[7] § 1001 and *Crane v. Comm.*, 47-1 USTC ¶9217, 35 AFTR 776, 331 U.S. 1 (USSC, 1947).

Any costs of acquiring property are included in basis. For stock and securities, commissions, transfer taxes, and other acquisition costs are included. For other property, many types of acquisition costs, including commissions, legal fees related to purchase, recording fees, title insurance, appraisals, sales taxes, and transfer taxes, are added to basis.[8] Any installation and delivery costs also are part of basis.

> **Example 8.** C purchased a new machine for his auto repair business during 1991. He paid $16,500 for the machine, $8,500 of which was made possible by a bank loan. In addition, C paid state sales taxes of $660, delivery charges of $325, and installation charges of $175. C's cost basis in the equipment is $17,660 ($16,500 purchase price + $660 sales taxes + $325 delivery charges + $175 installation charges).

Periodic operating costs such as interest and taxes are generally deducted in the year paid. However, a taxpayer may elect to *capitalize* (i.e., include in basis) certain taxes and interest related to unproductive and unimproved real property or related to real property during development or improvement rather than take a current tax deduction.[9]

> **Example 9.** T purchased a small parcel of unimproved land near a lake known for its excellent fishing. She uses the property as a weekend retreat and plans someday to build a log cabin. T annually pays $150 for local property taxes but does not itemize deductions. T should elect to capitalize the property taxes paid each year as a part of her basis in the land.

Identification Problems. Generally, the adjusted basis of property sold or otherwise transferred is easily traced to the acquisition of the property and certain subsequent events. However, identification of cost may be difficult if a taxpayer has multiple homogeneous assets. For example, if a taxpayer owns identical shares of stock in a corporation that were acquired in more than one transaction and sells less than his or her entire investment in that stock, it is necessary to identify which shares are sold. For tax purposes, the owner must use the *first-in, first-out* (FIFO) method of identification if it is impossible to identify which shares were sold. Specific identification of the shares sold is appropriate if the shares can be identified.[10]

---

[8] § 1012 and Reg. § 1.1012-1(a).

[9] § 266 and Reg. § 1.266-1(b)(1).

[10] Reg. § 1.1012-1(c).

Example 10.   K purchased the following lots of G Corporation stock:

50 shares	Purchased 1/10/89	Cost $5,500
75 shares	Purchased 8/15/89	Cost $9,000
40 shares	Purchased 6/18/90	Cost $4,600

K sold 60 shares of her G Corporation stock in 1991 for $8,700. Unless she can specifically identify the shares sold, her basis will be determined using the FIFO method. Therefore, her basis in 50 shares sold is $5,500 and her basis in 10 shares sold is $1,200 [10 shares $\times$ $120 ($9,000 $\div$ 75 shares)]. Her total gain is $2,000.

Example 11.   Assuming the same facts in *Example 10*, the gain would be different if K could specifically identify the shares sold. If she directed her broker to deliver to the buyer the shares purchased on 8/15/89, referring to them by certificate number and date of purchase, her gain would be $1,500 [$8,700 sales price $-$ $7,200 ($120 basis per share $\times$ 60)].

PROPERTY ACQUIRED BY GIFT

Generally, the basis of property received by gift is the same as the basis was to the donor.[11] This basis is *increased* by that portion of the gift tax paid by the donor, which is attributable to the appreciation in the property's value, if any, up to the date of the gift. The appreciation is measured by the difference between the fair market value of the property and the donor's adjusted basis in the property immediately before the gift.[12] The appropriate increase in basis for a given property is determined using the following formula:

$$\frac{\begin{array}{c}\text{Fair Market Value}\\\text{Date of Gift}\end{array} - \begin{array}{c}\text{Donor's Basis}\\\text{Date of Gift}\end{array}}{\begin{array}{c}\text{Fair Market Value}\\\text{Date of Gift}\end{array}} \times \text{Gift Taxes Paid}$$

Gift tax returns must be filed annually. If there is more than one gift on the annual gift tax return, then the taxes paid on a *particular gift* bear the same proportion to the total gift taxes for the year as the value of that taxable gift bears to the total taxable gifts for the year.[13]

Example 12.   In 1991, P received a diamond necklace as a gift from her grandmother. The necklace had an adjusted basis to her grandmother of $12,000 and had a fair market value of $36,000 on the date of the gift. Gift taxes of $9,000 were paid. P's basis in the necklace is $18,000, including an adjustment for gift taxes of $6,000 ($9,000 gift taxes paid $\times$ [($36,000 $-$ $12,000) $\div$ $36,000]. If P sells the necklace for $39,000 in 1992, her gain will be $21,000 ($39,000 $-$ $18,000).

---

[11]   § 1015(a).

[12]   § 1015(d)(6).

[13]   § 1015(d)(2).

Example 13.   If P, from the previous example, had sold the necklace for $15,000, she would have realized a loss of $3,000. The tax treatment of the loss depends on how she used the necklace. If she used the necklace for personal (rather than business or investment) purposes, then P would not be allowed to recognize the loss for tax purposes.

Loss Limitation Rule.   Where the fair market value of the property *at the time of the gift* is less than the donor's basis, special rules must be applied to determine the basis for the donee. Perhaps the clearest expression of the rules in this case is as follows: the basis for *determining gain* is the donor's basis, while the basis for *determining loss* is the lower of either (1) the donor's basis or (2) the property's fair market value at the date of the gift.[14] Due to the way the rule for determining loss is stated, the donee will not recognize any gain or loss if the property is disposed of for any amount that *is less than* the donor's basis *but greater than* the value of the property at the date of the gift. These rules are illustrated in the following examples.

Example 14.   S received 200 shares of X Corporation stock as a gift from his uncle. The stock had a basis to the uncle of $32,000 and a fair market value on the date of the gift of $29,000. Gift taxes of $1,400 were paid on the transfer.

During 1991, S sold all of the shares for $24,000. His loss realized on the sale is $5,000 ($24,000 sale price − $29,000 fair market value at date of gift). Note that S was not permitted to add any of the $1,400 gift taxes to his basis since such adjustments are allowed only if the fair market value is more than the donor's basis on the date of the gift (i.e., the property appreciated in the donor's hands).

Example 15.   Assuming the same facts as in *Example 14*, if S had sold his stock for $31,000 he would not realize gain or loss on the sale. His basis for gain is $32,000 (the donor's basis) and his basis for loss is limited to $29,000 (fair market value on the date of the gift). Since the $31,000 sales price does not exceed the gain basis and is not less than his loss basis, neither gain nor loss is realized on the sale.

Example 16.   Assuming the same facts as in *Example 14*, if S's stock had been sold for $36,000, his realized gain would have been $4,000 ($36,000 sales price − $32,000 gain basis). There is no adjustment for gift taxes paid because the property did not appreciate in the donor's hands.

---

[14]   § 1015(a). It also should be noted that total depreciation claimed using the gain basis for computation cannot exceed the property's fair market value at date of gift. Reg. § 1.167(g)-1.

Application of these special rules illustrates *three* important points. First, *any gain* realized by the donee on a subsequent sale of the property is limited to the amount of gain that the donor would have realized had he or she sold it at the donee's sales price. Second, *any loss* allowed on a subsequent sale of the property is limited to the decline in the property's value that occurs while owned by the donee. Third, although the payment of a gift tax may be required as a result of the gift, the donee is not allowed to adjust the donor's basis in the property by any gift taxes paid because there is no appreciation in value of the property in the donor's hands (i.e., the fair market value of the property at the time of the gift is less than the donor's basis).

Gifts before 1977.   For gifts before 1977, the addition to the basis of property acquired by gift is the entire amount of gift taxes paid. The gift taxes, however, cannot be used to raise the basis above the fair market value of the property on the date of the gift.

> **Example 17.**   B received a painting as a gift from her mother in 1975. The art work had a basis to her mother of $4,000 and a fair market value of $4,500. Gift taxes of $900 were paid on the gift. After further appreciation in the value of the painting, it was sold by B for $5,500 during the current year. Her realized gain is $1,000 [$5,500 sales price − $4,500 ($4,000 donor's basis + $500 of the gift taxes paid)].

> **Example 18.**   Assuming the same facts as in *Example 17*, if the painting had a fair market value of $5,000 on the date of the gift, the entire $900 gift taxes paid would be allowed as a basis adjustment. If B sold the painting for $5,500, her realized gain would now be $600 ($5,500 sales price − $4,900 basis).

PROPERTY ACQUIRED FROM A DECEDENT

The adjusted basis of property acquired from a decedent generally is its fair market value on the date of the decedent's death.[15] This also is the value used in determining the taxable estate for estate tax purposes.[16] The fiduciary (executor or administrator) of the estate may, however, *elect* to value the estate for estate tax purposes six months after the date of death.[17] This election is available only if (1) the estate is required to file a Federal estate tax return (Form 706), and (2) the alternate valuation reduces *both* the gross estate and the Federal estate tax.[18] If the fiduciary elects to use this alternate valuation date, the fair market value on the later date must also be used as the income tax basis to the heir or estate.[19]

---

[15]   § 1014(a).

[16]   § 2031(a).

[17]   § 2032(a).

[18]   § 2032(c).

[19]   § 1014(a)(2).

Example 19.   D inherited some gold jewelry from his grandmother during 1989. The fair market value of the jewelry on the date of her death was $4,000 and its adjusted basis to the grandmother was $3,050. If D sells the jewelry in 1991 for $4,350, his realized gain will be $350 ($4,350 sale price − $4,000 basis).

Example 20.   If D, from the previous example, sells the jewelry for $3,000, he will have a realized loss of $1,000 ($3,000 − $4,000).

Exceptions to this basis rule are provided for *income in respect of a decedent* under § 691[20] and for certain property acquired by the decedent by gift. Income in respect of a decedent (often referred to as IRD) includes all items of income that the decedent had earned or was entitled to as of the date of death, but which were not included in the decedent's final income tax return under his or her method of accounting. For example, if a cash basis individual performed all the services required to earn a $3,000 consulting fee but had not collected the fee before his or her death, the $3,000 would be income in respect of a decedent. All IRD items are includible in the decedent's gross estate at fair market value for Federal estate tax purposes. Whoever receives the right to collect these items of income must report them in the same manner as the decedent would have been required to report them had he or she lived to collect the income. As a result, IRD items generally are fully included in the gross income of the recipient when received.[21]

If appreciated property was acquired by the decedent by gift within one year before his or her death and the property passes *back* to the donor or the donor's spouse, the recipient's adjusted basis is the decedent's adjusted basis.[22]

Example 21.   H transferred a parcel of lake-front real estate to his elderly grandmother when the property had an adjusted basis to H of $3,000 and a fair market value of $40,000. No gift taxes were paid on the transfer.

H's grandmother died three months after the gift and left the lake-front property to H in her will. H's basis in the property is $3,000 (the rules used for gifted property apply rather than those for inherited property). If his grandmother had lived for more than a year after the gift was made, H's basis would have been determined under the general rule for property acquired from a decedent.

Another exception is provided in the case of real property subject to special use valuation for Federal estate tax purposes. In such cases, the basis to the heir is the special value used for estate tax purposes. This special use valuation applies only to certain real property used in a trade or business and held by the heir more than 10 years.[23]

---

[20]   § 1014(c).

[21]   § 691(a)(1).

[22]   § 1014(e).

[23]   § 2032A(b).

PROPERTY ACQUIRED IN A NONTAXABLE EXCHANGE

Most nontaxable exchanges provide deferral, rather than permanent nonrecognition of gain or loss. The mechanism for such deferral is typically an adjustment to the basis in some replacement property.[24] This adjustment is a reduction in basis in the case of a deferred gain and an increase in basis in the case of a deferred loss.

The specific rules for determining the basis of property acquired in nontaxable transactions, along with the requirements of each nontaxable transaction, are discussed in various parts of this text. Several such transactions are discussed in the next chapter. The following example illustrates one such transaction:

> **Example 22.**   G sold his principal residence at a gain of $12,000. G met all requirements for total nonrecognition of gain under § 1034. He purchased a replacement residence for $74,000. His basis in the new residence is $62,000 ($74,000 replacement cost − $12,000 deferred gain).

PROPERTY CONVERTED FROM PERSONAL USE TO BUSINESS USE

Losses on the disposition of personal use properties are clearly not deductible. Absent some provision to the contrary, business owners could simply convert personal use assets to business use before disposing of them in order to generate business deductions for losses on their sale. Accordingly, when property is converted from personal use to trade or business use, its basis is limited for determining realized loss and for depreciation purposes. For each of those purposes, fair market value on the date of conversion is used as the property's basis if it is less than its adjusted basis.[25]

> **Example 23.**   J owned a single-family home that had been her personal residence for four years. When J discontinued use of the house as her residence, she converted it to rental property. J's original basis in the property was $90,000, and the property was worth $86,000 on the date of conversion. J must determine any depreciation using the fair market value of $86,000, since it is less than her $90,000 adjusted basis. If the property is later sold, J's *gain basis* will be the original $90,000 adjusted basis reduced by the depreciation allowed after the conversion. Her *loss basis* will be the lower fair market value on the date of conversion, $86,000, reduced by the allowed depreciation. Note the similarity to the basis rules that would have applied if J had received the residence as a gift (see *Examples 14, 15, and 16*).

---

[24] See, for example, § 1034(e), dealing with the sale of a principal residence.

[25] Reg. § 1.167(g)-1.

PROPERTY CONVERTED FROM BUSINESS USE TO PERSONAL USE

Once property is converted from business use to personal use, it is treated as personal use property. Any loss on the disposition of such property would, therefore, be disallowed; and, in the event that the property was subsequently converted back to business use, the limitations discussed above would apply.

> **Example 24.** W has a photocopier used exclusively for business. The copier cost $4,000 and depreciation of $1,800 has been allowed, making its basis $2,200. If W converts the copier to personal and family use and later sells it for $500, no loss will be deductible. Of course, if W had immediately sold the copier at a loss rather than converting it to personal use, he would have a business loss.

ADJUSTMENTS TO BASIS

Regardless of the method used in determining a property's basis initially, certain adjustments are made to that basis. Generally, the adjustments can be broken down into three groups. Basis is *increased* by *betterments* or *improvements*[26] and *reduced* by *depreciation allowed* or *allowable*[27] and by *other capital recoveries*.[28]

Depreciation reduces basis regardless of whether it is actually deducted by the taxpayer. The *allowable depreciation* is determined using the straight-line method if no method is adopted by the taxpayer.[29]

Various types of *capital recoveries* also reduce a property's adjusted basis. The following are some of the specific items that reduce basis:

1. Certain dividend distributions that are treated as a return of basis[30]

2. Deductible losses with respect to property, such as casualty loss deductions[31]

3. Credits for rehabilitation expenditures related to older commercial buildings and certified historic structures[32]

Numerous other events have an impact on a property's adjusted basis. Many of them are discussed in the remaining chapters of this text, which deal with specific types of transactions.

Exhibit 14-4 summarizes the rules for determining a property's adjusted basis.

---

[26] § 1016(a)(1).

[27] § 1016(a)(2).

[28] See following examples.

[29] § 1016(a)(2).

[30] § 1016(a)(4).

[31] See Reg. § 1.1016-6 and Rev. Rul. 74-206, 1974-1 C.B. 198.

[32] See §§ 46(a), 48(q), and 1016(a)(22).

Exhibit 14-4
Determination of Adjusted Basis

Method of Acquisition	Basis	Exceptions
General Rule Purchase	Cost	See special rules
Special Rules Acquired by gift	Donor's basis + gift taxes paid on appreciation	If fair market value at date of gift is less than donor's basis, use fair market value to determine loss
Acquired from a decedent	Fair market value at date of death (or alternate valuation date, if elected)	1) Income in respect of a decedent 2) Property given to the decedent by the donor/heir within one year of decedent's death 3) Property subject to special valuation under § 2032A
Converted from personal use	Adjusted basis before conversion	For determining loss and depreciation, use fair market value date of conversion if lower than original adjusted basis
Acquired in a nontaxable exchange	Fair market value less any gain not recognized or plus any loss deferred	

Note: The basis as determined under any of the above methods is subject to adjustments as provided by other provisions of the Code. Basis is increased by betterments or improvements and reduced by depreciation allowed or allowable and by other capital recoveries.

EFFECT OF LIABILITIES ON AMOUNT REALIZED

Mention has been made of the fact that the amount realized in a sale or other disposition of property includes the amount of any liabilities of the seller assumed by the buyer plus any liabilities encumbering the transferred property that remain with the property.[33] The amount realized from a transaction is reduced by any liabilities assumed by the seller plus any liabilities encumbering property received in the transaction that remain with the property. The basis of any property received includes the portion of the cost represented by the liabilities assumed by the seller or encumbering the property.[34]

> **Example 25.** B exchanges a vacant lot with an adjusted basis of $20,000 for a mountain cabin worth $75,000. B's vacant lot has a fair market value of $50,000 and is subject to a $15,000 mortgage. The mountain cabin B receives is subject to a mortgage of $40,000. B assumes the $40,000 mortgage on the mountain cabin and the other party to the exchange assumes the $15,000 mortgage on the vacant lot.
>
> B's amount realized on this exchange is $50,000 ($75,000 fair market value of cabin received + $15,000 mortgage on vacant lot assumed by the other party − $40,000 mortgage on the mountain cabin assumed by B). If this exchange does not qualify for tax deferral, B has a realized and recognized gain of $30,000 ($50,000 amount realized − $20,000 adjusted basis of the vacant lot given up); and his basis in the mountain cabin is $75,000 (i.e., its fair market value).

> **Example 26.** D, the other party to the exchange in *Example 25*, had an adjusted basis in her mountain cabin of $65,000. D's amount realized on the exchange is $75,000 ($50,000 fair value of vacant lot received + $40,000 mortgage assumed by B − $15,000 mortgage on the vacant lot). If the exchange does not qualify for tax deferral, D has a realized and recognized gain of $10,000 ($75,000 amount realized − $65,000 adjusted basis in the mountain cabin given up); and her basis in the vacant lot is $50,000 (i.e., its fair market value).

The amount realized on a sale or exchange of property is affected by liabilities even though neither the buyer nor the seller is personally obligated for payment.[35] The rationale for such treatment is that the owner benefits from the nonrecourse liabilities as owner of the property because his or her basis in the property, or some other property, is properly increased because of the liability.[36]

---

[33] Reg. § 1.1001-2(a)(1).

[34] *Crane v. Comm.*, 47-1 USTC ¶9217, 35 AFTR 776, 331 U.S. 1 (USSC, 1947). Such liabilities are not included if they are contingent or not subject to valuation. Rev. Rul. 78-29, 1978-1 C.B. 62.

[35] *Ibid.*

[36] See *Tufts v. Comm.*, 83-1 USTC ¶9328, 51 AFTR2d 1983-1132, 461 U.S. 300 (USSC, 1983) for an excellent discussion of nonrecourse liabilities and their impact on basis.

CONCEPTS RELATED TO
REALIZATION AND RECOGNITION

SALE OR OTHER DISPOSITION

Realization of gain or loss occurs upon any sale or other disposition of property. Whether such an event has occurred generally is not difficult to ascertain. A typical sale or exchange obviously constitutes a sale or other disposition, but other transactions in which the taxpayer surrenders property other than cash also may be so classified. The timing of such realization is determined according to the taxpayer's method of accounting. Under the accrual method, realization generally occurs when a transaction is closed and the seller has an unqualified right to collect the sales price.[37] Under the cash method, the taxpayer realizes gain or loss upon the receipt of cash or cash equivalents.[38] In any case, a sale is consummated and realization occurs if beneficial title or possession of the burdens and benefits of ownership are transferred to the buyer.[39]

Transactions Involving Certain Securities. Generally, a sale or other disposition occurs any time a taxpayer surrenders property in exchange for some consideration. Accordingly, if a taxpayer exchanges securities of one type for securities of another type, a taxable event has occurred.[40]

> **Example 27.** F exchanged X Corporation 12% bonds with a face value of $100,000 for Z Corporation 9% bonds with a face value of $120,000. Each group of bonds was worth $105,000 at the time of the exchange. If the X Corporation bonds that F exchanged had a basis of $100,000, he has a $5,000 gain on the exchange.

Several exceptions to this scheme do exist. In some instances, the exchange of *substantially identical* bonds of state or municipal governments has been declared a nontaxable transfer.[41] The condition of being substantially identical is usually determined in terms of rate of return and fair market value. If the bonds received do not meet this test, the exchange may be taxable.[42]

---

[37] See *Alfred Scully*, 20 TCM 1272, T.C. Memo 1961-243 (1961), and Rev. Rul. 72-381, 1972-2 C.B. 581.

[38] See, for example, *Comm. v. Union Pacific R.R. Co.*, 36-2 USTC ¶9525, 18 AFTR 636, 86 F.2d 637 (CA-2, 1936).

[39] *Ibid.*

[40] Rev. Rul. 60-25, 1960-1 C.B. 283, and Rev. Rul. 78-408, 1978-2 C.B. 203.

[41] *Motor Products Corp. v. Comm.*, 44-1 USTC ¶9308, 32 AFTR 672, 142 F.2d 449 (CA-6, 1944), and Rev. Rul. 56-435, 1956-2 C.B. 506.

[42] See *Emery v. Comm.*, 48-1 USTC ¶9165, 36 AFTR 741, 166 F.2d 27 (CA-2, 1948), and Rev. Rul. 81-169, 1981-25 I.R.B. 17. Also, see *Mutual Loan and Savings Co. v. Comm.*, 50-2 USTC ¶9420, 39 AFTR 1034, 184 F.2d 161 (CA-5, 1950) for an example of nonrecognition where the state Supreme Court held the new bonds with a lower interest rate to be a mere continuation of the original issue.

It is clearly established that converting bonds into stock under a conversion privilege contained in the bond instrument does not result in the recognition of gain.[43] Similarly, the conversion of stock into some other stock of the same corporation pursuant to a right granted under the stock certificate does not result in recognition of gain or loss.[44]

Transfer Related to Taxpayer's Debt. When property is transferred to a creditor, the transfer may or may not be a disposition. The mere granting of a lien against property to secure a loan is not a disposition.[45] The transfer of property in satisfaction of a liability, however, is a taxable disposition.[46] Similarly, the loss of property in a foreclosure sale [47] and the voluntary transfer of mortgaged property to creditors in satisfaction of debt [48] are dispositions of property.

> **Example 28.** M purchased a commercial property for $20,000, paying $4,000 down and signing a note secured by a mortgage for the $16,000 difference. Three years later, when M had reduced the balance on the note to $7,000, the lender accepted 300 shares of T Corporation stock in satisfaction of the obligation. The T Corporation stock had a fair market value of $7,000 and an adjusted basis to M of $5,000. Because of this disposition of stock, M has a $2,000 realized gain. Note that this result is the same as if M had sold the stock for $7,000 cash and paid the balance on the note.

> **Example 29.** K purchased a warehouse for use in her business for $30,000, paying $5,000 down and signing a nonrecourse note (K is not personally liable) secured by a mortgage lien for the $25,000 difference. Over a three-year period, K's business suffered a decline and as a result she was able to make payments of only $3,000 on the note. During the same three-year period, K deducted depreciation of $12,000, thereby reducing her basis in the warehouse to $18,000.
>
> After the three years, K reduced the size of her business substantially and voluntarily transferred the warehouse to the lender. Upon the transfer, K's amount realized from the discharge of the remaining indebtedness is $22,000 ($25,000 original note − $3,000 payments). Since her basis in the warehouse was $18,000, K has a $4,000 realized gain on the disposition of the property.

Abandonment. The abandonment of property used in a business or income-producing activity, whether depreciable or not, results in realization of loss to the extent of the property's adjusted basis. A loss deduction is allowed if the taxpayer

---

43 Rev. Rul. 57-535, 1957-2 C.B. 513.

44 Ltr. Rul., 2-23-45, ¶76,130 P-H Fed. 1945.

45 See *Dorothy Vickers*, 36 TCM 391, T.C. Memo 1977-90.

46 *Carlisle Packing Co.*, 29 B.T.A. 514 (1933), and Rev. Rul. 76-111, 1976-1 C.B. 214 (1976).

47 *O'Dell & Sons Co., Inc.*, 8 T.C. 1165 (1947).

48 *Estate of Delman*, 73 T.C. 15 (1979).

takes action that demonstrates that he or she has no intention of retrieving the property for use, for sale, or other disposition in the future.[49]

Example 30. While working in a logging operation, R's truck became unoperational, and it was clear that the cost of having the truck moved to a repair site exceeded its value. R abandoned the truck with no intention of seeking its return. If R has a $2,500 adjusted basis in the truck, he is entitled to an abandonment loss deduction of $2,500.

Demolition. No deduction is allowed for expenses related to the demolition of a building or for a loss where the adjusted basis of the building exceeds any salvage value. Both the cost of the demolition and any disallowed loss are added to the basis of the land on which the building stood.[50]

Example 31. T purchased a rezoned commercial lot with a small house for $75,000. The structure was worth $2,000. In order to expedite construction of a new car wash, T simply razed the house at a cost of $1,500. No deduction is allowed for the loss of the house or the razing cost, and T's basis in the vacant lot is $76,500 ($73,000 lot + $2,000 house + $1,500 demolition costs).

Spousal Transfers. The transfer of property to one's spouse while married or as a result of dissolution of the marriage does not constitute a taxable event. This is true even if the transfer is in exchange for the release of marital rights under state law or for some other consideration. This rule applies to *any* transfer made to one's spouse during the marriage or within *one year* after the marriage is terminated. It also applies to later transfers to a former spouse if the transfers are made incident to the divorce (e.g., under a provision of the divorce decree).[51] In a consistent manner, the basis of the transferred property for the transferee (recipient) is the same as the transferor's basis.[52]

It is important to note that this nonrecognition provision applies to all transfers between spouses—including the sale of property at a fair market price. Additionally, the transferor is required to provide the transferee with records needed to determine the basis and holding period of the property.[53]

Example 32. H and W were divorced this year. Under the terms of their agreement, H received marketable securities with a basis of $16,000 and a value of $10,000. W received the house with a basis of $80,000, valued at $96,000 and subject to a mortgage of $60,000. No gain or loss is recognized by either party regardless of who owned the property before the transfer. H and W have bases in their separate properties of $16,000 and $80,000, respectively.

---

[49] Reg. §§ 1.165-2 and 1.167(a)-8.

[50] § 280B.

[51] §§ 1041(a) and (c).

[52] § 1041(b)(2).

[53] Temp. Reg. § 1.1041-1T(e).

Example 33.   Under an option provided in their divorce agreement, W (from the previous example) sold the house to H six months later (subject to the mortgage obligation) for $36,000. W still recognizes no gain and H's basis in the residence is $80,000.

Gift or Bequest.   A transfer of property by gift or bequest generally does not constitute a sale or other disposition. Accordingly, there is no gain or loss recognized by the donor or decedent, respectively. An exception exists, however, in the case of a sale of property at a price below its fair market value. In such a *part-gift* and *part-sale*, the donor recognizes gain *only* to the extent the sales price exceeds the adjusted basis of the property transferred.[54]

Example 34.   M sold her personal automobile to her brother for $4,000. She had a basis of $12,000 in the auto which was worth $6,000 on the date of sale. M has made a gift of $2,000 in this part-sale/part-gift transaction and she recognizes no gain or loss.

Example 35.   Assume the same facts above, except that M's basis in the auto had been reduced to $3,000 from depreciation deductions allowed in prior years. Although M has still made a $2,000 gift in this transaction, she must now recognize a $1,000 gain on the sale ($4,000 amount realized − $3,000 adjusted basis).

If the donee/buyer pays some cash and assumes debt of the donor/seller, or takes the property subject to encumbrances, the amount of the liabilities must be included by the donor/seller in the amount realized from the transaction.[55] Even if no cash changes hands, the part-gift and part-sale rules apply if there are liabilities associated with the transfer. Accordingly, if the donee assumes liabilities that exceed the donor's basis in the transferred property, the donor has taxable gain to the extent the liabilities exceed such basis.[56]   Also, the donee/purchaser will take as his or her basis in the property acquired the *greater* of the basis under the gift rules or the purchase (cost) basis.

Example 36.   F gave a duplex rental unit to her grandson for his 18th birthday so he could develop property management skills. The duplex had a basis to F of $22,000 and a fair market value on the date of the gift of $40,000. The property was subject to a mortgage of $25,000, for which the grandson is now responsible. F has an amount realized on the gift transaction of $25,000 (transfer of the mortgage). Since the adjusted basis of the duplex was $22,000, F has a $3,000 taxable gain. If no gift taxes were paid, the grandson's basis in the duplex will be $25,000, the greater of the basis under the gift rules ($22,000) or the purchase (cost) basis.

---

[54]   Reg. § 1.1015-4(d).

[55]   *Reginald Fincke*, 39 B.T.A. 510 (1939).

[56]   *Levine Est. v. Comm.*, 80-2 USTC ¶9607, 46 AFTR2d, 80-5349, 634 F.2d 12 (CA-2, 1980).

Example 37. If the property in the previous example had been subject to a mortgage of only $8,000, the general rule would have applied, and F would not have recognized gain or loss. The exception only applies when the discharged liabilities exceed the adjusted basis of the gifted property. Note also that the grandson's basis in the duplex would be $22,000, the same basis F had in the property.

Transfer of Property to Charities. The transfer of property to a charity generally is not treated as a sale or other disposition. Accordingly, no gain or loss is realized or recognized. However, an exception is provided for *bargain sales* of property to charities that result in a charitable contribution deduction to the seller. In such a case, the adjusted basis of the transferred property must be allocated between the sale portion and the contribution portion based on the fair market value of the property—and any resulting gain must be recognized.[57]

Example 38. P sold land to her church for $30,000. P had an adjusted basis in the land of $25,000. The land was appraised at $50,000 at the time of the bargain sale. P is entitled to a charitable contribution deduction of $20,000 ($50,000 fair market value − $30,000 sale price). She also has taxable gain of $15,000 on the sale ($30,000 amount realized − the $15,000 pro rata share of the adjusted basis allocable to the sale portion [($30,000 sale price ÷ $50,000 fair market value) × $25,000 basis].

A charitable contribution of encumbered property is also treated as a bargain sale. The amount realized includes the amount of cash and the fair market value of any other property received plus the amount of the liabilities transferred. Accordingly, the property's adjusted basis must be allocated between the sale portion (represented by the amount realized) and the contribution portion.[58] This is true even if no cash or other property is received by the taxpayer.[59]

Example 39. E made a gift of land to his alma mater. The land had a fair market value of $50,000 and was subject to a $22,000 mortgage which was assumed by the university. If the land is a long-term capital asset, E is entitled to a charitable contribution deduction of $28,000 ($50,000 fair market value reduced by the $22,000 mortgage).[60]

---

[57] § 1011(b); Reg. § 1.1011-2(a).

[58] See Reg. § 1.1011-2(a).

[59] *Winston Guest*, 77 T.C. 9 (1981) and Rev. Rul. 81-163, 1981-1 C.B. 433.

[60] See Chapter 11 for a discussion of charitable contributions involving long-term capital gain property.

Additionally, E's $20,000 adjusted basis in the property must be allocated between the contribution of $28,000 and the amount realized of $22,000. The basis allocated to the sale portion is $8,800 [$20,000 basis × ($22,000 amount realized ÷ $50,000 fair market value)]. The result of the bargain sale is a taxable gain to E of $13,200 ($22,000 amount realized − $8,800 allocated basis).

ALLOCATIONS OF PURCHASE PRICE AND BASIS

Properties purchased in a single transaction are often sold separately. In such a situation, the total basis must be allocated between the various items in order to determine gain or loss on the independent sales. Generally, relative fair market values at the time of acquisition are used to allocate the total basis among the various properties.[61] Similarly, allocation is necessary when a single sale involves properties acquired at different times in separate transactions. It may be necessary to allocate the sales price to individual assets; in such a situation, the relative fair market values on the date of sale are used for the allocation. Generally, an allocation in the sale agreement between buyer and seller will sufficiently establish the relative values unless it is shown that such assigned values were arbitrary or unreasonable.[62]

Example 40.   T purchased a commercial lot in 1984 for $30,000 and built a warehouse on the site in 1986 at a cost of $60,000. During the six years he used the warehouse in his business, T deducted depreciation of $32,000. The property was sold in 1991 for $110,000. T must allocate the $110,000 sale price between the building and the land to determine the gain or loss on each. If $40,000 is allocated to the land and $70,000 is allocated to the building based on relative fair market values, T has a gain of $10,000 ($40,000 − $30,000) and $42,000 [$70,000 − ($60,000 − $32,000)], respectively, on the properties.

Sale of a Business.   When a business operated as a sole proprietorship is sold, the sale is treated as a sale of each of the individual assets of the business. Accordingly, allocations of sales price and basis must be made to the individual assets of the business.[63] The various gains and losses have separate impact, according to their character, on the taxable income of the owner.

---

[61] See, for example, *Fairfield Plaza, Inc.*, 39 T.C. 706 (1963), and Rev. Rul. 72-255, 1972-1 C.B. 221.

[62] See *John B. Resler*, 38 TCM 153, T.C. Memo 1979-40.

[63] See Rev. Rul. 55-79, 1955-1 C.B. 370, and *Williams v. McGowan*, 46-1 USTC ¶9120, 34 AFTR 615, 152 F.2d 570 (CA-2, 1945).

Example 41. F has owned and operated a convenience store for 12 years. F's increased interest in her grandchildren and in fishing prompted her to sell the store and retire. The sales agreement with the buyer allocated the total sales price to the individual assets as follows:

	Value per Sales Agreement	F's Adjusted Basis
Inventory	$16,000	$18,000
Furniture and fixtures	14,000	6,000
Leasehold and leasehold improvements	20,000	3,000
Goodwill	0	0
Total	$50,000	$27,000

F has a $2,000 loss on the sale of inventory, and gains on the furniture and fixtures of $8,000 and on the leasehold and improvements of $17,000, each of which has its separate impact on taxable income.

The sale of an interest in a partnership or in a corporation that operates a business is generally treated as the sale of such interest, rather than of the underlying assets. Therefore, no allocation is necessary and gain or loss is recognized on the sale of the interest. For each type of entity, major exceptions to this treatment exist and are discussed in a later chapter.[64]

INSTALLMENT SALE METHOD

The general rule of Federal taxation is that all gains or losses are recognized in the year of sale or exchange. This rule could place a severe burden on taxpayers who sell their property for something other than cash, particularly deferred payment obligations. Without some relief, taxpayers would be required to pay their tax liability before obtaining the sale proceeds with which they could pay the tax. If the tax is substantial, a requirement to pay before sufficient cash collections occur might necessitate the sale of other assets the taxpayer wished to retain.

Because of the potential hardship placed on taxpayers from reporting gain without the corresponding receipt of cash, Congress enacted the installment sale method of reporting in 1926. The installment method has been significantly modified over the years, with each modification further restricting *both* the types of gains and the taxpayers eligible for its use. The eligibility requirements are discussed below.

---

[64]   See Chapter 19 for a discussion of corporate taxation and Chapter 22 for partnership taxation.

GENERAL RULES

The installment method is used to report *gains*—not losses—from qualifying installment sales of property. An *installment sale* is defined as any sale of property whereby the seller will receive at least one payment after the close of the tax year in which the sale occurs. Unfortunately, not all gains from installment sales qualify for installment reporting.

Ineligible Sales. Currently, use of the installment method is denied for reporting gains from sales of the following:[65]

1. Property held for sale in the ordinary course of the taxpayer's trade or business (e.g., inventories)

2. Depreciable property if the depreciation recapture rules require some or all of the gain to be reported as ordinary income (see Chapter 17 for a discussion of these rules)

3. Stocks or securities that are traded on an established securities market

Mandatory Reporting Requirement. Generally, gains from eligible sales *must* be reported under the installment method regardless of the taxpayer's method of accounting.[66] Thus, the installment method is considered to be *mandatory* rather than elective. However, Congress recognized the fact that for some taxpayers the installment method of reporting would not be the relief measure that it was intended to be. Consequently, taxpayers are allowed to *elect out* of the installment method simply by reporting the entire gain in the year of sale.[67]

ELECTION OUT OF INSTALLMENT REPORTING

There are various reasons why a taxpayer might wish to elect not to use the installment method of reporting gain from the sale of property. Such reasons might include the following:

1. The taxpayer's income in the year of sale is quite low and income is expected to be higher in subsequent years.

2. The taxpayer might have a large capital loss with which to absorb the capital gain in the year of sale.

3. The taxpayer might have an expiring net operating loss.

4. It might be necessary for the taxpayer to report the gain in order to utilize a tax credit carryover.

5. The burden of complying with the installment sale rules might outweigh the advantage of the installment reporting of the gain.

---

[65] §§ 453(b), (i), and (l). See § 453(l)(2) for certain limited exceptions.

[66] § 453(a).

[67] See § 453(d) and Temp. Reg. § 15a.453-1(d)(2)(ii).

If a taxpayer *elects not to use* the installment method for a given sale, the amount of gain must be computed under his or her usual method of accounting (i.e., cash or accrual) and reported in the year of sale.[68] A cash basis taxpayer must use the *fair market value* of any installment obligation received in determining the amount realized from the installment sale.[69] On the other hand, an accrual basis taxpayer must account for an installment obligation at its *face value* in computing the amount realized.[70]

Example 42. S, a cash basis taxpayer, sold land to B on December 15, 1991. S received $100,000 cash and a note from B payable in five equal annual installments of $80,000 (i.e., face value), bearing a 9% interest rate. The note has a fair market value of $300,000 and S has a $75,000 basis in the land. If S elects not to use the installment method, his gain to be reported in 1991 is computed as follows:

Amount realized:	
Cash received	$100,000
FMV of installment obligations	+ 300,000
	$400,000
Less: Basis of land	− (75,000)
Gain to be reported in 1991	$325,000

In addition to the interest income that S will recognize when the installment payments are collected, he must recognize additional income on the collection of each installment payment as follows:

Amount realized (installment payment)	$80,000
Less: Basis in each installment ($300,000 FMV of note ÷ 5 installments)	− (60,000)
Ordinary income to be reported	$20,000

[68] *Ibid.*

[69] § 1001(b).

[70] Rev. Rul. 79-292, 1979-2 C.B. 287.

Example 43.   Assume the same facts as in *Example 42*, except that S is an accrual basis taxpayer. His gain to be reported in the year of sale is computed as follows:

Amount realized:	
Cash received...........................	$100,000
Face value of installment obligations......	+ 400,000
	$500,000
Less: Basis in land......................	− (75,000)
Gain to be reported in 1991................	$425,000

In this case, S will not be required to report any income other than the interest received as each of the payments are collected because his basis in each installment obligation is $100,000 (i.e., its face amount).

GAIN REPORTED UNDER THE INSTALLMENT METHOD

The following *six* factors must be taken into account by a taxpayer using the installment method of reporting gain:

1. The gross profit on the sale

2. The total contract price

3. The gross profit percentage

4. The payments received in the year of sale

5. The gain to be reported in the year of sale

6. The gain to be reported in the following years

Determining Gross Profit.   A taxpayer's gross profit is nothing more than the total gain that will be reported (excluding interest) from the installment sale. It is determined by subtracting the *sum* of the seller's adjusted basis and expenses of sale from the selling price:[71]

Selling price.............................	$xxx,xxx
Less: Adjusted basis in property	
plus selling expenses.................	− xx,xxx
Gross profit on sale........................	$ xx,xxx

---

[71]   Temp. Reg. § 15a.453-1(b)(2)(v).

Determining the Total Contract Price. The total contract price is the total amount of cash (excluding interest) that the seller expects to collect from the buyer over the term of the installment sale. It is usually equal to the selling price less any liabilities of the seller that are transferred to the buyer. However, if the liabilities assumed by the buyer *exceed* the seller's adjusted basis in the property and the selling expenses, the excess must be treated as a *deemed payment* received in the year of sale. Because a deemed payment is treated as cash collected in the year of sale, it must be added to the contract price.[72]

Determining Gross Profit Percentage. The taxpayer's gross profit percentage is the percentage of each dollar received that must be reported as gain. It is equal to the gross profit divided by the total contract price.[73]

$$\frac{\text{Gross profit}}{\text{Total contract price}} = \text{Gross profit percentage}$$

Determining Payments Received in Year of Sale. Payments received in the year of sale include the following:[74]

1. Money received at the time of closing the sale, including any selling expenses *paid* by the buyer

2. Deemed payments (i.e., excess of seller's liabilities transferred over the property's adjusted basis plus selling expenses)

3. The fair market value of any third-party obligations received at the time of closing and the fair market value of any other property received

4. Installment payments received in the year of sale, excluding interest income

Gain Reported in Year of Sale. Gain reported in the year of sale is computed as follows:

$$\frac{\text{Gross profit}}{\text{Total contract price}} \times \text{Payments received} = \text{Recognized gain}$$

Gain Reported in Following Years. Gain to be reported in the years following the year of sale equals the taxpayer's gross profit percentage multiplied by the principal payments received on the purchaser's note in that year.

---

[72] § 453A(a)(2) and Temp. Reg. § 15a.453-1(b)(2)(ii).

[73] § 453(c) and Temp. Reg. § 15a.453-1(b)(2)(i).

[74] Temp. Reg. § 15a.453-1(b)(3)(i).

Example 44. T sold a 70-acre tract of land that she had held as an investment on March 1, 1991. The facts concerning the sale are as follows:

Sales price:		
Cash payment...........................	$120,000	
Mortgage assumed by buyer.............	200,000	
Buyer's notes payable to T..............	480,000	$800,000
Less: Selling expenses....................	$ 50,000	
T's basis in land...........................	250,000	(300,000)
Gross profit on sale........................		$500,000

The contract price is $600,000 ($800,000 sales price − $200,000 debt assumed by buyer). Assuming the $120,000 payment is the only payment received in 1991, T's gain to be reported for the year is computed as follows:

$$\frac{\$500,000 \text{ (gross profit)}}{\$600,000 \text{ (contract price)}} \times \$120,000 = \$100,000 \text{ gain to be recognized}$$

As T collects the remaining $480,000 of the total contract price, she will report the remaining $400,000 gross profit from the sale (i.e., $480,000 × $5/6$ gross profit percentage = $400,000).

Example 45. Assume the same facts as in *Example 44*, except that T's basis in the land is only $100,000. In this case, the gross profit on the sale is $650,000 [$800,000 − ($50,000 + $100,000)]. T's payments received in the year of sale are computed as follows:

Cash payment..............................		$120,000
Plus: deemed payment received:		
Mortgage assumed by buyer...........	$200,000	
Less: Selling expenses.................	(50,000)	
T's basis in land..................	(100,000)	50,000
Total payments received in 1991............		$170,000

The total contract price is $650,000 ($800,000 selling price − $200,000 mortgage transferred + $50,000 excess of mortgage assumed over T's basis in property and selling expenses). T's gain to be reported in 1991 is computed as follows:

$$\frac{\$650,000 \text{ (gross profit)}}{\$650,000 \text{ (contract price)}} \times \$170,000 \text{ payments} = \$170,000$$

Note that the excess of the mortgage transferred over T's basis in the land and the selling expenses (i.e., the deemed payment) causes the gross profit percentage to become 100%. This adjustment to *both* the total contract price and the payments received in the year of sale must be made to ensure that the entire gain from the sale is ultimately reported by the seller. As a result, all payments received by T in subsequent years (excluding interest) will be reported as gain from the sale [$650,000 total gross profit − $170,000 gain reported in year of sale = $480,000 gain to be reported in subsequent years ($480,000 buyer's notes × 100%)].

LIMITATIONS ON CERTAIN INSTALLMENT SALES

As mentioned earlier, the installment sales provisions have been modified over the years to limit or stop perceived taxpayer abuse of what was intended to be simply a relief from immediate taxation of all gain from deferred payment sales. These modifications have created the following problem areas:

1. Imputed interest rules

2. Related-party rules

3. Gain recognition on dispositions of installment notes

4. Required interest payments on deferred taxes

Each of these problem areas is discussed below.

Imputed Interest Rules. Without some limitation, a taxpayer planning a deferred payment sale of a capital asset could require the buyer to pay a higher sales price in return for a lower than prevailing market rate of interest on the deferred payments, thereby converting into capital gain what would have been ordinary (interest) income. The imputed interest rules were designed to prevent just such a scheme. Under these rules, any deferred payment sale of property with a selling price exceeding $3,000 must provide a *reasonable* interest rate.[75] Thus, in a deferred payment sale providing little or no interest, the selling price must be *restated* to equal the sum of payments received on the date of the sale and the discounted present value of the future payments. The difference between the face value of the future payments and this discounted value (i.e., the imputed interest) generally must be reported as interest income under the accrual method of accounting, regardless of the taxpayer's regular accounting method.[76]

If the sales contract does not provide for interest equal to the *applicable Federal rate* (AFR), interest will be imputed at that rate.[77] The AFR is the interest rate the Federal government pays on borrowed funds, and the actual rate varies with the terms of the loan. Loans are divided into short-term (not over three years), mid-term (over three years but not over nine years), and long-term (over nine years).[78]

---

[75] See §§ 483 and 1274.

[76] See §§ 1272(a), 1273(a), and 1274(a). Also see §§ 483 and 1274(c) for various exceptions to this requirement.

[77] § 1274(d)(1).

[78] These three Federal rates are published monthly by the IRS.

Example 46. S, a cash basis taxpayer, sold land held as an investment on July 1, 1991 for $1 million cash and a non–interest-bearing note (face value of $4 million) due on July 1, 1993. At the time of the sale, the short-term AFR was 10% (compounded semiannually). Because the sales contract did not provide for interest of at least the AFR, the selling price must be restated and interest must be imputed at 10% (compounded semiannually).

Sales price:	
Cash payment..........................	$1,000,000
Present value of $4,000,000 note due	
July 1, 1993 (0.8264 × $4,000,000)....	3,305,600
Recomputed sales price...................	$4,305,600

S must use this recomputed sales price in determining the total contract price, gross profit percentage, gain to be reported in the year of sale, and gain to be reported (excluding interest) when the $4 million deferred payment is received. In addition, S must report $165,280 of imputed interest income in 1991, computed as follows:

Period	Present Value	×	10% compounded semiannually	=	Imputed Interest
7/1/91 to 12/31/91	$3,305,600	×	0.05	=	$165,280

S must also compute and report her imputed interest for 1992 and 1993. When the $4 million note payable is collected on July 1, 1993, S will report only the gain on the sale remaining after that portion reported in 1991.

Related-Party Sales. Generally, installment sales between related parties are subject to the same rules as other such sales *except* (1) when the related-party purchaser resells the property before payment of the original sales price;[79] and (2) when the property sold is depreciable property.[80] The primary purpose of the *resale* rule is to prevent a related-party seller from deferring his or her gain on the first sale while the related-party purchaser enjoys the use of proceeds from its resale.

Example 47. M plans to sell a capital asset (basis $40,000) to B, an unrelated party, for $200,000. Instead of selling the asset to B, she sells it to her son, S, for $10,000 cash and a $190,000 note due in five years and bearing a reasonable interest rate. Shortly after his purchase, S sells the asset to B for $200,000.

[79] § 453(e). [80] § 453(g).

Without the resale rule, M would report a gain of $8,000 in the year of sale, computed as follows:

$$\frac{\$200,000 - \$40,000}{\$200,000} \times \$10,000 = \$8,000$$

M would have a deferred gain of $152,000 ($160,000 gross profit − $8,000 gain reported in year of sale). More importantly, S would have a cost basis of $200,000 in the asset and report no gain on the subsequent resale to B. The net result of the two transactions is a $152,000 deferred gain and the immediate use of the sales proceeds by a family member.

Under the resale rule, any proceeds collected by the related-party purchaser on the subsequent sale are treated as being collected by the related-party seller. Consequently, M must report her $152,000 deferred gain when S resells the property, even though she has not yet collected the $190,000 note.

For purposes of the resale rule, the term *related party* includes the spouse, children, grandchildren, and parents of the seller.[81] Any controlled corporation, partnership, trust, or estate in which the seller has an interest is also considered related under these rules.[82] It is also important to note that the resale rule does not apply when the second sale occurs (1) more than two years after the first sale, or (2) after the death of the related-party seller.[83]

The installment method is generally not allowed to be used to report a gain on the sale of depreciable property to an entity controlled by the taxpayer.[84] This rule is designed to prevent a related-party seller from deferring gain on a sale that will result in the purchaser's being able to use a higher (cost) basis to claim depreciation deductions. For this purpose, a *controlled entity* is a partnership or corporation in which the seller owns a more than 50 percent direct or indirect interest. Indirect ownership includes any interest owned by the seller's spouse and certain other family members.[85] It is important to note that this rule is based on a presumption that the related-party installment sale is motivated by tax avoidance. Thus, the related party seller can use the installment method of reporting the sale if he or she can establish that tax avoidance *was not* the principal motive of the transaction. This makes such a sale subject to a facts and circumstances review and approval of the Internal Revenue Service.

Dispositions of Installment Obligations. After deciding to report a deferred payment sale under the installment method, rather than *electing out*, sellers ordinarily collect the payments in due course and report the remaining gain in full. However, if this process is interrupted by a sale, gift, or other transfer of some or all of the installment obligations, rules require that any unreported gain be

---

[81] §§ 453(f) and 267(b).

[82] §§ 453(f) and 318(a).

[83] § 453(e)(2).

[84] *Supra*, footnote 80.

[85] §§ 1239(b) and (c).

reported at the time of the transfer. Consequently, if an installment obligation is satisfied at other than its face value or is distributed, transmitted, sold, or otherwise disposed of, the taxpayer is generally required to recognize gain or loss.

The amount of gain or loss is the difference between the obligation's basis and *either* the amount realized, if the obligation is satisfied at an amount other than its face value because it is sold or exchanged, *or* its fair market value when distributed, transmitted, or disposed of, if the transfer is not a sale or exchange.[86] The obligation's basis is its face amount less the amount of gain that would have been reported if the obligation had been satisfied in full.[87]

Taxable dispositions include most sales and exchanges. Also included are gifts, transfers to trusts, distributions by trusts and estates to beneficiaries, distributions from corporations to shareholders, net proceeds from the pledge of an installment obligation, and cancellation of the installment obligation.

The obvious purpose of the disposition rules is to prevent the seller from *either* shifting the income to another taxpayer (e.g., by gift) *or* enjoying the use of the sales proceeds prior to gain recognition (e.g., by pledging an installment obligation for borrowed funds). However, there are several exceptions to the requirement of immediate gain recognition. Transfers of installment obligations upon the death of the seller, transfers incident to divorce, transfers to or distributions from a partnership, certain transfers to controlled corporations, and certain transfers incident to corporate reorganization are among the exceptions to these rules.[88]

Required Interest Payments on Deferred Taxes. Another rule designed to reduce the benefits of installment reporting for certain taxpayers is the requirement to pay interest to the government on the deferred taxes. This rule applies if *two conditions* are met. First, the taxpayer must have outstanding installment obligations from the sale of property (other than farming property) for more than $150,000. Second, the outstanding obligations from such sales must exceed $5 million at the close of the tax year.[89] Only the deferred taxes attributable to the installment obligations in *excess* of $5 million are subject to this annual interest payment. The interest must be calculated using the tax underpayment rate in § 6621.

---

[86] § 453B(a).

[87] § 453B(b).

[88] See §§ 453B(c), (d), and (g).

[89] § 453A.

Example 48. T has $9 million of installment obligations outstanding on December 31, 1991. These obligations arose from the sale of a vacant lot located in the downtown area of Chicago. T's gross profit percentage on the installment sale was 40%. Assuming the underpayment rate in § 6621 is 10% and T's 1991 marginal tax rate is 28%, the required interest payment on the deferred taxes is computed as follows:

Outstanding installment obligations.............................	$9,000,000
Less: Amount not subject to rule.............................	(5,000,000)
Excess installment obligations.................................	$4,000,000
Times: Gross profit percentage..............................	× 40%
Deferred gross profit...	$1,600,000
Times: T's marginal tax rate.................................	× 28%
Deferred Federal income taxes...............................	$ 448,000
Times: § 6621 underpayment rate...........................	× 10%
Required interest payment.....................................	$ 44,800

Because taxpayers are allowed to have up to $5 million of installment obligations outstanding without being subject to the required interest payment rule, it is apparent that only those taxpayers with one or more substantial installment sales need be concerned with this rule.

REPORTING GAIN ON INSTALLMENT SALES

Taxpayers reporting gain on the installment sale method should attach Form 6252, Computation of Installment Sale Income, to the tax return for the year of sale and each subsequent year in which a payment is collected. A sample of this form is contained in Appendix B.

DISALLOWED LOSSES

Various limitations exist regarding gain and loss recognition in certain property transactions. Several such limitations have already been discussed. Recall that any losses on the sale of personal use assets are disallowed. Similarly, losses on the sale of property acquired by gift are limited to the decline in its value subsequent to the transfer by gift. This results because the basis for determining loss is the fair market value on the date of gift, if that fair market value is less than the donor's basis (which would otherwise be the donee's basis).[90] Likewise, a loss on the disposition of property that has been converted from personal use to business use is limited to the decline in its value subsequent to the conversion. In determining any loss on such a disposition, the adjusted basis is the lesser of the taxpayer's adjusted basis or the fair market value on the date of conversion.[91]

---

[90] § 1015(a).   [91] Reg. § 1.165-9(b).

There are several other limitations on the deductibility of losses arising from sales or other dispositions of property. As discussed in Chapter 7, losses incurred in sales between related taxpayers are not deductible. Also, certain losses incurred from the sale of stock or securities will not be allowed as a deduction.

WASH SALES

A *wash sale* occurs when a taxpayer sells stock or securities at a loss and reinvests in substantially identical stock or securities within 30 days before or after the date of sale. Any loss realized on such a wash sale is not deductible.[92] In essence, a taxpayer who has a wash sale has not had a *change* in economic position—thus the transaction resulting in a loss is ignored for tax purposes. The loss is, however, taken into consideration in determining the adjusted basis in the new shares.[93]

> **Example 49.** C, a calendar year taxpayer, owns 100 shares of X Corporation stock (adjusted basis of $4,000), all of which he sells for $3,000 on December 28, 1991. On January 7, 1992, C purchased another 100 shares of X Corporation stock for $3,500. C's realized loss of $1,000 in 1991 will not be deductible because it resulted from a wash sale. Instead, his basis in the 100 shares purchased in 1992 is increased to $4,500 ($3,500 purchase price + $1,000 disallowed loss).

The *numbers* of shares purchased and sold are not always the same. When the number of shares reacquired is less than the number sold, the deduction for losses is disallowed only for the number of shares purchased.[94] When the number of shares repurchased is greater than the number of shares sold, none of the loss is deductible and the basis in a number of shares equivalent to the number of shares sold is affected by the disallowed loss.[95]

Any loss also will be disallowed if the "substantially equivalent" stock or securities are acquired by certain related parties. For example, the U.S. Supreme Court held that the wash sale provisions apply if replacement stock is acquired by a taxpayer's spouse *and* they file a joint return for the tax year of the loss.[96]

SALES BETWEEN RELATED PARTIES

The Code places numerous limitations on gain or loss recognition from transactions between certain related parties. The purpose of such restrictions is to prevent related taxpayers from entering into various property transactions solely for the tax reduction possibilities. For example, a father could sell land to his daughter at a loss, deduct the loss, and the property would still remain within the

[92] § 1091(a).

[93] § 1091(d).

[94] Reg. § 1.1091-1(c).

[95] Reg. § 1.1091-1(d).

[96] *Helvering v. Taft*, 40-2 USTC ¶9888, 24 AFTR 1976, 311 U.S. 195 (USSC, 1940).

family unit. Similarly, a taxpayer could sell depreciable property to her spouse and report a long-term capital gain on their joint return. For many years thereafter, she and her husband could claim ordinary deductions for depreciation on this higher basis. To control such potentially abusive situations, Congress enacted Code §§ 267 and 1239.

Section 267 disallows deductions for any losses that result from the sale or exchange of property between related parties.[97] Such losses may, however, be used by the related purchaser to offset any gain realized from a subsequent disposition of the property.[98] For purposes of § 267, related parties include the following:[99]

1. Members of an individual's family—specifically, brothers and sisters (including by half-blood), spouses, ancestors (i.e., parents and grandparents), and lineal descendants (i.e., children and grandchildren)

2. A corporation owned more than 50 percent in value by the taxpayer (directly or indirectly)

3. Two corporations owned more than 50 percent in value by the taxpayer (directly or indirectly) if either corporation is a personal holding company or a foreign personal holding company in the tax year of the transaction

4. Various partnership, S corporation, grantor, fiduciary, and trust relationships with regular corporations and individual taxpayers

Example 50.   M sells stock (adjusted basis of $10,000) to her daughter, D, for its fair market value of $8,000. D sells the stock two years later for $11,000. M's $2,000 loss is disallowed as a deduction. However, D's realized gain of $3,000 ($11,000 sales price − $8,000 cost basis) is reduced by the $2,000 previously disallowed loss, and she will report only $1,000 of gain.

Note the similarity between the results in *Example 50* and the situation that would result if D had received the stock as a gift from M. First, D's basis for gain would be $10,000 (M's basis) if the stock had been received as a gift; its subsequent sale for $11,000 would have resulted in the same $1,000 recognized (reported) gain. Although the disallowance of a loss deduction might discourage many related-party transactions, some taxpayers prefer to sell rather than give property to a related party in order to avoid paying state or Federal gift taxes.

---

[97]   § 267(a)(1).

[98]   § 267(d).

[99]   See §§ 267(b) and (c).

Section 1239 provides that any gain realized from the sale of depreciable property between specified related parties will be taxed as ordinary income.[100] In effect, this statute precludes the possibility that any gain on the sale might be taxed as a long-term capital gain since the sale results in a higher basis in the depreciable property to a related party. Furthermore, recall that such related-party sales of depreciable property are not eligible for installment sale treatment.[101] Transactions subject to § 1239 treatment are discussed in greater detail in Chapter 19.

---

[100]   § 1239(a).   [101]   § 453(g).

TAX PLANNING CONSIDERATIONS

GIFT VERSUS BEQUEST

In devising a plan for transferring wealth from one family member to another, several considerations related to the income tax, the transfer taxes, and the wishes of the parties involved must be evaluated. If there is a desire to transfer properties, there are relative advantages and disadvantages to lifetime transfers as opposed to testamentary transfers (transfers by will). Some of the specific factors that should be considered are as follows:

1. The income tax rate of each individual (decedent and heirs) relative to the estate and gift tax rates.

2. Whether the property is highly appreciated. If so, a testamentary transfer may be preferred since the property's basis to the heirs or the estate will be its fair market value at date of death or alternate valuation date. If the property is gifted, its basis will be the donor's basis increased by a fraction of any gift taxes paid. If the property has declined in value, only the *original* owner (donor) can benefit from any tax loss by disposing of the property to an unrelated party, due to the basis for determination of loss under § 1015(a).

3. Whether the property is expected to appreciate rapidly in the foreseeable future. If so, a current gift might be considered because the amount subject to gift taxes would be the current market value. If the property were held until death, the higher fair market value at that time would be used in calculating estate taxes. This action is, of course, speculative in nature.

4. Whether the transferee is likely to hold the property for a long period of time. If so, the basis considerations are not as important as they would be if the property were to be sold immediately upon its receipt.

5. Whether the property is income-producing property. If the property produces income, and the owner (donor) is in a high income tax bracket, a lifetime transfer could result in the profits being taxed at a lower tax rate to another family member. If the donee is in a significantly lower income tax bracket, substantial income tax savings can be accomplished.

These factors, as well as the health of the parties involved and other personal considerations, must all be considered. It is possible that the personal factors will outweigh the tax factors, or that significant amounts of taxes cannot be saved.

**CHARITABLE TRANSFERS INVOLVING PROPERTY
OTHER THAN CASH**

Taxpayers who are considering making major charitable transfers and who have property other than cash that they would consider transferring must consider both the effects of any gain or loss if property is sold and the effects of any allowable charitable deduction. If a property has declined in value, its owner may benefit from selling the property and deducting the loss and later contributing the cash proceeds to the charity.

Planning can be even more important when the property is appreciated, since in certain instances a charitable deduction is allowed equal to the fair market value of the property. This is true when the property is long-term capital gain property that is used in the exempt function of the charity, is intangible, or is real estate (see Chapter 11). In such a case, the taxpayer will avoid paying tax on the property's unrealized appreciation and still receive full benefit from the charitable deduction.

CHANGES IN THE USE OF PROPERTY

A taxpayer who converts business property to personal use when its value is less than its adjusted basis should consider selling the asset in order to trigger a deduction for the loss. Also, a taxpayer who buys property that he or she intends to use in a business should think carefully before using the asset for personal purposes. For example, a taxpayer who purchases a new auto and drives it for personal purposes for two years before converting it to business use must use the fair value upon conversion in determining both depreciation and any loss on disposition.

SALES TO RELATED PARTIES

Care must be exercised to avoid the undesirable effects of transactions between related parties. If a loss on the sale of property to a related party is disallowed, the tax benefit of a loss deduction is permanently lost unless the value of the property subsequently increases. The only way to generate a tax deduction for the loss is for the original owner to sell the property to an unrelated party. Also, characterizing gain on the sale of depreciable property as ordinary income under § 1239 should normally be avoided.

USE OF INSTALLMENT SALES

Installment sale treatment provides an excellent opportunity for deferring the tax on gain (other than depreciation recapture) when a taxpayer is willing to accept an installment obligation in exchange for property. Actually, installment reporting may provide such attractive tax deferral and tax savings possibilities that the taxpayer is induced to accept an installment obligation, even though he or she would not do so otherwise. In short, this is a tax variable which must be considered by a prudent taxpayer in planning sales of property.

A taxpayer may benefit in at least two ways from the installment method. First, benefits accrue from the deferral of the tax. The time value of money works to the taxpayer's benefit, assuming the sales contract provides for a fair rate of interest. The second benefit from installment reporting is the spreading of the gain over more than one tax year. If the gain on a sale is unusual and moves the taxpayer into a higher tax bracket, spreading the gain over several years tends to allow the overall gain to be taxed in lower tax brackets.

It is important to remember, however, that taxpayers may face several limitations on certain installment sales. First, if a reasonable interest rate is not provided in the deferred payment sale, the seller will be required to impute interest at the appropriate Federal rate. Second, a taxpayer unaware of the rules relating to related-party sales may find that he or she is required to report all the gain on such a sale long before the actual collection of cash from the installment obligations. Third, taxpayers with installment obligations must be informed of the rules requiring immediate gain recognition on certain dispositions of such obligations. These rules include treating borrowed funds as collections on the installment notes if such notes are used as collateral for a loan. Finally, taxpayers with significant amounts of installment obligations outstanding at the end of a particular tax year (i.e., in excess of $5 million) may find that the required interest payment on the deferred income taxes is greater than the interest currently being collected.

PROBLEM MATERIALS

DISCUSSION QUESTIONS

14-1 *Realization vs. Recognition.* In a few sentences, distinguish realization from recognition.

14-2 *Return-of-Capital Principle.* What is the return-of-capital principle?

14-3 *Computing Amount Realized.* Reproduce the formula for computing the amount realized in a sale or exchange.

14-4 *Impact of Liabilities.* What impact do liabilities assumed by the buyer or liabilities encumbering property transferred have on the amount realized? How are they treated if both parties to the transaction incur new liabilities?

14-5 *Cost Basis.* How does one determine cost basis for property acquired? How is this basis affected if property other than money is transferred in exchange for the new property?

14-6 *Gift Basis.* Reproduce the formula for the general rule for determining the basis of property acquired by gift.

14-7 *Gift Basis Exception.* When does the general rule for determining basis of property acquired by gift (Question 14-6) not apply?

14-8 *Basis of Inherited Property.* The basis of property acquired from a decedent is generally fair market value at date of death. What are the two exceptions to this rule (do not include property subject to special use valuation)?

14-9 *Basis Adjustments.* List the three broad categories of adjustments to basis.

14-10 *Transfers Pursuant to Divorce.* In general, do transfers of property in a divorce action result in the realization of gain or loss? Under what circumstances might gain recognition be required?

14-11 *Part-Sale/Part-Gift.* When does a bargain sale to a donee (part-gift) result in gain to the donor? Does the assumption of the donor's liabilities by the donee have any impact? Explain.

14-12 *Bargain Sales.* How is a bargain sale of property to a charitable organization treated for tax purposes?

14-13 *Allocating Sales Price.* Allocations are generally necessary when a sole proprietorship is sold as a unit. What method is normally used for such allocation? What impact does the sales agreement have if it allocates the price to the individual assets?

14-14 *Installment Sales Method—General Rules.* What is the purpose of the installment sale method of reporting gains? Is it an elective provision? How does one elect out of the installment sale method? What sales do not qualify for installment sale treatment?

14-15 *Installment Sales Method—Key Terms.* Explain how each of the following factors related to an installment sale is determined.

    a.   Gross profit on deferred payment sale
    b.   Total contract price
    c.   Gross profit percentage
    d.   Payments received in the year of sale
    e.   Gain to be reported in the year of sale

14-16 *Imputed Interest Rules.* Under what circumstances must a taxpayer impute interest income from an installment sale? How is the applicable Federal rate (AFR) determined?

14-17 *Related-Party Installment Sales.* Under what circumstances will a taxpayer be faced with the related-party installment sale rules? Explain how a resale of the property by the related-party purchaser before the seller has collected the balance of the installment obligation affects the seller.

14-18 *Dispositions of Installment Obligations.* Your neighbor has $30,000 of installment obligations from a recent sale of land held for investment. He asks you for advice concerning his planned gift of these obligations to his children to be used for their future college expenses. An examination of Form 6252 attached to his most recent tax return reveals a gross profit percentage of 60% and a reasonable market rate of interest related to these installment obligations. What tax advice would you give regarding this plan?

14-19 *Wash Sale.* What is a wash sale? How is a wash sale treated for tax purposes?

14-20 *Timing of Recognition.* Under what circumstances is a realized gain actually recognized? What event generally controls the timing of gain recognition?

PROBLEMS

14-21 *Sale Involving Liabilities.* C sold a cottage in which his basis was $32,000, for cash of $12,000 and a note from the buyer worth $28,000. The buyer assumed an existing note of $30,000 secured by an interest in the property.

    a.   What is C's amount realized in this sale?
    b.   What is C's gain or loss realized on this sale?

14-22 *Exchange Involving Liabilities.* D exchanged a mountain cabin for a leisure yacht and $30,000 cash. The yacht was worth $25,000 and was subject to liabilities of $10,000, which were assumed by D. The cabin was subject to liabilities of $32,000, which were assumed by the other party.

    a.   How much is D's amount realized?
    b.   Assuming D's basis in the cabin was $42,000, what is his gain or loss realized?

14-23 *Identification of Stock Sold.* T purchased the following lots of stock in Z Corporation:

50 shares	1/12/82	Cost $1,200
100 shares	2/28/87	Cost $3,000
75 shares	10/16/88	Cost $2,500

T sold 75 shares on January 16, 1991 for $2,800. His only instruction to his broker, who actually held the shares for T, was to sell 75 shares.

     a.   How much gain or loss does T recognize on this sale?

     b.   How could this result be altered?

14-24 *Sale of Property Acquired by Gift.* J received a set of silver flatware as a gift from her grandmother in 1987, when the set was worth $5,000. The silver had a basis to the grandmother of $2,000, and gift taxes of $500 were paid.

     a.   How much gain does J recognize when she sells the set for $5,000 during the current year?

     b.   What would be your answer if the sales price were $4,200?

     c.   What would be your answer if the sales price were $1,500?

14-25 *Sale of Property Acquired by Gift.* For each of the following situations, determine the gain or loss realized by the taxpayer (donee), assuming the property was acquired by gift after 1976:

Case	Donor's Basis	Fair Market Value(*)	Gift Taxes Paid	Sales Price
A	$3,000	$4,000	$400	$4,100
B	3,000	2,500	500	3,200
C	1,200	1,400	280	1,100
D	2,000	1,600	400	1,700
E	2,400	3,000	600	2,600

* Date of gift

14-26 *Sale of Inherited Property.* D inherited two acres of commercial real estate from her grandmother, who had a basis in the property of $52,000, when it had a fair market value of $75,000. For estate tax purposes, the estate was valued as of the date of death, and estate and inheritance taxes of $8,250 were paid by the estate on this parcel of real estate.

     a.   How much gain or loss will be realized by D if she sells the property for $77,000?

     b.   What would be your answer if the sales price were $66,000?

14-27 *Basis of Inherited Property.* H inherited a parcel of real estate from his father. The property was valued for estate tax purposes at $120,000, and the father's basis was $45,000 immediately before his death. H had given the property to his father as a gift six weeks before his death. The proper portion of the gift taxes paid by H are included in his father's basis.

a. What is H's basis in the real estate?

b. What would be your answer if H had given the property to his father two years before his father's death?

14-28 *Basis of Converted Property.* K converted his 1989 sedan from personal use to business use as a delivery vehicle in his pizza business. The auto had an adjusted basis to K of $4,200 and a fair market value on the date of the conversion of $2,400. K properly deducted depreciation on the auto of $900 over two years before the auto was sold.

a. How much is K's gain or loss if he sells the auto for $800?

b. What would be your answer if the auto were sold for $3,500?

14-29 *Part-Sale/Part-Gift.* G sold a personal computer to his son for $2,000. The computer was worth $3,000, and G had a basis in the unit of $2,200. G has made a gift of $1,000 in this part-sale/part-gift.

a. How much gain, if any, must G recognize on this sale?

b. Would your answer differ if G's basis had been $1,700?

14-30 *Bargain Sale to Charity.* F sold a parcel of land to the city to be used as a location for a new art museum. The land had a market value of $70,000 and was sold for $40,000. F's adjusted basis in the property was $35,000. F is entitled to a charitable contribution deduction on this transfer. How much gain does F recognize on this sale?

14-31 *Installment Sale.* On July 1, 1991, G sold her summer cottage (basis $70,000) for $105,000. The sale contract provided for a payment of $30,000 at the time of sale and payment of the $75,000 balance in three equal installments due in July 1992, 1993, and 1994. Assuming a reasonable interest rate is charged on this deferred payment sale, compute each of the following:

a. Gross profit on the sale

b. Total contract price

c. Gain to be reported (excluding interest) in 1991

d. Gain to be reported (excluding interest) in 1992

e. Gain to be reported in 1991 if G elects not to use the installment method

14-32 *Imputed Interest on Installment Sale.* On January 1, 1991, S sold a 100-acre tract of land for $200,000 cash and an $800,000 non–interest-bearing note due on January 1, 1994. On the date of sale, the land had a basis of $400,000. Assuming the applicable Federal rate is 10% compounded semiannually, calculate the following:

a. Gain, excluding interest, to be reported in 1991

b. The imputed interest to be reported by S for 1991

c. Gain, excluding interest, to be reported in 1994

14-33 *Wash Sale*. R sold 100 shares of Y Corporation common stock for $3,000 on December 24, 1991. On November 30, 1991, R had purchased an additional 200 shares of Y Corporation's common stock for $5,800. His basis in the shares sold was $12,000.

    a.   What is R's loss realized?

    b.   How much of the loss realized by R is deductible (recognized)?

    c.   What is R's adjusted basis in the remaining 200 shares he owns?

14-34 *Related-Party Sale*. J sold 2,000 shares of T Corporation stock, in which he had an adjusted basis of $3,000, to his brother, F, for $1,200.

    a.   How much of the realized loss is recognized (reported) by J?

    b.   How much gain or loss to F if he subsequently sells the stock for $1,000? for $2,000?

14-35 *Property Settlements*. H was divorced from W this year. H was required to transfer stock, which was his separate property, to W in satisfaction of his obligation for spousal support. The stock was worth $5,700 and had an adjusted basis to H of $2,900.

    a.   How much gain, if any, does H recognize on the transfer?

    b.   How much gain or loss does W recognize? What is her basis in the property received?

14-36 *Property Tax Allocation*. J purchased a rental property during the current year for $45,000 cash. He was required to pay all of the property taxes for the year of sale, and under the law of the state $47 is allocable to the period before J purchased the property (see Chapter 11).

    a.   How much is J's property tax deduction if the total payment made during the tax year of acquisition is $700?

    b.   What is J's adjusted basis in the property?

14-37 *Sales of Inherited Properties*. Each of the following involves property acquired from a decedent. None of the properties include income in respect of a decedent. Determine the gain or loss for each.

Case	Decedent's Basis	Death Taxes Paid	Fair Market Value(*)	Sales Price
A	$3,000	$600	$4,000	$6,000
B	6,000	600	4,000	5,000
C	6,000	400	4,000	3,000

    * Date of decedent's death.

14-38 *Nontaxable Dividends*. M owned 300 shares of X Corporation common stock, in which her basis was $6,000 on January 1, 1991. With respect to her stock, during 1991 M collected dividends of $600 and tax-free distributions of $400. What is M's basis in the stock as of December 31, 1991?

RESEARCH PROBLEMS

14-39　*Gain Realized from Transferred Debt.*　H owns a small office building and commercial complex, which he purchased for $175,000 in 1986. H invested $20,000 and signed a nonrecourse note secured by an interest in the property for the difference. The note provided for 14 percent interest, compounded annually and payable quarterly.

After five years, H decided his property was not as good an investment as he had originally thought. He found a buyer who offered him $1,000 cash for the property, subject to the existing liabilities. H eventually accepted the offer and sold the property.

During the five years he owned the property, H made timely interest payments and no payments of principal. He was allowed depreciation deductions of $37,500, using an accelerated method.

Required:

1.　How much is H's gain or loss realized on this sale?
2.　Would your answer differ if H's building was only worth $150,000 and instead of selling the building he had voluntarily transferred it to the obligee on the note?

Partial list of research aids:

> Reg. § 1.1001-2.
> *Crane v. Comm.*, 47-1 USTC ¶9217, 35 AFTR 776, 331 U.S. 1 (USSC, 1947).
> *Tufts v. Comm.*, 83-1 USTC ¶9328, 51 AFTR2d 1983-1132, 461 U.S. 300 (USSC, 1983).
> *Millar v. Comm.*, 78-2 USTC ¶9514, 42 AFTR2d 78-4276, 577 F.2d 212, (CA-3, 1978).

14-40　*Bargain Sale to Charity.*　K sold a mountain cabin for $55,000 to State University (her alma mater) for use in an annual fund raising auction. The cabin was worth $85,000. K had purchased the cabin five years earlier as an investment for $40,000, and no depreciation has been allowed.

Required:

1.　What is K's charitable contribution deduction and her gain or loss realized on this bargain sale?
2.　Would your answers differ if the property were a painting instead of a mountain cabin?

Research aids:

> § 170(e)(1).
> § 1011(b).
> Reg. §§ 1.170A-4(a)(2) and (c)(2).
> Reg. § 1.1011-2.

COMPUTERIZED TAX ANALYSIS

14-41 *Sale of Property Acquired by Gift.* Assume the gift from the donor to the donee is made after 1976. Thus, calculations regarding the gift tax adjustment to the donee's basis are made using current tax law. Also assume the gift is not depreciable property in the hands of the donee. Use computer file T1401 for this problem.

a. For the independent situations listed below, compute the missing values.

	(1)	(2)	(3)	(4)	(5)	(6)
Donor's basis	$6,000	$6,000	$6,000	$6,000	$6,000	$6,000
Fair market value at date of gift	8,000	8,000	7,000	5,500	8,000	5,500
Gift taxes paid by donor	1,400	1,400	1,400	900	900	900
Sale price received by donee	9,000	6,250	6,250	6,250	5,100	5,900
Realized gain or (loss)	___	___	___	___	___	___
Gift tax basis adjustment	___	___	___	___	___	___
Basis for computing gain	___	___	___	___	___	___
Basis for computing (loss)	___	___	___	___	___	___

b. Explain the tax rules which cause the gift tax basis adjustment and basis for gain (loss) to remain the same in questions (a)(1) and (a)(2) even though the sale price changes.

c. Refer to questions (a)(2) and (a)(3). What is the impact on the realized gain (loss) from reducing the fair market value at the date of the gift by $1,000? Explain the tax rules which cause this result.

d. Explain the tax rules which cause the basis for computing gain to differ from the basis for computing loss in questions (a)(4) through (a)(6).

e. Explain the tax rules which prevent a gift tax basis adjustment in questions (a)(4) through (a)(6).

f. Why is there no gain (loss) realized for question (a)(6)?

LEARNING OBJECTIVES

Upon completion of this chapter you will be able to:

- Understand the rationale for deferral of gains and losses on certain property transactions

- Explain how gain or loss deferral is accomplished through adjustment to basis of the replacement property

- Apply the nonrecognition rules to the following transactions:

    - Sale of a taxpayer's principal residence

    - Involuntary conversion of property

    - Like-kind exchange of business or investment property

- Identify other common nontaxable transactions

- Recognize tax planning opportunities related to the more common types of gain-deferral transactions available to individual taxpayers

CHAPTER OUTLINE

Chapter **15**

NONTAXABLE EXCHANGES

INTRODUCTION

The Internal Revenue Code requires that any gain or loss realized on a sale or other disposition of property be recognized unless an exception is specifically provided. Generally, this means that gains or losses are considered in the determination of taxable income. However, there are certain exceptions to this rule. This chapter deals with the types of transactions the gain or loss from which is not recognized.

Nonrecognition can be either a permanent exclusion or a deferral of the gain or loss. In either case, the gain or loss is not included in the determination of taxable income for the year. If the nonrecognition is permanent—the gain or loss will *never* affect taxable income.

> **Example 1.** F, an elderly widow, sold her personal residence of 30 years for $92,000 (her basis in it was $21,000) and moved into a rented unit in a retirement community. F elected under Code § 121 to exclude her gain of $71,000 from gross income. Since the gain was excluded, F will never be required to pay tax on the gain from that residence.[1]

When the recognition of a gain or loss is deferred, it will be recognized later if the replacement property from the deferred transaction is sold in a taxable transaction. This deferral of the gain or loss is usually accomplished by adjusting the basis in the replacement property. A deferred gain results in a reduction to the basis in the replacement property, while a deferred loss results in an increase.

> **Example 2.** D exchanged a vacant lot in San Jose that had been held for investment for unimproved farm land near Fresno. The city lot had cost $35,000 fifteen years earlier and had not been improved. Both the city lot and the rural property were worth $120,000. D recognizes no gain on the exchange and his basis in the farm land is $35,000.[2] Of course, if D later sells the farm for $130,000, his recognizable gain will be $95,000, the gain on the farm of $10,000 plus the gain deferred from the city lot of $85,000.

---

[1] See discussion of § 121 following.   [2] See discussion of § 1031 following.

Recall that a loss realized on the sale of a personal use asset (e.g., residence, auto, or motorcycle) is never recognized for tax purposes. This type of loss is simply *disallowed* rather than deferred. Thus, if a taxpayer realizes such a loss and later purchases similar property as a replacement, the replacement property's basis is not affected by the previously disallowed loss.

TYPES OF NONTAXABLE EXCHANGES

There are several types of nontaxable exchanges allowed under the Internal Revenue Code. Three are discussed in detail in this chapter. The sale of a personal residence is covered initially. This includes both the exclusion of gain for persons 55 years of age or over and the deferral of gain by persons reinvesting in another principal residence. Separate discussions of the deferral of gain on involuntary conversions and the deferral of gain or loss on like-kind exchanges follow. Then several other types of nontaxable transactions are discussed briefly.

SALE OF A PERSONAL RESIDENCE

Since 1951, the Internal Revenue Code has provided for the deferral of gain on the sale of an individual's *principal* residence. Gain is deferred under § 1034 when a taxpayer who sells his or her residence reinvests in another principal residence within a specified time period. In order to defer all of the gain, the amount reinvested must equal or exceed the "adjusted sales price" of the old residence.

> **Example 3.** J sold her condominium, which she used as a principal residence, for $120,000. Her basis in the residence was $82,000 and her realized gain was $38,000 ($120,000 − $82,000). Eight months after the sale, J located a suitable tract home which she purchased for $135,000 and occupied as her principal residence. None of the $38,000 realized gain is recognized by J since she invested $135,000, which is more than the adjusted sales price of her old residence of $120,000.

In addition, homeowners who have reached the age of 55 may take advantage of a one-time exclusion of gain on the sale of their residence. A person who qualifies may exclude up to $125,000 of the gain from the sale of his or her residence from gross income under § 121. Gain in excess of $125,000 will be either recognized or deferred by reinvesting.

> **Example 4.** T, who is 63 years of age, sold his principal residence for $224,000 on July 22, 1991. His basis in the property was $109,000 and his realized gain on the sale is $115,000 ($224,000 − $109,000). T may elect to exclude all of the $115,000 in gain from his taxable income even if he chooses not to reinvest in another personal residence.

SECTION 1034

Section 1034 allows a taxpayer to postpone the recognition of gain on the sale of his or her *principal residence*. Generally, a principal residence is the one in which the taxpayer actually lives. An individual can have only *one* principal residence at a time. Therefore, a taxpayer selling two residences can only postpone gain on the *principal* residence, and a taxpayer purchasing two new residences can only treat the new *principal* residence as the replacement property.[3] Also, if an individual uses property that he or she is renting as the principal residence (e.g., a taxpayer rents an apartment and lives in it), then some other property which the taxpayer owns *will not* qualify as the taxpayer's principal residence for purposes of § 1034.[4]

> **Example 5.** Z moved out of his residence in New Jersey with no intention of returning, and offered it for rent. He immediately moved into a rented apartment in New York City. Several years later, Z sold the New Jersey residence and a year later purchased a house in Virginia that he used on weekends. Z continued to live in his New York City apartment. Neither the New Jersey residence nor the house in Virginia is Z's principal residence. Z's principal residence is the apartment in New York City. Z may not defer the gain on the sale of the New Jersey residence.

A taxpayer may still be able to use § 1034 if he or she *temporarily* rents the old residence before it is sold or rents the new residence before he or she occupies it.[5] The intent of the taxpayer is very important in such a situation. For example, if the property is rented only while the taxpayer is actively trying to sell it, then it will usually be considered the taxpayer's "principal" residence.

ADJUSTED SALES PRICE

No gain is recognized on the sale of the taxpayer's prior residence as long as the amount reinvested exceeds its adjusted sales price. If the amount invested in the replacement residence is less than the adjusted sales price of the prior residence, the gain recognized is the portion of the adjusted sales price that is not reinvested.[6]

---

[3] Rev. Rul. 66-114, 1966-1 C.B. 181.

[4] *Stolk v. Comm.*, 64-1 USTC ¶9228, 13 AFTR2d 535, 326 F.2d 760 (CA-2, 1964), *aff'g.*, 40 T.C. 345 (1963), *acq.* 1964-2 C.B. 7.

[5] Reg. § 1.1034-1(c)(3)(i).

[6] § 1034(a).

The *adjusted sales price* is the amount realized (see Exhibit 14-2) on the sale of the prior residence reduced by any fixing-up expenses.[7] *Fixing-up expenses* are costs incurred to assist in the sale which are neither capitalizable nor deductible and are incurred and paid within a specified time period. Painting and wallpapering are examples of items that may qualify as fixing-up expenses. The expenses must be for work that is performed during the 90-day period ending on the date a contract of sale is entered into and must be paid no later than 30 days after the date of sale.[8]

Example 6. X entered into a contract to sell her old principal residence on June 1, 1991. The sale was final on July 1, 1991 (date of closing). X incurred the following expenses in fixing up her home for sale.

Nature of Expense	Date Work Performed	Date Paid	Amount
Painted living room	February 15, 1991	March 2, 1991	$450
Shampooed carpets	April 1, 1991	April 1, 1991	231
Wallpapered bedrooms	May 22, 1991	July 7, 1991	176
Cleaned draperies	June 15, 1991	June 16, 1991	135

All of the above items would qualify as fixing-up expenses if the work is performed and is paid for within the required time periods. However, to qualify as fixing-up expenses the work must be performed during the 90-day period that ends on June 1, 1991 (March 3, 1991, through June 1, 1991), and must be paid within 30 days after July 1, 1991 (before July 31, 1991). Therefore, X's fixing-up expenses will be $407 (carpets shampooed and bedrooms wallpapered). The living room was painted before the 90-day period and the draperies were cleaned afterwards, so they do not qualify as fixing-up expenses.

It is important to remember that fixing-up expenses are only a reduction in determining *adjusted sales price*. They do not reduce the amount of the gain realized on the sale (see *Examples 8, 9,* and *10*).

Losses on the sale of a personal residence are never deductible since the property is personal use property.[9] Furthermore, such losses may not be deferred under § 1034 because this section applies to gains only.

REPLACEMENT PERIOD

The period during which a personal residence must be replaced in order to qualify for the deferral of gain under § 1034 begins two years before and ends two years after the date of sale of the old residence. The new residence must be purchased (or constructed) and used by the taxpayer as his or her principal residence within this period.[10]

---

[7] § 1034(b)(1).

[8] § 1034(b)(2); Reg. § 1.1034-1(b)(6).

[9] § 165(c).

[10] § 1034(a); Reg. § 1.1034-1(a).

Example 7.   M sold her principal residence and realized a gain on December 18, 1991. M can defer her gain if she reinvests in a qualifying replacement residence by December 18, 1993. If she purchased the replacement residence *before* selling her old residence, she also qualifies for gain deferral if the replacement was not purchased *before* December 18, 1989. In order to defer *all* of her gain in either case, however, she must reinvest at least as much as the adjusted sales price of the old residence.

A new residence purchased or constructed before the sale of the old residence will not qualify as a replacement residence if it is sold before the sale of the old residence.[11]

Constructed Residence.   The cost of a constructed residence which is occupied by the taxpayer within the time limits is treated the same as the cost of a purchased residence. Only those construction costs that are incurred within the time limits can be considered in determining the amount reinvested.[12]

Improvements to New Residence.   When a replacement residence is purchased, subsequent improvements made within the reinvestment period are also considered. Thus, the amount reinvested is the cost of the new home *plus* the eligible improvements.

Suspension of Reinvestment Period.   The reinvestment period is suspended, but not beyond a total of four years after the date of sale of the old residence, for members of the armed forces on active duty.[13]   A similar suspension is provided for U.S. taxpayers in a foreign residence.[14]

BASIS OF REPLACEMENT RESIDENCE

The basis in the replacement residence is its cost reduced by the portion of the realized gain that is postponed by § 1034.[15]   If none of the realized gain is postponed (i.e., the entire realized gain is recognized), then the basis of the replacement residence will be its cost. The cost of the new residence includes not only the purchase price and acquisition expenses, but also all capital expenditures for the construction, reconstruction, and improvement of the residence which were made during the replacement period.[16]

---

[11]   Reg. § 1.1034-1(d).

[12]   § 1034(c)(2).

[13]   § 1034(h). If any member of the armed forces is stationed outside the United States or required to reside in government quarters, the reinvestment period is suspended an additional four years (eight years in total).

[14]   § 1034(k).

[15]   § 1034(e).

[16]   Reg. § 1.1034-1(b)(7).

Example 8.   Richard Towns sold his principal residence for $96,000 on November 21, 1991. The residence had been purchased three years earlier for $73,000 and no improvements had been made. He did, however, pay $1,200 for painting and general repairs to the home on or about October 12, 1991 (which were paid for immediately), and $6,000 in realtor fees and other closing costs. Richard purchased another principal residence on December 20, 1991 for $102,000. Richard's adjusted sales price of the prior residence is $88,800 [$96,000 sale price − $7,200 ($6,000 selling expenses + $1,200 fixing-up expenses)].

Richard's realized gain on this sale is $17,000 [amount realized of $90,000 ($96,000 − $6,000) − his basis of $73,000]. None of the gain is recognized, however, because he reinvested at least $88,800, his adjusted sales price of the prior residence. His basis in the replacement residence will be $85,000 (its cost of $102,000 − the $17,000 realized gain not recognized).

Exhibit 15-1 is a completed Form 2119 using the information in *Example 8* above. (Note that a 1990 Form 2119 is used because the 1991 tax forms were not available on the publication date of this text.)

Example 9.   If Richard had reinvested only $85,000, he would recognize gain on the sale. The adjusted sales price of the former residence was $88,800 (the amount realized of $90,000 − fixing up expenses of $1,200). Richard's recognized gain would be $3,800 (the amount by which the $88,800 adjusted sales price exceeds the $85,000 reinvested). His basis in the replacement residence would be $71,800 (its $85,000 cost − the gain not recognized of $13,200).

Example 10.   If Richard's new residence cost $71,000, he would be required to recognize the entire gain realized of $17,000 ($90,000 amount realized − $73,000 basis) since the adjusted sales price minus the amount reinvested exceeds $17,000 ($88,800 − $71,000 = $17,800 > $17,000 gain recognition limit). His basis in the new residence would be its cost of $71,000, since no gain was deferred.

SALE OF NEW RESIDENCE

Section 1034 generally does not apply to a replacement residence that is sold within the replacement period for the original residence.[17] Accordingly, if a taxpayer sells his or her new residence within the replacement period for the former residence and gain is deferred from the old residence, the gain on the sale of the second residence does not qualify for deferral under § 1034.[18]

---

[17]   The holding period generally is two years.   [18]   § 1034(d)(1).
See §§ 1034(a) and 1034(c)(4).

Exhibit 15-1

Form **2119**	**Sale of Your Home**	OMB No. 1545-0072

Form **2119**
Department of the Treasury
Internal Revenue Service

Sale of Your Home
▶ Attach to Form 1040 for year of sale.
▶ See Separate Instructions. ▶ Please print or type.

OMB No. 1545-0072
1990
Attachment Sequence No. **20**

Your first name and initial (If joint, also give spouse's name and initial.): RICHARD
Last name: TOWNS
Your social security number: 567 89 0123

Fill in Your Address Only If You Are Filing This Form by Itself and Not With Your Tax Return

Present address: 4321 REVERSE BLVD.
Spouse's social security number:
City, town or post office, state, and ZIP code: ANNUITY, AL 33221

Part I General Information

1a Date your former main home was sold (month, day, year) ▶ 11/21/91

b Enter the face amount of any mortgage, note... 1b NONE

2 Have you bought or built a new main home? ☑ Yes ☐ No

3 Is or was any part of either main home rented out or used for business? ☐ Yes ☑ No

Part II Gain on Sale (Do not include amounts you deduct as moving expenses.)

4 Selling price of home. 4 96,000 00
5 Expense of sale. 5 6,000 00
6 Amount realized. Subtract line 5 from line 4 6 90,000 00
7 Basis of home sold. 7 73,000 00
8a Gain on sale. Subtract line 7 from line 6 8a 17,000 00

• If line 8a is zero or less, stop here...
• If you answered "Yes" on line 2, go to Part III or Part IV...

b If you haven't replaced your home, do you plan to do so within the replacement period? ☐ Yes ☐ No
• If "Yes," stop here...
• If "No," go to Part III or Part IV, whichever applies.

Part III One-Time Exclusion of Gain for People Age 55 or Older (If you are not taking the exclusion, go to Part IV now.)

9a Were you 55 or older on date of sale? ☐ Yes ☑ No
b Was your spouse 55 or older on date of sale? ☐ Yes ☑ No
If you did not answer "Yes" on either line 9a or 9b, go to Part IV now.
c Did the person who answered "Yes" on line 9a or 9b own and use the property... ☐ Yes ☐ No
d If you answered "Yes" on line 9c, do you elect to take the one-time exclusion?... ☐ Yes ☐ No
e At time of sale, who owned the home? ☐ You ☐ Your spouse ☐ Both of you
f Social security number of spouse at time of sale... ▶
g Exclusion. Enter the smaller of line 8a or $125,000 ($62,500, if married filing separate return). 9g

Part IV Adjusted Sales Price, Taxable Gain, and Adjusted Basis of New Home

10 Subtract the amount on line 9g, if any, from the amount on line 8a 10 17,000 00
• If line 10 is zero, stop here...
• If you answered "Yes" on line 2, go to line 11 now.
• If you are reporting this sale on the installment method...
• All others, stop here and enter the amount from line 10 on Schedule D...

11 Fixing-up expenses. 11 1,200 00
12 Adjusted sales price. Subtract line 11 from line 6 12 88,800 00
13a Date you moved into new home (month, day, year) ▶ 12/20/91 b Cost of new home 13b 102,000 00
14a Add the amount on line 9g, if any, and the amount on line 13b and enter the total 14a 102,000 00
b Subtract line 14a from line 12. If the result is zero or less, enter -0- 14b -0-
c Taxable gain. Enter the smaller of line 10 or line 14b 14c -0-
• If line 14c is zero, go to line 15 and attach this form to your return.
• If you are reporting this sale on the installment method...
• All others, enter the amount from line 14c on Schedule D...

15 Postponed gain. Subtract line 14c from line 10 15 17,000 00
16 Adjusted basis of new home. Subtract line 15 from line 13b 16 85,000 00

Sign Here Only If You Are Filing This Form by Itself and Not With Your Tax Return — Your signature / Date / Spouse's signature / Date
(If a joint return, both must sign.)

For Paperwork Reduction Act Notice, see separate Instructions. Form **2119** (1990)

Example 11.   J sold her principal residence (basis of $75,000) for $100,000 on January 15, 1991 and purchased a replacement for $105,000 on February 19, 1991. After becoming dissatisfied with the nearby schools, J sold the second residence for $112,000 on December 2, 1991 and purchased a third residence for $118,000 on January 26, 1992.

Since the third residence was purchased within the reinvestment period for the first residence, it is treated as the replacement. The $25,000 gain from the sale of the original residence is deferred, and the basis of the third residence is $93,000 ($118,000 cost − $25,000 deferred gain). Note that the $7,000 gain ($112,000 sale price − $105,000 cost) on the sale of the second residence does not qualify for deferral.

An exception to the above rule is provided for taxpayers who sell their homes in connection with beginning employment (or self-employment) at a new location. Gain on the sale of a second residence purchased and sold within the reinvestment period for the original residence may be deferred, but only if the relocation to a new place of work meets both the distance and time requirements for the moving expense deduction under § 217(c).[19]

Example 12.   Assume the same facts as in *Example 11* except that the second residence was sold because J was promoted and transferred from Philadelphia to Atlanta. In this situation, the gain on the sale of the second residence is also deferred. J's basis in the third residence would be $86,000 ($118,000 − $32,000 total deferred gain from sale of both houses).

OWNERSHIP BY HUSBAND AND WIFE

When a husband and wife sell a common, jointly owned principal residence, the rules generally are applied as usual so long as they reinvest in another common, jointly owned principal residence. However, if one spouse dies after a residence is sold, but before the replacement is purchased and occupied, a principal residence that the surviving spouse purchases and occupies may, at the election of the survivor, be treated as a replacement for purposes of deferring any gain.[20]

Although the gain on the sale of a principal residence generally may not be deferred when replacing it with two residences, the sale of a jointly owned residence by husband and wife who divorce or agree to live apart may be deferred into separate residences by each party. Each must reinvest at least his or her share of the adjusted sales price of the old residence in order to defer gain.[21]

---

[19]   § 1034(d)(2). See Chapter 8 for a discussion of these requirements.

[20]   § 1034(g).

[21]   Rev. Rul. 74-250, 1974-1 C.B. 202.

Similarly, if two individuals own separate residences before marrying, they may each sell their separate residences and defer the gain into a single residence. Each must invest an amount equal to the adjusted sales price of his or her separate residence in order to avoid recognizing any gain.[22]

> **Example 13.** R and S each own their own homes. They marry each other and decide to sell their separate homes and purchase a new home together. Assuming that the amount realized equals the adjusted sales price for each sale, the results are as follows:

	R's Residence	S's Residence
Amount realized (and adjusted sales price)	$40,000	$50,000
Less: Adjusted basis in residence	− 25,000	− 36,000
Realized gain	$15,000	$14,000

R and S purchased a new home for $102,000, of which R and S each invested $51,000. Since each invested at least the amount of their adjusted sales price, the requirements of § 1034 are met and R and S will not recognize their realized gains. However, if R and S had invested only $80,000 ($40,000 each), then S would have to recognize $10,000 of her realized gain. This is the amount of her adjusted sales price that she did not reinvest. R reinvested his entire adjusted sales price and therefore has no recognized gain.

Change in Ownership Percentage. When husband and wife own either the new residence or the old residence in some form of joint ownership (e.g., tenancy by the entirety), it is possible that their proportional interests in the two residences will be different and that gain would be recognized even though the new residence costs more than the adjusted sales price of the old. If both spouses use both the new residence and the old residence as their personal residence, they may elect to recognize gain only to the extent the adjusted sales price of the prior residence exceeds the amount reinvested. It is necessary, however, that they consent to reduce the basis of the new residence by the total amount of the gain not recognized.[23]

[22] Rev. Rul. 75-238, 1975-1 C.B. 257.   [23] § 1034(g).

Example 14. K owned a residence as a single individual which had an adjusted basis of $42,000. When she married M, he moved into the residence. Several years later, the residence was sold at an adjusted sales price of $70,000, resulting in a realized gain of $28,000. Within the two-year replacement period, K and M purchased a new residence for $92,000, which they own jointly.

Since K has in effect reinvested only $46,000 ($^1/_2$ of $92,000), she must recognize $24,000 of the realized gain ($70,000 adjusted sales price − $46,000 reinvested). The basis in the new residence will be $88,000 [$42,000 to K ($46,000 cost − $4,000 deferred gain) plus $46,000 to M]. However, if K and M elect under § 1034(g) to reduce the basis of their new residence by all of the realized gain from K's old residence, none of that gain will be currently taxed to K. The basis of the new residence would be $64,000 ($92,000 cost − $28,000 deferred gain).

Divorce. Section 1041 provides that no gain or loss shall be recognized upon the transfer of property to one's spouse any time during the marriage, within one year after a divorce, or even later if the transfer is related to the divorce. If a residence is sold jointly by divorcing individuals, either or both may defer their share of any gain by reinvesting in a separate residence. However, if the residence is transferred to one spouse and later sold, no gain or loss is recognized upon the transfer, and all of any gain realized on the sale will be the responsibility of the transferee spouse.[24] Of course, the selling spouse may defer the gain by reinvesting under § 1034.

SECTION 121 EXCLUSION OF GAIN

A taxpayer may exclude from gross income all of his or her gain (up to a statutory limit of $125,000) from the sale of a personal residence if he or she has reached age 55 on or before the date of sale.[25] In order to qualify, the residence must have been owned and used by the taxpayer as his or her principal residence for at least three years within the five years ending with the date of its sale.[26] To meet this test, the ownership and use as a principal residence must total 36 months or 1,095 days.[27]

The § 121 exclusion is elective and applies to any gain up to $125,000 ($62,500 for a married person filing separately). If the total gain *exceeds* the limit, then $125,000 (or $62,500) of the gain may be excluded from gross income. The exclusion may be used only once by a taxpayer. Once the election has been used by either a taxpayer or the taxpayer's spouse, he or she is unable to take advantage of the provision again.[28]

---

[24] See discussion and examples related to § 1041 in Chapter 14.

[25] §§ 121(a)(1) and 121(b)(1). Also see Rev. Rul. 77-382, 1977-2 C.B. 51, regarding sales on birthdays.

[26] § 121(a)(2).

[27] Reg. § 1.121-1(c).

[28] § 121(b)(2).

Example 15. L, age 64, sold her principal residence of 10 years during 1991 for $114,000 and she does not intend to reinvest in another residence. Her adjusted basis in the property was $56,000. L may exclude her gain of $58,000 ($114,000 − $56,000) under § 121; however, if she does, she can never benefit from this provision again.

Example 16. If the sales price of L's home had been $190,000, L's realized gain of $134,000 could be only partially excluded. The maximum of $125,000 could be excluded, and the remaining gain of $9,000 would be recognized in 1991.

Example 17. B, age 63, elected to exclude the gain, in the amount of $90,000, on the sale of her residence on March 19, 1986 because she never intended to own a home again. B later married H, age 64, who owned his own home. After they lived in H's home for five years, the residence was sold and no reinvestment took place. H may not elect to exclude any gain under § 121 (since B had previously benefited from a § 121 election) even though H had never benefited from the provision and the property was his separate property.

The election may, however, be made or revoked at any time before the statute of limitations expires for filing a refund claim for the year of sale. In the case of taxpayers who are married at the date of sale, both spouses must consent to the election or revocation.[29]

Example 18. P and Q, a married couple, ages 57 and 56, sold their old home and purchased a new but smaller one in 1991. Since they only reinvested a small portion of the adjusted sales price of the former residence, they elected to exclude their remaining gain from gross income under § 121. Two years later, they decided to sell the new home and rent an apartment. Since they are still within the time allowed by the statute of limitations for filing a refund claim for the 1991 year, they may, if they wish, revoke their § 121 election for 1991 and elect § 121 for the new sale in 1993. This action would be advisable if the gain on the sale of the old residence was less than the $125,000 allowed to be excluded *and* the tax on the sale of the new home was greater than the tax from the old residence.

---

[29] § 121(c).

Incapacitated Taxpayers. A taxpayer who purchases a residence and is soon forced to move to a rest home or similar facility may never be able to meet the time requirement for the § 121 exclusion. Fortunately, if a person in this situation lives in the residence for at least one year, he or she will be treated as having lived in that residence during any period of time that he or she has lived in a licensed facility for incapacitated individuals.[30] Thus, anyone at least 55 years of age who purchases a new home, lives in it one year, and spends two years in a rest home while still owning the home will meet all the tests for § 121.

Married Taxpayers. If only one spouse meets the age, holding, and use requirements, husband and wife will both be treated as meeting the requirements if they own the residence jointly and file a joint return for the year of sale.[31] Also, if a taxpayer's spouse is deceased and the decedent met the holding and use requirements, the taxpayer (i.e., survivor) will be treated as meeting the holding and use requirements as long as the deceased spouse had not benefited from the § 121 election previously.[32]

> **Example 19.** R married S in 1990 and moved into S's home which S had owned and lived in since 1982. In 1991 S died and left the home to R in her will. R, age 58, sold the home in December 1991. Because S met the three-year tests for ownership and use, and R meets the age test, then R may elect to exclude gain under § 121.

Involuntary Conversions. For purposes of § 121, an involuntary conversion of a qualifying residence will be treated as the sale of that residence.[33] Thus, a person who has attained the age of 55 and meets the use and ownership tests can exclude at least a portion of any gain from the destruction, theft, or condemnation of his or her residence. Involuntary conversions are discussed in detail later in this chapter.

Interaction of §§ 121, 1033, and 1034. When a taxpayer who has made a § 121 election has a gain greater than the $125,000 which may be excluded, then he or she may be able to defer the amount of gain in excess of $125,000 by using § 1034 (sale of a residence) or § 1033 (involuntary conversions). In this situation, the amount realized for purposes of §§ 1033 and 1034 is *reduced* by the gain excluded under § 121. This reduces the amount that must be reinvested in order to defer any remaining gain.[34]

---

[30] § 121(d)(9).

[31] § 121(d)(1).

[32] § 121(d)(2).

[33] § 121(d)(4).

[34] § 121(d)(7).

Example 20. D sold a principal residence that he had owned and occupied for 22 years for $276,000 during the current year. His selling expenses were $18,000 and he incurred no fixing-up expenses related to the sale. D was 66 years of age at the time and had purchased the residence for $86,000. Six months after the sale, D located and purchased a smaller home for $160,000.

Amount realized ($276,000 − $18,000)	$258,000
Less: Adjusted basis in old residence	− 86,000
Total gain realized on sale	$172,000
Less: Amount excluded per § 121	− 125,000
Remaining gain realized	$ 47,000
Amount realized on sale	$258,000
Less: § 121 exclusion	− 125,000
Amount realized for purposes of § 1034	$133,000
Less: Fixing-up expenses	− 0
Adjusted sales price	$133,000
Amount reinvested in new residence	$160,000

Since the entire (revised) adjusted sales price of $133,000 (amount realized of $133,000 − fixing-up expenses of zero) has been reinvested, none of the gain is recognized. D's basis in the new residence is $113,000 ($160,000 cost − the deferred gain of $47,000).

Example 21. Assume the same facts in *Example 20*. Had D reinvested only $110,000, he would have excluded gain of $125,000 and recognized the $23,000 difference between the adjusted sales price ($133,000) and the amount he reinvested. The only gain that would be deferred is $24,000 ($47,000 total gain − $23,000 recognized gain) and D's basis in his new residence would be $86,000 ($110,000 cost − the deferred gain of $24,000).

INVOLUNTARY CONVERSIONS

The Internal Revenue Code allows a gain to be deferred in certain instances when a taxpayer disposes of property involuntarily. Such an involuntary conversion occurs either due to condemnation by public authorities or due to casualty or theft. This deferral provision is elective and is allowed only if qualifying replacement property is acquired within the specified replacement period. Congress decided that the gain should be deferred when there is no real economic change and the conversion is beyond the control of the taxpayer.

Example 22.   J owned a sailing yacht held for rental. The yacht was totally destroyed in an unusual and unexpected hurricane. J had a basis in the destroyed craft of $40,000 (her cost of $62,000 less depreciation allowed of $22,000). When J collects the insurance proceeds of $75,000, based on the yacht's fair market value, she realizes a gain of $35,000. The gain may be deferred if J reinvests at least $75,000 for similar-use property within the allowable time period.

INVOLUNTARY CONVERSION DEFINED

An involuntary conversion is defined in the Code as the compulsory or involuntary conversion of property "as a result of its destruction in whole or in part, theft, seizure, or requisition or condemnation or threat or imminence thereof."[35] The terms *destruction* and *theft* have the same basic meaning as when they are used for casualty and theft losses. The IRS has ruled, however, that the destruction of property for purposes of § 1033 need not meet the *suddenness* test which has been applied to casualty loss deductions.[36]

Seizure, Requisition, or Condemnation.   It is not as simple to determine what qualifies as a "seizure, or requisition or condemnation" as it is to identify theft or destruction. The property must be taken without the taxpayer's consent and the taxpayer must be compensated.[37]

Not all types of forced dispositions will qualify. For example, a foreclosure sale[38] and a sale after continued insistence by a Chamber of Commerce[39] have been found not to constitute involuntary conversions by the courts. The IRS has ruled that the condemnation of rental properties due to structural defects or sanitary conditions does not constitute an involuntary conversion since the sale was made to avoid making property improvements necessary to meet a housing ordinance.[40]   Generally, a transfer must be made to an authority that has the power to actually condemn the property, and the property must be taken for a public use.

In the case of the conversion of part of a single economic unit, § 1033 applies not only to the condemned portion, but also to the part not condemned if it is *voluntarily sold*. When a truck freight terminal was rendered virtually useless because the adjoining parking lot for the trucks was condemned, a single economic unit was found to exist and § 1033 applied to the sale of the terminal

---

[35]   § 1033(a).

[36]   Rev. Rul. 59-102, 1959-1 C.B. 200.

[37]   See, for example, *Hitke v. Comm.*, 62-1 USTC ¶9114, 8 AFTR2d 5886, 296 F.2d 639 (CA-7, 1961).

[38]   *Cooperative Publishing Co. v. U.S.*, 40-2 USTC ¶9823, 25 AFTR 1123, 115 F.2d 1017 (CA-9, 1940).

[39]   *Davis Co.*, 6 B.T.A. 281 (1927), *acq.* VI-2 C.B. 2.

[40]   Rev. Rul. 57-314, 1957-2 C.B. 523.

as well as the condemnation of the parking area.[41] In a similar situation when a shopping center was partially destroyed by fire and the owner chose to sell the entire shopping center rather than reconstruct the destroyed portion, the IRS ruled that no conversion existed with respect to the remaining portion since the undamaged portion could still be used and the damaged portion repaired. The fire insurance proceeds, but not the sale proceeds, qualified for deferral under § 1033.[42]

Threat or Imminence of Condemnation. Voluntary sale due to threat or imminence of condemnation can qualify for involuntary conversion treatment. The fact that newspapers or magazines report that certain properties are being considered for condemnation by governmental authorities is not sufficient.[43]

Threat or imminence exists only after officials have communicated that they intend to condemn the property and the owner has good reason to believe they would. Threat or imminence also exists in the case of a sale to an agent of a disclosed principal, even if the agent does not have, but could readily acquire, the authority to condemn the property.[44] Accordingly, a sale to the county when the county had authorized the institution of condemnation proceedings was an involuntary conversion.[45] A similar result was reached when existing law authorized condemnation, but funds had not yet been appropriated.[46]

No threat or imminence was found when a taxpayer had not been notified of intended condemnation and could not reasonably infer from events that it would occur.[47] Similarly, the sale of land to a city before highway plans were completed and when condemnation was just a remote possibility did not qualify.[48]

It is not necessary, however, that the property be sold to the condemning authority in order to qualify as an involuntary conversion. The sale to a third party after the threat exists has also been approved.[49] If the third party realizes gain when the property is later sold to the condemning authority, the new transaction may also qualify for involuntary conversion treatment if the proceeds are reinvested in qualified property after the condemnation of the property, even though the threat existed before the property was acquired.[50]

---

[41] *Harry Masser*, 30 T.C. 741 (1958), *acq.* 1959-2 C.B. 5; Rev. Rul. 59-361, 1959-2 C.B. 183.

[42] Rev. Rul. 78-377, 1978-2 C.B. 208, distinguishing Rev. Rul. 59-361, Footnote 39.

[43] Rev. Rul. 58-557, 1958-2 C.B. 402.

[44] Rev. Rul. 74-8, 1974-1 C.B. 200.

[45] *Carson Estate Co.*, 22 TCM 425, T.C. Memo. 1963-090.

[46] Rev. Rul. 71-567, 1971-2 C.B. 309.

[47] *Edward Warner*, 56 T.C. 1126 (1971), *acq.* 1972-2 C.B. 3.

[48] *Rainer Companies, Inc.*, 61 T.C. 68 (1963), *acq.* 1974-1 C.B. 2.

[49] *Creative Solutions, Inc. v. U.S.*, 63-2 USTC ¶9615, 12 AFTR2d 5229, 320 F.2d 809 (CA-5, 1963); Rev. Rul. 81-180, 1981-2 C.B. 161.

[50] Rev. Rul. 81-181, 1981-2 C.B. 162.

Example 23. T has owned and operated a successful automobile dealership for many years. Upon receipt of legal notice from the City of New Orleans indicating that it planned to condemn his showroom and car lot for use as the site of a new convention center in approximately five years, T began searching for an acceptable new location. After finding a suitable location, T sold the old property to a person who could use it for just four or five years.

T's sale and reinvestment qualifies for involuntary conversion treatment and his gain can be deferred so long as all other requirements are met. When the property is finally purchased by the city, the new owner can also qualify for involuntary conversion treatment if he or she realizes a gain and the proceeds are reinvested in qualifying property within the replacement period.

REPLACEMENT PROPERTY

The Internal Revenue Code specifies that the replacement property in an involuntary conversion must be *similar or related in service or use* to the property which is converted.[51] The IRS and taxpayers often disagree as to what qualifies as replacement property. It is clear, however, that the new property must replace the converted property, and therefore, property that was already owned by the taxpayer will not qualify.[52]

Generally, the replacement property must serve the same functional use as that served by the converted property. This *functional use* test requires that the character of service or use be the same for both properties. For example, the IRS has ruled that the replacement of a bowling alley, destroyed by fire, with a billiard center did not qualify.[53]

The functional use test was met when a farm containing a leased residence was replaced with a farm with two residences, one of which was leased.[54] It was also met when a parking lot was replaced with improved real estate which was immediately converted into a parking lot,[55] and when a lessee of improved property used its share of condemnation proceeds to construct a building on owned land for use in the same business.[56]

---

[51]   § 1033(a).

[52]   § 1033(a)(1)(A)(i).

[53]   Rev. Rul. 76-319, 1976-2 C.B. 242.

[54]   Rev. Rul. 54-569, 1954-2 C.B. 144.

[55]   Rev. Rul. 58-245, 1958-1 C.B. 274.

[56]   *Davis Regulator Co.*, 36 B.T.A. 437 (1937), *acq.* 1937-2 C.B. 7.

A different and more liberal test has been applied to rental properties involved in involuntary conversions. This test is the *taxpayer use* test, which basically requires that the replacement property be used by the taxpayer as rental property regardless of the lessee's use.[57] Using this test, the replacement of land and a warehouse with a filling station,[58] and the replacement of condemned agricultural land with improvements to an industrial park have been found to be involuntary conversions.[59]

Control of Corporation. The replacement property in an involuntary conversion may be controlling stock in a corporation owning property that is "similar or related in use or service."[60] Control consists of owning at least 80 percent of all voting stock plus at least 80 percent of all other classes of stock.[61]

Condemned Real Estate. Congress provided special relief in the situation where real property is condemned by an outside authority. A more liberal interpretation of "similar or related in use" is allowed for the replacement of condemned real property if it is held by the taxpayer for use in a trade or business, or for investment. The Code provides that the *like-kind* test shall be applied.[62] This is the test used for § 1031 like-kind exchanges (discussed in the next section of this chapter); it allows any real property used in a trade or business or held for investment to qualify.

The like-kind test does not apply to the replacement of real property that is destroyed.[63] It also does not apply when the replacement property is stock in a controlled corporation.[64] In each of these situations, the general rule for "similar or related in use" would apply.

Conversion of Personal Residence. Section 1033 applies to the involuntary conversion of a principal residence. However, the taxpayer may choose between § 1033 and § 1034 in the case of a condemnation, or threat or imminence of condemnation.[65] Also, if he or she qualifies, a taxpayer may elect to use § 121 instead of, or along with, § 1033 for the involuntary conversion of a personal residence.[66]

Conversion of Livestock. Section 1033 includes certain special provisions related to sales of livestock. Livestock sold because of disease[67] or solely because of drought[68] are considered involuntarily converted. Furthermore, if livestock are sold because of soil contamination or environmental contamination and it is not feasible for the owner to reinvest in other livestock, then other farm property, including real property, will qualify as replacement property.[69]

---

[57] Rev. Rul. 64-237, 1964-2 C.B. 319.

[58] Rev. Rul. 71-41, 1971-1 C.B. 223.

[59] *Davis v. U.S.*, 79-1 USTC ¶9142, 43 AFTR2d 79-584, 589 F.2d 446 (CA-9, 1979).

[60] § 1033(a)(2)(A).

[61] § 1033(a)(2)(E)(i).

[62] § 1033(g)(1).

[63] § 1033(g)(1); Reg. § 1.1033(g)-1(a).

[64] § 1033(g)(2).

[65] § 1034(i).

[66] § 121(d)(4).

[67] § 1033(d).

[68] § 1033(e).

[69] § 1033(f).

REPLACEMENT PERIOD

The period during which the replacement property must be acquired is specified in Code § 1033(a). It usually begins on the date of disposition of the converted property; but in the case of condemnation or requisition, it begins at the earliest date of threat or imminence of the requisition or condemnation. The replacement period ends on the last day of the second taxable year after the year in which a gain is first realized,[70] but may be extended by the IRS if the taxpayer can show reasonable cause for being unable to replace within the specified time limit.[71]

In the case of condemned real property used in a trade or business or held for investment, the replacement period is extended. The extension is one year, causing the replacement period to remain open until the end of the third taxable year after the first year in which gain is first realized.[72]

> **Example 24.**   E's rental house was condemned for public use by the county during 1991. Her basis in the residence was $32,000 and the county paid her $46,000. E is a calendar year taxpayer and her replacement period begins the day of the condemnation, or threat thereof, and ends on December 31, 1994.

> **Example 25.**   If the residence in the previous example had been used as E's personal residence, the replacement period would end on December 31, 1993. The replacement period is extended *only* for real estate held for productive use or for investment.

ELECTION REQUIRED

Deferral of gain is mandatory in an involuntary conversion of property directly into property which is similar or related in use; however, the § 1033 deferral of gain is elective if the taxpayer receives money or other property in the conversion.[73] The election is made by not reporting any of the deferred gain on the tax return for the year in which the gain is realized.

The return for that year must include detailed information relating to the involuntary conversion,[74] and if the taxpayer has not yet reinvested when the return is filed, he or she is required to notify the IRS when replacement property has been acquired or that no replacement will occur.[75]

---

[70]   § 1033(a)(2)(B).

[71]   Reg. § 1.1033(a)-2(c)(3).

[72]   § 1033(g)(4).

[73]   § 1033(a).

[74]   Reg. § 1.1033(a)-2(c)(2).

[75]   Reg. § 1.1033(a)-2(c)(5).

If after an election has been made under § 1033 *and* the taxpayer fails to reinvest all of the required amount within the allowable period, the tax return for the year (or years) in which gain was realized must be *amended to include the recognized gain* and the tax deficiency must be paid. The period of limitations during which the IRS can assess tax deficiencies does not end until three years after the taxpayer has notified the IRS of failure to reinvest the required amount in replacement property.[76]

> **Example 26.**   The city condemned an apartment building owned by F on April 2, 1988. F sold the building to the city on May 15, 1988, and had a realized gain of $26,000. F's replacement period ends December 31, 1991 (three full tax years later). F replaced the building with other rental property on November 11, 1991, but did not notify the IRS of the replacement until February 23, 1993. The IRS may assess deficiencies (if any) related to this transaction until February 23, 1996 (three years after notification).

AMOUNT OF GAIN RECOGNIZED

No gain is recognized by an electing taxpayer on an involuntary conversion if the amount reinvested in replacement property equals or exceeds the amount realized from the converted property (i.e., the taxpayer does not "cash out" on the transaction). If the amount reinvested is less than the amount realized, the taxpayer has "cashed out" on the transaction and *must* recognize gain to the extent of the amount *not* reinvested.[77] No gain is recognized in a direct conversion.[78]

The *amount reinvested* is the *cost* of the replacement property. The property may not have been acquired by gift, inheritance, or any other method resulting in other than a cost basis.[79] The cost basis would include the amount of any debt incurred in the purchase.

The taxpayer will determine his or her basis in property acquired in an involuntary conversion by taking into consideration the deferred gain. In the case of a direct conversion, the basis of the replacement property is the same as the basis in the converted property. In conversions into money and other property, the basis in the replacement property is its cost *reduced* by the amount of gain realized but not recognized.[80]

---

[76] § 1033(a)(2)(C); Reg. § 1.1033(a)-2(c)(5).

[77] § 1033(a)(2)(A).

[78] § 1033(a)(1).

[79] Reg. § 1.1033(a)-2(c)(4).

[80] § 1033(b); Reg. § 1.1033(b)-1.

Example 27. *Comprehensive Example of Involuntary Conversion.* M owned a rented industrial equipment warehouse that was adjacent to a railway. The warehouse was destroyed by fire on January 15, 1991, and M received $240,000 from her insurance carrier on March 26, 1991. Her basis in the warehouse was $130,000. M constructed a wholesale grocery warehouse on the same site since the predicted demand for such space was superior to equipment storage. The new warehouse was constructed at a cost of $280,000 and was completed May 7, 1992.

Leased (rental) property is subject to the more liberal *taxpayer use* test, rather than the *functional use* test that is applied to other properties. Therefore, the new warehouse meets the similar or related in use test since it is rental property to M.

M reports no gain on her 1991 return since she reinvested a sufficient amount within the reinvestment period, which ends December 31, 1993. She is required to give the IRS the details of the conversion with her 1991 return and provide a description of the replacement property when it is completed. The basis in the replacement property is $170,000 (cost of $280,000 − the gain not recognized of $110,000).

Example 28. Assume the same facts in *Example 27*. If M had reinvested only $200,000, she would have been required to recognize a gain of $40,000 (her amount realized of $240,000 − the amount reinvested, or the amount she "cashed out") on an amended return for 1991. Her basis in the replacement property would be $130,000 [her cost of $200,000 − the gain not recognized of $70,000 ($110,000 realized gain − $40,000 recognized gain)].

LIKE-KIND EXCHANGES

Section 1031 of the Code provides that a taxpayer may exchange certain types of property *in kind* without the recognition of a taxable gain or loss. Specifically, no gain or loss is recognized when qualifying property is exchanged *solely* for other qualifying property that is of like-kind.

Example 29. E traded in his 1988 automobile that was worth $4,500 and was used entirely for business purposes and also paid $15,000 cash for a new auto worth $19,500. E's basis in the old auto was $8,200, based on an original cost of $16,000 less depreciation of $7,800. E recognizes no gain or loss on the transaction since it is a qualifying like-kind exchange. Her basis in the new auto is $23,200 ($8,200 basis of trade-in + $15,000 cash paid).

If property other than like-kind property—commonly called *boot*—is received in the exchange, a gain may be recognized.[81]

---

[81]   § 1031(b).

QUALIFIED PROPERTY

In order to qualify for like-kind exchange treatment, a property must be held *either* for use in a trade or business *or* for investment. A qualified exchange may, however, involve the transfer of investment property for trade or business property, or vice versa.[82] No personal use properties qualify.

Unqualified Properties. Certain properties are specifically excluded from like-kind exchange treatment. For example, stocks, bonds, notes, other securities or evidences of indebtedness, and interests in partnerships do not qualify.[83] In addition, inventory items and other properties held *primarily for sale* are not eligible. Whether an item is inventory (i.e., held primarily for sale to customers in the ordinary course of a trade or business) is discussed in Chapter 16. Several courts have interpreted the phrase *held for sale* to include any property which is acquired in an exchange only to be resold shortly thereafter.[84]

> **Example 30.** K exchanged a parcel of real estate held for investment for another parcel and immediately offered the parcel received for sale. The parcel was sold on the installment basis. Since K held the new property for sale rather than for use in a trade or business or for investment, the entire gain realized on the exchange must be recognized at the time of the exchange.

However, the Tax Court ruled that when a recipient of property in a like-kind exchange *gives* away (rather than sells) qualifying property received in the exchange shortly afterward, Code § 1031 still provides for the nonrecognition of gain.[85]

LIKE-KIND PROPERTY

The concept of *like-kind* refers to the nature or character of property. It is immaterial whether it is of the same class (e.g., rental property or property used in a trade or business). An exchange of real property for real property normally will qualify, while the exchange of real property for personal property will not.[86]

---

[82] Reg. § 1.1031(a)-1(a).

[83] § 1031(a)(2).

[84] *Ethel Black*, 35 T.C. 90 (1960); *George M. Bernard*, 26 T.C.M. 858, T.C. Memo. 1967-176.

[85] *Fred W. Wagensen*, 74 T.C. 653 (1980).

[86] Reg. § 1.1031(a)-1(b).

Real Estate. Generally, any exchange of realty for realty will meet the like-kind test. It is immaterial whether the real property is improved or unimproved.[87] The IRS has ruled that a lease of real property with a remaining term of at least 30 years will be treated as real property for purposes of determining whether a like-kind exchange has occurred.[88] Accordingly, a realized loss from the exchange of property that has declined in value for a lease interest in that property with a life of 30 years or more will result in a nondeductible (nonrecognized) loss.[89] Condemned real estate in an involuntary conversion is also subject to the like-kind test, as discussed previously.

Personalty. The like-kind test as applied to personalty is not as clear as for realty. When properties are substantially the same, like-kind exchange treatment generally has been allowed.[90] For example, exchanges of professional athletes' contracts have been determined by the IRS to be like-kind exchanges.[91] Similarly, a typical trade-in of business machinery qualifies for like-kind exchange treatment. Livestock used in a trade or business, but not held for sale, may qualify as like-kind;[92] however, livestock of different sexes is not like-kind property.[93]

> **Example 31.** W traded his camera, which he used in his profitable photographic business, for a newer, more sophisticated camera worth $975. In addition to his old camera, which was worth $500 and in which his basis was $100, W paid $475 cash for the new camera. No gain is recognized by W on this exchange as long as the new camera is used in his business. His basis in the new camera is $575 ($100 basis of trade-in + $475 cash paid).

---

[87] Reg. § 1.1031(a)-1(b). However, an exchange of realty located within the United States for realty located outside the United States is specifically denied like-kind exchange treatment—§ 1031(h). It is also important to note that § 1250 may supercede § 1031 and cause the recognition of gain. Effectively, § 1250 property (generally depreciable realty) must be acquired in an amount at least as great as the § 1250 recapture potential—§ 1250(d)(4)(C). See Chapter 17 for a discussion of § 1250 recapture of depreciation.

[88] Rev. Rul. 76-301, 1976-2 C.B. 241.

[89] *Century Electric Co. v. Comm.,* 51-2 USTC ¶9482, 41 AFTR 205, 192 F.2d 155 (CA-8, 1951).

[90] See, for example, *W.H. Hartman Co.,* 20 B.T.A. 302 (1930), *acq.* X-1 C.B. 27.

[91] Rev. Rul. 67-380, 1967-2 C.B. 291.

[92] *Leo A. Woodbury,* 49 T.C. 180 (1967), *acq.* 1969-2 C.B. xxv.

[93] § 1031(e).

Exchanges of bullion-type coins have been one area of controversy. The IRS has ruled that noncurrency, bullion-type coins of different countries constitute like-kind properties.[94] However, legal tender coins (currency) are not of like-kind with bullion-type noncurrency coins.[95]

Exchanges of tangible depreciable personalty (e.g., furniture, fixtures, and equipment) have been another area of controversy. Recently proposed Treasury regulations require that such properties must be exchanged for other tangible depreciable property that is of *like-class* in order to qualify for like-kind exchange treatment.[96] To qualify as like-class, the exchanged properties must be from the same *one* of the thirteen "general business asset" classes that have been established for depreciation purposes.[97]

If multiple properties are exchanged, as in an exchange of one business for another, the same proposed regulations require that the various assets be *matched* with those of the same kind or class. In addition, goodwill and going-concern value of similar businesses will be considered like-kind properties in rare and unusual circumstances. If the businesses are dissimilar, these intangibles will not qualify as like-kind properties.[98]

RECEIPT OF PROPERTY NOT OF A LIKE-KIND

No gain or loss is recognized as long as an exchange is for qualified like-kind property only. However, a transaction may qualify as a like-kind exchange under § 1031 even though property other than like-kind property changes hands. Section 1031(b) provides that any gain realized on the exchange will be recognized to the extent that other property, commonly called *boot*, is received in the exchange. For these purposes, *boot* includes any money received in the exchange *plus* the fair market value of any property that is either nonqualified or not like-kind. Under § 1031(c), the receipt of boot does not cause the recognition of any realized losses in such an exchange.

> **Example 32.** J transferred a vacant lot held as an investment and worth $8,000 to another party in exchange for a similar lot worth $6,000. J received $2,000 cash in addition to the new lot. J's basis in her old lot

---

[94] Rev. Rul. 76-214, 1976-1 C.B. 218.

[95] Rev. Rul. 79-143, 1979-1 C.B. 264; *California Federal Life Insurance Co. v. Comm.*, 82-2 USTC ¶9464, 50 AFTR2d 82-5271, 680 F.2d 85 (CA-9, 1982), *aff'g*. 76 T.C. 107 (1981). It is interesting that the Revenue Ruling states that U.S. gold coins are currency, while the courts in these cases state that they are more like "other property" than "money."

[96] Prop. Reg. § 1.1031(a)-1(b).

[97] See Rev. Proc. 87-56, 1987-2 C.B. 674, and Chapter 9 for a description of these general business asset classes.

[98] Prop. Reg. § 1.1031(a)-1(b). Because the proposed treatment of goodwill is extremely controversial, these regulations may not be finalized in their current form.

was $5,500. J's realized gain is $2,500 ($8,000 amount realized − $5,500 basis). If she holds the new lot as an investment, J still must recognize gain on this exchange in the amount of $2,000 because she received *cash boot* of $2,000.

Example 33. If J's basis in the property given up in the prior example had been $6,500, her realized gain would have been $1,500 ($8,000 amount realized − $6,500 basis). Although she received $2,000 of boot, J's recognized gain is $1,500 (recognized gain is *never* more than the realized gain).

Example 34. If J's basis in the vacant lot exchanged in the previous two examples had been $9,000, she would have a realized loss of $1,000 and a recognized loss of zero. Losses in like-kind exchanges are not recognized.

Installment Reporting. The installment sales provisions of § 453 provide that any gain to be recognized in a like-kind exchange—other than depreciation recapture—may be reported on the installment basis.[99] The gain in such an exchange is spread over the period in which the taxpayer collects the "boot." For purposes of installment reporting, the value of the like-kind property is not included in the contract price. The *gross profit percentage* is computed as follows:

$$\frac{\text{Gain to be recognized on like-kind exchange}}{\text{Contract price less value of like-kind property received}}$$

The boot, but not the like-kind property, is treated as a payment when received.

Example 35. F received a vacant lot worth $35,000 and an installment note for $25,000 with interest at 11% in exchange for his rental warehouse. F's adjusted basis in the warehouse, after straight-line depreciation, was $42,000. During the year of sale, F received the lot and no cash. His realized gain on the exchange is $18,000; but none is recognized since none of the boot was received. The contract price for purposes of the installment sales provisions is $25,000 ($60,000 amount realized − $35,000 value of like-kind property received).

Example 36. In 1991, F collects $10,000 principal and $2,750 interest on the note. He reports a gain on his 1991 return in the amount of $7,200 [(gross profit of $18,000 ÷ contract price of $25,000) × (payment received of $10,000)]. The $2,750 of interest is also reported as income in 1991.

---

[99] §§ 453(f)(6) and (7). See Chapter 17 for the treatment of installment sales where depreciation recapture is involved.

Liabilities as Boot. Liabilities discharged in a like-kind exchange are treated as boot received.[100] Thus, a taxpayer who is relieved of liabilities in an exchange will recognize any gain realized on the exchange to the extent of the liabilities.

However, if the taxpayer also incurs a debt obligation or assumes a liability in the exchange, then the result is not as harsh. Only the net increase or decrease in a taxpayer's liabilities is treated as boot paid or boot received, respectively.[101]

Liabilities are the *only* type of boot that may be netted. Other types of boot cannot be netted. In addition, other boot received cannot be offset by net liabilities incurred. However, other boot paid may be offset against liabilities discharged.[102]

Example 37. S exchanged a tractor worth $11,000 for a lighter duty tractor worth $9,000, both held for use in his landscaping business. The tractor given up was subject to a secured obligation of $8,000 and S incurred a liability secured by the new tractor of $6,000. S's basis in the tractor given up was $6,500, his cost of $13,500 less depreciation allowed of $7,000. S's realized gain on this exchange is $4,500, computed as follows:

Fair market value of property received......................	$ 9,000
Plus: Liabilities encumbering the property transferred....................................	+ 8,000
Less: Liabilities assumed by taxpayer....................	− 6,000
Amount realized...	$11,000
Less: Adjusted basis of property given up...............	− 6,500
Gain realized...	$ 4,500

S's recognized gain is $2,000 since the net liabilities discharged ($8,000 liability discharged − $6,000 liability assumed) are treated as boot.

Example 38. Use the facts in *Example 37*, but assume that instead of receiving a $9,000 tractor and incurring a $6,000 liability, S received a tractor worth $7,500 and paid $4,500 cash. S's realized gain is $4,500 computed as follows:

Fair market value of property received......................	$ 7,500
Plus: Liabilities encumbering the property transferred.............................	+ 8,000
Less: Amount of money given up........................	− 4,500
Amount realized...	$11,000
Less: Adjusted basis of property given up...............	− 6,500
Gain realized...	$ 4,500

S's recognized gain is $3,500, the amount of liabilities discharged ($8,000) less the other boot paid ($4,500 cash).

---

[100] § 1031(d).

[101] See Reg. §§ 1.1031(b)-1(c) and 1.1031 (d)-2. It is important to note that liabilities incurred in anticipation of a like-kind ex-change will not qualify for this netting treatment. See Prop. Reg. § 1.103(b)-1(c).

[102] Reg. § 1.1031(d)-2, Ex. 2.

Example 39. If S had received a tractor worth $3,000 and incurred no liabilities and paid no cash in the transaction, his realized gain is still $4,500, computed as follows:

Fair market value of property received......................	$ 3,000
Plus: Liabilities encumbering the property transferred............................	+ 8,000
Amount realized...	$11,000
Less: Adjusted basis of property given up................	− 6,500
Gain realized...	$ 4,500

The amount of boot received is $8,000, the amount of the liabilities discharged. The recognized gain is $4,500, since the gain is recognized to the extent of boot received, but never more than the gain realized.

BASIS IN PROPERTY RECEIVED

Exhibit 15-2 presents two ways of computing the basis of property received in a like-kind exchange. The first method (Method 1), prescribed by the Code, is based on the notion that the like-kind property received in the exchange is merely

---

Exhibit 15-2
Basis of Property Received in a Like-Kind Exchange

Method 1:

Adjusted basis of property given up.................			$xxx,xxx
Plus:	Gain recognized.......................	$xx,xxx	
	Boot paid.............................	x,xxx	
	Liabilities assumed by the taxpayer.......................	xx,xxx	
	Liabilities encumbering the property received	xx,xxx	+ xx,xxx
			$xxx,xxx
Less:	Boot received	$xx,xxx	
	Liabilities assumed by the other party (transferee).....................	xx,xxx	
	Liabilities encumbering the property transferred.................	xx,xxx	− xx,xxx
Basis of property received			$xxx,xxx

Method 2:

Fair market value of property received			$xxx,xxx
Less:	Deferred gain (realized gain − recognized gain)		− xx,xxx
Plus:	Realized loss (deferred)		+ xx,xxx
Basis of property received			$xxx,xxx

a continuation of the taxpayer's investment in the like-kind property given up. Thus, the basis of the property received should be the same as the property given up—a so-called *substituted* basis. This basis is *increased* by any gain recognized and by any additional consideration given or to be paid in the future, or *decreased* by the fair market value of any boot received and by any liabilities transferred.[103] The second method is derived from the basis determination method used for replacement property in involuntary conversions and sales of principal residences. Under this method, the fair market value of the like-kind property received (i.e., its cost if purchased) is *reduced* by a deferred gain or *increased* by deferred loss in determining its basis. This adjustment is made so that if the newly acquired property is later sold, any realized gain or loss that is not recognized (deferred amount) from the previous like-kind exchange will be automatically considered in the computation of the realized gain or loss. Under either method, the basis of any boot received is its fair market value.

The following example is a comprehensive review of the like-kind exchange rules.

Example 40. E exchanged a rental house for T's rental condominium. E's house was worth $36,000 and her adjusted basis was $27,000. The house was not subject to any liabilities. T's condominium was worth $82,000 and was subject to a mortgage of $54,000. T also transferred $8,000 worth of Alpha Corp. stock to E in order to equalize the transaction. T's adjusted basis in his condominium and the Alpha stock were $64,000 and $5,600, respectively. The gains realized by E and T are computed as follows:

$$\underline{E}$$

Fair market value of property received		
Rental condominium (like-kind property).................		$82,000
Alpha Corp. stock (boot received).......................		+ 8,000
		$90,000
Less: Liabilities (mortgage) assumed		
by taxpayer......................................		− 54,000
Amount realized...		$36,000
Less: Adjusted basis of rent house given up..............		− 27,000
Gain realized...		$ 9,000

$$\underline{T}$$

Fair market value of rental house received................		$36,000
Plus: Liabilities discharged (assumed by E)...............		+ 54,000
Amount realized...		$90,000
Less: Adjusted basis of properties given up:		
Rental condominium...........................	$64,000	
Alpha Corp. stock (boot paid)...................	5,600	− 69,600
Gain realized...		$20,400

[103] § 1031(d).

E's gain recognized is $8,000, the amount of boot (stock) received. The amount of boot received by T is $54,000 (the amount of liabilities discharged), which is reduced by his boot paid of $8,000 (fair market value of Alpha stock). Therefore, T's net liabilities discharged are $46,000. T's recognized gain, however, is $20,400, since recognized gain never exceeds realized gain. T's recognized gain consists of $2,400 ($8,000 fair market value − $5,600 basis) for the taxable exchange of the Alpha stock, and the remaining $18,000 is attributable to the exchange of his house.

E and T's bases in their like-kind property received are determined as follows:

	E's Condominium	T's House
Adjusted basis of like-kind property given up.................................	$27,000	$64,000
Plus: Gain recognized......................	+ 8,000	+ 20,400
Boot paid.............................	+ 0	+ 5,600
Liabilities assumed...................	+ 54,000	+ 0
Less: Boot received........................	− 8,000	− 0
Liabilities discharged.................	− 0	− 54,000
Basis of property received...................	$81,000	$36,000

E's basis in the Alpha Corp. stock is $8,000, its fair market value.[104] E and T could have computed their bases in the like-kind property received by using the alternative method (Method 2) discussed previously.

	E	T
Fair market value of like-kind property received:		
Rental house.............................		$36,000
Rental condominium......................	$82,000	
Less: Deferred gain........................	− 1,000	− 0
Basis of like-kind property received............	$81,000	$36,000

EXCHANGE REQUIREMENT

Generally, the determination of whether an exchange has occurred is not difficult. All that is required is a reciprocal transfer of qualifying properties. An exchange of one real estate investment for another would normally qualify. Similarly, a trade-in of a business auto along with some cash for another auto is a qualifying exchange. However, an argument can be made for collapsing seemingly independent transactions which might appear to be an exchange in substance.[105]

---

[104] Reg. §§ 1.1031(d)-1(c) and 1.1031 (d)-1(d).

[105] Rev. Rul. 61-119, 1961-1 C.B. 395.

Example 41.   B, a traveling salesperson, "sold" his business auto to a car dealership for $3,200 cash. Shortly thereafter, he purchased another auto from the same dealer for $12,000 cash. The IRS could collapse the *two* transactions (sale and purchase) between the same parties in *one* like-kind exchange. Thus, if B's basis in the old vehicle was $6,000, his loss would be disallowed, and his basis in the new auto would be $14,800 ($12,000 fair market value of new auto + $2,800 deferred loss).

Three-Corner Exchanges.   It is not always easy for two parties with properties of equal value, both of which are suitable to the other party, to get together. Even so, it may be possible for a taxpayer who cannot find an exchange partner to qualify for like-kind treatment through a three-corner exchange.

Several forms of multiple party exchanges have qualified for like-kind exchange treatment. The IRS has ruled that when three property owners entered into an exchange in which each gave up and received qualifying property, like-kind exchange treatment was appropriate.[106]   However, a three-corner exchange must be part of a single, integrated plan.[107]

Example 42.   X, Y, and Z each own rental property. They exchange the properties as follows:

> X gets Y's property, Y gets Z's property, and Z gets X's property. X, Y, and Z pay or receive boot in order to equalize the difference in the values of the properties.

This three-party transaction qualifies as a like-kind exchange under § 1031. Each party receiving boot must recognize gain up to the amount of the boot received.

In another common situation, one party to a like-kind exchange will purchase property (from a third party) to use in the exchange. The property purchased is often specified by the person who will receive it as a result of the like-kind exchange.

Example 43.   C owned rental property worth $70,000 (adjusted basis of $34,000) which she was willing to dispose of only if she could do so without recognizing any gain. B wanted to purchase C's property, but in order that C might defer her $36,000 realized gain, he agreed to purchase another rental property of equal value that was suitable to C. As long as she receives no boot, C would recognize no gain and her basis in the replacement

---

[106]   Rev. Rul. 57-244, 1957-1 C.B. 247; Rev. Rul. 73-476, 1973-2 C.B. 300.

[107]   Rev. Rul. 75-291, 1975-2 C.B. 332; Rev. Rul. 77-297, 1977-2 C.B. 304.

property would be $34,000 ($70,000 fair market value of property received − $36,000 deferred gain). B will not qualify for § 1031 treatment since he purchased the property specifically for the exchange and thus never held it for business use or investment.[108] However, B will not have any realized gain or loss as a result of the transaction since his amount realized of $70,000 (fair market value of rental property received from C) is equal to his cost basis of the property given up.

Delayed Exchanges. The property to be accepted by the taxpayer in a like-kind exchange need not be received *simultaneously* with the transfer of his or her property. However, in order to qualify for nonrecognition treatment, the property to be acquired must be

1. Identified within 45 days after the date the taxpayer surrenders his or her property; and

2. Received within 180 days of the transfer, but no later than the due date (including extensions) of the tax return for the year of transfer.[109]

Example 44. R has agreed to purchase any real property worth $120,000 that is acceptable to S if S will immediately transfer his commercial parking lot, which is adjacent to R's store, to R. S agrees to the plan. S later identifies a duplex worth $120,000 and directs R to purchase it for him. This delayed exchange will qualify under § 1031 if the duplex is specified as the replacement property within 45 days and is transferred to S within 180 days of the transfer of the parking lot to R.

TREATMENT MANDATORY

Like-kind exchange treatment is mandatory. Therefore, any transaction that meets the requirements will result in the recognition of no gain or loss. Since the provision also applies to losses, like-kind treatment may work to the disadvantage of a taxpayer and it may be to his or her benefit to avoid exchange status.[110]

Example 45. In a like-kind exchange, T had a realized loss of $3,000. T may not recognize the loss since loss recognition is prohibited under § 1031. However, the loss would have been recognized if it had been the result of a sale or other taxable transaction.

---

[108] *Biggs v. Comm.*, 81-1 USTC ¶9114, 47 AFTR2d 81-484, 632 F.2d 1171 (CA-5, 1980).

[109] § 1031(a)(3).

[110] § 1031(a).

HOLDING PERIOD

The holding period of like-kind property received in a § 1031 exchange includes the holding period of the property given up on the exchange.[111] This also applies to the holding period of replacement property in an involuntary conversion. However, the holding period of any property received as boot in a § 1031 exchange *begins* on the date of its receipt. In effect, when boot received is property other than money (or discharged liabilities), it is treated as if the taxpayer received money (equal to the property's fair market value) and used it to purchase the property. Consequently, the property's holding period starts on the day of the exchange *and* the basis of the property is its fair market value.

OTHER NONTAXABLE TRANSACTIONS

CHANGES IN FORM OF DOING BUSINESS

Several provisions in the Internal Revenue Code are intended to allow mere changes in the form of carrying on a continuing business activity without the recognition of gain or loss. Section 721, for example, allows the transfer of property to a partnership in exchange for a partnership interest without the recognition of taxable gain or loss. Section 351 allows a similar treatment when property is transferred to a corporation solely in exchange for its stock by persons possessing control, and § 355 provides for nontaxability in certain corporate reorganizations. These specific topics are addressed in subsequent chapters.

CERTAIN EXCHANGES OF STOCK IN SAME CORPORATION

No gain or loss is recognized by the shareholder who exchanges common stock for common stock or preferred stock for preferred stock in the same corporation under § 1036. The exchange may be voting stock for nonvoting stock, and it is immaterial whether the exchange is with another shareholder or with the issuing corporation.[112] If the exchange is not solely in kind, the rules of § 1031(b) (applicable to like-kind exchanges) are applied to determine the amount of any gain recognized.[113]

---

[111] § 1223(1).

[112] Reg. § 1.1036-1(a).

[113] Reg. § 1.1036-1(b).

CERTAIN EXCHANGES OF U.S. OBLIGATIONS

Gain may be deferred in the case of certain exchanges of U.S. obligations between the taxpayer and the U.S. Government. Section 1037 applies to exchanges of bonds of the Government issued under Chapter 31 of Title 31 (the Second Liberty Bond Act). The Treasury regulations for § 1037 discuss the application of this section.

REPOSSESSION OF REAL PROPERTY

Section 1038 provides that the seller of real property will recognize a gain on the repossession of real property only to the extent the sum of the money and other property besides the repossessed realty received exceeds the gain from the transaction previously reported. This provision applies only to repossessions to satisfy debt obligations received in exchange for the sold property (e.g., foreclosure for nonpayment of mortgage). Such purchase-money obligations must be secured by an interest in the property. If any part of these obligations has previously been deducted as a bad debt, the amount of such deductions is included in income in the year of the repossession.

ROLLOVER GAIN FROM LOW-INCOME HOUSING

The gain on the sale of "qualified housing projects" can be deferred if the property is sold to its tenants or occupants, or to a cooperative or other nonprofit organization formed solely for their benefit. To qualify, the sale must be approved by the Secretary of Housing and Urban Development.

Section 1039 provides that the owner may elect to defer the gain if another "qualified housing project" is purchased within specified time limits. The time limit may be extended by the IRS at the request of the taxpayer.

A *qualified housing project* is one subject to a mortgage insured by the Federal government under specified housing programs and, under such programs, is limited as to rates of return and occupancy charges. Properties that qualify for these guarantees provide housing for lower-income families.

CERTAIN EXCHANGES OF INSURANCE POLICIES

Section 1035 allows the deferral of gain on the exchange of a life insurance contract for another insurance policy. Additionally, it allows certain exchanges involving annuity contracts and endowment contracts.

TAX PLANNING CONSIDERATIONS

CURRENT RECOGNITION VERSUS DEFERRAL

A basic concept in tax planning, as discussed in earlier chapters, is the deferral of tax payments. Each of the provisions discussed in this chapter (as it relates to gains) is a perfect example of such a deferral. A taxpayer is usually better off by deferring any gain—unless he or she expects to be in a much higher effective tax bracket in the later year when the deferred gain would be recognized. Of course, a taxpayer is *always* better off if he or she can avoid tax altogether, as is the case under § 121. However, if a loss is deferred under § 1031, taxes are accelerated. Thus, if the adjusted basis of business or investment property being disposed of exceeds its fair market value, the nonrecognition treatment of § 1031 should be avoided.

CURRENT GAIN RESULTING IN FUTURE REDUCTIONS

In each case of deferred gain, the mechanism is a reduced basis in the replacement property. If this replacement property is depreciable property, the depreciation deductions will also be smaller. It may be advantageous to report a large gain *currently* if the tax cost is low, and reap the benefit of the larger depreciation deductions in later years.

> **Example 46.** W plans to dispose of a building which would result in capital gain if sold, and acquire similar property in a different location. W could defer gain by arranging an exchange, but his basis in the new property would be low. W also has a large capital loss carryforward that he has been deducting at the rate of $3,000 per year.
>
> If W sells the property, the gain would offset the capital loss carryforward and he would pay no tax. His basis in the new building would be its cost, resulting in larger future depreciation deductions.

SECTION 1034 CONSIDERATIONS

Qualifying for the deferral of gain on the sale of a principal residence under § 1034 involves several tax planning considerations. First, care must be exercised so that the timing requirements are met. If a taxpayer purchases a replacement residence before selling the prior residence, the later sale must occur within the two-year period.

Another use of the reinvestment period involves a situation where the taxpayer sells and reinvests an amount less than the adjusted sales price. Any improvements to the property are included in its cost if they are made prior to the expiration of the reinvestment period.

Example 47. F sold her residence for $90,000, resulting in an adjusted sales price of $87,000 after selling costs and fixing-up expenses. She purchased a new residence for $65,000 three months later. Based on these facts, F must recognize gain of $22,000 ($87,000 − $65,000). However, if F adds a garage and a swimming pool to the new residence for $24,000 (or any other improvements) within two years of selling the prior residence, her amount reinvested will be $89,000 and her entire gain will be deferred.

Sale of Replacement. A taxpayer who sells and reinvests, may not defer gain from the replacement residence if it is sold before the expiration of the two-year reinvestment period from the prior residence. A taxpayer who wishes to sell the replacement and would recognize a gain should wait until that period expires.

Example 48. G purchased his first home for $56,000 and sold it for $70,000 on April 1, 1990. He purchased a replacement on July 1, 1990 for $75,000, deferring all his gain. On October 1, 1991, G received an offer to purchase his replacement residence for $92,000. Even if G reinvests on a timely basis, he will recognize the $17,000 gain ($92,000 − $75,000) if he sells before April 1, 1992. If G waits until after March 31, 1992 to sell his replacement, he can defer all of the gain by reinvesting in another replacement residence.

Business Use of Home. If part of a home is used exclusively as an office or is otherwise dedicated to business use, the costs of that portion of the residence, including depreciation, may be deductible. However, that portion of the residence will not qualify as a principal residence and any gain on that portion of the residence cannot be deferred under §1034. A taxpayer who anticipates selling his or her residence may wish to convert the business portion of the residence to personal use prior to the sale so that the entire residence will qualify under §1034. In the case of an office in the home, one could begin to use the office for some nonbusiness uses (i.e., not use the office exclusively for business), resulting in disallowance of the office expenses.

SECTION 121 CONSIDERATIONS

It is often difficult to determine whether a taxpayer with a gain of less than $125,000 on the sale of a personal residence and who intends to reinvest should use his or her § 121 election. In at least two instances, the § 121 election can be very useful. *First*, it is useful when a residence is sold and the taxpayer does not anticipate ever owning another home. *Second*, it is useful when a person has a large gain and intends to invest in a significantly less expensive home. If the gain is less than $125,000, it totally escapes tax and there is no reduction in the basis of the new residence. If the gain is greater than $125,000, the amount that must be reinvested to defer all of the gain, the adjusted sales price, is reduced by the amount of gain excluded under § 121.

Age 55. To qualify under §121, the taxpayer must be at least 55 years of age on the date the property is sold. Accordingly, a taxpayer in his or her early fifties may wish to defer selling the residence until such time as all requirements are met. A taxpayer nearing his or her 55th birthday may wish to go ahead and offer the residence for sale, specifying that the sale cannot occur until after his or her birthday.

IMPORTANCE OF CAPITAL BUDGETING IN DECISION MAKING

In any decision of whether to defer taxes when subsequent tax years are affected, capital budgeting techniques are appropriate in making the decision. When considering possible investment opportunities, a taxpayer must *compare* current investment requirements and tax effects with the future returns from the investment and their tax effects. Some form of present-value analysis will help the taxpayer to make a sound decision. A similar analysis should be applied in deciding the appropriateness of entering into any nontaxable (tax-deferred) transaction.

PROBLEM MATERIALS

DISCUSSION QUESTIONS

15-1 *Deferral vs. Exclusion.*   In what way do deferred gains differ from excluded gains?

15-2 *Adjusted Sales Price.*   Write a formula for determining the adjusted sales price of a residence under § 1034 beginning with the gross sales price.

15-3 *Fixing-up Expenses.*   What are "fixing-up expenses"?

15-4 *Loss on Sale of Personal Assets.*   Y sold his principal residence and realized a $12,000 loss. What is the proper tax treatment of this loss?

15-5 *Basis Determination.*   How is the basis of a replacement residence determined under § 1034?

15-6 *Impact on Basis of Fixing-up Expenses.*   How do fixing-up expenses affect the tax treatment of the sale of a principal residence under § 1034?

15-7 *Replacement Period.*   T entered into a contract to sell on February 21, 1991, and sold her principal residence on April 2, 1991. What is the replacement period during which this residence must be replaced in order to defer gain from the sale?

15-8 *Required Election.*   How often may the § 121 election be made? Can the taxpayer change his or her mind about a § 121 election previously made? If so, under what circumstances might you advise such action?

15-9 *Tests for Gain Exclusion.*   What three tests must be met in order for a taxpayer to exclude gain on the sale of a personal residence under § 121?

15-10 *Interaction of §§ 121 and 1034.*   How does an election of the § 121 exclusion affect the computation of the gain recognized and the basis of the replacement property if gain is also deferred under § 1034?

15-11 *Condemnation.*   What is required in order to have "threat or imminence" of condemnation?

15-12 *Replacement Property Under § 1033.*   How does the concept of "similar or related in service or use" differ between an owner/user of property and an owner/lessor?

15-13 *Replacement Period.*   B's beauty salon was destroyed by fire. The building was covered by current value insurance, and B realized a gain of $70,000. When must B reinvest in order to defer this gain under § 1033?

15-14 *Making the § 1033 Election.*   How does a taxpayer elect to defer gain under § 1033 in involuntary conversions?

15-15 *Ineligible Property.*   Property "held for sale" is not eligible for like-kind exchange treatment. Elaborate.

15-16 *Real Property under § 1031.* K proposes to exchange a downtown office building she holds as rental property for a 450-acre ranch in Virginia that she would operate as a horse ranch. Will this transaction qualify for like-kind exchange treatment?

15-17 *Personal Property under § 1031.* What constitutes personal property of "like-kind"?

15-18 *Boot.* What is the meaning of "boot" in § 1031 like-kind exchanges?

15-19 *Liabilities.* Are liabilities discharged always treated as boot received in a like-kind exchange under § 1031? Explain.

15-20 *Basis of Property Received.* How is the basis in the property received in a like-kind exchange under § 1031 determined? What is the basis in any boot received?

15-21 *§ 1031 Elective or Mandatory.* Is like-kind exchange treatment elective with the taxpayer? If not, how could such treatment be avoided if the taxpayer was so inclined?

15-22 *Holding Period.* In the current year, R received a rental house and 300 shares of IBM common stock in exchange for a vacant lot he had held as an investment since April 16, 1989. When does the holding period for the rental house begin? For the IBM stock?

PROBLEMS

15-23 *Sale of Principal Residence.* B, age 46, sold his principal residence for $96,000 on March 16, 1991. His basis in the residence was $56,000, and he paid sales commissions on the sale of $6,720. He also spent $780 on general repairs one month before entering the contract of sale. On May 7, 1992, B purchased a new residence for $90,000.

    a.   What is B's "adjusted sales price" on the old residence?
    b.   How much gain, if any, does B recognize on the sale of the old residence? If any gain is to be recognized, when?
    c.   What is B's basis in his new residence?

15-24 *Sale of Principal Residence.* What would be your answers in Problem 15-23 if B had invested $80,000 in his new residence?

15-25 *Sale of Principal Residence.* What would be your answers to the questions in Problem 15-23 if B had reinvested $53,000?

15-26 *Sale of Principal Residence.* T realized a $66,000 gain on the sale of her personal residence. She incurred selling costs of $7,500 and allowable fixing-up expenses of $1,500 related to this sale. Assuming that T purchased a qualifying replacement residence for $187,000 and recognized a $2,000 gain, answer the following:

    a.   What were the sales price and adjusted basis of T's former residence?
    b.   What is T's basis in the replacement residence?

15-27   *Sale of Principal Residence.*   M sold her principal residence for $220,000 on April 17, 1991 and reinvested in a new residence costing $190,000 on June 23, 1991. She incurred the following expenses related to the sale: sales commissions, $12,000; paint for residence, $800; general repairs, $600; new roof, $1,200; and closing costs, $500. The cost of the old residence was $124,000. The expenditures for painting and general repairs qualify as fixing-up expenses under § 1034.

   a.   What is M's "adjusted sales price"?
   b.   How much gain does M recognize on the sale of the old residence?
   c.   What is M's basis in her new residence?

15-28   *Sale of Principal Residence.*   What would be your answers to Problem 15-27 if M had reinvested $208,000?

15-29   *Ownership by Husband and Wife.*   J owned, as her separate property, the residence that she and her husband R lived in for many years. The residence was sold for $80,000, and J and R reinvested in a jointly owned home costing $120,000. They own equal interests in the replacement residence.

   a.   How much gain must J recognize on this sale under the general rules? (Assume J's basis in the former residence was $54,000).
   b.   Is there any relief provision which could benefit J and R? Explain.

15-30   *Sale of Principal Residence.*   During the current year, H and W ended their stormy marriage of 20 years. They had jointly owned a residence valued at $330,000 with a basis of $95,000. As part of their divorce settlement, H sold his interest in the home to W for $165,000. Assuming that there were no selling costs or fixing-up expenses, answer the following:

   a.   How much must H reinvest in a new principal residence in order to defer his entire gain on this sale?
   b.   What is W's basis in the residence?

15-31   *Sales of Principal Residences.* Provide the missing information in each of the following independent situations. Assume that each case qualifies for § 1034 treatment and that the realized gain in each case is $15,000.

Case	Sales Price	Selling Expense	Fixing-up Costs	Adjusted Sales Price	Amount Reinvested	Gain Recognized
A	$40,000	$2,400	$3,600	$_____	$34,000	$_____
B	_____	3,000	500	46,500	_____	1,000
C	40,000	2,400	_____	36,600	31,000	_____
D	70,000	_____	0	65,800	53,500	_____
E	55,000	3,300	_____	51,500	35,000	_____

15-32   *Interaction of §§ 121 and 1034.* G, age 59, sold her home during 1991 for $320,000. The property had been her principal residence for the last 15 years and had a basis to G of $172,000. She incurred selling costs of $22,000 and eligible fixing-up expenses of $5,500.

a.   Assuming that G has no intention of reinvesting in a replacement residence, what is the least possible gain she may report from this sale during 1991?

b.   What would be your answer if G had reinvested $80,000 in another principal residence in 1991?

15-33   *Section 121 Election Limitation.*   B and C were married in 1988. B moved into C's house which C had owned and occupied for 10 years. The residence was sold at a large gain in 1991 when B and C decided to enjoy the peacefulness of renting. In each of the situations below, can any gain be excluded under § 121?

a.   C deferred the gain from a prior residence that he owned jointly with his deceased first spouse by reinvesting in the current residence. B has not elected § 121 before.

b.   B excluded gain on the sale of a prior residence under § 121, and B and C file jointly for 1991. C has not elected § 121 before.

c.   B excluded gain on the sale of a prior residence under § 121, and B and C file separately for 1991. C is the sole owner of the residence and has not elected § 121 before.

15-34   *Involuntary Conversion.*   L owned a leased warehouse that was totally destroyed by fire on October 31, 1991. The building had a basis to L of $45,000 and his insurance paid the replacement cost of $75,000. L completed construction of a new warehouse on the same land on December 2, 1993 at a cost of $80,000.

a.   How much gain must L recognize on this conversion?

b.   What is L's basis in the replacement warehouse?

c.   Summarize L's reporting requirements.

15-35   *Involuntary Conversion.*   How would your answers to Problem 15-34 differ if L had invested only $65,000 in the replacement property?

15-36   *Involuntary Conversion.*   Complete the following table involving certain involuntary conversions in which the taxpayer elects to defer gain. The property is converted into cash and the cash is invested in qualifying replacement property in each case. Each case is independent of the others.

Case	Amount Realized	Adjusted Basis	Amount Reinvested	Gain Recognized	Basis in Replacement
A	$3,000	$1,600	$1,200	$_____	$_____
B	3,000	1,300	1,400	$_____	$_____
C	6,000	4,000	5,500	$_____	$_____
D	7,500	3,400	7,900	$_____	$_____
E	8,400	9,000	8,700	$_____	$_____

15-37 *Like-Kind Exchange.* F traded in an automobile that was used 100 percent of the time for business for a new auto for the same use. F had fully depreciated the old auto. The auto received was worth $12,000 and F paid $5,000 cash in addition to giving up her old auto.

  a.   How much gain must F recognize on the trade-in?
  b.   What is F's adjusted basis in the new auto?

15-38 *Like-Kind Exchange.* T transferred his farm land (100% business) to V in exchange for a parcel of unimproved urban real estate held by V as an investment. The farm was valued at $400,000 and was subject to a mortgage obligation of $260,000. T's basis in the farm was $340,000. The urban real estate was valued at $450,000 and was subject to a mortgage of $310,000.

  a.   How much gain must T recognize on this exchange?
  b.   What is T's basis in the urban real estate received?

15-39 *Like-Kind Exchange.* Refer to Problem 15-38. Assume that V had a basis of $360,000 in the urban real estate transferred to T.

  a.   How much gain must V recognize on the exchange?
  b.   What is V's basis in the farm property received?

15-40 *Like-Kind Exchange: Installment Reporting.* D entered into an agreement on December 15, 1991, under which he will immediately receive an apartment complex worth $300,000 and an installment obligation of the buyer for $200,000 with interest at 12 percent annually. D is to give up another apartment complex in which he has a basis of $320,000.

  a.   What is the minimum gain that D must recognize on this exchange in 1991?
  b.   How much gain must D report when he receives his first principal installment of $20,000 in 1992?

15-41 *Like-Kind Exchanges.* Complete the following table for exchanges that qualify for like-kind exchange treatment under § 1031.

Case	Adjusted Basis of Property Given up	FMV of Property Received	Cash Boot Received	Cash Boot Paid	Gain or Loss Recognized	Basis of Property Received
A	$3,000	$2,500	$ 0	$ 0	$_____	$_____
B	5,000	5,000	0	1,000	$_____	$_____
C	4,000	6,000	1,000	0	$_____	$_____
D	7,000	5,900	600	0	$_____	$_____
E	5,000	4,000	2,500	0	$_____	$_____
F	3,000	3,200	200	0	$_____	$_____
G	4,000	3,600	500	0	$_____	$_____

RESEARCH PROBLEMS

15-42 *Sale of Principal Residence.*   R was transferred to a new location by his employer, so he attempted to sell his home for several months before moving. Concluding that there was nothing he could do to sell the home at a reasonable market value, R offered the property for rent and a tenant moved in the following week. The following represent the results of operations for the rental period:

Gross rental income...	$7,000
Cash rental expenses, excluding	
interest and taxes...	1,275
Interest and taxes..	6,345
Depreciation, assuming 100% rental use.........................	3,225

One year later, R again offered the home for sale, this time successfully. The home was sold and R purchased a new home at an adequate price at the new work location.

a.   Can R defer his gain under § 1034?

b.   What amount of the rental expenses for the year may R deduct against his taxable rental income?

15-43 *Like-Kind Exchange.*   L operates a profitable electronic game room located in a large shopping center. She owns most of the machines and the lease for the location of the business in the shopping center. These assets are substantially appreciated and L would like to avoid gain on disposition of the business. She would, however, like to exchange this business for another business in a suburban or rural location. She has located a potential business, a convenience store. The primary assets of that business are shelves and other fixtures.

Will an exchange of L's business for the convenience store qualify for like-kind exchange treatment? Would it matter if the exchange included the land on which the store is located?

Research aids:

Rev. Rul. 57-365, 1957-2 C.B. 521.
Rev. Rul. 59-229, 1959-2 C.B. 180.
Miller v. U.S., 63-2 USTC ¶9606, 12 AFTR2d 5244 (S.D. Ind., 1963).
Proposed Reg. § 1.1031(a)-1(b).

COMPUTERIZED TAX ANALYSIS

15-44 *Sale of Principal Residence.*   Use computer file T1501 for this problem.

a.   For the independent situations listed below, compute the missing values.

	(1)	(2)	(3)	(4)	(5)	(6)
Sale price of old residence	$400,000	$400,000	$400,000	$369,000	$350,000	$350,000
Selling expenses	12,000	12,000	12,000	12,000	12,000	12,000
Section 121 exclusion	0	0	125,000	125,000	125,000	125,000
Adjusted basis of old residence	60,000	60,000	60,000	60,000	60,000	325,000
Fixing up expenses	2,000	2,000	2,000	2,000	2,000	2,000
Cost of new residence	0	230,000	230,000	230,000	230,000	230,000
Gain recognized on sale						
Adjusted basis of new residence						
Gain realized						
Adjusted sales price						
Postponed gain						

b.   For situation (a)(1), explain the tax rule that causes all of the gain realized to be recognized.

c.   The difference between situation (a)(1) and (a)(2) is that the taxpayer purchased another residence for $230,000. The realized gain does not change, but the recognized gain declines. Explain the tax rules that cause this.

d.   The difference between situations (a)(2) and (a)(3) is the election under § 121. Explain the tax rules that cause the gain realized, gain recognized, and adjusted sales price to decline while the adjusted basis of the new residence and the postponed gain remain the same.

e.   The difference between situations (a)(3) and (a)(4) is a reduction in the sale price of $31,000. The gain realized, gain recognized, and adjusted sales price decline while the adjusted basis of the new residence and the postponed gain remain the same. Explain the tax rules that cause this.

f.   In situation (a)(5), the sale price drops another $19,000 from the amount in situation (a)(4). The gain realized and adjusted sales price decline, but not the gain recognized. Also, the postponed gain declines, yet the adjusted basis in the new residence increases. Explain the tax rules that cause the results regarding the gain recognized, gain postponed, and adjusted basis in the new residence.

g.   In situation (a)(6), how much gain would be recognized if the § 121 exclusion were not elected?

LEARNING OBJECTIVES

Upon completion of this chapter you will be able to:

- Define a capital asset and use this definition to distinguish capital assets from other types of property
- Explain the holding period rules for classifying a capital asset transaction as either short-term or long-term
- Apply the capital gain and loss netting process to a taxpayer's capital asset transactions
- Understand the differences in tax treatment of an individual's capital gains and losses
- Explain the differences in tax treatment of the capital gains and losses of a corporate taxpayer versus those of an individual taxpayer
- Identify various transactions to which capital gain or loss treatment has been extended
- Discuss the tax treatment of investments in corporate bonds and other forms of indebtedness

CHAPTER OUTLINE

Chapter 16

PROPERTY TRANSACTIONS
Capital Gains and Losses

Chapters 14 and 15 examined various income tax considerations related to transactions in property. They dealt primarily with the determination of gain or loss realized on the sale or other disposition of property and the recognition, or nonrecognition as the case might be, of gains and losses in such transactions. Other aspects of property transactions were also covered. This chapter deals with the special treatment accorded an individual's *recognized* gains and losses on dispositions of capital assets.

GENERAL REQUIREMENTS

Capital gain or loss treatment is appropriate only if each of several elements is present. The asset being transferred must be a *capital asset* and the disposition must constitute a *sale or exchange*. In addition, the exact treatment of any net gain or loss can be determined only after taking into consideration the *holding period* of the properties transferred. Each of these elements is discussed below.

CAPITAL ASSETS

DEFINITION OF A CAPITAL ASSET

A capital asset is defined in Code § 1221 as any asset *other than* one that falls into any one of five excluded classes. The five groups of *excluded* assets are as follows:

1. Inventory or property held primarily for sale to customers in the ordinary course of a trade or business

2. Accounts and notes receivable acquired in the ordinary course of a trade or business for services rendered or from the sale of inventory

3. Depreciable property and land used in a trade or business

4. A copyright, a literary, musical, or artistic composition, a letter or memorandum, or similar property held by the creator, or a letter or memorandum held by the person for whom the property was created; in addition, such property held by a taxpayer whose basis is determined by reference to the creator's basis (e.g., acquired by gift), or person for whom created

5. A publication of the United States Government that is received from the Government by any means other than purchase at the price at which it is offered to the public, and which is held by the taxpayer who received the publication or by a transferee whose basis is found with reference to the original recipient's basis (e.g., acquired by gift)

It is important to note that the classification of an asset as a capital asset may affect more than the character of the gain or loss on its sale. For example, the amount of a charitable contribution deduction also may be affected in certain instances. Recall that the deduction for charitable contributions of appreciated capital gain property is limited.[1]

INVENTORY

The inventory exception has been the subject of much litigation and controversy. Whether property is held primarily for sale is a question of fact. The Supreme Court decided in *Malat v. Riddell*[2] that the word "primarily" should be interpreted as used in an ordinary, everyday sense, and as such, means "principally" or of "first importance."

The determination of whether an item is inventory or not frequently arises in the area of sales of real property. In determining whether a taxpayer holds real estate, or a particular tract of real estate, primarily for sale, the courts seem to place the greatest emphasis on the frequency, continuity, and volume of sales.[3] Other important factors considered by the courts are subdivision and improvement,[4] solicitation and advertising,[5] purpose and manner of acquisition,[6] and reason for and method of sale.[7]

---

[1] See § 170(e)(1) and Chapter 11 for a discussion of these charitable contribution limitations.

[2] 66-1 USTC ¶9317, 17 AFTR2d 604, 383 U.S. 569 (USSC, 1966).

[3] See, for example, *Houston Endowment, Inc. v. U.S.*, 79-2 USTC ¶9690, 44 AFTR2d 79-6074, 606 F.2d 77 (CA-5, 1979) and *Reese v. Comm.*, 80-1 USTC ¶9350, 45 AFTR2d 80-1248, 615 F.2d 226 (CA-5, 1980).

[4] See, for example, *Houston Endowment, Inc.* (Footnote 3), and *Biedenharn Realty Co.,*

Inc. v. U.S., 76-1 USTC ¶9194, 37 AFTR2d 76-679, 526 F.2d 409 (CA-5, 1976).

[5] See, for example, *Houston Endowment, Inc.* (Footnote 3).

[6] See, for example, *Scheuber v. Comm.*, 67-1 USTC ¶9219, 19 AFTR2d 639, 371 F.2d 996 (CA-7, 1967), and *Biedenharn Realty Co., Inc. v. U.S.* (Footnote 4).

[7] See, for example, *Voss v. U.S.*, 64-1 USTC ¶9290, 13 AFTR2d 834, 329 F.2d 164 (CA-7, 1964).

In another area, the Supreme Court has determined that payments and adjustments arising out of an earlier capital gain or loss transaction will also result in capital asset treatment. In *Arrowsmith v. Comm.*,[8] it was held that a shareholder who had been allowed capital gain treatment upon the liquidation of a corporation had a capital loss when additional corporate taxes became due and were paid by him.

DISPOSITION OF A BUSINESS

The treatment of the sale of a business depends on the form in which the business is operated. Generally, the sale of a partnership interest or the sale of corporate stock is treated as the sale of an investment in an entity. Such investments are generally capital assets. However, major exceptions to the treatment of gains as capital gains are provided in the Code. These specifics are discussed in subsequent chapters, dealing with corporations (Chapters 19 and 20) and partnerships (Chapter 22).

The sale of a proprietorship is treated as the separate sale of each of the assets of the business.[9] Accordingly, the gains and losses from the sales of inventory items and receivables will be treated separately as ordinary gains and losses. Gains and losses from the sale of depreciable assets and land used in a trade or business will be given special treatment in a second category, and those from the sale of capital assets in a third. The specific treatment of depreciable assets and land used in a trade or business is covered later in this chapter.

SALE OR EXCHANGE REQUIREMENT

In order for capital gain or loss treatment to be allowed, the property must be disposed of in a "sale or exchange." An abandonment of property generally does not constitute a sale or exchange.[10] Accordingly, any loss on such a disposition would be an ordinary loss if deductible. Most other forms of dispositions, however, are treated as sales or exchanges, and normally there is no difficulty in determining whether one has occurred.

---

[8] 52-2 USTC ¶9527, 42 AFTR 649, 344 U.S. 6 (1952).

[9] *Williams v. McGowan*, 46-1 USTC ¶9120, 34 AFTR 615, 152 F.2d 570 (CA-2, 1945); Rev. Rul. 55-79, 1955-1 C.B. 370.

[10] Reg. §§ 1.165-2 and 1.167(a)-8.

WORTHLESS SECURITIES

A statutory exception is provided in the case of worthless stock or securities. Section 165(g) provides that worthless stocks or securities shall be treated as sold or exchanged on the last day of the taxable year in which they become worthless.

> **Example 1.** D owns 200 shares of ABC Paving, Inc. which he purchased for $4,500 in 1987. D was able to ascertain that the ABC stock became wholly worthless during 1991. Since this worthlessness is treated as a sale or exchange on the last day of D's taxable year, December 31, 1991, and he owned the stock for more than one year, his loss on worthlessness of $4,500 is a long-term capital loss.

The question of whether stock became worthless during a given year is a question of fact, and the burden of proof is on the taxpayer to show that the stock actually became worthless during the year in question.[11]

Another exception to the sale or exchange requirement involves the collection of the face value of a corporate bond (i.e., a bond redemption) at its maturity. These two exceptions are discussed in greater detail later in this chapter.

CERTAIN CASUALTIES AND THEFTS

Still another exception to the sale or exchange requirement involves *excess* casualty and theft gains from the involuntary conversion of *personal use assets*. As discussed in Chapter 10, § 165(h) provides that if personal casualty or theft gains *exceed* personal casualty or theft losses for any taxable year, each such gain and loss must be treated as a gain or loss from the sale or exchange of a capital asset. Each separate casualty or theft loss must be reduced by $100 before being netted with the personal casualty or theft gains.

> **Example 2.** T had three separate casualties involving personal-use assets during the year:

			Fair Market Value	
Casualty	Property	Adjusted Basis	Before Casualty	After Casualty
1. Accident	Personal Car	$12,000	$ 8,500	$ 6,000
2. Robbery	Jewelry	1,000	4,000	0
3. Hurricane	Residence	60,000	80,000	58,000

---

[11] *Young v. Comm.*, 41-2 USTC ¶9744, 28 AFTR 365, 123 F.2d 597 (CA-2, 1941). Code § 6511(d) extends the statute of limitations from three years to seven years be- cause of the difficulty of determining the specific tax year in which stock becomes worthless.

T received insurance reimbursements as follows: (1) $900 for repair of the car; (2) $3,200 for the theft of her jewelry; and (3) $21,500 for the damages to her home. Assuming T does not elect (under § 1033) to purchase replacement jewelry, her personal casualty gain exceeds her personal casualty losses by $300, computed as follows:

1. The loss for the car is $1,500 [(lesser of $2,500 decline in value or the $12,000 adjusted basis = $2,500) − $900 insurance recovery − $100 floor].

2. The gain for the jewelry is $2,200 ($3,200 insurance recovery − $1,000 adjusted basis).

3. The loss from the residence is $400 [(lesser of $22,000 decline in value or the $60,000 adjusted basis = $22,000) − $21,500 insurance recovery − $100 floor].

T must report each separate gain and loss as a gain or loss from the sale or exchange of a capital asset. The classification of each gain and loss as short-term or long-term depends on the holding period of each asset.

It is important to note that this exception *does not* apply if the personal casualty losses exceed the gains. In such case, the *net* loss, subject to the 10 percent limitation, is deductible *from* A.G.I. Recall, however, that casualty and theft losses are among those itemized deductions that are not subject to the three percent cut-back rule if the taxpayer's A.G.I. exceeds $100,000. (See Chapter 11 for a discussion of this cut-back rule.)

Example 3. Assume the same facts in *Example 2* except the insurance recovery from the hurricane damage to the residence was only $11,500. In this case, the loss from the hurricane is $10,400 ($22,000 − $11,500 − $100), and the personal casualty losses exceed the gain by $9,700 ($1,500 + $10,400 − $2,200). T must treat the $9,700 net loss as an itemized deduction subject to the 10% A.G.I. limitation, but not subject to the 3% cut-back rule.

HOLDING PERIOD

As mentioned previously, in order to determine the actual treatment of capital asset transactions, it is necessary to separate the long-term capital gains and losses from those that are short-term. This is done by determining the *holding period*, or the length of time each asset has been held. In order to have a long-term capital gain or loss, the capital asset must have been held *more than* one year. The short-term holding period is one year or less.[12]

---

[12] § 1222.

In computing the holding period, the day of acquisition is not counted but the day of sale is. The holding period is based on calendar months and fractions of calendar months, rather than on the number of days.[13] The fact that different months contain different numbers of days (i.e., 28, 30, or 31) is disregarded.

> **Example 4.** P purchased 10 shares of EX, Inc. on March 16, 1991. Her gain or loss on the sale is short-term *if* the stock is sold on or before March 16, 1992, but long-term if sold on or after March 17, 1992.

> **Example 5.** T purchased 100 shares of FMC Corp. stock on February 28, 1991. His gain or loss will be long-term if he sells the stock on or after March 1, 1992.

The holding period runs from the time property is acquired until the time it is disposed of. Property is generally considered *acquired* or *disposed of* when title passes from one party to another. State law usually controls the passage of title and must be consulted when questions arise.

STOCK EXCHANGE TRANSACTIONS

The holding period for securities traded on a stock exchange is determined in the same manner as for other property. The trade dates, rather than the settlement dates, are used as the dates of acquisition and sale.

Generally, both cash and accrual basis taxpayers must report (recognize) gains and losses on stock or security sales in the tax year of the trade, even though cash payment (settlement) may not be received until the following year. This requirement is imposed because the installment method of reporting gains is not allowed for sales of stock or securities that are traded on an established securities market.[14]

> **Example 6.** C, a cash basis calendar year taxpayer, sold 300 shares of ARA stock at a gain of $5,000 on December 29, 1991. The settlement date was January 3, 1992. C must report the gain in 1991 (the year of trade).

---

[13]   Rev. Rul. 66-7, 1966-1 C.B. 188.

[14]   § 453(j)(2). See Chapter 14 for a detailed discussion of the installment sale method.

SPECIAL RULES AND EXCEPTIONS

Section 1223 provides several special rules for determining the holding period of certain properties. The first exception provides that the holding period of property received in an exchange *includes* the holding period of the property given up in the exchange if the basis of the property is determined by reference, in whole or in part, to the basis in that property given up.[15] It is required that the property exchanged be a capital asset or a § 1231 asset at the time of the exchange. An involuntary conversion under § 1033 is to be treated as an exchange for purposes of this special rule.

Under this provision, the holding period of a property received in a like-kind exchange under § 1031 would begin when the property given up in the exchange was originally acquired if any gain or loss was deferred in the exchange. Similarly, the holding period of a principal residence with a reduced basis because of a deferred gain from another residence under § 1034 would include the holding period of the old residence.[16]

> **Example 7.** M sold his personal residence, which he had owned for nine months, for $122,500 and does not intend to purchase a new residence. M's basis in the residence sold is $70,500, its cost of $109,000 less $38,500 of gain that was deferred from the sale of a previous residence he had owned for six years. The basis of M's residence is determined partially by referring to his basis in the previous residence (by adjusting for the deferred gain from that sale). Thus, M's holding period for the residence he has just sold is six years plus nine months, and M's gain of $52,000 ($122,500 sales price − $70,500 basis) is a long-term capital gain.

Another exception provides that if a taxpayer's basis in property is the same basis as another taxpayer had in that property, in whole or in part, the holding period will include that of the other person.[17] Therefore, the holding period of property acquired by gift generally will include the holding period of the donor. This will not be true, however, if the property is sold at a loss and the basis in the property for determining the loss is fair market value on the date of the gift.

---

[15]   § 1223(1).   [17]   § 1223(2).

[16]   § 1223(7).

Example 8. G received a gold necklace from her elderly grandmother as a birthday gift on August 31, 1991. The necklace was worth $5,200 at that time and had a basis to the grandmother of $1,300. Grandmother had bought the necklace approximately 20 years earlier. Contrary to her grandmother's wishes, G sold the family heirloom for $5,000 on December 13, 1991. The $3,700 gain to G will be a long-term gain since her $1,300 basis is determined (under § 1015) by reference to her grandmother's basis, *and* her holding period includes the 20 years the necklace was held by her grandmother.

Example 9. If G's grandmother had a basis in the necklace of $6,000, G's basis for determining loss would be $5,200, the fair market value at the date of the gift (see discussion in Chapter 14). Because G's basis is *not* determined by reference to her grandmother's basis, the grandmother's holding period is not added to G's holding period. Since G only held the necklace for three months, she will have a $200 short-term capital loss ($5,200 basis − $5,000 sales price).

A special rule is provided for property acquired from a decedent. The holding period formally begins on the date of death. However, the Code provides that if the heir's basis in the property is its fair market value under § 1014 and the property is sold within one year after the decedent's death, the gain or loss will be treated as long-term.[18]

Example 10. P sold 50 shares of Xero Corp. stock for $11,200 on July 27, 1991. The stock was an inheritance from P's uncle who died on May 16, 1991, and it was included in the uncle's Federal estate tax return at a fair market value of $12,000. Since P's basis in the stock ($12,000) is determined under § 1014, the $800 loss on the sale will be a long-term capital loss. This would be the case even if P's uncle had purchased the stock within days of his death. The decedent's prior holding period is irrelevant.

There are various other provisions that contain special rules for determining holding periods. The holding period of stock acquired in a transaction in which a loss was disallowed under the "wash sale" provisions (§ 1091) is added to the holding period of the replacement stock.[19] Also, when a shareholder receives stock dividends or stock rights as a result of owning stock in a corporation, the holding period of the stock or stock rights includes the holding period of the stock already owned in the corporation.[20] The holding period of any stock acquired by exercising stock rights, however, begins on the date of exercise.[21]

---

[18] § 1223(11).

[19] § 1223(4); Reg. § 1.1223-1(d).

[20] § 1223(5); Reg. § 1.1223-1(e).

[21] § 1223(6); Reg. § 1.1223-1(f).

The holding period of property acquired by exercise of an option begins on the day after the option is exercised.[22] If a taxpayer sells the property acquired by option within one year after exercising the option, then he or she will have a short-term gain or loss.

> **Example 11.** N owned an option to purchase ten acres of land. She had owned the option more than one year when she exercised it and purchased the property. Her holding period for the property begins on the day after she exercises the option. Had she sold the option, her gain or loss would have been long-term. If she had sold the property immediately, her gain or loss would have been short-term.

The holding period of a commodity acquired in satisfaction of a commodity futures contract includes the holding period of the futures contract. However, the futures contract must have been a capital asset in the hands of the taxpayer.[23]

CAPITAL GAIN AND LOSS NETTING PROCESS

The netting process for capital gains and losses is not described as a process in the Code but is required implicitly under the definitions provided in § 1222. Gains and losses from sales or exchanges of capital assets must be combined in a particular order in determining the impact of the transactions on taxable income.

THE PROCESS

In the first step of the netting process, each taxpayer combines his or her short-term capital gains and losses and the result is either a *net* short-term capital gain (NSTCG) or a *net* short-term capital loss (NSTCL). Likewise, the taxpayer combines long-term capital gains and losses with a result of either a *net* long-term capital gain (NLTCG) or a *net* long-term capital loss (NLTCL). If the taxpayer has *both* a net short-term capital gain and a net long-term capital gain (i.e., NSTCG and NLTCG)—or a net short-term capital loss and a net long-term capital loss (i.e., NSTCL and NLTCL)—*no* further netting is allowed. However, if the taxpayer has *either* a net short-term capital gain and a net long-term capital loss (NSTCG and NLTCL), *or* a net short-term capital loss and a net long-term capital gain (NSTCL and NLTCG), these results are combined in the second stage of the netting process.

---

[22] See, for example, *Helvering v. San Joaquin Fruit & Inv. Co.*, 36-1 USTC ¶9144, 17 AFTR 470, 297 U.S. 496 (USSC, 1936), and *E.T. Weir*, 49-1 USTC ¶9190, 37 AFTR 1022, 173 F.2d 222 (CA-3, 1949).

[23] § 1223(8); Reg. § 1.1223-1(h).

THE RESULTS

The *three* possible results of the capital gain and loss netting process are defined as follows:

1. *Overall net short-term capital gain* (NSTCG)—either a net short-term capital gain with no further netting allowed, or the *excess* of a net short-term capital gain over a net long-term capital loss (i.e., NSTCG − NLTCL, if any)[24]

2. *Net capital gain* (NCG)—either a net long-term capital gain with no further netting allowed, or the *excess* of a net long-term capital gain over a net short-term capital loss (i.e., NLTCG − NSTCL, if any)[25]

3. *Net capital loss* (NCL)—either a net short-term capital loss or a net long-term capital loss with no further netting allowed (NSTCL or NLTCL), the *sum* of both net short-term and net long-term capital losses (NSTCL + NLTCL), the *excess* of a net short-term capital loss over a net long-term capital gain (NSTCL − NLTCG), or the *excess* of a net long-term capital loss over a net short-term capital gain (NLTCL − NSTCG)[26]

Note that a taxpayer could have *both* an overall net short-term capital gain (NSTCG) and a net long-term capital gain (NCG) at the end of the netting process. Unlike net losses, net short-term capital gains and net long-term capital gains are *not* combined. As discussed below, individual taxpayers with net long-term capital gains (NCG) may receive favorable tax treatment.

The results of the netting process are illustrated below. Also, note that married persons filing a joint return net their respective capital gains and losses together, even though the asset disposed of may have been separately owned.

Example 12.   The first step in the netting process is illustrated by the four independent cases below:

Case	STCG	STCL	LTCG	LTCL	Net Result	Description
A	$6,000	($2,000)			$4,000	NSTCG
B	3,000	(5,000)			(2,000)	NSTCL
C			$8,000	($1,000)	7,000	NLTCG
D			4,000	(7,000)	(3,000)	NLTCL

---

[24]   Unlike the other possible results, an overall NSTCG has no special name—and as discussed below, is not eligible for any special tax treatment.

[25]   § 1222(11).

[26]   § 1222(10).

A taxpayer with the net results of cases A and C *or* B and D above would have no further netting of capital gains and losses. The $4,000 NSTCG from case A would be classified as an overall net short-term capital gain (NSTCG). The $7,000 NLTCG from case C would be classified as a net capital gain (NCG). The $2,000 NSTCL from case B or the $3,000 NLTCL from case D would become a net capital loss (NCL). If a taxpayer had two results, like cases B and D, the two losses would be added together and become a $5,000 net capital loss.

If a taxpayer had the results of cases A and D *or* cases B and C, however, he or she would proceed to the second step of the netting process.

Example 13. Assume that individual K has all the capital gains and losses illustrated in cases A and D above. These results would be further combined as follows:

```
Case A: $6,000 STCG  −  $2,000 STCL  =  $4,000   NSTCG
Case D: $4,000 LTCG  −  $7,000 LTCL  =  (3,000)  NLTCL

Overall NSTCG (NSTCG − NLTCL)          $1,000
```

K's $3,000 NLTCL is offset (deducted) against her $4,000 NSTCG and the result is an overall net short-term capital gain (NSTCG) of $1,000.

Example 14. Assume that individual R has the capital gains and losses illustrated in cases B and C from *Example 12*. These results would be further combined as follows:

```
Case C: $8,000 LTCG  −  $1,000 LTCL  =  $7,000   NLTCG
Case B: $3,000 STCG  −  $5,000 STCL  =  (2,000)  NSTCL

Net capital gain (NLTCG − NSTCL)          $5,000  NCG
```

R's $2,000 NSTCL is offset (deducted) against his $7,000 NLTCG and the result is a $5,000 net capital gain.

TREATMENT OF CAPITAL GAINS

The tax treatment of capital gains depends on *both* the nature of the gains and the type of taxpayer (i.e., individual, corporation, trust, or estate) involved.

Overall Net Short-term Capital Gains. An overall net short-term capital gain is not eligible for any special tax treatment. Consequently, *all* taxpayers with this type of gain simply include it with any other ordinary taxable income in computing their tax liability.

Net Capital Gains. Regular corporations, trusts, and estates are required to treat net capital gains in the same manner as net short-term capital gains. That is, these gains are included with all other ordinary taxable income. *Individual taxpayers*, however, may be entitled to use a special tax computation in determining the tax on their net capital gains. The special tax computation is designed to ensure that an individual's net capital gain will (1) not be taxed at a rate greater than 28 percent, or (2) not be taxed at 28 percent when the gain falls in the 15 percent bracket.[27] Note that whenever an individual's *ordinary taxable income* exceeds the amount that would be taxed at 15 percent (e.g., $34,000 for joint returns), none of his or her net capital gain is taxed at 15 percent. In such case, the taxpayer computes the tax liability by first calculating the regular tax on ordinary taxable income and adding to that a tax of 28 percent on the net capital gain. On the other hand, if ordinary taxable income does not exceed the amount that is taxed at 15 percent, a portion of the net capital gain is taxed at the 15 percent rate, and the balance of the gain, if any, is taxed at a maximum rate of 28 percent. This special tax computation formula is presented in Exhibit 16-1.

The first step of the special tax computation formula simply seeks to determine whether the individual's ordinary taxable income is higher than the 15 percent

---

Exhibit 16-1
*Special Tax Computation for
Individual Taxpayers' Net Capital Gains*

Step 1. Determine the larger of
  a. Ordinary taxable income (taxable income − net capital gain)
  b. Amount of 15 percent bracket for *this* taxpayer's filing status

Step 2. Compute the regular tax on the *greater* of (a) or (b) in Step 1 above (i.e., the regular tax on the larger of ordinary taxable income or the amount taxed at 15 percent).

Step 3. Compute the tax on the balance of any net capital gains not taxed in Step 2 above as follows:

Taxable income (including ordinary taxable income and net capital gain)	$xxx,xxx
Less: Greater of (a) or (b) in Step 1 above	− xx,xxx
Balance:	$xxx,xxx
Times: Maximum tax rate for net capital gains	× 28%
Equals: Tax	$ xx,xxx

Step 4. Add the taxes computed in Steps 2 and 3 to determine the maximum tax.

Step 5. Compute the regular tax on total taxable income.

Step 6. Compare the taxes computed in Steps 4 and 5 and pay the smaller.

---

[27]   See § 1(h).

bracket amount (e.g., $20,350 for single taxpayers and $34,000 for joint returns in 1991). If so, the entire 15 percent bracket is absorbed by ordinary taxable income, and all of the net capital gain is taxed 28 percent. To obtain this result, Step 2 computes the regular tax on ordinary taxable income (taxable income *without* the net capital gain), and Step 3 computes the tax on the net capital gain at the 28 percent rate. Normally, the taxpayer's tax will be the sum of the tax on ordinary taxable income and the 28 percent tax on the net capital gain (i.e., the *sum* of the taxes obtained in Steps 2 and 3). However, if the tax computed in the normal fashion is lower, the lower tax applies (Steps 5 and 6).

On the other hand, if the individual taxpayer's ordinary taxable income does not exceed the 15 percent bracket amount (Step 1), the 15 percent bracket amount is not entirely absorbed by ordinary taxable income. As a result, ordinary taxable income and a portion of the net capital gain are taxed at 15 percent (Step 2). The balance of the net capital gain, if any, is taxed at 28 percent. This stepwise approach to computing the tax is illustrated in *Example 15*.

Example 15. Assuming a married taxpayer filing jointly has the following amounts of ordinary taxable income and net capital gain, the tax liability for 1991 is computed as shown.

	Case 1	Case 2	Case 3
Step 1:			
a. Ordinary taxable income			
Taxable income	$100,000	$100,000	$100,000
− Net capital gain	− 10,000	− 40,000	− 90,000
Ordinary taxable income	$ 90,000	$ 60,000	$ 10,000
b. Amount of 15% bracket for taxpayer's filing status	$ 34,000	$ 34,000	$ 34,000
Larger of (a) or (b) above	$ 90,000	$ 60,000	$ 34,000
Step 2:			
Regular tax on larger of (a) or (b) in *Step 1*	$ 21,016	$ 12,380	$ 5,100
Step 3:			
Total taxable income	$100,000	$100,000	$100,000
Less: Greater of (a) or (b)	− 90,000	− 60,000	− 34,000
Balance	$ 10,000	$ 40,000	$ 66,000
Times: 28% rate	× 28%	× 28%	× 28%
Tax	$ 2,800	$ 11,200	$ 18,480
Step 4:			
Tax computed in *Step 2*	$ 21,016	$ 12,380	$ 5,100
Plus: Tax computed in *Step 3*	+ 2,800	+ 11,200	+ 18,480
Maximum tax	$ 23,816	$ 23,580	$ 23,580
Step 5:			
Regular tax on total taxable income	$ 24,116	$ 24,116	$ 24,116
Step 6:			
1991 tax liability is lesser of amount from *Steps 4* or *5*	$ 23,816	$ 23,580	$ 23,580

In *Case 1*, the taxpayer's ordinary taxable income of $90,000 exceeds the 15% bracket amount of $34,000 for joint returns (Step 1). Consequently, the entire 15% bracket amount is absorbed by ordinary taxable income, and the net capital gain is taxed at the 28% rate. In effect, the taxpayer pulls the net capital gain out of taxable income (Step 1), computes the regular tax on $90,000 of ordinary income (Step 2 tax of $21,016), and adds to that a 28% tax on the $10,000 net capital gain (Step 3 tax of $2,800). The sum of these two taxes, $23,816 (Step 4), represents the maximum gross tax that the taxpayer will owe. The taxpayer then computes the regular tax on total taxable income of $100,000, resulting in a tax of $24,116 (Step 5). The final gross tax is $23,816 (Step 6), the lower of the regular tax of $24,116 and the maximum tax of $23,816. A similar analysis applies to *Case 2*.

In *Case 3*, the taxpayer's ordinary taxable income of $10,000 is less than the 15% bracket amount of $34,000 for joint returns (Step 1). As a result, all the $10,000 of ordinary taxable income and a portion of the $90,000 net capital gain, $24,000 ($34,000 − $10,000), a total of $34,000, is taxed at 15% (Step 2). The balance of the $90,000 net capital gain not taxed at 15%, $66,000 ($90,000 − $24,000), is taxed at 28% (Step 3). The sum of the taxes computed in Steps 2 and 3 (Step 4) is then compared to the regular tax (Step 5) to determine the final gross tax (Step 6). Note that the tax saving in *Case 2* and *Case 3* is the same ($24,116 − $23,580 = $536). This occurs because in both instances the same amount of net capital gain is removed from the 31% tax bracket ($100,000 taxable income − 28% bracket limit of $82,150 = $17,850 × 3% = $536).

TREATMENT OF CAPITAL LOSSES

There are important differences between individual and corporate taxpayers in the tax treatment of *net capital losses* [i.e., net short-term capital losses (NSTCL), net short-term capital losses in excess of net long-term capital gains (NSTCL − NLTCG), net long-term capital losses (NLTCL), and net long-term capital losses in excess of net short-term capital gains (NLTCL − NSTCG)]. Individuals are allowed a *capital loss deduction* in arriving at A.G.I. This deduction is limited to the lesser of (1) $3,000 ($1,500 in the case of a married individual filing a separate return), *or* (2) the net capital loss.[28] In either case, the capital loss deduction cannot exceed taxable income *before* the deduction.

In computing the capital loss deduction, a net short-term capital loss (NSTCL) or the excess of a net short-term capital loss over a net long-term capital gain (NSTCL − NLTCG) is taken into account first and offsets ordinary income up to the $3,000 limit.[29] In the absence of a net short-term capital loss *or*, if after deducting any existing net short-term capital loss the taxpayer has not reached the annual limit of the capital loss deduction, he or she will then be allowed to use any net long-term capital loss (or the excess of a net long-term

---

[28] § 1211(b).

[29] Reg. § 1.211-1(b)(4)(i).

capital loss over a net short-term capital gain) to reduce ordinary income up to the limit.[30] Any capital losses in excess of the capital loss deduction may be *carried forward* to subsequent years and offset against capital gains of the same character (i.e., short-term or long-term) or deducted within the same annual limitation. There is no limitation on an individual's capital loss carryover period.[31]

> **Example 16.**   After netting all of his capital gains and losses for 1991, individual T has *both* a $2,000 NSTCL and a $5,000 NLTCL. Combining these results, T has a $7,000 net capital loss.
>
> Assuming adequate taxable income, T will be entitled to a $3,000 capital loss deduction for 1991. In arriving at the $3,000 deduction, T must use his $2,000 NSTCL first and then use $1,000 of the NLTCL to reach the deduction limit. T must carry over to 1992 the remaining $4,000 NLTCL ($5,000 NLTCL available − $1,000 NLTCL used in the 1991 capital loss deduction). This capital loss carryover will be treated as a long-term capital loss in 1992, and must once again be put into the capital gain and loss netting process. If T has *only* the $4,000 NLTCL carryover in 1992, he will use $3,000 of the carryover amount to arrive at the $3,000 capital loss deduction for 1992 and carry over to 1993 the remaining $1,000 NLTCL.

> **Example 17.**   After netting all of her capital gains and losses for 1991, individual R has a net capital loss consisting of only a $7,000 NSTCL. Her taxable income before the capital loss deduction is $18,000. R is entitled to a capital loss deduction of $3,000 for 1991, and she must carry over to 1992 the $4,000 unused net short-term capital loss.
>
> If R has any short-term capital gains in 1992, she will include the $4,000 NSTCL carryover in the short-term capital gain and loss netting process. In the absence of short-term capital gains in 1992, R will then net the $4,000 NSTCL carryover against any 1992 net long-term capital gain. If any part of the carryover amount remains after this final step of the netting process, R can use it as a capital loss deduction for 1992 and carry over to 1993 any remaining NSTCL.

> **Example 18.**   After the first step in the netting process for 1991, individual S has an $8,000 NLTCL and a $2,000 NSTCG. S must continue the netting process by offsetting the $2,000 NSTCG against the $8,000 NLTCL, with the result being a net capital loss consisting of only a $6,000 NLTCL.
>
> Assuming adequate taxable income, S will be entitled to a $3,000 capital loss deduction for 1991 and will carry over to 1992 the remaining $3,000 NLTCL. If S has any long-term capital gains in 1992, he must *first* offset

---

[30] For years prior to 1987, individual taxpayers were required to use $2 of NLTCL to offset $1 of ordinary income.

[31] § 1212(b).

these gains with the $3,000 LTCL carryover. If any of the LTCL carryover remains, it is then used to offset any NSTCG for the year. Absent any net short-term capital gains, S can use the remaining LTCL carryover as a capital loss deduction for the year.

Unlike individual taxpayers, corporations are not allowed a capital loss deduction. A corporate taxpayer's capital losses can be used *only to reduce* its capital gains.[32] Any excess losses are first *carried back* to the three preceding years and offset against any capital gains. Absent any capital gains in the three prior years, or if the loss carried back exceeds any capital gains, the excess may be *carried forward* for five years.[33]

REPORTING CAPITAL GAINS AND LOSSES

Individual taxpayers report any capital gains or losses on Schedule D of Form 1040.[34] This form is designed to facilitate the netting process, with one part used for reporting short-term gains and losses and another part used to report long-term transactions. A third part of the form is available for the second step of the netting process in the event the taxpayer has either NSTCGs and NLTCLs *or* NLTCGs and NSTCLs.

Regular corporations must report capital gains and losses on Schedule D of Form 1120 in much the same manner as individual taxpayers. Partnerships and S corporations must also report capital gains and losses on a separate schedule (Schedule D of Form 1065 for partnerships and Schedule D of Form 1120S for S corporations). However, these conduit entities are limited to the *first* step of the netting process. Each owner (partner or S corporation shareholder) must include his or her share of the results from the entity with the appropriate capital transactions (i.e., short-term or long-term) being netted on the owner's Schedule D, Form 1040.

CAPITAL GAIN TREATMENT EXTENDED TO CERTAIN TRANSACTIONS

The Internal Revenue Code contains several special provisions related to capital asset treatment. In some instances the concept of capital asset is expanded and in others it is limited. Some of the provisions merely clarify the tax treatment of certain transactions.

---

[32] § 1211(a).

[33] § 1212(a). See Chapter 19 for a discussion of the unique tax treatment of a corporation's capital loss carryovers.

[34] See Appendix B for a sample of this form.

PATENTS

Section 1235 provides that certain transfers of patents shall be treated as transfers of capital assets held for more than one year. This virtually assures that a long-term capital gain will result if the patent is transferred in a taxable transaction, because the patent will have little, if any, basis since the costs of creating it are usually deducted under § 174 (research and experimental expenditures) in the tax year in which such costs are incurred. Any transfer, other than by gift, inheritance, or devise, will qualify as long as *all substantial rights* to the patent are transferred. All substantial rights have been described as all rights that have value at the time of the transfer. For example, the transfer must not limit the geographical coverage within the country of issuance or limit the time application to less than the remaining term of the patent.[35]

The transferor must be a *holder* as defined in § 1235(b). The term holder refers to the creator of the patented property or to an individual who purchased such property from its creator if such individual is neither the employer of the creator nor related to such creator.[36]

The sale of a patent will qualify for § 1235 treatment even if payments are made over a period that ends when the purchaser's use of the patent ceases or if payments are contingent on the productivity, use, or disposition of the patent.[37] It also is important to note that §§ 483 and 1274, which require interest to be imputed on certain sales contracts, do not apply to amounts received in exchange for patents qualifying under § 1235 that are contingent on the productivity, use, or disposition of the patent transferred.[38]

> **Example 19.** K, a successful inventor, sold a patent (in which she had a basis of zero) to Bell Corp. The sale agreement called for K to receive a percentage of the sales of the property covered by the patent. All of K's payments received in consideration for this patent will be long-term capital gain regardless of her holding period.

LEASE CANCELLATION PAYMENTS

Section 1241 allows the treatment of payments received in cancellation of a lease or in cancellation of a distributorship agreement as having been received in a sale or exchange. Therefore, the gains or losses will be treated as capital gains or losses if the underlying assets are capital assets.[39]

---

[35] Reg. § 1.1235-2(b).

[36] For definition of "relative," see § 1235(d).

[37] § 1235(a).

[38] §§ 483(d)(4) and 1274(c)(4)(E). See Chapter 14 for a discussion of the imputed interest rules.

[39] See Chapter 17 for treatment if the asset is a § 1231 asset.

SPECIAL TREATMENT
FOR SOME INVESTMENTS

WORTHLESS SECURITIES

General Rules.   As mentioned earlier, securities that become worthless during the taxable year receive special tax treatment.[40] This treatment applies only to those items satisfying the definition of securities. The term *security* means stock, stock rights, and bonds, notes, or other forms of indebtedness issued by a corporation or the government.[41] In addition, the security must be considered a capital asset before the special rules apply. In the event that a qualifying security becomes worthless at *any* time during the taxable year, the resulting loss is treated as having arisen from the sale or exchange of a capital asset on the *last* day of the taxable year. Therefore, losses from worthlessness are treated as either short-term or long-term capital losses. As discussed earlier, the deduction allowed for an individual's capital loss in any one year (without any capital gains) is limited to a maximum of $3,000.

> **Example 20.**   On November 1, 1990, J, a calendar year taxpayer, invested $10,000 in bonds issued by XYZ Corporation. On February 3, 1991, the XYZ Corporation declared bankruptcy and the bonds became worthless. J is treated as having a $10,000 capital loss arising from a hypothetical sale of the bonds on December 31, 1991, the last day of J's taxable year. Since J is considered as holding the bonds for more than one year before their sale (November 1, 1990 to December 31, 1991), the $10,000 loss is treated as a long-term capital loss. Without any capital gains, J's capital loss deduction for 1991 is limited to $3,000 and the remaining loss is carried over to future years.

Securities in Affiliated Corporations.   A modification to the general rule regarding worthless securities is made for a corporate taxpayer's securities in affiliated corporations.[42] A corporation is considered affiliated to a parent corporation if the parent owns at least 80 percent of the voting power of all classes of stock and at least 80 percent of each class of nonvoting stock of the affiliated corporation. To be treated as an affiliated corporation for purposes of worthless securities, the corporation also must have less than 10 percent of the aggregate of its gross receipts from passive sources such as royalties, rents, dividends, annuities, and gains from sales or exchanges of stock and securities. If securities of an affiliated corporation become worthless, the loss is treated as an *ordinary loss*. Therefore, there is no limitation on the deduction as is the case under the general rule.

Losses on Small Business Stock—§ 1244.   Without special rules, the limitation on deductions for capital losses would serve to discourage investment in new corporations. For example, if an individual invested $90,000 in stock of a new

---

[40]   § 165(g).

[41]   § 165(g)(2).

[42]   § 165(g)(3).

corporate venture, deductions for any loss from the investment would be limited to $3,000 annually.[43] Thus, where the stock becomes worthless it could take the investor as long as 30 years to recover the investment. This restriction on losses also is inconsistent with the treatment of losses resulting from investments by an individual in his or her sole proprietorship or in a partnership. In the case of a sole proprietorship or a partnership, losses generally may be used to offset the taxpayer's other income without limitation. In 1958 Congress eliminated these problems and encouraged the flow of capital into small corporations by enacting Code § 1244.

Under § 1244, losses on "Section 1244 stock" generally are treated as ordinary rather than capital losses.[44] Ordinary loss treatment normally is available *only to individuals* who are the original holders of the stock. If these individuals sell the stock at a loss or the stock becomes worthless, they may deduct up to $50,000 annually as an ordinary loss. Taxpayers who file a joint return may deduct up to $100,000 regardless of how the stock is owned (e.g., separately or jointly). When the loss in any one year exceeds the $50,000 or $100,000 limitation, the excess is considered a capital loss.

> **Example 21.** T, married, is one of the original purchasers of RST Corporation's stock, which qualifies as § 1244 stock. She separately purchased the stock two years ago for $150,000. During the year, she sold all of the stock for $30,000, resulting in a $120,000 loss. On her joint return for the current year, she may deduct $100,000 as an ordinary loss. The portion of the loss exceeding the limitation, $20,000 ($120,000 − $100,000), is treated as a long-term capital loss.

Stock issued by a corporation (including preferred stock issued after July 18, 1984) qualifies as § 1244 stock only if the issuing corporation meets certain requirements. The most important condition is that the corporation's total capitalization (amounts received for stock issued, contributions to capital, and paid-in surplus) must not exceed $1 million at the time the stock is issued.[45] This requirement effectively limits § 1244 treatment to those individuals who originally invest the first $1 million in money and property in the corporation.

> **Example 22.** In 1988 F provided the initial capitalization for MNO Corporation by purchasing 700 shares at a cost of $1,000 a share for a total cost of $700,000. In 1991 G purchased 500 shares at a cost of $1,000 per share or a total of $500,000. All of F's shares qualify as § 1244 stock. Only 300 of G's shares qualify for § 1244 treatment, however, since 200 of the 500 purchased were issued when the corporation's total capitalization exceeded $1 million.

---

[43] A taxpayer can offset any capital losses against capital gains, if any.

[44] § 1244(a).

[45] § 1244(c)(3)(A).

DEALERS IN SECURITIES

Securities dealers commonly hold stocks and bonds primarily for sale to customers in the ordinary course of their trade or business. Gains and losses from such sales are generally treated as ordinary gains and losses. However, securities dealers may also hold some stocks and bonds as investments that should be classified as capital assets, which, if sold, result in capital gain or loss treatment. Since ordinary loss treatment and capital gain treatment are generally preferred, some tendency to classify assets to provide the greatest tax benefit would exist. Section 1236 eliminates uncertainty as to the classification of securities held by securities dealers.

A security held by a dealer in securities is not considered a capital asset unless it is identified as a security held for investment in the dealer's records before the *end of the day* on which it is acquired. Furthermore, it may not have been held primarily for sale to customers in the ordinary course of his or her trade or business at any time after that day.[46] In no case may a loss from the sale of a security be considered an ordinary loss if the security has been identified at any time as held for investment.[47]

For dealers who are registered as "floor specialists" in particular securities on a stock exchange, the period for designating a security held for investment is extended to the seventh business day following the day of acquisition. The extended period only applies to securities for which the dealer is listed with the exchange as a specialist.[48]

For purposes of § 1236, the term *security* refers to any share of corporate stock plus any note, bond, debenture, or other evidence of indebtedness. It is extended to any evidence of interest in, or any right to subscribe to, any of the above.[49]

SUBDIVIDED REAL ESTATE

Section 1237 provides that real estate held by a noncorporate taxpayer shall not be treated as held primarily for sale to customers in the ordinary course of a trade or business solely because of subdivision activities. In order to qualify under § 1237, the property must never have been held primarily for sale to customers, no substantial improvements can have been made, and the property must have been held at least five years, except in the case of property acquired by inheritance. No other real property may be held by the taxpayer primarily for sale to customers during the same tax year.[50]

---

[46]   § 1236(a).

[47]   § 1236(b).

[48]   § 1236(d).

[49]   § 1236(c).

[50]   § 1237(a).

Special rules apply to the character of the gain on such sales if more than five lots or parcels are sold from the tract. A portion of the gain will be treated as ordinary income[51] and a portion of any selling expenses may be allowed as ordinary deductions.[52]

OTHER RELATED PROVISIONS

NONBUSINESS BAD DEBTS

Bad debt losses from nonbusiness debts are deductible as short-term capital losses. Nonbusiness bad debts are deductible only in the year they become totally worthless since no deduction is allowed for partially worthless debts.[53] These rules and others related to the allowable deduction for bad debts were discussed in Chapter 10.

FRANCHISE AGREEMENTS, TRADEMARKS, AND TRADE NAMES

Section 1253 includes specific guidelines for the treatment of both the transferee and the transferor of payments with respect to franchise, trademark, and trade name agreements. The transfer of such rights is *not* treated as the sale or exchange of a capital asset by the transferor *if* he or she retains significant power, right, or continuing interest with respect to the property.[54] Capital gain and loss treatment also is denied for periodic payments that are contingent on the productivity, use, or sale of the property.[55]

"Significant power, right, or continuing interest" is defined in the Code by example. Some of the characteristics listed in the Code as indicative of such power, right, or interest retained by the transferor of the franchise are as follows:[56]

1. The right to terminate the franchise at will;

2. The right to disapprove any assignment;

3. The right to prescribe quality standards;

4. The right to require that the transferee advertise only products of the transferor;

5. The right to require that the transferee acquire substantially all of his or her supplies or equipment from the transferor; and

6. The right to require payments based on the productivity, use, or sale of the property.

---

[51] § 1237(b)(1).

[52] § 1237(b)(2).

[53] See § 166(d) and related discussion in Chapter 10.

[54] § 1253(a).

[55] § 1253(c).

[56] § 1253(b)(2).

The transferee is allowed current deductions for amounts paid or accrued that are contingent on the productivity, use, or sale of the property transferred.[57] Other payments must be at least partially deferred. They generally are amortized over the shorter of 10 years or the period covered by the transfer agreement.[58]

> **Example 23.** M, Inc. and R enter into a franchise agreement that allows R to operate a hamburger establishment using the trade name and products of M, Inc. According to the contract, M, Inc. has retained all six rights that are listed above. R is required to pay M $50,000 upon entering the contract and 2% of all sales. The term of the contract is 25 years with provision for renewals. R must also pay for any supplies provided by M. Both the $50,000 payment and the percentage royalty payment are ordinary income to M, Inc.
>
> R may treat the royalty payments to M, Inc. as ordinary deductions incurred in his trade or business. The initial fee of $50,000 is amortized equally over 10 years beginning with the year in which the payment is made.

OPTIONS

The general rule for the sale or exchange of an option to purchase or to sell property or the failure to exercise such an option is that the gain or loss shall be of the same character as that of the property to which the option relates.[59] Accordingly, if a taxpayer sells an option to buy an asset that would be a capital asset in his or her hands if purchased, the gain or loss will be capital in nature. Losses from failure to exercise an option shall be treated as having been sold or exchanged on the date the option expired.[60]

> **Example 24.** D purchased for $5,000 an option to buy a piece of real estate. If D were to acquire the real estate, it would be a capital asset to him, held for investment. If, instead, D fails to exercise the option he will have a capital loss of $5,000 as of the date the option expires.

CORPORATE BONDS AND OTHER INDEBTEDNESS

Investments in corporate bonds and other forms of indebtedness present several unique problems that must be considered by taxpayers who choose this form of investment. Under the general rules, mere collection of principal payments does not constitute a sale or exchange and, therefore, a capital gain or capital loss cannot result. However, the Code creates an exception for certain forms of debt. This special rule provides that any amounts received by the holder on

---

[57] § 1253(d)(1).

[58] § 1253(d)(2).

[59] § 1234(a)(1).

[60] § 1234(a)(2).

retirement of any debt are considered as amounts received in exchange for the debt.[61] Consequently, capital gain or loss is normally recognized when the debt is redeemed or sold for more or less than the taxpayer's basis in the debt.

> **Example 25.** B purchased a $1,000, 10% bond issued by Z Corporation for $990. Assuming the bond is held to maturity and redeemed by the corporation, B will recognize a capital gain of $10. If B had sold the bond prior to redemption for $995, he would recognize a capital gain of $5.

A second and more difficult problem to be considered concerns the *interest element* that may be inherent in the purchase price of a corporate bond. For example, if the rate at which a bond pays interest—the stated rate—is less than the current market rate, the bond will sell for less than its face value, or at a discount. In this case, the *discount* effectively functions as a substitute for interest income. Conversely, if the stated rate exceeds the market rate, the bond will sell for more than its face value, or at a premium. Here, the *premium* essentially reduces the amount of interest income. Without special rules, the proper amount of interest income would not be captured and reported in a timely manner.

> **Example 26.** Several years ago when interest rates were 10%, T purchased a $10,000, 8% corporate bond for $8,000, or a $2,000 discount. This year the bond matured and T redeemed the bond for its par value of $10,000. Under normal accounting procedures, the redemption is treated as an exchange and the taxpayer would recognize a long-term capital gain of $2,000 ($10,000 − $8,000). In this case, the taxpayer would have converted the discount of $2,000, which from an economic view is ordinary interest income, to capital gain. Moreover, this income would be deferred until T sold the bond.

The example above illustrates the problems that the special tax rules governing bond transactions address. The provisions ensure that any premium or discount is not treated as part of the capital gain or loss realized on disposition of the bond, but rather is treated as an *adjustment* to the taxpayer's interest income received from the bond. In addition, the Code provides rules for determining how much of the premium or discount will affect interest income and *when* the additional interest income (in the case of discount) or the interest expense (in the case of premium) will be reported.

The Code provides a separate set of rules governing the treatment of premium and discount. In the case of discount, the rules differ depending on when the discount arises. One set applies when the bonds were *originally issued* at a discount (the "original issue discount" provisions) and another set applies if the discount arises when the bonds are purchased later in the open market (the "market discount" rules). The rules governing premium are the same regardless of when the premium arises.

---

[61]   § 1271.

ORIGINAL ISSUE DISCOUNT

When corporate bonds are *issued* at a price less than the stated redemption price at maturity (i.e., the bond's face value), the resulting discount is referred to as *original issued discount*, or more commonly OID. The amount of OID is easily computed as follows:

```
    Redemption price (face value) ................  $x,xxx
  − Issue price ...................................  −   xxx
  = Original issue discount .......................  $x,xxx
```

The OID provisions generally require the holder of the bond to amortize the discount and include it in income during the period the bond is held.[62]   For purposes of computing the gain or loss on disposition of the bond, the holder must increase the basis of the bond by the amount of any amortized discount. Any gain or loss on the disposition of the bond normally is capital gain. However, if at the time of issue there was an intention to call the bond before maturity, any gain on the bond is treated as ordinary income to the extent of any unamortized discount.[63]

Before examining the amortization methods, it should be emphasized that the Code furnishes a *de minimis* rule that may exempt the debt from the OID amortization requirements. OID is considered to be zero when the bond discount is less than one-fourth of one percent of the redemption price at maturity multiplied by the number of complete years to maturity.[64] This may be expressed as follows:

```
    Redemption price at maturity .................  $x,xxx
  × Percentage ...................................  × 0.25%
  × Number of complete years to maturity .........  ×     x
  = De minimis amount ............................  $x,xxx
```

In most cases, new bond issues do not create OID because the stated interest rate is set near the market rate so that the amount of discount that arises, if any, does not exceed the de minimis amount. As a result, no amortization is required.

For bonds issued after July 1, 1982, the discount is amortized into income using a technique similar to the effective interest method used in financial accounting.[65] To determine the includible OID, the OID attributable to an *accrual period* must be computed. This is done by multiplying the *adjusted issue price* at the beginning of the *accrual period* by the *yield to maturity* and reducing this amount by any interest payable on the bond during the period. The adjusted issue price is the bond's original issue price as increased for previously amor-

---

[62] §§ 1271–1275.

[63] § 1271(a)(2).

[64] § 1273(a)(3).

[65] § 1272(a). For bonds issued after July 1, 1982, and before January 1, 1985, the accrual period is one year.

tized OID. The accrual period is generally the six-month period ending on the anniversary date of the bond (date of original issue) and six months before such date. The yield to maturity must be determined using present value techniques or may be found in bond tables designed specifically for this purpose.[66]

Once the OID attributable to the entire bond period is computed, this amount is allocated ratably to each day in the bond period. The bondholder's includible OID is the sum of the daily portions of OID for each day during the taxable year that the owner held the bond.

Example 27.   On July 1, 1991, R purchased 100 newly issued 30-year, 8%, bonds with a face value of $1,000 for $800 each or $80,000. The bonds pay interest semiannually on July 1 and December 31. The OID rules apply since the $200 discount per bond exceeds the de minimis amount of $75.

Redemption price at maturity	$1,000
× Percentage	× 0.25%
× Number of complete years to maturity	× 30
= De minimis amount	$ 75

Using present value calculations, the annual yield to maturity for this bond is 10.14% (or 5.07% semiannually). The OID that R must include in income in 1991 and 1992 for all of the bonds is computed in the aggregate as follows.

	7/1–12/31 1991	1/1–6/30 1992	7/1–12/31 1992
Adjusted issue price	$80,000	$80,056**	$80,115
Semiannual yield	× 5.07%	× 5.07%	× 5.07%
Total effective interest.....................	$ 4,056	$ 4,059	$ 4,062
Less: Interest received	− 4,000*	− 4,000	− 4,000
Includible OID	$ 56	$ 59	$ 62

* $100,000 × 4% = $4,000
** $80,000 + $56 = $80,056

R would include the amount of OID in income in addition to the interest income actually received. Note that the issuer of the bond would include in its annual deduction for interest expense the amount of OID that must be amortized.

Example 28.   Assume the same facts as above, except that R sells all of the bonds for $85,000 on July 1, 1992. Assuming there was no intention to call the bonds when issued, R will report a capital gain of $4,885 ($85,000 − $80,115).

---

[66]   Given the issue price, the redemption price, and the number of periods to maturity, the yield to maturity may be approximated by reference to appropriate present value tables.

Additional computations are required when the purchase price exceeds the original issue price as increased by OID amortized by previous holders. As a practical matter, the issuer of the bond is obligated to provide the taxpayer a Form 1099-OID, Statement of Original Issue Discount, disclosing the amount of interest income to be reported annually. For those who do not receive such a form, the IRS provides a special publication with the necessary information.

For bonds issued before July 2, 1982, the OID is generally included in the income of the holder ratably over the term of the bond (i.e., a straight-line method is used).[67]

> **Example 29.**   Assume the bond in *Example 27* was issued prior to July 2, 1982. The original issue discount included annually would be $667 ($20,000 ÷ 30).

Although the OID rules are to apply to virtually all debt instruments, there are several notable exceptions:[68]

1. U.S. Savings Bonds (which are treated as discussed in Chapter 5)

2. Tax-exempt state and local obligations (although the discount income is not included as taxable income, the taxpayer increases the basis of the instrument)

3. Debt instruments that have a fixed maturity date not exceeding one year [unless held by certain parties identified in § 1281(b), including accrual basis taxpayers]

4. Obligations issued by individuals before March 2, 1984

5. Nonbusiness loans between individuals of $10,000 or less

In 1984 the coverage of the OID rules was substantially extended to help curb abuses that occurred when a taxpayer sold property and received a note in exchange. The application of the OID rules in this area was discussed in Chapter 14 in conjunction with unstated interest.

MARKET DISCOUNT

As previously noted, without special rules, amortization of discount would not be required where the security was treated as having no OID (e.g., where the discount on the bond when originally issued was small). For example, if a bond having a $10,000 face value bearing 10 percent interest over a 30-year term was issued for $9,500, there would be no OID since the discount is less than $750 (0.25% × 30 × $10,000). In subsequent years, however, interest rates might rise, causing the bond to sell at a substantially greater discount (i.e., lower value),

---

[67]   § 1272(a); for bonds issued before May 28, 1969, special rules apply. See § 1272(b).

[68]   §§ 1272(a)(2) and 1274(c)(2).

say $8,000 (e.g., if rates rose to 14% the bond's price might fall to $8,000). In such case, an investor could purchase the bond and ultimately report the built-in appreciation as capital gain—the $2,000 rise from the discounted price to face value at maturity—notwithstanding the fact that a portion of the increase in value actually represents interest income. Moreover, the investor could borrow amounts to purchase the investment and obtain an immediate deduction for interest on the debt, although the income from the bond was deferred until it was redeemed or sold. This highly publicized and extremely popular investment technique was foreclosed by the Deficit Reduction Act of 1984 for newly issued bonds.

Effective for bonds issued after July 18, 1984, Code § 1276 provides that any gain on the disposition of a bond is treated as interest income to the extent of any accrued *market discount*. Market discount, in contrast to OID, is measured at the time the purchaser acquires the bond. Hence, market discount is the excess of the stated redemption price over the basis of the bond immediately after *acquisition*.[69] Like OID, market discount is considered to be zero if it is less than one-fourth of one percent of the stated redemption price multiplied by the number of complete years to maturity after acquisition. The portion of market discount that is considered ordinary income upon disposition of the bond is computed assuming the discount accrues ratably over the number of days from the purchase of the bond to the bond's maturity date.

> **Example 30.** On January 1, 1990, T purchased a bond issued in 1989 having a face value of $10,000 for $8,000. The bond matures four years later on January 1, 1994. The market discount on the bond is $2,000, the difference between the stated redemption price of $10,000 and the tax-payer's $8,000 basis in the bond immediately after acquisition. The $2,000 is deemed to accrue on a daily basis over the 1,460 days remaining on the bond's term. Assuming T sells the bond for $9,000 on January 2, 1991, her gain is $1,000, of which $500 is ordinary interest income [$2,000 × (365 ÷ 1,460)] and the remaining $500 is long-term capital gain.

In lieu of using the daily method of computing the accrued market discount, the taxpayer may use the effective interest method similar to that used for amortizing OID. In addition, the taxpayer may elect to report accrued market discount in taxable income annually rather than at the date of disposition. If this election is made, the taxpayer increases the basis of the bond by the amount of market discount included in income.

Congress also enacted provisions limiting the taxpayer's interest deduction on loans to purchase market discount bonds. Section 1277 requires the taxpayer to defer the deduction for interest expense until that time when income from the bond is reported.

---

[69] § 1277(a)(2). If the bond also has OID, the market discount is reduced by the amortized portion of OID.

BOND PREMIUM

The treatment of premium depends in part on whether the interest income on the bond is taxable.[70] When the interest income is taxable, the taxpayer *may* elect to amortize and deduct the premium as interest expense and concomitantly reduce the basis in the bond. The interest expense in this case is considered investment interest and is, therefore, deductible as an itemized deduction to the extent of net investment income. If the taxpayer does not elect to amortize the premium, the unamortized premium is simply included as part of the taxpayer's basis in the bond and thus decreases the gain or increases the loss on disposition of the bond.

If the interest income on the bond is tax-exempt, the premium *must* be amortized and the bond's basis decreased. No deduction is allowed for the amortized premium since it merely represents an adjustment in the amount of nontaxable income received by the holder. In other words, no deduction for the premium is allowed since it represents interest expense related to producing tax-exempt income. Note that by requiring amortization of the premium, the taxpayer is prohibited from securing a deduction for the premium in the form of a capital loss or a reduced gain on the disposition of the bond.

> **Example 31.** V purchased a $1,000 tax-exempt bond for $1,100. If V holds the bond to maturity, all of the premium will be amortized and his basis in the bond will be $1,000. Therefore, on redemption of the bond for $1,000, no gain or loss is recognized. However, if amortization of the premium was not required, V would report a capital loss of $100 on redemption of the bond.

The method to be used for amortizing premium depends on when the bond was issued. If the bond was issued before September 28, 1985, the premium is amortized using the straight-line method over the number of months to maturity. Premium on bonds issued on or after that date must be amortized based on the bond's yield to maturity determined when the bond was issued.

---

[70]   § 171.

TAX PLANNING CONSIDERATIONS

TIMING OF CAPITAL ASSET TRANSACTIONS

A taxpayer with investments that he or she may wish to sell should pay careful attention to the timing of those sales, particularly near the end of a year. Since the netting process takes into consideration only the sales for the year under consideration plus any capital loss carryovers, the year into which a particular transaction falls may have significant impact on the total amount of taxes paid. The taxpayer must also consider market conditions, since he or she may believe that waiting to sell a particular asset may cost more than paying any additional tax.

Strictly from a tax planning perspective, a taxpayer should consider timing the recognition of year-end capital gains and losses under the following circumstances:

1. *No capital gains or losses currently*—recognize up to $3,000 STCL or LTCL to take advantage of the annual capital loss deduction.

2. *Currently have STCG*—recognize either STCL or LTCL to offset the STCG and more, if possible, to take advantage of the capital loss deduction.

3. *Currently have LTCG*—recognize either LTCL or STCL to offset the LTCG and more, if possible, to take advantage of the capital loss deduction.

4. *Currently have STCL*—if less than $3,000, recognize more STCL or LTCL to take advantage of the capital loss deduction. If more than $3,000, recognize either STCG or LTCG to offset the STCL in excess of $3,000.

5. *Currently have LTCL*—if less than $3,000, recognize more LTCL or STCL to take advantage of the capital loss deduction. If more than $3,000, recognize either STCG or LTCG to offset the LTCL in excess of $3,000.

SECTION 1244 STOCK

The importance of § 1244 should not be overlooked when making an investment.

> **Example 32.** Dr. G is extremely successful and consequently is often approached by friends, promoters, and others asking her to make an investment in one deal or another. If G loans $30,000 to a friend to start a business which ultimately fails, the loss would be governed by the worthless-security rules and thus treated as a capital loss. In such case, Dr. G's annual loss deduction is limited to the extent of her capital gains plus $3,000. If G has no capital gains (which are not necessarily easily found), it could take her as long as ten years to deduct her loss. However, if the investment had been in the form of § 1244 stock, the entire $30,000 loss would be deductible in the year incurred.

Under § 1244, the taxpayer is allowed to deduct up to $50,000 ($100,000 in the case of a joint return) of loss *annually*. Any loss in excess of this amount is treated as a capital loss and is subject to limitation. In light of these rules, a taxpayer who anticipates a loss on § 1244 stock that exceeds the annual limitation should attempt to limit the loss recognized in any one year to $50,000 (or $100,000).

> **Example 33.** C, a bachelor, invested $200,000 in Risky Corporation several years ago, receiving 1,000 shares of § 1244 stock. It now appears that Risky, true to its name, will fail and that C will receive at best $100,000 for his investment. If C sells all of his shares this year, $50,000 of the loss is completely deductible as an ordinary loss under § 1244, while the remaining $50,000 of the loss would be a capital loss of which only $3,000 could be deducted (assuming he has no capital gains). C should sell half of his shares this year and half of his shares next year. By so doing, his loss for each year will be $50,000. In such case, neither loss would exceed the annual limitation, and therefore both would be deductible in full.

PROBLEM MATERIALS

DISCUSSION QUESTIONS

16-1 *Capital Asset Defined.* Define a capital asset. How would you describe the way a capital asset is defined?

16-2 *Sale of a Business.* How is the sale of an operating business treated? Discuss the sale of sole proprietorships, partnerships, and corporations in general.

16-3 *Holding Period.* What is the holding period requirement for long-term capital gains and losses? How does one determine the holding period for purchased property?

16-4 *Holding Period.* What is the rule for determining the holding period for property acquired by gift?

16-5 *Holding Period.* What is the holding period of property acquired from a decedent?

16-6 *Holding Period—Stock Exchange Transactions.* T placed an order with her stock broker to sell 100 shares of Kent Electronics, Inc. stock on December 23, 1991. Because the sale order was received after the close of the market on the 23rd, the sale was executed at 9:00 A.M. on December 30, 1991. T received a settlement check from the brokerage house on January 5, 1992. What is the date of sale and what is the last date of T's holding period?

16-7 *Capital Gain and Loss Netting Process.* Describe the three possible results of the capital gain and loss netting process. How are the gains treated for tax purposes?

16-8 *Capital Gains Tax.* D is single and has taxable income for the current year of $72,000, including a net capital gain of $7,000. Describe how D will determine the tax on his income for the year.

16-9 *Capital Loss Deduction.* How is the capital loss deduction limited for individual taxpayers?

16-10 *Capital Loss Carryover.* Capital losses in excess of the annual limit can be carried forward to the subsequent year. How long may losses be carried forward by individual taxpayers? What is the character of the loss carryover and what happens if both long-term and short-term losses are carried forward?

16-11 *Patents.* What is necessary for a patent to qualify for capital gain or loss treatment under § 1235?

16-12 *Ordinary vs. Capital Loss Treatment.*   What are the tax consequences to P, a bachelor, of a $70,000 loss occurring on June 1 of the current year attributable to the following:

   a.   An uncollectible nonbusiness loan to XYZ Corporation
   b.   Worthless bonds of XYZ Corporation acquired on November 30 of the prior year
   c.   The sale of XYZ stock qualifying as § 1244 stock when acquired two years ago

16-13 *Section 1244 Stock.*   When is a taxpayer's stock considered § 1244 stock? Why is the designation significant?

16-14 *Dealers in Securities.*   How does a dealer in securities guarantee that a particular "investment" will qualify for capital gain or loss treatment?

16-15 *Original Issue Discount—Deep Discount Bonds.*   Financial consulting services often advise investment in so-called *deep discount bonds*, (e.g., a $1,000 par value bond maturing in 10 years with coupon rate of 6% that sells at a discounted price of $400). Explain how such an investment could provide any tax savings in light of the original issue discount rules.

16-16 *Bond Premium.*   This year, G purchased a $1,000 bond for $1,100. The bond matures in 1997 and pays interest at a rate of 10 percent. Interest is paid semi-annually on February 1 and August 1. Explain the treatment of the premium on the bond if the bond was issued by:

   a.   General Motors
   b.   City of Sacramento

PROBLEMS

16-17 *Identifying Capital Assets.*   Which of the following items are capital assets?

   a.   An automobile held for sale to customers by Midtown Motors, Inc.
   b.   An automobile owned and used by Sherry Hartman to run household errands
   c.   An automobile owned and used by Windowwashers, Inc.
   d.   The private residence of Robert Hamilton
   e.   Letters from famous U.S. President he wrote to Jane Doe. Jane Doe has the letters.
   f.   A warehouse owned and used by Holt Packing Company

16-18 *Identifying Capital Assets.*   Which of the following properties are capital assets? Briefly explain your answers.

   a.   A house built by a home-building contractor and used by her as her principal residence
   b.   A house, 80 percent of which is used as a residence and 20 percent of which is used to store business inventory
   c.   The same house in (b) above, used as stated for 10 years, and now used exclusively as a residence
   d.   Undeveloped land held for investment by a real estate broker
   e.   Stock held for investment by a stock broker

16-19 *Capital Gain Netting Process.*   D sold the following capital assets during 1991:

Description	Date Acquired	Date Sold	Sales Price	Adjusted Basis
100 shares XY Corp.	1/10/71	1/12/91	$14,000	$1,000
50 shares LM Inc.	9/14/90	1/12/91	1,900	4,000
140 shares CH Corp.	11/20/90	4/10/91	3,400	3,000
Gold necklace	4/22/79	6/30/91	5,000	1,300
Personal auto	5/10/88	8/31/91	4,000	6,500

Determine each of the following amounts:

a.   D's net long-term capital gain or loss
b.   D's net short-term capital gain or loss
c.   D's net capital gain, if any, and whether it is long- or short-term
d.   D's tax liability (before prepayments and credits), assuming she is single with no dependents and her taxable income before these capital transactions is $72,000

16-20 *Capital Gain Netting Process.*   Each of the following situations deals with capital gains and losses occurring during the calendar year 1991 for an individual taxpayer. For each case, determine the change in adjusted gross income and the maximum tax to be imposed on any net capital gain.

Note: NLTCG(L)   = Net long-term capital gain or (loss)
         NSTCG(L)   = Net short-term capital gain or (loss)

Case	NLTCG(L)	NSTCG(L)
A	$1,200	$1,200
B	1,600	(1,000)
C	(1,200)	1,800
D	4,500	(800)
E	2,400	1,800

16-21 *Capital Gain and Losses on Property Acquired by Gift.*   In each of the following situations, assume that the taxpayer received the capital asset as a gift on March 19, 1991, that the donor had held the property since 1961, and that the property was sold during 1991. No gift taxes were payable on the transfer. Determine the gain or loss recognized in each case and whether it is long- or short-term.

Case	Date of Sale	Sales Price	Donor's Basis	FMV Date of Gift
A	4/19	$1,000	$ 400	$ 600
B	6/3	1,000	1,400	1,200
C	11/20	1,000	900	1,100

16-22   *Capital Gains Tax.* R is a single, calendar year taxpayer. During 1991, R recognized net capital gains of $20,000. Calculate R's tax liability (before credits and prepayments) for each of the following levels of taxable income, assuming that the net capital gains have been included in the taxable income numbers.

a. $35,000
b. $50,000
c. $500,000

16-23   *Capital Gains Tax.*   H and J are married, calendar year taxpayers who elect to file jointly. Their income and deductions for 1991 are summarized below.

Salaries and wages	$105,000
Interest and dividend income	10,000
Short-term capital loss	5,000
Long-term capital gains	20,000
Standard deduction	5,700
Personal exemptions	2

Determine H and J's tax liability (before credits and prepayments).

16-24   *Effective Tax Rate on Net Capital Gains.*   T is a single, calendar year taxpayer. He provides more than one-half the support of his elderly mother, who is living in a nearby nursing home. T's income and deductions for 1991 are summarized below.

Salary	$95,000
Interest and dividend income	7,000
Itemized deductions (all subject to the 3% cut-back rule)	12,500
Personal and dependency exemptions	2

a.   Calculate T's taxable income and income tax liability (before credits and prepayments) for the year.
b.   How would your answers to (a) above change if T also had a $10,000 long-term capital gain in 1991?
c.   Is the additional income tax from the capital gain limited to $2,800 ($10,000 net capital gain × 28%)? If not, explain why.

16-25 *Netting Process and Capital Losses.* T, an unmarried taxpayer, sold the following capital assets during her calendar year 1991:

Description	Date Acquired	Date Sold	Sales Price	Adjusted Basis
100 shares CZ Corp.	1/10/91	9/17/91	$14,000	$18,000
75 shares PC, Inc.	7/6/91	9/17/91	5,200	4,300
Silver coins (held as an investment)	12/2/86	11/20/91	2,000	5,000

Complete each of the following requirements based on T's taxable income of $15,000 before capital gains and losses:

a. T's net long-term capital gain or loss
b. T's net short-term capital gain or loss
c. T's capital loss deduction in arriving at adjusted gross income
d. T's capital loss carryover to 1992 (describe amount and character)
e. How would your answers to (c) and (d) differ if T's basis in the PC stock had been $1,000?

16-26 *Capital Gains and Losses.* Each of the following involves capital gains and losses occurring during the calendar year 1991 for an unmarried individual taxpayer.

Note:	NLTCG(L)	= Net long-term capital gain or (loss)
	NSTCG(L)	= Net short-term capital gain or (loss)

Case	NLTCG(L)	NSTCG(L)
A	$1,200	($4,300)
B	(5,000)	200
C	(1,200)	(2,300)
D	(7,000)	200
E	(5,000)	(200)

a. Determine the amount deductible in arriving at adjusted gross income in each case for 1991.
b. Which, if any, of the above case(s) generate(s) a capital loss carryover to 1992? Give the amount and character (short- or long-term).

16-27 *Capital Loss Deduction and Capital Loss Carryover.* W, an unmarried calendar year individual, had numerous capital asset transactions during the years listed. Determine the amount deductible in each year and the amount and character of any carryover.

Year	NLTCG(L)	NSTCG(L)
1990	$(8,000)	$ 1,000
1991	(1,500)	(2,000)
1992	0	(4,000)
1993	2,000	(3,000)

16-28 *Capital Loss Deduction and Capital Loss Carryover.*   M, an unmarried calendar year individual, had numerous capital asset transactions during the years listed. Determine the amount deductible in each year and the amount and character of any carryover.

Year	NLTCG(L)	NSTCG(L)
1990	$1,000	($5,000)
1991	(6,000)	0
1992	3,000	(3,000)
1993	(3,000)	(3,000)

16-29 *Requirements for § 1244 Stock.*   During the year, X, who is single, sold stock and realized a loss. For each of the following situations, indicate whether § 1244 would apply to the taxpayer's stock loss. Unless otherwise indicated, Code § 1244 applies.

a.   The stock was that issued to X when she incorporated her business several years ago.

b.   The stock was that of General Motors Corporation and was purchased last year.

c.   X inherited the stock from her grandfather, who had started the company ten years ago.

d.   X is a corporate taxpayer.

e.   X acquired her stock interest in 1987. The other four owners had acquired their interest for $250,000 each in 1983.

f.   The loss was $60,000.

16-30 *Section 1244 Stock Computation.*   S is a bachelor. Durng the year, he sold stock in X Corporation that qualifies as § 1244 stock at a loss of $70,000. In addition, S sold stock in Y Corporation, realizing a $4,000 long-term capital gain. Compute the effect of these transactions on S's A.G.I.

16-31 *Worthless Securities.*   Several years ago, T was persuaded by his good friend W to invest in her new venture, Wobbly Corporation. T purchased 100 shares of Wobbly stock from W for $60,000. He also purchased Wobbly bonds, which had a face value of $20,000 for $18,000. This year, Wobbly declared bankruptcy and T's investment in Wobbly became worthless. What are the tax consequences to T?

16-32 *Sale of Stock.*   B owned 50 percent of the stock in a small incorporated dress shop. The business was successful for several years until a new freeway diverted nearly all of the traffic away from the location. The shop was moved, but to no avail, and the stock continued to quickly decline in value. Other than small interest payments, the income of the business came exclusively from sales of women's apparel.

The total paid-in capital of the corporation was $250,000, all in the form of cash. B's basis in the stock was always $125,000. In an attempt to prevent further losses, the shop was sold to a larger competitor during 1991. B received $50,000 for all of her stock.

a.   How will B report the loss on the joint return she files with her husband for 1991?

b.   How would your answer to (a) differ if the stock became totally worthless rather than being sold in 1991?

16-33 *Franchise Agreements.*   J entered into a franchise agreement with Box, Inc. under which J will operate a fast food restaurant bearing the trademark and using the products of Box. Box retained "significant power, right and continuing interest" related to the franchise agreement.

J made an initial payment under the contract of $40,000, which entitles him to the rights under the contract for 15 years with indefinite extensions at the agreement of both parties. J also is required to pay for all supplies used plus a royalty of 1.5 percent of gross sales. J's sales were $112,000 during the first year. All of the payments described, totaling $41,680, were made during the current year.

a.   How will J report these payments on his cash basis tax return for the current year?

b.   How would Box, Inc. treat the payments from J on its return for the current year? The corporation reports on the cash basis.

16-34 *Original Issue Discount.*   On January 1, 1991, B purchased from XYZ Corporation a newly issued, $1 million, 30-year, 4 percent bond for $300,000. The bond produces a semiannual yield to maturity of 7 percent. Interest is paid semiannually on January 1 and July 1. What is B's income with respect to the bond in 1991 and 1992?

16-35 *Market Discount.*   D purchased a $10,000, 7 percent bond, for $6,350 on January 1, 1991. The bond was issued at par on January 1, 1990, and matures January 1, 1995. On January 1, 1992, D sold the bond for $8,000. What is D's income from the sale?

RESEARCH PROBLEMS

16-36 *Transfer of Patents.*   G has just completed a successful invention of a new automotive fuel conservation device. He is willing to sell his patent rights for all areas of the United States east of the Rocky Mountains.

In 1991, G entered into an agreement with a marketing firm, giving them exclusive rights to market his invention anywhere east of the Rockies. In exchange, he received a principal sum and is to receive royalties based on sales volume.

Is G entitled to capital gain treatment on this sale under § 1235? Would it make any difference if the transferee of the patent was given exclusive rights to the patent and was given the right to "sublease" the patent?

Research aids:

Kueneman v. Comm., 80-2 USTC ¶9616, 46 AFTR2d 80-5677, 628 F.2d 1196 (CA-9, 1980).
Klein Est. v. Comm., 75-1 USTC ¶9127, 35 AFTR2d 75-457, 507 F.2d 617 (CA-7, 1974).
Rouverol v. Comm., 42 T.C. 186 (1964), *non. acq.,* 1965-2 C.B. 7.

16-37 *Sale of Subdivided and Improved Real Property.*   D, a full-time physician, has owned 15 acres of unimproved suburban real estate for 10 years. The property was originally purchased for $30,000 and has been held solely for investment. D is now interested in selling the property and has several alternatives. She has come to you for advice concerning the tax treatment of these alternatives. What is the proper tax treatment of each of the following?

a.   A sale of the entire acreage to an unrelated party in a single transaction for $150,000.

b.   Recording the property with the county as 30 single residential lots, adding roads and improvements at a cost of $100,000, and selling the lots for $25,000 each.

c.   Recording the property with the county as 30 single residential lots, and then selling them to an unrelated developer in a single transaction for $190,000.

d.   Recording the property with the county as 30 single residential lots and then selling them for $190,000 in a single transaction to a partnership in which D is a 40 percent partner. The partnership then adds roads and improvements at a cost of $100,000 and sells the lots for $25,000 each.

LEARNING OBJECTIVES

Upon completion of this chapter you will be able to:

- Trace the historical development of the special tax treatment allowed for dispositions of trade or business property

- Apply the § 1231 gain and loss netting process to a taxpayer's § 1231 asset transactions

- Determine the tax treatment of § 1231 gains and losses

- Explain the purpose of the depreciation recapture rules

- Compute depreciation recapture under §§ 1245 and 1250

- Explain the additional recapture rule applicable only to corporate taxpayers

- Identify tax planning opportunities related to sales or other dispositions of trade or business property

CHAPTER OUTLINE

Chapter **17**

PROPERTY
TRANSACTIONS:
DISPOSITIONS OF
TRADE OR
BUSINESS PROPERTY

INTRODUCTION

As discussed in the earlier chapters involving property transactions, the income tax treatment of gains or losses from the disposition of assets depends on the answers to the following issues:

1. The amount of gain or loss realized;

2. The amount of gain or loss to be recognized; and

3. The character of the recognized gain or loss.

It would seem logical to assume that the *entire* gain or loss to be recognized from the disposition of an asset is simply characterized as either capital or ordinary. Under this rationale, the recognized gains or losses from dispositions of capital assets would be characterized only as capital gains or losses—and the recognized gains or losses from any other assets would be treated as ordinary gains or losses. Since most assets used in a trade or business are specifically excluded from the definition of capital assets under § 1221, ordinary gain or loss recognition would appear to be the proper treatment on dispositions of such assets. Taxpayers with losses from dispositions of trade or business assets would prefer ordinary loss treatment. As illustrated in Chapter 16, however, high-income taxpayers with long-term gains should generally prefer capital rather than ordinary gain treatment. Fortunately, this "best of both worlds" treatment may be available under Code § 1231. Unfortunately, such favorable treatment does not come without a great deal of complexity. The purpose of this chapter is to explain how to cope with that complexity.

CODE § 1231 TREATMENT

In order to encourage new business investment and the replacement of obsolete or inefficient business assets, Congress decided years ago to allow a unique tax treatment for gains and losses arising from certain dispositions of business property. Originally, net gains received capital gain treatment, and net losses were treated as ordinary losses. Not unexpectedly, taxpayers took advantage of this favorable treatment by claiming ordinary deductions from depreciating assets as quickly as possible and reporting any gains realized on subsequent dispositions as capital gains. In order to limit this significant tax advantage, Congress modified the original rules so that some or all of the gain from sales or exchanges of depreciable assets must *now* be reported (i.e., recaptured) as ordinary income. Consequently, the once favorable treatment of gains from the disposition of depreciable assets has been significantly limited by the depreciation recapture rules of §§ 1245 and 1250. These recapture rules are discussed later in this chapter.

Despite the requirement to recapture a portion of any gain from the disposition of depreciable assets, § 1231 continues to offer the potential of limited capital gain treatment for some of these assets. More important, the original treatment of net gains remains available for nondepreciable business assets as well as for many other assets meeting the definition of § 1231 assets.

DEFINITION OF § 1231 ASSETS

The term § *1231 assets* refers to property held for *more than one year* and used in the taxpayer's trade or business or as rental property. This includes any depreciable property and land used in the taxpayer's business or rental activity. Code § 1231 specifically excludes the following assets (which also are excluded from the definition of capital assets under § 1221):

1. Property held primarily for sale to customers in the ordinary course of a trade or business, or includible in inventory, if on hand at the close of the tax year;

2. A copyright; a literary, musical, or artistic composition; a letter or memorandum; or similar property held by a taxpayer whose personal efforts created such property or by certain other persons; or

3. A publication of the United States Government received from the government other than by purchase at the price at which the publication is offered to the general public.[1]

---

[1] § 1231(b)(1).

OTHER § 1231 PROPERTY

The definition of § 1231 assets extends beyond trade or business property in certain instances. The following items are specifically included in § 1231 assets:

1. Timber, coal, and iron ore to which § 631 applies;[2]

2. Unharvested crops on land used in a trade or business and held for more than one year;[3] and

3. Certain livestock.[4]

Timber. Under § 631, the cutting of timber by the owner of the timber, or by a person who has the right to cut the timber and has held the timber or right more than one year, is to be treated, at his or her election, as a sale or exchange of the timber that is cut during the year. The timber must be cut for sale or for use in the taxpayer's trade or business. Gain or loss on the "sale" is the fair market value of the timber on the first day of the taxable year minus the timber's adjusted basis for depletion. For all subsequent purposes (i.e., the sale of the cut timber), the fair market value of the timber as of the beginning of the year will be treated as the cost of the timber. The term *timber* not only includes trees used for lumber and other wood products, but also includes evergreen trees that are more than six years old when cut and are sold for ornamental purposes (e.g., Christmas trees).[5]

> **Example 1.** B owned standing timber that he had purchased for $250,000 three years earlier. The timber was cut and sold to a lumber mill for $410,000 during 1991. The fair market value of the standing timber as of January 1, 1991 was $320,000. B has a § 1231 gain of $70,000 if he makes an election under § 631 ($320,000 fair market value of the timber on the first day of the taxable year less its $250,000 adjusted basis for depletion). The remainder of his gain on the *actual* sale of the timber, $90,000 ($410,000 selling price − $320,000 new "cost" of the timber), is ordinary income. Any expenses incurred by B in cutting the timber would be deductible as ordinary deductions.

An election under § 631 with respect to timber is binding on all timber owned by the taxpayer during the year of the election *and* in all subsequent years. The IRS may permit revocation of such election because of significant hardship. However, once the election is revoked, IRS consent must be obtained to make a new election.[6]

---

[2] § 1231(b)(2).

[3] § 1231(b)(4).

[4] § 1231(b)(3).

[5] § 631(a).

[6] *Ibid.*

Section 631 also applies to the sale of timber under a contract providing a retained economic interest (i.e., a taxpayer sells the timber, but keeps the right to receive a royalty from its later sale) for the taxpayer in the timber. In such a case, the transfer is considered a sale or exchange. The gain or loss is recognized on the date the timber is cut, or when payment is received, if earlier, at the election of the taxpayer.[7]

Coal and Iron Ore. When an owner disposes of coal or domestic iron ore under a contract that calls for a retained economic interest in the property, the disposition is treated as a sale or exchange of the coal or iron ore. The date the coal or ore is mined is considered the date of sale and since the property is § 1231 property, the gain or loss will be treated under § 1231.[8]

The taxpayer may not be a co-adventurer, partner, or principal in the mining of the coal or iron ore. Furthermore, the coal or iron ore may not be sold to certain related taxpayers.[9]

Unharvested Crops. When land used in a trade or business and held for more than one year *and* unharvested crops on that land are sold at the same time to the same buyer, the gain or loss is subject to § 1231 treatment.[10] Any deductions related to the production of the crop are not currently deductible. These expenses are added to the basis in the crop.[11]

Section 1231 applies to exchanges and involuntary conversions as well as to sales of such properties. It does not apply, however, to any transaction in which the taxpayer retains any right or option to reacquire the land the crop is on, other than a right customarily included in a mortgage or other security agreement.[12]

Livestock. Cattle and horses (regardless of age) held by the taxpayer for draft, breeding, dairy, or sporting purposes for 24 months or more are included as § 1231 assets. Other livestock (regardless of age) held 12 months or more also is included.[13] (Note, however, that poultry is not included.)

Trade or Business. Property is held for use in a trade or business if it is held primarily for productive use in a business venture;[14] however, any property that is inventory is not included. Properties held for rental purposes have consistently been treated as held for use in a trade or business for purposes of § 1231.[15]

Holding Period. The holding period for § 1231 assets is determined in the same manner as it is for capital assets. As previously discussed, § 1223 provides the rules for determining holding period.

---

[7] § 631(b).

[8] § 631(c).

[9] §§ 631(c)(1) and (2).

[10] § 1231(b)(4).

[11] § 268.

[12] Reg. § 1.1231-1(f).

[13] § 1231(b)(3).

[14] *Hollywood Baseball Association v. Comm.*, 70-1 USTC ¶9251, 25 AFTR2d 70-788, 423 F.2d 494 (CA-9, 1970).

[15] See, for example, *Mary Crawford*, 16 T.C. 678 (1951) A. 1951-2 C.B. 2, and *Gilford v. Comm.*, 53-1 USTC ¶9201, 43 AFTR 221, 201 F.2d 735 (CA-2, 1953).

SECTION 1231 NETTING PROCESS

The netting process under § 1231 involves three steps. *First*, all casualty and theft gains (after reduction for any depreciation recapture) and losses involving § 1231 assets *and* capital assets held in connection with a trade or business (including transactions entered into for profit) and held for more than one year are netted together. If the result is a net *loss*, the casualty and theft gains and losses are removed from the § 1231 netting process and treated separately. The gains are treated as ordinary income, and the losses on business use assets are deductible in arriving at adjusted gross income (i.e., deductions *for* A.G.I.). Any other casualty and theft losses are deductible *from* A.G.I. If the net result is a *gain*, it is treated as a § 1231 gain. This § 1231 gain is combined with other § 1231 transactions in the next step of the netting process.

The *second* step of the process is to combine any net casualty or theft gain from the first step with (1) gains (net of depreciation recapture) and losses from sales and taxable exchanges of § 1231 assets, and (2) gains (net of depreciation recapture) and losses from the seizure or condemnation (involuntary conversions) of § 1231 assets.

The *final* step in the § 1231 netting process is to characterize the resulting gain or loss. If the net result is a *loss*, this loss is treated as an ordinary deduction (i.e., not a capital loss). If the net result is a *gain*, this gain generally is treated as a long-term capital gain and taken to the capital gain and loss netting process. In an effort to prevent taxpayers from bunching § 1231 losses in one taxable year (to achieve ordinary deduction treatment) and § 1231 gains in a separate tax year (for LTCG treatment), Congress enacted the so-called *look-back rule* in 1984. Under this rule, a taxpayer with a net § 1231 gain in the current year must report the gain as ordinary income to the extent he or she has *unrecaptured* net § 1231 losses in the five most recent taxable years. Unrecaptured net § 1231 losses are defined as the excess of net § 1231 losses of the five preceding years over the amount of such losses that has been recaptured in the five prior taxable years.

The § 1231 netting process is illustrated in Exhibit 17-1 and *Examples 2, 3, and 4* which follow.

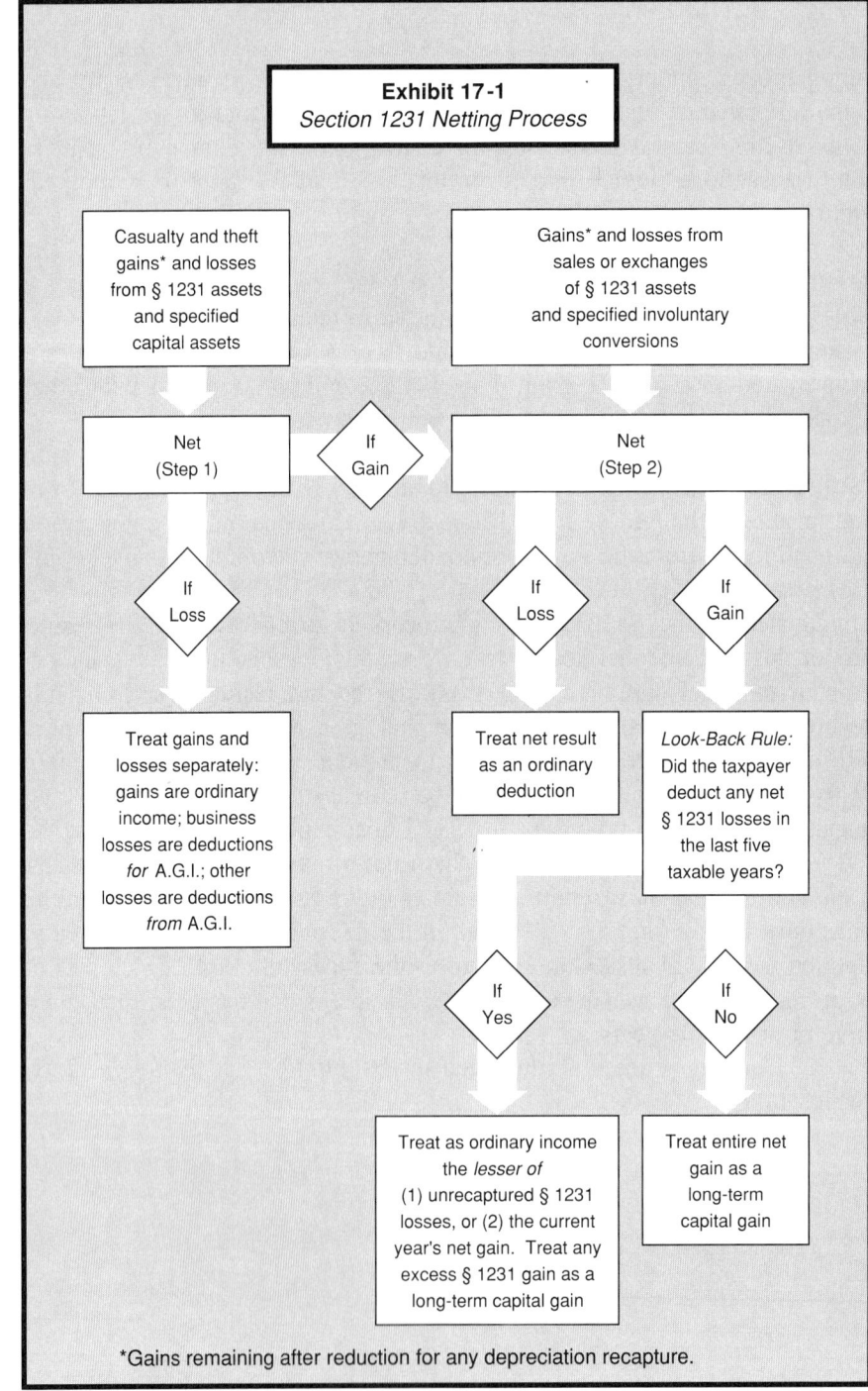

Exhibit 17-1
Section 1231 Netting Process

Casualty and theft gains* and losses from § 1231 assets and specified capital assets

Gains* and losses from sales or exchanges of § 1231 assets and specified involuntary conversions

Net (Step 1)

If Gain

Net (Step 2)

If Loss

If Loss

If Gain

Treat gains and losses separately: gains are ordinary income; business losses are deductions *for* A.G.I.; other losses are deductions *from* A.G.I.

Treat net result as an ordinary deduction

Look-Back Rule: Did the taxpayer deduct any net § 1231 losses in the last five taxable years?

If Yes

If No

Treat as ordinary income the *lesser of* (1) unrecaptured § 1231 losses, or (2) the current year's net gain. Treat any excess § 1231 gain as a long-term capital gain

Treat entire net gain as a long-term capital gain

*Gains remaining after reduction for any depreciation recapture.

Example 2.   During the current year, D sold a rental house for $45,000. She had purchased the house for $36,000 and had deducted depreciation of $8,400 using the straight-line method. D also sold a business car (held for more than one year) at a loss of $1,200. D's gain on the rental house is computed as follows:

Selling price......................................		$45,000
Cost...	$36,000	
Less: Depreciation...........................	− 8,400	
Adjusted basis................................		− 27,600
Gain realized and recognized....................		$17,400

D nets the gain and loss as follows:

Gain from sale of § 1231 asset............	$17,400
Loss from sale of § 1231 asset............	(1,200)
Net § 1231 gain for year...................	$16,200

Assuming D has not deducted § 1231 losses in any prior years, there are no unrecaptured losses in the look-back years. Thus, her entire net § 1231 gain of $16,200 is treated as a long-term capital gain. If she had other capital gains or losses during the year, they will be subject to the capital gain and loss netting process discussed in Chapter 16.

Example 3.   During 1991, R sold a business computer for $32,000. His basis at the time of the sale was $44,000. He also sold land used in his business at a gain of $1,400 and had an uninsured theft loss of works of art used to decorate his business offices (i.e., capital assets held in connection with a trade or business). R had purchased the artwork for $1,500 four years ago and it was valued at $5,000 before the burglary.

R nets his gains and losses as follows:

Step 1:   The net loss from the casualty is $1,500 (lesser of adjusted basis or fair market value). Since R has a net casualty loss, it is not treated as a § 1231 loss. Instead, the loss is treated as an ordinary loss (which is fully deductible for A.G.I since the art works were business property).

Step 2:   Combine gains and losses from sales of § 1231 assets:

Loss from sale of business computer..	($12,000)
Gain from sale of business land.......	1,400
Net § 1231 loss for year..............	($10,600)

Step 3:   A net § 1231 loss is treated as an ordinary deduction. Thus, R's $10,600 loss can be used to offset other ordinary income.

Note that the theft loss of the works of art is included in the first step of the netting process even though these items are capital assets. This loss would have offset, dollar for dollar, any casualty or theft gains (net of depreciation recapture) from § 1231 assets as well as any casualty or theft gains from other capital assets held in connection with R's business. Also note that the current year's deductible § 1231 loss may result in a change in the character of any net § 1231 gains in the next five years due to the look-back rule.

Example 4.   Assume the same facts in *Example 3*, except that R's 1991 net § 1231 loss is the only loss he has deducted in the past five years. In 1992 R has a $15,000 net § 1231 gain and is subject to the look-back rule. He must recapture (and report) as ordinary income $10,600 of the 1992 gain. The remaining net § 1231 gain of $4,400 ($15,000 − $10,600) is treated as a long-term capital gain. Should R have a net § 1231 gain in 1993, he will not be subject to the look-back rule since he has recaptured all prior years' net § 1231 losses.

DEPRECIATION RECAPTURE

HISTORICAL PERSPECTIVE

As stated earlier, the sole purpose of the depreciation recapture rules is to prevent taxpayers from taking advantage of the tax benefits of ordinary deductions from depreciation and the long-term capital gain treatment of § 1231 on the subsequent disposition of depreciable assets. Prior to 1962, there were no substantial statutory restrictions on the depreciation methods that could be adopted. Consequently, a taxpayer could elect to recover the basis of a depreciable asset under such rapid recovery methods as the double-declining-balance method or the sum-of-the-years'-digits method. If the property's value did not decline as quickly as its basis was being reduced by the depreciation deductions, a gain was ensured if the property was disposed of at a later date. The gain deferral rules of like-kind exchanges or involuntary conversions were *deliberately avoided* if the property was replaced, because the gain was favorably taxed as a long-term capital gain. In addition, the replacement property's higher cost basis could once again provide a series of ordinary deductions. This process of converting ordinary depreciation deductions into capital gains became a very popular tax shelter scheme.

Example 5.   T purchased a $50,000 piece of equipment in 1957 and de-ducted $43,520 of depcreciation over the next four years by using the 200% declining-balance method. Rather than accepting a $20,000 trade-in value for the equipment in 1961, T sold the asset for $18,500 and purchased new equipment for $65,000. By avoiding the tax deferral requirement of like-kind exchanges (i.e., § 1031), T was allowed to treat her $12,020 gain [$18,500 sales price − ($50,000 − $43,520 = $6,480 basis)] as a § 1231 gain.

If T had no other § 1231 transactions or capital losses in 1961, this gain was treated as a long-term capital gain and taxed at a rate substantially lower than the prevailing 87% top marginal tax rate for ordinary income. Also, T could begin a new tax shelter process by rapidly depreciating her higher cost basis of $65,000 in the new equipment rather than using the lower $45,000 basis that would be required under the like-kind exchange rules.

WHEN APPLICABLE

Before specific recapture rules are examined, there are two very important points to keep in mind. First, depreciable assets held for one year or less could not qualify for § 1231 treatment. Thus, any gain from the disposition of such assets is always reported as ordinary income. Second, the depreciation recapture rules *do not apply* if property is disposed of at a *loss*. Remember that losses from the sale or exchange of depreciable assets are treated as § 1231 losses if the long-term holding period requirement is met. In addition, casualty or theft losses of such property are included in the § 1231 netting process. Any loss from a depreciable asset held one year or less is an ordinary loss regardless of whether it was sold, exchanged, stolen, or destroyed.

TYPES OF DEPRECIATION RECAPTURE

There are essentially *three* depreciation recapture provisions in the Code. These are

1. Section 1245 Recapture—commonly called the *full recapture rule*, and applicable primarily to depreciable personalty (rather than realty)

2. Section 1250 Recapture—commonly called the *partial recapture rule*, and applicable to most depreciable realty if a method of depreciation other than straight-line was used

3. Section 291 Recapture—commonly called the *additional recapture rule*, and applicable *only* to corporate taxpayers.

Each of these recapture rules is discussed below.

FULL RECAPTURE—§ 1245

The first recapture provision passed by Congress was § 1245, which is generally effective for all depreciation taken on § 1245 property after 1961. Subsequent legislation extended the recapture rules to § 1250 property, which is discussed in the next section of this chapter.

Definition of § 1245 Property. Generally, § 1245 property is personalty owned by the taxpayer and subject to depreciation.[16] As such, it includes any depreciable machinery, equipment, and furniture. The definition is expanded to include the following:[17]

1. Property used as an integral part of manufacturing, production, or extraction, or in furnishing transportation, communications, electrical energy, gas, water, or sewage disposal services.

    a. However, any portion of a building or its structural components will not qualify.

    b. A research facility or a facility for the bulk storage of commodities related to an activity listed above also qualifies.

2. A single-purpose agricultural or horticultural structure.

3. A storage structure used in connection with the distribution of petroleum or any primary product of petroleum.

4. Any railroad grading or tunnel bore.

5. Certain other property that is subject to a special provision allowing rapid amortization (e.g., pollution control facilities and railroad rolling stock).

Section 1245 property is extended to include depreciable property that is expensed in the year of acquisition under § 179 and certain real property.[18]

Operation of § 1245. In order to determine the amount, if any, of § 1245 recapture (ordinary income), the gain realized and the recapture potential must be ascertained. The gain realized is the amount realized minus the adjusted basis in the property.[19]

---

[16]   § 1245(a)(3).

[17]   The definition parallels that of § 38 property, which qualified for the investment tax credit. § 48(a)(1).

[18]   § 1245(a)(3)(D) includes as "§ 1245 property" several other properties subject to unique expensing rules. In addition, the definition of § 1245 property has been expanded further to include certain nonresidential real property acquired between 1981 and the end of 1986 (i.e., subject to pre-1987 ACRS depreciation). If a taxpayer used one of the accelerated ACRS meth-

ods, his or her nonresidential real property is classified as § 1245 property. However, if the taxpayer elected to use the *alternative straight-line method*, the property is § 1250 property (rather than § 1245 property). As discussed in Chapter 9, the straight-line method is mandatory for all depreciable real property acquired after 1986. Thus, nonresidential real property acquired after 1986 *cannot* be classified as § 1245 property.

[19]   § 1001(a). See detailed discussion in Chapter 14.

Section 1245 *recapture potential* includes all depreciation or amortization allowed (or allowable) with respect to a given property—regardless of the method of depreciation used. This is why § 1245 is often called the full recapture rule. Recapture potential also includes adjustments to basis related to items that are expensed or where tax credits have been allowed under various sections of the Code.[20]

The process of determining the character of gain on the disposition of § 1245 property is as follows:

1. The gain is ordinary income to the extent of the *lesser* of the gain recognized or the § 1245 recapture potential (all depreciation allowed or allowable).[21]

2. Any recognized gain in excess of the recapture potential is usually treated as § 1231 gain.

Note that the depreciation recapture provision does not affect the amount of gain or loss, only the character of any gain to be recognized. There is no § 1245 depreciation recapture when a property is sold at a loss, so any loss is normally a § 1231 loss.

> **Example 6.** T owned a printing press that he used in his business. Its cost was $6,800 and T deducted depreciation in the amount of $3,200 during the three years he owned the press. T sold the press for $4,000 and his realized and recognized gain is $400 ($4,000 sales price − $3,600 adjusted basis). T's recapture potential is $3,200, the amount of depreciation taken on the property. Thus, the entire $400 gain is ordinary income under § 1245.

> **Example 7.** If T had sold his press for $7,000, his realized and recognized gain would have been $3,400 ($7,000 − $3,600). The ordinary income portion under § 1245 would be $3,200 (the amount of the recapture potential), and the remaining $200 of the gain is a § 1231 gain.

> **Example 8.** Assume the same facts as in *Example 6*, except that the printing press is sold for $3,000 instead of $4,000. In this case, T has a loss from the sale of $600 ($3,000 − $3,600 adjusted basis). Because there is a loss, there is no depreciation recapture. All of T's loss is a § 1231 loss.

---

[20] See § 1245(a)(2) for a listing of these adjustments and their related Code sections, including the basis adjustment related to the earned portion of any investment credit.

[21] § 1245(a).

Exceptions and Limitations.   Certain exceptions to the application of § 1245 are allowed. Gifts and inheritances, which generally are not taxable events, escape § 1245 recapture. Recapture of depreciation under § 1245 is required, however, to the extent § 691 applies (relating to income in respect to a decedent).[22]

In involuntary conversions and like-kind exchanges, the depreciation recapture under § 1245 is limited to the *gain recognized*.[23] Similarly, in nontaxable business adjustments such as the formation of partnerships, transfers to controlled corporations, and certain corporate reorganizations, § 1245 recapture is limited to the gain recognized under the controlling provisions.[24]

PARTIAL RECAPTURE—§ 1250

Section 1250 requires that a portion of any *accelerated* depreciation allowed with respect to *§ 1250 property* be recaptured as ordinary income if the property is disposed of at a gain. This section was first effective for depreciation deducted after 1963. Since it has been modified numerous times, one must be certain that the appropriate rules are applied.

Section 1250 Property.   Section 1250 property consists of depreciable real property that is not § 1245 property.[25] It therefore includes buildings and their structural components as well as most other depreciable real property.[26]

Depreciation of Real Property.   As a result of the Tax Reform Act of 1986, depreciable real property acquired after 1986 *must* be depreciated over a specified life using the straight-line method. Residential real property is assigned a 27.5-year recovery period, while nonresidential real property is assigned a recovery period of 31.5 years. In either case, the taxpayer may elect to use an optional 40-year life under the Alternative Depreciation System, and both types of property will be classified as § 1250 property.[27]

For real property acquired between 1981 and the end of 1986, the taxpayer could either use the accelerated depreciation method allowed under ACRS or elect an optional straight-line method. If the taxpayer used the accelerated method of recovering cost for *nonresidential real property*, the property is classified as § 1245 property and is subject to the full recapture rule of § 1245. If the accelerated method was used for *residential realty*, the property is classified as § 1250 property and is subject to the partial recapture rule under this section.

---

[22]   §§ 1245(b)(1) and (2).

[23]   § 1245(b)(4).

[24]   § 1245(b)(3). See Chapter 19 for further discussion of nontaxable business adjustments.

[25]   § 1250(c).

[26]   The term does not include nonresidential real property placed in service between 1981 and the end of 1986 that is being depreciated under ACRS using the accelerated method. It is important to note, however, that such properties *are* § 1250 property if the optional straight-line method is used. § 1245(a)(5).

[27]   § 168. See Chapter 9 for further details.

All depreciable real property acquired before 1981 is classified as § 1250 property. For such property acquired before 1981 (non-ACRS property), taxpayers were required to estimate useful lives and salvage values. The annual deduction (during the first two-thirds of the useful life) generally could not exceed that arrived at by using the following maximum rates and methods:[28]

Maximum Allowable Deduction Type of Property	Method/Rate
New residential real estate	Declining-balance using 200% of the straight-line rate
Used residential real estate:	
If estimated useful life at least 20 years	Declining-balance using 125% of the straight-line rate
If estimated useful life less than 20 years	Straight-line
New nonresidential real estate	Declining-balance using 150% of the straight-line rate
Used nonresidential real estate	Straight-line

Operation of § 1250. The two critical factors in determining the amount, if any, of § *1250 recapture* are the gain realized *and* the amount of *excess depreciation*. Excess depreciation refers to depreciation deductions in excess of that which would be deductible using the straight-line method. For property held one year or less, all depreciation is considered excess depreciation.[29]

In determining the excess depreciation, the same life and salvage value that were used to calculate the accelerated depreciation are used.[30] Under ACRS for 15, 18, and 19-year real property, the same is true. A salvage value of zero and a life of 19 (or 18 or 15) years are used in calculating the amount of excess depreciation. If the taxpayer depreciated the property using the straight-line method, there would be no excess depreciation. Because the § 1250 recapture provision applies *only* to any excess depreciation claimed by a taxpayer, it is often referred to as the partial recapture rule.

---

[28] § 167(j).

[29] § 1250(b).

[30] § 1250(b)(5).

The process of determining the character of gain on the disposition of § 1250 property is as follows:

1.   The gain is ordinary income to the extent of the *lesser* of the gain recognized or the § 1250 recapture potential (generally the excess depreciation allowed).[31]

2.   Any recognized gain in excess of the recapture potential is usually treated as § 1231 gain.

There is no § 1250 depreciation recapture when a property is sold at a loss, so any loss is normally a § 1231 loss.

Example 9.   During 1991, L sold a small office building for $38,000. The building had cost her $22,000 in 1979, and she had deducted depreciation of $7,000 using an accelerated method. Straight-line depreciation would have been $5,600. L's gain recognized on the sale is $23,000 ($38,000 amount realized − $15,000 adjusted basis). Of that amount, $1,400 ($7,000 − $5,600 = $1,400 excess depreciation) is ordinary income under § 1250 and the remainder, $21,600, is § 1231 gain.

Example 10.   M purchased a rental duplex during 1986 for $60,000. He deducted $20,880 depreciation from 1986 through 1990 using the 19-year realty ACRS tables. Depreciation using the straight-line recovery percentages for 19-year realty would have resulted in total depreciation of $15,342.

On January 3, 1991, M sold the property for $57,000. His gain is reported as follows:

Sales price...		$57,000
Less: Adjusted basis		
Cost...	$ 60,000	
Depreciation....................................	(20,880)	(39,120)
Gain to be recognized...................................		$17,880
Depreciation actually taken.............................		$20,880
Straight-line depreciation...............................		(15,342)
Excess depreciation subject to recapture................		$ 5,538
Character of gain:		
Ordinary income (partial recapture)		$ 5,538
§ 1231 gain...		12,342
Total gain recognized....................................		$17,880

---

[31]   See § 1250(a) and discussion below dealing with recapture of only a portion of the excess depreciation for certain properties.

Although M claimed a total of $20,880 depreciation, there is only partial depreciation recapture under § 1250 (i.e., the excess depreciation). M's remaining gain of $12,342 ($17,880 − $5,538) is a § 1231 gain.

Example 11.   Assume the same facts as in *Example 10*, except that M elected to recover his basis in the duplex using the 19-year straight-line method. In this case, there is no § 1250 depreciation recapture potential. Consequently, M's *entire* gain of $12,342 [$57,000 − ($60,000 − $15,342 = $44,658 basis)] is reported as a § 1231 gain.

Example 12.   Assume the same facts as in *Example 10*, except that the property is an office building rather than a duplex. In this case, the asset is treated as § 1245 property rather than § 1250 property. Thus, M is subject to full rather than partial depreciation recapture. The *entire* gain must be reported as ordinary income.

History of § 1250.   Over the years, § 1250 has been changed frequently, with a general trend toward an expanded scope. The generalizations made in the previous paragraphs apply to depreciation allowed on nonresidential property after 1969 and residential property (other than low-income housing) after 1975. Only a portion of any other excess depreciation on § 1250 property is included in the recapture potential. The following percentages are applied to the gain realized in the transaction or the excess depreciation taken during the particular period, whichever is less:

1. For all excess depreciation taken after 1963 and before 1970, 100 percent less 1 percent for each full month over 20 months the property is held.[32] Any sales after 1979 would result in no recapture of pre-1970 excess depreciation since this percentage when calculated is zero.

2. For all excess depreciation taken after 1969 and before 1976, as follows:

   a. In the case of low-income housing, 100 percent less 1 percent for each full month the property is held over 20 months.

   b. In the case of other residential rental property (e.g., an apartment building) and property that has been rehabilitated [for purposes of § 167(k)], 100 percent less 1 percent for each full month the property is held over 100 months.[33]

   All sales from this group of real property after August 1992 will have no recapture of excess depreciation claimed before 1976. For those assets sold before September 1992, only a small percentage will be recaptured.

---

[32] § 1250(a)(3).   [33] § 1250(a)(2).

3. For excess depreciation taken after 1975 on low-income housing and property that has been rehabilitated [for purposes of § 167(k)], 100 percent less 1 percent for each full month the property is held over 100 months.[34]

In summary, 100 percent of the excess depreciation allowed with respect to § 1250 property after 1963 is subject to recapture unless it falls into one of the above categories. The rules for the various categories are provided in § 1250(a).

Exceptions and Limitations under § 1250. Generally, the exceptions and limitations that apply under § 1245 also apply under § 1250. Thus, gifts, inheritances, and most nontaxable exchanges are allowed to occur without triggering recapture.[35] This exception is extended to any property to the extent it qualifies as a principal residence and is subject to deferral of gain under § 1034 or nonrecognition of gain under § 121.[36] In such nontaxable exchanges, the excess depreciation (that is not recaptured) taken prior to the nontaxable exchange on the property transferred carries over to the property received or purchased.[37] Similarly, in the case of gifts and certain nontaxable transfers in which the property is transferred to a new owner with a carryover basis, the excess depreciation carries over to the new owner.[38] In the case of inheritances in which basis to the successor in interest is determined under § 1014, no carryover of excess depreciation occurs.[39]

Certain like-kind exchanges and involuntary conversions may result in the recognition of gain solely because of § 1250 if insufficient § 1250 property is acquired. Since not all real property is depreciable, it is possible that the replacement property would not be § 1250 property and would still qualify for nonrecognition under the appropriate rules of §§ 1033 or 1034. In such situations, gain will be recognized to the extent the amount that would be recaptured exceeds the fair market value of the § 1250 property received (property purchased in the case of an involuntary conversion).[40]

---

[34] § 1250(a)(1).

[35] §§ 1250(d)(1) through (d)(4).

[36] § 1250(d)(7).

[37] Reg. §§ 1.1250-3(d)(5) and (h)(4).

[38] Reg. §§ 1.1250-3(a), (c), and (f).

[39] Reg. § 1.1250-3(b).

[40] § 1250(d)(4)(C). A similar rule is provided for rollovers (deferral) of gains from low-income housing under § 1039 [see § 1250(d)(8)].

Example 13. D completed a like-kind exchange in 1991 in which he transferred an apartment complex (§ 1250 property) for rural farmland (not § 1250 property). The apartment had cost D $175,000 in 1980 and depreciation of $69,000 has been taken under the 200% declining-balance method. D would have deducted $42,000 under the straight-line method.

The farm land was worth $200,000 at the time of the exchange. There were no improvements on the farm property. D's realized gain on the exchange is $94,000 ($200,000 amount realized − $106,000 adjusted basis in property given up). If there had been no § 1250 recapture, then D would have had no recognized gain. Because the property acquired was not § 1250 property, § 1250 supersedes (overrides) § 1031. D has a recognized gain of $27,000 (the amount of excess depreciation), which is all ordinary income under § 1250.

Exhibit 17-2 provides an overview of the handling of sales and exchanges of business property. A comprehensive example of sales and exchanges of trade or business property is presented below.

Exhibit 17-2
Stepwise Approach to Sales or Exchanges of Trade or Business Property—An Overview

Step 1: Recapture any *unearned* investment credit and make appropriate basis adjustments, if any.

Step 2: Calculate any depreciation recapture on the disposition of § 1245 property and § 1250 property sold or exchanged at a taxable *gain* during the year.

Step 3: For any remaining gain (after recapture) on depreciable property held for more than one year, add to other § 1231 gains and losses and complete the § 1231 netting process.

Step 4: Complete the netting process for capital assets, taking into consideration the net § 1231 gain, if any.

Example 14. Cheryl A. Reporter sold the following assets during the current year:

Description	Holding Period	Selling Price	Adjusted Basis
Land and building (straight-line depreciation)	3 years	$14,000	$9,000
Cost, $13,000			
Depreciation allowed, $4,000			
Photocopier	14 months	2,600	1,564
Cost, $2,500			
Depreciation allowed, $936			
Business auto	2 years	1,800	1,920
Cost, $4,000			
Depreciation allowed, $2,080			

First, any depreciation recapture must be considered. There is no recapture for the building since straight-line depreciation was used. The recapture on the photocopier is $936 (i.e., full recapture), and there is no recapture on the automobile since it is sold at a loss. Total recapture is $936.

The § 1231 gain of $5,000 on the sale of the land and building, the § 1231 gain on the sale of the photocopier of $100 ($1,036 total gain − $936 depreciation recapture), and the § 1231 loss of $120 on the sale of the car are netted for an overall § 1231 gain of $4,980. This "net gain" is treated as a long-term capital gain, assuming Cheryl has not deducted § 1231 losses in any of the prior five years. The recapture of $936 is ordinary income.

A Form 4797 containing the information from *Example 14* is included in Exhibit 17-3, which follows. (Note that a 1990 form is used because the 1991 form was not available.)

Exhibit 17-3
Completed Form 4797

Form **4797**

Sales of Business Property
(Also, Involuntary Conversions and Recapture Amounts Under Sections 179 and 280F)
▶ Attach to your tax return. ▶ See separate Instructions.

Department of the Treasury
Internal Revenue Service

OMB No. 1545-0184

19**90**

Attachment Sequence No. **27**

Name(s) shown on return: CHERYL A. REPORTER
Identifying number: 427-29-0121

Part I — Sales or Exchanges of Property Used in a Trade or Business and Involuntary Conversions From Other Than Casualty and Theft—Property Held More Than 1 Year

1 Enter here the gross proceeds from the sale or exchange of real estate reported to you for 1990 on Form(s) 1099-S (or a substitute statement) that you will be including on line 2, 10, or 20 . . . . **1**

(a) Description of property	(b) Date acquired (mo., day, yr.)	(c) Date sold (mo., day, yr.)	(d) Gross sales price	(e) Depreciation allowed or allowable since acquisition	(f) Cost or other basis, plus improvements and expense of sale	(g) LOSS ((f) minus the sum of (d) and (e))	(h) GAIN ((d) plus (e) minus (f))
2 AUTO	3-1-89	5-2-91	1,800	2,080	4,000	120	

3 Gain, if any, from Form 4684, Section B, line 21
4 Section 1231 gain from installment sales from Form 6252, line 22 or 30
5 Gain, if any, from line 32, from other than casualty and theft . . . | 5,100
6 Add lines 2 through 5 in columns (g) and (h). . . | (120) | 5,100
7 Combine columns (g) and (h) of line 6. Enter gain or (loss) here, and on the appropriate line as follows: . . | 4,980

Partnerships.—Enter the gain or (loss) on Form 1065, Schedule K, line 6. Skip lines 8, 9, 11, and 12 below.

S corporations.—Report the gain or (loss) following the instructions for Form 1120S, Schedule K, lines 5 and 6. Skip lines 8, 9, 11, and 12 below, unless line 7 is a gain and the S corporation is subject to the capital gains tax.

All others.—If line 7 is zero or a loss, enter the amount on line 11 below and skip lines 8 and 9. If line 7 is a gain and you did not have any prior year section 1231 losses, or they were recaptured in an earlier year, enter the gain as a long-term capital gain on Schedule D and skip lines 8, 9, and 12 below.

8 Nonrecaptured net section 1231 losses from prior years (see Instructions)
9 Subtract line 8 from line 7. If zero or less, enter -0-. Also enter on the appropriate line as follows (see instructions):
S corporations.—Enter this amount (if greater than zero) on Form 1120S, Schedule D, line 7, and skip lines 11 and 12 below.
All others.—If line 9 is zero, enter the amount from line 7 on line 12 below. If line 9 is more than zero, enter the amount from line 8 on line 12 below, and enter the amount from line 9 as a long-term capital gain on Schedule D.

Part II Ordinary Gains and Losses

10 Ordinary gains and losses not included on lines 11 through 16 (include property held 1 year or less):

11 Loss, if any, from line 7
12 Gain, if any, from line 7, or amount from line 8 if applicable
13 Gain, if any, from line 31 . . | 936
14 Net gain or (loss) from Form 4684, Section B, lines 13 and 20a
15 Ordinary gain from installment sales from Form 6252, line 21 or 29
16 Recapture of section 179 deduction for partners and S corporation shareholders from property dispositions by partnerships and S corporations (see Instructions)
17 Add lines 10 through 16 in columns (g) and (h) . . | ( ) | 936
18 Combine columns (g) and (h) of line 17. Enter gain or (loss) here, and on the appropriate line as follows: . . | 936
a For all except individual returns: Enter the gain or (loss) from line 18 on the return being filed.
b For individual returns:
(1) If the loss on line 11 includes a loss from Form 4684, Section B, Part II, column (b)(ii), enter that part of the loss here and on line 21 of Schedule A (Form 1040). Identify as from "Form 4797, line 18b(1)". See Instructions
(2) Redetermine the gain or (loss) on line 18, excluding the loss, if any, on line 18b(1). Enter here and on Form 1040, line 15 | 936

For Paperwork Reduction Act Notice, see page 1 of separate Instructions.
Form **4797** (1990)

Exhibit 17-3 Continued

Form 4797 (1990)   Page **2**

Part III Gain From Disposition of Property Under Sections 1245, 1250, 1252, 1254, and 1255

19 Description of section 1245, 1250, 1252, 1254, and 1255 property:	Date acquired (mo., day, yr.)	Date sold (mo., day, yr.)
A BUILDING AND LAND	1988	1991
B PHOTOCOPIER	1989	1991
C		
D		

Relate lines 19A through 19D to these columns ▶	Property A	Property B	Property C	Property D
20 Gross sales price (**Note:** *See line 1 before completing.*)	14,000	2,600		
21 Cost or other basis plus expense of sale	13,000	2,500		
22 Depreciation (or depletion) allowed or allowable	4,000	936		
23 Adjusted basis. Subtract line 22 from line 21	9,000	1,564		
24 Total gain. Subtract line 23 from line 20	5,000	1,036		
25 If section 1245 property:				
a Depreciation allowed or allowable from line 22		936		
b Enter the **smaller** of line 24 or 25a		936		
26 If section 1250 property: If straight line depreciation was used, enter zero on line 26g unless you are a corporation subject to section 291.				
a Additional depreciation after 12/31/75 (see Instructions)	– 0 –			
b Applicable percentage multiplied by the **smaller** of line 24 or line 26a (see Instructions)				
c Subtract line 26a from line 24. If line 24 is not more than line 26a, skip lines 26d and 26e.				
d Additional depreciation after 12/31/69 and before 1/1/76				
e Applicable percentage multiplied by the **smaller** of line 26c or 26d (see Instructions)				
f Section 291 amount (corporations only)				
g Add lines 26b, 26e, and 26f	–0–			
27 If section 1252 property: Skip this section if you did not dispose of farmland or if you are a partnership.				
a Soil, water, and land clearing expenses				
b Line 27a multiplied by applicable percentage (see Instructions)				
c Enter the **smaller** of line 24 or 27b				
28 If section 1254 property:				
a Intangible drilling and development costs, expenditures for development of mines and other natural deposits, and mining exploration costs (see Instructions)				
b Enter the **smaller** of line 24 or 28a				
29 If section 1255 property:				
a Applicable percentage of payments excluded from income under section 126 (see Instructions)				
b Enter the **smaller** of line 24 or 29a				

Summary of Part III Gains (Complete property columns A through D, through line 29b before going to line 30.)

30 Total gains for all properties. Add columns A through D, line 24	6,036
31 Add columns A through D, lines 25b, 26g, 27c, 28b, and 29b. Enter here and on line 13. (See the Instructions for Part IV if this is an installment sale.)	936
32 Subtract line 31 from line 30. Enter the portion from casualty and theft on Form 4684, Section B, line 15. Enter the portion from other than casualty and theft on Form 4797, line 5	5,100

Part IV Election Not to Use the Installment Method (Complete this part only if you elect out of the installment method and report a note or other obligation at less than full face value.)

33 Check here if you elect out of the installment method	▶ ☐	
34 Enter the face amount of the note or other obligation	▶ $	
35 Enter the percentage of valuation of the note or other obligation	▶	%

Part V Recapture Amounts Under Sections 179 and 280F When Business Use Drops to 50% or Less (See Instructions for Part V.)

	(a) Section 179	(b) Section 280F
36 Section 179 expense deduction or section 280F recovery deductions		
37 Depreciation or recovery deductions (see Instructions)		
38 Recapture amount. Subtract line 37 from line 36. (See Instructions for where to report.)		

Example 15. Assume that Cheryl Reporter, from the previous example, had the following capital asset transactions during the same year:

Description	Holding Period	Selling Price	Adjusted Basis	Description of Gain or (Loss)
100 shares XY Corp.	4 months	$ 3,200	$4,200	($1,000) STCL
100 shares GB Corp.	3 years	3,200	4,600	(1,400) LTCL
1 acre vacant land	5 years	12,000	5,000	7,000 LTCG

Taking into consideration the net § 1231 gain of $4,980 from *Example 14*, Cheryl has a net long-term capital gain of $10,580 [$4,980 § 1231 gain + ($7,000 LTCG − $1,400 LTCL)] and a net short-term capital loss of $1,000 after the first step in the capital gain and loss netting process. After the second step, Cheryl has a $9,580 net capital gain ($10,580 NLTCG − $1,000 NSTCL). This net capital gain *cannot* be taxed at a rate greater than 28%.

ADDITIONAL RECAPTURE—CORPORATIONS

Corporations generally compute the amount of §§ 1245 and 1250 ordinary income recapture on the sales of depreciable assets in the same manner as do individuals. However, Congress added Code § 291 to the tax law in 1982 with the intent of reducing the tax benefits of the accelerated cost recovery of depreciable § 1250 property available to corporate taxpayers. For sales or other taxable dispositions of § 1250 property, corporations must treat as ordinary income 20 percent of any § 1231 gain *that would have been* ordinary income if Code § 1245 rather than § 1250 had applied to the transaction.[41] The amount that is treated as ordinary income under § 291 is computed in the following manner:

Amount that would be treated as ordinary income under Code § 1245		$xx,xxx
Less:	Amount that would be treated as ordinary income under § 1250	(x,xxx)
Equals:	Difference between recapture amounts	$xx,xxx
Times:	Rate specified in § 291	× 20%
Equals:	Amount that is treated as ordinary income	$xx,xxx

---

[41] § 291(a)(1).

Example 16.   K Corporation sells residential rental property for $500,000 in 1991. The property was purchased for $400,000 in 1986, and K claimed ACRS depreciation of $140,000. Straight-line depreciation would have been $105,000. K Corporation's depreciation recapture and § 1231 gain are computed as follows:

Step 1:	Compute realized gain:		
	Sales price.........................		$500,000
	Less: Adjusted basis		
	Cost..........................	$400,000	
	ACRS depreciation............	(140,000)	(260,000)
	Realized gain........................		$240,000
Step 2:	Compute *excess* depreciation:		
	Actual depreciation................		$140,000
	Straight-line depreciation..........		(105,000)
	Excess depreciation.................		$ 35,000
Step 3:	Compute § 1250 depreciation recapture:		
	Lesser of realized gain of $240,000 or		
	Excess depreciation of $35,000		
	§ 1250 depreciation recapture.......		$ 35,000
Step 4:	Compute depreciation recapture if § 1245 applied:		
	Lesser of realized gain of $240,000 or		
	Actual depreciation of $140,000		
	Depreciation recapture if § 1245 applied...................		$140,000
Step 5:	Compute § 291 ordinary income: Depreciation recapture if		
	§ 1245 applied...................		$140,000
	§ 1250 depreciation recapture.......		(35,000)
	Excess recapture potential..........		$105,000
	Times: § 291 rate...............	×	20%
	§ 291 ordinary income..............		$ 21,000
Step 6:	Characterize recognized gain:		
	§ 1250 depreciation recapture.......		$ 35,000
	Plus: § 291 ordinary income........		21,000
	Ordinary income....................		$ 56,000
	Realized gain.......................		$240,000
	Less: Ordinary income.............		(56,000)
	§ 1231 gain		$184,000

Note that without the additional recapture required under § 291, K Corporation would have reported a § 1231 gain of $205,000 ($240,000 total gain − $35,000 § 1250 recapture). If the property had been subject to § 1245 recapture, K Corporation would have only a $100,000 § 1231 gain ($240,000 − $140,000 § 1245 recapture). Section 291 requires that the corporation report 20% of this difference ($205,000 − $100,000 = $105,000 × 20%), or $21,000, as *additional* recapture.

Example 17. Assume the same facts as in *Example 16*, except that the property is an office building rather than residential realty *and* straight-line depreciation was elected. An individual taxpayer would report the entire gain of $205,000 [$500,000 − ($400,000 basis − $105,000 straight-line depreciation)] as a § 1231 gain. However, the corporate taxpayer must recapture $21,000 (20% × $105,000 depreciation) as ordinary income under § 291. The remaining $184,000 ($205,000 − $21,000) would be a § 1231 gain.

OTHER RECAPTURE PROVISIONS

There are several more recapture provisions than those already discussed. They include the recapture of farmland expenditures,[42] recapture of intangible drilling costs,[43] and recapture of gain from the disposition of § 126 property (relating to government cost-sharing program payments for conservation purposes).[44] Another type of recapture is investment tax credit recapture.[45] This is discussed in detail in Chapter 13.

INSTALLMENT SALES OF TRADE OR BUSINESS PROPERTY

As discussed in Chapter 14, gains on sales of trade or business property may be deferred using the installment sale method. However, depreciation recapture does not qualify for installment sale treatment. Thus, ordinary income from depreciation recapture must be reported in the year of sale—*regardless* of whether the seller received any payment in that year.[46] Consequently, only the § 1231 gain from such sales will qualify for installment gain deferral.

---

[42] § 1252.

[43] § 1254.

[44] § 1255.

[45] § 47.

[46] § 453(i). See Chapter 14 for a detailed discussion of installment reporting.

TAX PLANNING CONSIDERATIONS

TIMING OF SALES AND OTHER DISPOSITIONS

Timing the sale of trade or business properties is very important, and from a tax perspective can be critical. In the simplest case, if a taxpayer has a tax loss or is in a lower tax bracket, any contemplated sales at a gain should be considered to take advantage of the favorable tax result under § 1231. If tax rates are particularly high in the current year, loss transactions should be considered. Any net § 1231 loss is treated as an ordinary deduction for A.G.I. and avoids the $3,000 deduction limit imposed on net capital losses.

In addition, a net § 1231 gain qualifies as a long-term capital gain. For high-income taxpayers with no capital asset transactions or with a net capital gain in the current year, the net § 1231 gain qualifies for the maximum capital gains tax rate of 28 percent. The benefit can be even greater for a taxpayer with substantial capital losses for the year. Because the losses in excess of $3,000 would otherwise be suspended, any net § 1231 gain can be currently recognized at no additional tax cost.

If a taxpayer has recognized or could recognize a § 1231 gain for the year and benefit from § 1231 treatment, additional sales of § 1231 property at a loss should be avoided. Because such losses must be netted against the gains, the favorable treatment of the gains is lost.

The look-back rule must be considered whenever a taxpayer is contemplating the timing of sales of § 1231 gain and loss assets. If no § 1231 losses have been recognized in the last five years, the gain assets should be sold in the current year to receive the favorable treatment of net § 1231 gains. The loss assets can then be sold in the next year and be treated as ordinary losses. This plan will not work, however, if the loss assets are sold first.

Finally, the timing of casualty and theft gains and losses should be considered. Obviously, a taxpayer cannot control the timing of such losses—not legally, anyway. However, the § 1033 gain deferral rules discussed in Chapter 15 may offer some tax planning opportunity. Because this deferral provision is generally elective, the taxpayer should consider existing § 1231 gains or losses before making a decision to defer gain. For example, a taxpayer with substantial capital losses may decide not to defer gain under § 1033 even though the involuntarily converted asset is to be replaced. Immediate recognition of the gain will not have any negative tax consequences because it can be offset by the existing capital losses. The replacement property will have a higher (cost) basis for future depreciation. This plan is much more important to corporate taxpayers because excess capital losses can be carried forward only five years.

SELECTING DEPRECIATION METHODS

The accelerated cost recovery system provides taxpayers with several choices of depreciation methods and conventions. For example, a taxpayer with depreciable personalty may elect to use the straight-line method and either the class life or a longer alternative life. For real estate, an alternative 40-year life may be used.

Effect of Recapture. Generally, a taxpayer should adopt the most rapid method of depreciation available because this results in a deferral of income taxes. Unless tax rates are expected to change significantly in the near future, the tax benefits produced by large depreciation deductions currently allow the taxpayer the use of the money that would otherwise have been used to pay income taxes. In addition, the availability of the like-kind exchange and involuntary conversion provisions eliminates the risk of depreciation recapture when the taxpayer plans to continue in business. It is also important to remember that, for noncorporate taxpayers, there is no depreciation recapture possibility for real estate placed in service after 1986. Because only the straight-line depreciation method can be used, there will be no excess depreciation.

Section 179. As discussed in Chapter 9, any § 179 expense amount is treated as depreciation allowed. As a result, the comments above may also apply in deciding whether to claim the option to expense the cost of qualifying property. If more than one qualifying asset is placed in service during the year and their total cost exceeds $10,000 (or reduced limit), the taxpayer must select the assets to be expensed. Obviously, only the assets not expected to be sold should be considered for this option. Given the time value of money, however, it seems unlikely that any taxpayer should forgo the § 179 expense option—unless the additional recordkeeping is considered to outweigh the current tax benefit.

INSTALLMENT SALES

Installment sales provide an excellent tax deferral possibility. Caution must be exercised, however, if trade or business property is to be sold under a deferred-payment arrangement. Because any depreciation recapture must be reported as income in the year of sale regardless of the amount of money received, taxpayers should require a cash down payment sufficient to pay any income taxes resulting from the depreciation recapture.

PROBLEM MATERIALS

DISCUSSION QUESTIONS

17-1 *Section 1231 Assets.* What are § 1231 assets? What is the required holding period? Does the § 1231 category of assets include § 1245 and § 1250 assets as well? Elaborate.

17-2 *Excluded Assets.* What type of property is excluded from § 1231 treatment?

17-3 *Section 1231 Netting Process.* Briefly describe the § 1231 netting process. Are personal use assets included in this process?

17-4 *Net § 1231 Gains.* What is the appropriate tax treatment of net § 1231 gains? Are they offset by short-term capital losses? Can they be offset by capital loss carryovers from prior years?

17-5 *Net § 1231 Losses.* What is the appropriate tax treatment of net § 1231 losses? Are they subject to any annual limitation? Can they be used to create or increase a net operating loss for the year?

17-6 *Certain Casualty or Theft Gains and Losses.* Which casualty or theft gains and losses are included in the § 1231 netting process? What is the proper treatment of a net casualty or theft gain? What is the proper treatment of a net casualty or theft loss?

17-7 *Section 1231 Look-Back Rule.* Describe how the § 1231 look-back rule operates. Why do you think Congress enacted such a rule?

17-8 *Section 1245 Property.* What category of trade or business property is subject to § 1245? What depreciable real property has been included in this category?

17-9 *Full Depreciation Recapture — § 1245.* What is meant by § 1245 recapture potential? Why is this rule sometimes called the full recapture rule? What is the lower limit of § 1245 recapture?

17-10 *Asset Classification.* When will the sale or other disposition of depreciable equipment be subject to both § 1231 and § 1245? What is the appropriate treatment of any loss from the sale of such equipment?

17-11 *Section 1245 Property.* F gave property with § 1245 recapture potential to his daughter, D. Will F be required to recapture any of the depreciation previously claimed? How must D characterize any gain she might recognize on a subsequent disposition of the property?

17-12 *Section 1245 Recapture Potential.* What happens to the § 1245 recapture potential when property is disposed of in a like-kind exchange?

17-13 *Section 179 Expense Treatment.* Explain the proper tax treatment of any gain recognized on the disposition of an asset that the taxpayer had earlier elected to expense under § 179. Does this mean that any amounts ever deducted under § 179 will always be subject to recapture? Explain.

17-14 *Section 1250 Property.*   Is land included in the definition of § 1250 property? Is any real property depreciated under the straight-line method included in this definition?

17-15 *Section 1250 Property.*   Is nonresidential real estate acquired after 1980 always § 1250 property? Explain.

17-16 *Section 1250 Property.*   Why will depreciable real property placed in service after 1986 never be subject to § 1250 recapture?

17-17 *Section 1250 Recapture Potential.*   Why is § 1250 sometimes called the partial recapture rule? Will the § 1250 recapture potential ever simply disappear? Explain.

17-18 *Additional Recapture—§ 291.*   Briefly describe the additional depreciation recapture rule of § 291. Which taxpayers are subject to this rule?

17-19 *Section 291 Recapture.*   Can a corporation that has always elected to use the straight-line depreciation method for all real property ever be subject to additional recapture under § 291? Explain.

17-20 *Reporting § 1231 Transactions.*   What tax form does a taxpayer use to report the results of § 1231 transactions? How is any depreciation recapture reported on this form?

17-21 *Planning § 1231 Transactions.*   Under what circumstances should a taxpayer with an involuntary conversion gain from business property consider not electing to defer the gain under § 1033?

17-22 *Planning § 1231 Transactions.*   A taxpayer plans to trade in depreciable property in order to acquire new property but is quite disappointed to find that his old equipment is worth less than its unrecovered cost basis. He is currently in the top marginal tax bracket and has no capital gains or losses or other § 1231 transactions for the year. What tax advice would you offer this taxpayer concerning the planned exchange?

17-23 *Installment Sales and Depreciation Recapture.*   Briefly describe how recapture is reported when either § 1245 property or § 1250 property is disposed of in an installment sale. What tax planning should a taxpayer undertake concerning such sales?

PROBLEMS

17-24 *Section 1231—Timber.*   A owns timber land that she purchased in 1981. During 1991, the timber was cut and A elected § 631 treatment for the gain. Her cost assignable to the timber was $25,000 and its fair market value on January 1, 1991 was $40,000. The actual sales price of the cut timber in 1992 was $55,000.

  a.   How much is A's gain or loss recognized and what is its character?
  b.   Can A deduct the costs of cutting the timber?

17-25   *Section 1231—Unharvested Crops.*   L sold her farmland, which she had owned for 20 years, during 1991. L had made minor improvements to the farm and had used straight-line depreciation to depreciate them. No personal property was sold with the farm.

The sales price was $80,000 and L's adjusted basis was $36,000. The unharvested crops on the land represented $8,000 of the sales price, and L had spent $3,200 in producing the crop to the point of sale.

a.   How does L report the gain or loss from the sale of the farm?
b.   If L has no other sales of trade or business property or of capital assets, how much of the gain is included in her taxable income?

17-26   *Section 1245 Recapture.*   During 1991, D sold a drill press he had used in his wood shop business for three years. D had purchased the press for $820 and had deducted depreciation of $476. Straight-line depreciation would have been $410. Determine the amount and character of gain or loss to D under each of the following circumstances below:

a.   The press is sold for $500.
b.   The press is sold for $100.
c.   The press is sold for $900.

17-27   *Section 1245 Recapture.*   During the calendar year 1991, N sold three different pieces of equipment used in her business. The units were as follows:

Description	Holding Period	Sales Price	Cost	Depreciation Allowed
Processing machine	3 years	$1,200	$1,400	$600
Work table	4 years	1,600	1,300	500
Automatic stapler	2 years	500	900	300

What is the amount and character of N's gain or loss from these transactions?

17-28   *Section 1245 Recapture.*   Fill in the missing information for each of the three independent sales of § 1245 assets identified below. Enter a dollar amount or n/a (for not applicable) in each blank space.

	Assets		
	A	B	C
Sales price.....................................	$105	$ 90	$___
Cost...	100	125	100
Depreciation allowed...........................	30	___	30
Depreciation recapture.........................	___	___	20
§ 1231 gain or (loss)...........................	___	(10)	___

17-29 *Section 1250 Recapture.*   Fill in the missing information for each of the three independent sales of § 1250 assets identified below. Enter a dollar amount or n/a (for not applicable) in each blank space.

	Assets		
	X	Y	Z
Sales price	$100	$___	$200
Cost	135	100	100
Depreciation allowed	55		30
Straight-line depreciation		20	
Depreciation recapture	0	10	___
§ 1231 gain or (loss)	___	30	120

17-30 *Basis Reductions.* Dr. T purchased a treadmill for use in his cardiology practice for $13,000 on August 14, 1989. T claimed § 179 expense of $10,000 and depreciation of $429 in 1989. The depreciation for 1990 and 1991 is scheduled to be $735 and $524, respectively. T sold the treadmill on January 13, 1991 for $3,500.

   a.   What are the amount and character of T's gain on the sale?

   b.   What would be your answer if the unit had been sold for $13,500?

17-31 *Real Property Acquired after 1986.*   V sold an office building in the current year that she had purchased for $60,000 in 1989. Depreciation of $4,127 was claimed before the building was sold for $75,000. What are the amount and character of V's gain on this sale?

17-32 *Section 1245, § 1250, and § 291 Recapture.*   K purchased a mini-warehouse unit on January 3, 1986 for $40,000. Using the tables under ACRS, K deducted depreciation of $15,295 for the period 1986–1991. The unit was sold on January 15, 1991 for $41,000.

   a.   How much is K's gain and what is its character?

   b.   If K had used the optional straight-line method and a 19-year life under ACRS, the depreciation deductions would have totaled $10,526. What would be the amount and character of K's gain using this method?

   c.   What would be your answer to (b) if K were a corporation?

17-33 *Section 1250 Recapture.*   Z sold an apartment unit during 1991 for $75,000. Z purchased the property for $42,000 in 1985 and has deducted depreciation of $22,000. Straight-line depreciation using the same life and salvage value would have been $16,000.

   a.   What is the amount and character of Z's gain if he receives the entire proceeds in 1991?

   b.   What would be the amount and character of gain reported by Z in 1991 and 1992 if the sale were under an installment contract with $15,000 down payment, $15,000 of principal payable in each year, and a reasonable interest rate?

17-34   *Section 1231 Gain and Look-Back Rule.*   R sold land and a building used in farming at a gain of $30,000 during 1991. No other sales or dispositions of § 1231 assets were made during the year, and the § 1250 depreciation recapture for the building was $4,500.

    a.   How is R's gain to be reported if he had a net § 1231 gain of $10,000 in 1988, a net § 1231 loss of $12,000 in 1989, and no § 1231 transactions in 1990?

    b.   How would your answer to (a) differ if the sale of the property had resulted in a loss of $7,500?

17-35   *Section 1231 and Depreciation Recapture.*   Fill in the missing information for each of the separate sales of § 1231 assets indicated below. Enter a dollar amount or n/a (for not applicable) in each blank space.

	Land	Building	Machine	Machine
Sales price	$100	$____	$ 90	$____
Cost	140	100	125	100
Depreciation allowed	____	30	____	30
Straight-line depreciation	____	20	____	____
Depreciation recapture	20	____	____	____
§ 1231 gain or (loss)	10	30	(10)	5

17-36   *Section 1231 Netting Process.*   T had three § 1231 transactions during the current year.

    1.   Theft of electric cart used on business premises. The cart was worth $600, originally cost $800, and had an adjusted basis of $425.

    2.   Sale of equipment used in manufacturing. The equipment sold for $5,500, originally cost $8,000, and had an adjusted basis of $4,250.

    3.   Sale of land and a small building used for storage. The property was sold for $60,000, originally cost $56,000, and had an adjusted basis of $42,500. Straight-line depreciation was claimed on the building.

Determine the amount of ordinary income or loss and capital gain or loss that T must report from these transactions for the current year.

17-37   *Section 1231 Transactions.*   K has the following business assets that she is interested in selling in either 1991 or 1992.

	Market Value	Basis
Manufacturing equipment	$220,000	$400,000
Factory building	350,000	220,000
Land used for factory	450,000	120,000

Straight-line depreciation was claimed on the factory. K has never sold any other § 1231 assets.

    a.   What are the tax results if K sells the land and building in 1991 and the equipment in 1992?

    b.   What are the tax results if K sells the equipment in 1991 and the land and building in 1992?

    c.   What are the tax results if K sells all the assets in 1991?

17-38   *Comprehensive Problem for Capital Asset and Trade or Business Property Trans-actions.* T owned a number of apartment units and sold several properties related to that trade or business during the current year as follows:

Description	Holding Period	Sales Price	Cost	Depreciation Allowed	Method
Apartment unit, including land (straight-line depreciation = $2,400)	3 years	$65,000	$24,000	$ 3,000	DB
Lawn tractor	5 years	1,000	3,000	2,600	SL
Spray painter	2 years	500	1,400	600	SL

During a severe winter storm, T also lost a depreciable motorscooter used in his business. The scooter, which was owned by T for two years and used exclusively in the business, had cost $2,600 and had an adjusted basis of $1,750. T has consistently followed a policy of claiming a reduced investment credit rather than making any required basis adjustment for depreciable assets. All investment credits claimed on these properties have been fully earned.

In addition, T sold several capital assets during the current year as follows:

Description	Holding Period	Sales Price	Adjusted Basis
100 shares LM Corp.	16 months	$2,000	$1,000
75 shares PL, Inc.	8 months	1,600	2,900
Silver ingots	6 years	2,600	6,000

Assuming T has never deducted § 1231 losses before, calculate the following amounts based on the above information:

a.   The amount of § 1245 recapture and § 1250 recapture, if any.
b.   The net § 1231 gain or loss.
c.   The net long-term capital gain or loss.
d.   The net short-term capital gain or loss.
e.   The overall impact of the above transactions on T's adjusted gross income.
       (*Hint:*   Set up as follows.)

```
Ordinary income:
    § 1245 recapture..............        $_____
    § 1250 recapture..............         _____
    Other: _____           _____
NSTCG(L)...................... $_____
NLTCG(L) ......................   _____
    Total/Difference...............         _____
Overall change in A.G.I..........    $_____
```

17-39 *Sections 1231 and 1245 Property.* The terms § *1231 property* and § *1245 property* are often used interchangeably. However, there are times when a specific asset can be classified as (1) *both* § 1231 and § 1245 property; (2) only § 1231 property; or (3) only § 1245 property. Based on the values assigned to the letters below, indicate the appropriate classification for each of the following mathematical expressions.

Let X = asset's original cost
Y = depreciation claimed
Z = asset's adjusted basis
T = amount realized on sale

a. If T < Z, asset is § _____ property.
b. If T > X, asset is § _____ property.
c. If X > T < Z, asset is § _____ property.
d. If Y > T > Z, asset is § _____ property.

17-40 *Section 1231 and § 1250 Property.* It is possible that (1) *both* § 1231 and § 1250 apply to the sale of depreciable real property, (2) only § 1250 applies, or (3) only § 1231 applies. Based on the values assigned to the letters below, indicate which Code sections apply for each of the following mathematical expressions.

Let X = asset's original cost
Y = depreciation claimed
Z = asset's adjusted basis
T = amount realized on sale
S = amount of straight-line depreciation

a. If $Y > S$ and $T < Z$, § _____ applies.
b. If $Y > S$ and $T > X$, § _____ applies.
c. If $Y = S$, § _____ applies.
d. If $Y > S$ and $(T - Z) < (Y - S)$, § _____ applies.

17-41 *Sale of Property Converted from Personal Use — Comprehensive Problem.* L owned and used a house as her personal residence since she purchased it in 1987 for $110,000. On February 11, 1989, when it was worth $85,000, L moved out and converted the property into a rental property. She rented the house until December 15, 1991, when it was sold for $104,500.

a. Determine L's depreciation deductions for the rental property from the time it was converted in 1989 until it was sold in 1991.
b. What is L's gain or loss to be recognized from the sale?

17-42   *Sale of Property Converted to Personal Use—Comprehensive Problem.*   Z purchased a computer system with peripherals for $14,500 on August 12, 1988. The system was used exclusively in his business. In October 1991, when the computer was worth $8,200, Z closed the business and began using the unit for personal purposes.

a.   Determine Z's depreciation deductions for the computer system from the time it was purchased until it was converted to personal use.

b.   Assume the computer system was sold for $5,400 on May 15, 1991 rather than being converted to personal use. What are the amount and character of Z's loss?

RESEARCH PROBLEMS

17-43   *Capital Assets versus § 1231 Assets.*   R inherited a residence that had been used exclusively by her grandmother as a principal residence for 30 years. Upon receiving the property, R immediately offered the property for rent and rented to several tenants.

After several months, R encountered an interesting potential business venture that would require a substantial capital investment. After an agonizing decision, she proceeded to sell her inherited rental unit. The unit was sold at a loss and R deducted the loss under § 1231. Since she had no § 1231 gains, the loss was deducted as an ordinary deduction.

Is the treatment R chose the appropriate treatment for the loss? Does the character of the property to her grandmother carryover to R, resulting in disallowance of the loss or capital loss treatment?

Research aids:

> *Campbell v. Comm.*, 5 T.C. 272 (1945).
> *Crawford v. Comm.*, 16 T.C. 678 (1951), *acq.* 1951-2 C.B. 2.

17-44   *Business Use of Personal Residence.*   J purchased a home in March 1978 for $120,000. Twenty percent of its cost was attributable to the land. From the date of purchase until March 1988, 20 percent of the house was used as a home-office, the costs of which were properly deducted annually (including depreciation). The home was used exclusively as J's residence from March 1988 until the house was sold for $325,000 on November 15, 1991.

a.   Assuming J used the declining-balance method at a 5 percent rate and a useful life of 25 years, what amount of depreciation did he claim over the 10-year period that the property was used as a home-office?

b.   Is there any depreciation recapture to be reported if gain is reported on the sale?

c.   Is there depreciation recapture to be reported if all or part of the gain is deferred under § 1034?

PART **VI**

EMPLOYEE COMPENSATION

CONTENTS

LEARNING OBJECTIVES

Upon completion of this chapter you will be able to:

- Distinguish between taxable and nontaxable employee fringe benefits

- Determine the tax consequences of the issuance and exercise of both nonqualified and qualified stock options

- Explain the advantages and disadvantages of nonqualified deferred compensation arrangements, including

  - The deferral of both the employee's recognition of income and the employer's deduction

  - The economic risk associated with unfunded arrangements

- Specify the two basic tax benefits of qualified retirement plans

- Distinguish between a defined benefit plan and a defined contribution plan

- Calculate the limitations on annual contributions to the various types of qualified plans

- Compute the annual amount of deductible contribution to an Individual Retirement Account

- Describe the characteristics of a Simplified Employee Pension

CHAPTER OUTLINE

Chapter **18**

EMPLOYEE COMPENSATION AND RETIREMENT PLANS

INTRODUCTION

For a large majority of individual taxpayers, compensation received for services rendered as an employee is the most significant, if not the only, source of taxable income. Because of this significance, the topic of taxation of employee compensation is of primary interest to the tax-paying public. Employee compensation consists not only of cash wage and salary payments but an incredible variety of compensation "packages" designed to accommodate the needs and desires of employer and employee alike.

The tax consequences to both the employer and employee of various types of employment compensation are examined in this chapter. Because the concept of compensation includes provisions for employee retirement income, the chapter also includes a discussion of the numerous types of retirement income plans available to both employees and self-employed taxpayers.

TAXATION OF CURRENT COMPENSATION

Under the broad authority of § 61, a taxpayer's gross income includes all compensation for services rendered including wages, salaries, fees, fringe benefits, sales commissions, customer tips, and bonuses. Compensatory payments may be made in a medium other than cash. For example, payment for services rendered may be made with property, such as marketable securities. In such cases, the fair market value of the property is the measure of the gross compensation income received.[1]

Payment for services performed by Taxpayer A for Taxpayer B could consist of services performed by Taxpayer B for Taxpayer A. For example, a lawyer might agree to draft a will for a carpenter, who in turn agrees to repair the lawyer's roof. As a result of such a *service swap*, both taxpayers must recognize gross income equal to the value of the services received.[2]

---

[1] Reg. § 1.61-2(d).   [2] *Ibid.*

STATUTORY FRINGE BENEFITS

As a general rule, any economic benefit bestowed on an employee by his or her employer that is intended to compensate the employee for services rendered represents gross income. This is true whether the benefit is in the form of a direct cash payment or an indirect noncash benefit that nonetheless improves the recipient's economic position.

Certain indirect or *fringe benefits*, however, are excludable from gross income under specific statutory authority. The following is a list of nontaxable fringe benefits and the authority for their exclusion from income. The details of these exclusions are discussed in Chapter 6.

1. Employer payment of employee group-term life insurance premiums (up to $50,000 of coverage)—§ 79

2. Employer contributions to employee accident or health plans—§ 106

3. Amounts paid to an employee under an employer's medical expense reimbursement plan—§ 105(b)

4. Employee meals or lodging furnished for the convenience of the employer—§ 119

5. Amounts received under an employer's group legal services program—§ 120

6. Amounts received under an employer's educational assistance program—§ 127

7. Amounts received under an employer's dependent care assistance program—§ 129

8. No-additional-cost services, qualified employee discounts, working condition fringes, and de minimis fringes—§ 132

The length of the above list demonstrates Congressional tolerance for the use of innovative fringe benefits to attract employees. Employers who want to design the most flexible compensation package for employees who have differing compensation needs may use a *cafeteria plan* of employee benefits. Under a cafeteria plan, an employee is allowed to choose among two or more benefits consisting of both cash and statutory nontaxable benefits.[3]

---

[3] § 125.

RECEIPT OF PROPERTY FOR SERVICES

From a corporate employer's point of view, any form of employee compensation that somehow strengthens that employee's commitment to the corporation is highly desirable. One such type of compensation is a payment made in the capital stock of the corporation itself. Such payment converts the employee into a stockholder and gives him or her an equity interest in the future prosperity of the corporation.

When stock in the corporate employer is used to compensate employees, it is typical for the employment contract to provide that the employee must continue to work for the corporation for some stated time period before he or she is given unrestricted ownership of the stock. If the employee leaves the job before the period expires, the stock received will be forfeited. In this situation, the tax consequences of the compensatory payment to both employee and employer are governed by § 83.

GENERAL RULE OF § 83

If in connection with the performance of services, property of any type is transferred to any person other than the person for whom such services are performed, § 83(a) provides that the fair market value of such property shall be included in the gross income of the person performing such services. If the recipient made any payment for the property, only the excess of the property's value over the amount of such payment is includible gross income. Such inclusion shall occur in the first taxable year in which the rights of the person having the beneficial interest in such property are *transferable* or are not subject to a *substantial risk of forfeiture*, whichever is applicable. If the property received for services is not immediately transferable by the recipient *or* is subject to risk of forfeiture, it is referred to as *restricted property*.

Regulation § 1.83-3(c)(1) explains that a substantial risk of forfeiture exists when the ownership of the transferred property is conditioned, directly or indirectly, upon the future performance (or refraining from performance) of substantial services by the recipient. The Regulation also states that the existence of a substantial risk of forfeiture can only be determined by examining the facts and circumstances of the specific situation.

Section 83(h) entitles the taxpayer for whom services were performed and who transferred property as compensation to a deduction equal to the fair market value of the property. The deduction must be taken in the taxable year in which (or with which) ends the taxable year in which the value of the property is recognized as gross income to the recipient.

> **Example 1.** Corporation M is on a fiscal year ending June 30. On November 1, 1988, the corporation gave employee E, a calendar year taxpayer, 100 shares of its own stock worth $100 per share as compensation for E's services to Corporation M. If E leaves M's employ for any reason during the three-year period beginning on November 1, 1988, he must return the shares. On November 2, 1991, E is still employed and the risk of forfeiture

of the stock lapses. On this date the stock is worth $120 per share. For his taxable year 1991, E must include $12,000 in gross income; his tax basis in his shares will also be $12,000. Corporation M has a deduction of $12,000 for its fiscal year ending June 30, 1992.

The Regulations make it clear that a deduction is available to the transferor of the property only if the transfer is an expense meeting the deductibility requirements of § 162 or § 212. If the transfer constitutes a capital expenditure, it must be capitalized rather than deducted.[4]

> **Example 2.** Refer to the facts in *Example 1*. If the shares were transferred to E because E performed organizational services for Corporation M, the corporation must capitalize the $12,000 amount included in E's gross income.

THE § 83(b) ELECTION

Section 83(b) gives a taxpayer who has performed services for *restricted* property an interesting option. Within 30 days of the receipt of the property, the taxpayer may choose to include its fair market value in his or her current year's gross income. This election accelerates the recognition of gross income to the taxpayer. However, the election could be beneficial if the property were rapidly appreciating in value and consequently would have a higher fair market value on the date the risk of forfeiture or other restrictions are scheduled to lapse.

> **Example 3.** In 1990 employee Z receives property worth $10,000 as payment for services rendered. The property is subject to a substantial risk of forfeiture, but Z elects to include the $10,000 value in her 1990 gross income. In 1992, when the risk of forfeiture lapses, the property is worth $25,000. However, Z has no gross income attributable to the property in 1992. Z will have a $10,000 basis in her stock, and Z's employer has a $10,000 deduction for its taxable year that includes December 31, 1990.

The election is not without risk. If the property depreciates during the forfeiture period, the election leads to a larger gross income inclusion as well as acceleration of tax recognition. And more costly still, if the property is in fact forfeited, the taxpayer receives no deduction for the original gross income inclusion.[5] Obviously, the decision to use the § 83(b) election requires a careful analysis of both the current and expected future value of the property, current and future marginal tax rates, and the nature of the restriction involved.

---

[4] Reg. § 1.83-6(a)(4).

[5] § 83(b)(1). This election is sometimes referred to as the "Las Vegas Election" because it can take the form of a gamble.

STOCK OPTIONS

As an alternative to the payment of compensation in the form of corporate stock, corporate employers may issue *options* to purchase stock at a specified price to employees whom the company wants to retain. As a general rule, stock options have no value on the date they are issued because the option price is equal to or greater than the market price of the stock. Consequently, the options will have value to the recipient (and become a cost to the employer) *only if* the market price of the shares increases.

If an option has no value upon date of grant to an employee, the employee obviously has not received taxable income. However, in certain unusual cases options may have a value at date of grant. If such value can be determined with reasonable accuracy under criteria provided in Regulation § 1.83-7(b)(2), the value represents compensation income to the recipient of the option. If an option is actively traded on an established market, it is deemed to have an ascertainable value at date of grant.[6]

> **Example 4.** Corporation C grants employee D an option to purchase 100 shares of C common stock for $10 a share at any time over the next ten years. If C stock is selling at $9 per share, D's option has no readily ascertainable value. Therefore, D has no taxable income at date of grant, and a zero tax basis in the option. If, however, D's option is actively traded on an established market and as a result can be valued at $5, D has received taxable compensation of that amount, and will have a $5 basis in the option.

OPTION EXERCISE

When the owner of a stock option that had no ascertainable value at date of grant exercises the option, the difference between the option price and the market price (bargain element) of the stock purchased represents ordinary income to the owner. If the option had an ascertainable value at date of grant, so that the recipient recognized taxable income upon receipt of the option, no additional income is recognized when the option is exercised.[7]

> **Example 5.** In 1989 employee M received certain stock options as part of her compensation from Corporation Q. At date of grant, the options had no ascertainable value. However, in 1991 M exercised the options and purchased 1,000 shares of Q stock, market value $90 per share, for the option price of $60 per share. In 1991 M must recognize $30,000 of ordinary income ($30 per share bargain element × 1,000 shares). M's tax basis in her shares is $90,000.

---

[6] Reg. § 1.83-7(b)(1).   [7] Reg. § 1.83-7(a).

From the employer's point of view, the value of a stock option can be taken as a deduction under the previously discussed rule of § 83(h). Generally, an employer will receive a deduction at date of grant if the option has a readily ascertainable value. If the option has no value at date of grant, the deduction will equal the income recognized by the owner of the option when the option is exercised.

INCENTIVE STOCK OPTIONS

In the past, Congress has experimented with a variety of *qualified stock options*— options afforded preferential tax treatment under § 421. Currently there is only a single type of qualified option, the Incentive Stock Option (ISO) of § 422A.[8]

Under § 421(a), the exercise of an ISO will not result in any income recognition to the owner. Correspondingly, the corporate employer who issued the option will never receive any deduction for the spread between option and market price at date of exercise. If and when the stock received upon exercise is sold, the employee will realize capital gain equal to the difference between the option price and selling price. The difference in tax consequences between a nonqualified stock option and an ISO is presented in the example below.

Example 6. Employee T was granted an option in 1986 to purchase *one* share of his corporate employer's stock at any time within the two succeeding calendar years. At the time the option was granted, the option price was $150 and the market price was $140. Assume that T exercised the option in 1988 when the stock had a market price of $200, and the stock acquired was sold in 1991 for $375. The tax consequences for each tax year would be as follows:

	Nonqualified Stock Option	Incentive Stock Option
1986	None	None
1988	Market price of $200 −$150 option price =$50 ordinary income and $200 basis in purchased stock ($150 cost + $50 income recognized). Employer deduction =$50	No income and $150 basis in purchased stock
1991	Sale price of $375 − $200 basis = $175 capital gain.	Sale price of $375 − $150 basis = $225 capital gain.

---

[8] The rules of § 422A apply to options granted on or after January 1, 1976 and outstanding on January 1, 1981.

HOLDING PERIOD REQUIREMENTS

For the beneficial rule of § 421(a) to apply, an individual may not dispose of the stock purchased upon exercise of the ISO within two years from the date of the granting of the option or within one year from the date of exercise.[9] Additionally, the individual must be an employee of either the corporation granting the ISO or a parent, subsidiary, or successor corporation from the date of grant until the day three months before the date of exercise.[10]

If an individual violates the holding period requirement by disposing of his or her stock too quickly after purchase, § 421(b) provides that the *compensation income* (ordinary income) the individual did not recognize at date of exercise must be recognized in the year of disposition. Any gain so recognized increases the cost basis of the stock.[11] In such a situation the employer will be entitled to a corresponding deduction.

> **Example 7.** Beta Corporation grants an ISO to employee Z on November 1, 1986. The option allows Z to purchase 500 shares of Beta stock at $3 per share. Z exercises the option on December 1, 1990, when Beta stock is selling for $7 per share. Z sells his 500 shares on March 1, 1991 for $9 per share. Because of the premature disposition (less than one year from date of exercise), Z must recognize $2,000 ordinary income [500 shares × $4 bargain price ($7 market price − $3 option price)] and a $1,000 capital gain in 1991. Additionally, Beta Corporation may claim a $2,000 deduction in 1991.

If the amount realized on a premature sale is less than the value of the stock at date of exercise, only the excess of the amount realized over the option price is recognized as ordinary income.[12]

> **Example 8.** Refer to the facts in *Example 7.* If Z sold his Beta stock for $6 rather than $9 a share, his ordinary income (and Beta's deduction) would be limited to $1,500 [500 shares × $3 bargain price ($6 selling price − $3 option price)].

---

[9] § 422A(a)(1).

[10] § 422A(a)(2).

[11] Reg. § 1.421-5(b)(2).

[12] § 422A(c)(2).

QUALIFICATION REQUIREMENTS

An employee stock option must meet a number of statutory requirements set forth in § 422A(b) to qualify as an ISO. The primary requirements are as follows:

1. The option is granted pursuant to a plan that specifies the total number of shares that may be issued under options and the class of employees eligible to receive the options. The shareholders of the corporation must approve the plan within twelve months before or after the date the plan is adopted.

2. The options are granted within ten years of the date of adoption or the date of shareholder approval, whichever is earlier.

3. The option price is not less than the market value of the stock at date of grant.

4. The option must be exercised within ten years of date of grant.

5. The option can only be exercised by the recipient employee during his or her lifetime and can only be transferred at the employee's death.

6. The recipient of the option does not own stock possessing more than 10 percent of the total combined voting power of all classes of stock of the employer corporation or of its parent or subsidiary corporation.[13]

A major restriction on the use of ISOs is the statutory requirement that the value of stock with respect to which ISOs are *exercisable* shall not exceed $100,000 per calendar year per employee. For purposes of this requirement, the value of the stock is determined at date of grant.[14]

> **Example 9.** In calendar year 1990, Corporation Q granted Employee F an ISO to purchase 1,000 shares of Q stock with a current aggregate value of $200,000. In calendar year 1991, Corporation Q granted Employee F a second ISO to purchase 1,200 shares of Q stock with a current aggregate value of $300,000. If Employee F decides to exercise any of her ISOs in 1991, she may only purchase 500 shares through exercise of her 1990 option or 400 shares through exercise of her 1991 option.

PLANNING FOR RETIREMENT INCOME

One of the central features of an individual's financial plan should be a provision for some source of retirement income. As the life span of the average American lengthens, the number of prospective retirement years increases. As a result, many individuals realize that some amount of current investment is necessary in order to ensure that their retirement years can be a period of financial security.

---

[13] § 422A(c)(6) waives this requirement in certain cases.

[14] § 422A(b)(7).

The remainder of this chapter will examine the variety of retirement plans available to individual taxpayers. In analyzing a particular plan, two basic questions must be answered:

1. Are payments into the plan deductible for Federal income tax purposes by the taxpayer?

2. To what extent are retirement benefits received from a plan includible in the recipient taxpayer's gross income?

FEDERAL RETIREMENT PLANS

Many working individuals are participants in some type of Federal retirement plan such as the Social Security System or the federal Railroad Retirement System. Both plans are funded by Federal payroll taxes imposed on employees and employers. These payroll taxes are not deductible by employees for Federal income tax purposes—but they are deductible by employers under § 164(a). Payments to retired taxpayers under these Federal plans generally are not included in the recipient's gross income.[15]

As discussed in Chapter 6, the Social Security Amendments Act of 1983 provides for a portion of social security benefits to be included as taxable income for high-income-bracket recipients. Under § 86, social security recipients must include in taxable income the lesser of (1) one-half the benefits received, *or* (2) one-half the excess *combined income* (adjusted gross income + interest on tax-exempt bonds + one-half of benefits received) over a specified base amount. The specified base is $32,000 for taxpayers who are married filing jointly, $0 for those married filing separately, and $25,000 for other individuals. Congress has earmarked all income tax generated by this new law for the social security trust fund.

PRIVATE RETIREMENT PLANS

As a supplement (or in some cases, an alternative) to a Federal retirement program, individuals may participate in retirement programs sponsored by their employers or designed by the individuals themselves. In the former situation an employee may make regular contributions (often in the form of a payroll deduction) to a retirement program established and managed by the employer, or the employer may contribute all or a part of the funds for the employee. In the latter situation, the individual may make contributions to an Individual Retirement Account (IRA) or a Keogh plan, or pay current premiums to a commercial annuity company to purchase an annuity contract under the terms of which the individual will receive a regular series of payments beginning in some designated future period.

---

[15] Reg. § 1.61-11(b).

If contributions are made to an employer-sponsored *qualified* retirement plan, the employer's contributions on behalf of an employee are not includible in the employee's gross income. While the employer is entitled to a current deduction for contributions to such plans, the employee will not include the retirement benefits in his or her gross income until the tax year of actual receipt. Qualified retirement plans, IRAs, and Keogh plans are discussed later in this chapter.

If the contributions or premiums are not made to a qualified plan, an employer's contribution on behalf of an employee is generally deductible by the employer and includible in the employee's gross income. The employee is not allowed a deduction for either current contributions to nonqualified plans or premiums paid for an annuity contract. Instead, these payments are viewed as investments made by the individual that will be recouped in the future when retirement benefits actually are paid to the individual. The taxation of employee annuities and similar investments is discussed in detail in Chapter 6.

RETIREMENT PLANNING USING DEFERRED COMPENSATION

For many years employers have designed total compensation packages for valued employees that combined both a current compensation element and a *deferred* compensation element. A deferred compensation arrangement typically is one in which the employee is compensated for current services rendered by the employer's promise to pay a certain amount at some future date. Through such an arrangement, an employee is providing for future (perhaps retirement) income. The two questions that must be answered about a deferred compensation arrangement are

1. When is the employee taxed on deferred compensation that is earned currently but will be received in a later year?

2. When is the employer entitled to a business deduction for deferred compensation that will be paid in a later year?

UNFUNDED DEFERRED COMPENSATION PLANS

If an employer contractually promises to pay deferred compensation to an employee and does not set aside current funds in some type of trust arrangement, the employee is put in the position of an unsecured creditor of the employer. If the employee is a cash basis taxpayer and does not have any current right to payment under the deferred compensation plan, there is no constructive receipt of the compensation and thus no current taxable income to the employee. The employee will not be taxed until the year in which the deferred compensation is actually paid.[16]

---

[16]   Rev. Rul. 69-649, 1969-2 C.B. 106.

From the employer's point of view, such unfunded arrangements are attractive because they do not require any current cash outflow from the business. However, neither a cash basis nor an accrual basis employer may take a deduction for deferred compensation until the deferred amount is includible in the employee's gross income.[17]

FUNDED DEFERRED COMPENSATION PLANS

Employees who agree to a deferred compensation arrangement normally prefer that their employers secure the promise of future compensation by transferring current funds into an independent trust for the employees' benefit. To this end, an employer can establish a *Rabbi trust* (so named because the first IRS ruling that approved this arrangement involved a rabbi) to fund deferred compensation plans. Employer funds contributed to a Rabbi trust are segregated from the employer's other business assets and cannot be reclaimed by the employer. However, if the employer gets into financial difficulty, the trust assets are subject to the claims of the employer's creditors. All income generated by trust assets is taxable to the employer.

The rules of § 83, discussed earlier in the chapter, apply to funded deferred compensation plans.[18] In the typical Rabbi trust arrangement, the rights of employees are forfeitable, so an employee will not recognize taxable income until he or she actually receives a distribution from the trust. If a deferred compensation arrangement provides that employees' rights in the retirement fund eventually become nonforfeitable (i.e., vested), an employee must recognize taxable income in the year his or her rights vest. In both cases, the employer will receive a deduction only in the taxable year in which the deferred compensation is includible in the gross income of the employee.[19]

> **Example 10.** As part of a deferred compensation arrangement, employer X agrees to place $10,000 annually into a trust account for employee Y. Y's right to the trust funds are forfeitable until he completes 10 years of service for X. In the year in which Y's risk of forfeiture lapses, the value of the trust funds is included in Y's gross income. Subsequent payments into the fund by X are fully taxable to Y.[20]

QUALIFIED RETIREMENT PLANS

Historically, Congress has viewed with favor the establishment of employer retirement plans as part of a total compensation package offered to employees. The existence of an employer-designed and administered plan encourages the young employee to think seriously about his or her retirement years and offers the employee a most convenient way to provide financially for such retirement.

---

[17] Rev. Rul. 69-650, 1969-2 C.B. 106.

[18] § 402(b).

[19] § 404(a)(5).

[20] Reg. § 1.402(b)-1(b).

Congress provided an extremely attractive set of tax benefits available to *qualified* employer retirement plans as part of the Internal Revenue Code of 1954. Since the enactment of the 1954 Code, the scope of the benefits has been periodically expanded, and Congress has made different forms of qualified plans available to an ever-increasing number of individual taxpayers. Before examining the various types of qualified plans and the specific features of each, it will be useful to analyze the two basic tax benefits associated with qualified plans for employees—the tax-free nature of employer contributions and the tax-free growth of these contributions.

TAX BENEFITS OF QUALIFIED PLANS

When an employer makes a current contribution to a *qualified* retirement plan on behalf of an employee, §§ 402(a) and 403(a) provide that the value of the contribution is not includible gross income to the employee, even though the employee has obviously received additional compensation in the form of the contribution. In contrast, if the contribution was made by the employer to a *nonqualified* retirement plan in which the employee had a vested interest, the employee would have additional gross income equal to the value of the contribution. As a result, the net amount saved toward retirement by the employee participating in a nonqualified plan is less than the amount saved by the employee participating in a qualified plan.

The second major benefit of qualified retirement plans is that the earnings generated by employer contributions are nontaxable. Sections 401(a) and 501(a) provide that a trust created to manage and invest employer contributions to a qualified retirement plan is exempt from tax.

The effect of these two benefits on the total amount of savings available to an employee at retirement is illustrated in Exhibit 18-1. The exhibit compares two retirement plans, A and B. The plans are identical in every respect but one—A is a nonqualified personal savings plan while B is a qualified employer's trust. The exhibit is based on the following assumptions:

1. The employer will make an annual $10,000 contribution to the plan on behalf of the employee.

2. The employee is in a 25 percent tax bracket. Therefore, the net amount saved by the employee in Plan A is only $7,500 ($10,000 − $2,500 tax on the current compensation represented by the contribution). The net amount saved in Plan B is $10,000.

3. Funds invested in both plans can earn a 12 percent before-tax return. The earnings from Plan A are taxable to the employee so that the plan's after-tax rate of return is 9 percent. Plan B is in the form of a qualified trust and therefore its earnings are tax-exempt.

Exhibit 18-1

Comparison of Nonqualified vs. Qualified Retirement Plans' Year-End Values of Employer Contributions

	Nonqualified Plan A	Qualified Plan B
Year 1...............	$ 7,500	$ 10,000
Year 2..............	15,675	21,200
Year 15.............	220,208*	372,800**

* $7,500 × 29.361 (factor for the sum of an annuity of $1.00 at 9% for 15 years)

** $10,000 × 37.280 (factor for the sum of an annuity of $1.00 at 12% for 15 years)

The difference in the amounts available to an employee after 15 years of participation in either plan is dramatic. It is not difficult to understand why qualified retirement plans have become such an attractive fringe benefit to employees concerned with providing for their retirement years. However, before the analysis presented in Exhibit 18-1 is complete, it is necessary to examine the general rule as to the taxability of benefits paid out of a qualified plan upon an employee's retirement.

When an employee begins to withdraw funds from a nonqualified retirement savings plan, such funds represent *after-tax* dollars, and he or she will not be taxed on these funds a second time. In comparison, benefits received by an employee out of a qualified plan funded solely by employer contributions are fully taxable to the employee. Even though the income tax on such benefits may be computed using a very beneficial method (discussed below), it is important to understand that the retirement dollars available under Plan A of Exhibit 18-1 are excludable (as a return of capital), while the retirement dollars available under Plan B are fully includible in the recipient's gross income.

TAXABILITY OF QUALIFIED PLAN LUMP SUM DISTRIBUTIONS

If an employee who has made no contributions to the employer's qualified retirement plan receives a distribution from the plan, the employee has no investment in the distribution and therefore must include the entire amount in adjusted gross income.[21] When the distribution is made by a series of payments (i.e., an annuity), the taxability of the distribution is spread over a number of years.[22] If

---

[21] If the employee has made contributions to the plan, he or she will have an investment in the plan which may be recovered tax-free under the rules of § 72.

[22] § 402(a).

the distribution is made in a lump sum, all the retirement income is taxed in one year.[23] Given the progressive rate structure of the Federal income tax, the normal tax on a large lump sum distribution could be prohibitive.

To mitigate this problem, Congress provided two relief provisions that benefit the recipient of a lump sum distribution from a qualified retirement plan. First, an employee could treat the portion of a distribution attributable to the employee's participation in the retirement plan prior to 1974 as long-term capital gain.[24] The Tax Reform Act of 1986 generally repealed such capital gain treatment. However, a taxpayer who was age 50 before January 1, 1986 may elect to utilize this relief provision. In such case, the long-term capital gain portion of a distribution will be taxed at a flat 20 percent rate.[25] For all other taxpayers, the pre-1974 portion of a lump sum distribution that may be treated as long-term capital gain will be systematically reduced, based on the following phase-out schedule.[26]

In the case of distributions during calendar year	The capital gain percentage is
1987	100
1988	95
1989	75
1990	50
1991	25

In 1992 no portion of a distribution attributable to pre-1974 participation may be considered long-term capital gain. During the phase-out period, any long-term capital gain portion of a distribution will be taxed in the same manner as other capital gains (i.e., not a flat 20% rate).

A second relief provision is a special procedure for computing the amount of current tax on a lump sum distribution. Prior to the Tax Reform Act of 1986, the procedure involved a 10-year forward averaging computation; for distributions made after December 31, 1986, the averaging period has been reduced to five years.[27] A taxpayer who was age 50 before January 1, 1986 may elect to use the 10-year forward averaging computation based on 1986 income tax rates for distributions received after 1986.[28]

Under current law, the averaging computation may be elected only for lump sum distributions received on or after the taxpayer has reached $59\frac{1}{2}$ years of age, and a taxpayer may only make one such election.[29] However, a taxpayer who was age 50 before January 1, 1986 may elect to use the forward averaging computation for lump sum distributions received prior to age $59\frac{1}{2}$.[30]

---

[23] § 402(e)(1).

[24] § 402(a)(2), repealed by the Tax Reform Act of 1986.

[25] Tax Reform Act of 1986, Act § 1122(h)(3).

[26] Tax Reform Act of 1986, Act § 112(h)(4).

[27] § 402(e).

[28] Tax Reform Act of 1986, Act § 1122(h)(5).

[29] § 402(e)(4)(B).

[30] Tax Reform Act of 1986, Act §§ 1122(h)(3) and (5).

The *five-year forward averaging* computation involves the following four steps:

1. Begin with the total lump sum distribution and subtract any available *minimum distribution allowance*.[31]

2. Divide the result into five equal portions.

3. Compute the tax on one portion using the rate schedule for single taxpayers.

4. Multiply the resulting tax by five.

A COMPREHENSIVE EXAMPLE

In 1991 employee E, age 64 and married, received a $90,000 lump sum distribution from a qualified retirement plan. His other taxable income for the year was $22,000. E's 1991 tax liability is computed as follows:

Tax on lump sum distribution:

Total distribution	$90,000
Less: Minimum distribution allowance (Step 1)[32]	− 0
Amount subject to five-year averaging........................	$90,000
$1/5$ of averageable amount (Step 2)	$18,000
Tax on 18,000 at single rates (Step 3)........................	$ 2,700
Tax multiplied by 5 (Step 4)....................................	$13,500
Tax on $22,000 taxable income:	
At rates for married, filing jointly..............................	$ 3,300
Total tax liability ($13,500 + $3,300)	$16,800

If E had simply computed his tax on $112,000 of taxable income, his total 1991 tax liability would be $27,836. Note that because E was age 50 prior to January 1, 1986, he could elect to treat the amount of the distribution attributable to any pre-1974 contributions as long-term capital gain taxable at 20 percent, *and* to use the 10-year forward averaging convention based on 1986 tax rates.

---

[31] § 402(e)(1)(C) defines the minimum distribution allowance as (1) the lesser of $10,000 or half the amount of the taxable lump sum distribution, (2) reduced by 20 percent of the amount by which the distribution exceeds $20,000. Thus, for lump sum distributions of $70,000 or more there is no minimum distribution allowance.

[32] The minimum distribution allowance is computed as follows: (1) lesser of $10,000 or $45,000 ($1/2 \times $90,000) = $10,000, (2) reduced by [20% × $70,000 ($90,000 − $20,000) = $14,000] = $0.

ADDITIONAL TAXES ON PREMATURE OR EXCESS DISTRIBUTIONS

Congress intended for the tax-favored status of qualified plans to serve as an inducement for taxpayers to provide for a source of retirement income. Therefore, if a taxpayer makes a premature withdrawal from a qualified plan, a 10 percent penalty tax is imposed on the amount of the distribution included in the taxpayer's gross income.[33] This penalty will not be imposed if the distribution occurs after the taxpayer has reached age 59½, or if the distribution is attributable to the death or permanent disability of the taxpayer.[34]

Congress has also decided that taxpayers who have used qualified retirement plans to accumulate substantial amounts of wealth should bear an extra tax burden for such privilege. Consequently, § 4980A imposes a 15 percent tax on an excess distribution received by an individual during any calendar year. An excess distribution is the total amount of distributions from qualified employer retirement plans and IRAs received during the year in excess of $150,000. The amount of tax is reduced by any premature withdrawal penalty imposed on the excess distribution.[35]

There are many situations in which taxpayers receive lump sum distributions from qualified plans prior to retirement. For example, a taxpayer who quits his job with his current employer to accept a position with a new employer may have a right to a distribution from his current employer's qualified plan. Any taxpayer who receives a qualified plan distribution but does not need additional disposable income can exclude the distribution from gross income (and thus avoid both the income tax and any penalty tax on the distribution) by making a *rollover contribution* of the distributed funds. A rollover contribution must be made into another qualified employer plan, a Keogh plan, or an IRA, and it must be made within 60 days of the receipt of the distribution.[36]

PLAN LOANS

Plan participants can avoid making taxable withdrawals from qualified plans while indirectly utilizing their retirement funds by borrowing money from their qualified plans. There is a very complex limit on the amount of a plan loan. In very general terms, a plan loan to a participant is limited to the lesser of (1) one-half the participant's vested accrued benefit (but not less than $10,000) or (2) $50,000. Any amount of a loan in excess of this limit is considered a taxable distribution.[37]

---

[33] § 72(t).

[34] For other exceptions to the penalty rule, see § 72(t)(2).

[35] Special rules apply to lump sum distributions and for retirement benefits accrued as of August 1, 1986.

[36] § 402(a)(5).

[37] § 72(p).

TYPES OF QUALIFIED PLANS

Qualified plans fall into two basic categories, defined benefit plans and defined contribution plans. A *defined benefit plan* is one designed to systematically provide for the payment of definitely determinable benefits to retired employees for a period of years or for life. The focus of the plan is on the eventual retirement benefit to be provided. The amount of the benefit is usually based on both an employee's compensation level and years of service to the company. Defined benefit plans are commonly referred to as pension plans. The current amount of employer contributions that are required to fund future pension benefits under a given plan must be determined actuarially.[38]

Defined contribution plans provide for annual contributions to each participating employee's retirement account. Upon retirement, an employee will be entitled to the balance accumulated in his or her account. Defined contribution plans are designed to allow employees to participate in the current profitability of the business. Generally, in profitable years, an employer will make a contribution to a qualified trust and such contribution will be allocated to each employee's retirement account. However, contributions may be made to a qualified profit sharing plan without regard to current or accumulated profits of the employer corporation.[39] Although the employer may have the discretion as to the dollar amount of an annual contribution, such contributions must be recurring and substantial if the plan is to be qualified.[40]

Many defined contribution plans constitute profit sharing arrangements. However, other types of defined contribution plans exist. Certain plans, such as money purchase pension plans, are based on contribution formulas for each individual employee with contributions used to purchase pension benefits. Stock bonus plans and Employee Stock Ownership Plans (ESOPS) are defined contribution plans that allow employees to acquire an ownership interest in the employer corporation upon retirement.

One of the most popular types of defined contribution plan is a § *401(k) plan* (also described as a salary-reduction plan or a cash-or-deferred arrangement). Under this type of plan, each participating employee can define his or her own contribution by specifying some amount of current salary to be paid into an employer-sponsored retirement plan. To the extent of the specified amount, the employee is converting currently taxable compensation to tax-deferred retirement income.[41]

---

[38]   Reg. § 1.401-1(b)(1)(i).

[39]   § 401(a)(27).

[40]   Reg. § 1.401-1(b)(1)(ii).

[41]   § 402(b)(8).

QUALIFICATION REQUIREMENTS

In order for a retirement plan to be *qualified* and therefore eligible for preferential tax treatment, it first must comply with a long list of requirements set forth in §§ 401 through 415. These requirements are extremely complex and can prove burdensome to the employer wishing to establish a qualified plan for his or her employees. The rigorous requirements are intended to ensure that a qualified retirement plan operates to benefit a company's employees in an impartial and nondiscriminatory manner.

The current requirements for plan qualification came into the law in 1974 with the enactment of the Employees Retirement Income Security Act (ERISA). Prior to ERISA, many qualified plans were designed to benefit only those employees who were officers of the company, shareholders, or highly compensated executives. Since the passage of ERISA, such discriminatory plans are no longer qualified.

EXISTENCE OF A QUALIFIED TRUST

Under § 401 and the accompanying Treasury Regulations, contributions made as part of a qualified plan must be paid into a domestic (U.S.) trust, administered by a trustee for the exclusive benefit of a company's employees. The plan must be in written form and its provisions must be communicated to all employees. The plan must be established by the employer. Any type of employer—sole proprietor, partnership, trust, or corporation—may establish a plan.

ANTI-DISCRIMINATION RULES

A retirement plan will not qualify if the contributions to or benefits from the plan discriminate in favor of the *prohibited group*. The prohibited group is defined as employees who are highly compensated or who are officers or shareholders of the company. If a plan provides for contributions or benefits to be determined under an equitable and reasonable formula, the fact that the prohibited group receives a greater dollar amount of contributions or benefits than employees in the nonprohibited group will not constitute discrimination.[42] However, if the formula is based on or makes reference to an employee's current compensation, only the first $200,000 (adjusted annually for inflation) of such compensation can be taken into account.[43]

> **Example 11.** Acme Inc.'s qualified profit sharing plan provides that the employer's total annual contribution will be allocated among the various plan participants based on the relative amount of each participant's current salary. Mr. J's annual salary is $275,000, but for purposes of the allocation formula only $200,000 of such salary can be taken into account for the allocation.

---

[42] §§ 401(a)(4) and (5).   [43] § 401(a)(17).

An important aspect of the statutory anti-discrimination rules for qualified plans is the fact that such plans may be integrated with public retirement benefits.[44] Thus the calculation of plan benefits may take into account the extent to which an employee is covered by Social Security or a state retirement program.

SCOPE OF PLAN PARTICIPATION AND COVERAGE

A qualified retirement plan must provide that a substantial portion of a company's employees are eligible to participate in the plan. Specifically, any employee who has reached age 21 must be eligible to participate after completing one year of service for the employer.[45] The plan may not exclude an employee from participation on the basis of a maximum age.[46]

In addition to these *minimum* and *maximum* age and service conditions, a qualified plan must meet complex minimum coverage requirements. For example, a plan will provide sufficient coverage if the plan benefits at least 70 percent of all employees who are not considered highly compensated employees.[47]

VESTING REQUIREMENTS AND FORFEITURES

Once an employee is participating in an employer-sponsored retirement plan, he or she may not be entitled to any benefits under the plan for a certain period of time. After the requisite period of time, the employee's benefits *vest* and become nonforfeitable regardless of his or her continued employee status.

Under a qualified plan, vesting must occur according to one of two statutory schedules designed to guarantee that an employee obtains a right to plan benefits within a reasonable time.[48] The simpler of the two schedules is the five-year rule, under which an employee must have a nonforfeitable right to all plan benefits after five years of service. The second schedule provides for cumulative 20 percent vesting from the third to the seventh year of service.

If an employee leaves the job before some or all of the retirement benefits have vested, he or she forfeits the right to such benefits. Previous employee contributions toward these forfeited benefits are not returned to the employer, but instead transfer to remaining plan participants in a nondiscriminatory manner.[49]

FUNDING AND CONTRIBUTION LIMITATIONS

Qualified retirement plans must be *funded*. Consequently, an employer is required to make current payments into a qualified trust. For a defined benefit plan, an actuarially determined minimum current contribution is required by statute.[50] For

---

[44] § 401(a)(5).

[45] § 410(a)(1).

[46] § 410(a)(2).

[47] § 410(b).

[48] § 411(a)(2).

[49] Rev. Rul. 71-149, 1971-1 C.B. 118.

[50] § 412.

a defined contribution plan, the annually determined contribution must be *paid* to the trustee. Because of these rules, an employer must back up its promises to the employees with actual plan contributions. Moreover, an employer has limits on the amount of contributions, and therefore, the benefits that may be provided to the employees under a qualified plan.

Under a defined benefit plan, the highest annual retirement benefit payable generally may not exceed the *lesser* of $90,000 (adjusted annually for inflation) or 100 percent of the employee's average earnings in his or her three highest compensation years.[51] Under a defined contribution plan, the annual addition to each employee's account generally cannot exceed the *lesser* of $30,000 or 25 percent of the employee's annual compensation.[52]

If the defined contribution plan is a § 401(k) plan, the amount of annual salary that an employee can designate as his or her tax-deferred contribution is limited to $7,000 (adjusted annually for inflation).[53] For an employee participating in both a defined benefit and a defined contribution plan, the statute provides a combined limitation.[54]

> **Example 12.** S is a participant in Summa Inc.'s qualified profit sharing plan. If S's annual salary is $275,000, her employer can make a maximum annual contribution for her of $30,000 (the *lesser* of $30,000 or 25% of S's first $200,000 of compensation).

> **Example 13.** If S's current salary is $95,000, the annual contribution is limited to $23,750 (the *lesser* of $30,000 or 25% of S's compensation).

TOP HEAVY PLANS

Section 416 contains additional requirements for qualified status of retirement plans that are deemed to be "top heavy." A *top heavy plan* is one in which more than 60 percent of the cumulative benefits provided by the plan are payable to *key employees*. Key employees include officers of the employer and highly compensated owner-employees. If a top heavy plan exists, § 416 provides an extra measure of assurance that the plan does not discriminate against non-key employees. To maintain qualified status a top heavy plan *must provide* a more rapid vesting schedule (generally 100% vesting after three years of service) and a minimum benefit to *all* employees regardless of social security or similar public retirement benefits.

---

[51]   § 415(b).

[52]   § 415(c).

[53]   § 402(g)(1).

[54]   § 415(e).

DEDUCTIBILITY OF CONTRIBUTIONS BY EMPLOYER

Section 404(a) allows a deduction for employer contributions to qualified retirement plans if the contributions represent an ordinary and necessary business expense. In addition, § 404 contains complex rules that limit the dollar amount of the annual deduction. (Note that the statutory limitations on employer deductions are independent of the previously discussed limitations on the amount of contributions.) For example, the deduction for an employer's contribution to a qualified profit sharing plan is subject to a general limitation of 15 percent of total annual compensation paid to participating employees.[55] If an employer makes a contribution that exceeds this percentage limitation, the excess may be carried forward and deducted in succeeding years (subject to the percentage limitation for each succeeding year).[56]

DETERMINATION LETTERS

At this point, it should be obvious to the beginning tax student that the qualification rules for employer-sponsored plans are many and complex. As a result, employers are well advised to request a determination letter from the IRS before a plan is put into effect. Such determination letter is a *written approval* of the plan verifying that the plan, as described to the IRS, complies with all requirements for qualified status. If a plan treated by an employer as qualified is disqualified in an IRS audit, the employer could be liable for a considerable amount of unwithheld income and payroll taxes on employer contributions.

QUALIFIED PLANS FOR INDIVIDUALS

Since the establishment of employer-qualified plans as part of the Internal Revenue Code of 1954, Congress has expanded the scope of the law to provide similar plans for individual taxpayers who are not covered by an employer plan or who wish to supplement their employer plan.

KEOGH (H.R. 10) PLANS

A self-employed individual who establishes an employer qualified retirement plan for his employees is not an employee eligible for participation in the plan. Self-employed individuals include sole proprietors and the partners in a business partnership. These taxpayers, however, may use the *Keogh* rules to obtain the tax benefits of a qualified plan.[57] A Keogh plan must benefit both the self-employed

---

[55] § 404(a)(3).

[56] *Ibid.*

[57] See § 410(c)(1). It is interesting to note that retirement plans for self-employed in-

dividuals often are referred to as Keogh *or* H.R. 10 plans. Actually, the descriptions are interchangeable since H.R. 10 designated the legislative bill introduced by Congressman Keogh and passed by Congress in 1962.

taxpayer and his or her employees in a nondiscriminatory manner under the wide range of rules for qualified plans previously discussed. In addition, the top heavy rules of § 416 apply to Keogh plans.[58]

Annual contributions to Keogh plans are generally subject to the same limitations that apply to employer plans. For a defined contribution plan, the annual contribution by a self-employed taxpayer is limited to the lesser of $30,000 or 25 percent of earned income.[59] However, earned income is defined as net earnings from self-employment *after* any deduction for the contribution.[60] This circular definition can be expressed by the following equation:

Allowable contribution = 0.25 (Net earnings less Allowable contribution)

The solution to this equation demonstrates that the actual limit on a self-employed taxpayer's annual contribution to a defined contribution Keogh plan is just 20 percent of net earnings.

> **Example 14.** During the current year, Mr. W earned $78,650 in his sole proprietorship. The maximum contribution he can make to his defined contribution Keogh plan is 25% of $78,650 *less* the contribution itself. Therefore, his maximum contribution will be $15,730 [25% of ($78,650 − $15,730) = $15,730]. Note that this contribution is actually only 20% of the net income generated by Mr. W's business.

An additional limitation applies if the Keogh plan is a purely discretionary profit sharing plan to which the self-employed individual is not required to make an annual contribution. In this case, § 404(a)(3) limits the deductible contribution to only 15 percent of net earnings from self-employment.[61] In order to make a deductible contribution equal to the maximum 20 percent, self-employed taxpayers typically adopt a defined contribution plan that combines a discretionary profit sharing plan with a money purchase pension plan requiring an annual contribution.

INDIVIDUAL RETIREMENT ACCOUNTS

Congress designed a qualified retirement plan for individuals called an Individual Retirement Account (IRA) in 1974 as part of ERISA. Currently, every taxpayer with earned income can establish an IRA with a commercial bank or savings and loan association. Even taxpayers who are participating in their employer's qualified retirement plan or who make contributions to a Keogh plan may establish an IRA. The annual contribution to an IRA is $2,000 or 100 percent of compensation, whichever is less.[62]

---

[58]   § 416(i)(3).

[59]   § 415(c)(1) and (3)(B).

[60]   § 401(c)(2).

[61]   Because this statutory 15 percent limit is applied to net earnings *after* deduction of the contribution, the actual limit is 13.043 percent.

[62]   § 219(b).

If a taxpayer with earned income has a spouse with minimal or no earned income, the taxpayer may establish a *spousal IRA* into which he or she may make annual contributions on behalf of the spouse. The total contribution into both IRAs is limited to $2,250 or 100 percent of compensation, with no more than $2,000 paid into either IRA.[63]

The deductibility of a taxpayer's annual IRA contribution is determined under a complex set of rules.[64]

1. For a taxpayer who is not an active participant in a qualified retirement plan, the full amount of the annual contribution is deductible.

2. For a taxpayer who is an active participant in a qualified retirement plan, but whose adjusted gross income is below an *applicable dollar amount*, the full amount of the annual contribution is deductible.

3. For a taxpayer who is an active participant in a qualified retirement plan, and whose adjusted gross income is in excess of an *applicable dollar amount*, the deductible amount of the annual contribution is reduced by a percentage. The percentage is calculated by dividing the excess of adjusted gross income (calculated before any deduction for an IRA contribution) over the applicable dollar amount by $10,000.

Once the excess adjusted gross income exceeds $10,000, no portion of a contribution to an IRA is deductible. However, if the excess is less than $10,000, the deductible portion of an IRA contribution shall not be reduced below $200.

The *applicable dollar amounts* are $40,000 for married taxpayers filing jointly, $25,000 for single taxpayers, and $0 for married taxpayers filing separately. On a joint return, the fact that either spouse is an active participant in a qualified plan will cause a reduction in the deductible IRA contributions of both spouses.

> **Example 15.** In the current year, Mr. and Mrs. W had compensation income of $27,000 and $21,000, respectively. Adjusted gross income on their jointly filed tax return was $48,000. During the year, neither Mr. or Mrs. W was an active participant in a qualified retirement plan. Mr. and Mrs. W may each contribute and deduct $2,000 to an IRA.

> **Example 16.** In the current year, Mr. and Mrs. X had compensation income of $17,000 and $8,000, respectively. Adjusted gross income on their jointly filed tax return was $25,000. During the year, Mr. X was an active participant in his employer's qualified pension plan. Mr. and Mrs. X may each contribute and deduct $2,000 to an IRA.

---

[63] § 219(c).

[64] § 219(g).

Example 17. In the current year, Mr. and Mrs. Y had compensation income of $20,000 and $28,000, respectively. Adjusted gross income on their jointly filed tax return was $48,000. During the year, Mr. Y was an active participant in his employer's qualified pension plan. Mr. and Mrs. Y may each contribute $2,000 to an IRA. However, the deductible amount of each contribution is *reduced* by $1,600 to $400.

$$\frac{\$8,000 \text{ (excess A.G.I. over applicable dollar amount)}}{\$10,000} \times \$2,000 = \frac{\$1,600 \text{ (reduction in deductible}}{\text{IRA contribution)}}$$

Example 18. In the current year, Mr. and Mrs. Z had compensation income of $20,000 and $28,000, respectively. During the year, Mr. Z was an active participant in his employer's qualified pension plan. Mr. and Mrs. Z filed separate tax returns on which adjusted gross income equaled compensation. Mr. and Mrs. Z may each contribute $2,000 to an IRA, and Mrs. Z may deduct the full amount of her contribution. However, no amount of the contribution made by Mr. Z is deductible because his excess adjusted gross income over the applicable dollar amount ($0) is more than $10,000.

Income earned in an IRA is tax-exempt, regardless of the deductibility of the contributions to the IRA.[65] When funds are withdrawn from an IRA, an amount of the withdrawal proportionate to any unrecovered non-deductible contributions in the account is not subject to tax; the balance of the withdrawal is fully includible in gross income.[66]

Example 19. In the current year, taxpayer A, age 61, withdrew $9,000 from his IRA, after which the account balance was $26,000. A has made $1,500 of unrecovered nondeductible contributions to the IRA. The nontaxable portion of the withdrawal is $386, computed as follows:

$$\frac{\$1,500 \text{ (nondeductible contributions)}}{\$26,000 + \$9,000 \text{ (account balance before withdrawal)}} \times \$9,000 \text{ withdrawal} = \$386$$

For subsequent years, A's unrecovered nondeductible contributions are $1,114 ($1,500 − $386).

One of the more common reasons for establishing an IRA is for the purpose of *rolling over* a lump sum distribution from a qualified retirement plan. However, a taxpayer who chooses to roll over a lump sum distribution foregoes the right to use any beneficial capital gain or forward averaging rules for computing the tax on the distribution when it is withdrawn from the IRA.

---

[65] § 408(c).   [66] § 408(d).

EXCESS CONTRIBUTIONS

The earnings generated by contributions into an IRA are tax deferred. Therefore, taxpayers might be tempted to contribute amounts in excess of the contribution limits so that the excess contribution could yield tax-free income. Unfortunately, a 6 percent penalty tax is imposed on any excess contribution left in an IRA after the close of the taxable year.[67]

SIMPLIFIED EMPLOYEE PENSIONS

The concept of a Simplified Employee Pension (SEP) was added to the law in 1978 to provide employers with a way to avoid the fearsome complexities involved in establishing and maintaining a qualified retirement plan. By following the relatively simple rules of § 408(k), which are designed to prevent discrimination in favor of the prohibited group, an employer may establish a SEP. This qualified plan allows the employer to make contributions directly into an employee's existing IRA, thereby avoiding the necessity of a qualified trust.

The annual limit on SEP contributions is the lesser of 15 percent of employee compensation or $30,000. Employer contributions to a SEP are excludable from an employee's gross income.[68]

Exhibit 18-2
Comparison of Maximum Annual Contribution to Qualified Retirement Plans

Plan Type:	Maximum Annual Contribution:
Defined benefit (pension) plan	Actuarially determined amount to fund an annual retirement benefit limited to the *lesser* of (1) $90,000 indexed for inflation or (2) 100% average earnings for the employee's three highest compensation years
Defined contribution profit sharing plan	The *lesser* of (1) $30,000 or (2) 25% of the employee's annual compensation
Section 401(k) salary-reduction plan	$7,000 indexed for inflation
Keogh plan for a self-employed individual	20% of net earnings from self-employment
Individual Retirement Account	The *lesser* of (1) $2,000 or (2) 100% compensation (deductibility depends upon "active participant" status and A.G.I.)
Simplified Employee Pension	The *lesser* of (1) $30,000 or (2) 15% of employee compensation

[67] § 4973. [68] § 402(h).

TAX PLANNING CONSIDERATIONS

The area of employment compensation and retirement planning offers tremendous opportunity for creative tax planning. During a taxpayer's productive years, he or she needs to be able to analyze and appreciate the tax consequences of the various types of compensation alternatives that may be offered. The taxpayer must be aware of the tradeoff between types of compensation that will be taxed currently and fringe benefits that may not be taxable upon receipt. Sophisticated forms of compensation such as § 83 property and incentive stock options should be considered in designing a specialized compensation package.

Taxpayers should also appreciate the necessity for long-range retirement planning. An understanding of the different tax consequences of qualified and non-qualified retirement plans is essential to effective planning for post employment years. The variety of tax-sheltered plans available today and the awesome legal complexities involved in establishing and maintaining such plans should prompt taxpayers to use tax advisers who can aid in designing the optimal plan for each individual's future.

PROBLEM MATERIALS

DISCUSSION QUESTIONS

18-1 *Taxation of Barter Transactions.* Your friend who is a practicing dentist tells you that he filled a tooth for a friend's child "for no payment" because the friend had prepared the dentist's income tax return for the previous year. Must the dentist recognize taxable income because of this arrangement? Explain.

18-2 *Taxation of Fringe Benefits.* Define the term *fringe benefit.* As a general rule are fringe benefits taxable?

18-3 *Taxation of Fringe Benefits.* Every year, Employer E gives each employee the choice of a turkey or ham as a Christmas "gift." Is the value of this fringe benefit taxable to the employees? Would your answer be different if each employee received a Christmas bonus of $500 cash?

18-4 *Fringe Benefits—Cafeteria Plans.* What is a cafeteria plan of employee benefits?

18-5 *Reasons for Stock Options.* How does a corporation benefit from compensating valuable employees with shares of stock in the corporation rather than a cash wage or salary?

18-6 *Receipt of Restricted Property for Services.* What factors should a taxpayer consider when deciding to make an election under § 83(b) with regards to restricted property?

18-7 *ISO Plans.* An ISO (incentive stock option) allows the recipient both a deferral of income and a conversion of ordinary income into capital gain. Explain.

18-8 *Funded versus Unfunded Deferred Compensation Arrangements.* Why would an employee normally prefer a funded rather than an unfunded deferred compensation arrangement? Which would the employer normally prefer?

18-9 *Deferred Compensation and the Constructive Receipt Doctrine.* Explain the doctrine of constructive receipt as it relates to a cash basis employee who has a deferred compensation arrangement with his or her employer.

18-10 *Tax Advantages of Qualified Retirement Plans.* Discuss the tax advantages granted to qualified retirement plans.

18-11 *Defined Benefit vs. Defined Contribution Plans.* Differentiate between a defined benefit retirement plan and a defined contribution retirement plan.

18-12 *Retirement Plan Qualification Requirements.* Any employee of Trion Ltd. Partnership can participate in the company's pension plan after they have been employed by Trion for 36 consecutive months. Can Trion's plan be a qualified retirement plan? Discuss.

18-13 *The Meaning of Vested Benefits.* Explain the concept of vesting as it relates to qualified retirement plans. How does it differ from the concept of participation?

18-14 *Profit Sharing Plans versus Pension Plans.* Many small, developing companies will choose to establish a qualified profit sharing plan rather than a pension plan. Why?

18-15 *Spousal IRAs.* Discuss the purpose of a spousal IRA (individual retirement account).

18-16 *Lump Sum Distribution Rollovers.* Why might an employee who receives a lump sum distribution from a qualified retirement plan choose to roll over the distribution into an IRA? What are the negative tax consequences of doing so?

PROBLEMS

18-17 *Receipt of Restricted Property for Services.* D, a calendar year taxpayer, is an employee of M Corporation, also on a calendar year for tax purposes. In 1991 M Corporation transfers 100 shares of its own common stock to D as a bonus for his outstanding work during the year. If D quits his job with M within the next three years, he must return the shares to the corporation. At date of transfer, the shares are selling on the open market at $35 per share. Three years later, when the risk of forfeiture lapses, the stock is selling at $100 per share.

    a.   Assume D does not make the election under § 83(b). How much income must he recognize in 1991 because of his receipt of the stock? In 1994 when his restriction lapses?

    b.   Assume D does elect under § 83(b). How much income must he recognize in 1991? In 1994?

    c.   Refer to questions (a) and (b). In each case how much of a deduction may M Corporation claim and in which year should the deduction be taken?

18-18 *Tax Consequences of a Nonqualified Stock Option Plan.* In 1991 Z Corporation grants a nonqualified stock option to employee M. The option allows M to purchase 100 shares of Z Corporation stock for $20 per share at any time during the next four years. Because the current market value of Z stock is $22 per share, the option has a readily ascertainable value of $200 ($2 per share bargain element × 100 shares) at date of grant. M exercises the option in 1993 when the market value of the Z stock has increased to $28 per share.

    a.   How much income does M recognize in 1991 because of the receipt of the option?

    b.   How much income does M recognize in 1993 upon exercise of the option?

    c.   What amount of deduction is available to Corporation Z because of the option granted to M? In what year is the deduction claimed?

18-19   *Tax Consequences of a Nonqualified Stock Option Plan.*   In 1991 X Corporation grants a nonqualified stock option to E, a valued employee, as additional compensation. The option has no value at date of grant, but entitles E to purchase 1,000 shares of X stock for $20 per share at any time during the next five years. E exercises the option in 1993, when X Corporation's stock is selling on the open market at $48 per share.

    a.   How much income does E recognize in 1991 because of her receipt of the option?

    b.   How much income does E recognize in 1993 upon exercise of the option?

    c.   What amount of deduction is available to X Corporation because of the option granted to E? In what year is the deduction claimed?

18-20   *Nonqualified Stock Option Plans.*   Refer to the facts in Problems 18-18 and 18-19. In each case, what tax basis does the employee have in the purchased corporate stock?

18-21   *Incentive Stock Options (ISO) versus Nonqualified Stock Options.*   Refer to the facts in Problem 18-19. If the stock option issued by X corporation had been an ISO rather than a nonqualified option, how much income would E recognize in 1993 upon option exercise?

18-22   *Incentive Stock Option Plans.*   In May 1990 employee N exercised an ISO that entitled him to purchase 50 shares of Clay Corporation common stock for $120 a share. The stock was selling on the open market for $210 per share. N sold the 50 shares in 1993 for $390 per share.

    a.   How much income must N recognize in 1990 upon exercise of the option?

    b.   How much income must N recognize in 1993 upon sale of the Clay stock?

18-23   *Incentive Stock Options—Early Disposition of Stock.*   Refer to the facts in Problem 18-22. What would be the tax consequences if N sold the Clay stock in August 1990 for $250 per share? For $190 per share?

18-24   *Tax Computation on Lump Sum Distributions.*   T participated in his employer's qualified profit sharing plan from 1980 until his retirement at age 64 in the current year. T made no contributions to the plan. In the current year, T received a lump sum distribution of $75,000 from the plan.

    a.   How much of the distribution is taxable to T in the current year?

    b.   Assuming T is single with no dependents, does not itemize deductions, and has only $13,000 of other taxable income, use the five-year forward averaging method to compute his current year tax liability.

18-25   *Tax Computation on Lump Sum Distributions.* In the current year, Mrs. Z, age 61, retired after a 35-year career with the same corporate employer. She received her entire $51,000 account balance from her employer's qualified profit-sharing plan. In the current year, Mrs. Z and her husband will file a joint return on which they will report $21,000 of other taxable income (net of all deductions and exemptions). If Mrs. Z elects five-year averaging, compute the tax liability on the joint return.

18-26 *Qualified Pension Plan—Maximum Annual Benefits.* During his last three years as president of R Corporation, G was paid $200,000, $230,000, and $280,000 as total compensation for his services. These were the three highest compensation years of his employment. What is the maximum retirement benefit payable to G from the corporation's qualified pension plan?

18-27 *Qualified Profit-Sharing Plans—Maximum Annual Contribution.* In the current year, Mr. W, a corporate vice-president, earned a base salary of $350,000. His corporate employer maintains a qualified retirement plan that provides for an annual contribution equal to 10 percent of each employee's base level of compensation. Based on these facts, compute the maximum current year contribution to Mr. W's retirement account.

18-28 *Additional Taxes on Plan Distributions.* In the current year, Mr. L, age 51 and in perfect health, resigns as President of Meta Industries, Inc. Mr. L receives a $300,000 lump sum distribution from Meta's qualified retirement plan. Before consideration of this distribution, Mr. L's taxable income for the year is over $200,000. If Mr. L decides not to "roll over" the contribution into another qualified plan or IRA, compute the net after-tax amount of the distribution that Mr. L will be able to spend.

18-29 *Maximum Annual Contributions to Keogh Plans.* H is a self-employed businessman with several employees. He has established a profit sharing plan for himself and his employees. The annual net earned income from his business is $132,000. What is the maximum amount of a deduction available to H for his contribution to the plan for the year?

18-30 *Maximum Annual Contributions to IRAs.* H and W file a joint tax return. W is a lawyer with current year earned income of $65,000. H works part-time as a landscape architect and earned $22,000 in the current year.

    a. Assume that W is an active participant in the firm's qualified profit sharing plan. How much may W and H contribute to their IRAs for the current year? How much of the contribution is deductible?

    b. Assume neither H nor W is an active participant in a qualified retirement plan. How does this assumption change your answers to (a) above?

18-31 *Maximum Deductible Contributions to IRAs.* In the current year, Ms. A, a single taxpayer, contributed $1,400 to her IRA. She also is an active participant in her employer's qualified money purchase pension plan. Ms. A's adjusted gross income (before any deduction for her IRA contribution) is $29,640. How much of the IRA contribution is deductible?

18-32 *Taxability of IRA Distributions.* Taxpayer B, age 66, makes his first withdrawal of $8,800 from his IRA in the current year and uses the money to make a downpayment on a sailboat. At the end of the year, B's IRA balance is $36,555. During previous years, B had made nondeductible contributions to the IRA totalling $13,400. Based on these facts, what amount of the $8,800 withdrawal must B include in current year gross income?

18-33 *Simplified Employee Pensions.* Z is an employee of a company that has established a SEP. Z's current year salary is $18,000.

    a. How much may Z's employer contribute to her IRA during the current year?

    b. May Z make any additional deductible contribution herself to her IRA?

RESEARCH PROBLEM

18-34   *Current vs. Deferred Compensation.*   Roy Hartman is a 55-year-old executive of the Robco Oil Tool Corporation. The corporation does not have any type of qualified pension or profit sharing plan, nor does it intend to adopt one in the near future. However, in an effort to ensure the continuing services of Mr. Hartman, Robco Corporation has offered him a choice between two different compensation arrangements. One pays $40,000 additional annual salary; and the other provides for $50,000 a year deferred compensation for 10 years beginning when Roy retires at age 65. Currently, Hartman's marginal tax rate is 28 percent. Roy does not expect to be in a lower tax bracket within his last 10 years of employment or after retirement. Since he does not need the $28,800 which would remain after paying current taxes on the $40,000 additional annual salary, Mr. Hartman asks you to evaluate his alternative compensation proposals. Assuming a 10 percent pre-tax return on savings will prevail over the entire 20 year period (10 years before and 10 years after retirement), and assuming that he would save the entire $28,800 annual after-tax salary under the $40,000 additional annual compensation arrangement, which alternative would you recommend? Why?

PART VII

CORPORATE TAXATION

CONTENTS

LEARNING OBJECTIVES

Upon completion of this chapter you will be able to:

- Define a corporation for Federal income tax purposes

- Compare and contrast corporate and individual taxation

- Compute the corporate income tax, including the tax for personal service corporations

- Describe the corporate tax forms and filing requirements

- Explain the basic tax consequences of forming a new corporation, including

  - Determination of the gain or loss recognized by the shareholders and the corporation

  - Determination of the basis of the shareholder's stock in the corporation and the corporation's basis in the property received

- Describe the requirements for qualifying a transfer to a corporation for tax-free treatment

- Understand the effects of transferring liabilities to an existing corporation

CHAPTER OUTLINE

Chapter 19

CORPORATIONS
Formation and Operation

INTRODUCTION

As discussed in Chapter 3, there are several types of taxable entities. The individual taxpayer has already been discussed at length. Various aspects of the corporate entity are covered in this chapter and the next two chapters. S corporations, partnerships, and fiduciaries are covered in later chapters.

WHAT IS A CORPORATION?

A corporation is an artificial "person" created under state law. The state may impose restrictions on the issuance of shares and the type of business conducted. The state also specifies the requirements for incorporation, such as the filing of articles of incorporation, the issuance of a corporate charter, and the payment of various fees (e.g., franchise taxes).

However, whether or not an entity meets the state's requirements as a corporation does not always govern its tax treatment. Congress stated in the Internal Revenue Code that "the term *corporation* includes associations, joint-stock companies, and insurance companies."[1] This broad definition has resulted in entities being taxed as corporations even though they are not considered corporations under applicable state law. It is also possible that an entity classified as a corporation under state law will not be taxed as a corporation for Federal income tax purposes.

---

[1] § 7701(a)(3).

ASSOCIATIONS

As mentioned above, an *association* is considered to be a corporation for Federal tax purposes. The Regulations define associations in terms of their corporate characteristics.[2] These characteristics, which are common to most corporations, are

1. Associates

2. A profit motive

3. Continuity of life

4. Centralized management

5. Limited liability

6. Free transferability of interests

In testing an entity to see if it is an association (and is therefore taxed as a corporation), the presence or absence of the above characteristics is considered. Because all business forms possess a profit motive, and all business organizations other than sole proprietorships have more than one owner (associates), an organization will be treated as an association if it possesses a *majority* of the remaining four corporate characteristics. If it does not possess a majority of these characteristics, it is taxed as either a partnership or a trust.

> **Example 1.**   Twenty persons form an organization in order to invest in real estate (associates). Their agreement states that the organization has a life of 24 years and that no member can dissolve the organization before that time (continuity of life). The organization is to be managed by five members elected by all the members (centralized management). Under local law, each member is personally liable for the organization's debts (there is *no* limited liability). The members may sell their interests in the organization (there is free transferability of interests). This organization has the following corporate characteristics not common to all business organizations:
>
> 1. Continuity of life
>
> 2. Centralized management
>
> 3. Free transferability of interests
>
> Since the organization has a majority of the four corporate characteristics not common to all business forms (3 out of 4), it may be treated as a corporation for Federal tax purposes *even though it is not a corporation under state law.*

---

[2]   Reg. § 301.7701-2.

SHAM CORPORATIONS

In some instances the IRS will ignore the fact that an entity is considered a corporation as defined by its state law. This may happen when a corporation's only purpose is to reduce taxes of its owners or to hold title to property. If the corporation has no real business or economic function, or if it conducts no activities, it may be a "sham" or "dummy" corporation.[3] Generally, as long as there is a business activity carried on, a corporation will be considered a separate taxable entity.[4]

> **Example 2.** M owns a piece of real estate. In order to protect it from his creditors, M forms X Corporation and transfers the land to it in exchange for all of X Corporation's stock. The only purpose of X Corporation is to hold title to the real estate, and X Corporation conducts no other business activities. It is properly incorporated under state law. The IRS, however, is likely to designate X Corporation as a sham corporation and to disregard its corporate status. Any income and expenses of X Corporation will be considered as belonging to M.
>
> If X Corporation had conducted some business activities (such as leasing the property and collecting rents), it is likely that it would not have been considered to be a sham corporation.

Generally the IRS, but not the taxpayer, is allowed to disregard the status of a corporation. The courts have frequently agreed that if a taxpayer has created a corporation, he or she should not be allowed to ignore its status (i.e., in order to reduce taxes). However, the Supreme Court recently ruled that a taxpayer could use a corporate entity as the taxpayer's agent in securing financing.[5] Thus, under certain conditions, taxpayers may use a corporation for a business purpose and not have it treated as a corporation for Federal tax purposes.

COMPARISON OF CORPORATE AND INDIVIDUAL INCOME TAXATION

A corporation's taxable income is computed by subtracting various deductions from its gross income. Although this appears to be the same basic computation as for individual taxpayers, there are numerous important differences. In order to highlight these differences, Exhibits 19-1 and 19-2 contain the tax formulas for corporate and individual taxpayers.

---

[3] See *Higgins v. Smith*, 40-1 USTC ¶9160, 23 AFTR 800, 308 U.S. 473 (USSC, 1940).

[4] *Moline Properties, Inc.*, 43-1 USTC ¶9464, 30 AFTR 1291, 319 U.S. 436 (USSC, 1943).

[5] *Jesse C. Bollinger*, 88-1 USTC ¶9233, 61 AFTR2d 88-793, 108 S. Ct. 1173 (USSC, 1988). See also *Joseph A. Roccaforte, Jr.*, 77 T.C. 263 (1981), and *Florenz R. Ourisman*, 82 T.C. 171 (1984).

Exhibit 19-1
Tax Formula for Corporate Taxpayers

Income (from whatever source)..	$xxx,xxx
Less: Exclusions from gross income...........................	− xx,xxx
Gross Income..	$xxx,xxx
Less: Deductions...	− xx,xxx
Taxable Income..	$xxx,xxx
Applicable tax rates...	xx%
Gross tax...	$xx,xxx
Less: Tax credits and prepayments...........................	− x,xxx
Tax due (or refund)...	$xx,xxx

Exhibit 19-2
Tax Formula for Individual Taxpayers

Total income (from whatever source).............		$xxx,xxx
Less: Exclusions from gross income.............		− xx,xxx
Gross Income......................................		$xxx,xxx
Less: Deductions **for** adjusted		
gross income..........................		− xx,xx
Adjusted gross income		$xxx,xxx
Less: 1. The larger of		
a. Standard deduction..................	$x,xxx	
or	*or*	− x,xxx
b. Total itemized deductions............	$x,xxx	
2. Number of personal and		
dependency exemptions		
× exemption amount...................		− x,xxx
Taxable income		$xxx,xxx
Applicable tax rates		
(from Tables or Schedules X, Y, or Z)..........		xx%
Gross tax..		$ xx,xxx
Less: Tax credits and prepayments.............		− x,xxx
Tax due (or refund)		$ xx,xxx

GROSS INCOME

The definition of gross income is the same for both corporations and individuals.[6] However, there are some differences in the exclusions from gross income. For example, capital contributions to a corporation (i.e., purchase of corporate stock by shareholders) are excluded from gross income.[7]

DEDUCTIONS

Corporations have no "Adjusted Gross Income." Thus, for corporations there are no "deductions for A.G.I." or "deductions from A.G.I." All corporate expenditures are either deductible or not deductible. All allowable deductions are subtracted from gross income in arriving at taxable income.

Corporations are considered to be "persons" only in a legal sense and are *not* entitled to the following "personal" deductions that are available for individuals:

1. Personal and dependency exemptions

2. Standard deduction

3. Itemized deductions

All activities of a corporation are considered to be business activities. Therefore, corporations usually deduct all their losses since they are considered business losses.[8] In addition, corporations do not have to reduce their casualty losses by either the $100 statutory floor or by 10 percent of adjusted gross income. (Corporations have no A.G.I., as mentioned.)

Corporations do not have "nonbusiness" bad debts, since all activities are considered business activities. All bad debts of a corporation are business bad debts.[9]

Several deductions are available only for corporations.[10] These are deductible in addition to the other business deductions and include the dividends-received deduction and the amortization of organizational expenditures.

DIVIDENDS-RECEIVED DEDUCTION

No doubt the most salient tax aspect of operating a business in the corporate form is that double taxation occurs when corporate profits are distributed in the form of dividends to the shareholders. The corporation is not allowed a deduction for the dividends paid, and an individual shareholder is not entitled to an exclusion.

---

[6] § 61(a).

[7] § 118(a).

[8] § 165(a). Like individuals, certain corporations are subject to the passive loss rules discussed in Chapter 12.

[9] § 166.

[10] § 241.

Therefore, when one corporation is a shareholder in another corporation, *triple* taxation might occur. To prevent this, Congress provided corporations with a deduction for dividends received.[11]

Generally, the dividends-received deduction (DRD) is 70 percent of the dividends received from taxable domestic (U.S.) corporations.[12] However, a corporation that owns at least 20 percent—but less than 80 percent—of the dividend paying corporation's stock is allowed to deduct *80* percent of the dividends received.[13] In addition, members of an *affiliated group* are allowed to deduct 100 percent of the dividends that are received from another member of the same group. A group of corporations is considered affiliated when at least 80 percent of the stock of each corporation is owned by other members of the group.[14]

Taxable Income Limitation. The 70 percent dividends-received deduction may not exceed 70 percent of the corporation's taxable income computed without the deduction for dividends received, net operating loss carryovers, and capital loss carrybacks.[15] However, if the dividends-received deduction adds to *or* creates a net operating loss for the current year, the 70 percent of taxable income limitation does not apply.

Like the dividends-received deduction percentage, the taxable income limitation percentage becomes *80* rather than 70 percent if the dividend-paying corporation is at least 20 percent owned by the recipient corporation. In the unlikely event a corporation receives dividends subject to *both* the 70 and 80 percent rules, a special procedure must be followed. First, the 80 percent limitation is applied by treating the "70 percent dividends" as other income. The 70 percent limitation is then applied by treating the "80 percent dividends" as if they had not been received.[16]

Exhibit 19-3 contains a format for the computation of the 70 percent dividends-received deduction, and *Examples 3, 4,* and *5* illustrate this computational procedure.[17]

Example 3. R Corporation has the following items of revenue and expenses for the year:

Dividends received from domestic corporations	$40,000
Revenue from sales	60,000
Cost of goods sold and operating expenses	54,000

---

[11] §§ 243 through 246.

[12] § 243(a)(1).

[13] § 243(c).

[14] §§ 243(a)(3), 243(b)(5), and 1504.

[15] § 246(b)(2).

[16] § 246(b)(3).

[17] To apply the 80 percent rules, simply substitute 80 for 70 percent in this exhibit and accompanying examples.

Exhibit 19-3
*Computation of Corporate
Dividends-Received Deduction*

Step 1:   Multiply the dividends received from taxable domestic (U.S.) corporations by 70 percent. This is the *tentative* dividends-received
deduction (DRD).

Step 2:   Compute the tentative taxable income for the current year, using
the *tentative* DRD (from Step 1):

      Total revenues (including dividend income)
        Less: Total expenses
      Equals: Taxable income (before DRD)
        Less: Tentative DRD (Step 1)
      Equals: Tentative taxable income (loss)

    If the tentative taxable income is *positive*, the taxable income
limitation may apply. Go to step 3.

    If the tentative taxable income is *negative*, there is no taxable
income limitation. The dividends-received deduction is the amount
computed in Step 1.

Step 3:   Compute the taxable income income limitation:

Taxable income (before DRD) (Step 2)
      Add: Any net operating loss carryovers from other years
               that are reflected in taxable income.
      Add: Any capital loss carrybacks from later years that
               are reflected in taxable income.
Equals: Taxable income, as adjusted
   Multiply by 70 percent
Equals: Taxable income limitation

Step 4:   Compare the tentative DRD (Step 1) to the taxable income limitation (Step 3). Choose the *smaller* amount. This is the corporate
dividends-received deduction.

The dividends-received deduction is computed as follows:

Step 1:
$40,000   dividends-received
× 70%
$28,000   *tentative* DRD

Step 2:

Dividend income	$ 40,000
Revenue from sales	+ 60,000
Total revenues	$100,000
Less: Total expenses	− 54,000
Taxable income (before DRD)	$ 46,000
Less: Tentative DRD	− 28,000
Tentative taxable income	$ 18,000

Since tentative taxable income is *positive*, the taxable income limitation may apply. Go to Step 3.

Step 3:
Compute the taxable income limitation:

Taxable income (before DRD)	$ 46,000
Multiply by 70 percent	× 70%
Taxable income limitation	$ 32,200

Step 4:
Compare the tentative DRD ($28,000) to the taxable income limitation ($32,200). Choose the *smaller* amount ($28,000). In this case, R Corporation's dividends-received deduction is $28,000 (not subject to limitation).

Example 4.   Assume the same facts as in *Example 3* except that the revenue from sales is $50,000. The dividends-received deduction is computed as follows:

Step 1:
$40,000   dividends-received
× 70%
$28,000   *tentative* DRD

Step 2:

Dividend income	$ 40,000
Revenue from sales	+ 50,000
Total revenues	$ 90,000
Less: Total expenses	− 54,000
Taxable income (before DRD)	$ 36,000
Less: Tentative DRD (Step 1)	− 28,000
Tentative taxable income	$ 8,000

Since tentative taxable income is *positive*, the taxable income limitation may apply. Go to Step 3.

Step 3: Compute the taxable income limitation:

Taxable income (before DRD)		$ 36,000
Multiply by 70%................................	×	70%
Taxable income limitation.........................		$ 25,200

Step 4: Compare the tentative DRD ($28,000) to the taxable income limitation ($25,200). Choose the smaller amount ($25,200). In this case, R Corporation's dividends-received deduction is $25,200 (limited to 70% of taxable income).

Example 5. Assume the same facts as in *Example 3* except that the revenue from sales is $41,000. The dividends-received deduction is computed as follows:

Step 1:
$40,000 dividends-received
× 70%
$28,000 *tentative* DRD

Step 2:

Dividend income	$ 40,000
Revenue from sales.............................	+ 41,000
Total revenues..................................	$ 81,000
Less: Total expenses..........................	− 54,000
Taxable income (before DRD)	$ 27,000
Less: Tentative DRD..........................	− 28,000
Tentative taxable income	($ 1,000)

Because the tentative taxable income (loss) is *negative,* there is no taxable income limitation. The dividends-received deduction is $28,000.

The taxable income limitation discussed above *does not* apply to dividends received from affiliated corporations that are subject to the 100 percent dividends-received deductions.[18]

Other Restrictions on Dividends-Received Deduction. The dividends-received deduction will be limited if the purchase price of the stock was debt-financed or the stock was refinanced and any portion of the debt remains unpaid during the period dividends are received on that stock.[19] In taxable years before 1984, a corporation could increase its cash flow and decrease its tax liability by purchasing stock with borrowed funds. Under prior law, the interest paid on the debt was fully deductible, whereas the dividends were only partially taxable because of the dividends-received deduction. Currently, corporations must reduce the dividends-received deduction if the stock was debt-financed. The dividends-received deduction for debt-financed stock equals the 70 percent deduction multiplied by the percentage of the stock price that is *not* debt-financed.[20]

[18] § 246(b)(1).

[19] § 246A.

[20] § 246A(a)(1); 80 percent in the case of any dividends received from a 20 percent or more owned corporation.

Example 6. T Corporation purchased 100 shares of XYZ stock for $100,000. T borrowed $60,000 of the purchase price. Therefore, the corporation used $40,000 of its own funds or 40% of the purchase price. The dividends-received deduction for dividends from XYZ will be limited to 28% (70% × 40%). As T Corporation *reduces* the debt, the dividends-received deduction will increase. For instance, if T reduces the debt to $50,000 before the next dividends are received from XYZ, the dividends-received deduction *increases* to 35% (70% × 50% of stock price no longer debt-financed). When the debt is retired, the dividends-received deduction is restored to the full 70%.

The dividends-received deduction may also cause a reduction in the basis of the stock. If a corporation receives an *extraordinary dividend* within the first two years that the stock is owned, the basis of the stock must be reduced by the nontaxable portion of the extraordinary dividend.[21] An extraordinary dividend is any dividend that equals or exceeds 10 percent of taxpayer's basis of common stock, or 5 percent of the basis of preferred stock.[22] If the taxpayer can prove the fair market value of the stock, then the taxpayer can use such value instead of basis to determine if the dividend is extraordinary.

Example 7. P Corporation purchases 100 shares of Y Corporation common stock on January 1, 1991 for $100,000. On December 31, 1991, Y Corporation declares and pays a $30,000 dividend to P. Since the dividend exceeds 10% of the basis of the stock, it is an extraordinary dividend. P Corporation must reduce its basis of the Y Corporation stock by $21,000 (70% × $30,000), the amount of the dividends-received deduction.

ORGANIZATIONAL EXPENDITURES

When a corporation is formed, various expenses directly related to the organization process are incurred, such as attorneys' fees, accountants' fees, and state filing charges. Although some of the attorneys' and accountants' fees may be ordinary and necessary business expenses which do not benefit future periods (and are therefore deductible), most of these expenditures will benefit future periods and are therefore capitalized as *organizational expenditures*. These organizational expenditures are intangible assets that have value for the life of the corporation.

---

[21] § 1059(a).

[22] Amounts distributed to corporate shareholders on certain preferred stock or as part of a partial liquidation or non–pro rata redemption which are treated as dividends are also considered extraordinary dividends. See Chapter 20 for a discussion of redemptions and partial liquidations.

Generally, assets with indefinite lives may not be amortized for Federal income tax purposes. However, Congress has given corporations the option of electing to *amortize* organizational expenditures.[23] If they elect, corporations may amortize (deduct) the costs ratably over a period of not less than 60 months (i.e., 60 months or longer). The 60-month period starts in the month in which the corporation begins business.

The Regulations give the following examples of organizational expenditures:[24]

1. Legal services incident to the organization of the corporation, such as drafting the corporate charter, by-laws, minutes of organizational meetings, and terms of original stock certificates

2. Necessary accounting services

3. Expenses of temporary directors and of organizational meetings of directors or stockholders

4. Fees paid to the state of incorporation

The Regulations also give several examples of items that are *not* considered organizational expenditures, such as costs of issuing stock.[25] The costs of issuing stock are considered to be selling expenses, and therefore are reductions in the proceeds from selling the stock. They reduce stockholders' equity and do not create any tax deduction.

> **Example 8.** N Corporation was formed and began business on July 1, 1991, and incurred and paid qualifying organizational expenditures of $3,000. N Corporation has chosen to use the calendar year for tax purposes. It has also elected to amortize the organizational expenditures over 60 months. On its first tax return (1991), N Corporation's amortization deduction will be $300, computed as follows:
>
> $$\frac{\text{Organizational expenditures}}{60 \text{ months}} = \text{Amortization per month}$$
>
> $$\frac{\$3,000}{60 \text{ months}} = \$50 \text{ Amortization per month}$$
>
> $$\$50 \times 6 \text{ months in 1991 (July–December)} = \underline{\$300}$$

The amortization deduction for organizational expenditures for 1992 will be $600 ($50 per month × 12 months).

---

[23] § 248.

[25] Reg. § 1.248-1(b)(3).

[24] Reg. § 1.248-1(b)(2).

An election to amortize organizational expenditures is made by attaching a statement to the corporation's first tax return.[26] If the election is not made, the organizational expenditures may not be amortized.

A similar election is available for the organizational costs of partnerships.[27] This will be discussed in Chapter 22.

NET OPERATING LOSS

Corporations, like individuals, are entitled to deduct net operating loss carryovers in arriving at taxable income. As discussed in Chapter 8, numerous modifications are considered in computing an individual's net operating loss. However, only two modifications are considered in computing a corporation's net operating loss. These two modifications are the net operating loss deductions[28] and the dividends-received deduction.[29] Net operating loss deductions for each year are considered separately. Therefore, the net operating loss deductions for other years are omitted from the computation of the current year's net operating loss. The modification relating to the dividends-received deduction is that the 70 percent (or 80%) taxable income limitation is ignored (i.e., the dividends-received deduction is allowed in full).

A corporate net operating loss may be carried back three years and carried forward 15 years.[30] The loss is first carried back to the earliest year. Any unabsorbed loss is carried to the second prior year, then the first prior year, the first year after the loss was created, and then forward until the loss is completely used or the 15-year period expires.

A corporation may elect not to carry the loss back.[31] If a corporation makes this election, the loss would be carried forward for 15 years. No loss would be carried back. This election is irrevocable.

Example 9.   T Corporation had the following items of revenue and expense for 1991:

Revenue from operations	$42,000
Dividends received from a less than 20% owned corporation	40,000
Expenses of operations	63,000

---

[26] Reg. § 1.248-1(c).

[27] § 709.

[28] § 172(d)(1).

[29] § 172(d)(5).

[30] § 172(b)(1).

[31] § 172(b)(3)(C).

T Corporation's net operating loss for 1991 is computed as follows:

Revenue from operations............................	$42,000
Dividend income....................................	40,000
Total revenue.......................................	$82,000
Less: Total expenses.............................	− 63,000
Less: Dividends-received deduction (ignore the taxable income limitation).............	− 28,000
Net operating loss (negative taxable income)........	($ 9,000)

The 1991 net operating loss is carried back three years to 1988. If T Corporation's taxable income for 1988 is $3,000, the 1991 net operating loss is treated as follows:

1988 taxable income.................................	$3,000
Less: NOL carryback..............................	− 9,000
NOL carryover to 1989..............................	($6,000)

A corporate net operating loss is carried back by filing either Form 1120X (Amended U.S. Corporation Income Tax Return) or Form 1139 (Corporation Application for Tentative Refund). T Corporation should receive a refund of its 1988 income tax paid.

CHARITABLE CONTRIBUTIONS

A corporation's charitable contribution deduction is much more limited than the charitable contribution deductions of individuals. As with individuals, the charitable contributions must be made to qualified organizations.[32] The amount that can be deducted in any year is the amount actually donated during the year plus, *if the corporation is on the accrual basis*, any amounts that are authorized during the year by the board of directors, provided the amounts are actually paid to the charity by the 15th day of the third month following the close of the tax year.[33]

Example 10. C Corporation donated $2,000 cash to United Charities (a qualified charitable organization) on June 3, 1991. On December 20, 1991 the board of directors of C Corporation authorized a $2,500 cash donation to United Charities. This $2,500 was actually paid to United Charities on March 12, 1992. C Corporation uses the calendar year as its accounting period.

If C Corporation is a *cash basis* corporation, only the $2,000 contribution to United Charities made in 1991 may be deducted in 1991. The additional $2,500 authorized contribution may not be deducted until 1992.

---

[32] § 170(c).   [33] §§ 170(a)(1) and (2).

If C Corporation is an *accrual basis* corporation, then $4,500 ($2,000 + $2,500) may be deducted in 1991.

> *Note:*   If the $2,500 donation authorized on December 20, 1991 had been paid after March 15, 1992, the $2,500 contribution deduction would not be allowed until 1992.

Contributions of Ordinary Income Property. The amount deductible when property is contributed generally is the fair market value of the property at the time it is donated. There are, however, several exceptions to this general rule. One exception involves donations of *ordinary income property.*[34] The Regulations define ordinary income property as property that would produce a gain *other than* long-term capital gain if sold by the contributing corporation for its fair market value. The charitable contribution deduction for ordinary income property generally may not exceed the corporation's basis in the property.

> **Example 11.**   G Corporation donates some of its inventory to a church. The inventory donated is worth $5,000 and has an adjusted basis to G Corporation of $2,000. G Corporation's deduction for this contribution is $2,000, its adjusted basis in the inventory.

There is an exception that permits corporate taxpayers to claim contribution deductions in excess of the basis of the ordinary income property. A corporation is allowed to deduct its basis *plus* one-half of the unrealized appreciation in value (not to exceed twice the basis) of any inventory item donated to a qualifying charity and used solely for the care of the ill, the needy, or infants.[35] This rule also applies to the gift to a college or university of a corporation's newly manufactured scientific equipment if the donee is the original user of the property and at least 80 percent of its use will be for research or experimentation.[36] In either case, the corporation is required to obtain a written statement from the charity indicating that the use requirement has been met.

Contributions of Capital Gain Property.   As discussed in Chapter 11, there are limitations on an individual's deduction for contributions of appreciated property (property which has increased in value). In *two* situations, a corporation also is limited in the amount of deduction when appreciated long-term capital gain property is contributed.[37] The *first* situation is when tangible personal property donated to a charity is put to a use that is not related to the charity's exempt purpose. The *second* situation in which a limitation will apply is the donation of appreciated property to certain private foundations. The limitation applied in these cases is that the fair market value of the property must be reduced by the unrealized appreciation (i.e., the deduction is limited to the property's adjusted basis). For other types of capital gain property, the contributions deduction is the fair market value of the property.

---

[34]   Reg. § 1.170A-4(b)(1).

[35]   § 170(e)(3).

[36]   § 170(e)(4).

[37]   § 170(e)(1).

Example 12. L Corporation donated a painting to a university. The painting was worth $10,000 and had an adjusted basis to L Corporation of $9,000. If the painting is placed in the university for display and study by art students, this is considered a use related to the university's exempt purpose.[38] The limitation mentioned above would not apply, and L Corporation's charitable contribution deduction would be $10,000, the fair market value of the painting.

If, however, the painting is immediately sold by the university, this is considered to be a use that is not related to the university's exempt purpose. L Corporation's contribution deduction would be limited to $9,000, its basis in the painting ($10,000 fair market value − $1,000 unrealized appreciation).

Annual Deduction Limitations. In addition to the limitations based on the type of property contributed, there is a maximum annual limitation. The limitation is 10 percent of the corporation's taxable income before certain deductions.[39] The 10 percent limitation is based on taxable income without reduction for charitable contributions, the dividends-received deduction, net operating loss carrybacks, and capital loss carrybacks. Amounts contributed in excess of this limitation may be carried forward and deducted in any of the five succeeding years.[40] In no year may the total charitable contribution deduction exceed the 10 percent limitation. In years in which there is *both* a current contribution and a carryover, the current contribution is deductible first. At the end of the five-year period, any carryover not deducted expires.

Example 13. M Corporation has the following for tax year 1991:

Net income from operations	$100,000
Dividends received (subject to 70% rules)	10,000
Charitable contributions made in 1991	8,000
Charitable contribution carryforward from 1990	5,000

M Corporation's contribution deduction for 1991 is limited to $11,000, computed as follows:

Net income from operations	$100,000
Dividends received	+ 10,000
Taxable income without the charitable contribution deduction and the dividend-received deduction	$110,000
Multiply by 10% limitation	× 10%
Maximum contribution deduction for 1991	$ 11,000

---

[38] Reg. § 1.170A-4(b)(3).

[39] § 170(b)(2).

[40] § 170(d)(2).

Taxable income for the year will be $92,000, computed as follows:

Net income from operations.....................		$100,000
Dividends received..............................		+ 10,000
		$110,000
Less: Special corporate deductions:		
Charitable contributions		
(maximum).........................	$11,000	
Dividends received		
(70% of $10,000)...................	+ 7,000	
Total special deductions...............		− 18,000
M Corporation's 1991 taxable income............		$ 92,000

Example 14. Based on the facts in *Example 13*, M Corporation has a $2,000 charitable contribution carryover remaining from 1990. The first $8,000 of the $11,000 allowed deduction for 1991 is considered to be from the current year's contributions, and the $3,000 balance is from the 1990 carryover. Thus, the remaining (unused) $2,000 of the 1990 contributions must be carried over to 1992.

CAPITAL GAINS AND LOSSES

Like individuals, corporate taxpayers receive special treatment for capital gains and losses. The definition of a capital asset, the determination of holding period, and the treatment of net short-term capital gains are the same for corporations as they are for individuals. Prior to 1988, corporate taxpayers could obtain favorable treatment for their net long-term capital gains by electing to tax such gains at an alternative rate. For example, in 1986, the alternative tax rate was 28 percent while the top rate applying to ordinary income was 46 percent. Beginning in 1988, however, a corporation's net long-term capital gain is taxed in the same manner as ordinary income. Although such treatment suggests that there is no reason to distinguish capital gains and losses from ordinary income, such is not the case. Like an individual, a corporation's deduction for capital losses is limited.

Net capital losses of corporations may *only* be used to offset corporate capital gains.[41] A corporation is never permitted to reduce income from operations or investment by a capital loss. As a result, corporations may not deduct their excess capital losses for the year. Instead, a corporation may carry back the excess capital losses for three years and forward for five years,[42] and use them to offset capital gains in those years. The losses are *first* carried back three years. They may reduce the amount of capital gains reported in the earliest year. Any amount not used to offset gain in the third previous year can offset gain in the

---

[41] § 1211(a).   [42] § 1212(a).

second previous year and then the first previous year. If the sum of the capital gains reported in the three previous years is less than the capital loss, the excess is carried forward. Losses carried forward may be used to offset capital gains recognized in the succeeding five tax years. Losses unused at the end of the five-year carryforward period expire.

Example 15. B Corporation has income, gains, and losses as follows:

	1988	1989	1990	1991
Ordinary income	$100,000	$100,000	$100,000	$100,000
Net capital gain or (loss)	4,000	3,000	2,000	(10,000)
Total income	$104,000	$103,000	$102,000	$ 90,000

B reported taxable income in years 1988, 1989, and 1990 of $104,000, $103,000, and $102,000, respectively, since net capital gains are added into taxable income. In 1991, B must report $100,000 taxable income because capital losses are nondeductible. However, B Corporation is entitled to carry the net capital loss back to years 1988, 1989, and 1990 and file a claim for refund of the taxes paid on the capital gains for each year. Because the 1991 capital loss carryback ($10,000) exceeds the sum of the capital gains in the prior three years ($9,000), B has a $1,000 capital loss carryforward. This loss carryforward can be used to offset the first $1,000 of capital gains recognized in years 1992 through 1996.

Corporations treat all capital loss carrybacks and carryovers as short-term losses. At the present, this has no effect on the tax due and it is often immaterial whether the carryover is considered long-term or short-term. However, if Congress ever reinstates special treatment for corporate long-term capital gains, keeping short-term and long-term carryovers separate will once again have meaning.

SALES OF DEPRECIABLE PROPERTY

Corporations generally compute the amount of § 1245 and § 1250 ordinary income recapture on the sales of depreciable assets in the same manner as do individuals. As discussed in Chapter 17, however, Congress added Code § 291 to the tax law in 1982 with the intent of reducing the tax benefits of the accelerated cost recovery of depreciable § 1250 property available to corporate taxpayers. As a result, corporations must treat as ordinary income 20 percent of any § 1231 gain *which would have been* ordinary income if Code § 1245 rather than § 1250 had applied to the transaction. In effect, a corporation must recapture 20 percent of the straight-line depreciation claimed on residential or nonresidential realty. Similar rules apply to amortization of pollution control facilities and intangible drilling costs incurred by corporate taxpayers.

Example 16. C Corporation sells residential rental property for $500,000 in 1991. The property was purchased for $400,000 in 1986, and C claimed ACRS depreciation of $120,000. Straight-line depreciation would have been $65,000. C Corporation's depreciation recapture and § 1231 gain are computed as follows:

Step 1:	Compute realized gain:		
	Sales price............................		$500,000
	Less: Adjusted basis		
	Cost......................	$400,000	
	ACRS depreciation........	− 120,000	− 280,000
	Realized gain...........................		$220,000
Step 2:	Compute *excess* depreciation:		
	Actual depreciation..................		$120,000
	Straight-line depreciation............		− 65,000
	Excess depreciation....................		$ 55,000
Step 3:	Compute § 1250 depreciation recapture:		
	Lesser of realized gain of $220,000 or		
	Excess depreciation of $55,000		
	§ 1250 depreciation recapture.....		$ 55,000
Step 4:	Compute depreciation recapture if § 1245 applied:		
	Lesser of realized gain of $220,000 or		
	Actual depreciation of $120,000		
	Depreciation recapture if § 1245 applied......................		$120,000
Step 5:	Compute § 291 ordinary income:		
	Depreciation recapture if § 1245 applied......................		$120,000
	§ 1250 depreciation recapture..........		− 55,000
	Excess recapture potential.............		$ 65,000
	Multipled by § 291 rate..............		× 20%
	§ 291 ordinary income.................		$ 13,000
Step 6:	Characterize recognized gain:		
	§ 1250 depreciation recapture..........		$ 55,000
	Plus: § 291 ordinary income.......		+ 13,000
	Ordinary income.......................		$ 68,000
	Realized gain..........................		$220,000
	Less: Ordinary income.............		− 68,000
	§ 1231 gain............................		$152,000

TRANSACTIONS BETWEEN CORPORATIONS AND THEIR SHAREHOLDERS

As discussed in Chapter 7, no deduction is allowed for a loss incurred in a transaction between related parties.[43] A corporation may be subjected to this rule. For example, a loss on the sale of the property from a corporation to a shareholder who owns more than 50 percent of the corporation is nondeductible. In such case, the unrecognized loss must be suspended and may be used by the shareholder to offset gain when the property is sold. A corporation also may be subjected to the prohibition of deductions for *accrued* but *unpaid* expenses incurred in transactions between related parties. For example, an accrual basis corporation will be denied a deduction for accrued expenses payable to cash basis related parties *until* the amount actually is paid.[44] In calculating ownership, stock owned by family members and other entities owned by the taxpayer are included.[45] With respect to the matching of income and deduction provisions only, the Tax Reform Act of 1986 expanded the definition of a related party in the case of a *personal service corporation* to include any employee that owns any of the corporation's stock. For this purpose, a personal service corporation is one where the principal activity of the corporation is the performance of personal services *and* such services are substantially performed by employee-owners. This rule applies to firms engaged in the performance of services in the fields of health, law, engineering, architecture, accounting, actuarial science, performing arts, or consulting.

The sale of property at a *gain* between a corporation and its controlling shareholders is not affected by the disallowance rules. Instead, the gain is *reclassified* as ordinary income rather than capital or § 1231 gain if the property is depreciable by the purchaser.[46] For purposes of this rule, a controlling shareholder is defined the same as under the disallowed loss rule (i.e., more than 50% ownership).[47] In addition, sales of depreciable property between a corporation and a more than 50 percent shareholder are ineligible for the installment method.[48]

COMPUTATION OF CORPORATE INCOME TAX

Like the tax rates for individuals, corporate tax rates were significantly modified by the Tax Reform Act of 1986. For the first time since the inception of the Federal income tax, the top rate applying to corporate taxable income exceeds

---

[43] § 267(a)(1).

[44] § 267(a)(2).

[45] §§ 267(b) and (c).

[46] § 1239(a).

[47] § 1239(c).

[48] § 453(g).

the top rate imposed on an individual's taxable income. The corporate tax rates for 1988 and subsequent years are as follows:[49]

Taxable Income	Tax Rate
$ 1 – $50,000	15%
50,001 – 75,000	25
Over $75,000	34

CORPORATE SURTAX

In an effort to restrict the tax benefit of the lower graduated rates to small corporate businesses with taxable incomes of $100,000 or less, a 5 percent *surtax* is imposed on corporate taxable income in excess of $100,000, up to a maximum surtax of $11,750—the net "savings" of having the first $75,000 of corporate income taxed at the lower rates rather than at 34 percent.[50]

Example 17. L Corporation has taxable income of $120,000 for its 1991 calendar year. Its tax liability is computed as follows:

15% ×	$50,000	=	$ 7,500
25% ×	25,000	=	6,250
34% ×	45,000	=	15,300

Tax liability before surtax..	$29,050
Plus: 5% surtax on $20,000 ($120,000 – $100,000)........	+ 1,000
Total tax liability for 1991......................................	$30,050

Example 18. P Corporation has taxable income of $335,000 for its 1991 tax year. Its tax liability is computed as follows:

15% ×	$ 50,000	=	$ 7,500
25% ×	25,000	=	6,250
34% ×	260,000	=	88,400

Tax liability before surtax....................................	$102,150
Plus: 5% surtax on $235,000...........................	+ 11,750
Total tax liability for 1991...................................	$113,900

Note that the 5% surtax on the $235,000 income in excess of $100,000 completely offsets the benefit of the lower graduated tax rates of 15 and 25%. Thus corporations with taxable income of $335,000 or more will have a flat tax rate of 34% ($335,000 × 34% = $113,900).

---

[49] § 11(b).   [50] *Ibid.*

Taking the 5 percent surtax into account, a corporate tax rate schedule applicable to *most* corporations would be as follows:

Taxable Income	Tax Rate
$ 1 – $ 50,000	15%
50,001 – 75,000	25
75,001 – 100,000	34
100,001 – 335,000	39
Over $335,000	34

This rate structure is not available to so-called personal service corporations or to certain related corporations. The specific rules applicable to these corporations are discussed below.

PERSONAL SERVICE CORPORATIONS

As described earlier, a personal service corporation (PSC) is a corporation where the principal activity is the performance of services in the fields of health, law, engineering, architecture, accounting, actuarial science, the performing arts, or consulting, *and* substantially all of the stock is owned by employees, retired employees, or their estates.[51] Apparently concerned that PSCs were being used to shield income from the employee-owners' higher individual tax rates, Congress denied the benefits of the lower tax rates to such corporations for taxable years after 1987. As a result, the taxable income of a PSC is subject to a flat rate of 34 percent.[52]

ALTERNATIVE MINIMUM TAX

As discussed in Chapter 13, corporations are subject to the alternative minimum tax. This tax is computed at a 20 percent rate on alternative minimum taxable income (AMTI) in excess of $40,000.[53] The $40,000 exemption is reduced by 25 percent of the amount of AMTI in excess of $150,000.[54] Consequently, the exemption is completely eliminated for AMTI in excess of $310,000.

Corporations are required to use many of the tax preferences and adjustments that individuals use in arriving at AMTI. However, there is one very important additional adjustment for corporations. The adjustment is 75 percent of the difference between adjusted current earnings (ACE) and alternative minimum taxable income.[55] In general, adjusted current earnings will equal current earnings and profits. The adjustment will be added to taxable income in arriving at AMTI.[56]

---

[51] § 448(d)(2).

[52] § 11(b)(2). Note that a PSC is not subject to the 5 percent surtax since it does not benefit from the lower corporate tax rates.

[53] See §§ 56(a) and (b).

[54] § 55(d)(3)(A).

[55] § 56(g).

[56] See Chapter 13 for a detailed discussion of the required adjustments and tax preferences used in computing the alternative minimum tax.

TAX CREDITS

Most of the same tax credits available to individuals are also available to corporations. However, corporations are not entitled to the earned income credit, the child care credit, or the credit for the elderly.[57]

ACCOUNTING PERIODS AND METHODS

A corporation is generally allowed to choose either a calendar year or fiscal year for its reporting period.[58] However, a personal service corporation (PSC) must use a calendar year for tax purposes unless it can satisfy IRS requirements that there is a business purpose for a fiscal year.[59] Special rules apply to deductions for year-end payments made by a fiscal year PSC to its employee-owners.[60] Like PSCs, S corporations generally must use a calendar year for tax purposes.[61] Exceptions to this rule are discussed in Chapter 23.

Unlike individuals, most corporations are denied the use of the cash method of accounting for tax purposes. There are *three* basic exceptions, however. The cash method may be used by the following:

1. Corporations with average annual gross receipts of $5 million or less in all prior taxable years

2. S corporations

3. Personal service corporations[62]

CORPORATE TAX FORMS AND FILING REQUIREMENTS

Corporations are required to report their income and tax liability on Form 1120 (or on Form 1120-A for those corporations with gross receipts, total income, and total assets *all* under $250,000). Page 1 of this form contains the summary of taxable income and tax due the Federal government or the refund due the corporation. There are separate schedules for the computation of cost of goods sold, bad debt deduction, compensation of officers, dividends-received deduction, and tax computation.

In addition to the computational schedules, Form 1120 also has several schedules that contain additional information. For example, Schedule L requires the corporation to provide a balance sheet as prepared for book purposes as of the beginning and end of the year. Form 1120 also contains *two* schedules of reconciliation, Schedules M-1 and M-2.

---

[57] §§ 32 and 22.

[58] § 441.

[59] § 441(i).

[60] § 280H.

[61] § 1378(b). But see § 444 for an exception, and Chapter 23 for further discussion.

[62] § 448.

Schedule M-1	Reconciliation of Income per Books With Income per Return (This schedule does not have to be completed if the total assets on line 15, column (d), of Schedule L are less than $25,000.)

Schedule M-1 Reconciliation of Income per Books With Income per Return (This schedule does not have to be completed if the total assets on line 15, column (d), of Schedule L are less than $25,000.)

1 Net income per books . . . .
2 Federal income tax . . . .
3 Excess of capital losses over capital gains . .
4 Income subject to tax not recorded on books this year (itemize): _____
_____
5 Expenses recorded on books this year not deducted on this return (itemize):
  a Depreciation . . . $ _____
  b Contributions carryover $ _____
  c Travel and entertainment . $ _____
_____
6 Total of lines 1 through 5 . . . .

7 Income recorded on books this year not included on this return (itemize):
  a Tax-exempt interest $ _____
_____
8 Deductions on this return not charged against book income this year (itemize):
  a Depreciation . . . $ _____
  b Contributions carryover $ _____
_____
_____
9 Total of lines 7 and 8 . . . . . .
10 Income (line 28, page 1)—line 6 less line 9 .

Schedule M-1 is a reconciliation of income per books and income per tax return. Both permanent and timing differences will appear in this schedule.

Schedule M-2 reconciles opening and closing retained earnings. This schedule uses *accounting* rather than tax data. Corporations without any special transactions will show an increase in retained earnings for net income and a decrease for distributions (i.e., dividends) as the major items in Schedule M-2. The use of these schedules is illustrated in an example of a corporate tax return presented later in this chapter.

FILING REQUIREMENTS

Form 1120 is required to be filed by the 15th day of the third month following the close of the corporation's tax year.[63] As mentioned previously, a corporation is permitted to elect either a calendar or fiscal year. The decision generally is unaffected by the tax years of its shareholders.[64] The selection is made by filing the first return by the appropriate due date. For calendar year corporations, the due date is March 15. The return must be signed by an officer or other authorized person.[65]

Schedule M-2 Analysis of Unappropriated Retained Earnings per Books (line 25, Schedule L) (This schedule does not have to be completed if the total assets on line 15, column (d), of Schedule L are less than $25,000.)

1 Balance at beginning of year . . . . . .
2 Net income per books . . . .
3 Other increases (itemize): _____
_____
_____
4 Total of lines 1, 2, and 3 . . . .

5 Distributions: a Cash . . . . .
             b Stock . . . . .
             c Property . . . .
6 Other decreases (itemize): _____
_____
7 Total of lines 5 and 6 . . . .
8 Balance at end of year (line 4 less line 7)

---

[63] § 6072(b).

[64] Although a regular corporation's selection of a calendar or fiscal year is not affected by the tax years of its shareholders, a corporation electing to be treated as a conduit

(flow-through) entity under Subchapter S of the Code generally is required to use the calendar year for tax purposes. See Chapter 23 for greater details.

[65] § 6062.

Corporations may obtain an automatic six-month extension of time to file the tax return.[66] The extension only covers the return—not the tax due. The request for extension (Form 7004) must be accompanied by the full amount of estimated tax due. The extension can be terminated by the government on ten days' notice.

ESTIMATED TAX PAYMENTS

Corporations are required to file and pay estimated tax (including any estimate AMT liability).[67] The estimates are due the 15th day of the 4th, 6th, 9th, and 12th months of the tax year. For a calendar year corporation, the payment dates for estimated taxes are April 15, June 15, September 15, and December 15. One-fourth of the estimated tax due is to be paid on each payment date.

To avoid a penalty for underpayment of the estimated tax, at least 90 percent of the corporation's tax due for the year must be paid as estimated taxes. Specifically, the corporation must pay *one-fourth* of this amount—$22\frac{1}{2}$ percent (90% ÷ 4) of the tax shown on its return—by the due date of each installment.[68] However, the underpayment penalty is normally not imposed where the installment for any period is

1. At least 25 percent of the tax shown on the prior year's return (if such return was for 12 months and showed a tax liability); or

2. Equal to 90 percent or more of the tax due for each quarter based on annualized taxable income.[69]

A so-called *large* corporation—one with taxable income of $1 million or more in any of its three preceding taxable years—is not allowed to use exception (2) above *except* for its first estimated tax payment of the year.[70] In addition, a corporation whose tax liability for the year is less than $500 is not subject to the underpayment penalty.[71] If a corporation does not qualify for any of the exceptions, its underpayment penalty is computed on Form 2220.

---

[66] § 6081(b).

[67] § 6655.

[68] § 6655(b).

[69] See §§ 6655(d) and (e) for these exceptions.

[70] § 6655(d)(2). Also note that the Technical and Miscellaneous Revenue Act of 1988 requires any corporation using exception (2) for estimate payments after 1988 must make up any shortfall (i.e., from 90% to 100%) from the last quarterly payment. § 6655(e)(1).

[71] § 6655(f).

EXAMPLE OF CORPORATE TAX RETURN

The next few pages contain an illustration of a corporation's annual Federal income tax return (Form 1120). This return is based on the following information:

R Corporation is a calendar year, cash method taxpayer, which operates as a men's clothing store. John Beyond owns 100% of R Corporation's stock and is employed as the company's only officer. The corporation had the following items of income and expense for the current year:

Gross sales	$390,000
Sales returns	2,000
Inventory at beginning of year	12,000
Purchases	110,000
Inventory at end of year	14,000
Salaries and wages	
Officers	40,000
Other	15,000
Rent expenses	12,000
Interest expense	5,000
Interest income:	
Municipal bonds	700
Other	1,000
Charitable contributions	7,900
Depreciation	11,000
Dividend income	3,000
Advertising expenses	5,000
Professional fees paid	2,000
Taxes paid (state income and payroll taxes)	4,000
Premiums paid on key-man life insurance policy	4,550

R Corporation timely paid $60,000 in estimated income tax payments based on its prior year's tax liability of $59,520. All dividends received by the corporation qualify for the 70% dividends-received deduction. The corporation declared and paid dividends of $6,500 to its sole shareholder. Additional information is provided in the balance sheets in Schedule L.

R Corporation's 1991 tax liability is computed as follows:

15%	×	$ 50,000	=	$ 7,500	
25%	×	25,000	=	6,250	
34%	×	105,000	=	35,700	
Surtax 5%	×	80,000	=	4,000	
				$53,450	Tax

Note: The sample corporate tax return is shown on 1990 tax forms because the 1991 forms were not available at the publication date of this text.

Form **1120**	U.S. Corporation Income Tax Return		OMB No. 1545-0123

Department of the Treasury / Internal Revenue Service
For calendar year 1990 or tax year beginning _____, 1990, ending _____, 19____
▶ Instructions are separate. See page 1 for Paperwork Reduction Act Notice.

1990

Check if a—
A Consolidated return ☐
B Personal holding co. ☐
C Personal service corp.(as defined in Temp. Regs. sec. 1.441-4T—see Instructions) ☐

Use IRS label. Otherwise, please print or type.

Name: **R CORPORATION**
Number, street, and room or suite no. (If a P.O. box, see page 2 of Instructions.): **123 JONES AVENUE**
City or town, state, and ZIP code: **ANYWHERE, USA 98765**

D Employer identification number: **74-0987650**
E Date incorporated: **1-1-80**
F Total assets (see Specific Instructions): $ **212,300**

G Check applicable boxes: (1) ☐ Initial return (2) ☐ Final return (3) ☐ Change in address

Income

1a	Gross receipts or sales **390,000**	b Less returns and allowances **2,000**	c Bal ▶ **1c** **388,000**
2	Cost of goods sold (Schedule A, line 7)		**2** **108,000**
3	Gross profit (line 1c less line 2)		**3** **280,000**
4	Dividends (Schedule C, line 19)		**4** **3,000**
5	Interest		**5** **1,000**
6	Gross rents		**6**
7	Gross royalties		**7**
8	Capital gain net income (attach Schedule D (Form 1120))		**8**
9	Net gain or (loss) from Form 4797, Part II, line 18 (attach Form 4797)		**9**
10	Other income (see Instructions—attach schedule)		**10**
11	**Total income**—Add lines 3 through 10 ▶		**11** **284,000**

Deductions (See Instructions for limitations on deductions.)

12	Compensation of officers (Schedule E, line 4)		**12** **40,000**
13a	Salaries and wages **15,000**	b Less jobs credit **-0-** c Balance ▶	**13c** **15,000**
14	Repairs		**14**
15	Bad debts		**15**
16	Rents		**16** **12,000**
17	Taxes		**17** **4,000**
18	Interest		**18** **5,000**
19	Contributions (**see Instructions for 10% limitation**)		**19** **7,900**
20	Depreciation (attach Form 4562)	**20** **11,000**	
21	Less depreciation claimed on Schedule A and elsewhere on return	**21a** **-0-**	**21b** **11,000**
22	Depletion		**22**
23	Advertising		**23** **5,000**
24	Pension, profit-sharing, etc., plans		**24**
25	Employee benefit programs		**25**
26	Other deductions (attach schedule) **PROFESSIONAL FEES**		**26** **2,000**
27	**Total deductions**—Add lines 12 through 26 ▶		**27** **101,900**
28	Taxable income before net operating loss deduction and special deductions (line 11 less line 27)		**28** **182,100**
29	**Less: a** Net operating loss deduction (see Instructions)	**29a**	
	b Special deductions (Schedule C, line 20)	**29b** **2,100**	**29c** **2,100**

Tax and Payments

30	**Taxable income**—Line 28 less line 29c		**30** **180,000**
31	**Total tax** (Schedule J, line 10)		**31** **53,450**
32	Payments: a 1989 overpayment credited to 1990 **32a**		
	b 1990 estimated tax payments **32b** **60,000**		
	c Less 1990 refund applied for on Form 4466 **32c** ( ) d Bal ▶ **32d**		
	e Tax deposited with Form 7004 **32e**		
	f Credit from regulated investment companies (attach Form 2439) **32f**		
	g Credit for Federal tax on fuels (attach Form 4136). See Instructions **32g**		**32h** **60,000**
33	Enter any **penalty** for underpayment of estimated tax—Check ▶ ☐ if Form 2220 is attached		**33**
34	**Tax due**—If the total of lines 31 and 33 is larger than line 32h, enter amount owed		**34**
35	**Overpayment**—If line 32h is larger than the total of lines 31 and 33, enter amount overpaid		**35** **6,550**
36	Enter amount of line 35 you want: Credited to 1991 estimated tax ▶ **6,550** Refunded ▶		**36** **NONE**

Please Sign Here

Under penalties of perjury, I declare that I have examined this return, including accompanying schedules and statements, and to the best of my knowledge and belief, it is true, correct, and complete. Declaration of preparer (other than taxpayer) is based on all information of which preparer has any knowledge.

Signature of officer: **John Beyond**   Date: **3/14**   Title: **PRESIDENT**

Paid Preparer's Use Only

Preparer's signature	**Sherry L. Hartman**	Date **3/10/91**	Check if self-employed ☐	Preparer's social security number **74-2735841**
Firm's name (or yours if self-employed) and address	**ROY W. HARTMAN & DAUGHTERS** **11318 KINGSLAND BLVD. SEALY, TX**		E.I. No. ▶	ZIP code ▶ **77540**

Form 1120 (1990)   Page **2**

Schedule A   Cost of Goods Sold (See Instructions for line 2, page 1.)

1 Inventory at beginning of year	1	12,000
2 Purchases	2	110,000
3 Cost of labor	3	
4a Additional section 263A costs (see Instructions—attach schedule)	4a	
b Other costs (attach schedule)	4b	
5 **Total**—Add lines 1 through 4b	5	122,000
6 Inventory at end of year	6	14,000
7 **Cost of goods sold**—Line 5 less line 6. Enter here and on line 2, page 1.	7	108,000

8a Check all methods used for valuing closing inventory:

  (i) ☐ Cost (ii) ☑ Lower of cost or market as described in Regulations section 1.471-4 (see Instructions)

  (iii) ☐ Writedown of "subnormal" goods as described in Regulations section 1.471-2(c) (see Instructions)

  (iv) ☐ Other (Specify method used and attach explanation.) ▶ _____

  b Check if the LIFO inventory method was adopted this tax year for any goods (if checked, attach Form 970) ☐

  c If the LIFO inventory method was used for this tax year, enter percentage (or amounts) of closing inventory computed under LIFO | 8c |

  d Do the rules of section 263A (with respect to property produced or acquired for resale) apply to the corporation? ☐ Yes ☑ No

  e Was there any change in determining quantities, cost, or valuations between opening and closing inventory? If "Yes," attach explanation ☐ Yes ☑ No

Schedule C   Dividends and Special Deductions (See Instructions.)

	(a) Dividends received	(b) %	(c) Special deductions: (a) × (b)
1 Dividends from less-than-20%-owned domestic corporations that are subject to the 70% deduction (other than debt-financed stock)	3,000	70	2,100
2 Dividends from 20%-or-more-owned domestic corporations that are subject to the 80% deduction (other than debt-financed stock)		80 see Instructions	
3 Dividends on debt-financed stock of domestic and foreign corporations (section 246A)			
4 Dividends on certain preferred stock of less-than-20%-owned public utilities		41.176	
5 Dividends on certain preferred stock of 20%-or-more-owned public utilities		47.059	
6 Dividends from less-than-20%-owned foreign corporations and certain FSCs that are subject to the 70% deduction		70	
7 Dividends from 20%-or-more-owned foreign corporations and certain FSCs that are subject to the 80% deduction		80	
8 Dividends from wholly owned foreign subsidiaries subject to the 100% deduction (section 245(b))		100	
9 **Total**—Add lines 1 through 8. See Instructions for limitation			2,100
10 Dividends from domestic corporations received by a small business investment company operating under the Small Business Investment Act of 1958		100	
11 Dividends from certain FSCs that are subject to the 100% deduction (section 245(c)(1))		100	
12 Dividends from affiliated group members subject to the 100% deduction (section 243(a)(3))		100	
13 Other dividends from foreign corporations not included on lines 3, 6, 7, 8, or 11			
14 Income from controlled foreign corporations under subpart F (attach Forms 5471)			
15 Foreign dividend gross-up (section 78)			
16 IC-DISC and former DISC dividends not included on lines 1, 2, or 3 (section 246(d))			
17 Other dividends			
18 Deduction for dividends paid on certain preferred stock of public utilities (see Instructions)			
19 **Total dividends**—Add lines 1 through 17. Enter here and on line 4, page 1. ▶	3,000		

20 **Total deductions**—Add lines 9, 10, 11, 12, and 18. Enter here and on line 29b, page 1 ▶ | 2,100 |

Schedule E   Compensation of Officers (See Instructions for line 12, page 1.)

Complete Schedule E only if total receipts (line 1a, plus lines 4 through 10, of page 1, Form 1120) are $500,000 or more.

(a) Name of officer	(b) Social security number	(c) Percent of time devoted to business	(d) Common	(e) Preferred	(f) Amount of compensation
1 JOHN BEYOND, PRESIDENT	451-54-6184	100 %	%	%	40,000
714 ENDELL CIRCLE		%	%	%	
ANYWHERE, USA 78765		%	%	%	
		%	%	%	
		%	%	%	

2 Total compensation of officers

3 **Less**: Compensation of officers claimed on Schedule A and elsewhere on return ( )

4 Compensation of officers deducted on line 12, page 1   40,000

Form 1120 (1990)   Page **3**

Schedule J	**Tax Computation**

1 Check if you are a member of a controlled group (see sections 1561 and 1563) . . . . ▶ ☐

2 If the box on line 1 is checked:

  a Enter your share of the $50,000 and $25,000 taxable income bracket amounts (in that order):

    (i) |$_____| **(ii)** |$_____|

  b Enter your share of the additional 5% tax (not to exceed $11,750) ▶ |$_____|

3 Income tax (see Instructions to figure the tax). Check this box if the corporation is a qualified personal service corporation (see Instructions on page 12). ▶ ☐ . . . . | **3** | 53,450 |

4a Foreign tax credit (attach Form 1118)	**4a**		
b Possessions tax credit (attach Form 5735)	**4b**		
c Orphan drug credit (attach Form 6765)	**4c**		
d Credit for fuel produced from a nonconventional source (see Instructions)	**4d**		
e General business credit. Enter here and check which forms are attached: ☐ Form 3800 ☐ Form 3468 ☐ Form 5884 ☐ Form 6478 ☐ Form 6765 ☐ Form 8586	**4e**		
f Credit for prior year minimum tax (attach Form 8801)	**4f**		

5 Total—Add lines 4a through 4f . . . . | **5** | -0-

6 Line 3 less line 5 . . . . | **6** | 53,450

7 Personal holding company tax (attach Schedule PH (Form 1120)) . . . . . . | **7** |

8 Recapture taxes. Check if from: ☐ Form 4255 ☐ Form 8611 . . . . . | **8** |

9a Alternative minimum tax (attach Form 4626). See Instructions . . . . | **9a** |

  b Environmental tax (attach Form 4626) . . . . | **9b** |

10 Total tax—Add lines 6 through 9b. Enter here and on line 31, page 1 . . . . | **10** | 53,450

Additional Information (See General Instruction F.)

Yes | No

H Refer to the list in the Instructions and state the principal:

  (1) Business activity code no. ▶ _5651_____

  (2) Business activity ▶ _____

  (3) Product or service ▶ _____

I (1) Did the corporation at the end of the tax year own, directly or indirectly, 50% or more of the voting stock of a domestic corporation? (For rules of attribution, see section 267(c).) . | | X

  If "Yes," attach a schedule showing: (a) name, address, and identifying number; (b) percentage owned; and (c) taxable income or (loss) before NOL and special deductions of such corporation for the tax year ending with or within your tax year.

  (2) Did any individual, partnership, corporation, estate, or trust at the end of the tax year own, directly or indirectly, 50% or more of the corporation's voting stock? (For rules of attribution, see section 267(c).) If "Yes," complete (a) through (c). . . . | | X

    (a) Attach a schedule showing name, address, and identifying number.

    (b) Enter percentage owned ▶ _100 %_____

    (c) Was the owner of such voting stock a foreign person? (See Instructions.) Note: If "Yes," the corporation may have to file Form 5472 . . . . | | X

    If "Yes," enter owner's country ▶ _____

J Was the corporation a U.S. shareholder of any controlled foreign corporation? (See sections 951 and 957.). . . . . . | | X

  If "Yes," attach Form 5471 for each such corporation.

Yes | No

K At any time during the tax year, did the corporation have an interest in or a signature or other authority over a financial account in a foreign country (such as a bank account, securities account, or other financial account)? . . . . | | X

  (See General Instruction F and filing requirements for form TD F 90-22.1.)

  If "Yes," enter name of foreign country ▶ _____

L Was the corporation the grantor of, or transferor to, a foreign trust that existed during the current tax year, whether or not the corporation has any beneficial interest in it? . . . . . . | | X

  If "Yes," the corporation may have to file Forms 3520, 3520-A, or 926.

M During this tax year, did the corporation pay dividends (other than stock dividends and distributions in exchange for stock) in excess of the corporation's current and accumulated earnings and profits? (See sections 301 and 316.) . . . . | | X

  If "Yes," file Form 5452. If this is a consolidated return, answer here for parent corporation and on **Form 851**, Affiliations Schedule, for each subsidiary.

N During this tax year, did the corporation maintain any part of its accounting/tax records on a computerized system? . . . . . | | X

O Check method of accounting:

  (1) ☐ Cash FOR ALL EXCEPT GROSS PROFIT

  (2) ☐ Accrual FOR GROSS PROFIT

  (3) ☐ Other (specify) ▶ HYBRID_____

P Check this box if the corporation issued publicly offered debt instruments with original issue discount . . . . . . ☐

  If so, the corporation may have to file Form 8281.

Q Enter the amount of tax-exempt interest received or accrued during the tax year ▶ |$_____|

R Enter the number of shareholders at the end of the tax year if there were 35 or fewer shareholders ▶

Form 1120 (1990)   Page **4**

Schedule L Balance Sheets

Assets	Beginning of tax year		End of tax year	
	(a)	(b)	(c)	(d)
1 Cash		3,000		32,000
2a Trade notes and accounts receivable . . .	18,000		21,000	
b Less allowance for bad debts	(—)	18,000	(—)	21,000
3 Inventories		12,000		14,000
4 U.S. government obligations				6,500
5 Tax-exempt securities (see Instructions) .				
6 Other current assets (attach schedule) . .				
7 Loans to stockholders				
8 Mortgage and real estate loans				
9 Other investments (attach schedule) . . .		20,000		104,800
10a Buildings and other depreciable assets . .	42,000		42,000	
b Less accumulated depreciation	(5,000)	37,000	(8,000)	34,000
11a Depletable assets				
b Less accumulated depletion	( )		( )	
12 Land (net of any amortization)				
13a Intangible assets (amortizable only) . . .				
b Less accumulated amortization	( )		( )	
14 Other assets (attach schedule)				
15 Total assets		90,000		212,300
Liabilities and Stockholders' Equity				
16 Accounts payable		15,000		11,000
17 Mortgages, notes, bonds payable in less than 1 year				
18 Other current liabilities (attach schedule) .				
19 Loans from stockholders				
20 Mortgages, notes, bonds payable in 1 year or more				
21 Other liabilities (attach schedule)				
22 Capital stock: a Preferred stock . . .				
b Common stock	1,000	1,000	1,000	1,000
23 Paid-in or capital surplus		9,000		9,000
24 Retained earnings—Appropriated (attach schedule)				
25 Retained earnings—Unappropriated . . .		65,000		191,300
26 Less cost of treasury stock		( )		( )
27 Total liabilities and stockholders' equity .		90,000		212,300

Schedule M-1 Reconciliation of Income per Books With Income per Return (This schedule does not have to be completed if the total assets on line 15, column (d), of Schedule L are less than $25,000.)

1 Net income per books	132,800	7 Income recorded on books this year not included on this return (itemize):		
2 Federal income tax	53,450	a Tax-exempt interest $ _700_		
3 Excess of capital losses over capital gains . .		MUNICIPAL BONDS		700
4 Income subject to tax not recorded on books this year (itemize): _____				
_____		8 Deductions on this return not charged against book income this year (itemize):		
5 Expenses recorded on books this year not deducted on this return (itemize):		a Depreciation . . . $ 8,000		
a Depreciation . . . $ _____		b Contributions carryover $ _____		
b Contributions carryover $ _____		_____		
c Travel and entertainment . $ _____		_____		8,000
PREMIUMS PAID ON KEY-MAN LIFE INSURANCE POLICY _____	4,550	9 Total of lines 7 and 8		8,700
6 Total of lines 1 through 5	190,800	10 Income (line 28, page 1)—line 6 less line 9 .		182,100

Schedule M-2 Analysis of Unappropriated Retained Earnings per Books (line 25, Schedule L) (This schedule does not have to be completed if the total assets on line 15, column (d), of Schedule L are less than $25,000.)

1 Balance at beginning of year	65,000	5 Distributions: a Cash		6,500
2 Net income per books	132,800	b Stock		
3 Other increases (itemize): _____		c Property		
_____		6 Other decreases (itemize): _____		
_____		_____		
		7 Total of lines 5 and 6		6,500
4 Total of lines 1, 2, and 3	197,800	8 Balance at end of year (line 4 less line 7)		191,300

CORPORATE FORMATION

When a corporation is formed, property generally is transferred to the corporation and the transferors receive stock in exchange for their property. If the fair market value of the stock received is more than the transferor's adjusted basis in the property transferred, that person has a *realized gain*. Without any special provisions in the Code, this realized gain would be recognized.[72] However, Congress did not wish to prevent or discourage incorporation because of tax reasons. Moreover, this treatment was justified since the taxpayer had not "cashed in" but continued to have an interest in the property transferred. Therefore, Congress enacted Code § 351 permitting the nonrecognition of gain or loss on incorporation.

Section 351(a) provides that

> No gain or loss shall be recognized if *property* is transferred to a corporation by *one or more persons solely* in exchange for *stock* in such corporation and immediately after the exchange such person or persons are in *control* of the corporation. (Emphasis added.)

This nonrecognition treatment is mandatory and not optional. Thus, if the transferor meets all the requirements, neither gain nor loss will be recognized. Only by failure to meet the prescribed conditions will there be recognition of gain or loss.

TRANSFER OF PROPERTY

The first requirement in § 351(a) is that *property* must be transferred to a corporation. The Code states that property does not include services rendered.[73] From this it is inferred that property includes money,[74] real property, and tangible and intangible personal property.

A person who receives stock in exchange for services is required to recognize income from services rendered. In this case, the corporation is entitled to deduct the amount as an expense or capitalize it depending on the nature of services rendered.

> **Example 19.** T incorporates his grocery store. He transfers all the assets for stock. The corporation issues additional stock to S, an attorney, in payment of her fee for legal services rendered in connection with the incorporation. T has neither gain nor loss recognized. S, however, is required to report the value of the stock as income. Note that this is the economic equivalent of paying S cash for her services followed by her investment of the amount received in stock of the corporation. The corporation must capitalize the value of the stock issued to S as an organization expense.

---

[72] § 1001(c).

[73] § 351(d)(1).

[74] Rev. Rul. 69-357, 1969-1 C.B. 101.

The rule that property but not services can be transferred under § 351 is applied to persons who transfer both. Such transferors are required to allocate the stock received between the property and services transferred and report the value of the stock received for services as income. Although the shareholder who contributes services is required to report some income, he or she can count *all* of the shares received in the determination of control.

BY ONE OR MORE PERSONS

For purposes of § 351(a), the term *persons* includes individuals, trusts, estates, partnerships, associations, corporations, or any combination of these.[75] Examples of transactions that might qualify for nonrecognition under § 351 include

1. Starting a new business

2. Incorporating a business already in existence

3. The formation of a subsidiary corporation by an existing corporation

4. Additional contributions to an existing corporation by an existing shareholder or a new shareholder

SOLELY FOR STOCK

Section 351 generally applies only if the transferor receives *solely* stock in exchange for property. The stock received by the transferor must be issued by the transferee (new) corporation. This requirement ensures that nonrecognition is granted only where the transferor has a continuing interest in the assets transferred. Stock may be common or preferred, voting or non-voting, participating or nonparticipating. Stock rights and warrants are not considered stock since these represent only the right to obtain an equity interest.[76]

CONTROL

One of the conditions imposed by § 351 is that the transferors be in *control* of the corporation immediately after the transfer. Under § 368(c), control exists if the transferor(s) own at least 80 percent of the total voting power and at least 80 percent of the total number of shares of all other classes of stock.[77]

The phrase "*immediately after the exchange*" has raised several questions. The first question is *when* to measure control. Transfers by two or more transferors do not have to be simultaneous to fall under this nonrecognition provision provided the transfers are part of one transaction. Therefore, control is measured at

---

[75] Reg. § 1.351-1(a)(1).

[76] Reg. § 1.351-1(a)(1)(ii).

[77] See Rev. Rul. 59-259, 1959-2 C.B. 115, for specific rules regarding voting power.

the conclusion of the intended transaction and not after each transfer. Another question that has been raised is whether the transferor must obtain control with the transfer or simply have control afterwards. The wording of § 351(a) indicates that the transferor(s) must simply have control *after* the exchange.

> **Example 20.**   B owns all the outstanding stock of R Corporation. In the current year he transfers real estate to the corporation as an additional capital contribution. B does not receive any additional stock from the corporation. The transfer qualifies, therefore, under § 351. B has control of R Corporation *after* the transfer. He did not have to acquire control as a result of the transfer. B did not receive anything other than stock or securities, but the fact that he did not receive anything is immaterial.

The final question raised by the phrase "immediately after the exchange" concerns the *loss of control* after the transfer. Is it necessary for the transferors to maintain control of the corporation or is it sufficient if they have control momentarily? There is no specified length of time for which the transferor must maintain control. Instead, the courts have looked at whether the loss of control is an integral part of the initial transfer.[78] As long as the transaction in which control is lost is not arranged and enforceable prior to the transfer, the receipt of the corporation's stock should be nontaxable. The subsequent transfer of stock and loss of control will be considered a separate transaction.

RECEIPT OF BOOT

Although § 351(a) states that the transferor(s) may receive only stock, § 351(b) deals with the receipt of property other than stock (e.g., money). This cash and other nonqualified property is referred to as *boot*. The receipt of boot does *not* invalidate the § 351(a) nonrecognition treatment. Section 351(a) still applies to the extent that stock is received. However, any realized gain must be recognized to the extent that boot is *received* by the transferor.[79] This treatment is similar to the receipt of nonqualifying property in a like-kind (§ 1031) exchange.

The amount of gain recognized is the lesser of the realized gain or the boot received. The receipt of boot does not cause the recognition of loss.[80] The gain recognized may be either long- or short-term. The nature of the gain is determined by the property transferred to the corporation. If the property was a capital asset in the hands of the transferor, the gain is capital. If the property was ordinary income property, the gain is ordinary.

[78] *American Bantam Car Co.*, 11 T.C. 397; aff'd., 49-2 USTC ¶9471, 38 AFTR 820, 177 F.2d 513 (CA-3, 1949).

[79] § 351(b)(1).

[80] § 351(b)(2).

Example 21. T transfers land to X Corporation in return for all of the common stock and $5,000 cash. T had purchased the land three years ago as a speculative investment for $40,000. At the time of transfer, the land was worth $100,000. The stock received is worth $95,000. The corporation plans on subdividing and selling the property.

T's realized and recognized gains are computed as follows:

Value of the stock received...........................	$ 95,000
Plus: Boot (cash) received.......................	+ 5,000
Amount realized.....................................	$100,000
Less: T's adjusted basis in the land..............	− 40,000
Realized gain.......................................	$ 60,000

Gain recognized equals *lesser* of

a.	Realized gain................................	$ 60,000
	or	
b.	Boot received................................	5,000

Thus, T's recognized gain is $5,000.

The gain is a long-term capital gain because the land was a capital asset for T. The fact that the land will be inventory to the corporation is immaterial. If no boot had been received by T, no gain would have been recognized.

ASSUMPTION OF LIABILITIES

Transfers to a corporation often include the transfer of liabilities as well as assets. Normally, the relief of a liability is treated the same as if cash had been received and the liability paid off. In a transaction otherwise qualifying under § 351, such treatment would result in the taxpayer receiving boot and having to recognize gain. However, for § 351 transactions, Code § 357(a) carves out a special *exception*.

The general rule of § 357(a) states that the following items will *not* be considered *boot*:

1. The assumption of the transferor's liability by the transferee corporation

2. The transfer by the transferor of property that is subject to liability

Therefore, under the general rule, the assumption of liabilities by the transferee corporation will not cause recognition of gain.

However, there are two exceptions to this general rule. First, if the reason for the transfer of any of the liabilities is *tax avoidance*, then the total amount of the liabilities transferred will be considered as boot received.[81]

---

[81] § 357(b).

Example 22.   K transferred land to a corporation in exchange for all of its common stock, worth $85,000. The land cost $40,000 and had a fair market value of $100,000. The day before the § 351 transfer, K mortgaged the land, receiving $15,000. The corporation assumed the $15,000 mortgage. The loan and its transfer was principally entered into to avoid tax.

K's realized gain is computed as follows:

Fair market value of stock received..................	$ 85,000
Plus: Liabilities assumed by transferee corporation..............................	+ 15,000
Amount realized.....................................	$100,000
Less: Basis in land transferred...................	− 40,000
Realized gain.......................................	$ 60,000

Because the primary purpose of the transfer was tax avoidance, the liabilities assumed by the transferee corporation are treated as boot received.

Gain recognized equals *lesser* of

a.	Realized gain.......................................	$60,000
	or	
b.	Boot received.......................................	15,000

Thus, K's recognized gain is $15,000.

The second exception to the general rule concerning the assumption of liabilities operates when the amount of the liabilities transferred *exceeds* the adjusted basis of all property (including money) transferred. This situation produces a recognized gain, computed as follows:

Liabilities assumed by the transferee corporation..........		$xx,xxx
Plus:	Liabilities that transferred property is subject to..............................	+ xx,xxx
Minus:	Adjusted basis of all property transferred (by that transferor) including money........	− xx,xxx
Equals:	Recognized gain..............................	$xx,xxx

Example 23.   N transfers land to a corporation in exchange for all of its common stock (worth $60,000). N's adjusted basis in the land is $10,000 and has a fair market value of $90,000. The land is subject to a $40,000 mortgage, which the corporation assumes. N's recognized gain is computed as follows:

Liabilities assumed by transferee corporation.............	$40,000
Minus: Adjusted basis in property transferred........	− 10,000
Recognized gain.......................................	$30,000

If tax avoidance is not the motivation, and the basis of the assets equals or exceeds the amount of the liabilities, the transferor will not be treated as having received boot.

EFFECT OF § 351 ON THE
TRANSFEREE CORPORATION

Section 1032 provides that a corporation will not recognize gain or loss when it issues its own stock in exchange for money or other property. Therefore, gain or loss is not recognized by the transferee corporation in a § 351 transfer.

BASIS TO SHAREHOLDERS

Following a transfer to which § 351 applies, the transferors (shareholders) must determine the basis of the stock and property received. To preserve the gain or loss not recognized on the transfer, the shareholder's basis in any stock received is generally the same as the basis of the property transferred (i.e., a substituted basis). Technically, the basis of the stock and other property received by a shareholder is determined under § 358, computed as follows:

	Basis of property transferred............................	$xxx,xxx
Plus:	Gain recognized by transferor..................	+ x,xxx
Less:	Money received by transferor	− x,xxx
	Fair market value of any other property (except stock) received by transferor................................	− x,xxx
	Liabilities assumed by transferee corporation...................................	− xx,xxx
	Liabilities encumbering the property transferred.................................	− xx,xxx
Equals:	Shareholder's (transferor's) basis in stock received..	$xxx,xxx

If several classes of stock are received, the total basis is allocated among the several classes based on the relative fair market value of the stock. The shareholder's basis in any other property (boot) received is its fair market value.[82] The holding period of the stock will include the holding period of the assets transferred to the corporation if the transferred property would have produced a capital or § 1231 gain on sale.[83] Otherwise, the holding period starts with the date of transfer.

> **Example 24.** J owns MNO, Inc. In the current year he transfers land and building to the corporation in return for 50 shares of common stock and 10 shares of preferred stock. The corporation also assumes a mortgage of $40,000. J's adjusted basis in the land is $10,000 and $90,000 in the

---

[82] § 358(a)(2).   [83] § 1223.

building. The land and building together have a current fair market value of $200,000. The common stock has a fair market value of $120,000, and the preferred stock has a value of $40,000.

J's basis in the stock received is

Basis of property transferred............................	$100,000
Less: Liabilities assumed by transferee corporation.................................	− 40,000
J's basis in the stock received...........................	$ 60,000

The $60,000 total basis is allocated based on the relative fair market value of the stock. Thus, J's basis in each class of stock is computed as follows:

Common stock:

$$\$60{,}000 \text{ total basis } \times \frac{\$120{,}000 \text{ value of common stock}}{\$160{,}000 \text{ value of all stock}} = \$45{,}000 \text{ basis}$$

Preferred Stock:

$$\$60{,}000 \text{ total basis } \times \frac{\$40{,}000 \text{ value of preferred stock}}{\$160{,}000 \text{ value of all stock}} = \$15{,}000 \text{ basis}$$

BASIS TO TRANSFEREE CORPORATION

The transferee corporation must also determine the basis of the property it has received from the transferor(s). This is computed under § 362 as follows:

Transferor's basis in property...........................	$xx,xxx
Plus: Gain recognized to transferor on transfer......	+ x,xxx
Equals: Transferee corporation's basis in property received...................................	$xx,xxx

DEPRECIATION RECAPTURE

If the transferor has no recognized gain in a § 351 transfer, then there will be no recapture of depreciation.[84] However, the transferee corporation is responsible for recapturing depreciation when the asset is later sold or disposed of in a taxable transaction. If there is gain recognized in a § 351 transfer, the depreciation recapture provisions apply to the recognized gain.

Exhibit 19-4 contains a summary of the computations required in a § 351 transfer. A comprehensive example of § 351 transfers follows Exhibit 19-4.

---

[84] §§ 1245(b)(3) and 1250(d)(3).

Exhibit 19-4
Computations in a § 351 Transfer

Step 1: Compute the amount realized by the transferor [§ 1001(b)].

Fair market value of stock received......................				$xxx,xxx
	Plus:	Amount of money received.................	$xx,xxx	
		Fair market value of other property received................................	xx,xxx	
		Liabilities assumed by transferee corporation.............................	xx,xxx	
		Liabilities encumbering the property transferred...............................	xx,xxx	+ xx,xxx
	Less:	Amount of money given up (paid)...........	$xx,xxx	
		Expenses of transfer.......................	x,xxx	
		Liabilities assumed by the transferor........	x,xxx	
		Liabilities encumbering any property received by the transferor................	xx,xxx	− xx,xxx
	Equals:	Amount realized		$xxx,xxx

Step 2: Compute gain realized by transferor [§ 1001(a)].

Amount realized...			$xxx,xxx
	Less:	Adjusted basis in property transferred.......	− xx,xxx
	Equals:	Gain realized	$ xx,xxx

Step 3: If any *boot* was *received*, compute transferor's gain recognized [§ 351(b)].

Gain recognized equals *lesser* of

a. Gain realized,
    or
b. Boot received

If no boot was received, then there is no gain recognized by the transferor.

Exhibit 19-4 Continued

Step 4:   Compute shareholder's basis in stock
received (§ 358).

Basis of property plus any money transferred			$ xx,xxx
Plus:	Gain recognized by transferor		+ x,xxx
Less:	Money received by transferor	$ x,xxx	
	Fair market value of any other property (except stock) received by transferor	x,xxx	
	Liabilities assumed by transferee corporation	x,xxx	
	Liabilities encumbering the property transferred	x,xxx	− x,xxx
Equals:	Shareholder's (transferor's) basis in stock received		$ xx,xxx

The shareholder's basis in any other property
(boot) received is its fair market value [see
§ 358(a)(2)].

Step 5:   Compute the transferee corporation's basis in
the property transferred to it (§ 362).

Transferor's basis in property		$ xx,xxx
Plus:	Gain recognized to transferor on transfer	+ x,xxx
Equals:	Transferee corporation's basis in property received	$ xx,xxx

Example 25.   R and S pooled their assets to form a new corporation, T, Incorporated.

R transferred the following:

1. Land (adjusted basis of $54,000, fair market value of $75,000).
2. A mortgage of $52,000 which the land was subject to.
3. Cash of $7,000.

S transferred the following:

1. Patent (adjusted basis of $24,000, fair market value $31,000).

R received the following:

50 shares of T Corporation stock, fair market value*	$30,000

S received the following:

50 shares of T Corporation stock, fair market value*	$30,000
$1,000 cash	

* The value of the T Corporation stock is computed as follows:

R's investment:

Land, FMV	$75,000
Less: Mortgage	(52,000)
Cash paid	7,000

S's investment:

Patent, FMV	31,000
Less: Cash received	(1,000)
Value of T Corporation stock	$60,000

Step 1: Compute amount realized.

	R	S
FMV of stock received	$30,000	$30,000
Plus: Money received	0	1,000
Liabilities assumed by transferee corporation	52,000	0
Less: Amount of money given up.	(7,000)	0
Amount realized	$75,000	$31,000

Step 2: Compute gain realized.

	R	S
Amount realized	$75,000	$31,000
Less: Adjusted basis in property transferred	(54,000)	(24,000)
Gain realized	$21,000	$ 7,000

Step 3: Compute gain recognized.

	R	S
Gain recognized equals lesser of		
a. Gain realized............	$21,000	$ 7,000
b. Boot received	0	1,000
Gain recognized is.................	$ 0	$ 1,000

Step 4: Compute shareholder's basis in property received.

	R	S
Basis of property and money transferred ($54,000 + $7,000)..........	$61,000	$24,000
Plus: Gain recognized...........	0	1,000
Less: Money received...........	0	(1,000)
Less: Liabilities assumed by the transferee...................	(52,000)	0
Shareholder's basis in stock received	$ 9,000	$24,000

Step 5: Compute corporation's basis in property received.

	R	S
Transferor's basis in property........	$54,000	$24,000
Plus: Gain recognized to transferor on transfer...........	0	1,000
Basis in land received	$54,000	
Basis in patent received		$25,000

CAPITAL CONTRIBUTIONS

MADE BY SHAREHOLDERS

A corporation recognizes neither gain nor loss on the issuance or sale of its stock.[85] It is immaterial whether the stock is a newly authorized issue, previously unissued stock, or treasury stock that the corporation had previously acquired. If it is treasury stock that was purchased for a price different from its sale price, the difference is merely an increase or decrease in the stockholders' equity. If it is a new sale of stock, the discount or premium also is a stockholders' equity adjustment. The contingent liability associated with issuing par value stock at a discount has no counterpart in tax.[86] The sale of stock at a discount is treated as the issuance of stock for the amount received. This provision, however, does not prevent a corporation deducting as an expense the value of stock issued for services. However, no gain or loss is recognized.

---

[85] § 1032.

[86] In many states, it is *illegal* for a corporation to issue its own stock below par value.

The provision against recognizing gain or loss afforded a corporation applies only to the issuance or sale of the corporation's own stock. Sale or exchange of stock in another corporation will be treated as any other sale or exchange of an asset. The difference between cost and sale price will produce realized gain or loss. This realized gain or loss will be recognized unless the transaction comes under the involuntary conversion or like-kind exchange nonrecognition provisions, or unless it qualifies as a tax-free corporate reorganization.[87] This general rule applies to stock acquired as a short-term investment as well as stock in related corporations.

In addition to the exclusion of gain or loss on the issuance of stock, contributions to capital are excluded from the corporation's income.[88] This exclusion applies to contributions from shareholders and nonshareholders. Although nonshareholder contributions are not as frequent as shareholder contributions, communities occasionally donate land and/or buildings in return for the relocation of a corporation's facilities.

MADE BY NONSHAREHOLDERS

There are special rules for contributions by nonshareholders.[89] Property contributed by a nonshareholder will have a *zero* basis. This prevents a corporation from obtaining a tax deduction either through depreciation or expense for the property. The provision was placed in the law because the value of the property is not treated as income to the corporation. This provision also guarantees that any amount received by the corporation upon sale of the property will be a taxable gain. The exclusion from income applies only to the receipt of property by the corporation as a contribution to capital, however.

If the property received by the corporation is money, the above rule does not apply. It is impossible to assign a zero basis to cash. Instead, the corporation is required to reduce the basis of property purchased using the cash by the amount of the contribution.[90] If the corporation does not acquire property with the contributed cash within 12 months, it is required to reduce the basis of property it already owns by the amount of the contribution.

---

[87] See §§ 354 and 361.

[88] § 118.

[89] § 362(c)(1).

[90] § 362(c)(2).

PROBLEM MATERIALS

DISCUSSION QUESTIONS

19-1 *What is a Corporation?*   Although an entity may be a corporation under state law, what characteristics must the entity possess to be treated as a corporation for Federal tax purposes? What difference will it make on the Federal tax classification if the entity possesses *all* or only a few of these characteristics?

19-2 *Disregard of Corporate Form.*   Why might the IRS try to disregard the corporate status of an entity that meets the state law requirements for a corporation? Under what circumstances might shareholders try to use the corporate form but attempt to disregard it for Federal tax purposes?

19-3 *Corporate vs. Individual Taxation.*   What are the differences in income tax treatment of corporations and individuals for the items below?

a. Dividends received
b. Classification of deductions
c. Casualty losses
d. Charitable contribution limitations
e. Capital loss deduction
f. Capital loss carryovers and carrybacks
g. Gain on sale of depreciable realty

19-4 *Dividends-Received Deduction.*   Why is a corporation allowed a dividends-received deduction? Under what circumstances is the recipient corporation allowed an 80 percent rather than the usual 70 percent dividends-received deduction?

19-5 *Limitations on Dividends-Received Deduction.*   What are the limitations imposed on a corporation's dividends-received deduction? Under what circumstances can one of these limitations be disregarded?

19-6 *Charitable Contribution Carryovers.*   Under what circumstances must a corporation carry over its qualifying contributions to subsequent years? If contributions are made in the current year and the corporation has a contribution carryover from a prior year, which contributions are deducted first? Why do you suppose Congress imposes this ordering of contribution deductions?

19-7 *Five Percent Surtax.*   Which corporations are subject to the 5 percent surtax? What is the marginal tax rate on the last dollar of taxable income of a corporation with taxable income of $170,000? What is the flat tax rate imposed on a corporation with taxable income of $335,000?

19-8 *Property Requirement of § 351.*   What constitutes property for purposes of § 351? If an individual receives stock for both property and services, what are the tax consequences?

19-9 *What are Transferring Persons?*   What types of entities are "persons" for purposes of § 351? When might such "person" or "persons" make use of the § 351 nonrecognition provision?

19-10 *Solely for Stock.* What is considered stock for purposes of § 351? Why do you suppose Congress imposes as a requirement for nonrecognition treatment the receipt of only stock by the transferor?

19-11 *Control Requirement.* What is the control requirement for purposes of § 351? What is the meaning of the term "immediately" when used to qualify the control requirement?

19-12 *Taxable § 351 Transfers.* Under what circumstances may a transferor be subject to gain recognition even though his or her transfer is subject to § 351?

19-13 *Transfer of Liabilities.* Unlike Code § 1031 transactions (like-kind exchanges), the transfer (discharge) of a liability generally is not treated as boot for purposes of Code § 351. Explain.

19-14 *Transfer of Liabilities and Tax Avoidance.* A transferor is considering whether to receive some cash in addition to stock when she transfers appreciated property to a corporation, or to mortgage the property for a similar amount of money and then transfer the property and the liability to the corporation. What difference will either alternative make?

19-15 *Basis of Stock Received.* How does a shareholder determine basis in stock received in a § 351 transfer? If both common stock and preferred stock are received, how is basis in each determined?

19-16 *Corporation's Basis.* What is the corporation's basis in property received in a § 351 transfer? If due to his current tax situation a transferor will not incur additional income taxes on any gain recognized, would it benefit the corporation to have a partially taxable § 351 transfer? Explain.

19-17 *Depreciation Recapture.* How do the depreciation recapture rules (i.e., §§ 1245, 1250, and 291) apply to a § 351 transfer?

PROBLEMS

19-18 *Comparison of Corporate vs. Individual Taxation.* In each of the situations below, explain the tax consequences if taxpayer T were either a corporation or a single individual.

   a. For the current year, T has gross income of $60,000, including $10,000 dividends from Ford Motor Company. Without regard to taxable income, how much of the dividend income will be subject to tax?

   b. During the current year, T sustains a total loss of an asset. The asset was valued at $2,000 shortly before the loss and had an adjusted basis of $2,700. If the casualty loss were incurred by T as an individual, it would be a personal rather than business loss. Without regard to any taxable income limitation, what is the measure of the casualty loss deduction?

   c. During 1991, T had $8,000 of long-term capital gains and $3,000 of short-term capital gains. During 1990, the only prior year with capital asset transactions, T had a short-term capital loss of $6,000. How much of T's 1991 gross income will consist of capital gains?

    d.   T's taxable income for 1991, before any deduction for charitable contributions, is $50,000. If T were an individual, adjusted gross income would be $60,000. If T made cash contributions of $40,000 during the year, what is the maximum amount that could be claimed as a deduction for 1991?

19-19   *Dividends-Received Deduction.*   K Corporation has the following items of revenue and expense for the current year:

Sales revenue, net of returns...........................	$100,000
Cost of sales..	30,000
Operating expenses....................................	40,000
Dividends (subject to 70% rules).......................	20,000

    a.   What is K Corporation's dividends-received deduction for the current year?

    b.   Assuming that K Corporation's operating expenses were $72,000 instead of $40,000, what is its dividends-received deduction for the current year?

19-20   *Dividends-Received Deduction.*   During 1991, R Corporation (a cash method, calendar year taxpayer) has the following income and expenses:

Revenue from operations................................	$170,000
Operating expenses.....................................	178,000
Dividends (subject to 70% rules)........................	40,000

    a.   What is R Corporation's 1991 dividends-received deduction?

    b.   Assuming R Corporation's 1991 tax year has not yet closed, what would be the effect on its dividends-received deduction if R accelerated to 1991 $5,000 of operating expenses planned for 1992?

19-21   *Organizational Expenditures.*   G Corporation incurred and paid $4,800 of qualifying organizational expenditures in 1991. Assuming G Corporation makes an election under § 248 to amortize these costs, what is the maximum amount that may be deducted for each of the following years if G Corporation adopts a calendar tax year?

    a.   For 1991, during which G Corporation began business on September 1?

    b.   Calendar year 1992?

    c.   Calendar year 1996?

19-22   *Charitable Contributions Deductions.*   T Corporation has the following for tax year 1991:

Net income from operations...............................	$600,000
Dividends received (subject to 70% rules).................	100,000

    a.   What is T Corporation's maximum charitable contribution deduction for 1991?

    b.   Assuming T Corporation made charitable contributions of $68,000 during 1991 and had a $10,000 charitable contribution carryover from 1990, how much of its 1990 contributions will be carried over to 1992?

19-23   *Computation of Corporate Tax Liability.*   L Corporation had taxable income of $150,000 for 1991. What is L Corporation's 1991 income tax liability before credits or prepayments?

19-24   *Corporate Tax Computation.*   T Corporation had the following items of income for its calendar year 1991:

Net income from operations...............................	$150,000
Dividends received (subject to 70% rules).................	10,000
Charitable contributions....................................	30,000
Net operating loss carryover from 1990....................	30,000
Long-term capital gains....................................	8,000
Long-term capital losses..................................	6,000
Short-term capital gains...................................	3,000
Capital loss carryover from 1990..........................	9,000

    a.   Compute T Corporation's 1991 income tax liability before credits or prepayments.

    b.   What is the nature and amount of any carryovers to 1992?

19-25   *Corporate Formation.*   Individuals J and R form the JR Corporation. J transfers land with a basis of $50,000 and a fair market value of $100,000. R transfers all the depreciable property from his former business, which has a basis of $80,000 and a fair market value of $70,000. In order to be an equal shareholder, R also transfers cash of $30,000 to the corporation. J and R each receive 100 shares of JR Corporation stock.

    a.   What is J's realized gain or loss? Recognized gain or loss?

    b.   What is R's realized gain or loss? Recognized gain or loss?

    c.   What basis will J have in the JR Corporation stock?

    d.   What basis will JR Corporation have in the land?

    e.   What basis will R have in the JR Corporation stock?

    f.   What basis will JR Corporation have in the depreciable property?

19-26   *Corporate Formation.*   Individuals K, L, and M form the KLM Corporation. K transfers land with a basis of $30,000, with fair market value of $100,000, and which is subject to a $20,000 mortgage in exchange for 80 shares of KLM common stock. L transfers $50,000 cash and equipment with a basis of $25,000 and fair market value of $40,000 in exchange for 90 shares of KLM common stock. M transfers $18,000 cash and renders services incident to the organization of KLM Corporation in exchange for 30 shares of its common stock.

Net of the mortgage transferred by K and assumed by the corporation, KLM issued 188 shares of common stock in exchange for money and other property with a net fair market value of $188,000 [$80,000 from K ($100,000 fair market value of land − $20,000 mortgage) + $90,000 from L ($50,000 cash + $40,000 fair market value of equipment) + $18,000 cash from M]. The additional 12 shares of common stock issued to M were in exchange for services.

a.   What is K's realized and recognized gain?
b.   What basis will K have in the KLM stock?
c.   What basis will KLM Corporation have in the land?
d.   How much gain must L recognize?
e.   What basis will L have in the KLM stock?
f.   What basis will KLM Corporation have in the equipment?
g.   How much income, if any, must M recognize?
h.   What basis will M have in the KLM stock?
i.   Assume that KLM Corporation incurred and paid $600 of organizational costs, in addition to its payment of stock in exchange for M's services incident to organization. If the corporation begins business on October 1, 1991, adopts a calendar tax year, and elects to amortize its organizational expenditures over 60 months, what amount can KLM Corporation amortize for 1991?

19-27   *Transfer of Liabilities.*   Each of the transfers below qualify as a § 351 transaction, and in each case the transferee corporation assumes liabilities involved in the transfer. For each transfer, compute the transferor shareholder's recognized gain, the transferor's basis in any stock or securities received, and the transferee corporation's basis in any property received.

a.   T transfers land with a basis of $60,000 and subject to a mortgage of $20,000 in exchange for stock worth $55,000.
b.   A transfers machinery with a basis of $4,000 and subject to a mortgage of $9,000 in exchange for stock worth $6,000. The $9,000 mortgage was created two weeks before the transfer and A used the loan proceeds to take her husband on a vacation trip to Europe.
c.   Assume the same facts in (b) except that the $9,000 liability is the balance remaining on a five-year $40,000 mortgage loan created to acquire the machinery transferred to A.
d.   X transfers equipment with a basis of $30,000 and subject to a liability of $10,000 in exchange for stock worth $80,000 and a $20,000 security (bond) maturing in 10 years and paying 15 percent interest annually.

RESEARCH PROBLEMS

19-28   *Corporate Formation.*   T, an individual taxpayer, plans to incorporate his farming and ranching activities currently operated as a sole proprietorship. His primary purpose of incorporating is to transfer a portion of his ownership in land to his son and daughter. T believes that gifts of stock rather than land will keep his business intact. T's current thought is to incorporate and immediately transfer 40 percent of the corporate stock to his two children. In fact, he has promised his children that he would make the stock gifts as soon as the corporation is created. What potential tax problems might result if T pursues his current plans? Would it make any difference if T received all voting stock and had the new corporation transfer nonvoting stock to the children?

Research Aid:

   Rev. Rul. 59-259, 1959-2 C.B. 115

19-29   *Admission of New Shareholder.*   RST Corporation is currently owned by three individuals, R, S, and T. The corporation has a net worth of $300,000 and has 500 shares (1,000 shares authorized) of common stock outstanding. R owns 200 shares (40%), and S and T each own 150 shares (30%). Individual E owns land worth $90,000 which the corporation could use as a new plant site. However, E is not interested in selling the land now because it would result in a large capital gain tax. E is willing to transfer the land to the corporation in exchange for 60 shares of its common stock or securities of equivalent value, but only if the transfer will be nontaxable. How would you advise the parties to structure the transaction?

Research aids:

   Rev. Rul. 73-472, 1973-2 C.B. 115.
   Rev. Proc. 76-22, 1976-1 C.B. 562.
   Reg. § 1.351-1(a)(1)(ii).

COMPUTERIZED TAX ANALYSIS

19-30 *Corporate Net Operating Loss Carryovers.* Use computer file T1901 for this exercise.

    a.   Compute the present value of the tax savings from the net operating loss carryovers for the table below:

	After-tax discount rates				
	0%	5%	10%	15%	20%
Carryback/carryforward options:					
1. Carry back 3 years and forward 15 years	_____	_____	_____	_____	_____
2. Carry forward 15 years	_____	_____	_____	_____	_____

    b.   Why does the present value of the tax savings from the net operating loss *carryback* (option 1) remain constant regardless of the discount rate?

    c.   Why is the second option (carry forward) better for the taxpayer than the first option when the discount rate is 0? Refer to the corporation's tax bracket levels in your answer.

    d.   Why does the carryforward option become sub-optimal as the discount rate rises?

LEARNING OBJECTIVES

Upon completion of this chapter you will be able to:

- Determine the tax consequences of dividend distributions to shareholders and the distributing corporation

- Compute a corporation's earnings and profits

- Identify the more common types of constructive dividends

- Explain the tax consequences of taxable and nontaxable stock dividends

- Define a redemption and distinguish it from other types of nonliquidating distributions

- Explain the tax consequences of a redemption to a shareholder and the distributing corporation

- Define a liquidation and determine its tax consequences to shareholders and the liquidating corporation

- Discuss the special rules that apply when a corporation liquidates a subsidiary

CHAPTER OUTLINE

Chapter 20

CORPORATE DISTRIBUTIONS, REDEMPTIONS, AND LIQUIDATIONS

INTRODUCTION

The life cycle of a corporation starts with its formation. This is followed by a period of operation and growth. During the growth stage, the corporation generally makes distributions to its shareholders, called *dividends*. Shareholders not only expect to receive dividends, but also expect their stock to appreciate in value. Following the growth phase, the corporation enters a period of maturity. In the maturity stage profits may stabilize, but eventually business may start to decline. A decline may force the corporation to redeem stock, reorganize, or possibly liquidate.

This chapter deals with the Federal income tax aspects of corporate dividends, redemptions of stock, and liquidations as they relate to both the shareholders and the corporations.

DIVIDENDS

A distribution by a corporation of cash or property to a shareholder is income to the shareholder to the extent it is a *dividend*.[1] A dividend is defined as a distribution by a corporation out of either its accumulated earnings and profits since 1913 (the inception of corporate income tax) or its earnings and profits for the current year.[2] If the distribution exceeds the corporation's earnings and profits, the excess is treated as a nontaxable reduction of the shareholder's basis in his or her stock. If the distribution exceeds both the corporation's earnings and profits and the shareholder's adjusted basis in his or her stock, the excess is treated as a gain on the sale of the shareholder's stock.

---

[1] § 301.

[2] § 316(a).

Example 1. J purchased 100 shares of M Corporation common stock on January 1, 1985 for $1,000. On February 3, 1991, M Corporation distributed to J $5,000 with respect to its stock, of which $2,300 is a dividend. (The amount of M Corporation's earnings and profits allocable to J is $2,300.) J is required to include this $2,300 of dividend income in gross income. The remaining $2,700 is applied first to reduce the $1,000 basis of J's stock to zero, and the rest ($1,700) is treated as a gain on the sale of his stock. It will be a long-term capital gain since he has held the stock for more than one year. J still has the 100 shares of stock, but his basis is reduced to zero.

EARNINGS AND PROFITS

The term *earnings and profits* (also referred to as "E&P") is not defined in either the Internal Revenue Code or the Regulations. Instead, the effect of certain transactions on earnings and profits is described.[3] From an examination of these transactions, however, it is possible to create a general definition of earnings and profits. Basically, corporate earnings and profits equal taxable income *increased* by nontaxable income and *decreased* by nondeductible expenses. Although earnings and profits are similar to retained earnings as used in financial accounting, there are often significant differences between the two. These differences are caused by differences in the treatment of various items (e.g., stock dividends) for financial accounting purposes as opposed to the items' tax treatment. Therefore, the computation of earnings and profits should be completely independent of any computation of retained earnings.

As mentioned previously, earnings and profits generally consist of taxable income plus nontaxable income minus nondeductible expenses. Exhibit 20-1 contains a partial list of the adjustments that must be made to determine earnings and profits for a taxable year.

Although most are self-explanatory, several items in Exhibit 20-1 require further clarification. For example, while there is an adjustment for tax-exempt interest income, there is no adjustment for the portion of a gain that is realized but not recognized in a like-kind exchange. A gain on the sale of assets affects earnings and profits only to the extent that the gain is recognized.[4]

Depreciation. The use of accelerated depreciation is not permitted in computing earnings and profits.[5] The corporation generally must use the straight-line method. However, depreciation for E&P purposes must be computed under the Alternative Depreciation System (ADS), using the straight-line method and the property's class life. Since taxable income reflects any accelerated methods used, an adjustment in determining earnings and profits is to add to taxable income the excess of the accelerated depreciation over straight-line.

---

[3] § 312.

[4] § 312(f)(1).

[5] § 312(k)(1).

Example 2. N Corporation uses the 150% declining balance method to compute the depreciation on its warehouse. (Assume that all other assets are depreciated using the straight-line method and that there are no other adjustments to earnings and profits.) The depreciation claimed on the warehouse for the current year (1991) was $7,350. Straight-line depreciation using ADS on the warehouse would have been $5,000. N Corporation's taxable income for 1991 was $19,000. Earnings and profits for 1991 are computed as follows:

Taxable income for 1991......................		$19,000
Plus: Excess of accelerated over straight-line depreciation:		
Accelerated depreciation.............	$7,350	
Straight-line depreciation............	(5,000)	+ 2,350
Earnings and profits for 1991..................		$21,350

Code § 179 Expense. If a corporation has elected the immediate expensing option of § 179, E&P adjustments are made for the year in which the asset is expensed and also for the four following years.[6] The effect of a § 179 election on earnings and profits is that the amount expensed is an earnings and profits deduction in equal installments over the five-year period.

Example 3. X Corporation elected to expense a $5,000 asset under § 179 in 1991. X Corporation's taxable income for 1991 was $20,000. Although the entire $5,000 deduction is reflected in X Corporation's taxable income, the amount that affects E&P is $1,000 per year for five years. Therefore, taxable income must be adjusted as follows (assume there are no other adjustments to earnings and profits):

1991 Taxable income	$20,000
Plus: $4/5$ of immediate expensing deduction ($4/5$ of $5,000)	4,000
1991 Earnings and profits.................................	$24,000

In 1992 through 1995, $1,000 per year ($1/5$ of the 1990 immediate expensing deduction) is subtracted when computing E&P.

Adjustments to More Accurately Reflect Income. Over the years, Congress has required additional adjustments to be made in the computation of a corporation's earnings and profits in an attempt to have E&P more accurately reflect the corporation's current economic gain or loss.[7] One of the most important of these adjustments affects corporations using the LIFO method of inventory valuation. These firms must adjust E&P for the *difference* between the inventory as valued by LIFO and the value the inventory would have if FIFO had been used.[8]

---

[6] § 312(k)(3)(B).

[7] § 312(n).

[8] § 312(n)(5).

Exhibit 20-1
*Partial List of Adjustments Used
in Computing Current Earnings and Profits*

Taxable Income

Plus:

Tax-exempt interest income
Deferred gain on installment sales
Dividends-received deduction
Excess of accelerated depreciation over straight-line depreciation
Excess of ACRS depreciation over straight-line depreciation
  [§ 312(k)(3)]
Excess of LIFO cost of goods sold over FIFO cost of goods sold
Four-fifths ($^4/_5$) of deduction for immediate expensing of assets under § 179
  taken during the current year [§ 312(k)(3)(B)]
Excess of depletion taken over cost depletion
Increases in cash surrender value of life insurance when the cor-
  poration is the beneficiary (directly or indirectly)
Proceeds of life insurance when the corporation is the beneficiary
  (directly or indirectly)
Net operating loss deductions carried over from other years
Federal income tax refunds
Recoveries of bad debts and other deductions, but only if they are
  not included in taxable income under the tax benefit doctrine
Income based on the percentage-of-completion rather than the completed
  contract method
In the year they are reflected in taxable income: charitable contribu-
  tion carryovers, capital loss carryovers, and other timing differences
  (since they reduced E&P in the year that they originated)

Minus:

    Federal income taxes
    Nondeductible expenses:
        Penalties and fines
        Payments to public officials not reflected in taxable income
        Expenses between related parties not deductible under § 267
        Interest expense related to the production of tax-exempt income
        Life insurance premiums when the corporation is the beneficiary
          (directly or indirectly)
        Travel, entertainment, and gift expenses that do not meet the
          substantiation requirements of § 247(d)
        Other expenses disallowed to the corporation as the result
          of an IRS audit
    Nondeductible losses between related parties under § 267
    Charitable contributions in excess of the 10 percent limitation
    Excess capital losses for the year that are not deductible
    Gains on sales of depreciable property to the extent that accelerated
      depreciation or ACRS exceeds the straight-line depreciation method
      used for computing increases in E&P
    Gains on sales of depletable property to the extent that depletion taken
      exceeds cost depletion
    One-fifth ($^{1}/_{5}$) of any immediate expensing deduction under § 179 taken
      during the previous four years [§ 312(k)(3)(B)]
    Foreign taxes paid that have been treated as credits on the corpora-
      tion's tax return

Equals: ***Current Earnings and Profits***

Note: This exhibit does not include the effect of corporate distributions and dividends on E&P, which is discussed later in the
chapter.

Another similar adjustment applies to corporations that use the installment method for any asset sale. The corporation's E&P must include the full amount of the gain in the year of sale as if the corporation had not used the installment method.[9]

DISTRIBUTIONS FROM EARNINGS AND PROFITS

A special approach has been designed for determining whether a distribution is made out of E&P and therefore treated as a dividend. This approach treats E&P as consisting of two distinctly separate pools of earnings from which distributions may be made: current E&P and accumulated E&P. Using this approach, the law creates a presumption that any distribution made during the year is deemed to come *first* from any current E&P that may exist.[10] If distributions during the year *exceed* current E&P, the distribution is treated as having been paid from any accumulated E&P. Note that under this "two-pot" process, it is possible for a distribution to be a taxable dividend out of current E&P even though the corporation has a deficit in accumulated E&P that, in fact, exceeds current E&P. In addition, a distribution may be treated as a taxable dividend even though it is distributed at a time during the year when the firm had a current loss. This result can occur because current E&P is computed at the close of the taxable year, without reduction for any distributions.

> **Example 4.** T Corporation distributed $10,000 cash on February 1 and $10,000 on November 1. The corporation has $25,000 of current earnings and profits and $15,000 of accumulated earnings and profits. The entire $20,000 distributed is a taxable dividend from current earnings and profits, since distributions are considered to come first from current earnings and profits and then from accumulated earnings and profits.

> **Example 5.** Assume the same facts as in *Example 4* except that there is a deficit in accumulated earnings and profits of $15,000. The $20,000 distributed is still a taxable dividend since there are current earnings and profits of $25,000. Accumulated earnings and profits will still have a deficit of $15,000.

> **Example 6.** R Corporation made a $15,000 distribution to its shareholders on December 31. R Corporation has $3,000 earnings and profits for the current year and $18,000 accumulated earnings and profits. The entire $15,000 distribution is a taxable dividend. Accumulated earnings and profits are reduced to $3,000 as a result of the distribution.

---

[9]   § 312(n)(6).   [10]   Reg. § 1.316-2(a).

In applying this basic scheme to determine whether a distribution is in fact a dividend, the following additional rules must be observed:[11]

1. Current E&P is allocated among *all* distributions made during the year on a pro rata basis, as follows:

$$\frac{\text{Amount of the distribution}}{\text{Total current distributions}} \times \frac{\text{Amount of}}{\text{current E\&P}} = \frac{\text{Distribution's share}}{\text{of current E\&P}}$$

Example 7.   During the current year, P Corporation distributed $12,000 to its shareholders on March 1 and another $12,000 to its shareholders on October 1. Current E&P was only $10,000. Each distribution would be treated as consisting of $5,000 of current E&P [($12,000 ÷ $24,000) × $10,000]. The balance of each distribution would be deemed to come from any accumulated E&P that may exist at the time of the distribution.

2. Accumulated E&P is allocated among distributions made during the year in *chronological* order.

Example 8.   Same facts as in *Example 7*. In addition, the corporation had accumulated E&P of $7,000. Earnings and profits are allocated as follows:

	$12,000 March Distribution	$12,000 October Distribution	Total
Current earnings and profits [allocated pro rata to all distributions: ($12,000 ÷ $24,000) × $10,000 current E&P = $5,000]	$5,000	$5,000	$10,000
Accumulated earnings and profits (allocated in chronological order: first to the March distribution and then to the October distribution)............................	7,000	0	7,000
Taxable dividend.........................	$12,000	$5,000	$17,000

The entire amount of the March distribution ($12,000) is a taxable dividend, but only $5,000 of the October distribution is a taxable dividend to the shareholders. The remaining $7,000 of the October distribution is a return of capital to the shareholders and will first be applied to reduce their bases in their stock. Any amount in excess of their stock bases will be treated as a gain from the sale of their stock.

---

[11]   Reg. § 1.316-2.

This allocation process becomes especially important if there is a change of ownership during the year, since each shareholder is concerned with how much of each distribution he or she receives is taxable as dividends. However, the *total* amount of taxable dividends is not affected by the allocations.

3. If there is a deficit in current E&P for the year (e.g., a current operating loss), it is treated as occurring *ratably* during the year (unless it can be shown that the loss did not occur evenly during the year).[12] Accordingly, the loss is allocated on a daily basis against any accumulated E&P.

Example 9. T Corporation distributed $10,000 to its shareholders on February 1 and $10,000 to its shareholders on October 1. T Corporation had a $6,000 loss for its current calendar tax year and accumulated earnings and profits from prior years of $20,000. The $6,000 loss is assumed to have occurred evenly throughout the year (assume $500 per month). The tax treatment of the distributions is determined as follows:

February Distribution: Since there are no current earnings and profits, the distribution is presumed to come from accumulated earnings and profits. Accumulated earnings and profits as of February 1 are considered to be $19,500 [$20,000 − $500 (one month of the current loss)]. The entire February distribution of $10,000 is a taxable dividend since accumulated earnings and profits are applied chronologically.

The balance in accumulated earnings and profits after the February distribution is $9,500 ($20,000 − $500 − $10,000).

October distribution: Since there are no current earnings and profits, the next step is to look at accumulated earnings and profits. Accumulated earnings and profits as of October 1 are $5,500 [$9,500 remaining after the February 1 distribution − $4,000 (8 months of current loss @ $500 per month) from February through September]. Therefore, $5,500 of the October distribution is a taxable dividend to the shareholders. The remaining $4,500 is a return of capital to the shareholders. After the October 1 distribution, the balance in accumulated earnings and profits is zero.

At the end of the year, the balance in accumulated earnings and profits is a deficit of $1,500 (the remaining 3 months of current loss at $500 per month).

---

[12]   *Ibid.*

CASH DIVIDENDS

Shareholders are required to include in income the amount of any distribution that is a dividend. If the distribution is cash, the amount of the distribution is simply the amount of the cash. As demonstrated in the above examples, earnings and profits are reduced by the amount of the cash distribution, but not below zero.[13]

PROPERTY DIVIDENDS

Corporations make distributions of property as well as distributions of cash. Code § 317(a) defines property as "money, securities, and any other property," but excludes from the definition stock and stock rights in the distributing corporation. Special rules must be followed when a property distribution is made. Basically, the thrust of the property distribution rules is to treat the corporation and shareholders as if the corporation had sold the property and distributed to the shareholders the cash proceeds from the sale.

Code § 311 provides that a corporation must recognize gain—*but not loss*—upon the distribution of property other than its own obligations.[14] Thus, when a corporation distributes property that has a value exceeding its basis, gain must be recognized. In contrast, a corporation is not allowed to recognize loss on a distribution of property whose value is less than its basis. This rule prohibits a corporation and its shareholders from circumventing the gain recognition requirement by distributing loss property that would offset the gain on appreciated property. When the corporation distributes appreciated property and recognizes gain, its E&P is first increased by the gain and then reduced by the fair market value of the property distributed.[15] In contrast, if the corporation distributes depreciated property, no loss is recognized and the corporation decreases its E&P by the basis of the property distributed.[16]

The Code provides a somewhat intricate set of rules governing the treatment of shareholders who receive property distributions. In light of changes made in 1986, however, the thrust of these rules is quite straightforward. Both corporate and noncorporate shareholders that receive a distribution of property report the *fair market value* of the property as a dividend to the extent it is out of the corporation's E&P.[17] The shareholder's basis in the property is also its fair market value.[18]

> **Example 10.** P Corporation distributed land worth $100,000 (basis $20,000) and equipment worth $30,000 (basis $45,000) to its sole shareholder, individual X. The corporation must recognize the $80,000

---

[13] § 312(a)(1).

[14] §§ 311(a) and (b).

[15] § 312(b).

[16] § 312(a)(3).

[17] §§ 301(b)(1)(A) and (B).

[18] § 301(d).

($100,000 − $20,000) gain realized on the distribution of the land. Although P also realizes a loss on the distribution of the equipment, the loss is not recognized. Assuming the corporation has adequate E&P, X reports a dividend of $130,000 (the fair market values of the property, $100,000 + $30,000). X's basis in the land and equipment is $100,000 and $30,000, respectively. The net effect of the distribution on the corporation's E&P is to decrease it by $65,000 ($80,000 gain − $100,000 value of the land − $45,000 basis of the equipment).

Adjustments for Liabilities. The above discussion ignores the possibilities that the property may be distributed subject to a liability or that the shareholder may assume a liability in conjunction with the property distribution. In such case, the rules regarding the amount of the distribution and the adjustment to E&P must be modified to account for any liabilities.[19] When a liability is distributed in connection with property, the amount of the distribution is decreased by the liability. Similarly, the reduction in E&P is decreased (i.e., E&P is increased by the amount of the liability). There is no adjustment to the basis of the property to the shareholder.

CONSTRUCTIVE DIVIDENDS

In addition to actual distributions of cash and property, a shareholder can be charged with the *constructive receipt* of a dividend. For example, excessive salaries to the shareholder or a member of the shareholder's family can be treated as a dividend. The corporation is limited to deducting only those salaries that are reasonable. The amount in excess of the reasonable standard will be considered a constructive dividend. Other transactions that have given rise to constructive dividends are

1. Loans to shareholders where there is no intent to repay the amounts loaned

2. Bargain purchases and rentals of corporate property by shareholders

3. Excess payment for corporate use of shareholder property

4. Payment of shareholder's loans or expenses by the corporation

5. Personal use by shareholder of corporate assets

As indicated by the above types of transactions, constructive dividends usually arise in closely held corporations, especially those with only one or two shareholders. Constructive dividends are not planned by the corporations. They usually arise in an IRS audit as the result of lack of formality in dealing with the corporate entity and a lack of transactions at "arm's length" (for fair market value). Therefore, it is possible for a shareholder to be considered as having received a dividend even though the corporation did not declare one.

---

[19] § 301(b)(2).

As with other dividends, the corporation must have sufficient earnings and profits for a constructive dividend to be taxable to the shareholders. Also, the dividends-received deduction is available to corporate shareholders with respect to constructive dividends.

STOCK DIVIDENDS AND STOCK RIGHTS

Occasionally, a corporation may want to pay a dividend but does not have sufficient cash or property to distribute. In this situation, the corporation may declare a dividend of its stock or of rights to acquire its stock.

Stock Dividends. As a general rule, a shareholder does not have any income as the result of receiving a distribution of the distributing corporation's own stock.[20] Instead, the shareholder simply allocates the basis of his or her old stock between the old stock and the new stock. There are several exceptions to this general rule, however. If the shareholder is given a choice between receiving stock or receiving property or money, the distribution will be taxable.[21] It does not matter which form of distribution the shareholder actually selects. The ability to select makes the distribution taxable. In fact, the ability of *any* of the shareholders to select property or stock will make the distribution taxable to all of the shareholders.[22]

Another case in which a stock dividend will be taxable is if the distribution is *disproportionate*.[23] The Code defines *disproportionate* in this situation as the receipt of cash or other property by some shareholders with an increase in the proportionate interests of other shareholders in the corporation. The determination as to whether or not a distribution is disproportionate is made at the end of the distribution or series of distributions and is made based on the result of the transactions.

Distributions of preferred stock to common stockholders are covered by the general rule of nontaxability. However, a distribution or a series of distributions that results in some shareholders receiving common and others receiving preferred is a taxable transaction.[24] In addition, any distribution (e.g., common stock) to a preferred stockholder is taxable.[25] A special rule applies for distributions of convertible preferred stock. The distribution will be taxable unless it can be shown that the result will not be disproportionate[26] (see above for definition of disproportionate).

Taxable stock dividends can be either actual or deemed dividends.[27] Actual dividends require distributions of stock. Deemed-dividend transactions include changes in conversion ratios, changes in redemption price, an excess redemption price over issue price, or any other transaction that increases the proportionate

---

[20]   § 305(a).

[21]   § 305(b)(1).

[22]   Reg. § 1.305-2.

[23]   § 305(b)(2).

[24]   § 305(b)(3).

[25]   § 305(b)(4).

[26]   § 305(b)(5).

[27]   § 305(c).

ownership of one or more shareholders. Deemed dividends can be totally unintentional. For example, in a corporate reorganization the issuance of preferred stock with a redemption value greater than its current issue price is a possible taxable stock dividend.[28]

Nontaxable Stock Dividends. If the taxpayer receives a nontaxable distribution of stock, the basis of the shares received is determined by allocation. The basis of the shares upon which the dividend is received is allocated between the old stock and the new stock based on their relative fair market values at the time of distribution.[29] If the shares received are identical to the shares owned (i.e., both the old and new stock are the same class of common stock), the allocation can be accomplished simply by dividing the basis of the old stock by the total number of shares owned after the distribution. If the type of shares received differs from the shares originally owned (e.g., old stock was common stock and new stock is preferred stock), the allocation of basis between the old stock and new stock is computed based on relative fair market value. The holding period of the new stock includes the holding period of the old stock.[30]

Example 11. Q owned 100 shares of common stock of V Corporation. His basis in the V Corporation stock was $1,300 ($13 per share). Q received a stock dividend of 25 additional shares of V Corporation common stock in a nontaxable distribution. Q's $1,300 basis in the old stock is allocated between his old stock (100 shares) and his new stock (25 shares) as follows:

$$\frac{\text{Basis in old stock}}{\text{Number of shares after distribution}} = \frac{\$1,300}{125 \text{ shares}} = \underline{\$10.40} \text{ per share}$$

Q's basis in his stock is still $1,300, which is $10.40 per share, since he now has 125 values of V Corporation common stock.

Example 12. Assume the same facts as in *Example 11* except that Q received 25 shares of preferred stock instead of common stock. On the date of distribution, the fair market value of V Corporation common stock was $15 per share and the fair market value of V Corporation preferred stock was $5 per share. Q's $1,300 basis in his stock is allocated between the old stock and the new stock as follows:

Step 1: Determine fair market value of stock:

Fair market value of Q's common stock (100 shares × $15)	$1,500
Fair market value of Q's preferred stock (25 shares × $5)	125
Total fair market value of Q's stock	$1,625

---

[28] See Rev. Rul. 83-119, 1983-2 C.B. 57.

[30] § 1223(5).

[29] Reg. § 1.307-1.

Step 2: Compute basis in each type of stock based on relative fair market value:

(a) $\dfrac{\text{Fair market value of Q's common stock}}{\text{Total fair market value of Q's stock}} \times \text{Old basis} = \begin{array}{l}\text{New basis in} \\ \text{common stock}\end{array}$

$\dfrac{\$1,500}{\$1,625} \times \$1,300 = \underline{\underline{\$1,200}} \quad \begin{array}{l}\text{New basis in} \\ \text{common stock}\end{array} \quad (\$12 \text{ per share})$

(b) $\dfrac{\text{Fair market value of Q's preferred stock}}{\text{Total fair market value of Q's stock}} \times \text{Old basis} = \begin{array}{l}\text{Basis in} \\ \text{preferred stock}\end{array}$

$\dfrac{\$125}{\$1,625} \times \$1,300 = \underline{\underline{\$100}} \quad \begin{array}{l}\text{Basis in} \\ \text{preferred stock}\end{array} \quad (\$4 \text{ per share})$

A nontaxable stock dividend *does not affect* the earnings and profits of the distributing corporation.[31]

Taxable Stock Dividends. A taxable distribution of stock is treated as a property distribution. If a stock distribution is taxable, the shareholder has dividend income equal to the fair market value of the stock received.[32] The basis of the stock received is the amount of income reported (fair market value of the stock received).[33] The holding period of the shares received would start on the date of distribution. The basis of the original stock is not affected by a taxable stock dividend. Taxable stock dividends have the same effect on the earnings and profits of a corporation as property dividends.

Stock Rights. Instead of stock, corporations may distribute stock rights to their shareholders. The taxation of the receipt of stock rights is governed by the same general principles as stock dividends.[34] In determining whether the distribution is taxable, it is often easier to assume that the stock that can be acquired by exercise of the rights was distributed instead of the rights. If the distribution of the stock to which the stock rights apply would have been taxable, the rights are taxable. If a distribution of the related stock would not have been taxable, the rights are not taxable.

> **Example 13.** N Corporation had 100 shares of common stock and 100 shares of nonvoting preferred stock outstanding. The corporation distributed rights to acquire a new issue of nonvoting preferred stock to all of its existing shareholders. The common shareholders have received a nontaxable distribution, whereas the preferred shareholders have received a taxable distribution. Since the distribution of the new preferred stock to the common shareholders would have been nontaxable, the rights received by the common shareholders are nontaxable. However, since preferred shareholders receive only taxable stock dividends, the rights received by the preferred shareholders also are taxable.

---

[31] § 312(d)(1).

[32] Reg. § 1.305-1(b)(1); Code §§ 301(b) and 316(a).

[33] § 301(d).

[34] § 305(a).

Nontaxable Stock Rights. If the stock rights are not taxable, there is a basis allocation similar to the one for stock dividends.[35] The basis of the old stock is allocated between the old stock and the new rights based on the relative fair market values at the date of distribution. There is no allocation of basis to the rights if the shareholder allows them to lapse[36] (and consequently no recognized loss on the lapse of the rights). Therefore, although the allocation uses the fair market values as of the date of distribution, the actual allocation generally is not made until the rights are sold or exercised.

Example 14. T Corporation distributed nontaxable stock rights to its shareholders on January 3. C received 100 rights on the 100 shares of common stock he purchased three years ago for $1,000. On the date of distribution, T Corporation's common stock had a value of $15 per share and the rights had a value of $5 each. On March 1, C sold the rights for $7 each. The stock had a value of $17 per share on March 1. C allocates the basis of his old stock between the stock and the rights based on their relative fair market values as of January 3, the date of the distribution. The March 1 value of the stock is irrelevant. The basis allocation is computed as follows:

Step 1:   Fair market value of C's common stock (100 × $15) $1,500
Fair market value of C's stock rights (100 × $5)   500

Total fair market value of stock and stock rights $2,000

(a) $\dfrac{\text{Fair market value of C's common stock}}{\text{Total fair market value of stock and stock rights}} \times \text{Old basis}$

$= \dfrac{\$1,500}{\$2,000} \times \$1,000 = \underline{\$750}$ ($7.50 per share)

(b) $\dfrac{\text{Fair market value of C's stock rights}}{\text{Total fair market value of stock and stock rights}} \times \text{Old basis}$

$= \dfrac{\$500}{\$2,000} \times \$1,000 = \underline{\$250}$ ($2.50 per stock right)

C's gain on the sale of his stock rights is computed as follows:

Selling price of stock rights (100 × $7) $700
Less: Basis in stock rights . . . .   −250

Gain on sale of stock rights $450

Example 15. Assume the same facts as in *Example 14* except that C does not sell the stock rights, but allows them to lapse on June 1. Since the stock rights lapsed, rather than being exercised or sold, there is no basis allocated to them. C has no recognized loss (since the rights have no basis) and the basis of the old shares remains $1,000.

---

[35] § 307(a).   [36] Reg. § 1.307-1(a).

If the taxpayer sells or exercises his or her rights, basis is allocated to the rights. The holding period of the rights includes the holding period of the old stock.[37] The fair market value of stock rights is frequently small in relation to the value of the stock on which it was distributed. As a result, an allocation of basis between the old stock and the new rights would produce a very small basis in the stock rights. For this reason, there is an exception to the rule regarding allocation of basis.

If the fair market value of the stock rights is *less than* 15 percent of the value of the stock at the date of distribution, no basis is *required* to be allocated to the rights.[38] The basis of the rights is zero and the basis of the old stock remains unchanged. However, even though the basis of the rights is zero, the holding period of the rights includes the holding period of the old stock.[39] If a taxpayer wishes, he or she may elect to allocate basis to the rights even though there is no requirement to allocate basis to the rights under this 15 percent rule.[40] This election to allocate is made by filing a statement with the taxpayer's tax return for the year in which the rights are received. The election applies to all the stock rights received in the distribution and is irrevocable.

> **Example 16.** Assume the same facts as in *Example 14* except that the fair market values of the stock and rights on January 3 were $19 and $1, respectively. Since the value of the rights ($100) is less than 15% of the value of the stock (15% of $1,900 = $285), no allocation is required. C would have a $700 gain on the sale of the stock rights since their basis was zero. The gain would be long-term since the holding period of the rights includes the holding period of the stock.

> **Example 17.** Assume the same facts as in *Example 16* except that C elects to allocate basis between the stock and the stock rights. The basis of the rights is computed as follows:

$$\frac{\text{Fair market value of stock rights}}{\text{Fair market value of stock and stock rights}} \times \text{Old basis}$$

$$= \frac{(100 \text{ rights} \times \$1)}{(100 \text{ rights} \times \$1) + (100 \text{ shares} \times \$19)} \times \underline{\underline{\$1,000}} \text{ Old basis}$$

$$= \frac{\$100}{\$2,000} \times \$1,000 = \underline{\underline{\$50}} \text{ basis in stock rights}$$

In this situation, the sale of the rights for $700 would result in a $650 gain.

---

[37] § 1223(5).

[38] § 307(b)(1).

[39] § 1223(5).

[40] § 307(b)(2) and Reg. § 1.307-2.

Taxable Stock Rights. The taxable receipt of stock rights, like a taxable stock dividend, is treated as a property dividend. The shareholder would have dividend income equal to the fair market value of the rights on date of receipt.[41] The rights would have a basis equal to the fair market value[42] and the holding period starts on the date of distribution. If the rights lapse, the taxpayer will have a loss equal to the basis of the rights. Stock rights have the same effect on a corporation's earnings and profits as stock dividends.

NONDEDUCTIBILITY OF DIVIDENDS TO CORPORATION

A corporation is not permitted a deduction for distributions to its shareholders with respect to its stock. It does not matter whether the distribution is cash, property, stock, or stock rights. As mentioned in Chapter 19, this produces "double taxation." The shareholders are taxed individually on dividends (distributed corporate earnings and profits), but the distributing corporation may not take a corresponding deduction for the dividends.

STOCK REDEMPTIONS

Corporations occasionally will acquire their own shares. Sometimes the acquisition is motivated by a desire to eliminate an issue of stock. In these cases the corporation might cancel the stock after its acquisition. Alternatively, the corporation might reacquire its own shares in order to issue the shares as additional compensation to hire or retain qualified employees or to acquire additional assets or even a whole business. The stock may be kept as treasury stock until needed. Such an acquisition is called a *stock redemption*. A redemption is defined in the Code as the acquisition by a corporation of its own stock from its shareholders in exchange for cash or other property, regardless of whether the shares are cancelled, retired, or held as treasury stock.[43]

IN GENERAL

The taxation of the acquisition of the shares from an existing shareholder could take either of two forms. It could be treated as a sale of stock, with the corporation treated as an independent purchaser. This generally would result in a capital gain or loss for the shareholder. Alternatively, the sales price could be treated as a distribution. In this situation, the shareholder would have dividend income. Generally, the key factor as to whether a stock redemption is treated as a sale or a dividend distribution is whether or not the shareholder's proportionate interest in the corporation is significantly reduced.

---

[41] Reg. § 1.305-1(b)(1); Code §§ 301(b) and 316(a).

[42] § 301(d).

[43] § 317(b).

As a general rule, if a shareholder's interest is basically the same or nearly the same after a redemption, the redemption is treated as a distribution. The tax treatment is based on whether the distribution is of cash or other property. The taxability of cash and property dividends was discussed previously in this chapter.

There are *five* situations in which stock redemptions are treated as a sale by the shareholder instead of as a dividend distribution. These five situations are as follows:

1. Redemptions not equivalent to dividends [§ 302(b)(1)]

2. Substantially disproportionate redemptions of stock [§ 302(b)(2)]

3. Terminations of shareholders' interests [§ 302(b)(3)]

4. Redemptions from noncorporate shareholders in partial liquidation [§ 302(b)(4)]

5. Distributions in redemption of stock to pay death taxes (§ 303)

In the above five situations, a shareholder recognizes gain or loss equal to the difference between the redemption proceeds and the basis of the stock surrendered.

REDEMPTIONS NOT EQUIVALENT TO DIVIDENDS

The Code states that a stock redemption is treated as a sale or exchange of the shareholder's stock "if the redemption is not essentially equivalent to a dividend."[44] The Regulations refer to *dividend equivalency* as meaning that the redemption has "the same effect as a distribution without any redemption of stock."[45] Several cases have helped to further clarify this provision. The most significant litigation over this issue was *U.S. v. Davis,*[46] decided by the Supreme Court in 1970. The case involved the redemption of all of the corporation's outstanding preferred stock from the sole shareholder (directly and indirectly)[47] of the corporation. The Court ruled that the redemption was a distribution and not a sale. In reaching this decision, the Court rejected the taxpayer's argument that since there was a business purpose for the issuance and redemption of the preferred stock, the transaction was not equivalent to a dividend. Instead, the Court decided that to meet the requirement of § 302(b)(1), there must be a meaningful reduction in the shareholder's interest in the corporation. There are *no other* relevant considerations. One of the outgrowths of this decision is that no redemption

---

[44] § 302(b)(1).

[45] Reg. § 1.302-2(a).

[46] 70-1 USTC ¶9289, 25 AFTR2d 70-827, 397 U.S. 301 (USSC, 1970).

[47] The provisions regarding constructive ownership of stock are discussed later in this chapter.

from a sole shareholder will qualify as being "not equivalent to a dividend." A sole shareholder remains a 100 percent owner after *any* redemption. Therefore, there can never be a meaningful reduction in a sole shareholder's interest.

Following the decision in *Davis,* it was generally felt that the "not essentially equivalent to a dividend" exception was effectively cancelled. Subsequent litigation has shown that this is not so. Taxpayers have been successful in those cases in which they were able to convince the court that there was a meaningful reduction in their interest in the corporation. Unfortunately, no precise definition of "meaningful reduction" has emerged from the litigation. Consequently, all subsequent taxpayers must prove the significance of the reduction based on the facts and circumstances of each specific case.

When a stock redemption is determined to be essentially equivalent to a dividend, the shareholder's basis in the stock redeemed is *added* to the basis of the stock that was not redeemed.[48]

> **Example 18.** R owned 1,000 shares (100%) of the common stock of T Corporation. (T Corporation had no other classes of stock outstanding). R's basis in the stock was $20,000 ($20 per share). T Corporation redeemed 500 shares of R's common stock for $15,000. Since R owned 100% of T Corporation, *both* before and after the redemption, the redemption was essentially the same as a dividend. (There was no meaningful reduction in R's interest in the corporation.) R, therefore, has a distribution of $15,000, a taxable dividend if T Corporation has sufficient earnings and profits. R's basis of $10,000 ($20 per share) in the 500 shares redeemed is added to the basis in his remaining 500 shares. After the redemption, R's basis in his remaining 500 shares is $20,000 ($40 per share).

SUBSTANTIALLY DISPROPORTIONATE REDEMPTIONS

A stock redemption is treated as a sale if it is *substantially disproportionate.*[49] In order for a redemption to be substantially disproportionate with respect to a shareholder, the shareholder must, after the redemption, own less than 80 percent of the voting stock owned prior to the redemption and own less than 80 percent of the common stock owned prior to the redemption.[50] By requiring the shareholder's ownership of both *voting* and *common stock* to be less than 80 percent of his or her former ownership, the law prevents redemption of solely preferred stock from meeting the § 302(b)(2) requirements. Redemptions of preferred stock may qualify only if there is also a redemption of common stock. In addition to the above requirements, a shareholder is not eligible for sale or exchange treatment unless the shareholder's ownership of voting stock after the redemption is less than 50 percent of the total voting stock.[51]

---

[48] Reg. § 1.302-2(c).

[49] § 302(b)(2).

[50] § 302(b)(2)(C).

[51] § 302(b)(2)(B).

Example 19. M owned 100 shares of Q Corporation's voting common stock. M's basis in this stock was $500 ($5 per share). Q Corporation had 200 shares of common stock (its only class of stock) issued and outstanding. The corporation redeemed 40 shares of M's stock for $300. The tax treatment of the redemption is determined as follows:

Test 1:   Does M own less than 80% of the voting stock that she owned prior to the redemption?

Before the redemption M owned 50% of the voting stock. $(\frac{100}{200})$

After the redemption M owned 37.5% of the outstanding voting stock. $(\frac{60}{160})$

$$\frac{\text{M's percentage interest in the voting stock after the redemption}}{\text{M's percentage interest in the voting stock prior to the redemption}} = \frac{37.5\%}{50\%} = \underline{\underline{75\%}}$$

(Alternative Computation: 80% of 50% = 40%; therefore, Test 1 is met because 37.5% is less than 40%).

Test 2:   Does M own less than 80% of the common stock that she owned prior to the redemption? Since the voting stock in this example is the same as the common stock, Test 2 is a repetition of Test 1. Therefore, Test 2 is also met.

Test 3:   Is M's ownership of voting stock after the redemption less than 50% of the total voting stock? (This is measured in voting *power* if different classes of stock have unequal voting rights.)

$$\frac{\text{Number of shares of voting stock owned by M after the redemption}}{\text{Total number of shares of voting stock after the redemption}} = \frac{60}{160} = \underline{\underline{37.5\%}}$$

37.5% is less than 50% of the voting stock, so Test 3 is met.

(Alternative Computation: 160 shares × 50% = 80 shares; therefore, Test 3 is met since 60 shares is less than 80 shares).

All three tests must be met in order for a stock redemption to be "substantially disproportionate." Since all three tests are met in this example, the redemption of 40 shares of M's stock meets the requirements of § 302(b)(2) and is, therefore, treated as a sale or exchange of the stock. M's gain is computed as follows:

Proceeds from redemption............................	$300
Less: M's basis in the 40 shares redeemed (40 × $5)........................	(200)
Gain from redemption.................................	$100

The gain will be long-term or short-term depending on how long the stock was held.

> **Note:** All computations regarding ownership after the redemption were made using 160 shares, the number of shares outstanding after 40 of the 200 originally outstanding shares had been redeemed by Q Corporation.

Example 20. X owned 150 of the 200 outstanding shares of W Corporation's voting common stock. (W Corporation has no other classes of stock.) The corporation redeemed 100 shares of X's stock. The tax treatment of the redemption is determined as follows:

Test 1: Does X own less than 80% of the voting stock that he owned prior to the redemption?

Before the redemption X owned 75% of the voting stock. $(\dfrac{150}{200})$

After the redemption X owned 50% of the voting stock. $(\dfrac{50}{100})$

$$\dfrac{50\%}{75\%} = \underline{\underline{67\%}}$$

67% is less than 80%, so Test 1 is met.

Test 2: Does X own less than 80% of the common stock that he owned prior to the redemption? Since the voting stock in this example is the same as the common stock, Test 2 is a repetition of Test 1. Therefore, Test 2 is also met.

Test 3: Is X's ownership of voting stock after the redemption less than 50% of the total voting stock?

$$\dfrac{50\%}{100\%} = \underline{\underline{50\%}}$$

Exactly 50% is *not* less than 50%. Therefore, Test 3 is *not* met.

Because *all three tests* must be met in order for a stock redemption to be "substantially disproportionate," the redemption is treated as a distribution, not a sale. Any proceeds from the redemption are treated as a dividend to the extent of earnings and profits, and X's basis in the 100 shares redeemed is added to the basis in his remaining 50 shares.

To prevent abuses in cases of multiple redemptions, the law requires that the tests be applied at the end of the series of redemptions if the redemptions are all part of one plan. Without this limitation, it would be possible to meet the substantially disproportionate rules after each redemption while leaving the redeeming shareholders' relative interests unaffected at the close of the intended transactions.[52]

---

[52] § 302(b)(2)(D).

Example 21. A, B, and C each owned 50 shares ($^1/_3$) of F Corporation's common stock. There are no other classes of stock. On January 2, pursuant to an overall plan, the corporation redeemed 40 shares of stock from A. On February 1, pursuant to the same plan, the corporation redeemed 40 shares from B. Finally, on March 3, the corporation redeemed 40 shares from C. Independently, each redemption is disproportionate. However, combining the series, A, B, and C each end up with the same $^1/_3$ ownership of F Corporation. Consequently, the redemptions are not substantially disproportionate.

TERMINATION OF A SHAREHOLDER'S INTEREST

The third case in which a redemption can qualify as a sale is if the redemption completely terminates the shareholder's interest.[53] A *complete termination* requires the corporation to redeem all of the shares that the stockholder owns. If a shareholder is completely terminating his or her interest in a corporation in which various close relatives own stock, special rules apply to the termination of the shareholder's interest.[54] These special rules regarding constructive ownership of stock are discussed later in this chapter.

REDEMPTION FROM NONCORPORATE SHAREHOLDER IN PARTIAL LIQUIDATION

The fourth case in which a redemption can qualify as a sale is a redemption from a noncorporate shareholder in partial liquidation.[55] A *partial liquidation* is a distribution that is not essentially equivalent to a dividend, determined at the corporate level rather than at the shareholder level.[56] To qualify, the distribution must be made in accordance with a plan of partial liquidation and made either in the year the plan is adopted or in the following year.

The Code specifically provides that a distribution in partial liquidation shall include (but not be limited to) distributions attributable to the termination of a business.[57] To satisfy this test, the distribution must be the result of the corporation ceasing to conduct a trade or business that had been in existence for at least five years prior to the distribution. The corporation, following the distribution, must be conducting a trade or business that also has been in existence for at least five years. Neither the continuing nor the terminated business may have been acquired during the five-year period in a transaction in which a gain or loss was recognized.[58] This provision was included to prevent the corporation from purchasing a business in order to convert a dividend into a partial liquidation.

---

[53] § 302(b)(3).

[54] § 302(c)(2).

[55] § 302(b)(4).

[56] § 302(e)(1).

[57] § 302(e)(2).

[58] § 302(e)(3).

There is no exact definition of a "trade or business." The Regulations state that a trade or business consists of a group of activities that includes every step in the process of earning income.[59] Owning investment assets or real estate used in a trade or business is not a trade or business by itself. The Regulations are helpful but do not eliminate all the questions as to what constitutes a trade or business.

REDEMPTIONS OF STOCK TO PAY DEATH TAXES

The fifth provision in the Code that classifies a redemption as a sale rather than as a distribution deals with the redemption of stock to pay death taxes.[60] This provision only applies to stock included in a decedent's gross estate and was designed to provide a way to obtain cash needed for the administration of an estate. It permits the redemption of stock in an amount equal to the taxes imposed as a result of decedent's death and to the funeral and administration expenses deductible by the estate.[61] There is no restriction in the law that the redemption proceeds actually be used to pay taxes or expenses. The limitation refers simply to the maximum amount that can be redeemed under the provision. The tax treatment of any amount redeemed in excess of the amount of the above expenses is determined by applying the rules previously discussed regarding taxability of stock redemptions.

In order to be eligible to redeem stock using this provision, the value of the stock that the decedent owned in the redeeming corporation must exceed 35 percent of the value of the decedent's gross estate reduced by expenses and losses of the estate.[62] This condition effectively limits the use of this exception to estates of which the stock of the redeeming corporation is a substantial part. It is also possible to use this provision when two or more corporations comprise a substantial part of a decedent's estate. In this situation, if 20 percent or more of the value of the outstanding stock of each of two or more corporations is included in the decedent's gross estate, the corporations are treated as a single corporation for the purpose of determining the 35 percent requirement.[63]

CONSTRUCTIVE OWNERSHIP OF STOCK

As demonstrated above, one of the primary factors distinguishing a stock redemption qualifying for sale or exchange treatment from a dividend distribution is whether there has been a change in the taxpayer's proportionate interest in the corporation. Ownership in a corporation refers to both *actual* and *constructive* ownership.[64]

---

[59] Reg. § 1.355-1(c).

[60] § 303(a).

[61] *Ibid.*

[62] § 303(b)(2)(A).

[63] § 302(b)(2)(B).

[64] § 318.

Under the rules of constructive ownership of stock, a taxpayer is considered to own not only those shares of stock he or she personally owns, but also to own those shares of stock owned by certain relatives and entities in which the taxpayer has an interest. The only family members considered relatives for these constructive ownership rules are the taxpayer's spouse, children, grandchildren, and parents.[65] Excluded from the list are siblings (i.e., brothers and sisters) and grandparents.

> **Example 22.** F, an individual, owns 60% of the stock of G Corporation. The remaining 40% is owned by S, F's son. F is considered to own 100% of G Corporation, 60% directly and 40% by the application of the constructive ownership rules.

> **Example 23.** H is married to W. They have one son, C, and a grandchild, G. H owns 100 shares of ABC Corporation. Either W or C can be considered to constructively own H's stock. G is not considered to be a constructive owner of H's stock, since an individual is not considered to constructively own his or her grandparent's stock.

Under the constructive ownership rules (also called the *attribution rules*), a person is deemed to own a proportionate share of the stock owned by a partnership, estate, or trust in which he or she has an interest.[66] Partnerships, estates, and trusts are also deemed to own the stock owned by persons who have an ownership interest in them.[67]

> **Example 24.** Y and Z are equal (50% each) partners in the YZ Partnership. The YZ Partnership owns 300 shares of A Corporation. Since Y and Z each own one-half of the partnership, they are each considered to constructively own one-half of the 300 shares of A Corporation owned by the YZ Partnership, or 150 shares each.

> **Example 25.** Assume the same facts as in *Example 24* except that the 300 shares of A Corporation stock are owned by Y instead of by the partnership. Since a partnership is considered to constructively own all of the stock of its partners, the YZ Partnership is deemed to own the entire 300 shares of A Corporation stock. Z does not constructively own any of the stock unless Y and Z are related family members.

---

[65] § 318(a)(1).

[66] §§ 318(a)(2)(A) and (B).

[67] §§ 318(a)(3)(A) and (B).

In order for there to be attribution (constructive ownership) between a shareholder and a corporation, the shareholder must own, actually or constructively, at least 50 percent of the value of the corporation's stock.[68] Once this requirement is met, a shareholder is deemed to own a proportionate share of the stock owned by the corporation.

> **Example 26.** C Corporation is owned 60% by B and 40% by W. C Corporation owns 1,000 shares of Z Corporation stock. B constructively owns 600 (1,000 shares × 60%) shares of the Z Corporation stock. W does not constructively own any shares of Z Corporation stock since he does not own at least 50% of C Corporation.

A corporation is deemed to own all of the stock owned by shareholders who have a 50 percent or more interest in the corporation.[69]

There are rules against *double* attribution. Specifically, stock may not be attributed to a family member from a family member and then reattributed to another family member.[70] In addition, stock attributed to an entity from an owner may not then be attributed to another owner.[71] These rules prevent attribution between unrelated individuals.

> **Example 27.** P has two children, R and S. R owns 100 shares of H Corporation. Therefore, P constructively owns R's 100 shares of H Corporation. Without the rules against double attribution, the 100 shares could be reattributed from P to S, resulting in sibling attribution, which is not authorized by the definition of relatives.

Complete Termination of Interest. The stock attribution rules could make it very difficult for a redemption by a family-owned corporation to qualify as a complete termination of interest under § 302(b)(3). Any constructively owned stock would prevent the shareholder from qualifying as having completely terminated his or her interest. To eliminate this problem, the Code permits the redeeming shareholder to ignore the family attribution rules (but not attribution from other entities) in determining whether there has been a complete termination of the shareholder's interest.[72] To qualify for this provision, the shareholder must not have any interest in the corporation after the redemption other than that of a creditor. Specifically, the shareholder may not be an officer, director, or even an employee of the corporation. In addition, the shareholder must not acquire one of the prohibited interests in the corporation during the 10 years following the redemption. This provision makes it much easier for a shareholder to qualify a redemption as a complete termination of interest.

---

[68]   § 318(a)(2)(C).

[69]   § 318(a)(3)(C).

[70]   § 318(a)(5)(B).

[71]   § 318(a)(5)(C).

[72]   § 302(c)(2).

REDEMPTIONS THROUGH RELATED CORPORATIONS

As stated earlier, a stock redemption is defined as the acquisition by a corporation of its own stock. The limitations on sale treatment discussed thus far could be avoided by an individual who controls two or more corporations. Instead of having a corporation redeem its stock, the shareholder could *sell* the stock of one controlled corporation to another controlled corporation. To prevent this type of transaction from avoiding the redemption limitations, Code § 304 reclassifies the "sale" of one controlled corporation's stock to another controlled corporation as a stock redemption.[73] Two different transactions are included in the reclassification provision. First, the sale of stock of a corporation controlled by one or more persons to another corporation controlled by the *same persons* is reclassified as a redemption.[74] Control is defined as ownership of either 50 percent or more of the combined voting power *or* 50 percent or more of the value of the outstanding stock.[75] The second reclassified transaction is the sale of stock of a parent corporation to its controlled subsidiary.[76]

> **Example 28.** A, B, and C, unrelated individuals, each own equal shares of T Corporation's outstanding stock. These same individuals own 100% of V Corporation's stock. If either A, B, or C sells shares of T Corporation to V Corporation, the transaction will be treated as a stock redemption.

> **Example 29.** Individual D owns all of the stock of P Corporation. P Corporation owns all of the stock of S Corporation. If D sells some of her P Corporation stock to S Corporation, the transaction will be treated as a stock redemption.

The fact that a transaction is reclassified as a stock redemption does not mean that the shareholder will be denied sale treatment. Instead, it requires that the selling shareholder meet one of the special rules relating to stock redemptions in § 302 (i.e., being not essentially equivalent to a dividend, substantially disproportionate, a complete termination of an interest, or a partial liquidation from a noncorporate shareholder) to qualify for sale treatment. In measuring the change in ownership under § 302, the stock of the issuing corporation—not the purchasing corporation—is used.[77] In addition, stock owned by attribution is counted.

> **Example 30.** Individual G owns 80 of the 100 shares of X Corporation and 90 of the 100 shares of Y Corporation. G "sells" 10 shares of X Corporation stock to Y Corporation. Since G controls both corporations, the transaction

---

[73] § 304.

[74] § 304(a)(1).

[75] § 304(c)(1).

[76] § 304(a)(2).

[77] § 304(b)(1).

is reclassified as a redemption. Before the transaction, G owns 80% of X Corporation. After the transaction, G owns 79% of X, computed as follows:

Actual ownership (70 × 100 shares)	70%
Constructive ownership:	
(90% ownership of Y Corporation times	
Y Corporation's 10% ownership of X Corporation)	9%
Total direct and indirect ownership	79%

Since G's ownership of X Corporation has only declined from 80% to 79%, the redemption does not meet any of the tests for sale treatment. Consequently, G must treat the "sale" proceeds as a dividend.

If the transaction is treated as a dividend rather than a sale, the amount of dividend income is measured by the earnings and profits of *both* the issuing corporation and the purchasing corporation.[78] This deemed dividend is considered as having been paid first from the E&P of the purchasing (acquiring) corporation to the extent thereof, and then from the E&P of the issuing corporation.

> **Example 31.**   Assume the same facts as in *Example 30*. Since the transaction is treated as a dividend, it is considered to come from Y Corporation's E&P first and then, if necessary, from X Corporation's E&P.

EFFECT OF REDEMPTIONS ON REDEEMING CORPORATION

In a stock redemption, the stockholders are concerned with whether the redemption is treated for tax purposes as a sale or as a distribution. The redeeming corporation, however, is concerned with whether or not it has income on the redemption and what effect there is on earnings and profits.

Gain or Loss.   The tax effect of redemption distributions on the corporation is identical to that arising from property distributions discussed earlier. As previously explained, the corporation must recognize gain—but not loss—on the distribution of property.[79]

Effect of Redemption on E&P.   The E&P of a corporation must be adjusted to reflect any redemption distributions. First, if the corporation must recognize gain on the distribution under § 311, E&P must be increased for the gain. The amount of the reduction of E&P on account of the distribution depends on whether the distribution qualifies for sale treatment. If the distribution does not qualify for sale treatment but rather is treated as a dividend, the rules discussed earlier for cash and property dividends must be followed. If the redemption qualifies for sale treatment, only a portion of the distribution is charged against E&P. In such case, E&P is reduced by the redeemed stock's proportionate share of E&P but not by more than the amount of the redemption distribution.[80]

---

[78]   § 304(b)(2).

[79]   § 311.

[80]   § 312(n)(7).

Example 32. B Corporation had the following capital accounts on January 2:

Common stock...	$100,000
Paid-in capital in excess of par.............................	300,000
Earnings and profits..	500,000

The common stock outstanding consisted of 1,000 shares of $100 par value stock. On January 2, B Corporation redeemed 100 shares for $700 per share (a total of $70,000). The corporation therefore redeemed 10% of its stock (100 ÷ 1,000). Of the $70,000 paid for the shares, B Corporation must charge $50,000 to its earnings and profits (10% × $500,000). The remaining $20,000 is charged to the capital accounts [$10,000 to common stock (10% × $100,000) and the remaining $10,000 to paid-in capital in excess of par].

Note: This example assumes that this redemption meets the requirements for sale or exchange treatment.

COMPLETE LIQUIDATIONS

INTRODUCTION

As discussed earlier in the chapter, in a partial liquidation or stock redemption the corporation redeems only a portion of its stock. In these situations, the corporation continues to operate all or part of its business. In other situations, however, a corporation may wish to terminate its existence by liquidating completely. A complete liquidation of a corporation occurs when, under a plan of complete liquidation, the corporation redeems *all* of its stock using a series of distributions.[81] In addition, the corporation must be in a status of liquidation throughout the life of the liquidation. The Regulations state that a status of liquidation exists when a corporation ceases to be a going concern and is engaged in activities whose sole function is the winding up of the business affairs.[82] There is one set of rules that governs most liquidations and one special set of rules that governs liquidations of a subsidiary.

COMPLETE LIQUIDATIONS: THE GENERAL RULES

Shareholder Gain or Loss. When a shareholder receives a liquidating distribution, the treatment of the shareholder—except where a parent liquidates a subsidiary—is governed solely by Code § 331. This rule provides that shareholders treat property received in liquidation of a corporation as full payment for

---

[81] § 346(a).   [82] Reg. § 1.332-2(c).

their stock. Therefore, the shareholder must recognize gain or loss equal to the difference between the *net* fair market value of the property received (fair market value of the assets received less any liabilities assumed by the shareholder) and the basis of the stock surrendered. Special rules must be followed where a shareholder receives an installment note arising from a sale by the corporation within the 12-month period after the corporation has adopted a plan of liquidation.[83] If the stock was purchased at different times and for different amounts, the gain or loss is computed on each separate lot. The gain or loss normally is capital gain or loss since the shareholder's stock is usually a capital asset.

Basis to Shareholder.   When a shareholder uses the general rule of § 331 to determine gain or loss on the liquidation, the shareholder's basis in the property received in the liquidation is its fair market value on the date of distribution.[84]

> **Example 33.**   K owned 100 shares of stock in L Corporation. K's adjusted basis in the stock was $400. L Corporation completely liquidated and distributed to K $200 cash and office equipment worth $700 in exchange for his stock. K's recognized gain is computed as follows:
>
> | | |
> |---|---:|
> | Cash received by K... | $200 |
> | Fair market value of property distributed to K................ | 700 |
> | Amount realized... | $900 |
> | Less: K's adjusted basis in his stock...................... | (400) |
> | Realized gain... | $500 |

K's entire realized gain of $500 is recognized under § 1001(c). K's basis in the cash received is, of course, $200. K's basis in the office equipment received is $700, its fair market value on the date of distribution.

Gain or Loss to the Liquidating Corporation.   A corporation generally must recognize gain *and* loss on the distribution of property as part of a complete liquidation.[85] The gain or loss is computed as if such property were sold to the shareholder for its fair market value.

> **Example 34.**   Sleepwaves Corporation, a waterbed retailer, fell on hard times and decided to dissolve the business. During the year, the corporation adopted a plan of liquidation and completely liquidated. The furniture that the corporation was unable to move in their going-out-of-business sale was distributed to its sole shareholder. This inventory was worth $5,000 (basis $1,000). In addition, the corporation distributed land held for investment worth $8,000 (basis $10,000). The corporation must recognize $4,000 of ordinary income ($5,000 − $1,000) on the distribution of the inventory and a $2,000 capital loss ($8,000 − $10,000) on the distribution of the land.

---

[83]   § 453(h).

[84]   § 334(a).

[85]   § 336.

If the shareholder assumes a corporate liability or takes the property subject to a liability, the fair market value of the property is treated as being no less than the liability.[86] Therefore, where the liability exceeds the value of the property, gain must be recognized to the extent the liability exceeds the basis of the property.

> **Example 35.** T Corporation's only asset is a building with a basis of $100,000 and which is subject to a liability of $400,000. The low basis is attributable to accelerated depreciation. The property is currently worth $250,000. During 1991, T distributed the land to its sole shareholder, R. T Corporation must recognize a gain of $300,000 ($400,000 liability − $100,000 basis). Had the liability been $200,000, T would have ignored the liability and recognized a gain of $150,000 ($250,000 value − $100,000 basis).

The treatment of distributions in liquidation differs from that of nonliquidating distributions in that the corporation is normally allowed to recognize loss on a liquidating distribution. This is not true for all liquidating distributions, however. As with nonliquidating distributions, Congress was concerned that taxpayers might use the loss recognition privilege to circumvent the gain recognition rule. To prohibit possible abuse, § 336(d) provides two exceptions concerning the treatment of losses.

The first exception prohibits the deduction of the loss if certain conditions are satisfied. Section 336(d)(1) provides that the liquidating corporation cannot recognize any loss on the distribution of property to a *related party* if the distribution is either (1) non–pro rata or (2) the property was acquired by the corporation during the five-year period prior to the distribution, either in a nontaxable transfer under § 351 (relating to transfers to a controlled corporation) or as a contribution to capital. For this purpose, a related party is the same as that defined in Code § 267 (e.g., an individual who owns either directly or constructively more than 50% of the distributing corporation).

> **Example 36.** J is the sole shareholder of Z Corporation. In anticipation of the corporation's liquidation, J contributed a dilapidated warehouse to the corporation, with a built-in loss of $100,000 (value $200,000, basis $300,000). Shortly thereafter, Z Corporation distributed the warehouse along with land worth $90,000 (basis $20,000). Absent the special rule, the corporation would recognize a loss of $100,000, which would offset the $70,000 gain on the land that it must recognize ($90,000 − $20,000). Under the exception, however, no loss is recognized since the distribution is to a related party, J, and the property was acquired as a contribution to capital within five years of the liquidation.

---

[86] § 336(b).

The second provision concerning losses limits the amount of loss that can be deducted—assuming the loss is not disallowed entirely under the related-party rule above. Under § 336(d)(2), the amount of loss recognized by a liquidating corporation on the sale, exchange, or distribution of any property acquired in a § 351 transaction or as a contribution of capital is reduced. This rule applies only if the principal purpose for the acquisition was the recognition of a loss by the corporation in connection with the liquidation. It is generally presumed that any property acquired in the above manner during the two-year period prior to the date on which a plan of liquidation is adopted was acquired for the purpose of recognizing a loss. When the tax-avoidance motive is found, the rule effectively limits the loss deduction to the decline in value that occurs while the property is in the hands of the corporation. In other words, any built-in loss existing at the time of contribution is not deductible. To ensure that any built-in loss is not deducted, the Code provides a special computation. For purposes of determining the *loss* on the disposition of the tainted property, the basis of such property is reduced (but not below zero) by the amount of the built-in loss (i.e., the excess of the property's basis over its value at the time the corporation acquired it). By reducing the basis, any subsequent loss recognized is reduced.

Example 37.   R, S, T, and U own the stock of Q Corporation. Knowing that the corporation planned to liquidate, R contributed land to the corporation with a built-in loss of $100,000 (value $200,000, basis $300,000) in exchange for shares of Q stock that qualified for nonrecognition under § 351. During the liquidation, the corporation sold the property for $160,000. Under the general rule, the corporation would recognize a loss of $140,000 ($160,000 amount realized − $300,000 carryover basis). However, since the property was acquired in a § 351 exchange and the principal purpose of the transaction was to recognize loss on the property in liquidation, the special rule applies. The loss recognized is limited to that which occurred in the hands of the corporation $40,000 ($200,000 value at contribution − $160,000 amount realized). In other words, the loss computed in the normal manner, $140,000, must be reduced by the built-in loss of $100,000. Technically, Q Corporation would compute the loss by reducing its basis in the property by the amount of built-in loss as follows:

Amount realized			$160,000
Adjusted basis:			
Carryover basis		$300,000	
− Basis reduction:			
Carryover basis	$300,000		
− Value at contribution	− 200,000		
Built-in loss		− 100,000	
Adjusted basis			(200,000)
Loss recognized			($40,000)

LIQUIDATION OF A SUBSIDIARY

A parent corporation generally recognizes no gain or loss on property it receives from the liquidation of a subsidiary corporation.[87] In order to qualify to use this provision (Code § 332), the parent corporation must own at least 80 percent of the voting power and this stock must have a value of at least equal to 80 percent of the total value of the subsidiary corporation's stock.[88] For purposes of these computations, nonvoting preferred stock is excluded.[89] This minimum amount of stock must be owned on the date of adoption of the plan of liquidation and at all times thereafter until the liquidation is completed. All of the property of the subsidiary must be distributed in complete cancellation of the subsidiary's stock within three years following the close of the tax year in which the first distribution takes place.[90] It also is important to note that Code § 332 is not elective. If the above conditions are met, no gain or loss is recognized.

Effect on Subsidiary. Under § 337, a subsidiary recognizes no gain or loss on the distribution of its assets to its parent in a liquidation under § 332.[91] This rule only applies to property transferred to the parent corporation in the liquidation. Property transferred to minority shareholders will result in the recognition of gain but not loss.[92]

Ordinarily, when one taxpayer is indebted to another and the debt is cancelled, the indebted taxpayer has income to the extent of the debt due to the relief of the indebtedness. Section 337(b) contains an exception to this general rule. The exception states that when a subsidiary corporation is indebted to its parent corporation and the subsidiary liquidates under § 332, no gain or loss is recognized when the subsidiary transfers property to the parent to satisfy the debt.

Basis of Assets—General Rule. When a subsidiary is liquidated by its parent corporation, the basis of the assets transferred from the subsidiary to the parent must be determined. Generally, the basis of each of the assets transferred is the same for the parent corporation as it had been for the subsidiary.[93] This rule applies not only to property transferred in cancellation of the subsidiary's stock, but also to property transferred in order to satisfy the subsidiary's debt to the parent.[94] The amount of the parent's investment in the subsidiary's stock is ignored. The parent's basis is determined solely by the subsidiary's basis.

> **Example 38.** T Corporation had assets with a basis of $1 million and no liabilities. P Corporation bought all of the stock of T Corporation for $1.2 million. Several years later, when T Corporation's assets had a basis of $800,000, P Corporation liquidated T Corporation in a tax-free liquidation under § 332. P Corporation's basis in the assets received from T Corpora-

---

[87]   § 332.

[88]   §§ 332(b)(1) and 1504(a)(2).

[89]   § 1504(a)(4).

[90]   § 332(b)(3).

[91]   § 337(a).

[92]   §§ 337(a) and 336(d)(3).

[93]   § 334(b)(1).

[94]   § 334(b)(2).

tion is $800,000, the same basis as T Corporation had in the assets. The $400,000 difference between the basis of the assets and P Corporation's basis in the stock of T Corporation is lost.

Example 39.   Assume the same facts as in *Example 38* except that P Corporation had paid $700,000 (instead of $1,200,000) for T Corporation's stock. P Corporation's basis in the assets received from T Corporation is still $800,000, the same as T Corporation's basis in the assets. In this example, rather than losing a $400,000 investment, P Corporation received a $100,000 tax-free increase in its basis in T Corporation and its assets ($800,000 basis in T Corporation's assets − $700,000 basis that P Corporation had in T Corporation's stock).

As demonstrated above, this carryover of the basis of assets from a subsidiary to its parent can be either beneficial (*Example 39*) or detrimental (*Example 38*) to the parent corporation.

Basis of Assets—Exception.   The carryover basis rule was challenged in the case of *Kimbell-Diamond Milling Co. v. Commissioner.*[95] In this case, Kimbell-Diamond's plant was destroyed by fire. The corporation wished to purchase replacement property to avoid recognizing gain on the involuntary conversion. The only plant that they wanted was owned by a corporation that would not sell. To acquire the asset, Kimbell-Diamond purchased the corporation's stock and then liquidated the corporation. Kimbell-Diamond used the basis of the assets of the liquidated corporation as its basis for the assets. The amount that Kimbell-Diamond paid for the stock of the corporation was *much less* than the liquidated corporation's basis in the assets, so that by using the carryover basis, Kimbell-Diamond received much larger depreciation deductions (and therefore had much smaller taxable income) than if it had actually purchased the plant. Upon review, however, the IRS reclassified the transaction as a purchase of assets, rather than a purchase of stock followed by a separate liquidation. The Tax Court agreed with IRS that the two transactions should be treated as one. This decision created the *Kimbell-Diamond* exception. Under this exception, if the original purpose of the stock acquisition was to acquire assets, the purchaser's basis in the assets acquired was the cost of the stock rather than the liquidated corporation's basis.

Congress incorporated the Kimbell-Diamond exception into the Internal Revenue Code,[96] effectively allowing an acquiring corporation such as Kimbell-Diamond to select the basis to be used for the subsidiary's assets: either a basis equal to the purchase price of the assets or the same basis as that of the subsidiary. As might be expected, many acquiring corporations attempted to take advantage of this latitude provided by the Code. Consequently, to curb potential abuses, Congress enacted § 338 in 1982. Although § 338 is still a codification of the *Kimbell-Diamond* exception, its requirements are much more specific than the previous law.

[95]   14 T.C. 74 (1950), *affd.*, 51-1 USTC ¶9201, 40 AFTR 328, 187 F2d 718 (CA-5, 1951).

[96]   The *Kimbell-Diamond* exception was formerly § 334(b)(2).

Code § 338—Purchase of Assets.   To qualify for a purchase price basis offered under § 338, the parent corporation must purchase stock having at least 80 percent of the voting power and at least 80 percent of the value of all stock (except nonvoting, nonparticipating, preferred stock).[97] To qualify as a purchase, the stock may not be acquired from a related party, in a transaction that qualifies under Code § 351, or in any transaction that will result in the purchaser using a carryover basis.[98] This acquisition of control may occur in a series of transactions; however, no more than 12 months may elapse between the first purchase and the acquisition of the required 80 percent control.[99]

If the parent corporation meets the purchase requirement, it must elect to treat the acquisition as an asset purchase by the 15th day of the ninth month following the month of acquisition.[100] The election, once made, is irrevocable. Failure to make the election results in the parent being treated as having purchased stock and thus prohibits the subsidiary from adjusting the basis of its assets. After the election, the subsidiary generally increases or decreases the basis of its assets to their fair market value.

Code § 338 does not require a liquidation. As a result, both the parent and the subsidiary may continue to exist. Section 338 takes a *two-step* approach to achieve the basis step-up. First, the subsidiary is treated as having sold in a single transaction all of its assets at fair market value on the close of the acquisition date. Any gain or loss realized on this hypothetical sale must be recognized *and* reported on the subsidiary's final tax return. Second, the subsidiary is treated as a new corporation that is deemed to have purchased all of the assets of the old subsidiary (i.e., the acquired or target corporation) on the day after the date the parent obtained the necessary control. For purposes of determining the subsidiary's new basis in its assets, the deemed purchase price is generally equal to the price the parent corporation paid for the subsidiary's stock adjusted for ownership less than 100 percent (i.e., the portion not owned by the parent) as well as liabilities of the subsidiary and other relevant items.[101] Note that in increasing the purchase price of the stock for liabilities of the subsidiary, such liabilities include the tax liability attributable to income arising from the deemed sale.

> **Example 40.**   During 1991, P Corporation purchased all of the stock of T Corporation for $1 million. T's only asset is land with a basis of $200,000. It had no liabilities. Assuming P makes the appropriate election under § 338, T is deemed to have sold its assets, in this case the land, for its fair market value, $1 million. Thus, T must recognize a gain of $800,000 ($1,000,000 − $200,000). The tax liability arising from the deemed sale is

---

[97]   § 338(d)(3).

[98]   § 338(h)(3).

[99]   § 338(d) and (h).

[100]   § 338(g).

[101]   § 338(a). § 338(b) provides that the basis is the sum of the grossed-up basis of stock purchased during the 12-month acquisition and the basis of stock not purchased during the period, adjusted as necessary.

$272,000 ($800,000 × 34%). After the hypothetical sale and repurchase, P's basis in the land is $1,272,000, its purchase price of the stock ($1 million) increased by the liability arising on the deemed sale of $272,000. Note that P, as the new owner of T, bears the economic burden of the tax liability. Consequently, assuming the value of the land is truly $1 million, P would no doubt desire to reduce the purchase price of the stock by the liability that arises with a § 338 election; that is, it probably would try to buy the stock for $728,000 ($1,000,000 − $272,000). If P did buy the stock for $728,000, presumably the gain on the deemed sale would still be $800,000, since the land is considered sold for its value of $1 million. In such case, the tax liability would still be $272,000 and the basis of the land under § 338 would be $1 million ($728,000 purchase price of the stock + $272,000 tax liability). Note that the effect of these rules is to reduce the value of the target subsidiary by an amount equal to the tax liability that would arise if § 338 is elected.

Under § 338, the subsidiary is considered to have purchased all of its assets from itself at the deemed price. The subsidiary must increase or decrease the basis of its assets so that its new basis in its assets equals the deemed purchase price. The method of allocating the basis among the assets is outlined by the Regulations.[102]

Allocation of Deemed Purchase Price. The temporary regulations under Code § 338 provide that the deemed purchase price of the stock is to be allocated to the subsidiary's assets using the "residual value" approach.[103] Under this technique, assets must be grouped into four classes for purposes of making the allocation:

1. *Class I:* Cash, demand deposits, and other cash equivalents

2. *Class II:* Certificates of deposit, U.S. government securities, readily marketable securities, and other similar items

3. *Class III:* All assets other than those in Classes I, II, or IV, such as accounts receivable, inventory, plant, property, and equipment

4. *Class IV:* Intangible assets in the nature of goodwill and going-concern value

According to the system, the purchase price is first allocated to Class I assets in proportion to their relative fair market values as determined on the date following the acquisition. Because Class I assets are either cash or cash equivalents, the basis assigned to them is their face value. Once this allocation is made, any excess of the purchase price over the amount allocated to Class I assets is allocated to Class II assets, again based on relative fair market values. Any excess purchase price remaining after making the allocation to Class II assets is allocated to Class

---

[102]   § 338(b)(3).   [103]   Temp. Reg. § 1.338(b)-2T.

III assets based on relative values. In allocating such excess to Class II and Class III assets, the amount allocated *cannot exceed the fair market value* of the asset. Thus, any purchase price which remains after the allocation to Class I, II, and III assets is assigned to Class IV assets—hence the reason for calling this method the *residual* value approach. By limiting the allocation to Class I, II, and III assets to the assets' fair market values, the rules generally seek to ensure that corporate taxpayers allocate the proper amount to goodwill.

For the purpose of these allocation rules, the temporary regulations provide that the fair market value of the asset is its gross value computed without regard to any mortgages, liens, or other liabilities related to the property. These rules are illustrated in the following example.

> **Example 41.** P Corporation purchases from an unrelated person 100% of the stock of T Corporation on June 1, 1991. Assume the purchase price adjusted for all relevant items is $100,000. T's assets at acquisition date are as follows:

	Basis	Fair Market Value
Cash	$10,000	$10,000
Accounts receivable	20,000	20,000
Inventory	25,000	55,000
Total	$55,000	$85,000

> The purchase price is first allocated to cash in the amount of $10,000. This leaves $90,000 to be allocated. Since there are no Class II assets, the allocation is to Class III. If the residual approach was not required, the taxpayer might allocate all of the remaining $90,000 to the receivables and inventory, despite the fact that their value is only $75,000. If this were allowed, income from the sale of the inventory would be reduced and a loss would result when the receivables were collected. However, since the remaining purchase price ($90,000) exceeds the fair market value of the Class III assets, the basis of the assets in this class is their fair market value, $20,000 for the receivables and $55,000 for the inventory. This leaves $15,000 of the purchase price which has not been allocated. It is all assigned to goodwill.

If the parent corporation owns less than 100 percent of the subsidiary, the deemed price must be "grossed up" to take into account the minority interest. The adjustment for a minority interest results in a deemed purchase price called the "grossed-up basis." This grossed-up basis is obtained by multiplying the actual purchase price of the stock by a ratio, the numerator being 100 percent and the denominator equal to the percentage of the subsidiary stock owned by the parent.[104] This computation can be expressed as follows:

$$\begin{array}{l} \text{Grossed-up} \\ \text{basis} \end{array} = \begin{array}{c} \text{Parent corporation's basis in the} \\ \text{subsidiary's stock on} \\ \text{the acquisition date} \end{array} \times \dfrac{100\%}{\begin{array}{c} \text{Percentage of subsidiary's} \\ \text{stock held by parent on the} \\ \text{acquisition date} \end{array}}$$

Example 42.   P Corporation purchased 90% of the outstanding stock of T Corporation for $900,000. T Corporation had only one asset, land with a basis of $900,000. Assume there are no liabilities or other relevant items that affect the deemed purchase price. Since P owns less than 100% of T, a grossed-up basis must be calculated. The result is $1 million [$900,000 purchase price × (100 ÷ 90, the percentage of T owned by P)]. If P elects § 338, T's basis for the land is $1 million. Note, however, that it is likely that the Regulations require the deemed sales price to be increased by any liabilities of the subsidiary. In such case, the deemed purchase price here would include the tax liability resulting from the fact that P purchased less than 100% of the stock, which in turn causes T to recognize income.

Section 338 not only entitles the subsidiary to a stepped-up basis for its assets, it also treats the subsidiary as a new corporation in every respect. As a result, the subsidiary may adopt any tax year it chooses, unless it files a consolidated return with the parent corporation, in which case it must adopt the parent's tax year. It may adopt new accounting methods if it desires. MACRS depreciation may be used for all of the hypothetically purchased property—the anti-churning rules being inapplicable since the old and new subsidiary are considered unrelated. The new subsidiary acquires none of the other attributes of the old subsidiary. The earnings and profits of the old subsidiary are eliminated and any net operating loss carryovers of the old subsidiary are unavailable to the new subsidiary.

In most situations, the target subsidiary has some assets that have appreciated in value (i.e., fair market value exceeds the asset's basis) and other assets where the value is less than the asset's basis. In such cases the acquiring corporation, desiring the highest possible basis for the assets, might first purchase the appreciated property, then purchase the subsidiary's stock and liquidate the subsidiary under § 332. By so doing, the acquiring corporation would obtain the best of both worlds: a basis for the appreciated property equal to its fair market value and a carryover basis for the other assets. In the latter case, the basis is higher than it would have been had the assets themselves been purchased or the stock purchased followed by an election under § 338. To prohibit the acquiring corporation from effectively selecting the basis that is most desirable for each separate

---

[104]   § 338(b)(2). This approach is modified where the parent holds stock not acquired during the 12-month period.

asset, the Code contains the so-called "consistency" provisions. According to these rules, an acquiring corporation is deemed to have made an election under § 338 to treat the stock purchase as an acquisition of assets—thus precluding a carryover basis—if it purchased any of the target subsidiary's assets during the consistency period. This period begins one year before the date of the first acquisition that comes within § 338 and ends one year after the acquisition date (i.e., the date on which the corporation obtains 80% control).

> **Example 43.**   P Inc. purchased 60% of T Corporation's stock on March 7, 1991 and the remaining 40% on December 4, 1991. The consistency period runs from March 7, 1990 through December 4, 1992. If P acquires any assets of T during this period, it is deemed to have made a § 338 election, in effect causing all of the subsidiary's assets to reflect the purchase price of the stock.

Similar rules exist requiring consistency for acquisitions where affiliated members of either the parent or subsidiary's group are involved.

As mentioned above, § 338 is an elective provision. If the election is not made and the subsidiary is liquidated, § 332, the general rule for the nontaxable liquidation of a subsidiary, applies. If § 332 is used, the parent corporation carries over the subsidiary's basis for its assets, whereas under § 338 the basis of the assets is their deemed purchase price (based upon the parent corporation's investment in the subsidiary).

PROBLEM MATERIALS

DISCUSSION QUESTIONS

20-1 *Dividends.* Define the term *dividend*.

20-2 *Earnings and Profits.* What are "earnings and profits"? Are earnings and profits the same as "retained earnings"? Why or why not?

20-3 *Earnings and Profits.* In addition to taxable income, what types of items affect earnings and profits?

20-4 *Earnings and Profits.* How does the use of an accelerated method of depreciation affect a corporation's earnings and profits?

20-5 *Earnings and Profits.* How does the § 179 immediate expensing option affect a corporation's earnings and profits?

20-6 *Distributions.* Is it possible for a distribution to be a taxable dividend even if there is a *deficit* in accumulated earnings and profits? If so, how?

20-7 *Cash Dividends.* What is the amount of distribution when cash is distributed?

20-8 *Property Dividends.* What is the amount of the distribution when property other than cash is distributed?

20-9 *Property Dividends and Liabilities.* What effect does a liability have on the amount and basis of property distributed if the property is subject to the liability?

20-10 *Constructive Dividends.* What are constructive dividends? When do they arise?

20-11 *Effect of Property Dividend on the Corporation.* In what situations must a corporation recognize income as a result of a distribution?

20-12 *Effect of Property Dividends on Earnings and Profits.* How do property dividends affect earnings and profits?

20-13 *Stock Dividends.* What is a stock dividend?

20-14 *Stock Dividends.* In what situations may a stock dividend be taxable? When is it not taxable?

20-15 *Stock Dividends.* How is the shareholder's basis in a stock dividend determined?

20-16 *Stock Dividends.* How do stock dividends affect earnings and profits?

20-17 *Stock Rights.* What are stock rights? How does their tax treatment differ from stock dividends?

20-18 *Dividends.* What is the effect of a dividend on the distributing corporation's taxable income?

20-19 *Stock Redemptions.* What is a stock redemption?

20-20 *Stock Redemptions.* List the situations in which a stock redemption will be treated as a sale of stock.

20-21 *Constructive Ownership.* What is constructive ownership of stock? How may stock be constructively owned?

20-22 *Effect of Redemption on Redeeming Corporation.* How do stock redemptions affect the redeeming corporation? In what situations must gain or loss be recognized when stock is redeemed? How do stock redemptions affect earnings and profits?

20-23 *Complete Liquidations.* What is a complete liquidation?

20-24 *Code § 331.* Generally explain the treatment of the shareholders in a complete liquidation.

20-25 *Code § 336.* Generally explain the treatment of the liquidating corporation in a complete liquidation.

20-26 *Liquidation of a Subsidiary.* What conditions must be met in order for § 332 to apply to the liquidation of a subsidiary?

20-27 *Liquidation of a Subsidiary—Basis.* What is the general rule for determining the parent corporation's basis in the assets received from its liquidated subsidiary?

20-28 Kimbell-Diamond *Exception.* What is the *Kimbell-Diamond* exception?

20-29 *Code § 338—Purchase of Assets.* When does § 338 apply to the liquidation of a subsidiary? How does it differ from the general rule for determining basis in the liquidation of a subsidiary?

PROBLEMS

20-30 *Dividends.* A's basis in his 50 shares of Q Corporation stock is $3,000. A purchased the Q Corporation stock in 1984. On November 11, 1991, Q Corporation distributed $8,000 to A with respect to the Q Corporation stock. The portion of Q Corporation's earnings and profits allocable to A is $3,500. What is the tax treatment of the $8,000 distribution to A?

20-31   *Earnings and Profits.*   D Corporation's taxable income for the year was computed as follows:

Gross income from operations................		$1,000,000
Less: Operating expenses...................		(900,000)
Net income from operations...................		$ 100,000
Dividend income.............................		20,000
Long-term capital gain.......................	$15,000	
Less: Capital loss carryover................	(7,000)	8,000
Income before special deductions.............		$ 128,000
Net operating loss carryover.................	$ 9,000	
Dividends-received deduction.................	16,000	
Total of special deductions...................		(25,000)
Taxable income...............................		$ 103,000

Additional information:

1.   The corporation received $5,000 in tax-exempt interest income.
2.   Included in operating expenses is depreciation of $130,000. Straight-line depreciation of the depreciable assets would have been $50,000.

Compute the earnings and profits of D Corporation for the current year.

20-32   *Earnings and Profits.*   V Corporation's taxable income for the year included the following items:

1.   A $12,000 charitable contributions deduction. Actual charitable contributions made by V Corporation were $20,000, but only $12,000 was deductible this year due to the 10 percent charitable contributions limitation.
2.   An 80 percent dividends-received deduction of $8,000. The amount of dividend income received by V Corporation was $10,000.
3.   Percentage depletion of $4,000 was deducted by V Corporation. Cost depletion would have been $800.
4. $2,000 of assets purchased by V Corporation this year were expensed using the § 179 immediate expensing option.
5.   ACRS depreciation of $1,500 was taken on a new heavy duty truck (5-year property) purchased this year. The cost of the automobile was $10,000.

Compute the effect of the above items on V Corporation's current earnings and profits.

20-33 *Distributions.* For each of the following independent situations, compute the amount of dividend income to the shareholder as a result of the distribution(s), and specify the source of each distribution (current and/or accumulated earnings and profits).

Distributions

	April 1	October 1	Current E&P	Accumulated E&P
a.	$5,000	$5,000	$15,000	$10,000
b.	9,000	9,000	15,000	10,000
c.	2,000	4,000	7,000	(20,000)
d.	6,000	2,000	0	11,000
e.	3,000	5,000	(12,000)	30,000
f.	3,000	2,000	1,000	0
g.	1,000	3,000	(6,000)	8,000

20-34 *Cash and Property Dividends.* A Corporation is owned by J (an individual) and B Corporation. A Corporation declared and paid the following dividends: $10,000 cash and a printing press with a fair market value of $10,000 and an adjusted basis of $6,000. A Corporation's current and accumulated earnings and profits exceed $20,000. Consider each alternative independently.

  a.   If B Corporation received the cash and J received the printing press, how much dividend income would each report?

  b.   If J received the cash and B Corporation received the printing press, how much dividend income would each report?

  c.   What are the tax consequences to A Corporation of the distribution?

  d.   What is the effect of the distribution on corporate earnings and profits?

20-35 *Property Dividends—Installment Obligations.* G Corporation distributed installment notes with a face value of $20,000 to its shareholders. The gross profit percentage of the notes was 20 percent, and the fair market value of the notes was $18,000 when they were distributed. Compute G Corporation's recognized gain on the distribution of the installment notes.

20-36 *Stock Dividends.* P owns 100 shares of Z Corporation common stock, which she purchased in 1975 for $50 a share. Z Corporation declared and paid a 100 percent stock dividend to all common stockholders. At the date of record, the selling price of a share of common stock was $200. Immediately following the distribution, the stock was selling for $225 per share.

  a.   How much income must P recognize on the receipt of the 100 shares of common stock as a dividend?

  b.   What is the basis of the dividend shares?

  c.   Assume that P received the dividend on June 1 and sold 50 shares of stock (25 new and 25 old) on July 1 for $150 per share. What is P's recognized gain or loss? Is it long-term or short-term?

20-37 *Stock Dividends.*   R owns 50 shares of A Corporation common stock, which he purchased in 1980 for $100 per share. On January 1 of the current year, A Corporation declared a dividend of one share of new preferred stock for each share of common. The shares were distributed on March 1. On that date, the common stock was selling for $150 per share and the preferred stock had a value of $50 per share.

a.   How much income must R recognize on the receipt of the preferred stock?

b.   What is R's basis in the preferred stock?

c.   On June 1, R sells 25 shares of common stock for $175 per share and 25 shares of preferred stock for $75 per share. What is R's recognized gain or loss? Is it long-term or short-term?

20-38 *Stock Dividends.*   N owns 200 shares of M Corporation preferred stock. She purchased the stock for $200 per share in 1983. On February 1 of the current year, the corporation declared and paid a 50 percent stock dividend. At date of declaration, the preferred stock was selling for $220 per share. Immediately following the distribution (June 1), the preferred stock was selling for $150 per share.

a.   How much income will N have as a result of the dividend?

b.   What is her basis of the dividend shares?

c.   If N sells 25 shares of the old and 25 shares of the new for $180 per share on August 1, what is her recognized gain or loss? Is it long-term or short-term?

20-39 *Stock Rights.*   Y Corporation's profits had taken a deep dive in recent years. To encourage purchase of its stock, the corporation issued one stock right for each share of outstanding common stock. The rights allow the holder to purchase a share of stock for $1. The common stock was selling for $1.50 when the rights were issued (June 1). The value of the stock rights on June 1 were $0.50 each. A owns 1,000 shares of common stock for which he paid $20 per share 10 years ago, and therefore received 1,000 stock rights. A sold 100 rights on July 1 for $175. He exercised 100 rights on August 1 when the stock was selling for $1.80 per share. The remaining rights lapsed on December 30.

a.   How much dividend income must A recognize?

b.   How much gain or loss must A recognize on the July 1 sale of the stock rights? Is it long-term or short-term?

c.   What is A's recognized loss when the remaining rights lapse?

d.   What is the basis of the original 1,000 shares on December 31?

20-40 *Stock Redemptions.*   B owned 100 shares (100%) of the common stock of C Corporation. C Corporation has no other classes of stock outstanding. B's basis in his 100 shares was $3,000 ($30 per share). C Corporation redeemed 20 of B's shares for $1,000.

a.   What is B's recognized gain or loss on the redemption? What is the character of B's recognized gain or loss?

b.   What is B's basis in his remaining shares of C Corporation stock?

20-41 *Stock Redemptions.* W has owned 500 shares of X Corporation's 1,000 outstanding shares of voting common stock since 1984. X Corporation has no other classes of stock outstanding. W's basis in her 500 shares was $1,500 ($3 per share). X Corporation redeemed 200 shares of W's stock for $800.

   a. Is this redemption treated as a sale or a distribution?
   b. What is W's recognized gain or loss on the redemption? What is the character of W's recognized gain or loss?
   c. What is the basis of W's remaining shares after the redemption?

20-42 *Stock Redemptions.* Assume the same facts as in Problem 20-41 except that X Corporation redeemed 100 shares of W's stock instead of 200 shares. Answer the above questions a, b, and c for this situation.

20-43 *Stock Redemptions.* T Corporation is owned by the following unrelated individuals:

K	60 shares
L	20 shares
M	10 shares
N	10 shares
Total	100 shares

If T Corporation redeems 30 shares owned by K, will the transaction qualify as a sale? Why or why not?

20-44 *Stock Redemptions—Constructive Ownership.* Use the same facts as in Problem 20-43. Would this redemption qualify as a sale if L is K's son? Why or why not?

20-45 *Constructive Ownership of Stock.* Q, an individual, owns 20 percent of A Corporation. Mrs. Q owns 60 percent of A Corporation and 50 percent of BC Partnership. R, Q's daughter, owns 30 percent of BC Partnership and 10 percent of A Corporation. What is Q's ownership (directly and indirectly) in A Corporation and BC Partnership, if the constructive ownership rules of § 318 apply?

20-46 *Constructive Ownership of Stock.* D is a 30 percent partner in DE Partnership. DE Partnership owns 10 percent of F Corporation. Using the § 318 constructive ownership rules, what percentage of F Corporation is D considered to own?

20-47 *Constructive Ownership of Stock.* G owns 200 shares of H Corporation stock. G is a 50 percent partner in GJ Partnership. Using the § 318 constructive ownership rules, how many shares of H Corporation is the GJ Partnership considered to own?

20-48 *Liquidations—General Rule (§§ 331 and 336).*   S, an individual, owns all of the stock of B Corporation. S purchased the stock 10 years ago for $300,000. S decided to completely liquidate B Corporation, and all of the assets of B Corporation were distributed to S. The balance sheet for B Corporation immediately prior to the liquidation was as follows:

		Basis	Fair Market Value
Cash		$ 40,000	$ 40,000
Marketable securities (acquired after 1953)		40,000	80,000
Equipment.............................	$300,000		
Less: Accumulated depreciation	(150,000)	150,000	200,000
Land.................................		520,000	880,000
Total assets		$750,000	$1,200,000
Retained earnings.....................		$450,000	$ 0
Common stock		300,000	1,200,000
Total equity..........................		$750,000	$1,200,000

a.   What is S's recognized gain or loss?

b.   What is S's basis in the assets received?

c.   How much, if any, income or loss will B Corporation recognize as a result of the liquidation?

20-49 *Liquidations (§ 332).*   Assume the same facts as in Problem 20-48 except that the stock is owned by S, Inc.

a.   How much, if any, gain or loss must S, Inc. recognize?

b.   What is the basis of the assets received by S, Inc.?

c.   How much, if any, income must B Corporation recognize as a result of the liquidation?

20-50 *Section 338 Election.*   Assume the same facts as in Problem 20-48 except that all the stock was purchased by Z Corporation during the last 12 months for $1 million. Assume Z makes a § 338 election and pays taxes at a 34 percent rate.

a.   What is Z's recognized gain or loss?

b.   What, if any, income must B recognize?

c.   What is the total basis of the assets to B after the election?

Upon completion of this chapter you will be able to:

- Understand the rationale for the two corporate penalty taxes: the accumulated earnings tax and the personal holding company tax

- Identify the circumstances that must exist before the accumulated earnings tax will apply

- Recognize when earnings have accumulated beyond the reasonable needs of the business

- Explain how the accumulated earnings tax is computed

- Indicate when the personal holding company tax applies

- Apply the stock ownership and income tests to determine if a corporation is a personal holding company

- Explain how the personal holding company tax is computed and how it might be avoided

■ CHAPTER OUTLINE ■

Chapter 21

TAXATION OF CORPORATE ACCUMULATIONS

INTRODUCTION

In addition to the regular tax, a corporation may be subject to two penalty taxes—the *accumulated earnings tax* and the *personal holding company tax*. As the label "penalty" suggests, the primary goal of these taxes is not to raise revenues but rather to prohibit certain activities. The objective of the accumulated earnings tax and the personal holding company tax is to discourage individual taxpayers from using the corporate entity solely for tax avoidance. These taxes contend with potential abuse by imposing limitations on the amount of earnings a corporation may retain without penalty. The rationale for these taxes is readily apparent when some of the opportunities for tax avoidance using the corporate structure are considered.

Perhaps the best illustration of how the corporate entity could be used to avoid taxes involves the 70 percent dividends-received deduction. As discussed in Chapter 19, this deduction is available only to corporate taxpayers. Nevertheless, individuals could take advantage of the deduction by establishing a corporation and transferring their dividend-paying stocks to it. By so doing, all dividend income would be taxable to the corporation instead of the individual. Using this arrangement, the corporation would pay tax on dividends at an effective rate of 10.2 percent or lower [$34\% \times (100\% - 70\%)$] in 1991. Most individual taxpayers with taxable dividend income would reap substantial tax savings from this arrangement since all individual marginal rates are 15 percent or higher. This is but one of the alluring features of the corporate entity.

Another corporate advantage that individuals may use to avoid taxes concerns the difference between individual and corporate tax rates. Prior to the enactment of the Tax Reform Act of 1986, the top individual tax rate had perennially exceeded the top corporate tax rate—at one time by as much as 64 percentage points. Individuals could capitalize on this disparity by shifting their ordinary income to a corporate entity. By so doing, they could obtain substantial tax savings. Although the 1986 Act reversed this longstanding relationship between corporate and individual tax rates, an individual can still obtain savings at lower levels of taxable income by splitting income between the individual and his or her corporation. For example, in 1991 the average corporate tax rate applying to $50,000 of taxable income is 15 percent while that for an individual is 20.4 percent. The savings obtained by utilizing this disparity, the dividends-received deduction, and other advantages of the corporate entity, illustrate that individuals could achieve wholesale tax avoidance if not for some provision denying or discouraging such plans.

The two penalty taxes battle avoidance schemes such as those above by attacking their critical component: the accumulation. This can be seen by examining the two previous examples. The fate of both tax savings schemes rests on whether the shareholder can reduce or totally escape the second tax normally incurred when the income is ultimately received. In other words, the success of these arrangements depends on the extent to which double taxation is avoided. Herein lies the role of corporate accumulations. As long as the earnings are retained in the corporation, the second tax is avoided and the taxpayer is well on the way to obtaining tax savings. To foil such schemes, Congress enacted the accumulated earnings tax and the personal holding company tax. Both taxes are imposed on unwarranted accumulations of income—income that normally would have been taxable to the individual at individual tax rates if it had been distributed. By imposing these taxes on unreasonable accumulations, Congress hoped to compel distributions from the corporation and thus prevent taxpayers from using the corporate entity for tax avoidance.

Although these penalty taxes are rarely incurred, each serves as a strong deterrent against possible taxpayer abuse. This chapter examines the operation of both the accumulated earnings tax and the personal holding company tax.

Mitigation of the double tax penalty and any resulting tax savings are not achieved solely through corporate accumulations. The effect of double taxation can be reduced or avoided in other ways. The most common method used to avoid double taxation is by making distributions that are deductible. Typical deductible payments include compensation for services rendered to the corporation, rent for property leased to the corporation by the shareholder, and interest on funds loaned to the corporation. All of these payments are normally deductible by the corporation (thus effectively eliminating the corporate tax) and taxable to the shareholder. Avoidance of the double tax penalty does not ensure tax savings, however. All of these payments are taxable to the shareholder; thus, savings through use of the corporate entity may or may not result. For example, savings could occur if the payments are made to shareholders after they have dropped to a tax bracket lower than the one in which they were when the earnings were initially realized by the corporation. In addition, even if the shareholder's tax bracket remains unchanged, deferral of the tax could be beneficial.

> **Example 1.** L operates a home improvement company, specializing in kitchen renovations. He is in the 28% bracket in 1991. Assume that he incorporates his business in 1991 and it earns $100,000, of which $50,000 is paid to him as a salary and $50,000 is accumulated. In 1991 L saves $6,500 [(28% − 15%) × $50,000] in taxes on the $50,000 not distributed. However, if the $50,000 accumulated is distributed to L as a salary in 1996 when he is still in the 28% bracket, the $6,500 of taxes originally saved is lost. Although no taxes have been saved, L continues to benefit because he has been able to postpone the $6,500 in tax for five years. Assuming

his after tax rate of return is 10%, the present value of the $6,500 tax is reduced to $4,035—a savings of $2,465, or almost 38%. Note that the savings would have increased if the distribution had been made to L when his tax bracket dropped below 28%.

ACCUMULATED EARNINGS TAX

The accumulated earnings tax, unlike most taxes previously discussed, is not computed by a corporation when filing its annual income tax return. There is no form to file to determine the tax. Normally, the issue arises during an audit of the corporation. Consequently, the actual tax computation is made only after it has been determined that the penalty must be imposed.

AN OVERVIEW

The accumulated earnings tax applies whenever a corporation is "formed or availed of" for what is generally referred to as the *forbidden purpose*, that is, "for the purpose of avoiding the income tax with respect to its shareholders ... by permitting earnings and profits to accumulate instead of being ... distributed."[1] Whether a corporation is in fact being used for the forbidden purpose and thus subject to penalty is an elusive question requiring a determination of the taxpayer's *intent*. Without guidance from the law, ascertaining the taxpayer's intent might prove impossible. However, the Code states that the required intent is deemed present whenever a corporation accumulates earnings beyond its reasonable needs unless the corporation can prove to the contrary by a preponderance of evidence.[2] The problems concerning intent are considered in detail below.

Not all corporations risk the accumulated earnings tax. The Code specifically exempts tax-exempt corporations, personal holding companies, and passive foreign investment companies.[3] In addition, the tax normally does not apply to an S corporation since it does not shield shareholders from tax. An S corporation's earnings are taxed to its shareholders annually.

If it applies, the accumulated earnings tax is imposed on the annual increment to the corporation's total accumulated earnings, *not* on the total accumulated earnings balance. This annual addition is referred to as *accumulated taxable income*. The tax is 28 percent of the corporation's accumulated taxable income.[4] This tax does not replace any other taxes (e.g., the corporate income tax or the alternative minimum tax) but is imposed in addition to these taxes.

---

[1] § 532(a).

[2] § 533(a).

[3] § 532.

[4] § 531. The Revenue Reconciliation Act of 1990 did not change this rate to conform with the top marginal tax rate imposed on individuals.

Example 2.   In an audit of P Corporation, it was determined that the company had accumulated earnings beyond the reasonable needs of its business. In addition, the corporation's accumulated taxable income was $150,000. Since evidence of the forbidden purpose is present and the corporation has accumulated taxable income, the accumulated earnings tax must be paid. P Corporation's accumulated earnings tax is $42,000 ($150,000 × 28%).

In short, the corporation actually pays the accumulated earnings tax only if the forbidden purpose is found and it has accumulated taxable income. The following sections examine the determination of the taxpayer's intent and the computation of accumulated taxable income.

INTENT

The accumulated earnings tax is imposed only if the corporation is formed or used for the purpose of avoiding income tax on its shareholders by accumulating earnings.[5] Unfortunately, the Code provides no objective, mechanical test for determining whether a corporation is in fact being used for the forbidden purpose. As a result, application of the accumulated earnings tax rests on a subjective assessment of the shareholders' intent. The Code and regulations offer certain guidelines for making this assessment. Section 533 provides that a corporation is deemed to have been formed or used for the purpose of avoiding tax on its shareholders in two situations:

1.   If the corporation has accumulated earnings beyond the reasonable needs of the business

2.   If the corporation is a mere holding or investment company

The first situation is the most common cause of an accumulated earnings tax penalty. Consequently, avoidance of the accumulated earnings tax normally rests on whether the corporation can prove that its balance (i.e., that in excess of the $250,000 or $150,000 threshold) in accumulated earnings and profits is required by the reasonable needs of the business. Before discussing what constitutes a "reasonable need" of the business, it should be noted that other circumstances may indicate that the forbidden purpose does or does not exist.

According to the Regulations, the following factors are to be considered in determining whether the corporation has been used to avoid tax:[6]

1.   Loans to shareholders or expenditures that benefit shareholders personally

2.   Investments in assets having no reasonable connection with the corporation's business

3.   Poor dividend history

---

[5] § 532(a).

[6] Reg. § 1.533-1(a)(2).

Although these factors are not conclusive evidence, their presence no doubt suggests improper accumulations.

In determining whether the requisite intent exists, the courts have considered not only the criteria mentioned above but also whether the corporation's stock is widely held. As a general rule, the accumulated earnings tax does not apply to publicly held corporations. Publicly held corporations normally are protected since the number and variety of their shareholders usually preclude the formation of a dividend policy to minimize shareholder taxes. Nevertheless, the tax has been applied to publicly held corporations in which management was dominated by a small group of shareholders who were able to control dividend policy for their benefit.[7] Moreover, in 1984, Congress eliminated any doubts as to whether publicly held corporations are automatically exempt from the penalty tax. Section 532(c) currently provides that the tax be applied without regard to the number of shareholders of the corporation. Thus, the tax may be imposed on a publicly held corporation if the situation warrants.

While publicly held corporations usually are immune from the penalty tax, closely held corporations are particularly vulnerable since dividend policy is easily manipulated to meet shareholders' desires. Indeed, it may be a formidable task to prove that the corporation was not used for tax avoidance in light of the *Donruss* decision.[8] In that case, the Supreme Court held that the tax avoidance motive need not be the primary or dominant motive for the accumulation of earnings before the penalty tax is imposed. Rather, if tax avoidance is but one of the motives, the tax may apply.

As a practical matter, it is difficult, if not impossible, to determine the actual intent of the corporation and its shareholders. For this reason, the presumption created by § 533(a) looms large in virtually all accumulated earnings tax cases. Under this provision, a tax avoidance purpose is deemed to exist if earnings were accumulated beyond the reasonable needs of the business.[9] As might be expected, most of the litigation in this area has concerned what constitutes a reasonable need of the business. In fact, many cases do not even mention intent, implying that the accumulated earnings tax will be applied in all cases in which the accumulation exceeds business needs. Except in the unusual case in which a corporation's intent can be demonstrated, a corporation should be prepared to justify the accumulations based on the needs of the business.

---

[7] See *Trico Products*, 42-2 USTC ¶9540, 31 AFTR 394, 137 F.2d 424 (CA-2, 1943). In *Golconda Mining Corp.*, 58 T.C. 139 (1972), the Tax Court held that the tax applied where management controlled 17 percent of the outstanding stock of a publicly held corporation but the Ninth Circuit reversed, suggesting the tax should be applied solely to closely held corporations, 74-2 USTC ¶9845, 35 AFTR2d 75-336, 507 F.2d 594 (CA-9, 1974). Tax applied to publicly held corporation in *Alphatype Corporation v. U.S.* 76-2 USTC ¶9730, 38 AFTR2d 76-6019 (Ct. Cls., 1976). In Rev. Rul. 73-305, 1975-2 C.B. 228 the IRS confirmed its position that it will apply the tax to publicly held corporations.

[8] *U.S. v. Donruss*, 69-1 USTC ¶9167, 23 AFTR2d 69-418, 393 U.S. 297 (USSC, 1969).

[9] § 533(a).

REASONABLE NEEDS OF THE BUSINESS

The Code does not define the term "reasonable needs of the business." Instead it states that the reasonable needs of the business include the *reasonably anticipated needs* of the business.[10] The Regulations clarify the term reasonably anticipated needs.[11] First, the corporation must have specific, definite, and feasible plans for the use of the accumulation. The funds do not have to be expended in a short period of time after the close of the year. In fact, the plans need only require that the accumulations be expended within a *reasonable* time in the future. However, if the plans are postponed indefinitely, the needs will not be considered reasonable. As a general rule, the plans must not be vague and uncertain. If the plans are based on specific studies containing dollar estimates and are approved by the board of directors, the corporation is in a better position to prove that the plans qualify as reasonable business needs.

In addition to reasonably anticipated needs, the Code and Regulations identify certain specific reasons for accumulations that are considered to be reasonable needs of the business.[12] Several of these are discussed below.

Stock Redemptions from an Estate. A corporation is allowed to temporarily accumulate earnings in order to redeem the stock of a deceased shareholder in conjunction with Code § 303 (discussed in Chapter 20).[13] The accumulations may commence *only after* the death of a shareholder. The fact that a shareholder dies after accumulations have been made and the corporation redeems his or her stock under § 303 is ignored in evaluating pre-death accumulations.[14] If the shareholder owned stock in two or more corporations, each corporation is entitled to accumulate only a portion of the total redeemable amount unless the estate's executor or administrator has indicated that more shares of one of the corporations will be offered for redemption than will those of another corporation.[15] The requirements of § 303 (relating to redemption of stock to pay death taxes) must be met in order for this provision to apply.

Product Liability Loss Reserves. The Code also allows accumulations to cover product liability losses.[16] Product liability is defined as damages for physical or emotional harm as well as damages and loss to property as a result of the use of a product sold, leased, or manufactured by taxpayer.[17] The amount accumulated can cover *both* actual and reasonably anticipated losses.

Business Expansion or Plant Replacement. Perhaps the most common reason for accumulating earnings that the Regulations specifically authorize is for

---

[10]   § 537(a)(1).

[11]   Reg. § 1.537-1(b).

[12]   See § 537(a) and (b), and Reg. § 1.537-2.

[13]   § 537(b)(1).

[14]   § 537(b)(5).

[15]   Reg. § 1.537-1(c)(3).

[16]   § 537(b)(4).

[17]   § 172(j).

bona fide expansion of business or replacement of plant.[18] This provision includes the purchase or construction of a building.[19] It also includes the modernization, rehabilitation, or replacement of assets.[20] However, this provision does not shield a corporation which has not adequately specified and documented its expansion needs.[21]

Acquisition of a Business Enterprise. A second reason offered in the Regulations for accumulating earnings is for the acquisition of a business enterprise through the purchase of stock or assets.[22] This appears to encourage business expansion, since the Regulations state that the business for which earnings can be accumulated includes any line of business the corporation wishes to undertake, and not just the line of business previously carried on.[23] However, this provision for accumulation is limited by the statement in the Regulations that investments in properties or securities that are *unrelated* to the activities of the business of the corporation are unacceptable reasons for accumulations.[24] The statements in the Regulations raise a question as to the validity of accumulations for diversification. On one hand the corporation can acquire an enterprise or expand its business into any field. On the other hand the acquisition should be related to the corporation's activities. This apparent conflict in the Regulations is reflected in court decisions. A corporation that manufactured automobile clutches was permitted to accumulate income to acquire a business that would make use of the corporation's metal-working expertise, whereas a corporation in the printing business was not permitted to accumulate income to acquire real estate.[25] The extent to which a corporation can diversify is uncertain. It appears that diversification into passive investments is unacceptable whereas diversification into an operating business, no matter how far removed from the original line of business, is acceptable.

Retirement of Indebtedness. The Regulations also provide for the accumulation of earnings to retire business indebtedness.[26] The debt can be to either a third party or a shareholder as long as it is a *bona fide* business debt.

---

[18]   Reg. § 1.537-2(b)(1).

[19]   *Sorgel v. U.S.*, 72-1 USTC ¶9427, 29 AFTR2d 72-1035, 341 F. Supp. 1 (D. Ct. Wisc., 1972).

[20]   *Knoxville Iron*, 18 TCM 251, T.C. Memo 1959-54.

[21]   *I.A. Dress Co.*, 60-1 USTC ¶9204, 5 AFTR2d 429, 273 F.2d 543 (CA-2, 1960), affg. 32 T.C. 93; *Herzog Miniature Lamp Works, Inc.*, 73-2 USTC ¶9593, 32 AFTR2d 73-5282, 273 F.2d 543, (CA-2, 1973).

[22]   Reg. § 1.537-2(b)(2).

[23]   Reg. § 1.537-3(a).

[24]   Reg. § 1.537-2(c)(4).

[25]   *Alma Piston Co.*, 22 TCM 948, T.C. Memo 1963-195; *Union Offset*, 79-2 USTC ¶9550, 44 AFTR2d 79-5652, 603 F.2d 90 (CA-9, 1979).

[26]   Reg. § 1.537-2(b)(3).

Investments or Loans to Suppliers or Customers. The Regulations state that earnings may be accumulated to provide for investments or loans to suppliers or customers.[27] However, loans to shareholders, friends and relatives of shareholders, and corporations controlled by shareholders of the corporation making the loan indicate that earnings are possibly being accumulated beyond reasonable business needs.[28]

Contingencies. Although the Regulations do not specifically allow accumulations for contingencies, they do imply approval of such accumulations as long as the contingencies are not unrealistic.[29] Unfortunately, the distinction between realistic and unrealistic contingencies is difficult to define. However, the more specific the need, the more detailed the cash estimate, and the more likely the occurrence, the easier it will be to prove the accumulation is reasonable.

Redemption of Stock. As noted above, accumulations to redeem stock from a decedent's estate under § 303 constitute a reasonable need of the business. This provision does not cover any other stock redemption. Several cases have held that a redemption may be a reasonable need provided the redemption is for the benefit of the corporation and not the shareholder.[30] For example, the redemption of a dissenting minority shareholder's stock can be for the corporation's benefit whereas the redemption of a majority shareholder's stock would be for the shareholder's benefit. It might also be possible to prove that the redemption was necessary to reduce or eliminate disputes over management or conduct of the business.

Working Capital. Another reason mentioned in the Regulations for a reasonable accumulation of earnings and profits is the need for working capital.[31] This is one of the primary justifications corporations use for the accumulation of earnings. A corporation is permitted to retain earnings to provide necessary working capital. Initially, the courts tried to measure working capital sufficiency by using rules of thumb. A current ratio of 2.5 to 1 generally meant that the corporation had not accumulated income unreasonably.[32] The courts considered a current ratio more than 2.5 to 1 an indication of unreasonable accumulation.

In the 1965 case of *Bardahl Mfg. Corp.*, the Tax Court utilized a formula to compute the working capital needs of a corporation.[33] Under this approach (called the *Bardahl* formula), the working capital needed for one operating cycle is computed. This amount in essence represents the cash *needed* to meet expenses incurred during the operating cycle—the period required for a business to convert

---

[27]   Reg. § 1.537-2(b)(5).

[28]   Reg. §§ 1.537-2(c)(1), (2), and (3).

[29]   Reg. § 1.537-2(c)(5).

[30]   See *John B. Lambert & Assoc. v. U.S.*, 38 AFTR2d 6207 (Ct. Cls., 1976); *C.E. Hooper, Inc. v. U.S.*, 38 AFTR2d 5417, 539 F.2d 1276 (Ct. Cls., 1976); *Mountain State Steel Foundries, Inc. v. Comm.*, 6 AFTR2d 5910, 284 F.2d 737 (CA-4, 1960); and *Koma, Inc. v. Comm.*, 40 AFTR 712, 189 F.2d 390 (CA-10, 1951).

[31]   Reg. § 1.537-2(b)(4).

[32]   *J. Scripps Newspaper*, 44 T.C. 453 (1965).

[33]   *Bardahl Mfg. Corp.*, 24 TCM 1030, T.C. Memo 1965-200.

cash into inventory, sell the merchandise, convert the customer's accounts receivable into cash, and pay its accounts payable. This necessary working capital is then compared to actual working capital. If necessary working capital is greater than actual working capital, an accumulation of earnings to meet the necessary working capital requirements is justified. If actual working capital is greater than the working capital needed, the corporation must show other reasons for the accumulation of earnings in order to avoid the accumulated earnings tax.

The initial step of the *Bardahl* formula is to calculate the inventory, accounts receivable, and accounts payable cycle ratios. These ratios are computed as follows:

$$1.\ \textit{Inventory cycle ratio} = \frac{\text{Average inventory}}{\text{Cost of goods sold}}$$

$$2.\ \textit{Accounts receivable cycle ratio} = \frac{\text{Average accounts receivable}}{\text{Net sales}}$$

$$3.\ \textit{Accounts payable cycle ratio} = \frac{\text{Average accounts payable}}{\text{Purchases}}$$

The ratios resulting from these calculations represent the cycle expressed as a percentage of the year. In other words, if the accounts receivable cycle ratio is 10 percent, then it normally takes about 36 days (10% × 365) to collect a receivable once it has been generated by a sale.

Instead of using the *average* inventory and the *average* receivables, a corporation can use *peak values* if it is in a seasonal business. If the corporation uses peak values for the other ratios, it may be required to use peak payables.

Once computed, the three ratios are combined. The result represents the number of days—expressed as a fraction of the year—during which the corporation needs working capital to meet its operating expenses. The operating cycle ratio is computed as follows:

$$\begin{array}{l} \text{Inventory cycle ratio} \\ + \ \text{Accounts receivable cycle ratio} \\ - \ \underline{\text{Accounts payable cycle ratio}} \\ = \ \text{Operating cycle ratio} \end{array}$$

The operating cycle ratio is multiplied by the *annual operating expenses* to compute the necessary working capital. Operating expenses are defined as the cost of goods sold plus other annual expenses (i.e., general, administrative, and selling expenses). The operating expense category does not include depreciation since depreciation does not require the use of cash. However, the category can include income taxes if the corporation pays estimated taxes and will make a tax payment during the next operating cycle.[34] Other expenses should be included if they will require the expenditure of cash during the next operating cycle.

---

[34] *Empire Steel*, 33 TCM 155, T.C. Memo 1974-34.

The required working capital computed by the *Bardahl* formula is compared to actual working capital to determine if there have been excess accumulations. Since the computed working capital is based on accounting data, it is normally compared to actual working capital (current assets − current liabilities) computed from the corporation's financial statements. There are exceptions to this rule. Financial statements are not used if they do not clearly reflect the company's working capital. The Supreme Court authorized the use of fair market value instead of historical cost to value a firm's current assets in *Ivan Allen Co.*[35] The assets in question were marketable securities that had appreciated. The decision is broad enough to permit the Internal Revenue Service to determine actual working capital based on current value anytime there is a significant difference between cost and market.

Any corporation whose actual working capital does not exceed required working capital (per the *Bardahl* formula) should be exempt from the accumulated earnings tax. If the actual working capital exceeds required working capital, the excess is considered an indication of unreasonable accumulations. This excess is compared to the reasonable needs of the business (other than working capital) to determine if the accumulations are unreasonable. To the extent that the corporation has needs, it may accumulate funds. If all of the excess working capital is not needed, the tax is imposed. The tax is based on the accumulated taxable income and not the excess working capital.

> **Example 3.**   K owns and operates K's Apparel, Inc. (KAI). After hearing that a friend's corporation was recently slapped with an accumulated earnings tax penalty, she asked her accountant to determine the vulnerability of her own business. The following is a balance sheet and income statement for 1990 and 1991 for KAI.

---

[35]   *Ivan Allen Co. v. U.S.*, 75-2 USTC ¶9557, 36 AFTR2d 75-5200, 422 U.S. 617 (USSC, 1975).

Balance Sheet

	1990	1991
Current Assets:		
Cash	$ 55,000	$ 67,000
Marketable securities	10,000	8,000
Accounts receivable (net)	45,000	55,000
Inventory	30,000	20,000
Total Current Assets	$140,000	$150,000
Property, plant, and equipment (net)	300,000	425,000
Total Assets	$440,000	$575,000
Current Liabilities:		
Notes payable	$ 5,000	$ 4,000
Accounts payable	50,000	30,000
Accrued expenses	8,000	16,000
Total Liabilities	$ 63,000	$ 50,000
Long-term debt	37,000	40,000
Total Current Liabilities	$100,000	$ 90,000
Stockholders' Equity:		
Common stock	10,000	10,000
Earnings and profits	330,000	475,000
Total Liabilities and Stockholders' Equity	$440,000	$575,000

Income Statement

	1990	1991
Sales	$400,000	$500,000
Cost of goods sold:		
Beginning inventory	$ 40,000	$ 30,000
Purchases	300,000	320,000
Ending inventory	(30,000)	(20,000)
Total	$310,000	$330,000
Gross profit	$ 90,000	$170,000
Other expenses:		
Depreciation	$ 40,000	$ 55,000
Selling expenses	10,000	15,000
Administrative	20,000	50,000
Total	$ 70,000	$120,000
Net income before taxes	$ 20,000	$ 50,000
Income tax expense	(2,000)	(5,000)
Net income	$ 18,000	$ 45,000

In addition to this information, K indicated that at the end of 1991 the securities were worth $15,000 more than their book value, or $23,000. K also estimates that her reasonable needs for the current year 1991 amount to $20,000.

Under the *Bardahl* formula, her working capital needs are determined as follows:

Step 1: Operating cycle expressed as a fraction of the year (in thousands):

$$\text{Inventory cycle} = \frac{\text{Average inventory}}{\text{Cost of goods sold}} = [(30 + 20) \div 2] \div 330 = 0.0758$$

$$+ \text{ Receivable cycle} = \frac{\text{Average receivables}}{\text{Sales}} = [(45 + 55) \div 2] \div 500 = 0.1000$$

$$- \text{ Payables cycle} = \frac{\text{Average payables}}{\text{Purchases}} = [(50 + 30) \div 2] \div 320 = (0.1250)$$

= Operating cycle expressed as percentage of the year   = 0.0508

Step 2: Computation of operating expenses:

Operating expenses:	
Cost of goods sold	$330,000
Selling expenses	15,000
Administrative expenses	50,000
Taxes	5,000
Total operating expenses	$400,000

Step 3: Working capital needs:

Operating expenses (Step 2)	$400,000
× Operating cycle (Step 1)	× 0.0508
= Working capital needs	$ 20,320

K's working capital needs, $20,320, must be compared to actual working capital using the assets' fair market value. Any excess of actual working capital over required working capital must be compared to the current year's needs to determine if unwarranted accumulations exist. Assuming the marketable securities are actually worth $23,000, the comparison is made as follows:

Actual working capital:		
Current assets		
($150,000 + $15,000)	$165,000	
− Current liabilities	(50,000)	
= Actual working capital		$115,000
− Required working capital (Step 3)		(20,320)
= Excess working capital		$ 94,680
− Reasonable needs		(20,000)
= Accumulations beyond current needs		$ 74,680

The accumulated earnings tax focuses on whether the corporation has accumulated liquid assets beyond its reasonable needs that could be distributed to shareholders. In this case, actual working capital exceeds required working capital and other needs of the business by $74,680, implying that the accumulated earnings tax applies. If so, the actual penalty tax is computed using accumulated taxable income, as explained below.

COMPUTATION OF THE ACCUMULATED EARNINGS TAX

The purpose of the accumulated earnings tax is to penalize taxpayers with unwarranted accumulations. To accomplish this, a 28 percent tax is imposed on what the Code refers to as *accumulated taxable income*. Accumulated taxable income is designed to represent the amount that the corporation could have distributed after funding its reasonable needs. In essence, the computation attempts to determine the corporation's dividend-paying capacity. Exhibit 21-1 shows the formula for computing accumulated taxable income.[36]

Exhibit 21-1
Accumulated Taxable Income[37]

Taxable income:

Plus:
1. The dividends-received deduction
2. Any net operating loss deduction that is reflected in taxable income
3. Any capital-loss carryovers from other years that are reflected in taxable income

Minus:
1. Federal income taxes for the year, but not the accumulated earnings tax or the personal holding company tax
2. The charitable contributions for the year in excess of the 10 percent limitation
3. Any net capital loss incurred during the year reduced by net capital gain deductions of prior years that have not previously reduced any net capital loss deduction
4. Any net capital gain (net long-term capital gain − the net short-term capital loss) for the year minus the taxes attributable to the gain and any net capital losses of prior years that have not reduced a net capital gain deduction in determining the accumulated earnings tax

Equals: **Adjusted taxable income**

Minus:
1. Accumulated earnings credit (see Exhibit 21-2)
2. Dividends paid deduction (see Exhibit 21-3)

Equals: **Accumulated taxable income**

---

[36] § 535.

[37] § 535. Several additional adjustments are required for computing accumulated taxable income of a holding or investment company.

The computation of accumulated taxable income begins with an imperfect measure of the corporation's ability to pay dividends—taxable income. To obtain a more representative measure of the corporation's dividend-paying capacity, taxable income is modified to arrive at what is often referred to as *adjusted taxable income*.[38] For example, the deduction allowed for dividends received is added back to taxable income since it has no effect on the corporation's ability to pay dividends. The same rationale can be given for the net operating loss deduction. In contrast, charitable contributions in excess of the 10 percent limitation may be deducted in determining adjusted taxable income since the corporation does not have the nondeductible amount available to pay dividends. For the same reason, Federal income taxes may be deducted in computing adjusted taxable income.

The deduction for capital gains stems from the assumption that these earnings are used to fund the corporation's needs and consequently may be accumulated with impunity. Capital losses are deductible since these amounts are unavailable for payment of dividends and are not reflected in taxable income. As shown in Exhibit 21-1, however, the deductions for capital gains as well as capital losses must be modified.

Prior to 1984, corporations were entitled to reduce taxable income not only by the amount of their net capital gains (reduced by related taxes) but also by the full amount of their net capital losses, depending on whether a net capital gain or loss occurred. Consequently, there was an advantage in recognizing capital gains in one year and capital losses in another year in order to avoid netting and thus permit both gains and losses to be deductible in full. For example, if the corporation had a capital loss of $1,000 this year and a capital gain of $5,000 next year (ignoring taxes), both could be deducted in full each year in computing adjusted taxable income. However, if they occurred in the same year, the deduction would be limited to $4,000. To eliminate this planning opportunity, corporations are now required to reduce their net capital losses by any net capital gain deductions that have been used to arrive at adjusted taxable income in prior years. Under these rules, it is immaterial in what order or in what year gains and losses are recognized. In effect, taxable income is reduced only by the overall net gain or loss that the corporation has recognized to date.

[38] This term is not found in the Code; it is used here solely for purposes of exposition.

Example 4. T Corporation has the following income and deductions for 1991:

Income from operations............................	$150,000
Dividend income (from less than 20% owned corporations)......................................	40,000
Charitable contributions............................	25,000

T Corporation computes its taxable income as follows:

Income from operations......................		$150,000
Dividend income............................		40,000
Income before special deductions............		$190,000
Special deductions:		
Charitable contribution (limited)..........	$19,000	
Dividend-received deduction.............	28,000	
Total special deductions.................		(47,000)
Taxable income.............................		$143,000

T Corporation's Federal income taxes for 1991 are $39,020. T Corporation's adjusted taxable income is computed as follows:

Taxable income............................		$143,000
Plus: Dividend-received deduction.......		28,000
		$171,000
Minus the sum of		
Federal income taxes....................	$39,020	
Actual charitable contributions for the year minus the charitable contribution deduction reflected in taxable income ($25,000 − $19,000).................	6,000	(45,020)
Equals: Adjusted taxable income...........		$125,980

Two additional deductions are permitted in computing accumulated taxable income: the dividends-paid deduction and the accumulated earnings credit. The deduction allowed for dividends is consistent with the theory that the tax should be imposed only on income that has not been distributed. The accumulated earnings credit allows the taxpayer to accumulate without penalty $250,000 or an amount equal to the reasonable needs of the business, whichever is greater.

ACCUMULATED EARNINGS CREDIT

In creating the accumulated earnings tax, Congress realized that a corporation should not be penalized for keeping enough of its earnings to meet legitimate business needs. For this reason, in computing accumulated taxable income, a corporation is allowed—in effect—a reduction for the amount out of current year's earnings necessary to meet such needs. This reduction is the *accumulated earnings credit*.[39] Note that despite its name, the credit actually operates as a deduction. As a practical matter, it is this credit that insulates most corporations from the accumulated earnings tax.

Specifically, the credit is the greater of two amounts as described in Exhibit 21-2 and discussed further below. Generally, however, the credit for the current year may be determined as follows:

Reasonable business needs (or $250,000 if larger)	$xxx,xxx
Less: Beginning Accumulated E&P	(xx,xxx)
Accumulated earnings credit.	$xxx,xxx

Part 1 of Exhibit 21-2 contains the general rule authorizing accumulations. It permits corporations to accumulate earnings to the extent of their reasonable needs without penalty.[40] In determining the amount of the earnings and profits for the taxable year that have been retained to meet the reasonable needs of the business, it is necessary to consider to what extent the accumulated earnings and profits are available to cover these needs.[41] In effect, prior accumulations reduce the amount that can be retained in the current year. If the corporation's accumulated earnings and profits are sufficient to meet the reasonable needs of the business, *none* of the current earnings and profits will be considered to be retained to meet the reasonable needs of the business.

Exhibit 21-2
Accumulated Earnings Credit[42]

The accumulated earnings credit is the greater of

1. *General Rule:* Earnings and profits for the taxable year that are retained to meet the reasonable needs of the business, minus the net capital gain for the year (reduced by the taxes attributable to the gain),

or

2. *Minimum Credit:* $250,000 ($150,000 for personal service corporations) minus the accumulated earnings and profits of the corporation at the close of the *preceding* taxable year, adjusted for dividends paid in the current year *deemed* paid in the prior year.

---

[39]   § 535(c).

[40]   § 535(c)(1).

[41]   Reg. § 1.535-3(b)(1)(ii).

[42]   § 535(c)(1).

Part 2 of Exhibit 21-2 is the so-called *minimum credit*.[43] For most corporations the amount of the minimum credit is $250,000. For personal service corporations, the minimum credit is $150,000. Personal service corporations are corporations that provide services in the area of health, law, engineering, architecture, accounting, actuarial science, performing arts, or consulting. The lower credit for personal service corporations reflects the fact that their capital needs are relatively small when compared to retail or manufacturing businesses.

To determine the amount of the minimum credit available for the current year, the base amount, $250,000 ($150,000), must be reduced by the accumulated earnings and profits at the close of the preceding tax year. For purposes of this computation, the accumulated earnings and profits at the close of the preceding year are reduced by the dividends that were paid by the corporation within $2\frac{1}{2}$ months after the close of the preceding year.[44]

> **Example 5.** X Corporation, a calendar year retail department store, had current earnings and profits for 1991 of $75,000. Its accumulated earnings and profits at the close of 1990 were $200,000. X Corporation has paid no dividends for five years. X Corporation's taxable income for 1991 included a net capital gain of $20,000. [The taxes related to this net capital gain were $6,800 (34% × $20,000).] The reasonable needs of X Corporation are estimated to be $240,000. The amount of X Corporation's current earnings and profits that are retained to meet reasonable business needs is computed as follows:
>
> | | |
> |---|---:|
> | Estimated reasonable needs of X Corporation | $240,000 |
> | Less: Accumulated earnings and profits as of 12/31/90 | (200,000) |
> | Extent to which current earnings and profits are needed to cover the reasonable needs of the business | $ 40,000 |

Even though the current earnings and profits are $75,000, only $40,000 of the current earnings and profits are needed to meet the reasonable needs of the business.

---

[43] § 535(c)(2).   [44] § 535(c)(4).

The accumulated earnings credit is the greater of

1.	Current earnings and profits to meet the reasonable needs of the business.............................		$ 40,000
	Minus: Net capital gain.............	$20,000	
	Reduced by the taxes attributable to the gain...	(6,800)	(13,200)
	General rule credit......................		$ 26,800

or

2.	$250,000...............................	$250,000
	Minus: Accumulated earnings and profits as of 12/31/90..........	(200,000)
	Minimum credit.........................	$ 50,000

X Corporation's accumulated earnings credit is $50,000, the greater of the general rule credit ($26,800) or the minimum credit ($50,000).

Example 6. Assume the same facts as in *Example 5*, except that X Corporation is an engineering firm. The general rule credit would still be $26,800, but the minimum credit would be computed as follows:

$150,000...	$150,000
Minus: Accumulated earnings and profits as of 12/31/90..................	(200,000)
Minimum credit (the minimum credit cannot be a negative number)...................	$ 0

In this situation the accumulated earnings credit is $26,800, the greater of the general rule credit ($26,800) or the minimum credit ($0).

Two aspects of the accumulated earnings credit deserve special mention. First, the minimum credit has a very limited role. Since the $250,000 (or $150,000 for service corporations) is reduced by the prior accumulations, the minimum credit will always be zero for firms that have greater than $250,000 of accumulated earnings. In other words, accumulations in excess of $250,000 must be justified by business needs.

The second aspect involves capital gains. As discussed previously, capital gains (net of related taxes) are subtracted from taxable income in arriving at adjusted taxable income. Therefore, a corporation can accumulate all of its capital gains without the imposition of the accumulated earnings tax. At the same time, however, capital gains are subtracted from business needs in arriving at the general credit (see Exhibit 21-2). As a result, a capital gain may cause accumulations of ordinary income to be subject to the special tax even though the capital gain itself escapes penalty. In effect, the computations are based on the assumption that business needs are funded first from capital gains and then from income from operations.

DIVIDENDS-PAID DEDUCTION

Exhibit 21-1 indicated that both the accumulated earnings credit and the dividends-paid deduction are adjustments in computing accumulated taxable income. Exhibit 21-3 lists the types of dividends that constitute the dividends-paid deduction.

To qualify for the dividend deduction, the distribution must constitute a "dividend" as defined in § 316.[45] As previously discussed, § 316 limits dividends to distributions out of current earnings and profits and accumulated earnings and profits since 1913. Property distributions qualify only to the extent of their adjusted basis.[46]

Throwback Dividends. The dividends-paid deduction includes not only dividends paid during the year, but also so-called *throwback dividends*, dividends paid during the 2 1/2 months following the close of the tax year.[47] Amounts paid during the 2 1/2 month period *must* be treated as if paid in the previous year.[48] This treatment is mandatory and not elective by the shareholders or the corporation.

Consent Dividends. In addition to actual dividends paid, the corporation is entitled to a deduction for consent dividends.[49] Sometimes a corporation may have a large amount of accumulated earnings, but insufficient cash or property to make a dividend distribution. In order to avoid the accumulated earnings tax, the

---

Exhibit 21-3
Dividends-Paid Deduction[50]

1. Dividends paid during the taxable year,[51]

2. Dividends paid within 2 1/2 months after the close of the taxable year,[52]

3. Consent dividends,[53] plus

4. Liquidating distributions.[54]

Equals: **Dividends-Paid Deduction**

---

[45] § 562(a).

[46] Reg. § 1.562-1(a).

[47] § 563.

[48] Reg. § 1.563-1.

[49] § 565.

[50] §§ 561 through 565.

[51] § 561(a)(1).

[52] § 563(a).

[53] § 565.

[54] § 562(b)(1).

corporation may obtain a dividends-paid deduction by using consent dividends— so called because the shareholders consent to treat a certain amount as a taxable dividend on their tax returns even though there is no distribution of cash or property. Not only are the shareholders deemed to receive the amount to which they consent, but they also are treated as having reinvested the amount received as a contribution to the corporation's capital.

To qualify a dividend as a consent dividend, the shareholders must file a consent form (Form 972) with the corporate income tax return. The consents must be filed by the due date (including extensions) of the corporate tax return for the year in which the dividend deduction is requested. Only shareholders who own stock on the last day of the tax year need file consent forms. On the forms, each shareholder must specify the amount of the consent dividend and then include this amount as a cash distribution by the corporation on his or her individual income tax return. Consent dividends are limited to the amount that would have qualified as a dividend under Code § 316 had the dividend been distributed in cash.[55] Only shareholders of common and participating preferred stock may consent to dividends.[56]

Liquidating Distributions. If the distribution is in liquidation, partial liquidation, or redemption of stock, the portion of the distribution chargeable to earnings and profits is included in the dividend deduction.[57] For partial liquidations and redemptions, this is the redeemed stock's proportionate share of accumulated E&P. For complete liquidations, any amount distributed within the two years following the adoption of a plan of liquidation and that is pursuant to the plan is included in the dividends-paid deduction, but not to exceed the corporation's current earnings and profits for the year of distribution.[58]

PERSONAL HOLDING COMPANY TAX

As mentioned earlier in this chapter, the accumulated earnings tax is not the only penalty tax applicable to corporations. Congress has also enacted the personal holding company tax. This tax evolved in 1934 from the need to stop the growing number of individuals who were misusing the corporate entity despite the existence of the accumulated earnings tax. The personal holding company tax was designed to thwart three particular schemes prevalent during that period.

The first two schemes specifically aimed to take advantage of the disparity between individual and corporate tax rates. At that time, the maximum individual tax rates were approximately 45 percentage points higher than the maximum corporate rates. A typical plan used to take advantage of this differential involved the formation of a corporation to hold an individual's investment portfolio. This

---

[55]   Reg. § 1.565-2(a).

[56]   § 565(f).

[57]   § 562(b)(1).

[58]   § 562(b)(1)(B).

plan allowed an individual's interest and dividends to become taxable to the corporation rather than to the individual and consequently to be taxed at the lower corporate rates. Another, somewhat more sophisticated, technique enabled the transfer of an individual's service income to a corporation. The blueprint for this plan required the formation of a corporation by an individual (e.g., movie star) who subsequently became an employee of the corporation. With the corporation in place, parties seeking the individual's services were forced to contract with the corporation rather than with the individual. The individual would then perform the services, but the corporation would receive the revenue. Finally, the corporation would pay the individual a salary which was less than the revenue earned. Through this plan, the individual succeeded in transferring at least some of the revenue to the corporation, where it would be taxed at the lower corporate rates.

The final scheme was not specifically designed to take advantage of the lower corporate rates. Instead, its attraction grew from the practical presumption that all corporate activities are business activities. Given this presumption, an individual would transfer his or her personal assets (e.g., a yacht, race car, or vacation home) along with other investments to the corporation. Under the veil of the corporation, the expenses relating to the personal assets, such as maintenance of a yacht, would be magically transformed from nondeductible personal expenses to deductible business expenses which could offset the income produced by the investments. In short, by using the corporate form, individuals were able to disguise their personal expenses as business expenses and deduct them.

Although the Internal Revenue Service tried to curb these abuses using the accumulated earnings tax, attempts often failed. These failures normally could be attributed to the problem of proving that the individuals actually intended to avoid taxes. Aware of this problem, Congress formulated the personal holding company tax, which could be applied without having to prove that the forbidden purpose existed. In contrast to the accumulated earnings tax, which is imposed only after a subjective assessment of the individual's intentions, the personal holding company tax automatically applies whenever the corporation satisfies two objective tests.

Not all corporations that meet the applicable tests are subject to the penalty tax, however. The Code specifically exempts certain corporations. These include S corporations, tax-exempt corporations, banks, life insurance companies, surety companies, foreign personal holding companies, lending and finance companies, and several other types of corporations.[59]

If the personal holding company tax applies, the tax is 28 percent of undistributed personal holding company income.[60] Like the accumulated earnings tax, the personal holding company tax is levied in addition to the regular tax.[61] The personal holding company tax differs from the accumulated earnings tax,

---

[59] § 542(c).   [61] *Ibid.*

[60] § 541.

however, in that the corporation is required to compute and remit any personal holding tax due at the time it files its annual return. Form 1120-PH is used to compute the tax and must be filed with the corporation's annual Form 1120. In those cases where both the accumulated earnings tax and the personal holding company tax are applicable, only the personal holding company tax is imposed.[62]

PERSONAL HOLDING COMPANY DEFINED

The personal holding company tax applies only if the corporation is considered a personal holding company (PHC). As might be expected in light of the schemes prevalent at the time the tax was enacted, a corporation generally qualifies as a personal holding company if it is closely held and a substantial portion of its income is derived from passive sources or services. Specifically, the Code provides that a corporation is deemed to be a personal holding company if it satisfies both of the following tests.[63]

1. *Ownership*—At any time during the last half of the taxable year, more than 50 percent of the value of the corporation's outstanding stock is owned by five or fewer individuals.[64]

2. *Passive income*—At least 60 percent of the corporation's adjusted ordinary gross income consists of personal holding company income (PHCI).[65]

Before each of these tests is examined in detail, the distinction between the personal holding company tax and the accumulated earnings tax should be emphasized. The accumulated earnings tax applies only when it is proven that it was the shareholder's intention to use the corporation to shield income from individual tax rates. In contrast, application of the personal holding company tax requires only that two mechanical tests be satisfied. As a result, a corporation may fall victim to the personal holding company tax where there was no intention to avoid tax by misusing the corporation. For example, consider a closely held corporation in the process of liquidating. During liquidation, the corporation may have income from operations and passive income from temporary investments (investments made pending final distributions). If the passive income is substantial—60 percent or more of the corporation's total income—the corporation will be treated as a personal holding company subject to the penalty tax even though there was no intention by the shareholders to shelter the passive income. As this example illustrates, the mechanical nature of the personal holding company tax, unlike the subjective nature of the accumulated earnings tax, presents a trap for those with the noblest of intentions.

---

[62] § 532(b)(1).

[63] § 542.

[64] § 542(a)(2).

[65] § 542(a)(1).

PHC OWNERSHIP TEST

As indicated above, the first part of the two-part test for personal holding company status concerns ownership. Apparently it was Congressional belief that the tax-saving schemes described above succeeded primarily in those cases where there was a concentration of ownership. For this reason, the ownership test is satisfied only if five or fewer individuals own more than 50 percent of the value of the corporation's outstanding shares of stock at any time during the last half of the taxable year.[66] As a quick study of this test reveals, a corporation having less than ten shareholders always meets the ownership test since there will always be a combination of five or fewer shareholders owning more than 50 percent of the stock (e.g., $100\% \div 9 = 11\%$; $11\% \times 5 > 50\%$). Thus, it becomes apparent that closely held corporations are extremely vulnerable to the tax.

In performing the stock ownership test, the shareholder's *direct* and *indirect* ownership must be taken into account.[67] Indirect ownership is determined using a set of constructive ownership rules designed specifically for the personal holding company area.[68] According to these rules, a taxpayer is considered owning indirectly the following:

1. Stock owned directly or indirectly by his or her family, including his or her brothers, sisters, spouse, ancestors, and lineal descendents[69]

2. His or her proportionate share of any stock owned by a corporation, partnership, estate, or trust in which he or she has ownership (or of which he or she is a beneficiary in the case of an estate or trust)[70] and

3. Stock owned indirectly or directly by his or her partner in a partnership[71]

In using these rules, the following guidelines must be observed: (1) stock attributed from one family member to another cannot be reattributed to yet another member of the family,[72] (2) stock attributed from a partner to the taxpayer cannot be reattributed to a member of his or her family or to yet another partner,[73] (3) stock on which the taxpayer has an option is treated as being actually owned,[74] and (4) convertible securities are treated as outstanding stock.[75] In addition, Code § 544 contains other rules that may affect an individual's stock ownership.

---

[66] § 542(a)(2).

[67] *Ibid.*

[68] § 544.

[69] § 544(a)(2).

[70] § 544(a)(1).

[71] § 544(a)(2).

[72] § 544(a)(5).

[73] *Ibid.*

[74] § 544(a)(3).

[75] § 544(b).

INCOME TEST

Although the stock ownership test may be satisfied, a corporation is not considered a personal holding company unless it also passes an income test. In general terms, this test is straightforward: at least 60 percent of the corporation's income must be derived from either passive sources or certain types of services. Unfortunately, the technical translation of this requirement is somewhat more complicated. According to the Code, at least 60 percent of the corporation's *adjusted ordinary gross income* must be *personal holding company income*.[76] This relationship may be expressed numerically as follows:

$$\frac{\text{Personal holding company income}}{\text{Adjusted ordinary gross income}} \geq 60\%$$

As will be seen below, the definition of each of these terms can be baffling. However, the general theme of each term and the thrust of the test should not be lost in the complexity. Personal holding company income is generally passive income, while adjusted ordinary gross income is just that, ordinary gross income with a few modifications. Performing the income test is, in essence, a matter of determining whether too much of the corporation's income (adjusted ordinary gross income) is passive income (personal holding company income).

> **Example 7.** K, a high-bracket taxpayer, wished to reduce her taxes. Upon the advice of an old friend, she transferred all of her stocks and bonds to a newly formed corporation of which she is the sole owner. During the year, the corporation had dividend income of $40,000 and interest income of $35,000. In this case, the corporation is treated as a personal holding company because *both* the stock ownership test and the income test are satisfied. The stock ownership test is met since K owned 100% of the stock in the last half of the year. The income test is also met since all of the corporation's income is passive income—or more specifically, its personal holding company income, $75,000 ($40,000 dividends + $35,000 interest) exceeds 60% of its adjusted ordinary gross income, $45,000 (60% of $75,000).

The technical definitions of adjusted ordinary gross income and personal holding income are explored below.

ADJUSTED ORDINARY GROSS INCOME

The first quantity that must be determined is adjusted ordinary gross income (AOGI).[77] As suggested above, the label given to this quantity is very appropriate since the amount which must be computed is just what the phrase implies; that

---

[76]   § 542(a)(1).

[77]   § 543(b)(2).

is, it includes only the ordinary gross income of the corporation with certain adjustments. In determining AOGI, the following amounts must be computed: (1) gross income, (2) ordinary gross income, and (3) the adjustments to ordinary gross income to arrive at AOGI. Therefore, the starting point for the calculation of AOGI is gross income.

Gross Income. The definition of gross income for purposes of the personal holding company provisions varies little from the definition found in § 61. Accordingly, gross income includes all income from whatever source except those items specifically excluded. In addition, gross income is computed taking into consideration cost of goods sold. The only departure from the normal definition of gross income concerns property transactions. Only the net gains from the sale or exchange of stocks, securities, and commodities are included in gross income.[78] Net losses involving these assets do not reduce gross income. Similarly, any loss arising from the sale or exchange of § 1231 property is ignored and does not offset any § 1231 gains.

Ordinary Gross Income. In applying the income test, capital-gain type items are ignored and consequently have no effect on whether the corporation is treated as a personal holding company. Therefore, since the quantity desired is adjusted "ordinary" gross income, the second step of the calculation requires the removal of capital-gain type items from gross income. As seen in Exhibit 21-4, all capital gains and § 1231 gains are subtracted from gross income to arrive at ordinary gross income.[79] It should be noted that this amount, "ordinary gross income," is not simply a subtotal in arriving at AOGI. As discussed below, ordinary gross income (OGI) is an important figure in determining whether certain types of income are treated as personal holding company income.

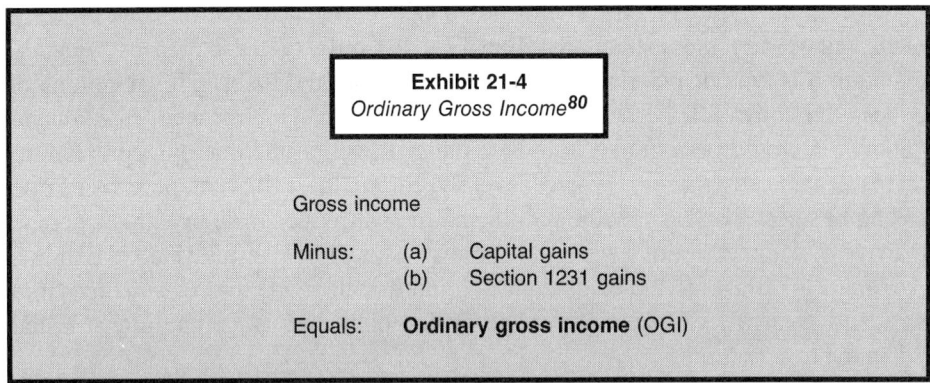

Exhibit 21-4
Ordinary Gross Income[80]

Gross income

Minus: (a)   Capital gains
          (b)   Section 1231 gains

Equals: **Ordinary gross income** (OGI)

---

[78]   Prop. Reg. § 1.543-12(a). Also see Reg.   [80]   *Ibid.*
        §§ 1.542-2 and 1.543-2.

[79]   § 543(b)(1).

Adjustments to OGI. For many years, OGI generally served as the denominator in the income-test fraction shown above. In 1964, however, modifications were necessary to discourage the use of certain methods taxpayers and their advisors had forged to undermine the income test. The popular schemes capitalized on the fact that $1 of gross rental income could shelter 60 cents of passive personal holding company income. This particular advantage could be obtained even though the rental activity itself was merely a break-even operation. Consequently, a taxpayer could easily thwart the income test and reap the benefits of the corporate entity by investing in activities that produced substantial gross rents or royalties, notwithstanding the fact that these activities were not economically sound investments.

> **Example 8.**   Refer to the facts in *Example 7*. Absent special rules, K could circumvent the income test by purchasing a coin-operated laundry which generated gross rents of more than $50,000 (e.g., $51,000) and transferring it to the corporation. In such case, assuming the rents would not be treated as personal holding income, the personal holding company income would still be $75,000 (dividends of $40,000 + interest of $35,000). However, when the laundry rents are combined with the personal holding company income to form the new AOGI, personal holding company income would be less than 60% of this new AOGI [$75,000 < 60% × ($40,000 + $35,000 + $51,000) = $75,600]. Although the laundry business might not show a profit, this would be irrelevant to K since she would have gained the advantage of the dividend received deduction and avoided personal holding company status.

To deter the type of scheme illustrated above, the calculation now requires rental and royalty income to be reduced by the bulk of the expenses typically related to this type of income: depreciation, interest, and taxes. This requirement reduces the ability of the activities to shelter income. For instance, in *Example 8* above, K would be required to reduce the gross rental income by depreciation, interest, and taxes—which would severely curtail the utility of purchasing the leasing business.[81] The specific modifications that reduce ordinary gross income to arrive at adjusted ordinary gross income are shown in Exhibit 21-5.[82] Exhibits 21-6 and 21-7 illustrate the adjustments required to be made to gross income from rents and mineral, oil, and gas royalties for purposes of computing adjusted ordinary gross income.

---

[81]   Under current law, it is also likely that the rents would be treated as PHCI, thus further spoiling the plan.

[82]   § 543(b)(2).

Exhibit 21-5
Adjusted Ordinary Gross Income[83]

Ordinary gross income (OGI)

Minus: (a) Depreciation, property taxes, interest expense, and rents paid related to gross rental income. These deductions may not exceed gross rental income. (Gross rental income is income for the use of corporate property and interest received on the sales price of real property held as inventory.)

(b) Depreciation and depletion, property and severance taxes, interest expense, and rents paid related to gross income from mineral, oil, and gas royalties. These deductions may not exceed the gross income from the royalties.

(c) Interest on tax refunds, on judgments, on condemnation awards, and on U.S. obligations (only for a dealer in the obligations).

Equals: **Adjusted ordinary gross income** (AOGI)

Exhibit 21-6
Adjusted Income from Rents[84]

Gross rental income

Minus: (a) Depreciation
(b) Property taxes
(c) Interest expense
(d) Rents paid

Equals: **Adjusted income from rents**

[83] *Ibid.*   [84] *Ibid.*

Exhibit 21-7
*Adjusted Income from Mineral,
Oil, and Gas Royalties*[85]

Gross income from mineral, oil, and gas royalties (including production payments and overriding royalties)

Minus: (a) Depreciation and depletion
         (b) Property and severance taxes
         (c) Interest expense
         (d) Rents paid

Equals: **Adjusted income from mineral, oil, and gas royalties**

PERSONAL HOLDING COMPANY INCOME (PHCI)

Following the computation of AOGI, the corporation's personal holding company income must be measured to determine whether it meets the 60 percent threshold. Although personal holding company income can be generally characterized as passive income and certain income from services, the Code identifies eight specific types of income which carry the personal holding company taint.[86] These are listed in Exhibit 21-8. Selected items of PHCI are discussed below.

Dividends, Interest, Royalties, and Annuities. The most obvious forms of PHCI are those usually considered passive in nature: dividends, interest, royalties, and annuities.[87] Generally, identification and classification of these items present little problem. The most noteworthy exception concerns royalties. Mineral, oil, gas, copyright, and computer software royalties generally are included in this category of PHCI. However, as seen in Exhibit 21-8, items b, c, and d, these royalties are not treated as PHCI if certain additional tests are satisfied.

Example 9. B Corporation has three stockholders. Its income consisted of

Gross income from a grocery	$52,000
Interest income	38,000
Capital gain	6,000

B Corporation's OGI (see Exhibit 21-4) is $90,000, computed as follows:

Gross income ($52,000 + $38,000 + $6,000)	$96,000
Minus: Capital gains	(6,000)
OGI	$90,000

---

[85] § 543(b)(4).

[86] § 543.

[87] § 543(a)(1).

Exhibit 21-8
Personal Holding Company Income (PHCI)

Dividends, interest, royalties (except mineral, oil, or gas royalties, copyright royalties, and certain software royalties), and annuities.

Plus: (a) Adjusted income from rents, *but* the adjusted income from rents is not added to PHCI *if*

1. The adjusted income from rents is 50 percent or more of AOGI, and
2. The dividends paid, the dividends considered paid, and the consent dividends equal or exceed

 (i) PHCI computed without the adjusted income from rents
 (ii) Minus 10 percent of OGI.

(b) Adjusted income from mineral, oil, and gas royalties, *but* the adjusted income from these royalties is *not* added to PHCI *if*

1. The adjusted income from the royalties is 50 percent or more of AOGI,
2. PHCI computed without the adjusted income from these royalties does not exceed 10 percent of OGI, and
3. The § 162 trade or business deductions equal or exceed 15 percent of AOGI.

(c) Copyright royalties, *but* the copyright royalties are *not* added to PHCI *if*

1. The copyright royalties are 50 percent or more of OGI,
2. PHCI computed without the copyright royalties does not exceed 10 percent of OGI, and
3. The § 162 trade or business deductions related to the copyright royalties equal or exceed 25 percent of

 (i) The OGI minus the royalties paid, plus
 (ii) The depreciation related to the copyright royalties.

In this example, AOGI is the same as OGI since the amounts which are subtracted from OGI to arrive at AOGI are zero (see Exhibit 21-5).

B Corporation's PHCI is $38,000, the amount of the interest income (see Exhibit 21-8). Since the corporation's PHCI ($38,000) is not 60 percent or more of its $90,000 AOGI ($90,000 × 60% = $54,000), it does not meet the income requirement.

Although B Corporation meets the stock ownership requirement since it has only three shareholders, it does not meet *both* the ownership requirement and the income requirement. As a result, it is not a personal holding company and is not subject to the personal holding company tax.

Exhibit 21-8 Continued

(d) Software royalties, but these are *not* added to PHCI *if*

    1. The royalties are received in connection with the licensing of computer software by a corporation which is actively engaged in the business of developing, manufacturing, or production of such software,

    2. The software royalties are 50 percent or more of OGI,

    3. Research and experimental expenditures, § 162 business expenses, and § 195 start-up expenditures allocable to the software business are generally 25 percent or more of OGI computed with certain adjustments, and

    4. Dividends paid, considered paid, and the consent dividends equal or exceed

        (i) PHCI computed without the software royalties and certain interest income

        (ii) Minus 10 percent of OGI.

(e) Produced film rents, *but* the produced film rents are *not* added to PHCI *if* the produced film rents equal or exceed 50 percent of OGI.

(f) Rent (for the use of tangible property) received by the corporation from a shareholder owning 25 percent or more of the value of the corporation's stock. This rent is only included in PHCI if PHCI computed without this rent and without the adjusted income from rents exceeds 10 percent of OGI.

(g) Income from personal service contracts *but only if*

    1. Someone other than the corporation has the right to designate who is to perform the services or if the person who is to perform the services is named in the contract, and

    2. At some time during the taxable year, 25 percent or more of the value of the corporation's outstanding stock is owned by the person performing the services.

(h) Income of estates and trusts taxable to the corporation.

Equals: *Personal holding company income (PHCI)*

Example 10. Assume the same facts as in *Example 9* except that B Corporation had received $88,000 of interest income.

B Corporation's OGI and AOGI would be computed as follows:

Gross income ($52,000 + $38,000 + $6,000)	$146,000
Minus: Capital gains	(6,000)
OGI (also AOGI)	$140,000

B Corporation's PHCI is now $88,000, the amount of the interest income. Since the corporation's $88,000 of PHCI is more than 60% of the $140,000 AOGI ($140,000 × 60% = $84,000), it meets the income requirement.

Since B Corporation meets both the ownership requirement and the income requirement, *it is* a personal holding company.

Adjusted Income from Rents. Rental income presents a special problem for the personal holding company provisions. Normally, rents—generally defined as compensation for the use of property—represent a passive type of income. However, for many corporations, most notably those involved in renting real estate and equipment, rental operations are not merely a passive investment but represent a true business activity. If all rental income were considered personal holding income, closely held corporations involved in the rental business could not escape PHC status. To provide these corporations with some relief, rental income is not treated as PHCI under certain circumstances.

The amount of rental income potentially qualifying as PHCI is referred to as the *adjusted income from rents*.[88] As seen in Exhibit 21-6, adjusted income from rents consists of the corporation's gross rental income reduced by the adjustments required for determining AOGI—depreciation, property taxes, interest expense, and rental payments related to such income (e.g., ground lease payments). The corporation's adjusted income from rents is treated as PHCI unless it can utilize the relief measure suggested above. Specifically, adjusted income from rents is PHCI unless: (1) it is 50 percent or more of the corporation's AOGI, and (2) the corporation's dividends during the taxable year as well as dividends paid within the first $2 \frac{1}{2}$ months of the following year *and* consent dividends are not less than the amount by which nonrental PHCI (e.g., dividends and interest) exceeds 10 percent of OGI.[89]

These relationships may be expressed as follows:

1. Adjusted income from rents $\geq$ (50% × AOGI); *and*

2. Dividends $\geq$ [nonrental PHCI − (10% × OGI)].

As the latter expression indicates, when rents represent a substantial portion of OGI relative to nonrental PHCI (as typically would be the case where a corporation is truly in the rental "business"), no dividends are required. In other words, as long as nonrental income is not a major portion of the corporation's total income—does not exceed 10 percent of the corporation's OGI—dividends are unnecessary. Otherwise, a corporation in the rental business is forced to make dividend distributions to avoid penalty.

[88] § 543(b)(3).   [89] *Ibid.*

Example 11. D Corporation had four shareholders in 1991 and therefore met the stock ownership requirement. The following information is available for D corporation for 1991:

Interest income	$10,000
Gross rental income	25,000
Depreciation, property taxes, and interest expense	
related to rental income	24,000
Maintenance and utilities related to rental income	3,000
Dividends paid during 1991	8,000

OGI (Exhibit 21-4) is $35,000 ($10,000 + $25,000). AOGI (see Exhibit 21-5) is computed as follows:

OGI	$35,000
Minus: Depreciation, property taxes, and interest expense related to rental income	(24,000)
AOGI	$11,000

D Corporation's adjusted income from rents is computed as follows (see Exhibit 21-6):

Gross rental income	$25,000
Minus: Depreciation, property taxes, and expense related to rental income	(24,000)
Adjusted income from rents	$ 1,000

Note that in determining AOGI and adjusted income from rents, the maintenance and utility expenses are ignored. Such expenses are also not taken into account in determining gross income or OGI. The next step is to determine if the adjusted income from rents is to be added to PHCI. It is *not* added to PHCI if *both* of the following tests are met.

Test 1   (50% test): Is the adjusted income from rents 50% or more of AOGI?

The adjusted income from rents ($1,000) is *not* 50% or more of AOGI ($11,000), so Test 1 is *not* met.

The adjusted income from rents is excluded from PHCI only if *both* Test 1 and Test 2 are met. Since Test 1 is not met, the adjusted income from rents *is* included in PHCI, and there is no need to go on to Test 2. However, Test 2 is done here for illustrative purposes.

Test 2   (10% test): Does the total of the dividends paid, the dividends considered paid, and the consent dividends equal or exceed PHCI (computed without the adjusted income from rents) reduced by 10% of OGI? This can also be expressed as:

Dividends $\geq$ [nonrental PHCI $-$ (OGI $\times$ 10%)]. Nonrental PHCI is $10,000 (interest income). OGI $\times$ 10% = $35,000 $\times$ 10% = $3,500. Therefore, nonrent PHCI ($10,000) minus OGI $\times$ 10% ($3,500) is $6,500. Since the total dividends ($8,000) were more than $6,500, Test 2 *is* met.

However, as mentioned above, *both* Test 1 and Test 2 must be met if the adjusted income from rents is to be excluded from PHCI. Therefore, the adjusted income from rents *is part of PHCI*.

D Corporation's PHCI is computed as follows (see Exhibit 21-8):

Interest income..	$10,000
Adjusted income from rents...........................	1,000
PHCI...	$11,000

D Corporation's $11,000 PHCI is more than 60% of the $11,000 AOGI. In this example, in fact, PHCI is 100% of AOGI since all of the income is personal holding company income. D Corporation, therefore, meets *both* the ownership requirement and the income requirement, and thus is a personal holding company.

The rules relating to mineral, oil, gas, copyright, and software royalties are very similar to those discussed above for rents. See Exhibits 21-7 and 21-8, items b, c, and d.

Income from Personal Service Contracts. The shifting of service income to a corporation by highly compensated individuals, such as actors and athletes, is sharply curtailed by the personal holding company provisions. The PHC provisions attack the problem by treating service income as PHCI under certain conditions. Generally, amounts received by a corporation for services provided are treated as PHCI if the party desiring the services can designate the person who will perform the services and that person owns 25 percent of the corporation's stock[90] (see Exhibit 21-8, item g).

> **Example 12.** T Corp., a producer of motion pictures, wanted RK to act in a new movie it was producing. Assume that RK's services could be obtained only by contracting with his wholly owned corporation, RK Inc. Accordingly, a contract is drafted providing that RK Inc. will provide the services of RK to T Corp. for $500,000. All of the income is PHCI to RK Inc. since RK owns at least 25% of the corporation *and* he is actually designated in the contract to perform the services.

---

[90] § 543(a)(7).

Given the general rule, it would appear that virtually all service corporations are likely candidates for the PHC tax. This problem was considered in Revenue Ruling 75-67.[91] According to the facts of the ruling, a corporation's primary source of income was attributable to the services of its only employee, a doctor, who also owned 80 percent of the corporation's stock. In this case, all the facts suggested that the income would be PHCI. The only question was whether the doctor's patients formally designated him as the one to perform the services. Although a formal designation was lacking, it was implicit since the doctor was the only employee of the corporation and the patients never expected someone other than the doctor to perform the services. Despite evidence to the contrary, the IRS ruled that the income was not PHCI on the theory that there was no indication that the corporation was obligated to provide the services of the doctor in question. In addition, the ruling emphasized that the services to be performed were not so unique as to prohibit the corporation from substituting someone else to perform them. The Service also relied on the uniqueness rationale in situations involving a CPA who had incorporated his or her practice and a musical composer who had incorporated his or her song-writing activities.[92] Apparently, as long as the services are not so unique as to preclude substitution and there is no formal designation of the individual who will perform the services, a service business can escape PHC status.

COMPUTATION OF THE PHC TAX

The personal holding company penalty tax is 28 percent of the *undistributed personal holding company income*. Undistributed personal holding company income is defined as adjusted taxable income minus the dividends-paid deduction.[93] The computation of adjusted taxable income and undistributed PHCI is shown in Exhibit 21-9.

Like the computation of accumulated taxable income, the calculation attempts to determine the corporation's dividend-paying capacity. As a practical matter, the tax is rarely paid because of a deduction allowed for "deficiency dividends" which can be made once it has been determined the PHC tax applies.

---

[91]   Rev. Rul. 75-67, 1975-1 C.B. 169.

[92]   Rev. Rul. 75-290, 1975-1 C.B. 172; Rev. Rul. 75-249, 1975-1 C.B. 171; and Rev. Rul. 75-250, 1975-1 C.B. 179.

[93]   § 545(a). The term "adjusted taxable income" is not found in the Code.

Exhibit 21-9
Undistributed Personal Holding Company Income[94]

Taxable income

Plus: (a) Dividends-received deduction.
  (b) Net operating loss deduction (but not a net operating loss of the preceding year computed without the dividends received deduction).
  (c) The amount by which the § 162 (trade or business) deductions and the § 167 (depreciation) deductions related to rental property exceed the income produced by the rental property, unless it can be shown that the rent received was the highest possible and that the rental activity was carried on as a bona fide business activity.

Minus: (a) Federal income taxes (but not the accumulated earnings tax or the personal holding company tax).
  (b) The amount by which actual charitable contributions exceeds the charitable contributions deduction reflected in net income.
  (c) Net capital gain reduced by the taxes attributable to the net capital gain.

Equals: *Adjusted taxable income*

Minus: Dividends-Paid Deduction

Equals: **Undistributed Personal Holding Company Income**

Dividends-Paid Deduction.   The dividends-paid deduction for personal holding companies is similar to the one for the accumulated earnings tax. It includes the following types of distributions:

1.   Dividends paid during the taxable year

2.   Throwback dividends: dividends paid within $2\,^1/_2$ months after the close of the taxable year (but subject to limitation as discussed below)

3.   Consent dividends

4.   Liquidating distributions and

5.   Deficiency dividends

Note that this list of qualifying distributions is identical to that provided in Exhibit 21-3 for the accumulated earnings tax, except for the special deficiency dividend. In addition, personal holding companies are entitled to a dividend carryover, which is not available for accumulated earnings tax purposes.[95]

---

[94]   § 545.   [95]   § 561(a)(3).

Throwback dividends. As in the accumulated earnings tax computation, a personal holding company is allowed a deduction for throwback dividends (i.e., dividends paid within $2\frac{1}{2}$ months after the close of the taxable year).[96] However, the PHC throwback dividend differs from that for the accumulated earnings tax in two ways. First, it is included in the dividends-paid deduction only if the corporation makes an *election* at the time the corporate tax return is filed to treat them as applying to the previous year.[97] Second, the amount treated as a throwback dividend is limited to the smaller of the following:[98]

1. Twenty percent of the dividends actually paid during the taxable year in question

2. Undistributed PHCI (computed without the dividends paid during the $2\frac{1}{2}$-month period)

Consent dividends. The rules for consent dividends are the same for personal holding companies as for the accumulated earnings tax.[99] As mentioned previously, a consent dividend is an amount that a shareholder agrees to consider as having been received as a dividend even though never actually distributed by the corporation. Consent dividends are limited to shareholders who own stock on the last day of the tax year. Their shares must be either common stock or *participating* preferred stock. Consent dividends do not include preferential dividends. A shareholder who consents to a dividend is treated as having received the amount as a cash dividend and contributing the same amount to the corporation's capital on the last day of the year.

Dividend carryover. A personal holding company is also entitled to a *dividend carryover* as part of its dividends-paid deduction.[100] If the dividends paid in the two prior years exceed the adjusted taxable incomes (see Exhibit 21-9) for those years, the excess may be used as a dividend carryover (and therefore as part of the dividends-paid deduction) for the year in question.

Deficiency dividends. Once a determination has been made that a corporation is subject to the personal holding company tax, the tax can still be abated by the use of a *deficiency dividend*.[101] Following the determination of the personal holding company tax, the corporation is given 90 days to pay a deficiency dividend. This must be an *actual cash dividend* which the corporation elects to treat as a distribution of the personal holding company income for the year at issue, and it is taxable to the shareholders. It does not reduce the personal holding company income of any year other than the year at issue. A deficiency dividend effectively reduces the amount of the penalty tax. However, interest and penalties are still imposed as if the deduction were not allowed. Thus, the corporation may be able

---

[96]   § 563.

[97]   § 563(b).

[98]   *Ibid.*

[99]   § 565.

[100]   § 564.

[101]   § 547.

to escape the tax itself—but not any interest or penalties related to such tax. It should also be noted that the deficiency dividend is available *only* to reduce the personal holding company tax. This escape is not available to those subject to the accumulated earnings tax.

Example 13. C Corporation determined that it was a personal holding company and had to file Form 1120-PH. Its records for 1991 reveal the following:

Gross profit from operations	$150,000
Dividend income	400,000
Interest income	350,000
Long-term capital gain	30,000
Gross income	$930,000
Compensation	(30,000)
Selling and administrative	(100,000)
	$800,000
Dividends-received deduction	(280,000)
Charitable contributions	(80,000)
Taxable income	$440,000
Federal income tax @ 34%	$149,600

Charitable contributions actually made during the year were $90,000, but are limited to $80,000 (10% × $800,000 taxable income before the deductions for contributions and dividends received). C paid dividends of $20,000 in 1991 and $10,000 during the first 2½ months of 1992, which it *elects* to throw back to 1991 in computing the dividends-paid deduction. The personal holding company tax is computed as follows:

Taxable income	$440,000
+ Dividends-received deduction	280,000
− Excess charitable contributions	(10,000)
− Federal income taxes	(149,600)
− Long-term capital gain net of tax	
[$30,000 − (34% × $30,000)]	(19,800)
Adjustable taxable income	$540,600
− Dividends paid deduction:	
1991	(20,000)
1992 Throwback (Limited to 20% of 1990 dividends)	(4,000)
UPHCI	$516,600
Times: PHC tax rate	× 28%
PHC tax	$144,648

C Corporation's tax liability for 1991 is $294,248 ($149,600 regular tax + $144,648 PHC tax). The PHC tax could be avoided by paying a deficiency dividend equal to UPHCI ($516,600). However, the payment of the dividend would not eliminate any penalties or interest that might be assessed on the $144,648 PHC tax due if Form 1120-PH is not filed in a timely manner.

TAX PLANNING

ACCUMULATED EARNINGS TAX

For taxpayers wanting to use the corporate form to shield their income from individual taxes, the accumulated earnings tax represents a formidable obstacle. Although there is an obvious cost if the tax is incurred, that cost may be far more than expected. This often occurs because the imposition of the tax for one year triggers an audit for all open years. In addition, the IRS usually takes the position that the negligence penalty of Code § 6653 should be imposed whenever the accumulated earnings tax is applicable. Moreover, in contrast to the personal holding company tax which can normally be averted using the deficiency dividend procedure, the accumulated earnings tax, once levied, cannot be avoided. At the time of the audit, it is too late for dividend payments or consent dividends!

Despite the potential cost of the tax, the rewards from avoidance—or at least the deferral—of double taxation are often so great that the shareholders are willing to assume the risk of penalty. Moreover, many practitioners believe that with proper planning the risk of incurring the accumulated earnings tax is minimal, particularly since the tax is not self-assessed but dependent on the audit lottery. In addition, it is possible to shift the burden of proof to the IRS. The discussion below examines some of the means for reducing the taxpayer's exposure to the accumulated earnings tax.

LIQUID ASSETS AND WORKING CAPITAL

Normally, the accumulated earnings tax is not raised as an issue unless the corporation's balance sheet shows cash, marketable securities, or other liquid assets that could be distributed easily to shareholders. The absence of liquid assets indicates that any earnings that have been retained have been reinvested in the business rather than accumulated for the forbidden purpose. It is a rare occasion, however, when such assets do not exist. Consequently, most IRS agents routinely assess whether the level of the corporation's working capital is appropriate by applying the *Bardahl* formula.

The courts have made it clear that the *Bardahl* formula serves merely as a guideline for determining the proper amount of working capital. In *Delaware Trucking Co., Inc.*, the court held that the amount needed using the *Bardahl* formula could be increased by 75 percent due to the possibility of increased labor and other operating costs due to inflation.[102] Nevertheless, in those in-

---

[102]   32 TCM 104, T.C. Memo 1973-29.

stances where working capital appears excessive, the Internal Revenue Manual directs agents to require justification of such excess. Therefore, the corporation should closely control its working capital to ensure that it does not exceed the corporation's reasonable needs.

One way to reduce working capital is to increase shareholder salaries, bonuses, and other compensation. Since these payments are deductible, double taxation is avoided. This technique also has the benefit of reducing taxable income, which in turn reduces the accumulated earnings tax should it apply. However, this method of reducing working capital may not be feasible if the compensation paid exceeds a reasonable amount. To the extent that the compensation is unreasonable, the payments are treated as dividends and double taxation results. In addition, if the unreasonable compensation is not pro rata among all shareholders, the dividend will be considered preferential and no deduction will be allowed for the dividend in computing adjusted taxable income.

Another method for reducing working capital is for the corporation to invest in additional assets. However, the taxpayer must be careful to avoid investments that are of a passive nature or that could be considered unrelated to the corporation's existing or projected business. With respect to the latter, the courts have rules that the business of a controlled subsidiary is the business of the parent while the business of a sister corporation normally is not the business of its brother.[103]

REASONABLE NEEDS

The courts have accepted a variety of reasons as sufficient justification for the accumulation of earnings. On the one hand, the needs deemed reasonable have been both certain and well-defined, such as the repayment of corporate debt. On the other hand, the courts have approved needs as contingent and unknown as those arising from possible damage from future floods.

One contingency that seemingly could be asserted by all corporations as a basis for accumulating funds is the possibility of a business reversal, depression, or loss of major customer. Interestingly, the courts have often respected this justification for accumulations, notwithstanding the fact that it is a risk assumed by virtually all business entities. Acceptance of this need, however, appears to be dependent on the taxpayer's ability to establish that there is at least some chance that a business reversal could occur that would affect the taxpayer. For example, in *Ted Bates & Co.*, the corporation was in the advertising business and received 70 percent of its fees from only five clients.[104] In ruling for the taxpayer, the court held that the corporation was allowed to accumulate amounts necessary to cover its fixed costs for a period following the loss of a major client. Much of the court's opinion was based on its view that the advertising business was extremely competitive and the possibility of losing a client was not unrealistic. A similar decision was reached where a manufacturer sold all its products to

---

[103] For example, see *Latchis Theatres of Keene, Inc. v. Comm.*, 54-2 USTC ¶9544, 45 AFTR 1836, 214 F.2d 834 (CA-1, 1954).

[104] 24 TCM 1346, T.C. Memo 1965-251.

one customer and had to compete with others for that customer's business. The court believed that accumulations were necessary to enable the corporation to develop new markets if it lost its only customer. Relying on a possible downturn in business as a basis for accumulations has not always sufficed. In *Goodall*, the company accumulated earnings in light of the prospect that military orders would be lost.[105] The court upheld the penalty tax, indicating that even if the loss occurred, it would not have a significant effect because the corporation's business was expanding.

Although the courts have sustained various reasons for accumulations, a review of the cases indicates that the taxpayer must demonstrate that the need is realistic. This was made clear in *Colonial Amusement Corp.*[106] In this case, the corporation's accumulations were not justified when it wanted to construct a building on adjacent land and building restrictions existed that prohibited construction.

In establishing that a need is realistic, a taxpayer's self-serving statement normally is not convincing. Proper documentation of the need is critical. This is true even when the need is obvious and acceptable. In *Union Offset*, the corporation stated at trial that its accumulations were necessary to retire outstanding corporate debt, a legitimate business need.[107] To the taxpayer's dismay, however, the Tax Court still imposed the tax because the corporation had failed to document in any type of written record its plan to use the accumulations in the alleged manner. In this case, a simple statement in the Board of Directors' minutes concerning the proposed use of the funds would no doubt have saved the taxpayer from penalty.

S CORPORATION ELECTION

In those cases where it is difficult to justify accumulations, the shareholders may wish to elect to be treated as an S corporation. Since the earnings of an S corporation are taxed to the individual shareholders rather than the corporation, S corporations cannot be used to shelter income and thus are immune to the accumulated earnings tax. However, the election insulates the corporation only prospectively (i.e., only for that period for which it is an S corporation). Prior years open to audit are still vulnerable. In addition, the S election may raise other problems. The shareholders will be required to report and pay taxes on the income of the corporation even though it may not be distributed to them. As a result, cash flow problems may occur. Further, because the corporation has accumulated earnings and profits, the excess passive income tax specifically designed for C corporations that have elected S status may apply.[108] For these reasons, an S election should be carefully considered.

---

[105] *Robert A. Goodall Estate v. Comm.*, 68-1 USTC ¶9245, 21 AFTR2d 813, 391 F.2d 775, (CA-8, 1968).

[106] 7 TCM 546.

[107] 79-2 USTC ¶9550, 603 F.2d 90 (CA-9, 1979).

[108] See Chapter 23 for a discussion of this special tax imposed on S corporations with excessive passive income.

PERSONAL HOLDING COMPANY TAX

The personal holding company tax, like the accumulated earnings tax, is clearly a tax to be avoided. Unfortunately, the personal holding company tax differs from the accumulated earnings tax in that it is not reserved solely for those whose intent is to avoid taxes. Rather, it is applied on a mechanical basis, regardless of motive, to all corporations that fall within its purview. For this reason, it is important to closely monitor the corporation's activities to ensure that it does not inadvertently become a PHC.

One important responsibility of a practitioner is to recognize potential personal holding company problems so that steps can be taken to avoid the tax or the need to distribute dividends. This responsibility not only concerns routine operations but extends to advice concerning planned transactions that could cause the corporation to be converted from an operating company to an investment company. For example, a corporation may plan to sell one or all of its businesses and invest the proceeds in passive type assets. Similarly, a planned reorganization (discussed in Chapter 20) may leave the corporation holding stock of the acquiring corporation. Failure to identify the possible personal holding company difficulty which these and other transactions may cause can lead to serious embarrassment.

Although the thrust of most tax planning for personal holding companies concerns how to avoid the tax, there are certain instances when a planned PHC can provide benefits. Both varieties of personal holding companies, the planned and the unplanned, are discussed below.

PHC CANDIDATES

All corporations could fall victim to the PHC tax. However, some corporations are more likely candidates than others. For this reason, their activities and anticipated transactions should be scrutinized more carefully than others.

Potential difficulties often concern corporations that are involved in rental activities and those that have some passive income. In this regard, it should be noted that the term "rent" is defined as payments received for the use of property. As a result, "rental companies" include not only those that lease such items as apartments, offices, warehouses, stadiums, equipment, vending machines, automobiles, trucks, and the like, but also those that operate bowling alleys, roller and ice skating rinks, billiards parlors, golf courses, and any other activity for which a payment is received for use of the corporation's property. All of these corporations are at risk since each has rental income which could be considered passive personal holding company income unless it satisfies the special two-prong test for rental companies.

There are several other types of corporations that must be concerned with PHC problems. Investment companies—corporations formed primarily to acquire income producing assets such as stock, bonds, rental properties, partnership interests, and similar investments—clearly have difficulties. Corporations that derive most of their income from the services of one or more of their shareholders also are vulnerable. In recent years, however, the Service has taken a liberal view toward the professional corporations of doctors, accountants, and several others. Another group of corporations that are probable targets of the PHC tax includes those that collect royalty income. The royalty income might arise from the corporation's development and licensing of a product (e.g., patent on a food processor or franchises to operate a restaurant). Other logical candidates for the PHC tax are banks, savings and loans, and finance companies since the majority of their income is interest income from making loans and purchasing or discounting accounts receivables and installment obligations. Banks and savings and loans need not worry, however, since they are specifically excluded from PHC status. Finance companies are also exempt from the penalty tax, but only if certain tests—not discussed here—are met. Consequently, those involved with finance companies should review their situation closely to ensure such tests are satisfied.

AVOIDING PHC STATUS

In general, if a corporation is closely held *and* 60 percent of its income is derived from passive sources or specified personal services, the PHC tax applies. Thus, to avoid the PHC tax *either* the stock ownership test or the income test must be failed.

STOCK OWNERSHIP TEST

The stock ownership test is satisfied if five or fewer persons own more than 50 percent of the stock. This test is the most difficult to fail since it requires dilution of the current shareholders' ownership. Moreover, dilution is very difficult to implement in practice due to the constructive ownership rules. The rules make it virtually impossible to maintain ownership in the family since stock owned by one family member or an entity in which the family member has an interest is considered owned by other family members. Therefore, to fail the ownership test, sufficient stock must be owned by unrelated parties to reduce the ownership of the five largest shareholders to 50 percent or less. Unfortunately, it is often impossible to design an arrangement that meets these conditions yet is still desirable from an economic viewpoint.

PASSIVE INCOME TEST

The corporation is deemed to satisfy the passive income test if 60 percent of its adjusted ordinary gross income (AOGI) is personal holding company income (PHCI)—income from dividends, interest, annuities, rents, royalties, or specified shareholder services. The potential for failing this test is perhaps more easily seen when this test is expressed mathematically:

$$\frac{PHCI}{AOGI} \geq 60\%$$

The steps that can be taken to fail this test fall into three categories: (1) increasing operating income or AOGI, (2) reducing PHCI, and (3) satisfying the exceptions to remove the PHC taint from the income.

Increasing Operating Income.   One way to fail the 60 percent test is to increase the denominator in the income test fraction, AOGI, without increasing the numerator. This requires the corporation to increase its operating income without any corresponding increase in its passive income. Obtaining such an increase is not easy since it is essentially asking that the corporation generate more gross income. This does not necessarily mean that sales must increase, however. The corporation might consider increasing its profit margin. Although this could reduce sales, the resulting increase in gross income could be sufficient to fail the test. Alternatively, the corporation might consider expanding the operating portion of the business. Expansion not only increases AOGI but also may have the effect of reducing PHCI if the investments generating the PHCI are sold to invest in the expansion.

Reducing Personal Holding Income.   Failing the income test normally is accomplished by reducing personal holding company income. It is sometimes asserted that merely reducing PHCI is not sufficient since both the numerator and the denominator in the test fraction are reduced by the same amounts. (This occurs because AOGI includes PHCI.) A mathematical check of this statement shows that it is incorrect and that a simple elimination of PHCI aids the taxpayer.

> **Example 14.**   Z Corporation has $100,000 of AOGI, including $70,000 of interest income which is PHCI. Substituting these values into the test fraction reveals that the corporation has excessive passive income.
>
> $$\frac{\text{PHCI}}{\text{AOGI}} = \frac{\$70,000}{\$100,000} = 70\%$$
>
> If Z Corporation simply reduces its interest income by $30,000, the corporation would fail the income test despite the fact that both the numerator and the denominator are reduced by the same amounts.
>
> $$\frac{\text{PHCI}}{\text{AOGI}} = \frac{\$40,000}{\$70,000} = 57.1\%$$

One way a corporation could eliminate part of its PHCI is by paying out as shareholder compensation the amounts that otherwise would be invested to generate PHCI. Alternatively, the corporation could eliminate PHCI by switching its investments into growth stocks where the return is generated from capital appreciation rather than dividends. Of course, the taxpayer would not necessarily want to switch completely out of dividend-paying stocks since the advantage of the dividends-received deduction would be lost.

The corporation could also reduce its PHCI by replacing it with tax-exempt income, capital gains, or § 1231 gains. This would have the same effect as simply eliminating the PHCI altogether.

Example 15. Same as *Example 14* above except the corporation invests in tax-exempt bonds which generate $20,000 of tax-exempt, rather than taxable, interest. In addition, the corporation realizes a $10,000 capital gain instead of taxable interest. The effect of replacing the taxable interest of $30,000 with capital gains of $10,000 and tax-exempt income of $20,000 would produce results identical to those above. This derives from the fact that the tax-exempt interest and capital gains are excluded from both the numerator, PHCI, and the denominator, AOGI, creating fractions identical to those shown above.

REMOVING THE PHC TAINT

In some situations, income which is normally considered PHCI (e.g., rental income) is not considered tainted if certain tests are met. For example, the Code provides escape hatches for rental income; mineral, oil, and gas royalties; copyright royalties; and rents from the distribution and exhibition of produced films. Although additional tests must be met to obtain exclusion for these types of income, there is one requirement common to each. *Generally*, if a corporation's income consists predominantly (50% or more) of only one of these income types, exclusion is available. More importantly, this condition can normally be obtained without great difficulty. To satisfy the 50 percent test, the taxpayer should take steps to ensure that a particular corporation receives only a single type of income. This may require forming an additional corporation that receives only one type of income, but by so doing the 50 percent test is met and the PHC tax may be avoided.

With proper control of their income, these corporations will have no difficulty in satisfying the income test since at least 50 percent of their AOGI is from one source. For corporations with rental income, however, dividends equal to the amount that their nonrental PHC income exceeds 10 percent of their OGI still must be paid. Note, however, that if a corporation has little or no nonrental PHC income, no dividends are necessary to meet the test. Also note that each additional dollar of gross rents, unreduced by expenses, decreases the amount of dividend that must be paid.

Example 16. G Corporation has $60,000 of OGI, including $53,000 of rental income and $7,000 of dividend income. In this case, dividends of only $1,000 are necessary since nonrental PHCI exceeds the 10% threshold by only $1,000 [$7,000 − (10% of OGI of $60,000)]. If the taxpayer wants to avoid distributing dividends, consideration should be given to increasing gross rents. Note how an increase of $10,000 in gross rents to $63,000 would increase OGI and concomitantly eliminate the need for a dividend. This increase in gross rents would be effective even if the typical adjustments for depreciation, interest, and taxes reduce the taxpayer's net profit to zero or a loss. This is true because such adjustments are not included in determining OGI, but only AOGI. Thus, an incentive exists for the corporation to invest in breakeven or unprofitable activities as a means to eliminate the dividend.

REDUCING THE PHC TAX WITH DIVIDENDS

If the tests for PHC status cannot be avoided, the penalty can be eliminated or minimized by the payment of dividends. Although a similar opportunity exists for the accumulated earnings tax, the treatment of dividends differs in several important respects.

On the one hand, the PHC tax requires quicker action than the accumulated earnings tax. For accumulated earnings tax purposes, all dividends paid within the $2^{1}/_{2}$-month period after the close of the taxable year are counted as paid for the previous year. However, for purposes of the PHC tax, the after-year-end dividends are limited to 20 percent of the amount actually paid during the year. Thus, if no dividends are paid during the year, then none can be paid during the $2^{1}/_{2}$-month period. On the other hand, the PHC tax can almost always be avoided through payment of a deficiency dividend, which is not available for the accumulated earnings tax. The deficiency dividend may come at a high price, however. As previously mentioned, any interest and penalties that would have been imposed had the penalty tax applied must be computed and paid as if the PHC tax were still due.

PLANNED PERSONAL HOLDING COMPANIES

Treatment of a corporation as a personal holding company is normally considered a dire consequence. Yet, in certain cases, PHC status may not be detrimental and at times can be beneficial. Two of these situations are outlined below.

Certain taxpayers seeking the benefits of the corporate form are unable to avoid characterization as a personal holding company. For example, an athlete or movie celebrity may seek the benefits reserved solely for employees, such as group-term life insurance, health and accident insurance, medical reimbursement plans, and better pension and profit-sharing plans. In these situations, if the individual incorporates his or her talents, the corporation will be considered a PHC since all of the income for services will be PHCI. This does not mean that the PHC tax must be paid, however. The PHC tax is levied only upon undistributed PHCI. In most cases, all of the undistributed PHCI can be eliminated through the payments of deductible compensation directly to the individual or deductible contributions to his or her pension plan. As a result, the individual can obtain the benefits of incorporation without concern for the PHC tax. This technique was extremely popular prior to 1982, when the benefits of corporate pension plans were significantly better than those available to the self-employed (i.e., Keogh plans).

Over the years, personal holding companies have been used quite successfully in estate planning in reducing the value of the taxpayer's estate and obtaining other estate tax benefits. Under a typical plan, a taxpayer with a portfolio of securities would transfer them to a PHC in exchange for preferred stock equal to their current value and common stock of no value. The exchange would be tax free under Code § 351. The taxpayer would then proceed to give the common stock to his or her children at no gift tax cost since its value at the time is zero. The taxpayer would also begin a gift program, transferring $10,000 of preferred stock annually to heirs which would also escape gift tax due to the annual gift tax exclusion. There were several benefits arising from this arrangement.

First and probably foremost, any appreciation in the value of the taxpayer's portfolio would accrue to the owners of the common stock and thus be successfully removed from the taxpayer's estate, avoiding both gift and estate taxes. Second, the corporation's declaration of dividends on the common stock would shift the income to the lower-bracket family members. Dividends on the preferred stock would also be shifted to the extent that the taxpayer has transferred the preferred stock. The dividends paid would in part aid in eliminating any PHC tax. Third, the taxpayer's preferred stock in the PHC would probably be valued at less than the value of the underlying assets for estate and gift tax purposes. Although the IRS takes the position that the value of the stock in the PHC is the same as the value of the corporation's assets, the courts have consistently held otherwise. The courts have normally allowed a substantial *discount* for estate and gift tax valuation, holding that an investment in a closely held business is less desirable than in the underlying shares since the underlying securities can easily be traded in the market while the PHC shares cannot.[109]

---

[109] For example, see *Estate of Maurice Gustane Heckscher*, 63 T.C. 485 (1974). Also, see Chapter 26 for possible limitations on this estate planning technique.

PROBLEM MATERIALS

DISCUSSION QUESTIONS

21-1 *Double Taxation.* List four approaches that corporations use to avoid the effects of double taxation.

21-2 *Accumulated Earnings Tax.* What is the purpose of the accumulated earnings tax?

21-3 *Accumulated Earnings Tax.* What is the accumulated earnings tax rate? Why do you suppose Congress chose this particular tax rate?

21-4 *Accumulated Taxable Income.* What is the difference between accumulated taxable income and taxable income?

21-5 *Accumulated Earnings Credit.* What is the accumulated earnings credit? How does it affect the accumulated earnings tax?

21-6 *Dividends-Paid Deduction.* What constitutes the dividends-paid deduction for purposes of the accumulated earnings tax?

21-7 *Throwback Dividend.* What is a throwback dividend?

21-8 *Consent Dividends.* What is a consent dividend? What is its purpose?

21-9 *Intent of Accumulations.* What situations are considered to indicate the intent of a corporation to unreasonably accumulate earnings?

21-10 *Reasonable Needs.* List six possible reasons for accumulating earnings that might be considered reasonable needs of the business.

21-11 *Reasonable Needs—The* Bardahl *Formula.* What is the *Bardahl* formula? How is it used?

21-12 *Personal Holding Company Tax.* What is the purpose of the personal holding company tax?

21-13 *Personal Holding Company.* What requirements must be met by a corporation in order for it to be a personal holding company?

21-14 *Ownership Requirement.* What is the ownership requirement for personal holding companies? What constructive ownership rules apply?

21-15 *Income Requirement.* What is the income requirement for personal holding companies? What terms must be defined in order to determine if a corporation meets the income requirement?

21-16 *Income Requirement.* What tests must be met in order to determine whether the adjusted income from rents is included in personal holding company income?

21-17 *Computing the Personal Holding Company Tax.* How is the personal holding company penalty tax computed?

21-18 *Adjusted Taxable Income*. How does adjusted taxable income differ from taxable income?

21-19 *Dividends-Paid Deduction*. How does the dividends-paid deduction for personal holding company tax purposes differ from the dividends-paid deduction for accumulated earnings tax purposes?

21-20 *Deficiency Dividends*. What is a deficiency dividend? What is its purpose? What effect does it have on the personal holding company tax?

PROBLEMS

21-21 *Computing the Accumulated Earnings Tax*. Z Corporation had accumulated taxable income of $180,000 for the current year. Calculate Z Corporation's accumulated earnings tax liability.

21-22 *Computing Adjusted Taxable Income*. R Corporation has the following income and deductions for the current year:

Income from operations	$200,000
Dividend income	60,000
Charitable contributions	40,000

Compute R Corporation's adjusted taxable income.

21-23 *Minimum Accumulated Earnings Tax Credit*. B Corporation, a calendar year manufacturing company, had accumulated earnings and profits at the beginning of the current year of $60,000. If the corporation's earnings and profits for the current year are $270,000, what is B Corporation's minimum accumulated earnings tax credit?

21-24 *Accumulated Earnings Tax Credit*. Assume the same facts in Problem 21-23 above, except that B Corporation has estimated reasonable business needs of $300,000 at the end of the current year.

a. Compute B Corporation's accumulated earnings tax credit for the current year.
b. Would your answer differ if B Corporation was an incorporated law practice owned and operated by one person? If so, by how much?

21-25   *Computing the Accumulated Earnings Tax.* T Corporation had accumulated earnings and profits at the beginning of 1991 of $300,000. It has never paid dividends to its shareholders and does not intend to do so in the near future. The following facts relate to T Corporation's 1990 tax year:

Taxable income..................................	$200,000
Federal income tax.............................	61,250
Dividends received (from less than	
20% owned corporations)...................	40,000
Reasonable business needs as of 12/31/91	356,850

     a.   What is T Corporation's accumulated earnings tax?

     b.   If T Corporation's sole shareholder wanted to avoid the accumulated earnings tax, what amount of consent dividends would be required?

21-26   *Dividends-Paid Deduction.* J Corporation, a small oil tool manufacturer, projects adjusted taxable income for the current year of $200,000. Its estimated reasonable business needs are $500,000; and the corporation has $380,000 of prior years' accumulated earnings and profits as of the beginning of the current year. Using this information, answer the following:

     a.   Assuming no dividends-paid deduction, what is J Corporation's accumulated earnings tax for the current year?

     b.   If J Corporation paid $50,000 of dividends during the year, what is J Corporation's accumulated earnings tax liability?

     c.   If J Corporation's shareholders are willing to report more dividends than the $50,000 actually received during the year, what amount of consent dividends is necessary to avoid the accumulated earnings tax?

     d.   If the corporation's shareholders are not interested in paying taxes on hypothetical dividends, what other possibility is available to increase the dividends-paid deduction?

21-27   *Working Capital Needs—The* Bardahl *Formula.* X Corporation wishes to use the *Bardahl* formula to determine the amount of working capital it can justify if the IRS agent currently auditing the company's records raises the accumulated earnings tax issue. For the year under audit, X Corporation had the following:

Annual operating expenses......................	$285,000
Inventory cycle ratio.............................	.41
Accounts receivable cycle ratio...................	.61
Accounts payable cycle ratio	.82

     a.   How much working capital can X Corporation justify based on the above facts?

     b.   If X Corporation's turnover ratios are based on annual averages, what additional information would you request before computing working capital needs based on the *Bardahl* formula?

21-28 *Working Capital Needs*—Bardahl *Formula.* B owns and operates BKA Inc., which is a retail toy store. One Wednesday morning in January, 1992, she noticed in the *Wall Street Journal*'s tax column an anecdote about a small corporation that was required to pay the accumulated earnings tax. Concerned, B presented the following information to her tax advisor to evaluate her exposure as of the end of 1991.

Balance Sheet

	1990	1991
Current Assets:		
Cash...	$ 15,000	$ 30,000
Marketable securities (cost).........................	10,000	23,000
Accounts receivable (net)..........................	55,000	45,000
Inventory...	30,000	50,000
Property, plant, and equipment (net).................	500,000	552,000
Total Assets......................................	$610,000	$700,000
Current Liabilities:		
Accounts payable..................................	$ 13,000	$ 31,000
Long-term debt....................................	147,000	119,000
Common stock.....................................	50,000	50,000
Earnings and profits...............................	400,000	500,000
	$610,000	$700,000

Income Statement

Sales..		$400,000
Cost of goods sold:		
Beginning inventory................................	$ 30,000	
Purchases..	220,000	
Ending inventory..................................	(50,000)	
Total...		(200,000)
Gross profit..		$200,000
Other Expenses:		
Depreciation......................................	$ 70,000	
Selling expenses and administrative................	25,000	
Interest...	5,000	
Total...		(100,000)
Net income before taxes.............................		$100,000
Income taxes..		(25,750)
Net income..		$ 74,250

B noted that the market value of the securities was $40,000 as of December 31, 1991. In addition, B estimates the future expansion of the business (excluding working capital) will require $25,000. Determine whether the accumulated earnings tax will apply to B.

21-29 *Personal Holding Company—Income Requirement.* K Corporation is equally owned and operated by three brothers. K Corporation's gross income for the current year is $80,000, which consists of $10,000 of dividend income, interest income of $40,000, and a long-term capital gain of $30,000.

  a.   Calculate ordinary gross income.
  b.   Calculate adjusted ordinary gross income.
  c.   Is K Corporation a personal holding company?

21-30 *Personal Holding Company—Rent Exclusion.* T Corporation has gross income of $116,000, which consists of gross rental income of $86,000, interest income of $20,000, and dividends of $10,000. Depreciation, property taxes, and interest expense related to the rental property totaled $16,000. Assuming T Corporation has seven shareholders and has no dividends-paid deduction, answer the following:

  a.   What is T Corporation's ordinary gross income?
  b.   Adjusted ordinary gross income?
  c.   Does the rental income constitute personal holding company income?
  d.   Is T Corporation a personal holding company?

21-31 *Personal Holding Company Income.* V Corporation is equally owned by two shareholders. The corporation reports the following income and deductions for the current year.

Dividend income	$30,000
Interest income	15,000
Long-term capital gain	10,000
Rental income (gross)	80,000
Rental expenses:	
Depreciation	10,000
Interest on mortgage	9,000
Property taxes	3,000
Real estate management fees	8,000

  a.   Calculate ordinary gross income.
  b.   Calculate adjusted ordinary gross income.
  c.   Calculate adjusted income from rentals.
  d.   Calculate personal holding company income.
  e.   Is V Corporation a personal holding company?
  f.   If V Corporation paid $3,000 of dividends to each of its two shareholders during the current year, how would this affect your answers to (d) and (e) above?

21-32 *Items of PHC Income.* Indicate whether the following would be considered personal holding company income.

a.   Income from the sales of inventory
b.   Interest income from AT&T bond
c.   Interest income from State of Texas bond
d.   Dividend income from IBM stock
e.   Long-term capital gain
f.   Short-term capital gain
g.   Rental income from lease of office building (100% of the corporation's income is from rents)
h.   Fees paid to the corporation for the services of Jose Greatfoot, internationally known soccer player.

21-33 *PHC Income Test.* All of the stock of C Corporation is owned by B. Next year, the corporation expects the following results from operations:

Sales	$500,000
Costs of goods sold	200,000
Other operating expenses	40,000
Interest income	10,000

What is the maximum amount of dividend income that the corporation can have without being classified as a personal holding company?

21-34 *Computing the Personal Holding Company Tax.* P Corporation is owned by five individuals. For the current year P had the following:

Taxable income	$200,000
Federal income tax	60,750
Dividends received	40,000
Long-term capital gain	10,000

Compute P Corporation's personal holding company tax assuming P meets the income test and that the long-term capital gain was taxed at 34 percent.

21-35 *Personal Holding Company—Dividend Deduction.* H, a personal holding company, anticipates having undistributed personal holding company income of $120,000 before any dividend deduction for 1991. The company wishes to distribute all of its income to avoid the penalty. Because of cash flow problems, it wishes to pay as much of this dividend as it can in the 2 1/2 months after the close of the tax year.

a.   What is the *maximum* amount that H can distribute during 1992 to accomplish its task if dividends of $50,000 were paid during 1991?
b.   What is the *minimum* amount that H must distribute during 1991 and still be able to defer until 1992 the payment of any additional dividends?

21-36 *Personal Holding Company—Service Income.* J, an orthopedic surgeon, is the sole owner of J Inc. The corporation employs surgical nurses and physical therapists in addition to J. The nurses assist Dr. J on all operations, and the therapists provide all follow-up treatment. J Inc. bills all clients for all services rendered and pays the employees a stated salary. Will any of J Inc.'s fee be personal holding company income?

21-37 *PHC Dividends-Paid Deduction.* Indicate whether the following distributions would qualify for the personal holding company dividends-paid deduction for 1991.

   a.   Cash dividends paid on common stock in 1991.
   b.   Dividend distribution of land (value $20,000, basis $5,000) paid on common stock in 1991.
   c.   Cash dividends paid on common stock March 3, 1992.
   d.   Cash dividends paid on common stock in 1990.
   e.   Consent dividend; the 1991 corporate tax return was filed on March 3, 1992; the consents were filed on May 15, 1992.
   f.   Cash dividend paid in 1994 shortly after it was determined that the corporation was a personal holding company.
   g.   The corporation adopted a plan of liquidation in 1989 and the final liquidating distribution was made during 1991.

21-38 *Accumulated Earnings Tax Dividends-Paid Deduction.* Indicate whether the distributions identified in problem 21-37 would qualify for the accumulated earnings tax dividends-paid deduction for 1991.

21-39 *Understanding the PHC Tax.* Indicate whether the following statements regarding the personal holding company tax are true or false.

   a.   The PHC tax is self-assessed and, if applicable, must be paid in addition to the regular income tax.
   b.   An S corporation or partnership may be subject to the PHC tax.
   c.   A corporation that can prove that its shareholders did not intend to use it as a tax shelter is not subject to the PHC tax.
   d.   A publicly traded corporation normally would not be subject to the PHC tax.
   e.   A corporation that derives virtually all of its income from leasing operations does not risk the PHC tax, even though such income is normally considered passive.
   f.   Federal income taxes reduce the base on which the PHC tax is assessed.
   g.   Long-term capital gains are not subject to the PHC tax.
   h.   A corporation that consistently pays dividends normally would not be subject to the PHC tax.
   i.   Throwback dividends are available to reduce the corporation's potential liability without limitation.
   j.   Corporations without cash or property that they can distribute cannot benefit from the dividends-paid deduction.
   k.   The PHC tax is not truly a risk because of the deficiency dividend procedure.
   l.   A corporation may be required to pay both the accumulated earnings tax and the personal holding company tax in the same year.

21-40 *Understanding the Accumulated Earnings Tax.* Indicate whether the statements in problem 21-39 are true or false regarding the accumulated earnings tax.

RESEARCH PROBLEMS

21-41   H Corporation is owned and operated by William and Wilma Holt. The corporation's principal source of income for the past few years has been net rentals from five adjacent rent houses located in an area that the city has condemned in order to expand its freeway system. The Holts anticipate a condemnation award of approximately $400,000, and a resulting gain of $325,000. Although convinced that they will have the corporation reinvest the proceeds in other rental units, the Holts would like to invest the corporation's condemnation proceeds in a high-yield certificate of deposit for at least three years. They have come to you for advice.

   a.   What advice would you give concerning the reinvestment requirements of Code § 1033?

   b.   If H Corporation will have substantial interest income in the next few years, could the § 541 tax be a possibility?

   c.   If the Holts have considered liquidating the corporation and reinvesting the proceeds in rental units, what additional information would you need in order to advise them?

21-42   Stacey Caniff is the controlling shareholder of Cotton, Inc., a textile manufacturer. She inherited the business from her father. In recent years earnings have fluctuated between $0.50 and $3.00 per share. Dividends have remained at $0.10 per share for the last ten years with a resulting increase in cash. On audit, the IRS agent has raised the accumulated earnings tax issue. In your discussion with Stacey, she has indicated that the dividends are so low because she is afraid of losing the business (as almost happened to her father during the depression), of decreased profitability from foreign competition, and of the need to modernize if OSHA were to enforce the rules concerning cotton dust. Evaluate the possibility of overcoming an accumulated earnings tax assessment.

PART VIII

FLOW-THROUGH ENTITIES

CONTENTS

LEARNING OBJECTIVES

Upon completion of this chapter you will be able to:

- Define a partnership and a partner for Federal income tax purposes
- Explain the basic tax consequences of forming a new partnership, including
  - Determination of any gain to be recognized by the partners
  - Determination of the basis of the partner's interest in the partnership and the partnership's basis in the property received
  - How partnership liabilities affect a partner's basis
- Compute the net operating income or loss for a partnership and the impact of partnership operations on partners' taxable income and self-employment taxes
- Recognize transactions between partners and their partnerships that are subject to special treatment
- Determine the appropriate taxable year for a partnership
- Explain the advantages and problems involving special allocations available to partnerships
- Explain the unique concepts relevant to family partnerships
- Identify the advantages and problems of limited partnerships and their partners
- Determine the tax consequences of current and liquidating partnership asset distributions, including
  - Determination of the basis of each asset and of the partnership interest to the partners
- Calculate gain or loss when partnership interests are sold
- Understand the benefits and disadvantages of special partnership optional adjustments to basis

CHAPTER OUTLINE

Chapter 22

TAXATION OF PARTNERSHIPS AND PARTNERS

Subchapter K of the Internal Revenue Code (§§ 701 through 761) governs many of the activities of partnerships and their interactions with partners. When first included in the 1954 Code, Congress intended that Subchapter K should be simple and provide partners with considerable flexibility.[1] These objectives continue today with a few exceptions. Nevertheless, some attempts to achieve equity while retaining the traditional freedom of activity have resulted in considerable complexity. In most instances, the partnership form still provides greater flexibility in a simple manner for its owners than does the corporate form under either Subchapter C or Subchapter S.

DEFINITIONS OF PARTNERSHIP AND PARTNER

WHAT IS A PARTNERSHIP?

The Uniform Partnership Act defines a partnership quite simply as "an association of two or more persons to carry on as co-owners a business for profit."[2] This definition is extended in the Code to include a syndicate, group, pool, joint venture, or other unincorporated organization.[3] Determining whether an organization qualifies as a partnership for federal income tax purposes usually does not present a problem. When co-owners intend to actively participate in a *trade or business for profit as partners*, the activity generally qualifies as a partnership.[4] This *excludes* agreements to simply share expenses, investments such as rental and leasing activities not conducted as a trade or business, and co-owners who

---

[1] See *David A. Foxman*, 41 T.C. 535 (1964), *aff'd.* in 65-2 USTC ¶9737, 16 AFTR2d, 5931, 352 F.2d 466 (CA-3, 1965).

[2] Uniform Partnership Act, § 6(1).

[3] §§ 761.

[4] See Reg. §§ 1.761-1(a) and 301.7701-3(a); *Fred P. Fiore*, 39 TCM 64, T.C. Memo 1979-360; and *William N. Gurtman*, 34 TCM 475, T.C. Memo 1975-96.

have no intention of forming a partnership. As in most areas of taxation, there are some exceptions to the general requirements. For example, it is possible for an unincorporated association to be taxed as a corporation if it possesses more corporate than partnership attributes.[5] This possibility is discussed in Chapter 19.

AVOIDING PARTNERSHIP STATUS

Not all co-owners of unincorporated activities want to be treated as members of a partnership. The Regulations permit owners of *investment property* to elect that Subchapter K not apply to their ventures if the following requirements are met:[6]

1. They are not actively conducting a trade or business.

2. The activities qualify as investments or production, extraction, or use of property.

3. Taxable income is determinable for each owner without resorting to computations required for a partnership.

4. Each owner retains a separate but undivided ownership interest in the acquisition, operation, and disposition of the property.

Activities meeting the above requirements are treated as *joint tenancies*. In some situations, joint tenancies allow owners to operate with greater simplicity and flexibility than they could by using the partnership form. This is primarily because special elections such as depreciation methods are made by each owner rather than for the group of owners, and because joint tenancies are not required to file annual partnership tax returns.

WHAT IS A PARTNER?

The definition of a partner is, of course, related to that of a partnership. If an organization qualifies as a partnership, it must have at least two partners. The Code and Regulations are not helpful beyond recognizing this relationship. It is simply stated that the word *partner* "means a member of a partnership."[7] Characteristics commonly associated with partners are (1) an intent to be a partner, (2) sharing in net profits and losses, (3) contributing capital or services, (4) participating in management, (5) personal liability for partnership debts, and (6) ability to liquidate an ownership interest. The absence of one or more of these elements does not necessarily mean a partner relationship does not exist. Partner status is determined based on all the facts and circumstances.

---

[5] See Reg. § 301.7701-2(a); *Morrisey v. Comm.*, 36-1 USTC ¶9020, 16 AFTR 1274, 296 U.S. 344 (USSC, 1935); *Phillip G. Larson*, 66 T.C. 159 (1978), *acq.* in 1979-1 C.B. 1; and *Zuchman v. U.S.*, 75-2 USTC ¶9778, 36 AFTR2d 75-6193, 524 F.2d 729 (Ct. Cls., 1975).

[6] Reg. §§ 1.761-2(a) and (b); and, see Rev. Rul. 68-344, 1968-1 C.B. 569. The method of election is described in Reg. § 1.761-2(b)(i).

[7] § 761(b) and Reg. § 1.761-1(b).

There are no restrictions on who may own a partnership interest. Individuals, corporations, trusts, estates, and even other partnerships may qualify as partners. Determining partner status is dependent, however, on whether the activity is organized as a *general* partnership or as a *limited* partnership. There are four major differences separating general and limited partnerships.

1. General partnerships are owned solely by general partners, whereas limited partnerships must have one or more general partners and one or more limited partners.

2. General partners have unlimited liability for partnership debt, whereas limited partners usually are liable only up to the amount of their contribution plus any personally guaranteed debt.

3. General partners participate in the management and control of the partnership, whereas limited partners are not allowed to participate in these activities.

4. General partners are subject to self-employment taxes on partnership earnings even though they do not perform services, whereas limited partners are not.

ENTITY AND AGGREGATE CONCEPTS

Most rules governing the taxation of partnerships are based on either the *aggregate* or the *entity* concept of a partnership.[8] According to the entity concept, partnerships are considered entities distinct and separate from their owners. As such, partnerships may enter into taxable transactions with partners, may own property in their own names, are not legally liable for debts of partners, are required to file annual tax returns (Form 1065) that report the result of operations, and are required to make tax elections for partnership activities that are applicable to all partners. Many other partnership issues are decided according to the aggregate concept which treats partnerships as conduits, primarily operating for the convenience of partners. Consequently, a partnership is viewed as merely a collection of individual taxpayers. For example, this concept provides that partnership revenues, expenses, gains, losses, and credits retain their character and "flow through" to be reported on the partners' own returns. The aggregate concept also prevents the recognition of gain or loss for several types of transactions between partners and partnerships, including the exchange of assets for a capital interest. In some instances, both the entity and aggregate concepts apply to the same transaction. This often occurs when a partner's interest is liquidated, as discussed in the latter part of this chapter.

The inconsistent application of the entity and aggregate concepts significantly complicates taxation of partnerships and partners. Generally, if an individual can

---

[8] For an interesting historical discussion of the development of this conflict, see Arthur B. Willis, John S. Pennell, and Philip F. Postlewaite, *Partnership Taxation* (Colorado Springs, Co.: Shepard's, Inc.), Chapter 2.

determine which concept governs a particular issue, the solution is relatively easy. But if it is not clear which concept is applicable to a given situation, the solution is elusive since the two concepts are diametrically opposed. As taxpayers and their advisers seek answers to partnership tax questions, they must first determine whether the entity or the aggregate concept is applicable. Only then can they use their reasoning power to solve the problems and engage in meaningful tax planning.

FORMING A PARTNERSHIP

The partnership form of doing business is frequently ignored by many attorneys and accountants. This is partly because they are less comfortable with the rules of Subchapter K than they are with the corporate requirements of Subchapter C and Subchapter S. As a result, many small businesses are operating as corporations when the simplicity and flexibility of a partnership arrangement might serve them better. One of the major reasons given for incorporating is the limited liability provision. However, this provision is of little or no benefit to many small businesses since owners often are either required to personally guarantee corporate debts or have most of their capital invested in the business. These incorporated businesses rarely seek outside capital, are frequently subjected to double taxation, and their owners commonly violate the separate entity concept by transacting business for and with the corporation, giving little attention to the legal and tax requirements. The courts are replete with cases where owners have carelessly abused the corporate form and pay a severe penalty for their actions. Many of these activities would have been acceptable with the partnership form. (See Exhibit 22-1 for a summary of the transactions in this section of the chapter.)

CONTRIBUTIONS OF PROPERTY

Like any business, a partnership may be formed by contributing cash, noncash assets, or services in exchange for a *capital interest*. The simplest procedure involves the contribution of cash. There are no current tax consequences involved in this transaction.

When property other than cash is contributed in exchange for a capital interest, the basis of this property to the contributing partner generally differs from its fair market value. Whether this difference results in taxable gain or loss depends on whether the entity or aggregate concept governs. Basically, § 721 applies the aggregate concept to this type of transaction. Therefore, the transfer is considered tax-free and no gain or loss is recognized by either the contributing partner or the partnership.[9] The partner's *initial basis* in the partnership is the total amount

---

[9] § 721 and Reg § 1.721-1. There is one exception. Gain or loss is recognized if the partnership qualifies as an investment company. § 721(b).

Exhibit 22-1
*Summary of Tax Effects
for Partnership Formations*

Transaction	Effect on Partnership	Effect on Partner
1. Contribution of cash or property for a capital interest (no boot received)	Nontaxable; partner's basis becomes partnership's basis in contributed assets	Nontaxable; partner's basis in contributed assets becomes partner's basis in the partnership
2. Partner assumes partnership liabilities	No effect	Increases partner's basis in partnership, based on P&L ratio
3. Partner's share of liabilities decreases	No effect	Decreases partner's basis in partnership, based on P&L ratio; includible income to the extent this "cash distribution" exceeds the partner's basis in the partnership
4. Special allocation of depreciation, depletion, gain, loss, and income attributable to contributed assets	Required for contributions after 3/84 Optional for contributions before 4/84	Required for contributions after 3/84 Optional for contributions before 4/84
5. Taint on contributed property		
a. Accrued losses on capital assets (for five years)	Capital losses when recognized	Capital losses flow through to the contributing partner
b. Accrued gains on inventory (for five years)	Ordinary gains when recognized	Ordinary gains flow through to the contributing partner
c. Gains or losses on unrealized receivables	Ordinary gains or losses when recognized	Ordinary gains and losses flow through to the contributing partner

of cash plus the adjusted basis of noncash assets contributed.[10] This is referred to as a *substituted basis* (i.e., the basis of the transferred property is substituted as the partner's basis in the partnership interest received). The partner's basis for each asset becomes the partnership's basis for each asset.[11] This is referred to as a *carryover basis* (i.e., the transferring partner's basis is carried over and used as the partnership's basis). There is one exception to this transfer of basis rule. Assets previously held for personal use transfer at the *lower* of market value or basis. When an asset's basis exceeds its market value, the transferring partner has a non-deductible personal loss and a basis in the partnership equal to the asset's market value.

In some instances, the entity concept applies to part or all of a transfer for a capital interest, and a partner is required to recognize gain. When this occurs, the partner's recognized gain increases the partnership's basis in the assets, but only if the partnership makes a special election.[12] (These exceptions and the election are discussed later in this chapter.)

When contributing either capital assets or § 1231 assets, the partner's *holding period* for these assets becomes the holding period for the capital interest in the partnership.[13] For all other contributions, the partner's holding period begins with the date the partnership interest is acquired.[14] The partnership's holding period for its contributed assets includes the holding period of the contributing partner.[15]

> **Example 1.** A contributes $50,000 cash to the AB Partnership, and B contributes investment land (a capital asset) with a fair market value of $50,000. B acquired the land three years ago for $30,000. A and B are equal partners. From an economic viewpoint, the AB Partnership has two newly acquired assets each worth $50,000, and B has a realized gain of $20,000. This approach also follows generally accepted accounting principles. However, for tax purposes, the transfer of land by B is treated as a tax-free exchange. This results in B's basis in the land being carried over to the partnership, causing the partnership's bases in the two assets to be unequal. Cash has a $50,000 basis but land has a $30,000 basis and is treated as held by the partnership for three years. Similarly, A has a $50,000 substituted basis in the partnership but B has a $30,000 substituted basis in the partnership. A's holding period for his partnership interest is just beginning, but B's holding period is three years.

---

[10] § 722.

[11] § 723.

[12] §§ 754 and 734(b) and Rev. Rul. 84-15, 1984-1 C.B. 158. There is one exception. Regardless of the election, gain or loss increases the partnership's basis in the assets if the partnership qualifies as an investment company.

[13] § 1231(a). But recall that an asset does not qualify under § 1231 until it has been held for more than six months.

[14] Reg. § 1.1223-1(a).

[15] § 1223(2) and Reg. § 1.1223-1(b).

Example 2. C contributes proprietorship equipment (a § 1231 asset) with a fair market value of $50,000 to the AB Partnership for a one-third capital interest. The equipment was purchased last year for $70,000, and depreciation of $10,000 was deducted for the proprietorship last year. This transfer also constitutes a tax-free exchange. Therefore, C's $60,000 basis ($70,000 − $10,000) carries over to the partnership as well as her one-year holding period. C's substituted basis in her partnership interest is $60,000 and her holding period is also one year. (Note: The answer is the same regardless of the fair market value of the equipment.)

As noted previously, an exception to this approach would apply if the equipment had been held for personal use. If this is the situation, the partnership's basis for the equipment is $50,000. C has a nondeductible personal loss and her basis in the partnership is $50,000. The holding period also transfers if the equipment qualified as a capital asset to C. (Note that property held for personal use is not a § 1231 asset.)

The tax-free exchange provisions apply to all *property* contributed, including installment receivables, contracts, accounts receivable, and property created by the contributing party.[16] In contrast, transactions involving (1) the right to use property, such as use through rental or lease agreements, or (2) services performed in exchange for a capital interest, are taxable as ordinary income to the contributing partner.[17] The partnership either has a deductible expense or a capital expenditure, depending on the nature of the services.

EFFECT OF LIABILITIES

Partners, other than limited partners, are collectively and individually liable for all partnership debts unless specifically stated otherwise. Consequently, liabilities are an important factor in taxation of partners. First, a general partner's basis in the partnership is increased by his or her share of partnership liabilities (e.g., accounts payable, accrued expenses, and long-term debt).[18] Liabilities included in the computation are *recourse* debt (those for which these partners are personally liable) plus nonrecourse debt (those for which no partner is personally liable).[19] Generally, each partner's share of liabilities is based on his or her individual *loss sharing ratio* in the case of *recourse debt* and *profit sharing ratio* in the case of *nonrecourse debt*.[20] (See the discussion on partner's basis at the end of this chapter for additional information on recourse and nonrecourse notes.) Second, when a partner's share of debt is decreased, the reduction is treated as a *cash*

---

[16] Property is not defined under § 721 but the definition for § 351 transfers to corporations generally is applied to partnerships. Also see Reg. §§ 1.721-1(a) and 1.453-9(c)(2).

[17] Reg. § 1.721-1(b)(1).

[18] § 752(a). Accrued expenses of a cash ba-sis partnership, however, are not included in a partner's basis. Temp. Reg. § 1.752-1T(g).

[19] § 465.

[20] Reg. § 1.752-1(e).

distribution from the partnership.[21] If the reduction in the partner's share of liabilities exceeds the partner's basis in the partnership, the excess is a taxable gain.[22] This same principle applies when (1) both debt and assets are contributed to the partnership in exchange for a capital interest, *and* (2) the portion of this debt allocable to other partners exceeds the basis of the assets being contributed.

All cash distributions reduce a partner's basis in the partnership but *never below zero*. Thus, when the partner's share of a reduction in liabilities exceeds his or her partnership basis, the excess has no effect on this basis.[23]

> **Example 3.**   D contributes land with a fair market value of $125,000 and transfers full responsibility for a mortgage on the land of $60,000 to a new partnership in exchange for a one-fourth capital interest. He acquired the land 10 years ago for $35,000. D's one-fourth partnership share of the mortgage is $15,000. Therefore, his basis in the partnership interest is $35,000 plus $15,000 or a total of $50,000. The $60,000 mortgage assumed by the partnership is treated as a cash distribution to D from the partnership. The $60,000 exceeds his basis of $50,000 by $10,000. As a result, D must recognize gain of $10,000 on the contribution and the basis in his partnership interest is reduced to (but not below) zero. The partnership's basis for the land is $35,000 and it has a $60,000 mortgage payable. (As discussed later in this chapter, a special election under § 754 allows the partnership to increase the basis in the land by D's $10,000 recognized gain to $45,000.) The other partners' bases in the partnership are increased by their share of the $60,000 debt.

> **Example 4.**   Assume the same facts as in *Example 3*, except that partnership liabilities before D's contribution are $28,000. D's one-fourth share of these liabilities ($7,000) is included in his basis before recognized gain is determined. In this situation, the $60,000 exceeds his basis of $57,000 ($35,000 + $15,000 + $7,000) by $3,000. Thus, he has a recognized gain of $3,000. His basis in the partnership interest is zero and the partnership's basis in the land is $35,000 (or $38,000 with a § 754 election).

RECAPTURE PROVISIONS

The contribution of depreciated property in a tax-free exchange for a capital interest does not trigger the §§ 1245 or 1250 depreciation recapture provisions.[24] In such instances, the partner's holding period, basis, and potential recapture of depreciation are transferred to the partnership.[25]

---

[21]   This allocation of debt may be overridden if the actual economic risk for the loss is different. For example, the entire amount of debt incurred after January 30, 1989 is assigned to the basis of a partner who has personal liability for it. Temp. Reg. §§ 1.752-1T and 4T.

[22]   §§ 731(a)(1) and 741.

[23]   § 733.

[24]   §§ 1245(b)(3) and 1250(d)(3).

[25]   Reg. §§ 1.1245-2(c)(2) and 1.1250-3(c)(3).

SPECIAL ALLOCATIONS

The nonrecognition principle of § 721 generally is quite beneficial for individuals who wish to exchange property for a partnership interest. Without this special treatment, many taxpayers would be reluctant to contribute appreciated assets to a partnership. As previously discussed, tax-free contributions result in a carryover of the partner's basis to the partnership. This basis *must* be used for depreciation and depletion purposes and for determining gain or loss on a subsequent disposition of these assets. Generally, all allocations of income, deductions, gains, and losses must be made according to the partners' profit and loss ratios (unless they have agreed to special allocations, as discussed later in this chapter).[26] However, if this rule is followed when the market value and carryover basis of contributed assets differ, partners report more income (or less loss) than they would if the market value of the assets could be used. Although this may be acceptable to the individual contributing appreciated property, it is inequitable to the other partners. This inequity is remedied in most situations with a *mandatory* special allocation. The special allocation is required for depreciation, depletion, gain, and loss accrued at the date the property is transferred to the partnership.[27] Its purpose is to ensure that precontribution gains and losses are assigned to the partner who contributed the property.

> **Example 5.** T and E formed a partnership with capital interests of 80% and 20%, respectively. E contributed land in exchange for her 20% capital interest. The land had a fair market value of $40,000 and a basis to E of $20,000. Thus, the partnership received an asset with an economic value of $40,000 and a tax basis of $20,000. If the land is sold December 31, 1990 for $48,000, the gain is $28,000 ($48,000 − $20,000). This includes appreciation of $20,000 while owned by E and $8,000 while owned by the partnership. Without a special allocation, E would recognize 20% of the gain, $5,600, and the remaining $22,400 gain would be recognized by T. However, the special allocation rules for precontribution gain require E to recognize the first $20,000 of gain, and the remaining gain is allocated among all partners based on their profit charing ratios. Thus, E recognizes $21,600 ($20,000 + 20% of $8,000) and T recognizes $6,400 (80% of $8,000).

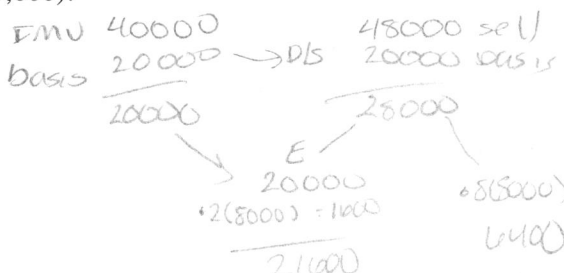

---

[26] § 704(c)(1).

[27] § 704(c). The requirement for special allocations is not applicable for property contributed before April 1984.

Example 6. Refer to *Example 5*. In addition to the land, E contributed a building with a market value of $63,000 to obtain her 20% capital interest. E had purchased the building six years earlier for $90,000 and deducted $36,000 depreciation, based on the straight-line method and a 15-year life ($90,000 ÷ 15 years = $6,000 × 6 years). Thus, the building's basis at contribution was $54,000 ($90,000 − $36,000 accumulated depreciation). The partnership continues to use E's depreciation method but must apply it to the carryover basis of $54,000. Consequently, annual depreciation is $6,000 ($54,000 ÷ 9 years). T's share of the deduction is $5,600 ($63,000 ÷ 9 years = $7,000 × 80%), and E's share is $400 ($6,000 maximum deduction − $5,600 allocated to T).

Note that if the building's market value had exceeded $67,500, T could not be allocated his full share. For example, if the building's value had been $72,000, T's share is $6,400 ($72,000 ÷ 9 years = $8,000 × 80%). However, since the partnership's depreciation is $6,000, T cannot be allocated more than $6,000.

Example 7. Refer to *Example 6*. Assume the special allocation is made to T and the building is sold for $50,000 after it was depreciated seven years as a partnership asset. The building's basis is $12,000 [$90,000 − ($6,000 × 7 = $42,000 + $36,000 prepartnership depreciation = $78,000)] and gain is $38,000 ($50,000 − $12,000). The gain should be allocated as follows:

Partnership	T (80%)	E (20%)	Total
Beginning basis[1]	$50,400	$ 3,600	$54,000
Less: Depreciation.	(39,200)	(2,800)	(42,000)
Basis when sold	$11,200	$ 800	$12,000
Sales proceeds	$40,000	$10,000	$50,000
Less: Basis	(11,200)	(800)	(12,000)
Section 1231 gain	$28,800	$ 9,200	$38,000

[1]$63,000 market value × 80% = $50,400 and $54,000 transfer basis − $50,400 = $3,600

Since this is a building with straight-line depreciation, there is no recapture gain. If this had been equipment, the § 1245 recapture depreciation would be $28,000 (the smaller of the $28,000 gain or the potential recapture of $12,000 partnership depreciation + $36,000 proprietorship depreciation = $48,000).

In addition to the required special allocation, the character of one type of gain and one type of loss accrued at the time of transfer remain with the contributed property for five years. Specifically, losses on capital assets will be capital losses (up to the amount accrued at date of transfer) and *any* gains on inventory will be ordinary income.[28] (Similar rules apply to unrealized receivables discussed later in this section of the chapter.) Consequently, these assets are referred to as being *tainted*. To prevent partnerships from avoiding this capital loss and ordinary income treatment, the taint remains with both this property *and* all assets (except corporate stock) received in any future tax-free exchange for the tainted property.

Example 8. On November 1, 1991, D exchanges land held for investment ($7,000 market value, $9,000 basis) and proprietorship inventory ($4,000 market value, $3,500 basis) for a 20% interest in a partnership. These assets will be used in the partnership business, and therefore qualify as § 1231 assets. Three years later, the partnership sells the land for $6,700 resulting in a loss of $2,300 ($6,700 − $9,000 basis). At the same time, the partnership sells the items previously qualifying as D's inventory for $5,600, resulting in a gain of $2,100 ($5,600 − $3,500 basis). All losses and gains accrued as of November 1, 1991 ($2,000 loss for the land, $500 gain for the inventory) must be allocated to D. The remaining losses ($300 for the land) and gains ($1,600 for the inventory) are divided among the partners according to their profit and loss ratios. Since these assets were sold before the required five-year period elapsed, the character (capital loss for the land and ordinary income for the inventory) is retained. Although these assets were converted by the partnership to business assets, the *entire* gain on the sale of the inventory is ordinary income. In contrast, the capital loss on the sale of the land is limited to the $2,000 precontribution amount. Thus, D has the following gains and losses to report:

Land:	Loss to 11/1/91 (100%)	$2,000 capital loss
	Loss after 10/31/91 (20%)	60 § 1231 loss
Inventory:	Gain to 11/1/91 (100%)	500 ordinary income
	Gain after 10/31/91 (20%)	320 ordinary income

If these same sales had occurred *more than* five years after the assets had been contributed, the numbers would be the same but all gains and losses would be § 1231 gains and losses. Regardless of the date of sale, the other partners have a $240 ($300 − $60) § 1231 loss for the land since the $2,000 precontribution loss is allocated to D. However, unless the inventory is held for more than five years before its sale, the other partners' share of the gain ($1,600 − $320 = $1,280) will be ordinary income.

The taint provisions also apply to the gain or loss on unrealized receivables (e.g., the unrecognized income from trade receivables of a cash basis business or the unrecognized ordinary income on installment sales contributed to the partnership).[29] Any gain or loss on these receivables is ordinary, regardless of when the income or loss is realized. Similar rules apply to the payables of a cash basis business contributed to a partnership.

---

[28] §§ 724 and 751(c) and (d)(2).   [29] § 724(a).

There are a number of options other than contributing the appreciated (or depreciated) property to a partnership that may be more acceptable to parties involved. For example, the property could be sold to the partnership with all gain or loss being recognized by the property owner.[30] This approach may have additional benefit when the owner has capital gains (to offset individual capital losses) on property that will be depreciated by the partnership. The larger future depreciation deductions may more than offset the present taxation of capital gains. Alternatively, the property could be leased to the partnership and cash or a note given for the capital interest. In any event, the most important point is that all partners should be aware of the problems and satisfied with the solution.

COMPARED WITH CORPORATE FORMATION

Many, but not all, of the rules applicable to contributions of assets for a partnership interest also exist under § 351 when assets are exchanged for corporate stock. Three rules discussed in this chapter are different, however, when contributions are made for a partnership interest rather than for corporate stock.

1. The tax-free exchange provisions apply to all partners regardless of their percentage ownership of the partnership, whereas § 351 applies only to contributing shareholders who, as a group, own at least 80 percent of the corporation's stock after the contribution.

2. Special allocations for depreciation, depletion, gains, and losses on contributed property are not available with the corporate form.

3. A partner's basis in the partnership is increased by his or her share of liabilities, whereas liabilities have no effect on a shareholder's basis in stock.

ORGANIZATION COSTS AND SYNDICATION FEES

Both organization costs and syndication fees for a partnership must be capitalized. An election is available at the partnership level to amortize *organization costs* (e.g., legal fees for drafting a partnership agreement) on a straight-line basis over a period of 60 months or longer.[31] In contrast, *syndication fees* paid or accrued to promote or sell a partnership interest may not be amortized at any time.[32] They remain on the books as intangible assets until the partnership is liquidated. Syndication fees generally are not incurred except for widely owned limited partnerships that are established as tax shelters.

---

[30]   § 707(a).

[31]   § 709(b).

[32]   § 709(a) and Reg. § 1.709-2(b).

OPERATING THE PARTNERSHIP

Federal Income Tax Form 1065 must be filed for a partnership by the 15th day of the fourth month following the end of its tax year. This means an April 15 due date when a calendar year is selected for the partnership. In contrast with most corporations, trusts, and estates, a partnership is not a taxable entity. Instead, it primarily serves as a *conduit* for accumulating income, expenses, gains, losses, and credits that *flow through* to its owners, based on their capital interests or some other allocation method adopted by them. Following the aggregate concept, all incidence of taxation passes to the partners who must report their share of these items on their own tax returns. In most instances, each item retains its original character. For example, interest on tax-exempt state bonds earned by a partnership flows through to owners as tax-exempt income. Because of this flow through concept, the primary purpose of the partnership return is to provide information about the nature and amount of income, expenses, gains, losses, and credits and how they are allocated to each partner.

DETERMINING PARTNERSHIP NET INCOME

Partnership information is divided into two categories: (1) includible income and deductible expenses that result in net *ordinary income or loss* that is not subject to special tax treatment by *any* taxpayer, and (2) all other income, expenses, gains, losses, and credits. This division is basic to preparing the partnership tax return. (See Exhibit 22-2 for an illustration of a partially completed Form 1065 and the accompanying Schedules K and K-1. The information is taken from the example in the Appendix to Chapter 23—S Corporations.) Classification of an item for reporting purposes is determined at the partnership level. For example, gain on the sale of business land is § 1231 gain to all partners, even if one of them is a real estate broker, or if one of them held a capital interest in the partnership for less than one year.[33]

A partnership is generally allowed to use either the cash or the accrual method of accounting for determining its income. However, the cash method of accounting *cannot* be used by any partnership that is a tax shelter (discussed later in this chapter).[34] Similarly, any partnership that has a C corporation as a partner must use the accrual basis, unless the partnership (1) is in the farming or timber business, (2) has average annual gross receipts of no more than $5 million for each of the prior three taxable years, or (3) has a corporate partner that is a qualified personal service corporation. A qualified personal service corporation generally is one that provides professional services and is owned substantially (95% in value) by employees who perform services in the fields of health, law,

---

[33] Rev. Rul. 67-188, 1967-1 C.B. 216. Also see *U.S. v. Basye*, 73-1 USTC ¶9250, 31 AFTR2d 73-802, 410 U.S. 441 (USSC, 1973); and Rev. Rul. 68-79, 1968-1 C.B. 310.

[34] § 448.

Exhibit 22-2

Form **1065**	U.S. Partnership Return of Income	OMB No. 1545-0099
Department of the Treasury Internal Revenue Service	For calendar year 1990, or tax year beginning _____, 1990, and ending _____, 19___ ► See separate instructions.	**19 90**

A Principal business activity RETAIL	Use IRS label. Other- wise, please print or type.	Name T COMPANY	**D** Employer identification number 88-9138761
B Principal product or service CLOTHING		Number, street, and room or suite no. (If a P.O. box, see page 9 of the instructions.) 8122 SOUTH S STREET	**E** Date business started 1-1-90
C Business code number 5651		City or town, state, and ZIP code NORFOLK, VA 23508	**F** Total assets (see Specific Instructions) $ 322,000 00

		Yes	No
G Check applicable boxes: (1) ☑ Initial return (2) ☐ Final return (3) ☐ Change in address (4) ☐ Amended return	**Q** Has this partnership filed, or is it required to file, **Form 8264**, Application for Registration of a Tax Shelter?		✓
H Check accounting method: (1) ☐ Cash (2) ☑ Accrual (3) ☐ Other (specify) ► _____	**R** Was there a distribution of property or a transfer (for example, by sale or death) of a partnership interest during the tax year? If "Yes," see the instructions concerning an election to adjust the basis of the partnership's assets under section 754		✓

		Yes	No
I Number of partners in this partnership ► 2			
J Is this partnership a limited partnership?			✓
K Are any partners in this partnership also partnerships?. .			✓
L Is this partnership a partner in another partnership? . .			✓
M Is this partnership subject to the consolidated audit procedures of sections 6221 through 6233? If "Yes," see "Designation of Tax Matters Partner" on page 2			✓
N Does this partnership meet **all** the requirements shown in the instructions for **Question N**?			✓
O Does this partnership have any foreign partners? . . .			✓
P Is this partnership a publicly traded partnership as defined in section 469(k)(2)?			✓

S At any time during the tax year, did the partnership have an interest in or a signature or other authority over a financial account in a foreign country (such as a bank account, securities account, or other financial account)? (See the instructions for exceptions and filing requirements for form TD F 90-22.1.) If "Yes," enter the name of the foreign country. ► _____ — No ✓

T Was the partnership the grantor of, or transferor to, a foreign trust which existed during the current tax year, whether or not the partnership or any partner has any beneficial interest in it? If "Yes," you may have to file Forms 3520, 3520-A, or 926 . . . . . — No ✓

Caution: Include **only** trade or business income and expenses on lines 1a through 21 below. See the instructions for more information.

Income					
1a Gross receipts or sales		**1a** 470,000			
b Less returns and allowances		**1b** -0-		**1c**	470,000
2 Cost of goods sold (Schedule A, line 7)				**2**	300,000
3 Gross profit—Subtract line 2 from line 1c				**3**	170,000
4 Ordinary income (loss) from other partnerships and fiduciaries *(attach schedule)*				**4**	
5 Net farm profit (loss) *(attach Schedule F (Form 1040))*				**5**	
6 Net gain (loss) from Form 4797, Part II, line 18				**6**	
7 Other income (loss) (see instructions) *(attach schedule)*				**7**	
8 Total income (loss)—Combine lines 3 through 7				**8**	170,000

Deductions (see instructions for limitations)					
9a Salaries and wages (other than to partners)		**9a** 48,000			
b Less jobs credit		**9b** -0-		**9c**	48,000
10 Guaranteed payments to partners				**10**	24,000
11 Rent				**11**	
12 Interest				**12**	3,300
13 Taxes				**13**	7,000
14 Bad debts				**14**	
15 Repairs				**15**	12,000
16a Depreciation (see instructions)		**16a** 15,000			
b Less depreciation reported on Schedule A and elsewhere on return		**16b** -0-		**16c**	15,000
17 Depletion **(Do not deduct oil and gas depletion.)**				**17**	
18a Retirement plans, etc.				**18a**	
b Employee benefit programs . LIFE INS.				**18b**	1,400
19 Other deductions *(attach schedule)* TELE.= $2,500; OFFICE SUPPLIES = $1,100; INSURANCE COSTS = $3,100 UTILITIES				**19**	6,700
20 Total deductions—Add lines 9c through 19				**20**	117,400
21 Ordinary income (loss) from trade or business activities—Subtract line 20 from line 8				**21**	52,600

Please Sign Here
Under penalties of perjury, I declare that I have examined this return, including accompanying schedules and statements, and to the best of my knowledge and belief, it is true, correct, and complete. Declaration of preparer (other than general partner) is based on all information of which preparer has any knowledge.

► Signature of general partner   ► Date

Paid Preparer's Use Only	Preparer's signature ►		Date	Check if self-employed ► ☐	Preparer's social security no.
	Firm's name (or yours if self-employed) and address ►			E.I. No. ►	
				ZIP code ►	

For Paperwork Reduction Act Notice, see page 1 of separate instructions.   Form **1065** (1990)

Exhibit 22-2 Continued

Form 1065 (1990)   Page **2**

Schedule A — Cost of Goods Sold (a)

1 Inventory at beginning of year	1	
2 Purchases less cost of items withdrawn for personal use	2	
3 Cost of labor	3	
4a Additional section 263A costs (see instructions) (attach schedule)	4a	
b Other costs (attach schedule)	4b	
5 Total—Add lines 1 through 4b	5	
6 Inventory at end of year	6	
7 Cost of goods sold—Subtract line 6 from line 5. Enter here and on page 1, line 2	7	300,000

8a Check all methods used for valuing closing inventory:
(i) ☑ Cost   (ii) ☐ Lower of cost or market as described in Regulations section 1.471-4
(iii) ☐ Writedown of "subnormal" goods as described in Regulations section 1.471-2(c)
(iv) ☐ Other (specify method used and attach explanation) ▶ ....
b Check this box if the LIFO inventory method was adopted this tax year for any goods (if checked, attach Form 970) . . . ▶ ☐
c Do the rules of section 263A (with respect to property produced or acquired for resale) apply to the partnership? . . ☐ Yes ☑ No
d Was there any change in determining quantities, cost, or valuations between opening and closing inventory? . . . ☐ Yes ☑ No
If "Yes," attach explanation.

Schedule L — Balance Sheets

Caution: Read the instructions for Question N on page 9 of the instructions before completing Schedules L and M.

Assets	Beginning of tax year (a)	(b)	End of tax year (c)	(d)
1 Cash				
2a Trade notes and accounts receivable				
b Less allowance for bad debts				
3 Inventories				
4 U.S. government obligations				
5 Tax-exempt securities				
6 Other current assets (attach schedule)				
7 Mortgage and real estate loans				
8 Other investments (attach schedule)				
9a Buildings and other depreciable assets				
b Less accumulated depreciation				
10a Depletable assets				
b Less accumulated depletion				
11 Land (net of any amortization)				
12a Intangible assets (amortizable only)				
b Less accumulated amortization				
13 Other assets (attach schedule)				
14 Total assets				322,000
Liabilities and Capital				
15 Accounts payable				
16 Mortgages, notes, bonds payable in less than 1 year				
17 Other current liabilities (attach schedule)				
18 All nonrecourse loans				
19 Mortgages, notes, bonds payable in 1 year or more				
20 Other liabilities (attach schedule)				
21 Partners' capital accounts				
22 Total liabilities and capital				322,000

Schedule M — Reconciliation of Partners' Capital Accounts
(Show reconciliation of each partner's capital account on Schedule K-1 (Form 1065), Item K.)

(a) Partners' capital accounts at beginning of year	(b) Capital contributed during year	(c) Income (loss) from lines 1, 2, 3c, and 4 of Schedule K	(d) Income not included in column (c), plus nontaxable income	(e) Losses not included in column (c), plus unallowable deductions	(f) Withdrawals and distributions	(g) Partners' capital accounts at end of year (combine columns (a) through (f))
		58,900 (b)	O	(7,700 (c))	(19,000 (d))	

Designation of Tax Matters Partner (See instructions.)
Enter below the general partner designated as the tax matters partner (TMP) for the tax year of this return:
Name of designated TMP ▶
Identifying number of TMP ▶
Address of designated TMP ▶

(a) LINES 1 THROUGH 6 MUST BE COMPLETED BEFORE THE RETURN IS FILED.
(b) $52,600 ORD. INC. + $3,300 INTEREST INC. + $2,000 DIVIDENDS + $1,000 NLTCG = $58,900.
(c) $7000 CHARITABLE CONT. + $700 LIFE INS. = $7,700.
(d) $12,000 CASH + $7,000 P/S BASIS IN LAND = $19,000.
SCHEDULE L & M MUST BE COMPLETED BEFORE THE RETURN IS FILED.

Exhibit 22-2 Continued

Form 1065 (1990)

Page 3

Schedule K — Partners' Shares of Income, Credits, Deductions, Etc.

	(a) Distributive share items		(b) Total amount
Income (Loss)	**1** Ordinary income (loss) from trade or business activities (page 1, line 21)	1	52,600
	2 Net income (loss) from rental real estate activities *(attach Form 8825)*	2	
	3a Gross income from other rental activities . . . . . [3a]		
	b Less expenses *(attach schedule)* . . . . [3b]		
	c Net income (loss) from other rental activities	3c	
	4 Portfolio income (loss) (see instructions):		
	a Interest income	4a	
	b Dividend income	4b	2,000
	c Royalty income	4c	
	d Net short-term capital gain (loss) *(attach Schedule D (Form 1065))*	4d	
	e Net long-term capital gain (loss) *(attach Schedule D (Form 1065))* $2,200−$1,200	4e	1,000
	f Other portfolio income (loss) *(attach schedule)*	4f	
	5 Guaranteed payments to partners	5	24,000
	6 Net gain (loss) under section 1231 (other than due to casualty or theft) *(attach Form 4797)*	6	
	7 Other income (loss) *(attach schedule)* INTEREST PAID TO T	7	3,300
Deductions	**8** Charitable contributions (see instructions) *(attach list)*	8	7,000
	9 Section 179 expense deduction *(attach Form 4562)*	9	
	10 Deductions related to portfolio income (see instructions) (itemize)	10	
	11 Other deductions *(attach schedule)*	11	
Investment Interest	**12a** Interest expense on investment debts	12a	
	b (1) Investment income included on lines 4a through 4f above	12b(1)	
	(2) Investment expenses included on line 10 above	12b(2)	
Credits	**13a** Credit for income tax withheld	13a	
	b Low-income housing credit (see instructions):		
	(1) From partnerships to which section 42(j)(5) applies for property placed in service before 1990	13b(1)	
	(2) Other than on line 13b(1) for property placed in service before 1990	13b(2)	
	(3) From partnerships to which section 42(j)(5) applies for property placed in service after 1989	13b(3)	
	(4) Other than on line 13b(3) for property placed in service after 1989	13b(4)	
	c Qualified rehabilitation expenditures related to rental real estate activities *(attach Form 3468)*	13c	
	d Credits (other than credits shown on lines 13b and 13c) related to rental real estate activities (see instructions)	13d	
	e Credits related to other rental activities (see instructions)	13e	
	14 Other credits (see instructions) REHABILITATION CREDIT	14	2,000
Self-Employment	**15a** Net earnings (loss) from self-employment $52,600 + $24,000	15a	76,600
	b Gross farming or fishing income	15b	
	c Gross nonfarm income	15c	
Adjustments and Tax Preference Items	**16a** Accelerated depreciation of real property placed in service before 1987	16a	
	b Accelerated depreciation of leased personal property placed in service before 1987 . . .	16b	
	c Depreciation adjustment on property placed in service after 1986	16c	
	d Depletion (other than oil and gas)	16d	
	e (1) Gross income from oil, gas, and geothermal properties	16e(1)	
	(2) Deductions allocable to oil, gas, and geothermal properties	16e(2)	
	f Other adjustments and tax preference items *(attach schedule)*	16f	
Foreign Taxes	**17a** Type of income ▶ ------------------------------		
	b Foreign country or U.S. possession ▶ ---------------------		
	c Total gross income from sources outside the U.S. *(attach schedule)*	17c	
	d Total applicable deductions and losses *(attach schedule)*	17d	
	e Total foreign taxes (check one): ▶ ☐ Paid ☐ Accrued	17e	
	f Reduction in taxes available for credit *(attach schedule)*	17f	
	g Other foreign tax information *(attach schedule)*	17g	
Other	**18a** Total expenditures to which a section 59(e) election may apply	18a	
	b Type of expenditures ▶		
	19 Other items and amounts required to be reported separately to partners (see instructions) *(attach schedule)*		

Analysis	**20a** Total distributive income/payment items—Combine lines 1 through 7 above . . .	20a				
	b Analysis by type of partner:	(a) Corporate	(b) Individual		(c) Partnership	(d) Exempt organization	(e) Nominee/Other
			i. Active	ii. Passive			
	(1) General partners		82,900				
	(2) Limited partners						

Exhibit 22-2 Continued

SCHEDULE K-1 (Form 1065)	**Partner's Share of Income, Credits, Deductions, Etc.** ► See separate instructions.	OMB No. 1545-0099
Department of the Treasury Internal Revenue Service	For calendar year 1990 or tax year beginning _____ , 1990, and ending _____ , 19 ___	19**90**

Partner's identifying number ► 467-63-5052	Partnership's identifying number ► 88-9138761
Partner's name, address, and ZIP code	Partnership's name, address, and ZIP code
ADOLPH Z.T. 1291 MAPLE DRIVE NORFOLK, VA 23508	T COMPANY 8122 SOUTH S STREET NORFOLK, VA 23508

A   Is this partner a general partner? . . . ☒ Yes ☐ No

B   Partner's share of liabilities (see instructions):
Nonrecourse *DATA NOT IN EXAMPLE* . . . $ _____
Qualified nonrecourse financing . . $ ___40,000___
Other . . . . $ _____

C   What type of entity is this partner? ► _____

D   Is this partner a ☐ domestic or a ☐ foreign partner?

E   Enter partner's percentage of:
	(i) Before change or termination	(ii) End of year
Profit sharing *NOT IN EXAMPLE*	100 %	100 %
Loss sharing *NOT IN EXAMPLE*	80 %	80 %
Ownership of capital *EXAMPLE*	80 %	80 %

F   IRS Center where partnership filed return ► MEMPHIS, TN

G(1) Tax shelter registration number ► N/A
(2) Type of tax shelter ► _____

H(1) Did the partner's ownership interest in the partnership change after Oct. 22, 1986? . . . . ☐ Yes ☒ No
If "Yes," attach statement. (See Form 1065 Instructions.)
(2) Did the partnership start or acquire a new activity after Oct. 22, 1986? . . . . ☐ Yes ☒ No
If "Yes," attach statement. (See Form 1065 Instructions.)

I   Check here if this partnership is a publicly traded partnership as defined in section 469(k)(2) . . . . ☐

J   Check applicable boxes: (1) ☐ Final K-1 (2) ☐ Amended K-1

K   Reconciliation of partner's capital account:

(a) Capital account at beginning of year	(b) Capital contributed during year	(c) Income (loss) from lines 1, 2, 3, and 4 below	(d) Income not included in column (c), plus nontaxable income	(e) Losses not included in column (c), plus unallowable deductions	(f) Withdrawals and distributions	(g) Capital account at end of year (combine columns (a) through (f))
58,900 (a)	0			(7,700 (b))	(19,000 (c))	

	(a) Distributive share item		(b) Amount	(c) 1040 filers enter the amount in column (b) on:
Income (Loss)	1	Ordinary income (loss) from trade or business activities . . .	1	52,600	⎫ (See Partner's Instructions for Schedule K-1 (Form 1065))
	2	Net income (loss) from rental real estate activities	2		
	3	Net income (loss) from other rental activities	3		
	4	Portfolio income (loss):			
	a	Interest	4a		Sch. B, Part I, line 1
	b	Dividends	4b	2,000	Sch. B, Part II, line 5
	c	Royalties	4c		Sch. E, Part I, line 4
	d	Net short-term capital gain (loss)	4d		Sch. D, line 5, col. (f) or (g)
	e	Net long-term capital gain (loss)	4e	1,000	Sch. D, line 12, col. (f) or (g)
	f	Other portfolio income (loss) (attach schedule)	4f		(Enter on applicable line of your return)
	5	Guaranteed payments to partner	5	24,000	⎫ (See Partner's Instructions for Schedule K-1 (Form 1065))
	6	Net gain (loss) under section 1231 (other than due to casualty or theft)	6		
	7	Other income (loss) (attach schedule) INTEREST . . .	7	3,300	(Enter on applicable line of your return)
Deductions	8	Charitable contributions	8	7,000	Sch. A, line 14 or 15
	9	Section 179 expense deduction (attach schedule)	9		⎫ (See Partner's Instructions for Schedule K-1 (Form 1065))
	10	Deductions related to portfolio income (attach schedule) . . .	10		
	11	Other deductions (attach schedule)	11		
Investment Interest	12a	Interest expense on investment debts	12a		Form 4952, line 1
	b	(1) Investment income included on lines 4a through 4f above .	b(1)		⎫ (See Partner's Instructions for Schedule K-1 (Form 1065))
		(2) Investment expenses included on line 10 above	b(2)		
Credits	13a	Credit for income tax withheld	13a		(See Partner's Instructions for Schedule K-1 (Form 1065))
	b	Low-income housing credit:			
		(1) From section 42(j)(5) partnerships for property placed in service before 1990	b(1)		⎫ Form 8586, line 5
		(2) Other than on line 13b(1) for property placed in service before 1990	b(2)		
		(3) From section 42(j)(5) partnerships for property placed in service after 1989	b(3)		
		(4) Other than on line 13b(3) for property placed in service after 1989	b(4)		
	c	Qualified rehabilitation expenditures related to rental real estate activities (see instructions)	13c		⎫ (See Partner's Instructions for Schedule K-1 (Form 1065))
	d	Credits (other than credits shown on lines 13b and 13c) related to rental real estate activities (see instructions)	13d		
	e	Credits related to other rental activities (see instructions) . . .	13e		
	14	Other credits (see instructions) REHABILITATION CREDIT .	14	2,000	

For Paperwork Reduction Act Notice, see Form 1065 Instructions.   Schedule K-1 (Form 1065) 1990

a) $52,600 ORD. INC. + $3,300 INTEREST INC. + $2,000 DIVIDENDS + $1,000 NLTCG = $58,900.

b) $7,000 CHARITABLE CONT. + $700 LIFE INS. = $7,700.

c) $12,000 CASH + $7,000 P/S BASIS IN LAND = $19,000.

SECTION K MUST BE COMPLETED BEFORE THE RETURN IS FILED.

(handwritten margin note:) One Partner = all income? — not realistic

Exhibit 22-2 Continued

Schedule K-1 (Form 1065) 1990   Page **2**

	(a) Distributive share item	(b) Amount	(c) 1040 filers enter the amount in column (b) on:
Self-em-ployment 15a	Net earnings (loss) from self-employment **15a**	76,600	Sch. SE, Section A or B
b	Gross farming or fishing income **15b**		} (See Partner's Instructions for Schedule K-1 (Form 1065))
c	Gross nonfarm income **15c**		
Adjustments and Tax Preference Items 16a	Accelerated depreciation of real property placed in service before 1987 . . . . **16a**		
b	Accelerated depreciation of leased personal property placed in service before 1987 . . . . **16b**		(See Partner's Instructions for Schedule K-1 (Form 1065) and Form 6251 Instructions)
c	Depreciation adjustment on property placed in service after 1986 **16c**		
d	Depletion (other than oil and gas) **16d**		
e	(1) Gross income from oil, gas, and geothermal properties . . **e(1)**		
	(2) Deductions allocable to oil, gas, and geothermal properties . **e(2)**		
f	Other adjustments and tax preference items *(attach schedule)* . **16f**		
Foreign Taxes 17a	Type of income ▶ _____		Form 1116, Check boxes
b	Name of foreign country or U.S. possession ▶ _____		Form 1116, Part I
c	Total gross income from sources outside the U.S. *(attach schedule)* **17c**		Form 1116, Part I
d	Total applicable deductions and losses *(attach schedule)* . . . **17d**		Form 1116, Part I
e	Total foreign taxes (check one): ▶ ☐ Paid ☐ Accrued . . **17e**		Form 1116, Part II
f	Reduction in taxes available for credit *(attach schedule)* . . . **17f**		Form 1116, Part III
g	Other foreign tax information *(attach schedule)* **17g**		See Form 1116 Instructions
Other 18a	Total expenditures to which a section 59(e) election may apply . **18a**	700	(See Partner's Instructions for Schedule K-1 (Form 1065))
b	Type of expenditures ▶ *LIFE INSURANCE* _____		
19	Recapture of low-income housing credit:		
a	From section 42(j)(5) partnerships **19a**		} Form 8611, line 8
b	Other than on line 19a **19b**		

Recapture of Tax Credits 20	Investment credit properties:	A	B	C	
a	Description of property (State whether recovery or nonrecovery property. If recovery property, state whether regular percentage method or section 48(q) election used.) .				Form 4255, top
b	Date placed in service .				Form 4255, line 2
c	Cost or other basis . .				Form 4255, line 3
d	Class of recovery property or original estimated useful life .				Form 4255, line 4
e	Date item ceased to be investment credit property				Form 4255, line 8

Supplemental Information

21   Supplemental information required to be reported separately to each partner *(attach additional schedules if more space is needed):*

$700 LIFE INSURANCE

_____

_____

_____

_____

accounting, engineering, architecture, actuarial science, performing arts, or consulting. When the accrual method is required, however, amounts that are not expected to be collected and that carry no interest or penalty for late payment need not be accrued.[35]

NET ORDINARY INCOME OR LOSS

All includible income and deductible expenses in determining net *ordinary* income or loss are reported on page 1 of Form 1065. Includible income is listed on lines 1 through 7. In addition to gross receipts from services and gross profit from merchandise sales, ordinary income includes net income or loss from other partnerships, and fiduciaries; net income or loss from farming operations; net gains from the recapture provisions of § 1245 and §§ 1250 through 1254; and other income or loss. Deductible expenses are recorded on lines 9 through 19. In general, the list includes employee salaries, rent, interest, taxes, bad debts, repairs, depreciation, depletion, retirement plans, and employee benefit programs. All other deductible ordinary expenses such as utilities, insurance, advertising, and entertainment are accumulated on a separate schedule and reported in total on line 19. Partnership net ordinary income or loss is determined next by subtracting the listed deductible expenses from the includible income. Partners are required to report their share of the net amount. This approach relieves them of the burden of reporting their share of each item affecting partnership ordinary net income or loss. Nevertheless, their share of each item is treated as flowing through the partnership to them.[36] This distinction can be important in some instances. For example, the statute of limitations increases from three to six years when taxpayers omit more than 25 percent of their *gross* income.[37] Partners' gross income for this determination includes their individual share of partnership gross income even though they only report their share of net ordinary income.

Page 2 of Form 1065 contains information relating to the cost of goods sold, balance sheet accounts, and a reconciliation of partners' capital accounts. Page 3 (Schedule K) is used to report the partners' shares of income or loss, deductions, credits, self-employment income, tax preferences, investment interest, and foreign taxes. (See Exhibit 22-3 for a summary of the tax effects in this section of the chapter.)

SEPARATELY REPORTED ITEMS

All income, expenses, gains, losses, and credits that *may* be subject to special tax treatment by one or more partners are reported separately on Schedule K, which is filed with Form 1065. These items include rental income and

expenses, dividends, portfolio interest, capital gains and losses, § 1231 gains

---

[35]   § 448(d)(5).   [37]   § 6501(e).

[36]   §§ 702(b) and (c).

Exhibit 22-3
*Summary of Tax Effects
for Operating the Partnership*

Event	Effect on Partnership	Effect on Partner
1. Net ordinary income	Reported on Form 1065	Distributive share flows through and increases the basis in the partnership; it is includible ordinary income
2. Net ordinary loss	Same as above	Distributive share flows through to the extent of each partner's basis and decreases the basis in the partnership; it is deductible ordinary loss to the extent of the flow through and other restrictions; losses in excess of basis are carried forward until the partner's basis is positive
3. Other income, expenses, gains, losses, and credits	Reported on Schedules K (if more than 10 partners) and K-1	Same as above; character flows through with all items
4. Self-employment income:		
a. General partner	Same as above	Distributive share of ordinary net income (adjusted) plus guaranteed payments
b. Limited partner	Same as above	Guaranteed payment for services performed
5. Partnership elections	All but three must be made by the partnership	Section 703 lists three elections to be made individually by each partner

and losses, charitable contributions, qualifying foreign taxes, deductions for the limited expensing election, and any other income, deductions, gains, losses, or credits subject to special tax treatment.[38] These other items include tax credits, itemized deductions attributable to partners, payments to Keogh and Individual Retirement Act plans for partners, and oil and gas depletion. In addition, any specially allocated items such as depreciation and gain or loss on contributed property must be reported separately.

Each partner's distributive share of partnership ordinary income or loss and other Schedule K items is reported on Schedule K-1. One copy of Schedule K-1 prepared for each partner is filed with Form 1065 and one is given to the partner. In this way, the Internal Revenue Service and each partner receive detailed partnership information necessary in determining both the partner's income tax and self-employment tax liability.

SELF-EMPLOYMENT INCOME

Income derived by a partner from a partnership may qualify as self-employment income. Generally, self-employment income for a partner is composed of the partner's (1) distributive share of partnership ordinary income (Form 1065, page 1) adjusted to eliminate all gains, losses, and passive income not earned in the course of the partnership's trade or business, *plus* (2) guaranteed payments (defined later in this chapter).[39] Passive income, gains, and losses include interest income (other than that on accounts and notes receivable), dividends, net rents, and net § 1245 and § 1250 gains. This computation generally is applicable to all partners, regardless of whether any of them perform services for the partnership.[40] However, there are three exceptions. Only *guaranteed payments* for *services performed* are self-employment income for (1) limited partners;[41] (2) partners who liquidated their ownership interests in a prior year but are being paid from current partnership profits;[42] and (3) partners of partnerships that are not engaged in a trade or business.[43]

---

[38] § 702.

[39] § 1402 and Reg. § 1.707-1(c). But see Rev. Rul. 64-220, 1964-2 C.B. 335, where guaranteed payments to manage the partnership's rental property were not self-employment income.

[40] *William J. Ellsasser, Est.,* 61 T.C. 241 (1973). The amount from this computation, however, does not necessarily qualify as earned income for Individual Retirement Accounts [see Code §§ 219(f)(1) and 401(c)(2)]. The same computation is applicable in community property states even though half the partner's distributable share of partnership income may be taxed to his or her spouse.

[41] § 1402(a)(12).

[42] Rev. Rul. 79-34, 1979-1 C.B. 285.

[43] Rev. Ruls. 75-525, 1975-2 C.B. 350 and 79-53, 1979-1 C.B. 286.

Example 9. The K-10 partnership reports the following information for the year:

Sales...		$200,000
Cost of goods sold		(89,000)
Interest income on trade receivables............		3,000
Interest income from corporate bonds...........		5,000
Gross rents....................................	$20,000	
Rental expenses................................	(22,000)	(2,000)
Guaranteed payment to X.......................		(17,000)
Other deductions (expenses)...................		(30,000)
Net ordinary income...........................		$ 70,000
Net capital gain...............................		$ 10,000

The partnership's profits and losses are divided as follows: 40% to X, 35% to Y, and 25% to Z. X and Y are general partners and Z is a limited partner.

The partnership's adjusted ordinary income for self-employment calculations is $67,000 ($70,000 − $5,000 interest income from corporate bonds + $2,000 net rental loss). X's self-employment income is $43,800 ($67,000 × 40% = $26,800 + $17,000 guaranteed payment). Y's self-employment income is $23,450 ($67,000 × 35%). But Z, the limited partner, has no self-employment income. If X were a limited partner, her self-employment income would be just the guaranteed payment of $17,000.

PARTNERSHIP ELECTIONS

Form 1065 and Schedule K-1 are prepared according to the aggregate concept. The partnership return simply serves as a conduit for the convenience of the partners. The aggregate concept, however, does not extend to special *elections* generally available to taxpayers. With few exceptions, all such elections follow the entity concept and must be made at the partnership level.[44] Consequently, all partners are required to use the same methods for reporting their share of partnership income, deductions, gains, losses, and credits. Uniformity, for example, is required for elections concerning the method of determining inventories and depreciation expenses, as well as for determining whether income is reported on the installment basis, and whether certain items are capitalized or expensed. Partners are not, however, required to use these same methods for their other business interests.[45]

Application of the entity concept to partnership elections has cost some partners considerable taxes since an election made by the wrong party is invalid. When the error is discovered, it usually is too late to be corrected. For example, a co-owner of condemned property electing to defer the gain under § 1033 (an

---

[44] See § 703(b) for the three elections that must be made by each partner rather than the partnership.

[45] Reg. § 1.703-1(b).

involuntary conversion) was unexpectedly taxed on the gain. The Tax Court held that the co-ownership arrangement qualified as a partnership and only the partnership could make the § 1033 election. Since the co-owners did not realize they were partners, no partnership election was made.[46]

RELATIONSHIP BETWEEN A PARTNERSHIP AND ITS PARTNERS

Different types of relationships frequently exist between a partnership and its partners. How these relationships between a partner and the partnership are treated depends on whether the aggregate or the entity concept applies. Since these concepts are employed consistently throughout Subchapter K, all partners must be aware of the tax consequences when they interact with the partnership. (See Exhibit 22-4 for a summary of the transactions in this section of the chapter.)

INTERMINGLING OF DEBT RESPONSIBILITIES

A partnership should be operated financially separate from its partners. Unfortunately, this often does not occur in practice. It is not uncommon to find a partner's debts paid with partnership funds. In such instances, the *aggregate* theory applies and both the amount and character of the payment flow through to the partner.

> **Example 10.** Partner F's property taxes of $2,000 are paid with partnership funds. The $2,000 is separately reported on F's Schedule K-1 as "Deductions—Other" and flows through as a distribution to F. This allows F to record the $2,000 property tax as an itemized deduction on her personal return.

In contrast, the *entity* theory applies when partnership debts are paid by partners. Thus, if the partner uses personal funds to pay partnership debts such as entertainment expenses, neither party is allowed the deduction.[47] The partner is not allowed a deduction because the expense was not his or her liability. The partnership is not allowed a deduction because it did not pay the expense. Such unfavorable results may be avoided if the partnership agreement contains a provision that certain expenses are to be borne by the partners personally without reimbursement from the partnership. An agreement of this type has the effect of transferring the responsibility for the debt to the partner.[48] Otherwise, the

---

[46] *Mihran and Mabel Demirjian*, 54 T.C. 1691, *aff'd.* in 72-1 USTC ¶9281, 29 AFTR2d 72-741, 457 F2d 1 (CA-3, 1972).

[47] *Tonkoff v. Comm.*, 73-2 USTC ¶9690, 32 AFTR2d 6038 (DC-Wash., 1973), *aff'd.* in unpublished opinion (CA-9, 1975).

[48] *Robert J. Wallendal,* 31 T.C. 1249 (1959), and *Frederick S. Klein*, 25 T.C. 1045 (1956), *acq.* in 1956-2 C.B. 6.

Exhibit 22-4
*Summary of Tax Effects
for Partner/Partnership Relations*

	Transaction	Effect on Partnership	Effect on Partner
1.	Partnership pays partner's debt (not the partnership's debt)	No deduction; Schedules K and K-1 withdrawl	Amount and character flow through to that partner
2.	Partner pays partnership's debt (not the partner's debt)	No deduction	No deduction — a personal expense
3.	Partner as an employee	Not applicable — a partner cannot be an employee of a partnership	Not applicable
4.	Partner compensation treated as a guaranteed payment	Deductible or capitalized, depending on the type of service performed	Includible ordinary income as of partnership's year-end
5.	Partner compensation based on partnership profits	Distribution of profits	Same as above
6.	Other payments to a partner in a nonpartner status (e.g., interest on debt, rent, and royalty payments)	Deductible when the payment is includible by the partner	Includible as though received from an unrelated party
7.	Losses on sales to partnership (partner owns more that 50% of partnership with constructive ownership rules)	FMV is basis; future gain is not recognized to the extent of the partner's disallowed losses	No deduction
8.	Capital gain on sales to partnership (partner owns more than 50% of partnership with constructive ownership rules)	Treated as a purchase from a nonpartner	All gain is ordinary income if asset is not a capital or § 1231 asset in the hands of the purchaser
9.	Sale of depreciable property to partnership (partner owns more than 50% of partnership with constructive ownership rules)	Same as above	Same as above

partnership must reimburse the partner before the deduction can be taken. If reimbursement occurs, the partnership has a deduction and the partner has includible income for the reimbursement less a deduction for the expense. The net effect is a reduction of partnership net income.

EMPLOYER/EMPLOYEE RELATIONSHIP

The aggregate concept dictates that an employer/employee relationship cannot exist between a partnership and its principal partners.[49] Even though partners may receive compensation for performing services similar to those of nonpartner employees, they are *not* employees for purposes of withholding taxes,[50] receiving excludable employer-provided meals and lodging,[51] nor receiving any other employee benefits deductible by the partnership such as group-term insurance, accident and health plans, or employee death benefits.[52] In contrast, however, a partner may qualify as an owner-employee for participation in a retirement plan.[53]

GUARANTEED PAYMENTS

Compensation to a partner may be classified as either a *guaranteed payment* or a distribution of partnership profits, depending on the terms of payment. If compensation is determined *without regard to the partnership's income*, payments qualify as a guaranteed payment.[54] Such amounts are (1) either deductible expenses or capital expenditures for the partnership,[55] and (2) includible ordinary income to the compensated partner as of the partnership's year-end in which the compensation was deducted or capitalized.

All compensation determined with regard to the partnership's gross or net income is treated as the partner's distributive share of partnership profits and not as a guaranteed payment. Examples include payments that are based on a percentage of net income, or payments that are not made unless the partnership has sufficient net income. These amounts qualify as withdrawals that are not deductible by the partnership but are includible income to the partner as of the partnership's year-end. In most instances, partners' taxable incomes (and their self-employment incomes) are unaffected whether these payments are classified as a guaranteed salary or a distribution of profits.

---

[49] A partner with a 5 percent capital interest was found to be an employee in *Armstrong v. Phinney*, 68-1 USTC ¶9355, 21 AFTR2d 1260, 394 F.2d 661 (CA-5, 1968).

[50] Reg. § 1.707-1(c) and Rev. Rul. 69-184. 1969-1 C.B. 256.

[51] § 119.

[52] Rev. Rul. 72-596, 1972-2 C.B. 395.

[53] §§ 401(a)(10)(A) and 401(c)(3); but see the special restrictions placed on these owner-employees at § 401(d).

[54] § 707(c).

[55] Rev. Rul. 75-214, 1975-1 C.B. 185; and *Cagle v. Comm.*, 63 T.C. 86 (1974), *aff'd.* in 76-2 USTC ¶9672, 38 AFTR2d 76-5834, 539 F.2d 409 (CA-5, 1976).

Example 11. N receives $20,000 as compensation for services rendered and his distributive share of profits and losses is 40%. Partnership ordinary income before deducting N's compensation is $100,000. If the $20,000 is payable regardless of the partnership's net income, it is a guaranteed payment. If this payment qualifies as a deductible expense, the partnership's ordinary income is $80,000 ($100,000 − $20,000) and N's includible ordinary income is $52,000 ($20,000 + 40% of $80,000).

However, if N's compensation is set at 20% of ordinary income before guaranteed payments are deducted plus a 40% distributive share of remaining partnership profits and losses, the entire $52,000 is a distribution of income since the payments are based on partnership income. In both situations, N has includible ordinary income of $52,000 and the remaining $48,000 is includible ordinary income to the other partner(s).

The partner's profit and loss ratio is the same whether the amount received is characterized as a guaranteed payment or a distribution of income. As a result, in *Example 11*, N's ratio is 52 percent ($52,000 distributed to N ÷ $100,000 total partnership income) even though it is recorded as 40 percent or as a series of 20 and 40 percent.

There are instances when the distinction between a guaranteed payment and a distribution of income does result in a different tax effect on the partners. For example, a guaranteed payment received by a partner performing services in a foreign country qualifies as foreign source income whereas a distributive share from a U.S. partnership does not.[56] This determination can either decrease includible income or increase the amount of foreign tax credit allowed the partner.[57] (See Chapter 26 for a discussion.) In addition, a guaranteed payment is an ordinary deduction (unless capitalized) that decreases ordinary income or increases (or even creates) ordinary loss of the partnership. A guaranteed payment may result in the compensated partner reporting ordinary income and other partners reporting ordinary losses from the partnership.

Example 12. Assume the same facts as in *Example 11*, except that the partnership's ordinary income before deducting N's $20,000 compensation is $3,000. If the $20,000 compensation is a deductible guaranteed payment, the partnership has an ordinary loss of $17,000 ($3,000 − $20,000). N had includible ordinary income of $20,000 and ordinary loss of $6,800 (40% of $17,000) for net includible income of $13,200. Other partners report an ordinary loss of $10,200 ($17,000 − $6,800).

In contrast with the above, if N's $20,000 compensation is guaranteed but only up to the amount of partnership net income, N would receive $3,000 and all of it would be a distribution of income. Other partners would have no ordinary gain or loss.

---

[56] *Carey v. U.S.*, 70-1 USTC ¶9455, 25 AFTR2d 70-1395, 427 F.2d 763 (Ct. Cls., 1970) compared with *Foster v. Comm.*, 64- 1 USTC ¶9362, 21 AFTR2d 859, 329 F.2d 727 (CA-2, 1964).

[57] § 911.

Whether partner compensation is a guaranteed payment or a distribution of ordinary income does not affect the amount or character of partnership items that may be subject to special tax treatment. For example, items such as capital gains and losses, qualifying dividends, and tax credits are computed without regard to the partnership's ordinary income or loss.[58]

> **Example 13.** A partnership has $5,000 net ordinary income before deducting guaranteed payments of $30,000 paid to H and a net capital gain of $12,000. H's distributive share is 10%. The partnership has a net ordinary loss of $25,000 ($5,000 − $30,000) and a net capital gain of $12,000. H has ordinary income of $30,000 and her 10% distributive share is $2,500 of ordinary loss and $1,200 of net capital gains.

Interest payable on a partner's capital account is treated in a manner similar to compensation for services. Therefore, interest on capital, computed without regard to partnership income (i.e., guaranteed payments), is deductible by the partnership and includible interest income for the partner.[59] In contrast, interest payments based on partnership income are nondeductible by the partnership and includible income to the partner as a distribution of profits, not as interest income. This latter distinction is relevant, for example, in determining the amount of interest income a partner has for the limitation on investment interest expense deductions.

TRANSACTIONS BETWEEN PARTNERSHIPS AND PARTNERS

Taxation of interest on *debt* differs from that of interest on capital when the partnership adopts the accrual method and the partner uses the cash method. Recall that guaranteed payments are deductible by the partnership and includible by the partner as of the *partnership's year-end* in which the payments were deducted or capitalized. In contrast, interest on debt is deductible by the partnership and includible by the partner when *received* by the partner.[60] This same rule applies to all payments that do not qualify as guaranteed payments.

> **Example 14.** At the end of 1991, an *accrual* basis partnership on the calendar year owes K, a 30% cash basis partner, a guaranteed payment of $4,000, and $1,500 interest on a note. Both amounts are paid January 8, 1992. Partnership net income before these two accruals are considered is $20,000 in 1991 and $30,000 in 1992. The partnership and K apply the partnership's accrual method for the guaranteed payment and record it in 1991. In contrast, they both apply K's cash method for the interest on

---

[58] Rev. Rul. 69-180, 1969-1 C.B. 183.

[59] § 707(c).

[60] §§ 267(a)(2) and (e). This same rule applies to C corporations and their greater than 50 percent shareholders and to S corporations and all of their shareholders, regardless of the ownership interest.

debt and record it in 1992. Based on these rules, the partnership has net income of $16,000 ($20,000 − $4,000) in 1991 and $28,500 ($30,000 − $1,500) in 1992. K increases includible compensation by $4,000 in 1991 and includible interest by $1,500 in 1992.

Transactions in a Nonpartner Capacity. Most other transactions between a partnership and its partners are governed by the entity concept of partnership taxation. Thus, the effect for all parties is the same as that which would occur in a similar transaction between the partnership and a nonpartner. Two important factors must be present for the entity concept to apply. First, the partner must be participating in the transaction with the partnership in some capacity other than that of a partner (e.g., a partner who is an attorney might perform legal work for the partnership).[61] Second, the price must be based on a fair market value that would be used by two unrelated parties.[62] In all instances, however, the entity concept does not apply to the partnership for accrued expenses to a cash basis partner. Thus, as discussed above for interest, a partnership cannot deduct expenses to a partner until they are reported as income by the partner.

Sales between Partner and Partnership. There are *three* types of situations when the aggregate, rather than the entity, concept applies to sales between a partnership and its partner even though the two above requirements are met. *First*, losses realized on the sale are disallowed when the partner owns directly or indirectly more than 50 percent of the capital or profits interest in the partnership.[63] In these instances, no deduction is allowed for the losses. This is not a deferral; therefore, there is no carryover of basis or holding period. However, if this property is sold later at a gain, the gain is offset by the previously disallowed losses.[64] Similar treatment applies when the sale occurs between two partnerships and the same partners own directly or indirectly more than 50 percent of the capital or profits interest of both partnerships.[65]

> **Example 15.** T sells land to his partnership for $40,000. His basis for the land is $50,000. T owns a 60% capital interest in the partnership. Since he owns more than 50%, his $10,000 loss is disallowed and the partnership's basis for the land is $40,000. If the partnership later sells the land to an unrelated party for $52,000, its gain of $12,000 ($52,000 − $40,000) is reduced by the previously disallowed $10,000 loss, leaving a $2,000 recognized gain. Notice that any sales price between $40,000 and $50,000 would result in no recognized gain or loss. However, a sales price below $40,000 would result in a recognized loss (e.g., a sale for $38,000 results in a $2,000 recognized loss).

---

[61] § 707(a). This restriction also is applicable when the business is a corporation under § 267.

[62] § 482.

[63] § 707(b)(1)(A).

[64] § 267(d).

[65] § 707(b)(1)(B).

Example 16.   Assume the same facts as *Example 15*, except that T has a 45% capital interest in the partnership. Since T's capital interest does not exceed 50%, the $10,000 loss is recognized by him. In addition, any future gain on the land must be reported by the partnership without reduction.

A *second* type of situation in which the aggregate concept applies to sales between a partnership and its partners occurs when the sale results in a capital gain. If the seller owns directly or indirectly more than 50 percent of the capital or profits interest and the property will *not* qualify as a capital asset to the buyer, all recognized gain is ordinary income to the seller. This treatment also occurs when a sale is between two partnerships and the same partners meet the 50 percent capital or profits requirement for both partnerships.[66]

Example 17.   M purchased land as an investment in 1975 for $25,000. She sells the land to a partnership for its $100,000 fair market value. The land will be developed, subdivided, and sold in one-acre plots. If M directly or indirectly owns no more than 50% of the partnership's capital and profits, she has a capital gain of $75,000. However, if her interest exceeds 50%, she has ordinary income of $75,000.

The *third* situation when the aggregate concept applies occurs with sales of depreciable property between a partnership and its partners. If the partner owns directly or indirectly more than 50 percent of the capital or profits interest, all gain on the depreciable property is ordinary income.[67] This treatment overrides both §§ 1245 and 1250.

Constructive Ownership.   In determining whether a partner has a *direct* or *indirect* interest of more than 50 percent for the first two exceptions above (i.e., related party sales with a loss or a capital gain), the constructive ownership rules of § 267 apply.[68] Basically, these rules state that a partner *indirectly* owns his or her proportionate share of any partnership interest owned by or for a corporation, other partnership, estate, or trust in which he or she has an interest. In addition, a partner indirectly owns the partnership interest that is directly or indirectly owned by or for his or her spouse, brothers, sisters, ancestors, and lineal descendants. An interest constructively owned by an individual through these family members, however, is not again attributed to another person.

---

[66]   § 707(b)(2). A similar provision applies to corporations. See § 1239.

[67]   This restriction is also applicable when the business is a corporation. § 1239.

[68]   Reg. § 1.707-1(b)(3) and §§ 267(c)(1), (2), (4), and (5).

Example 18.   The WHEAT Partnership is owned as follows:

30% by H;
5% by W, H's wife;
30% by A who is not related to any other partner;
15% by E, W's mother; and
20% by T, a corporation whose stock is owned 60% by W, 30% by H, and 10% by unrelated parties.

H directly owns 30% and indirectly owns 23% of the WHEAT Partnership for a total of 53%. The 23% is composed of 5% owned by his wife, W, plus 12% indirectly owned by W (60% × 20%) and 6% owned by H (30% × 20%) through T Corporation.

W directly owns 5% and indirectly owns 63% of the partnership for a total of 68%. The 63% is composed of the 30% owned by H and the 15% owned by E (W's mother) plus the 12% indirectly owned by W and 6% indirectly owned by H through T Corporation.

E directly owns 15% and indirectly owns 17% for a total of 32%. The 17% is composed of 5% owned by her daughter W directly and 12% owned by W through T Corporation.

As a result of these attribution rules, both H and W constructively own more than 50% of the WHEAT Partnership.

REPORTING PARTNERSHIP RESULTS

With few exceptions, partners must report their distributive shares of partnership income, expenses, gains, losses, and credits as of the partnership's year-end, regardless of when distributions of assets are actually made.[69] This timing requirement, based on the entity concept, makes the selection of a partnership's taxable year an important tax planning issue.

SELECTING A PARTNERSHIP'S TAXABLE YEAR

Generally, it is a tax advantage to defer all includible income as long as possible but to accelerate the deduction of all expenses, losses, and credits. The basic rule, of course, is dependent on the current and future tax positions of the partners. If operations are expected to result in net losses in the early years, the greatest benefit would be achieved by electing a partnership year that coincides with that of the partners. In this way, partners would be able to maximize their distributive shares of partnership losses currently. However, this benefit would be reversed in years when operations result in net income. In these years, the ideal partnership year would end one month after that of the partners.

---

[69]   § 706(a).

Example 19. A partnership is organized October 1, 1991. Its net ordinary income for the first 15 months is as follows:

October 1, 1991–December 31, 1991	$ 20,000
January 1–31, 1992	10,000
February 1, 1992–December 31, 1992	135,000

All partners report on the calendar year. If the partnership's year-end also is December 31, the partners have includible income of $20,000 in 1991 and includible income of $145,000 ($10,000 + $135,000) in 1992. However, if the partnership's year-end is January 31, the partners have no includible income in 1991 and includible income of $30,000 ($20,000 + $10,000) in 1992. Consequently, the income for October 1 through December 31—the deferral period—is shifted to the following year. The $135,000 will be combined with the net income or loss for January 1993 and reported in 1993.

Unfortunately, partners usually do not have the freedom to elect the ideal year-end for their partnerships.

Generally, a partnership can adopt only the taxable year of those owning a *majority interest* in the partnership.[70] For example, assume a fiscal year corporation owns 15 percent of a partnership while the remaining 85 percent is owned by 10 individuals who report on the calendar year. Since individuals using the calendar year own more than 50 percent of the partnership, the partnership *must* adopt the calendar year. If those having the same taxable year do not own a majority interest, the partnership must adopt the tax year of its *principal* partners—those partners owning at least 5 percent or more of the partnership. If the principal partners have different tax years, however, the calendar year must be used.

A partnership may select another taxable year, subject to IRS approval. The IRS normally gives its approval only if the taxpayer can establish a valid business purpose for the particular taxable year.[71] For example, a summer resort hotel might satisfy this requirement if it establishes that its natural business year ends during September.

NET LOSSES

The benefit of the aggregate theory is particularly significant when partnership operations result in a net loss. Based on the flow through concept, partners include their distributive shares of the net loss in their taxable income. Unlike the flow through of net income, however, each partner's distributive share of net

---

[70] § 706(b) and Reg. § 1.706-1(b).

[71] § 706(b)(1)(C). Also see Rev. Proc. 83-25, 1983-1 C.B. 689, in which the IRS allows a partnership that recognizes 25 percent or more of its gross receipts in the last two months of a 12-month period for three consecutive years to adopt an alternative 12-month period as its fiscal year.

losses may not exceed that partner's basis in the ownership.[72] Any losses that exceed a partner's basis may be carried forward indefinitely to be distributed to the partner when the basis is increased.

> **Example 20.** A partnership has a net loss for 1991 of $50,000. L, a 40% owner, has a basis in the partnership of $17,000. Although 40% of the partnership loss is $20,000, L's distributive share is limited to his basis of $17,000. He reports the $17,000 loss on his 1991 tax return. His basis in the partnership, reduced by the distributed loss, is $0. If his basis increases to $2,000 at the end of 1992, he reports the $2,000 loss on his 1992 tax return and his basis in the partnership once again is $0. The remaining excess loss of $1,000 is carried forward.

When there is more than one type of partnership loss and the partner's basis is insufficient to absorb all of it, an allocation is made to determine how much of each type of loss flows through to the partner.

> **Example 21.** Refer to *Example 20* except the partnership has an ordinary loss of $40,000 and a capital loss of $10,000. L's 40% share is $16,000 and $4,000, respectively. His distributive share is $13,600 ($16,000 ÷ $20,000 × $17,000) ordinary loss and $3,400 ($17,000 − $13,600) capital loss. The remaining $2,400 ordinary loss and $600 capital loss are carried forward.

The flow through of partnership losses is considered to be the last event to occur during a partnership's taxable year. Thus, all asset distributions and contributions and changes in partnership liabilities are recorded first. This is generally an advantage to partners whose bases are insufficient to absorb their share of partnership losses. When asset distributions have been made, this rule maximizes the carryover of excess losses. In addition, it provides a tax planning opportunity for the partners. Year-end actions can be taken to increase a partner's basis. An individual partner may contribute additional assets to the partnership or the partnership may increase its liabilities.[73] It is possible that these year-end actions will be disallowed, however, unless there is a business purpose for them.[74] The reverse actions can be taken to reduce the basis of a partner who wishes to defer the losses to a future year when marginal tax rates are expected to be higher.

> **Example 22.** A partnership has a net loss for the current year of $60,000. D is a 40% owner. Her basis at the beginning of the year was $22,000. She received a cash distribution of $6,000 in June. Year-end partnership liabilities exceed beginning liabilities by $10,000. D's basis before the loss

---

[72] § 704(d). There is one exception; charitable contributions flow out to partners even if they exceed a partner's basis.

[73] Reg. § 1.704-1(d).

[74] A partner generally must have personal liability for the partnership debts to be included in his or her basis for loss purposes. § 465.

is distributed equals $20,000 [$22,000 − $6,000 + (40% of $10,000)]. If no action is taken before the partnership year ends, her distributive share of the loss is limited to her $20,000 basis and the remaining $4,000 will be carried forward. However, if she makes a capital contribution that increases her basis by $4,000 before the partnership year ends, her basis becomes $24,000 and she may report her entire share of partnership losses. The same result is achieved if partnership debts are increased an additional $10,000. In contrast, D may reduce her basis and current year distributive share of losses by withdrawing assets from the partnership or if partnership liabilities are paid before the year ends.

SPECIAL ALLOCATIONS

Partners' distributive shares of partnership income, gains, losses, deductions, and credits usually are determined by their ownership interests.[75] Earlier in this chapter, however, a deviation from this approach was discussed for special allocations with depreciation, depletion, gains, and losses on property contributed in exchange for a capital interest.[76] Similar allocations may be made for other partnership items, including net income or loss. In order for a special allocation to qualify, it must have a *substantial economic effect*.[77] This requirement is designed to prohibit arbitrary allocations of tax benefits without the accompanying economic consequences.

According to the Regulations, an allocation generally has economic effect if four tests are satisfied:[78]

1. The allocation is actually reflected as an appropriate increase or decrease in the partner's capital account.

2. Liquidation proceeds are to be distributed in accordance with the partners' capital account balances.

3. Partners with a deficit in their capital account following the distribution of liquidation proceeds must be required to restore all capital accounts deficits to the partnership.

4. The shift in tax consequences due to the allocation is not disproportionately large in relation to the shift of economic consequences.

---

[75] § 704(a).

[76] § 704(c). These allocations are mandatory after March, 1984.

[77] § 704(b)(2) and Reg § 1.704-1(b).

[78] Reg. § 1.704-1(b)(2). These tests are based on the landmark case of *Stanley C. Orrisch,* 55 T. C. 395 (1971), *aff'd* in 31 AFTR2d 1069 (CA-9, 1973).

Example 23. B and K are equal partners. Each partner has a basis of $24,000 and a partnership capital account of $18,000. Current year operations result in a capital gain of $6,000 and a net ordinary loss of $20,000. If no special allocation is made, the distribution to each partner is $3,000 capital gain and $10,000 net ordinary loss. After the distribution, each partner will have a basis of $17,000 ($24,000 + $3,000 − $10,000) and a capital account balance of $11,000 ($18,000 + $3,000 − $10,000). Assume, however, that B and K agree to allocate all of the loss to B. The results of this special allocation are as follows:

	B	K
Net ordinary loss	$(20,000)	$ 0
Net capital gain	3,000	3,000
Basis (1)	7,000	27,000
Capital account (2)	1,000	21,000

(1) Basis for B is $24,000 + $3,000 − $20,000 = $7,000 and for K is $24,000 + $3,000 = $27,000.

(2) The capital account for B is $18,000 + $3,000 − $20,000 = $1,000 and for K is $18,000 + $3,000 = $21,000.

The first three regulation requirements listed above—concerning the "economic effect" of the allocation—are illustrated in *Example 23* above, when the liquidation of the partnership was not in accordance with the capital accounts. The fourth requirement—the *substantial test*—is considered in the following example.

Example 24. R and S are equal partners. The partnership *expects* to receive $10,000 tax-exempt interest income and other taxable income in excess of $10,000. The partnership agreement states that the $10,000 of tax-exempt income is to be allocated to R while S is to be allocated $10,000 of taxable income. Any remaining income is to be allocated equally between them. The partnership agreement also states that the allocations are to be made to the capital accounts that serve as the basis for distributing liquidating proceeds. Despite the fact that the allocation has economic effect (i.e., the capital accounts are increased), it is not considered substantial because it has no economic consequences since R and S will receive the same amount of income.

The above discussion represents a brief summary of the voluminous regulations that have been issued on the subject of allocations. The regulations establish numerous other conditions that must be observed if a special allocation is to be recognized.

RETROACTIVE ALLOCATIONS

New partners cannot be allocated any partnership items that occurred before they acquired their ownership interests.[79] Despite this basic rule, methods have been devised—primarily by tax shelter promoters—that enable taxpayers to claim a substantial portion of a partnership's net losses even though their capital interests are not purchased until late in the year. One way of achieving this has been with a cash basis partnership that pays much of its expenses at the end of the year.

> **Example 25.** A calendar year partnership on the cash basis reports a net loss of $10,000 for the first 11 months of 1991 and an additional net loss of $60,000 for December 1991. G purchases a 10 percent capital and profits interest December 1, 1991. G's share of the $70,000 loss is $6,000 (10% × $60,000). However, G could be specially allocated up to $60,000 of the loss if the substantial economic effect requirements are met. Under no circumstances may G report any of the loss that occurred before December 1, 1991.

Concerned about cash basis partnerships that delay payment of expenses to attract year-end investors, Congress enacted requirements governing the allocation of certain expenses of cash basis partnerships that have a change in ownership during the year.[80] Specifically, taxpayers must apply the accrual method to deductible payments made during the taxable year for (1) interest, (2) taxes, (3) use of property, (4) services, and (5) any other item necessary to avoid significant misstatements of income by the partners. Thus, an equal amount of these items is to be assigned to each day during the period covered by the expenses. The IRS also provides that assignment may be made on a semimonthly basis: (1) if the partnership uses the interim closing of the books method rather than a proration, and (2) no partner completely terminated a partnership interest that month. Since these periods will vary considerably in most partnerships, the record-keeping requirements could be burdensome even if the semimonthly rather than daily proration is used. Of course, only those years in which there is a change in ownership interests are affected.

It is further provided that any deductible payments made during the year that are attributable (1) to a *prior year* are assigned to the *first day* of the current tax year (i.e., January 1 for a calendar year partnership); and (2) to a *future year* are assigned to the *last day* of the current tax year (i.e., December 31 for a calendar year partnership).[81]

---

[79] §§ 706(c)(2)(B) and (d), and *Rodman v. Comm.*, 76-2 USTC ¶9710, 38 AFTR2d 76-5840, 542 F.2d 845 (CA-2, 1976), *rev'g.* and *rem'g.* 32 TCM 1307 T.C. Memo 1973-277 and *Cecil R. Richardson*, 76 T.C. 512 (1981).

[80] § 706(d)(2).

[81] §§ 706(d)(2)(C) and (D).

Example 26. Refer to *Example 25* except that $12,000 of interest expense, covering the six-month period of August 1, 1991 through January 31, 1992, was paid in December 1991 and is included in the $60,000 loss. For simplicity, assume the IRS allows a monthly proration. Under the accrual method, the interest is assigned as follows: $2,000 ($12,000 ÷ 6 months) to each of the five months in 1991 and next January's $2,000 is assigned to December 31, 1991. Based on this adjustment, G's share of the $70,000 is $5,200 ($60,000 loss for December = $8,000 interest reassigned to August through November − $52,000 × 10% ownership). G could be specially allocated up to $52,000 of the loss.

Similar to the changes made for the treatment of contributed property discussed earlier, these rules are primarily directed toward taxpayers using a partnership to shift taxable income and losses among partners. However, many small businesses will be affected unless they are exempted by the regulations.

The situation when one partnership is a partner in a second partnership is also addressed. An approach similar to that developed for the cash basis partnership discussed above is established. That is, basically, the first partnership's share of the second partnership's items is to be allocated throughout the taxable years. Thus, new partners who acquire their interests in the first partnership at the end of the year cannot be allocated any items from either partnership that occurred before their ownership interests were acquired.[82]

ADJUSTMENTS TO PARTNER'S BASIS

The *partner's basis* in the partnership is referred to repeatedly in this chapter. Numerous examples of items affecting basis are given. The purpose here is to provide a comprehensive summary of items that affect partners' bases. In all computations of basis, there is one important limitation—basis cannot be negative, not even temporarily.[83]

Generally, basis begins with a partner's contribution of assets or services in exchange for a capital interest. As indicated earlier, a partner's *initial basis* is the total of cash contributed plus the partner's basis for noncash contributions and less any liabilities transferred to the partnership.[84] If the partnership interest is received as a gift or is inherited, however, the general rules applicable to basis in these situations are used.

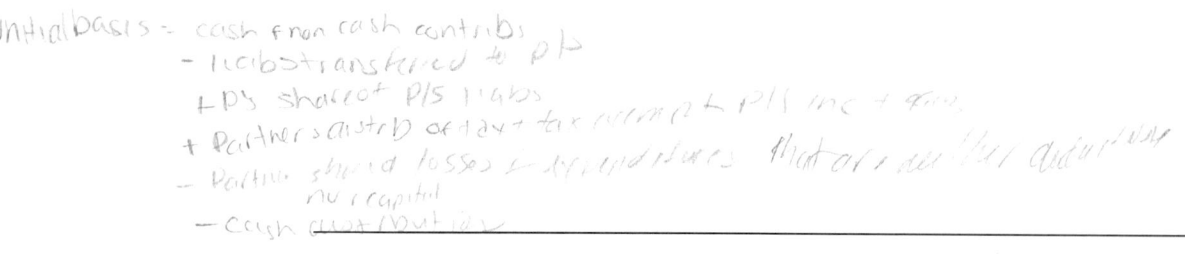

[82] § 706(d)(3).

[83] §§ 705(a)(2) and 722. Basis also is increased by the amount of recognized gain

when the contribution is to an investment partnership. § 721(b).

[84] §§ 722 and 752(b).

Basis is *increased* by the partner's share of partnership liabilities.[85] A general partner's basis includes his or her share of recourse debts (according to the loss sharing ratio) *and* nonrecourse debts (according to the profit sharing ratio). In contrast, a limited partner's basis includes only his or her share of nonrecourse debts (according to the profit sharing ratio). Basis must be adjusted annually to reflect fluctuations that occurred during the year in the partnership's debts and in the partner's share of these debts. Basis also is increased by a partner's distributive share of taxable and tax-exempt partnership income and gains. When partnership net income has been reduced by percentage depletion deducted in excess of the depletable property's basis, this excess is added back to each partner's basis.[86]

A partner's distributive share of losses and expenditures that are neither deductible nor capitalized *reduces* basis. Recall that deductible losses are distributed to each partner only to the extent of that partner's basis.[87] Percentage and cost depletion for oil and gas wells are deductible at the partner level rather than by the partnership. Any of these deductions taken by the partner also reduce basis. However, these deductions may not reduce the partner's basis in the partnership below zero.[88]

Finally, cash distributions, including decreases in partnership liabilities that are deemed to be cash distributions, decrease basis. As will be explained later in this chapter, a basis reduction is also required when other property is distributed. (For a detailed listing of a partner's basis compared with an S corporation shareholder's basis, see Exhibit 23-2 in Chapter 23.)

Example 27. The TU Partnership owns a shopping center with the following selected account balances for 1991 and 1992.

	1990	1991	1992
Recourse liabilities	$ 70,000	$ 80,000	$ 67,000
Nonrecourse liabilities	418,000	400,000	430,000
Net ordinary income (or loss)		(40,000)	8,000
Tax exempt interest income		4,000	0
Section 1231 gains		12,000	0
Cash distributions to partners		14,000	16,000

[85] §§ 465 and 752(b). But see exceptions to the method of determining a partner's share of debt. Temp. Reg. §§ 1.752-1T and 4T.

[86] § 705(a)(1).

[87] § 705(a)(2).

[88] §§ 613A(c)(7)(D) and 705(a)(3).

Although T and U share profits and losses equally, T is a general partner and U is a limited partner. At the end of 1990, T's basis in the partnership is $200,000 and U's basis is $130,000. Bases at the end of 1991 and 1992 are computed as follows:

	T	U
Basis 12/31/90	$200,000	$130,000
Increase in recourse debt	+ 10,000	0
Decrease in nonrecourse debt	− 9,000	− 9,000
Tax exempt income	+ 2,000	+ 2,000
Section 1231 gains	+ 6,000	+ 6,000
Cash distributions	− 7,000	− 7,000
Net ordinary loss	− 20,000	− 20,000
Basis 12/31/91	$182,000	$102,000
Decrease in recourse debt	− 13,000	0
Increase in nonrecourse debt	+ 15,000	+ 15,000
Net ordinary income	+ 4,000	+ 4,000
Cash distributions	− 8,000	− 8,000
Basis 12/31/92	$180,000	$113,000

When partners cannot practically determine their bases in a partnership, the IRS may allow them to forgo the detailed calculations previously discussed in this chapter.[89] The alternative is to determine their share of the partnership's basis in total assets plus or minus any appropriate adjustments. This method may be used, however, only if the IRS accepts the results as being a reasonable approximation of the basis that would result from the more detailed calculations.[90] It is not to be used as a substitute for acceptable records.[91]

FAMILY PARTNERSHIPS

Family owned and operated businesses play an important role in our economy and society. Quite often, a partnership is the most suitable form for operating a family business. Members of the same family form partnerships for a variety of reasons. Frequently there is a sound business purpose and the partnership is operated similar to ones owned by unrelated individuals. That is, each partner contributes property and/or services to the partnership in exchange for a capital interest and participates in the management of the partnership. Generally, these family partnerships are subject to the same tax provisions as other partnerships. However, when the arrangements of family partnerships deviate from that of other partnerships, they may be subject to additional requirements.

---

[89] § 705(b).

[90] Reg. § 1.705-1(b).

[91] *Eugene Coloman*, 33 TCM 411, T.C. Memo 1974-78, *aff'd.* in 76-2 USTC ¶9581, 38 AFTR2d 76-5523, 540 F.2d 427 (CA-9, 1976).

TAX SAVINGS POTENTIAL

In some instances, family partnerships are formed primarily for tax reasons. The most common example is the partnership that includes both a parent and one or more otherwise dependent children as partners. The basic tax structure provides considerable incentive for this type of arrangement when the child is at least 14 years of age.[92]

Although a family may be one economic unit, each member is a separate individual for tax purposes. The tax rate of each person at least 14 years old is determined by his or her taxable income. Consequently, marginal tax rates often are lower for some family members than they are for others. For example, a taxpayer's children who are full-time students usually have little or no taxable income. When a difference in tax rates exists, there may be opportunities for income splitting that reduce the total tax borne by the family unit. Partnerships frequently have been used to obtain these benefits.[93]

A large percentage of the income in our society today is earned by personal service businesses. That is, fees, commissions, or other types of compensation are received for personal services provided by individuals such as entertainers, physicians, beauticians, attorneys, plumbers, consultants, and public accountants. Many of these businesses require minimal capital investment. It has long been held that earned income is taxable to the individual who earns it and cannot be assigned to another.[94] As a result, these businesses seldom provide tax-splitting opportunities through the use of family partnerships.

Another axiom of tax law is that income earned on property is taxable to the owner of such property.[95] This is true even if the property (e.g., a partnership capital interest) is received as a tax-motivated gift from a relative.[96] A capital interest in a partnership is defined as an interest in the assets of the partnership.[97] Thus, when capital is "a material income-producing factor,"[98] a partnership may provide considerable tax savings by splitting income among family members who are partners. The Regulations state that if substantial investments in assets such as inventories, plant, machinery, and equipment are necessary to the business, capital ordinarily will be considered a material income-producing factor.[99] However, when the income of the business consists principally of fees, commissions,

---

[92] Recall that after 1986, much of the income-splitting advantages with children under 14 years of age are eliminated.

[93] However, the child may be subject to self-employment taxes on the partnership income (as discussed earlier in this chapter).

[94] *Lucas v Earl*, 2 USTC ¶496, 8 AFTR 10287, 281 U.S. 111 (USSC, 1930); and *Helvering v. Eubank*, 40-2 USTC ¶9788, 24 AFTR 1063, 311 U.S. 122 (USSC, 1940), *rev'g.* 40-1 USTC ¶9334, 24 AFTR 767, 110 F.2d 737 (CA-2, 1940), *rev'g.* 39 B.T.A. 583 (1939).

[95] *Helvering v. Horst*, 40-2 USTC ¶9787, 24 AFTR 1058, 311 U.S. 112 (USSC, 1940).

[96] *Blair*, 37-1 USTC ¶9083, 18 AFTR 1132, 300 U.S. 5 (USSC, 1937).

[97] Reg. § 1.704-1(e)(1)(v).

[98] § 704(e)(1).

[99] Reg. § 1.704-1(e)(1)(iv).

or other compensation for personal services, the Regulations state that capital is not a material income-producing factor. It should be noted that in this context income refers to *gross income* (i.e., gross receipts less cost of goods sold). Therefore, a partnership may satisfy this test even though it has a net loss for the year.

For nonservice partnerships, investments in many other assets necessary to the business may qualify as well as those listed in the Regulations.[100] For example, working capital often requires a significant investment in assets.[101] In one instance, the court held that a partnership's existing good-will was an asset for this purpose.[102] However, the Tax Court, in a split decision, ruled that when most of the partnership assets were acquired with debt, contributed capital was not a material income-producing factor.[103] Thus, in this case, capital meant ownership equity rather than debt equity.

The Code does not mention family partnerships when capital is not a material income-producing factor. Most businesses, including those that only provide services, require some capital. In these situations, case law may still allow the family partnership some income-splitting benefits.[104] Alternatively, the family members could own these assets directly or in a second partnership and lease them to the service business.

INCOME ALLOCATION RULES

To prevent abuses of the income-splitting opportunities, Congress established special income allocation rules for family partnerships.[105] The rules apply when an individual (the donee) receives a partnership interest as a gift from a family member (the donor). The same donee/donor relationship can be deemed to exist, however, when the ownership interest is purchased from the family member and even if a fair market price is paid. This occurs if the purchase does not meet the requirements for an arm's length business transaction.[106] For purposes of this statute, family members only include a spouse, ancestors, and lineal descendants and any trusts created for their primary benefit.[107] The donee partner's distributive share of partnership income is subject to two limitations.[108]

---

[100] For example, see *Jeremiah J. O'Donnell, Jr.,* 23 TCM 210, T.C. Memo 1964-38 (1964), and *Jelindo A. Tiberti,* 21 TCM 961, T.C. Memo 1962-174 (1962).

[101] For example, see *Sanford H. Hartman,* 43 T.C. 105 (1964), and *James G. Bennett,* 21 TCM 903, T.C. Memo 1962-163.

[102] *Bateman v. U.S.,* 74-1 USTC ¶9176, 33 AFTR2d, 74-483, 490 F.2d 549 (CA-9, 1973), *aff'g.* 71-2 USTC ¶9546, 28 AFTR2d 71-5306 (D.C. Calif., 1971).

[103] *Carriage Square, Inc.,* 69 T.C. 119 (1977).

[104] *Comm. v. Culbertson,* 49-1 USTC ¶9232, 37 AFTR 1391, 337 U.S. 733 (USSC,

1949), *rev'g.* and *rem'g.* 48-2 USTC ¶9324, 36 AFTR 1168, 168 F.2d 979 (CA-5, 1948), *rev'g* 6 TCM 692, T.C. Memo 1947-168, on *rem.* 52-1 USTC ¶9233, 41 AFTR 850, 194 F.2d 581 (CA-5, 1952), *rev'g.* 9 TCM 647, T.C. Memo 1950-187.

[105] § 704(e).

[106] § 704(e)(3) and Reg. § 1.704-1 (3)(ii)(b).

[107] § 704(e)(3); Reg. §§ 1.704-1(e)(3) and (4).

[108] § 704(e)(2) and Reg. § 1.704-1 (e)(3)(i)(b). These two requirements are essentially the same as those added by the Revenue Act of 1951.

1. Reasonable compensation must be allocated to the *donor* partner for all services performed for the partnership. (Note that there is no similar requirement that reasonable compensation be allocated to any other partner, including the donee.)

2. Allocations to the *donee* partner cannot represent a greater return on capital than that allocated to the *donor* partner. (There is no similar requirement that prevents allocating a greater share to any other partner, including the donor, or even to a donee partner compared with partners other than the donor.)

Unless both requirements are met, partnership income may be reallocated between the donee and donor, based on these two requirements. Note that the above provisions do not affect the distributive shares of any other partners.

> **Example 28.**   A partnership is owned equally by a father and his 15-year-old daughter. Their capital accounts are maintained in the same ratio. The daughter received her ownership interest as a gift from her father. Partnership income of $120,000 for the year is distributed to them equally, $60,000 to each. If the father performed services during the year valued at $20,000, partnership income to the father and daughter may be reallocated by the IRS. The first $20,000 would be allocated to him and one-half (or $50,000) of the remaining $100,000 would be allocated to each of them. His portion becomes $70,000 ($20,000 + $50,000) and hers becomes $50,000.

> **Example 29.**   Assume the same facts as in *Example 28*, except that the partnership is owned equally by a father, his 15-year old daughter, and a friend. The $120,000 is allocated to them equally, $40,000 to each. If the IRS requires a reallocation, only the father and daughter are affected. Their combined share of $80,000 will be allocated as $50,000 to him ($20,000 compensation + one-half of the remaining $60,000) and $30,000 to her (one-half the $60,000). The friend's share remains unchanged at $40,000.

Although reasonable compensation is not defined for family partnerships, the definition developed for compensation of corporate employees should be applicable.[109] The partnership requirements do state, however, that compensation must consider (1) the possibility that one partner may have more managerial responsibility than another, and (2) the fact that a general partner has unlimited liability, whereas a limited partner does not.[110]

Note that allocations *among* donees do not appear to be covered by these rules.[111] Presumably, the intent of the allocation provisions is to limit the donees' income to the amount earned on the capital. In reality, this may not occur. Since the full value of the donor partner's services is guaranteed up to the amount of net income, the return on capital may be understated or even nonexistent when the business is unsuccessful and overstated when it is successful.

---

[109]   § 162(a)(1).

[110]   Reg. § 1.704-1(e)(3)(i)(c) and (ii)(c).

[111]   § 704(e)(2).

LIMITED PARTNERSHIPS

The option for taxpayers to form and operate as limited partnerships has been available for many years. However, their popularity increased significantly during the 1970s and early 1980s. This interest paralleled the growth of syndicated tax shelters. Although the limited partnership form is available to all businesses and can be a distinct advantage in several types of situations, it is most closely identified with tax shelters.

When evaluating whether to establish a general or a limited partnership, there are several important differences to consider. First, limited partnerships must have at least one general partner. Second, all limited partners have limited liability. That is, their potential liability for partnership debts does not extend beyond the assets contributed plus any additional amounts they are obligated by the partnership agreement to contribute. Third, limited partners may not participate in management. A limited partner who participates in management may cause his or her status to be changed to that of a general partner. Fourth, the death, insanity, or retirement of a limited partner does not dissolve the partnership. Fifth, limited partners' interests often are transferable, as are corporate ownership interests. Sixth, limited partners do not have self-employment income from the partnership except to the extent of guaranteed compensation. Seventh, a limited partner's basis is increased by his or her share of nonrecourse but not recourse debt. A holder of *nonrecourse debt* has a claim against specified assets only and not against other partnership assets or any personal assets of a general or limited partner. In contrast, a holder of *recourse debt* has a claim against partnership assets and the personal assets of *general partners* but not limited partners. Recall that partners' shares of partnership liabilities generally are determined by their individual ratios for profits in the case of nonrecourse debt and ratios for losses in the case of recourse debt.[112]

DISTRIBUTIONS OF PARTNERSHIP ASSETS

Distributions of partnership assets are classified as either current or liquidating. Distributions are considered *current*, and thus nonliquidating, when the partners receiving the property retain all or part of their capital interest. Even if a significant percentage of a partner's capital interest in the partnership is liquidated, the distribution still qualifies as current. Therefore, distributions are *liquidating* only when a partner's entire interest in the partnership is relinquished. The tax treatment is identical in many instances for all distributions, whether current or liquidating. However, as is often the case in taxation, exceptions do exist.

---

[112] Temp. Reg. §§ 1.752-1T through 4T add an "economic risk of loss analysis" require- ment which is beyond the scope of this text.

CURRENT DISTRIBUTIONS—PROPORTIONATE

Partnerships frequently make current distributions of cash to their owners. A *current distribution* is one that does not liquidate a partner's capital interest nor is a part of a series of distributions that will liquidate the interest. Recall that all decreases in a partner's share of partnership liabilities also are treated as though they are distributions of cash.[113] In most instances, cash distributions are nontaxable. There is, however, one exception. At no time may a partner's basis in the partnership be reduced below zero.[114] Consequently, any cash distributed in excess of a partner's basis is taxable income to the partner.[115]

In determining whether cash distributions exceed a partner's basis, all distributions are deemed to have been made on the last day of the partnership's taxable year regardless of when they actually occurred. Thus, a partner has the opportunity to offset the distributions with current year profits, any year-end capital contributions, and increases in partnership liabilities.

> **Example 30.** On January 1 of the current year, A's basis in a calendar year partnership was $30,000 and B's basis was $5,000. Each partner received $20,000 in cash July 2. Partnership taxable income for the year was $24,000. A and B share profits equally. Neither of them made any contributions to the partnership, nor did their share of partnership liabilities change during the year. A's includible income is $12,000 (50% of $24,000) and her basis is $22,000 [($30,000 + $12,000) − $20,000]. B's taxable income is $15,000, composed of $12,000 partnership taxable income and $3,000 gain recognized on the distribution to avoid a negative basis in the partnership [($5,000 + $12,000) − $20,000]. B could have avoided the additional $3,000 taxable income from excess distributions if he had contributed $3,000 to the partnership or if the partnership's debt had increased $6,000 by the end of the year.

Distributions of noncash assets follow the aggregate concept and are tax-free as long as they do not alter the partners' *proportionate interest* in § 751 assets.[116] Section 751 assets consist of *unrealized receivables* and *substantially appreciated inventory*. In many instances, the tax treatment of these distributions is quite similar to the treatment applicable to the reverse situation, when partners contribute property to the partnership for a capital interest. That is, (1) neither the partnership nor the partners recognize gain or loss, (2) the partnership's holding period for capital assets and § 1231 assets carries over to the partners, and (3) the partnership's basis in the assets carries over to the partners.[117]

---

[113]   § 752(b).

[114]   § 733.

[115]   § 731(a)(1).

[116]   § 731(a).

[117]   § 732(a).

Example 31. K's basis in the partnership at the end of the year, before distributions are considered, is $60,000. The partnership uses the cash method. Proportionate distributions were made during the year to all partners. K's share was as follows:

	Partnership's Basis	Fair Market Value
Cash	$ 7,000	$ 7,000
Receivables	0	12,000
Land	15,000	39,000
Investment stock	30,000	32,000
Total assets	$52,000	$90,000

The distribution qualifies as a nontaxable transfer. The partnership reduces (debits) K's capital account for $52,000 ($7,000 + $0 + $15,000 + $30,000) and reduces (credits) each of the assets for their respective bases. K's basis in the partnership of $60,000 exceeds the partnership's basis in the assets. Thus, his basis in the assets is (1) $7,000 cash, (2) $0 receivables, (3) $15,000 land, and (4) $30,000 stock. His basis in the partnership is reduced to $8,000 ($60,000 − $52,000).

The tax treatment of property distributions differs from property contributions in one important manner. The partnership's basis in the assets carries over to the distributee partner only to the extent of the partner's basis in the partnership.[118] Thus, when a partner's basis is *less than* that of the property received, the partner's basis must be allocated in the following order:[119]

1. To all cash received, including cash deemed received when partnership liabilities are decreased.

2. To all assets received that are *not* capital assets or § 1231 assets (generally defined as unrealized receivables and inventory, discussed later in this chapter).

3. To any capital assets and § 1231 assets received.

A second allocation is then required to assign the basis among the assets received in the last two categories. In contrast with the common tax allocation method using relative fair market values, this calculation uses the partnership's *relative bases* for the assets.[120] After all allocations are completed, the partner's basis in the partnership is zero.[121]

---

[118] § 732(a)(2).

[119] Reg. §§ 1.731-1(a)(1)(i) and 1.732-1.

[120] § 732(c).

[121] § 733.

Example 32. Assume the same facts as in *Example 31* (i.e., K's share of partnership basis is $7,000 cash, $0 receivables, $15,000 land, and $30,000 investment stock) except that K's basis in the partnership is $37,000 (rather than $60,000). Generally, this change has no effect on the partnership but does affect K's situation, since his basis in the partnership is $15,000 less than the partnership's basis in the assets ($37,000 − $52,000).[122] K must allocate his $37,000 basis in the partnership among the assets as follows: (1) $7,000 cash, (2) $0 receivables, (3) $10,000 land [($37,000 basis − $7,000 = $30,000) × ($15,000 ÷ $45,000)], and (4) $20,000 stock (calculated the same as land, except substituting $30,000 for $15,000 in the numerator of the fraction). The $15,000 excess of partnership basis over K's basis is lost to K forever. (Note that fair market values were not used in either example.)

LIQUIDATING DISTRIBUTIONS—PROPORTIONATE

Liquidating distributions that do not alter the partners' proportionate interest in § 751 assets are treated as discussed above for current distributions, with two exceptions. First, when a partner's basis in the partnership *exceeds* the partnership's basis in the distributed assets, the excess must be allocated among the § 1231 and capital assets received. Again, the allocation is determined by the partnership's relative bases in the assets.

Example 33. Assume the same facts as in *Example 31,* except that this is a liquidating distribution. Recall that K's basis in the partnership is $60,000 and his share of proportionate distributions was

	Partnership's Basis	Fair Market Value
Cash...	$ 7,000	$ 7,000
Receivables................................	0	12,000
Land...	15,000	39,000
Investment stock............................	30,000	32,000
Total assets..............................	$52,000	$90,000

K's $60,000 basis in the partnership is allocated as follows: (1) $7,000 cash, (2) $0 receivables, (3) $17,667 land [($60,000 − $7,000 = $53,000) × ($15,000 ÷ $45,000)], and (4) $35,333 stock (calculated the same as land except substituting $30,000 for $15,000 in the numerator of the fraction).

---

[122] The partnership, however, will be allowed to increase the bases of certain assets it holds by the $15,000 basis lost by K, *if* a § 754 election is in effect. See discussion later in this chapter.

A second difference in tax treatment of liquidating and nonliquidating distributions occurs when (1) no § 1231 or capital assets are distributed, and (2) a partner's basis in the partnership exceeds the partnership's basis in the distributed assets (including the unrealized receivables and inventory). In a nonliquidating distribution, the difference is simply the partner's remaining basis in the partnership. However, in a liquidating distribution, this difference is treated as a loss since there are no assets to which the basis may be assigned and the partner's interest terminates. Since a partnership interest is considered a capital asset, the loss is a capital loss. Note that when unrealized receivables or inventory is distributed, the basis assigned to these assets cannot exceed the partnerships basis for them.

> **Example 34.** Assume the same facts as in *Example 33*, except that the land and stock are inventory items A and B that qualify as § 751 assets and that this is a liquidating distribution. K's $60,000 basis in the partnership is allocated as follows: (1) $7,000 cash, (2) $0 receivables, (3) $15,000 inventory A, and (4) $30,000 inventory B. The remaining basis of $8,000 is a capital loss.

When § 751 assets are received as a current or liquidating distribution, the partnership's potential for ordinary gain or loss carries over to the partners.[123] Thus, the collection of unrealized trade receivables by the distributee partners results in ordinary income to them. Similarly, any gain on the sale of inventory is also ordinary income, with one exception. If the inventory is held by a distributee partner for more than five years, the partnership "taint" is eliminated. Whether the gain or loss after five years is capital or ordinary is determined by the character of the assets in the hands of the particular partner.[124] The Code suggests the rules apply only to a *distributee partner*. Consequently, it may be possible to avoid the taint by transferring the inventory in a tax-free gift to a family member or in a tax-free exchange to a corporation. Then, if the property is a capital asset to the new owners, a sale of the property should result in capital gain or loss.

SECTION 751 ASSETS

Section 751 assets, often referred to as "tainted" or "hot" assets, are defined as unrealized receivables and substantially appreciated inventory. *Unrealized receivables* include all amounts due from the sale or exchange of property other than capital assets and from the performance of services that have not been included in income previously.[125] Common examples of unrealized receivables

---

[123]   § 735(a).

[124]   *Ibid.*

[125]   § 751(c).

are trade receivables of partnerships reporting on the cash or installment method. Unexpectedly, *unrealized receivables* are also defined to include the recapture provisions of § 1245 and §§ 1250 through 1254.[126]

The term *inventory* in § 751 is misleading since it includes most partnership property other than cash. Capital assets and § 1231 assets are excluded from the definition, however, *if* they are also capital assets or § 1231 assets to the partners receiving them.[127] For the inventory to be considered *substantially appreciated*, two tests must be met.[128]

1. The fair market value of the inventory must exceed 120 percent of the partnership's basis in the inventory. In this calculation, the fair market value of inventory refers to its replacement cost, not its resale value.

2. The fair market value of the inventory must exceed 10 percent of the fair market value of all noncash partnership property.

If neither or only one test is met, none of the inventory qualifies as § 751 property.

Example 35. A partnership has the following assets:

	Partnership's Basis	Fair Market Value
Cash	$ 5,000	$ 5,000
Receivables	30,000	30,000
Inventory	40,000	70,000
Land	60,000	80,000
Section 1231 assets	225,000	235,000
Total assets	$360,000	$420,000

Assume there is no § 1245 or § 1250 potential depreciation recapture. Both substantially appreciated inventory tests are met *if* the land and § 1231 assets will be capital assets or § 1231 assets to the partner receiving them. Therefore, inventory qualifies as a § 751 asset. In the first test, the fair market value of the inventory items of $100,000 ($30,000 + $70,000) exceeds 120% of their basis or $84,000 [($30,000 + $40,000 = $70,000) × 120%]. In the second test, the fair market value of the inventory items of $100,000 exceeds 10% of the fair market value of all noncash property or $41,500 [($420,000 − $5,000 = $415,000) × 10%].

[126] Reg. § 1.751-1(c)(4). The definition also includes lesser known § 617(f)(2) sales of mining property and § 955(c) sales of stock of a Domestic International Sales Corporation.

[127] § 751(d) and Reg. § 1.751-1(d).

[128] § 751(d)(1).

In contrast, if the land and § 1231 assets will *not* be capital assets or § 1231 assets to the partner receiving them, inventory is not substantially appreciated since the first test is not met: $420,000 − $5,000 = $415,000, which does not exceed $360,000 − $5,000 = $355,000 × 120% = $426,000.

Land, building, and equipment are not capital assets or § 1231 assets when they qualify as inventory. Consequently, they are treated as inventory at the partnership level for the two tests if they qualify as inventory at the partner level.

In some situations, the partners can take actions to prevent inventory from qualifying as substantially appreciated. An analysis of the two tests suggests several possibilities. First, current purchases of inventory would increase both the basis and market value of the inventory items by the same amount, thus narrowing the percentage difference between the two numbers in the first test. Second, cash could be temporarily invested in securities. This action increases total noncash property for the 10 percent calculation in the second test. Similarly, a partnership loan could be obtained and temporarily invested in securities. Third, unrealized receivables affect both tests. If some of the receivables can be collected before distribution, the increased ordinary income on their collection may be more than offset if inventory is prevented from being substantially appreciated.

DISPROPORTIONATE DISTRIBUTIONS

As previously discussed, proportionate distributions of partnership property generally do not result in taxable income, regardless of whether they are liquidating or nonliquidating transfers. In contrast, both liquidating and nonliquidating *disproportionate distributions* generally do result in taxable income. The solution is based on the aggregate concept for § 751 assets and the entity concept for all other assets distributed. Generally, a partner receiving a disproportionate distribution of § 751 assets is treated as though a sale has been made between the partnership and the partner. Gain is recognized on the disproportionate amount as though a sale of these assets actually occurred between the partnership and the partner. The character of the gain depends on the character of the assets deemed sold. Section 751 and the Regulations provide a detailed analysis (which is beyond the scope of this chapter) of the computations to be made when a disproportionate distribution occurs.

SALES OF PARTNERSHIP
CAPITAL INTERESTS

Based on the entity theory, an ownership interest in a partnership is a capital asset. Consequently, in keeping with the general rule, gains and losses on the sale of all or a part of that capital asset should result in a capital gain or loss. It does, with one exception.[129] Any part of the gain attributable to a selling partner's share of § 751 assets is ordinary gain.[130] This departure from the common treatment of capital assets follows an aggregate-concept argument. That is, if the selling partners had continued their ownership interests, income from these assets would have been ordinary income to them. This one aspect can be a disadvantage of the partnership form when compared with the corporate form. Also recall that losses cannot be recognized on a sale or exchange of any asset between related parties.[131] Thus, any loss realized on the sale of a partnership interest to a relative is not deductible.

ALLOCATION OF SALES PROCEEDS

The tax treatment governing sales of partnership capital interests combines the aggregate and entity theories in a manner similar to that of disproportionate distributions. When a partner sells all or part of the capital interest, two calculations are required.

1. The partner's share of § 751 ordinary gain must be determined as previously discussed.

2. The partner's share of capital gain or loss must be determined. (This computation also can be made by subtracting the partner's basis in the partnership from the amount realized to arrive at the gain or loss on the sale. This gain or loss less the § 751 gain equals the partner's capital gain or loss.)

The amount realized on the sale of a partnership interest is determined as it is for any other sale. It is the sum of (1) cash, (2) the market value of property received, and (3) the amount of the seller's liabilities assumed by the purchaser.[132] Liabilities, in the sale of a partnership interest, are composed of the seller's share of partnership debt.[133] Recall that a general partner's share of partnership liabilities is based on total debt, whereas a limited partner's share is restricted to nonrecourse debt.

It is possible for a partner to report both ordinary income and either capital gain or capital loss on the single transaction of selling a capital interest.

---

[129] § 741.

[130] § 751(a).

[131] § 267(b).

[132] § 1001(b) and Reg. § 1.1001-2(a) (1).

[133] § 752(d).

Example 36. D sells her 25% partnership interest to E for $20,000 cash. The amount realized is $30,000 ($20,000 cash + 25% × $40,000 liabilities). D's basis is $20,000. The partnership records indicate the following:

	Partnership's Basis	Fair Market Value
Cash...	$10,000	$10,000
Receivables.................................	0	24,000
Section 1231 assets..........................	70,000	86,000
Total assets...............................	$80,000	$120,000
Liabilities...................................	$40,000	$40,000
Capital accounts.............................	40,000	80,000
Total equities..............................	$80,000	$120,000

Assume there is no § 1245 or § 1250 potential depreciation recapture. D has ordinary gain of $6,000 (25% of $24,000 receivables), and the remaining $4,000 gain is capital gain ($30,000 amount realized − $20,000 basis − $6,000 ordinary gain). If D's basis in the partnership is $25,000 rather than $20,000, she still has ordinary gain of $6,000 *but* now has a capital loss of $1,000 ($5,000 gain − $6,000 ordinary gain).

OPTIONAL ADJUSTMENT TO BASIS

The Internal Revenue Code combines the entity and aggregate concepts in determining the taxability of partnership distributions and sales of partnership capital interests. In some situations, there is no taxable gain or loss to the partners; in some, there is only capital gain or loss; and in others, there is both ordinary gain and either capital gain or loss.

Unless specifically elected otherwise, any gain or loss reported by a partner has no effect on the partnership or on the other partners.[134] This follows the entity concept and is identical to the tax treatment of a corporation and its stockholders. However, because the aggregate or conduit concept is used to calculate net operating income, this applicability of the entity concept can create inequities. These are particularly evident when a capital interest in a partnership with appreciated assets is sold. The selling partner reports gain on the sale, but the purchasing partner must accept the old basis of the assets for purposes of depreciation, amortization, depletion, and gain or loss. This results in the new partner reporting more net income (or less loss) from the partnership. Further confusing the situation, this partner's *outside basis* (basis in the partnership interest) exceeds his or her *inside basis* (basis in the partnership's assets).

---

[134] §§ 734(a) and 743(a).

Example 37. A partnership has the following information:

	Partnership's Basis	Fair Market Value
Cash	$10,000	$10,000
Section 1231 assets	80,000	140,000
Total assets	$90,000	$150,000
Liabilities	$21,000	$21,000
Capital accounts	69,000	129,000
Total equities	$90,000	$150,000

R purchases T's one-third interest in the partnership for $43,000 and assumes responsibility for her share of existing liabilities. T's basis, including partnership liabilities, is $30,000. Recall from the previous discussion that she will report a gain of $20,000 ($43,000 + $7,000 liabilities − $30,000). If $45,000 of the $60,000 difference in § 1231 assets qualifies as potential depreciation recapture, her ordinary income is $15,000 (one-third of $45,000) and her capital gain is $5,000 ($20,000 − $15,000). R's basis in the partnership is his purchase price of $43,000 plus his $7,000 share of the partnership liabilities, for a total outside basis of $50,000. His inside basis is T's inside basis of $30,000 (one-third of $90,000). The difference between R's outside and inside basis is equal to the gain reported by T. R's annual partnership net income will be determined in the same manner as the other partners. That is, depreciation, gain, and loss on § 1231 assets will be calculated on the $80,000 basis.

REQUIRED ELECTION

The inequities encountered by the new partner are quite similar to those that exist when a partner contributes appreciated property in exchange for a capital interest. As discussed previously, these inequities can be alleviated with the use of special allocations. However, the Code provides an alternative that is often more attractive in the present type of situation. A partnership may elect that the basis of its property will be adjusted when partners sell a capital interest and when property is distributed to partners.[135] The initial election is included with the annual partnership return.[136] In the case of a sale, the partnership property is adjusted for the difference between the purchasing partner's outside basis and inside basis. The benefit of this adjustment accrues solely to the purchasing partner.[137]

[135] §§ 754, 743(a), and 734(a).

[136] Reg. § 1.754-1.

[137] § 743(b).

Example 38. Assume the same facts as in *Example 37*, except that the partnership has made the adjustment to basis election. This election has no effect on T, the selling partner, or on the other partners. It does affect the partnership's basis in the assets but only with respect to R, the purchasing partner. The partnership's basis in the § 1231 assets is increased by the $20,000 difference between R's outside and inside bases to $100,000. R's inside basis in the partnership is increased by this same $20,000 to $50,000, and now equals his outside basis. For purposes of depreciation, gain, and loss relating to the § 1231 assets, R's share is computed on a basis of $46,667 [($\frac{1}{3}$ of $80,000) + the $20,000 adjustment], while computations for the other partners remain as they were before T's sale to R. That is, they are computed on a basis of $53,333 ($\frac{2}{3}$ of $80,000).

The discussion and examples above pertain to sales when gains result. The reverse occurs when losses result. That is, the basis of the partnership's assets are decreased with respect to the purchasing partner.

Once the optional adjustment to basis election is made it applies to all sales, distributions, and partner deaths in the year of election and in future years unless the partnership is given permission to revoke the election.[138] If a request for revocation is filed within 30 days after the year-end, it may be retroactively applied to the preceding year. Reasons considered acceptable for approval include a change in the nature of the partnership's business, a substantial increase or change in character of the partnership's assets, or frequent transactions requiring adjustments that result in an administrative burden for the partnership. Approval will not be given when the primary purpose of the revocation is to avoid decreasing the basis of the partnership assets.[139]

Adjustments to basis are more difficult when distributions of partnership property are involved. Increases to basis include (1) all gain recognized by the partners receiving the property, plus (2) the amount of the partnership's basis for the property in excess of the basis of this property to the partners receiving it. Decreases to basis include (1) all losses recognized by the partners receiving the property, plus (2) the amount of the basis for the property to the partners receiving it in excess of the partnership's basis for the property when it qualifies as a *liquidating* distribution. The increases or decreases are made to the partnership's remaining property. Allocations of the adjustments among the various properties are beyond the scope of this discussion.[140]

---

[138]   § 754.

[139]   Reg. § 1.754-2(c).

[140]   § 755 and Reg. § 1.755.

TAX PLANNING WITH A PARTNERSHIP

Congressional intent that Subchapter K allow partners considerable flexibility in forming, operating, and liquidating their partnerships also provides numerous tax planning opportunities for partners. Many of these were discussed throughout this chapter. Although tax planning opportunities are too extensive and too personalized to prepare an exhaustive list, some additional ones are mentioned here to encourage the student of taxation to analyze tax situations continually with an eye for tax planning. The thoughtful but imaginative tax adviser who is able to provide clients with planning options that meet their needs is in much demand in today's tax conscious society.

ORGANIZING A PARTNERSHIP

Before a business is organized, all relevant factors should be evaluated to determine the type of organization that best meets the needs of the parties involved. The first step is to prepare a list of these needs and arrange them in order of their importance. For example, questions relevant to determining the owners' needs include the following: (1) Is limited liability important or will the owners be required to guarantee most of the business debt? (2) Will all owners participate in the management of the business? (3) Do the owners desire special allocations of specific business items? (4) Is the business expected to have net profits or net losses in the early years? (5) Do the owners expect to withdraw most of the business profits? (6) Are employee benefits such as deferred compensation plans and health insurance important to one or more of the owners who intend to work in the business? After the owners are satisfied with the list and its order, the tax adviser must evaluate the items in terms of the types of available organizations. This process requires both qualitative and quantitative measures. It should include an analysis of the tax effects on each owner under each type of organization based on projected business activities. Some firms have computer programs to aid in this evaluation. The analysis should be prepared in a form such that the owners can understand the options available to them with minimal explanation. The owners should be given ample opportunity to study the options, ask questions of the tax adviser, and arrive at an informed decision.

After the legal form is selected, the process should be repeated in a similar manner to determine the most desirable operational form. For example, relevant questions include (1) How will profits and losses be split? (2) What assets will each owner contribute and how will they be valued? (3) What are the current and future objectives and goals of the business? (4) What are the responsibilities of each owner? (5) Are any special allocations, guaranteed payments (e.g., compensation), or interest on capital balances desired? (6) What restrictions should be placed on the transfer of an ownership interest? Once the decision process concerning these factors is completed, a detailed agreement should be prepared. The more the owners are involved in the entire process, the greater are their chances for a satisfying business relationship.

The situation of any taxpayer planning to contribute property in exchange for a partnership interest should be evaluated. In some instances, it may be in the individual's best interest to seek an alternate method of obtaining an ownership interest. For example, property with a basis in excess of its market value may provide the owner greater benefits if leased to the partnership. The effects on the other partners and the availability of special allocations discussed in the chapter should also be considered.

Partners purchasing an interest in a partnership that owns appreciated assets should determine if the partnership has a § 754 election in effect. If not, the partners would possibly be willing to agree to such an election. The absence of a § 754 election means the partner's purchase price will exceed the asset bases for purposes of depreciation, depletion, amortization, gains, and losses. Therefore, it is quite possible that the purchase price should be adjusted below market value when no election exists. This, of course, is quite important to the selling partner as well.

OPERATING THE PARTNERSHIP

The flexibility of the partnership allows partners to determine, up until the tax return filing date, how various partnership items will be allocated among them. Thus, partners may wait until all the numbers are known before they decide how to allocate partnership profits and losses. Recall, however, that these special allocations must have an economic effect. This is achieved if the allocations affect the capital accounts and the partnership agreement states that liquidation will be based on capital account balances and that partners must restore any capital account deficits.

Year-end tax planning checklists should be developed for all partners and partnerships. This is particularly important for the partner whose basis is low. It might be necessary for this partner to take year-end actions to avoid reporting income when actual and deemed distributions exceed basis. The partnership's year-end planning is dependent on whether it reports on the cash or accrual basis and whether its partners' positions suggest its objectives should be to maximize or to minimize net income or net losses.

Partnerships provide excellent income-splitting opportunities among family members. Children can be employees of their parents' partnership. The amount of salary paid is, of course, dependent on the work performed. Significant tax savings can be achieved through family partnerships. The benefits and difficulties of dependent children as partners were discussed in the chapter.

DISPOSING OF PARTNERSHIP INTERESTS

The liquidation of a partnership interest results in ordinary gain under § 751 to the extent of unrealized receivables (including depreciation recapture) and substantially appreciated inventory. In some instances, it may be beneficial for the exiting partner to negotiate an installment sale. This allows the partner to defer recognition of a portion of the gain until proceeds are received. One negative factor, however, is that the partner's share of partnership debt is included in the amount realized and also in the amount received at the time of sale.

Partners are not taxed when they receive a pro rata distribution of § 751 assets. Thus, tax benefits may occur if a partnership makes a pro rata distribution of § 751 assets and of non–§ 751 assets to liquidating partners. This can occur whether the partnership is being liquidated or not. Gain is avoided, however, only as long as the distributed assets are not sold by the partners. The § 751 ordinary income taint is removed from the substantially appreciated inventory after five years but is removed from the unrealized receivables only on the death of the partner. In any case, partners may obtain deferral benefits by disposing of these assets over time or on an installment contract. Capital gains treatment does not adhere to the non–§ 751 assets. Capital gains are available only if these assets continue to qualify for capital gains treatment in the hands of the distributee partner. Although distribution of noncash assets can be complicated, the benefits may warrant the extra planning necessary. In many instances, a partnership can make adjustments that result in inventory being classified as a non-§ 751 asset. This was discussed in the chapter, but it is sufficiently important and overlooked so often that it is worth repeating.

When one or more partners plan to dispose of at least 50 percent of a partnership's capital and profits interests, tax planning can be very important for those partners retaining an interest in the partnership. Under § 708, a partnership terminates for all partners when 50 percent or more of its capital and profits interest is transferred (other than by death of a partner) within a 12-month period. Unless the 50 percent requirement is met, the partnership's year closes for terminating partners but not for continuing partners. Consequently, it is usually in the continuing partners' best interest to avoid a 50 percent transfer within 12 months. It is advisable to include a provision in the partnership agreement to this effect.

PROBLEM MATERIALS

DISCUSSION QUESTIONS

22-1 *Aggregate/Conduit vs. Entity.* How does the aggregate/conduit theory differ from the entity theory? Discuss how the transactions below would be treated under (a) the aggregate/conduit theory, and (b) the entity theory.

   a. A contributes appreciated land in exchange for a capital interest.
   b. B performs services in exchange for a capital interest.
   c. C contributes a patent with a market value in excess of basis in exchange for a capital interest.
   d. D, a 40 percent partner, sells equipment to the partnership for a loss.
   e. E, a 60 percent partner, sells equipment to the partnership for a loss.
   f. F, a 20 percent partner, performs services and is paid a guaranteed payment by the partnership.
   g. G, a 20 percent partner in a CPA firm, sells the partnership interest to Z.
   h. H receives a cash distribution that exceeds H's basis in the partnership interest.
   i. A liquidating partnership distributes the inventory to its owners according to their profit and loss sharing ratios. Neither the basis nor the value of the inventory exceeds any of the partners' bases in the partnership.

22-2 *Contribution of Property—Basis.* Generally, a contribution of property in exchange for a partnership interest results in a carryover of basis of the property from the contributing partner to the partnership. Give an example of when the partnership's basis in the property is the property's market value.

22-3 *Contributions of Property—Taxable.* Generally, a contribution of property in exchange for a partnership interest is nontaxable. Give an example of when a contributing partner recognizes gain on the exchange.

22-4 *Formation.* How is the allocation of depreciation, gain, and loss treated for appreciated properties contributed to a partnership in the current year?

22-5 *Special Allocations—Contributed Property.* Explain the Congressional and other equity reasons for the special allocation of precontribution gains and losses on contributed property.

22-6 *Partnership vs. Corporation.* List tax and nontax advantages of the partnership form of business compared with the corporate form.

22-7 *Organization Costs vs. Syndication Fees.* Compare the tax effects of organization costs with syndication fees.

22-8 *Operations.* Transactions between a partnership and a partner acting in a nonpartner capacity may be treated as though they occurred between the partnership and a nonpartner.

   a. Give examples of when this occurs.
   b. Give examples of when this cannot occur.

22-9   *Partner/Employee.*   May a partner be treated as an employee of the partnership? Explain.

22-10 *Timing.*   At what point in time does a cash basis partner have includible income or loss for the following?

a.   Distributive share of partnership net income
b.   Guaranteed payments for personal services
c.   Interest income on a loan
d.   Guaranteed payments on partner's capital account
e.   Cash distributions in excess of partnership basis

22-11 *Partnership's Taxable Year.*   What choices are available to a partnership when selecting a taxable year? If a partnership elects a fiscal year different from the tax year generally required, what additional requirements are imposed on the partnership?

22-12 *Allocations.*   What are the requirements for allocating partnership income, deductions, gains, and losses for contributed property and for other partnership activities?

22-13 *Partner's Basis.*   Indicate whether the following (a) increase, (b) decrease, or (c) have no effect on a general partner's basis. Assume all liabilities are recourse liabilities.

a.   The partnership borrows cash that is to be repaid in two years.
b.   The partnership earns interest on short-term municipal bonds.
c.   The partnership has a net loss for the year.
d.   The partnership has a net ordinary income for the year but none of it is paid to the partners.
e.   Partnership liabilities total $50,000 at the beginning of the year and $35,000 at the end of the year.
f.   A proportionate, nonliquidating distribution of property is made to the partners.

22-14 *Family Partnerships.*   Why are family partnerships subject to special rules? How do the tax effects for a family partnership differ from those of other partnerships?

22-15 *Limited Partnerships.*   Under what circumstances is a limited partnership more beneficial than a general partnership? Explain.

22-16 *Distributions—Current.*   Under what circumstances do nonliquidating partnership distributions to partners result in gain or loss to the partners?

22-17 *Distributions—Liquidating.*   Under what circumstances do liquidating partnership distributions to partners result in gain or loss to the partners?

22-18 *Inside vs. Outside Basis.*   How can the inside and outside bases of a partner be different? What are the potential inequities of this difference?

PROBLEMS

22-19 *Formation.* The A-E Partnership is being formed by five individuals who contribute assets in exchange for a 20 percent capital and profit/loss interest each. Calculate the following: (1) the recognized gain or loss, (2) each partner's basis in the partnership, (3) the partnership's bases in the assets, and (4) the holding period of the partnership interest and the property. Assume all contributed assets will be used in the partnership's trade or business. [Items (a) through (e) are to be treated as a group rather than as independent transactions. Accept all numbers given as correct and do not attempt to verify them.]

    a.   A contributes proprietorship equipment with a fair market value of $10,000. The equipment cost $16,000 when it was purchased four years ago and A deducted $11,000 depreciation as a proprietorship expense during the four years.

    b.   B contributes proprietorship equipment with a market value of $10,000. The equipment cost $20,000 when purchased two years ago and B's basis for the equipment is $12,000.

    c.   C contributes equipment identical to B's equipment. C's equipment also has a market value of $10,000. In fact, C and B purchased their equipment at the same time, at the same cost of $20,000, and used the equipment in the same manner. The only difference is that C used the equipment for personal, not business, purposes.

    d.   D contributes land with a market value of $16,000. The land was acquired 10 months ago for $9,000 cash and a $6,000 note payable (recourse debt). The $6,000 note payable is also transferred to the partnership.

    e.   E contributes land with a market value of $18,000. E received the land three years ago as a gift from a relative and has a basis of $5,000. In addition, E transfers an $8,000 mortgage (recourse debt) on the land to the partnership.

22-20 *Formation.* F and G form a cash basis partnership and will share profits and losses equally. F contributes cash basis proprietorship accounts receivable of $11,000. The partners agree that approximately $1,000 of the accounts will not be collected. G performs services for the partnership in exchange for a capital interest. One-fourth of the services constitute activities that must be capitalized, but the rest may be deducted in the current year. Calculate each partner's recognized gain and basis in the partnership. When does each partner's holding period for the partnership capital interest begin?

22-21 *Contributed Property—Allocations.*   The H and I Equal Partnership was formed at the beginning of the year. H contributed cash of $40,000 and I contributed equipment with a market value of $40,000 and a basis of $25,000. The equipment cost $35,000. I had used the equipment in a proprietorship for three years and did not recapture any depreciation or investment tax credit when it was transferred to the partnership. For the sake of simplicity, assume the partnership's depreciation rate for the current year on this equipment is 20 percent. The partnership's net ordinary income, excluding deductions for the equipment, is $60,000.

    a.   Calculate H's distributive share of partnership net ordinary income (after depreciation is deducted) and determine H's share of the investment tax credit recapture now or in an early disposition of the equipment.

    b.   H asks you what the tax consequences would have been if the partnership had sold the equipment for $39,000 only five months after I transferred it to the partnership.

22-22 *Sale of Contributed Property.*   Z and N are equal partners. Z's interest was obtained by contributing proprietorship assets in a tax-free exchange. One of these assets was used in his proprietorship for one year and in the Z and N partnership for two years. The records show:

Asset Cost	Proprietorship Depreciation	Partnership Depreciation	Sale Proceeds
$20,000	$3,000	$8,600	$13,000

The asset's market value at the time of contribution was $19,000 and $4,800 of the $8,600 partnership depreciation was allocated to N and $3,800 to Z. Calculate the amount and type of gain or loss to be reported by Z and N in the year of sale.

22-23 *Sale of Contributed Property—Allocations.*   Two years ago, individual X contributed an inventory asset from his sole proprietorship to D Partnership in exchange for a one-third interest in partnership profits and losses. At the date of contribution, the asset had a basis of $120,000 and a value of $145,000. The asset was used in the partnership's business as a nondepreciable §1231 asset. In the current year, the partnership sold the asset for $160,000.

    a.   Calculate the amount and character of the taxable gain recognized on the sale that is allocable to X.

    b.   How would the answer for (a) change if the sale occurred six years rather than two years after contribution?

    c.   How would the answer for (a) change if the asset had been sold for $100,000 rather than $160,000?

22-24   *Net Income and Self-Employment Income.*   An accrual basis partnership reports the following information for its calendar year.

Sales		$500,000
Cost of goods sold		(220,000)
Interest income from tax-exempt bonds		22,000
Interest income on trade receivables		18,000
Gross rental income	$30,000	
Rental expenses	(26,000)	4,000
Guaranteed payment to W		(24,000)
Interest expense to W on a loan		(6,000)
Other deductions (expenses)		(70,000)
Net capital loss		(4,000)

W is a 30 percent cash basis partner. All but $1/12$ of the guaranteed payment and interest were paid to W during the current year. The $1/12$ was paid the following April 25. W is single and has no other includible income or deductions.

a.   Calculate the partnership's net ordinary income.
b.   Calculate partner W's AGI.
c.   Calculate W's self-employment income assuming she is a general partner.
d.   Calculate W's self-employment income assuming she is a limited partner.

22-25   *Taxation of Partners.*   An accrual basis partnership has net income of $40,000 before deducting the following amounts due to P, a 20 percent partner: a $12,000 guaranteed payment for services and $5,000 interest on a loan from P. P reports on the cash basis and received no assets from the partnership during the year. Calculate P's includible income for the current year.

22-26   *Partner's Distributive Shares.*   R is a partner in a three-person partnership, RHS. The partnership agreement states that R is to receive 15 percent of the partnership's net income before deducting any payments to partners. In addition, each partner is allocated one-third of all profits and losses after R receives his compensation. The partnership had $50,000 of net income before any payments to partners.

a.   What is the amount of R's guaranteed payment?
b.   What is R's total taxable income from RHS?
c.   What is H's total taxable income from RHS?

22-27   *Payments for Partner's Services.*   The LLB Partnership has a September 30 taxable year-end. Partner B, a calendar year, cash basis individual, received a guaranteed payment for services rendered to the partnership of $4,500 a month for the partnership's year ending September 30, 1991. The partnership agreed to increase the payment to $6,000 a month for the next fiscal year. On October 12, 1991, B also received a $12,000 payment from the partnership for professional services; B performs such professional services for a variety of clients in his sole proprietorship business. How much income attributable to these payments should B report in 1991?

22-28 *Guaranteed Payments.* B and G are partners in DR partnership. B oversees the daily operations of the business and therefore receives compensation of $50,000, regardless of the amount of the partnership's net income. In addition, his distributive share of profits and losses is 50 percent.

  a. If the partnership had $75,000 ordinary income before any payments to partners, what are the amount and character of B's total income?

  b. Same as (a), but assume the partnership had $30,000 ordinary income before payments to partners.

  c. Same as (a), except assume the partnership had $25,000 ordinary income and $50,000 long-term capital gain before payments to partners.

22-29 *Guaranteed Payments.* At the end of the current year, the three partners in the ABC partnership had the following pre-closing balances in their capital accounts.

Partner A.....................	$ 70,000
Partner B.....................	89,000
Partner C.....................	105,000

The ABC partnership agreement provides that (1) each partner will receive an annual cash distribution equal to 6 percent of the pre-year-end closing balance in his or her capital account and (2) any remaining income or loss for the year will be allocated equally among the partners. Before accounting for any distributions to the partners, ABC had $54,600 of taxable income for the current year. How much taxable income is allocated to each partner?

22-30 *Related Party Transactions.* S Partnership is owned by four individuals: W and X (each owns a 30 percent interest in capital and profits) and Y and Z (each owns a 20 percent interest in capital and profits). W and X are brothers, and Y and Z are not related to any other partner. During the current year, W sells an asset to the partnership for $22,000. The basis of the asset to W is $35,000.

  a. How much of the $13,000 realized loss on the sale may W recognize for tax purposes?

  b. How would the answer for (a) change if partner Y rather than W made the sale?

22-31 *Transactions.* V, a 60 percent partner, sells land to the partnership for $8,000. V's basis in the land is $9,000 and his basis in the partnership is $45,000.

  a. Determine (1) V's recognized gain or loss, (2) V's basis in the partnership, and (3) the partnership's basis in the land after the transaction.

  b. Determine V's recognized gain or loss (personally and share of partnership's gain or loss) if the partnership sells the land six months later for (1) $7,500, (2) $8,600, or (3) $9,300.

  c. How would your answers to (a) and (b) differ if V were a 40 percent partner?

22-32 *Operations.* T is a 30 percent partner who works in the partnership business. Both T and the partnership use the calendar year for tax purposes. The partnership's records for the current year show the following:

Gross profit	$240,000
Guaranteed payment to T	20,000
Keogh contributions for T	7,000
Health insurance premium for T	500
Operating expenses	60,000
Charitable contributions	5,000
Net capital gain	10,000

T is single, has no other income, and has $4,500 personal itemized deductions (including $600 deductible medical expenses). T received the $20,000 guaranteed payment for services and withdrew an additional $10,000 during the year. T's basis in the partnership was $40,000 at the beginning of the year.

a. Calculate the partnership's ordinary income (Form 1065, page 1) for the year.

b. Calculate T's taxable income for the year.

c. Calculate T's basis in the partnership at the end of the year.

22-33 *Partnership Year-End.* R, S, and T each owned a retail store as sole proprietors. R and S have a December 31 year-end, and T has a January 31 year-end. In order to take advantage of certain economies of scale, they combined their operations by forming a partnership on December 1, 1991. Each partner has a one-third interest in partnership profits. The partnership's net income was as follows:

December 1 — December 31, 1991	$30,000
January 1 — January 31, 1992	10,000
February 1 — November 30, 1992	50,000
December 1 — December 31, 1992	25,000

a. Assuming no special elections, what tax year-end must the partnership adopt?

b. Assuming the partnership adopts a December 31 year-end, how much income from the partnership will T report on her tax return for her year ending January 31, 1992?

c. What tax year(s) may the partnership adopt with IRS permission or with special elections?

d. Assuming the partnership could adopt a January 31 year-end, how much income from the partnership will R report on his December 31, 1991 tax return? On his December 31, 1992 return?

22-34 *Partnership Net Losses.*   XYZ partnership has three general partners. At the beginning of the year, X had a basis in his partnership interest of $20,000, and Y and Z had bases of $40,000 each in their partnership interests. X and Y receive 30 percent of partnership profits and losses, and Z receives 40 percent. During the year, the partnership incurred a $90,000 ordinary loss.

    a.   How much income or loss will each partner report on his or her individual return and what is each partner's basis in his or her partnership interest at the end of the year? Assume no distributions to or contributions by partners during the year.

    b.   Same as (a) but assume the partnership incurs a $70,000 ordinary loss and a $30,000 capital loss.

22-35 *Basis and Losses.*   A partnership has the following balance sheet information:

Cash	$ 30,000	Nonrecourse loans	$200,000
Land	100,000	Recourse loans	300,000
Rental buildings	500,000	Partners' capital	130,000

The nonrecourse liabilities are payable to qualified lenders.

On September 1, W contributes $50,000 cash to the partnership. The agreement states that W is to be allocated 20 percent of all profits and losses. During the year, the partnership has net ordinary losses of $10,000 each month and, thus, a $120,000 loss for the calendar year.

    a.   Calculate W's basis in the partnership as of September 1, if W is a general partner in a general partnership.

    b.   Calculate W's basis in the partnership as of September 1, if W is a limited partner in a limited partnership.

    c.   If all partners agree, what is the maximum amount of net ordinary loss that can be allocated to W for the year? Explain.

22-36 *Retroactive Allocation.*   A cash basis, calendar year real estate partnership reported quarterly net losses of $20,000, $24,000, $15,000, and $40,000, respectively. The losses were partly due to $14,000 interest prepaid in the fourth quarter for the following January and $18,000 property taxes paid July 1 for the previous year. T sold his entire 20 percent interest to V on June 30. Assume the IRS allows a monthly proration. Calculate the loss to be reported by each of the two partners

    a.   If no special allocation is made.

    b.   If a special allocation is made to maximize the loss reported by V.

22-37 *Basis and Taxation of Partners.* The TVX Partnership, formed in 1990, owns several office rental buildings. Selected year-end information for its first five years reveals the following:

	1990	1991	1992	1993	1994
Recourse liabilities........	$100,000	$120,000	$130,000	$150,000	$160,000
Nonrecourse liabilities........	500,000	400,000	300,000	250,000	200,000
Net income or (loss)..........	(300,000)	(200,000)	(110,000)	(40,000)	70,000
Cash distributed to partners.....	50,000	100,000	150,000	100,000	0

The nonrecourse liabilities are payable to qualified lenders.

Partner A contributed property with a basis of $50,000 and a market value of $75,000. Nine other partners contributed $75,000 cash each. A is a general partner and the other nine partners are limited partners. They share profits and losses equally—10 percent each. Prepare a schedule showing: (a) the distributive share of profits and losses, and (b) the basis in the partnership each year for the general partner and for one of the limited partners.

22-38 *Allocation of Partnership Liabilities.* In the current year, individuals M, N, and O form a general partnership, making no initial capital contributions. The three partners share partnership profits and losses in the following manner: 10 percent to M, 45 percent to N, and 45 percent to O. The partnership borrows $50,000 cash on a fully recourse basis. The partnership also borrows $180,000 on a fully nonrecourse basis. The nonrecourse debt is secured by investment land purchased by the partnership at a total cost of $200,000 ($20,000 cash plus the $180,000 proceeds of the nonrecourse debt). Calculate the effect of the two partnership liabilities on each partner's basis in the partnership.

22-39 *Family Partnership.* W, A, and E are members of a partnership and share profits and losses equally. Capital is a material income-producing factor for this partnership. Ordinary income for the year is $100,000. Although W is the only partner working in the partnership, no compensation is paid or distributed to W. The value of W's work is approximately $30,000. Partners' capital account balances before the current year's income are $50,000 for W and $25,000 each for A and E. Assume you are an IRS agent auditing the partnership return. How much of the $100,000 would you deem taxable to W, to A, and to E, assuming (a) W, A, and E are unrelated, (b) A and E are W's children, 14 and 15 years old, and that a donor/donee relationship exists, or (c) same as (b) except E is a cousin to W?

22-40 *Current Distributions—Proportionate.* X is a 50 percent partner in XY, a calendar year partnership. X had a basis in her partnership interest of $10,000 at the beginning of the year. On October 1, she and the other partner withdrew $15,000 each. The partnership net earnings for the year are $60,000.

    a.   How much gain or loss must X recognize on October 1?

    b.   What is X's taxable income for the year, and what is her basis in her partnership interest at the end of the year?

    c.   How would the answers to (a) and (b) change if partnership earnings had been $6,000 instead of $60,000?

22-41 *Current Distribution—Proportionate.* B Partnership proposes making a proportionate current distribution to each of its two equal partners of *either* (a) $50,000 cash or (b) partnership inventory ($50,000 market value and $28,000 basis). Prior to any distribution, K's basis in his partnership interest is $40,000. The partnership has no unrealized receivables or substantially appreciated inventory. Based on these facts, what are the tax consequences of the alternative distributions, and what factors should K consider in deciding which alternative to accept?

22-42 *Current Distribution—Proportionate.* During the current year, partner J received a proportionate distribution from HIJK Partnership, consisting of $13,000 cash and some marketable securities (investment assets to the partnership). The securities had a basis to the partnership of $20,000 and an FMV of $33,000. Prior to the distribution, J's basis in his partnership interest was $40,000. The distribution had no effect on J's profit and loss sharing ratio.

    a.   How much gain or loss must J recognize because of this distribution? What basis will J have in the securities? What basis will J have in his partnership interest after the distribution?

    b.   Does the partnership recognize any gain for the distribution of the appreciated securities to J?

    c.   How would the answer to (a) change if J's basis in his interest prior to distribution had been $25,000 rather than $40,000?

22-43 *Liquidating Distribution—Proportionate.* The FN Partnership is liquidating. Before liquidation, the records show the following:

	Partnership's Basis	Fair Market Value
Cash	$ 40,000	$ 40,000
§ 1231 land	10,000	30,000
Equipment	100,000	70,000
Accumulated depreciation	(60,000)	
Owners capital	90,000	140,000

F, a 50 percent owner, receives one-half of the assets. F's basis in the partnership is $45,000. Calculate F's ordinary gain and capital gain or loss on the distribution and F's basis for each asset.

22-44 *Substantially Appreciated Inventory.*   A partnership has the following assets:

	Partnership's Basis	Fair Market Value
Cash......................................	$10,000	$10,000
Accounts receivable.........................	15,000	15,000
Inventory...................................	30,000	38,000
Capital assets..............................	40,000	46,000

a.   According to the Regulations, is the inventory substantially appreciated?

b.   How would the answer to (a) change if the inventory had a $25,000 basis instead of $30,000?

22-45 *Sale of a Partnership Interest.*   M is an equal partner in a three-person accrual basis partnership that has the following assets at year-end:

	Partnership's Basis	Fair Market Value
Cash......................................	$100,000	$100,000
Accounts receivable.........................	100,000	100,000
Land.......................................	130,000	160,000
Notes payable..............................	(60,000)	(60,000)
Net assets.................................	$270,000	$300,000

M sells her entire partnership interest (basis of $110,000) to J for $100,000. Each partner has a capital account with a $90,000 basis and a $100,000 market value.

a.   Calculate M's ordinary and capital gain on the sale.

b.   What are J's outside basis and inside basis in his partnership interest if the partnership does not have a §754 election in effect?

22-46 *Sale of a Partnership Interest.*   Partnership records of a CPA firm show the following:

	Partnership's Basis	Fair Market Value
Cash	$ 8,000	$ 8,000
Accounts Receivable	0	40,000
§ 1231 assets	130,000	100,000
Accumulated depreciation	(50,000)	0
	$ 88,000	$148,000
Liabilities	$ 28,000	$ 28,000
Owners' capital	60,000	120,000
	$ 88,000	$148,000

[handwritten: 375 / -unrealized receivables]

There is potential § 1245 and § 1250 gain of $4,000. M, a 25 percent owner, has a basis in the partnership of $21,000 (including 25% of partnership liabilities). M sells the 25 percent interest to J for $30,000.

a.   Calculate M's ordinary gain and capital gain or loss on the sale.

b.   How would your answers differ if M's basis in the partnership had been $28,000?

22-47 *Optional Adjustment to Basis.*   Refer to Problem 22-46. During the first month after J purchases a 25 percent interest in the partnership, 50 percent of the accounts receivable ($20,000) are collected. Calculate (1) J's distributive share, and (2) the other partners' distributive shares of ordinary income or capital gain as a result of this collection under each of the assumptions below:

a.   Assume there is no special election under § 754 for partnership assets to be adjusted for the sale in Problem 22-46.

b.   Assume there is a special election under § 754 for partnership assets to be adjusted for the sale in Problem 22-46.

22-48 *Tax Return Problem.*   P and K formed the P&K General Partnership on March 1, 1981 to provide computer consulting services. They share all profits, losses, and capital, with 60 percent going to P and 40 percent to K. The business code and employer identification numbers are 1370 and 24-3897625, respectively. The business office is located at 3010 East Apple Street, Atlanta, Georgia 30304. P and K live nearby at 1521 South Elm Street and 3315 East Apple Street, respectively. Their social security numbers are 403-16-5110 for P and 518-72-9147 for K.

The calendar year, cash basis partnership's December 31, 1990 balance sheet and December 31, 1991 trial balance (both prepared for tax purposes) contain the following information:

	Balance Sheet 12/31/90		Trial Balance 12/31/91	
	Debit	Credit	Debit	Credit
Cash.........................	$ 12,000		$ 22,000	
Note receivable (1)............	14,000		14,000	
Equipment (2, 3)..............	150,000		190,000	
Accumulated depreciation......		$ 38,000		$ 63,500
Recourse notes payable (3, 4).		58,000		87,200
Nonrecourse notes payable (4)		36,000		30,000
P, Capital.....................		28,000		28,000
P, Drawing....................			25,400	
K, Capital.....................		16,000		16,000
K, Drawing			17,000	
Revenues.....................				235,000
Interest income (1).............				1,400
§ 1245 gain (2)................				3,500
Compensation (5)..............			110,000	
Rent expense..................			12,000	
Interest expense..............			16,600	
Tax expense...................			13,800	
Repair expense................			5,800	
Depreciation expense..........			29,200	
Health insurance expense (6)..			1,600	
Property insurance expense ...			1,500	
Office supplies expense			3,000	
Utility expense.................			2,200	
Charitable contribution.........			500	
Totals.......................	$176,000	$176,000	$464,600	$464,600

1. The note receivable is from K and is due December 31, 1996. The annual interest rate is 10 percent; K paid $1,400 on December 28, 1991.
2. Equipment was sold May 12, 1991 for $9,800. It was purchased new on May 1, 1989 for $10,000, and its basis when sold was $6,300.
3. New equipment was purchased March 1, 1991 with $5,000 cash and a $45,000 three-year recourse note payable. The first note payment is March 1, 1992.
4. Notes payable are long-term except for $20,000 of the recourse note to be paid next year. The nonrecourse notes are payable to qualified lenders.
5. Compensation is composed of guaranteed payments of $30,000 each to P and to K and $50,000 to unrelated employees.
6. Health insurance premiums paid where $400 for P, $400 for K, and $800 for unrelated employees.

Prepare Form 1065, Schedule K, Schedules L and M (even though not required by the IRS instructions to Form 1065), and Schedule K-1 for P. Complete all pages, including responses to all questions. If any necessary information is missing in the problem, assume a logical answer and record it. Do not prepare Schedule K-1 or other required supplemental forms for partner K at this time. Be sure to calculate the self-employment income and record the amounts on Schedules K and K-1.

RESEARCH PROBLEMS

22-49 *Family Partnership.* B operates a proprietorship that manufactures and sells utility tables. Net ordinary income has been increasing approximately 20 percent each year. Last year, net ordinary income was $60,000 on net assets of $225,000. B needs $75,000 to expand the business. Although B's daughter is only 13 years old, she plans to join her father in the business at some point in the future. B is considering forming a partnership with his daughter. His ownership interest would be 75 percent and hers would be 25 percent. If the daughter's interest is held in trust until she reaches 18, can B serve as the trustee without disqualifying the partnership arrangement?

Suggested research materials:

§ 704 and accompanying Regulations
Stern, 15 T.C. 521 (1950)
Bateman v. U.S., 74-1 USTC ¶9176, 33 AFTR2d 74-483, 490 F.2d 549 (CA-9, 1973)
Ginsberg v. Comm., 74-2 USTC ¶9660, 34 AFTR2d 74-5760, 502 F.2d 965 (CA-6, 1974)

22-50 *Corporate Partners.* M and Z are attorneys who wish to combine their proprietorship business activities. They intend to expand their activities and hire six employees. Some problems arise in their negotiations. First, they cannot agree on several tax elections. Second, they want to maximize the tax-deductible retirement contributions for themselves but do not want to include the six employees in the plan, even though this would violate the nondiscriminatory requirements for such plans. They ask you if they can avoid their two problems by taking the following actions:

a.   Transfer M's proprietorship assets to a newly created professional corporation controlled by M. The corporation will employ M.
b.   Transfer Z's proprietorship assets to a newly created professional corporation controlled by Z. The corporation will employ Z.
c.   The two newly created corporations form a partnership. The partnership hires the six employees and conducts all of the business activities. The assets remain in the corporations.

LEARNING OBJECTIVES

Upon completion of this chapter you will be able to:

- Identify the requirements necessary to elect S status

- Recognize the actions that terminate S status

- Compute the net operating income or loss for an S corporation and the impact of S corporate operations on shareholders' taxable income

- Recognize transactions between shareholders and their S corporations that are subject to special treatment

- Determine the shareholders' basis in the S corporation stock

- Determine the appropriate taxable year for an S corporation

- Explain the unique concepts relevant to family members

- Calculate gain or loss for the S corporation and its shareholders when asset distributions are made and the S corporation (1) has no AE&P or (2) has AE&P

- Calculate the special taxes on excessive passive income and on built-in gains

- Understand how dispositions of S corporate stock differ from those of C corporate stock

- Compare the four business organizations—proprietorships, partnerships, S corporations, and C corporations (see Appendix)

CHAPTER OUTLINE

Chapter 23

S CORPORATIONS

INTRODUCTION

Congress added Subchapter S to the Internal Revenue Code in 1958, giving birth to a unique tax entity: the S corporation. The S corporation is taxed in a manner very similar to a partnership, while retaining the legal characteristics of a corporation. In providing this distinctive treatment, Congressional intent was to allow small businesses to have "the advantages of the corporate form of organization without being made subject to the possible tax disadvantages of the corporation."[1] As this statement suggests, Congress recognized that many taxpayers who normally would incorporate their businesses to secure limited liability were reluctant to do so because of the possibility of double taxation. Accordingly, one of the major objectives of the Subchapter S legislation was to minimize taxes as a factor in the selection of the form of business organization. To accomplish this objective, a complete set of special rules were designed, most of which are contained in Subchapter S.

Although the treatment of S corporations was intended to be identical to that for partnerships, this goal was not achieved under the 1958 legislation. As originally written, the rules governing S corporations (or Subchapter S corporations as they were initially called) bore little resemblance to partnership rules. Many of these differences were eliminated, however, with the substantial modifications introduced by the Subchapter S Revision Act of 1982. Under the revised rules, Federal income tax treatment of S corporations and their shareholders is similar to that of partnerships and their partners. The S corporation is not subject to the corporate *Federal income tax*. Rather, like a partnership, the S corporation is merely a conduit. The income, deductions, gains, losses, and credits of the S corporation flow through to its shareholders. An S corporation, however, may be subject to a special tax such as the tax on excessive passive income or on built-in gains.

Even though the Federal income tax treatment of an S corporation resembles that of a partnership, the corporation is subject to many rules that apply to regular corporations. For example, since an S corporation is formed in the same manner as a regular corporation, the basic rules governing organization (i.e., the nonrecognition rules contained in § 351 concerning transfers to a controlled

---

[1] S. Rept. No. 1622, 83rd Cong., 2d Sess., 119 (1954).

corporation discussed in Chapter 19) of all corporations also apply to S corporations. Similarly, redemptions of an S corporation's stock, as well as liquidation and reorganization of an S corporation, generally are taxed according to the rules applying to regular corporations. As a practical matter, however, each provision must be closely examined to determine whether special treatment is provided S corporations.

S CORPORATION ELIGIBILITY REQUIREMENTS

The special tax treatment provided for S corporations is available only if the corporation is a *small business corporation*, and all of its shareholders *consent* to the corporation's election to be taxed under Subchapter S. A corporation is considered a small business corporation if it:[2]

1. Is an *eligible domestic* corporation;

2. Does not have more than thirty-five *eligible* shareholders; and

3. Has only *one class of stock* outstanding.

All of these requirements must be met when the election is made and at all times thereafter. Failure at any time to qualify as a small business corporation terminates the election, and as of the date of termination, the corporation is taxed as a regular corporation (hereafter referred to as a C corporation).[3]

The phrase *small business corporation* is clearly a misnomer. As the requirements for this status indicate, the sole restriction on the size of the corporation is the limitation imposed on the *number* of shareholders. Corporations are not denied use of Subchapter S due to the amount of their assets, income, net worth, or any other measure of size. In addition, the S corporation is not required to conduct an active business. Merely holding assets does not bar the corporation from Subchapter S.

ELIGIBLE CORPORATIONS

Subchapter S status is reserved for *eligible domestic corporations*.[4] Thus, foreign corporations do not qualify. In order for a domestic corporation to be eligible, it cannot be a member of an affiliated group. Consequently, an S corporation is prohibited from having an 80 percent owned subsidiary.[5] An important exception,

---

[2] § 1361.

[3] § 1362(d)(2).

[4] § 1361(b); Reg. § 1.1371-1(b) includes any U.S. territory as well as states.

[5] § 1361(b)(2)(A).

however, permits an S corporation to own 80 percent or more of an *inactive* subsidiary.[6] A subsidiary is generally considered inactive if (1) it has not begun business during the parent's taxable year, and (2) it has no gross income during the parent's taxable year.[7] This provision enables an S corporation to establish one or more inactive affiliates that may be used in the future.

> **Example 1.** An S corporation owns and operates a chain of restaurants in Arkansas. The restaurants have been so successful that the corporation is considering expanding to other states. In anticipation of expansion, the corporation established subsidiaries in each of the surrounding states to ensure that the company's name cannot be used by others. Although the corporation is a member of an affiliated group, the S election is not invalidated as long as the subsidiaries are inactive.

Other ineligible corporations include financial institutions, insurance companies, Domestic International Sales Corporations, and corporations electing Code § 936 Puerto Rico and United States Possessions tax credits.[8]

SHAREHOLDER REQUIREMENTS

Subchapter S imposes several restrictions on S corporation shareholders. Not only is the total number of shareholders limited to thirty-five, but certain parties are prohibited from owning stock of the corporation.

Type of Shareholder. The stock of an S corporation may be owned only by individuals who are citizens or resident aliens of the United States, estates, and certain trusts. Nonresident aliens (i.e., generally foreign citizens residing outside the United States), corporations, partnerships, and certain trusts are not allowed to hold stock in an S corporation. This prohibition is directly related to the limitation on the number of shareholders. Absent this prohibition, the thirty-five shareholder restriction could easily be defeated, for example, by allowing a partnership with more than thirty-five partners to own the S corporation stock. A similar result could be obtained if a trust with more than thirty-five beneficiaries were to own the stock. Consequently, acquisition of an S corporation's stock by any one of these parties terminates the election. Rules denying trusts as shareholders have been relaxed over the years. Four types of trusts may be shareholders: (1) grantor and § 678 trusts, (2) qualified Subchapter S trusts (QSSTs), (3) certain testamentary trusts, and (4) voting trusts.[9]

---

[6] § 1361(c)(6).

[7] §§ 1361(c)(6)(A) and (B).

[8] § 1361(b)(2).

[9] § 1361(c)(2). See Chapter 25 for a detailed discussion of trusts.

Number of Shareholders. As a general rule, a corporation does not qualify as an S corporation if the number of shareholders exceeds 35 at any moment during the taxable year. After being altered several times over the past few years, this limitation on number of shareholders is identical to the private placement exemption of Federal securities laws.[10]

For purposes of counting the number of shareholders in an S corporation, stock owned by a husband and wife is treated as owned by one shareholder. This rule applies whether the stock is owned by the spouses separately or jointly. Consequently, it is possible for an S corporation to have 70 shareholders if all stock is owned by married couples. This treatment is not extended to couples who are divorced but continue to own the stock jointly. Similarly, other persons who are co-owners of the stock but who are not married are counted as separate shareholders.

When a permissible trust is a shareholder of the S corporation, the number of shareholders counted depends on the type of trust. For grantor and § 678 trusts, there is one deemed owner who is considered to be the shareholder. For testamentary trusts, the estate is deemed to be the sole shareholder rather than the beneficiaries. In the case of a QSST, there is one beneficiary who is treated as a shareholder. For a voting trust, each beneficiary is treated as a shareholder. Consequently, all qualifying trusts, *except* voting trusts, represent one shareholder.

When stock is held in the name of a nominee, agent, guardian, or custodian, the beneficial owner of the stock is treated as the shareholder.

> **Example 2.** XYZ Bank and Trust, a corporation, holds legal title to stock in an S corporation. The corporation holds the stock for the benefit of R, a minor child. In this case, R, the beneficial owner, is treated as the shareholder rather than XYZ. As a result, the S corporation is not denied the benefits of Subchapter S because of a corporate shareholder.

> **Example 3.** F holds stock in an S corporation as custodian for his two minor children. For purposes of counting shareholders, F is ignored and the children are counted as two separate shareholders.

ONE CLASS OF STOCK

In order to minimize the problems of allocating income of the S corporation among shareholders, the corporation is allowed only one class of stock outstanding. Stock that is authorized but unissued does not invalidate the election. For example, an S corporation may have authorized but unissued preferred stock. Similarly, outstanding stock rights, options, or convertible debentures may be issued without affecting the election.

---

[10]   Offerings of securities to 35 parties or fewer are exempt from registration under Federal securities laws.

Outstanding shares generally must provide identical rights to all shareholders. Differences in rights such as the amount of dividends a shareholder is entitled to or the amount that the shareholder would receive on liquidation are considered as creating a second class of stock, which causes the S election to be terminated. However, differences in *voting rights* are expressly authorized by the Code.[11] This exception enables control of the organization to be exercised in a manner that differs from stock ownership and income allocation.

> **Example 4.** R organized MND, an S corporation. MND issued two classes of common stock to R: class A voting and class B nonvoting stock. The rights represented by the stock are identical except for voting rights, and thus, do not invalidate the S election. Shortly after the organization of the corporation, R gives the class B nonvoting stock to her two children. Although R has shifted income and future appreciation of the stock to her children (assuming certain other requirements are satisfied), she has retained all of the voting control of the corporation.

Debt that does not meet certain rules may be reclassified as stock and thus terminate the S election. Safe-harbor rules provide that *straight debt* is not treated as a second class of stock if[12]

1. The interest rate and interest payment dates are not contingent on either the corporation's profits, management's discretion, or similar factors;

2. The instrument cannot be converted into stock; and

3. The creditor is an individual, estate, or trust that is eligible to hold stock in an S corporation.

Straight debt is defined as any written unconditional promise to pay on demand, or on a specified date, a certain sum of money.

Proposed regulations for § 1361 were issued October 15, 1990 with a *retroactive* effective date, which makes them applicable to all years after 1982. The proposed regulations provide that "non-conforming distributions" to shareholders generally will be treated as a distribution on stock. As a result, stock owned by the shareholders(s) receiving the "non-conforming distribution" will be reclassified as a second class of stock that automatically terminates the S election. Since distributions from S corporate earnings are required to be the same for each share of outstanding stock, a distribution is non-conforming when a stockholder's percentage of the distribution exceeds his or her ownership percentage. Consequently, if an S corporation erroneously paid a shareholder's expense in 1983 (or a later date), the S election was lost at that point and the corporation is

---

[11] § 1361(c)(4).   [12] § 1361(c)(5).

subject to taxation as a C corporation for the remainder of that year and for all future years, or until the S election is reinstated. At this writing, the S Corporation Taxation Committee of the AICPA is drafting comments to be submitted to the IRS requesting that changes be made to the proposed regulations, including a deferral of the effective date.

ELECTION OF S CORPORATION STATUS

A corporation that qualifies as a small business corporation is taxed according to the rules of Subchapter S only if the corporation elects to be an S corporation. This election exempts the business from the corporate income tax and all other Federal income taxes normally imposed on corporations except for (1) the tax on excessive passive investment income, (2) the tax on built-in gains, and (3) the tax from the recapture of investment credits claimed by the corporation prior to the election. In addition, the corporation normally is exempt from the personal holding company tax and the accumulated earnings tax. Although the S corporation generally avoids taxation as a regular corporation, most rules governing regular corporations such as those concerning organization, redemptions, and liquidations apply.

MAKING THE ELECTION: MANNER AND PERIOD OF EFFECT

In order for a corporation to be taxed according to the rules of Subchapter S, an election must be filed on Form 2553. The effective date of the election, as well as the required shareholder consents that must be evidenced on the form, generally depend on when the election is filed.

Current-Year Election. To be effective for the corporation's current taxable year, the election must be filed by the fifteenth day of the third month of the corporation's taxable year (e.g., March 15 for a calendar year S corporation).[13] In addition, consent to the election must be obtained not only from all shareholders holding stock at the time of election, but also from former shareholders who have held stock during the earlier portion of that taxable year.[14] The consent of former shareholders is required since they will be allocated a share of the income, losses, and other items applicable to the time they held the stock. If only the consent of former shareholders is lacking, the election is effective for the following taxable year. Similarly, if the corporation fails to meet any of the Subchapter S requirements during the pre-election portion of the year, the election is effective for the following taxable year.

---

[13] §§ 1362(b)(1)(B) and (b)(2).

[14] §§ 1362(a)(2) and (b)(2)(B)(ii). Although the election must be filed timely, the IRS may grant an extension for filing the consent forms if reasonable cause can be shown. Reg. § 18.1362-2(c).

Example 5.   At the beginning of 1991, D, E, and F owned the stock of GHI Corporation, a calendar year taxpayer. On February 15, 1991, F sold all of her shares in GHI to C. On March 1, 1991, an S corporation election is desired. In order for the election to be effective for 1991, all shareholders on the date of election (C, D, and E), as well as any shareholders in the pre-election portion of the year (F), must consent. Failure to obtain F's consent would cause the election to become effective for 1992.

Election Effective for Subsequent Years.   Elections made after the first two and one-half months of the current taxable year are effective for the following taxable year.[15] When the election becomes effective in the following taxable year, only shareholders holding stock on the date of election must consent. The consent of shareholders who acquire stock after the election is not required.[16] As noted above, an election made within the first two and one-half months of the year without the consent of former shareholders or without satisfaction of the requirements causes the election to be effective for the following taxable year.

TERMINATION OF THE ELECTION

An election to be taxed as an S corporation is effective until it is terminated. The election may be terminated when the corporation[17]

1. Revokes the election;

2. Fails to satisfy the requirements; or

3. Receives excessive passive income.

Revocation.   The S corporation election may be revoked if shareholders holding a *majority* of the shares of stock (voting and nonvoting) consent.[18] A revocation filed by the fifteenth day of the third month of the taxable year (e.g., March 15 for a calendar year corporation) normally is effective for the current taxable year.[19] In contrast, if the revocation is filed after this two and one-half month period has elapsed, it usually becomes effective for the following taxable year.[20] In both situations, however, a date on or after the date of revocation may be specified for the termination to become effective.[21]

---

[15]   § 1362(b)(3).

[16]   As noted later in the discussion, however, a shareholder owning more than 50 percent of stock may terminate the election.

[17]   § 1362(d).

[18]   § 1362(d)(1)(B).

[19]   § 1362(d)(1)(C)(i).

[20]   § 1362(d)(1)(C)(ii).

[21]   § 1362(d)(1)(D).

Example 6. A calendar year S corporation is owned equally by C, D, and E. On February 12, 1992 C and D consent to revoke the S corporation election. Since C and D own a majority of the outstanding shares of stock, the election is effective beginning on January 1, 1992 unless the revocation specifies February 12, 1992 or some later date.

Example 7. Same as *Example 6* above except the revocation was made on May 3, 1992. The election is effective for the following taxable year beginning January 1, 1993. If the revocation had specified, however, that the termination was to become effective November 2, 1992, the S corporation year would end on November 1, 1992.

As currently designed, the revocation rules allow a new shareholder to terminate the election only if he or she acquires a majority of the shares of stock.

Example 8. An S corporation has 100 shares of outstanding stock, 75 owned by J and 25 owned by B. On June 1 of this year, J sold 60 of her shares to D. Since D owns a majority of the outstanding shares, he may revoke the election.

Failure to Meet the Requirements. If the S corporation fails to satisfy any of the Subchapter S requirements at any time, the election is terminated on the date the disqualifying event occurred.[22] In such case, the corporation is treated as an S corporation for the period ending prior to the date of termination. This often causes the corporation to have two short taxable years: one as an S corporation and one as a C corporation. As a result, income and loss for the entire year must be allocated between the two years. The methods for making these allocations are discussed later in this chapter. The tax returns for both the short S year and short C year must be filed by the *original* due date of the short year C corporate return.[23]

Example 9. C, D, and E own a calendar year S corporation. On June 3 of this year, E sold her stock to a corporation. The S corporation's year ends on June 2. The same result would be obtained if the sale had been to a partnership or to an individual who became the 36th shareholder. The S short year includes January 1 through June 2. The C short year is June 3 through December 31.

S shareholders report their proportionate share of all S short year items in the same manner as they would for a complete year, except computations are made as of the last day the business qualified as an S corporation. The C corporate tax liability, however, must be annualized.[24]

---

[22] § 1362(d)(2).

[23] § 1362(e)(6)(B).

[24] §§ 443(b)(1) and 1362(e)(5)(A).

When termination is *inadvertent*, the Code authorizes the IRS to allow a corporation to continue its S status if the disqualifying action is corrected.[25] It is possible, for example, that if stock is transferred to an ineligible shareholder, the IRS might allow the corporation to correct the violation and continue its S status uninterrupted.

> **Example 10.** On the advice of his attorney, a majority shareholder transferred his S corporation shares to an ineligible trust. When the shareholder discovered the transfer terminated the S corporation election, the error was corrected. The IRS has ruled, under similar circumstances, that the S election was not lost since termination was inadvertent, it occurred as the result of advice from counsel, and it was corrected as soon as the violation of S status was discovered.[26]

Excessive Passive Income. Under the passive income test, the election is terminated if the corporation has[27]

1. Passive investment income exceeding 25 percent of its gross receipts for three consecutive years, and

2. C corporation accumulated earnings and profits (AE&P) at the end of each of the three consecutive years.

If both of these conditions are satisfied, the termination becomes effective at the beginning of the first year following the end of the three-year period.[28]

As reflected in the second condition above, the excessive passive income test is reserved *solely* for corporations that were C corporations prior to becoming S corporations. In addition, the test applies to these former C corporations only if they have AE&P from C years. Accordingly, corporations that have never been C corporations as well as corporations that have distributed all AE&P cannot be terminated because of passive investment income.

Passive investment income generally is defined as gross receipts from royalties, rents, dividends, interest (including tax-exempt interest but excluding interest on notes from sales of inventory), annuities, and gains on sales or exchanges of stock or securities.[29] For this purpose, rents are not considered passive income if significant services are provided (e.g., room rents paid to a hotel).[30] In computing total gross receipts, costs of goods sold, returns and allowances, deductions, and returns of basis are ignored; receipts from the sale of capital assets are

---

[25] § 1362(f).

[26] Rev. Rul. 86-110, 1986-38 I.R.B. 4. Also, see Ltr. Ruls. 8550033 and 8608006.

[27] § 1362(d)(3).

[28] § 1362(d)(3)(A)(ii).

[29] § 1362(d)(3)(D).

[30] Reg. § 1.1372-4(b)(5)(vi).

included but only to the extent of net gains (i.e., capital gains less capital losses). Consequently, there are no gross receipts when the sale of a capital asset results in a net loss.[31]

> **Example 11.** OBJ, an S corporation, was a C corporation for several years before it elected to be taxed under Subchapter S beginning in 1990. For 1990 and 1991, the corporation had excessive passive income. In addition, at the close of 1990 and 1991, OBJ reported a balance in its AE&P that was attributable to its years as a C corporation. OBJ's income and expenses for 1992 are shown below. No distributions from its AE&P were made during the year. The corporation's passive investment income and total gross receipts, based on its reported items, are determined as follows:

	Reported	Gross Receipts	Passive Income
Sales...........................	$200,000	$200,000	$ 0
Cost of goods sold..............	(150,000)	0	0
Interest income.................	30,000	30,000	30,000
Dividends......................	15,000	15,000	15,000
Rental income (passive).........	40,000	40,000	40,000
Rental expenses................	(28,000)	0	0
Gain on sale of stock...........	15,000	15,000	15,000
Total.........................		$300,000	$100,000

Because OBJ's passive investment income exceeds 25% of its gross receipts [$100,000 > (25% × $300,000 = $75,000)] for the third consecutive year and it also has a balance of AE&P at the end of each of those years, the election is terminated beginning on January 1, 1993.

Even though a corporation may avoid having its election terminated by failing the excessive passive income test once every three years, a corporation still may be required to pay a tax on its excessive passive investment income. This tax is explained in detail later in this chapter.

ELECTION AFTER TERMINATION

When the election is terminated, whether voluntarily through revocation or involuntarily through failure to satisfy the Subchapter S or passive income requirements, the corporation normally may not make a new election until the fifth taxable year following the year in which the termination became effective.[32] The five-year wait is unnecessary, however, if the IRS consents to an earlier election. Consent usually is given in two instances: (1) when the corporation's ownership

---

[31] §§ 1362(d)(3)(C) and 1222(9).   [32] § 1362(g).

has changed such that more than 50 percent of the stock is owned by persons who did not own the stock at the time of termination, or (2) when the termination was attributable to an event that was not within the control of the corporation or its majority shareholders.[33]

Example 12. KLZ, an S corporation, was wholly owned by G. The corporation revoked its S election effective on July 17, 1991. KLZ may not make an election until 1996 unless it obtains permission from the IRS. Permission to reelect S status prior to 1996 would be denied since the termination was completely under the control of G. A similar conclusion would be reached if KLZ issued a second class of stock.

Example 13. Same facts as in *Example 12* above. Assume F purchased all of the corporation's stock in 1992 and desired to reelect S status. Since more than 50 percent of the stock is owned by someone who did not own stock during the year the termination took place, the IRS would probably waive the waiting period.

OPERATING THE S CORPORATION

Federal Income Tax Form 1120S must be filed for an S corporation within two and one-half months following the end of its year. For a calendar year S corporation, the due date is March 15. This requirement coincides with that of the C corporation and is one month less than the period allowed a partnership. However, an automatic six-month extension may be obtained by filing Form 7004. This is the same form and privilege granted C corporations. Since the S corporation is a nontaxable entity that serves as a conduit to its owners, a delayed Form 1120S creates problems for all of its shareholders. These problems occur because the S corporation performs the same role as the partnership. That is, it accumulates income, expenses, gains, losses, and credits that flow through to its owners, based on their ownership interests.[34] Unlike the partnership, there is no provision for special allocations among owners. Thus, the one class of stock requirement means that allocations must be identical for each share of stock outstanding.[35] This can be a significant disadvantage when compared with the more flexible rules governing special allocations for partners.[36]

---

[33] Reg. § 1.1372-5(a).

[34] § 1366(a).

[35] § 1377(a).

[36] §§ 704(b)(2) and (c).

Consistent with the aggregate concept that is applied to partnerships, all incidence of taxation (with the exceptions discussed later in this chapter) passes to the stockholders who must report their share of the S corporation items on their own tax returns.[37] The character of the items is retained.[38] Consequently, Form 1120S is an information return that summarizes the income, deductions, credits, gains, and losses to be reported by the shareholders.

Also consistent with the partnership provisions, most special elections are made by the S corporation and not by each shareholder. The exceptions to this general approach are the same as those for the partnership and affect few taxpayers.[39]

DETERMINING S CORPORATION NET INCOME

S corporations generally compute net income, gains, and losses in the same manner as a partnership. There are several important differences, however. Three of these are discussed below.

Payments to Shareholder-Employees.   S corporation shareholders who work for the corporation qualify as employees. As a result, salary paid to a shareholder-employee as well as payroll taxes related to the salary are deductible by the S corporation. Recall from Chapter 22 that partnerships can deduct guaranteed payments for compensation paid to partners. However, these payments are not subject to withholding or payroll taxes.[40]   Instead, a partner's compensation is treated as self-employment income.

> **Example 14.**   An owner who works for the business is paid a $20,000 salary during 1991. Net income *before* the salary and any payroll taxes on it is $60,000. If the business is an S or C corporation, the salary is subject to withholding taxes and the corporation must pay FICA and unemployment taxes on it. Corporate taxes are $1,530 FICA (7.65% × $20,000) and $434 unemployment taxes (6.2% on the first $7,000). Corporate net income is $38,036 ($60,000 − $20,000 − $1,530 − $434). If, however, the business is a partnership, there are no payroll taxes for owner compensation and partnership net income is $40,000 ($60,000 − $20,000), which usually qualifies as self-employment income and is subject to that tax at the partner level.

Section 291 Recapture.   Certain S corporations are subject to the special depreciation recapture rules of § 291(a)(1), while a partnership is not.[41]   Recall from Chapter 19 that § 291 reclassifies some of a corporation's § 1231 gains on depreciable realty from capital gain to ordinary income.

---

[37]   § 1363(a).

[38]   § 1366(b).

[39]   § 1363(c).

[40]   Reg. § 1.707-1(c) and Rev. Rul. 69-148, 1969-1 C.B. 256.

[41]   An S corporation that was a C corporation for any of the three immediately preceding taxable years is subject to § 291. See § 1363(b)(4).

Accounting Methods. Certain entities are prohibited from using the cash method of accounting, and consequently are required to use the accrual method. A C corporation normally cannot use the cash method unless its annual gross receipts average $5 million or less or it is a qualified personal service corporation. In contrast, an S corporation or partnership can use the cash method unless the entity is considered a tax shelter [under § 461(i)] or, in the case of a partnership, has a corporate partner. However, even a partnership with a C corporate partner may use the cash method if the corporate partner meets the annual gross receipts test or is a qualified personal service corporation. (Since an S corporation is prohibited from having a C corporation as an owner, the latter restriction is inapplicable to an S corporation.)

The above exceptions should not be considered all inclusive. As will be seen, there are other differences in the taxation of S corporations and partnerships, many of which are significant.

Reporting S Corporation Income. The similarity between the taxation of S corporations and partnerships becomes readily apparent when Forms 1120S and 1065 are compared. (See Exhibit 23-1 for an illustration of Form 1120S. The numbers are taken from the last example in the Appendix to this chapter.) There is one major difference in computing the net ordinary income on page one of the two tax forms, however. Unlike Form 1065, Form 1120S has a section for computing any taxes due on excessive passive investment income and Schedule D built-in gains (both are discussed in a later section of this chapter).

All income, expenses, gains, losses, and credits that may be subject to special treatment by one or more of the shareholders are reported separately on Schedule K, which is filed with Form 1120S.[42] Schedule K-1 is then prepared for the shareholders' use. (See Exhibit 23-1 for an illustration. The numbers are taken from the last example in the Appendix to this chapter.) Again, these schedules are quite similar to the schedules applicable to partnerships and partners. There are three major differences. Two partnership items are not relevant to S corporations. Since S shareholders can be employees of the corporation, the listing of guaranteed payments on the partnership schedule is inapplicable to the S corporation. In addition, the listing for self-employment income on the partnership schedule is omitted from the S corporation schedule. A shareholder does *not* have self-employment income from the business. Neither a shareholder's salary nor any portion of the corporate net income qualifies as self-employment income.[43] Finally, the S corporation schedule includes a section for reporting distributions. These are divided into two categories: (1) distributions from earnings of the S corporation, and (2) if it has been operated as a C corporation in previous years, distributions from earnings of the C corporation. (Distributions are discussed in a later section of this chapter.)

---

[42]   § 1366(a)(1)(A).

[43]   This is consistent with the C corporation. Note, however, an individual cannot escape FICA taxes completely by receiving "dividends" from the corporation. The IRS takes the position that in such case, a portion *or* all of the purported dividends would be compensation subject to withholding and FICA. See Rev. Rul. 74-44, 1974-1 C.B. 287.

Exhibit 23-1

Form 1120S
Department of the Treasury
Internal Revenue Service

U.S. Income Tax Return for an S Corporation

For calendar year 1990, or tax year beginning _____, 1990, and ending _____, 19 ___.
► See separate instructions.

OMB No. 1545-0130

1990

A Date of election as an S corporation	Use IRS label. Other-wise, please print or type.	Name	C Employer identification number
1-1-90		T COMPANY	88-9138761
B Business code no. (see Specific Instructions)		Number, street, and room or suite no. (If a P.O. box, see page 7 of the instructions.)	D Date incorporated
5651		8122 SOUTH S STREET	1-1-90
		City or town, state, and ZIP code	E Total assets (see Specific Instructions)
		NORFOLK, VA 23508	$ 322,000

F Check applicable boxes: (1) ☑ Initial return   (2) ☐ Final return   (3) ☐ Change in address   (4) ☐ Amended return

G Check this box if this is an S corporation subject to the consolidated audit procedures of sections 6241 through 6245 (see instructions before checking this box) . . ► ☐

H Enter number of shareholders in the corporation at end of the tax year

Caution: Include **only** trade or business income and expenses on lines 1a through 21. See the instructions for more information.

Income

1a Gross receipts or sales	470,000	**b** Less returns and allowances –0– c Bal ► **1c** 470,000
2 Cost of goods sold (Schedule A, line 7)	**2**	300,000
3 Gross profit (subtract line 2 from line 1c)	**3**	170,000
4 Net gain (loss) from Form 4797, Part II, line 18	**4**	
5 Other income (see instructions) (attach schedule)	**5**	
6 **Total** income (loss)—Combine lines 3 through 5 . . . . . . ►	**6**	170,000

Deductions (See instructions for limitations.)

7 Compensation of officers	**7**	24,000
8a Salaries and wages 48,000 **b** Less jobs credit –0– c Bal ►	**8c**	48,000
9 Repairs	**9**	12,000
10 Bad debts	**10**	
11 Rents	**11**	
12 Taxes PROPERTY TAXES = $3,000 ; PAYROLL TAXES = $6,000.	**12**	9,000
13 Interest	**13**	3,300
14a Depreciation (see instructions) **14a** 15,000		
b Depreciation reported on Schedule A and elsewhere on return . . **14b** –0–		
c Subtract line 14b from line 14a	**14c**	15,000
15 Depletion (**Do not deduct oil and gas depletion. See instructions.**) .	**15**	
16 Advertising	**16**	
17 Pension, profit-sharing, etc., plans	**17**	
18 Employee benefit programs LIFE INS.	**18**	1,400
19 Other deductions (attach schedule) UTILITIES TELE. = $2,500 ; OFFICE SUPPLIES = $1,100 ; INSURANCE COSTS = $3,100 . ►	**19**	6,700
20 **Total** deductions—Add lines 7 through 19 . . . . ►	**20**	119,400
21 Ordinary income (loss) from trade or business activities—Subtract line 20 from line 6	**21**	50,600

Tax and Payments

22 **Tax:**		
a Excess net passive income tax (attach schedule) **22a**		
b Tax from Schedule D (Form 1120S) **22b**		
c Add lines 22a and 22b (see instructions for additional taxes)	**22c**	NONE
23 **Payments:**		
a 1990 estimated tax payments **23a**		
b Tax deposited with Form 7004 . . . . **23b**		
c Credit for Federal tax on fuels (attach Form 4136) . . **23c**		
d Add lines 23a through 23c	**23d**	
24 Enter any **penalty** for underpayment of estimated tax—Check ► ☐ if Form 2220 is attached .	**24**	
25 **Tax due**—If the total of lines 22c and 24 is larger than line 23d, enter amount owed. See instructions for depositary method of payment . . . . ►	**25**	NONE
26 **Overpayment**—If line 23d is larger than the total of lines 22c and 24, enter amount overpaid ►	**26**	
27 Enter amount of line 26 you want: **Credited to 1991 estimated tax** ► **Refunded** ►	**27**	

Please Sign Here

Under penalties of perjury, I declare that I have examined this return, including accompanying schedules and statements, and to the best of my knowledge and belief, it is true, correct, and complete. Declaration of preparer (other than taxpayer) is based on all information of which preparer has any knowledge.

► _____ Signature of officer   Date   ► _____ Title

Paid Preparer's Use Only

Preparer's signature ►	Date	Check if self-employed ► ☐	Preparer's social security number
Firm's name (or yours if self-employed) and address ►		E.I. No. ►	
		ZIP code ►	

For Paperwork Reduction Act Notice, see page 1 of separate instructions.   Form **1120S** (1990)

Exhibit 23-1 Continued

Form 1120S (1990)   Page **2**

Schedule A   **Cost of Goods Sold** (See instructions.)   *(a)*

1 Inventory at beginning of year	**1**	
2 Purchases	**2**	
3 Cost of labor	**3**	
4a Additional section 263A costs (see instructions) *(attach schedule)*	**4a**	
b Other costs *(attach schedule)*	**4b**	
5 Total—Add lines 1 through 4b	**5**	
6 Inventory at end of year	**6**	
7 Cost of goods sold—Subtract line 6 from line 5. Enter here and on line 2, page 1	**7**	300,000

8a Check all methods used for valuing closing inventory:
   (i) ☑ Cost
   (ii) ☐ Lower of cost or market as described in Regulations section 1.471-4
   (iii) ☐ Writedown of "subnormal" goods as described in Regulations section 1.471-2(c)
   (iv) ☐ Other (specify method used and attach explanation) ▶ ------------------------------

   b Check this box if the LIFO inventory method was adopted this tax year for any goods *(if checked, attach Form 970)* . . . ▶☐

   c If the LIFO inventory method was used for this tax year, enter percentage (or amounts) of closing inventory computed under LIFO **8c**

   d Do the rules of section 263A (with respect to property produced or acquired for resale) apply to the corporation? . . . ☐ Yes ☑ No

   e Was there any change in determining quantities, cost, or valuations between opening and closing inventory? . . . . ☐ Yes ☑ No
     If "Yes," attach explanation.

Additional Information Required (continued from page 1)

	Yes	No
I Did you at the end of the tax year own, directly or indirectly, 50% or more of the voting stock of a domestic corporation? For rules of attribution, see section 267(c). If "Yes," attach a schedule showing: **(1)** name, address, and employer identification number; and **(2)** percentage owned.		✓
J Refer to the list in the instructions and state your principal: **(1)** Business activity ▶ *5651* **(2)** Product or service ▶ *CLOTHING-RETAIL*		
K Were you a member of a controlled group subject to the provisions of section 1561?		✓
L At any time during the tax year, did you have an interest in or a signature or other authority over a financial account in a foreign country (such as a bank account, securities account, or other financial account)? (See instructions for exceptions and filing requirements for form TD F 90-22.1.)		✓
If "Yes," enter the name of the foreign country ▶		
M Were you the grantor of, or transferor to, a foreign trust that existed during the current tax year, whether or not you have any beneficial interest in it? If "Yes," you may have to file Forms 3520, 3520-A, or 926		✓
N During this tax year did you maintain any part of your accounting/tax records on a computerized system?		✓

O Check method of accounting: **(1)** ☐ Cash   **(2)** ☑ Accrual   **(3)** ☐ Other (specify) ▶ ---------------------------

P Check this box if the S corporation has filed or is required to file **Form 8264,** Application for Registration of a Tax Shelter   ▶☐

Q Check this box if the corporation issued publicly offered debt instruments with original issue discount . . . . . ▶☐
   If so, the corporation may have to file **Form 8281,** Information Return for Publicly Offered Original Issue Discount Instruments.

R If the corporation: **(1)** filed its election to be an S corporation after 1986, **(2)** was a C corporation before it elected to be an S corporation **or** the corporation acquired an asset with a basis determined by reference to its basis (or the basis of any other property) in the hands of a C corporation, and **(3)** has net unrealized built-in gain (defined in section 1374(d)(1)) in excess of the net recognized built-in gain from prior years, enter the net unrealized built-in gain reduced by net recognized built-in gain from prior years (see instructions) . . . . ▶ $ -----------------

S Check this box if the corporation had subchapter C earnings and profits at the close of the tax year (see instructions) ▶☐

Designation of Tax Matters Person (See instructions.)

Enter below the shareholder designated as the tax matters person (TMP) for the tax year of this return:

Name of designated TMP ▶   Identifying number of TMP ▶

Address of designated TMP ▶ _____

(a) lines 1 through 6 must be completed before the return is filed.

Exhibit 23-1 Continued

Form 1120S (1990)   Page **3**

Schedule K	Shareholders' Shares of Income, Credits, Deductions, Etc.		
	(a) Pro rata share items		**(b) Total amount**

Income (Loss)	1	Ordinary income (loss) from trade or business activities (page 1, line 21)	1	50,600
	2	Net income (loss) from rental real estate activities *(attach Form 8825)*	2	
	3a	Gross income from other rental activities . . . . [3a]		
	b	Less expenses *(attach schedule)* . . . . [3b]		
	c	Net income (loss) from other rental activities	3c	
	4	Portfolio income (loss):		
	a	Interest income	4a	3,300
	b	Dividend income	4b	2,000
	c	Royalty income	4c	
	d	Net short-term capital gain (loss) *(attach Schedule D (Form 1120S))* $3,000 + $2,200	4d	
	e	Net long-term capital gain (loss) *(attach Schedule D (Form 1120S))* -$1200	4e	4,000
	f	Other portfolio income (loss) *(attach schedule)*	4f	
	5	Net gain (loss) under section 1231 (other than due to casualty or theft) *(attach Form 4797)*	5	
	6	Other income (loss) *(attach schedule)*	6	
Deductions	7	Charitable contributions (see instructions) *(attach list)*	7	7,000
	8	Section 179 expense deduction *(attach Form 4562)*	8	
	9	Deductions related to portfolio income (loss) (see instructions) (itemize) . . .	9	
	10	Other deductions *(attach schedule)*	10	
Investment Interest	11a	Interest expense on investment debts	11a	
	b	(1) Investment income included on lines 4a through 4f above . . .	11b(1)	
		(2) Investment expenses included on line 9 above	11b(2)	
Credits	12a	Credit for alcohol used as a fuel *(attach Form 6478)*	12a	
	b	Low-income housing credit (see instructions):		
		(1) From partnerships to which section 42(j)(5) applies for property placed in service before 1990.	12b(1)	
		(2) Other than on line 12b(1) for property placed in service before 1990	12b(2)	
		(3) From partnerships to which section 42(j)(5) applies for property placed in service after 1989	12b(3)	
		(4) Other than on line 12b(3) for property placed in service after 1989	12b(4)	
	c	Qualified rehabilitation expenditures related to rental real estate activities *(attach Form 3468)*	12c	
	d	Credits (other than credits shown on lines 12b and 12c) related to rental real estate activities (see instructions)	12d	
	e	Credits related to other rental activities (see instructions)	12e	
	13	Other credits (see instructions) *REHABILITATION CREDIT*	13	2,000
Adjustments and Tax Preference Items	14a	Accelerated depreciation of real property placed in service before 1987 . .	14a	
	b	Accelerated depreciation of leased personal property placed in service before 1987 . . .	14b	
	c	Depreciation adjustment on property placed in service after 1986	14c	
	d	Depletion (other than oil and gas)	14d	
	e	(1) Gross income from oil, gas, or geothermal properties	14e(1)	
		(2) Deductions allocable to oil, gas, or geothermal properties . . .	14e(2)	
	f	Other adjustments and tax preference items *(attach schedule)*	14f	
Foreign Taxes	15a	Type of income ▶		
	b	Name of foreign country or U.S. possession ▶		
	c	Total gross income from sources outside the U.S. *(attach schedule)* . . .	15c	
	d	Total applicable deductions and losses *(attach schedule)*	15d	
	e	Total foreign taxes (check one): ▶ ☐ Paid ☐ Accrued	15e	
	f	Reduction in taxes available for credit *(attach schedule)*	15f	
	g	Other foreign tax information *(attach schedule)*	15g	
Other Items	16a	Total expenditures to which a section 59(e) election may apply	16a	
	b	Type of expenditures ▶		
	17	Total property distributions (including cash) other than dividends reported on line 19 below	17	22,000 (a)
	18	Other items and amounts required to be reported separately to shareholders (see instructions) *(attach schedule)*		
	19	Total dividend distributions paid from accumulated earnings and profits . . .	19	
	20	Income (loss) (Required only if Schedule M-1 must be completed.)—Combine lines 1 through 6 in column (b). From the result subtract the sum of lines 7 through 11a, 15e, and 16a . . .	20	

(a) $12,000 CASH + $10,000 FAIR MKT. VALUE OF LAND = $22,000.

Exhibit 23-1 Continued

Form 1120S (1990) — Page 4

Schedule L — Balance Sheets

Assets	Beginning of tax year (a)	(b)	End of tax year (c)	(d)
1 Cash				
2a Trade notes and accounts receivable				
b Less allowance for bad debts				
3 Inventories				
4 U.S. government obligations				
5 Tax-exempt securities				
6 Other current assets (attach schedule)				
7 Loans to shareholders				
8 Mortgage and real estate loans				
9 Other investments (attach schedule)				
10a Buildings and other depreciable assets				
b Less accumulated depreciation				
11a Depletable assets				
b Less accumulated depletion				
12 Land (net of any amortization)				
13a Intangible assets (amortizable only)				
b Less accumulated amortization				
14 Other assets (attach schedule)				
15 Total assets				322,000

Liabilities and Shareholders' Equity

	(a)	(b)	(c)	(d)
16 Accounts payable				
17 Mortgages, notes, bonds payable in less than 1 year				
18 Other current liabilities (attach schedule)				
19 Loans from shareholders				
20 Mortgages, notes, bonds payable in 1 year or more				
21 Other liabilities (attach schedule)				
22 Capital stock				
23 Paid-in or capital surplus				
24 Retained earnings				
25 Less cost of treasury stock		( )		( )
26 Total liabilities and shareholders' equity				322,000

Schedule M-1 — Reconciliation of Income per Books With Income per Return (You are not required to complete this schedule if the total assets on line 15, column (d), of Schedule L are less than $25,000.)

1 Net income per books
2 Income included on Schedule K, lines 1 through 6, not recorded on books this year (itemize): _____
3 Expenses recorded on books this year not included on Schedule K, lines 1 through 11a, 15e, and 16a (itemize):
  a Depreciation $ _____
  b Travel and entertainment $ _____
4 Total of lines 1 through 3

5 Income recorded on books this year not included on Schedule K, lines 1 through 6 (itemize):
  a Tax-exempt interest $ _____
6 Deductions included on Schedule K, lines 1 through 11a, 15e, and 16a, not charged against book income this year (itemize):
  a Depreciation $ _____
7 Total of lines 5 and 6
8 Income (loss) (Schedule K, line 20)—Line 4 less line 7

Schedule M-2 — Analysis of Accumulated Adjustments Account, Other Adjustments Account, and Shareholders' Undistributed Taxable Income Previously Taxed (c) (See instructions.)

	(a) Accumulated adjustments account	(b) Other adjustments account	(c) Shareholders' undistributed taxable income previously taxed
1 Balance at beginning of tax year	50,600		
2 Ordinary income from page 1, line 21	9,300 (a)		
3 Other additions			
4 Loss from page 1, line 21	( )		
5 Other reductions	( )	( )	
6 Combine lines 1 through 5			
7 Distributions other than dividend distributions	29,700 (b)		
8 Balance at end of tax year—subtract line 7 from line 6			

(a) $3,300 INTEREST INC. + $2,000 DIVIDENDS + $4,000 NLTCG = $9,300.

(b) $12,000 CASH + $10,000 FAIR MKT. VALUE LAND + $7,000 CHARITABLE CONTRIBUTION + $700 T's LIFE INS. = $29,700.

(c) SCHEDULES L AND M MUST BE COMPLETED BEFORE THE RETURN IS FILED.

Exhibit 23-1 Continued

SCHEDULE K-1 (Form 1120S) Department of the Treasury Internal Revenue Service	**Shareholder's Share of Income, Credits, Deductions, Etc.** ▶ See separate instructions. For calendar year 1990 or tax year beginning , 1990, and ending , 19	OMB No. 1545-0130 19**90**

Shareholder's identifying number ▶	Corporation's identifying number ▶
Shareholder's name, address, and ZIP code ADOLPH Z. T. 1291 MAPLE DRIVE NORFOLK, VA 23508	Corporation's name, address, and ZIP code T COMPANY 8122 SOUTH S STREET NORFOLK, VA 23508

A Shareholder's percentage of stock ownership for tax year (see Instructions for Schedule K-1) . . . . ▶ _100_ %
B Internal Revenue Service Center where corporation filed its return ▶ _MEMPHIS, TN_
C (1) Tax shelter registration number (see Instructions for Schedule K-1) . . . . ▶ ....
     (2) Type of tax shelter ▶ ....
D If the shareholder acquired corporate stock after 10/22/86, check here ▶ ☐ and enter the shareholder's weighted percentage increase in stock ownership for 1990 (see Instructions for Schedule K-1) . . . . ▶ .... %
E If any activity for which income or loss is reported on line 1, 2, or 3, was started or acquired by the corporation after 10/22/86, check here ▶ ☐ and enter the date of start up or acquisition in the date space on line 1, 2, or 3 **below.**
F Check applicable boxes: **(1)** ☐ Final K-1   **(2)** ☐ Amended K-1

	(a) Pro rata share items		(b) Amount	(c) Form 1040 filers enter the amount in column (b) on:
Income (Loss)	**1** Ordinary income (loss) from trade or business activities. If applicable, enter date asked for in item E . . . . ▶ _1-1-90_	**1**	_50,600_	See Shareholder's Instructions for Schedule K-1 (Form 1120S).
	2 Net income (loss) from rental real estate activities. If applicable, enter date asked for in item E . . . . ▶	**2**		
	3 Net income (loss) from other rental activities. If applicable, enter date asked for in item E . . . . ▶	**3**		
	4 Portfolio income (loss):			
	a Interest	**4a**	_3,300_	Sch. B, Part I, line 1
	b Dividends	**4b**	_2,000_	Sch. B, Part II, line 5
	c Royalties	**4c**		Sch. E, Part I, line 4
	d Net short-term capital gain (loss)	**4d**		Sch. D, line 5, col. (f) or (g)
	e Net long-term capital gain (loss)	**4e**	_4,000_	Sch. D, line 12, col. (f) or (g)
	f Other portfolio income (loss) *(attach schedule)*	**4f**		(Enter on applicable line of your return.)
	5 Net gain (loss) under section 1231 (other than due to casualty or theft)	**5**		See Shareholder's Instructions for Schedule K-1 (Form 1120S).
	6 Other income (loss) *(attach schedule)*	**6**		(Enter on applicable line of your return.)
Deductions	**7** Charitable contributions	**7**	_7,000_	Sch. A, line 14 or 15
	8 Section 179 expense deduction *(attach schedule)*	**8**		See Shareholder's Instructions for Schedule K-1 (Form 1120S).
	9 Deductions related to portfolio income (loss) *(attach schedule)* .	**9**		
	10 Other deductions *(attach schedule)*	**10**		
Investment Interest	**11a** Interest expense on investment debts	**11a**		Form 4952, line 1
	b (1) Investment income included on lines 4a through 4f above .	**b(1)**		See Shareholder's Instructions for Schedule K-1 (Form 1120S).
	(2) Investment expenses included on line 9 above	**b(2)**		
Credits	**12a** Credit for alcohol used as fuel	**12a**		Form 6478, line 10
	b Low-income housing credit:			
	(1) From section 42(j)(5) partnerships for property placed in service before 1990	**b(1)**		Form 8586, line 5
	(2) Other than on line 12b(1) for property placed in service before 1990 .	**b(2)**		
	(3) From section 42(j)(5) partnerships for property placed in service after 1989 .	**b(3)**		
	(4) Other than on line 12b(3) for property placed in service after 1989 .	**b(4)**		
	c Qualified rehabilitation expenditures related to rental real estate activities (see instructions) _CREDIT_	**12c**		
	d Credits (other than credits shown on lines 12b and 12c) related to rental real estate activities (see instructions)	**12d**		See Shareholder's Instructions for Schedule K-1 (Form 1120S).
	e Credits related to other rental activities (see instructions) . . .	**12e**		
	13 Other credits (see instructions) _REHABILITATION CREDIT_ . .	**13**	_2,000_	

For Paperwork Reduction Act Notice, see Form 1120S Instructions.   Schedule K-1 (Form 1120S) 1990

ALLOCATIONS TO SHAREHOLDERS

All S corporation items are allocated among the shareholders based on their *ownership percentage* of the outstanding stock on each day of the year.[44] Thus, a shareholder owning 20 percent of the outstanding stock all year is deemed to have received 20 percent of *each item*. The allocation rate can be changed only by increasing or decreasing the percentage of stock ownership. This precludes shareholders from dividing net income or losses in any other manner. Of course, a certain amount of special allocation can be achieved through salaries and other business payments to owners. If there is no change in stock ownership during the year, each item to be allocated is multiplied by the percentage of stock owned by each shareholder. There is *one* exception: actual distributions of assets are assigned to the shareholder who receives them.

> **Example 15.** M owns 100 of an S corporation's 1,000 shares of common stock outstanding. Neither the number of shares outstanding nor the number owned by M has changed during the year. The S corporation items for its calendar year are allocated to M, based on her 10% ownership interest, as follows:
>
> | | Totals on Schedule K | M's 10% on Schedule K-1 |
> | --- | --- | --- |
> | Ordinary income (from page 1) | $70,000 | $7,000 |
> | Net capital gain | 2,000 | 200 |
> | Charitable contributions | 4,000 | 400 |
>
> In addition, cash distributions from S earnings are $20 for each 1% stock ownership, paid on the last day of each month. Thus, M received $2,400 ($20 × 12 months × 10 units of 1%).

If the ownership of stock changes during the year, there are two methods for determining the allocations for those shareholders whose interests have changed. These are: (1) the *per day allocation method*, and (2) the *interim closing of books* method. The per day allocation method must be used unless the shareholder completely terminates his or her interest in the S corporation. When an owner's interest is terminated, shareholders may elect to use either method. It should be noted that these same methods apply when the S election is terminated and items must be prorated between the former S corporation and the new C corporation.

---

[44]   §§ 1366(a) and 1377(a).

Per-Day Allocation. This method assigns an equal amount of the S items to each day of the year.[45] When a shareholder's interest changes, the shareholder must report a pro rata share of each item for each day that the stock was owned. This computation may be expressed as follows:

$$\text{Percentage of shares owned} \times \text{Percentage of year stock was owned} = \text{Portion of item to be reported}$$

Example 16. Assume the same facts as in *Example 15*, except that M sold all of her shares on August 8. Since the S corporation uses the calendar year, M has held 100 shares for 219 days or 60% of the year (219 ÷ 365). (The day of sale is not an ownership day for M.) Based on the per day allocation method, M's share of the S corporation items is as follows:

	Totals on Schedule K	M's 10% on Schedule K-1
Ordinary income (from page 1)................	$70,000	$4,200
Net capital gain..............................	2,000	120
Charitable contributions.......................	4,000	240
Total distributions (from S earnings)...........	24,000	1,400

The computations for M's share are the totals on Schedule K *multiplied by* her 10% ownership interest *multiplied by* her ownership period of 219 days, or 60% of the year. For example, $70,000 × 10% = $7,000 × 60% = $4,200. M received cash distributions of $1,400 ($20 × 7 months × 10 units).

The per day allocation method also is applicable for a shareholder whose stock interest varies during the year.

Example 17. Assume the same facts as in *Example 16*, except M only sold 20 shares on August 8. Thus, she owned 10% of the business the first 219 days and 8% the remaining 146 days. Based on the per day allocation method, her share of the S corporation items is as follows:

	Totals on Schedule K	M's Share 10%	M's Share 8%	Schedule K-1
Ordinary income (from page 1)...............	$70,000	$4,200	$2,240	$6,440
Net capital gain................	2,000	120	64	184
Charitable contributions.........	4,000	240	128	368
Total distributions (from S earnings)............	24,000	1,400	800	2,200

---

[45]   § 1377(a)(1).

The computations for the last 146 days are the totals on Schedule K *multiplied by* her 8% ownership interest *multiplied by* her ownership period of 146 days, or 40% (146 ÷ 365) of the year. For example, $70,000 × 8% = $5,600 × 40% = $2,240. The amount on Schedule K-1 is M's 10% share *plus* her 8% share. For example, $4,200 + $2,240 = $6,440.

Interim Closing of the Books.   As noted above, the per day method must be used unless the shareholder's interest completely terminates. If there is a complete termination of a shareholder's interest, an election may be made to use the interim closing of books method instead of the per day allocation method.[46] This election means the S corporation's taxable year ends when the shareholder's interest is terminated. As a result, the year is divided into two short taxable years and all owners report the actual dollar amounts that were accumulated while they owned their shares. A valid election requires that all parties who owned a share of stock during either part of the year must agree to the election.

Example 18.   Assume the same facts as in *Example 16*, except the interim closing of books method is elected. Since M sells all of her shares on August 8, the S corporation's year ends the day before on August 7. Corporate records show the following amounts for the first 219 days, for the last 146 days, and M's share for the first 219 days.

	First 219 days	Last 146 days	M's 10% on Schedule K-1
Ordinary income (from page 1)	$15,000	$55,000	$1,500
Net capital gain........................	1,000	1,000	100
Charitable contributions................	0	4,000	0
Total distributions (from S earnings)....	14,000	10,000	1,400

The computations for M's share are the amounts for the first 219 days *multiplied by* her 10% ownership interest.

It is also possible for an S corporation to have an ordinary loss for part of the year and ordinary income for the remaining period.

The differences in the tax effect of the two methods of dividing S corporation items between exiting shareholders and successor shareholders can be substantial. As a result, the method used could have an impact on the value of the stock being sold or exchanged. All parties involved should be aware of the risks being taken under either method. For example, the exiting shareholder has considerable risk under the per day allocation method. If the S corporation is more profitable than expected in the remaining portion of the year, the former shareholder reports more income than expected while the benefits of these additional profits accrue to the new owner. Of course, the reverse also can be true.

---

[46]   §§ 1377(a)(2) and 302(a)(2)(A)(i).

Although the interim closing of the books method can be elected only when a shareholder's interest is completely terminated, there are other times when it might be preferred to the per day allocation method. For example, it might be desirable when stock is issued to a new shareholder. Fortunately, this may be accomplished through tax planning. First, note that *any* termination of a shareholder's interest qualifies regardless of the number of shares involved. Therefore, when possible, S corporations should have a shareholder who owns just one share of stock. Then, when a complete termination is desired, the interest of this shareholder can be terminated rather easily. To prevent any unexpected results, the shareholder's agreement should clearly define when the interim closing of books method is to be elected.[47]

LOSSES OF THE S CORPORATION

One of the most common reasons a corporation elects Subchapter S status is because of the tax treatment for corporate losses. Recall that the C corporation's benefits are limited to those available from carrying the losses to another year to offset income. Refunds may be obtained to the extent *prior* year income is offset while losses carried to future years reduce the taxes due in those years. Frequently, these carryover benefits provide little or no value to the corporation. For example, many businesses report losses in the first few years, meaning that the carryback privilege would be useless. In addition, many new businesses are never successful. But, even those that are successful receive no tax benefit from their losses currently—generally when the need is the greatest. *Future* tax savings do not provide cash to pay present bills. When the cash for the tax savings is finally received, its purchasing power is diminished because of the time value of money.

The aggregate theory that is applied to S corporations can be a significant advantage when a corporation has a net loss. Based on the flow through concept, shareholders include their distributive shares of the S corporation's losses in their taxable income currently. Thus, the deduction for losses is transferred to the shareholder and generally results in tax savings for the current year. Even if a shareholder is unable to use the loss currently, carryover provisions also apply to an individual's net operating losses (including those from S corporations, partnerships, proprietorships, personal casualties and thefts, and suspended passive business losses—see discussion in Chapter 22). Of course, net capital losses can only be carried forward by individuals.

---

[47] Lorence L. Bravenec, "The Subchapter S Revision Act of 1982 (Part II)," *The Tax Adviser* 14 (May, 1983), p. 281.

Limitations. Each shareholder's distributive share of net losses may not exceed that shareholder's basis in the corporation. Any losses that exceed a shareholder's basis may be carried forward indefinitely to be used when the shareholder's basis is increased.[48] When basis is insufficient and there is more than one item that reduces basis, the flow through of each item is determined in a pro rata manner. In addition, any items that increase basis flow through to the owner before any items that reduce basis, including distributions on stock.[49]

Example 19. G owns 200 of an S corporation's 1,000 shares of common stock outstanding. Neither the number of shares outstanding nor those owned by G has changed during the year. The S corporation items for its calendar year are allocated to G, based on his 20% ownership interest, as follows:

	Totals on Schedule K	G's 20% on Schedule K-1
Ordinary loss (from page 1)............	($70,000)	($14,000)
Net capital loss.......................	(5,000)	(1,000)
Section 1231 gain....................	10,000	2,000

First, G's basis is increased by the $2,000 § 1231 gain. If G's basis in the S corporation after the $2,000 increase is at least $15,000, all of the ordinary loss and capital loss flow through to be reported on his personal return. However, if his basis after the $2,000 increase is $12,000, only $12,000 of the loss is deductible, and it must be prorated. G may report ordinary loss of $11,200 ($14,000 ÷ $15,000 × $12,000 basis) and net capital loss of $800 ($12,000 − $11,200). The remaining ordinary loss of $2,800 and net capital loss of $200 are carried forward to be used at the end of the first year that G's basis increases.

The above allocation of losses is applicable to all losses and separate deductions (e.g., charitable contributions and state income taxes) for owners of both the S corporation and the partnership.

Generally, no carryovers from a C corporation may be used during the years it is taxed as an S corporation (or vice versa). For example, a C corporation with a net operating loss may not use it to offset income in an S year. There is one

---

[48] § 1366(d)(2). Losses may also be subject to limitation under § 465 at-risk rules and § 469 passive activity rules.

[49] § 1366(d)(1).

exception: C corporate NOLs may be used to offset the S corporation's built-in gains (discussed later in this chapter).[50] The S years are counted, however, when determining the expiration period of the carryover. Thus, a carryback of three years means three fiscal or calendar years regardless of whether the corporation was taxed under Subchapter C or S.[51]

RELATIONSHIP BETWEEN AN S CORPORATION AND ITS SHAREHOLDERS

The S corporation is a legal entity, distinctly separate from its owners. As a result, transactions between an S corporation and its shareholders are treated as though occurring between unrelated parties unless otherwise provided. Of course, these transactions must be conducted in an arm's-length manner, based on market values that would be used by unrelated parties.

TRANSACTIONS BETWEEN S CORPORATIONS AND THEIR SHAREHOLDERS

Contributions of property for stock follow the C corporate rules (see Chapter 19). That is, they are nontaxable *only if* the persons involved in the transaction own at least 80 percent of the corporation after the transfer is completed.[52] This generally means a new corporation can be formed with nontaxable exchanges of assets for stock. However, this restriction often results in taxable transfers for similar exchanges when the corporation has been in existence for some time.

Owners may engage in *taxable transactions* with their S corporations. For example, shareholders may lend money, rent property, or sell assets to their S corporations (or vice versa). With few exceptions, owners include the interest income, rent income, or gain or loss from these transactions on their tax returns. Meanwhile, the S corporation is allowed a deduction for the interest, rent, or depreciation expense on assets purchased (if applicable).

> **Example 20.** During the year, K received the following amounts from an S corporation in which she owns 30% of the stock outstanding:
>
> 1. $2,750 interest on a $25,000 loan made to the corporation;
>
> 2. $3,600 rental income from a storage building rented to the corporation; and
>
> 3. $6,300 for special tools sold to the corporation; the tools were acquired for personal use two years ago for $5,800.

---

[50] § 1374(b)(2).

[51] §§ 1371(b) and 1362(e)(6)(A).

[52] § 351. See Chapter 19 for the requirements of tax-free transfers to controlled corporations.

Assume that the S corporation's net ordinary income, excluding the above items, is $40,000, and the depreciation deduction for the tools is $900. Thus, net income for the corporation, after the above three items are considered, is $32,750 ($40,000 − $2,750 − $3,600 − $900). K's income is $2,750 interest, $3,600 rental income, $500 capital gain on sale of a nonbusiness asset ($6,300 − $5,800), and $9,825 ordinary income from the S corporation (30% × $32,750).

There is a restriction, however, on when an S corporation may deduct expenses owed but not paid to a shareholder. An accrual basis business (whether an S corporation or partnership) may not deduct expenses owed to a cash basis owner until the amount is paid.[53]

> **Example 21.**   Assume the same facts as in *Example 20*, except that $2,000 of the $2,750 interest is accrued but not paid at the end of 1990, the S corporation is on the accrual basis, and K is on the cash basis. The interest owed is paid as follows: $600, March 1, 1991; $400, August 10, 1991; $550, October 15, 1991; and $450, January 10, 1992. K reports the interest when received and the S corporation deducts the interest when paid. Assuming both use the calendar year, the amounts are $750 in 1990, $1,550 ($600 + $400 + $550) in 1991, and $450 in 1992.

Two special rules governing related party transactions affect all business forms. Both are discussed in Chapter 22. *First*, realized *losses* on sales between related parties are disallowed.[54] This is not a deferral; therefore, there is no carryover of basis or holding period. However, if this property is later sold at a gain, the gain is offset by the previously disallowed losses.[55] *Second*, recognized gains on sales between related parties of *property* that will be *depreciable* to the new owner are taxed as ordinary income.[56] A related party is defined as one who owns directly or indirectly more than 50 percent of the business when losses are disallowed or when depreciable property is involved. (See the discussion and examples in Chapter 22 regarding these transactions and the definitions of related parties.) A *third* restriction, affecting transactions between partners and their 50 percent owned partnerships, is *not* applicable to either S or C corporations. For these partners, recognized gains on sales of capital assets that will not be capital assets to the partnership are taxed as ordinary income.[57] In contrast, shareholders may sell capital assets to their more than 50 percent owned S or C corporations and the gain is capital, as long as the assets will not be depreciable property to the corporation.

---

[53] §§ 267(a)(2) and 267(e). This same restriction applies to a C corporation if its cash basis shareholders own more than 50 percent of its stock. § 267(b)(10).

[54] §§ 267 and 707(b)(1).

[55] § 267(d).

[56] § 1239.

[57] § 707(b)(2).

DETERMINING SHAREHOLDER BASIS

A shareholder's basis in the S corporation is computed in much the same way as the partner's basis in the partnership.[58] There are three important exceptions, however (see Exhibit 23-2 for a comparison of the partner's basis in the partnership with the shareholder's basis in the S corporation).

First, recall that an S shareholder's contribution of appreciated assets for stock is tax-free with a carryover of basis *only if* the 80 percent of stock ownership rule is met.[59] If it is not met, basis begins with a taxable exchange, and thus is equal to the market value of noncash assets (i.e., basis of the assets plus gain recognized on the contribution).

Second, an S shareholder's basis does *not* include a proportionate share of corporate debt nor does it include any personal guarantees of corporate debt. Instead, it includes all corporate debt owed to this particular shareholder (i.e., this shareholder's receivables from the S corporation).[60] Annual adjustments to basis are required for any increases or decreases in these receivables but no adjustments (nor gain recognition) are required for changes in corporate debt owed to anyone else. To properly apply the rules, shareholders must compute their basis in S stock separately from their basis in the receivables. Most adjustments that affect a shareholder's basis are made to the *stock*. A shareholder's basis in the receivables is adjusted *only* (1) when the actual indebtedness itself changes, (2) when corporate net losses exceed the shareholder's basis in S stock, and (3) to restore any basis reduction due to the flow through of net losses. The third adjustment can be made only with net income and gains earned in subsequent years. The receivable/debt basis is the last to be reduced *but* the first to be restored.

> **Example 22.** An S corporation incurs a net operating loss of $30,000 in 1991. L, its sole shareholder, has a basis in the stock of $24,000 and a note due him from the corporation totals $10,000. The $30,000 loss flows through to L, first to the extent of his $24,000 stock basis and the remaining $6,000 because of the $10,000 note owed to him. After the appropriate adjustments, his basis is zero for the stock and $4,000 ($10,000 − $6,000) for the note. (If the 1991 loss had been $36,000, only $34,000 would be deductible by L, reducing his basis in both items to zero. The remaining $2,000 loss would be carried forward indefinitely until a positive basis occurs in either item.)

> **Example 23.** Refer to *Example 22*. The S corporation has net income of $3,000 in 1992 and $8,000 in 1993. L reports the $3,000 in 1992 and increases his basis in the note to $7,000 ($4,000 + $3,000). L reports the $8,000 in 1993 and increases his basis in the note to its face amount of $10,000 ($7,000 + $3,000) and in the stock to $5,000 ($8,000 − $3,000 to the note).

---

[58]   § 1367.

[59]   §§ 351 and 358.

[60]   § 1367(b)(2).

Exhibit 23-2
Adjustments to Ownership Basis
(with emphasis added to highlight differences)

Partner's Basis in the Partnership	*Shareholder's Basis in the S Corporation*
Initial investment	Initial investment
Plus: 1. Basis of additional capital contributions	**Plus:** 1. Same as partner
2. *Share of partnership liabilities* (adjusted annually)	2. None *except total receivables due from the corporation* (adjusted annually) can be used for distributions of losses.
3. Share of taxable income	3. Same as partner
4. Share of separately stated income and gains	4. Same as partner but also *including gain recognized on distribution of noncash assets*
5. Share of nontaxable income and gains	5. Same as partner
6. Gain recognized by the partner (when cash received exceeds basis)	6. Same as partner
Less: 1. Cash distributions received (including *share of decreases in partnership liabilities*)	**Less:** 1. Cash distributions received (and for distributions of losses and *decreases in debt owed to this shareholder*)
2. *Basis* of noncash distributions received *(but not to exceed basis)*	2. *Market value* of noncash distributions received *(any amount in excess of basis is recognized capital gain)*
3. Share of net loss (but not to exceed basis)	3. Same as partner
4. Share of separately stated expenses and losses (but not to exceed basis)	4. Same as partner
5. Share of nondeductible expenses and losses (but not to exceed basis and not a capital expenditure)	5. Same as partner
6. Dispositions of ownership interest	6. Same as partner

After a shareholder's basis in the indebtedness is reduced, repayments of the debt in excess of basis result in includible income. If the debt is a note, bond, or other written debt instrument, the shareholder recognizes capital gain to the extent the payment exceeds basis.[61] If the debt is an *open* account, the shareholder recognizes ordinary income.[62] This ordinary income can be recharacterized as capital gain by converting the open account to a capital contribution; no gain is recognized for this conversion, even if the open account has been reduced by net losses (i.e., its basis is less than its face or market value).[63]

Third, as illustrated later, the distribution of noncash assets (i.e., property) requires the S corporation to recognize gain to the extent that market value exceeds an asset's basis.[64] The basis of the appreciated property to the recipient shareholders is its market value. Thus, a shareholder's basis in the S corporation is increased by his or her proportionate share of the recognized gain and decreased by the market value of assets received. If the market values of these assets exceed the owner's basis in the business, the excess is capital gain from the sale of stock (illustrated later in this chapter with distributions).[65]

OUTSIDE VERSUS INSIDE BASIS

When a shareholder sells his or her interest in the S corporation, any gain or loss reported by the seller has no effect on the business or the purchaser. This can create an inequity for the purchaser, especially if the S corporation has appreciated assets. In this situation, the purchase price is based on the market value of the assets but the new owner must accept the seller's basis in the assets for calculating depreciation, amortization, depletion, and gain or loss. This causes the new owner to report more net income (or less loss) from the S corporation. Further confusing the situation, this shareholder's *outside basis* (basis in the S corporation stock) exceeds his or her *inside basis* (share of the corporation's basis in its net assets). This situation is similar to the one encountered in a partnership.

Example 24. An S corporation (or a partnership) has the following information:

	Basis	Market Value
Cash	$10,000	$ 10,000
Equipment	80,000	140,000
Capital accounts	$90,000	$150,000

---

[61] § 1232 and Rev. Rul. 64-162, 1964-1 C.B. 304.

[62] Rev. Rul. 68-537, 1968-2 C.B. 372 and *Cornelius v. U.S.*, 74-1 USTC ¶9446, 33 AFTR2d 74-1331, 494 F.2d 465 (CA-5, 1974).

[63] §§ 108(e)(6) and (d)(7)(C).

[64] §§ 311(b) and 336(a).

[65] § 1368(b).

R purchases T's one-third interest for $50,000. If T's basis is $30,000, she will recognize a gain of $20,000 ($50,000 − $30,000). R's basis in the business is his purchase price of $50,000. However, his share of the corporation's (or partnership's) basis in the net assets is $30,000 (one-third of $90,000). R's annual net income will be determined in the same manner as that of the other owners. That is, depreciation, gain, and loss on the equipment will be calculated on the $80,000 basis.

The inequities encountered by the new owner are quite similar to those that exist when an owner contributes appreciated property in a nontaxable exchange for a capital interest. Since there is no provision for correcting these inequities, the new shareholder should be aware of their impact before the transactions are completed. In contrast, recall that there is a special allocation available to partnerships for correcting both types of inequities (see Chapter 22). These two differences can be a significant disadvantage for the S corporation when compared with the partnership form.

SELECTING A TAXABLE YEAR

With few exceptions, owners report their share of S corporation (or partnership) income, deductions, and credits as of the business's year-end regardless of when distributions of assets are actually made.[66] This timing requirement makes the selection of a year-end for the owners and the business an important tax planning decision.

Generally, it is a tax advantage to defer all includible income as long as possible but to accelerate the deduction of all expenses, losses, and credits. The basic rule is, of course, dependent upon the current and future tax positions of the owners. If operations are expected to result in net losses in the early years, the greatest benefit would be achieved by electing a business year that coincides with that of the owners. In this way, owners would be able to recognize their distributive shares of the losses currently. This benefit, of course, would be reversed in years when operations result in net income. When there is net income, the ideal business year would end one month after that of the owners. However, owners do not always have the freedom to elect the ideal year-end for their S corporations.

S corporations, like partnerships, generally are restricted to two types of taxable years.[67] First, an S corporation may use the calendar year.[68] Second, a fiscal year that is a *natural business year* may be used. This second option requires that, during the three previous years, more than 25 percent of the gross business receipts must have been earned the last two months of the selected fiscal year.

---

[66] §§ 706(a) and 1378.

[67] § 1378(b).

[68] § 1378.

Example 25. An S corporation is organized November 1, 1991. Its net ordinary income for the first 14 months is as follows:

November 1, 1991–December 31, 1991	$ 20,000
January 1, 1992–October 31, 1992	200,000
November 1, 1992–December 31, 1992	40,000

All shareholders report on the calendar year. If the S corporation's year-end also is December 31, the owners have includible income of $20,000 in 1991 and $240,000 ($200,000 + $40,000) in 1992. Based on the second option listed above, if the S corporation receives permission for an October 31 year-end, the owners have no includible income in 1991 but have includible income of $220,000 ($20,000 + $200,000) in 1992. The $40,000 will be combined with the net income or loss for the first ten months in 1993 and reported in 1993.

As discussed in Chapter 22, the Revenue Act of 1987 introduced a third option in the selection of a taxable year for a partnership or an S corporation. Either entity may elect to adopt or change its tax year to any fiscal year that does not result in a deferral period longer than three months—or, if less, the deferral period of the year currently in use.[69] Recall, however, that such an election requires that the electing partnership or S corporation make a single tax payment on or before May 15 of each year computed at the highest tax rate imposed on individual taxpayers for the prior year *plus* one percent (e.g., 32 percent if the prior year is 1991) on the prior year's deferred income.[70] In essence, the partnership or S corporation must maintain a non–interest-bearing deposit of the income taxes that would have been deferred without this requirement. Since this option eliminates any tax benefits of income deferral, few S corporations made the election.

S corporations have a fourth year-end option when IRS permission is obtained. Thus, with IRS approval, a fiscal year may be adopted if it is identical to that of owners holding a *majority* of the stock.[71] This option also is available when a majority of the shareholders are currently changing to the same tax year requested or held by the S corporation.

Since restrictions on C corporation year-end choices are much more lenient than those for S corporations, an election by a fiscal year C corporation to become an S corporation also may require a change in the corporate year-end. This new year is applicable to all future years, even if the Subchapter S election is canceled and the business reverts to a C corporation.

---

[69]   § 444. Partnerships and S corporations in existence before 1987 are allowed to continue their fiscal years even if the deferral period exceeds three months.

[70]   § 7519 and Reg § 1.7519-2T(a)(4)(ii).

[71]   Rev. Proc. 87-32, 1987-2 C.B. 396.

FAMILY OWNERSHIP

Many of the benefits available to family businesses from *income splitting* are dependent on which organizational form is selected. Some income splitting, however, may be achieved by employing relatives in the business regardless of the organizational form. For example, owners may hire their children to work for them. All reasonable salaries are deductible business expenses and includible salary income to the children. In addition to the tax benefits, some owners believe this provides personal advantages, including encouraging the children to take an interest in the business at an early age.

In some instances, family businesses are formed primarily for tax reasons. The most common example includes both a parent and one or more otherwise dependent children as owners. The basic tax rate structure provides considerable incentive for this type of arrangement when the child is at least 14 years of age.[72]

Rules similar to those affecting the family partnership (discussed in Chapter 22) are applicable to family S corporations.[73] Thus, if reasonable compensation is not paid for services performed or for the use of capital contributed by a family member, the IRS may reallocate S corporation income or expenses.[74] Unlike the partnership, this rule extends to all family members, including those who are *not* owners and when there is no donee/donor relationship.

> **Example 26.** At the beginning of the year, F made an interest-free loan of $10,000 to an S corporation owned by his daughter. The loan is not repaid by the end of the year. Assume an arm's length interest rate of 12% would have been charged by a commercial lender. The IRS may make an adjustment of $1,200 interest income to F and of $1,200 interest expense to the S corporation. However, the IRS is not compelled to make this adjustment. Note that the IRS has the same options if F is a shareholder along with his daughter in the S corporation.

Two important advantages of using the S corporate form instead of a *general* partnership are that (1) shareholders are not required to participate in management, and (2) corporate stock may have different voting rights. In contrast with the general partnership, the parent can retain management control of an S corporation or a limited partnership without violating other family members' rights of participation. This is an important point since it has been a major problem for many general partnerships.

---

[72] Recall that after 1986 many of the income-splitting advantages with children under 14 years of age are eliminated.

[73] § 1366(e) and Reg. § 1.1373-1(a)(2).

[74] Family member, as defined by the Code, is the same for the partnership and the S corporation. §§ 704(e)(3) and 1366(e).

CURRENT DISTRIBUTIONS OF CORPORATE ASSETS

Rules governing current (i.e., nonliquidating) distributions of S corporate assets are unique although they include some characteristics of partnerships and C corporations. Several factors affect the tax treatment. First, it is relevant if an S corporation has accumulated earnings and profits (AE&P) from previous years when it was operated as a C corporation (see Chapter 20 for a definition of AE&P).[75] Second, there is a difference if distributions include property (i.e., noncash assets). Third, special rules cover distributions made during a qualifying period after the Subchapter S status is terminated (referred to as the post-termination period).

Unlike the partnership, it is not necessary to determine if distributions are proportionate (i.e., representative of § 751 and non–§ 751 assets). Instead, all asset distributions in excess of the S shareholder's basis in the stock are capital gains (unless they qualify under the collapsible corporation provisions discussed in Chapter 20).[76] The amount of distributions is equal to cash plus the market value of all other assets. Recall that, in all situations other than the allocation of net losses, an S shareholder's basis *excludes* receivables or other obligations of the S corporation. Computations for basis and determination of whether distributions exceed basis occur at the end of the taxable year.

DISTRIBUTIONS IN GENERAL

Distributions from an S corporation generally represent accumulated income that has been previously taxed to the shareholder. Consistent with the principles underlying Subchapter S, this income should not be taxed again when it is distributed. Therefore, distributions normally are considered nontaxable to the extent of the shareholder's basis. For a corporation that has been an S corporation from inception, this will always be the case. However, when a regular C corporation elects S status, distributions may represent earnings and profits that were accumulated during C years and that are taxed again when distributed.

S CORPORATIONS WITH NO AE&P

All cash distributions by S corporations that have no AE&P are nontaxable unless they exceed the shareholder's basis in the stock.[77] (Property distributions are discussed later in this chapter.)

---

[75]   § 312.

[76]   §§ 1368(b) and 341.

[77]   § 1368(b).

Example 27. D and F have been equal owners of an S corporation for five years. D's basis in the stock is $15,000 and F's basis is $4,000. Corporate net ordinary income for the year totals $10,000 and cash distributions total $22,000. D reports $5,000 (50% × $10,000) ordinary income and has a basis in the stock of $9,000 ($15,000 + $5,000 − $11,000). F reports $5,000 ordinary income and $2,000 capital gain because the $11,000 cash received exceeds her $9,000 basis ($4,000 + $5,000).

When it is known that distributions will exceed a shareholder's basis, the recognition of capital gain can be avoided if the shareholder increases his or her stock basis before the year ends. This may be done by (1) contributing capital to the S corporation, or (2) having debt owed this shareholder converted to capital.

As discussed later in this chapter, realized gains (but not losses) on assets distributed by the S corporation to its shareholders must be recognized by the corporation and passes through to the owners.[78] The basis of the property received by the shareholders is its fair market value (FMV). In addition, unlike the partnership rules, owners must recognize gain when the FMV of the assets received exceeds their basis in the corporate *stock*.[79] This is treated as a partial sale and, consequently, is a capital gain.

Example 28. After using the following equipment for four of its five year ACRS life, an S corporation distributes it to H, its sole owner.

Asset	Cost	Accumulated Depreciation	Basis	Fair Market Value
Equipment	$10,000	$7,900	$2,100	$4,300

Assume H's basis, after all adjustments except the equipment distribution, is $1,800. The S corporation must recognize a § 1245 gain of $2,200 ($4,300 − $2,100). The $2,200 gain flows through to H. H's basis in the equipment is its $4,300 FMV. He must also recognize a $300 capital gain since the $4,300 FMV of the equipment exceeds his $4,000 basis ($1,800 + $2,200).

S CORPORATIONS WITH AE&P

S corporations with accumulated E&P have *three* types of corporate level accounts that determine the treatment of a distribution. The three equity accounts are the Accumulated Adjustments Account, the Accumulated E&P account for S years before 1983, and the Accumulated E&P account for years that the corporation was a regular C corporation.

---

[78] §§ 311(b) and 336(a).   [79] § 1368(b).

Accumulated Adjustments Account. The *accumulated adjustments account* (AAA) is the initial reference point for determining the source of a distribution and therefore its treatment. The AAA represents post-1982 income of the S corporation that has been taxed to shareholders but has not been distributed. Consequently, distributions from the account are a *nontaxable* return of the shareholder's basis in his or her stock. Distributions from the AAA that exceed the shareholder's stock basis are capital gain.[80]

The AAA is a corporate level equity account that is maintained only if the S corporation has accumulated E&P from years when it was operated as a C corporation.[81] The AAA is the cumulative total of the S corporation's post-1982 income and gains (other than tax-exempt income) as reduced by all expenses and losses (both deductible and nondeductible other than those related to tax-exempt income) and any distributions deemed to have been made from the account. The specific formula for computing the balance in the AAA is shown in Exhibit 23-3. Note that the adjustments to the AAA are identical to those made by shareholders to their basis in their stock with *three* exceptions:[82]

1. Tax-exempt income increases the shareholder's stock basis but has no effect on the AAA.

2. Expenses and losses related to tax-exempt income decrease the shareholder's stock basis but have no effect on the AAA. [However, some nondeductible expenditures reduce the AAA as they do the shareholder's stock basis (e.g., the 20% of meal and entertainment expenses that is not deductible, fines, and penalties).]

3. The various adjustments to the AAA (other than distributions) could create either a positive or negative balance in the AAA account. In contrast, the shareholder's stock basis can never be negative. Note that distributions that decrease the shareholder's stock basis have no effect on the AAA once the AAA's balance is exhausted.

Example 29. In 1975, T formed ABC Inc. and operated it as a calendar-year C corporation until 1983 when it elected to be treated as an S corporation. T has owned 100% of the stock since the corporation's inception. T's basis in his stock at the beginning of 1991 was $10,000. Other information related to the S corporation for 1991 is shown in the following.

Net ordinary income for 1991	$50,000
Charitable contribution	9,000
Tax-exempt interest income	10,000
Expenses related to tax-exempt interest income	1,000
Disallowed portion of meal expenses	2,000
Cash distributions	20,000
Accumulated adjustments account	10,000

[80] § 1368(b).

[81] § 1368(c).

[82] § 1368(e)(1).

Exhibit 23-3
*Accumulated Adjustments Account
Computations*

Beginning Balance (S years beginning after 1982)

\+ Taxable income (but not tax-exempt income)

\+ Separately stated items of income and gain

− Net loss

− Separately stated expenses and losses

− Nondeductible expenses and losses (other than expenses related to
   tax-exempt income)

− Cash distributions

− Market value of property distributions

= Accumulated Adjustment Account Balance

The first five items listed above flow through to T. Of these, T must include the $50,000 of ordinary taxable income on his 1991 tax return. In addition, T is allowed to report the $9,000 charitable contribution made by the corporation as an itemized deduction on his return.

T's basis and the balance in the AAA account at the end of the year are computed in the following manner:

	Basis	AAA
Beginning balance	$10,000	$10,000
Net ordinary income for 1991	50,000	50,000
Tax-exempt interest income	10,000	—
Charitable contribution	(9,000)	(9,000)
Disallowed portion of meal expenses	(2,000)	(2,000)
Expenses related to tax-exempt income	(1,000)	—
Cash distribution	(20,000)	(20,000)
Total	$38,000	$29,000

Note that the $9,000 ($38,000 − $29,000) difference between the increase in T's basis in his stock and the corporation's AAA is attributable to the tax-exempt interest income of $10,000 less the $1,000 of expenses related to this income, neither of which affects the AAA.

As noted above, distributions from the AAA are nontaxable to the shareholders unless they exceed the shareholder's stock basis. However, it is rare for shareholders to receive distributions from the AAA that exceed the basis in their stock. Most of the time, the aggregate basis of the shareholders will equal or exceed the AAA (e.g., see *Example 29* above). Nevertheless, the AAA can exceed the shareholder's basis.

> **Example 30.** Same facts as in *Example 29* above. T died on January 1, 1992 and willed all of his stock to his daughter, D. At the time of his death, T's shares were worth $15,000. As a result, D's basis will be $15,000 which is substantially less than the balance in the AAA account of $29,000.

> **Example 31.** Same facts as in *Example 29* above. Due to losses in the stock market, T was forced to sell his shares in ABC. In January 1992, T sold all of his shares to B for $10,000. In this case, B's basis will be less than the $29,000 balance in the AAA. Note that the AAA is a corporate-level account and is unaffected by shareholder transactions.

Previously Taxed Income. The second account from which a distribution may come consists of the AE&P for S years before 1983, commonly referred to as previously taxed income (PTI). As a practical matter, this account may be viewed as the AAA for years prior to 1983. The balance in this account represents taxable income that was earned by the corporation while it was an S corporation prior to 1983 and which has not been distributed to shareholders. Distributions from this account, like those from the AAA, are considered a nontaxable return of the shareholder's basis in his or her stock.

Accumulated E&P of C Years. The third account from which a distribution may come represents earnings and profits accumulated in years when the corporation was a C corporation. Distributions from AE&P are taxable as dividend income.

Other Adjustments Account. Schedule M of Form 1120S creates a fourth classification, entitled *other adjustments account* (OAA). The OAA represents post-1982 tax-exempt income and expenses related to tax-exempt income that do not flow into the AAA. Thus, the OAA is used to show amounts that affect shareholder bases but not the AAA.

Schedule M. Schedule M on page 4 of Form 1120S is a reconciliation of the beginning and ending balances in these corporate accounts: shareholders' undistributed taxable income previously taxed, the AAA, and the OAA.

Example 32. Same facts as in *Example 29* above. The corporation's Schedule M for the year would appear as follows:

Schedule M-2	Analysis of Accumulated Adjustments Account, Other Adjustments Account, and Shareholders' Undistributed Taxable Income Previously Taxed (See instructions.)	(a) Accumulated adjustments account	(b) Other adjustments account	(c) Shareholders' undistributed taxable income previously taxed
1	Balance at beginning of tax year.	10,000		
2	Ordinary income from page 1, line 21 . . .	50,000		
3	Other additions		10,000	
4	Loss from page 1, line 21	( )		
5	Other reductions	(11,000 *)	(1,000)	
6	Combine lines 1 through 5	49,000	9,000	
7	Distributions other than dividend distributions	20,000		
8	Balance at end of tax year—subtract line 7 from line 6	29,000	9,000	

* CHARITABLE CONTRIBUTIONS = $9,000 +
   DISALLOWED MEAL EXPENSE = $2,000
                                    $11,000

Source of Distribution. Cash distributions by S corporations that have AE&P must follow five specific steps:[83]

1. Nontaxable to the extent of AAA (unless they exceed a shareholder's basis in the stock)

2. Nontaxable to the extent of PTI (unless they exceed a shareholder's basis in the stock)

3. Dividend income to the extent of AE&P

4. A return of capital to the extent of the shareholder's basis in the stock (as adjusted by increases or decreases in the OAA)

5. Capital gain for all remaining amounts (including distributions in steps 1 and 2 above in excess of stock basis), determined as though the stock had been sold

All nontaxable distributions (steps 1, 2, and 4 above) decrease a shareholder's basis whereas the taxable ones (steps 3 and 5) do not.

Example 33. J and W have been equal owners of a calendar year S corporation for several years. It has been operated as a C and an S corporation in the past. Balances at the beginning of the year are shown below in the schedule. Operations for the year show $12,000 net ordinary income,

---

[83] § 1368(c).

$2,000 tax-exempt interest income, and $24,000 cash distributions. Based on the five steps listed above, the $24,000 cash distribution offsets (1) all of the $18,000 AAA, (2) all of the $4,000 PTI, and (3) $2,000 ($24,000 − $18,000 − $4,000) of the AE&P. The balances at the end of the year are determined as follows:

	Corporate Accounts				Stock Basis	
	AAA	PTI	AE&P	OAA	J	W
Beginning balances.......	$ 6,000	$4,000	$3,000	$ 0	$10,000	$6,000
Net ordinary income......	12,000				6,000	6,000
Tax-exempt interest income................				2,000	1,000	1,000
Cash distributions:						
Step 1..................	(18,000)				(9,000)	(9,000)
Step 2..................		(4,000)			(2,000)	(2,000)
Step 3..................			(2,000)			
Ending balances..........	0	0	$1,000	$2,000	$ 6,000	$2,000

Both J and W have $6,000 net ordinary income (from S operations) and $1,000 dividend income (from AE&P). Note that J and W recognize dividend income because tax-exempt income does not increase AAA. Also note that there is no longer any need to maintain an account for PTI once the corporation has distributed its PTI.

Example 34. Refer to *Example 33*. Operations for the following year show $10,000 net ordinary income, $600 net capital loss, and $16,000 cash distributions. The balances at the end of this year are determined as follows:

	Corporate Accounts				Stock Basis	
	AAA	AE&P	OAA	Return of Capital	J	W
Beginning balances.......	$ 0	$1,000	$2,000		$6,000	$2,000
Net ordinary income......	10,000				5,000	5,000
Net capital loss..........	(600)				(300)	(300)
Cash distributions:						
Step 1..................	(9,400)				(4,700)	(4,700)
Step 2..................		(1,000)				
Step 3..................			(2,000)		(1,000)	(1,000)
Step 4..................				3,600	(1,800)	(1,000)
Step 5..................						(800)
Ending balances	0	0	0	$3,600	$3,200	0

Both J and W have $5,000 net ordinary income, $300 capital loss, and $500 dividend income. In addition, W has $800 capital gain since the distributions that reduce basis exceed her basis in the stock by $800. Because this S corporation no longer has AE&P, any future distributions will be nontaxable unless they exceed a shareholder's basis in the stock. Also note that the first $2,000 of the $5,600 return of capital distribution was charged to the OAA, reducing its balance to zero.

DISTRIBUTIONS OF PROPERTY

Although most distributions consist solely of cash, an S corporation may distribute property. Rules governing property distributions of an S corporation are a unique blend of both the partnership and C corporation provisions.

An S corporation, like a C corporation, must recognize gain—but not loss—on the distribution of appreciated property. Any gain recognized by the S corporation on the distribution passes through to be reported by the shareholders. In addition, this gain increases each shareholder's stock basis. Upon receipt of the distribution, the shareholder reduces his or her basis by the fair market value of the property received (but not below zero). Any amount in excess of the shareholder's basis is capital gain. The shareholder's basis in the property is its fair market value.

Noncash distributions follow the same five steps as cash distributions except that step 2—PTI—is omitted.[84]

> **Example 35.** Assume the same facts as *Example 33*, except the distribution is of property with a $24,000 market value and a basis of $21,000. Further assume the $3,000 is depreciation recapture and is included in the $12,000 net ordinary income. The balances at the end of the year are determined as follows:

	Corporate Accounts				Stock Basis	
	AAA	PTI	AE&P	OAA	J	W
Beginning balances.......	$ 6,000	$4,000	$3,000	$ 0	$10,000	$6,000
Net ordinary income......	12,000				6,000	6,000
Tax-exempt interest						
income................				2,000	1,000	1,000
Cash distributions:						
Step 1..................	(18,000)				(9,000)	(9,000)
Step 2..................		0				
Step 3..................			(3,000)			
Step 4..................				(2,000)	(1,500)	(1,500)
Ending balances	0	$4,000	0	0	$ 6,500	$2,500

Both J and W have $6,000 net ordinary income and $1,500 dividend income.

Shareholders may *elect* to omit step 1, distributions from AAA.[85] Although this action may increase includible distributions from AE&P, the advantage is that it accelerates the elimination of AE&P. S corporations with no AE&P avoid several potentially negative rules (such as the tax on excess passive investment income which is discussed in the next section of this chapter). The election requires the consent of all shareholders.

---

[84] Reg. 1.1375-4 (b).   [85] § 1368(e)(3).

Recall that taxation of property distributions for C corporations (see Chapter 20) and partnerships (see Chapter 22) differs from that of S corporations. A comparison of the taxation of property distributions for these three business forms is illustrated in the following example.

Example 36.   A business distributes property to its owners with a $15,000 market value and a $9,000 basis. The owners' basis in the business totals $8,000, before the distribution. An S corporation must recognize the $6,000 gain. The character of the gain (i.e., ordinary or capital) is determined in the same manner as any other taxable transaction. This $6,000 gain then flows through to be reported by the owners. The shareholders' basis in the property is $15,000. Since the $15,000 exceeds the shareholders' $14,000 ($8,000 + $6,000) basis in the stock, the $1,000 difference is recognized as a capital gain. The C corporation also recognizes $6,000 gain, which increases its E&P. Assuming the C corporation has at least $15,000 of E&P, its shareholders have $15,000 dividend income, a $15,000 basis in the property, and no change in their stock bases. In contrast, this is a nontaxable distribution for the partnership and the partner. The partnership's $9,000 basis in the property would be the partners' bases except it is limited to the partners' $8,000 bases. A summary of this information follows.

	S Corporation	C Corporation	Partnership
Gain recognized by the business..............	$ 6,000	$ 6,000	$ 0
Business' gain reported by owners............	6,000	0	0
Gain recognized by owners on property received...........................	1,000	15,000	0
Basis in property received....................	15,000	15,000	8,000
Basis in ownership interest...................	0	14,000	0

POST-TERMINATION DISTRIBUTIONS

When an S corporation election terminates, the business is immediately treated as a C corporation. Without special rules, this treatment could be particularly severe. Recall that distributions for a C corporation are dividends to the extent of E&P.[86] This is true even though the C corporation may have undistributed nontaxable income from S years. In addition, S corporate net losses that did not flow through to a shareholder because his or her basis was zero expire when Subchapter S status is terminated. To alleviate some of the harshness of these rules, a post-termination period is created to allow shareholders to transact certain S corporate activities after the S corporation no longer exists.

---

[86] §§ 301(c)(1) and 316(a).

The post-termination transaction period begins the day after the S corporation's final tax year and ends on whichever occurs *last*:[87]

1. The date one year later

2. The due date, including extensions, for the S corporation's final return

3. The date 120 days after a final court decision, a closing agreement, or some other agreement between the S corporation and the IRS determining that the S corporation terminated in a prior year

During the post-termination period, nontaxable *cash* (but not property) distributions may be made from AAA.[88] If the S corporation had no AE&P but the C corporation has current E&P, the treatment of cash distributions in excess of AAA is uncertain. However, the wording of the Code indirectly suggests that only cash distributions to the extent of AAA qualify for the special post-termination treatment. If this is true, any cash distributions in excess of AAA are dividends from E&P.

NET LOSSES

The post-termination period also can be used by a shareholder to increase his or her basis in *stock* (but not debt/receivables). This allows the flow through of any net loss carryovers that were not available to the shareholder previously because the basis in the S corporation stock plus debt/receivables was zero.[89] *First*, any corporate debt owed the shareholder should be exchanged for stock (but see previous discussion). *Second*, the shareholder should contribute cash or other assets to the C corporation or exchange them for additional stock. It should be noted, however, that gain on any appreciated assets in the exchange may be recognized if the 80 percent ownership rules of § 351 are not met.

TAXES IMPOSED ON THE S CORPORATION

S corporations, like partnerships, normally are considered nontaxable entities. Unlike partnerships, however, S corporations may be required to pay one of the following taxes:

1. Excessive passive investment income tax

2. Tax on built-in gains

3. Investment credit recapture tax

---

[87]   § 1377(b).   [89]   § 1366(d)(3).

[88]   § 1371(e).

TAX ON EXCESSIVE PASSIVE INCOME

When Congress revised Subchapter S in 1982, it was concerned that C corporations with a potential accumulated earnings tax or personal holding company tax, particularly those that are mere holding companies (i.e., those whose principal assets are investment properties such as stocks, securities, and real estate projects), would attempt to escape these penalty taxes by electing to be treated as S corporations. Subchapter S can provide a refuge for these corporations since S corporations normally are exempt from both penalty taxes.[90] To guard against this possibility, two steps were taken. First, as previously explained, when a corporation has AE&P *and* excessive passive income in three consecutive years, the corporation's S election is terminated.[91] Second, an S corporation must pay a special tax on its passive income if it has (1) AE&P at the close of its tax year, *and* (2) passive investment income exceeds 25 percent of its gross receipts that year.[92] Note that similar to the termination provision for excessive passive income (discussed early in this chapter), the tax only applies to corporations that have been operated as C corporations and have AE&P at the end of the taxable year. Consequently, the tax is not imposed on corporations that have distributed all of their AE&P or that have never been C corporations.

The tax on excessive passive income is equal to the maximum corporate rate for the year (34%) multiplied by *excess net passive income* (ENPI). ENPI is computed as follows:

$$\text{ENPI} = \begin{array}{c} \text{Net} \\ \text{passive} \\ \text{income} \end{array} \times \frac{\begin{array}{c}\text{Passive investment income} - \\ 25\% \text{ of gross receipts}\end{array}}{\text{Passive investment income}}$$

In computing the tax, several rules must be observed.

1. For any taxable year, ENPI cannot exceed the corporation's taxable income.[93]

2. Passive investment income is defined the same as it is for the termination provisions of § 1362(d) discussed previously:[94] generally gross receipts from dividends, interest, rents, royalties, and annuities, and gains from sales of capital assets.

---

[90] The accumulated earnings tax and the personal holding company tax do not apply to S corporations because income is not sheltered within the corporate entity but flows through to the shareholders.

[91] § 1362(d)(3).

[92] § 1375(a).

[93] § 1375(b)(1)(B).

[94] §§ 1375(b)(3) and 1362(d)(3)(D)(i).

3. Net passive income is passive investment income reduced by any allowable deductions directly connected with the production of this income. These deductions include such expenses as property taxes and depreciation related to rental property but exclude such deductions as the dividends-received deduction.[95]

The amount of any tax paid reduces the amount of each item of passive investment income that flows through to shareholders. The tax is allocated proportionately based on passive investment income.[96]

> **Example 37.**   PTC is owned equally by R and S. At the close of the year, PTC, an S corporation, reports gross receipts of $200,000 and a balance in its AE&P account of $24,000. Gross receipts include $25,000 interest and $50,000 rent. Deductions directly attributable to rents were $30,000, including depreciation, maintenance, insurance, and property taxes. Since the corporation has passive investment income exceeding 25% of its gross receipts [$75,000 > (25% × $200,000 = $50,000)] *and* it has AE&P at the end of the taxable year, the tax on passive income is imposed. Excessive net passive income of $15,000 is computed as follows:
>
> $$(\$75,000 - \$30,000) \times \frac{\$75,000 - (25\% \times \$200,000)}{\$75,000} = \$15,000$$
>
> PTC's excessive passive investment income tax is $5,100 (34% × $15,000). Of this amount, $1,700 ($5,100 × $25,000 ÷ $75,000) is attributed to the interest and the remainder of $3,400 ($5,100 − $1,700) to rent. Since 50% of the passive income flows through to each shareholder, both of them reduce the amount of passive income that they report by their share of the tax, $2,550 (50% × $5,100), or $850 for interest and $1,700 for rent. Thus, each shareholder reports interest of $11,650 ($12,500 − $850) and rent of $23,300 ($25,000 − $1,700) less $15,000 rent expense, or $8,300.

Shareholders of an S corporation that has an ownership in a partnership must be alert to the fact that each partner is deemed to be distributed a percentage of every partnership item, including each item of gross receipts (unless a special allocation is in effect). As a result, the excessive passive investment tax can be triggered by partnership activities.

---

[95]   § 1375(b)(2).   [96]   § 1366(f)(3).

TAX ON BUILT-IN GAINS

Without special rules, C corporations planning sales or distributions of appreciated property (e.g., as a dividend or in liquidation) could avoid double taxation by electing S status before making the distributions.

> **Example 38.**   R, a regular C corporation, owns land worth $50,000 (basis $10,000). If R Corporation distributes the land to its sole shareholder, D, as a dividend, the corporation recognizes a gain of $40,000 ($50,000 − $10,000) and D recognizes dividend income of $50,000. Therefore, two taxes are imposed. In contrast, compare the result that occurs if R Corporation has S status. R still recognizes a $40,000 gain. However, that gain is not taxed at the corporate level, but flows through to D to be taxed. In addition, D increases his basis in his stock by $40,000. On receipt of the property, D does not report any income but simply reduces the basis in his stock. As a result, there is only a *single tax* if R Corporation has S status.

To eliminate the tax-avoidance possibility of electing S status before the distribution (or a sale), Congress enacted § 1374. This section imposes a special corporate level tax—the *built-in gains tax*—on gains recognized by an S corporation that accrued while it was a C corporation. The built-in gains tax generally applies only to corporations that "convert" from C to S status (i.e., operate as a C corporation and then elect S status) after 1986.[97] The tax applies *only* to gains recognized during the 10-year period following the S election.

Under § 1374, it is presumed that *any* gain recognized on the sale or distribution of any property by a "converted" S corporation is subject to the built-in gains tax. However, the corporation may rebut this presumption and avoid the tax by proving either of the following: (1) the asset sold or distributed was not held on the date that the corporation elected S status; or (2) the gain had not accrued at the time of the election. As a practical matter, this approach requires every C corporation electing S status to have an independent appraisal of its assets in order to rebut the presumption. Note that for purposes of this tax, built-in gains include the unrealized receivables of a cash basis taxpayer as well as any gain on a long-term contract that has not been recognized (e.g., the taxpayer uses the completed contract method of accounting) and any goodwill.

As a general rule, the special tax applies only to S corporations having a *net unrealized built-in gain*. This is defined as the difference between the value and basis of all assets held on the first day the S election is effective. This represents the *maximum* amount that may be subject to the built-in gains tax.

---

[97]   Qualified small corporations electing S status after 1986 are subject to the built-in gains tax only on their ordinary income items.

Example 39. On November 3, 1991, T Corporation made an S election. The election was effective for calendar year 1992. On January 1, 1992, its balance sheet revealed the following assets.

	Adjusted Basis	Fair Market Value	Built-in Gain (Loss)
Inventory	$ 50,000	$ 75,000	$25,000
Land	30,000	70,000	40,000
Stock	20,000	15,000	(5,000)
	$100,000	$160,000	$60,000

T Corporation's net unrealized built-in gain is $60,000. Note that the built-in loss on the stock effectively reduces the taxpayer's future exposure to the built-in gains tax.

Only the *net recognized built-in gain* is subject to tax.[98] This gain is the difference between any built-in gains and built-in losses recognized during the year. In effect, the corporation may offset any built-in gains recognized during the year with built-in losses that are also recognized. Built-in losses include not only accrued losses on property held at the time of conversion but also any amount that is allowable as a deduction and is attributable to pre-S periods (e.g., a cash basis taxpayer's routine payables). In contrast with built-in gains, it is presumed that any loss recognized on the sale of property or any deduction arising from the payment of an expense is *not* a built-in loss. However, the corporation may rebut the presumption by establishing that the fair market value of the property was less than its basis on the first day of the first S year, or that an unrealized payable existed on that date.

Example 40. Refer to the facts in *Example 39*. During 1992, T Corporation sold the inventory and the stock for $77,000 and $15,000, respectively. Although T recognizes a gain of $27,000 ($77,000 − $50,000) on the sale of the inventory, T's built-in gain recognized is limited to the amount accrued on the date of conversion from a C corporation to S status, $25,000. T's net recognized built-in gain that is potentially subject to tax is $20,000 (the built-in gain of $25,000 less the $5,000 built-in loss recognized.)

If T Corporation had sold the land at a gain of $40,000 instead of selling the stock, the total gain for 1992 would have been $67,000 ($40,000 gain from land + $27,000 gain from inventory). However, only $60,000 of this gain would be subject to the § 1374 tax because T's $60,000 net unrealized built-in gain is the maximum amount subject to the tax.

---

[98] § 1374(b). If a C corporation uses the LIFO inventory method, it must recognize the excess of the FIFO inventory value over the LIFO inventory value. This amount recognized by the C corporation will not be included in built-in gains for the S corporation.

The built-in gains tax is computed by multiplying the top tax rate applicable to regular C corporations (i.e., 34%) times the *lesser* of (1) the net built-in gain recognized, or (2) the S corporation's taxable income determined as if the corporation were a C corporation (except a dividends-received deduction is not allowed).[99] The latter amount provides relief for taxpayers who may have large built-in gains during the year but small taxable incomes. The lesser of these two amounts is then reduced by any NOL and capital loss carryforward from C corporate years. In addition, business tax credit carryforwards arising in a C year can be used to reduce the tax.[100] Any net recognized built-in gain not subject to tax because of this limitation is carried over to the following year and treated as if it occurred in that year.[101] The calculation of the tax is summarized below.

	Lesser of built-in gain or taxable income	$x,xxx
−	NOL carryforward from C year	(xxx)
=	Tax base...	$x,xxx
×	Top corporate tax rate................................. ×	xx%
=	Potential tax	$x,xxx
−	Business credit carryforward from C year...............	(xxx)
=	Tax...	$x,xxx

Example 41. Refer to the facts in *Example 39*. Assume that T sold the land for $70,000 in 1993, recognizing a $40,000 gain, which is also the total amount of its net realized built-in gain for the year. Also assume that the corporation's taxable income, including this $40,000 gain and a $3,000 NOL carryforward from C years, is $10,000. T's built-in gains tax is computed as follows:

Lesser of:		
	Net recognized built-in gains..........................	$40,000
	Taxable income (before NOL)...........................	13,000
		$13,000
NOL..		(3,000)
Taxable built-in gain....................................		$10,000
Highest corporate rate..................................		× 34%
Built-in gains tax.......................................		$3,400

Note that the $30,000 of net recognized built-in gain that was not taxed due to the limitation is carried over to the following year and treated as if it were recognized in that year, along with any other built-in gains and losses.

---

[99] §1374(b)(1).

[100] §§1374(b)(2) and (3).

[101] This amount escapes the tax for S corporations electing S status before March 1, 1988.

INVESTMENT CREDIT RECAPTURE

For years beginning after 1983, an S corporation election is treated as a mere change in form of conducting a trade or business.[102] As a result, the electing corporation is not required to recapture unearned investment credits because of the election. When the election is made, however, the S corporation assumes the liability for any recapture tax that may arise for credits claimed during years when the corporation was not an S corporation.[103]

ESTIMATED TAXES

After 1989, S corporations are required to pay estimated taxes for (1) excessive passive investment income taxes (§ 1375), (2) taxes on built-in gains (§ 1374), and (3) investment credit recapture taxes [§ 1371(d)(2)]. The computations of estimated taxes generally follow the rules applicable to C corporations.[104]

DISPOSITION OF OWNERSHIP INTEREST

Based on the entity theory, sales of stock by shareholders of a corporation electing Subchapter S result in capital gain or loss.[105] This, of course, is identical to how stock sales of a nonelecting corporation are treated. However, the amount of the gain or loss will differ since an S shareholder's basis is adjusted for S corporate items whereas a C shareholder's basis is not. All other stock transfers also follow the rules of an exchange or gift of a capital asset.[106] This is a significant advantage for the S (or C) corporate shareholder when compared with the complicated and often unfavorable rules of the partnership. However, recall from the earlier discussion, shareholders who sell or otherwise dispose of their stock must report their share of the S corporation's current year items, based either on the per day allocation method or the interim closing of books method.

As discussed earlier, any debt owed the shareholder with a reduced basis because of net loss flow throughs will result in capital gain when paid if it is a note, bond, or other written debt instrument or ordinary income if it is an open account.[107] Consequently, this is the last chance for a shareholder who is disposing of all the stock to convert the debt to capital and avoid ordinary income when the open accounts are paid.

---

[102] § 1371(d)(1).

[103] § 1371(d)(2).

[104] See § 6655 for estimated taxes applicable to C corporations.

[105] If certain oil and gas properties are held by the S corporation, ordinary income may result from the sale of its stock. § 1254(b)(2).

[106] § 1221.

[107] § 1232; Rev. Ruls. 64-162, 1964-1 C.B. 304 and 68-537, 1968-2 C.B. 372; and *Cornelius v. U.S.*, 74-1 USTC ¶9446, 33 AFTR2d 74-1331, 494 F.2d 465 (CA-5, 1974).

WORTHLESS SECURITIES

S and C shareholders who hold worthless securities, including stock and debt, are subject to the same provisions with one exception. The S corporation's flow through rules apply *before* the deduction for worthless stock or debt. The loss on worthless securities is treated as though it occurred on the last day of the *shareholder's* taxable year (not the S corporation's year) from the sale or exchange of a capital asset. Thus, it is possible for stock to become worthless before corporate activities are completed. In addition, if the S corporation's year ends *after* the stockholder's year ends, worthlessness could occur before the flow through is available. This potential loss of deduction could be a serious disadvantage to shareholders.

The deduction for worthless stock is a capital loss unless the stock qualifies for ordinary loss treatment under § 1244.[108] Bad debts also are capital losses unless the shareholder can establish that they are business bad debts.[109] For example, the debts may have arisen as a result of a business transaction or the shareholder's employment status with the corporation. Business bad debts are ordinary losses.

CORPORATE LIQUIDATION

Generally, provisions governing liquidations and reorganizations for C corporations are applicable to S corporations (see Chapter 20).

---

[108] Compare §§ 165(g) and 1367(b)(3) with § 1244(a).

[109] Compare §§ 166(a) and (d).

TAX PLANNING

There are numerous tax planning opportunities available to a business regardless of the form of organization selected. Many of these were discussed throughout this and previous chapters. Although tax planning opportunities are too extensive and too personalized to prepare an exhaustive list, a brief comparison of the S corporation, partnership, and C corporation is mentioned here to encourage the student of taxation to continually analyze tax situations with an eye to tax planning. The thoughtful but imaginative tax adviser who is able to provide clients with planning options that meet their needs is in much demand in today's tax-conscious society.

The situation of any taxpayer planning to contribute property in exchange for an ownership interest should be evaluated. In some instances, it may be in the individual's best interest to seek an alternate method of obtaining an ownership interest. For example, property with a basis in excess of its market value may provide the owner greater benefits if leased to the business.

Taxpayers purchasing an interest in a business that owns appreciated assets should be aware that no adjustment to the business's assets can be made except in the partnership, and then only if a special election is in effect. This is particularly relevant to the purchasing partner or S shareholder. When the election cannot be made, the purchase price will exceed the asset bases for purposes of depreciation, depletion, amortization, gains, and losses. Therefore, it is quite possible the purchase price should be adjusted below market value when no election exists. This, of course, is quite important to the seller.

BASIC PRINCIPLES

The S corporation has many of the same advantages and disadvantages as a partnership. Unlike general partners, however, S shareholders have limited liability. This factor often is the major reason for incorporating a business. Some of this protection, however, may be lost if shareholders are required to guarantee corporate liabilities. Regardless of the restrictions, shareholders are protected from a number of debts that are not guaranteed. To achieve this benefit, owners must give up much of the flexibility available to the partnership and are subject to more filing requirements and other formalities.

Two significant advantages of the partnership are not available with any other organizational form. One is the ability to specially allocate partnership items among the partners. This can be particularly useful in alleviating inequities and for tax planning when marginal rates differ among the owners. A second unique attribute of the partnership is the ability to adjust the basis of the assets when a capital interest is sold and when gain is recognized on distribution of partnership assets. An important disadvantage of the partnership is that an owner cannot be an employee. As a result, owner/employee benefits are not deductible by the partnership and the owner has self-employment income. After 1987, owner/employee benefits are nondeductible for an S corporation as well.

In addition to limited liability for its shareholders, the C corporation's major advantage is that it is a separate taxable entity. As a result, owner/employee benefits are deductible expenses. In addition, business income is not taxable to owners until distributed to them. As is often the case, the major advantage also can be a disadvantage. The separate taxable entity concept results in double taxation when corporate profits are distributed to shareholders. It also means that neither losses nor the character of income or deductions flows through to shareholders.

The corporate form may be a disadvantage for businesses with sales of depreciable realty. Section 291(a)(1) serves to reclassify some of a § 1231 gain of C corporations and certain S corporations from capital gain to ordinary income. This section, however, is not applicable to a partnership.

Generally, newly formed businesses provide greater benefits if organized as a partnership or S corporation. This is because operations in the early years often produce net losses. In these two types of businesses, losses are deductible by the owners (subject to the limitation on passive business losses). In contrast, a C corporation's losses must be carried back or forward to offset corporate income in those years. If losses are incurred in the first years, no tax savings will be obtained from these losses until sometime in the future, and then most likely at the lowest corporate rates. Another situation where the flow through concept is important occurs when owners need to have earnings distributed to cover their current living expenses. This, of course, is dependent on the marginal rates of all taxpayers and the percentage and amount of earnings distributed.

Family businesses provide excellent income-splitting opportunities among family members. For example, children can be employees of their parents' businesses. The amount of salary paid is, of course, dependent on the work performed, but significant tax savings can be achieved. The benefits and difficulties of dependent children as general partners were discussed in Chapter 22.

The corporate form often is an advantage for owners who are selling their interests. Stock sales result in capital gains when the business is successful but often qualify for ordinary loss treatment if unsuccessful. The partner may have the opposite effect. That is, gain is ordinary income to the extent of unrealized receivables, substantially appreciated inventory, and depreciation recapture. But sales at amounts below basis are capital losses. This may be an important consideration when establishing a new business or investing in a business for a limited period of time. From this perspective, the S corporation combines the advantage of the flow through concept with the capital gain/ordinary loss benefit when the ownership interest is sold.

APPENDIX: SELECTING A FORM OF DOING BUSINESS

In summary, S corporations and their shareholders are taxed in a manner similar to that of C corporations and their shareholders in the beginning (when the businesses are being formed or stock is being acquired) and in the end (when the businesses are being liquidated or reorganized or the shareholder is disposing of the stock). However, the tax effects while the S corporation is being operated generally conform more closely to those of the partnership. In some instances, S corporation provisions are unique with no counterpart among the C corporation or partnership provisions. Consequently, these three organizational forms offer an important choice to owners of a business. To illustrate some of the differences that should be considered, a comprehensive summary, in a comparative format, is presented in *Example 42* and Exhibit 23-4.

Example 42.   T Company, organized January 1, 1990, has the following information for 1991, its second calendar year:

Gross profit
Sales...	$470,000
Cost of goods sold............................	300,000

Operating Expenses
Salary (or compensation) to T, the owner........	24,000	
Salaries to others (2 nonowners).................	48,000	
Payroll taxes for T..............................	(1)	
Payroll taxes for others.........................	4,000	(1)
Employee benefits: (2)		
Life insurance for T...........................	700	(3)
Life insurance for others......................	1,400	(3)
Utilities and telephone..........................	2,500	
Office expenses.................................	1,100	
Insurance.......................................	3,100	
Interest to T ($300 not paid until 2/1/92).........	3,600	
Property taxes..................................	3,000	
Repairs..	12,000	
Depreciation...................................	15,000	
Charitable contributions.........................	7,000	

Other items
Dividend income (from 25% owned corporation)	2,000	
Capital gain (CG)...............................	2,200	
Capital loss (CL)...............................	1,200	
Rehabilitation investment credit..................	2,000	
Cash distributed to owner T.....................	12,000	
Land distributed to owner T (basis).............	7,000	(4)

1. Each employee was paid $2,000 per month. FICA is 7.65% × $24,000 = $1,836 and unemployment taxes are 6.2% × $7,000 = $434 for each employee and $2,270 for both taxes. This is rounded to $4,000 to simplify the illustration. If the company is a corporation, payroll taxes for T are $2,000 (rounded). If the company is a proprietorship or partnership, there are no payroll taxes for T. Instead, T is subject to self-employment taxes on his personal tax return.

2. Assume T has agreed to reimburse the business for any expenses that cannot be deducted because he is an owner.

3. Life insurance is group-term life insurance of $50,000 for T and each of the other two employees.

4. Market value of the land distributed is $10,000. It was purchased for the $7,000 on May 2, 1990.

If the business is a proprietorship, T is the owner. For the sake of comparison, assume T is allocated all of the partnership items and is the sole shareholder of the S or C corporation. The Ts (Mr. and Mrs. T) file a joint return, have two exemptions, and $8,000 of personal itemized deductions of interest, taxes, and charitable contributions. They have no other includible income or deductible expenses for the year. On December 31, 1990, T's basis was $100,000.

A.   The taxable business income for each of the four organizational
     forms is computed below.

	Proprietorship	Partnership	S Corporation	C Corporation
Income				
Sales......................	$470,000	$470,000	$470,000	$470,000
Cost of goods sold.........	(300,000)	(300,000)	(300,000)	(300,000)
Gross profit..............	$170,000	$170,000	$170,000	$170,000
Dividend income...........	0	0	0	2,000
Net capital gain...........	0	0	0	4,000 [1]
Total income............	$170,000	$170,000	$170,000	$176,000
Deductions				
Salary (or compensation) to T	0	24,000	24,000	24,000
Salaries to others..........	48,000	48,000	48,000	48,000
Payroll taxes for T.........	0	0	2,000	2,000
Payroll taxes for others	4,000	4,000	4,000	4,000
Life insurance for T........	0	0	0 [2]	700
Life insurance for others...	1,400	1,400	1,400	1,400
Utilities and telephone	2,500	2,500	2,500	2,500
Office supplies.............	1,100	1,100	1,100	1,100
Insurance..................	3,100	3,100	3,100	3,100
Interest to T	0	3,300 [3]	3,300 [3]	3,300 [3]
Property taxes.............	3,000	3,000	3,000	3,000
Repairs....................	12,000	12,000	12,000	12,000
Depreciation..............	15,000	15,000	15,000	15,000
Charitable contributions....	0	0	0	5,590 [4]
Dividend deduction	0	0	0	1,600
Total deductions.........	$ 90,100	$117,400	$119,400	$127,290
Taxable income..........	$ 79,900	$ 52,600	$ 50,600	$ 48,710
Tax liability.................				$ 7,306 [5]
Rehabilitation credit........				2,000
Tax due.................				$ 5,306

1. The C corporation must recognize the $3,000 ($10,000 − $7,000) § 1231 gain on the
    land distributed which is treated as capital gain. Thus, $3,000 + $2,200 − $1,200 =
    $4,000 net capital gain.

2. Since the corporation was formed after 1982 and T owns more than 2% of the stock, the
    S corporation cannot deduct his employee benefits. Thus, from note 2 on the previous
    page, this is a loan to T of $700.

3. Accrued expenses to a cash-basis related party are not deductible until paid. The $300
    is deductible in 1992.

4. Charitable contributions may not exceed 10% of taxable income computed before the
    dividends-received deduction, charitable contribution deduction, and net operating and
    capital loss carrybacks ($48,710 + $5,590 + $1,600 = $55,900 × 10% = $5,590). The
    $1,410 ($7,000 − $5,590) is carried forward.

5. 15% × $48,710 = $7,306.

B.   The Ts' Federal income tax for each of the organizational forms is computed below.

	Proprietorship	Partnership	S Corporation	C Corporation
Net business income.........	$79,000	$52,600	$50,600	$ 0
Business dividend income....	2,000	2,000	2,000	0
Net capital gain.............	1,000 (1)	1,000 (1)	4,000 (1)	0
Salary income	0	24,000	24,000	24,000
Interest income	0	3,300	3,300	3,300
Cash distribution............	0	0	0	12,000
Land distribution	0	0	0	10,000
Adjusted gross income ..	$82,900	$82,900	$83,900	$49,300
Itemized deductions from the business:				
Charitable contributions....	7,000	7,000	7,000	0
Other itemized deductions(2)..	8,000	8,000	8,000	8,000
Exemptions..................	4,300	4,300	4,300	4,300
Deductions from A.G.I......	19,300	19,300	19,300	12,300
Taxable income............	$63,600	63,600	64,600	$37,000
Federal income tax(3).........	$13,388	$13,388	$13,668	$ 5,940
Self-employment tax(4)	7,687	7,605	0	0
Rehabilitation credit..........	(2,000)	(2,000)	(2,000)	0
Tax due...................	$19,075	$18,993	$11,668	$ 5,940

1.   Net capital gains for the proprietor and the partner total $2,200 capital gain − $1,200 capital loss = $1,000. The S corporation must recognize the $3,000 ($10,000 − $7,000) gain on the land distributed. This $3,000 capital gain also flows out to T. Thus, the S shareholder's net capital gains total $1,000 + $3,000 = $4,000.

2.   Itemized deductions exceed the standard deduction.

3.   1991 tax rates used: (15% × $34,000 = $5,100) + (28% × remaining taxable income). The surtax is not assessed since taxable income is below the surtax requirement.

4.   The self-employment tax for T is [$5,694.58 ($53,400 × 10.664%)] + [$1,992.71 ($79,900 × 2.494%) for the proprietorship and $1,910.40 ($52,600 + $24,000 = $76,600 × 2.494%) for the partnership] = $7,687.29 for the proprietorship and $7,604.98 for the partnership. The 10.664 percent and 2.494 percent are the effective rates for an individual with a 28 percent marginal rate because 50 percent of the self-employment tax is deductible [12.4% − (12.4% × 50% = 6.2% × 28% = 1.736%) = 10.664%] and [2.9% − (2.9% × 50% = 1.45% × 28% = 0.406%) = 2.494%]. The 1991 maximum base is $53,400 and $125,000, respectively, for the two calculations.

C. The combined taxes on income, self-employment, and owner salary
    for T and each of the organizational forms is computed below.

	Proprietorship	Partnership	S Corporation	C Corporation
Employee taxes on T's salary	$ 0	$ 0	$ 2,000	$ 2,000
FICA taxes paid by T.......	0	0	2,000	2,000
Corporate Federal income tax......................	0	0	0	5,306
T's Federal income and self-employment tax......	19,075	18,993	11,668	5,940
Total tax.................	$19,075	$18,993	$15,668	$15,246

No conclusion should be drawn from this comparison and applied to other situations. For
example, the self-employment tax is a substantial cost in the illustration. An owner who
has salary income from another source would avoid all or part of the self-employment
tax. Different cash and property distributions also would affect the total taxes. In addition,
a proprietor and partner would have a $7,000 basis in the land whereas the S and C
shareholders would have a $10,000 basis in the land.

D. T's basis in the business or stock for the organizational forms is
    computed below.

	Partnership	S Corporation	C Corporation
Basis 12/31/90............	$100,000	$100,000	$100,000
Net business income	52,600	50,600	0
Dividend income..........	2,000	2,000	0
Net capital gain.....	1,000	4,000	0
Life insurance....	(700)	0 [(1)]	0
Charitable contributions..	(7,000)	(7,000)	0
Cash distributed..........	(12,000)	(12,000)	0
Property distributed... ...	(7,000)	(10,000)	0
Basis 12/31/91............	$128,900	$127,600	$100,000

The proprietor has a basis in each asset and liability, not in the business
itself.

1. T's basis is indirectly reduced by the $700 in premiums since he
    owes the S corporation this amount.

	Exhibit 23-4
	Comparative Analysis of Business Forms

Basic Concepts

Items for Comparison	*Proprietorship/ Proprietor*	*Partnership/ Partner*	*S Corporation/ Shareholder*	*C Corporation/ Shareholder*
1. What are the restrictions on the number of owners or who may be an owner?	1. One owner who must be an individual	1. None, except there must be at least two owners	1. No more than 35 shareholders (and some states set a minimum number) who must be individuals, estates, or certain trusts	1. None, except some states set a minimum number of shareholders
2. Are owners liable for business debts that they have not personally guaranteed?	2. Yes.	2. Yes, for general partners but no for limited partners	2. No	2. No
3. What are the appropriate tax forms and schedules and who files them?	3. Schedules C, SE, and all supporting schedules and forms are filed with proprietor's Form 1040	3. Form 1065 and Schedules K-1 are prepared at the partnership level; partners report their shares on Schedules E, SE, and other supporting schedules and file them with their Form 1040s	3. Same as partnership except Form 1120S and its Schedules K-1 are prepared at the S corporation level	3. Form 1120 and all supporting schedules are filed for the C corporation; shareholders report dividend income on Schedule B and file it with their Form 1040s

Exhibit 23-4 Continued:

	Items for Comparison	Proprietorship/ Proprietor	Partnership/ Partner	S Corporation/ Shareholder	C Corporation/ Shareholder
Basic Concepts Continued	4. Who is the taxpayer?	4. Proprietor	4. Partners (but the partnership may be subject to tax if a year-end different from the partners is used)	4. Shareholders (but the S corporation may be subject to a special tax on certain built-in gains and excess passive investment income or if a year-end different from the shareholders is used)	4. C corporation and shareholders are taxed on dividend income when corporate earnings are distributed
	5. Do owners have self-employment income from the business?	5. Yes, the net income from Schedule C	5. Yes, each *general* partner's share of net ordinary income less passive income from Form 1065 plus his or her guaranteed payments; but for *limited* partners, only their guaranteed payments from services provided to the partnership	5. No	5. No
	6. Must the business's taxable year be the same as the majority owners?	6. Yes	6. Generally, but a different year may be used if the partnership pays a tax on the deferred income	6. Same as partnership	6. No, any generally accepted accounting period may be used

Exhibit 23-4 Continued:

	Items for Comparison	Proprietorship/ Proprietor	Partnership/ Partner	S Corporation/ Shareholder	C Corporation/ Shareholder
Asset Transfers between Owners and Their Business	1. Are contributions of assets for an ownership interest taxable transactions?	1. No, tax-free exchange, all tax attributes transfer to the business except the lower of basis or market value must be used for nonbusiness assets transferred; the term "ownership interest" is not applicable	1. No, same as proprietorship except ownership (capital) interest is applicable	1. No, same as partnership *if* parties to the exchange own more than 80 percent of the corporation after the contribution, but otherwise, a taxable exchange with no carryover of tax attributes	1. Same as S corporation
	2. Are distributions of cash includible income to owners?	2. No.	2. No, except a distribution in excess of the partner's basis in the partnership is treated as a partial sale of the ownership interest	2. No, same as partnership except shareholders' basis for this purpose is their basis in stock and not in corporate debt owed to them	2. Yes, they are nondeductible distributions by the corporation and dividend income to shareholders if from the C corporation's earnings and profits; otherwise it may be same as S corporation in certain situations that are beyond the scope of this chapter

Exhibit 23-4 Continued:

Asset Transfers between Owners and Their Business Continued:	Items for Comparison	Proprietorship/ Proprietor	Partnership/ Partner	S Corporation/ Shareholder	C Corporation/ Shareholder
	3. Do distributions of property result in includible income to either the business or the owners?	3. No, same as contributions except the reverse	3. No, same as proprietorship except the transfer of basis in the assets is limited to the partner's basis in the partnership	3. Yes, S corporation must recognize all realized gain; shareholder receives the assets at their market value with no transfer of tax attributes and any market value in excess of the shareholder's basis in stock (not debt) is treated as a partial sale of the stock	3. Yes, C corporation must recognize realized gain—but not loss—if a nonliquidating distribution; shareholders have dividend income equal to the market value of the assets
	4. May an owner enter into taxable transactions (sales, loans, lease arrangements, etc.) with the business?	4. No	4. Yes, when acting in a nonpartner capacity, but subject to related party restrictions	4. Yes, subject to related party restrictions	4. Same as S corporation
	5. May an accrual basis business deduct accrued expenses to cash basis owners?	5. No, not applicable	5. No, deductible only when paid (except see 6 below)	5. Same as partnership	5. Same as partnership and S corporation

Exhibit 23-4 Continued:

Asset Transfers between Owners and Their Business Continued:	Items for Comparison	Proprietorship/ Proprietor	Partnership/ Partner	S Corporation/ Shareholder	C Corporation/ Shareholder
	6. Are accrued expenses of the business includible income to cash basis owners? If yes, when?	6. No, not applicable	6. Yes, when received, except guaranteed salary and interest on capital are includible when accrued to a partner whose capital interest exceeds 5 percent	6. Yes, when received	6. Yes, when received
	7. Can owners be employees of the business and be paid salaries subject to employment taxes and withholding?	7. No.	7. No, unless partner's capital interest does not exceed 5 percent	7. Yes	7. Yes
	8. Are fringe benefits for owner/ employees deductible expenses?	8. No	8. No, unless partner's capital interest does not exceed 5 percent	8. No, except for a 2 percent or less shareholder; cost is a debt owed by the shareholder to the S corporation	8. Yes
	9. May the business use the cash method?	9. Yes	9. Yes, unless it qualifies as a tax shelter or has a C corporation as a partner	9. Yes, unless it qualifies as a tax shelter	9. No, unless gross receipts do not exceed $5 million or it qualifies under "type of business" exception

Exhibit 23-4 Continued:

Income,
Deductions,
and
Credits

Items for Comparison	Proprietorship/ Proprietor	Partnership/ Partner	S Corporation/ Shareholder	C Corporation/ Shareholder
1. Is the business a conduit with the original character of the items flowing through to its owners as of the last day of the business's taxable year?	1. Yes	1. Yes	1. Yes	1. No, the business is an entity and the flow through concept is not applicable
2. How are capital gains and losses treated?	2. As though received by the proprietor	2. Flow through to each partner	2. Same as partnership	2. Net capital gain includible in corporate taxable income and taxed at regular rates; net capital losses are subject to the carryover rules (back 3 years and forward 5 years) and deductible against capital gains
3. How is dividend income treated?	3. Includible income as though received by the proprietor	3. Flow through to each partner as dividend income	3. Same as partnership	3. Includible income with a 70 percent dividend deduction (80% if at least 20% of the distributing corporation's stock is owned; 100 % if from an affiliated corporation)

Exhibit 23-4 Continued:

Income, Deductions, and Credits Continued:	Items for Comparison	Proprietorship/ Proprietor	Partnership/ Partner	S Corporation/ Shareholder	C Corporation/ Shareholder
	4. How are charitable contributions treated?	4. An itemized deduction as though contributed by the proprietor	4. Flow through to each partner as an itemized deduction	4. Same as partnership	4. Deductions may not exceed 10 percent of taxable income before certain deductions
	5. Who pays state and local income taxes on the business net income and how are they treated?	5. Proprietor; an itemized deduction as though paid by the proprietor	5. Each partner; an itemized deduction	5. Same as partnership, except some state and local income taxes are assessed on the S corporation and are a deductible expense	5. Deductible expense
	6. How are tax credits treated?	6. As though the credit was earned	6. Qualifying credits flow through to each partner subject to any limitations applicable at the partner level	6. Same as partnership	6. Computed at the corporate level and reduces corporate tax liability
	7. How is net ordinary income treated?	7. Includible with proprietor's A.G.I.	7. Flows through to each partner	7. Same as partnership	7. Included in corporate taxable income
	8. How is net ordinary loss treated?	8. Includible as a reduction of proprietor's A.G.I.	8. Flows through to each partner up to that partner's basis in the partnership; any excess is carried forward	8. Same as partnership	8. Subject to carryover rules (back 3 years and forward 15 years or forward 15 years only) and deductible against net ordinary income

Exhibit 23-4 Continued:

Income, Deductions, and Credits Continued:

Items for Comparison	Proprietorship/ Proprietor	Partnership/ Partner	S Corporation/ Shareholder	C Corporation Shareholder
9. Is § 291(a)(1) applicable?	9. No	9. No	9. Yes, if C corporation for any of 3 prior tax years	9. Yes
10. How are items allocated among the owners?	10. Not applicable	10. According to profit and loss ratio or may be specially allocated	10. According to stock ownership ratio	10. Not applicable
11. Is the basis of business assets adjusted when an ownership interest is sold?	11. Not applicable	11. Yes, if the partners have elected the optional adjustment to basis	11. No	11. No

Basis in the Business

Items for Comparison	Proprietorship/ Proprietor	Partnership/ Partner	S Corporation/ Shareholder	C Corporation Shareholder
1. Is basis affected by business liabilities?	1. Not applicable	1. Yes, a general partner's basis includes his or her share of partnership liabilities but a limited partner's basis does not	1. No, except a shareholder's basis is increased by the amount of debt owed to him or her for loss flow through	1. No.
2. Is basis affected by business income, gains, deductions, and losses?	2. Not applicable	2. Yes, all income and gains increase basis and all expenses and losses (that flow through) decrease basis	2 . Yes, same as partnership	2. No

Exhibit 23-4 Continued:

Sale of a Business Interest

Items for Comparison	Proprietorship/ Proprietor	Partnership/ Partner	S Corporation/ Shareholder	C Corporation Shareholder
1. What is the character of gains and losses on the sale of a business interest?	1. Each asset is treated as sold individually and the character of the gain or loss is dependent on that asset	1. Capital gain or loss except ordinary income to the extent of partner's share of unrealized receivables, depreciation recapture, and substantially appreciated inventory	1. Capital gains and losses, except losses may qualify as § 1244 ordinary losses if the corporation meets certain requirements	1. Same as S corporation

Family Ownership

Items for Comparison	Proprietorship/ Proprietor	Partnership/ Partner	S Corporation/ Shareholder	C Corporation Shareholder
1. Must all owners participate in the management of the business?	1. No	1. Yes, all general partners but limited partners cannot	1. No	1. No
2. Must a reasonable salary be allocated to family members performing services for the business?	2. No	2. Yes	2. Yes	2. No
3. May minors be owners of the business?	3. Yes, if they are the sole proprietor	3. Yes	3. Yes	3. Yes

PROBLEM MATERIALS

DISCUSSION QUESTIONS

23-1 *Eligibility Requirements.* May the following corporations elect Subchapter S? If not, explain why.

    a.   A corporation is 90 percent owned by another corporation.

    b.   A corporation has 36 shareholders, including Mr. and Mrs. V and Mr. and Mrs. Z.

    c.   A corporation has 60 percent of its revenues from exports to Europe.

    d.   A family corporation is owned by a father and his three children. Since the children are under age 18, their shares are held in a trust fund.

    e.   A corporation has 1,000 shares of common stock outstanding and 500 shares of authorized but unissued preferred stock.

23-2 *Stock Requirements.* A mother wishes to establish an S corporation with her two children. However, she is concerned about the one class of stock requirement. She does not want to provide her children with voting control but does wish to give them 60 percent of the stock. Can she achieve her wishes? Explain.

23-3 *Election.* F, M, and T are shareholders of a calendar year corporation. On February 15, 1991, they are advised they should elect Subchapter S status. All agree to the election. However, they state that they purchased a 10 percent ownership interest from V on January 4, 1991. V sold his interest because he said he never wanted to have any contact with F, M, or T again. Can they elect Subchapter S for 1991? Explain.

23-4 *Termination of the Election.* Compare the effects of an intentional revocation, an unintentional violation of the eligibility requirements, and a termination due to the receipt of excessive passive investment income.

23-5 *Termination of the Election.* A calendar year S corporation unexpectedly receives a government contract on April 3, 1991. The profits from the contract in 1991 will be substantial. The three equal shareholders wish to revoke the election for 1991. Can they? Explain.

23-6 *Passive Investment Income.* An S corporation with AE&P of $5,000 is expected to receive 30 percent of its gross income from rents but only 18 percent of its net income from these rents. Will the excess passive investment income test be violated? Assume the S corporation's taxable year does not end for seven months and all income is earned equally over the year. Can any action be taken during the next seven months to ensure the test will not be violated?

23-7 *Employee-Owner.* Which of the three organizational forms—S corporation, C corporation, or partnership—treats owners who work for the business in the following manner?

    a.   The owner's compensation is a deductible business expense.

    b.   The owner's compensation is subject to FICA withholding.

    c.   The employee benefits are deductible expenses.

23-8 *Schedule K-1.* Why must each shareholder of an S corporation be provided with a Schedule K-1?

23-9 *Business Income.* How are each of the following items treated by an S corporation?

a.   Dividend income
b.   Accrued rental expense to a shareholder
c.   Net capital gain
d.   Distribution of assets with a market value in excess of basis

23-10 *Family Ownership.* A taxpayer operates a retail store as an S corporation. He has a 16-year-old daughter and a 12-year-old son.

a.   Can he employ either or both of them in the business and deduct their salaries?
b.   Can they be shareholders in the S corporation?
c.   Can a trust be formed to hold the shares of stock owned by a minor child?

23-11 *Stock Basis.* What is outside basis? What is inside basis? Why is it a problem if the outside basis exceeds the inside basis?

23-12 *Property Distributions.* What effect do noncash distributions have on the S corporation and on the shareholder if the S corporation has no AE&P, and:

a.   The property's market value exceeds its basis, or
b.   The property's basis exceeds its market value?

23-13 *Distributions.* When do cash distributions result in includible income to the S shareholder?

23-14 *Post-Termination Period.* What is a post-termination period? How is it useful?

23-15 *Basic Comparison.* List the tax advantages and the tax disadvantages of an S corporation when compared with:

a.   A partnership.
b.   A C corporation.

PROBLEMS

23-16 *Termination of Election.* T, the sole shareholder and president of T, Inc., had operated a successful automobile dealership as a regular C corporation for many years. In 1986, however, the corporation elected to be taxed as an S corporation. After T's unexpected heart attack in 1987, the corporation sold most of its assets and retained only a small used car operation. In 1989 and 1990, T, Inc. had paid the tax on excessive passive income and had AE&P (from its C corporation years) at the end of both years. In 1991, the corporation paid no dividends and had the following income and expenses:

Interest income	$50,000
Dividend income	5,000
Gain from prior installment sale	30,000
Used car sales	40,000
Cost of sales	20,000

Is the S election terminated, and if so, when?

23-17 *Consequences of Revocation of an S Election.* In July 1991, the shareholders of S Inc., a calendar year corporation, unanimously vote to revoke their corporation's S election as of August 1, 1991. The corporation's taxable income for January through December 1991 is $432,000, and the shareholders do not elect to perform an interim closing of the corporate books.

a.   What tax return(s) must S file for 1991, and what are the due dates of the return(s)?

b.   Compute S's corporate taxable income for the 1991 short year for the (1) S corporation and (2) C corporation.

23-18 *Net Income from Operations.* A and B are MDs in the AB partnership. Because of limited liability considerations, their attorney has advised them to incorporate. A typical year for the MDs (who are equal partners) is as follows:

Revenues	$400,000
Operating expenses	190,000
Charitable contributions	10,000
Owner compensation	200,000

a.   Calculate AB's ordinary net income if it is taxed as (1) a partnership or (2) an S corporation.

b.   Ignoring limited liability considerations, should the partners incorporate and elect S status?

23-19 *Net Income.* A calendar year S corporation, organized in 1988, has the following information for the current taxable year:

Sales...	$180,000
Cost of goods sold..............................	(70,000)
Dividend income	5,000
Net capital loss.................................	(4,000)
Salary to Z......................................	12,000
Life insurance for Z.............................	500
Other operating expenses.......................	40,000
Cash distributions to owners....................	20,000

Assume Z is single and her only other income is $30,000 salary from an unrelated employer. She is a 20 percent owner with a $10,000 basis in the S stock. Calculate the S corporation's net ordinary income and Z's adjusted gross income and ending basis in the S corporation stock.

23-20 *Net Losses.* A calendar year S corporation, organized in 1988, has the following information for the current taxable year:

Sales...	$180,000
Cost of goods sold..............................	(130,000)
Net capital gain	(6,000)
Salary to Z......................................	18,000
Charitable contributions	1,000
Other operating expenses.......................	65,000
Dividend income	4,000

Assume Z is single and her only other income is $30,000 salary from an unrelated employer. She is a 40 percent owner with a $10,000 basis in the S stock and no corporate debt owed to her. Calculate the S corporation's net ordinary loss, Z's adjusted gross income, and the character and amount of S corporate items that flow through to her.

23-21 *Allocations.* V owns 500 shares of stock of an S corporation with 2,000 shares outstanding. The calendar year S corporation's records show the following information:

Net ordinary income	$200,000
Net capital loss..................................	(10,000)
Distributions from S earnings...................	30,000

Calculate V's share of the items if on March 15 he sells:

a. 200 of his shares of stock;

b. All 500 shares of his stock and the per day allocation method is used; or

c. All 500 shares of his stock and the interim closing of the books method is used. The records reveal that through March 15, net ordinary income was $60,000, net capital loss was $10,000, and distributions from earnings were $15,000.

23-22   *Basis*.   A calendar year business reports the following information as of the end of 1990 and 1991:

	1990	1991
Accounts payable to suppliers..........	$10,000	$11,000
Note payable to City Bank..............	40,000	37,000
Note payable to H.....................	12,000	10,000
Cash distributions to owners...........		20,000
Net ordinary income...................		15,000

H, a 30 percent owner, had a basis in the business at the end of 1990 of $9,000. Calculate H's basis at the end of 1991 assuming the business is

a.   A partnership
b.   An S corporation

23-23   *Deductibility of Losses by Shareholders*. B, Inc. was incorporated in 1988, and its shareholders made a valid Subchapter S election for B's first taxable year. At the beginning of 1991, Shareholder Z had a basis of $14,500 in his B stock and held a $10,000 note receivable from B with a $10,000 basis. For 1991, Z was allocated a $32,000 ordinary loss and a $4,000 capital loss from the corporation. B did not make any distributions to its shareholders during the current year.

a.   How much of each allocated loss may Z deduct in 1991?
b.   How much basis will Z have in his B stock and his note receivable at the end of 1991?

23-24   *Basis Adjustments*. Refer to the facts in Problem 23-23 above. In 1992, Z is allocated $7,000 of ordinary income and $5,500 of tax-exempt income from B. B did not make any distributions to its shareholders during the year. What effect will these income allocations have on Z's basis in his B stock and note receivable?

23-25   *Losses and Basis*. J, Inc. is an S corporation that reported the following selected items as of December 31, 1991.

Ordinary loss (from Form 1120S, page 1).........	$30,000
Long-term capital gain...........................	500
Tax-exempt interest income......................	1,000
Notes payable to banks	30,000
(1/1/91 balance = $20,000)	
Notes payable to LJ.............................	5,000
(1/1/91 balance = $0)	

The corporation is owned 60 percent by LJ and 40 percent by RS. At the beginning of the year, they had a basis in their *stock* of $12,000 and $10,000, respectively. How much income or loss will each of the shareholders report for 1991?

23-26   *Basis*.   M, a 40 percent owner, has a basis in the S corporate stock of $15,000 and in a note receivable from the S corporation of $8,000. Compute the basis of the stock and the note and the amount of the ordinary loss and income that flow through to M in 1991 and 1992.

a.   The S corporation has a net operating loss of $45,000 in 1991.
b.   The S corporation has a net operating income of $20,000 in 1992.

23-27 *Basis.* A calendar year S corporation has the following information for 1991 and 1992:

	1991	1992
Net ordinary income (or loss)............	$(50,000)	$10,000
Dividend income........................	5,000	2,000

X, an unmarried 60 percent shareholder, has a basis in the stock on January 1, 1991 of $18,000 and a note receivable from the corporation for $12,000. X's only other income is salary from an unrelated business.

a. Calculate X's basis in the stock and in the note after the above income and loss distributions are recorded for 1991.

b. Calculate X's basis in the stock and in the note after the above income distributions are recorded for 1992.

c. Assume the corporation paid the $12,000 note on April 3, 1992. Calculate X's basis in the stock after the above income distributions are recorded for 1992, and calculate the effect on X's adjusted gross income for all 1992 items, including the payment of the note.

23-28 *Inside and Outside Basis.* XYZ is an S corporation owned equally by three shareholders. X has often disagreed with the other shareholders over business matters and now believes he should withdraw from the corporation. X's basis in his stock is $50,000. The corporation's balance sheet appears as follows:

Cash...	$100,000
Accounts receivable.............................	50,000
Land...	30,000
Equipment (net).................................	10,000
Accounts payable...............................	30,000
Note payable to X...............................	10,000
Capital accounts................................	150,000

The equipment's market value is approximately the same as its net book value, but the land is now valued at $60,000. X sells all of his stock to W for $60,000.

a. How much gain must X recognize?

b. What is W's "inside" stock basis? What is her "outside" basis?

23-29 *Family Ownership.* K operates a small retail store as a proprietorship. Annual net ordinary income is expected to be $60,000 next year. The estimated value of her services to the business is $25,000. K's 14-year-old son is interested in the business. She is considering giving him a 30 percent ownership interest in the business. If she does this, she will be paid a salary of $25,000. K files as head of household and does not itemize deductions. Neither she nor her son has any other includible income. Ignore all payroll and self-employment taxes in the following computations.

a. Determine next year's tax savings that will be achieved if K establishes an S corporation with her son at the beginning of the year compared with continuing the business as a proprietorship.

b. Will K or her son have any includible income if they exchange the appreciated proprietorship assets for the 70 and 30 percent ownership interests, respectively, in the S corporation?

c. What advice should you give K on establishing and operating the S corporation?

23-30 *Property Distributions.* M receives the following equipment from an S corporation as a distribution of profits.

Asset	Cost	Accumulated Depreciation	Basis	Fair Market Value
Equipment	$10,000	$7,900	$2,100	$2,280

The equipment was used in the business for four years of its five-year ACRS life and will be a nonbusiness asset to M. M is a 60 percent owner and has a basis in the stock of $11,000 before the property distribution. Calculate the following amounts.

a. The S corporation's recognized gain

b. M's basis in the equipment

c. The effect on M's basis in the stock

d. The effect on M's adjusted gross income

23-31 *Property Distributions.* Refer to Problem 23-30. Calculate the same amounts if M's basis in the S corporation, before the distribution, is $1,200 instead of the $11,000.

23-32   *Computation of AAA and Basis.*   J formed R Corporation in 1977. The corporation operated as a C corporation from 1977 until 1986, when it elected to be taxed as an S corporation. At the beginning of the current year, J had a basis in his stock of $20,000. The corporation's balance in the AAA at the beginning of the current year was $30,000. R's records for the current year reveal the following information:

Sales..	$300,000
Cost of goods sold.................................	120,000
Miscellaneous operating expenses	50,000
Salary to J..	40,000
Nondeductible portion of entertainment..............	4,000
Tax-exempt interest income.........................	13,000
Expenses related to tax-interest income.......	3,000
Capital gain.......................................	7,000
Capital loss.......................................	2,000
Charitable contribution.............................	5,000
Cash distribution to J..............................	10,000

Compute J's basis in his stock and the corporation's balance in the AAA as of the end of the taxable year.

23-33   *Cash and Property Distributions.*   S, Inc. had previously been a regular C corporation, but elected to be taxed as an S corporation in 1981. It is owned equally by J and G, who have a basis in their stock of $100,000 each at the beginning of the current year. Also at the beginning of the current year, the corporation had the following balances:

Accumulated adjustments account................	$50,000
Previously taxed income.........................	40,000
Accumulated earnings and profits	30,000
Other adjustments account.......................	0

During the current year, the corporation had ordinary income of $35,000 and distributed IM stock worth $75,000 to J and cash of $75,000 to G. The stock was purchased four years ago for $50,000.

a.   What are the tax effects of the distribution on the corporation?

b.   What are the consequences to each of the shareholders?

23-34   *Cash Distributions—AE&P.*   A calendar year S corporation has the following balance on January 1, 1991:

Accumulated adjustments account.................	$13,000
Previously taxed income..........................	2,000
Accumulated earnings and profits.................	6,000
Other adjustments account........................	0

The S corporation records show $12,000 net ordinary income, $4,000 tax-exempt income net of related expenses, and $55,000 cash distributions for 1991. Y owns 70 percent of the stock. Her basis in the stock on January 1, 1991 was $7,000, and she has a note receivable from the corporation of $5,000. Y is single, and her only other income is salary from an unrelated business.

a.   Calculate the balances in the corporate accounts as of December 31, 1991.

b.   Calculate the effect on Y's adjusted gross income for 1991.

c.   Calculate the basis in Y's stock and note as of December 31, 1991.

23-35 *Property Distributions—AE&P.* Assume the same facts as in Problem 23-34 except the distribution is stock held more than one year as an investment with a market value of $55,000 and a basis of $53,000.

    a.   Calculate the balances in the corporate accounts as of December 31, 1991.
    b.   Calculate the effect on Y's adjusted gross income for 1991.
    c.   Calculate the basis in Y's stock and note as of December 31, 1991.

23-36 *Distributions from an S Corporation.* D, Inc. was incorporated in 1986, and its shareholders made a valid S election for D's 1989 calendar year. At the end of the current year but before the distribution is considered, D had $19,000 of accumulated earnings and profits from 1986 through 1988, and an accumulated adjustments account of $11,000. D made only one cash distribution of $20,000 during the year, $5,000 of which was paid to shareholder M, who owns 25 percent of D's stock. After all adjustments *except* any required for the distribution, M's basis in his stock was $18,000.

    a.   What are the tax consequences of the distribution to M, and what is M's basis in his D stock after the distribution?
    b.   What are the balances in D's accumulated earnings and profits account and accumulated adjustments account after the distribution?

23-37 *Excess Passive Investment Income.* A calendar year S corporation has AE&P of $15,000 from years when it was operated as a C corporation. Its records show the following:

Sales	$100,000
Cost of goods sold	(55,000)
Operating expenses	(15,000)
Dividend income	20,000
Rental income	40,000
Rental expenses	(25,000)

The corporation is owned equally by three brothers. Determine the tax effect on the S corporation and on each brother.

23-38 *Tax on Built-in Gains.* A corporation, organized in 1971, was operated as a C corporation until Subchapter S was elected as of January 1, 1988. Assets held on that date ($80,000 market value and $50,000 basis) are distributed in 1991 when the market value is $90,000. Calculate the 1991 tax on built-in gains if 1991 taxable income, based on computations for a C corporation, is

    a. $60,000
    b. $20,000

23-39 *Tax on Built-in Gains.*   On February 5, 1991 L Corporation, a cash basis calendar year C corporation, elected S status effective for January 1, 1991. On January 1, L's balance sheet revealed the following assets:

	Adjusted Basis	Fair Market Value
Inventory	$20,000	$85,000
Land	30,000	70,000
Equipment	45,000	15,000

During the year, L sold all of the inventory and the equipment for $90,000 and $12,000, respectively. In addition, during the year the corporation paid $3,000 of routine operating expenses incurred in the previous year. Compute the corporation's built-in gains tax assuming that its taxable income, if it were a C corporation, would have been $100,000 (including the transactions above).

23-40 *Worthless Securities.*   A calendar year S corporation is bankrupt. E, a 60 percent owner for several years, will not receive any assets from the business. His basis in the stock as of January 1, 1991 was $70,000, and he has a note receivable of $25,000 from the corporation. Both are determined to be uncollectible July 1, 1991. The S corporation has a net ordinary loss during 1991 of $30,000; $20,000 before July 1 and $10,000 after July 1. E lent the corporation the $20,000 last year and $5,000 four months ago in an effort to protect his ownership interest in the business. Calculate E's adjusted gross income and capital loss carryovers if his adjusted gross income from other sources totals $120,000.

23-41 *Comprehensive Comparison.*   A service business has the following information for the current calendar year:

Revenues from services.........................	$200,000
Operating expenses:	
Depreciation.................................	22,000
Insurance.....................................	1,400
Office supplies..............................	1,800
Repairs.......................................	2,300
Salary (or compensation) to owners/employee W	25,000
Payroll taxes for W...........................	(1)
Salary to nonowner employees................	50,000
Payroll taxes for nonowner employees.........	4,600
Group-term life insurance premiums:	
For W[2].....................................	750
For nonowner employees...................	1,320
Utilities and telephone........................	7,900
Charitable contributions.......................	1,100
Rent expense[3]	4,800
Other items:	
Capital gain..................................	2,000
Capital loss[4]	5,000
Dividend income (from 10% owned corporation)	6,000
Cash distributions to owners..................	30,000
Rehabilitation credit..........................	3,000

(1)   Payroll taxes for W are $2,300 ($25,000 × 7.65% = $1,912.50 FICA + $434 unemployment taxes = $2,346.50, rounded to $2,300 for simplicity) if the business is an S or C corporation.

(2)   Assume W has agreed to reimburse the business for any expenses that cannot be deducted because W is an owner.

(3)   The rent expense is for a building rented from W. $400 of the rent expenses was accrued at the end of the year but not paid until January of the next year.

(4)   There have been no capital gains in prior years.

W is a 90 percent owner and has a basis in the business, before the above information is considered, of $50,000. W has no other includible income, files as married joint, has four exemptions, and has other itemized deductions of $8,500 (including no medical expenses and no miscellaneous deductions).

a.   Calculate the net business income for the partnership and the S corporation, and calculate the taxable income and tax liability for the C corporation.

b.   Calculate W's Federal income tax liability and self-employment tax liability for each of the three organizational forms.

c.   Calculate W's basis in the partnership, S corporation, and C corporation after all information is considered for the year.

23-42 *Tax Return Problem.* Individuals P and K formed P&K Corporation on March 1, 1982 to provide computer consulting services. The company has been an S corporation since its formation, and the stock ownership is divided as follows: 60 percent to P and 40 percent to K. The business code and employer identification numbers are 7389 and 24-3897625, respectively. The business office is located at 3010 East Apple Street, Atlanta, Georgia 30304. P and K live nearby at 1521 South Elm Street and 3315 East Apple Street, respectively. Their social security numbers are 403-16-5110 for P and 518-72-9147 for K.

The calendar year, cash basis corporation's December 31, 1990 balance sheet and December 31, 1991 trial balance contain the following information:

	Balance Sheet 12/31/90		Trial Balance 12/31/91	
	Debit	Credit	Debit	Credit
Cash	$ 12,000		$ 22,000	
Note receivable[1]	14,000		14,000	
Equipment[2,3]	150,000		190,000	
Accumulated depreciation......		$ 38,000		$ 63,500
Notes payable[3,4]		94,000		117,200
Capital stock...................		10,000		10,000
Accumulated adjustments account		34,000		34,000
Cash distributed to P			25,440	
Cash distributed to K			16,960	
Revenues......................				235,000
Interest income[1]				1,400
§ 1245 gain....................				3,500
Salary expense[5]			110,000	
Rent expense..................			12,000	
Interest expense..............			16,600	
Tax expenses (property and payroll)			13,800	
Repair expense................			5,800	
Depreciation expense..........			29,200	
Health insurance expense[6] ...			1,600	
Property insurance expense.....................			1,500	
Office supplies expense			3,000	
Utility expense................			2,200	
Charitable contributions........			500	
Totals.......................	$176,000	$176,000	$464,600	$464,600

(1) The note receivable is from K and is due December 31, 1996. The annual interest rate is 10 percent and K paid $1,400 on December 28,1991.

(2) Equipment was sold May 12, 1991 for $9,800. It was purchased new on May 1, 1989 for $10,000 and its basis when sold was $6,300.

(3) New equipment was purchased March 1, 1991 with $5,000 cash and a $45,000 three-year note payable. The first note payment is March 1, 1992.

(4) Notes payable are long-term except for $20,000 of the note to be paid next year.

(5) Salary expense is composed of salary of $30,000 each to P and to K and $50,000 to unrelated employees.

(6) Health insurance premiums paid were for the unrelated employees.

Prepare Form 1120S (including Schedules K, L, and M), and Schedule K-1 for shareholder P. Complete all six pages, including responses to all questions. If any necessary information is missing in the problem, assume a logical answer and record it. Do not prepare Schedule K-1 for shareholder K or other required supplemental forms at this time.

23-43   *Tax Return Problem.* During 1990, Lisa Cutter and Jeff McMullen decided they would like to start their own gourmet hamburger business. Lisa and Jeff believed that the public would love the recipes used by Lisa's mom, Tina Woodbrook. They also thought that they had the necessary experience to enter this business, since Jeff currently owned a fast-food franchise business while Lisa had experience operating a small bakery. After doing their own market research, they established Slattery's Inc. and elected to be taxed as an S corporation. The company's address is 5432 Partridge Pl., Tulsa, Oklahoma 74105 and its employer identification number is 88-7654321.

The company started modestly. After refurbishing an old gas station that it had purchased, the company opened for business on February 25, 1991. Shortly after business began, however, business boomed. By the end of 1991, the company had established two other locations.

Slattery's has three shareholders who own stock as follows:

Shareholder	Shares
Lisa Cutter................	500
Jeff McMullen.............	200
Tina Woodbrook..........	300
Total outstanding	1,000

Slattery's was formed on February 1, 1991. On that date, shareholders made contributions as follows:

> Lisa Cutter contributed $30,000 in cash and 200 shares of MND stock, a publicly held company, which had a fair market value of $20,000. Lisa had purchased the MND stock on October 3, 1986 for $8,000.
> Jeff McMullen contributed equipment worth $35,000 and with a basis of $29,000.
> Tina Woodbrook contributed $30,000 in cash.

Assume 1991 depreciation for tax purposes is $10,560.

The company is on the accrual basis and has chosen to use the calendar year for tax purposes. Its adjusted trial balance for *financial accounting* purposes reveals the following information:

	Debit	Credit
Cash	$279,800	
Ending inventory	16,000	
Equipment	35,000	
Land	10,000	
Building	15,000	
Improvements to building	55,000	
Accumulated depreciation		$ 9,000
Notes payable		93,000
Accounts payable		40,000
Taxes payable		8,000
Salaries payable		20,000
Capital stock		100,000
Sales		400,000
Gain on sale of MND stock		18,000
Dividend from MND Corporation		2,000
Cost of goods sold	84,000	
Legal expenses	500	
Accounting expenses	400	
Miscellaneous expenses	2,100	
Premium on key-man life insurance policy	800	
Advertising	8,600	
Utilities	8,000	
Payroll taxes	12,500	
Salary expenses	120,000	
Insurance	9,000	
Repairs	6,500	
Charitable contributions	17,600	
Depreciation per books	9,000	
Interest expense	200	

The company has provided additional information below.

The company took a physical count of inventory on December 31, 1991 and determined that ending inventory was $16,000.

On February 9, 1991, the corporation purchased an old gas station for $25,000 to house the restaurant. Of the $25,000 purchase price, $10,000 was allocated to the land while $15,000 was allocated to the building. Prior to opening, the old gas station was renovated. Improvements to the structure were made during February at a cost of $55,000.

The legal costs were for work done by Slattery's attorney in February for drafting the articles of incorporation and by-laws. Accounting fees were paid in May for setting up the books and the accounting system. Miscellaneous expenses included a one-time $100 fee paid in February to the State of Oklahoma to incorporate.

The MND stock was sold for $38,000 on April 3, 1991. Shortly before the sale, MND had declared and paid a dividend. Slattery's received $2,000 on April 1, 1991. MND was incorporated in Delaware.

The corporation purchased refrigeration equipment (7-year property) on February 15, 1991 for $15,000.

Slattery's has elected not to use the limited expensing provisions of Code § 179. In addition, it claimed the maximum depreciation with respect to all other assets. Any other elections required to minimize the corporation's tax liability were made.

Lisa Cutter (Social Security No. 447-52-7943) is president of the corporation and spends 90 percent of her working time in the business. She received a salary of $60,000. No other officers received compensation. Social security numbers are 306-28-6192 for Jeff and 403-34-6771 for Tina. The key-man life insurance policy covers Lisa's life and the corporation is the beneficiary.

Prepare Form 1120S and other appropriate forms and schedules for Slattery's. On separate schedule(s), show all calculations used to determine all reported amounts except those for which the source is obvious or which are shown on a formal schedule to be filed with the return.

Note: This problem is based on the tax return problem that appears at the end of Chapters 2 and 10.

RESEARCH PROBLEMS

23-44 *Incorporating a Proprietorship or Partnership.* E and F have operated competing businesses for several years. Recently, they agreed to combine their assets and form a corporation. They plan to transfer appreciated property to the newly organized corporation in exchange for stock and notes. The net assets have a market value of $320,000 and a basis to the owners of $175,000. After the exchange, each of them will own stock valued at $100,000 and long-term notes with a face value of $60,000 and an annual interest rate of 10 percent. The term of the notes has not been established yet but E and F are considering making a third of them ($20,000 to E and $20,000 to F) payable at the end of three years, a third payable at the end of five years, and the remainder payable at the end of 10 years. Based on their present plans, will the transfer of appreciated property to the corporation for stock and notes qualify as a nontaxable exchange?

Some suggested research materials:

§ 351 and accompanying Regulations.
Pinellas Ice & Cold Storage Co. v. Comm., 3 USTC ¶1023, 11 AFTR 1112, 287
    U.S. 462 (1933).
Camp Wolters Enterprises, Inc., 22 T.C. 737 (1955) *aff'd* in 56-1 USTC
    ¶9314, 49 AFTR 283, 230 F.2d 555 (CA-5, 1956).
Robert W. Adams, 58 T.C. 41 (1972).

23-45 *Expanding an S Corporation.* L Inc., an S corporation, manufactures computers. Most of its computers are sold through individually owned retail computer stores. This year it decided it wanted to expand its operations into the retail market. To this end, it has decided to acquire Micros Unlimited, which operates a chain of computer retail stores nationwide. According to the proposed plan, L will purchase all of the stock of Micros and then completely liquidate the newly acquired corporation. It will then operate all of the stores of Micro as a separate division of the company. Advise L regarding any problems you foresee in this plan.

Hint: Read the requirements that must be satisfied in order for a corporation to operate as an S corporation.

PART IX

FAMILY TAX PLANNING

CONTENTS

LEARNING OBJECTIVES

Upon completion of this chapter you will be able to:

- Characterize the types of transfers that are subject to the Federal gift tax
- Compute a donor's total taxable gifts for the current year, including
    - Determination of all available $10,000 exclusions
    - Calculation of any available marital or charitable deduction
- Explain the mechanics of the calculation of the gift tax, including the role of the unified credit
- List the three basic steps involved in the computation of a decedent's taxable estate
- Specify the various types of property interests that must be valued for inclusion in a decedent's gross estate
- Describe any deductions from the gross estate
- Explain the mechanics of the calculation of the estate tax, including the role of the unified credit
- Discuss the purpose of the generation-skipping transfer tax

CHAPTER OUTLINE

Chapter 24

THE FEDERAL TRANSFER TAXES

INTRODUCTION

Unlike the Federal income tax, the Federal transfer taxes are not significant revenue producers. For example, in 1988 collection of the Federal transfer taxes represented less than 2 percent of Federal income.[1] Historically, the primary function of these taxes has been to inhibit the accumulation of wealth by family units. Thus, the goal of wealth redistribution underlies the design of the Federal gift, estate, and generation-skipping transfer taxes that are examined in this chapter.

A BRIEF HISTORY

In 1916, Congress enacted the first Federal law designed to tax the transfer of property triggered by the death of an individual. The value of the transfer was measured by the fair market value of the various assets included in the decedent's taxable estate.

Because an individual could avoid the estate tax simply by gifting away his or her property before death, a transfer tax on gifts payable by the donor was deemed necessary to prevent full scale avoidance of the estate tax. The first Federal gift tax was enacted in 1924. Until 1976, the gift tax was computed on the basis of a separate (and less expensive) rate schedule than that of the estate tax. A unique feature of the gift tax is the fact that it is computed on the cumulative amount of gifts made by an individual during his or her lifetime. Because of the progressive transfer tax rates, every gift is more expensive in terms of tax dollars than the last.

Congress enacted several substantial changes in the structure of the transfer tax system in 1976. The first change was the integration of the gift and estate taxes. The two separate rate schedules were replaced by a single, unified transfer tax rate schedule used to compute both the gift and the estate tax. After 1976, a decedent's taxable estate is treated as an individual's *final* taxable gift and is

---

[1] Commissioner of Internal Revenue, *1988 Annual Report*, IRS Publication 55.

taxed on a cumulative basis with actual gifts made during the decedent's life. In addition, a single, *unified* credit was substituted for the $30,000 gift tax exemption and the $60,000 estate tax exemption. The credit is "unified" in the sense that whatever amount is used to offset the gift tax is unavailable to offset the estate tax.

Another change made in 1976 was the introduction of a third Federal transfer tax on generation-skipping transfers. This tax, designed to complement the gift and estate taxes, is quite complex and highly controversial. It is discussed later in this chapter.

The Economic Recovery Tax Act of 1981 (ERTA 1981) continued the restructuring of the transfer tax system begun in 1976. The most important feature of this legislation was the unlimited marital deduction. This deduction makes gifts between spouses completely nontaxable and allows the first spouse to die to leave the family wealth to the surviving spouse at no Federal transfer tax cost. Thus, after 1981, the taxable unit for the imposition of the gift or estate tax is no longer the individual but the marital unit.

PROPERTY INTERESTS

Since the estate and gift taxes concern transfers of property, understanding the two taxes requires an appreciation of the nature of property interests and the different forms of property ownership. In the United States, each of the 50 states has its own system of *property law*—statutory rules that govern an individual's right to own and convey both real and personal property during his or her lifetime. Unfortunately, the specific property laws of each state vary considerably and therefore generalizations about property laws can be dangerous. However, the various state legal systems can be divided into two basic categories: *common law systems* and *community property systems*. The common law system, derived from English laws of property ownership, focuses on individual ownership of assets, regardless of the marital status of the individual. This system has been adopted in 41 states. The community property system is a derivation of Spanish property law and is followed in nine states: Arizona, California, Idaho, Louisiana, Nevada, New Mexico, Texas, Washington, and Wisconsin. Under either system, an individual may own property alone or jointly with another. In addition, an individual may own only a partial interest in the property such as an income interest. The different forms of co-ownership and various types of partial interests are considered below.

FORMS OF CO-OWNERSHIP

The consequences of holding property jointly with another can vary substantially, depending on the type of co-ownership. There are four forms of co-ownership: (1) tenancy in common, (2) joint tenancy, (3) tenancy by the entirety, and (4) community property ownership.

Tenancy in Common. A tenancy in common exists when two or more persons hold title to property, each owning an undivided fractional interest in the whole. The percentage of the property owned by one tenant need not be the same as the other co-tenants but can differ as the co-tenants provide. The most important feature of this type of property interest is that it is treated in virtually all respects like property that is owned outright. Thus, the interest can be sold, gifted, willed, or, when there is no will, passed to the owner's heirs according to the laws of the state. Another important characteristic of a tenancy in common is the *right of partition*. This right permits co-owners who disagree over something concerning the property to go to court to secure a division of the property among the owners. In some cases, however, a physical division is impossible (e.g., 50 acres of land where each acre's value is dependent on the whole), and consequently, the property must be sold with the proceeds split between the owners.

Joint Tenancy. Under a joint tenancy arrangement, two or more persons hold title to property, each owning the same fractional interest in the property. Joint tenancy normally implies the right of survivorship (joint tenancy with right of survivorship, or JTWROS). This means that upon the death of one joint tenant, the property automatically passes to the surviving joint tenants. Consequently, the disposition of the property is not controlled by the decedent's will. Like tenants in common, joint tenants have the right to sever their interest in the property. This is a particularly valuable right since the tenant may wish to disinherit the other joint tenants.

Tenancy by the Entirety. A tenancy by the entirety is a JTWROS between husband and wife. The critical difference between a tenancy by the entirety and a JTWROS is that in most states a spouse cannot sever his or her interest without the consent of the other spouse. In addition, in some states the husband has full control over the property while alive and is entitled to all the income from it.

Community Property. In a community property system, married individuals own an equal, undivided interest in all wealth acquired during the course of the marriage, regardless of which spouse made any individual contribution to the marital wealth. In addition to a half interest in such "community property," a spouse may also own property in an individual capacity as "separate property." Generally, assets acquired prior to marriage and assets received by gift or inheritance are separate property. However, in all nine community property states there exists a strong legal presumption that all property possessed during marriage is community, and that presumption can only be overcome by convincing proof of the property's separate nature.

Marital Property. Before leaving the subject of joint ownership, the concept of marital property deserves attention. Except in community property states, it is a common mistake to assume that all property acquired during marriage is jointly held. State laws vary widely on this issue. In some states, only property specifically titled as JTWROS is treated as jointly held. In these and other states, it is not unusual that property acquired during marriage belongs to the husband regardless of whose earnings were used to acquire the property. In other states, each spouse is deemed to own that which can be traced to his or her own earnings. Because of the problems with marital property, transfers of such property should be evaluated carefully to ensure that the rights of either spouse are not violated.

PROPERTY INTERESTS: LIFE ESTATES, REVERSIONS, AND REMAINDERS

Persons who own property outright have virtually unlimited rights with respect to their property. They can sell it, mortgage it, or transfer it as they wish. In addition, they can divide the ownership of the property in any number of ways. In this regard, it is not uncommon for property owners to transfer ownership in property to someone temporarily. During the period of temporary ownership, the beneficiary could have the right to use, possess, and benefit from the income of the property. Assuming that the beneficiary's interest is limited to the income from the property, he or she would be treated as having an *income interest*. The time to which the beneficiary is entitled to the income from the property could be specified in any terms, such as common measures of time: days, weeks, months, or years. Alternatively, the time period could be determined by reference to the occurrence of a specific event. For example, when an individual has an income interest for life, the interest is referred to as a *life estate*. In this case, the person entitled to the life estate is called the *life tenant*.

The owner of property has the right to provide for one or more temporary interests, subject only to the *rule against perpetuities*. This rule requires that the property pass outright to an individual within a certain time period after the transfer. Normally, ownership of the property must vest at a date no later than 21 years after the death of persons alive at the time the interest is created. After any temporary interests have been designated, the owner has the right to provide for the outright transfer of the property. If the owner specifies that the property should be returned to the owner or his or her estate, the interest following the temporary interest is referred to as a *reversionary interest*. If the property passes to someone other than the owner, the interest is called a *remainder interest*. The holder of the remainder interest is the *remainderman*.

Life estates, remainders, and reversions are property interests which can be transferred, sold, and willed (except for life estates) like other types of property. These interests can also be reached by creditors in satisfaction of their claims. However, a person can establish a trust with so-called *spendthrift* provisions, which prohibit the beneficiary from assigning or selling his or her interest (e.g., a life estate) or using the assets to satisfy creditors.

THE GIFT TAX

The statutory provisions regarding the Federal gift tax are contained in §§ 2501 through 2524 of the Internal Revenue Code. These rules provide the basis for the gift tax formula found in Exhibit 24-1. The various elements of this formula are discussed below.

Exhibit 24-1
Computation of Federal Gift Tax Liability

Fair market value of all gifts made in the current year..............		$xxx,xxx
Less the sum of		
Annual exclusions ($10,000 per donee).................	$xx,xxx	
Marital deduction................	xx,xxx	
Charitable deduction............	x,xxx	− xx,xxx
Taxable gifts for current year........		$xxx,xxx
Plus: All taxable gifts made in prior years................		+ xx,xxx
Taxable transfers to date............		$xxx,xxx
Tentative tax on total transfers to date.........		$ xx,xxx
Less the sum of		
Gift taxes computed at current rates on prior years' taxable gifts.......	$ x,xxx	
Unified transfer tax credit.........	x,xxx	− xx,xxx
Gift tax due on current gifts..........		$ xx,xxx

TRANSFERS SUBJECT TO TAX

Section 2511 states that the gift tax shall apply to transfers in trust or otherwise, whether the gift is direct or indirect, real or personal, tangible or intangible. The gift tax is imposed only on transfers of property; gratuitous transfers of services are not subject to tax.[2] The types of property interests to which the gift tax applies are virtually unlimited. The tax applies to transfers of such common items as money, cars, stocks, bonds, jewelry, works of art, houses, and every other type of item normally considered property. It should be emphasized that no property is specifically excluded from the gift tax. For example, the transfer of municipal bonds is subject to the gift tax, even though the income from the bonds is tax free.

The gift tax reaches transfers of partial interests as well. One example is a transfer of property in trust where the income interest is given to someone—the income beneficiary—for his or her life, while the trust property or remainder interest is given to another person—the remainderman—upon the income beneficiary's death. In this case, the donor would be treated as having made two separate gifts, a gift of the income interest and a gift of the remainder interest.

---

[2] Rev. Rul. 56-472, 1956-2 C.B. 21.

The application of the gift tax to both direct and indirect gifts ensures that the tax reaches all transfers regardless of the method of transfer. Direct gifts encompass the common types of outright transfers (e.g., father transfers bonds to daughter, or grandmother gives cash to grandson). On the other hand, indirect gifts are represented primarily by transfers to trusts and other entities. When a transfer is made to a trust, it is considered a gift to the beneficiaries of the trust. Similarly, a transfer to a corporation or partnership is considered a gift to the shareholders or partners. However, if the donor owns an interest in a partnership or corporation, he or she is not treated as making a gift to the extent it would be a gift to himself or herself. An individual may also be treated as making a gift if he or she refuses to accept property and the property passes to another person on account of the refusal.

Most taxpayers understand that the gift tax is imposed on transfers of property motivated by affection and generosity. However, the tax may also be imposed on a transfer of property not intended as a gift within the commonly accepted definition of the word. The tax is intended to apply to any transfer of wealth by an individual that reduces his or her potential taxable estate. Therefore, § 2512 provides that any transfer of property, in return for which the transferor receives *less than adequate or full consideration* in money or money's worth, is a transfer subject to the gift tax.

Adequate Consideration.   Revenue Ruling 79-384 provides an excellent example of a transfer for insufficient consideration.[3]   The taxpayer in the ruling was a father, who had made an oral promise to his son to pay him $10,000 upon the son's graduation from college. The son graduated but the father refused to pay him the promised amount. The son then successfully sued the father, who was forced to transfer the $10,000. The IRS ruled that the father had received no consideration in money or money's worth for the transfer and therefore had made a taxable gift to his son.

Revenue Ruling 79-384 illustrates two important concepts. First, *donative intent* on the part of a transferor of property is not necessary to classify the transfer as a taxable gift.[4]   Second, anything received by the transferor in exchange for the property must be subject to valuation in monetary terms if it is to be consideration within the meaning of § 2512.[5]   The father did receive the satisfaction resulting from his son's graduation, and this consideration was sufficient to create an enforceable oral contract between father and son. However, because the consideration could not be objectively valued in dollar terms it was irrelevant for tax purposes.

---

[3]   1979-2 C.B. 12.

[4]   Reg. § 25.2511-1(g)(1).

[5]   Reg. § 25.2512-8.

The question of sufficiency of consideration normally arises when transfers of assets are made between family members or related parties. When properties are transferred or exchanged in a bona fide business transaction, the Regulations specify that sufficiency of consideration will be presumed because of the arm's-length negotiation between the parties.[6]

Transfers of wealth to dependent family members that represent support are not taxable gifts. The distinction between support payments and gifts is far from clear, particularly when the transferor is not legally obligated to make the payments. Section 2503(e) specifies that amounts paid on behalf of any individual for tuition to an educational organization or for medical care shall not be considered taxable gifts to such individual.

Payments that a divorced taxpayer is legally required to make for the *support* of his or her former spouse are not taxable gifts.[7] However, Regulation § 25.2512-8 specifies that payments made prior to or after marriage in return for the recipient's relinquishment of his or her *marital property rights* are transfers for insufficient consideration and subject to the gift tax. Section 2516 provides an exception to this rule. If a transfer of property is made under the terms of a written agreement between spouses and the transfer is (1) in settlement of the spouse's marital property rights, or (2) to provide a reasonable allowance for support of any minor children of the marriage, no taxable gift will occur. For the exception to apply, divorce must occur within the three-year period beginning on the date one year before such agreement is entered into.

Retained Interest. The final criterion of a taxable transfer is that the transfer must be complete. A transfer is considered complete only if the donor has surrendered all control over the property. For this reason, when the donor alone retains the right to revoke the transfer, the transfer is incomplete and the gift tax does not apply. Similarly, the donor must not be able to redirect ownership of the property in the future; nonetheless, to have a completed gift it is not necessary that the donees have received the property or that the specific donees even be identified.[8]

> **Example 1.** Donor D transfers $1 million into an irrevocable trust with an independent trustee. The trustee has the right to pay the income of the trust to beneficiaries A, B, or C *or* to accumulate the income. After 15 years, the trust will terminate and all accumulated income and principle will be divided among the surviving beneficiaries. Because D has parted with all control over the $1 million, it is a completed gift, even though neither A, B, or C has received or is guaranteed any specified portion of the money.

---

[6] *Ibid.*

[7] Rev. Rul. 68-379, 1968-2 C.B. 414.

[8] Reg. § 25.2511-2(a).

VALUATION AND BASIS

The value of a transfer subject to the Federal gift tax is measured by the fair market value of the property transferred less the value of any consideration received by the transferor. Determining fair market value can be the most difficult aspect of computing a gift tax due. Fair market value is defined in the Regulations as "the price at which such property would change hands between a willing buyer and a willing seller, neither being under any compulsion to buy or to sell, and both having reasonable knowledge of relevant facts."[9]

The determination of an asset's fair market value must be made on the basis of all relevant facts and circumstances. The Regulations under § 2512 are quite detailed and extremely useful in that they prescribe methods for valuation of a variety of assets.

> **Example 2.** Donor S transfers 10 shares of the publicly traded common stock of XYZ Corporation on June 8, 1991. On that date, the highest quoted selling price of the stock was $53 per share. The lowest quoted selling price was $48 per share. Regulation § 25.2512-2(b)(1) specifies that the fair market value of the XYZ stock on June 8, 1990 shall be the mean between the highest and lowest quoted selling price [($53 + $48) ÷ 2], or $50.50 per share.

The valuation of a gift of a partial interest in property is a particularly difficult matter. As part of the Revenue Reconciliation Act of 1990, Congress enacted a set of complex valuation rules that may apply if a donor gives away part of his or her interest in property while retaining an interest in the same property. The general effect of these new rules is to assign a zero value to the donor's retained interest unless such interest is "qualified" by meeting a strict set of statutory requirements. Note that when a retained interest is not a qualified interest, the value of the gifted interest equals the entire value of the property.

> **Example 3.** In the current year Donor D transfers property worth $100,000 into a trust, retaining the right to receive all the income generated by the property for the next 20 years. At the end of the 20-year period, the trust property will be distributed to D's children. Clearly the discounted present value of the children's right to receive the property in 20 years is substantially less than $100,000. However, under the new § 2702 valuation rules, a retained income interest is not a qualified interest, so the value of D's gift to his children upon formation of the trust is $100,000.

The basis of an asset in the hands of a donee is calculated under the rules of § 1015. Generally, the basis of property received as a gift is the basis of the

---

[9] Reg. § 25.2512-1.

asset in the hands of the donor, increased by the amount of any gift tax paid attributable to the excess of fair market value over the donor's basis at the date of gift. This general rule applies only if the asset is sold at a gain by the donee. If the carryover basis rule would result in a realized loss upon subsequent sale, the basis of the asset will be considered the *lesser* of the carryover basis (donor's basis) *or* the asset's fair market value at date of gift. If the asset is sold at a price greater than the fair market value at date of gift but less than its carryover basis, no gain or loss is recognized.

THE GIFT TAX EXCLUSION

When computing taxable gifts made during a current year, a donor may exclude the first $10,000 of gifts made to any donee. This is an *annual exclusion*, subject to the single requirement that a gift eligible for the exclusion must be a gift of a *present* or *current interest* in property.[10] Regulation § 25.2503-3(b) defines a present interest as one that gives the donee "an unrestricted right to the immediate use, possession, or enjoyment of property or the income from property." Therefore, the $10,000 annual exclusion is not available for a gift that can only be enjoyed by the donee at some future date, even if the donee does receive a current ownership interest in the gift.

> **Example 4.** Donor D gifts real estate to donees M and N. M is given *a life estate* (the right to the income from the property for as long as M lives). N receives *the remainder interest* (complete ownership of the property upon the death of M). Although both M and N have received legal property interests, D may claim only one exclusion for his gift to M. The gift to N is a gift of a future rather than a current interest.

Securing the obvious tax benefit of the $10,000 annual exclusion can be difficult if the gift in question is made to a minor or an incapacitated donee. In such cases the donor may be reluctant to give an unrestricted current interest in the donated property. A complete discussion of strategies for making gifts to minors or incapacitated donees is included in Chapter 26.

GIFT SPLITTING

Because of the progressivity of the gift tax and the availability of the annual $10,000 exclusion, gift taxes on a transfer can be minimized by increasing the number of donors. A gift made by a married individual residing in a community property state may have two donors (husband and wife) because of state property law. Property laws in the forty-one non–community property states do not produce this *two donor* result. To compensate for this difference, § 2513 provides a *gift splitting* election to a married donor.

---

[10] § 2503(b).

If a donor makes the proper election on his or her current gift tax return, one-half of all gifts made during the year will be considered to have been made by the donor's spouse. Both spouses must consent to gift splitting for the election to be valid. Since evidence of the spouse's consent is necessary when gift splitting is used, a gift tax return must be filed.

> **Example 5.** In the current year, husband H makes two gifts of $100,000 each to his son and daughter. His wife, W, makes a gift of $5,000 to their daughter. H and W elect gift splitting on their current gift tax returns. As a result, H will report a gift to the daughter of $52,500 and a gift to the son of $50,000, and will claim two $10,000 gift tax exclusions. W will report exactly the same gifts and claim two $10,000 exclusions.
>
> Without gift splitting, H would still be entitled to $20,000 of exclusions, but W could only claim an exclusion of $5,000 for her gift to the daughter.

GIFTS TO POLITICAL AND CHARITABLE ORGANIZATIONS

Code § 2501(a)(5) excludes gifts of money or other property to a political organization from the statutory definition of taxable transfers. If a gratuitous donation is made to a qualified charitable organization, § 2522 provides a deduction for such gift from the donor's taxable gifts for the calendar year. Thus, transfers made without sufficient consideration to qualifying political or charitable groups are not subject to the Federal gift tax.

THE GIFT TAX MARITAL DEDUCTION

Because of the 1981 changes in § 2523, gifts to spouses made after December 31, 1981 are fully deductible by the donor. The marital deduction is permitted only if certain requirements are satisfied. A full discussion of these requirements is considered in conjunction with the discussion of the marital deduction for estate tax purposes.

The gift tax marital deduction allows an individual to make tax-free transfers of wealth to his or her spouse. This opportunity to equalize the wealth owned by husband and wife plays an essential role in family tax planning, a role that will be discussed in Chapter 26.

COMPUTATION AND FILING

Unlike the income tax, which is computed on annual taxable income, the Federal gift tax is *computed cumulatively* on taxable gifts made during a donor's lifetime. This is done by adding taxable gifts for the current year to all taxable gifts made in prior years, calculating the gross tax on the sum of cumulative gifts, and subtracting the amount of gift tax calculated on prior years' gifts.[11]

---

[11] § 2502(a). The amount of gift tax calculated on prior years' gifts is based on current gift tax rates, *regardless* of the rates in effect when the gifts were actually made.

The transfer tax rate schedule in effect for 1984 through 1992 is reproduced in Exhibit 24-2. Exhibit 24-3 contains the transfer tax rate schedule applicable to transfers made after December 31, 1992. Note that the only difference in these two rate structures is at the highest transfer tax rates of 50 and 55 percent.

Exhibit 24-2
Unified Transfer Tax Rate Schedule

For Gifts Made and for Deaths before 1993

If the amount with respect to which the tentative tax to be computed is	The tentative tax is
Not over $10,000	18 percent of such amount
Over $10,000 but not over $20,000	$1,800 plus 20 percent of the excess of such amount over $10,000
Over $20,000 but not over $40,000	$3,800 plus 22 percent of the excess of such amount over $20,000
Over $40,000 but not over $60,000	$8,200 plus 24 percent of the excess of such amount over $40,000
Over $60,000 but not over $80,000	$13,000 plus 26 percent of the excess of such amount over $60,000
Over $80,000 but not over $100,000	$18,200 plus 28 percent of the excess of such amount over $80,000
Over $100,000 but not over $150,000	$23,800 plus 30 percent of the excess of such amount over $100,000
Over $150,000 but not over $250,000	$38,800 plus 32 percent of the excess of such amount over $150,000
Over $250,000 but not over $500,000	$70,800 plus 34 percent of the excess of such amount over $250,000
Over $500,000 but not over $750,000	$155,800 plus 37 percent of the excess of such amount over $500,000
Over $750,000 but not over $1,000,000	$248,300 plus 39 percent of the excess of such amount over $750,000
Over $1,000,000 but not over $1,250,000	$345,800 plus 41 percent of the excess of such amount over $1,000,000
Over $1,250,000 but not over $1,500,000	$448,300 plus 43 percent of the excess of such amount over $1,250,000
Over $1,500,000 but not over $2,000,000	$555,800 plus 45 percent of the excess of such amount over $1,500,000
Over $2,000,000 but not over $2,500,000	$780,800 plus 49 percent of the excess of such amount over $2,000,000
Over $2,500,000 but not over $3,000,000	$1,025,800 plus 53 percent of the excess of such amount over $2,500,000
Over $3,000,000	$1,290,800 plus 55 percent of the excess of such amount over $3,000,000

Exhibit 24-3
Unified Transfer Tax Rate Schedule

For Gifts Made and for Deaths after 1992

If the amount with respect to which the tentative tax to be computed is	*The tentative tax is*
Not over $10,000	18 percent of such amount
Over $10,000 but not over $20,000	$1,800 plus 20 percent of the excess of such amount over $10,000
Over $20,000 but not over $40,000	$3,800 plus 22 percent of the excess of such amount over $20,000
Over $40,000 but not over $60,000	$8,200 plus 24 percent of the excess of such amount over $40,000
Over $60,000 but not over $80,000	$13,000 plus 26 percent of the excess of such amount over $60,000
Over $80,000 but not over $100,000	$18,200 plus 28 percent of the excess of such amount over $80,000
Over $100,000 but not over $150,000	$23,800 plus 30 percent of the excess of such amount over $100,000
Over $150,000 but not over $250,000	$38,800 plus 32 percent of the excess of such amount over $150,000
Over $250,000 but not over $500,000	$70,800 plus 34 percent of the excess of such amount over $250,000
Over $500,000 but not over $750,000	$155,800 plus 37 percent of the excess of such amount over $500,000
Over $750,000 but not over $1,000,000	$248,300 plus 39 percent of the excess of such amount over $750,000
Over $1,000,000 but not over $1,250,000	$345,800 plus 41 percent of the excess of such amount over $1,000,000
Over $1,250,000 but not over $1,500,000	$448,300 plus 43 percent of the excess of such amount over $1,250,000
Over $1,500,000 but not over $2,000,000	$555,800 plus 45 percent of the excess of such amount over $1,500,000
Over $2,000,000 but not over $2,500,000	$780,800 plus 49 percent of the excess of such amount over $2,000,000
Over $2,500,000	$1,025,800 plus 50 percent of the excess of such amount over $2,500,000

Example 6. In 1987, X made his first taxable gift of $100,000. Tax (before credits) on this amount was $23,800. X made a second taxable gift of $85,000 in 1991. The tax (before credits) on the second gift is $26,200, computed as follows:

1987 taxable gift	$100,000
1991 taxable gift	+ 85,000
Cumulative gifts	$185,000
Tax on $185,000	$ 50,000
Less: Tax on 1987 taxable gift	− 23,800
Tax on 1991 gift	$ 26,200

This cumulative system of gift taxation *and* the progressive rate schedule of § 2001 cause a higher tax on the 1991 gift, even though the 1991 gift was $15,000 *less* than the 1987 gift.

A 5 percent surtax applies to any amount of a donor's taxable gifts or a decedent's taxable estate exceeding $10 million, but not in excess of $21,040,000 ($18,340,000 for transfers made after 1992). The purpose of the surtax is to gradually eliminate the tax benefit of both the progressive transfer tax rate structure *and* the unified credit of §§ 2505 and 2010.

Example 7. In 1991, Z makes his first taxable gift of $14 million. Tax before credits on this amount is $7,540,800, computed as follows:

55% on amount of gift in excess of $3,000,000	$6,050,000
Plus: Tax on first $3,000,000 of the gift	1,290,800
Plus: 5% surtax on amount of gift in excess of $10,000,000	200,000
Total tax before credits	$7,540,800

Unified Credit. Only a single credit is available to offset the Federal gift tax—the unified credit authorized by § 2505. The amount of this lifetime credit is currently $192,800. This amount of credit offsets the tax on $600,000 of taxable transfers. Thus, an individual may make substantial transfers of wealth before any tax liability is incurred. The unified credit must be used when available—a taxpayer may not decide to postpone use of the credit if he or she makes a taxable gift during the current year.[12]

---

[12] Rev. Rul. 79-398, 1979-2 C.B. 338.

Example 8. In 1987, Y made her first taxable gift of $350,000. The tax calculated on this gift is $104,800, and Y must use $104,800 of her available unified credit so that the actual gift tax due is reduced to zero. In 1991, Y makes her second taxable gift of $650,000. The tax on this gift is $153,000, computed as follows:

Taxable gift for 1991		$ 650,000
Plus: 1987 taxable gift		+ 350,000
Taxable transfers to date		$1,000,000
Tentative tax on total transfers to date (see Exhibit 24-2)		$ 345,800
Less: Gift taxes calculated on 1987 gift		− 104,800
Tentative tax on 1991 gift		$ 241,000
Less: Remaining unified transfer tax credit:		
Total credit available for 1991	$192,800	
Less: Unified transfer tax credit used in 1987	− 104,800	− 88,000
Gift tax due on 1991 gift		$ 153,000

Filing Requirements. The Federal gift tax return, Form 709, is filed annually on a calendar year basis. The due date of the return is the April 15th after the close of the taxable year. If a calendar year taxpayer obtains any extension to file his or her Federal income tax return, such extension automatically applies to any gift tax return due. If the donor dies during a taxable year for which a gift tax return is due, the gift tax return must be filed by the due date (nine months after death) plus any extensions of the donor's Federal estate tax return.[13]

THE OVERLAP BETWEEN THE GIFT AND ESTATE TAXES

A beginning student of the Federal transfer tax system might reasonably assume that an inter vivos (during life) transfer of property that is considered complete and therefore subject to the gift tax would also be considered complete for estate tax purposes, so that the transferred property would not be included in the decedent's taxable estate. This, however, is not the case. The gift tax and the estate tax are not mutually exclusive; property gifted away in earlier years can be included in the donor's taxable estate. The relationship between the two taxes is illustrated in the following diagram:

---

[13] § 6075(b).

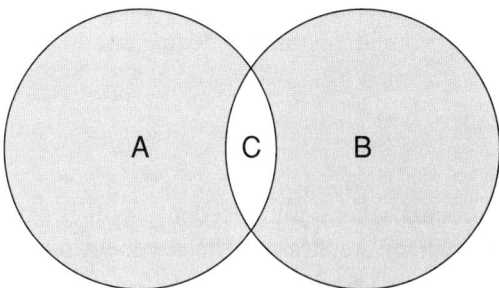

Circle A represents property transferred by the decedent during his or her lifetime and subject to the gift tax. Circle B represents the decedent's taxable estate. Overlap area C represents property already subject to a gift tax that is nevertheless included in the donor/decedent's taxable estate.

Examples of transfers that fall into the overlap area above will be presented later in the chapter. At this point, however, it is important to note that any gift tax paid on a transfer which is considered incomplete for estate tax purposes reduces the amount of estate tax payable.[14]

TRANSFERS OF PROPERTY AT DEATH

ROLE OF A WILL

Each of the 50 states gives its citizens the right to transfer the ownership of their property at death by means of a valid will. State law provides various formal requirements for valid wills, and as a result great care must be taken that a will is drafted in strict accordance with such requirements. There are few restrictions on the right of an individual to dispose of property at death in any manner he or she chooses. The most common restriction is the right under state law of a surviving spouse to receive a specified statutory share of the deceased individual's wealth. The statutory share rules effectively prevent an individual from completely disinheriting a surviving spouse.[15]

INTESTACY

When a person dies with no will or an invalid will, the transfer of his or her wealth is determined under the intestacy laws of the deceased's state of residence. Again, the particulars of the intestacy laws of each state are different. As a general rule, property will pass in order in prescribed shares to a decedent's surviving

---

[14]   § 2001(b)(2).

[15]   Modern statutory share laws have their origins in the English common law property concepts of the "dower" rights of a widow and the "curtesy" rights of a widower.

spouse, children and lineal descendants, parents and lineal ascendants, collateral relatives, and finally, if no relatives of any degree can be located, to the state of residence itself.

PROBATE

Probate is the legal process whereby a decedent's will is established as genuine and valid, and during which creditors of the decedent may submit their claims for payment from the estate. A decedent's probate estate consists of property interests owned at death that will pass under the terms of a decedent's will (or under the laws of intestacy if no valid will exists). It is extremely important for an individual engaged in estate planning to be aware of any property interests that he or she owns but which will *not* be included in the probate estate at death. A major example of such a property interest is a joint tenancy with right of survivorship (JTWROS). As previously explained, upon the death of one of the joint tenants, ownership of the asset automatically shifts to the surviving joint tenant or tenants. This is true *regardless* of the provisions of the deceased joint tenant's will. Similarly, survivor benefits, such as those from a life insurance policy or an annuity, or payments from pension and profit sharing plans, pass directly to the beneficiary and are not controlled by the will.

It should be apparent that those individuals who have amassed any amount of wealth and who wish to control the disposition of that wealth at death should have a validly executed will. However, there are compelling reasons why *every* responsible adult should have a will. When an individual dies intestate (without a valid will), the resulting legal and administrative complications can cause unnecessary hardship and confusion for the surviving family. Finally, one of the most critical functions of a will is to name a guardian for the decedent's minor children; failure to have a will to do so can result in years of family discord and distress.

THE TAXABLE ESTATE

Code §§ 2001 through 2056 contain the statutory rules providing for the imposition of a tax on the transfer of the taxable estate of every decedent who is a citizen or resident of the United States. Sections 2101 through 2108 provide for an estate tax on the value of assets located within the United States owned by a nonresident alien decedent. Discussion of this latter tax is beyond the scope of an introductory text.

Computation of a decedent's taxable estate involves three basic steps:

1. Identification and valuation of assets includible in the gross estate

2. Identification of deductible claims against the gross estate and deductible expenses of estate administration

3. Identification of any deductible bequests out of the gross estate

THE GROSS ESTATE CONCEPT

Section 2031 broadly states that "the value of the gross estate of the decedent shall be determined by including to the extent provided for in this part the value at the time of his death of all property, real or personal, tangible or intangible, wherever situated." The Regulations under this section make it clear that property located in a foreign country is included in this definition.[16]

Sections 2033 through 2044 identify the various types of property that are includible in a decedent's gross estate. Section 2033 is the most commonly applied of these Code sections. It requires the inclusion of any property interest owned by the decedent at date of death. The property interests specified in § 2033 correspond to the legal concept of a decedent's *probate estate*, property interests that will pass to the beneficiaries under the terms of the decedent's will.[17] If the decedent dies without a valid will, these interests will be distributed to the decedent's heirs under the state intestacy laws.

All individuals are, in a sense, on the accrual method of accounting for estate tax purposes. Any legal claim to or interest in an asset that exists at death is includible in the gross estate. For example, a cash basis taxpayer who performed substantial services and was to be paid $20,000 would not report the fee as income until collected. However, if death occurred before collection, the decedent is considered to have owned a $20,000 asset, the right to the fee, which would be includible in his or her gross estate.

The concept of the gross estate is much broader than the legal probate estate. Exhibit 24-4 lists the various types of property interests and assets includible in the gross estate and the statutory authority for each inclusion. These various inclusions are discussed in more detail later in the chapter.

Although the estate tax reaches virtually all types of property interests, it does not extend to property in which the decedent had a life estate created by another. Section 2033 does not require inclusion of such property, since the decedent's only interest in the property terminated upon death.

> **Example 9.** Upon W's death, she transferred stock worth $300,000 in trust, giving her son a life estate and the remainder to her grandson. When the son subsequently dies, his estate does not include the stock, since his interest terminates at his death and he is not transferring the property to the grandson.

The above example illustrates why the life estate is one of the most important devices used in estate planning. Note that the son is entitled to use the property for his life, yet the property escapes taxation in his estate. The 1976 Tax Reform Act addressed this problem in one respect with the generation-skipping transfer tax, discussed later in this chapter. These changes, however, have not eliminated all of the benefits of using the life estate.

---

[16] Reg. § 20.2031-1(a).   [17] Reg. § 20.2031-1(a)(1).

Exhibit 24-4
*Property Included in
the Gross Estate*

Property	*Statutory Authority*
Any property interest owned by the decedent at death	Section 2033

Includes
  cash
  stocks, bonds, other investments securities
  personal assets
  personal residence
  collectibles (antiques, etc.)
  investment real estate
  business interests (sole proprietorship, partner-
  ship interest)	

Certain gifts made within three years of death (limited application after 1981)	Section 2035
Assets transferred during life in which the decedent retained an income interest or control over the enjoyment of the assets or the income therefrom	Section 2036
Assets transferred during life in which the decedent retained more than a 5 percent reversionary interest and possession of which could only be obtained by surviving the decedent	Section 2037
Assets transferred during life if, at death, the decedent possessed the right to alter, amend, revoke, or terminate the terms of the transfer	Section 2038
Certain survivor benefits and annuities	Section 2039
Joint tenancies with right of survivorship	Section 2040
Assets over which the decedent held a *general* power of appointment	Section 2041

Insurance proceeds on the decedent's life if
 	
  (1) payable to the decedent's estate; *or*
  (2) the decedent possessed any incident of
      ownership in the policy at death.
	Section 2042

Assets in a QTIP trust in which the decedent had the income interest	Section 2044

VALUATION OF GROSS ESTATE AND BASIS

Once an asset is identified as part of the gross estate, its fair market value at date of death must be determined. Practically, valuation of assets is the most difficult and subjective problem in computing a decedent's gross estate. Many assets, such as capital stock in a closely held corporation, have no readily ascertainable fair market value. Fortunately the estate tax Regulations, like their gift tax counterparts, provide detailed guidelines to the valuation of many types of assets.[18]

In the 41 common law states, a surviving spouse may have a legally enforceable claim against assets owned by a decedent that cannot be defeated by the terms of the decedent's will. Section 2034 states that the value of property included in the decedent's gross estate is not diminished by such a claim. In the nine community property states, most property owned by a married individual is community property in which both spouses have equal interests. Only one-half the value of such community property is included in a decedent's gross estate.

Although the gross estate is normally valued as of the decedent's date of death, § 2032 allows the executor to elect an alternative valuation date of six months after death. If the election is made, the alternative valuation date must be used for every asset in the gross estate. If an asset is disposed of within six months of death, its value at date of disposition is used. This choice of two possible dates for valuation gives the executor some flexibility in minimizing the value of the gross estate and any estate tax liability.

For income tax purposes, the basis of property in the hands of a person acquiring the property from a decedent is the property's fair market value at date of death or on the alternate valuation date under Code § 2032.[19] Under § 1223(11), assets acquired from a decedent are presumed to have a holding period in excess of six months. In the case of community property, the adjustment to fair market value is available for the *entire property* rather than just the one-half interest that is included in the gross estate of the decedent spouse.[20]

In situations in which the Federal estate tax to be imposed on a particular estate is minimal, an executor might actually elect the alternate valuation date in order to increase the valuation of assets included in the gross estate, thus achieving maximum step-up in the basis of the assets for income tax purposes. Section 2032(c) eliminates this particular tax planning option by providing that no § 2032 election may be made unless such election will decrease the value of the gross estate *and* the amount of the Federal estate tax imposed.

---

[18] See Reg. § 20.2031.

[19] § 1014(a). This rule does not apply to items of property that constitute income in respect of a decedent. § 1014(c). For a com-

plete discussion of income in respect of a decedent, see Chapter 25.

[20] § 1014(b)(6).

SPECIAL USE VALUATION: § 2032A

The requirement that property in a decedent's gross estate be valued at fair market value can create hardship if a principal estate asset is real property used in a family business. The value of such real property as it is used in the business may be considerably less than its potential selling price on the open market. As a result, an estate might be forced to sell the real estate and terminate the family business in order to pay the Federal estate tax.

Section 2032A allows that qualifying real estate used in a closely held business may be valued based on its business usage rather than market value. The requirements for qualification under this section are formidable. For example, the fair market value of the real estate in question and any related personal property must equal or exceed 50 percent of the gross estate (within certain adjustments) before the special use valuation of Code § 2032A may be elected. In addition, the real estate alone must comprise 25 percent of the adjusted gross estate. During at least five of the eight years preceding the decedent's death, the real estate must have been used by the decedent or the decedent's family for farming purposes or in a trade or business. If these requirements are satisfied, the maximum reduction from fair market value of qualifying real estate is $750,000.

> **Example 10.** Decedent F owned a large farm south of a major urban center. As farming property, F's real estate was worth $4 million; however, developers wanting to acquire the real estate for future use as commercial and residential property had offered F $7 million for the real estate. If all the qualifications of § 2032A can be met, F's real property would be valued at $6.25 million in his gross estate, and would take an income tax basis of $6.25 million.

The estate tax savings offered by the election of qualified-use valuation is conditional upon the continued use of the qualified real property in the family farm or other business. If the heirs of the decedent dispose of the real property or discontinue its qualified use within 10 years of the decedent's death, Code § 2032A(c) requires that the heirs repay the estate tax saved by the original use of the § 2032A election.

GROSS ESTATE INCLUSIONS

The Federal estate tax is not a property tax levied on the value of property owned at death. Instead, it is a transfer tax levied on the value of any shift in a property interest that occurs because of a decedent's death. As a result, a decedent's gross estate may include assets not owned by a decedent at death, the transfer of which is not controlled by the terms of the decedent's will.

INSURANCE ON THE LIFE OF THE DECEDENT

The proceeds of an insurance policy on the life of a decedent do not come into existence until the death of the insured and are paid to the beneficiaries specified in the insurance contract, not the beneficiaries named in the decedent's will. However, § 2042 provides that such proceeds shall be included in the decedent's gross estate if either of the following is true:

1. The decedent's estate is the beneficiary,

2. The decedent, at his or her death, possessed any incident of ownership in the life insurance policy, alone or in conjunction with any other person.

The term *incident of ownership* implies any economic interest in the policy and is broadly interpreted by the IRS. The Regulations under § 2042 list the power to change the policy's beneficiary, the right to cancel or assign the policy, and the right to borrow against the policy as incidents of ownership.[21]

> **Example 11.**   In 1982, T purchased an insurance policy on his own life. Under the terms of the policy, beneficiary B would receive $150,000 upon T's death. In 1983, T transferred the ownership of the policy to his wife, W, retaining none of the incidents of ownership in the policy. In 1991, T died. The $150,000 paid to B is not includible in T's gross estate. Had T retained the right to change the beneficiary, however, the proceeds would have been included in his gross estate.

Note in *Example 11* that if W had predeceased her husband, the fair market value of the insurance policy (approximately its cash surrender value, if any) would be includible in W's gross estate under § 2033 as an asset owned at death.

SURVIVOR BENEFITS

Section 2039 requires that the value of an annuity or any payment receivable by a beneficiary by reason of surviving a decedent be included in the decedent's gross estate. This rule only applies to the extent that the value of the annuity or payment is attributable to contributions made by the decedent or the decedent's employer. A second condition for applicability is that the payment or annuity be payable to the decedent or that the decedent possess the right to payment at death. For example, social security death benefits paid to a decedent's family are not covered by § 2039 because the decedent had no right to the payments during his or her lifetime.

The value of an annuity includible under § 2039 is the replacement cost to the beneficiary of a comparable commercial annuity.[22]

---

[21]   Reg. § 20.2042-1(c)(2).   [22]   Reg. § 20.2031-8(a).

Example 12.   H purchased a self and survivor annuity contract that was to pay him $1,500 a month for his life and, upon his death, $1,000 a month to his widow, W. At the date of H's death, W would have to pay $24,000 to purchase a $1,000 a month lifetime annuity for herself. Under § 2039, the value of the annuity received by W, $24,000, is includible in H's gross estate.

JOINT INTERESTS

Nonspousal Joint Tenancies.   As discussed earlier in the chapter, a joint tenancy with right of survivorship is a form of equal co-ownership of an asset that causes full ownership of the asset to vest automatically in the survivor when the first joint tenant dies. The decedent's will cannot change this result; property owned in joint tenancy is not included in a decedent's probate estate. Some portion of the value of this property may be includible in the decedent's gross estate, however. Under § 2040, it is necessary to determine the proportion of the decedent's original contribution toward the acquisition of the asset. This same proportion of the value of the asset at date of death must be included in the decedent's gross estate.

Example 13.   Brothers A and B decided to purchase a tract of real estate as equal joint tenants with right of survivorship. A contributed $40,000 and B contributed $10,000 toward the $50,000 purchase price. At A's death, the real estate was worth $150,000. A's gross estate must include $120,000, 80% [$40,000 ÷ ($40,000 + $10,000)] of the real estate's value. If B had died before A, only $30,000, 20% of the real estate's value, would be includible in B's gross estate.

Note in *Example 13* that in the year the real estate was acquired, A made a taxable gift to B of $15,000, the difference between half the value of the asset when purchased, $25,000, and B's $10,000 contribution. In spite of this completed gift, a portion of the property is taxed in A's gross estate under the authority of § 2040 if he dies before B.

Spousal Joint Tenancies.   If a husband and wife own property as joint tenants with right of survivorship, § 2040(b) contains a rule that requires 50 percent of the value of the property to be included in the gross estate of the first spouse to die, regardless of the original contribution of that spouse.

GENERAL POWERS OF APPOINTMENT

A *power of appointment* is a right to dispose of property that the holder of the power does not legally own. It is normally created by the will of a decedent in conjunction with a transfer of property in trust. Typically, the decedent's will provides for the transfer of property in trust, giving an individual a life estate and a power to appoint the remainder interest during his or her life or at death through a will. By so doing, the decedent transfers the ability to control the property's disposition to the holder of the power, even though the holder does not own the property. In effect, a power of appointment gives a person the right to fill in the blanks of another person's will.

A power of appointment may be *specific*, meaning that the holder of the power may only give the property to members of a specified eligible group of recipients which does *not* include the holder. Alternatively, the power may be *general*, so that the holder may appoint the property to himself or herself, or his or her creditors, estate, or creditors of that estate. The terms of the power should specify to whom ownership of the property will go if the holder deliberately or inadvertantly fails to exercise the power.

A *general power of appointment* over property is tantamount to actual ownership of the property. If the holder appoints the property to another person, the exercise is treated as a taxable gift per § 2514.[23] Section 2041 provides that if a decedent holds a general power over property at his or her death, the value of the property must be included in the gross estate.

> **Example 14.** Individual I has the right to appoint ownership of certain real estate to any of I's children or grandchildren. He may exercise the right during life or by will. Upon I's death, his will appoints the property to his daughter, D. Because I held only a *specific power*, the value of the appointed property is *not* included in D's gross estate.

> **Example 15.** Individual M has the right to appoint ownership of certain real estate to *himself* or any of his brothers and sisters. He may exercise the right during life or by will. However, M dies without exercising the power. The terms of the power provide that if the power is not exercised the property shall go to M's uncle. Because M possessed a *general power* of appointment, the date of death value of the property must be included in M's gross estate.

Nontaxable Powers. As indicated above, a specific power of appointment over property will not result in inclusion of the property in the holder's gross estate. There are other situations where a power does not cause taxation. If the holder's power to appoint property for his or her benefit is limited to an *ascertainable standard*, it is not a general power of appointment and inclusion is not required. A power is considered limited to a standard if appointments of property may be made solely for the holder's health, education, maintenance, or support in his or her accustomed manner of living. The language used to describe the scope of the holder's power is extremely important. For example, a power is not considered limited if it permits appointments for the holder's comfort, happiness, or well-being.

---

[23] If the holder of a general power releases the power or allows it to lapse, the transfer of ownership is still considered a taxable gift made by the holder. See §§ 2514(b) and (e).

Example 16. H's will provided for the transfer of $600,000 in trust, giving his wife a life estate and a power to appoint the property to herself for her support. Upon the wife's death, nothing is included in her gross estate since she does not have a general power of appointment. The power does not cause inclusion since it is limited to an ascertainable standard.

TRANSFERS TAKING EFFECT AT DEATH

Taxpayers who are reluctant to give away property during life but who also want to minimize the tax burden on their estate have designed a variety of inter vivos gifts with "strings attached." Such gifts are subject to a condition or restriction that enables the donor to continue to benefit from or enjoy the property until death. Such a transfer may be complete for gift tax purposes. Nevertheless, for estate tax purposes it may be classified as a transfer taking effect at death, with the result that the date of death value of the property is includible in the donor's gross estate.

Code §§ 2036, 2037, and 2038 govern transfers taking effect at death. Because these three sections were added to the Code at different times, there is a confusing amount of overlap in their coverage. The sections' requirements are very complex and difficult to apply. However, a brief description of each section can give the beginning tax student an idea of their general functions.

One important rule to remember is that all three sections can only require the inclusion in a decedent's gross estate of property that was originally owned by the decedent. A second rule is that the sections are inapplicable if the transfer of the property by the decedent was for sufficient consideration.

Code § 2036. This section requires that the value of any property given away by the decedent, but to which the decedent retained the right to the property's income or the right to designate who may possess or enjoy the property, shall be included in the decedent's gross estate. Section 2036 also specifies that the retention of the voting rights of shares of stock in a controlled corporation represents a retention of enjoyment.[24]

Example 17. In 1987, F made a completed gift of rental property to his son, S, subject to the condition that F was to receive the net rent from the property for the rest of his life. Upon F's death in 1991, the date of death value of the rent property must be included in F's gross estate, even though S is the owner of the property.

---

[24] § 2036(b)(2) defines a controlled corporation as a corporation in which the decedent controlled (directly or indirectly) at least 20 percent of the voting power of all classes of stock.

Example 18. In 1991, M transferred assets into an irrevocable trust for the sole benefit of her grandchildren. Under the terms of the trust instrument, M reserved the right to designate which of the grandchildren should receive the annual income of the trust. Because M retained the right to designate the persons who shall possess the income from the trust assets, the value of the trust assets will be included in M's gross estate upon her death.

The IRS is very aggressive in applying § 2036. For example, in a situation in which a parent gifts a family residence to a child but continues to occupy the residence rent free, the parent is considered to have retained a beneficial interest in the residence, with the result that the value of the residence will be includible in the parent's gross estate.[25]

Code § 2037. This statute requires inclusion in a decedent's gross estate of the value of previously transferred property if two conditions are met:

1. Possession or enjoyment of the property can only be obtained by surviving the decedent,

2. The decedent owns a reversionary interest in the property, the value of which exceeds 5 percent of the value of the property. The value of the reversion is computed as of the moment immediately before death, based on actuarial tables.[26]

Regulation § 20.2037-1(e) gives the following example of the application of Code § 2037.

Example 19. The decedent transferred property in trust, with the income payable to his wife for life and with the remainder payable to the decedent or, if he is not living at his wife's death, to his daughter or her estate. The daughter cannot obtain possession or enjoyment of the property without surviving the decedent. Therefore, if the decedent's reversionary interest immediately before death exceeded 5% of the value of the property, the value of the property less the value of the wife's outstanding life estate is includible in the decedent's gross estate.

Note in *Example 19* that the decedent's reversionary interest was extinguished at death and did not constitute an interest in property that would be transferred under the terms of the decedent's will. However, it is the event of the decedent's death that completes the transfer of the remainder interest in the trust to the daughter or her estate.

---

[25] Rev. Rul. 70-155, 1970-1 C.B. 189; and *Estate of Linderme*, 52 T.C. 305 (1966).

[26] Reg. § 20.2037-1(c)(3).

Code § 2038. If, on the date of death, the decedent had the power to alter, amend, or revoke the enjoyment of any property previously given away by the decedent, § 2038 requires that the date of death value of the property be included in the decedent's gross estate. Obviously, a revocable transfer falls within § 2038. However, the scope of the section is broad enough to apply to much less obvious types of powers.

> **Example 20.** Individual Z creates an irrevocable trust for the benefit of her children and names the trust department of a national bank as trustee. The only right retained by Z allows her to replace the trustee with a different trust department. Upon Z's death, Revenue Ruling 79-353 [27] states that Code § 2038 applies and the value of the trust corpus must be included in Z's gross estate.

GIFTS IN CONTEMPLATION OF DEATH

For many years, Code § 2035 required that the date of death value of any gift made by the decedent during the three years prior to death, plus the amount of any gift tax paid on such gifts, be included in the decedent's gross estate. In 1981, Congress drastically altered this section so that it currently applies only to gifts of interests described in the sections governing transfers taking effect at death (§§ 2036, 2037, and 2038) and § 2042, relating to gifts of life insurance. In addition, § 2035 applies for determining the applicability of provisions such as § 2032A, concerning special use valuation (e.g., any property given away within three years of death is added back to the gross estate in applying the 50 and 25% tests). Notwithstanding the limited application of the general rule, § 2035(c) continues to require the inclusion in the gross estate of any gift tax paid within three years of death.

> **Example 21.** Refer to the facts in *Example 17*. Assume that in 1990, one year prior to his death, F made a gift of his retained income interest in the rental property to his granddaughter, D. Section 2035 applies to the transfer of the income interest, with the result that the date of death value of the rental property and any gift tax paid on the 1990 gift are included in F's gross estate.

TRANSFERS FOR INSUFFICIENT CONSIDERATION

A transfer for which the donor received consideration less than the value of the transferred property is vulnerable to the application of §§ 2035, 2036, 2037, or 2038 upon the donor's death. However, § 2043 does allow the estate an offset for the consideration received.[28]

---

[27] 1979-2 C.B. 325.   [28] See Reg. § 20.2043-1(a).

Example 22. Individual A transferred her 100 shares of stock in Famco Corporation to her daughter, D, subject to the condition that A would retain the voting rights in the shares. At date of transfer, the fair market value of the stock was $500,000, and D paid A only $300,000 cash in exchange. The transfer constituted a taxable gift of $200,000. Upon A's death, the value of the stock, $1.2 million, is includible in A's gross estate under § 2036. However, A's estate may reduce this value by $300,000, the amount of the consideration received by A.

The § 2043 consideration offset equals the value of the consideration at date of receipt. Therefore, in *Example 22* only 40 percent ($200,000 ÷ $500,000) of the value of the property was transferred without consideration, but 75 percent [($1.2 million − $300,000) ÷ $1.2 million] of the date of death value of the property must be included in the gross estate.

DEDUCTIONS FROM THE GROSS ESTATE

Not all of the value of a decedent's gross estate will be available for transfer to estate beneficiaries or other individuals. Some of the value must first be used to pay off debts of the decedent and other claims against the estate. The second step in computing an individual's taxable estate is to identify the debts and claims that are deductible against the gross estate.

CODE §§ 2053 AND 2054

Section 2053 authorizes deductions for unpaid mortgages or liens on property included in the gross estate and for personal debts of the decedent. In computing these deductions, a decedent is on the accrual basis, so that liabilities accrued at death but not yet paid are deductible for estate tax purposes.[29]

Also deductible are the decedent's funeral expenses and administrative expenses of the estate. Administrative expenses include legal, accounting, and other professional fees and expenses of selling estate assets to provide necessary funds. In addition, expenses incurred in preserving the estate, including the costs of maintaining and storing property (e.g., utility bills on the decedent's home) are deductible. These expenses can only be taken as an estate tax deduction if they are not also claimed as income tax deductions by the estate.[30]

Losses incurred during the settlement of an estate that are caused by casualty or theft and are not compensated for by insurance are deductible under § 2054. If deducted on the estate tax return, a loss may not be deducted again on the estate's income tax return.[31]

---

[29]   Reg. § 20.2053-4.

[30]   § 642(g).

[31]   *Ibid.*

The gross estate less §§ 2053 and 2054 deductions represents the net estate available for transfer to beneficiaries or other individuals. Dispositions of the net estate to a qualified charity or the decedent's surviving spouse can result in further deductions on the estate tax return.

CHARITABLE CONTRIBUTIONS

An estate may deduct the value of any transfer of assets to a qualified charitable organization under § 2055. Qualifying organizations are specifically defined in the statute. If an individual is willing to leave his or her entire estate for public, charitable, or religious use, there will be no taxable estate.

For a charitable contribution to be deductible, it must consist of the decedent's entire interest in the underlying property. For example, if a decedent bequeaths a life interest in real estate to his son and the remainder interest in the property to charity, the value of the remainder interest is not deductible. Alternatively, if the decedent bequeaths the interest in the real estate to a charity for a term of years (e.g., 20 years), and the remainder to his son, the value of the income interest is not deductible. However, this restriction does not apply if the transfer is in a specific statutory form: a *charitable lead trust*, where an income interest is given to the charity, or a *charitable remainder trust*, where a remainder interest is given to the charity.[32] A detailed description of such trusts is beyond the scope of this text, but they do allow a decedent to create both a charitable and a noncharitable interest in the same property and secure a deduction for the charitable interest. The restriction also is inapplicable to a charitable contribution of a remainder interest in a personal residence or farm and to certain contributions for conservation purposes.[33]

If an individual taxpayer is considering making bequests to charity upon his or her death, his or her tax adviser should certainly explore the possibility of having the individual make such charitable contributions during his or her life. Such inter vivos contributions would serve a dual purpose: The donated assets would be removed from the individual's potential taxable estate, and the donation would create a deduction for income tax purposes.

THE MARITAL DEDUCTION

Code § 2056 provides an unlimited deduction for the value of property passing to a surviving spouse. If a married taxpayer, no matter how wealthy, is willing to leave all his or her property to the surviving spouse, no transfer tax will be imposed on the estate.[34] Only upon the subsequent death of the spouse will the couple's wealth be subject to taxation. Planning for maximizing the benefit of the unlimited marital deduction is discussed in Chapter 26.

---

[32] § 2055(e)(2).

[33] *Ibid.*

[34] No marital deduction is allowed for the value of property passing to a surviving spouse who is not a U.S. citizen unless the property is placed in a "qualified domestic trust." §§ 2056(d) and 2056A.

In certain instances, interests transferred to the surviving spouse are not deductible—so-called *nondeductible terminable interests*. If a decedent leaves an interest in property to his or her spouse that can or will terminate at a future date *and* if after termination another person receives an interest in the property from the decedent, the value of the interest passing to the spouse is ineligible for the marital deduction.[35] Absent this rule, the interest would escape taxation entirely, since it terminates prior to or with the death of the surviving spouse and thus is not included in his or her gross estate.

> **Example 23.**   Decedent M leaves a life estate in real property to his surviving spouse, S, with the remainder after S's death left to M's granddaughter. The interest passing to S is a terminable interest ineligible for the marital deduction.

The property need not pass directly to the surviving spouse to qualify for the marital deduction. Section 2056(b)(5) generally allows the deduction if the surviving spouse is entitled to annual payments of all of the income from the property for life and has a general power of appointment over the property exercisable during life or at death. In this case, the entire value of the property will be included in the estate of the surviving spouse because of his or her general power of appointment.

Under § 2056(b)(7), a marital deduction is also available for the value of *qualifying terminable interest property* left to a surviving spouse. Qualifying terminable interest property is property from which the entire income must be paid to the spouse at least annually. During the spouse's lifetime, no one else must be able to receive any interest in the property. Upon the spouse's death, the property may pass to anyone. If the executor elects, the entire value of the property is deductible on the decedent's estate tax return.

Section 2044 requires that when the surviving spouse dies, the entire value of the qualifying terminable interest property at that time must be included in the spouse's gross estate. If the surviving spouse gives away the income interest during life, § 2519 requires that the gift will consist of the entire value of the property. The rationale for this exception, along with the planning opportunities it creates, are discussed in Chapter 26.

COMPUTATION OF THE ESTATE TAX

Once the value of the taxable estate has been determined, the first step in computing the estate tax liability is to add the taxable estate to the amount of the decedent's *adjusted taxable gifts*. Adjusted taxable gifts are defined in Code § 2001(b) as the total amount of taxable gifts (after any available exclusion or

---

[35]   § 2056(b).

deduction) made after December 31, 1976 *other than* gifts includible in the gross estate of the decedent.

The transfer tax rates of § 2001(c) are then applied to the sum of the taxable estate plus adjusted taxable gifts. The tentative tax calculated is then reduced by any gift taxes payable at current rates for gifts made after December 31, 1976. The result is the amount of Federal estate tax liability *before* credits.[36]

ESTATE TAX CREDITS

The major credit available to reduce the Federal estate tax is the unified credit of Code § 2010. This credit is identical in amount to the § 2505 unified gift tax credit described earlier. The § 2010 credit may be used by the estate of every decedent, regardless of prior usage of the gift tax credit. However, the mechanics of the estate tax calculation ensure that the decedent's estate benefits from the credit only to the extent that it was not used to offset any gift tax during his or her lifetime. It is important to understand that the two credits combined will shelter a maximum of $600,000 of transfers from the imposition of any Federal transfer tax.

All other estate tax credits have a single underlying purpose—to reduce or eliminate the effect of multiple taxation of a single estate. Sections 2011 and 2014 provide a credit against the Federal estate tax for the death taxes imposed by the state in which the decedent resided or by a foreign government. Section 2012 authorizes a credit for pre-1977 gift taxes paid by the decedent on property that must be included in the gross estate and therefore is subject to the estate tax.

If two family members die within a short period of time, the same property may be included in both taxable estates and be subject to two rounds of estate taxation in rapid succession. Section 2013 provides a credit to the estate of the second decedent to mitigate this excessive taxation. The credit generally is computed as a percentage of the amount of tax attributable to the inclusion of property in the estate of the first decedent. The percentage is based on the number of years between the two deaths as follows:

0–2 years	100%
3–4 years	80%
5–6 years	60%
7–8 years	40%
9–10 years	20%

---

[36] Estates of decedents dying after December 31, 1986 will be liable for an additional amount of estate tax equal to 15 percent of the decedent's "excess retirement accumulation" per § 4981A(d).

If the second decedent outlived the first by more than 10 years, no § 2013 credit is allowed.

> **Example 24.** Individual A died in March 1989. Under the terms of his will, A left $1 million in assets to his younger sister, B. B died unexpectedly in December 1991 and the assets inherited from A were included in B's taxable estate. The amount of tax paid by A's estate that is attributable to the assets is calculated at $100,000. The § 2013 credit available to B's estate is $80,000 (80% × $100,000).

The formula for computing the estate tax is presented in Exhibit 24-5.

Exhibit 24-5
Estate Tax Formula

Gross estate (§§ 2031 through 2046)........		$x,xxx,xxx
Less the sum of		
Expenses, indebtedness,		
and taxes (§ 2053)..................	$ xx,xxx	
Losses (§ 2054)......................	x,xxx	
Charitable bequests (§ 2055)..........	xx,xxx	
Marital deduction (§ 2056).............	xxx,xxx	− xxx,xxx
Taxable estate(§ 2051).....................		$ xxx,xxx
Plus: Taxable gifts made after		
December 31,1976 [§ 2001(b)]...		+ xx,xxx
Total taxable transfers......................		$ xxx,xxx
Tentative tax on total transfers (§ 2001).....		$ xxx,xxx
Less the sum of		
Gift taxes paid on post-1976		
taxable gifts (§ 2001)................	$ x,xxx	
Unified transfer tax credit (§ 2010)......	xx,xxx	
Other tax credits (§§ 2011 through 2016)	x,xxx	− xx,xxx
Estate tax liability		$ xx,xxx

A COMPREHENSIVE EXAMPLE

The following example will illustrate the complete computation of the Federal estate tax.

In 1987, taxpayer M makes his first taxable gift to his son S. The fair market value of the property transferred is $200,000. The gift tax is computed as follows:

Value of gift	$200,000
Less: Annual exclusion	− 10,000
Taxable gift	$190,000
Gift tax before credits	$ 51,600
Less: Unified credit	− 51,600
Gift tax liability for 1987	$ 0

In 1988, M makes gifts to son S and daughter D. The value of each transfer is $250,000.

Value of gifts	$500,000
Less: Annual exclusions	− 20,000
Taxable gifts for 1988	$480,000
Plus: 1987 taxable gift	+ 190,000
Taxable transfers to date	$670,000
Tentative tax on total transfers to date	$218,700
Less: Tax on 1987 gift	− 51,600
Less: 1988 Unified credit	
($192,800 − $51,600)	− 141,200
1988 gift tax liability	$ 25,900

M dies in 1991, leaving a taxable estate valued at $1.6 million. The estate tax is computed as follows:

Taxable estate		$1,600,000
Plus: Taxable gifts made in prior years		+ 670,000
Total taxable transfers		$2,270,000
Tentative tax on total transfers		$ 913,100
Less the sum of		
Gift taxes paid on post-1976		
taxable gifts (on 1988 gift)	$ 25,900	
Unified credit	192,800	− 218,700
Estate tax liability		$ 694,400

PAYMENT OF THE ESTATE TAX

The Federal estate tax return, Form 706, is due nine months after the date of the decedent's death, and any tax liability shown is payable with the return. However, Congress appreciates the fact that the payment of the estate tax is often unforeseen, and has provided for a variety of relief measures for the estate with a substantial tax liability and insufficient liquidity to pay the tax nine months after death.

Section 6161 authorizes the Secretary of the Treasury to extend the time of payment of the estate tax for up to 10 years past the normal due date. To obtain an extension, the executor must show reasonable cause for the delay in payment. For example, the fact that the executor of an estate requires additional time to sell a particularly illiquid asset to generate the cash with which to pay the estate tax might be accepted as reasonable cause for an extension of the payment date for the estate tax.

Section 6166 allows an estate to pay a portion of its estate tax liability in installments if a substantial portion of the estate consists of the decedent's interest in a closely held business.[37] An estate is eligible if more than 35 percent of the *adjusted gross estate* (gross estate less §§ 2053 and 2054 deductions for debts of the decedent, funeral and administrative expenses, and losses) consists of the value of such an interest. The percentage of the estate tax liability that can be deferred is based on the ratio of the value of the closely held business to the value of the adjusted gross estate.

If a decedent owned an interest in more than one closely held business, the values of the interests can be combined to meet the 35 percent *if* the decedent's interest represents 20 percent or more of the total value of the business.

Example 25.   The taxable estate of decedent X is composed of the following:

		Value
Sole proprietorship		$ 400,000
40% interest in closely held		
corporation		500,000
Other assets		1,400,000
Gross estate		$2,300,000
Less sum of		
Code §§ 2053 and 2054 deductions	$300,000	
Code § 2055 charitable deduction	500,000	– 800,000
Taxable estate		$1,500,000

The decedent owned 100% of the value of the sole proprietorship and 40% of the value of the closely held corporation. The combined values of these interests, $900,000, represents 45% of the adjusted gross estate of $2,000,000. Therefore, the executor may elect to defer payment on 45% of the estate tax liability.

---

[37]   § 6166(b) provides specific definition of the phrase "interest in a closely held business."

The tax deferred under § 6166 is payable in 10 equal annual installments. The first installment is payable five years and nine months after death. The IRS does charge the estate interest on the unpaid balance for the entire 15-year period.[38] If the estate disposes of 50 percent or more of the value of the qualifying closely held interest, any outstanding amount of deferred estate tax must be paid immediately.

THE GENERATION-SKIPPING TRANSFER TAX

As part of the Tax Reform Act of 1976, Congress added a third type of transfer tax to the Internal Revenue Code. The *generation-skipping transfer tax* (GSTT) was designed to "plug a loophole" in the coverage of the gift and estate taxes. The original version of the GSTT was intimidatingly complex, and was criticized by tax practitioners from the moment of enactment.

The Tax Reform Act of 1986 retroactively repealed the 1976 version of the GSTT and replaced it with a new tax applicable to testamentary transfers occurring after the date of enactment and to inter vivos transfers made after September 25, 1985. Any tax actually paid under the 1976 GSTT is fully refundable. Only time will tell if the new version of the GSTT is any more workable than the old version.

A traditional generation-skipping transfer involves at least three generations of taxpayers. For example, Grandfather G could create a trust, income payable to Son S for S's life with the trust assets passing to Grandson GS upon S's death. G would pay a gift tax upon the transfer of assets into trust. However, upon S's death his income interest terminates and S, according to § 2035, is not considered to own a property interest in the trust assets at the time of his death. Although the enjoyment of the trust assets is transferred from the second generation (S) to the third generation (GS), neither the Federal gift or estate tax is imposed on the value of the transfer. In addition to this type of generation-skipping transfer, which benefits at least two generations of taxpayers, the 1986 version of the GSTT also applies to certain "direct skips," outright transfers of wealth for the sole benefit of a person at least two generations younger than the transferor.[39]

Generally, the value of property transferred in a taxable generation-skipping transaction is subject to a flat-rate tax of 55 percent until 1992, and 50 percent for subsequent taxable years.[40] However, each transferor is allowed a lifetime exemption of $1 million for generation-skipping transfers of any type.[41]

---

[38] See § 6601(j) for applicable interest rate.

[39] § 2612.

[40] § 2641.

[41] § 2631.

TAX PLANNING CONSIDERATIONS

The statutory rules of Federal gift, estate, and generation-skipping taxes have been examined in this chapter. Any individual taxpayer who desires to maximize the accumulated wealth available to family members will want to minimize the burden of these three transfer taxes. Tax planning for transfer taxes would be incomplete, however, without consideration of any interrelated Federal income taxes. Many gifts are made by transfers to a trust, and the income taxation of the trust entity and its beneficiaries may have a significant impact upon the original tax minimization plan. For this reason, the Federal income taxation of trusts, estates, and beneficiaries is discussed in the next chapter (Chapter 25). The tax planning considerations for transfer taxes and any attendant income taxes are incorporated in Chapter 26, *Family Tax Planning*.

PROBLEM MATERIALS

DISCUSSION QUESTIONS

24-1 *Interrelation of Federal Estate and Gift Taxes.* Discuss the various reasons why the Federal gift and estate taxes can be considered as a single, unified transfer tax.

24-2 *Entity for Transfer Tax Purposes.* Why can the married couple rather than each individual spouse be considered the taxable entity for transfer tax purposes?

24-3 *What Constitutes a Gift?* Businessperson B offers X $40,000 for an asset owned by X. Although X knows the asset is worth $60,000, he is in desperate need of cash and agrees to sell. Has X made a $20,000 taxable gift to B? Explain.

24-4 *Adequate Consideration.* During the current year, K offered to pay $50,000 to his only son, S, if S would agree to live in the same town as K for the rest of K's life. K is very elderly and frail and desires to have a relative close at hand in case of emergency. Does the $50,000 payment constitute a taxable gift made by K?

24-5 *When Is a Gift Complete?* Wealthy Grandmother G wants to provide financial support for her Grandson GS. She opens a joint checking account with $20,000 of cash. At any time, G or GS may withdraw funds from this account. Has G made a completed gift to GS by opening this account? At what point is the gift complete?

24-6 *Cumulative Nature of Transfer Taxes.* The Federal income tax is computed on an annual basis. How does this contrast to the computation of the Federal gift tax?

24-7 *Purpose of Unified Transfer Tax Rates.* A decedent's taxable estate can be considered the last taxable gift the decedent makes. Why?

24-8 *Incomplete Transfers.* The Federal gift tax and estate tax are not mutually exclusive. Give examples of transfers that may be treated as taxable gifts but that do not remove the transferred assets from the donor's gross estate.

24-9 *Computation of Taxable Estate.* What are the three steps involved in computing the taxable estate of a decedent?

24-10 *Probate Estate vs. Gross Estate.* How can the value of a decedent's probate estate differ from the value of his or her gross estate for tax purposes?

24-11 *Special Use Valuation of § 2032A.* The gross estate of decedent F consists of a very successful farming operation located 80 miles east of an expanding metropolitan area. The estate includes 2,000 acres of real estate worth $400,000 as agricultural land. However, a real estate developer is willing to pay $1.5 million for the property because of its potential for suburban development. Discuss the utility of § 2032A to F's estate.

24-12 *Powers of Appointment.* What are some *nontax* reasons for the creation of a power of appointment? What is the difference between a specific and a general power?

24-13 *Gifts in Contemplation of Death.* Discuss the scope of § 2035 concerning gifts made within three years of death after the enactment of ERTA 1981.

24-14 *Estate Tax Credits.* With the exception of the unified credit of § 2010, what is the basic purpose of the various estate tax credits?

24-15 *Due Date of Estate Tax Return and Payment.* Why is the tax law particularly lenient in authorizing extensions for payment of the Federal estate tax?

24-16 *Unified Transfer Tax Credit.* Section 2010 appears to allow a second $192,800 credit against the Federal estate tax (in addition to the credit allowed for gift tax purposes under § 2505). Is this the case?

24-17 *Generation-Skipping Transfers.* Decedent T's will created a trust, the income from which is payable to T's invalid daughter D for her life. Upon D's death, the trust assets will be paid to T's two sons (D's brothers) in equal shares. Has T made a generation-skipping transfer? Explain.

PROBLEMS

24-18 *Gift Splitting.* During the current year, Mr. and Mrs. Z make the following cash gifts to their adult children:

Mr. Z:
to son M	$30,000
to daughter N	8,000
Total	$38,000

Mrs. Z:
to son M	$ 2,000
to daughter N	12,000
to daughter O	18,000
Total	$32,000

a. Assume Mr. and Mrs. Z do *not* elect to split their gifts per § 2513. Compute the total taxable gifts after exclusions for each.

b. How does the amount of taxable gifts change if Mr. and Mrs. Z *elect* to split their gifts?

24-19 *Computing Gift Tax Liability.* B, a single individual, made a cash gift of $200,000 to his niece C in 1988. In the current year, B gives C an additional $200,000 and nephew D $450,000. Compute B's gift tax liability for the current year.

24-20 *Computing Taxable Gifts.*   C, a single individual, makes the following transfers during the current year.

	Fair Market Value
Cash to sister D	$13,000
Real estate:	
Life estate to brother B	28,000
Remainder to nephew N	21,000
Cash to First Baptist Church	25,000

What is the total amount of taxable gifts C must report?

24-21 *Computing Taxable Gifts.*   During the current year, L, a widower, makes the following transfers:

	Fair Market Value
Tuition payment to State College for	
nephew N, age 32	$ 6,000
New automobile to nephew N	9,000
Cash to a local qualified political committee	15,000

What is the total amount of taxable gifts L must report?

24-22 *Computing Taxable Gifts.*   During the current year, Z, a widow, makes the following transfers:

	Fair Market Value
Real estate located in France to son J	$500,000
City of Philadelphia municipal bonds to	
daughter K	120,000
Payment to local hospital for medical	
expenses of brother-in-law M	18,000

What is the total amount of taxable gifts Z must report?

24-23 *Basis of Gifted Assets.*   During the current year, L received a gift of land from his grandmother. The land had a basis to the grandmother of $100,000 and a fair market value of $250,000 on the date of the gift. A gift tax of $30,000 was paid on the transfer.

    a.   If L subsequently sells the land for $300,000, how much gain or loss will he recognize?

    b.   What would be the amount of L's recognized gain or loss on the sale if the land had a tax basis of $325,000 (rather than $100,000) to the grandmother?

24-24 *Marital Deduction.* F died during the current year, leaving a gross estate valued at $5 million. F's will specifically provided that *no* amount of her wealth was to be left to her estranged husband, G. However, under applicable state law, G is legally entitled to $1 million of his deceased wife's assets. How does the payment of $1 million affect the value of

    a.   F's *gross* estate,

    b.   F's *taxable* estate?

24-25 *Gross Estate Inclusions.* Q was a cash basis taxpayer who died in the current year. On the date of Q's death, he owned corporate bonds, principal amount of $50,000, with accrued interest of $3,950. On the date of death, the bonds were selling on the open market for $54,000. Six months later the market price of the bonds had dropped to $51,500; there was $3,200 of accrued interest on the bonds as of this date. Neither market price includes any payment for accrued interest.

    a.   Assuming the executor of Q's estate does not elect the alternate valuation date, what amounts should be included in Q's gross estate because of his ownership of the bonds?

    b.   Assuming the executor does elect the alternate valuation date, what amounts should be included in Q's gross estate?

24-26 *Interests in Trusts Included in Gross Estate.* M's mother left property in trust (Trust A), with the income payable to M for M's lifetime and the remainder to M's daughter. At M's death, Trust A was worth $6.5 million. M's grandfather created a trust (Trust B), with the income payable to M's father for his lifetime. Upon the father's death, the remainder in Trust B was payable to M or M's estate. At M's death, his 82-year-old father was still living and Trust B was worth $2.1 million. Assuming a 9.8% interest rate, what are the values of the inclusions in M's gross estate attributable to M's interests in Trust A and Trust B? (See Table A, contained in Appendix A.)

24-27 *Computing Gross Estate.* Upon A's death, certain assets were valued as follows:

	Fair Market Value
Probate estate	$ 750,000
Insurance proceeds on a policy on A's life. The policy has always been owned by A's niece, the beneficiary	150,000
Corpus of Trust A. A possessed the right to give the ownership of the corpus to herself or any of her family. In her will she left the corpus to cousin K	15,000,000

Based on these facts, what is the value of A's gross estate?

24-28   *Computing Gross Estate.*   Upon G's death, the following assets were valued:

	Fair Market Value
Probate estate	$ 350,000
Social security benefits payable to G's widow	38,000
Annuity payable to G's widow out of G's employer's pension plan	20,000
Corpus of revocable trust created by G for the benefit of his children 10 years prior to death. Upon G's death, the trust becomes irrevocable	1,000,000

What is the value of G's gross estate?

24-29   *Gifts Included in Gross Estate.*   Donor D, age 66, makes a gift in trust for his grandchildren K and L. Under the terms of the trust instrument, D will receive the income from the trust for the rest of his life. Upon his death, the trust assets will be distributed equally between K and L.

   a.   D's assets transferred into trust are worth $1 million. Assuming that D's income interest is not a "qualified interest" within the meaning of § 2702(b), what is the amount of the taxable gift to K and L?

   b.   Upon the date of D's death, at age 77, the value of the trust assets is $2.5 million. What amount, if any, is included in D's gross estate?

24-30   *Gifts in Contemplation of Death.*   In 1990, S made a taxable gift of marketable securities to his nephew and paid a gift tax of $14,250. In 1991, S gave an income interest in trust property to the same nephew and paid a gift tax of $5,000. S originally created the trust in 1978, retaining the income interest for life and giving the remainder to another family member. S died in 1992 when the marketable securities were worth $300,000 and the trust property was worth $972,000. Based on these facts, what amounts, if any, are included in S's gross estate?

24-31   *Gifts Included in Gross Estate.*   In 1975, F transferred real estate into a trust, the income from which was payable to M during her lifetime. Upon M's death, the trust property will be distributed in equal portions among M's children. However, the trust instrument gives F the right to change the remainder beneficiaries at any time. F dies in the current year without ever having changed the original trust provisions. At date of death, the trust property is worth $3.9 million and M is 60 years old. Assuming a 10% interest rate, determine the amount, if any, to be included in F's gross estate. (See Table A, contained in Appendix A.)

24-32   *Including Insurance in Gross Estate.*   Decedent R left a probate estate of $3,000,000. Two years prior to his death, R gave all incidents of ownership in an insurance policy on his own life to his daughter S, the policy beneficiary. Because the policy had a substantial cash surrender value, R paid a gift tax of $77,000 on the transfer. Upon death, the insurance policy paid $5,000,000 to S. What is the value of R's gross estate?

24-33 *Joint Tenancy.*   In 1985, individual Q pays $500,000 for an asset and takes title with his brother R as joint tenants with right of survivorship. R makes no contribution toward the purchase price. In the current year, when the asset is worth $1.2 million, Q dies and ownership of the asset vests solely in R.

    a.   What are the gift tax consequences of the creation of the joint tenancy?

    b.   How much of the date of death value of the asset must be included in Q's gross estate?

    c.   How much would be included in the gross estate of R if R, rather than Q, died in the current year?

24-34 *Computing Taxable Estate.*   Decedent T left a gross estate for tax purposes of $1.1 million. T had personal debts of $60,000 and his estate incurred funeral expenses of $12,000 and legal and accounting fees of $35,000. T's will provided for $100,000 bequest to the American Cancer Society, with all other assets passing to his grandchildren. Compute T's taxable estate.

24-35 *Sections 2053 and 2054 Expenses.*   Decedent D died on July 1 of the current year. D owned a sailboat valued at $85,000 as of the date of death. However, on December 1 of the current year, the boat was destroyed in a storm, and the estate was unable to collect any insurance to compensate for the loss. In December, the executor of D's estate received a $2,200 bill from the company that had stored the sailboat from January 1 through December 1 of the current year.

    a.   If the executor does not elect the alternate valuation date, will the $85,000 value of the boat be included in D's gross estate? D's taxable estate?

    b.   May any portion of the $2,200 storage fee be deducted on D's Federal estate tax return? On the first income tax return filed by the estate?

24-36 *Marital Deduction Assets.*   J, who was employed by Gamma Inc. at the date of his death, had been an active participant in Gamma's qualified retirement plan. Under the terms of the plan, J's widow will receive an annuity of $1,500 per month for the next 20 years. The replacement value of the annuity is $145,000. In his will, J left his interest in a patent worth $50,000 to his widow; the patent will expire in 8 years. To what extent will these transfers qualify for a marital deduction from J's gross estate?

24-37 *Qualified Terminable Interest Trust.*   Under the will of decedent H, all his assets (fair market value of $10 million) are to be put into trust. His widow, W, age 64, will be paid all the income from the trust every quarter for the rest of her life. Upon W's death, all the assets in the trust will be distributed to the couple's children and grandchildren. During W's life, no part of the trust corpus can be distributed to anyone but W.

    a.   What amount of marital deduction is available on H's estate tax return?

    b.   W dies eight years after H and under the terms of H's will the trust assets are distributed. What percentage, if any, of the value of these assets must be included in W's gross estate?

24-38   *Deferring Estate Tax Payments.*   Decedent X has the following taxable estate:

Sole proprietorship		$ 900,000
Ten percent interest in a		
closely held corporation		100,000
Other assets		600,000
Gross estate		$1,600,000
Less sum of		
§§ 2053 and 2054 deduction	$400,000	
§ 2056 marital deduction	200,000	− 600,000
Taxable estate		$1,000,000

Assume the estate tax liability on this estate is $300,000.

a.   How much of the liability may be deferred under § 6166?

b.   If X died in November 1991, when is the first installment payment of tax due?

24-39   *Computing Estate Tax Liability.*   Decedent Z dies in the current year and leaves a taxable estate of $1.4 million. During his life, Z made the following unrestricted gifts:

	Fair Market Value
1988: Gift of 2,000 shares of Acme stock	
to son S	$900,000
1989: Gift of cash to daughter D	600,000
1989: Gift of cash to wife W	700,000

Compute Z's estate tax liability after utilization of the available unified credit.

24-40   *Gifts Included in Gross Estate.*   In 1967, P transferred $500,000 of assets into an irrevocable trust for the exclusive benefit of his children. Under the terms of the trust agreement, annual income must be distributed among the children according to P's direction. When the youngest child attains the age of 25 years, the trust corpus will be distributed equally among the living children. P dies in the current year while the trust is still in existence and the corpus has a fair market value of $3,200,000. How much, if any, of the corpus must be included in P's gross estate?

24-41   *Powers of Appointment.*   In 1980, donor D transferred $100,000 of assets into an irrevocable trust for the exclusive benefit of her minor grandchildren. Under the terms of the trust agreement, the grandchildren will receive the annual income from the trust, and when the youngest grandchild attains the age of 21, the trust corpus will be divided among the living grandchildren as S, D's only child, so directs. S dies in the current year while the trust is still in existence and the corpus has a fair market value of $400,000. S's valid will directs that the corpus of the trust will go entirely to grandchild Q. How much, if any, of the corpus must be included in S's gross estate?

RESEARCH PROBLEMS

24-42 In 1974, JW gifted 30 percent of her stock in W Corporation to her favorite nephew, N. Although she retained a 50 percent interest in W Corporation and her husband owned the remaining 20 percent of the outstanding stock, JW was concerned that the family might eventually lose control of the firm. To reassure JW, the three stockholders agreed to restrict transferability of their stock by signing an agreement that any shareholder wishing to dispose of W Corporation stock must offer the stock to the corporation for a formula price based on the average net earnings per share for the three previous years. The corporation would then be obligated to purchase the stock at the formula price. At the time the buy-sell agreement was entered into, this formula resulted in a price very close to the stock's actual fair market value.

JW died in the current year at a time when the value of her W Corporation stock was substantially depreciated because of certain unfavorable local economic conditions. Several independent appraisals of the stock valued JW's 50 percent interest at $650,000. However, the formula under the 1974 buy-sell agreement resulted in a value of only $150,000 for the decedent's 50 percent interest. What is the correct value of the 50 percent interest in the corporation for estate tax purposes?

Some suggested research materials:

Rev. Rul. 59-60, 1959-1 C.B. 237.
Estate of Littick, 31 T.C. 181 (1958), *acq.* 1959-2 C.B. 5.
Code § 2703 (enacted by the Revenue Reconciliation Act of 1990).

24-43 In 1979, Mr. and Mrs. B (residents of a common law state) created two trusts for the benefit of their children. Mr. B transferred $600,000 of his own property into trust, giving the income interest to his wife for her life, and the remainder interest to the children. Mrs. B transferred $640,000 of her own property into trust, giving the income interest to her husband for his life, and the remainder interest to the children. In the current year, Mrs. B dies. How much, if any, of the current value of the corpus of the 1979 trust created by Mrs. B will be included in her gross estate?

Some suggested research materials:

United States v. Estate of Grace, 69-1 USTC ¶12,609,
    23 AFTR2d 69-1954, 395 U.S. 316 (USSC, 1969).

LEARNING OBJECTIVES

Upon completion of this chapter you will be able to:

- Compute fiduciary accounting income and determine the required allocation of such income among the various beneficiaries of the fiduciary

- Identify the special rules that apply to the computation of fiduciary taxable income

- Explain the concept of income and deductions in respect of a decedent

- Compute both the taxable and nontaxable components of a fiduciary's distributable net income

- Describe the defining characteristics of a simple and a complex trust, including

  - The computation of the deduction for distributions to beneficiaries for both types of trusts

  - The distinction between tier one and tier two distributions from a complex trust

- Determine the tax consequences of fiduciary distributions to the recipient beneficiaries

CHAPTER OUTLINE

Chapter 25

INCOME TAXATION OF ESTATES AND TRUSTS

INTRODUCTION

Trusts and estates are taxable entities subject to a specialized set of tax rules contained in Subchapter J of the Internal Revenue Code (§§ 641 through 692). The income taxation of trusts and estates (commonly referred to as fiduciary taxpayers) and their beneficiaries is the subject of this chapter. Grantor trusts, a type of trust not recognized as a taxable entity and therefore not subject to the rules of Subchapter J, are discussed in Chapter 26.

THE FUNCTION OF ESTATES AND TRUSTS

ESTATES

An estate as a legal entity comes into existence upon the death of an individual. During the period of time in which the decedent's legal affairs are being settled, assets owned by the decedent are managed by an executor or administrator of the estate. Once all legal requirements have been satisfied, the estate terminates and ownership of all estate assets passes to the decedent's beneficiaries or heirs.

During its existence, the decedent's estate is a taxable entity that files a tax return and pays Federal income taxes on any income earned.[1] Normally an estate is a transitional entity that bridges the brief gap in time between the death of an individual taxpayer and the distribution of that individual's wealth to other taxpayers. However, estates as taxpayers may continue in existence for many years if the correct distribution of a decedent's wealth is in question. If the administration of a decedent's estate is unreasonably prolonged, the IRS may treat the estate as terminated for tax purposes after a reasonable amount of time for settlement of the decedent's affairs has elapsed.[2]

---

[1] § 641(a)(3).

[2] Reg. § 1.641(b)-3(a).

TRUSTS

A trust is a legal arrangement in which an individual, the *grantor*, transfers legal ownership of assets to one party, the *trustee*, and the legal right to enjoy and benefit from those assets to a second party, the *beneficiary* (or beneficiaries). Such an arrangement is usually designed for the protection of the beneficiary. Often trust beneficiaries are minor children or family members incapable of competently managing the assets themselves.

The terms of the trust, the duties of the trustee, and the rights of the various beneficiaries are specified in a legal document, the *trust instrument*. The assets put into trust are referred to as the trust *corpus*.

The role of the trustee is that of a fiduciary; he or she is required to act in the best interests of the trust beneficiaries rather than for his or her own interests. The position of trustee is usually filled by the professional trust department of a bank or a competent friend or family member. Professional trustees receive an annual fee to compensate them for services rendered.

The purpose of a trust is to protect and conserve trust assets for the sole benefit of the trust beneficiaries, not to operate a trade or business. A trust that becomes involved in an active, profit-making business activity runs the risk of being classified as an *association* for Federal tax purposes, with the unfavorable result that it will be taxed as a corporation rather than under the rules of Subchapter J.[3]

TRUST BENEFICIARIES

An individual who desires to establish a trust has virtually unlimited discretion as to the identity of the trust beneficiaries and the nature of the interest in the trust given to each beneficiary. For example, assume grantor A creates a trust consisting of $1 million of assets. A could specify in the trust instrument that individual B is to receive all the income of the trust for B's life, and upon B's death the assets in the trust are to be distributed to individual C. In this example, both B and C are trust beneficiaries. B owns an *income interest* in the trust, while C owns a *remainder interest* (the right to the trust corpus at some future date).

A grantor can give trust beneficiaries any mix of rights to trust income or corpus (trust assets) that will best accomplish the goals of the trust. In the previous example, if grantor A decided that the trust income might be insufficient to provide for B, the trust document could specify that B also will receive a certain amount of trust corpus every year. Alternatively, if A believed that B might not need all the trust income annually, the trust document could provide that the trustee could accumulate income to distribute to B at some later point. As the student can see, a trust can be a wonderfully flexible arrangement for providing for the needs of specific beneficiaries.

---

[3]   See *Morrissey v. Comm.*, 36-1 USTC ¶9020,
16 AFTR 1274, 296 U.S. 344 (USSC, 1936),
for this result.

FIDUCIARY ACCOUNTING INCOME

The income of an estate or trust for legal and accounting purposes is determined by reference to the governing instrument (the decedent's valid will or trust instrument) and applicable state law. In many cases such fiduciary accounting income is different from the concept of taxable income as defined in the Internal Revenue Code. The administrator or trustee will always refer to fiduciary accounting income rather than taxable income in carrying out his or her duties.

One major difference between fiduciary accounting income and taxable income is the classification of fiduciary capital gains. Typically, capital gains represent an increase in the value of the corpus of the fiduciary and are not available for distribution to income beneficiaries. Of course, for Federal tax purposes capital gains represent taxable income. Similarly, stock dividends are often regarded as an increase in corpus rather than trust income, even though the dividend may be taxable income under the Internal Revenue Code.

Trustee fees are generally deductible for tax purposes. However, for fiduciary accounting purposes such fees may be charged *either* to trust income or to trust corpus.

The following items of trust receipts and disbursements illustrate the concept of fiduciary accounting income:

Receipts:

Dividends	$10,000
Interest from municipal bonds	12,000
Long-term capital gain allocable to corpus under state law	6,500
Stock dividend allocable to corpus under the trust instrument	4,000
Total receipts	$32,500

Disbursements:

Trustee fee (half allocable to trust income; half allocable to corpus under the trust instrument)	$ 3,000

Based on the above, the accounting income of the trust would be $20,500, computed as follows:

Dividends	$10,000
Interest from municipal bonds	12,000
	$22,000
Less: One-half of the trustee fee ($3,000 ÷ 2)	(1,500)
Trust accounting income	$20,500

If the trustee of this particular trust was required to distribute the entire amount of trust income to a particular group of beneficiaries, the trustee would make a payment of $20,500. Note that this amount bears little relationship to the *taxable income* generated by the trust's activities.

INCOME TAXATION OF FIDUCIARIES

For Federal tax purposes, fiduciaries are taxable entities.[4] Every estate that has annual gross income of $600 or more and every trust that has either annual gross income of $600 or more *or* any taxable trust income must file an income tax return. Furthermore, if a fiduciary has a beneficiary who is a nonresident alien, that fiduciary must file a return regardless of the amount of its gross or taxable income for the year.[5]

Form 1041, the fiduciary income tax return, must be filed by the 15th day of the fourth month following the close of the fiduciary's taxable year (see Appendix B for sample Form 1041). An estate may adopt a calendar or any fiscal taxable year. However, the taxable year of a trust must be a calendar year.[6] In the case of an estate, the first taxable year begins on the day following the date of death of the decedent.[7] In the case of a trust, the date of creation as specified in the controlling trust instrument marks the beginning of the first taxable year.

Fiduciaries generally must make quarterly estimated tax payments in the same manner as individuals. However, no estimated taxes must be paid by an estate or a grantor trust to which the residual of the grantor's estate is distributed for any taxable year ending within the two years following the decedent's death.[8] A trustee may *elect* to treat any portion of an excess estimated tax payment made by a trust as a payment of estimated tax made by a beneficiary. If the election is made, the payment is considered as having been distributed to the beneficiary on the last day of the trust's taxable year and then remitted to the government as estimated tax paid by the beneficiary on January 15th of the following year.[9]

> **Example 1.**   On April 15, 1991, Trust T made an estimated tax payment of $14,000. However, later in the year, the trustee decided to distribute all 1991 trust income to beneficiary B. Because Trust T will have no 1991 tax liability, the trustee may elect to treat the $14,000 payment as a cash distribution made to beneficiary B on December 31, 1991. Beneficiary B will report the $14,000 as part of his 1991 estimated tax payment made on January 15, 1992.

Section 641(b) provides that "the taxable income of an estate or trust shall be computed in the same manner as in the case of an individual, except as otherwise provided in this part." Thus many of the rules governing the taxation of individuals apply to fiduciaries. Before examining the specific rules unique to fiduciary income taxation, it will be useful to look at the basic formula for computing fiduciary taxable income.

---

[4]   See §§ 7701(a)(6) and 641(a).

[5]   § 6012(a)(3), (4), and (5).

[6]   § 645. This requirement does not apply to tax-exempt and charitable trusts.

[7]   See Reg. §§ 1.443-1(a)(2), and 1.461-1(b).

[8]   § 6654(l).

[9]   § 643(g).

Step One: Compute fiduciary accounting income and identify any receipts and disbursements allocated to corpus (under either the trust instrument or state law).

Step Two: Compute fiduciary taxable income *before* the deduction for distributions to beneficiaries authorized by Code §§ 651 and 661.

Step Three: Compute the deduction for distributions to beneficiaries. This step will require a computation of fiduciary "distributable net income" (DNI).

Step Four: Subtract the deduction for distributions to arrive at *fiduciary taxable income*.

Step One, the computation of fiduciary accounting income, was discussed earlier. Detailed discussions of Steps Two and Three constitute most of the remainder of this chapter.

FIDUCIARY TAXABLE INCOME

Unless otherwise modified, the fiduciary computes its taxable income in a manner identical to that of an individual taxpayer. The principal difference is the deduction granted for distributions made to beneficiaries, explained later in this chapter. In addition, § 642 contains a number of special provisions that must be followed in computing fiduciary taxable income and the final tax. These unique aspects of estate and trust taxation are considered below.

FIDUCIARY TAX RATES

The tax rates for estates and trusts for 1991 are shown in Exhibit 25-1. Note that there is very little progressivity in the fiduciary rate schedule; taxable income in excess of $10,350 is taxed at the highest 31 percent rate. However, under § 1(j), any component of fiduciary taxable income consisting of net long-term capital gain is taxed at a maximum 28 percent rate.

Exhibit 25-1
Income Tax Rates for Estates and Trusts

For Taxable Years Beginning after 1990

If taxable income is		The tax is	Of the amount
Over—	But not over—		over—
$ 0	$ 3,450	15%	$ 0
3,450	10,350	$ 517.50 + 28%	3,450
10,350	—	2,449.50 + 31%	10,350

Example 2. Estate E has taxable income for calendar year 1991 of $70,000, $20,000 of which is net long-term capital gain. E's tax liability for the year is $14,741 ($2,449.50 + 31% of the excess of $50,000 over $10,350) *plus* $5,600 (28% of the $20,000 capital gain), for a total liability of $20,341.

In determining their final tax liability, fiduciaries are subject to the alternative minimum tax provisions.[10] Generally, the alternative minimum tax is computed with any items of tax preference allocated between the fiduciary and the beneficiaries.

STANDARD DEDUCTION AND PERSONAL EXEMPTION

Unlike individual taxpayers, fiduciaries are not entitled to a standard deduction.[11] However, a fiduciary, like an individual taxpayer, is entitled to a personal exemption. The amount of the exemption depends on the type of fiduciary. The personal exemption for an estate is $600. The exemption for a trust that is required by the trust instrument to distribute all trust income currently is $300. The exemption for any trust not subject to this requirement is $100.[12]

LIMITATIONS ON DEDUCTIBILITY OF FIDUCIARY EXPENSES

Because fiduciaries generally do not engage in the conduct of a business, the gross income of a fiduciary usually consists of investment income items such as dividends, interest, rents, and royalties. Fiduciary expenses are normally deductible under the authority of § 212, which provides for the deduction of ordinary and necessary expenses paid for the management, conservation, or maintenance of property held for the production of income.

Before specific fiduciary expenses can be deducted, they must be allocated among the various income items received by the fiduciary. Expenses directly attributable to taxable fiduciary income are fully deductible. For example, rent expenses are directly attributable to rent income and are deductible by the fiduciary. However, expenses that cannot be *directly connected* with any specific type of income must be allocated proportionately to each item of distributable income. Any amount of expenses allocated to distributable tax-exempt income is not deductible by the fiduciary.[13]

Example 3. During the year, Estate E receives $9,000 of tax-exempt interest and $36,000 of taxable interest, and recognizes a $10,000 capital gain allocable to corpus. The estate pays $3,000 of administrative fees that are not directly attributable to any item of income. Those fees must be proportionally allocated to the various items of *distributable* income; therefore,

---

[10] § 59(c).

[11] § 63(c)(6)(D).

[12] § 642(b).

[13] Reg. § 1.652(b)-3(b).

20% of the fee ($9,000 tax-exempt income ÷ $45,000 total distributable income) must be allocated to tax-exempt income, and only $2,400 ($3,000 × 80%) of the fee is deductible by the estate.

Section 642(g) provides a second major limitation on the deductibility of fiduciary expenses. If an administrative expense is claimed as a deduction on the estate tax return of a decedent, it may not also be claimed as a deduction on an income tax return of the decedent's estate or subsequent trust. However, administrative expenses that could be deducted for either estate tax or income tax purposes can be divided between the two returns in whatever portions achieve maximum tax benefit.[14]

Section 67(a) limits certain miscellaneous itemized deductions, including the § 212 deduction for investment expenses. Such itemized deductions are allowed only to the extent they exceed 2 percent of adjusted gross income. Section 67(e) provides that the deduction for expenses paid or incurred in connection with the administration of a fiduciary that would have been avoided if the property were not held by the fiduciary shall be allowable in computing the adjusted gross income of the fiduciary. In other words, fiduciary expenses such as trustee fees which are incurred only because of the choice of the trust form are not considered itemized deductions subject to the 2 percent floor. The § 68 overall limitation on itemized deductions, enacted by the Revenue Reconciliation Act of 1990, is *not* applicable to fiduciaries.

CHARITABLE CONTRIBUTIONS

Section 642(c) authorizes an unlimited charitable deduction for any amount of gross income paid by a fiduciary to a qualified charitable organization. Fiduciaries are given a great deal of flexibility as to the timing of charitable contributions; if a contribution is paid after the close of one taxable year but before the close of the next taxable year, the fiduciary may elect to deduct the payment in the earlier year.[15]

If a fiduciary receives tax-exempt income that is available for charitable distribution, its deduction for any charitable contribution made normally must be reduced by that portion of the contribution attributable to tax-exempt income.[16]

> **Example 4.** During the current year, Trust T receives $30,000 of tax-exempt interest, $25,000 of taxable interest, and $45,000 of taxable dividends. The trust makes a charitable contribution of $20,000 during the year. Because 30% of the trust's income available for distribution is nontaxable, 30% of the charitable distribution is nondeductible and the trust's deduction for charitable contributions is limited to $14,000.

[14] Reg. § 1.642(g)-2.

[15] § 642(c)(1). See Reg. § 1.642(c)-1(b) for the time and manner in which such an election is to be made.

[16] Reg. § 1.642(c)-3(b).

DEPRECIATION, DEPLETION, AND AMORTIZATION

The total allowable amount of depreciation, depletion, and amortization that may be deducted by the fiduciary (or passed through to the beneficiaries) is determined in the normal manner. However, a fiduciary is not entitled to expense any portion of the cost of eligible property under § 179.

Deductions for depreciation and depletion available to a fiduciary depend upon the terms of the controlling will or trust instrument. If the controlling instrument authorizes a reserve for depreciation or depletion, any *allowable* (deductible) tax depreciation or depletion will be deductible by the fiduciary to the extent of the specified reserve. If the allowable tax depreciation or depletion exceeds the reserve, the excess deduction is allocated between the fiduciary and beneficiaries based upon the amount of fiduciary income allocable to each.[17]

> **Example 5.** Trust R owns rental property with a basis of $300,000. The trust instrument authorizes the trustee to maintain an annual depreciation reserve of $15,000 (5% of the cost of the property). For tax purposes, however, the current year's depreciation deduction is $22,000. The trust instrument provides that one-half of annual trust income including rents will be distributed to the trust beneficiaries. For the current year, the trust is entitled to a depreciation deduction of $18,500 (5% of $300,000 + one-half the tax depreciation in excess of $15,000).

Note that if the controlling instrument is silent, depreciation and depletion deductions are simply allocated between fiduciary and beneficiaries on the basis of fiduciary income allocable to each. If a fiduciary is entitled to statutory amortization, the amortization deduction also will be apportioned among fiduciary and beneficiaries on the basis of income allocable to each.[18]

FIDUCIARY LOSSES

Because the function of a trust generally is to conserve and protect existing wealth rather than to engage in potentially risky business activities, it is unusual for a trust to incur a net operating loss. It is not unusual, however, for an estate that includes a business interest owned by a decedent to incur this type of loss. In any case, if a net operating loss does occur, a fiduciary may carry the loss back 3 years and forward for 15.[19] Capital losses incurred by a fiduciary are deductible against capital gains; a maximum of $3,000 of net capital loss may be deducted against other sources of income.[20] Nondeductible net capital losses are carried forward to subsequent taxable years of the fiduciary.[21]

---

[17] Reg. § 1.167(h)-1; Reg. § 1.611-1(c)(4).

[18] Reg. § 1.642(f)-1.

[19] § 172(b)(1).

[20] § 1211(b).

[21] § 1212(b).

Fiduciaries are also subject to the limitations imposed on passive activity losses and credits by § 469.[22] Therefore, a fiduciary may only deduct current losses from passive activities against current income from passive activities. Any nondeductible loss is suspended and carried forward to subsequent taxable years. If an interest in a passive activity is distributed by a fiduciary to a beneficiary, any suspended loss of the activity is added to the tax basis of the distributed interest.[23]

Unlike the net losses of a partnership or an S corporation, fiduciary losses do not flow through to beneficiaries. An exception to this rule applies for the year in which a trust or estate terminates. If the terminating fiduciary has net operating losses, capital loss carryforwards, or current year deductions in excess of current gross income, § 642(h) provides that such unused losses and excess deductions become available to the beneficiaries succeeding to the property of the fiduciary.

Casualty losses of a fiduciary are subject to the rules pertaining to individual taxpayers. For casualty losses, the limitation of the deduction to that amount in excess of 10 percent of adjusted gross income applies, although the concept of adjusted gross income is normally not associated with trusts or estates.[24] In addition, § 642(g) prohibits the deduction by a fiduciary of any loss that has already been claimed as a deduction on an estate tax return.

INCOME AND DEDUCTIONS IN RESPECT OF A DECEDENT

The death of an individual taxpayer can create a peculiar timing problem involving the reporting of income items earned or deductible expenses incurred by the taxpayer prior to death. For example, if a cash basis individual had performed all the services required to earn a $5,000 consulting fee but had not collected the fee before death, by whom shall the $5,000 of *income in respect of a decedent* (IRD) be reported? The individual taxpayer who earned the income never received payment, but the recipient of the money, the individual's estate, is not the taxpayer who earned it. Section 691(a) gives a statutory solution to this puzzling question by providing that any income of an individual not properly includible in the taxable period prior to the individual's death will be included in the gross income of the recipient of the income, typically the estate of the decedent or a beneficiary of the estate. Common IRD items include unpaid salary or commissions, rent income or interest accrued but unpaid at death, and the amount of a § 453 installment obligation that would have been recognized as income if payment had been received by the decedent prior to death.

Certain expenses incurred by a decedent but not properly deductible on the decedent's final return because of nonpayment are afforded similar statutory treatment. Under § 691(b), these *deductions in respect of a decedent* (DRD) are

---

[22]   § 469(a)(2)(A).

[23]   § 469(j)(12).

[24]   See Form 4684 and its instructions for this computation.

deducted by the taxpayer who is legally required to make payment. Allowable DRD items include business and income-producing expenses, interest, taxes, and depletion.

ESTATE TAX TREATMENT AND THE § 691(c) DEDUCTION

Items of IRD and DRD represent assets and liabilities of the deceased taxpayer. As such, these items will be included on the decedent's estate tax return. Because IRD and DRD also have future income tax consequences, special provisions in the tax law apply to these items. First, even though the right to IRD is an asset acquired from a decedent, the basis of an IRD item does not become the item's fair market value at date of death. Instead, under § 1014(c), the basis of the item to the decedent carries over to the new owner. This special rule preserves the potential income that must be recognized when the IRD item is eventually collected. The character of IRD also is determined by reference to the decedent taxpayer.

Secondly, items of DRD that are deducted as § 2053 expenses on an estate tax return are *not* subject to the rule prohibiting a deduction on a subsequent income tax return.[25] Finally, a taxpayer who recognizes an item of IRD as income may be entitled to an income tax deduction [authorized by § 691(c)] for the amount of the Federal estate tax imposed on the value of the item. The deduction is a percentage of the estate tax attributable to the total *net* IRD included in an estate based on the ratio of the recognized IRD item to all IRD items. Estate tax attributable to net IRD is the excess of the actual tax over the tax computed without including the IRD in the taxable estate.

> **Example 6.** Taxpayer T's estate tax return included total IRD items valued at $145,000. DRD items totaled $20,000. If the *net* IRD of $125,000 had not been included in T's estate, the Federal estate tax liability would have decreased by $22,000. During the current year, the estate of T collected half ($72,500) of all IRD items and included this amount in estate gross income. T's estate is entitled to a § 691(c) deduction of $11,000.

THE DISTRIBUTION DEDUCTION AND THE TAXATION OF BENEFICIARIES

The central concept of Subchapter J is that income recognized by a fiduciary will be taxed *either* to the fiduciary itself or to the beneficiaries of the fiduciary. The determination of the amount of income taxable to each depends upon the amount of annual distributions from the fiduciary to the beneficiary. Conceptually, distributions to beneficiaries represent a flow-through of trust income that will be

[25] § 642(g).

taxed to the beneficiary. Under §§ 651 and 661, the amount of the distribution will then be available as a *deduction* to the fiduciary, reducing the taxable income the fiduciary must report. Income that flows through the fiduciary to a beneficiary retains its original character; therefore, the fiduciary acts as a *conduit,* similar to a partnership in this respect.[26]

All distributions made from a fiduciary are considered to be distributions of fiduciary income to the extent thereof. Distributions of income can be made in both cash and property. However, § 663(a)(1) provides that specific gifts or bequests properly distributed from a fiduciary to a beneficiary under the terms of the governing instrument do not represent distributions of income. Correspondingly, the fiduciary does not recognize gain or loss upon the distribution of a specific property bequest.

> **Example 7.** During the current year, the Estate of Z recognized $30,000 of income, all of which is taxable. During the year, the executor of the estate distributed a pearl necklace to beneficiary B. The necklace had a fair market value of $6,000. If the will of decedent Z specifically provided for the distribution of the necklace to B, no estate income will be taxed to her. Alternatively, if there were no such specific bequest and B received the necklace as part of her general interest in estate assets, she will have received an income distribution.

The amount of income associated with a property distribution from a fiduciary depends upon the tax treatment of the distribution *elected* by the fiduciary. Section 643(e)(3) provides an election under which the fiduciary recognizes gain or loss on the distribution of appreciated or depreciated property as if the property had been sold at its fair market value. In this case, the amount of fiduciary income carried by the property distribution and the basis of the property in the hands of the beneficiary equals the property's fair market value. If the election is not made, the distribution of property produces no gain or loss to the fiduciary, and the amount of fiduciary income carried by the distribution is the lesser of the basis of such property in the hands of the fiduciary or the property's fair market value.[27] In the case where the election is not made, the basis of the property in the hands of the fiduciary will carry over as the basis of the property in the hands of the beneficiary.[28]

> **Example 8.** During the current year, Trust T distributes property to beneficiary B. The distribution is not a specific gift of property. On the date of distribution, the property has a basis to the trust of $10,000 and a fair market value of $17,000. If the trust so elects, it will recognize a $7,000 gain on the distribution, and B will be considered to have received a $17,000 income distribution and will have a $17,000 basis in the property. If the

---

[26] §§ 652(b) and 662(b).

[27] § 643(e)(2).

[28] § 643(e)(1).

trustee does not make the election, it will not recognize any gain upon distribution of the property. B will be considered to have received only a $10,000 income distribution and will have only a $10,000 basis in the property.

When a beneficiary is entitled to a specific gift or bequest of a sum of money (a pecuniary gift or bequest), and the fiduciary distributes property in satisfaction of such gift or bequest, any appreciation or depreciation in the property is recognized as a gain or loss to the fiduciary.[29]

> **Example 9.** Under the terms of E's will, beneficiary M is to receive the sum of $60,000. E's executor distributes 600 shares of corporate stock to M to satisfy this pecuniary bequest. At the time of distribution, the stock has a fair market value of $100 a share and a basis to E's estate of $75 a share. Upon distribution, the estate must recognize a capital gain of $15,000 (600 shares × $25 per share appreciation). Note that because this distribution represents a specific bequest, it is not an income distribution to M and the § 643(e)(3) election is inapplicable. The basis of the stock to M will be its fair market value.

In any case in which the distribution of depreciated property by a trust to a beneficiary results in the recognition of loss, § 267 disallows any deduction of the loss by the trust. However, § 267 does not disallow such losses recognized by an estate.

THE ROLE OF DISTRIBUTABLE NET INCOME

To calculate the distribution deduction available to a fiduciary and the amount of fiduciary income taxable to beneficiaries, it is first necessary to calculate the *distributable net income* (DNI) of the fiduciary. DNI represents the net income of a fiduciary available for distribution to income beneficiaries.

DNI has several important characteristics. First, it does not include taxable income that is unavailable for distribution to income beneficiaries. For example, in most states capital gains realized upon the sale of fiduciary assets are considered to represent a part of *trust corpus* and are not considered *fiduciary income*. Such capital gains, while taxable, are not included in DNI. Secondly, DNI may include nontaxable income that is available for distribution to income beneficiaries.

At this point, it would appear that the amount of DNI is the same amount as fiduciary accounting income. However, there is an important difference between the two concepts. All expenses that are deductible *for tax purposes* by the fiduciary enter into the DNI calculation, even if some of these expenses are chargeable to corpus and not deducted in computing fiduciary accounting income.

---

[29] Reg. § 1.661(a)-2(f)(1).

A beneficiary who receives a distribution from a fiduciary with both taxable and nontaxable DNI is considered to have received a proportionate share of each.[30]

> **Example 10.** Trust A has DNI of $80,000, $30,000 of which is nontaxable. During the year, beneficiary X receives a distribution of $16,000. This distribution consists of $10,000 of taxable DNI [$16,000 distribution × ($50,000 taxable DNI ÷ $80,000 total DNI)] and $6,000 of nontaxable DNI.

The amount of a fiduciary's *taxable* DNI represents *both* the maximum income that may be taxed to beneficiaries and the maximum deduction for distributions available to the fiduciary in computing its own taxable income.[31]   Therefore, computing DNI is crucial to the correct computation of the taxable incomes of both beneficiary and fiduciary. Note that in *Example 10* Trust A is entitled to a deduction for distributions to beneficiaries of $10,000.

THE COMPUTATION OF DNI

Section 643 defines DNI as fiduciary taxable income before any deduction for distributions to beneficiaries, adjusted as follows:

1. No deduction for a personal exemption is allowed.

2. No deduction against ordinary income for net capital losses is allowed.

3. Taxable income allocable to corpus and not available for distribution to income beneficiaries is excluded.

4. Tax-exempt interest reduced by expenses allocable thereto is included.

> **Example 11.** A trust that is not required to distribute all income currently has the following items of income and expense during the current year:

Tax exempt interest	$10,000
Dividends	5,000
Rents	20,000
Long-term capital gains allocable to corpus	8,000
Rent expense	6,700
Trustee fee allocable to income	3,500

---

[30]   Reg. § 1.662(b)-1.   [31]   §§ 651(b) and 661(c).

The trust's taxable income before any deduction for distributions to beneficiaries is $23,700, computed as follows:

Dividends...		$ 5,000
Rents..		20,000
Capital gain...		8,000
		$33,000
Less: Rent expense.................................	$6,700	
Trustee fee allocable to *taxable*		
trust income*.............................	2,500	
Exemption....................................	100	(9,300)
Taxable income before		
distribution deduction...............................		$23,700

*$3,500 fee $\times \dfrac{\$25,000 \text{ taxable trust income}}{\$35,000 \text{ total trust income}}$

The trust's DNI is $24,800, computed as follows:

Trust taxable income before distribution	
deduction...	$23,700
Add back exemption..	100
	$23,800
Exclude: Nondistributable capital gain........................	(8,000)
Include: *Net* tax exempt interest	
($10,000 total − $1,000	
allocable to trustee fee)**........................	9,000
Distributable net income (DNI)...............................	$24,800

**$3,500 fee $\times \dfrac{\$10,000 \text{ tax-exempt income}}{\$35,000 \text{ total trust income}}$

SIMPLE TRUSTS

Section 651 defines a *simple trust* as one that satisfies these conditions:

1. Distributes all trust income currently

2. Does not take a deduction for a charitable contribution for the current year

3. Does not make any current distributions out of trust corpus

Because of the requirement that a simple trust distribute all trust income to its beneficiaries, all taxable DNI of a simple trust is taxed to the beneficiaries, based upon the relative income distributable to each.

Example 12.   Trust S is required to distribute 40% of trust income to beneficiary A and 60% of trust income to B. The trust's DNI for the current year is $100,000, of which $20,000 is nontaxable. For the current year, beneficiary A must report $32,000 of trust income (40% of *taxable* DNI) and B must report $48,000 of trust income (60% of *taxable* DNI). Trust S's deduction for distributions to beneficiaries is $80,000.

In *Example 12,* the tax results would not change if the trustee had failed to make actual distributions to the beneficiaries. In the case of a simple trust, the taxability of income to beneficiaries is not dependent upon cash flow from the trust.[32]

COMPLEX TRUSTS AND ESTATES

Any trust that does not meet all three requirements of a simple trust is categorized as a *complex trust.* The categorization of a trust may vary from year to year. For example, if a trustee is required to distribute all trust income currently but also has the discretion to make distributions out of trust corpus, the trust will be *simple* in any year in which corpus is not distributed, but *complex* in any year in which corpus is distributed.

Computing the taxable income of complex trusts and estates generally is more difficult than computing the taxable income of a simple trust. Complex trusts and estates potentially may distribute amounts of cash and property that are less than or in excess of DNI.

If distributions to beneficiaries are less than or equal to DNI, each beneficiary is required to report the amount of the distribution representing *taxable DNI* in his or her gross income. Taxable DNI remaining in the fiduciary is taxed to the fiduciary.

> **Example 13.** In the current year, Trust C has DNI of $50,000, of which $20,000 is nontaxable. During the year, the trustee makes a $5,000 distribution to both beneficiary M and beneficiary N. M and N will each report $3,000 of income from Trust C [$5,000 distribution × ($30,000 taxable DNI ÷ $50,000 total DNI)]. Trust C is allowed a $6,000 deduction for distributions to beneficiaries.[33] As a result, $24,000 of taxable DNI will be reported by (and taxed to) Trust C.

When distributions to beneficiaries exceed DNI, the entire taxable portion of DNI will be reported as income by the beneficiaries. However, it may be necessary to allocate DNI among a number of beneficiaries who have received distributions during the taxable year. To make the proper allocation, distributions to beneficiaries must be categorized as *tier one* or *tier two* distributions. A tier one distribution is any distribution of fiduciary income *required to be paid currently.* A tier two distribution is any other distribution properly made to a beneficiary.[34]

Fiduciary DNI is first allocated proportionally to any first-tier distributions; if any DNI remains, it is then allocated proportionally to second-tier distributions.[35]

---

[32] § 652(a).

[33] § 661(c).

[34] §§ 662(a)(1) and (2).

[35] § 662(a)(2). For purposes of determining DNI available for first-tier distribution only, no charitable contribution deduction is allowed.

Example 14.   In the current year, Trust F has DNI of $90,000, all of which is taxable. Under the terms of the trust instrument, the trustee is required to make a $50,000 distribution of income to beneficiary A. The trustee also has discretion to distribute additional amounts of income or corpus to beneficiaries A, B, or C. During the current year, the trustee distributes $60,000 to A, $25,000 to B, and $25,000 to C. The first $50,000 of DNI is allocated to A because of the $50,000 *first-tier distribution* A received. The remaining $40,000 of DNI is allocated proportionally to the *second-tier distributions* received by A, B, and C. This allocation is $6,666, $16,667 and $16,667, respectively.

Note that all Trust F's DNI is allocated and taxed to the three beneficiaries; none is taxed to the trust. Beneficiary A received $60,000 from the trust, of which $56,666 is taxable ($50,000 first-tier distribution + $6,666 second-tier distribution). B and C each received $25,000, of which $16,667 is taxable. Trust F's deduction for distributions to beneficiaries is limited to $90,000, its taxable DNI for the year.

REPORTING REQUIREMENTS FOR BENEFICIARIES

A beneficiary who receives a distribution from a fiduciary will receive a summary of the tax consequences of the distribution in the form of a Schedule K-1 from the executor or trustee. The K-1 will tell the beneficiary the amounts and character of the various items of income that constitute the taxable portion of the distribution.

A beneficiary also may be entitled to depreciation or depletion deductions and various tax credits because of distributions of fiduciary income. Such items are also reflected on the Schedule K-1.

If the taxable year of a beneficiary is different from that of the fiduciary, the amount of fiduciary income taxable to the beneficiary is included in the beneficiary's tax year within which the fiduciary's year ends.[36]

Example 15.   For tax purposes, Estate E is on a fiscal year ending January 31. During its fiscal year ending January 31, 1991, but prior to December 31, 1990, the estate made cash distributions to beneficiary Z, a calendar year taxpayer. Because of these distributions, Z must report income of $8,000. However, this income will be reported on Z's 1991 individual tax return.

THE SEPARATE SHARE RULE

In certain circumstances, the rules governing the taxation of beneficiaries of a complex trust can lead to an inequitable result. Assume a grantor created a single trust with two beneficiaries, A and B. The grantor intended that each beneficiary

---

[36]   §§ 652(c) and 662(c).

have an equal interest in trust income and corpus. The trustee has considerable discretion as to the timing of distributions of income and corpus. Consider a year in which beneficiary A was in exceptional need of funds and, as a result, the trustee distributed $15,000 to A as A's half of trust income for the year *plus* $10,000 out of A's half of trust corpus. Because B had no need of current funds, the trustee distributed neither income nor corpus to B.

If the trust's DNI was $30,000 for the year, the normal rules of Subchapter J would dictate that A would have to report and pay tax on $25,000 of trust income. However, the clear intent of the grantor is that A only be responsible for half of trust income and no more. To reflect such intent, § 663(c) provides the following rule: If a single trust contains substantially separate and independent shares for different beneficiaries, the trust shall be treated as separate trusts for purposes of determining DNI. Therefore, using this separate share rule, beneficiary A's *separate trust* would have DNI of only $15,000, the maximum amount taxable to A in the year of distribution. This rule is inapplicable to estates.

A COMPREHENSIVE EXAMPLE

The AB Trust is a calendar year taxpayer. In the current year, the trust books show the following:

Gross rental income	$25,000
Taxable interest income	10,000
Tax-exempt interest income	15,000
Long-term capital gain	8,000
Trustee fee	6,000
Rent expenses	3,000
Contribution to charity	1,500
Distributions to	
Beneficiary A	20,000
Beneficiary B	20,000

Under the terms of the trust instrument the capital gain and one-third of the trustee fee are allocable to corpus. The trustee is required to maintain a reserve for depreciation on the rental property equal to one-tenth of annual gross rental income. (For tax purposes, assume actual tax depreciation is $1,300.) The trustee is required to make an annual distribution to beneficiary A of $12,000 and has the discretion to make additional distributions to A or beneficiary B.

Based on these facts, the computation of the income taxable to the trust and the beneficiaries is as follows:

Step One: Compute fiduciary accounting income.

Gross rental income	$25,000
Taxable interest income	10,000
Tax-exempt interest income	15,000
	$50,000
Trustee fee charged against income	(4,000)
Rent expenses	(3,000)
Depreciation ($1/_{10} \times$ $25,000)	(2,500)
Fiduciary accounting income	$40,500

Step Two: Compute fiduciary taxable income before the § 661 deduction for distributions to beneficiaries.

Gross rental income	$25,000
Taxable interest income	10,000
Long-term capital gain	8,000
	$43,000
Deductible trustee fee	(4,200)*
Deductible rent expense	(3,000)
Deductible depreciation allocable to fiduciary	(1,300)
Deductible charitable contribution	(1,050)*
Exemption	(100)
Taxable income before § 661 deduction	$33,350

* $35,000 ÷ $50,000 of gross fiduciary accounting income is taxable; thus, only 70% of both the $6,000 trustee fee and $1,500 charitable contribution is deductible.

Step Three: Compute DNI and the § 661 deduction for distributions to beneficiaries.

Taxable income from Step Two	$33,350
Add back:	
Exemption	100
Net tax-exempt income	12,750*
Subtract:	
Capital gain allocable to corpus	(8,000)
Distributable net income (DNI)	$38,200

* $15,000 tax-exempt interest less 30% of the $6,000 trustee fee and $1,500 charitable contribution.

Because distributions to beneficiaries exceeded DNI, the trust will deduct the entire amount of taxable DNI, $25,450 ($38,200 − $12,750).

Step Four: Subtract the § 661 deduction for distributions to beneficiaries.

Taxable income before deduction	$33,350
Section 661 deduction	(25,450)
Trust taxable income	$ 7,900

Tax Consequences to Beneficiaries: The $40,000 cash distribution to beneficiaries exceeds the total DNI of $38,200; thus, the entire amount of DNI must be allocated to the beneficiaries.

Total DNI...	$38,200
Allocation to first-tier	
distribution to Beneficiary A.................................	(12,000)
DNI available for allocation to	
second-tier distributions.....................................	26,200

	Second-tier Distributions	DNI Allocation
Beneficiary A......................	$ 8,000 (29%)	$ 7,483
Beneficiary B......................	20,000 (71%)	18,717
Total.............................	$28,000(100%)	$26,200

The composition of DNI is as follows:

	Rent	Taxable Interest	Tax-exempt Interest	Total
Gross receipts..........	$25,000	$10,000	$15,000	$50,000
Rent expense..........	(3,000)			(3,000)
Depreciation............	(1,300)			(1,300)
Trustee fee*............		(4,200)	(1,800)	(6,000)
Charitable				
contribution**........	(750)	(300)	(450)	(1,500)
Total...................	$19,950	$ 5,500	$12,750	$38,200

* The trustee fee allocable to taxable income may be arbitrarily allocated to **any** item of taxable income. Reg. § 1.652(b)-3(b).
** In the absence of a specific provision in the trust instrument, the charitable contribution is allocated proportionally to each class of income. Reg. § 1.642(c)-3(b)(2).

Each beneficiary should report the following:

	Rent	Taxable Interest	Tax-exempt Interest	Total DNI Allocated
Beneficiary A...........	$10,175*	$2,805	$ 6,503	$19,483
Beneficiary B..........	9,775	2,695	6,247	18,717
Total...................	$19,950	$5,500	$12,750	$38,200

* Beneficiary A's proportionate share of DNI ($12,000 first-tier distribution + $7,483 second-tier distribution = $19,483 ÷ $38,200 total DNI) multiplied times $19,950 total rent income included in DNI equals Beneficiary A's share of rent income. This same procedure is used to determine each beneficiary's share of all other items.

A completed Form 1041 for the AB Trust and a Schedule K-1 for Beneficiary A are shown on the following pages.

Form 1041 Department of the Treasury—Internal Revenue Service
U.S. Fiduciary Income Tax Return 1990

For the calendar year 1990 or fiscal year beginning	, 1990, and ending	, 19	OMB No. 1545-0092

Check applicable boxes:
☐ Decedent's estate
☐ Simple trust
☐ Complex trust
☐ Grantor type trust
☐ Bankruptcy estate
☐ Family estate trust
☐ Pooled income fund

Name of estate or trust (grantor type trust, see instructions)
A B Trust

Name and title of fiduciary

Number, street, and room or suite no. (If a P.O. box, see page 5 of Instructions.)

City, state, and ZIP code

Employer identification number

Date entity created

Nonexempt charitable and split-interest trusts, check applicable boxes (see instructions):
☐ Described in section 4947(a)(1)
☐ Not a private foundation
☐ Described in section 4947(a)(2)

Number of Schedules K-1 attached (see instructions) . ▶

Check applicable boxes: ☐ First return   ☐ Final return   ☐ Amended return
Change in Fiduciary's ▶   ☐ Name or   ☐ Address

Income

1	Interest income	1	10,000
2	Dividends	2	
3	Income (or losses) from partnerships, other estates, or other trusts (see instructions)	3	
4	Net rental and royalty income (or loss) (attach Schedule E (Form 1040))	4	20,700
5	Net business and farm income (or loss) (attach Schedules C and F (Form 1040))	5	
6	Capital gain (or loss) (attach Schedule D (Form 1041))	6	8,000
7	Ordinary gain (or loss) (attach Form 4797)	7	
8	Other income (state nature of income) _____	8	
9	**Total** income (combine lines 1 through 8) ▶	9	38,700

Deductions

10	Interest	10			
11	Taxes	11			
12	Fiduciary fees	12	4,200		
13	Charitable deduction (from Schedule A, line 6)	13	1,050		
14	Attorney, accountant, and return preparer fees	14			
15a	Other deductions NOT subject to the 2% floor (attach schedule)	15a			
b	Allowable miscellaneous itemized deductions subject to the 2% floor	15b			
c	Add lines 15a and 15b	15c			
16	**Total** (add lines 10 through 15c)			16	5,250
17	Adjusted total income (or loss) (subtract line 16 from line 9). Enter here and on Schedule B, line 1 . ▶			17	33,450
18	Income distribution deduction (from Schedule B, line 17) (see instructions) (attach Schedules K-1 (Form 1041))			18	25,450
19	Estate tax deduction (including certain generation-skipping transfer taxes) (attach computation)			19	
20	Exemption			20	100
21	**Total deductions** (add lines 18 through 20) ▶			21	25,550
22	Taxable income of fiduciary (subtract line 21 from line 17)			22	7,900
23	**Total tax** (from Schedule G, line 7) ▶			23	1,504

Please attach check or money order here
Tax and Payments

24a	Payments: 1990 estimated tax payments and amount applied from 1989 return	24a	
b	Treated as credited to beneficiaries	24b	
c	Subtract line 24b from line 24a	24c	
d	Tax paid with extension of time to file: ☐ Form 2758 ☐ Form 8736 ☐ Form 8800	24d	
e	Federal income tax withheld	24e	
	Credits: f Form 2439 ....; g Form 4136 ....; h Other ....; Total ▶	24i	
25	**Total payments** (add lines 24c through 24e, and 24i) ▶	25	
26	**Penalty** for underpayment of estimated tax (see instructions)	26	
27	If the total of lines 23 and 26 is larger than line 25, enter **TAX DUE**	27	1,504
28	If line 25 is larger than the total of lines 23 and 26, enter **OVERPAYMENT**	28	
29	Amount of line 28 to be: a Credited to 1991 estimated tax ▶ ....; b Refunded ▶	29	

Please Sign Here
Under penalties of perjury, I declare that I have examined this return, including accompanying schedules and statements, and to the best of my knowledge and belief, it is true, correct, and complete. Declaration of preparer (other than fiduciary) is based on all information of which preparer has any knowledge.

▶ _____ Signature of fiduciary or officer representing fiduciary   Date   ▶ EIN of fiduciary (see instructions)

Paid Preparer's Use Only

Preparer's signature ▶	Date	Check if self-employed ▶ ☐	Preparer's social security no.
Firm's name (or yours if self-employed) and address ▶		E.I. No. ▶	
		ZIP code ▶	

For Paperwork Reduction Act Notice, see page 1 of the separate Instructions.

Form **1041** (1990)

Form 1041 (1990) Page **2**

Schedule A Charitable Deduction—Do not complete for a simple trust or a pooled income fund.

1	Amounts paid or permanently set aside for charitable purposes from current year's gross income	1	1,500
2	Tax-exempt interest allocable to charitable distribution (see instructions)	2	450
3	Subtract line 2 from line 1	3	1,050
4	Enter the net short-term capital gain and the net long-term capital gain of the current tax year allocable to corpus paid or permanently set aside for charitable purposes (see instructions)	4	
5	Amounts paid or permanently set aside for charitable purposes from gross income of a prior year (see instructions)	5	
6	**Total** (add lines 3 through 5). Enter here and on page 1, line 13	6	1,050

Schedule B Income Distribution Deduction (see instructions)

1	Adjusted total income (from page 1, line 17) (see instructions)	1	33,450
2	Adjusted tax-exempt interest (see instructions)	2	12,750
3	Net gain shown on Schedule D (Form 1041), line 17, column (a). (If net loss, enter zero.)	3	
4	Enter amount from Schedule A, line 4	4	
5	Long-term capital gain included on Schedule A, line 1	5	
6	Short-term capital gain included on Schedule A, line 1	6	
7	If the amount on page 1, line 6, is a capital loss, enter here as a positive figure	7	
8	If the amount on page 1, line 6, is a capital gain, enter here as a negative figure	8	(8,000)
9	Distributable net income (combine lines 1 through 8)	9	38,200
10	Amount of income for the tax year determined under the governing instrument (accounting income) 10	40,500	
11	Amount of income required to be distributed currently (see instructions)	11	12,000
12	Other amounts paid, credited, or otherwise required to be distributed (see instructions)	12	28,000
13	Total distributions (add lines 11 and 12). (If greater than line 10, see instructions.)	13	40,000
14	Enter the amount of tax-exempt income included on line 13	14	12,750
15	Tentative income distribution deduction (subtract line 14 from line 13)	15	27,250
16	Tentative income distribution deduction (subtract line 2 from line 9)	16	25,450
17	Income distribution deduction. Enter the smaller of line 15 or line 16 here and on page 1, line 18	17	25,450

Schedule G Tax Computation (see instructions)

1	Tax: **a** Tax rate schedule 1,504 ; **b** Other taxes ; Total ▶	1c	1,504
2a	Foreign tax credit (attach Form 1116) — 2a		
b	Credit for fuel produced from a nonconventional source. — 2b		
c	General business credit. Check if from: ☐ Form 3800 or ☐ Form (specify) ▶ — 2c		
d	Credit for prior year minimum tax (attach Form 8801) — 2d		
3	**Total** credits (add lines 2a through 2d) ▶	3	
4	Subtract line 3 from line 1c	4	1,504
5	Recapture taxes. Check if from: ☐ Form 4255 ☐ Form 8611	5	
6	Alternative minimum tax (attach Form 8656)	6	
7	**Total** tax (add lines 4 through 6). Enter here and on page 1, line 23 ▶	7	1,504

Other Information (see instructions)

		Yes	No
1	Did the estate or trust receive tax-exempt income? (If "Yes," attach a computation of the allocation of expenses.) Enter the amount of tax-exempt interest income and exempt-interest dividends ▶ $ 15,000	✓	
2	Did the estate or trust have any passive activity losses? (If "Yes," enter these losses on **Form 8582**, Passive Activity Loss Limitations, to figure the allowable loss.)		✓
3	Did the estate or trust receive all or any part of the earnings (salary, wages, and other compensation) of any individual by reason of a contract assignment or similar arrangement?		✓
4	At any time during the tax year, did the estate or trust have an interest in or a signature or other authority over a financial account in a foreign country (such as a bank account, securities account, or other financial account)? (See the instructions for exceptions and filing requirements for Form TD F 90-22.1.) If "Yes," enter the name of the foreign country ▶		✓
5	Was the estate or trust the grantor of, or transferor to, a foreign trust which existed during the current tax year, whether or not the estate or trust has any beneficial interest in it? (If "Yes," you may have to file Form 3520, 3520-A, or 926.)		✓
6	Check this box if this entity has filed or is required to file **Form 8264**, Application for Registration of a Tax Shelter ▶ ☐		
7	Check this box if this entity is a complex trust making the section 663(b) election ▶ ☐		
8	Check this box to make a section 643(e)(3) election (attach Schedule D (Form 1041)) ▶ ☐		
9	Check this box if the decedent's estate has been open for more than 2 years ▶ ☐		
10	Check this box if the trust is a participant in a Common Trust Fund that was required to adopt a calendar year ▶ ☐		

SCHEDULE D (Form 1041)	Capital Gains and Losses	OMB No. 1545-0092
Department of the Treasury Internal Revenue Service	▶ File with Form 1041. See the separate Form 1041 instructions.	1990

Name of estate or trust *A B TRUST*	Employer identification number

Do not report section 644 gains on Schedule D (See Form 1041 instructions for line 1b, Schedule G.)

Part I Short-Term Capital Gains and Losses—Assets Held One Year or Less

(a) Description of property (Example, 100 shares 7% preferred of ''Z'' Co.)	(b) Date acquired (mo., day, yr.)	(c) Date sold (mo., day, yr.)	(d) Gross sales price	(e) Cost or other basis, as adjusted, plus expense of sale (see instructions)	(f) Gain (or loss) (col. (d) less col. (e))
1					

2 Short-term capital gain from installment sales from Form 6252	2	
3 Net short-term gain (or loss) from partnerships, S corporations, and other fiduciaries	3	
4 Net gain (or loss) (combine lines 1 through 3)	4	
5 Short-term capital loss carryover (see instructions)	5 (	)
6 Net short-term gain (or loss) (combine lines 4 and 5). Enter here and on line 15 below ▶	6	

Part II Long-Term Capital Gains and Losses—Assets Held More Than One Year

7					8,000

8 Long-term capital gain from installment sales from Form 6252	8	
9 Net long-term gain (or loss) from partnerships, S corporations, and other fiduciaries	9	
10 Capital gain distributions	10	
11 Enter gain, if applicable, from Form 4797	11	
12 Net gain (or loss) (combine lines 7 through 11)	12	8,000
13 Long-term capital loss carryover (see instructions)	13 (	)
14 Net long-term gain (or loss) (combine lines 12 and 13). Enter here and on line 16 below ▶	14	8,000

Part III Summary of Parts I and II

	(a) Beneficiaries	(b) Fiduciary	(c) Total
15 Net short-term gain (or loss) from line 6, above 15			
16 Net long-term gain (or loss) from line 14, above 16		8,000	8,000
17 Total net gain (or loss) (combine lines 15 and 16) ▶ 17		8,000	8,000

If line 17, column (c), is a net gain, enter the gain on Form 1041, line 6, and DO NOT complete Parts IV and V. If line 17, column (c), is a net loss, complete Parts IV and V, as necessary.

For Paperwork Reduction Act Notice, see page 1 of the Instructions for Form 1041.   Schedule D (Form 1041) 1990

SCHEDULE K-1	Beneficiary's Share of Income, Deductions, Credits, Etc.—1990	OMB No. 1545-0092
(Form 1041)	for the calendar year 1990, or fiscal year	1990
Department of the Treasury Internal Revenue Service	beginning ...., 1990, ending ...., 19 ..... Complete a separate Schedule K-1 for each beneficiary.	

Name of estate or trust	☐ Amended K-1 ☐ Final K-1

Beneficiary's identifying number ▶	Estate's or trust's employer identification number ▶
Beneficiary's name, address, and ZIP code	Fiduciary's name, address, and ZIP code
BENEFICIARY A	*A B TRUST*

Reminder: *If you received a short year 1987 Schedule K-1 that was from a trust required to adopt a calendar year, be sure to include one-fourth of those amounts reported as income, in addition to the items reported on this Schedule K-1, on the appropriate lines of your 1990 Form 1040 and related schedules.*

(a) Allocable share item	(b) Amount	(c) Calendar year 1990 Form 1040 filers enter the amounts in column (b) on:
1 Interest	2,805	Schedule B, Part I, line 1
2 Dividends		Schedule B, Part II, line 5
3a Net short-term capital gain		Schedule D, line 5, column (g)
b Net long-term capital gain		Schedule D, line 12, column (g)
4a Other taxable income: (itemize)		Schedule E, Part III
(1) Rental, rental real estate, and business income from activities acquired before 10/23/86		
(2) Rental, rental real estate, and business income from activities acquired after 10/22/86	10,175	
(3) Other passive income		
b Depreciation, including cost recovery (itemize):		
(1) Attributable to line 4a(1)		
(2) Attributable to line 4a(2)		
(3) Attributable to line 4a(3)		
c Depletion (itemize):		
(1) Attributable to line 4a(1)		
(2) Attributable to line 4a(2)		
(3) Attributable to line 4a(3)		
d Amortization (itemize):		
(1) Attributable to line 4a(1)		
(2) Attributable to line 4a(2)		
(3) Attributable to line 4a(3)		
5 Income for minimum tax purposes	12,980	
6 Income for regular tax purposes (add lines 1 through 4a) . .	12,980	
7 Adjustment for minimum tax purposes (subtract line 6 from line 5)		Form 6251, line 4t
8 Estate tax deduction (including certain generation-skipping transfer taxes) (attach computation)		Schedule A, line 26
9 Excess deductions on termination (attach computation) . .		Schedule A, line 21
10 Foreign taxes (list on a separate sheet)		Form 1116 or Schedule A (Form 1040), line 7
11 Tax preference items (itemize):		
a Accelerated depreciation		(Include on the applicable
b Depletion		line of Form 6251)
c Amortization		
12 Other (itemize):		
a Trust payments of estimated taxes credited to you . . .	6,503	Form 1040, line 56
b Tax-exempt interest		Form 1040, line 8b
c Short-term capital loss carryover		Schedule D, line 6, column (f)
d Long-term capital loss carryover		Schedule D, line 15, column (f)
e		(Include on the applicable line
f		of appropriate tax form)
g		

For Paperwork Reduction Act Notice, see page 1 of the Instructions for Form 1041.   Schedule K-1 (Form 1041) 1990

SPECIALIZED TRUST PROBLEMS

A complete discussion of the taxation of fiduciaries should include the following specialized problem areas:

1. The § 644 special tax on certain trusts;

2. Accumulation distributions; and

3. The sixty-five day rule.

While a technical exploration of these complex areas is beyond the scope of this text, the following paragraphs will provide a conceptual introduction to the areas.

SPECIAL TAX COMPUTATION—CODE § 644

An individual planning to sell an appreciated asset might be tempted to utilize an existing trust or to create a new trust for the purpose of reducing the tax bill upon sale. Because trusts are taxable entities, a transfer of the appreciated asset to the trust prior to sale would appear to cause the gain on sale to be taxed to the trust. If the marginal tax rate of the trust was lower than that of the individual transferor, a net tax savings would be achieved.

To discourage this assignment of income scheme, Congress enacted § 644. This statute provides that if an appreciated asset is transferred into trust *and* the trust sells or exchanges the asset *within two years* of the transfer, the trust's tax on the gain recognized is computed in an unusual way. The amount of the gain not in excess of the amount of the appreciation in the asset at date of transfer to the trust is taxed as if the transferor rather than the trust made the sale.[37] Although the gain is taxed to the trust, the tax is computed based on the marginal rate of the transferor.

> **Example 16.** In 1990, individual X transfers real property (basis $100,000, fair market value $250,000) into a family trust. X pays no gift tax on the transfer. In 1991, the trust sells the real property for $330,000. The tax on $150,000 of the gain recognized upon sale will be computed as if such gain were included in X's 1991 taxable income. The tax on the remaining $80,000 of recognized gain is taxed under normal Subchapter J rules. The entire tax is paid by the trust.

In a tax regime in which there is only minimal progressivity, there is scant potential for the type of abuse that § 644 was designed to prevent. Since 1986, the tax rates imposed on the income of a trust have been higher than those imposed on the income of an individual. As a result, the deliberate assignment of income to a trust from an individual offers no opportunity for tax savings, and § 644 has little current vitality.

---

[37] § 644(a)(2).

ACCUMULATION DISTRIBUTIONS

The trustee of a complex trust may have the discretion whether or not to distribute trust income to trust beneficiaries. In a year in which the marginal tax rate of the beneficiaries is higher than that of the trust (an historic rather than a current possibility), and the beneficiaries are not in immediate need of trust funds, the trustee might be tempted to accumulate income in the trust so that it would be taxed at the cheaper trust rates. Then in a later year, the accumulated income, net of taxes, could be distributed as nontaxable corpus to the beneficiaries.

Congress decided to curb this abuse of the complex trust in 1969 and enacted what are now §§ 665 through 668 of Subchapter J. These sections, referred to as the *throwback rules*, are very complex and require a series of intricate computations. However, the theory underlying this part of the tax law is not difficult to understand.

If a complex trust fails to distribute all of its DNI for one or a series of taxable years and instead pays tax at the trust level on the DNI, the accumulated DNI after taxes is referred to as *undistributed net income* (UNI).[38] In a subsequent tax year in which the trust distributes amounts to beneficiaries in excess of its current DNI, such excess is deemed to be a distribution of any trust UNI.[39] The amount of distributed UNI *plus* the taxes originally paid by the trust attributable to the UNI is taxed as an *accumulation distribution* to the recipient beneficiary.[40]

The tax rate imposed on an accumulation distribution is computed under a complex averaging formula that uses three earlier tax years of the recipient beneficiary as a base. If the tax liability computed by use of this formula is greater than the tax already paid by the trust, the beneficiary must pay the excess in the year the distribution is received. If the formula results in a tax liability less than the taxes already paid, *no refund* is available to the beneficiary.[41]

Accumulation distributions are reported by a trust on Schedule J, Form 1041. This form is reproduced in Appendix B.

The accumulation distribution rules do not apply to simple trusts and estates. Also, income accumulated by a trust on behalf of a beneficiary who has not yet attained the age of twenty-one is not subject to the throwback rules.[42]

---

[38] § 665(a).

[39] § 665(b).

[40] § 667(a).

[41] § 666(e).

[42] § 665(b).

THE SIXTY-FIVE DAY RULE

Many trustees want to avoid accumulating DNI at the trust level because of the complexity of the throwback rules and the expense of compliance. Because DNI is often not calculated until after the close of the trust's taxable year, a trustee may not know the amount of current distributions necessary to avoid accumulation. To alleviate this timing problem, § 663(b) provides that a trustee *may elect* that any distribution made within the first 65 days of a taxable year will be considered paid to the beneficiary on the last day of the preceding taxable year.[43] This rule allows a trustee to make distributions after the close of a year to eliminate any accumulations of DNI for that year.

---

[43] See Reg. § 1.663(b)-2 for the manner and time for making such an election.

TAX PLANNING CONSIDERATIONS

The tax planning considerations for the use of trusts are discussed in Chapter 26, *Family Tax Planning*.

PROBLEM MATERIALS

DISCUSSION QUESTIONS

25-1 *Trusts and Estates as Conduits.* What does it mean to describe a fiduciary as a *conduit* of income? To what extent does a fiduciary operate as a conduit?

25-2 *Purpose of Trusts.* Trusts are usually created for nonbusiness purposes. Give some examples of situations in which a trust could be useful.

25-3 *Trust as a Separate Legal Entity.* A trust cannot exist if the only trustee is also sole beneficiary. Why not?

25-4 *Trust Expenses Allocable to Corpus.* For what reason might the grantor of a trust stipulate that some amount of trust expenses be paid out of trust corpus rather than trust income?

25-5 *Use of Fiduciaries to Defer Income Taxation.* Although a trust must adopt a calendar year for tax purposes, an estate may adopt any fiscal year, as well as a calendar year, for reporting taxable income. Why is Congress willing to allow an estate more flexibility in the choice of taxable year?

25-6 *Trust Accounting Income vs. Taxable Income.* Even though a trustee may be required to distribute all trust income currently, the trust may still have to report taxable income. Explain.

25-7 *Deductibility of Administrative Expenses.* Explain any options available to the executor of an estate with regard to the deductibility of administrative expenses incurred by the estate.

25-8 *Capital Loss Deductions.* To what extent may a fiduciary deduct any excess of capital losses over capital gains for a taxable year?

25-9 *Operating Losses of a Fiduciary.* How does the tax treatment of operating loss incurred by a fiduciary differ from the treatment of such losses by a partnership or an S corporation?

25-10 *Purpose of DNI.* Discuss the function of DNI from the point of view of the fiduciary and the point of view of beneficiaries who receive distributions from the fiduciary.

25-11 *Taxable vs. Nontaxable DNI.* Why is it important to correctly identify any nontaxable component of DNI?

25-12 *Charitable Deductions.* Enumerate the differences in the charitable deduction allowable to a fiduciary and the charitable deduction allowable to an individual.

25-13 *Timing Distributions from an Estate.* Why might a beneficiary of an estate prefer *not* to receive an early distribution of property from the estate?

25-14 *Simple vs. Complex Trusts.* All trusts are complex in the year of termination. Why?

25-15 *Trust Reserves for Depreciation.*   Discuss the reason why a grantor of a trust would require the trustee to maintain a certain reserve for depreciation of trust assets.

25-16 *Purpose of Accumulation Distribution Tax.*   It has been stated that Congress intended that *all* ordinary income earned by trust be taxed to trust beneficiaries. Discuss. (Review the rules on the taxation of accumulation distributions.)

25-17 *Accumulations for Minors and the Throwback Rules.*   What reasons can you identify for the exclusion of accumulations of income for minor beneficiaries from the "throwback" rules?

PROBLEMS

25-18 *Computation of Fiduciary Accounting Income.*   Under the terms of the trust instrument, the annual fiduciary accounting income of Trust MNO must be distributed in equal amounts to individual beneficiaries M, N, and O. The trust instrument also provides that capital gains or losses realized on the sale of trust assets are allocated to corpus, and that 40 percent of the annual trustee fee is to be allocated to corpus. For the current year, the records of the trust show the following:

Dividend income	$38,000
Tax-exempt interest income	18,900
Taxable interest income	12,400
Capital loss on sale of securities	(2,500)
Trustee fee	5,000

Based on these facts, determine the required distribution to each of the three trust beneficiaries.

25-19 *Tax Consequences of Property Distributions.*   During the taxable year, beneficiary M receives 100 shares of Acme common stock from Trust T. The basis of the stock is $70 per share to the trust, and its fair market value at date of distribution is $110 per share. The trust's DNI for the year is $60,000, all of which is taxable. There were no other distributions made or required to be made by the trust.

a. Assume the stock distribution was in satisfaction of an $11,000 pecuniary bequest to M. What is the tax result to M? To Trust T? What basis will M have in the Acme shares?

b. Assume the distribution did not represent a specific bequest to M, and that Trust T did not make a § 643(e)(3) election. What is the tax result to M? To Trust T? What basis will M have in the Acme shares?

c. Assume now that Trust T did make a § 643(e)(3) election with regards to the distribution of the Acme shares. What is the tax result to M? To Trust T? What basis will M have in the Acme shares?

25-20 *Trust's Depreciation Deduction.*   Under the terms of the trust instrument, Trustee K is required to maintain a reserve for depreciation equal to $3,000 per year. All trust income, including rents from depreciable trust property, must be distributed currently to trust beneficiaries.

   a.   Assume allowable depreciation for tax purposes is $2,000. What is the amount of the depreciation deduction available to the trust? To the trust beneficiaries?

   b.   Assume allowable depreciation for tax purposes is $7,000. What is the amount of the depreciation deduction available to the trust? To the trust beneficiaries?

25-21 *Trust Losses.*   Complex Trust Z has the following receipts and disbursements for the current year:

Receipts:	
Rents..	$ 62,000
Proceeds from sale of securities	
(basis of securities = $55,000).......................	48,000
Dividends..	12,000
Total receipts...	$120,000
Disbursements:	
Rent expenses...	$ 70,000
Trustee fee (100 percent	
allocable to income)..................................	4,000
Total disbursements.....................................	$ 74,000

The trustee made no distributions to any beneficiaries during the current year. Based on these facts, compute trust taxable income for the current year.

25-22 *Deductibility of Funeral and Administrative Expenses.*   Decedent L died on May 12 of the current year, and her executor elected a calendar taxable year for L's estate. Prior to December 31, L's estate paid $4,800 of funeral expenses, $19,900 of legal and accounting fees attributable to the administration of the estate, and a $6,100 executor's fee. Before consideration of any of these expenses, L's estate has taxable income of $60,000 for the period May 13 to December 31. Decedent L's taxable estate for Federal estate tax purposes is estimated at $1,700,000.

   a.   To what extent are the above expenses deductible on L's estate tax return (Form 706) or on the estate's income tax return (Form 1041) for the current year? On which return would the deductions yield the greater tax benefit?

   b.   Assume that L was married at the time of her death and that all the property included in her gross estate was left to her surviving spouse. Does this fact change your answer to (a)?

25-23 *Amount of Distribution Taxable to Beneficiary.*   During the current year, Trust H has DNI of $50,000, of which $30,000 is nontaxable. The trustee made a $10,000 cash distribution to beneficiary P during the year; no other distributions were made.

   a.   How much taxable income must P report?

   b.   What deduction for distributions to beneficiaries may Trust H claim?

25-24 *Deductibility of Trust Expenses.* Trust A has the following receipts and disbursements for the current year:

Receipts:	
Nontaxable interest	$ 40,000
Taxable interest	30,000
Rents	30,000
Total receipts	$100,000
Disbursements:	
Charitable donation	$ 10,000
Rent expense	6,500
Trustee fee	5,000
Total disbursements	$ 21,500

    a.   What is Trust A's deduction for charitable contributions for the current year?

    b.   How much of the trustee fee is deductible?

    c.   How much of the rent expense is deductible?

25-25 *Computation of DNI and Trust's Tax Liability.* Trust M has the following receipts and disbursements for the current year:

Receipts:	
Nontaxable interest	$ 4,000
Taxable interest	25,000
Rents	11,000
Long-term capital gain allocable	
to corpus	9,000
Total receipts	$49,000
Disbursements:	
Rent expense	$ 2,400
Trustee fee	1,000
Total disbursements	$ 3,400

The trustee is required to distribute all trust income to beneficiary N on a quarterly basis.

    a.   Compute Trust M's DNI for the current year.

    b.   Compute Trust M's taxable income for the current year.

    c.   Compute Trust M's tax liability for the current year.

25-26 *Taxation of Trust and Beneficiaries.*   Trust B has the following receipts and disbursements for the current year:

Receipts:	
Nontaxable interest.....................................	$10,000
Dividends...	10,000
Rents..	30,000
Long-term capital gain allocable	
to corpus..	15,000
Total receipts...	$65,000

Disbursements:	
Rent expense..	$ 7,500
Trustee fee...	5,000
Total disbursements....................................	$12,500

During the year, the trustee distributes $20,000 to beneficiary C and $10,000 to beneficiary D. None of these distributions is subject to the throwback rule. The trust and both beneficiaries are calendar year taxpayers.

a. Compute Trust B's DNI for the current year.
b. Compute Trust B's taxable income for the current year.
c. How much taxable income must each beneficiary report for the current year?

25-27 *Distributions from Complex Trusts.*   Under the terms of the trust instrument, the trustee of Trust EFG is required to make an annual distribution of 50 percent of trust accounting income to beneficiary E. The trustee can make additional discretionary distributions out of trust income or corpus to beneficiaries E, F, or G. During the current year, the trust accounting income of $85,000 equaled taxable DNI.

a. Assume that the trustee made current distributions of $60,000 to E and $10,000 to G. How much taxable income must each beneficiary report for the current year? What is the amount of the trust's deduction for distributions to beneficiaries?
b. Assume that the trustee made current distributions of $80,000 to E and $40,000 to G. How much taxable income must each beneficiary report for the current year? What is the amount of the trust's deduction for distributions to beneficiaries?

25-28 *First- and Second-Tier Distributions.*   For the current year, Trust R has DNI of $100,000, of which $25,000 is nontaxable. The trustee is required to make an annual distribution of $60,000 to beneficiary S. Also during the year, the trustee made discretionary distributions of $40,000 to beneficiary T and $30,000 to beneficiary U. None of these distributions is subject to the throwback rules. How much taxable income must each beneficiary report?

25-29 *Accumulation Distribution.* In 1989 and 1990, complex Trust C had taxable DNI of $18,000 and $28,500, respectively. No distributions were made to beneficiaries in either year and the trust paid income taxes totaling $13,041 for the two years. In 1991, trust DNI was $33,000 and the trustee distributed $100,000 to beneficiary W.

    a.   What is the amount of the accumulation distribution received by W in 1991?

    b.   Explain how such distribution is taxed.

25-30 *Special Tax Computation of § 644.* In 1990, individual J transferred land into existing trust H. The beneficiaries of the trust are all members of J's family. At date of transfer, the basis of the land to J was $50,000 and its fair market value was $125,000. The trust sold the land in 1991 for $150,000. Explain how the $100,000 gain on the sale is taxed.

25-31 *Income in Respect of a Decedent.* Individual K is a self-employed business consultant. In the current year, K performed services for a client and billed the client for $14,500. Unfortunately, K died on October 10 of the current year, before he received payment for his services. A check for $14,500 was received by K's executor on November 18. At the date of K's death, he owed a local attorney $1,600 for legal advice concerning a child custody suit in which K was involved. K's executor paid this bill on December 15.

    a.   Assuming that K was a cash basis taxpayer, describe the tax consequences of the $14,500 receipt and the $1,600 payment by K's executor.

    b.   How would your answer change if K had been an accrual basis taxpayer?

25-32 *Income in Respect of a Decedent.* Early in 1991, Z (an unmarried cash basis taxpayer) sold investment land with a basis of $50,000 for $200,000. In payment, Z received an installment note for $200,000, payable over the next ten years. Z died on December 1, 1991. As of the date of death, Z had received no principal payments on the note. Accrued interest on the note as of December 1, 1991 was $18,000, although the first interest payment was not due until early in 1992.

    a.   Assuming that no election is made to avoid installment sale treatment, how much of the $150,000 gain realized by Z will be included on her final income tax return? How much of the accrued interest income will be included?

    b.   In 1992, the estate of Z collects the first annual interest payment on the note of $19,700, and the first principal payment of $20,000. What are the income tax consequences to the estate of these collections?

    c.   Assume that the amount of estate tax attributable to the inclusion of the IRD represented by the installment note and the accrued interest in Z's taxable estate is $10,000, and that there are no other IRD or DRD items on the estate tax return. Compute the § 691(c) deduction available on the estate's 1992 income tax return.

TAX RETURN PROBLEM

25-33   The MKJ trust is a calendar year, cash basis taxpayer. For 1990, the trust's books and records reflect these transactions:

Income:		
Dividends		$ 30,000
Gross rents		25,000
Interest:		
Bonds of the City of New York	$25,000	
U.S. government bonds	20,000	45,000
Capital gains:		
General Motors stock received from estate of MKJ:		
Sales price—December 2, 1990	48,000	
Less: Basis (FMV on date of death)	(30,000)	18,000
Total income		$118,000
Expenses:		
Trustee commissions (allocable to income)		$ 4,000
Legal fee		28,800
Contribution-American Cancer Society (paid out of corpus)		12,000
Depreciation—rental property		2,000
Real estate tax—rental property		4,000
Repairs and maintenance—rental property		4,200
Total expenses		$ 55,000
Net income for 1990		$ 63,000

The legal fee was a legitimate trust expense, allocated by the trustee to the various income classes as follows:

Dividends	$ 9,400
Taxable interest	6,600
Tax-exempt interest	6,000
Rents	6,800
Total legal fee	$28,800

The propriety of this allocation is *not* in question. Under the terms of the trust instrument, the $2 000 depreciation reserve equals the available tax depreciation deduction for the year. The trust instrument also specifies that all capital gains are allocable to corpus and that the trustee has discretion as to the amount of trust income distributed to BTJ, the sole trust beneficiary. During 1990, the trustee distributes $24,000 of income to BTJ.

Required:

Complete Form 1041 and Schedule D for the MKJ trust. **Note:** If the student is required to complete a Schedule K-1 for beneficiary BTJ, he or she should refer to Reg. §§ 1.661(b)-1, 1.661(c)-2, and 1.661(c)-4, and the comprehensive example in this chapter in order to determine the character of any income distributed to the beneficiary.

RESEARCH PROBLEM

25-34   In 1987 N transferred $600,000 of assets into an irrevocable trust for the benefit of her mother, M. The independent trustee, T, is required to distribute annually all income to M. The trust instrument also provides that any capital gains or losses realized upon the sale of trust assets are to be allocated to trust corpus. In 1988 and 1990, the trustee sold trust assets and distributed an amount equal to the capital gain realized to M, in addition to the required distribution of trust income. During the current year, T sold certain trust securities and realized a net gain of $25,000. The trust also earned $10,000 of other income. During the year, $35,000 was distributed to M. Should the DNI of the trust for the current year include the $25,000 capital gain?

Suggested research materials:

§ 643 and accompanying Regulations
Rev. Rul. 68-392, 1968-2 C.B. 284

LEARNING OBJECTIVES

Upon completion of this chapter you will be able to:

- Explain the concept of income shifting and the judicial constraints on this tax planning technique

- Describe the marriage penalty and the singles penalty and identify the taxpayer situations in which either might occur

- Identify different planning techniques that achieve tax savings by the shifting of income among family members

- Characterize a regular corporation, an S corporation, and a partnership in terms of their viability as intrafamily income-shifting devices

- Explain how the "kiddie tax" is computed on the unearned income of a minor child

- Understand the role of a trust as a vehicle for intrafamily income shifting

- Distinguish between a grantor trust and a taxable trust

- Specify the tax advantages of *inter vivos* gifts as compared to testamentary transfers of wealth

- Explain the potential tax advantages and disadvantages of the estate tax marital deduction

CHAPTER OUTLINE

Chapter 26

FAMILY TAX PLANNING

INTRODUCTION

Under the United States system of taxation, individuals are viewed as the basic unit of taxation. However, most individuals who are members of a nuclear family tend to regard the family as the economic and financial unit. For example, the individual wage earner with a spouse and three children must budget his or her income according to the needs of five people rather than one individual. Similarly, the family that includes a teenager who has received a college scholarship may perceive the scholarship as a financial benefit to all its members.

The concept of family tax planning is a product of this family-oriented economic perspective. Such planning has as its goal the minimization of taxes paid by the family unit as opposed to the separate taxes paid by individual members. Minimization of the total annual income tax bill of a family results in greater consumable income to the family unit. Minimization of transfer taxes on shifts of wealth among family members increases the total wealth that can be enjoyed by the family as a whole.

Before beginning a study of family tax planning, it is important to remember that such planning is only one aspect of the larger issue of family financial planning. Nontax considerations may often be more important to a family than the tax consequences of a course of action. For example, a family that faces the possibility of large medical expenses might be more concerned with their short-term liquidity needs than minimization of their current tax bill. A competent tax adviser must always be sensitive to the family's nontax goals and desires before he or she can design a tax plan that is truly in the family's best interests.

FAMILY INCOME SHIFTING

A general premise in tax planning holds that, given a single amount of income, two taxpayers are always better than one. This premise results from the progressive structure of the United States income tax. As one taxpayer earns an increasing amount of income, the income is taxed at an increasing marginal rate. If the income can be diverted to a second taxpayer with less income of his or her own, the diverted amount will be taxed at a lower marginal rate. The reductions in the individual tax rates enacted as part of the Tax Reform Act of 1986 substantially decrease the progressivity of the income tax. However, even under a progressive tax structure consisting only of three rates (15%, 28%, and 31%), opportunities for tax savings through family income shifting still exist.

A family unit composed of several individuals theoretically represents a single economic unit which nonetheless is composed of separate taxpayers. A shift of income from one of these taxpayers to another has no effect economically. However, if the shift moves the income from a high tax bracket to a low tax bracket, the family has enjoyed a tax savings. A simple example can illustrate this basic point.

> **Example 1.** Family F is composed of a father and his 15-year-old daughter. The father earns taxable income of $50,000 a year, an amount that represents total family income. During the summer, the daughter needs $5,000 for various personal expenses. To earn the money, she agrees to work for her father for a $5,000 salary, payment of which represents a deductible expense to him. The tax bill on the father's $45,000 income is $6,736 (1990 head-of-household rates, $4,750 standard deduction, two $2,050 exemptions). The tax bill on the daughter's $5,000 income is $263 (1990 single rates, $3,250 standard deduction, no exemption). The total family tax bill is $6,999. If the father had simply agreed to pay the daughter's personal expenses rather than shifting income to her, the family tax bill based on $50,000 of taxable income would be $8,136.

The tax savings in the above example is attributable to two factors. First, the daughter as a taxpayer with earned income is entitled to a $3,250 standard deduction, which shelters $3,250 of the income shifted to her from any taxation at all.[1] Second, the income taxable to the daughter is subject to a 15 percent tax rate; if this income had been taxed on the father's return, it would have been subject to a 28 percent tax rate.

The fact that the daughter is a taxpayer does not prevent the father from qualifying as a head of household for filing purposes. However, because the daughter is claimed as a dependent on her father's return, she is not entitled to a personal exemption on her own return.[2]

JUDICIAL CONSTRAINTS ON INCOME SHIFTING

The Federal courts have consistently recognized that the United States system of taxation cannot tolerate arbitrary shifting of income from one family member to another. The decisions in a number of historic cases have established clear judicial doctrine that limits the assignment of income from one taxpayer to another.

---

[1] § 63(c)(5).   [2] § 151(d)(2).

The 1930 Supreme Court case of *Lucas v. Earl*[3] involved a husband and wife who entered into a contract providing that the earnings of either spouse should be considered as owned equally by each. The contract was signed in 1901, twelve years before the first Federal income tax law was written, and was legally binding upon the spouses under California law.

The taxpayers contended that because of the contract certain attorney fees earned by Mr. Earl should be taxed in equal portions to Mr. and Mrs. Earl. However, the Supreme Court agreed with the government's argument that the intent of the Federal income tax law was to tax income to the individual who earns it, an intent that cannot be avoided by anticipatory arrangements to assign the income to a different taxpayer. The decision of the Court ended with the memorable statement that the tax law must disregard arrangements "by which the fruits are attributed to a different tree from that on which they grew."[4]

The Supreme Court followed the same logic in its 1940 decision in *Helvering v. Horst*.[5] This case involved a father who owned corporate coupon bonds and who detached the negotiable interest coupons from the bonds shortly before their due date. The father then gifted the coupons to his son, who collected the interest upon maturity and reported the income on his tax return for the year.

The Court's decision focused on the fact that ownership of the corporate bonds themselves created the right to the interest payments. Because the father owned the bonds, he alone had the right to and control over the interest income. In exercising his control by gifting the interest coupons to his child, the father realized the economic benefit of the income represented by the coupons and therefore was the individual taxable on the income.

These two cases illustrate the two basic premises of the assignment of income doctrine. Earned income must be taxed to the individual who performs the service for which the income is paid. Investment income must be taxed to the owner of the investment capital that generated the income. All legitimate efforts to shift income from one individual to another must take into account these judicial constraints.

JOINT FILING AND THE SINGLES PENALTY

The most obvious candidates for intrafamily income shifting are a husband and wife, one of whom has a much larger income than the other. However, since 1948 married couples have been allowed to file a joint income tax return, which reports the total income earned by the couple and taxes the income on the basis of one progressive rate schedule.[6]

---

[3] 2 USTC ¶496, 8 AFTR 10287, 281 U.S. 111 (USSC, 1930).

[4] *Ibid.*, 281 U.S. 115.

[5] 40-2 USTC ¶9787, 24 AFTR 1058, 311 U.S. 112 (USSC, 1940).

[6] § 6013. Married individuals may choose to file separate returns, but they must use the rate schedule of § 1(d), which simply halves the tax brackets of the married filing jointly rate schedule of § 1(a). As a general rule, separate filing results in a greater tax than joint filing and such filing status is elected only for nontax reasons.

Joint filing originally was intended as a benefit to married couples. Prior to 1969, the joint filing tax rates were designed to tax one-half of total marital income at the tax rates applicable to single individuals. The resultant tax was then doubled to produce the married couple's tax liability. This perfect split and the corresponding tax savings were perceived as inequitable by unmarried taxpayers, who felt they were paying an unjustifiable "singles penalty."

To illustrate, consider the situation of a single taxpayer with taxable income of $24,000. In 1965 this taxpayer owed $8,030 of income tax, with the last dollar of income taxed at a 50 percent marginal tax rate. A married couple with the same 1965 taxable income owed only $5,660 and faced a marginal tax rate of only 32 percent.

THE MARRIAGE PENALTY

In 1969 Congress attempted to alleviate the singles penalty by enacting a new (and lower) rate schedule for single taxpayers.[7] While this action did reduce (but not eliminate) the singles penalty, it also created a marriage penalty for certain individuals. To illustrate both types of penalties, consider taxpayers J and S and the following situations.

Initially, assume J is single and has a taxable income (after a $3,250 standard deduction and $2,050 personal exemption) of $30,000. His 1990 tax liability as a single taxpayer is $5,872. If J marries S during the year and S has no taxable income of her own, the couple may file a joint tax return reflecting a $5,450 standard deduction and two exemptions totaling $4,100. Their 1990 tax liability as a married couple will be only $3,863. In this situation, marriage has saved J $2,009 of tax and a *singles penalty* can be said to exist.

Now assume that S also earns a salary that results in $30,000 of taxable income to her as a single taxpayer. If she and J remain single, each will pay a tax of $5,872, for a total tax bill of $11,744. However, if they choose to marry, their combined taxable income will increase to $61,050 because of the loss of $1,050 of standard deduction. Their tax liability as a married couple is $12,876, and J and S are paying a *marriage penalty* of $1,132.

Generally, a singles penalty may occur when *one* income can be taxed at married, rather than single, rates. A marriage penalty may occur when *two* incomes are combined and taxed at married, rather than singles, rates. Today, two-income families have become the rule rather than the exception, and the marriage penalty has received considerable publicity. Because marital status is determined as of the last day of the taxable year,[8] couples have attempted to avoid the marriage penalty by obtaining a technically legal divorce shortly before year end. When

---

[7] Act. § 803(a), P.L. 91-172, Dec. 30, 1969.   [8] § 7703(a).

a couple has immediately remarried and the only purpose of the divorce was to enable the husband and wife to file as single taxpayers, the IRS and the courts have had little trouble in concluding that the divorce was a sham transaction and therefore ineffective for tax purposes.[9]

INCOME SHIFTING TO CHILDREN AND OTHER FAMILY MEMBERS

Because a married couple is considered one rather than two taxpayers for Federal tax purposes, intrafamily income shifting usually involves a transfer of income from parents to children (or, less commonly, other family members) who are considered taxpayers in their own right.

The fact that children are taxpayers separate and distinct from their parents is recognized by § 73, which states "amounts received in respect of the services of a child shall be included in his gross income and not in the gross income of the parent, even though such amounts are not received by the child." The Regulations elaborate by stating that the statutory rule applies even if state law entitles the parent to the earnings of a minor child.[10]

Because children typically will have little or no income of their own, a shift of family income to such children can cause the income to be taxed at a lower marginal rate. The income shifted from parent to child also represents wealth that is owned by the child rather than the parent. Thus, the future taxable estate of the parent will not include the accumulated income that is already in the hands of younger-generation family members.

INCOME-SHIFTING TECHNIQUES

The next section of this chapter explores a variety of techniques whereby income can be successfully shifted to family members in a lower marginal tax bracket. The circumstances of each particular family situation will dictate the specific technique to be used.

FAMILY MEMBERS AS EMPLOYEES

The first technique for intrafamily income shifting is for a low-bracket family member to become an employee of a family business. This technique does not involve the transfer of a capital interest in the business, so the family member who owns the business does not dilute his or her ownership by this technique.

In the simplest case in which the family business is a sole proprietorship, any family members who become employees must actually perform services the value

---

[9]   Rev. Rul. 76-255, 1976-2 C.B. 40; and *Boyter v. Comm.*, 82-1 USTC ¶9117, 49 AFTR2d 451, 668 F.2d 1382 (CA-4, 1981).

[10]   Reg. § 1.73-1(a).

of which equates to the amount of compensation received. This requirement implies that the employee is both capable and qualified for his or her job and devotes an appropriate amount of time to the performance of services.

> **Example 2.** F owns a plumbing contracting business as a sole proprietorship. During the current year, F employs his son S as an apprentice plumber for an hourly wage of $10. The total amount paid to S for the year is $9,000.

If the father can prove to the satisfaction of the IRS that his son performed services worth $10 per hour and that the son actually worked 900 hours during the year, the father may deduct the $9,000 as wage expense on his tax return and the son will report $9,000 of compensation income on his own return.

If, on the other hand, the IRS concludes that the son was not a legitimate employee of his father's business, the transfer of $9,000 to the son would be recharacterized as a gift. As a result, the father would lose the business deduction, and no income shift from father to son would occur.

Obviously, the legitimacy of the employment relationship between father and son can only be determined by an examination of all relevant facts and circumstances. Facts to be considered would include the age of the son, his prior work experience and technical training, and his actual participation on contracted jobs requiring an apprentice plumber.

When a family member is an employee of a family business, any required payroll taxes on his or her compensation must be paid. However, compensation paid to an employer's children under the age of 18 is not subject to Federal payroll tax.[11]

FAMILY EMPLOYEES OF PARTNERSHIPS AND CORPORATIONS

If a family member wants to work as an employee of a family business that is in partnership or corporate form, the requirement that the value of his or her services equate to the amount of compensation received does not change. If the employment relationship is valid, the partnership or corporation may deduct the compensation paid to the family member. If the family member is not performing services that justify the salary he or she is drawing from the business, the IRS may recharacterize the payment.

In the case of a partnership, the payment may be recharacterized as a constructive cash withdrawal by one or more partners followed by a constructive gift of the cash to the pseudo-employee.

---

[11]   §§ 3121(b)(3)(A) and 3306(c)(5).

Example 3. Brothers X, Y, and Z are equal partners in Partnership XYZ. The partnership hires S, the sister of the partners, to act as secretary-treasurer for the business. S's salary is $20,000 per year. Assume that S has no business or clerical training and performs only minimal services for the business on a very sporadic basis. As a result, the IRS disallows a deduction to the partnership for all but $5,000 of the payment to the sister. The nondeductible $15,000 will be treated as a withdrawal by the partners that was transferred as a gift to the sister.

Constructive cash withdrawals from a partnership could have adverse tax consequences to the partners. If the withdrawal exceeds a partner's basis in his or her partnership interest, the excess constitutes capital gain to the partner.[12] Similarly, a constructive gift to a family member could result in an unexpected gift tax liability.

When the employer is a family corporation and a salary or wage paid to a nonshareholder family member is disallowed, the tax results can be extremely detrimental. Not only does the corporation lose a deduction, but the payment could be recharacterized as a constructive dividend to the family members who are shareholders, followed by a constructive gift to the family member who actually received the funds.[13] Thus, the corporate shareholders would have dividend income without any corresponding cash, and a potential gift tax liability.

The lesson to be learned from the preceding discussion should be clear. If an intrafamily income shift is to be accomplished by hiring a family member as an employee of a family business, the family member must perform as a legitimate employee. If the employment relationship has no substance, the unintended tax consequences to the family could be costly indeed.

FAMILY MEMBERS AS OWNERS OF THE FAMILY BUSINESS

A second technique for intrafamily income shifting is to make a low-bracket family taxpayer a part owner of the family business. By virtue of his or her equity or capital interest, the family member is then entitled to a portion of the income generated by the business. This is a more extreme technique in that it involves an actual transfer of a valuable asset. Moreover, the disposition of a partial ownership interest may cause dilution of the original owner's control of the business. These and other negative aspects of this technique will be discussed in greater detail later in the chapter.

The gratuitous transfer of an equity interest in a business will constitute a taxable gift to the original owner.

---

[12] § 731(a).

[13] *Duffey v. Lethert*, 63-1 USTC ¶9442, 11 AFTR2d 1317 (D.Ct. Minn., 1963).

Example 4. M runs a very successful business as a sole proprietorship. She wants to bring her son S into the business as an equal general partner. Under the terms of a legally binding partnership agreement, she contributes her business, valued at $1 million, to the partnership. Although the son will have a 50% capital interest in the partnership, he contributes nothing. As a result, M has made a $500,000 taxable gift to S.

Of course, if the transfer of the equity interest is accomplished by sale rather than gift, no initial gift tax liability will result. But in a typical family situation, the equity interest is being transferred to a family member without significant income or wealth, so that family member lacks the funds to purchase the interest. Also, the income tax consequences of a sale could be more expensive than gift tax consequences, depending upon the facts and circumstances. The prudent tax adviser should explore both possible methods of transfer when designing a particular plan.

FAMILY PARTNERSHIPS

A family partnership can be used as a vehicle for the co-ownership of a single business by a number of family members. As a partner, each family member will report his or her allocable share of partnership income (or loss) on his or her individual tax return.[14] Therefore, through use of a partnership, business income can be shifted to family members with relatively low marginal tax brackets.

If the family partnership is primarily a service business, only a family member who performs services can receive an allocation of partnership income. In such service partnerships the physical assets of the business (the capital of the partnership) are not a major factor of income production. Rather, it is the individual efforts and talents of the partners that produce partnership income. An attempt to allow a family member who cannot perform the appropriate services to participate in partnership income is an unwarranted assignment of earned income.

If the family partnership is one in which capital is a major income-producing factor, the mere ownership of a capital interest will entitle a family member to participate in partnership income. The determination of whether or not capital is a material income-producing factor is made by reference to the facts of each situation. However, capital is ordinarily a material income-producing factor if the operation of the business requires substantial inventories or investment in plant, machinery, or equipment.[15]

Section 704(e)(1) specifies that a family member will be recognized as a legitimate partner if he or she owns a capital interest in a partnership in which capital is a material income-producing factor. This is true even if the family member received his or her interest as a gift. However, § 704(e)(2) limits the amount of partnership income that can be shifted to such a donee partner. Under this statute, the income allocated to the partner cannot be proportionally greater than his or her interest in partnership capital.

---

[14]　§ 702(a).

[15]　Reg. § 1.704-1(e)(1)(iv).

Example 5.   Grandfather F is a 50% partner in Magnum Partnership. At the beginning of the current year, F gives his grandson G a 20% capital interest in Magnum (leaving F with a 30% interest). For the current year Magnum has taxable income of $120,000. The *maximum* amount allocable to G is $24,000 (20% × $120,000). If F wanted to increase the dollar amount of partnership income shifted to G, he must give G a greater equity interest in the partnership.

Section 704(e)(2) contains a second restriction on income allocation. A donor partner who gifts a capital interest must receive reasonable compensation for any services he or she renders to the partnership before any income can be allocated to the donee partner.

Example 6.   Refer to the facts in *Example 5*. During the current year, F performs services for Magnum worth $15,000 but for which he receives no compensation. Half of the $120,000 partnership income is still allocable to F and G with respect to their combined 50% capital interests; however, the maximum amount allocable to G decreases to $ 18,000 [($60,000 − $15,000 allocated to F as compensation for services) × 40%].

Note that in the above example, Grandfather F might be willing to forgo any compensation for the services performed for Magnum in order to increase the amount of partnership income shifted to his grandson. Unfortunately, § 704(e)(2) effectively curtails this type of indirect assignment of earned income.

Family members are not able to avoid the dual limitations of § 704(e) by arranging a transfer of a capital interest to a lower-bracket family member by sale rather than by gift. Under § 704(e)(3), a capital interest in a partnership purchased by one member of a family from another is considered to be created by gift from the seller. In this context the term *family* includes an individual's spouse, ancestors, lineal descendants, and certain family trusts.

REGULAR CORPORATIONS

Family businesses are frequently owned as closely held corporations. There are a number of business reasons why the corporate form is popular. For example, shareholders in a corporation have limited liability so that creditors of the corporation cannot force the shareholders to pay the debts of the corporation out of the shareholders' personal assets. There are also tax benefits to the corporate form of business. The owners of the business can function as employees of the corporate entity. As employees, they may participate in a wide variety of tax-favored employee benefit plans, such as employer-sponsored medical reimbursement plans. If the family business were in sole proprietorship or partnership form, the owners of the business would be self-employed and ineligible to participate in such employee benefit plans.

The corporate form of business must be regarded as a mixed blessing from a tax point of view. The incorporation of a family business does result in the creation of a new taxable entity, separate and distinct from its owners. Business income has been shifted to the corporate taxpayer, and because corporate tax rates are progressive, a net tax savings to the business can be the result.[16]

> **Example 7.** Individual T owns a sole proprietorship that produces $100,000 of net income before taxes. Ignoring the availability of any deductions or exemptions, T's 1990 tax on this income is $24,862 (Schedule Y). If T incorporates the business and draws a salary of $50,000, he will pay an individual tax of only $9,782. The corporation also will have income of $50,000 ($100,000 net income − $50,000 salary to T). The corporate tax on $50,000 is $7,500. Therefore, the *total* tax on the business income has decreased to $17,282 ($9,782 + $7,500).

The tax savings to T's business ($7,580) achieved by incorporation is certainly dramatic. However, the potential problem created by the incorporation of T's business is that the after-tax earnings of the business are now in the corporation rather than in T's pocket. If T needs or wants more than $40,218 ($50,000 salary − $9,782 tax liability) of after-tax personal income, he may certainly have his corporation pay out some of its after-tax earnings to him as a dividend. But any dividends paid must be included in T's gross income and taxed at the individual level.

This double taxation of corporate earnings paid to shareholders as dividends can quickly offset the tax savings resulting from using a corporation as a separate entity. Therefore, shareholders in closely held corporations usually become very adept in drawing business income out of their corporations as deductible business expenses rather than nondeductible dividends.

Shareholders who are also employees will usually try to maximize the amount of compensation they receive from the corporation. Section 162(a)(1) authorizes the corporation to deduct a *reasonable* allowance for salaries or other compensation paid. If the IRS determines that the compensation paid to an owner employee is unjustifiably high and therefore *unreasonable,* the excessive compensation can be reclassified as a dividend. As a result, the corporation loses the deduction for the excessive compensation, and to a corresponding extent, business earnings are taxed twice.

---

[16] Because of the 5 percent surtax on taxable income between $100,000 and $335,000, corporations with taxable income in excess of $335,000 face a flat 34 percent tax rate rather than a progressive rate. Qualified personal service corporations pay a flat 34 percent of their total taxable income. § 11(b)(2).

Other types of deductible payments from corporations to shareholders include rents paid for corporate use of shareholder assets and interest on loans made to the corporation by shareholders. The arrangements between corporation and shareholder that give rise to such rent or interest payments will be subject to careful scrutiny by the IRS. If an arrangement lacks substance and is deemed to be a device to camouflage the payments of dividends to shareholders, the corporate deduction for the payments will be disallowed.

Because it is a taxpayer in its own right, a regular corporation cannot be effectively used to shift business income to low-bracket family members. If such family members are made shareholders in the corporation and have no other relationship to the corporate business (employee, creditor, etc.), the only way to allocate business earnings to them is by paying dividends on their stock. As previously discussed, dividend payments are usually considered prohibitively costly from a tax standpoint.

Closely held regular corporations do have tremendous utility in other areas of tax planning. However, for purposes of intrafamily income shifting, the S corporation is a highly preferable alternative to a regular corporation.

S CORPORATIONS

The complex set of statutory provisions that govern the tax treatment of S corporations is explained in Chapter 23. For family tax planning purposes, the most important characteristic of an S corporation is that the corporate income escapes taxation at the corporate level and is taxed to the corporation's shareholders. This characteristic makes an S corporation a very useful mechanism for intrafamily income shifting.

Section 1366(a) provides that the taxable income of an S corporation is allocated to the shareholders on a pro rata basis. Thus, any individual who is a shareholder will report a proportionate share of the corporate business income on his or her personal tax return for the year with or within which the S corporation's taxable year ends.

> **Example 8.**   Individual M owns a sole proprietorship with an annual net income before taxes of $200,000. Ignoring the availability of any itemized deductions or exemptions, M's personal tax on this income is $56,000 (Schedule Y). If at the beginning of 1990 M incorporates the business, gives each of his four unmarried children 20 percent of the stock, and has the shareholders elect S status for the corporation, the corporate income of $200,000 will be taxed in equal amounts to the five shareholders. Ignoring other deductions or exemptions, the 1990 tax bill on the business income will be $41,670 [$6,982 from Schedule Y + (4 × $8,672 from Schedule X)].

A shareholder who is also an employee of a family-owned S corporation will not be able to divert corporate income to other shareholders by forgoing any compensation for services rendered to the corporation. Code § 1366(e) provides that if such a shareholder employee does not receive reasonable compensation from the S corporation, the IRS may reallocate corporate income to the shareholder employee so as to accurately reflect the value of his or her services.

Because shareholders of an S corporation are taxed on all the taxable income earned by the corporation, subsequent cash withdrawals of this income by shareholders are tax free.[17] However, the technical requirements for cash withdrawals from an S corporation are dangerously complicated. Because of the complexity of these requirements and many other tax aspects of S corporations, family tax plans involving their use should be carefully designed and monitored by the family tax adviser.

NEGATIVE ASPECTS OF OWNERSHIP TRANSFERS

A high-bracket taxpayer who desires to shift income to low-bracket family members by making such members co-owners of the taxpayer's business must reconcile himself or herself to several facts. First, the transfer of the equity interest in the business must be complete and legally binding so that the recipient of the interest has "dominion and control" over his or her new asset. A *paper* transfer by which the transferor creates only the illusion that a family member has been given an equity interest in a business will be treated as a sham transaction, ineffective for income shifting purposes.[18]

As a general rule, the recipient of an ownership interest in a family business is free to dispose of the interest, just as he or she is free to dispose of any asset he or she owns. If the recipient is a responsible individual and supportive of the family tax planning goals, his or her legal right to assign the interest may not be a problem. But if the recipient is a spendthrift in constant need of ready cash, he or she may sell the interest to a third party, thereby completely subverting the family tax plan.

One popular technique that can prevent an unexpected and undesired disposition of an interest in a family business is a buy-sell agreement. A taxpayer can transfer an equity interest to a low-bracket family member on the condition that should the family member desire to sell the interest he or she must first offer the interest to its original owner at an independently determined market value. Such an agreement is in no way economically detrimental to the family member, yet affords a measure of protection for both the original owner and the family tax plan.

---

[17]   § 1368(b).   [18]   For example, see Reg. § 1.704-1(e)(2).

A related aspect of the requirement that the taxpayer must legally surrender the ownership of the business interest transferred is that the transfer is irrevocable. Ownership of the interest cannot be regained if future events cause the original tax plan to become undesirable. For example, an estrangement between family members could convert a highly satisfactory intrafamily income shifting plan into a bitterly resented trap. A father who has an ill-favored son as an employee can always fire him. It is another matter entirely if the son is a 40 percent shareholder in the father's corporation.

A change in economic circumstances could also cause a taxpayer to regret a transfer of a business interest. Consider a situation in which a formerly high-income taxpayer suffers a severe financial downturn. A tax plan that is shifting income *away* from such a taxpayer could suddenly become an economic disaster.

PRESERVATION OF CONTROL OF THE BUSINESS

A taxpayer who is contemplating transferring an ownership interest in a business to one or more family members should also consider any resultant dilution of his or her control of the business. The taxpayer may be willing to part with an equity interest in order to shift business income to low-bracket family members, but may be very reluctant to allow such family members to participate in the management of the business.

A limited partnership can be used to bring family members into a business without allowing them a voice in management. A family member who owns a capital interest as a limited partner in a partnership may be allocated a share of business income, subject to the family partnership rules, and yet be precluded from participating in management of the business.

If the family business is in corporate form, various classes of stock with differing characteristics can be issued. For example, nonvoting stock can be given to family members without any dilution of the original owner's voting power, and hence control, over the business. If the original owner does not want to draw any dividends out of the corporate business but is willing to have dividends paid to low-bracket family members, nonvoting preferred stock can be issued to such family members.

Unfortunately, this flexibility in designing a corporate capital structure that maximizes income-shifting potential while minimizing loss of control is not available to S corporations. To qualify for S status a corporation may have only one class of stock outstanding.[19] Thus, all outstanding shares of stock in an S corporation must be identical with respect to the rights they convey in the profits and assets of the corporation. However, shares of stock in S corporations may have different *voting rights* without violating the single class of stock requirement.[20]

---

[19] § 1361(b)(1)(D).   [20] § 1361(c)(4).

SHIFTS OF INVESTMENT INCOME

In many ways the shifting of investment income to family members is simpler than the shifting of business income. Questions of forms of co-ownership and control are not as difficult to resolve if the income-producing asset to be transferred is in the form of an investment security rather than a business interest.

The simplest means to shift investment income from one taxpayer to another is an outright gift of the investment asset. Even gifts to minors who are under legal disabilities with regard to property ownership can be accomplished under state Uniform Gifts to Minors Acts. By using a custodian to hold the property for the benefit of a minor, the donor has shifted the investment income to the minor's tax return.[21]

Although gifting of investment property is a relatively simple technique, the donor must be aware that the transfer must be complete. The asset (and the wealth it represents) is irrevocably out of the donor's hands. If the donor attempts to retain an interest in or control over the asset, the gift may be deemed incomplete and the attempted income shift ineffectual.

If a donee receives an unrestricted right to a valuable investment asset, there is always the worry that he or she will mismanage it, or worse, assign it to a third party against the wishes of the donor. Because of these negative aspects of outright gifts, the private trust has become a very popular vehicle for the transfer of investment assets, especially when minor children are involved. A subsequent section of the chapter explores the use of trusts in family tax planning.

TAXATION OF UNEARNED INCOME OF MINOR CHILDREN

The Tax Reform Act of 1986 significantly limited the ability of parents to shift investment income to their children. Section 1(i) provides that any *net unearned income* of a minor child in excess of a $500 base is taxed at the marginal rate applicable to the income of the child's parents.[22] A minor child is one who has not obtained the age of 14 by the close of the taxable year and who has at least one living parent on that date.

Net unearned income is generally defined as passive investment income such as interest and dividends, reduced by the $500 standard deduction available against unearned income of a dependent.[23] The amount of net unearned income for any taxable year may not exceed the child's taxable income for the year. The *source* of the unearned income is irrelevant for purposes of this so-called "kiddie tax."

---

[21] Rev. Rul. 56-484, 1956-2 C.B. 23. However, income earned by the custodian account used for the support of the minor will be taxed to the person legally responsible for such support (i.e., the parent).

[22] In the case of parents who are not married, the child's tax is computed with reference to the tax rate of the custodial parent. If the parents file separate tax returns, the tax rate of the parent with the *greater* taxable income is used. § 1(i)(5).

[23] § 63(c)(5).

Example 9.   In 1989 grandchild G, age 10, received a gift of investment securities from her grandparents. G's current year dividend income from the securities totaled $7,189. G had no other income or deductions for the year. G's parents claimed G as a dependent and reported taxable income of $215,000 on their joint return. G's taxable income is $6,689 ($7,189 gross income − a $500 standard deduction) and her net unearned income to be taxed at her parents' rates is $6,189 ($7,189 − the $500 base − a $500 standard deduction). If this income had been included on G's parents' return, it would have been taxed at a marginal rate of 31% and the resulting tax liability would have been $1,919. Therefore, G's tax liability is 15% of $500 (G's taxable income − her net unearned income) plus $1,919, a total of $1,994.

In certain cases parents may elect to include a dependent's unearned income on their return, rather than filing a separate return and making the "kiddie tax" calculation.

THE TRUST AS A TAX PLANNING VEHICLE

As discussed in Chapter 25, a private trust is a legal arrangement whereby the ownership and control of property is vested in a trustee while the beneficial interest in the property is given to one or more beneficiaries. The trustee has a fiduciary responsibility to manage the property for the sole benefit of the beneficiaries.

ADVANTAGES OF THE TRUST FORM

The use of a trust has many nontax advantages. If an individual desires to make a gift of property to a donee who is not capable of owning or managing the property, the gift can be made in trust so that a competent trustee can be selected to manage the property free from interference from the donee-beneficiary.

The trust form of property ownership is very convenient in that it allows the legal title to property to be held by a single person (the trustee) while allowing the beneficial enjoyment of the property to be shared by a number of beneficiaries. If legal ownership of the property were fragmented among the various beneficiaries, they would all have to jointly participate in management decisions regarding the property. This cumbersome and oftentimes impractical co-ownership situation is avoided when a trustee is given sole management authority over the property.

If a donor would like to give property to several donees so that the donees have sequential rather than concurrent rights in the property, the trust form for the gift is commonly the solution.

Example 10.   Individual K owns a valuable tract of income-producing real estate. She would like ownership of the real estate to ultimately pass to her three minor grandchildren. She also would like to give her invalid brother an interest in the real estate so as to provide him with a future source of income. K can transfer the real estate into trust, giving her brother an income interest for a designated time period. Upon termination of the time period, ownership of the real estate will go to K's grandchildren.

TAX CONSEQUENCES OF TRANSFERS INTO TRUST

The use of the trust form can have distinct income tax advantages to a family because both the trust itself and any beneficiaries who receive income from the trust are taxpayers in their own right.

Example 11.   F, a high-bracket taxpayer, transfers income-producing assets into a trust of which his four grandchildren are discretionary income beneficiaries. In the current year, the trust assets generate $100,000 of income of which the trustee distributes $24,000 to each child. The $100,000 of investment income will be taxed to five relatively low-bracket taxpayers, the four grandchildren and the trust itself.

It is important to remember that unearned income *distributed* from a trust to a beneficiary who is under the age of 14 is subject to the rule of § 1(i). The income will be taxed at the marginal rate applicable to the beneficiary's parents, even if the parents did not create the trust.

The accumulation distribution rules of §§ 665 through 668 severely limit arbitrary shifting of income between a trust and its beneficiaries. Under these rules, income that is accumulated by (and therefore taxed to) a trust and then distributed in a later year to a beneficiary will be taxed to the beneficiary in the year of distribution. This tax is computed by a complex set of rules intended to simulate the tax the beneficiary would have paid if the trust income had originally been distributed rather than accumulated.[24]

The purpose of the accumulation distribution rules is to prevent a trust from being used as a tax shelter in a year in which the trust's marginal tax rate is less than that of the income beneficiaries. However, the rules do not apply to accumulations of income made before the appropriate income beneficiary reaches the age of 21.[25]

---

[24] See Chapter 25 for a discussion of these "throwback" rules.

[25] § 665(b)(2).

GIFT-LEASEBACKS

A popular and controversial method for family income shifting through use of a trust involves a technique known as a gift-leaseback. Typically, a taxpayer who owns assets that he or she uses in a trade or business transfers the assets as a gift in trust for the benefit of the taxpayer's children (or other low-bracket family members). The independent trustee then leases the assets back to the taxpayer for their fair rental value. The rent paid by the taxpayer to the trust is deducted as a § 162 ordinary and necessary business expense and becomes income to the taxpayer's children because of their status as trust beneficiaries.

The IRS has refused to recognize the validity of gift-leaseback arrangements and has consistently disallowed the rent deduction to the transferor of the business assets under the theory that the entire transaction has no business purpose. However, if the trust owning the leased assets has an independent trustee and the leaseback arrangement is in written form and requires payment to the trust of a reasonable rent, the Tax Court and the Second, Third, Seventh, Eighth, and Ninth Circuits have allowed the transferor to deduct the rent paid.[26] To date, the Fourth and Fifth Circuits have supported the government's position that gift-leaseback transactions are shams to be disregarded for tax purposes.[27] Given this split between the appellate courts, the future of gift-leasebacks as income-shifting devices will probably be determined by the Supreme Court.

GIFT TAX CONSIDERATIONS

The obvious income tax advantage of a family trust, such as the one described in *Example 11* above, can be offset if the original gift of property into the trust is subject to a substantial gift tax. Thus, the first step in designing a family trust is the minimization of any front-end gift tax. If the fair market value of the transferred property is less than the taxable amount sheltered by the unified credit of § 2505, no gift tax will be paid. However, the reader should bear in mind that the use of the credit against inter vivos gifts reduces the future shelter available on the donor's estate tax return.

An essential element in the minimization of any gift tax for transfers into trust is securing the $10,000 annual exclusion (§ 2503) for the amount transferred to each beneficiary-donee. This can be difficult when certain of the donees are given only a prospective or future interest in the trust property.

---

[26] See *May v. Comm.*, 76 T.C. 7(1981), *aff'd.* 84-1 USTC ¶9166, 53 AFTR2d 84-626 (CA-9, 1984).

[27] See *Mathews v. Comm.*, 75-2 USTC ¶9734, 36 AFTR2d 75-5965, 520 F.2d 323 (CA-5, 1975).

Example 12. Donor Z transfers $100,000 into trust. The independent trustee has the discretion to distribute income currently among Z's five children, or she may accumulate it for future distribution. Upon trust termination, the trust assets will be divided equally among the children. Because the five donees have only future interests in the $100,000, Z may not claim any exclusions in computing the amount of the taxable gift.[28]

SECTION 2503(c) AND CRUMMEY TRUSTS

One method of securing the exclusion for transfers into trust is to rely on the *safe harbor* rules of § 2503(c). Under this subsection a transfer into trust will not be considered a gift of a future interest if

1. The property and income therefrom may be expended for the benefit of the donee-beneficiary before he or she reaches age 21; and

2. If any property or income is not so expended, it will pass to the donee-beneficiary at age 21 or be payable to his or her estate if he or she dies before that age.

One drawback to the "§ 2503(c) trust" is that the trust assets generally must go to the beneficiaries at age 21. Many parent-donors would prefer to postpone trust termination until their children-donees attain a more mature age. This goal can be accomplished through the use of a *Crummey trust*.[29]

A Crummey trust is one in which the beneficiaries are directly given only a future right to trust income or corpus. The term of the trust may extend well beyond the time when the beneficiaries reach age 21. However, the trust instrument contains a clause (the Crummey clause) which authorizes any beneficiary or his or her legal representative to make a current withdrawal of any current addition to the trust of up to $10,000. The withdrawal right is made noncumulative from year to year. As long as the beneficiary is given notification of this right within a reasonable period before it lapses for the year, the donor will be entitled to an exclusion for the current transfers into trust.[30] It should be noted that most donors anticipate that their donees will never exercise their withdrawal right; the Crummey clause is included in the trust instrument for the *sole purpose* of securing the $10,000 exclusion for gift tax purposes.

---

[28] Reg. § 25.2503-3(c), Ex. 3.

[29] The amusing designation comes from the court case which established the validity of the technique—*Crummey v. Comm.,* 68-2 USTC ¶12, 541, 22 AFTR2d 6023, 397 F.2d 82 (CA-9, 1968). The IRS *acquiesced* to this decision in Rev. Rul. 73-405, 1973-2 C.B. 321.

[30] Rev. Rul. 81-7, 1981-1 C.B. 27.

GRANTOR TRUSTS

In certain cases a taxpayer may desire to transfer property into trust but does not want to surrender complete control over the property. Alternatively, the taxpayer may want to dispose of the property (and the right to income from the property) for only a limited period of time. Prior to the enactment of the 1954 Internal Revenue Code there was no statutory guidance as to when the retention of powers over a trust by the grantor (transferor) would prevent the trust from being recognized as a separate taxable entity. Nor was there statutory guidance as to the tax status of a reversionary trust, the corpus of which reverted to the grantor after a specified length of time.

The judicial attitude toward these *grantor* trusts was reflected in the Supreme Court decision of *Helvering v. Clifford*.[31] This case involved a taxpayer who transferred securities into trust for the exclusive benefit of his wife. The trust was to last for five years, during which time the taxpayer as trustee would manage the trust corpus as well as decide how much, if any, of the trust income was to be paid to his wife. Upon trust termination, corpus was to return to the taxpayer while any accumulated income was to go to the wife.

In reaching its decision, the Court noted the lack of a precise standard or guide supplied by statute or regulations. As a result, the Court turned to a subjective evaluation of all the facts and circumstances of this particular short-term trust arrangement and held that "the short duration of the trust, the fact that the wife was the beneficiary, and the retention of control over the corpus by respondent all lead irresistably to the conclusion that the respondent continued to be the owner."[32] As a result, the trust income was held to be taxable to the grantor rather than the trust or its beneficiary.

The authors of the 1954 Internal Revenue Code recognized that the uncertainty regarding the tax treatment of grantor trusts was undesirable and supplanted the subjective *Clifford* approach with a series of code sections (§§ 671 through 679) containing more objective rules as to the taxability of such trusts. The basic operative rule is contained in § 671—if §§ 673 through 679 specify that the grantor (or another person) shall be treated as the owner of any portion of a trust, the income, deductions, or credits attributable to that portion of the trust shall be reported on the grantor's (or other person's) tax return. If §§ 673 through 679 are inapplicable, the trust shall be treated as a separate taxable entity under the normal rules of Subchapter J (see Chapter 25).

---

[31] 40-1 USTC ¶9265, 23 AFTR 1077, 309 U.S. 331 (1940).

[32] *Ibid.,* 309 U.S. 332.

REVERSIONARY TRUSTS

Section 673 provides that the grantor shall be treated as the owner of any portion of a trust in which he or she has a reversionary interest, if upon creation of the trust the value of the reversion exceeds 5 percent of the value of the assets subject to reversion.[33]

> **Example 13.** In the current year, grantor G transfers assets worth $500,000 into trust. Niece N, age 20, will receive the income from the trust for 15 years, after which the trust will terminate and the assets returned to G. On the date the trust is created, the reversion is properly valued at $121,000. Because the reversion is worth more than 5% of $500,000, the income will be taxed to G, even though it will be distributed to N.

> **Example 14.** If in the previous example, N had been given the income from the trust for her life, the proper value of G's reversion would only be $13,000. Because this reversionary interest is worth only 2.6% of the value of the trust assets, the trust is not a grantor trust and the income will be taxed to N.

In the case of a trust in which a lineal descendant of the grantor (child, grandchild, etc.) is the income beneficiary, and the grantor owns a reversionary interest that takes effect only upon the death of the beneficiary prior to the age of 21, the trust *will not* be considered a grantor trust.[34]

INTEREST-FREE LOANS

Through use of a reversionary trust, a taxpayer may divert income to low-bracket family members only if he or she is willing to part with control of the trust corpus for a significant period of time. For many years the use of an interest-free demand loan between family members seemed to provide an alternative to a reversionary trust. A taxpayer could loan a sum of money to a family member on a demand basis and the money could be invested to earn income for that family member. Because the loan was interest-free, the creditor-taxpayer had no income from the temporary shift of wealth and could call the loan (demand payment) at any time.

---

[33] The Tax Reform Act of 1986 repealed the popular Clifford trust device, whereby the transfer of assets into a reversionary trust which lasted at least 10 years resulted in an income shift to the beneficiaries. However, Clifford trusts in existence on or before March 1, 1986 will not be considered grantor trusts under the new law.

[34] § 673(b).

The IRS was understandably hostile to such loans and argued that the creditor was making a gift of the use of the money to the borrower and that the amount of the gift equaled the interest that the creditor would have charged an unrelated borrower. On February 22, 1984 the Supreme Court agreed with the IRS position in *Dickman v. Commissioner.*[35]

Before the ink on the *Dickman* decision had dried, Congress addressed the problem by enacting Code § 7872, concerning below-interest and no-interest loans. The thrust of this provision is to impute interest income to the creditor-donor and correspondingly allow an interest deduction for the borrower-donee. Therefore, the creditor-donor is effectively treated as having received interest income and then gifting such income to the borrower. The deemed transfer is subject to the gift tax to the extent the interest exceeds the annual exclusion. As a result, interest-free loans are no longer an effective device for shifting income.

> **Example 15.** On January 1 of the current year, father F lent $175,000 to his daughter, S. The loan was interest-free and F may demand repayment at any time. The current interest rate as determined by the IRS is 10% per annum. On December 31 of the current year, S is considered to have paid $17,500 of deductible interest to F, and F is considered to have received $17,500 of taxable interest income from S. On the same date, F is considered to have made a $17,500 gift to S which is eligible for the $10,000 annual gift tax exclusion.

POWER TO CONTROL BENEFICIAL ENJOYMENT

Section 674(a) contains the general rule that a grantor shall be treated as the owner of any portion of a trust of which the grantor, a nonadverse party, or both, controls the beneficial enjoyment. However, if the exercise of such control requires the approval or consent of an *adverse party,* the general rule shall not apply. An adverse party is defined in § 672(a) as any person who has a substantial beneficial interest in the trust that would be adversely affected by the exercise of the control held by the grantor.

> **Example 16.** F transfers income-producing property into trust with City Bank as independent trustee. F's two children are named as trust beneficiaries. However, F retains the unrestricted right to designate which of the children is to receive annual distributions of trust income. This is a grantor trust with the result that all trust income is taxed to F.

---

[35] 84-1 USTC ¶13, 560, 53 AFTR2d 84-1608, 104 S.Ct. 1086 (USSC, 1984).

Example 17.   Refer to the facts in *Example 16*. Assume that the trust instrument provides that the trust income will be paid out on an annual basis in equal portions to F's two children. However, F retains the right to adjust the amount of the income distributions at any time with the consent of the older child C. Because C is an adverse party with respect to the one-half of the income to which he is entitled, only the other half of the income is considered subject to F's control. As a result, only half the trust property is deemed owned by F and only half the trust income is taxable directly to him.[36]

The general rule of § 674(a) is subject to numerous exceptions contained in §§ 674(b), (c), and (d). Any tax adviser attempting to avoid the grantor trust rules should be aware of these exceptions. For example, § 674(c) provides that the power to distribute income within a class of beneficiaries will not cause the grantor trust rules to apply if the power is solely exercisable by an independent trustee.

Example 18.   M transfers income-producing property into trust and names Midtown Bank as independent trustee. The trustee has the right to *sprinkle* (distribute) the annual income of the trust among M's three children in any proportion the trustee deems appropriate. Even though the power to control the enjoyment of the income is held by a nonadverse party, such party is independent of the grantor and the trust is not a grantor trust.

OTHER GRANTOR TRUSTS

Section 675 provides that the grantor shall be treated as the owner of any portion of a trust in respect of which he or she holds certain administrative or management powers.

Example 19.   T transfers 60% of the common stock in his closely held corporation into trust with City National Bank as independent trustee. All income of the trust must be paid to T's only grandchild. However, T retains the right to vote the transferred shares. Because T has retained an administrative power specified in § 675(4), he will be taxed on the income generated by the corporate stock.

If a grantor, a nonadverse party, or both have the right to revest in the grantor the ownership of any portion of trust property, § 676 provides that such portion of the trust is considered to be owned by the grantor. Therefore, revocable trusts are grantor trusts for income tax purposes.

---

[36]   Reg. § 1.672(a)-1(b).

Under § 677, a grantor also is treated as owner of any portion of a trust the income of which *may be* distributed to the grantor or spouse without the approval of any adverse party. This rule also applies if trust income may be used to pay premiums for insurance on the life of the grantor and spouse. This provision is inapplicable if the beneficiary of the policy is a charitable organization.

> **Example 20.** Individual J transfers income-producing assets into trust and designates Second National Bank as independent trustee. Under the terms of the trust instrument, the trustee may distribute trust income to either J's spouse or J's brother. In the current year the trustee distributes all trust income to J's brother. Since a nonadverse party (the trustee) could have distributed the trust income to J's spouse, this is a grantor trust and all income is taxed to J.

If trust income may be expended to discharge a legal obligation of the grantor, § 677 applies,[37] subject to two important exceptions. Section 682 creates an exception for *alimony trusts*. In certain divorce situations an individual who is required to pay alimony may fund a reversionary trust, the income from which will be paid to the grantor's former spouse in satisfaction of the alimony obligation. Under § 682, the recipient of the trust income rather than the grantor will be taxed on the income regardless of the applicability of any other of the grantor trust rules.

As a second exception, § 677(b) specifies that if trust income may be distributed for the support or maintenance of a beneficiary (other than the grantor's spouse) whom the grantor is legally obligated to support, such a provision by itself will not cause the trust to be a grantor trust. However, to the extent trust income is actually distributed for such purposes, it will be taxed to the grantor.

The final type of trust that is not recognized as a separate taxable entity is described in § 678. Under this provision, a person *other than* the grantor may be treated as the owner of a portion of a trust if such person has an unrestricted right to vest trust corpus or income in himself or herself. Section 678 shall not apply to the situation in which a person, in the capacity of trustee, has the right to distribute trust income to a beneficiary whom the person is legally obligated to support. Only to the extent that trust income is actually so expended will the income be taxed to the person.

> **Example 21.** Grantor G creates a trust with an independent corporate trustee and names his children and grandchildren as beneficiaries. The trust instrument also provides that G's sister S has the unrestricted right to withdraw up to one-third of trust corpus at any time. S is considered the owner of one-third of the trust and will be taxed on one-third of the income, regardless of the fact that such income is not distributable to her.

---

[37]   Reg. § 1.677(a)-1(d).

GRANTOR TRUSTS AND THE TRANSFER TAX RULES

As a general rule, a transfer of assets into trust that is incomplete for income tax purposes, so that the grantor is taxed on trust income, is also incomplete for gift and estate tax purposes.

> **Example 22.**   M transfers income-producing properties into a trust but retains the right to designate which of the specified trust beneficiaries will receive a distribution of trust income. The arrangement is a grantor trust per § 674. Under the gift tax Regulations, M has not made a completed gift of the income interest in the trust, and per § 2036 the value of the trust corpus will be included in M's gross estate upon his death.

However, it should be emphasized that the general rule doesn't always hold.

> **Example 23.**   Grantor G transfers assets into a reversionary trust that will last only eight years. During the existence of the trust, all income must be paid to G's cousin, C. For income tax purposes, this is a grantor trust and all trust income is taxable to G. However, for gift tax purposes G has made a completed gift of the income interest to C.

TRANSFER TAX PLANNING

The first part of this chapter dealt with a variety of techniques to shift income within a family group and thereby minimize the family's income tax burden. The second part of the chapter focuses on family tax planning techniques designed to reduce any transfer tax liability on intrafamily shifts of wealth. At this point, the student should be cautioned against thinking of income tax planning and transfer tax planning as two separate areas; both types of planning should be considered as highly interrelated aspects of a single integrated family tax plan.

A second aspect of transfer tax planning of which any tax adviser should be aware is that a client's nontax estate planning goals may conflict with an optimal tax-oriented estate plan. From a client's point of view, an orderly disposition of wealth that benefits the heirs in the precise manner that the client desires may be the primary planning objective, regardless of the tax cost. A client planning for his or her own death may be most concerned with his or her own emotional and psychological needs as well as those of other family members. Minimization of the Federal estate tax levied on the estate simply may not be a central concern. A tax adviser who fails to appreciate the client's priorities and who designs an estate plan that fails to reflect the client's nontax needs is not acting in the best interest of that client.

TAX PLANNING WITH INTRAFAMILY GIFTS

Before enactment of the Tax Reform Act of 1976, the Federal transfer tax savings associated with gifting assets to family members during the donor's life rather than transferring the assets at death were obvious. The gift tax rates were only 75 percent of the estate tax rates, and because of the progressive nature of both rate schedules, inter vivos gifts could shift an individual's wealth out of a high marginal estate tax bracket into a lower marginal gift tax bracket.

The Tax Reform Act of 1976 integrated the gift and estate taxes by providing a single rate schedule for both taxes and by including in the estate tax base the amount of post 1976 gifts made by a decedent.[38] Thus, any inter vivos gift made by a decedent after 1976 has the effect of boosting his or her taxable estate into a higher tax bracket.

> **Example 24.**   In 1987, D makes a taxable gift of $400,000, her only taxable inter vivos transfer. D dies in the current year, leaving a taxable estate of $1,500,000. The base for computing D's estate tax is $1.9 million, her taxable estate plus the $400,000 taxable gift.

Because of the integration of the gift and estate taxes, the tax benefit of inter vivos giving has been reduced but certainly not eliminated. The following advantages of making gifts have survived the integration process.

1.   All appreciation in value of the transferred property that occurs after the date of gift escapes taxation in the donor's gross estate. Refer to *Example 24*. If the value of the gifted asset increased from $400,000 in 1987 to $700,000 in the current year, the $300,000 appreciation is not taxed in D's estate. It should be noted that inter vivos transfers of appreciating assets do have a potentially serious negative income tax consequence. The basis of such assets to the donee will be a carryover basis from the donor, increased by the amount of any gift tax paid attributable to the difference between the value of the gift and the donor's tax basis.[39] If the donor retained the property until death, the basis of the property would be stepped up to its fair market value at date of death.[40] Thus, a transfer of the asset during life rather than at death preserves rather than eliminates pre-death appreciation in the value of the asset that will be subject to income taxation on subsequent sale.

---

[38] § 2001(b).

[39] § 1015.

[40] § 1014.

2. Future income generated by property that the donor has transferred will be accumulated by younger generation family members rather than in the estate of the donor.

3. The availability of the annual $10,000 exclusion allows a donor to give away a substantial amount of wealth completely tax free.

4. All other factors being equal, it is cheaper to pay a gift tax rather than an estate tax. This is true because the dollars used to pay a gift tax are never themselves subject to a Federal transfer tax. However, dollars used to pay an estate tax have been included in the taxable estate and are subject to the estate tax.

"FREEZING" THE VALUE OF ASSETS IN THE GROSS ESTATE

A long-range plan of inter vivos giving from older generation to younger generation family members is a basic component of most family tax plans. However, elderly individuals can be very reluctant about making substantial gifts of their wealth, even when they fully understand the tax advantages in doing so. Psychologically it is difficult to part with wealth that is the result of a lifetime of endeavor. Elderly individuals often fear that gifts of property might leave them without sufficient income or capital to provide for their future comfort and security. They may even worry that their children and grandchildren might "desert" them if the offspring were given the family wealth too soon.

For these and many other reasons it may be difficult for the tax adviser to persuade an older client to transfer existing wealth during his or her lifetime. However, the same client may be much more amenable to simply "freezing" the value of his or her current estate, so that future accumulations of wealth are somehow transferred to younger members of the family and therefore not subject to estate tax upon the client's death.

One of the simplest techniques for freezing the value of an asset in a taxpayer's estate is for the taxpayer to sell the asset to a younger generation family member.

> **Example 25.**   Grandfather G owns several acres of undeveloped real estate with a current value of $1 million. The land is located near a rapidly growing metropolitan area and its value is expected to triple over the next decade. If G sells the real estate to his granddaughter D for $1 million cash, the value of his current estate is unchanged. However, the future increase in the value of the land has been removed from G's estate and will belong to D.

An attractive variation of the selling technique illustrated in *Example 25* is an installment sale to the granddaughter. If D does not have $1 million of cash readily available (a most realistic assumption), G could simply accept his granddaughter's bona fide installment note as payment for the land. If the note is to be paid off over 20 years, G could use the installment sale method of reporting any taxable gain on the sale. If G had no need for cash during the term of the note, he could forgive his granddaughter's note payments and interest as they become due. Such forgiveness of indebtedness would not change the income tax consequences of the installment sale to G and would represent a gift to D eligible for the annual $10,000 exclusion.[41]

SELECTED DISPOSITIONS OF ASSETS AT DEATH

Only two types of gratuitous dispositions of assets at death give rise to a deduction for purposes of computing the taxable estate. The first type is a disposition of assets to a qualified charity. Section 2055 authorizes an *unlimited* charitable deduction for the value of such dispositions. If a wealthy taxpayer desires to transfer a portion of his or her estate to a qualified charity under the terms of a will, he or she may do so at no transfer tax cost. However, from a tax planning perspective it is preferable for the taxpayer to make a charitable donation during life rather than at death. Not only will the donated property be removed from the donor's potential estate, but the donation will give rise to an income tax deduction under § 170.

The second type of disposition that can result in a reduction of the transferor's gross estate is a bequest to a surviving spouse. Under § 2056(a) the value of any qualifying interest in property included in a decedent's gross estate that passes to the decedent's surviving spouse constitutes a deduction (the *marital deduction*) from the gross estate. Thus, if a decedent leaves his or her entire estate to the surviving spouse, the taxable estate of the decedent will be zero.

At first glance, it would appear that all of a decedent's property should be left to his or her spouse to avoid estate taxes. However, using the marital deduction to reduce a decedent's taxable estate to zero could result in a waste of the decedent's unified credit under § 2010. Moreover, all of the property would be taxed as part of the surviving spouse's estate to the extent it is not consumed or given away. For these reasons, an effective estate plan will attempt to leave a *taxable estate* exactly equal to the tax shelter provided by this credit.

TAX ADVANTAGES OF THE UNLIMITED MARITAL DEDUCTION

The unlimited marital deduction permits a deferral of any estate tax on the wealth accumulated by a married couple until the death of the second spouse. This deferral can be highly advantageous even if the bequest to the surviving spouse causes the wealth to be subsequently taxed at a higher marginal tax rate.

---

[41] See Rev. Rul. 77-299, 1977-2 C.B. 343 for the IRS's negative reaction to this tax plan.

To illustrate, assume that W has a net estate of $1.4 million. W's will provides that all her wealth in excess of the amount sheltered by the available § 2010 credit shall pass to her husband, H. W dies in 1991, when the credit will shelter a taxable estate of $600,000; therefore, $800,000 of her estate is transferred to her husband and becomes a marital deduction against W's gross estate. No estate tax is due upon W's death. If H has $2 million of wealth in addition to his $800,000 inheritance from W, and if he outlives his wife by five years, the estate tax upon his death will be $983,000 (the § 2001 tax on $2.8 million less the unified credit of $192,800).[42]

If W had not left any of her estate to H, the estate tax payable on her death would have been $320,000, computed at a marginal rate of 43 percent. However, because of the marital bequest, her estate was "stacked" on that of her surviving spouse. As a result, the actual tax on her estate was $395,000 computed at a marginal rate of 50 percent.[43] But the actual tax payment was deferred for five years. Using a conservative discount rate of 8 percent, the present value of a $395,000 tax paid at the end of five years is only $268,995. Thus, the use of the unlimited marital deduction saved the family of H and W approximately $51,000 in estate taxes.[44]

In addition to the deferral of tax available through use of the unlimited marital deduction, the postponement of tax until the death of the second spouse increases the length of time during which estate planning objectives can be accomplished. The surviving spouse can continue or even accelerate a program of inter vivos giving to younger generation family members. Deferral also provides the surviving spouse with the opportunity to seek advice about areas of estate planning neglected before the death of the first spouse.

QUALIFYING TERMINAL INTEREST PROPERTY

Section 2056(b) denies a marital deduction for an interest in property that passes to a surviving spouse if the interest will terminate at some future date and if after termination someone other than the surviving spouse will receive an interest in the property. This restriction was designed to ensure that assets escaping taxation in the estate of the first spouse by virtue of a marital deduction do, in fact, become the property of the surviving spouse includible in that spouse's taxable estate.

---

[42] For simplicity's sake, this example assumes no appreciation in assets between the two deaths.

[43] $395,000 is the difference between $983,000 (the tax on H's estate including his inheritance from W) and $588,000 (the tax on H's estate without an inheritance from W).

[44] $320,000 (current tax on W's estate without a marital deduction) minus $268,995 (present value of actual tax of $395,000 to be paid at the end of five years assuming an 8% discount rate).

Prior to the enactment of the Economic Recovery Tax Act of 1981 (ERTA 1981), a wealthy taxpayer desiring to secure the tax savings offered by the use of the marital deduction had to be willing to entrust to his or her surviving spouse the ultimate disposition of the assets passing to that spouse. Because of § 2056(b), the surviving spouse had to receive control over the transferred assets sufficient to pull the assets into that spouse's gross estate. This generally required an outright transfer of the property to the surviving spouse, or transfer in trust giving the spouse a general power of appointment. In certain situations wealthy taxpayers were reluctant to accept this condition. For example, a taxpayer with children from a previous marriage might be concerned that his surviving second wife might not leave the marital deduction assets to these children upon her death. As a result, the taxpayer might not take advantage of the marital deduction in order to leave his wealth directly to his children.

To increase the utility of the marital deduction, Congress added § 2056(b)(7) to the law as part of ERTA 1981. This paragraph allows a marital deduction equal to the value of *qualifying terminable interest property.* Such property is defined as property in which the surviving spouse is entitled to all the income, payable at least annually for life. During the life of the spouse, no one may have a power to appoint any part of the property to any one other than the spouse.

> **Example 26.**   Under the will of X, $1 million worth of assets are transferred into trust. X's surviving spouse, S, must be paid the entire trust income on a quarterly basis. During S's life, no person has any power of appointment over trust corpus, and upon S's death, trust corpus will be divided equally among X's living grandchildren. Because the assets are qualifying terminable interest property, X's estate may claim a marital deduction of $1 million.

Upon the death of the surviving spouse, the entire date of death value of the qualifying terminable interest property must be included in the surviving spouse's gross estate per § 2044. Thus, even though the property is passing to a recipient chosen by the first spouse to die, it is taxed in the estate of the second spouse.[45]

LIQUIDITY PLANNING

The Federal estate tax is literally a once-in-a-lifetime event. Because taxpayers do not have to pay the tax on a regular recurring basis, many individuals give little thought to the eventual need for cash to pay the tax.

---

[45]   If the surviving spouse gives away the income interest in the qualifying terminable interest property during life, § 2519 requires that the entire value of the property constitute a taxable gift. When either § 2044 or § 2519 applies, § 2207(A) allows the estate or donor to recover an appropriate amount of transfer tax from the party receiving the actual property.

When an individual dies leaving a large estate but little cash with which to pay death taxes and other expenses, serious problems can result. The family may be forced to sell assets at distress prices just to obtain cash. In a severe situation, a decedent's carefully designed dispositive plan may be shattered because of the failure to anticipate the liquidity needs of the estate.

One of the functions of a competent tax adviser is to foresee any liquidity problem of his or her client's potential estate and to suggest appropriate remedies. The remainder of this chapter covers some of the common solutions to the problem of a cash poor estate.

SOURCE OF FUNDS

An excellent source of funds with which to pay an estate tax is insurance on the life of the potential decedent. For a relatively small cash outlay, a taxpayer can purchase enough insurance coverage to meet all the liquidity needs of his or her estate. It is absolutely vital that the insured individual does not possess any incidents of ownership in the policies and that his or her estate is not the beneficiary of the policies. If these two rules are observed, the policy proceeds will not be included in the insured's estate and needlessly subjected to the estate tax.[46]

A second source of funds is any family business in which the decedent owned an interest. Under the terms of a binding buy-sell agreement, the business could use its cash to liquidate the decedent's interest. If the business is in corporate form, a redemption of the decedent's interest under § 303 can be a highly beneficial method of securing funds. If the fairly straightforward requirements of § 303 are met, the corporation can purchase its own stock from the decedent's estate without danger of the payment being taxed as a dividend. Because the estate's basis in the stock has been stepped up to its fair market value at date of death, the estate normally will realize little or no taxable gain on sale. The amount of the corporate distribution protected by § 303 cannot exceed the amount of death taxes and funeral and administrative expenses payable by the estate.[47]

In order for a redemption of stock to qualify under § 303, the value of the stock must exceed 35 percent of the value of the gross estate less § 2053 and § 2054 expenses.[48] Careful pre-death planning may be necessary to meet this requirement.

> **Example 27.** C owns a 100% interest in F Corporation, a highly profitable business with substantial cash flow. However, the value of the F stock is only 29% of the value of C's projected estate. As C's tax adviser, you could recommend that C (1) gift away other assets to reduce the estate, or (2) transfer assets into F Corporation as a contribution to capital in order to increase the stock's value.

---

[46] § 2042.

[47] § 303(a).

[48] § 303(b)(2)(A).

FLOWER BONDS

Certain issues of Treasury bonds known as *flower bonds* may be used to pay the Federal estate tax at their par value plus accrued interest.[49] Because these bonds have very low interest rates, they are obtainable on the open market at a price well below their par value. Thus, an estate can satisfy its Federal tax liability with bonds that cost much less than the amount of that liability. The bonds must be included in the decedent's estate at their par, rather than market value.[50]

PLANNING FOR DEFERRED PAYMENT OF THE ESTATE TAX

Under § 6166, an estate may be entitled to pay its Federal estate tax liability on an installment basis over a 15-year period. This provision can be a blessing for an illiquid estate. However, only estates that meet the requirements of § 6166 may use the installment method of payment. As a result, pre-death planning should be undertaken to ensure qualification.

Basically, only an amount of estate tax attributable to a decedent's interest in a closely held business may be deferred.[51] In addition, the value of the closely held business must exceed 35 percent of the gross estate minus Code § 2053 and § 2054 deductions. If a deferral of estate tax is desirable in a specific situation, the tax adviser should make certain that such requirements are met on a prospective basis.

CONCLUSION

This chapter has introduced the reader to one of the most fascinating and satisfying areas of tax practice—family tax planning. Such planning involves arrangements whereby family income can be shifted to low-bracket members so as to reduce the income taxes paid by the family unit. The use of trusts also has been discussed, and grantor trusts whose income is taxed not to the trust or its beneficiaries but to the grantor have been described.

Transfer tax planning techniques for reducing the family transfer tax burden have been introduced. Such techniques include long-range programs of inter vivos giving, asset freezes, selective use of the marital deduction, and liquidity planning. The family tax planner should never lose sight of the basic premise of family tax planning: only a plan that meets the subjective nontax goals and desires of a family as well as the objective goal of tax minimization is a truly well-designed plan.

---

[49] § 6312 provided the authorization for such usage. However, the section was repealed with respect to bonds issued after March 3, 1971. Bonds issued before this date and still outstanding continue to be eligible for payment of the estate tax.

[50] Rev. Rul. 69-489, 1969-2 C.B. 172.

[51] § 6166(a)(2).

PROBLEM MATERIALS

DISCUSSION QUESTIONS

26-1 *Assignment of Income Doctrine.* Explain the assignment of income doctrine as it relates to earned income. How does the doctrine apply to investment income?

26-2 *Income Shifting.* Assignment of income from one taxpayer to another can result in a tax savings only in a tax system with a progressive rate structure. Discuss.

26-3 *Family Employees.* List some of the factors the IRS might consider in determining whether a particular family member is a bona fide employee of a family business.

26-4 *Shareholder/Employee.* Discuss the tax consequences if the IRS determines that a family member is receiving an amount of unreasonable compensation from a family-owned corporation if that family member is a shareholder. What if the family member is not a shareholder?

26-5 *Gift of Business Interest.* An individual who transfers an equity interest in his or her business to a family member may be accomplishing an income shift to that family member. What are some nontax risks associated with such an equity transfer?

26-6 *Buy-Sell Arrangements.* How may a buy-sell agreement be utilized when an intrafamily transfer of an equity interest in a business is contemplated?

26-7 *Regular Corporation vs. S Corporation.* As a general rule, a regular corporation is an inappropriate vehicle by which to shift business income to low-bracket family members. Discuss.

26-8 *Limitation on Using S Corporations.* An S corporation may have only a single class of common stock outstanding. How does this fact limit the utility of the S corporation in many family tax plans?

26-9 *Use of Grantor Trusts.* Grantor trusts are ineffective as devices for shifting income to trust beneficiaries. However, such trusts may be very useful in achieving nontax family planning goals. Explain.

26-10 *Crummey Trusts.* What is a Crummey trust and why might a grantor prefer a Crummey trust to a § 2503(c) trust?

26-11 *Reversionary Trusts and Interest-Free Loans.* Can a trust in which the grantor has the right to receive his or her property back after a specified period of time be considered a valid trust for tax purposes so that the income is taxed to the beneficiaries rather than the grantor? Can an interest-free demand loan achieve an income shift from the lender to the debtor?

26-12 *Inter Vivos Gifts.* Why are inter vivos gifts beneficial from a transfer tax planning viewpoint?

26-13 *Limitations of Inter Vivos Gifts.*   For what reasons might an elderly taxpayer be reluctant to make inter vivos gifts?

26-14 *Estate Freezes.*   Define an "asset freeze" as the term relates to estate planning.

26-15 *Current vs. Testamentary Contributions.*   Is it preferable to make a charitable contribution during a taxpayer's life or at his or her death under the terms of his or her will?

26-16 *Marital Deduction.*   Discuss the tax benefits associated with the unlimited marital deduction of § 2056.

26-17 *Limiting Estate Taxes.*   Why is it generally inadvisable for a taxpayer to plan to reduce his or her taxable estate to zero? What can be considered an "optimal" size for a decedent's taxable estate?

26-18 *Qualifying Terminable Interests.*   In what circumstances would a taxpayer desire to make a bequest to a surviving spouse in the form of qualifying terminable interest property? What are the tax consequences of such a bequest?

PROBLEMS

26-19 *Using Family Employees.*   F runs a carpet installation and cleaning business as a sole proprietorship. In the current year, the business generates $83,000 of net income.

    a.   Assume F is married, has three children (all under the age of 19), does not have any other source of taxable income and does not itemize deductions. What is his current year tax liability?

    b.   Assume F can use all three children in his business as legitimate part-time employees. He pays each child $6,000 per year, but continues to provide more than one-half of their support. Compute the family's total tax bill for the current year.

26-20 *Sole Proprietorship vs. Corporation.*   Single individual K owns a sole proprietorship that is K's only source of income. In the current year, the business has net income of $130,000.

    a.   If K does not itemize deductions, what is her current year tax liability?

    b.   If K incorporates the business on January 1 and pays herself a $40,000 salary (and no dividends), by how much will she have reduced the tax bill on her business income? (Assume the corporation will not be a personal service corporation.)

26-21 *Sole Proprietorship vs. Corporation.*   Mr. and Mrs. C own their own business, which they currently operate as a sole proprietorship. Annual income from the business averages $400,000. Mr. and Mrs. C are considering incorporating the business. They estimate that each of them could draw a reasonable annual salary of $75,000. In order to maintain their current standard of living, they would also have to draw an additional $50,000 cash out of the business annually in the form of dividends. Based on these facts, compute the income tax savings or cost that would result from the incorporation. In making your calculation, ignore any deductions or exemptions available on the C's joint return.

26-22   *Singles Penalty.*   Single taxpayer S has current year taxable income of $35,000 (after all available deductions and exemptions). His fiance F has a taxable income of $6,000. Should F and S marry before or after December 31? Support your conclusion with calculations.

26-23   *Marriage Penalty.*   Taxpayers H and W are married and file a joint return. Both are professionals and earn salaries of $28,000 and $39,000, respectively. Assuming H and W have no other income, and do not itemize deductions, compute any *marriage penalty* they will pay.

26-24   *Married vs. Head-of-Household.*   Refer to the facts in Problem 26-23. Assume H and W are not married and H has a child by a previous marriage that entitles him to file as a head-of-household. If H and W marry, will the marriage penalty they incur be more or less than in Problem 26-23?

26-25   *Unearned Income of a Minor Child.*   In the current year, taxpayer M receives $12,000 of interest income and earns a salary of $2,500 from a summer job. M has no other income or deductions. M is 13 years old and is claimed as a dependent on his parents' jointly filed tax return. His parents report taxable income of $200,000. Based on these facts, compute M's income tax liability.

26-26   *Sheltering Unearned Income of a Minor Child.*   Taxpayer P made a gift of investment securities to his 13-year-old dependent daughter, D, under the Uniform Gift to Minors Act. The securities generate annual dividend income of $4,000. P is considering a second gift to D that would generate an additional $3,000 of investment income annually. Calculate the amount of tax savings to the family if P could employ D in his business and pay her an annual salary of $3,000, rather than making the second gift. In making your calculation, assume P is in a 31 percent tax bracket.

26-27   *Family Partnerships.*   F owns a 70 percent interest in Mako Partnership, in which capital is a material income-producing factor. On January 1 of the current year, F gives his son S a 35 percent interest in Mako (leaving F with a 35% interest). For the current year, Mako has taxable income of $200,000.

    a.   Assume F does not perform any services for Mako. What is the maximum amount of partnership income allocable to S?
    b.   Assume F performs services for Mako for which he normally would receive $30,000. However, F has not charged the partnership for his services. Based on these facts, what is the maximum amount of partnership income allocable to S in the current year?

26-28   *Gift of S Corporation Stock.*   Grandfather G owns all 100 shares of the outstanding stock of Sigma, Inc., a calendar year S corporation. On January 1 of the current year, G gives 10 shares of Sigma stock to each of his four minor grandchildren under the Uniform Gift to Minors Act. For the current year, Sigma reports taxable income of $70,000. To whom is this income taxed?

26-29　*Gift-Leaseback.*　Taxpayer B owns land used in his sole proprietorship with a tax basis of $75,000 and a fair market value of $100,000. B gives this land to an irrevocable simple trust for the equal benefit of his three children (ages 14, 16, and 19) and leases back the land from the trust for a fair market rental of $9,000 per year.

　　a.　Assuming that all three children are B's dependents and have no other source of income, calculate the tax savings to the family of this gift-leaseback arrangement. In making your calculation, assume B is in a 31 percent tax bracket.

　　b.　What are the gift and estate tax consequences of this transaction to B and his family? Assume that B has made no prior taxable gifts and that he is married.

26-30　*Use of Trusts.*　Grandfather Z is in the habit of giving his 26-year-old grand-child, A, $10,000 annually as a gift. Z's taxable income is consistently over $200,000 per year, and A has no income. If Z creates a valid trust with invest-ment assets just sufficient to yield $12,000 of income a year and specifies in the trust instrument that A is to receive the trust income annually, what will be the net tax savings to the family? (For purposes of this problem, *ignore* the fact that A may be claimed as a dependent on the return of another taxpayer.)

26-31　*Reversionary Trusts.*　Grantor G transfers $100,000 of assets into a trust that will last for 10 years, after which time the assets will revert to G or his estate. During the trust's existence all income must be paid to beneficiary M on a current basis. For the current year, ordinary trust income is $18,000 and the trust recognizes a capital gain of $3,000. To whom are these amounts taxed?

26-32　*Reversionary Trusts.*　Refer to the facts in Problem 26-31. Assume that under the terms of the trust agreement the trust will last for M's lifetime. Upon M's death, the trust corpus will revert to G or his estate. On the date the trust is created, M is 25 years old. For the current year, ordinary trust income is $18,000 and the trust recognizes a capital gain of $3,000. To whom are these amounts taxed?

26-33　*Irrevocable Trusts.*　F transfers assets into an irrevocable trust and designates First City Bank as independent trustee. F retains no control over the trust assets. The trustee may distribute income to either of F's two adult brothers or to S, F's minor son whom F is legally obligated to support. During the year, the trustee distributed all of the trust income to one of F's brothers. To whom will the income be taxed?

26-34　*Irrevocable Trusts.*　M transfers assets into an irrevocable trust and appoints National Bank independent trustee. M retains no control over trust assets. Under the terms of the trust agreement, M's sister N is given the right to determine which of M's three children will receive trust income for the year. N herself is not a trust beneficiary. During the year, N directs that trust income be divided equally between M's three children. To whom will the income be taxed?

26-35   *Irrevocable Trusts.*   Grantor B transfers assets into an irrevocable trust and designates Union State Bank independent trustee. B retains no control over trust assets. Under the terms of the trust instrument the trustee must use trust income to pay the annual insurance premium on a policy on B's life. Any remaining income must be distributed to B's grandson, GS. For the current year, trust income totals $60,000, of which $9,000 is used to pay the required insurance premium. To whom will the income be taxed?

26-36   *Grantor Trusts.*   Although T is not a beneficiary of the ABC Trust, T does have the right under the terms of the trust instrument to appoint up to 10 percent of the trust assets to himself or any member of his family. T has never exercised this right. For the current year, the trust income of $80,000 is distributed to the income beneficiaries of the trust.

a.   To whom will the income be taxed?

b.   If T dies before exercising his right to appoint trust corpus, will the possession of the right have any estate tax consequences?

26-37   *Gift Splitting.*   Every year D gives each of her nine grandchildren $15,000 in cash to be used toward their education.

a.   If D is unmarried, what is the amount of her annual taxable gift?

b.   If D is married and she and her husband elect to "gift split," what is the amount of her annual taxable gift?

26-38   *Terminable Interest Trusts.*   Taxpayer Q dies in the current year and leaves a net estate of $3 million. Under the terms of his will, $2.4 million of the estate will be put into trust. Q's widow W will be paid trust income annually and during W's life no person has the right to appoint any of the trust corpus. Upon W's death, the trust corpus will be divided among Q's offspring from a previous marriage. The remaining $600,000 of Q's estate is to be paid to unrelated friends named in Q's will.

a.   What is the amount of Q's taxable estate?

b.   What is the estate tax liability on Q's taxable estate? (Q made no taxable gifts during his lifetime.)

c.   W outlives Q by only eight years. If the value of the corpus of the trust created for W's benefit by Q is $6.3 million at the date of W's death, what amount must be included in W's gross estate?

26-39 *Inter Vivos Gifts.*   Decedent T died in the current year and left the following taxable estate:

	Fair Market Value
Investment real estate	$1,000,000
Cash and securities	3,500,000
Gross estate	$4,500,000
Less: §2053 and §2054 expenses	(500,000)
Taxable estate	$4,000,000

After payment of all death taxes, the estate will be divided equally among T's five surviving married children.

a.   If T has never made any inter vivos gifts, compute the estate's Federal estate tax liability (before credit for any state death tax paid).

b.   How much tax could have been saved if T had made cash gifts equal to the maximum annual exclusion under § 2503 to each of his children and their spouses in each of the 10 years preceding his death?

26-40 *Liquidity Planning.*   Decedent D left the following taxable estate:

	Fair Market Value
Life insurance proceeds from policy on D's life (D owned the policy at his death)	$ 500,000
Real estate	1,300,000
Stock in Acme Corporation (100% owned by D)	650,000
Gross estate	$2,450,000
Less: §2053 and §2054 expenses	(450,000)
Taxable estate	$2,000,000

a.   If D has never made any inter vivos gifts and dies in the current year, what is the estate's Federal estate tax liability (before credit for any state death tax paid)?

b.   How much tax could have been avoided if D had *not* been the owner of the life insurance policy?

c.   Can the Acme stock qualify for a § 303 redemption? What if the life insurance proceeds were not included in the gross estate?

RESEARCH PROBLEMS

26-41   In 1986, P, a resident of St. Louis, Missouri, created an irrevocable trust for the benefit of his teenage son, S, and his brother, B. The independent trustee, T, has discretionary power to use the trust income for the "payment of tuition, books, and room and board at any institution of higher learning that S chooses to attend." After an 11-year period, the trust will terminate with any accumulated income payable to S and the trust corpus payable to B. In the current year, S received an income distribution of $7,000 from the trust, which he used to attend a state-supported school, the University of Missouri. To whom will the $7,000 of trust income be taxed?

Some suggested research aids:

> § 677 and accompanying regulations
> *Morrill, Jr. v. United States,* 64-1 USTC ¶9463, 13 AFTR2d 1334, 228
>   F.Supp. 734 (D. Ct. Maine, 1964).
> *Braun, Jr.,* 48 TCM 210, T.C. Memo 1984-285.

26-42   Decedent D died on January 19, 1990. Under the terms of D's will, D's sister S, age 57, is to receive $500,000 as a specific bequest. The remainder of D's estate will be distributed to D's various grandchildren. On June 8, 1991, S decides to join a religious community and take a vow of poverty. She makes written notification to the executor of D's estate that she will not accept her bequest from her late sister, and that the $500,000 should be added to the amount to be distributed to the grandchildren. What are the transfer tax consequences of S's action?

Suggested research aid:

> § 2518

APPENDICES

CONTENTS

Appendix **A**

TAX RATE SCHEDULES AND TABLES

A-1   1990 Income Tax Rate Schedules

1990 Tax Rate Schedules

Caution: *Use ONLY if your taxable income (Form 1040, line 37) is $50,000 or more. If less, use the **Tax Table.** (Even though you cannot use the tax rate schedules below if your taxable income is less than $50,000, we show all levels of taxable income so that taxpayers can see the tax rate that applies to each level.)*

Schedule X—Use if your filing status is **Single**

If the amount on Form 1040, line 37, is: Over—	But not over—	Enter on Form 1040, line 38	of the amount over—
$0	$19,450	. . . . . . .15%	$0
19,450	47,050	**$2,917.50 + 28%**	19,450
47,050	97,620	**10,645.50 + 33%**	47,050
97,620	. . . .	Use **Worksheet** below to figure your tax.	

Schedule Z—Use if your filing status is **Head of household**

If the amount on Form 1040, line 37, is: Over—	But not over—	Enter on Form 1040, line 38	of the amount over—
$0	$26,050	. . . . . . .15%	$0
26,050	67,200	**$3,907.50 + 28%**	26,050
67,200	134,930	**15,429.50 + 33%**	67,200
134,930	. . . .	Use **Worksheet** below to figure your tax.	

Schedule Y-1—Use if your filing status is **Married filing jointly or Qualifying widow(er)**

If the amount on Form 1040, line 37, is: Over—	But not over—	Enter on Form 1040, line 38	of the amount over—
$0	$32,450	. . . . . . .15%	$0
32,450	78,400	**$4,867.50 + 28%**	32,450
78,400	162,770	**17,733.50 + 33%**	78,400
162,770	. . . .	Use **Worksheet** below to figure your tax.	

Schedule Y-2—Use if your filing status is **Married filing separately**

If the amount on Form 1040, line 37, is: Over—	But not over—	Enter on Form 1040, line 38	of the amount over—
$0	$16,225	. . . . . . .15%	$0
16,225	39,200	**$2,433.75 + 28%**	16,225
39,200	123,570	**8,866.75 + 33%**	39,200
123,570	. . . .	Use **Worksheet** below to figure your tax.	

Worksheet (Keep for your records)

1. If your filing status is:
   - Single, enter $27,333.60
   - Head of household, enter $37,780.40
   - Married filing jointly or Qualifying widow(er), enter $45,575.60
   - Married filing separately, enter $36,708.85   . . . . 1. _____

2. Enter your taxable income from Form 1040, line 37   . . . . 2. _____

3. If your filing status is:
   - Single, enter $97,620
   - Head of household, enter $134,930
   - Married filing jointly or Qualifying widow(er), enter $162,770
   - Married filing separately, enter $123,570   . . . . 3. _____

4. Subtract line 3 from line 2. Enter the result. (If the result is zero or less, use the schedule above for your filing status to figure your tax. DO NOT use this worksheet.)   4. _____

5. Multiply the amount on line 4 by 28% (.28). Enter the result   . . . . 5. _____

6. Multiply the amount on line 4 by 5% (.05). Enter the result   . . . . 6. _____

7. Multiply $574 by the number of exemptions claimed on Form 1040, line 6e. (If married filing separately, see the **Note** below.) Enter the result   . . . . 7. _____

8. Compare the amounts on lines 6 and 7. Enter the **smaller** of the two amounts here   . . . . 8. _____

9. **Tax.** Add lines 1, 5, and 8. Enter the total here and on Form 1040, line 38   . . . . 9. _____

Note: *If married filing separately and you did **not** claim an exemption for your spouse, multiply $574 by the number of exemptions claimed on Form 1040, line 6e. Add $574 to the result and enter the total on line 7 above.*

A-2 1990 Income Tax Tables

1990 Tax Table

Use if your taxable income is less than $50,000. If $50,000 or more, use the Tax Rate Schedules.

Example: Mr. and Mrs. Brown are filing a joint return. Their taxable income on line 37 of Form 1040 is $25,300. First, they find the $25,300–25,350 income line. Next, they find the column for married filing jointly and read down the column. The amount shown where the income line and filing status column meet is $3,799. This is the tax amount they must write on line 38 of their return.

At least	But less than	Single	Married filing jointly *	Married filing separately	Head of a household
			Your tax is—		
25,200	25,250	4,535	3,784	4,954	3,784
25,250	25,300	4,549	3,791	4,968	3,791
25,300	25,350	4,563	(3,799)	4,982	3,799
25,350	25,400	4,577	3,806	4,996	3,806

If line 37 (taxable income) is— / And you are—

At least	But less than	Single	Married filing jointly *	Married filing separately	Head of a household
			Your tax is—		
$0	$5	$0	$0	$0	$0
5	15	2	2	2	2
15	25	3	3	3	3
25	50	6	6	6	6
50	75	9	9	9	9
75	100	13	13	13	13
100	125	17	17	17	17
125	150	21	21	21	21
150	175	24	24	24	24
175	200	28	28	28	28
200	225	32	32	32	32
225	250	36	36	36	36
250	275	39	39	39	39
275	300	43	43	43	43
300	325	47	47	47	47
325	350	51	51	51	51
350	375	54	54	54	54
375	400	58	58	58	58
400	425	62	62	62	62
425	450	66	66	66	66
450	475	69	69	69	69
475	500	73	73	73	73
500	525	77	77	77	77
525	550	81	81	81	81
550	575	84	84	84	84
575	600	88	88	88	88
600	625	92	92	92	92
625	650	96	96	96	96
650	675	99	99	99	99
675	700	103	103	103	103
700	725	107	107	107	107
725	750	111	111	111	111
750	775	114	114	114	114
775	800	118	118	118	118
800	825	122	122	122	122
825	850	126	126	126	126
850	875	129	129	129	129
875	900	133	133	133	133
900	925	137	137	137	137
925	950	141	141	141	141
950	975	144	144	144	144
975	1,000	148	148	148	148
1,000					
1,000	1,025	152	152	152	152
1,025	1,050	156	156	156	156
1,050	1,075	159	159	159	159
1,075	1,100	163	163	163	163
1,100	1,125	167	167	167	167
1,125	1,150	171	171	171	171
1,150	1,175	174	174	174	174
1,175	1,200	178	178	178	178
1,200	1,225	182	182	182	182
1,225	1,250	186	186	186	186
1,250	1,275	189	189	189	189
1,275	1,300	193	193	193	193
1,300	1,325	197	197	197	197
1,325	1,350	201	201	201	201
1,350	1,375	204	204	204	204
1,375	1,400	208	208	208	208

At least	But less than	Single	Married filing jointly *	Married filing separately	Head of a household
1,400	1,425	212	212	212	212
1,425	1,450	216	216	216	216
1,450	1,475	219	219	219	219
1,475	1,500	223	223	223	223
1,500	1,525	227	227	227	227
1,525	1,550	231	231	231	231
1,550	1,575	234	234	234	234
1,575	1,600	238	238	238	238
1,600	1,625	242	242	242	242
1,625	1,650	246	246	246	246
1,650	1,675	249	249	249	249
1,675	1,700	253	253	253	253
1,700	1,725	257	257	257	257
1,725	1,750	261	261	261	261
1,750	1,775	264	264	264	264
1,775	1,800	268	268	268	268
1,800	1,825	272	272	272	272
1,825	1,850	276	276	276	276
1,850	1,875	279	279	279	279
1,875	1,900	283	283	283	283
1,900	1,925	287	287	287	287
1,925	1,950	291	291	291	291
1,950	1,975	294	294	294	294
1,975	2,000	298	298	298	298
2,000					
2,000	2,025	302	302	302	302
2,025	2,050	306	306	306	306
2,050	2,075	309	309	309	309
2,075	2,100	313	313	313	313
2,100	2,125	317	317	317	317
2,125	2,150	321	321	321	321
2,150	2,175	324	324	324	324
2,175	2,200	328	328	328	328
2,200	2,225	332	332	332	332
2,225	2,250	336	336	336	336
2,250	2,275	339	339	339	339
2,275	2,300	343	343	343	343
2,300	2,325	347	347	347	347
2,325	2,350	351	351	351	351
2,350	2,375	354	354	354	354
2,375	2,400	358	358	358	358
2,400	2,425	362	362	362	362
2,425	2,450	366	366	366	366
2,450	2,475	369	369	369	369
2,475	2,500	373	373	373	373
2,500	2,525	377	377	377	377
2,525	2,550	381	381	381	381
2,550	2,575	384	384	384	384
2,575	2,600	388	388	388	388
2,600	2,625	392	392	392	392
2,625	2,650	396	396	396	396
2,650	2,675	399	399	399	399
2,675	2,700	403	403	403	403

At least	But less than	Single	Married filing jointly *	Married filing separately	Head of a household
2,700	2,725	407	407	407	407
2,725	2,750	411	411	411	411
2,750	2,775	414	414	414	414
2,775	2,800	418	418	418	418
2,800	2,825	422	422	422	422
2,825	2,850	426	426	426	426
2,850	2,875	429	429	429	429
2,875	2,900	433	433	433	433
2,900	2,925	437	437	437	437
2,925	2,950	441	441	441	441
2,950	2,975	444	444	444	444
2,975	3,000	448	448	448	448
3,000					
3,000	3,050	454	454	454	454
3,050	3,100	461	461	461	461
3,100	3,150	469	469	469	469
3,150	3,200	476	476	476	476
3,200	3,250	484	484	484	484
3,250	3,300	491	491	491	491
3,300	3,350	499	499	499	499
3,350	3,400	506	506	506	506
3,400	3,450	514	514	514	514
3,450	3,500	521	521	521	521
3,500	3,550	529	529	529	529
3,550	3,600	536	536	536	536
3,600	3,650	544	544	544	544
3,650	3,700	551	551	551	551
3,700	3,750	559	559	559	559
3,750	3,800	566	566	566	566
3,800	3,850	574	574	574	574
3,850	3,900	581	581	581	581
3,900	3,950	589	589	589	589
3,950	4,000	596	596	596	596
4,000					
4,000	4,050	604	604	604	604
4,050	4,100	611	611	611	611
4,100	4,150	619	619	619	619
4,150	4,200	626	626	626	626
4,200	4,250	634	634	634	634
4,250	4,300	641	641	641	641
4,300	4,350	649	649	649	649
4,350	4,400	656	656	656	656
4,400	4,450	664	664	664	664
4,450	4,500	671	671	671	671
4,500	4,550	679	679	679	679
4,550	4,600	686	686	686	686
4,600	4,650	694	694	694	694
4,650	4,700	701	701	701	701
4,700	4,750	709	709	709	709
4,750	4,800	716	716	716	716
4,800	4,850	724	724	724	724
4,850	4,900	731	731	731	731
4,900	4,950	739	739	739	739
4,950	5,000	746	746	746	746

* This column must also be used by a qualifying widow(er).

Continued on next page

1990 Tax Table—Continued

5,000 – 8,000 – 11,000

If line 37 (taxable income) is— At least	But less than	Single	Married filing jointly *	Married filing separately	Head of a household
5,000					
5,000	5,050	754	754	754	754
5,050	5,100	761	761	761	761
5,100	5,150	769	769	769	769
5,150	5,200	776	776	776	776
5,200	5,250	784	784	784	784
5,250	5,300	791	791	791	791
5,300	5,350	799	799	799	799
5,350	5,400	806	806	806	806
5,400	5,450	814	814	814	814
5,450	5,500	821	821	821	821
5,500	5,550	829	829	829	829
5,550	5,600	836	836	836	836
5,600	5,650	844	844	844	844
5,650	5,700	851	851	851	851
5,700	5,750	859	859	859	859
5,750	5,800	866	866	866	866
5,800	5,850	874	874	874	874
5,850	5,900	881	881	881	881
5,900	5,950	889	889	889	889
5,950	6,000	896	896	896	896
6,000					
6,000	6,050	904	904	904	904
6,050	6,100	911	911	911	911
6,100	6,150	919	919	919	919
6,150	6,200	926	926	926	926
6,200	6,250	934	934	934	934
6,250	6,300	941	941	941	941
6,300	6,350	949	949	949	949
6,350	6,400	956	956	956	956
6,400	6,450	964	964	964	964
6,450	6,500	971	971	971	971
6,500	6,550	979	979	979	979
6,550	6,600	986	986	986	986
6,600	6,650	994	994	994	994
6,650	6,700	1,001	1,001	1,001	1,001
6,700	6,750	1,009	1,009	1,009	1,009
6,750	6,800	1,016	1,016	1,016	1,016
6,800	6,850	1,024	1,024	1,024	1,024
6,850	6,900	1,031	1,031	1,031	1,031
6,900	6,950	1,039	1,039	1,039	1,039
6,950	7,000	1,046	1,046	1,046	1,046
7,000					
7,000	7,050	1,054	1,054	1,054	1,054
7,050	7,100	1,061	1,061	1,061	1,061
7,100	7,150	1,069	1,069	1,069	1,069
7,150	7,200	1,076	1,076	1,076	1,076
7,200	7,250	1,084	1,084	1,084	1,084
7,250	7,300	1,091	1,091	1,091	1,091
7,300	7,350	1,099	1,099	1,099	1,099
7,350	7,400	1,106	1,106	1,106	1,106
7,400	7,450	1,114	1,114	1,114	1,114
7,450	7,500	1,121	1,121	1,121	1,121
7,500	7,550	1,129	1,129	1,129	1,129
7,550	7,600	1,136	1,136	1,136	1,136
7,600	7,650	1,144	1,144	1,144	1,144
7,650	7,700	1,151	1,151	1,151	1,151
7,700	7,750	1,159	1,159	1,159	1,159
7,750	7,800	1,166	1,166	1,166	1,166
7,800	7,850	1,174	1,174	1,174	1,174
7,850	7,900	1,181	1,181	1,181	1,181
7,900	7,950	1,189	1,189	1,189	1,189
7,950	8,000	1,196	1,196	1,196	1,196

If line 37 (taxable income) is— At least	But less than	Single	Married filing jointly *	Married filing separately	Head of a household
8,000					
8,000	8,050	1,204	1,204	1,204	1,204
8,050	8,100	1,211	1,211	1,211	1,211
8,100	8,150	1,219	1,219	1,219	1,219
8,150	8,200	1,226	1,226	1,226	1,226
8,200	8,250	1,234	1,234	1,234	1,234
8,250	8,300	1,241	1,241	1,241	1,241
8,300	8,350	1,249	1,249	1,249	1,249
8,350	8,400	1,256	1,256	1,256	1,256
8,400	8,450	1,264	1,264	1,264	1,264
8,450	8,500	1,271	1,271	1,271	1,271
8,500	8,550	1,279	1,279	1,279	1,279
8,550	8,600	1,286	1,286	1,286	1,286
8,600	8,650	1,294	1,294	1,294	1,294
8,650	8,700	1,301	1,301	1,301	1,301
8,700	8,750	1,309	1,309	1,309	1,309
8,750	8,800	1,316	1,316	1,316	1,316
8,800	8,850	1,324	1,324	1,324	1,324
8,850	8,900	1,331	1,331	1,331	1,331
8,900	8,950	1,339	1,339	1,339	1,339
8,950	9,000	1,346	1,346	1,346	1,346
9,000					
9,000	9,050	1,354	1,354	1,354	1,354
9,050	9,100	1,361	1,361	1,361	1,361
9,100	9,150	1,369	1,369	1,369	1,369
9,150	9,200	1,376	1,376	1,376	1,376
9,200	9,250	1,384	1,384	1,384	1,384
9,250	9,300	1,391	1,391	1,391	1,391
9,300	9,350	1,399	1,399	1,399	1,399
9,350	9,400	1,406	1,406	1,406	1,406
9,400	9,450	1,414	1,414	1,414	1,414
9,450	9,500	1,421	1,421	1,421	1,421
9,500	9,550	1,429	1,429	1,429	1,429
9,550	9,600	1,436	1,436	1,436	1,436
9,600	9,650	1,444	1,444	1,444	1,444
9,650	9,700	1,451	1,451	1,451	1,451
9,700	9,750	1,459	1,459	1,459	1,459
9,750	9,800	1,466	1,466	1,466	1,466
9,800	9,850	1,474	1,474	1,474	1,474
9,850	9,900	1,481	1,481	1,481	1,481
9,900	9,950	1,489	1,489	1,489	1,489
9,950	10,000	1,496	1,496	1,496	1,496
10,000					
10,000	10,050	1,504	1,504	1,504	1,504
10,050	10,100	1,511	1,511	1,511	1,511
10,100	10,150	1,519	1,519	1,519	1,519
10,150	10,200	1,526	1,526	1,526	1,526
10,200	10,250	1,534	1,534	1,534	1,534
10,250	10,300	1,541	1,541	1,541	1,541
10,300	10,350	1,549	1,549	1,549	1,549
10,350	10,400	1,556	1,556	1,556	1,556
10,400	10,450	1,564	1,564	1,564	1,564
10,450	10,500	1,571	1,571	1,571	1,571
10,500	10,550	1,579	1,579	1,579	1,579
10,550	10,600	1,586	1,586	1,586	1,586
10,600	10,650	1,594	1,594	1,594	1,594
10,650	10,700	1,601	1,601	1,601	1,601
10,700	10,750	1,609	1,609	1,609	1,609
10,750	10,800	1,616	1,616	1,616	1,616
10,800	10,850	1,624	1,624	1,624	1,624
10,850	10,900	1,631	1,631	1,631	1,631
10,900	10,950	1,639	1,639	1,639	1,639
10,950	11,000	1,646	1,646	1,646	1,646

If line 37 (taxable income) is— At least	But less than	Single	Married filing jointly *	Married filing separately	Head of a household
11,000					
11,000	11,050	1,654	1,654	1,654	1,654
11,050	11,100	1,661	1,661	1,661	1,661
11,100	11,150	1,669	1,669	1,669	1,669
11,150	11,200	1,676	1,676	1,676	1,676
11,200	11,250	1,684	1,684	1,684	1,684
11,250	11,300	1,691	1,691	1,691	1,691
11,300	11,350	1,699	1,699	1,699	1,699
11,350	11,400	1,706	1,706	1,706	1,706
11,400	11,450	1,714	1,714	1,714	1,714
11,450	11,500	1,721	1,721	1,721	1,721
11,500	11,550	1,729	1,729	1,729	1,729
11,550	11,600	1,736	1,736	1,736	1,736
11,600	11,650	1,744	1,744	1,744	1,744
11,650	11,700	1,751	1,751	1,751	1,751
11,700	11,750	1,759	1,759	1,759	1,759
11,750	11,800	1,766	1,766	1,766	1,766
11,800	11,850	1,774	1,774	1,774	1,774
11,850	11,900	1,781	1,781	1,781	1,781
11,900	11,950	1,789	1,789	1,789	1,789
11,950	12,000	1,796	1,796	1,796	1,796
12,000					
12,000	12,050	1,804	1,804	1,804	1,804
12,050	12,100	1,811	1,811	1,811	1,811
12,100	12,150	1,819	1,819	1,819	1,819
12,150	12,200	1,826	1,826	1,826	1,826
12,200	12,250	1,834	1,834	1,834	1,834
12,250	12,300	1,841	1,841	1,841	1,841
12,300	12,350	1,849	1,849	1,849	1,849
12,350	12,400	1,856	1,856	1,856	1,856
12,400	12,450	1,864	1,864	1,864	1,864
12,450	12,500	1,871	1,871	1,871	1,871
12,500	12,550	1,879	1,879	1,879	1,879
12,550	12,600	1,886	1,886	1,886	1,886
12,600	12,650	1,894	1,894	1,894	1,894
12,650	12,700	1,901	1,901	1,901	1,901
12,700	12,750	1,909	1,909	1,909	1,909
12,750	12,800	1,916	1,916	1,916	1,916
12,800	12,850	1,924	1,924	1,924	1,924
12,850	12,900	1,931	1,931	1,931	1,931
12,900	12,950	1,939	1,939	1,939	1,939
12,950	13,000	1,946	1,946	1,946	1,946
13,000					
13,000	13,050	1,954	1,954	1,954	1,954
13,050	13,100	1,961	1,961	1,961	1,961
13,100	13,150	1,969	1,969	1,969	1,969
13,150	13,200	1,976	1,976	1,976	1,976
13,200	13,250	1,984	1,984	1,984	1,984
13,250	13,300	1,991	1,991	1,991	1,991
13,300	13,350	1,999	1,999	1,999	1,999
13,350	13,400	2,006	2,006	2,006	2,006
13,400	13,450	2,014	2,014	2,014	2,014
13,450	13,500	2,021	2,021	2,021	2,021
13,500	13,550	2,029	2,029	2,029	2,029
13,550	13,600	2,036	2,036	2,036	2,036
13,600	13,650	2,044	2,044	2,044	2,044
13,650	13,700	2,051	2,051	2,051	2,051
13,700	13,750	2,059	2,059	2,059	2,059
13,750	13,800	2,066	2,066	2,066	2,066
13,800	13,850	2,074	2,074	2,074	2,074
13,850	13,900	2,081	2,081	2,081	2,081
13,900	13,950	2,089	2,089	2,089	2,089
13,950	14,000	2,096	2,096	2,096	2,096

* This column must also be used by a qualifying widow(er).

Continued on next page

1990 Tax Table—Continued

If line 37 (taxable income) is— At least	But less than	Single	Married filing jointly *	Married filing separately	Head of a household
			Your tax is—		
14,000					
14,000	14,050	2,104	2,104	2,104	2,104
14,050	14,100	2,111	2,111	2,111	2,111
14,100	14,150	2,119	2,119	2,119	2,119
14,150	14,200	2,126	2,126	2,126	2,126
14,200	14,250	2,134	2,134	2,134	2,134
14,250	14,300	2,141	2,141	2,141	2,141
14,300	14,350	2,149	2,149	2,149	2,149
14,350	14,400	2,156	2,156	2,156	2,156
14,400	14,450	2,164	2,164	2,164	2,164
14,450	14,500	2,171	2,171	2,171	2,171
14,500	14,550	2,179	2,179	2,179	2,179
14,550	14,600	2,186	2,186	2,186	2,186
14,600	14,650	2,194	2,194	2,194	2,194
14,650	14,700	2,201	2,201	2,201	2,201
14,700	14,750	2,209	2,209	2,209	2,209
14,750	14,800	2,216	2,216	2,216	2,216
14,800	14,850	2,224	2,224	2,224	2,224
14,850	14,900	2,231	2,231	2,231	2,231
14,900	14,950	2,239	2,239	2,239	2,239
14,950	15,000	2,246	2,246	2,246	2,246
15,000					
15,000	15,050	2,254	2,254	2,254	2,254
15,050	15,100	2,261	2,261	2,261	2,261
15,100	15,150	2,269	2,269	2,269	2,269
15,150	15,200	2,276	2,276	2,276	2,276
15,200	15,250	2,284	2,284	2,284	2,284
15,250	15,300	2,291	2,291	2,291	2,291
15,300	15,350	2,299	2,299	2,299	2,299
15,350	15,400	2,306	2,306	2,306	2,306
15,400	15,450	2,314	2,314	2,314	2,314
15,450	15,500	2,321	2,321	2,321	2,321
15,500	15,550	2,329	2,329	2,329	2,329
15,550	15,600	2,336	2,336	2,336	2,336
15,600	15,650	2,344	2,344	2,344	2,344
15,650	15,700	2,351	2,351	2,351	2,351
15,700	15,750	2,359	2,359	2,359	2,359
15,750	15,800	2,366	2,366	2,366	2,366
15,800	15,850	2,374	2,374	2,374	2,374
15,850	15,900	2,381	2,381	2,381	2,381
15,900	15,950	2,389	2,389	2,389	2,389
15,950	16,000	2,396	2,396	2,396	2,396
16,000					
16,000	16,050	2,404	2,404	2,404	2,404
16,050	16,100	2,411	2,411	2,411	2,411
16,100	16,150	2,419	2,419	2,419	2,419
16,150	16,200	2,426	2,426	2,426	2,426
16,200	16,250	2,434	2,434	2,434	2,434
16,250	16,300	2,441	2,441	2,448	2,441
16,300	16,350	2,449	2,449	2,462	2,449
16,350	16,400	2,456	2,456	2,476	2,456
16,400	16,450	2,464	2,464	2,490	2,464
16,450	16,500	2,471	2,471	2,504	2,471
16,500	16,550	2,479	2,479	2,518	2,479
16,550	16,600	2,486	2,486	2,532	2,486
16,600	16,650	2,494	2,494	2,546	2,494
16,650	16,700	2,501	2,501	2,560	2,501
16,700	16,750	2,509	2,509	2,574	2,509
16,750	16,800	2,516	2,516	2,588	2,516
16,800	16,850	2,524	2,524	2,602	2,524
16,850	16,900	2,531	2,531	2,616	2,531
16,900	16,950	2,539	2,539	2,630	2,539
16,950	17,000	2,546	2,546	2,644	2,546

If line 37 (taxable income) is— At least	But less than	Single	Married filing jointly *	Married filing separately	Head of a household
			Your tax is—		
17,000					
17,000	17,050	2,554	2,554	2,658	2,554
17,050	17,100	2,561	2,561	2,672	2,561
17,100	17,150	2,569	2,569	2,686	2,569
17,150	17,200	2,576	2,576	2,700	2,576
17,200	17,250	2,584	2,584	2,714	2,584
17,250	17,300	2,591	2,591	2,728	2,591
17,300	17,350	2,599	2,599	2,742	2,599
17,350	17,400	2,606	2,606	2,756	2,606
17,400	17,450	2,614	2,614	2,770	2,614
17,450	17,500	2,621	2,621	2,784	2,621
17,500	17,550	2,629	2,629	2,798	2,629
17,550	17,600	2,636	2,636	2,812	2,636
17,600	17,650	2,644	2,644	2,826	2,644
17,650	17,700	2,651	2,651	2,840	2,651
17,700	17,750	2,659	2,659	2,854	2,659
17,750	17,800	2,666	2,666	2,868	2,666
17,800	17,850	2,674	2,674	2,882	2,674
17,850	17,900	2,681	2,681	2,896	2,681
17,900	17,950	2,689	2,689	2,910	2,689
17,950	18,000	2,696	2,696	2,924	2,696
18,000					
18,000	18,050	2,704	2,704	2,938	2,704
18,050	18,100	2,711	2,711	2,952	2,711
18,100	18,150	2,719	2,719	2,966	2,719
18,150	18,200	2,726	2,726	2,980	2,726
18,200	18,250	2,734	2,734	2,994	2,734
18,250	18,300	2,741	2,741	3,008	2,741
18,300	18,350	2,749	2,749	3,022	2,749
18,350	18,400	2,756	2,756	3,036	2,756
18,400	18,450	2,764	2,764	3,050	2,764
18,450	18,500	2,771	2,771	3,064	2,771
18,500	18,550	2,779	2,779	3,078	2,779
18,550	18,600	2,786	2,786	3,092	2,786
18,600	18,650	2,794	2,794	3,106	2,794
18,650	18,700	2,801	2,801	3,120	2,801
18,700	18,750	2,809	2,809	3,134	2,809
18,750	18,800	2,816	2,816	3,148	2,816
18,800	18,850	2,824	2,824	3,162	2,824
18,850	18,900	2,831	2,831	3,176	2,831
18,900	18,950	2,839	2,839	3,190	2,839
18,950	19,000	2,846	2,846	3,204	2,846
19,000					
19,000	19,050	2,854	2,854	3,218	2,854
19,050	19,100	2,861	2,861	3,232	2,861
19,100	19,150	2,869	2,869	3,246	2,869
19,150	19,200	2,876	2,876	3,260	2,876
19,200	19,250	2,884	2,884	3,274	2,884
19,250	19,300	2,891	2,891	3,288	2,891
19,300	19,350	2,899	2,899	3,302	2,899
19,350	19,400	2,906	2,906	3,316	2,906
19,400	19,450	2,914	2,914	3,330	2,914
19,450	19,500	2,925	2,921	3,344	2,921
19,500	19,550	2,939	2,929	3,358	2,929
19,550	19,600	2,953	2,936	3,372	2,936
19,600	19,650	2,967	2,944	3,386	2,944
19,650	19,700	2,981	2,951	3,400	2,951
19,700	19,750	2,995	2,959	3,414	2,959
19,750	19,800	3,009	2,966	3,428	2,966
19,800	19,850	3,023	2,974	3,442	2,974
19,850	19,900	3,037	2,981	3,456	2,981
19,900	19,950	3,051	2,989	3,470	2,989
19,950	20,000	3,065	2,996	3,484	2,996

If line 37 (taxable income) is— At least	But less than	Single	Married filing jointly *	Married filing separately	Head of a household
			Your tax is—		
20,000					
20,000	20,050	3,079	3,004	3,498	3,004
20,050	20,100	3,093	3,011	3,512	3,011
20,100	20,150	3,107	3,019	3,526	3,019
20,150	20,200	3,121	3,026	3,540	3,026
20,200	20,250	3,135	3,034	3,554	3,034
20,250	20,300	3,149	3,041	3,568	3,041
20,300	20,350	3,163	3,049	3,582	3,049
20,350	20,400	3,177	3,056	3,596	3,056
20,400	20,450	3,191	3,064	3,610	3,064
20,450	20,500	3,205	3,071	3,624	3,071
20,500	20,550	3,219	3,079	3,638	3,079
20,550	20,600	3,233	3,086	3,652	3,086
20,600	20,650	3,247	3,094	3,666	3,094
20,650	20,700	3,261	3,101	3,680	3,101
20,700	20,750	3,275	3,109	3,694	3,109
20,750	20,800	3,289	3,116	3,708	3,116
20,800	20,850	3,303	3,124	3,722	3,124
20,850	20,900	3,317	3,131	3,736	3,131
20,900	20,950	3,331	3,139	3,750	3,139
20,950	21,000	3,345	3,146	3,764	3,146
21,000					
21,000	21,050	3,359	3,154	3,778	3,154
21,050	21,100	3,373	3,161	3,792	3,161
21,100	21,150	3,387	3,169	3,806	3,169
21,150	21,200	3,401	3,176	3,820	3,176
21,200	21,250	3,415	3,184	3,834	3,184
21,250	21,300	3,429	3,191	3,848	3,191
21,300	21,350	3,443	3,199	3,862	3,199
21,350	21,400	3,457	3,206	3,876	3,206
21,400	21,450	3,471	3,214	3,890	3,214
21,450	21,500	3,485	3,221	3,904	3,221
21,500	21,550	3,499	3,229	3,918	3,229
21,550	21,600	3,513	3,236	3,932	3,236
21,600	21,650	3,527	3,244	3,946	3,244
21,650	21,700	3,541	3,251	3,960	3,251
21,700	21,750	3,555	3,259	3,974	3,259
21,750	21,800	3,569	3,266	3,988	3,266
21,800	21,850	3,583	3,274	4,002	3,274
21,850	21,900	3,597	3,281	4,016	3,281
21,900	21,950	3,611	3,289	4,030	3,289
21,950	22,000	3,625	3,296	4,044	3,296
22,000					
22,000	22,050	3,639	3,304	4,058	3,304
22,050	22,100	3,653	3,311	4,072	3,311
22,100	22,150	3,667	3,319	4,086	3,319
22,150	22,200	3,681	3,326	4,100	3,326
22,200	22,250	3,695	3,334	4,114	3,334
22,250	22,300	3,709	3,341	4,128	3,341
22,300	22,350	3,723	3,349	4,142	3,349
22,350	22,400	3,737	3,356	4,156	3,356
22,400	22,450	3,751	3,364	4,170	3,364
22,450	22,500	3,765	3,371	4,184	3,371
22,500	22,550	3,779	3,379	4,198	3,379
22,550	22,600	3,793	3,386	4,212	3,386
22,600	22,650	3,807	3,394	4,226	3,394
22,650	22,700	3,821	3,401	4,240	3,401
22,700	22,750	3,835	3,409	4,254	3,409
22,750	22,800	3,849	3,416	4,268	3,416
22,800	22,850	3,863	3,424	4,282	3,424
22,850	22,900	3,877	3,431	4,296	3,431
22,900	22,950	3,891	3,439	4,310	3,439
22,950	23,000	3,905	3,446	4,324	3,446

* This column must also be used by a qualifying widow(er).

Continued on next page

1990 Tax Table—Continued

If line 37 (taxable income) is—		And you are—			
At least	But less than	Single	Married filing jointly *	Married filing separately	Head of a household

Your tax is—

23,000

At least	But less than	Single	MFJ	MFS	HoH
23,000	23,050	3,919	3,454	4,338	3,454
23,050	23,100	3,933	3,461	4,352	3,461
23,100	23,150	3,947	3,469	4,366	3,469
23,150	23,200	3,961	3,476	4,380	3,476
23,200	23,250	3,975	3,484	4,394	3,484
23,250	23,300	3,989	3,491	4,408	3,491
23,300	23,350	4,003	3,499	4,422	3,499
23,350	23,400	4,017	3,506	4,436	3,506
23,400	23,450	4,031	3,514	4,450	3,514
23,450	23,500	4,045	3,521	4,464	3,521
23,500	23,550	4,059	3,529	4,478	3,529
23,550	23,600	4,073	3,536	4,492	3,536
23,600	23,650	4,087	3,544	4,506	3,544
23,650	23,700	4,101	3,551	4,520	3,551
23,700	23,750	4,115	3,559	4,534	3,559
23,750	23,800	4,129	3,566	4,548	3,566
23,800	23,850	4,143	3,574	4,562	3,574
23,850	23,900	4,157	3,581	4,576	3,581
23,900	23,950	4,171	3,589	4,590	3,589
23,950	24,000	4,185	3,596	4,604	3,596

24,000

At least	But less than	Single	MFJ	MFS	HoH
24,000	24,050	4,199	3,604	4,618	3,604
24,050	24,100	4,213	3,611	4,632	3,611
24,100	24,150	4,227	3,619	4,646	3,619
24,150	24,200	4,241	3,626	4,660	3,626
24,200	24,250	4,255	3,634	4,674	3,634
24,250	24,300	4,269	3,641	4,688	3,641
24,300	24,350	4,283	3,649	4,702	3,649
24,350	24,400	4,297	3,656	4,716	3,656
24,400	24,450	4,311	3,664	4,730	3,664
24,450	24,500	4,325	3,671	4,744	3,671
24,500	24,550	4,339	3,679	4,758	3,679
24,550	24,600	4,353	3,686	4,772	3,686
24,600	24,650	4,367	3,694	4,786	3,694
24,650	24,700	4,381	3,701	4,800	3,701
24,700	24,750	4,395	3,709	4,814	3,709
24,750	24,800	4,409	3,716	4,828	3,716
24,800	24,850	4,423	3,724	4,842	3,724
24,850	24,900	4,437	3,731	4,856	3,731
24,900	24,950	4,451	3,739	4,870	3,739
24,950	25,000	4,465	3,746	4,884	3,746

25,000

At least	But less than	Single	MFJ	MFS	HoH
25,000	25,050	4,479	3,754	4,898	3,754
25,050	25,100	4,493	3,761	4,912	3,761
25,100	25,150	4,507	3,769	4,926	3,769
25,150	25,200	4,521	3,776	4,940	3,776
25,200	25,250	4,535	3,784	4,954	3,784
25,250	25,300	4,549	3,791	4,968	3,791
25,300	25,350	4,563	3,799	4,982	3,799
25,350	25,400	4,577	3,806	4,996	3,806
25,400	25,450	4,591	3,814	5,010	3,814
25,450	25,500	4,605	3,821	5,024	3,821
25,500	25,550	4,619	3,829	5,038	3,829
25,550	25,600	4,633	3,836	5,052	3,836
25,600	25,650	4,647	3,844	5,066	3,844
25,650	25,700	4,661	3,851	5,080	3,851
25,700	25,750	4,675	3,859	5,094	3,859
25,750	25,800	4,689	3,866	5,108	3,866
25,800	25,850	4,703	3,874	5,122	3,874
25,850	25,900	4,717	3,881	5,136	3,881
25,900	25,950	4,731	3,889	5,150	3,889
25,950	26,000	4,745	3,896	5,164	3,896

26,000

At least	But less than	Single	MFJ	MFS	HoH
26,000	26,050	4,759	3,904	5,178	3,904
26,050	26,100	4,773	3,911	5,192	3,915
26,100	26,150	4,787	3,919	5,206	3,929
26,150	26,200	4,801	3,926	5,220	3,943
26,200	26,250	4,815	3,934	5,234	3,957
26,250	26,300	4,829	3,941	5,248	3,971
26,300	26,350	4,843	3,949	5,262	3,985
26,350	26,400	4,857	3,956	5,276	3,999
26,400	26,450	4,871	3,964	5,290	4,013
26,450	26,500	4,885	3,971	5,304	4,027
26,500	26,550	4,899	3,979	5,318	4,041
26,550	26,600	4,913	3,986	5,332	4,055
26,600	26,650	4,927	3,994	5,346	4,069
26,650	26,700	4,941	4,001	5,360	4,083
26,700	26,750	4,955	4,009	5,374	4,097
26,750	26,800	4,969	4,016	5,388	4,111
26,800	26,850	4,983	4,024	5,402	4,125
26,850	26,900	4,997	4,031	5,416	4,139
26,900	26,950	5,011	4,039	5,430	4,153
26,950	27,000	5,025	4,046	5,444	4,167

27,000

At least	But less than	Single	MFJ	MFS	HoH
27,000	27,050	5,039	4,054	5,458	4,181
27,050	27,100	5,053	4,061	5,472	4,195
27,100	27,150	5,067	4,069	5,486	4,209
27,150	27,200	5,081	4,076	5,500	4,223
27,200	27,250	5,095	4,084	5,514	4,237
27,250	27,300	5,109	4,091	5,528	4,251
27,300	27,350	5,123	4,099	5,542	4,265
27,350	27,400	5,137	4,106	5,556	4,279
27,400	27,450	5,151	4,114	5,570	4,293
27,450	27,500	5,165	4,121	5,584	4,307
27,500	27,550	5,179	4,129	5,598	4,321
27,550	27,600	5,193	4,136	5,612	4,335
27,600	27,650	5,207	4,144	5,626	4,349
27,650	27,700	5,221	4,151	5,640	4,363
27,700	27,750	5,235	4,159	5,654	4,377
27,750	27,800	5,249	4,166	5,668	4,391
27,800	27,850	5,263	4,174	5,682	4,405
27,850	27,900	5,277	4,181	5,696	4,419
27,900	27,950	5,291	4,189	5,710	4,433
27,950	28,000	5,305	4,196	5,724	4,447

28,000

At least	But less than	Single	MFJ	MFS	HoH
28,000	28,050	5,319	4,204	5,738	4,461
28,050	28,100	5,333	4,211	5,752	4,475
28,100	28,150	5,347	4,219	5,766	4,489
28,150	28,200	5,361	4,226	5,780	4,503
28,200	28,250	5,375	4,234	5,794	4,517
28,250	28,300	5,389	4,241	5,808	4,531
28,300	28,350	5,403	4,249	5,822	4,545
28,350	28,400	5,417	4,256	5,836	4,559
28,400	28,450	5,431	4,264	5,850	4,573
28,450	28,500	5,445	4,271	5,864	4,587
28,500	28,550	5,459	4,279	5,878	4,601
28,550	28,600	5,473	4,286	5,892	4,615
28,600	28,650	5,487	4,294	5,906	4,629
28,650	28,700	5,501	4,301	5,920	4,643
28,700	28,750	5,515	4,309	5,934	4,657
28,750	28,800	5,529	4,316	5,948	4,671
28,800	28,850	5,543	4,324	5,962	4,685
28,850	28,900	5,557	4,331	5,976	4,699
28,900	28,950	5,571	4,339	5,990	4,713
28,950	29,000	5,585	4,346	6,004	4,727

29,000

At least	But less than	Single	MFJ	MFS	HoH
29,000	29,050	5,599	4,354	6,018	4,741
29,050	29,100	5,613	4,361	6,032	4,755
29,100	29,150	5,627	4,369	6,046	4,769
29,150	29,200	5,641	4,376	6,060	4,783
29,200	29,250	5,655	4,384	6,074	4,797
29,250	29,300	5,669	4,391	6,088	4,811
29,300	29,350	5,683	4,399	6,102	4,825
29,350	29,400	5,697	4,406	6,116	4,839
29,400	29,450	5,711	4,414	6,130	4,853
29,450	29,500	5,725	4,421	6,144	4,867
29,500	29,550	5,739	4,429	6,158	4,881
29,550	29,600	5,753	4,436	6,172	4,895
29,600	29,650	5,767	4,444	6,186	4,909
29,650	29,700	5,781	4,451	6,200	4,923
29,700	29,750	5,795	4,459	6,214	4,937
29,750	29,800	5,809	4,466	6,228	4,951
29,800	29,850	5,823	4,474	6,242	4,965
29,850	29,900	5,837	4,481	6,256	4,979
29,900	29,950	5,851	4,489	6,270	4,993
29,950	30,000	5,865	4,496	6,284	5,007

30,000

At least	But less than	Single	MFJ	MFS	HoH
30,000	30,050	5,879	4,504	6,298	5,021
30,050	30,100	5,893	4,511	6,312	5,035
30,100	30,150	5,907	4,519	6,326	5,049
30,150	30,200	5,921	4,526	6,340	5,063
30,200	30,250	5,935	4,534	6,354	5,077
30,250	30,300	5,949	4,541	6,368	5,091
30,300	30,350	5,963	4,549	6,382	5,105
30,350	30,400	5,977	4,556	6,396	5,119
30,400	30,450	5,991	4,564	6,410	5,133
30,450	30,500	6,005	4,571	6,424	5,147
30,500	30,550	6,019	4,579	6,438	5,161
30,550	30,600	6,033	4,586	6,452	5,175
30,600	30,650	6,047	4,594	6,466	5,189
30,650	30,700	6,061	4,601	6,480	5,203
30,700	30,750	6,075	4,609	6,494	5,217
30,750	30,800	6,089	4,616	6,508	5,231
30,800	30,850	6,103	4,624	6,522	5,245
30,850	30,900	6,117	4,631	6,536	5,259
30,900	30,950	6,131	4,639	6,550	5,273
30,950	31,000	6,145	4,646	6,564	5,287

31,000

At least	But less than	Single	MFJ	MFS	HoH
31,000	31,050	6,159	4,654	6,578	5,301
31,050	31,100	6,173	4,661	6,592	5,315
31,100	31,150	6,187	4,669	6,606	5,329
31,150	31,200	6,201	4,676	6,620	5,343
31,200	31,250	6,215	4,684	6,634	5,357
31,250	31,300	6,229	4,691	6,648	5,371
31,300	31,350	6,243	4,699	6,662	5,385
31,350	31,400	6,257	4,706	6,676	5,399
31,400	31,450	6,271	4,714	6,690	5,413
31,450	31,500	6,285	4,721	6,704	5,427
31,500	31,550	6,299	4,729	6,718	5,441
31,550	31,600	6,313	4,736	6,732	5,455
31,600	31,650	6,327	4,744	6,746	5,469
31,650	31,700	6,341	4,751	6,760	5,483
31,700	31,750	6,355	4,759	6,774	5,497
31,750	31,800	6,369	4,766	6,788	5,511
31,800	31,850	6,383	4,774	6,802	5,525
31,850	31,900	6,397	4,781	6,816	5,539
31,900	31,950	6,411	4,789	6,830	5,553
31,950	32,000	6,425	4,796	6,844	5,567

* This column must also be used by a qualifying widow(er).

Continued on next page

1990 Tax Table—Continued

If line 37 (taxable income) is— At least	But less than	Single	Married filing jointly *	Married filing separately	Head of a household
32,000					
32,000	32,050	6,439	4,804	6,858	5,581
32,050	32,100	6,453	4,811	6,872	5,595
32,100	32,150	6,467	4,819	6,886	5,609
32,150	32,200	6,481	4,826	6,900	5,623
32,200	32,250	6,495	4,834	6,914	5,637
32,250	32,300	6,509	4,841	6,928	5,651
32,300	32,350	6,523	4,849	6,942	5,665
32,350	32,400	6,537	4,856	6,956	5,679
32,400	32,450	6,551	4,864	6,970	5,693
32,450	32,500	6,565	4,875	6,984	5,707
32,500	32,550	6,579	4,889	6,998	5,721
32,550	32,600	6,593	4,903	7,012	5,735
32,600	32,650	6,607	4,917	7,026	5,749
32,650	32,700	6,621	4,931	7,040	5,763
32,700	32,750	6,635	4,945	7,054	5,777
32,750	32,800	6,649	4,959	7,068	5,791
32,800	32,850	6,663	4,973	7,082	5,805
32,850	32,900	6,677	4,987	7,096	5,819
32,900	32,950	6,691	5,001	7,110	5,833
32,950	33,000	6,705	5,015	7,124	5,847
33,000					
33,000	33,050	6,719	5,029	7,138	5,861
33,050	33,100	6,733	5,043	7,152	5,875
33,100	33,150	6,747	5,057	7,166	5,889
33,150	33,200	6,761	5,071	7,180	5,903
33,200	33,250	6,775	5,085	7,194	5,917
33,250	33,300	6,789	5,099	7,208	5,931
33,300	33,350	6,803	5,113	7,222	5,945
33,350	33,400	6,817	5,127	7,236	5,959
33,400	33,450	6,831	5,141	7,250	5,973
33,450	33,500	6,845	5,155	7,264	5,987
33,500	33,550	6,859	5,169	7,278	6,001
33,550	33,600	6,873	5,183	7,292	6,015
33,600	33,650	6,887	5,197	7,306	6,029
33,650	33,700	6,901	5,211	7,320	6,043
33,700	33,750	6,915	5,225	7,334	6,057
33,750	33,800	6,929	5,239	7,348	6,071
33,800	33,850	6,943	5,253	7,362	6,085
33,850	33,900	6,957	5,267	7,376	6,099
33,900	33,950	6,971	5,281	7,390	6,113
33,950	34,000	6,985	5,295	7,404	6,127
34,000					
34,000	34,050	6,999	5,309	7,418	6,141
34,050	34,100	7,013	5,323	7,432	6,155
34,100	34,150	7,027	5,337	7,446	6,169
34,150	34,200	7,041	5,351	7,460	6,183
34,200	34,250	7,055	5,365	7,474	6,197
34,250	34,300	7,069	5,379	7,488	6,211
34,300	34,350	7,083	5,393	7,502	6,225
34,350	34,400	7,097	5,407	7,516	6,239
34,400	34,450	7,111	5,421	7,530	6,253
34,450	34,500	7,125	5,435	7,544	6,267
34,500	34,550	7,139	5,449	7,558	6,281
34,550	34,600	7,153	5,463	7,572	6,295
34,600	34,650	7,167	5,477	7,586	6,309
34,650	34,700	7,181	5,491	7,600	6,323
34,700	34,750	7,195	5,505	7,614	6,337
34,750	34,800	7,209	5,519	7,628	6,351
34,800	34,850	7,223	5,533	7,642	6,365
34,850	34,900	7,237	5,547	7,656	6,379
34,900	34,950	7,251	5,561	7,670	6,393
34,950	35,000	7,265	5,575	7,684	6,407

If line 37 (taxable income) is— At least	But less than	Single	Married filing jointly *	Married filing separately	Head of a household
35,000					
35,000	35,050	7,279	5,589	7,698	6,421
35,050	35,100	7,293	5,603	7,712	6,435
35,100	35,150	7,307	5,617	7,726	6,449
35,150	35,200	7,321	5,631	7,740	6,463
35,200	35,250	7,335	5,645	7,754	6,477
35,250	35,300	7,349	5,659	7,768	6,491
35,300	35,350	7,363	5,673	7,782	6,505
35,350	35,400	7,377	5,687	7,796	6,519
35,400	35,450	7,391	5,701	7,810	6,533
35,450	35,500	7,405	5,715	7,824	6,547
35,500	35,550	7,419	5,729	7,838	6,561
35,550	35,600	7,433	5,743	7,852	6,575
35,600	35,650	7,447	5,757	7,866	6,589
35,650	35,700	7,461	5,771	7,880	6,603
35,700	35,750	7,475	5,785	7,894	6,617
35,750	35,800	7,489	5,799	7,908	6,631
35,800	35,850	7,503	5,813	7,922	6,645
35,850	35,900	7,517	5,827	7,936	6,659
35,900	35,950	7,531	5,841	7,950	6,673
35,950	36,000	7,545	5,855	7,964	6,687
36,000					
36,000	36,050	7,559	5,869	7,978	6,701
36,050	36,100	7,573	5,883	7,992	6,715
36,100	36,150	7,587	5,897	8,006	6,729
36,150	36,200	7,601	5,911	8,020	6,743
36,200	36,250	7,615	5,925	8,034	6,757
36,250	36,300	7,629	5,939	8,048	6,771
36,300	36,350	7,643	5,953	8,062	6,785
36,350	36,400	7,657	5,967	8,076	6,799
36,400	36,450	7,671	5,981	8,090	6,813
36,450	36,500	7,685	5,995	8,104	6,827
36,500	36,550	7,699	6,009	8,118	6,841
36,550	36,600	7,713	6,023	8,132	6,855
36,600	36,650	7,727	6,037	8,146	6,869
36,650	36,700	7,741	6,051	8,160	6,883
36,700	36,750	7,755	6,065	8,174	6,897
36,750	36,800	7,769	6,079	8,188	6,911
36,800	36,850	7,783	6,093	8,202	6,925
36,850	36,900	7,797	6,107	8,216	6,939
36,900	36,950	7,811	6,121	8,230	6,953
36,950	37,000	7,825	6,135	8,244	6,967
37,000					
37,000	37,050	7,839	6,149	8,258	6,981
37,050	37,100	7,853	6,163	8,272	6,995
37,100	37,150	7,867	6,177	8,286	7,009
37,150	37,200	7,881	6,191	8,300	7,023
37,200	37,250	7,895	6,205	8,314	7,037
37,250	37,300	7,909	6,219	8,328	7,051
37,300	37,350	7,923	6,233	8,342	7,065
37,350	37,400	7,937	6,247	8,356	7,079
37,400	37,450	7,951	6,261	8,370	7,093
37,450	37,500	7,965	6,275	8,384	7,107
37,500	37,550	7,979	6,289	8,398	7,121
37,550	37,600	7,993	6,303	8,412	7,135
37,600	37,650	8,007	6,317	8,426	7,149
37,650	37,700	8,021	6,331	8,440	7,163
37,700	37,750	8,035	6,345	8,454	7,177
37,750	37,800	8,049	6,359	8,468	7,191
37,800	37,850	8,063	6,373	8,482	7,205
37,850	37,900	8,077	6,387	8,496	7,219
37,900	37,950	8,091	6,401	8,510	7,233
37,950	38,000	8,105	6,415	8,524	7,247

If line 37 (taxable income) is— At least	But less than	Single	Married filing jointly *	Married filing separately	Head of a household
38,000					
38,000	38,050	8,119	6,429	8,538	7,261
38,050	38,100	8,133	6,443	8,552	7,275
38,100	38,150	8,147	6,457	8,566	7,289
38,150	38,200	8,161	6,471	8,580	7,303
38,200	38,250	8,175	6,485	8,594	7,317
38,250	38,300	8,189	6,499	8,608	7,331
38,300	38,350	8,203	6,513	8,622	7,345
38,350	38,400	8,217	6,527	8,636	7,359
38,400	38,450	8,231	6,541	8,650	7,373
38,450	38,500	8,245	6,555	8,664	7,387
38,500	38,550	8,259	6,569	8,678	7,401
38,550	38,600	8,273	6,583	8,692	7,415
38,600	38,650	8,287	6,597	8,706	7,429
38,650	38,700	8,301	6,611	8,720	7,443
38,700	38,750	8,315	6,625	8,734	7,457
38,750	38,800	8,329	6,639	8,748	7,471
38,800	38,850	8,343	6,653	8,762	7,485
38,850	38,900	8,357	6,667	8,776	7,499
38,900	38,950	8,371	6,681	8,790	7,513
38,950	39,000	8,385	6,695	8,804	7,527
39,000					
39,000	39,050	8,399	6,709	8,818	7,541
39,050	39,100	8,413	6,723	8,832	7,555
39,100	39,150	8,427	6,737	8,846	7,569
39,150	39,200	8,441	6,751	8,860	7,583
39,200	39,250	8,455	6,765	8,875	7,597
39,250	39,300	8,469	6,779	8,892	7,611
39,300	39,350	8,483	6,793	8,908	7,625
39,350	39,400	8,497	6,807	8,925	7,639
39,400	39,450	8,511	6,821	8,941	7,653
39,450	39,500	8,525	6,835	8,958	7,667
39,500	39,550	8,539	6,849	8,974	7,681
39,550	39,600	8,553	6,863	8,991	7,695
39,600	39,650	8,567	6,877	9,007	7,709
39,650	39,700	8,581	6,891	9,024	7,723
39,700	39,750	8,595	6,905	9,040	7,737
39,750	39,800	8,609	6,919	9,057	7,751
39,800	39,850	8,623	6,933	9,073	7,765
39,850	39,900	8,637	6,947	9,090	7,779
39,900	39,950	8,651	6,961	9,106	7,793
39,950	40,000	8,665	6,975	9,123	7,807
40,000					
40,000	40,050	8,679	6,989	9,139	7,821
40,050	40,100	8,693	7,003	9,156	7,835
40,100	40,150	8,707	7,017	9,172	7,849
40,150	40,200	8,721	7,031	9,189	7,863
40,200	40,250	8,735	7,045	9,205	7,877
40,250	40,300	8,749	7,059	9,222	7,891
40,300	40,350	8,763	7,073	9,238	7,905
40,350	40,400	8,777	7,087	9,255	7,919
40,400	40,450	8,791	7,101	9,271	7,933
40,450	40,500	8,805	7,115	9,288	7,947
40,500	40,550	8,819	7,129	9,304	7,961
40,550	40,600	8,833	7,143	9,321	7,975
40,600	40,650	8,847	7,157	9,337	7,989
40,650	40,700	8,861	7,171	9,354	8,003
40,700	40,750	8,875	7,185	9,370	8,017
40,750	40,800	8,889	7,199	9,387	8,031
40,800	40,850	8,903	7,213	9,403	8,045
40,850	40,900	8,917	7,227	9,420	8,059
40,900	40,950	8,931	7,241	9,436	8,073
40,950	41,000	8,945	7,255	9,453	8,087

* This column must also be used by a qualifying widow(er).

Continued on next page

1990 Tax Table—Continued

Headers for each panel: "If line 37 (taxable income) is—" (At least / But less than) and "And you are—" (Single / Married filing jointly* / Married filing separately / Head of a household). Your tax is—

41,000 / 44,000 / 47,000

At least	But less than	Single	Married filing jointly*	Married filing separately	Head of a household	At least	But less than	Single	Married filing jointly*	Married filing separately	Head of a household	At least	But less than	Single	Married filing jointly*	Married filing separately	Head of a household
41,000	41,050	8,959	7,269	9,469	8,101	44,000	44,050	9,799	8,109	10,459	8,941	47,000	47,050	10,639	8,949	11,449	9,781
41,050	41,100	8,973	7,283	9,486	8,115	44,050	44,100	9,813	8,123	10,476	8,955	47,050	47,100	10,654	8,963	11,466	9,795
41,100	41,150	8,987	7,297	9,502	8,129	44,100	44,150	9,827	8,137	10,492	8,969	47,100	47,150	10,670	8,977	11,482	9,809
41,150	41,200	9,001	7,311	9,519	8,143	44,150	44,200	9,841	8,151	10,509	8,983	47,150	47,200	10,687	8,991	11,499	9,823
41,200	41,250	9,015	7,325	9,535	8,157	44,200	44,250	9,855	8,165	10,525	8,997	47,200	47,250	10,703	9,005	11,515	9,837
41,250	41,300	9,029	7,339	9,552	8,171	44,250	44,300	9,869	8,179	10,542	9,011	47,250	47,300	10,720	9,019	11,532	9,851
41,300	41,350	9,043	7,353	9,568	8,185	44,300	44,350	9,883	8,193	10,558	9,025	47,300	47,350	10,736	9,033	11,548	9,865
41,350	41,400	9,057	7,367	9,585	8,199	44,350	44,400	9,897	8,207	10,575	9,039	47,350	47,400	10,753	9,047	11,565	9,879
41,400	41,450	9,071	7,381	9,601	8,213	44,400	44,450	9,911	8,221	10,591	9,053	47,400	47,450	10,769	9,061	11,581	9,893
41,450	41,500	9,085	7,395	9,618	8,227	44,450	44,500	9,925	8,235	10,608	9,067	47,450	47,500	10,786	9,075	11,598	9,907
41,500	41,550	9,099	7,409	9,634	8,241	44,500	44,550	9,939	8,249	10,624	9,081	47,500	47,550	10,802	9,089	11,614	9,921
41,550	41,600	9,113	7,423	9,651	8,255	44,550	44,600	9,953	8,263	10,641	9,095	47,550	47,600	10,819	9,103	11,631	9,935
41,600	41,650	9,127	7,437	9,667	8,269	44,600	44,650	9,967	8,277	10,657	9,109	47,600	47,650	10,835	9,117	11,647	9,949
41,650	41,700	9,141	7,451	9,684	8,283	44,650	44,700	9,981	8,291	10,674	9,123	47,650	47,700	10,852	9,131	11,664	9,963
41,700	41,750	9,155	7,465	9,700	8,297	44,700	44,750	9,995	8,305	10,690	9,137	47,700	47,750	10,868	9,145	11,680	9,977
41,750	41,800	9,169	7,479	9,717	8,311	44,750	44,800	10,009	8,319	10,707	9,151	47,750	47,800	10,885	9,159	11,697	9,991
41,800	41,850	9,183	7,493	9,733	8,325	44,800	44,850	10,023	8,333	10,723	9,165	47,800	47,850	10,901	9,173	11,713	10,005
41,850	41,900	9,197	7,507	9,750	8,339	44,850	44,900	10,037	8,347	10,740	9,179	47,850	47,900	10,918	9,187	11,730	10,019
41,900	41,950	9,211	7,521	9,766	8,353	44,900	44,950	10,051	8,361	10,756	9,193	47,900	47,950	10,934	9,201	11,746	10,033
41,950	42,000	9,225	7,535	9,783	8,367	44,950	45,000	10,065	8,375	10,773	9,207	47,950	48,000	10,951	9,215	11,763	10,047

42,000 / 45,000 / 48,000

At least	But less than	Single	Married filing jointly*	Married filing separately	Head of a household	At least	But less than	Single	Married filing jointly*	Married filing separately	Head of a household	At least	But less than	Single	Married filing jointly*	Married filing separately	Head of a household
42,000	42,050	9,239	7,549	9,799	8,381	45,000	45,050	10,079	8,389	10,789	9,221	48,000	48,050	10,967	9,229	11,779	10,061
42,050	42,100	9,253	7,563	9,816	8,395	45,050	45,100	10,093	8,403	10,806	9,235	48,050	48,100	10,984	9,243	11,796	10,075
42,100	42,150	9,267	7,577	9,832	8,409	45,100	45,150	10,107	8,417	10,822	9,249	48,100	48,150	11,000	9,257	11,812	10,089
42,150	42,200	9,281	7,591	9,849	8,423	45,150	45,200	10,121	8,431	10,839	9,263	48,150	48,200	11,017	9,271	11,829	10,103
42,200	42,250	9,295	7,605	9,865	8,437	45,200	45,250	10,135	8,445	10,855	9,277	48,200	48,250	11,033	9,285	11,845	10,117
42,250	42,300	9,309	7,619	9,882	8,451	45,250	45,300	10,149	8,459	10,872	9,291	48,250	48,300	11,050	9,299	11,862	10,131
42,300	42,350	9,323	7,633	9,898	8,465	45,300	45,350	10,163	8,473	10,888	9,305	48,300	48,350	11,066	9,313	11,878	10,145
42,350	42,400	9,337	7,647	9,915	8,479	45,350	45,400	10,177	8,487	10,905	9,319	48,350	48,400	11,083	9,327	11,895	10,159
42,400	42,450	9,351	7,661	9,931	8,493	45,400	45,450	10,191	8,501	10,921	9,333	48,400	48,450	11,099	9,341	11,911	10,173
42,450	42,500	9,365	7,675	9,948	8,507	45,450	45,500	10,205	8,515	10,938	9,347	48,450	48,500	11,116	9,355	11,928	10,187
42,500	42,550	9,379	7,689	9,964	8,521	45,500	45,550	10,219	8,529	10,954	9,361	48,500	48,550	11,132	9,369	11,944	10,201
42,550	42,600	9,393	7,703	9,981	8,535	45,550	45,600	10,233	8,543	10,971	9,375	48,550	48,600	11,149	9,383	11,961	10,215
42,600	42,650	9,407	7,717	9,997	8,549	45,600	45,650	10,247	8,557	10,987	9,389	48,600	48,650	11,165	9,397	11,977	10,229
42,650	42,700	9,421	7,731	10,014	8,563	45,650	45,700	10,261	8,571	11,004	9,403	48,650	48,700	11,182	9,411	11,994	10,243
42,700	42,750	9,435	7,745	10,030	8,577	45,700	45,750	10,275	8,585	11,020	9,417	48,700	48,750	11,198	9,425	12,010	10,257
42,750	42,800	9,449	7,759	10,047	8,591	45,750	45,800	10,289	8,599	11,037	9,431	48,750	48,800	11,215	9,439	12,027	10,271
42,800	42,850	9,463	7,773	10,063	8,605	45,800	45,850	10,303	8,613	11,053	9,445	48,800	48,850	11,231	9,453	12,043	10,285
42,850	42,900	9,477	7,787	10,080	8,619	45,850	45,900	10,317	8,627	11,070	9,459	48,850	48,900	11,248	9,467	12,060	10,299
42,900	42,950	9,491	7,801	10,096	8,633	45,900	45,950	10,331	8,641	11,086	9,473	48,900	48,950	11,264	9,481	12,076	10,313
42,950	43,000	9,505	7,815	10,113	8,647	45,950	46,000	10,345	8,655	11,103	9,487	48,950	49,000	11,281	9,495	12,093	10,327

43,000 / 46,000 / 49,000

At least	But less than	Single	Married filing jointly*	Married filing separately	Head of a household	At least	But less than	Single	Married filing jointly*	Married filing separately	Head of a household	At least	But less than	Single	Married filing jointly*	Married filing separately	Head of a household
43,000	43,050	9,519	7,829	10,129	8,661	46,000	46,050	10,359	8,669	11,119	9,501	49,000	49,050	11,297	9,509	12,109	10,341
43,050	43,100	9,533	7,843	10,146	8,675	46,050	46,100	10,373	8,683	11,136	9,515	49,050	49,100	11,314	9,523	12,126	10,355
43,100	43,150	9,547	7,857	10,162	8,689	46,100	46,150	10,387	8,697	11,152	9,529	49,100	49,150	11,330	9,537	12,142	10,369
43,150	43,200	9,561	7,871	10,179	8,703	46,150	46,200	10,401	8,711	11,169	9,543	49,150	49,200	11,347	9,551	12,159	10,383
43,200	43,250	9,575	7,885	10,195	8,717	46,200	46,250	10,415	8,725	11,185	9,557	49,200	49,250	11,363	9,565	12,175	10,397
43,250	43,300	9,589	7,899	10,212	8,731	46,250	46,300	10,429	8,739	11,202	9,571	49,250	49,300	11,380	9,579	12,192	10,411
43,300	43,350	9,603	7,913	10,228	8,745	46,300	46,350	10,443	8,753	11,218	9,585	49,300	49,350	11,396	9,593	12,208	10,425
43,350	43,400	9,617	7,927	10,245	8,759	46,350	46,400	10,457	8,767	11,235	9,599	49,350	49,400	11,413	9,607	12,225	10,439
43,400	43,450	9,631	7,941	10,261	8,773	46,400	46,450	10,471	8,781	11,251	9,613	49,400	49,450	11,429	9,621	12,241	10,453
43,450	43,500	9,645	7,955	10,278	8,787	46,450	46,500	10,485	8,795	11,268	9,627	49,450	49,500	11,446	9,635	12,258	10,467
43,500	43,550	9,659	7,969	10,294	8,801	46,500	46,550	10,499	8,809	11,284	9,641	49,500	49,550	11,462	9,649	12,274	10,481
43,550	43,600	9,673	7,983	10,311	8,815	46,550	46,600	10,513	8,823	11,301	9,655	49,550	49,600	11,479	9,663	12,291	10,495
43,600	43,650	9,687	7,997	10,327	8,829	46,600	46,650	10,527	8,837	11,317	9,669	49,600	49,650	11,495	9,677	12,307	10,509
43,650	43,700	9,701	8,011	10,344	8,843	46,650	46,700	10,541	8,851	11,334	9,683	49,650	49,700	11,512	9,691	12,324	10,523
43,700	43,750	9,715	8,025	10,360	8,857	46,700	46,750	10,555	8,865	11,350	9,697	49,700	49,750	11,528	9,705	12,340	10,537
43,750	43,800	9,729	8,039	10,377	8,871	46,750	46,800	10,569	8,879	11,367	9,711	49,750	49,800	11,545	9,719	12,357	10,551
43,800	43,850	9,743	8,053	10,393	8,885	46,800	46,850	10,583	8,893	11,383	9,725	49,800	49,850	11,561	9,733	12,373	10,565
43,850	43,900	9,757	8,067	10,410	8,899	46,850	46,900	10,597	8,907	11,400	9,739	49,850	49,900	11,578	9,747	12,390	10,579
43,900	43,950	9,771	8,081	10,426	8,913	46,900	46,950	10,611	8,921	11,416	9,753	49,900	49,950	11,594	9,761	12,406	10,593
43,950	44,000	9,785	8,095	10,443	8,927	46,950	47,000	10,625	8,935	11,433	9,767	49,950	50,000	11,611	9,775	12,423	10,607

* This column must also be used by a qualifying widow(er).

50,000 or over—use tax rate schedules

A-3   Unified Transfer Tax Rate Schedules

Unified Transfer Tax Rate Schedule

For Gifts Made and For Deaths Before 1993

If the amount with respect to which the tentative tax to be computed is:	*The tentative tax is:*
Not over $10,000	18 percent of such amount.
Over $10,000 but not over $20,000	$1,800 plus 20 percent of the excess of such amount over $10,000
Over $20,000 but not over $40,000	$3,800 plus 22 percent of the excess of such amount over $20,000
Over $40,000 but not over $60,000	$8,200 plus 24 percent of the excess of such amount over $40,000
Over $60,000 but not over $80,000	$13,000 plus 26 percent of the excess of such amount over $60,000
Over $80,000 but not over $100,000	$18,200 plus 28 percent of the excess of such amount over $80,000
Over $100,000 but not over $150,000	$23,800 plus 30 percent of the excess of such amount over $100,000
Over $150,000 but not over $250,000	$38,800 plus 32 percent of the excess of such amount over $150,000
Over $250,000 but not over $500,000	$70,800 plus 34 percent of the excess of such amount over $250,000
Over $500,000 but not over $750,000	$155,800 plus 37 percent of the excess of such amount over $500,000
Over $750,000 but not over $1,000,000	$248,300 plus 39 percent of the excess of such amount over $750,000
Over $1,000,000 but not over $1,250,000	$345,800 plus 41 percent of the excess of such amount over $1,000,000
Over $1,250,000 but not over $1,500,000	$448,300 plus 43 percent of the excess of such amount over $1,250,000
Over $1,500,000 but not over $2,000,000	$555,800 plus 45 percent of the excess of such amount over $1,500,000
Over $2,000,000 but not over $2,500,000	$780,800 plus 49 percent of the excess of such amount over $2,000,000
Over $2,500,000 but not over $3,000,000	$1,290,800 plus 53 percent of the excess of such amount over $2,500,000
Over $3,000,000	$1,290,800 plus 55 percent of the excess of such amount over $3,000,000

Unified Transfer Tax Rate Schedule

For Gifts Made and For Deaths After 1992

If the amount with respect to which the tentative tax to be computed is: **The tentative tax is:**

Not over $10,000	18 percent of such amount.
Over $10,000 but not over $20,000	$1,800 plus 20 percent of the excess of such amount over $10,000
Over $20,000 but not over $40,000	$3,800 plus 22 percent of the excess of such amount over $20,000
Over $40,000 but not over $60,000	$8,200 plus 24 percent of the excess of such amount over $40,000
Over $60,000 but not over $80,000	$13,000 plus 26 percent of the excess of such amount over $60,000
Over $80,000 but not over $100,000	$18,200 plus 28 percent of the excess of such amount over $80,000
Over $100,000 but not over $150,000	$23,800 plus 30 percent of the excess of such amount over $100,000
Over $150,000 but not over $250,000	$38,800 plus 32 percent of the excess of such amount over $150,000
Over $250,000 but not over $500,000	$70,800 plus 34 percent of the excess of such amount over $250,000
Over $500,000 but not over $750,000	$155,800 plus 37 percent of the excess of such amount over $500,000
Over $750,000 but not over $1,000,000	$248,300 plus 39 percent of the excess of such amount over $750,000
Over $1,000,000 but not over $1,250,000	$345,800 plus 41 percent of the excess of such amount over $1,000,000
Over $1,250,000 but not over $1,500,000	$448,300 plus 43 percent of the excess of such amount over $1,250,000
Over $1,500,000 but not over $2,000,000	$555,800 plus 45 percent of the excess of such amount over $1,500,000
Over $2,000,000 but not over $2,500,000	$780,800 plus 49 percent of the excess of such amount over $2,000,000
Over $2,500,000	$1,025,800 plus 50 percent of the excess of such amount over $2,500,000

A-4 Estate and Gift Tax Valuation Tables

Table A

Single Life Remainder Factors
Various Interest Rates
(See Notes to Table A)

Age	9.8%	10.0%	10.2%	Age	9.8%	10.0%	10.2%
0	.01954	.01922	.01891	25	.02902	.02784	.02673
1	.00834	.00801	.00770	26	.03052	.02928	.02811
2	.00819	.00784	.00751	27	.03219	.03088	.02965
3	.00832	.00795	.00760	28	.03403	.03264	.03134
4	.00862	.00822	.00786	29	.03604	.03458	.03322
5	.00904	.00862	.00824	30	.03825	.03671	.03527
6	.00954	.00910	.00869	31	.04067	.03905	.03753
7	.01013	.00966	.00923	32	.04329	.04160	.04000
8	.01081	.01031	.00986	33	.04616	.04438	.04269
9	.01159	.01107	.01059	34	.04926	.04738	.04561
10	.01249	.01194	.01142	35	.05260	.05063	.04877
11	.01351	.01293	.01239	36	.05617	.05411	.05215
12	.01463	.01402	.01345	37	.05999	.05783	.05578
13	.01582	.01517	.01457	38	.06407	.06180	.05965
14	.01698	.01630	.01567	39	.06841	.06604	.06379
15	.01810	.01738	.01672	40	.07303	.07055	.06820
16	.01917	.01842	.01772	41	.07794	.07535	.07288
17	.02018	.01940	.01866	42	.08312	.08041	.07784
18	.02118	.02035	.01958	43	.08858	.08576	.08308
19	.02218	.02131	.02050	44	.09434	.09141	.08861
20	.02320	.02229	.02143	45	.10042	.09736	.09445
21	.02424	.02328	.02238	46	.10680	.10363	.10060
22	.02532	.02430	.02336	47	.11352	.11022	.10707
23	.02644	.02538	.02438	48	.12055	.11713	.11386
24	.02767	.02655	.02550	49	.12787	.12433	.12094

(Continued)

Table A *(Continued)*

Age	9.8%	10.0%	10.2%	Age	9.8%	10.0%	10.2%
50	.13548	.13182	.12831	80	.53248	.52705	.52171
51	.14342	.13963	.13600	81	.55035	.54499	.53974
52	.15172	.14780	.14405	82	.56796	.56270	.55753
53	.16038	.15635	.15247	83	.58523	.58007	.57500
54	.16940	.16524	.16124	84	.60218	.59713	.59216
55	.17878	.17450	.17039	85	.61886	.61392	.60906
56	.18854	.18414	.17991	86	.63511	.63030	.62555
57	.19870	.19419	.18984	87	.65071	.64602	.64139
58	.20927	.20464	.20018	88	.66574	.66117	.65666
59	.22024	.21551	.21093	89	.68045	.67601	.67163
60	.23158	.22674	.22206	90	.69502	.69071	.68646
61	.24325	.23831	.23353	91	.70921	.70504	.70093
62	.25524	.25020	.24532	92	.72267	.71864	.71466
63	.26754	.26240	.25742	93	.73524	.73135	.72750
64	.28016	.27493	.26987	94	.74680	.74303	.73931
65	.29317	.28787	.28271	95	.75727	.75362	.75001
66	.30663	.30124	.29601	96	.76657	.76303	.75953
67	.32053	.31508	.30978	97	.77504	.77160	.76819
68	.33488	.32937	.32401	98	.78267	.77931	.77599
69	.34961	.34405	.33863	99	.78971	.78644	.78319
70	.36468	.35907	.35361	100	.79624	.79304	.78987
71	.38000	.37436	.36886	101	.80245	.79932	.79622
72	.39558	.38991	.38439	102	.80892	.80586	.80283
73	.41143	.40575	.40021	103	.81577	.81279	.80983
74	.42763	.42195	.41639	104	.82338	.82048	.81760
75	.44424	.43856	.43301	105	.83282	.83003	.82726
76	.46129	.45563	.45009	106	.84659	.84397	.84137
77	.47873	.47311	.46761	107	.86676	.86443	.86211
78	.49652	.49094	.48548	108	.90020	.89840	.89660
79	.51488	.50897	.50356	109	.95537	.95455	.95372

Notes to Table A:

1. These single life remainder factors are excerpts from Notice 89-60, 1989-22 I.R.B. (May 30, 1989). The IRS released tables for various interest rates beginning at 8.2 percent and incrementing by 0.2 percent up to 12.0 percent. Only three different rates are illustrated here.

2. These single life remainder factors can be used to determine the appropriate income factor for valuation of an income interest by using the following formula:

$$\text{Income factor} = 1.000000 - \text{Remainder factor}$$

Table B

Term Certain Remainder Factors
Various Interest Rates

Number of Years	9.8%	10.0%	10.2%	Number of Years	9.8%	10.0%	10.2%
1	.910747	.909091	.907441	31	.055122	.052099	.049246
2	.829460	.826446	.823449	32	.050202	.047362	.044688
3	.755428	.751315	.747232	33	.045722	.043057	.040552
4	.688003	.683013	.678069	34	.041641	.039143	.036798
5	.626597	.620921	.615307	35	.037924	.035584	.033392
6	.570671	.564474	.558355	36	.034539	.032349	.030301
7	.519737	.513158	.506674	37	.031457	.029408	.027497
8	.473349	.466507	.459777	38	.028649	.026735	.024952
9	.431101	.424098	.417221	39	.026092	.024304	.022642
10	.392624	.385543	.378603	40	.023763	.022095	.020546
11	.357581	.350494	.343560	41	.021642	.020086	.018645
12	.325666	.318631	.311760	42	.019711	.018260	.016919
13	.296599	.289664	.282904	43	.017951	.016600	.015353
14	.270127	.263331	.256719	44	.016349	.015091	.013932
15	.246017	.239392	.232957	45	.014890	.013719	.012642
16	.224059	.217629	.211395	46	.013561	.012472	.011472
17	.204061	.197845	.191828	47	.012351	.011338	.010410
18	.185848	.179859	.174073	48	.011248	.010307	.009447
19	.169260	.163508	.157961	49	.010244	.009370	.008572
20	.154153	.148644	.143340	50	.009330	.008519	.007779
21	.140395	.135131	.130073	51	.008497	.007744	.007059
22	.127864	.122846	.118033	52	.007739	.007040	.006406
23	.116452	.111678	.107108	53	.007048	.006400	.005813
24	.106058	.101562	.097195	54	.006419	.005818	.005275
25	.096592	.092296	.088198	55	.005846	.005289	.004786
26	.087971	.083905	.080035	56	.005324	.004809	.004343
27	.080119	.076278	.072627	57	.004849	.004371	.003941
28	.072968	.069343	.065905	58	.004416	.003974	.003577
29	.066456	.063039	.059804	59	.004022	.003613	.003246
30	.060524	.057309	.054269	60	.003663	.003284	.002945

Note: Like Table A, this table contains excerpts from Notice 89-60, but only 3 different interest rates are illustrated. The Table B from Notice 89-60 contains factors for 8.2 percent through 12.0 percent.

Appendix **B**

TAX FORMS

B-1 Form 1040A U.S. Individual Income Tax Return

Form
1040A

Department of the Treasury—Internal Revenue Service
**U.S. Individual
Income Tax Return 1990**

OMB No. 1545-0085

**Step 1
Label**
(See page 14.)

Use IRS label. Otherwise, please print or type.

L A B E L H E R E	Your first name and initial	Last name	Your social security no.
	If a joint return, spouse's first name and initial	Last name	Spouse's social security no.
	Home address (number and street). (If you have a P.O. box, see page 14.)	Apt. no.	
	City, town or post office, state, and ZIP code. (If you have a foreign address, see page 14.)		

**For Privacy Act
and Paperwork
Reduction Act
Notice, see page 3.**

Presidential Election Campaign Fund (see page 15)
Do you want $1 to go to this fund? . . . . □ Yes □ No
If joint return, does your spouse want $1 to go to this fund? □ Yes □ No

Note: *Checking "Yes" will not change your tax or reduce your refund.*

**Step 2
Check your
filing status**
(Check only one.)

1 □ Single. (See page 16 to find out if you can file as head of household.)
2 □ Married filing joint return (even if only one had income)
3 □ Married filing separate return. Enter spouse's social security number above and spouse's full name here ▶
4 □ Head of household (with qualifying person). (See page 16.) If the qualifying person is your child but not your dependent, enter this child's name here ▶
5 □ Qualifying widow(er) with dependent child (year spouse died ▶ 19____). (See page 17.)

**Step 3
Figure your
exemptions**
(See page 17.)

If more than 7 dependents, see page 20.

6a □ **Yourself** If your parent (or someone else) can claim you as a dependent on his or her tax return, do not check box 6a. But be sure to check the box on line 18b on page 2.
6b □ **Spouse**

| c Dependents:
1. Name (first, initial, and last name)	2. Check if under age 2	3. If age 2 or older, dependent's social security number	4. Dependent's relationship to you	5. No. of months lived in your home in 1990

No. of boxes checked on 6a and 6b

No. of your children on 6c who:
● lived with you
● didn't live with you due to divorce or separation (see page 21)

No. of other dependents listed on 6c

d If your child didn't live with you but is claimed as your dependent under a pre-1985 agreement, check here . . . . ▶ □
e Total number of exemptions claimed.

Add numbers entered on lines above

**Step 4
Figure your
total income**

Attach Copy B of your Forms W-2 and W-2P here.

Attach check or money order on top of any Forms W-2 or W-2P.

7 Wages, salaries, tips, etc. This should be shown in Box 10 of your W-2 form(s). (Attach Form(s) W-2.) | 7
8a **Taxable** interest income (see page 23). (If over $400, also complete and attach Schedule 1, Part I.) | 8a
b **Tax-exempt** interest. (DO NOT include on line 8a.) 8b
9 Dividends. (If over $400, also complete and attach Schedule 1, Part II.) | 9
10a Total IRA distributions. 10a | 10b Taxable amount (see page 24). | 10b
11a Total pensions and annuities. 11a | 11b Taxable amount (see page 25). | 11b
12 Unemployment compensation (insurance) from Form(s) 1099-G. | 12
13a Social security benefits. 13a | 13b Taxable amount (see page 28). | 13b
14 Add lines 7 through 13b (far right column). This is your **total income.** ▶ 14

**Step 5
Figure your
adjusted
gross
income**

15a Your IRA deduction from applicable worksheet. 15a
b Spouse's IRA deduction from applicable worksheet. 15b
Note: *Rules for IRAs begin on page 30.*
c Add lines 15a and 15b. These are your **total adjustments.** 15c
16 Subtract line 15c from line 14. This is your **adjusted gross income.** (If less than $20,264, see "Earned income credit" on page 38.) ▶ 16

1990   Form 1040A   Page 2

Step 6

17 Enter the amount from line 16.   17

18a Check ⎰ ☐ **You** were 65 or older ☐ Blind ⎱ **Enter number of**
     if: ⎱ ☐ **Spouse** was 65 or older ☐ Blind ⎰ **boxes checked** . ▶18a

b If your parent (or someone else) can claim you as a dependent,
     check here . . . . ▶18b ☐

Figure your
standard
deduction,

c If you are married filing separately and your spouse files Form
     1040 and itemizes deductions, see page 34 and check here . . . ▶18c ☐

19 Enter your standard deduction. See page 35 for the chart (or worksheet)
     that applies to you. Be sure to enter your standard deduction here.   19

exemption
amount, and

20 Subtract line 19 from line 17. (If line 19 is more than line 17, enter -0-.)   20

21 Multiply $2,050 by the total number of exemptions claimed on line 6e.   21

taxable
income

22 Subtract line 21 from line 20. (If line 21 is more than line 20, enter -0-.)
     This is your **taxable income.**   ▶ 22

Step 7

23 Find the tax on the amount on line 22. Check if from:
     ☐ Tax Table (pages 49–54) or ☐ Form 8615 (see page 36)   23

Figure your
tax,
credits,
and
payments

24a Credit for child and dependent care expenses.
      Complete and attach Schedule 2.   24a
b Credit for the elderly or the disabled.
      Complete and attach Schedule 3.   24b
c Add lines 24a and 24b. These are your **total credits.**   24c

If you want IRS
to figure your
tax, see the
instructions for
line 22 on page
36 .

25 Subtract line 24c from line 23. (If line 24c is more than line 23, enter -0-.) 25

26 Advance earned income credit payments from Form W-2.   26

27 Add lines 25 and 26. This is your **total tax.**   ▶ 27

28a Total Federal income tax withheld. (If any is
      from Form(s) 1099, check here ▶ ☐ .)   28a
b 1990 estimated tax payments and amount
      applied from 1989 return.   28b
c **Earned income credit.** See page 38 to find
      out if you can take this credit.   28c
d Add lines 28a, 28b, and 28c. These are your **total payments.** ▶ 28d

Step 8

29 If line 28d is more than line 27, subtract line 27 from line 28d.
     This is the amount you **overpaid.**   29

Figure your
refund
or amount
you owe

30 Amount of line 29 you want **refunded to you.**   30

31 Amount of line 29 you want **applied to your**
     1991 estimated tax.   31

Attach check or
money order on
top of Form(s)
W-2, etc. on
page 1.

32 If line 27 is more than line 28d, subtract line 28d from line 27. This is the
     amount you owe. Attach check or money order for full amount payable to
     "Internal Revenue Service." Write your name, address, social security
     number, daytime phone number, and "1990 Form 1040A" on it.   32

33 Estimated tax penalty (see page 42).   33

Step 9

Sign your
return

Under penalties of perjury, I declare that I have examined this return and accompanying schedules and statements, and to the best of my knowledge
and belief, they are true, correct, and complete. Declaration of preparer (other than the taxpayer) is based on all information of which the preparer has
any knowledge.

Keep a copy of
this return for
your records.

Your signature ▶	Date	Your occupation
Spouse's signature (if joint return, BOTH must sign)	Date	Spouse's occupation

Paid
preparer's
use only

Preparer's signature ▶	Date	Check if self-employed ☐	Preparer's social security no.
Firm's name (or yours if self-employed) and address ▶		E.I. No.	
		ZIP code	

Schedule 1
(Form 1040A)
(0)

Department of the Treasury—Internal Revenue Service
Interest and Dividend Income
for Form 1040A Filers   **1990**

OMB No. 1545-0085

Name(s) shown on Form 1040A

Your social security number

Part I

Interest Income
(See pages 23 and 44.)

Complete this part and attach Schedule 1 to Form 1040A if:
● You have over $400 in taxable interest, or
● You are claiming the exclusion of interest from series EE U.S. savings bonds issued after 1989.

If you are claiming the exclusion or you received, as a nominee, interest that actually belongs to another person, see page 45.

Note: *If you received a Form 1099-INT, Form 1099-OID, or substitute statement, from a brokerage firm, enter the firm's name and the total interest shown on that form.*

1 List name of payer		Amount	
	1		
2 Add the amounts on line 1.	2		
3 Enter the excludable savings bond interest, if any, from Form 8815, line 14. Attach Form 8815 to Form 1040A.	3		
4 Subtract line 3 from line 2. Enter the result here and on Form 1040A, line 8a.	4		

Part II

Dividend Income
(See pages 24 and 45.)

Complete this part and attach Schedule 1 to Form 1040A if you received over $400 in dividends.

If you received, as a nominee, dividends that actually belong to another person, see page 45.

Note: *If you received a Form 1099-DIV, or substitute statement, from a brokerage firm, enter the firm's name and the total dividends shown on that form.*

5 List name of payer		Amount	
	5		
6 Add amounts on line 5. Enter the total here and on Form 1040A, line 9.	6		

For Paperwork Reduction Act Notice, see the Form 1040A instructions.

Schedule 1 (Form 1040A) 1990

☆ U.S. GPO 1990—265-425

B-2   Form 1040EZ   Income Tax Return for Single Filers With No Dependents

Department of the Treasury - Internal Revenue Service

Form 1040EZ

Income Tax Return for Single Filers With No Dependents   **1990**

OMB No. 1545-0675

Name & address

Use IRS label (see page 9). If you don't have one, please print.

LABEL HERE

Print your name (first, initial, last)

Home address (number and street). (If you have a P.O. box, see page 9.)   Apt. no.

City, town or post office, state, and ZIP code. (If you have a foreign address, see page 9.)

Please print your numbers like this:

Your social security number

Please see instructions on the back. Also, see the Form 1040EZ booklet.

Presidential Election Campaign (see page 9)
Do you want $1 to go to this fund?

Note: Checking "Yes" will not change your tax or reduce your refund. ▶

Yes No   **Dollars**   **Cents**

Report your Income

1 Total wages, salaries, and tips. This should be shown in Box 10 of your W-2 form(s). (Attach your W-2 form(s).)   1

Attach Copy B of Form(s) W-2 here. Attach tax payment on top of Form(s) W-2.

2 Taxable interest income of $400 or less. If the total is more than $400, you cannot use Form 1040EZ.   2

3 Add line 1 and line 2. This is your **adjusted gross income.**   3

Note: You must check Yes or No.

4 Can your parents (or someone else) claim you on their return?
☐ **Yes.** Do worksheet on back; enter amount from line E here.
☐ **No.** Enter 5,300.00. This is the total of your standard deduction and personal exemption.   4

5 Subtract line 4 from line 3. If line 4 is larger than line 3, enter 0. This is your **taxable income.**   5

Figure your tax

6 Enter your Federal income tax withheld from Box 9 of your W-2 form(s).   6

7 **Tax.** Use the amount on **line 5** to find your tax in the tax table on pages 14–16 of the booklet. Enter the tax from the table on this line.   7

Refund or amount you owe

8 If line 6 is larger than line 7, subtract line 7 from line 6. This is your **refund.**   8

9 If line 7 is larger than line 6, subtract line 6 from line 7. This is the **amount you owe.** Attach your payment for full amount payable to "Internal Revenue Service." Write your name, address, social security number, daytime phone number, and "1990 Form 1040EZ" on it.   9

Sign your return

Keep a copy of this form for your records.

I have read this return. Under penalties of perjury, I declare that to the best of my knowledge and belief, the return is true, correct, and complete.

Your signature   Date

X

For IRS Use Only—Please do not write in boxes below.

For Privacy Act and Paperwork Reduction Act Notice, see page 4 in the booklet.   Form 1040EZ (1990)

1990   Instructions for Form 1040EZ

Use this form if
- Your filing status is single.
- You do not claim any dependents.
- You were under 65 and not blind at the end of 1990.
- Your taxable income (line 5) is less than $50,000.

- You had **only** wages, salaries, tips, and taxable scholarships or fellowships, and your taxable interest income was $400 or less. *Caution: If you earned tips (including allocated tips) that are not included in Box 13 of your W-2, you may not be able to use Form 1040EZ. See page 10 in the booklet.*

If you are not sure about your filing status, see page 5 in the booklet. If you have questions about dependents, see Tele-Tax *(topic no. 155)* on page 23 in the booklet.

If you can't use this form, see Tele-Tax *(topic no. 152)* on page 23 in the booklet.

Completing your return
Please print your numbers inside the boxes. Do not type your numbers. Do not use dollar signs.

Most people can fill out the form simply by following the instructions on the front. But you will have to use the booklet if you received a scholarship or fellowship or tax-exempt interest income (such as on municipal bonds). Also use the booklet if you received a 1099-INT showing income tax withheld (backup withholding) or if you had two or more employers and your total wages were more than $51,300.

Remember, you must report your wages, salaries, and tips even if you don't get a W-2 form from your employer. You must also report all your taxable interest income, including interest from savings accounts at banks, savings and loans, credit unions, etc., even if you don't get a Form 1099-INT.

If you paid someone to prepare your return, that person must also sign it and show other information. See page 13 in the booklet.

Standard deduction worksheet for dependents who checked "Yes" on line 4

If you checked "Yes" because someone can claim you as a dependent, fill in this worksheet to figure the amount to enter on line 4.

A. Enter the amount from line 1 on front. A._____

B. Minimum amount. B._____500.00

C. **Compare** the amounts on lines A and B above. Enter the LARGER of the two amounts here. C._____

D. Maximum amount. D._____3,250.00

E. **Compare** the amounts on lines C and D above. Enter the SMALLER of the two amounts here and on line 4 on front. E._____

If you checked "No" because no one can claim you as a dependent, enter 5,300.00 on line 4. This is the total of your standard deduction (3,250.00) and personal exemption (2,050.00).

Avoid common mistakes
This checklist is to help you make sure that your form is filled out correctly.

1. Are your name, address, and social security number on the label correct? If not, did you correct the label?
2. If you didn't get a label, did you enter your name, address (including ZIP code), and social security number in the spaces provided on page 1 of Form 1040EZ?
3. Did you check your computations (additions, subtractions, etc.) especially when figuring your refund or amount you owe?
4. If your parent (or someone else) can claim you as a dependent on his or her tax return, did you check the "Yes" box on line 4?
5. If you checked the "Yes" box on line 4, did you fill out the worksheet above to figure the amount to enter on line 4? If you checked the "No" box, did you enter 5,300.00 on line 4?
6. Did you use the amount from **line 5** to find your tax in the tax table? Did you enter the correct tax on line 7?
7. Did you attach your W-2 form(s) to the left margin of your return?
8. Did you sign and date Form 1040EZ?

Mailing your return
Mail your return by **April 15, 1991.** Use the envelope that came with your booklet. If you don't have that envelope, see page 17 in the booklet for the address to use.

B-3   Form 1040   U.S. Individual Income Tax Return and Schedules

Form **1040**   Department of the Treasury—Internal Revenue Service
U.S. Individual Income Tax Return 19**90**

For the year Jan.–Dec. 31, 1990, or other tax year beginning _____, 1990, ending _____, 19 ___   OMB No. 1545-0074

Label
(See Instructions on page 8.)

Use IRS label. Otherwise, please print or type.

L A B E L   H E R E

Your first name and initial _____ Last name _____   Your social security number _____

If a joint return, spouse's first name and initial _____ Last name _____   Spouse's social security number _____

Home address (number and street). (If you have a P.O. box, see page 9.)   Apt. no. ___

City, town or post office, state, and ZIP code. (If you have a foreign address, see page 9.)

For Privacy Act and Paperwork Reduction Act Notice, see Instructions.

Presidential Election Campaign (See page 9.)

Do you want $1 to go to this fund? . . . .   Yes ▨ No
If joint return, does your spouse want $1 to go to this fund? . .   Yes ▨ No

Note: Checking "Yes" will not change your tax or reduce your refund.

Filing Status

Check only one box.

1 ☐ Single. (See page 10 to find out if you can file as head of household.)
2 ☐ Married filing joint return (even if only one had income)
3 ☐ Married filing separate return. Enter spouse's social security no. above and full name here. ▶ _____
4 ☐ Head of household (with qualifying person). (See page 10.) If the qualifying person is your child but not your dependent, enter this child's name here. ▶ _____
5 ☐ Qualifying widow(er) with dependent child (year spouse died ▶ 19___). (See page 10.)

Exemptions

(See Instructions on page 10.)

If more than 6 dependents, see Instructions on page 11.

6a ☐ **Yourself** If your parent (or someone else) can claim you as a dependent on his or her tax return, do not check box 6a. But be sure to check the box on line 33b on page 2
b ☐ **Spouse**

c **Dependents:** (1) Name (first, initial, and last name)	(2) Check if under age 2	(3) If age 2 or older, dependent's social security number	(4) Dependent's relationship to you	(5) No. of months lived in your home in 1990
_____		:		
_____		:		
_____		:		
_____		:		
_____		:		
_____		:		

No. of boxes checked on 6a and 6b ___
No. of your children on 6c who:
• lived with you ___
• didn't live with you due to divorce or separation (see page 11) ___
No. of other dependents on 6c ___

d If your child didn't live with you but is claimed as your dependent under a pre-1985 agreement, check here ▶ ☐
e Total number of exemptions claimed . . . .

Add numbers entered on lines above ▶ ___

Income

Attach Copy B of your Forms W-2, W-2G, and W-2P here.

If you do not have a W-2, see page 8.

Attach check or money order on top of any Forms W-2, W-2G, or W-2P.

7	Wages, salaries, tips, etc. (attach Form(s) W-2)	7
8a	**Taxable** interest income (also attach Schedule B if over $400)	8a
b	**Tax-exempt** interest income (see page 13). DON'T include on line 8a 8b ___	▨
9	Dividend income (also attach Schedule B if over $400)	9
10	Taxable refunds of state and local income taxes, if any, from worksheet on page 14	10
11	Alimony received	11
12	Business income or (loss) (attach Schedule C)	12
13	Capital gain or (loss) (attach Schedule D)	13
14	Capital gain distributions not reported on line 13 (see page 14)	14
15	Other gains or (losses) (attach Form 4797)	15
16a	Total IRA distributions . 16a ___ 16b Taxable amount (see page 14)	16b
17a	Total pensions and annuities 17a ___ 17b Taxable amount (see page 14)	17b
18	Rents, royalties, partnerships, estates, trusts, etc. (attach Schedule E)	18
19	Farm income or (loss) (attach Schedule F)	19
20	Unemployment compensation (insurance) (see page 16)	20
21a	Social security benefits . 21a ___ 21b Taxable amount (see page 16)	21b
22	Other income (list type and amount—see page 16)	22
23	Add the amounts shown in the far right column for lines 7 through 22. This is your **total income** ▶	23

Adjustments to Income

(See Instructions on page 17.)

24a	Your IRA deduction, from applicable worksheet on page 17 or 18 . 24a ___	▨
b	Spouse's IRA deduction, from applicable worksheet on page 17 or 18 . 24b ___	▨
25	One-half of self-employment tax (see page 18) . . . . . 25 ___	▨
26	Self-employed health insurance deduction, from worksheet on page 18 26 ___	▨
27	Keogh retirement plan and self-employed SEP deduction . . 27 ___	▨
28	Penalty on early withdrawal of savings . . . . . 28 ___	▨
29	Alimony paid. Recipient's SSN ▶ _____ 29 ___	▨
30	Add lines 24a through 29. These are your **total adjustments** . . . . ▶	30

Adjusted Gross Income

31 Subtract line 30 from line 23. This is your **adjusted gross income**. If this amount is less than $20,264 and a child lived with you, see page 23 to find out if you can claim the "Earned Income Credit" on line 57 . . . . ▶   31

Form 1040 (1990)   Page **2**

	32 Amount from line 31 (adjusted gross income)	32

Tax Computation

If you want IRS to figure your tax, see Instructions on page 19.

33a Check if: ☐ **You** were 65 or older ☐ Blind; ☐ **Spouse** was 65 or older ☐ Blind.

Add the number of boxes checked above and enter the total here . . . . ▶ 33a

b If your parent (or someone else) can claim you as a dependent, check here . . . ▶ 33b ☐

c If you are married filing a separate return and your spouse itemizes deductions, or you are a dual-status alien, see page 19 and check here . . . . ▶ 33c ☐

34 Enter the larger of:
- Your **standard deduction** (from the chart (or worksheet) on page 20 that applies to you), **OR**
- Your **itemized deductions** (from Schedule A, line 27). If you itemize, attach Schedule A and check here. . . ▶ ☐

	34	
	35 Subtract line 34 from line 32	35
	36 Multiply $2,050 by the total number of exemptions claimed on line 6e	36
	37 **Taxable income.** Subtract line 36 from line 35. (If line 36 is more than line 35, enter -0-.) . . .	37
	38 Enter tax. Check if from: **a** ☐ Tax Table, **b** ☐ Tax Rate Schedules, or **c** ☐ Form 8615 (see page 21) (If any is from Form(s) 8814, enter that amount here ▶ **d** _____ .) . . .	38
	39 Additional taxes (see page 21). Check if from: **a** ☐ Form 4970 **b** ☐ Form 4972 . . .	39
	40 Add lines 38 and 39 . . . . ▶	40

Credits

(See Instructions on page 21.)

41	Credit for child and dependent care expenses (attach Form 2441)	41	
42	Credit for the elderly or the disabled (attach Schedule R) . . .	42	
43	Foreign tax credit (attach Form 1116)	43	
44	General business credit. Check if from: **a** ☐ Form 3800 or **b** ☐ Form (specify) _____ .	44	
45	Credit for prior year minimum tax (attach Form 8801)	45	

46 Add lines 41 through 45 . . . . ▶	46	
47 Subtract line 46 from line 40. (If line 46 is more than line 40, enter -0-.) . . . . . . ▶	47	

Other Taxes

48 Self-employment tax (attach Schedule SE)	48	
49 Alternative minimum tax (attach Form 6251)	49	
50 Recapture taxes (see page 22). Check if from: **a** ☐ Form 4255 **b** ☐ Form 8611 . . .	50	
51 Social security tax on tip income not reported to employer (attach Form 4137)	51	
52 Tax on an IRA or a qualified retirement plan (attach Form 5329)	52	
53 Advance earned income credit payments from Form W-2	53	
54 Add lines 47 through 53. This is your **total tax** . . . . ▶	54	

Payments

Attach Forms W-2, W-2G, and W-2P to front.

55	Federal income tax withheld (**If any is from Form(s) 1099, check ▶ ☐**)	55	
56	1990 estimated tax payments and amount applied from 1989 return	56	
57	**Earned income credit** (see page 23)	57	
58	Amount paid with Form 4868 (extension request)	58	
59	Excess social security tax and RRTA tax withheld (see page 24) .	59	
60	Credit for Federal tax on fuels (attach Form 4136)	60	
61	Regulated investment company credit (attach Form 2439) . . .	61	

62 Add lines 55 through 61. These are your **total payments** . . . . ▶	62	

Refund or Amount You Owe

63 If line 62 is more than line 54, enter amount **OVERPAID** . . . . ▶	63	
64 Amount of line 63 to be **REFUNDED TO YOU** . . . . ▶	64	
65 Amount of line 63 to be **APPLIED TO YOUR 1991 ESTIMATED TAX** ▶	65	
66 If line 54 is more than line 62, enter **AMOUNT YOU OWE.** Attach check or money order for full amount payable to "Internal Revenue Service." Write your name, address, social security number, daytime phone number, and "1990 Form 1040" on it . . . . ▶	66	
67 Estimated tax penalty (see page 25) . . . . ▶	67	

Sign Here

Keep a copy of this return for your records.

Under penalties of perjury, I declare that I have examined this return and accompanying schedules and statements, and to the best of my knowledge and belief, they are true, correct, and complete. Declaration of preparer (other than taxpayer) is based on all information of which preparer has any knowledge.

Your signature	Date	Your occupation
Spouse's signature (if joint return, BOTH must sign)	Date	Spouse's occupation

Paid Preparer's Use Only

Preparer's signature	Date	Check if self-employed ☐	Preparer's social security no.
Firm's name (or yours if self-employed) and address		E.I. No.	
		ZIP code	

SCHEDULES A&B
(Form 1040)

Department of the Treasury
Internal Revenue Service

Schedule A—Itemized Deductions

(Schedule B is on back)

▶ Attach to Form 1040. ▶ See Instructions for Schedules A and B (Form 1040).

OMB No. 1545-0074

1990

Attachment
Sequence No. **07**

Name(s) shown on Form 1040

Your social security number

Medical and Dental Expenses	**Caution:** *Do not include expenses reimbursed or paid by others.*		
	1 Medical and dental expenses. (See page 27 of the Instructions.)	1	
	2 Enter amount from Form 1040, line 32 . **2**		
	3 Multiply the amount on line 2 by 7.5% (.075). Enter the result .	3	
	4 Subtract line 3 from line 1. Enter the result. If less than zero, enter -0- . . . ▶	4	
Taxes You Paid (See Instructions on page 27.)	5 State and local income taxes	5	
	6 Real estate taxes	6	
	7 Other taxes. (List—include personal property taxes.) ▶	7	
	8 Add the amounts on lines 5 through 7. Enter the total . . . . . . ▶	8	
Interest You Paid (See Instructions on page 27.)	9a Deductible home mortgage interest paid to financial institutions and reported to you on Form 1098. Report deductible points on line 10 .	9a	
	b Other deductible home mortgage interest. (If paid to an individual, show that person's name and address.) ▶		
		9b	
	10 Deductible points. (See Instructions for special rules.) . . .	10	
	11 Deductible investment interest (attach Form 4952 if required). (See page 28.)	11	
	12a Personal interest you paid. (See page 28.) **12a**		
	b Multiply the amount on line 12a by 10% (.10). Enter the result .	12b	
	13 Add the amounts on lines 9a through 11, and 12b. Enter the total . . . . ▶	13	
Gifts to Charity (See Instructions on page 29.)	**Caution:** *If you made a charitable contribution and received a benefit in return, see page 29 of the Instructions.*		
	14 Contributions by cash or check	14	
	15 Other than cash or check. (You **MUST** attach Form 8283 if over $500.)	15	
	16 Carryover from prior year	16	
	17 Add the amounts on lines 14 through 16. Enter the total . . . . . ▶	17	
Casualty and Theft Losses	18 Casualty or theft loss(es) (attach Form 4684). (See page 29 of the Instructions.) . ▶	18	
Moving Expenses	19 Moving expenses (attach Form 3903 or 3903F). (See page 30 of the Instructions.). ▶	19	
Job Expenses and Most Other Miscellaneous Deductions (See Instructions on page 30 for expenses to deduct here.)	20 Unreimbursed employee expenses—job travel, union dues, job education, etc. (You **MUST** attach Form 2106 if required. See Instructions.) ▶	20	
	21 Other expenses (investment, tax preparation, safe deposit box, etc.). List type and amount ▶	21	
	22 Add the amounts on lines 20 and 21. Enter the total	22	
	23 Enter amount from Form 1040, line 32. **23**		
	24 Multiply the amount on line 23 by 2% (.02). Enter the result .	24	
	25 Subtract line 24 from line 22. Enter the result. If less than zero, enter -0- . . . ▶	25	
Other Miscellaneous Deductions	26 Other (from list on page 30 of Instructions). List type and amount ▶		
		26	
Total Itemized Deductions	27 Add the amounts on lines 4, 8, 13, 17, 18, 19, 25, and 26. Enter the total here. Then enter on Form 1040, line 34, the **LARGER** of this total or your standard deduction from page 20 of the Instructions . . . . ▶	27	

For Paperwork Reduction Act Notice, see Form 1040 Instructions.

Schedule A (Form 1040) 1990

Schedules A&B (Form 1040) 1990

Name(s) shown on Form 1040. (Do not enter name and social security number if shown on other side.)

OMB No. 1545-0074   Page **2**

Your social security number

Schedule B—Interest and Dividend Income

Attachment Sequence No. **08**

Part I Interest Income	If you received more than $400 in taxable interest income, or you are claiming the exclusion of interest from series EE U.S. savings bonds issued after 1989 (see page 31), you must complete Part I. List ALL interest received in Part I. If you received more than $400 in taxable interest income, you must also complete Part III. If you received, as a nominee, interest that actually belongs to another person, or you received or paid accrued interest on securities transferred between interest payment dates, see page 31.

(See Instructions on pages 13 and 30.)

Interest Income	Amount
1 Interest income. (List name of payer—if any interest income is from seller-financed mortgages, see Instructions and list that interest first.) ▶	

Note: If you received a Form 1099-INT, Form 1099-OID, or substitute statement, from a brokerage firm, list the firm's name as the payer and enter the total interest shown on that form.

1	
2 Add the amounts on line 1. Enter the total	**2**
3 Enter the excludable savings bond interest, if any, from Form 8815, line 14. Attach Form 8815 to Form 1040	**3**
4 Subtract line 3 from line 2. Enter the result here and on Form 1040, line 8a . ▶	**4**

Part II Dividend Income	If you received more than $400 in gross dividends and/or other distributions on stock, you must complete Parts II and III. If you received, as a nominee, dividends that actually belong to another person, see page 31.

(See Instructions on pages 13 and 31.)

Dividend Income	Amount
5 Dividend income. (List name of payer—include on this line capital gain distributions, nontaxable distributions, etc.) ▶	

Note: If you received a Form 1099-DIV, or substitute statement, from a brokerage firm, list the firm's name as the payer and enter the total dividends shown on that form.

5	
6 Add the amounts on line 5. Enter the total	**6**
7 Capital gain distributions. Enter here and on Schedule D* .	**7**
8 Nontaxable distributions. (See the Inst. for Form 1040, line 9.) .	**8**
9 Add the amounts on lines 7 and 8. Enter the total . . . . . . ▶	**9**
10 Subtract line 9 from line 6. Enter the result here and on Form 1040, line 9 . . ▶	**10**

If you received capital gain distributions but do not need Schedule D to report any other gains or losses, see the Instructions for Form 1040, lines 13 and 14.

Part III Foreign Accounts and Foreign Trusts	If you received more than $400 of interest or dividends, OR if you had a foreign account or were a grantor of, or a transferor to, a foreign trust, you must answer both questions in Part III.	Yes	No

(See Instructions on page 31.)

		Yes	No
11a	At any time during 1990, did you have an interest in or a signature or other authority over a financial account in a foreign country (such as a bank account, securities account, or other financial account)? (See page 31 of the Instructions for exceptions and filing requirements for Form TD F 90-22.1.)		
b	If "Yes," enter the name of the foreign country ▶		
12	Were you the grantor of, or transferor to, a foreign trust that existed during 1990, whether or not you have any beneficial interest in it? If "Yes," you may have to file Form 3520, 3520-A, or 926		

For Paperwork Reduction Act Notice, see Form 1040 Instructions.

Schedule B (Form 1040) 1990

SCHEDULE C (Form 1040)
Department of the Treasury
Internal Revenue Service

Profit or Loss From Business
(Sole Proprietorship)

Partnerships, Joint Ventures, Etc., Must File Form 1065.

▶ Attach to Form 1040 or Form 1041. ▶ See Instructions for Schedule C (Form 1040).

OMB No. 1545-0074
19**90**
Attachment Sequence No. 09

Name of proprietor

Social security number (SSN)

A Principal business or profession, including product or service (see Instructions)

B Enter principal business code (from page 2) ▶

C Business name and address ▶ (include suite or room no.)

D Employer ID number (Not SSN)

E Accounting method: (1) ☐ Cash (2) ☐ Accrual (3) ☐ Other (specify) ▶

F Method(s) used to value closing inventory: (1) ☐ Cost (2) ☐ Lower of cost or market (3) ☐ Other (attach explanation) (4) ☐ Does not apply (if checked, go to line H)

	Yes	No
G Was there any change in determining quantities, costs, or valuations between opening and closing inventory? (If "Yes," attach explanation.)		
H Are you deducting expenses for business use of your home? (If "Yes," see Instructions for limitations.)		
I Did you "materially participate" in the operation of this business during 1990? (If "No," see Instructions for limitations on losses.)		

J If this is the first Schedule C filed for this business, check here ▶ ☐

Part I Income

1 Gross receipts or sales. *Caution: If this income was reported to you on Form W-2 and the "Statutory employee" box on that form was checked, see the Instructions and check here* ▶ ☐	**1**	
2 Returns and allowances	**2**	
3 Subtract line 2 from line 1. Enter the result here	**3**	
4 Cost of goods sold (from line 38 on page 2)	**4**	
5 Subtract line 4 from line 3 and enter the **gross profit** here	**5**	
6 Other income, including Federal and state gasoline or fuel tax credit or refund (see Instructions)	**6**	
7 Add lines 5 and 6. This is your **gross income** ▶	**7**	

Part II Expenses

8 Advertising	**8**		**21** Repairs and maintenance	**21**	
9 Bad debts from sales or services (see Instructions)	**9**		**22** Supplies (not included in Part III)	**22**	
10 Car and truck expenses (attach **Form 4562**)	**10**		**23** Taxes and licenses	**23**	
11 Commissions and fees	**11**		**24** Travel, meals, and entertainment:		
12 Depletion	**12**		**a** Travel	**24a**	
13 Depreciation and section 179 expense deduction (not included in Part III) (see Instructions)	**13**		**b** Meals and entertainment		
14 Employee benefit programs (other than on line 19)	**14**		**c** Enter 20% of line 24b subject to limitations (see Instructions)		
15 Insurance (other than health)	**15**		**d** Subtract line 24c from line 24b	**24d**	
16 Interest:			**25** Utilities	**25**	
a Mortgage (paid to banks, etc.)	**16a**		**26** Wages (less jobs credit)	**26**	
b Other	**16b**		**27a** Other expenses (**list type and amount**):		
17 Legal and professional services	**17**				
18 Office expense	**18**				
19 Pension and profit-sharing plans	**19**				
20 Rent or lease (see Instructions):					
a Vehicles, machinery, and equip.	**20a**				
b Other business property	**20b**		**27b** Total other expenses	**27b**	

28 Add amounts in columns for lines 8 through 27b. These are your **total expenses** ▶	**28**	
29 Net profit or (loss). Subtract line 28 from line 7. If a profit, enter here and on Form 1040, line 12. Also enter the net profit on Schedule SE, line 2 (statutory employees, see Instructions). If a loss, you MUST go on to line 30 (fiduciaries, see Instructions)	**29**	

30 If you have a loss, you MUST check the box that describes your investment in this activity (see Instructions).
30a ☐ All investment is at risk.
30b ☐ Some investment is not at risk.

If you checked 30a, enter the loss on Form 1040, line 12, and Schedule SE, line 2 (statutory employees, see Instructions). If you checked 30b, you MUST attach **Form 6198.**

For Paperwork Reduction Act Notice, see Form 1040 Instructions.

Schedule C (Form 1040) 1990

Schedule C (Form 1040) 1990   Page **2**

Part III Cost of Goods Sold (See Instructions.)

31	Inventory at beginning of year. (If different from last year's closing inventory, attach explanation.)	31
32	Purchases less cost of items withdrawn for personal use	32
33	Cost of labor. (Do not include salary paid to yourself.)	33
34	Materials and supplies	34
35	Other costs	35
36	Add lines 31 through 35	36
37	Inventory at end of year	37
38	**Cost of goods sold.** Subtract line 37 from line 36. Enter the result here and on page 1, line 4	38

Part IV Principal Business or Professional Activity Codes

Locate the major category that best describes your activity. Within the major category, select the activity code that most closely identifies the business or profession that is the principal source of your sales or receipts. **Enter this 4-digit code on page 1, line B.** *For example, a grocery store is under the major category of "Retail Trade," and the code is "3210." (Note: If your principal source of income is from farming activities, you should file Schedule F (Form 1040), Farm Income and Expenses.)*

Construction

Code
0018 Operative builders (for own account)

General contractors
0034 Residential building
0059 Nonresidential building
0075 Highway and street construction
3889 Other heavy construction (pipe laying, bridge construction, etc.)

Building trade contractors, including repairs
0232 Plumbing, heating, air conditioning
0257 Painting and paper hanging
0273 Electrical work
0299 Masonry, dry wall, stone, tile
0414 Carpentering and flooring
0430 Roofing, siding, and sheet metal
0455 Concrete work
0885 Other building trade contractors (excavation, glazing, etc.)

Manufacturing, Including Printing and Publishing
0638 Food products and beverages
0653 Textile mill products
0679 Apparel and other textile products
0695 Leather, footware, handbags, etc.
0810 Furniture and fixtures
0836 Lumber and other wood products
0851 Printing and publishing
0877 Paper and allied products
1032 Stone, clay, and glass products
1057 Primary metal industries
1073 Fabricated metal products
1099 Machinery and machine shops
1115 Electric and electronic equipment
1883 Other manufacturing industries

Mining and Mineral Extraction
1511 Metal mining
1537 Coal mining
1552 Oil and gas
1719 Quarrying and nonmetallic mining

Agricultural Services, Forestry, Fishing
1933 Crop services
1958 Veterinary services, including pets
1974 Livestock breeding
1990 Other animal services
2113 Farm labor and management services
2212 Horticulture and landscaping
2238 Forestry, except logging
0836 Logging
2246 Commercial fishing
2469 Hunting and trapping

Wholesale Trade—Selling Goods to Other Businesses, Etc.

Durable goods, including machinery, equipment, wood, metals, etc.
2618 Selling for your own account
2634 Agent or broker for other firms— more than 50% of gross sales on commission

Nondurable goods, including food, fiber, chemicals, etc.
2659 Selling for your own account

2675 Agent or broker for other firms— more than 50% of gross sales on commission

Retail Trade—Selling Goods to Individuals and Households
3012 Selling door-to-door, by telephone or party plan, or from mobile unit
3038 Catalog or mail order
3053 Vending machine selling

Selling From Showroom, Store, or Other Fixed Location

Food, beverages, and drugs
3079 Eating places (meals or snacks)
3086 Catering services
3095 Drinking places (alcoholic beverages)
3210 Grocery stores (general line)
0612 Bakeries selling at retail
3236 Other food stores (meat, produce, candy, etc.)
3251 Liquor stores
3277 Drug stores

Automotive and service stations
3319 New car dealers (franchised)
3335 Used car dealers
3517 Other automotive dealers (motorcycles, recreational vehicles, etc.)
3533 Tires, accessories, and parts
3558 Gasoline service stations

General merchandise, apparel, and furniture
3715 Variety stores
3731 Other general merchandise stores
3756 Shoe stores
3772 Men's and boys' clothing stores
3913 Women's ready-to-wear stores
3921 Women's accessory and specialty stores and furriers
3939 Family clothing stores
3954 Other apparel and accessory stores
3970 Furniture stores
3996 TV, audio, and electronics
3988 Computer and software stores
4119 Household appliance stores
4317 Other home furnishing stores (china, floor coverings, etc.)
4333 Music and record stores

Building, hardware, and garden supply
4416 Building materials dealers
4432 Paint, glass, and wallpaper stores
4457 Hardware stores
4473 Nurseries and garden supply stores

Other retail stores
4614 Used merchandise and antique stores (except motor vehicle parts)
4630 Gift, novelty, and souvenir shops
4655 Florists
4671 Jewelry stores
4697 Sporting goods and bicycle shops
4812 Boat dealers
4838 Hobby, toy, and game shops
4853 Camera and photo supply stores
4879 Optical goods stores
4895 Luggage and leather goods stores
5017 Book stores, excluding newsstands
5033 Stationery stores
5058 Fabric and needlework stores
5074 Mobile home dealers
5090 Fuel dealers (except gasoline)
5884 Other retail stores

Finance, Insurance, Real Estate, and Related Services
5520 Real estate agents or brokers
5579 Real estate property managers
5710 Subdividers and developers, except cemeteries
5538 Operators and lessors of buildings, including residential
5553 Operators and lessors of other real property
5702 Insurance agents or brokers
5744 Other insurance services
6064 Security brokers and dealers
6080 Commodity contracts brokers and dealers, and security and commodity exchanges
6130 Investment advisors and services
6148 Credit institutions and mortgage bankers
6155 Title abstract offices
5777 Other finance and real estate

Transportation, Communications, Public Utilities, and Related Services
6114 Taxicabs
6312 Bus and limousine transportation
6361 Other highway passenger transportation
6338 Trucking (except trash collection)
6395 Courier or package delivery services
6510 Trash collection without own dump
6536 Public warehousing
6551 Water transportation
6619 Air transportation
6635 Travel agents and tour operators
6650 Other transportation services
6676 Communication services
6692 Utilities, including dumps, snowplowing, road cleaning, etc.

Services (Personal, Professional, and Business Services)

Hotels and other lodging places
7096 Hotels, motels, and tourist homes
7211 Rooming and boarding houses
7237 Camps and camping parks

Laundry and cleaning services
7419 Coin-operated laundries and dry cleaning
7435 Other laundry, dry cleaning, and garment services
7450 Carpet and upholstery cleaning
7476 Janitorial and related services (building, house, and window cleaning)

Business and/or personal services
7617 Legal services (or lawyer)
7633 Income tax preparation
7658 Accounting and bookkeeping
7518 Engineering services
7682 Architectural services
7708 Surveying services
7245 Management services
7260 Public relations
7286 Consulting services
7716 Advertising, except direct mail
7732 Employment agencies and personnel supply
7799 Consumer credit reporting and collection services

7856 Mailing, reproduction, commercial art and photography, and stenographic services
7872 Computer programming, processing, data preparation, and related services
7922 Computer repair, maintenance, and leasing
7773 Equipment rental and leasing (except computer or automotive)
7914 Investigative and protective services
7880 Other business services

Personal services
8110 Beauty shops (or beautician)
8318 Barber shop (or barber)
8334 Photographic portrait studios
8532 Funeral services and crematories
8714 Child day care
8730 Teaching or tutoring
8755 Counseling (except health practitioners)
8771 Ministers and chaplains
6882 Other personal services

Automotive services
8813 Automotive rental or leasing, without driver
8839 Parking, except valet
8953 Automotive repairs, general and specialized
8896 Other automotive services (wash, towing, etc.)

Miscellaneous repair, except computers
9019 TV and audio equipment repair
9035 Other electrical equipment repair
9050 Reupholstery and furniture repair
2881 Other equipment repair

Medical and health services
9217 Offices and clinics of medical doctors (MDs)
9233 Offices and clinics of dentists
9258 Osteopathic physicians and surgeons
9241 Podiatrists
9274 Chiropractors
9290 Optometrists
9415 Registered and practical nurses
9431 Other health practitioners
9456 Medical and dental laboratories
9472 Nursing and personal care facilities
9886 Other health services

Amusement and recreational services
8557 Physical fitness facilities
9597 Motion picture and video production
9688 Motion picture and tape distribution and allied services
9613 Videotape rental
9639 Motion picture theaters
9670 Bowling centers
9696 Professional sports and racing, including promoters and managers
9811 Theatrical performers, musicians, agents, producers, and related services
9837 Other amusement and recreational services

8888 Unable to classify

SCHEDULE D

(Form 1040)

Department of the Treasury
Internal Revenue Service

Capital Gains and Losses

(And Reconciliation of Forms 1099-B for Bartering Transactions)

▶ Attach to Form 1040.   ▶ See Instructions for Schedule D (Form 1040).

▶ For more space to list transactions for lines 2a and 9a, get Schedule D-1 (Form 1040).

OMB No. 1545-0074

19 90

Attachment
Sequence No. **12A**

Name(s) shown on Form 1040

Your social security number

1   Enter the total sales of stocks, bonds, other securities, and real estate transactions reported to you for 1990 on Forms 1099-B and 1099-S (or on substitute statements). If this total is not the same as the total of lines 2c and 9c, column (d), attach a statement explaining the difference. (Do not include on this line amounts from Form 1099-S if you reported them on another form or schedule.) **See Instructions for line 1** **1**

Part I   Short-Term Capital Gains and Losses—Assets Held One Year or Less

(a) Description of property (Example, 100 shares 7% preferred of "Z" Co.)	(b) Date acquired (Mo., day, yr.)	(c) Date sold (Mo., day, yr.)	(d) Sales price (see Instructions)	(e) Cost or other basis (see Instructions)	(f) LOSS If (e) is more than (d), subtract (d) from (e)	(g) GAIN If (d) is more than (e), subtract (e) from (d)
2a Stocks, Bonds, Other Securities, and Real Estate. Include Form 1099-B and 1099-S Transactions. See Instructions.						
2b Amounts from Schedule D-1, line 2b (attach Schedule D-1) .						
2c Total of All Sales Price Amounts. Add column (d) of lines 2a and 2b . . . . ▶ **2c**						

2d Other Transactions (Do NOT include real estate transactions from Forms 1099-S. Report them on line 2a.)

3 Short-term gain from sale or exchange of your home from Form 2119, line 10 or 14c .	**3**		
4 Short-term gain from installment sales from Form 6252, line 22 or 30	**4**		
5 Net short-term gain or (loss) from partnerships, S corporations, and fiduciaries . .	**5**		
6 Short-term capital loss carryover from 1989 Schedule D, line 29	**6**		
7 Add lines 2a, 2b, 2d, and 3 through 6, in columns (f) and (g)	**7** (	)	
8 **Net short-term gain or (loss).** Combine columns (f) and (g) of line 7		**8**	

Part II   Long-Term Capital Gains and Losses—Assets Held More Than One Year

9a Stocks, Bonds, Other Securities, and Real Estate. Include Form 1099-B and 1099-S Transactions. See Instructions.

9b Amounts from Schedule D-1, line 9b (attach Schedule D-1) .						
9c Total of All Sales Price Amounts. Add column (d) of lines 9a and 9b . . ▶ **9c**						

9d Other Transactions (Do NOT include real estate transactions from Forms 1099-S. Report them on line 9a.)

10 Long-term gain from sale or exchange of your home from Form 2119, line 10 or 14c .	**10**		
11 Long-term gain from installment sales from Form 6252, line 22 or 30	**11**		
12 Net long-term gain or (loss) from partnerships, S corporations, and fiduciaries . .	**12**		
13 Capital gain distributions	**13**		
14 Gain from Form 4797, line 7 or 9	**14**		
15 Long-term capital loss carryover from 1989 Schedule D, line 36	**15**		
16 Add lines 9a, 9b, 9d, and 10 through 15, in columns (f) and (g)	**16** (	)	
17 **Net long-term gain or (loss).** Combine columns (f) and (g) of line 16		**17**	

For Paperwork Reduction Act Notice, see Form 1040 Instructions.   Schedule D (Form 1040) 1990

Schedule D (Form 1040) 1990   Attachment Sequence No. **12A**   Page **2**

Name(s) shown on Form 1040. (Do not enter name and social security number if shown on other side.)   Your social security number

Part III — Summary of Parts I and II

18 Combine lines 8 and 17, and enter the net gain or (loss) here. If the result is a gain, **stop here** and also enter the gain on Form 1040, line 13 . . . . **18**

19 If line 18 is a (loss), enter here and as a (loss) on Form 1040, line 13, the **smaller** of:
a The (loss) on line 18; **or**
b ($3,000) or, if married filing a separate return, ($1,500) . . . . **19** (   )
  Note: *When figuring whether line 19a or 19b is* **smaller**, *treat both numbers as if they were positive.*
  Go on to Part IV if the loss on line 18 is more than $3,000 ($1,500, if married filing a separate return), OR if taxable income on Form 1040, line 37, is zero.

Part IV — Capital Loss Carryovers from 1990 to 1991

Section A.—Carryover Limit

20 Enter taxable income from Form 1040, line 37. **(If Form 1040, line 37 is zero, see Instructions for amount to enter.)** **20**
  Note: *For lines 21 through 36, enter all amounts as positive numbers.*
21 Enter the loss on line 19 . . . . **21**
22 Enter the amount on Form 1040, line 36 . . . . **22**
23 Combine lines 20, 21, and 22. If zero or less, enter -0- **23**
24 **Carryover Limit.** Enter the **smaller** of line 21 or line 23 . . . . **24**

Section B.—Short-Term Capital Loss Carryover to 1991
(Complete this section only if there is a loss on both line 8 and line 19. Otherwise, go on to Section C.)

25 Enter the loss on line 8 . . . . **25**
26 Enter the gain, if any, on line 17 . . . . **26**
27 Enter the amount on line 24 . . . . **27**
28 Add lines 26 and 27. . . . . **28**

29 **Short-term capital loss carryover to 1991.** Subtract line 28 from line 25. If zero or less, enter -0- . . **29**

Section C.—Long-Term Capital Loss Carryover to 1991
(Complete this section only if there is a loss on both line 17 and line 19.)

30 Enter the loss on line 17 . . . . **30**
31 Enter the gain, if any, on line 8 . . . . **31**
32 Enter the amount on line 24 . . . . **32**
33 Enter the amount, if any, on line 25. . . . . **33**
34 Subtract line 33 from line 32. If zero or less, enter -0- **34**
35 Add lines 31 and 34. . . . . **35**

36 **Long-term capital loss carryover to 1991.** Subtract line 35 from line 30. If zero or less, enter -0- . **36**

Part V — Election Not to Use the Installment Method (Complete this part only if you elect out of the installment method and report a note or other obligation at less than full face value.)

37 Check here if you elect out of the installment method . . . . ▶ ☐
38 Enter the face amount of the note or other obligation . . . . ▶ ....
39 Enter the percentage of valuation of the note or other obligation . . . . ▶

Part VI — Reconciliation of Forms 1099-B for Bartering Transactions
(Complete this part if you received one or more Forms 1099-B or substitute statements reporting bartering income.)

Amount of bartering income from Form 1099-B or substitute statement reported on form or schedule

40 Form 1040, line 22 . . . . **40**
41 Schedule C (Form 1040) **41**
42 Schedule D (Form 1040) **42**
43 Schedule E (Form 1040) **43**
44 Schedule F (Form 1040) **44**
45 Other form or schedule (identify) (if nontaxable, indicate reason—attach additional sheets if necessary):
  ....
  ....
  .... **45**

46 Total (add lines 40 through 45) **46**
  Note: *The amount on line 46 should be the same as the total bartering income on all Forms 1099-B and substitute statements received for bartering transactions.*

SCHEDULE E
(Form 1040)

Department of the Treasury
Internal Revenue Service

Supplemental Income and Loss

(From rents, royalties, partnerships, estates, trusts, REMICs, etc.)
▶ Attach to Form 1040 or Form 1041.
▶ See Instructions for Schedule E (Form 1040).

OMB No. 1545-0074

19**90**

Attachment
Sequence No. **13**

Name(s) shown on return

Your social security number

Part I **Income or Loss From Rentals and Royalties** Note: *Report farm rental income or loss from* **Form 4835** *on page 2, line 39.*

1 Show the kind and location of each **rental property**:

A ....

B ....

C ....

		Yes	No
2 For each rental property listed on line 1, did you or your family use it for personal purposes for more than the greater of 14 days or 10% of the total days rented at fair rental value during the tax year? (See Instructions.)	A		
	B		
	C		

Rental and Royalty Income:		Properties			D Totals
		A	B	C	(Add columns A, B, and C)
3 Rents received	3				3
4 Royalties received	4				4
Rental and Royalty Expenses:					
5 Advertising	5				
6 Auto and travel	6				
7 Cleaning and maintenance . . .	7				
8 Commissions	8				
9 Insurance	9				
10 Legal and other professional fees .	10				
11 Mortgage interest paid to banks, etc. (see Instructions)	11				11
12 Other interest	12				
13 Repairs	13				
14 Supplies	14				
15 Taxes	15				
16 Utilities	16				
17 Wages and salaries	17				
18 Other (list) ▶	18				
19 Add lines 5 through 18	19				19
20 Depreciation expense or depletion (see Instructions)	20				20
21 Total expenses. Add lines 19 and 20	21				
22 Income or (loss) from rental or royalty properties. Subtract line 21 from line 3 (rents) or line 4 (royalties). If the result is a (loss), see Instructions to find out if you must file **Form 6198**	22				
23 Deductible rental loss. **Caution:** *Your rental loss on line 22 may be limited. See Instructions to find out if you must file Form 8582*	23	(	)(	)(	)
24 **Income.** Add rental and royalty income from line 22. Enter the total income here				24	
25 **Losses.** Add royalty losses from line 22 and rental losses from line 23. Enter the total losses here . . .				25	( )
26 Total rental and royalty income or (loss). Combine amounts on lines 24 and 25. Enter the result here. If Parts II, III, IV, and line 39 on page 2 do not apply to you, enter the amount from line 26 on Form 1040, line 18. Otherwise, include the amount from line 26 in the total on line 40 on page 2.				26	

For Paperwork Reduction Act Notice, see Form 1040 Instructions.   Schedule E (Form 1040) 1990

Schedule E (Form 1040) 1990   Attachment Sequence No. **13**   Page **2**

Name(s) shown on return. (Do not enter name and social security number if shown on other side.)   Your social security number

Note: *If you report amounts from farming or fishing on Schedule E, you must include your gross income from those activities on line 41 below.*

Part II   Income or Loss From Partnerships and S Corporations

If you report a loss from an at-risk activity, you MUST check either column **(e)** or **(f)** of line 27 to describe your investment in the activity. See Instructions. If you check column **(f)**, you must attach **Form 6198**.

27	(a) Name	(b) Enter P for partnership; S for S corporation	(c) Check if foreign partnership	(d) Employer identification number	(e) All is at risk	(f) Some is not at risk
A						
B						
C						
D						
E						

	Passive Income and Loss		Nonpassive Income and Loss		
	(g) Passive loss allowed (Attach Form 8582 if required)	(h) Passive income from Schedule K-1	(i) Nonpassive loss from Schedule K-1	(j) Section 179 expense deduction from Form 4562	(k) Nonpassive income from Schedule K-1
A					
B					
C					
D					
E					
28a Totals					
b Totals					

29 Add amounts in columns (h) and (k) of line 28a. Enter the total income here . . . . | **29** |

30 Add amounts in columns (g), (i), and (j) of line 28b. Enter the total here . . . . | **30** ( )

31 Total partnership and S corporation income or (loss). Combine amounts on lines 29 and 30. Enter the result here and include in the total on line 40 below . . . . | **31**

Part III   Income or Loss From Estates and Trusts

32	(a) Name	(b) Employer identification number
A		
B		
C		

	Passive Income and Loss		Nonpassive Income and Loss	
	(c) Passive deduction or loss allowed (Attach Form 8582 if required)	(d) Passive income from Schedule K-1	(e) Deduction or loss from Schedule K-1	(f) Other income from Schedule K-1
A				
B				
C				
33a Totals				
b Totals				

34 Add amounts in columns (d) and (f) of line 33a. Enter the total income here . . . . | **34** |

35 Add amounts in columns (c) and (e) of line 33b. Enter the total here . . . . | **35** ( )

36 Total estate and trust income or (loss). Combine amounts on lines 34 and 35. Enter the result here and include in the total on line 40 below . . . . | **36**

Part IV   Income or Loss From Real Estate Mortgage Investment Conduits (REMICs)—Residual Holder

37	(a) Name	(b) Employer identification number	(c) Excess inclusion from Schedules Q, line 2c (see Instructions)	(d) Taxable income (net loss) from Schedules Q, line 1b	(e) Income from Schedules Q, line 3b

38 Combine amounts in columns (d) and (e) only. Enter the result here and include in the total on line 40 below. . . . . | **38** |

Part V   Summary

39 Net farm rental income or (loss) from **Form 4835**. (Also complete line 41 below.) . . . . | **39** |

40 TOTAL income or (loss). Combine amounts on lines 26, 31, 36, 38, and 39. Enter the result here and on Form 1040, line 18 . . . . ▶ | **40** |

41 **Reconciliation of Farming and Fishing Income:** Enter your **gross** farming and fishing income reported in Parts II and III, and on line 39 (see Instructions) . . . . | **41** | |

SCHEDULE F
(Form 1040)

Department of the Treasury
Internal Revenue Service

Farm Income and Expenses

▶ Attach to Form 1040, Form 1041, or Form 1065.

▶ See Instructions for Schedule F (Form 1040).

OMB No. 1545-0074

1990

Attachment
Sequence No. **14**

Name of proprietor

Social security number (SSN)

A Principal product. (Describe in one or two words your principal crop or activity for the current tax year.)

B Enter principal agricultural activity code (from page 2) ▶

C Accounting method: ☐ Cash   ☐ Accrual

D Employer ID number (Not SSN)

E Did you make an election in a prior year to include Commodity Credit Corporation loan proceeds as income in that year? . ☐ Yes ☐ No

F Did you "materially participate" in the operation of this business during 1990? (If "No," see Instructions for limitations on losses.) ☐ Yes ☐ No

G Do you elect, or did you previously elect, to currently deduct certain preproductive period expenses? (See Instructions.) ☐ Does not apply ☐ Yes ☐ No

Part I Farm Income—Cash Method—Complete Parts I and II (Accrual method taxpayers complete Parts II and III, and line 11 of Part I.)

Do not include sales of livestock held for draft, breeding, sport, or dairy purposes; report these sales on Form 4797.

1 Sales of livestock and other items you bought for resale	1
2 Cost or other basis of livestock and other items you bought for resale .	2
3 Subtract line 2 from line 1	3
4 Sales of livestock, produce, grains, and other products you raised	4
5a Total cooperative distributions (Form(s) 1099-PATR)	5a	5b Taxable amount	5b
6a Agricultural program payments (see Instructions)	6a	6b Taxable amount	6b
7 Commodity Credit Corporation (CCC) loans:		
a CCC loans reported under election (see Instructions)	7a
b CCC loans forfeited or repaid with certificates .	7b	7c Taxable amount	7c
8 Crop insurance proceeds and certain disaster payments (see Instructions):		
a Amount received in 1990	8a	8b Taxable amount	8b
c If election to defer to 1991 is attached, check here ▶ ☐ 8d Amount deferred from 1989 . .	8d
9 Custom hire (machine work) income	9
10 Other income, including Federal and state gasoline or fuel tax credit or refund (see Instructions) . .	10
11 Add amounts in the right column for lines 3 through 10. If accrual method taxpayer, enter the amount from page 2, line 51. This is your **gross income** . . . . ▶	11

Part II Farm Expenses—Cash and Accrual Method (Do not include personal or living expenses such as taxes, insurance, repairs, etc., on your home.)

12 Breeding fees	12	24 Labor hired (less jobs credit) .	24
13 Chemicals	13	25 Pension and profit-sharing plans	25
14 Conservation expenses (you must attach **Form 8645**)	14	26 Rent or lease (see Instructions):	
		a Vehicles, machinery, and equip.	26a
15 Custom hire (machine work)	15	b Other (land, animals, etc.) . .	26b
16 Depreciation and section 179 expense deduction not claimed elsewhere (see Instructions)	16	27 Repairs and maintenance . .	27
		28 Seeds and plants purchased . .	28
		29 Storage and warehousing . . .	29
17 Employee benefit programs other than on line 25 . .	17	30 Supplies purchased	30
		31 Taxes	31
18 Feed purchased	18	32 Utilities	32
19 Fertilizers and lime	19	33 Veterinary fees and medicine .	33
20 Freight and trucking . . .	20	34 Other expenses (specify):	
21 Gasoline, fuel, and oil . . .	21	a _____	34a
22 Insurance (other than health) .	22	b _____	34b
23 Interest:		c _____	34c
a Mortgage (paid to banks, etc.) .	23a	d _____	34d
b Other	23b	e _____	34e

35 Add amounts on lines 12 through 34e. These are your **total expenses** . . . . ▶	35	
36 Net farm profit or (loss). Subtract line 35 from line 11. If a profit, enter on Form 1040, line 19, and on Schedule SE, line 1. If a loss, you MUST go on to line 37. (Fiduciaries and partnerships, see Instructions.)	36	

37 If you have a loss, you MUST check the box that describes your investment in this activity (see Instructions).

If you checked 37a, enter the loss on Form 1040, line 19, and Schedule SE, line 1.
If you checked 37b, you MUST attach **Form 6198.**

37a ☐ All investment is at risk.
37b ☐ Some investment is not at risk.

For Paperwork Reduction Act Notice, see Form 1040 Instructions.

Schedule F (Form 1040) 1990

Schedule F (Form 1040) 1990   Page **2**

Part III Farm Income—Accrual Method

Do not include sales of livestock held for draft, breeding, sport, or dairy purposes; report these sales on Form 4797 and do not include this livestock on line 46 below.

38 Sales of livestock, produce, grains, and other products during year	**38**	
39a Total cooperative distributions (Form(s) 1099-PATR) **39a** | | **39b** Taxable amount	**39b**	
40a Agricultural program payments (see Instructions) **40a** | | **40b** Taxable amount	**40b**	
41 Commodity Credit Corporation (CCC) loans:		
a CCC loans reported under election (see Instructions)	**41a**	
b CCC loans forfeited or repaid with certificates **41b** | | **41c** Taxable amount	**41c**	
42 Crop insurance proceeds	**42**	
43 Custom hire (machine work) income	**43**	
44 Other income, including Federal and state gasoline or fuel tax credit or refund (see Instructions) . . .	**44**	
45 Add amounts in the right column for lines 38 through 44	**45**	
46 Inventory of livestock, produce, grains, and other products at beginning of year **46**		
47 Cost of livestock, produce, grains, and other products purchased during year **47**		
48 Add lines 46 and 47 . . . . **48**		
49 Inventory of livestock, produce, grains, and other products at end of year . **49**		
50 Cost of livestock, produce, grains, and other products sold. Subtract line 49 from line 48*	**50**	
51 Subtract line 50 from line 45. Enter the result here and on page 1, line 11. This is your **gross income** ▶	**51**	

*If you use the unit-livestock-price method or the farm-price method of valuing inventory and the amount on line 49 is larger than the amount on line 48, subtract line 48 from line 49. Enter the result on line 50. Add lines 45 and 50. Enter the total on line 51.

Part IV Principal Agricultural Activity Codes

Select one of the following codes and write the 3-digit number on page 1, line B. **(Note:** *If your principal source of income is from providing agricultural services such as soil preparation, veterinary, farm labor, horticultural, or management for a fee or on a contract basis, you should file* **Schedule C** *(Form 1040), Profit or Loss From Business.)*

120 **Field crop,** including grains and nongrains such as cotton, peanuts, feed corn, wheat, tobacco, Irish potatoes, etc.

160 **Vegetables and melons,** garden-type vegetables and melons, such as sweet corn, tomatoes, squash, etc.

170 **Fruit and tree nuts,** including grapes, berries, olives, etc.

180 **Ornamental floriculture and nursery products**

185 **Food crops grown under cover,** including hydroponic crops

211 **Beefcattle feedlots**

212 **Beefcattle,** except feedlots

215 **Hogs, sheep, and goats**

240 **Dairy**

250 **Poultry and eggs,** including chickens, ducks, pigeons, quail, etc.

260 **General livestock,** not specializing in any one livestock category

270 **Animal specialty,** including fur-bearing animals, pets, horses, etc.

280 **Animal aquaculture,** including fish, shellfish, mollusks, frogs, etc., produced within confined space

290 **Forest products,** including forest nurseries and seed gathering, extraction of pine gum, and gathering of forest products

300 **Agricultural production,** not specified

Schedule R
(Form 1040)

Department of the Treasury
Internal Revenue Service

Credit for the Elderly or the Disabled

▶ For Paperwork Reduction Act Notice, see Form 1040 Instructions.
▶ Attach to Form 1040.   ▶ See separate Instructions for Schedule R.

OMB No. 1545-0074

19**90**

Attachment
Sequence No. **16**

Name(s) shown on Form 1040   Your social security number

You may be able to use Schedule R to reduce your tax if by the end of 1990:

● You were 65 or older, **OR**

● You were under 65, you retired on **permanent and total** disability, and you received taxable disability income.

But you must also meet other tests. See the separate Instructions for Schedule R.

Note: *In most cases, IRS can figure the credit for you. See page 19 of the Form 1040 Instructions.*

Part I   **Check the Box That Applies to Your Filing Status and Age** (Check only one box.)

If your filing status is:	And by the end of 1990:	Check box:
Single*	**1** You were 65 or older	**1** ☐
	2 You were under 65 and you retired on permanent and total disability	**2** ☐

* Includes head of household and qualifying widow(er) with dependent child

	3 Both spouses were 65 or older	**3** ☐
Married filing a joint return	**4** Both spouses were under 65, but only one spouse retired on permanent and total disability	**4** ☐
	5 Both spouses were under 65, and both retired on permanent and total disability	**5** ☐
	6 One spouse was 65 or older, and the other spouse was under 65 and retired on permanent and total disability .	**6** ☐
	7 One spouse was 65 or older, and the other spouse was under 65 and **NOT** retired on permanent and total disability	**7** ☐
Married filing a separate return	**8** You were 65 or older and you did not live with your spouse at any time in 1990	**8** ☐
	9 You were under 65, you retired on permanent and total disability, and you did not live with your spouse at any time in 1990	**9** ☐

Note: *If you checked Box 1, 3, 7, or 8, skip Part II and complete Part III on the back. All others, complete Parts II and III.*

Part II   **Statement of Permanent and Total Disability** (Complete **only** if you checked Box 2, 4, 5, 6, or 9 above.)

IF: 1 You filed a physician's statement for this disability for 1983 or an earlier year, or you filed a statement for tax years after 1983 and your physician signed line B on the statement, **AND**

     2 Due to your continued disabled condition, you were unable to engage in any substantial gainful activity in 1990, check this box . ▶ ☐

If you checked this box, you do not have to file another statement for 1990. If you did **not** check this box, have your physician complete the following statement:

Physician's Statement

I certify that _____
                             Name of disabled person

was permanently and totally disabled on January 1, 1976, or January 1, 1977, **OR** was permanently and totally disabled on the date he or she retired. If retired after December 31, 1976, enter the date retired. ▶ _____

Physician: Sign your name on **either** line A or B below.

A The disability has lasted, or can be expected to last, continuously for at least a year. . . . . _____
                Physician's signature   Date

B There is no reasonable probability that the disabled condition will ever improve . . . . _____
                Physician's signature   Date

Physician's name _____   Physician's address _____

Instructions for Physician's Statement

Taxpayer

If you retired after December 31, 1976, enter the date you retired in the space provided in Part II.

Physician

A person is permanently and totally disabled when—

● He or she cannot engage in any substantial gainful activity because of a physical or mental condition; and

● A physician determines that the disability:

1. has lasted, or can be expected to last, continuously for at least a year; or

2. can be expected to lead to death.

(Continued on back)   **Schedule R (Form 1040) 1990**

Part III Figure the Amount of Your Credit

10 If you checked (in Part I):   Enter:

Box 1, 2, 4, or 7 . . . . $5,000

Box 3, 5, or 6 . . . . $7,500   } **10**

Box 8 or 9 . . . . $3,750

Caution: *If you checked Box 2, 4, 5, 6, or 9 in Part I, you **MUST** complete line 11 below. Otherwise, skip line 11 and enter the amount from line 10 on line 12.*

11 If you checked Box 6 in Part I, enter on line 11 the taxable disability income of the spouse who was under age 65 **PLUS** $5,000. Otherwise, enter on line 11 your taxable disability income (and also your spouse's if you checked Box 5 in Part I) that you reported on Form 1040. (For more details on what to include, see the Instructions.) **11**

12 If you completed line 11 above, compare the amounts on lines 10 and 11, and enter the smaller of the two amounts here. Otherwise, enter the amount from line 10 . . . . **12**

13 Enter the following pensions, annuities, or disability income that you (and your spouse if you file a joint return) received in 1990 (see Instructions):

a Nontaxable part of social security benefits; and

Nontaxable part of railroad retirement benefits treated as } . . . **13a**
social security.

b Nontaxable veterans' pensions; and

Any other pension, annuity, or disability benefit that is } . . . **13b**
excluded from income under any other provision of law.

c Add lines 13a and 13b. (Even though these income items are not taxable, they **must** be included here to figure your credit.) If you did not receive any of the types of nontaxable income listed on line 13a or 13b, enter -0- on line 13c **13c**

14 Enter the amount from Form 1040, line 32 **14**

15 If you checked (in Part I):   Enter:

Box 1 or 2 . . . . . $7,500

Box 3, 4, 5, 6, or 7 . . . $10,000 } **15**

Box 8 or 9 . . . . . $5,000

16 Subtract line 15 from line 14. Enter the result. If line 15 is more than line 14, enter -0- **16**

17 Divide the amount on line 16 by 2. Enter the result **17**

18 Add lines 13c and 17. Enter the total **18**

19 Subtract line 18 from line 12. Enter the result. If the result is zero or less, stop here; you **cannot** take the credit. Otherwise, go to line 21 . . . . **19**

20 Decimal amount used to figure the credit . . . . **20** × .15

21 Multiply the amount on line 19 by the decimal amount (.15) on line 20. Enter the result here and on Form 1040, line 42. **Caution:** *If you file Schedule C, D, E, or F (Form 1040), your credit may be limited. See the Instructions for line 21 for the amount of credit you can claim.* **21**

<table>
<tr><td>**SCHEDULE SE**
(Form 1040)
Department of the Treasury
Internal Revenue Service</td><td>**Social Security Self-Employment Tax**
▶ See Instructions for Schedule SE (Form 1040).
▶ **Attach to Form 1040.**</td><td>OMB No. 1545-0074
19**90**
Attachment
Sequence No. **17**</td></tr>
</table>

Name of person with **self-employment** income (as shown on Form 1040)	Social security number of person with **self-employment** income ▶	

Who Must File Schedule SE

You must file Schedule SE if:

- Your net earnings from self-employment were $400 or more; **OR**
- You were an employee of an electing church or church-controlled organization that paid you wages (church employee income) of $100 or more;

          AND

- Your wages (subject to social security or railroad retirement tax) were less than $51,300.

Exception: If your only self-employment income was from earnings as a minister, member of a religious order, or Christian Science practitioner, AND you filed **Form 4361** and received IRS approval not to be taxed on those earnings, DO NOT file Schedule SE. Instead, write "Exempt–Form 4361" on Form 1040, line 48.

For more information about Schedule SE, see the Instructions.

Note: *Most people can use the short Schedule SE on this page. But, you may have to use the longer Schedule SE on the back.*

Who MUST Use the Long Schedule SE (Section B)

You must use Section B if ANY of the following apply:

- You elect the "optional method" to figure your self-employment tax (see Section B, Part II, and the Instructions);
- You are a minister, member of a religious order, or Christian Science practitioner and you received IRS approval (from **Form 4361**) not to be taxed on your earnings from these sources, but you owe self-employment tax on other earnings;
- You had church employee income of $100 or more that was reported to you on Form W-2;
- You had tip income that is subject to social security tax, but you did not report those tips to your employer; OR
- You were a government employee with wages subject ONLY to the 1.45% Medicare part of the social security tax (Medicare qualified government wages) AND the total of **all** of your wages (subject to social security, railroad retirement, or the 1.45% Medicare tax) plus **all** your earnings subject to self-employment tax is **more** than $51,300.

Section A—Short Schedule SE (Read above to see if you must use the long Schedule SE on the back (Section B).)

1	Net farm profit or (loss) from Schedule F (Form 1040), line 36, and farm partnerships, Schedule K-1 (Form 1065), line 15a	1	
2	Net profit or (loss) from Schedule C (Form 1040), line 29, and Schedule K-1 (Form 1065), line 15a (other than farming). See Instructions for other income to report.	2	
3	Combine lines 1 and 2. Enter the result	3	
4	Multiply line 3 by .9235. Enter the result. If the result is less than $400, **do not** file this schedule; you **do not** owe self-employment tax . . . . ▶	4	
5	Maximum amount of combined wages and self-employment earnings subject to social security or railroad retirement (tier 1) tax for 1990	5	$51,300 00
6	Total social security wages and tips (from Form(s) W-2) and railroad retirement compensation (tier 1). **Do not** include Medicare qualified government wages on this line	6	
7	Subtract line 6 from line 5. Enter the result. If the result is zero or less, **do not** file this schedule; you **do not** owe self-employment tax . . . . ▶	7	
8	Enter the **smaller** of line 4 or line 7	8	
9	Rate of tax	9	×.153
10	**Self-employment tax.** If line 8 is $51,300, enter $7,848.90. Otherwise, multiply the amount on line 8 by the decimal amount on line 9 and enter the result. Also enter this amount on Form 1040, line 48 . **Note:** *Also enter one-half of this amount on Form 1040, line 25.*	10	

For Paperwork Reduction Act Notice, see Form 1040 Instructions.   Schedule SE (Form 1040) 1990

Schedule SE (Form 1040) 1990   Attachment Sequence No. **17**   Page **2**

Name of person with **self-employment** income (as shown on Form 1040)	Social security number of person with **self-employment** income ▶

Section B—Long Schedule SE (Before completing, see if you can use the short Schedule SE on the other side (Section A).)

A   If you are a minister, member of a religious order, or Christian Science practitioner, AND you filed **Form 4361,** but you had $400 or more of **other** earnings subject to self-employment tax, continue with Part I and check here   . . . . ▶ ☐

B   If your only income subject to self-employment tax is church employee income and you are not a minister or a member of a religious order, skip lines 1 through 4b. Enter -0- on line 4c and go to line 6a. But **do not** include your church employee income on line 6a.

Part I   Social Security Self-Employment Tax

1	Net farm profit or (loss) from Schedule F (Form 1040), line 36, and farm partnerships, Schedule K-1 (Form 1065), line 15a. (**Note:** *Skip this line if you elect the farm optional method. See requirements in Part II below and in the Instructions.*)	**1**	
2	Net profit or (loss) from Schedule C (Form 1040), line 29, and Schedule K-1 (Form 1065), line 15a (other than farming). See Instructions for other income to report. **Do not** include church employee income from Form W-2 on this line. (**Note:** *Skip this line if you elect the nonfarm optional method. See requirements in Part II below and in the Instructions.*)	**2**	
3	Combine lines 1 and 2. Enter the result	**3**	
4a	If line 3 is more than zero, multiply line 3 by .9235. Otherwise, enter the amount from line 3 here . .	**4a**	
b	If you elected one or both of the optional methods, enter the total of lines 12 and 14 here	**4b**	
c	Combine lines 4a and 4b. If less than $400, **do not** file this schedule; you **do not** owe self-employment tax. (**Exception:** *If less than $400 and you had church employee income, enter -0- and continue.*) . ▶	**4c**	
5	Maximum amount of combined wages and self-employment earnings subject to social security or railroad retirement (tier 1) tax for 1990	**5**	$51,300 00
6a	Total social security wages and tips (from Form(s) W-2) and railroad retirement compensation (tier 1). **Do not** include Medicare qualified government wages or church employee income on this line **6a**		
b	Unreported tips subject to social security tax (from Form 4137, line 9) or railroad retirement tax (tier 1) **6b**		
c	Add lines 6a and 6b. Enter the total	**6c**	
7a	Subtract line 6c from line 5. If zero or less, **do not** file this schedule; you **do not** owe self-employment tax . . . . ▶	**7a**	
b	Enter your church employee income from Form W-2 of $100 or more . . **7b**		
c	Multiply line 7b by .9235 (if the result is less than $100, enter -0-) . . . **7c**		
d	Add lines 4c and 7c. Enter the total . . . . ▶	**7d**	
8	Enter the **smaller** of line 7a or line 7d	**8**	
9	Enter your Medicare qualified government wages. See Instructions to see if you must use the worksheet in the Instructions to figure your self-employment tax . **9**		
10	Self-employment tax. If line 8 is $51,300, enter $7,848.90. Otherwise, multiply line 8 by .153 and enter the result. Also enter this amount on Form 1040, line 48	**10**	
	Note: *Also enter one-half of this amount on Form 1040, line 25.*		

Part II   Optional Method To Figure Net Earnings (See "Who Can File Schedule SE" in the Instructions.)

See Instructions for limitations. Generally, you may use this part **only** if:

A   Your **gross** farm income[1] was not more than $2,400; **or**

B   Your **gross** farm income[1] was more than $2,400 and your **net** farm profits[2] were **less** than $1,733; **or**

C   Your **net** nonfarm profits[3] were **less** than $1,733 and also **less** than two-thirds (⅔) of your **gross** nonfarm income.[4]

11	Maximum income for optional methods	**11**	$1,600 00
12	**Farm Optional Method**—If you meet test **A** or **B** above, enter the **smaller** of: two-thirds (⅔) of gross farm income[1] **or** $1,600. Also include this amount on line 4b above	**12**	
13	Subtract line 12 from line 11. Enter the result	**13**	
14	**Nonfarm Optional Method**—If you meet test **C** above, enter the **smallest** of: two-thirds (⅔) of gross nonfarm income[4] or $1,600; **or,** if you elected the farm optional method, the amount on line 13. Also include this amount on line 4b above	**14**	

[1]From Schedule F (Form 1040), line 11, and Schedule K-1 (Form 1065), line 15b.   [3]From Schedule C (Form 1040), line 29, and Schedule K-1 (Form 1065), line 15a.
[2]From Schedule F (Form 1040), line 36, and Schedule K-1 (Form 1065), line 15a.   [4]From Schedule C (Form 1040), line 7, and Schedule K-1 (Form 1065), line 15c.

For Paperwork Reduction Act Notice, see Form 1040 Instructions.   **Schedule SE (Form 1040) 1990**

1990 Earned Income Credit Table

Caution: *This Is Not A Tax Table*

To find your earned income credit: Read down the column titled "If line 5 or 6 of the worksheet is—" and find the appropriate amount from the Earned Income Credit Worksheet on page 24. Read across to the right and find the amount of the earned income credit. Enter that amount on line 7 or 8 of the worksheet, whichever applies.

If line 5 or 6 of the worksheet is—		Your earned income credit is—	If line 5 or 6 of the worksheet is—		Your earned income credit is—	If line 5 or 6 of the worksheet is—		Your earned income credit is—	If line 5 or 6 of the worksheet is—		Your earned income credit is—	If line 5 or 6 of the worksheet is—		Your earned income credit is—
At least	But less than		At least	But less than		At least	But less than		At least	But less than		At least	But less than	
$1	$25	$2	$1,600	$1,625	$226	$3,200	$3,225	$450	$4,800	$4,825	$674	$6,400	$6,425	$898
25	50	5	1,625	1,650	229	3,225	3,250	453	4,825	4,850	677	6,425	6,450	901
50	75	9	1,650	1,675	233	3,250	3,275	457	4,850	4,875	681	6,450	6,475	905
75	100	12	1,675	1,700	236	3,275	3,300	460	4,875	4,900	684	6,475	6,500	908
100	125	16	1,700	1,725	240	3,300	3,325	464	4,900	4,925	688	6,500	6,525	912
125	150	19	1,725	1,750	243	3,325	3,350	467	4,925	4,950	691	6,525	6,550	915
150	175	23	1,750	1,775	247	3,350	3,375	471	4,950	4,975	695	6,550	6,575	919
175	200	26	1,775	1,800	250	3,375	3,400	474	4,975	5,000	698	6,575	6,600	922
200	225	30	1,800	1,825	254	3,400	3,425	478	5,000	5,025	702	6,600	6,625	926
225	250	33	1,825	1,850	257	3,425	3,450	481	5,025	5,050	705	6,625	6,650	929
250	275	37	1,850	1,875	261	3,450	3,475	485	5,050	5,075	709	6,650	6,675	933
275	300	40	1,875	1,900	264	3,475	3,500	488	5,075	5,100	712	6,675	6,700	936
300	325	44	1,900	1,925	268	3,500	3,525	492	5,100	5,125	716	6,700	6,725	940
325	350	47	1,925	1,950	271	3,525	3,550	495	5,125	5,150	719	6,725	6,750	943
350	375	51	1,950	1,975	275	3,550	3,575	499	5,150	5,175	723	6,750	6,775	947
375	400	54	1,975	2,000	278	3,575	3,600	502	5,175	5,200	726	6,775	6,800	950
400	425	58	2,000	2,025	282	3,600	3,625	506	5,200	5,225	730	6,800	10,750	953
425	450	61	2,025	2,050	285	3,625	3,650	509	5,225	5,250	733	10,750	10,775	950
450	475	65	2,050	2,075	289	3,650	3,675	513	5,250	5,275	737	10,775	10,800	948
475	500	68	2,075	2,100	292	3,675	3,700	516	5,275	5,300	740	10,800	10,825	945
500	525	72	2,100	2,125	296	3,700	3,725	520	5,300	5,325	744	10,825	10,850	943
525	550	75	2,125	2,150	299	3,725	3,750	523	5,325	5,350	747	10,850	10,875	940
550	575	79	2,150	2,175	303	3,750	3,775	527	5,350	5,375	751	10,875	10,900	938
575	600	82	2,175	2,200	306	3,775	3,800	530	5,375	5,400	754	10,900	10,925	935
600	625	86	2,200	2,225	310	3,800	3,825	534	5,400	5,425	758	10,925	10,950	933
625	650	89	2,225	2,250	313	3,825	3,850	537	5,425	5,450	761	10,950	10,975	930
650	675	93	2,250	2,275	317	3,850	3,875	541	5,450	5,475	765	10,975	11,000	928
675	700	96	2,275	2,300	320	3,875	3,900	544	5,475	5,500	768	11,000	11,025	925
700	725	100	2,300	2,325	324	3,900	3,925	548	5,500	5,525	772	11,025	11,050	923
725	750	103	2,325	2,350	327	3,925	3,950	551	5,525	5,550	775	11,050	11,075	920
750	775	107	2,350	2,375	331	3,950	3,975	555	5,550	5,575	779	11,075	11,100	918
775	800	110	2,375	2,400	334	3,975	4,000	558	5,575	5,600	782	11,100	11,125	915
800	825	114	2,400	2,425	338	4,000	4,025	562	5,600	5,625	786	11,125	11,150	913
825	850	117	2,425	2,450	341	4,025	4,050	565	5,625	5,650	789	11,150	11,175	910
850	875	121	2,450	2,475	345	4,050	4,075	569	5,650	5,675	793	11,175	11,200	908
875	900	124	2,475	2,500	348	4,075	4,100	572	5,675	5,700	796	11,200	11,225	905
900	925	128	2,500	2,525	352	4,100	4,125	576	5,700	5,725	800	11,225	11,250	903
925	950	131	2,525	2,550	355	4,125	4,150	579	5,725	5,750	803	11,250	11,275	900
950	975	135	2,550	2,575	359	4,150	4,175	583	5,750	5,775	807	11,275	11,300	898
975	1,000	138	2,575	2,600	362	4,175	4,200	586	5,775	5,800	810	11,300	11,325	895
1,000	1,025	142	2,600	2,625	366	4,200	4,225	590	5,800	5,825	814	11,325	11,350	893
1,025	1,050	145	2,625	2,650	369	4,225	4,250	593	5,825	5,850	817	11,350	11,375	890
1,050	1,075	149	2,650	2,675	373	4,250	4,275	597	5,850	5,875	821	11,375	11,400	888
1,075	1,100	152	2,675	2,700	376	4,275	4,300	600	5,875	5,900	824	11,400	11,425	885
1,100	1,125	156	2,700	2,725	380	4,300	4,325	604	5,900	5,925	828	11,425	11,450	883
1,125	1,150	159	2,725	2,750	383	4,325	4,350	607	5,925	5,950	831	11,450	11,475	880
1,150	1,175	163	2,750	2,775	387	4,350	4,375	611	5,950	5,975	835	11,475	11,500	878
1,175	1,200	166	2,775	2,800	390	4,375	4,400	614	5,975	6,000	838	11,500	11,525	875
1,200	1,225	170	2,800	2,825	394	4,400	4,425	618	6,000	6,025	842	11,525	11,550	873
1,225	1,250	173	2,825	2,850	397	4,425	4,450	621	6,025	6,050	845	11,550	11,575	870
1,250	1,275	177	2,850	2,875	401	4,450	4,475	625	6,050	6,075	849	11,575	11,600	868
1,275	1,300	180	2,875	2,900	404	4,475	4,500	628	6,075	6,100	852	11,600	11,625	865
1,300	1,325	184	2,900	2,925	408	4,500	4,525	632	6,100	6,125	856	11,625	11,650	863
1,325	1,350	187	2,925	2,950	411	4,525	4,550	635	6,125	6,150	859	11,650	11,675	860
1,350	1,375	191	2,950	2,975	415	4,550	4,575	639	6,150	6,175	863	11,675	11,700	858
1,375	1,400	194	2,975	3,000	418	4,575	4,600	642	6,175	6,200	866	11,700	11,725	855
1,400	1,425	198	3,000	3,025	422	4,600	4,625	646	6,200	6,225	870	11,725	11,750	853
1,425	1,450	201	3,025	3,050	425	4,625	4,650	649	6,225	6,250	873	11,750	11,775	850
1,450	1,475	205	3,050	3,075	429	4,650	4,675	653	6,250	6,275	877	11,775	11,800	848
1,475	1,500	208	3,075	3,100	432	4,675	4,700	656	6,275	6,300	880	11,800	11,825	845
1,500	1,525	212	3,100	3,125	436	4,700	4,725	660	6,300	6,325	884	11,825	11,850	843
1,525	1,550	215	3,125	3,150	439	4,725	4,750	663	6,325	6,350	887	11,850	11,875	840
1,550	1,575	219	3,150	3,175	443	4,750	4,775	667	6,350	6,375	891	11,875	11,900	838
1,575	1,600	222	3,175	3,200	446	4,775	4,800	670	6,375	6,400	894	11,900	11,925	835

1990 Earned Income Credit Table *(continued)* **Caution:** *This is Not a Tax Table*

If line 5 or 6 of the worksheet is—		Your earned income credit is—	If line 5 or 6 of the worksheet is—		Your earned income credit is—	If line 5 or 6 of the worksheet is—		Your earned income credit is—	If line 5 or 6 of the worksheet is—		Your earned income credit is—	If line 5 or 6 of the worksheet is—		Your earned income credit is—
At least	But less than		At least	But less than		At least	But less than		At least	But less than		At least	But less than	
$11,925	$11,950	$833	$13,625	$13,650	$663	$15,325	$15,350	$493	$17,025	$17,050	$323	$18,725	$18,750	$153
11,950	11,975	830	13,650	13,675	660	15,350	15,375	490	17,050	17,075	320	18,750	18,775	150
11,975	12,000	828	13,675	13,700	658	15,375	15,400	488	17,075	17,100	318	18,775	18,800	148
12,000	12,025	825	13,700	13,725	655	15,400	15,425	485	17,100	17,125	315	18,800	18,825	145
12,025	12,050	823	13,725	13,750	653	15,425	15,450	483	17,125	17,150	313	18,825	18,850	143
12,050	12,075	820	13,750	13,775	650	15,450	15,475	480	17,150	17,175	310	18,850	18,875	140
12,075	12,100	818	13,775	13,800	648	15,475	15,500	478	17,175	17,200	308	18,875	18,900	138
12,100	12,125	815	13,800	13,825	645	15,500	15,525	475	17,200	17,225	305	18,900	18,925	135
12,125	12,150	813	13,825	13,850	643	15,525	15,550	473	17,225	17,250	303	18,925	18,950	133
12,150	12,175	810	13,850	13,875	640	15,550	15,575	470	17,250	17,275	300	18,950	18,975	130
12,175	12,200	808	13,875	13,900	638	15,575	15,600	468	17,275	17,300	298	18,975	19,000	128
12,200	12,225	805	13,900	13,925	635	15,600	15,625	465	17,300	17,325	295	19,000	19,025	125
12,225	12,250	803	13,925	13,950	633	15,625	15,650	463	17,325	17,350	293	19,025	19,050	123
12,250	12,275	800	13,950	13,975	630	15,650	15,675	460	17,350	17,375	290	19,050	19,075	120
12,275	12,300	798	13,975	14,000	628	15,675	15,700	458	17,375	17,400	288	19,075	19,100	118
12,300	12,325	795	14,000	14,025	625	15,700	15,725	455	17,400	17,425	285	19,100	19,125	115
12,325	12,350	793	14,025	14,050	623	15,725	15,750	453	17,425	17,450	283	19,125	19,150	113
12,350	12,375	790	14,050	14,075	620	15,750	15,775	450	17,450	17,475	280	19,150	19,175	110
12,375	12,400	788	14,075	14,100	618	15,775	15,800	448	17,475	17,500	278	19,175	19,200	108
12,400	12,425	785	14,100	14,125	615	15,800	15,825	445	17,500	17,525	275	19,200	19,225	105
12,425	12,450	783	14,125	14,150	613	15,825	15,850	443	17,525	17,550	273	19,225	19,250	103
12,450	12,475	780	14,150	14,175	610	15,850	15,875	440	17,550	17,575	270	19,250	19,275	100
12,475	12,500	778	14,175	14,200	608	15,875	15,900	438	17,575	17,600	268	19,275	19,300	98
12,500	12,525	775	14,200	14,225	605	15,900	15,925	435	17,600	17,625	265	19,300	19,325	95
12,525	12,550	773	14,225	14,250	603	15,925	15,950	433	17,625	17,650	263	19,325	19,350	93
12,550	12,575	770	14,250	14,275	600	15,950	15,975	430	17,650	17,675	260	19,350	19,375	90
12,575	12,600	768	14,275	14,300	598	15,975	16,000	428	17,675	17,700	258	19,375	19,400	88
12,600	12,625	765	14,300	14,325	595	16,000	16,025	425	17,700	17,725	255	19,400	19,425	85
12,625	12,650	763	14,325	14,350	593	16,025	16,050	423	17,725	17,750	253	19,425	19,450	83
12,650	12,675	760	14,350	14,375	590	16,050	16,075	420	17,750	17,775	250	19,450	19,475	80
12,675	12,700	758	14,375	14,400	588	16,075	16,100	418	17,775	17,800	248	19,475	19,500	78
12,700	12,725	755	14,400	14,425	585	16,100	16,125	415	17,800	17,825	245	19,500	19,525	75
12,725	12,750	753	14,425	14,450	583	16,125	16,150	413	17,825	17,850	243	19,525	19,550	73
12,750	12,775	750	14,450	14,475	580	16,150	16,175	410	17,850	17,875	240	19,550	19,575	70
12,775	12,800	748	14,475	14,500	578	16,175	16,200	408	17,875	17,900	238	19,575	19,600	68
12,800	12,825	745	14,500	14,525	575	16,200	16,225	405	17,900	17,925	235	19,600	19,625	65
12,825	12,850	743	14,525	14,550	573	16,225	16,250	403	17,925	17,950	233	19,625	19,650	63
12,850	12,875	740	14,550	14,575	570	16,250	16,275	400	17,950	17,975	230	19,650	19,675	60
12,875	12,900	738	14,575	14,600	568	16,275	16,300	398	17,975	18,000	228	19,675	19,700	58
12,900	12,925	735	14,600	14,625	565	16,300	16,325	395	18,000	18,025	225	19,700	19,725	55
12,925	12,950	733	14,625	14,650	563	16,325	16,350	393	18,025	18,050	223	19,725	19,750	53
12,950	12,975	730	14,650	14,675	560	16,350	16,375	390	18,050	18,075	220	19,750	19,775	50
12,975	13,000	728	14,675	14,700	558	16,375	16,400	388	18,075	18,100	218	19,775	19,800	48
13,000	13,025	725	14,700	14,725	555	16,400	16,425	385	18,100	18,125	215	19,800	19,825	45
13,025	13,050	723	14,725	14,750	553	16,425	16,450	383	18,125	18,150	213	19,825	19,850	43
13,050	13,075	720	14,750	14,775	550	16,450	16,475	380	18,150	18,175	210	19,850	19,875	40
13,075	13,100	718	14,775	14,800	548	16,475	16,500	378	18,175	18,200	208	19,875	19,900	38
13,100	13,125	715	14,800	14,825	545	16,500	16,525	375	18,200	18,225	205	19,900	19,925	35
13,125	13,150	713	14,825	14,850	543	16,525	16,550	373	18,225	18,250	203	19,925	19,950	33
13,150	13,175	710	14,850	14,875	540	16,550	16,575	370	18,250	18,275	200	19,950	19,975	30
13,175	13,200	708	14,875	14,900	538	16,575	16,600	368	18,275	18,300	198	19,975	20,000	28
13,200	13,225	705	14,900	14,925	535	16,600	16,625	365	18,300	18,325	195	20,000	20,025	25
13,225	13,250	703	14,925	14,950	533	16,625	16,650	363	18,325	18,350	193	20,025	20,050	23
13,250	13,275	700	14,950	14,975	530	16,650	16,675	360	18,350	18,375	190	20,050	20,075	20
13,275	13,300	698	14,975	15,000	528	16,675	16,700	358	18,375	18,400	188	20,075	20,100	18
13,300	13,325	695	15,000	15,025	525	16,700	16,725	355	18,400	18,425	185	20,100	20,125	15
13,325	13,350	693	15,025	15,050	523	16,725	16,750	353	18,425	18,450	183	20,125	20,150	13
13,350	13,375	690	15,050	15,075	520	16,750	16,775	350	18,450	18,475	180	20,150	20,175	10
13,375	13,400	688	15,075	15,100	518	16,775	16,800	348	18,475	18,500	178	20,175	20,200	8
13,400	13,425	685	15,100	15,125	515	16,800	16,825	345	18,500	18,525	175	20,200	20,225	5
13,425	13,450	683	15,125	15,150	513	16,825	16,850	343	18,525	18,550	173	20,225	20,250	3
13,450	13,475	680	15,150	15,175	510	16,850	16,875	340	18,550	18,575	170	20,250	20,264	1
13,475	13,500	678	15,175	15,200	508	16,875	16,900	338	18,575	18,600	168			
13,500	13,525	675	15,200	15,225	505	16,900	16,925	335	18,600	18,625	165	**$20,264 or more**—you cannot take the credit		
13,525	13,550	673	15,225	15,250	503	16,925	16,950	333	18,625	18,650	163			
13,550	13,575	670	15,250	15,275	500	16,950	16,975	330	18,650	18,675	160			
13,575	13,600	668	15,275	15,300	498	16,975	17,000	328	18,675	18,700	158			
13,600	13,625	665	15,300	15,325	495	17,000	17,025	325	18,700	18,725	155			

B-4 Form 1041 U.S. Fiduciary Income Tax Return

Form 1041 Department of the Treasury—Internal Revenue Service
U.S. Fiduciary Income Tax Return 1990

For the calendar year 1990 or fiscal year beginning _____ , 1990, and ending _____ , 19 ___ OMB No. 1545-0092

Check applicable boxes:
- ☐ Decedent's estate
- ☐ Simple trust
- ☐ Complex trust
- ☐ Grantor type trust
- ☐ Bankruptcy estate
- ☐ Family estate trust
- ☐ Pooled income fund

Name of estate or trust (grantor type trust, see instructions)

Name and title of fiduciary

Number, street, and room or suite no. (If a P.O. box, see page 5 of Instructions.)

City, state, and ZIP code

Employer identification number

Date entity created

Nonexempt charitable and split-interest trusts, check applicable boxes (see instructions):
- ☐ Described in section 4947(a)(1)
- ☐ Not a private foundation
- ☐ Described in section 4947(a)(2)

Number of Schedules K-1 attached (see instructions) . ▶

Check applicable boxes: ☐ First return ☐ Final return ☐ Amended return
Change in Fiduciary's ▶ ☐ Name or ☐ Address

Income

1	Interest income	1
2	Dividends	2
3	Income (or losses) from partnerships, other estates, or other trusts (see instructions)	3
4	Net rental and royalty income (or loss) (attach Schedule E (Form 1040))	4
5	Net business and farm income (or loss) (attach Schedules C and F (Form 1040))	5
6	Capital gain (or loss) (attach Schedule D (Form 1041))	6
7	Ordinary gain (or loss) (attach Form 4797)	7
8	Other income (state nature of income)	8
9	**Total income** (combine lines 1 through 8) ▶	9

Deductions

10	Interest	10	
11	Taxes	11	
12	Fiduciary fees	12	
13	Charitable deduction (from Schedule A, line 6)	13	
14	Attorney, accountant, and return preparer fees	14	
15a	Other deductions NOT subject to the 2% floor (attach schedule)	15a	
b	Allowable miscellaneous itemized deductions subject to the 2% floor	15b	
c	Add lines 15a and 15b	15c	
16	**Total** (add lines 10 through 15c)		16
17	Adjusted total income (or loss) (subtract line 16 from line 9). Enter here and on Schedule B, line 1 . ▶		17
18	Income distribution deduction (from Schedule B, line 17) (see instructions) (attach Schedules K-1 (Form 1041))		18
19	Estate tax deduction (including certain generation-skipping transfer taxes) (attach computation)		19
20	Exemption		20
21	**Total deductions** (add lines 18 through 20) ▶		21

Tax and Payments

22	Taxable income of fiduciary (subtract line 21 from line 17)		22
23	**Total tax** (from Schedule G, line 7) ▶		23
24a	Payments: 1990 estimated tax payments and amount applied from 1989 return		24a
b	Treated as credited to beneficiaries		24b
c	Subtract line 24b from line 24a		24c
d	Tax paid with extension of time to file: ☐ Form 2758 ☐ Form 8736 ☐ Form 8800		24d
e	Federal income tax withheld		24e
	Credits: f Form 2439 _____ ; g Form 4136 _____ ; h Other _____ ; Total ▶		24i
25	**Total payments** (add lines 24c through 24e, and 24i) ▶		25
26	**Penalty** for underpayment of estimated tax (see instructions)		26
27	If the total of lines 23 and 26 is larger than line 25, enter **TAX DUE**		27
28	If line 25 is larger than the total of lines 23 and 26, enter **OVERPAYMENT**		28
29	Amount of line 28 to be: **a Credited to 1991 estimated tax** ▶ _____ ; **b Refunded** ▶		29

Please Sign Here

Under penalties of perjury, I declare that I have examined this return, including accompanying schedules and statements, and to the best of my knowledge and belief, it is true, correct, and complete. Declaration of preparer (other than fiduciary) is based on all information of which preparer has any knowledge.

▶ Signature of fiduciary or officer representing fiduciary Date ▶ EIN of fiduciary (see instructions)

Paid Preparer's Use Only

Preparer's signature ▶ Date Check if self-employed ▶ ☐ Preparer's social security no.

Firm's name (or yours if self-employed) and address ▶ E.I. No. ▶ ZIP code ▶

For Paperwork Reduction Act Notice, see page 1 of the separate Instructions. Form **1041** (1990)

Form 1041 (1990)   Page **2**

Schedule A	**Charitable Deduction—Do not complete for a simple trust or a pooled income fund.**			
1	Amounts paid or permanently set aside for charitable purposes from current year's gross income . . .	1		
2	Tax-exempt interest allocable to charitable distribution (see instructions)	2		
3	Subtract line 2 from line 1	3		
4	Enter the net short-term capital gain and the net long-term capital gain of the current tax year allocable to corpus paid or permanently set aside for charitable purposes (see instructions)	4		
5	Amounts paid or permanently set aside for charitable purposes from gross income of a prior year (see instructions)	5		
6	**Total** (add lines 3 through 5). Enter here and on page 1, line 13	6		

Schedule B	**Income Distribution Deduction (see instructions)**			
1	Adjusted total income (from page 1, line 17) (see instructions)	1		
2	Adjusted tax-exempt interest (see instructions)	2		
3	Net gain shown on Schedule D (Form 1041), line 17, column (a). (If net loss, enter zero.)	3		
4	Enter amount from Schedule A, line 4	4		
5	Long-term capital gain included on Schedule A, line 1	5		
6	Short-term capital gain included on Schedule A, line 1	6		
7	If the amount on page 1, line 6, is a capital loss, enter here as a positive figure	7		
8	If the amount on page 1, line 6, is a capital gain, enter here as a negative figure	8		
9	Distributable net income (combine lines 1 through 8)	9		
10	Amount of income for the tax year determined under the governing instrument (accounting income) | 10 |			
11	Amount of income required to be distributed currently (see instructions)	11		
12	Other amounts paid, credited, or otherwise required to be distributed (see instructions)	12		
13	Total distributions (add lines 11 and 12). (If greater than line 10, see instructions.)	13		
14	Enter the amount of tax-exempt income included on line 13	14		
15	Tentative income distribution deduction (subtract line 14 from line 13)	15		
16	Tentative income distribution deduction (subtract line 2 from line 9)	16		
17	Income distribution deduction. Enter the smaller of line 15 or line 16 here and on page 1, line 18 . . .	17		

Schedule G	**Tax Computation (see instructions)**			
1	Tax: **a** Tax rate schedule . . . . ; **b** Other taxes . . . . ; . . . . Total ▶	1c		
2a	Foreign tax credit (attach Form 1116)	2a		
b	Credit for fuel produced from a nonconventional source.	2b		
c	General business credit. Check if from: ☐ Form 3800 or ☐ Form (specify) ▶	2c		
d	Credit for prior year minimum tax (attach Form 8801)	2d		
3	**Total** credits (add lines 2a through 2d) . . . . ▶	3		
4	Subtract line 3 from line 1c	4		
5	Recapture taxes. Check if from: ☐ Form 4255 ☐ Form 8611	5		
6	Alternative minimum tax (attach Form 8656)	6		
7	**Total** tax (add lines 4 through 6). Enter here and on page 1, line 23 . . . . ▶	7		

Other Information (see instructions)		**Yes**	**No**
1	Did the estate or trust receive tax-exempt income? (If "Yes," attach a computation of the allocation of expenses.) . . . Enter the amount of tax-exempt interest income and exempt-interest dividends ▶ $		
2	Did the estate or trust have any passive activity losses? (If "Yes," enter these losses on **Form 8582**, Passive Activity Loss Limitations, to figure the allowable loss.)		
3	Did the estate or trust receive all or any part of the earnings (salary, wages, and other compensation) of any individual by reason of a contract assignment or similar arrangement?		
4	At any time during the tax year, did the estate or trust have an interest in or a signature or other authority over a financial account in a foreign country (such as a bank account, securities account, or other financial account)? (See the instructions for exceptions and filing requirements for Form TD F 90-22.1.) . . . . If "Yes," enter the name of the foreign country ▶		
5	Was the estate or trust the grantor of, or transferor to, a foreign trust which existed during the current tax year, whether or not the estate or trust has any beneficial interest in it? (If "Yes," you may have to file Form 3520, 3520-A, or 926.) .		
6	Check this box if this entity has filed or is required to file **Form 8264**, Application for Registration of a Tax Shelter . ▶ ☐		
7	Check this box if this entity is a complex trust making the section 663(b) election . . . . ▶ ☐		
8	Check this box to make a section 643(e)(3) election (attach Schedule D (Form 1041)) . . . . ▶ ☐		
9	Check this box if the decedent's estate has been open for more than 2 years . . . . ▶ ☐		
10	Check this box if the trust is a participant in a Common Trust Fund that was required to adopt a calendar year . . ▶ ☐		

SCHEDULE J
(Form 1041)

Department of the Treasury
Internal Revenue Service

Trust Allocation of an Accumulation Distribution
(Under Code Section 665)

▶ File with Form 1041.
▶ See the separate Form 1041 instructions.

OMB No. 1545-0092

1990

Name of trust | Employer identification number

Part I Accumulation Distribution in 1990

For definitions and special rules, see the regulations under sections 665-668 of the Internal Revenue Code.
See the Form 4970 instructions for certain income that minors may exclude and special rules for multiple trusts.

1 Enter amount from Schedule B (Form 1041), line 12, for 1990 . . . . **1**

2 Enter amount from Schedule B (Form 1041), line 9, for 1990 . . . . **2**

3 Enter amount from Schedule B (Form 1041), line 11, for 1990 . . . . **3**

4 Subtract line 3 from line 2. If line 3 is more than line 2, enter zero **4**

5 Accumulation distribution for 1990. (Subtract line 4 from line 1.) **5**

Part II Ordinary Income Accumulation Distribution (Enter the applicable throwback years below.)

If the distribution is thrown back to more than five years (starting with the earliest applicable tax year beginning after December 31, 1968), attach additional schedules. (If the trust was a simple trust, see Regulations section 1.665(e)-1A(b).)		Throwback year ending 19	Throwback year ending 19	Throwback year ending 19	Throwback year ending 19	Throwback year ending 19 ....
6 Distributable net income (see instructions)	6					
7 Distributions (see instructions) .	7					
8 Undistributed net income (subtract line 7 from line 6) . . .	8					
9 Enter amount from page 2, line 25 or line 31, as applicable . .	9					
10 Subtract line 9 from line 8 . .	10					
11 Enter amount of prior accumulation distributions thrown back to any of these years	11					
12 Subtract line 11 from line 10 .	12					
13 Allocate the amount on line 5 to the earliest applicable year first. Do not allocate an amount greater than line 12 for the same year (see instructions) . .	13					
14 Divide line 13 by line 10 and multiply result by amount on line 9	14					
15 Add lines 13 and 14	15					
16 Tax-exempt interest included on line 13 (see instructions) . . .	16					
17 Subtract line 16 from line 15 .	17					

For Paperwork Reduction Act Notice, see page 1 of the Instructions for Form 1041.   Schedule J (Form 1041) 1990

Schedule J (Form 1041) 1990   Page **2**

Part III Taxes Imposed on Undistributed Net Income (Enter the applicable throwback years below.)

If more than five throwback years are involved, attach additional schedules. If the trust received an accumulation distribution from another trust, see the regulations under sections 665-668 of the Internal Revenue Code.

If the trust elected the alternative tax on capital gains, **OMIT** lines 18 through 25 **AND** complete lines 26 through 31.		Throwback year ending 19	Throwback year ending 19	Throwback year ending 19	Throwback year ending 19	Throwback year ending 19 ....
(The alternative tax on capital gains was repealed for tax years beginning after December 31, 1978.)						
18 Tax (see instructions)	18					
19 Net short-term gain (see instructions)	19					
20 Net long-term gain (see instructions)	20					
21 Total net capital gain (add lines 19 and 20)	21					
22 Taxable income (see instructions)	22					
23 Enter percent (divide line 21 by line 22, but not more than 100%)	23	%	%	%	%	%
24 Multiply amount on line 18 by the percentage on line 23	24					
25 Tax on undistributed net income. (Subtract line 24 from line 18. Enter here and on page 1, line 9.)	25					
Complete lines 26 through 31 only if the trust elected the alternative tax on long-term capital gain.						
26 Tax on income other than long-term capital gain (see instructions)	26					
27 Net short-term gain (see instructions)	27					
28 Taxable income less section 1202 deduction (see instructions)	28					
29 Enter percent (divide line 27 by line 28, but not more than 100%)	29	%	%	%	%	%
30 Multiply amount on line 26 by the percentage on line 29	30					
31 Tax on undistributed net income. (Subtract line 30 from line 26. Enter here and on page 1, line 9.)	31					

Part IV Allocation to Beneficiary

Complete Part IV for each beneficiary. If the accumulation distribution is allocated to more than one beneficiary, attach an additional Schedule J with Part IV completed for each additional beneficiary. If more than five throwback years are involved, attach additional schedules.

Beneficiary's name   Identifying number

Beneficiary's address (number and street including apartment number or rural route)

City, state, and ZIP code

		Enter amount from line 13 allocated to this beneficiary (a)	Enter amount from line 14 allocated to this beneficiary (b)	Enter amount from line 16 allocated to this beneficiary (c)
32 Throwback year 19	32			
33 Throwback year 19	33			
34 Throwback year 19	34			
35 Throwback year 19	35			
36 Throwback year 19	36			
37 Total (add lines 32 through 36)	37			

SCHEDULE K-1
(Form 1041)

Department of the Treasury
Internal Revenue Service

Beneficiary's Share of Income, Deductions, Credits, Etc.—1990

for the calendar year 1990, or fiscal year
beginning ...., 1990, ending ...., 19 .....
Complete a separate Schedule K-1 for each beneficiary.

OMB No. 1545-0092

1990

Name of estate or trust

☐ Amended K-1
☐ Final K-1

Beneficiary's identifying number ▶

Estate's or trust's employer identification number ▶

Beneficiary's name, address, and ZIP code

Fiduciary's name, address, and ZIP code

Reminder: *If you received a short year 1987 Schedule K-1 that was from a trust required to adopt a calendar year, be sure to include one-fourth of those amounts reported as income, in addition to the items reported on this Schedule K-1, on the appropriate lines of your 1990 Form 1040 and related schedules.*

(a) Allocable share item	(b) Amount	(c) Calendar year 1990 Form 1040 filers enter the amounts in column (b) on:
1 Interest		Schedule B, Part I, line 1
2 Dividends		Schedule B, Part II, line 5
3a Net short-term capital gain		Schedule D, line 5, column (g)
b Net long-term capital gain		Schedule D, line 12, column (g)
4a Other taxable income: (itemize)		Schedule E, Part III
(1) Rental, rental real estate, and business income from activities acquired before 10/23/86		
(2) Rental, rental real estate, and business income from activities acquired after 10/22/86		
(3) Other passive income		
b Depreciation, including cost recovery (itemize):		
(1) Attributable to line 4a(1)		
(2) Attributable to line 4a(2)		
(3) Attributable to line 4a(3)		
c Depletion (itemize):		
(1) Attributable to line 4a(1)		
(2) Attributable to line 4a(2)		
(3) Attributable to line 4a(3)		
d Amortization (itemize):		
(1) Attributable to line 4a(1)		
(2) Attributable to line 4a(2)		
(3) Attributable to line 4a(3)		
5 Income for minimum tax purposes		
6 Income for regular tax purposes (add lines 1 through 4a)		
7 Adjustment for minimum tax purposes (subtract line 6 from line 5)		Form 6251, line 4t
8 Estate tax deduction (including certain generation-skipping transfer taxes) (attach computation)		Schedule A, line 26
9 Excess deductions on termination (attach computation)		Schedule A, line 21
10 Foreign taxes (list on a separate sheet)		Form 1116 or Schedule A (Form 1040), line 7
11 Tax preference items (itemize):		
a Accelerated depreciation		Include on the applicable line of Form 6251
b Depletion		
c Amortization		
12 Other (itemize):		
a Trust payments of estimated taxes credited to you		Form 1040, line 56
b Tax-exempt interest		Form 1040, line 8b
c Short-term capital loss carryover		Schedule D, line 6, column (f)
d Long-term capital loss carryover		Schedule D, line 15, column (f)
e		Include on the applicable line of appropriate tax form
f		
g		

For Paperwork Reduction Act Notice, see page 1 of the Instructions for Form 1041.

Schedule K-1 (Form 1041) 1990

B-5   Form 1120   U.S. Corporation Income Tax Return

Form 1120

Department of the Treasury
Internal Revenue Service

U.S. Corporation Income Tax Return

For calendar year 1990 or tax year beginning _____, 1990, ending _____, 19 ____

▶ Instructions are separate. See page 1 for Paperwork Reduction Act Notice.

OMB No. 1545-0123

1990

Check if a—

A Consolidated return ☐
B Personal holding co. ☐
C Personal service corp.(as defined in Temp. Regs. sec. 1.441-4T—see Instructions) ☐

Use IRS label. Otherwise, please print or type.

Name

Number, street, and room or suite no. (If a P.O. box, see page 2 of Instructions.)

City or town, state, and ZIP code

D Employer identification number

E Date incorporated

F Total assets (see Specific Instructions)

$

G Check applicable boxes: (1) ☐ Initial return (2) ☐ Final return (3) ☐ Change in address

Income

1a	Gross receipts or sales _____ **b** Less returns and allowances _____	**c** Bal ▶	1c
2	Cost of goods sold (Schedule A, line 7).		2
3	Gross profit (line 1c less line 2)		3
4	Dividends (Schedule C, line 19)		4
5	Interest		5
6	Gross rents		6
7	Gross royalties		7
8	Capital gain net income (attach Schedule D (Form 1120)) . . .		8
9	Net gain or (loss) from Form 4797, Part II, line 18 (attach Form 4797) . . .		9
10	Other income (see Instructions—attach schedule).		10
11	**Total income**—Add lines 3 through 10 . . . . ▶		11

Deductions (See Instructions for limitations on deductions.)

12	Compensation of officers (Schedule E, line 4)		12
13a	Salaries and wages _____ **b** Less jobs credit _____ **c** Balance ▶		13c
14	Repairs		14
15	Bad debts		15
16	Rents		16
17	Taxes		17
18	Interest		18
19	Contributions (**see Instructions for 10% limitation**)		19
20	Depreciation (attach Form 4562)	20	
21	Less depreciation claimed on Schedule A and elsewhere on return . .	21a	21b
22	Depletion		22
23	Advertising		23
24	Pension, profit-sharing, etc., plans		24
25	Employee benefit programs		25
26	Other deductions (attach schedule)		26
27	**Total deductions**—Add lines 12 through 26. . . . . ▶		27
28	Taxable income before net operating loss deduction and special deductions (line 11 less line 27) .		28
29	**Less: a** Net operating loss deduction (see Instructions)	29a	
	b Special deductions (Schedule C, line 20)	29b	29c

30	**Taxable income**—Line 28 less line 29c		30
31	**Total tax** (Schedule J, line 10)		31

Tax and Payments

32	Payments: **a** 1989 overpayment credited to 1990	32a		
	b 1990 estimated tax payments . .	32b		
	c Less 1990 refund applied for on Form 4466	32c ( ) **d** Bal ▶	32d	
	e Tax deposited with Form 7004		32e	
	f Credit from regulated investment companies (attach Form 2439) . .		32f	
	g Credit for Federal tax on fuels (attach Form 4136). See Instructions .		32g	32h
33	Enter any **penalty** for underpayment of estimated tax—Check ▶ ☐ if Form 2220 is attached .			33
34	**Tax due**—If the total of lines 31 and 33 is larger than line 32h, enter amount owed			34
35	**Overpayment**—If line 32h is larger than the total of lines 31 and 33, enter amount overpaid . .			35
36	Enter amount of line 35 you want: **Credited to 1991 estimated tax** ▶	Refunded ▶		36

Please Sign Here

Under penalties of perjury, I declare that I have examined this return, including accompanying schedules and statements, and to the best of my knowledge and belief, it is true, correct, and complete. Declaration of preparer (other than taxpayer) is based on all information of which preparer has any knowledge.

▶ Signature of officer   Date   ▶ Title

Paid Preparer's Use Only

Preparer's signature ▶	Date	Check if self-employed ☐	Preparer's social security number
Firm's name (or yours if self-employed) and address ▶		E.I. No. ▶	
		ZIP code ▶	

Form 1120 (1990)   Page **2**

Schedule A Cost of Goods Sold (See Instructions for line 2, page 1.)

1 Inventory at beginning of year	**1**	
2 Purchases	**2**	
3 Cost of labor	**3**	
4a Additional section 263A costs (see Instructions—attach schedule)	**4a**	
b Other costs (attach schedule)	**4b**	
5 **Total**—Add lines 1 through 4b	**5**	
6 Inventory at end of year	**6**	
7 **Cost of goods sold**—Line 5 less line 6. Enter here and on line 2, page 1.	**7**	

8a Check all methods used for valuing closing inventory:

    (i) ☐ Cost **(ii)** ☐ Lower of cost or market as described in Regulations section 1.471-4 (see Instructions)

    (iii) ☐ Writedown of "subnormal" goods as described in Regulations section 1.471-2(c) (see Instructions)

    (iv) ☐ Other (Specify method used and attach explanation.) ▶ _____

    b Check if the LIFO inventory method was adopted this tax year for any goods (if checked, attach Form 970) . . . . . . ☐

    c If the LIFO inventory method was used for this tax year, enter percentage (or amounts) of closing inventory computed under LIFO **8c**

    d Do the rules of section 263A (with respect to property produced or acquired for resale) apply to the corporation? . . ☐ Yes ☐ No

    e Was there any change in determining quantities, cost, or valuations between opening and closing inventory? If "Yes," attach explanation . . . . ☐ Yes ☐ No

Schedule C Dividends and Special Deductions (See Instructions.)

	(a) Dividends received	(b) %	(c) Special deductions: (a) × (b)
1 Dividends from less-than-20%-owned domestic corporations that are subject to the 70% deduction (other than debt-financed stock)		70	
2 Dividends from 20%-or-more-owned domestic corporations that are subject to the 80% deduction (other than debt-financed stock)		80 see Instructions	
3 Dividends on debt-financed stock of domestic and foreign corporations (section 246A)			
4 Dividends on certain preferred stock of less-than-20%-owned public utilities . . .		41.176	
5 Dividends on certain preferred stock of 20%-or-more-owned public utilities		47.059	
6 Dividends from less-than-20%-owned foreign corporations and certain FSCs that are subject to the 70% deduction		70	
7 Dividends from 20%-or-more-owned foreign corporations and certain FSCs that are subject to the 80% deduction		80	
8 Dividends from wholly owned foreign subsidiaries subject to the 100% deduction (section 245(b))		100	
9 **Total**—Add lines 1 through 8. See Instructions for limitation	▨	▨	
10 Dividends from domestic corporations received by a small business investment company operating under the Small Business Investment Act of 1958		100	
11 Dividends from certain FSCs that are subject to the 100% deduction (section 245(c)(1))		100	
12 Dividends from affiliated group members subject to the 100% deduction (section 243(a)(3))		100	
13 Other dividends from foreign corporations not included on lines 3, 6, 7, 8, or 11			▨
14 Income from controlled foreign corporations under subpart F (attach Forms 5471)			▨
15 Foreign dividend gross-up (section 78)			▨
16 IC-DISC and former DISC dividends not included on lines 1, 2, or 3 (section 246(d))			▨
17 Other dividends			▨
18 Deduction for dividends paid on certain preferred stock of public utilities (see Instructions)	▨	▨	
19 **Total dividends**—Add lines 1 through 17. Enter here and on line 4, page 1. ▶		▨	▨

20 **Total deductions**—Add lines 9, 10, 11, 12, and 18. Enter here and on line 29b, page 1 . . . . ▶

Schedule E Compensation of Officers (See Instructions for line 12, page 1.)

Complete Schedule E only if total receipts (line 1a, plus lines 4 through 10, of page 1, Form 1120) are $500,000 or more.

(a) Name of officer	(b) Social security number	(c) Percent of time devoted to business	Percent of corporation stock owned		(f) Amount of compensation
			(d) Common	(e) Preferred	
1		%	%	%	
		%	%	%	
		%	%	%	
		%	%	%	
		%	%	%	

2 Total compensation of officers		
3 **Less:** Compensation of officers claimed on Schedule A and elsewhere on return	(	)
4 Compensation of officers deducted on line 12, page 1		

Form 1120 (1990)   Page **3**

Schedule J   Tax Computation

1. Check if you are a member of a controlled group (see sections 1561 and 1563) . . . . . . ▶ ☐
2. If the box on line 1 is checked:
   a. Enter your share of the $50,000 and $25,000 taxable income bracket amounts (in that order):
      (i) |$ _____ | | **(ii)** |$ _____ | |
   b. Enter your share of the additional 5% tax (not to exceed $11,750) ▶ |$ _____ | |
3. Income tax (see Instructions to figure the tax). Check this box if the corporation is a qualified personal service corporation (see Instructions on page 12). ▶ ☐ **3**
4a. Foreign tax credit (attach Form 1118) **4a**
   b. Possessions tax credit (attach Form 5735) **4b**
   c. Orphan drug credit (attach Form 6765) **4c**
   d. Credit for fuel produced from a nonconventional source (see Instructions) **4d**
   e. General business credit. Enter here and check which forms are attached:
      ☐ Form 3800   ☐ Form 3468   ☐ Form 5884
      ☐ Form 6478   ☐ Form 6765   ☐ Form 8586 . . . . . . **4e**
   f. Credit for prior year minimum tax (attach Form 8801) **4f**

5. **Total**—Add lines 4a through 4f **5**

6. Line 3 less line 5 . . . . **6**
7. Personal holding company tax (attach Schedule PH (Form 1120)) **7**
8. Recapture taxes. Check if from: ☐ Form 4255 ☐ Form 8611 . . . . . **8**
9a. Alternative minimum tax (attach Form 4626). See Instructions **9a**
   b. Environmental tax (attach Form 4626) **9b**

10. **Total tax**—Add lines 6 through 9b. Enter here and on line 31, page 1 . . . . **10**

Additional Information (See General Instruction F.)   Yes | No

H Refer to the list in the Instructions and state the principal:
  (1) Business activity code no. ▶ _____
  (2) Business activity ▶ _____
  (3) Product or service ▶ _____

I (1) Did the corporation at the end of the tax year own, directly or indirectly, 50% or more of the voting stock of a domestic corporation? (For rules of attribution, see section 267(c).) . .
  If "Yes," attach a schedule showing: (a) name, address, and identifying number; (b) percentage owned; and (c) taxable income or (loss) before NOL and special deductions of such corporation for the tax year ending with or within your tax year.

  (2) Did any individual, partnership, corporation, estate, or trust at the end of the tax year own, directly or indirectly, 50% or more of the corporation's voting stock? (For rules of attribution, see section 267(c).) If "Yes," complete (a) through (c) . . . .
  (a) Attach a schedule showing name, address, and identifying number.
  (b) Enter percentage owned ▶ _____
  (c) Was the owner of such voting stock a foreign person? (See Instructions.) **Note:** *If "Yes," the corporation may have to file Form 5472* . . . .
  If "Yes," enter owner's country ▶ _____

J Was the corporation a U.S. shareholder of any controlled foreign corporation? (See sections 951 and 957.). . . . .
  If "Yes," attach Form 5471 for each such corporation.

K At any time during the tax year, did the corporation have an interest in or a signature or other authority over a financial account in a foreign country (such as a bank account, securities account, or other financial account)? . . . .
(See General Instruction F and filing requirements for form TD F 90-22.1.)
If "Yes," enter name of foreign country ▶ _____

L Was the corporation the grantor of, or transferor to, a foreign trust that existed during the current tax year, whether or not the corporation has any beneficial interest in it? . . . . . .
If "Yes," the corporation may have to file Forms 3520, 3520-A, or 926.

M During this tax year, did the corporation pay dividends (other than stock dividends and distributions in exchange for stock) in excess of the corporation's current and accumulated earnings and profits? (See sections 301 and 316.) . . . .
If "Yes," file Form 5452. If this is a consolidated return, answer here for parent corporation and on **Form 851**, Affiliations Schedule, for each subsidiary.

N During this tax year, did the corporation maintain any part of its accounting/tax records on a computerized system? . . . . .

O Check method of accounting:
  (1) ☐ Cash
  (2) ☐ Accrual
  (3) ☐ Other (specify) ▶ _____

P Check this box if the corporation issued publicly offered debt instruments with original issue discount . . . . . . ☐
If so, the corporation may have to file Form 8281.

Q Enter the amount of tax-exempt interest received or accrued during the tax year ▶ |$ _____ | |

R Enter the number of shareholders at the end of the tax year if there were 35 or fewer shareholders ▶

Form 1120 (1990)
Page **4**

Schedule L — Balance Sheets

Assets	Beginning of tax year (a)	(b)	End of tax year (c)	(d)
1 Cash				
2a Trade notes and accounts receivable				
b Less allowance for bad debts	( )		( )	
3 Inventories				
4 U.S. government obligations				
5 Tax-exempt securities (see Instructions)				
6 Other current assets (attach schedule)				
7 Loans to stockholders				
8 Mortgage and real estate loans				
9 Other investments (attach schedule)				
10a Buildings and other depreciable assets				
b Less accumulated depreciation	( )		( )	
11a Depletable assets				
b Less accumulated depletion	( )		( )	
12 Land (net of any amortization)				
13a Intangible assets (amortizable only)				
b Less accumulated amortization	( )		( )	
14 Other assets (attach schedule)				
15 Total assets				
Liabilities and Stockholders' Equity				
16 Accounts payable				
17 Mortgages, notes, bonds payable in less than 1 year				
18 Other current liabilities (attach schedule)				
19 Loans from stockholders				
20 Mortgages, notes, bonds payable in 1 year or more				
21 Other liabilities (attach schedule)				
22 Capital stock: a Preferred stock				
b Common stock				
23 Paid-in or capital surplus				
24 Retained earnings—Appropriated (attach schedule)				
25 Retained earnings—Unappropriated				
26 Less cost of treasury stock		( )		( )
27 Total liabilities and stockholders' equity				

Schedule M-1 — Reconciliation of Income per Books With Income per Return
(This schedule does not have to be completed if the total assets on line 15, column (d), of Schedule L are less than $25,000.)

1 Net income per books		7 Income recorded on books this year not included on this return (itemize):	
2 Federal income tax		a Tax-exempt interest $ _____	
3 Excess of capital losses over capital gains		_____	
4 Income subject to tax not recorded on books this year (itemize): _____		_____	
_____		8 Deductions on this return not charged against book income this year (itemize):	
5 Expenses recorded on books this year not deducted on this return (itemize):		a Depreciation $ _____	
a Depreciation $ _____		b Contributions carryover $ _____	
b Contributions carryover $ _____		_____	
c Travel and entertainment $ _____		_____	
_____		9 Total of lines 7 and 8	
6 Total of lines 1 through 5		10 Income (line 28, page 1)—line 6 less line 9	

Schedule M-2 — Analysis of Unappropriated Retained Earnings per Books (line 25, Schedule L)
(This schedule does not have to be completed if the total assets on line 15, column (d), of Schedule L are less than $25,000.)

1 Balance at beginning of year		5 Distributions: a Cash	
2 Net income per books		b Stock	
3 Other increases (itemize): _____		c Property	
_____		6 Other decreases (itemize): _____	
_____		_____	
4 Total of lines 1, 2, and 3		7 Total of lines 5 and 6	
		8 Balance at end of year (line 4 less line 7)	

Form **1120-W** **(WORKSHEET)** Department of the Treasury Internal Revenue Service	**Corporation Estimated Tax** (Keep for Your Records—Do *Not* Send to the Internal Revenue Service)	OMB No. 1545-0975 **1991**

1	Taxable income expected in the tax year	**1**
	Qualified personal service corporations (defined in Instructions): Skip lines 2 through 9 and enter 34% of line 1 on line 10.	
2	Enter the smaller of line 1 or $50,000 (members of a controlled group, see Instructions)	**2**
3	Subtract line 2 from line 1	**3**
4	Enter the smaller of line 3 or $25,000 (members of a controlled group, see Instructions)	**4**
5	Subtract line 4 from line 3	**5**
6	Enter 15% of line 2	**6**
7	Enter 25% of line 4	**7**
8	Enter 34% of line 5	**8**
9	If line 1 is greater than $100,000, enter the lesser of: 5% of the excess over $100,000; or $11,750 (members of a controlled group, see Instructions)	**9**
10	Add amounts on lines 6 through 9	**10**
11	Estimated tax credits	**11**
12	Subtract line 11 from line 10	**12**
13	Recapture of: **a** Investment credit and **b** Low-income housing credit	**13**
14a	Alternative minimum tax	**14a**
b	Environmental tax	**14b**
15	Total—Add lines 12 through 14b	**15**
16	Credit for Federal tax on fuels (see Instructions)	**16**
17	Total—Subtract line 16 from line 15. **Note:** *If the amount on this line is less than $500, the corporation is not required to make estimated tax payments*	**17**

18a	Enter 90% of line 17	**18a**
b	Enter the tax shown on your 1990 return *(Caution: See Instructions before completing this line.)*	**18b**
c	**Estimated tax.**—Enter the lesser of line 18a or line 18b	**18c**

		(a)	(b)	(c)	(d)
19	Installment due dates (see Instructions)	**19**				
20	**Required installments.** Enter 25% of line 18c in columns (a) through (d) unless **a** or **b** below applies to the corporation:					
a	If you use the annualized income installment method and/or the adjusted seasonal installment method, complete Schedule A and enter the amounts from line 45 in each column of line 20.					
b	If you are a "large corporation," see the Instructions for the amount to enter in each column of line 20	**20**				

For Paperwork Reduction Act Notice, see Instructions.   Form **1120-W** (1991)

Form 1120-W (WORKSHEET) 1991   Page **2**

Schedule A	Required Installments Using the Annualized Income Installment Method or the Adjusted Seasonal Installment Method Under Section 6655(e)

Part I—Annualized Income Installment Method		**(a)**	**(b)**	**(c)**	**(d)**
		Period			
			First 3 months	First 6 months	First 9 months
(1) Enter your taxable income for each period.	1				
(2) Annualization amounts.	2		4	2	1.33333
(3) Multiply line 1 by line 2.	3				
		Period			
		First 3 months	First 5 months	First 8 months	First 11 months
(4) Enter your taxable income for each period.	4				
(5) Annualization amounts.	5	4	2.4	1.5	1.09091
(6) Multiply line 4 by line 5.	6				
(7) Annualized taxable income. In column (a), enter the amount from line 6, column (a). In columns (b), (c), and (d), enter the **lesser** of the amounts in each column on line 3 or line 6.	7				
(8) Figure your tax on the amount in each column on line 7 in the same manner as you figured line 10, Form 1120-W.	8				
(9) Enter other taxes for each payment period (see Instructions).	9				
(10) Total tax. Add lines 8 and 9.	10				
(11) For each period, enter the same type of credits as allowed on Form 1120-W, lines 11 and 16 (see Instructions).	11				
(12) Total tax after credits. Subtract line 11 from line 10. If less than zero, enter zero.	12				
(13) Applicable percentage.	13	22.5%	45%	67.5%	90%
(14) Multiply line 12 by line 13.	14				
(15) Enter the total of amounts in all preceding columns of line 45.	15				
(16) Subtract line 15 from line 14. If less than zero, enter zero.	16				

Part II—Adjusted Seasonal Installment Method (Caution: *You may use this method only if the base period percentage for any 6 consecutive months is at least 70%. See the Schedule A Instructions for more information.)*

		(a)	**(b)**	**(c)**	**(d)**
		Period			
		First 3 months	First 5 months	First 8 months	First 11 months
(17) Enter your taxable income for the following periods:					
a Tax year beginning in 1988	17a				
b Tax year beginning in 1989	17b				
c Tax year beginning in 1990	17c				
(18) Enter your taxable income for each period for your tax year beginning in 1991.	18				
		Period			
		First 4 months	First 6 months	First 9 months	Entire year
(19) Enter your taxable income for the following periods:					
a Tax year beginning in 1988	19a				
b Tax year beginning in 1989	19b				
c Tax year beginning in 1990	19c				
(20) Divide the amount in each column on line 17a by the amount in column (d) on line 19a.	20				
(21) Divide the amount in each column on line 17b by the amount in column (d) on line 19b.	21				
(22) Divide the amount in each column on line 17c by the amount in column (d) on line 19c.	22				

Form 1120-W (WORKSHEET) 1991   Page **3**

		(a)	(b)	(c)	(d)
(23)	Add lines 20 through 22.	23				
(24)	Base period percentage for months before filing month. Divide line 23 by 3.	24				
(25)	Divide line 18 by line 24.	25				
(26)	Figure your tax on the amount on line 25 in the same manner as you figured line 10, Form 1120-W.	26				
(27)	Divide the amount in columns (a) through (c) on line 19a by the amount in column (d) on line 19a.	27				
(28)	Divide the amount in columns (a) through (c) on line 19b by the amount in column (d) on line 19b.	28				
(29)	Divide the amount in columns (a) through (c) on line 19c by the amount in column (d) on line 19c.	29				
(30)	Add lines 27 through 29.	30				
(31)	Base period percentage for months through and including filing month. Divide line 30 by 3.	31				
(32)	Multiply the amount in columns (a) through (c) of line 26 by the amount in the corresponding column of line 31. In column (d), enter the amount from line 26, column (d).	32				
(33)	Enter other taxes for each payment period (see Instructions).	33				
(34)	Total tax. Add lines 32 and 33.	34				
(35)	For each period, enter the same type of credits as allowed on Form 1120-W, lines 11 and 16 (see Instructions).	35				
(36)	Total tax after credits. Subtract line 35 from line 34. If less than zero, enter zero.	36				
(37)	Multiply line 36 by 90%.	37				
(38)	Enter the total of amounts in all preceding columns of line 45.	38				
(39)	Subtract line 38 from line 37. If less than zero, enter zero.	39				

Part III—Required Installments

			1st installment	2nd installment	3rd installment	4th installment
(40)	If you completed one of the above parts, enter the amounts in each column from line 16 or line 39. (If you completed both parts, enter the lesser of the amounts in each column from line 16 or line 39.)	40				
(41)	Divide line 18c, Form 1120-W, by 4 and enter the result in each column. (**Note:** *"Large corporations" see line 20b Instructions on page 5 for the amount to enter.*)	41				
(42)	Enter the amount from line 44 for the preceding column.	42				
(43)	Add lines 41 and 42 and enter the total.	43				
(44)	If line 43 is more than line 40, subtract line 40 from line 43. Otherwise, enter zero.	44				
(45)	**Required installments.**—Enter the lesser of line 40 or line 43 here and on Form 1120-W, line 20.	45				

General Instructions

(Section references are to the Internal Revenue Code unless otherwise noted.)

Paperwork Reduction Act Notice.—Your use of this form is optional. It is provided to aid you in determining your tax liability.

The time needed to complete this form will vary depending on individual circumstances. The estimated average time is:

Form	Recordkeeping	Learning about the law or the form	Preparing the form
1120-W	6 hrs., 56 min.	1 hr., 12 min.	1 hr., 21 min.
1120-W, Sch. A (Pt. I)	11 hrs., 43 min.	6 min.	17 min.
1120-W, Sch. A (Pt. II)	24 hrs., 23 min.	-------	24 min.
1120-W, Sch. A (Pt. III)	5 hrs., 16 min.	-------	5 min.

If you have comments concerning the accuracy of these time estimates or suggestions for making this form more simple, we would be happy to hear from you. You can write to both the **Internal Revenue Service,** Washington, DC 20224, Attention: IRS Reports Clearance Officer, T:FP; and the **Office of Management and Budget,** Paperwork Reduction Project (1545-0975), Washington, DC 20503. **DO NOT** send the tax form to either of these offices. Instead, keep the form for your records.

A. Who Must Make Estimated Tax Payments.—Generally, a corporation must make estimated tax payments if it expects its estimated tax (income tax less credits) to be $500 or more. S corporations must also make estimated tax payments for certain taxes. See the Instructions for **Form 1120S,** U.S. Income Tax Return for an S Corporation, to figure the estimated tax payments of an S corporation.

In addition, tax-exempt corporations filing **Form 990-T,** Exempt Organization Business Income Tax Return, must make estimated tax payments for their unrelated business income tax. Tax-exempt corporations use **Form 990-W,** Estimated Tax on Unrelated Business Taxable Income for Tax-Exempt Organizations, to figure their estimated tax.

B. Underpayment of Estimated Tax.—A corporation that does not pay estimated tax when due may be charged an underpayment penalty for the period of underpayment (section 6655), at a rate determined under section 6621.

C. Overpayment of Estimated Tax.—A corporation that has overpaid its estimated tax may apply for a "quick refund" if the overpayment is:

(1) At least 10% of its expected income tax liability, **and**

(2) At least $500.

To apply, the corporation must file **Form 4466,** Corporation Application for Quick Refund of Overpayment of Estimated Tax, after the end of its tax year, but before the 16th day of the 3rd month thereafter, and before it files its tax return.

D. Depositary Method of Tax Payment.—Deposit corporation income tax payments and estimated tax payments with a Federal Tax Deposit (FTD) Coupon. Be sure to darken the "1120" box on Form 8109. Make these tax deposits with either a financial institution qualified as a depositary for Federal taxes or the Federal Reserve bank or branch servicing the geographic area where the corporation is located. **Do not** submit deposits directly to an IRS office; otherwise, the corporation may be subject to a failure to deposit penalty. Records of deposits will be sent to the IRS for crediting to the corporation's account. See the instructions contained in FTD Coupon Book **(Form 8109)** and **Pub. 583,** Taxpayers Starting a Business, for more information.

To help ensure proper crediting to your account, write your employer identification number, "Form 1120" (or applicable form), and the tax period to which the deposit applies on your check or money order.

E. Amended Estimated Tax.—If after the corporation figures and deposits estimated tax, it finds that its tax liability for the year is much more or less than originally estimated because its economic condition has changed, it may have to refigure its required installments. If earlier installments were underpaid, the corporation may owe a penalty for underpayment of estimated tax.

An immediate "catch-up" payment should be made to reduce the amount of any penalty resulting from the underpayment of any earlier installments, whether caused by a change in estimate, failure to make a deposit, or a mistake.

Specific Instructions

Qualified personal service corporations.—A qualified personal service corporation is taxed at a flat rate of 34% on its taxable income. For this purpose, a qualified personal service corporation is any corporation: **(a)** substantially all of the activities of which involve the performance of services in the fields of health, law, engineering, architecture, accounting, actuarial science, performing arts, or consulting, and **(b)** at least 95% of the stock of which is owned by employees performing the services, retired employees who had performed the services listed above, any estate of an employee or retiree described above, or any person who acquired stock of the corporation as a result of the death of an employee or retiree described above, if the acquisition occurred within 2 years of death. See Temporary Regulations section 1.448-1T(e) for details.

Lines 2 and 4.—Members of a controlled group enter on line 2 the lesser of the amount on line 1 or their share of the $50,000 amount. Members of a controlled group enter on line 4 the lesser of the amount on line 3 or their share of the $25,000 amount.

If no apportionment plan is adopted, the members of the controlled group must divide the amount in each taxable income bracket equally among themselves. For example, controlled group AB consists of corporation A and corporation B. They do not elect an apportionment plan. Therefore, corporation A is entitled to $25,000 (one-half of $50,000) in the $50,000 taxable income bracket, and $12,500 (one-half of $25,000) in the $25,000 taxable income bracket. Corporation B is also entitled to $25,000 in the $50,000 taxable income bracket and $12,500 in the $25,000 taxable income bracket.

Members of a controlled group may elect an unequal apportionment plan and divide the amounts in each taxable income bracket in any way they want. They need not divide each taxable income bracket in the same way. For example, if controlled group AB above elects an unequal apportionment plan, any member of the controlled group may be entitled to all, some, or none of the $50,000 amount in the first taxable income bracket, as long as the total for all members of the controlled group is not more than $50,000. Similarly, any member may be entitled to all, some, or none of the $25,000 amount in the second taxable income bracket, as long as the total for all members of the controlled group is not more than $25,000.

Line 9.—Members of a controlled group of corporations are treated as one corporation for purposes of figuring the applicability of the additional 5% tax. If the taxable income of the controlled group exceeds $100,000, enter on line 9 the portion of the lesser of: 5% of the excess over $100,000; or $11,750.

Line 11.—The estimated tax credits include the sum of any credits against tax provided by Part IV of Subchapter A of Chapter 1 (except the credits shown on line 16).

Line 14a.—Alternative minimum tax is generally the excess of tentative minimum tax over regular tax. See section 55 for definitions of tentative minimum tax and regular tax. A limited amount of the foreign tax credit may be used to offset the minimum tax. See sections 55 through 59 for more information on alternative minimum tax.

Line 14b.—Environmental tax is 0.12 percent of the excess of modified alternative minimum taxable income over $2 million. See section 59A and **Pub. 542,** Tax Information on Corporations, for more information.

Line 16.—Include on line 16 any credit the corporation is claiming for ozone depleting chemicals used in the manufacture of rigid foam insulation under section 4681(a)(1).

Line 18b.—Figure your 1990 tax in the same manner that line 17 of this worksheet was determined, using the taxes and credits from your 1990 tax return. If you did not file a return showing at least some amount of tax for the 1990 tax year, or if your 1990 tax year was for less than 12 months, do not complete this line. Instead, enter the amount from line 18a on line 18c.

Line 19.—*Calendar year taxpayers:* Enter 4-15-91, 6-17-91, 9-16-91, and 12-16-91, respectively, in columns (a) through (d).

Fiscal year taxpayers: Enter the 15th day of the 4th, 6th, 9th, and 12th months of your tax year in columns (a) through (d). If any date falls on a Saturday, Sunday, or legal holiday, substitute the next regular workday.

Line 20.—When making payments of estimated tax, be sure to take into account any 1990 overpayment that the corporation chose to credit against its 1991 tax.

Line 20a.—Annualized Income Installment Method or Adjusted Seasonal Installment Method: If the corporation's income is expected to vary during the year because, for example, it operates its business on a seasonal basis, it may be able to lower the amount of one or more required installments by using the annualized income installment method or the adjusted seasonal installment method. For example, a ski shop, which receives most of its income during the winter months, may be able to benefit from using one or both of these methods in figuring one or more of its required installments.

To use one or both of these methods to figure one or more required installments, use Schedule A on pages 2 and 3. If you use Schedule A for any payment date, you must use it for **all** payment due dates. To arrive at the amount of each required installment, Schedule A automatically selects the smallest of: **(a)** the annualized income installment, **(b)** the adjusted seasonal installment (if applicable), or **(c)** the regular installment under section 6655(d) (increased by any reduction recapture under section 6655(e)(1)(B)).

Line 20b.—Large corporations: A "large corporation" is one that had, or its predecessor had, taxable income of $1 million or more for any of the 3 tax years immediately preceding the tax year involved. For this purpose, taxable income is modified to exclude net operating loss or capital loss carrybacks or carryovers. Members of a controlled group, as defined in section 1563, must divide the $1 million amount among themselves in accordance with rules similar to those in section 1561.

If you are not using the annualized income installment method or adjusted seasonal installment method, follow the instructions below to figure the amounts to enter on line 20. (If you are using the annualized income installment method and/or the adjusted seasonal installment method, these instructions apply to line 41 of Schedule A.)

If line 18a is less than line 18b: Enter 25% of line 18a in columns (a) through (d) of line 20.

If line 18b is less than line 18a: In column (a) of line 20, enter 25% of line 18b. In column (b), determine the amount to enter by: (i) subtracting line 18b from line 18a, (ii) adding the result to the amount on line 18a, and (iii) multiplying the total by 25%. In columns (c) and (d), enter 25% of line 18a.

Schedule A Instructions

If you are using only the annualized income installment method (Part I), complete Parts I and III of Schedule A. If you are using only the adjusted seasonal installment method (Part II), complete Parts II and III of Schedule A. If you are using both methods, complete all 3 parts of Schedule A. Enter in each column on line 20 of page 1 the amounts from the corresponding column of line 45 of Schedule A.

Caution: *If you use Schedule A, do not attempt to figure any required installment until after the end of the month preceding the due date for that installment.*

For each part that applies to you, complete each column in its entirety before going to the next column. For example, if Parts I and III are required, complete column (a) lines 1 through 16, and column (a) lines 40 through 45, before starting column (b).

Part I—Annualized Income Installment Method

Line 9.—Enter the taxes the corporation owed because of events that occurred during the months shown in the headings used to figure annualized taxable income. Include the same taxes used to figure line 15 of Form 1120-W.

Compute the alternative minimum tax and environmental tax by figuring alternative minimum taxable income and modified alternative minimum taxable income based on the corporation's income and deductions during the months shown in the column headings used to figure annualized taxable income. Multiply the alternative minimum taxable income and modified alternative minimum taxable income by the annualization amounts used to figure annualized taxable income (on line 2 or line 5) before subtracting the exemption amounts (see sections 55(d) and 59A(a)(2)).

Line 11.—Enter the credits to which you are entitled because of events that occurred during the months shown in the column headings used to figure annualized taxable income.

Part II—Adjusted Seasonal Installment Method

Do **not** complete this part unless the corporation's base period percentage for any six consecutive months of the tax year equals or exceeds 70%. The term "base period percentage" for any period of six consecutive months is the average of the three percentages figured by dividing the taxable income for the corresponding six consecutive-month period in each of the 3 preceding tax years by the taxable income for each of their respective tax years.

Example: An amusement park that has a calendar year as its tax year receives the largest part of its taxable income during the six-month period from May through October. To compute its base period percentage for the period May through October 1991, it must figure its taxable income for the period May through October in each of the following years: 1988, 1989, and 1990. The taxable income for each May-through-October period is then divided by the total taxable income for the tax year in which the period is included, resulting in the following quotients: .69 for May through October 1988, .74 for May through October 1989, and .67 for May through October 1990. Since the average of .69, .74, and .67 is .70, the base period percentage for May through October 1991 is 70%. Therefore, the amusement park qualifies for the adjusted seasonal installment method.

Line 33.—Enter the taxes the corporation owed because of events that occurred during the months shown in the column headings above line 17 of Part II. Include the same taxes used to figure line 15 of Form 1120-W.

Compute the alternative minimum tax and environmental tax by figuring alternative minimum taxable income and modified alternative minimum taxable income based on the corporation's income and deductions during the months shown in the column headings above line 17 of Part II. Divide the alternative minimum taxable income and modified alternative minimum taxable income by the amounts shown on line 24 before subtracting the exemption amounts (see sections 55(d) and 59A(a)(2)). For columns (a) through (c) only, multiply the alternative minimum tax and environmental tax so determined by the amounts shown on line 31.

Line 35.—Enter the credits to which you are entitled because of events that occurred during the months shown in the column headings above line 17 of Part II.

B-6   Form 1120S   U.S. Income Tax Return for an S Corporation

Form **1120S**	**U.S. Income Tax Return for an S Corporation**	OMB No. 1545-0130
Department of the Treasury Internal Revenue Service	For calendar year 1990, or tax year beginning _____, 1990, and ending _____, 19___ . ▶ See separate instructions.	**1990**

A Date of election as an S corporation	Use IRS label. Otherwise, please print or type.	Name	**C** Employer Identification number
B Business code no. (see Specific Instructions)		Number, street, and room or suite no. (If a P.O. box, see page 7 of the instructions.)	**D** Date incorporated
		City or town, state, and ZIP code	**E** Total assets (see Specific Instructions) $

F Check applicable boxes: (1) ☐ Initial return (2) ☐ Final return (3) ☐ Change in address (4) ☐ Amended return

G Check this box if this is an S corporation subject to the consolidated audit procedures of sections 6241 through 6245 (see instructions before checking this box) . . ▶ ☐

H Enter number of shareholders in the corporation at end of the tax year . . . . ▶

Caution: *Include only trade or business income and expenses on lines 1a through 21. See the instructions for more information.*

Income

1a	Gross receipts or sales |_____| **b** Less returns and allowances |_____| **c** Bal ▶	**1c**	
2	Cost of goods sold (Schedule A, line 7) .	**2**	
3	Gross profit (subtract line 2 from line 1c) .	**3**	
4	Net gain (loss) from Form 4797, Part II, line 18 .	**4**	
5	Other income (see instructions) *(attach schedule)* .	**5**	
6	**Total** income (loss)—Combine lines 3 through 5 . . . . ▶	**6**	

Deductions (See instructions for limitations.)

7	Compensation of officers	**7**	
8a	Salaries and wages |_____| **b** Less jobs credit |_____| **c** Bal ▶	**8c**	
9	Repairs	**9**	
10	Bad debts	**10**	
11	Rents	**11**	
12	Taxes	**12**	
13	Interest	**13**	
14a	Depreciation (see instructions) **14a**		
b	Depreciation reported on Schedule A and elsewhere on return . **14b**		
c	Subtract line 14b from line 14a	**14c**	
15	Depletion (**Do not deduct oil and gas depletion.** See instructions.)	**15**	
16	Advertising	**16**	
17	Pension, profit-sharing, etc., plans	**17**	
18	Employee benefit programs	**18**	
19	Other deductions *(attach schedule)*	**19**	
20	**Total** deductions—Add lines 7 through 19 . . . . ▶	**20**	
21	Ordinary income (loss) from trade or business activities—Subtract line 20 from line 6	**21**	

Tax and Payments

22	**Tax:**		
a	Excess net passive income tax *(attach schedule)* **22a**		
b	Tax from Schedule D (Form 1120S) **22b**		
c	Add lines 22a and 22b (see instructions for additional taxes)	**22c**	
23	**Payments:**		
a	1990 estimated tax payments **23a**		
b	Tax deposited with Form 7004 . . . . . . **23b**		
c	Credit for Federal tax on fuels *(attach Form 4136)* **23c**		
d	Add lines 23a through 23c	**23d**	
24	Enter any **penalty** for underpayment of estimated tax—Check ▶ ☐ if Form 2220 is attached .	**24**	
25	**Tax due**—If the total of lines 22c and 24 is larger than line 23d, enter amount owed. See instructions for depositary method of payment . . . . ▶	**25**	
26	**Overpayment**—If line 23d is larger than the total of lines 22c and 24, enter amount overpaid ▶	**26**	
27	Enter amount of line 26 you want: **Credited to 1991 estimated tax** ▶ |_____| **Refunded** ▶	**27**	

Please Sign Here

Under penalties of perjury, I declare that I have examined this return, including accompanying schedules and statements, and to the best of my knowledge and belief, it is true, correct, and complete. Declaration of preparer (other than taxpayer) is based on all information of which preparer has any knowledge.

▶ Signature of officer	Date	▶ Title

Paid Preparer's Use Only	Preparer's signature ▶	Date	Check if self-employed ▶ ☐	Preparer's social security number
	Firm's name (or yours if self-employed) and address ▶		E.I. No. ▶	
			ZIP code ▶	

For Paperwork Reduction Act Notice, see page 1 of separate instructions.   Form **1120S** (1990)

Form 1120S (1990)   Page **2**

Schedule A   **Cost of Goods Sold** (See instructions.)

1 Inventory at beginning of year **1**		
2 Purchases **2**		
3 Cost of labor **3**		
4a Additional section 263A costs (see instructions) *(attach schedule)* **4a**		
b Other costs *(attach schedule)* **4b**		
5 Total—Add lines 1 through 4b **5**		
6 Inventory at end of year **6**		
7 Cost of goods sold—Subtract line 6 from line 5. Enter here and on line 2, page 1 . . . . **7**		

8a Check all methods used for valuing closing inventory:
  (i) ☐ Cost
  (ii) ☐ Lower of cost or market as described in Regulations section 1.471-4
  (iii) ☐ Writedown of "subnormal" goods as described in Regulations section 1.471-2(c)
  (iv) ☐ Other (specify method used and attach explanation) ▶ ....

b Check this box if the LIFO inventory method was adopted this tax year for any goods *(if checked, attach Form 970)* . . . ▶ ☐

c If the LIFO inventory method was used for this tax year, enter percentage (or amounts) of closing inventory computed under LIFO . . . . **8c** |

d Do the rules of section 263A (with respect to property produced or acquired for resale) apply to the corporation? . . . ☐ Yes   ☐ No

e Was there any change in determining quantities, cost, or valuations between opening and closing inventory? . . . . ☐ Yes   ☐ No
If "Yes," attach explanation.

Additional Information Required (continued from page 1)

	Yes	No
I Did you at the end of the tax year own, directly or indirectly, 50% or more of the voting stock of a domestic corporation? For rules of attribution, see section 267(c). If "Yes," attach a schedule showing: **(1)** name, address, and employer identification number; and **(2)** percentage owned.		
J Refer to the list in the instructions and state your principal: **(1)** Business activity ▶ .... **(2)** Product or service ▶		
K Were you a member of a controlled group subject to the provisions of section 1561?		
L At any time during the tax year, did you have an interest in or a signature or other authority over a financial account in a foreign country (such as a bank account, securities account, or other financial account)? (See instructions for exceptions and filing requirements for form TD F 90-22.1.) . . . . If "Yes," enter the name of the foreign country ▶		
M Were you the grantor of, or transferor to, a foreign trust that existed during the current tax year, whether or not you have any beneficial interest in it? If "Yes," you may have to file Forms 3520, 3520-A, or 926		
N During this tax year did you maintain any part of your accounting/tax records on a computerized system?		
O Check method of accounting: **(1)** ☐ Cash ▶ **(2)** ☐ Accrual **(3)** ☐ Other (specify) ▶		
P Check this box if the S corporation has filed or is required to file **Form 8264,** Application for Registration of a Tax Shelter . . . . ▶ ☐		
Q Check this box if the corporation issued publicly offered debt instruments with original issue discount . . . . . ▶ ☐ If so, the corporation may have to file **Form 8281,** Information Return for Publicly Offered Original Issue Discount Instruments.		
R If the corporation: **(1)** filed its election to be an S corporation after 1986, **(2)** was a C corporation before it elected to be an S corporation **or** the corporation acquired an asset with a basis determined by reference to its basis (or the basis of any other property) in the hands of a C corporation, and **(3)** has net unrealized built-in gain (defined in section 1374(d)(1)) in excess of the net recognized built-in gain from prior years, enter the net unrealized built-in gain reduced by net recognized built-in gain from prior years (see instructions) . . . . . . ▶ $		
S Check this box if the corporation had subchapter C earnings and profits at the close of the tax year (see instructions) ▶ ☐		

Designation of Tax Matters Person (See instructions.)

Enter below the shareholder designated as the tax matters person (TMP) for the tax year of this return:

Name of designated TMP ▶ _____   Identifying number of TMP ▶ _____

Address of designated TMP ▶ _____

Form 1120S (1990)   Page **3**

Schedule K   Shareholders' Shares of Income, Credits, Deductions, Etc.

	(a) Pro rata share items		(b) Total amount
Income (Loss)	**1** Ordinary income (loss) from trade or business activities (page 1, line 21)	**1**	
	2 Net income (loss) from rental real estate activities *(attach Form 8825)*	**2**	
	3a Gross income from other rental activities . . . . . . `3a`		
	b Less expenses *(attach schedule)* . . . . `3b`		
	c Net income (loss) from other rental activities	**3c**	
	4 Portfolio income (loss):		
	a Interest income	**4a**	
	b Dividend income	**4b**	
	c Royalty income	**4c**	
	d Net short-term capital gain (loss) *(attach Schedule D (Form 1120S))*	**4d**	
	e Net long-term capital gain (loss) *(attach Schedule D (Form 1120S))*	**4e**	
	f Other portfolio income (loss) *(attach schedule)*	**4f**	
	5 Net gain (loss) under section 1231 (other than due to casualty or theft) *(attach Form 4797)*	**5**	
	6 Other income (loss) *(attach schedule)*	**6**	
Deductions	**7** Charitable contributions (see instructions) *(attach list)*	**7**	
	8 Section 179 expense deduction *(attach Form 4562)*	**8**	
	9 Deductions related to portfolio income (loss) (see instructions) (itemize)	**9**	
	10 Other deductions *(attach schedule)*	**10**	
Investment Interest	**11a** Interest expense on investment debts	**11a**	
	b (1) Investment income included on lines 4a through 4f above	**11b(1)**	
	(2) Investment expenses included on line 9 above	**11b(2)**	
Credits	**12a** Credit for alcohol used as a fuel *(attach Form 6478)*	**12a**	
	b Low-income housing credit (see instructions):		
	(1) From partnerships to which section 42(j)(5) applies for property placed in service before 1990.	**12b(1)**	
	(2) Other than on line 12b(1) for property placed in service before 1990	**12b(2)**	
	(3) From partnerships to which section 42(j)(5) applies for property placed in service after 1989	**12b(3)**	
	(4) Other than on line 12b(3) for property placed in service after 1989	**12b(4)**	
	c Qualified rehabilitation expenditures related to rental real estate activities *(attach Form 3468)*	**12c**	
	d Credits (other than credits shown on lines 12b and 12c) related to rental real estate activities (see instructions)	**12d**	
	e Credits related to other rental activities (see instructions)	**12e**	
	13 Other credits (see instructions)	**13**	
Adjustments and Tax Preference Items	**14a** Accelerated depreciation of real property placed in service before 1987	**14a**	
	b Accelerated depreciation of leased personal property placed in service before 1987 . . .	**14b**	
	c Depreciation adjustment on property placed in service after 1986	**14c**	
	d Depletion (other than oil and gas)	**14d**	
	e (1) Gross income from oil, gas, or geothermal properties	**14e(1)**	
	(2) Deductions allocable to oil, gas, or geothermal properties	**14e(2)**	
	f Other adjustments and tax preference items *(attach schedule)*	**14f**	
Foreign Taxes	**15a** Type of income ▶ ---		
	b Name of foreign country or U.S. possession ▶ ---------------------------		
	c Total gross income from sources outside the U.S. *(attach schedule)*	**15c**	
	d Total applicable deductions and losses *(attach schedule)*	**15d**	
	e Total foreign taxes (check one): ▶ ☐ Paid ☐ Accrued	**15e**	
	f Reduction in taxes available for credit *(attach schedule)*	**15f**	
	g Other foreign tax information *(attach schedule)*	**15g**	
Other Items	**16a** Total expenditures to which a section 59(e) election may apply	**16a**	
	b Type of expenditures ▶ --		
	17 Total property distributions (including cash) other than dividends reported on line 19 below	**17**	
	18 Other items and amounts required to be reported separately to shareholders (see instructions) *(attach schedule)*		
	19 Total dividend distributions paid from accumulated earnings and profits	**19**	
	20 Income (loss) (Required only if Schedule M-1 must be completed.)—Combine lines 1 through 6 in column (b). From the result subtract the sum of lines 7 through 11a, 15e, and 16a	**20**	

Form 1120S (1990)   Page **4**

Schedule L   Balance Sheets

Assets	Beginning of tax year		End of tax year	
	(a)	(b)	(c)	(d)
1 Cash				
2a Trade notes and accounts receivable . .				
b Less allowance for bad debts				
3 Inventories				
4 U.S. government obligations				
5 Tax-exempt securities				
6 Other current assets (attach schedule) . . .				
7 Loans to shareholders				
8 Mortgage and real estate loans				
9 Other investments (attach schedule) . . .				
10a Buildings and other depreciable assets . .				
b Less accumulated depreciation				
11a Depletable assets				
b Less accumulated depletion				
12 Land (net of any amortization)				
13a Intangible assets (amortizable only) . . .				
b Less accumulated amortization . . .				
14 Other assets (attach schedule)				
15 Total assets				
Liabilities and Shareholders' Equity				
16 Accounts payable				
17 Mortgages, notes, bonds payable in less than 1 year				
18 Other current liabilities (attach schedule) . .				
19 Loans from shareholders				
20 Mortgages, notes, bonds payable in 1 year or more				
21 Other liabilities (attach schedule)				
22 Capital stock				
23 Paid-in or capital surplus				
24 Retained earnings				
25 Less cost of treasury stock		( )		( )
26 Total liabilities and shareholders' equity . .				

Schedule M-1   Reconciliation of Income per Books With Income per Return (You are not required to complete this schedule if the total assets on line 15, column (d), of Schedule L are less than $25,000.)

1 Net income per books		5 Income recorded on books this year not included on Schedule K, lines 1 through 6 (itemize):	
2 Income included on Schedule K, lines 1 through 6, not recorded on books this year (itemize): _____		a Tax-exempt interest $ _____	
_____		_____	
3 Expenses recorded on books this year not included on Schedule K, lines 1 through 11a, 15e, and 16a (itemize):		6 Deductions included on Schedule K, lines 1 through 11a, 15e, and 16a, not charged against book income this year (itemize):	
a Depreciation $ _____		a Depreciation $ _____	
b Travel and entertainment $ _____		_____	
_____		7 Total of lines 5 and 6	
4 Total of lines 1 through 3		8 Income (loss) (Schedule K, line 20)—Line 4 less line 7	

Schedule M-2   Analysis of Accumulated Adjustments Account, Other Adjustments Account, and Shareholders' Undistributed Taxable Income Previously Taxed (See instructions.)

	(a) Accumulated adjustments account	(b) Other adjustments account	(c) Shareholders' undistributed taxable income previously taxed
1 Balance at beginning of tax year			
2 Ordinary income from page 1, line 21 . . .			
3 Other additions			
4 Loss from page 1, line 21	( )		
5 Other reductions	( )	( )	
6 Combine lines 1 through 5			
7 Distributions other than dividend distributions			
8 Balance at end of tax year—subtract line 7 from line 6			

SCHEDULE K-1
(Form 1120S)
Department of the Treasury
Internal Revenue Service

Shareholder's Share of Income, Credits, Deductions, Etc.
▶ See separate instructions.
For calendar year 1990 or tax year
beginning _____, 1990, and ending _____, 19 ▶

OMB No. 1545-0130

1990

Shareholder's identifying number ▶ | Corporation's identifying number ▶

Shareholder's name, address, and ZIP code | Corporation's name, address, and ZIP code

A Shareholder's percentage of stock ownership for tax year (see Instructions for Schedule K-1) . . . . ▶ _____ %
B Internal Revenue Service Center where corporation filed its return ▶ ....
C **(1)** Tax shelter registration number (see Instructions for Schedule K-1) . . . . . . ▶ ....
  (2) Type of tax shelter ▶ ....
D If the shareholder acquired corporate stock after 10/22/86, check here ▶ ☐ and enter the shareholder's weighted percentage increase in stock ownership for 1990 (see Instructions for Schedule K-1) . . . . ▶ _____ %
E If any activity for which income or loss is reported on line 1, 2, or 3, was started or acquired by the corporation after 10/22/86, check here ▶ ☐ and enter the date of start up or acquisition in the date space on line 1, 2, or 3 **below.**
F Check applicable boxes: **(1)** ☐ Final K-1   **(2)** ☐ Amended K-1

		(a) Pro rata share items		(b) Amount	(c) Form 1040 filers enter the amount in column (b) on:
Income (Loss)	1	Ordinary income (loss) from trade or business activities. If applicable, enter date asked for in item E . . . . ▶ _____	1		See Shareholder's Instructions for Schedule K-1 (Form 1120S).
	2	Net income (loss) from rental real estate activities. If applicable, enter date asked for in item E . . . . ▶ _____	2		
	3	Net income (loss) from other rental activities. If applicable, enter date asked for in item E . . . . ▶ _____	3		
	4	Portfolio income (loss):			
	a	Interest	4a		Sch. B, Part I, line 1
	b	Dividends	4b		Sch. B, Part II, line 5
	c	Royalties	4c		Sch. E, Part I, line 4
	d	Net short-term capital gain (loss)	4d		Sch. D, line 5, col. (f) or (g)
	e	Net long-term capital gain (loss)	4e		Sch. D, line 12, col. (f) or (g)
	f	Other portfolio income (loss) (attach schedule)	4f		(Enter on applicable line of your return.)
	5	Net gain (loss) under section 1231 (other than due to casualty or theft)	5		See Shareholder's Instructions for Schedule K-1 (Form 1120S)
	6	Other income (loss) (attach schedule)	6		(Enter on applicable line of your return.)
Deductions	7	Charitable contributions	7		Sch. A, line 14 or 15
	8	Section 179 expense deduction (attach schedule) . .	8		See Shareholder's Instructions for Schedule K-1 (Form 1120S).
	9	Deductions related to portfolio income (loss) (attach schedule) . .	9		
	10	Other deductions (attach schedule)	10		
Investment Interest	11a	Interest expense on investment debts	11a		Form 4952, line 1
	b	(1) Investment income included on lines 4a through 4f above	b(1)		See Shareholder's Instructions for Schedule K-1 (Form 1120S).
		(2) Investment expenses included on line 9 above	b(2)		
Credits	12a	Credit for alcohol used as fuel	12a		Form 6478, line 10
	b	Low-income housing credit:			
		(1) From section 42(j)(5) partnerships for property placed in service before 1990	b(1)		Form 8586, line 5
		(2) Other than on line 12b(1) for property placed in service before 1990 .	b(2)		
		(3) From section 42(j)(5) partnerships for property placed in service after 1989 .	b(3)		
		(4) Other than on line 12b(3) for property placed in service after 1989	b(4)		
	c	Qualified rehabilitation expenditures related to rental real estate activities (see instructions)	12c		See Shareholder's Instructions for Schedule K-1 (Form 1120S).
	d	Credits (other than credits shown on lines 12b and 12c) related to rental real estate activities (see instructions)	12d		
	e	Credits related to other rental activities (see instructions) . . .	12e		
	13	Other credits (see instructions)	13		

For Paperwork Reduction Act Notice, see Form 1120S Instructions.   **Schedule K-1 (Form 1120S) 1990**

Schedule K-1 (Form 1120S) (1990)   Page **2**

(a) Pro rata share items		(b) Amount	(c) Form 1040 filers enter the amount in column (b) on:
Adjustments and Tax Preference Items	**14a** Accelerated depreciation of real property placed in service before 1987 **14a**		See Shareholder's Instructions for Schedule K-1 (Form 1120S) and Form 6251 Instructions.
	b Accelerated depreciation of leased personal property placed in service before 1987. **14b**		
	c Depreciation adjustment on property placed in service after 1986 . **14c**		
	d Depletion (other than oil and gas) **14d**		
	e (1) Gross income from oil, gas, or geothermal properties . . . **e(1)**		
	(2) Deductions allocable to oil, gas, or geothermal properties . . **e(2)**		
	f Other adjustments and tax preference items *(attach schedule)* . . **14f**		
Foreign Taxes	**15a** Type of income ▶		Form 1116, Check boxes
	b Name of foreign country or U.S. possession ▶		Form 1116, Part I
	c Total gross income from sources outside the U.S. *(attach schedule)* **15c**		Form 1116, Part I
	d Total applicable deductions and losses *(attach schedule)* **15d**		Form 1116, Part I
	e Total foreign taxes (check one): ▶ ☐ Paid ☐ Accrued . . . **15e**		Form 1116, Part II
	f Reduction in taxes available for credit *(attach schedule)* **15f**		Form 1116, Part III
	g Other foreign tax information *(attach schedule)* **15g**		See Form 1116 Instructions
Other Items	**16a** Total expenditures to which a section 59(e) election may apply . . **16a**		See Shareholder's Instructions for Schedule K-1 (Form 1120S).
	b Type of expenditures ▶		
	17 Property distributions (including cash) other than dividend distributions reported to you on Form 1099-DIV. **17**		
	18 Amount of loan repayments for "Loans from Shareholders" . . . **18**		

			A	B	C	
Recapture of Tax Credits	**19**	Recapture of low-income housing credit:				
	a	From section 42(j)(5) partnerships **19a**				} Form 8611, line 8
	b	Other than on line 19a **19b**				
	20	Investment credit properties:	**A**	**B**	**C**	
	a	Description of property (State whether recovery or non-recovery property. If recovery property, state whether regular percentage method or section 48(q) election is used.)				Form 4255, top
	b	Date placed in service .				Form 4255, line 2
	c	Cost or other basis . .				Form 4255, line 3
	d	Class of recovery property or original estimated useful life .				Form 4255, line 4
	e	Date item ceased to be investment credit property				Form 4255, line 8

Supplemental Information	**21** Supplemental information required to be reported separately to each shareholder *(attach additional schedules if more space is needed):*

B-7   Amended Tax Return Forms

Form 1040X (Rev. October 1990)

Department of the Treasury—Internal Revenue Service

Amended U.S. Individual Income Tax Return

▶ See separate Instructions.

OMB No. 1545-0091
Expires 10-31-93

This return is for calendar year ▶ 19___ , OR fiscal year ended ▶ ___ , 19___

Please print or type

| Your first name and initial | Last name | Your social security number |

| If a joint return, spouse's first name and initial | Last name | Spouse's social security number |

Home address (number and street). (If you have a P.O. box, see Instructions.)   Apt. no.   Telephone number (optional) (   )

City, town or post office, state, and ZIP code. (If you have a foreign address, see Instructions.)

For Paperwork Reduction Act Notice, see page 1 of separate Instructions.

Enter name and address as shown on original return (if same as above, write "Same"). If changing from separate to joint return, enter names and addresses from original returns.

A Service center where original return was filed

B Has original return been changed or audited by IRS? . . . . ☐ Yes ☐ No
If "No," have you been notified that it will be? . . . . . . ☐ Yes ☐ No
If "Yes," identify IRS office ▶

C Are you amending your return to include any item (loss, credit, deduction, other tax benefit, or income) relating to a tax shelter required to be registered? . . . . ☐ Yes ☐ No
If "Yes," you **MUST** attach **Form 8271,** Investor Reporting of Tax Shelter Registration Number.

D Filing status claimed. (**Note:** You cannot change from joint to separate returns after the due date has passed.)
On original return ▶ ☐ Single ☐ Married filing joint return ☐ Married filing separate return ☐ Head of household ☐ Qualifying widow(er)
On this return ▶ ☐ Single ☐ Married filing joint return ☐ Married filing separate return ☐ Head of household ☐ Qualifying widow(er)

Income and Deductions (see Instructions)
(*Note: Be sure to complete page 2*)

		A. As originally reported or as adjusted (see Instructions)	B. Net change—Increase or (Decrease)—explain on page 2	C. Correct amount
1 Total income	1			
2 Adjustments to income	2			
3 Adjusted gross income (subtract line 2 from line 1)	3			
4 Itemized deductions or standard deduction	4			
5 Subtract line 4 from line 3	5			
6 Exemptions	6			
7 Taxable income (subtract line 6 from line 5)	7			
8 Tax (see Instructions). (Method used in col. C ____)	8			
9 Credits (see Instructions)	9			
10 Subtract line 9 from line 8. Enter the result, but not less than zero	10			
11 Other taxes (such as self-employment tax, alternative minimum tax)	11			
12 Total tax (add lines 10 and 11)	12			
13 Federal income tax withheld and excess FICA and RRTA tax withheld	13			
14 Estimated tax payments	14			
15 Earned income credit	15			
16 Credits for Federal tax on fuels, regulated investment company, etc	16			
17 Amount paid with Form 4868, Form 2688, or Form 2350 (application for extension of time to file)	17			
18 Amount paid with original return, plus additional tax paid after it was filed	18			
19 Add lines 13 through 18 in column C	19			

Tax Liability (lines 8–12); **Payments** (lines 13–19)

Refund or Amount You Owe

20 Overpayment, if any, as shown on original return (or as previously adjusted by IRS)	20	
21 Subtract line 20 from line 19 (see Instructions)	21	
22 **AMOUNT YOU OWE.** If line 12, col. C, is more than line 21, enter difference. Please pay in full with this return	22	
23 **REFUND** to be received. If line 12, column C, is less than line 21, enter difference	23	

Please Sign Here

Under penalties of perjury, I declare that I have filed an original return and that I have examined this amended return, including accompanying schedules and statements, and to the best of my knowledge and belief, this amended return is true, correct, and complete. Declaration of preparer (other than taxpayer) is based on all information of which the preparer has any knowledge.

▶ Your signature   Date   ▶ Spouse's signature (if joint return, BOTH must sign)   Date

Paid Preparer's Use Only

Preparer's signature ▶   Date   Check if self-employed ☐   Preparer's social security no.

Firm's name (or yours if self-employed) and address ▶   E.I. No.   ZIP code

Form 1040X (Rev. 10-90)   Page **2**

Part I   Exemptions (see Form 1040 or Form 1040A Instructions)

If you are not changing your exemptions, do not complete Part I.
If claiming more exemptions, complete lines 24–30 and, if applicable, line 31.
If claiming fewer exemptions, complete lines 24–29.

		A. Number originally reported	**B.** Net change	**C.** Correct number
24 Yourself and spouse	24			
Caution: *If your parent (or someone else) can claim you as a dependent, you cannot claim an exemption for yourself.*				
25 Your dependent children who lived with you	25			
26 Your dependent children who did not live with you due to divorce or separation	26			
27 Other dependents	27			
28 Total number of exemptions (add lines 24 through 27)	28			
29 For tax year 1990, multiply $2,050 by the number of exemptions claimed on line 28. For tax year 1989, use $2,000; for tax year 1988, use $1,950; for tax year 1987, use $1,900. Enter the result here and on page 1, line 6 . .	29			

30 Dependents (children and other) not claimed on original return:

(a) Dependent's name (first, initial, and last name)	**(b)** Check if under age 2 (under age 5 if a 1987 or 1988 return)	**(c)** If age 2 or older (age 5 or older if a 1987 or 1988 return), dependent's social security number	**(d)** Dependent's relationship to you	**(e)** No. of months lived in your home
		: :		
		: :		
		: :		
		: :		

No. of your children on line 30 who lived with you ► ☐

No. of your children on line 30 who didn't live with you due to divorce or separation (see Instructions) ► ☐

No. of other dependents listed on line 30 ► ☐

31 If your child listed on line 30 didn't live with you but is claimed as your dependent under a pre-1985 agreement, check here ► ☐

Part II   Explanation of Changes to Income, Deductions, and Credits

Enter the line number from page 1 for each item you are changing and give the reason for each change. **Attach all supporting forms and schedules for items changed. Be sure to include your name and social security number on any attachments.**

If the change pertains to a net operating loss carryback or a general business credit carryback, attach the schedule or form that shows the year in which the loss or credit occurred. See the Instructions. Also, check here . . . . ► ☐

_____

_____

_____

_____

_____

_____

_____

_____

_____

_____

_____

_____

_____

Part III   Presidential Election Campaign Fund

Checking below will not increase your tax or reduce your refund.

If you did not previously want to have $1 go to the fund, but now want to . . . . check here ► ☐
If joint return and your spouse did not previously want to have $1 go to the fund, but now wants to . . . . check here ► ☐

Department of the Treasury
Internal Revenue Service

Instructions for Form 1040X
(Revised October 1990)
Amended U.S. Individual Income Tax Return

(Section references are to the Internal Revenue Code.)

General Instructions

Paperwork Reduction Act Notice

We ask for the information on this form to carry out the Internal Revenue laws of the United States. You are required to give us this information. We need it to ensure that you are complying with these laws and to allow us to figure and collect the right amount of tax.

The time needed to complete and file this form will vary depending on individual circumstances. The estimated average time is:

Recordkeeping . . . . . .1 hr., 12 min.

**Learning about the
law or the form** . . . . 20 min.

Preparing the form . . . .1 hr., 11 min.

**Copying, assembling, and
sending the form to IRS** . . . 35 min.

If you have comments concerning the accuracy of these time estimates or suggestions for making this form more simple, we would be happy to hear from you. You can write to both the **Internal Revenue Service,** Washington, DC 20224, Attention: IRS Reports Clearance Officer, T:FP; and the **Office of Management and Budget,** Paperwork Reduction Project (1545-0091), Washington, DC 20503. **DO NOT** send the tax form to either of these offices. Instead, see **Where to File** on page 2.

Purpose of Form

Use Form 1040X to correct **Form 1040, Form 1040A,** or **Form 1040EZ.** Please note that it often takes 2 to 3 months to process Form 1040X. If you are changing your Federal return, you may also have to change your state return.

Filing Form 1045

You may use **Form 1045,** Application for Tentative Refund, instead of Form 1040X if:

• you are applying for a refund resulting from a net operating loss or credit carryback (other than a foreign tax credit carryback), AND

• less than one year has elapsed since the end of the year in which the loss or credit arose.

See the instructions for Form 1045 for more information about filing that form instead of Form 1040X.

Carryback Claims

You must attach copies of the following to Form 1040X if it is used as a carryback claim.

• Pages 1 and 2 of Form 1040 and Schedules A and D (if applicable) for the year in which the loss or credit originated. At the top of these forms write "Attachment to Form 1040X— Copy Only—Do Not Process."

• Any Schedules K-1 you received from any partnership, S corporation, estate, or trust for the year of the loss or credit which contribute to the loss or credit carryback.

• Any form or schedule from which the carryback results (such as Form 3800 or Schedule C or F).

• The forms or schedules for items refigured in the carryback year (such as Form 6251, Form 3468, or Schedule A).

All information described above must be attached to your Form 1040X, if applicable, or your Form 1040X will be returned for the attachments.

Note: *If you filed a joint return (or a separate return) for some, but not all, of the years involved in figuring the loss or credit carryback, you may have to allocate your income, deductions, and credits. For details, get the publication that explains the type of carryback you are claiming. For example, get Pub. 536, Net Operating Losses, if you are claiming a net operating loss carryback, or Pub. 514, Foreign Tax Credit for Individuals, for a foreign tax credit carryback.*

Net Operating Loss

Attach a computation of your net operating loss using **Schedule A (Form 1045).**

A refund based on a net operating loss should not include the refund of any self-employment tax reported on line 11 of Form 1040X. For more information, get **Pub. 536.**

Other Claims

Attach to Form 1040X any schedule or form related to the item changed. For example, if you are amending your return to change amounts reported on **Schedule D (Form 1040),** attach the corrected Schedule D.

Injured Spouse Claim. Do **not** use Form 1040X to file an injured spouse claim. Instead, file only **Form 8379,** Injured Spouse Claim and Allocation.

Information on Income, Deductions, etc.

If you have questions, such as what income is taxable or what expenses are deductible, the instructions for the return you are amending may help you. Be sure to use the Tax Table or Tax Rate Schedules for the right year to figure the corrected tax. The related schedules and forms may also help you.

Death of Taxpayer

If you are filing a Form 1040X for a deceased person, write **"DECEASED,"** the deceased's name, and the date of death across the top of Form 1040X.

If you are filing Form 1040X as a surviving spouse filing a joint return with the deceased write "Filing as surviving spouse" in the area where you sign the return.

If someone else is the personal representative, he or she must also sign.

Claiming a Refund for a Deceased Person. If you are claiming a refund as a surviving spouse filing a joint return with the deceased, file only Form 1040X to claim the refund. If you are a court-appointed representative, file Form 1040X **AND** attach a copy of the certificate that shows your appointment. All other filers requesting the deceased taxpayer's refund should file Form 1040X and attach **Form 1310,** Statement of Person Claiming Refund Due a Deceased Taxpayer.

For more details, get **Pub. 559,** Tax Information for Survivors, Executors, and Administrators.

When To File

File Form 1040X after you file your original return. Generally, Form 1040X must be filed within 3 years after the date the original return was filed, or within 2 years after the date the tax was paid, whichever is later. A return filed early is considered filed on the date it was due.

A Form 1040X based on a bad debt or worthless security must generally be filed within 7 years after the due date of the return for the tax year in which the debt or security became worthless. For more details, see section 6511.

A Form 1040X based on a net operating loss carryback, or a general business credit carryback, generally must be filed within 3 years after the due date of the return for the tax year of the net operating loss or unused credit.

Where To File

Please use the address for your state. Mail your return to the **Internal Revenue Service Center** for the place where you live. No street address is needed.

If you live in:	Use this address:
Florida, Georgia, South Carolina	Atlanta, GA 39901
New Jersey, New York (New York City and counties of Nassau, Rockland, Suffolk, and Westchester)	Holtsville, NY 00501
New York (all other counties), Connecticut, Maine, Massachusetts, New Hampshire, Rhode Island, Vermont	Andover, MA 05501
Illinois, Iowa, Minnesota, Missouri, Wisconsin	Kansas City, MO 64999
Delaware, District of Columbia, Maryland, Pennsylvania, Virginia	Philadelphia, PA 19255
Indiana, Kentucky, Michigan, Ohio, West Virginia	Cincinnati, OH 45999
Kansas, New Mexico, Oklahoma, Texas	Austin, TX 73301
Alabama, Arkansas, Louisiana, Mississippi, North Carolina, Tennessee	Memphis, TN 37501
Alaska, Arizona, California (counties of Alpine, Amador, Butte, Calaveras, Colusa, Contra Costa, Del Norte, El Dorado, Glenn, Humboldt, Lake, Lassen, Marin, Mendocino, Modoc, Napa, Nevada, Placer, Plumas, Sacramento, San Joaquin, Shasta, Sierra, Siskiyou, Solano, Sonoma, Sutter, Tehama, Trinity, Yolo, and Yuba), Colorado, Idaho, Montana, Nebraska, Nevada, North Dakota, Oregon, South Dakota, Utah, Washington, Wyoming	Ogden, UT 84201
California (all other counties), Hawaii	Fresno, CA 93888
American Samoa	Philadelphia, PA 19255
Guam	Commissioner of Revenue and Taxation 855 West Marine Dr. Agana, GU 96910
Puerto Rico (or if excluding income under section 933)	Philadelphia, PA 19255
Virgin Islands: Nonpermanent residents	
Virgin Islands: Permanent residents	V.I. Bureau of Internal Revenue Lockharts Garden No. 1A Charlotte Amalie, St. Thomas, VI 00802
Foreign country: U.S. citizens and those filing Form 2555 or Form 4563	Philadelphia, PA 19255
All A.P.O. and F.P.O. addresses.	Philadelphia, PA 19255

Preparer Information

If you fill in your own return, the Paid Preparer's space should remain blank. If someone else prepares your return and does not charge you, that person should **not** sign your return.

Generally, anyone you pay to prepare your return must sign it. A preparer who signs your return must sign it by hand in the space provided (signature stamps or labels cannot be used) and give you a copy of the return for your records.

Line-by-Line Instructions

Page 1

Above your name, enter the calendar year or fiscal year of the return you are amending.

Name and Social Security Number

If amending a joint return, list your names and social security numbers in the same order as shown on the original return.

If changing from a separate to joint return and your spouse did not file an original return, enter your name and social security number first.

P.O. Box

If your post office does not deliver mail to your home and you have a P.O. box, enter your P.O. box number instead of your home address.

Foreign Address

If your address is outside of the United States or its possessions or territories, enter the information on the line for "City, town or post office, state, and ZIP code" in the following order: city, province or state, postal code, and the name of the country. Do **not** abbreviate the country name.

Line D—Filing Status

If you are changing from separate returns to a joint return, both of you must sign Form 1040X. If there is any tax due, it must be paid in full.

Column A

Enter the amounts from your return as originally filed or as you later amended it. If your return was changed or audited by IRS, enter the amounts as adjusted.

Column B

Enter the net increase or net decrease for each line you are changing. Show all decreases in parentheses. Explain each change on page 2, Part II, and attach any related schedule or form. For example, if you are amending your return to itemize deductions, attach **Schedule A (Form 1040).** If you need more space, show the required information on an attached statement.

Column C

Add the increase in column B to the amount in column A, or subtract the column B decrease from column A. Show the result in column C. For any item you do not change, enter the amount from column A in column C.

Note: *If you are changing only credits or other taxes, skip lines 1–7 and start with line 8. If changing only payments, skip lines 1–11 and start with line 12.*

Line 1

To figure this amount, add income from all sources, such as wages, taxable interest, dividends, and net profit from business. On Form 1040 for 1987, use line 22. For 1988–1990, use line 23.

On Form 1040A for 1987, use line 10. For 1988 and 1989, use line 11. For 1990, use line 14.

On Form 1040EZ, use line 3.

If you are correcting wages or other employee compensation, attach the first copy or Copy B of all additional or corrected Forms W-2 that you got after you filed your original return.

Line 2

Enter all adjustments to income, such as an IRA deduction or alimony paid. On Form 1040 for 1987, use lines 23–28. For 1988 and 1989, use lines 24–29. For 1990, use lines 24a–29. Be sure to include as an adjustment to income any write-in adjustment. For more details, see your Form 1040 instructions.

On Form 1040A for 1987, use lines 11a and 11b. For 1988 and 1989, use lines 12a and 12b. For 1990, use lines 15a and 15b.

Note: *If you are amending your Form 1040 or Form 1040A to change the amount of your IRA deduction, write in Part II on page 2 of Form 1040X "IRA deduction" and the amount of the increase or decrease.*

Line 4

Itemized Deductions. If you itemize deductions on **Schedule A (Form 1040),** enter on line 4 your total itemized deductions. On Schedule A (Form 1040) for 1987–1989, use line 26. For 1990, use line 27.

Standard Deduction. If amending your return and you do **not** itemize, enter on line 4 your standard deduction. On Form 1040 for 1987, use line 33b. For 1988–1990, use line 34.

On Form 1040A for 1987, use line 14d. For 1988 and 1989, use line 16. For 1990, use line 19.

On Form 1040EZ for 1987 and 1988, use line 4. For 1989 and 1990, if you checked the "Yes" box on Form 1040EZ, line 4, enter the amount from line 4 of Form 1040EZ on line 4 of Form 1040X. If you checked the "No" box for 1989, enter $3,100 on line 4 of Form 1040X. If you checked the "No" box for 1990, enter $3,250.

Caution: Some changes you make to income or deductions can cause other amounts to increase or decrease. For example, increasing your income may decrease your medical expense deduction or your miscellaneous itemized deductions It also may increase the allowable deduction for charitable contributions or the amount of social security benefits that is taxable. You should refigure these items whenever you change your return.

Page 2

Line 6

If you are changing your exemptions, complete the applicable lines in Part I on page 2 to figure the amounts to enter on line 6. If you are not changing your exemptions, enter in columns A and C of line 6 the amount you claimed for exemptions on your original return. On Form 1040 for 1987, use line 35. For 1988–1990, use line 36.

On Form 1040A for 1987, use line 16. For 1988 and 1989, use line 18. For 1990, use line 21.

On Form 1040EZ for 1987 and 1988, use line 6. For 1989 and 1990, enter -0- on line 6 if you checked the "Yes" box on Form 1040EZ, line 4. If you checked the "No" box for 1989, enter $2,000 on line 6 of Form 1040X. If you checked the "No" box for 1990, enter $2,050.

Line 8

Enter your income tax before subtracting any credits. Show on this line the method you use in column C to figure your tax. For example, if you use the Tax Rate Schedules, write "TRS." If, for 1987, you use Part IV of **Schedule D (Form 1040)**, write "Sch. D."

Figure the tax on the taxable income you reported on line 7, column C. Attach the appropriate schedules or forms. Include on line 8 any additional taxes from **Form 4970 or Form 4972.** Include any section 72 tax in the total for line 11 of Form 1040X. The forms and instructions for the right year will help you with line 8.

Line 9

Enter your total credits, such as the credit for the elderly or for the disabled, credit for child and dependent care expenses, or, for 1988–1990, credit for prior year minimum tax. On Form 1040 for 1987, use lines 40, 41, 44, and 45. For 1988–1990, use lines 41–45. Include as a credit any write-in credit. For more details, see your Form 1040 instructions.

On Form 1040A for 1987, use line 19. For 1988 and 1989, use line 21. For 1990, use lines 24a and 24b.

Line 11

Include other taxes, such as tax from recapture of investment credit, alternative minimum tax, self-employment tax, advance earned income credit payments, or, for 1988–1990, recapture of low-income housing credit. On Form 1040 for 1987-1989, use lines 48–52. For 1990, use lines 48–53. Be sure to include any write-in tax. For more details, see your Form 1040 instructions.

On Form 1040A, use advance earned income credit (EIC) payments received.

Lines 13–17

Enter on the applicable lines your payments and credits. On Form 1040 for 1987 and 1988, use lines 54–60. For 1989, use lines 56-62. For 1990, use lines 55–61. Also include any credit for overpaid windfall profit tax on line 16 of Form 1040X and write "OWPT" in the space to the left of line 16.

On Form 1040A for 1987, use lines 21a and 21b. For 1988, use lines 23a and 23b. For 1989, use lines 25a and 25b. For 1990, use lines 28a–28c. Also, for 1990, be sure to include as a payment any write-in payment. For more details, see your 1990 Form 1040A instructions.

On Form 1040EZ for 1987 and 1988, use lines 8. For 1989 and 1990, use line 6.

Line 13

If you change these amounts, attach the first copy or Copy B of all additional or corrected Forms W-2 that you got after you filed your original return.

Line 14

Enter the estimated tax payments you claimed on your return. If you filed Form 1040C, include the amount you paid as the balance due with the return.

Line 18

Enter the amount you paid on the "Amount You Owe" reported on your original return. Also include any additional tax that may have resulted if your original return was changed or examined. **Do not include payments of interest or penalties.**

Line 20

Enter the overpayment from your original return. On Form 1040 for 1987–1990, it is called "amount overpaid." On Form 1040A and Form 1040EZ for 1987 and 1988, it is called "amount of your refund." For 1989, it is called "refund." For 1990, it is called "amount you overpaid" on Form 1040A; on Form 1040EZ it is called "refund." That amount must be considered in preparing Form 1040X since any refund you have not yet received from your original return will be refunded separately from any additional refund claimed on your Form 1040X. If your original return was changed or audited by IRS and, as a result of the change or audit, there was an additional overpayment of tax, also include that amount on line 20. **Do not** include any interest you received on any refund.

Lines 21 and 22

Caution: If line 21 is a minus figure, add it to line 12, column C, instead of subtracting. Enter the result on line 22.

Attach your check or money order for the full amount you owe. Make it payable to the "Internal Revenue Service." Write your name, address, social security number, and daytime phone number on it. Also write on your payment the year and type of return you are amending. For example, "1989 Form 1040." We will figure the interest due and send you a bill.

Line 23

If you are entitled to a larger refund than you claimed on your original return, show only the additional amount due you. This will be refunded separately from the amount claimed on your original return (see the instructions for line 20). We will figure the interest and include it in your refund.

Page 2

Part I—Exemptions

If you are claiming more exemptions, complete lines 24–31, as they apply. If you are claiming fewer exemptions, complete lines 24–29.

In column A, enter the number of exemptions claimed on your original return. In column B, enter any changes to exemptions claimed on your original return. Enter in column C the corrected number of exemptions you are claiming.

Line 30

If you are amending your return to claim an exemption for a dependent, you may be required to enter the dependent's social security number in column (c) of line 30. For 1987 and 1988, you must enter the social security number of any dependent who was age 5 or older on December 31 of the year you are amending. For 1989 and 1990, you must enter the social security number of any dependent who was age 2 or older on December 31 of the year you are amending. If you don't enter the number, or if the number entered is incorrect, you may have to pay a $50 penalty. If your dependent does not have a social security number, see your 1990 Form 1040 or 1040A instructions for line 6c.

If you are claiming more than five additional dependents, show the information requested in columns (a) through (e) on an attached statement. When entering the total number of dependents in the boxes to the right of line 30, be sure to include these dependents.

If you are claiming a child who didn't live with you under the special rules for children of divorced or separated parents, you **must** do one of the following :

● Check the box on line 31 if your divorce decree or written separation agreement was in effect before 1985 and it states that you can claim the child as your dependent.

● Attach **Form 8332,** or similar statement. If your divorce decree or separation agreement went into effect after 1984 and it states that you can claim the child as your dependent, you may attach a copy of the following pages from the decree or agreement instead of Form 8332:

1. Cover page (write the other parent's social security number on this page), and

2. The page that states you can claim the child as your dependent, and

3. Signature page showing the date of agreement.

For more details, see your 1990 Form 1040 or Form 1040A instructions for line 6c.

Part III—Presidential Election Campaign Fund

You may use Form 1040X to have $1 go to the Presidential Election Campaign Fund if you (or your spouse on a joint return) did not do so on your original return. This **must** be done within 20½ months after the original due date for filing the return. For the calendar year 1990, this period ends on December 31, 1992.

Note: A "Yes" designation cannot be changed.

Page 3

Form **1120X**
(Rev. June 1988)
Department of the Treasury
Internal Revenue Service

**Amended U.S. Corporation
Income Tax Return**

OMB No. 1545-0132
Expires 6-30-91

For tax year ending in
▶ - - - - - - - - - - - - - - - - - -
(Enter month and year)

Name	Employer identification number
Number and street (or P.O. box number if mail is not delivered to street address)	
City or town, state, and ZIP code	Telephone number (optional) ( )

**Please
Type
or
Print**

Enter name and address used on original return (if same as above, write "Same")

Internal Revenue Service Center
where original return was filed ▶

Fill in Applicable Items and Use Part II To Explain Any Changes

Part I	Income and Deductions	(a) As originally reported or as adjusted (See Specific Instructions)	(b) Net change (Increase or Decrease— explain in Part II)	(c) Correct amount
1	Total income (line 11 of Form 1120 or 1120-A)			
2	Total deductions (total of lines 27 and 29c, Form 1120, or lines 23 and 25c, Form 1120-A)			
3	Taxable income (subtract line 2 from line 1)			
4	Tax (line 31, Form 1120, or line 27, Form 1120-A)			

Payments and Credits

5a	Estimated tax payments (include overpayment in prior year allowed as a credit)			
b	Amount of refund applied for on Form 4466			
c	Subtract line 5b from line 5a			
6	Tax deposited with Form 7004 (automatic extension of time to file).			
7	Credit from regulated investment companies			
8	Credit for Federal tax on fuels			
9	Other payment or refundable credit (specify) ▶- - - - - - - - - - - -			
	- -			
10	Tax deposited or paid with (or after) the filing of the original return			
11	Total of lines 5c through 10, column (c)			
12	Overpayment, if any, as shown on original return or as later adjusted			
13	Subtract line 12 from line 11			

Tax Due or Refund

14	**Tax due** (subtract line 13 from line 4, column (c)). Make check payable to Internal Revenue Service (see instructions) . . . . ▶	
15	**Refund** (subtract line 4, column (c), from line 13)	

**Please
Sign
Here**

Under penalties of perjury, I declare that I have filed an original return and that I have examined this amended return, including accompanying schedules and statements, and to the best of my knowledge and belief, this amended return is true, correct, and complete. Declaration of preparer (other than taxpayer) is based on all information of which preparer has any knowledge.

▶	▶	▶
Signature of officer	Date	Title

**Paid
Preparer's
Use Only**

Preparer's signature ▶	Date	Check if self-employed ▶ ☐	Preparer's social security no.
Firm's name (or yours if self-employed) and address ▶		E.I. No. ▶	
		ZIP code ▶	

For Paperwork Reduction Act Notice, see instructions on back.   Form **1120X** (Rev. 6-88)

Form 1120X (Rev. 6-88)   Page **2**

Part II **Explanation of Changes to Income, Deductions, Credits, Etc.** Enter the line reference from page 1 for which a change is reported, and give the reason for each change. Show any computation in detail. Attach any schedules needed.

Check here ▶ ☐ if the change is due to a net operating loss carryback, a capital loss carryback, a general business credit carryback, or for tax years beginning before 1986, a research credit carryback.

General Instructions

(Section references are to the Internal Revenue Code.)

Paperwork Reduction Act Notice.—We ask for this information to carry out the Internal Revenue laws of the United States. The information is used to ensure that taxpayers are complying with these laws and to allow us to figure and collect the correct amount of tax. You are required to give us this information.

Purpose of Form.—Use Form 1120X to correct **Form 1120**, U.S. Corporation Income Tax Return, or **Form 1120-A**, U.S. Corporation Short-Form Income Tax Return, as you originally filed it or as it was later adjusted by an amended return, claim for refund, or an examination. Please note that it often takes 3 to 4 months to process Form 1120X.

    Do not use this form to apply for a tentative refund or a quick refund of estimated tax.

● For a quick refund of estimated tax, file **Form 4466**, Corporation Application for Quick Refund of Overpayment of Estimated Tax. File Form 4466 only within 2½ months after the end of the tax year and before the corporation files its tax return.

● For a tentative refund due to the carryback of a net operating loss, a net capital loss, unused credits, or overpaid tax resulting from a claim-of-right adjustment under section 1341(b)(1), file **Form 1139**, Corporation Application for Tentative Refund. You may use Form 1139 only if one year or less has passed since the tax year in which the carryback or adjustment occurred. For additional information on net operating losses and a worksheet to help figure the corporation's net operating loss deduction in a carryback year, see **Publication 536**, Net Operating Losses.

When To File.—File Form 1120X only after the corporation has filed its original return. Generally, Form 1120X must be filed within 3 years after the date the original return was due or 3 years after the date the corporation filed it, whichever was later. A Form 1120X based on a net operating loss carryback, a capital loss carryback, a general business credit carryback, or for tax years beginning before 1986, a research credit carryback, generally must be filed within 3 years after the due date of the return for the tax year of the net operating loss, capital loss, or unused credit. Other claims for refund must be filed within 3 years after the date the original return

was due, 3 years after the date the corporation filed it, or 2 years after the date the tax was paid, whichever is later.

What To Attach.—If you are amending your return to include any item (loss, credit, deduction, other tax benefit, or income) relating to a tax shelter required to be registered, you must attach **Form 8271**, Investor Reporting of Tax Shelter Registration Number.

Information on Income, Deductions, Tax Computation, etc.—Refer to the instructions for the Form 1120 and related schedules and forms, for the year being amended, concerning the taxability of certain types of income, the allowability of certain expenses as deductions from income, computation of tax, etc.

Note: *Deductions for such items as charitable contributions and dividends received may have to be refigured due to changes made to items of income or expense.*

Where To File.—Mail this form to the Internal Revenue Service Center where the corporation filed its original return.

Specific Instructions

Tax Year.—In the space above the employer identification number, enter the ending month and year of the calendar or fiscal year for the tax return you are amending.

Column (a)

Enter the amounts from your return as originally filed or as you later amended it. If your return was changed or audited by IRS, enter the amounts as adjusted.

Column (b)

Enter the net increase or net decrease for each line you are changing. Bracket all decreases. Explain the increase or decrease in Part II. If the change involves an item of income, deduction, or credit that the corporation income tax return or its instructions requires the corporation to support with a schedule, statement, or form, attach the appropriate schedule, statement, or form to Form 1120X.

Column (c)

Lines 1 and 2.—Add the increase in column (b) to the amount in column (a) or subtract the column (b) decrease from column (a). Report the result in column (c). For any item not changed, enter the amount from column (a) in column (c).

Line 4.—Figure the new amount of tax using the taxable income on line 3, column (c). Use Schedule J, Form 1120, or Part I, Form 1120-A, of the original return to make the necessary tax computation.

Line 6.—If you are amending a tax year prior to 1983 for which you filed Form 7005, include on line 6 the amount you deposited with Form 7005.

Line 12—Overpayment.—Enter the amount of overpayment received (or expected to be received) or the amount to be credited to estimated tax, as shown on the original return. That amount must be considered in preparing Form 1120X since any refund due from the original return will be refunded separately (or credited to estimated tax) from any additional refund claimed on Form 1120X.

Line 14—Tax due.—Make the check payable to ''Internal Revenue Service'' for the amount shown on line 14 and attach it to this form. Do not use the depositary method of payment.

Line 15—Refund.—If the corporation is entitled to a refund larger than the amount claimed on the original return, line 15 will show only the additional amount of refund. This additional amount will be refunded separately from the amount claimed on the original return.

Signature.—The return must be signed and dated by the president, vice president, treasurer, assistant treasurer, chief accounting officer, or any other corporate officer (such as tax officer) authorized to sign. A receiver, trustee, or assignee must sign and date any return required to be filed on behalf of a corporation.

Preparer.—If a corporate officer filled in Form 1120X, the Paid Preparer's space should remain blank. If someone prepares Form 1120X and does not charge the corporation, that person should not sign the return. Certain others who prepare Form 1120X should not sign. See the Form 1120 instructions and **Publication 1045**, Information for Tax Practitioners, for more information on preparers and their responsibilities.

Note: *IRS will figure any interest due and will either include it in the refund or bill the corporation for the interest.*

★ U.S.GPO:1988-0-205-236

B-8   Application for Extension of Time to File Income Tax Returns

Form **4868** Department of the Treasury Internal Revenue Service	**Application for Automatic Extension of Time To File U.S. Individual Income Tax Return**	OMB No. 1545-0188 19**90**

Please Type or Print	Your first name and initial	Last name	Your social security number
	If a joint return, spouse's first name and initial	Last name	Spouse's social security number
	Present home address (number, street, and apt. no. or rural route). (If you have a P.O. box, see the instructions.)		
	City, town or post office, state, and ZIP code		

Note: *File this form with the Internal Revenue Service Center where you are required to file your income tax return, and pay any amount(s) you owe.* **This is not an extension to pay your tax.**

I request an automatic 4-month extension of time to August 15, 1991, to file Form 1040A or Form 1040 for the calendar year 1990 (or if a fiscal year Form 1040 to _____, 19_____, for the tax year ending _____, 19_____).

1 Total tax liability for 1990. This is the amount you expect to enter on line 27 of Form 1040A, or line 54 of Form 1040. If you do not expect to owe tax, enter zero (-0-) **1**
Caution: You **MUST** enter an amount on line 1 or your extension will be denied. You can estimate this amount; but be as exact as you can with the information you have. If we later find that your estimate was not reasonable, the extension will be null and void.

2 Federal income tax withheld **2**
3 1990 estimated tax payments (include 1989 overpayment allowed as a credit) . **3**
4 Other payments and credits you expect to show on Form 1040A or Form 1040 . **4**

5 Add lines 2, 3, and 4 . . . . **5**
6 **BALANCE DUE** (subtract line 5 from line 1). *In order to get this extension, you* **MUST** *pay in full the balance due with this form.* (If line 5 is more than line 1, enter zero (–0–) . . . . ▶ **6**

Complete line 7 (and 8a or 8b if applicable) only if you expect to owe gift or generation-skipping transfer (GST) tax. Do not include income tax on these lines. (See the instructions.)

7 If you or your spouse expect to file a gift tax return (Form 709 or 709-A) for 1990, ⎱ Yourself . ▶ ☐
generally due by April 15, 1991, see the instructions and check here . . . ⎰ Spouse . ▶ ☐
8a Enter the amount of gift or GST tax that *you* are paying with this form **8a**
b Enter the amount of gift or GST tax that *your spouse* is paying with this form **8b**

Signature and Verification

Under penalties of perjury, I declare that I have examined this form, including accompanying schedules and statements, and to the best of my knowledge and belief, it is true, correct, and complete; and, if prepared by someone other than the taxpayer, that I am authorized to prepare this form.

Signature of taxpayer ▶ _____ Date ▶ _____

Signature of spouse ▶ _____ Date ▶ _____
(If filing jointly, BOTH must sign even if only one had income)

Signature of preparer other than taxpayer ▶ _____ Date ▶ _____

If correspondence regarding this extension is to be sent to you at an address other than that shown above, or to an agent acting for you, please enter the name of the agent and/or the address where it should be sent.

Please Type or Print	Name	
	Number and street (or P.O. box number if mail is not delivered to street address)	
	City, town or post office, state, and ZIP code	

General Instructions

Paperwork Reduction Act Notice.—We ask for the information on this form to carry out the Internal Revenue laws of the United States. You are required to give us this information. We need it to ensure that you are complying with these laws and to allow us to figure and collect the right amount of tax.

The time needed to complete and file this form will vary depending on individual circumstances. The estimated average time is: **Recordkeeping,** 26 minutes; **Learning about the law or the form,** 11 minutes; **Preparing the form,** 20 minutes; and **Copying, assembling, and sending the form to IRS,** 20 minutes.

If you have comments concerning the accuracy of these time estimates or

suggestions for making this form more simple, we would be happy to hear from you. You can write to both the **Internal Revenue Service,** Washington, DC 20224, Attention: IRS Reports Clearance Officer, T:FP; and the **Office of Management and Budget,** Paperwork Reduction Project (1545-0188), Washington, DC 20503.

DO NOT send the tax form to either of these offices. Instead, see the instructions below for information on where to file.

Form **4868** (1990)

Form 4868 (1990)

Purpose

Use Form 4868 to ask for 4 more months to file **Form 1040A** or **Form 1040**. You do not have to explain why you are asking for the extension. We will contact you only if your request is denied.

To get the extra time you **MUST:**
1. Fill in Form 4868 correctly, **AND**
2. File it by the due date of your return, **AND**
3. Pay ALL of the amount shown on line 6.

If you already had 2 extra months to file because you were "out of the country" (see below) when your return was due, then use this form to ask for an additional 2 months to file.

Do **not** file Form 4868 if you want IRS to figure your tax, or are under a court order to file your return by the regular due date.

Note: *An extension to file your 1990 calendar year income tax return also extends the time to file a gift tax return (Form 709 or 709-A) for 1990.*

If the automatic extension does not give you enough time, you can later ask for additional time. But you'll have to give a good reason, and it must be approved by IRS. To ask for the additional time, you must:
1. File **Form 2688,** Application for Additional Extension of Time To File U.S. Individual Income Tax Return, OR
2. Explain your reason in a letter. Mail it to the address under **Where To File.**

File Form 4868 **before** you file Form 2688 or write a letter asking for more time. Only in cases of undue hardship will we approve your request for more time without first receiving Form 4868. If you need this extra time, ask for it early so that you can still file your return on time if your request is not approved.

When To File Form 4868

File Form 4868 by April 15, 1991. If you are filing a fiscal year Form 1040, file Form 4868 by the regular due date of your return. If you had 2 extra months to file your return because you were out of the country, file this form by June 17, 1991, for a 1990 calendar year return.

Where To File

Mail this form to the **Internal Revenue Service Center** for the place where you live.

If you are located in:	Use this address:
Florida, Georgia, South Carolina	Atlanta, GA 39901
New Jersey, New York (New York City and counties of Nassau, Rockland, Suffolk, and Westchester)	Holtsville, NY 00501
New York (all other counties), Connecticut, Maine, Massachusetts, New Hampshire, Rhode Island, Vermont	Andover, MA 05501
Illinois, Iowa, Minnesota, Missouri, Wisconsin	Kansas City, MO 64999
Delaware, District of Columbia, Maryland, Pennsylvania, Virginia	Philadelphia, PA 19255
Indiana, Kentucky, Michigan, Ohio, West Virginia	Cincinnati, OH 45999
Kansas, New Mexico, Oklahoma, Texas	Austin, TX 73301

Alaska, Arizona, California (counties of Alpine, Amador, Butte, Calaveras, Colusa, Contra Costa, Del Norte, El Dorado, Glenn, Humboldt, Lake, Lassen, Marin, Mendocino, Modoc, Napa, Nevada, Placer, Plumas, Sacramento, San Joaquin, Shasta, Sierra, Siskiyou, Solano, Sonoma, Sutter, Tehama, Trinity, Yolo, and Yuba), Colorado, Idaho, Montana, Nebraska, Nevada, North Dakota, Oregon, South Dakota, Utah, Washington, Wyoming	Ogden, UT 84201
California (all other counties), Hawaii	Fresno, CA 93888
Alabama, Arkansas, Louisiana, Mississippi, North Carolina, Tennessee	Memphis, TN 37501
American Samoa	Philadelphia, PA 19255
Guam	Commissioner of Revenue and Taxation 855 West Marine Drive Agana, GU 96910
Puerto Rico (or if excluding income under section 933) Virgin Islands: Nonpermanent residents	Philadelphia, PA 19255
Virgin Islands: Permanent residents	V.I. Bureau of Internal Revenue Lockharts Garden No. 1 A Charlotte Amalie, St. Thomas, VI 00802
Foreign countries: U.S. citizens and those filing Form 2555 or Form 4563	Philadelphia, PA 19255
A.P.O. or F.P.O. addresses	Philadelphia, PA 19255

Filing Your Tax Return

You may file Form 1040A or Form 1040 any time before the extension of time is up. But remember, Form 4868 does not extend the time to pay taxes. If you do not pay the amount due by the regular due date, you will owe interest. You may also be charged penalties.

Interest.—You will owe interest on tax not paid by the regular due date of your return. The interest runs until you pay the tax. Even if you had a good reason not to pay on time, you will still owe interest.

Late payment penalty.—Generally, the penalty is ½ of 1% of any tax (other than estimated tax) not paid by the regular due date. It is charged for each month, or part of a month, that the tax is unpaid. The most you have to pay is 25%. You might not owe this penalty if you have a good reason for not paying on time. Attach a statement to your return explaining the reason.

Late filing penalty.—A penalty is usually charged if your return is filed after the due date (including extensions). It is usually 5% of the tax not paid by the regular due date for each month, or part of a month, that your return is late. Generally, the most you have to pay is 25%. If your return is more than 60 days late, the penalty will not be less than $100 or the balance of tax due on your return, whichever is smaller. You might not owe the penalty if you have a good reason for filing late. Attach a full explanation to your return if you file late.

How to claim credit for payment made with this form.—When you file your return, show the amount of any payment (line 6) sent with Form 4868. Form 1040A filers should include the payment on line 28d and write "Form 4868" in the space to the left. Form 1040 filers should enter it on line 58.

If you and your spouse each filed a separate Form 4868, but later file a joint return for 1990, then enter the total paid with the two Forms 4868 on the correct line of your joint return.

If you and your spouse jointly filed Form 4868, but later file separate returns for 1990, you may enter the total amount paid with Form 4868 on either of your separate returns. Or, you and your spouse may divide the payment in any agreed amounts. Be sure each separate return has the social security numbers of both spouses.

Specific Instructions

Name, address, and social security numbers.—Enter your name(s), address, social security number, and spouse's social security number if filing a joint return. If your post office does not bring mail to your street address and you have a P.O. box, enter your P.O. box number instead of your street address.

Note: *If you changed your mailing address after you filed your last return, you should use Form 8822, Change of Address, to notify IRS of your new address. You can order Form 8822 by calling 1-800-TAX-FORM (1-800-829-3676).*

Fiscal year filers.—Below your address, enter the date your 4-month extension will end and the date your tax year ends.

Out of the country.—If you already had extra months to file because you were a U.S. citizen or resident and were out of the country on the due date of your return, write **"Taxpayer Abroad"** across the top of this form.

For this purpose, "out of the country" means you meet one of the following conditions: (1) You live outside the U.S. and Puerto Rico, AND your main place of work is outside the U.S. and Puerto Rico; or (2) You are in military or naval service outside the U.S. and Puerto Rico.

Line 7.—If you or your spouse are also using the extra 4 months to file a 1990 gift tax return, check whichever box applies on line 7. However, if your spouse files a separate Form 4868, do not check the box for your spouse.

Lines 8a and 8b.—Enter the amount you (or your spouse) expect to owe on these lines. If your spouse files a separate Form 4868, enter on your form only the total gift tax and GST tax you expect to owe. Pay in full with this form to avoid interest and penalties. If paying gift and GST taxes on time would cause you undue hardship (not just inconvenience), attach an explanation to this form.

Your signature.—This form must be signed. If you plan to file a joint return, both of you should sign. If there is a good reason why one of you cannot, then the other spouse may sign for both. Attach an explanation why the other spouse cannot sign.

Others who can sign for you.—Anyone with a power of attorney can sign. But the following can sign for you without a power of attorney:
• Attorneys, CPAs, and enrolled agents, or
• A person in close personal or business relationship to you who is signing because you cannot. There must be a good reason why you cannot sign (such as illness or absence). Attach an explanation to the form.

Form **2688**

Department of the Treasury
Internal Revenue Service

Application for Additional Extension of Time To File
U.S. Individual Income Tax Return

(See back for filing instructions. Be sure to complete all items.)

OMB No. 1545-0066

19**90**

Attachment
Sequence No. **59**

Please type or print.

File the original and one copy by the due date for filing your return.

Your first name and initial	Last name	Your social security number
If a joint return, spouse's first name and initial	Last name	Spouse's social security number

Present home address (number, street, and apt. no. or rural route). (If you have a P.O. box, see the instructions.)

City, town or post office, state, and ZIP code

1   I request an extension of time until _____, 19 _____ , to file Form 1040A or Form 1040 for the calendar year 1990, or other tax year ending _____, 19 _____.

2   Have you previously requested an extension of time to file for this tax year? . . . . ☐ Yes   ☐ No

3   Explain why you need an extension _____

_____
_____
_____
_____
_____
_____
_____
_____
_____
_____
_____

Complete line 4 only if you expect to owe gift or generation-skipping transfer (GST) tax.

4   If you or your spouse expect to file a gift tax return (Form 709 or 709-A) for 1990, generally due by April 15, 1991, see the instructions and check here . . . . } **Yourself** . . ▶ ☐
Spouse . . ▶ ☐

Signature and Verification

Under penalties of perjury, I declare that I have examined this form, including accompanying schedules and statements, and to the best of my knowledge and belief, it is true, correct, and complete; and, if prepared by someone other than the taxpayer, that I am authorized to prepare this form.

Signature of taxpayer ▶ _____ Date ▶ _____

Signature of spouse   ▶ _____ Date ▶ _____
(If filing jointly, BOTH must sign even if only one had income)

Signature of preparer
other than taxpayer ▶ _____ Date ▶ _____

File original and one copy. IRS will show below whether or not your application is approved and will return the copy.

Notice to Applicant—To Be Completed by IRS

☐ We **HAVE** approved your application. (Please attach this form to your return.)

☐ We **HAVE NOT** approved your application. (Please attach this form to your return.)
However, because of your reasons stated above, we have granted a 10-day grace period from the date shown below or due date of your return, whichever is later. This grace period is considered to be a valid extension of time for elections otherwise required to be made on returns filed on time.

☐ We **HAVE NOT** approved your application. After considering your reasons stated above, we cannot grant your request for an extension of time to file. (We are not granting the 10-day grace period.)

☐ We cannot consider your application because it was filed after the due date of your return.

☐ We **HAVE NOT** approved your application. The maximum extension of time allowed by law is 6 months.

☐ Other _____

Director

By: _____

_____
Date

For Paperwork Reduction Act Notice, see back of form.   Form **2688** (1990)

Form 2688 (1990)   Page **2**

If the copy of this form is to be returned to you at an address other than that shown on page 1 or to an agent acting for you, please enter the name of the agent and/or the address where the copy should be sent.

Please	Name
Type	Number and street (or P.O. box number if mail is not delivered to street address)
or	
Print	City, town or post office, state, and ZIP code

General Instructions

Paperwork Reduction Act Notice.—We ask for the information on this form to carry out the Internal Revenue laws of the United States. You are required to give us this information. We need it to ensure that you are complying with these laws and to allow us to figure and collect the right amount of tax.

The time needed to complete and file this form will vary depending on individual circumstances. The estimated average time is:

Learning about the law or the form . . . . 7 min.

Preparing the form . . . . . 10 min.

Copying, assembling, and sending the form to IRS . . . 20 min.

If you have comments concerning the accuracy of these time estimates or suggestions for making this form more simple, we would be happy to hear from you. You can write to both the **Internal Revenue Service,** Washington, DC 20224, Attention: IRS Reports Clearance Officer, T:FP; and the **Office of Management and Budget,** Paperwork Reduction Project (1545-0066), Washington, DC 20503.

DO NOT send the tax form to either of these offices. Instead, see the instructions below for information on where to file.

Purpose

Use Form 2688 to ask for more time to file **Form 1040A** or **Form 1040.** Use it only if you already asked for more time on **Form 4868,** and that time was not enough. (Form 4868 is the "automatic" extension form.)
To get the extra time you MUST:
1. File Form 2688 on time, AND
2. Have a good reason why the first 4 months were not enough. Explain the reason on line 3.

Generally, we will not give you more time to file just for the convenience of your tax return preparer. However, if the reasons for being late are beyond his or her control, or if despite a good effort you cannot get professional help in time to file, we will usually give you the extra time.

We usually do not approve Form 2688 unless Form 4868 is filed first. We will make an exception to this rule only for undue hardship. You must clearly explain this reason on line 3.

You cannot have IRS figure your tax if you file after the regular due date of your return.

Note: *An extension to file a 1990 calendar year income tax return also extends the time to file a gift tax return for 1990.*

If you live abroad.—U.S. citizens or resident aliens living abroad may qualify for special tax treatment if they meet the required residence or presence tests. If you do not expect to meet either of those tests by the due date of your return, request an extension to a date after you expect to qualify. Ask for it on **Form 2350,** Application for Extension of Time To File U.S. Income Tax Return. See **Pub. 54,** Tax Guide for U.S. Citizens and Resident Aliens Abroad.

Total Time Allowed

We cannot extend the due date of your return for more than 6 months. This includes the 4 extra months allowed by Form 4868. (There may be an exception if you live abroad. See previous discussion.)

When To File Form 2688

File Form 2688 by the due date of your return (April 15, 1991, for a calendar year return), or extended due date if you filed Form 4868. For most taxpayers, this is by August 15, 1991.

Be sure to file Form 2688 early, so that if your request is not approved, you can still file your return on time.

Out of the country.—You may have been allowed 2 extra months to file if you were a U.S. citizen or resident out of the country on the due date of your return. For this purpose, "out of the country" means you meet one of the following conditions: (1) You live outside the U.S. and Puerto Rico, AND your main place of work is outside the U.S. and Puerto Rico; or (2) You are in military or naval service outside the U.S. and Puerto Rico.

Where To File

Make an extra copy of Form 2688. **Mail both the original and the copy** to the IRS address where you send your return.

Filing Your Tax Return

You may file Form 1040A or Form 1040 any time before your extension of time is up. But remember, Form 2688 does not extend the time to pay these taxes. If you do not pay the amount due by the regular due date, you will owe interest. If you do not make a reasonable estimate of taxes due, you may also be charged penalties.

Interest.—You will owe interest on tax not paid by the regular due date of your return. The interest runs until you pay the tax. Even if you had a good reason not to pay on time, you will still owe interest.

Late payment penalty.—Generally, the penalty is ½ of 1% of any tax (other than estimated tax) not paid by the regular due date. It is charged for each month, or part of a month, that the tax is unpaid. The most you have to pay is 25%. You might not owe this penalty if you have a good reason for not paying on time. Attach a statement to your return explaining the reason.

Late filing penalty.—A penalty is usually charged if your return is filed after the due date (including extensions). It is usually 5% of the tax not paid by the regular due date for each month, or part of a month, that your return is late. Generally, the most you have to pay is 25%. If your return is more than 60 days late, the penalty will not be less than $100 or the balance of tax due on your return, whichever is smaller. You might not owe the penalty if you have a good reason for filing late. Attach a full explanation to your return if you file late.

How to claim credit for payment made with this form.—When you file your return, show the amount of any payment sent with Form

2688. Form 1040A filers should include the payment on line 28d and write "Form 2688" in the space to the left. Form 1040 filers should enter it on line 58.

If you and your spouse each filed a separate Form 2688, but later file a joint return for 1990, then enter the total paid with the two Forms 2688 on the correct line of your joint return.

If you and your spouse jointly filed Form 2688, but later file separate returns for 1990, you may enter the total amount paid with Form 2688 on either of your separate returns. Or, you and your spouse may divide the payment in any agreed amounts. Be sure each separate return has the social security numbers of both spouses.

Specific Instructions

Name, address, and social security numbers.—Enter your name(s), address, social security number, and spouse's social security number if filing a joint return .If the post office does not bring mail to your street address and you have a P.O. box, enter your P.O. box number instead of your street address.

Note: *If you changed your mailing address after you filed your last return, you should use* **Form 8822,** *Change of Address, to notify IRS of your new address. You can order Form 8822 by calling 1-800-TAX-FORM (1-800-829-3676).*

Line 3.—Clearly describe the reasons that will delay your return. We cannot accept incomplete reasons, such as "illness" or "practitioner too busy," without adequate explanations. If it is clear that you have no important reason, but only want more time, we will deny your request. The 10-day grace period will also be denied.

If because of undue hardship you are filing Form 2688 without filing Form 4868 first, clearly explain why on line 3. Attach any information you have that helps explain the hardship.

Caution: *If we give you more time to file and later find that the statements made on this form are false or misleading, the extension is null and void. You will owe the late filing penalty, explained above.*

Line 4.—If you or your spouse expect to file **Form 709** or **709-A** for 1990, check whichever box applies. However, if your spouse files a separate Form 2688, do not check the box for your spouse.

Your signature.—This form must be signed. If you plan to file a joint return, both of you should sign. If there is a good reason why one of you cannot, then the other spouse may sign for both. Attach an explanation why the other spouse cannot sign.

Others who can sign for you.—Anyone with a power of attorney can sign, but the following can sign for you without a power of attorney:
● Attorneys, CPAs, and enrolled agents, or
● A person in close personal or business relationship to you who is signing because you cannot. There must be a good reason why you cannot sign (such as illness or absence). Attach an explanation to the form.

Form 7004
(Rev. September 1989)
Department of the Treasury
Internal Revenue Service

Application for Automatic Extension of Time
To File Corporation Income Tax Return

OMB No. 1545-0233
Expires 8-31-92

Name of corporation

Employer identification number

Number and street (or P.O. box number if mail is not delivered to street address)

City or town, state, and ZIP code

Check type of return to be filed:

- ☐ Form 1120
- ☐ Form 1120-A
- ☐ Form 1120-DF
- ☐ Form 1120F
- ☐ Form 1120-FSC
- ☐ Form 1120-H
- ☐ Form 1120L
- ☐ Form 1120-ND
- ☐ Form 1120-PC
- ☐ Form 1120-POL
- ☐ Form 1120-REIT
- ☐ Form 1120-RIC
- ☐ Form 1120S
- ☐ Form 990-C
- ☐ Form 990-T

Form 1120F filers: Check here ▶ ☐ if you do not have an office or place of business in the U.S.

1a I request an automatic 6-month extension of time until ...., 19 ......, to file the income tax return of the corporation named above for ▶ ☐ calendar year 19 ......, or ▶ ☐ tax year beginning..............................., 19 ......, and ending.............................., 19 ....

b If this tax year is for less than 12 months, check reason:
☐ Initial return   ☐ Final return   ☐ Change in accounting period   ☐ Consolidated return to be filed

2 If this application also covers subsidiaries to be included in a consolidated return, complete the following:

Name and address of each member of the affiliated group	Employer identification number	Tax period

3 Tentative tax (see instructions)	**3**		
4 **Credits:**			
a Overpayment credited from prior year . .	**4a**		
b Estimated tax payments for the tax year	**4b**		
c Less refund for the tax year applied for on Form 4466	**4c** ( ) Bal ▶	**4d**	
e Credit from regulated investment companies		**4e**	
f Credit for Federal tax on fuels		**4f**	
5 Total—Add lines 4d through 4f	**5**		
6 **Balance due**—Line 3 less line 5. **Deposit this amount with a Federal Tax Deposit (FTD) Coupon** (see instructions)	**6**		

Signature.—Under penalties of perjury, I declare that I have been authorized by the above-named corporation to make this application, and to the best of my knowledge and belief, the statements made are true, correct, and complete.

_____   _____   _____
(Signature of officer or agent)   (Title)   (Date)

Form **7004** (Rev. 9-89)

B-9   Underpayment of Estimated Tax

Form **2210**		
Department of the Treasury Internal Revenue Service	**Underpayment of Estimated Tax by Individuals and Fiduciaries** ► See separate instructions. ► Attach to Form 1040, Form 1040A, or Form 1041.	OMB No. 1545-0140 **1990** Attachment Sequence No. **44**

Name(s) shown on tax return	Identifying number

A Change To Note

In response to many requests to simplify Form 2210, IRS has developed a new **Short Method** to figure the penalty. To see if you can use the short method, read the instructions on this page. Then, if you can use it, complete only Parts I and II below.

Purpose of Form

Use Form 2210 to see if you owe a penalty for underpaying your estimated tax and, if you do, to figure the amount of the penalty.

If you prefer, IRS will figure the penalty for you and send you a bill. But see **Lowering Your Penalty**, below. If you want IRS to figure the penalty for you, leave the penalty line on your return blank; do not file Form 2210.

Lowering Your Penalty

If any of the conditions below applies to you, you may be able to lower the amount of your penalty. But you must complete and attach Form 2210 to your tax return to do so. In the space next to the penalty amount on your tax return, you **must** write the letter (**A, B,** or **C**) that corresponds to any of the following conditions that applies to you.

A. You claim a **waiver**. See page 1 of the separate instructions.

B. Your income varied during the year and you use the **annualized income installment method** to figure your required installment payments. See the instructions for line 20.

C. You had Federal income tax withheld from your wages and you treat it as being paid when it was **actually withheld** (instead of in four equal amounts). See the instructions for line 21.

Short Method

If you made estimated tax payments, you may use the short method **only** if:
● You paid your estimated tax in four equal amounts; **and**
● You paid your estimated tax on the due dates.

You may also use the short method if you made no payments at all, or your only credit for payment was due to Federal income tax withholding.

Note: *If you made estimated tax payments, the short method will give the precise penalty amount only if your payments were made exactly on the due dates. If any payment was made early, using the short method may cause you to pay a larger penalty than the regular method. If the payment is only a few days early, the difference will generally be small.*

Although line 17 of the short method requires a five-place decimal computation, it will relieve you of making the more complicated computations under the regular method.

Do not use the short method if you made any of your estimated tax payments late.

You must use the regular method if **B** or **C** under **Lowering Your Penalty** applies. But if **A** applies, and you meet the conditions above, you may use the short method.

Regular Method

Use the regular method to figure the penalty if you did not pay your estimated tax payments on the due dates or in four equal amounts. To use the regular method, complete Part I below and Part III on the back.

Part I	**Required Annual Payment**—All filers must complete this part.		
1	Enter your 1990 tax after credits (from Form 1040, line 47; Form 1040A, line 25; or Form 1041, Schedule G, line 4)	1	
2	Other taxes (see instructions)	2	
3	Add lines 1 and 2	3	
4	Earned income credit 4		
5	Credit for Federal tax on fuels 5		
6	Add lines 4 and 5	6	
7	Current year tax. Subtract line 6 from line 3	7	
8	Multiply line 7 by 90% (.90) and enter the result 8		
9	Withholding taxes from 1990 Form 1040, lines 55 and 59; Form 1040A, line 28a; or Form 1041, line 24e. Include any credit from Form 4469. (Do **not** include any estimated tax payments on this line)	9	
10	Subtract line 9 from line 7. If the result is less than $500, stop here; **do not** complete or file this form. You do not owe the penalty	10	
11	Enter your prior year (1989) tax. (**Caution:** *See instructions.*)	11	
12	**Required annual payment.** Enter the **smaller** of line 8 or line 11 (see instructions)	12	
	Note: *If line 9 is equal to or more than line 12, stop here. You do not owe the penalty.*		

Part II	**Short Method**—If you made estimated tax payments, use this method only if they were paid on the due dates and in four equal amounts. Otherwise, use the regular method (Part III) on the back.		
13	Enter the amount, if any, from line 9 above 13		
14	Enter the total amount, if any, of estimated tax payments you made 14		
15	Add lines 13 and 14	15	
16	**Total underpayment for year.** Subtract line 15 from line 12. (If the result is zero or less, stop here; you do not owe the penalty.)	16	
17	Multiply line 16 by .07315 and enter the result	17	
18	● If the amount on line 16 was paid **on or after** 4/15/91, enter -0-. ● If the amount on line 16 was paid **before** 4/15/91, make the following computation to find the amount to enter on line 18. Amount on line 16 × Number of days paid before 4/15/91 × .0003	18	
19	**PENALTY.** Subtract line 18 from line 17. Enter the result here and on Form 1040, line 67; Form 1040A, line 33; or Form 1041, line 26 . . . . ►	19	

For Paperwork Reduction Act Notice, see page 1 of separate instructions.   Form **2210** (1990)

Form 2210 (1990)   Page **2**

Part III   Regular Method

Section A—Figure Your Underpayment

		Payment Due Dates			
		(a) 4/15/90	**(b)** 6/15/90	**(c)** 9/15/90	**(d)** 1/15/91
20	**Required Installment.** Divide line 12 by 4 and enter the result in each column. **Exception:** If you use the annualized income installment method, see the Instructions and check this box . . . . . . ▶ ☐ **20** *Complete lines 21 through 28 of one column before going to the next column.*				
21	Estimated tax paid and tax withheld. (See Instructions.) For column (a) only, also enter the amount from line 21 on line 25 . . . . **21** *If line 21 is equal to or more than line 20 for all payment periods, stop here; you do not owe the penalty. But see "Lowering Your Penalty" on page 1.*				
22	Enter amount, if any, from line 28 of previous column . . **22**				
23	Add lines 21 and 22 . . . . **23**				
24	Add amounts on lines 26 and 27 of the previous column. Enter the total here **24**				
25	Subtract line 24 from line 23. If zero or less, enter -0-. For column (a) only, enter the amount from line 21 . . **25**				
26	Remaining underpayment from previous period. If the amount on line 25 is -0-, subtract line 23 from line 24 and enter the result. Otherwise, enter -0-. **26**				
27	**Underpayment.** If line 20 is equal to or more than line 25, subtract line 25 from line 20. Then go to line 21 of next column. Otherwise, go to line 28 . . . . . . ▶ **27**				
28	Overpayment. If line 25 is more than line 20, subtract line 20 from line 25. Then go to line 21 of next column . . **28**				

Section B—Figure the Penalty (Complete lines 29 and 30 of one column before going to the next column.)

		4/15/90	6/15/90	9/15/90	1/15/91
29	Number of days FROM the date shown above line 29 TO the date the amount on line 27 was paid **or** 4/15/91, whichever is earlier **29**	*Days:*	*Days:*	*Days:*	*Days:*
30	$\dfrac{\text{Number of days on line 29}}{365} \times .11 \times \text{underpayment on line 27}$ (see Instructions) ▶ **30**	$	$	$	$
31	**PENALTY.** Add the amounts in each column of line 30. Enter the total here and on Form 1040, line 67; Form 1040A, line 33; or Form 1041, line 26 . . . . ▶ **31**				$

Form **2220**	**Underpayment of Estimated Tax by Corporations**	OMB No. 1545-0142
Department of the Treasury Internal Revenue Service	▶ See separate Instructions. ▶ Attach to your tax return.	19**90**

Name	Employer identification number

Note: *In most cases, IRS can figure the penalty and the corporation will not have to complete this form. See the separate Instructions for more information.*

Part I   **Figuring The Underpayment**

1 Total tax (see Instructions) **1**

2a Personal holding company tax included on line 1 (Schedule PH (Form 1120), line 27) . **2a**

  b Credit for Federal tax on fuels (see Instructions) **2b**

  c Total—Add lines 2a and 2b **2c**

3 Subtract line 2c from line 1. If the result is less than $500, **do not** complete or file this form. The corporation does not owe the penalty **3**

4a Enter 90% of line 3 . . . . **4a**

  b Enter the tax shown on the corporation's 1989 tax return. **(Caution:** *See Instructions before completing this line.)* **4b**

  c **Estimated tax.** Enter the **smaller** of line 4a or line 4b **4c**

		(a)	(b)	(c)	(d)
5	**Installment due dates.** Enter in columns (a) through (d) the 15th day of the 4th, 6th, 9th, and 12th months of the corporation's tax year . . . . ▶ **5**				
6	**Required installments.** Enter 25% of line 4c in columns (a) through (d) unless a or b below applies to the corporation:				
a	If the corporation uses the annualized income installment method and/or the adjusted seasonal installment method, complete the worksheet in the Instructions and enter the amounts from line 45 in each column of line 6. Also check this box ▶ ☐ and attach a copy of the worksheet.				
b	If the corporation is a "large corporation," check this box ▶ ☐ and see the Instructions for the amount to enter in each column of line 6 . . . . **6**				
	Complete lines 7 through 14 for one column before completing the next column.				
7	Amount paid or credited for each period. (See Instructions.) (For column (a) only, enter the amount from line 7 on line 11.) **7**				
8	Enter amount, if any, from line 14 of previous column . . **8**				
9	Add lines 7 and 8 . . . . **9**				
10	Add amounts on lines 12 and 13 of the previous column and enter the result. **10**				
11	Subtract line 10 from line 9. If less than zero, enter zero. (For column (a) only, enter the amount from line 7.) **11**				
12	Remaining underpayment from previous period. If the amount on line 11 is zero, subtract line 9 from line 10 and enter the result. Otherwise, enter zero **12**				
13	**UNDERPAYMENT.** If line 11 is less than or equal to line 6, subtract line 11 from line 6 and enter the result. Then go to line 7 of the next column. Otherwise, go to line 14 . . . **13**				
14	**OVERPAYMENT.** If line 6 is less than line 11, subtract line 6 from line 11 and enter the result. Then go to line 7 of the next column **14**				

Go to Part II on the back to figure the penalty.

For Paperwork Reduction Act Notice, see page 1 of the separate Instructions.   Form **2220** (1990)

Form 2220 (1990)   Page **2**

Part II   Figuring the Penalty

		(a)	(b)	(c)	(d)
15 Enter the date of payment or the 15th day of the 3rd month after the close of the tax year, whichever is earlier. *(Form 990-PF and Form 990-T filers:* Use 5th month instead of 3rd month.)	**15**				
16 Number of days from due date of installment on line 5 to the date shown on line 15	**16**				
17 Number of days on line 16 after 4/15/90 and before 4/1/91 .	**17**				
18 Number of days on line 16 after 3/31/91 and before 7/1/91 .	**18**				
19 Number of days on line 16 after 6/30/91 and before 10/1/91	**19**				
20 Number of days on line 16 after 9/30/91 and before 1/1/92 .	**20**				
21 Number of days on line 16 after 12/31/91 and before 2/16/92 . .	**21**				
22 $\frac{\text{Number of days on line 17}}{365} \times 11\% \times$ the underpayment on line 13 . .	**22**				
23 $\frac{\text{Number of days on line 18}}{365} \times$ *% $\times$ the underpayment on line 13 . .	**23**				
24 $\frac{\text{Number of days on line 19}}{365} \times$ *% $\times$ the underpayment on line 13 . .	**24**				
25 $\frac{\text{Number of days on line 20}}{365} \times$ *% $\times$ the underpayment on line 13 . .	**25**				
26 $\frac{\text{Number of days on line 21}}{366} \times$ *% $\times$ the underpayment on line 13 . .	**26**				
27 Add lines 22 through 26	**27**				

28 **PENALTY.** Add columns (a) through (d), line 27. Enter here and on line 33, Form 1120; line 29, Form 1120-A; or comparable line for other income tax returns   .   .   .   . | **28** |

*If the corporation's tax year ends after December 31, 1990, see the Instructions for lines 23 through 26.

19**90**

 **Department of the Treasury
Internal Revenue Service**

Instructions for Form 2220

Underpayment of Estimated Tax by Corporations

(Section references are to the Internal Revenue Code unless otherwise noted.)

Paperwork Reduction Act Notice

We ask for the information on this form to carry out the Internal Revenue laws of the United States. You are required to give us this information. We need it to ensure that you are complying with these laws and to allow us to figure and collect the right amount of tax.

The time needed to complete and file this form will vary depending on individual circumstances. The estimated average time is:

Form	Recordkeeping	Learning about the law or the form	Preparing the form	Copying, assembling, and sending the form to IRS
2220	18 hrs., 11 min.	1 hr., 32 min.	3 hrs., 46 min.	32 min.
Worksheet, Pt. I	11 hrs., 43 min.	6 min.	17 min.	...
Worksheet, Pt. II	24 hrs., 23 min.	...	24 min.	...
Worksheet, Pt. III	5 hrs., 16 min.	...	5 min.	...

If you have comments concerning the accuracy of these time estimates or suggestions for making this form more simple, we would be happy to hear from you. You can write to both the IRS and the Office of Management and Budget at the addresses listed in the instructions for the tax return with which this form is filed. **DO NOT** send the tax form to either of these offices. Instead, see the instructions in your income tax return for information on where to file.

Purpose of Form

Corporations (including S corporations), tax-exempt organizations subject to the unrelated business income tax, and private foundations use Form 2220 to determine whether they are subject to the penalty for underpayment of estimated tax and, if so, the amount of the penalty.

Who Must Pay the Underpayment Penalty

If the corporation did not pay enough estimated tax by any due date for paying estimated tax, it may be charged a penalty. This is true even if the corporation is due a refund when its return is filed. The penalty is figured separately for each installment due date. Therefore, the corporation may owe a penalty for an earlier installment due date, even if it paid enough tax later to make up the underpayment.

Generally, a corporation is subject to the penalty if its tax liability is $500 or more and it did not timely pay the lesser of 90% of its tax liability for 1990, or 100% of its tax liability for 1989 (if it filed a 1989 return showing at least some amount of tax and the return covered a full 12 months). However, a "large corporation" (defined in the instructions for line 6b) may base only its first required installment on 100% of the prior year's tax liability. A corporation may be able to reduce or eliminate the penalty by using the annualized income installment method or the adjusted seasonal installment method.

IRS May Be Able To Figure the Penalty for the Corporation

Generally, the corporation does not have to file this form because IRS can figure the amount of any penalty and bill the corporation. However, complete and attach this form if:

a. The annualized income installment method and/or the adjusted seasonal installment method is used (see the instructions for line 6),

b. The corporation is a "large corporation" computing its first required installment based on the prior year's tax, or

c. An insurance company requests a waiver of the penalty as discussed in the instructions for line 13 under **Waiver of Penalty for Insurance Companies.**

How To Use This Form

Complete Part I of Form 2220 to determine the underpayment for any of the four installment due dates. If there is an underpayment on line 13 (column (a), (b), (c), or (d)), go to Part II to figure the penalty. Attach Form 2220 to the income tax return and check the box on line 33, page 1, of Form 1120; line 29 of Form 1120-A; or the comparable line of any other income tax return the corporation is required to file (e.g., Form 990-C, 1120L, 1120S, etc.).

Part I. Figuring The Underpayment

Complete lines 1 through 14 in Part I. Follow the instructions below.

Line 1.—Enter the tax from line 31, Form 1120; line 27, Form 1120-A; or the comparable line for other income tax returns (except as noted below).

Interest due under the look-back method for completed long-term contracts is not treated as an increase in tax for purposes of computing the estimated tax penalty. Do not include on line 1 any interest due under the look-back method included in tax on the corporation's income tax return. Instead, write on the dotted line to the left of the entry space, "From Form 8697" and the amount of interest due in brackets.

Filers of Forms 990-PF, 990-T, 1120L, 1120-PC, 1120-REIT, 1120-RIC, and 1120S: See the instructions for the appropriate tax return for the definition of tax for purposes of the estimated tax provisions.

Line 2b.— Enter the amount of the credit(s) from line 32g, Form 1120; line 28g, Form 1120-A; or the comparable line for other income tax returns.

Line 4b.—All filers other than S corporations.—Figure the corporation's 1989 tax in the same manner as the amount on line 3 of this form was determined, using the taxes and credits from its 1989 tax return. Skip line 4b and enter the amount from line 4a on line 4c if either of the following apply: **(1)** the corporation did not file a tax return for 1989 that showed at least some amount of tax; **or (2)** the corporation had a 1989 tax year of less than 12 months.

S corporations.—Enter on line 4b the sum of: (i) 90% of the sum of the investment credit recapture tax and the built-in gains tax (or the tax on certain capital gains) shown on the return for the 1990 tax year, and (ii) 100% of any excess net passive income tax shown on the S corporation's return for the 1989 tax year. If the 1989 tax year was for less than 12 months, do not complete this line. Instead, enter the amount from line 4a on line 4c.

Line 6.— (a) Annualized Income Installment Method or Adjusted Seasonal Installment Method: If the corporation's income varied during the year because, for example, it operated its business on a seasonal basis, it may be able to lower the amount of one or more required installments by using the annualized income installment method or the adjusted seasonal installment method. For example, a ski shop, which receives most of its income during the winter months, may benefit from using one or both of these methods in figuring its required installments. The annualized income installment or adjusted seasonal installment may be less than the required installment under the regular method for one or more due dates, thereby reducing or eliminating the penalty for those due dates.

To use one or both of these methods to figure one or more required installments, use the worksheet on pages 3 and 4 of these instructions. If the worksheet is used for any payment due date, it must be used for **all** payment due dates. To arrive at the amount of each required installment, the worksheet automatically selects the smallest of: (a) the annualized income installment, (b) the adjusted seasonal installment (if applicable), or (c) the regular installment under section 6655(d) (increased by any reduction recapture under section 6655(e)(1)(B)).

If the corporation is using only the annualized income installment method, it must complete Parts I and III of the worksheet. If it is using only the adjusted seasonal installment method, it must complete Parts II and III of the worksheet. If the corporation is using both methods, it must complete the entire worksheet. Enter in each column on line 6 of Form 2220 the amounts from the corresponding column of line 45 of the worksheet. Also attach a copy of the worksheet to Form 2220 and check the box on line 6a.

(b) "Large corporations": A "large corporation" is a corporation (other than an S corporation) that had, or its predecessor had, taxable income of $1 million or more for any of the 3 tax years immediately preceding the tax year involved. For this purpose, taxable income is modified to exclude net operating loss or capital loss carrybacks or carryovers. Members of a controlled group, as defined in section 1563, must divide the $1 million amount among themselves in accordance with rules similar to those in section 1561.

If the annualized income installment method or adjusted seasonal installment method is not used, follow the instructions below to figure the amount to enter on line 6. Also check the box on line 6b. (If the corporation is using the annualized income installment method and/or the adjusted seasonal installment method, these instructions apply to line 41 of the worksheet.)

If line 4a is less than line 4b: Enter 25% of line 4a in columns (a) through (d) on line 6. *If line 4b is less than line 4a:* Enter 25% of line 4b in column (a) on line 6. In column (b), determine the amount to enter by: (i) subtracting line 4b from line 4a, (ii) adding the result to the amount on line 4a, and (iii) multiplying the total by 25%. In columns (c) and (d), enter 25% of line 4a.

Line 7.—In column (a), enter the estimated tax payments deposited by the 15th day of the 4th month of the corporation's tax year; in column (b), enter payments made after the 15th day of the 4th month through the 15th day of the 6th month of the tax year; in column (c), enter payments made after the 15th day of the 6th month through the 15th day of the 9th month of the tax year; and, in column (d), enter payments made after the 15th day of the 9th month through the 15th day of the 12th month of the tax year.

Include in the estimated tax payments any overpayment of tax from the corporation's 1989 return that was credited to the corporation's 1990 estimated tax.

Line 13.—If line 13 shows an underpayment, complete Part II to figure the penalty.

Waiver of Penalty for Insurance Companies.—The Revenue Reconciliation Act of 1990 (Act) changed the way an insurance company handles the amortization of policy acquisition expenses and the treatment of salvage. No penalty will be imposed on any underpayment of estimated tax attributable to the changes made by the Act to IRC sections 807(e), 832(b)(4), 832(b)(5), and 848, for any period before March 16, 1991. Accordingly, for any installment due date before March 16, 1991, if an insurance company has an underpayment on line 13 which is due to changes made by the Act, the penalty for that underpayment will be waived.

To claim the waiver, affected companies should compute the penalty by refiguring Form 2220 through line 27 on the basis of the law in effect before the changes were made and write the word "WAIVER" on the

Page 2

bottom margin of page 1. Also write "Waiver-$(amount)" on the dotted line to the left of line 28. Subtract the waiver amount from the total of columns (a) through (d), line 27, to arrive at the amount to be entered on line 28. Attach an explanation showing your computation of the amount of the penalty to be waived.

Part II. Figuring The Penalty

Complete lines 15 through 28 to determine the amount of the penalty. The penalty is figured for the period of underpayment determined under section 6655 at a rate determined under section 6621. For underpayments paid after March 31, 1991, see the instructions for lines 23 through 26.

Line 15.—A payment of estimated tax is applied against underpayments of required installments in the order that installments are required to be paid, regardless of which installment the payment pertains to. For example, a corporation has an underpayment for the April 15 installment of $1,000. The June 15 installment requires a payment of $2,500. On June 10, the corporation deposits $2,500 to cover the June 15 installment. However, $1,000 of this payment is considered to be for the April 15 installment. The penalty for the April 15 installment is figured to June 10 (56 days). The underpayment for the June 15 installment will then be $1,500.

If the corporation has made more than one payment for a required installment, attach a separate computation for each payment.

Line 23.—For underpayments paid after March 31, 1991, and before July 1, 1991, use the interest rate that the IRS will determine in January 1991.

Line 24.—For underpayments paid after June 30, 1991, and before October 1, 1991, use the interest rate that the IRS will determine in April 1991.

Line 25.—For underpayments paid after September 30, 1991, and before January 1, 1992, use the interest rate that the IRS will determine in July 1991.

Line 26.—For underpayments paid after December 31, 1991, use the interest rate that the IRS will determine in October 1991.

Instructions for Worksheet
Part I—Annualized Income Installment Method

Line 4.—*Filers of Forms 990-PF and 990-T:* The period to be used to figure taxable income for each column is as follows: Column (a), first 2 months; column (b), first 4 months; column (c), first 7 months; and column (d), first 10 months.

Line 5.—*Filers of Forms 990-PF and 990-T:* The annualization amount to be used in each column is as follows: Column (a), 6; column (b), 3; column (c), 1.71429; and column (d), 1.2.

Line 9.—Enter the taxes the corporation owed because of events that occurred during the months shown in the column headings used to figure annualized taxable income. Include the same taxes used to figure line 1 of Form 2220, but do not include the personal holding company tax.

Figure the alternative minimum tax and environmental tax on **Form 4626,**

Alternative Minimum Tax–Corporations. Figure alternative minimum taxable income and modified alternative minimum taxable income based on the corporation's income and deductions during the months shown in the column headings used to figure annualized taxable income. Multiply the alternative minimum taxable income and modified alternative minimum taxable income by the annualization amounts used to figure annualized taxable income (on line 2 or line 5) before subtracting the exemption amounts (see sections 55(d) and 59A(a)(2)).

Line 11.—Enter the credits allowed due to events that occurred during the months shown in the column headings used to figure annualized taxable income.

Line 15.—Before completing line 15 in columns (b) through (d), complete line 16; Part II (if applicable); and lines 40 through 45, in each of the preceding columns. For example, complete line 16, lines 17 through 39 (if using the adjusted seasonal installment method), and lines 40 through 45, in column (a) before completing line 15 in column (b).

Part II—Adjusted Seasonal Installment Method

Do **not** complete this part unless the corporation's base period percentage for any six consecutive months of the tax year equals or exceeds 70%. The term "base period percentage" for any period of six consecutive months is the average of the three percentages figured by dividing the taxable income for the corresponding six consecutive month period in each of the 3 preceding tax years by the taxable income for each of their respective tax years.

Example: An amusement park that has a calendar year as its tax year receives the largest part of its taxable income during the six-month period from May through October. To compute its base period percentage for the period May through October 1990, it must figure its taxable income for the period May through October in each of the years: 1987, 1988, and 1989. The taxable income for each May-through-October period is then divided by the total taxable income for the tax year in which the period is included, resulting in the following quotients: .69 for May through October 1987, .74 for May through October 1988, and .67 for May through October 1989. Since the average of .69, .74, and .67 is equal to .70, the base period percentage for May through October 1990 is 70%. Therefore, the amusement park qualifies for the adjusted seasonal installment method.

Line 33.—Enter the alternative minimum tax the corporation owed because of events that occurred during the months shown in the column headings above line 17. Include the same taxes used to figure line 1 of Form 2220, but do not include the personal holding company tax.

Figure the alternative minimum tax and environmental tax on Form 4626. Figure alternative minimum taxable income and modified alternative minimum taxable income based on the corporation's income and deductions during the months shown in the column headings above line 17. Divide the alternative minimum taxable income and modified alternative minimum taxable income by the amounts shown on line 24 before subtracting the exemption amounts (see sections 55(d) and 59A(a)(2)). For columns (a) through (c) only, multiply the alternative minimum tax and environmental tax so determined by the amounts shown on line 31.

Line 35.—Enter the credits allowed due to events that occurred during the months shown in the column headings above line 17.

Line 38.—Before completing line 38 in columns (b) through (d), complete lines 39 through 45 in each of the preceding columns. For example, complete lines 39 through 45 in column (a) before completing line 38 in column (b).

Worksheet to Figure Required Installments Using the Annualized Income or Adjusted Seasonal Installment Methods Under Section 6655(e)

Note to Form 1120S filers.—*For purposes of lines 1, 4, 17, 18, and 19, below, "taxable income" refers to excess net passive income or the amount on which tax is imposed under section 1374(a) (or the corresponding provisions of prior law), whichever applies.*

Part I Annualized Income Installment Method		(a)	(b)	(c)	(d)
		Period			
			First 3 months	First 6 months	First 9 months
(1) Enter taxable income for each period.	1				
(2) Annualization amounts.	2		4	2	1.33333
(3) Multiply line 1 by line 2.	3				
Form 990-PF and Form 990-T filers: *Do not use the periods shown directly above line 4 or the annualization amounts shown on line 5 when figuring lines 4 and 6. Instead, see the Instructions for Worksheet lines 4 and 5.*		**Period**			
		First 3 months	First 5 months	First 8 months	First 11 months
(4) Enter taxable income for each period.	4				
(5) Annualization amounts.	5	4	2.4	1.5	1.09091
(6) Multiply line 4 by line 5.	6				
(7) Annualized taxable income. In column (a), enter the amount from line 6, column (a). In columns (b), (c), and (d), enter the **smaller** of the amounts in each column on line 3 or line 6.	7				
(8) Figure tax on the amount in each column on line 7 using the Instructions for Form 1120, Schedule J, line 3 (or the comparable line of the tax return).	8				
(9) Enter other taxes for each payment period (see Instructions).	9				
(10) Total tax. Add lines 8 and 9.	10				
(11) For each period, enter the same type of credits as allowed on Form 2220, lines 1 and 2b (see Instructions).	11				
(12) Total tax after credits. Subtract line 11 from line 10. If less than zero, enter zero.	12				
(13) Applicable percentage.	13	22.5%	45%	67.5%	90%
(14) Multiply line 12 by line 13.	14				
(15) Enter the combined amounts of line 45 from all preceding columns (see Instructions).	15				
(16) Subtract line 15 from line 14. If less than zero, enter zero.	16				

Part II Adjusted Seasonal Installment Method (**Caution:** *Use this method only if the base period percentage for any 6 consecutive months is at least 70%. See the Instructions for more information.*)

		(a)	(b)	(c)	(d)
		Period			
		First 3 months	First 5 months	First 8 months	First 11 months
(17) Enter taxable income for the following periods:					
a Tax year beginning in 1987	17a				
b Tax year beginning in 1988	17b				
c Tax year beginning in 1989	17c				
(18) Enter taxable income for each period for the tax year beginning in 1990.	18				

Page 3

		(a)	(b)	(c)	(d)
		\multicolumn{4}{c}{Period}			
		First 4 months	First 6 months	First 9 months	Entire year
(19)	Enter taxable income for the following periods: **a** Tax year beginning in 1987	**19a**				
	b Tax year beginning in 1988	**19b**				
	c Tax year beginning in 1989	**19c**				
(20)	Divide the amount in each column on line 17a by the amount in column (d) on line 19a.	**20**				
(21)	Divide the amount in each column on line 17b by the amount in column (d) on line 19b.	**21**				
(22)	Divide the amount in each column on line 17c by the amount in column (d) on line 19c.	**22**				
(23)	Add lines 20 through 22.	**23**				
(24)	Base period percentage for months before filing month. Divide line 23 by 3.	**24**				
(25)	Divide line 18 by line 24.	**25**				
(26)	Figure tax on the amount on line 25 using the Instructions for Form 1120, Schedule J, line 3 (or the comparable line of the return).	**26**				░░░
(27)	Divide the amount in columns (a) through (c) on line 19a by the amount in column (d) on line 19a.	**27**				░░░
(28)	Divide the amount in columns (a) through (c) on line 19b by the amount in column (d) on line 19b.	**28**				░░░
(29)	Divide the amount in columns (a) through (c) on line 19c by the amount in column (d) on line 19c.	**29**				░░░
(30)	Add lines 27 through 29.	**30**				
(31)	Base period percentage for months through and including the filing month. Divide line 30 by 3.	**31**				
(32)	Multiply the amount in columns (a) through (c) of line 26 by the percentage in the corresponding column of line 31. In column (d), enter the amount from line 26, column (d).	**32**				
(33)	Enter other taxes for each payment period (see Instructions).	**33**				
(34)	Total tax. Add lines 32 and 33.	**34**				
(35)	For each period, enter the same type of credits as allowed on Form 2220, lines 1 and 2b (see Instructions).	**35**				
(36)	Total tax after credits. Subtract line 35 from line 34: If less than zero, enter zero.	**36**				
(37)	Multiply line 36 by 90%.	**37**				
(38)	Enter the total of amounts in all preceding columns of line 45.	**38**	░░░			
(39)	Subtract line 38 from line 37. If less than zero, enter zero.	**39**				

Part III Required Installments

			1st installment	2nd installment	3rd installment	4th installment
(40)	If only one of the above parts was completed, enter the amounts in each column from line 16 or line 39. (If both parts were completed, enter the lesser of the amounts in each column from line 16 or line 39.)	**40**				
(41)	Divide line 4c, Form 2220, by 4 and enter the result in each column. (**Note:** "large corporations" see line 6(b) Instructions on page 2 for the amount to enter.)	**41**				
(42)	Enter the amount from line 44 for the preceding column.	**42**	░░░			
(43)	Add lines 41 and 42 and enter the total.	**43**				
(44)	If line 43 is more than line 40, subtract line 40 from line 43. Otherwise, enter zero.	**44**				
(45)	**Required installments.**—Enter the lesser of line 40 or line 43 here and on Form 2220, line 6.	**45**				░░░

Page 4   ★U.S.GPO:1990-0-265-301

B-10 Forms for Computation of Minimum Tax

Form **4626**	**Alternative Minimum Tax—Corporations**	OMB No. 1545-0175
Department of the Treasury Internal Revenue Service	**(including environmental tax)** ▶ See separate instructions. ▶ Attach to your tax return.	19**90**

Name		Employer identification number

1	Taxable income or (loss) before net operating loss deduction. (**Important:** See instructions if you are subject to the environmental tax.)		1
2	**Adjustments:**		
a	Depreciation of tangible property placed in service after 1986	2a	
b	Amortization of certified pollution control facilities placed in service after 1986	2b	
c	Amortization of mining exploration and development costs paid or incurred after 1986	2c	
d	Amortization of circulation expenditures paid or incurred after 1986 (personal holding companies only)	2d	
e	Basis adjustments in determining gain or loss from sale or exchange of property	2e	
f	Long-term contracts entered into after February 28, 1986	2f	
g	Installment sales of certain property	2g	
h	Merchant marine capital construction funds	2h	
i	Section 833(b) deduction (Blue Cross, Blue Shield, and similar type organizations only)	2i	
j	Tax shelter farm activities (personal service corporations only)	2j	
k	Passive activities (closely held corporations and personal service corporations only)	2k	
l	Certain loss limitations	2l	
m	Other adjustments	2m	
n	Combine lines 2a through 2m		2n
3	**Tax preference items:**		
a	Depletion	3a	
b	Tax-exempt interest from private activity bonds issued after August 7, 1986	3b	
c	Appreciated property charitable deduction	3c	
d	Intangible drilling costs	3d	
e	Reserves for losses on bad debts of financial institutions	3e	
f	Accelerated depreciation of real property placed in service before 1987	3f	
g	Accelerated depreciation of leased personal property placed in service before 1987 (personal holding companies only)	3g	
h	Amortization of certified pollution control facilities placed in service before 1987	3h	
i	Add lines 3a through 3h		3i
4	Pre-adjustment AMTI. Combine lines 1, 2n, and 3i		4
5	**Adjusted current earnings adjustment:**		
a	Enter your adjusted current earnings	5a	
b	Subtract line 4 from line 5a (even if one or both of these figures is a negative number). Enter zero if the result is zero or less (see instructions for examples)	5b	
c	Multiply line 5b by 75%		5c
6	Combine lines 4 and 5c. If zero or less, stop here (you are not subject to the alternative minimum tax)		6
7	Alternative tax net operating loss deduction. (Do not enter more than 90% of line 6.)		7
8	Alternative minimum taxable income (subtract line 7 from line 6)		8
9	**Exemption phase-out computation (members of a controlled group, see instructions for lines 9a through 9c):**		
a	Tentative exemption amount. Enter $40,000	9a	
b	Enter $150,000	9b	
c	Subtract line 9b from line 8. If zero or less, enter zero	9c	
d	Multiply line 9c by 25%	9d	
e	Exemption. Subtract line 9d from line 9a. If zero or less, enter zero		9e
10	Subtract line 9e from line 8. If zero or less, enter zero		10
11	Multiply line 10 by 20%		11
12	Alternative minimum tax foreign tax credit (see instructions for limitation)		12
13	Tentative minimum tax (subtract line 12 from line 11)		13
14	Regular tax liability before all credits except the foreign tax credit and possessions tax credit		14
15	**Alternative minimum tax**—Subtract line 14 from line 13. If the result is zero or less, enter zero. Also enter the result on line 9a, Schedule J, Form 1120, or on the comparable line of other income tax returns		15
16	**Environmental tax**—Subtract $2,000,000 from line 6 (computed without regard to your environmental tax deduction), and multiply the result, if any, by 0.12% (.0012). Enter on line 9b, Schedule J, Form 1120, or on the comparable line of other income tax returns (members of a controlled group, see instructions)		16

For Paperwork Reduction Act Notice, see separate instructions.

Form **4626** (1990)

19**90**

 **Department of the Treasury
Internal Revenue Service**

Instructions for Form 4626

Alternative Minimum Tax—Corporations

(Section references are to the Internal Revenue Code unless otherwise noted.)

General Instructions

Paperwork Reduction Act Notice.—We ask for the information on this form to carry out the Internal Revenue laws of the United States. You are required to give us this information. We need it to ensure that you are complying with these laws and to allow us to figure and collect the right amount of tax.

The time needed to complete and file this form will vary depending on individual circumstances. The estimated average time is:

Recordkeeping . . . . . 10 hrs., 31 min.

**Learning about the law
or the form** . . . . . . 11 hrs., 49 min.

**Preparing and sending the
form to IRS** . . . . . . 12 hrs., 31 min.

If you have comments concerning the accuracy of these time estimates or suggestions for making this form more simple, we would be happy to hear from you. You can write to both the IRS and the Office of Management and Budget at the addresses listed in the instructions for the tax return with which this form is filed.

Changes you should note:

(1) Lines 5 through 5c were modified to reflect the change from the book income adjustment to the adjusted current earnings adjustment.

(2) Line 14 of the 1989 Form 4626, which was entitled "general business credit allowed against alternative minimum tax," was deleted. This amount is now requested as a "write-in" entry on the dotted line to the left of the entry space on line 9a, Schedule J, Form 1120 (or on the comparable line of other income tax returns).

Who Must File.—You must file this form if your taxable income or (loss) before the net operating loss **(NOL)** deduction when combined with your adjustments and tax preference items (including the adjusted current earnings adjustment) totals more than the lesser of: (a) $40,000, or (b) your allowable exemption amount.

Short Period Return.—If this is a short period return, use the formula in section 443(d) to determine your alternative minimum taxable income **(AMTI)** and your alternative minimum tax **(AMT).**

Apportionment of Differently Treated Items in Case of Certain Entities.—If you are preparing Form 4626 for a regulated investment company, real estate investment trust, or a common trust fund, see section 59(d).

Credit for Prior Year Minimum Tax.—See **Form 8801,** Credit for Prior Year Minimum Tax, for details concerning the computation of the credit.

Line-by-Line Instructions

Line 1.—Enter your taxable income or (loss) before the NOL deduction. For example, if you file Form 1120, subtract line 29b from line 28.

Important: *If you are subject to the environmental tax, you will generally need to figure that tax on line 16 before completing line 1 (see instructions for line 16).*

Line 2a—Depreciation of tangible property placed in service after 1986 (or after 7/31/86 if you made the transitional election under section 203(a)(1)(B) of the Tax Reform Act of 1986).

Caution: *If you have a depreciation adjustment attributable to a passive activity or a tax shelter farm activity, do not include that adjustment on line 2a. Instead, include the adjustment on line 2j or 2k.*

The depreciation expense allowable for regular tax purposes under section 167 with respect to any tangible property placed in service after 1986 must be recomputed for AMT purposes under the alternative depreciation system **(ADS)** described in section 168(g) as follows:

(1) For any real property described in section 1250(c) (generally nonresidential real and residential rental), use the straight line method over 40 years using the same mid-month convention you used for regular tax purposes;

(2) For any tangible property (other than the real property described in (1) above) with respect to which depreciation for regular tax purposes is determined using the straight line method, recompute your depreciation expense using the straight line method over the property's "class life" using the same convention you used for regular tax purposes;

(3) For all tangible property other than property described in (1) or (2) above, use the 150% declining balance method, switching to the straight line method the first tax year it gives a larger deduction, over the property's class life. Use the same convention you used for regular tax purposes.

In applying the above rules:

(1) The "class life" to be used for AMT purposes has a different meaning than the recovery period used for regular tax purposes (although these periods could possibly be the same in some instances). The class lives you need to use for AMT purposes can be found in Rev. Proc. 87-56, 1987-2 C.B. 674, or in **Publication 534,** Depreciation. Use 12 years for any tangible personal property that does not have an assigned class life;

(2) See Rev. Proc. 87-57, 1987-2 C.B. 687, for optional tables (14 through 18) that can be used in computing depreciation for AMT purposes. (These optional tables have been reproduced in Publication 534.);

(3) Do not make an adjustment for:
(a) property for which you made a section 168(g)(7) election (to use the ADS of section 168(g)) for regular tax purposes, **(b)** property expensed under section 179 for regular tax purposes, or **(c)** property described in sections 168(f)(1) through (4); and

(4) You must take into consideration the transitional rules (described in section 56(a)(1)(C)) and the normalization rules (described in section 56(a)(1)(D)).

Subtract your recomputed AMT expense from the depreciation expense you claimed for regular tax purposes and enter the result on line 2a. If the total recomputed AMT expense exceeds the depreciation expense you claimed for regular tax purposes, enter the difference as a negative amount.

Note: *Depreciation that is capitalized to inventory under the uniform capitalization rules must be refigured using the rules described above.*

Line 2b—Amortization of certified pollution control facilities placed in service after 1986.—The amortization deduction you claimed for regular tax purposes is not allowed for AMT purposes.

For AMT purposes, you must use the ADS described in section 168(g). As such, use the straight line method over the facility's class life (which may be found in Rev. Proc. 87-56 or in Publication 534). **Note:** *Section 168(g) applies to 100% of the asset's amortizable basis. Do not reduce your AMT basis by the 20% section 291 adjustment that applied for regular tax purposes.*

Subtract your recomputed AMT expense from the expense you claimed for regular tax purposes and enter the result on line 2b. If your recomputed AMT expense is greater than the expense you claimed for regular tax purposes, enter the difference as a negative amount.

Line 2c—Amortization of mining exploration and development costs paid or incurred after 1986.—*If, for regular tax purposes, you elected the optional 10-year writeoff under section 59(e) for all assets in this category, skip this line (no adjustment is necessary).*

The deduction you claimed for regular tax purposes under sections 616(a) and 617(a) is not allowed for AMT purposes. Instead, you must capitalize such costs and amortize them ratably over a 10-year period beginning with the tax year in which you made them. **Note:** *The 10-year amortization applies to 100% of the mining development and exploration costs paid or incurred during the tax year. Do not reduce your AMT basis by the 30% section 291 adjustment that applied for regular tax purposes.*

Subtract your recomputed AMT expense from the expense you claimed for regular tax purposes and enter the result on line 2c. If your recomputed AMT expense is greater than the expense you claimed for regular tax purposes, enter the difference as a negative amount. See section 56(a)(2)(B) if you had a loss with respect to any mine or other natural deposit (other than an oil, gas, or geothermal well).

Line 2d—Amortization of circulation expenditures paid or incurred after 1986 (personal holding companies only).—*If, for regular tax purposes, you elected the optional 3-year writeoff under section 59(e) for all of these expenditures, skip this line (no adjustment is necessary).*

The deduction you claimed for regular tax purposes (under section 173) for these expenditures incurred after 1986 is not allowed for AMT purposes. For AMT purposes, you must capitalize these expenditures and amortize them ratably over a 3-year period beginning with the tax year in which you made them.

Subtract your recomputed AMT expense from the expense you claimed for regular tax purposes and enter the result on line 2d. If your recomputed AMT expense is greater than the expense you claimed for regular tax purposes, enter the difference as a negative amount. See section 56(b)(2)(B) if you had a loss with respect to circulation expenditures deducted under section 173.

Line 2e—Basis adjustments in determining gain or loss from sale or exchange of property.—*If, during the tax year, you disposed of property for which you are making (or have previously made) any of the adjustments described in lines 2a through 2d above, you must recompute the property's adjusted basis for AMT purposes. You must then recompute the property's gain or loss.*

For AMT purposes, the property's adjusted basis is its cost less all applicable depreciation or amortization deductions allowed during the current tax year and previous tax years for AMT purposes. This recomputed basis is subtracted from the sales price to arrive at gain or loss for AMT purposes. **Note:** *You may also have gains or losses from lines 2j, 2k, and 2l that must be taken into consideration on line 2e. For example, if for regular tax purposes, you report a loss from the disposition of an asset used in a passive activity, you include the loss in your computations for line 2j to determine whether any passive activity loss is limited for AMT purposes. You then include the portion of the AMT passive activity loss allowed* that pertains to the disposition of the asset on line 2e in determining your AMT basis adjustment. In this respect, it may be helpful to refigure Form 8810 and related worksheets and Schedule D (Form 1120), Form 4684 (Section B), or Form 4797 for AMT purposes.

Enter the difference between the gain or loss reported on your tax return for regular tax purposes and your recomputed gain or loss for AMT purposes. If the gain recomputed for AMT purposes is less than the gain computed for regular tax purposes OR if the loss recomputed for AMT purposes is more than the loss computed for regular tax purposes OR if you recomputed a loss for AMT purposes and computed a gain for regular tax purposes, enter the difference as a negative amount.

Line 2f—Long-term contracts entered into after February 28, 1986.—For AMT purposes, you must use the percentage of completion method rules described in section 460(b) to determine the taxable income from any "long-term contract" (defined in section 460(f)) you entered into after 2/28/86. However, this rule does not apply to: **(1)** any "home construction contract" (as defined in section 460(e)(6)) you entered into after 6/20/88 with respect to which you meet the "small" home construction contract requirements of section 460(e)(1)(B) or **(2) any** home construction contract you entered into in a tax year beginning after 9/30/90, regardless of whether you meet the "small" home construction contract requirements of section 460(e)(1)(B).

Note: In the case of a contract described in section 460(e)(1), the percentage of the contract completed is to be determined using the simplified procedures for allocating costs outlined in section 460(b)(4).

Subtract the income you reported for regular tax purposes from the income you recomputed for AMT purposes and enter the difference on line 2f. If the recomputed AMT income is less than the income you reported for regular tax purposes, enter the difference as a negative amount.

Line 2g—Installment sales of certain property.—With respect to any disposition of inventory (as defined in section 1221(1)) after 3/1/86, the installment method of accounting cannot be used in determining income for AMT purposes (except for certain dispositions of timeshares or residential lots for which you elected to pay interest under section 453(l)(2)(B)).

Application of rules in computing adjustment:

(1) Dealer dispositions: For dealer dispositions occurring after 3/1/86 but before 1/1/88, you will have adjustments if you used the installment method for regular tax purposes but were required for AMT purposes to report the entire gain in the year of disposition. In such cases, enter the income you reported for regular tax purposes for the current year with respect to those dispositions on line 2g as a negative amount.

For dealer dispositions occurring after 1987, generally no adjustments are necessary since the installment method of accounting generally cannot be used for either regular tax purposes or for AMT purposes.

(2) Nondealer dispositions: For nondealer dispositions occurring after 3/1/86 but before the first day of your tax year that began in 1987, you will have adjustments if you used the installment method for regular tax purposes but were required for AMT purposes to report the entire gain in the year of disposition. In such cases, enter the income you reported for regular tax purposes for the current year with respect to those dispositions on line 2g as a negative amount.

For nondealer dispositions occurring on or after the first day of your tax year that began in 1987, generally no adjustments are necessary since you are allowed to use the installment method of accounting for both regular tax purposes and AMT purposes.

Line 2h—Merchant marine capital construction funds.—Amounts deposited in these funds (established under section 607 of the Merchant Marine Act of 1936) after 1986 are not deductible

for AMT purposes. Furthermore, earnings on these funds are not excludable from gross income for AMT purposes. Therefore, if you deducted these amounts or excluded them from income for regular tax purposes, you must add them back on line 2h. See section 56(c)(2) for more information.

Line 2i—Section 833(b) deduction (Blue Cross, Blue Shield, and similar type organizations only).—This deduction is not allowed for AMT purposes. Therefore, if you took this deduction for regular tax purposes, you must add it back on line 2i.

Line 2j—Tax shelter farm activities (personal service corporations only).—Complete line 2j only if you have a gain or loss from a tax shelter farm activity (as defined in section 58(a)(2)) that is **not** a passive activity. If the tax shelter farm activity **is** a passive activity, you must include the gain or loss in your computations for line 2k below.

Recompute all gains and losses you reported for regular tax purposes from tax shelter farm activities by taking into account your AMT adjustments and tax preference items. **Important:** To avoid duplication, any AMT adjustment or tax preference item taken into account on line 2j must not be included in the amounts to be entered on any other line of this form.

Determine your tax shelter farm activity gain or loss for AMT purposes using the same rules you used for regular tax purposes with the following modification: No recomputed loss is allowed, except to the extent the personal service corporation is insolvent (see section 58(c)(1)). Furthermore, a recomputed loss may not be used in the current tax year to offset gains from other tax shelter farm activities. Instead, any recomputed loss must be suspended and carried forward indefinitely until: **(1)** you have a gain in a subsequent tax year from that same tax shelter farm activity, OR **(2)** the activity is disposed of.

Note: The amount of any tax shelter farm activity loss that is not deductible (and is therefore carried forward) for AMT purposes is likely to differ from the amount (if any) that is carried forward for regular tax purposes. Therefore, it is essential that you retain adequate records for both AMT purposes and regular tax purposes.

Enter on line 2j the difference between the gain or loss you recomputed for AMT purposes and the gain or loss you reported for regular tax purposes. If you reported a loss for AMT purposes and a gain for regular tax purposes OR if you recomputed a loss for AMT purposes that exceeds the loss you reported for regular tax purposes OR if you reported a gain for regular tax purposes that exceeds the gain you recomputed for AMT purposes, enter the difference as a negative amount.

Line 2k—Passive activities (closely held corporations and personal service corporations only).—Recompute all passive activity gains and losses you reported for regular tax purposes by taking into account your AMT adjustments, tax preference items, and AMT prior year unallowed losses.

Important: To avoid duplication, any AMT adjustment or tax preference item taken into account on line 2k must not be included in the amounts to be entered on any other line of this form.

Determine your passive activity gain or loss for AMT purposes using the same rules you used for regular tax purposes with the following modifications: **(1)** Do not use the phase-in of disallowance rules of section 469(m); and **(2)** If the corporation is insolvent, see section 58(c)(1).

Disallowed losses of a personal service corporation are suspended until the corporation has income from that (or any other) passive activity or until the passive activity is disposed of (i.e., its passive losses cannot offset "net active income" (defined in section 469(e)(2)(B)) or "portfolio income"). Disallowed losses of a closely held corporation that is not a personal service corporation are treated the same except that, in addition, they may be used to offset "net active income."

Note: The amount of any passive activity loss that is not deductible (and is therefore carried forward) for AMT purposes is likely to differ from the amount (if any) that is carried forward for regular tax purposes. Therefore, it is essential that you retain adequate records for both AMT purposes and regular tax purposes.

Enter on line 2k the difference between the gain or loss you recomputed for AMT purposes and the gain or loss you reported for regular tax purposes. If you reported a loss for AMT purposes and a gain for regular tax purposes OR if you recomputed a loss for AMT purposes that exceeds the loss you reported for regular tax purposes OR if you reported a gain for regular tax purposes that exceeds the gain you recomputed for AMT purposes, enter the difference as a negative amount.

Tax shelter farm activities that are passive activities.—Recompute all gains and losses you reported for regular tax purposes by taking into account your AMT adjustments, tax preference items, and AMT prior year unallowed losses.

Important: To avoid duplication, any AMT adjustment or tax preference item taken into account here must not be included in the amounts to be entered on any other line of this form. These recomputed gains and losses should enter into the determination of your passive activity gain or loss for AMT purposes described above. Use the same rules outlined above, with the following additional modification: Recomputed gains from tax shelter farm activities that are passive activities may be used to offset recomputed losses from other passive activities; however, recomputed losses from tax shelter farm activities that are passive activities may not be used to offset recomputed gains from other passive activities. (Recomputed losses from tax shelter farm activities that are passive activities are disallowed and must be suspended and carried forward as explained in the instructions for line 2j.)

Line 2l—Certain loss limitations.—Recompute gains and losses you reported for regular tax purposes from at-risk activities and partnerships by taking into account your AMT adjustments and tax preference items. If you have recomputed losses that must (in accordance with section 59(h)) be limited for AMT purposes by section 465 or by section 704(d) OR if, for regular tax purposes, you reported losses from at-risk activities or partnerships that were limited by those sections, compute the difference between the loss limited for AMT purposes and the loss limited for regular tax purposes with respect to each applicable at-risk activity or partnership. If the loss limited for regular tax purposes exceeds the loss limited for AMT purposes, enter the difference as a negative amount.

Line 2m—Other adjustments.—Include on this line:

(1) Income eligible for the possessions tax credit—The corporation's AMTI is not to include any income (from the sources described in section 936(a)(1)) that is eligible for the possessions tax credit of section 936. Therefore, if you included this type of income in your taxable income for regular tax purposes, enter the amount on line 2m as a negative amount.

(2) Income with respect to the alcohol fuel credit—The corporation's AMTI is not to include any amount with respect to the alcohol fuel credit that was included in your gross income in accordance with section 87. Therefore, if you included this type of income in your income for regular tax purposes, enter the amount on line 2m as a negative amount.

(3) Income as a beneficiary of an estate or trust—If the corporation is a beneficiary, enter the amount from Schedule K-1 (Form 1041), line 7.

Line 3a—Depletion.—In the case of mines, wells, and other natural deposits, enter the amount by which your depletion deduction under section 611 exceeds the adjusted basis of the property at the end of your tax year. In computing the year-end adjusted basis, use the rules of section 1016; however, do not reduce basis by the current year's depletion deduction.

Page 2

Figure the excess separately for each property. If the depletion deduction for any property does not exceed the property's year-end adjusted basis, the shortfall is not to be considered on line 3a. (In other words, do not use a shortfall for one property to offset the excess of depletion deduction over adjusted basis for any other property.)

Note: *In the case of iron ore and coal (including lignite), the section 291 adjustment is to be applied before figuring this tax preference item.*

Line 3b—Tax-exempt interest from private activity bonds issued after August 7, 1986.—Enter the interest you earned on "specified private activity bonds" reduced by any deduction that would have been allowable if the interest were includible in gross income for regular tax purposes. Generally, the term "specified private activity bonds" means any private activity bond (as defined in section 141) issued after 8/7/86. See section 57(a)(5) for exceptions and for more information.

Line 3c—Appreciated property charitable deduction.—Enter the amount by which your contribution deduction allowable under section 170 would be reduced if all capital gain and section 1231 property were taken into account at its adjusted basis (rather than its fair market value).

Line 3d—Intangible drilling costs.—*If, for regular tax purposes, you elected the optional 60-month writeoff under section 59(e) for all assets in this category, skip this line (no adjustment is necessary).*

Intangible drilling costs (**IDCs**) from oil, gas, and geothermal properties are a tax preference item to the extent that "excess IDCs" exceed 65% of the "net income" from the properties. The tax preference item is computed separately for geothermal deposits, and for oil and gas properties that are not geothermal deposits.

"Excess IDCs" are the excess of: (**1**) the amount of IDCs you paid or incurred with respect to oil, gas, or geothermal properties that you elected to expense for regular tax purposes under section 263(c) (not including any section 263(c) deduction for nonproductive wells) reduced by the section 291 adjustment for integrated oil companies; over (**2**) the amount that would have been allowed had you amortized that amount over a 120-month period starting with the month the well was placed in production. **Note:** *If you prefer not to use the 120-month period, you can elect to use any method that is permissible in determining cost depletion.*

"Net income" is the gross income you received or accrued from all oil, gas, and geothermal wells less the deductions allocable to these properties (reduced by the excess IDCs).

Line 3e—Reserves for losses on bad debts of financial institutions.—Enter the excess of: (**1**) the deduction allowable for a reasonable addition to a reserve for bad debts of a financial institution to which section 593 applies (reduced by the section 291 adjustment) over (**2**) the amount that would have been allowable had the financial institution maintained its bad debt reserve for all tax years on the basis of actual experience.

Line 3f—Accelerated depreciation of real property placed in service before 1987.—Enter the excess of the depreciation claimed for the property for regular tax purposes over the depreciation allowable for AMT purposes as refigured using the straight line method. Figure this amount separately for each property and include only positive adjustments on line 3f. For 15-, 18-, or 19-year real property, use the straight line method over 15, 18, or 19 years, respectively. For low-income housing property, use the straight line method over 15 years.

Line 3g—Accelerated depreciation of leased personal property placed in service before 1987 (personal holding companies only).—For leased personal property, other than recovery property, enter the excess of the depreciation claimed for the property for regular tax purposes over the depreciation allowable for AMT purposes

as refigured using the straight line method. Figure this amount separately for each property and include only positive adjustments on line 3g.

For leased recovery property, other than 15-, 18-, or 19-year real property, or low-income housing, enter the amount by which your depreciation deduction determined for regular tax purposes is more than the deduction allowable for AMT purposes using the straight line method over the following recovery period:

3-year property	. 5 years
5-year property	. 8 years
10-year property	15 years
15-year public utility property . . .	22 years

Line 3h—Amortization of certified pollution control facilities placed in service before 1987.—If, for regular tax purposes, you made an election under section 169 to amortize the basis of a certified pollution control facility over a 60-month period, your tax preference with respect to each such facility is computed as follows:

(**1**) Reduce the current year amortization deduction by the 20% section 291 adjustment;

(**2**) Reduce the result in (1) above by the deduction you would have been allowed under section 167; and

(**3**) Multiply the result in (2) above by 59 ⅚%. Include only positive adjustments on line 3h.

Line 5a—Adjusted current earnings.—*If you are preparing Form 4626 for a regulated investment company or a real estate investment trust, skip lines 5a through 5c (they do not apply).*

If you are preparing Form 4626 for an affiliated group that has filed a consolidated tax return for the current tax year under the rules of section 1501, you must determine adjusted current earnings (ACE) on a consolidated basis.

Your ACE is your line 4 pre-adjustment AMTI, with the following additional adjustments:

(**1**) ACE depreciation adjustment. This adjustment is computed in the following two steps:

(**a**) Add back all current year depreciation expense you deducted for AMT purposes in arriving at your line 4 pre-adjustment AMTI.

(**b**) Subtract your current year ACE depreciation expense, which is computed as follows: For each asset, compute your current year depreciation expense for ACE purposes based on the method of depreciation described after the appropriate classification (see (i) through (iv) below) for such asset:

(**i**) Property placed in service after 1989. Depreciate the basis of such property using the ADS described in section 168(g).

(**ii**) Property placed in service in a tax year beginning before 1990 to which the modified accelerated cost recovery system (**MACRS**) applies (i.e., generally property placed in service in tax years beginning after 1986 and before 1990). Depreciate the adjusted basis of such property (which, for these purposes, is the adjusted basis of such property for AMT purposes as of the close of the last tax year beginning before 1990) using the straight line method over the remainder of the recovery period applicable to such property under the ADS of section 168(g). In doing so, use the applicable convention that would have applied to the property under section 168(g).

(**iii**) Property placed in service in a tax year beginning before 1990 to which the original accelerated cost recovery system (**ACRS**) applies (i.e., generally property placed in service in tax years beginning after 1980 and before 1987). Depreciate the adjusted basis of such property (which, for these purposes, is the adjusted basis of such property for regular tax purposes as of the close of the last tax year beginning before 1990) using the straight line method over the remainder of the recovery period applicable to such property under the ADS of section 168(g). In doing so, use the convention that would have applied to the property under section 168(g).

(**iv**) Property placed in service before 1981 and property described in sections 168(f)(1) through (4). Use the depreciation expense you claimed for regular tax purposes.

(**2**) Adjustments based on general rules for computing earnings and profits (**E & P**):

(**a**) Any income item that is not "taken into account" (defined below) in determining your line 4 pre-adjustment AMTI but that is "taken into account" in determining your ACE must be included in determining your ACE. Any such income item may be reduced by all items that relate to such income item and that would be deductible in computing your pre-adjustment AMTI if the income items to which they relate were included in your pre-adjustment AMTI for the tax year. Examples of adjustments for such income items include: (**i**) interest income from tax-exempt obligations excluded under section 103 less any costs incurred in carrying such tax-exempt obligations; and (**ii**) proceeds of life insurance contracts excluded under section 101 less the basis in the contract for purposes of ACE.

Note: *Do not make an adjustment for any income from discharge of indebtedness excluded from gross income under section 108 (or any corresponding provision of prior law repealed by the Bankruptcy Tax Act of 1980).*

An income item is considered "taken into account" without regard to the timing of its inclusion in your pre-adjustment AMTI or your E&P. Therefore, only income items that are "permanently excluded" from your pre-adjustment AMTI are included in your ACE. An income item will not be considered "taken into account" merely because the proceeds from that item might eventually be reflected in your pre-adjustment AMTI (for example, that of a shareholder) on the liquidation or disposal of a business.

Adjustment for buildup in life insurance contracts. Include in your ACE the income on life insurance contracts (as determined under section 7702(g)) for the tax year less the portion of any premium that is attributable to insurance coverage.

(**b**) Generally, no deduction is allowed in computing your ACE for items not "taken into account" (defined below) for purposes of computing your E&P for the tax year. Therefore, these amounts increase your ACE to the extent they are deductible in computing your line 4 pre-adjustment AMTI (i.e., they would be positive adjustments to your line 4 pre-adjustment AMTI in arriving at your ACE). However, there are exceptions. Do not add back: (**i**) any deduction allowable under section 243 or 245 for any dividend that qualifies for a 100% dividends-received deduction under section 243(a), 245(b), or 245(c); and (**ii**) any dividend received from a "20-percent owned corporation" (as defined in section 243(c)(2)), but only to the extent such dividend is attributable to income of the paying corporation that is subject to federal income tax. Also see sections 56(g)(4)(C)(iii) and (iv) for special rules for dividends from section 936 companies and certain dividends received by certain cooperatives.

An item is considered "taken into account" without regard to the timing of its deductibility in computing your line 4 pre-adjustment AMTI or your E&P. Therefore, only deduction items that are "permanently disallowed" in computing your E&P are disallowed in computing your ACE.

(**c**) Generally, no deduction is allowed for an item in computing your ACE if the item is not deductible in computing your line 4 pre-adjustment AMTI (even if the item is deductible for purposes of computing your E&P). The only exceptions to this general rule are the related reductions to an income item described in the second sentence of item (2)(a) above. Deductions that are not allowed in computing your ACE include: (**i**) capital losses in excess of capital gains; (**ii**) bribes, fines, and penalties disallowed under section 162; (**iii**) charitable

Page 3

contributions in excess of the limitations of section 170; (iv) expenditures for meals and entertainment in excess of the limitations of section 274; (v) Federal taxes disallowed under section 275; and (vi) golden parachute payments in excess of the limitation of section 280G. **Note:** *No adjustment is necessary for these items since they were not allowed in computing your line 4 pre-adjustment AMTI.*

(3) Other adjustments based on specific rules for computing E&P:

(a) Intangible drilling costs. For purposes of computing your ACE, determine your deduction for intangible drilling costs (as defined in section 263(c)) in the manner provided in section 312(n)(2)(A).

(b) Certain amortization provisions do not apply. For purposes of computing your ACE, section 173 (relating to circulation expenditures) and section 248 (relating to organizational expenditures) do not apply to amounts paid or incurred in tax years beginning after 1989.

(c) LIFO inventory adjustments. The adjustments provided in section 312(n)(4) apply in computing your ACE.

(d) Installment sales. For any installment sale in a tax year beginning after 1989, you generally cannot use the installment method for purposes of computing your ACE. However, the installment method may be used with respect to the applicable percentage (as determined under section 453A) of the gain from any installment sale to which section 453A(a)(1) applies.

(4) Disallowance of loss on exchange of debt pools. For purposes of computing your ACE, you may not recognize any loss on the exchange of any pool of debt obligations for another pool of debt obligations having substantially the same effective interest rates and maturities.

(5) Acquisition expenses of certain life insurance companies. For purposes of computing your ACE, acquisition expenses of life insurance companies (other than "small insurance companies," defined below) must be capitalized and amortized in accordance with the treatment generally required under generally accepted accounting principles (and in such a manner as if this rule applied to all applicable tax years). A "small insurance company" is any insurance company that meets the requirements of section 806(a)(3), except that section 806(c)(2) does not apply. **Note:** *This adjustment was repealed by the Revenue Reconciliation Act of 1990; however, it applies in full to tax years beginning after December 31, 1989 but before September 30, 1990, and in part to tax years that include September 30, 1990 (see section 11301(d)(2)(B) for a special proration rule for tax years that include September 30, 1990).* See new section 848(i) for a special rule for the treatment of qualified foreign contracts under the ACE adjustment.

(6) Depletion. For purposes of computing your ACE, the allowance for depletion with respect to any property placed in service in a tax year beginning after 1989 must be determined under the cost depletion method of section 611.

(7) Treatment of certain ownership changes. If a corporation undergoes an ownership change (within the meaning of section 382) in a tax year beginning after 1989, and such corporation has a net unrealized built-in loss (within the meaning of section 382(h)), then the adjusted basis of each asset of such corporation (immediately after the ownership change) must be adjusted to its proportionate share (determined on the basis of respective fair market values) of the fair market value of the assets of such corporation (determined under section 382(h)) immediately before the ownership change. For purposes of determining whether you have a built-in loss, you must use the aggregate adjusted basis of your assets that is used in computing ACE. **Note:** *These new adjusted bases must be subsequently*

Page 4

used for all ACE calculations (such as depreciation and gain or loss on disposition of an asset).
Line 5b.—*If you are preparing Form 4626 for an affiliated group that has filed a consolidated tax return for the current tax year under the rules of section 1501, you must figure line 5b on a consolidated basis.*

The following examples illustrate the calculation to be performed on line 5b:
Example 1: Corporation C determines its line 5a ACE to be $25,000. If its line 4 pre-adjustment AMTI were $10,000, it would enter the $15,000 difference on line 5b. If its line 4 amount were instead $30,000, it would enter zero on line 5b since the difference is less than zero. Finally, if its line 4 amount were a negative $100,000, it would enter the difference of $125,000 on line 5b.
Example 2: Corporation D determines its line 5a ACE to be a negative $25,000. If its line 4 pre-adjustment AMTI were a negative $30,000, it would enter the difference of $5,000 on line 5b.
Line 7—Alternative tax net operating loss deduction.— Your alternative tax net operating loss deduction **(ATNOLD)** is the NOL you determined for regular tax purposes under section 172, except that:

(1) In the case of a loss year beginning after 1986, the NOL you determined for regular tax purposes from such year must be: (a) reduced by the positive AMT adjustments and increased by the negative AMT adjustments provided in sections 56 and 58, and (b) reduced by the tax preference items you determined under section 57 (but only to the extent they increased the NOL you determined for regular tax purposes).

(2) In applying the rules outlined in section 172(b)(2) (regarding the determination of the amount of carrybacks and carryovers), you must use the modification to those rules described in section 56(d)(1)(B)(ii).

(3) If, for any tax year beginning before 1987, you had minimum tax that was deferred under section 56(b) (as in effect before the enactment of the Tax Reform Act of 1986) and that deferred tax has not been paid, the amount of NOL carryovers that you may carry over to this year for AMT purposes must be reduced by your tax preference items that gave rise to the deferred add-on minimum tax. (Section 701(f)(2)(B) of the Tax Reform Act of 1986.)

(4) Your ATNOLD is limited to 90% of your AMTI computed without regard to your ATNOLD. Therefore, enter on line 7 the smaller of the ATNOLD or 90% of the amount on line 6.

Note: *The amount of any NOL that is not deductible for AMT purposes may be carried back or carried over in accordance with the rules outlined in section 172(b). The amount carried back or carried over for AMT purposes is likely to differ from the amount (if any) that is carried back or carried over for regular tax purposes; therefore, it is essential that you retain adequate records for both AMT purposes and regular tax purposes.*

Line 9a. Tentative exemption amount .—All members of a controlled group of corporations are limited to one $40,000 exemption, which must be divided equally among the members (unless all of the members consent to an unequal allocation). If you are preparing Form 4626 for a member of a controlled group, enter such member's share of the $40,000 exemption on line 9a.

Lines 9b and 9c .—In computing the reduction of the tentative exemption amount, the line 8 AMTI of all members of a controlled group of corporations must be taken into account and any decrease of the tentative exemption amount must be divided equally among the members (unless all of the members consent to an unequal allocation). If you are preparing Form 4626 for a member of a controlled group, enter such member's share of the $150,000 floor on line 9b, and subtract that line 9b amount from such member's share of the combined line 8 AMTI of all members of the controlled group of corporations and enter the difference on line 9c. See section 1561 for additional information.

Line 12—Alternative minimum tax foreign tax credit.—Refigure the foreign tax credit you claimed for regular tax purposes as follows:

(1) For each separate limitation, recompute both the numerator (foreign source taxable income) and the denominator (worldwide taxable income) of the limitation fraction by taking into account your AMT adjustments and tax preference items;

(2) Substitute line 11 of Form 4626 for the "total U.S. income tax against which the credit is allowed";

(3) For each separate limitation, multiply the fraction in (1) above by the amount in (2) above to determine your recomputed limitation;

(4) For each separate limitation, take the lesser of the total foreign taxes paid with respect to that separate limitation and the recomputed limitation from (3) above; and

(5) Add the credits you recomputed for each separate limitation and enter the result on line 12.
Note: *For purposes of determining whether any income is high-taxed in applying the separate income category limitations for the AMT foreign tax credit, the AMT rate is to be used instead of the regular rate.*

Your AMT foreign tax credit is subject to a 90% limit (i.e., the credit cannot be more than the amount on line 11 less 10% of the amount that would be on that line if Form 4626 were recomputed using zero on line 7). For tax years beginning after March 31, 1990, the 90% limit does not apply to certain corporations that meet the requirements of section 59(a)(2)(C). For tax years that include March 31, 1990, these corporations should see section 7612 of the Revenue Act of 1989 for a special proration rule.

Note: *With respect to any separate limitation, any AMT foreign tax credit you cannot claim (because of the limitation fraction or the 90% limit discussed above) may be carried back or carried over in accordance with the rules outlined in section 904(c). However, foreign taxes paid or accrued in a tax year beginning after 1986 that were carried back (for regular tax purposes) to offset tax in a tax year beginning before 1987 may not be used in computing the AMT foreign tax credit for the current tax year.*

Note also: *The amount of any foreign tax credit that you cannot claim (and is therefore carried back or carried over) for AMT purposes is likely to differ from the amount (if any) that is carried back or carried over for regular tax purposes. Therefore, it is essential that you retain adequate records for both AMT purposes and regular tax purposes.*
Line 14.—Enter your regular tax liability for the tax year (as defined in section 26(b)) less your foreign tax credit and your possessions tax credit. Be sure to **include** any tax on accumulation distribution of trusts you computed on Form 4970. **Do not include** any recapture of investment credit you computed on Form 4255 or any recapture of low-income housing credit you computed on Form 8611. If you file Form 1120, this is line 3, Schedule J, minus the sum of lines 4a and 4b, Schedule J.
Line 16— Environmental tax.—*If you are preparing Form 4626 for a regulated investment company or a real estate investment trust, skip line 16 (it does not apply).*
Compute your environmental tax as follows:
(1) Complete line 1 of Form 4626 without taking into account any environmental tax deduction.
(2) Complete lines 2a through 6 of Form 4626.
(3) Skip lines 7 through 15 and compute your environmental tax on line 16 of Form 4626.
Note: If you are completing line 16 for a member of a controlled group of corporations, all members of the controlled group are limited to one $2,000,000 exemption, which must be divided equally among the members (unless all of the members consent to an unequal allocation). See section 1561 for additional information.
Then compute your AMT as follows: Complete line 1 of Form 4626 taking into account any deduction you are allowed with respect to the environmental tax. Then complete lines 2a through 15 of Form 4626.

Form **6251**

Department of the Treasury
Internal Revenue Service

Alternative Minimum Tax—Individuals

▶ See separate Instructions.

▶ Attach to Form 1040 or Form 1040NR. Estates and trusts, use Form 8656.

OMB No. 1545-0227

1990

Attachment
Sequence No. **32**

Name(s) shown on Form 1040

Your social security number

1	Taxable income from Form 1040, line 37. (If Form 1040, line 37 is zero, see Instructions.)	**1**	
2	Net operating loss deduction, if any, from Form 1040, line 22. (Enter as a positive amount.)	**2**	
3	Combine lines 1 and 2	**3**	
4	**Adjustments:** (See Instructions before completing.)		
a	Standard deduction, if any, from Form 1040, line 34	**4a**	
b	Personal exemption amount from Form 1040, line 36	**4b**	
c	Medical and dental expenses	**4c**	
d	Miscellaneous itemized deductions from Schedule A (Form 1040), line 25	**4d**	
e	Taxes from Schedule A (Form 1040), line 8	**4e**	
f	Refund of taxes	**4f** ( )	
g	Personal interest from Schedule A (Form 1040), line 12b	**4g**	
h	Other interest adjustments	**4h**	
i	Reserved	**4i**	
j	Depreciation of tangible property placed in service after 1986	**4j**	
k	Circulation and research and experimental expenditures paid or incurred after 1986	**4k**	
l	Mining exploration and development costs paid or incurred after 1986	**4l**	
m	Long-term contracts entered into after 2/28/86	**4m**	
n	Pollution control facilities placed in service after 1986	**4n**	
o	Installment sales of certain property	**4o**	
p	Adjusted gain or loss	**4p**	
q	Certain loss limitations	**4q**	
r	Tax shelter farm loss	**4r**	
s	Passive activity loss	**4s**	
t	Beneficiaries of estates and trusts	**4t**	
u	Combine lines 4a through 4t	**4u**	
5	**Tax preference items:** (See Instructions before completing.)		
a	Appreciated property charitable deduction	**5a**	
b	Tax-exempt interest from private activity bonds issued after 8/7/86	**5b**	
c	Depletion	**5c**	
d	Accelerated depreciation of real property placed in service before 1987	**5d**	
e	Accelerated depreciation of leased personal property placed in service before 1987	**5e**	
f	Amortization of certified pollution control facilities placed in service before 1987	**5f**	
g	Intangible drilling costs	**5g**	
h	Add lines 5a through 5g	**5h**	
6	Combine lines 3, 4u, and 5h	**6**	
7	Alternative tax net operating loss deduction. (Do not enter more than 90% of line 6.) See Instructions	**7**	
8	Alternative minimum taxable income. Subtract line 7 from line 6. If married filing a separate return, see Instructions	**8**	
9	Enter: $40,000 ($20,000 if married filing separately; $30,000 if single or head of household)	**9**	
10	Enter: $150,000 ($75,000 if married filing separately; $112,500 if single or head of household)	**10**	
11	Subtract line 10 from line 8. If zero or less, enter -0- here and on line 12 and go to line 13	**11**	
12	Multiply line 11 by 25% (.25)	**12**	
13	Subtract line 12 from line 9. If zero or less, enter -0-. If completing this form for a child under age 14, see Instructions for amount to enter	**13**	
14	Subtract line 13 from line 8. If zero or less, enter -0- here and on line 19 and skip lines 15 through 18	**14**	
15	Multiply line 14 by 21% (.21)	**15**	
16	Alternative minimum tax foreign credit. See Instructions	**16**	
17	Tentative minimum tax. Subtract line 16 from line 15	**17**	
18	Enter your tax from Form 1040, line 38, minus any foreign tax credit on Form 1040, line 43. If an amount is entered on line 39 of Form 1040, see Instructions	**18**	
19	**Alternative minimum tax.** Subtract line 18 from line 17. If zero or less, enter -0-. Enter this amount on Form 1040, line 49. If completing this form for a child under age 14, see Instructions for amount to enter	**19**	

For Paperwork Reduction Act Notice, see separate Instructions.

Form **6251** (1990)

19**90**   Department of the Treasury Internal Revenue Service

Instructions for Form 6251

Alternative Minimum Tax—Individuals

(Section references are to the Internal Revenue Code.)

Paperwork Reduction Act Notice.—We ask for the information on this form to carry out the Internal Revenue laws of the United States. You are required to give us this information. We need it to ensure that you are complying with these laws and to allow us to figure and collect the right amount of tax.

The time needed to complete and file this form will vary depending on individual circumstances. The estimated average time is:

Recordkeeping	2 hrs., 17 min.
Learning about the law or the form	1 hr., 10 min.
Preparing the form	1 hr., 20 min.
Copying, assembling, and sending the form to IRS	20 min.

If you have comments concerning the accuracy of these time estimates or suggestions for making this form more simple, we would be happy to hear from you. You can write to both the IRS and the Office of Management and Budget at the addresses listed in the instructions of the tax return with which this form is filed.

General Instructions

Who Must File.—Complete Form 6251 to see if the alternative minimum tax (AMT) applies to you. Attach it to your return only if:

● You are liable for the AMT; or

● Line 6 (computed without regard to any negative adjustments on line 4) is more than line 9, and

(a) you have one or more adjustments on line 4h and lines 4j through 4t; or

(b) you have tax preference items on line 5.

Also, certain credits are limited by the amount shown on line 15, or in some cases, line 17. If this applies to you, Form 6251 must be attached to your return. The forms used to figure these credits have information on the tentative minimum tax limit.

Additional Information.—For more details, get **Pub. 909,** Alternative Minimum Tax for Individuals.

Recordkeeping.—For AMT purposes, certain items of income, deductions, etc., receive different tax treatment than for regular tax purposes. Therefore, for the AMT you need to recompute items that you figured for the regular tax. In some cases, you may wish to do this by completing the applicable tax form a second time. If you do complete another form, do not attach it to your tax return.

For the regular tax, some deductions and credits may result in carrybacks or carryforwards to other tax years. Examples are investment interest expense, a net operating loss, a capital loss, and the foreign tax credit. Because you may have to refigure these items for the AMT, the carryback or carryforward amount may be different for the AMT than for the regular tax. Therefore, you should keep records of these different amounts for the AMT and the regular tax. An AMT carryforward amount will be important in completing Form 6251 for the following year.

Partners, Shareholders, etc.—If you are a member of a partnership or a shareholder in an S corporation, the partnership or S corporation will give you information on any adjustments or tax preference items relating to it that you have to take into account for Form 6251.

Nonresident Alien Individuals.—If you disposed of U.S. real property interests at a gain, see the instructions for line 45 of **Form 1040NR,** U.S. Nonresident Alien Income Tax Return. You may have to enter a different figure on line 15 of Form 6251 if the amount figured in the worksheet in the instructions for line 45 of Form 1040NR is more than the tentative amount you figured on line 15 of Form 6251.

Credit For Prior Year Minimum Tax.—Get **Form 8801,** Credit for Prior Year Minimum Tax, if you paid AMT for 1989, or if you had a minimum tax credit carryforward on line 28 of your 1989 Form 8801.

Earned Income Credit.—If you have an earned income credit, you must reduce the credit by any AMT.

Optional Write-off for Certain Adjustments and Tax Preference Items (section 59(e)).—For the regular tax, you may elect to deduct certain adjustment and preference items ratably over a period of time, instead of treating them as adjustments or tax preference items on Form 6251. These items are: circulation expenditures under section 173, research and experimental expenditures under section 174(a), intangible drilling and developmental expenditures under section 263(c), development expenditures under section 616(a), and mining exploration expenditures under section 617(a). You may elect to deduct circulation expenditures over 3 years, intangible drilling and development expenditures over 60 months, and the other items over 10 years.

The election is made in the year of the expenditure. You can revoke it only with the consent of IRS. If you made the election for one of the above items, do not make an adjustment for that item on Form 6251. See section 59(e) for more details.

Specific Instructions

Line 1—Taxable income.—Enter the amount from Form 1040, line 37. If line 37 is zero, subtract line 36 from line 35 and enter the result as a negative amount.

If your taxable income includes an amount from the alcohol fuel credit under section 87, reduce your taxable income by the amount of the credit included in income.

Lines 4a through 4t—Adjustments.—Enter all adjustments on lines 4a through 4t as positive amounts, unless otherwise indicated.

Line 4c—Medical and dental expenses.—If you have an entry on line 4 of Schedule A (Form 1040), figure this adjustment as follows:

Step 1.—Multiply your adjusted gross income (line 32 of Form 1040) by 2½% (.025).

Step 2.—Compare the amount from Step 1 to the amount on line 4 of Schedule A (Form 1040), and enter the smaller amount.

Line 4f—Refund of taxes.—Include any refund from line 10 of Form 1040 that is attributable to state or local income taxes deducted in a tax year after 1986.

Also include on this line any refunds received in 1990 attributable to state or local personal property taxes, or foreign income or real property taxes, deducted in a tax year after 1986. If you include such amounts, you **must** write a description of the amount on the dotted line to the left of line 4f. For example, if you include a refund of real property taxes, write "real property" to the left of the entry space.

Line 4h—Other interest adjustments.—Include on this line home mortgage interest from line 9a, 9b, or 10 of Schedule A (Form 1040) that:

● is for a mortgage whose proceeds were not used to buy, build, or substantially rehabilitate your main home or qualified dwelling; **AND**

● if the mortgage was taken out before 7/1/82, the mortgage was not secured by property that was your main home or a qualified dwelling used by you or a member of your family at the time the mortgage was taken out. (A qualified dwelling is any house, apartment, condominium, or mobile home not used on a transient basis. See section 163(h)(4).)

See Regulations section 1.56A.

Investment Interest Expense.—If you completed **Form 4952,** Investment Interest Expense Deduction, you may have an adjustment on this line. Refigure your investment interest expense on another Form 4952 as follows:

Step 1.—Complete lines 1 and 2 of Form 4952. Follow the Form 4952 instructions for lines 1 and 2, but add to line 1 any interest expense that is included on line 4h of Form 6251 as a mortgage interest adjustment that is paid or accrued on indebtedness properly attributable to property held for investment within the meaning of section 163(d)(5). An example is interest on a home equity loan whose proceeds were invested in preferred stock, which is deductible as home mortgage interest expense for regular tax purposes, but not for alternative minimum tax purposes. Add to this amount any interest expense that would have been deductible if interest earned on specified private activity bonds issued after 8/7/86 had been includible in gross income.

When completing line 2, recompute your gross investment income, any net gain attributable to the disposition of property held for investment, and any investment expenses taking into account all AMT adjustments and tax preference items that apply. Include any interest income and investment expenses from private activity bonds issued after 8/7/86.

Step 2.—Enter -0- on line 3 and complete lines 4 and 5.

Step 3.—Skip lines 6 through 12 and enter the amount from line 5 on line 13.

Step 4.—Complete lines 14 through 24. When entering your disallowed investment interest expense from 1989 on line 17, use your AMT disallowed investment interest expense from 1989.

To figure your adjustment, find the difference between line 24 of your AMT Form 4952 and line 24 of the Form 4952 completed for regular tax purposes. If your investment interest expense allowed for the AMT is more than that allowed for the regular tax, enter the difference as a negative amount on line 4h.

Note: *If you took the standard deduction instead of itemizing your deductions, and you had investment interest expense, do not enter an amount on line 4h unless you reported investment interest expense on Schedule E. If you did, follow the instructions on page 1 for completing Form 4952. Allocate the investment interest expense allowed on line 24 of the AMT Form 4952 in the same way you did for the regular tax. Enter on line 4h the difference between the amount allowed on Schedule E for the regular tax and the amount allowed on Schedule E for the AMT.*

Line 4i—Reserved.—This line is reserved for future use.

Line 4j—Depreciation of tangible property placed in service after 1986 (or after 7/31/86 if election was made under the transitional provision of section 203(a)(1) of the Tax Reform Act of 1986).—

Caution: *Do not include on this line any depreciation adjustment from: (1) an activity for which you are not at risk; (2) amounts received from a partnership or an S corporation if the basis limitations under section 704(d) or 1366(d) apply; (3) a passive activity; or (4) a tax shelter farm activity. Instead, take these depreciation adjustments into account when figuring the amount to enter on line 4q, 4r, or 4s, whichever applies.*

For the AMT, the depreciation deduction must be recomputed using the alternative depreciation system (ADS) described in section 168(g) for tangible property as follows:

(1) For any real property described in section 1250(c) (generally nonresidential real and residential rental), use the straight line method over 40 years.

(2) For any tangible property (other than the property described in (1) above) which is depreciated using the straight line method for regular tax purposes, recompute your depreciation using the straight line method over the property's class life (explained below).

(3) For all other tangible property, use the 150% declining balance method over the property's class life, switching to the straight line method in the first tax year it yields a larger deduction.

In applying the above rules:

(1) Use the same convention you used for regular tax purposes;

(2) The "class life" to be used for AMT purposes has a different meaning than the recovery period used for regular tax purposes (although these periods could be the same in some instances). The class lives you need to use for AMT purposes can be found in Rev. Proc. 87-56, 1987-2 C.B. 674 or in **Pub. 534,** Depreciation. Use 12 years for any tangible personal property that does not have an assigned class life;

(3) See Rev. Proc. 87-57, 1987-2 C.B. 687 for optional tables (14 through 18) that can be used in computing depreciation for AMT purposes. (These optional tables have been reproduced in Pub. 534.); and

(4) Do not make an adjustment for property depreciated under the unit-of-production method, or any other method not expressed in terms of years. See section 168(f)(1), (2), (3), or (4).

Subtract the recomputed depreciation for AMT purposes from the depreciation deducted for regular tax purposes. If the depreciation

figured for the AMT is more than the depreciation deducted for the regular tax, enter the difference as a negative amount on line 4j.

If depreciation is capitalized to inventory under the uniform capitalization rules, refigure the inventory using the rules discussed above.

Line 4k—Circulation expenditures and research and experimental expenditures paid or incurred after 12/31/86.—

Caution: *Skip this line, if for regular tax purposes, you elected to take the optional 3-year write-off period for circulation expenditures, or the optional 10-year write-off period for research and experimental expenditures under section 59(e).*

Circulation expenditures incurred after 1986.—For regular tax purposes, section 173 allows circulation expenditures to be deducted in full in the tax year they were paid or incurred. However, for the AMT these expenditures must be amortized over 3 years beginning with the year the expenditures were paid or incurred. Refigure these circulation expenditures for the AMT. Subtract your recomputed AMT expense from the expense claimed for regular tax purposes and enter the result on line 4k. If the current year deduction for the AMT is more than that figured for the regular tax, enter the difference as a negative amount.

Research and experimental expenditures incurred after 1986.—Research and experimental expenditures deducted during the current year for the regular tax under section 174(a) must be amortized over 10 years for the AMT. Refigure these expenditures for the AMT and enter the adjustment on line 4k. Figure the adjustment in the same manner as described above for circulation expenditures.

If you had a loss on property for which a deduction for circulation or research and experimental expenditures was allowed for regular tax purposes, see section 56(b)(2)(B).

Line 4l—Mining exploration and development costs paid or incurred after 12/31/86.—

Caution: *Skip this line if, for the regular tax, you elected to take the optional 10-year write-off under section 59(e).*

The deduction you claimed for regular tax purposes under sections 616(a) and 617(a) is not allowed for AMT purposes. Instead, you must capitalize such costs and amortize them ratably over a 10-year period beginning with the tax year in which they were paid or incurred.

Subtract your recomputed AMT expense from the expense you claimed for regular tax purposes and enter the result on line 4l. If your recomputed AMT expense is greater than the expense you claimed for regular tax purposes, enter the difference as a negative amount.

If you had a loss on property for which a deduction for mining exploration and development costs was allowed for regular tax purposes, see section 56(a)(2)(B).

Line 4m—Long-term contracts entered into after 2/28/86.—For AMT purposes, you must use the percentage of completion method rules described in section 460(b) to determine your taxable income from any "long-term contract" (defined in section 460(f)) you entered into after 2/28/86. However, this rule does not apply to any "home construction contract" (as defined in section 460(e)(6)) you entered into after 6/20/88 if you meet the 2-year estimated completion requirement of section 460(e)(1)(B)(i) and the $10 million ceiling on average annual gross receipts requirement of section 460(e)(1)(B)(ii).

Note: *In the case of a contract described in section 460(e)(1), use the simplified procedures for allocating costs outlined in section 460(b)(4) to determine the percentage of completion.*

Subtract the income you reported for regular tax purposes from the income you recomputed for AMT purposes and enter the result on line 4m. If the amount reportable for the AMT is less than that reported for the regular tax, enter the difference as a negative amount on line 4m.

Line 4n—Pollution control facilities placed in service after 12/31/86.—The election under section 169 to amortize the basis of a certified pollution control facility over a 60-month period is not available for AMT purposes.

Instead, the deduction is determined using the ADS and the class life asset depreciation range for the facility under the straight line method.

Subtract your recomputed AMT deduction from the deduction you claimed under section 169 for regular tax purposes. If the amount allowed for AMT is more than the amount allowed for regular tax, enter the difference as a negative amount on line 4n.

Line 4o—Installment sales of certain property.—For any disposition of inventory (as defined in section 1221(1)) after 3/1/86, the installment method of accounting cannot be used in determining income for AMT purposes (except for certain dispositions of timeshares or residential lots if you made an election to pay interest under section 453(l)(2)(B)).

Application of rules in computing adjustment:

Dealer dispositions.— For dealer dispositions occurring after 3/1/86 but before 1/1/88, you will have adjustments for those dispositions if you used the installment method for regular tax purposes but were required for AMT purposes to report the entire gain in the year of disposition. Enter the income you reported for regular tax purposes for the current year for those dispositions on line 4o as a negative amount.

For dealer dispositions occurring after 1987, generally no adjustments are necessary because the installment method generally cannot be used for either regular tax purposes or for AMT purposes.

Nondealer dispositions.—For nondealer dispositions occurring after 3/1/86, but before the first day of your tax year that began in 1987, you will have adjustments for those dispositions if you used the installment method for regular tax purposes but were required for AMT purposes to report the entire gain in the year of disposition. Enter the income you reported for regular tax purposes for the current year for those dispositions on line 4o as a negative amount.

For nondealer dispositions occurring on or after the first day of your tax year that began in 1987, generally no adjustments are necessary since you are allowed to use the installment method of accounting for both regular tax purposes and AMT purposes.

Line 4p—Adjusted gain or loss.—Use this line to report:

(a) Any AMT adjustment resulting from the recomputation of a gain or loss from the sale or exchange of property during the year, or from the recomputation of a casualty gain or loss to business or income-producing property; and

(b) Any AMT adjustment from the exercise of incentive stock options after 12/31/87.

Page 2

Recomputed gain or loss.—For item (a) above, this line can apply only if you reported gain or loss on **Form 4797,** Sale of Business Property, Schedule D (Form 1040), or Section B of **Form 4684,** Casualties and Thefts. Recompute your gain or loss for those forms. When figuring your adjusted basis, take into account any AMT adjustment you made this year or in previous years for items related to lines 4j, 4k, 4l, and 4n, of Form 6251. On line 4p, enter the difference between the gain or loss reported for the regular tax, and that figured for the AMT.

If the gain recomputed for AMT purposes is less than the gain computed for regular tax purposes, **OR** if the loss recomputed for AMT purposes is more than the loss computed for regular tax purposes, **OR** if you recomputed a loss for AMT purposes and computed a gain for regular tax purposes, enter the difference as a negative amount.

Incentive stock options.—The rules of section 421 that give favorable tax treatment to incentive stock options do not apply for AMT purposes to stock received from options exercised after 12/31/87. Instead, the rules of section 83 apply. Include as an adjustment on line 4p the difference between the amount reported as income for regular tax purposes, if any, from the exercise of these options, and that reportable as income under section 83.

If you acquired stock by exercising an incentive stock option and you disposed of that stock in the same year, the regular tax and AMT treatments are the same.

Line 4q—Certain loss limitations.— Caution: *If the loss is from a passive activity, use line 4s instead. If the loss is from a tax shelter farm activity (that is not passive), use line 4r.*

Refigure your gains and losses from activities for which you are not at risk and basis limitations applicable to partnerships and S corporations by taking into account your AMT adjustments and tax preference items. See sections 59(h), 465, 704(d), and 1366(d).

Enter on line 4q the difference between the amount that would be reported for the activity on Schedule C, E, F, or **Form 4835,** Farm Rental Income and Expenses, for AMT purposes and the amount that was reported for the activity on that form or schedule for regular tax purposes.

Enter any adjustment for amounts reported on Schedule D, Form 4684 or Form 4797 for the activity on line 4p instead of line 4q. See Instructions for line 4p.

Line 4r—Tax shelter farm loss.—Complete line 4r only if you have a gain or loss from a tax shelter farm activity (as defined in section 58(a)(2)) that is **not** a passive activity. If the tax shelter farm activity **is** a passive activity, you must include the gain or loss with your other passive activities on line 4s below.

Recompute all gains and losses you reported for regular tax purposes from tax shelter farm activities by taking into account your AMT adjustments and tax preference items. **Caution:** *To avoid duplication, any AMT adjustment or tax preference item taken into account on line 4r should not be taken into account in figuring the amount to enter on any other line of this form.*

Determine your tax shelter farm activity gain or loss for AMT purposes using the same rules you used for regular tax purposes with the following modifications. No recomputed loss is allowed, except to the extent you are insolvent (see section 58(c)(1)). A recomputed loss may not be used in the current tax year to offset gains from other tax shelter farm activities.

Instead, any recomputed loss must be suspended and carried forward indefinitely until: **(1)** you have a gain in a subsequent tax year from that same tax shelter farm activity, **or (2)** the activity is disposed of.

Note: *The amount of any tax shelter farm activity loss that is not deductible (and is therefore carried forward) for AMT purposes is likely to differ from the amount (if any) that is carried forward for regular tax purposes. Therefore, it is essential that you keep adequate records for both AMT purposes and regular tax purposes.*

Enter on line 4r the difference between the amount that would be reported for the activity on Schedule E, F, or Form 4835 for AMT purposes and the amount that was reported for the activity on that form or schedule for regular tax purposes.

Enter any adjustment for amounts reported on Schedule D, Form 4684, or Form 4797 for the activity on line 4p instead of line 4r. See Instructions for line 4p.

Line 4s—Passive activity loss.—Your passive activity gains and losses must be refigured for the AMT by taking into account all AMT adjustments, tax preference items, and AMT prior year unallowed losses that apply to that activity. You may wish to fill out a second **Form 8582,** Passive Activity Loss Limitations, to determine your passive activity loss allowed for AMT purposes, but do not file the second Form 8582. When refiguring your passive activity loss, no phase-in under section 469(m) is allowed. Skip lines 10 through 15 of Form 8582 when filling out an AMT Form 8582.

Example. Assume you are a partner in a partnership and the Schedule K-1 (Form 1065) you received shows the following:

● A passive activity loss of ($4,125),

● A depreciation adjustment of $500 on property placed in service after 12/31/86, and

● A tax preference item of $225 for accelerated depreciation on property placed in service before 1/1/87.

Because the depreciation adjustment and the depreciation tax preference item are deductions that are not allowed for the AMT, you must first reduce the passive activity loss by those amounts. The result is a passive activity loss for the AMT of ($3,400). You would then enter this amount on Worksheet 2 of the AMT Form 8582 and refigure the allowable passive activity loss for AMT purposes.

Note: *The amount of any passive activity loss that is not deductible (and is therefore carried forward) for AMT purposes is likely to differ from the amount (if any) that is carried forward for regular tax purposes. Therefore, it is essential that you keep adequate records for both AMT purposes and regular tax purposes.*

Enter on line 4s the difference between the amount that would be reported for the activity on Schedule C, E, F, or Form 4835 for AMT purposes and the amount that was reported for the activity on that form or schedule for regular tax purposes.

Enter any adjustment for amounts reported on Schedule D, Form 4684, or Form 4797 for the activity on line 4p instead of line 4s. See Instructions for line 4p.

Caution: *To avoid duplication, any AMT adjustment or tax preference item taken into account on this line should not be taken into account in figuring the amounts to enter on any other line of this form.*

Publicly Traded Partnership (PTP).—If you had losses from a PTP, you will have to refigure the loss using any AMT adjustments,

tax preference items, and any AMT prior year unallowed loss. Any phase-in amount allowed on pre-enactment activities for regular tax purposes is not allowed for AMT purposes.

Tax shelter passive farm activities.— Refigure any gain or loss from a tax shelter passive farm activity taking into account all AMT adjustments, tax preference items, and AMT prior year unallowed losses. If the amount is a gain, it can be included on the AMT Form 8582, but if it is a loss, the adjustment for the tax shelter passive farm activity is the loss you reported for regular tax purposes. The AMT loss to carry forward is the refigured AMT loss.

Insolvency.—If at the end of the tax year, your liabilities exceed the fair market value of your assets, increase your passive activity loss allowed by that excess (but not more than your total loss). See section 58(c)(1).

Line 4t—Beneficiaries of estates and trusts.—Enter on this line the amount from line 7 of your Schedule K-1 (Form 1041). This is your share of the distributable alternative minimum taxable income from the estate or trust.

Lines 5a through 5g—Tax preference items.—Enter all tax preference items on lines 5a through 5g as positive amounts. When you figure an item for AMT, and the AMT amount is more than that figured for the regular tax, do not enter an amount on the line.

Line 5a—Appreciated property charitable deduction.—Enter the amount by which your contribution deduction would be reduced if all capital gain and section 1231 property was taken into account at its cost or other basis (rather than its fair market value).

Do not make an adjustment for carryforwards of charitable contributions made before 8/16/86. Also, do not include property for which you elected under section 170(b)(1)(C)(iii) to figure the contribution deduction using the property's adjusted basis rather than its fair market value.

Line 5b—Tax-exempt interest from private activity bonds issued after 8/7/86.—Enter interest you earned on "specified private activity bonds" reduced by any deduction that would have been allowable if the interest were includible in gross income for regular tax purposes. Generally, the term "specified private activity bonds" means any private activity bond (as defined in section 141) issued after 8/7/86. See section 57(a)(5) for exceptions and more details.

Exempt-interest dividends paid by a regulated investment company are treated as interest on a specified private activity bond to the extent the company received interest on the bond.

If you are filing **Form 8814,** Parent's Election To Report Child's Interest and Dividends, any tax-exempt interest from line 1b of that form that is a tax preference item must be included on line 5b.

Line 5c—Depletion.—In the case of mines, wells, and other natural deposits, enter the amount by which your depletion deduction under section 611 exceeds the adjusted basis of the property at the end of your tax year. In computing your year-end adjusted basis, use the rules of section 1016. However, do not reduce the adjusted basis by the current year's depletion.

Figure the excess amount separately for each property. If the depletion deduction for any property does not exceed the adjusted basis at year end, do not include a tax preference amount for that property.

Page 3

Line 5d—Accelerated depreciation of real property placed in service before 1987.— For AMT purposes, you must use the straight line method to figure depreciation on this property. Enter on line 5d the excess of the depreciation taken on this property for the regular tax over the depreciation as refigured for the AMT (using the straight line method). Figure this amount separately for each property and include only positive amounts on line 5d. For 15-year, 18-year, or 19-year real property, use the straight line method over 15, 18, or 19 years. For low-income housing property, use the straight line method over 15 years.

Line 5e—Accelerated depreciation of leased personal property placed in service before 1987.— For AMT purposes, you must use the straight line method to figure depreciation on this leased property. Enter on line 5e the excess of the depreciation taken for the regular tax over the depreciation as refigured for the AMT (using the straight line method). Figure this amount separately for each property and include only positive amounts on line 5e.

For leased recovery property, other than 15-year, 18-year, or 19-year real property, or low-income housing, enter the amount by which your depreciation deduction figured for the regular tax exceeds the deduction allowable using the straight line method with a half-year convention, no salvage value, and the following recovery period:

3-year property	5 years
5-year property	8 years
10-year property	15 years
15-year public utility property .	22 years

Line 5f—Amortization of certified pollution control facilities placed in service before 1987.— The election under section 169 to amortize the basis of a certified pollution control facility over a 60-month period is not available for AMT purposes. If the election was made for regular tax purposes, compute the adjustment by subtracting the depreciation deduction you would have been allowed under section 167 from the current year amortization deduction.

Line 5g—Intangible drilling costs.— *If, for regular tax purposes, you elected the optional 60-month write-off under section 59(e) for all property in this category, skip this line. No adjustment is necessary.*

Intangible drilling costs (IDCs) from oil, gas, and geothermal wells are a tax preference item to the extent that the "excess IDCs" exceed 65% of the "net income" from the wells. The tax preference item is computed separately for oil and gas properties and geothermal properties.

Excess IDCs are computed as follows: Figure the amount of your IDCs allowed for regular tax purposes under section 263(c), but do not include any section 263(c) deduction for nonproductive wells. Then, subtract the amount that would have been allowed had you amortized that amount over a 120-month period starting with the month the well was placed in production.

Note: *If you prefer not to use the 120-month period, you can elect to use any method that is permissible in determining cost depletion.*

Net income is determined by taking the gross income that you received or accrued during the tax year from all oil, gas, and geothermal wells and reducing it by the deductions allocable to these properties (reduced by the excess IDCs).

Note: *When refiguring net income, use only income and deductions allowed for AMT purposes.*

Line 7—Alternative tax net operating loss deduction (ATNOLD).— The ATNOLD is the aggregate of the alternative minimum tax net operating loss (ATNOL) carryovers and carrybacks to the tax year limited to 90% of alternative minimum taxable income (AMTI) determined without regard to the ATNOLD. Your ATNOLD is figured as follows:

For loss years beginning after 1986, your ATNOL is the excess of the deductions allowed for computing AMTI (excluding the ATNOLD) over the income included in computing the AMTI. This excess is computed with the modifications contained in section 172(d), taking into account the adjustments in sections 56 and 58 and the preferences in section 57 (i.e., the section 172(d) modifications should be separately computed in figuring the ATNOLD). For example, the limitation of nonbusiness deductions to the amount of nonbusiness income must be separately computed in figuring the ATNOL, using only nonbusiness income and deductions that are included in computing AMTI.

For loss years beginning before 1987, see section 56(d)(2)(B) to refigure your ATNOLD.

Enter on line 7 the smaller of the ATNOLD or 90% of the amount shown on line 6 of Form 6251. If the 90% amount is smaller, the unused NOL can be carried back or forward according to section 172(b). The treatment of NOLs for AMT purposes does not affect the amount of your NOL for regular tax purposes.

Note: *If you elected under section 172(b)(3)(C) to forego the carryback period for regular tax purposes, the election will also apply for the AMT.*

Line 8—Alternative minimum taxable income.— If you are married filing a separate return and the amount on line 8 is more than $155,000, you must enter the amount from line F below on line 8 instead.

A.	Enter amount from line 8 .	_____
B.	Maximum amount	$155,000
C.	Subtract line B from line A .	_____
D.	Multiply line C by 25% (.25)	_____
E.	Enter the **smaller** of line D or $20,000	_____
F.	Add lines A and E. Enter here and replace the amount on line 8 of Form 6251 with this amount . .	_____

Line 13.— If you are completing this form for a child who was under age 14 on January 1, 1991, and at least one of the child's parents was alive on December 31, 1990, use the worksheet below to figure the amount to enter on line 13. To the left of the entry space on line 13, write "Exemption Worksheet."

Line 13 Worksheet For Computing Minor Child's Alternative Minimum Tax Exemption

A.	Enter amount from line 9 .	_____
B.	Enter amount from line 12 .	_____
C.	Subtract line B from line A. If zero or less, enter -0-. .	_____
D.	Enter the child's earned income. See below . . .	_____
E.	Enter the greater of $1,000 or the child's share of the unused parental minimum tax exemption, if any. See below	_____
F.	Add lines D and E . . .	_____
G.	Enter the **smaller** of line C or line F here and on line 13	_____

Line D.— Earned income includes wages, tips, and other payments received for personal services performed. Generally, earned income is the amount reported on Form 1040, line 7; Form 1040A, line 7; or Form 1040NR, lines 8, 13, and 20. Earned income also includes the amount from line 29 of Schedule C for statutory employees. See the Instructions for Schedule C (Form 1040).

Note: *If the child is self-employed, earned income also includes the amount from Schedule SE, Part I, line 3, or Part II, lines 3 and 4b, minus any amount reported on Form 1040, line 25.*

Line E.— The unused parental minimum tax exemption is the excess, if any, of the parent's minimum tax exemption over the parent's AMTI. The child's share is determined by dividing the child's AMTI by the sum of the AMTI of all of the parent's children under age 14 and multiplying the result by the unused parental minimum tax exemption. See section 59(j).

If the child's parents are married and file separate returns, the above rule applies to the parent with the greater AMTI. If the child's parents are not married, the above rule applies to the custodial parent.

Line 16—Alternative minimum tax foreign tax credit.— Your AMT foreign tax credit is your foreign tax credit refigured as follows:

(1) Complete and attach a separate **Form 1116,** Foreign Tax Credit, for each separate limitation specified at the top of Form 1116 to help you determine your AMT foreign tax credit. Write across the top of each Form 1116–"Alt. Min. Tax."

(2) Complete Part I using only income and deductions allowed for AMT purposes attributable to sources outside the U.S.

(3) Complete Part III, but do not enter on line 9 any taxes taken into account in a tax year beginning after 12/31/86 that are treated under section 904(c) as paid or accrued in a tax year beginning before 1987. Enter on line 10 of Form 1116 your alternative minimum foreign tax credit carryover, and on line 17 of Form 1116, enter the alternative minimum taxable income from line 8 of Form 6251. On line 19 of Form 1116, enter the amount from line 15 of Form 6251.

(4) Complete Part IV of Form 1116. The foreign tax credit from line 32 of Form 1116 used for AMT purposes is limited to the tax on line 15 of Form 6251 minus 10% of what the tax on line 15 would have been if line 7 of Form 6251 had been zero. If you have no entry on line 7 of Form 6251, enter on line 16 of Form 6251 the smaller of 90% of line 15 of Form 6251 or the amount from line 32 of Form 1116. If line 7 of Form 6251 has an amount, for purposes of this line, recompute what your tax on line 15 would have been if line 7 were zero. Multiply that amount by 10% and subtract the result from the tax on line 15. Enter the smaller of that amount or the amount from line 32 of Form 1116 on line 16 of Form 6251.

If your foreign tax credit is limited for AMT purposes, the unused amount can be carried back or forward according to section 904(c).

Line 18—Tax.— Enter the amount from Form 1040, line 38 plus any tax from Form 4970 entered on line 39 of Form 1040. Subtract from that amount any foreign tax credit entered on line 43 of Form 1040. Enter the result on line 18.

Line 19.— If you are completing this form for a child who was under age 14 on January 1, 1991, (the line 13 worksheet was completed) and line 17 is more than line 18, get **Form 8803,** Limit on Alternative Minimum Tax for Children Under Age 14. Using Form 8803 may reduce or eliminate the child's AMT if:

● the child's parent has regular tax that is more than the parent's tentative minimum tax (line 18 is more than line 17 if the parent completed Form 6251); **or**

● another child of the parent who was under age 14 on January 1, 1991, has regular tax that is more than that child's tentative AMT.

Page 4

B-11 Forms for Tax Credits

Form **1116** Department of the Treasury Internal Revenue Service	**Foreign Tax Credit** Individual, Fiduciary, or Nonresident Alien Individual ▶ Attach to Form 1040, 1040NR, 1041, or 990-T. ▶ See separate Instructions.	OMB No. 1545-0121 19**90** Attachment Sequence No. **19**

Name	Identifying number as shown on page 1 of your tax return

Use a separate Form 1116 for each category of income listed below. Check only **one** box. Before you check a box, read **Categories of Income** on page 2 of the Instructions. This form is being completed for credit for taxes on:

☐ Passive income   ☐ Shipping income   ☐ Lump-sum distributions (see Instructions before completing form)

☐ High withholding tax interest   ☐ Dividends from a DISC or former DISC

☐ Financial services income   ☐ Certain distributions from a foreign sales corporation (FSC) or former FSC   ☐ General limitation income—all other income from sources outside the United States (including income from sources within U.S. possessions)

Resident of (name of country) ▶

Note: If you paid taxes to one foreign country or U.S. possession, use column A in Part I and line A in Part II. If you paid taxes to **more than one** foreign country or U.S. possession, use a separate column and line for each country or possession.

Part I   Taxable Income or Loss From Sources Outside the United States for Separate Category Checked Above

	Foreign Country or U.S. Possession			Total
	A	B	C	(Add Cols. A, B, and C)
Enter the name of the foreign country or U.S. possession . . . . ▶				
1 Gross income from sources within country shown above and of the type checked above. (See Instructions.):				**1**
Applicable deductions and losses (See Instructions.):				
2 Expenses directly allocable to the income on line 1 (attach schedule)				
3 Pro rata share of other deductions not directly allocable:				
a Certain itemized deductions or standard deduction. (See Instructions.)				
b Other deductions (attach schedule)				
c Add lines 3a and 3b				
d Total foreign source income. (See Instructions.) .				
e Gross income from all sources. (See Instructions.)				
f Divide line 3d by line 3e				
g Multiply line 3c by line 3f				
4 Pro rata share of interest expense. (See Instructions.):				
a Home mortgage and personal interest from line 7 of the worksheet on page 3 of the Instructions				
b Other interest				
5 Losses from foreign sources				
6 Add lines 2, 3g, 4a, 4b, and 5				**6**
7 Subtract line 6 from line 1. Enter the result here and on line 14 . . . . ▶				**7**

Part II   Foreign Taxes Paid or Accrued (See Instructions.)

Country	Credit is claimed for taxes (you must check one): ☐ Paid ☐ Accrued	Foreign taxes paid or accrued								
		In foreign currency				In U.S. dollars				
		Taxes withheld at source on:			(d) Other foreign taxes paid or accrued	Taxes withheld at source on:			(h) Other foreign taxes paid or accrued	(i) Total foreign taxes paid or accrued (add cols. (e) through (h))
	Date paid or accrued	(a) Dividends	(b) Rents and royalties	(c) Interest		(e) Dividends	(f) Rents and royalties	(g) Interest		
A										
B										
C										

8   Add lines A through C, column (i). Enter the total here and on line 9 . . . . ▶ **8**

For Paperwork Reduction Act Notice, see page 1 of separate Instructions.   Form **1116** (1990)

Form 1116 (1990)   Page **2**

Part III Figuring the Credit

9 Enter amount from line 8. This is the total foreign taxes paid or accrued for the category of income checked above Part I . . . . . . | **9** |

10 Carryback or carryover (attach detailed computation) . . . . . . | **10** |

11 Add lines 9 and 10 . . . . | **11** |

12 Reduction in foreign taxes. (See Instructions.) . . . . | **12** |

13 Subtract line 12 from line 11. This is the total amount of foreign taxes available for credit . . . . | **13** |

14 Enter amount from line 7. This is your taxable income or (loss) from sources outside the United States (before adjustments) for the category of income checked above Part I. (See Instructions.) . . . . | **14** |

15 Adjustments to line 14. (See Instructions.) . . . . | **15** |

16 Combine the amounts on lines 14 and 15. This is your net foreign source taxable income. (If the result is zero or less, you have no foreign tax credit for the type of income you checked on page 1. Skip lines 17 through 21.) . . . . | **16** |

17 **Individuals:** Enter amount from Form 1040, line 35. If you are a nonresident alien, enter amount from Form 1040NR, line 33. **Estates and trusts:** Enter your taxable income without the deduction for your exemption . . . . | **17** |

18 Divide line 16 by line 17. (If line 16 is more than line 17, enter the figure "1.") . . . . | **18** |

19 **Individuals:** Enter amount from Form 1040, line 40, **less** any amounts on Form 1040, lines 41 and 42. If you are a nonresident alien, enter amount from Form 1040NR, line 38, **less** any amount on Form 1040NR, line 39. **Estates and trusts:** Enter amount from Form 1041, Schedule G, line 1c, or Form 990-T, line 8 . . . . | **19** |

20 Multiply line 19 by line 18. (Maximum amount of credit) . . . . | **20** |

21 Enter the amount from line 13 or line 20, whichever is smaller. (If this is the only Form 1116 you are completing, skip lines 22 through 29 and enter this amount on line 30. Otherwise, complete the appropriate lines in Part IV.) . . . . ▶ | **21** |

Part IV Summary of Credits From Separate Parts III (See Instructions.)

22 Credit for taxes on passive income . . . . | **22** |

23 Credit for taxes on high withholding tax interest . . . . | **23** |

24 Credit for taxes on financial services income . . . . | **24** |

25 Credit for taxes on shipping income . . . . | **25** |

26 Credit for taxes on dividends from a DISC or former DISC . . . . . | **26** |

27 Credit for taxes on certain distributions from a FSC or former FSC . . | **27** |

28 Credit for taxes on lump-sum distributions . . . . | **28** |

29 Credit for taxes on general limitation income (all other income from sources outside the U.S.) . . . . | **29** |

30 Add lines 22 through 29 . . . . | **30** |

31 Reduction of credit for international boycott operations. (See "Reduction of Credit for International Boycott Operations" in instructions for line 12.) . . . . | **31** |

32 Subtract line 31 from line 30. This is your foreign tax credit. Enter here and on Form 1040, line 43; Form 1040NR, line 40; Form 1041, Schedule G, line 2a; or Form 990-T, line 9a . . . . . . ▶ | **32** |

Form **2441**	**Child and Dependent Care Expenses**	OMB No. 1545-0068
	▶ Attach to Form 1040.	19**90**
Department of the Treasury Internal Revenue Service	▶ See separate Instructions.	Attachment Sequence No. 21

Name(s) shown on Form 1040	Your social security number

- If you are claiming the child and dependent care credit, complete Parts I and II below. But if you received employer-provided dependent care benefits, first complete Part III on the back.
- If you are not claiming the credit but you received employer-provided dependent care benefits, only complete Part I, below, and Part III on the back.

Part I — Persons or Organizations Who Provided the Care—You must complete this part. (See the Instructions. If you need more space, attach a statement.)

1	(a) Name	(b) Address (number, street, city, state, and ZIP code)	(c) Identifying number (SSN or EIN)	(d) Amount paid (see Instructions)

2 Add the amounts in column (d) of line 1 and enter the total. . . . . | **2** |

Note: *If you paid cash wages of $50 or more in a calendar quarter to an individual for services performed in your home, you must file an employment tax return. Get **Form 942** for details.*

Part II — Credit for Child and Dependent Care Expenses

3 Enter the number of qualifying persons who were cared for in 1990. (See the Instructions for the definition of qualifying persons.) **Caution:** *To qualify, the person(s) **must** have shared the same home with you in 1990* . . ▶ | |

4 Enter the amount of **qualified** expenses you incurred and actually paid in 1990. See the Instructions to find out which expenses qualify. **Caution:** *If you completed Part III on page 2, do **not** include on this line any excluded benefits shown on line 25* . . . . | **4** |

5 Enter $2,400 ($4,800 if you paid for the care of two or more qualifying persons) . . . . | **5** | |

6 If you completed Part III on page 2, enter the **excluded benefits,** if any, from line 25 . . . . | **6** | |

7 Subtract line 6 from line 5 and enter the result. (If the result is zero or less, skip lines 8 through 13. Enter zero on line 14, and go to line 15.) . . . . | **7** |

8 Compare the amounts on lines 4 and 7. Enter the **smaller** of the two amounts here . . . . . . | **8** |

9 You **must** enter your **earned income**. (See the Instructions for the definition of earned income.) . . | **9** |

10 If you are married filing a joint return, you **must** enter your spouse's earned income. (If your spouse was a full-time student or disabled, see the Instructions for the amount to enter.). . . . . . | **10** |

11 If you are married filing a joint return, compare the amounts on lines 9 and 10. Enter the **smaller** of the two amounts here . . . . | **11** |

12 ● If you are married filing a joint return, compare the amounts on lines 8 and 11. Enter the **smaller** of the two amounts here. } . . . . | **12** |
   ● All others, compare the amounts on lines 8 and 9. Enter the **smaller** of the two amounts here.

13 Enter the decimal amount from the table below that applies to the **adjusted gross income** on Form 1040, line 32 . . . . | **13** | × |

If line 32 is:	Decimal amount is:	If line 32 is:	Decimal amount is:
Over— But not over—		Over— But not over—	
$0—10,000	.30	$20,000—22,000	.24
10,000—12,000	.29	22,000—24,000	.23
12,000—14,000	.28	24,000—26,000	.22
14,000—16,000	.27	26,000—28,000	.21
16,000—18,000	.26	28,000	.20
18,000—20,000	.25		

14 Multiply the amount on line 12 by the decimal amount on line 13 and enter the result . . . . . | **14** |

15 Multiply any child and dependent care expenses for 1989 that you paid in 1990 by the decimal amount that applies to the adjusted gross income on your 1989 Form 1040, line 32, or Form 1040A, line 14. Enter the result. (You must complete Part I and attach a statement. See the Instructions.) | **15** |

16 Add the amounts on lines 14 and 15. See the Instructions for the amount of credit you can claim . . | **16** |

For Paperwork Reduction Act Notice, see separate Instructions.   Form **2441** (1990)

Form 2441 (1990)   Page **2**

Part III   **Employer-Provided Dependent Care Benefits**—Complete this part only if you received employer-provided dependent care benefits. Also, be sure to complete Part I.

17	Enter the total amount of employer-provided dependent care benefits you received for 1990. (This amount should be shown in Box 15 of your W-2 form(s).) Do **not** include amounts that were reported to you as wages in Box 10 of Form(s) W-2 . . . . **17**	
18	Enter the amount forfeited, if any. **Caution:** *See the Instructions.* **18**	
19	Subtract line 18 from line 17 and enter the result **19**	
20	Enter the total amount of qualified expenses incurred in 1990 for the care of a qualifying person. (See the Instructions.) **20**	
21	Compare the amounts on lines 19 and 20. Enter the **smaller** of the two amounts here **21**	
22	You **must** enter your **earned income.** (See the Instructions for lines 9 and 10 for the definition of earned income.) **22**	
23	If you were married at the end of 1990, you **must** enter your spouse's earned income. (If your spouse was a full-time student or disabled, see the Instructions for lines 9 and 10 for the amount to enter.) **23**	
24	• If you were married at the end of 1990, compare the amounts on lines 22 and 23. Enter the **smaller** of the two amounts here. • If you were unmarried, enter the amount from line 22 here. } **24**	
25	**Excluded benefits.** Enter here the **smallest** of the following: • The amount from line 21, or • The amount from line 24, or • $5,000 ($2,500 if married filing a separate return). } **25**	
26	**Taxable benefits.** Subtract line 25 from line 19. Enter the result, but not less than zero. Also include this amount in the total on Form 1040, line 7. On the dotted line next to line 7, write "DCB" . . . **26**	

Note: *If you are also claiming the child and dependent care credit, fill in Form 1040 through line 40. Then complete Part II of this form.*

19**90**

Department of the Treasury
Internal Revenue Service

Instructions for Form 2441

Child and Dependent Care Expenses

General Instructions

Paperwork Reduction Act Notice.—We ask for the information on this form to carry out the Internal Revenue laws of the United States. You are required to give us this information. We need it to ensure that you are complying with these laws and to allow us to figure and collect the right amount of tax.

The time needed to complete and file this form will vary depending on individual circumstances. The estimated average time is: **Recordkeeping,** 20 minutes; **Learning about the law or the form,** 13 minutes; **Preparing the form,** 38 minutes; and **Copying, assembling, and sending the form to IRS,** 25 minutes.

If you have comments concerning the accuracy of these time estimates or suggestions for making this form more simple, we would be happy to hear from you. You can write to both the IRS and the Office of Management and Budget at the addresses listed in the Instructions for Form 1040.

Purpose

Child care credit.—Use Parts I and II of Form 2441 to figure the credit for child and dependent care expenses. You may be able to take this credit if you paid someone to care for your child or other qualifying person so you (and your spouse if you were married) could work or look for work in 1990. But you must have had earned income to do so. See the instructions for lines 9 and 10 for the definition of earned income.

Employer-provided dependent care benefits.—If you received benefits for 1990 under your employer's dependent care plan, use Parts I and III of Form 2441 to figure the amount, if any, of the benefits you may exclude from your income on Form 1040, line 7. (The benefits should be shown in Box 15 of your W-2 form(s).)

Additional Information

For more details, get **Pub. 503,** Child and Dependent Care Expenses.

Who May Take the Credit or Exclude Employer-Provided Dependent Care Benefits?

You may take the credit or the exclusion if **all five** of the following apply:
1. The care was provided so you (and your spouse if you were married) could work or look for work (but see **Spouse who was a full-time student or disabled,** on page 2).
2. You and the qualifying person(s) lived in the same home. See the instructions for line 3 for the definition of a qualifying person.
3. You (and your spouse if you were married) paid over half the cost of keeping up your home. The cost includes: rent; mortgage

interest; property taxes; utilities; home repairs; and food eaten at home.
4. The person who provided the care was not your spouse or a person whom you can claim as a dependent. If your child provided the care, he or she must have been age 19 or older by the end of 1990.
5. You report the required information about the care provider on line 1.

If you were married at the end of 1990, you generally must file a joint return to take the credit. But you will be treated as unmarried and still be eligible to take the credit if:

a. You were legally separated; or

b. You lived apart from your spouse during the last 6 months of the year, the qualifying person lived with you in your home over 6 months, and you provided over half the cost of keeping up your home.

Specific Instructions

Part I

Line 1

Complete columns **(a)** through **(d)** for each person or organization that provided the care. You can use **Form W-10,** Dependent Care Provider's Identification and Certification, or any of the other sources listed in its instructions to get the information from the care provider.

If you do not give correct or complete information, your credit (and exclusion, if applicable) may be disallowed, unless you can show you used due diligence in attempting to provide the required information.

Due diligence. You can show due diligence by keeping in your records a Form W-10 properly completed by the care provider or one of the other sources of information listed in the instructions for Form W-10. If the provider does not comply with your request for one of these items, complete the entries you can, such as the provider's name and address. Write "See attached" in the columns for which you do not have the information. Attach a statement that you requested the information from the care provider, but the provider did not comply with your request.

Columns (a) and (b).—Enter the care provider's name and address. If you were covered by your employer's dependent care plan and your employer furnished the care (either at your workplace or by hiring a care provider), enter your employer's name in column **(a),** write "See W-2" in column **(b),** and leave columns **(c)** and **(d)** blank. But if your employer paid a third party (not hired by your employer) on your behalf to provide the care, you must give information on the third party in columns **(a)** through **(d).**

Column (c).—If the care provider is an individual, enter his or her social security number (SSN). For other than an individual,

enter the provider's employer identification number (EIN). If the provider is a tax-exempt organization, enter "Tax-Exempt."

Column (d).—Enter the total amount you *actually paid* in 1990 to the care provider. Also include amounts your employer paid on your behalf to a third party. It does not matter when the expenses were incurred. Do not reduce this amount by any reimbursement you received.

Part II

Line 3

A **qualifying person** is:

• Any child **under age 13** whom you can claim as a dependent (but see **Exception for children of divorced or separated parents,** below). If the child turned 13 during the year, the child is a qualifying person for the part of the year he or she was under age 13.

• Your disabled spouse who is not able to care for himself or herself.

• Any disabled person who is not able to care for himself or herself whom you can claim as a dependent (or could claim as a dependent except that the person had gross income of $2,050 or more).

Exception for children of divorced or separated parents.—If you were divorced, legally separated, or lived apart from your spouse during the last 6 months of 1990, you may be able to take the credit or the exclusion even if your child is not your dependent. If your child is not your dependent, he or she is a qualifying person if **all five** of the following apply:

1. You had custody of the child for a longer time in 1990 than the other parent.

2. One or both of the parents provided over half of the child's support.

3. One or both of the parents had custody of the child for more than half of 1990.

4. The child was under age 13, or was disabled and could not care for himself or herself.

5. The other parent claims the child as a dependent because—

   a. As the custodial parent, you signed **Form 8332,** or a similar statement, agreeing not to claim the child's exemption for 1990; or

   b. Your divorce decree or written agreement that was in effect before 1985 states that the other parent can claim the child as a dependent and the other parent gave at least $600 for the child's support in 1990. But this rule does not apply if your decree or agreement was changed after 1984 to specify that the other parent cannot claim the child as a dependent.

If you can take the credit because of this exception, enter your child's name on the dotted line on line 3. If you can take the exclusion because of this exception, enter your child's name on the dotted line next to line 20.

Line 4

Qualified expenses include amounts paid for household services and care of the qualifying person while you worked or looked for work. Child support payments are **not** qualified expenses.

Household services.—These services must be needed to care for the qualifying person as well as to run the home. They include, for example, the services of a cook, maid, babysitter, housekeeper, or cleaning person if the services were partly for the care of the qualifying person. Do not include services of a chauffeur or gardener.

Qualified expenses also include your share of the employment taxes paid on wages for qualifying child and dependent care services.

Note: *If you paid cash wages of $1,000 or more for household services in any calendar quarter in 1989 or 1990, you should file a* **Form 940** *or* **Form 940-EZ** *for 1990 by January 31, 1991.*

Care of the qualifying person.—Care includes the cost of services for the qualifying person's well-being and protection. It does not include the cost of clothing or entertainment.

You may count care provided outside your home if the care was for your dependent under age 13, or any other qualifying person who regularly spends at least 8 hours a day in your home.

Generally, care does not include food or schooling expenses. But, if these items are included as part of the total care, and they are incident to, and cannot be separated from, the total cost, you may include the total cost. You may not include the cost of schooling for a child in the first grade or above, or the expenses for sending your child to an overnight camp.

Medical expenses.—Some disabled spouse and dependent care expenses may qualify as medical deductions if you itemize deductions on **Schedule A** (Form 1040). See Pub. 503 for details.

Note: *Do not include on line 4 expenses you incurred in 1990 but did not pay until 1991. You may be able to increase your 1991 credit when you pay the 1990 expenses in 1991.*

Lines 9 and 10

The amount of your qualified expenses may not be more than your earned income or, if married filing a joint return, the smaller of your earned income or your spouse's earned income.

Earned income generally means wages, salaries, tips, and other employee compensation. This is usually the amount shown on Form 1040, line 7. If you were self-employed, it also includes the amount shown on **Schedule SE** (Form 1040), line 3, minus any deduction you claimed on Form 1040, line 25. If you filed Schedule C to report income as a statutory employee, also include as earned income the amount from line 29 of that Schedule C. You must reduce your earned income by any loss from self-employment.

Note: *If you can use the optional method to figure self-employment tax, you may be able to increase your earned income for this credit. (Get Pub. 533, Self-Employment Tax, for details.) In this case, subtract any deduction you claimed on Form 1040, line 25, from the total of the amounts on Schedule SE, Section B, lines 3 and 4b, to figure earned income.*

If you are **married filing a joint return,** disregard community property laws. Enter your earned income on line 9 and your spouse's earned income on line 10. If your spouse died in 1990 and had no earned income, see Pub. 503.

Spouse who was a full-time student or disabled.—If your spouse was a full-time student or was disabled in 1990, figure your spouse's earned income on a monthly basis to determine your spouse's earned income for the year. For each month, or part of a month, that your spouse was disabled or a full-time student, your spouse is considered to have worked and earned income of not less than $200 a month ($400 a month if more than one qualifying person was cared for in 1990). But if your spouse also worked during any month and earned more than that amount, use his or her actual earned income.

For any month that your spouse was not disabled or a full-time student, use your spouse's actual earned income if your spouse worked during the month.

To be a full-time student your spouse must be enrolled in a school for the number of hours or classes that the school considers full time. He or she must also have been enrolled during any 5 months in 1990.

If, in the same month, both you and your spouse were full-time students and did not work, you may not use any amount paid that month to figure the credit. The same applies to a couple who did not work because neither was capable of self-care.

Line 15

If you had qualified expenses for 1989 that you did not pay until 1990, you may be able to increase the amount of credit you can take in 1990. To do this, multiply the 1989 expenses you paid in 1990 by the decimal amount from the table on line 13 that applies to the adjusted gross income shown on your 1989 Form 1040, line 32, or Form 1040A, line 14. Your 1989 expenses must be within the 1989 limits. Attach a computation showing how you figured the increase.

Line 16

In certain cases, the amount of credit you figured on line 16 may be limited. Some people will need to complete **Form 6251,** Alternative Minimum Tax—Individuals, because the computation of this limit uses an amount from line 15 of that form. Others, however, will not be affected by the limit and will not need Form 6251. The following will help you determine if you need Form 6251.

First, complete line 1 of the worksheet on this page.

Get Form 6251 if:
● You filed Schedule C, D, E, or F (Form 1040); **OR**
● The amount you entered on line 1 of the worksheet on this page is more than $150,000 ($112,500 if single or head of household; $75,000 if married filing separately).

If **either** of the above applies to you, complete Form 6251 through line 15. Skip lines 2 through 6 of the worksheet and go directly to line A of the worksheet.

If **neither** of the above applies to you, continue with line 2 of the worksheet. You may still need to get Form 6251.

Worksheet (Keep for your records)

1. Enter the amount from Form 1040, line 23 . . . . _____
   (Add to line 1 any tax-exempt interest from private activity bonds issued after August 7, 1986, and any net operating loss deduction.)
2. Enter $40,000 ($30,000 if single or head of household; $20,000 if married filing separately) . . . _____
3. Subtract line 2 from line 1. If the result is zero or less, **STOP HERE** and enter on Form 1040, line 41, the amount of your credit shown on line 16 of Form 2441. Otherwise, go to line 4 . . . . _____
4. Enter the amount from Form 1040, line 40 . . . . _____
5. Multiply line 3 by .21 . . . _____
6. Subtract line 5 from line 4 (if zero or less, enter -0-) . . . . . _____

Compare line 6 of the worksheet above with the amount of credit shown on Form 2441, line 16.

● **If line 6 above is more than your credit,** you do not have to complete Form 6251. Enter on Form 1040, line 41, the amount of your credit shown on Form 2441, line 16.

● **If your credit is more than the amount on line 6 above,** get Form 6251 and complete it through line 15. Then figure the limit on your credit as follows:

A. Enter the amount from Form 1040, line 40 . . . . _____
B. Enter the amount from Form 6251, line 15 . . . . _____
C. Maximum credit. Subtract line B from line A (if zero or less, enter -0-) . . . . _____

Compare the credit you first figured on line 16 of Form 2441 with line C above. Enter the **smaller** of the two amounts on line 16 of Form 2441, and on Form 1040, line 41. If line C above is the smaller amount, also write "AMT" in the left margin next to line 41.

Part III

Line 18

If you had a flexible spending account, any amount included on line 17 that you did not receive because you did not incur the expense is considered forfeited. Enter the forfeited amount on line 18. Do **not** include amounts you expect to receive at a future date.

Example. Under your employer's dependent care plan, you elected to have your employer set aside $5,000 to cover your 1990 dependent care expenses. The $5,000 is shown in Box 15 of your W-2 form. In 1990, you incurred and were reimbursed for $4,950 of qualified expenses. You would enter $5,000 on line 17 and $50, the amount forfeited, on line 18.

Line 20

Enter the total of all qualified expenses (see the instructions for line 4) incurred in 1990 for the care of your qualifying person(s). It does not matter when the expenses were paid.

Example. You received $2,000 in cash under your employer's dependent care plan for 1990. The $2,000 is shown in Box 15 of your W-2 form. During 1990 only $900 of qualified expenses were incurred for the care of your 5-year-old dependent child. You would enter $2,000 on line 17 and $900 on line 20.

Page 2

Form **3468**	**Investment Credit**	OMB No. 1545-0155
Department of the Treasury Internal Revenue Service	▶ Attach to your return. ▶ See separate Instructions.	19**90** Attachment Sequence No. **52**
Name(s) as shown on return		Identifying number

Part I   **Current Year Investment Credit**

Note: *Generally, you cannot claim the regular investment credit for property placed in service after December 31, 1985 (see Instructions).*

A If you are claiming credit under section 46(g) for "qualified withdrawals" with respect to "certain vessels" (see Instructions), check here . . . . ▶ ☐

1 Regular credit—Enter amount from Schedule A, line 4 . . . . **1**

2 Qualified rehabilitation expenditures for transitional rehabilitation property and certain rehabilitation projects—Enter qualified investment and multiply by percentage shown:

 a 30-year-old buildings . . . . _____ × 10% **2a**

 b 40-year-old buildings . . . . _____ × 13% **2b**

 c Certified historic structures (attach NPS certificate) . . . . . _____ × 25% **2c**

   Enter NPS number assigned or the flow-through entity's identifying number (see Instructions). . . . . _____

3 Qualified rehabilitation expenditures not includible in line 2 above:

 a Pre-1936 buildings . . . . _____ × 10% **3a**

 b Certified historic structures (attach NPS certificate) . . . . . _____ × 20% **3b**

   Enter NPS number assigned or the flow-through entity's identifying number (see Instructions). . . . . _____

4 Credit from cooperatives—Enter unused regular investment credit from cooperatives **4**

5 Business energy investment credit—Enter amount from Schedule B, line 6 . . . . **5**

6 Current year investment credit—Add lines 1 through 5 . . . . **6**

See General Instruction B, "When To File Form 3800, General Business Credit."

Part II   **Current Year Investment Credit Tax Liability Limitation**

7a Individuals—Enter amount from Form 1040, line 40 . . . . ⎫

 b Corporations—Enter amount from Form 1120, Schedule J, line 3 (or Form 1120-A, Part I, line 1) ⎬ **7**

 c Other filers—Enter regular tax before credits from your return . . . . ⎭

8 Credits that reduce regular tax before the investment credit:

 a Credit for child and dependent care expenses (Form 2441) . . **8a**

 b Credit for the elderly or the disabled (Schedule R, Form 1040) . **8b**

 c Foreign tax credit (Form 1116 or Form 1118) **8c**

 d Possessions tax credit (Form 5735) **8d**

 e Mortgage interest credit (Form 8396) **8e**

 f Credit for fuel from a nonconventional source (see instructions) **8f**

 g Orphan drug credit (Form 6765) **8g**

 h Total credits that reduce regular tax before the investment credit. Add lines 8a through 8g . . . **8h**

9 Net regular tax—Subtract line 8h from line 7 . . . . **9**

10 Tentative minimum tax:

 a Individuals—Enter amount from Form 6251, line 17 . . . . ⎫

 b Corporations—Enter amount from Form 4626, line 13 . . . . ⎬ **10**

 c Estates and Trusts—Enter amount from Form 8656, line 37 . . . . ⎭

11 Net income tax:

 a Individuals—Add line 9 above and line 19 of Form 6251. Enter the total . . . . ⎫

 b Corporations—Add line 9 above and line 15 of Form 4626. Enter the total . . . . . . ⎬ **11**

 c Other filers—See Instructions . . . . ⎭

12 If line 9 is more than $25,000, enter 25% of the excess (see Instructions) **12**

13 Subtract line 10 or line 12, whichever is greater, from line 11. Enter the result. If less than zero, enter zero **13**

14 Total allowed credit—Enter the smaller of line 6 or line 13. This is your **General Business Credit** for 1990. Enter here and on Form 1040, line 44; Form 1120, Schedule J, line 4e; Form 1120-A, Part I, line 2a; or on the corresponding line of other income tax returns **14**

For Paperwork Reduction Act Notice, see separate Instructions.   Form **3468** (1990)

Form 3468 (1990)   Page **2**

Schedule A—Current Year Regular Investment Credit

1   Enter on lines 1a through 1h your qualified investment in transition property (see Instructions).

Type of Property	Line	(1) Class of Recovery Property or Useful Life of Nonrecovery Property	(2) Basis or Cost	(3) Applicable Percentage	(4) Qualified Investment (column 2 x column 3)
New Recovery	a	20-year or more		100	
	b	Other			
Used Recovery	c	20-year or more		100	
	d	Other			
New Nonrecovery	e	20-year or more		100	
	f	Other			
Used Nonrecovery	g	20-year or more		100	
	h	Other			

2   Transition property—Enter qualified investment (from lines 1a through 1h, column (4)) and multiply by percentage shown . . _____ × 6.5%   **2**

3   Qualified timber property—Enter qualified investment (see Instructions for limitations) and multiply by percentage shown . _____ × 10%   **3**

4   Current year regular investment credit. Add lines 2 and 3. Enter here and on line 1 of page 1 . . .   **4**

Schedule B—Business Energy Investment Credit

1   Enter on lines 1a through 1e your qualified investment in business energy property.

Type of Property	Line	(1) Class of Property or Life Years	(2) Code	(3) Basis	(4) Applicable Percentage	(5) Qualified Investment (column 3 × column 4)
Recovery	a	3-year			60	
	b	Other			100	
Nonrecovery	c	3 or more/less than 5			33⅓	
	d	5 or more/less than 7			66⅔	
	e	7 or more			100	

2   Total qualified investment—Add lines 1a through 1e, column (5) **2**

3   Enter in column (1) the portion of the line 2 amount attributable to the following types of property:

	Line	(1) Qualified Investment	(2) Credit Percentage	(3) Investment Credit (column 1 × column 2)
a Solar energy property (see Instructions)	a		10	
b Geothermal property (see Instructions)	b		10	
c Ocean thermal property (see Instructions)	c		15	

d   Current year credit for investment in business energy property. Add lines 3a through 3c, column (3) **3d**

4   Certain other property. (See Instructions.) Enter qualified investment and multiply by percentage shown:

a   Certain long-term section 46(b)(2)(C) projects under way before 1983 . . . . _____ × 6.5%   **4a**

b   Hydroelectric generating property placed in service before 1989 (if an application has been docketed with the Federal Energy Regulatory Commission by 12-31-85). . . . . _____ × 7.15%   **4b**

5   Cooperative credit—Enter unused business energy investment credit from cooperatives. . . .   **5**

6   Tentative business energy investment credit—Add lines 3d through 5. Enter here and on line 5 of page 1 . . . .   **6**

1990

 Department of the Treasury
Internal Revenue Service

Instructions for Form 3468

Investment Credit

(Section references are to the Internal Revenue Code unless otherwise noted.)

Paperwork Reduction Act Notice.—We ask for the information on this form to carry out the Internal Revenue laws of the United States. You are required to give us the information. We need it to ensure that you are complying with these laws and to allow us to figure and collect the right amount of tax.

The time needed to complete and file this form will vary depending on individual circumstances. The estimated average time is:

Recordkeeping . . . . . . 22 hrs.

**Learning about
the law or the form** . . . . 7 hrs., 3 min.

**Preparing and sending
the form to IRS** . . . . 7 hrs., 43 min.

If you have comments concerning the accuracy of these time estimates or suggestions for making this form more simple, we would be happy to hear from you. You can write to both the IRS and the Office of Management and Budget at the addresses listed in the instructions of the tax return with which this form is filed.

Items You Should Note

Section 11813 of the Revenue Reconciliation Act of 1990 eliminated expired or obsolete investment tax credit provisions, generally effective for property placed in service after December 31, 1990. Code section references in these instructions do **not** reflect changes made by this "deadwood" provision.

Generally, you cannot claim an investment credit for property placed in service after December 31, 1985. However, you may claim a current year investment credit for "section 38 property" (as defined in section 48(a)) that is:

● Transition property (see Specific Instructions for Schedule A) placed in service before January 1, 1991;

● Progress expenditure property that is transition property when placed in service (see Specific Instructions for Schedule A);

Note: *Except for qualified timber property and properties listed in paragraphs (8) and (12) of section 204(a) of the Tax Reform Act of 1986, the regular percentage investment credit expires for property placed in service after December 31, 1990.*

● Qualified timber property (see Specific Instructions for Schedule A);

● Certain building rehabilitation property (see Specific Instructions for Part I, lines 2 and 3); or

● Business energy property (see Specific Instructions for Schedule B).

The business energy investment credit for solar energy property and geothermal property has been extended through

December 31, 1991. The business energy credit for ocean thermal property expired for property placed in service after September 30, 1990.

Energy property must meet the same requirements as regular investment credit property, except that the provisions of sections 48(a)(1) and 48(a)(3) do not apply. The property must be acquired new. See sections 46(b)(2) and 48(l)(1) through (17) for details.

See section 48(l)(17) for special rules on public utility property, and section 48(l)(11) for special rules on property financed by industrial development bonds.

General Instructions

A. Purpose of Form.—Use Form 3468 to claim a regular, rehabilitation, or business energy investment credit. If you are a partner of a partnership, beneficiary of an estate or trust, shareholder in an S corporation, or lessee, use Form 3468 to figure the credit based on your share of the investment that was allocated to you by the partnership, estate, trust, S corporation, or lessor.

Caution: *You may have to refigure the credit and recapture all or a portion of it if:*

● *you dispose of the property before the end of the property class life or life years;*

● *you change the use of the property;*

● *the business use of the property decreases so that it no longer qualifies (in whole or in part) as investment credit property;*

● *you reduce your proportionate interest in a partnership or other "pass-through" entity that had claimed a credit; or*

● *you returned leased property (on which you had taken a credit) to the lessor before the end of the recapture period or useful life.*

For more information, see **Form 4255,** Recapture of Investment Credit.

For more details on investment credit, see the regulations under sections 46 and 48.

B. Who Must File Form 3800, General Business Credit.— The general business credit consists of the investment credit, jobs credit, credit for alcohol used as fuel, credit for increasing research activities, low-income housing credit and disabled access credit. If you have:

(1) more than one of these credits for 1990, **(2)** a carryback or a carryforward of any of these credits, or **(3)** an investment credit for a passive activity, do not complete Part II. Instead, attach the appropriate credit forms and summarize them on Form 3800. C corporations that are required to file **Form 4626,** Alternative Minimum Tax —Corporations, may also use Schedule A of Form 3800 to determine if they are entitled to additional general business credit under section 38(c)(2).

C. How To Figure the Credit.—For recovery property (i.e., property that is depreciated under the Accelerated Cost Recovery System (ACRS)), the class of property determines the percentage qualifying for investment credit. For nonrecovery property (i.e., property that is not depreciated under ACRS), the useful life of the property for investment credit must be the same as the useful life for depreciation.

See section 48 for special rules on movie and television films, sound recordings, and sale-leasebacks.

D. Investment Credit Property.—You may claim an investment credit for property placed in service only if it qualifies as one of the items listed above under "Items You Should Note." Enter only the business part if property is for both business and personal use.

Exceptions.—You **cannot** claim an investment credit for property that is:

(1) Used mainly outside the U.S.;

(2) Used by a tax-exempt organization (other than a section 521 farmers' cooperative) unless the property is used mainly in an unrelated trade or business;

(3) Used by governmental units and foreign persons and entities;

(4) Used for lodging or for furnishing the lodging (see section 48(a)(3) for exceptions, i.e., hotel or motel furnishings);

(5) Amortized or depreciated under section 167(k), 184, or 188; or

(6) Acquired or constructed with "excluded cost-sharing payments" from grants under any program listed in section 126(a) or by grants under the Energy Security Act.

E. Election for Certain Leased Property.—If you lease property to someone else, you may elect to treat all or part of your investment in new property as if it were made by the person who is leasing it from you. Lessors and lessees should see section 48(d) and related regulations for rules on making this election. For limitations, see sections 46(e)(3) and 48(d)(6).

F. At-Risk Limitation for Individuals and Closely Held Corporations.—The cost or basis of property for investment credit purposes may be limited if you borrowed against the property and are protected against loss, or if you borrowed money from a person who is related or who has other than a creditor interest in the business activity. The cost or basis must be reduced by the amount of this "nonqualified nonrecourse financing" related to the property as of the close of the tax year in which it is placed in service. See sections 46(c)(8) and 465 for details. If there is an increase during a later year of this nonqualified nonrecourse financing, you may have to refigure the credit on Form 4255.

Specific Instructions

Partnerships, S Corporations, Estates, and Trusts.— To figure the cost or basis of property to pass through to the individual partners, shareholders, or beneficiaries, complete only the following lines:

● item A in Part I;

● columns (2) and (4) (and column (3) if applicable) for line 1 of Schedule A;

● the qualified investment on lines 2 and 3 of Part I;

● the qualified investment on line 3 of Schedule A; and

● columns (2), (3), and (5) for line 1, Schedule B (you should also inform the partners, shareholders, or beneficiaries how much of the column (5) amount to enter on lines 3 or 4 of Schedule B).

Attach the completed form to the partnership, S corporation, estate, or trust income tax return to show the total cost or basis (or unused credit from a cooperative) that is passed through.

Part I—Current Year Investment Credit

Item A. Shipbuilders that make "qualified withdrawals" (described in section 46(g)(1)) from a capital construction fund for the acquisition, construction, or reconstruction of a qualified vessel are deemed to have made (at the time of the withdrawal) a qualified investment of 50% of the "applicable percentage" (specified in section 46(c)(2)) of the qualified withdrawal. If you are claiming credit under section 46(g)(3), check the box in item A.

Lines 2 and 3—Rehabilitation Expenditures.—You may take credit for certain capital costs incurred for additions or improvements to qualified existing buildings and for rehabilitation of certified historic structures. The expenditures must be: added to the basis of the building; depreciated by the straight-line method; and incurred in connection with the rehabilitation of a qualified rehabilitated building. The applicable percentage for qualified rehabilitation expenditures is 100%.

Decrease the depreciable basis by the allowed credit.

For filers placing property in service in 1990, the expenditures must be for either:

(1) nonresidential real property,

(2) residential rental property, or

(3) real property that has a class life of more than 12½ years.

Your building must also meet the following requirements:

(1) The building must be substantially rehabilitated.

(2) The building must have been placed in service before the beginning of rehabilitation. This requirement is met if the building was placed in service by any person at any time before the rehabilitation begins.

(3) At least 75% of the external walls must be retained with 50% or more kept in place as external walls. Also, at least 75% of the existing internal structural framework of the building must be retained in place. This does not apply to certified historic structures.

Page 2

A building is considered to be "substantially rehabilitated" if your rehabilitation expenses during a 24-month period that you select and that ends with or within your tax year are more than:

(1) $5,000, or

(2) Your adjusted basis in the building and its structural components, if this amount is more than $5,000.

Figure your adjusted basis on the first day of the 24-month period or the first day of your holding period, whichever is later.

If you are rehabilitating the building in phases under a written architectural plan and specifications that were completed before the rehabilitation began, substitute "60-month period" for "24-month period."

Enter on the applicable entry space under line 2 the qualified rehabilitation expenditures for transitional rehabilitation property and certain rehabilitation projects. See section 251(d) of the Tax Reform Act of 1986 for details on the transition rules and certain rehabilitation projects.

Enter on the applicable entry space under line 3 the qualified expenditures for any other rehabilitation property. This is property that is not covered by the transition rules. To qualify for the credit, the building must have been originally placed in service before 1936 or must be a certified historic structure. See section 48(g) for details.

If you are claiming a credit for a certified historic structure on line 2c or 3b, you must attach a copy of your request for final National Park Service (NPS) certification (NPS Form 10-168c). Enter the building number assigned by the NPS in the space provided. If the credit is a flow-through from a partnership, S corporation, estate, or trust, enter the identifying number of the flow-through entity in the space provided.

Limitations for lines 2 and 3 of Part I, line 12 of Part II, and lines 1a through 2 of Schedule A.—Mutual savings institutions, regulated investment companies, and real estate investment trusts are subject to special limitations for the amounts to be entered on these lines. See Regulations section 1.46-4.

Line 4—Credit from Cooperative.— Section 1381(a) cooperative organizations may claim the investment credit. If the cooperative cannot use any of the credit because of its tax liability limitation, the unused credit must be allocated to the patrons of the cooperative. The recapture provisions of section 47 apply as if the cooperative had kept the credit and not allocated it. Patrons should enter their unused regular investment credit from a cooperative on line 4.

Part II—Current Year Investment Credit Tax Liability Limitation

Do not complete Part II (instead go to Form 3800) if item (1), (2), or (3) listed in General Instruction B, "When To File Form 3800, General Business Credit," on page 1 applies.

Line 8f.—Corporations enter the nonconventional source fuel credit from Form 1120, Schedule J, line 4d. For individuals, the credit is included in the total for line 46 of Form 1040 (report only the portion of line 46 of Form 1040 that is the

nonconventional source fuel credit). Other filers enter the credit from the appropriate line of their returns.

Line 11c—Other Filers.—Enter the sum of line 9 and your alternative minimum tax from the alternative minimum tax form you file.

Line 12.—If a husband and wife file separate returns, each must use $12,500 instead of $25,000. But if one of them has *no* investment credit (or no carryforwards or carrybacks to the current year), then the other may use the entire $25,000.

A member of a controlled group enters only its apportioned share of the $25,000.

A mutual savings institution, a regulated investment company, or a real estate investment trust should see the Specific Instructions for "Limitations for lines 2 and 3 of Part I, line 12 of Part II, and lines 1a through 2 of Schedule A" above.

For estates and trusts, the $25,000 limitation is reduced by the same proportionate share of income that was allocated to the beneficiaries.

Carryback and Carryforward of Unused Credits.—If you cannot use all of the credit because line 6 is greater than line 13, you may carry the excess back 3 years and then forward 15 years. See General Instruction B on page 1.

Schedule A

Generally, the regular investment credit is not allowed for property placed in service after December 31, 1985. However, you may claim regular investment credit for the current year for "section 38 property" (as defined in section 48(a)) that is:
(a) transition property, (b) progress expenditure property, or (c) qualified timber property.

(a) Transition property.—Generally, transition property that is placed in service before January 1, 1991, is eligible for the regular investment credit in this year if:

(1) the property has a class life of 20 years or more and was constructed, reconstructed, or acquired under a written contract that was binding on December 31, 1985;

(2) you began construction or reconstruction of property (that has a class life of 20 years or more) by December 31, 1985, and you incurred or committed the lesser of $1,000,000 or 5% of the cost of such property;

(3) you began construction of an equipped building or "plant facility" (as defined in section 203(b)(4) of the Tax Reform Act of 1986) that has a class life of 20 years or more by December 31, 1985, under a written specific plan and you have incurred or committed more than one-half of the cost of such property by such date;

(4) the property is part of specific projects listed in section 204(a) of the Tax Reform Act of 1986.

Transition property (except for the properties described in paragraphs (8) and (12) of section 204(a) of the Tax Reform Act of 1986) must be placed in service before January 1, 1991.

Note: *The term "class life" (as used above) is defined in section 203(b)(2)(C) of the Tax Reform Act of 1986.*

You must reduce the basis for depreciation by the full amount of the credit claimed.

See section 49(e) for additional information.

(b) Progress Expenditure Property.—Property for which qualified progress expenditures (QPEs) were claimed in prior years must be placed in service before January 1, 1991. Investment credit is not allowed for QPEs in the year property is placed in service or for the year in which recapture is required for the property.

The allowable credit for the year the property is placed in service is based on the entire qualified investment in the property reduced by the QPEs included as qualified investment in earlier tax years.

If the property is not placed in service before January 1, 1991, all post-1985 QPEs must be recaptured. See section 46(d) and related regulations for more information.

You must reduce the depreciable basis of progress expenditure property by the full amount of the credit claimed, even if you made a section 48(q)(4) election in a prior year. See section 49(d) for additional information.

(c) Qualified Timber Property.—Regular investment credit may be claimed for the portion of the basis of "qualified timber property" that qualifies for amortization under section 194. You may not claim regular investment credit for the portion of such amortizable basis attributable to the capitalization of depreciation or cost recovery on property that already qualifies for the investment credit.

Only direct costs for planting and seeding can be amortized. These include costs for site preparation, seed, seedlings, labor, tools, and depreciation on equipment such as tractors, trucks, and tree planters used in planting or seeding. Depreciation is a direct cost only for the period of time the equipment is used in these activities. However, in figuring the amount qualifying for investment credit, you cannot include depreciation on equipment that itself qualifies for the investment credit.

You cannot claim more than $10,000 (or $5,000 in the case of a married person filing a separate return) of investment on line 3, Schedule A. For more information, see Regulations sections 1.194-2 and 1.48-1(p).

For timber property you must reduce the amortizable basis by one-half of the credit taken.

Lines 1a through 1d—Recovery Property.—Enter the basis of recovery property in column (2). This is generally the cost of the property reduced by any personal-use factor and by any portion that was expensed under section 179. It includes all items properly included in the depreciable basis, such as installation and freight costs. *Recovery property* is tangible personal property used in a trade or business or held for the production of income, and depreciated under the Accelerated Cost Recovery System (ACRS).

Lines 1e through 1h—Nonrecovery Property.—Nonrecovery property includes:

- property you elect to depreciate using a method not expressed in terms of years;
- property you elect to amortize (e.g., leasehold improvements);
- property transferred or acquired merely to bring the property under ACRS;
- property acquired in certain nonrecognition transactions;
- certain property used outside the U.S.;
- public utility property if you do not use the normalization method of accounting.

Enter the amortizable basis in forestation and reforestation expenditures on line 3 of Schedule A.

See section 46(c)(5) for rules for certain pollution control facilities.

Lines 1c, 1d, 1g, and 1h—Used Property Dollar Limitation.—In general, you may not take into account more than $150,000 of the cost of used property in any one year. This does not include the basis of any property traded in unless the trade-in caused the recapture of all or part of an investment credit allowed earlier or a reduction in an investment credit carryback or carryforward. Determine the $150,000 amount before applying the percentages based on the class of property or useful life. Enter the cost (subject to the dollar limitation) of used property placed in service during the year. Property inherited, received as a gift, or acquired from certain related persons does not qualify for the investment credit.

If a husband and wife file separate returns, each may claim up to $75,000. If one of them has *no* qualifying used property, the other may claim up to $150,000.

The $150,000 limitation applies to a partnership, S corporation, estate, or trust. The $150,000 must be divided among the estate or trust and its beneficiaries based on the income of the estate or trust allocable to each beneficiary. A $150,000 limitation also applies to each partner, shareholder, or beneficiary. Controlled corporate groups must apportion the limitation among all its members. See section 48(c) and related regulations.

Lines 1b, 1d, 1f, and 1h—Other.—Use these lines to claim a credit for any transition property with a class life of fewer than 20 years. Enter the applicable percentage for the property in column (3).

Line 2.—You must reduce the regular 10% credit for transition property by 35%, thus making the credit for this type of property 6.5%. If you use **all** of the transition credit in the current year, then none of the reduction may be carried to any other year.

If you are able to use **only a portion** of the reduced credit in the current year because line 13, Part II is smaller than line 6, Part I, you may carry forward to your next tax year the unused portion of the reduced credit and a corresponding portion of the 35% reduction.

If, for example, you are able to use half of the reduced credit in 1990, you may carry forward the other half of the reduced credit and half of the reduction.

If you are **not** able to use **any** of the reduced credit because of the tax liability limitations, you may carry forward to your next tax year the entire credit (both the reduced credit and the reduction).

Schedule B

Line 1—Column (2).—Use the code letters from the following list to indicate the kind of property for which you are claiming a credit. If you enter more than one kind of property on a line, enter the code letter for each kind of property in column (2) and the code letter and dollar amount of each kind of property in the right hand margin.

The code letters are:

a. Solar energy property
b. Geothermal property
c. Ocean thermal property

See sections 48(l)(4) and 48(l)(3)(A)(viii) and (ix) for definitions and special rules that apply to these kinds of property.

Lines 3a, 3b, and 3c.—The business energy investment credit for ocean thermal property expired for property placed in service after September 30, 1990. If property was under construction before October 1, 1990, see section 48(m) for transitional rules.

Lines 4a and 4b.—You must reduce the basis for depreciation by the full amount of the credit claimed.

If the installed capacity of hydroelectric generating property is more than 25 megawatts, the energy credit on line 4b is allowed for only part of the qualified investment. See section 48(l)(13)(C).

In the margin to the left of line 4b, enter the megawatt capacity of the generator as shown on its nameplate.

You must reduce the 10% credit on line 4a and the 11% credit on line 4b by 35%, thus making the credit for this type of property 6.5% and 7.15%, respectively.

If you use **all** of the reduced credit in the current year, none of the reduction may be carried to any other year.

If you are able to use **only a portion** of the reduced credit in the current year because line 13, Part II is smaller than line 6, Part I, you may carry forward to your next tax year the unused portion of the reduced credit and a corresponding portion of the 35% reduction. If, for example, you are able to use half of the reduced credit in 1990, you may carry forward the other half of the reduced credit and half of the reduction.

If you are **not** able to use **any** of the reduced credit because of the tax liability limitations, you may carry forward to your next tax year the entire credit (both the reduced credit and the reduction).

Form **3800**

Department of the Treasury
Internal Revenue Service

General Business Credit

▶ Attach to your tax return.
▶ See separate Instructions.

OMB No. 1545-0895

1990

Attachment
Sequence No. **22**

Name(s) as shown on return

Identifying number

Part I   Tentative Credit

1	Current year investment credit (Form 3468, Part I)	**1**	
2	Current year jobs credit (Form 5884, Part I)	**2**	
3	Current year credit for alcohol used as fuel (Form 6478)	**3**	
4	Current year credit for increasing research activities (Form 6765, Part III)	**4**	
5	Current year low-income housing credit (Form 8586, Part I)	**5**	
6	Current year disabled access credit (Form 8826, Part I)	**6**	
7	**Current year general business credit**—Add lines 1 through 6	**7**	
8	Passive activity credits included on lines 1 through 6 (see Instructions)	**8**	
9	Subtract line 8 from line 7	**9**	
10	Passive activity credits allowed in 1990 (see Instructions)	**10**	
11	Carryforward of general business credit, WIN credit or ESOP credit to 1990 (see Instructions).	**11**	
12	Carryback of general business credit to 1990	**12**	
13	Tentative general business credit—Add lines 9 through 12	**13**	

Part II   General Business Credit Limitation Based on Amount of Tax

14a	Individuals—Enter amount from Form 1040, line 40	⎫		
b	Corporations—Enter amount from Form 1120, Schedule J, line 3 (or Form 1120-A, Part I, line 1)	⎬	**14**	
c	Other filers—Enter regular tax before credits from your return	⎭		
15	Credits that reduce regular tax before the general business credit—			
a	Credit for child and dependent care expense (Form 2441)	**15a**		
b	Credit for the elderly or the disabled (Schedule R, Form 1040) . .	**15b**		
c	Foreign tax credit (Form 1116 or Form 1118).	**15c**		
d	Possessions tax credit (Form 5735)	**15d**		
e	Mortgage interest credit (Form 8396)	**15e**		
f	Credit for fuel from a nonconventional source	**15f**		
g	Orphan drug credit (Form 6765)	**15g**		
h	Total credits that reduce regular tax before the general business credit. Add lines 15a through 15g and enter here		**15h**	
16	Net regular tax—Subtract line 15h from line 14		**16**	
17	Tentative minimum tax:			
a	Individuals—Enter amount from Form 6251, line 17	⎫		
b	Corporations—Enter amount from Form 4626, line 13	⎬	**17**	
c	Estates and Trusts—Enter amount from Form 8656, line 37	⎭		
18	Net income tax:			
a	Individuals—Add line 16 above and line 19 of Form 6251. Enter the total	⎫		
b	Corporations—Add line 16 above and line 15 of Form 4626. Enter the total	⎬	**18**	
c	Other filers—See Instructions	⎭		
19	If line 16 is more than $25,000, enter 25% of the excess		**19**	
20	Subtract line 17 or line 19, whichever is greater, from line 18. Enter the result. If less than zero, enter zero		**20**	
21	**General business credit**—Enter the smaller of line 13 or line 20. Also enter this amount on Form 1040, line 44; Form 1120, Schedule J, line 4e; Form 1120-A, Part I, line 2a; or on the appropriate line of your return. (Individuals, estates, and trusts, see instructions if the credit for increasing research activities is claimed. C corporations, see instructions for Schedule A if the investment credit is claimed or if the corporation has undergone a post-1986 "ownership change.")		**21**	

For Paperwork Reduction Act Notice, see page 1 of the separate Instructions to this form.

Form **3800** (1990)

B-12   Other Tax Forms

Form **2106**	**Employee Business Expenses**	OMB No. 1545-0139
Department of the Treasury Internal Revenue Service	▶ See separate Instructions. ▶ Attach to Form 1040.	**1990** Attachment Sequence No. **54**

Your name	Social security number	Occupation in which expenses were incurred

Part I   Employee Business Expenses and Reimbursements

STEP 1 Enter Your Expenses		Column A Other Than Meals and Entertainment	Column B Meals and Entertainment
1 Vehicle expense from line 22 or line 29	1		
2 Parking fees, tolls, and local transportation, including train, bus, etc. . . .	2		
3 Travel expense while away from home overnight, including lodging, airplane, car rental, etc. **Do not** include meals and entertainment . . .	3		
4 Business expenses not included on lines 1 through 3. **Do not** include meals and entertainment	4		
5 Meals and entertainment expenses. (See the separate Instructions.) . .	5		
6 Add lines 1 through 5 and enter the **total expenses** here	6		

Note: *If you were not reimbursed for any expenses in Step 1, skip line 7 and enter the amount from line 6 on line 8.*

STEP 2   Enter Amounts Your Employer Gave You For Expenses Listed In STEP 1

7 Enter amounts your employer gave you that were **not** reported to you in Box 10 of Form W-2. Include any amount reported under code "L" in Box 17 of your Form W-2. (See Instructions.)	7		

STEP 3   Figure Expenses To Deduct on Schedule A (Form 1040)

8 Subtract line 7 from line 6	8		
Note: *If **both columns** of line 8 are zero, **stop here.** If column A is less than zero, report the amount as income and enter -0- on line 10, column A. See the separate Instructions for how to report.*			
9 Enter 20% (.20) of line 8, Column B	9		
10 Subtract line 9 from line 8	10		
11 Add the amounts on line 10 of both columns and enter the total here. **Also enter the total on Schedule A (Form 1040), line 20.** (Qualified performing artists and individuals with disabilities, see the separate Instructions for special rules on where to enter the total.) . . . . ▶	11		

For Paperwork Reduction Act Notice, see the separate Instructions.   Form **2106** (1990)

Form 2106 (1990)   Page **2**

Part II Vehicle Expenses (See Instructions to find out which sections to complete.)

Section A.—General Information

			(a) Vehicle 1	(b) Vehicle 2
12	Enter the date vehicle was placed in service	12	/ /	/ /
13	Total mileage vehicle was used during 1990	13	miles	miles
14	Miles included on line 13 that vehicle was used for business	14	miles	miles
15	Percent of business use (divide line 14 by line 13)	15	%	%
16	Average daily round trip commuting distance	16	miles	miles
17	Miles included on line 13 that vehicle was used for commuting	17	miles	miles
18	Other personal mileage (add lines 14 and 17 and subtract the total from line 13).	18	miles	miles

19   Do you (or your spouse) have another vehicle available for personal purposes? . . . . ☐ Yes   ☐ No

20   If your employer provided you with a vehicle, is personal use during off duty hours permitted? . . ☐ Yes   ☐ No   ☐ Not applicable

21a   Do you have evidence to support your deduction?   ☐ Yes   ☐ No.   **21b**   If "Yes," is the evidence written?   ☐ Yes ☐ No

Section B.—Standard Mileage Rate (Use this section only if you own the vehicle.)

22	Multiply line 14 by 26¢ (.26). Enter the result here and on line 1. (Rural mail carriers, see the separate Instructions.).	22	

Section C.—Actual Expenses

			(a) Vehicle 1		(b) Vehicle 2	
23	Gasoline, oil, repairs, vehicle insurance, etc..	23	░░░		░░░	
24a	Vehicle rentals.	24a		░░░		░░░
b	Inclusion amount	24b				
c	Subtract line 24b from line 24a	24c	░░░		░░░	
25	Value of employer-provided vehicle (applies only if 100% annual lease value was included on Form W-2. See Instructions.)	25	░░░		░░░	
26	Add lines 23, 24c, and 25	26	░░░		░░░	
27	Multiply line 26 by the percentage on line 15	27	░░░		░░░	
28	Enter amount from line 38 below	28				
29	Add lines 27 and 28. Enter total here and on line 1.	29	░░░		░░░	

Section D.—Depreciation of Vehicles (Use this section only if you own the vehicle.)

			(a) Vehicle 1		(b) Vehicle 2	
30	Enter cost or other basis. (See Instructions.)	30		░░░		░░░
31	Enter amount of Section 179 deduction. (See Instructions.)	31		░░░		░░░
32	Multiply line 30 by line 15. (See Instructions if you elected the Section 179 deduction.)	32		░░░		░░░
33	Enter depreciation method and percentage. (See Instructions.)	33				
34	Multiply line 32 by the percentage on line 33. (See Instructions.)	34	░░░		░░░	
35	Add lines 31 and 34	35				
36	Enter the limitation amount from the table in the line 36 instructions.	36		░░░		░░░
37	Multiply line 36 by the percentage on line 15.	37	░░░		░░░	
38	Enter the **smaller** of line 35 or line 37. Also enter it on line 28 above.	38	░░░		░░░	

1990

 Department of the Treasury
Internal Revenue Service

Instructions for Form 2106

Employee Business Expenses

Paperwork Reduction Act Notice

We ask for the information on this form to carry out the Internal Revenue laws of the United States. You are required to give us this information. We need it to ensure that you are complying with these laws and to allow us to figure and collect the right amount of tax.

The time needed to complete and file this form will vary depending on individual circumstances. The estimated average time is:

Recordkeeping . . . . 1 hr., 38 min.
**Learning about the law
or the form** . . . . 18 min.
Preparing the form . . . 1 hr., 14 min.
**Copying, assembling, and
sending the form to IRS** . . . 42 min.

If you have comments concerning the accuracy of these time estimates or suggestions for making this form more simple, we would be happy to hear from you. You can write to both IRS and the Office of Management and Budget at the addresses listed in the instructions for Form 1040.

A Change You Should Note

New rules apply to the calculation of expenses for the business use of your vehicle. If you use the standard mileage rate method for calculating these expenses, you may apply one rate to all business miles. The limitation of 15,000 miles to which the maximum rate applied, and special provisions for fully depreciated vehicles, have been eliminated.

Purpose of Form

Use Form 2106 if you are an employee and are deducting expenses attributable to your job.

Items To Note

● If your employer provided a vehicle for your business use and included 100% of its annual lease value on your Form W-2, see the instructions for line 25, Part II. You may be able to deduct a portion of the annual lease value if you use your actual expenses to figure your vehicle expense deduction.
● If a vehicle was used more than 50% for business in the year it was placed in service, and used 50% or less in a later year, part of the depreciation and Section 179 deduction

may have to be recaptured. Figure the depreciation and Section 179 deduction recapture on **Form 4797,** Sales of Business Property.

Additional Information

If you need more information about employee business expenses, you will find the following publications helpful:
Pub. 463, Travel, Entertainment, and Gift Expenses
Pub. 529, Miscellaneous Deductions
Pub. 534, Depreciation
Pub. 587, Business Use of Your Home
Pub. 907, Tax Information for Persons With Handicaps or Disabilities
Pub. 917, Business Use of a Car

Line-by-Line Instructions

**Part I.—Employee Business
Expenses and Reimbursements**

Fill out ALL of Part I if you were reimbursed for employee business expenses. If you were not reimbursed for your expenses, fill out only Steps 1 and 3 of Part I.

Who Must File Form 2106

A Were you an employee during the year? [Yes] [No] → Do not file Form 2106. See the instructions for Schedule C, E, or F.

B Did you have job-related business expenses? [Yes] [No] → Do not file Form 2106.

C Were you reimbursed for any of your business expenses? [Yes] [No] → **D** Are you claiming travel, transportation, meals, or entertainment expenses OR are you a **qualified performing artist** or an **individual with a disability claiming impairment-related work expenses** (see the line 11 instructions for definitions)?

E If you used the same vehicle in your job in 1990 and any prior year, did you use the actual expense method in the first year you used your vehicle, OR did you use a depreciation rate other than straight line for this vehicle in a prior year? (Skip Step E if you did not use a vehicle in your job in 1990.) [No] [Yes] → File Form 2106.

[Yes] → File Form 2106 (but see **Notes** below).

[No] → Do not file Form 2106. Enter expenses on Schedule A, line 20.

F Are your deductible expenses more than your reimbursements (count only reimbursements your employer did **not** include in Box 10 of your Form W-2)? For rules covering employer reporting of reimbursed expenses, see the instructions for line 7. [Yes] [No] → Do not file Form 2106.

File Form 2106 (but see **Notes** below).

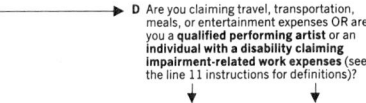

Notes

● Generally, employee expenses are deductible only if you itemize your deductions on Schedule A (Form 1040). But **qualified performing artists** and **individuals with disabilities** should see the special instructions for line 11 for where to deduct employee expenses.
● Do not file Form 2106 if none of your expenses are deductible because of the 2% limit on Schedule A (Form 1040) (that is, Schedule A, line 25 is zero).

Step 1.—Enter Your Expenses

Line 1.—Enter your vehicle expenses from Part II, line 22 or line 29.

Line 2.—Enter parking fees, etc., that did not involve overnight travel. Do not include transportation expenses for commuting to and from work. See the line 17 instructions for the definition of **commuting.**

Line 3.—Enter expenses for lodging and transportation connected with overnight travel away from your **tax home.** Do not include expenses for meals and entertainment.

Generally, your **tax home** is your main place of business or post of duty, regardless of where you maintain your family home. If you do not have a regular or main place of business because of the nature of your work, then your tax home is the place where you regularly live. If you do not fit either of these categories, you are considered an itinerant and your tax home is wherever you work. As an itinerant, you are not away from home and cannot claim a travel expense deduction. For more details on tax home, get Pub. 463.

Line 4.—Enter any other job-related expenses not listed on any other line on this form. Include expenses for business gifts, education (tuition and books), home office, trade publications, etc. If you are deducting home office expenses, get Pub. 587 for special instructions on how to report your expenses. If you are deducting depreciation on a cellular telephone or other similar telecommunications equipment, get **Form 4562,** Depreciation and Amortization, to figure the depreciation. Enter the depreciation on line 4.

Do not include expenses for meals and entertainment, taxes, or interest. Deductible taxes and interest are entered on lines 5 through 13 of Schedule A.

Line 5.—Enter your allowable meals and entertainment expense. Include meals while away from your tax home overnight and other business meals and entertainment. Instead of actual cost, you may include your expenses for meals while away from your tax home overnight at the maximum rate authorized to be paid by the Federal government for meals and incidental expenses in the locality where the travel was performed. For more information, including the maximum rate, see Pub. 463.

Step 2.—Enter Amounts Your Employer Gave You for Expenses Listed in Step 1

Line 7.—Enter the amounts your employer (or third party) gave you for expenses shown in Step 1 that were NOT reported to you in Box 10 of your Form W-2. This includes any amount reported under code "L" in Box 17 of Form W-2. Amounts reported under code "L" are certain reimbursements you received for business expenses that were not included as wages on Form W-2 because the expenses were treated as meeting specific IRS substantiation requirements.

Generally, when your employer pays for your expenses, the payments should not be included in Box 10 of your Form W-2 if, within a reasonable period of time, you (1) accounted to your employer for the expenses, AND (2) were required to return, and did return, any payments not spent (or considered not spent) for business expenses. If these payments were included in Box 10, ask your employer for a corrected Form W-2.

Accounting to your employer means that you gave your employer documentary evidence and an account book, diary, or similar statement to verify the amount, time, place, and business purpose of each expense. You are also treated as having accounted for your expenses if either of the following applies:

● Your employer gave you a fixed travel allowance that is similar in form to the per diem allowance specified by the Federal government and you verified the time, place, and business purpose of each expense. See Pub. 463 for more details.

● Your employer reimbursed you for vehicle expenses at the standard mileage rate or according to a flat rate or stated schedule, and you verified the date of each trip, mileage, and business purpose of the vehicle use. Get Pub. 917 for more details.

Allocating Your Reimbursement. If your employer paid you a single amount that covers both meals and entertainment, as well as other business expenses, you must allocate the reimbursement so that you know how much to enter in Column A and Column B of line 7. Use the following worksheet to figure this allocation.

Worksheet

1. Enter the total amount of reimbursements your employer gave you that were **not** reported to you in Box 10 of Form W-2 . . . . _____
2. Enter the total amount of your expenses for the periods covered by this reimbursement . . . . . _____
3. Of the amount on line 2, enter your total expense for meals and entertainment . . . . _____
4. Divide line 3 by line 2. Enter the result as a decimal (to at least two places) _____
5. Multiply line 1 by line 4. Enter the result here and in Column B, line 7 _____
6. Subtract line 5 from line 1. Enter this result here and in Column A, line 7 _____

Step 3.—Figure Expenses To Deduct on Schedule A (Form 1040)

Line 8.—If line 8, Column A, is less than zero, you have an excess reimbursement that must be reported as income. In this case, include the excess reimbursement in wages on Form 1040, line 7.

Line 11.—If you are a qualified performing artist (defined below), include your performing-arts-related expenses in the total on Form 1040, line 30. Write "Form 2106" and the amount in the space to the left of line 30. Your performing-arts-related business expenses are deductible whether or not you itemize deductions on Schedule A. The expenses are not subject to the 2% limit that applies to most other employee business expenses.

A **qualified performing artist** is an individual who (1) performed services in the performing arts as an employee for at least two employers during the tax year, (2) received at least $200 from each of these employers, (3) had allowable business expenses attributable to the performing arts of more than 10% of gross income from the performing arts, and (4) had adjusted gross income of $16,000 or less before deducting expenses as a performing artist.

Get Pub. 529 for more information.

If you are an **individual with a disability** and are claiming impairment-related work expenses (defined below), enter the line 11 amount on Schedule A, line 26, instead of

on Schedule A, line 20. Your impairment-related work expenses are not subject to the 2% limit that applies to most other employee business expenses.

Impairment-related work expenses are the allowable expenses of an individual with physical or mental disabilities for attendant care at his or her place of employment. They also include other expenses in connection with the place of employment that enable the employee to work.

Get Pub. 907 for more information.

Part II.—Vehicle Expenses

There are two methods for computing vehicle expenses—the Standard Mileage Rate and the Actual Expense Method. In some cases, you must use the Actual Expense Method instead of the Standard Mileage Rate. Use the following two flowcharts to see which method you should use. Rural mail carriers should see the line 22 instructions instead of using the flowcharts for special rules that apply to them.

If you have the option of using either the Standard Mileage Rate or Actual Expense Method, you should calculate your expenses using each method, and use the method most advantageous to you.

For Vehicles Placed in Service After 1980

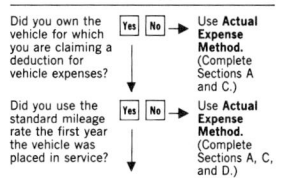

Use either the:
Standard Mileage Rate.
(Complete Sections A and B.)
OR
Actual Expense Method.
(Complete Sections A, C, and D.)

For Vehicles Placed in Service Before 1981

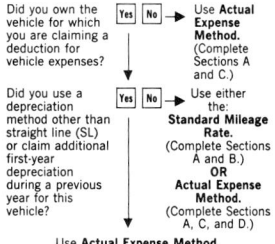

Use **Actual Expense Method.**
(Complete Sections A, C, and D.)

Section A.—General Information

All individuals claiming vehicle expenses must complete Section A.

If you used two vehicles for business during the year, use a separate column for each vehicle in Sections A, C, and D. If you used more than two, attach a computation using the format in Sections A, C, and D.

Line 12.—Date placed in service is generally the date you first start using your vehicle. However, if you first start using your vehicle for personal use and later convert it to business use, the vehicle is treated as placed in service on the date you started using it for business.

Line 13.— Enter the total mileage each vehicle was driven for all purposes during the year. If you changed your job during the year to one in which you started using a vehicle, enter only the total mileage for the months the vehicle was used in your new job.

Line 14.—Do not include commuting mileage on this line; it is not business mileage.

Line 15.—Divide line 14 by line 13 to figure your business use percentage. If you changed your job during the year to one in which you used your vehicle for business, multiply this percentage by the number of months the car was used in your new job, and divide the result by 12.

Line 16.—Enter your average daily round trip commuting distance. If you go to a different business location each day, figure the average.

Line 17.—Figure your commuting mileage by multiplying the number of days during the year that you used each vehicle to drive to and from your regular place of business by the average roundtrip commuting mileage. If you go to more than one regular place of business, figure the average. **Commuting mileage** is the mileage between your home and any location at which you work or perform services on a regular basis, even if you do not go to the same location each day. However, mileage between your home and a location at which you perform services on an irregular or short-term basis (generally a matter of days or weeks) is not commuting mileage. If you changed jobs (see line 13), enter the commuting mileage for the period of time you used your vehicle for business in the new job.

Section B.—Standard Mileage Rate

If you do not own the vehicle, skip Section B and go to Section C.

You may use the standard mileage rate instead of actual expenses to figure the deductible costs of operating a passenger car, including a van, pick-up, or panel truck. If you want to use the standard mileage rate for a car placed in service after 1980, you must do so in the first year you place your car in service. In later years you may deduct actual expenses, but you may not use a depreciation method other than straight line. If you do not use the standard mileage rate in the first year, you may not use it for that car for any subsequent year.

You may also deduct state and local personal property taxes and 10% of the interest on car loans in 1990. Include state and local personal property taxes on

Schedule A, line 7, and car loan interest on Schedule A, line 12a.

Line 22.—If you are a rural mail carrier (defined below) and you use the standard mileage rate to figure your vehicle expense, multiply the number of miles on line 14 by 39 cents (.39) instead of 26 cents.

You may use the higher mileage rate if you (1) were an employee of the U.S. Postal Service in 1990, (2) used your own vehicle to collect and deliver mail on a rural route, and (3) did not claim depreciation for the vehicle for any tax year beginning after 1987.

If you are also claiming the standard mileage rate for mileage driven in another business activity, you must figure the deduction for that mileage on a separate Form 2106.

See Pub. 917 for more information.

Section C.—Actual Expenses

Line 23.—Enter your total annual expenses for gasoline, oil, repairs, insurance, tires, license plates, or similar items. Do not include state and local personal property taxes or interest expense you paid. Include state and local personal property taxes on Schedule A, line 7, and car loan interest on Schedule A, line 12a.

Line 24a.—If you rented or leased a vehicle during the year instead of using one you own, enter the cost of renting. Also, include on this line any temporary vehicle rentals not included on line 3, such as when your car was being repaired.

Line 24b.—If you leased a vehicle for a term of 30 days or more after June 18, 1984, you may have to reduce your deduction for vehicle lease payments by an amount called the **inclusion amount.** You may have to enter the inclusion amount on line 24b if—

The lease term began:	And the vehicle's fair market value on the first day of the lease exceeded:
After 12/31/86	$12,800
After 12/31/85 but before 1/1/87	$23,000
After 4/2/85 but before 1/1/86 .	$28,000
After 12/31/84 but before 4/3/85	$34,500
After 6/18/84 but before 1/1/85.	$40,500

However, if you leased a vehicle during 1986, and 1990 is the first tax year you used the vehicle 50% or less for business, you will need to figure an additional inclusion amount. You must figure this additional amount even if you had no inclusion amount using the table shown above.

See Pub. 917 for instructions on how to figure the inclusion amount and the additional inclusion amount. Enter the total of these amounts on line 24b. If you have no inclusion amount or additional inclusion amount, leave line 24b blank.

Line 25.—If during 1990 your employer provided a vehicle for your business use, and included 100% of its annual lease value in Box 10 of your Form W-2, enter this amount

on line 25. If less than 100% of the annual lease value was included in Box 10 of your Form W-2, do not include this amount here. Instead, include the value of the business use on line 7 if you are claiming a deduction for vehicle expenses.

Section D.—Depreciation of Vehicles

Depreciation is an amount you can deduct to recover the cost or other basis of your vehicle over a certain number of years. In some cases, you may elect to expense, under Internal Revenue Code Section 179, part of the cost of your vehicle in the year of purchase. For more details, see Pub. 917.

Line 30.—Enter the vehicle's actual cost or other basis (unadjusted for prior years' depreciation). If you traded in your vehicle, your basis is the adjusted basis of the old vehicle (figured as if 100% of the vehicle's use had been for business purposes) plus any additional amount you pay for your new vehicle. Reduce your basis by any diesel fuel tax credit. For any vehicle purchased after 1986, add to basis any sales tax paid on the vehicle.

If you converted the vehicle from personal use to business use, your basis for depreciation is the smaller of the vehicle's adjusted basis or its fair market value on the date of conversion.

Line 31.—If 1990 is the first year your vehicle was placed in service and the percentage on line 15 is more than 50%, you may elect to deduct as an expense a portion of the cost (subject to a yearly limit). To calculate the Section 179 deduction, multiply the part of the cost of the vehicle that you choose to expense by the percentage on line 15. The total of your depreciation and Section 179 deduction may not exceed $2,660 multiplied by the percentage on line 15. Your Section 179 deduction for the year may be no greater than the excess of the income over the other deductions from any active trade or business on your Form 1040.

Caution: *If you placed more than $200,000 of Section 179 property in service during the year, use Form 4562 to figure your Section 179 deduction. Enter the amount of the Section 179 deduction allocable to your vehicle (from Form 4562, line 12) on Form 2106, line 31.*

Note: *For Section 179 purposes, the cost of the new vehicle does not include the adjusted basis of the vehicle you traded in.*

Example:

Cost including taxes	$15,000
Adjusted basis of trade-in . . .	– $ 2,000
Section 179 basis, ...	= $13,000
Limit on depreciation and Section 179 deduction	$ 2,660

Smaller of:

Section 179 basis, or Limit on depreciation and Section 179 deduction	$ 2,660
Percentage on line 15	x 75%
Section 179 deduction	= $ 1,995

Line 32.—To figure the basis for depreciation, multiply line 30 by the percentage on line 15. From that result, subtract the full amount of any Section 179 deduction (and half of any investment credit taken before 1986, unless you took the reduced credit.)

Line 33.—Use the chart below to find the depreciation method and percentage to enter on line 33. (For example, if you placed a car in service on December 1, 1990, and you use the method and percentage in column (a), enter "200 DB 5%" on line 33.) To use the chart, first find the date you placed the vehicle in service (line 12). Then select the depreciation method and percentage from column (a), (b), (c), or (d). For vehicles placed in service before 1990, use the same method and percentage you used on last year's return, unless a decline in your business use requires a change to the straight line method. For vehicles placed in service during 1990, select the depreciation method and percentage after reading the explanation for each column below.

   Column (a).—You may use column (a) only if the business use percentage on line 15 is more than 50%. The method in this column, the 200% declining balance method, will give you the largest deduction in the year your vehicle is placed in service. This column is also used for vehicles placed in service before 1987 and depreciated under ACRS (accelerated cost recovery system).

   Column (b).—You may use column (b) only if the business use percentage on line 15 is more than 50%. The method in this column, the 150% declining balance method, will give you a smaller depreciation deduction than in column (a) for the first three years. However, you will not have a "depreciation adjustment" on this item for alternative minimum tax purposes. This may result in a smaller tax liability if you must file **Form 6251,** Alternative Minimum Tax—Individuals.

   Column (c).—You must use column (c), or column (d) if applicable, if the business use percentage on line 15 is 50% or less. The method in this column is the straight line method over 5 years. It is optional if the business use percentage on line 15 is more than 50%.

Note: *If your vehicle was used more than 50% for business in the year it was placed in service, and used 50% or less in a later year, part of the depreciation and Section 179 deduction previously claimed may have to be added back to your income in the later year. Figure the amount to be included in income on Form 4797.*

   Column (d).—You must use column (d) if you placed your vehicle in service before 1987 and you elected the straight line method over a recovery period of 12 years.

Caution: *If you placed other business property in service during the year you placed your vehicle in service (for any year after 1986), you may not be able to use the chart shown below. See Pub. 917 for the proper depreciation rate to use.*

Depreciation Method Chart

Date Placed in Service	(a)	(b)	(c)	(d)
Oct. 1—Dec. 31, 1990	200 DB 5%	150 DB 3.75%	SL 2.5%	
Jan. 1—Sept. 30, 1990	200 DB 20%	150 DB 15%	SL 10%	
Oct. 1—Dec. 31, 1989	200 DB 38%	150 DB 28.88%	SL 20%	
Jan. 1—Sept. 30, 1989	200 DB 32%	150 DB 25.5%	SL 20%	
Oct. 1—Dec. 31, 1988	200 DB 22.8%	150 DB 20.21%	SL 20%	
Jan. 1—Sept. 30, 1988	200 DB 19.2%	150 DB 17.85%	SL 20%	
Oct. 1—Dec. 31, 1987	200 DB 13.68%	150 DB 16.4%	SL 20%	
Jan. 1—Sept. 30, 1987	200 DB 11.52%	150 DB 16.66%	SL 20%	
Jan. 1—Dec. 31, 1986	ACRS*		SL 20%	SL 8.333%
Jan. 1—Dec. 31, 1985	ACRS*		SL 10%	SL 8.333%
June 19—Dec. 31, 1984	ACRS*		SL*	SL 8.333%
Jan. 1, 1981—June 18, 1984				SL 8.333%

   *Enter your unrecovered basis, if any, on line 34. See Pub. 917 for more information.

Line 34.—If during the year you sold or exchanged your vehicle that was placed in service before 1987, enter -0- on line 34 for that vehicle.

Line 36.—Using the chart below, find the date you placed your vehicle in service. Then enter on line 36 the corresponding amount from the **Limitation** column. If your vehicle was placed in service before June 19, 1984, skip lines 36 and 37 and enter on line 38 the amount from line 35.

Date Vehicle Was Placed in Service	Limitation
Jan. 1—Dec. 31, 1990	$2,660
Jan. 1—Dec. 31, 1989	$4,200
Jan. 1—Dec. 31, 1988	$2,450
Jan. 1—Dec. 31, 1987	$1,475
Jan. 1—Dec. 31, 1986	$4,800
Apr. 3—Dec. 31, 1985	$4,800
Jan. 1—Apr. 2, 1985	$6,200
June 19—Dec. 31, 1984	$6,000

Form **2119**	**Sale of Your Home**	OMB No. 1545-0072
Department of the Treasury Internal Revenue Service	▶ Attach to Form 1040 for year of sale. ▶ See Separate Instructions. ▶ Please print or type.	**1990** Attachment Sequence No. **20**

Your first name and initial (If joint, also give spouse's name and initial.)	Last name	Your social security number
Fill in Your Address Only If You Are Filing This Form by Itself and Not With Your Tax Return	Present address (no., street, and apt. no., rural route, or P.O. box no. if mail is not delivered to street address)	Spouse's social security number
	City, town or post office, state, and ZIP code	

Part I   General Information

1a Date your former main home was sold (month, day, year) . . . . ▶   /   /

b Enter the face amount of any mortgage, note (e.g., second trust), or other financial instrument on which you will receive periodic payments of principal or interest from this sale (see Instructions) . . | **1b**

2 Have you bought or built a new main home? . . . . ☐ Yes   ☐ No

3 Is or was any part of either main home rented out or used for business? (If "Yes," see Instructions.) . . . . . . ☐ Yes   ☐ No

Part II   Gain on Sale *(Do not include amounts you deduct as moving expenses.)*

4 Selling price of home. (Do not include personal property items that you sold with your home.) . . . | **4**

5 Expense of sale. (Include sales commissions, advertising, legal, etc.) . . . . | **5**

6 Amount realized. Subtract line 5 from line 4 . . . . | **6**

7 Basis of home sold. (See Instructions.) . . . . | **7**

8a **Gain on sale.** Subtract line 7 from line 6 . . . . | **8a**

   ● If line 8a is zero or less, stop here and attach this form to your return.

   ● If you answered "Yes" on line 2, go to Part III or Part IV, whichever applies. Otherwise, go to line 8b.

b If you haven't replaced your home, do you plan to do so within the replacement period (see Instructions)? . . . . ☐ Yes   ☐ No

   ● If "Yes," stop here, attach this form to your return, and see Instructions under **Additional Filing Requirements.**

   ● If "No," go to Part III or Part IV, whichever applies.

Part III   One-Time Exclusion of Gain for People Age 55 or Older *(If you are not taking the exclusion, go to Part IV now.)*

9a Were you 55 or older on date of sale? . . . . ☐ Yes   ☐ No

b Was your spouse 55 or older on date of sale? . . . . ☐ Yes   ☐ No

   If you did not answer "Yes" on either line 9a or 9b, go to Part IV now.

c Did the person who answered "Yes" on line 9a or 9b own and use the property as his or her main home for a total of at least 3 years (except for short absences) of the 5-year period before the sale? (If "No," go to Part IV now.) . . . ☐ Yes   ☐ No

d **If you answered "Yes" on line 9c, do you elect to take the one-time exclusion?** (If "No," go to Part IV now.) . . ☐ Yes   ☐ No

e At time of sale, who owned the home? . . . . ☐ You   ☐ Your spouse   ☐ Both of you

f Social security number of spouse at time of sale if you had a different spouse from the one above at time of sale. (Enter "None" if you were not married at time of sale.) . . . . ▶

g **Exclusion.** Enter the **smaller** of line 8a or $125,000 ($62,500, if married filing separate return) . . | **9g**

Part IV   Adjusted Sales Price, Taxable Gain, and Adjusted Basis of New Home

10 Subtract the amount on line 9g, if any, from the amount on line 8a . . . . | **10**

   ● If line 10 is zero, stop here and attach this form to your return.

   ● If you answered "Yes" on line 2, go to line 11 now.

   ● If you are reporting this sale on the installment method, stop here and see line 1b Instructions.

   ● All others, stop here and enter the amount from line 10 on Schedule D, line 3 or line 10.

11 Fixing-up expenses. (See Instructions for time limits.) . . . . | **11**

12 **Adjusted sales price.** Subtract line 11 from line 6 . . . . | **12**

13a Date you moved into new home (month, day, year) ▶   /   /   **b** Cost of new home . | **13b**

14a Add the amount on line 9g, if any, and the amount on line 13b and enter the total . . . . . | **14a**

b Subtract line 14a from line 12. If the result is zero or less, enter -0- . . . . | **14b**

c **Taxable gain.** Enter the **smaller** of line 10 or line 14b . . . . | **14c**

   ● If line 14c is zero, go to line 15 and attach this form to your return.

   ● If you are reporting this sale on the installment method, see line 1b Instructions and go to line 15.

   ● All others, enter the amount from line 14c on Schedule D, line 3 or line 10, and go to line 15.

15 Postponed gain. Subtract line 14c from line 10 . . . . | **15**

16 **Adjusted basis of new home.** Subtract line 15 from line 13b . . . . | **16**

Sign Here Only If You Are Filing This Form by Itself and Not With Your Tax Return	Under penalties of perjury, I declare that I have examined this form, including attachments, and to the best of my knowledge and belief, it is true, correct, and complete.			
	Your signature	Date	Spouse's signature	Date
▶	(If a joint return, both must sign.)	▶		

For Paperwork Reduction Act Notice, see separate Instructions.   Form **2119** (1990)

 **19**90

 Department of the Treasury
Internal Revenue Service

Instructions for Form 2119

Sale of Your Home

(Section references are to the Internal Revenue Code.)

Paperwork Reduction Act Notice.— We ask for the information on this form to carry out the Internal Revenue laws of the United States. You are required to give us the information. We need it to ensure that you are complying with these laws and to allow us to figure and collect the right amount of tax.

The time needed to complete and file this form will vary depending on individual circumstances. The estimated average time is:

Recordkeeping . . . . 46 min.
Learning about the
law or the form . . . . 13 min.
Preparing the form . . . . . 45 min.
Copying, assembling,
and sending the form
to IRS . . . . 20 min.

If you have comments concerning the accuracy of these time estimates or suggestions for making this form more simple, we would be happy to hear from you. You can write to both the **Internal Revenue Service,** Washington, DC 20224, Attention: IRS Reports Clearance Officer, T:FP; and the **Office of Management and Budget,** Paperwork Reduction Project (1545-0072), Washington, DC 20503. **Do not** send this form to either of these offices. Instead, see **When and Where To File,** below.

General Instructions

Purpose of Form

Use Form 2119 to report the sale of your main home. If you replaced your main home, use Form 2119 to postpone all or part of the gain. Form 2119 is also used by people who were age 55 or older on the date of sale to elect a one-time exclusion of the gain on the sale.

Main Home.—Your main home is the one you live in most of the time. It can be a house, houseboat, housetrailer, cooperative apartment, condominium, etc.

You may want to get **Pub. 523,** Tax Information on Selling Your Home, for more details.

Who Must File

You must file Form 2119 with Form 1040 for the year in which you sell your main home, even if the sale resulted in a loss or you are electing the one-time exclusion for people age 55 or older. There may be additional filing requirements as well. See **When and Where To File,** below.

If part of your home was rented out or used for business in the year of sale, report that part of the sale on **Form 4797,** Sales of Business Property. See the instructions for line 3.

If you sold your home on the installment method, complete Form 2119 and **Form 6252,** Installment Sale Income.

If your home was damaged by fire, storm, or other casualty, see **Form 4684,** Casualties and Thefts, and its separate Instructions, and **Pub. 547,** Nonbusiness Disasters, Casualties, and Thefts.

If your home was condemned for public use, you can choose to postpone gain under the rules for a condemnation, or you can choose to treat the transaction as a sale of your home. For details, see Pub. 523.

Which Parts To Complete

Parts I and II.—You must complete Parts I and II.

Part III.—Complete this part only if you qualify for the **One-Time Exclusion for People Age 55 or Older** (see below), and you want to make the election for this sale.

Part IV.—Complete line 10 even if you did not take the exclusion in Part III. Complete lines 11 through 16 only if line 10 is more than zero and you answered "Yes" on line 2.

When and Where To File

File Form 2119 with your tax return for the year of sale.

Additional Filing Requirements.—If you have not replaced your home, but plan to do so within the replacement period (defined on page 2), you will also have to complete a second Form 2119.

● You must file the second Form 2119 by itself if:

1. You planned to replace your home within the replacement period, **and**

2. You later replaced your home within the replacement period, **and**

3. Your taxable gain (line 14c on the second Form 2119) is zero.

If your taxable gain is zero, no tax is due, but you must still file the second Form 2119 to show that you replaced your home within the replacement period. Enter your name and address, and sign and date the second form. If a joint return was filed for the year of sale, both you and your spouse must sign the second Form 2119. Send the form to the place where you would file your next tax return based on the address where you now live.

● You must file **Form 1040X,** Amended U.S. Individual Income Tax Return, for the year of sale with the second Form 2119 attached if:

1. You planned to replace your home when you filed your tax return, you later replaced your home within the replacement period, **and** you had a taxable gain on line 14c of the second Form 2119; **or**

2. You planned to replace your home when you filed your tax return, but did **not** do so within the replacement period; **or**

3. You did **not** plan to replace your home when you filed your tax return and included the gain in income, but later you did replace your home within the replacement period.

Report the correct amount of gain from Form 2119 on Schedule D (Form 1040) and attach both forms to Form 1040X. Interest will be charged on any additional tax due. If tax is to be refunded to you, interest will be included with the refund.

One-Time Exclusion for People Age 55 or Older

Generally, you can elect to exclude from your income up to $125,000 ($62,500 if married filing a separate return) of the gain from one sale of any main home you choose. To make the election for this sale, complete Part III and answer "Yes" on line 9d. You qualify to make the election if you meet **ALL** of the following tests:

1. You or your spouse were age 55 or older on the date of sale,

2. Neither you nor your spouse have ever excluded gain on the sale of a home after July 26, 1978, and

3. The person who was age 55 or older owned and lived in the home for periods adding up to at least 3 years within the 5-year period ending on the date of sale.

For purposes of test 3, if you were physically or mentally unable to care for yourself, count as time living in your main home any time during the 5-year period that you lived in a facility such as a nursing home. The facility must be licensed by a state (or political subdivision) to care for people in your condition. For this rule to apply, you must have owned and used your residence as your main home for a total of at least 1 year during the 5-year period. See Pub. 523 for more details.

The gain excluded is never taxed. But, if the gain is more than the amount excluded, the excess gain is either included in your income or postponed, as explained on page 2. Generally, you can make or revoke the election within 3 years from the due date of your return (including extensions) for the year of sale. To make or revoke the election, file Form 1040X with Form 2119 attached.

Married Taxpayers.—If you and your spouse owned the property jointly and file a joint return, only one of you must meet the age, ownership, and use tests to be able to make the election. If you did not own the property jointly, the spouse who owned the property must meet these tests.

If you were married at the time of sale, both you and your spouse must agree to exclude the gain. If you do not file a joint return with that spouse, your spouse must agree to exclude the gain by signing a statement saying, "I agree to the Part III election." The statement and signature may be made on a separate piece of paper or in the bottom margin of Form 2119.

If you sell a home while you are married, and one spouse already made the election prior to the marriage, neither of you can exclude gain on the sale.

The election to exclude gain does not apply separately to you and your spouse. If you elect to exclude gain during marriage and later divorce, neither of you can make the election again.

Postponing Gain

If you buy or build another main home and move into it within the replacement period (defined below), you must postpone all or part of the gain in most cases. The amount of gain postponed is shown on line 15.

If one spouse dies after the old home is sold and before the new home is purchased, the gain from the sale of the old home is postponed if the above requirements are met, the spouses were married on the date of death, and the surviving spouse uses the new home as his or her main home. This rule applies regardless of whether the title of the old home is in one spouse's name or is held jointly. For more details, see Pub. 523.

If you bought more than one main home during the replacement period, only the last one you bought qualifies as your new main home for postponing gain. If you sold more than one main home during the replacement period, any sale after the first one does not qualify for postponing gain. However, these rules do not apply if you sold your home because of a job change that qualifies for a moving expense deduction. If this is the case, file a Form 2119 for each sale, for the year of the sale, and attach an explanation for each sale (except the first) to Form 2119. For more details on qualifications for moving expenses, get **Pub. 521,** Moving Expenses.

Replacement Period.—Generally, the replacement period starts 2 years before and ends 2 years after the date you sell your former main home. The replacement period may be longer if you are on active duty in the U.S. Armed Forces for more than 90 days, or if you live and work outside the U.S. For more details, see Pub. 523.

Applying Separate Gain to Basis of New Home.—If you are married and the old home was owned by only one spouse, but you and your spouse own the new home jointly, you and your spouse may elect to divide the gain and the adjusted basis. If

you owned the old home jointly, and you now own new homes separately, you may elect to divide the gain to be postponed. In either situation, you both must:

1. Use the old and new homes as your main homes, and

2. Sign a statement that says, "We agree to reduce the basis of the new home(s) by the gain from selling the old home." This statement can be made in the bottom margin of Form 2119 or on an attached sheet.

If you both do not meet these two requirements, you must report the gain in the regular way without allocation.

Line-by-Line Instructions

You may not take double benefits. For example, you cannot use the moving expenses that are part of your moving expense deduction on **Form 3903,** Moving Expenses, to lower the amount of gain on the sale of your old home or to add to the cost of your new home.

Line 1b.—If you report the gain from the sale of your home on Form 6252 using the installment method, complete Form 2119 first. When completing Form 6252, be sure to enter the total of lines 9g and 15 of Form 2119 on line 11 of Form 6252. Do not enter the gain from Form 2119 on Schedule D (Form 1040).

Note: *Report interest you receive on a note (or other financial instrument) as interest income for the tax year in which you receive it.*

Line 3.—If any part of either home was rented out or used for business for which a deduction is allowed, check "Yes."

• If part of your former main home was rented out or used for business in the year of sale, treat the sale as two separate sales. Report the part of the sale that applies to the rental or business use on Form 4797. Report only the part of the sale that represents your main home on Form 2119. You must allocate the sales price, expense of sale, and the basis of the property sold between Forms 2119 and 4797.

Note: *Only the part of the fixing-up expenses that applies to your main home may be included on line 11. These amounts are not allowed on Form 4797.*

Attach a statement showing the total selling price of the property and the method used to allocate the amounts between Forms 2119 and 4797. You cannot postpone or take the one-time exclusion on the part of the gain that is reported on Form 4797.

• If part of your new main home is rented out or used for business, enter on line 13b only the part of the total cost of the property that is allocable to your new main home. Attach a statement showing the total cost of the property and the allocation between the part that is your new main home and the part that is rented out or used for business.

For more details, see Pub. 523.

Line 4—Selling Price of Home.—Enter the gross sales price of your old home. Generally, this includes the amount of money you received, plus all notes, mortgages, or other debts that are part of the sale, and the fair market value of any other property you received.

Line 5—Expense of Sale.—Enter your expense of sale, such as commissions, advertising expenses, and attorney and legal fees, that you paid in selling your old home. Loan charges, such as points charged to the seller, are also selling expenses. Do not include fixing-up expenses on this line, but see the instructions for line 11.

Line 7—Basis of Home Sold.—If you filed a Form 2119 when you originally bought your old home (to postpone gain on a previous sale of a home), use the adjusted basis of the new home from the last line of that Form 2119 as the starting point to figure the basis of your old home. If you did not file a Form 2119 to postpone gain when you originally bought your old home, use the cost of the home including any expenses incurred to buy the home as the starting point.

Add the cost of any capital improvements, and subtract any depreciation, casualty losses, or energy credits you reported on your tax return(s) that were related to your old home. For more details, get **Pub. 551,** Basis of Assets.

If you acquired your home other than by purchase, such as by gift, inheritance, or trade, see Pub. 523 and Pub. 551 to figure the basis.

Line 11—Fixing-up Expenses.—Enter the amount paid for work performed on your old home in order to help sell it. Do not include amounts that are otherwise deductible, or selling expenses included on line 5. The expenses must be for work performed within 90 days before the contract to sell the home was signed and paid within 30 days after the sale. Do not include expenses for permanent improvements or replacements, which should be added to the basis of the property sold.

Line 13b—Cost of New Home.—The cost of your new home includes one or more of the following:

1. Cash payments,

2. The amount of any mortgage or other debt on the new home,

3. Commissions and other purchase expenses you paid that were not deducted as moving expenses, and

4. Any capital expenses incurred within 2 years before or 2 years after the sale of your old home.

If you build your new home, include all construction costs incurred within 2 years before and 2 years after the sale of the old home. Do not include the value of your own labor.

Form **2120**
(Rev. August 1988)

Department of the Treasury—Internal Revenue Service

Multiple Support Declaration

OMB No. 1545-0071
Expires 6-30-91

Attachment
Sequence No. **50**

During the calendar year 19 _____ , I paid more than 10% of the support of

_____
(Name of person)

I could have claimed this person as a dependent except that I did not pay more than 50% of his or her support. I understand that this person is being claimed as a dependent on the income tax return of

_____
(Name)

_____
(Address)

I agree not to claim an exemption for this person on my Federal income tax return for any tax year that began in this calendar year.

_____
(Your signature)

_____
(Your social security number)

_____
(Date)

_____
(Address)

For Paperwork Reduction Act Notice, see back of form.

Form **2120** (Rev. 8-88)

Form 2120 (Rev. 8-88)

Page **2**

Instructions

Paperwork Reduction Act Notice.—We ask for this information to carry out the Internal Revenue Laws of the United States. We need it to ensure that taxpayers are complying with these laws and to allow us to figure and collect the right amount of tax. You are required to give us this information.

The estimated average time needed to complete this form, depending on individual circumstances, is 5 minutes. If you have comments concerning the accuracy of this time estimate or suggestions for making this form more simple, we would be happy to hear from you. You can write either IRS or the Office of Management and Budget at the addresses listed in the instructions of the tax return with which this form is filed.

Purpose.—When two or more persons together pay over 50% of a dependent's support, Form 2120 is used to allow one person to claim the dependent for tax purposes.

General Information.—To claim an exemption for a dependent, you must pay over 50% of the person's living expenses (support). However, sometimes no one person pays over 50%. Instead, two or more people do as a group. If each could have claimed the dependent but for the 50% support rule, then one person in the group can still claim the dependent.

All people who paid more than 10% of the support should decide who will claim the dependent. If you are chosen, you can claim the dependent if:
- you paid over 10% of the support, AND
- all others who paid over 10% agree not to claim the dependent.

How to File.—The people who agree not to claim the dependent do so by each signing Form 2120. They give the signed forms to the person who does claim the dependent.

If you are the one who claims the dependent, attach all Forms 2120 from the others to YOUR return. You must meet all of the other rules for claiming dependents. See **Pub. 501,** Exemptions, Standard Deduction, and Filing Information.

⭐U.S. GPO: 1988-205-399   23-0916750

Form **3903**	**Moving Expenses**	OMB No. 1545-0062
Department of the Treasury Internal Revenue Service	▶ **Attach to Form 1040.** ▶ **See separate Instructions.**	19**90** Attachment Sequence No. **6 2**

Name(s) shown on Form 1040	Your social security number

1	Enter the number of miles from your **old** home to your **new** workplace	**1**
2	Enter the number of miles from your **old** home to your **old** workplace	**2**
3	Subtract line **2** from line **1**. Enter the result (but not less than zero) . . . . ▶	**3**

If line **3** is 35 or more miles, complete the rest of this form. If line 3 is less than 35 miles, you may not deduct your moving expenses. This rule does not apply to members of the armed forces.

Part I   Moving Expenses

Section A.—Transportation of Household Goods

4	Transportation and storage for household goods and personal effects	**4**

Section B.—Expenses of Moving From Old To New Home

5	Travel and lodging **not** including meals	**5**	
6	Total meals	**6**	
7	Multiply line **6** by 80% (.80).	**7**	
8	Add lines 5 and 7	**8**	

Section C.—Pre-move Househunting Expenses and Temporary Quarters (for any 30 days in a row after getting your job)

9	Pre-move travel and lodging **not** including meals	**9**	
10	Temporary quarters expenses **not** including meals	**10**	
11	Total meal expenses for both pre-move househunting and temporary quarters	**11**	
12	Multiply line 11 by 80% (.80)	**12**	
13	Add lines 9, 10, and 12	**13**	

Section D.—Qualified Real Estate Expenses

14	Expenses of (check one): **a** ☐ selling or exchanging your old home; or **b** ☐ if renting, settling an unexpired lease . . .	**14**	
15	Expenses of (check one): **a** ☐ buying your new home; or **b** ☐ if renting, getting a new lease	**15**	

Part II   Dollar Limits

16	Enter the amount from line 13	**16**	
17	Enter the **smaller** of line 16 or $1,500 ($750 if married filing a separate return, and at the end of 1990 you lived with your spouse who also started work during 1990)	**17**	
18	Add lines 14, 15, and 17	**18**	
19	Enter the **smaller** of line 18 or $3,000 ($1,500 if married filing a separate return, and at the end of 1990 you lived with your spouse who also started work during 1990)	**19**	
20	Add lines 4, 8, and 19. This is your moving expense deduction. **Enter here and on Schedule A (Form 1040), line 19. (Note:** *Any payments your employer made for any part of your move (including the value of any services furnished in kind) should be included on Form W-2. Report that amount on **Form 1040, line 7.** See **Reimbursements** in the Instructions.)*. . . . . ▶	**20**	

For Paperwork Reduction Act Notice, see separate Instructions.   Form **3903** (1990)

Instructions for Form 3903

Moving Expenses

Paperwork Reduction Act Notice

We ask for the information on this form to carry out the Internal Revenue laws of the United States. You are required to give us this information. We need it to ensure that you are complying with these laws and to allow us to figure and collect the right amount of tax.

The time needed to complete and file this form will vary depending on individual circumstances. The estimated average time is:

Recordkeeping	1 hr., 5 min.
Learning about the law or the form	7 min.
Preparing the form	32 min.
Copying, assembling, and sending the form to IRS	20 min.

If you have comments concerning the accuracy of these time estimates or suggestions for making this form more simple, we would be happy to hear from you. You can write to both the IRS and the Office of Management and Budget at the addresses listed in the instructions for Form 1040.

Purpose of Form

Use Form 3903 if you moved to a new principal workplace within the United States or its possessions and you qualify to deduct your moving expenses.

Note: *Use* **Form 3903F,** *Foreign Moving Expenses, instead of this form if you are a U.S. citizen or resident alien who moved to a new principal workplace outside the United States or its possessions.*

Additional Information

For more information about moving expenses, please get **Pub. 521,** Moving Expenses.

Who May Deduct

If you moved to a different home because of a change in the location of your job, you may be able to deduct your moving expenses. You may qualify for a deduction whether you are self-employed or an employee. However, you must meet certain tests explained in the next column.

Distance Test.—Your new principal place of work (workplace) must be at least 35 miles farther from your old home than your old workplace was. For example, if your old workplace was 3 miles from your old home, your new workplace must be at least 38 miles from that home. If you did not have an old workplace, your new workplace must be at least 35 miles from your old home. (The distance between two points is the shortest of the more commonly traveled routes between the points.)

Time Test.—If you are an employee, you must work full time in the general area of your new workplace for at least 39 weeks during the 12 months right after you move. If you are self-employed, you must work full time in the general area of your new workplace, for at least 39 weeks during the first 12 months and a total of at least 78 weeks during the 24 months right after you move.

You may deduct your moving expenses for 1990 even if you have not met the time test before your 1990 return is due. You may do this if you expect to meet the 39-week test by the end of 1991 or the 78-week test by the end of 1992. If you have not met the test by then, you will have to do one of the following:

● Amend your 1990 tax return on which you deducted moving expenses. To do this, use **Form 1040X,** Amended U.S. Individual Income Tax Return; or

● In the year you cannot meet the test, report as income on your tax return the amount of your 1990 moving expense deduction that reduced your 1990 income tax. For more information, see **Time Test** in Pub. 521.

If you do not deduct your moving expenses on your 1990 return and you later meet the time test, you may take the deduction by filing an amended return for 1990. To do this, use Form 1040X.

Exceptions to the Distance and Time Tests.—You do not have to meet the time test in case of death, if your job ends because of disability, if you are transferred for your employer's benefit, or if you are laid off or discharged for a reason other than willful misconduct.

You do not have to meet the time test if you meet the requirements for retirees

or survivors living outside the United States, as explained on this page.

If you are in the armed forces, you do not have to meet the distance and time tests if the move is due to a permanent change of station. A permanent change of station includes a move in connection with and within 1 year of retirement or other termination of active duty. In figuring your moving expenses, do not deduct any moving expenses for moving services that were provided by the military or that were reimbursed to you and that you did not include in income. However, you may deduct your unreimbursed moving expenses, subject to the dollar limits. If you and your spouse and dependents are moved to or from different locations, treat the moves as a single move.

Qualified Retirees or Survivors Living Outside the United States

If you are a retiree or survivor who moved to a U.S. home and you meet the requirements below, you are treated as if you moved to a new workplace located in the United States. You are subject to the distance test and other limitations explained on this form. Use this form instead of Form 3903F to claim your moving expenses.

Retirees.—You may deduct moving expenses for a move to a new home in the United States when you actually retire if both your old principal workplace and your old home were outside the United States.

Survivors.—You may deduct moving expenses for a move to a home in the United States if you are the spouse or dependent of a person whose principal workplace at the time of death was outside the United States. In addition, the expenses must be: (1) for a move that begins within 6 months after the decedent's death; and (2) must be from a former home outside the United States that you lived in with the decedent at the time of death.

Moving Expenses in General

You may deduct most of the reasonable expenses you incur in moving your family and dependent household members. These include your costs to move to the new location (Part I, Sections A and B), pre-move househunting expenses and expenses of temporary quarters once you arrive in the new location (Section C), and certain qualified real estate expenses (Section D).

You MAY NOT deduct expenses of a loss on the sale of your home, mortgage penalties, refitting draperies and carpets, or quitting club memberships. Neither can you deduct expenses for employees such as a servant, governess, or nurse.

Reimbursements

You must include any reimbursement of, or payment for, moving expenses in gross income as compensation for services. If your employer paid for any part of your move, you must report that amount as income on **Form 1040, line 7.** Your employer should include the amount paid in your total income on Form W-2. However, if you are not sure that the reimbursements have been included in your Form W-2, check with your employer. Your employer must give you a statement showing a detailed breakdown of reimbursements or payments for moving expenses. Your employer may use **Form 4782,** Employee Moving Expense Information, to give you the required breakdown of reimbursements, or your employer may use his or her own form.

You may choose to deduct moving expenses in the year you are reimbursed by your employer, even though you paid for the moving expenses in a different year. However, special rules apply. See **How to Report** in Pub. 521.

Meal Expenses

Only 80% of your meal expenses are deductible. This limit is figured on lines 7 and 12 in Sections B and C, respectively.

No Double Benefit

You may not take double benefits. For example, you may not use the moving expenses on line 14 that are part of your moving expense deduction to lower the amount of gain on the sale of your old home. In addition, you may not use the moving expenses on line 15 that are part of your moving expense deduction to add to the cost of your new home. (Use **Form 2119,** Sale of Your Home, to figure the gain, if any, you must report on the sale of your old home and the adjusted cost of the new one.)

Part I Instructions

We have provided specific instructions for most of the form. The lines that do not appear in these instructions are self-explanatory.

Section A.—Enter on line 4 the actual cost to pack, crate, move, store in transit, and insure your household goods and personal effects.

Section B.—Enter the costs of travel from your old home to your new home. These include transportation, meals, and lodging on the way. Include costs for the day you arrive. *Show your meal expenses separately on line 6.* You may only include expenses for one trip. However, not all the members of your household have to travel together or at the same time.

If you use your own car, you may figure the expenses in either of the following two ways:

● Actual out-of-pocket expenses for gas and oil (keep records to verify the amounts); or
● At the rate of 9 cents a mile (keep records to verify your mileage).

You may add parking fees and tolls to the amount claimed under either method.

Section C.—Include the costs of travel to look for a new home before you move and temporary quarters expenses after you move. Report pre-move househunting travel and lodging on line 9, temporary quarters expenses on line 10, and the combined cost of meals on line 11.

Pre-move househunting expenses are deductible only if:

● You took the trip after you got the job; **and**
● You returned to your old home after looking for a new one; **and**
● You traveled to the new work area primarily to look for a new home.

There is no limit on the number of househunting trips taken, and you do not have to be successful to qualify for this deduction. If you used your own car, figure transportation costs the same way as you did in Section B. If you are self-employed, you may deduct househunting costs only if you had already made substantial arrangements to begin work in the new location.

You may deduct the cost of meals and lodging while occupying temporary quarters in the area of your new workplace. You may include the costs for any period of 30 days in a row after you get the job, but before you move into permanent quarters. If you are self-employed, you may count

these expenses only if you had already made substantial arrangements to begin work in the new location.

Section D.—You may include most of the costs to sell or buy a home or to settle or get a lease. Examples of qualified real estate expenses you MAY include are:

● Sales commissions;
● Advertising costs;
● Attorney's fees;
● Title and escrow fees;
● State transfer taxes; and
● Costs to settle an unexpired lease or to get a new lease.

Examples of expenses you MAY NOT include are:

● Costs to improve your home to help it sell;
● Charges for payment or prepayment of interest; and
● Payments or prepayments of rent.

Check the appropriate box, **a** or **b,** for lines 14 and 15 when you enter the amounts for these two lines.

Part II Instructions

The following dollar limits apply to the expenses shown in Part I.

Line 16.—Enter the total of your househunting and temporary quarters expenses (line 13). These expenses are limited to $1,500 (on line 17).

Line 18.—Enter the amount from line 17 plus your qualified real estate expenses (lines 14 and 15). This total is limited to $3,000 (on line 19).

There are some special situations:

● If both you and your spouse began work at new workplaces and shared the same new home at the end of 1990, you must treat this as one move rather than two. If you file separate returns, each of you is limited to a total of $750 on line 17, and to a total of $1,500 on line 19.

● If both you and your spouse began work at new workplaces but each of you moved to separate new homes, this is treated as two separate moves. If you file a joint return, line 17 is limited to a total of $3,000; and line 19 is limited to a total of $6,000. If you file separate returns, each of you is limited to a total of $1,500 on line 17; and a total of $3,000 on line 19.

Note: *If you checked box **a** on **line 14,** any amount on line 14 that you cannot deduct because of the dollar limit should be used on Form 2119 to decrease the gain on the sale of your old home. If you checked box **a** on **line 15,** use any amount on line 15 that you cannot deduct because of the limit to increase the basis of your new home.*

Form **4562**	**Depreciation and Amortization**	OMB No. 1545-0172
Department of the Treasury Internal Revenue Service	**(Including Information on Listed Property)** ► See separate instructions. ► Attach this form to your return.	**1990** Attachment Sequence No. **67**

Name(s) shown on return	Identifying number

Business or activity to which this form relates

Part I **Election To Expense Certain Tangible Property (Section 179)** (**Note:** *If you have any "Listed Property," also complete Part V.*)

1 Maximum dollar limitation (see instructions)	1	$10,000
2 Total cost of section 179 property placed in service during the tax year (see instructions)	2	
3 Threshold cost of section 179 property before reduction in limitation	3	$200,000
4 Reduction in limitation—Subtract line 3 from line 2, but do not enter less than -0-	4	
5 Dollar limitation for tax year—Subtract line 4 from line 1, but do not enter less than -0-	5	

(a) Description of property	(b) Cost	(c) Elected cost	
6			

7 Listed property—Enter amount from line 26	7	
8 Total elected cost of section 179 property—Add amounts in column (c), lines 6 and 7	8	
9 Tentative deduction—Enter the lesser of line 5 or line 8	9	
10 Carryover of disallowed deduction from 1989 (see instructions)	10	
11 Taxable income limitation—Enter the lesser of taxable income or line 5 (see instructions)	11	
12 Section 179 expense deduction—Add lines 9 and 10, but do not enter more than line 11	12	
13 Carryover of disallowed deduction to 1991—Add lines 9 and 10, less line 12 ►	13	

Note: *Do not use Part II or Part III below for automobiles, certain other vehicles, cellular telephones, computers, or property used for entertainment, recreation, or amusement (listed property). Instead, use Part V for listed property.*

Part II **MACRS Depreciation For Assets Placed in Service ONLY During Your 1990 Tax Year (Do Not Include Listed Property)**

(a) Classification of property	(b) Mo. and yr. placed in service	(c) Basis for depreciation (Business use only—see instructions)	(d) Recovery period	(e) Convention	(f) Method	(g) Depreciation deduction
14 General Depreciation System (GDS) (see instructions):						
a 3-year property						
b 5-year property						
c 7-year property						
d 10-year property						
e 15-year property						
f 20-year property						
g Residential rental property			27.5 yrs.	MM	S/L	
			27.5 yrs.	MM	S/L	
h Nonresidential real property			31.5 yrs.	MM	S/L	
			31.5 yrs.	MM	S/L	
15 Alternative Depreciation System (ADS) (see instructions):						
a Class life					S/L	
b 12-year			12 yrs.		S/L	
c 40-year			40 yrs.	MM	S/L	

Part III **Other Depreciation (Do Not Include Listed Property)**

16 GDS and ADS deductions for assets placed in service in tax years beginning before 1990 (see instructions).	16	
17 Property subject to section 168(f)(1) election (see instructions)	17	
18 ACRS and other depreciation (see instructions)	18	

Part IV **Summary**

19 Listed property—Enter amount from line 25	19	
20 Total—Add deductions on line 12, lines 14 and 15 in column (g), and lines 16 through 19. Enter here and on the appropriate lines of your return. (Partnerships and S corporations—see instructions) . .	20	
21 For assets shown above and placed in service during the current year, enter the portion of the basis attributable to section 263A costs (see instructions).	21	

For Paperwork Reduction Act Notice, see page 1 of the separate instructions.   Form **4562** (1990)

Form 4562 (1990), Page 2

Form 4562 (1990) — Page 2

Form **4684**

Department of the Treasury
Internal Revenue Service

Casualties and Thefts

► See separate Instructions.
► Attach to Form 1040, 1041, 1065, 1120, etc.
► Use a separate Form 4684 for each different casualty or theft.

OMB No. 1545-0177

19**90**

Attachment
Sequence No. **26**

Name(s) shown on tax return

Identifying number

Note: *Use Section A for casualties and thefts of personal use property and Section B for business and income-producing property.*

SECTION A.—Personal Use Property *(Casualties and thefts of property **not** used in a trade or business or for income-producing purposes.)*

1 Description of properties. (Show kind, location, and date of purchase for each.)
   Property **A**...
   Property **B**...
   Property **C**...
   Property **D**...

		Properties (Use a separate column for each property lost or damaged from one casualty or theft.)		
		A	**B**	**C**	**D**

		A	B	C	D
2 Cost or other basis of each property	**2**				
3 Insurance or other reimbursement (whether or not you submitted a claim). See Instructions. . **Note:** *If line 2 is **more** than line 3, skip line 4.*	**3**				
4 Gain from casualty or theft. If line 3 is **more than** line 2, enter the difference here and skip lines 5 through 9 for that column. (If line 3 includes an amount that you did not receive, see Instructions.)	**4**				
5 Fair market value **before** casualty or theft . .	**5**				
6 Fair market value **after** casualty or theft . . .	**6**				
7 Subtract line 6 from line 5	**7**				
8 Enter the **smaller** of line 2 or line 7	**8**				
9 Subtract line 3 from line 8 (if result is zero or less, enter zero)	**9**				

10 Casualty or theft loss. Add the amounts on line 9. Enter the total **10**

11 Enter the amount from line 10 or $100, whichever is **smaller** **11**

12 Subtract line 11 from line 10 . . . . **12**
   Caution: *Use only one Form 4684 for lines 13 through 18.*

13 Add the amounts on line 12 of all Forms 4684, Section A **13**

14 Combine the amounts from line 4 of all Forms 4684, Section A **14**

15 ● If line 14 is **more than** line 13, enter the difference here and on Schedule D. Do not complete the rest of this Section. (See instructions.)
   ● If line 14 is **less than** line 13, enter zero here and continue with form.   **15**
   ● If line 14 is **equal to** line 13, enter zero here. Do not complete the rest of this Section.

16 If line 14 is **less than** line 13, enter the difference **16**

17 Enter 10% (.10) of your adjusted gross income (Form 1040, line 32). Estates and trusts, see Instructions **17**

18 Subtract line 17 from line 16. If result is zero or less, enter zero. Also enter result on Schedule A (Form 1040), line 18. Estates and trusts, enter on the "Other deductions" line of your tax return **18**

For Paperwork Reduction Act Notice, see page 1 of separate Instructions.

Form **4684** (1990)

Form 4684 (1990)   Attachment Sequence No. **26**   Page **2**

Name(s) shown on tax return. (Do not enter name and identifying number if shown on other side.) | Identifying number

SECTION B.—Business and Income-Producing Property *(Casualties and thefts of property used in a trade or business or for income-producing purposes.)*

Part I   Casualty or Theft Gain or Loss (Use a separate Part I for each different casualty or theft.)

1   Description of properties. (Show kind, location, and date of purchase for each.)
Property **A**...
Property **B**...
Property **C**...
Property **D**...

		Properties (Use a separate column for each property lost or damaged from one casualty or theft.)			
		A	B	C	D
2	Cost or adjusted basis of each property . . .	**2**				
3	Insurance or other reimbursement (whether or not you submitted a claim). See Instructions. . **Note:** *If line 2 is **more** than line 3, skip line 4.*	**3**				
4	Gain from casualty or theft. If line 3 is **more than** line 2, enter the difference here and on line 11 or line 16, column (c). However, see Instructions for line 15. Also, skip lines 5 through 9 for that column. (If line 3 includes an amount that you did not receive, see the instructions for Section A, line 4.)	**4**				
5	Fair market value **before** casualty or theft . .	**5**				
6	Fair market value **after** casualty or theft . . .	**6**				
7	Subtract line 6 from line 5	**7**				
8	Enter the **smaller** of line 2 or line 7 . . .	**8**				
	Note: *If the property was totally destroyed by casualty, or lost from theft, enter on line 8 the amount from line 2.*					
9	Subtract line 3 from line 8 (if zero or less, enter zero) . .	**9**				

10   Casualty or theft loss. Add the amounts on line 9. Enter the total here and on line 11 **or** line 16. (See instructions.) **10**

Part II   Summary of Gains and Losses (From separate Parts I)

(a) Identify casualty or theft	(b) Losses from casualties or thefts		(c) Gains from casualties or thefts includible in income
	(i) Trade, business, rental or royalty property	(ii) Income-producing property	

Casualty or Theft of Property Held One Year or Less

11				
12	Totals. Add the amounts on line 11 . . . . **12**			

13   Combine line 12, columns (b)(i) and (c). Enter the net gain or (loss) here and on Form 4797, Part II, line 14. (If Form 4797 is not otherwise required, see Instructions.) **13**

14   Enter the amount from line 12, column (b)(ii) here and on Schedule A (Form 1040), line 21. Partnerships, S corporations, estates and trusts, see Instructions **14**

Casualty or Theft of Property Held More Than One Year

15	Casualty or theft gains from Form 4797, Part III, line 32 . . . . **15**			
16				
17	Total losses. Add amounts on line 16, columns (b)(i) and (b)(ii). . . **17**			/////

18   Total gains. Add lines 15 and 16, column (c) **18**

19   Add amounts on line 17, columns (b)(i) and (b)(ii). **19**

20   If the loss on line 19 is **more than** the gain on line 18:

  a Combine line 17, column (b)(i) and line 18, and enter the net gain or (loss) here. Partnerships and S corporations see the note below. All others enter this amount on Form 4797, Part II, line 14. (If Form 4797 is not otherwise required, see Instructions.) **20a**

  b Enter the amount from line 17, column (b)(ii) here. Partnerships and S corporations see the note below. Individuals enter this amount on Schedule A (Form 1040), line 21. Estates and trusts, enter on the "Other deductions" line of your tax return   .   . **20b**

21   If the loss on line 19 is **equal to** or **less than** the gain on line 18, combine these lines and enter here. Partnerships see the note below. All others enter this amount on Form 4797, Part I, line 3   .   .   .   .   . **21**

  Note: *Partnerships, enter the amount from line 20a, 20b, or line 21 on Form 1065, Schedule K, line 7. S corporations, enter the amount from line 20a or 20b on Form 1120S, Schedule K, line 6.*

 **90**

Department of the Treasury
Internal Revenue Service

Instructions for Form 4684

Casualties and Thefts

General Instructions

Paperwork Reduction Act Notice.—We ask for the information on this form to carry out the Internal Revenue laws of the United States. You are required to give us this information. We need it to ensure that you are complying with these laws and to allow us to figure and collect the right amount of tax.

The time needed to complete and file this form will vary depending on individual circumstances. The estimated average time is:

Recordkeeping . . . . . 1 hr., 12 min.
Learning about the law or the form . . . . 10 min.
Preparing the form . . . . . 58 min.
Copying, assembling, and sending the form to IRS . . . . 35 min.

If you have comments concerning the accuracy of these time estimates or suggestions for making this form more simple, we would be happy to hear from you. You can write to both the IRS and the Office of Management and Budget at the addresses listed in the Instructions of the tax return with which this form is filed.

Purpose of Form

If you had a gain or loss from a casualty or theft, you must use Form 4684 to figure the amount to report.

Who Must File

Form 4684 is completed to report gains and losses from casualties and thefts. Attach Form 4684 to your tax return.

Deductible Losses

You may deduct losses arising from fire, storm, shipwreck, or other casualty, or theft (for example, larceny, embezzlement, and robbery).

If your property is covered by insurance, you must file a timely insurance claim for reimbursement of your loss. Otherwise, you cannot deduct this loss as a casualty or theft loss. However, the portion of the loss that is not covered by insurance is still deductible.

If the amount you receive in insurance or other compensation is more than the cost or other basis of property, you have a casualty or theft gain.

Related expenses.—The related expenses you have due to a casualty or theft, such as expenses for the treatment of personal injuries or for the rental of a car, are not deductible as casualty or theft losses.

Costs for protection against future casualties are not deductible but should be capitalized as permanent improvements. An example would be the cost of a levee to stop flooding.

Which Sections To Complete

Section A, page 1, is for figuring casualty or theft gains and losses to property that **is not** used in a trade or business or for income-producing purposes.

Section B, page 2, is for figuring casualty or theft gains and losses to property that **is** used in a trade or business or for income-producing purposes.

If property is partly used in a trade or business, and partly for personal purposes, such as a personal home with a rental unit, figure the personal part in Section A and the business part in Section B.

Additional Information

Get the following publications for more information:

Pub. 225, Farmer's Tax Guide;
Pub. 334, Tax Guide for Small Business;
Pub. 529, Miscellaneous Deductions;
Pub. 534, Depreciation;
Pub. 547, Nonbusiness Disasters, Casualties, and Thefts;
Pub. 550, Investment Income and Expenses;
Pub. 551, Basis of Assets; and
Pub. 584, Nonbusiness Disaster, Casualty, and Theft Loss Workbook.

When To Deduct a Loss

Deduct the part of your casualty or theft loss that is not reimbursable. Deduct it in the tax year the casualty occurred or the theft was discovered. However, a disaster loss and a loss from deposits in insolvent or bankrupt financial institutions may be treated differently. See **Special Rule for Disaster Losses** and **Special Treatment for Losses on Deposits in Insolvent or Bankrupt Financial Institutions,** below.

If you are not sure whether part of your casualty or theft loss will be reimbursed, do not deduct that part until the tax year when you are reasonably certain that it will not be reimbursed.

If you are reimbursed for a loss you deducted in an earlier year, include the reimbursement in your income in the year you received it, but only to the extent the deduction reduced your tax in an earlier year.

If property is destroyed or lost by casualty or theft and replaced with similar property, the gain, if any, may be partially or wholly nontaxable. Report on this form only the part of the gain that is taxable.

See Pub. 547 for special rules on when to deduct losses from casualties and thefts to leased property.

Special Rule for Disaster Losses

A disaster loss is a loss that occurred in an area determined by the President of the United States to warrant Federal disaster assistance.

If your home was located in a disaster area and your state or local government ordered you to tear it down or move it because it was no longer safe to use as a home, the loss from tearing it down or moving it is treated as a disaster loss. The order for you to tear down or move the home must have been issued within 120 days after the area was officially declared a disaster area.

Use the value of your home before you moved it or tore it down as its fair market value after the casualty for purposes of figuring the disaster loss.

You may elect to deduct a disaster loss in the prior tax year as long as the loss would otherwise be allowed as a deduction in the year it occurred.

This election must be made by filing your return or amended return for the prior year, and claiming your disaster loss on it, by the later of the following two dates:

(1) The due date for filing your original return (without extensions) for the tax year in which the disaster actually occurred.

(2) The due date for filing your original return (including extensions) for the tax year immediately before the tax year in which the disaster actually occurred.

You may revoke your election within 90 days after making it by returning to the Internal Revenue Service any refund or credit you received from the election. If you revoke your election before receiving a refund, you must repay the refund within 30 days after receiving it.

The return claiming the disaster loss should specify the date or dates of the disaster and the city, town, county, and state in which the damaged or destroyed property was located.

Note: *To determine the amount to deduct for a disaster loss, you must take into account as reimbursements any benefits you received from Federal or state programs to restore your property.*

Special Treatment for Losses on Deposits in Insolvent or Bankrupt Financial Institutions

If you incurred a loss from a deposit in a bank, credit union, or other financial institution because it became insolvent or bankrupt, and meet all the qualifications explained in Pub. 547, you can choose to deduct the loss as:

● A nonbusiness bad debt on Schedule D; or

● A casualty loss to personal use property on Form 4684; or

● An ordinary loss (miscellaneous itemized deduction) on Schedule A (Form 1040), line 21. Get Pub. 529 for details.

Get Pub. 547 for more information on the choice of tax treatment and how to figure the amount of the deductible loss.

A nonbusiness bad debt is deducted as a short-term capital loss. You must wait until the actual loss is determined before you can deduct the loss as a nonbusiness bad debt. See Pub. 550 for details.

If you are a 1% or more owner, an officer of the financial institution, or related to any such owner or officer, you cannot deduct the loss as a casualty loss or as an ordinary loss. See Pub. 550 for the definition of "related."

You **cannot** choose the ordinary loss deduction if any part of the deposits related to the loss is federally insured.

You can decide to deduct the loss as a casualty loss or as an ordinary loss in any year in which you can reasonably estimate how much of your total deposits in a qualified institution you have lost. If you make this choice, and have more than one account in the same financial institution, you must include all your accounts. Once you make the choice, you cannot change it without permission from the Internal Revenue Service.

To choose to deduct the loss as a casualty loss, complete Form 4684 as follows: In Section A, line 1, show the name of the financial institution and write "Insolvent Financial Institution." Skip lines 2 through 9. Enter the amount of the loss on line 10, and complete the rest of Section A.

If, in a later year, you recover an amount you deducted as a loss, you may have to include the amount recovered in your income for that year. See Pub. 547 for details.

Line-by-Line Instructions
Section A, Personal Use Property
Use a separate column for lines 1 through 9 to show each item lost or damaged from a single casualty or theft. If more than four items were lost or damaged, use additional sheets following the format of lines 1 through 9.

Use a separate Section A of Form 4684 through line 12 for each different casualty or theft occurrence involving property not used in a trade or business or for income-producing purposes.

Do not include any loss previously deducted on an estate tax return.

If you are liable for casualty or theft losses to property you **lease** from someone else, see Pub. 547.

Line 2.—Cost or other basis usually means original cost plus improvements. Subtract any postponed gain from the sale of a previous main home. Special rules apply to property received as a gift or inheritance.

Line 3.—Enter on this line the amount of insurance or other reimbursement you received or expect to receive for each property. Include on this line your insurance coverage, whether or not you are submitting a claim for reimbursement. For example, your car worth $2,000 is totally destroyed in a collision. You are insured with a $500 deductible, but decide not to report it to your insurance company because you are

afraid the insurance company will cancel your policy. In this case, enter $1,500 on this line.

See the instructions for Section B, line 3, for other kinds of reimbursements you should consider.

Line 4.—Although you cannot deduct a loss for any part of a casualty or theft for which you did not claim reimbursement to which you are entitled, you cannot realize a gain from a reimbursement you did not claim. Therefore, in figuring a gain on line 4, subtract your cost or other basis in the property (line 2) only from the amount of reimbursement you actually received. Enter the result on line 4, but do not enter less than zero. If you filed a claim for reimbursement but did not receive it until after the year of the casualty or theft, see Pub. 547 for information on how to report the reimbursement.

Lines 5, 6, and 7.—Fair market value is the price at which the property would change hands between a willing buyer and a willing seller, each having a knowledge of the relevant facts. The difference between the fair market value immediately before the casualty or theft and the fair market value immediately thereafter represents the decrease in fair market value because of the casualty or theft.

The fair market value of property after a theft is zero if the property is not recovered.

Fair market value is generally determined by competent appraisal. The appraiser's knowledge of sales of comparable property about the same time as the casualty or theft, knowledge of your property before and after the occurrence, and the methods of determining fair market value are important elements in proving your loss.

The appraised value of property immediately after the casualty must be adjusted (increased) for the effects of any general market decline that may occur at the same time as the casualty or theft. For example, the value of all nearby property may become depressed because it is in an area where such occurrences are commonplace. This general decline in market value is not part of the property's decrease in fair market value as a result of the casualty or theft.

Replacement cost or the cost of repairs is not necessarily fair market value. However, you may be able to use the cost of repairs to the damaged property as evidence of loss in value if:

(a) The repairs are necessary to restore the property to the condition it was in immediately before the casualty;

(b) The amount spent for repairs is not excessive;

(c) The repairs only correct the damage caused by the casualty; and

(d) The value of the property after the repairs is not, as a result of the repairs, more than the value of the property immediately before the casualty.

To figure a casualty loss to real estate not used in a trade, business, or for income-producing purposes, measure the decrease in value of the property as a whole. All improvements, such as buildings, trees, and shrubs, are considered together as one

item. Figure the loss separately for other items. For example, figure the loss separately for each piece of furniture.

Line 15.—If there is a net gain on this line, combine your short-term gains with your short-term losses, and enter the net short-term gain or loss on your Schedule D. Combine your long-term gains with your long-term losses and enter the net long-term gain or loss on your Schedule D. In both cases write "Form 4684, Schedule A."

Line 17.—Estates and trusts, figure adjusted gross income in the same way as individuals, except that the costs of administration are allowed in figuring adjusted gross income.

Section B, Business and Income-Producing Property
Use a separate column of Part I, lines 1 through 9, to show each item lost or damaged from a single casualty or theft. If more than four items were lost or damaged, use additional sheets following the format of Part I, lines 1 through 9.

Use a separate Section B, Part I, of Form 4684 for each different casualty or theft occurrence involving property used in a trade or business or for income-producing purposes. Use one Section B, Part II, to combine all Sections B, Part I.

For further information on the treatment of casualties or thefts to business or income-producing property, including rules on the loss of inventory through casualty or theft, see Pub. 334.

Note: A gain or loss from a casualty or theft of property used in a passive activity is not taken into account in determining the loss from a passive activity unless losses similar in cause and severity recur regularly in the activity. See Form 8582, Passive Activity Loss Limitations, for more information.

Line 2.—Cost or adjusted basis usually means original cost plus improvements, minus depreciation allowed or allowable (including any deduction taken under section 179), amortization, depletion, etc. Special rules apply to property received as a gift or inheritance. See Pub. 551 for details.

Line 3.—Enter on line 3, insurance or other reimbursement you received or expect to receive for each property.

If you expect to be reimbursed, but have not yet received payment, you must still enter the expected reimbursement from the loss. If, in a later tax year, you determine with reasonable certainty that you will not be reimbursed for all or part of the loss, you can deduct for that year the amount of the loss that is not reimbursed.

Kinds of reimbursements.—Insurance is the most common way in which to be reimbursed for a casualty or theft loss, but if:

(a) Part of a federal disaster loan under the Disaster Relief Act is forgiven, the part you do not have to pay back is considered a reimbursement.

(b) The person who leases your property must make repairs or must repay you for any part of a loss, the repayment and the cost of the repairs are considered reimbursements.

Page 2

(c) A court awards you damages for a casualty or theft loss, the amount you are able to collect, minus lawyers' fees and other necessary expenses, is a reimbursement.

(d) You accept repairs, restoration, or cleanup services provided by relief agencies, it is considered a reimbursement.

(e) A bonding company pays you for a theft loss, the payment is also considered a reimbursement.

Lump-sum reimbursement.—If you have a casualty or theft loss of several assets at the same time and you receive a lump-sum reimbursement, you must divide the amount you receive among the assets according to the fair market value of each asset at the time of the loss.

Grants, gifts, and other payments.—Grants and other payments you receive to help you after a casualty are considered reimbursement only if they are specifically designated to repair or replace your property. Such payments, if so designated, will reduce your casualty loss deduction. If there are no conditions on how you have to use the money you receive, it is not a reimbursement.

Use and occupancy insurance.—If insurance reimburses you for your loss of business income, it does not reduce your casualty or theft loss. The reimbursement is income, however, and is taxed in the same manner as your business income.

Line 4.—See the instructions for Section A, line 4.

Lines 5, 6, and 7.—See the instructions for Section A, lines 5, 6, and 7, for details on determining fair market value.

Loss on each item figured separately.—Unlike a casualty loss to personal use real estate, in which all improvements are considered one item, a casualty loss to business or income-producing property must be figured separately for each item. For example, if casualty damage occurs to both a building and to trees on the same piece of property, measure the loss separately for the building and for the trees.

Line 8.—If you have business or income-producing property that is completely lost (becomes totally worthless) because of a casualty or theft, figure your loss without taking into account any decrease in fair market value.

Line 10.—If the amount on line 10 consists of losses on items of property held one year or less, and on items held for more than one year, you must allocate the amount between lines 11 and 16 according to how long you held each item.

Lines 11 and 16.—Enter on line 11 all gains and losses to property held 1 year or less. Enter on line 16 all gains and losses to property held more than 1 year. However, see the instructions for line 15, below.

Part II, Column (a).—Use a separate line for each different casualty or theft.

Part II, Column (b)(i).—Enter the part of line 10 from trade, business, rental, or royalty property.

Part II, Column (b)(ii).—Enter the part of line 10 from income-producing property.

Line 13.—If **Form 4797,** Sales of Business Property, is not otherwise required, enter the amount from this line on page 1 of your tax return, on the line identified as from Form 4797. Write "Form 4684."

Line 14.—Estates and trusts, enter on the "Other deductions" line of your tax return. Partnerships, enter on Schedule K (Form 1065), line 11. S corporations, enter on Schedule K (Form 1120S), line 10. Write "Form 4684."

Line 15.—If you had a casualty or theft gain from certain trade, business, or income-producing property held more than 1 year, you may have to recapture part or all of the gain as ordinary income. See the Instructions for Form 4797, Part III, for more information on the types of property subject to recapture. If recapture applies, complete Form 4797, Part III, and this line, instead of Form 4684, line 16.

Line 20a.—Taxpayers, other than partnerships and S corporations, if Form 4797 is not otherwise required, enter amount from this line on page 1 of your tax return, on the line identified as from Form 4797. Write "Form 4684."

Page 3

Form **4797**	**Sales of Business Property**	OMB No. 1545-0184
Department of the Treasury Internal Revenue Service	(Also, Involuntary Conversions and Recapture Amounts Under Sections 179 and 280F) ▶ Attach to your tax return. ▶ See separate Instructions.	19**90** Attachment Sequence No. **27**

Name(s) shown on return | Identifying number

Part I Sales or Exchanges of Property Used in a Trade or Business and Involuntary Conversions From Other Than Casualty and Theft—Property Held More Than 1 Year

1 Enter here the gross proceeds from the sale or exchange of real estate reported to you for 1990 on Form(s) 1099-S (or a substitute statement) that you will be including on line 2, 10, or 20 . . . . | **1** |

(a) Description of property	(b) Date acquired (mo., day, yr.)	(c) Date sold (mo., day, yr.)	(d) Gross sales price	(e) Depreciation allowed or allowable since acquisition	(f) Cost or other basis, plus improvements and expense of sale	(g) LOSS ((f) minus the sum of (d) and (e))	(h) GAIN ((d) plus (e) minus (f))
2							

3 Gain, if any, from Form 4684, Section B, line 21 . . . .

4 Section 1231 gain from installment sales from Form 6252, line 22 or 30 . . . .

5 Gain, if any, from line 32, from other than casualty and theft . . . . ( )

6 Add lines 2 through 5 in columns (g) and (h) . . . .

7 Combine columns (g) and (h) of line 6. Enter gain or (loss) here, and on the appropriate line as follows: . . . .

   Partnerships.—Enter the gain or (loss) on Form 1065, Schedule K, line 6. Skip lines 8, 9, 11, and 12 below.

   S corporations.—Report the gain or (loss) following the instructions for Form 1120S, Schedule K, lines 5 and 6. Skip lines 8, 9, 11, and 12 below, unless line 7 is a gain and the S corporation is subject to the capital gains tax.

   All others.—If line 7 is zero or a loss, enter the amount on line 11 below and skip lines 8 and 9. If line 7 is a gain and you did not have any prior year section 1231 losses, or they were recaptured in an earlier year, enter the gain as a long-term capital gain on Schedule D and skip lines 8, 9, and 12 below.

8 Nonrecaptured net section 1231 losses from prior years (see Instructions) . . . .

9 Subtract line 8 from line 7. If zero or less, enter -0-. Also enter on the appropriate line as follows (see instructions): . . . . .

   S corporations.—Enter this amount (if greater than zero) on Form 1120S, Schedule D, line 7, and skip lines 11 and 12 below.

   All others.—If line 9 is zero, enter the amount from line 7 on line 12 below. If line 9 is more than zero, enter the amount from line 8 on line 12 below, and enter the amount from line 9 as a long-term capital gain on Schedule D.

Part II Ordinary Gains and Losses

10 Ordinary gains and losses not included on lines 11 through 16 (include property held 1 year or less):

11 Loss, if any, from line 7 . . . .

12 Gain, if any, from line 7, or amount from line 8 if applicable . . . .

13 Gain, if any, from line 31 . . . .

14 Net gain or (loss) from Form 4684, Section B, lines 13 and 20a . . . .

15 Ordinary gain from installment sales from Form 6252, line 21 or 29 . . . .

16 Recapture of section 179 deduction for partners and S corporation shareholders from property dispositions by partnerships and S corporations (see Instructions) . . . . ( )

17 Add lines 10 through 16 in columns (g) and (h) . . . .

18 Combine columns (g) and (h) of line 17. Enter gain or (loss) here, and on the appropriate line as follows: . . . .
   a For all except individual returns: Enter the gain or (loss) from line 18 on the return being filed.
   b For individual returns:
     (1) If the loss on line 11 includes a loss from Form 4684, Section B, Part II, column (b)(ii), enter that part of the loss here and on line 21 of Schedule A (Form 1040). Identify as from "Form 4797, line 18b(1)". See Instructions . . . .
     (2) Redetermine the gain or (loss) on line 18, excluding the loss, if any, on line 18b(1). Enter here and on Form 1040, line 15

For Paperwork Reduction Act Notice, see page 1 of separate Instructions.   Form **4797** (1990)

Form 4797 (1990)   Page **2**

Part III Gain From Disposition of Property Under Sections 1245, 1250, 1252, 1254, and 1255

19 Description of section 1245, 1250, 1252, 1254, and 1255 property:

		Date acquired (mo., day, yr.)	Date sold (mo., day, yr.)
A			
B			
C			
D			

Relate lines 19A through 19D to these columns ►	Property A	Property B	Property C	Property D
20 Gross sales price (**Note:** *See line 1 before completing.*)				
21 Cost or other basis plus expense of sale				
22 Depreciation (or depletion) allowed or allowable				
23 Adjusted basis. Subtract line 22 from line 21				
24 Total gain. Subtract line 23 from line 20.				
25 **If section 1245 property:**				
a Depreciation allowed or allowable from line 22				
b Enter the **smaller** of line 24 or 25a				
26 **If section 1250 property:** If straight line depreciation was used, enter zero on line 26g unless you are a corporation subject to section 291.				
a Additional depreciation after 12/31/75 (see Instructions)				
b Applicable percentage multiplied by the **smaller** of line 24 or line 26a (see Instructions)				
c Subtract line 26a from line 24. If line 24 is not more than line 26a, skip lines 26d and 26e.				
d Additional depreciation after 12/31/69 and before 1/1/76				
e Applicable percentage multiplied by the **smaller** of line 26c or 26d (see Instructions)				
f Section 291 amount (corporations only)				
g Add lines 26b, 26e, and 26f				
27 **If section 1252 property:** Skip this section if you did not dispose of farmland or if you are a partnership.				
a Soil, water, and land clearing expenses				
b Line 27a multiplied by applicable percentage (see Instructions)				
c Enter the **smaller** of line 24 or 27b				
28 **If section 1254 property:**				
a Intangible drilling and development costs, expenditures for development of mines and other natural deposits, and mining exploration costs (see Instructions)				
b Enter the **smaller** of line 24 or 28a				
29 **If section 1255 property:**				
a Applicable percentage of payments excluded from income under section 126 (see Instructions)				
b Enter the **smaller** of line 24 or 29a				

Summary of Part III Gains (Complete property columns A through D, through line 29b before going to line 30.)

30 Total gains for all properties. Add columns A through D, line 24	
31 Add columns A through D, lines 25b, 26g, 27c, 28b, and 29b. Enter here and on line 13. (See the Instructions for Part IV if this is an installment sale.)	
32 Subtract line 31 from line 30. Enter the portion from casualty and theft on Form 4684, Section B, line 15. Enter the portion from other than casualty and theft on Form 4797, line 5	

Part IV Election Not to Use the Installment Method (Complete this part only if you elect out of the installment method and report a note or other obligation at less than full face value.)

33 Check here if you elect out of the installment method . . . . ▶ ☐

34 Enter the face amount of the note or other obligation . . . . ▶ $ _____

35 Enter the percentage of valuation of the note or other obligation . . . . ▶ _____ %

Part V Recapture Amounts Under Sections 179 and 280F When Business Use Drops to 50% or Less
(See Instructions for Part V.)

	(a) Section 179	(b) Section 280F
36 Section 179 expense deduction or section 280F recovery deductions		
37 Depreciation or recovery deductions (see Instructions)		
38 Recapture amount. Subtract line 37 from line 36. (See Instructions for where to report.).		

Form **4952**
Department of the Treasury
Internal Revenue Service

Investment Interest Expense Deduction
▶ See separate Instructions.
▶ Attach to your tax return.

OMB No. 1545-0191

19**90**

Attachment
Sequence No. **72**

Name(s) shown on return

Identifying number

1 Investment interest expense paid or accrued in 1990. See Instructions		**1**
2 Investment income minus investment expenses. See Instructions	**2**	
3 Phase-in adjustment from passive activities. See Instructions	**3**	
4 **Net investment income.** Subtract line 3 from line 2. If zero or less, enter -0-		**4**
5 Subtract line 4 from line 1. If zero or less, enter -0- here and on line 13, and skip lines 6 through 12 . . .		**5**
6 Enter the amount from line 1, minus the interest expense from certain trade or businesses. See Instructions		**6**
7 Enter the amount from line 2, without the income or expenses from certain trade or businesses. See Instructions	**7**	
8 Phase-in ceiling amount:		

8 Phase-in ceiling amount:
Individuals (not married filing separately) and estates, enter $10,000 ⎫
Married individuals filing separately, enter $5,000 . . . . ⎬ . **8**
Trusts, enter -0- . . . . ⎭

9 Add lines 7 and 8		**9**
10 Subtract line 9 from line 6. If zero or less, enter -0-		**10**
11 Subtract line 10 from line 5. If zero or less, enter -0-		**11**
12 Multiply line 11 by 90% (.9)		**12**
13 Add lines 10 and 12		**13**
14 Enter the amount from line 1	**14**	
15 Enter the **smaller** of line 5 or line 13	**15**	
16 Subtract line 15 from line 14	**16**	
17 Disallowed investment interest expense from 1989 Form 4952, line 23. If zero, enter -0- here and on lines 21 and 22, and skip lines 18 through 20		**17**
18 Enter the amount from line 4. If line 4 is zero, enter -0- here and on line 20 and skip line 19	**18**	
19 Enter the amount from line 1	**19**	
20 Subtract line 19 from line 18. If zero or less, enter -0- . .	**20**	
21 Enter the **smaller** of line 17 or line 20		**21**
22 Subtract line 21 from line 17		**22**
23 **Disallowed investment interest expense to be carried forward to 1991.** Add lines 15 and 22		**23**
24 **Investment interest expense deduction.** Add lines 16 and 21. See Instructions		**24**

For Paperwork Reduction Act Notice, see page 1 of separate Instructions.

Form **4952** (1990)

*U.S. Government Printing Office: 1990 — 265-346

Form **4970**	**Tax on Accumulation Distribution of Trusts**	OMB No. 1545-0192
Department of the Treasury Internal Revenue Service	▶ Attach to beneficiary's tax return. ▶ See instructions on back.	**1990** Attachment Sequence No. **73**

Name(s) as shown on return	Social security number
Name and address of trust	Employer identifying number

| Type of trust:
☐ Domestic ☐ Foreign | Beneficiary's date of birth | Enter number of trusts from which you received accumulation distributions in this tax year. . . . ▶ | |

Part I Average Income and Determination of Computation Years

1	Amount of current distribution that is considered distributed in earlier tax years. (From Schedule J (Form 1041), line 37, column (a)).	1
2	Distributions of income accumulated before you were born or reached age 21	2
3	Subtract line 2 from line 1	3
4	Taxes imposed on the trust on amounts from line 3. (From Schedule J (Form 1041), line 37, column (b))	4
5	Total (add lines 3 and 4).	5
6	Tax-exempt interest included on line 5. (From Schedule J (Form 1041), line 37, column (c)).	6
7	Taxable part of line 5 (subtract line 6 from line 5)	7
8	Number of trust's earlier tax years in which amounts on line 7 are considered distributed	8
9	Average annual amount considered distributed (divide line 3 by line 8)	9	
10	Multiply line 9 by .25	10	
11	Number of earlier tax years to be taken into account (see instructions)	11
12	Average amount for recomputing tax (divide line 7 by line 11). Enter here and in each column on line 15 .	12

13	Enter your taxable income before this distribution for the 5 immediately preceding tax years	**1989**	**1988**	**1987**	**1986**	**1985**

Part II Computation of Tax Attributable to the Accumulation Distribution

			(a) 19....	(b) 19....	(c) 19....
14	Enter the amounts from line 13, eliminating the highest and lowest taxable income years.	14			
15	Enter amount from line 12 in each column	15			
16	Recomputed taxable income (add lines 14 and 15)	16			
17	Income tax on amounts on line 16	17			
18	Income tax before credits on line 14 income	18			
19	Additional tax before credits (subtract line 18 from line 17) . . .	19			
20	Tax credit adjustment	20			
21	Subtract line 20 from line 19	21			
22	Minimum and alternative minimum tax adjustments	22			
23	Combine lines 21 and 22	23			

24	Add columns (a), (b), and (c), line 23	24
25	Divide the amount on line 24 by three	25
26	Multiply the amount on line 25 by the number of years on line 11	26
27	Enter the amount from line 4	27
28	Partial tax (subtract line 27 from line 26) (If line 27 is more than line 26, enter zero.)	28
29	Interest charge on accumulation distribution from foreign trusts	29
30	Add lines 28 and 29	30

For Paperwork Reduction Act Notice, see back of form.   Form **4970** (1990)

General Instructions

(Section references are to the Internal Revenue Code.)

Paperwork Reduction Act Notice.— We ask for the information on this form to carry out the Internal Revenue laws of the United States. You are required to give us the information. We need it to ensure that taxpayers are complying with these laws and to allow us to figure and collect the right amount of tax.

The time needed to complete and file this form will vary depending on individual circumstances. The estimated average time is:

Recordkeeping	1 hr., 12 mins.
Learning about the law or the form	16 mins.
Preparing the form	1 hr., 30 mins.
Copying, assembling, and sending the form to the IRS	20 mins.

If you have comments concerning the accuracy of these time estimates or suggestions for making this form more simple, we would be happy to hear from you. You can write to both the IRS and the Office of Management and Budget at the addresses listed in the instructions of the tax return with which this form is filed.

Purpose of Form.—If you are the beneficiary of a trust that accumulated its income , instead of distributing it currently, use Form 4970 to figure the partial tax under section 667. The fiduciary notifies the beneficiary of an "accumulation distribution" by completing Part IV of Schedule J (Form 1041).

Thus, if you received a distribution for this tax year from a trust that accumulated its income, instead of distributing it each year (and the trust paid taxes on that income), you must complete Form 4970 to compute any additional tax liability. The trustee must give you a completed Part IV of Schedule J (Form 1041) so you can complete this form.

If you received accumulation distributions from more than one trust during the current tax year, prepare a separate Form 4970 for each trust from which you received an accumulation distribution. You can arrange the distributions in any order you want them considered to have been made.

Definitions

Undistributed net income (UNI).— Undistributed net income is the distributable net income (DNI) of the trust for any tax year less: (1) the amount of income required to be distributed currently and any other amounts properly paid or credited or required to be distributed to beneficiaries in the tax year; and (2) the taxes imposed on the trust attributable to such DNI.

Accumulation distribution.—An accumulation distribution is the amount by which amounts properly paid, credited, or required to be distributed currently for the tax year exceed the DNI of the trust reduced by the amount of income required to be distributed currently.

Generally, except for tax-exempt interest, the distribution loses its character upon distribution to the beneficiary. See section 667(d) for special rules for foreign trusts.

Line-by-Line Instructions

Line 1.—For a nonresident alien or foreign corporation, include only your share of the accumulation distribution that is attributable to U.S. sources or is effectively connected with a trade or business carried on in the U.S.

Line 2.—Enter any amount from line 1 that represents UNI of a domestic trust considered to have been distributed before you were born or reached age 21. However, if the multiple trust rule applies, see the instructions for line 4.

Line 4—Multiple Trust Rule.—If you received accumulation distributions from two or more other trusts that were considered to have been made in any of the earlier tax years in which the current accumulation distribution is considered to have been made, do not include on line 4 the taxes attributable to the current accumulation distribution considered to have been distributed in the same earlier tax year(s).

For this special rule only count as trusts those trusts for which the sum of this accumulation distribution and any earlier accumulation distributions from the trust, which are considered under section 666(a) to have been distributed in the same earlier tax year, is $1,000 or more.

If the trust is a foreign trust, see section 665(d).

Line 8.—You can determine the number of years which the UNI is deemed to have been distributed by counting the "throwback years" for which there are entries on lines 32 through 36 of Part IV of Schedule J (Form 1041).These throwback rules apply even if you would not have been entitled to receive a distribution in the earlier tax year if the distribution had actually been made then. **Note:** *There can be more than five "throwback years."*

Line 11.—From the number of years entered on line 8, subtract any year in which the distribution from column (a), Part IV of Schedule J (Form 1041) is less than the amount on line 10 of Form 4970. If the distribution for each throwback year is more than line 10, then enter the same number on line 11 as you entered on line 8.

Line 13.—Enter your taxable incomes for years 1985–1989, even if less than five years of the trust had accumulated income after the beneficiary became 21. Use the taxable income as reported, amended by you, or as changed by IRS. Include in the taxable income amounts considered distributed as a result of prior accumulation distributions whether from the same or another trust, and whether made in an earlier year or the current year.

If you are not an individual, and your taxable income as adjusted is less than zero, enter zero.

If you are an individual, and your taxable income as adjusted for 1985–1986 is less than your zero bracket amount, enter your zero bracket amount. For 1987-1989, enter the amount of your taxable income, but not less than zero.

Line 17.—Figure the income tax (not including any minimum tax or alternative minimum tax) on the income on line 16 using the tax rates in effect for your particular earlier tax year shown in each of the three columns. You may use the Tax Rate Schedules, etc., as applicable. You can get the Tax Rate Schedules and earlier year forms from many IRS offices.

Line 18.—Enter your income tax (not including any minimum tax or alternative minimum tax) as originally reported, corrected, or amended, before reduction for any credits for your particular earlier year shown in each of the three columns.

Line 20.—Nonrefundable credits that are limited to tax liability, such as the general business credit, may be changed because of an accumulation distribution. If the total allowable credits for any of the three computation years increases, enter the increase on line 20. However, do not treat as an increase the part of the credit that was allowable as a carryback or carryforward credit in the current or any preceding year other than the computation year.

To refigure these credits, you must consider changes to the tax before credits for each of the three computation years due to previous accumulation distributions.

If the accumulation distribution is from a domestic trust that paid foreign income taxes, the limitation on the foreign tax credit under section 904 is applied separately to the accumulation distribution. If the distribution is from a foreign trust, see sections 667(d) and 904(f)(4) for special rules.

Attach the proper form for any credit you refigure. The amount determined for items on this line is limited to tax law provisions in effect for those years involved.

Line 22.—Use and attach a separate **Form 4626, Form 6251**, or **Form 8656** to recompute the minimum and alternative minimum tax for each earlier year and show any change in those taxes in the bottom margin of the forms. Enter the adjustments on this line.

Line 28.—For estate taxes and generation-skipping transfer taxes, reduce the partial tax by the estate tax or generation-skipping transfer tax attributable to the accumulation distribution. See section 667(b)(6) for the computation.

Line 29.—For an accumulation distribution from a foreign trust, an interest charge must be added to the partial tax. This interest charge is not deductible under any section and is figured as follows:

(1) Figure 6% of line 28.

(2) Total the number of years from the year(s) of allocation to the year of distribution (including the year of distribution, but not the year of allocation, but not the year of distribution).

(3) Divide the number in step (2) by the total years of allocation (line 8).

(4) Multiply the answer in step (1) by the decimal in step (3).

(5) Subtract line 28 from line 1. This is the maximum interest.

(6) Enter on line 29 the amount from step (4) or step (5), whichever is less.

If this form is not being used for distributions from a foreign trust, enter zero on line 29.

Line 30—Individuals.—Enter the amount from this line on line 39, Form 1040.

Estates and Trusts.—Include the amount on line 1b, Schedule G, Form 1041.

Other filers.—Add the result to the total tax liability before credits on your income tax return for the year of the accumulation distribution. Attach this form to that return.

Form **6252**	**Installment Sale Income**		OMB No. 1545-0228
Department of the Treasury Internal Revenue Service	▶ See separate Instructions. ▶ Attach to your tax return. Use a separate form for each sale or other disposition of property on the installment method.		**1990** Attachment Sequence No. **79**

Name(s) shown on tax return	Identifying number

A   Description of property ▶ _____

B   Date acquired (month, day, and year) ▶ ___/___/___   **C**   Date sold (month, day, and year) ▶ ___/___/___

D   Was the property sold to a related party after May 14, 1980? (See Instructions.) . . . . ☐ Yes   ☐ No

E   If the answer to D is "Yes," was the property a marketable security? (If "Yes," complete Part III. If "No," complete Part III for the year of sale and for 2 years after the year of sale.) . . . . ☐ Yes   ☐ No

Part I   **Gross Profit and Contract Price** *(Complete this part for the year of sale only.)*

1 Selling price including mortgages and other debts. (Do not include interest whether stated or unstated.) .		**1**	
2 Mortgages and other debts the buyer assumed or took the property subject to, but not new mortgages the buyer got from a bank or other source	**2**		
3 Subtract line 2 from line 1	**3**		
4 Cost or other basis of property sold	**4**		
5 Depreciation allowed or allowable	**5**		
6 Adjusted basis. Subtract line 5 from line 4	**6**		
7 Commissions and other expenses of sale	**7**		
8 Income recapture from Form 4797, Part III. See Instructions	**8**		
9 Add lines 6, 7, and 8		**9**	
10 Subtract line 9 from line 1. If zero or less, do not complete the rest of this form		**10**	
11 If the property described in question A above was your main home, enter the total of lines 9g and 15 from Form 2119. Otherwise, enter -0-		**11**	
12 Gross profit. Subtract line 11 from line 10.		**12**	
13 Subtract line 9 from line 2. If zero or less, enter -0-		**13**	
14 Contract price. Add line 3 and line 13		**14**	

Part II   **Installment Sale Income** *(Complete this part for the year of sale and any year you receive a payment or have certain debts you must treat as a payment on installment obligations.)*

15 Gross profit percentage. Divide line 12 by line 14. (For years after the year of sale, see Instructions.) . .		**15**	
16 For year of sale only—enter amount from line 13 above; otherwise, enter -0-		**16**	
17 Payments received during year. See Instructions. (Do not include interest whether stated or unstated.)		**17**	
18 Add lines 16 and 17		**18**	
19 Payments received in prior years. See Instructions. (Do not include interest whether stated or unstated.)	**19**		
20 Installment Sale Income. Multiply line 18 by line 15		**20**	
21 Part of line 20 that is ordinary income under recapture rules. See Instructions		**21**	
22 Subtract line 21 from line 20. Enter here and on Schedule D or Form 4797		**22**	

Part III   **Related Party Installment Sale Income** *(Do not complete if you received the final payment this tax year.)*

F   Name, address, and taxpayer identifying number of related party _____

G   Did the related party, during this tax year, resell or dispose of the property ("second disposition")? . . . . ☐ Yes   ☐ No

H   If the answer to question G is "Yes," complete lines 23 through 30 below unless one of the following conditions is met (check only the box that applies).

☐   The second disposition was more than two years after the first disposition (other than dispositions of marketable securities). If this box is checked, enter the date of disposition (month, day, year) . . . . ▶ ___/___/___

☐   The first disposition was a sale or exchange of stock to the issuing corporation.

☐   The second disposition was an involuntary conversion where the threat of conversion occurred after the first disposition.

☐   The second disposition occurred after the death of the original seller or buyer.

☐   It can be established to the satisfaction of the Internal Revenue Service that tax avoidance was not a principal purpose for either of the dispositions. If this box is checked, attach an explanation. See Instructions.

23 Selling price of property sold by related party		**23**	
24 Enter contract price from line 14 for year of first sale		**24**	
25 Enter the **smaller** of line 23 or line 24		**25**	
26 Total payments received by the end of your 1990 tax year. Add lines 18 and 19		**26**	
27 Subtract line 26 from line 25. If zero or less, enter -0-		**27**	
28 Multiply line 27 by the gross profit percentage on line 15 for year of first sale		**28**	
29 Part of line 28 that is ordinary income under recapture rules. See Instructions		**29**	
30 Subtract line 29 from line 28. Enter here and on Schedule D or Form 4797		**30**	

For Paperwork Reduction Act Notice, see separate Instructions.   Form **6252** (1990)

19**90**  Department of the Treasury Internal Revenue Service

Instructions for Form 6252

Installment Sale Income

General Instructions

(Section references are to the Internal Revenue Code unless otherwise noted.)

Paperwork Reduction Act Notice

We ask for the information on this form to carry out the Internal Revenue laws of the United States. You are required to give us the information. We need it to ensure that you are complying with these laws and to allow us to figure and collect the right amount of tax.

The time needed to complete and file this form will vary depending on individual circumstances. The estimated average time is:

Recordkeeping . . . . 1 hr., 25 min.

Learning about the law or the form . . . . 35min.

Preparing the form . . . . 56 min.

Copying, assembling, and sending the form to IRS . . 20 min.

If you have comments concerning the accuracy of these time estimates or suggestions for making this form more simple, we would be happy to hear from you. You can write to both IRS and the Office of Management and Budget at the addresses listed in the instructions for the tax return with which this form is filed.

Purpose of Form

Use Form 6252 to report income from casual sales of real or personal property (other than inventory) if you will receive any payments in a tax year after the year of sale.

If any part of an installment payment you received is for interest, be sure to report that interest on the appropriate form or schedule. Do not report interest received, carrying charges received, or unstated interest on this form. Get **Pub. 537**, Installment Sales, for details on unstated interest.

You cannot use the installment method for sales after 1986 of stock or securities traded on an established securities market. See section 453(k).

Do not use Form 6252 if you elect not to report the sale on the installment method. To elect out, see the Instructions for **Schedule D (Form 1040),** Capital Gains and Losses, or **Form 4797,** Sales of Business Property. If you do not use the installment method, report the sale on Schedule D or Form 4797, whichever applies.

Note: *Generally, once you file Form 6252, you cannot later elect out of the installment method. See Pub. 537 for details.*

Report the ordinary income from sections 1245, 1250, 179, and 291 in full in the year of sale even if no payments were received. Figure the ordinary income to be recaptured on Form 4797, Part III.

Which Parts To Complete

For the Year of Sale—Complete questions A through E, Part I, and Part II.

For Years After the Year of Sale—Complete questions A through E, and Part II, for any year you receive a payment from an installment sale.

Related Party Sales—If you sold marketable securities to a related party, complete Form 6252 for each year of the installment agreement even if you did not receive a payment. See **Installment Sales to Related Party,** below, for the definition of a related party. For a year after the year of sale, complete questions A through E, and Part III. (If you received a payment, also complete Part II.)

If you sold property other than marketable securities to a related party, complete the form for the year of sale and for 2 years after the year of sale even if you did not receive a payment. If during this 2-year period you did not receive an actual or deemed payment, complete questions A through E, and Part III. After this 2-year period, see "For Years After the Year of Sale," above.

Installment Sales to Related Party

A related party is your spouse, child, grandchild, parent, brother, sister, or a related corporation, S corporation, partnership, estate, or trust.

The term "related persons" includes two or more partnerships in which the same persons own, directly or indirectly, more than 50% of the capital or profits interests. This provision is generally effective for sales of depreciable property after October 22, 1986.

Use of the installment method is disallowed for transactions where the rules of section 453A otherwise would be avoided through the use of related persons, passthrough entities, or intermediaries. This is generally effective for dispositions in tax years that begin after 1986.

See Pub. 537 for other related party rules that apply to sales after October 22, 1986.

If one of the exceptions in Part III applies, check the appropriate box. Do not complete lines 23 through 30. If you can establish that tax avoidance was not a principal purpose for either disposition, attach an explanation. See Pub. 537 for exceptions where tax avoidance is not a principal purpose.

Sale of Depreciable Property to Related Party

If you sell depreciable property to a related party (as defined in section 1239(b)), the installment sale rules do not apply, unless it is established to the satisfaction of the Internal Revenue Service that tax avoidance was not a principal purpose for the sale.

See Pub. 537 and the regulations under section 453 for more details, including single sales of several assets, disposition of installment obligations, like-kind exchanges, and changes in selling price. Also see section 453(g) for new rules that apply to sales after October 22, 1986, if any of the payments are contingent as to amount and the fair market value cannot be readily determined.

Pledge Rule

If an installment obligation from a nondealer disposition of real property used in a trade or business or held for the production of rental income with a sales price over $150,000 is pledged as security on debt after December 17, 1987, the net proceeds of the secured debt must be treated as a payment on the installment obligation. The amount treated as a payment cannot exceed the excess of the total contract price over any payments received under the contract before the secured debt was obtained.

The pledge rule does not apply to pledges made after December 17, 1987, if the debt is incurred to refinance the principal amount of a debt that was outstanding on December 17, 1987, AND was secured by nondealer real property installment obligations on that date and at all times after that date until the refinancing occurred. However, this exception does not apply to the extent that the principal amount of the debt resulting from the refinancing exceeds the principal amount of the refinanced debt immediately before the refinancing.

Also, the pledge rule does not affect refinancing due to the calling of a debt by the creditor as long as the debt is then refinanced by a person other than this creditor or someone related to the creditor. However, the pledge rule includes all types of property sold after December 31, 1988, except personal use property disposed of by an individual, or farm property.

Interest on Deferred Tax

Interest must be paid on the deferred tax from certain installment obligations. (The rules generally apply to dispositions of real property after December 31, 1987, and to dispositions of personal property after December 31, 1988.) The interest applies to any installment obligation arising from the disposition of any property under the installment method if:

- the property had a sales price over $150,000; AND

- the aggregate balance of those obligations arising during, and outstanding at the close of, the tax year is more than $5 million.

Exception: *These rules do not apply to dispositions of farm property or to dispositions of personal use property by an individual.*

Interest must be paid in subsequent years if installment obligations, which originally required interest to be paid, are still outstanding at the close of a tax year.

How To Report the Interest.—The interest is not figured on Form 6252. See section 453A to figure the interest. Enter the interest as an additional tax on your tax return. Include it in the amount to be entered on the total tax line after credits and other taxes. For individuals, this is line 54 of the 1990 Form 1040. For corporations, it is line 10 of Schedule J (Form 1120). Write "Section 453A(c) interest" to the left of the amount.

How To Deduct the Interest.—This additional tax may be deductible as interest in the year it is paid or accrued. For individuals, it is treated as "personal interest." Ten percent of personal interest paid in 1990 is deductible on 1990 Schedule A (Form 1040). Personal interest paid in 1991 is not deductible.

Specific Instructions

Partnerships and S corporations that pass through a section 179 expense deduction to their partners or shareholders should not include this amount on lines 5 and 8.

For the Year of Sale.—If this is the year of sale and you sold section 1245, 1250, 1252, 1254, or 1255 property, you may have ordinary income. Complete Part III of Form 4797 to figure the ordinary income. See the instructions for Part IV of Form 4797 before starting Part I of Form 6252.

Line 1—Selling price.—Enter the total of any money, face amount of the installment obligation, and the fair market value of other property, such as the buyer's note, that you received or will receive in exchange for the property sold. Include on line 1 any existing mortgage or other debt the buyer assumed or took the property subject to.

If there is no stated maximum selling price, such as in a contingent sale, attach a schedule showing the computation of gain. Enter the taxable part on line 20 (and also line 28 if Part III applies). See Regulations section 1.453.

Line 2—Mortgage and other debts.—Enter only mortgages (or other debts) the buyer assumed from the seller or took the property subject to. Do not include new mortgages the buyer gets from a bank, the seller, or other sources.

Line 4—Cost or other basis of property sold.—Enter the original cost and other expenses you incurred in buying the property. Add the cost of improvements, etc., and subtract any casualty losses previously allowed. For more details, get **Pub. 551,** Basis of Assets.

Line 5—Depreciation allowed or allowable.—Enter all depreciation or amortization you deducted or should have deducted from the date of purchase until the date of sale. Add any deduction you took under section 179 and the section 48(q)(1) downward basis adjustment, if any. Subtract 50% of any investment tax credit recaptured if the basis of the property was reduced under section 48(q)(1) and any section 179 or 280F recapture amount included in gross income in a prior tax year. See section 48(q)(3) for a special rule that applies to qualified rehabilitated buildings.

Line 7—Commissions and other expenses of sale.—Enter sales commissions, advertising expenses, attorney and legal fees, etc., in selling the property.

Line 8—Ordinary income recapture.—See the Instructions for Parts III and IV of Form 4797 to figure the recapture. Enter the part of the gain from the sale of depreciable property recaptured under sections 1245 and 1250 (including sections 179 and 291) here and on line 13 of Form 4797.

Line 15—Gross profit percentage.—Enter the gross profit percentage determined for the year of sale even if you did not file Form 6252 for that year.

Line 17—Payments received during the year.—Enter all money and the fair market value of any property you received in 1990. Include as payments any amount withheld to pay off a mortgage or other debt, such as broker and legal fees. Do not include the buyer's note, any mortgage, or other liability assumed by the buyer. If you did not receive any payments in 1990, enter -0-.

If in prior years an amount was entered on the equivalent of line 25 of the 1990 form, do not include it on this line. Instead, enter it on line 19.

See **Pledge Rule** beginning on page 1 for details about proceeds that must be treated as payments on installment obligations.

Line 19—Payments received in prior years.—Enter all money and the fair market value of property you received before 1990 from the sale. Include allocable installment income and any other deemed payments from prior years.

Lines 21 and 29.—Report on line 21 or line 29 any ordinary income recapture remaining from prior years on section 1245 and 1250 property sold before June 7, 1984. Also report on these lines any ordinary income recapture on section 1252, 1254, and 1255 property regardless of when it was sold. This includes ordinary income recapture in the year of sale or any remaining recapture from a prior year sale. See section 453(i). Do not enter ordinary income from a section 179 deduction. If this is the year of sale, see the instructions for Part IV of Form 4797.

The amount on these lines should not exceed the total of the amounts on lines 20 and 28.

Lines 22 and 30—Trade or business property.—Enter this amount on Form 4797, line 4, if the property was held more than 1 year. If the property was held 1 year or less, or if you have an ordinary gain from a noncapital asset, even if the holding period is more than 1 year, enter the amount on Form 4797, line 10, and write "From Form 6252."

Capital assets.—Enter this amount on Schedule D as a short-term or long-term gain. Use the lines identified as from Form 6252.

Line 23.—If the related party sold all or part of the property from the original sale in 1990, enter the selling price of the part resold. If part was sold in an earlier year and part was sold this year, enter the cumulative amount of the selling price.

Page 2

Form **8582**	**Passive Activity Loss Limitations**	OMB No. 1545-1008
Department of the Treasury Internal Revenue Service	► See separate Instructions. ► Attach to Form 1040 or Form 1041.	**1990** Attachment Sequence No. **88**

Name(s) shown on return	Identifying number

Part I   Computation of 1990 Passive Activity Loss

Caution: *See the Instructions for Worksheets 1 and 2 on page 7 before completing Part I.*

Rental Real Estate Activities With Active Participation (For the definition of active participation see **Active Participation in a Rental Real Estate Activity** in the Instructions.)

Activities acquired before 10-23-86 (Pre-enactment):

1a	Activities with net income (from Worksheet 1, Part 1, column (a)). .	1a	
1b	Activities with net loss (from Worksheet 1, Part 1, column (b)) . . .	1b	
1c	Combine lines 1a and 1b	1c	

Activities acquired after 10-22-86 (Post-enactment):

1d	Activities with net income (from Worksheet 1, Part 2, column (a)). .	1d	
1e	Activities with net loss (from Worksheet 1, Part 2, column (b)) . . .	1e	
1f	Combine lines 1d and 1e	1f	
1g	Net income or (loss). Combine lines 1c and 1f	1g	
1h	Prior year unallowed losses (from Worksheet 1, Parts 1 and 2, column (c))	1h	
1i	Combine lines 1g and 1h	1i	

All Other Passive Activities

Activities acquired before 10-23-86 (Pre-enactment):

2a	Activities with net income (from Worksheet 2, Part 1, column (a)). .	2a	
2b	Activities with net loss (from Worksheet 2, Part 1, column (b)) . . .	2b	
2c	Combine lines 2a and 2b.	2c	

Activities acquired after 10-22-86 (Post-enactment):

2d	Activities with net income (from Worksheet 2, Part 2, column (a)). .	2d	
2e	Activities with net loss (from Worksheet 2, Part 2, column (b)) . . .	2e	
2f	Combine lines 2d and 2e	2f	
2g	Net income or (loss). Combine lines 2c and 2f	2g	
2h	Prior year unallowed losses (from Worksheet 2, Parts 1 and 2, column (c))	2h	
2i	Combine lines 2g and 2h	2i	
3	Combine lines 1i and 2i. If the result is net income or -0-, see the Instructions for line 3. If this line and line 1c or line 1i are losses, go to line 4. Otherwise, enter -0- on lines 8 and 9 and go to line 10 . . .	3	

Note: *Treat all numbers entered in Parts II and III as positive amounts. (See Instructions on page 8 for examples.)*

Part II   Computation of the Special Allowance for Rental Real Estate With Active Participation

4	Enter the **smaller** of the loss on line 1i or the loss on line 3. If line 1i is -0- or net income, enter -0- and complete lines 5 through 9	4	
5	Enter $150,000. If married filing separately, see the Instructions .	5	
6	Enter modified adjusted gross income, but not less than -0- (see instructions) .	6	

Note: *If line 6 is equal to or greater than line 5, skip line 7, enter -0- on lines 8 and 9, and then go to line 10. Otherwise, go to line 7.*

7	Subtract line 6 from line 5	7	
8	Multiply line 7 by 50% (.5). **Do not** enter more than $25,000. If married filing separately, see Instructions	8	
9	Enter the **smaller** of line 4 or line 8	9	

Part III   Computation of Passive Activity Loss Allowed

10	Combine lines 1c and 2c. If the result is net income or -0-, skip to line 16. (See Instructions.) . . .	10	
11	If line 1c shows income, has no entry, or shows -0-, enter -0-. Otherwise, enter the **smaller** of line 1c or line 8 .	11	
12	Subtract line 11 from line 10. If line 11 is equal to or greater than line 10, enter -0-	12	
13	Subtract line 9 from line 3	13	
14	Enter the **smaller** of line 12 or line 13	14	
15	Multiply line 14 by 10% (.1) and enter the result	15	
16	Enter the amount from line 9	16	
17	**Passive activity loss allowed for 1990.** Add lines 15 and 16	17	
18	Add the income, if any, on lines 1a, 1d, 2a, and 2d and enter the total	18	
19	**Total losses allowed from all passive activities for 1990.** Add lines 17 and 18. See the Instructions to find out how to report the losses on your tax return.	19	

For Paperwork Reduction Act Notice, see separate Instructions.   Form **8582** (1990)

Form **8615**	**Tax for Children Under Age 14**	OMB No. 1545-0998
Department of the Treasury Internal Revenue Service	**Who Have Investment Income of More Than $1,000** ▶ See instructions below and on back. ▶ Attach ONLY to the Child's Form 1040, Form 1040A, or Form 1040NR.	 Attachment Sequence No. **33**

General Instructions

Purpose of Form. For children under age 14, investment income (such as taxable interest and dividends) over $1,000 is taxed at the parent's rate if the parent's rate is higher than the child's rate.

Do not use this form if the child's investment income is $1,000 or less. Instead, figure the tax in the normal manner on the child's income tax return. For example, if the child had $900 of taxable interest income and $200 of wages, Form 8615 is not required to be completed and the child's tax should be figured on Form 1040A using the Tax Table.

If the child's investment income is more than $1,000, use this form to see if any of the child's investment income is taxed at the parent's rate and, if so, to figure the

child's tax. For example, if the child had $1,100 of taxable interest income and $200 of wages, complete Form 8615 and attach it to the child's Form 1040A.

Investment Income. As used on this form, "investment income" includes all taxable income other than earned income as defined on page 2. It includes income such as taxable interest, dividends, capital gains, rents, royalties, etc. It also includes pension and annuity income and income (other than earned income) received as the beneficiary of a trust.

Who Must File. Generally, Form 8615 must be filed for any child who was under age 14 on January 1, 1991, and who had more than $1,000 of investment income. If neither parent was alive on December 31,

1990, do not use Form 8615. Instead, figure the child's tax based on his or her own rate.

Note: *The parent may be able to elect to report the child's investment income on his or her return. If the parent makes this election, the child will not have to file a return or Form 8615. For more details, see the Instructions for Form 1040 or Form 1040A, or get* **Form 8814,** *Parent's Election To Report Child's Interest and Dividends.*

Additional Information. For more information about the tax on investment income of children, please get **Pub. 929,** Tax Rules for Children and Dependents.

(Instructions continue on back.)

Child's name shown on return	Child's social security number

A Parent's name (first, initial, and last). **(Caution:** See instructions on back before completing.)	B Parent's social security number

C   Parent's filing status (check one):
☐ Single, ☐ Married filing jointly, ☐ Married filing separately, ☐ Head of household, or ☐ Qualifying widow(er)

D   Enter number of exemptions claimed on parent's return. (If the parent's filing status is married filing separately, see the instructions.) ▶ ☐

Step 1	**Figure child's net investment income**		
1	Enter the child's investment income, such as taxable interest and dividend income (see the instructions). (If this amount is $1,000 or less, stop here; do not file this form.)	1	
2	If the child DID NOT itemize deductions on Schedule A (Form 1040 or Form 1040NR), enter $1,000. If the child ITEMIZED deductions, see the instructions	2	
3	Subtract the amount on line 2 from the amount on line 1. Enter the result. (If zero or less, stop here; do not complete the rest of this form but ATTACH it to the child's return.)	3	
4	Enter the child's **taxable** income (from Form 1040, line 37; Form 1040A, line 22; or Form 1040NR, line 35) .	4	
5	Compare the amounts on lines 3 and 4. Enter the **smaller** of the two amounts here . . . . . . ▶	5	
Step 2	**Figure tentative tax based on the tax rate of the parent listed above**		
6	Enter the parent's **taxable** income (from Form 1040, line 37; Form 1040A, line 22; Form 1040EZ, line 5; or Form 1040NR, line 35). But if the parent transferred property to a trust, see the instructions . .	6	
7	Enter the total, if any, of the net investment income from Forms 8615, line 5, of ALL OTHER children of the parent. (Do not include the amount on line 5 above.)	7	
8	Add the amounts on lines 5, 6, and 7. Enter the total	8	
9	Tax on the amount on line 8 based on the **parent's** filing status	9	
10	Enter the parent's tax (from Form 1040, line 38; Form 1040A, line 23; Form 1040EZ, line 7; or Form 1040NR, line 36)	10	
11	Subtract the amount on line 10 from the amount on line 9. Enter the result. (If no amount is entered on line 7, enter the amount from line 11 on line 13; skip lines 12a and 12b.)	11	
12a	Add the amounts on lines 5 and 7. Enter the total	12a		
b	Divide the amount on line 5 by the amount on line 12a. Enter the result as a decimal (rounded to two places) .	12b	× .
13	Multiply the amount on line 11 by the decimal amount on line 12b. Enter the result . . . . . . ▶	13	
Step 3	**Figure child's tax**		
	Note: *If the amounts on lines 4 and 5 are the same, skip to line 16.*		
14	Subtract the amount on line 5 from the amount on line 4. Enter the result .	14		
15	Tax on the amount on line 14 based on the **child's** filing status	15	
16	Add the amounts on lines 13 and 15. Enter the total	16	
17	Tax on the amount on line 4 based on the **child's** filing status	17	
18	Compare the amounts on lines 16 and 17. Enter the **larger** of the two amounts here and on Form 1040, line 38; Form 1040A, line 23; or Form 1040NR, line 36. Be sure to check the box for "Form 8615" . ▶	18	

For Paperwork Reduction Act Notice, see back of form.   Form **8615** (1990)

Form 8615 (1990)

Paperwork Reduction Act Notice. We ask for the information on this form to carry out the Internal Revenue laws of the United States. You are required to give us the information. We need it to ensure that you are complying with these laws and to allow us to figure and collect the right amount of tax.

The time needed to complete and file this form will vary depending on individual circumstances. The estimated average time is:

Recordkeeping . . . . . . 13 min.
Learning about the law or the form . . . . 11 min.
Preparing the form . . . . 37 min.
Copying, assembling, and sending the form to IRS . . . 17 min.

If you have comments concerning the accuracy of these time estimates or suggestions for making this form more simple, we would be happy to hear from you. You can write to both the IRS and the Office of Management and Budget at the addresses listed in the instructions of the tax return with which this form is filed.

Incomplete Information for Parent. If a parent or guardian of a child cannot obtain the necessary information to complete Form 8615 before the due date of the child's return, reasonable estimates of the parent's taxable income or filing status and the net investment income of the parent's other children may be made. The appropriate line of Form 8615 must be marked "Estimated." For more information, see Pub. 929.

Line-by-Line Instructions

We have provided specific instructions for most of the lines on the form. Those lines that do not appear in these instructions are self-explanatory.

Lines A and B. If the child's parents were married to each other and filed a joint return, enter the name and social security number of the parent who is listed first on the joint return. For example, if the father's name is listed first on the return and his social security number is entered in the block labeled "Your social security number," enter his name on line A and his social security number on line B.

If the parents were married but filed separate returns, enter the name and social security number of the parent who had the **higher** taxable income. If you do not know which parent had the higher taxable income, see Pub. 929.

If the parents were unmarried, treated as unmarried for Federal income tax purposes, or separated either by a divorce or separate maintenance decree, enter the name and social security number of the parent who had custody of the child for most of the year (the custodial parent). **Exception.** If the custodial parent remarried and filed a joint return with his or her spouse, enter the name and social security number of the

person who is listed first on the joint return, even if that person is not the child's parent. If the custodial parent and his or her spouse filed separate returns, enter the name and social security number of the person with the **higher** taxable income, even if that person is not the child's parent.

Note: *If the parents were unmarried but lived together during the year with the child, enter the name and social security number of the parent who had the **higher** taxable income.*

Line D. If the parent's filing status is married filing separately and the parent claimed an exemption for his or her spouse, write "Spouse" in the space above the box on line D.

Line 1. If the child had no earned income (defined below), enter the child's adjusted gross income (from Form 1040, line 32; Form 1040A, line 17; or Form 1040NR, line 31).

If the child had earned income, use the following worksheet to figure the amount to enter on line 1. However, if any of the following applies, use the worksheet in Pub. 929 instead of the one below to figure the amount to enter on Form 8615, line 1:

● The child files **Form 2555,** Foreign Earned Income.

● The child had a net loss from self-employment.

● The child claims a net operating loss deduction.

Worksheet (keep for your records)

1. Enter the amount from the child's Form 1040, line 23; Form 1040A, line 14; or Form 1040NR, line 23, whichever applies . . _____

2. Enter the child's **earned income** (defined below) plus any deduction the child claims on Form 1040, line 28, or Form 1040NR, line 27, whichever applies . . _____

3. Subtract the amount on line 2 from the amount on line 1. Enter the result here and on Form 8615, line 1 . . _____

Earned income includes wages, tips, and other payments received for personal services performed. Generally, earned income is the total of the amounts reported on Form 1040, lines 7, 12, and 19; Form 1040A, line 7; or Form 1040NR, lines 8, 13, and 20.

Line 2. If the child itemized deductions on **Schedule A** (Form 1040 or 1040NR), enter on line 2 the **greater** of:

● $500 plus the portion of the amount on Schedule A (Form 1040), line 27 (or Schedule A (Form 1040NR), line 10), that

is directly connected with the production of the investment income on Form 8615, line 1; OR

● $1,000.

Line 6. Enter the taxable income shown on the tax return of the parent identified on line A of Form 8615. If the parent's taxable income is less than zero, enter zero on line 6.

If the parent filed a joint return, enter the taxable income shown on that return even if the parent's spouse is not the child's parent.

If the parent transferred property to a trust which sold or exchanged the property during the year at a gain, include any gain that was taxed to the trust under Internal Revenue Code section 644 in the amount entered on line 6. Write "Section 644" and the amount on the dotted line next to line 6. Also, see the instructions for line 10 below.

Line 7. If the individual identified as the parent on this Form 8615 is also identified as the parent on any other Form 8615, add the amounts, if any, from line 5 on each of the other Forms 8615 and enter the total on line 7.

Lines 9, 15, and 17. Figure the tax using the Tax Table or Tax Rate Schedules, whichever applies.

Line 10. Enter the tax shown on the tax return of the parent identified on line A of Form 8615. If the parent filed a joint return, enter the tax shown on that return even if the parent's spouse is not the child's parent.

If line 6 includes any gain taxed to a trust under Internal Revenue Code section 644, add the tax imposed under section 644(a)(2)(A) to the tax shown on the parent's return. Enter the total on line 10 instead of entering the tax from the parent's return. Write "Section 644" on the dotted line next to line 10.

Line 18. Compare the amounts on lines 16 and 17 and enter the **larger** of the two amounts on line 18. Be sure to check the box for "Form 8615" on the appropriate line of the child's tax return even if the amount on line 17 is the larger of the two amounts.

Amended Return. If after the child's return is filed, the parent's taxable income is changed or the net investment income of any of the parent's other children is changed, the child's tax must be refigured using the adjusted amounts. If the child's tax is changed as a result of the adjustment(s), file **Form 1040X,** Amended U.S. Individual Income Tax Return, to correct the child's tax.

Alternative Minimum Tax. A child whose tax is figured on Form 8615 may be subject to the alternative minimum tax. Get **Form 6251,** Alternative Minimum Tax—Individuals, and its instructions to see if the child owes this tax.

Form **8814**

Department of the Treasury
Internal Revenue Service

Parent's Election To Report Child's Interest and Dividends
▶ See instructions below and on back.
▶ Attach to Parent's Form 1040 or Form 1040NR.

OMB No. 1545-1128

1990

Attachment
Sequence No. **40**

General Instructions

Purpose of Form.—Use this form if you are a parent and choose to report the income of your child on your return. If you do, the child will not have to file a return. You can file this form only if your child:

● Was under age 14 on January 1, 1991;
● Had income only from interest and dividends (including Alaska Permanent Fund dividends);
● Had gross income for 1990 that was more than $500 but less than $5,000;

● Had no estimated tax payments for 1990;
● Did not have any overpayment of tax shown on his or her 1989 return applied to the 1990 return; AND
● Had no Federal income tax withheld from his or her income (backup withholding).

The parent(s) must also qualify as explained on page 2 of these instructions.

Step 1 is used to figure the amount of the child's income to report on the parent's return. **Step 2** is used to figure an additional tax that must be added to the parent's tax.

A separate Form 8814 must be filed for each child whose income the parent chooses to report.

Caution: *The Federal income tax on your child's income may be less if you file a tax return for the child instead of making this election. This is because you cannot take certain deductions that your child would be entitled to on his or her own return. For details, see **Deductions You May Not Take** on page 2.*

(Instructions continue on back.)

Name(s) shown on parent's return	Your social security number
Child's name (first, initial, and last)	Child's social security number

Caution: If more than one Form 8814 is attached, check here . . . . ▶ ☐

Step 1   Figure amount of child's interest and dividend income to report on your return

1a Enter your child's **taxable** interest income. If this amount is different than the amounts shown on the child's Forms 1099-INT and 1099-OID, see the instructions **1a**

b Enter your child's **tax-exempt** interest income. Do **NOT** include this amount on line 1a **1b**

2a Enter your child's gross dividends (including any Alaska Permanent Fund dividends). If none, enter zero on line 2c and go to line 3. If your child received any capital gain distributions or dividends as a nominee, see the instructions **2a**

b Enter your child's nontaxable distributions (from Form 1099-DIV, Box 1d) included on line 2a **2b**

c Subtract line 2b from line 2a. Enter the result **2c**

3 Add lines 1a and 2c. Enter the total. If the total is $1,000 or less, skip lines 4 and 5 and go to line 6. If the total is $5,000 or more, **do not** file this form. Your child **must** file his or her own return to report the income **3**

4 Base amount . . . . **4** | 1,000 | 00

5 Subtract line 4 from line 3. Enter the result. (If filing more than one Form 8814, see the instructions.) Also include this amount in the total on Form 1040, line 22, or Form 1040NR, line 22. In the space next to line 22, write "Form 8814" and show the amount. Go on to line 6 ▶ **5**

Step 2   Figure your tax on the first $1,000 of child's interest and dividend income

6 Amount not taxed . . . . **6** | 500 | 00

7 Subtract line 6 from line 3. Enter the result. If the result is zero or less, enter zero **7**

8 **Tax.** ● If the amount on line 7 is $500 or more, enter $75 here. (Also, see the **Note** below for where to enter it on your tax return.)
● If the amount on line 7 is less than $500, multiply the amount on line 7 by 15% (.15). Enter the result here. (Also, see the **Note** below for where to enter it on your tax return.) } **8**

Note: *Include the amount from line 8 in the tax you enter on Form 1040, line 38, or Form 1040NR, line 36. On Form 1040, also enter the amount from line 8 in the space provided next to line 38. On Form 1040NR, enter the amount from line 8 and "Form 8814" next to line 36. (If filing more than one Form 8814, see the instructions.)*

For Paperwork Reduction Act Notice, see back of form.   Form **8814** (1990)

General Instructions

(continued)

Parents Who Qualify To Make the Election.—You qualify to make this election if you file Form 1040 or Form 1040NR and any of the following applies to you:

• You and the child's other parent were married to each other and you are filing a joint return for 1990.

• You and the child's other parent were married to each other but you file separate returns for 1990 AND you had the **higher** taxable income. (If you do not know if you had the higher taxable income, get **Pub. 929,** Tax Rules for Children and Dependents.)

• You were unmarried, treated as unmarried for Federal income tax purposes, or separated from the child's other parent by a divorce or separate maintenance decree. You must have had custody of your child for most of the year (you were the custodial parent). If you were the custodial parent and you remarried, you may make the election on a joint return with your new spouse. But if you and your new spouse (your child's stepparent) do not file a joint return, you qualify to make the election only if you had **higher** taxable income than your new spouse.

Note: *If you and the child's other parent were not married but you lived together during the year with the child, you qualify to make the election only if you are the parent with the* **higher** *taxable income.*

Deductions You May Not Take.—If you elect to report your child's income on your return, you may not reduce that income by any of the following deductions that your child would be entitled to on his or her own return.

• Standard deduction of $1,300 for a blind child.

• Penalty on early withdrawal of child's savings.

• Itemized deductions (such as child's investment expenses or charitable contributions).

If any of the above applies to your child, you should figure the tax on the child's income as if he or she is filing a return and as if you are electing to report the income on your return to find out which results in the lowest amount of tax.

How To Make the Election.—To make the election, complete and attach Form 8814 to your tax return and file your return by the due date (including extensions).

Additional Information.—For more information about the election, see Pub. 929.

Line-by-Line Instructions

Parent's Name and Social Security Number.—Enter the name(s) shown on your return. If filing a joint return, enter the social security number of the person whose name is shown first on the return.

Line 1a.—Enter **ALL** taxable interest income received by your child in 1990. If your child received a **Form 1099-INT** for tax-exempt interest, such as from municipal bonds, write the amount and "Tax-exempt interest" on the dotted line next to line 1a. Be sure to include this interest on line 1b but do **not** include it in the total for line 1a.

If your child received, as a **nominee,** interest that actually belongs to another person, write the amount and "ND" (for nominee distribution) on the dotted line next to line 1a. Do **not** include amounts received as a nominee in the total for line 1a.

If your child had accrued interest that was paid to the seller of a bond, amortizable bond premium (ABP) allowed as a reduction to interest income, or if any original issue discount (OID) included on line 1a is less than the amount shown on your child's **Form 1099-OID,** follow the instructions above for nominee interest to see how to report the nontaxable amounts. But, on the dotted line next to line 1a, write the nontaxable amount and "Accrued interest," "ABP adjustment," or "OID adjustment," whichever applies. Do **not** include any nontaxable amounts in the total for line 1a.

Line 1b.—If your child received any tax-exempt interest income, such as interest on certain state and municipal bonds, enter the total tax-exempt interest on line 1b. Also include any exempt-interest dividends your child received as a shareholder in a mutual fund or other regulated investment company. Do **not** include this interest on lines 1a or 3.

Note: *If line 1b includes tax-exempt interest (or exempt-interest dividends paid by a regulated investment company) from private activity bonds, see* **Alternative Minimum Tax** *on this page.*

Line 2a.—Enter gross dividends received by your child in 1990, including capital gain distributions and nontaxable distributions. **Form 1099-DIV** shows gross dividends in Box 1a. Also include dividends your child received through a partnership, an S corporation, or an estate or trust.

If line 2a includes any **capital gain distributions** (from Form 1099-DIV, Box 1c), and you have gains or losses to report on Schedule D, part or all of your child's capital gain distributions should be reported on your Schedule D instead of on Form 8814, line 5. Before you enter an amount on line 5, see Pub. 929 for details on how to figure the amount to report on your Schedule D.

If your child received, as a **nominee,** dividends that actually belong to another person, write the amount and "ND" (for nominee distribution) on the dotted line next to line 2a. Do **not** include amounts received as a nominee in the total for line 2a.

Line 5.—If you are filing more than one Form 8814, add the amounts from line 5 of ALL your Forms 8814 and include the total on Form 1040, line 22 (or Form 1040NR, line 22).

Be sure to write "Form 8814" and show the total of the line 5 amounts in the space next to line 22 on your return.

Line 8.—If you are filing more than one Form 8814, add the amounts from line 8 of ALL your Forms 8814 and include the total on Form 1040, line 38 (or Form 1040NR, line 36).

On Form 1040, be sure to enter the total of the line 8 amounts in the space provided next to line 38. On Form 1040NR, be sure to write "Form 8814" and the total of the line 8 amounts next to line 36.

Alternative Minimum Tax.—If your child received any tax-exempt interest (or exempt-interest dividends paid by a regulated investment company) from certain private activity bonds, you must take this into account in determining if you owe the alternative minimum tax. Get **Form 6251,** Alternative Minimum Tax—Individuals, and its instructions for more information.

Foreign Accounts and Foreign Trusts.—If your child had a foreign financial account or was the grantor of, or transferor to, a foreign trust, Part III of **Schedule B** (Form 1040) would have to be completed and attached to the child's return if he or she was filing a return. If Part III of Schedule B had been completed for your child, would either the question on line 11a or line 12 have been answered "Yes"? If so, you must file Schedule B with your return and answer "Yes" to the question(s). Also complete line 11b if applicable. Write "Form 8814" on the dotted line next to line 11a or line 12, whichever applies, on your Schedule B.

Change of Address.—If your child filed a return for a year before 1990 and the address shown on the last return your child filed is not his or her current address, be sure to notify IRS, in writing, of your child's new address. To do this, you may use **Form 8822,** Change of Address, or you may write to the Internal Revenue Service Center where your child's last return was filed, or to the Chief, Taxpayer Service Division, in your local IRS district office.

Paperwork Reduction Act Notice.—We ask for the information on this form to carry out the Internal Revenue laws of the United States. You are required to give us this information. We need it to ensure that you are complying with these laws and to allow us to figure and collect the right amount of tax.

The time needed to complete and file this form will vary depending on individual circumstances. The estimated average time is:

Recordkeeping	20 minutes
Learning about the law or the form	8 minutes
Preparing the form	16 minutes
Copying, assembling, and sending the form to IRS	35 minutes

If you have comments concerning the accuracy of these time estimates or suggestions for making this form more simple, we would be happy to hear from you. You can write to both the IRS and the Office of Management and Budget at the addresses listed in the instructions of the tax return with which this form is filed.

*U.S. Government Printing Office: 1990 — 265-410

Appendix **C**

MODIFIED ACRS AND ORIGINAL ACRS TABLES

Modified ACRS Accelerated Depreciation Percentages
Using the Half-Year Convention
for 3-, 5-, 7-, 10-, 15-, and 20-Year Property
Placed in Service after December 31, 1986

Recovery Year	Property Class					
	3-Year	5-Year	7-Year	10-Year	15-Year	20-Year
1	33.33	20.00	14.29	10.00	5.00	3.750
2	44.45	32.00	24.49	18.00	9.50	7.219
3	14.81	19.20	17.49	14.40	8.55	6.677
4	7.41	11.52	12.49	11.52	7.70	6.177
5		11.52	8.93	9.22	6.93	5.713
6		5.76	8.92	7.37	6.23	5.285
7			8.93	6.55	5.90	4.888
8			4.46	6.55	5.90	4.522
9				6.56	5.91	4.462
10				6.55	5.90	4.461
11				3.28	5.91	4.462
12					5.90	4.461
13					5.91	4.462
14					5.90	4.461
15					5.91	4.462
16					2.95	4.461
17						4.462
18						4.461
19						4.462
20						4.461
21						2.231

Source: Rev. Proc. 87-57, Table 1.

Modified ACRS Depreciation Rates
for Residential Real Property
Placed in Service after December 31, 1986

Recovery Year	Month Placed in Service					
	1	2	3	4	5	6
1	3.485	3.182	2.879	2.576	2.273	1.970
2	3.636	3.636	3.636	3.636	3.636	3.636
3	3.636	3.636	3.636	3.636	3.636	3.636
4	3.636	3.636	3.636	3.636	3.636	3.636
5	3.636	3.636	3.636	3.636	3.636	3.636
6	3.636	3.636	3.636	3.636	3.636	3.636
7	3.636	3.636	3.636	3.636	3.636	3.636
8	3.636	3.636	3.636	3.636	3.636	3.636
9	3.636	3.636	3.636	3.636	3.636	3.636
10	3.637	3.637	3.637	3.637	3.637	3.637
11	3.636	3.636	3.636	3.636	3.636	3.636
12	3.637	3.637	3.637	3.637	3.637	3.637
13	3.636	3.636	3.636	3.636	3.636	3.636
14	3.637	3.637	3.637	3.637	3.637	3.637
15	3.636	3.636	3.636	3.636	3.636	3.636
16	3.637	3.637	3.637	3.637	3.637	3.637
17	3.636	3.636	3.636	3.636	3.636	3.636
18	3.637	3.637	3.637	3.637	3.637	3.637
19	3.636	3.636	3.636	3.636	3.636	3.636
20	3.637	3.637	3.637	3.637	3.637	3.636
21	3.636	3.636	3.636	3.636	3.636	3.636
22	3.637	3.637	3.637	3.637	3.637	3.637
23	3.636	3.636	3.636	3.636	3.636	3.636
24	3.637	3.637	3.637	3.637	3.637	3.637
25	3.636	3.636	3.636	3.636	3.636	3.636
26	3.637	3.637	3.637	3.637	3.637	3.637
27	3.636	3.636	3.636	3.636	3.636	3.636
28	1.970	2.273	2.576	2.879	3.182	3.485
29	0.000	0.000	0.000	0.000	0.000	0.000

Recovery Year	Month Placed in Service					
	7	8	9	10	11	12
1	1.667	1.364	1.061	0.758	0.455	0.152
2	3.636	3.636	3.636	3.636	3.636	3.636
3	3.636	3.636	3.636	3.636	3.636	3.636
4	3.636	3.636	3.636	3.636	3.636	3.636
5	3.636	3.636	3.636	3.636	3.636	3.636
6	3.636	3.636	3.636	3.636	3.636	3.636
7	3.636	3.636	3.636	3.636	3.636	3.636
8	3.636	3.636	3.636	3.636	3.636	3.636
9	3.636	3.636	3.636	3.636	3.636	3.636
10	3.636	3.636	3.636	3.636	3.636	3.636
11	3.637	3.637	3.637	3.637	3.637	3.637
12	3.636	3.636	3.636	3.636	3.636	3.636
13	3.637	3.637	3.637	3.637	3.637	3.637
14	3.636	3.636	3.636	3.636	3.636	3.636
15	3.637	3.637	3.637	3.637	3.637	3.637
16	3.636	3.636	3.636	3.636	3.636	3.636
17	3.637	3.637	3.637	3.637	3.637	3.637
18	3.636	3.636	3.636	3.636	3.636	3.636
19	3.637	3.637	3.637	3.637	3.637	3.637
20	3.636	3.636	3.636	3.636	3.636	3.636
21	3.637	3.637	3.637	3.637	3.637	3.637
22	3.636	3.636	3.636	3.636	3.636	3.636
23	3.637	3.637	3.637	3.637	3.637	3.637
24	3.636	3.636	3.636	3.636	3.636	3.636
25	3.637	3.637	3.637	3.637	3.637	3.637
26	3.636	3.636	3.636	3.636	3.636	3.636
27	3.637	3.637	3.637	3.637	3.637	3.637
28	3.636	3.636	3.636	3.636	3.636	3.636
29	0.152	0.455	0.758	1.061	1.364	1.667

Source: Rev. Proc. 87-57, Table 7.

Modified ACRS Depreciation Percentages
for Nonresidential Real Property
Placed in Service after December 31, 1986

Recovery Year	Month Placed in Service					
	1	*2*	*3*	*4*	*5*	*6*
1	3.042	2.778	2.513	2.249	1.984	1.720
2	3.175	3.175	3.175	3.175	3.175	3.175
3	3.175	3.175	3.175	3.175	3.175	3.175
4	3.175	3.175	3.175	3.175	3.175	3.175
5	3.175	3.175	3.175	3.175	3.175	3.175
6	3.175	3.175	3.175	3.175	3.175	3.175
7	3.175	3.175	3.175	3.175	3.175	3.175
8	3.175	3.174	3.175	3.174	3.175	3.174
9	3.174	3.175	3.174	3.175	3.174	3.175
10	3.175	3.174	3.175	3.174	3.175	3.174
11	3.174	3.175	3.174	3.175	3.174	3.175
12	3.175	3.174	3.175	3.174	3.175	3.174
13	3.174	3.175	3.174	3.175	3.174	3.175
14	3.175	3.174	3.175	3.174	3.175	3.174
15	3.174	3.175	3.174	3.175	3.174	3.175
16	3.175	3.174	3.175	3.174	3.175	3.174
17	3.174	3.175	3.174	3.175	3.174	3.175
18	3.175	3.174	3.175	3.174	3.175	3.174
19	3.174	3.175	3.174	3.175	3.174	3.175
20	3.175	3.174	3.175	3.174	3.175	3.174
21	3.174	3.175	3.174	3.175	3.174	3.175
22	3.175	3.174	3.175	3.174	3.175	3.174
23	3.174	3.175	3.174	3.175	3.174	3.175
24	3.175	3.174	3.175	3.174	3.175	3.174
25	3.174	3.175	3.174	3.175	3.174	3.175
26	3.175	3.174	3.175	3.174	3.175	3.174
27	3.174	3.175	3.174	3.175	3.174	3.175
28	3.175	3.174	3.175	3.174	3.175	3.174
29	3.174	3.175	3.174	3.175	3.174	3.175
30	3.175	3.174	3.175	3.174	3.175	3.174
31	3.174	3.175	3.174	3.175	3.174	3.175
32	1.720	1.984	2.249	2.513	2.778	3.042
33	0.000	0.000	0.000	0.000	0.000	0.000

Recovery Year	Month Placed in Service					
	7	8	9	10	11	12
1	1.455	1.190	0.926	0.661	0.397	0.132
2	3.175	3.175	3.175	3.175	3.175	3.175
3	3.175	3.175	3.175	3.175	3.175	3.175
4	3.175	3.175	3.175	3.175	3.175	3.175
5	3.175	3.175	3.175	3.175	3.175	3.175
6	3.175	3.175	3.175	3.175	3.175	3.175
7	3.175	3.175	3.175	3.175	3.175	3.175
8	3.175	3.175	3.175	3.175	3.175	3.175
9	3.174	3.175	3.175	3.175	3.174	3.175
10	3.175	3.174	3.175	3.174	3.175	3.174
11	3.174	3.175	3.174	3.175	3.174	3.175
12	3.175	3.174	3.175	3.174	3.175	3.174
13	3.174	3.175	3.174	3.175	3.174	3.175
14	3.175	3.174	3.175	3.174	3.175	3.174
15	3.174	3.175	3.174	3.175	3.174	3.175
16	3.175	3.174	3.175	3.174	3.175	3.174
17	3.174	3.175	3.174	3.175	3.174	3.175
18	3.175	3.174	3.175	3.174	3.175	3.174
19	3.174	3.175	3.174	3.175	3.174	3.175
20	3.175	3.174	3.175	3.174	3.175	3.174
21	3.174	3.175	3.174	3.175	3.174	3.175
22	3.175	3.174	3.175	3.174	3.175	3.174
23	3.174	3.175	3.174	3.175	3.174	3.175
24	3.175	3.174	3.175	3.174	3.175	3.174
25	3.174	3.175	3.174	3.175	3.174	3.175
26	3.175	3.174	3.175	3.174	3.175	3.174
27	3.174	3.175	3.174	3.175	3.174	3.175
28	3.175	3.174	3.175	3.174	3.175	3.174
29	3.174	3.175	3.174	3.175	3.174	3.175
30	3.175	3.174	3.175	3.174	3.175	3.174
31	3.174	3.175	3.174	3.175	3.174	3.175
32	3.175	3.174	3.175	3.174	3.175	3.174
33	0.132	0.397	0.661	0.926	1.190	1.455

Source: Rev. Proc. 87-57, Table 7.

Modified ACRS Accelerated Depreciation Percentages
Using the Mid-Quarter Convention
for 3-, 5-, 7-, 10-, 15-, and 20-Year Property
Placed in Service after December 31, 1986

3-Year Property:

Recovery Year	Quarter Placed in Service			
	1	2	3	4
1	58.33	41.67	25.00	8.33
2	27.78	38.89	50.00	61.11
3	12.35	14.14	16.67	20.37
4	1.54	5.30	8.33	10.19

5-Year Property:

	1	2	3	4
1	35.00	25.00	15.00	5.00
2	26.00	30.00	34.00	38.00
3	15.60	18.00	20.40	22.80
4	11.01	11.37	12.24	13.68
5	11.01	11.37	11.30	10.94
6	1.38	4.26	7.06	9.58

7-Year Property:

	1	2	3	4
1	25.00	17.85	10.71	3.57
2	21.43	23.47	25.51	27.55
3	15.31	16.76	18.22	19.68
4	10.93	11.37	13.02	14.06
5	8.75	8.87	9.30	10.04
6	8.74	8.87	8.85	8.73
7	8.75	8.87	8.86	8.73
8	1.09	3.33	5.53	7.64

10-Year Property:

	1	2	3	4
1	17.50	12.50	7.50	2.50
2	16.50	17.50	18.50	19.50
3	13.20	14.00	14.80	15.60
4	10.56	11.20	11.84	12.48
5	8.45	8.96	9.47	9.98
6	6.76	7.17	7.58	7.99
7	6.55	6.55	6.55	6.55
8	6.55	6.55	6.55	6.55
9	6.56	6.56	6.56	6.56
10	0.82	6.55	6.55	6.55
11		2.46	4.10	5.74

Recovery Year	Quarter Placed in Service			
	1	2	3	4

15-Year Property:

	1	2	3	4
1	8.75	6.25	3.75	1.25
2	9.13	9.38	9.63	9.88
3	8.21	8.44	8.66	8.89
4	7.39	7.59	7.80	8.00
5	6.65	6.83	7.02	7.20
6	5.99	6.15	6.31	6.48
7	5.90	5.91	5.90	5.90
8	5.91	5.90	5.90	5.90
9	5.90	5.91	5.91	5.90
10	5.91	5.90	5.90	5.91
11	5.90	5.91	5.91	5.90
12	5.91	5.90	5.90	5.91
13	5.90	5.91	5.91	5.90
14	5.91	5.90	5.90	5.91
15	5.90	5.91	5.91	5.90
16	.74	2.21	3.69	5.17

20-Year Property:

	1	2	3	4
1	6.563	4.688	2.813	0.938
2	7.000	7.148	7.289	7.430
3	6.482	6.612	6.742	6.872
4	5.996	6.116	6.237	6.357
5	5.546	5.658	5.769	5.880
6	5.130	5.233	5.336	5.439
7	4.746	4.841	4.936	5.031
8	4.459	4.478	4.566	4.654
9	4.459	4.463	4.460	4.458
10	4.459	4.463	4.460	4.458
11	4.459	4.463	4.460	4.458
12	4.460	4.463	4.460	4.458
13	4.459	4.463	4.461	4.458
14	4.460	4.463	4.460	4.458
15	4.459	4.462	4.461	4.458
16	4.460	4.463	4.460	4.458
17	4.459	4.462	4.461	4.458
18	4.460	4.463	4.460	4.459
19	4.459	4.462	4.461	4.458
20	4.460	4.463	4.460	4.459
21	.557	1.673	2.788	3.901

Source: Rev. Proc. 87-57.

Alternative Depreciation System
Recovery Periods

General Rule: Recovery period is the property's class life unless:

1. There is no class life (see below), or
2. A special class life has been designated (see below).

Type of Property	Recovery Period
Personal property with no class life	12 years
Nonresidential real property with no class life	40 years
Residential rental property with no class life	40 years
Cars, light general purpose trucks, certain technological equipment, and semiconductor manufacturing equipment	5 years
Computer-based telephone central office switching equipment	9.5 years
Railroad track	10 years
Single purpose agricultural or horticultural structures	15 years
Municipal waste water treatment plants, telephone distribution plants	24 years
Low-income housing financed by tax-exempt bonds	27.5 years
Municipal sewers	50 years

Modified ACRS and ADS Straight-Line Depreciation Percentages
Using the Half-Year Convention
for 3-, 5-, 7-, 10-, 15-, and 20-Year Property
Placed in Service after December 31, 1986

Recovery Year	Property Class					
	3-Year	*5-Year*	*7-Year*	*10-Year*	*15-Year*	*20-Year*
1	16.67	10.00	7.14	5.00	3.33	2.50
2	33.33	20.00	14.29	10.00	6.67	5.00
3	33.33	20.00	14.29	10.00	6.67	5.00
4	16.67	20.00	14.28	10.00	6.67	5.00
5		20.00	14.29	10.00	6.67	5.00
6		10.00	14.28	10.00	6.67	5.00
7			14.29	10.00	6.67	5.00
8			7.14	10.00	6.66	5.00
9				10.00	6.67	5.00
10				10.00	6.66	5.00
11				5.00	6.67	5.00
12					6.66	5.00
13					6.67	5.00
14					6.66	5.00
15					6.67	5.00
16					3.33	5.00
17						5.00
18						5.00
19						5.00
20						5.00
21						2.50

Source: Rev. Proc. 87-57.

ADS Straight-Line Depreciation Percentages
Real Property
Using the Mid-Month Convention
for Property Placed in Service after December 31, 1986

Month Placed	Recovery Year		
In Service	1	2-40	41
1	2.396	2.500	0.104
2	2.188	2.500	0.312
3	1.979	2.500	0.521
4	1.771	2.500	0.729
5	1.563	2.500	0.937
6	1.354	2.500	1.146
7	1.146	2.500	1.354
8	0.938	2.500	1.562
9	0.729	2.500	1.771
10	0.521	2.500	1.979
11	0.313	2.500	2.187
12	0.104	2.500	2.396

Source: Rev. Proc. 87-57, Table 13.

Original ACRS
Accelerated Recovery Percentages
for 3-, 5-, 10-, and 15-Year Public Utility Property

Personalty Placed in Service after 1980 and before 1987

	Property Class			
Recovery Year	3-Year	5-Year	10-Year	15-Year Public Utility
1	25%	15%	8%	5%
2	38	22	14	10
3	37	21	12	9
4		21	10	8
5		21	10	7
6			10	7
7			9	6
8			9	6
9			9	6
10			9	6
11				6
12				6
13				6
14				6
15				6

Original ACRS
Accelerated Recovery Percentages
for 15-Year Realty

Placed in Service after 1980 and before March 16, 1984

Recovery Year	\	\	\	\	Month Placed in Service	\	\	\	\	\	\	\
	1	2	3	4	5	6	7	8	9	10	11	12
1	12	11	10	9	8	7	6	5	4	3	2	1
2	10	10	11	11	11	11	11	11	11	11	11	12
3	9	9	9	9	10	10	10	10	10	10	10	10
4	8	8	8	8	8	8	9	9	9	9	9	9
5	7	7	7	7	7	7	8	8	8	8	8	8
6	6	6	6	6	7	7	7	7	7	7	7	7
7	6	6	6	6	6	6	6	6	6	6	6	6
8	6	6	6	6	6	6	5	6	6	6	6	6
9	6	6	6	6	5	6	5	5	5	6	6	6
10	5	6	6	6	5	5	5	5	5	5	6	5
11	5	5	5	5	5	5	5	5	5	5	5	5
12	5	5	5	5	5	5	5	5	5	5	5	5
13	5	5	5	5	5	5	5	5	5	5	5	5
14	5	5	5	5	5	5	5	5	5	5	5	5
15	5	5	5	5	5	5	5	5	5	5	5	5
16			1	1	2	2	3	3	4	4	4	5

Original ACRS
Accelerated Recovery Percentages
for Low-Income Housing

Placed in Service after 1980 and before March 16, 1984

Recovery Year	Month Placed in Service											
	1	2	3	4	5	6	7	8	9	10	11	12
1	13	12	11	10	9	8	7	6	4	3	2	1
2	12	12	12	12	12	12	12	13	13	13	13	13
3	10	10	10	10	11	11	11	11	11	11	11	11
4	9	9	9	9	9	9	9	9	10	10	10	10
5	8	8	8	8	8	8	8	8	8	8	8	9
6	7	7	7	7	7	7	7	7	7	7	7	7
7	6	6	6	6	6	6	6	6	6	6	6	6
8	5	5	5	5	5	5	5	5	5	5	6	6
9	5	5	5	5	5	5	5	5	5	5	5	5
10	5	5	5	5	5	5	5	5	5	5	5	5
11	4	5	5	5	5	5	5	5	5	5	5	5
12	4	4	4	5	4	5	5	5	5	5	5	5
13	4	4	4	4	4	4	5	4	5	5	5	5
14	4	4	4	4	4	4	4	4	4	5	4	4
15	4	4	4	4	4	4	4	4	4	4	4	4
16			1	1	2	2	2	3	3	3	4	4

Original ACRS
Accelerated Recovery Percentages
for 18-Year Realty

Realty Placed in Service after March 15, 1984 and before May 9, 1985

Recovery Year	Month Placed in Service											
	1	2	3	4	5	6	7	8	9	10	11	12

The applicable percentage is:

Recovery Year	1	2	3	4	5	6	7	8	9	10	11	12
1	9	9	8	7	6	5	4	4	3	2	1	0.4
2	9	9	9	9	9	9	9	9	9	10	10	10.0
3	8	8	8	8	8	8	8	8	9	9	9	9.0
4	7	7	7	7	7	8	8	8	8	8	8	8.0
5	7	7	7	7	7	7	7	7	7	7	7	7.0
6	6	6	6	6	6	6	6	6	6	6	6	6.0
7	5	5	5	5	6	6	6	6	6	6	6	6.0
8	5	5	5	5	5	5	5	5	5	5	5	5.0
9	5	5	5	5	5	5	5	5	5	5	5	5.0
10	5	5	5	5	5	5	5	5	5	5	5	5.0
11	5	5	5	5	5	5	5	5	5	5	5	5.0
12	5	5	5	5	5	5	5	5	5	5	5	5.0
13	4	4	4	5	4	4	5	4	4	4	5	5.0
14	4	4	4	4	4	4	4	4	4	4	4	4.0
15	4	4	4	4	4	4	4	4	4	4	4	4.0
16	4	4	4	4	4	4	4	4	4	4	4	4.0
17	4	4	4	4	4	4	4	4	4	4	4	4.0
18	4	3	4	4	4	4	4	4	4	4	4	4.0
19		1	1	1	2	2	2	3	3	3	3	3.6

Original ACRS
Accelerated Cost Recovery Percentages
for 19-Year Real Property

Realty Placed in Service after May 8, 1985 and before 1987

Recovery Year	Month Placed in Service											
	1	2	3	4	5	6	7	8	9	10	11	12
The applicable percentage is:												
1	8.8	8.1	7.3	6.5	5.8	5.0	4.2	3.5	2.7	1.9	1.1	0.4
2	8.4	8.5	8.5	8.6	8.7	8.8	8.8	8.9	9.0	9.0	9.1	9.2
3	7.6	7.7	7.7	7.8	7.9	7.9	8.0	8.1	8.1	8.2	8.3	8.3
4	6.9	7.0	7.0	7.1	7.1	7.2	7.3	7.3	7.4	7.4	7.5	7.6
5	6.3	6.3	6.4	6.4	6.5	6.5	6.6	6.6	6.7	6.8	6.8	6.9
6	5.7	5.7	5.8	5.9	5.9	5.9	6.0	6.0	6.1	6.1	6.2	6.2
7	5.2	5.2	5.3	5.3	5.3	5.4	5.4	5.5	5.5	5.6	5.6	5.6
8	4.7	4.7	4.8	4.8	4.8	4.9	4.9	5.0	5.0	5.1	5.1	5.1
9	4.2	4.3	4.3	4.4	4.4	4.5	4.5	4.5	4.5	4.6	4.6	4.7
10	4.2	4.2	4.2	4.2	4.2	4.2	4.2	4.2	4.2	4.2	4.2	4.2
11	4.2	4.2	4.2	4.2	4.2	4.2	4.2	4.2	4.2	4.2	4.2	4.2
12	4.2	4.2	4.2	4.2	4.2	4.2	4.2	4.2	4.2	4.2	4.2	4.2
13	4.2	4.2	4.2	4.2	4.2	4.2	4.2	4.2	4.2	4.2	4.2	4.2
14	4.2	4.2	4.2	4.2	4.2	4.2	4.2	4.2	4.2	4.2	4.2	4.2
15	4.2	4.2	4.2	4.2	4.2	4.2	4.2	4.2	4.2	4.2	4.2	4.2
16	4.2	4.2	4.2	4.2	4.2	4.2	4.2	4.2	4.2	4.2	4.2	4.2
17	4.2	4.2	4.2	4.2	4.2	4.2	4.2	4.2	4.2	4.2	4.2	4.2
18	4.2	4.2	4.2	4.2	4.2	4.2	4.2	4.2	4.2	4.2	4.2	4.2
19	4.2	4.2	4.2	4.2	4.2	4.2	4.2	4.2	4.2	4.2	4.2	4.2
20	0.2	0.5	0.9	1.2	1.6	1.9	2.3	2.6	3.0	3.3	3.7	4.0

Original ACRS
Straight-Line Recovery Percentages
for 3-, 5-, 10-, and 15-Year Public Utility Property

Personalty Placed in Service before 1987

Recovery Year	Optional Recovery Period in Years							
	3	5	10	12	15	25	35	45

The applicable percentage is:

Recovery Year	3	5	10	12	15	25	35	45
1	17	10	5	4	3	2	1	1.1
2	33	20	10	9	7	4	3	2.3
3	33	20	10	9	7	4	3	2.3
4	17	20	10	9	7	4	3	2.3
5		20	10	9	7	4	3	2.3
6		10	10	8	7	4	3	2.3
7			10	8	7	4	3	2.3
8			10	8	7	4	3	2.3
9			10	8	7	4	3	2.3
10			10	8	7	4	3	2.3
11			5	8	7	4	3	2.3
12				8	6	4	3	2.2
13				4	6	4	3	2.2
14					6	4	3	2.2
15					6	4	3	2.2
16					3	4	3	2.2
17						4	3	2.2
18						4	3	2.2
19						4	3	2.2
20						4	3	2.2
21						4	3	2.2
22						4	3	2.2
23						4	3	2.2
24						4	3	2.2
25						4	3	2.2
26						2	3	2.2
27							3	2.2
28							3	2.2
29							3	2.2
30							3	2.2
31							3	2.2
32							2	2.2
33							2	2.2
34							2	2.2
35							2	2.2
36							1	2.2
37								2.2
38								2.2
39								2.2
40								2.2
41								2.2
42								2.2
43								2.2
44								2.2
45								2.2
46								1.1

Original ACRS
Straight-Line Recovery Percentages
for 18-Year Realty

Realty Placed in Service after March 15, 1984 and before May 9, 1985

Recovery Year	Month Placed in Service					
	1-2	3-4	5-7	8-9	10-11	12
	The applicable percentage is:					
1	5	4	3	2	1	0.2
2	6	6	6	6	6	6.0
3	6	6	6	6	6	6.0
4	6	6	6	6	6	6.0
5	6	6	6	6	6	6.0
6	6	6	6	6	6	6.0
7	6	6	6	6	6	6.0
8	6	6	6	6	6	6.0
9	6	6	6	6	6	6.0
10	6	6	6	6	6	6.0
11	5	5	5	5	5	5.8
12	5	5	5	5	5	5.0
13	5	5	5	5	5	5.0
14	5	5	5	5	5	5.0
15	5	5	5	5	5	5.0
16	5	5	5	5	5	5.0
17	5	5	5	5	5	5.0
18	5	5	5	5	5	5.0
19	1	2	3	4	5	5.0

Original ACRS
Straight-Line Recovery Percentages
for 19-Year Realty

Realty Placed in Service after May 8, 1985 and before 1987

Recovery Year	Month Placed in Service											
	1	2	3	4	5	6	7	8	9	10	11	12
The applicable percentage is:												
1	5.0	4.6	4.2	3.7	3.3	2.9	2.4	2.0	1.5	1.1	.7	.2
2	5.3	5.3	5.3	5.3	5.3	5.3	5.3	5.3	5.3	5.3	5.3	5.3
3	5.3	5.3	5.3	5.3	5.3	5.3	5.3	5.3	5.3	5.3	5.3	5.3
4	5.3	5.3	5.3	5.3	5.3	5.3	5.3	5.3	5.3	5.3	5.3	5.3
5	5.3	5.3	5.3	5.3	5.3	5.3	5.3	5.3	5.3	5.3	5.3	5.3
6	5.3	5.3	5.3	5.3	5.3	5.3	5.3	5.3	5.3	5.3	5.3	5.3
7	5.3	5.3	5.3	5.3	5.3	5.3	5.3	5.3	5.3	5.3	5.3	5.3
8	5.3	5.3	5.3	5.3	5.3	5.3	5.3	5.3	5.3	5.3	5.3	5.3
9	5.3	5.3	5.3	5.3	5.3	5.3	5.3	5.3	5.3	5.3	5.3	5.3
10	5.3	5.3	5.3	5.3	5.3	5.3	5.3	5.3	5.3	5.3	5.3	5.3
11	5.3	5.3	5.3	5.3	5.3	5.3	5.3	5.3	5.3	5.3	5.3	5.3
12	5.3	5.3	5.3	5.3	5.3	5.3	5.3	5.3	5.3	5.3	5.3	5.3
13	5.3	5.3	5.3	5.3	5.3	5.3	5.3	5.3	5.3	5.3	5.3	5.3
14	5.2	5.2	5.2	5.2	5.2	5.2	5.2	5.2	5.2	5.2	5.2	5.2
15	5.2	5.2	5.2	5.2	5.2	5.2	5.2	5.2	5.2	5.2	5.2	5.2
16	5.2	5.2	5.2	5.2	5.2	5.2	5.2	5.2	5.2	5.2	5.2	5.2
17	5.2	5.2	5.2	5.2	5.2	5.2	5.2	5.2	5.2	5.2	5.2	5.2
18	5.2	5.2	5.2	5.2	5.2	5.2	5.2	5.2	5.2	5.2	5.2	5.2
19	5.2	5.2	5.2	5.2	5.2	5.2	5.2	5.2	5.2	5.2	5.2	5.2
20	.2	.6	1.0	1.5	1.9	2.3	2.8	3.2	3.7	4.1	4.5	5.0

Appendix D

INSTRUCTIONS FOR LOTUS-BASED COMPUTERIZED TAX ANALYSIS PROBLEMS

Editors' Note to Students: If you have been assigned any of the Computerized Tax Analysis problems, you will need a copy of a master disk containing the Lotus-based template files referred to in these problems before you can begin an assignment. See your instructor for his or her directions in obtaining a copy of the master disk.

Instructions for Loading A Computerized Tax Analysis File into Lotus 1-2-3

Three disks are necessary to use a Computerized Tax Analysis file (template, spreadsheet). The first is IBM-DOS (IBM disk operating system). The second is the Lotus system disk, and the third is the Computerized Tax Analysis disk. The following instructions indicate how to "load" (read, store) a file into the Lotus program. After the file is loaded, you can use it for your analyses.

Steps to follow if your IBM-PC is currently turned off

Note: If you can hear a humming sound made by the internal fan, then the microcomputer is on. If it is on, skip to the next section of instructions.

1. Lift the flap (disk drive door) on the front of the A: disk drive. This disk drive is located on the left, or on the top for microcomputers with stacked disk drives.

2. Remove the IBM-DOS disk from its envelope with the label facing up and held by your fingers. Be sure not to touch the unprotected portions of the disk located in the center and toward the non-labeled end.

3. With the label facing up, gently slide the end that is furthest from your fingers into drive A: Then close the disk drive door.

4. An orange on/off switch is located on the right side of the microprocessing unit. Put the switch in the "on" (up) position. When most microcomputers are turned on, they perform a self-test before the user can begin computing. This is also true for the IBM-PC. Depending on the amount of the microcomputer's internal memory, this self-test can take from 30 seconds to two minutes. After the self-test is completed, IBM-DOS is automatically loaded into the computer's memory. The red disk drive light is on when information on the disk is being accessed (read). Never open the disk drive door when the light is on.

5. Some monitors (screens) have an on/off switch and some do not. If your monitor has an on/off switch, turn it to the "on" position.

6. After IBM-DOS has finished loading, the read light on the disk drive will go off. Remove the IBM-DOS disk from the disk drive and place it back into its envelope. In its place (in drive A:), insert the Lotus system disk. Close the disk drive door and type the following:

lotus

Then press the [Return] key. Continue to press the [Return] key until you see a blank spreadsheet. The blank spreadsheet will have letters across the top of the screen and numbers down the left side of the screen.

7. Insert the Computerized Tax Analysis disk into the B: disk drive. This is the drive located on the right, or on the bottom for microcomputers with stacked disk drives. (Actually, this step can be done at any time up to this point.)

8. Press the following three keys, one at a time

/ f r

Note that the [/] key is on the lower right side of the keyboard. For the [f] and [r] keys, you can use upper or lower case. This is true for all Lotus commands. If you press a wrong key by mistake, press the [Esc] key in the upper left corner of the keyboard to "back up" to where you were before you made the error. This "back up" technique can be used for steps 9–11 also.

You should now see file names listed horizontally just above the column letters of the worksheet (names such as T101, T1001). If you do not see file names, press the following four keys, one at a time:

[Esc] b : [Return]

9. Now you are ready to tell Lotus which file you wish to use. You can do this in either of two ways. You can type in the file name and then press the [Return] key. Alternatively, you can move the cursor along the

horizontal menu of file names (by using the arrowed keys) until you arrive at the file you need, then press the [Return] key. If you do not see the file name among those listed, keep moving the cursor to the right. Either of these two methods will load the file into the Lotus program.

10. If, after using the file you have selected, you wish to load another file, go back to step 8.

11. After you have *finished* using Lotus, press the following keys, one at a time:

/ q y e y

12. Gently remove both disks from the disk drives and place them back into their envelopes. Remember to close the disk drive flaps (doors). The IBM-PC should be left on.

Steps to follow if your IBM-PC is currently turned on

1. Lift the flap (disk drive door) on the front of the A: disk drive. This disk drive is located on the left, or on the top for microcomputers with stacked disk drives.

2. Remove the IBM-DOS disk from its envelope with the label facing up and held by your fingers. Be sure not to touch the unprotected portions of the disk located in the center and toward the non-labeled end.

3. With the label facing up, gently slide the end furthest from your fingers into drive A:. Then close the disk drive door.

4. Press at the same time the [Ctrl], [Alt], and [Del] keys to automatically load IBM-DOS into the computer's memory. The red disk drive light is on when information on the disk is being accessed (read). Never open the disk drive door when the light is on.

5. Now that DOS is loading, you may go to step 5 above for the rest of your instructions.

Appendix E

TWO INDIVIDUAL COMPREHENSIVE TAX RETURN PROBLEMS FOR 1990

1. David R. and Susan L. Holman

   a. David and Susan Holman are married and file a joint return. David is 38 years of age and Susan is 36. David is a self-employed certified real estate appraiser (C.R.E.), and Susan is employed by Wells Fargo Bank as a trust officer. They have two children: Richard Lawrence, age 7, and Karen Ann, age 4. The Holmans currently live at 5901 W. 75th Street, Los Angeles, California 90034, in a home they purchased and occupied on September 6, 1990.

   Until August 12, 1990 the Holman family lived in Dallas, Texas, where David was employed by a real estate appraisal company and Susan was a bank officer for First National Bank. They sold their home in Dallas and moved to Los Angeles so that Susan could assume her new job as a trust officer and David could become self-employed.

   b. David and Susan sold their home in Dallas for $95,000 and incurred the following expenses:

Sales commission	$5,700
Attorney's fee	300
Title insurance	450
Document preparation fee	60
Recording fee	10
Pest inspection fee	80
Prepayment penalty for early retirement of home mortgage (3 points)	1,500

   The Holmans had purchased the Dallas home on March 4, 1983 and never held it for rent or used it for business purposes. The home originally cost $62,500, and they had paid $1,200 for a cedar fence and $300 for landscaping. Within seven weeks of receiving a contract of sale on their house, the Holmans paid $800 for interior and exterior painting and $200 for steam-cleaning of the carpets. The sale was closed on August 1, 1990 and the Holmans were required to move out of the home by August 15, 1990.

c. In moving from Dallas to Los Angeles, the Holmans incurred the following expenses, none of which were reimbursed:

Cost of moving household goods................	$6,250
Meals...	100
Lodging..	250
House-hunting expenses (including $150 for meals)..............................	1,000
Temporary living expenses (20 days; including meals costing $400)................	1,700

Not included in any of the above expenses are the costs for driving two automobiles from Dallas to Los Angeles. David and Susan each drove a car, taking turns driving with the children. Although neither one of them kept receipts, Susan noted that her auto mileage was 1,500 miles. In addition, David noted that the number of miles from their old home to their old workplace was 24 miles, and the number of miles from their old home to their new workplace is 1,514 miles.

d. The Holmans purchased their new home for $230,000 by making a $30,000 down payment and financing the remaining balance with a 30-year, 10% conventional mortgage loan from California Federal Savings and Loan. They were required to prepay 2 points ($4,000) in return for the favorable mortgage terms. New furniture and drapes cost an additional $7,500.

e. The Holmans received the following Forms W-2, reporting their salaries for 1990:

1) David R. Holman, Social Security No. 452-64-5837:

Gross salary...	$45,000
Federal income taxes withheld.........................	6,750
F.I.C.A. taxes withheld.................................	3,380

2) Susan L. Holman, Social Security No. 467-32-5452:

	First Nat'l Bank	Wells Fargo Bank	Total
Gross salary...........................	$17,500	$24,000	$41,500
Federal income taxes withheld......................	1,100	3,150	4,250
F.I.C.A. taxes..........................	1,314	1,802	3,116
California income taxes withheld......................	—	700	700

f. On October 1, 1990 David rented office space at 5510 Wacker Drive, Los Angeles, California 90025. The terms of the one-year lease agreement called for a monthly rent of $800, with the first and last month's rent paid in advance.

David decided to operate his business in the name of "David R. Holman, Certified Real Estate Appraiser," and he elected to use the cash method of accounting for his revenues and expenses. The following items relate to his business for 1990:

Gross receipts	$35,000
Expenses:	
Advertising	250
Bank service charges	50
Dues and publications	450
Insurance	600*
Interest	275
Professional services	525
Office rent	3,200**
Office supplies	700
Meals and entertainment	500
Miscellaneous expenses	75

*Three months of coverage
**Includes prepayment of rent for September, 1991

David drove his personal automobile 5,000 miles for business purposes from October 1 through December 31. Rather than keeping receipts, he elected to use the automatic mileage method (27.5 cents per mile) for determining his auto expenses.

On October 3, 1990 David purchased the following furniture and equipment for use in his business:

Office furniture	$7,000
Copying machine	2,800
Computer	4,500
Laser printer	1,500
Phone answering machine	200

David elects to expense the maximum amount allowed under the optional expensing rules of § 179. He also elects to compute the maximum depreciation allowance using the appropriate MACRS percentages.

g. The Holmans received interest income during 1990 from the follow-
    ing:

U.S. Treasury bills	$1,475
First National Bank, Dallas	625
Wells Fargo Bank	400
Tarrant County municipal bonds	800

h. David and Susan received the following dividends during 1990:

Ford Motor Company	$ 300
Eastman Kodak Company	575
IBM Corporation	125
General Motors stock dividend (20 new shares of stock valued at $60 per share, received March 9, 1990)	1,200

i. The Holmans have never maintained foreign bank accounts or created
    foreign trusts.

j. The Holmans report the following stock transactions for 1990:

    1) Sold 100 shares of IBM stock for $120 per share on August 1,
        1990. David had inherited 500 shares of IBM stock from his
        uncle on July 18, 1988, and the stock was valued at $170 per
        share on the date of his uncle's death (the value used for estate
        tax purposes).

    2) Sold 400 shares of General Motors stock for $78 per share on
        September 20, 1990. Susan had received 1,000 shares of General
        Motors stock as a wedding present from her grandfather on June
        3, 1982. Her grandfather had purchased the stock for $35 per
        share on May 7, 1967, and the stock was valued at $50 per share
        on the date of the gift. Susan's grandfather paid gift taxes of
        $10,000 as a result of the gift.

    3) Sold 300 shares of Eastman Kodak stock for $40 per share on
        December 28, 1990, but did not receive the sales proceeds until
        January 3, 1991. The Holmans had paid $25 per share for the
        stock on October 21, 1989.

k.   Susan has summarized the following cash expenditures for 1990 from canceled checks, mortgage company statements, and other documents:

Prescription medicines and drugs	$ 982
Medical insurance premiums	2,830
Doctors' and hospital bills (net of	
reimbursements)	1,535
Contact lenses for David	218
Real estate taxes paid on	
Dallas residence	1,400
Los Angeles residence	2,600
Sales taxes paid on new auto	1,485
Ad valorem taxes paid on both autos	350
Interest paid for	
Dallas home mortgage	3,250*
Los Angeles home mortgage	7,200**
Credit card interest	480
Personal car loan	620
Cash contributions to	
United Methodist Church	3,000
American Heart Fund	200
United Way Campaign	300
George Bush Re-election Campaign Fund	250
Susan's unreimbursed employee expenses	470***
David's unreimbursed employee expenses	360***
Tax return preparation fee	375

*Does not include the mortgage prepayment penalty identified in item (b) above.
**Does not include the interest points charged for the new mortgage identified in item (d) above.
***Does not include any costs for meals or entertainment.

Susan also noted that she and David had driven their personal automobiles 500 miles to receive medical treatment for themselves and their children. She also has a receipt for 100 shares of General Motors stock that she gave to her alma mater, Southern Methodist University, on November 12, 1990. The stock was valued at $70 per share on the date of the gift and was from the block of General Motors stock Susan had received as a wedding present from her grandfather [see item (j)(2) above for details].

l.   The Holmans paid the following child care expenses during 1990:

1)	Kindergarten School	$2,800
	1177 Valley View	
	Dallas, Texas 75210	
	EIN: 74-0186254	
2)	Happy Trails Day Center	2,200
	3692 Airport Blvd.	
	Los Angeles, California 90034	
	EIN: 78-0593676	

m. While reading an article in the *Los Angeles Times*, Susan became aware of the requirement to report the social security number of any person claimed as a dependent on a Federal income tax return. She applied for and received the following social security numbers for the children:

> Richard L. Holman, Social Security No. 582-60-4732
> Karen A. Holman, Social Security No. 582-60-5840

n. David and Susan made timely estimated Federal income tax payments of $5,000 for the year ($1,250 each quarter).

o. The Holmans have always directed that $2 go to the Presidential Election Campaign by checking the "yes" box on their Form 1040.

Required:

Complete the Holmans' Federal income tax return for 1990. If they have a refund due, they would prefer having it credited against their 1991 taxes.

2. Richard M. and Anna K. Wilson

a. Richard and Anna Wilson are married and file a joint return. Richard is 47 years of age and Anna is 46. Richard is employed by Telstar Corporation as its controller and Anna is self-employed as a travel agent. They have three children: Michael, age 20; Lisa, age 17; and Laura, age 14. Michael is a full-time student at Rutgers University. Lisa and Laura both live at home and attend school full-time. The Wilsons currently live at 3721 Chestnut Ridge Road, Montvale, New Jersey 07645, in a home they have owned since July, 1976.

Richard and Anna provided over half of the support of Anna's mother, who currently lives in a nursing home in Mahwah, New Jersey. They also provided over half of the support of their son, Michael, who earned $2,750 during the summer as an accounting student intern for a national accounting firm.

b. Richard received a Form W-2 from his employer reporting the following information for 1990:

Richard M. Wilson, Social Security No. 294-38-6249:

Gross wages and taxable benefits	$63,000.00
Federal income taxes withheld	12,400.00
F.I.C.A. taxes withheld	3,604.80
State income taxes withheld	1,850.00

The taxable benefits reported on his W-2 Form include $2,700 ($0.275 per mile) for Richard's personal use of the company car provided by his employer.

c. Anna operates her business under the name "Wilson's Travel Agency," located at 7200 Treeline Drive, Montvale, NJ 07645. Anna has one full-time employee, and her federal employer identification number is 74-2638596.

Anna uses the cash method of accounting for her business, and her records for 1990 show the following:

Fees and commissions	$114,000
Expenses:	
Advertising	1,425
Bank service charges	75
Dues and subscriptions	560
Insurance	1,100
Interest on furniture loan	960
Professional services	700
Office rent	6,000
Office supplies	470
Meals and entertainment	1,000
Payroll taxes	2,170
Utilities and telephone	3,480
Wages paid to full-time employee	22,800
Miscellaneous expenses	20

Automobile expenses and amounts paid to her children are not included in the above expenses. Anna paid her daughters Lisa and Laura $750 and $450, respectively, for working part-time during the summer. Since she did not withhold or pay any Federal income or employment taxes on these amounts, Anna is not certain that she is allowed a deduction. She does feel that the amounts paid to her children were reasonable, however.

Anna purchased a new automobile in November of last year, and her tax accountant used the actual cost method in determining the deductible business expenses for her 1989 Federal tax return. Because the deductible amount seemed so small, she is not certain whether she should claim actual expenses (including depreciation), or simply use the automatic mileage method. She has the following records relating to the business auto:

Original cost (including sales tax and auto title)	$18,000
Depreciation claimed in 1989	900
Gas, oil, and repairs in 1990	1,790
Parking and tolls paid in 1990	410
Insurance for 1990	650
Interest on car loan	750

Anna drove the auto 20,000 miles for business purposes and 5,000 miles for personal purposes during the year. The above expenses for 1990 have not been reduced to reflect her personal use of the vehicle.

In January, 1990 Anna purchased the following items for use in her business:

Office furniture	$2,900
Copying machine	1,700
Zenith portable computer	1,500
Printer	600
Fax machine	1,300

Anna wishes to claim the maximum amount of depreciation deductions allowed on the office furniture and equipment.

d. Richard attended an accounting convention in Washington, D.C. for three days in October. He incurred the following unreimbursed expenses related to the trip:

Air fare (round-trip)	$270
Registration fee for meeting	425
Hotel cost	375
Meals	130
Taxis	20
Airport parking	18
Road tolls	2

e. Richard and Anna received Forms 1099-INT reporting interest income earned during 1990 from the following:

Series EE savings bonds	$845
Montvale National Bank	900
Telstar Employees' Credit Union	755

f. The Wilsons received the following dividends during 1990:

Telstar Corporation	$300
Exxon Coporation	200

g. The Wilsons have never had a foreign bank account or created a foreign trust.

h. The Wilsons had the following property transactions for 1990:

1. Anna sold 300 shares of Exxon Corporation stock on September 9, 1990 in order to pay for Michael's fall semester of college. She received a check in the amount of $14,950 from Shearson Lehman on September 16, 1990. The stock was from a block of 1,000 shares that Richard and Anna had purchased for $35 per share on February 1, 1967.

2. They gave each of the children 100 shares of Exxon stock on December 30, 1990, when the stock was valued at $62.50 per share. The stock was from the same block of stock purchased for $35 per share in February, 1967. No gift taxes were paid on these gifts.

3. They gave 100 shares of Exxon stock to Richard's alma mater, Rider College, on December 29, 1990. The average trading price of Exxon stock on that day was $61.25. This stock was also from the original block of 1,000 shares the Wilsons had purchased for $35 per share in 1967.

4. On May 17, 1990, Richard and Anna were notified by the bankruptcy judge handling the affairs of Bubbling Crude Oil Company in Houston, Texas that the company's shareholders would not receive anything for their stock ownership because all of the assets were used to satisfy claims of creditors. Richard had purchased 2,000 shares of the stock for $6 per share on April 1, 1981. Unfortunately, the stock did not meet the requirements of § 1244.

i. Richard and Anna own a rental condominium located at 7777 Boardwalk in Atlantic City, New Jersey. The unit was purchased in July, 1989 for $25,000 cash and a $125,000 mortgage. The following items relate to the rental unit for 1990:

Gross rents	$15,400
Expenses:	
Management fee	2,310
Cleaning and maintenance	1,200
Insurance	840
Property taxes	2,750
Interest paid on mortgage	13,675
Utilities	150

Although the unfurnished unit was vacant for 11 weeks during the year, the Wilsons never used the property for personal purposes. When the property is rented, the tenant is required to pay for all utilities, and the Wilsons are charged a management fee equal to 15 percent of the rents collected.

j. The Wilsons have prepared the following summary of their other expenditures for 1990:

Prescription medicines and drugs	$ 425
Medical insurance premiums	1,595
Doctors' and hospital bills (net of reimbursements)	805*
Dentist	2,750**
Real estate taxes paid on home	1,625
State income taxes paid during 1990	2,100***
Interest paid for	
Original home mortgage	2,690
Home equity loan	6,410****
Credit card interest	275
Personal car loan	725
Cash contributions to church	1,200
Fee for preparation of 1989 tax return	450

> *Does not include $1,485 of doctor bills paid by Richard and Anna for medical treatment provided to Anna's mother at the nursing home. Also not included is $115 that Anna paid for a new pair of eyeglasses for her mother.
> **$2,350 of this amount represents a prepayment for Laura's braces. The dentist requried the prepayment before he would begin the two-year dental program involved.
> ***Does not include amounts withheld from Richard's wages.
> ****Represents interest paid on a $75,000 home equity loan made by the Wilsons in 1989.

k. Anna contributed $11,500 to her Keogh plan on December 15, 1990.

l. Richard paid the following unreimbursed employee business expenses:

Professional dues	$450
Professional journals	385
New briefcase	115

m. The Wilsons received a state income tax refund of $130 in 1990. They itemized their deductions for 1989.

n. Richard and Anna made timely estimated Federal income tax payments of $9,000 for the year ($2,250 each quarter).

o. Social security numbers for Anna, the children, and Anna's mother are provided below:

	Number
Anna K. Wilson	296-48-2385
Michael D. Wilson	256-83-4421
Lisa M. Wilson	257-64-7573
Laura D. Wilson	258-34-2894
Ruth Knapp	451-38-3790

p. The Wilsons have always checked the "no" box on their Form 1040 regarding the Presidential Election Campaign fund contribution.

Required:

Complete the Wilsons' Federal income tax return for 1990. If they have a refund due, they would prefer having it credited against their 1991 taxes.

Appendix F

GLOSSARY OF TAX TERMS

—A—

A. (*see* Acquiescence).

Accelerated Cost Recovery System (ACRS). An alternate form of depreciation enacted by the Economic Recovery Tax Act of 1981 and significantly modified by the Tax Reform Act of 1986. The cost of a qualifying asset is recovered over a set period of time. Salvage value is ignored. § 168.

Accelerated Depreciation. Various depreciation methods that produce larger depreciation deductions in the earlier years of an asset's life than straight-line depreciation. Examples: double-declining balance method (200% declining balance) and sum-of-the-years'-digits method. § 167 (*see also* Depreciation).

Accounting Method. A method by which an entity's income and expenses are determined. The primary accounting methods used are the accrual method and the cash method. Other accounting methods include the installment method; the percentage-of-completion method (for construction); and various methods for valuing inventories, such as FIFO and LIFO. §§ 446 and 447 (*see also specific accounting methods*).

Accounting Period. A period of time used by a taxpayer in determining his or her income, expenses, and tax liability. An accounting period is generally a year for tax purposes, either a calendar year, a fiscal year, or a 52–53 week year. §§ 441 and 443.

Accrual Method of Accounting. The method of accounting that reflects the income earned and the expenses incurred during a given tax period. However, unearned income of an accrual basis taxpayer must generally be included in an entity's income in the year in which it is received, even if it is not actually earned by the entity until a later tax period. § 446.

Accumulated Adjustment Account (AAA). A summary of all includible income and gains, expenses, and losses of an S corporation for taxable years after 1982, except those that relate to excludable income, distributions, and redemptions of an S corporation. Distributions from the AAA are generally not taxable to the shareholders. §§ 1368(c)(1) and (e)(1).

Accumulated Earnings Credit. A reduction in arriving at a corporation's accumulated taxable income (in computing the Accumulated Earnings Tax). Its purpose is to avoid penalizing a corporation for retaining sufficient earnings and profits to meet the reasonable needs of the business. § 535(c).

Accumulated Earnings Tax.   A penalty tax on the unreasonable accumulation of earnings and profits by a corporation. It is intended to encourage the distribution of earnings and profits of a corporation to its shareholders. §§ 531–537.

Accumulated Taxable Income.   The amount on which the accumulated earnings tax is imposed. §§ 531 and 535.

Accuracy-Related Penalty.   Any of the group of penalties that includes negligence or disregard of rules or regulations, substantial understatement of income tax, substantial valuation misstatement for income tax purposes, substantial overstatement of pension liabilities, and substantial estate or gift valuation understatement. § 6662.

Acquiescence.   The public endorsement of a regular Tax Court decision by the Commissioner of the Internal Revenue Service. When the Commissioner acquiesces to a regular Tax Court decision, the IRS generally will not dispute the result in cases involving substantially similar facts (*see also* Nonacquiescence).

Ad Valorem Tax.   A tax based on the value of property.

Adjusted Basis.   The basis (i.e., cost or other basis) of property plus capital improvements minus depreciation allowed or allowable. See § 1016 for other adjustments to basis. § 1016 (*see also* Basis).

Adjusted Gross Income.   A term used with reference to individual taxpayers. Adjusted gross income consists of an individual's gross income less certain deductions and business expenses. § 62.

Adjusted Ordinary Gross Income (AOGI).   A term used in relation to personal holding companies. Adjusted ordinary gross income is determined by subtracting certain interest expense and certain expenses related to rents and mineral, oil, and gas royalties from ordinary gross income. § 543(b)(2).

Administrator.   A person appointed by the court to administrate the estate of a deceased person. If named to perform these duties by the decedent's will, this person is called an executor (executrix).

AFTR (American Federal Tax Reports).   Published by Prentice Hall, these volumes contain the Federal tax decisions issued by the U.S. District Courts, U.S. Claims Court, U.S. Circuit Courts of Appeal, and the U.S. Supreme Court (*see also* AFTR2d).

AFTR2d (American Federal Tax Reports, Second Series).   The second series of the American Federal Tax Reports. These volumes contain the Federal tax decisions issued by the U.S. District Courts, U.S. Claims Court, U.S. Circuit Courts of Appeal, and the U.S. Supreme Court (*see also* AFTR).

Alternate Valuation Date.   The property contained in a decedent's gross estate must be valued at either the decedent's date of death or the alternate valuation date. The alternate valuation date is six months after the decedent's date of death, or, if the property is disposed of prior to that date, the particular property disposed of is valued as of the date of its disposition. § 2032.

Alternative Minimum Tax.   A tax imposed on taxpayers only if it exceeds the "regular" tax of the taxpayer. Regular taxable income is adjusted by certain timing differences, then increased by tax preferences to arrive at alternative minimum taxable income.

Amortization.   The systematic write-off (deduction) of the cost or other basis of an intangible asset over its estimated useful life. The concept is similar to depreciation (used for tangible assets) and depletion (used for natural resources) (*see also* Goodwill; Intangible Asset).

Amount Realized.   Any money received, plus the fair market value of any other property or services received, plus any liabilities discharged on the sale or other disposition of property. The determination of the amount realized is the first step in determining realized gain or loss. § 1001(b).

Annual Exclusion.   The amount each year that a donor may exclude from Federal gift tax for each donee. Currently, the annual exclusion is $10,000 per donee per year. The annual exclusion does not generally apply to gifts of future interests. § 2503(b).

Annuity.   A fixed amount of money payable to a person at specific intervals for either a specific period of time or for life.

Appellate Court.   A court to which other court decisions are appealed. The appellate courts for Federal tax purposes include the Courts of Appeals and the Supreme Court.

Arm's-Length Transaction.   A transaction entered into by unrelated parties, all acting in their own best interests. It is presumed that in an arm's-length transaction the prices used are the fair market values of the properties or services being transferred in the transaction.

Articles of Incorporation.   The basic instrument filed with the appropriate state agency when a business is incorporated.

Assessment of Tax.   The imposition of an additional tax liability by the Internal Revenue Service (i.e., as the result of an audit).

Assignment of Income.   A situation in which a taxpayer assigns income or income-producing property to another person or entity in an attempt to avoid paying taxes on that income. An assignment of income or income-producing property is generally not recognized for tax purposes, and the income is taxable to the assignor.

Association.   An entity that possesses a majority of the following characteristics: associates; profit motive; continuity of life; centralized management; limited liability; free transferability of interests. Associations are taxed as corporations. §§ 7701(a)(3); Reg. § 301.7701-2.

At-Risk Limitation.   A provision that limits a deduction for losses to the amounts "at risk." A taxpayer is generally not "at risk" in situations where nonrecourse debt is used. § 465.

Attribution.   (*see* Constructive Ownership).

Audit.   The examination of a taxpayer's return or other taxable transactions by the Internal Revenue Service in order to determine the correct tax liability. Types of audits include correspondence audits, office audits, and field audits (*see also* Correspondence Audit; Field Audit; Office Audit).

—B—

Bad Debt.   An uncollectible debt. A bad debt may be classified either as a business bad debt or a nonbusiness bad debt. A business bad debt is one that has arisen in the course of the taxpayer's business (with a business purpose). Nonbusiness bad debts are treated as short-term capital losses rather than as ordinary losses. § 166.

Bargain Sale, Rental, or Purchase.   A sale, rental, or purchase of property for less than its fair market value. The difference between the sale, rental, or purchase price and the property's fair market value may have its own tax consequences, such as consideration as a constructive dividend or a gift.

Bartering.   The exchange of goods and services without using money.

Basis.   The starting point in determining the gain or loss from the sale or other disposition of an asset, or the depreciation (or depletion or amortization) on an asset. For example, if an asset is purchased for cash, the basis of that asset is the cash paid. §§ 1012, 1014, 1015, 334, 358, 362.

Beneficiary.   Someone who will benefit from an act of another, such as the beneficiary of a life insurance contract, the beneficiary of a trust (i.e., income beneficiary), or the beneficiary of an estate.

Bequest.   A testamentary transfer (by will) of personal property (personalty).

Board of Tax Appeals (B.T.A.)   The predecessor of the United States Tax Court, in existence from 1924 to 1942.

Bona Fide.   Real; in good faith.

Boot.   Cash or property that is not included in the definition of a particular type of nontaxable exchange [see §§ 351(b) and 1031(b)]. In these nontaxable exchanges, a taxpayer who receives boot must recognize gain to the extent of the boot received or the realized gain, whichever is less.

Brother-Sister Corporations.   A controlled group of two or more corporations owned (in certain amounts) by five or fewer individuals, estates, or trusts. § 1563(a)(2).

Burden of Proof.   The weight of evidence in a legal case or in a tax proceeding. Generally, the burden of proof is on the taxpayer in a tax case. However, the burden of proof is on the government in fraud cases. § 7454.

Business Purpose.   An actual business reason for following a course of action. Tax avoidance alone is not considered to be a business purpose. In areas such as corporate formation and corporate reorganizations, business purpose is especially important.

—C—

Capital Asset.   All property held by a taxpayer (e.g., house, car, clothing) except for certain assets that are specifically excluded from the definition of a capital asset, such as inventory and depreciable and real property used in a trade or business.

Capital Contribution.   Cash, services, or property contributed by a partner to a partnership or by a shareholder to a corporation. Capital contributions are not income to the recipient partnership or corporation. §§ 721 and 118.

Capital Expenditure.   Any amount paid for new buildings or for permanent improvements; any expenditures that add to the value or prolong the life of property or adapt the property to a new or different use. Capital expenditures should be added to the basis of the property improved. § 263.

Capital Gain.   A gain from the sale or other disposition of a capital asset. § 1222.

Capital Loss.   A loss from the sale or other disposition of a capital asset. § 1222.

Cash Method of Accounting.   The method of accounting that reflects the income received (or constructively received) and the expenses paid during a given period. However, prepaid expenses of a cash basis taxpayer that benefit more than one year may be required to be deducted only in the periods benefited (e.g., a premium for a three-year insurance policy may have to be spread over three years).

CCH.   (*see* Commerce Clearing House).

C Corporation.   A so-called regular corporation that is a separate tax-paying entity and subject to the tax rules contained in Subchapter C of the Internal Revenue Code (as opposed to an S corporation, which is subject to the tax rules of Subchapter S of the Code).

Certiorari.   A Writ of Certiorari is the form used to appeal a lower court (U.S. Court of Appeals) decision to the Supreme Court. The Supreme Court then decides, by reviewing the Writ of Certiorari, whether it will accept the appeal or not. The Supreme Court generally does not accept the appeal unless a constitutional issue is involved or the lower courts are in conflict. If the Supreme Court refuses to accept the appeal, then the certiorari is denied (cert. den.).

Claim of Right Doctrine.   If a taxpayer has an unrestricted claim to income, the income is included in that taxpayer's income when it is received or constructively received, even if there is a possibility that all or part of the income may have to be returned to another party.

Closely Held Corporation.   A corporation whose voting stock is owned by one or a few shareholders and is operated by this person or closely knit group.

Collapsible Corporation.   A corporation that liquidates before it has realized a substantial portion of its income. Shareholders treat the gain on these liquidating distributions as ordinary income (rather than dividend income or capital gains). § 341.

Commerce Clearing House.   A publisher of tax materials, including a multi-volume tax service, volumes that contain the Federal courts' decisions on tax matters (USTC) and the Tax Court regular (T.C.) and memorandum (TCM) decisions.

Community Property.   Property that is owned together by husband and wife, where each has an undivided one-half interest in the property due to their marital status. The nine community property states are Arizona, California, Idaho, Louisiana, Nevada, New Mexico, Texas, Washington, and Wisconsin.

Complex Trust.   Any trust that does not meet the requirements of a simple trust. For example, a trust will be considered to be a complex trust if it does not distribute the trust income currently, if it takes a deduction for a charitable contribution for the current year, or if it distributes any of the trust corpus currently. § 661.

Condemnation.   The taking of private property for a public use by a public authority, an exercise of the power of eminent domain. The public authority compensates the owner of the property taken in a condemnation. (see also Involuntary Conversion).

Conduit Principle.   The provisions in the tax law that allow specific tax characteristics to be passed through certain entities to the owners of the entity without losing their identity. For example, the short-term capital gains of a partnership would be passed through to the partners and retain their character as short-term capital gains on the tax returns of the partners. This principle applies in varying degrees to partnerships, S corporations, estates, and trusts.

Consent Dividend.   A term used in relation to the accumulated earnings tax and the personal holding company tax. A consent dividend occurs when the shareholders consent to treat a certain amount as a taxable dividend on their tax returns even though there is no distribution of cash or property. The purpose of this is to obtain a dividends-paid deduction. § 565.

Consolidated Return.   A method used to determine the tax liability of a group of affiliated corporations. The aggregate income (with certain adjustments) of the group is viewed as the income of a single enterprise. § 1501.

Consolidation.   The statutory combination of two or more corporations in a new corporation. § 368(a)(1)(A).

Constructive Dividends.   The constructive receipt of a dividend. Even though a taxable benefit was not designated as a dividend by the distributing corporation, a shareholder may be designated by the IRS as having received a dividend if the benefit has the appearance of a dividend. For example, if a shareholder uses corporate property for personal purposes rent-free, he or she will have a constructive dividend equal to the fair rental value of the corporate property.

Constructive Ownership.   In certain situations the tax law attributes the ownership of stock to persons "related" to the person or entity that actually owns the stock. The related party is said to constructively own the stock of that person. For example, under § 267(c) a father is considered to constructively own all stock actually owned by his son. §§ 267, 318, and 544(a).

Constructive Receipt.   When income is available to a taxpayer, even though it is not actually received by the taxpayer, the amount is considered to be constructively received by the taxpayer and should be included in income (e.g., accrued interest on a savings account). However, if there are restrictions on the availability of the income, it is generally not considered to be constructively received until the restrictions are removed (e.g., interest on a six-month certificate of deposit is not constructively received until the end of the six-month period if early withdrawal would result in loss of interest or principal).

Contributions to the Capital of a Corporation.   (see Capital Contributions).

Controlled Foreign Corporation. A foreign corporation in which more than 50 percent of its voting power is controlled directly or indirectly at any time during the year by U.S. stockholders who individually control at least 10 percent of the voting power. U.S. shareholders are taxed on their share of the income as it is earned, rather than when it is distributed. §§ 951–964.

Corpus. The principal of a trust, as opposed to the income of the trust. Also called the *res* of the trust.

Correspondence Audit. An IRS audit conducted through the mail. Generally, verification or substantiation for specified items is requested by the IRS, and the taxpayer mails the requested information to the IRS (*see also* Field Audit; Office Audit).

Cost Depletion. (*see* Depletion).

Court of Appeals. The U.S. Federal court system has 13 circuit Courts of Appeals which consider cases appealed from the U.S. Claims Court, the U.S. Tax Court, and the U.S. District Courts. A writ of certiorari is used to appeal a case from a Court of Appeals to the U.S. Supreme Court (*see also* Appellate Court).

Creditor. A person or entity to whom money is owed. The person or entity who owes the money is called the debtor.

—D—

Death Tax. A tax imposed on property upon the death of the owner, such as an estate tax or inheritance tax.

Debtor. A person or entity who owes money to another. The person or entity to whom the money is owed is called the creditor.

Decedent. A deceased person.

Deductions in Respect of a Decedent (DRD). Certain expenses that are incurred by a decedent but are not properly deductible on the decedent's final return because of nonpayment. Deductions in respect of a decedent are deducted by the taxpayer who is legally required to make payment. § 691(b).

Deficiency. An additional tax liability owed to the IRS by a taxpayer. A deficiency is generally proposed by the IRS through the use of a Revenue Agent's Report.

Deficit. A negative balance in retained earnings or in earnings and profits.

Dependent. A person who derives his or her primary support from another. In order for a taxpayer to claim a dependency exemption for a person, there are five tests that must be met: support test, gross income test, citizenship or residency test, relationship or member of household test, and joint return test. § 152.

Depletion. As natural resources are extracted and sold, the cost or other basis of the resource is recovered by the use of depletion. Depletion may be either cost or percentage (statutory) depletion. Cost depletion has to do with the recovery of the cost of natural resources based on the units of the resource sold. Percentage depletion uses percentages given in the Internal Revenue Code multiplied by the gross income from the interest, subject to limitations. §§ 613 and 613A.

Depreciation.   The systematic write-off of the basis of a tangible asset over the asset's estimated useful life. Depreciation is intended to reflect the wear, tear, and obsolescence of the asset (*see also* Amortization; Depletion).

Depreciation Recapture.   The situation in which all or part of the realized gain from the sale or other disposition of depreciable business property could be treated as ordinary income. See text for discussion of §§ 291, 1245, and 1250.

Determination Letter.   A written statement regarding the tax consequences of a transaction issued by an IRS District Director in response to a written inquiry by a taxpayer that applies to a particular set of facts. Determination letters are frequently used to state whether a pension or profit-sharing plan is qualified or not, to determine the tax-exempt status of nonprofit organizations, and to clarify employee status.

Discretionary Trust.   A trust in which the trustee or another party has the right to determine whether to accumulate or distribute the trust income currently, and/or which beneficiary is to receive the trust income.

Discriminant Function System (DIF).   The computerized system used by the Internal Revenue Service in identifying and selecting returns for examination. This system uses secret mathematical formulas to select those returns that have a probability of tax errors.

Dissent.   A disagreement with the majority opinion. The term is generally used to mean the explicit disagreement of one or more judges in a court with the majority decision on a particular case.

Distributable Net Income (DNI).   The net income of a fiduciary that is available for distribution to income beneficiaries. DNI is computed by adjusting an estate's or trust's taxable income by certain modifications. § 643(a).

Distribution in Kind.   A distribution of property as it is. For example, rather than selling property and distributing the proceeds to the shareholders, the property itself is distributed to the shareholders.

District Court.   A trial court in which Federal tax matters can be litigated; the only trial court in which a jury trial can be obtained.

Dividend.   A payment by a corporation to its shareholders authorized by the corporation's board of directors to be distributed pro rata among the outstanding shares. However, a constructive dividend does not need to be authorized by the shareholders (*see also* Constructive Dividend).

Dividends-Paid Deduction.   A deduction allowed in determining the amount that is subject to the accumulated earnings tax and the personal holding company tax. §§ 561–565.

Dividends-Received Deduction.   A deduction available to corporations on dividends received from a domestic corporation. The dividends-received deduction is generally 70 percent of the dividends received. If the recipient corporation owns 20 percent or more of the stock of the paying corporation, an 80 percent deduction is allowed. The dividends-received deduction is 100 percent of the dividends received from another member of an affiliated group, if an election is made. §§ 243–246.

Domestic Corporation.   A corporation created or organized in the United States or under the law of the United States or of any state. § 7701(a)(4).

Domestic International Sales Corporation (DISC).   A U.S. corporation that derives most of its income from exports. A portion of the income taxes on a DISC's income is deferred as long as the DISC requirements are met. §§ 991–997.

Donee.   The person or entity to whom a gift is made.

Donor.   The person or entity who makes a gift.

Double Taxation.   A situation in which income is taxed twice. For example, a regular corporation pays tax on its taxable income, and, when this income is distributed to the corporation's shareholders, the shareholders are taxed on the dividend income.

—E—

Earned Income.   Income from personal services. § 911(d)(2).

Earnings and Profits (E&P).   The measure of a corporation's ability to pay dividends to its shareholders. Distributions made by a corporation to its shareholders are dividends to the extent of the corporation's earnings and profits. §§ 312 and 316.

Eminent Domain.   (*see* Condemnation).

Employee.   A person in the service of another, where the employer has the power to specify how the work is to be performed (*see also* Independent Contractor).

Employee Achievement Award.   An award of tangible personalty that is made for length of service achievement or safety achievement. § 274(j).

Encumbrance.   A liability.

Entity.   For tax purposes, an organization that is considered to have a separate existence, such as a partnership, corporation, estate, or trust.

Escrow.   Cash or other property that is held by a third party as security for an obligation.

Estate.   All of the property owned by a decedent at the time of his or her death.

Estate Tax.   A tax imposed on the transfer of a decedent's taxable estate. The estate, not the heirs, is liable for the estate tax. §§ 2001–2209 (*see also* Inheritance Tax).

Estoppel.   A bar or impediment preventing a party from asserting a fact or a claim in court that is inconsistent with a position he or she had previously taken.

Excise Tax.   A tax imposed on the sale, manufacture, or use of a commodity or on the conduct of an occupation or activity; considered to include every Internal Revenue Tax except the income tax.

Executor.   A person appointed in a will to carry out the provisions in the will and to administer the estate of the decedent. (Feminine of executor is executrix.)

Exempt Organization.   An organization (such as a charitable organization) that is exempt from Federal income taxes. §§ 501–528.

Exemption.   A deduction allowed in computing taxable income. Personal exemptions are available for the taxpayer and his or her spouse. Dependency exemptions are available for the taxpayer's dependents. §§ 151–154 (*see also* Dependent).

Expatriate (U.S.).   U.S. citizen working in a foreign country.

—F—

F.2d (Federal Reporter, Second Series).   Volumes in which the decisions of the U.S. Claims Court and the U.S. Courts of Appeals are published.

F. Supp. (Federal Supplement).   Volumes in which the decisions of the U.S. District Courts are published.

Fair Market Value.   The amount a willing buyer would pay a willing seller in an arm's-length transaction.

Fed. (Federal Reporter).   Volumes in which the decisions of the U.S. Claims Court and the U.S. Courts of Appeals are published.

FICA (Federal Insurance Contributions Act).   The law dealing with Social Security taxes and benefits. §§ 3101–3126.

Fiduciary.   A person or institution who holds and manages property for another, such as a guardian, trustee, executor, or administrator. § 7701(a)(6).

Field Audit.   An audit conducted by the IRS at the taxpayer's place of business or at the place of business of the taxpayer's representative. Field audits are generally conducted by Revenue Agents (*see also* Correspondence Audit; Office Audit).

FIFO (First-in, First-out).   A method of determining the cost of an inventory. The first inventory units acquired are considered to be the first sold. Therefore, the cost of the inventory would consist of the most recently acquired inventory.

Filing Status.   The filing status of an individual taxpayer determines the tax rates that are applicable to that taxpayer. The filing statuses include Single, Head of Household, Married Filing Jointly, Married Filing Separately, and Surviving Spouse (Qualifying Widow or Widower).

Fiscal Year.   A period of 12 consecutive months, other than a calendar year, used as the accounting period of a business. § 7701(a)(24).

Foreign Corporation.   A corporation that is not organized under U.S. laws, other than a domestic corporation. § 7701(a)(5).

Foreign Personal Holding Company (FPHC).   A foreign corporation in which five or fewer U.S. citizens or residents owned more than 50 percent of the value of its outstanding stock during the taxable year and at least 50 percent of its gross income (or 60 percent if it was not an FPHC in the previous year) is foreign personal holding company income. §§ 551–558.

Foreign Sales Corporation (FSC). A corporation created or organized under the laws of a U.S. possession (other than Puerto Rico) or certain foreign countries that has no more than 25 shareholders at any time, has no outstanding preferred stock, maintains a set of records at an office outside the United States and certain records inside the United States, has at least one non–U.S. resident member of the board of directors, is not a member of a controlled group that has a DISC as a member, makes a timely FSC election, and meets foreign management and foreign economic process tests. §§ 921–927.

Foreign Source Income. Income derived from sources outside the United States. The source of earned income is determined by the place where the work is actually performed. Unearned income usually qualifies as foreign source income when it is received from a foreign resident or for property used in a foreign country and not effectively connected with U.S. sources.

Foreign Tax Credit. A credit available against taxes for foreign income taxes paid or deemed paid. A deduction may be taken for these foreign taxes as an alternative to the foreign tax credit. §§ 27 and 901–905.

Fraud. A willful intent to evade tax. For tax purposes, fraud is divided into civil fraud and criminal fraud. The IRS has the burden of proof of proving fraud. Civil fraud has a penalty of 75 percent of the underpayment [§ 6653(b)]. Criminal fraud requires a greater degree of willful intent to evade tax (§§ 7201–7207).

Freedom of Information Act. The means by which the public may obtain information held by Federal agencies.

Fringe Benefits. Benefits received by an employee in addition to his or her salary or wages, such as insurance and recreational facilities.

FUTA (Federal Unemployment Tax Act). A tax imposed on the employer on the wages of the employees. A credit is generally given for amounts contributed to state unemployment tax funds. §§ 3301–3311.

Future Interest. An interest in which the possession or enjoyment of which will come into being at some point in the future. The annual exclusion for gifts applies only to gifts of present interests, as opposed to future interests.

—G—

General Partner. A partner who is jointly and severally liable for the debts of the partnership. A general partner has no limited liability (*see* Limited Partner).

Generation-Skipping Tax. A transfer tax imposed on a certain type of transfer involving a trust and at least three generations of taxpayers. The transfer generally skips a generation younger than the original transferor. The transfer therefore results in the avoidance of one generation's estate tax on the transferred property. §§ 2601–2622.

Gift. A transfer of property or money given for less than adequate consideration in money or money's worth.

Gift-Splitting.   A tax provision that allows a married person who makes a gift of his or her property to elect, with the consent of his or her spouse, to treat the gift as being made one-half by each the taxpayer and his or her spouse. The effect of gift-splitting is to take advantage of the annual gift tax exclusions for both the taxpayer and his or her spouse. § 2513.

Gift Tax.   A tax imposed on the donor of a gift. The tax applies to transfers in trust or otherwise, whether the gift is direct or indirect, real or personal, tangible or intangible. §§ 2501–2524.

Goodwill.   An intangible asset that has an indefinite useful life, arising from the difference between the purchase price and the value of the assets of an acquired business. Goodwill is not amortizable since it has no ascertainable life. § 263(b).

Grantor.   The person who creates a trust.

Grantor Trust.   A trust in which the transferor (grantor) of the trust does not surrender complete control over the property. Generally, the income from a grantor trust is taxable to the grantor rather than to the person who receives the income. §§ 671–677.

Gross Estate.   The value of all property, real or personal, tangible or intangible, owned by a decedent at the time of his or her death. §§ 2031–2046.

Gross Income.   Income that is subject to Federal income tax. All income from whatever source derived, unless it is specifically excluded from income (e.g., interest on state and local bonds). § 61.

Guaranteed Payment.   A payment made by a partnership to a partner for services or the use of capital, without regard to the income of the partnership. The payment generally is deductible by the partnership and taxable to the partner. § 707(c).

—H—

Half-Year Convention.   When a taxpayer is using ACRS, personalty placed in service at any time during the year is treated as placed in service in the middle of the year, and personalty disposed of or retired at any time during the year is treated as disposed of in the middle of the year. However, if more than 40 percent of all personalty placed in service during the year is placed in service during the last three months of the year, the mid-quarter convention applies. § 168(d)(4)(A).

Heir.   One who inherits property from a decedent.

Hobby.   An activity not engaged in for profit. § 183.

Holding Period.   The period of time that property is held. Holding period is used to determine whether a gain or loss is short-term or long-term. §§ 1222 and 1223.

H.R. 10 Plans.   (see Keogh Plans).

—I—

Incident of Ownership. Any economic interest in a life insurance policy, such as the power to change the policy's beneficiary, the right to cancel or assign the policy, and the right to borrow against the policy. § 2042(2).

Income Beneficiary. The person or entity entitled to receive the income from property. Generally used in reference to trusts.

Income in Respect of a Decedent (IRD). Income that had been earned by a decedent at the time of his or her death, but is not included on the final tax return because of the decedent's method of accounting. Income in respect of a decedent is included in the decedent's gross estate and also on the tax return of the person who receives the income. § 691.

Independent Contractor. One who contracts to do a job according to his or her own methods and skills. The employer has control over the independent contractor only as to the final result of his or her work (*see also* Employee).

Indirect Method. A method used by the IRS in order to determine whether a taxpayer's income is correctly reported when adequate records do not exist. Indirect methods include the Source and Applications of Funds Method and the Net Worth Method.

Information Return. A return that must be filed with the Internal Revenue Service even though no tax is imposed, such as a partnership return (Form 1065), Form W-2, and Form 1099.

Inheritance Tax. A tax imposed on the privilege of receiving property of a decedent. The tax is imposed on the heir.

Installment Method. A method of accounting under which a taxpayer spreads the recognition of his or her gain ratably over time as the payments are received. §§ 453, 453A, and 453B.

Intangible Asset. A nonphysical asset, such as goodwill, copyrights, franchises, or trademarks.

Inter Vivos Transfer. A property transfer during the life of the owner.

Intercompany Transaction. A transaction that occurs during a consolidated return year between two or more members of the same affiliated group.

Internal Revenue Service. Part of the Treasury Department, it is responsible for administering and enforcing the Federal tax laws.

Intestate. No will existing at the time of death.

Investment Tax Credit. A credit against tax that was allowed for investing in depreciable tangible personalty before 1986. The credit was equal to 10 percent of the qualified investment. §§ 38 and 46–48.

Investment Tax Credit Recapture. When property on which an investment credit has been taken is disposed of prior to the full time period required under the law to earn the credit, then the amount of unearned credit must be added back to the taxpayer's tax liability—this is called recapture of the investment tax credit. § 47.

Involuntary Conversion.   The complete or partial destruction, theft, seizure, requisition, or condemnation of property. § 1033.

Itemized Deductions.   Certain expenditures of a personal nature that are specifically allowed to be deductible from an individual taxpayer's adjusted gross income. Itemized deductions (e.g., medical expenses, charitable contributions, interest, taxes, moving expenses, and miscellaneous itemized deductions) are deductible if they exceed the taxpayer's standard deduction.

—J—

Jeopardy Assessment.   If the IRS has reason to believe that the collection or assessment of a tax would be jeopardized by delay, the IRS may assess and collect the tax immediately. §§ 6861–6864.

Joint and Several Liability.   The creditor has the ability to sue one or more of the parties who have a liability, or all of the liable persons together. General partners are jointly and severally liable for the debts of the partnership. Also, if a husband and wife file a joint return, they are jointly and severally liable to the IRS for the taxes due.

Joint Tenancy.   Property held by two or more owners, where each has an undivided interest in the property. Joint tenancy includes the right of survivorship, which means that upon the death of an owner, his or her share passes to the surviving owner(s).

Joint Venture.   A joining together of two or more persons in order to undertake a specific business project. A joint venture is not a continuing relationship like a partnership, but may be treated as a partnership for Federal income tax purposes. § 761(a).

—K—

Keogh Plans.   A retirement plan available for self-employed taxpayers. § 401.

"Kiddie" Tax.   Unearned income of a child under age 14 is taxed at the child's parent's marginal tax rate. § 1(i).

—L—

Leaseback.   A transaction in which a taxpayer sells property and then leases back the property.

Lessee.   A person or entity who rents or leases property from another.

Lessor.   A person or entity who rents or leases property to another.

Life Estate.   A trust or legal arrangement by which a certain person (life tenant) is entitled to receive the income from designated property for his or her life.

Life Insurance.   A form of insurance that will pay the beneficiary of the policy a fixed amount upon the death of the insured person.

LIFO (Last-in, First-out). A method of determining the cost of an inventory. The last inventory units acquired are considered to be the first sold. Therefore, the cost of the inventory would consist of the earliest acquired inventory.

Like-Kind Exchange. The exchange of property held for productive use in a trade or business or for investment (but not inventory, stock, bonds, or notes) for property that is also held for productive use or for investment (i.e., realty for realty; personalty for personalty). No gain or loss is generally recognized by either party unless boot (other than qualifying property) is involved in the transaction. § 1031.

Limited Liability. The situation in which the liability of an owner of an organization for the organization's debts is limited to the owner's investment in the organization. Examples of taxpayers with limited liability are corporate shareholders and the limited partners in a limited partnership.

Limited Partner. A partner whose liability for partnership debts is limited to his or her investment in the partnership. A limited partner may take no active part in the management of the partnership according to the Uniform Limited Partnership Act (*see* General Partner).

Limited Partnership. A partnership with *one* or more general partners *and* one or more limited partners. The limited partners are liable only up to the amount of their contribution plus any personally guaranteed debt. Limited partners cannot participate in the management or control of the partnership.

Liquidation. The cessation of all or part of a corporation's operations or the corporate form of business and the distribution of the corporate assets to the shareholders. §§ 331–337.

Lump Sum Distribution. Payment at one time of an entire amount due, or the entire proceeds of a pension or profit-sharing plan, rather than installment payments.

—M—

Majority. Of legal age (*see* Minor).

Marital Deduction. Upon the transfer of property from one spouse to another, either by gift or at death, the Internal Revenue Code allows a transfer tax deduction for the amount transferred.

Market Value. (*see* Fair Market Value).

Material Participation. Occurs when a taxpayer is involved in the operations of an activity on a regular, continuous, and substantial basis. § 469(h).

Mid-Month Convention. When using ACRS, realty placed in service at any time during a month is treated as placed in service in the middle of the month, and realty disposed of or retired at any time during a month is treated as disposed of in the middle of the month. § 168(d)(4)(B).

Mid-Quarter Convention. Used for all personalty placed in service during the year if more than 40 percent of all personalty placed in service during the year is placed in service during the last three months of the year. § 168(d)(4)(C).

Merger.   The absorption of one corporation (target corporation) by another corporation (acquiring corporation). The target corporation transfers its assets to the acquiring corporation in return for stock or securities of the acquiring corporation. Then the target corporation dissolves by exchanging the acquiring corporation's stock for its own stock held by its shareholders.

Minimum Tax.   (*see* Alternative Minimum Tax).

Minor.   A person who has not yet reached the age of legal majority. In most states, a minor is a person under 18 years of age.

Mortgagee.   The person or entity that holds the mortgage; the lender; the creditor.

Mortgagor.   The person or entity that is mortgaging the property; the debtor.

—N—

NA.   (*see* Nonacquiescence).

Negligence Penalty.   An accuracy-related penalty imposed by the IRS on taxpayers who are negligent or disregard the rules or regulations (but are not fraudulent), in the determination of their tax liability. § 6662.

Net Operating Loss (NOL).   The amount by which deductions exceed a taxpayer's gross income. § 172.

Net Worth Method.   An indirect method of determining a taxpayer's income used by the IRS when adequate records do not exist. The net worth of the taxpayer is determined for the end of each year in question, and adjustments are made to the increase in net worth from year to year for nontaxable sources of income and nondeductible expenditures. This method is often used when a possibility of fraud exists.

Ninety-Day Letter.   (*see* Statutory Notice of Deficiency).

Nonacquiescence.   The public announcement that the Commissioner of the Internal Revenue Service disagrees with a regular Tax Court decision. When the Commissioner nonacquiesces to a regular Tax Court decision, the IRS generally will litigate cases involving similar facts (*see also* Acquiescence).

Nonresident Alien.   A person who is not a resident or a citizen of the United States.

—O—

Office Audit.   An audit conducted by the Internal Revenue Service on IRS premises. The person conducting the audit is generally referred to as an Office Auditor (*see also* Correspondence Audit; Field Audit).

Office Auditor.   An IRS employee who conducts primarily office audits, as opposed to a Revenue Agent, who conducts primarily field audits (*see also* Revenue Agent).

Ordinary Gross Income. A term used in relation to personal holding companies. Ordinary gross income is determined by subtracting capital gains and § 1231 gains from gross income. § 543(b)(1).

—P—

Partial Liquidation. A distribution that is not essentially equivalent to a dividend, or a distribution that is attributable to the termination of one of two or more businesses (that have been active businesses for at least five years). § 302(e).

Partner. (*see* General Partner; Limited Partner).

Partnership. A syndicate, group, pool, joint venture, or other unincorporated organization, through or by means of which any business, financial operation, or venture is carried on, and which is not a trust, estate, or corporation. §§ 761(a) and 7701(a)(2).

Passive Activity. Any activity that involves the conduct of any trade or business in which the taxpayer does not materially participate. Losses from passive activities generally are deductible only to the extent of passive activity income. § 469.

Passive Investment Income. A term used in relation to S corporations. Passive investment income is generally defined as gross receipts derived from royalties, rents, dividends, interest, annuities, and gains on sales or exchanges of stock or securities. § 1362(d)(3)(D).

Pecuniary Bequest. Monetary bequest (*see also* Bequest).

Percentage Depletion. (*see* Depletion).

Percentage of Completion Method of Accounting. A method of accounting that may be used on certain long-term contracts in which the income is reported as the contract reaches various stages of completion.

Personal Holding Company. A corporation in which five or fewer individuals owned more than 50 percent of the value of its stock at any time during the last half of the taxable year and at least 60 percent of the corporation's adjusted ordinary gross income consists of personal holding company income. § 542.

Personal Property. All property that is not realty; personalty. This term is also often used to mean personal use property (*see also* Personal Use Property; Personalty).

Personal Use Property. Any property used for personal, rather than business, purposes. Distinguished from "personal property."

Personalty. All property that is not realty (e.g., automobiles, trucks, machinery, and equipment).

P.H. (*see* Prentice Hall).

Portfolio Income. Interest and dividends. Portfolio income, annuities, and royalties are not considered to be income from a passive activity for purposes of the passive activity loss limitations. § 469(e).

Power of Appointment. A right to dispose of property that the holder of the power does not legally own.

Preferred Stock Bailout. A scheme by which shareholders receive a nontaxable preferred stock dividend, sell this preferred stock to a third party, and report the gain as a long-term capital gain. This scheme, therefore, converts what would be ordinary dividend income to capital gain. Section 306 was created to prohibit use of this scheme.

Prentice Hall. A publisher of tax materials, including a multi-volume tax service and volumes that contain the Federal courts' decisions on tax matters (AFTR, AFTR2d.).

Present Interest. An interest in which the donee has the present right to use, possess, or enjoy the donated property. The annual exclusion is available for gifts of present interests, but not for gifts of future interests (*see also* Future Interest).

Previously Taxed Income (PTI). A term used to refer to the accumulated earnings and profits for the period in which a Subchapter S election was in effect prior to 1983. Distributions from PTI are not taxable to the shareholders.

Private Letter Ruling. A written statement from the IRS to a taxpayer in response to a request by the taxpayer for the tax consequences of a specific set of facts. The taxpayer who receives the Private Letter Ruling is the only taxpayer that may rely on that specific ruling in case of litigation.

Probate. The court-directed administration of a decedent's estate.

Prop. Reg. (Proposed Regulation). Treasury (IRS) Regulations are generally issued first in a proposed form in order to obtain input from various sources before the regulations are changed (if necessary) and issued in final form.

Pro Rata. Proportionately.

—Q—

Qualified Pension or Profit-Sharing Plan. A pension or profit-sharing plan sponsored by an employer that meets the requirements set forth by Congress in § 401. §§ 401–404.

Qualified Residence Interest. Interest on indebtedness that is secured by the principal residence or one other residence of a taxpayer. §§ 162(h)(3) and (5)(A).

Qualified Terminable Interest Property (QTIP). Property that passes from the decedent in which the surviving spouse has a qualifying income interest for life. An election to treat the property as qualified terminable interest property has been made. § 2056(b).

—R—

RAR. (*see* Revenue Agent's Report).

Real Property. (*see* Realty).

Realized Gain or Loss. The difference between the amount realized from the sale or other disposition of an asset and the adjusted basis of the asset. § 1001.

Realty. Real estate; land, including any objects attached thereto that are not readily movable (e.g., buildings, sidewalks, trees, and fences).

Reasonable Needs of the Business. In relation to the accumulated earnings tax, a corporation may accumulate sufficient earnings and profits to meet its reasonable business needs. Examples of reasonable needs of the business include working capital needs, amounts needed for bona fide business expansion, and amounts needed for redemptions for death taxes. § 537.

Recapture. The recovery of the tax benefit from a previously taken deduction or credit. The recapture of a deduction results in its inclusion in income, and the recapture of a credit results in its inclusion in tax (see also Depreciation Recapture; Investment Credit Recapture).

Recognized Gain or Loss. The amount of the realized gain or loss that is subject to income tax. § 1001.

Redemption. The acquisition by a corporation of its own stock from a shareholder in exchange for property. § 317(b).

Reg. (see Regulations).

Regulations (Treasury Department Regulations). Interpretations of the Internal Revenue Code by the Internal Revenue Service.

Related Party. A person or entity that is related to another under the various code provisions for constructive ownership. §§ 267, 318, and 544(a).

Remainder Interest. Property that passes to a remainderman after the life estate or other income interest expires on the property.

Remainderman. The person entitled to the remainder interest.

Remand. The sending back of a case by an appellate court to a lower court for further action by the lower court. The abbreviation for "remanding" is "rem'g."

Reorganization. The combination, division, or restructuring of a corporation or corporations.

Resident Alien. A person who is not a citizen of the United States, and who is a resident of the United States or meets the substantial presence test. § 7701(b).

Revenue Agent. An employee of the Internal Revenue Service who performs primarily field audits.

Revenue Agent's Report (RAR). The report issued by a Revenue Agent in which adjustments to a taxpayer's tax liability are proposed. (IRS Form 4549; Form 1902 is used for office audits.)

Revenue Officer. An employee of the Internal Revenue Service whose primary duty is the collection of Tax. (As opposed to a Revenue Agent, who audits returns.)

Revenue Procedure. A procedure published by the Internal Revenue Service outlining various processes and methods of handling various matters of tax practice and administration. Revenue Procedures are published first in the Internal Revenue Bulletin and then compiled annually in the Cumulative Bulletin.

Revenue Ruling. A published interpretation by the Internal Revenue Service of the tax law as applied to specific situations. Revenue Rulings are published first in the Internal Revenue Bulletin and then compiled annually in the Cumulative Bulletin.

Reversed (Rev'd.). The reverse of a lower court's decision by a higher court.

Reversing (Rev'g.). The reversing of a lower court's decision by a higher court.

Revocable Transfer. A transfer that may be revoked by the transferor. In other words, the transferor keeps the right to recover the transferred property.

Rev. Proc. (*see* Revenue Procedure).

Rev. Rul. (*see* Revenue Ruling).

Right of Survivorship. (*see* Joint Tenancy).

Royalty. Compensation for the use of property, such as natural resources or copyrighted material.

—S—

S Corporation. A corporation that qualifies as a small business corporation and elects to have §§ 1361–1379 apply. Once a Subchapter S election is made, the corporation is treated similarly to a partnership for tax purposes. An S corporation uses Form 1120S to report its income and expenses. (*see* C Corporation).

Section 38 Property. Property subject to the investment tax credit (*see also* Investment Tax Credit).

Section 751 Assets. Unrealized receivables and appreciated inventory items of a partnership. A disproportionate distribution of § 751 assets generally results in taxable income to the partners.

Section 1231 Property. Depreciable property and real estate used in a trade or business held for more than one year. Section 1231 property may also include timber, coal, domestic iron ore, livestock, and unharvested crops.

Section 1244 Stock. Stock of a small business corporation issued pursuant to § 1244. A loss on § 1244 stock is treated as an ordinary loss (rather than a capital loss) within limitations. § 1244.

Section 1245 Property. Property that is subject to depreciation recapture under § 1245.

Section 1250 Property. Property that is subject to depreciation recapture under § 1250.

Securities. Evidences of debt or of property, such as stock, bonds, and notes.

Separate Property. Property that belongs separately to only one spouse (as contrasted with community property in a community property state). In a community property state, a spouse's separate property generally includes property acquired by the spouse prior to marriage, or property acquired after marriage by gift or inheritance.

Severance Tax. At the time they are severed or removed from the earth, a tax on minerals or timber.

Sham Transaction. A transaction with no substance or bona fide business purpose that may be ignored for tax purposes.

Simple Trust. A trust that is required to distribute all of its income currently and does not pay, set aside, or use any funds for charitable purposes. § 651(a).

Small Business Corporation. There are two separate definitions of a small business corporation, one relating to S corporation, and one relating to § 1244. If small business corporation status is met under § 1361(b), a corporation may elect Subchapter S. If small business corporation status is met under § 1244(c)(3), losses on § 1244 stock may be deducted as ordinary (rather than capital) losses, within limitations.

Special Use Valuation. A special method for valuing real estate for estate tax purposes. The special use valuation allows that qualifying real estate used in a closely held business may be valued based on its business usage rather than its market value. § 2032A.

Specific Bequest. A bequest made by a testator in his or her will giving an heir a particular piece of property or money.

Spin-off. A type of divisive corporate reorganization in which the original corporation transfers some of its assets to a newly formed subsidiary in exchange for all the subsidiary's stock, which it then distributes to its shareholders. The shareholders of the original corporation do not surrender any of their ownership in the original corporation for the subsidiary's stock.

Split-off. A type of divisive corporate reorganization in which the original corporation transfers some of its assets to a newly formed subsidiary in exchange for all the subidiary's stock, which it then distributes to some or all of its shareholders in exchange for some portion of their stock.

Split-up. A type of divisive corporate reorganization in which the original corporation transfers some of its assets to one newly created subsidiary and the remainder of the assets to another newly created subsidiary. The original corporation then liquidates, distributing the stock of both subsidiaries in exchange for its own stock.

Standard Deduction. A deduction that is available to most individual taxpayers. The standard deduction or total itemized deductions, whichever is larger, is subtracted in computing taxable income. §§ 63(c) and (f).

Statute of Limitations. Law provisions that limit the period of time in which action may be taken after an event occurs. The limitations on the IRS for assessments and collections are included in §§ 6501–6504, and the limitations on taxpayers for credits or refunds are included in §§ 6511–6515.

Statutory Depletion. (*see* Depletion).

Stock Option.   A right to purchase a specified amount of stock for a specified price at a given time or times.

Subchapter S.   Sections 1361–1379 of the Internal Revenue Code (*see also* S Corporation).

Substance vs. Form.   The essence of a transaction as opposed to the structure or form that the transaction takes. For example, a transaction may formally meet the requirements for a specific type of tax treatment, but if what the transaction is actually accomplishing is different from the form of the transaction, the form may be ignored.

Surtax.   An additional tax imposed on corporations with taxable income in excess of $100,000. The surtax is 5 percent of the corporation's taxable income in excess of $100,000 up to a maximum surtax of $11,750. § 11(b).

—T—

Tangible Property.   Property that may be touched (e.g., machinery, automobile, desk) as opposed to intangibles which may not be touched (e.g., goodwill, copyrights, patents).

Tax Avoidance.   Using the tax laws to avoid paying taxes or to reduce one's tax liability (*see also* Tax Evasion).

Tax Benefit Rule.   The doctrine by which the amount of income that a taxpayer must include in income when the taxpayer has recovered an amount previously deducted is limited to the amount of the previous deduction that produced a tax benefit.

Tax Court (United States Tax Court).   One of the three trial courts that hears cases dealing with Federal tax matters. A taxpayer need not pay his or her tax deficiency in advance if he or she decides to litigate the case in Tax Court (as opposed to the District Court or Claims Court).

Tax Credits.   An amount that is deducted directly from a taxpayer's tax liability, as opposed to a deduction, which reduces taxable income.

Tax Evasion.   The illegal evasion of the tax laws. § 7201 (*see also* Tax Avoidance).

Tax Preference Items.   Those items specifically designated in § 57 that may be subject to a special tax (*see also* Alternative Minimum Tax).

Tax Shelter.   A device or scheme used by taxpayers either to reduce taxes or to defer the payment of taxes.

Taxable Estate.   Gross estate reduced by the expenses, indebtedness, taxes, losses, and charitable contributions of the estate and by the marital deduction. § 2051.

Taxable Gifts.   The total amount of gifts made during the calendar year, reduced by charitable gifts and the marital deduction. § 2503.

T.C. (Tax Court: United States Tax Court).   This abbreviation is also used to cite the Tax Court's Regular Decisions (*see also* Tax Court; T.C. Memo).

T.C. Memo.   The term used to cite the Tax Court's Memorandum Decisions (*see also* Tax Court; T.C.).

Tenancy by the Entirety.   A form of ownership between a husband and wife wherein each has an undivided interest in the property, with the right of survivorship.

Tenancy in Common.   A form of joint ownership whereby each owner has an undivided interest in the property, with no right of survivorship.

Testator.   A person who makes or has made a will; one who dies and has left a will.

Thin Corporation.   A corporation in which the amount of debt owed by the corporation is high in relationship to the amount of equity in the corporation. § 385.

Treasury Regulations.   (*see* Regulations).

Trial Court.   The first court to consider a case, as opposed to an appellate court.

Trust.   A right in property that is held by one person or entity for the benefit of another. §§ 641–683.

—U—

Unearned Income.   Income that is not earned or is not yet earned. The term is used to refer to both prepaid (not yet earned) income and to passive (not earned) income.

Unearned Income of a Minor Child.   (*see* "Kiddie" tax).

Unified Transfer Tax.   The Federal tax that applies to both estates and gifts after 1976.

Unified Transfer Tax Credit.   A credit against the unified transfer tax that allows a taxpayer to make a certain amount of gifts and/or have a certain size estate without incurring any Federal estate or gift tax.

Uniform Gift to Minors Act.   An Act that provides a way to transfer property to minors. A custodian manages the property on behalf of the minor, and the custodianship terminates when the minor achieves majority.

USSC (U.S. Supreme Court).   This abbreviation is used to cite U.S. Supreme Court cases.

U.S. Tax Court.   (*see* Tax Court).

USTC (U.S. Tax Cases).   Published by Commerce Clearing House. These volumes contain all the Federal tax-related decisions of the U.S. District Courts, the U.S. Claims Court, the U.S. Courts of Appeals, and the U.S. Supreme Court.

—V—

Valuation.   (*see* Fair Market Value).

Vested.   Fixed or settled; having the right to absolute ownership, even if ownership will not come into being until some time in the future.

INDEX

— T —

Corporate Tax Rate Schedule

If taxable income is:		The tax is:	Of the amount
Over—	But not over—		over—
$ 0	$ 50,000	15%	$ 0
50,000	75,000	$ 7,500 + 25%	50,000
75,000	100,000	13,750 + 34%	75,000
100,000	335,000	22,250 + 39%	100,000
335,000	—	113,900 + 34%	335,000

Income Tax Rates for Estates and Trusts

For Taxable Years Beginning after 1990

If taxable income is:		The tax is:	Of the amount
Over—	But not over—		over—
$ 0	$ 3,450	15%	$ 0
3,450	10,350	$ 517.50 + 28%	3,450
10,350	—	2,449.50 + 31%	10,350